BUSINESS LAW

PRINCIPLES, CASES, AND POLICY

SIXTH EDITION

MARK E. ROSZKOWSKI

PROFESSOR OF BUSINESS LAW
UNIVERSITY OF ILLINOIS AT URBANA-CHAMPAIGN

CONTRIBUTING AUTHOR
Christie L. Roszkowski
ASSOCIATE PROFESSOR OF BUSINESS LAW
EASTERN ILLINOIS UNIVERSITY

To My Parents,
Stanley and Catherine Roszkowski

ISBN: 1-58874-557-0

Library of Congress Cataloging-in-Publication Data applied for.

CONTENTS

PART ONE

INTRODUCTION TO LAW AND THE LEGAL SYSTEM 1

CHAPTER 1

LAW AND COURTS 3

CHAPTER 2

CIVIL DISPUTE RESOLUTION 27

iii

PART FOUR

NEGOTIABLE INSTRUMENTS   397

PART SEVEN

BUSINESS ORGANIZATIONS   723

CHAPTER 40

CHAPTER 41

CHAPTER 42

Business Law: Principles, Cases, and Policy, Sixth Edition, is a comprehensive introduction to the legal principles governing business, the legal system within which business operates, and the role of government in regulating business conduct.

Key Features

1. The text is designed to provide complete substantive business law coverage, coupled with the flexibility to adapt to the needs of many different educational institutions, their teachers, and students. Specifically, this text is written and organized not only to reinforce and supplement principles developed in the classroom, but also to permit teachers with limited lecture or class discussion time to cover topics through readings assigned from the text.

2. The organization of the book (59 chapters organized into 9 parts) leads the reader logically through each subject by starting with basic definitions, concepts, and principles. This approach minimizes confusion, allows the teacher to choose the level of coverage, and permits efficient coverage of detailed topics.

3. To enhance student understanding of complex topics, hypothetical examples and textual discussion of actual cases are used throughout the text to illustrate legal principles. In addition, the text explains not only the substance and derivation of legal rules, but also the rationale or policy behind them. The text also carefully defines and explains legal terminology. This approach promotes student understanding and retention of the legal concepts and principles.

4. The text also allows the teacher to pick and choose among a variety of topics to design a course, or courses, tailored to a particular curriculum and the needs of particular students.

New to This Edition

Since the publication of the fifth edition, significant changes have been made in many of the legal subjects covered in the text. This sixth edition incorporates those changes while retaining coverage of the fundamental rules and principles of business law. Specifically, this edition retains the overall organization, chapter format, and pedagogical features of the first five editions, and incorporates a number of important revisions and additions:

1. To reflect changes in the law since the fifth edition was written, many new topics are covered and many existing substantive law discussions have been revised and updated. Listed below are some of the important changes and additions:

- Expanded coverage of federal diversity jurisdiction (Chapter 1).
- Expanded coverage of personal jurisdiction (Chapter 2).
- New coverage of 2005 federal class action amendments (Chapter 2).
- Additional coverage of removal jurisdiction (Chapter 2).
- Revised text reflecting Revised Article 1 of Uniform Commercial Code (Chapter 6 and all other Article 1 references in the text).
- New coverage of Incoterms 2000 shipping terms published by the International Chamber of Commerce (Chapter 16 and Appendix B).
- Expanded coverage of the check collection process (Chapter 27).
- Expanded coverage of Fair Credit Reporting Act as amended in 2003 (Chapter 28).
- Revision of the bankruptcy material to reflect major changes made by 2005 amendments (Chapter 30).
- Revision of the documents of title material to reflect the 2003 revision of UCC Article 7 (Chapter 35).
- Coverage of the 2001 revised Uniform Limited Partnership Act (Chapter 44).
- Coverage of 2004 and 2005 amendments to the Model Business Corporation Act regarding duties of officers and directors of public companies (Chapter 47).
- Revision of the securities regulation material to reflect changes in public offering rules adopted by the SEC in 2005 (Chapter 49).
- Expanded coverage of insider trading (Chapter 49).
- New coverage of the Sarbanes-Oxley Act of 2002 (Chapter 49).

2. New cases—twenty new cases have been added to improve and update the case coverage.

3. Glossary—The glossary has been updated, revised and expanded to include new terms and additional cross references to definitions of related terms.

Content Features

Some of the unique or distinctive features of this text's coverage include the following:

1. *Constitutional Framework of Government Regulation of Business:* Chapter 4, The Constitution and Business Regulation, explains the constitutional framework of government regulation of business. This chapter provides the background for the detailed coverage of securities regulation, antitrust law, employment and labor law, and environmental law contained in Part Eight of the text (Government Regulation of Business, Chapters 49–55).

2. *Property and the UCC:* Chapter 6, Introduction to Property and the Uniform Commercial Code, discusses property and the Uniform Commercial Code (UCC), topics important to a complete understanding of the comprehensive contracts, sales, negotiable instruments, debtor-creditor, and property coverage in Parts Two through Six of the text (Chapters 7–39).

3. *Careful Integration of Sales Contract Material:* Coverage of Article 2 of the Uniform Commercial Code, governing contracts for the sale of goods, is carefully integrated into the basic contracts material (Chapters 7–15). This approach minimizes needless duplication in coverage, and compares and contrasts Code and common-law contracts principles on a topic-by-topic basis.

4. *Tort Law Focus:* Four separate chapters, Chapter 5, Tort Law; Chapter 20, Products Liability; Chapter 41, Agency and Torts; and Chapter 56, Accountants' Liability, focus on this important topic.

5. *Extensive Consumer Protection Coverage:* The text includes discussion of unconscionability and contracts of adhesion, fraud, warranty (including the Magnuson-Moss Warranty Act), Federal Trade Commission holder in due course rule, Consumer Credit Protection Act, consumer bankruptcy under Chapters 7 and 13 of the Bankruptcy Code, warranty of habitability in residential leases, and consumer protection under the Federal Trade Commission Act.

6. *CPA Examination Coverage:* All topics tested on the Uniform Certified Public Accountants Examination are covered, including accountants' liability, insurance law, and principal and income allocation.

7. *International Legal Problems:* Chapter 58 is devoted to this important topic, and cases and textual discussions involving international issues are integrated throughout the text.

8. *Technology Law:* Chapter 59 includes extensive coverage of intellectual property, computers and the law, the Internet and E-commerce, and the Uniform Electronic Transactions Act.

Pedagogical Aids

Each chapter begins with a listing of major topics and concludes with a summary of the principles covered in the chapter. Legal case excerpts are integrated into the chapters and questions and problems follow each chapter. Additional pedagogical aids include:

1. Cases are chosen to illustrate and reinforce legal concepts discussed in the text. Some cases supplement textual material by explaining or developing the history or rationale for a legal principle. Cases have been edited to retain the court's reasoning and policy and the court's application of its holding to the facts of the case. The facts are summarized in sufficient detail to give the reader a clear understanding of the events underlying the controversy. These features facilitate using the cases for class discussion and promote student understanding. The cases represent a mix of classic and recent cases and are drawn from both the state and federal court systems.

2. Within chapters, key terms and concepts are boldfaced where defined or first discussed and compiled in a list at the end of the chapter. In addition, key terms are defined in the author-prepared glossary that contains 1,185 entries and hundreds of definitional and statutory cross-references.

3. At the end of each chapter are a series of questions and problems. Some of the questions review the concepts discussed in the text, while others expand the focus to address related subjects or issues not covered in the text. In many instances, the questions are based on actual court cases.

4. A guide to reading the legal case excerpts presented in the text follows the preface.

5. A glossary, a table of cases, and a subject index are included at the end of the text.

Ancillary Package

To enhance student learning and to facilitate instruction, an expanded ancillary package is available.

1. *Instructor's Manual.* Prepared by the author and Christie L. Roszkowski, the completely revised and updated instructor's manual contains teaching outlines, briefs of cases included in the text, and discussion of questions and problems appearing at the end of each chapter.

2. *Study Guide.* Prepared by Gregory J. Naples of Marquette University, this completely revised study guide includes chapter outlines, chapter review tests, as well as other activity-based material.

3. *Test Bank.* Prepared by Gregory J. Naples of Marquette University, the test bank contains over 1,500 true/false, multiple choice, fill-in, and short answer questions correlated to each chapter in *Business Law: Principles, Cases, and Policy.*

4. *Business Law for the CPA Candidate* (8th ed. 2005) Prepared by Mark E. Roszkowski, this volume contains a selection of questions from the Uniform CPA Examinations from 1974 through 2003. These questions are organized into outlines that correspond to the organization of the text chapters.

Acknowledgments

As in previous editions, I have been assisted in this revision by contributing author Christie L. Roszkowski, Associate Professor of Business Law at Eastern Illinois University, who selected and edited many of the cases and drafted many discussion questions and text discussions. I also would like to thank Gregory J. Naples, Marquette University, who wrote the study guide and test bank. Finally, I would like to thank Carol Nelson, who, since June 1983, has expertly typed every draft of the text and the instructor's manual.

Mark E. Roszkowski
January 2006

Case Format

Edited opinions of actual cases are reprinted throughout this text to illustrate how rules of law are applied to factual situations. The following information will help you understand the format of each edited opinion.

Name of Case

The formal name of the case is reprinted at the beginning of the case; for example, *Smith v. Jones, California v. Brown, Acme Corporation v. Motor Company.* Only the listed first party on each side is shown in the case name. For example, if Johnson and Green sued Banks, Inc., the case name would be *Johnson v. Banks, Inc.*

Sometimes the case name may include a procedural phrase. For example, *ex rel.* (meaning "on the relation of" or "on behalf of") may be used as follows: *California ex rel. Washington v. ABC Co.* This phrase indicates the state of California is acting on behalf of the party named Washington in a suit against ABC Co. Another frequently used phrase is *In re* which generally means "in the matter of." A case entitled *In re Will of Garcia* concerns a legal proceeding involving the will of Garcia. Bankruptcy cases also are prefaced with the term *In re.*

Citation to Legal Reporter (including court of decision and date)

Decisions of court cases are published in volumes known as reporters. West Publishing Company has developed a national reporter system of state and federal court opinions. Table 1 provides a list of the reporters (including the courts covered by each reporter).

All citations are listed in the same format: volume, abbreviated name of reporter, first page of opinion. Thus, for example, 377 P.2d 897 indicates that the case is printed in Volume 377 of the Pacific Reporter, Second Series, at page 897.

Following the citation, the court of decision and the date of the decision are listed in parentheses. For state court opinions, only the name of the state is shown if the decision was written by the state's highest court. If, however, the decision was rendered by an intermediate appellate court, the abbreviation "App." (meaning Appellate Court) follows the state name. To illustrate, (Mich. 1986) indicates that the decision was rendered by the Supreme Court of Michigan in 1986. (Fla. App. 1975) indicates an opinion rendered by an intermediate appellate court of Florida in 1975.

For federal court cases, the name of the federal appellate court or district is listed with the date of decision in parentheses following the citation. United States Supreme Court cases show only the date in parentheses. For example (2d Cir. 1982), indicates that the decision was rendered by the federal Second Circuit Court of Appeals in 1982. "(S.D.N.Y. 1964)" means that the decision was written by the federal district court for the Southern District of New York in 1964. Decisions rendered by a federal bankruptcy court list "Bkrtcy." and the federal district. For example, "(Bkrtcy., N.D. Ill. 1986)" indicates an opinion written by the Bankruptcy Court for the Northern District of Illinois in 1986. For cases without national reporter system citations, citations to online legal databases are used.

Summary of Facts and Prior Legal Proceedings

Following the citation, the facts underlying the dispute and a history of the proceedings in the lower court or courts are presented. This summary has been written by the author and includes the facts pertinent to the reprinted portion of the opinion.

Edited Court Opinion

The name of the judge who wrote the decision precedes the opinion. An ellipse (. . .) indicates that part of the decision or a citation to legal authority has been edited or deleted. Brackets ([ ]) indicate material inserted by the author.

Disposition

At the conclusion of the opinion, the court's disposition of the case usually is stated in brackets. "Affirmed" means the court has upheld the decision of the lower court. "Reversed"

Table 1	Coverage of National Reporter System	

Reporter Abbreviation	Reporter	Courts Covered
Federal Courts		
S.Ct.	Supreme Court Reporter	U.S. Supreme Court
F. F.2d F.3d	Federal Reporter Federal Reporter, 2d Series Federal Reporter, 3d Series	U.S. Circuit Courts of Appeals
Fed. Appx.	Federal Appendix	U.S. Circuit Courts of Appeals (cases not published in Federal Reporter series)
F.Supp. F.Supp.2d	Federal Supplement Federal Supplement, 2d Series	U.S. District Courts
F.R.D.	Federal Rules Decisions	U.S. District Courts
B.R.	Bankruptcy Reporter	Bankruptcy cases from U.S. Bankruptcy Courts and other federal courts
Cl. Ct.	Claims Court Reporter	U.S. Claims Court and other federal courts reviewing Claims Court decisions
M.J.	Military Justice Reporter	United States Court of Military Appeals; courts of military review
State Courts		
A. A.2d	Atlantic Reporter Atlantic Reporter, 2d Series	Connecticut, Delaware, Maine, Maryland, New Hampshire, New Jersey, Pennsylvania, Rhode Island, Vermont, District of Columbia
N.E. N.E.2d	North Eastern Reporter North Eastern Reporter, 2d Series	Illinois, Indiana, Massachusetts, New York, Ohio
N.W. N.W.2d	North Western Reporter North Western Reporter, 2d Series	Iowa, Michigan, Minnesota, Nebraska, North Dakota, South Dakota, Wisconsin
P. P.2d P.3d	Pacific Reporter Pacific Reporter, 2d Series Pacific Reporter, 3d Series	Alaska, Arizona, California, Colorado, Hawaii, Idaho, Kansas, Montana, Nevada, New Mexico, Oklahoma, Oregon, Utah, Washington, Wyoming
S.E. S.E.2d	South Eastern Reporter South Eastern Reporter, 2d Series	Georgia, North Carolina, South Carolina, Virginia, West Virginia
S.W. S.W.2d S.W.3d	South Western Reporter South Western Reporter, 2d Series South Western Reporter, 3d Series	Arkansas, Kentucky, Missouri, Tennessee, Texas
So. So.2d	Southern Reporter Southern Reporter, 2d Series	Alabama, Florida, Louisiana, Mississippi
Cal.Rptr. Cal.Rptr.2d Cal.Rptr.3d	California Reporter California Reporter, 2d Series California Reporter, 3d Series	California Supreme Court and intermediate appellate courts
N.Y.S. N.Y.S.2d	New York Supplement New York Supplement, 2d Series	All New York state courts

indicates that the lower court's decision was voided. "Remanded" means the case was sent back to a lower court.

Studying a Case

Analyze each case to ensure that you understand its ruling. Every student develops a method of analyzing a case but that analysis at least should include consideration of the following factors.

1. What is the legal issue presented to the court? The facts present a question of law to the court and you should identify this issue.

2. What is the holding of the case? In other words, what is the court's conclusion of law that resolves the issue? The court's holding determines the legal effect of the facts of the case.

3. What is the court's reasoning? Most of the edited opinions include the court's explanation of the reasons for reaching its holding. In some cases the judge will comment on some rule of law that is not necessarily involved in, or essential to the determination of, the case under consideration. Or, the court may enunciate a legal principle or rule for purposes of illustration, analogy, or argument. These comments are known as *dicta* (from the Latin *obiter dictum* meaning "a remark by the way"). Although *dicta* is not part of the court's holding, it may provide insight into the court's reasoning.

4. What is the effect of the court's holding on the factual controversy under review? Consider how the rule of law resolves the factual dispute and determine which party won the case.

Read the following case. At the conclusion, the case is analyzed in the manner suggested above.

E. I. du Pont deNemours & Company, Inc. v. Christopher

431 F.2d 1012 (5th Cir. 1970)

Plaintiff E. I. du Pont deNemours & Company, Inc. (DuPont) was constructing a plant for production of methanol in Beaumont, Texas. After DuPont employees noticed an airplane circling over the construction site, DuPont investigated and discovered that defendants Rolfe and Gary Christopher were taking aerial photographs of the site. The Christophers told DuPont that they had been hired to take the photographs but refused to disclose their client's name.

DuPont sued the Christophers alleging that they had wrongfully appropriated DuPont's trade secrets by taking the photographs. DuPont claimed that it had developed a secret process for producing methanol and that photographs of the construction site would enable a skilled person to deduce the secret process. The Christophers alleged that under Texas law, photographing the construction site did not constitute wrongful appropriation of trade secrets. Following a hearing, the trial court ruled that Texas law recognized a claim for wrongful appropriation of trade secrets based on the facts alleged by DuPont. Prior to holding a trial or further proceedings, the trial court allowed the Christophers to appeal the ruling.

Goldberg, Circuit Judge

. . . The question . . . is whether aerial photography of plant construction is an improper means of obtaining another's trade secret. We conclude that it is and that the Texas courts would so hold. . . .

We think . . . that the Texas rule is clear. One may use his competitor's secret process if he discovers the process by reverse engineering applied to the finished product; one may use a competitor's process if he discovers it by his own independent research; but one may not avoid these labors by taking the process from the discoverer without his permission at a time when he is taking reasonable precautions to maintain its secrecy. To obtain knowledge of a process without spending the time and money to discover it independently is *improper* unless the holder voluntarily discloses it or fails to take reasonable precautions to ensure its secrecy.

In the instant case the Christophers deliberately flew over the DuPont plant to get pictures of a process which DuPont had attempted to keep secret. The Christophers delivered their pictures to a third party who was certainly aware of the means by which they had been acquired and who may be planning to use the information contained therein to manufacture methanol by the DuPont process. The third party has a right to use this process only if he obtains this knowledge through his own research efforts, but thus far all information indicates that the third party has gained this knowledge solely by taking it from DuPont at a time when DuPont was making reasonable efforts to preserve its secrecy. In such a situation DuPont has a valid cause of action to prohibit the Christophers from improperly discovering its trade secret and to prohibit the undisclosed third party from using the improperly obtained information. . . .

In taking this position we realize that industrial espionage of the sort here perpetrated has become a popular sport in some segments of our industrial community. However, our devotion to free wheeling industrial competition must not force us into accepting the law of the jungle as the standard of morality expected in our commercial relations. Our tolerance of the espionage game must cease when the protections required to prevent another's spying cost so much that the spirit of inventiveness is dampened. Commercial privacy must be protected from espionage which could not have been reasonably anticipated or prevented. We do not mean to imply, however, that everything not in plain view is within the protected vale, nor that all information obtained through every extra optical extension is forbidden. Indeed, for our industrial competition to remain healthy there must be breathing room for observing a competing industrialist. A competitor can and must shop his competition for pricing and examine his products for quality, components, and methods of manufacture. Perhaps ordinary fences and roofs must be built to shut out incursive eyes, but we need not require the discover of a trade secret to guard against the unanticipated, the undetectable, or the unpreventable methods of espionage now available.

In the instant case DuPont was in the midst of constructing a plant. Although after construction the finished plant would have protected much of the process from view, during the period of construction the trade secret was exposed to view from the air. To require DuPont to put a roof over the unfinished plant to guard its secret would impose an enormous expense to prevent nothing more than a school boy's trick. We introduce here no new or radical ethic since our ethos has never given moral sanction to piracy. The market place must not deviate far from our mores. We should not require a person or corporation to take unreasonable precautions to prevent another from doing that which he ought not do in the first place. Reasonable precautions against predatory eyes we may require, but an impenetrable fortress is an unreasonable requirement, and we are not disposed to burden industrial inventors with such a duty in order to protect the fruits of their efforts. "Improper" will always be a word for many nuances, determined by time, place, and circumstances. We therefore need not proclaim a catalogue of commercial improprieties. Clearly, however, one of its commandments does say "thou shall not appropriate a trade secret through deviousness under circumstances in which countervailing defenses are not reasonably available." . . .

[T]he espionage was an improper means of discovering DuPont's trade secret.

[Judgment affirmed and remanded for further proceedings.]

---

1. Issue: Whether aerial photography of a plant under construction is an improper means of obtaining trade secrets.

2. Holding: Aerial photography of a plant under construction is an improper means of obtaining trade secrets.

3. Reasoning: Trade secrets properly may be obtained by reverse engineering or independent research. Other methods of obtaining trade secrets are improper unless the holder voluntarily discloses the secrets or fails to take reasonable precautions to ensure secrecy. To protect the spirit of inventiveness, holders of trade secrets must be protected from industrial espionage not reasonably anticipated or prevented.

4. Effect: Judgment for plaintiff DuPont affirmed. DuPont took reasonable efforts to preserve the secrecy of its methanol production method; therefore, third parties were not entitled to take aerial photographs of the site. DuPont may prohibit the defendants Rolfe and Gary Christopher from taking photographs of its plant and from disclosing the information to third parties.

PART ONE

INTRODUCTION TO LAW AND THE LEGAL SYSTEM

LAW AND COURTS

- an introduction to law, including the relationship between law and business, and law and ethics
- methods of classifying law
- sources of law in the United States including constitutions, statutes, and the common law
- jurisdiction, organization, and relationship between state and federal courts
- how courts determine the appropriate law to apply to cases

The news media regularly highlight stories about business and the law. Billion dollar mergers of multinational corporations, criminal convictions of business officers, multi-million dollar judgments awarded to parties injured by defective products, and corporate bankruptcies affecting thousands of employees and investors, have captured headlines and the public interest in recent years. Unfortunately, many people conceive of business law only in terms of such extraordinary cases. Although controversial or newsworthy court actions do raise complex and interesting issues, they also contribute to a conception of business law as a discipline largely removed from the everyday lives of individuals. In fact, however, business laws shape virtually all commercial activities and relationships. Whether involved in marketing, accounting, finance, production, or administration, business managers rely every day upon the intricate framework of the law. The study of that intricate framework initially requires an understanding of the nature and sources of law and the workings of the court system.

Introduction to Law and Business Law

In its most basic sense, **law** is the body of rules and principles of conduct that are enforceable through sanctions. Within every society, rules of conduct have evolved to maintain harmony and order. In more primitive societies these rules consist only of customs and norms that are enforceable through informal social sanctions. As societies increase in size and complexity, however, rules of conduct become formalized, usually through a government that adopts and enforces the rules for the society. The law of the United States, for example, consists of rules and principles of conduct that are enacted or adopted by the government, and are embodied in constitutions, statutes, and judicial decisions.

Although law preserves peace and stability, thus allowing members of society to pursue economic and social activities, it is ineffectual unless the society also develops a **legal system**—institutions and processes for enforcing the law. In the United States, the legal system consists primarily of the courts, which are a part of the government. Legal systems provide forums and processes that serve two important functions for society:

1. Government punishment of those who fail to conform to the rules of law that outline minimum socially acceptable standards of conduct; and
2. Resolution of disputes of private individuals (or entities) who cannot resolve the disputes on their own.

In performing these functions, the courts apply rules of law previously established by the government or, in the absence of such rules, develop new legal principles to maintain order. Once a court renders a decision, it has the power, with the backing of the government, to force compliance. Courts thus impose sanctions against those who fail to follow legal rules. The threat of these sanctions usually is sufficient to induce compliance with the law.

Law and Business

In the United States, the law governs the conduct of all persons, including **artificial persons** (such as corporations) as well as **natural persons** (human beings). Because businesses are considered persons and, thus, members of society, many of the legal rules and principles affecting business are merely general laws that affect all persons. For example, the rights and duties of a property owner are established by general property law, whether the property is a factory owned by a business or a private residence owned by an individual. The principles of contract law enable both individuals and businesses to rely upon agreements—for example, to purchase a home or raw material for manufacturing—by providing a private legal remedy to persons injured by another's failure to perform an agreement. Other legal rules have been established specifically to govern the conduct of businesses and business relationships. The securities laws regulate the sale and trading of the stocks and bonds issued only by businesses. Antitrust laws enacted to protect competition affect only those in business.

Law both restricts and facilitates business operations. Some laws, such as those prohibiting price-fixing or requiring a safe workplace, clearly limit business practices. In contrast, other legal rules are designed to foster or encourage business activities. Few businesses,

for example, could operate without reliable and enforceable principles of contract law that allow the sale, purchase, and exchange of goods and services. Businesses would not invest in plants and equipment without the assurance that their property rights in these items will be protected by law. Intellectual property law encourages businesses to engage in research and development. Even modern business expansion and efficiencies of scale would have been impossible without principles of agency and corporate law.

Although American law clearly affects the operation of businesses, business also influences the development of the law. For instance, the law of negligence developed initially to provide compensation for injuries resulting indirectly from the emergence of a modern, industrialized society. As businesses increased production of goods, the law of products liability developed to determine whether manufacturers and distributors should be responsible for injuries caused by their products. Entire new areas of law—such as antitrust, securities regulation, and environmental law—have been created in response to changing business activities. Today, new laws address legal issues evolving from e-commerce, computers, and other business technology. In short, business and law engage in a dynamic process, each shaping and influencing the development of the other.

Law and Ethics

Despite the law's importance as a source of rules of conduct, few societies could function effectively if they depended solely on law as a basis for social conduct. The morals—principles of right, good, and fairness—of individual members of a society provide a more informal and pervasive basis for standards of conduct. From norms, beliefs, and values, individuals develop **ethics,** systems of moral standards and beliefs, that address the most fundamental issues of social conduct, such as honesty, loyalty, fair treatment of others, and respect for human life and dignity. Like law, ethics provide standards of conduct for individuals. Unlike law, however, ethics are not imposed or enforced by an external authority such as the government. Rather, ethical standards derive from an individual's internalized moral principles and are applied by the individual. Thus, through law society imposes and enforces legal standards of conduct applicable to all of its members, while through ethics individuals develop and apply their own moral standards of conduct. The purpose of law, then, is to govern the conduct of all members of society, while ethics provide guidance for individual conduct.

Although law and ethics derive from different authorities and for different purposes, they often are related, especially in a democratic society such as the United States in which the people are the source of power. Law generally reflects basic moral principles shared by members of society because people will not long comply with a body of rules that they consider wrong or evil. Thus, a law prohibiting murder not only preserves order, but also reflects a widely held ethical belief that human life should be protected. In other cases, however, legal rules are morally neutral—for example, the law's requirement that all vehicles be driven on the right side of the road. In still other cases, the law may partially reflect moral principles but may not fully incorporate an ethical standard as the legal standard. Most people would agree, for example, that lying is immoral, but under American law, lying is illegal only in limited circumstances, such as when it constitutes perjury or fraud. Similarly, most individuals believe that it is unethical to break promises, but American law enforces only those promises that meet the requirements of a legal contract. In the following excerpt,[1] Oliver Wendell Holmes, Jr., noted legal philosopher and Associate Justice of the United States Supreme Court from 1902 to 1932, articulates his view of the distinction between law and morals:

> The first thing for a business-like understanding of the [law] is to understand its limits, and therefore I think it desirable at once to point out and dispel a confusion between morality and law. . . . You can see very plainly that a bad man has as much reason as a good one for wishing to avoid an encounter with the public force, and therefore you can see the practical importance of the distinction between morality and law. A man who cares nothing for an ethical rule which is believed and practised by his neighbors is likely nevertheless to care a good deal to avoid being made to pay money, and will want to keep out of jail if he can.
>
> I take it for granted that no hearer of mine will misinterpret what I have to say as the language of cynicism. The law is the witness and external deposit of our moral life. Its history is the history of the moral development of the race. The practice of it, in spite of popular jests, tends to make good citizens and good men. When I emphasize the differ-

[1]Holmes, *The Path of the Law,* 10 HARV. L. REV. 457, 459–460 (1897).

ence between law and morals I do so with reference to a single end, that of learning and understanding the law. . . .

> If you want to know the law and nothing else, you must look at it as a bad man, who cares only for the material consequences which such knowledge enables him to predict, not as a good one, who finds his reasons for conduct, whether inside the law or outside of it, in the vaguer sanctions of conscience. . . . The law is full of phraseology drawn from morals, and by the mere force of language continually invites us to pass from one domain to the other without perceiving it, as we are sure to do unless we have the boundary constantly before our minds. The law talks about rights, and duties, and malice, and intent, and negligence, and so forth, and nothing is easier, or I may say, more common in legal reasoning, than to take these words in their moral sense, at some stage of the argument, and so to drop into fallacy. For instance, when we speak of the rights of man in a moral sense, we mean to mark the limits of interference with individual freedom which we think are prescribed by conscience, or by our ideal, however reached. Yet it is certain that many laws have been enforced in the past, and it is likely that some are enforced now, which are condemned by the most enlightened opinion of the time, or which at all events pass the limit of interference as many consciences would draw it. Manifestly, therefore, nothing but confusion of thought can result from assuming that the rights of man in a moral sense are equally rights in the sense of the Constitution and the law. No doubt simple and extreme cases can be put of imaginary laws which the statute-making power would not dare to enact, even in the absence of written constitutional prohibitions, because the community would rise in rebellion and fight; and this gives some plausibility to the proposition that the law, if not a part of morality, is limited by it. But this limit of power is not coextensive with any system of morals. . . .

Understanding the distinction between law and morals is important in studying business law. Historically businesses often have used legal standards as the sole basis for determining appropriate social conduct. This perspective is reflected in the following statement by the chief executive of a company accused of using a cheap—and possibly harmful—form of alcohol in manufacturing mouthwash:

> We broke no law. We're in a highly competitive industry. If we're going to stay in business, we have to look for profit wherever the law permits. We don't make the laws. We obey them. Then why do we have to put up

with this "holier than thou" talk about ethics? It's sheer hypocrisy. We're not in business to promote ethics. Look at the cigarette companies, for God's sake! If the ethics aren't embodied in the laws by the men who made them, you can't expect businessmen to fill the lack. Why, a sudden submission to Christian ethics by businessmen would bring about the greatest economic upheaval in history![2]

As suggested by this quotation, many businesspeople believe that establishing standards of commercial conduct is the responsibility not of businesses but of the government through its power to make laws. Others believe ethical matters are beyond the scope of business decisions, arguing instead that the common good is best served by strict adherence to the free market theory of competition. This viewpoint was expressed by economist Milton Friedman as follows:

> The view has been gaining widespread acceptance that corporate officials and labor leaders have a "social responsibility" that goes beyond serving the interest of their stockholders or their members. This view shows a fundamental misconception of the character and nature of a free economy. In such an economy, there is one and only one social responsibility of business—to use its resources and engage in activities designed to increase its profits so long as it stays within the rules of the game, which is to say, engages in open and free competition, without deception or fraud. . . . Few trends could so thoroughly undermine the very foundations of our free society as the acceptance by corporate officials of a social responsibility other than to make as much money for their stockholders as possible.[3]

More recently, however, as businesses have grown in both size and influence, many people recognize that businesses are social as well as economic entities. This dual economic and social aspect of business is especially evident in large corporations whose conduct affects not only shareholders but also suppliers, customers, consumers, employees, and sometimes even entire communities. In contrast to the position articulated by Milton Friedman, many people now suggest that businesses, which operate as distinct, but artificial persons, have the same obligations as natural persons to

develop and apply ethical standards. This point of view is summarized as follows:

> A corporation can and should have a conscience. The language of ethics does have a place in the vocabulary of an organization. . . . Organizational agents such as corporations should be no more and no less morally responsible (rational, self-interested, altruistic) than ordinary persons. . . . Legal systems of rules and incentives are insufficient, even though they may be necessary, as frameworks for corporate responsibility. Taking conceptual cues from the features of moral responsibility normally expected of the person in our opinion deserves practicing managers' serious consideration.[4]

Even businesses that acknowledge an obligation to act ethically or morally have had difficulty in developing and implementing procedures to meet this obligation. Part of the difficulty stems from a growing realization that moral issues can arise from all aspects of business operations. Traditionally, discussion of business ethics was restricted to topics such as deceptive advertising, honesty in contract negotiations, and bribery. Today, however, ethical considerations affect all areas of business:

1. Marketers regularly encounter ethical dilemmas such as: establishing fair prices, copying ideas of competitors and suppliers, determining whether to sell dangerous products, and increasing sales through planned obsolescence of products.
2. Operations managers routinely take into account moral factors, such as employee safety, environmental impact, and product quality in developing processes for producing goods and services.
3. Financial managers—when analyzing or implementing plant closings, mergers, acquisitions, and restructurings—need to consider ethical implications because of potential impact on both shareholders and stakeholders.
4. Human resource professionals need to consider the fairness of hiring, firing, and promotion practices; the ethics of employee monitoring; and health and safety issues that may affect employees.
5. Accountants and others who control business data face ethical considerations in determining whether information is presented fairly.

---

[2]Carr, *Is Business Bluffing Ethical?* HARV. BUS. REV. (Jan.–Feb. 1968) at 143, 148.
[3]FRIEDMAN, CAPITALISM AND FREEDOM 133 (1962).

---

[4]Goodpaster & Matthews, *Can a Corporation Have a Conscience?* HARV. BUS. REV. (Jan.–Feb. 1982) at 132, 133, 138.

In short, almost all business decisions, but especially those with uncertain and extended consequences that affect many individuals, other organizations, and even government operations, can present significant ethical questions.

Codes of ethics, similar to those used by attorneys, physicians, engineers, and other professionals, can provide guidance for business decision-making. No ethical code has been developed to cover all businesses, but many industries and trade associations have adopted codes applicable to their members. Similarly, corporations increasingly are developing formal codes of ethics or conduct to help guide employees in considering ethical issues during the decision-making process.

Although legal standards should not be equated with moral standards for purposes of ethical inquiry, the principles of business law discussed in this text provide an opportunity to examine both ethical issues and legal issues. In many cases, for example, the rule of law provides an ethical minimum to which a business should at least adhere. Knowledge of the rule of law can help frame issues and establish basic premises. Finally, because business ethics is an area of applied ethics, the factual situations presented in the legal cases reprinted throughout the text provide a concrete basis for ethical inquiry.

Classifications of Law

Legal study encompasses a wide variety of subjects. Before examining specific topics, it is helpful to examine the broad general characteristics of legal rules and principles. These characteristics, common to many legal systems, provide a basis for classifying or categorizing the various areas of law. The following sections discuss traditional methods of classifying law.

Substantive and Procedural Law. Law may be classified as either substantive or procedural. **Substantive law** defines the rights to which a person is entitled and the duties a person is obligated to perform. Rights and duties are correlative: for each right there exists a corresponding duty. A person's right to freedom of speech, for example, imposes a corresponding duty on the government not to restrain that freedom. The rules of substantive law compose what most people consider the law. This text primarily concerns the substantive legal rules that govern business transactions including property, contracts, commercial paper, debtor-creditor relations, business organizations, and government regulation of business.

Procedural law establishes the mechanisms to enforce the rights and duties created by substantive law. Because the courts are the primary forum for applying and enforcing the law, much procedural law concerns the process by which rights and duties may be enforced in courts. Procedural law includes the rules for initiating a lawsuit, conducting a trial, and appealing a judgment.

Substantive and procedural law are interdependent, as illustrated in the following example. The rules of substantive property law grant a landowner the right to exclude others from entering on his or her land; all persons have a duty not to enter on land that is owned by others. Violation of this duty is known as "trespass." Assume that Doaks and Jones are adjoining landowners and recently Jones has driven her car over Doaks's land as a shortcut to her own property. Despite Doaks's request that Jones stay off his land, she has refused.

Procedural law provides a method by which Doaks may enforce his right and Jones's duty. Doaks may file a lawsuit against Jones in the local court and may request a judge to order Jones to stay off his land and to pay for any damages that Jones has caused. If the judge finds that Jones committed trespass, the judge may order her to cease entering on Doaks's land and to pay for damage to the land. If Jones refuses to comply with the judge's orders, the judge, after further procedures, may impose sanctions to force compliance.

Thus, substantive and procedural law are complementary. Without the enforcement mechanisms of the procedural law, substantive rights and duties are illusory. Without the substantive law, however, procedural law is unnecessary because there are no rights and duties to enforce.

Criminal and Civil Law. Both substantive and procedural law may be further classified as either criminal or civil law. **Criminal law** consists of principles and rules that protect society as a whole by establishing certain minimum standards of acceptable conduct and punishing those who fail to meet those standards. Criminal law thus creates duties owed to the community or public at large and is penal in nature. Substantive criminal law defines the classes of conduct deemed particularly injurious to the public welfare—such as murder, robbery, or assault—and establishes a penalty—such as a fine, prison term, or even capital punishment—for those who are found guilty of committing the acts. Procedural criminal law establishes the rules for legal proceedings (prosecutions) that determine the guilt or innocence of those who allegedly have violated the substantive criminal law. In criminal proceedings, the government acts on behalf of society by initiating prosecutions, and society as a whole benefits from the penalty imposed on convicted wrongdoers.

In contrast, **civil law** concerns relations between individuals and is remedial in nature. Although both criminal and civil law establish standards of conduct, civil law is enforced not by the government, but by the party who was injured by the violation of the civil law. The injured party brings the dispute to court, seeking a personal remedy from the alleged wrongdoer. If a court finds that the person violated the rules of civil law, the wrongdoer is held liable—or responsible—for the resulting injuries. The injured party then is entitled to a judicial remedy, usually the payment of money, to compensate for the injury.

Some conduct may violate both civil and criminal law. Criminal law, for example, requires an automobile driver who exceeds the maximum speed limit to pay a penalty. The government may prosecute the driver, who must pay a fine if found guilty. If the driver also caused an accident while driving over the speed limit, he may have violated a civil law that prohibits negligent (careless) conduct. A person injured in the accident might sue the driver who, if a court finds negligence, may be held liable for the negligently caused injuries. In this situation, the criminal law serves to protect society: a maximum speed limit reduces the likelihood of an automobile accident that would interfere with safe and peaceful travel on thoroughfares. The civil law protects the individual by creating a source of compensation to someone injured by another's carelessness.

Public and Private Law. Legal subjects often are designated as either public or private. **Public law** consists of principles and rules that involve the government in its capacity of representing society. In public law, the government or an agency of the government participates and acts on behalf of society. For example, in criminal law, which is one area of public law, the government as a representative of society brings the wrongdoer to court. Other areas of public law include constitutional and administrative law.[5]

Private law consists of rules and principles that involve persons (whether artificial or natural) as private individuals. Much of civil law is private law. Private law cases may involve the government, but in its capacity as a member of society rather than as a representative of society. Traditionally, private law has encompassed three areas of law: torts, property, and contracts, all of which are discussed later in the text.[6]

Derivation of American Legal Systems

The general classifications and functions of law described above provided a basis for establishing a legal system in the United States at the time the colonies won their independence from England. At that time, two general legal systems existed in Western Europe: common law (in England) and civil law (in most other countries). The civil law system, which evolved from Roman law, establishes all basic principles of law in a code, a collection of statutes adopted by a parliamentary body. The founders chose to base the American legal system on English common law. Today, common law systems are used in all states but Louisiana, which has established a civil law system.

Under a traditional common law system, the basic principles of law are set forth in case law, decisions written by judges to resolve specific cases. The common law historically is based on custom. When resolving disputes, the judges of the court refer to prior cases to ascertain how similar disputes were resolved and apply the customary law derived from the preceding cases to resolve the current dispute.

Many familiar elements of American law originated in the English common law courts. The use of a jury in both criminal and civil cases was a common law practice. The adversarial system in which each party to a dispute presents its case to the court was characteristic of the common law courts. These courts also employed the remedy of awarding money damages (the "remedy at law") to injured parties in civil cases.

---

[5]Criminal law is discussed above and in Chapter 3. Constitutional law issues are discussed throughout the introductory chapters, particularly Chapters 3 and 4. Administrative law is discussed in Chapter 4.

[6]Tort law is introduced in Chapter 5. Property law is introduced in Chapter 6 and is discussed in Part VI. Contract law is discussed in Parts II and III.

The American legal system also adopted principles and procedures from a complementary English court system known as **courts of chancery** or **courts of equity**. This separate court system developed in England, under the supervision of the chancellor (a clergyman who served as an advisor to the monarch), during a period in which the common law courts had become inflexible because of rigid procedural rules. The common law courts, for example, were prohibited from recognizing new types of claims and were limited to providing only damages (that is, monetary awards) as a remedy to injured parties. The principal purpose of the courts of chancery was to provide fair and equitable resolution of disputes without being restricted by inflexible procedures.

Unlike the common law courts, the courts of equity operated without juries and used broad concepts of fairness and justice, rather than custom or prior case law, to resolve disputes. An important contribution of the chancery courts was creation of new remedies—called "equitable remedies"—that could be used when money damages were not adequate. Perhaps the most significant of these remedies was the injunction, an order requiring a party to do or refrain from doing some act. Other equitable remedies included rescission (an order voiding contracts obtained unfairly), and specific performance (an order requiring a party to perform contractual obligations). Equitable remedies continue to be available today in American courts but only if, in the discretion of the court (judge), money damages provide an inadequate remedy.

The Role of an Attorney

An **attorney** (attorney at law, lawyer, counselor at law) is a person who has been authorized by one or more states to practice law on behalf of clients. The attorney plays an important role in the American legal system. The American Bar Association has summarized the general functions of the attorney as follows:

> As advisor, a lawyer provides a client with an informed understanding of the client's legal rights and obligations and explains their practical implications. As advocate, a lawyer zealously asserts the client's position under the rules of the adversary system. As negotiator, a lawyer seeks a result advantageous to the client but consistent with requirements of honest dealing with others. As an evaluator, a lawyer acts by examining a client's legal

affairs and reporting about them to the client or to others.[7]

The specific functions of an attorney depend on the wants and needs of the individual client. Lawyers representing business clients frequently draft documents (such as contracts, trusts, partnership agreements, corporate charters and bylaws) as well as act as advisor, advocate, or negotiator. Some business clients routinely seek an attorney's advice prior to making major business decisions; others consult an attorney only if they recognize that a question of law or a legal dispute has arisen. Large businesses increasingly have employed "in-house counsel"—lawyers who work solely for the business—to participate in day-to-day business operations and provide legal advice.

American law requires attorneys to comply with a variety of ethical and professional duties and responsibilities. Although the specific duties may vary from state to state, attorneys are required to maintain the highest standard of ethics and conduct in relation to a client. A lawyer is required to exercise independent professional judgment on behalf of a client and to represent a client competently and zealously within the bounds of the law. An attorney also must preserve the confidence and secrets revealed by a client while seeking legal advice.

To encourage complete and open communications between lawyer and client, all states recognize an attorney-client privilege that prevents an attorney from disclosing communications made with a client while seeking legal advice. A client may, however, waive the privilege and consent to the disclosure. Although the privilege covers a client's admission of previous criminal acts, it does not extend to a client's proposed criminal or fraudulent acts. In general, an attorney is required to discourage a client from committing criminal or fraudulent acts and, if unsuccessful, may be required to reveal the proposed unlawful conduct to the proper authorities.

The American Bar Association and many states maintain committees that render confidential opinions to attorneys who are uncertain of their ethical duties in a specific situation. If a client believes an attorney has breached his or her ethical duties, most states—through the judiciary, bar association, or licensing authority—provide a procedure to review alleged misconduct. An

---

[7]MODEL RULES OF PROFESSIONAL CONDUCT Preamble: A Lawyer's Responsibilities (2002).

attorney who has violated ethical or professional duties is subject to discipline, including loss of the privilege to practice law, by state authorities.

Sources of Law in the United States

Under the democratic form of government in the United States, the people are considered the sovereign and, thus, are the source of all powers, including the power to establish law. The American people have adopted a republican form of government in which elected representatives exercise these powers. In general, therefore, the government in its representative capacity is the source of law in the United States.

The United States operates under a system of federalism with two levels of government. At the national level, the federal government adopts and enforces laws that are binding on the citizens of all states. Additionally, each of the 50 states that compose the United States enacts laws that are effective within that state. The governments at both the state and federal levels are organized in accordance with the doctrine of separation of powers so that governmental powers are divided among the three branches of government, each possessing checks upon the powers of the others. The legislative branch adopts written laws called "statutes," which are executed by the executive branch of the government. The judicial branch of government enforces the law in specific cases and controversies presented to the courts. The laws applied by the judiciary derive from three principal sources: constitutions, statutes, and the common law.

Constitutions

A **constitution** establishes the basic principles, governmental structure, and law of a state or nation. Each of the United States has adopted its own written constitution and all of the states have ratified the federal Constitution and have agreed to comply with its provisions.

United States Constitution. The United States Constitution is the written agreement that binds the states together as a federation. It consists of seven articles adopted in 1787 and 27 amendments adopted between 1791 and 1992. The Constitution serves three important functions: (1) it limits the powers of the states and their governments; (2) it enumerates the powers that the states have delegated to the federal government; and (3) it guarantees certain rights to the people of the United States.

Limitation on States' Powers. As a sovereign entity, each state has the inherent power to enact and enforce its own laws. The federal Constitution, however, restricts this power by making state law subordinate to federal law. The **Supremacy Clause** of Article VI of the Constitution provides:

> This Constitution, and the Laws of the United States which shall be made in Pursuance thereof; and all Treaties made, or which shall be made, under the Authority of the United States shall be the supreme Law of the Land; and the Judges in every State shall be bound thereby, any Thing in the Constitution or Laws of any State to the Contrary notwithstanding.

The Supremacy Clause requires a court to invalidate and refuse to enforce any state law that conflicts with the federal Constitution, federal statutes, or federal treaties. The Supremacy Clause provides a general limitation on state powers, but other provisions of the Constitution more specifically restrict state powers. These provisions, for example, prohibit the states from entering into treaties with foreign nations, taxing imports and exports, impairing contractual obligations, and coining money.

Enumeration of Federal Powers. Unlike the states, the federal government has no inherent powers but possesses only those powers that the states have delegated to it. The Constitution enumerates those delegated powers; the states have retained all other powers.

Article I of the Constitution establishes Congress (consisting of the House of Representatives and the Senate) as the legislative branch of government and sets forth the congressional powers. Congress is empowered, for example, to impose taxes, to regulate interstate commerce and commerce with foreign countries, to issue currency, to appropriate money, to reduce or expand the number of courts, and to provide for the national defense. Congress exercises its powers by enacting federal statutes. The House of Representatives also has the power, in appropriate cases, to impeach judicial and executive officers, and the Senate has the power to try all impeachments.

Article II of the Constitution vests the executive powers of the federal government in the president, who appoints executive officers, including a cabinet, to assist in performing executive duties. In addition to executing federal laws, the president serves as commander-in-chief of the armed forces. As a check on the legislative power, the president has the power to veto acts of Congress, which Congress may override only by a two-thirds vote of both houses. The president also has the power, with the advice and consent of the Senate, to make treaties with foreign nations and to appoint ambassadors and Supreme Court justices.

Article III of the Constitution grants federal judicial power to the United States Supreme Court and other federal courts established by Congress. The federal courts can hear only limited types of cases, which are discussed in detail later in this chapter. Under the **doctrine of judicial review,** federal courts have the power to determine whether the acts of the legislative and executive branches of government comply with the Constitution and to refuse to enforce those acts that violate it. Although this doctrine, which imposes a significant limitation on the powers of the other branches, is not explicitly stated in the Constitution, the United States Supreme Court asserted its existence in the following landmark case.

Marbury v. Madison

5 U.S. (1 Cranch) 137 (1803)

In the election of 1800, Thomas Jefferson, a Republican, defeated the incumbent president John Adams, a Federalist. Following the election, President Adams appointed Federalists to fill 42 vacancies as federal justices of the peace and initiated the formal appointment procedure that required the secretary of state to deliver sealed commissions to the appointees. All of the commissions, however, were not delivered prior to the inauguration of Jefferson, and the new secretary of state, James Madison, refused to deliver the remaining commissions. William Marbury, an appointee who had not received his commission, filed suit in the Supreme Court requesting a writ of mandamus ordering Madison to deliver the commissions. (A writ of mandamus is an order issued by a court commanding a public official to perform a specific act or duty.) Marbury asserted his right to bring his suit in the Supreme Court based on the Judiciary Act of 1789, a federal statute that authorized the Supreme Court "to issue writs of mandamus . . . to persons holding office under the authority of the United States."

Although the case was fraught with political issues, the Supreme Court focused on a narrow issue: whether the provisions of the Judiciary Act of 1789 violated the Constitution. The Constitution enumerates the types of cases that may be brought to the Supreme Court and these cases do not include disputes seeking a writ of mandamus to federal officials. The Supreme Court concluded that Congress's attempt to expand the types of cases that the Court may hear to include those cases not listed in the Constitution was "repugnant" to the Constitution. The Court then considered whether it should follow the law established by the Judiciary Act of 1789.

Chief Justice Marshall

. . . The question, whether an act, repugnant to the constitution can become the law of the land, is a question deeply interesting to the United States. . . .

The powers of the legislature are defined and limited; and that those limits may not be mistaken, or forgotten, the constitution is written. To what purpose are powers limited, and to what purpose is that limitation committed to writing, if these limits may, at any time, be passed by those intended to be restrained? . . . The constitution is either a superior paramount law, unchangeable by ordinary means, or it is on a level with ordinary legislative acts, and, like other acts, is alterable when the legislative shall please to alter it. If the former part of the alternative be true, then a legislative act contrary to the constitution is not law: if the latter part be true, then written constitutions are absurd attempts, on the part of the people, to limit a power in its own nature illimitable. Certainly all those who have framed written constitutions contemplate them as forming the fundamental and paramount law of the nation, and, consequently, the theory of every such government must be, that an act of the legislature, repugnant to the constitution, is void. . . .

If an act of the legislature, repugnant to the constitution, is void, does it, notwithstanding its invalidity, bind the courts, and oblige them to give it effect? Or, in other words, though it be not law, does it constitute a rule as operative as if it was a law? . . .

It is emphatically the province and duty of the judicial department to say what the law is. Those who apply the rule to particular cases, must of necessity expound and interpret that rule. If two laws conflict with each other, the courts must decide on the operation of each. So if a law be in opposition to the constitution; if both the law and the constitution apply to a particular case, so that the court must either decide that case conformably to the law, disregarding the constitution; or conformably to the constitution, disregarding the law; the court must determine which of these conflicting rules governs the case. This is of the very essence of judicial duty. If, then, the courts are to regard the constitution, and the constitution is superior to any ordinary act of the legislature, the constitution, and not such ordinary act, must govern the case to which they both apply. . . .

The judicial power of the United States is extended to all cases arising under the constitution. Could it be the intention of those who gave this power, to say that in using it the constitution should not be looked into? That a case arising under the constitution should be decided without examining the instrument under which it arises? This is too extravagant to be maintained. In some cases, then, the constitution must be looked into by the judges. And if they can open it at all, what part of it are they forbidden to read or to obey? . . . [T]he framers of the constitution contemplated that instrument as a rule for the government of courts, as well as of the legislature. . . .

It is also not entirely unworthy of observation, that in declaring what shall be the supreme law of the land, the constitution itself is first mentioned; and not the laws of the United States generally, but those only which shall be made in pursuance of the constitution, have that rank. Thus, the particular phraseology of the constitution of the United States confirms and strengthens the principle, supposed to be essential to all written constitutions, that a law repugnant to the constitution is void; and that courts, as well as other departments, are bound by that instrument.

Guarantee of Individual Rights. In addition to limiting the powers of the states and enumerating the powers of the three branches of the federal government, the Constitution delineates certain rights that are guaranteed to United States citizens. Most of these rights are set forth in the Bill of Rights, the first ten amendments to the Constitution. Included in the Bill of Rights are the people's rights to freedom of speech and religion, to freedom from unreasonable searches and seizures, to a speedy and public trial by an impartial jury in criminal prosecutions, and to due process of law. The Constitution imposes a duty on the government not to infringe on these rights of individuals.

State Constitutions. In addition to the federal Constitution, each state has adopted its own constitution. Although the provisions of these constitutions vary, each generally outlines the principles and organization of the state's government and the rights guaranteed to citizens of the state, and divides the state powers among executive, legislative, and judicial branches of government. All state constitutions establish multilevel state judicial systems with trial courts for resolution of disputes and controversies and one or more appellate courts to review the decisions rendered by the trial courts. State court systems are discussed in more detail later in this chapter.

Statutes

Statutes—written laws enacted by the legislature—are the second source of law in the United States. Congress adopts federal statutes and the legislative body of each state enacts state statutes. Federal and state statutes must comply with the federal Constitution. A state's statutes also must be consistent with its constitution. Many states also authorize other governmental units, such as counties or cities, to enact statutes, usually called "ordinances," which are effective within the local units. Both federal and state legislatures may authorize administrative agencies to issue rules and regulations that clarify or explain statutes. These administrative rules and regulations, though not equivalent to statutes, are generally interpreted and applied by the courts in a manner similar to statutes.

Federal and State Codes. Statutes are compiled in official codes. All federal statutes are codified in the **United States Code (U.S.C.),** which is divided into various "titles." For example, federal bankruptcy law is codified in Title 11 of the U.S.C. Title 15, "Commerce and Trade," contains the antitrust laws and a number of other important statutes affecting business. The states maintain their own official codes, which are published under a variety of names, such as "Illinois Compiled Statutes," "Code of Georgia," "Oregon Revised Statutes," and "Pennsylvania Consolidated Statutes." Rules and regulations issued by administrative agencies are usually compiled in volumes separate from the official codes. For example, federal regulations are compiled in the **Code of Federal Regulations (C.F.R.).**

Uniform State Laws and Model Acts. Except as limited by the United States Constitution and its own state constitution, each state legislature has the power to enact statutes that it deems appropriate for the welfare of its citizens. As a result, the substance of state statutes can vary from state to state. Differences among state statutes have limited impact when they affect matters of only local interest. Inconsistencies among state laws, however, can hinder interstate activities. As technological changes in communication and transportation increased the scope of commercial activities during the nineteenth century, businesses and individuals began to demand more consistent state laws.

In 1892, in an effort to facilitate interstate activities, seven states organized the Conference of State Boards of Commissioners on Promoting Uniformity of Law in the United States and in 1915 the Conference reorganized as the National Conference of Commissioners on Uniform State Laws. Today, each state, the District of Columbia, and Puerto Rico appoint at least one commissioner to the organization. The commissioners consider the areas of law requiring uniformity, draft legislation known as **uniform codes, acts,** or **laws,** and encourage their adoption by each of the states. The individual state legislatures consider a uniform act as they do any other legislative bill. If a uniform act is passed by the legislature, it becomes a part of the state's statutes.

The National Conference has drafted more than 250 uniform acts, many of which address areas of business law. The Uniform Commercial Code (UCC), which is discussed in detail throughout this book, has been adopted by all states except Louisiana, which has adopted only part of it. Other uniform laws that will be discussed later in the book include the Revised Uniform Partnership Act, the Revised Uniform Limited Partnership Act, the Uniform Fraudulent Transfer Act, the Uniform Trade Secrets Act, the Uniform Principal and Income Act, and the Uniform Probate Code.

The National Conference, as well as other organizations, also drafts model acts that serve as guidelines to state legislatures in drafting other types of legislation. Although model acts do not necessarily concern subjects requiring uniformity among the states, the expertise of the commissioners, especially in complex areas of the law, facilitates enactment of well-drafted legisla-

tion. As with uniform laws, model acts that are adopted by a state become a part of the state statutes.

Case Law

Another source of law in the United States is case law, also known as the **common law**—rules and principles of law embodied in cases previously decided by the courts. When an issue is presented to a court for resolution, it looks first to constitutions and statutes to ascertain whether they provide a rule of law to resolve the issue. If neither provides such a rule, the court will apply the rules of the common law. Thus, the three major sources of law stand in an hierarchical relationship. Statutes must comply with any relevant constitutional provision, and the common law is subordinate both to constitutions and statutes. Areas of law discussed in this text that are based largely upon common law principles include torts, contracts, restitution, suretyship, property, trusts, and agency.

Precedent and the Doctrine of Stare Decisis. Use of the common law as a source of law is based on the **doctrine of** *stare decisis,* which derives its name from the Latin phrase *stare decisis et non quieta movere,* meaning "to adhere to precedents and not to unsettle things established." The doctrine of *stare decisis* provides that courts will adhere to and apply principles of law decided in prior cases to later cases involving substantially the same facts. The **holding**—the rule of law that resolved the issues of the prior case—serves as authority or **precedent** for resolution of the issues of subsequent cases that involve the same or similar facts. A court, therefore, applies one rule of law to all cases involving the same or similar facts and issues.

To illustrate the doctrine of *stare decisis,* assume Andrews promised to make a gift of $500 to the Cancer Society of America. Andrews later refused to fulfill his promise and the Cancer Society sued him alleging breach of promise. The court ruled in favor of Andrews, holding that a promise to make a gift is not legally enforceable. Ten years later, the Heart Disease Institute sues Baker alleging that she had breached her promise to give $1,000 to the Institute. The two cases are substantially the same: each involves breach of a promise to make a gift. The court in the second case would use the precedent of the first case to hold that Baker's promise is not legally enforceable.

The doctrine of *stare decisis* and its use of precedent facilitate consistency, fairness, and predictability in the application of the law. William Rehnquist, former Chief Justice of the United States Supreme Court, explained the doctrine as follows:

> *Stare decisis* is the preferred course because it promotes the evenhanded, predictable, and consistent development of legal principles, fosters reliance on judicial decisions, and contributes to the actual and perceived integrity of the judicial process. Adhering to precedent is usually the wise policy, because in most matters it is more important that the applicable rule of law be settled than it be settled right. Nevertheless, when governing decisions are unworkable or are badly reasoned, this Court has never felt constrained to follow precedent. *Stare decisis* is not an inexorable command; rather, it is a principle of policy and not a mechanical formula of adherence to the latest decision. This is particularly true in constitutional cases, because in such cases correction through legislative action is practically impossible. Considerations in favor of *stare decisis* are at their acme in cases involving property and contract rights, where reliance interests are involved.[8]

Methods of Creating and Changing Precedent.
Despite the need for consistency and predictability, sometimes the use of precedent is not appropriate. In some cases, no applicable rule of law has been announced in the common law. In such cases, the court considers the issue to be one of *first impression* and reaches a holding that serves as a new rule of law under the common law.

Cases involving completely new factual situations are rare. Prior cases usually involve similar but not identical facts. If a court is convinced that the facts of the current case significantly differ from those of prior cases, the court may distinguish the case on its facts and issue a new rule of law. As a result, the common law retains its vitality and flexibility to accommodate changing times.

Sometimes the facts of a new case may not be distinguishable from those of a prior case; yet, the rule of law of the earlier case may no longer be valid because of changed social conditions. In such circumstances, a court may overrule the precedent, declaring the preexisting rule of law to be invalid, and issue a new rule. Overruling precedent is a drastic measure that courts try to avoid because it creates uncertainty and unpredictability.

---

[8]Payne v. Tennessee, 111 S. Ct. 2597, 2609-2610 (1991) (internal quotation marks and citations omitted).

An alternative way of changing common law precedent is by legislative act. The legislature can invalidate common law principles by adopting statutes that create a different rule of law. A statute that repeals or abolishes a common law principle is said to be in "derogation" of the common law.

In the following case, the court considers whether to overrule a common law doctrine.

Beattie v. Beattie
630 A.2d 1096 (Del. 1993)

> In 1991, plaintiff Margaret Beattie, while a passenger in a car driven by her husband, defendant Michael Beattie, was seriously injured in an automobile accident in Delaware. As a result of her injuries, the plaintiff was rendered a quadriplegic and incurred medical expenses in excess of $286,000. The plaintiff sued the defendant for negligence seeking damages for her injuries. If the defendant had been found liable for negligence, the plaintiff would have been entitled to proceeds of a substantial automobile liability insurance policy carried by the defendant. The trial court, however, granted judgment for the defendant. The plaintiff appealed to the Delaware Supreme Court.

Veasey, Chief Justice

. . . The trial court properly followed the prior precedents of this Court and relied on the common law doctrine of interspousal immunity ("the Doctrine") which prevents one spouse from suing the other in tort. We have concluded, however, that the Doctrine is no longer a viable concept and no longer meets the needs of modern society. . . .

This antiquated doctrine was first applied by Delaware courts in the seminal case of *Plotkin v. Plotkin,* [125 A. 455 (Del. 1924)]. In *Plotkin,* the Superior Court adopted the Doctrine primarily on the belief that upon marriage, the identity of the wife merged with that of the husband. The Doctrine's continued existence in Delaware since 1924 has been justified as a means of promoting family harmony and discouraging collusion and fraud upon insurance companies. . . . After most recently reviewing the Doctrine in 1979, this Court held that "it retains sufficient merit to warrant continued adherence." *Alfree v. Alfree,* [410 A.2d 161, 162 (Del. 1979)]. . . .

It is well settled that the judiciary has the power to overturn judicially-created doctrine, so long as that doctrine has not been codified in a statute. . . . Furthermore, it is the duty of this Court to review common law rules to ensure that the conditions and policy objectives that justify the rules remain relevant and valid. . . . In the present case, there is no statute that directly applies to the Doctrine. Therefore, it is within the authority of this Court to abrogate the common law doctrine if it no longer merits recognition. . . .

In our view, the Doctrine is more likely to have the effect of disrupting family harmony rather than preserving it. Denying a person compensation for injuries arising from the negligence of his or her spouse can be very disruptive (*e.g.,* large medical bills and loss of wages often result from serious accidents). Under the Doctrine, the married couple will have to pay these huge expenses, instead of relying on insurance proceeds. This added financial burden could well promote marital discord. . . . Any destruction of family harmony that is prevented by the Doctrine is likely to be minimal due to the prevalence of liability insurance. In addition, the Doctrine may actually promote divorces because a person who suffers an injury at the hands of his or her spouse, but who has since divorced the spouse, may maintain a tort action against the former spouse. . . . Accordingly, it is conceivable that spouses may decide to divorce solely to bypass the restrictions of a Doctrine which putatively is designed to preserve marital harmony. Such a result is repugnant to public policy.

Because of the prevalence of liability insurance, Husband argues that collusion and fraud will increase if spouses are able to sue each other. It is true that the adversarial system may be subject to tension because it is in the defendant spouse's interest for his or her injured spouse to receive some compensation, especially when the insurance company is the "real" party being sued. Such tension could potentially lead to a threat of corruption. Although the possibility of collusion exists in various situations such as intrafamily cases and suits between friends, the judicial system is adept at ferreting out frivolous and unfounded cases. It is unnecessary and unwise to deny legitimate claims in order to prevent fraudulent and collusive suits because the judicial system contains numerous safeguards and deterrents against fraudulent claims such as perjury charges and modern discovery procedures. . . .

The conclusion that the abrogation of the Doctrine will not lead to the destruction of family harmony or the proliferation of fraudulent suits is amply supported by empir-

ical evidence. Delaware is the only state in the nation which recognizes the doctrine solely on common law grounds. Four other states also recognize the Doctrine, but do so pursuant to a statute or a perceived statutory prohibition of judicial abrogation of the Doctrine. . . .

We find that the Doctrine is a relic from the common law that is no longer a viable concept and no longer meets the needs of modern society. The overwhelming majority of states in this nation have already abrogated the Doctrine without negative repercussions. Accordingly, we overrule *Alfree* and reject the Doctrine as a defense in this case.

[Judgment reversed and remanded.]

Interpretation of Constitutions and Statutes. The common law is a source of precedent for rules and principles of law not set out in a statute or constitution. Prior case law also provides precedent for the interpretation of a constitution or statute. That is, a body of case law has developed under most constitutional provisions and statutes interpreting what their language (which is often general) means as applied to specific fact situations. For example, §1 of the Sherman Act, the major federal antitrust statute, declares illegal "every contract, combination, . . . or conspiracy, in restraint of trade. . . . " The specific business conduct that violates this prohibition is found not in the Sherman Act, but in the voluminous body of cases decided under the Act since it was enacted in 1890. Thus, even in areas of law governed by a statute or constitutional provision, prior court decisions often are an important, and often the major, source of legal rules. The case law interpreting statutes and constitutions develops through the doctrine of *stare decisis* in much the same manner as the common law.

When initially interpreting a statute, a court usually applies the "plain meaning rule," which provides that a statute should be interpreted according to the literal meaning of its words. Using this rule, the court examines only the statute as written, without reviewing any other sources. Although the plain meaning rule is appealing in its simplicity and minimizes "judicial legislation," most courts do not rely solely on this rule to interpret a statute. Often a legislature adopts a statute without considering all ramifications, so that use of the plain meaning rule can lead to absurd results if the law is applied literally. Moreover, the inherent nature of language creates ambiguity due to various definitions and connotations of words. Supreme Court Justice Oliver Wendell Holmes summarized these problems by stating:

> A word is not a crystal, transparent and unchanged, it is the skin of a living thought and may vary greatly in color and content according to the circumstances and the time in which it is used.[9]

In addition to examining the plain meaning, many courts also consider a provision's legislative history—such as previous drafts of the statute, committee reports, and transcripts of floor debates—to help ascertain its meaning. Often these sources provide evidence of the statute's purpose or of the legislators' intent that helps clarify the meaning. The legislative history, however, may not address these issues. Moreover, statutes often are the product of compromises, making it likely that all legislators did not intend the same meaning.

After determining the meaning of the statutory language, the court then renders a written opinion explaining its reasoning and resolving the case before the court. That case then serves as precedent for later cases involving the same statutory provision. If the legislature believes that the courts have misinterpreted its language, the legislature can revise the statute to ensure that in subsequent cases courts reach the desired interpretation. Although similar principles govern interpretation of constitutional provisions, the method for correcting an inappropriate judicial interpretation (constitutional amendment) is much more difficult than revising a statute.

State and Federal Common Law. Each state has its own body of case law comprised of decisions of its courts, including substantive rules of law in areas not covered by statute or constitution, and the court's interpretations of statutes and constitutions. Generally, the precedents of one state are not binding on the courts of other states. Nevertheless, a state court may look to decisions in other states for guidance when adopting a new principle of law in a case of first impression or in a case overruling an outmoded rule of law.

The federal courts also have a body of case law that includes the decisions of all federal courts. Federal case law, however, includes rules of law interpreting only federal statutes and the Constitution. There is no body of federal substantive common law that is applied in the absence of a federal statute or constitutional provision. Rather, in such cases, the federal courts generally use the common law of the state in which the court is located. These topics will be further discussed later in this chapter.

Restatement of the Law. When considering an issue of first impression or outdated precedent, a court also may consult legal treatises and scholarly works for guidance to determine the appropriate rule of law to adopt. A major civil law treatise, widely used by the courts, is the **Restatement of the Law** (often simply called "the Restatement"), which is published by a national organization of attorneys, law professors, and judges known as the American Law Institute. The Restatement provides a unique perspective on the law because its purpose is to state "the law as it would be decided today by the great majority of courts."[10] Therefore, the Restatement does not necessarily reflect the rules of the common law as they have been adopted by the courts. Rather, it contains the principles of common law that the American Law Institute believes would be adopted if all courts reexamined their common law rules.

Although the entire work is called the *Restatement of the Law,* it is usually referred to by its individual topics (for example, *Restatement of Torts, Restatement of Contracts*). Those parts of the Restatement that have been revised since their initial adoption are referred to by addition of the word "Second" to the title—for example, the *Restatement (Second) of Contracts.*

When a court must decide an issue of first impression, it frequently adopts the rule of law of the Restatement. The Restatement also has been instrumental in providing a basis for overruling outmoded principles of the common law. As a result, many of the cases reprinted in this book cite the Restatement for rules of common law and the text discusses the rules of the Restatement as examples of common law principles. The Restatement itself is not a part of the common law, but if a court adopts a rule promulgated by the Restatement, that rule becomes a part of the state's common law.

American Court Systems

The judicial branch of government is responsible for applying and interpreting the law. The courts that com-

---

[9]Towne v. Eisner, 38 S. Ct. 158, 159 (1918).

[10]Restatement in the Courts, Permanent Edition 12 (1945).

pose the judicial branch, therefore, serve a crucial function in maintaining law and order in the United States. They provide a forum for the peaceful resolution of civil disputes and serve as a tribunal for the impartial enforcement of criminal laws in a fair and consistent manner. A court cannot initiate judicial action. Private individuals, businesses, or other branches of the government must present a case or controversy to the court before it can interpret and apply the law. Legal cases are initiated by a party known as the **plaintiff** who seeks some form of judicial remedy from or penalty against another, known as the **defendant.**

Jurisdiction

A court also is restricted to hearing cases that lie within its jurisdiction. **Jurisdiction** is the power and authority to render a binding decision of law. A court's jurisdiction is established in the statute or constitution that created the court. Unless a legal case is within a court's jurisdiction, the court lacks the legal authority to resolve the case.

Original and Appellate Jurisdiction. Courts may possess original or appellate jurisdiction. A court of **original jurisdiction** has the power to render the initial decision in a case. In other words, the court is the proper forum in which the parties commence the lawsuit and first obtain a legal ruling resolving the case. In the court of original jurisdiction, a trial is held, evidence is presented, and the judge enters an order determining a party's liability in a civil case or guilt or innocence in a criminal case.

Courts of **appellate jurisdiction** are empowered to review cases that have been tried by a court of original jurisdiction. The courts of appellate jurisdiction correct and revise legal errors that were made in the prior proceedings. Trials are not conducted in these courts. Instead, courts of appellate jurisdiction merely review the trial that was held in the court of original jurisdiction. Some courts have both original and appellate jurisdiction. The United States Supreme Court, for example, has original jurisdiction over cases between two or more states, but also has appellate jurisdiction over other types of cases.

Subject Matter Jurisdiction. The statute or constitution that creates a court also establishes its **subject matter jurisdiction.** A court of general subject matter jurisdiction is authorized to hear all types of disputes, including civil and criminal cases and cases at law and at equity. In contrast, a court of limited subject matter jurisdiction has the power to hear only certain categories of disputes. The federal bankruptcy courts, for example, are courts of limited subject matter jurisdiction; they have the power only to resolve cases concerning federal bankruptcy law.

State Court Systems

Every state in the United States has established its own court system. Although the structures of these systems differ, most states have created inferior courts, trial courts, and appellate courts.

State Inferior Courts. Some states have established courts of original and limited subject matter jurisdiction to handle cases of a specialized nature. These courts include probate courts (sometimes called "surrogate" or "orphans" courts) for cases involving wills and distribution of a deceased person's property, traffic courts for prosecution of violations of traffic laws, and municipal courts for minor criminal cases in larger cities.

Additionally, many states have established small claims courts, which are courts of original jurisdiction that are restricted to hearing civil cases involving a limited dollar amount, usually less than $2,500. Small claims courts provide simple and quick resolution of minor civil cases and relieve the trial courts of substantial workload. Many of these courts operate on weekends or during evening hours, use informal rules of procedure, or allow the parties to represent themselves rather than employ an attorney.

State Trial Courts. For the majority of cases, a state trial court is the court of original jurisdiction. Most state trial courts are courts of general subject matter jurisdiction and are empowered to hear all civil and criminal cases. Depending on the state, the trial courts may be called "circuit courts," "courts of common pleas," or "district courts." Trial courts usually are located in larger cities within the state or in the county seats.

As suggested by its name, the trial court is the forum in which the trial occurs to establish the facts underlying the case. A judge presides over the trial to make rulings of law and a jury may be employed to make factual determinations. Trials are discussed more fully in Chapters 2 and 3.

State Appellate Courts. All states have established appellate courts with jurisdiction to review the decisions of the inferior and trial courts. Due process of law entitles a party to a lawsuit to one appeal of right. By following procedures established by state law, a person dissatisfied with the ruling made by the court of original jurisdiction may obtain review by an appellate court. Some states have only one appellate court, usually called "the supreme court," while other states have an intermediate appellate court, usually called "the court of appeals" or "appellate court," and a supreme court.

Intermediate Appellate Courts. In states with an intermediate appellate court, a party's appeal of right generally is to that court. Some of the more populous states have subdivided the state into districts and have established an intermediate appellate court in each district. The district serves a number of counties or circuits and, therefore, hears intermediate appeals only from trial courts within those counties or circuits.

State Supreme Courts. In states without an intermediate appellate court, appeals of right are taken to the state supreme court. In states with an intermediate appellate court, the state supreme court provides another review of cases already reviewed by the court of appeals. In those states, the supreme court usually has the power to select the cases it wants to review from petitions filed by parties following the intermediate appeal. For most cases tried within the state court system, the state supreme court is the court of last resort. The United States Supreme Court, however, may provide further review of some cases as discussed later in this chapter.

Function of Appellate Courts. The function of the appellate courts is to review inferior trial court decisions to determine whether reversible error has occurred. In contrast to the trial court, where only one judge presides over a case, appellate cases usually are reviewed by a panel of three or more judges who reach a decision by majority vote. The appellate court does not retry a case; it merely reviews the record of the trial, the briefs provided by the parties, and oral arguments made by the attorneys of the parties. Generally, appellate courts are restricted to reviewing issues of law; the appellate court ordinarily accepts the facts as found by the trial court unless they are clearly erroneous. If an appellate court determines that reversible error occurred in the lower court, it will reverse the case and correct the error or send the case back to the lower court for further proceedings.

Federal Court System

Article III, Section 1 of the Constitution provides:

> The judicial Power of the United States, shall be vested in one supreme Court, and in such inferior Courts as the Congress may from time to time ordain and establish.

Thus, the only constitutionally mandated federal court is the Supreme Court, but Congress has established a federal court system composed of three main tiers: the United States District Courts, the United States Courts of Appeals, and the United States Supreme Court. In addition, Congress has established several other courts to hear special cases.

Specialized Federal Courts. For some cases, the court of original federal jurisdiction is a specialized court with limited subject matter jurisdiction. These specialized courts include, for example, the United States Claims Court, which has jurisdiction over cases involving claims against the United States arising from government contracts, and the Court of International Trade, which has jurisdiction over cases involving import transactions.

United States District Courts. The United States District Courts, the trial courts of the federal judicial system, are the courts of original jurisdiction for most federal cases. Under federal statute, the country is divided into 94 judicial districts, each of which has a district court. Every state has at least one district; those states with larger populations have more than one district within their boundaries. Federal district court judges are appointed for life by the president with the advice and consent of the Senate.

Unlike most state trial courts, federal district courts are courts of limited subject matter jurisdiction. The majority of the district court cases are based on federal question jurisdiction and diversity of citizenship jurisdiction.

Federal Question Jurisdiction. Under **federal question jurisdiction,** a district court is authorized to resolve cases arising under the U.S. Constitution, federal statutes, or treaties. Someone challenging the constitutionality of a state or federal law, for example, may file the case in federal district court because the case arises under the Constitution. The federal government also initiates suits in district courts to enforce federal statutes or treaties. By statute, a few types of federal question cases (such as bankruptcy cases, prosecutions of federal crimes, and federal antitrust law violations) can be tried only in federal courts. Unless so restricted, most cases involving federal questions may be brought in either federal or state court.

Diversity Jurisdiction. Federal district courts also have **diversity jurisdiction,** the power to try civil cases in which the plaintiff and defendant demonstrate diversity of citizenship and the amount in controversy exceeds $75,000. Diversity of citizenship exists if the plaintiff and defendant are citizens of different states or if one party is a citizen of the United States and the other is the citizen of a foreign nation.

The purpose of diversity jurisdiction is to provide a forum free from bias that might occur in a state trial court. If, for example, a citizen of Illinois sued a citizen of Ohio in an Illinois state court, the judge's or the jury's prejudice could deny the out-of-state citizen a fair trial in the state court. The federal court is an alternative forum that may be free of local bias.

Diversity jurisdiction is based upon the citizenship of the parties. Natural persons (human beings) generally are citizens of their "domicile"—the fixed, permanent home to which they intend to return after an absence.[11] By statute,[12] a corporation is a citizen of (1) any state in which it is incorporated, and (2) the state in which its principal place of business is located. A corporation's "principal place of business" is the state "where the bulk of the corporate activity takes place."[13] If a corporation operates in more than one state, and no one state meets this test, then the location of the corporation's home office is used.[14] Citizenship of an unincorporated association, such as a partnership or limited liability company, is determined by the citizenship of its individual partners or members. For example, assume A, B, and C are partners in a construction business. A is a citizen of Illinois, B is a citizen of Wisconsin, and C is a citizen

of Indiana. For diversity purposes, the partnership is a citizen of all three states.

In cases involving multiple parties, the Supreme Court has held that "complete" diversity is required to trigger federal diversity jurisdiction.[15] This means that each plaintiff's citizenship must differ from each defendant's citizenship. For example, assume A, a citizen of Illinois, and B, a citizen of Indiana, join to sue C, a citizen of Missouri, and D, a citizen of Kansas, for damages arising from an auto accident or breach of contract. This case could be brought in federal court, but could not if, for example, C or D was a citizen of Illinois or Indiana.

Note finally that citizenship is determined when the lawsuit is filed, not when the facts giving rise to the lawsuit occurred. For example, assume X wants to sue Y for injuries sustained in an auto accident that occurred while both X and Y were Illinois residents. Shortly after the accident, Y moves to Maine. X can sue Y in federal court based on diversity.

United States Courts of Appeals. While the United States district courts serve as the trial courts of the federal judicial system, the federal circuit courts of appeals are the intermediate courts with appellate jurisdiction. A party to a federal lawsuit generally is entitled to one appeal of right to the appropriate court of appeals. Federal law divides the country into 12 judicial circuits, each encompassing several districts. The court of appeals for each circuit has the power to review district court decisions from districts within the circuit. For example, the Second Circuit encompasses New York, Connecticut, and Vermont. The Second Circuit Court of Appeals can review decisions only from federal district courts within those three states. Additionally, a thirteenth federal appellate court, called the United States Court of Appeals for the Federal Circuit, has appellate jurisdiction over cases from the United States Patent and Trademark Office, the United States Court of Federal Claims, and the Court of International Trade; some decisions of federal agencies; and patent cases decided in the various federal district courts. Figure 1.1 indicates the states and territories within each of the federal judicial circuits.

The justices of the courts of appeals are appointed by the president with the advice and consent of the Senate. Most cases are reviewed by a panel of three justices who issue a written decision representing the ruling of a majority of the panel. In certain cases, usually involving

---

[11]Wright, Federal Courts 161 (5th ed. 1994).

[12]28 U.S.C. §1332(c)(1).

[13]Wright, Federal Courts 168 (5th ed. 1994).

[14]*Id.*

[15]Strawbridge v. Curtiss, 7 U.S. (3 Cranch) 267 (1806).

Figure 1.1	**The Thirteen Federal Judicial Circuits**

very important issues, all justices for the circuit review the case, a procedure called *en banc* review. Again, a written decision is rendered representing the majority opinion. As in the state appellate courts, the federal courts of appeals generally review only the law and do not retry the facts as found by the district court. Attorneys for the parties may submit legal briefs and present oral arguments to the court of appeals.

United States Supreme Court. The court of last resort in this country is the United States Supreme Court, a court composed of a chief justice and eight associate justices, all of whom are appointed by the president with the advice and consent of the Senate. The Supreme Court is primarily a court of appellate jurisdiction with the power to review cases from both the federal courts

of appeals and the state supreme courts. Generally, the Supreme Court retains discretion whether to accept a case for review. A party seeking Supreme Court review must file a petition summarizing the issues of the case. If the Supreme Court justices exercise their discretion to review the case, the Court will issue a **writ of certiorari** granting the petitioning party the right to Supreme Court review. According to the Court's rules, a "[r]eview on writ of certiorari is not a matter of right, but of judicial discretion. A petition for a writ of certiorari will be granted only for compelling reasons."[16] As a result, the Court grants a writ of certiorari in only a few cases although thousands of petitions are filed each year.

---

[16]SUP. CT. R. 10.

The Supreme Court also is a court of original jurisdiction for a very few types of cases. If a lawsuit is between two or more states, the Supreme Court not only is the court of original jurisdiction but is also the exclusive forum for resolution of the dispute. Additionally, the Supreme Court is a court of original but not exclusive jurisdiction for cases in which a foreign ambassador, public minister (an upper-level diplomatic representative), or consul is a party; cases between the United States and a state; and cases in which a state sues citizens of another state or aliens. Because federal district courts also have original jurisdiction over these types of cases, the Supreme Court rarely exercises original jurisdiction.

Relationship Between State and Federal Courts

Each state court system and the federal court system are independent of one another. Generally, once a suit is begun in a court of original jurisdiction in one system, the case and subsequent appeals remain within that system. A case filed in a California trial court, for example, must be appealed through the California appellate courts, rather than through the appellate courts of another state or of the federal government. One exception to the independent functioning of state and federal courts is the United States Supreme Court's power to review cases from the highest state courts.

For many civil cases, a number of courts will have subject matter jurisdiction over the case. The plaintiff is entitled to select the court of original jurisdiction in which to file the claim; the defendant usually has no voice in selecting the court.[17] If, however, a plaintiff sues a defendant in a state trial court, but the case could have been filed in a federal district court, the defendant may have the case transferred to the federal district court for the district and division in which the state court is located. The federal court's power to transfer the case is known as "removal jurisdiction." For example, if Garcia, a resident of Ohio, wishes to sue Evans, a resident of Kentucky, for damages for breach of contract in excess of $75,000, the case could be brought in a state trial court with general subject matter jurisdiction or in a federal district court on the basis of diversity jurisdiction. If Garcia chose to file the suit in an Ohio trial court, Evans could request that the case be transferred to a federal district court. The defendant, however, does not have the option of having the case transferred to another state court; removal may be made only to federal court. This rule allows a nonresident defendant the opportunity to avoid possible prejudice in the state court through removal to federal court. Removal is discussed in more detail in the next chapter. Figure 1.2 indicates the general organization of the federal and state court systems.

Applicable Law

The function of a court is to apply the appropriate law to cases presented to it for resolution. A court, therefore, must determine what substantive law is applicable to each case. Regardless of the source of substantive law, a court always applies its own procedural law.

State Courts. In general, a state court applies the law of its own state. In civil cases, not governed by constitution or statute, the state's common law is the appropriate source of law. If a case in the state court involves a federal statute or the federal Constitution, the Supremacy Clause of the Constitution requires the judge to apply these federal laws, following the interpretations announced in the federal case law.

Conflict of Laws in State Courts. Because state courts operate independently of one another, the law of one state generally is inapplicable in the courts of other states. If, however, the events giving rise to a lawsuit occur in a state other than the state in which the lawsuit is brought, the court may be required by its own law to apply the law of that state. Each state, through its common law, has adopted rules of law to determine when and how its courts will apply another state's law, an area of law known as **conflict of laws.**

Consider, for example, an automobile accident that occurs in New York City between driver A and driver B, both residents of New Jersey. A sues B for negligence in the state court of New Jersey. Should the New Jersey court apply New Jersey negligence law or New York negligence law? To resolve this question, the judge of the case must look to New Jersey's conflicts of law. (The judge uses the conflicts of law rules of the state in which the court is sitting.) In an effort to maintain consistent and predictable law, most states' conflicts of law rules require the court to apply the law of the state in which the events underlying the dispute occurred. Thus, New Jersey's conflicts of law would require that the

---

[17]As a practical matter, the plaintiff's choice may be restricted by the court's jurisdiction over the defendant, which will be discussed in Chapter 2.

| **Figure 1.2** | **The Federal and State Court Systems** |

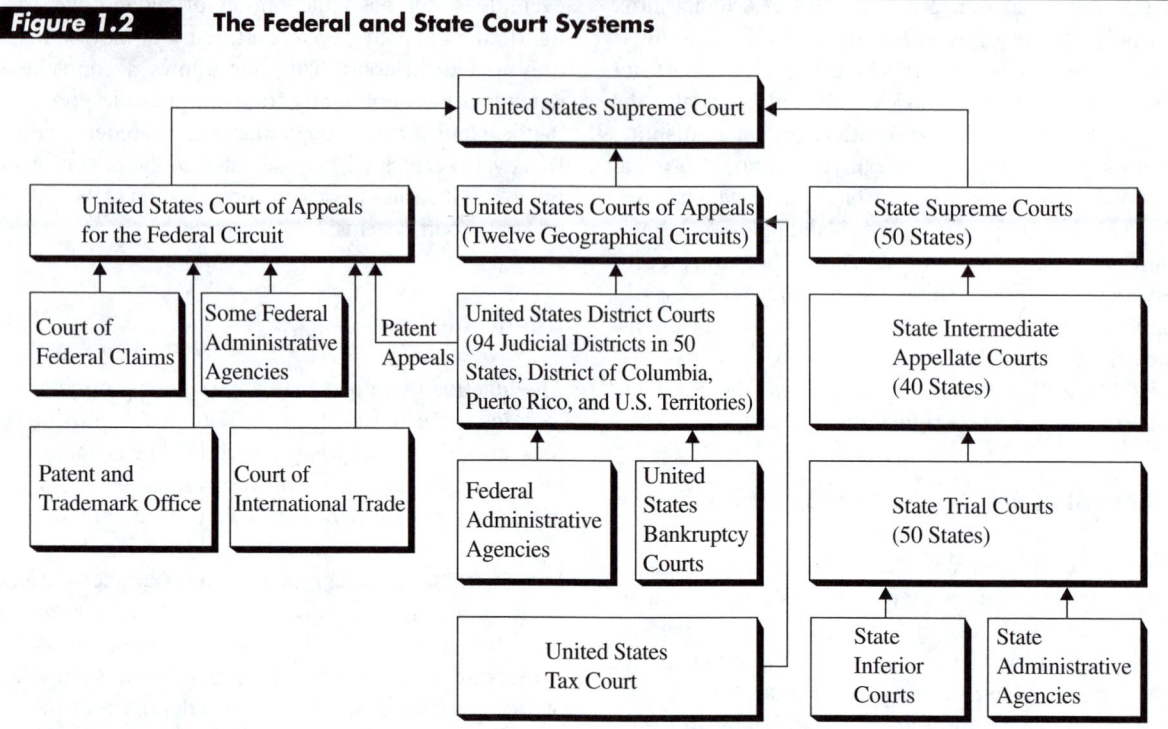

New Jersey court apply the rules of negligence of the state in which the accident occurred—that is, New York negligence law. The rules of conflicts of law are especially important when the states have different laws that may affect the outcome of the case. One purpose served by the law of conflicts of law is to prevent the plaintiff from *forum shopping*—choosing to sue in a particular state because its laws are more advantageous.

Federal Courts. As previously noted, two types of cases are brought in federal district courts: cases involving federal law and cases involving diversity of the parties. In federal question cases, the federal courts apply federal law, including federal case law interpretations of the statutes, Constitution, or treaties.

In cases involving diversity jurisdiction, however, the federal courts apply the substantive law of the state in which the court is sitting. For example, a federal district court located in Illinois hearing a case based upon diversity of citizenship applies Illinois law. Therefore, the federal court must follow local substantive constitutional, statutory, and common law in diversity jurisdiction cases. Although federal courts always applied state constitutional law and statutes when appropriate, for many years the federal courts developed their own body of substantive common law for diversity cases. In 1938,

the United States Supreme Court overruled the holdings of prior cases that had allowed the federal courts to ignore state common law and held that federal courts exercising diversity jurisdiction also were required to apply the substantive common law of the local state.

Erie Railroad Co. v. Tompkins
58 S. Ct. 817 (1938)

While walking along a pathway next to defendant Erie Railroad Co.'s railroad tracks in Pennsylvania, plaintiff Tompkins was struck and injured by a train owned by Erie. Tompkins, a citizen of Pennsylvania, sued Erie, a New York corporation, for damages in a federal district court located in New York. Pennsylvania common law provided that persons using pathways along a railroad right of way were trespassers and that railroad companies were liable to trespassers only if the railroad had acted wantonly or willfully. Erie argued that the Pennsylvania common law rule should be applied. Tompkins argued that the federal court should disregard the Pennsylvania law and adopt a rule holding the railroad company liable if it had acted negligently. The trial court held that the Pennsylvania common law was inapplicable and Tompkins was awarded $30,000 in damages; the Second Circuit Court of Appeals affirmed. Erie was granted a petition of certiorari to the United States Supreme Court.

Justice Brandeis

. . . The question for decision is whether the oft-challenged doctrine of *Swift v. Tyson* shall now be disapproved. . . .

First. Swift v. Tyson, [41 U.S. (16 Pet.) 1 (1842)], held that federal courts exercising jurisdiction on the ground of diversity of citizenship need not, in matters of general jurisprudence, apply the unwritten law of the State as declared by its highest court; that they are free to exercise an independent judgment as to what the common law of the State is—or should be. . . .

Second. Experience in applying the doctrine of *Swift v. Tyson* had revealed its defects, political and social; and the benefits expected to flow from the rule did not accrue. Persistence of state courts in their own opinions on questions of common law prevented uniformity; and the impossibility of discovering a satisfactory line of demarcation between the province of general law and that of local law developed a new well of uncertainties.

On the other hand, the mischievous results of the doctrine had become apparent. Diversity of citizenship jurisdiction was conferred in order to prevent apprehended discrimination in state courts against those not citizens of the State. *Swift v. Tyson* introduced grave discrimination by non-citizens against citizens. It made rights enjoyed under the unwritten "general law" vary according to whether enforcement was sought in the state or in the federal court; and the privilege of selecting the court in which the right should be determined was conferred upon the non-citizen. Thus, the doctrine rendered impossible equal protection of the law. In attempting to promote uniformity of law throughout the United States, the doctrine had prevented uniformity in the administration of the law of the State. . . .

The injustice and confusion incident to the doctrine of *Swift v. Tyson* have been repeatedly urged as reasons for abolishing or limiting diversity of citizenship jurisdiction. Other legislative relief has been proposed. If only a question of statutory construction were involved, we should not be prepared to abandon a doctrine so widely applied throughout nearly a century. But the unconstitutionality of the course pursued has now been made clear and compels us to do so.

Third. Except in matters governed by the Federal Constitution or by Acts of Congress, the law to be applied in any case is the law of the State. And whether the law of the State shall be declared by its Legislature in a statute or by its highest court in a decision is not a matter of federal concern. There is no federal general common law. Congress has no power to declare substantive rules of common law applicable in a State whether they be local in their nature or "general," be they commercial law or a part of the law of torts. And no clause in the Constitution purports to confer such a power upon the federal courts. . . .

The fallacy underlying the rule declared in *Swift v. Tyson* is made clear by Mr. Justice Holmes. The doctrine rests upon the assumption that there is "a transcendental body of law outside of any particular State but obligatory within it unless and until changed by statute," that federal courts have the power to use their judgment as to what the rules of common law are; and that in the federal courts "the parties are entitled to an independent judgment on matters of general law":

> "But law in the sense in which courts speak of it today does not exist without some definite authority behind it. . . . the authority and only authority is the State, and if that be so, the voice adopted by the State as its own [whether it be of its Legislature or of its Supreme Court] should utter the last word." [*Black & White Taxicab & Transfer Co. v. Brown & Yellow Taxicab & Transfer Co.,* 48 S. Ct. 404, 409 (1928).]

Thus the doctrine of *Swift v. Tyson* is, as Mr. Justice Holmes said, "an unconstitutional assumption of powers by courts of the United States which no lapse of time or respectable array of opinion should make us hesitate to correct." [*Black & White Taxicab & Transfer Co. v. Brown & Yellow Taxicab & Transfer Co.,* 48 S. Ct. 404, 408 (1928).] . . .

The Circuit Court of Appeals ruled that the question of liability is one of general law; and on that ground declined to decide the issue of state law. As we hold this was error, the judgment is reversed and the case remanded to it for further proceedings in conformity with our opinion.

Since the *Erie* decision, the federal courts in exercising diversity jurisdiction apply the substantive common law of the state in which the court is located. In later decisions, the Court held that the substantive common law includes the rules of conflicts of law. As a result, in diversity cases the federal courts apply the same law that would have governed had the case been tried in the state courts.

Sometimes the federal courts must decide a case presenting an issue not previously resolved by the state courts. In these cases, the federal court may review related state law and decide the issue as it believes the state court would if it had had the opportunity to establish a rule of law. Nevertheless, the federal court may follow the "abstention" doctrine by which the court allows the state courts to rule on the issues prior to deciding the federal case. Because the abstention doctrine often results in protracted litigation, some states have adopted a procedure known as "certification of issues of law" that allows the federal court to obtain a ruling on the appropriate law from the state supreme court and then apply that law to the case before it.

Statutes of Limitation

Even if a court has jurisdiction over a particular case, the operation of a statute of limitations may prevent the court from exercising that jurisdiction. A **statute of limitation** requires the plaintiff to file a lawsuit within a specified period of time after the legal claim arises. A plaintiff who fails to file suit within the statute of limitation loses the right to recover on the claim. The typical statutory period runs from the date the legal claim arises to the date the suit is filed. How long it takes to ultimately dispose of the suit after filing is irrelevant. The purpose of a statute of limitation is to protect a defendant's rights by preventing persons from filing "stale claims," those that are so old that witnesses may have forgotten the relevant facts, may have died or moved out of the jurisdiction, or may have lost or destroyed relevant documents.

Statutes of limitation have been enacted by both the federal and state legislatures for most civil and criminal cases. For example, federal law provides a four-year statute of limitations for civil cases based on any federal statute that does not contain its own explicit limitations period.[18] The UCC provides a four-year statute of limitations for claims involving contracts for the sale of goods.[19] States commonly provide a 20-year statute of limitation on actions to recover possession of land. Cases seeking recovery for personal injury, sustained in an automobile accident, for example, are commonly governed by a two-year statute of limitations.

At both the state and federal level, criminal actions for very serious crimes such as murder may generally be commenced at any time without limitation.[20] Limitation periods for other criminal offenses vary. For example, prosecution of most federal crimes must be commenced within five years after the offense was committed.[21]

A statute of limitations should be distinguished from a **statute of repose**. A statute of repose sets a fixed outside time limit for filing without regard to when the legal claim arises or the plaintiff's awareness that a claim exists. For example, as discussed in Chapter 49, a lawsuit seeking damages for securities fraud must be filed within two years after the plaintiff discovers the facts constituting the violation, and within five years after the violation occurred.[22] The five year limitation is a statute of repose.

In cases within a court's equity jurisdiction, the doctrine of "laches" serves a purpose similar to that of a statute of limitations. Laches allows the court to deny recovery to a plaintiff who unreasonably delays in presenting an equitable claim to the court.

Summary

1. In the United States, law is the body of principles and rules applied and enforced by the courts. Substantive law defines the rights and duties of members of society while procedural law establishes the mechanisms for enforcing rights and duties. Criminal law protects society as a whole by imposing penalties on those who violate minimum standards of socially acceptable conduct, whereas civil law protects individuals by providing remedies to those injured by the unlawful conduct of others. Public law involves the government in its capacity as a representative for all of society, while private law concerns persons in their individual capacities.

2. In the United States, both the individual state and the federal governments create law, and are organized under the doctrine of separation of powers by which governmental powers are divided among the legislative, executive, and judicial branches. The three primary sources of law in the United States are constitutions, statutes, and the common law. A written constitution is a document that establishes the basic principles, governmental structure, and law of a state or nation. Statutes are written laws enacted by the federal or state legislatures. The common law consists of the body of cases previously decided by the courts.

3. The United States Constitution serves three important functions: (1) it limits the powers of the states; (2) it enumerates the powers the states have delegated to the federal government; and (3) it guarantees certain rights of the people of

---

[18]28 U.S.C. §1658. This provision applies only to federal statutes enacted after December 1, 1990.

[19]UCC §2–725. See discussion in Chapter 18.

[20]See, for example, 18 U.S.C. §3281.

[21]18 U.S.C. §3282.

[22]28 U.S.C. §1658(b).

the United States. The doctrine of judicial review, first articulated in *Marbury v. Madison,* empowers the courts to review the acts of the executive and legislative branches of government and to refuse to enforce acts of those branches that violate the Constitution.

4. Under the doctrine of *stare decisis,* the courts follow the precedent found in the common law to resolve cases involving the same or similar facts. Precedent may be changed by a court's overruling the prior case or by the legislature's enacting statutes in derogation of the common law.

5. Courts interpret statutes in accordance with previous interpretations found in the case law. To assist in interpreting statutes in cases of first impression, the courts usually apply the "plain meaning rule" and may look to legislative history.

6. A court is empowered to render binding decisions of law only in cases within the court's jurisdiction. Courts of original jurisdiction have the power to render the initial decision in the case. Courts of appellate jurisdiction are authorized only to review cases that have been tried in a court of original jurisdiction. Courts of general subject matter jurisdiction are empowered to hear all types of cases while courts of limited subject matter jurisdiction have authority to hear only specific types of cases.

7. State court systems generally include inferior courts, trial courts, and appellate courts. State trial courts usually are courts of general subject matter jurisdiction.

8. The federal court system consists of specialized inferior courts, United States district courts, courts of appeals, and the Supreme Court. Federal district courts, which are courts of limited subject matter jurisdiction, predominantly hear cases based on federal law and on diversity of citizenship of the parties. The Supreme Court is the ultimate appellate court in the United States and reviews cases from both the state and federal court systems.

9. Generally, state courts apply the law of their own state. Federal courts apply federal law in cases based on federal question jurisdiction and the law of the state in which the court is sitting in cases based on diversity jurisdiction. The rules of law establish the applicable law in both state and federal court cases in which state law from different states is involved.

10. To prevent persons from filing "stale" claims, state and federal statutes of limitation require the plaintiff to file a suit within a specified period of time after occurrence of the facts entitling the plaintiff to recover.

Key Terms

law
legal system
artificial persons
natural persons
ethics
attorney
substantive law
procedural law
criminal law
civil law
public law
private law
courts of chancery (courts of equity)
constitution
Supremacy Clause
doctrine of judicial review
statute
United States Code
Code of Federal Regulations
uniform codes, acts, or laws
model acts
common law
doctrine of *stare decisis*
holding
precedent
Restatement of the Law
plaintiff
defendant
jurisdiction
original jurisdiction
appellate jurisdiction
subject matter jurisdiction
federal question jurisdiction
diversity jurisdiction
writ of certiorari
conflict of laws
statute of limitation
statute of repose

Questions and Problems

1.1 Discuss the differences and similarities between law and ethics. Do you agree with the economist Milton Friedman and the unnamed company executive that businesses only are obligated to make lawful decisions or do you agree with Professors Goodpaster and Matthews that businesses also should make ethical decisions? Explain.

1.2 Yellow Rose Co. (YRC), a corporation that has manufactured gizmos at a large factory in Central City, Texas, for more than 50 years, is the largest employer in western Texas. Following adoption of the North American Free Trade Agreement, YRC began considering moving its manufacturing operations to Mexico. Two important considerations have made Mexico seem attractive: YRC will be able to pay lower wages because the federal and Texas minimum wage statutes will not apply, and YRC's manufacturing costs will decrease because it will not have to comply with U.S. environmental laws. Assume that you are an officer of YRC and have been asked for your recommendation on whether the factory should be moved to Mexico.
(a) Based on legal considerations, what issues are important to your recommendation? Explain.
(b) Based on ethical considerations, what issues are important to your recommendation? Explain.

1.3 The legislature of the state of Illinois enacted an antitrust statute that included the following provision: "When the language of this Act is the same or similar to the language of federal antitrust law, the courts of this state in construing this Act shall follow the construction given to the federal law by the federal courts." In a lawsuit based on the state law, a party raised the issue that this provision violated the doctrine of separation of powers. Do you agree? Explain.

1.4 Under the common law, judges "make law." Is the use of the common law system in the United States consistent with the republican form of government and the doctrine of separation of powers? Explain.

1.5 Professor Karl Llewellyn, in discussing the common law and *stare decisis,* stated:

> In the large, disregarding for the moment peculiarities of our law and legal doctrine—in the large precedent consists in an official doing over again under similar circumstances substantially what has been done by him or his predecessor before. The foundation, then, of precedent is the official analogue of what, in society at large, we know as folkways, or as institutions, and of what in the individual, we know as habit. And the things which make for precedent in this broad sense are the same which make for habit and for institutions. It takes time and effort to solve problems. Once you have solved one it seems foolish to reopen it. Indeed you are likely to be quite impatient with the notion of reopening it. Both inertia and convenience speak for building further on what you have already built; for incorporating the decision once made, *the solution once worked out,* into your operating technique *without reexamination* of what *earlier went into* reaching your solution. [Llewellyn, *The Bramble Bush* 64–65 (1951)]

In the preceding quotation, is Professor Llewellyn indicating the advantages or the disadvantages of the doctrine of *stare decisis* and the use of precedent? Explain.

1.6 Reconsider the example in the text in which the court held that a promise to make a gift is not legally enforceable.

(a) Assume in the example that Andrews orally promised to make a gift but in the subsequent case Baker's promise to make a gift was in writing. Should the court follow the holding of the Andrews case? Explain.

(b) Assume that a third case arises in which Chang promises to make a gift of $1 million to the Metropolitan Art Museum on April 1. Relying on that promise, the museum enters into a contract to purchase a Van Gogh painting for $1 million. The museum must pay the seller of the painting on April 15 and intends to use Chang's gift for that purpose. On April 1, Chang notifies the museum that he will not make the gift and the museum sues Chang for breach of promise. Should the court follow the precedent of the Andrews case? Why or why not?

1.7 Federal law provides that federal judges are appointed to their positions for life although they may be removed from office for misconduct. Suggest reasons why this law was adopted. Many state judges are elected by the general electorate and, therefore, must run for reelection on a periodic basis. Suggest reasons for these state laws. Do you think appointment or election of judges is a better policy? Explain.

1.8 XYZ Corporation breached a contract to manufacture and deliver certain machinery to Fred, a resident of California. Fred sued XYZ in a trial court of the state of California, a court of general subject matter jurisdiction. XYZ is a Delaware corporation with its principal place of business located in Arizona.

(a) Does the trial court have subject matter jurisdiction over this case? Why or why not? Do other state trial courts in the United States have subject matter jurisdiction? Explain.

(b) XYZ would prefer to have this case tried in a federal court. Would a federal district court have subject matter

jurisdiction over the case? Explain. Could XYZ have the case transferred to a federal district court? Explain.

1.9 Assume that the legislature of the state of Alaska adopted the following statute, entitled the Alaska Motor Vehicle Mileage Act, in 2004:

> I.   Any person who sells a car, truck, or other motor vehicle in the state of Alaska shall provide to the buyer of the vehicle a written statement correctly showing the mileage of the vehicle.
>
> II.   The seller shall provide said written mileage statement to the buyer no later than one day before the seller transfers the vehicle to the buyer.
>
> III.   Any person who buys a vehicle in the state of Alaska and does not receive said written mileage statement from the seller shall be entitled to sue the seller and to receive damages or rescission of contract.

(a) Identify at least one duty and one right created by the Alaska Motor Vehicle Mileage Act.

(b) Is the Alaska Motor Vehicle Mileage Act a criminal statute or a civil statute? Explain.

(c) Super Motors Co. is a corporation that sells automobiles at retail in Alaska. Is Super Motors Co. required to comply with the Alaska Motor Vehicle Mileage Act? Explain.

(d) In 1999 Smith purchased an automobile from Seward. Although the odometer on the car showed 15,000 miles, it had been out of order for several months and the true mileage of the car was 40,000 miles. Smith sued Seward alleging that Seward had committed fraud by failing to tell Smith the correct mileage. In the 2000 case of *Seward v. Smith,* the Alaska Supreme Court held that the seller of a car has no obligation to notify the buyer of the car's mileage unless the buyer first asks the seller. What effect will the Alaska Motor Vehicle Mileage Act have on the holding of *Seward v. Smith?* Explain.

1.10 Assume that the federal Congress adopts a statute called the Federal Mileage Act, which states:

> I.   Any person who sells a car, truck, or other motor vehicle in the United States shall provide to the buyer of the vehicle a written statement correctly showing the mileage of the vehicle.
>
> II.   The seller shall provide said written mileage statement to the buyer no later than three days before the seller transfers the vehicle to the buyer.
>
> III.   Any person who is found guilty in a court of law of violating sections 1 and 2 of the Federal Mileage Act shall be sentenced to serve not more than 6 months in a federal penitentiary and/or to pay a fine not to exceed $1,000.

(a) Is the Federal Mileage Act a criminal statute or a civil statute? Explain.

(b) Stella Seller, a resident of Alaska, contracted to sell her truck to Bernie Buyer and the transfer is scheduled to occur on March 15. Seller has read both the Alaska Motor Vehicle Mileage Act (see previous question) and the Federal Mileage Act but she is uncertain when to provide the written mileage statement to Buyer. Should she provide the statement at least three days before March 15 or at least one day before March 15? Explain.

CIVIL DISPUTE RESOLUTION

Almost all the day-to-day activities of a business create potential for a civil dispute: a supplier may fail to deliver goods under a contract; a customer may refuse to pay a bill; one of the business's products may injure a consumer; an employee may be injured in a manufacturing plant; a marketing plan may restrain trade. Although good business managers attempt to minimize the potential for disputes through careful planning, even the best-run businesses cannot avoid them.

A business that becomes engaged in a legal dispute may resort to **litigation,** contesting the claim in court, to resolve it. Because litigation can be time-consuming and costly, however, it often is not the best method for resolving a business dispute. The formal procedures of litigation, which are discussed later in this chapter, can require a business and its employees to devote valuable time to collecting and reviewing evidence, meeting with attorneys, and attending court hearings. Further costs are incurred to retain attorneys, who must draft documents, attend court hearings, review evidence and legal precedent, interview witnesses, and otherwise plan for trial. Additionally, litigation rarely resolves a dispute quickly. Because of pretrial proceedings and the volume of cases in the courts, even simple civil lawsuits may not come to trial until one to two years after they have been initiated, and complicated cases involving multiple parties or complex issues may not come to trial for many years. Complex business issues may further protract proceedings because the judge or jury is not familiar with economic, scientific, or other specialized information. Even after trial, the case may be prolonged by appeal. Litigation also often creates hostility between the parties, a result that is especially detrimental if the parties must maintain a business relationship, such as a long-term contract or employer-employee relationship. Moreover, because court proceedings and documents generally are open to the public, a litigated case may produce adverse publicity for a business or the opportunity for its competitors to obtain valuable information. In addition, a successful plaintiff does not have the benefit of the damage award until the case is resolved and the judgment collected. Finally, even a strong case can be lost, and uncertainty regarding the outcome of a case often adversely affects both parties' ability to plan operations.

Alternative Dispute Resolution

Because of the expense, delay, and uncertainty of litigation, most civil disputes involving businesses are resolved using alternative dispute resolution (ADR) processes. ADR encompasses a variety of procedures, including time-tested techniques such as negotiation, mediation, and arbitration, as well as more recent innovations, such as mini-trials and private trials. Although ADR is available to resolve any legal controversy, many ADR techniques are particularly suitable for resolving business disputes.

ADR techniques are intended to achieve quick resolution of disputes using informal procedures. Because the parties avoid crowded court dockets and the protracted appellate process, the delays associated with litigation generally are eliminated. Further time and expense can be avoided by using ADR methods that employ experts as decision makers or facilitators to resolve complex business problems not readily understood by judges or juries. The informal procedures of ADR, as well as its emphasis on quick resolution, tend to minimize the hostility and frustration that can arise during a dispute, so ADR is especially suitable for resolving disputes between businesses that must maintain long-term relationships. Most ADR processes also are conducted in private, free from scrutiny by competitors or the public.

Various methods of alternative dispute resolution are discussed in the following sections. The appropriate method for resolving a specific dispute depends on a number of factors, including the nature of the dispute and the relationship of the parties.

Negotiation

The vast majority of business disputes are resolved through negotiation, a process by which two parties with differing demands reach an agreement generally through compromise and concession. Whether negotiation is informal (for instance, one or more telephone conversations between two businesspeople), or formally structured (such as a meeting or meetings scheduled solely to resolve the dispute), the negotiation process generally follows a similar format. After defining their positions and communicating them to one another, the parties usually engage in a period of discussion, oral or in writing, in which they analyze the strengths and weaknesses of the other. Eventually one or both of the parties propose solutions requiring compromise by each. If the parties can mutually agree on appropriate concessions, the dispute will be resolved. Without agreement, the parties eventually become deadlocked and resort to more formal dispute resolution techniques.

Negotiation is the simplest and most efficient method of dispute resolution, provided the parties truly desire to resolve their differences. Negotiation is such a common practice in business relationships that the parties often do not consciously realize that they are engaging in a dispute resolution technique. Although effective negotiating skills and strategies are important, negotiating parties also should be knowledgeable about the legal principles underlying their dispute. Many businesses, therefore, either consult with their attorneys throughout the negotiation process or refer the matter to their attorneys, who then negotiate the dispute on behalf of their clients.

Mediation

Disputing parties who are deadlocked may seek the assistance of a third party to resolve the controversy. **Mediation** is a relatively informal process in which a neutral third party, the mediator, helps resolve a dispute. A mediator generally has no power to impose a resolution. In many respects, therefore, mediation can be considered as structured negotiation in which the mediator facilitates the process. The mediator usually initiates the process by meeting with the disputing parties, either individually or jointly, to explain the mediation process and to gather information about the parties and their dispute. The mediator then attempts to define the issues, establish an agenda for mediation, and preserve an atmosphere conducive to communication. Throughout the process, the mediator assists in generating and assessing options for settlement. Finally, the mediator helps the parties reach concessions and compromises that will lead to a final settlement. If a resolution is reached, the mediator may help reduce the agreement to writing and work with the parties to implement the agreement.

Mediation, like negotiation, rarely is successful unless both parties truly desire to resolve their differences. Parties often voluntarily agree to retain a mediator after a dispute has arisen, but some contractual agreements (such as a collective bargaining agreement between a business and a union) may require mediation of any disputes arising under the contract. Mediation long has been a popular technique for resolving labor-management conflicts and international business disputes, particularly those involving parties from Eastern Asian countries. More recently, mediation has been used successfully to settle relatively minor consumer claims and landlord-tenant disputes, family matters relating to divorce and child custody, and environmental law problems involving numerous parties. Many courts now offer mediation services to help parties settle lawsuits prior to trial.

Mediation can resolve business disputes quickly and inexpensively because good faith negotiation often improves with the presence of a neutral third party. A good mediator also employs strategies and techniques to facilitate communication, minimize distrust, and help develop alternatives when the parties are unable to achieve these goals without guidance. A mediator with expertise in the subject area of the dispute can expedite a fair resolution. The primary disadvantage of mediation is the mediator's lack of power to impose a binding resolution. Therefore, time and effort may be devoted to mediation without reaching a solution. To protect the legal interests of their clients, many attorneys participate in mediation, if only to review the final agreement reached through the process.

Arbitration

Like mediation, **arbitration** uses a neutral third party to resolve a dispute. Unlike the mediator, however, an arbitrator generally is empowered to impose a binding decision that resolves the dispute and is enforceable by a court if the parties fail to comply. Arbitrators derive their power to impose a binding decision from a contract, the arbitration agreement, between the parties. Frequently, parties to a contract include a provision requiring any disputes arising under the contract to be resolved through arbitration. Alternatively, parties may enter into an arbitration agreement, sometimes called an **ad hoc** agreement, after a dispute arises. Some arbitration agreements provide for a panel of arbitrators, who reach a decision by majority vote, while others use a single arbitrator.

The arbitration contract may establish all of the rules for the arbitration process, including selection of the arbitrator, designation of the arbitration site, procedures for presenting evidence, and deadlines for hearings and the decision. Rather than develop these rules for each

agreement, parties may simply incorporate rules previously developed by existing arbitration organizations, such as the American Arbitration Association, the International Chamber of Commerce, or the United Nations Commission on International Trade Law. The American Arbitration Association, a not-for-profit organization specializing in arbitration and other ADR methods since 1926, suggests the following standard clause for insertion in commercial contracts:

> Any controversy or claim arising out of or relating to this contract, or the breach thereof, shall be settled by arbitration administered by the American Arbitration Association under its Commercial Arbitration Rules, and judgment on the award rendered by the arbitrator(s) may be entered in any court having jurisdiction thereof.[1]

Although the exact process depends on the agreement, arbitration typically follows a standard procedure. The following discussion is based on the Commercial Arbitration Rules of the American Arbitration Association.

To initiate the process, one or both parties notify the arbitrator or arbitration association that the dispute is being submitted to arbitration. If the agreement does not specify the arbitrator, selection often is made from a roster of arbitrators, many of whom have expertise or specialize in certain types of disputes. After appointment, the arbitrator generally assumes responsibility for the arbitration process and schedules a hearing with notice to the parties. The arbitrator also may schedule an administrative conference or preliminary hearing with the parties to arrange the production and exchange of pertinent evidence or to discuss any matters that could expedite the proceedings. At the arbitration hearing, each party presents its claims, evidence, and witnesses subject to the arbitrator's determination of relevancy and materiality. Generally, legal rules of evidence do not apply. Following the hearing, the arbitrator may allow the parties to submit written briefs. The arbitrator then renders a written decision, known as an "award," that resolves the dispute and grants any remedy deemed just by the arbitrator. Although the award may explain the reasons for the decision, a formal opinion is not required and the award usually need not follow legal precedent.

---

[1]AMERICAN ARBITRATION ASSOCIATION, COMMERCIAL DISPUTE RESOLUTION CLAUSES (2004).

If the arbitration is binding, the parties must comply with the award. To ensure enforcement, most arbitration agreements provide for entry of a judgment on the award in a court where it then may be enforced in the same manner as a judgment rendered by the court. At the request of one or both of the parties, the court may provide a limited review of the award generally restricted to a determination that the arbitration proceedings were fair and unbiased. The court, however, will not review the merits of the case. As illustrated in the following case, courts generally defer to the arbitrator when reviewing issues relating to the arbitration.

Advanced Micro Devices, Inc. v. Intel Corporation

885 P.2d 994 (Cal. 1994)

Two computer chip manufacturers, Intel Corporation and Advanced Micro Devices, Inc. (AMD), entered into a 10-year contract to exchange technical information so that each could make products that could be substituted for the other's products. The contract required arbitration of "disagreements arising under this Agreement" and authorized the arbitrator to "grant any remedy or relief which the Arbitrator deems just and equitable and within the scope of the agreement of the parties." In 1987, AMD claimed that Intel had breached the contract and requested arbitration. After four and one-half years of arbitration, that included 355 days of hearings, the arbitrator found that Intel had breached the contract. Paragraphs 5 and 6 of the arbitrator's award ordered Intel to allow AMD to use certain patents, trade secrets, and copyrights owned by Intel. Intel petitioned the California trial court to vacate paragraphs 5 and 6 of the award. The trial court confirmed the full award, but the California Court of Appeal ruled that the remedies in paragraphs 5 and 6 were improper. AMD appealed to the California Supreme Court.

Werdegar, Justice

. . . [O]ur decisions teach that courts should generally defer to an arbitrator's finding that determination of a particular question is within the scope of his or her contractual authority. . . .

Although [California Law] permits the court to vacate an award that exceeds the arbitrator's powers, the deference due an arbitrator's decision on the merits of the controversy requires a court to refrain from substituting its judgment for the arbitrator's in determining the contractual scope of those powers. . . . The decision to arbitrate disputes is motivated in part by the desire to avoid the delay and cost of judicial trials and appeals. . . . A rule of judicial review under which courts would independently redetermine the scope of an arbitration agreement already interpreted by the arbitrator would invite frequent and protracted judicial proceedings, contravening the parties' expectations of finality. . . .

Deference to the arbitrator is also required by the character of the remedy decision itself. Fashioning remedies for a breach of contract or other injury is not always a simple matter. . . . It may require, . . . as in this case, finding a way of approximating the impact of a breach that cannot with any certainty be reduced to monetary terms. Passage of time and changed circumstances may have rendered any remedies suggested by the contract insufficient or excessive. As the United States Supreme Court explained in the leading case on review of arbitral remedies in the collective bargaining context, the arbitrator is required "to bring his informed judgment to bear to reach a fair solution of a problem. . . . There the need is for flexibility in meeting a wide variety of situations. . . ." [*Steelworkers v. Enterprise Corp.,* 80 S. Ct. 1358, 1361 (1960).]

The choice of remedy, then, may at times call on any decisionmaker's flexibility, creativity and sense of fairness. In private arbitrations, the parties have bargained for the relatively free exercise of those faculties. . . . Were courts to reevaluate independently the merits of a particular remedy, the parties' contractual expectation of a decision according to the arbitrators' best judgment would be defeated.

Independent reevaluation by a court, moreover, is unlikely to be either expeditious or accurate. Arbitrations may, as this case demonstrates, be lengthy and complicated. The proceedings may be informal and a complete stenographic record may not be prepared. A reviewing court is thus not in a favorable position to substitute its judgment for that of the arbitrator as to what relief is most just and equitable under all the circumstances. Further, independent review of remedies, no less than of other arbitrated questions, would tend to increase the cost and delay involved. . . .

We do not, by the above, intend to suggest an arbitrator's exercise of discretion in ordering relief is unrestricted or unreviewable. Such an extreme position enjoys no support in our statutes or cases. The powers of an arbitrator derive from, and are limited by, the agreement to arbitrate. . . . [T]he courts retain the ultimate authority to overturn awards as beyond the arbitrator's powers, whether for an unauthorized remedy or decision on an unsubmitted issue. . . .

In *Ethyl Corp. v. United Steelworkers of America,* [768 F.2d 180, 184–85 (7th Cir. 1985)], . . . [t]he court explained an award does not exceed the arbitrator's powers if it is based on an interpretation— "unsound though it may be"—of the contract: "It is only when the arbitrator *must* have based his award on some body of thought, feeling, or policy, or law that is outside the contract . . . that the award can be said not to 'draw its essence from the collective bargaining agreement'. . . ."

We distill from these cases what we believe is a meaningful, workable and properly deferential framework for reviewing an arbitrator's choice of remedies. Arbitrators are not obliged to read contracts literally, and an award may not be vacated merely because the court is unable to find the relief granted was authorized by a specific term of the contract. . . . The remedy awarded, however, must bear some rational relationship to the contract and the breach. . . . Where the damage is difficult to determine or measure, the arbitrator enjoys correspondingly broader discretion to fashion a remedy. . . . The award will be upheld so long as it was even arguably based on the contract; it may be vacated only if the reviewing court is *compelled* to infer the award was based on an extrinsic source. . . . In close cases the arbitrator's decision must stand. . . .

[S]ection 42 of the rules of arbitration agreed upon by the parties authorized the arbitrator to grant "any remedy or relief which the Arbitrator deems just and equitable and within the scope of the agreement. . . ." Section 42 is identical to a provision of the Commercial Arbitration Rules of the American Arbitration Association (AAA). . . . Nothing in the contract's arbitration clause, section 42 of the rules adopted here, or the order of reference indicates an intent to place any special restrictions on the arbitrator's discretion to fashion remedies. . . .

Paragraphs 5 and 6 of the award did not exceed the arbitrator's power under the standard previously stated. The contested items of relief were rationally drawn from the arbitrator's conception of the contract's subject matter and the effects on AMD of Intel's breach. The available facts do not compel the conclusion [that] the arbitrator fashioned a remedy by reaching outside the contract to some extrinsic source. . . . We conclude the challenged portions of the arbitrator's award were within his authority to fashion remedies for a breach of contract. . . .

[Judgment reversed.]

Historically, American courts viewed arbitration agreements as an infringement on the judicial function and often refused to enforce them. More recently, however, courts have recognized that arbitration of civil disputes can be an effective way for courts to reduce their caseloads, and for the parties to avoid the expense and delay of litigation. The **Federal Arbitration Act**[2] provides that arbitration agreements generally "shall be valid, irrevocable, and enforceable, save upon such grounds as exist at law or in equity for the revocation of any contract."[3] Relying on the Arbitration Act, the Supreme Court has upheld a variety of arbitration agreements, including those resolving claims based on alleged violations of federal statutes, such as the federal securities and antitrust laws.

The success of private arbitration has led many state and federal courts to establish court-annexed arbitration programs. Under these programs, a trial court may require the parties to a civil suit to submit their dispute to nonbinding arbitration, which permits subsequent litigation if either party is dissatisfied with the arbitration proceedings. Jurisdictions using court-annexed arbitration have reported a reduction in both court congestion and court costs because many parties have been willing to forgo the litigation option and accept the arbitrator's award.

Other ADR Methods

Other ADR methods that are especially useful to businesses include neutral evaluation (sometimes called early neutral evaluation), the mini-trial, and the private trial.

---

[2]9 U.S.C. §1 *et seq.*
[3]9 U.S.C. §2.

In neutral evaluation, the parties retain an impartial third person (the neutral), who often has expertise in the legal or technical issues of the case, to assess the strengths and weaknesses of their cases. After the parties and their attorneys make informal presentations of their evidence and legal arguments, the neutral provides an evaluation of both parties' cases and a prediction of the results if the case goes to trial. The neutral also may assist the parties to reach an agreement or settlement.

The mini-trial is a more structured format in which the parties' attorneys present a summary of the evidence and law of the dispute to upper level executives of the parties who have the authority to settle the dispute. A neutral advisor or moderator generally presides over the proceedings. Following the presentation, the executives meet (without attorneys or support staff) to try to reach a settlement. In some cases, the advisor may provide assistance in helping the executives reach an agreement. Both neutral evaluation and the mini-trial encourage the parties to resolve their dispute as a business decision.

A private trial (also known as a private judging) is a form of litigation in which the parties agree to have the case resolved by a retired judge with the authority to try cases under state law. Private trials, which must be authorized by state law, require the judge to follow procedural rules used in court trials. The parties often try to select a judge with expertise in the issues of their case. Unlike other forms of ADR, the decisions of a private trial may be appealed to a higher court like other judicial cases. Nevertheless, private trials are advantageous to businesses because the trial usually can be scheduled quickly and the likelihood of legal error is minimized due to the judge's expertise.

In recent years, both state and federal courts have encouraged parties involved in lawsuits to take advantage of ADR to resolve their civil disputes. Federal law now requires federal district courts to make ADR methods available to litigants and to authorize their use.[4] ADR has proved important in saving time and money, in providing more flexible, and often private, methods of resolving disputes, and in relieving court congestion. Yet, alternative dispute resolution will not replace the judicial system because litigation serves important purposes that cannot be achieved by private means. Table 2.1 briefly compares the various methods of civil dispute resolution.

Litigation—Pretrial Proceedings

In litigation, a dispute is resolved in a court of law by a neutral judge who applies principles of law set forth in constitutions, statutes, and the common law. Courts generally apply law in a consistent manner using the doctrine of *stare decisis*. The court system also provides parties the opportunity to litigate new issues of law in order to develop rules that can be used for guidance in determining future conduct. Perhaps the most important advantage of litigation is that the parties are guaranteed due process of law. The Fifth and Fourteenth Amendments to the Constitution prohibit the federal and state governments from depriving a person of life, liberty, or property without due process of law. Because the courts, as one branch of the government, are empowered in civil cases to deprive a person of property—for example, by granting a remedy requiring one party to pay money damages to the other—they must comply with the constitutional due process mandate in resolving civil disputes.[5]

Due process of law (specifically "procedural due process") entitles a party to a civil lawsuit to receive notice of the alleged violation of law and a hearing in which the party may defend its actions. To implement this guarantee, courts have adopted rules of civil procedure to be followed in lawsuits. Each state, as well as the federal government, has its own rules of civil procedure; yet, they generally are very similar. Thus, lawsuits proceed in three broad stages: the pleadings stage, the discovery stage, and the trial. Some cases include a fourth stage, the appeal. At any time during this process, the parties may agree to settle their case, and at certain points the court may terminate the case as a matter of law. As a result, few civil lawsuits actually reach trial.

Pleadings Stage

Pleadings are written documents that summarize the facts and establish the legal issues of a lawsuit. These documents are filed with the court and are served on the parties to the lawsuit. Generally, pleadings must be signed by the party or her attorney. To discourage frivolous lawsuits or baseless claims, courts maintain the

---

[4]Alternative Dispute Resolution Act of 1998, 28 U.S.C. §§651-658.

[5]Criminal proceedings also must comply with the requirements of due process (see Chapter 3).

Table 2.1	Comparison of Methods of Civil Dispute Resolution*			
	Litigation	**Arbitration**	**Mediation**	**Negotiation**
Private/Public	Public	Private	Private	Private
Third-Party Involvement	Judge: neutral decision maker imposed on parties; generally no expertise in subject of dispute.	Arbitrator: neutral decision maker usually selected by parties; generally has expertise in subject of dispute.	Mediator: facilitator selected by parties; generally has expertise in subject of dispute.	None.
Procedural Characteristics	Very formal; applies procedural and substantive rules set by law.	Formal; procedural and substantive rules may be set by parties.	Usually informal; unstructured.	Usually informal; unstructured.
Presentation of Evidence	Each party may present evidence and arguments, generally limited by rules of relevance.	Each party may present evidence and arguments, generally limited by rules of relevance.	Each party may present evidence and arguments, usually without limitations.	Each party may present evidence and arguments, usually without limitations.
Final Outcome	Judgment, sometimes supported by opinion.	Award, sometimes supported by opinion.	Parties seek mutually acceptable agreement.	Parties seek mutually acceptable agreement.
Enforceability	Binding, subject to appellate review.	Generally binding, subject to limited judicial review.	If agreement reached, may be enforced as contract.	If agreement reached, may be enforced as contract.
Variations	Private trial.	Court-annexed arbitration.	Neutral evaluation; mini-trial.	

*This table is adapted from Goldberg, Green, and Sander, *Dispute Resolution* 8–9 (1985).

power to impose sanctions against attorneys or parties who file pleadings that do not have a sound basis in fact or law. The pleadings include the complaint, the answer, counterclaims, crossclaims, third-party complaints, and answers to the counterclaims, crossclaims, and third-party complaints.

The Complaint. A lawsuit begins when the plaintiff files a **complaint** against a defendant.[6] The complaint includes a statement of the basis for the court's jurisdiction, allegations of fact, and a prayer or demand for relief. The allegations of fact are the plaintiff's statement of the facts underlying the dispute and must present a **cause of action:** facts that, if proven, entitle the plaintiff to judicial relief. Statutory law and the common law establish the elements of a cause of action. A cause of action for breach of contract, for example,

requires that the facts establish the following elements: the existence of a contract, the defendant's duty to perform some act under the contract, the defendant's failure to perform, and an injury to the plaintiff resulting from the defendant's failure to perform. If the plaintiff bases a claim on more than one cause of action, the facts supporting each cause of action are listed in separate counts within the complaint.

Following the allegations in each count, the plaintiff requests the court to provide a remedy for the alleged wrong in a statement called the prayer or demand for relief. Usually, the plaintiff requests **damages,** a monetary award. Damages are known as the "legal remedy" or "remedy at law" because a monetary award was the traditional remedy available in courts of law. Several types of damages are recognized. General damages (also called compensatory or actual damages) are intended to compensate the plaintiff for direct and immediate losses caused by the defendant's conduct. Special (or consequential) damages are requested for extraordinary injuries peculiar to the plaintiff. Punitive

[6]In some states, or in certain types of cases, the initial pleading is called a petition; the party filing the suit is called the petitioner; and the party being sued is called the respondent.

(or exemplary) damages are a monetary award in excess of the plaintiff's actual losses designed to punish the defendant for aggravated misconduct.[7] The type of damages sought by the plaintiff depends on the nature of the case. If damages are not adequate, the plaintiff might request an equitable remedy such as an injunction or specific performance of a contract.

Many lawsuits involve only two parties, but in other cases, multiple parties may be involved. If two or more persons join together to bring a lawsuit, they are called "co-plaintiffs." Similarly, the plaintiff or plaintiffs may sue more than two or more persons who become "co-defendants." State and federal statutory law authorize a special type of lawsuit known as a **class action** for cases involving numerous plaintiffs. In a class action one or more persons file a lawsuit on their own behalf and on behalf of all persons (the class) having claims based on the same issues of fact and law. A class action might be appropriate, for example, if a large group of consumers purchased a defective product from a manufacturer. The class action serves to prevent multiple suits that might result in inconsistent judgments and facilitates litigation of matters in which no individual plaintiff has a claim large enough to justify the expenses of litigation.

Note that, by statute enacted in 2005, many class actions formerly maintained in state courts, are now tried in federal court under diversity jurisdiction. Specifically, federal district courts have original jurisdiction over any class action in which: (1) 100 or more plaintiffs seek damages totaling more than $5 million; and (2) any member of the plaintiff class is a citizen of a state different from any defendant ("minimal" diversity).[8] Any class action filed in state court that meets these criteria may, at the defendant's request, be removed (transferred) to federal court.[9]

Service of Process. After the plaintiff files the complaint, the defendant must be provided notice of the suit by **service of process**—formal delivery of the complaint and a summons to the defendant. The **summons** orders the defendant to appear in court on a certain date or to answer the complaint within a specified number of days. The proper method of service of process varies from state to state but, generally, requires the sheriff to personally serve the defendant with the summons and complaint. In some cases, service of process may be made by mailing or delivering the complaint and summons to the defendant's residence. The sheriff usually provides a written record of service of process to the court.

Personal Jurisdiction. Service of process is effective only if the court has personal jurisdiction over the defendant. **Personal jurisdiction** (or *in personam* jurisdiction) is a court's power and authority to issue a judgment that is binding on the parties.[10] The plaintiff, by filing the lawsuit with the court, voluntarily submits to its jurisdiction, thereby agreeing to be bound by the court's judgment of the case.

Personal jurisdiction over the defendant, however, depends on the relationship of the defendant to the state in which the court is located. A state court has personal jurisdiction over all persons who reside in the state and who are properly served with the summons and complaint. A defendant who is not a resident of the state is subject to a state court's personal jurisdiction if the defendant, while present in the state, is properly served with the summons and complaint ("transient" jurisdiction). A nonresident also may consent to the court's personal jurisdiction, thereby waiving the right to challenge the authority of the court to issue a judgment binding on him.

If, however, an out-of-state resident does not consent or is not served within the state, a state court has personal jurisdiction only over a defendant who has had certain *minimum contacts* with the state so that permitting the suit "does not offend traditional notions of fair play and substantial justice."[11] In other words, a nonresident defendant who has certain contacts, ties, or relations with the state may be subject to the personal jurisdiction of that state's courts. To determine whether an out-of-state defendant has had minimum contacts with the state, the court examines the nature and extent of the activities that the defendant has conducted within the state. The court determines whether the defendant has

---

[7]Special damages are discussed in detail in Chapters 15 and 19; punitive damages are discussed in Chapters 5 and 15.
[8]28 U.S.C. §1332(d)(2).
[9]28 U.S.C. §1453.

[10]Personal jurisdiction should not be confused with a court's subject matter jurisdiction—the statutory or constitutional grant of power to a court authorizing it to resolve certain types of cases. Personal jurisdiction concerns whether a court with subject matter jurisdiction over a case can exercise that authority over parties to a specific dispute.
[11]International Shoe Company v. State of Washington, 66 S. Ct. 154, 158 (1945).

in some way enjoyed the protection and benefits of the state's laws so that he should be obligated to submit to the state court's jurisdiction.

Corporations and other organizations that conduct business activities in more than one state are required to defend lawsuits filed against them only in those states with which they have had minimum contacts. In the landmark 1945 case *International Shoe Co. v. State of Washington,* the United States Supreme Court first examined the minimum contacts that subject an out-of-state corporation to the personal jurisdiction of a state court. International Shoe Co., a corporation with its principal place of business in Missouri, employed salespeople who lived in the state of Washington and solicited orders there. The corporation had no offices in Washington and all merchandise was shipped from St. Louis. The state of Washington sued International Shoe Co. in a Washington court for failure to pay unemployment taxes for several of its salespeople who worked in the state. Service of process was made by delivering the notice of assessment to a salesman in Washington and mailing a copy by registered mail to International Shoe's offices in St. Louis. In holding that the Washington state court had personal jurisdiction over International Shoe Co., the Supreme Court noted:

> [The Due Process Clause] does not contemplate that a state may make binding a judgment *in personam* against an individual or corporate defendant with which the state has no contacts, ties, or relations. . . . But to the extent that a corporation exercises the privilege of conducting activities within a state, it enjoys the benefits and protection of the laws of that state. The exercise of that privilege may give rise to obligations, and, so far as those obligations arise out of or are connected with the activities within the state, a procedure which requires the corporation to respond to a suit brought to enforce them can, in most instances, hardly be said to be undue. . . .
>
> Applying these standards, the activities carried on in behalf of appellant in the State of Washington were neither irregular nor casual. They were systematic and continuous throughout the years in question. They resulted in a large volume of interstate business, in the course of which appellant received the benefits and protection of the laws of the state, including the right to resort to the courts for the enforcement of its rights. The obligation which is here sued upon arose out of those very activities. It is evident that these operations establish sufficient contacts or ties with the state of the forum to make it reasonable and just, according to our traditional conception of fair play and

substantial justice, to permit the state to enforce the obligations which appellant has incurred there. Hence we cannot say that the maintenance of the present suit in the State of Washington involves an unreasonable or undue procedure. . . .[12]

Long Arm Statutes. Since the Supreme Court's holding in *International Shoe Co.,* most states have enacted **long arm statutes** to codify the minimum contacts that subject a nonresident defendant to a state court's jurisdiction. Generally, these statutes provide that a court has personal jurisdiction over a defendant in cases arising from the defendant's:

1. transacting any business in the state;
2. contracting to supply goods or services in the state;
3. contacting to insure any person, property, or risk located in the state;
4. committing a tort in the state or causing injury as a result of business transacted or solicited in the state; or
5. owning, using, or possessing real property interests in the state.

Although long arm statutes give a court personal jurisdiction over a nonresident defendant, service of process still must be made. Usually, the long arm statutes require that the summons and complaint be delivered to the out-of-state defendant or to an agent of the defendant located within the state. States generally require a corporation to appoint an in-state agent upon whom service of process may be made as a condition of doing business within the state.

When jurisdiction over a defendant is based solely upon a long arm statute, only claims arising from acts listed in the statute may be asserted against the defendant. In such cases, the court is said to have *specific* personal jurisdiction over the defendant. Because the defendant has a limited relationship with the state, the court may only consider claims that arise from the specific contacts that the defendant has had with the state. So, for example, if the defendant's minimum contact with the state is ownership of a building (real property), the state's courts have jurisdiction over the defendant only in cases arising from the ownership of the building. Unrelated contracts or torts that do not meet the requirements of the long-arm statute cannot be litigated in the state.

---

[12]66 S. Ct. at 160.

Sometimes, however, a non-resident defendant may have extensive contacts with a state. The Supreme Court has ruled that when a defendant has contacts with a state that are "substantial"[13] and "continuous and systematic,"[14] the state's courts have *general* personal jurisdiction over the defendant. In such cases, the court may resolve any claims against the defendant, not just claims that arose from the defendant's specific contact with the state. In the following case, the court analyzes the differences between specific personal jurisdiction and general personal jurisdiction.

American Type Culture Collection, Inc. v. Coleman

83 S.W.3d 801 (Tex. 2002)

American Type Culture Collection, Inc. ("ATCC") is a repository for living microorganisms, viruses, and cell lines used in research. ATCC sells biological research material to research institutes and commercial manufacturers throughout the United States and in forty-five countries. Plaintiff Marshall Coleman and approximately 1,800 veterans of the Persian Gulf War sued ATCC claiming that they had been injured by biological and chemical weapons made from material, equipment, and technology that ATCC had sold to Iraq. The plaintiffs sued ATCC in Texas seeking damages allegedly caused by ATCC's negligence and sale of defective products. ATCC moved to dismiss the lawsuit arguing that it was not subject to the personal jurisdiction of Texas courts. The trial court and court of appeals denied ATCC's motion holding that jurisdiction was proper due to ATCC's "numerous and repetitive" sales in Texas. ATCC appealed to the Texas Supreme Court.

Jefferson, Justice

. . . Texas courts may assert personal jurisdiction over a nonresident defendant only if the Texas long-arm statute authorizes jurisdiction and the exercise of jurisdiction is consistent with federal and state due process standards. . . . Under the Due Process Clause of the Fourteenth Amendment, jurisdiction is proper if a non-

resident defendant established "minimum contacts" with Texas and maintenance of the suit does not offend "traditional notions of fair play and substantial justice." *International Shoe Co. v. Washington,* [66 S. Ct. 154, 160 (1945)]. The purpose of the minimum-contacts analysis is to protect the defendant from being haled into court when its relationship with Texas is too attenuated to support jurisdiction. . . . Accordingly, we focus upon the defendant's activities and expectations in deciding whether it is proper to call it before a Texas court.

The minimum-contacts analysis requires that a defendant "purposefully avail" itself of the privilege of conducting activities within Texas, thus invoking the benefits and protections of our laws. *Burger King Corp. v. Rudzewicz,* [105 S. Ct. 2174 (1985)]. The defendant's activities, whether they consist of direct acts within Texas or conduct outside Texas, must justify a conclusion that the defendant could reasonably anticipate being called into a Texas court. . . . A defendant is not subject to jurisdiction here if its Texas contacts are random, fortuitous, or attenuated. . . . Nor can a defendant be haled into a Texas court for the unilateral acts of a third party. It is the quality and nature of the defendant's contacts, rather than their number, that is important to the minimum-contacts analysis. . . .

A defendant's contacts with a forum can give rise to either specific or general jurisdiction. For a court to exercise specific jurisdiction over a nonresident defendant, two requirements must be met: (1) the defendant's contacts with the forum must be purposeful, and (2) the cause of action must arise from or relate to those contacts. . . . General jurisdiction, which the plaintiffs assert here, on the other hand, allows a forum to exercise jurisdiction over a defendant even if the cause of action did not arise from or relate to a defendant's contacts with the forum. . . . General jurisdiction is present when a defendant's contacts with a forum are "continuous and systematic," a more demanding minimum-contacts analysis than specific jurisdiction. *Guardian Royal Exch. Assur., Ltd. v. English China Clays, P.L.C.,* 815 S.W.2d 223, 228 (Tex. 1991).

The plaintiff bears the initial burden of pleading allegations sufficient to bring a nonresident defendant within the provisions of the long-arm statute. . . . Because Coleman alleges that general personal jurisdiction exists, we examine whether ATCC met its burden of establishing that its contacts with Texas were not continuous and systematic. The pertinent jurisdictional facts are set out below.

---

[13]Perkins v. Benguet Consolidated Mining Co., 72 S. Ct. 413, 419 (1952).

[14]Helicopteros Nacionales de Colombia, S.A. v. Hall, 104 S. Ct. 1868, 1873 (1984).

ATCC is organized under District of Columbia laws and its principal place of business is Rockville, Maryland. ATCC advertises in national and international journals and its catalogues are sent only upon request. The majority of its sales are made by phone or written orders received in Maryland and are sent free-on-board ("F.O.B.") Rockville, Maryland. Title to the goods passes to buyers in Maryland. . . . (Free on Board "means that title to property passes from the seller to buyer at the designated FOB point."). ATCC invoices all of its sales and receives all payments in Maryland.

ATCC is not authorized to do business in Texas and does not have offices, distributors, employees, real property, or telephone listings in Texas. ATCC is not required to and does not have a registered agent in Texas. It does not make unsolicited mailings to Texas customers, it does not recruit employees in Texas, and it does not advertise in Texas journals. Nevertheless, the record reveals that ATCC has had contacts with Texas. We examine these contacts to determine whether they are "continuous and systematic."

ATCC has sold its products to Texas residents for at least eighteen years. At the commencement of this suit, ATCC's Texas sales accounted for 3.5 percent of its total annual sales and five percent of its total U.S. sales, generating approximately $350,000 in revenue. Although Coleman argues to the contrary, the record establishes ATCC's contention that the sales were shipped F.O.B. from Rockville, Maryland.

In addition to selling goods to Texas residents, ATCC also serves as a repository for Texas researchers seeking microorganism patents. For the fifteen to twenty-year period before this suit, nearly 2.7 percent of the 13,000 patents in ATCC's Maryland repository came from Texas residents. In connection with these services, interested customers shipped their materials to Maryland and entered into customer safe-deposit agreements. All the services related to the safe-deposit agreements were performed by ATCC in Maryland.

Similarly, in 1991, ATCC contracted with the University of Texas Southwestern Medical Center to propagate and test cell-lines. The contract was signed by ATCC in Maryland. And like its other agreements with Texas residents, ATCC performed all the services related to the contract in Maryland.

Over a five-year period, ATCC purchased approximately $378,000 of supplies from thirty-three Texas vendors. Some of the goods were sent F.O.B. from Texas. And from 1987 to 1994, ATCC representatives attended five scientific conferences in Texas. At four

conferences, ATCC had an exhibit booth and distributed corporate publications.

The court of appeals stated that ATCC's volume of Texas sales was the "bedrock" fact that supported jurisdiction. . . . We disagree. In *Bearry v. Beech Aircraft Corp.,* 818 F.2d 370 (5th Cir. 1987), the Fifth Circuit [Court of Appeals] discounted the fact that Beech Aircraft sold over $72 million of airframe assemblies to a Texas company because the goods were delivered "F.O.B. Wichita." The court stated:

> Beech exercised its right to structure its affairs in a manner calculated to shield it from the general jurisdiction of the courts of other states such as Texas, carefully requiring the negotiation, completion, and performance of all contracts in Kansas. Beech has not afforded itself the benefits and protections of the laws of Texas, but instead has calculatedly avoided them . . . . We are not aware that other courts have disregarded the structure of transactions in support of general jurisdiction. And, we have held such 'technicalities' relevant in analyzing general personal jurisdiction questions.

Id. at 375-76. We are persuaded by this analysis. General jurisdiction is premised on the notion of consent. That is, by invoking the benefits and protections of a forum's laws, a nonresident defendant consents to being sued there. When a nonresident defendant purposefully structures transactions to avoid the benefits and protections of a forum's laws, the legal fiction of consent no longer applies. Thus, title passing outside of Texas is a factor that weighs against a finding that Texas has general jurisdiction over a nonresident defendant such as ATCC. As a result, ATCC's Texas sales cannot properly be characterized as a "bedrock" fact that supports jurisdiction.

ATCC contends that its purchases from Texas vendors "do not provide evidence warranting the exercise of general jurisdiction over ATCC." We agree. In *Helicopteros Nacionales De Colombia, S.A. v. Hall,* [104 S. Ct. 1868 (1984)], the United States Supreme Court stated that "mere purchases, even if occurring at regular intervals, are not enough to warrant a State's assertion of in personam jurisdiction over a nonresident corporation in a cause of action not related to those purchase transactions." . . . Accordingly, ATCC's purchases from Texas vendors will not alone support the exercise of general jurisdiction.

Moreover, because ATCC signed and performed in Maryland its repository contracts and its contract with the University of Texas Southwestern Medical Center, those contracts do not support a finding of general jurisdiction. . . . Similarly, ATCC's attendance at the five Texas conferences does not support the exercise of general jurisdiction. The record reflects that the scientific community, not ATCC, selected the conference locations. . . .

However, for general jurisdictional purposes, we do not view each contact in isolation. All contacts must be carefully investigated, compiled, sorted, and analyzed for proof of a pattern of continuing and systematic activity. . . . Thus, we must determine whether ATCC's contacts establish a pattern of continuing and systematic activity. . . .

The Court in *Helicopteros,* analyzing facts somewhat similar to those presented here, concluded there was no basis for the assertion of personal jurisdiction. In that case, Helicol, a helicopter company from Colombia, contracted to provide helicopter services in Peru. . . . Four United States citizens were killed in a helicopter crash in Peru. Their representatives filed suit against Helicol in Texas. Helicol filed a motion to dismiss for lack of personal jurisdiction. The motion was denied and ultimately the Supreme Court granted certiorari to determine whether a Texas court could lawfully exercise general jurisdiction over Helicol.

The Court found Helicol's contacts with Texas insufficient to support the exercise of general jurisdiction, even though Helicol had ventured to Texas and negotiated a contract for transportation in Texas, purchased approximately eighty percent of its helicopter fleet (worth over $4 million) and other related equipment from Texas vendors at regular intervals, and had sent pilots and other personnel to Texas for training. . . .

Although the quantity of ATCC's contacts may suggest that ATCC had a significant relationship with Texas, we are not concerned with the quantity of contacts. Instead, we must look to the quality of those contacts. And in this case, we are not persuaded that the quality of ATCC's contacts support general jurisdiction as defined by the United States Supreme Court. ATCC does not advertise in Texas, has no physical presence in Texas, performs all its business services outside Texas, and carefully constructs its contracts to ensure it does not benefit from Texas laws. . . . Under these circumstances, we must conclude that ATCC's contacts with Texas were not continuous and systematic. . . .

In sum, because ATCC did not have sufficient minimum contacts with Texas, it is not subject to *in personam* jurisdiction. Accordingly, we reverse the court of appeals' judgment and render judgment dismissing the case against ATCC for lack of personal jurisdiction.

[Judgment reversed and remanded.]

Personal Jurisdiction in Federal Courts. The federal government has adopted rules similar to those of the states to govern service of process for cases brought in federal district courts.[15] If the defendant is an individual or corporation, federal law also allows service of the summons and complaint to be made according to the rules of the state in which the federal court is located. A federal district court has personal jurisdiction over a defendant who is properly served and a resident of the state, or who is served within the state, or who is subject to the state's long arm statute. In certain cases involving multiple parties, a federal district court may also obtain personal jurisdiction over a defendant properly served who resides within 100 miles of the court, even in another state. In addition, specific federal statutes often permit service of federal court process beyond the territorial limits of the state in cases brought under those statutes. In the federal courts, service of process generally is made by a United States marshal.

Answer to the Complaint. After receiving service of process, a defendant who intends to contest the lawsuit must respond, by filing either a motion to dismiss or an answer to the complaint within the time period specified in the summons. If the defendant fails to respond, the court may enter **default judgment**—a ruling in favor of the plaintiff granting the relief requested in the complaint. To contest the lawsuit on its merits, the defendant files an **answer** to the complaint within the time specified in the summons. In the answer, the defendant must reply to each allegation of the complaint by admitting or denying the truth of the allegation. If the defendant does not know whether the allegation is true or false, and so states, the statement has the same effect as a denial. The answer also must list any affirmative defenses that the defendant intends to prove at trial. An **affirmative defense** is an allegation of facts that the law recognizes as a bar to the plaintiff's claim. Affirmative defenses are discussed further in later chapters but include matters such as expiration of

---

[15]Fed. R. Civ. P. 4.

the statute of limitations, discharge of the claim by bankruptcy, or prior adjudication of the claim.

The complaint and answer establish the issues of the case. Every allegation of the complaint not admitted in the answer must be proved by the plaintiff; all facts admitted are accepted as established when the trial occurs.

Counterclaims, Crossclaims, and Third-Party Complaints.

At the same time the defendant answers the complaint, she also may file additional pleadings. A **counterclaim** is a complaint filed by the defendant against the plaintiff. Counterclaims are either compulsory or permissive. In most jurisdictions, the law requires the defendant to file all compulsory counterclaims: legal claims arising from the same facts alleged in the original complaint. A defendant who fails to do so may be barred from suing on the claim in the future. Permissive counterclaims are any that the defendant is not required to file. Permissive counterclaims usually concern facts not related to the plaintiff's cause of action.

The defendant also may file appropriate **crossclaims**—complaints against other parties listed as defendants in the lawsuit. Crossclaims generally must arise from the same occurrence underlying the original complaint. The defendant named in the original complaint also may sue other persons not named as parties in the original suit by filing a pleading called a **third-party complaint.**

Assume that an automobile accident occurs involving separate cars driven by Alfred, Betty, and Charlie. Alfred as plaintiff files a complaint naming Betty and Charlie as defendants and alleging that each of them negligently caused the accident. Betty, who believes that the accident was caused by Alfred and Charlie, could file a counterclaim for negligence against Alfred and a crossclaim for negligence against Charlie. Assume further that Betty believes the accident also was caused in part by Donna, a bicyclist who rode into the street in front of the cars. Betty could file a third-party complaint against Donna.

Counterclaims, crossclaims, and third-party complaints are treated procedurally as complaints. That is, the counterdefendant, crossdefendant, or third-party defendant must be served with the counterclaim, crossclaim, or third-party complaint. Each party then has the opportunity to answer and assert other claims against the named parties or third parties. In a complicated lawsuit, the filing of pleadings may continue for several months until all appropriate persons are brought into the lawsuit.

Motions.

A **motion** is an application to the court to issue an order on a matter of law. Motions—either written or oral—are made during pretrial proceedings and throughout a trial. After a party makes a motion, the judge may allow oral or written arguments in support of or in opposition to the motion. The judge rules either by granting or by denying the motion. During the pleadings stage, the parties may file various types of motions, including a motion to dismiss the complaint, a motion for judgment on the pleadings, and a motion for change of venue or "place of trial."

Motion to Dismiss the Complaint. A **motion to dismiss the complaint** is filed by the defendant, usually instead of answering the complaint. The motion may request the court to dismiss the lawsuit on the grounds that the court does not have the power or authority to hear the case or to provide the remedy requested by the plaintiff. For example, the defendant may file a motion to dismiss on the grounds that the court lacks subject matter jurisdiction over the case or lacks personal jurisdiction over the defendant. Another basis for a motion to dismiss is that the complaint fails to state a claim for which judicial relief may be granted (sometimes called a "general demurrer"). This motion basically asserts that even if the plaintiff could prove all of the allegations of fact, the facts do not establish a legally recognized cause of action entitling the plaintiff to a judicial remedy.

If the judge grants a motion to dismiss, the case is dismissed, effectively ending the lawsuit. If, however, the judge denies the motion, the defendant then must answer the complaint and the pleadings process continues.

Motion for Judgment on the Pleadings. After all pleadings have been filed, one or both of the parties may file another motion, called a **motion for judgment on the pleadings,** which is similar to a general demurrer and allows the court to rule as a matter of law that one of the parties is entitled to judgment. Because the pleadings generally reveal many disputed facts, this motion is granted infrequently.

Motion for Change of Venue. Another motion that may be made by the defendant is a motion for change of venue, or "place of trial." Venue is sometimes confused with jurisdiction so that the distinction between the two should be carefully noted. **Venue** rules are stated in statutes or rules of civil procedure and determine which particular court among those having subject matter and personal jurisdiction *should* hear the case.

In state cases, proper venue generally is the county where any defendant resides or the county where the transaction causing the dispute occurred. Similarly, in federal civil cases (diversity and federal question), proper venue generally is the judicial district in which any defendant resides, if all defendants reside in the same state. Alternatively, the case may be tried in any judicial district where most of the events giving rise to the claim occurred or where most of the property involved in the dispute is located.[16]

A defendant who believes the case has been brought in an improper venue may make a motion for change of venue. Generally, the defendant must make a motion for change of venue prior to commencement of the trial. If the court grants the motion, the court simply transfers the case to the proper venue. If not, the case proceeds as usual and the judgment entered by the court is binding on the parties. Thus, improper venue does not affect the court's jurisdiction.

Removal. Although the plaintiff chooses the court in which to litigate, that choice is limited by the court's subject matter jurisdiction, and, more importantly, the chosen court's ability or inability to obtain personal jurisdiction over the defendant, discussed above. Another factor limiting the plaintiff's choice is the defendant's right of removal, introduced in Chapter 1.

Specifically, federal statute[17] provides that a defendant may remove or transfer a case filed in state court to the federal court (for the judicial district where the state court is located) if the case originally could have been filed in federal court. The defendant initiates the removal process by filing a "notice of removal" with the federal court within 30 days after receiving service of process from the state court. If the federal court finds removal appropriate, it will so notify the state court, which will proceed no further, and the case will then continue in the federal court.

If the case involves a federal question, the defendant may remove without regard to the citizenship of the parties. As previously noted, state courts often have concurrent jurisdiction with the federal courts to try federal question cases. In diversity cases, removal is allowed only if the defendant is not a resident of the forum state.[18] For example, assume Paul, a citizen of Illinois

sues David, a citizen of Indiana, in Illinois state court for $100,000 in damages arising out of an auto accident occurring in Illinois. The state court has both subject matter jurisdiction (as a court of general jurisdiction) and can obtain personal jurisdiction over David under the Illinois longarm statute (David allegedly committed a tort in Illinois). Because this case also could have been tried in federal court (as a diversity of citizenship case with an amount in controversy over $75,000), David has the option of removing the case to the federal court in Illinois. Had David instead sued Paul in Illinois state court for the same accident, Paul could not remove to federal court because he is a resident of Illinois.

Discovery Stage

After all pleadings are filed, the judge fixes a time period for **discovery,** a process in which the parties collect potential evidence for the case. During discovery, the parties and witnesses must cooperate in disclosing pertinent information. Courts have established five primary discovery tools—interrogatories, depositions, requests for production of documents and things, physical and mental examinations, and requests for admission—to assist in the process. During the discovery stage, each party is entitled to use these tools, which are described in detail below, to uncover relevant evidence.

The federal courts have adopted a rule requiring parties in all cases to disclose certain information even if not requested by the other party.[19] This information includes the name and, if known, address and telephone number of all persons likely to have relevant discoverable information; a copy or description of all relevant documents or other tangible things within the party's control; and any pertinent insurance agreements. To supplement these initial disclosures in federal court or to obtain all information in state courts without mandated disclosures, the parties can use the following discovery tools.

Discovery Tools. **Interrogatories** are written questions submitted by one party to another party who must provide written answers under oath. Interrogatories provide an efficient means to ascertain general information relevant to the case including the names of witnesses and the location of documents and other evidence. The

---

[16]28 U.S.C. §1391.
[17]28 U.S.C. §1441.
[18]28 U.S.C. §1441(b).

---

[19]Fed. R. Civ. P. 26(a).

parties often use other discovery tools to obtain more detailed information about data discovered through interrogatories.

A **deposition** is the testimony under oath of a person (the deponent) who is examined (deposed) out of court. The party requesting a deposition notifies the deponent and other parties of the time and place of the deposition and all parties may attend and ask questions of the deponent. The proceedings generally are recorded, and a transcript is available for a fee to parties who request it. If the deponent is not a party to the suit and will not attend voluntarily, the court will issue a **subpoena,** a court order commanding the deponent to appear and present testimony.

Depositions provide an opportunity not only to obtain information, but also to determine whether the deponent would be a credible and convincing witness at trial. Most jurisdictions also allow written depositions, although they are much less effective in eliciting pertinent information. If, however, the deponent resides far away from the parties, a written deposition may be necessary.

A third discovery tool is the **request for production of documents and things,** a party's written request to another party to produce specified materials in her possession or control for examination and copying. Generally, the items must be described with some specificity. If the items are immovable or difficult to transport, the party may request access to allow inspection of the items.

If the physical or mental condition of a party is at issue in a lawsuit, the judge may order the person to submit to a physical or mental examination by a physician. The judge makes such an order only if requested by one of the parties and the judge deems that cause has been shown for an examination—for example, when one party has claimed physical or mental injury by an opposing party.

The final tool available during the discovery stage is the **request for admission,** a written request from either party asking the other party to admit certain facts or opinions of facts or the genuineness of specified documents. Admissions, which are made under oath, are considered to be established, thereby eliminating the necessity of proving the matter at trial.

Discovery is conducted outside the court by the parties and their attorneys, who are required to comply with procedural rules on discovery. If the parties violate these rules, a judge may order compliance and, if the violations are serious, may impose sanctions including fines or even order imprisonment for contempt of court.

Purpose of Discovery. Discovery is designed to help the parties uncover relevant facts prior to trial. The discovery tools were developed to provide a relatively inexpensive means to collect this information so that wealthier litigants, with greater resources for investigation, would not have an unfair advantage. Thus, the major purpose of discovery is to ensure that civil cases are decided on their merits, not on the investigative or rhetorical skills of the parties or their attorneys. Discovery also substantially reduces the number of cases that actually go to trial. Based on information obtained during discovery, the parties usually evaluate the strengths and weaknesses of their claims and often settle the case without a trial.

The scope of discovery generally is very broad. Federal law, for example, provides:

> Parties may obtain discovery regarding any matter, not privileged, that is relevant to the claim or defense of any party, including the existence, description, nature, custody, condition, and location of any books, documents, or other tangible things and the identity and location of persons having knowledge of any discoverable matter. . . . Relevant information need not be admissible at the trial if the discovery appears reasonably calculated to lead to the discovery of admissible evidence.[20]

State discovery laws vary, but are similar to the federal rule. Excluded from discovery are materials that are the work product of the parties' attorneys and privileged information, such as information protected by attorney-client, doctor-patient, or priest-penitent privilege.

Although the discovery process is effective in helping parties uncover relevant evidence and witnesses, it has been criticized for unduly delaying, and increasing the costs of, litigation. The discovery process has been abused, for example, by parties and attorneys who conduct unnecessary or excessive discovery or who fail properly to respond to discovery requests in an effort to prolong a case or to force a settlement. Courts have made efforts to remedy these problems by adopting rules to simplify discovery and by imposing sanctions for abuses.

Motion for Summary Judgment. During the discovery stage many cases are settled and others are disposed of through a **motion for summary judgment.** The party

---

[20]FED. R. CIV. P. 26(b)(1).

who makes this motion must establish that no relevant facts are in dispute, thereby allowing the judge to decide the case as a matter of law. Unlike the motion for judgment on the pleadings, the summary judgment motion must be supported by statements under oath that prove the lack of factual controversy. Information obtained by deposition, interrogatories, mental or physical examination, or request for admissions is used to establish these facts. Summary judgment ends the case without trial but the judge's decision can be appealed.

Trial

If a case proceeds beyond the pleadings or discovery stage, the judge sets it for **trial,** a formal proceeding in court in which the issues established in the pleadings are resolved. Two types of trials are available, jury trial or bench trial.

Jury Trials and Bench Trials

In a jury trial, a **petit jury** (or simply a jury)—a body of disinterested persons—is selected to determine all issues of fact. After hearing factual evidence offered by the parties, the jury decides what actually happened. The judge advises the jury of the pertinent law in the case and the jury then applies the law to the facts to determine which party wins the case. In other words, in a jury trial, the judge decides issues of law and the jury determines issues of fact.

The Seventh Amendment of the United States Constitution guarantees a right to a jury trial in common law cases in the federal courts and most state constitutions create a similar right in state courts. In cases based on a statutory cause of action, the parties are entitled to a jury trial only if the statute so provides. The parties do not have the right to a jury trial in equity cases.

Even if the right to jury trial is guaranteed, a party generally must take some affirmative step to assert that right. For example, in federal courts a party must demand a jury trial in writing during the pleadings stage. Similar rules have been adopted by the states. A party who fails to assert the right to a jury trial may lose it.

Traditionally, a jury was composed of twelve men selected from the citizens of the community in which the court was located. Today, juries include both men and women and statutes allow fewer than twelve jurors. Although many states still employ twelve-person juries,

the Supreme Court has upheld the constitutionality of a jury in civil cases with as few as six persons.[21]

The alternative to a jury trial is a bench trial, which is used if the parties waive their right to a jury trial or in cases for which there is no right to a jury trial. In a bench trial, the judge determines all issues of fact and decides all issues of law.

Burden of Proof

The function of the trial is to allow the trier of fact—the jury in a jury trial, the judge in a bench trial—to resolve the issues of the case. The parties to the lawsuit present the facts of the case through **evidence**—legally admissible testimony of witnesses and documents or other pertinent tangible items offered to prove the facts alleged in the pleadings.

The rules of substantive law establish which party bears the **burden of proof**—the duty or obligation to prove the disputed fact or facts constituting a cause of action or affirmative defense. Generally, the plaintiff bears the burden of proving the facts of the complaint that have not been admitted by the defendant. At a minimum, the plaintiff must establish a "prima facie" case—some evidence supporting each allegation of the complaint that, unless contradicted or rebutted by other evidence, would entitle the plaintiff to recover. In other words, the defendant automatically prevails without producing any evidence, unless the plaintiff proves a prima facie case. Once the plaintiff establishes a prima facie case, the defendant then bears the burden of proving the facts alleged in any affirmative defenses. In addition, the defendant has the opportunity to present pertinent evidence rebutting the plaintiff's evidence. Similarly, the plaintiff may rebut the evidence offered by the defendant to prove the affirmative defenses.

The duty of the party bearing the burden of proof in most civil cases is to establish by a preponderance of the evidence (it is more probable or likely than not) that his allegations are true. In other words, the party bearing the burden of proof must provide evidence that is more persuasive or convincing than that provided by the opposing party. After considering all evidence presented by the parties, the trier of fact determines which allegations of fact are true based on the credibility of the witnesses and the quality of the evidence.

---

[21]Colgrove v. Battin, 93 S. Ct. 2448 (1973).

The Trial Process

Courts follow statutory rules of procedure that facilitate the organized presentation of evidence at the trial. Most trials, therefore, follow a similar order of proceeding: selection of the jury, opening statements, presentation of evidence, closing arguments, and instructions to the jury.

Jury Selection. A jury trial begins with the selection of the jury through *voir dire* **examination,** a procedure by which the potential jurors are questioned under oath to determine whether they are suitable to serve on the jury for the particular case. The judge requests a group of persons selected randomly from a pool of potential jurors to appear in the courtroom to answer a series of questions designed to elicit potential jurors' bias or prejudice against any of the parties. To dismiss a potential juror, a party exercises a challenge that excuses an individual from serving on the jury. Generally, each party is entitled to an unlimited number of *challenges for cause*—disqualification of the potential juror because of business or personal ties to a party or attorney or because of demonstrated bias concerning the merits of the case—and to a limited number of *peremptory challenges*—disqualification of the potential juror for which the party need not state a reason.[22] The *voir dire* examination continues until the appropriate number of jurors has been selected.

Opening Statements. At the beginning of the trial, each party may make an opening statement, a general explanation of the case and of the facts that the party will try to prove. Opening statements are not evidence; they serve to clarify the case and to provide a framework so that the jury will better understand the evidence presented later in the trial.

Presentation of Evidence. Following the opening statements, the plaintiff presents evidence usually through the testimony of witnesses who are under oath. A witness who is called by the plaintiff is first subject to **direct examination** by which the plaintiff asks questions that are answered by the witness. The defendant is then entitled to **cross-examination** of the witness, further questions concerning the testimony elicited on direct examination. Evidence also may be presented through tangible items such as documents, records, charts, or other items relevant to the case. Tangible items are admitted as evidence only if a witness attests that they are genuine and establishes the relevancy of the items to the issues of the case. The items then are labeled as **exhibits** and become a part of the evidence. After the plaintiff has called all witnesses and entered all exhibits that she believes meet the burden of proving the allegations of the complaint, the plaintiff rests her case.

Generally, the defendant then will make a **motion for directed verdict** requesting the court to rule as a matter of law that the defendant is entitled to judgment in his favor. The judge will grant the motion only if the plaintiff has failed to meet her burden of proof, that is, if the plaintiff has not presented a prima facie case. If the motion is granted, the judge rules in favor of the defendant and the trial ends. Usually, however, the motion is denied and the defendant has the opportunity to present evidence.

The procedure followed by the defendant is similar to that of the plaintiff. The defendant generally provides evidence to rebut the plaintiff's evidence. In addition, the defendant must prove the facts of any affirmative defenses that were pled. After presenting all of his evidence, the defendant rests his case.

The plaintiff then has the opportunity to offer rebuttal evidence in response to evidence provided by the defendant. Rebuttal evidence is limited to matters raised by the defendant's evidence; the plaintiff cannot use rebuttal to introduce new matters that should have been raised during plaintiff's cause. Following rebuttal, the defendant may offer evidence in rejoinder to rebut facts presented by plaintiff's rebuttal evidence.

During the presentation of evidence, the parties are limited by rules of evidence that allow only evidence that is relevant, probative, and not unduly prejudicial. A party who believes that certain evidence will violate the rules of evidence objects to its admission. If the objection is sustained, the evidence is excluded; if the objection is overruled, the evidence is allowed.

Following the presentation of the evidence both parties generally make a motion for directed verdict. This motion requests the court to rule as a matter of law that the moving party is entitled to judgment in his favor.

---

[22]The Supreme Court has ruled that parties in civil trials may not use peremptory challenges to engage in purposeful discrimination on the basis of race or gender. A party who appears to be discriminating in excluding jurors may be required to articulate a neutral explanation (a reason unrelated to race or gender) or abandon the challenge. Edmonson v. Leesville Concrete Co. Inc., 111 S. Ct. 2077 (1991); J.E.B. v. Alabama *ex. rel.* T.B., 114 S. Ct. 1419 (1994).

Because granting the motion removes the fact-finding from the jury, such motions are seldom granted.

Closing Arguments. After all evidence has been presented, each party is entitled to make closing arguments, statements to assist the trier of fact—especially in a jury trial—to analyze the evidence of the case. Like the opening statement, the closing argument is not evidence and the parties may analyze only the presented evidence; no arguments may be made concerning information that was not presented in evidence.

Jury Instructions. At the close of a jury trial, the judge provides **jury instructions** or **charges** to the jury. These instructions explain the rules of law pertinent to the case, including the burden of proof, definitions of preponderance of the evidence, and a summary of the elements of the cause of action. Using these instructions, the jury must determine the facts of the case and apply the rules of law to them to resolve the dispute.

The Verdict. After receiving the jury instructions, the jury retires to the jury room and elects a foreman. After a period of discussion and analysis, the jurors usually reach a **verdict,** a formal decision of the issues of the case. Although at common law the verdict was the unanimous decision of the jurors, the laws of some states now allow verdicts that are not unanimous. If the jury cannot reach a verdict, it is called a "hung jury" and upon request of one or both of the parties, a new trial will be held with another jury.

Usually, the judge requests a "general" verdict in which the jury makes a general finding for the plaintiff or the defendant and assesses the amount of damages. In some cases, however, the judge may request a "special" verdict in which the jury merely makes a finding of fact on each issue of the case. The judge then applies the law to these facts to resolve the dispute. If a special verdict is used, the jury instructions usually are limited to defining the necessary legal terms without full explanation of the law applicable to the case. Special verdicts simplify the jury's role and reduce the possibility of error. Nevertheless, most cases are still resolved by general verdicts.

After announcement of the verdict, the losing party usually files a motion for **judgment notwithstanding the verdict** (or judgment *non obstante veredicto* or judgment *n.o.v.*) requesting the court to find as a matter of law that the jury's verdict was incorrect and to enter judgment in favor of the moving party. If granted, the court enters judgment for the plaintiff even though the jury has returned a verdict for the defendant, or vice versa. The motion is similar to the motion for directed verdict and the judge will grant the motion only if the evidence was insufficient to support the jury's verdict.

In bench trials, of course, the judge decides both issues of fact and of law. As a result, no jury instructions are prepared. Following closing arguments, the judge makes findings of fact and conclusions of law and determines the appropriate remedy.

Entry of Judgment. At the conclusion of the case, the judge pronounces the decision of the case that is entered into the court's records. Because the case may be terminated at any time during the litigation process, entry of judgment does not necessarily occur only after the trial. If, for example, the defendant fails to answer the complaint, judgment by default will be entered. In addition, judgment is entered in favor of the moving party if the court grants a motion for judgment on the pleadings, a motion for summary judgment, a motion for directed verdict, or a motion for judgment notwithstanding the verdict. In some cases, even if the parties voluntarily settle the case during the litigation process, they may agree to a judgment by consent, which will be entered in the court's records.

Post-Trial Proceedings

Further legal proceedings sometimes follow entry of judgment. A party dissatisfied with the judgment may seek review of the case by an appellate court. Or, further assistance of the trial court may be needed to secure enforcement of a judgment.

Appellate Review

After judgment is entered by the trial court, the parties have the right to appeal the case to the appropriate appellate court. Generally, appeal may be taken only after final judgment, but occasionally a court order that does not terminate the case may be grounds for an appeal. The appellate process commences when the **appellant** (usually, but not necessarily, the party who lost at trial) files a *notice of appeal* with the trial court. The notice, which is served on all parties, must be filed within a time period set by statute or the right to appeal is waived. Enforcement of judgment may be postponed pending appellate review if the party seeking the appeal posts a bond.

Brief. The appellant then prepares a **brief,** a written document summarizing the legal errors for which the appellant requests review. The brief also includes citations to precedent and to statutory and constitutional law to support the appellant's contentions of legal error. The brief then is served on the opposing party who is called the **appellee.** The appellee may file a reply brief, a written document containing arguments and legal citations in opposition to those in the appellant's brief. The trial court also sends the appellate court a copy of the record, which includes pleadings, discovery documents, and a written transcript of the trial.

Oral Argument. Upon receipt of these documents, the appellate court may schedule oral arguments at which the appellant and the appellee may make oral presentations before a panel of judges of the appellate court. During oral arguments, the appellate judges ask questions of the attorneys for clarification and elucidation of points presented in the briefs. After review of the record, briefs, and oral arguments, the appellate court publishes a written opinion in which it decides the issues raised on appeal.

Decision. The appellate court generally does not retry the facts of the case. Rather, it reviews the proceedings to determine whether the trial court committed *prejudicial error,* a legal error that substantially affected the parties' right to a fair trial. An appellate court may find that a trial court committed *harmless error,* an error that did not affect the fairness of the trial. If the appellate court determines that no prejudicial error occurred, it **affirms** the trial court's judgment. If, however, the trial court committed prejudicial error, the appellate court **reverses** or sets aside the judgment entered by the trial court. When the appellate court reverses a judgment, the court also **remands**—sends back—the case to the trial court. If the record provides sufficient evidence to determine how the case should have been decided, the appellate court orders the trial court to enter the correct judgment on remand. If, however, the record does not provide a basis for determining the correct outcome, the appellate court orders a new trial or other legal proceedings on remand.

As discussed in Chapter 1, a party may be able to obtain further appellate review by a higher state appellate court or by the United States Supreme Court. Like the intermediate appellate court, the higher court usually writes an opinion to explain the legal reasoning underlying its decision that is published and becomes a part of the common law of the jurisdiction.

Effect of Judgment

A case concludes when *final judgment* is entered in the trial court's records. If no appeal was taken in the case, judgment becomes final when the time for appeal expires. If the case was appealed, final judgment occurs after all appellate review is completed. Once final judgment is entered, further litigation of the dispute is limited by the doctrine of *res judicata* and the Full Faith and Credit Clause of the United States Constitution.

Res Judicata and Collateral Estoppel. The common law doctrine of *res judicata* ("the thing has been decided") provides that final judgment by a court of competent jurisdiction is conclusive on the parties and prevents relitigation of the cause of action. The doctrine is designed to prevent a dissatisfied party from beginning a new lawsuit to try to obtain a more favorable ruling on the same dispute. Thus, after the appellate process has been completed (or the time to file an appeal has expired), the parties may not relitigate the case. If a party does file a subsequent lawsuit on the same cause of action, the defendant asserts *res judicata* as an affirmative defense and the second suit will be dismissed during the pleadings stage.

Closely related to *res judicata* is the doctrine of **collateral estoppel.** It provides that issues actually decided in one lawsuit are conclusively determined for later lawsuits between the same parties involving different causes of action. Collateral estoppel usually is invoked when an issue that is critical to the second suit was litigated in a previous suit. If the issue was fully litigated and necessary to the outcome of the prior decision, the adversely affected party is estopped or precluded from relitigating the issue. Thus, whereas *res judicata* prevents successive suits based on the same claim, collateral estoppel prevents relitigation of issues common to two or more claims between the parties.

Full Faith and Credit. Article IV, Section 1, of the United States Constitution provides that: "Full Faith and Credit shall be given in each State to the . . . judicial Proceedings of every other State." The **Full Faith and Credit Clause** prevents relitigation of cases previously decided in other states. Once a court of competent jurisdiction enters judgment on a cause of action in one state, other states must recognize the judicial proceedings and apply the doctrine of *res judicata.*

The Full Faith and Credit Clause also enables a plaintiff to obtain enforcement of a judgment in other

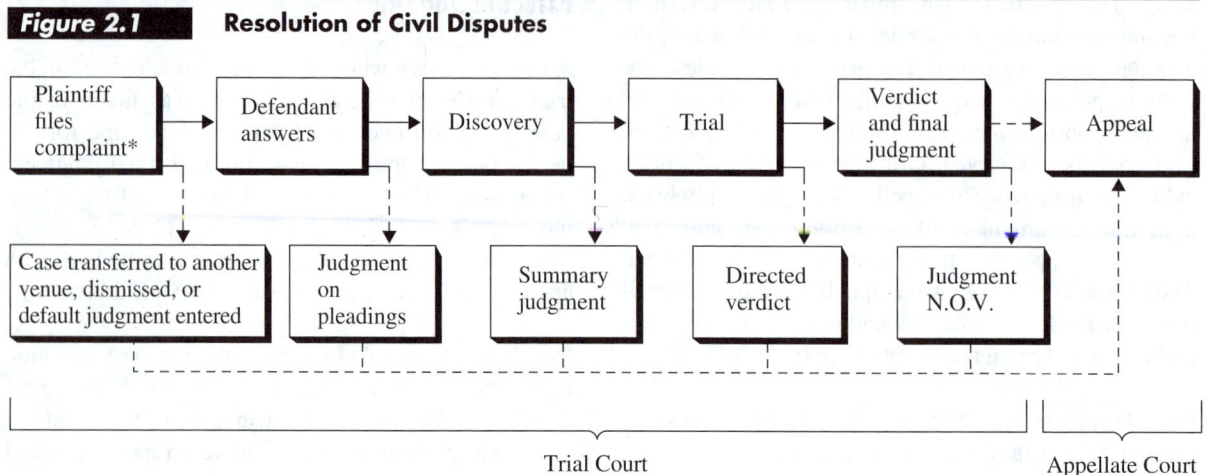

Figure 2.1 **Resolution of Civil Disputes**

*At any stage, the parties may agree to resolve their dispute outside of court.

states. Thus, for example, if a court of California enters judgment against a defendant who lives in Oregon, the plaintiff may enforce the judgment in Oregon where the defendant is likely to maintain assets. Generally, the plaintiff first must register the judgment in the state where he seeks enforcement. As a part of the registration process, the state may require one of its trial courts to review out-of-state judicial proceedings to determine that the court rendering the judgment had subject matter jurisdiction over the case and personal jurisdiction over the defendant. If the court finds that the out-of-state court did have jurisdiction, the judgment will be registered in the court's records and may be enforced like any other judgment.

Enforcement of Judgment

A final judgment awarding damages becomes a debt of the defendant. Every state provides a number of judicial remedies to assist creditors (persons to whom a debt is owed) to collect debts from unwilling debtors. Using these remedies, a creditor can locate and seize the debtor's assets and apply them to the unpaid debt. The remedies are designed to reach assets held by the debtor and by third parties, such as banks and employers, indebted to the debtor. They also reach assets transferred by the debtor to third parties with the intent to hinder, delay, or defraud creditors. State debt collection remedies are discussed in more detail in Chapter 29.

Because a judgment is effective only for a limited time, usually five to ten years depending on state law, a plaintiff who fails to secure prompt payment of the judgment may later be prohibited from collecting it. Nevertheless, a court has the discretion to renew the judgment if the plaintiff can establish a legitimate reason for failing to collect the damages.

Figure 2.1 summarizes the principles of civil dispute resolution discussed in this chapter.

Summary

1. Civil disputes are common among both businesses and individuals. Although most disputes are resolved by negotiation, mediation, or arbitration, many disputes are litigated, or resolved in court. A lawsuit consists of three general parts: the pleadings stage, the discovery stage, and the trial.

2. A lawsuit begins with the filing of pleadings that establish the disputed issues of a case. Pleadings consist of the complaint, the answer, counterclaims, crossclaims, third-party complaints, and answers to counterclaims, crossclaims, and third-party complaints.

3. To satisfy the constitutional requirements of due process, a defendant must be notified of the lawsuit through service of process that can be made properly only if a court has personal jurisdiction over the defendant. A state court obtains personal jurisdiction over the defendant in four instances: (1) the defendant is a resident of the state in which the court is located; (2) the defendant is served while present in the state in which the court is located; (3) the defendant consents to the court's jurisdiction; or (4) the defendant has had "minimum contacts" with the state in which the court is located. A federal court has personal jurisdiction over defendants who are subject to the state court's jurisdiction, certain defendants residing within 100 miles of the federal district court, and defendants subject to specific federal statutes.

4. The parties to a lawsuit gather evidence prior to trial by using the discovery methods that include depositions, interrogatories, requests for production of documents and things, physical and mental examinations, and requests for admission.

5. The trial is a formal proceeding in court in which the issues established in the pleadings are resolved. At a trial, the party bearing the burden of proof must provide evidence by testimony and exhibits to prove the cause of action by a preponderance of the evidence. In a jury trial, the jury determines issues of fact and applies the facts to the law, and the judge determines issues of law. In a bench trial, the judge resolves issues of both fact and law.

6. Prior to or during the trial, the parties to a lawsuit obtain rulings on questions of law by filing motions. Common motions include the motions to dismiss the complaint, for judgment on the pleadings, for change of venue, for summary judgment, for directed verdict, and for judgment notwithstanding the verdict.

7. At the conclusion of the trial, a party who is dissatisfied with the trial court's judgment may obtain review of the case by the appellate court. The appellate courts review trial proceedings to determine whether prejudicial error occurred. Appellate courts issue written opinions that become a part of the common law of the jurisdiction.

8. Following entry of final judgment, the doctrine of *res judicata* precludes relitigation of a cause of action and the doctrine of collateral estoppel prevents litigation of the same issues in other lawsuits. Further, the Full Faith and Credit Clause of the Constitution requires state courts to recognize valid judgments rendered in other states.

Key Terms

litigation
mediation
arbitration
Federal Arbitration Act
due process of law

pleadings
complaint
cause of action
damages
class action

service of process
summons
personal jurisdiction
long arm statute
default judgment
answer
affirmative defense
counterclaim
crossclaims
third-party complaint
motion
motion to dismiss the complaint
motion for judgment on the pleadings
venue
discovery
interrogatories
deposition
subpoena
request for production of documents and things
request for admission

motion for summary judgment
trial
petit jury
evidence
burden of proof
voir dire examination
direct examination
cross-examination
exhibits
motion for directed verdict
jury instructions or charges
verdict
judgment notwithstanding the verdict
appellant
brief
appellee
affirm
reverse
remand
res judicata
collateral estoppel
Full Faith and Credit Clause

Questions and Problems

2.1 A study comparing litigation to arbitration found that 95 percent of the court cases were settled prior to a full trial while fewer than 50 percent of the cases submitted to arbitration were settled prior to resolution by the arbitrator. Suggest reasons for this disparity.

2.2 Neither mediation nor arbitration generally requires adherence to rules of substantive law. Thus, precedent may be ignored. Discuss the effect of this policy on society, giving consideration to the reasons that courts use precedent.

2.3 Web Company designs and manages websites for more than 1,000 large companies. Its contracts usually extend for at least 5 years. Web Company created an e-commerce website for International Computer Company (ICC) but failed to properly manage security on the site. As a result, some financial information (bank account and credit card numbers) of ICC's customers may have been stolen. When ICC discovered the problem, it demanded that Web Company pay ICC over $5 million. Web Company admits that it made a mistake, but because the financial information of very few customers was compromised, believes that $5 million is excessive. Web Company and ICC cannot reach agreement on how to resolve this dispute.
(a) Suggest reasons why both Web Company and ICC would prefer not to have this dispute litigated.
(b) Would arbitration or mediation be a better ADR method for resolving this dispute?

2.4 Major Motor Co., an automobile manufacturer, has determined that because producing engines for its cars is too expensive, it will purchase engines from Common Engine, Inc. The two companies will enter into a multimillion dollar contract extending over five years. Major Motor would like to include a provision requiring arbitration if any problems arise during the course of the contract, but prefers not to use the rules or clauses developed by the AAA. Draft the arbitration clause. Would you include some method for selecting an arbitrator? Why or why not? Include a provision that describes the method for choosing the arbitrator.

2.5   In each of the following cases determine whether the trial court has personal jurisdiction over the defendant. Explain the reasons for your answer.

(a) Phillip sues Denise in a California trial court. Denise is a resident of California but is attending college in Arizona. The local sheriff makes service of process on Denise in Arizona.

(b) Harry, a resident of New York, purchased a new car from State Auto Sales, Inc., a retail dealership that operates in New York and New Jersey. After being transferred by his employer to Arizona, Harry moved from New York and drove his car to Arizona. The car broke down in Oklahoma. Harry had the car repaired and completed the drive to Arizona. Harry wants to sue State Auto for breach of contract. Assume that service of process is properly made on State Auto.
   (1) Would an Oklahoma trial court have personal jurisdiction over State Auto?
   (2) Would an Arizona trial court have personal jurisdiction over State Auto?

(c) Claire, a resident of Massachusetts, receives materials from the National Council of Hypnotists advertising a professional conference to be held at Quality Inn in California. The materials included a brochure published by Quality Inn highlighting the hotel and the special rates it offered for conference attendees. Using the phone number provided in the materials, Claire contacted Quality Inn and made reservations. Quality Inn specializes in conferences and markets its services directly—including meeting rooms, restaurants, and hotel rooms—to large companies and organizations. Although Quality Inn does not advertise in Massachusetts, it has hosted conferences for at least ten businesses that operate primarily in Massachusetts. While staying at Quality Inn, Claire was seriously injured and has sued Quality Inn in a Massachusetts trial court. The sheriff has made service of process on Quality Inn's agent in California.

(d) Plaintiff sues defendant, a resident of Tennessee, in the federal district court of Arkansas. Defendant has not had minimum contacts with the state of Arkansas. A federal marshal serves the summons and complaint on defendant on an airplane flight from Memphis to Dallas while the plane is flying directly over Arkansas.

(e) Ernie Umpire sues On Deck, Inc., a New Jersey corporation, in Minnesota state trial court. On Deck manufactures bat weights, which are doughnut-shaped metal rings that are slipped over a baseball bat while the batter takes warm-up swings. By contract, On Deck sells its products to independent distributors who market the bat weights throughout North America and Latin America. The distributors generally sell the bat weights to large retail chains including Sears, K-mart, and Wal-Mart. On Deck also hires baseball players who demonstrate the bat weights across the United States. While umpiring a baseball game in Minnesota, Ernie Umpire was seriously injured by a bat weight that slipped off a bat and hit him in the head. On Deck has no offices, property, or employees in Minnesota. The batter who had been using the bat weight found it at a local baseball diamond. An independent distributor sold On Deck bat weights to stores in Minnesota, more than 1,000 of the bat weights had been sold in Minnesota, and the local K-mart store sells On Deck bat weights.

2.6   James Mesalic, a New Jersey resident, contracted to purchase a custom-built boat for $235,000 from Fiberfloat Corp., a Florida corporation. Mesalic had traveled to Fiberfloat's principal place of business in Florida to order the boat but had told Fiberfloat that he intended to use it in New Jersey. While the boat was under construction, the parties communicated by telephone, Fiberfloat sent four letters to Mesalic in New Jersey, and Mesalic inspected and test drove the boat several times in Florida. At Mesalic's request, Fiberfloat delivered the completed boat to New Jersey. After the boat failed to operate properly, Fiberfloat twice sent a mechanic to New Jersey to try to repair it. When the boat still did not operate, Mesalic sued Fiberfloat for breach of contract in the New Jersey federal district court.

(a) Does the New Jersey federal district court have subject matter jurisdiction over this case? Explain.

(b) Does the New Jersey federal district court have personal jurisdiction over Fiberfloat Corp.? Explain.

2.7   When drafting contracts, the parties often include a provision—called a choice of forum clause—that specifies the jurisdiction in which lawsuits arising under the contract must be litigated. For example, a choice of forum clause might provide that any cases arising under the contract must be tried in New York state court.

(a) Why would parties to a contract want to include a choice of forum clause?

(b) Suggest reasons why a choice of forum clause should not be enforced.

2.8   The pretrial stages (the pleadings and discovery stages) of litigation have been criticized for complicating and prolonging lawsuits.

(a) What are the purposes of pleadings and discovery?

(b) What are the disadvantages of pleadings and discovery?

(c) Suggest ways that these stages could be improved and made more efficient while still meeting their purposes.

2.9   Plaintiff was injured by an explosion that occurred at a power plant operated by Central Gas and Electric Co. Plaintiff is uncertain as to the exact cause of the explosion or the source of his injuries. An expert has suggested that the explosion could have been caused by a faulty generator, improper installation of the generator, poor installation of power or gas lines, faulty design of the plant, or improper construction of the plant. The expert suggests that plaintiff must obtain the design and construction plans for the plant and must talk with the various people who constructed the plant and installed the equipment. Plaintiff has learned from a friend that at least three architects designed the plant, several contractors supervised construction, and at least fifteen companies performed installation as subcontractors. Plaintiff has sued Central Gas and Electric. Explain in some detail how the discovery tools could be used to obtain the information necessary to prove his case.

2.10   Johnny Plaintiff, a child, was injured when the pajamas he was wearing caught fire and rapidly burned. Plaintiff sued the manufacturer, Seabuck Co., alleging that the pajamas were unreasonably dangerous. Plaintiff filed a request that Seabuck produce a record of all complaints and communications concerning injuries or deaths allegedly caused by the burning of children's nightwear manufactured by Seabuck. Seabuck objected to the request arguing that obtaining the information was an impossible task because the company filed all of its claims alphabetically by name of claimant rather than by type of claim. Seabuck offered to allow the plaintiff's attorney to visit its home office in Chicago where she could try to locate the documents.

(a) Are the documents sought by Plaintiff subject to discovery?

(b) How should the court rule on Seabuck's objection?

2.11   In mediation and arbitration hearings, witnesses often explain their evidence in narrative form rather than by the question and answer technique used in courts. Suggest reasons for the use of direct and cross-examination in court. What problems might arise if witnesses simply told their story? Are there any types of cases for which such a technique might be appropriate? Explain.

2.12   Why do appellate courts usually accept the facts as determined in the trial court rather than reviewing issues of fact?

CHAPTER 3

CRIMINAL LAW AND PROCEDURE

Major Topics

- **the definition and classification of crimes and the sources of criminal law**
- **the elements of a crime and an introduction to criminal offenses and responsibility**
- **an introduction to business crimes, including principles of corporate criminal liability**
- **the law of criminal procedure, including an introduction to the constitutional limitations on criminal procedure, and an explanation of the various stages in the criminal process**

Unlike civil law, which is designed primarily to resolve individual disputes and provide compensation, criminal law is designed to protect society from harm by preventing certain undesirable conduct by members of society. The criminal law attempts to induce individuals and businesses to conform their conduct to socially accepted norms by punishing or threatening to punish those who violate the minimum standards of acceptable behavior outlined in the criminal law.

Criminal law is a broad subject encompassing two major fields of study: substantive criminal law and criminal procedure. **Substantive criminal law** defines the acts and omissions that constitute crimes as well as the punishment for those crimes. Criminal defenses, that excuse a person from liability for otherwise crimi-

nal acts, also are defined in the substantive criminal law. **Criminal procedure** is the law governing the various steps of a criminal proceeding from preliminary investigation to arrest to trial through termination of punishment. This chapter reviews the basic elements of substantive criminal law and criminal procedure, with special emphasis on crimes relevant to business.

Substantive Criminal Law

A **crime** is an act or failure to act, which is injurious to the public welfare, that violates a law prohibiting or commanding the act, and subjects the offender to punishment prescribed by law. Punishment for criminal conduct may include one or a combination of the following sanctions: death, imprisonment, fine, removal from office, or disqualification to hold a given office. Crimes first were defined in the English common law to protect individuals or their property and to deter conduct disruptive of social order. In the United States, each state has enacted a criminal or penal "code" defining and punishing criminal conduct within the state. Many of these statutes are patterned after the Model Penal Code, drafted by the American Law Institute and published in 1962. Although some states still recognize common law crimes, most substantive criminal law is statutory.

The federal government also has enacted criminal statutes, codified in Title 18 of the United States Code entitled "Crimes and Criminal Procedure." Federal law does not recognize common law crimes. Because both the state and federal governments have enacted criminal statutes, the same conduct in some cases may constitute more than one crime. For example, bank robbery is a violation of both state and federal criminal law and the offender may be prosecuted and punished by both sovereigns.

Crimes are classified in three general categories: felonies, misdemeanors, and treason. Felonies and misdemeanors also are known as **offenses.** The more serious offenses are **felonies,** commonly defined as crimes punishable by death or imprisonment in a penitentiary. **Misdemeanors,** the less serious offenses, are crimes that are punishable by imprisonment in a local jail, a fine, or both. Some criminal statutes distinguish felony and misdemeanor according to the length rather than, or in addition to, the place of imprisonment. For example, any offense punishable by death or imprisonment for a term exceeding one year is a felony; any other offense is a misdemeanor.

Treason involves attempting by overt acts to overthrow the government of the sovereign to which the offender owes allegiance, or betraying the sovereign into the hands of a foreign power.[1] Treason, of course, represents only a small percentage of criminal prosecutions.

Elements of a Crime

Most crimes include two elements: a criminal act (the *actus reus,* guilty act, or deed of crime) and the state of mind that accompanies or concurs with the act or omission (the *mens rea* or guilty mind, that is, the criminal intent). A few crimes, known as strict liability crimes, consist only of a criminal act; no criminal intent is necessary.

The Criminal Act. The criminal act may be one of commission—a voluntary bodily movement—or may be an act of omission—a failure to perform an act required by law. Most crimes are perpetrated by acts of commission (for example, aiming a gun and pulling the trigger). Possession is the criminal act in such common crimes as possession of illegal drugs or stolen property.

Other crimes are specifically defined in terms of failure to act; that is, the criminal statute imposes a duty to act and makes breach of that duty a crime. Such criminal acts of omission include, for example, failure to file a tax return or to register for the military draft.

State of Mind. The second element of most crimes defines the state of mind that must accompany the criminal act. Whereas the physical elements vary widely among crimes, crimes are classified according to their mental element or state of mind as either crimes requiring that the defendant be at *fault* (subjectively or objectively) or crimes imposing liability without fault.

Subjective Fault. Criminal law characterizes three types of mental culpability as subjective fault: (1) intention, (2) knowledge, and (3) recklessness. These states of mind are known as "subjective" because they describe the actual state of mind of the criminal who must have a "bad" or "guilty" mind. Consider, for example, the following definition of larceny:

> A person steals property and commits larceny when, with intent to deprive another of property . . . , he wrongfully takes, obtains or withholds such property from an owner thereof.[2]

The criminal act described in this statute is taking, obtaining, or withholding another person's property. A person commits the crime of larceny, however, only if this act is accompanied by subjective fault: "with *intent* to deprive another of property." Subjective fault also is required in a statute imposing liability upon a person receiving stolen property "knowing it to be stolen." Similarly, subjective fault is required for conviction of reckless homicide, for example, killing an individual through reckless driving of a motor vehicle.

Objective Fault. Some crimes define the criminal state of mind objectively, requiring, for example, that the defendant act "negligently," "carelessly," or "with reason to know." In these crimes, the mental element focuses on the state of mind of a reasonable person in the defendant's position, not the defendant's actual state of mind. Objective fault, for example, is required under a statute imposing criminal liability upon a person who receives property "having reason to know" that it had been stolen. That is, in this case criminal responsibility

---

[1]Black's Law Dictionary 1501 (6th ed. 1990).

[2]This illustration is based upon New York Penal Law §155.05.

results if a reasonable person would have known the property was stolen, whether or not the defendant, *in fact,* knew it was stolen.

Strict Liability Crimes. Crimes imposing liability without any requirement of fault are commonly known as "strict liability" or "absolute liability" crimes. Criminal responsibility requires only the act; no concurrent mental state is required. That is, a strict liability crime is one imposing criminal penalties upon "whoever does or omits to do . . ." rather than upon "whoever (intentionally, knowingly, recklessly, or negligently) does or omits to do. . . ." Usually, strict liability crimes are misdemeanors carrying relatively light penalties. Strict criminal liability is commonly imposed for violations of pure food and drug laws, illegal sales of intoxicating liquor, sales of misbranded articles, and minor violations of traffic and motor vehicle laws.

Offenses and Responsibility

Categories of Offenses. The Model Penal Code recognizes five basic categories of substantive criminal offenses:

1. Offenses involving danger to the person. These offenses include criminal homicide (murder, manslaughter, and negligent homicide), assault, kidnapping, false arrest, and sex offenses such as rape.
2. Offenses against property. This category includes arson, burglary, robbery, theft (larceny), forgery, and fraudulent business practices.
3. Offenses against the family. These include, for example, incest, bigamy, and polygamy.
4. Offenses against public administration. Examples of such offenses are bribery, perjury, obstruction of justice, resisting arrest, and escape.
5. Offenses against public order and decency. In this category are disorderly conduct, public drunkenness, loitering, and prostitution.

In addition, both the states and the federal government regulate the possession, use, manufacture, and distribution of commodities such as dangerous drugs and firearms. Violations of these statutes often are serious criminal offenses.

Inchoate Crimes. An important class of criminal offenses are the **inchoate crimes,** so named because the conduct they prohibit is designed to culminate in the commission of another crime but has failed to do so. The major inchoate offenses are attempt, solicitation, and conspiracy to commit crimes.

The crime of **attempt** is committed if a person, with the intent to commit some other crime, performs an act or acts constituting a substantial step (going beyond mere preparation) toward the commission of that crime. In many attempts, the defendant does all acts necessary to commit the substantive crime but is unsuccessful because of an extraneous or fortuitous circumstances. For example, a person who, with intent to kill, fires a gun at the intended victim and misses (or pulls the trigger and the firing mechanism malfunctions) is guilty of attempted murder. Note, however, that an act constituting criminal attempt need not be the last or ultimate step toward commission of the substantive crime.

Solicitation is committed when a person, with intent that a crime be committed, asks, orders, or otherwise encourages another to commit that crime. Solicitation is illegal even if the crime solicited is never committed. For example, assume A desires to kill B and asks C to perform the murder. A is guilty of solicitation, whether or not C consents or ever attempts to kill B.

The crime of **conspiracy** occurs if a person, with the intent that a crime be committed, agrees with another or others to the commission of that offense. Thus, agreement is the essence of a criminal conspiracy. Conspiracy statutes are among the most potent and frequently used weapons in criminal law enforcement. Under the general federal conspiracy statute,[3] criminal liability may be imposed for conspiracies to defraud the United States or its agencies and conspiracies to commit any offense against the United States. Criminal conspiracy under federal law requires an agreement between two or more persons to achieve an illegal objective, coupled with one or more overt acts in furtherance of the conspiracy.

All inchoate offenses involve conduct that is preliminary to the commission of some criminal act. Inchoate offenses serve several important functions in criminal law: (1) they permit timely intervention by law enforcement officials to prevent commission of completed offenses, (2) they allow arrest and punishment of those who have indicated a clear disposition toward criminal conduct, and (3) they allow punishment of persons who are unable to achieve their criminal objectives due solely to circumstances beyond their control. The law of

---

[3]18 U.S.C. §371.

conspiracy serves an additional function: it protects the public against the grave and continuing danger inherent in group criminal activity.

Defenses. A defendant who has committed a crime may escape liability by proving one of the various defenses recognized by the criminal law. These defenses involve unusual or extraordinary circumstances in which the purposes of the criminal law would not be served by convicting the defendant. For example, a defendant charged with homicide may be excused if he can prove that he killed the victim in self-defense. A person charged with selling illegal drugs may escape liability if he can prove entrapment—that a law enforcement official or agent, in order to obtain evidence to prosecute the defendant, incited or induced the defendant to commit a crime that he was not, absent the inducement, predisposed to commit. Persons who have not achieved a minimum age (generally 13) also may not be held criminally responsible. Another defense that may be raised by the defendant is the so-called insanity defense. Unlike other defenses, which if proven result in release of the defendant, a defendant found not guilty by reason of insanity ordinarily is committed to a mental institution.

Criminal Liability. A person is responsible for her own criminal acts and, under some circumstances, for criminal acts committed by others. Co-conspirators, for example, may be held liable for foreseeable crimes committed by others in furtherance of the conspiracy.

The Model Penal Code and many state statutes also hold a person accountable for conduct of an accomplice. Generally, an **accomplice** is a person who, with the purpose of promoting or facilitating commission of a crime, solicits another to commit it, or aids or agrees or attempts to aid the other in planning or committing it.[4] For federal crimes, §2(a) of Title 18 of the United States Code imposes criminal liability on a person who directly commits an offense and upon one who "aids, abets, counsels, commands, induces or procures its commission."

Business Crimes

Types of Offenses. Although violent crimes such as murder, rape, and armed robbery remain serious concerns of the criminal justice system, an increasing amount of crime is committed by individuals or corporations in the conduct of business operations. Such "white-collar" or business crime includes bribery (including illegal rebates, kickbacks, and bribery of foreign officials), criminal fraud, illegal political contributions, income tax evasion, criminal antitrust violations (primarily price-fixing and bid-rigging), and criminal violation of other regulatory statutes such as food and drug laws. Of course, traditional crimes such as forgery, embezzlement, and theft also occur in business. In addition to these offenses and violations of the federal conspiracy statute, other federal criminal statutes of particular importance to business include criminal federal securities law violations (discussed in Chapter 49), the Racketeer Influenced and Corrupt Organizations Act (RICO)[5], and the federal mail and wire fraud statutes.[6]

RICO was enacted by Congress primarily to prevent and punish financial infiltration and corrupt operation of legitimate business operations through patterns of racketeering activity. For example, the Act prohibits using racketeering income to acquire an interest in a business enterprise or to establish or operate an enterprise.[7] Though its primary purpose was to eradicate organized crime and corruption, RICO is not limited to persons connected with traditional organized crime or to activities commonly considered racketeering, such as extortion, gambling, property theft rings, drug trafficking, and loan sharking. Rather, the Act defines "racketeering activity" expansively to include also securities fraud; mail and wire fraud; bankruptcy fraud; embezzlement of pension, welfare, or union funds; obstruction of justice; and violations of currency transaction reporting laws.[8] Although many white-collar crimes committed by legitimate business enterprises are therefore potential RICO violations, most criminal prosecutions involve traditional racketeering: drug offenses, gambling, and extortion. Penalties are severe, including fines, imprisonment, or both, and forfeiture of property derived from racketeering activity.

Federal law also imposes criminal liability for mail and wire fraud. Conviction generally requires proof that the defendant devised a scheme to defraud and used the mails, telephone, radio, or television to further or execute the scheme. The fraudulent scheme need not itself constitute a crime or a violation of federal law.

---

[4]MODEL PENAL CODE §2.06.

[5]18 U.S.C. §§1961–1968.
[6]18 U.S.C. §§1341, 1343.
[7]18 U.S.C. §1962(a).
[8]18 U.S.C. §1961(1).

Violators are subject to fines, imprisonment, or both. The mail and wire fraud statutes have been used to reach a wide variety of deceptive schemes, including mail order frauds and schemes involving kickbacks or bribes paid to corporate employees or public officials.

Corporate Criminal Liability. The corporation is the dominant form of business organization in the United States. As discussed in Chapter 45, a corporation is a legal entity, an "artificial" person created by complying with state incorporation laws. A corporation, however, can act only through agents such as its officers and employees. Crimes committed in the corporate setting involve two important issues: (1) the liability of the corporation for the crimes of its agents, and (2) the liability of an individual corporate agent for crimes committed by the agent or others during the course of the agent's employment.

Liability of the Corporation. Since the early twentieth century, United States courts have recognized that a corporation may be criminally responsible for acts committed by the corporation's employees. In general, a corporation is responsible for crimes committed by any agent who acts within the scope of employment and with intent to benefit the corporation.[9] The following case illustrates the application of this rule.

United States v. Hilton Hotels Corporation
467 F.2d 1000 (9th Cir. 1972)

The operators of various hotels, restaurants, and other businesses in Portland, Oregon, formed an association to attract conventions to the city. The members then agreed to boycott or curtail purchases from suppliers who refused to contribute to the association. The Hilton Hotel in Portland, a member of the association, was operated by Hilton Hotels Corporation, which had a policy of purchasing supplies only on the basis of price, quality, and service. On two occasions, the manager and assistant manager of the Portland Hilton told its purchasing agent not to participate in the boycott and to follow the corporate policy. Despite these instructions, the purchasing agent threatened a supplier with loss of the hotel's business unless the supplier contributed to the association. The purchasing agent

---

[9]Note, *Developments in the Law—Corporate Crime: Regulating Corporate Behavior Through Criminal Sanctions,* 92 HARV. L. REV. 1227, 1247 (1979).

admitted that he made the threat because of personal anger toward the supplier's representative.

An agreement among competitors to boycott a supplier or to threaten to refuse to deal with a supplier is a criminal violation of the federal Sherman Act. The federal government charged the appellant Hilton Hotels Corporation with violation of the Sherman Act and the jury returned a guilty verdict. Hilton Hotels Corporation appealed, arguing that it could not be held guilty for the acts of its employees that were contrary to corporate policy and to the corporation's instructions to the employees.

Browning, Circuit Judge

. . . Congress may constitutionally impose criminal liability upon a business entity for acts or omissions of its agents within the scope of their employment. . . . Such liability may attach without proof that the conduct was within the agent's actual authority, and even though it may have been contrary to express instructions. . . .

The intention to impose such liability is sometimes express . . . but it may also be implied. The text of the Sherman Act does not expressly resolve the issue. For the reasons that follow, however, we think the construction of the Act that best achieves its purpose is that a corporation is liable for acts of its agents within the scope of their authority even when done against company orders. . . .

Because of the nature of Sherman Act offenses and the context in which they normally occur, the factors that militate against allowing a corporation to disown the criminal acts of its agents apply with special force to Sherman Act violations.

Sherman Act violations are commercial offenses. They are usually motivated by a desire to enhance profits. They commonly involve large, complex, and highly decentralized corporate business enterprises, and intricate business processes, practices, and arrangements. More often than not they also involve basic policy decisions, and must be implemented over an extended period of time.

Complex business structures, characterized by decentralization and delegation of authority, commonly adopted by corporations for business purposes, make it difficult to identify the particular corporate agents responsible for Sherman Act violations. At the same time, it is generally true that high management officials, for whose conduct the corporate directors and stockholders are the most clearly responsible, are likely to have participated in the policy decisions underlying Sherman Act violations, or at least to have become aware of them.

Violations of the Sherman Act are a likely consequence of the pressure to maximize profits that is commonly imposed by corporate owners upon managing agents and, in turn, upon lesser employees. In the face of that pressure, generalized directions to obey the Sherman Act, with the probable effect of foregoing profits, are the least likely to be taken seriously. And if a violation of the Sherman Act occurs, the corporation, and not the individual agents, will have realized the profits from the illegal activity.

In sum, identification of the particular agents responsible for a Sherman Act violation is especially difficult, and their conviction and punishment is peculiarly ineffective as a deterrent. At the same time, conviction and punishment of the business entity itself is likely to be both appropriate and effective.

For these reasons we conclude that as a general rule a corporation is liable under the Sherman Act for the acts of its agents in the scope of their employment, even though contrary to general corporate policy and express instructions to the agent.

Thus, the general policy statements of appellant's president were no defense. Nor was it enough that appellant's manager told the purchasing agent that he was not to participate in the boycott. The purchasing agent was authorized to buy all of the appellant's supplies. Purchases were made on the basis of specifications, but the purchasing agent exercised complete authority as to source. He was in a unique position to add the corporation's buying power to the force of the boycott. Appellant could not gain exculpation by issuing general instructions without undertaking to enforce those instructions by means commensurate with the obvious risks. . . .

[Judgment affirmed.]

Liability of Corporate Agents. Individual officers or agents also may be held responsible for employment-related criminal acts under several theories. First, individuals are liable for their own criminal conduct, whether or not committed in a corporate capacity. Thus, corporate agents who commit crimes are not insulated from criminal liability simply because they acted on behalf of the business organization. Second, a corporate official may be liable as an accomplice by directing, authorizing, participating in, or acquiescing in the criminal activity of others. Third, responsible corporate officers who violate a statutory duty to discover and correct criminal violations within the corporation committed by subordinates may themselves be criminally responsible. The following case illustrates the application of the "responsible corporate officer" doctrine.

U.S. v. Hong
242 F.3d 528 (4th Cir. 2001)

The U.S. government charged defendant James Ming Hong with 13 violations of the federal Clean Water Act. Following a trial before a magistrate judge, Hong was convicted on all counts and was fined $1.3 million and sentenced to 36 months imprisonment. Hong appealed to the federal district court which affirmed the convictions and the prison sentence but reduced the fine to $300,000. Hong then appealed to the U.S. Court of Appeals for the Fourth Circuit.

Wilkins, Circuit Judge

James Ming Hong appeals his convictions and sentence for violating the . . . Clean Water Act (CWA). . . . In September 1993, Hong acquired a wastewater treatment facility at Second and Maury Streets in Richmond, Virginia from Environmental Restoration Company, Inc. Hong initially operated the facility under the name ERC-USA but subsequently made several changes to the company name, eventually calling it Avion Environmental Group (Avion). Hong also moved the company's operations to a new facility on Stockton Street in Richmond. Hong avoided any formal association with Avion and was not identified as an officer of the company. Nevertheless, he controlled the company's finances and played a substantial role in company operations. For example, Hong negotiated the lease for the Stockton Street facility, participated in the purchase of a wastewater treatment system (discussed further below), reviewed marketing reports, urged Avion employees to make the company successful through the use of various marketing strategies, and controlled the payment of Avion's various expenses. Hong maintained an office at Avion from which he conducted business.

In late 1995, Hong and Robert Kirk, Avion's general manager, began to investigate the possibility of obtaining a carbon-filter treatment system for the Stockton Street facility, which lacked a system to treat wastewater. Hong and Kirk were specifically advised that the treatment system they were considering was designed only as a final step in the process of treating wastewater; it was not intended for use with completely untreated wastewater. Nevertheless, after purchasing the system, Avion used it as the sole means of treating wastewater. The system quickly became clogged. Hong was advised of the problem by Avion employees and inspected the treatment system himself on at least one occasion. Additionally, Bruce Stakeman, who sold the filtration media necessary for the system, advised Hong that the treatment system would not function properly unless it was preceded by an additional filtration mechanism. No additional filtration media were purchased, nor was an additional filtration system installed.

In May 1996, Avion employees began discharging untreated wastewater directly into the Richmond sewer system in violation of Avion's discharge permit. Untreated wastewater was discharged numerous other times during the remainder of 1996. . . .

The provision of the CWA under which Hong was convicted applies to "any person who" negligently violates pretreatment requirements. 33 U.S.C.A. §1319(c)(1)(A). The CWA defines "person" generally as "an individual, corporation, partnership, association, State, municipality, commission, or political subdivision of a State, or any interstate body." 33 U.S.C.A. §1362(5) (West 1986). For purposes of §1319(c), "person" is further defined to include "any responsible corporate officer." 33 U.S.C.A. §1319(c)(6) (West Supp. 2000). . . . Hong argues that the Government failed to prove that he was a responsible corporate officer. Specifically, he maintains that the Government failed to prove that he was a formally designated corporate officer of Avion and that, even if such proof was not required, the Government failed to prove that he exerted sufficient control over the operations of Avion to be held responsible for the improper discharges. We disagree with both contentions.

The "responsible corporate officer" doctrine was first articulated by the Supreme Court in *United States v. Dotterweich,* [64 S. Ct. 134 (1943)]. . . . In *Dotterweich,* the president and general manager of a drug company argued that he could not be held criminally liable for the company's violations of the Federal Food, Drug, and Cosmetic Act. . . . The Supreme Court rejected this contention, holding that all who had "a responsible share" in the criminal conduct could be held accountable for corporate violations of the law. . . .

The Court revisited the responsible corporate officer doctrine in *United States v. Park,* [95 S. Ct. 1903

(1975)]. In elaborating on the concept of a "responsible share" in a violation that the defendant did not personally commit, the Court stated that the Government may satisfy its burden of proof by introducing "evidence sufficient to warrant a finding by the trier of the facts that the defendant had, by reason of his position in the corporation, responsibility and authority either to prevent in the first instance, or promptly to correct, the violation complained of, and that he failed to do so." [*Id.* at 1912.] The Court explicitly rejected the argument that the defendant must have brought the violation about through some "wrongful action." [*Id.; See United States v. Iverson,* 162 F.3d 1015, 1025 (9th Cir. 1998)] ("Under the CWA, a person is a 'responsible corporate officer' if the person has authority to exercise control over the corporation's activity that is causing the discharges. There is no requirement that the officer in fact exercise such authority or that the corporation expressly vest a duty in the officer to oversee the activity.").

It is evident from these principles that the Government was not required to prove that Hong was a formally designated corporate officer of Avion. The gravamen of liability as a responsible corporate officer is not one's corporate title or lack thereof; rather, the pertinent question is whether the defendant bore such a relationship to the corporation that it is appropriate to hold him criminally liable for failing to prevent the charged violations of the CWA.

Regarding that question, Hong contends that the Government failed to prove that his relationship to Avion was such that he possessed authority to prevent the illegal discharges. Ample evidence supports the magistrate judge's finding of guilt, however. The evidence indicated that although Hong went to great lengths to avoid being formally associated with Avion, in fact he substantially controlled corporate operations. Furthermore, Hong was involved in the purchase of the filtration system and was aware, in advance, that the filtration media would quickly be depleted if used as Hong intended. And, the evidence supported a finding that Hong was in control of Avion's finances and refused to authorize payment for additional filtration media. Finally, Hong was regularly present at the Avion site, and discharges occurred openly while Hong was present. Accordingly, we affirm Hong's convictions. . . .

[Judgment affirmed.]

Criminal Procedure

The executive branch of government is responsible for enforcing the criminal law by investigating crimes, arresting and charging persons suspected of committing crimes, and prosecuting those suspects in courts of law. A legal proceeding that determines the guilt or innocence of a person charged with a crime is known as a **prosecution.** Because criminal law is designed to protect society generally, criminal prosecutions are maintained by public officials on behalf of the people of a state or the United States. Therefore, the plaintiffs in criminal prosecutions are, for example, the "People of the State of ___," or the "State of __," or the "United States." The defendant in a criminal case is the person charged with a violation of substantive criminal law. Every state and the federal government have adopted rules of criminal procedure that establish the process by which executive officers bring an accused person to court for a determination of guilt or innocence.

Enforcement of Criminal Law

State law enforcement agencies, including local and state police departments, bureaus of investigation, and specialized crime units, investigate suspected violations of state criminal laws. After gathering evidence, the investigators refer cases to the "state's attorney," "district attorney," or other attorney under the supervision of the state attorney general for prosecution.

At the federal level, over 50 federal agencies, including the Federal Bureau of Investigation, are responsible for investigating violations of federal criminal statutes. United States attorneys, who are appointed by the president, prosecute federal criminal cases. The attorney general supervises the prosecutors and the Justice Department may provide additional support.

Cases involving violations of state law are prosecuted in state courts, either in the trial courts or in specialized felony courts, misdemeanor courts, or traffic courts. Federal criminal cases generally are tried in the federal district courts. The judiciary of both the federal and state courts employ officers known as "magistrates" or "commissioners" to perform judicial functions such as issuing warrants and setting bail.

Criminal Jurisdiction and Venue

As in civil cases, in criminal prosecutions the court must have jurisdiction both over the subject matter and the person. Generally, state trial courts have subject matter jurisdiction over state offenses committed either wholly or partly within the state. In state cases, the proper venue (place of trial) usually is the county in which the offense was committed. The federal district courts have original jurisdiction, to the exclusion of any state court, to try all federal criminal offenses.[10] Proper venue for federal cases is generally the federal district (for example, Northern District of Illinois or Eastern District of New York) in which the offense was committed.[11]

Jurisdiction over the person (the defendant) in criminal cases is obtained by arrest. If the arrest is made in a state other than the one in which the offense was committed, extradition of the defendant is required. **Extradition** is the surrender by one state (or country) of an individual accused of a crime to another state or country having jurisdiction to try the offender. The duty of one state to extradite criminals sought in other states is contained in Article IV, Section 2, Clause 2, of the Constitution, which provides:

> A Person charged in any State with Treason, Felony, or other Crime, who shall flee from Justice, and be found in another State, shall on demand of the executive Authority of the State from which he fled, be delivered up, to be removed to the State having Jurisdiction of the Crime.

The legal machinery to execute the Extradition Clause is contained in both federal statutes[12] and in the Uniform Criminal Extradition Act, which has been enacted in virtually all states. The Supreme Court has held that the Extradition Clause creates a mandatory duty to deliver up fugitives on a proper demand, and that the federal courts have authority under the Constitution to compel state officials to perform this ministerial duty of delivery.[13] In addition to extradition among the various states, the United States has entered into bilateral treaties of extradition with more than 90 countries.

The Constitution and Criminal Procedure

Over half of the rights guaranteed by the Bill of Rights in the U.S. Constitution are designed to protect individuals accused of crimes. Some of these rights apply to

---

[10]18 U.S.C. §3231.

[11]FED. R. CRIM. P. 18. The court may grant a change of venue if local prejudice or pretrial publicity prevent the defendant from receiving a fair trial in the original venue.

[12]18 U.S.C. §3181 *et seq.*

[13]Puerto Rico v. Branstad, 107 S. Ct. 2802 (1987).

the trial stage of the criminal process. Others safeguard the rights of a suspect prior to the trial and affect the methods by which police investigate criminal activity, collect evidence, and treat a suspect prior to trial. Because criminal procedure is essentially a branch of constitutional law, the U.S. Supreme Court, which interprets the Constitution, plays a pivotal role in developing and applying principles of criminal procedure. The various Bill of Rights provisions relating to criminal procedure are shown in Table 3.1.

The Due Process Clause. The Fifth Amendment (applicable to the federal government) and Fourteenth Amendment (applicable to the states) prohibit both federal and state governments from depriving a person of

"life, liberty, or property, without due process of law." As noted in Chapter 2, this provision has long been interpreted to require "procedural" due process—notice and hearing—before life, liberty, or property is taken. The rules of criminal procedure discussed later in this chapter are designed to protect the accused's due process rights.

In addition, the Due Process Clause of the Fourteenth Amendment plays an important role in determining the specific constitutional guarantees available to the accused in a *state* prosecution. The Bill of Rights was enacted solely to limit the power of the federal government. Accordingly, the specific rights guaranteed to the criminally accused, by the terms of the Bill of Rights, apply only in *federal* prosecutions. The Supreme Court has held, however, that the Due Process Clause of the Fourteenth Amendment, which is applicable to the states, guarantees all rights that are fundamental principles of liberty and justice. If the court determines that a given Bill of Rights guarantee is fundamental, it is then incorporated and applied to the states through the Due Process Clause of the Fourteenth Amendment. Through this process of "selective incorporation," occurring in a series of cases decided primarily since 1961, the Supreme Court has held fundamental, and therefore applicable to the states, most of the Bill of Rights criminal procedure provisions.

The following material discusses constitutional guarantees important in the early stages of the criminal process: the right to be secure from unreasonable searches and seizures, the privilege against self-incrimination, and the right to the assistance of counsel. Other guarantees applicable in the trial stage and beyond are discussed later in the chapter.

Table 3.1	**Bill of Rights Provisions Related to Criminal Procedure**

Fourth Amendment

- Prohibits unreasonable searches and seizures

Fifth Amendment

- Guarantees right to grand jury indictment for capital and other "infamous" crimes
- Prohibits double jeopardy
- Guarantees privilege against self-incrimination
- Requires due process of law

Sixth Amendment

- Guarantees specific rights in all criminal prosecutions:
  - Right to speedy trial
  - Right to public trial
  - Right to jury trial
  - Right to be informed of nature and cause of accusation
  - Right to confront opposing witnesses
  - Right to compulsory process to obtain witnesses
  - Right to assistance of counsel

Eighth Amendment

- Prohibits excessive bail
- Prohibits cruel and unusual punishment

Right to Be Secure from Unreasonable Searches and Seizures. The Fourth Amendment provides:

> The right of the people to be secure in their persons, houses, papers, and effects, against unreasonable searches and seizures, shall not be violated, and no Warrants shall issue, but upon probable cause, supported by Oath or affirmation, and particularly describing the place to be searched, and the persons or things to be seized.

This amendment serves as limitation on the powers of the government in arresting (seizing) a person suspected of committing a crime and in obtaining evidence (search and seizure of things) to be used in criminal trials.

Arrests. The Supreme Court has indicated that to comply with the Fourth Amendment the police should obtain an arrest warrant prior to arresting a suspect. An **arrest warrant** is a writ issued by a magistrate or other appropriate official authorizing the police to take a specified person into custody. To obtain an arrest warrant, the police must provide to the magistrate a sworn statement of facts. If the magistrate determines that the statement establishes probable cause—that is, a substantial probability—that a criminal offense has been committed and that the person to be arrested committed the offense, he will issue a warrant for the suspect's arrest.

Despite the preference for an arrest warrant, the courts have recognized that an arrest without a warrant sometimes may be lawful. Generally, arrest without a warrant is legal if the police officer has reasonable grounds to believe that the arrestee has committed a felony, or if the arrestee commits a misdemeanor or felony in the officer's presence.

Searches. Although the Fourth Amendment appears to protect only "persons, houses, papers, and effects," the Supreme Court has liberally construed the scope of the amendment's protection. Recognizing that the purpose of the amendment is to protect people, the Court has held that anything that a person justifiably seeks to preserve as private is protected from unreasonable searches. Thus, a person's home, as well as his office, hotel room, and automobile may not be subjected to unreasonable searches.

Because the Fourth Amendment prohibits only "unreasonable searches," many cases have attempted to define under what conditions a search is reasonable. Generally, a search by a police officer is reasonable if it is made pursuant to a proper search warrant or with proper consent.

Prior to conducting a search, a police officer may obtain a **search warrant** from a magistrate or other appropriate official by providing a sworn statement of the facts that justify the request to search a specified place to obtain specified items. If the statement establishes probable cause—substantial evidence that the items are located in the place to be searched and that the items are connected with illegal activities—the magistrate will issue a warrant describing the place to be searched and the items to be seized.

Police searches conducted without a warrant or consent may be reasonable (and, therefore, lawful) under certain circumstances. For example, a search made incident to a lawful arrest may be reasonable. Generally, such a search is limited to the person of the arrestee and to the area of his immediate control, for the purpose of locating a weapon or to prevent the destruction of evidence. Police seizure of items "in plain view" also is reasonable if a police officer is lawfully present in a place and observes an item he knows to be related to criminal activity.

Privilege Against Self-Incrimination. The Fifth Amendment provides that no person shall be "compelled in any criminal case to be a witness against himself." Thus, a defendant cannot be required to testify, and a person cannot be required to provide self-incriminating evidence at the trial of another person. To compel testimony from a witness who might refuse to testify because of self-incrimination, the government may grant immunity from prosecution to the witness.

The privilege against self-incrimination also limits the power of the police in obtaining confessions or other information from a person accused of a crime. As discussed later in this chapter, such statements are considered to have been lawfully obtained only if certain procedural safeguards have been provided.

Right to Counsel. The Sixth Amendment provides that "In all criminal prosecutions, the accused shall enjoy the right . . . to have the Assistance of Counsel for his defence." Many of the cases interpreting the Sixth Amendment concern the right of an indigent defendant to have legal counsel appointed to represent him at government expense. Generally, an indigent defendant is entitled to representation in all felony cases and in misdemeanor cases punishable by a prison sentence[14] at any "critical stage" following the initiation of adversary judicial proceedings. A stage in the criminal proceedings is critical if potential substantial prejudice to the defendant's rights is inherent in the particular confrontation and counsel may be able to help avoid that prejudice.[15] The summary of the criminal process that follows indicates the critical stages at which legal counsel should be made available.

Exclusionary Rule. Although the Bill of Rights guarantees the right to be secure from unreasonable searches

---

[14]If a court fails to provide counsel in a misdemeanor case, no prison sentence may be imposed. Although the Supreme Court has not established that counsel in such cases is constitutionally mandated, some states have extended the right to counsel to all criminal cases.

[15]Coleman v. Alabama, 90 S. Ct. 1999 (1970).

and seizures, the privilege against self-incrimination, and the right to counsel, the Constitution does not specify how these rights are to be enforced. To help safeguard these rights, the Supreme Court has adopted the **exclusionary rule,** which provides that evidence obtained in violation of the Fourth Amendment, the Fifth Amendment self-incrimination privilege, and the Sixth Amendment right to counsel must be excluded in a criminal prosecution of the person whose rights were violated. Because the excluded evidence frequently is crucial to establishing guilt, application of the exclusionary rule may lead to the acquittal or other discharge of a criminal defendant who clearly is guilty of a crime. As a result, many advocate abolition or less stringent application of the rule. Proponents of the exclusionary rule, however, argue that it is the only effective method of deterring the police from unlawful violation of the Constitution.

Stages in the Criminal Process

The individual states and the federal government have enacted rules of criminal procedure. Procedures vary somewhat among the various jurisdictions and also may differ depending on the nature of the crime. Offenses committed by persons under a minimum age (for example, 17 years) generally are handled through the juvenile court system rather than the criminal justice system. The text that follows provides a brief description of the criminal process applicable to adult offenders.

Arrest. Most criminal cases begin when the police arrest a suspect—take him into custody for the purpose of charging him with a crime. The suspect then is taken to the police station for **booking,** an administrative procedure during which the suspect's name, time of arrest, and alleged crime are recorded in the police records, and the defendant may be photographed or fingerprinted. In the landmark case *Miranda v. Arizona,*[16] the U.S. Supreme Court ruled that government authorities must advise suspects of their Fifth and Sixth Amendment rights (the "Miranda warning") prior to interrogation:

> [W]hen an individual is taken into custody or otherwise deprived of his freedom by the authorities in any significant way and is subjected to questioning, the privilege against self-incrimination is jeopardized. Procedural safe-

guards must be employed to protect the privilege, and unless other fully effective means are adopted to notify the person of his right of silence and to assure that the exercise of the right will be scrupulously honored, the following measures are required. He must be warned prior to any questioning that he has the right to remain silent, that anything he says can be used against him in a court of law, that he has the right to the presence of an attorney, and that if he cannot afford an attorney one will be appointed for him prior to any questioning if he so desires. Opportunity to exercise these rights must be afforded to him throughout the interrogation. After such warnings have been given, and such opportunity afforded him, the individual may knowingly and intelligently waive these rights and agree to answer questions or make a statement. But unless and until such warnings and waiver are demonstrated by the prosecution at trial, no evidence obtained as a result of interrogation can be used against him.[17]

At issue in the following case was whether Congress had the power to overrule the *Miranda* decision by statute.

Dickerson v. United States
120 S. Ct. 2326 (2000)

> Charles Dickerson, who had been indicted for bank robbery and other federal crimes, moved to suppress a statement that he had made at a Federal Bureau of Investigation office. The trial court granted his motion ruling that Dickerson had not received the "Miranda warnings" before he was interrogated. The federal government argued that Dickerson's statement was admissible under 18 U.S.C. §3501, a federal statute, that states in part:
>
> > In any criminal prosecution brought by the United States or by the District of Columbia, a confession . . . shall be admissible in evidence if it is voluntarily given. . . . The trial judge in determining the issue of voluntariness shall take into consideration all the circumstances surrounding the giving of the confession, including (1) the time elapsing between arrest and arraignment of the defendant making the confession, if it was made after arrest and before arraignment, (2) whether such defendant knew the nature of the offense with which he was charged or of which he was suspected at the time of making the confession, (3) whether or not such defendant was advised or knew that he was not required to make

---

[16]86 S. Ct. 1602 (1966).

[17]*Id.* at 1630.

any statement and that any such statement could be used against him, (4) whether or not such defendant had been advised prior to questioning of his right to the assistance of counsel, and (5) whether or not such defendant was without the assistance of counsel when questioned and when giving such confession.

The presence or absence of any of the above-mentioned factors to be taken into consideration by the judge need not be conclusive on the issue of voluntariness of the confession.

The federal court of appeals held that Dickerson's statement was admissible under §3501. The United States Supreme Court granted Dickerson's petition for review.

Chief Justice Rehnquist

. . . We begin with a brief historical account of the law governing the admission of confessions. Prior to *Miranda,* we evaluated the admissibility of a suspect's confession under a voluntariness test. . . . Over time, our cases recognized two constitutional bases for the requirement that a confession be voluntary to be admitted into evidence: the Fifth Amendment right against self-incrimination and the Due Process Clause of the Fourteenth Amendment. . . .

[F]or the middle third of the 20th century our cases based the rule against admitting coerced confessions primarily, if not exclusively, on notions of due process. . . . Those cases refined the test into an inquiry that examines "whether a defendant's will was overborne" by the circumstances surrounding the giving of a confession. [*Schneckcloth v. Bustamonte,* 93 S. Ct. 2041, 2047 (1973).] The due process test takes into consideration "the totality of all the surrounding circumstances—both the characteristics of the accused and the details of the interrogation." *Id.* . . .

In *Miranda,* we noted that the advent of modern custodial police interrogation brought with it an increased concern about confessions obtained by coercion. . . . Because custodial police interrogation, by its very nature, isolates and pressures the individual, we stated that "[e]ven without employing brutality, the 'third degree' or [other] specific stratagems, . . . custodial interrogation exacts a heavy toll on individual liberty and trades on the weakness of individuals." [*Miranda v. Arizona,* 86 S. Ct. 1602, 1618 (1966).] We concluded that the coercion inherent in custodial interrogation blurs the line between voluntary and involuntary statements, and thus heightens the risk that an individual will not be "accorded his privilege under the Fifth Amendment . . . not to be compelled to incriminate himself." [*Id.* at 1609.] Accordingly, we laid down "concrete constitutional guidelines for law enforcement agencies and courts to follow." [*Id.* at 1611.] Those guidelines established that the admissibility in evidence of any statement given during custodial interrogation of a suspect would depend on whether the police provided the suspect with four warnings. These warnings (which have come to be known colloquially as "*Miranda* rights") are: a suspect "has the right to remain silent, that anything he says can be used against him in a court of law, that he has the right to the presence of an attorney, and that if he cannot afford an attorney one will be appointed for him prior to any questioning if he so desires." [*Id.* at 1630.]. . . .

Given §3501's express designation of voluntariness as the touchstone of admissibility, its omission of any warning requirement, and the instruction for trial courts to consider a nonexclusive list of factors relevant to the circumstances of a confession, we agree with the Court of Appeals that Congress intended by its enactment to overrule *Miranda.* . . . Because of the obvious conflict between our decision in *Miranda* and §3501, we must address whether Congress has constitutional authority to thus supersede *Miranda.* . . .

The law in this area is clear. This Court has supervisory authority over the federal courts, and we may use that authority to prescribe rules of evidence and procedure that are binding in those tribunals. . . . Congress retains the ultimate authority to modify or set aside any judicially created rules of evidence and procedure that are not required by the Constitution. . . . But Congress may not legislatively supersede our decisions interpreting and applying the Constitution. . . . This case therefore turns on whether the *Miranda* Court announced a constitutional rule or merely exercised its supervisory authority to regulate evidence in the absence of congressional direction. . . .

[F]irst and foremost of the factors . . . [indicating] that *Miranda* is a constitutional decision is that both *Miranda* and two of its companion cases applied the rule to proceedings in state courts—to wit, Arizona, California, and New York. . . . Since that time, we have consistently applied *Miranda*'s rule to prosecutions arising in state courts. . . . It is beyond dispute that we do not hold a supervisory power over the courts of the several States. . . . With respect to proceedings in state courts, our "authority is limited to enforcing the commands of the United States Constitution." [*Mu'Min v. Virginia,* 111 S. Ct. 1899 (1991).] . . .

The *Miranda* opinion itself begins by stating that the Court granted certiorari "to explore some facets of the problems . . . of applying the privilege against self-incrimination to in-custody interrogation, *and to give concrete constitutional guidelines for law enforcement agencies and courts to follow.*" [86 S. Ct. at 1611. (emphasis added).] In fact, the majority opinion is replete with statements indicating that the majority thought it was announcing a constitutional rule. Indeed, the Court's ultimate conclusion was that the unwarned confessions obtained in the four cases before the Court in *Miranda* "were obtained from the defendant under circumstances that did not meet constitutional standards for protection of the privilege." [*Id.* at 1636.] . . .

In *Miranda,* the Court noted that reliance on the traditional totality-of-the-circumstances test raised a risk of overlooking an involuntary custodial confession, . . . a risk that the Court found unacceptably great when the confession is offered in the case in chief to prove guilt. The Court therefore concluded that something more than the totality test was necessary. . . . [Section] 3501 reinstates the totality test as sufficient. Section 3501 therefore cannot be sustained if *Miranda* is to remain the law.

Whether or not we would agree with *Miranda*'s reasoning and its resulting rule, were we addressing the issue in the first instance, the principles of *stare decisis* weigh heavily against overruling it now. . . . "[E]ven in constitutional cases, the doctrine carries such persuasive force that we have always required a departure from precedent to be supported by some 'special justification.'" *United States v. International Business Machines Corp.,* [116 S. Ct. 1793, 1801 (1996).] We do not think there is such justification for overruling *Miranda. Miranda* has become embedded in routine police practice to the point where the warnings have become part of our national culture. . . . While we have overruled our precedents when subsequent cases have undermined their doctrinal underpinnings, . . . we do not believe that this has happened to the *Miranda* decision. If anything, our subsequent cases have reduced the impact of the *Miranda* rule on legitimate law enforcement while reaffirming the decision's core ruling that unwarned statements may not be used as evidence in the prosecution's case in chief.

The disadvantage of the *Miranda* rule is that statements which may be by no means involuntary, made by a defendant who is aware of his "rights," may nonetheless be excluded and a guilty defendant go free as a result. But experience suggests that the totality-of-the-circumstances test which §3501 seeks to revive is more difficult than *Miranda* for law enforcement officers to conform to, and for courts to apply in a consistent manner. . . .

In sum, we conclude that *Miranda* announced a constitutional rule that Congress may not supersede legislatively. Following the rule of *stare decisis,* we decline to overrule *Miranda* ourselves. . . .

[Judgment reversed.]

Initial Appearance. Following an arrest, the prosecutor generally determines whether to charge the suspect with an offense. If charges are filed, the prosecutor prepares a complaint listing the offenses allegedly committed and the complaint is signed either by the police officer or a complaining witness. The police then must take the accused without unreasonable delay for the initial appearance before the magistrate, who notifies the accused of the charges of the complaint and of his constitutional rights. If the case involves a minor misdemeanor and the accused pleads guilty, the magistrate may have the authority to try the case and impose the sentence immediately. Other misdemeanor cases are set for trial. In misdemeanor cases punishable by imprisonment, the initial appearance is considered a critical stage entitling the accused to legal counsel if the accused is required to enter a plea.

If the charge is a felony, however, the magistrate sets the matter for a preliminary hearing and may set bail. **Bail** is a security or obligation given by the accused or another to obtain the accused's release from custody. The purpose of bail is to ensure that the accused will appear at the scheduled court proceed-ings. A person who posts bail is released, but forfeits the bail if he or she fails to appear at the subsequent proceedings.

Preliminary Hearing. The **preliminary hearing** is a proceeding held before the magistrate to protect the accused from unwarranted prosecution. At the hearing, the prosecutor presents evidence through witnesses who are subject to cross-examination by the accused's counsel. The prosecution generally must introduce evidence sufficient to establish that there is probable cause to believe that a felony has been committed, and that the accused committed it. If the magistrate determines that probable cause exists, the magistrate "binds over" the accused for prosecution. If the magistrate determines that probable cause has not been established, the accused is discharged. Generally, the preliminary hearing is a critical stage giving rise to the right to legal counsel.

Formal Charge. The next step in the criminal process is to file formal charges against the accused by either an indictment issued by a grand jury or an information filed by the prosecutor without the intervention of a grand jury. A **grand jury** is a group of citizens whose function is to consider evidence of criminal conduct presented by the prosecutor and to determine whether the accused should be required to stand trial for a criminal offense. Unlike the petit jury, whose function is to decide facts, the grand jury is an accusatory and investigatory body that determines probable cause — whether sufficient evidence exists that an offense has been committed and the accused committed it. Although the size varies according to state or federal law, grand juries traditionally are composed of 23 persons with the affirmative vote of a majority (12) required for indictment (a "true bill"). If the grand jury finds no probable cause it returns a "no bill." If the grand jury does find probable cause, the prosecutor prepares an **indictment,** a written accusation setting forth the facts and charging the accused of violation of specific statutes. The indictment is signed by the foreman of the grand jury and then is filed with the court.

Under the Fifth Amendment to the U.S. Constitution and the federal rules of criminal procedure, prosecution of *federal* offenses punishable by death or imprisonment for a term exceeding one year must be prosecuted by grand jury indictment. Any other federal offense may be prosecuted either by indictment or information.[18] An **information,** a written accusation setting forth the facts and charging violation of the criminal statutes, is prepared and signed by the prosecutor and then filed with the court.

The Supreme Court has held that commencing prosecution by grand jury indictment is not fundamental, and is therefore not binding on the states through the Fourteenth Amendment Due Process Clause.[19] Accordingly, only about half of the states require that felony prosecutions be initiated by grand jury indictment. The remaining states permit the prosecutor to proceed either by information or indictment. In these states, information is the almost exclusive method of initiating prosecution. Misdemeanor prosecutions are almost always commenced by information.

The grand jury was designed to provide a buffer between the prosecutor and the accused, exercising independent judgment concerning whether or not to prosecute. Because only prosecution evidence is presented, however, the grand jury is often criticized as merely a rubber stamp wielded by the prosecutor. As one commentator noted: "[T]he prosecutor . . . if he is candid, will concede that he can indict anybody, at any time, for almost anything, before any grand jury."[20] Despite these criticisms, the grand jury is a very useful tool for investigating major criminal activity such as organized crime or public corruption because its proceedings are conducted in secret. Further, the grand jury has subpoena power allowing it to compel testimony and obtain evidence.

Filing the information or indictment starts the formal court proceedings in a criminal case just as the filing of the complaint commences the court proceedings in a civil suit. The procedural steps preceding the information or indictment serve to protect the rights of the accused prior to the involvement of the judiciary.

Arraignment. Following the formal filing of charges the case is set for **arraignment,** a hearing before the court at which the indictment or information is read to the defendant. The arraignment serves to fulfill the constitutional requirement that the accused "be informed of the nature and cause of the accusation." The arraignment is a critical stage entitling the defendant to legal counsel if desired.

The defendant may file motions objecting to the charges on procedural grounds, seeking suppression of evidence obtained in violation of his constitutional rights, or alleging a bar to the proceeding such as a statute of limitations. The defendant also may move for a change of venue, especially if the case has received substantial publicity. Finally, the defendant may file a *bill of particulars,* a request for detailed information explaining the facts or the charges. Because there is very little pretrial discovery in criminal cases, the bill of particulars serves as a tool to discover the evidence of the prosecution.

If the judge does not dismiss the case as a result of the motions, the defendant is required to answer the charges by entering a *plea* of not guilty, guilty, or *nolo contendere* (no contest). If the defendant pleads not guilty, the case is set for trial. If the defendant pleads guilty, the judge may sentence the defendant or set a later hearing for sentencing.

---

[18]FED. R. CRIM. P. 7(a).
[19]Hurtado v. California, 4 S. Ct. 111 (1884).

[20]Campbell, *Eliminate the Grand Jury,* 64 J. CRIM. L. & CRIMINOLOGY 174 (1973).

In the federal courts and in some state courts the defendant may enter a plea of **nolo contendere** rather than pleading guilty or not guilty. The legal effect of a plea of *nolo contendere* is the same as that of a guilty plea: the defendant may be sentenced as if found guilty. The plea of *nolo contendere,* however, may not be used as an admission of guilt in other court proceedings. This result is especially important in certain cases, such as antitrust law, where the defendant's conduct could result in civil liability. Acceptance of a *nolo contendere* plea is discretionary with the judge.

The defendant usually enters a plea of guilty or *nolo contendere* as a result of *plea bargaining,* negotiations with the prosecutor in which the defendant agrees to enter a plea in exchange for the prosecutor's promise to drop or reduce some of the charges or to recommend a particular sentence. The judge, though not bound by any promises made by the prosecutor, usually follows the prosecutor's recommendations. Plea bargaining reduces the case load of the trial courts and allows prosecutors to devote more time to major cases. It is appealing to a defendant who will receive a predictable and limited sentence rather than face the uncertain result of a trial.

Trial.   The Sixth Amendment entitles the defendant to a speedy and public trial by an impartial jury. If the government unduly delays the trial, the court may dismiss the case. The federal government and most states have adopted statutes prescribing the time limits within which a case must be brought to trial.

Right to Jury Trial.   The Sixth Amendment explicity guarantees the right to a jury[21] trial in "all criminal prosecutions." The Supreme Court has, however, held that this right does not apply to trials for "petty offenses," generally those punishable by less than six months imprisonment. In federal prosecutions, juries are composed of 12 persons and verdicts must be by unanimous vote of the jurors.[22] To ensure that the jury trial is fair, the Supreme Court has established that a jury must be selected from a cross section of the community.

The right to jury trial in *state* criminal cases is usually guaranteed by state constitutions and has also been applied to the states through the Fourteenth Amendment Due Process Clause.[23] In *state* cases, however, the Supreme Court has upheld less than 12-person juries and less than unanimous verdicts.

In general, a defendant may waive the right to trial by jury, although some states prohibit waiver or allow waiver only if the prosecution agrees. Similarly, in federal prosecutions, the defendant may waive the right to jury trial only with approval of the court and consent of the government.[24] If the right is waived, a bench trial is held.

Conduct of Trial.   A criminal trial is similar to a civil trial. If the defendant has not waived the right to a jury trial, jurors are selected by *voir dire* examination. Both the prosecution and defendant may exercise an unlimited number of challenges for cause to excuse potential jurors who demonstrate bias during voir dire. Both parties also may use a limited number of peremptory challenges to excuse jurors without stating a reason for the challenge.[25]

Once the jury is chosen, the attorneys make opening statements and the prosecution presents its case through the testimony of witnesses and tangible evidence. Witnesses are subject to cross-examination by the defendant's attorney, which satisfies the Sixth Amendment provision entitling the defendant to confront witnesses against him.

In a criminal trial, the prosecution bears the burden of proving beyond a "reasonable doubt" that the defendant committed all elements of the crime. The prosecution bears a greater burden of proof in a criminal case than a civil plaintiff, who generally need only prove his case by a "preponderance of the evidence." The defendant is not required to present evidence, is not required to testify, and bears no burden of proof in criminal proceedings. Nevertheless, the defendant may offer evidence through his own witnesses, who are subject to cross-examination by the prosecutor. At the conclusion of the evidence, closing arguments are presented and instructions are read to the jury.

As in a civil trial, the jury retires to the jury room to deliberate and reach a verdict. If the jury cannot reach a verdict—a "hung jury"—the court will dismiss the jury and order a new trial. If the jury returns a verdict of not

---

[21]The jury referred to in the Constitution is the petit jury that determines issues of fact and should not be confused with the grand jury.

[22]FED. R. CRIM. P. 23, 31.

[23]Duncan v. Louisiana, 88 S. Ct. 1444 (1968).

[24]FED. R. CRIM. P. 23(a).

[25]The Supreme Court has held, however, that neither the prosecution nor the defendant may use peremptory challenges to engage in purposeful racial discrimination during jury selection. A party who appears to be discriminating on the basis of race in excluding jurors may be required to articulate a racially neutral explanation (a reason unrelated to race) or abandon the challenge. Batson v. Kentucky, 106 S. Ct. 1712 (1986); Powers v. Ohio, 111 S. Ct. 1364 (1990); Georgia v. McCoullum, 112 S. Ct. 2348 (1992).

guilty, the defendant is acquitted: the court enters judgment in favor of the defendant, who then is released.

If the jury returns a verdict of guilty, the judge usually enters judgment in accordance with the jury's findings. Prior to judgment, however, the defendant may make posttrial motions requesting judgment n.o.v. or a new trial. A motion for judgment n.o.v. is granted only if the judge determines that the jury could not reach a verdict of guilty beyond a reasonable doubt in light of the evidence. The judge will grant a motion for a new trial if he or she determines that a material error prejudicial to the defendant occurred during the proceedings. If the court denies the defendant's motion, the judge will sentence the defendant, sometimes at a later hearing.

Appellate Review. Following entry of judgment, a convicted defendant is entitled to one appeal of right, usually to the intermediate appellate court or, in states with only one appellate court, the state supreme court, to that court. In some cases (for example, those in which the defendant has been sentenced to death), state law often provides for direct appeal to the state supreme court bypassing the intermediate court. In criminal cases the state is not entitled to appeal a judgment of acquittal. The Supreme Court has held that the Sixth Amendment right to counsel applies to the defendant's appeal of right.

The procedure for appellate review is similar to that in civil cases. Depending on the issues raised in the appeal of right, the defendant may in some cases obtain further appellate review by the state supreme court or the U.S. Supreme Court.

Post-Conviction Remedies. In addition to the direct attack of a judgment through the *appellate* courts, the defendant also may attempt a "collateral" attack by filing a petition in the *trial* courts. The best-known form of collateral attack is an application for **writ of *habeas corpus.*** The writ is a judicial order that directs a government official (for example, the warden) to produce the prisoner in order to test the legality of the imprisonment. The availability of the writ is guaranteed by Article 1, Section 9, Clause 2, of the U.S. Constitution and by state constitutions.

Usually, applications for writs of *habeas corpus* are directed to the federal courts by persons in state custody. Under federal law, the defendant must allege that the imprisonment violates the Constitution, federal law, or treaties, and must first exhaust state remedies.[26] The federal court reviews the state court proceedings, and

may discharge the defendant or order a new trial if federal law has been violated. The large majority of habeas corpus proceedings are unsuccessful. Following the federal district court's ruling, the defendant may appeal the judgment.

If a prisoner is held by federal officials, federal law provides a statutory remedy similar to that provided for those in state custody.[27] The scope of review of a federal case may be narrower because the court does not have to review alleged constitutional violations previously raised at trial or on appeal.

Finally, most states provide a statutory basis for collateral attack to persons imprisoned by state officials. These statutory remedies provide an opportunity for a state court to review the basis for imprisonment and to determine whether the prisoner's constitutional rights have been violated.

Double Jeopardy. The Fifth Amendment provides that no person shall "be subject for the same offence to be twice put in jeopardy of life or limb." This provision, frequently referred to as prohibiting **double jeopardy,** has been interpreted to mean that a person cannot be subjected to a second trial for the same offense (1) after a conviction, (2) after an acquittal, or (3) after "jeopardy attaches." In a criminal case heard by a jury, jeopardy attaches when the jury is impaneled and sworn. In a bench trial, jeopardy attaches when evidence is introduced. The Double Jeopardy Clause also prohibits prosecution appeals if the defendant would have to be retried if the prosecution wins the appeal.

Retrial is, however, permitted with the defendant's consent or for a "legally sufficient reason." For example, a defendant may be retried if a mistrial is granted on the defendant's motion, or if an appellate court orders a new trial as a result of the defendant's appeal of a guilty verdict. In these cases, the subsequent trials are deemed to be with the defendant's consent. Retrials also are permitted for legally sufficient reasons such as death of a judge or juror, a hung jury, or other conditions making a fair trial impossible.

The Double Jeopardy Clause does not prohibit successive prosecutions by the state and federal governments for the same conduct. For example, bank robbery is both a state and federal crime and the defendant can be tried and punished separately by each sovereign. The Double Jeopardy Clause merely prohibits multiple prosecutions by the same sovereign.

---

[26] 28 U.S.C. §2254.

[27] 28 U.S.C. §2255.

Summary

1. Criminal law is designed to protect society by setting minimum standards of socially acceptable conduct and punishing those who violate those standards. A crime is an act or failure to act in violation of a law prohibiting or commanding the act, which is injurious to the public welfare and subjects the offender to punishment prescribed by law. Substantive criminal law defines, generally by statute, which acts or omissions are crimes and prescribes the punishment to be imposed. Crimes generally are classified into three categories: treason, felonies, and misdemeanors.

2. Most crimes require two elements: a criminal act and a state of mind concurrent with the act. Although the criminal act varies widely among crimes, crimes are classified according to state of mind as either requiring that the defendant be at fault or imposing liability without fault. Four types of mental culpability are recognized for crimes requiring fault: intention, knowledge, recklessness, and negligence. In crimes imposing liability without fault, so-called strict liability crimes, criminal responsibility requires only the act; no concurrent mental state is required.

3. A number of specific criminal offenses are recognized under state and federal law, including "inchoate" crimes (such as attempt, solicitation, and conspiracy), so named because the conduct they prohibit is designed to culminate in commission of another crime but has failed to do so. A person who commits a crime may escape liability if he or she is able to prove one of the various extraordinary defenses, such as insanity, to criminal responsibility. Under principles of accomplice and conspiracy liability, a person may be convicted of criminal acts committed by others.

4. Although traditional violent crimes, such as murder, rape, and armed robbery, remain serious concerns of the criminal justice system, an increasing amount of crime is committed by individuals or corporations in the conduct of business operations. In such business or "white-collar" crime, the law must frequently determine when a corporation should be held liable for crimes of its agents, and when corporate agents should be held liable for crimes committed during the course of their employment.

5. Although the legislature enacts substantive criminal statutes, the executive branch is responsible for enforcing them. Various state and federal law enforcement agencies are responsible for investigating alleged violations of the criminal law. Criminal proceedings, known as "prosecutions," are maintained by public officials on behalf of the people of a state or the United States. Criminal jurisdiction and venue are determined by principles much simpler than those applied to civil cases. The law of criminal procedure governs the various steps of a criminal proceeding from preliminary investigation through termination of punishment.

6. The U.S. Constitution guarantees a number of specific rights to persons accused of a crime. These rights are contained in the Fourth, Fifth, Sixth, and Eight Amendments. Rules of criminal procedure, both state and federal, must therefore conform with interpretations of these provisions by the U.S. Supreme Court.

7. The usual stages of a criminal proceeding include arrest, the defendant's initial appearance, the preliminary hearing, formal charge (either by grand jury indictment or by information prepared by the prosecutor), arraignment, trial, appellate review, and, in some cases, post-conviction remedies. The defendant is entitled to trial by jury in most criminal prosecutions. Further, under the "double jeopardy" provision of the Fifth Amendment, a defendant generally may not be subjected to a second trial for the same offense.

Key Terms

substantive criminal law	arrest warrant
criminal procedure	search warrant
crime	exclusionary rule
treason	booking
offense	bail
felony	preliminary hearing
misdemeanor	grand jury
inchoate crimes	indictment
attempt	information
solicitation	arraignment
conspiracy	*nolo contendere* plea
accomplice	writ of *habeas corpus*
prosecution	double jeopardy
extradition	

Questions and Problems

3.1 Why have statutes almost totally supplanted the common law as the source of substantive criminal law? Why are strict liability crimes usually limited to relatively minor offenses? Why does the law punish inchoate crimes?

3.2 The Model Penal Code defines theft as follows:

> A person is guilty of theft if he [or she] takes, or exercises unlawful control over, movable property of another with purpose to deprive him [or her] thereof.

(a) What is the criminal act described in this statute?
(b) What is the state of mind necessary to commit the crime of theft?

3.3 The Model Penal Code also defines the crime of theft by deception, which includes the following:

A person is guilty of theft if he [or she] obtains property of another by deception. A person deceives if he [or she] purposely:

(a) creates or reinforces a false impression, including false impressions as to law, value, intention or other state of mind; . . . or

(b) prevents another from acquiring information which would affect his [or her] judgment of a transaction. . . .

Marilyn owns and operates Marilyn's Luxury Automobiles, a retailer of fine cars. Consider whether Marilyn has committed the crime of theft by deception in each of the following cases:

(a) Ronald, a devoted fan of the famous, but now deceased, celebrity Rock Star, purchased a pre-owned Rolls Royce from Marilyn for $75,000. During the sales negotiations, she tells him that Rock Star previously owned the car. Marilyn had purchased the car from Rock Star's personal agent who told her that the car had been Rock Star's favorite possession. In truth, the automobile formerly belonged to the agent's mother and Rock Star had never used it.

(b) Marilyn sells an Italian sports car to Mario for $60,000. She describes the car upholstery as "Italian Butterleather," which, as Marilyn knows, is a trade name for a new type of plastic upholstery that looks exactly like leather. Just prior to showing the car to Mario, Marilyn sprayed the interior with "Leather Scent," a commercial spray that smells like leather. As Marilyn o0ened the door for Mario, she sniffed the air and stated, "Don't you just love the smell of real leather?" In fact, leather seats are an option on the automobile and cost an additional $8,000.

3.4 Mary, an ambitious employee of BFC Co., offered an illegal bribe to a government official to obtain preferential treatment for BFC. The government charged both Mary and BFC with violation of a criminal statute prohibiting bribery. Explain under what circumstances you believe BFC could be held guilty for the criminal acts committed by Mary.

3.5 For many years the courts and legislatures have struggled to find an appropriate penalty for corporate crimes. The problem is especially difficult when employees commit "white-collar crimes" not for their own enrichment but for the benefit of the corporation. Traditionally, the courts have fined the corporation and the employee, or both, for such criminal activities. Suggest alternatives that might be more effective both as a deterrent to corporate crime and as punishment for those committing unlawful activities. Discuss the advantages and disadvantages of these alternatives.

3.6 Historically, defendants guilty of crimes committed in the business setting such as tax evasion, embezzlement, bribery, or fraud have received lighter sentences than those convicted of "street" crimes such as burglary or theft even if the business crimes involved larger sums of money. Suggest reasons for this disparity in sentencing. Do you believe that in general a person guilty of business crime should receive a lighter sentence than someone guilty of a crime like burglary? Explain.

3.7 In the last few years, increased attention has been paid to a variety of white-collar crimes that have been committed by employees of corporations. In some cases, the employees commit the crime for the benefit of the corporation although the employee also may benefit incidentally. If, for example, a salesperson illegally bribes an official to receive preferential treatment for purchases of the corporation's products, the corporation may benefit by increased sales but the salesperson also may benefit by receiving higher commissions or favorable job reviews leading to promotion. In other cases, an employee may use opportunities arising within the course of his or her employment to commit criminal acts that benefit the employee with little or no benefit to the corporation. A stockbroker, for example, may illegally use inside information obtained through her employment to purchase stocks for her own account and to personally profit from the transaction.

(a) Does a corporation have a legal or ethical obligation to prevent employees from engaging in illegal practices for the benefit of the corporation?

(b) Does a corporation have a legal or ethical obligation to prevent employees from engaging in illegal conduct for their own benefit?

(c) What, if anything, should a corporation do to prevent criminal wrongdoing by its employees? Why?

3.8 Jones, an employee of Film Recovery Systems, Inc., a film processing company, died of cyanide poisoning as a result of working with cyanide on a daily basis in his job at the processing plant. Subsequently, an investigation established that conditions in the plant were totally unsafe and in violation of state and federal occupational health and safety laws. The corporation's president was well aware of the dangers of working with cyanide and admitted that he knew that other workers had become ill before Jones died of acute cyanide poisoning resulting from an on-the-job exposure. The state criminal code provides:

A person who kills an individual without lawful justification commits murder if, in performing the acts which cause the death:

1. He either intends to kill or do great bodily harm to that individual or another, or knows that such acts will cause death to that individual or another; or

2. He knows that such acts create a strong probability of death or great bodily harm to that individual or another. . . .

A person who unintentionally kills an individual without lawful justification commits involuntary manslaughter if his acts whether lawful or unlawful which cause the death are such as are likely to cause death or great bodily harm to some individual, and he performs them recklessly. . . .

A person who causes bodily harm to or endangers the bodily safety of an individual by any means, commits reckless conduct if he performs recklessly the acts which cause the harm or endanger safety, whether they otherwise are lawful or unlawful. . . .

A person is reckless or acts recklessly, when he consciously disregards a substantial and unjustifiable risk that circumstances exist or that a result will follow, described by the statute defining the offense; and such disregard constitutes a gross deviation from the standard of care which a reasonable person would exercise in the situation.

Of what crime or crimes, if any, should the corporation's president be convicted?

3.9   Riverton Motors is a retail automobile dealership that sells General Motors (GM) cars. To help auto sales, GM advertised that it would provide rebates on cars bought before March 15. To secure the rebate, the purchaser had to submit a signed application to GM which then sent a check to the dealership. At Riverton Motors, Phil, the sales manager, supervised the rebate program. On March 20, Linden purchased a new car from Phil. Without telling Linden, Phil prepared a rebate application postdated to March 14, forged Linden's signature, and submitted it to GM. GM subsequently mailed a rebate check for $500 to Riverton Motors. Linden accidentally learned of the rebate application when a GM marketing representative called to see if Linden was satisfied with his purchase. Linden reported the matter to the state's attorney who charged both Riverton Motors and Phil with criminal forgery and theft.

(a) Assume that Phil had pocketed the $500 check by again forging the necessary signatures. Do you think that Riverton Motors should be held criminally responsible? Explain.

(b) Assume instead that Riverton Motors received and kept the $500 check. Do you think that Phil should be held criminally responsible? Explain.

3.10   The exclusionary rule has been strongly criticized for many years by judges, lawyers, police officers, politicians, and the public.

(a) Discuss the purposes of the exclusionary rule and the disadvantages of its use.

(b) Suggest other methods of achieving the purposes of the rule that would minimize its disadvantages.

3.11   In criminal cases the extensive discovery procedures used in civil cases are not employed. Why?

3.12   Discuss the advantages and disadvantages of the grand jury system.

CHAPTER 4

THE CONSTITUTION AND BUSINESS REGULATION

Major Topics

■ the sources and scope of federal and state power to regulate business and commerce

■ constitutional limitations on federal and state powers to regulate business and commerce

■ the nature and scope of administrative agencies' powers to regulate business

The proper relationship between government and business has been debated throughout American history. The economic and political issues underlying this controversy have yet to be resolved. Those who favor the *laissez-faire* theory argue that any government regulation of business creates undesirable interference with the free market and competition. Others assert that complete regulation of business is necessary to prevent monopolization, to allocate scarce resources, and to protect the public safety and health. The laws of the United States generally have reflected a compromise between these two extreme viewpoints. Since the founding of the United States, businesses have been subject to some, but not total, regulation by both federal and state government.

This chapter examines the sources of governmental powers to enact laws that regulate business and constitutional restrictions on those powers. The chapter concludes with a discussion of administrative agencies created by the government to implement and enforce regulatory laws.

Governmental Power to Regulate Business and Commerce

Both state and federal governments regulate business. States control business activity through two inherent powers: the state police power and the power to tax. The federal government regulates business by exercising specific powers delegated to it by the states in the Constitution. Most important among these is the power to regulate interstate commerce.

State Powers to Regulate Business

Police Power. A state's **police power** is its inherent authority to establish laws for the protection of the health, safety, morals, and general welfare of its citizens. In the late 1800s, states first began using the police power to enact statutes to protect their citizens from social and economic problems created by rapidly growing businesses and corporations. Today, state police powers are the source of laws regulating a broad spectrum of business activities including, for example, building codes; fire, health, and safety standards for restaurants, retail, and manufacturing operations; workers' compensation; and business and professional licensing. In some cases, the states have used the police power to limit certain business activities regionally or statewide. Zoning laws, for example, usually allow manufacturing operations only in specified areas of a city or county. Some states even use the police power to prohibit entire industries, such as liquor or gambling operations. Although the police power is an expansive authority for state regulation of businesses, it is limited by constitutional provisions discussed later in this chapter.

Power to Tax. A second inherent power of the states is the **power to tax:** the authority to require financial contributions to state government. Although the primary purpose of taxation is to provide revenues to support the operations of government, such as fire and police protection, taxation is also a form of indirect regulation due to its economic impact on business activities. Most states impose income and property taxes on businesses as well as individuals. Other taxes, such as corporate franchise and license taxes are paid solely by business.

A business that is organized as a corporation must pay an initial franchise tax to obtain a corporate charter from the state and an annual franchise tax to maintain its corporate status. Some states require a license to engage in a specific type of business and require payment of a license tax to secure and maintain the license. A license often is required, for example, to operate a retail store or restaurant or to practice medicine or law. License taxes often provide a regulatory effect. The amount of the license tax, for example, often effectively limits the number of businesses that are engaged in the licensed activity.

Many other forms of taxation are used by the states, including sales taxes, death taxes, use taxes, and excise taxes on specified goods or services. Like the police power, the power to tax is subject to constitutional restrictions.

Federal Power to Regulate Business: The Commerce Clause

Under the Articles of Confederation, which governed the federal union prior to adoption of the Constitution, the federal government had no authority to control business activities among the states. During this period,

individual states established trade barriers and taxes that severely limited interstate trade. States with major ports imposed taxes on goods from foreign nations. Some states adopted laws to protect their citizens from out-of-state competition. These trade restrictions created a national economic crisis marked by a shortage of necessary goods and a lack of markets for goods produced in the states. A major objective of the Constitutional Convention in 1787 was to improve commercial relations among the states.

The **Commerce Clause** of the Constitution was adopted in an effort to resolve these problems and today it is the primary source of the federal government's power to regulate business. The Commerce Clause provides:

> The Congress shall have Power . . . to regulate Commerce with foreign Nations, and among the several States, and with the Indian Tribes.[1]

Of the three subjects covered by the Commerce Clause—international commerce, interstate commerce, and commerce with the Indian tribes—interstate commerce has produced the most significant legal and political problems. One difficult issue has been to define the scope of Congress's Commerce Clause authority; in other words, to define the business activities that are considered interstate commerce subject to regulation by the federal government.

This issue first became important during the period of business growth and industrialization following the Civil War. Congress began using the power to regulate interstate commerce to adopt statutes that controlled business activities. Businesses challenged these statutes alleging that Congress was exceeding its authority and impinging on activities better regulated by the states. During this period, the Supreme Court usually upheld the constitutionality of federal statutes that regulated commercial activities directly related to trade between the states. The Court, however, tended to strike down laws that controlled activities that were more local in nature even if they affected interstate commerce. Thus, the Court held that the Commerce Clause enabled Congress to regulate railroad rates because railroads were used for interstate transportation.[2] In contrast, the

---

[1]U.S. Const. art. 1, §8, cl. 3.
[2]Shreveport Rate Cases, 34 S. Ct. 833 (1914).

Supreme Court held that a federal law prohibiting the interstate shipment of goods manufactured in factories employing children was unconstitutional.[3] The Court perceived manufacturing and employer-employee relations to be matters for state and local regulation and beyond the scope of federal regulation. The Court also struck down statutes that appeared to reflect a Congressional intent to regulate public health, morals, or welfare, subjects more appropriately regulated by the states under their police powers. In general, then, the Supreme Court initially narrowly construed the federal power to regulate interstate commerce and, as a result, federal regulation of business was limited.

The Court's interpretation of the scope of federal power to regulate interstate commerce underwent a dramatic change during the 1930s. Following the election of 1932, President Franklin D. Roosevelt perceived a public mandate that the federal government resolve the nationwide economic and social problems of the Great Depression. Beginning in 1933, Congress, pursuant to its powers under the Commerce Clause, enacted many of Roosevelt's "New Deal" programs designed to end the Depression. During Roosevelt's first term, the Supreme Court, using a variety of theories, consistently held the legislation to be unconstitutional and beyond the scope of Congress's Commerce Clause powers. In 1937, however, the Court reversed itself and began to uphold the constitutionality of federal statutes regulating economic conditions. During the years that followed, the Court increasingly held that the federal government's powers under the Commerce Clause were broad and not narrowly restricted to regulating actual trade between states.

Because the Supreme Court continues to interpret the Commerce Clause power broadly, Congress today has extensive authority to regulate interstate commerce. The Supreme Court has identified three general types of activity subject to Congressional regulation:

> First, Congress may regulate the use of the channels of interstate commerce. . . . Second, Congress is empowered to regulate and protect the instrumentalities of interstate commerce, or persons or things in interstate commerce, even though the threat may come only from intrastate activities. . . . Finally, Congress' commerce authority includes the power to regulate those activities having a substantial relation to interstate commerce, . . .

i.e., those activities that substantially affect interstate commerce.[4]

This power extends even to intrastate business activities—those that occur in only one state—if the business activity has a substantial effect on interstate commerce or if the activity in combination with other similar activities might have a cumulative effect on interstate commerce.

In modern Commerce Clause cases, the courts generally defer to Congress's judgment regarding the policy and purposes of legislation. Once the relationship between the regulation and interstate commerce has been established, the courts do not even require that the legislation have a commercial purpose. The federal Civil Rights Act of 1964, for example, prohibits racial discrimination in public accommodation (for example, hotels and restaurants) if the operation of the establishment "affects commerce." Clearly, at least one purpose of this statute is to prevent racial discrimination, a moral consideration generally within the purview of the police power of the states. Nevertheless, the Supreme Court has upheld the validity of the Civil Rights Act.

In the case that follows, the Supreme Court considers the scope of federal authority under the Commerce Clause.

McLain v. Real Estate Board of New Orleans, Inc.
100 S. Ct. 502 (1980)

The petitioner James McLain, on behalf of persons who had employed real state brokers in New Orleans, filed suit against the respondent Real Estate Board of New Orleans, Inc. and other respondents including six real estate firms and a group of real estate brokers. Petitioner alleged that the respondents had engaged in a price-fixing conspiracy to control real estate broker commissions, a violation of the federal Sherman Act adopted by Congress pursuant to its Commerce Clause power to regulate interstate commerce.

The trial court dismissed petitioner's complaint on the ground that "brokerage activities are wholly intrastate in nature and . . . they neither occur in nor substantially affect interstate commerce." The court of appeals affirmed and the petitioner was granted a writ of certiorari by the Supreme Court.

---

[3]Hammer v. Dagenhart, 38 S. Ct. 529 (1918).

[4]U.S. v. Lopez, 115 S. Ct. 1624, 1629–1630 (1995).

Chief Justice Burger

. . . The broad authority of Congress under the Commerce Clause has, of course, long been interpreted to extend beyond activities actually *in* interstate commerce to reach other activities that, while wholly local in nature, nevertheless substantially *affect* interstate commerce. . . .

Although the cases demonstrate the breadth of Sherman Act prohibitions, jurisdiction may not be invoked under that statute unless the relevant aspect of interstate commerce is identified; it is not sufficient merely to rely on identification of a relevant local activity and to presume an interrelationship with some unspecified aspect of interstate commerce. . . . [A] plaintiff must allege . . . [and prove] either that the defendants' activity is itself in interstate commerce or, if it is local in nature, that it has an effect on some other appreciable activity demonstrably in interstate commerce. . . . To establish the jurisdictional element of a Sherman Act violation it would be sufficient for petitioners to demonstrate a substantial effect on interstate commerce generated by respondents' brokerage activities. . . .

It is clear that an appreciable amount of commerce is involved in the financing of residential property in the Greater New Orleans area and in the insuring of titles to such property. The presidents of two of the many lending institutions in the area stated in their deposition testimony that those institutions committed hundreds of millions of dollars to residential financing during the period covered by the complaint. The testimony further demonstrates that this appreciable commercial activity has occurred in interstate commerce. Funds were raised from out-of-state investors and from interbank loans obtained from interstate financial institutions. Multistate lending institutions took mortgages insured under federal programs which entailed interstate transfers of premiums and settlements. Mortgage obligations physically and constructively were traded as financial instruments in the interstate secondary mortgage market. Before making a mortgage loan in the Greater New Orleans area, lending institutions usually, if not always, required title insurance, which was furnished by interstate corporations.

To establish federal jurisdiction in this case, there remains only the requirement that respondents' activities which allegedly have been infected by a price-fixing conspiracy be shown "as a matter of practical economics" to have a not insubstantial effect on the interstate commerce involved. . . . It is clear, as the record shows, that the function of respondent real estate brokers is to bring the buyer and seller together on agreeable terms. For this service the broker charges a fee generally calculated as a percentage of the sale price. Brokerage activities necessarily affect both the frequency and the terms of residential sales transactions. Ultimately, whatever stimulates or retards the volume of residential sales, or has an impact on the purchase price, affects the demand for financing and title insurance, those two commercial activities that on this record are shown to have occurred in interstate commerce. Where, as here, the services of respondent real estate brokers are often employed in transactions in the relevant market, petitioners at trial may be able to show that respondents' activities have a not insubstantial effect on interstate commerce. . . .

[Judgment vacated and remanded.]

Constitutional Limitations on Federal and State Regulation of Business

Although state police and taxing powers and the federal Commerce Clause powers are broad, they are subject to limitations imposed by the Constitution. The following sections discuss constitutional restrictions on state and federal powers to regulate business activities.

Limitations on the State Police and Taxing Powers

Federal Preemption. Under the Supremacy Clause of the Constitution, federal law preempts (overrides) conflicting state laws.[5] When a federal statute conflicts directly with state law, the courts do not hesitate to strike down the state law as unconstitutional. The effect of the Supremacy Clause is less clear, however, if no *direct* conflict exists between state and federal law. As federal regulation expanded during the twentieth century, businesses increasingly became subject to both federal and state laws. In an effort to avoid dual regulation, businesses often argue that the federal laws preempt state regulation even when there is no direct conflict between the two laws.

---

[5]The Supremacy Clause, contained in Article VI of the Constitution, is introduced in Chapter 1.

The Supreme Court, however, has ruled that federal law preempts state regulation only if Congress clearly has demonstrated its intent to preempt. Congress may explicitly state its intent by statute. The federal statute governing aviation, for example, specifically preempts state regulation of airlines by prohibiting states from enacting or enforcing any "law, regulation, or other provision having the force and effect of law related to a price, route, or service of an air carrier."[6] The Supreme Court held, therefore, that this statute expressly prohibited the states from setting standards for advertising airline fares.[7] Even if Congress does not explicitly preempt state regulation, the Supreme Court has ruled that it may infer Congress's intent to preempt if: (1) the federal law is so pervasive that state regulation must be excluded; (2) national uniformity is required; or (3) state laws interfere with achieving Congress's objectives.

The Commerce Clause. The Supreme Court has interpreted the Commerce Clause not only as a grant of power to the federal government, but also as a limitation on the powers of the states. Under the Commerce Clause provisions relating to international commerce and trade with the Indian tribes, the federal government's power essentially is exclusive. As a result, the states generally cannot regulate trade either with foreign nations or Indian tribes. Interpretation of the states' powers to regulate interstate commerce, however, is more complicated.

As interpreted by the Supreme Court, the federal government does not have exclusive power to regulate interstate commerce. While *direct* state regulation of interstate commerce is prohibited, some *indirect* regulation by the states is permissible. Historically, states sometimes have attempted to directly regulate interstate commerce to protect local businesses from competition. The Supreme Court consistently has ruled that such state laws are unconstitutional under the Commerce Clause. In the following case, the Court explains the reasons for invalidating such state laws.

Granholm v. Heald
125 S. Ct. 1885 (2005)

By statute, both Michigan and New York establish a three-tier distribution system to regulate marketing of alcoholic

beverages. Under these systems, producers of beer, wine, and liquor may sell their products only to wholesalers that are licensed by the state. Wholesalers then may distribute the alcoholic beverages only to licensed retailers who then sell to consumers.

Under Michigan law, wineries located in Michigan were allowed to ship their wines directly to consumers without using the state distribution system. Several Michigan residents and a California winery challenged the Michigan law asserting that it violated the Commerce Clause of the United States Constitution by discriminating in favor of Michigan wine producers. The U.S. Court of Appeals for the Sixth Circuit held that the Michigan law was unconstitutional.

New York law also exempted certain wineries from complying with the three-tier distribution system. The New York law did not prohibit out of state wineries from shipping to New York customers but allowed those shipments only if the out of state winery obtained a New York licensed winery. To do so, however, the winery was required to establish a "branch factory, office or storeroom in the state of New York." This law was challenged in a lawsuit filed by several New York residents and wineries in Virginia and California. The United States Court of Appeals for the Second Circuit ruled that the New York law did not violate the U.S. Constitution.

After granting certiorari, the U.S. Supreme Court consolidated the two cases and issued the following opinion.

Justice Kennedy

. . . Time and again this Court has held that, in all but the narrowest circumstances, state laws violate the Commerce Clause if they mandate "differential treatment of in-state and out-of-state economic interests that benefits the former and burdens the latter." *Oregon Waste Systems, Inc. v. Department of Environmental Quality of Oregon,* [114 S. Ct. 1345 (1994)]. . . . This rule is essential to the foundations of the Union. The mere fact of nonresidence should not foreclose a producer in one State from access to markets in other States. . . . States may not enact laws that burden out-of-state producers or shippers simply to give a competitive advantage to in-state businesses. This mandate "reflects a central concern of the Framers that was an immediate reason for calling the Constitutional Convention: the conviction that in order to succeed, the new Union would have to avoid the tendencies toward economic Balkanization that had plagued relations among the Colonies and later among the States under the Articles of Confederation." *Hughes v. Oklahoma,* [99 S. Ct. 1727 (1979)].

The rule prohibiting state discrimination against interstate commerce follows also from the principle that States should not be compelled to negotiate with each

---

[6]49 U.S.C. §41713(b)(1).
[7]Morales v. Trans World Airlines, Inc., 112 S. Ct. 2031 (1992).

other regarding favored or disfavored status for their own citizens. States do not need, and may not attempt, to negotiate with other States regarding their mutual economic interests. . . . Rivalries among the States are thus kept to a minimum, and a proliferation of trade zones is prevented. . . .

Laws of the type at issue in the instant cases contradict these principles. They deprive citizens of their right to have access to the markets of other States on equal terms. The perceived necessity for reciprocal sale privileges risks generating the trade rivalries and animosities, the alliances and exclusivity, that the Constitution and, in particular, the Commerce Clause were designed to avoid. State laws that protect local wineries have led to the enactment of statutes under which some States condition the right of out-of-state wineries to make direct wine sales to in-state consumers on a reciprocal right in the shipping State. California, for example, passed a reciprocity law in 1986. . . . Prior to 1986, all but three States prohibited direct-shipments of wine. The obvious aim of the California statute was to open the interstate direct-shipping market for the State's many wineries. . . . The current patchwork of laws—with some States banning direct shipments altogether, others doing so only for out-of-state wines, and still others requiring reciprocity—is essentially the product of an ongoing, low-level trade war. Allowing States to discriminate against out-of-state wine "invites a multiplication of preferential trade areas destructive of the very purpose of the Commerce Clause." *Dean Milk Co. v. Madison,* [71 S. Ct. 295 (1951)]. . . .

The discriminatory character of the Michigan system is obvious. Michigan allows in-state wineries to ship directly to consumers, subject only to a licensing requirement. Out-of-state wineries, whether licensed or not, face a complete ban on direct shipment. The differential treatment requires all out-of-state wine, but not all in-state wine, to pass through an in-state wholesaler and retailer before reaching consumers. These two extra layers of overhead increase the cost of out-of-state wines to Michigan consumers. The cost differential, and in some cases the inability to secure a wholesaler for small shipments, can effectively bar small wineries from the Michigan market.

The New York regulatory scheme differs from Michigan's in that it does not ban direct shipments altogether. Out-of-state wineries are instead required to establish a distribution operation in New York in order to gain the privilege of direct shipment. This, though, is just an indirect way of subjecting out-of-state wineries,

but not local ones, to the three-tier system. New York and those allied with its interests defend the scheme by arguing that an out-of-state winery has the same access to the State's consumers as in-state wineries: All wine must be sold through a licensee fully accountable to New York; it just so happens that in order to become a licensee, a winery must have a physical presence in the State. There is some confusion over the precise steps out-of-state wineries must take to gain access to the New York market, in part because no winery has run the State's regulatory gauntlet. New York's argument, in any event, is unconvincing.

The New York scheme grants in-state wineries access to the State's consumers on preferential terms. . . . In-state producers, with the applicable licenses, can ship directly to consumers from their wineries. . . . Out-of-state wineries must open a branch office and warehouse in New York, additional steps that drive up the cost of their wine. . . . For most wineries, the expense of establishing a bricks-and-mortar distribution operation in one State, let alone all fifty, is prohibitive. It comes as no surprise that not a single out-of-state winery has availed itself of New York's direct-shipping privilege. . . .

We have no difficulty concluding that New York, like Michigan, discriminates against interstate commerce through its direct-shipping laws. . . . The two States, however, contend their statutes are saved by §2 of the Twenty-first Amendment, which provides: "The transportation or importation into any State, Territory, or possession of the United States for delivery or use therein of intoxicating liquors, in violation of the laws thereof, is hereby prohibited." The States' position is inconsistent with our precedents and with the Twenty-first Amendment's history. Section 2 does not allow States to regulate the direct shipment of wine on terms that discriminate in favor of in-state producers. . . .

The aim of the Twenty-first Amendment was to allow States to maintain an effective and uniform system for controlling liquor by regulating its transportation, importation, and use. The Amendment did not give States the authority to pass nonuniform laws in order to discriminate against out-of-state goods, a privilege they had not enjoyed at any earlier time. . . .

Our more recent cases, furthermore, confirm that the Twenty-first Amendment does not supersede other provisions of the Constitution and, in particular, does not displace the rule that States may not give a discriminatory preference to their own producers. . . . The instant cases . . . involve straightforward attempts to discriminate in favor of local producers. The discrimination is contrary to the Commerce Clause and is not saved by the Twenty-first Amendment.

States have broad power to regulate liquor under §2 of the Twenty-first Amendment. This power, however, does not allow States to ban, or severely limit, the direct shipment of out-of-state wine while simultaneously authorizing direct shipment by in-state producers. If a State chooses to allow direct shipment of wine, it must do so on evenhanded terms. Without demonstrating the need for discrimination, New York and Michigan have enacted regulations that disadvantage out-of-state wine producers. Under our Commerce Clause jurisprudence, these regulations cannot stand.

[Judgment of the Court of Appeals for the Sixth Circuit affirmed; judgment of the Court of Appeals for the Second Circuit reversed and remanded.]

Direct regulation of interstate commerce occurs when a state law explicitly treats business products from out-of-state differently from in-state products. The Michigan law discussed in Granholm is an example of direct regulation of interstate commerce because the state law expressly gave more favorable treatment to Michigan wineries.

The New York law discussed in *Granholm* is an example of indirect regulation of interstate commerce. Indirect regulation of interstate commerce occurs when a state regulatory law affects both in-state and out-of-state businesses. Under the New York law, any winery—whether located in New York or in another state—could obtain favorable treatment (that is, ship directly to consumers) provided that it obtained a New York license. Although the Court held that the New York law was unconstitutional because of its discriminatory effect, indirect regulation of interstate commerce sometimes is permissible under the Commerce Clause. Unless a federal law expressly preempts state regulation, the courts generally apply the following standard to determine whether a state law indirectly regulating interstate commerce is constitutional:

> Where the statute regulates evenhandedly to effectuate a legitimate local public interest, and its effects on interstate commerce are only incidental, it will be upheld unless the burden imposed on such commerce is clearly excessive in relation to the putative local benefits.[8]

This standard requires a legitimate purpose for the state statute: for example, a need to protect the health, safety, or welfare of local citizens. The statute also must apply evenhandedly to both intrastate and interstate commerce. Statutes, such as the New York law described in *Granholm,* that attempt to protect local industry from out-of-state competition are illegal. Finally, in applying this standard, the court weighs the benefits of the regulation to the state against the burdens on interstate commerce. If the benefits outweigh the burdens, the state legislation usually is upheld unless the court determines that the benefits could be achieved through other forms of regulation less burdensome on interstate commerce.

State Taxation Statutes Affecting Interstate Commerce. Just as states may use the police power to regulate some activities that affect interstate commerce, states also may impose taxes that affect interstate commerce. Direct state taxation of goods in interstate commerce is illegal, but incidental taxation of interstate commerce or of businesses engaged in interstate commerce is generally permissible if the state can establish some nexus (connection) between the tax and the state. This connection may be established for property taxes if there is a taxable situs in the state—that is, if the property is located within the state. Income taxes may be imposed on businesses if there is a nexus between the business transactions conducted in the state and the tax. For example, the states may impose income taxes on businesses domiciled within the state or engaged in commercial activities within the state. Nevertheless, income taxes must be apportioned in a manner that bears a reasonable relationship to the business activities conducted within the state. Taxes that are based on an actual nexus to the state and are properly apportioned generally do not violate the Commerce Clause.

Import-Export Clause. State taxation of goods in international commerce is limited by the **Import-Export Clause** of the Constitution, which states:

> No State shall, without the Consent of the Congress, lay any Imposts or Duties on Imports or Exports, except what may be absolutely necessary for executing its inspection Laws. . . . [9]

---

[8]Pike v. Bruce Church, Inc., 90 S. Ct. 844, 847 (1970).

[9]U.S. Const. art. I, §10, cl. 2.

This provision prohibits a state from imposing a direct tax on imports or exports solely because the goods have been received from or are bound for a foreign country. The provision, however, does not prohibit assessment of a nondiscriminatory tax before or after the goods are in transit.

In *Michelin Tire Corporation v. Wages,* the Supreme Court considered the validity of a Georgia tax imposed on all personal property in the state. Michelin challenged assessment of the tax on its inventory of goods made in France and held in a Georgia warehouse for distribution in the United States. The Court upheld the tax assessment against Michelin and stated:

> . . . [S]uch property taxes are taxes by which a State apportions the cost of such services as police and fire protection among the beneficiaries according to their respective wealth; there is no reason why an importer should not bear his share of these costs along with his competitors handling only domestic goods. The Import-Export Clause clearly prohibits state taxation based on the foreign origin of imported goods, but it cannot be read to accord imported goods preferential treatment that permits escape from uniform taxes imposed without regard to foreign origin for services which the State supplies. . . . [10]

A similar rule applies to incidental taxation of exports. Until domestic goods bound for foreign countries are placed in transit or begin their "physical entry into the stream of exportation,"[11] they may be subject to nondiscriminatory taxation by the states.

The Import-Export Clause applies only to state taxation of imports and exports. The Constitution also prohibits the federal government from taxing exports but allows direct federal taxation of imports.

Privileges and Immunities Clause. The Constitution places further restrictions on the states' police and taxing powers by the **Privileges and Immunities Clause,** which provides:

> The Citizens of each State shall be entitled to all Privileges and Immunities of Citizens in the several States.[12]

This provision prohibits states from unreasonable discrimination against out-of-state citizens. As explained by the Supreme Court, "one of the privileges which the clause guarantees to citizens of State A is that of doing business in State B on terms of substantial equality with the citizens of that State."[13] The Privileges and Immunities Clause, however, protects only the rights of individuals. For purposes of the clause, corporations are not considered to be citizens.

The Court, for example, has held unconstitutional a state statute requiring state residents to pay $25 for a commercial fishing license and nonresidents to pay $2,500 for the same license.[14] Similarly, the Privileges and Immunities Clause prohibits unreasonable discriminatory income taxation. For instance, a New York income tax that allowed exemptions for resident taxpayers and their dependents but allowed no exemptions for out-of-state residents was held to violate the Privileges and Immunities Clause.[15]

The Contract Clause. The Constitution prohibits the states from passing any "Law impairing the Obligation of Contracts."[16] The original purpose of this provision, known as the **Contract Clause,** was to prevent states from enacting debtor relief laws, a practice that had occurred in several states following the American Revolution. To encourage credit arrangements necessary for economic growth, the drafters of the Constitution provided creditors some assurance that their existing contracts would not be adversely modified by state law. Under the Clause, however, states can adopt statutes to regulate contracts that are made *after* enactment of the statute.

The Supreme Court has interpreted the Contract Clause as restricting the states' ability to adopt laws that retroactively affect private contracts, holding that ". . . it must be understood to impose some limits upon the power of a State to abridge existing contractual relationships, even in the exercise of its otherwise legitimate police power."[17] A state, however, may adopt statutes that substantially modify *existing* contracts—that is, contracts made before enactment of the law—only if the

---

[10]Michelin Tire Corporation v. Wages, 96 S. Ct. 535, 541 (1976).

[11]Kosydar v. National Cash Register Co., 94 S. Ct. 2108, 2114 (1974).

[12]U.S. CONST. art. IV, §2, cl. 1. The Fourteenth Amendment contains a provision prohibiting the states from abridging "the privileges or immunities of citizens of the United States." Courts have interpreted this clause to protect the rights accruing to a citizen of the United States—for example, the right to vote in federal elections or to interstate travel. The clause has not been used to protect rights of state citizenship.

[13]Toomer v. Witsell, 68 S. Ct. 1156, 1162 (1948).

[14]*Id.*

[15]Travis v. Yale & Towne Mfg. Co., 40 S. Ct. 228 (1920).

[16]U.S. CONST. art. I, §10, cl. 1.

[17]Allied Structural Steel Company v. Spannaus, 98 S. Ct. 2716, 2721 (1978).

legislation is necessary to meet an important and wide-spread problem. The state law is more likely to be held constitutional if it only temporarily alters the contractual relationship or affects a field that the state has previously regulated. For example, the Supreme Court held that a state statute placing a moratorium on mortgage foreclosures during the Depression did not violate the Contract Clause.[18] Although the statute modified existing mortgage contracts, the Court found that the need to protect homeowners from loss of their homes justified the moratorium. In contrast, in a more recent case, the Court held that a state statute that permanently modified private contractual pension plans violated the Contract Clause.[19] The Court noted that the statute, designed to protect the interest of employees who participated in certain private pension plans, was not directed at a broad societal interest and severely and permanently changed the private contractual arrangements.

Bill of Rights and Fourteenth Amendment Limitations

The Supreme Court has ruled that the Bill of Rights and the Fourteenth Amendment not only guarantee certain rights to individuals, but also protect some rights of businesses. The following sections briefly discuss the limitations that the First, Fourth, Fifth, and Fourteenth Amendments impose on both state and federal regulation of business.

Freedom of Speech. The First Amendment, as interpreted by the Supreme Court, prohibits federal and state governments from adopting laws abridging freedom of speech. **Freedom of speech** is interpreted broadly to include freedom of expression in oral and written communications, as well as nonverbal actions with symbolic value (for example, saluting a flag, wearing an armband).

Under the First Amendment, the government generally cannot restrain someone from engaging in free expression or punish a person for having engaged in free expression if the restraint or punishment is based on the content of the speech. For example, if the federal government refused to allow any public speech on the subject of nuclear war, the government's action would violate the First Amendment because the basis for restraining the speech is its content, that is, the subject of nuclear war.

Freedom of expression, however, is not absolute. Defamatory speech and obscenity, for example, are considered to be unprotected speech subject to regulation and punishment by the government. The government also may impose reasonable time, place, and manner regulations on expression. The government, for example, may prohibit all demonstrations or parades unless the participants first obtain a governmental license or permit. If, however, the state required a permit only if the demonstration or speech concerned a specific topic (for example, nuclear war), the regulation would be illegal because the content of the speech was the basis for the regulation.

If a type of communication is subject to First Amendment protection, then the expression is protected whether its source is an individual or a business such as a corporation.[20] For many years, the courts considered **commercial speech** (such as advertisements for products or services) to be unprotected. More recently, however, the Supreme Court has held that although commercial speech is subject to regulation (for example, truth in advertising), it is entitled to some protection from governmental regulation. The following case illustrates First Amendment protection of commercial speech.

Thompson v. Western States Medical Center
122 S. Ct. 1497 (2002)

Since 1938, the federal government has regulated the pharmaceutical industry by requiring approval of the federal Food and Drug Administration before a new drug can be marketed in the United States. For many years, however, compounded drugs—drugs custom made by a pharmacist to meet the needs of a specific patient—were not subject to the FDA approval. Compounding generally is used to prepare medicines that are not commercially available, for example, a medication for someone who is allergic to a mass-produced drug. Learning to compound drugs is part of a pharmacist's training and compounded drugs can be provided only if the patient has a valid prescription from a

---

[18]Home Building & Loan Assn. v. Blaisdell, 54 S. Ct. 231 (1934).

[19]Allied Structural Steel Company v. Spannaus, 98 S. Ct. 2716 (1978).

[20]First National Bank of Boston v. Bellotti, 98 S. Ct. 1407 (1978).

physician. The Food and Drug Administration Modernization Act (FDAMA), a federal statute enacted in 1997, modified federal drug regulation. The law continued to exempt compounded drugs from the lengthy FDA approval process, but imposed new regulations that prohibited the advertising or promotion of drug compounding.

Plaintiffs, a group of licensed pharmacists specializing in drug compounding, filed a lawsuit claiming that the FDAMA's restriction on advertising violated the First Amendment of the United States Constitution. The government asserted that the restriction was necessary to justify excluding compounded drugs from the FDA approval process. The federal trial court ruled that the provision was unconstitutional, and the Ninth Circuit Federal Court of Appeals affirmed. The United States Supreme Court agreed to review the case.

Justice O'Connor

The parties agree that the advertising and soliciting prohibited by the FDAMA constitute commercial speech. In *Virginia Bd. of Pharmacy v. Virginia Citizens Consumer Council, Inc.,* [96 S. Ct. 1817, 1827 (1976)], the first case in which we explicitly held that commercial speech receives First Amendment protection, we explained the reasons for this protection: "It is a matter of public interest that [economic] decisions, in the aggregate, be intelligent and well-informed. To this end, the free flow of commercial information is indispensable." Indeed, we recognized that a "particular consumer's interest in the free flow of commercial information . . . may be as keen, if not keener by far, than his interest in the day's most urgent political debate." [*Id.,* at 1826.] We have further emphasized:

> The commercial marketplace, like other spheres of our social and cultural life, provides a forum where ideas and information flourish. Some of the ideas and information are vital, some of slight worth. But the general rule is that the speaker and the audience, not the government, assess the value of the information presented. Thus, even a communication that does no more than propose a commercial transaction is entitled to the coverage of the First Amendment. *Edenfield v. Fane,* [113 S. Ct. 1792, 1798 (1993)].

Although commercial speech is protected by the First Amendment, not all regulation of such speech is unconstitutional. . . . In *Central Hudson Gas & Elec. Corp. v. Public Serv. Comm'n of N. Y.,* [100 S. Ct. 2343 (1980)], we articulated a test for determining whether a particular commercial speech regulation is constitutionally permissible. Under that test we ask as a threshold matter whether the commercial speech concerns unlawful activity or is misleading. If so, then the speech is not protected by the First Amendment. If the speech concerns lawful activity and is not misleading, however, we next ask "whether the asserted governmental interest is substantial." [*Id.* at 2351.] If it is, then we "determine whether the regulation directly advances the governmental interest asserted," and, finally, "whether it is not more extensive than is necessary to serve that interest." [*Id.*] Each of these latter three inquiries must be answered in the affirmative for the regulation to be found constitutional. . . .

The Government does not attempt to defend the FDAMA's speech-related provisions under the first prong of the *Central Hudson* test; that is, it does not argue that the prohibited advertisements would be about unlawful activity or would be misleading. Instead, the Government argues that the FDAMA satisfies the remaining three prongs of the *Central Hudson* test.

The Government asserts that three substantial interests underlie the FDAMA. The first is an interest in "preserving the effectiveness and integrity of the FDCA's new drug approval process and the protection of the public health that it provides." *Brief for Petitioners* 19. The second is an interest in "preserving the availability of compounded drugs for those individual patients who, for particularized medical reasons, cannot use commercially available products that have been approved by the FDA." *Id.,* at 19-20. Finally, the Government argues that "achieving the proper balance between those two independently compelling but competing interests is itself a substantial governmental interest." *Id.,* at 20. . . .

Preserving the effectiveness and integrity of the FDCA's new drug approval process is clearly an important governmental interest, and the Government has every reason to want as many drugs as possible to be subject to that approval process. The Government also has an important interest, however, in permitting the continuation of the practice of compounding so that patients with particular needs may obtain medications suited to those needs. And it would not make sense to require compounded drugs created to meet the unique needs of individual patients to undergo the testing required for the new drug approval process. Pharmacists do not make enough money from small-scale compounding to make safety and efficacy testing of their compounded drugs economically feasible, so requiring such testing would force pharmacists to stop providing compounded drugs. Given this, the

Government needs to be able to draw a line between small-scale compounding and large-scale drug manufacturing. That line must distinguish compounded drugs produced on such a small scale that they could not undergo safety and efficacy testing from drugs produced and sold on a large enough scale that they could undergo such testing and therefore must do so.

The Government argues that the FDAMA's speech-related provisions provide just such a line, that is, that, in the terms of *Central Hudson,* they "directly advance the governmental interests asserted." [100 S. Ct. at 2352.] Those provisions use advertising as the trigger for requiring FDA approval—essentially, as long as pharmacists do not advertise particular compounded drugs, they may sell compounded drugs without first undergoing safety and efficacy testing and obtaining FDA approval. If they advertise their compounded drugs, however, FDA approval is required. . . . The Government argues that advertising particular products is useful in a broad market but is not useful when particular products are designed in response to an individual's "often unique needs." . . .

Assuming it is true that drugs cannot be marketed on a large scale without advertising, the FDAMA's prohibition on advertising compounded drugs might indeed "directly advance" the Government's interests. . . . Even assuming that it does, however, the Government has failed to demonstrate that the speech restrictions are "not more extensive than is necessary to serve [those] interests." In previous cases addressing this final prong of the *Central Hudson* test, we have made clear that if the Government could achieve its interests in a manner that does not restrict speech, or that restricts less speech, the Government must do so. . . .

Several non-speech-related means of drawing a line between compounding and large-scale manufacturing might be possible here. . . . For example, the Government could ban the use of "commercial scale manufacturing or testing equipment for compounding drug products." *1992 FDA Compliance Policy Guide.* . . . It could prohibit pharmacists from "offering compounded drugs at wholesale to other state licensed persons or commercial entities for resale." *Id.* Another possibility . . . would be capping the amount of any particular compounded drug, either by drug volume, number of prescriptions, gross revenue, or profit that a pharmacist or pharmacy may make or sell in a given period of time. It might even be sufficient to rely solely on the non-speech-related provisions of the FDAMA, such as the requirement that compounding only be conducted in response to a prescription or a history of receiving a prescription. . . .

The Government has not offered any reason why these possibilities, alone or in combination, would be insufficient to prevent compounding from occurring on such a scale as to undermine the new drug approval process. Indeed, there is no hint that the Government even considered these or any other alternatives. . . .The Government simply has not provided sufficient justification here. If the First Amendment means anything, it means that regulating speech must be a last—not first—resort. Yet here it seems to have been the first strategy the Government thought to try. . . .

[Judgment affirmed.]

Guarantee of Due Process. The Fifth and Fourteenth Amendments prohibit the federal and state governments from depriving a person of life, liberty, or property without due process of law. For purposes of the Due Process Clauses, "persons" include both natural persons and corporations. As applied to business regulation, procedural due process generally requires that the government must engage in a fair decision-making process prior to depriving a business of property. Most regulatory statutes establish certain standards with which a business must comply. Failure to comply with those standards may subject the business to criminal penalties or to civil liability. If the statutes are enforceable through the judicial system, a business is entitled to the procedural due process available in court proceedings—notice by a complaint, indictment, or information and the right to a trial in which the business may defend itself.[21]

Some business regulations, however, are enforceable in hearings conducted by an administrative agency.[22] If a business may suffer loss of property through the administrative hearing, the business is entitled to procedural due process: notice of the alleged violation and the right to defend itself at the hearing.

Guarantee of Equal Protection. The Fourteenth Amendment provides in part that "No State shall . . . deny to any person within its jurisdiction the equal protection of the laws."[23] This provision, known as the

---

[21]See the discussion of procedural due process in Chapters 2 and 3.
[22]These hearings will be discussed in greater detail later in this chapter.
[23]U.S. CONST. amend. XIV, §1.

Equal Protection Clause, explicitly limits the powers of the states, and the Supreme Court's interpretation of the Due Process Clauses requires that the federal government also provide equal protection. The guarantee of equal protection extends to both individuals and businesses.

Equal protection limits the way the government may classify persons for purposes of regulation. Laws often establish classifications. Liquor laws, for example, classify individuals based on age: most states prohibit individuals under the age of 21 from purchasing alcoholic beverages, while those over age 21 legally can purchase alcohol. Under the Equal Protection Clause, the government can estalish classifications, but they must relate to a proper governmental purpose. In determining whether a governmental classification complies with the equal protection guarantee, the courts examine the purpose of the statute and then consider whether the method of classification bears a sufficient relationship to that purpose. If the governmental classification is not properly related to an appropriate purpose or if the classification is arbitrary or based on impermissible criteria, the classification violates equal protection.

In lawsuits alleging that a statute violates the Equal Protection Clause, the courts use three types of analysis. Under *strict scrutiny analysis,* a statute is considered to be constitutional only if the government can prove that a compelling governmental interest necessitates the type of classification used in the statute. Strict scrutiny analysis is used only in cases challenging classifications based on race or ancestry or affecting the exercise of fundamental rights such as voting. It is extremely difficult for the government to meet the standard of proof required under strict scrutiny analysis. As a result, statutes examined under strict scrutiny analysis usually are found to be unconstitutional. Statutes using other types of classifications are not examined as closely by the courts. Courts use *intermediate scrutiny analysis* when examining statutes that classify individuals on the basis of gender or that affect important, but not fundamental, rights. Under this analysis, the statute is invalidated unless the government can prove that the classification is substantially related to an important government objective.[24] The government's burden of proof under intermediate scrutiny analysis is rigorous, but less difficult than that required by strict scrutiny.

Economic and social legislation generally is evaluated under the *rational basis analysis,* the third type of analysis used by courts to evaluate the constitutionality of statutes alleged to violate the Equal Protection Clause. Statutes examined under the rational basis test are presumed to be valid and are upheld by the court so long as the law is rationally related to a legitimate governmental purpose. Most statutes examined under rational basis analysis are found to be constitutional. Because statutes regulating businesses generally are for economic or social purposes, these laws rarely are found to be a violation of the Equal Protection Clause.

Administrative Agencies

Today, state and federal administrative agencies have assumed primary responsibility for implementing and enforcing much state and federal legislation. Hundreds of agencies are involved in the regulation of business and industry, including the major federal administrative agencies summarized in Table 4.1. The remainder of this chapter provides an introduction to federal administrative agencies. Most of the general principles that govern federal agencies also apply to state agencies.

An "administrative agency" is a unit of government that is responsible for executing and enforcing statutes. Two types of administrative agencies operate at the federal level: independent agencies and executive agencies. Independent agencies, which are designed to minimize political influence and pressure on agency action, are created by Congress and are governed by a commission or board appointed by the president, subject to Senate confirmation. These commissioners or board members serve fixed terms in office and cannot be removed except for cause. Almost all independent agencies are free-standing governmental units that exist organizationally outside the three branches of government—that is, they are not a part of the legislative, executive, or judicial branch—so they sometimes are described as the "fourth branch" of government. Independent agencies, such as the Federal Trade Commission and the Securities and Exchange Commission, include some of the largest and most influential agencies that regulate business and the economy.

In contrast, executive agencies are units within the executive branch of government and the heads of these agencies generally are appointed by the president. Although some of the appointments require Senate

---

[24]See, for example, Craig v. Boren, 97 S. Ct. 451 (1976).

Table 4.1 Major Federal Administrative Agencies Responsible for Business Regulation

Agency	Area of Regulation
Antitrust Division, Department of Justice	Enforcement of federal antitrust laws
Commodity Futures Trading Commission (CFTC)	Commodity and financial futures and options; futures and options markets
Consumer Product Safety Commission (CPSC)	Safety of consumer products
Environmental Protection Agency (EPA)	Air, water, and land environment; pollution control
Equal Employment Opportunity Commission (EEOC)	Employment laws prohibiting discrimination based on race, color, national origin, sex, religion, age, and disability
Federal Aviation Administration (FAA) Department of Transportation	Navigable airspace, air commerce, and air safety
Federal Communications Commission (FCC)	Interstate and international communications (radio, television, wire, cable, and satellite)
Federal Deposit Insurance Corporation (FDIC)	Insurance of deposits in banks and thrift institutions; banks
Federal Energy Regulatory Commission (FERC) Department of Energy	Interstate transmission of electricity, natural gas, and oil; hydroelectric projects
Federal Reserve Board (FRB)	National credit and monetary affairs
Federal Trade Commission (FTC)	Antitrust, corporate mergers, unfair trade practices, and unfair methods of competition
Food and Drug Administration (FDA), Department of Health and Human Services	Safety of food, drugs, cosmetics, biological products, and medical devices
Internal Revenue Service (IRS) Department of Treasury	Federal tax laws
National Labor Relations Board (NLRB)	Labor laws, unions, and collective bargaining
Nuclear Regulatory Commission (NRC)	Civilian use of nuclear energy
Office of Comptroller of Currency Department of Treasury	National banks
Occupational Safety and Health Administration (OSHA) Department of Labor	Workplace safety and health
Overseas Private Investment Corporation (OPIC)	Private investment in developing countries and emerging markets
Patent and Trademark Office (PTO) Department of Commerce	Patents and trademarks
Securities and Exchange Commission (SEC)	Federal securities laws
Social Security Administration (SSA)	Social Security contributions and benefits
United States International Trade Commission (USITC)	International trade policies; tariffs
Wage and Hour Division Department of Labor	Enforcement of federal labor laws governing minimum wage, overtime pay, and employment of minors

approval, the head of an executive agency usually is subject to removal by the president. Most executive agencies are located within Cabinet departments; for example, the National Highway Traffic Safety Administration is located within the Department of Transportation and the Food and Drug Administration is part of the Department of Health and Human Services. Executive agencies generally have more restricted powers than independent agencies and the scope of their authority often is narrower or limited to one industry. Yet, some executive agencies, such as the Internal Revenue Service and the Social Security Administration, are very powerful and play a major role in business regulation. Since its creation in 1970, the Environmental Protection Agency, the only executive agency not located within a Cabinet department, has become one of the largest federal agencies and its regulatory authority affects almost all industries.

Powers of Administrative Agencies

Congress has delegated a variety of powers to administrative agencies. In general, these powers are analogous to those exercised by the three branches of government. Like the executive branch, some agencies are authorized to investigate and prosecute violations of federal law. Other agencies have the power to engage in rule-making, a process of adopting rules and regulations that are enforced like statutes enacted by the legislature. Some administrative agencies also are responsible for adjudicating individual cases involving issues of fact and law through administrative hearings that resemble court cases tried by the judiciary. Individual federal statutes that create an agency or that establish the activities subject to the agency's regulation also define the powers—investigative, prosecutorial, rule-making, or adjudicative—granted to the agency. Additionally, Congress has adopted the **Administrative Procedure Act,**[25] a comprehensive statute that sets forth the procedures agencies must follow when engaging in rule-making or adjudication and that regulates dissemination of information gathered by agencies.

Investigation and Prosecution. Many administrative agencies possess the power to investigate and prosecute—functions traditionally exercised by the executive branch of government. Some administrative agencies are authorized to engage in investigation of specific

individuals or businesses suspected of violating the law. If authorized by statute, such agencies may compel disclosure of information. The Federal Trade Commission, for example, has the following powers:

> . . . the [Federal Trade] Commission, or its duly authorized agent or agents, shall at all reasonable times have access to, for the purpose of examination, and the right to copy any documentary evidence of any person, partnership, or corporation being investigated or proceeded against; and the Commission shall have power to require by subpoena the attendance and testimony of witnesses and the production of all such documentary evidence relating to any matter under investigation.[26]

An administrative agency may demand only information relevant to legitimate investigations within the scope of the agency's authority. Further, requests for information generally must be reasonable, that is, not unduly vague or oppressive, and may not include privileged information. If a business subpoenaed by an agency wishes to contest the request, the business may seek a judicial order to quash the subpoena, but if the business merely fails to comply with the request, the agency may seek a judicial order including a penalty for contempt. In either case, judicial review minimizes the possibility of agency abuse of its investigative powers.

Some administrative agencies with investigatory powers also are authorized to prosecute violations of federal law. If an agency seeks criminal penalties, the case must be prosecuted in federal court generally with the assistance of the federal Department of Justice. In other cases involving only civil laws or regulations, Congress has authorized some agencies to try the matter within the agency through an administrative hearing.[27]

Administrative Searches. Some statutes authorize administrative agencies to conduct inspections of a business as a method of investigating compliance with regulations. The Supreme Court has held that such inspections, even when conducted only in conjunction with civil violations, constitute "searches" and are subject to the Fourth Amendment's prohibition against unreasonable searches and seizures. These **administrative searches** are a practical means to enforce laws relating to safety and health such as food and drug

---

[25]5 U.S.C. §§551–559, 701–706.

[26]15 U.S.C. §49.
[27]Administrative hearings are discussed later in this chapter.

preparation and handling, pollution controls, and building and workplace safety and fire codes. The owner or manager of the premises may consent to an administrative search, but if consent is refused, an administrative search is valid only if the government obtains a warrant by demonstrating probable cause either that conditions on the premises violate the law or that the search is made pursuant to reasonable legislative or administrative standards.[28] These standards, for example, might provide that the sites are selected for inspection on a random or periodic basis. The Supreme Court has, however, recognized a limited exception to the warrant requirement for "pervasively regulated business[es],"[29] and for "closely regulated" industries "long subject to close supervision and inspection."[30] These industries, such as liquor and firearms, have such a history of government regulation and oversight that proprietors enjoy no reasonable expectation of privacy.

Information Gathering. Most investigations conducted by agencies are for the purpose of prosecution. Administrative agencies, however, also engage in a broad spectrum of information-gathering activities for other purposes. An agency may gather and analyze data to provide information for public and private policy making. The Commerce Department, for example, collects a variety of economic and business information that is made available to other governmental units, to businesses, and to the general public. Much of this information is acquired from public sources or is disclosed voluntarily by businesses and individuals. Other information collected by agencies is provided by businesses or individuals in compliance with federal law. Sometimes a business provides data to secure a governmental benefit such as a government contract, a license to operate, or approval to market a product. Regulations of the Food and Drug Administration, for example, require a manufacturer who proposes to market a new drug to submit information about its composition, method of manufacture, recommended labeling, as well as test data demonstrating its safety and effectiveness. Other federal laws require businesses to gather and keep specified information and records. The Occupational Safety and Health Act, for example, requires businesses to maintain records of employee accidents and illnesses

and exposure to hazardous substances. Agencies generally may mandate specified record keeping or submission of reports on matters relating to the agency's area of regulation if authorized by statute.

Freedom of Information Act. Administrative agencies possess vast amounts of information and data that have been accumulated through their investigative and information-gathering powers. In response to claims that government information was inaccessible, Congress amended the Administrative Procedure Act by enacting the **Freedom of Information Act (FOIA)**.[31] The FOIA requires federal agencies to make agency records available for examination or copying to any person who requests the records. Under the FOIA, the requesting party need not provide a reason for access, but some records are exempt from disclosure. The Act establishes nine categories of exempt documents, including certain national defense and foreign policy secrets, internal personnel matters, items exempted from disclosure by other statutes, and certain inter-agency and intra-agency memoranda. Exemption 4 of the FOIA provides that the Act "does not apply to matters that are . . . trade secrets and commercial or financial information obtained from a person and privileged or confidential."[32] This exemption has been especially important to businesses that have provided information to the government but desire to prevent competitors from gaining access to the information. When an FOIA request is made for data submitted by a business, most agencies notify the business and may allow it to comment on whether exemption 4 should apply.

Rule-Making. Many federal agencies possess rule-making power, the authority to adopt rules and regulations to carry out the provisions of statutes enforced by the agency. Rule-making enables an agency to clarify its policies, procedures, and interpretation of statutes subject to the agency's regulation. When authorized by statute, the agency also can adopt legislative or substantive rules that fill in the gaps or add details to federal statutes. For example, the federal Clean Water Act, which regulates water pollution, delegates to the Environmental Protection Agency (EPA) the authority to set specific standards for each type of pollutant that may be discharged into navigable waters. Thus, the leg-

---

[28]Marshall v. Barlow's Inc., 98 S. Ct. 1816, 1824–1825 (1978).
[29]United States v. Biswell, 92 S. Ct. 1593, 1596 (1972).
[30]Colonnade Catering Corp. v. United States, 90 S. Ct. 774, 777 (1970).

[31]5 U.S.C. §552.
[32]5 U.S.C. §552(b)(4).

islative rules of the EPA, rather than the provisions of the Clean Water Act, actually regulate pollution control. Legislative rules cannot contradict the provisions of a statute and generally are enforced like statutes.

Rules and regulations that have been adopted by federal agencies are added to the Code of Federal Regulations. Before adopting legislative rules, however, an agency must comply with procedures established in the Administrative Procedure Act. Two types of procedures are outlined in the Act: formal rule-making and informal rule-making. When Congress grants rule-making authority to an agency, the statute specifies whether the agency must use either the formal or informal procedures. An agency initiates formal rule-making by publishing a notice of its proposed rule in the Federal Register and then must allow all interested parties to submit written responses. The agency, members of its governing board, or an administrative law judge must conduct a formal hearing at which evidence is presented, subject to cross-examination and rebuttal, in support of the rule. A full record of the hearing must be maintained and the final rule must be based exclusively on information presented in the record. Formal rule-making, which in many ways resembles a trial, can be time-consuming, expensive, and inefficient and is required by only a few federal statutes.

Most legislative rules, therefore, are adopted under informal rule-making procedures, which also begin with Federal Register publication of a notice of the proposed rule. After an opportunity for interested parties to submit written data and arguments, the agency may adopt a final rule with a "concise general statement of [its] basis and purpose."[33] Although most agencies prepare a record in support of the rule, the contents of the record are not prescribed by law, so often all data received by the agency is not included. Informal rule-making allows an agency greater flexibility to adapt the rule-making process to its own needs. Some agencies, for example, will hold public hearings or will solicit information from certain parties, such as the regulated industries, even if not required by law. Nevertheless, the informal rule-making process has been criticized for allowing agencies to disregard options or to ignore conflicting information.

Agencies maintain even broader discretion in adopting regulations that are not considered to be legislative or substantive. The Administrative Procedure Act establishes no procedure for interpretive rules, policy statements, or rules of agency procedure. Interpretive rules, which explain an agency's construction of statutory language, and policy statements are important because, although they do not have the legal force of a statute, courts generally defer to an agency's expertise in interpreting statutes.

The authority to adopt rules is one of the most important powers delegated to administrative agencies. Rule-making relieves Congress from having to enact detailed statutes that are sufficiently comprehensive to cover all aspects of a subject. Because each agency develops expertise in its area of regulation, agency adoption of rules and standards often provides effective and practical regulation that accomplishes the goals of Congress.

Adjudication. Some administrative agencies possess powers, similar to those of the judiciary, to apply and enforce statutes, rules, and regulations in administrative hearings. These proceedings, conducted by an administrative law judge, determine factual matters, secure compliance with specified laws or regulations, resolve claims of private individuals or businesses, or determine whether the government will issue a license. The administrative law judges are employees of the agency who have expertise in the laws administered by the agency.

Administrative hearings, which must meet the requirement of procedural due process, follow procedures similar to those of a trial. The proceeding usually is initiated by filing a complaint that is answered by the respondent. Most complaints are filed by the agency itself, although private businesses or individuals sometimes may initiate the proceeding. Following a period for discovery, evidence is presented, witnesses are examined and cross-examined, rulings are made on motions, and an order is issued by the administrative law judge.

The **administrative order,** like a judgment in a court trial, terminates the hearings. If the administrative law judge finds that a party violated the law, the judge may issue a **cease and desist order** that commands the wrongdoer to stop the illegal practice. Most agencies do not have the power to enforce the orders of administrative law judges. Rather, if a party fails to comply with a cease and desist order, the agency must bring a suit in federal court to obtain judicial enforcement.

As in court trials, a dispute may be settled prior to completion of an administrative hearing. The adminis-

---

[33]5 U.S.C. §553(c).

trative law judge may issue **a consent order** in which the party, without admitting guilt, agrees to stop the allegedly illegal practice. Consent orders usually require public notice prior to becoming effective. A consent order may be enforced like a cease and desist order.

Administrative hearings resemble bench trials in the courts. The administrative law judge makes findings of both fact and law. Generally, procedure in an agency hearing is less formal than at a trial; for example, complaints may be served by mail and rules of evidence may not apply. Although the parties usually have the right to counsel, many parties do not retain attorneys. Moreover, an administrative law judge does not have the power to impose criminal penalties or to award civil damages.

Administrative hearings reduce the caseload of federal courts and generally save parties time and money. Due to the specialization and expertise of an administrative law judge, adjudication by an agency often is more efficient and may result in a more pragmatic approach than judicial resolution.

Government Control of Administrative Agencies

Despite the broad powers that have been delegated to administrative agencies, they remain subject to control by all three branches of the government. These controls help to minimize abuse of power by an agency.

Executive Control. Generally, the president has the power to appoint and remove the heads of executive administrative agencies. Although the president also appoints the commissioners who head independent agencies, statutes restrict the presidential power. Commissioners usually are appointed to staggered terms for an established number of years, and the president must await expiration of a commissioner's term before appointing a new commissioner. Federal law also requires that some commissions be politically balanced. For example, no more than three of the five commissioners of the Securities and Exchange Commission may belong to the same political party. The authority to appoint officers and commissioners allows the president to staff administrative agencies with people who support and implement his policies.

The executive exercises further control of agencies through the budget process. Prior to submitting budgets to the Congress, appropriations for administrative agencies are reviewed and revised by the Office of Management and Budget (OMB), which is under the president's control. Although Congress is not required to adopt OMB's budget, it does influence congressional allocations. The scope of an administrative agency's activities, of course, depends on the amount of funding it receives.

Legislative Control. Congress creates administrative agencies and retains the power to terminate them. Congress rarely exercises this power because of political pressures from interested parties, and most agencies virtually become permanent. The legislature, however, still retains important controls. For example, it can expand or restrict the powers of an administrative agency. If Congress does not approve of an agency rule, it can change the rule by statute. Through the budgetary process, Congress can limit financial appropriations and effectively diminish the agency's powers. Finally, the legislature retains some control over personnel by requiring Senate approval of the appointment of some agency heads and commissioners.

At issue in the following case was whether a federal administrative agency had exceeded its statutory authority.

Food and Drug Administration v. Brown & Williamson Tobacco Corporation
120 S. Ct. 1291 (2000)

In 1996, the federal Food and Drug Administration (FDA), citing health risks and the need to curb tobacco use by minors, issued administrative rules restricting the sale and advertising of tobacco products. Maintaining that nicotine is a drug, the FDA asserted its power to regulate tobacco based on the Food, Drug, and Cosmetic Act (FDCA), which authorizes the FDA to control the sale and advertising of drugs. Brown & Williamson Tobacco Corporation and other tobacco manufacturers, retailers, and advertisers sued the FDA, arguing that the agency lacked the authority to regulate tobacco products. The trial court ruled in favor of the FDA, but the Fourth Circuit Court of Appeals reversed. The U.S. Supreme Court granted the FDA's petition for review.

Justice O'Connor

. . . Because this case involves an administrative agency's construction of a statute that it administers, . . . a reviewing court must first ask "whether Congress has directly spoken to the precise question at issue." [*Chevron U.S.A. Inc. v. Natural Resources Defense Council, Inc.,* 104 S. Ct. 2778, 2781 (1984).] If Congress has done so, the inquiry is at an end; the court "must give effect to the unambiguously expressed intent of Congress." *Id.* . . . But if Congress has not specifically addressed the question, a reviewing court must respect the agency's construction of the statute so long as it is permissible. . . . With these principles in mind, we find that Congress has directly spoken to the issue here and precluded the FDA's jurisdiction to regulate tobacco products.

Viewing the FDCA as a whole, it is evident that one of the Act's core objectives is to ensure that any product regulated by the FDA is "safe" and "effective" for its intended use. . . . [T]he Act generally requires the FDA to prevent the marketing of any drug or device where the "potential for inflicting death or physical injury is not offset by the possibility of therapeutic benefit." *United States v. Rutherford,* [99 S. Ct. 2470, 2477 (1979)].

In its rulemaking proceeding, the FDA quite exhaustively documented that "tobacco products are unsafe," "dangerous," and "cause great pain and suffering from illness." . . . It found that the consumption of tobacco products "presents extraordinary health risks," and that "tobacco use is the single leading cause of preventable death in the United States." . . . It stated that "[m]ore than 400,000 people die each year from tobacco-related illnesses, such as cancer, respiratory illnesses, and heart disease, often suffering long and painful deaths," and that "[t]obacco alone kills more people each year in the United States than acquired immunodeficiency syndrome (AIDS), car accidents, alcohol, homicides, illegal drugs, suicides, and fires, combined." Indeed, the FDA characterized smoking as "a pediatric disease," . . . because "one out of every three young people who become regular smokers . . . will die prematurely as a result." . . . [See 61 Fed. Reg. 44396 (1996).]

These findings logically imply that, if tobacco products were "devices" under the FDCA, the FDA would be required to remove them from the market. Consider, first, the FDCA's provisions concerning the misbranding of drugs or devices. The Act prohibits "[t]he introduction or delivery for introduction into interstate commerce of any food, drug, device, or cosmetic that is adulterated or misbranded." 21 *U.S.C.* §331(a). In light of the FDA's findings, two distinct FDCA provisions would render cigarettes and smokeless tobacco misbranded devices. First, §352(j) deems a drug or device misbranded "[i]f it is dangerous to health when used in the dosage or manner, or with the frequency or duration prescribed, recommended, or suggested in the labeling thereof." The FDA's findings make clear that tobacco products are "dangerous to health" when used in the manner prescribed. Second, a drug or device is misbranded under the Act "[u]nless its labeling bears . . . adequate directions for use . . . in such manner and form, as are necessary for the protection of users," except where such directions are "not necessary for the protection of the public health." §352(f)(l). Given the FDA's conclusions concerning the health consequences of tobacco use, there are no directions that could adequately protect consumers. That is, there are no directions that could make tobacco products safe for obtaining their intended effects. Thus, were tobacco products within the FDA's jurisdiction, the Act would deem them misbranded devices that could not be introduced into interstate commerce. . . . The FDCA's misbranding and device classification provisions therefore make evident that were the FDA to regulate cigarettes and smokeless tobacco, the Act would require the agency to ban them. . . .

Congress, however, has foreclosed the removal of tobacco products from the market. A provision of the United States Code currently in force states that "[t]he marketing of tobacco constitutes one of the greatest basic industries of the United States with ramifying activities which directly affect interstate and foreign commerce at every point, and stable conditions therein are necessary to the general welfare." 7 *U.S.C.* §1311(a). More importantly, Congress has directly addressed the problem of tobacco and health through legislation on six occasions since 1965. . . . When Congress enacted these statutes, the adverse health consequences of tobacco use were well known, as were nicotine's pharmacological effects. . . . Nonetheless, Congress stopped well short of ordering a ban. Instead, it has generally regulated the labeling and advertisement of tobacco products, expressly providing that it is the policy of Congress that "commerce and the national economy may be . . . protected to the maximum extent consistent with" consumers "be[ing] adequately informed about any adverse health effects." 15 *U.S.C.* §1331. Congress' decisions to regulate labeling and advertising and to adopt the express policy of protecting "commerce and the national economy . . . to the maximum extent" reveal its intent that tobacco products remain on the market. Indeed, the collective premise of these statutes is that cigarettes and smokeless tobacco will continue to be sold in the United States. A ban of tobacco products by the FDA would therefore plainly contradict congressional policy. . . .

Considering the FDCA as a whole, it is clear that Congress intended to exclude tobacco products from the FDA's jurisdiction. A fundamental precept of the FDCA is that any product regulated by the FDA — but not banned — must be safe for its intended use. . . . That is, the FDA must determine that there is a reasonable assurance that the product's therapeutic benefits outweigh the risk of harm to the consumer. According to this standard, the FDA has concluded that, although tobacco products might be effective in delivering certain pharmacological effects, they are "unsafe" and "dangerous" when used for these purposes. Consequently, if tobacco products were within the FDA's jurisdiction, the Act would require the FDA to remove them from the market entirely. But a ban would contradict Congress' clear intent as expressed in its more recent, tobacco-specific legislation. The inescapable conclusion is that there is no room for tobacco products within the FDCA's regulatory scheme. If they cannot be used safely for any therapeutic purpose, and yet they cannot be banned, they simply do not fit. . . .

Congress has persistently acted to preclude a meaningful role for *any* administrative agency in making policy on the subject of tobacco and health. Moreover, the substance of Congress' regulatory scheme is, in an important respect, incompatible with FDA jurisdiction. Although the supervision of product labeling to protect consumer health is a substantial component of the FDA's regulation of drugs and devices, . . . the Federal Cigarette Labeling and Advertising Act and the Comprehensive Smokeless Tobacco Health Education Act of 1986 explicitly prohibit any federal agency from imposing any health-related labeling requirements on cigarettes or smokeless tobacco products. . . .

Owing to its unique place in American history and society, tobacco has its own unique political history. Congress, for better or for worse, has created a distinct regulatory scheme for tobacco products, squarely rejected proposals to give the FDA jurisdiction over tobacco, and repeatedly acted to preclude any agency from exercising significant policymaking authority in the area. Given this history and the breadth of the authority that the FDA has asserted, we are obliged to defer not to the agency's expansive construction of the statute, but to Congress' consistent judgment to deny the FDA this power. . . .

By no means do we question the seriousness of the problem that the FDA has sought to address. The agency has amply demonstrated that tobacco use, particularly among children and adolescents, poses perhaps the single most significant threat to public health in the United States. Nonetheless, no matter how "important, conspicuous, and controversial" the issue, and regardless of how likely the public is to hold the Executive Branch politically accountable, . . . an administrative agency's power to regulate in the public interest must always be grounded in a valid grant of authority from Congress . . . Reading the FDCA as a whole, as well as in conjunction with Congress' subsequent tobacco-specific legislation, it is plain that Congress has not given the FDA the authority that it seeks to exercise here. . . .

[Judgment affirmed.]

Judicial Control. Judicial review of the actions of administrative agencies provides a third form of control. Although the courts may review both an agency's rule-making and administrative orders, they generally limit review to procedural aspects of these decisions.

Prior to reviewing an administrative agency decision, the court requires the complaining party to establish that it has *standing to sue*. Standing exists if the party has been injured in fact by an agency decision and is "arguably within the zone of interests to be protected or regulated by the statute or constitutional guarantee in question."[34] The standing requirement ensures that a legitimate controversy exists and prevents suits by persons who disagree with agency decisions merely on political or philosophical grounds.

The courts also require a party who seeks judicial review of an agency decision to exhaust all administrative remedies prior to undertaking a court case. In other words, the party must use remedies offered by an agency before going to the courts. The purpose of this requirement is to limit court review only to those issues that have

---

[34] Association of Data Processing Service Organizations, Inc. v. Camp, 90 S. Ct. 827, 830 (1970).

been thoroughly considered by the agency and to decisions that clearly represent a final position of the agency.

Under Securities and Exchange Commission (SEC) procedures, for example, a party dissatisfied with an administrative order issued by an administrative law judge can request the SEC commissioners to review the decision. If, however, the party instead files suit in court seeking reversal of the order, the court will dismiss the suit and order the party to exhaust his administrative remedies— that is, obtain review by the commissioners. The commissioners might reverse or change the order, thereby eliminating the need for judicial review or restructuring the issues that ultimately may be reviewed by the court.

Judicial Review of Agency Rule-Making. Even if a party establishes standing and exhausts his administrative remedies, a court usually provides only limited review of an agency's rule-making. When a party challenges a rule promulgated by an administrative agency the court traditionally considers two issues: (1) whether the agency has acted within the scope of authority validly delegated by the legislature and (2) whether the agency rule-making process provided due process of law.

If an agency adopts a rule that exceeds the authority that Congress has granted to the agency, the rule is said to be *ultra vires* (beyond one's power) and is invalid. Because Congress has delegated such broad authority to administrative agencies, a court rarely holds a rule to be *ultra vires*. Most judicial review of agency rule-making therefore concerns due process of law. If, for example, an agency has failed to follow the appropriate procedure (notice and a hearing) or has acted arbitrarily or capriciously, the court can invalidate the rule.

Judicial Review of Administrative Hearings. In reviewing decisions of administrative law judges or other hearing officers, the courts generally perform appellate-type review, determining only whether any errors of law occurred. For example, the court may review whether the agency acted within the scope of its statutory authority, whether the hearing procedure complied with procedural due process, and whether the decision violated any constitutional provisions. A few statutes, however, do allow the court to obtain further evidence if the judge deems it appropriate.

In most cases, the court will accept the administrative law judge's findings of fact if they are supported by substantial evidence, "such relevant evidence as a reasonable mind might accept as adequate to support a conclu-

sion."[35] In determining whether the record of the hearing provides substantial evidence to support the administrative law judge's findings, the court must consider both evidence supporting and contradictory to the findings.[36]

Administrative Agencies—Problems and Reforms

Administrative agencies are an integral part of federal government regulation. They perform important tasks that would be difficult for the executive, legislative, and judicial branches of government to undertake in a systematic manner. As the size and number of agencies have grown, so too have their functions. This continued growth, including the expanding power of agencies, often generates much criticism from the public, government officials, and particularly the business community. Even the strongest supporters of administrative agencies recognize that they could operate more efficiently. Despite numerous efforts to streamline federal regulation, criticism of federal agencies continues.

The relationship between agencies and the businesses they regulate creates additional problems. Frequently, the president selects administrators who have worked in the field subject to the agency's regulation. Although such an arrangement ensures some familiarity and expertise in that field, critics suggest that it may undermine the independence of the agency. Similarly, after terminating their employment with the government, officials often find employment in the industry they formerly regulated. To minimize potential conflicts of interest, Congress enacted the Ethics in Government Act,[37] which restricts some former upper-level government officials from lobbying their former agencies after leaving office.

Reforms of government agencies are likely to continue in the future as the executive and legislative branches try to find effective but efficient ways to regulate business. Yet, despite strong criticism, administrative agencies will continue to play a central role in the regulation of business because of the crucial functions they perform.

---

[35]Consolidated Edison Co. v. National Labor Relations Board, 59 S. Ct. 206, 217 (1938).
[36]Universal Camera Corp. v. National Labor Relations Board, 71 S. Ct. 456 (1951).
[37]18 U.S.C. §207.

Summary

1. States regulate business activities through the exercise of two inherent powers: the state police power and the power to tax. Federal regulation is based upon specific powers enumerated in the U.S. Constitution, most notably the Commerce Clause. Although the Supreme Court formerly adopted a narrow construction of federal powers under the Commerce Clause, today Congress may regulate virtually any activity that has an effect on interstate commerce.

2. Under the Commerce Clause and the Supremacy Clause, the federal government may preempt state legislation in a specific area of commerce either explicitly or implicitly through comprehensive regulation. Absent federal preemption, state regulation of business that has an incidental effect on interstate commerce is permissible if the regulation serves a legitimate state purpose and the benefit of the regulation outweighs the burden on interstate commerce.

3. In addition to the Commerce Clause, other constitutional provisions impose limitations on state police and taxing power. For example, the Import-Export Clause prohibits state taxation of imports and exports in the stream of commerce. The Privileges and Immunities Clause prohibits the states from unreasonably discriminating against out-of-state residents. The Contract Clause limits the power of the states to abridge existing contractual relationships.

4. The Constitution imposes various limitations upon both federal and state powers to regulate business. The First Amendment restricts government from prohibiting commercial speech but allows limited regulation of commercial speech. The Fourth Amendment limits state and federal governments' powers to conduct administrative searches. The Fifth and Fourteenth Amendments provide the guarantees of due process and equal protection.

5. The federal and state governments create administrative agencies to implement and enforce regulatory laws governing specified industries or areas of commerce. Administrative agencies perform various functions including investigation and prosecution, rule-making, and adjudication by administrative hearing.

6. The three branches of government exercise control over administrative agencies. The executive branch has the power to appoint heads of the agencies and to influence budget appropriations. The legislative branch has the power to create and terminate agencies, and to expand and restrict their powers or budgets. The judicial branch has the power to review agency rule-making and adjudication to determine whether the agency has complied with statutory and constitutional law.

Key Terms

state police power	commercial speech
state power to tax	Equal Protection Clause
Commerce Clause	Administrative Procedure Act
Import-Export Clause	administrative search
Privileges and Immunities Clause	Freedom of Information Act
Contract Clause	administrative order
freedom of speech	cease and desist order
	consent order

Questions and Problems

4.1 Several landfills containing hazardous waste—chemical and toxic products that can cause cancer, birth defects, physical disabilities, and death—are located in Alabama. The landfills include waste from within the state of Alabama as well as waste shipped there from other states. Over a five-year period, the amount of hazardous waste located in these landfills more than doubled; more than 90 percent of the hazardous waste had been shipped from out of state. The Alabama legislature adopted a statute imposing new fees for dumping hazardous waste in its landfills. Waste generated within Alabama was subject to a fee of $100 per ton. To dump waste shipped from other states required payment of a fee of $300 per ton. For many years, Chemical Waste Management, Inc. (CWMI) has transported hazardous waste generated by its customers in Illinois to landfills located in Alabama. The new dumping fees will substantially affect CWMI's business.

    (a) Suggest reasons why Alabama adopted its new fee statute. What state powers might justify adoption of the statute?

    (b) The Alabama statute probably is unconstitutional. Explain why.

    (c) Suggest how the state of Alabama could revise its statute so that it would be constitutional.

4.2 An ordinance of the city of Madison, Wisconsin, prohibited the sale of milk unless it had been processed and bottled in a licensed plant within a five-mile radius of the city. The legislative history of the ordinance shows that it was adopted to protect the health of local citizens. Because the city of Madison could control the production standards of milk from nearby plants by inspection of the plants, the ordinance served to protect citizens from contaminated milk. A milk producer from Illinois who operates a milk plant outside the five-mile radius sues the city of Madison alleging that the ordinance discriminates against interstate commerce. How should the court rule? Explain.

4.3 The city of Burbank, California, adopted an ordinance prohibiting jets from taking off or landing at the local airport between the hours of 11:00 P.M. and 7:00 A.M. The Federal Aviation Administration previously had granted Pacific

Southwest Airlines the right to operate a flight that landed at 11:30 P.M. Pacific Southwest sues the city of Burbank.
  (a) What grounds might Pacific Southwest allege to establish that the local ordinance is invalid?
  (b) How should the court rule?

4.4   Section 4 of the federal Public Health Cigarette Smoking Act requires all cigarettes sold in the United States to include a label warning that states: CAUTION: CIGARETTE SMOKING MAY BE HAZARDOUS TO YOUR HEALTH. The Act also includes the following provisions captioned "Preemption":

> (1)   No statement relating to smoking and health, other than the statement required by section 4 of this Act shall be required on any cigarette package.
> (2)   No requirement or prohibition based on smoking and health shall be imposed under State law with respect to the advertising or promotion of any cigarettes the packages of which are labeled in conformity with the provisions of this Act.

Rose Cipollone developed lung cancer after smoking cigarettes for many years. She sued Liggett Group, Inc., a cigarette manufacturer, alleging that the defendant had failed to provide adequate warnings of the dangers of cigarette smoking and had manufactured a defectively designed product. Liggett filed for dismissal of the case asserting that Cipollone's suit was pre-empted by the Public Health Cigarette Smoking Act. How should the court rule?

4.5   The state of North Carolina imposes a property tax on all tobacco present in the state on January 1 of each year. The RJRT Company objected to the state's applying this tax to tobacco imported from foreign countries that RJRT was storing in North Carolina warehouses on January 1. Assuming that RJRT intended to use this tobacco in cigarettes that primarily would be consumed in the United States, would application of the tax to the foreign goods be unconstitutional? What if RJRT intended to ship the tobacco to France where it would be made into cigars?

4.6   The state of Montana requires hunters to obtain a license to hunt elk and other game in the state. The fee charged to out-of-state residents is $225 while in-state residents paid a fee of only $30. Does the statute comply with the Constitution? Explain.

4.7   A Virginia statute prohibits pharmacists from advertising the price of prescription drugs. Pharmacists who violate the law may be penalized by fine or by suspension of their licenses.
  (a) Under what power could the state of Virginia adopt this statute? Suggest reasons why the state might have adopted the law.
  (b) A group of consumers has filed suit challenging the constitutionality of the statute. Does the statute violate the U.S. Constitution? Explain.

4.8   Massachusetts enacted a statute prohibiting corporations from making contributions or expenditures "for the purpose of . . . influencing or affecting the vote on any question submitted to the voters, other than one materially affecting any of the property, business or assets of the corpo-

ration." The statute explicitly states that income tax matters do not materially affect corporations.
  (a) What purpose would this statute serve?
  (b) Assume you are employed by a corporation that wishes to publicize its views on a public referendum to increase income taxes. Suggest reasons why the statute may be unconstitutional.

4.9   The state of Alaska has adopted a statute that requires all companies to grant preference to Alaska residents when hiring new employees. To qualify as a resident, a person must reside in the state for at least one year. Is the statute constitutional? Explain.

4.10   A common complaint of the business community is that the government (federal and state) imposes too many regulations on business.
  (a) Explain why businesses generally oppose regulation.
  (b) Are there any instances in which a business would favor regulation by the government? Explain.
  (c) Assuming that either the state or federal government will regulate businesses, is a Fortune 500 corporation more likely to prefer regulation by the state or federal government? What type of regulation would a small business operating only in one locality prefer? Explain.

4.11   In *Ferguson v. Skrupa*, 83 S. Ct. 1028, 1030–1031 (1963), Justice Hugo Black stated:

> Under the system of government created by our Constitution, it is up to legislatures, not courts, to decide on the wisdom and utility of legislation. . . . [C]ourts do not substitute their social and economic beliefs for the judgment of legislative bodies, who are elected to pass laws.

  (a) Consider the standards used by the courts in cases challenging federal statutes for alleged violations of the Commerce Clause. Do those standards contradict or support Justice Black's statement? Explain.
  (b) Assume that a business opposes the economic purposes of a federal statute. If courts refrain from invalidating such statutes, what recourse does a business have? Explain.

4.12   Justice Benjamin Cardozo stated that the Constitution "was framed upon the theory that the peoples of the several states must sink or swim together, and that in the long run prosperity and salvation are in union and not division." (*Baldwin v. G.A.F. Seelig, Inc.,* 55 S. Ct. 497, 500 (1935)).
  (a) Explain the meaning of this statement.
  (b) Explain how the Commerce Clause, the Privileges and Immunities Clause, and the Import-Export Clause, as interpreted by the Supreme Court, effectuate the theory referred to by Justice Cardozo.

4.13   From time to time, politicians, businesspersons, and others have suggested that administrative agencies should be abolished. What effect would such an action have on the three branches of government?

4.14   What purposes are served by requiring administrative agencies to follow informal rule-making procedures? Explain.

TORT LAW

The law of torts is a pervasive area of law imposing liability for intentional and unintentional conduct, and affecting individuals, businesses, and governmental bodies. Tort law imposes liability for injuries caused by automobile accidents and airline crashes, by dangerous conditions on land, by fraud or defamation, by defective products, or by medical or other professional malpractice. Potential tort liability is a fundamental consideration in prudent personal and business planning and is a major reason for insurance. Indeed, the perceived risk of tort liability often determines what goods or services businesses provide, the form those goods or services take, and the design and maintenance of buildings and equipment used in manufacturing, wholesaling, retailing, and service operations.

Introduction to Tort Law

A **tort** (Latin *tortus:* "twisted") is "a private or civil wrong or injury, other than breach of contract, for which the court will provide a remedy in the form of an action for damages."[1] Whereas contract law is designed to compensate one person for injuries caused by another's failure to perform a special form of promise, a contract, tort law provides compensation for legal wrongs committed against a person or her property arising independently of any contract between the parties. A person who commits a tort is known as **a tort-feasor,** and acts or omissions constituting torts are said to be "tortious."

Torts and Crimes Distinguished

The nature of a tort can be clarified somewhat by comparing it to another form of wrong, a crime, discussed in Chapter 3. A crime is an offense or wrong committed against the public generally, for which the public vindicates its rights through a criminal prosecution. A criminal prosecution is maintained by the sovereign (state or federal government) and punishes the defen-

---

[1]BLACK'S LAW DICTIONARY 1489 (6th ed. 1990); PROSSER & KEETON, THE LAW OF TORTS 2 (5th ed. 1984).

dant's conduct by imposing a fine, prison term, or both. Criminal law is contained in statutes, both state and federal, that define the prohibited conduct and outline the penalties imposed. Criminal law is not generally designed to compensate individuals injured by criminal conduct.

In contrast, tort actions are maintained by the injured individual seeking compensation from the defendant for the injury caused by the defendant's conduct. Tort law is derived from state common law, developed by the courts on a case-by-case basis. Thus, tort and criminal actions differ in three important respects: (1) the identity of the plaintiff (the public generally versus an injured individual), (2) the nature of the relief sought (punishment versus compensation), and (3) the source of the law (statute versus common law).

Assume A punches B, breaking B's nose. In this case, the state may take criminal action under its criminal code against A for assault and battery, leading to a fine or prison sentence. In addition, B may file a tort action against A using common law tort principles to recover damages to compensate for the injuries.

As indicated previously, although the same conduct may be both a crime and a tort, most torts are not crimes. Torts are simply those wrongs, other than breach of contract, for which the law provides compensation through a civil action.

Grounds of Tort Liability

Tort actions, like other civil actions, begin when a person injured by another's act or omission files a complaint in an appropriate court alleging that the defendant has committed a tort and requesting damages. All tort actions require the plaintiff to prove (1) the existence of a legal duty owed by the defendant to the plaintiff, (2) breach of that duty, and (3) injury or damage as a proximate result of the defendant's breach.

Tort liability is imposed on three basic grounds: intent, negligence, and strict liability. In intentional torts, the tort-feasor acts deliberately with the desire to harm the plaintiff. The *Restatement (Second) of Torts* finds a person's conduct **intentional** if he either "desires to cause the consequences of his act, or . . . believes that the consequences are substantially certain to result from it."[2] As the probability that the harmful consequences will follow decreases to less than substantial *certainty,* the conduct is no longer inten-

tional, but becomes reckless, or ultimately merely negligent, conduct that increases the *risk* of harm.

Thus, in intentional and negligent torts, the law imposes liability because of the defendant's "fault" in causing the plaintiff's harm. Intent and negligence simply represent differing degrees of fault. In strictly liability torts, on the other hand, the defendant is held liable in the absence of either negligence or an intent to interfere with the plaintiff's legally protected interests. That is, the defendant is held strictly liable—liable without fault.

Tort law recognizes certain defenses that extinguish or reduce the defendant's liability. That is, even if a plaintiff establishes all the elements of a tort, a defendant may prove facts constituting a legitimate defense to the plaintiff's recovery. A defense may be complete (the defendant is released from all liability) or partial (the defendant's liability is reduced). A number of important defenses to tort actions are discussed later in this chapter.

Damages in Tort Actions

Tort law enables an injured party to recover damages for injuries caused by the defendant's tortious conduct. Generally, the plaintiff is entitled to compensatory damages, a monetary award designed to compensate the plaintiff for the injuries caused by the defendant. Compensatory damages include, for example, payment for medical bills, property damage, loss of income, total or partial disability, and in some cases "pain and suffering."

In some cases, the defendant also may be assessed **punitive** or **exemplary damages,** a monetary award designed to punish the defendant and to deter similar conduct by the defendant or others in the future. Through punitive damages, tort law uses a criminal law concept—punishment—to supplement the basic compensatory purpose of tort actions. Punitive damages are awarded only in cases involving a defendant's intentional and deliberate disregard for others' rights. Punitive damages may be awarded for many of the intentional torts discussed in this chapter, for fraud (discussed in Chapter 11), and for the sale of unreasonably dangerous products (discussed in Chapter 20).

The amount of damages, like the issue of liability, usually is determined by the trier of fact, normally the jury. Compensatory damage awards must be supported by evidence (for example, medical bills). If the plaintiff seeks punitive damages, the jury must be carefully instructed regarding the purpose of punitive damages and the circumstances justifying them. If properly instructed,

---

[2]RESTATEMENT (SECOND) OF TORTS §8A.

a jury's punitive damage award need bear no relation to actual compensatory damages, and often greatly exceeds them. The U.S. Supreme Court, however, has held that "grossly excessive" punitive damage awards may be an unconstitutional violation of due process.[3]

The majority of states place some limits on punitive damage awards. As a part of tort reform legislation adopted by many states, punitive damages often are subject to a "cap"—either a maximum dollar amount or a maximum proportion of compensatory damages. Other states use bifurcated trials that allow juries to hear evidence concerning punitive damages only after the jury has found the defendant liable and computed compensatory damages.

Multiple Defendants in Tort Actions

Frequently, a plaintiff's injury is caused by tortious conduct of more than one person. In such cases, the plaintiff generally sues all persons whose conduct was a factor in causing the injury. If the defendants acted in concert, they are considered to be joint tort-feasors and are held jointly and severally liable for damages: all defendants together are responsible to pay the damages (joint liability) and each defendant individually is responsible to pay the full amount of damages (several liability). So, for example, if Punch and Judy, acting in concert, commit the tort of battery and a jury awards damages of $1,000, the plaintiff may collect a total of $1,000 from Punch and Judy or $1,000 from either Punch or Judy. The plaintiff's recovery is limited, however, to the total damage award, so she could not recover $1,000 from Punch and $1,000 from Judy. Generally, joint tort-feasors who act in concert are not entitled to receive contribution from the other defendants. Thus, for example, if Punch paid the full $1,000, he would have no right to obtain partial or full repayment from Judy.

In many cases, multiple defendants do not act in concert but each independently commits an act that contributes to the plaintiff's injuries. In an automobile accident, for example, two drivers may commit separate negligent acts that combine to injure the plaintiff. If a distinct injury is caused by each defendant, or if the injuries reasonably can be apportioned among the defendants, damages will be assessed against each defendant individually. If, however, no reasonable basis exists for apportioning damages, states traditionally have imposed joint and several liability on all defendants. Under joint and several liability, each defendant is responsible for all damages even if his conduct alone might not have caused the entire injury.

Imposing joint and several liability on multiple defendants is based on the policy that an innocent plaintiff should not be denied recovery from defendants who partially caused the injury merely because the plaintiff cannot prove the extent of injury caused by each defendant. Generally, a defendant subject to joint and several liability who pays the judgment is entitled to obtain contribution from the other tort-feasors if they did not act in concert. Wealthy defendants or parties carrying insurance, however, may be forced to pay the full amount of the judgment and then be unable to obtain contribution from poorer or uninsured defendants. In some cases defendants whose conduct only minimally contributed to a plaintiff's injuries have been required to pay for all damages.

The rules of joint and several tort liability can be unfair to businesses, that often have more assets than individuals or carry liability insurance, and to governmental bodies with significant financial resources. As a result, many states have modified or abolished the traditional rule imposing joint and several liability when two or more defendants do not act in concert. For example, under comparative fault principles (discussed later in this chapter) adopted in many states, each of several defendants may be held liable only for the percentage of the plaintiff's damages caused by that defendant's negligence.

Intentional Torts

Intentional torts may be classified according to the interest protected. A person may be held liable in tort for intentionally interfering with another's person, property, or business relations.

Intentional Interference with the Person

Various tort actions are designed to protect a person's physical or emotional well-being against intentional interference. Tort law protects a person against harmful or offensive bodily contacts (and apprehension of such contacts), and confinement. It also protects intangible emotional interests, such as a person's peace of mind, reputation, or right to be left alone. The torts safeguarding these interests include assault, battery, false imprisonment, intentional infliction of emotional distress, defamation, and invasion of privacy.

---

[3]BMW of North America, Inc. v. Gore, 116 S.Ct. 1589 (1996).

Assault and Battery. The related torts of assault and battery protect a person against intentionally inflicted harmful bodily contact and threat of such contact. A **battery** is a harmful or offensive *contact* with a person which is intended by the actor to cause such a contact. A battery may be committed by a direct use of force, such as a punch, or indirectly, such as by placing a trip-wire across a path used by the plaintiff. Battery liability may be imposed whether or not the contact causes physical injury.

In contrast, an **assault** occurs if a person, intending to cause a harmful or offensive contact, acts in a manner that places another in imminent *apprehension* of such a contact. That is, an assault amounts to a threat to use force, which would convince a reasonable person of the actor's ability and opportunity to carry it out. Although both assault and battery are often present in the same case, not all batteries require a prior assault. For example, it is battery but not assault to strike a person from behind. A person injured by an assault or battery is entitled to recover damages to compensate for the physical illness or injury sustained. Even if no physical injury occurs, damages may be awarded for mental injury. In addition, punitive damages often are appropriate because assault and battery involve an intent to injure. Assault and battery also are crimes, subjecting the defendant to punishment under state criminal law.

A defendant in an assault or battery case may avoid liability by proving that she acted reasonably in self-defense or in the defense of others. The defendant may use force likely to cause death or serious injury, however, only if she reasonably believes that such force is necessary to prevent death or serious injury to herself or another, or to prevent the commission of a forcible felony. Similarly, although one may use reasonable force in the protection of property, there is no privilege to use deadly force unless there is also a threat to the property owner's personal safety that would justify the use of such force in self-defense. This rule applies even if the plaintiff is a trespasser. Finally, the plaintiff's consent to the assault or battery is a complete defense.

False Imprisonment. Tort law safeguards an individual's freedom of movement by imposing liability for **false imprisonment** (or **false arrest**). A person who intentionally confines another within fixed boundaries has committed false imprisonment. Although the "confinement" must be total and complete, offering no reasonable means of escape, actual incarceration or imprisonment is not required. Thus, a person may be confined not only by physical barriers (for example, by being locked in a room), but also by physical force, threat of physical force, or other forms of duress.

Many false imprisonment cases involve improper arrests by police officers or other officials. In the business setting, a retailer's detention of a suspected shoplifter may give rise to a false imprisonment claim. In recognition of the serious problems posed by shoplifting, most states have adopted statutes (sometimes called merchant protection legislation or shopkeeper's privilege statutes) that relieve a merchant from liability for false imprisonment if the merchant acts reasonably in detaining and confining suspected shoplifters. Compliance with such a statute is a complete defense to a claim of false imprisonment. The following case illustrates a false imprisonment suit brought by a suspected shoplifter.

Adams v. Zayre Corporation
499 N.E.2d 678 (Ill. App. 1986)

> Plaintiff Mary Adams sued defendant Zayre Corporation for false imprisonment as a result of events that occurred at a retail store operated by Zayre. After shopping in various departments for about 30 minutes, Adams purchased two blankets for which she paid cash at a checkout counter near the front of the store. As Adams and her daughter exited the store, they were detained by two members of Zayre's security staff who escorted the women to a security room in the store. According to testimony from Adams and her daughter, the security officers grabbed them and held each by the arm as they returned to the store. The security officers testified that they had asked Adams and her daughter to return to the store and that the women had done so voluntarily. The security manager further testified that she had seen Adams place a radio in her purse while she was shopping, but the radio was not found in Adams's or her daughter's possession in the security room. After being detained for approximately 30 minutes, Adams and her daughter were allowed to leave.
>
> Following a trial, the jury found Zayre liable for false imprisonment and awarded Adams compensatory damages of $2,500 and punitive damages of $30,000. Zayre appealed.

Strouse, Justice

. . . False imprisonment consists of the unlawful restraint, against a person's will, of that individual's personal liberty or freedom of locomotion. . . . Defendant is, however, afforded protection by sections 16A-5 and 16A-6 of the [Illinois] Criminal Code. . . . The statute empowers a merchant who has reasonable grounds to believe that a person has committed retail theft to detain such person in a reasonable manner for a reasonable length of time. . . .

A review of the record reveals that plaintiff's case in chief presents a case of false imprisonment. She testified that the security guard grabbed her by the arm after she exited the store. A minor struggle ensued, after which she was forcibly led back into the store and ushered to a security area. Four witnesses testified that she was under their forcible control.

Defendant had the burden of proving that it fell within the scope of sections 16A-5 and 16A-6, *i.e.,* that the actions of its security force were reasonable. This factual determination was for the jury. . . .

The record reflects that the jury could have found defendant's actions to be unreasonable—both in manner of execution and time of detention. "The use of unnecessary force on suspected shoplifters by store personnel, as well as rudeness and harassment of the suspects, have been factors upon which the courts have determined either that the manner of detention was not reasonable as intended by the statute or that a finding to that effect was supportable." (Annot., 47 A.L.R.3d 998, 1020 (1973).) There was also corroborated testimony that defendant detained plaintiff for one-half hour—15 minutes of which was after they had concluded their search and investigation and determined that there were no grounds to continue holding the plaintiff. Further, based on the disputed testimony, the jury could have found that no reasonable grounds existed for holding the plaintiff. We therefore cannot say that the jury's verdict as to general damages was against the manifest weight of the evidence.

We last address defendant's contention that punitive damages are inappropriate. Punitive damages are permitted where an arrest is effected recklessly, oppressively, insultingly or willfully, with a design to oppress and injure. . . . The manner of plaintiff's apprehension has already been described. This apprehension was conducted in violation of the store's own guidelines as to the manner in which a suspect is observed and detained. These guidelines provide that a store security officer making an arrest must have continual and unbroken surveillance of a subject after the alleged taking, up to the actual apprehension of the subject. The officer must follow the suspect in such a manner as to have "both the subject and the merchandise under observation *at all times. If the subject gets out of sight even for a moment the apprehension cannot be made unless another theft act is witnessed.*" Since the security officers thoroughly searched the plaintiff and found no radio, it can only be concluded that even if plaintiff had taken a radio, it was not in her possession at the time she left the store and she should not have been detained.

Also, the store guidelines for approaching suspected shoplifters were violated. The store policy as to approaching suspects is as follows:

"Again, when the suspect reaches the sidewalk (outside the store) and the officer is sure of his case, this approach is suggested: 'Excuse me, my name is Sandy Smith, Store Security (showing I.D.). May I examine your cash register receipt for (describe the article or articles concealed).' When identification of the article has been established and examination of the receipt shows no ringup, ask the suspect to return to the store to privately discuss the incident. If at all possible avoid touching the suspect. There are circumstances where this is necessary, sometimes the person needs to be coached along with the hand placed under an arm for direction and guidance through the store. But Rough Tactics Must Be Avoided."

The testimony of plaintiff and others was that this apprehension was conducted in a reckless, oppressive, insulting, and willful manner. . . . Here, the jury found a factual basis for the punitive award and we cannot say that the jury's award of punitive damages was against the manifest weight of the evidence. . . .

[Judgment affirmed.]

Intentional Infliction of Emotional Distress. Mental pain and anxiety have long been recognized as an element of damages in other personal torts such as assault, battery, and false imprisonment. Perhaps because of the difficulty of proof and fear of false or trivial claims, tort law was slow to recognize intentional infliction of mental injury as a separate tort theory. Modern courts, however, allow compensation in tort for intentionally imposed severe emotional distress and the resulting bodily injury if the defendant's conduct is "extreme and outrageous." To recover, the plaintiff must prove (1) outrageous conduct by the defendant, (2) the defendant's intent to cause (or reckless disregard of the probability of causing) emotional distress, and (3) the plaintiff's suffering extreme and severe emotional distress caused by the defendant's conduct.

Clearly, this test is imprecise and does not permit recovery for most insults, threats, annoyances, bad manners, rudeness, or other realities of modern life. Its application depends upon the particular circumstances of each case. Courts have allowed recovery, for example, for (1) spreading a false rumor that the plaintiff's spouse or child had been seriously injured or committed suicide, (2) bullying tactics by insurance adjusters seeking to force a settlement, (3) threats or verbal abuse of particularly susceptible persons, such as invalids or children, and (4) mishandling or mutilation of dead bodies by funeral directors, hospitals, and others.

Defamation. The law has long protected, through a tort action for **defamation,** a person's reputation and good name. To recover for defamation, the plaintiff must prove that a false and defamatory statement was made and communicated or "published" to a third party, and that the defendant was at fault in disseminating the defamatory statement. The law recognizes two forms of action for defamatory publications, libel and slander. **Libel** involves the publication of a defamatory statement by written or printed words (as in a newspaper, book, or magazine), by its embodiment in other physical form (as in a picture or statue), or by radio or television communication. **Slander,** on the other hand, involves communication of the defamatory statement by spoken words or gestures, such as the nod of the head, a wink, or hand gesture.

False and Defamatory Statement. A communication is defamatory if it "tends so to harm the reputation of another as to lower him in the estimation of the community or to deter third persons from associating or dealing with him."[4] Liability for defamation requires the statements to be *false* and defamatory. Truth is an absolute defense to a defamation action, even if the statement is inspired solely by ill will toward the plaintiff and for the purpose of injuring or destroying his reputation.

A defamatory communication may be a statement of fact: Betty says to Carol, "Andy is a liar, a drunk, an adulterer, and a thief." Or it may be a statement of opinion, if the comment creates the impression that the opinion is based upon undisclosed defamatory facts: Bob says to Carol, "I think my next door neighbor, Alice, is involved in drug dealing." The jury might find that this is not a mere expression of opinion, but implies that Bob knows undisclosed facts which justify the opinion. In this case, Bob's opinion is defamatory.

Defamatory statements can be directed against a particular living individual, a group, or a class. An individual member of a group may recover if the group is small enough so that the statement can be reasonably interpreted as referring to a particular member, or if the circumstances clearly indicate that the statement refers to that particular member. Assume Robert, at a party, states

"all doctors are incompetent and dishonest." Charles, one of 100 local doctors, has not been defamed. If, however, Charles was at the party and the only doctor present, persons present might reasonably believe Robert was specifically referring to Charles. A corporation or partnership may also be defamed if the statement discredits the way it does business or deters others from dealing with it. Though a corporation or partnership has no reputation in a personal sense, it has a business reputation that is entitled to protection. Thus, defamatory statements concerning a business's credit, honesty, or efficiency are actionable.

Fault in Defamation Actions. Generally, a defendant in a defamation lawsuit is considered to be "at fault" if he acts negligently. In other words, the defendant is at fault by failing to act reasonably to determine whether the defamatory statement was false. The U.S. Supreme Court, however, has determined that in certain cases, a higher standard of fault is required to protect the defendant's rights under the First Amendment, which prohibits laws abridging freedom of speech and the press. In *New York Times Company v. Sullivan,*[5] the Supreme Court held that a public official, such as an elected official or government employee, is prohibited "from recovering damages for a defamatory falsehood relating to his official conduct unless he proves that the statement was made with 'actual malice'—that is, with knowledge that it was false or with reckless disregard of whether it was false or not."[6] Under this test, the defendant is not liable for negligently or inadvertently publishing a defamatory statement (such as by failing to adequately check sources). Actual knowledge of falsity or reckless disregard of the truth is required. Subsequent Supreme Court decisions have extended this "knowledge-reckless disregard" rule to candidates for public office and public figures. "Public figures" include both persons who have achieved pervasive fame or notoriety (who are public figures for all purposes in all contexts) and those who voluntarily inject themselves into a particular public controversy (who become public figures for a limited range of issues).

This rule is designed to prevent use of defamation actions to deter free discussion and criticism of public issues and persons by the press. As noted by the Court in the *New York Times* case,

> [W]e consider this case against the background of a profound national commitment to the principle that debate on public issues should be uninhibited, robust, and wide-

---

[4] RESTATEMENT (SECOND) OF TORTS §559.

[5] 84 S. Ct. 710 (1964).

[6] *Id.* at 726; RESTATEMENT (SECOND) OF TORTS §580A.

open, and that it may well include vehement, caustic, and sometimes unpleasantly sharp attacks on government and public officials.[7]

Liability for defamation is expanded if the defamatory statement relates to a private person or to a public figure or official concerning a purely private matter. Like public officials and public figures, private individuals may recover for statements made with knowledge of falsity or reckless disregard of the truth. Private plaintiffs, however, also may recover for false and defamatory statements published merely as a result of the defendant's negligence.[8] Thus, the press is insulated from defamation actions for nonnegligent mistakes reporting newsworthy events concerning private individuals.

In the following case, a private plaintiff sought to recover damages for defamatory statements made in an employment reference.

Sigal Construction Corporation v. Stanbury

586 A.2d 1204 (D.C. App. 1991)

Defendant Sigal Construction Corporation employed plaintiff Kenneth Stanbury as a construction project manager from May 1984 to June 1985 when Sigal terminated his employment. According to Sigal's personnel manager, Stanbury was fired because "he was not doing his job correctly," but Stanbury was told that the reason was "lack of work or reduction in work." Sometime later, Daniel Construction offered to hire Stanbury to manage a construction project subject to the approval of the project's owner, Lincoln Properties. William Janes of Lincoln Properties investigated Stanbury's employment references by calling Paul Littman, a Sigal project executive. During their conversation Littman told Janes that Stanbury seemed "detail oriented to the point of losing sight of the big picture." Littman indicated that Stanbury was knowledgeable and had experience on large projects and that with a large staff he might be a competent manager, but Littman concluded by noting, "Obviously he no longer worked for us [Sigal] and that might say enough." After Lincoln Properties expressed its disapproval of Stanbury, he was not hired by Daniel Construction.

Stanbury sued Sigal alleging that it had defamed him while giving the employment reference. Following a trial, a jury ruled in favor of Stanbury and he was awarded damages of $250,000. Sigal appealed.

---

[7]84 S. Ct. at 721.

[8]Gertz v. Robert Welch, Inc., 94 S. Ct. 2997, 3010–3011 (1974); RESTATEMENT (SECOND) OF TORTS §580B; Discussion of negligence law begins later in this chapter.

Ferren, Associate Judge

. . . [A]ny statement—even one expressed as an "opinion"—can amount to actionable defamation, unprotected by the First Amendment, if it reasonably implies a false assertion of fact. . . .

Sigal does not contest, on appeal, either that the statements were false or were negligently made. Sigal does contend, however—and Stanbury does not dispute—that Littman's negligent statements were subject to a "qualified privilege." . . . According to the Virginia Supreme Court:

A communication, made in good faith, on a subject matter in which the person communicating has an interest, or owes a duty, legal, moral, or social, is qualifiedly privileged if made to a person having a corresponding interest or duty.

[*Great Coastal Express, Inc. v. Ellington,* 334 S.E.2d 846, 853 (Va. 1985).] . . .

Once the privilege applies, the plaintiff has the burden of proving the defendant has abused, and thus lost, it. . . .

There was sufficient evidence at trial, viewed in the light most favorable to Stanbury, from which a reasonable jury could find by clear and convincing evidence that Littman and Sigal had abused the qualified privilege under Virginia law by acting with "such gross indifference or recklessness as to amount to wanton and willful disregard of the rights of Stanbury." [*Great Coastal,* at 854.] . . . Littman testified, and Stanbury's testimony confirmed, that Littman had never supervised, worked with, evaluated, or read an evaluation of Stanbury. Moreover, Littman testified that he had not received information from anyone in particular, let alone anyone who had had a work-related relationship with Stanbury. Littman's sources for his statements to Janes were observations in the company's halls and general office contacts with unnamed third parties, perhaps at "casual lunches" or "project executive meetings" or "over beer on a Friday afternoon." But he could recall none of the conversations or otherwise provide any concrete support for his statements, whether first-hand information or hearsay. Littman admitted that he had no facts to support any of his statements to Janes and that he had never sought to verify the information before giving his evaluation. Littman also testified that he knew Janes wanted to speak with someone who had "interacted" with Stanbury at Sigal, and yet Littman further testified that he did not tell Janes he had never done so. Nor did Littman tell Janes the altogether vague sources of his statements. To make matters worse, according to Janes' testimony, Littman told Janes that he had worked with Stanbury on a project.

In short, this is a case of pure "rumor" or "gossip" or "scuttlebutt" conveyed as fact, without any disclaimer or explanation, coupled with Littman's erroneously leading the prospective employer to believe he had worked on a project with Stanbury. . . .

In sustaining the conclusion that Sigal (through Littman) abused the qualified privilege, we do not mean to imply that employers are at serious risk when providing employment references in the normal course of business. Nor are we suggesting that employers, when providing such references, may not rely on information from the employee's co-workers, even when hearsay. Our analysis here is limited to an office gossip situa-tion where the rec-ommender (1) has conveyed information which cannot be traced to anyone with personal knowledge of the employee whose reputation is at stake, (2) has not quali-fied his statements by disclosing the nebulous source of his information, and (3) has led the prospective employer to believe he has worked on a project with the employee and thus has first-hand information. . . .

Cases holding there was no abuse of the qualified privi-lege are easily distinguishable. This is not a case, for exam-ple, where an employee's supervisor, who has worked directly with the employee, provides a negative reference based on personal experience. . . . Nor is this a case where the reference is based on a careful, thorough investi-gation, . . . or on the employee's own admission. . . .

On this record, therefore, the jury could find wanton, willful, or reckless conduct that amounted to abuse of the qualified privilege. . . .

[Judgment affirmed.]

Invasion of Privacy. In the early twentieth century, courts began to recognize invasions of privacy as com-pensable in a tort action. The **right to privacy** is gener-ally defined as simply the right to be left alone. For example, an invasion of privacy action may provide compensation for the following types of interference:

1. Intentional intrusions, highly offensive to a rea-sonable person, into a person's solitude or private affairs. For example, a person may recover for another's spying through windows, tapping telephone wires, or making harassing phone calls or visits.

2. Wrongful appropriation of another's name or likeness. For example, a person may be held liable for using another's name or picture to promote the defen-dant's product, business, or other commercial venture.

3. Publicity portraying a person in an objection-ably false light if the defendant knows the portrayal is false or that it recklessly disregards the truth. If the false publicity given to the plaintiff is also defamatory, an invasion of privacy action provides an additional or alternative remedy.

Intentional Interference with Property

Interests in property are classified as either real or per-sonal (see Chapter 6). Real property includes interests in land, and personal property includes anything else that can be owned. Personal property with tangible physical existence, such as automobiles, clothing, and appliances, is commonly known as a "chattel." Tort law protects against interference with an owner's right to possess and use real property through an action for trespass and nui-sance. The right to use and possess personal property is protected primarily through an action for conversion.

Trespass. A person commits **trespass** by intentionally interfering with another's right to exclusive possession of real property. Trespass occurs if, without permission or legal privilege, a person intentionally: (1) enters land possessed by another, (2) causes anything or anyone to enter onto the land, (3) remains on the land, or (4) fails to remove from the land a thing which he is under a duty to remove. Liability may be imposed even though the trespasser's presence causes no harm to the land, its possessor, or other thing or person on the land. Thus, an intentional intrusion upon another's land is a trespass even if the actor is mistaken concerning the right or privilege to enter. Assume Beth reasonably mistakes the location of the property line between her property and her neighbor, Ann. As a result, Beth occupies a six-foot strip of Ann's land. Beth is liable to Ann for trespass.

Nuisance. The legal term **nuisance** refers to a human activity conducted on land or a physical condition of land that is harmful or annoying to neighboring landowners or members of the public generally. Under some circumstances, a person responsible for creating or maintaining a nuisance may be subject to criminal sanctions. In other cases, the person responsible for a nuisance may be liable in tort for injuries caused by the nuisance. The nature and extent of the liability depends on whether a "public" (or "common") nuisance or "private" nuisance is involved.

Public Nuisance. A **public nuisance** involves invasion of public rights, those common to all members of the public. It is essentially a catchall minor criminal offense encompassing a wide range of miscellaneous conduct offensive to public health, safety, or morals. All states have statutes declaring certain specified conduct or conditions to be public nuisances. Examples include buildings used in commission of criminal offenses (such as prostitution or storage of contraband); maintenance of diseased animals or other conditions injurious to public health (such as a pond breeding mosquitoes); pollution of air or water; and excessively loud or continuous noises. In addition to criminal sanctions, members of the public who suffer particular harm, distinct from that suffered by members of the public in general, may maintain a separate private tort action for damages.

Private Nuisance. Unlike the public nuisance, a **private nuisance** is a strictly private *tort* remedy, closely related to the tort of trespass. Private nuisance is designed to protect against invasions of the private interest in the *use and enjoyment of land,* whereas trespass protects against wrongful interference with *possession of land.* Private "use and enjoyment" refers to that use of land a person is privileged to make as an individual, not as a member of the general public.

The types of conduct constituting a private nuisance are infinitely variable. The activity involved may interfere with the physical condition of the land itself, such as vibration due to blasting or manufacturing, destruction of trees or crops, flooding, or polluting water. It may affect the possessor's comfort or enjoyment by the intrusion of loud noises (for example, due to barking dogs or a manufacturing process), excessive smoke, gas, light, heat, fumes, or odors. Or, it may simply affect the possessor's peace of mind or threaten future injury (such as a neighbor keeping a vicious dog or storing explosives or other dangerous materials). Most nuisances are intentional only in the sense that the defendant has created or continued a condition with knowledge that an interference with plaintiff's interest will occur or has occurred.

Not all intentional interference with the private use and enjoyment of land is actionable. The law of nuisance represents an attempt to balance the conflicting interests of landowners. These interests are, on one hand, the general principle that a person should be able to use his property as he sees fit, and, on the other, the opposing principle that a person is bound to use his property in such a manner as not to unreasonably interfere with the use and enjoyment of neighboring property. The court must, therefore, make a comparative evaluation of these competing interests to determine whether or not tort liability should be imposed.

This comparative evaluation is made by testing the "reasonableness" of the defendant's conduct. In other words, an intentional interference with the use and enjoyment of another's land is actionable as a private nuisance only if the invasion is both substantial and *unreasonable.* An intentional interference is unreasonable if the gravity (seriousness) of the harm outweighs the utility (meritoriousness) of the actor's conduct.[9]

Conversion. Unreasonable interference with use and possession of tangible personal property is compensable in tort through an action for conversion. **Conversion** occurs when one person intentionally exercises control over a chattel belonging to another, which so seriously interferes with the owner's right to control it that the possessor "may justly be required to pay the other the full value of the chattel."[10] In other words, a person who has "converted" another's goods to his own use is effectively forced to buy them from the owner.

Conversion occurs in various ways, including dispossessing the owner—taking the chattel from his possession without his consent or through fraud or duress, destroying or altering the property, or using it in a manner that seriously interferes with the owner's right of use. Whether the interference is serious enough to constitute conversion is a matter of degree, dependent upon the circumstances of the particular case. Assume Ted entrusts his car to Bill, a used car dealer, to be sold. Bill drives the car once for ten miles on a personal errand. Bill has not converted the car. If, however, he drives the car 5,000 miles, a conversion occurs, requiring him to pay Ted the value of the car. The same result occurs if Bill substantially alters the car, destroys it, or refuses to return it at Ted's request.

---

[9]Some of the factors considered in weighing the *gravity of the harm* are: (1) the extent of the harm, (2) the character of the harm, and (3) the social value of the type of use or enjoyment invaded. Factors relevant in ascertaining the *utility* of the conduct include: (1) the social value of the conduct attacked as a nuisance, (2) the suitability of the conduct to the character of the locality, and (3) the impracticability of preventing or avoiding the invasion.

[10]RESTATEMENT (SECOND) OF TORTS §222A(1).

Although conversion is always an *intentional* exercise of control over another's property, the converter merely must intend to exercise control over the chattel; no intent to interfere with another's rights is required. Thus, a defendant who mistakenly believes that she has the right to possession or consent of the owner is not relieved of liability. For example, a person who innocently buys stolen goods is liable to their owner for conversion.

Intentional Interference with Business Relations

A contract is a legally enforceable promise or set of promises. Contract law, which forms the basis of many business relationships, is a distinct and well-developed area of law that is discussed in detail in Chapters 7 through 19 of this text. Tort law extends protection to contracts by imposing liability for intentional interference with the performance of contracts, a tort now recognized by almost all states. Under §766 of the *Restatement (Second) of Torts,* a person who "intentionally and improperly interferes with the performance of a contract" between two other persons "by inducing or otherwise causing" one of them not to perform is liable in tort for damages to the other party to the broken contract. Some states also extend protection to advantageous business relationships or expectancies not amounting to contracts through the tort of intentional interference with prospective contractual relations.

To establish a claim for intentional interference with the performance of a contract, the plaintiff must prove that the defendant knew that the plaintiff had entered into a contract with another party and that the defendant improperly or unjustifiably caused that party to breach (not to perform) the contract. A defendant who induces the breach through illegal or otherwise tortious conduct clearly acts improperly. Assume, for example, that Chris contracts to deliver goods to Barbara and that Fred, with knowledge of this contract, intentionally destroys the goods. Fred would be liable to Barbara for intentional interference with contract. Many cases, however, involve conduct that is not so clearly wrongful, requiring courts to apply a balancing test that considers the nature of the defendant's conduct and motive, the nature of the contract, and the interests and relations of the parties. Since the classic English case *Lumley v. Gye* (1853),[11] courts have allowed recovery even if the means to induce the breach were not illegal or tortious. Thus, for example, if ABC Co. knowingly induces Robin to breach her employment contract with XYZ, Inc. by offering her a higher salary, ABC Co. may be held liable to XYZ, Inc. for intentional interference with contract.

The tort of intentional interference with prospective contractual relation is not as clearly defined in the case law. Section 766B of *Restatement (Second) of Torts* provides that a defendant intentionally and improperly interferes with the plaintiff's prospective contractual relation by inducing or otherwise causing another not to enter into or continue the prospective relation, or by preventing another from acquiring or continuing the prospective relation. If, for example, Arnold and Juanita are negotiating a contract and Leonard unjustifiably tells Juanita that he will sue her if she enters into the contract, Leonard may be held liable to either Arnold or Juanita for interference with the prospective contractual relation. As in intentional interference with contract, many cases involve a defendant who engages in tortious or illegal conduct, such as defamation or antitrust law violations, to prevent others from entering into a contract. In such cases, courts usually hold the defendant liable for intentional interference with prospective contractual relation. In other cases, courts use the same balancing test described above to evaluate the defendant's conduct. Additionally, several defenses are available to the defendant including, most importantly, competition. Generally, if a competitor interferes with a prospective contract, the competitor is not liable if the competitor is acting in its own interest and does not act tortiously or illegally. So, for example, if Robin is negotiating an employment contract with ABC Co. and XYZ, Inc., a competitor, offers her a higher salary which Robin accepts, XYZ would not be liable for interference with the prospective contract. If, however, XYZ acted wrongfully, for instance by slandering Robin causing ABC to discontinue negotiations, XYZ may be liable.

Negligence

Negligence law compensates those who are injured because of a person's *careless*—rather than intentional—conduct that creates an *unreasonable risk* of harm. **Negligence** occurs when a person does something that a reasonable person would not do or fails to do something that a reasonable person would do under the circumstances.[12]

---

[11]2 El. & Bl. 216, 118 Eng. Rep. 749 (Q.B. 1853).

[12]Blyth v. Birmingham Waterworks Co., 11 Ex. 781, 784, 156 Eng. Rep. 1047, 1049 (Ex. 1856).

Negligence alone, however, does not subject a person to tort liability. To recover damages for the tort of negligence, the plaintiff must prove that:

1. the defendant owed the plaintiff a legal duty not to be negligent,
2. the defendant breached that duty by failing to act as a reasonable person would act under the circumstances,
3. the defendant's negligence was the "proximate" or "legal" cause of an injury suffered by the plaintiff, and
4. the plaintiff suffered actual loss, damage, or injury as a result of the defendant's conduct.

The law of negligence is of fairly recent origin; it was first recognized as a separate tort only during the early part of the nineteenth century. It grew dramatically in importance when it was used to compensate for injuries caused by the industrial revolution and early railroads. Today, the law of negligence is the dominant legal theory to provide compensation for accidental injury.

Duty and Breach of Duty

Negligence law creates a duty to act with reasonable care. To avoid liability for negligence, a person must conform his conduct to that of a "reasonable person" under similar circumstances. A person whose conduct falls below this objective standard breaches the duty and is considered to be negligent. The **reasonable person** is a hypothetical, fictitious person who possesses characteristics of attentiveness, knowledge, intelligence, and judgment required by society for the protection of others. The reasonable person is therefore a personification of the community ideal of reasonable behavior.

Although the reasonable person generally represents a uniform standard, certain persons are judged by more lenient standards. Generally, a person's insanity or other mental illness does not relieve her from liability for conduct unbecoming a reasonable person, but physical disability may. A person who is ill or otherwise physically disabled therefore, must conform her conduct to that of a reasonable person under a similar disability. To avoid liability for negligence, children, as well, need only conform their conduct to that of a reasonable child of similar age, intelligence, and experience under the circumstances. On the other hand, persons with superior skill or competence, such as doctors, attorneys, architects, engineers, or accountants, avoid negligence liability only by exercising the amount of care that is reasonable in light of their superior learning, experience, or ability.

The standard of conduct of a reasonable person may be determined in various ways. Initially, a statute or administrative regulation may establish a minimum level of conduct and provide that a violation is negligence. Even in the absence of express provision for tort liability, courts often adopt the requirements of a statute or regulation to define negligence. In this case, an unexcused violation of the statute or regulation is negligent in itself (negligent *per se*); no further evidence of negligence is required. Courts have used this approach, for example, to impose liability upon defendants for injuries to employees, hotel guests, restaurant patrons, and members of the public caused by violations of fire codes, workplace safety regulations, food laws, and other statutes designed for the protection of others.

If no legislative enactment establishes a standard of conduct, appellate court decisions often define the reasonable person standard applicable to specific fact situations. In the absence of statute or judicial decision governing the particular facts of the case, the court (judge) may determine on its own whether the defendant was negligent. Usually, the court will instruct the jury in the law of negligence, and let the jury compare the defendant's conduct to that of a reasonable person under the circumstances. The reasonable person standard provides flexibility, allowing the jury to consider the particular circumstances and individuals of the case, while furnishing, as far as possible, a uniform standard of conduct.

Proximate Cause and Injury

To recover in an action for negligence, the plaintiff must prove some reasonable connection between the defendant's conduct and the injury sustained by the plaintiff. In legal terms, courts state that the defendant's conduct must be the "proximate" or "legal" cause of the injury. The concept of **proximate cause** encompasses a number of legal issues focusing on whether the causal connection between the defendant's negligence and the plaintiff's injury is sufficiently strong to justify holding the defendant liable. Determining proximate cause generally requires resolving two questions: (1) Did the defendant's negligence *in fact* cause the injury, and (2) if so, was the injury to the plaintiff foreseeable? These two questions are discussed in the following paragraphs.

Causation in Fact. At its most basic level, proximate causation requires proof that the defendant's negligent conduct in fact caused the plaintiff's injury. That is, the law must determine whether the defendant's negligent act or omission triggered a sequence of events that ultimately resulted in the plaintiff's injury. The issue generally is a matter for the trier of fact, usually the jury, to decide. Courts have developed two rules to determine causation in fact.

"But-for" or "Sine Qua Non" Test. Under this test, the defendant's conduct is the proximate cause of the injury if the injury would not have occurred *but for* that conduct. If the event would have occurred whether or not the defendant had been negligent, the defendant's negligence is not the proximate cause of the harm. For example, assume Don owns a car in need of brake repair. Despite the long stopping distances required, he continues to drive the car, a negligent act. While Don is driving the car slowly in a residential neighborhood, Phillip, a child, darts from behind a parked car and is hit and seriously injured by Don's car. Evidence at trial proves that even if the brakes had been in the best of condition, Don could not have stopped in time to avoid hitting Phillip. Don's negligence is not the proximate cause of Phillip's injury.

"Substantial-Factor" Test. The "but-for" test resolves most causation questions but proves inadequate when two or more acts of negligence bring about the injury. To resolve this case, many courts use the *substantial factor* test. Under this test, when separate acts of negligence combine to produce a single injury, each tort-feasor is responsible for the entire result even if her act alone might not have caused it. That is, a defendant's negligence need not be the only cause, or the last or nearest cause. Liability is imposed upon any defendant whose negligence is a substantial factor in causing the plaintiff's injury.[13]

Foreseeability of Harm. Even if causation in fact is established, the defendant is not necessarily liable. Negligent conduct may injure one or thousands of people in various ways and trigger a chain of events causing injuries far removed in time and place from the original negligent act. The second proximate cause requirement, foreseeability, determines whether the defendant should be liable to all potential plaintiffs for all consequences of his negligent conduct or whether some limitation on the extent of liability should be recognized.

The classic case addressing this issue is *Palsgraf v. Long Island Railroad Company* (1928).[14] In this case, a passenger carrying a package was attempting to board a train operated by defendant Long Island Railroad as the train left the station. The railroad's employees, while helping the passenger board the train, negligently knocked the package from the passenger's arms and it landed on the track. The package contained fireworks, which exploded. Either the explosion or the stampede of frightened passengers knocked over some heavy scales at the other end of the platform, which struck and injured the plaintiff Palsgraf. She sued the railroad, alleging that the negligent conduct of its employees caused her injury.

On these facts, Judge Benjamin Cardozo, speaking for the majority, found the railroad not liable because there had been no negligence toward the plaintiff. In his opinion negligence, based upon the relation between the parties, required foreseeability of harm to the person in fact injured. The court ruled that the employees had been negligent toward the holder of the package, but had not been negligent to the plaintiff, standing far away, outside the zone of apparent danger. As noted by Judge Cardozo: "The plaintiff sues in her own right for a wrong personal to her, and not as the vicarious beneficiary of a breach of duty to another."[15]

The rule of *Palsgraf*—that there is no liability for negligence to the unforeseeable plaintiff—has been criticized by many courts and commentators, including three dissenting judges in *Palsgraf* itself. As noted by Judge Andrews in dissent:

> Due care is a duty imposed on each one of us to protect society from unnecessary danger, not to protect A, B, or C alone. . . .
>
> The proposition is this: Every one owes to the world at large the duty of refraining from those acts that may unreasonably threaten the safety of others. Such an act occurs. Not only is he wronged to whom harm might reasonably be expected to result, but he also who is in fact injured, even if he be outside what would generally be thought the danger zone.[16]

---

[13]In determining whether a given defendant's negligence is a substantial factor in causing injury, the following circumstances are considered: (1) the number of other factors contributing to the injury, (2) whether the defendant's conduct has created a force in continuous operation up to the time of injury or has created a harmless situation unless acted upon by forces beyond his control, and (3) lapse of time. RESTATEMENT (SECOND) OF TORTS §433.

[14]162 N.E. 99 (N.Y. 1928).

[15]*Id.* at 100.

[16]*Id.* at 102–103.

The modern law of "foreseeability," which follows Judge Andrews's dissent, is stated in Section 435 of the *Restatement (Second) of Torts*. Under this rule, the fact that the negligent defendant "neither foresaw nor should have foreseen the extent of the harm or the manner in which it occurred does not prevent him from being liable."[17] Further, the foreseeability is a matter of hindsight, measured from the court's point of view looking back upon events which in fact occurred, not from what the defendant should have foreseen at the time of the accident. Under this test, the defendant is relieved of liability only if "looking back from the harm to the actor's negligent conduct, it appears to the court *highly extraordinary* that it should have brought about the harm."[18] This test is extremely difficult for a negligent defendant to meet. For example, in one case, a person negligently driving his car crashed into and knocked over a power line pole; the downed power line shut off power to a traffic control box at a remote intersection causing traffic signals to stop functioning; as a result two cars collided at the uncontrolled intersection. On these facts, the accident was held to be a foreseeable consequence of the defendant's negligence.[19] The cases involving what consequences are or are not foreseeable are difficult to reconcile. It is clear, however, that under modern foreseeability principles, few cases actually "restrict liability short of holding" the defendant liable "for all the harm of which his negligence is a substantial cause."[20]

Intervening Causes. Although the defendant is negligent, the ultimate injury may occur as a result of a *later* independent cause for which the defendant is not responsible—an intervening cause or force. If the later event is judged a "supervening" or "superceding" cause, the defendant is relieved of liability for negligence. In determining whether an intervening force is a supervening cause, various factors are considered. These include whether the injury is different in kind from that which would otherwise have resulted from the defendant's negligence, whether the intervening force operates independently of the original negligence or is a normal result of that negligence, and whether the intervening force is due to the act of a third party and the character (negligent, intentional, or criminal) of that act. In short, the test is similar to that previously dis-

cussed: the defendant is liable if the intervening cause is "foreseeable"; if not, the defendant's liability is "superceded" by the subsequent event. Most intervening causes including the later negligence of a third party meet this foreseeability requirement. For example, a person who negligently breaks another's leg is also liable for the subsequent negligent treatment of the leg by a doctor. If, however, the injury is caused by a subsequent *intentionally tortious* or *criminal* act of a third party, which is not within the scope of risk created by the original negligence, the defendant is relieved of liability. Assume Gene, a contractor, digs a trench near a public sidewalk to run a gas pipe. Gene negligently fails to erect a barrier next to the trench. Donna, passing Louise on the sidewalk, negligently bumps into her, causing Louise to fall into the trench. Gene is liable to Louise. Had Donna intentionally pushed Louise into the trench, Gene would be relieved of liability.

The following case illustrates principles of proximate causation in a negligence case.

Hairston v. Alexander Tank and Equipment Co.
311 S.E.2d 559 (N.C. 1984)

John Hairston purchased a new automobile from Haygood Lincoln-Mercury, Inc. (Haygood). After installing new wheels, Haygood delivered the car to Hairston. As Hairston was approaching a bridge on Interstate 85 approximately 3½ miles from the dealership, the left rear wheel came off the car. Because there was no shoulder on the road, he stopped the car in the far right lane. A passing motorist driving a van stopped his vehicle about 20 feet behind Hairston's car, set the hand brake, turned on his emergency flashers, and telephoned for assistance on his mobile telephone. Traffic continued to pass on the road using the left lane to avoid the stopped vehicles. A flatbed truck owned by Alexander Tank and Equipment Co. (Alexander Tank) and driven by Robert Alexander, struck the van knocking it into the rear of the Hairston automobile. Hairston, who had been standing between his car and the van, was killed.

Plaintiff Bettye Hairston sued both Haygood and Alexander Tank and Equipment Co. for damages alleging that their negligence had caused her husband's death. The evidence established that Haygood had failed to tighten the lug nuts on the wheels thereby causing the wheel to fall off Hairston's car. The evidence also showed that Alexander's negligence caused him to collide with the van that struck and killed Hairston. The jury found that both Haygood and Alexander Tank had acted negligently. The trial court, however, granted Haygood's motion for judg-

[17]RESTATEMENT (SECOND) OF TORTS §435(1).
[18]RESTATEMENT (SECOND) OF TORTS §435(2). Emphasis added.
[19]Ferroggiaro v. Bowline, 315 P.2d 446 (Cal. App. 1957).
[20]RESTATEMENT (SECOND) OF TORTS, Chapter 16, at 449.

ment notwithstanding the verdict and held that Alexander's negligence had been the proximate cause of Hairston's death. Upon the appeal of Bettye Hairston and Alexander Tank, the court of appeals affirmed. The North Carolina Supreme Court granted certiorari.

Martin, Justice

. . . In order to establish actionable negligence, plaintiff must show (1) that there has been a failure to exercise proper care in the performance of some legal duty which defendant owed to plaintiff under the circumstances in which they were placed; and (2) that such negligent breach of duty was a proximate cause of the injury. . . .

We agree with the Court of Appeals that the record clearly reveals sufficient evidence from which a jury could find the first requisite of liability, negligence. That Haygood violated a legal duty to this plaintiff in failing to tighten the lug bolts on the left rear wheel and in failing to check the new car before delivery is self-evident.

For reasons which follow, however, it is also our opinion that from the evidence presented at trial the jury could reasonably infer that defendant's negligence was a proximate cause of Hairston's death. The jury could further infer from the facts in this case that while the subsequent negligence of defendant Alexander Tank joined with Haygood's original negligence in proximately causing the death of Hairston, it did not supercede the negligent acts of Haygood and thereby relieve Haygood of liability.

Proximate cause is a cause which in natural and continuous sequence, unbroken by any new and independent cause, produced the plaintiff's injuries, and without which the injuries would not have occurred, and one from which a person of ordinary prudence could have reasonably foreseen that such a result, or consequences of a generally injurious nature, was probable under all the facts as they existed. . . . Foreseeability is thus a requisite of proximate cause, which is, in turn, a requisite for actionable negligence. . . .

It is well settled that the test of foreseeability as an element of proximate cause does not require that defendant should have been able to foresee the injury in the precise form in which it actually occurred. . . .

The law requires only reasonable prevision. A defendant is not required to foresee events which are merely possible but only those which are reasonably foreseeable. . . .

There may be more than one proximate cause of an injury. When two or more proximate causes join and concur in producing the result complained of, the author of each cause may be held for the injuries inflicted. The defendants are jointly and severally liable. . . .

Applying the foregoing to the facts of this case to determine whether the negligence of defendant Haygood was a proximate cause of decedent's death, the decisive question is one of foreseeability. Under the circumstances here disclosed, we believe a jury could find that a reasonably prudent person should have foreseen that Haygood's negligence in failing to tighten the lugs on the wheel of the new automobile could cause the car to be disabled on the highway and struck by another vehicle, causing harm to the driver. Absent Haygood's original negligence, the tragic series of events on I-85 would not have occurred; the danger was foreseeable. Proximate causation is thus established and, with it, defendant's liability.

We turn now to the question whether the evidence in this case is susceptible of the single inference by the jury that Haygood's negligence ceased to be the proximate cause of decedent's death and that it was superseded and insulated by the subsequent negligence of defendant Alexander Tank.

The Court of Appeals found that Alexander was negligent in failing to keep a proper lookout for vehicles stopped on the highway and in failing to keep his vehicle under proper control. "These negligent acts of Alexander—new and independent of any negligent acts of Haygood—constitute the proximate cause of injury and the death of plaintiff's intestate, and the negligence of Haygood was shielded by the subsequent acts of negligence by Alexander." [299 S.E.2d at 795.]

We do not agree with the conclusion of the Court of Appeals. Under the applicable law summarized above, the negligent acts of Alexander quite properly may be found to be a proximate cause of the injury and death in this case: Without Alexander's negligence, the collision would not have occurred; the injury was clearly foreseeable, given the failure to keep a proper lookout. It is also true, of course, that Alexander's unfortunate lack of attention to the road acted independently of Haygood's earlier carelessness. These facts, however, do not of themselves absolve defendant Haygood from his liability.

Insulating negligence means something more than a concurrent and contributing cause. It is not to be invoked as determinative merely upon proof of negligent conduct on the part of each of two persons, acting independently, whose acts unite to cause a single injury. . . . Contributing negligence signifies contribution rather than independent or sole proximate cause. . . .

We hold that on the facts of this case a jury might readily find that defendant Haygood could have reasonably foreseen the subsequent acts of Alexander and the resultant harm to Hairston that occurred on I-85, barely six minutes and 3.5 miles away from the Haygood dealership. Alexander's negligence in driving was, as the Court of Appeals noted, inexcusable. It was not, however, so highly improbable and extraordinary an occurrence in this series of events as to bear no reasonable connection to the harm threatened by Haygood's original negligence. . . . The area of risk created by the negligence of Haygood included the subsequent events and wrongful death of John Hairston. . . .

[Reversed and remanded for entry of judgment in accordance with the jury's verdict.]

Defenses to Negligence

Even after the plaintiff has proven negligence, the defendant may raise one or more defenses, based on the plaintiff's conduct, that can reduce or extinguish liability. These include contributory negligence, assumption of the risk, and comparative negligence.

Contributory Negligence. **Contributory negligence** is negligence on the plaintiff's part which, combining with the defendant's negligence, causes the plaintiff harm. Traditionally, the plaintiff's contributory negligence was a complete bar to recovery against a defendant who would otherwise be liable to the plaintiff for negligence.

Assumption of Risk. A defendant establishes **assumption of the risk** by proving that the plaintiff voluntarily assumed the risk of harm caused by the defendant's negligent conduct. Assumption of the risk, therefore, rests upon the plaintiff's consent (express or implied) to encounter a known unreasonable danger created by the defendant's conduct. By voluntarily proceeding in the face of a known danger, the plaintiff may be acting reasonably or unreasonably. If he or she is acting unreasonably, the conduct also constitutes contributory negligence. Thus, the two defenses will often overlap and the plaintiff may be denied recovery on either basis. Assume Pat continues to drive a car after she discovers its brakes

are dangerously defective because they were negligently repaired by Joe's Brake Service. Pat is subsequently injured when the brakes fail. When sued by her for negligence, Joe may defend himself on the basis that Pat was either contributorily negligent or had assumed the risk.

Assumption of the risk is determined according to a subjective standard; that is, did this plaintiff know, understand, and appreciate the risk. In contrast, contributory negligence is determined according to an objective standard; that is, did the plaintiff fail to use the amount of care a reasonable person would exercise for his own safety under similar circumstances.

Comparative Fault. The "all-or-nothing" rule of contributory negligence may lead to harsh results. A slightly negligent plaintiff may be denied recovery from a substantially more culpable defendant. In addition, though the rule theoretically promotes caution by making the plaintiff responsible for his own conduct, it may in fact promote negligence by allowing careless defendants to escape liability for their conduct.

For these reasons, the contributory negligence doctrine has been replaced (either by statute or judicial decision) in most American jurisdictions by a rule of **comparative fault,** in which the negligent plaintiff, instead of being denied recovery altogether, is awarded damages reduced in proportion to his fault (negligence) in causing the injury. In the following case, the Tennessee Supreme Court rejects contributory negligence in favor of comparative fault.

McIntyre v. Balentine
833 S.W.2d 52 (Tenn. 1992)

Plaintiff Harry McIntyre and Defendant Clifford Balentine were involved in a vehicle collision when Balentine's Peterbilt tractor collided with McIntyre's pickup truck on Highway 69 near Savannah, Tennessee. The plaintiff sued the defendant for negligence. The plaintiff's evidence at trial indicated that Balentine had been drinking and was driving in excess of the posted speed limit at the time of the accident. The defendant's evidence showed that the plaintiff also had been drinking and had a blood alcohol level of 0.17 after the accident. The jury's verdict stated: "We, the jury, find the plaintiff, and the defendant equally at fault in this accident; therefore, we rule in favor of the defendant." The plaintiff appealed asserting that the trial court should have instructed the jury on comparative negligence. After the Court of Appeals affirmed, the Tennessee Supreme Court granted the plaintiff's request for appeal.

Drowota, Justice

The common law contributory negligence doctrine has traditionally been traced to Lord Ellenborough's opinion in *Butterfield v. Forrester, 11 East 60, 103 Eng. Rep. 926 (1809)*. There, plaintiff, "riding as fast as his horse would go," was injured after running into an obstruction defendant had placed in the road. Stating as the rule that "one person being in fault will not dispense with another's using ordinary care," plaintiff was denied recovery on the basis that he did not use ordinary care to avoid the obstruction. . . .

The contributory negligence bar was soon brought to America as part of the common law, . . . and proceeded to spread throughout the states. . . . This strict bar may have been a direct outgrowth of the common law system of issue pleading; issue pleading posed questions to be answered "yes" or "no," leaving common law courts, the theory goes, no choice but to award all or nothing. . . . A number of other rationalizations have been advanced in the attempt to justify the harshness of the "all-or-nothing" bar. Among these: the plaintiff should be penalized for his misconduct; the plaintiff should be deterred from injuring himself; and the plaintiff's negligence supersedes the defendant's so as to render defendant's negligence no longer proximate. . . . In Tennessee, . . . we have continued to follow the general rule that a plaintiff's contributory negligence completely bars recovery. . . .

Between 1920 and 1969, a few states began utilizing the principles of comparative fault in all tort litigation. . . . Then, between 1969 and 1984, comparative fault replaced contributory negligence in 37 additional states. In 1991, South Carolina became the 45th state to adopt comparative fault, leaving Alabama, Maryland, North Carolina, Virginia, and Tennessee as the only remaining common law contributory negligence jurisdictions. . . .

After exhaustive deliberation that was facilitated by extensive briefing and argument by the parties, amicus curiae, and Tennessee's scholastic community, we conclude that it is time to abandon the outmoded and unjust common law doctrine of contributory negligence and adopt in its place a system of comparative fault. Justice simply will not permit our continued adherence to a rule that, in the face of a judicial determination that others bear primary responsibility, nevertheless completely denies injured litigants recompense for their damages. . . .

Two basic forms of comparative fault are utilized by 45 of our sister jurisdictions, these variants being commonly referred to as either "pure" or "modified." In the "pure" form, a plaintiff's damages are reduced in proportion to the percentage negligence attributed to him; for example, a plaintiff responsible for 90 percent of the negligence that caused his injuries nevertheless may recover 10 percent of his damages. In the "modified" form, plaintiffs recover as in pure jurisdictions, but only if the plaintiff's negligence either (1) does not exceed ("50 percent" jurisdictions) or (2) is less than ("49 percent" jurisdictions) the defendant's negligence. . . .

Although we conclude that the all-or-nothing rule of contributory negligence must be replaced, we nevertheless decline to abandon totally our fault-based tort system. We do not agree that a party should necessarily be able to recover in tort even though he may be 80, 90, or 95 percent at fault. We therefore reject the pure form of comparative fault.

We recognize that modified comparative fault systems have been criticized as merely shifting the arbitrary contributory negligence bar to a new ground. . . . However, we feel the "49 percent rule" ameliorates the harshness of the common law rule while remaining compatible with a fault-based tort system. . . . We therefore hold that so long as a plaintiff's negligence remains less than the defendant's negligence the plaintiff may recover; in such a case, plaintiff's damages are to be reduced in proportion to the percentage of the total negligence attributable to the plaintiff. . . .

Turning to the case at bar, the jury found that "the plaintiff and defendant [were] equally at fault." Because the jury, without the benefit of proper instructions by the trial court, made a gratuitous apportionment of fault, we find that their "equal" apportionment is not sufficiently trustworthy to form the basis of a final determination between these parties. Therefore, the case is remanded for a new trial in accordance with the dictates of this opinion. . . .

[Judgment reversed and remanded.]

Premises Liability

In modern times, automobile and industrial accidents, product-related injuries, and professional malpractice form the bulk of negligence litigation. Another area of negligence that has generated many lawsuits is premises liability, the liability of land and building owners and occupiers (such as tenants) for injuries occurring on their property.

Under the traditional common law rules, premises liability is based on the duty owed to the person injured. Generally, the duty owed depends upon the *status* of the injured person as a trespasser, licensee, or invitee. A **trespasser** is a person who enters or remains upon another's property without a privilege to do so. A **licensee** is a person privileged to enter or remain upon the land only because the possessor consents. Licensees include members of the possessor's household, social guests,[21] and those present on the property solely for their own purposes and to whom the privilege of entering was extended as a mere personal favor. An **invitee** is one of two types: a public invitee or a business invitee. A **public invitee** is a member of the public invited to enter or remain on the property for a purpose for which it is held open to the public (such as a person entering a museum or library to examine the exhibits or read a book). A **business invitee** is a person invited to enter or remain on the premises to conduct business with the possessor of the property (a patron of a retail store).

Liability to Trespassers. Generally, a property owner or occupier has no duty to exercise reasonable care to make the property safe for trespassers or to conduct activities on the land in a manner that will not endanger them. The sole duty owed to a trespasser is to refrain from "willfully and wantonly" injuring him. This rule is subject to a number of exceptions that significantly limit its availability as a defense to actions by the trespasser.

Although most of these exceptions, if applicable, merely impose a duty upon the possessor to warn or to exercise reasonable care to avoid injury to the trespasser, a special exception, applicable when trespassers are *children,* may impose additional duties. Under §339 of the *Restatement (Second) of Torts,* if a possessor (1) maintains an artificial condition upon the land around which he or she knows or should know children are likely to trespass, and (2) the condition poses an unreasonable risk of death or injury to such children who, because of their youth, are unable to discover the danger or realize the risk presented, and (3) the utility to the possessor in maintaining the condition and the burden of eliminating the danger are slight when compared to the risk involved, then the possessor is liable for injury to the trespassing children caused by the condition if he or she fails to exercise reasonable care to *eliminate the danger or otherwise protect the children.* Note that this special duty to children generally is imposed only for "artificial" conditions (those created or maintained by the possessor), such as buildings, cranes, railroad tracks, turntables, and switchyards. The possessor's duty may be fulfilled in some cases by a mere warning, but in others more may be required such as building fences, boarding up, locking up, or tearing down offending structures, or filling in a dangerous pit.

The foregoing rule is called the **turntable doctrine,** because it originated in 1873 in *Sioux City & Pacific R. Co. v. Stout,*[22] involving a child injured while playing upon a railroad turntable. It also is frequently called the **attractive nuisance** doctrine, although this designation is somewhat misleading because there is generally no requirement that the children be allured or enticed onto the premises by the condition that causes injury. Most cases imposing liability involve children less than 12 years of age, although courts generally reject any fixed age limit. The basic test is whether the child is still too young to appreciate the particular danger presented.

Liability to Licensees. A licensee, unlike a trespasser, is upon the property with the possessor's consent. Consent to enter the premises alone, however, generally gives the licensee no right to expect that the possessor will conduct its activities differently or remedy dangerous conditions to assure the licensee's safety. Thus, as a general rule, a possessor has a duty to conduct activities with reasonable care for the safety of licensees or make dangerous conditions safe only if (1) the possessor should expect that the licensee will not discover or realize the danger, and (2) the licensee is unaware of the activities or conditions and the risks involved. Under this approach, once the licensee knows (through knowledge or observation, or by the possessor's warning) of the nature of the business or other activity conducted on the premises, he or she then assumes the risk involved upon entering the premises.

Liability to Invitees. The invitee, unlike a licensee, is a person who enters or remains on the property by invitation that includes an implied representation that the possessor has used reasonable care to prepare the premises and make them safe for the invitee. A possessor, therefore, must generally exercise reasonable care to protect invitees against both dangerous activities conducted and dangerous conditions occurring on the property or at least to discover the dangerous condition or activity and give an adequate warning. What constitutes adequate

---

[21]In some states social guests now are treated as invitees.

[22]84 U.S. (17 Wall.) 657 (1873).

preparation for the invitee's protection depends primarily on the nature of the property and the purposes for which it is used. Invitees may recover for their injuries, however, only if the possessor knows or should know that the activity or condition poses an unreasonable risk of injury.

Modern Approaches. The traditional tests outlined previously impose liability based solely on the circumstances of the injured party's entry onto the property—that is, his or her status as trespasser, licensee, or invitee. This approach has been criticized as awkward, complex, and mechanical in its application, and unduly protecting property interests at the expense of human safety. For these reasons, some states have abandoned the traditional tripartite classification and instead apply ordinary principles of negligence in determining possessor's liability. Under this approach an owner or occupier of land or buildings "must act as a reasonable person in maintaining his property in a reasonably safe condition in view of all the circumstances, including the likelihood of injury to others, the seriousness of the injury, and the burden on the respective parties of avoiding the risk."[23] The status of the injured party is simply one factor to be considered in assessing the possessor's reasonable care.

An alternative approach is to eliminate the distinction between licensees and invitees and impose a duty of reasonable care under the circumstances to such entrants. Under this approach, the duty owed to trespassers continues to be governed by the traditional test previously discussed.

The following case illustrates the modern approach to the difficult task of proving negligence in business invitee cases.

Lanier v. Wal-Mart Stores, Inc.
99 S.W.3d 431 (Ky. 2003)

> While shopping at a Wal-Mart Superstore in Hopkinsville, Kentucky, plaintiff Barbara Lanier slipped on a clear liquid on the floor, fell, and injured her head. Lanier sued defendant Wal-Mart Stores, Inc. for negligence seeking damages for her injuries. The trial court granted summary judgment to Wal-Mart and the court of appeals affirmed. Lanier appealed to the Kentucky Supreme Court.

---

[23]Webb v. City and Borough of Sitka, 561 P.2d 731, 733 (Alaska 1977).

Cooper, Justice

. . . "Slip and fall" cases are traditionally based on the duty of care that a possessor of land owes to an invitee. . . .

> A possessor of land is subject to liability for physical harm caused to his invitees by a condition on the land if, but only if, he: (a) knows or by the exercise of reasonable care would discover the condition, and should realize that it involves an unreasonable risk of harm to such invitees; and (b) should expect that they will not discover or realize the danger, or will fail to protect themselves against it; and (c) fails to exercise reasonable care to protect them against the danger.

[*Restatement (Second) of Torts* §343.] And, if the possessor of the property holds it open to the public for entry for his business purposes, he is subject to liability to members of the public while they are on the property for business purposes for physical harm caused by the accidental, negligent, or intentionally harmful acts of third persons if the possessor failed to exercise reasonable care to either: a) discover that such acts are being done or are likely to be done, or b) give warning adequate to enable the business visitors to avoid the harm, or otherwise protect them against it. . . . *Id.* §344.

Under these common law principles, the business owner has an affirmative duty to exercise reasonable care to inspect for hazardous conditions. . . . These general principles relate only to the duty owed by a business proprietor to his customers and not to the burden of proof as to whether that duty has been violated. . . .

[Kentucky law] requires a plaintiff in this type of action to plead and prove . . . that the proprietor or his employees either caused the foreign substance to be on the floor or, by the exercise of reasonable care, could have discovered it and either removed it or warned of its presence before the accident occurred. . . .

Lanier admits that she cannot prove how long the clear liquid substance was on the floor or that Wal-Mart's employees either spilled it there or had actual or constructive notice of its presence for a sufficient time to have removed it before she fell. In the face of this evidentiary insufficiency, Lanier is forced to contend—in effect—that the spill should be presumed attributable to Wal-Mart because of its self-service method of retail sales. She observes that customers of all ages and abilities are encouraged by Wal-Mart to handle its merchandise and to move it about the store either by hand or by way of shopping baskets and carts that are provided by the store for that purpose. She argues that this method of self-service sales facilitates the creation of hazardous conditions which it is reasonably foreseeable will result in harm to innocent customers. . . .

Wal-Mart's Hopkinsville Superstore contains more than two acres of self-service shopping areas consisting of a number of departments, including the grocery department where Lanier fell. There were fourteen management and eighty-four hourly employees on duty when the accident occurred. None claims to have seen Lanier fall, or to have discovered the clear liquid substance that caused her to fall, or to know what caused it to be on the floor where she fell. Two employees who observed the substance after Lanier fell speculated that it could have been shampoo that might have dripped from another customer's shopping cart. The exact nature and source of the substance was never established.

The inherent inequity in our present approach to the burden of proof in premises liability cases of this kind was discussed at length in the concurring opinion in *Smith v. Wal-Mart Stores, Inc.,* [6 S.W.3d 829 (Ky. 1999)].

. . . [A]bsent proof that the proprietor or his employees caused the substance/object to be on the floor, the injured customer is faced with the daunting burden of proving how long the substance/object had been on the floor before the accident and whether that was a sufficient length of time for notice and correction to have taken place. Presumably, had the customer had personal knowledge of the presence of the substance/object before the accident, he would not have stepped on it. Absent his own knowledge . . . , the customer must either produce a witness who saw the substance or object on the floor prior to [the] accident or face either summary judgment or a directed verdict. Placing this virtually insurmountable burden of proof on the customer is inconsistent with the proposition that a proprietor of a place of business has a duty to keep his premises in a reasonably safe condition for normal use by his customers. . . .

[*Id.,* at 831-32.] . . . [T]he Supreme Court of Florida in *Owens v. Publix Supermarkets, Inc.,* 802 So. 2d 315 (Fla. 2001) [has ruled]:

We hold that the existence of a foreign substance on the floor of a business premises that causes a customer to fall and be injured is not a safe condition and the existence of that unsafe condition creates a rebuttable presumption that the premises owner did not maintain the premises in a reasonably safe condition.

Thus, once the plaintiff establishes that he or she fell as a result of a transitory foreign substance, a rebuttable

presumption of negligence arises. At that point, the burden shifts to the defendant to show by the greater weight of evidence that it exercised reasonable care in the maintenance of the premises under the circumstances. The circumstances could include the nature of the specific hazard and the nature of the defendant's business.

Id., at 331. . . .

The modern self-service form of retail sales encourages the business's patrons to obtain for themselves from shelves and containers the items they wish to purchase, and to move them from one part of the store to another in baskets and shopping carts as they continue to shop for other items, thus increasing the risk of droppage and spillage. . . .

It is also common knowledge that modern merchandising techniques employed by self-service retail stores are specifically designed to attract a customer's attention to the merchandise on the shelves and, thus, away from any hazards that might be on the floor. This fact is exemplified by photographs in this record showing the layout of aisle 8 of the grocery department of the Wal-Mart Superstore where Lanier fell. Under these circumstances, it is unreasonable to require the customer to prove how a foreign substance was caused to be on the floor and/or how long it had been there. Most importantly, however, both logic and fairness mandate that, as between two apparently innocent parties, one being a business proprietor having a duty to maintain his premises in a reasonably safe condition for the use of his customers, and the other being the invited customer, the burden of proof with respect to the cause of an unsafe condition of the premises should be on the one with the duty to prevent it.

Thus, we now depart from our previous approach imposing the burden on the injured customer to prove how the foreign substance came to be on the floor and/or how long it had been there and adopt the burden-shifting approach. . . . Insofar as our previous cases hold that the entire burden of proof rests on the injured customer, they are overruled.

By adopting the burden-shifting approach to premises liability, we . . . impose a rebuttable presumption that shifts the burden of proving the absence of negligence, that is, the exercise of reasonable care, to the party who invited the injured customer to its business premises.

Our holding does not make the operator of a self-service grocery store an insurer against all accidents on the premises.

The proprietor is guilty of negligence only if he fails to use reasonable care under the circumstances to discover the foreseeable dangerous condition and to correct it or to warn customers of its existence. We believe, however, that it is unrealistic to require the victim of a fall resulting from a dangerous condition in a self-service grocery store to present evidence of the absence of reasonable care by the storekeeper. The steps the storekeeper took to discover the condition and to correct or warn of it are peculiarly within his own knowledge.

Safeway Stores, Inc. v. Smith, [658 P.2d 255, 258 (Colo.1983)].

[Judgment reversed and remanded.]

Strict Liability

In certain cases, tort liability is imposed in the absence of both negligence and an intent to interfere with the plaintiff's legally protected interests. Such liability is known as **strict liability,** or liability without fault. In other words, a person is said to be "strictly liable" if legal responsibility is imposed even though he or she has not acted intentionally and has exercised the utmost care to prevent the harm. Two types of strict liability, imposed upon possessors of animals and those who conduct abnormally dangerous activities, are discussed below. Two other forms of strict liability, imposed upon suppliers of defective products that cause personal injury or property damage and upon common carriers for goods lost or damaged in transit, are covered in detail in Chapters 20 and 35, respectively.

Possessors of Animals

People who own or possess wild or domestic animals often are held strictly liable for damages caused when their animals trespass upon another's land, or inflict other injuries, such as bites.

Trespassing Livestock. A possessor of livestock, such as horses, cattle, pigs, sheep, and poultry, has traditionally been held strictly liable for personal injury and property damage caused if the livestock escape and trespass upon another's land. If permitted to run at large, these animals often do substantial harm by eating grass or other plants, trampling crops, or injuring persons or animals. Strict liability generally does not extend to animals, such as dogs and cats, that are not ordinarily kept under confinement and are unlikely to do significant damage by their trespass. Many states regulate animal trespass liability by statutes that often alter the common law rules.

Liability Apart from Trespass. Trespass is not the only damage done by privately owned animals. Numerous cases involve dog bites and other injuries inflicted by pets. Liability of the owner generally depends upon whether the kept animal is domestic or wild.[24] Examples of the former are dogs, cats, sheep, cattle, and horses, and of the latter wolves, rattlesnakes, monkeys, and raccoons. The possessor of a wild animal is strictly liable for personal injury to another or another's animal caused by a dangerous propensity characteristic of animals of that type. On the other hand, the law imposes strict liability for injuries caused by domestic animals only if the possessor knows or has reason to know of the particular animal's abnormally dangerous characteristics. Under this test, an owner may be held strictly liable for the first attack by a dog that previously has exhibited vicious tendencies.

Abnormally Dangerous Activities

A person who carries on an abnormally dangerous or ultrahazardous activity is strictly liable for personal injury and property damage resulting from that activity. An activity is abnormally dangerous if it is highly dangerous even when carefully performed and is not one, such as driving a car, that is commonly undertaken. Examples of conditions and activities meeting this test are: (1) blasting or pile driving, (2) storing explosives, inflammable liquids, dangerous chemicals, or dangerous gases in quantity, (3) collecting water in a dangerous place, (4) producing, transporting, and using nuclear material, and (5) emitting noxious gases or fumes. Liability for damages caused by these activities also is often imposed on theory of nuisance discussed earlier in this chapter. In fact, the rule of strict liability outlined above is applied by many courts under the name "absolute nuisance."

In the following case the court traces the development of the law governing strict liability for abnormally dangerous activities and considers whether such liability should be imposed for damages caused by toxic waste storage.

---

[24]A "domestic" animal is one "by custom devoted to the service of mankind at the time and in the place in which it is kept." A "wild" animal is one not so devoted. RESTATEMENT (SECOND) OF TORTS §506.

State Department of Environmental Protection v. Ventron Corporation

468 A.2d 150 (N.J. 1983)

Over a period of about 50 years, several businesses engaged in mercury processing operations on a 40-acre tract of land known as Berry's Creek, located near the Meadowlands in New Jersey. These operations created an estimated 268 tons of toxic waste, primarily mercury pollution, that contaminated Berry's Creek and adjacent land and groundwaters with lethal mercury and threatened the environment, marine life, and human health and safety. The mercury processing plant at Berry's Creek was operated from 1929 to 1960 by F. W. Berk and Company, Inc. (which went out of business in 1960) and from 1960 to 1974 by Wood Ridge Chemical Corporation (which first operated as a subsidiary of Velsicol Chemical Corporation and later was sold to Ventron Corporation). The plaintiff New Jersey Environmental Protection Agency sued numerous defendants including Wood Ridge, Velsicol, and Ventron to recover damages for cleanup of the area. The trial court found the defendants strictly liable for "unleashing a dangerous substance during non-natural use of the land." The appellate court affirmed and the corporate defendants appealed to the New Jersey Supreme Court.

Pollock, Justice

. . . We believe it is time to recognize expressly that the law of liability has evolved so that a landowner is strictly liable to others for harm caused by toxic wastes that are stored on his property and flow onto the property of others. Therefore, we . . . adopt the principle of liability originally declared in *Rylands v. Fletcher* [L.R. 3 H.L. 330 (1868)]. The net result is that those who use, or permit others to use, land for the conduct of abnormally dangerous activities are strictly liable for resultant damages. Comprehension of the relevant legal principles, however, requires a more complete explanation of their development. . . .

[I]n 1868, the English courts decided *Rylands v. Fletcher*. In that case, defendants, mill owners in a coal-mining region, constructed a reservoir on their property. Unknown to them, the land below the reservoir was riddled with the passages and filled shafts of an abandoned coal mine. The waters of the reservoir broke through the old mine shafts and surged through the passages into the working mine of the plaintiff. . . .

The Exchequer Chamber . . . held the mill owners liable, relying on the existing rule of strict liability for damage done by trespassing cattle. The rationale was stated:

> We think that the true rule of law is that the person who for his own purposes brings on his land and collects and keeps there anything likely to do mischief if it escapes, must keep it at his peril, and if he does not do so, is *prima facie* answerable for all damage which is the natural consequence of its escape. [*Rylands v. Fletcher,* L.R. 1 Ex. 265, 279–80 (1866), aff'd, L.R. 3 H.L. 330 (1868)].

On appeal, the House of Lords limited the applicability of this strict liability rule to "nonnatural" uses of land. Consequently, if an accumulation of water had occurred naturally, . . . strict liability would not be imposed. . . .

More recently, the *Restatement (Second) of Torts* reformulated the standard of landowner liability. . . . [T]his standard incorporates the theory developed in *Rylands v. Fletcher*. Under the *Restatement* analysis, whether an activity is abnormally dangerous is to be determined on a case-by-case basis, taking all relevant circumstances into consideration. As set forth in the *Restatement:*

> In determining whether an activity is abnormally dangerous, the following factors are to be considered:
>
> (a) existence of a high degree of risk of some harm to the person, land or chattels of others;
> (b) likelihood that the harm that results from it will be great;
> (c) inability to eliminate the risk by the exercise of reasonable care;
> (d) extent to which the activity is not a matter of common usage;
> (e) inappropriateness of the activity to the place where it is carried on; and
> (f) extent to which its value to the community is outweighed by its dangerous attributes.

[*Restatement (Second) of Torts* §520 (1977)].

Pollution from toxic wastes that seeps onto the land of others and into streams necessarily harms the environment. . . . Determination of the magnitude of the damage includes recognition that the disposal of toxic waste may cause a variety of harms, including ground water contamination via leachate, surface water contamination via runoff or overflow, and poison via the food chain. . . . The lower courts found that each of those hazards was present as a result of the contamination of the entire tract. . . . Further, as was the case here, the waste dumped may react synergistically with elements in the environment, or other waste elements, to form an even more toxic compound. . . . With respect to the ability to eliminate the risks involved in disposing of hazardous wastes by the exercise of reasonable care, no safe way exists to dispose of mercury by simply dumping it onto land or into water.

The disposal of mercury is particularly inappropriate in the Hackensack Meadowlands, an environmentally sensitive area where the arterial waterways will disperse the pollution through the entire ecosystem. Finally, the dumping of untreated hazardous waste is a critical societal problem in New Jersey, which the Environmental Protection Agency estimates is the source of more hazardous waste than any other state. . . . From the fore-

going, we conclude that mercury and other toxic wastes are "abnormally dangerous," and the disposal of them, past or present, is an abnormally dangerous activity. . . .

Our examination leads to the conclusion, consistent with that of the lower courts, that defendants have violated long-standing common-law principles of landowner liability. . . . That activity has poisoned the land and Berry's Creek. Even if they did not intend to pollute or adhered to the standards of the time, all of these parties remain liable. Those who poison the land must pay for its cure. . . .

[Judgment affirmed.]

Summary

1.   A "tort" is defined as a private or civil wrong or injury, other than breach of contract, for which the law provides a remedy in the form of an action for damages. Tort law is designed to compensate the injured party and is based generally upon state common law.

2.   Tort liability is imposed on three basic grounds: (1) because the defendant *intentionally* interfered with a legally protected interest of the plaintiff, or (2) because the defendant was *negligent,* or (3) because the defendant was *strictly liable,* that is, liable in the absence of either negligence or an intent to interfere with the plaintiff's interests.

3.   Intentional torts are those in which the tort-feasor knows that invasion of a legally protected interest is certain, or substantially certain, to result from his or her act. Intentional torts are generally classified according to the interest protected. For example, the torts of assault, battery, false imprisonment, intentional infliction of emotional distress, defamation, and invasion of privacy protect against intentional interference with a person's physical or emotional well-being. The torts of trespass, nuisance, and conversion protect against interference with the use, possession, or enjoyment of property. Business or economic interests are protected, for example, by allowing recovery for intentional interference with performance of a contract or prospective contractual relation.

4.   Most tort liability is not based upon conduct intended to cause injury; rather it is imposed for negligence—conduct that creates an unreasonable risk of injury. To avoid liability for negligence, a person must conform his or her conduct to that of a reasonable person under like circumstances.

5.   To recover in an action for negligence, the plaintiff must prove some reasonable connection between the defendant's negligent conduct and the plaintiff's injury, or as is usually stated, the defendant's negligence must be the "proximate" or "legal" cause of the injury. The proximate cause requirement is actually a number of interrelated legal issues that collectively limit the defendant's liability for the consequences of his or her negligent acts.

6.   When sued on the basis of negligence, defenses based upon the plaintiff's conduct may be available to the defendant to reduce or extinguish liability to the plaintiff. Traditionally, these included contributory negligence and assumption of the risk. The contributory negligence doctrine has been supplanted in most states today by a system of comparative fault under which the negligent plaintiff is awarded damages in proportion to his fault (negligence) in causing the injury.

7.   An important area of law based upon negligence concerns premises liability, the liability of land and building owners and occupiers for injuries occurring on their property. Under the traditional common law rule, premises liability is based upon the duty owed to the person injured. Generally, the duty owed depends upon the *status* of the injured person as a (1) trespasser, (2) licensee, or (3) invitee. Some courts have abandoned this traditional tripartite classification system and instead impose liability for injuries caused by the possessor's failure to exercise reasonable care under all the circumstances.

8.   Tort liability may be imposed in the absence of both intent and negligence. Such "strict liability," or liability without fault, is imposed for certain damage caused by possessors

of animals and for damages caused by abnormally dangerous or ultrahazardous activities.

Key Terms

tort	conversion
tort-feasor	negligence
intent	reasonable person
punitive (exemplary) damages	proximate cause
battery	contributory negligence
assault	assumption of the risk
false imprisonment (false arrest)	comparative fault
defamation	trespasser
libel	licensee
slander	invitee
right to privacy	public invitee
trespass	business invitee
nuisance	turntable (attractive
public nuisance	nuisance) doctrine
private nuisance	strict liability

Questions and Problems

5.1   Tort liability, like criminal liability, may be imposed either because of the defendant's fault (intentional or negligent torts) or in the absence of fault (strict liability torts). What considerations justify imposing tort responsibility in absence of fault? Do any considerations justify a more liberal use of strict liability as a basis for liability in tort rather than criminal cases?

5.2   Sticks and Stones, an accounting firm with high employee turnover, is concerned about its potential liability for defamation. The firm requires every supervisor to maintain an individual file for each employee. If an employee quits or is terminated, the supervisor notes the reason for the employee's leaving in the file. Supervisors may add other information to the files including copies of the employee's annual evaluations. The firm has no policy concerning references for former employees. Instead, each supervisor determines whether or not to provide a reference.

(a) Discuss potential problems with the firm's policies in light of the law of defamation.

(b) Recommend changes in the firm's policies that would better protect it from liability for defamation.

5.3   Consumer advocate Ralph Nader had been a vocal critic of General Motors products for many years. Nader filed a complaint against GM alleging that it had committed invasion of his privacy by the following acts:

1. Interviewing Nader's acquaintances and "casting aspersions upon [his] political, social, . . . racial and religious views; . . . his integrity; his sexual proclivities and inclinations; and his personal habits";
2. Keeping him under surveillance;

3. Making threatening, harassing, and obnoxious telephone calls to him;
4. Tapping his telephone; and
5. Conducting a harassing investigation of him.

Assuming that Nader can prove his allegations, would GM's conduct constitute invasion of privacy? Why or why not?

5.4   Bertha inherited farmland that included an unoccupied house. Although she kept the house boarded up to discourage intruders and posted "no trespass" signs, trespassers broke into the house several times. Bertha and her husband Ed decided to set a "shotgun trap" to protect the property from the trespassers. They tied a loaded 20-gauge shotgun to a bed in the house and rigged a wire from the doorknob to the trigger so that the gun would fire when the door was opened. Marvin, who lived in a town near the farmhouse, thought the house had been abandoned and frequently collected antique bottles from the premises. Marvin returned to the farmhouse and entered the building by removing a board from a window. When he opened the bedroom door, the gun went off causing serious injury to his leg. Marvin sued Bertha and Ed for damages. In defense they alleged that they were entitled to use a spring gun to protect their property from trespassers and burglars. How should the court rule? Explain.

5.5   Distinguish trespass and private nuisance. Why aren't all private nuisance actionable in tort? What are the advantages of using both legal (money damages) and equitable (injunction) remedies in nuisance cases?

5.6   What social or public policies justify allowing recovery for negligently caused injury? Negligence liability is imposed for injuries caused by failure to conform conduct to that of a "reasonable person." Why are juries particularly adept at applying this standard? Could the judge acting alone perform it better?

5.7   Everett Company chartered a ship for two years and agreed to make monthly payments of $25,000 to Michaels, the owner of the ship. Every month Everett wired a telex message to his bank to transfer the monthly payment to Michaels. One month, the bank failed to act on Everett's instructions and did not transfer payment. Under the charter contract, Michaels could cancel the contract if Everett failed to make a monthly payment. Michaels canceled the contract. As a result Everett lost profits of about $2 million because it was unable to charter another ship. Everett sued the bank and the evidence proved that the bank had acted negligently in failing to make the payment as instructed by Everett.

(a) What injury was suffered by Everett?

(b) Was the bank's negligence the proximate cause of the injury?

(c) If so, should the bank be held liable for damages of $2 million? Explain.

5.8   In each of the following cases, determine the proximate cause of the plaintiff's injuries. From whom should the plaintiff be entitled to recover?

(a) Plaintiff was dining at the Concord Cafeteria when a man ran into the restaurant, poured gasoline on the floor, and lit a match to the gasoline. During the ensuing fire, plaintiff suffered smoke inhalation and broken bones when other patrons trampled over her while trying to escape the fire. An inspection of Concord Cafeteria revealed that there were an insufficient number of fire exits and the existing exits were not adequately marked.

(b) Joe's Liquor Store sold a fifth of tequila to Randy who was 17 years old. Randy shared the liquor with Dave and the plaintiff. Several hours later while Dave was driving his car, he made an illegal left turn and collided with another car. Dave's blood alcohol level at the time of the accident was 0.134. Plaintiff was seriously injured in the accident.

5.9 Jones works as a clerical worker at a chemical plant operated by Kelco, Inc. Although many chemicals used in the plant are dangerous, Kelco stores them in unlocked rooms accessible to all plant workers. After having a nasty argument with Henry, Jones took some sulfuric acid from a Kelco storeroom and threw the acid in Henry's face. Henry was seriously injured and sued Kelco for negligence.

(a) Assume that Henry is not an employee of Kelco and was injured when Jones came to Henry's house. Should Kelco be held liable for Henry's injuries?

(b) Assume instead that Henry is a co-worker of Jones who injured Henry at the plant. Should Kelco be held liable for Henry's injuries? Explain.

5.10 Andy was taking care of his children and cooking dinner. After placing a quiche in the oven, Andy picked up his son and walked into an adjacent room. Suddenly, the oven exploded. Andy was so startled he dropped the baby, who suffered a broken arm. His other child was hit by flying debris and began bleeding. Andy grabbed both children and rushed them to the hospital. While he was gone, the house caught fire from the explosion. The flames spread to a neighbor's house and the neighbor telephoned the fire department. En route to the fire, the truck was involved in a collision causing property damage and personal injury to two firefighters and to the driver of another automobile. Because of the delay, both houses burned to the ground before another firetruck arrived. Meanwhile, back at the hospital, while Andy's children were being treated, he began to suffer chest pains. Andy was hospitalized for a heart attack, which the doctors attributed to stress and to a preexisting heart condition.

Assume the oven was negligently designed and manufactured. Specifically, an improperly designed gas valve had caused the explosion. For which of the foregoing personal injury and property damage should the manufacturer be held liable? Explain.

5.11 Alice was seriously injured while riding a bumper car ride at Worldwide Amusement Park. The accident occurred when a bumper car being driven by Walt violently collided with a car driven by Alice. Alice sued Worldwide and Walt in a Florida court, seeking damages of $100,000. Florida imposes joint and several liability on all defendants who are liable for plaintiff's injuries. The jury found that Alice's negligence was 14 percent responsible for the accident, Worldwide's negligence was 1 percent responsible, and Walt's negligence was 85 percent responsible. The jury also found that Alice's total damages were $100,000.

(a) Assume that Florida follows the doctrine of contributory negligence. What is the total amount of damages for which the defendants may be held liable?

(b) Assume that Florida follows the doctrine of comparative fault. What is the total amount of damages for which the defendants may be held liable? Further assume that Walt is a penniless pauper and that Alice will be unable to recover any damages from him. What is the total amount of damages that she could collect from Worldwide?

(c) Since the development of the doctrine of comparative fault, most states have reconsidered whether to retain joint and several liability. Why would the doctrine of comparative fault influence joint and several liability?

5.12 Yummy Burger is a fast food restaurant located on a busy street in Los Angeles, California. Ed Munch has sued Yummy for damages resulting from gunshot wounds that he suffered at Yummy. He has alleged that Yummy was negligent for failing to provide security guards at the restaurant. Discuss whether Yummy should be held liable under each of the following situations.

(a) Ed purchased a hamburger from Yummy and returned to his car on Yummy's parking lot. An assailant pulled a gun on Ed and demanded his money. When Ed cried for help, the assailant shot him in the leg. Although several burglaries had occurred in the neighborhood during the preceding three years, only one other person had been assaulted.

(b) Ed entered the restaurant while a robbery was in progress and was shot by one of the robbers. During the preceding three years, ten armed robberies had occurred at Yummy.

5.13 Joan was walking on a public street outside a public housing project when she was accosted by a man wielding a knife. He ordered her into a nearby unlocked apartment building, where she was robbed and sexually assaulted. The New York City Housing Authority, the owner of the apartment building, had negligently failed to keep the building's security system in good repair. May the Housing Authority be held liable to Joan because its negligence facilitated commission of a crime begun on a public street? Explain.

CHAPTER 6

INTRODUCTION TO PROPERTY AND THE UNIFORM COMMERCIAL CODE

Major Topics

- the definition of property
- the nature and characteristics of property interests including the distinction between "real" and "personal" property
- an introduction to the organization and coverage of the Uniform Commercial Code

This chapter introduces two fundamental topics in business law: property and the Uniform Commercial Code (UCC). A substantial portion of business law concerns the creation, protection, transfer, and enforcement of interests in property. The UCC, the most ambitious and successful uniform state law, governs many important aspects of commercial transactions. Although the two topics are discussed in great detail throughout the text, they are introduced together at this point because both subjects are necessary prerequisites to a complete understanding of the law of contracts and sales (Chapters 7–20).

These topics are important to contract study because property principles help resolve a basic contracts issue: what law to apply to the transaction. Contract law is derived primarily from two sources: the common law and the UCC. Uniform Commercial Code contracts are limited to "transactions in goods," whereas the common law governs, among other things, contracts for the sale of land, personal service contracts, and construction contracts. Therefore, the initial determination in *every* contract case is whether the contract is governed by the common law or the UCC. Because the applicable law differs depending upon the type of property involved, the student must, *before* studying contract law, obtain a firm grasp of property in general and the specific property classified as goods. In addition, rights created by contract are themselves property, further underscoring the need for a property background.

Introduction to Property

"Property" Defined

Property is generally defined as either (1) a thing in which legal relations between persons exist, or (2) the legal relations themselves. When asked to define property, people generally mention a house, an automobile, a television set, or any other *thing* having tangible, physical existence. This definition, however, fails to account for a share of stock, a patent, a copyright, the goodwill of a business, or a person's right to another's performance of a contract. Legally speaking, these things are property, even though they have no physical existence except, perhaps, a piece of paper evidencing them.

It therefore becomes necessary to adopt the broader, and legally correct, view of property represented by the second definition. Briefly stated, **property** denotes the sum of the various legal relationships existing between identifiable persons with respect to a thing, tangible or intangible. Specifically, property concerns the relationships between the person possessing a legally protected interest in the thing, the property *owner,* and other members of society. For example, the "property" of a homeowner is not the bricks, mortar, and wood composing the physical structure, it is the extent to which the law protects the owner in his possession, transfer, use, and enjoyment of the house against appropriation, interference, or destruction by others. Thus, if the owner's neighbor carelessly damages the house, or interferes with the owner's possession, the law provides a remedy to compensate the owner for the loss. As noted in Chapter 5, this remedy is often provided by the law of torts.

In the preceding example, property exists in a tangible object (a house). Physical existence of the thing is not, however, a prerequisite to property. Assume that on June 1, a seller and a buyer enter into a contract under which the seller promises to deliver and transfer title to an automobile to the buyer on July 1, and the buyer promises to pay $2,000 to the seller on that date. The contract is the property of both the seller and the buyer. Each has the legally protected right to the other's performance of his promise. In short, all property, but not necessarily the things in which it exists, is intangible.

Property and Law

Property represents the legal relations between persons with respect to a thing. Without a system of laws designed to protect the legal relationships composing property, property would not exist. If X destroys Y's automobile, infringes upon her patent, or trespasses upon her land, the law recognizes that X has interfered with Y's property, and therefore affords Y a legal remedy. As one commentator noted,

> Property and law are born together, and die together. Before laws were made there was no property; take away laws, and property ceases.[1]

The concept of property is so firmly rooted in law that interests in property are explicitly protected by the U.S. Constitution. Specifically, the Fifth and Fourteenth Amendments provide that no person may be deprived of life, liberty, or *property* without due process of law. The Fifth Amendment further provides that the government may not take private property for a public use, such as a park or a highway, without providing just compensation to the owner.

Property therefore requires legal sanctions protecting property rights. Without such sanctions, physical possession of tangible objects, protected only by brute force, would be all that remained. Intangibles such as contracts, stocks, bonds, checks, notes, patents, and copyrights would not exist. Modern society, in which such intangibles represent an increasing percentage of total wealth, would give way to a law of the jungle.

Although property law normally confers exclusive rights in property (for example, of possession, use, and enjoyment) upon the owner, these rights are certainly not absolute. That is, the owner's rights are limited by a corresponding policy designed to protect other members of the community. For example, although a landowner may ordinarily use his property as he sees fit, local zoning ordinances or environmental protection regulations may restrict uses of the property. Similarly, the law prohibits (through principles of "nuisance") the use of property that interferes unreasonably with the right of adjoining landowners and occupiers to use their property.

In sum, property represents a set of relations, defined by law, involving both rights and limitations. As explained by one commentator, property represents a

> complex system of recognized rights and duties with reference to the control of valuable objects . . . linked with basic economic processes . . . validated by traditional beliefs, attitudes and values and sanctioned in custom and law.[2]

Nature and Characteristics of Property Interests

Property is often characterized as a bundle of sticks possessed by the owner. Collectively, this bundle of sticks is known as **ownership.** In common and legal

---

[1]Bentham, Theory of Legislation, Principles of the Civil Code Part I, 113 (Dumont ed., Hildreth trans. 1871).

[2]Hallowell, *The Nature and Function of Property as a Social Institution,* 1 J. Legal & Pol. Soc. 115 (1943).

speech the word **title** frequently is used to signify ownership. Property law is therefore the study of ownership, with property including everything recognized by law as capable of ownership.

An owner, or a number of owners, may possess one, or several, or all of the sticks representing full ownership and each owner is said to have an "interest" in the property. In addition, he or she may create new property interests in others by relinquishing (for example, by sale, will, or gift) one or more of the sticks to others. Commonly included in the bundle of sticks representing full ownership of a thing is the right

1. to possess it;
2. to exclude others from possession;
3. to use and enjoy it;
4. to be free from unreasonable interference by others with its use and enjoyment;
5. to dispose of it (for example, by sale, will, or gift);
6. to change its nature (for example, to make a cabinet out of an oak board);
7. to take its fruits (for example, crops from land or offspring from animals); and
8. to destroy it.

Possession is probably the most important stick in the bundle representing property ownership. The term has major significance in many branches of law including gifts, bailments, adverse possession, secured transactions, landlord and tenant, and original acquisition. Further, both criminal and tort law protect against interference with an owner's possession, and criminal liability is imposed for possessing certain things such as illegal drugs or stolen property. Possession generally requires a combination of two factors: 1) physical control of the thing, coupled with 2) intent to exert control. Possession additionally includes the legally protected power to exclude others from control of the thing possessed.

As previously noted, the entire bundle of sticks constituting ownership may be held by one person or may be divided in various ways that allow many people to have an interest in a given piece of property. The permissible interests existing in property may differ in duration, the extent of the interest held by the owner, the time of possession, and the number of persons concurrently holding an ownership interest. Taken collectively, the various types of interests existing in property and the rights and obligations of the parties thereto form the basis for studying property law in Chapters 34 through 39.

The Distinction Between Real and Personal Property

Though property is intangible in nature, property rules differ depending on the physical character (or lack thereof) of the thing in which the property exists. Property law recognizes a fundamental distinction between real and personal property. **Real property** generally includes:

1. land (such as unimproved real estate);
2. things permanently attached to land (such as a house, a barn, or a factory);
3. certain things affixed or annexed to land ("fixtures");
4. things growing on land in certain situations; and
5. things belonging to or incidental to land (such as an easement for a driveway across neighboring property).

In short, real property includes land, structures, objects, and other interests attached to or closely associated with it.

Personal property, on the other hand, is everything else capable of ownership. Personal property is commonly designated either tangible (when the thing in which property rights exist has a physical existence) or intangible (when the thing has no physical existence but instead represents a valuable claim against a third person or persons). Tangible personal property includes a car, a television set, a book, a dog, or any other movable object. Intangible personal property includes patents, copyrights, trademarks, royalty rights, documents of title, negotiable instruments, stocks and bonds, goodwill, accounts receivable, bank accounts, security interests, or other contract rights. The foregoing are designated intangible even though their existence may be evidenced by a document (for example, such as a share of stock or promissory note).

Since early times, the terms **choses** (things) **in possession** and **choses in action** have been used to distinguish these two types of personal property. Choses in possession refers to rights in tangible physical objects. Choses in action, on the other hand, refers to property rights which, although they may be evidenced by a piece of paper, are essentially intangible because they can ultimately be claimed or enforced only by action (a legal proceeding), not by taking physical possession.

The term "personal property" does not mean that the property must be personally or individually owned, but that the property is not real property. For example, an automobile is personal property whether it is in the hands of an individual, partnership, corporation, or governmental body. The term **chattel** is frequently used to designate an article of personal property.[3] Though the term "chattel" may designate both types of personal property, its use is ordinarily limited to tangible, movable objects.

The United States legal system is substantially derived from that of England,[4] and the real-personal property dichotomy evolved from early English common law. The distinction between movables (personal property) and immovables (real property) is, however, recognized to some extent in all legal systems.

Introduction to the Uniform Commercial Code (UCC)

The Background of the UCC

Business law is derived primarily from the common law and statutes, including a number of important "uniform state laws." As discussed in Chapter 1, the National Conference of Commissioners on Uniform State Laws periodically promulgates and promotes the passage of these uniform laws. The most ambitious and successful of the uniform state laws is the **Uniform Commercial Code** (UCC or Code).[5] Its official text, which was completed in 1962, represents a substantial and comprehensive modernization and expansion of prior uniform laws relating to commercial transactions. Amendments periodically have been made to portions of the text, and new articles were added in 1987 and 1989.

The Code's reception in the various state legislatures was overwhelming. By 1968, 49 states and the District of Columbia had enacted it. The lone holdout, Louisiana, now has adopted a significant portion of the Code.

General Organization of the UCC

The UCC is divided into 13 articles. The first 11 articles contain the substantive provisions, summarized below and discussed in detail at various points throughout the text. Articles 10 and 11 address the mechanics of enact-

ing the Code, such as effective date, repeal of conflicting statutes, and transition between repealed statutes and the Code. The 11 substantive articles are:

Article 1	General Provisions
Article 2	Sales
Article 2A	Leases
Article 3	Negotiable Instruments
Article 4	Bank Deposits and Collections
Article 4A	Funds Transfers
Article 5	Letters of Credit
Article 6	Bulk Sales
Article 7	Documents of Title
Article 8	Investment Securities
Article 9	Secured Transactions

All Articles, except 5 and 6, are divided into two or more "parts" that govern differing issues within the major subject matter area. Each part is then divided into "sections" (abbreviated §). Sections are then numbered in a manner that indicates both the Article and part from which the section is taken. For example, §2–302, entitled "Unconscionable Contract or Clause," is contained in part 3 (General Obligation and Construction of Contract) of Article 2 (Sales). Thus, the first number indicates the Article and the second number the part.

After each section, the official text of the Code includes "Official Comments" on that section. These Comments, generally prepared by the drafters, state

1. the prior uniform statute or statutes, if any, from which the section is derived;
2. the purpose of the section—here the underlying legal or factual problem is commonly stated, important prior cases or statutes are sometimes discussed, and the intent, theory, and rationale of the section is outlined and explained;
3. cross references to related Code sections and definitions.

The various state legislatures enacted into law only the text of the statute, not the Official Comments. Courts have, however, consistently attached great weight to the Official Comments in resolving Code disputes. They have proven to be valuable aids to construction, and promote uniformity of interpretation—a stated purpose of the Code.

---

[3]"Chattel" is derived from "cattle," the most common form of non-landed, personal wealth in early England.

[4]The law of the state of Louisiana is an exception because it is based upon the French Civil Law.

[5]The UCC was jointly sponsored by the National Conference and the American Law Institute.

Introduction to Specific Articles

The following material provides an overview of the scope and coverage of the UCC's 11 substantive Articles.

Article 1—General Provisions. Article 1, amended in 2001 and entitled "General Provisions," contains various general principles, rules of construction, and definitions applicable to the remainder of the Code.

Section 1–103(a) initially states that the UCC is to be "liberally construed and applied to promote its underlying purposes and policies." Those purposes and policies are

1. to simplify, clarify and modernize the law governing commercial transactions;
2. to permit the continued expansion of commercial practices through custom, usage and agreement of the parties; and
3. to make uniform the law among the various jurisdictions.

Thus, the Code initially exhorts the judiciary, which must interpret and apply it, to give the UCC a liberal construction allowing it to develop to cover possibly unforeseen circumstances, to resolve situations not explicitly covered, or to create new remedies.

Variation by Agreement. Although the UCC resolves a substantial number of legal issues, its provisions are not mandatory. That is, freedom of contract is a basic principle of the Code embodied in §1–302 that provides:

> Except as otherwise provided . . . , the effect of provisions of the Uniform Commercial Code may be varied by agreement.

In other words, Code provisions often are referred to as "default" rules or "gap-fillers." That is, the Code provides a rule to resolve a litigated dispute between the parties if and only if they have failed previously to agree to a contrary rule by contract.

Applicability of Supplementary Principles of Law. The UCC is not a comprehensive and exhaustive treatment of the entire commercial law area. It does not govern transfers of, or security interests in, real property. It does not govern bankruptcy or suretyship. It is inapplicable to many types of commercial contracts (such as insurance, employment, or construction contracts), and does not address all issues presented by the contracts it does govern. Section 1–103(b), therefore, provides that the substantial body of law existing both before and outside the Code must therefore be used to supplement its provisions. In other words, the Code supersedes prior legal principles only to the extent it explicitly covers a specific area or issue. Situations not covered by the UCC are resolved by reference to relevant pre-Code or non-Code law.

Commercial law therefore is governed primarily by the UCC, supplemented by a variety of common law principles (drawn primarily from the law of contracts, agency, and property) and statutes (such as the Bankruptcy Code). In addition, Code provisions may be supplemented by the "law merchant," a system of rules, customs, or usages generally recognized and adopted by merchants, which either alone or as modified by common law or statute, regulate commercial transactions and the resolution of controversies.[6] Thus, custom and trade usage also may supplement Code provisions. Of course, because the parties are generally free to alter the effect of Code provisions, much commercial law is based on private agreement, not mandated by either the Code or supplementary legal principles.

Obligation of Good Faith. Another important principle underlying the entire Code is the obligation of good faith, a fundamental principle running through law generally. The UCC makes the obligation explicit in §1–304, which states:

> Every contract or duty within the Uniform Commercial Code imposes an obligation of good faith in its performance and enforcement.

The term **good faith** is defined in §1–201(20) as "honesty in fact and the observance of reasonable commercial standards of fair dealing."

Good faith therefore generally is governed by both a "subjective" and an "objective" standard. That is, the law inquires into subjective honesty—whether the person whose good faith is questioned was in fact (in his or her own mind) dealing honestly with the other party to

---

[6] BLACK'S LAW DICTIONARY 886, 986 (6th ed. 1990).

the transaction. It then compares the actor's conduct to an objective standard—reasonable commercial standards of fair dealing in the trade. Under either test, good faith "emphasizes faithfulness to an agreed common purpose and consistency with the justified expectations of the other party; it excludes a variety of types of conduct characterized as involving 'bad faith' because they violate community standards of decency, fairness, and reasonableness."[7]

General Definitions. Section 1–201, which defines 43 terms, is the general definitional section for the entire UCC. In addition, each of the remaining Articles includes one or more sections defining terms specifically applicable to that Article. The terms defined in §1–201 and other definitional sections are explained throughout the remainder of this text as needed for an understanding of the underlying discussion. Access to a particular term can be obtained by using the index or the glossary.

Code provisions frequently require that actions, such as delivery or notice, be taken within a "reasonable time." Under §1–205, what constitutes a reasonable time is a question of fact dependent upon the nature, purpose, and circumstance of the action, including custom or trade usage and prior conduct of the parties. Thus, because the determination depends upon the facts of the individual case, no precise period can generally be fixed as reasonable. The UCC also commonly requires an action to be taken "seasonably." This term means that the required act must be taken at or within the time called for by the contract, or if no time is agreed on, then at or within a reasonable time.

Article 2—Sales. Article 2 of the UCC, entitled "Sales," governs contracts for the sale of "goods." Article 2 occupies a central position in the study of business law. Its provisions form much of the basis of Part II of this text (Contracts) and virtually all of Part III (Sales). Article 2 was revised in 2003, but the revised version has not been widely adopted.

Article 2A—Leases. In 1987, the National Conference and American Law Institute added Article 2A, entitled "Leases," to the Uniform Commercial Code. Article 2A governs personal property leasing (for example, a lease

by a business of its trucks or manufacturing equipment) and is designed to fill the gap between Article 2, which focuses primarily on sales, rather than lease, transactions involving personal property, and Article 9, which governs only those leases intended for security. Article 2A, which was amended in 1990, is discussed in more detail in Chapter 16.

Article 3—Negotiable Instruments. Article 3, entitled "Negotiable Instruments," governs specialized commercial instruments payable in money, including drafts, checks, certificates of deposit, and promissory notes. The issues addressed include the creation and transfer of such instruments and the rights and liability of various parties thereto. Article 3 is based on the concept of "negotiability," which is designed to enhance the marketability and promote free transferability of the paper. Article 3, which was amended in 1990, is treated in detail in Part IV of this text.

Article 4—Bank Deposits and Collections. Article 4, entitled "Bank Deposits and Collections," contains the principal rules of the bank collection process. Ordinarily, a holder of a check deposits it in an account in his own bank. This bank (the "depositary" bank) must then undertake to collect the check from the bank on which it is drawn (known as the "drawee" or "payor" bank) through one or a series of "intermediary" banks.

Issues covered by Article 4 include the bank collection process in general, and the rights, duties, and liabilities of a checking account depositor and her bank arising from payment or nonpayment of checks. Included in this latter category are rules governing wrongful dishonor, overdrafts, stale checks, death or incompetence of the depositor, stop payment orders, attachment and other legal process, and forgery and alteration. Article 4, which was amended in 1990, is discussed in Chapter 27.

Article 4A—Funds Transfers. Checks, credit cards, and consumer electronic fund transfers provide alternative methods for paying debts through the banking system. Another method is the wholesale wire transfer used primarily by businesses and financial institutions to transfer large sums of money. To provide a comprehensive body of law to govern such transfers, Article 4A, entitled "Funds Transfers," was added to the UCC in 1989. Article 4A is discussed in Chapter 27.

---

[7]RESTATEMENT (SECOND) OF CONTRACTS §205 comment a.

Article 5—Letters of Credit. A letter of credit is a financing, payment, and security device used in many forms in a variety of transactions. Letters of credit were originally developed and are still primarily used to finance international sales transactions between buyers and sellers not commercially acquainted with each other. In this context, the letter of credit assures payment for a sale of goods or other obligation, while providing some assurance that the obligation for which payment is requested has been performed. The letter of credit achieves this result by substituting the credit of financial institutions, such as banks, for the credit of the parties to the contract (such as a buyer and seller in a contract for the sale of goods).

Article 5, which was revised in 1995, provides a system of rules governing the complicated letter of credit field. Since its enactment, the use of letters of credit has burgeoned throughout the country to include a significant number of both domestic and international applications. Letters of credit are explained in more detail in Chapter 35.

Article 6—Bulk Transfers; Bulk Sales. Article 6, originally entitled "Bulk Transfers," is designed to protect creditors of a merchant who sells his entire stock in trade out of the ordinary course of business (the "bulk transfer") to an innocent purchaser, pockets the proceeds, and then disappears, leaving his creditors unpaid. Article 6 provides that such a transfer in bulk is ineffective against creditors of the seller unless they are notified of the sale in advance. Once notified, the creditors can then take steps to protect themselves prior to consummation of the sale.

Article 6 has long been criticized for being poorly drafted and insufficiently specific. In addition, many commentators believe that technological improvements in credit reporting services and communications, and modern debt collection law, have reduced the need for bulk sales legislation. For these reasons, the Code drafters recommended in 1988 that states either repeal Article 6 or adopt a substantially revised version, entitled "Bulk Sales." The operation of Article 6 and its 1988 revision are covered in more detail in Chapter 29.

Article 7—Documents of Title. Article 7 is concerned with an important part of many sales transactions: the shipment or storage of goods. Although these functions may be performed by the parties, more commonly professionals such as common carriers or commercial warehouses perform them. The instruments issued by these specialists upon receipt of goods for shipment or storage ("documents of title") governed by Article 7 simultaneously serve three functions:

1. they act as the receipt for the goods delivered to the carrier or warehouse;
2. they contain the terms of the contract of carriage or storage between the owner and the professional; and
3. in the case of "negotiable" documents, they are a symbol standing in place of the goods, allowing a transfer of the goods simply by transferring the document.

The most common documents of title are the bill of lading (issued by carrier in exchange for goods shipped) and the warehouse receipt (issued by a warehouse in exchange for goods stored). The rules of Article 7 are similar in many respects to those stated in Article 3, Negotiable Instruments. The fundamental difference is that whereas Article 3 instruments, primarily notes and checks, are payable in money, Article 7 paper is payable in goods. Article 7 is discussed in more detail in Chapter 35.

Article 8—Investment Securities. Article 8 governs the rights and duties of persons dealing with "investment securities." Although the stocks and bonds commonly traded on securities exchanges or in the "over the counter" market are the most common type of investment security, Article 8 also covers anything else that securities markets regard as suitable for trading. Article 8 determines the relative rights in investment paper of issuers, owners, purchasers, and creditors regarding transfer of the paper, notice of claims to it, registration of interests, and other issues. It therefore serves the same purpose for investment securities that Article 3 serves for promissory notes, drafts, checks, and certificates of deposit, and that Article 7 serves for documents of title. Note that Article 8 is concerned with rights in the security itself, and is not designed to prevent fraud or require disclosure in securities trading; that is the function of federal and state "securities regulation" statutes, discussed in detail in Chapter 49. Article 8, which was revised in 1994, is discussed in Chapter 46.

Article 9—Secured Transactions. A secured creditor enjoys a favored position upon default by a debtor, enjoying a preferred claim against specific assets of the debtor. Upon default, a secured creditor may proceed without judgment against those assets and apply them to the unpaid debt to the exclusion of other creditors. Article 9 governs all *consensual security interests in personal property* and fixtures; and all sales of accounts and chattel paper (basically a secured account receivable). Prior to the adoption of Article 9, security interests in personal property were governed by a fragmented, nonuniform assortment of devices including chattel mortgages, pledges, conditional sales contracts, factor's liens, trust receipts, and assignments of accounts receivable. Article 9 replaces these devices with a comprehensive scheme governing the creation, perfection, and foreclosure of security interests in personal property that applies without regard to the type or form of security device used by the parties. Article 9 as amended in 2000 is discussed in Chapters 31–32 as part of the coverage of debtor-creditor relations. The scope and coverage of the Code's 11 substantive articles are summarized in Table 6.1.

Table 6.1	Summary of the Coverage of the Uniform Commercial Code
Article	**Coverage**
Article 1 **General Provisions**	General principles, rules of construction, and definitions applicable to the rest of the Code.
Article 2 **Sales**	Contracts for the sale of goods.
Article 2A **Leases**	Leases of goods.
Article 3 **Negotiable Instruments**	Negotiable instruments payable in money, primarily promissory notes and checks.
Article 4 **Bank Deposits** **and Collections**	Bank collection process and the legal relationship between a bank and its checking account customer.
Article 4A **Funds Transfers**	Wholesale wire transfers.
Article 5 **Letters of Credit**	Rights and obligations of parties to a letter of credit, a financing device used primarily in international trade.
Article 6 **Bulk Sales**	Protection for creditors of a merchant who sells his entire stock in trade not in the ordinary course of business.
Article 7 **Documents of Title**	Rights and duties of parties to documents of title issued in exchange for the carriage or storage of goods.
Article 8 **Investment Securities**	Rules for transfer of stocks, bonds, and other securities traded on exchanges or in other organized markets.
Article 9 **Secured Transactions**	Security interests in personal property created by agreement of the parties and all sales of accounts, chattel paper, payment intangibles, and promissory notes.

Summary

1.   Property is defined as the sum of legal relations between persons with respect to a thing. The owner of a property interest is protected by law against interference with or destruction of that interest by others. Property is commonly classified as real or personal. Real property includes land, and structures, objects, and other interests closely associated with it. Personal property, on the other hand, includes everything else capable of ownership. Personal property is often classified as tangible (a chose in possession, good, or chattel) or intangible (a chose in action).

2.   The Uniform Commercial Code is a widely enacted state statute governing many aspects of commercial transactions in 11 substantive articles. Article 2 of the Code explicitly governs contracts for the sale of goods and is therefore integral to the study of contract law generally. Article 2A governs the burgeoning personal property leasing field. The Code also is the source of law governing many types of documents commonly used in business transactions including notes, checks, bills of lading, warehouse receipts, stocks, bonds, and letters of credit. Article 4A governs wholesale wire transfers. The Code also addresses two issues regarding debtor-creditor relations. First, its bulk transfer provisions are designed to protect a merchant's creditors when the merchant sells its entire inventory in bulk to a third party. Second, Article 9 of the UCC provides a comprehensive framework governing all consensually created security interests in personal property.

3.   The UCC is neither mandatory nor comprehensive in its coverage. Generally, the parties are free to alter the effect of Code provisions by agreement. Further, the Code, to the extent it does not address a specific issue, is liberally supplemented by legal principles existing outside the UCC.

Key Terms

property	choses in possession
ownership	choses in action
title	chattel
possession	Uniform Commercial Code
real property	good faith
personal property	

Questions and Problems

6.1   Harry recently purchased a new house and three acres of adjacent land. In discussing the purchase with a friend Harry states, "It feels so good to own this property. I am king of the roost and nobody can tell me what I can or cannot do with my property." The friend replies, "You are wrong, Harry; property rights are not absolute." Who is right? Explain.

6.2   Review the definition of property and the bundle of rights constituting property. Are stolen goods property in the hands of the thief? Of anyone? Are illegal drugs, such as heroin or cocaine, property? Are human beings property?

6.3   Al, who is dining at the Corner Cafe, checks his coat at the restaurant's hatcheck room. Jesse, after robbing the First National Bank, runs into the Corner Cafe and stashes the money in Al's coat. After conducting a search of the restaurant, the police discover the money in Al's coat and find Jesse hiding near the check room. Possession of stolen goods is a crime. Jesse, however, asserts that the stolen goods are not located on his person. The restaurant owner states that he does not have the goods—they are in Al's coat. Al protests that he was not even aware of the stolen goods. Which, if any, of the above parties is liable for possession of stolen goods? Explain.

6.4   Under a trust, Joe Butler was "beneficial owner" of a ranch in South Dakota. As beneficial owner, Butler owned all personal property rights in the land but the trustee owned all real property rights. A scientist discovered a dinosaur skeleton embedded in the land on the ranch. In exchange for $5,000, Butler sold the dinosaur to the scientist who then excavated and moved ten tons of bones to a nearby laboratory to restore the fossil. After learning that the dinosaur was one of the most valuable fossils ever discovered, the trustee claimed ownership. The trustee argued that the dinosaur had become part of the land and, therefore, was real property. The scientist argued that the dinosaur was personal property that Butler was authorized to sell. Who owns the dinosaur?

6.5   UCC §1–302 provides that most UCC provisions may be varied by agreement of the parties to a contract. Why was §1–302 included in the Code? Does it not defeat the Code purpose of making commercial law uniform nationwide?

6.6.   Professors James J. White and Robert S. Summers have noted that §1-103(b) "is probably the most important single provision in the Code." (WHITE & SUMMERS, UNIFORM COMMERCIAL CODE 6 (3d ed. 1988)) What basis might they offer to support this assertion?

CONTRACTS

INTRODUCTION TO CONTRACTS

No aspect of modern life is free from contractual relationships. The ordinary consumer who buys a house, purchases a television or other good, borrows money, leases an apartment, rents a car, or insures his or her property or life, acquires rights and obligations based on contract. Businesspeople purchasing raw materials or equipment, building a plant or retail store, selling goods or services to customers, borrowing money, selling stocks or bonds, or insuring their property are involved in contracts. Contract law provides the certainty, stability, and predictability required for the smooth and efficient performance of these and many other essential transactions.

The Law of Contracts

In its most general sense, the law of contracts concerns the legal effect of promise-making, determining when performance of a promise is legally required, and governing the relationship between parties to a contractual promise. Promises and their legal consequences are therefore the basis of contract study.

That certain promises are legally binding is fundamental to modern society. As eloquently stated by the noted legal scholar Roscoe Pound:

> In a developed economic order the claim to promised advantages is one of the most important of the individual interests that press for recognition. . . . Credit is a principal form of wealth. It is a presupposition of the whole economic order that promises will be kept. Indeed, the matter goes deeper. The social order rests upon the stability and predictability of conduct, of which keeping promises is a large item.[1]

In other words, the basic premise of contract law, expressed in the Latin phrase *pacta sunt servanda* (agreements shall be kept), reflects a more fundamental premise of human conduct generally.

The policy favoring performance of promises is supported on many theoretical grounds. Historically, giving a promise or concluding an agreement constituted a solemn commitment, based upon religious, moral, or

---

[1]3 POUND, JURISPRUDENCE 162 (1959).

127

ethical grounds, to perform. This "sanctity of contract" approach is bolstered by the law's general recognition of private autonomy in contract matters. Under the principle of "freedom of contract," the law allows individuals to regulate their own affairs by private agreement by recognizing the promises embodied in the agreement as legally binding. Yet another approach supports enforcement of contracts on grounds that a promise, once made, induces others to rely upon it, creating an expectation of performance. Finally, and perhaps most important, promises are enforced because the needs of modern business and society generally require recognition of binding promises. Because all of the foregoing considerations—personal responsibility or morality, individual autonomy, fairness, and economic efficiency—support enforcement of promises, it is no surprise that contract principles are among the most firmly rooted in law.

Although the law generally allows individuals to order their conduct by private agreement, "freedom of contract" is certainly not absolute. Increasingly in recent years, the law has imposed limitations upon private contract to prevent abuse in the bargaining process and enforcement of agreements that are illegal or otherwise contrary to public policy. These various limitations are discussed extensively throughout the contracts material.

Contract law is the basic framework of all commercial law. Therefore, although contracts are discussed here as a separate and distinct topic, many later topics are merely refined applications of contract principles. For example, rights and duties in property, negotiable instruments, agency, partnership, corporations, suretyship, secured transactions, and insurance frequently are determined on the basis of contractual relationships. Even when a transaction is governed by statute—such as the Uniform Commercial Code or the Uniform Partnership Act—the statutory rules may, in many cases, be changed by a contract between the parties.

Promise and Contract

Promise Defined. In legal terms, a **promise** is simply a commitment or undertaking that something will or will not happen in the future. The person making the promise is the **promisor,** and the person to whom the promise is made is the **promisee.** For example, if Sam promises to sell goods to Betty and to deliver them in 30 days, Sam is the promisor and Betty the promisee. Sam indicates that something *will* happen in the future; goods will be delivered. Alternatively, the promisor can indicate that something will *not* happen in the future. Suppose, for example, that Sam, in exchange for an agreed sum of money, indicates that he *will not* file a lawsuit against Betty. The definition of a promise includes both types of commitments.

Contract Defined. People make promises all the time: to show up on a date, to pay back a loan, to obey certain rules. Contract law is concerned with a special class of promises, for a **contract** is "a promise or a set of promises for the breach of which the law gives a remedy, or the performance of which the law in some way recognizes as a duty."[2] Thus, not all promises are contracts. What distinguishes contractual from noncontractual promises are the consequences of failure to perform. A promisor who fails to perform a noncontractual promise incurs no legal liability. If, however, a promise is contractual, the promisee is generally entitled to a contract remedy in the event of the promisor's nonperformance or *breach.* The most common remedy available for breach of contract is an award of dollar damages. If, in the opinion of the court, money is an inadequate remedy, the court may force the promisor actually to *perform* the breached promise—a remedy known as *specific performance.*

For example, assume a seller and buyer enter into a contract on March 1 for the sale of 500 fountain pens for $2,000. Delivery of the pens and payment of the price are to occur on June 1. If the seller fails to deliver on June 1, the buyer is entitled to a contract remedy—dollar damages, or, in an appropriate case, specific performance, which would require actual delivery of the 500 pens for $2,000.

Joint and Several Promises. An indefinite number of people may contract with one another. Promises may be made by or to individuals or groups acting together. If there is more than one promisor in a contract, some or all of them may promise the same performance. Rights and duties created by multiple promises of the same performance are commonly stated to be "joint," "several," or "joint and several." If two or more persons are **jointly liable** on a contract, each promisor undertakes the duty to render the same performance. In joint liability, all copromisors are liable for the entire perfor-

---

[2]RESTATEMENT (SECOND) OF CONTRACTS §1.

mance, even though one or more others are also liable to perform the same duty. A joint promisor is therefore effectively liable for the performance of each one of his copromisors.

Liability of copromisors is several if (1) each promises a separate performance to be rendered respectively by each of them, or (2) each makes a separate promise that the same performance will be rendered. Therefore, the term **severally liable** means that each party is liable alone or individually. Because several liability is separate and distinct, a lawsuit to enforce the contract may be brought against each several promisor independently, without joining other copromisors. For example, if Albert and Bob each promise to pay Charles $500, making a total of $1,000, their promises are several. If Albert and Bob together promise to pay Charles a total of $1,000, each to be fully responsible for the entire debt, their promises are joint.

Promises made by two or more parties can be both **joint and several** if the promisors bind themselves jointly as one party and also severally as separate parties. For example, if Albert and Bob both together and individually promise to pay Charles $1,000, their liability is joint and several. Thus, in a joint and several contract, there is one more contract (the joint contract) than there are promisors. Whether liability is joint, several, or joint and several is dependent upon the parties' intent, determined from the language used.[3]

Enforceable and Unenforceable Contracts

Contract law makes promises legally **enforceable.** A contract is legally enforceable if the promisee is entitled to a contract remedy if the promisor fails to perform. Generally speaking, a promise is enforceable as a contract if it meets two fundamental requirements:

1. *Agreement*—An enforceable contract requires an agreement or bargain between the parties. An agreement generally is created when an offer made by one party is accepted by the other.
2. *Consideration*—A promise must generally be supported by consideration to be enforceable as a contract. Consideration refers to a promise or a performance that is bargained for and given in exchange for the promise.

Taken collectively, offer, acceptance, and consideration form a conceptual unit commonly known as "contract formation." Contract formation is discussed in Chapters 8 and 9.

The existence of an agreement supported by consideration does not necessarily guarantee the enforceability of the promises contained therein. One or more formation "defects" may be present. These "defects" are generally divided into four categories: (1) lack of contractual capacity of one or both parties, (2) lack of genuine assent to the bargain due to factors such as fraud, misrepresentation, mistake, duress, or undue influence, (3) a contractual purpose that is illegal or otherwise contrary to public policy, or (4) lack of proper formality when legal formalities are required. These defects render contractual promises either *unenforceable* or *voidable.*

If a contract is **unenforceable** no contract remedy (either damages or specific performance) is available for its breach. A contract may be unenforceable, for example, because its performance would be illegal or otherwise contrary to public policy, or because it does not comply with the Statute of Frauds that requires that certain types of contracts (for example, a land-sale contract) be evidenced by a writing. Therefore, an *oral* agreement to sell land is unenforceable: A court will not award a contract remedy to either the seller or buyer if the other fails to perform.

Void and Voidable Contracts

Literally, a **void promise** or contract is one that is totally without legal force or effect. The term is, however, often used imprecisely, often simply referring to an unenforceable promise. To avoid confusion, therefore, "void" should be used to designate only those promises having no legal force or binding effect. That is, a promise is void when it lacks one of the elements of contract formation—agreement and consideration. For example, a promise to make a gift in the future is void because it is not supported by consideration.

A void contract must also be carefully distinguished from a **voidable** contract. A voidable contract is one in which one or more parties have the power, by electing to do so, to avoid the legal relations created by the contract. Avoidance of a voidable contract is commonly

---

[3]The joint liability concept appears at various other points throughout the text including multiple tort-feasors (see Chapter 5), cosuretyship (see Chapter 33), the liability of partners for tort, breach of trust, and contract (see Chapter 43), and the liability of two or more persons signing a negotiable instrument (see Chapter 25).

designated "disaffirmance." A voidable contract is perfectly binding and enforceable unless and until the party with the power to disaffirm elects to do so. That is, a person with a power to avoid a contract may choose instead to be bound. Such a **ratification** extinguishes that person's power of avoidance and makes the contract enforceable against her. Conversely, disaffirmance discharges the contractual duty and terminates the power of ratification. This power of ratification distinguishes a voidable from an unenforceable contract.

In most voidable contracts, only one party possesses the power to avoid, meaning that one party is bound and the other may elect whether or not to be bound. Voidable contracts of this type include those in which one party is a minor and contracts procured through fraud, misrepresentation, mistake, or duress. Assume that Michael, a minor, contracts to sell land to Anne, an adult, for $25,000. The contract is perfectly binding upon Anne if Michael wishes to enforce it. However, Michael's promise is voidable because he is a minor; that is, Michael has the power to extinguish his own right to the money and Anne's duty to pay it, and may avoid his obligation to convey the property. Although the ability to avoid usually is confined to one party, occasionally the contract may be voidable by either. Examples include contracts formed under a mutual mistake or in which both parties are minors.

Types of Contracts

Formal and Informal Contracts

Most contracts discussed in this part of the text are **informal** or **simple** contracts. If the basic elements of an enforceable contract are present, the promises involved are binding. With few exceptions,[4] no particular formalities need be observed.

On the other hand, certain contracts are governed by special rules that result from the contract's formal characteristics. The rules governing these **formal** contracts often differ from those applicable to contracts in general. Three types of formal contracts are the contract under seal, the recognizance, and the negotiable contract.

Contracts Under Seal. Since medieval times, the law has enforced promises under seal. Such promises generally lack consideration, basic to an enforceable informal contract, but are enforced because of the formality of their creation. Generally those formalities are a writing, a seal (historically, a wax seal with an impression upon it affixed to the paper), and delivery of the writing to the promisee. In many states the legal effect of the seal has been modified or abolished by statute.

Recognizance. Recognizance involves a promise in court by the promisor (recognizor) to make a certain payment unless a specified event occurs. Recognizances are used primarily to secure the recognizor's appearance in court or payment of bail.

Negotiable Contracts. Although the promise under seal and recognizance have little commercial utility, negotiable contracts are pervasive and fundamental in business. Negotiable contracts are of three types: (1) negotiable instruments (for example, notes and checks), (2) documents of title (for example, bills of lading and warehouse receipts), and (3) investment securities (for example, stocks and bonds). These contracts are governed by Articles 3, 7, and 8, respectively, of the Uniform Commercial Code.[5]

Unilateral and Bilateral Contracts

A contractual obligation, as noted above, results from a "promise or a set of promises." Thus, a contract may involve: (1) a single promise made from a promisor to a promisee, (2) a mutual exchange of promises by two persons, or (3) any other combination of persons and promises. At least two parties are essential to a contract, but there may be an indefinitely greater number of promisors and promisees.

A contract containing only one promise is said to be **unilateral** ("one-sided"). That is, a unilateral contract involves a promise in exchange for performance of an act. For example, assume Art loses his antique gold watch and places a newspaper advertisement promising to pay a $100 reward for its return. Betty finds and returns the watch to Art. Art's promise to pay a $100 reward is binding as a contract. In this case, only Art

---

[4]An exception to this rule exists for contracts subject to the "Statute of Frauds," which requires that some contracts be evidenced by a writing. The Statute of Frauds is discussed in Chapter 12.

[5]Negotiable instruments are the subject of Part IV. Documents of title are discussed in Chapter 35 and investment securities are discussed in Chapter 46. The general scope of the various UCC articles is discussed in Chapter 6.

makes a promise; Betty never promises to return the watch. Unilateral contracts therefore result when only one of the parties makes a promise.

In contrast, most contracts are **bilateral** ("two-sided"), involving at least two promises in which each party is both simultaneously a promisor and a promisee. Bilateral contracts, therefore, involve a promise in exchange for a return promise. For example, assume Seller and Buyer have a contract for the sale of an automobile. Seller promises to deliver and transfer title to a 1955 Chevrolet on June 1. In exchange, Buyer promises to pay $5,000 on that date. Seller is both a promisor (of the promise to deliver and transfer title to the car) and a promisee (of Buyer's promise to pay $5,000). Conversely, Buyer is a promisor (of the promise to pay $5,000) and a promise (of Seller's promise to deliver and transfer title to the car). Bilateral contracts result from a mutual exchange of promises. Figure 7.1 summarizes the differences between unilateral and bilateral contracts.

The unilateral-bilateral distinction is important in understanding the manner in which an offer to contract may be accepted, a topic discussed in Chapter 8.

Express and Implied Contracts

Express Contracts or Terms. Contracts often are characterized as either express or implied. A contract is **express** if it arises from the language, either oral or written, of the parties. Assume S states to B, "I offer to sell you my motorcycle for $1,500," and B responds, "I accept." In this case the promises involved are express.

Contracts or Terms Implied in Fact. A promise also may be inferred from conduct other than language. In this case, the contract is said to be **implied in fact.**[6] Suppose A brings his television to B's shop for repair. A informs B of the problem and requests that he fix it. B agrees. Even though the parties are silent on the point, a promise by A to pay the cost of the repair would be inferred. Thus, a contract implied in fact is an actual contract. The intent of the parties is ascertained and enforced by the court based upon the actions of the parties, not upon their oral or written statements.

Contract Terms Supplied by Law. In addition to those arising expressly or by inference from conduct, contract terms also may be supplied by the common law. For example, contract law generally imposes a duty of good faith and fair dealing upon the parties. Thus, a duty to act in good faith is an implied term in all contracts. Statutes also are a fertile source of implied contract terms. Certain statutes and administrative regulations, for example, prescribe standard forms for contracts such as insurance policies and bills of lading. In addition, in contracts involving goods, the Uniform Commercial Code often supplies a contract term if the parties fail to address a particular matter in their express agreement. Assume Seller agrees to sell and Buyer to buy 100 dishwashers. No other express terms are included. Article 2 of the UCC (Sales) supplies a myriad of additional "gap filling" terms including price, time, place, and manner of delivery, warranties, passage of title and risk of loss, and remedies.

Contracts Implied in Law. In contrast to the contract implied in fact, a contract also may be "implied in law." Such a **quasi-contract** is not really a contract at all, but a form of the remedy of restitution discussed in detail in Chapter 15. Quasi-contract is designed to provide a remedy when a benefit is conferred by one party upon another, who retains the benefit. If necessary to prevent unjust enrichment of the benefited party, the law implies or imposes a promise (the quasi-contract) to pay the reasonable value of the benefit conferred. To illustrate, assume Wilson owes Carr $100. Wilson pays Carr by check but inadvertently makes it payable for $1,000.

---

[6]More accurately, "inferred from fact."

Figure 7.1 — Unilateral and Bilateral Contracts

Unilateral Contract

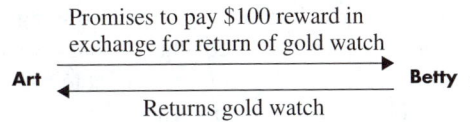

Bilateral Contract

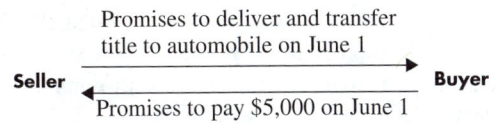

To prevent a windfall to Carr, the court may imply a promise by Carr (the quasi-contract) to pay $900 to Wilson.

The following case illustrates the distinction between express and implied contracts.

Eaton v. Engelcke Manufacturing, Inc.
681 P.2d 1312 (Wash. App. 1984)

The defendant Engelcke Manufacturing, Inc. asked its employee, plaintiff John Eaton, whether he could design an electronic schematic for "Whizball," an electronic game that Engelcke planned to design and manufacture. After Eaton stated that he estimated he could design the game in three months at a cost of $1,200 to $1,500, Engelcke asked him to proceed and told him the compensation would be determined when the project was complete. As Eaton worked on the design, Engelcke made several changes necessitating redesign of the electronics and circuitry. During the course of the project, Eaton and Engelcke had numerous conversations concerning additional compensation because of the increased length and complexity and Engelcke repeatedly assured Eaton that he would be paid for the work. After Eaton had worked on the project for 11 months during his off-duty hours and the schematic was 90 percent complete, Engelcke terminated Eaton's employment and refused to pay him for the design project.

Eaton sued Engelcke for breach of contract and the trial court awarded him damages of $5,415. On appeal, Engelcke argued that it had entered into an express contract with Eaton for production of a completed schematic design and, because Eaton had not produced the design, Engelcke owed him nothing.

Ringold, Judge

. . . The various contentions concerning liability and damages may be resolved by a careful definition of the terms involved. An express contract is one where the intentions of the parties and the terms of the agreement are expressed by the parties in writing or orally at the time it is entered into. . . . The law recognizes two classes of implied contracts: those implied in fact and those implied in law. . . . A contract implied in fact

is an agreement depending for its existence on some act or conduct of the party sought to be charged and arising by implication from circumstances which, according to common understanding, show a mutual intention on the part of the parties to contract with each other. The services must be rendered under such circumstances as to indicate that the person rendering them expected to be paid therefor, and that the recipient expected, or should have expected, to pay for them.

Johnson v. Nasi [309 P.2d 380 (Wash. 1957)]. A true implied contract, or contract implied in fact, does not describe a legal relationship which differs from an express contract: only the mode of proof is different. . . . A contract implied in law, or "quasi contract," on the other hand, arises from an implied duty of the parties not based on a contract, or on any consent or agreement. Recovery is quasi contract and is based on the prevention of unjust enrichment. . . .

With these definitions in mind, we turn to the specific contentions raised by Engelcke. Its arguments against liability are premised upon the claim that the parties had an express oral contract.

The burden of proving an express contract is on the party asserting it, who must prove that the parties expressly agreed to each essential fact, including the price, time and manner of performance. . . . The trial court's findings indicate that the parties did not expressly agree to these elements. These unchallenged findings are verities on appeal, . . . and support the conclusion that the parties did not have an express contract for the design of the schematic.

In other unchallenged findings, the court found that Eaton's services in designing the prototype were rendered at Engelcke's request. The findings demonstrate that the services were "rendered under such circumstances as to indicate that the person rendering them expected to be paid therefor, and that the recipient expected, or should have expected, to pay for them." *Johnson v. Nasi, supra.* . . . These findings, in turn, support the court's legal conclusion that the parties had an enforceable implied in fact contract to pay Eaton the reasonable value of the services rendered. . . .

Engelcke also challenges Eaton's recovery on the ground that Engelcke received nothing of value from Eaton. This argument mistakenly assumes that the court held Engelcke liable in quasi contract and awarded damages so as to prevent Engelcke's unjust enrichment. . . . As previously indicated, Engelcke's liability was based on an implied in fact contract. The proper measure of recovery is not the benefit obtained but the reasonable value of the services rendered. . . . Eaton presented expert testimony that the reasonable value of his services was $7800. The court's award of $5415 is within the range of evidence presented at trial and will not be disturbed on appeal. . . .

[Judgment affirmed.]

Executed and Executory Contracts

As defined above, a contract consists of a legally enforceable promise or set of promises. Yet, contracting parties ordinarily do not bargain merely for promises; they seek *performance* of those promises. Thus, the ordinary contract involves an exchange of promises followed on a later date by an exchange of performances. To indicate a contract's stage of performance, the law uses the terms executory and executed.

A promise or contract is **executed** if it has been completed or performed and **executory** if it is yet to be performed. At any given time a contract may be partially executed and partially executory. Assume that on December 1, Seller contracts to sell goods to Buyer for $500. Delivery is to be made on January 1 with payment to follow on January 30. On December 1, the contract is wholly executory, yet to be performed on both sides. As of the date of delivery, the contract is partially executed (the goods have been delivered) and partially executory (the purchase price is yet to be paid). Once the money is paid, the contract is wholly executed.

If a contract is fully performed as agreed, the contractual duties are said to be discharged. To **discharge** a contractual obligation is to extinguish or terminate it. As a noun, the term discharge is sometimes used to designate the act, event, or instrument terminating the binding force of the contract. Most commonly, contractual duties are discharged by full performance by both parties. Contractual obligations may, however, be discharged prior to full performance (that is, while the contract is wholly or partially executory). A party's duty may be discharged, for example, through impracticability of performance, a mutual agreement to rescind the contract, a substitute or compromise contract, or the other party's breach. The various circumstances under which enforceable contract duties are discharged are discussed throughout the contracts chapters, most notably in the material on performance of contracts.

Scope and Organization of Contract Study

The Chronology of a Contract

Contract issues occur along a time continuum from preliminary negotiations through contract formation to performance. In the preliminary negotiation stage, the parties communicate, sometimes extensively, about the subject matter of the proposed contract. Possible contract terms are suggested and accepted, rejected, or modified. Ultimately, the parties reach agreement concerning both the desire to enter into a contract and the terms of that contract. That is, the parties decide what each will do or promise to do in exchange for the return promise or performance of the other. This process of contract formation is covered in Chapters 8 and 9.

Although the law usually enforces the promises made by the parties at the conclusion of their bargaining, certain factors, discussed in Chapters 10 through 12, may render otherwise binding promises either voidable or unenforceable. Chapter 10 covers contracts void or voidable because one or both parties lacks (or has limited) contractual capacity as well as contracts unenforceable in whole or in part as illegal or otherwise contrary to public policy. Chapter 11 discusses contracts voidable due to fraud, misrepresentation, mistake, duress, or undue influence in the bargaining process. Chapter 12 covers the Statute of Frauds, which requires that certain contracts be evidenced by a writing to be enforceable.[7] In short, an agreement reached by competent parties, free from illegality, fraud, misrepresentation, mistake, or duress, and meeting any necessary writing requirements is binding as a contract.

Assuming binding contractual promises are created, the law must then determine who is entitled to enforce and who is required to perform them. Ordinarily, the promisors and the promisees of the various contractual promises, known as the **parties,** are required to perform and entitled to enforce them. Occasionally, however, third parties may have rights or obligations under a contract. Simply defined, a **third party** is a person other than one of the contracting parties who is affected by the contract in question. Rights and obligations of third parties in contract are discussed in Chapter 13.

---

[7]Also discussed in Chapter 12 are other issues involving written contracts, including contract construction and interpretation, and the legal effect of the adoption of a writing.

Figure 7.2   Life Cycle of a Contract

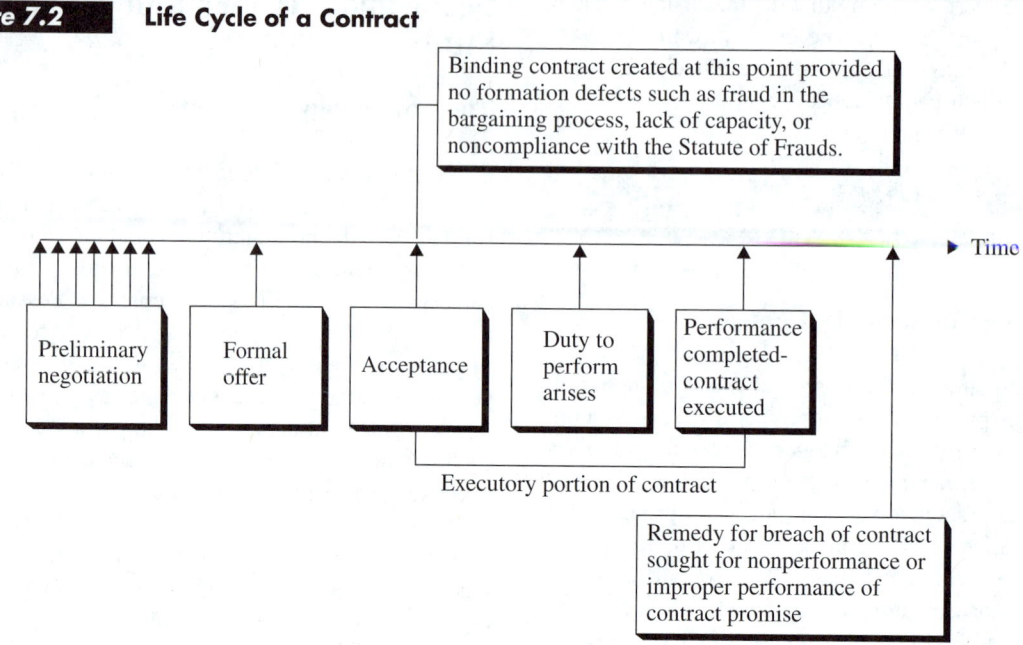

Once the foregoing issues have been resolved, a duty to perform the enforceable promises ultimately arises. This duty is breached if either party fails to perform when agreed or in some cases when a party repudiates or renounces his duty prior to the time of agreed performance. Issues arising during the performance of a contract are treated in Chapter 14.

A party who breaches a binding contractual promise is liable to the other for a contract remedy. Remedies are therefore inextricably tied to issues of performance and nonperformance. For this reason, remedies are covered in Chapter 15, immediately following the performance material. Figure 7.2 illustrates the life cycle of a contract.

Common Law and Code Contracts

Sources of Contract Law. As noted in Chapter 6, Article 2 of the Uniform Commercial Code (Sales) occupies an important position in the overall study of contract law. The scope of Article 2 and its relationship to contract law generally must therefore be carefully noted. Section 2–102 provides that

> Unless the context otherwise requires, this Article applies to *transactions in goods;* it does not apply to any transaction which although in the form of an unconditional con-

tract to sell or present sale is intended to operate only as a security transaction. . . .

By removing security interests in goods from the "transactions" covered,[8] the basic scope of Article 2 becomes *contracts for the sale of goods.*

Of course many contracts, such as those for the sale of land, employment and other personal services, insurance, and building construction, do not involve a sale of goods. Being outside the scope of Article 2, these contracts are governed by the vast common law of contracts. Hence, a fundamental distinction exists in contract law between "Code" and "common law" contracts.

Although code and common law contracts are governed by two different bodies of law, there is a significant overlap between them for two reasons. First, the Code is not exhaustive in the coverage of its subjects. As discussed in Chapter 6, various legal principles and doctrines existing outside the Code often supplement its provisions. For example, Article 2 includes several sections concerning formation of sales contracts, but leaves the remaining formation issues to the common law of contracts. Thus, with respect to issues not specifically addressed by the Code, common law rules govern both types of contracts. Second, courts have exhibited an

---

[8]These are governed by Article 9 of the Code.

increasing tendency in recent years to apply Article 2 rules by analogy to common law contracts. This trend is evidenced by the fact that the *Restatement (Second) of Contracts,* published in 1979, has adopted many Code rules as now applicable to common law contracts. In other words, Article 2 has significantly affected the development of the common law of contracts. Although a combination of these factors provides more consistency between Code and common law rules, significant differences remain.

Goods Defined. As indicated above, if the contract in question involves a sale of goods, it is governed primarily by Article 2. If not, the common law of contracts provides the rules of law applicable to the transaction. Thus, resolving the initial issue in any contracts question (is this a Code or a common law contract?) requires a knowledge of what types of property are classified as goods.

Section 2–105(1) states the general rule that **goods**

> means all things (including specially manufactured goods) which are movable at the time of identification[9] to the contract for sale. . . .

Because the definition of goods is based on movability, real property (which, of course, is immovable) is not a good and therefore not within the scope of Article 2. Also excluded from the definition of goods are the money in which the price of the goods is to be paid, investment securities (such as stocks and bonds), and other intangibles. Thus, simply stated, goods are *tangible personal property:* television sets, automobiles, manufacturing equipment, appliances, clothing, books, furniture, stereo equipment, or virtually anything else sold at your local grocery store or shopping center. Living animals also are goods, as are their unborn young (in gestation) and the products of animals (for example, eggs, milk, wool). Further, money qualifies as a good if it is the commodity being sold, such as a coin collection. Growing crops, timber, fixtures, and minerals are also goods in most cases if they are to be removed and sold apart from the land to which they are attached. Article 2, therefore, governs a vast number of transactions between people in business (for example, a contract for raw materials or equipment used in manufacture), between retail merchants and consumers (for example, the sale of a refrigerator or television set), and between individuals not engaged in business (for example, the sale of a bicycle through a classified newspaper advertisement).

Merchant Defined. The term **merchant** is another important term used in Article 2. Under §2–104(1) a merchant is a person

1. who deals in goods of the kind; or
2. who otherwise (by her occupation or employment of an agent, broker, or other intermediary) holds herself out as having knowledge or skill peculiar to the business practices or goods involved in the transaction.

A transaction is deemed to be "between merchants" when *both* parties possess the knowledge or skill of a merchant.

Because Article 2 governs transactions in goods, its coverage is not limited only to transactions involving merchant buyers or sellers. As long as a sale of *goods* is involved, Article 2 applies, whether or not the parties are merchants. Many separate Code sections, however, discussed in the following contracts and sales chapters, apply different or specialized rules when one or both parties are merchants. The reason for this approach is that transactions between professionals or experts in a particular field require special rules not necessarily applicable to a casual or inexperienced buyer or seller.[10]

Note that the definition of merchant includes not only persons who deal in goods of the same kind—for example, the appliance dealer, hardware store, department store, or other seller out of inventory—but also includes persons who hold themselves out as having knowledge peculiar to the goods or practices involved in the transaction. Under the *goods* aspect of the definition, for example, an auto mechanic selling a car would be a merchant. Under the *practices* aspect, almost any person in business is a merchant if goods are the subject matter of the transaction, because the practices referred to are ordinary business practices, such as answering mail. Under this portion of the definition, banks or universities may be merchants.[11]

---

[9]The term "identification" is the process by which the particular goods to which the contract refers are designated or specified. Many important legal consequences depend upon whether or not goods have been identified to the contract. The effect of identification is discussed in Chapter 17.

[10]UCC §2–104, Official Comment 1.

[11]UCC §2–104, Official Comment 2.

The various merchants' provisions do not necessarily apply to all types of merchants listed above. The nature and purpose of the particular provision determines which merchants are included within its coverage. Table 7.1 lists the thirteen merchants' provisions contained in Article 2 and indicates where each is discussed in the text. The first four provisions apply only to persons who deal in goods of the kind. The remaining provisions apply to persons who qualify as merchants under any aspect of the definition.

Table 7.1	Article 2—Merchants' Provisions	
Provision	**Subject**	**Chapter**
§2–312(3)	Merchant sellers' warranty against infringement	Chapter 19 (The Sales Contract—Warranties)
§2–314(1)	Implied warranty of merchantability	Chapter 19 (The Sales Contract—Warranties)
§2–402(2)	Rule applying to merchant sellers who retain goods sold	Chapter 17 (The Sales Contract—Title and Risk of Loss)
§2–403(2)	Effect of entrusting goods to a merchant	Chapter 17 (The Sales Contract—Title and Risk of Loss)
§2–201(2)	Statute of Frauds exception between merchants	Chapter 12 (Written Agreements)
§2–205	Firm offers by merchants	Chapter 8 (Contract Formation—Agreement)
§2–207(2)	Effect of additional terms in an acceptance between merchants	Chapter 8 (Contract Formation—Agreement)
§2–209(2)	Rule as between merchants giving effect to a provision on a form contract precluding modification unless in writing	Chapter 12 (Written Agreements)
§2–327(1)(c)	Obligations of a merchant buyer in a sale on approval	Chapter 17 (The Sales Contract—Title and Risk of Loss)
§2–509(3)	Special residual risk of loss provision applicable to merchant sellers	Chapter 17 (The Sales Contract—Title and Risk of Loss)
§2–603	Merchant buyer's duties with respect to rightfully rejected goods	Chapter 18 (The Sales Contract—Remedies)
§2–605(1)(b)	Rule between merchants creating waiver of buyer's objections after rejecting goods	Chapter 18 (The Sales Contract—Remedies)
§2–609(2)	Standard for reasonableness of insecurity and assurance of performance between merchants	Chapter 14 (Performance of the Contract)

Summary

1. Contract law is concerned with the legal implications of promise-making. That certain promises are made to be kept is a basic premise of contract law, consistent with human conduct generally, and necessary to the efficient operation of modern society.

2. A promise is simply a person's undertaking that something will or will not happen in the future. The person making the promise is the promisor, and the person to whom it is directed is the promisee. A contract is a promise or set of promises for breach of which the law gives a remedy or the performance of which the law recognizes as a duty. If a contractual promise is not performed, the injured promisee may recover a contract remedy.

3. Contracts commonly are classified according to their various characteristics. Contracts may be categorized as formal or informal, express or implied, unilateral or bilateral, enforceable or unenforceable, void or voidable, and executory or executed.

4. The life cycle of a contract occurs along a time continuum starting with preliminary negotiations and ending with full performance. This chronology provides a useful organizational basis for studying contracts.

5. Contract law is derived primarily from two sources: the common law and Article 2 of the Uniform Commercial Code. Code contracts are those involving sales of goods, generally meaning tangible personal property. Although all sales of goods are governed by Article 2, special rules are often applied to merchant buyers and sellers. Common law contracts include among others those involving land, employment and other services, and building construction. The distinction between the two types is important because Code rules of law differ from common law principles in many important respects.

Key Terms

promise	unilateral contract
promisor	bilateral contract
promisee	express contract
contract	implied in fact contract
joint liability	quasi-contract (implied in
several liability	law contract)
joint and several liability	executed contract
enforceable contract	executory contract
unenforceable contract	discharge
void promise	party
voidable contract	third party
ratification	goods
informal (simple) contract	merchant
formal contract	

Questions and Problems

7.1 Contracts is the body of law making certain promises legally enforceable. It occupies a pivotal place in the study of commercial law generally. Why is it necessary to have a law of contract? What purposes do contracts serve?

7.2 Seller promises to sell Buyer a machine to be used in Buyer's factory, for which Buyer promises to pay $10,000. If later a dispute arises regarding the terms of this contract, the court may utilize several sources to determine the contract terms. What are these sources?

7.3 Eric, an adult, signs a written contract by which he promises to sell his guitar to Jimmy, a minor, for $500. Before the transaction takes place, however, another adult, Mick, offers Eric $700 for the guitar. When Eric tells Mick of the contract with Jimmy, Mick says "Don't worry. Contracts with minors are void." In fact, the law of the state in which Eric resides provides that contracts with minors are voidable by the minor.
  (a) Has Mick correctly summarized the law by stating, "Contracts with minors are void"?
  (b) Jimmy later tenders $500 to Eric, Eric says, "I'm sorry, Jimmy; our contract is unenforceable," Jimmy sues. Will the court enforce the contract?

7.4 Alice and Gertrude operate a restaurant and want to hire Snow Linen Co. to launder all of the restaurant's linens. At Snow Linen's request, Alice and Gertrude sign the following to evidence their agreement:

> 1. Snow Linen hereby agrees to pick up and launder all linens used by the Alice and Gertrude Restaurant from June 1 to October 1, at such times as agreed by the parties.
> 2. Alice and Gertrude jointly and each of them hereby agree to pay Snow Linen the sum of $200 per month for the services described in paragraph 1, payment to be made on the first day of July and the first day of each month thereafter.

Snow Linen provides laundering services during the months of June and July, but Alice and Gertrude fail to pay.
  (a) Is the agreement a bilateral or unilateral contract? What is (are) the promise(s) made in this agreement? Identify the promisor and promisee of each promise.
  (b) On August 1, is the contract executory or executed? Explain.
  (c) If Snow Linen decides to sue for the $400 due under the contract, who can it sue?
  (d) Assume that Alice has moved out of the country and Snow Linen sues only Gertrude. What is the maximum amount for which she can be held liable?

7.5 Tex, owner of the Silver Spur Bar and Lounge, hired Donald to manage operations beginning on January 1. They orally agreed that Donald would pay all operating and fixed costs and would retain the net revenues as his compensation. On April 1, Donald notified Tex to find a new manager because the arrangement was generating monthly net revenues of only $300. Tex offered Donald a 49 percent owner-ship interest in the bar if he would remain for two more years. When Donald rejected this offer, Tex asked Donald to continue to serve as manager while Tex investigated other alternatives. Donald continued to act as manager, receiving net revenues of about $300 per month as his only compensation. Whenever he asked Tex whether he had a new plan for compensation, Tex replied, "Don't you worry, we're going to make things right." On November 1, Tex hired a new manager and terminated Donald's employment. Donald sued Tex for breach of contract. An expert witness testified that reasonable compensation for management of the Silver Spur was $1,000 per month. When asked why he had not left the job earlier, Donald told the court that Tex's reassurances had convinced him that a satisfactory arrangement would be worked out.

(a) Did Donald and Tex have an express contract? Explain.
(b) Did Donald and Tex have an implied in fact contract? Explain.
(c) Assume that the court has found that a contract existed. How much should Donald be awarded as compensation?

7.6   For over 25 years, Hirsch Department Stores had purchased paper bags imprinted with its name and logo from Smith Paper Co. When Hirsch needed bags, it ordered them from Smith by telephone and paid after delivery. To ensure that the bags were readily available, Smith kept a supply of Hirsch bags in stock. Hirsch was aware of this arrangement and annually provided Smith with an estimate of the bags it would need. In 1995, Hirsch temporarily purchased bags from another manufacturer but paid for all of the bags that Smith had in stock. In 1996, Hirsch resumed doing business with Smith under the previous arrangement. In 2005, Hirsch decided to go out of business. After hearing rumors of the closings, Smith telephoned Hirsch's president requesting assurance that Hirsch would buy the preprinted bags in Smith's inventory. The president became outraged and said, "I cannot believe that you would question my integrity after all these years. I always honor my commitments." Several months later, Smith sent Hirsch a bill for the bags it held in stock. When Hirsch failed to pay, Smith sued for breach of contract. Did a contract exist between Smith and Hirsch? Explain.

7.7   Determine whether the following are sales of "goods" as defined in the Uniform Commercial Code:
(a) water sold by a city to its residents;
(b) electricity sold by a utility company to consumers.

7.8   A problem under §2–104, which has proven difficult for courts to resolve, is whether or not a farmer is a merchant to which the various Article 2 merchants' provisions should apply. Should a farmer be treated as a merchant under any aspect of definition stated in UCC §2–104(1)? Explain.

CONTRACT FORMATION—AGREEMENT

Contract formation is the process by which binding promises are created. It generally requires two elements: (1) mutual assent, or agreement, to an exchange, and (2) consideration, what each party gives up in exchange for the return promise or performance of the other. The first element, agreement, is covered in this chapter. Consideration is the subject of Chapter 9.

Because most contracts are enforced without regard to form, the contract formation process usually is an informal process starting with preliminary inquiries or expressions of interest by one of the parties. These preliminary communications are often followed by more detailed inquiry, negotiation, or dickering over specific terms of the proposed contract, including price, quali-

ties, and characteristics of any property or services involved, time or times for performance, and other rights and obligations of the parties. Specific contract terms are determined only after this often laborious process of give and take, inclusion and exclusion, proposal and counterproposal. Although not all contracts require extensive precontract negotiation, many do.

Agreement ultimately is reached when an offer is made by one party (the offeror) and accepted by the other (the offeree). Agreement analysis therefore is generally divided into two parts, offer and acceptance. This chapter follows a similar organizational approach, although offer and acceptance issues are closely intertwined. Further, as noted above, the offer, the traditional starting point in contract formation analysis, often occurs well into the life cycle of the contract.

The Offer

"Offer" Defined

An **offer** is a conditional promise made by the offeror to the offeree, giving the offeree the power of acceptance, or the power to create a contract. Or, as defined in the *Restatement (Second) of Contracts,*

An offer is the manifestation of willingness to enter into a bargain, so made as to justify another person in understanding that his assent to that bargain is invited and will conclude it.[1]

Suppose a neighbor says to you, "I offer to sell you my antique china cabinet for $2,000." The neighbor has made an offer. The offer gives you, the offeree, the power to convert your neighbor's promise into a contractual obligation. If you accept and the other elements of contract formation are present, appropriate contract remedies may be recovered in the event either party fails to perform. Thus, by making an offer, the offeror agrees to be bound contractually if (that is, on the condition that) the offeree accepts.

Master of the Offer Rule

The offeror is the **master of the offer,** which means that the offeree must accept according to the terms of the offer. The requirements of the offer might include not only the requested promise or performance, but also the time, place, and manner of acceptance. For example, if the offer states that acceptance must take place by noon on January 10, any acceptance attempted after that time is ineffective. If the offer states how an acceptance must be communicated—perhaps by telephone, e-mail, or letter—the offeree must use the prescribed means. In short, the offeror as the master of the offer dictates the terms under which the offer is to be accepted. Any deviation by the offeree from those terms generally results in no contract. Because the offeror incurs contract liability upon acceptance, the master of the offer rule allows the offeror to control the terms upon which she is willing to assume that liability. This concept forms the basis of several rules discussed in this chapter.

The Objective Theory of Contract

Even though the offeror is the master of the offer, the terms of the offer are judged by an *objective,* not a subjective, test. Under this test the offeror's subjective intention is generally irrelevant; rather, whatever meaning the offeror conveys either intentionally or negligently to the offeree is used. Therefore, the existence and terms of an offer are judged from the point of view of a reasonable person in the position of the offeree.

For example, assume a fellow student sends you a letter offering to sell you her car. Although the student actually *intends* the offering price to be $2,500, she inadvertently types $2,000 in the letter. Upon receipt of the letter, a reasonable person in your position as the offeree would assume that an offer for sale has been made at $2,000. If you accept the offer without reason to know that a mistake has been made, a contract exists at $2,000. Thus, to have a binding agreement, there need be no actual "meeting of the minds" or subjective agreement between the parties. As long as there is an outward manifestation of mutual assent, a contract exists. A party is not generally allowed to assert that his subjective intention differs from his outward manifestation. This rule is known as the **objective theory of contract,** which protects the stability of contractual relationships by allowing a party to act upon reasonable appearance rather than be subject to a hidden, uncommunicated intention of the other.

The objective theory often is used to test the legal effect of various communications between the parties during the negotiating stage. Each statement is analyzed from the viewpoint of the person to whom it is made to determine whether it amounts to an offer or is merely an expression of interest, solicitation of an offer, request for clarification, or request for a better or alternative contract term. The prior relationship or conduct of the parties often is important to this inquiry. Circumstances may indicate, for instance, that a person made the alleged "offer" in jest or while intoxicated, making it difficult to construe the communication as a true "manifestation of willingness to enter into a bargain." Making this determination is often a difficult issue, as the following classic case illustrates.

Lucy v. Zehmer
84 S.E.2d 516 (Va. 1954)

Plaintiff W. O. Lucy sued defendants A. H. Zehmer and Ida S. Zehmer, requesting that the court enforce the following written agreement: "We hereby agree to sell to W. O. Lucy the Ferguson Farm complete for $50,000.00, title satisfactory to buyer." The agreement, which was dated and signed by A. H. Zehmer and his wife, Ida S. Zehmer, had been written by Zehmer in a restaurant during a conversation with Lucy. The Zehmers asserted that the writing had been drawn up while Zehmer was under the influence of alcohol and had been intended as a joke.

---

[1]RESTATEMENT (SECOND) OF CONTRACTS §24.

Lucy maintained that he believed the agreement was a valid contract.

The trial court held that the agreement was not legally binding and denied specific performance. Lucy appealed.

Buchanan, Justice

. . . The defendants insist that the evidence was ample to support their contention that the writing sought to be enforced was prepared as a bluff or dare to force Lucy to admit that he did not have $50,000; that the whole matter was a joke; that the writing was not delivered to Lucy and no binding contract was ever made between the parties.

It is an unusual, if not bizarre, defense. When made to the writing admittedly prepared by one of the defendants and signed by both, clear evidence is required to sustain it.

In his testimony, Zehmer claimed that he "was high as a Georgia pine," and that the transaction "was just a bunch of two doggoned drunks bluffing to see who could talk the biggest and say the most." That claim is inconsistent with his attempt to testify in great detail as to what was said and what was done. It is contradicted by other evidence as to the condition of both parties, and rendered of no weight by the testimony of his wife that when Lucy left the restaurant she suggested that Zehmer drive him home. The record is convincing that Zehmer was not intoxicated to the extent of being unable to comprehend the nature and consequences of the instrument he executed, and hence that instrument is not to be invalidated on that ground. . . .

The evidence is convincing also that Zehmer wrote two agreements, the first one beginning "I hereby agree to sell. . . ."

The appearance of the contract, the fact that it was under discussion for forty minutes or more before it was signed; Lucy's objection to the first draft because it was written in the singular, and he wanted Mrs. Zehmer to sign it also; the rewriting to meet that objection and the signing by Mrs. Zehmer; the discussion of what was to be included in the sale, the provision for the examination of the title, the completeness of the instrument that was executed, the taking possession of it by Lucy with no request or suggestion by either of the defendants that he give it back, are facts which furnish persuasive evidence that the execution of the contract was a serious business transaction rather than a casual, jesting matter as defendants now contend. . . .

Not only did Lucy actually believe, but the evidence shows he was warranted in believing, that the contract represented a serious business transaction and a good faith sale and purchase of the farm.

In the field of contracts, as generally elsewhere, "We must look to the outward expression of a person as manifesting his intention rather than to his secret and unexpressed intention. The law imputes to a person an intention corresponding to the reasonable meaning of his words and acts." [*First Nat. Exchange Bank of Roanoke v. Roanoke Oil Co.,* 192 S.E. 764, 770 (Va. 1937).]

At no time prior to the execution of the contract had Zehmer indicated to Lucy by word or act that he was not in earnest about selling the farm. . . .

The mental assent of the parties is not requisite for the formation of a contract. If the words or other acts of one of the parties have but one reasonable meaning, his undisclosed intention is immaterial except when an unreasonable meaning which he attaches to his manifestations is known to the other party. . . .

An agreement or mutual assent is of course essential to a valid contract but the law imputes to a person an intention corresponding to the reasonable meaning of his words and acts. If his words and acts, judged by a reasonable standard, manifest an intention to agree, it is immaterial what may be the real but unexpressed state of his mind. . . .

So a person cannot set up that he was merely jesting when his conduct and words would warrant a reasonable person in believing that he intended a real agreement. . . .

Whether the writing signed by the defendants and now sought to be enforced by the complainants was the result of a serious offer by Lucy and a serious acceptance by the defendants, or was a serious offer by Lucy and an acceptance in secret jest by the defendants, in either event it constituted a binding contract of sale between the parties. . . .

[Judgment reversed and remanded.]

Intent and Definiteness

Elements of an Offer. To be an offer, a communication must meet two criteria: (1) it must indicate an intention by the offeror to be contractually bound upon acceptance, and (2) the terms of the offer must be reasonably certain or definite. Both issues are determined by a close analysis of the language of the communication involved and the surrounding circumstances.

The communication must first be examined to determine whether it evidences a serious intention to be legally obligated or is merely an expression of opinion, statement of intention, invitation to commence negotiation, or solicitation of an offer. Suppose Smith says to Jones: "I'm thinking of selling my house, and I'd like to get $150,000 for it." In this case, no offer for sale at $150,000 has been made to Jones. Smith is merely making a statement of intention, or at most, soliciting offers. A reasonable person in Jones's position would not assume that Smith has made a commitment to him to sell at $150,000.

Intent to be bound, by itself, is not enough. An offer must also be sufficiently definite and explicit so that, if accepted, a court in a subsequent dispute has a reasonably certain basis upon which to determine the existence of a breach and to award an appropriate remedy. In other words, this **definiteness** (or certainty) requirement means that the agreement must contain certain minimum terms. The minimum terms necessary for enforcement vary with the type of contract involved.[2]

Advertisements and Catalog Quotations. Both intent and definiteness issues are present in disputes involving the legal effect of advertisements and catalog quotations. For example, does a newspaper advertisement hawking dishwashers for $600 each constitute an offer to sell? Most courts hold that the ordinary newspaper or other advertisement is a mere invitation to make an offer, not a binding offer to sell at the price stated in the advertisement. This result is supported on two grounds. First, the advertiser ordinarily does not intend that legal consequences result from merely placing the advertisement. Neither the advertiser nor the reader contemplates closing a deal without further action by the seller. Rather, the reasonable inference ordinarily drawn from the advertisement is that readers are invited to come in and examine and negotiate. After such further communication and negotiation, an offer may be made and

accepted, resulting in a sale of specific goods or services at an agreed price. The second reason for refusing to treat advertisements as offers is that an advertisement is generally too indefinite to constitute an offer, because it commonly omits many essential terms, most notably the *quantity*.

Offers, however, may be made by advertisement. If an advertisement is sufficiently definite and explicit to indicate an intention on the part of the advertiser to enter into a contract on those terms, courts have construed the advertisement as an offer. For example, in *Lefkowitz v. Great Minneapolis Surplus Store,*[3] the defendant store published the following advertisement in the newspaper:

> Saturday 9 A.M.
> 2 Brand New Pastel
> Mink 3-Skin Scarfs
> Selling for $89.50
> Out they go
>
> Saturday. Each . . . $1.00
> 1 Black Lapin Stole
> Beautiful, worth $139.50 . . . $1.00
> First Come,
> First Served.

Lefkowitz, the plaintiff, was the first person in the store on Saturday, and tendered $1 for the black lapin (rabbit) stole. Defendant refused to sell on the basis of its "house rule" that only women were qualified to receive the bargains advertised. The court held that the advertisement was clear, definite, explicit, and left nothing open for negotiation, and thus constituted an offer. The limitation of the offer to women only, because not stated in the offer itself, was not binding on the plaintiff. Having complied with the terms of the offer, the plaintiff was therefore entitled to performance. Note that this advertisement contains two factors not present in the ordinary newspaper advertisement: the quantity is stated and promissory language indicating an intent to be legally bound is present ("First come, First served").

At issue in the following case was whether a newspaper advertisement constituted an offer.

---

[2]The UCC generally follows the principles outlined above for contracts involving goods. Section 2–204(3) provides that a contract will not fail for indefiniteness even if one or more terms are left open if (1) the parties have *intended* to make a contract, and (2) there is a *reasonably certain* basis for giving an appropriate remedy. As explained in Chapter 16, many of the omitted terms are supplied by the Code.

[3]86 N.W.2d 689 (Minn. 1957).

Chang v. First Colonial Savings Bank

410 S.E.2d 928 (Va. 1991)

On November 18, 1985, defendant First Colonial Savings Bank ran an advertisement in the Richmond, Virginia, newspapers that read in part:

> Saving at First Colonial is a very rewarding experience. In appreciation for your business we have Great Gifts for you to enjoy NOW—and when your investment matures you get your entire principal back PLUS GREAT INTEREST.

> Deposit $14,000 and receive two gifts: a Remington Shotgun and GE CB Radio OR an RCA 200 Color-Trac TV and $20,136.12 upon maturity in 3¹/₂ years.

Plaintiffs Chia and Shin Chang, after reading the advertisement, deposited $14,000 with First Colonial and received a television and certificate of deposit from the bank. When the Changs returned three and a half years later to liquidate their certificate of deposit, First Colonial paid them only $18,823.93. According to the bank, the newspaper advertisement contained a typographical error and a deposit of $15,000 was necessary to receive $20,136.12 upon maturity. The Changs sued First Colonial for breach of contract. The trial court ruled in favor of the Changs and awarded damages of $1,312.19. The court of appeals reversed, holding that the newspaper advertisement was not a valid offer. The Virginia Supreme Court granted the Changs' petition for review.

Hassell, Justice

. . . The general rule followed in most states, and which we adopt, is that newspaper advertisements are not offers, but merely invitations to bargain. . . . However, there is a very narrow and limited exception to this rule. "[W]here the offer is clear, definite, and explicit, and leaves nothing open for negotiation, it constitutes an offer, acceptance of which will complete the contract." *Lefkowitz v. Great Minneapolis Surplus Store, Inc.*, . . . 86 N.W.2d 689, 691 (Minn. 1957). . . . As Professor Williston observed:

> In any event there can be no doubt that a positive offer may be made even by an advertisement or general notice. . . . The only general test which can be submitted as a guide is an inquiry whether the facts show that some performance was promised in positive terms in return for something requested.

1 Williston on Contracts §27, p. 65 (3d ed. 1957).

Applying these principles to the facts before us, we hold that the advertisement constituted an offer which was accepted when the Changs deposited their $14,000 with the Bank for a period of three and one-half years. A plain reading of the advertisement demonstrates that First Colonial's offer of the television and $20,136.12 upon maturity in three and one-half years was clear, definite, and explicit and left nothing open for negotiation.

Even though the Bank's advertisement upon which the Changs relied may have contained a mistake caused by a typographical error, under the unique facts and circumstances of this case, the error does not invalidate the offer. First Colonial did not inform the Changs of this typographical error until after it had the use of the Changs' $14,000 for three and one-half years. Additionally, applying the general rule to which there are certain exceptions not applicable here, a unilateral mistake does not void an otherwise legally binding contract. . . .

When the Changs tendered their $14,000 to First Colonial for three and one-half years, they complied with all of the conditions in First Colonial's offer. Hence, there was a meeting of the minds and an enforceable contract. . . .

[Judgment reversed and remanded.]

Communication, Effectiveness, and Duration of the Offer

Communication of the Offer. Once an offer is made, it must be communicated to the offeree, and to create a contract, the act or promise constituting acceptance must be done or made in response to the offer. In other words, the offer must *induce* the acceptance. To illustrate, suppose Sonia loses her watch, and places an advertisement in the newspaper offering a reward for its return. Bryan finds the watch and returns it to Sonia without knowledge of the reward offer. Bryan is not entitled to the reward. Because the offer has not been communicated to the offeree, his act of returning the watch does not constitute acceptance.

Not only must the offer be communicated to the offeree, it must also be communicated by the offeror or his or her authorized agent and in the manner chosen by the offeror. This requirement is merely an application of the master of the offer rule. Assume Smith directs her secretary to type a letter to Bates, offering to sell a warehouse to Bates for $1.5 million. Prior to mailing the letter, the secretary sees Bates in the hallway and informs her of the offer. No offer has been made because the offer was not communicated either by the offeror or a person authorized by the offeror to communicate it. Assume further that after being informed of the offer, Bates walks into Smith's office and sees the letter on Smith's desk. Bates may not accept because the offer has not been communicated to Bates in the medium chosen by the offeror, the mails. In these cases, however, an attempted acceptance by Bates is itself an offer, which Smith may accept if she chooses.

Effectiveness and Duration of the Offer. An offer is not effective until properly communicated to the offeree. For example, if an offer is mailed on January 1 and received on January 4, it is effective on January 4. Once an offer is effective, the offeree obtains power of acceptance—the power to create a contract. The duration of that power depends upon how long the offer is held open. The offer may state that it will be held open for a stipulated period—for example, 30 days. In this case—the offer remains open for the stipulated period, which runs from the date of the offer's effectiveness (the date of the receipt). The offeror as master of the offer, however, can provide that the time period runs from the date the offer was sent or from any other date. If no period is stipulated, the offer remains open for a reasonable time. What constitutes a "reasonable time" is a question of fact dependent upon the nature of the subject matter and all the circumstances under which the offer was made.

Termination of the Offer Before Acceptance

Once an offer has been made, it can either be terminated prior to acceptance, or accepted, thereby creating a contract. The offer may terminate prior to acceptance because it has lapsed according to its terms or after a reasonable time has passed. In the following material, three additional situations terminating the offer before acceptance are discussed: termination by the offeror (revocation), termination by the offeree (rejection), and

termination by operation of law. In studying the following contract formation issues, pay special attention to the effective dates of the various communications between the offeror and the offeree. Whether an offer results in a contract or is terminated before acceptance is determined by comparing the effective dates of each communication.

Termination by the Offeror—Revocation

Generally, an offeror may revoke an offer at any time before the offeree's acceptance becomes effective. A **revocation** is simply the offeror's statement or other conduct after the offer is made, indicating that he or she no longer intends to enter into the proposed contract. The revocation is effective when it is communicated to the offeree. In other words, the objective theory of contract applies to revocations as well as offers. It is not enough that the offeror no longer *intends* to enter into a contract. That intention must be made known to the other party.

Unlike the offer, however, the revocation may be communicated either directly or indirectly to the offeree. That is, the revocation need not be communicated by the *offeror* to become effective. Assume Smith offers to sell a car to Bates for $1,500, but before Bates accepts the offer, Smith sells the car to Jones. Revoca-tion would be effective if Jones notifies Bates that the car has been sold. Effective revocation occurs when the offeree receives reliable information from a third party that would inform a reasonable person of the offeror's intent to withdraw the offer. Note that the information received must be inconsistent with the offeror's keeping the offer open. For example, no revocation occurs if Bates merely learns that Smith has offered the car to others.

A revocation made by mail or other written communication is effective when it comes into the offeree's possession, or into the possession of some person authorized by the offeree to receive it, or when it is deposited in some authorized place, such as a post office box. Therefore, the offeree cannot avoid the revocation by failing to open or read the mail.

An offer made to the general public (such as a reward offer) may be revoked by giving equal publicity to the revocation. A reward offer made by newspaper could therefore be revoked by publishing the revocation in the same newspaper, provided no better means of notification is reasonably available.

Situations in Which the Offeror Cannot Revoke. An ordinary offer is freely revocable by the offeror at any time prior to the effectiveness of the offeree's acceptance. The law, however, recognizes several situations in which an offer cannot be revoked. Two such situations, option contracts and "firm offers" under the UCC, are discussed in the following material. A third situation, based upon the doctrine of promissory estoppel, is discussed in Chapter 9.

Option Contracts. An **option** is a contract to keep an offer open for a specified period of time. In an option contract, one party promises to hold an offer open in exchange for some consideration, usually payment by the other of a specified sum of money. An option is therefore a contract limiting the offeror's (promisor's) power to revoke an offer. Unless an option contract exists, a promise by the offeror to keep an offer open is not generally binding; it is not supported by consideration from the offeree-promisee, thus lacking a basic element of an enforceable contract. In other words, a person is usually bound to perform a promise (including one to hold an offer open) only if that promise is enforceable as a contract. Assume Stevens offers to sell Bryant a tract of land for $5,000, and promises to keep the offer open for 30 days. Stevens may revoke the offer at any time prior to the expiration of the 30-day period because his promise to keep the offer open is not supported by consideration, and is therefore not a contract. If, however, Bryant had given Stevens $5—consideration—in exchange for Stevens's promise to hold the offer open, an option contract would have been created, precluding Stevens's from revoking the offer prior to expiration of the stipulated period.

When an option exists, two contracts are actually contemplated: one contract (the option contract) to keep the offer open for the specified period of time and the underlying contract that comes into existence if the option is exercised. To "exercise" an option means to accept the offer embodied in the option. In the preceding example, therefore, Bryant exercises the option by accepting Stevens's offer to sell the land at $5,000.

Firm Offers—UCC §2–205. Section §2–205 of the UCC contains an exception to the general rule that a promise to hold an offer open needs consideration, or something exchanged, to be binding. Under the **firm offer rule,** a written, signed offer to buy or sell goods made by a merchant stating that it will be held open is binding without consideration for the period stated. If no period is stated, the offer remains open for a reasonable time, not to exceed three months. In other words, such a written firm offer is treated as an option contract for a limited period even though no consideration supports the promise.

For the rule to apply, the offer must relate to the purchase or sale of *goods* (contracts governed by Article 2 of the UCC), the offer must be made by a *merchant,* and the offer must be made in a *signed writing.* If the term providing for irrevocability is contained in a form provided by the *offeree,* the term must be separately signed by the offeror (commonly by initialing the clause involved). This rule protects the offeror against inadvertently signing a firm offer contained in a form prepared by the offeree.

The firm offer rule supports the promise on the basis of a formality (a signed writing) as a substitute for consideration usually required to support an option. The rule applies only to current short-term, firm offers and not to long-term options. An outside time limit of three months is set. A promise made for a longer period binds the offeror only during the first three months. The promise may be renewed, and if it ever becomes supported by consideration it may continue as long as the parties provide.

Termination by the Offeree—Rejection

Rejection is the *offeree's* statement or other conduct indicating an intention not to accept the offer. Like a revocation, a rejection is effective to terminate the offer when it is received by the offeror directly or indirectly; the rejection need not be communicated by the offeree to be effective. Because a rejection terminates an offer, the offeree may not later reconsider and accept unless the offeror revives the offer. If the offeree tries to accept after initially rejecting the offer, his purported "acceptance" simply operates as a new offer, in effect, a counteroffer.

An explicit rejection (for example, the offeree says, "I reject your offer") clearly terminates the offer. In other cases, the offeree's language and other conduct must be carefully scrutinized to determine whether a reasonable person in the offeror's position would believe that a rejection has been made. For example, no rejection occurs if an offeree merely demonstrates an intention to consider the offer further. Assume Smith offers to sell a coin collection to Bates for $2,000. Bates replies, "The price seems a little high, but let me think about it." Bates has not rejected Smith's offer.

Under an option contract, the power of acceptance is generally not terminated by the offeree's rejection. The offeror is contractually obligated not to withdraw the offer during the option period. Thus, an offeree who indicates an intent not to exercise an option may nevertheless reconsider and accept within the option period unless the offeror changes position in reliance upon the previous rejection. For example, if, after the rejection, the offeror sells the subject matter of the option to a third party, the offeree is prevented from accepting.

The "Mirror Image" Rule—Rejection by Counter-offer.

Frequently the offer is not expressly rejected. Instead, the terms of the acceptance differ from or add to the terms of the offer. The traditional common law rule differs from the UCC treatment of this situation.

Under the common law, the so-called **mirror image rule** governs—the acceptance must exactly conform to (or mirror) the terms of the offer. Any deviation between an attempted acceptance and the terms of the offer is deemed a rejection of the original offer and a counteroffer[4] on the new terms.

A counteroffer, like an express rejection, terminates the offeree's power to accept the original offer. Assume Smythe offers to sell his house to Burns for $130,000. Burns responds, "I accept, but at $120,000," or, "I'll pay $120,000." In effect, Burns is rejecting Smythe's $130,000 offer and counteroffering at $120,000. Burns cannot change her mind later and accept Smythe's $130,000 offer, because the original offer no longer exists. If Burns simply makes an inquiry regarding different terms, requests better terms, or comments on the terms of the offer, she does not make a counteroffer. For example, if Burns had stated, "Won't you consider less?" "Is the house air-conditioned?" or "The price seems a bit high," the original offer remains effective.

The following case illustrates the application of basic common law principles of revocation and rejection by counteroffer.

---

[4]A counteroffer is an offer made by the offeree relating to the same subject matter proposing a substituted bargain that differs from that proposed by the original offer. RESTATEMENT (SECOND) OF CONTRACTS §39.

Normile v. Miller
326 S.E.2d 11 (N.C. 1985)

On August 4, 1980, Richard Byer, a real estate broker with Gallery of Homes, showed a piece of real estate owned by Hazel Miller to Michael Normile and Wawie Kurniawan. After viewing the property, Normile and Kurniawan prepared a written offer to purchase that included a provision stating, "Time is of the essence, therefore this offer must be accepted on or before Aug. 5th 1980." Byer delivered the offer to Miller, who signed it after making several changes in the terms. The major changes were an increase in the earnest money deposit from $100 to $500; an increase in the down payment from $875 to $1,000; and a reduction from 25 to 20 years for the term of a loan to be made by the seller. On the evening of August 4, Byer delivered the revised document to Normile and Kurniawan, who advised the broker that they intended to wait a while before making a decision. In the early afternoon of August 5, Miller entered into a contract to sell the real estate to Lawrence Segal. At about 2:00 p.m. on that day, Byer informed Normile of the contract stating, "You snooze, you lose; the property has been sold." Prior to 5:00 p.m. on August 5, Normile and Kurniawan initialed the changes on the purchase form signed by Miller and delivered it and a $500 deposit to the Gallery of Homes office.

Normile and Kurniawan (plaintiff-appellants) and Segal (plaintiff-appellee) sued defendant Miller demanding performance of the contract. The trial court ruled in favor of Segal and ordered Miller to perform the contract and convey the real estate to Segal. The Court of Appeals affirmed and Normile and Kurniawan appealed to the North Carolina Supreme Court.

Frye, Justice

. . . [W]e begin with a brief description of how a typical sale of real estate is consummated. The broker whose primary duty is to secure a ready, willing, and able buyer for the seller's property, generally initiates a potential sale by procuring the prospective purchaser's signature on an offer to purchase instrument. . . . This instrument contains the prospective purchaser's "offer" of the terms he wishes to propose to the seller. . . .

In the instant case, the offerors, plaintiff-appellants, submitted their offer to purchase defendant's property. This offer contained a Paragraph 9, requiring that "this offer must be accepted on or before 5:00 P.M. Aug. 5th 1980." Thus the offeree's, defendant-seller's, power of acceptance was controlled by the duration of time for acceptance of the offer. . . . "The offeror is the creator of the power, and before it leaves his hands, he may fashion it to his will . . . if he names a specific period for its existence, the offeree can accept only during this period." Corbin, *Offer and Acceptance, and Some of the Resulting Legal Relations,* 26 Yale L.J. 169, at 183 (1917). . . .

This offer to purchase remains only an offer until the seller accepts it on the terms contained in the original offer by the prospective purchaser. . . . If the seller does accept the terms in the purchaser's offer, he denotes this by signing the offer to purchase at the bottom, thus forming a valid, binding, and irrevocable purchase contract between the seller and purchaser. However, if the seller purports to accept but changes or modifies the terms of the offer, he makes what is generally referred to as a qualified or conditional acceptance. . . . Such a reply from the seller is actually a counteroffer and a rejection of the buyer's offer. . . .

The question then becomes, did defendant-seller accept plaintiff-appellants' offer prior to the expiration of the time limit contained within the offer? We conclude that she did not. The offeree, defendant-seller, changed the original offer in several material respects, most notably in the terms regarding payment of the purchase price. . . . This qualified acceptance was in reality a rejection of the plaintiff-appellants original offer because it was coupled with certain modifications or changes that were not contained in the original offer. . . . Additionally, defendant-seller's conditional acceptance amounted to a counteroffer to plaintiff-appellants. . . .

In substance, defendant's conditional acceptance modifying the original offer did not manifest any intent to accept the terms of the original offer, including the time-for-acceptance provision, unless and until the original offeror accepted the terms included in defendant's counteroffer. The offeree, by failing to unconditionally assent to the terms of the original offer and instead qualifying his acceptance with terms of his own, in effect says to the original offeror, "I will accept your offer; provided you [agree to my proposed terms]." *Rucker v. Sanders,* [109 S.E. 857, 858 (N.C. 1921)]. Thus, the time-for-acceptance provision contained in plaintiff-appellants' original offer did not become part of the terms of the counteroffer. And, of course, if they had accepted the counteroffer from defendant, a binding purchase contract, which would have included the terms of the original offer and counteroffer, would have then resulted. . . .

Plaintiff-appellants argue that the counteroffer made by Defendant Miller to plaintiff-appellants became a binding and irrevocable option to purchase within the time for acceptance contained in their original offer to purchase. . . .

It is generally recognized that "[a]n 'option' is a contract by which the owner agrees to give another the exclusive right to buy property at a fixed price within a specified time." 8A G. Thompson, *Commentaries on the Modern Law of Real Property,* §4443 (1963). . . . In effect, an owner of property agrees to hold his offer open for a specified period of time. . . .

[W]e conclude that defendant-seller made no promise or agreement to hold her offer open. Thus, a necessary ingredient to the creation of an option contract, *i.e.,* a promise to hold an offer open for a specified time, is not present. Accordingly, we hold that defendant's counteroffer was not transformed into an irrevocable offer for the time limit contained in the original offer because the defendant's conditional acceptance did not include the time-for-acceptance provision as part of its terms and because defendant did not make any promise to hold her counteroffer open for any stated time. . . .

[T]he next question is did plaintiff-appellants, the original offerors, accept or reject defendant-seller's counteroffer?. . . . [P]laintiff-appellants did not manifest any intent to agree to or accept the terms contained in defendant's counteroffer. . . .

It is evident from the record that after plaintiff-appellants failed to accept defendant's counteroffer, there was a second purchaser, Plaintiff-appellee Segal, who submitted an offer to defendant that was accepted. This offer and acceptance between the latter parties, together with consideration in the form of an earnest money deposit from plaintiff-appellee, ripened into a valid and binding purchase contract.

By entering into the contract with Plaintiff-appellee Segal, defendant manifested her intention to revoke her previous counteroffer to plaintiff-appellants. . . . The revocation of an offer terminates it, and the offeree has no power to revive the offer by any subsequent attempts to accept. . . .

Generally, notice of the offeror's revocation must be communicated to the offeree to effectively terminate the offeree's power to accept the offer. It is enough that the offeree receives reliable information, even indirectly, "that the offeror had taken definite action inconsistent with an intention to make the contract." E. Farnsworth, [*Contracts,* §3.17 (1982).] . . .

In this case, plaintiff-appellants received notice of the offeror's revocation of the counteroffer in the afternoon of August 5, when Byer saw Normile and told him, "[Y]ou snooze, you lose; the property has been sold." Later that afternoon, plaintiff-appellants initialed the counteroffer and delivered it to the Gallery of Homes, along with their earnest money deposit of $500. These subsequent attempts by plaintiff-appellants to accept defendant's revoked counteroffer were fruitless, however, since their power of acceptance had been effectively terminated by the offeror's revocation. . . . Since defendant's counteroffer could not be revived, the practical effect of plaintiff-appellants' initialing defendant's counteroffer and leaving it at the broker's office before 5:00 P.M. on August 5 was to resubmit a new offer. This offer was not accepted by defendant since she had already contracted to sell her property by entering into a valid, binding, and irrevocable purchase contract with Plaintiff-appellee Segal. . . .

[Judgment modified and affirmed.]

UCC Change—§2–207. Section 2–207 of the UCC alters the strict effect of the mirror image rule in contracts for the sale of goods. Under §2–207(1), a definite and seasonable[5] expression of acceptance, or a written confirmation sent within a reasonable time, operates as an acceptance resulting in a contract even though the acceptance or confirmation states terms different from, or in addition to, the offer. No contract results, however, if the acceptance is expressly made conditional on assent to the additional or different terms.

The primary reason for the Code's departure from strict compliance with the mirror image rule is the Code's attempt to resolve the "battle of the forms" problem. The UCC drafters found that in commercial sales contracts, the buyer and seller usually explicitly agree upon major terms such as the quantity and price of the goods sold, their quality, and the time and manner of delivery. The parties then exchange preprinted forms such as the buyer's "purchase order" and the seller's "confirmation" or "acknowledgment." Other terms, not

explicitly considered or agreed upon, are usually contained under a heading such as "terms and conditions" in the fine print on the standard forms. These terms commonly govern remedies, warranties and limitations upon warranties, time limits for notice of defects in goods shipped, credit terms, and the like. Because these forms are drafted by the respective parties, the preprinted terms usually favor the drafting party. As a result, when placed side-by-side, certain terms contained in the purchase order and acknowledgment form do not correspond. Therefore, if the forms are treated as the offer and acceptance, a strict adherence to the common law mirror image rule would result in no contract even though the obvious intent of the parties is to enter into a contract, and they nevertheless proceed with the transaction.

Section 2–207 is primarily designed to enforce the intent of the parties. Neither party is allowed to escape contractual obligation because of minor discrepancies between preprinted forms. If compliance with an unnegotiated term is important, the offeree can protect itself by making acceptance expressly conditional upon the offeror's assent to the term.

In addition to the battle of the forms, §2–207 governs the written confirmation. In this case, an agreement is reached either orally—for example, by telephone—or by informal correspondence. Subsequently, a formal writing—the confirmation—is sent by one or both parties embodying the agreement but adding terms not discussed.

In both the battle of the forms and written confirmation cases, the Code relaxes somewhat the effect of the mirror image rule by making contract formation turn upon the existence of a "definite and seasonable expression of acceptance" by the offeree, or the timely dispatch of a written confirmation, rather than the offeree's literal compliance with the terms of the offer. The effect of the mirror image rule on Code contracts is further reduced by §2–207(3). Under this provision, even if the writings exchanged by the parties do not establish an agreement, *conduct* by the parties that recognizes the existence of a contract is sufficient.

To illustrate the general operation of Section 2–207, assume S, a manufacturer of nuts, bolts, and other fasteners, and B, an appliance manufacturer, negotiate for the sale of large quantities of fasteners for use in B's manufacturing operation. The parties ultimately agree upon the quantity, assortment, price, quality, and delivery terms. These terms are typed on B's purchase order form, which is sent to S, who responds with S's

---

[5]Under the UCC, an action is taken "seasonably" if it is taken at or within the time called for by the contract, or if no time is stated, then at or within a reasonable time. UCC §1–205.

preprinted confirmation form. The forms exchanged, though agreeing on the basic dickered terms, conflict somewhat in the fine print. S's form states its standard credit terms: 1/10, net 30; B's form provides 2/10, net 30. S's form states that notice of defects in deliveries must be given within 10 days; B's form allows 21 days. S's form provides for interest on overdue invoices; B's form is silent on the point. S's form contains a provision requiring arbitration of disputes arising out of the contract. B's form is silent on the point. S's form contains a provision disclaiming warranties and limiting the buyer's remedies to repair or replacement of defective goods. B's form provides that the seller makes all warranties and the buyer possesses all remedies for breach provided in Article 2 of the UCC. Despite these discrepancies, which would defeat contract formation under a strict application of the mirror image rule, a contract is formed under §2–207.

Terms of the Contract. Section 2–207 not only determines when a contract exists if an apparent acceptance varies the terms of the offer, but also determines the terms of that contract. Under §2–207(2), the additional terms are construed as proposals for addition to the contract. In other words, a contract is created on the *offeror's* terms, and additional terms are treated as proposals by the offeree for inclusion. In contracts between merchants, however, the additional terms become part of the contract unless

1. the offer expressly limits acceptance to the terms of the offer,
2. the additional terms materially alter the offer, or
3. the offeror notifies the offeree of his or her objection to them within a reasonable time.

Thus, between merchants, a contract exists on the *offeree's* terms, but the offeror may be protected through the application of one of the exceptions listed above.

Section 2–207's rules determining the terms of the contract have generated a significant volume of litigation. The reason is that §2–207 treats the forms as offers and acceptances, even though the parties do not. (That is, the parties previously have reached agreement over the phone, by an exchange of business letters, or by face to face meeting.) As a result, cases often are resolved based on the order in which the forms are sent, a fortuitous event. As noted UCC commentators have concluded: "We see no way to apply §2–207 that does not sometimes give an unearned and unfair advantage to the

person who happens to send the first, or in some cases the second, document."[6] In addition, because the forms are ignored by the parties during negotiations, but have significant legal consequences under §2–207 in litigation, each party attempts to draft its form, not to reflect the parties' actual agreement, but to assure that its non-negotiated terms will govern any subsequent dispute. As a result a dispute over a term on which the forms conflict often requires litigation to resolve, litigation which under §2–207 binds one party to a term in the other's form that has not been considered, much less agreed upon, by the parties.

Termination by Operation of Law

As noted above, offers are often terminated by the language or other conduct of either the offeror (revocation) or the offeree (rejection). In certain circumstances, the offer may be terminated automatically by operation of law upon the occurrence of an event without further action by the offeror or offeree. The term **operation of law** is a general legal concept used to describe the manner in which a party's rights or duties are determined automatically by the application of a rule of law to a given set of facts, without the act or cooperation of the party.[7]

An offer is terminated by operation of law if before acceptance

1. either party dies;
2. either party is deprived of contractual capacity due, for example, to a physical disability or mental illness; or
3. the subject matter of the proposed contract becomes illegal or is destroyed.

Note that these terminations become effective automatically without notice to the other party. Assume Seller offers to sell land to Buyer on January 1, dies on January 2, and Buyer learns of the death on January 3. The offer is terminated by operation of law on January 2, even though Buyer does not learn of the death until January 3. Similarly, assume that on June 1, Seller offers to sell his antique Rolls-Royce to Buyer. On June 2, while Buyer is still considering the offer, the car is destroyed by fire. The offer is terminated by operation of law on June 2.

---

[6]White & Summers, Uniform Commercial Code 24 (4th ed. 1995).
[7]Black's Law Dictionary 1092 (6th ed. 1990).

It is important to note that although *offers* are terminated on death, *contracts* generally are not. That is, a contract is ordinarily unaffected by the death of one or both parties. To illustrate, assume Small makes an offer on June 1 to sell land to Brinkley, and agrees to hold the offer open until June 30. If Small dies on June 15, the offer is automatically revoked by Small's death; Brinkley may not accept it between the fifteenth and the thirtieth. If, however, an option contract had been created, Small's death on the fifteenth would not terminate Brinkley's ability to exercise the option. Brinkley still has 15 days in which to accept the offer (exercise the option), and if he elects to do so, Small's estate is bound by Brinkley's acceptance and would be required to perform the contract.

Acceptance

The offer creates the power of acceptance, the power to create a contract, in the offeree. To this point the text has discussed events terminating the offer, resulting in no contractual relationship between the parties. The following material discusses **acceptance** of the offer, by which the offeree unequivocally manifests assent to the terms of the offer in the manner prescribed or authorized by the offeror. Upon acceptance, the promise or promises contemplated by the offer become binding as a contract.

A number of previously considered topics are closely related to acceptance. For instance, the material relating to counteroffer, mirror image, and "battle of the forms" often concerns the legal effect of an attempted, though defective, acceptance. As these topics and the following case indicate, it is often difficult to determine whether an offeree's response to an offer constitutes an acceptance.

Wucherpfennig v. Dooley
351 N.W.2d 443 (N.D. 1984)

Plaintiff Donald Wucherpfennig and his sister, defendant Elizabeth Dooley, each owned an undivided interest in their family farm. On January 4, 1979, Dooley sent to Robert Case, an attorney handling the farm, a letter that stated in part, "Now if Don wants to buy my share of the real estate, I will sell it to him for $200 an acre, provided it is a cash deal and handled promptly." By letter dated January 13, 1979, Case notified Dooley that Wucherpfennig was interested and on February 17, 1979, Case sent Dooley the following letter:

Donald has made arrangements with the Federal Land Bank to secure funds to purchase your interest in the estate farmland and we are therefore ready to proceed with this transaction. Please let me know the exact dollar amount that you expect to receive for your interest in the land.

I must know also if you are willing to sign the agreement relating to Special Use Valuation.

Please let me hear from you regarding these matters.

Dooley did not respond to the letter, but by letter dated March 9, 1979, she revoked her offer to sell the land to Donald for $200 per acre. Wucherpfennig sued Dooley for breach of contract seeking the remedy of specific performance. The trial court found that no contract had been formed and ruled in favor of Dooley. Wucherpfennig appealed to the North Dakota Supreme Court.

Sand, Justice

. . . The acceptance of an offer must be absolute, unequivocal, and unconditional, and it may not introduce additional terms or conditions. . . . In order to form a contract, the offer and acceptance must express assent to the same thing. . . . A valid acceptance must be unequivocally expressive of an intent to create thereby, *without more,* a contract. . . .

There is no dispute that Elizabeth offered to sell the property for $200 per acre. Donald claims that Case's letter of 17 February unequivocally accepted that offer. However, Case's letter merely states that Donald "has made arrangements . . . to secure funds" and that they were "ready to proceed with this transaction." In the next sentence of the letter, Case asks Elizabeth to let him know the exact dollar amount that she expected to receive for the land.

The language of the 17 February letter does not embody an absolute, unequivocal, and unconditional acceptance of Elizabeth's offer, and is not expressive of an intent to create, without more, a contract. The terms of the letter appear to be more in the nature of negotiations with a view toward reaching an agreement in the future. Case states that Donald is "ready to proceed" and asks what amount Elizabeth expects to receive for her interest in the property. These are hardly the words of an unequivocal, unconditional acceptance of Elizabeth's offer.

In addition, the testimony of Donald at trial lends further support to the conclusion that the parties never assented to the same terms. In response to a question by Elizabeth's counsel asking why an exact dollar amount was not included in the 17 February letter, Donald stated:

> The exact dollar amount would have been $37,200.00. And that would have been somewhat less than she would have thought she was entitled to. And had we sent a contract at that time with the $37,200.00 in it, I'm sure she wouldn't have signed it.

The parties can hardly be said to have mutually assented to the terms of a contract when Donald admits that he believed Elizabeth was expecting more than $37,200, the amount he intended to pay, and that she would not have agreed to that amount.

We conclude that Donald did not accept Elizabeth's offer prior to her revocation of the offer on 9 March 1979, and thus there is no contract between the parties. . . .

[Judgment affirmed.]

Manner of Acceptance

An offer may invite acceptance either by the offeree's *promise to perform* (that is, a promise to do or refrain from doing an act) resulting in a *bilateral* contract, or by the offeree's *performance* of the act requested by the offer creating a *unilateral* contract. A bilateral contract contains two promises—the offeror's promise in exchange for the offeree's return promise. In a bilateral contract, each party is both a promisor, a person making a promise, and a promisee, a person to whom a promise is made. Assume Zach says to Rod, "If you promise to paint my house, I promise to pay you $2,000." Rod says, "I accept. I promise to paint your house." A bilateral contract is created, under which Rod promises to paint the house, and Zach promises to pay $2,000. Most contracts are bilateral in nature.

In contrast, a unilateral offer requests an act rather than a return promise. An offer that says, "I promise to pay you $25 after you have completed mowing my lawn," is an offer for a unilateral contract. The offeror is not requesting a return promise (the *promise* to mow the lawn); he is requesting an act (mowing the lawn). The offeree must perform the act to accept the offer. Only one promise, the offeror's, is present. This promise is binding upon the offeror only after the offeree has completed the requested act (accepted the offer). Because the offeree makes no promise, he generally incurs no liability to the offeror for failure to perform the act requested in the offer.

Both unilateral and bilateral offers can be accepted only by a person to whom the offer has been directed, either individually, or as a member of a class (for example, an offer for a reward). For example, assume Sam offers to sell his boat to Betty for $15,000. John overhears Sam making the offer and says, "I accept." No contract results. Similarly, Betty could not assign or transfer Sam's offer to John or anyone else. This result again illustrates the general principle that the offeror is the master of the offer.

Specific Problems of Unilateral Contracts

Unilateral contracts present unique problems for the law of offer and acceptance including (1) the effect of the offeree's commencing performance without knowledge of the offer, (2) the revocability of unilateral offers after performance has commenced, and (3) the effect of ambiguous offers, offers that fail to clearly indicate whether a promise or performance is requested.

Commencing Performance Without Knowledge of Offer. The offer must be communicated to the offeree before acceptance can occur. If a unilateral offer is made, however, the offeree may accept even though she *started* performance without knowledge of the offer. She must only *complete* performance with knowledge of the offer. In other words, the offer need only induce completion of performance, not necessarily the entire act. Assume Audrey loses her watch and places an advertisement in the newspaper offering a reward for its return. Barbara finds the watch without knowledge of the offer. She later learns of the offer and returns the watch to Audrey. Barbara is entitled to the reward.

Revocation After Performance Commenced. The principle that unilateral offers can be accepted only by performance poses a problem commonly illustrated by the following hypothetical situation involving the Brooklyn Bridge. Suppose the offeror says to the offeree, "After you have completed walking across the Brooklyn Bridge, I promise to pay you $10." The offeree then starts walking across the bridge, and as he nears the other side, the offeror yells, "I revoke." Because an offeror may generally revoke an offer prior to the effectiveness of the acceptance, and a unilateral offer is not accepted until completion of the act, one may argue that the offeror is free to revoke a unilateral offer at any time before the offeree completes performance. This is true even if, as in the above example, the offeree substantially completes performance before revocation. The rationale for this argument is that because the offeree makes no enforceable promise, the offeror should be free to withdraw before full performance.

Obviously, this result works an injustice upon an offeree who has substantially completed performance. Most courts resolve the problem by finding that once the offeree has substantially commenced performance of a unilateral contract, he must be given a reasonable opportunity to complete performance. That is, after the offeree commences performance, an option is created, making the offer irrevocable by the offeror. If the offeree completes performance within the time allowed, the offeror is bound to the promise.

Ambiguous Offers. Under the master of the offer rule, the offeror may require any mode of acceptance—promise or performance. Ordinarily, however, the offeror invites acceptance in a reasonable manner, and in case of doubt, an offer is construed as inviting the offeree to choose between promise and performance. Under both the common law and the UCC, "unless otherwise unambiguously indicated by the language or circumstances . . . an offer to make a contract shall be construed as inviting acceptance in any manner . . . reasonable in the circumstances."[8] Thus, if an offer is ambiguous or indifferent regarding the manner of acceptance, the offeree may choose either promise or performance. If the offeree chooses a promise, a bilateral contract is created. If the offeree chooses performance, §62 of the *Restatement (Second) of Contracts* provides that the offeree's commencement of perfor-

mance constitutes an acceptance, and such an acceptance operates as a promise to render complete performance. Under this approach, a bilateral contract is created, rendering the offeree liable for breach of contract for failure to complete performance.

Expressly Unilateral Offers—UCC Approach. Under the UCC, an offer that is expressly *unilateral* may be accepted by a promise or performance. Assume B sends S an order stating, "Ship 100 dishwashers, Model 100, at once." The order is an offer for a unilateral contract, requesting shipment, not a promise to ship. However, §2–206(1)(b) provides that "an order or other offer to buy goods for prompt or current shipment" may be accepted either by a prompt promise to ship or the prompt shipment of the goods. That is, the expressly unilateral offer ("ship at once") may be accepted either by the act, shipment, or by a promise to ship.

The "Unilateral Contract Trick." If the offeree-seller elects to ship, the UCC provides that acceptance occurs by the "prompt or current shipment of conforming or non-conforming goods." By making shipment of nonconforming goods an acceptance, the Code prevents what has been called the "unilateral contract trick." To illustrate, assume Bendix orders Star, Inc., to "ship at once, 100 'deluxe' model electric window fans." Star is out of the deluxe model, but ships instead the cheaper "standard" model. Bendix rejects the shipment and sues for breach of contract. Star defends by asserting that acceptance of a unilateral offer requires performance of the requested act, here, shipment of "deluxe" fans. Because "standard" fans were shipped instead, Star has not performed the act contemplated by the offer, and has therefore not accepted the offer. Because there has been no acceptance, there is no contract, and consequently no breach—the unilateral contract trick. The Code eliminates this argument by making Star's shipment of "standard" fans (nonconforming goods) acceptance of the offer. Thus, Star's shipment simultaneously constitutes both an acceptance and a breach.

Accommodating Substitution. Occasionally, a seller will not have goods ordered by a buyer, but will ship substitute goods instead as an accommodation to the buyer. If the buyer can use them, a contract is made and the accommodation is successful; if not, the buyer simply returns them without legal consequence. To

---

[8]UCC §2–206(1)(a); *See also* RESTATEMENT (SECOND) OF CONTRACTS §§30, 32.

prevent the accommodating substitution from operating as an acceptance and breach under the rule outlined above, §2–206(1)(b) provides that "a shipment of non-conforming goods does not constitute an acceptance if the seller seasonably notifies the buyer that the shipment is offered only as an accommodation to the buyer." Thus, by notifying the buyer of its intention, the seller can avoid the usual consequences of a nonconforming shipment.

The net effect of the above rules is that most offers may be accepted by a promise to perform (bilateral) or are ultimately treated as bilateral contracts. The rationale for this result is that the unilateral-bilateral distinction is essentially an artificial one, leading both the common law and the UCC to limit the importance of the dichotomy, and to treat most contracts as bilateral. Unilateral offers now include primarily reward offers, offers requesting a forebearance (for example, when the offer asks the offeree to refrain from doing an act, such as drinking, smoking, swearing), or other situations in which the offer unambiguously indicates that full performance, as opposed to a promise or commencement of performance, is requested.

Notification of Acceptance

Notification is a concept appearing throughout contracts, and law generally. A person notifies or gives notice to another person by taking whatever steps are reasonably necessary to inform the other in the usual course of events. Provided these reasonable steps are taken, the notice is effective whether or not the other person actually learns of it. A person receives a notice or notification when it comes to his or her attention or is properly delivered at a place used for receipt of such communications, such as a place of business, post office box, or residence.

Generally speaking, and subject to the rules on effectiveness of an acceptance outlined below, an effective acceptance by promise—the "bilateral" contract—requires that the offeree notify the offeror of acceptance. If an offer invites acceptance by rendering a performance—the "unilateral" contract—no notification is generally necessary to make the acceptance effective. In most cases, the offeror promptly learns of the offeree's performance, thus negating any need for notification. Notice *may,* however, be required if the offer itself requires it or if the offeror has no adequate means of learning of the per-

formance. Note that in any unilateral contract case, notification does not create the contract; performance or beginning performance does. Lack of notification *may,* however, discharge the offeror's duty. Notice therefore protects the offeree, who is relying upon the offer, by preventing the offeror's discharge while the offeree is performing. As previously noted, the offeree's commencement of performance often constitutes an acceptance, thereby binding him to complete performance.

The Uniform Commercial Code addresses this issue in §2–206(2) by providing that "Where the beginning of a requested performance is a reasonable mode of acceptance an offeror who is not notified of acceptance within a reasonable time may treat the offer as having lapsed before acceptance." To illustrate, assume Buyer sends Seller a written order for goods to be specially manufactured for Buyer, requesting that Seller begin at once, because manufacture will take several months. As previously discussed, acceptance may be complete when Seller begins manufacture, but Buyer's duty to pay is discharged and he may treat the offer as having lapsed before acceptance unless within a reasonable time Seller sends Buyer a notification of acceptance or unless the offer or prior dealing indicates that notice is not required. The following classic English case illustrates notification of acceptance of a unilateral offer.

Carlill v. Carbolic Smoke Ball Company
[1893] 1 Q.B. 256 (C.A.)

Defendant Carbolic Smoke Ball Company (Carbolic) published the following advertisement in several British newspapers during November 1891:

100£ reward will be paid by the Carbolic Smoke Ball Company to any person who contracts the increasing epidemic influenza, colds, or any disease caused by taking cold, after having used the ball three times daily for two weeks according to the printed directions supplied with each ball. 1,000£ is deposited with the Alliance Bank, Regent Street, showing our sincerity in the matter.

During the last epidemic of influenza, many thousand carbolic smoke balls were sold as preventives against this disease, and in no ascertained case was the disease contracted by those using the carbolic smoke ball.

One carbolic smoke ball will last a family several months, making it the cheapest remedy in the world at the price, 10s post free. The ball can be refilled at a cost of 5s. Address,

Carbolic Smoke Ball Company, 27 Princess Street, Hanover Square, London.

Plaintiff Carlill, relying on the advertisement, purchased one of the smoke balls. After using it according to the printed directions for two weeks, she contracted influenza. When she attempted to claim the 100£ reward, Carbolic refused to pay. Carlill sued Carbolic and the trial court ruled in favor of Carlill. Carbolic appealed.

Lindley, Lord Justice

. . . The first observation I would make is that we are not dealing with any inferences of fact. We are dealing with an express promise to pay 100£ in certain events. There can be no mistake about that at all. Read this advertisement how you will, and twist it about as you will, here is a distinct promise expressed in language which is perfectly unmistakable: "100£ reward will be paid by the Carbolic Smoke Ball Company to any person who contracts the influenza after having used the ball three times daily," and so on.

Now one must look at it a little further, and see if this is intended to be a promise at all, or whether it is a mere puff—a sort of thing which means nothing. Is that the meaning of it? My answer to that question is No, and I base my answer upon this passage: "1,000£ is deposited with the Alliance Bank, shewing our sincerity in the matter." Now, what is that deposited for? What is that put in for, except to negative the suggestion that this is a mere puff, and means nothing at all? The deposit is called in aid by the advertiser as proof of his sincerity in the matter—that is, of his intention to pay this 100£ in the events which he has specified. I make that remark, as I say, for the purpose of giving point to the observation that we are not inferring the promise from ambiguous language. Here it is, as plain as words can make it.

Then it is said that it is not binding. In the first place, it is said that it is not made with anybody in particular. Now that point is common to the words of this advertisement, as to the words of all other advertisements offering rewards. They make offers to anybody who performs the conditions named in the advertisement, and anybody who does perform the conditions accepts the offer. I take it, if you look at this advertisement, in point of law, it is an offer to pay 100£ to anybody who will perform these conditions, and the performance of the conditions is the acceptance of the offer. . . .

But then it is said, "Well, supposing that the performance of the condition is an acceptance of the offer, that acceptance ought to be notified." Unquestionably, as a general proposition, when an offer is made, you must have it not only accepted, but the acceptance notified. But is that so in cases of this kind? I apprehend that this is rather an exception to that rule, or, if not an exception, it is open to the observation that the notification of the acceptance need not precede the performance. This offer is a continuing offer; it was never revoked, and if notice of acceptance is required . . . , the person who makes the offer gets the notice of acceptance contemporaneously with his notice of the performance of the condition. Anyhow, if notice is wanted, he gets it before his offer is revoked, which is all you want in principle; but I doubt very much whether the true view is not in a case of this kind that the person who makes the offer shows by his language and from the nature of the transaction that he does not expect, and does not require, notice of the acceptance apart from notice of the performance.

We have, therefore, all the elements which are necessary to form a binding contract enforceable in point of law. . . .

[Judgment affirmed.]

Silence as Acceptance. Generally, the offeree's failure to respond to the offer does not constitute acceptance. For example, suppose Seth offers to sell land to Roger stating, "If I don't hear from you by noon tomorrow, I will assume you have accepted my offer." By failing to respond, Roger has not accepted the offer. Receipt of the offer does not limit the offeree's freedom to act or refuse to act and may not require him to speak.

The offeree's explicit statements, trade custom, express agreement, or prior course of dealing between the parties may, however, lead the offeror to assume justifiably that silence is acceptance. Using the above example, suppose Roger stated to Seth, "If you don't hear from me by noon tomorrow, you can assume I have accepted." Roger's failure to respond would constitute acceptance. Or, assume Roger joins a book club. The agreement provides that the club will send a card every month indicating the current month's selection. If Roger fails to return the card, he receives the book. In this case, Roger's silence (failure to return) is an acceptance because of the prior agreement by the parties that silence operates as acceptance. Such an agreement may arise either expressly or as a result of prior dealing between the parties. Acceptance also may be inferred from silence when a person knowingly receives and accepts benefits from another while in a position to reject them. In this case, a contract implied in fact is created. That is, silence is merely one form of conduct through which a promise may be made.[9]

Effectiveness of Acceptance: "Mailbox Acceptance Rule"

The effective date of an acceptance is often governed by the doctrine known as the **mailbox acceptance rule,** or "deposited acceptance rule." This rule applies when the parties are communicating at a distance, generally by mail. Under these circumstances, an acceptance is normally effective when *sent;* that is, when the offeree relinquishes control over his acceptance. For instance, a mailed acceptance is usually effective when it is placed in the mailbox, whether or not it ever reaches the offeror.[10]

For the rule to apply, the offeree must use the means of acceptance authorized by the offeror. Assume S sends B a letter offering to sell S's farm for $1 million. Assume the offer states, "You must accept by U.S. mail," or the offer says nothing about the manner or medium of acceptance. In the first situation, if the acceptance is sent by e-mail, no contract is created. If sent by mail, a contract is created when the letter is placed in the mailbox. In the second situation, an acceptance by mail or commercial overnight letter would be effective when sent because the offeror, in the absence of evidence to the contrary, authorizes the means used in communicating the offer. She also impliedly authorizes any other means customarily used in similar transactions. The UCC retains the mailbox rule, but divorces the rule from authorization. Under the Code, an acceptance made "by any medium reasonable in the circumstances" is effective when sent.[11]

If an unauthorized or unreasonable means of acceptance is used, the acceptance is effective when received (provided the offeror has not dictated the means which must be used). Additionally, an acceptance sent by mail or otherwise is not effective unless it is properly addressed, with postage or cost of transmission provided for, and with any other precautions necessary to insure a proper transmission of similar messages.[12]

The rationale for the mailbox rule is that because the offer is freely revocable by the offeror, an offeree who decides to accept needs to know precisely when an enforceable contract exists. The rule allows the offeree to rely upon the existence of the contract when he sends his acceptance. Any revocation received after this point is ineffective. Assume Sally makes an offer to sell her farm to Bob by mail on June 1. Bob accepts by mail on June 3, received by Sally on June 6. On June 4, Sally gets a better offer for the farm from Mary and telephones Bob revoking the offer. Sally's revocation is ineffective because a contract was made on June 3. Note that the rule also precludes the offeree from speculating at the offeror's expense while the acceptance is in transit. That is, the offeree's attempt to retract an acceptance after mailing is ineffective.

The rule is further justified by the fact that the offeror, being the master of the offer, can stipulate that any attempted acceptance will not be effective until actually received. In this case, the offeree cannot rely upon the contract until learning that the offeror has received the acceptance. Further, the risk of losing the acceptance in transit and the risk of a revocation becoming effective before the acceptance is received are borne by the offeree. The mailbox rule places these burdens on the offeror who was originally in a position to protect herself and failed to do so.

The mailbox rule does not apply to acceptance of offers held open under option contracts. Thus, an acceptance under an option contract is not effective until actually received by the offeror. Because the offer in an option contract is irrevocable by the offeror, the protection against revocation afforded the offeree by the mailbox rule is not necessary. Assume Sally grants Bob a 30-day option to buy Sally's farm. Bob must actually notify Sally of his intent to exercise the option within the 30-day period. Notification sent but not received within that period is ineffective.

The mailbox rule also may be inapplicable if the offeree sends both an acceptance and a rejection. For example, assume that in response to Sally's offer, Bob sends the following communications:

---

[9]Contracts implied in fact are discussed in Chapter 7.

[10]Of course, if the parties are dealing face-to-face, or by telephone or other medium of substantially instantaneous two-way communication, the time of sending and receiving are the same.

[11]UCC §2–206(1)(a).

[12]Under both the common law and the Code, however, even if an unreasonable means is used, or if the instrument is improperly dispatched, the acceptance is effective when sent if actually received within the time at which it would have arrived if properly sent.

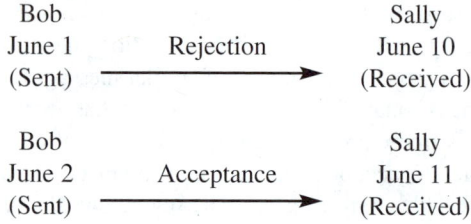

Bob		Sally
June 1	Rejection	June 10
(Sent)	——————→	(Received)

Bob		Sally
June 2	Acceptance	June 11
(Sent)	——————→	(Received)

Because rejections are effective when received and acceptances are effective when sent, it appears that a contract exists on June 2. Because the offeror may rely on the rejection of June 10, however, the law recognizes an exception to the mailbox rule. On these facts, Bob's acceptance is effective when received. If received after receipt of the rejection (the case here), it is treated as a counteroffer. If received before the rejection arrives, a contract is created, because the offeror cannot rely on a rejection until received.

In the above example, the rejection is sent before the acceptance. If the acceptance is sent first, the mailbox rule still applies. To illustrate, assume that Bob responds as follows to Sally's offer:

Bob		Sally
June 1	Acceptance	June 10
(Sent)	——————→	(Received)

Bob		Sally
June 2	Rejection	June 9
(Sent)	——————→	(Received)

On these facts, the acceptance is effective when sent. Bob's June 2 communication is merely an attempt to retract an already binding acceptance. However, if Sally changes her position in reliance on the rejection (for example, by selling the goods she offered to Bob elsewhere upon learning of the rejection), Bob may not enforce the contract.

Summary

1. The first element of contract formation is an agreement embodying mutual assent to an exchange. Ordinarily, agreement is reached, after preliminary dickering or negotiation, when an offer made by one party is accepted by the other.

2. Offer and acceptance issues may be divided into three categories: (1) the existence, terms, and effectiveness of the offer; (2) events terminating an offer prior to acceptance; and (3) acceptance of the offer.

3. An offer is a conditional promise raising the power of acceptance, the power to create a contract, in the offeree. Because the offeror is contractually bound upon acceptance, the offeror is allowed to control the terms, duration, and manner of acceptance. This "master of the offer" rule protects the offeror by allowing him to dictate the terms on which he is willing to deal.

4. The contents of the offer and most other communications between the parties is governed by the "objective theory of contract." Under this theory the terms of a communication are determined not by the subjective intention of the communicating party, but instead by the reasonable impression the communication makes upon the other party. Judged by this test, a communication is treated as an offer if it is sufficiently definite to indicate an intention on the part of the offeror to be contractually bound and contains sufficient minimum terms.

This "definiteness" requirement affords a court in a later dispute a basis to determine whether a contract exists and has been breached, and to award an appropriate remedy.

5. Once made, an offer may be terminated before acceptance, resulting in no contract. Termination may occur by act of the offeror or offeree, or by operation of law.

6. The offeror may generally terminate an offer by revoking it. An offer is generally freely revocable prior to acceptance unless the offer is itself a contract, an option, or is a "firm offer" made by a merchant to buy or sell goods in a signed writing.

7. The offeree may terminate an offer by rejecting it, including either an express rejection or counteroffer. Under the traditional common law rule, any attempted acceptance must be the "mirror image" of the offer and any variation between the two constitutes a rejection of the offer and a counteroffer on the new terms. The UCC alters this result somewhat for contracts involving goods by providing that a definite expression of acceptance or timely written confirmation operates as an acceptance even though it contains terms different from or in addition to the offer.

8. The offer may also be terminated by operation of law, most commonly upon the death of either party.

9. The offer, if not terminated, may be accepted, resulting in a contract. The offer may invite acceptance either by the offeree's return promise, creating a bilateral contract, or by the offeree's performance of an act, resulting in a unilateral contract. In general, the offeror must be notified of acceptance in a bilateral contract, although in limited circumstances the offeree's silence operates as an acceptance. In a unilateral contract, notice is usually provided by the offeree's performance of the act requested by the offer.

10. In determining the effectiveness of the various communications between offeror and offeree, the following rules apply: (1) offers, rejections (including counteroffers), and revocations are effective when received by the person to whom directed; (2) termination of an offer by operation of law is effective immediately (for example, on death) with no notice to the other party required; and (3) subject to various exceptions, acceptances are effective when sent under the "mailbox acceptance rule." By comparing the effective dates of the various communications (for example, acceptance versus revocation), the existence or nonexistence of a contract is determined.

Key Terms

offer	rejection
master of the offer	mirror image rule
objective theory of contract	operation of law
definiteness	acceptance
revocation	notification
option contract	mailbox acceptance rule
firm offer rule	

Questions and Problems

8.1 Explain the rationale for the master of the offer rule. Is this rule consistent with the objective theory of contract?

8.2 From time to time a business may want to sell a piece of used equipment or a tract of land. The sale usually is unrelated to the firm's ordinary business activities. Although the seller may want to inform a segment of the public of the availability of the property, it also may not want such information construed as an offer. Why would a seller, who clearly wants to sell property, not want communication intended as informational to be considered an offer?

If the seller already knows the terms it is willing to accept (for example, price, financing, delivery) and wants to convey this information, it runs a greater risk that the information it communicates will be considered an offer. How can the seller protect itself from this risk?

8.3 After purchasing a new computer system, City University published a notice in the newspaper on November 1 offering to sell its used computer system to the highest bidder. The notice described the system and requested all interested parties to submit firm bids in writing to the university. Falco, a used computer dealer, submitted a letter on November 18 stating that it would purchase the system for $300,000 and that its bid would remain open through December 18.

(a) Who is the offeror? the offeree?

(b) On December 9, after learning that its bank would not lend it the money to purchase the system, Falco telephoned City University and revoked its bid. Nevertheless, on December 10, City University unequivocally accepted Falco's bid. Has a contract been formed? Explain.

8.4 In each of the following cases, the offeror argued that no contract had been formed because the attempted acceptance was not made in the manner required by the offeror. How should the court rule in each of these cases?

(a) The Electric Cooperative, Inc. provided electric power to the town of Lindsay pursuant to a contract that expired on June 1, 2005. On March 1, 2005, the Cooperative proposed a new contract to the town. Following a vote of the city council the mayor wrote a letter dated April 1, 2005, to the Cooperative stating that the town was offering the Cooperative the right to provide electricity to Lindsay if the Cooperative would pay an annual fee of $200. The letter concluded, "This agreement shall take effect upon the Cooperative's filing a written acceptance within 30 days." The Cooperative paid the $200 fee but did not file a written acceptance. On August 1, 2005, the town entered into a contract with The Peoples' Power Co. by which Peoples agreed to provide electric power to Lindsay. Electric Cooperative sued the town of Lindsay alleging that it had a contract to provide power. What result?

(b) Sea Coast Steel sells and delivers steel to automobile manufacturers. On January 4, 2005, USA Motors ordered 565 tons of steel from Sea Coast by submitting a purchase order. The final paragraph of the purchase order stated, "All deliveries to be made on or before January 15, 2005. Delivery of any item covered by this order or written approval of the order shall constitute acceptance." Sea Coast began making purchases to fill the contract. Because steel was in short supply, USA Motors wrote Sea Coast authorizing delivery on or before February 1. On January 25, Sea Coast phoned USA Motors to notify it that delivery could be made only on January 28, a Saturday. USA Motors told Sea Coast that its loading dock was closed on Saturdays so that Sea Coast should cancel the order. Sea Coast sued for breach of contract. What result?

(c) Bob Brown had been negotiating to purchase a house from Rhonda Underman. On October 12, Bob Brown made a valid written offer to purchase the house on a uniform purchase agreement form. At the bottom of the form was the following statement: "ACCEPTANCE ON REVERSE SIDE." On the reverse side was a line reading "I hereby accept the foregoing offer" and a line for the offeree's signature. At Underman's request, Brown delivered the offer to the office of Underman's attorney,

Sam Wurd. On October 14, Brown received the following letter written and signed by Wurd: "This letter is written on behalf of Rhonda Underman who hereby accepts your offer of October 12." Enclosed was a copy of Brown's written offer. On October 16, Brown delivered a letter to Underman in which he revoked his offer of October 12. When Brown refused to buy the house, Underman sued for breach of contract. Brown argued that no contract had been made because Underman had not accepted the offer as prescribed by the offeror. How should the court rule?

8.5   On January 1, Franny granted Johnny a 30-day option to purchase a farm. Johnny paid $100 for the option, which gave him the right to purchase the farm for $50,000. Determine how the court should rule in each of the following cases.

(a) On January 15, Johnny tells Franny that he is moving out of state and would not buy the farm. On January 25, Johnny tenders $50,000 to Franny, telling her he has changed his mind. Franny refuses to sell him the farm. Johnny sues.

(b) On January 10, Howard offers to purchase Franny's farm for $60,000. Franny promptly notifies Johnny that she is revoking the option unless Johnny agrees to pay $60,000. Johnny does not respond immediately but on January 22, Franny dies. On January 23, Johnny exercises his option to purchase at $50,000, but Franny's estate refuses to sell. Johnny sues.

(c) Would your answers to (a) and (b) change if Johnny had not paid $100 for the option? Explain.

(d) If the option had been for the purchase of a tractor, rather than a farm, would your answers to (a), (b), and (c) change? Explain.

8.6   (a) On February 1, Joshua received a letter from Treasure magazine in a window envelope that permitted Joshua to read the following through the window: "JOSHUA, I'LL GIVE YOU A VERSATILE NEW CALCULATOR WATCH FREE JUST FOR OPENING THIS ENVELOPE BEFORE FEBRUARY 15." Joshua immediately opened the envelope and discovered that the letter continued "AND MAILING THIS CERTIFICATE TODAY!" By mailing the certificate, Joshua would be required to purchase a subscription to Treasure magazine. Has an offer been made? Has an acceptance been made? Has a contract been formed? Explain.

(b) Amos Driver was playing golf at the Fairview Golf Course. At the tee of the ninth hole, Amos saw a brand-new Cadillac next to a large sign which stated, "HOLE IN ONE wins this Cadillac courtesy of Lewis Car Dealer." Amos shot a hole in one and attempted to collect his prize. Lewis refused to deliver the car explaining that it had offered the car as a prize in a charity tournament held the previous day at Fairview Golf Course. Driver sued Lewis Car Dealer for breach of contract. How should the court rule? Explain.

8.7   On May 20, J. W. Worth was visiting his neighbors Joe and Olive Twist when the conversation turned to taxes. Joe stated that he and his wife were considering selling some of their real estate because the taxes were too high. At Worth's request, J. W. brought out maps showing where his properties were located. Worth was especially interested in Bear Ranch and asked Joe how much he expected to sell that ranch for, and Joe replied, "for the assessed value." As Worth was leaving, Olive promised to send him more information about their land sales.

On June 17, Worth received a letter from the Twists that stated in part, "Enclosed is the information about the ranch sales that we discussed previously." The enclosure read as follows:

Joe and Olive Twist
R. R. 1
Hometown, Oregon

Selling Bear Ranch—approximately 2,933 acres in Grant County near Seneca, Oregon, at the assessed market value:

Land	$306,409
Buildings	18,010
Total	$324,419

Terms available: Buyer pays 25% down, balance over 5 years at 8% interest. Can negotiate sale date. Available after crops harvested and seller removes all equipment.
    ALSO selling 250 head of cattle now located on ranch.

(a) Assume that on May 20, during his conversation with Joe Twist, Worth had stated, "I accept your offer to sell Bear Ranch for the assessed value." Would a contract have been formed at that point? Explain.

(b) Assume instead that on June 21. Worth sent a letter to the Twists stating, "Re Bear Ranch. I accept your offer of June 17." Would a contract have been formed at that point? Explain. Would your answer be different if, during their meeting on May 20, the Twists had told Worth that they would sell the land only if the purchaser also agreed to buy the cattle? Explain.

(c) Assume that upon receipt of Worth's letter of June 21 (see (b) above), the Twists wrote a letter in response that stated in part, "You have misconstrued our prior negotiations concerning Bear Ranch. Our letter of June 17 was not intended as an offer. In fact, we sent similar letters to three other neighbors who are also interested in the property. We are open to further negotiations." Would a contract have been formed on June 21? Explain.

(d) Assume that Worth sent his letter of June 21 but that another neighbor of the Twists also sent them a letter on June 21 accepting the offer of sale. Both Worth and the neighbor sue the Twists demanding performance of the contract. How would a court resolve the dispute?

(e) Assume that upon receipt of Worth's letter of June 21, the Twists agreed that a contract had been formed. What are the terms of the contract?

8.8   Because year-end car sales were slow, Mighty Motors needed to sell some of its inventory to make room for the new 1995 model cars. Mighty Motors placed the following advertisement in the newspaper.

BUY NOW! Buy a 2005 United Motors car now and when the 2006 models come out, we'll trade even for your '05. Your '06 car will be the same model, accessory group, etc. as the '05 that you buy now. A sure thing for you—a gamble for us, but we'll risk it!

HURRY! This offer good only during September. Buyer responsible for taxes and license fees.

Mr. and Mrs. Johnson saw the ad and visited Mighty Motors. On September 20, they bought a 2005 United Motors Stingbird. When the 2006 cars came out, the Johnsons went back to Mighty Motors and requested that Mighty Motors trade in the '05 Stingbird for a new 2006 model. Mighty Motors refused stating that the Johnsons had not notified Mighty Motors in September that their purchase was being made on the terms of the advertisement. The salesman pointed out that the Johnsons had not even mentioned or discussed the ad. Mr. and Mrs. Johnson sue requesting that the court order Mighty Motors to accept their 2005 car in trade for a 2006 car.

(a) Mighty Motors alleged that the advertisement was not intended as an offer but was an invitation to make an offer and to come in to the dealership to bargain. Do you agree?

(b) Mr. and Mrs. Johnson alleged that the newspaper ad was an offer. If the ad was an offer, was it accepted? Was the acceptance communicated to Mighty Motors? Explain.

8.9   After learning that Barbara was interested in buying a business, Arnold told her that he knew of an opportunity to purchase a liquor store. Several days later, Barbara called Arnold to request further information and mentioned that she also would need financing. Arnold promised to help her but added, "Under the circumstances I would expect to be compensated if you work out a deal." Barbara responded that she would appreciate further information. After contacting Sam, a friend who owned a liquor store, Arnold acted as a go-between and eventually arranged the sale of Sam's store to Barbara for $150,000. Arnold also introduced Barbara to Peter, a local investor who financed the transaction. When Arnold requested compensation from Barbara, she replied that she could not afford to pay him. Arnold sued Barbara, alleging that she had breached an oral contract, and requested the court to award him a finder's fee of $7,500. Was a contract formed? Explain.

8.10   Purcell Tire Co. contacted Computer Network Ltd. (CNL), a computer dealer, about purchasing a computer system for its chain of 15 stores. After several weeks of discussions, a representative of CNL sent Purcell the following letter:

Please let this letter serve as written confirmation of our previous conversations regarding the purchase by Purcell Tire of 21 IBM PCs over the next 12 months. The configuration of the systems you are to purchase are as follows:

IBM PC 356K (50 MG hard disk)	$1,200.00
Color Monitor	335.00
Hayes Smart Modern	599.00
Okidata Printer w/cable	400.00
Microsoft DOS	56.00
Total	$2,590.00
Less 10% discount	(259.00)
	$2,331.00

As per our understanding, we have placed two machines on order for immediate delivery. If this is in accordance with your understanding, please sign the enclosed copy of this letter and return. If this is not in accordance with your understanding, please let me know as soon as possible.

The president of Purcell signed and returned a copy of the letter. CNL delivered and Purcell paid for nine computer systems during the next six months. In some cases, different components were substituted based on availability and cost. As a result, the prices of the systems varied between $1,500 and $2,331. When CNL telephoned for instructions on delivery of 12 more systems. Purcell stated that they did not need the systems. CNL has sued for breach of contract. CNL offered the signed copy of the letter as proof of the contract for 21 computers but Purcell argued that the letter was an agreement for only two computers. How should the court rule? Explain.

8.11   Don owned a farm that he wanted to sell. On June 1, he mailed a letter to Barbara, who lived in a neighboring state, offering to sell the property for $100,000. The offer stipulated it would remain open for 30 days, but did not state a prescribed means of acceptance. Barbara received the offer on June 3 and immediately wrote back stating, "I accept your offer, but at $90,000; that's the most I can borrow from the bank." Don received Barbara's letter on June 10. Meanwhile, on June 3, Ed offered to buy the land from Don for $150,000. Don then promptly revoked the offer in a letter written to Barbara on June 3. On that day, Don gave the letter to his son, Jack, to mail, but Jack placed the letter in his glove compartment and forgot about it. On June 8 Don sold the land to Ed for $150,000.

On June 5, Barbara, fearing the property would be sold elsewhere if she failed to meet Don's asking price, wrote Don a letter stating, "I accept your offer of the 1st." Don received Barbara's letter on June 9. On June 7, Barbara saw Jack at a cattle auction. Jack then remembered the letter in his glove compartment and handed it to her. Infuriated by the revocation, Barbara immediately called Don on the phone and stated, "You said the offer would remain open for 30 days. As far as I'm concerned the offer is still open. I hereby accept the offer."

Barbara sues Don for breach of contract. What result? Analyze the legal effect of the various communications between the parties to determine whether or not Don's offer was terminated prior to acceptance or was accepted while still effective resulting in a contract.

8.12   Mr. and Mrs. Brewer agreed to buy a house owned by Jane. At the same time, Jane offered to sell them some of the furnishings that the Brewers had admired. Because the Brewers were leaving on vacation, Jane agreed to provide a written statement of the furnishings she was willing to sell. Jane sent the Brewers the following:

I am willing to sell the following articles:

Antique grandfather's clock	$1,500
Spinet piano	2,000
Queen Anne chairs	1,500
Oriental rug	1,000

All of the furnishing will be left in the house. Payment of $3,000 due upon acceptance; balance of $3,000 due within 60 days. If the above is satisfactory, please sign below and return one copy with the first payment.

Six weeks later the Brewers sent the following letter to Jane:

Our trip was great! Enclosing a $3,000 check. We've misplaced the contract. Can you send another? We're moving into the house in two weeks. Please include the red secretary in the entrance foyer on the contract.

Mr. and Mrs. Brewer

After receiving the letter and $3,000 check, Jane sent the Brewers a copy of her previous letter adding the red secretary to the list of furnishings.

After the Brewers moved into the house, they asked Jane to remove the grandfather's clock and Queen Anne chairs. She refused and demanded that the Brewers pay the balance of $3,000 plus $500 for the red secretary.

(a) Jane insists that she and the Brewers had entered into a contract. Review §2–207 of the UCC and determine whether she is correct.

(b) Assuming a contract has been made, is the red secretary included in the sale? If so, at what price?

(c) The Brewers assert that no contract resulted because they did not sign and return one copy of the contract as requested by Jane. Is this argument correct? See UCC §2–206.

CONTRACT FORMATION—CONSIDERATION

The second element required for contract formation is consideration. **Consideration** is what each contracting party bargains for and gives in exchange for the return promise or performance of the other party. The consideration in the form of property, services, or other conduct promised or performed provides the inducement to each party to enter into the contract.

The Doctrine of Consideration

Although the law enforces certain promises without consideration,[1] it is the primary legal doctrine determining when a promise is binding as a contract. As eloquently stated by one court:

> It is clear that not every promise is legally enforceable. Much of the vast body of law in the field of contracts is concerned with determining which promises should be legally enforced. On the one hand, in a civilized community men must be able to assume that those with whom they deal will carry out their undertakings according to reasonable expectations. On the other hand, it is neither practical nor reasonable to expect full performance of every assurance given, whether it be thoughtless, casual and gratuitous, or deliberately and seriously made.
>
> The test that has been developed by the common law for determining the enforceability of promises is the doctrine of consideration. This is a crude and not altogether successful attempt to generalize the conditions under which promises will be legally enforced.[2]

Thus, consideration generally distinguishes contractual promises, which are binding on the promisor, from gratuitous or casual promises, which are not. For example, assume Sam promises to give Bill an antique gold watch in 30 days. If Sam fails to transfer the watch to

---

[1]"Promissory estoppel," discussed later in this chapter, is perhaps the most important doctrine used to enforce promises lacking consideration

[2]Baehr v. Penn-O-Tex Oil Corporation, 104 N.W.2d 661, 665 (Minn. 1960).

Bill as promised, Sam incurs no liability because Bill has furnished no consideration to "support" the promise—that is, to make it enforceable. Sam's promise is not a contract.

Form of Consideration

Consideration capable of supporting a promise may be either (1) a promise to do something or refrain from doing something, or (2) a performance. For example, if Seth contracts to sell Bill a snowmobile for $500, Bill's promise to pay $500 provides consideration for Seth's promise to transfer title to the snowmobile. Conversely, Seth's promise to transfer title furnishes consideration for Bill's promise to pay $500. Or, suppose that Cal, as part of the sale of his restaurant to Ben for $50,000, promises *not* to open a restaurant in competition with Ben for five years. Ben's promise to pay $50,000 supports Cal's promise to transfer the restaurant's assets or stock as well as Cal's promise not to compete with Ben. Note that, as this example indicates, a single promise (or performance) may support any number of return promises.

Consideration in the form of performance may be (1) an act other than a promise, (2) a forbearance, or (3) the creation, modification, or destruction of a legal relation.[3] To illustrate, suppose Al promises to pay Bob $500. In exchange for this promise, Bob alternatively paints Al's house, refrains from smoking cigarettes for one year, or transfers title to Bob's 1955 Chevrolet to Al. In all three cases, Bob's performance is consideration for Al's promise. Keep in mind that if the consideration supporting a promise is a return promise, a bilateral contract is created; if the consideration is a performance, a unilateral contract is created.

Requirement of a Bargain

To constitute consideration, the promise or performance involved must be **bargained for.** As defined in the *Restatement (Second) of Contracts:*

> A performance or return promise is bargained for if it is sought by the promisor in exchange for his promise, and is given by the promisee in exchange for that promise.[4]

In other words, consideration requires not only that a promise be made or a performance rendered, but also that the respective promises or performances be given in *exchange* for each other. One court explained the rationale for the bargain requirement as follows:

> Consideration requires that a contractual promise be the product of a bargain. However, in this usage, "bargain" does not mean an exchange of things of equivalent, or any, value. It means a negotiation resulting in the voluntary assumption of an obligation by one party upon condition of an act or forbearance by the other. Consideration thus insures that the promise enforced as a contract is not accidental, casual, or gratuitous, but has been uttered intentionally as the result of some deliberation, manifested by reciprocal bargaining or negotiation. . . . In substance, a contractual promise must be of the logical form: "If . . . (consideration is given) . . . then I promise that. . . . [5]

Regarding the social utility of enforcing bargains, the *Restatement (Second) of Contracts* notes:

> Bargains are widely believed to be beneficial to the community in the provision of opportunities for freedom of individual action and exercise of judgment and as a means by which productive energy and product are apportioned in the economy. The enforcement of bargains rests in part on the common belief that enforcement enhances that utility.[6]

Ordinarily, the consideration is furnished by the promisee to the promisor. For example, if Smith promises to sell his guitar to Barker for $500, Barker, the promisee, furnishes the consideration (a promise to pay $500) supporting Smith's promise to transfer title to the guitar. The performance or return promise constituting consideration may, however, be given *to* a person other than the promisor, and may be given *by* a person other than the promisee. In other words, consideration may run from or to a third person. Assume that Doaks is negotiating for a loan from Carter. To induce Carter to make the loan, Smith promises to pay the obligation if Doaks fails to do so. Carter subsequently makes the loan to Doaks. Carter's loan to Doaks is consideration for *Smith's* promise, even though the consideration runs not to the promisor, Smith, but to a third party, Doaks.

---

[3]RESTATEMENT (SECOND) OF CONTRACTS §71(3).
[4]RESTATEMENT (SECOND) OF CONTRACTS §71(2).

[5]Baehr v. Penn-O-Tex Oil Corporation, 104 N.W.2d 661, 665–666 (Minn. 1960).
[6]RESTATEMENT (SECOND) OF CONTRACTS §72 comment b.

The following case illustrates general consideration principles in the context of an employment contract.

McInerney v. Charter Golf, Inc.

680 N.E.2d 1347 (Ill. 1997)

In 1988, defendant Charter Golf, Inc. hired plaintiff Dennis McInerney to sell its golf apparel and supplies in Illinois. The following year, Hickey-Freeman, manufacturer of a competing line of golf clothing, offered to employ McInerney as an exclusive sales representative. After learning of the Hickey-Freeman job offer, Charter Golf's president offered McInerney his sales position for "the remainder of his life" subject to termination only for dishonesty or disability. McInerney accepted the president's offer and turned down the Hickey-Freeman job. In 1992, Charter Golf fired McInerney, who then sued Charter Golf alleging that it had breached his lifetime contract. The trial court dismissed the lawsuit, and the court of appeals affirmed holding that "a promise to forbear another job opportunity was insufficient consideration to convert an existing employment-at-will relationship into a contract for lifetime employment." The Illinois Supreme Court granted McInerney's petition for review.

Heiple, Justice

. . . Employment contracts in Illinois are presumed to be at-will and are terminable by either party; this rule, of course, is one of construction which may be overcome by showing that the parties agreed otherwise. . . . As with any contract, the terms of an employment contract must be clear and definite . . . and the contract must be supported by consideration. . . .

What is consideration? Under the prevailing view, embodied in the *Restatement (Second) of Contracts,* consideration is the bargained-for exchange of promises or performances, and may consist of a promise, an act, or a forbearance. . . . Thus, a promise for a promise is, without more, enforceable. . . . In past cases, this court has recognized this basic precept, *i.e.,* mutual assent and an exchange of promises provides consideration to support the formation of a contract. . . .

While this court has never directly addressed the specific requirements to establish a permanent employment contract, it has held more generally that the employment relationship is governed by the law of contract. Existence of an employment contract, express or implied, is essential to the employer-employee relationship. . . . As with any contract, it is not possible for a contract of employment to exist without consent of the parties. . . .

Although the rules of contract law are well-established and straightforward, a conflict has emerged in the appellate court decisions on the subject of consideration in the context of a lifetime employment contract. Several decisions have held that a promise of lifetime employment, which by its terms purports to alter an employment-at-will contract, must be supported by "additional" consideration beyond the standard employment duties. . . . These cases have held that an employee's rejecting an outside job offer in exchange for a promised guarantee of lifetime employment is not sufficient consideration to alter an employment-at-will relationship. . . . The premise underlying these cases is that the employee simply weighs the benefits of the two positions, and by accepting one offer the employee necessarily rejects the other. As such, these cases have reasoned that the employee has not given up anything of value, and thus there is no consideration to support the promise of lifetime employment. . . .

One case, however, has taken issue with this analysis. In *Martin v. Federal Life Insurance Co.,* [440 N.E.2d 998 (Ill. App. 1982)], the appellate court held that an enforceable contract for lifetime employment was formed when an employee relinquished a job offer in exchange for a promise of permanent employment from his current employer. The *Martin* court recognized that there was consideration in an exchange of prom-ises: the employer promised to give up his right to terminate the employee at-will, and in exchange the employee agreed to continue working for his current employer and to forgo a lucrative opportunity with a competitor.

In the instant case, Charter Golf argues that an employee's promise to forgo another employment offer in exchange for an employer's promise of lifetime employment is not sufficient consideration. But why not? The defendant has failed to articulate any principled reason why this court should depart from traditional notions of contract law in deciding this case. While we recognize that some cases have indeed held that such an exchange is "inadequate" or "insufficient" consideration to modify an employment-at-will relationship, we believe that those cases have confused the conceptual element of consideration with more practical problems of proof. As we discussed above, this court has held that a promise for a promise constitutes consideration to support the existence of a contract. To hold otherwise in the instant case would ignore the economic realities underlying the case.

Here McInerney gave up a lucrative job offer in exchange for a guarantee of lifetime employment; and in exchange for giving up its right to terminate McInerney at will, Charter Golf retained a valued employee. Clearly both parties exchanged bargained-for benefits in what appears to be a near textbook illustration of consideration. . . .

[Decision of the Court of Appeals affirmed on other grounds.]

Consideration issues can be divided into two broad areas: the nature of the promise or performance providing the consideration, and the existence of a "bargained-for exchange." This discussion begins with the nature of consideration, embodied in the concept of legal detriment. Note that throughout the chapter, various substitutes for or alternatives to consideration also are discussed. In these cases, the law enforces certain promises, (commonly because of formality, public policy, or reliance) that are not supported by consideration under traditional analysis.

Legal Detriment

Both parties to a contract must provide consideration. Generally, in a bilateral contract each party's promise supports the return promise of the other. In a unilateral contract, the offeree's performance of the requested act supplies the consideration to support the offeror's promise, the only promise made. Thus, the offeree of a unilateral contract and each party to a bilateral contract must ask, "Is the other party bound to his or her promise as a result of what I have done or promised to do?" The answer is "yes" if the party's promise or performance constitutes a **legal detriment.** A legal detriment is incurred if the promisee either

1. refrains (or promises to refrain) from doing something that he or she has a legal right to do, or
2. does (or promises to do) something that he or she is not legally obligated to do.

The legal detriment concept is helpful in understanding a number of consideration issues and is well illustrated by a New York Court of Appeals case, *Hamer v. Sidway,*[7] decided in 1891. In this case, an uncle

promised to pay his 15-year-old nephew the sum of $5,000 if the nephew would refrain from drinking, using tobacco, swearing, and playing cards or billiards for money until he became 21. The nephew agreed to the terms of his uncle's promise and fully performed the conditions; in other words he accepted the unilateral offer by performance. The uncle died, however, without paying the $5,000 to the nephew. When the nephew attempted to enforce the contract against his uncle's estate, the executor refused to pay on the basis that the uncle's promise was not supported by consideration. The executor asserted that the promisee (the nephew) was benefited rather than harmed by refraining from the use of liquor and tobacco. Because he had done what was best for him independently of his uncle's promise, the executor asserted, the promise should not be binding unless the promisor (uncle) also was benefited.

The court rejected this argument, and held that the test of consideration is not whether the promisor or any other person benefits, but whether the promisee has incurred a detriment. The court reasoned that the nephew had a legal right to drink liquor and use tobacco. He abandoned that right for a period of years upon the strength of his uncle's promise. His forbearance, therefore, was consideration to support his uncle's promise to pay $5,000.[8]

Thus, when analyzing an alleged contract for the presence of consideration, one must examine each promise individually (the offeror's promise in a unilateral contract and both parties' promises in a bilateral contract). Look then to the promisee of that promise, and ask, "Has the promisee incurred a *detriment* in exchange for this promise?" If so, the promise is ordinarily supported by consideration and is therefore binding on the promisor.[9] Assume Fred promises to make a gift of a ring to Louise in 30 days. Fred is not contractually bound to perform his promise because the promisee, Louise, has incurred no detriment—done or promised to do something she is not legally obligated to do, or refrained or promised to refrain from doing something she has a legal right to do—in exchange for it. On the other hand, assume that Fred promises to sell a specified tract of land to Louise in exchange for Louise's promise to pay $10,000. To determine whether Fred's promise is binding, look to the promisee, Louise.

---

[7]27 N.E. 256 (N.Y. 1891).

[8]*Id.* at 257.

[9]As previously noted, a third party may supply the consideration to support a promise. In that case, ask whether the third party has incurred a detriment in exchange for the promise.

Here, Louise has incurred a detriment in exchange for Fred's promise. She has done something she is not legally obligated to do: promised to pay Fred $10,000. Conversely, Louise's promise is supported by a detriment to the promisee, Fred, who promised to convey land to Louise, something, prior to the contract, he was under no legal obligation to do. Thus, both promises are supported by consideration and are binding upon the parties.

The following material discusses adequacy of consideration, preexisting duty, and contract modification. These important contracts issues are all resolved, at least in part, by applying the legal detriment concepts outlined above.

Adequacy of Consideration

Contract law is based upon the principle of freedom of contract: the parties are generally free to determine the terms of their contract through private negotiation, subject primarily to public policy limitations. One of the terms left to private determination is the value placed upon the consideration exchanged.

For this reason, as a general rule, courts do not inquire into the adequacy of the consideration. As long as a detriment is incurred, it is irrelevant whether or not the economic value of the consideration exchanged is equivalent. In fact, the disparity may be very great. The rationale for this rule is that, in the absence of fraud, duress, or other extraordinary circumstances, the court should not intrude on the parties' freedom of contract to rescue a person from the consequences of a bad bargain. Assume Don purchases an old rocking chair from Steve at a garage sale for $25. After stripping off the old paint, Don discovers that the chair is a valuable antique, worth $1,000. Steve may not avoid the contract on the basis that the consideration is inadequate. Freedom of contract means freedom to make a bad as well as a good bargain.

Further, if courts became involved in comparing relative values, the adequacy of consideration would be an issue in every contract case, regardless of the underlying basis of the dispute. A party seeking to avoid performance of a contract would always assert the inadequacy of the consideration. Value determination, therefore, is left to the parties, who are in a better position than others to evaluate the circumstances of their particular agreement.

Note that the relative equivalence of the values exchanged is not totally irrelevant. Gross differences in economic value may offer strong circumstantial evidence of fraud, duress, mistake, unconscionability, lack of con-

tractual capacity, or lack of a bargained-for exchange. These topics are considered later in the contracts material.

Preexisting Legal Duties

The Preexisting Duty Rule. Once made, most contracts are performed according to their original terms. The parties may, however, before or during performance desire to modify or even extinguish the obligations imposed by the contract. Perhaps the most fundamental principle based upon the legal detriment concept is the **preexisting duty rule** governing contract modification.

Under the rule, the promise to perform (or performance of) a preexisting legal or public duty does not furnish consideration to support a return promise. The rule is designed to prevent enforcement of promises that are supported by nothing more than the other party's promise to perform an existing legal duty. Such promises are often obtained by express or implied threat to withhold performance of the preexisting legal duty. To prevent a contracting party from threatening breach to secure a change in the contract he or she could not secure during contract formation, the law simply provides that promising to do (or doing) what one is already legally obligated to do does not support an additional return promise.

Suppose an actor contracts with a producer to perform in a play for $10,000. At the last moment, the actor refuses to perform unless the producer promises to pay an additional $5,000. The producer reluctantly agrees. The producer is not bound to pay the extra $5,000 because the actor has furnished no consideration (incurred no further detriment) to support the producer's promise. Thus, assuming the actor performs as agreed, the producer is bound to pay the agreed $10,000, but is not obligated on his additional $5,000 promise coerced by the actor's threat of breach.

In addition to contractual duties, the preexisting duty rule applies to legal duties owed by public officials to members of the general public. Suppose a banker offers a reward for return of certain stolen property. A police officer who recovers the property, while acting within the scope of his duties, may not enforce the banker's promise as a contract. The officer's performance of his preexisting public duty is not consideration for the banker's promise.

Enforceable Contract Modification—Common Law. The preexisting duty rule prevents enforcement of promises supported solely by a promise to perform (or performance of) a preexisting duty. It therefore follows that in both the contract and public duty cases a promise may be enforceable if the promisee incurs an additional detriment. To illustrate, using the examples in the preceding section, the police officer would be entitled to the reward if he was permitted to, and was using his free time, to work on a crime outside the scope of his official responsibilities. Similarly, the producer's promise is binding if the actor changes his duty in some respect. Assume that the original contract requires the actor to perform in the play for two weeks. If the actor agrees to do one more performance in return for the $5,000, the detriment requirement is satisfied. As previously discussed, the value of the new consideration exchanged need not be equal; there must simply be some additional detriment, which reflects more than a pretense of a bargain, to support the promise.[10]

Under the preexisting duty rule, therefore, an agreement to modify an existing common law contract—for example, contracts involving land, personal services, construction, or employment—requires consideration for the modification on both sides. In other words, a promise by one party altering his rights or duties is not binding unless the other party also incurs a further detriment. If both parties change their rights or duties, the consideration requirement is met because each has incurred a detriment. Under this analysis, mutual agreements to rescind are binding, because each party has given up the right to demand performance from the other.

The following case illustrates the principles governing modification of common law contracts.

Zhang v. Sorichetti
103 P.3d 20 (Nev. 2004)

By written contract dated February 1, 2004, plaintiff Lanlin Zhang agreed to purchase defendant Frank Sorichetti's house for $532,500. On February 3, Sorichetti notified Zhang that he was terminating the sale but stated that he would sell her the house if she would pay more money. After Zhang agreed, they signed a new contract dated February 3 with a purchase price of $578,000. This contract extended the closing date by one month and added that the sale would include the drapes. On February

16, Sorichetti told Zhang that a murder had occurred in the house several years earlier and offered to allow Zhang to cancel the contract. Zhang declined but Sorichetti later notified her that he was rescinding the contract so that he could "use and/or dispose of my home as I wish."

Zhang sued Sorichetti seeking damages and performance of the February 1 contract. The trial court dismissed the lawsuit ruling that the February 1 contract was no longer binding because it had been replaced by the contract dated February 3. Zhang appealed.

Per Curiam

The primary issue we decide is whether a real property purchase agreement is enforceable when it is executed by the buyer only because the seller would not perform under an earlier purchase agreement for a lesser price. We conclude that such a modified agreement is not supported by consideration and is therefore unenforceable. . . .

Zhang alleged in her complaint that, on February 3, Sorichetti announced that he would not sell his home under the February 1 contract because "he was not satisfied with the deal." This allegation demonstrates an actionable anticipatory breach of contract, which is a "clear, positive, and unequivocal" repudiation of the duties arising under or imposed by agreement. [*Covington Bros. v. Valley Plastering, Inc.*, 566 P.2d 814, 817 (Nev. 1977).] That Zhang subsequently agreed on February 3 to pay more money to obtain Sorichetti's performance does not substitute the February 3 agreement in place of the February 1 agreement. As noted in *Williston on Contracts* [569-73 (4th ed. 1992)]:

> Where two parties have entered into a bilateral agreement, it will often occur that one of the parties, having become dissatisfied with the contract, will refuse to perform or to continue performance unless he is promised or paid a greater compensation than that provided in the original agreement. . . . The question arises whether the new [agreement to pay more money] is enforceable. . . . As a matter of principle, the second agreement must be held invalid, for the performance by the recalcitrant contractor is no legal detriment to him whether actually given or merely promised, since, at the time the second agreement was entered into, he was already bound to do the [performance]. . . .

This principle is commonly known as the preexisting duty rule and is recognized in Nevada. Consequently, Zhang's execution of the February 3 agreement does not relieve Sorichetti of liability under the February 1 agreement. . . .

---

[10]RESTATEMENT (SECOND) OF CONTRACTS §73.

Contrary to Sorichetti's suggestion, consideration for the February 3 agreement cannot be found in the purported rescission of the February 1 agreement. It is true that some courts have avoided the preexisting duty rule's effect by finding new consideration unnecessary when contract modification follows rescission of the original contract. But the better reasoned approach is articulated in the *Restatement (Second) of Contracts* and *Corbin on Contracts,* which reject the notion that rescission of a contract that is executory on both sides supplies consideration for a simultaneous new agreement differing in terms of promised compensation. These authorities reason that a contrary view requires a court to argue in "a circle" in order to support the new agreement, as "the validity of the new agreement depends upon the rescission while the validity of the rescission depends upon the new agreement." [2 J. Perillo & H. Bender, *Corbin on Contracts* 408 (rev. ed. 1995).] Further, the *Restatement* and *Corbin* express concern that overlooking the preexisting duty rule for a simultaneous rescission/modification might permit fraudulent or unfair modifications. . . .

The Iowa Supreme Court addressed these principles in *Recker v. Gustafson,* [279 N.W.2d 744 (Iowa 1979)]. In Recker, the issue was whether a $290,000 agreement for the sale of a farm was enforceable, given that the buyers later agreed to purchase the farm for $300,000. The court declined to employ the fiction criticized by Corbin and the Restatement that allows increases in contract compensation without new consideration. Instead, the court concluded that, as the new agreement arose solely from the seller's desire for more money, rather than a wholesale rescission of the earlier sales agreement, the price increase was merely an attempted modification, unsupported by consideration.

Recker is indistinguishable from the instant case. Zhang alleged in her complaint that the February 3 agreement originated from Sorichetti's desire for more money, rather than any desire to end his dealings with Zhang. Consequently, consideration for the February 3 agreement cannot be found in the purported simultaneous rescission of the February 1 agreement. Nor can consideration be found elsewhere, as Zhang alleges in her complaint a lack of "additional consideration" to support the February 3 agreement. . . .

[Judgment reversed and remanded.]

Contract Modification Under the UCC. The Uniform Commercial Code alters the preexisting duty rule for contracts for the sale of goods in §2–209(1) by providing that "an agreement modifying a contract within this Article needs no consideration to be binding." Assume S contracts to sell his car to B for $10,000. Prior to delivery or payment, the parties modify the contract. S agrees to include a CD player with the car with no change in price. S is obligated to include the CD player even though B has incurred no additional detriment, for instance, by agreeing to pay more money or include added property. That is, the modification needs no consideration to be binding. If both S and B had changed their duties, consideration would exist on both sides, and it would not be necessary to rely upon §2–209(1) to enforce the new agreement. It applies, as above, to make modifications binding in which one party alters his duty and the other does not. Note that nothing in §2–209 forces either party to grant a modification. It merely states that *if* a contract modification is granted by one party it needs no consideration to be binding.

As discussed in Chapter 6, an obligation of good faith is imposed upon every contract or duty governed by the UCC, including modifications under §2–209. Therefore, coercion of a modification without legitimate commercial reason is ineffective as a violation of the duty to act in good faith.[11] In this manner, the Code, while doing away with the preexisting duty rule for *commercially justified* contract modifications, preserves a basic advantage of the rule—the prevention of coerced contract modifications.

Contract Modifications—Unforeseen Difficulties. Section 2–209 enforces commercially justified contract modifications without consideration. A growing number of courts have applied a similar analysis to enforce modifications of common law contracts necessitated by unforeseen difficulties arising during performance of the contract. For example, the *Restatement (Second) of Contracts* provides that an agreement to modify a contract executory on both sides is binding without consideration if the modification is fair and equitable in light of circumstances that were not anticipated by the parties when the contract was made.[12]

---

[11]UCC §2–209, Official Comment 2.
[12]RESTATEMENT (SECOND) OF CONTRACTS §89.

Bargained-for Exchange

The second major element of consideration is that the promises or performances involved be given in exchange for each other. In other words, the existence of a detriment alone is insufficient. The promisor must make the promise because he or she wishes to exchange it for the detriment (promise or performance) incurred by the promisee and the promisee must make the promise or render a performance in order to exchange it for the promise made by the promisor. The following material examines this element of exchange required for enforcement of a promise.

Past Consideration

Typically, the promise and the consideration that supports it stand in a reciprocal relationship; the consideration induces the making of the promise and the promise induces the furnishing of the consideration. Therefore, if a promise is made or performance rendered before the return promise is made, the return promise is unenforceable because it has not been bargained for. The earlier act or promise is referred to as **past consideration.** To illustrate, if

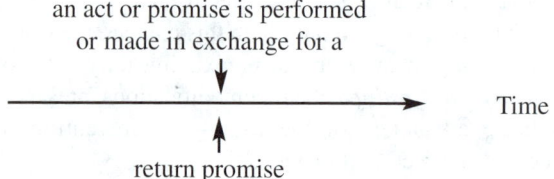

the return promise is bargained for and binding upon the promisor.

If however,

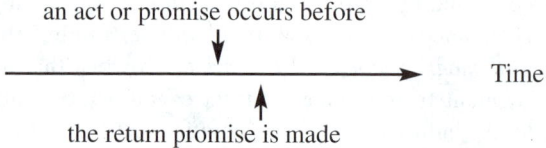

then there is no bargain for the return promise. Because no act or promise is given in exchange, the promise is not binding upon the promisor. In the eyes of the law, therefore, past consideration is no consideration. The following case illustrates an application of the past consideration principle.

Passante v. McWilliam
62 Cal. Rptr. 2d 298 (Cal. App. 1997)

In March 1988, Upper Deck Company was formed to produce baseball trading cards. To purchase materials for its first run of cards, Upper Deck needed to secure $100,000 before August 1. Upper Deck's directors were unsuccessful in obtaining financing; however, Anthony Passante, an advisor to Upper Deck, was able to arrange a $100,000 loan from an acquaintance on July 26. After learning of the availability of the loan, Boris Korbel, one of Upper Deck's directors, asked Passante to attend a special board meeting on the evening of July 29. On the morning of July 29, the lender wired $100,000 to Korbel. At the meeting, Upper Deck's board of directors voted to accept the loan and agreed to transfer 3% of Upper Deck's stock to Passante in return for arranging the loan. Upper Deck, however, never transferred the stock to Passante. Within a few years, Upper Deck had become a multimillion-dollar corporation. In 1990, Passante sued Upper Deck and its directors in 1990 demanding 3% of the corporation's stock. A jury awarded Passante damages of $32 million, but the trial judge overruled the verdict and entered judgment in favor of Upper Deck and the directors. Passante appealed.

Sills, Presiding Justice

. . . The board had a clear moral obligation to honor its promise to Passante. He had, as the baseball cliché goes, stepped up to the plate and homered on the Upper Deck's behalf. And if this court could enforce such moral obligations, we would advise the company even yet to pay something in honor of its promise. . . .

Passante asserts that "[a]n enforceable contract requires only a promise capable of being enforced and consideration to support the promise." As framed, the assertion is incomplete. Consideration must also be given in exchange for the promise. Past consideration cannot support a contract. . . . As a matter of law, any claim by Passante for breach of contract necessarily founders on the rule that consideration must result from a bargain. . . .

But a close reading of the facts shows that the stock had not been bargained for in exchange for arranging the loan; Passante had already arranged the loan (even though the loan had not been formally accepted by the board) before the idea of giving him stock was ever brought up. There is no evidence that Passante had any expectation that he be given stock in return for arranging the $100,000 loan. Clearly, all of Passante's services had already been rendered by the time the idea of giving Passante some stock was proposed. As the court in [*Dow v. River Farms Co.*, 243 P.2d 95, 99 (Cal. App. 1952)] plainly stated, ". . . if there was no expectation of payment by either party when the services were rendered, the promise is a mere promise to make a gift and not enforceable."

The promise of 3 percent of the stock . . . was simply . . . an inchoate gift—that is, an unenforceable promise from a grateful corporate board. . . .

[Judgment affirmed.]

Obligations barred by operation of law provide exceptions to the past consideration rule. A subsequent promise for instance, to pay a contractual debt barred by the statute of limitations is binding without additional consideration. Suppose Don owes Chris $500. Chris may no longer sue Don to recover because the statute of limitations has run on the claim. However, if Don later promises Chris in writing to pay the $500, then Don's promise is binding.

Promises to perform previously voidable duties also are binding. Induced by Seller's fraud, Buyer promises to pay Seller $100 for defective merchandise. Buyer's promise is voidable. After discovering the fraud, Buyer promises to pay as agreed. Buyer's promise is binding.

Moral Consideration

One of the most common applications of the past consideration doctrine is the moral obligation case. Suppose Alice saves Stan's life, but is seriously injured while doing so. Stan, in gratitude to Alice, later promises to pay Alice $1000 a month for life or pay her medical bills. Stan is not bound by his promise, because nothing has been given in exchange for it. The act giving rise to his promise (Alice saving his life) occurred before the promise was made. The past consideration provided by Alice does not support Stan's return promise. Because Stan's promise rests upon a moral but not legal obligation, past consideration in this context is often referred to as **moral consideration.**

Promises based upon moral obligations are, however, sometimes enforced. A number of courts, either by statute or through a refined application of the doctrine of quasi-contract,[13] enforce promises arising out of ben-efits previously conferred by the promisee upon the promisor to the extent necessary to prevent injustice or unjust enrichment of the promisor. The promises are clearly not "bargained for," but are enforced for public policy reasons. In these situations, however, the promises are not binding if their value is disproportionate to the benefit conferred.[14]

Nominal Consideration

Occasionally, a contract will state that property or services are to be exchanged "for $1 and other valuable consideration" or similar language. Such a statement is referred to as a recited or **nominal consideration.** Nominal consideration is often used in an effort to make gratuitous promises enforceable. The issue thus presented is whether a nominal consideration accomplishes that purpose.

Courts look generally for the existence of a bargain, not the relative equivalence of the values exchanged. Nevertheless, great disparity in value may sometimes indicate that a purported exchange is not in fact bargained for, but is a mere formality. If so, a recited or nominal consideration does not support the return promise.

Assume Mark promises to paint Bob's house, a job worth $2,000. Mark's promise is stated to be "in consideration of $1 paid to me by Bob, the receipt of which is hereby acknowledged." If the recited amount is not paid and no other bargained for consideration is given (that is, the recital of consideration is a "sham"), the promise is unenforceable. Even if the nominal amount is paid, however, many courts still find no consideration if the return promise is not otherwise bargained for, that is, if the promise was made with the intent to make a gift.

The rules stated above concern the enforceability of *promises* supported by nominal consideration. Performance of the promise, however, may create a valid gift. That is, though a promise to make a gift is unenforceable, a gift once validly made is irrevocable by the donor.[15]

---

[13]Quasi-contract is introduced in Chapter 7 and covered in more detail in Chapter 15.

[14]RESTATEMENT (SECOND) OF CONTRACTS §86. The rule making promises arising out of benefits previously conferred enforceable in certain instances does not apply to benefits conferred as a gift or under other circumstances not involving unjust enrichment of the promisor.

[15]Gifts are discussed in Chapter 34.

Options and Suretyship Promises. Not all promises supported solely by a nominal or recited consideration are unenforceable. Under the view taken by many courts and adopted by the *Restatement (Second) of Contracts,* an option (a promise to keep an offer open), or a suretyship promise (a promise guaranteeing payment of another's debt) is binding if it (1) is in writing, (2) is signed by the promisor, and (3) recites a purported consideration.[16] Additionally, in the case of an option, the promise must propose an exchange on fair terms within a reasonable time. That is, nominal consideration paid or promised will support a bargained for short-term option. For example, assume S, in a signed writing, "in consideration of $1 paid," grants B a 30-day option to purchase a tract of land for $15,000, a fair price. The offer is irrevocable even if the $1 is not in fact paid.[17] The rationale for enforcing written short-term options and suretyship promises in the absence of consideration is that such promises are often a necessary preliminary step to the conclusion of a socially useful bargain (for example, a sale of land or loan of money). Further, the formality of a signed writing executed in a commercial setting provides adequate evidence of the signer's intent to be contractually bound while minimizing the possibility of fraud.

Settlement of Claims

Accord and Satisfaction

As noted in Chapter 2, compromise is certainly the most common method of resolving disputes. An important contracts issue, grounded upon consideration analysis, concerns the legal effect of a compromise agreement reached to settle a preexisting obligation. The creation and performance of the compromise agreement is known as an **accord and satisfaction.**

An accord is a contract in which a party entitled to a performance (the "creditor" below) promises to accept an alternative stated performance in full satisfaction of the original duty owed him. The effect of an accord is: (1) until performance of the accord agreement, the cred-

itor's right to sue on the original obligation is suspended; (2) the performance of the accord agreement (satisfaction) discharges both the original duty and the duty under the accord; and (3) if the accord agreement is breached, the original duty survives and the creditor may sue on either the accord or the original duty.

In determining whether an accord and satisfaction has been created, a distinction must be made between obligations that are undisputed and liquidated, on one hand, and those that are unliquidated in amount. A claim is **disputed** if one party is contesting the *existence* of the obligation. Assume that S asserts that B promised to pay $500 for certain goods to be delivered by S. B admits talking to S, but denies any agreement concerning the goods was made. S's claim against B is disputed.

A claim, though undisputed, may be liquidated or unliquidated. A **liquidated claim** is simply one that is fixed in amount. Thus, in the preceding example, assume that B admits that an agreement to purchase the goods was made, but asserts that the price was to be left open pending further negotiation. In this case the claim is undisputed, but unliquidated. If both parties agree that a contract exists at $500, S's claim against B is both undisputed and liquidated.

If an obligation is *liquidated* and *undisputed,* courts traditionally apply the preexisting duty rule to find that a part payment does not discharge the entire debt, even if the reduced amount is bargained for in satisfaction of the obligation. Here, the debtor is merely doing what (or in this case less than) he is already legally obligated to do. Assume Seller contracts to sell Buyer a tract of land for $4,000, payable in monthly installments over a five-year period. Two years later, Seller agrees to reduce the price to $2,500, which is ultimately paid by Buyer. In this case, Seller is not bound to his promise to accept the reduced amount in satisfaction of the $4,000 debt.

On the other hand, if a *good faith* dispute arises concerning either the existence of a claim or the amount owing, a compromise agreement to pay any definite sum of money (or render any other performance) is binding (supported by consideration) and creates an accord contract. In addition, even a liquidated and undisputed obligation may be discharged by compromise agreement involving performance significantly different from that originally agreed upon. In other words, the creditor's promise to accept substituted performance in satisfaction of the original duty is supported by consideration either because (1) the debtor's

---

[16]RESTATEMENT (SECOND) OF CONTRACTS §§87(1)(a), 88(a). Options are discussed in Chapter 8. Suretyship is covered in Chapter 33.

[17]This result is consistent with UCC §2–205 discussed in Chapter 8. Under that provision, short-term options to buy or sell *goods* granted by a merchant in a signed writing are binding without consideration.

performance differs significantly from that required by the original duty (thus it is not merely performance of a preexisting legal duty), or (2) the existence or amount of the original duty is in doubt. The following examples illustrate the operation of an accord and satisfaction.

Using the land sale example above, assume that the Buyer, in addition to paying $2,500, agreed to paint Seller's house or transfer a fishing boat to Seller.[18] Here Buyer has substantially altered his duty, and therefore the agreement to pay money and also to provide services or property is an accord. Until Buyer performs the accord, Seller's right to sue on the original $4,000 obligation is suspended. If Buyer breaches the accord, Seller may sue either on the underlying $4,000 debt or on the accord. If Buyer properly performs the accord, both the $4,000 original debt and the accord are discharged. Or, assume that A owes B $10,000. A and B agree that A will deliver a machine to B in 30 days, which B will accept in full satisfaction of the debt. The contract is an accord. A's debt is suspended and both the debt and the accord are discharged if A delivers the machine in 30 days.

Both of the preceding examples involve undisputed, liquidated claims. To illustrate the operation of accord and satisfaction upon a disputed or unliquidated obligation, assume that Ralph performs remodeling work on Freda's house. No agreement on price is reached before work is commenced. Ralph subsequently sends Freda a bill for $1,000. Freda, thinking the bill is too high, sends a letter explaining that she thinks the amount is excessive and offering $800 in full satisfaction. Ralph accepts and Freda subsequently pays $800. An accord and satisfaction is created, discharging Ralph's claim for $1,000.

Settling Claims by Conditional Check

An accord and satisfaction commonly is created by **conditional check,** a device well illustrated by *Nardine v. Kraft Cheese Company.*[19] In this case, Kraft had shipped longhorn cheese to Nardine, a grocery store owner, on open account. A dispute developed concerning the cheese. Nardine contended that it was spoiled

when received and that Kraft should take it back. Kraft asserted that the cheese was spoiled by Nardine's attempt to force cure it. In attempting to reconcile the dispute, Nardine discovered other discrepancies in the account. Finally, Nardine sent Kraft a check for approximately $146 with the notation on the check. "This pays my account in full to date." Kraft certified the check and proceeded to sue Nardine for the additional sum of approximately $88 that it alleged to be still owing. In refusing to allow Kraft to recover the claimed deficiency, the court applied the now well-settled common law rule that when a bona fide dispute exists as to either the existence or the amount of a money debt, a check tendered in full satisfaction of the claim (marked "paid in full" or the like), which is cashed (or certified) by the other party, discharges the claim. The tender of the check is regarded as an offer for an accord. Cashing the check is simultaneous acceptance of the offer for an accord and satisfaction, which discharges both the accord and the disputed debt. Therefore, the accord and satisfaction is a defense to any subsequent suit by the creditor to collect the balance of its claim.

The creditor cannot alter this result by (1) crossing out the words "paid in full" on the check and then cashing it, (2) notifying the debtor that the payment is being applied on account and not in full satisfaction, or (3) by depositing the check indorsed "under protest," "without prejudice," "with reservation of rights," or similar language. Because the offeror is the master of the offer, the offeree may not alter its terms and create a contract on the altered terms by acceptance, as the following case illustrates.

County Fire Door Corporation v. C. F. Wooding Company
520 A.2d 1028 (Conn. 1987)

Defendant C. F. Wooding Company (Wooding) ordered several metal doors from the plaintiff County Fire Door Corporation for use at a construction site known as the Upjohn Project. After receiving the doors, Wooding informed County Fire Door that it would not pay the full sales price because of additional installation expenses that Wooding had incurred due to late delivery of the doors. After Wooding indicated its intention to pay $416.88 as the balance due on the account, County Fire Door notified Wooding that full payment of $2,618.88 was due. Wooding wrote County Fire Door reiterating its intention

---

[18]Note that a promise to provide services or property would create a binding accord even if those services or the property were not worth $1,500. Once again, courts generally do not inquire into adequacy of consideration.

[19]52 N.E.2d 634 (Ind. App. 1944).

to pay only $416.88 and subsequently sent County Fire Door a check in the amount of $416.88 with the following statement on the reverse side: "By its endorsement, the payee accepts this check in full satisfaction of all claims against the C. F. Wooding Co. arising out of or relating to the Upjohn Project under Purchase Order #3302, dated 11/17/81." County Fire Door crossed out the statement and added the following: "This check is accepted under protest and with full reservation of rights to collect the unpaid balance for which this check is offered in settlement."

County Fire Door indorsed the check, deposited it in its account, and later sued Wooding for the balance of approximately $2,200. The trial court ruled in favor of County Fire Door and Wooding appealed.

Peters, Chief Justice

. . . When there is a good faith dispute about the existence of a debt or about the amount that is owed, the common law authorized the debtor and the creditor to negotiate a contract of accord to settle the outstanding claim. Such a contract is often initiated by the debtor, who offers an accord by tendering a check as "payment in full" or "in full satisfaction." If the creditor knowingly cashes such a check, or otherwise exercises full dominion over it, the creditor is deemed to have assented to the offer of accord. Upon acceptance of the offer of accord, the creditor's receipt of the promised payment discharges the underlying debt and bars any further claim relating thereto, if the contract of accord is supported by consideration. . . .

A contract of accord and satisfaction is sufficiently supported by consideration if it settles a monetary claim that is unliquidated in amount. This court has had numerous occasions to decide whether, in the context of accord and satisfaction, a claim is unliquidated when the debtor tenders payment in an amount that does not exceed that to which the creditor is concededly entitled. "Where it is admitted that one of two specific sums is due, but there is a dispute as to which is the proper amount, the demand is regarded as unliquidated, within the meaning of that term as applied to the subject of accord and satisfaction. . . . Where the claim is unliquidated any sum, given and received in settlement of the dispute, is a sufficient consideration." *Hanley Co. v. American Cement Co.,* [143 A. 566 (Conn. 1928)]. . . .

Application of these settled principles to the facts of this case establishes, as the defendant maintains, that the parties entered into a valid contract of accord and satisfaction. The defendant offered in good faith to settle an unliquidated debt by tendering, in full satisfac-

tion, the payment of an amount less than that demanded by the plaintiff. Under the common law, the plaintiff could not simultaneously cash such a check and disown the condition on which it had been tendered. . . .

Under prevailing common law principles, . . . the parties in this case negotiated a contract of accord whose satisfaction discharged the defendant from any further monetary obligation to the plaintiff. The plaintiff might have avoided this result by returning the defendant's check uncashed, but could not simultaneously disregard the condition on which the check was tendered and deposit its proceeds in the plaintiff's bank account. . . .

[Judgment reversed and remanded.]

In determining whether a binding accord and satisfaction exists, it is irrelevant who is right or wrong in the underlying dispute; the law simply requires that a bona fide dispute exist at the time the check is tendered in full payment. In *Nardine,* for example, the court found a binding accord and satisfaction despite its additional finding that Nardine was in fact responsible for spoiling the cheese.[20] Therefore, whenever accord and satisfaction is alleged on a disputed or unliquidated claim, the good faith of the party asserting the dispute is crucial. One cannot avoid a legitimate obligation merely by insisting dishonestly that a dispute exists and then tendering a part payment marked "paid in full."

In sum, if a creditor is involved in a good faith contract dispute over the existence or amount of a money debt, and a check is tendered by the debtor marked "paid in full," he should not cash or certify the check unless he agrees to the terms under which the check is tendered.

Conditional Check and the UCC

Revised Article 3 of the Uniform Commercial Code, which governs checks and other negotiable instruments,[21] provides additional rules governing accord and satisfaction by conditional check. Initially, §§3–311 (a)

---

[20] *Id.* at 635.

[21] Article 3 is discussed in detail in Part IV of the text.

and (b) codify the common law rules previously discussed by providing that if a claim is unliquidated or subject to a bona fide dispute, the claim is discharged if the creditor obtains payment of an instrument conspicuously tendered in good faith by the debtor in full satisfaction of the claim.

Sections 3–311(c) and (d), however, recognize two important exceptions to the foregoing principles. These exceptions are designed to prevent inadvertent accord and satisfaction, and thus cannot apply if the debtor proves that the creditor (or an agent of the creditor having direct responsibility for the disputed obligation) in fact knew that the instrument, when tendered, was offered in full satisfaction of the disputed debt.

1. Section 3–311(c)(1) provides that an organization, such as a department store or public utility, may send its debtors in advance of any dispute a notice that communications concerning disputed debts (including full satisfaction checks) must be sent to a designated person, office, or place. If a full payment check is sent to the designated office and is paid, an accord and satisfaction results. If the check is sent to another address (for example, the creditor's check processing center used for receiving and recording ordinary payments on account) and paid, no accord and satisfaction results.

2. Section 3–311(c)(2) provides an exception that may be used by individual creditors and organizations that choose not to send a notice as described above. Under this provision, a creditor that inadvertently cashes a full satisfaction check, may prevent an accord and satisfaction by repaying the amount of the check to the debtor within 90 days after the check was paid.

Mutuality of Consideration

The term **mutuality of consideration** simply means that both parties to a contract must provide consideration. Each party to a bilateral contract incurs a bargained-for detriment, and it is this detriment that supports the return promise of the other. The doctrine of mutuality applies to unilateral contracts as well, even though only one promise is involved. Mutuality requires that both parties provide *consideration,* not that both parties be mutually *obligated.* In a unilateral contract, the offeror's promise becomes binding upon the offeree's performance of the requested act. Thus, both parties provide consideration. The offeree's per-

formance is a detriment that is bargained for in exchange for the offeror's promise, making it enforceable. A contract exists despite the fact that the offeree is never obligated to perform.[22]

Illusory Promises

Because both promises in a bilateral contract must be supported by consideration, the entire contract fails if one party's promise makes his or her performance entirely optional. In this case, the promissory language is known as an **illusory promise.** An illusory promise is not a promise at all, and therefore does not furnish consideration for a return promise. It, in effect, says, "I'll perform if I want to perform." Suppose Seller and Buyer enter into a contract in which Buyer promises to purchase "as many bicycles as I shall choose to order within the next 30 days." The buyer's "promise" is illusory, stating in effect, "I will buy as many bicycles as I want from you, but if I don't want them, I am not obligated to take them." Performance is entirely optional with the "promisor," Buyer. In other words, Buyer has incurred no detriment. Thus, Seller's promise to deliver bicycles at fixed prices is not binding.

The following material examines a number of important contracts issues in which one contracting party seeks to avoid performance for lack of mutuality (asserting that the other party's promise is illusory).

Conditional Promises

A condition is an event that must occur before a contracting party is required to perform her promise. If a promise is subject to a condition and the condition fails to occur, no duty to perform the promise arises, and the promisor incurs no liability for failure to perform. Although conditions are discussed in detail in Chapter 14, conditional promises present a number of mutuality issues.

For example, a contract may provide that one party's duty to perform arises only if she is "satisfied" with the performance of the other. A condition of "satisfaction" or "complete satisfaction" appears to render the promise illusory because the party whose satisfaction is

---

[22]Under the rules discussed in Chapter 8, the offeree may become bound after she commences performance or if she treats an ambiguous offer as a bilateral offer.

required may avoid her obligation by merely stating, "I'm not satisfied." Such promises, however, are not illusory. The party whose satisfaction is required must act in *good faith* and in accordance with standards of fair dealing. That is, she must be *honestly* dissatisfied and therefore may not reject the other party's performance as a means to avoid performing her own promise.

As the preceding discussion indicates, a party's duty to perform may be conditional upon the occurrence of a given event (for example, in the above case, satisfaction of the promisor). If the occurrence or nonoccurrence of the condition is outside the control of the promisor, his or her conditional promise clearly supports a return promise. For example, assume S contracts to sell land to B for $50,000. The buyer's promise is subject to a condition that an independent appraisal must reveal that the market value of the property is at least equal to the purchase price. B's promise supports S's return promise to convey the property, because the occurrence of the condition is not within B's control.

A promise also may be made conditional upon the occurrence or nonoccurrence of an uncertain or fortuitous event. In this situation, the promise is referred to as **aleatory.** A common aleatory promise is made in an insurance contract. Assume an insurance company promises to pay you up to $40,000 per occurrence for fire losses to your house sustained within one year. This promise supports your promise to pay the premium, even if no loss occurs within the stated period. That is, even though the company incurred no actual detriment, the possibility of a detriment is sufficient. Similarly, a promise is not rendered illusory because the promisor makes his duty to perform conditional upon the nonoccurrence of strikes, fires, accidents, riots, wars, floods or other Acts of God, damage or destruction of production facilities, unforeseen shutdown of sources of supply, or any other circumstances over which the promisor has no control. Such provisions (known as *force majeure* clauses) are common in contracts requiring manufacture and delivery of goods or construction of a building or other project by a stated date. A conditional promise is, however, not consideration if, at the time the promise is made, the promisor knows that the condition cannot occur.

A promise may be capable of supporting a return promise even if conditional upon occurrence of an event within the control of the promisor. For example, contracts for the sale of real estate frequently provide that the buyer's duty to perform is conditional upon her

acquiring mortgage financing for the purchase in a specified amount with a given term and interest rate. At first glance, the buyer's promise to pay the purchase price seems illusory; that is, she may avoid it by failing to apply for the loan. Courts, however, find consideration in these cases by *implying a promise* on the part of the buyer to use his or her "best efforts" to obtain the financing (that is, to bring about occurrence of the condition).

A similar problem exists in exclusive dealing contracts. For example, a seller may grant a buyer an exclusive right to market the seller's products within a certain geographic area. The buyer may not be required, under the terms of the contract, to sell any products, making his promise appear "illusory." The UCC, which adopts the common law rule, finds consideration to support the seller's promise by imposing a "best efforts" requirement in the sale or promotion of the goods upon the buyer. A similar requirement to supply the goods is imposed upon the seller.[23]

Rights of Termination

A contract may contain a provision that the contract shall continue in force for a given period of time or continue indefinitely, subject to termination at the option of one or both parties. Because a party may avoid any further obligation under the contract at any time, such a promise appears illusory. Frequently, however, the right to terminate is conditional upon giving advance notice to the other party—for example, 30, 60, or 90 days. If a prior notice requirement exists, consideration exists, because each party has agreed to provide goods or services (or to purchase them) for at least the notice period. For example, if Seller agrees to provide Buyer with goods for a three-year period subject to cancellation on 30-days notice by either party, both parties are bound to either buy or sell goods for at least 30 days. By doing something they are not legally required to do (buying or selling for 30 days), the requirement of legal detriment is met.

If either party has the right to terminate at will, or upon mere notification without any advance waiting period, early courts found the promises illusory. More recent cases, however, have found consideration in the act of giving reasonable advance notice in cases in which mere notice is required, or by implying a promise

---

[23]UCC §2–306(2).

to give a reasonable notice of termination if a notice requirement is not explicitly stated in the contract. The UCC adopts this approach by providing in §2–309(3):

> Termination of a contract by one party except on the happening of an agreed event requires that reasonable notification be received by the other party and an agreement dispensing with notification is invalid if its operation would be unconscionable.[24]

This provision recognizes that principles of good faith and sound commercial practice normally require that sufficient notice be given to allow the other party a reasonable time within which to make a substitute arrangement.[25] It also appears to make contracts that are terminable at will by either party enforceable, because the obligation to give "reasonable notification" before termination would satisfy the consideration requirement.

In conclusion, as the entire mutuality discussion indicates, courts tend to enforce contracts despite the fact that one or both promises appear "illusory." They achieve this result by imposing an obligation to act in good faith (for example, conditions of satisfaction) or by implying a promise (for example, to use "best efforts," or to give "reasonable" notification). This tendency, exhibited in both common law decisions and by statutes such as the UCC, represents the belief by courts and legislatures that enforcement best effectuates the *intent* of the parties to enter into a *contractual* relationship. In other words, when parties make an agreement, they intend legal consequences to follow. They do not view their bargain as void, having no legal force or effect.

Promissory Estoppel

The preceding material discusses a number of situations in which the law enforces promises not otherwise supported by consideration under traditional analysis. Examples include firm offers under the UCC, promises to perform obligations barred by operation of law, and certain promises to pay for benefits previously conferred. One final exception to the consideration require-

ment is provided by the promissory estoppel doctrine. Under this theory a promise not otherwise binding as a contract is enforced because of the promisee's *justifiable reliance* upon it.

Estoppel is the legal principle by which a person is prevented (estopped) from asserting a position that is inconsistent with his prior conduct, if injustice would thereby result to a person who has changed position in justifiable reliance upon that conduct. Promises that are not otherwise supported by consideration may be enforceable through application of the **promissory estoppel** doctrine. Its requirements are stated in §90(1) of the *Restatement (Second) of Contracts,* which forms the basis of virtually all judicial adoptions of the doctrine:

> A promise which the promisor should reasonably expect to induce action or forbearance on the part of the promisee or a third person and which does induce such action or forbearance is binding if injustice can be avoided only by enforcement of the promise. The remedy granted for breach may be limited as justice requires.

Thus, if a promisor makes a promise knowing that the promisee or a third person will rely upon it, and the promisee or third person changes position in reliance upon the promise by acting or forbearing to act, then the promisor is bound to perform to the extent necessary to avoid injustice to the reliant party.

The promise is binding upon the promisor, not because it is supported by consideration (which it is not), but because the promisor by her conduct is precluded (estopped or prevented) from asserting a contrary position. In other words, the promise is binding without consideration because of the promisee's change of position in reliance upon it. Note that the promisor is only affected by reliance that she does or should foresee. Further, enforcement of the promise must be necessary to avoid injustice. In determining this issue, factors such as the reasonableness and character of the promisee's reliance, the formality with which the promise is made, and the possibility of unjust enrichment are considered.[26]

"Promissory" estoppel should be distinguished from **equitable estoppel** (or estoppel *in pais*). Equitable estoppel results when a person relies upon another's statement of fact (which may be made expressly, or inferred from silence or other conduct) resulting in

---

[24]Unconscionability is discussed in Chapter 10. Under the UCC, "termination occurs when either party pursuant to a power created by agreement or law puts an end to the contract *otherwise than for its breach.*" §2–106(3). (Emphasis added.)

[25]UCC §2–309, Official Comment 8. No notice is required if the contract provides for termination upon the occurrence of an agreed event.

---

[26]RESTATEMENT (SECOND) OF CONTRACTS §90 comment b.

injury. Equitable estoppel, for example, is the basis of the law of fraud and misrepresentation (discussed in Chapter 11), and the doctrine of apparent authority in the law of agency (discussed in Chapter 40). In promissory estoppel, the injured party relies upon a promise, not upon a statement of fact. Equitable estoppel prevents a party from asserting facts (including the truth) which differ from his prior representations. Promissory estoppel makes a promise binding upon the promisor, though unsupported by consideration.

In the following case the court was required to determine whether a promise should be enforced on the basis of promissory estoppel.

Hayes v. Plantations Steel Company
438 A.2d 1091 (R.I. 1982)

In January 1972 plaintiff Edward Hayes, who had been employed by Plantations Steel Company since 1947, announced his intention to retire in July 1972. Although Plantations maintained no formal pension plan, Hayes anticipated receiving a pension from his employer. Approximately one week before Hayes's retirement, Hugo Mainelli, Jr., an officer and shareholder of Plantations, talked briefly with Hayes and told him that the company "would take care" of him. After Hayes retired, Plantations paid him an annual pension of $5,000 until 1977 when, following several poor business years, Plantations changed ownership and management and discontinued the payments to Hayes.

Hayes sued Plantations alleging that the company was contractually obligated to continue paying the pension for his life. The trial court ruled that Plantations was required to pay Hayes a yearly pension of $5,000 on the basis of an implied in fact contract and that Hayes had demonstrated detrimental reliance sufficient to support promissory estoppel in lieu of consideration for the contract. Plantations appealed.

Shea, Justice

. . . Assuming for the purpose of this discussion that Plantations in legal effect made a promise to Hayes, we must ask whether Hayes did supply the required consideration that would make the promise binding? And, if Hayes did not supply consideration, was his alleged reliance sufficiently induced by the promise to estop defendant from denying its obligation to him? We answer both questions in the negative. . . .

Contracts implied in fact require the element of consideration to support them as is required in express contracts. The only difference between the two is the manner in which the parties manifest their assent. . . . In this jurisdiction, consideration consists either in some right, interest, or benefit accruing to one party or some forbearance, detriment, or responsibility given, suffered, or undertaken by the other. . . . Valid consideration furthermore must be bargained for. It must induce the return act or promise. To be valid, therefore, the purported consideration must not have been delivered before a promise is executed, that is, given without reference to the promise. . . . Consideration is therefore a test of the enforceability of executory promises . . . and has no legal effect when rendered in the past and apart from an alleged exchange in the present. . . .

In the case before us, Plantations's promise to pay Hayes a pension is quite clearly not supported by any consideration supplied by Hayes. Hayes had announced his intent to retire well in advance of any promise, and therefore the intention to retire was arrived at without regard to any promise by Plantations. Although Hayes may have had in mind the receipt of a pension when he first informed Plantations, his expectation was not based on any statement made to him or on any conduct of the company officer relative to him in January 1972. In deciding to retire, Hayes acted on his own initiative. Hayes's long years of dedicated service also is legally insufficient because his service too was rendered without being induced by Plantation's promise. . . .

Clearly then this is not a case in which Plantations's promise was meant to induce Hayes to refrain from retiring when he could have chosen to do so in return for further service. . . . Nor was the promise made to encourage long service from the start of his employment. . . . Instead, the testimony establishes that Plantations's promise was intended "as a token of appreciation for [Hayes's] many years of service." As such it was in the nature of a gratuity paid to Hayes for as long as the company chose. . . .

Hayes urges that in the absence of a bargained-for promise the facts require application of the doctrine of promissory estoppel. He stresses that he retired voluntarily while expecting to receive a pension. He would not have otherwise retired. Nor did he seek other employment.

We disagree with this contention largely for the reasons already stated. One of the essential elements of the doctrine of promissory estoppel is that the promise must *induce* the promisee's action of forbearance. The particular act in this regard is plaintiff's decision whether or not to retire. As we stated earlier, the record indicates that he made the decision on his own initiative. In other words, the conversation between Hayes and Mainelli which occurred a week before Hayes left his employment cannot be said to have induced his decision to leave. He had reached that decision long before. . . .

In *Feinberg v. Pfeiffer Co.,* 322 S.W.2d 163 (Mo.App.1959), the plaintiff-employee had worked for her employer for nearly forty years. The defendant corporation's board of directors resolved, in view of her long years of service, to obligate itself to pay "retirement privileges" to her. The resolution did not require the plaintiff to retire. Instead, the decision whether and when to retire remained entirely her own. The board then informed her of its resolution. The plaintiff worked for eighteen months more before retiring. She sued the corporation when it reduced her monthly checks seven years later. The court held that a pension contract existed between the parties. Although continued employment was not a consideration to her receipt of retirement benefits, the court found sufficient reliance on the part of the plaintiff to support her claim. . . . [T]hat is, the defendant informed the plaintiff of its plan, and the plaintiff in reliance thereon, retired. . . .

However, the important distinction between *Feinberg* and the case before us is that in *Feinberg* the employer's decision definitely shaped the thinking of the plaintiff. In this case the promise did not. It is not reasonable to infer from the facts that Hugo R. Mainelli, Jr., expected retirement to result from his conversation with Hayes. Hayes had given notice of his intention seven months previously. Here there was thus no inducement to retire which would satisfy the demands of §90 of the restatement. . . . These circumstances do not lead to a conclusion that injustice can be avoided only by enforcement of Plantations's promise. . . .

[Judgment reversed and remanded.]

Irrevocable Offers

As discussed in Chapter 8, an offer is generally revocable by the offeror at any time prior to the effectiveness of the acceptance, unless the promise to hold the offer open is supported by consideration (creating an option contract) or subject to the "firm offer" rule of the UCC.

Promissory estoppel provides a third exception to the general rule of revocability.

Ordinarily an offeree is not entitled to rely upon an offer prior to acceptance. An offeree who desires protection should secure an option or promptly accept the offer to prevent the possibility of a timely revocation. In some cases, however, the offeree may be justified in relying upon an offer prior to acceptance. For example, to obtain building construction contracts, competing general contractors often submit bids (offers) to a property owner (often a governmental body), which usually awards the contract to the lowest bidder. To compute its overall bid, each general contractor solicits and uses the lowest competing bids from various subcontractors (for example, for the electrical, plumbing, heating and air conditioning, masonry, and excavation work). In many cases, subcontractors who have submitted mistaken low bids have sought to revoke their bids after the general contract has been awarded but before the successful general contractor has formally accepted the subcontractor's bid. To protect the general contractor, who relied on the mistaken subcontractor's bid and is now bound to perform at a price including that bid, courts often apply promissory estoppel principles to prevent the subcontractor from revoking its bid before the successful general contractor has had a reasonable opportunity to accept it.[27] Note that as in other promissory estoppel cases, the doctrine is used to convert a noncontractual promise (here an offer, the bid) into a contract (here an option).

Charitable Subscriptions

Another common application of the promissory estoppel doctrine occurs in charitable subscriptions. Although a basic purpose of the consideration doctrine is to prevent enforcement of a promise to make a gift, an exception is generally recognized for promises made to charitable institutions. Some courts have sustained a charitable promise by treating it as an offer for a unilateral contract, accepted by the charity's acts in reliance. Other courts have used basic promissory estoppel principles. Under the approach followed by many courts and adopted by the *Restatement (Second) of Contracts,* a promise made to a charitable institution, which is

---

[27]The landmark case adopting this approach is *Drennan v. Star Paving Company,* 333 P.2d 757 (Cal. 1958).

expected to induce reliance upon it, is enforceable, even without a showing of actual reliance by the institution.[28] A mere probability of reliance is sufficient. Assume Doaks, a millionaire, promises to give $1 million to the University of Illinois for expansion of the chemistry building. The university, in reliance upon

Doaks's pledge and similar pledges, proceeds with the expansion plan by spending and obligating itself to spend large sums of money on the project. Doaks's promise is binding.[29] Under the *Restatement* approach, the promise would be binding even without a showing of actual reliance upon it.

Summary

1. Consideration, the second element of contract formation, is what is given or promised by each party in exchange for and to induce the return promise or performance of the other. Consideration is the test developed by the law to determine which promises are legally enforceable as contracts.

2. A promise is supported by consideration and therefore binding upon the promisor if two requirements are met. First, the promisee of the promise must incur "legal detriment" by rendering a performance or making a promise. Second, the detriment incurred must be "bargained for."

3. A promise incurs a legal detriment in exchange for a promise if she either refrains or promises to refrain from doing something that she has a legal right to do, or does or promises to do something she is under no legal obligation to do. Assuming a detriment exists, courts do not examine the relative equivalence of the values exchanged. That is, the value of the consideration is determined by the parties.

4. A promise to perform or performance of a preexisting public or statutory duty does not furnish consideration to support a return promise. This preexisting duty rule is a direct application of the legal detriment concept, and effectively requires that modifications of existing common law contracts be supported by consideration. The UCC, however, abolishes the preexisting duty rule for contracts involving goods by providing that a modification of a Code contract needs no consideration to be binding. Though no consideration is required, coerced contract modifications are prohibited as a violation of the duty of good faith.

5. Legal detriment analysis also forms the basis of the law governing compromise agreements reached to settle preexisting obligations. Under principles of accord and satisfaction, a compromise agreement reached to settle a disputed or unliquidated obligation is binding. The doubt regarding either the existence or amount of the original duty—the existence of a good faith dispute—provides the consideration to support the compromise (accord) agreement.

Further, even a liquidated and undisputed obligation may be discharged by a compromise agreement involving performance significantly different from that originally agreed upon.

6. To constitute consideration, the detriment must be bargained for in exchange for the promise. That is, it must be sought by the promisor in exchange for his promise and given by the promise in exchange for that promise. For this reason if a promise is made or performance rendered before a return promise is made, the return promise is unenforceable because it has not been bargained for. In other words, such "past consideration" is no consideration. Similarly, a promise purportedly given in exchange for nominal consideration is often unenforceable for lack of a bargain. In these cases, the promise usually evidences a promise to make a gift, not a contract.

7. Under the doctrine of mutuality, both parties to a contract must provide consideration. If one party's promise is illusory, making his or her performance entirely optional, no detriment is incurred, rendering any return promise unenforceable. Various types of promises including satisfaction required and other conditional promises have survived attack on grounds that they were illusory. Courts sustain these promises on various grounds, such as by imposing an obligation of good faith or implying a promise.

8. The law enforces certain promises not supported by consideration under traditional analysis. Perhaps the most important of these consideration exceptions is the promissory estoppel doctrine under which the promise is enforced because of the promisee's justifiable reliance upon it. Under the doctrine, if a promise is made with the reasonable expectation that it will be relied upon and the promisee acts or refrains from acting in reliance on the promise, then the promise is enforceable to the extent necessary to avoid injustice.

---

[28]RESTATEMENT (SECOND) OF CONTRACTS §90(2).

[29]See In re Field's Estate, 172 N.Y.S.2d 740 (N.Y. Surrogate Ct. 1958).

Key Terms

consideration
bargained-for exchange
legal detriment
preexisting duty rule
past consideration
moral consideration
nominal consideration
accord and satisfaction
disputed claim

liquidated claim
conditional check
mutuality of consideration
illusory promise
aleatory promise
estoppel
promissory estoppel
equitable estoppel

Questions and Problems

9.1 Most people would agree that ethical individuals and businesses keep their promises. In the United States, and in most other countries, however, not all promises are legally enforceable.

(a) Should the law make all promises legally enforceable? Why or why not?

(b) Suggest policy reasons supporting the general rule of law that only those promises supported by consideration are enforceable.

(c) Name three exceptions to the general rule that only promises supported by consideration are enforceable. What are the policy reasons for these exceptions?

(d) Often, businesspeople or businesses will perform a promise even if it is not legally enforceable. Why? If you were a business manager, under what circumstances would you recommend performance of an unenforceable promise?

(e) Throughout this text, you will see examples of legally enforceable promises that are breached. If a person or business fails to perform a promise, is that conduct unethical? Explain.

9.2 Bob owned a vacant lot that had been appraised at $10,000. Susan owned a truck with an appraised value of $4,000. After reviewing both of the appraisals, they entered into a written agreement by which Bob agreed to sell the lot to Susan in exchange for the truck and $1,000 cash. Susan delivered the truck and money; however, Bob refused to convey the lot to her. Susan sued. Bob alleged that the contract was unenforceable because of insufficient consideration. He offered copies of the appraisals as evidence. Should the court enforce the agreement? Explain.

9.3 Al worked as a foreman for Constructo, a construction company. Al was paid on an hourly basis and had no specific term of employment. On a particular construction project, Constructo offered to pay Al a bonus equal to one-half of the difference between the estimated and actual cost of the project. In order to earn the bonus, Al was required to remain in Constructo's employ until completion of the project and to use his extra efforts to induce workers under him to exceed union standards in construction. Al performed his duties efficiently and as a result over $30,000 in estimated labor costs were saved. Is Al entitled to a $15,000 bonus? Explain.

9.4 In the following cases, determine whether the conduct of the parties would be considered an accord and satisfaction.

(a) Ann hired Tom's Tree Service (TTS) to cut down and remove a dead tree located in her front yard. TTS satisfactorily removed the tree and sent Ann a bill for $500. When Ann received the bill she was shocked at the high price. She sent the bill back to TTS after writing across it in red ink. "This bill is outrageous!" Ann enclosed a check in the amount of $150 and wrote the following on the back of the check. "In complete payment for services rendered in tree removal." TTS cashed the check then sued Ann for the unpaid $350.

(b) J. C. Nickels operates a national chain of department stores. Wilbur visited the Nickels store in Joplin, Missouri, where he saw a water heater advertised for $200. Wilbur ordered the water heater and requested Nickels to deliver and install it. After receiving a bill for $300, Nickels contacted the Joplin store manager who explained that the additional $100 was for delivery and installation. Wilbur replied that he believed the $200 purchase price included delivery and installation. Wilbur and the Joplin store manager discussed the matter several times without resolving the dispute. Finally, Wilbur wrote a check to Nickels for $200 and wrote on the back of the check, "In full satisfaction of all outstanding claims. Negotiation of this check discharges payor of all liability for amounts owed to J. C. Nickels." Wilbur mailed the check to Nickel's regional billing center in Chicago in a preaddressed envelope provided by Nickels with its bill. Nickels cashed the check and then sued Wilbur for the unpaid $100.

9.5 Seller contracts to sell a tract of land to Buyer. The land is fairly appraised at $50,000. Buyer promises to pay "$10 and other good and adequate consideration" for the land. Buyer pays the $10 but provides no other consideration. Seller subsequently refused to perform the contract. Should the court enforce it? Why or why not? Would your answer change if the $10 was never paid? Explain. Does resolution of this question turn primarily upon the existence of a "detriment" or the presence of a "bargained-for" exchange?

9.6 Aunt Sarah owns a valuable antique silver service. Aunt Sarah telephones her niece, Lucille, and tells her, "Come over to my house and I will give you my silver service." If Lucille goes to Aunt Sarah's house, would Aunt Sarah's statement become a legally enforceable contract? Explain.

9.7 Silas, a wealthy man, gave his friend Abraham a valuable stamp collection. As a result of some poor investments, Silas later lost all of his assets. Abraham, in an effort to help his friend, offered to pay $5,000 for the stamp collection and Silas reluctantly accepted the offer. If Abraham fails to pay, will Silas be able to enforce the agreement? Explain.

9.8 Consider the following fact situations:

(a) Seller sells his restaurant to Buyer. To protect Buyer's goodwill, Seller promises to pay $5,000 "if I open a competing restaurant within three years." Is Seller's promise illusory or is it sufficient consideration to support Buyer's return promise to pay money? Explain.

(b) A is negotiating to purchase a ship from X. A promises B, "If I decide to buy the ship, I will charter it to you." B accepts the charter. Is A's promise illusory? What has A promised to do? Has a valid enforceable contract been created?

9.9   Billie Jean is a world famous tennis player whose endorsements of tennis balls, rackets, and shoes are valuable for marketing purposes. Billie Jean and Otis enter into an agreement by which Billie Jean grants Otis the exclusive right to use her name and to license her name in conjunction with the sale of tennis products. Otis agrees to pay Billie Jean 75 percent of all profits received from the licensing agreements.

Several weeks later another agent offers Billie Jean a similar deal. The agent suggests that he be given the exclusive right to license her name and in return he will pay her 90 percent of the profits. Billie Jean explains that she already has entered such a contract. After reviewing the contract, the agent concludes that it is not an enforceable contract. He points out that Otis has not promised to do anything and that, therefore, it is an illusory contract. Is the agent correct? Explain.

9.10   The U.S. government solicited bids to provide materials for a construction project at an airport. Sylvan Company submitted a bid to provide gravel of a specified quality at $5 per ton. The bid was submitted on a government form that stated in part, "If this bid is accepted, the bidder promises to supply the materials as required and shall deliver the materials to the site upon request of the procurement office. The U.S. Government reserves the right to cancel this contract at any time."

Sylvan's bid was accepted. Although Sylvan was willing and able to deliver the rock, the procurement office never requested delivery. Two years later, the U.S. government canceled the contract. Sylvan sued the government alleging that the government's failure to request delivery within a reasonable time constituted a breach of contract. The government alleged that no contract existed arguing that its power to cancel at any time rendered the contract illusory. How should the court rule? Explain.

9.11   Hoffman, who owned and operated a bakery, wanted to establish a Red Owl franchise grocery store. Hoffman contacted Red Owl and after several discussions a Red Owl representative told Hoffman that if he invested $18,000, Red Owl would build and stock a store in Chilton, Wisconsin. Hoffman told the representative that he could raise the $18,000, part of which would be a loan from his father-in-law. With the advice of the representative, Hoffman bought a lot for the store in Chilton, paying $1,000 down. Hoffman and his family sold their bakery business and moved to Chilton. The Red Owl representative was aware of and encouraged all of the actions taken by Hoffman. Several weeks later, the representative increased the investment needed by Hoffman to $24,100

based on new project financial statements. Two weeks later Red Owl said it was prepared to proceed if Hoffman could raise another $2,000 for promotional purposes. After Red Owl again revised the figures and said it would require Hoffman's father-in-law to sign an agreement that his loan was a gift to Hoffman, negotiations broke off. Hoffman sues Red Owl for damages alleging that he had acted in reliance on Red Owl's promise to build a store for him. Is Hoffman entitled to recover? Explain.

9.12   Since 1900, All American Steel Corporation has operated two large steel mills in Ohio that employ over 3,500 people. Amid speculation that the mills were going to be closed, All American issued a press release stating in part:

> In response to many rumors, we wish to tell you that All American has no immediate plans to permanently shut down our Ohio mills. However, steps must be taken to improve these plants' profitability. Serious profit problems have been created by heavy imports of foreign steel, higher energy costs, higher taxes, and environmental expenditures. Continued operation of these plants is absolutely dependent upon their being profit-makers. In the months ahead, we will be calling for the full support of each and every one of you. Your cooperation and assistance are absolutely necessary if our facilities are to continue to operate.

During the following six months, employees of the plants worked diligently to improve productivity. They agreed to new working hours, assumed new duties when jobs were eliminated, and some, who had been seeking other employment, gave up new job opportunities. Within a few months productivity improved significantly and gross profit margins showed a small profit. The next year, however, All American announced that it would close the two plants. While recognizing improved productivity, company management noted that according to net profits the plants were operating at a loss.

The employees of the two mills sued All American alleging that the company was obligated to the employees, under principles of promissory estoppel, to keep the plants open if they operated at a profit. How should the court rule?

9.13   Brash worked as a salesman for Sand, Inc. After receiving several memos critical of his work, Brash began to search for a new job. Brash received a job offer from Quatro Co. and notified Sand that he planned to resign to work for Quatro. Sand's president scheduled a meeting with Brash and informed him that Sand was very satisfied with his work and that the critical memos were intended only to motivate him. After further discussion, the president promised Brash that if he stayed with Sand, the company would consider raising his salary and would not terminate his employment so long as he continued to meet his sales quotas. Brash agreed and rejected Quatro's offer. Six months later, Sand fired Brash even though he had met all sales quotas. Brash sued Sand for breach of contract. Sand argued that its promise not to terminate Brash was unenforceable because it was not supported by consideration. Should the court enforce Sand's promise? Explain.

CHAPTER 10

CAPACITY AND LEGALITY

Major Topics

■ the definition of contractual capacity and the legal effects of incapacity
■ the principles governing contracts made by minors and persons who are mentally ill or intoxicated
■ the types of contracts that are unenforceable on public policy grounds
■ the problems created by standardized form contracts and the legal principles, most notably unconscionability, that the law has developed to resolve them
■ the standards governing enforceability of contracts in restraint of trade

Ordinarily, the courts will enforce a bargain evidencing mutual assent supported by consideration. Nevertheless, certain bargains, although they may meet the requisites of contract formation, are rendered either voidable or unenforceable for a variety of reasons, including: (1) a lack of contractual capacity on the part of one or both parties, (2) circumstances under which enforcement of the contract would be contrary to public policy, (3) fraud, misrepresentation, mistake, duress, or undue influence, or (4) noncompliance with certain formalities (for example, a writing) required by law for the enforcement of certain types of contracts. By treating promises made under these circumstances as either voidable or unenforceable, the law imposes special limitations on promissory liability. These limitations are treated in detail in this and the following two chapters.

Contractual Capacity

Generally, the term *capacity* refers to the ability of a person to create or enter into a legal relationship. In order to be bound to a contract both parties must have **contractual capacity.** Usually, any natural[1] person has full legal capacity to incur contractual duties. Certain classes of individuals, however, possess some special characteristic that limits, or in some cases extinguishes, their contractual capacity. Examples include minors (persons under legal age), persons suffering from a mental illness or defect, and intoxicated persons. The law of contractual capacity is designed to protect these people from the effects of their own immaturity, inexperience, and lack of judgment, and to prevent another party from taking unfair advantage of them.

Lack of capacity usually renders a person's contractual obligations voidable. As previously discussed,[2] a

---

[1]Contractual capacity of a corporation, an artificial person, is discussed in Chapter 45.
[2]Voidable contracts are defined in Chapter 7.

voidable contract is one in which one or more parties have the power, by electing to do so, to avoid the legal relations created by the contract. After making the contract, the persons with limited capacity may elect either to be bound by the contract (to ratify it), or to avoid it. The election to avoid a contractual duty is commonly referred to as a *disaffirmance.* The other party to the contract, unless also lacking capacity or having some other grounds for avoidance, is ordinarily bound pending the election to disaffirm.

Minors' (Infants') Contracts

Most contracts voidable on capacity grounds are minors' (or infants') contracts. A **minor** or **infant** is a person who has not yet reached the age of contractual capacity. The age at which a person achieves full contractual capacity (referred to as **majority**) is determined by state statute or constitutional provision. Although the age of majority was traditionally 21 years, it has now been reduced in nearly all states to 18, the voting age. A lower age of majority (for example, 15 years) often is provided for certain types of contracts, such as life, health, or accident insurance, and student loans.

Contracts made by a minor are voidable. The minor's right to disaffirm exists whether or not the agreement is reasonable or fair to the minor and whether or not the adult knew that he was dealing with a minor. In many jurisdictions, the right to disaffirm also extends to emancipated minors. **Emancipation** occurs when the parent surrenders the right to control the minor, including the right to the care, custody, services, and earnings of the child, and renounces parental duties. In many states, emancipation also occurs by operation of law when the minor marries.

Time of Disaffirmance; Ratification. Contracts made during minority are voidable by the minor prior to reaching legal age and for a reasonable time thereafter. In other words, a minor's power of avoidance is not extinguished immediately upon reaching majority. What constitutes a "reasonable time" is a question of fact dependent on all facts and circumstances. Some states, by statute, limit the minor's power of avoidance to a fixed period (for example, one year) after attaining legal age.

A minor may, after reaching majority, elect to be bound upon the previously voidable obligation. As discussed in Chapter 7, such an election, known as **ratifi-**

cation, extinguishes the power of disaffirmance. Ratification may be express or implied. For example, after reaching majority a minor may communicate directly with the adult to indicate her intent to be bound on a contract made during minority. Usually, however, ratification occurs through conduct other than express statements. Such conduct frequently includes retaining and continuing to use the subject matter of the contract for more than a reasonable time after reaching majority, and failing to disaffirm within a reasonable time after reaching majority. Whether a ratification has occurred is a question of fact to be decided by the trier of fact, normally the jury, if the issue is disputed.

Restitution in Executed or Partially Executed Transactions. If a contract is wholly executory, no particular problems arise if the minor elects to avoid. If the minor disaffirms a partially or totally executed bargain, however, the law must determine to what extent the parties (particularly the adult) are entitled to be returned to their precontract positions. To resolve this issue, courts must weigh the policy protecting minors from improvident bargains against the risk of forfeiture[3] by the adult and unjust enrichment of the minor.

If a minor purchases goods or services from an adult on credit, the minor may plead infancy as a defense to enforcement of the contract. Generally, however, he must return any consideration passing from the adult that he still retains. He must also return any identifiable proceeds of the sale or other exchange of the consideration. Assume Andy, an adult, sells a television set to Mike, a minor, on credit. Mike may assert his infancy as a defense against Andy's action for the price, but must return the set if he still has it. Although the minor must return any consideration retained, the minor is not liable to the adult for (1) damage caused to the property, (2) depreciation in value of the property while in the minor's possession through normal wear and tear, (3) the rental value of the property, or (4) any profit derived by the minor from its use (for example, when goods are bought for use in the minor's business operation).

A minor who is unable to return the consideration because it has been squandered, lost, stolen, or negligently destroyed may still generally avoid the obliga-

---

[3]"Forfeiture" in contract law refers to the denial of compensation that results when a person entitled to performance (here the adult) loses that right (upon the minor's disaffirmance) after relying substantially (through preparation or performance) on the contract. RESTATEMENT (SECOND) OF CONTRACTS §229 comment b.

tion to pay. Assume Seller sells a car to Buyer, a minor, on credit. The car is destroyed in a traffic accident while being driven by Buyer. Buyer may avoid her obligation to pay for the car, even though she cannot return the car or its proceeds to Seller. This result is supported by the reasoning that the same immaturity or lack of foresight that induces the minor to make the contract initially also leads to the loss or destruction of the consideration. Therefore, to force minors to return the consideration before disaffirming would deprive them of the defense, grounded in public policy, designed to protect them against the results of their indiscretion.

The rules discussed above often result in a windfall to the minor and a substantial loss to the adult. They also, in the opinion of some critics, tend to promote dishonesty by minors. For these reasons, many courts have taken steps to provide more protection for the adult when the minor disaffirms. For example, as the following case illustrates, a growing number of courts have adopted a rule requiring the minor, upon disaffirmance, to compensate the adult for the value of the use and depreciation of the article while in the minor's possession.

Dodson by Dodson v. Shrader
824 S.W.2d 545 (Tenn. 1992)

In April 1987, plaintiff Joseph Dodson paid $4,900 in cash to purchase a used pickup truck from Shrader's Auto Sales, a business owned by the defendants Burns and Mary Shrader. Although Dodson was only 16 years of age, none of the parties discussed his age at the time of the purchase. In December 1987, the truck developed mechanical problems and Dodson consulted a mechanic who suggested the problem was a burnt valve inside the engine. Without having the truck repaired, Dodson continued to drive it until the engine "blew up" in January. Dodson then sued the Shraders seeking rescission of the contract. The trial court granted rescission and ordered the Shraders to reimburse the $4,900 to Dodson. After the court of appeals affirmed, the Shraders appealed to the Tennessee Supreme Court.

O'Brien, Justice

. . . [Tennessee has adopted] "the modern rule that contracts of infants are not void but only voidable and subject to be disaffirmed by the minor either before or after attaining majority . . . " [*Human v. Hartsell*, 148 S.W.2d 634, 636 (1940).]

[T]he rule in Tennessee . . . is in accord with the majority rule on the issue among our sister states. This rule is based upon the underlying purpose of the "infancy doctrine" which is to protect minors from their lack of judgment and "from squandering their wealth through improvident contracts with crafty adults who would take advantage of them in the marketplace." *Halbman v. Lemke,* [298 N.W.2d 562, 564 (Wis. 1980)].

There is, however, a modern trend among the states, either by judicial action or by statute, in the approach to the problem of balancing the rights of minors against those of innocent merchants. As a result, . . . minority rules have developed which allow the other party to a contract with a minor to refund less than the full consideration paid in the event of rescission. . . . [One] rule holds that the minor's recovery of the full purchase price is subject to a deduction for the minor's "use" of the consideration he or she received under the contract, or for the "depreciation" or "deterioration" of the consideration in his or her possession. . . .

Upon serious reflection we are convinced that a modified form of [this] rule should be adopted in this State concerning the rights and responsibilities of minors in their business dealings. . . .

We state the rule to be followed hereafter, in reference to a contract of a minor, to be where the minor has not been overreached in any way, and there has been no undue influence, and the contract is a fair and reasonable one, and the minor has actually paid money on the purchase price, and taken and used the article purchased, that he ought not to be permitted to recover the amount actually paid, without allowing the vendor of the goods reasonable compensation for the use of, depreciation, and willful or negligent damage to the article purchased, while in his hands. If there has been any fraud or imposition on the part of the seller or if the contract is unfair, or any unfair advantage has been taken of the minor inducing him to make the purchase, then the rule does not apply. Whether there has been such an overreaching on the part of the seller, and the fair market value of the property returned, would always, in any case, be a question for the trier of fact. This rule will fully and fairly protect the minor against injustice or imposition, and at the same time it will be fair to a business person who has dealt with such minor in good faith.

This rule is best adapted to modern conditions under which minors are permitted to, and do in fact, transact a great deal of business for themselves, long before they have reached the age of legal majority. Many young people work and earn money and collect it and spend it oftentimes without any oversight or restriction. The law does not question their right to buy if they have the money to pay for their purchases. It seems intolerably burdensome for everyone concerned if merchants and business people cannot deal with them safely, in a fair and reasonable way. Further, it does not appear consistent with practice of proper moral influence upon young people, tend to encourage honesty and integrity, or lead them to a good and useful business future, if they are taught that they can make purchases with their own money, for their own benefit, and after paying for them, and using them until they are worn out and destroyed, go back and compel the vendor to return to them what they have paid upon the purchase price. Such a doctrine can only lead to the corruption of principles and encourage young people in habits of trickery and dishonesty.

In view of the foregoing considerations, we conclude that the rule, as we have indicated, . . . will henceforth be the rule to be utilized in this State. . . .

[Judgment reversed and remanded.]

Misrepresentation of Age. A related issue concerns the rights of the parties when the minor misrepresents his or her age to the adult. Assume Sara negotiates with Beverly, a minor, for the sale of a new car. Beverly knows Sara will not deal with a minor. Therefore, to induce Sara to sell, Beverly misrepresents her age, indicating she has reached majority.

Under the majority rule, the fact that a minor misrepresents her age does not affect the power to avoid the contract. Other courts additionally protect the adult in this situation by applying the estoppel doctrine or by allowing the adult to sue the minor for fraudulent misrepresentation. Courts applying the estoppel principle hold that when the minor's fraudulent misstatement of age induces the adult to enter into the contract, an equitable estoppel (estoppel *in pais*) results to prevent the minor from exercising the power of avoidance. Courts allowing recovery on the basis of fraud rely upon the basic proposition that minors, although not liable in contract, are liable for their torts. A misstatement of age, if relied upon, and causing injury, constitutes fraud, a tort. Thus, the court does not enforce the contract, but holds the minor liable in tort for damages.

The legislation in most states lowering the age of majority from 21 to 18 has largely relieved the misrep-

resentation of age problem. Persons under age 18 are more easily recognized as minors, and substantially fewer people (those between 18 and 21) may now avoid their contractual obligations.

Liability for "Necessaries." Though able to avoid contractual obligations, a minor may be held liable for the reasonable value of **necessaries** furnished to him. This liability, although protecting the adult supplier, is imposed to insure that the minor will be able to acquire goods and services necessary for his and his dependents' support. The minor's liability in these cases is based, not upon the contract, but on restitutionary quasi-contract grounds.[4] Because the minor's obligation is grounded in restitution, not contract, the minor's liability is limited to the reasonable value of the benefit conferred, not necessarily the contract price. In addition, a minor is liable only for necessaries actually furnished, not an executory agreement to furnish necessaries.

Traditionally, courts have held basic items such as food, clothing, shelter, medical care, and a certain amount of education to be necessaries. Modern courts have expanded this concept of necessaries to include

> . . . such articles of property and such services as are reasonably necessary to enable the infant to earn the money required to provide the necessities of life for himself and those who are legally dependent upon him. . . .[5]

Under this test, for example, attorneys' fees, employment agency fees, and automobiles might be necessaries. Courts, however, have not applied a fixed meaning to the term. Rather, the determination is based upon the particular facts and circumstances of each case including the minor's health, marital status, and standard of living. Thus, a necessary for one minor may not be so for another.

Because a parent is liable for the support of a child, a minor is not liable upon contracts for necessaries if he has a parent or guardian who is supplying (or is willing to supply) them. A minor is liable only if the parent or

---

[4]The law of restitution implies a promise to pay (a quasi-contract or contract implied in law) the reasonable value of benefits conferred by one party upon another when required to prevent "unjust enrichment." In the necessaries case, the implied promise runs from the minor to the party furnishing the goods or services. Restitution is discussed in Chapter 15.

[5]Gastonia Personnel Corporation v. Rogers, 172 S.E.2d 19, 24 (N.C. 1970).

guardian refuses, neglects, or is unable to supply necessaries. However, a parent who neglects the duty to support may be liable on quasi-contract grounds to a person who furnishes necessaries to his child. In other words, the person who supplies necessaries has conferred a benefit upon the delinquent parent for which the law implies a promise by the parent to pay.

Mental Illness and Intoxication

In addition to infancy, contractual capacity may be restricted or extinguished due to a mental illness or defect. Contractual capacity may be affected, for example, by mental retardation, senility, brain damage resulting from accident or disease, or mental illness. Because the cause and severity of mental incompetency varies widely, the law must balance the incompetent's need for protection against the reasonable expectations of persons dealing with her.

Mental Illness. Certain persons suffering from a mental illness or defect have no contractual capacity and their contracts are void, rather than voidable. For example, severe mental or physical disability may prevent formation of the necessary intent to contract.

A person for whom a guardian has been appointed also has no contractual capacity. A **guardian** is a person appointed by the court to manage, subject to court supervision, the affairs and property of a person (referred to as a **ward**) who is considered incapable of administering her own affairs. The guardian may be appointed, for example, as a result of a person's insanity, senility, or addiction to alcohol or other drugs. The purpose of the guardianship is to protect the ward's rights and to prevent her from squandering or improvidently using her property. The guardianship proceedings provide public notice of the ward's incapacity. Thus, persons dealing with the ward are bound by the ward's incapacity, even without actual knowledge of the guardianship.[6]

Although a mental infirmity may render a contract void, it more commonly renders the obligation merely voidable. Courts have developed two tests to determine when a contract is voidable due to mental incompetency. The first is the traditional "cognitive" test used by most courts under which the contract is voidable if the person is substantially incapable of understanding and

appreciating the nature and consequences of the transaction. The second "motivational" or "affective" test is a more recent judicial development adopted in some states to supplement the cognitive test. It permits avoidance of contracts by persons who know and understand what they are doing but, due to mental illness, cannot rationally control their behavior. Under the motivational test, avoidance is allowed only if the other party to the transaction has reason to know of the mental condition.[7]

If a mentally incompetent person's contract has been partly or fully performed, it generally may be avoided by restoring the parties to their original positions, including restitution for any benefits retained by the incompetent. The court may, however, refuse to allow avoidance if the previous positions cannot be restored or if avoidance would be otherwise inequitable.

Intoxication. Contracts made by persons intoxicated through alcohol or other drug use also may be voidable. The same competency standards applied to mental illness also apply in intoxication cases. Extreme intoxication may prevent contract formation altogether. Less extreme intoxication provides a defense only if the other party has reason to know of it. Courts have, however, been less sympathetic to avoidance claims based upon intoxication than those based upon other mental infirmity.[8]

Unenforceability on Public Policy Grounds

Contract Enforcement and Public Policy

Not all agreements made by competent parties and supported by consideration are enforceable. The courts will not enforce a promise or contract term that, either in its formation or performance: (1) violates an applicable civil or criminal statute, (2) constitutes the commission of or inducement to commit a tort, or (3) is otherwise contrary to public policy. Contracts unenforceable on this basis have traditionally been analyzed as **illegal bargains.** The concept is, however, broader than illegality — for example, a contract that violates a criminal

---

[6] Restatement (Second) of Contracts §13 and comment a.

[7] The approach allowing avoidance under either test has been adopted by the *Restatement (Second) of Contracts* §15.

[8] See Restatement (Second) of Contracts §16; for a case presenting an intoxication issue, see *Lucy v. Zehmer* in Chapter 8.

statute. Also included are other transactions in which the interest in freedom of contract is outweighed by an overriding public interest against judicial recognition of the contract or contract term. In other words, the issue is whether the promise will be *enforced,* not necessarily whether the law has made the act of making or performing it illegal. In this manner, the law discourages certain types of promises by refusing to allow the judicial system to be used as a means to enforce them. The following material examines contracts unenforceable because they violate a statute, and those unenforceable on public policy grounds in the absence of statute.

Contracts Violating a Statute. Some contracts or contract terms are unenforceable because they violate either the letter or the policy of a state or federal statute. Only infrequently—as in the gambling or usurious contracts discussed below—will legislation explicitly provide that a contract or contract provision is unenforceable. More commonly, the statute merely prohibits certain conduct and provides a penalty, such as a fine, for a violation. Thus, in ruling upon the enforceability of a contract that violates the statute, the court is required to balance the policy of the statute in protecting some aspect of the public welfare against the parties' interest in enforcing their promises. Frequently, to further the statutory policy, the court will find the contract wholly or partially unenforceable.

Gambling Contracts. In many states, statutes make wagering a crime and provide that gambling contracts are unenforceable. Assume that Tom and Margaret reside in such a state, but they agree to wager $1,000 on the outcome of the Illinois-Michigan basketball game. Tom promises to pay Margaret $1,000 if Illinois wins and Margaret promises to pay Tom $1,000 if Michigan wins. In accordance with the state statute, both of their promises are unenforceable.

Usurious Contracts. **Usurious contracts** are those in which interest rates greater than the maximum legal rate are charged. Usury statutes vary widely among the states, regarding both maximum interest rates and penalties. In some states neither principal nor interest may be recovered by the creditor if the interest rate is usurious. On the other hand, some states merely hold that interest in excess of the maximum rate is uncollectible.

A Contract to Commit a Crime. A contract to commit a murder or theft, or to give or receive a bribe, is unenforceable. The parties also are subject to criminal liability for their conduct. The following case illustrates the judicial approach to enforceability of a contract violating a criminal statute.

Kunz v. Lobo Lodge, Inc.
990 P.2d 1219 (Idaho App. 1999)

Under a 10-year contract made in December 1990, Lobo Lodge, Inc. leased part of its land to Donrey Outdoor Advertising. Donrey intended to use two billboards on the property. Before the contract took effect, however, the city enacted an ordinance making it a crime to maintain billboards on certain types of property, including that owned by Lobo Lodge. The ordinance also required a permit and payment of a fee for all billboards. Sometime later, Donrey assigned its contract with Lobo Lodge to Gregory Kunz who maintained the two billboards but never obtained the city permits or paid the city fee. In 1995, while negotiating to sell its property, Lobo Lodge notified Kunz that it was terminating the contract. Kunz refused to remove his billboards and sued Lobo Lodge for breach of contract. The trial court granted Lobo Lodge's motion for summary judgment, refusing to enforce the contract because it was in violation of a city ordinance.

Schwartzman, Judge

. . . Kunz asserts that the district court failed to perform a necessary balancing of competing public policies to determine if the lease agreements should be enforced. However, this case is not about a contract in possible violation of public policy. Rather, this case concerns leases made in direct contravention of a municipal criminal ordinance and a party who knowingly took assignment of and maintained said leases. . . .

Contracts to do acts forbidden by law are void and cannot be enforced. . . . In *Hancock v. Elkington,* [186 P.2d 494, 498 (Idaho 1947)], the Idaho Supreme Court stated that:

No principle of law is better settled than that a party to an illegal contract cannot come into a court of law and ask to have his illegal objects carried out; . . . the law in short will not aid either party to an illegal contract; it leaves the parties where it finds them. The general rule is the same at law and in equity, and whether the contract is executory or executed.

When Kunz took assignment of the leases from Donrey, it had knowledge of the continuing illegality of the leases' purpose. . . . Kunz does not dispute that it had knowledge of the leases' claimed illegality. Kunz continued to maintain the prohibited uses without securing the required permits or paying the mandated fees. Kunz assumed the risks inherent in an ongoing illegal agreement. Kunz argues that Lobo Lodge should also not be permitted to benefit from the illegal contract. However,

> This rule is made for the protection of the public and not for the benefit of the parties; its object in refusing relief to either party where the contract is executed is not to give validity to the transaction but to deprive the parties of all right to have either enforcement of, or relief from, the illegal agreement. In such cases the defense of illegality prevails, not as a protection to defendant, but as a disability in plaintiff. . . . While it may not always seem an honorable thing to do, yet a party to an illegal agreement is permitted to set up the illegality as a defense. [17 *C.J.S. Contracts* § 272 (1963)]

Additionally, if we were to adopt Kunz's analysis (requiring a balancing of public policy concerns every time the court encounters a contract made in contravention of a municipal criminal ordinance), the laws of Idaho's municipalities as well as those of Idaho itself would fall into disarray. If parties knew that they could enter into contracts in direct contravention of law and then seek judicial relief if and when the transaction went awry, then citizens would be encouraged to conduct a risk-benefit analysis before entering into such illegal contracts. If a contract's economic benefit substantially outweighs the penalties the party could be subject to, then such party has an incentive to make the agreement in conflict with existing regulatory laws, hoping that it could still have its contract enforced by the judiciary.

By ruling as we do today, citizens will have no incentive to knowingly enter into contracts in direct contravention of regulatory criminal ordinances. On the facts of this case, we adopt the rule generally applicable to illegal contracts and leave the parties where we find them, i.e. with no enforceable agreement.

[Judgment affirmed.]

Contracts Violating Licensing Statutes. City, state, and federal statutes often require that persons providing certain goods or services be licensed. A contract made by an unlicensed individual to furnish the regulated goods or services is generally unenforceable if (1) the statute has a regulatory (as opposed to merely a revenue raising) purpose, and (2) the public policy of the licensing or registration requirement clearly outweighs the interest in enforcement.[9]

One case of this type involves statutes requiring licensing of professionals such as physicians, dentists, and attorneys. Applying the foregoing principles, courts in these cases generally refuse to allow unlicensed practitioners to recover for their services. Assume Jones, who is not admitted to the bar, and Smith, an unlicensed physician, render services to Cox, who promises to pay for them. Cox's promises to Jones and Smith are unenforceable. This result fosters the basic regulatory purpose of professional licensing statutes: to protect the public against professional practice by incompetent or unqualified individuals.

Unenforceability in the Absence of Statute. Even in the absence of statute, the court frequently is required to balance public against private interests to determine enforceability. Examples of contracts or terms which have been held unenforceable on this basis include the following.

Contracts Constituting or Inducing a Tort. Courts generally do not enforce a contract or contract term that requires either party to commit a tort. Assume that A promises to pay B, who owns a newspaper, $1,000 if B will print a defamatory statement about C which both A and B know to be false. B promises to do so. Both promises are unenforceable. A's promise induced the commission of a tort and performance of B's promise would constitute commission of a tort, libel.

Promises Involving Violation of Fiduciary Duty. A fiduciary relationship is one in which one person is bound to act solely in the interest of another concerning matters within the scope of the relation. The concept is important in many areas of the law, including trusts, agency, partnership, and corporations. A fiduciary must refrain from acting for her private benefit or otherwise against the interests of the person or persons to whom

---

[9] Restatement (Second) of Contracts §181.

she owes the fiduciary duty. Therefore, a promise to violate a fiduciary duty, or a promise made as inducement to violate that duty, is unenforceable. For example, a corporate director stands in a fiduciary relationship to a corporation. Assume X, in her capacity as director of ABC Corporation, learns trade secrets relating to ABC's manufacturing process. X promises to disclose the secrets to Y in exchange for Y's promise to pay $10,000. Because X's disclosure of the trade secrets will violate her fiduciary duty to ABC, both promises are unenforceable on grounds of public policy.

Promises Interfering with Another's Contractual Relationship. As discussed in Chapter 5, a person who intentionally and unjustifiably interferes with the performance of a contract by inducing or otherwise causing one of the parties not to perform is liable in tort to the nonbreaching party for damages resulting from the breach of the contract.[10] In other words, a contractual relationship is recognized by the law as a property right. The unjustifiable destruction of that right is a tort for which judicial relief is available.

Because intentional interference with a contractual relationship is a tort, both a promise that tortiously induces a breach, and the return promise to commit the breach, are unenforceable on grounds of public policy. Assume A contracts to employ B full time for three years. C, with knowledge of the existing contract and with the intent to induce B to breach it, offers B a substantially larger salary if B will begin work immediately. B accepts. Both promises are unenforceable.[11]

Exculpatory Clauses. A contract term that exempts a person from liability for his or her own torts is known as an **exculpatory clause.** An exculpatory term that seeks to excuse a person for liability for *intentional* or *reckless* conduct is always unenforceable. In contrast, parties generally may exempt themselves from liability for *negligence,* that is, failure to exercise reasonable care. This general rule is subject to several exceptions. First, state statutes frequently make exculpatory clauses unenforceable in specific types of contracts. For example, in many states, a provision in a lease that exempts a landlord from liability for damages caused by the negligence of the landlord or his employees is unenforceable

as contrary to public policy. Second, courts have recognized a number of specific exceptions as a matter of general contract law. For example, an employer may not contractually relieve itself of liability to an employee for job-related injuries caused by the employer's negligence. Similarly, most courts refuse to permit a party who performs a public service, such as a common carrier or public utility, to contractually avoid liability for negligence to persons it serves.[12] At issue in the following case was whether an exculpatory clause could relieve a defendant from liability for its allegedly reckless (grossly negligent) conduct.

The New Light Company, Inc. v. Wells Fargo Alarm Services
525 N.W.2d 25 (Neb. 1994)

Defendant Wells Fargo Alarm Services contracted with plaintiff The New Light Company (New Light) to install and maintain a fire alarm system in a building where New Light owned and operated a restaurant. A fire later extensively damaged the building and restaurant. The fire started in a basement laundry room adjacent to the electrical room in which Wells Fargo had installed the alarm communication system. Because Wells Fargo had not installed fire-sensing devices in the laundry room or electrical room, the fire destroyed the alarm communication system before it activated sensing devices in other areas of the building.

New Light sued Wells Fargo, alleging gross negligence in the design, installation, and maintenance of the alarm system. Wells Fargo claimed that it was not liable due to an exculpatory clause in its contract with New Light. That clause provided that Wells Fargo would not be liable

> for any loss or damage, irrespective of origin, to persons or property whether directly or indirectly caused by performance or nonperformance of any obligation imposed by [the agreement] or by negligent acts or omissions of Wells Fargo Alarm, its agents, or employees.

In the alternative, Wells Fargo argued that another provision of the contract limited damages resulting from failure of the alarm system to the lesser of "the annual charge under the contract or $10,000." The trial court dismissed

---

[10]RESTATEMENT (SECOND) OF TORTS §766. See discussion in Chapter 5.
[11]RESTATEMENT (SECOND) OF CONTRACTS §194 and ill. 1.

[12]RESTATEMENT (SECOND) OF CONTRACTS §195.

the lawsuit based on the exculpatory clause, New Light appealed, arguing that both the exculpatory clause and limitation of damages provision violated public policy. After the appellate court affirmed the dismissal, the Nebraska Supreme Court granted New Light's petition for review.

Wright, Justice

. . . In determining whether the language of a particular exculpatory clause in a contract is a clear contravention of public policy, we must consider each agreement on the basis of the particular facts surrounding the agreement. We have defined public policy as

[t]hat principle of the law which holds that no subject can lawfully do that which has a tendency to be injurious to the public or against the public good. . . . The principle under which the freedom of contract or private dealings is restricted by law for the good of the community. [*OB-GYN v. Blue Cross,* 361 N.W.2d 550, 553 (Neb. 1985)]. . . .

Whether a particular exculpatory clause in a contractual agreement violates public policy depends upon the facts and circumstances of the agreement and the parties involved. The right of contract may be restricted for the public good. The greater the threat to the general safety of the community, the greater the restriction on the party's freedom to contractually limit the party's liability. For example, a contractual agreement to dig a ditch does not have the same public policy considerations as would the installation of a fire alarm system in a school, hospital, nursing home, restaurant, or other heavily occupied building. Common sense tells us that the greater the risk to human life and property, the stronger the argument in favor of voiding attempts by a party to insulate itself from damages caused by that party's gross negligence or willful and wanton misconduct.

In the factual setting in this case, when we balance the parties' right to contract against the protection of the public, we find a sufficiently compelling reason to prevent Wells Fargo from insulating itself by contractual agreement from damages caused by its own gross negligence or willful and wanton misconduct. Such an agreement would have a tendency to be injurious to the public. This limitation on the freedom to contract is imposed by law because of the potential risks to human life and property and is, therefore, independent of the agreement of the parties.

A similar exculpatory clause was determined to be contrary to public policy in *Sommer v. Federal Signal Corp.,* [593 N.E.2d 1365 (N.Y. 1992)]. The New York Court of Appeals stated that it was the public policy of the state that a party could not insulate itself from damages caused by grossly negligent conduct. . . . The court found that this policy would apply equally to contract clauses purporting to exonerate a party from liability and to clauses limiting damages to a nominal sum. We agree with the New York court that public policy with regard to gross negligence and willful and wanton misconduct applies both to clauses attempting to exculpate liability and clauses attempting to limit damages to a nominal sum. . . .

[Judgment reversed and remanded.]

Restitution in Executed and Partially Executed Transactions. If an agreement unenforceable on grounds of public policy has been partially or wholly performed, one party may seek restitution for any benefits conferred upon the other pursuant to the unenforceable bargain. The general rule is that the court leaves the parties as it finds them, regardless of the extent to which the contract has been performed. The court will not aid the promisee either by enforcing the promise or by granting him restitution of the benefit conferred upon the other, even if the other also is a wrongdoer. Because the rule denying restitution may result in an unjust enrichment of one party coupled with a forfeiture by the other, courts have made several exceptions to the general rule if necessary to do justice. For example, restitution has been granted (1) if denial of restitution would effect a disproportionate forfeiture, (2) if the party claiming restitution was excusably unaware of the facts or of minor legislation, but for which the promise would be enforceable, (3) if the party claiming restitution is not equally in the wrong *(in pari delicto)* with the party from whom he seeks restitution, or (4) if the party seeking restitution withdraws from the transaction in time to prevent the accomplishment of the illegal or improper purpose for which the bargain was created. This is known as the doctrine of *locus poenitentiae,* which means literally "a place for repentance." These exceptions provide the flexibility necessary to do justice in a variety of fact situations presenting widely varying degrees of culpable behavior.[13]

Contracts of Adhesion and Unconscionability: Problems of Standardized Form Contracts

Contracts of Adhesion. Standardized form contracts, commonly known as **contracts of adhesion,** play an essential role in modern business, which requires mass production and distribution of goods and services. Form contracts can be tailored to specific transaction types, eliminating needless and repetitive detail in each individual contract, saving time and money, and allowing the parties to focus upon important particulars such as quantity and price. The forms themselves are often adapted to office routines and business machines and may be used for recordkeeping or supervisory purposes.[14]

Most contracts entered into by consumers are adhesion contracts. Examples include insurance policies, agreements for the sale or lease of personal or real property, mortgages, installment sales contracts and other agreements creating security interests, and checking and savings account agreements.

Despite their obvious utility, adhesion contracts present a major problem area in contract law. In these agreements, one party dictates many of the contract terms to the other (the "adhering" party) who generally stands in a substantially inferior bargaining position. Because the contract is drafted solely by one party and is given to the other on a "take it or leave it" basis, its terms are often unreasonably favorable to the drafting party. Contract law generally is premised upon the existence of an agreement negotiated by the parties at "arm's length." An *arm's length transaction* is one negotiated by unrelated parties, each acting in his or her own self-interest. This premise is not ordinarily present in adhesion contracts. The "adhering" party frequently must either accept the terms as written or forgo the goods or services involved, because similar provisions are used by all drafting parties. The following material discusses the doctrine of unconscionability and other means developed by courts and legislatures to resolve the problems created by this disparity in bargaining power.

Unconscionability. The doctrine of **unconscionability** is an important tool used to address the problems created by adhesion contracts. The doctrine is a general principle of contract law, adopted by both the UCC and the common law. As stated in the UCC, §2–302(1), if a court as a matter of law[15] finds a contract or clause of a contract to have been unconscionable at the time it was made, the court may (1) refuse to enforce the contract, (2) enforce the remainder of the contract without the unconscionable provision, or (3) limit the effect of the unconscionable provision to avoid any unconscionable result.

Unconscionability is not specifically defined, but Official Comment 1 to §2–302 indicates that:

> The basic test is whether, in the light of the general commercial background and the commercial needs of the particular trade or case, the clauses involved are so one-sided as to be unconscionable under the circumstances existing at the time of the making of the contract. . . . The principle is one of the prevention of *oppression and unfair surprise.* . . . (Emphasis added.)

Oppression or **substantive unconscionability** is present when a contract or provision is unreasonably harsh or unfair, generally extracted by a party with vastly superior bargaining power. Such contracts or terms are unenforceable as contrary to public policy. *Unfair surprise* or **procedural unconscionability** frequently occurs when a person signs a standardized form contract containing a provision, commonly in fine print, that substantially alters his or her reasonable expectations under the agreement. If procedural unconscionability is involved, enforcement is denied on the basis that the informed, voluntary mutual assent essential to a binding contract is not present. In virtually all cases in which the courts have found a contract or term unconscionable, elements of both substantive and procedural unconscionability were present.

In adhesion contracts, unconscionability may arise out of gross disparity in the values exchanged or if the form contract binds only the person who signs. Other provisions that may be unconscionable include warranty and liability disclaimers, penalties, or terms granting substantial advantages in enforcement and remedy to the drafting party. The effect of such provisions is aggravated when the person signing has limited intelli-

---

[13]Restatement (Second) of Contracts §§197–199.
[14]Restatement (Second) of Contracts §211 comment a.

[15]Because the issue is a matter of *law,* relief on the basis of unconscionability is granted in the discretion of the court, not as a question of fact for the jury to decide.

gence, financial resources, education, or knowledge of the English language.

In the following case the court was required to determine whether a limitation of liability clause was unconscionable.

Fotomat Corporation of Florida v. Chanda
464 So.2d 626 (Fla. App. 1985)

Plaintiff Joseph Chanda, a physician, brought 28 rolls of Super-8 movie film to an outlet operated by defendant Fotomat Corporation of Florida to have the films transferred to a videotape to prevent deterioration of the pictures. The films, which were of great sentimental value, included movies from his honeymoon, graduation from medical school, his son's birth and childhood, and other important family events. Upon delivery of the film, the store clerk asked Chanda to read and sign the order form which included a limitation of liability clause stating in part:

> By depositing film or other material with Fotomat, customer acknowledges and agrees that Fotomat's liability for any loss, damage, or delay to film during the processing service will be limited to the replacement cost of a non-exposed roll of film and/or a blank cassette of similar size. . . . Except for such replacement, Fotomat shall not be liable for any other loss or damage, direct, consequential, or incidental, arising out of customer's use of Fotomat's services.

The clause was printed in bold type in a conspicuous place on the order form. After reading the clause and asking the clerk about it, Chanda signed the form. While in Fotomat's possession, the films were lost prior to transfer to the videotape.

Chanda sued Fotomat for breach of contract seeking damages of $9,500, but Fotomat argued that damages should be limited to replacement of 28 rolls of unexposed Super-8 film. The trial court ruled that Fotomat's limitation of liability clause was unconscionable and ordered the jury to disregard it in determining damages. The jury found for Chanda and awarded damages of $9,500. Fotomat appealed.

Orfinger, Judge

. . . In the seminal case of *Williams v. Walker-Thomas Furniture Company*, 350 F.2d 445, 449 (D.C. Cir. 1965), . . . the court discussed unconscionability in terms of its elements:

Unconscionability has generally been recognized to include an absence of meaningful choice on the part of one of the parties together with contract terms which are unreasonably favorable to the other party. Whether a meaningful choice is present in a particular case can only be determined by consideration of all the circumstances surrounding the transaction. In many cases the meaningfulness of the choice is negated by a gross inequality of bargaining power. The manner in which the contract was entered is also relevant to this consideration. Did each party to the contract, considering his obvious education or lack of it, have a reasonable opportunity to understand the terms of the contract, or were the important terms hidden in a maze of fine print and minimized by deceptive sales practices? Ordinarily, one who signs an agreement without full knowledge of its terms might be held to assume the risk that he has entered a one-sided bargain. But when a party of little bargaining power, and hence little real choice, signs a commercially unreasonable contract with little or no knowledge of its terms, it is hardly likely that his consent, or even an objective manifestation of his consent, was ever given to all the terms. In such a case the usual rule that the terms of the agreement are not to be questioned should be abandoned and the court should consider whether the terms of the contract are so unfair that enforcement should be withheld.

Florida has long recognized the principle that the courts are not concerned with the wisdom or folly of contracts . . . but where it is perfectly plain to the court that one party has overreached the other and has gained an unjust and undeserved advantage which it would be inequitable to permit him to enforce, a court will grant relief even though the victimized parties owe their predicament largely to their own stupidity. . . .

In *Kohl v. Bay Colony Club Condominium, Inc.,* [398 So.2d 865 (Fla. App. 1981)], the court reviewed the authorities on the subject and concluded that:

> The authorities appear to be virtually unanimous in declaring (or assuming) that two elements must coalesce before a case for unconscionability is made out. The first is referred to as substantive unconscionability and the other procedural unconscionability. . . . A case is made out for substantive unconscionability by alleging and proving that the terms of the contract are unreasonable and unfair. . . . Procedural unconscionability, on the other hand, speaks to the individualized circumstances surrounding each contracting party at the time the contract was entered into. . . .

Applying the substantive prong of the test here, it cannot be said, as a matter of law, that the limitation clause here was unreasonable, when viewed in its commercial setting and when considering its purpose and effect. The charge for the processing service here was $31.00. The videocassette was priced at $18.95, and there was an additional $2.00 charge for an item not identified. There was unrebutted defense testimony that the limitation of liability provision was standard in the industry because, although loss and damage of film was relatively low in view of the tremendous volume of work done, no film processor would expose itself to liability for the unknown content of film without having to so greatly increase the cost to the public as to price the service out of the market. This is clearly a commercially reasonable consideration. . . .

The reasonableness of the clause is demonstrated by the huge loss claimed by Dr. Chanda, compared to the cost of the service. Without a doubt the film had peculiar value to the plaintiff. Some of it was irreplaceable and all of it was of great sentimental value, but that unknown "tiger" is the very reason for the inclusion of the limitation of liability provision in the transaction. There is no way the processor can conceive of the risk it takes in accepting film for processing absent an explicit agreement to accept such risk. When the customer is made aware of the provision for limitation of liability and nevertheless proceeds with the transaction he has assented to an agreement for which there is a commercial need, if the cost of the service is to be made reasonable.

Neither can we perceive that plaintiff satisfied the procedural prong of the test. The evidence reflects that Dr. Chanda saw and read the clause in question, asked a question about it and was apparently satisfied with the answer because he signed it. He had previously suffered the loss of film at a different place of business, and it had been replaced by new film. He was a doctor, well educated, experienced in business transactions, and well aware of what he was signing. While he was given no opportunity to negotiate the terms of this agreement, he did not attempt to determine if anyone else could provide this service. Thus, the evidence falls short of showing procedural unconscionability. If, as indicated by the official comment to Section 2–302 of the Uniform Commercial Code, the principle involved in the section "is one of the prevention of oppression and unfair surprise . . . and not of disturbance of allocation of risks because of superior bargaining power," no such oppression or unfair surprise is shown here. . . .

It is clear from the record here that the trial court refused to consider and apply the procedural/substantive test to determine the issue of unconscionability. Neither was any other objective analysis applied, but instead, the court appeared to view the unfairness of the agreement in retrospect, because of the result. The contract should have been reviewed in the light of the circumstances that existed when it was made. The judgment for plaintiff is reversed, and the cause is remanded to the trial court with directions to enter judgment for plaintiff for the cost of 28 rolls of unexposed Super-8 movie film.

[Judgment reversed and remanded.]

Unconscionability Between Merchants. The unconscionability doctrine has been most often applied to relieve a consumer from the effects of an unreasonably unfair contract. Courts have, however, been much more hesitant to apply the doctrine when the parties involved are *merchants* for two reasons. First, many commercial contracts are negotiated arm's length bargains, not the adhesion contracts used in consumer transactions. Secondly, the gross disparity in bargaining position characterizing many consumer transactions usually is not present between merchants, which often are sophisticated business entities represented by counsel.

Assent to Terms Not Bargained For. Traditionally, a person, by signing her name to a contract, manifests her assent to its terms and may not later assert that she had not read or did not understand its contents. This rule is generally stated as imposing a **duty to read** upon a person who signs a contract. In an adhesion contract, however, the party signing affirmatively assents to a few terms, commonly those that are inserted in the blanks on the standardized contract. She neither reads nor understands the printed terms contained in the remainder of the form. This fact is generally known to the drafting party. The party signing relies on the other's good faith and upon the implied representation that like terms are being accepted by others. The issue thus presented is: To what extent should the "adhering" party be bound to the unknown terms?

The *Restatement (Second) of Contracts* answers this question by providing that although the person signing a standardized agreement is bound to its terms, even without reading or understanding them, he or she is not bound to "unknown terms which are beyond the range of reasonable expectation."[16] In other words, a party who signs an adhesion contract does not assent to a term if the drafting party has reason to believe that the signer would not have agreed to it had he known about it. The drafting party has "reason to believe" if the term is oppressive, or substantially and adversely alters the nonstandard terms explicitly negotiated, or eliminates the dominant purpose of the transaction. Note that this approach addresses the problem of unconscionability by "unfair surprise" by refusing to enforce provisions that are contrary to reasonable expectations, indicating a lack of assent to those terms.

The unconscionability doctrine and the *Restatement* approach to nonnegotiated terms will continue to provide relief from the more onerous effects of adhesion contracts. Nevertheless, these approaches provide protection only after a person has signed an unreasonably unfair contract and is seeking to avoid its consequences in a subsequent lawsuit. They do not prevent the inclusion of such provisions initially. Additional statutory relief has been directed to this end. Many states, for example, have adopted residential landlord and tenant statutes defining rights and duties of both parties to protect tenants from the effects of one of the most troublesome adhesion contracts, the residential lease (particularly in multiunit dwellings). States have passed statutes regulating insurance policies, bills of lading, retail installment sales, and small loans. Additionally, statutes frequently provide that certain contract provisions are unenforceable for public policy reasons. At the federal level, statutes such as the Truth-in-Lending Act protect consumers in credit transactions. The Magnuson-Moss Warranty Act regulates the form and content of written warranties covering consumer goods. Statutes such as these, when coupled with diligent court policing through the unconscionability doctrine, have provided significantly greater protection to persons signing standardized form contracts.

Covenants Not to Compete

Promises in Restraint of Trade. Both the common law and the antitrust laws have long limited enforcement of promises in **restraint of trade.** A promise is in restraint of trade if its performance would limit competition in any business or restrict the promisor in the exercise of any gainful occupation. A promise unreasonably in restraint of trade is unenforceable on grounds of public policy. For example, assume A is considering opening a store that would compete with B's business in the same locality. B promises to pay A $10,000 in exchange for A's promise not to open a competing business. Both promises are unenforceable. Similarly, an agreement between A and B to fix the prices at which they will sell, or to divide up the existing market, are unenforceable. Such promises, which are also violations of federal and state antitrust law, are commonly designated **naked restraints** of trade, because they have no purpose other than to suppress or eliminate competition.

Despite this general prohibition, some promises in which the promisor agrees to refrain from competition with the promisee are enforceable. To be enforceable, a promise to refrain from competition must be **ancillary** to an otherwise valid transaction or relationship. To be ancillary, as opposed to naked, a restraint must be imposed *as part of* the otherwise valid transaction. Even if a promise not to compete is ancillary to a valid transaction, it will be enforced only if

1. the restraint is reasonably necessary to protect a legitimate interest of the promisee, and
2. the promisee's interest is not outweighed either by (a) hardship to the promisor, or (b) likely injury to the public.[17]

The most common types of promises that are judged under this test include promises (1) by the seller of a business not to compete with his buyer, (2) by an employee not to compete with his employer after termination of employment, and (3) by a partner not to compete with his former partnership.

Covenants Ancillary to Sale of a Business. A promise by a seller not to compete with his buyer is quite common when an ongoing business is sold. Such promises are enforceable under the test stated above if they are reasonable in light of the buyer's need to protect the value of the goodwill that he has purchased. Assume Seller has contracted to sell her bakery to Buyer. The bakery has been in business for many years and has a reputation for excellence in the community. Therefore, a significant portion of the purchase price represents

---

[16]RESTATEMENT (SECOND) OF CONTRACTS §211 comment f.

[17]RESTATEMENT (SECOND) OF CONTRACTS §188(1).

goodwill.[18] On these facts, if Seller, after the sale, immediately opens a competing bakery in the same locality, the value of Buyer's goodwill is likely to be destroyed. Rather than receiving an established business of excellent reputation with the expectation of continuing profitability, the value of the purchase may now be limited to the leasehold or the building and equipment.

To prevent this result, contracts for sale of a business often include a promise by the seller that she will not compete with the buyer in a certain business activity for a stated time period in a given geographic area. Such promises are generally enforceable as ancillary to an otherwise legal transaction (the sale of a business) and necessary to protect a legitimate interest of the promisee-buyer (the value of the goodwill acquired). Effectively, the seller is promising not to act in a manner that will diminish the value of what she has sold. Note, however, that the restraint must be reasonable in light of the interest it protects, so as not to impose an undue hardship upon the promisor.

As noted above, the extent of the restraint is measured by the activity it prohibits, its geographic scope, and its time duration. All these elements must be reasonable before the promise will be enforced. What is reasonable depends upon all circumstances including the nature and size of the business sold. To illustrate, using the preceding example, if Seller's bakery operated only in Champaign, Illinois, a restriction which included the entire state probably would be unreasonable and therefore unenforceable. Had the bakery operated interstate, however, a limitation involving the entire United States might be reasonable.

Even if the covenant is overly broad, circumstances may justify enforcement of a more narrowly drawn term. In such cases, the court, applying equitable principles, may reduce the term's scope to that which is reasonable under the circumstances, and then enforce it. Assume Seller, ancillary to the sale of the bakery, agrees not to compete with Buyer within a radius of 50 miles. The promise is fairly bargained for. Seller's promise is unreasonable because the business extends only over a two-mile radius. Although part of Seller's promise is unreasonable (from two to 50 miles), it is enforceable to the extent of two miles. Or, on the same facts, assume that the contract provides that Seller will not compete in the "bakery or other business" in the same town for three years. The term is too broad

because Seller's business consisted only of a bakery. It is enforceable, however, to the extent it precludes competition in the bakery business.

Covenants Ancillary to Employment Relationships. Employment contracts and partnership agreements also sometimes use covenants not to compete. Under these covenants, the employee (or partner) agrees that upon termination of employment (or withdrawal from the partnership), he or she will not work for a competing employer or open a competing firm for a stated period of time, if ever. In many cases, the employer's reason for exacting such a promise is to prevent disclosure to a competing employer of trade secrets or confidential information acquired by the employee. Additionally, the employee may have acquired the means to lure customers away from the former employer. For example, the employee may have access to confidential customer lists, or gained the trust and confidence of existing customers, who are likely to follow the employee to a new business.

Courts generally are more reluctant to enforce such covenants in employment relationships than in sales of businesses for several reasons. First, they are frequently imposed by the employer who stands in a superior bargaining position, often on the employer's standardized form contract, and may bear no substantial relationship to any information or skill peculiar to the employer's business that the employee may acquire. Second, the employer's (promisee's) interest in enforcement may be outweighed by the potential hardship upon the employee (promisor) or likely injury to the public. For example, the restraint may effectively deny the employee the means of earning a living, restrict his upward economic mobility, or deprive the public of a person whose skills are in short supply. For these reasons, some states, by statute, provide that covenants not to compete contained in employment contracts are unenforceable. At issue in the following case was the enforceability of a covenant not to compete in an employment contract.

BDO Seidman v. Hirshberg
712 N.E.2d 1220 (N.Y. 1999)

Plaintiff BDO Seidman (BDO), a national accounting firm with 40 offices in the United States, employed defendant Jeffrey Hirshberg as an accountant in its Buffalo, New

---

[18]That is, the purchase price exceeds the value of the assets, such as land, equipment, fixtures, inventory, and leasehold.

York office. After working at BDO for five years, the defendant was promoted to manager. As a condition of the promotion, he signed an agreement promising that, if his employment with BDO terminated, he would compensate BDO if he provided services to any former client of BDO's Buffalo office. In October 1993, defendant resigned from BDO. In January 1995, BDO sued defendant seeking enforcement of the agreement based on BDO's allegations that he had provided services to 100 of BDO's former clients. Defendant asserted that some of the clients identified by BDO were personal clients that he had brought to the firm, and he had not serviced others while working at BDO. After finding that the agreement was overbroad and unenforceable, the trial court granted summary judgment to the defendant. The appellate court affirmed and further ruled that the entire agreement was unenforceable. The New York Court of Appeals granted BDO's request for review.

Levine, Judge

. . . [The agreement] defendant signed does not prevent him from competing for new clients, nor does it expressly bar him from serving BDO clients. Instead, it requires him to pay "for the loss and damages" sustained by BDO in losing any of its clients to defendant within 18 months after his departure, an amount equivalent to $1^1/_2$ times the last annual billing for any such client who became the client of defendant. Nonetheless, it is not seriously disputed that the agreement, in its purpose and effect, is a form of ancillary employee anti-competitive agreement that will be carefully scrutinized by the courts. . . .

The modern, prevailing common-law standard of reasonableness for employee agreements not to compete applies a three-pronged test. A restraint is reasonable only if it: (1) is no greater than is required for the protection of the legitimate interest of the employer, (2) does not impose undue hardship on the employee, and (3) is not injurious to the public. . . . [*Restatement (Second) of Contracts* §188.] A violation of any prong renders the covenant invalid. New York has adopted this prevailing standard of reasonableness in determining the validity of employee agreements not to compete. . . .

Close analysis of . . . the agreement under the first prong of the common-law rule, to identify the legitimate interest of BDO and determine whether the covenant is no more restrictive than is necessary to protect that interest, leads us to conclude that the covenant as written is overbroad in some respects. . . . Professor Blake, in his seminal article in the Harvard Law Review, explains that the legitimate purpose of an employer in connection with employee restraints is "to prevent competitive use, for a time, of information or relationships which pertain peculiarly to the employer and which the employee acquired in the course of the employment," [Blake, *Employee Agreements Not To Compete,* 73 Harv. L. Rev. 625, 647 (1960) (emphasis supplied).] Protection of customer relationships the employee acquired in the course of employment may indeed be a legitimate interest. . . . "The risk to the employer reaches a maximum in situations in which the employee must work closely with the client or customer over a long period of time, especially when his services are a significant part of the total transaction" (id., at 661). . . .

It follows from the foregoing that BDO's legitimate interest here is protection against defendant's competitive use of client relationships which BDO enabled him to acquire through his performance of accounting services for the firm's clientele during the course of his employment. . . . Extending the anti-competitive covenant to BDO's clients with whom a relationship with the defendant did not develop through assignments to perform direct, substantive accounting services would, therefore, violate the first prong of the common-law rule: it would constitute a restraint "greater than is needed to protect" these legitimate interests. . . .

To the extent, then, that . . . the agreement requires defendant to compensate BDO for lost patronage of clients with whom he never acquired a relationship through the direct provision of substantive accounting services during his employment, the covenant is invalid and unenforceable. By a parity of reasoning, it would be unreasonable to extend the covenant to personal clients of defendant who came to the firm solely to avail themselves of his services and only as a result of his own independent recruitment efforts, which BDO neither subsidized nor otherwise financially supported as part of a program of client development. Because the goodwill of those clients was not acquired through the expenditure of BDO's resources, the firm has no legitimate interest in preventing defendant from competing for their patronage. Indeed, enforcement of the restrictive covenant as to defendant's personal clients would permit BDO to appropriate goodwill created and maintained through defendant's efforts, essentially turning on its head the principal justification to uphold any employee agreement not to compete based on protection of customer or client relationships.

Except for the overbreadth in the foregoing two respects, the restrictions in [the agreement] do not violate the tripartite common-law test for reasonableness.

The restraint on serving BDO clients is limited to 18 months, and to clients of BDO's Buffalo office. The time constraint appears to represent a reasonably brief interlude to enable the firm to replace the client relationship and goodwill defendant was permitted to acquire with some of its clients. Defendant is free to compete immediately for new business in any market and, if the overbroad provisions of the covenant are struck, to retain his personal clients and those clients of BDO's that he had not served to any significant extent while employed at the firm. He has averred that BDO's list of lost accounts contains a number of clients in both categories. Thus, there is scant evidence suggesting that the covenant, if cured of overbreadth, would work an undue hardship on defendant.

Moreover, given the likely broad array of accounting services available in the greater Buffalo area, and the limited remaining class of BDO clientele affected by the covenant, it cannot be said that the restraint, as narrowed, would seriously impinge on the availability of accounting services in the Buffalo area from which the public may draw, or cause any significant dislocation in the market or create a monopoly in accounting services in that locale. . . .

We conclude that the Appellate Division erred in holding that the entire covenant must be invalidated, and in declining partially to enforce the covenant to the extent necessary to protect BDO's legitimate interest. . . . The issue of whether a court should cure the unreasonable aspect of an overbroad employee restrictive covenant through the means of partial enforcement or severance has been the subject of some debate among courts and commentators. . . . A legitimate consideration against the exercise of this power is the fear that employers will use their superior bargaining position to impose unreasonable anti-competitive restrictions, uninhibited by the risk that a court will void the entire agreement, leaving the employee free of any restraint. . . . The prevailing, modern view rejects a per se rule that invalidates entirely any overbroad employee agreement not to compete. Instead, when, as here, the unenforceable portion is not an essential part of the agreed exchange, a court should conduct a case specific analysis, focusing on the conduct of the employer in imposing the terms of the agreement. . . . Under this approach, if the employer demonstrates an absence of overreaching, coercive use of dominant bargaining power, or other anti-competitive misconduct, but has in good faith sought to protect a legitimate business interest, consistent with reasonable standards of fair dealing, partial enforcement may be justified. . . .

Here, the undisputed facts and circumstances militate in favor of partial enforcement. The covenant was not imposed as a condition of defendant's initial employment, or even his continued employment, but in connection with promotion to a position of responsibility and trust just one step below admittance to the partnership. There is no evidence of coercion or that the . . . agreement was part of some general plan to forestall competition. Moreover, no proof was submitted that BDO imposed the covenant in bad faith, knowing full well that it was overbroad. . . . Thus, we conclude that severance is appropriate, rendering the restrictive covenant partially enforceable. . . .

[Judgment reversed in part and remanded.]

Summary

1. A variety of factors may render an otherwise binding promise either unenforceable or voidable. One such factor is lack of contractual capacity. Certain persons possess special characteristics that limit, or in some cases extinguish, their contractual capacity. Examples include minors, persons suffering from a mental illness or defect, and intoxicated persons. Although lack of capacity may render a contract totally void, it more commonly renders the obligation merely voidable.

2. Minors, or infants, are persons who have not yet reached the age of contractual capacity, known as majority. A minor's contract is voidable by the minor prior to reaching legal age, usually 18 years, and for a reasonable time thereafter. After reaching majority, however, the minor may ratify, and thereby make binding, a contract made during minority. Though not liable in contract, a minor may be held liable in restitution for the reasonable value of "necessaries," such as food, clothing, and shelter furnished to him.

3. Upon disaffirmance, the minor must generally return any consideration he still retains. If the consideration has been squandered or destroyed, the minor may nevertheless avoid

the contract and recover the money or other consideration paid. In this case, however, a substantial minority of courts require the minor to account to the adult for the lost consideration. A similar duty to account is often imposed if the minor has misrepresented his age to the adult.

4.   Contractual capacity also may be extinguished or limited by mental illness or defect. Persons for whom a court has appointed a guardian have no contractual capacity. If no guardian has been appointed, a contract is nevertheless voidable if made by a person who, due to a mental infirmity, is unable to reasonably understand the nature and consequences of the transaction. Some states also permit avoidance by persons who understand what they are doing but are unable to rationally control their behavior. Similar competency standards are applied to persons incapacitated due to alcohol or other drug intoxication.

5.   Even if made by competent parties, a contract is rendered unenforceable if it violates an applicable criminal or civil statute, constitutes the commission of or inducement to commit a tort, or is otherwise contrary to public policy. Examples of contracts that have been held unenforceable because they violate a statute include gambling contracts, usurious contracts, contracts made in violation of a licensing requirement, contracts to commit crimes, and unconscionable contracts or terms.

6.   The unconscionability doctrine, embodied in §2–302 of the UCC, is used primarily to address problems created by standardized form contracts. Such "adhesion" contracts are drafted by one party usually with superior bargaining power and are given to the other on a "take it or leave it" basis. Because of the disparity in bargaining power, the contract may contain terms unreasonably favorable to the drafting party. To police against such terms, the unconscionability doctrine allows a court, as matter of law, to refuse to enforce or to limit the effect of any contract or term it finds to be unconscionable. Unconscionability is not explicitly defined but is characterized by an absence of meaningful choice by one party coupled with a contract or contract term that is unreasonably favorable to the other.

7.   Even in the absence of a governing statute, courts are often required to balance private against public interests to determine enforceability. Examples of promises which have been held unenforceable on this basis include contracts involving the commission of a tort, contracts made by a fiduciary in violation of duty, promises interfering with another's contractual relation, exculpatory clauses, and promises in restraint of trade.

8.   A promise is in restraint of trade if it limits competition in any business or restrains the promisor in the exercise of any gainful occupation. So-called naked restraints, those having no purpose other than to restrain competition, are always unenforceable and are also violations of federal and state antitrust law. A restraint imposed as part of, or "ancillary" to, an otherwise valid transaction, however, is enforceable if reasonably necessary to protect a legitimate business interest of the promisee. Common promises judged under this test include promises by the seller of a business not to compete with his buyer, by an employee not to compete with an employer after termination of employment, and by a partner not to compete with his former partnership.

Key Terms

contractual capacity	exculpatory clause
minor (infant)	adhesion contract
majority	unconscionability
emancipation	substantive unconscionability
ratification	procedural unconscionability
necessaries	duty to read
guardian	restraint of trade
ward	naked restraint
illegal bargain	ancillary restraint
usurious contract	

Questions and Problems

10.1   As noted in the text, the parties' freedom to contract is limited by public policy and contracts contrary to public policy are unenforceable.

(a) What is the "public policy" or the "public interest"? Is it capable of precise definition? Does the term "good faith" as discussed in Chapter 6 assist in defining the parameters of public policy?

(b) Why does contract law prevent enforcement of promises contrary to public policy? If such promises truly violate public policy, wouldn't other substantive legal areas, such as criminal or tort law, provide adequate protection?

10.2   As noted in the text, contracts by minors and others with limited contractual capacity are voidable. In modern society, do minors need protection against their own improvidence, inexperience, or lack of good judgment, allowing them to back out of a contract with an adult who is acting in good faith? Is such protection desirable, or as noted by one court, does it "lead to the corruption . . . of principles and encourage . . . habits of trickery and dishonesty"? Suggest ways that the avoidance power given minors and other incompetents actually harms, rather than benefits, them.

10.3

(a) Billy, a 17-year-old-minor, was married and the father of a child. Billy entered into a contract to purchase a station wagon for $1,000 from Okay Used Autos. Two weeks later, the automobile began to evidence mechanical problems. After Okay refused to repair the car, Billy wrote to Okay to notify it that he was disaffirming the contract and demanding return of his $1,000. Okay did not respond so Billy sued seeking recovery of $1,000. How should the court rule? Explain.

(b) Billy also needed a job to support himself and his dependents. Billy entered into an agreement with Gaston Employment Agency by which he agreed to pay a fee if Gaston found him a job. Gaston secured employment for Billy and he accepted the job. Billy then refused to pay the agency's fee. Should a court enforce Billy's agreement with Gaston?

(c) Susie, a 17-year-old minor, and Byte Computer School entered into a contract in which Susie agreed to pay $50 per month for three years for a correspondence course in computer programming offered by Byte. After receiving her first lesson in the mail, Susie notified Byte that she no longer was interested in the course. Nevertheless, she paid four monthly billing statements submitted by Byte; three of the payments were made after she reached the age of majority on her eighteenth birthday. Susie made no further payments and Byte sued her for breach of contract. Susie asserted that she had disaffirmed the contract but Byte argued that she had ratified the contract by making payments after her eighteenth birthday. Should the court enforce the contract? Explain.

10.4   In recent years, federal and state governments have discouraged institutionalization of people with mental disabilities. As a result, many people who suffer from mental illness, senility, or mental retardation now live outside institutions and need to purchase many of the items needed for everyday life.

(a) If a person technically lacks mental capacity but lives outside an institution, should that person be able to avoid contractual obligations?

(b) Assume that you are a salesperson who suspects that a potential customer lacks mental capacity. Are there any measures you can take to protect yourself from entering into a contract with someone who is incompetent? Are protective measures available if you suspect the customer is a minor?

10.5   Asdourian and Araj entered into a written contract by which Asdourian agreed to remodel a garage. After Asdourian had completed substantial work, Araj refused to pay. Asdourian sued, and Araj defended by asserting that a state statute prohibits a contractor from filing suit for compensation unless the contractor was duly licensed during the performance of the contract. At the time he performed the remodeling work, Asdourian did not hold a contractor's license in his own name, though he previously had obtained a contractor's license for his unincorporated contracting business. Because Asdourian had signed the contract in his own name, however, Araj argued that Asdourian should be barred from recovery. Is Araj correct? What factors should the court consider in determining whether Asdourian's failure to obtain a license should bar his recovery in this case? Explain.

10.6   Joe, a resident of Idaho, was unemployed and behind in paying his child support. Because he was concerned that the state might seize his house to pay for his child support obligations, Joe made a written agreement with his sister Evelyn in which he agreed to transfer ownership of his house to her and she agreed to transfer the house back to him in the future if he

paid her $1,000. Joe transferred his house to his sister and one year later sent her a check for $1,000 and asked her to transfer the house to him. After Evelyn returned the check and refused to transfer the house to Joe, he sued her for breach of contract. Under Idaho state law, it is illegal to transfer property to avoid paying child support. Evelyn argued that because the contract with Joe was illegal, the contract was void and the court should not enforce it. Joe argued that by allowing Evelyn to keep the house, she would benefit from the illegal contract. How should the court resolve this dispute?

10.7   The unconscionability doctrine gives the court broad discretion in refusing to enforce or limiting the application of unconscionable contracts or terms. According to Official Comment 1 to §2–302, this discretion is "intended to make it possible for the courts to *police explicitly* against the contracts or clauses which they find to be unconscionable." (Emphasis added.) What does the quoted language mean? How would such "policing" be done in the absence of an unconscionability doctrine?

10.8   It is generally stated that contracting parties have a "duty to read" contracts they sign. Is this a contractual "duty"? What is the effect of a failure to read? Explain the relationship between the unconscionability doctrine and the duty to read.

10.9   The Yellow Pages telephone directory is an effective advertising outlet used by many local businesses. In most cities, only one company publishes the Yellow Pages. Dr. Kathleen Schwarz, a psychologist, annually purchased a display advertisement in the Yellow Pages. One year, the Yellow Pages Co., publisher of the directory, inadvertently printed the wrong telephone number in the advertisement. Dr. Schwarz sued the Yellow Pages Co. for breach of contract alleging damages of $25,000. She is able to prove that in prior years over half of her new patients initially learned of her business through the Yellow Pages. Dr. Schwarz also can establish that her contract with Yellow Pages Co. is a form contract prepared by Yellow Pages. Yellow Pages denies liability based on the following provision in that contract: "The customer agrees that Yellow Pages Co. shall not be liable for errors and omissions of the directory beyond the amount paid for the directory advertising." Yellow Pages Co. offers to reimburse Dr. Schwarz for the cost of the advertisement.

(a) Is the contract with Yellow Pages Co. an adhesion contract?

(b) How should the court rule on Dr. Schwarz's case? Explain.

10.10   Duane was an experienced farmer who annually purchased seeds from Joseph Seed Co. Each year a Joseph Seed salesperson visited Duane and prepared his order on a form supplied by Joseph Seed. The form included a limitation of liability provision that stated in part:

> Joseph Seed Co. warrants that seeds it sells conform to the label description. If for any reason, the seeds fail to perform as expected, Joseph Seed Co. will refund the purchase price. IN ANY EVENT JOSEPH SEED CO.'s LIABILITY FOR BREACH OF ANY WARRANTY OR CONTRACT WITH

RESPECT TO SEEDS IT SELLS IS LIMITED TO THE PUR-
CHASE PRICE OF THE SEEDS.

In 2005, Duane purchased cabbage seeds from Joseph Seed
and planted them as usual. His cabbage crop failed when a
fungus infected the entire crop. The fungus was caused by
Joseph Seed's failure to treat the cabbage seed with a hot
water process that would have killed the fungus. Duane sues
Joseph Seed for damages equal to his lost profits, arguing that
the limitation of liability clause is unconscionable. Duane
alleges that he had not read the clause. How should the court
rule in light of the following facts?

(a) In past years, Joseph Seed always had used the hot
water process that would have killed the fungus. Duane
did not know how cabbage seed was processed and was
unaware that Joseph Seed had changed its procedures.

(b) During the visit with Duane, the Joseph Seed salesperson told Duane that Joseph Seed had decided not to use
the hot water process for treating the cabbage seed in
2005.

(c) During the visit with Duane, the Joseph Seed salesperson pointed out the limitation of liability clause and
asked Duane whether he had any questions about
Joseph Seed's policies. The salesperson did not discuss
the hot water process.

10.11 Harold operated an automobile repair and tow shop in
St. Paul, Minnesota. After accepting a job in another city,
Harold closed the shop and sold his tow trucks to Robert and
Bess Delmar who opened a business called St. Paul Towing
Co. The contract for the tow trucks included the following
provision:

> Covenant Not to Compete. Seller agrees not to engage in the
> business of towing or to commit any other act detrimental to the
> business operated by the Buyers.

Harold soon became dissatisfied with his job and returned to
St. Paul.

(a) Assume that Harold opened a towing business called
Harold Tow Services. The Delmars sue him for violation of the covenant not to compete. Should the court
enforce the agreement? Explain.

(b) Assume instead that Harold opened an automobile
repair shop called Harold's Auto Repair and that he
occasionally towed disabled vehicles to his shop for
repairs. The Delmars sue him for violation of the

covenant not to compete. How should the court rule?
Explain.

(c) Before signing the contract, the Delmars asked your
advice on improving the covenant not to compete. What
recommendations would you make? Explain.

10.12 Why are courts more hesitant to enforce covenants not
to compete in an employment contract than in a sale of a business? Is not the same legal test applied to determine enforceability in either case?

10.13 While serving in the military, Donovan was trained to
install glass on automobiles. Following his military discharge,
Donovan accepted a job as a glass installer at Glass Specialty
Co. in Kansas City, Missouri, and signed an employment contract that stated in part:

> I acknowledge that I will have access to confidential customer
> lists of Glass Specialty Co. and that Glass Specialty Co.'s auto
> glass installation business covers the entire state of Missouri and
> that I promise during the period of three years from and after
> termination of my employment, for any reason, with Glass
> Specialty Co. I will not associate myself with or engage in any
> business in competition with Glass Specialty Co. or in any other
> manner work for or assist any competitive automotive glass
> installation business in the state of Missouri.

One year later Donovan resigned from Glass Specialty Co.
and, because he had no other marketable skills, he took a job
as a glass installer at Custom Glass. Glass Specialty Co. sued
Donovan alleging that he violated the covenant not to compete
of his employment contract.

(a) Assume that Custom Glass is located in Kansas City.
Should the court enforce the covenant not to compete?

(b) At trial, Donovan proved that he had no access to confidential customer lists at Glass Specialty Co. While at
Glass Specialty Co. he had worked merely as an artisan,
installing glass as requested by his supervisor. Would
your answer to the preceding question change?

(c) Although Glass Specialty Co. agreed that Donovan had
no access to customer lists, Specialty proved that
Donovan had frequent contact with customers, including discussions of the optimal way to perform glass
repairs. Would your answers to questions (a) or (b)
change?

(d) Assume instead that Custom Glass is located in St.
Louis, Missouri, which is approximately 300 miles from
Kansas City. How should the court rule?

GENUINE ASSENT

The preceding chapter discussed contracts that are voidable or unenforceable due to either lack of contractual capacity or conflict with public policy. This chapter examines additional formation defects that can render contracts voidable: fraud and misrepresentation, mistake, and duress and undue influence. Contracts involving fraud and misrepresentation are voidable because one party misleads the other concerning a fact material to the transaction. In addition, fraud is a tort for which damages are recoverable. The law of mistake concerns contracts voidable by one or both parties because of mistakes of fact not caused by the other party to the

transaction. Finally, cases of duress and undue influence address problems of coercion and unfair persuasion in the bargaining process.

Fraud (Deceit) and Misrepresentation

A **misrepresentation** is an assertion that is not in accord with existing facts. That is, words or conduct asserting the existence of a fact constitute a misrepresentation if the fact does not exist. Assume Sam and Bob are negotiating for the sale of Sam's car. Sam tells Bob that the car's brakes have just been overhauled. In fact, the brakes have 75,000 miles on them. Sam has made a misrepresentation.

A misrepresentation is **fraudulent** if it is made with knowledge of its untrue character. The term **scienter** is frequently used by the courts when referring to the defendant's knowledge of falsity.

Scienter may be established in several ways. First, the statement may be made with actual knowledge of, or belief in, its falsity. Suppose S is negotiating with B for sale of S's house. In order to induce B to buy, S states, "The furnace is in perfect working order." In fact, as S is well aware, the furnace is in need of major repairs. The scienter requirement is met, because the statement is knowingly false.

Second, scienter may be inferred if the statement is made without belief in its truth or with reckless disregard of its truth or falsity. That is, a person may not actually know her assertion is false. She simply has no basis upon which to represent it as true. For example, if an auditor gives an unqualified opinion to financial statements that she has not audited, she may be liable for fraud to reliant third parties who are injured because the statements are materially misleading. The auditor may not know that the statements are incorrect. However, because she has not examined them, she knows that she has no basis upon which to assert that they fairly reflect the client's financial position. Thus, a misrepresentation may be fraudulent if the maker knows that she has neither knowledge nor belief in the existence of the matter she asserts as fact.

Not all misrepresentations are fraudulent. A person may, either negligently or innocently, make a false or inaccurate statement, believing it to be true. The legal consequences following such a nonfraudulent misrepresentation are not, as outlined below, as harsh as those imposed upon makers of fraudulent misrepresentations.

If a material misrepresentation made by one party to a contract induces the other to enter into a contract in justifiable reliance upon it, two legal consequences result. First, the contract is voidable by the reliant party on grounds of misrepresentation. Second, if the misrepresentation is fraudulent the party making the misrepresentation may be liable for damages for the tort of **fraud** (also known as "deceit" or "fraud in the inducement"). Thus, a misrepresentation has legal ramifications derived both from the law of contracts and from the law of torts.

Elements of Fraud

The party making the misrepresentation is liable for fraud if the plaintiff is able to prove the following elements:

1. the defendant made a fraudulent misrepresentation, with the intent to induce the plaintiff to act in reliance upon it;
2. the misrepresentation related to a material existing fact;
3. the plaintiff justifiably relied upon and acted upon the misrepresentation; and
4. the plaintiff suffered injury as a result of the reliance.[1]

---

[1]RESTATEMENT (SECOND) OF TORTS §525.

No defenses are available to the defendant in fraud cases. To avoid liability, the defendant must refute one or more elements of the plaintiff's claim. Each of these elements is discussed in more detail later in this chapter. The following case illustrates the elements of a fraud claim in the context of the sale of a used car.

Miller v. Triangle Volkswagen, Inc.
286 S.E.2d 608 (N.C. App. 1982)

After telephoning defendant Triangle Volkswagen, Inc. (Triangle) and discussing the purchase of a used car, plaintiff James Miller visited Triangle's used car lot to examine a 1971 Monte Carlo. Don Harmon, a salesman, told Miller that the Monte Carlo had low mileage and that Triangle had purchased it from another dealer, Phil's Auto Sales, which had purchased the car at an auction for $1,635. Nevertheless, Triangle offered to sell the car to Miller for $1,600. Plaintiff agreed to pay $1,600 for the car and $45 for a safety inspection and lubrication. Triangle delivered the car to Miller with an odometer statement indicating the car had been driven approximately 24,000 miles.

In fact, Phil's Auto Sales had paid only $850 for the car at a private sale. Phil's had sold the Monte Carlo to Triangle for $1,065, and the correct mileage was 124,000 miles. Additionally, Triangle had not performed the safety inspection or lubrication.

Miller sued, alleging common law fraud. The trial court granted summary judgment in favor of Triangle and Miller appealed.

Martin, Judge

. . . In order to prove that defendant was guilty of fraud the plaintiff at trial must prove: (1) that a defendant made a representation relating to some material fact; (2) that the representation was false; (3) that the defendant knew it was false or made it recklessly without any knowledge of its truth and as a positive assertion; (4) that the defendant made the representation with the intention that it should be acted upon by the plaintiff; (5) that the plaintiff reasonably relied upon the misrepresentation and acted upon it; and (6) that the plaintiff suffered injury. . . .

In this case plaintiff presented evidence on each element of fraud sufficient to withstand a motion for summary judgment. Plaintiff's evidence tended to show that the defendant through its agent, Harmon, made the material misrepresentations to the plaintiff that the car was a low mileage vehicle, with a wholesale value of $1635.00 and that Triangle had performed a safety inspection and minor repairs on the car worth $45.00. Harmon gave to plaintiff an odometer statement which verified the mileage as approximately 24,000 miles.

The plaintiff further presented evidence that these representations were false and that defendant knew they were false or made them recklessly. Phil McLamb [of Phil's Auto Sales], in his deposition, stated that he told Harmon that the car had travelled approximately 124,000 miles, not 24,000 miles. Plaintiff also presented evidence that the automobile was worth less than $1635.00, and that the safety inspection and minor repairs were not performed by defendant.

Plaintiff's evidence tended to show that defendant made these misrepresentations with the intention that they should be acted on by the plaintiff. The statements were made in a business context for the purpose of selling the car to plaintiff and the salesman Harmon took plaintiff's money on the basis of those representations.

The plaintiff purchased the automobile and drove it to Pennsylvania. This tends to show that plaintiff relied and acted upon defendant Harmon's representations.

Finally, the plaintiff's evidence indicates that he suffered injury. Defendant knew that plaintiff wanted a low mileage car. Plaintiff paid for a car that he believed had 24,000 miles, not 124,000 miles, and he paid for minor repairs and inspection of the car in the amount of $45. Plaintiff got less than he bargained for because of the misrepresentations about the car. . . .

[Judgment reversed.]

Fraud and Misrepresentation Distinguished

A plaintiff who is unable to prove fraud may nevertheless be able to avoid the contract on misrepresentation grounds. A contract is voidable on misrepresentation grounds if three elements are established:

1. the misrepresentation must be either fraudulent or material;
2. it must induce the recipient to enter into the contract; and
3. the recipient's reliance upon the misrepresented fact must be justified.[2]

---

[2]RESTATEMENT (SECOND) OF CONTRACTS §164.

If a contract procured through a fraudulent or material misrepresentation is avoided, the reliant party simply rescinds the contract, returns the subject matter, and obtains restitution of any benefit conferred upon the other party.

Note that the requirements for avoidance of the contract are less stringent than those applicable to fraud. Under tort law, fraud liability is not imposed unless the representation is both fraudulent and material, whereas contract law makes the contract voidable if the representation is either fraudulent or material. Thus, a contracting party who is unable to prove fraud may nevertheless avoid the contract if he can prove that he justifiably relied upon (1) a nonfraudulent misrepresentation of a material fact, or (2) a fraudulent misstatement not relating to a material fact. Assume S and B are negotiating for the sale of a machine to be used in B's manufacturing process. To induce B to buy, S states his good faith belief that the machine is capable of producing 100 units per hour. In fact, the machine produces only 50 units per hour. B buys the machine in reliance upon S's misrepresentation. Although B may not recover from S for fraud (because the misrepresentation is not fraudulent), he may nevertheless avoid the contract.

The following material examines the various elements of fraud and misrepresentation in more detail, including the manner in which misrepresentations may be made, the various types of misrepresentations having legal consequences, when reliance upon a misrepresentation is justified, and the remedies available to a party injured by fraud or misrepresentation.[3]

Manner in Which Misrepresentation May Be Made

A misrepresentation may be made expressly, by conduct, or in some cases, by silence (nondisclosure).

Express Misrepresentation. Because a misrepresentation is a false assertion of fact, it is commonly made expressly; that is, through use of spoken or written words. For example, to induce B to buy his automobile, S states, "This car has never been involved in an accident." In fact, S knows that the car has been involved in a major accident and handles poorly as a result. S has made an express misrepresentation.

---

[3]Chapter 56 (Accountants' Liability) is based in part upon the law of fraud and negligent misrepresentation. The following material, therefore, provides the framework for understanding accountants' legal liability to third parties at common law.

Misrepresentation by Conduct (Concealment). Frequently, conduct other than express statements constitutes a misrepresentation. That is, action by one person that is intended or likely to prevent the other from learning of a fact is equivalent to an assertion that the fact does not exist. In this situation, misrepresentation is made by **concealment.** Assume S, an auto dealer, in order to induce B to buy a used car, turns back the odometer from 75,000 to 35,000 miles. S's conduct is a misrepresentation. Or, assume S, to induce B to purchase her house, hides the fact that her basement floods after rainstorms by painting over a section of the basement wall to conceal water marks caused by the flooding. This concealment is equivalent to an assertion that the basement does not flood, a misrepresentation. Note that if B, while inspecting the basement asks S, "Does the basement flood after a rainstorm?" and S answers, "No," S makes an express misrepresentation.

In addition to active concealment situations discussed above, a party may make a misrepresentation by successfully preventing or frustrating the other's investigation that would lead to disclosure of the fact. For example, one party may send the other searching for information on a "wild goose chase" to a person or place where he knows it cannot be found. Similarly, a misrepresentation is made if one party falsely denies that he has the knowledge or information requested, and the other is thereby led to believe that the facts do not exist or cannot be discovered.

Misrepresentation by Silence (Nondisclosure). Generally, a party to an arm's length business transaction is not liable for fraud simply for failing to disclose facts to the other—even facts that she knows the other would regard as material. Mere nondisclosure should be distinguished from concealment. Concealment obviously involves an element of nondisclosure, but it also involves action by one party that prevents the other from learning the fact and it is this action that constitutes the misrepresentation. On the other hand, a mere failure to speak (silence or nondisclosure) amounts to a fraudulent misrepresentation only in certain limited situations, discussed below, in which the law has imposed a duty to disclose the matter in question.

1. A person may make a statement that, when made, was true or believed to be true. Later, however, the maker may learn that the assertion was originally false or that subsequent events have rendered it false. In this situation, a person who remains silent, with knowledge that the person to whom the statement was made is

relying upon it, is in the same position as if the statement had been knowingly false when made. For example, Smith and Brown are negotiating for the sale of a machine to be used in Brown's manufacturing operation. To induce Brown to buy, Smith states her good faith belief that the machine is capable of producing 100 units per hour. Smith subsequently discovers that the machine will produce only 50 units per hour. In this case, Smith is under a duty to correct her prior misrepresentation. Her failure to do so, with knowledge that Brown is relying upon her original assertion, constitutes a fraudulent misrepresentation that the machine is capable of producing 100 units per hour.

2. If the parties stand in a fiduciary or other relation of trust and confidence, the law imposes a duty to disclose all relevant facts. Thus, when a fiduciary duty is imposed, silence may constitute a fraudulent misrepresentation. Some of the relationships in which a person has the right to expect disclosure on this basis include those existing between (1) a trustee and the beneficiaries of a trust, (2) an agent and principal, (3) partners, (4) a director and the corporation and its shareholders, (5) a creditor and a surety, (6) an attorney and client, (7) a physician and patient, (8) a priest and parishioner, (9) a guardian and ward, (10) tenants in common, and (11) family members.

3. A growing number of courts, following §551 of the Restatement (Second) of Torts, impose a duty to disclose under certain circumstances if one party to an agreement knows that the other is mistaken with respect to facts that are basic to the transaction. A "basic" fact goes to the substance or essence of what is bargained for. Assume that S, in order to induce B to purchase her house, fails to disclose that the house is infested with termites, a fact unknown to B. The fact withheld is basic to the transaction.

Generally, superior knowledge, skill, and experience are legitimate business advantages. A party to contract negotiations generally is not required to compensate for the other's deficiencies in investigation, experience, or judgment. For example, a buyer of property ordinarily is not expected to disclose facts to the seller that indicate that the property is more valuable than the seller believes. The *Restatement* rule, however, somewhat limits a party's ability to take advantage of the other's ignorance. It requires a party to disclose "facts basic to the transaction" if he or she knows that the other party (1) is about to enter into the transaction while mistaken concerning those facts, and (2) would reasonably expect disclosure of basic facts that would substantially and adversely affect the value of the exchange. The expectation of disclosure may arise out of the relationship between the parties, customs or standards of fair dealing in the trade, or other objective circumstances. Assume Sara is negotiating with Betty for sale of Sara's house. The house is constructed over a landfill and, as a result, the foundation and other walls periodically crack. All existing cracks have been repaired, but the condition is certain to recur. In order to induce Betty to buy, Sara fails to disclose the problem. Sara knows that Betty is unaware of this fact, that it could not be discovered by inspection, and that Betty would not buy if she knew it. Sara also knows that Betty regards her as an honest person who would disclose such a fundamental problem. Sara's nondisclosure here constitutes a fraudulent misrepresentation.

Material Existing Fact

To be actionable on the basis of fraud or misrepresentation, the misrepresentation must relate to a material existing fact. A misrepresentation is **material** if either a reasonable person would attach importance to the existence or nonexistence of the fact represented, or the person making the misrepresentation knows or should know that the other party is likely to regard the fact as important, even though it would not be important to a reasonable person.[4] In other words, both an objective and subjective test of materiality are used. Even if the matter misrepresented would not influence a reasonable person (an objective test), it is material if the maker knows that it would influence the person to whom it is made (a subjective test).

Facts include not only the existence or characteristics of a tangible thing or the occurrence of a given event or the relationship between particular persons or things, but also a state of mind, such as a statement of intention or opinion. The following material examines the various types of factual misrepresentations recognized by the courts.

Misrepresentation of Intention. Existing facts include past events as well as present circumstances, but generally do not include future events. Assume Sam contracts to sell a thoroughbred to Bill. During the negotiations, Sam asserts, "This horse will win the Kentucky Derby." Sam generally has no liability to Bill if the horse subsequently finishes last in the race. A statement relating to the future, however, may imply a representation concerning an existing fact. The most common application of this principle concerns a person's statement of intention.

A person's assertion that he does or does not intend to do a particular thing indicates his state of mind at the time the statement is made. In the words of one court, the state of a person's mind is as much a fact as the state of his or her digestion. Thus, even though a statement of intention relates to a future event, a false representation of intent may form the basis of a fraud action, if, at the time the statement is made, the maker does not have that intention.

This rule is commonly applicable to misrepresentations of intention to perform an agreement. Normally, a person who fails to perform a contractual promise is liable for breach of contract, not fraud. For example, assume Steve agrees to sell and deliver a vacuum cleaner to Bill in 30 days in exchange for Bill's $100 cash payment. If Steve later fails to deliver because of a shortage of supply or because the agreement has become unprofitable, Steve is liable for breach of contract to Bill.

A promisor, however, by making a promise, impliedly represents to the promisee an intent to perform it. Therefore, a promise made without such intent is fraudulent. This result follows even if the promise is not legally binding as a contract—for example, if the promise is not supported by consideration. If the promise is contractually binding, however, the promisee has an action both in tort (fraud) and contract. To illustrate, using the preceding example, assume that Steve, with the intent to induce Bill to pay him $100, promises to deliver the vacuum cleaner to Bill in 30 days. Steve, when making the promise, has no intent to perform it. In fact, immediately after making the promise, Steve leaves town with the money. Steve is liable for fraud as well as breach of contract to Bill.

Misrepresentation of Opinion. Like a statement of intention, a person's opinion is a fact. It represents a particular state of mind concerning the matter to which the opinion relates. Statements of opinion may take two forms. First, a person may express a *belief,* without professing actual knowledge, concerning the existence or nonexistence of a fact. Second, the person may express a *judgment* about quality, value, authenticity, or other similar matters. Thus, in an opinion, a person, rather than making a positive assertion ("this is true"), states only a belief or judgment regarding its truth ("I think this is true but I am not sure").[5]

It is sometimes stated, erroneously, that relief on the basis of fraud is granted for misrepresentations of fact, not

---

[4]Restatement (Second) of Torts §538.

[5]Restatement (Second) of Torts §538A and comment b.

false statements of opinion. This blanket statement apparently is derived from the general rule that when both parties possess approximately equal competence and information with respect to the subject matter, each must trust his own judgment and, generally, neither is justified in relying upon the opinion of the other. Thus, if an ordinary commodity is sold, the purchaser is generally not entitled to rely upon the seller's opinion of its quality or worth.

The rationale for this result is the common knowledge that a seller will express a glowing opinion of whatever he has to sell. When the seller praises wares in general terms without specific representations or reference to facts, a reasonable person realizes that he or she is not entitled to rely literally on the seller's statement. This seller's hype or buildup is commonly known as "puffing" or "seller's talk." Thus, no action for fraud lies against the used car dealer who knowingly describes a defective car as a "honey," a "dandy," "the pride of the line," "a best buy," "a good little car," or the like. A court may also find that such statements are not "material" and deny recovery on that basis. Note, however, that the more specific the seller's talk becomes, the more likely a court may be to interpret the statement as a fact (that is, knowledge as opposed to opinion) supporting a fraud action. Therefore, a statement that the car is "mechanically perfect" or "in A–1 condition" may result in liability if the car is not as represented.[6]

Outside the puffing case, misrepresentations of opinion can support fraud actions. A person's opinion is a fact—her state of mind. In puffing situations recovery is denied not because the opinion is true, but because the law does not protect those who *rely* upon it. Reliance is often justified upon opinions rendered under the circumstances outlined in the following paragraphs.

In the preceding discussion, the parties are assumed to be on an equal footing concerning the information and knowledge forming the basis of the opinion. A party may, however, assert an opinion concerning facts that are not disclosed or otherwise known to the other. Such an opinion, in certain circumstances, includes an implied representation that the maker knows facts that are sufficient to justify the opinion, or at least that he knows no facts inconsistent with it. In other words, when the parties do not possess equal information, the statement of opinion may include an implied representation of facts sufficient to support the opinion or belief.

This implied representation is particularly strong when the person rendering the opinion possesses special skill, knowledge, or judgment concerning the subject matter not possessed by the other. Thus, a misstatement of opinion by an expert may be grounds for a fraud action if the facts known to the expert do not justify the opinion. For example, Andrew, who knows nothing about jewelry, employs Joanne, a jeweler, to appraise an antique diamond ring that Andrew is considering purchasing. Joanne states that, in her opinion, the ring is worth $1,000. In this case, Joanne is expressing more than her personal belief. In giving her opinion regarding the value of the ring, she is also giving a summary of information she has concerning the qualities and characteristics of diamonds affecting their value, as compared to the qualities of this particular ring. Thus, the statement of the jeweler is both an expression of her opinion and a conclusion of fact. The conclusion is that she has the kind of information that would justify a reasonable expert in believing that the ring is worth $1,000. If she does not possess this information, either because she has not examined the ring or has intentionally understated or overstated its value, her false opinion may subject her to liability for fraud. Therefore, when an opinion is rendered by an expert necessarily requiring a conclusion of fact supporting the opinion, the party without the special skill or expertise is entitled to rely upon the honesty of the expert's opinion and attach to it the importance warranted by the other's superior competence. Note that liability is imposed here on the basis of the *difference* in the information possessed by the respective parties.

Misrepresentations of Law. Early courts stated, as a general rule of law, that in cases involving fraud, everyone is presumed to know the law, and, therefore, cannot be deceived by a misrepresentation of it. Under this approach, no fraud liability can result from a misrepresentation of law. The rule is apparently an extension of the principle that ignorance of the law is not a defense in a *criminal* prosecution. As the following discussion indicates, the modern approach is to treat misrepresentations of law in the same manner as any other misrepresentation.

A misrepresentation of law may be either a statement of fact or a statement of opinion. Therefore, a statement that a statute has been enacted or repealed or that a court has rendered a particular decision in a given fact situation is an assertion of fact. On the other hand, a statement of a person's judgment concerning the legal

---

[6] Under UCC §2–313(1)(a), any *affirmation of fact* or promise that relates to the goods and becomes part of the basis of the bargain creates an *express warranty* that the goods will conform to the affirmation or promise. Thus, even if the seller's false statements of fact do not result in fraud liability (for example, they were not made with knowledge of falsity), the seller may be liable to the buyer for breach of express warranty. Warranties are covered in Chapter 19.

effect of a particular set of facts is a statement of opinion and is governed by the same principles applicable to other misrepresentations of opinion. Thus, as between two bargaining adversaries with equal knowledge of the facts, there can be ordinarily no justifiable reliance by one party on the other's opinion as to the legal effect of those facts. If, however, all facts are not known to both parties, a statement of opinion may carry with it the implication that the maker knows facts that justify his opinion or is unaware of facts incompatible with it. Assume a seller of real property states to a prospective buyer, "I have good title to the property." The seller's statement here is a conclusion of law. However, the buyer may be justified in interpreting the statement as the seller's assertion that she knows facts supporting her opinion (for example, she is in possession of a deed to the property and has title insurance or an attorney's opinion indicating she has good title) and that she has no information that would cause a reasonable person not to entertain the opinion expressed (for example, if the seller knows she is only a tenant under a long-term lease).

The same reasoning applies to statements of legal opinion rendered by lawyers or others who have a superior legal training, information, or expertise. Thus, a layman who requests a lawyer's opinion on a point of law is entitled to an honest opinion. He may reasonably assume the lawyer's professional honesty. The party rendering the opinion need not, however, be a lawyer. A layman dealing with an insurance agent or real estate broker is entitled to rely upon opinions of law relating to common problems related to those fields. Once again, it is the difference in the information, expertise, or skill possessed by the respective parties that makes reliance upon certain statements of opinion justified. In these cases, the opinion represents a shorthand description of the information possessed by one party over and above that possessed by the other.

Justifiable Reliance

In order to recover for loss resulting from a fraudulent misrepresentation, the party to whom it is made must rely upon the misrepresentation in acting or forbearing to act, and that reliance must be justified. Reliance upon a fraudulent misrepresentation is not justified unless the misrepresentation relates to a material matter.[7]

The recipient of the fraudulent misrepresentation must *in fact* rely upon it in order to recover. It is not nec-

essary, however, that reliance upon the truth of the assertion be the sole or decisive factor in influencing the decision. The misrepresentation need only play a substantial part. Assume S, in order to induce B to buy his house, makes three representations concerning the property. Two are true, but the third is false and fraudulent. B buys the property, relying in substantial part upon the truth of all three statements. S is subject to liability for fraud to B.

Because reliance upon the misrepresentation is required, no fraud liability results if the recipient relies upon her own independent investigation concerning the matter to which the false assertion relates. Generally, a person who makes an investigation is deemed to rely upon it as to facts that it disclosed, and as to obvious facts uncovered during its course. The fraudulent party escapes liability, however, only if the other party relies solely upon the investigation and not upon the misrepresentation. That is, if reliance is partly upon the investigation and partly upon the false assertion, liability results.

The defrauded party need not only rely upon the misrepresentation, the reliance also must be justified. A person is, therefore, not justified in relying upon a statement she knows to be false or whose falsity is obvious to anyone upon a cursory examination or inspection. Additionally, early courts imposed a duty to independently investigate the truth of statements made by the other party. This view has, however, given way to the modern approach that the recipient of a fraudulent misrepresentation is justified in relying upon its truth, without undertaking an investigation, even though an investigation might have uncovered its falsity. This is true even if an investigation would be reasonable in the circumstances, could be made without unreasonable expense, trouble, or delay, and even if the fact misrepresented is a matter of public record. For example, assume Susan fraudulently asserts to Dave that her land is free of all encumbrances. In fact, the land is subject to an unsatisfied mortgage, which is recorded. Dave could easily ascertain this fact by walking across the street and checking with the county recorder of deeds office. Dave, however, fails to do so and buys the land in reliance upon Susan's misrepresentation. Dave's reliance is justified. Thus, the law generally imposes no duty to investigate the truth of statements made by the other party.

The rationale for this rule is that, if a duty to investigate is imposed, the wrongdoer escapes liability for fraud as a result of the other's gullibility, credulity, or negligence. Thus, the persons with the greatest need for

---

[7]As previously discussed, however, a fraudulent assertion concerning even an immaterial matter is grounds for avoidance of the contract.

protection from fraud are denied recovery. The Vermont Supreme Court, in ruling upon this issue, stated:

> The defendant insists that the false representations must have been such as to deceive a man of ordinary care and prudence; i.e., if a man is not endowed with those faculties he is at the mercy of every swindler who makes him his prey, excluding from the benefits of the law the very class around whom its arm should be thrown, thus protecting the strong and robbing the weak. As well adopt Rob Roy's rule: "That they should take who have the power, and they should keep who can." No rogue should enjoy his ill-gotten plunder for the simple reason that his victim is by chance a fool.[8]

As the preceding quotation forcefully indicates, whether or not a person's reliance is justified is not judged by comparing his conduct to that of a "reasonable person" in the circumstances—an objective test. It is determined in a subjective manner, taking into account any peculiar characteristics of the plaintiff as well as the particular facts of the case. The following case illustrates the principles concerning misrepresentation of law and reliance in fraud cases.

Cao v. Nguyen
607 N.W.2d 528 (Neb. 2000)

Defendants Huan Nguyen and Nega Pham (sellers) sold a building located at 2223 R Street in Lincoln, Nebraska to plaintiffs Lee and Louann Cao (buyers). The buyers, responding to the sellers' advertisement for the sale of a duplex, inspected the property several times. They told the sellers that they planned to operate the building as a two-family rental property. The parties signed an agreement describing the property as a duplex. After purchasing the building, the buyers applied for a building permit to make repairs. City officials informed them that the property could not be used as a duplex because the lot was not wide enough to meet municipal code requirements for a two-family dwelling. The buyers sought rescission of the contract alleging that the sellers had committed fraud. The trial court dismissed the suit and the buyers appealed.

Wright, Justice

. . . In order to maintain an action for fraudulent misrepresentation, a plaintiff must allege and prove the fol-

---

[8]Chamberlin v. Fuller, 9 A. 832, 836 (Vt. 1887).

lowing elements: (1) that a representation was made; (2) that the representation was false; (3) that when made, the representation was known to be false or made recklessly without knowledge of its truth and as a positive assertion; (4) that it was made with the intention that the plaintiff should rely upon it; (5) that the plaintiff reasonably did so rely; and (6) that the plaintiff suffered damage as a result. . . .

In dismissing the buyers' petition, the district court concluded that the sellers' representations that the home was a duplex were representations of law and not representations of fact. The court also concluded that the buyers' reliance upon such representations was not reasonable. The court found that the buyers should have questioned the sellers' assurances that the property could be rented as a duplex because only one unit was actually rented; the purchase price was about half the expected price, given the predicted rentals; and one of the units was in need of repair. The court concluded that ordinary prudence under these circumstances would have required the buyers to contact the city building and safety department. We disagree with both of these conclusions. . . .

Here, the district court incorrectly characterized the misrepresentations as misrepresentations of law. The buyers informed the sellers that they intended to use the house as rental property, and upon inspection, the buyers saw that the property consisted of two separate apartments and had two front doors, two mailboxes, and two gas meters. The buyers were told by the sellers that the house was divided into two units, and the sellers admitted that the house had been rented to two separate families in the past. The statement that the home could be rented to two families is a representation of fact, and not a representation of law. . . .

The district court's findings suggest it concluded that the buyers' reliance on the representation was unreasonable, since a search of public records would have revealed the falsity of the representations. Standing alone, this fact is insufficient to constitute unreasonable reliance. In *Foxley Cattle Co. v. Bank of Mead,* [241 N.W.2d 495 (Neb. 1976)], we stated that generally, fraud may be predicated on false representations although the truth could have been ascertained by an examination of public records.

We also conclude that the buyers' reliance was not unreasonable. . . . [I]n the zoning district where the property is located, a lot containing a two-family dwelling must be 50 feet wide. The lot at 2223 R Street is 40 feet wide, and therefore, the property does not comply with the minimum width requirement for a two-family dwelling. . . .

[H]ere, the means of discovering the truth were not in the buyers' hands. The buyers were not provided with any information which would have placed them on notice that the home did not meet the municipal code requirement for a two-family dwelling. The sellers informed the buyers that the house had been rented to two families in the past. The physical layout of the property suggested that it was divided into two units. The buyers were told by the sellers that the property had been divided into two units, the advertisement for the property described it as a duplex, and the initial contract signed by the parties described the property as a duplex. Although one unit was not rented at the time of inspection, there was no indication that it could not be rented in the future.

In order to prove the sellers' representations were false, the buyers would have had to contact the city, research the public records, and compare the building code to the actual structure of the home. Therefore, the buyers' reliance was reasonable.

We conclude . . . that the sellers made representations that the property could be used as a two-family dwelling, that such representations were false, and that when such representations were made, they were known to be false or were made recklessly without knowledge of the truth and as positive assertions. We also find that the sellers intended for the buyers to rely upon such representations, the buyers did in fact so rely upon the representations, and the buyers were damaged as a result. Thus, the buyers have proved each of the elements of fraudulent misrepresentations . . .

[Judgment reversed and remanded.]

Remedies for Fraud and Misrepresentation

To recover in deceit, the defrauded party must both rely upon the misrepresentation and suffer loss as a result of the reliance. That is, a fraud plaintiff may only recover for monetary injury that could reasonably be expected to result from reliance upon the misrepresentation. Assume S misrepresents the financial position of ABC Co. in order to induce B to buy his shares of stock. B buys in reliance upon the misrepresentation. Subsequently, the value of the stock deteriorates when ABC's production facilities are destroyed by fire. S is not liable for fraud to B. Although the misrepresentation caused the loss (that is, without it B would not have purchased the stock), the loss did not result from the

misrepresented financial condition, but from a subsequent event unrelated to the misrepresentation. Of course, had the stock value declined as a result of ABC's impending bankruptcy, S would be liable.

In computing the amount of damages available to the injured party for fraud, most courts utilize a "benefit of the bargain test" similar to that applied in determining damages for breach of contract generally. Under this approach, the court awards the injured plaintiff the difference between the value of what the plaintiff actually received and the value of what the plaintiff would have received had the property, services, or other performance been as represented. In other words, the plaintiff recovers as if the false statements had, in fact, been true. The benefit of the bargain rule has been adopted by the great majority of courts as the measure of damages in fraud actions. It is also used to determine damages in fraud and misrepresentation cases arising out of contracts for the sale of goods under Article 2 of the UCC.[9]

Although commonly arising in the contract context, fraud is an intentional tort. As such, courts frequently award *punitive* damages to the plaintiff in fraud actions in addition to compensatory damages.

A person who merely elects to *avoid* the contract, as opposed to seeking recovery in tort for fraud, need not prove actual harm from reliance upon the misrepresentation. Rescission of the contract does not, however, bar recovery of any other damages sustained, including losses suffered as a consequence of using or preparing the subject matter of the contract prior to discovering the misrepresentation.[10]

Mistake

A **mistake** is simply a belief that is inconsistent with existing facts. Liability for fraud and misrepresentation results when one party acts or refrains from acting while under a mistake of fact *caused* by the other's misrepresentation. Occasionally, one or both parties to a

---

[9]UCC §2–721 provides that remedies for fraud and material misrepresentation include all remedies for nonfraudulent breach. Under §2–313(1)(a), a seller's misrepresentation of fact concerning his wares constitutes breach of an express warranty. Under §2–714(2), the basic measure of damages for breach of warranty is the difference between ". . . the value of the goods accepted and *the value they would have had if they had been as warranted* . . ." (Emphasis added.) Warranties and remedies for breach of warranty are discussed in more detail in Chapter 19.

[10]Remedies including punitive damages are discussed in detail in Chapter 15.

contract will be mistaken about relevant facts but for reasons not dependent upon the assertions of either party. This type of mistake is the subject of the following discussion.

As in misrepresentation, the basic remedy available in mistake cases is avoidance of the contract.[11] The availability of this remedy is closely limited by certain basic premises of contract law. Ordinarily, a contracting party bears the risk that existing facts are not as he believes them to be and also that events subsequent to contract formation will make performance more expensive or burdensome. That is, freedom of contract includes the freedom to make bad bargains as well as good ones. For example, courts ordinarily do not provide relief for mistaken belief concerning the value of the subject matter. To illustrate, assume Smith contracts to sell land to Bernard at a price based upon Smith's mistaken assumption that the property is suitable only for farming. Subsequently, valuable mineral deposits are discovered on the land. Smith may not avoid the contract.

Similarly, courts generally do not grant relief for mistakes relating to the difficulty or expense of performance. Assume Alice contracts to dig a foundation for Walter's house at an agreed price, based upon Alice's mistaken assumption that the ground contains only ordinary clay and small rocks. However, during excavation, Alice discovers solid rock which substantially increases her costs, causing her to lose money on the bargain. Alice may not avoid the contract. The same result follows if Alice had underestimated the labor costs on the job or if heavy rains had made performance more expensive. To allow a party to avoid his obligation on grounds of mistake in these situations would substantially impair a basic purpose of contract law: to make promises legally enforceable. In other words, a person should not be able to avoid a contract simply because it was entered into on the mistaken belief that it was a good bargain. The certainty, stability, and predictability that contractual promises provide would no longer be present. It is therefore reasonable to allocate the risk of such mistakes to the adversely affected party (Smith or Alice in the preceding examples). Additionally, the contract may expressly allocate the risk to one party, or may do so by implication, as

when one party undertakes to perform, knowing he has only limited knowledge concerning facts to which the mistake relates.

Unilateral Mistake

In some situations, like those discussed above, one but not both parties are mistaken regarding a basic assumption upon which the contract is made. Generally, in such a **unilateral mistake,** courts do not provide relief to the mistaken party unless the nonmistaken party knows or has reason to know of (or was at fault in causing) the mistake. Suppose Seller and Buyer enter into a contract for sale of a machine to be used in Buyer's manufacturing process. Buyer assumes that the machine will produce 100 units per hour. In fact, the machine is capable of producing only 50 units per hour. Seller is unaware of Buyer's mistaken assumption and has made no warranties concerning the machine. Buyer may not avoid the contract. If, however, Seller knows of Buyer's mistaken belief and says nothing, Buyer may avoid the contract, not on the basis of mistake, but on the basis of fraud. The rationale for the courts' hesitancy to allow rescission on grounds of unilateral mistake is that because mistake is the exception rather than the rule, evidence of the mistake must be fairly convincing, particularly because avoidance on this ground substantially alters the reasonable expectations of the nonmistaken party. Courts have, however, shown a growing willingness to allow rescission when the consequences of the mistake are so onerous that enforcement of the contract would be unconscionable.

The most common type of unilateral mistake involves clerical errors or omissions in the computation of bids for construction contracts. Assume Forbes solicits bids for construction of a building pursuant to stated specifications. Turner submits a bid of $150,000. However, Turner has (a) added incorrectly, (b) omitted an item from the total, or (c) misunderstood Forbes's specifications. The bid should be $200,000. If Forbes has reason to know of the mistake (for example, all other bids range between $215,000 and $275,000), he cannot accept Turner's offer. If, however, Forbes has no reason to know of the mistake and accepts, Turner may not avoid the contract *unless* the court finds that enforcement of the contract would be unconscionable. This issue will be decided in the discretion of the court based upon the extent of the loss to be incurred by Turner. If, because of the mistake, Turner will incur a $20,000 loss instead of making a $30,000 profit, the

---

[11]If the mistake occurs in reducing the parties' oral agreement to a writing, appropriate relief is afforded by reformation. Reformation is an equitable remedy in which the court essentially rewrites the contract to conform to the parties' actual agreement. If the mistake can be corrected by reformation, avoidance of the contract is unavailable. Reformation is discussed in Chapter 15.

court may grant rescission. But if Forbes will make $10,000 instead of $60,000 on the contract as a result of the mistake, the court may refuse to allow rescission.

Mutual Mistake

When both parties, at the time of the contract, are mistaken concerning a basic assumption upon which the contract is made, the contract is voidable by the adversely affected party if (1) the mistake has a material effect on the agreed exchange of performance, and (2) the risk of the mistake has not been allocated to her.[12] Such **mutual mistakes** occur in many different contexts. The parties may be mistaken regarding the existence, identity, quantity, or other qualities or characteristics of the subject matter. They may also be mistaken concerning the law applicable to the transaction. In all cases, the contract is voidable, if the foregoing test is met.

To illustrate, assume Sharp and Bailey enter into a contract for sale of Sharp's 1955 Chevrolet. Both parties believe that the car is still in existence, but in fact it has been destroyed by fire. The contract is voidable by Bailey. The parties here are mistaken concerning the *existence* of the subject matter.

The parties may also be mistaken as to the *identity* or *quantity* of the subject matter. Suppose S and B enter into a contract for sale of S's farm for $1,500,000. Both parties believe that the tract contains 500 acres, based upon a survey by X. X's survey is inaccurate; the farm contains only 400 acres. B may avoid the contract. If the farm actually contains 600 acres, S may avoid the contract.

Mistakes also may arise concerning the qualities or characteristics of the subject matter. In the well-known case of *Sherwood v. Walker,*[13] the seller contracted to sell a cow that both parties believed to be sterile. Because the cow was of a breed ordinarily used as breeding stock, the agreed price of the cow was substantially lower than could otherwise be commanded. Before delivery, the cow was discovered to be fertile and the seller sought to avoid the contract. The court allowed rescission on the basis that a barren cow is substantially different from a fertile one and thus the mistake went to the very nature of the thing sold. Because the facts were substantially

different from those upon which the parties based their bargain, rescission was allowed.

A mistake of law providing a basis for rescission may be illustrated by the following example. Assume Tate leases commercial property from Levy for use as a fertilizer plant. As both parties know, such a use requires an unrestricted zoning classification. Both parties acting in good faith mistakenly believe that the land is located in an unrestricted zone. In fact, the land is zoned for light industrial use only, and is totally unsuitable for Tate's purposes, even with substantial additional investment. The contract is voidable by Tate. The following case explains the circumstances under which the law allocates the risk of a mutual mistake to one of the parties.

Estate of Nelson v. Rice
12 P.3d 238 (Ariz. App. 2000)

When Martha Nelson died in 1996, Edward Franz and Kenneth Newman were appointed to act as representatives of Nelson's estate ("the Estate"). To prepare for an estate sale, the representatives hired an expert in Native American art to appraise Nelson's collection of Indian art. They also hired Judith McKenzie-Larson to appraise the other estate property. McKenzie-Larson told them she had no expertise in appraising fine art. Based on her appraisal, the Estate representatives priced Nelson's property and sold it at public sale. Defendants Carl and Anne Rice purchased two framed oil paintings at the sale paying the asking price of $60. After later discovering that the paintings were by the artist Martin Johnson Heade, the Rices sold the paintings through the New York auction house Christie's for $1,072,000. Arguing that the parties had made a mutual mistake, the Estate sued the Rices seeking rescission of their contract purchasing the paintings for $60. The trial court granted judgment in favor of the Rices and the Estate appealed.

Espinosa, Chief Judge

. . . A party seeking to rescind a contract on the basis of mutual mistake must show by clear and convincing evidence that the agreement should be set aside. . . . A contract may be rescinded on the ground of a mutual mistake as to a basic assumption on which both parties made the contract. . . . Furthermore, the parties' mutual mistake must have had "such a material effect on the agreed

---

[12]RESTATEMENT (SECOND) OF CONTRACTS §152 (1).
[13]33 N.W. 919 (Mich. 1887).

exchange of performances as to upset the very bases of the contract." *Restatement (Second) of Contracts* §152, comment a. However, the mistake must not be one on which the party seeking relief bears the risk under the rules stated in §154(b) of the *Restatement*. . . .

In concluding that the Estate was not entitled to rescind the sale, the trial court found that, although a mistake had existed as to the value of the paintings, the Estate bore the risk of that mistake under §154(b) of the *Restatement*. . . . Section 154(b) states that a party bears the risk of mistake when "he is aware, at the time the contract is made, that he has only limited knowledge with respect to the facts to which the mistake relates but treats his limited knowledge as sufficient." In explaining that provision, the Washington Supreme Court stated, "In such a situation there is no mistake. Instead, there is an awareness of uncertainty or conscious ignorance of the future." [*Bennett v. Shinoda Floral, Inc.*, 739 P.2d 648, 653-54 (Wash. 1987).] . . .

The Estate contends neither party bore the risk of mistake, arguing that §154 and comment a are not applicable to these facts. In the example in comment a, the risk of mistake is allocated to the seller when the buyer discovers valuable mineral deposits on property priced and purchased as farmland. Even were we to accept the Estate's argument that this example is not analogous, comment c clearly applies here and states:

> Conscious ignorance. Even though the mistaken party did not agree to bear the risk, he may have been aware when he made the contract that his knowledge with respect to the facts to which the mistake relates was limited. If he was not only so aware that his knowledge was limited but undertook to perform in the face of that awareness, he bears the risk of the mistake. It is sometimes said in such a situation that, in a sense, there was not mistake but "conscious ignorance."

. . . McKenzie-Larson told them that she did not appraise fine art and that, if she saw any, they would need to hire an additional appraiser. McKenzie-Larson did not report finding any fine art, and relying on her silence and her appraisal, Newman and Franz priced and sold the Estate's personal property. . . . In his deposition, Newman testified that he had not been concerned that McKenzie-Larson had no expertise in fine art, believing the Estate contained nothing of "significant value" except the house and the Indian art collection. Despite the knowledge that the Estate contained framed art other than the Indian art, and that McKenzie-Larson was not qualified to appraise fine art, the personal representatives relied on her to notify them of any fine art or whether a fine arts appraiser was needed. Because McKenzie-Larson did not say they needed an additional appraiser, Newman and Franz did not hire anyone qualified to appraise fine art. By relying on the opinion of someone who was admittedly unqualified to appraise fine art to determine its existence, the personal representatives consciously ignored the possibility that the Estate's assets might include fine art, thus assuming that risk. . . . Accordingly, the trial court correctly found that the Estate bore the risk of mistake as to the paintings' value.

The Estate asserts that the facts here are similar to those in *Renner v. Kehl*, [722 P. 2d 262 (Ariz. 1986)], in which real estate buyers sued to rescind a contract for acreage upon which they wished to commercially grow jojoba after discovering the water supply was inadequate for that purpose. The supreme court concluded that the buyers could rescind the contract based upon mutual mistake because both the buyers and the sellers had believed there was an adequate water supply, a basic assumption underlying formation of the contract. The parties' failure to thoroughly investigate the water supply did not preclude rescission when "the risk of mistake was not allocated among the parties." [*Id.* at 265.]. The Estate's reliance on *Renner* is unavailing because, as stated above, the Estate bore the risk of mistake based on its own conscious ignorance.

Furthermore, under *Restatement* §154(c), the court may allocate the risk of mistake to one party "on the ground that it is reasonable in the circumstances to do so." In making this determination, "the court will consider the purposes of the parties and will have recourse to its own general knowledge of human behavior in bargain transactions." *Restatement* §154 comment. d. Here, the Estate had had ample opportunity to discover what it was selling and failed to do so; instead, it ignored the possibility that the paintings were valuable and attempted to take action only after learning of their worth as a result of the efforts of the Rices. Under these circumstances, the Estate was a victim of its own folly and it was reasonable for the court to allocate to it the burden of its mistake.

[Judgment affirmed.]

Effect of Misunderstanding

A problem closely related to mutual mistake concerns the effect of misunderstanding between the parties occurring in the bargaining process. Although under the objective theory of contract the parties are ordinarily bound by their outward manifestations, the parties may attach materially different meanings to those manifestations. Material differences in meaning are a major cause of contract disputes. To resolve these disputes, courts must interpret the parties' language and other conduct in light of the surrounding circumstances. The problem is illustrated by the famous case of *Raffles v. Wichelhaus,*[14] commonly known as the "Peerless" case. In this case the plaintiff (seller) agreed to sell cotton to the defendant (buyer). According to the contract the cotton was to arrive by the steamer *Peerless* from Bombay. By coincidence there happened to be two ships named *Peerless* sailing from Bombay, one in October and the other in December. The seller intended *Peerless* #2 (December) and the buyer intended *Peerless* #1 (October). When the seller tendered delivery from *Peerless* #2, the buyer refused to accept or pay for the goods, resulting in the seller's suit. Because both parties attached materially different meanings to the term "Peerless," and neither party knew or had reason to know that different ships were intended, the court held that no contract had been created. The same result would occur if both seller and buyer knew or had reason to know that each party meant a different ship. In other words, no contract is created if the parties attach conflicting and irreconcilable meanings to an important term that could have either but not both meanings.[15] Note that unlike the ordinary mistake cases, which may render a contract voidable, the misunderstanding outlined above prevents formation of the contract initially. The following case provides a modern example of the effect of misunderstanding.

Konic International Corporation v. Spokane Computer Services, Inc.
708 P.2d 932 (Idaho App. 1985)

David Young, an employee of defendant Spokane Computer Services, was instructed by his employer to obtain a surge protector to safeguard the firm's computers from damaging surges of electric current. Young considered several protectors priced from $50 to $200 but, because none was appropriate for Spokane's needs, he contacted plaintiff Konic International Corp. Following a discussion with a Konic engineer, Young selected a protector and requested a price quote from a Konic salesman who replied "fifty-six twenty." The salesman meant $5,620; Young understood him to mean $56.20. Young ordered the device and it was installed in Spokane's office. When Spokane's president saw the device the next day, he realized it was a very expensive model and immediately had it disconnected. Konic refused return of the surge protector and, after Spokane failed to pay, Konic sued for breach of contract. The trial court ruled in favor of Spokane and Konic appealed.

Walters, Chief Judge

. . . Basically what is involved here is a failure of communication between the parties. A similar failure to communicate arose over 100 years ago in the celebrated case of *Raffles v. Wichelhaus,* . . . which has become better known as the case of the good ship "Peerless." . . . The *Peerless* rule . . . has now evolved into section 20 of Restatement (Second) of Contracts (1981). Section 20 states in part:

> (1) There is no manifestation of mutual assent to an exchange if the parties attach materially different meanings to their manifestations and
>   (a) neither knows or has reason to know the meaning attached by the other. . . .

In the present case, both parties attributed different meanings to the same term, "fifty-six twenty." Thus, there was no meeting of the minds of the parties. With a hundred fold difference in the two prices, obviously price was a material term. Because the "fifty-six twenty" designation was a material term expressed in an ambiguous form to which two meanings were obviously applied, we conclude that no contract between the parties was ever formed. . . . The mutual misunderstanding of the parties was so basic and so material that any agreement the parties thought they had reached was merely an illusion. . . .

[Judgment affirmed.]

---

[14]2 Hurl. & C. 906, 159 Eng. Rep. 375 (Ex. 1864).
[15]RESTATEMENT (SECOND) OF CONTRACTS §20(1).

Duress and Undue Influence

The preceding discussion concerns contracts voidable on grounds of mistake, whether induced by the other party (fraud and misrepresentation) or otherwise. The following material examines contracts void or voidable due to an element of compulsion or coercion (duress) or unfair persuasion (undue influence) in the bargaining process. Contracts procured through duress or undue influence are generally voidable by the injured party. Unlike fraud, however, duress and undue influence are not themselves torts for which dollar damages are recoverable.

Duress

Duress may result from two forms of conduct: physical coercion and improper threat. Physical coercion ordinarily renders an obligation void (as opposed to voidable) because it lacks the manifestation of assent required for a contract. For example, assume Barry, placing a loaded gun to Short's head, forces Short to sign an instrument purportedly conveying Short's farm to Barry. Short has no knowledge of the instrument's contents. No contract is created and Short's obligation under the instrument is void.

More often duress results from a threat, not physical compulsion. In such cases, the coerced consent (rather than as above, absence of consent) renders the contract voidable. Threats may be made expressly or by other conduct including past acts or events. Threats constituting duress are usually made by one contracting party to the other. Nevertheless, neither the person making the threat nor the person threatened need be a party to the contract, as long as the threat induces the making of the contract.

Improper threats take many forms. A threat is improper if the act threatened is itself a crime or a tort. Common examples include threats of physical violence or of wrongful seizure or retention of land or goods.

Threats of criminal prosecution also are generally improper. Either the person induced to contract or some third person (for example, a relative of the recipient) may be the object of the threatened prosecution. Threats of prosecution are usually deemed an abuse of the criminal process solely for private benefit. Assume Adams embezzles money in his capacity as Philip's agent. Philip discovers the embezzlement and threatens to file a criminal complaint against Adams unless Adams signs a promissory note for the amount stolen. Adams

signs, induced by the threat. The contract is voidable by Adams. In this case, Philip has a legal right to report Adam's crime to the police. His threat to do so for private benefit is a misuse of that right. In addition, as is commonly the case, Philip may agree not to file a criminal complaint in exchange for Adams's promise. Such a promise to suppress a criminal prosecution is itself unenforceable as contrary to public policy, and may subject Philip to criminal liability.

Because the law favors free access to the courts, a threat to file a civil (rather than criminal) suit is ordinarily not improper. For example, assume Don owes Carol money for accounting services rendered by Carol. Don refuses to pay Carol's bill, thinking the amount is too high. Carol threatens to file a civil suit against Don unless Don contracts to discharge the claim at a fixed sum. To avoid going to court, Don makes the contract. Carol's threat is not improper and the contract may not be avoided by Don.

Although contracts made under threat of a civil action ordinarily are not voidable, the threat must be made in good faith. That is, a threat to pursue an action known to be without legal basis is made in bad faith and is an abuse of the judicial process. The threat is therefore improper.

To constitute duress, the threat must both be improper and induce the making of the contract. Two points regarding inducement should be noted. First, to render a contract voidable, the victim of the threat must be left with no reasonable alternative to making the contract. Second, as in cases of fraud, a subjective test of inducement is applied. That is, the threat need only induce action by the person to whom directed. The law does not require that a reasonable or prudent person (representing an objective standard) would be so induced.

As the following case illustrates, duress in modern commercial contracts often takes the form of "economic duress" or "business compulsion."

Totem Marine Tug & Barge, Inc. v. Alyeska Pipeline Service Company
584 P.2d 15 (Alaska 1978)

Plaintiff Totem Marine Tug & Barge, Inc. (Totem) and defendant Alyeska Pipeline Service Company (Alyeska) entered into an agreement by which Totem agreed to transport construction materials from Houston, Texas, to Alaska via the Panama Canal. Because of unforeseen delays, Alyeska terminated the contract and took possession of the materials at Long Beach, California. Totem then submitted a bill of approximately $300,000 to Alyeska. The bill remained unpaid for almost two months during which Totem faced bankruptcy because it lacked cash to pay its creditors. Alyeska offered to settle the bill for $97,500 if Totem would sign an agreement releasing Alyeska from all claims by Totem. Totem accepted the offer, but later sued for damages equal to the unpaid balance on the bill. Totem also requested rescission of the release agreement alleging that it had been forced to sign the agreement under duress. The trial court granted summary judgment in favor of Alyeska. Totem appealed.

Burke, Justice

. . . This court has not yet decided a case involving a claim of economic duress or what is also called business compulsion. At early common law, a contract could be avoided on the ground of duress only if a party could show that the agreement was entered into for fear of loss of life or limb, mayhem or imprisonment. . . . The threat had to be such as to overcome the will of a person of ordinary firmness and courage. . . . Subsequently, however, the concept has been broadened to include myriad forms of economic coercion which force a person to involuntarily enter into a particular transaction. The test has come to be whether the will of the person induced by the threat was overcome rather than that of a reasonably firm person. . . .

At the outset it is helpful to acknowledge the various policy considerations which are involved in cases involving economic duress. Typically, those claiming such coercion are attempting to avoid the consequences of a modification of an original contract or of a settlement and release agreement. On the one hand, courts are reluctant to set aside agreements because of the notion of freedom of contract and because of the desirability of having private dispute resolutions be final. On the other hand, there is an increasing recognition of the law's role in correcting inequitable or unequal exchanges between parties of disproportionate bargaining power and a greater willingness to not enforce agreements which were entered into under coercive circumstances.

There are various statements of what constitutes economic duress. . . . Under [the standard used by many courts], duress exists where: (1) one party involuntarily accepted the terms of another, (2) circumstances permitted no other alternative, and (3) such circumstances were the result of coercive acts of the other party. . . .

As the above indicates, one essential element of economic duress is that the plaintiff show that the other party by wrongful acts or threats, intentionally caused him to involuntarily enter into a particular transaction. Courts have not attempted to define exactly what constitutes a wrongful or coercive act, as wrongfulness depends on the particular facts in each case. This requirement may be satisfied where the alleged wrongdoer's conduct is criminal or tortious but an act or threat may also be considered wrongful if it is wrongful in the moral sense. . . .

In many cases, a threat to breach a contract or to withhold payment of an admitted debt has constituted a wrongful act. . . . Implicit in such cases is the additional requirement that the threat to breach the contract or withhold payment be done in bad faith. . . .

Economic duress does not exist, however, merely because a person has been the victim of a wrongful act; in addition, the victim must have no choice but to agree to the other party's terms or face serious financial hardship. Thus, in order to avoid a contract, a party must also show that he had no reasonable alternative to agreeing to the other party's terms, or, as it is often stated, that he had no adequate remedy if the threat were to be carried out. . . . What constitutes a reasonable alternative is a question of fact, depending on the circumstances of each case. . . .

Turning to the instant case, we believe that Totem's allegations, if proved, would support a finding that it executed a release of its contract claims against Alyeska under economic duress. Totem has alleged that Alyeska deliberately withheld payment of an acknowledged debt, knowing that Totem had no choice but to accept an inadequate sum in settlement of that debt; that Totem was faced with impending bankruptcy; that Totem was unable to meet its pressing debts other than by accepting the immediate cash payment offered by Alyeska; and that through necessity, Totem thus involuntarily accepted an inadequate settlement offer from Alyeska and executed a release of all claims under the contract. If the release was in fact executed under these circumstances, we think that under the legal principles discussed above, that this would constitute the type of wrongful conduct and lack of alternatives that would render the release voidable by Totem on the ground of economic duress. . . .

[Judgment reversed and remanded.]

Undue Influence

Contracts formed under duress are tainted by the presence of coercion in various forms and degrees. Contracts voidable for **undue influence** are characterized by a subtler type of overreaching: unfair persuasion. The cases divide themselves into two broad categories. In the first, one person so psychologically dominates another that the dominant party is able to induce the other's assent to an unreasonably unfair or disadvantageous bargain. In the second, a relation of trust and confidence exists between the parties, but it is abused by one who uses that position to unfairly persuade the other to make the contract. Examples of such confidential relationships include parent-child, husband-wife, trustee-beneficiary, guardian-ward, attorney-client, and physician-patient.

Most undue influence cases result in an unusual or uncharacteristic transaction, conferring a disproportionate benefit upon the persuading party. Commonly, the victim of the persuasion is deceased at the time of trial. Cases, therefore, usually arise between the benefited party and the relatives or the estate of the deceased, who seek to recover property transferred during life, or in some cases, to set aside a will. Because the victim of undue influence usually is unavailable to testify, circumstantial evidence of unfair persuasion is usually required including, for example, evidence of the relationship between the parties, the unfairness of the resulting contract, and the susceptibility of the person influenced.

Summary

1.   Various defects in the formation process such as fraud and misrepresentation, mistake, duress, and undue influence may render otherwise binding contracts voidable.

2.   A misrepresentation is an assertion that is not in accord with existing fact. A misrepresentation, made with *scienter,* is fraudulent if made with knowledge of its falsity or reckless disregard of the truth. If one party is induced to enter into a contract because of a misrepresentation by the other, the contract is voidable by the recipient. Additionally, if the misrepresentation is fraudulent, dollar damages may be recovered by the reliant party in tort for fraud.

3.   Liability for fraud is imposed if one party makes a fraudulent material misrepresentation of existing fact upon which the other justifiably relies to his injury. The misrepresentation may be made by language (an express misrepresentation), by other conduct intended or likely to prevent the other from learning of the fact (concealment), or by silence (nondisclosure) in a limited class of cases in which the law imposes a duty to speak. Facts which may be misrepresented include not only the existence or characteristics of a tangible thing, the occurrence of an event, or the relationship between particular persons or things, but also a state of mind, such as a person's intention or opinion.

4.   Regardless of the manner or content of the misrepresentation, the recipient must justifiably rely upon it. Thus, a person who knows a statement to be false or conducts an independent investigation which uncovers its falsity has not relied upon it. An independent investigation into the truth of statements made by the other party is not, however, required, and whether reliance is justified is determined by considering any peculiar characteristics of the reliant party and the particular facts of the case. This approach protects persons who are gullible or negligent, those with the greatest need for protection from fraud.

5.   A party seeking merely to avoid a contract on misrepresentation grounds may do so by proving that the misrepresentation was either fraudulent or material. The plaintiff need not prove actual harm resulting from reliance upon it. To recover for fraud, however, the plaintiff must prove that the misrepresentation relied upon was both fraudulent and material, and that he suffered monetary injury as a result. Most courts apply a "benefit of the bargain" test in computing damages in fraud actions. Under this test the plaintiff recovers the difference between what he actually received under the contract and what he would have received had the false statements, in fact, been true.

6.   Liability for fraud and misrepresentation results from a mistake of fact caused by one of the parties. Occasionally, one of both parties are mistaken concerning a relevant fact for reasons not dependent upon the assertion of either party. Relief for such mistakes, in the form of avoidance of the contract, is given under very limited circumstances. For example, avoidance by the adversely affected party is allowed if both parties are mistaken (a mutual mistake) concerning the existence, identity, quantity, or other qualities or characteristics of the subject matter. Avoidance is not available simply because one party is mistaken concerning the value of the subject matter or the difficulty or expense of performance. Similarly, other unilateral mistakes, such as errors in computing an offer, do not provide grounds for avoidance, unless the nonmistaken party knows or should know of the mistake.

7.   Contracts may also be voidable due to an element of compulsion or coercion (duress) or unfair persuasion (undue influence) in the bargaining process. Duress takes two forms,

physical compulsion and improper threat. Undue influence usually results either from psychological domination of one party by the other or from abuse of a relationship of trust and confidence between the parties.

Key Terms

misrepresentation	mistake
fraudulent	unilateral mistake
scienter	mutual mistake
fraud (deceit)	duress
concealment	undue influence
material	

Questions and Problems

11.1   Denise owned an appliance store that she wanted to sell. Because the business had been a perennial money loser she falsified the financial statements to indicate that the business was profitable. Claude purchased the business for $20,000, a fair price on the basis of the information supplied. Shortly thereafter he discovered the true financial picture indicating the business was worth $5,000.

   (a) Assuming Claude can prove that Denise altered the financial statements, upon what legal theory should he sue her?

   (b) What possible remedies could Claude obtain?

   (c) If Claude attempts to prove that Denise has made a misrepresentation, could Denise defend on the ground that no misrepresentation was made because she merely supplied the financial statements, but never talked to him?

   (d) The facts indicate that Claude relied upon the false financial statements. What standard is utilized to determine whether or not a person's reliance upon a representation is justified? Was Claude's reliance justifiable?

11.2   Consider whether, and under what circumstances, a fraud action could be maintained by Bob in the following situations.

   (a) Sam, in order to induce Bob to buy his 100 shares of XYZ Corporation stock, states to Bob, "This stock will pay dividends within five years that will equal or exceed the purchase price I am asking." Partly in reliance upon Sam's statement, Bob purchases the stock. XYZ Corporation subsequently goes bankrupt without paying any dividends.

   (b) Helen, in need of money, is negotiating for a loan from Bob. Helen tells Bob that she intends to use the money to expand her business and purchase new equipment. Helen's actual intention is to use the money to invest heavily in the commodities market and speculative mining stocks. Partly in reliance on Helen's statement, Bob loans her $50,000. Helen loses everything in the commodities market.

   (c) Joan and Bob are negotiating for the sale of Joan's XYZ Corporation stock. Both parties have equal access to information on the earnings of XYZ and corporate earn-

ings generally. Joan tells Bob that in her opinion XYZ stock is a "first-class security" and "worth $100 per share." In reliance on Joan's statement, Bob buys the stock, which proves to be worthless.

   (d) Sam is negotiating the sale of his commercial building to Bob. Tom is a tenant in the building under a long-term lease. Sam, in order to induce Bob to buy, states that, in his opinion, Tom is a "good" tenant. In fact, as Sam knew, Tom had been consistently delinquent in rent payments and had damaged the premises in the past. Partially in reliance upon Sam's statement, Bob purchased the building. Tom moved out shortly thereafter, leaving the premises in a shambles and a substantial amount of rent unpaid.

11.3   Julie Murdoch was interested in buying a house offered for sale by Greg and Beth Puckett. During a tour of the house, Murdoch noticed an apparatus labeled "water conditioner" in the basement and asked, "What kind of water do you have here?" Mrs. Puckett replied, "It's good. It's fine. It's a little hard but this system takes care of it." Mr. Puckett, who also was present, remained silent. Murdoch bought the house and after moving in, she discovered that the water on the property came from a well that contained sulfur water that smelled strongly of rotten eggs. Although the water was "a little hard," the sulfur was unrelated to the water hardness. After treatment for drinking, the water tasted like sulfur and chlorine and still smelled bad. Murdoch hired a plumber who arranged hookup to the water system of a nearby town at a cost of $5,000. Murdoch sued Beth and Greg Puckett for fraud. Did either or both of the defendants commit fraud? Explain.

11.4   Mr. and Mrs. Mortimer were interested in purchasing a house in Woodlane Acres, a subdivision developed by Wood Brothers, Inc. The Mortimers visited Wood Brothers' office and told the salesman that they wanted a house in a quiet area away from traffic. The salesman provided complete materials about the subdivision and told them that the state planned to extend Highway C, a busy state highway, along the west side of Woodlane. After examining an aerial photograph of the subdivision provided by the salesman and visiting several houses, the Mortimers contracted to buy a house on the east side of Woodlane Acres. Three years later, the state constructed the Highway C extension on the east side of Woodlane Acres adjacent to the Mortimers' house. The Mortimers sued Wood Brothers requesting rescission of their contract.

   (a) Based on these facts, do you believe that the Mortimers are entitled to rescission of the contract? Explain.

   (b) At trial, Wood Brothers presented the aerial photograph that the Mortimers had examined prior to their purchase. On the photograph, the planned Highway C extension was clearly highlighted with bright yellow tape and was located on the east side of the subdivision exactly where it later was constructed. What effect, if any, does the photograph have on the Mortimers' case? Explain.

11.5   Monarch Label Co. received a written order for three types of custom printed labels from Reed Photo Mart. A sample of each label was affixed to the order form, which included a column for the quantity. For two of the labels, the quantity was listed as "2M"; the quantity for the third label was marked "4MM." According to custom and usage in the trade, the term "M" means one thousand and the term "MM" means one million. Monarch printed the labels and shipped them to Reed. Reed refused delivery of the third set of labels, which weighed over 600 pounds, and telephoned Monarch claiming "a terrible mistake has been made." Reed explained that he had intended to order four thousand, not four million, of the third label. Monarch sued Reed for payment and Reed argued that the contract was voidable because of unilateral mistake. How should the court rule?

11.6   Mildred owned 23 acres of land at the edge of a large city. Because she was having difficulty paying the expenses of the property, Mildred entered into a contract with Robert, a real estate developer. Mildred agreed to transfer half of the property to Robert who agreed to pay some of the expenses of the property. They further agreed to develop the property into a condominium project from which Mildred and Robert would share profits. Immediately after they signed the agreement, interest rates rose causing the costs of construction to skyrocket. Additionally, the city widened a street making the property less desirable for residential units. As a result, no condominium project was built. Mildred sued Robert and requested the court to rescind the contract on the grounds that the parties had entered into the agreement under the mutual mistake that the property could be profitably developed. Should the court grant rescission? Explain.

11.7   Review the case *Raffles v. Wichelhaus* discussed in the text and then answer the following questions.
 (a) Assume that, although there were two ships named *Peerless,* both parties had intended the same ship *Peerless.* Would a contract have been formed? Would it make any difference whether or not the parties knew or had reason to know that there were two ships? Explain.
 (b) Assume instead that the seller knew that two ships named *Peerless* were sailing on different dates. Would a contract have resulted if the seller had known that the buyer intended *Peerless* #1 (October) and that the buyer was unaware that two ships existed? Why or why not? If a contract was formed, which ship was to be used? Explain.

11.8   In January 2003, Quinn, a stockbroker employed by Humphrey Co., convinced Emma to buy 250 shares of a mutual fund by threatening her with bodily violence if she refused to buy. Emma bought the shares. Several months later Quinn was arrested on another matter and subsequently was fired by his employer. Emma continued to hold the shares of the mutual fund and received dividends until 2005 when she sold them for a loss of $35,000. Emma sued Humphrey Co. for damages based on the fact that she had been forced by duress into purchasing the shares. How should the court rule? Explain.

11.9   Beatty, a Montana rancher, sold a portion of his land to the U.S. government. The government needed the land for a reservoir to be constructed in conjunction with a dam on the Missouri River. After the sale, Beatty sued the government seeking to avoid the contract alleging that he had been induced to sell the land through fear and duress. Beatty claimed that the government agents had threatened to have the property condemned through legal proceedings if he refused to sell at the price offered by the agents. Although Beatty would have received the fair market value of the land if the property were condemned, the agents stated that Beatty's attorneys' fees would consume the amount paid for the property and that Beatty might not receive payment until 25 years later.

The agents knew that these statements were false. Is the government liable for duress? What factors should the court consider in resolving the dispute?

11.10 Jack Pond owns an office building in the downtown area of a large city. For over ten years, Pond has leased most of the building to Lincoln Co., a major national corporation. The lease had a term of three years but included an option for renewal with a rental increase at each renewal. The original rent was $50,000 per year, but was scheduled to increase to $100,000 at the next renewal. Lincoln notified Pond that it would not renew the lease but offered to enter into a new lease for eight years at $50,000 per year, a rental rate that barely covered Pond's expenses. Lincoln refused Pond's efforts to negotiate saying only that the company would move if its offer was not accepted. Because of a severe economic recession. Pond's efforts to find a new tenant were unsuccessful and he reluctantly entered into the lease with Lincoln. Within a year, the economy had improved and several companies expressed an interest in renting Pond's building for more than $100,000 per year. Pond sued Lincoln alleging that Lincoln had coerced him into making the lease by economic duress. Is the lease voidable? Explain.

11.11 Jewell, an elderly widow, owned several parcels of real estate. Jewell's closest relative was her nephew, Hoyt. Upon Hoyt's recommendation, Jewell executed two contracts by which she promised to sell her real property to her nephew. The contracts were prepared by Jewell's attorney. Jewell later sued to have the contracts rescinded. Although each document was clearly marked "Contract to Sell Property," she alleged that her nephew had led her to believe the documents were merely power of attorney forms. Jewell further alleged that she and her nephew stood in a confidential relationship that her nephew had exploited by exercising undue influence to induce her to sign the contracts. Is Jewell correct in asserting that undue influence is the appropriate grounds for rescission? Do the facts suggest that other grounds for rescission might exist? Explain.

WRITTEN AGREEMENTS

Contrary to popular belief, contracts generally are not required to be written to be enforceable. Both the common law and the Uniform Commercial Code (UCC) recognize and enforce a wide variety of oral contracts. A formal written contract, however, has distinct advantages over an oral contract because the writing can substantiate the existence and terms of the agreement in a dispute. A writing is particularly valuable in ongoing business relationships, such as agency and employment, partnership and corporations, or when a business is sold. The use of written contracts, incorporating all agreed terms and addressing all anticipated contingencies, is a sound business practice. The more comprehensive the writing, the more legal protection the parties have, because once a dispute arises, agreement on any issue may be impossible. In addition, the parties fre-

quently can avoid costly litigation, because rights and duties of the parties are determined in advance, and potential misunderstandings may be uncovered during the process of reducing the agreement to writing.

A written contract, however, is no insurance against controversy. In both oral and written agreements, misunderstandings, missing terms, and ambiguous language often make it difficult to determine the scope and extent of the parties' contractual undertaking. Various legal principles aid the courts in determining the meaning of a contract or term.

A common interpretation question concerns the legal effect of the adoption of a writing. Contracting parties frequently conduct lengthy preliminary negotiations ultimately incorporated into a written contract. Disputes often arise when preliminary understandings conflict with the contents of the writing. The court must then determine the terms of the contract in light of conflicting evidence presented by the parties. This issue is governed by the parol evidence rule, which generally prevents admission of evidence of preliminary negotiations or prior agreements to contradict a writing adopted as the final expression of an agreement.

Although many agreements are reduced to writing, as a general rule no writing is required for legal recognition of a contract. Contracts subject to the Statute of Frauds provide a major exception to this rule. The

Statute of Frauds requires that certain types of contracts be evidenced by a writing to be enforceable. This chapter discusses general principles of contract interpretation, the parol evidence rule, and the various types of oral contracts rendered unenforceable by the Statute of Frauds.

Contract Interpretation

Interpretation is the process by which a court ascertains the meaning of a contract or contract term. Courts must interpret contracts when the parties become deadlocked concerning the scope of their contractual undertakings. In these cases, the court must examine a variety of evidence in order to ascertain the *intention* of the parties, the primary inquiry in contract interpretation.

If the contract is oral, the court's interpretation process is extremely perilous. The terms of the contract must be proven by oral testimony of the parties or others and circumstantial evidence including the parties' conduct before or after making the alleged contract. Testimony on the term or issue in dispute is certain to be self-serving or ambiguous, a situation often leading the court to find that the parties had not reached agreement on the matter in question. The court, if it wishes to enforce the contract, is then required to supply the missing or disputed terms.[1]

Although a carefully drafted, comprehensive written contract unquestionably prevents countless contract disputes, potential pitfalls remain. The disputed issue may not be covered in the writing (again requiring the court to supply a term) and even if it is, the words used may be ambiguous or their meaning may be affected by the context (technical or other), by trade usage, or by typographical errors. Terms may be inadvertently included or excluded. And, even if the language is clear, the parties' subsequent conduct may indicate a modification of the term outlined in the writing.

Courts every day are required to resolve these and many other interpretation problems in a wide variety of oral and written contracts. The law has developed various guidelines to aid courts in interpreting contracts. Initially, public policy and considerations of fairness provide a general guide to courts in determining the scope of a contractual undertaking. For example, the duty of good faith pervades contracts generally and forms the background against which all contracts are interpreted. Similarly, unconscionability and other public policy restrictions limit the range of permissible contract obligations. Interpretation standards also are derived from general contract theory, most notably the objective theory of contracts. That is, in ascertaining the extent of a contractual obligation, the courts examine the impression each party created in the other—each party's objective manifestation of assent—rather than any subjective or hidden intention.

Against this framework, the law supplies more specific interpretation aids:

1. Generally, a contract is interpreted as a whole and in a manner designed to give a lawful and reasonable meaning to all terms. Words or other conduct are interpreted by taking all circumstances into account, particularly the purpose and intention of the parties when making the bargain. Language usually is given its general meaning. If, however, the transaction arises in an industry or discipline using technical terms, such terms are interpreted according to their technical meaning.

2. Language within the contract is interpreted according to common sense priorities. Specific language takes precedence over conflicting general language. Separately negotiated terms or terms added to the basic bargain are preferred over conflicting language in a standardized contract.

3. Because the party choosing the language used commonly protects its own interest, any ambiguity in that language commonly is interpreted according to the other party's meaning. This principle is particularly applicable to standardized form ("adhesion") contracts in which one party drafts the entire contract and offers it to the other on a "take it or leave it" basis. In adhesion contracts, construction against the draftsman is often intertwined with the courts' refusal to enforce, as unconscionable, the term or clause involved.

4. A contract is to be interpreted in light of all circumstances including not only the express terms of the contract, but also the conduct of the parties, including performance under the disputed contract or other contracts. Additionally, any customs or conventions of the particular trade or business involved are considered.[2] In the following case, the court was required to resolve a

---

[1]Contract terms supplied by the court in absence of agreement are discussed throughout the contracts and sales material. The most notable source of such "gap fillers" is Article 2 of the UCC.

[2]The effect of course of performance, course of dealing, and usage of trade upon contract interpretation and the standards of preference among them are discussed later in this chapter.

dispute over the meaning of the language of a written contract.

RCI Northeast Services Division v. Boston Edison Company

822 F.2d 199 (1st Cir. 1987)

In response to a request for bids from defendant Boston Edison Company (Edison), plaintiff RCI Northeast Services Division (RCI) submitted a bid to perform construction at Edison's nuclear power plant. RCI described its bid as a "cost plus percentage fee" proposal and enclosed various schedules setting forth its labor costs and equipment charges. The page describing labor costs included the following provision: "Labor cost rates include all costs, burdens, insurances and taxes applicable, based on current labor rates and are subject to escalation." Edison selected RCI to perform the contract and issued a series of purchase orders stating that the work was to be performed on a "cost plus fee basis" and that billings were to be "in accordance with the [RCI] proposal on file with Edison." RCI submitted periodic billings while performing the work in 1981 and 1982. In December 1983, 18 months after completion of the project, RCI submitted a final bill in the amount of $185,535 for workers' compensation insurance on the project.

After Edison refused to pay the final bill, RCI sued. The evidence established that RCI's insurer required RCI to pay estimated premiums during the project but that actual premium costs were determined following completion of the project based on job-related injuries that occurred during the construction. RCI established that this type of insurance policy was not uncommon in the industry and had been used in contracts with other utility companies. The trial court ruled in favor of RCI and awarded damages of $185,535. Edison appealed.

Selya, Circuit Judge

. . . The issue in this case is a straightforward one. From RCI's standpoint, the contract documents specifically protected it against mounting insurance costs, thus shifting the burden of the retrospective workers' compensation premium hike to Edison. The defendant reads the same language quite differently: the base labor rate alone was subject to change, and the associated "burdens," including compensation insurance, would fluctuate only in direct proportion to, and in the same percentage as, the base labor rate itself. In short,

Edison maintains that the contract price was not meant to change in accordance with increases in raw insurance costs. . . .

We start our discussion of the merits with the disputed sentence itself. We repeat it here for ease in reference:

> Labor cost rates include all costs, burdens, insurances and taxes applicable, based on current labor rates and are subject to escalation.

The least forced reading of the language is to the effect that "labor cost rates" include a variety of components — "costs, burdens, insurances and taxes" — and that these components, as well as the labor rates themselves, "are subject to escalation." Whatever may be said, pro and con, as to whether this is the *only* reasonable construction of the clause, it is surely a plausible interpretation. . . .

> If the language of the contract is susceptible of more than one interpretation, the court should construe the contract in the light of the situation and relation of the parties at the time it was made, and, if possible, accord it a reasonable and sensible meaning, consonant with its dominant purpose.

Continental Bus System, Inc. v. NLRB, 325 F.2d 267, 273 (10th Cir. 1963). . . . And, as the Court has instructed,

> The intention of the parties is to be gathered, not from [a] single sentence . . . , but from the whole instrument read in the light of the circumstances existing at the time of negotiations leading up to its execution.

Miller v. Robertson, . . . 45 S. Ct. 73, 76 . . . 1924).

Here, it was Edison that determined to let the contract on the basis of the vendor's costs, supplemented by a reasonable profit. It was Edison which, in its purchase orders, stated that RCI was to perform the work "on a cost plus fee basis." The notion that RCI should absorb increases in its insurance costs for the job, rather than pass such increases along to the owner, is at odds with the "dominant purpose" of the cost-plus arrangement. . . . Although it would have been possible for the parties to have limited the pass-through of insurance expense in some artificial way, there is nothing in the language of the contract, the relationship of the parties, or the situation as a whole which suggests such was the case.

Defining the contours of the escalator in terms of real cost increases rather than in the palpably obscure manner suggested by [Edison] fits much more comfortably into the everyday context of the deal. . . .

There would be scant utility in any further analysis. In the arena of commerce, it avails us little to stand language on its ear in an effort to rescue a firm from a sinkhole of its own design. It is no appropriate part of judicial business to rewrite contracts freely entered into between sophisticated business entities. Rather, the courts must give effect to the language of such agreements and to their discernible meaning. That is exactly what has occurred: the district judge adopted the most natural reading of the disputed sentence, ascertained that the parties intended the clause to operate in precisely that way, and decided the case accordingly. His finding that, under the purchase orders, RCI was entitled to recoup from Edison the augmented costs attributable to the retrospective insurance premium increases enjoys adequate record support. . . .

[Judgment affirmed.]

Effect of Adoption of a Writing: The Parol Evidence Rule

Despite the protection written contracts provide, they create special interpretation problems. For example, courts frequently must determine the legal effect of a writing adopted by the parties as a final expression of their agreement. To illustrate the problem, assume Bill, a banker, is considering construction of a new, expanded bank building. Bill contacts Sam, a contractor, and the two begin preliminary negotiations for a contract to construct the building. Over a period of months, the parties meet several times to discuss various issues such as building materials, price, financing, and completion schedule. Various understandings are reached, some oral, others incorporated in informal memoranda and business correspondence. Ultimately, the parties reach final agreement and reduce their construction contract to a writing signed by both parties. Some of the previous understandings are incorporated into the writing, others are not. Some of the preliminary understandings are modified by the writing, which also includes terms not previously discussed.

If a dispute later arises concerning the terms of the construction contract, the court is often required to determine the relationship between the writing and the prior understandings and negotiations it incorporates. The basic question is to what extent, if at all, parol evidence may be admitted in court to supplement or contradict the terms contained in the writing. **Parol evidence** includes oral or written evidence of prior or contemporaneous (occurring at the same time as the final writing) agreements or negotiations and more generally anything not contained in the writing itself. The principles governing the legal effect of the writing and the admissibility of parol evidence to supplement or contradict it are embodied in the parol evidence rule.

The Parol Evidence Rule

The **parol evidence rule** provides that if the parties adopt a writing that is intended to be a final expression of some or all terms of their agreement, then all prior or contemporaneous, oral or written, agreements are discharged to the extent that they are within the scope of, or are inconsistent with, the writing. Courts commonly state that such prior agreements and negotiations are "merged" into the finalized writing. Because, under the rule, the writing effectively *becomes* the agreement, parol evidence is not admissible in court to vary or contradict the terms of the writing. The rule, however, has no application whatsoever to a subsequent modification of the final writing, whether that modification be oral or written. Figure 12.1 illustrates the application of the rule.

The parol evidence rule is designed to protect the integrity of the final writing, which is adopted to provide

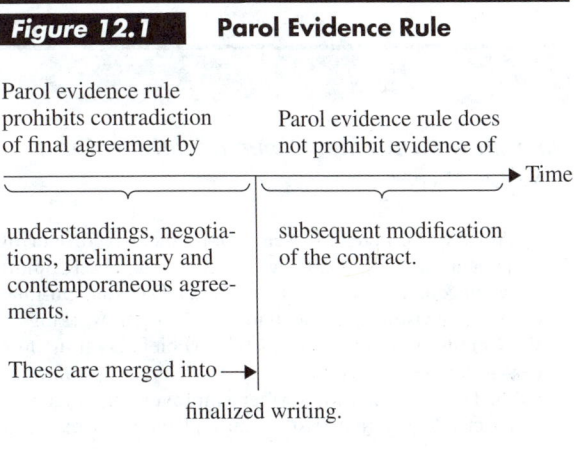

Figure 12.1 **Parol Evidence Rule**

Parol evidence rule prohibits contradiction of final agreement by

Parol evidence rule does not prohibit evidence of

→ Time

understandings, negotiations, preliminary and contemporaneous agreements.

subsequent modification of the contract.

These are merged into → finalized writing.

reliable evidence of the existence and terms of the contract, against contradiction by evidence of prior understandings, negotiations, or agreements of the parties. The rule limits what can be admitted as evidence to establish the terms of the contract in a lawsuit between the parties. It does not determine the interpretation placed upon that evidence by the trier of fact, generally the jury. In other words, when the terms of a written contract are in dispute, the jury will consider the writing together with any other evidence the court admits and reach its own conclusion concerning the scope of the parties' contractual undertaking.

"Integration" Defined. The parol evidence rule applies only to writings that constitute a final written expression of one or more terms of the agreement. This finalized writing is referred to as an **integrated agreement.** Integration may be **complete** (a complete and exclusive statement of the terms of the agreement) or **partial** (conclusive on some but not all issues). Because integration frequently is difficult to ascertain, parol evidence is admissible to establish, as a question of fact, whether or not the writing constitutes an integrated agreement and, if so, whether the integration is partial or complete.

If the court finds the writing to be only a partial integration, evidence of agreements not covered by the writing is admissible. That is, because the entire agreement has not been reduced to a writing, parol evidence may be admitted, not to vary or contradict the writing, but to establish other terms or agreements necessary to ascertain the entire contract of the parties.

The following case illustrates the operation of the parol evidence rule.

Davison v. FastComm Communications, Inc.
46 Va. Cir. 25 (1998)

> In April 1994, Peter Madsen, chief executive officer of defendant FastComm Communications, Inc. (FastComm) began negotiations to hire plaintiff Gary Davison. On June 6, 1994, Davison signed a contract and began working as FastComm's senior vice president and chief operating officer. After being terminated by FastComm in October 1995, Davison sued his former employer for breach of contract alleging that FastComm had failed to pay him quarterly bonuses required under the employment contract. Following a trial, the jury ruled in favor of Davison. FastComm filed a motion to set aside the verdict arguing that it was inconsistent with Virginia law.

Klein, Judge

This dispute arises from Davison's employment tenure with FastComm as a high-level executive. . . . As part of Davison's proposed compensation package, Madsen initially agreed to confer certain stock options, along with a base salary and other incentives. Madsen and Davison also orally agreed to a bonus plan, whereby Davison was to receive an unconditional $25,000 quarterly bonus. The basic proposed terms of employment were written by Madsen on a napkin or business card during a luncheon meeting. Madsen's notes were then passed on to the Human Resources department at FastComm so that an appropriate written offer could be drafted. On April 28, 1994, Madsen signed and presented to Davison a letter setting forth the proposed terms of employment for Davison with FastComm (the "Contract"). The Contract provided, inter alia, that "During the first 30 days [of Davison's employment], we will jointly develop an incentive bonus plan based on performance milestones."

Between April 28, 1994, and June 6, 1994, the parties had numerous discussions about the wording of the Contract. Davison refused to commence his employment with FastComm until the parties reached agreement on each of the terms of the Contract. During those discussions, Madsen assured Davison that the bonuses provision of the Contract was consistent with the terms upon which they had previously agreed. On June 6, 1994, Davison signed the Contract and commenced his employment with FastComm. Over the ensuing months, Davison and Madsen discussed potential "performance milestones," but no agreement on any such milestone was reached. No bonuses were paid to Davison until March 6, 1995, when he received a $25,000 bonus. This bonus was not described as a quarterly bonus, nor was it linked to any performance milestone as it was paid during FastComm's worst financial quarter of Davison's employment tenure. Davison's employment was terminated by FastComm in October 1995. No other bonuses were paid to Davison during his employment with FastComm. . . .

The parol evidence rule is a basic principle of contract law, which provides that prior or contemporaneous negotiations or stipulations are not admissible to vary or contradict the terms of a complete and unambiguous written instrument. . . . The parol evidence rule applies to both oral and written prior or contemporaneous stipulations. . . . Where a writing is clear and complete on its face, it is considered the whole contract between the parties, and no additional evidence will be allowed to construe the agreement. . . . The Virginia Supreme Court, however, has recognized certain exceptions to the rule. Under the "partial integration doctrine," parol evidence may be admissible to show additional terms "not inconsistent with or contrary to" the writing, if the contract does not embody all prior or contemporaneous negotiations. [*Durham v. National Pool Equipment Co.,* 138 S.E.3d 55 (Va. 1964).] . . .

FastComm argues that the Contract is a clear and unambiguous recitation of the parties' agreement on the bonuses issue. As such, FastComm asserts that under the parol evidence rule, any evidence of prior or contemporaneous discussions or stipulations, in writing or otherwise, cannot be considered by the Court. . . . Even if the Court were to conclude that the Contract is incomplete or ambiguous, FastComm further contends that the Court, under Virginia law, cannot consider parol evidence which is inconsistent with or contrary to the terms of the Contract. FastComm asserts that the alleged discussions between Madsen and Davison concerning an unconditional $25,000 per quarter bonus are inconsistent with and contrary to the plain language of the Contract. . . .

Davison initially replies that parol evidence regarding the prior discussions between Madsen and Davison is admissible to supplement the terms of the Contract in order to establish the intent of the parties because the written contract was an incomplete recordation of the parties' agreement. Davison argues that any parol evidence establishing an agreement by FastComm to confer unconditional $25,000 quarterly bonuses was consistent with the Contract, as evidenced by Madsen's assurances between April 28, 1994, and Davison's execution of the Contract on June 6, 1994, that the bonuses provision in the Contract was consistent with their prior understanding. . . .

This Court need not determine whether the bonuses provision in the Contract is incomplete or ambiguous as a matter of law, because, even if it were, parol evidence could only be admitted to supplement or explain the provision, not to contradict it. . . . The plain language utilized by the parties in the Contract tied bonuses to "performance milestones." At trial, Davison himself unequivocally testified that the parties "never finalized any performance milestones," . . . and that, "we didn't set any kind of performance milestones, no, but he did give me a bonus." . . . Davison is bound by his own admission that no performance milestones were ever set. . . . Therefore, he can only recover on his bonuses claim if he was entitled to bonuses that were unrelated to any performance milestones. The parol evidence adduced at trial upon which Davison now relies, clearly contradicts the express language of the Contract. Consequently, the jury's verdict on the bonuses claim cannot be upheld on the basis that it may have reflected the intent of the parties. . . .

This Court is not unmindful of the jury's obvious determination that the testimony of Davison and his witnesses was more credible than the testimony of FastComm's witnesses. However, the parol evidence rule "is a principle founded in wisdom, and cannot be too carefully guarded. Upon its enforcement the certainty and sanctity of written contracts depend, and its violation would be destructive of the most solemn transactions of life." *May v. Bradley,* [110 S.E.2d 520 (Va. 1959)]. . . . To allow the jury's verdict on the bonuses issue to stand would require this Court to ignore one of the most basic tenets of Virginia substantive law. The Court declines to do so. Accordingly, FastComm's motion to set aside the verdict is granted as to the bonuses claim. . . .

Complete Integration; Collateral Contracts. If the parties adopt a partial integration, parol evidence is admissible to establish the remaining terms of the contract. Similarly, evidence of an agreement not within the scope of a completely integrated writing is admissible. In other words, the rule does not bar proof of a collateral contract—one related to but not part of the integrated contract, and which is not inconsistent with it. This rule, commonly referred to as the **collateral contract doctrine,** is illustrated by the following classic case.

High Knob, Incorporated v. Allen
138 S.E.2d 49 (Va. 1964)

George Allen and J. R. Roberson, Jr. entered into separate written contracts to purchase lots in a residential subdivision developed by High Knob, Incorporated. The contracts were silent concerning the source of water for residences to be built on the lots, but a provision in the deeds provided that no well could be drilled on the property. Both Roberson and Allen testified, however, that during the course of the negotiations, Mr. McElroy, High Knob's secretary, orally stated that High Knob had a water system and would furnish water to the houses to be constructed in the subdivision for a $200 hookup fee, which would be the only consideration paid for water service. Partially on the basis of this representation, Allen and Roberson were induced to purchase lots. After building their houses, Allen and Roberson connected to the water main and tendered the $200 fee, which was refused. Six months later, High Knob tendered a water service contract to Allen and Roberson that both refused to sign because it was not in accordance with the original oral agreement. High Knob then severed their water connections by installing cutoff valves.

Allen and Roberson sued to have water service restored. After considering all the evidence, including testimony concerning the alleged oral agreement, the trial court permanently restrained High Knob from cutting off Allen's and Roberson's supply of water. High Knob appealed, asserting that testimony concerning the oral contract should be inadmissible under the parol evidence rule because it varied the terms of the written sales contracts.

I'anson, Justice

. . . It is universally accepted that parol or extrinsic evidence will be excluded when offered to add to, subtract from, vary, or contradict the terms of a written contract. But there are well-recognized exceptions to the rule. Where the entire agreement has not been reduced to writing, parol evidence is admissible, not to contradict or vary its terms, but to show additional independent facts contemporaneously agreed upon, in order to establish the entire contract between the parties. This is generally referred to as the partial integration doctrine. . . .

Another exception to the rule, which is similar in many respects to the partial integration doctrine, is the collateral contract doctrine. Under this doctrine the parol evidence rule does not exclude parol proof of a prior or contemporaneous oral agreement that is independent of, collateral to and not inconsistent with the written contract, and which would not ordinarily be expected to be embodied in the writing. . . .

In the present case, the written contracts for the sale of the lots were silent as to how Allen and Roberson were to obtain water for their homes. The covenants in the deeds forbidding them from drilling a well or in any other manner taking water from the ground for use in their dwellings, indicate that since [Allen and Roberson] were unable to take water from the ground there must of necessity have been some independent, collateral agreement for obtaining water. It is inconceivable that Allen and Roberson would covenant not to take water from the ground on their own property unless there had been an agreement to obtain it from another source. The written contracts dealt with the sale of property, and since there was to be an additional consideration paid for connecting to the water system, and this subject would not ordinarily be included in a contract for the sale of land, there is a strong indication that the parties were dealing with this question in collateral agreements. The oral agreements were not inconsistent with the written sales contracts and did not vary or contradict their terms. Even High Knob recognized that the question of furnishing water was to be covered in an independent collateral agreement when it submitted water service contracts to Allen and Roberson. Thus the evidence was admissible to prove the oral agreements, and did not violate the parol evidence rule. . . .

[Judgment affirmed.]

Complete Integration; Effect of Merger Clause. In many cases, the parties adopt a complete integration. If the writing is specific, detailed, comprehensive, and carefully drafted, the court may find that it evidences the final and complete expression of the agreement. Under the common law rule, a writing apparently complete on its face is presumed to be a complete integration in the absence of contrary evidence.

The parties sometimes explicitly indicate their intention that the writing operate as a complete integration by using a **merger** or **integration clause.** These clauses expressly state that the writing is the entire agreement of the parties, and that there are no understandings, promises, or representations except those contained therein. Merger clauses generally are enforceable and are used to prevent the court from finding that the writing is not a complete integration. The clause is especially useful when the parties are involved in extended negotiations, in which many proposals are made, altered, or withdrawn. When an agreement is finally reached and reduced to writing, a merger clause is included to prevent either party from offering evidence of prior proposals or negotiations to contradict the writing.

A merger clause provides strong evidence that the writing is a complete integration, but does not necessarily resolve the issue. All relevant evidence is considered, particularly when the clause is not the result of arm's length bargaining but is imposed by one party in a standardized form (adhesion) contract. For example, merger clauses in form contracts frequently disclaim liability for statements made by the seller's agents or employees not contained in the writing. The clause in this case is inserted to protect the seller against liability for unauthorized oral representations made by an overzealous salesperson. When used in consumer transactions, however, giving literal effect to the clause may defeat the reasonable expectations of the adhering party. For example, assume a salesperson makes representations or promises to a buyer to induce her to buy a product. When the buyer signs the seller's form contract to purchase, the representations are not included in the writing, which contains a merger clause. In these cases, the clause should be ineffective unless actually agreed upon.

Exceptions to the Parol Evidence Rule

Modern courts have adopted a fairly liberal attitude concerning the admissibility of parol evidence. Courts apparently believe that the risk in hearing such evidence—the possibility, for instance, that a contract or provision based upon perjured testimony will be enforced—is outweighed by a desire to enforce the entire agreement, including terms not stated in the writing. Further, as previously noted, the inapplicability of the rule does not dictate inclusion of any term, but merely affords a party the chance to prove its existence. Courts have therefore recognized several exceptions to the parol evidence rule, which, when combined with evidence admitted under principles of integration outlined above, substantially limit the actual effect of the rule. These exceptions are discussed next.

1. Parol evidence may be admitted to establish fraud, duress, undue influence, illegality, or any other factor undermining the validity of the integrated writing.

For example, if Seller and Buyer have a comprehensive written contract for the sale of land, Buyer may introduce evidence of a prior oral or written statement made by the seller that defrauded Buyer. In this case, Buyer is not trying to alter the terms of the written contract, but is attempting to show its voidable nature by virtue of fraud.

2. Parol evidence is admissible to show that the writing is subject to an oral condition. Assume a written contract requires Sam to convey land and Beth to pay the purchase price. Beth may introduce evidence that her duty was conditional upon her ability to obtain adequate mortgage financing, or subject to approval of an independent third party. In other words, evidence of the existence of the condition is not subject to the rule.

3. Parol evidence may always be admitted to clarify ambiguous terms in the integrated writing. Ambiguity may arise either from the language used in the writing or in its application to a particular fact situation. Assume Seller and Buyer have a contract for sale of goods to be manufactured by Seller. The parties have adopted a writing in which Buyer agrees to pay Seller's "total cost." Evidence of previous negotiations of the parties is admissible to determine the meaning of "total cost."

UCC Parol Evidence Rule—§2–202

The UCC retains the parol evidence rule for Code contracts. Section 2–202(a) provides that terms of a contract for the sale of goods

1. upon which the confirmatory memoranda of the parties agree, or
2. which are otherwise set forth in a writing intended by the parties as a final expression of their agreement with respect to the terms included in the writing,

may not be contradicted by evidence of any prior agreement or of a contemporaneous oral agreement. Under the Code, however, the contract terms may be *explained or supplemented* by (1) course of dealing, (2) usage of trade, or (3) course of performance.

A **course of dealing** is a sequence of conduct between the parties prior to the agreement establishing a common basis of understanding for interpreting their expressions and other conduct.[3] For example, previous contracts between the parties may establish a pattern of conduct useful in interpreting the disputed contract. A

---

[3]UCC §1–303(b); RESTATEMENT (SECOND) OF CONTRACTS §223.

usage of trade is any regularly observed practice or method of dealing in a trade, place, or location.[4] For example, in the lumber industry the description "2 by 4" means a board with dimensions approximately $1\frac{1}{2}$ inches by $3\frac{1}{2}$ inches, not 2 inches by 4 inches. The expression "2 by 4" is a usage of trade.

Course of performance is action taken by the parties pursuant to a contract involving repeated occasions for performance, such as an installment contract. In this situation, if either party has knowledge of the nature of the other's performance and an opportunity to object to it, any course of performance accepted without objection is relevant to determine the meaning of the agreement.[5]

Whenever possible in interpreting the contract, the court construes express terms as consistent with any course of performance, course of dealing, and usage of trade. If a conflict arises, however, and such a construction is unreasonable, the contract meaning is ascertained according to the following rules. The express terms control any course of performance. Course of performance controls both course of dealing and usage of trade. Course of dealing controls usage of trade.[6]

Under §2–202(b), evidence of *consistent additional terms* also is admissible to explain or to supplement the writing unless the court finds that the writing was intended by both parties to be a complete and exclusive statement of the terms of the agreement—a complete integration.[7]

The Statute of Frauds

One of the most important and frequently litigated contracts issues is the applicability of the **Statute of Frauds,** which simply requires that certain types of contracts be evidenced by a writing to be enforceable. The term "Statute of Frauds" originally was derived from the English or "common law" statute, but now generally is used to describe any statute imposing a writing requirement. Unless subject to some Statute of Frauds provision, a contract is enforceable without a writing.

The primary purpose of the Statute of Frauds is *evidentiary;* that is, "to require reliable evidence of the existence and terms of the contract, and to prevent enforcement through fraud or perjury of contracts never in fact made."[8] Certain Statute of Frauds provisions also perform a *cautionary* function; that is, the requirement of a writing provides additional protection to the promisor against enforcement of ill-considered, imprudent bargains. The statute also performs a *channeling* function, creating a climate in which the parties do not regard agreements as binding until put into writing and signed.

The original Statute of Frauds (formally entitled "An Act for the Prevention of Frauds and Perjuries"), usually referred to as the "common law" statute, originally was enacted in England in 1677.[9] The statute was passed when contract law was in its early developmental stages. In the fourteenth century, English courts began to enforce oral promises, commonly on the strength of oral testimony of witnesses. No distinct system of rules for excluding evidence, however, had yet been devised, and the power of courts to set aside jury verdicts contrary to the evidence was just beginning to be recognized. Further, neither the parties to the action nor persons having an interest in the outcome were competent to testify. These procedural deficiencies facilitated fraud through the use of perjured testimony to bind persons to oral promises never in fact made. To illustrate, assume Brown falsely asserts that Smith has agreed to sell his farm to Brown. Brown induces Doaks to perjure himself (known as "subornation" of perjury) by saying that he had witnessed Smith's oral promise to convey. On these facts, at early common law, Smith could not testify that he made no such promise. Nor could Brown be called to testify in an effort to expose the fraud upon cross-examination.

To prevent this result, the Statute of Frauds was enacted to provide that certain *types* of contracts were unenforceable "unless the agreement . . . or some memorandum or note thereof, shall be in writing, and signed by the party to be charged. . . ."[10] A contract subject to the Statute of Frauds writing requirement is said to be "within the statute." The types of contracts within the statute, discussed below, include:

1. suretyship contracts—promises to answer for the debt or duty of another;
2. contracts for the sale of land or interests in land; and
3. contracts that cannot be performed within one year.

---

[4]UCC §1–303(c); Restatement (Second) of Contracts §222.

[5]UCC §§1–303(a),(d).

[6]UCC §1–303(e). Restatement (Second) of Contracts §§202(5), 203(b).

[7]This rule is followed for common law contracts by the *Restatement (Second) of Contracts* §216.

[8]Restatement (Second) of Contracts §131 comment c.

[9]29 Car. 2, ch. 3(1677).

[10]Language of §4 of the original English statute.

Both parties need not sign the writing evidencing the contract, but the contract only is enforceable against a party who signs it. Thus, prior to a dispute, no one can determine which party's signature may be necessary. Each party, therefore, should be aware that it is the other party's signature that is important to enforceability. Assume S and B have a contract for the sale of land evidenced in a writing signed by S. B can enforce the contract against S, but S cannot enforce it against B.

The Statute of Frauds has been widely criticized as perpetrating far more fraud than it prevents. Even though the common law disability of a party to testify has long been removed, the statute has traditionally been interpreted as an absolute defense to enforceability. Under this approach, no matter how convincing the oral evidence may be, the contract is unenforceable if the statute's requirements are not met. Thus, parties have been able to avoid genuine bargains by hiding behind the statute, even while admitting the existence of the oral contract in court. The Statute of Frauds also has been criticized because the voluminous case law and numerous judge-made exceptions it has generated create uncertainty and unpredictability in the law. Further, a substantial amount of litigation has focused upon the sufficiency of the writing to the exclusion of the basic issue in dispute.

Though the original Statute of Frauds was repealed in England in 1954, statutes based upon it remain in effect in virtually all American jurisdictions. Further, additional writing requirements have been adopted, as indicated by the inclusion of several Statute of Frauds provisions in the UCC. Legislatures apparently continue to believe that writing requirements accomplish their desired purpose — to prevent the use of perjured testimony in contract cases. Additionally, because they create a climate in which written contracts are preferred, parties are induced, and therefore more likely, to put their deals in writing. The benefit derived from a writing in the vast bulk of cases in preventing misunderstanding and litigation may offset the occasional case in which the Statute of Frauds produces an unjust result. A writing requirement also seems to comport with the layperson's conception about the enforceability of important contracts; that is, agreement is tentative until put into writing and signed.

The Common Law Statute

Suretyship Contracts—Promises to Answer for the Debt or Duty of Another. In a suretyship contract, one party (the surety) promises another (the creditor) to pay a debt owing from a debtor (or principal) to the creditor, if the debtor does not. Under the Statute of Frauds, the promise by a surety to a creditor guaranteeing performance of a duty owed by a debtor to the creditor must be evidenced by a writing to be enforceable. Some states require that the writing state the consideration for the promise. Although the primary purpose of the Statute of Frauds is evidentiary, in suretyship contracts it also serves a cautionary function protecting the surety, who is commonly acting gratuitously and merely as a favor to the debtor, against ill-considered action.

A separate provision of the Statute of Frauds governs suretyship contracts made by executors or administrators. A promise by an executor or administrator of an estate to pay a debt of the deceased out of his own property is within the statute. This is merely a specialized application of the rule applicable to suretyship promises generally.

The Main Purpose Rule. The **main purpose** or **leading object rule** provides an exception to the general rule requiring a writing for suretyship promises. Under the main purpose rule, a surety's oral promise is enforceable if it is made to benefit the surety's personal economic interest, rather than to aid the debtor. When the surety guarantees a debt to advance his own economic or business interests, the gratuitous element often present in suretyship is eliminated, and the commercial setting ordinarily provides evidentiary safeguards. Thus, the cautionary and evidentiary protection of the statute is not required, rendering an oral promise enforceable.[11]

To illustrate, assume Shaw has a long-term contract with Bird to specially manufacture and deliver goods to Bird. Shaw encounters financial difficulty, resulting in a refusal by Shaw's suppliers to deliver additional raw materials. Bird, to ensure continued delivery from Shaw, orally promises the suppliers that if they will continue shipping to Shaw, Bird will pay if Shaw fails to do so. Bird's promise is not required to be evidenced by a writing because its primary purpose is to benefit Bird, not to accommodate Shaw. In this case, most courts would hold Bird's oral promise enforceable whether it related to past or future deliveries or both.

Assume, however, on these same facts that Shaw believes that with a little time she can extricate herself from her financial difficulties. Several of her creditors,

---

[11]RESTATEMENT (SECOND) OF CONTRACTS §116 comment a.

however, are threatening legal proceedings that would force a closure of her business. Frost, a friend of Shaw, learns of her precarious financial position. In an effort to prevent Shaw's financial ruin, Frost promises the creditors that if they will postpone legal action for three months, he will pay Shaw's debts to them, if Shaw fails to do so. Frost's promise must be evidenced in writing because the consideration received for his promise (the forbearance to sue) primarily benefited Shaw. That is, the promise was made as an accommodation to Shaw; its purpose was not to further Frost's economic or business interests. In short, for the rule to apply, the circumstances must justify a conclusion that the surety's primary motive in making the promise is to advance his own interests.

The following case illustrates the application of the main purpose rule.

Graybar Electric Co. v. Sawyer
485 A.2d 1384 (Me. 1985)

Pine Tree Electrical Company, Inc. (Pine Tree), an electrical contracting firm, purchased supplies from Graybar Electric Co. (Graybar). In 1980, Hollis Sawyer invested $100,000 in Pine Tree and subsequently became vice president of the company. Later that year, Graybar cut off credit to Pine Tree because it was delinquent in paying its account. In September, Sawyer met with Graybar's finance manager and told him that if Pine Tree failed to pay its account, Sawyer would arrange to have it paid. Sawyer also provided a list of telephone numbers where he could be reached if problems arose. Graybar then wrote Sawyer a letter — which he denied having received — that stated, "Based on your willingness to have us contact you directly and your personal guarantee of payment, we will be happy to continue shipments to Pine Tree Electric." In June 1981, Pine Tree went bankrupt.

Graybar sued Sawyer for payment of Pine Tree's account. The jury found that Sawyer had agreed to guarantee the Pine Tree account and held him liable. Sawyer appealed, alleging that Graybar's suit was barred by Maine's Statute of Frauds, which requires a signed writing in a case against a person who has promised to answer for the debt of another.

McKusick, Chief Justice

. . . [T]he Statute of Frauds has . . . long been subject to an exception in a case where the promisor's main purpose in making his promise is to secure some benefit for himself. . . .

The benefit that a promisor must expect to receive under the main purpose rule in order to be held to his promise must be substantial, immediate, and pecuniary, though it may flow to the promisor through benefit to the principal obligor. . . . That is, although the promisor need not receive cash in hand from the promisee, the path of benefits flowing to the promisor must not be so circuitous or uncertain that obtaining those benefits cannot be said to have been his main purpose in making the promise. As a matter of practicality, the promisor's advantage must be served in a straightforward way in order for the main purpose rule to apply. . . .

The evidence before the jury amply supports its finding, under the instructions, that Sawyer intended by his promise to procure an immediate and substantial benefit flowing directly to himself. Sawyer had outstanding loans to Pine Tree of almost $300,000. He admitted in testimony that he needed to keep the business going in order to be paid back. The activities he undertook to get the business back on its feet financially were extensive. He followed upon his initial loan of $100,000 by lending Pine Tree further larger sums of money with the obvious purpose of keeping jobs going. . . . He guaranteed letters of credit necessary for Pine Tree to obtain two other jobs. He elected himself vice president, and had an active hand in rejecting jobs and meeting with suppliers, and he maintained his involvement even while he was in Florida for substantial periods of time. He received interest on his loans to Pine Tree through the fall and winter of 1980 and the spring of 1981. He also received $18,000 in April of 1981 in partial repayment of the principal amount of the loans. He testified at length about his desire to increase Pine Tree's profitability so that he could be paid back. . . . Sawyer also stood to benefit in his capacity as sole preferred stockholder from any increase in the net worth of the company and from the quarterly dividends that Pine Tree was required to pay to him.

In view of the necessity of maintaining the flow of supplies to Pine Tree in order to keep the business going, and the necessity of its staying in business if Sawyer was to be repaid, the jury could reasonably find that Sawyer's oral promise, given to avoid serious difficulties for Pine Tree, was intended to confer on him a direct and substantial benefit. . . .

[T]he present case . . . falls within the accepted ambit of the main purpose doctrine.

[Judgment affirmed.]

Contracts for the Sale of Land or Interests in Land. A contract to buy or sell any interest in real property must be evidenced by a writing to be enforceable. Therefore, agreements to transfer fee simple title as well as more limited interests such as mortgages, easements, and leases are within the Statute of Frauds. Contracts creating other present or future interests such as life estates or remainders also are covered. Most Statutes of Frauds, however, exempt oral leases with a term of less than one year from the writing requirement. Some states enforce oral leases for longer terms, while others do not recognize an exception for short-term leases. The Statute of Frauds applies to any executory promise to buy or sell interests in real property regardless of the nature of the consideration exchanged—for example, money, personal property, services, or other real estate.

The "Part Performance" Doctrine. The **part performance doctrine,** which is based upon estoppel principles, provides an exception to the writing requirement for land sale contracts. For the doctrine to apply, the party seeking enforcement must show that he or she has changed position in reasonable reliance upon the oral contract. If necessary to avoid injustice, the court, exercising its equitable powers, will order performance of the contract.

The doctrine is usually applied when a seller of property refuses to convey it after the buyer has substantially relied upon an oral contract to sell that exists between the parties. The buyer's reliance may take several forms including, for example: (1) payment of part or all of the purchase price, (2) taking possession of the property, and (3) making valuable improvements to the property. Generally, payment of the purchase price alone is insufficient, because returning the payment to the buyer in these cases is often an adequate remedy. Return of the price may, however, be inadequate because of an additional change in position by the buyer. Ordinarily, some combination of payment, possession, and improvements brings the doctrine into play. Assume S and B enter into an oral contract for sale of a tract of land owned by S. S. allows B to take possession of the property, who pays part of the purchase price and constructs a house on the land. Two years later a dispute arises over the amount still owing and S repudiates the contract. Upon suit by B, the court may enforce the oral contract by ordering S to convey the land to B.

The following case illustrates the application of the part performance doctrine.

Sullivan v. Porter
861 A. 2d 625 (Me. 2004)

In 1999, plaintiff Joan Sullivan began managing a horse stable located on property owned by defendants Merval and Susan Porter in Bar Harbor, Maine. In August 2000, the Porters, after telling Sullivan that they planned to move, offered to sell their property to Sullivan and plaintiff David Andrews. Sullivan and Andrews orally accepted the offer and the parties agreed to the general terms of sale including a purchase price of $350,000, financing provided by the sellers at an interest rate between five and seven percent for a period of 20–30 years, and a down payment of $20,000. Porter told Sullivan and Andrews that he would have his attorney prepare the paperwork. When the Porters moved in September 2000, they gave the keys to Sullivan and Andrews. In November 2000, Merval Porter returned to the property with a real estate agent. After explaining that someone had expressed an interest in buying the property, Merval told Sullivan that the Porters intended to honor their agreement with her and Andrews. The following day, Sullivan tried to give the Porters $10,000 in partial payment of the down payment but they would accept only $3,000 until the paperwork was completed. During the months that followed, Sullivan and Andrews began renovation of the property and continued operation of their business. In July 2001, the Porters offered to sell the property to Sullivan and Andrews for $450,000 with a $50,000 down payment.

Sullivan and Andrews sued the Porters requesting enforcement of the oral agreement made in August 2000. The Porters argued that the oral agreement was unenforceable because the Maine statute of frauds required land contracts to be in writing. After a jury found that the parties had made an oral agreement that had been performed in part by Sullivan and Andrews, the court ordered the Porters to perform the August 2000 agreement. The Porters appealed.

Saufley, Chief Judge

. . . We begin with the axiom that, absent extraordinary circumstances, a contract for the sale of land must be in writing to be enforceable. . . . A transfer of real property without a written instrument may be enforced only if the party seeking to enforce the contract proves by clear and convincing evidence that an oral contract exists and that an exception to the statute of frauds applies. . . . One exception to the statute of frauds is found in the part performance doctrine. . . .

The part performance doctrine requires the party seeking to enforce the contract to establish both that she acted in partial performance of her contractual duties and that the other party made misrepresentations that induced that partial performance. . . . Thus, to remove the contract from the operation of the statute of frauds pursuant to this doctrine, the party seeking to enforce the contract must establish by clear and convincing evidence (1) that the parties did enter into a contract; (2) that the party seeking to enforce the contract partially performed the contract; and (3) that the performance was induced by the other party's misrepresentations, which may include acquiescence or silence. . . .

1. Existence of a Contract

Because any action to enforce a contract depends on the existence of the contract itself, we begin by addressing the Porters' argument that there was insufficient evidence for the jury to find the existence of a contract for the sale of their farm to Sullivan and Andrews. . . .

A review of the record supports the jury's findings that there was a meeting of the minds between the Porters and Sullivan and Andrews. The parties' agreement in August 2000 embodied the essential material terms for a contract to sell the farm, including the identification of the property, the parties to the sale, the purchase price, the amount of the down payment, and the type of financing. . . . Specifically, the parties agreed to the essential elements of a contract by identifying: (1) the property to be sold as "Lakewood Farm"; (2) the parties to the transaction, the Porters as the sellers and Sullivan and Andrews as the buyers; (3) the purchase price of $350,000; (4) the $20,000 down payment; and (5) the arrangement for owner financing. The parties also established within a finite range the term of the mortgage (twenty to thirty years) and the interest rate (five to seven percent). Although the rate and duration of the loan were expressed within a range, this is not unusual in a purchase and sale agreement and did not create an unaddressed element. . . . This evidence was sufficient for the jury to determine the existence of a contract and to fix the legal liabilities of the parties. . . .

2. Part Performance

In addition to arguing that there was insufficient evidence to support the existence of the contract, the Porters also argue that Sullivan and Andrews failed to prove part performance. The part performance doctrine is grounded in the principle of equitable estoppel. . . . Equitable estoppel, also referred to as estoppel in pais, "involves misrepresentations, including misleading statements, conduct, or silence, that induce detrimental reliance." [*Cottle Enterprises, Inc. v. Town of Farmington,* 693 A.2d 330, 335-36 (Maine 1997).] "After having induced or knowingly permitted another to perform in part an agreement, on the faith of its full performance by both parties and for which he could not well be compensated except by specific performance, the other shall not insist that the agreement is void." *Woodbury v. Gardner,* [77 Me. 68, 70 (Me. 1885)]. . . . Accordingly, the party asserting partial performance must demonstrate not only meaningful partial performance, but also the other party's inducement of that performance through misrepresentation.

a. Proof of Performance

Sullivan and Andrews took possession of the farm in September 2000 with the understanding that Merval would begin the necessary paperwork to effectuate the sale of the farm. Sullivan and Andrews made extensive repairs to the farmhouse, stables, and grounds . . . which included removing four tons of horsehair plaster from the walls and replacing it with insulation and sheetrock, rewiring the electricity, installing new plumbing, erecting new fencing, and removing trash. They also started their new business, joined the chamber of commerce, repaired horse trails, began giving riding lessons and rehabilitating horses, placed advertisements in the local newspaper, and paid for an appraisal of the property. During the renovation process, Merval visited the property regularly and received updates about the renovations. . . . They also offered $10,000 toward the down payment, $3,000 of which the Porters actually accepted, and devoted time and money to their new business on the property. This evidence supports a conclusion that Sullivan and Andrews partially performed their contractual obligations.

b. Proof of Inducement by Misrepresentation

The evidence also supports the finding that the Porters induced Sullivan and Andrews's partial performance by misrepresentation. The Porters relinquished possession of the farm to Sullivan and Andrews. They remained silent upon learning that Sullivan and Andrews planned to refinance their home to obtain the funds for the agreed upon down payment. After accepting $3,000 as a partial down payment for the farm, the Porters remained silent while they observed Sullivan and Andrews beginning extensive renovations and building their business on the property. Merval also repeatedly represented that he was having his lawyer draw up the paperwork for the sale of the farm. Taken collectively, the Porters' actions and silent acquiescence resulted in a misrepresentation that induced Sullivan and Andrews to partially perform their contractual obligations in faith that the Porters were going to perform the contract.

In sum, the evidence supports the findings that (1) the Porters entered into a contract with Sullivan and Andrews to sell the farm; (2) Sullivan and Andrews partially performed their duties under the contract; and (3) the Porters made misrepresentations through their actions and omissions that induced Sullivan and Andrews's partial performance. We therefore affirm the court's finding, consistent with the jury's advisory finding on the issue, that the parties' oral contract for the sale of land was removed from the statute of frauds based on the part performance doctrine. . . .

[Judgment affirmed.]

Contracts That Cannot Be Performed Within One Year.

The Statute of Frauds also applies to "any agreement that is not to be performed within the space of one year from the making thereof."[12] To determine whether or not a contract falls within this "one-year provision," three questions must be answered: (1) When does the one-year period commence? (2) Is the contract one that *cannot* be performed within that period? and (3) Has one party to the contract completed his performance? The answers to these questions are discussed in the following paragraphs.

Commencement of the One-Year Period. Regarding the first question, the one-year period begins to run from the date the contract is made—when the offer is accepted—not the date on which performance is to begin. Assume A and B enter into a contract on January 1. Performance is to begin on February 1 and continue for one year from that date. The contract must be evidenced by a writing to be enforceable because the one-year period runs from January 1, not February 1. Similarly, a contract entered into on June 1, 2000, calling for performance from June 9 to June 10, 2001, must be evidenced by a writing.[13] The completion date, not the duration of performance, is relevant.

Oral leases provide an exception to the rule that the one-year period runs from the date of the contract. As previously noted, in most states an oral lease is enforceable if the term is shorter than one year. In these cases, the one-year period generally runs from the date the term begins, not the date of the agreement. For example, on June 1, L orally agrees to lease certain premises to T for one year commencing July 1. The agreement need not be in writing to be enforceable because the one-year period runs from July 1.

Possibility of Performance Within One Year. To be within the statute, the contract *by its terms* must be incapable of performance within one year. Therefore, if there is any possibility that the contract can be performed within a year of its making, it is not subject to the Statute of Frauds even though the actual performance takes more than one year. Typical illustrations include contracts calling for performance "on or before," "within," or "not later than" a certain date. For example, if S agrees to paint B's house within 13 months, no writing is necessary because, on the date of the contract, there was a possibility of performance within one year. In determining the applicability of the statute, subsequent actual performance is not considered.

The following case discusses the rationale for this principle.

C. R. Klewin, Inc. v. Flagship Properties, Inc.
600 A.2d 772 (Conn. 1991)

Plaintiff C. R. Klewin, Inc. applied to serve as construction manager of a $120 million project, developed by defendant Flagship Properties, Inc., involving construction of 20 industrial buildings, a 280-room hotel and convention center, and housing for 592 graduate students and faculty near the University of Connecticut. Following a meeting in March 1986 to discuss the project, Flagship's representative shook hands with Klewin's agent and stated, "You've got the job. We've got a deal." Klewin began construction of the first phase in May 1987. By October, Flagship was dissatisfied with Klewin's work and in March 1988, Flagship retained another contractor to complete the next phase of the project.

Klewin sued Flagship for breach of contract in federal district court. Flagship argued that their oral agreement was not enforceable because it violated the Connecticut Statute of Frauds. Although the parties had not specified the term of the project in their agreement, the court ruled in favor of Flagship finding that the project "as a matter of

---

[12]Language of §4 of the original English statute.

[13]The one-year period ends at midnight on the anniversary of the day on which the contract was made. For example, a contract entered into on December 1, 2006, requires a writing if it cannot be performed by midnight of December 1, 2007.

law could not possibly have been performed within one year." Klewin appealed to the Second Circuit Court of Appeals, which requested that the Supreme Court of Connecticut issue a ruling of law interpreting the Connecticut Statute of Frauds.

Peters, Chief Justice

. . . The Connecticut statute of frauds has its origins in a 1677 English statute entitled "An Act for the prevention of Fraud and Perjuries." . . . Although the British Parliament repealed most provisions of the statute, including the one-year provision, in 1954, . . . the statute nonetheless remains the law virtually everywhere in the United States.

Modern scholarly commentary has found much to criticize about the continued viability of the statute of frauds. . . . It is, however, the one-year provision that is at issue in this case that has caused the greatest puzzlement among commentators. As Professor Farnsworth observes, "of all the provisions of the statute, it is the most difficult to rationalize.

"If the one-year provision is based on the tendency of memory to fail and of evidence to go stale with the passage of time, it is ill-contrived because the one-year period does not run from the making of the contract to the proof of the making, but from the making of the contract to the completion of performance. If an oral contract that cannot be performed within a year is broken the day after its making, the provision applies though the terms of the contract are fresh in the minds of the parties. But if an oral contract that can be performed within a year is broken and suit is not brought until nearly six years (the usual statute of limitations for contract actions) after the breach, the provision does not apply, even though the terms of the contract are no longer fresh in the minds of the parties. . . ." 2 E. Farnsworth, Contracts (2d Ed. 1990) §6.4. . . .

In any case, the one-year provision no longer seems to serve any purpose very well, and today its only remaining effect is arbitrarily to forestall the adjudication of possibly meritorious claims. For this reason, the courts have for many years looked on the provision with disfavor, and have sought constructions that limited its application. . . .

Our case law in Connecticut, like that in other jurisdictions, has taken a narrow view of the one-year provision of the statute of frauds. . . . In *Russell v. Slade,* 12 Conn. 455, 460 (1838), this court held that "it has been repeatedly adjudged, that unless it appear *from the agreement itself,* that it is *not* to be performed within a

year, the statute does not apply. . . . The statute of frauds plainly means an agreement *not* to be performed within the space of a year, and *expressly* and *specifically* so agreed." . . .

More recently, in *Finley v. Aetna Life & Casualty Co.,* [520 A.2d 208 (Conn. 1987)], we stated that "[u]nder the prevailing interpretation, the enforceability of a contract under the one year provision does not turn on the actual course of subsequent events, nor on the expectations of the parties as to the probabilities. Contracts of uncertain duration are simply excluded; the provision covers *only* those contracts whose performance *cannot possibly* be completed within a year." (Emphasis added.) 1 Restatement (Second), Contracts. . . .

In light of this unbroken line of authority, the legislature's decision repeatedly to reenact the provision in language virtually identical to that of the 1677 statute suggests legislative approval of the restrictive interpretation that this court has given to the one-year provision. . . .

Our case law makes no distinction, with respect to exclusion from the statute of frauds, between contracts of uncertain or indefinite duration and contracts that contain no express terms defining the time for performance. . . . [The] issue can be framed as follows: in the exclusion from the statute of frauds of all contracts except those "whose performance cannot possibly be completed within a year"; . . . what meaning should be attributed to the word "possibly"? One construction of "possibly" would encompass only contracts whose completion within a year would be inconsistent with the express terms of the contract. An alternate construction would include as well contracts such as the one involved in this case, in which, while no time period is expressly specified, it is (as the district court found) realistically impossible for performance to be completed within a year. We now hold that the former and not the latter is the correct interpretation. . . .

We therefore hold that an oral contract that does not say, in express terms, that performance is to have a specific duration beyond one year is, as a matter of law, the functional equivalent of a contract of indefinite duration for the purposes of the statute of frauds. Like a contract of indefinite duration, such a contract is enforceable because it is outside the proscriptive force of the statute regardless of how long completion of performance will actually take. . . .

Effect of Performance. If one party has fully performed, the one-year provision does not prevent enforcement of the remaining promises. The rule is applicable to contracts fully performed on one side when the contract is made, such as a loan of money. It also applies to any other contract fully performed on one side subsequent to its making, even if that performance takes longer than one year. If, however, either party's performance cannot be completed within a year, statute applies to all promises in the contract, including those that can or are required to be performed within a year.[14] Suppose a creditor loans money to a debtor to be repaid in installments extending beyond one year. The debtor's promise is enforceable even if not evidenced by a writing because the creditor has fully performed. Or, assume Seller and Buyer enter into an oral agreement on July 1, 2000. In exchange for Seller's promise to deliver goods on September 1, 2000, Buyer promises to pay the purchase price in three equal installments payable on January 1, 2001, July 1, 2001 and January 1, 2002. Until Seller performs, the contract is not enforceable against either Seller or Buyer because Buyer's promise cannot be performed within one year. This is true even if, as here, Seller's promise can be (in fact is required to be) performed within one year. Once Seller performs, however, Buyer's promises become enforceable even though oral.

Finally, it is important to note that the one-year provision applies independently of other Statute of Frauds requirements. For example, assume Seller and Buyer orally contract for the sale of land to be performed in two years. The requirements of both the land sale and one-year provisions of the statute must be fulfilled.

Uniform Commercial Code Statute — Goods (§2 – 201)

Rather than classifying contracts according to types, as in the common law statute, the UCC adopts a minimum dollar limitation with respect to contracts for the sale of goods. Section 2 – 201(1) provides that a contract for the sale of goods for the price of $500 or more is not enforceable unless there is some writing sufficient to indicate that a contract for sale has been made between the parties, stating a quantity term, which is signed by the party to be charged or his authorized agent.

Exceptions to the Writing Requirement Under the Code. The Code recognizes four major exceptions to the writing requirements outlined above.

Part Performance — §2 – 201(3)(c). Under UCC §2 – 201(3)(c), an oral contract for the sale of goods subject to the Statute of Frauds is nevertheless enforceable with respect to goods:

1. for which payment has been made (by the buyer) and accepted (by the seller), or
2. which have been received and accepted (by the buyer).

Part performance by the buyer requires delivery of something to the seller, accepted by him as a partial performance. Thus, the buyer's part performance may consist of money, a check, services, or property that has been delivered to and accepted by the seller. In the case of the buyer, "receipt" means taking physical possession of the goods.[15] "Acceptance" is the buyer's indication of her intention to keep them, which may be made expressly, by silence, or other conduct.[16] The "part performance" exception is based upon the premise that the evidentiary function of the Statute of Frauds is satisfied by the conduct of the parties.

To illustrate the operation of this provision, assume Stein and Barth have an oral contract for the sale of auto parts for $2,000. Stein delivers parts worth $500 to Barth, and Barth accepts the goods; or alternatively, Barth makes a part payment of $500, which is accepted by Stein. In either case, to the extent of the partial performance, the contract is enforceable, even though otherwise required to be evidenced by a writing under §2 – 201(1). In this example, with respect to the $500 already paid or delivered, neither party can assert Statute of Frauds as a defense.

Note that part performance serves as a substitute for a writing only to the extent that payment has been made and accepted or the goods have been received and accepted. That is, part performance does not take the entire contract out of the statute. Thus, in the previous example, either party may rely upon the statute as a defense to enforcement of the remaining $1,500 of the contract. This is true even if the remaining portion is less than $500. Whether or not a writing is required is determined by reference to the original amount, in this case $2,000.

---

[14]Restatement (Second) of Contracts §130 comment d.

[15]UCC §2 – 103(1)(c).
[16]UCC §2 – 606.

This rule prevents one party from using a small *executed* oral contract to take his *fraudulent* assertion that a larger contract exists out of the Statute of Frauds. To illustrate, using the preceding example, assume Stein and Barth actually have an oral contract for $500 that has been performed. However, because the price is particularly advantageous to Barth, she fraudulently asserts that the actual agreement was $2,000, not merely $500. On these facts, the Code protects Stein by allowing him to assert the Statute of Frauds as a defense to enforcement of the fraudulently alleged contract.

Merchants' Exception—§2–201(2). Section 2–201(2) provides a special rule applicable when both parties to the contract are merchants, and one sends a writing in confirmation of the contract to the other satisfying the Statute of Frauds against the sending merchant. In this case, the confirmation satisfies the statute against the receiving merchant, unless he gives written notice of objection to its contents within ten days after receipt of the confirmation. Note that §2–201(2) is not really an exception to the writing requirement, but is instead an exception to the general rule that the writing is only enforceable against the person who signs it. If §2–201(2) applies, the Statute of Frauds is nevertheless also satisfied against the nonsigning merchant. Note that both parties must be merchants and the writing in confirmation of the contract must be sufficient to bind the sender; that is, it must be signed and state the quantity term. Further, the confirmation must be received within a reasonable time after the contract is made and written notice of objection must be given within ten days after receipt. Notice of objection is effective as long as it is sent, even though not received, within ten days after receipt of the confirmation.

Section 2–201(2) is designed to prevent a type of fraud that can occur when two merchants make an oral contract over the phone. Suppose Seller and Buyer in a telephone conversation enter into a contract for sale of goods for $1,000, calling for delivery in 30 days. Seller then sends Buyer a signed written confirmation restating the terms of the agreement. Under traditional Statute of Frauds rules, the memorandum is sufficient against Seller, but not Buyer, because only Seller has signed. Because Seller is bound and Buyer is not, Buyer can back out of the contract if the market price falls below the contract price on the date of delivery, but may hold Seller liable if the market price rises. To prevent this type of speculation, the Code provides that the statute is satisfied against the nonsigning merchant as well unless he gives timely notice of objection after receiving the confirmation. The rule also encourages sending written confirmations by eliminating the obvious disadvantage to the sender. Additionally, it protects the rights of both parties without requiring a second signed writing—that is, signed by Buyer.

Specially Manufactured Goods—§2–201(3)(a). Under §2–201(3)(a), an oral contract for sale of goods to be **specially manufactured** for the buyer and not suitable for sale to others in the ordinary course of the seller's business is enforceable regardless of dollar amount. This rule applies, however, only if the seller, before repudiation by the buyer, has changed her position in reliance on the contract. Reliance is shown if the seller substantially begins manufacture or makes commitments to obtain the goods under circumstances reasonably indicating that the goods are for the buyer. Therefore, the seller need not be the manufacturer to be protected by this provision.

Admission in Pleading, Testimony, or Otherwise in Court—§2–201(3)(b). As discussed previously, a major criticism of the common law statute was the injustice caused when a person asserted the statute as a defense to enforcement, even while admitting the existence of the oral contract in court. The Code prevents this result in §2–201(3)(b) by denying the Statute of Frauds as a defense to a party who admits in his *pleading, testimony, or otherwise in court* that a contract for sale was made. If an admission is made, however, the contract is not enforceable beyond the *quantity* of goods admitted.

Therefore, under the Code, the Statute of Frauds may be used as a defense only if the defendant denies the existence of the contract. If she admits its existence, either voluntarily or inadvertently—for example, in his pleadings or testimony—or involuntarily—while being cross-examined by the other party—the evidentiary function of the statute is met.

§2–201—*Exclusive Versus Cumulative Application.*
In some cases, a contract for the sale of goods will, by its terms, require performance extending beyond one year. In such cases, courts often have been required to determine whether §2–201 alone is the appropriate Statute of Frauds provision, or whether in addition the contract must comply with the requirements of the common law statute's one-year provision. The issue is important because §2–201 contains exceptions to its application not found in the common law statute and, as

developed later in this chapter, has more liberal requirements regarding the sufficiency of the writing. Unfortunately, courts are split on the issue, some holding that §2–201 alone controls, and others requiring compliance with both statutes. Accordingly, parties to long-term contracts for the sale of goods should make sure that their contract is evidenced by a writing that satisfies both Statute of Frauds provisions.

Other Statutes of Frauds

A security interest is an interest in personal property (the collateral) created to secure payment or performance of an obligation, usually the repayment of a money debt. Security interests in personal property are governed by Article 9 of the UCC. Under §9–203(b), an agreement that creates or provides for a security interest (a security agreement) must be in a record to be enforceable against the debtor or third parties. A "record" includes both traditional writings discussed in the next section, and information stored in an electronic or other medium that can be retrieved in perceivable form. The agreement must contain a description of the collateral and be signed (or "authenticated" in the case of an electronic record) by the debtor. However, no record is required if, under the terms of the agreement, the secured party takes possession of the collateral.

In addition to those previously discussed, most states impose several additional Statute of Frauds requirements. Some common examples include promises to pay debts barred by the statute of limitations, to pay a commission to a real estate broker, to make a testamentary disposition (that is, in a will), or to pay a debt contracted in infancy.

Sufficiency of the Writing

The primary purpose of the Statute of Frauds is evidentiary—to provide reliable evidence of the existence of a contract and prevent enforcement of fraudulently asserted contracts. The memorandum (writing) required by the Statute of Frauds need not satisfy rigorous formal standards. It must simply indicate that a contract has been made between the parties (or offered by the signer to the other party), state certain minimum terms, and be signed by the party to be bound—the defendant in the contract action. Generally, for contracts subject to the "common law" statute, the memorandum must (1) iden-

tify the parties, (2) reasonably identify the subject matter, and (3) state the essential terms of the unperformed promises of the contract with reasonable certainty.[17]

The writing need not be made as a memorandum of a contract. Generally, any writing, formal or informal, is sufficient provided it meets the requirements stated above. A **writing** for purposes of the Statute of Frauds includes handwriting, printing, typewriting, or any other intentional reduction to tangible form.[18] The writing may be made or signed at any time before or after contract formation. Therefore, the Statute of Frauds may be satisfied in a will, a notation on a check, a newspaper advertisement, a receipt, an informal letter, an entry in a diary, or the minutes of a meeting. Additionally, a signed, written offer, communicated by the offeror to the offeree, and subsequently accepted orally, is sufficient to bind the offeror. A writing that has been lost or destroyed may still satisfy the statute provided its existence and terms can be proven—for example, by an unsigned copy or oral evidence.

The statute also may be satisfied in a series of documents, even though no individual writing, by itself, would be sufficient. In this case, at least one writing must be signed, and all writings taken collectively must clearly indicate that they are part of the same transaction.

In the following case, the court was required to decide whether a series of related writings constituted a sufficient memorandum under the Statute of Frauds.

Crabtree v. Elizabeth Arden Sales Corp.
110 N.E.2d 551 (N.Y. 1953)

Plaintiff Nate Crabtree sued defendant Elizabeth Arden Sales Corp., a cosmetics company, for breach of contract. The evidence adduced at trial established that in 1947 the company began negotiations to hire Crabtree as sales manager. He requested a three-year contract at $25,000 per year because he would be giving up a secure position and believed the new position might require several years to master. After further negotiations, Elizabeth Arden, the president of Elizabeth Arden Sales Corp., offered Crabtree

---

[17]RESTATEMENT (SECOND) OF CONTRACTS §131.
[18]UCC §1–201(b)(43). The same definition applies when used elsewhere in this text, particularly in the negotiable instruments material (Chapters 21–27).

a two-year contract on terms that were summarized in the following writing prepared by Arden's personal secretary:

EMPLOYMENT AGREEMENT WITH NATE CRABTREE
Date Sept. 26, 1947
At 681 — 5th Ave   6: PM

Begin 20000.
6 months 25000.
6 months 30000.

5000. per year expense money
[2 years to make good]
Arrangement with Mr. Crabtree by Miss Arden
Present Miss Arden
    Mr. Johns
    Mr. Crabtree
    Miss O'Leary

The memorandum was not signed by any of the parties.

Several days later Crabtree telephoned Robert P. Johns, the vice president and general manager of the company, and telegraphed Arden to accept the position. When Crabtree began employment, a payroll card was made up, initialed by Johns and sent to the payroll department. The card recited that it had been prepared on September 30, 1947, was to be effective as of October 22, listed Crabtree's job classification, and contained the following notation:

This employee is to be paid as follows:

First six months of employment $20,000. per annum

Next six months of employment 25,000. per annum

After one year of employment 30,000. per annum

Approved by RPJ [initialed]

After six months of employment, Crabtree's salary was increased from $20,000 to $25,000. When Crabtree did not receive an increase at the end of a year, he discussed the issue with Johns and the comptroller. The comptroller prepared and signed a payroll change card that stated there was to be a "salary increase from $25,000 to $30,000 per contractual agreement with Miss Arden." Arden, however, refused to authorize the increase, and after further fruitless discussion, Crabtree left Arden's employ and commenced an action for breach of contract.

At the trial, Elizabeth Arden Sales Corp. denied the existence of an agreement to employ Crabtree for two years. The company further alleged that if there had been an agreement, the Statute of Frauds barred its enforcement because it had not been reduced to a written contract. The trial court ruled in favor of Crabtree and awarded $14,000 in damages. Elizabeth Arden Sales Corp. appealed.

Fuld, Judge

. . . Since the contract relied upon was not to be performed within a year, the primary question for decision is whether there was a memorandum of its terms, subscribed by defendant, to satisfy the statute of frauds. . . .

The statute of frauds does not require the "memorandum . . . to be in one document. It may be pieced together out of separate writings, connected with one another either expressly or by the internal evidence of subject-matter and occasion." [*Marks v. Cowdin,* 123 N.E. 139, 141 (N.Y. 1919)]. . . . Where each of the separate writings has been subscribed by the party to be charged, little if any difficulty is encountered. . . . Where, however, some writings have been signed, and others have not — as in the case before us . . . this court has on a number of occasions approved the rule, and we now definitively adopt it, permitting the signed and unsigned writings to be read together, provided that they clearly refer to the same subject matter or transaction. . . .

The [Statute of Frauds] . . . does not impose the requirement that the signed acknowledgment of the contract must appear from the writings alone, unaided by oral testimony. The danger of fraud and perjury, generally attendant upon the admission of parol evidence, is at a minimum in a case such as this. None of the terms of the contract are supplied by parol. All of them must be set out in the various writings presented to the court, and at least one writing, the one establishing a contractual relationship between the parties, must bear the signature of the party to be charged, while the unsigned document must on its face refer to the same transaction as that set forth in the one that was signed. Parol evidence — to portray the circumstances surrounding the making of the memorandum — serves only to connect the separate documents and to show that there was assent, by the party to be charged, to the contents of the one unsigned. If that testimony does not convincingly connect the papers, or does not show assent to the unsigned paper, it is within the province of the judge to conclude, as a matter of law, that the statute has not been satisfied. True, the possibility still remains that, by fraud or perjury, an agreement never in fact made may occasionally be enforced under the subject matter or transaction test. It is better to run that risk, though, than to deny enforcement to all agreements, merely because the signed document made no specific mention of the unsigned writing. . . .

Turning to the writings in the case before us—the unsigned office memo, the payroll change form initialed by the general manager Johns, and the paper signed by the comptroller Carstens—it is apparent, and most patently, that all three refer on their face to the same transaction. The parties, the position to be filled by plaintiff, the salary to be paid him, are all identically set forth; it is hardly possible that such detailed information could refer to another or a different agreement. . . . Under such circumstances, the courts below were fully justified in finding that the three papers constituted the "memorandum" of their agreement within the meaning of the statute.

Nor can there be any doubt that the memorandum contains all of the essential terms of the contract. . . . Only one term, the length of the employment, is in dispute. The September 26th office memorandum contains the notation, "2 years to make good." What purpose, other than to denote the length of the contract term, such a notation could have, is hard to imagine. . . . Quite obviously, as the courts below decided, the phrase signifies that the parties agreed to a term, a certain and definite term, of two years, after which, if plaintiff did not "make good", he would be subject to discharge. And examination of other parts of the memorandum supports that construction. . . . Having in mind the relations of the parties, the course of the negotiations and plaintiff's insistence upon security of employment, the purpose of the phrase—or so the trier of the facts was warranted in finding—was to grant plaintiff the tenure he desired.

[Judgment affirmed.]

Sufficiency Under the UCC. As previously noted, the Statute of Frauds is often criticized for perpetrating far more fraud than it prevents. One reason for this criticism is the requirement imposed by the common law statute that the writing contain all material terms of the contract. As a result, a substantial amount of litigation under the statute has focused upon the sufficiency of the writing, even when the existence of the underlying contract was not in dispute. The UCC attempts to correct this problem by providing less rigorous requirements for the sufficiency of the writing for contracts for the sale of goods.

Under the Code, the writing is sufficient even though it omits or incorrectly states any agreed term. The con-

tract is not enforceable, however, beyond the *quantity* of goods shown in the writing. Therefore, only three definite and invariable requirements regarding the sufficiency of the memorandum are imposed by §2–201: (1) the writing must evidence a contract for the sale of goods; (2) it must be signed by the party to be charged; and (3) it must specify a quantity term. If the price is payable in goods rather than money, the quantity of goods must be stated.

Beyond these minimal requirements, the writing need not state any other terms, and terms stated (other than quantity) are not conclusive. As noted in Official Comment 1 to §2–201: "All that is required is that the writing afford a basis for believing that the offered oral evidence rests on a real transaction." Therefore, once the Statute of Frauds is satisfied, the party seeking enforcement will offer evidence regarding other agreed terms. Terms omitted from an uncontradicted writing or not otherwise proven are supplied by the Code.

The Signature Requirement. Under both the common law and the UCC, the writing satisfying the Statute of Frauds must be signed. A **signature** includes any symbol executed or adopted by a party with the present intention to adopt or accept a writing as her own.[19] The signature requirement is not rigorous. That is, a formal signature handwritten in ink is not required. A signature may be printed, stamped, or written and may be made by initials or even a fingerprint. It may appear on any part of the document and in some cases may be found in a billhead or letterhead.[20]

Electronic Transactions. The traditional rules governing the writing and signature requirement assume that the parties use paper documents. Of course, many modern business transactions are conducted through electronic forms of communication, such as e-mail. The legal effect of transactions conducted through electronic media is discussed in detail in Chapter 59 (Technology Law). The basic principles as they apply to Statute of Frauds requirements are discussed below.

The Uniform Electronic Transactions Act (UETA) and its federal counterpart, the Electronic Signatures in

---

[19]UCC §1–201(b)(37), which follows the common law rule.
[20]UCC §1–201, Official Comment 37.

Global and National Commerce Act, are designed to assure that records and documents existing solely in electronic form have the same legal effect as paper-based documents. To this end, the UETA provides generally that "the medium in which a record, signature, or contract is created, presented, or retained does not affects its legal significance."[21]

Under the UETA and UCC, a "record" includes both information "inscribed on a tangible medium" and information that is "stored in an electronic or other medium and is retrievable in perceivable form."[22] An "electronic signature" includes "an electronic sound, symbol, or process attached to or logically associated with a record and executed or adopted by a person with the intent to sign the record."[23] As applied to Statute of Frauds requirements, Section 7 of the UETA provides:

1. If a law requires a record to be in writing, an electronic record satisfies the law.
2. If a law requires a signature, an electronic signature satisfies the law.

Thus, under these principles, the Statute of Frauds writing and signature requirements discussed in this chapter may be satisfied in either tangible or electronic form.

Effect of Performance, Rescission, and Modification

Full Performance. Noncompliance with the Statute of Frauds generally renders a contract "unenforceable," not "void." Oral contracts subject to the statute frequently are made and performed. If the contract has been fully performed on both sides, courts have unanimously held that the Statute of Frauds has no effect upon the legal relations of the parties. That is, after full performance, neither party can maintain an action for rescission on the basis that the contract was unenforceable under the statute. The evidentiary function of the statute is clearly satisfied and the parties are in the same position as if the contract had been originally enforceable.

A commonly encountered problem concerns the extent to which the Statute of Frauds applies to a subsequent rescission or modification by the parties of a contract originally within the statute. Two basic issues are

presented: (1) Must an agreement to rescind a contract be in writing if the underlying contract is within the statute? and (2) To what extent does the Statute of Frauds apply to a contract modifying but not rescinding a prior contract?

Effect of Rescission. An executory written contract subject to the Statute of Frauds may be rescinded orally. For example, assume A and B have a written contract in which A agrees to employ B for two years. Subsequently, the parties orally agree to rescind the contract. The oral agreement is effective to rescind the written contract.

Effect of Modification. The parties may, subsequent to formation of the contract, agree to modify its terms. In determining whether or not the Statute of Frauds applies to the contract modifying but not rescinding the original agreement, the second contract is treated as containing the originally agreed terms *as modified.* The UCC reaches the same result in §2–209(3) that provides: "The requirements of the statute of frauds section of this Article (§2–201) must be satisfied if the contract as modified is within its provisions." In other words, the Statute of Frauds is applied to the new contract that contains terms found in both the original and the modifying contract.

The following examples illustrate the operation of this rule, using both common law and UCC contracts. Assume A, in a written contract, agrees to employ B for two years at $3,000 per month. When B begins work, the parties orally agree to modify the contract to provide a salary of $3,500 per month for six months. The second contract is enforceable even though oral (because not subject to the one-year provision) and discharges the written contract. Had the converse been true—for example, an oral contract with a six-month term modified to two years—the contract as modified would now be within the statute, requiring a writing for enforceability. Of course, if the contract had been outside the statute both before and after the modification—a six-month contract modified to nine months—no writing is required in any event. Conversely, a writing is required if the contract is within the statute both before and after the modification—a two-year contract modified to three years.

To illustrate the modification rules using UCC §2–201, assume that S and B have an oral contract for the sale of 500 cardboard shipping boxes at $.95 each ($475). The oral contract is enforceable because the

---

[21]UETA §7, comment 1.
[22]UETA §2(13); UCC §1–201(b)(31).
[23]UETA §2(8).

price is less than $500. The parties orally agree to increase the price to $1.05 without changing the quantity. The contract as modified is within the statute requiring a writing for enforceability because the price is now $525. On the other hand, if the modification had reduced the price from $1.05 to $.95, the modified contract would no longer be subject to §2–201 and would be enforceable even if oral. Once again, if the contract price is below $500 both before and after the modification, §2–201 is inapplicable both to the original contract and the modification. If the price is $500 or more both before and after the modification, a writing satisfying §2–201 is required.

The preceding discussion concerns the application of the Statute of Frauds to modifications of contracts: (1) outside the statute both before and after the modification, (2) outside the statute originally but brought within it by the modification, and (3) within the statute before but not after the modification. A particularly thorny question concerns the fourth and perhaps most common modification possibility: a contract within the statute both before and after the modification. Under the rules previously discussed, some writing satisfying the statute for the modified contract is required. The common law statute requires that all material terms be stated in the writing. As such, courts have generally held that an oral agreement modifying a material term of a contract within the statute is unenforceable unless a writing complying with requisite formalities accompanies the modification. That is, the writing satisfying the statute for the original contract does not satisfy it for the modification. A separate writing incorporating the modified term is required. The modification agreement, therefore, must satisfy the statute to the same extent as the original agreement.

Many courts considering the issue have applied this common law rule to modifications of Code contracts as well. Nevertheless, a different rule apparently should apply to contracts for the sale of goods because §2–201, as previously noted, is designed to make the writing requirement less rigorous than that imposed by the common law statute. Under the Code (§2–209(3)), if the parties modify a contract within the statute (involving goods of a price of $500 or more) both before and after the modification, parol evidence should be admissible to prove any modification *except an increase in quantity,* because the original memorandum continues to satisfy §2–201 for the contract "as modified." Because §2–201 prohibits a party from enforcing a contract beyond the quantity specified in the original memoran-

dum, the party seeking to enforce a modification increasing quantity needs a new memorandum complying with the requirements of §2–201, specifying the new quantity in order to prevail. All other types of modifications, including a reduction in quantity, may be proven by parol evidence. In these cases, the original memorandum continues to satisfy §2–201, which is all that §2–209(3) demands. That is, both before and after the modification the contract is evidenced by a writing which: (1) indicates a contract for sale has been made, (2) is signed by the party to be charged, and (3) states a quantity term.

Under the UCC, the parties are effectively permitted to make their own statute of frauds regarding subsequent rescission or modification of a written contract for the sale of goods. Section 2–209(2) states that a signed written agreement (whether or not subject to §2–201) may provide that any future modification or rescission must be evidenced by a signed writing. If such a term is included, an oral modification or rescission is ineffective. If, however, the term is contained in a form contract (contract of adhesion) supplied by a *merchant* to a consumer, it is not binding on the consumer unless he signs the provision separately.[24]

Effect of Alteration

As a general rule of contract law, if a person who is owed a contractual duty fraudulently and materially alters a writing that (1) is a complete or partial integration of the agreement or (2) satisfies the Statute of Frauds with respect to the contract, then the duty of the other party is discharged.[25] A writing may be altered by addition, deletion, unauthorized completion of a blank space in the writing, or other change. Fraudulent material alteration of a writing deprives the party responsible of the right to enforce the obligation even in its original form. That is, a duty discharged by alteration may not be revived unless the alteration is forgiven by the innocent party.[26] These rules are designed to prevent tampering with writings that determine the content or enforceability of contract duties.

---

[24]Note that as *between* merchants, a term in a form contract supplied by one of them preventing modification without a writing is binding without a separate signing by the other.

[25]Restatement (Second) of Contracts §286.

[26]Restatement (Second) of Contracts §287(2).

An alteration that is not both fraudulent and material does not discharge the duty, and the contract remains enforceable according to its original terms. In addition, no discharge occurs if the alteration is made by a person who is not a party to the contract, even if the alteration is both fraudulent and material. As used in this context, an alteration is "material" if it varies the legal relations of any party with the maker of the alteration or with third parties. The meaning of the term "fraudulent" is discussed in detail in Chapter 11.

Summary

1.   As a general rule, contracts need not be written to be enforceable. Nevertheless, written contracts have distinct advantages, both in preventing misunderstandings and omissions that cause contract disputes and in proving contract terms when a dispute does arise.

2.   In both oral and written agreements, courts are often required to determine the meaning or content of a contract tendered uncertain by ambiguous language, misunderstanding, or simply because the parties failed to anticipate the contingency causing the dispute. The law has developed various principles to aid courts in interpreting contracts.

3.   When contracting parties reduce their agreement to writing, disputes often arise concerning whether evidence of preliminary negotiations and agreements (parol evidence) may be admitted in evidence in a subsequent contract dispute. The parol evidence rule generally prevents admission of evidence regarding preliminary negotiations or prior agreements to contradict a writing, known as an integration, adopted by the parties as the final expression of their agreement. An integration may be complete (a complete and exclusive statement of all terms of the agreement) or partial (conclusive on some but not all issues). If an integration is merely partial, evidence of terms not governed by the writing is admissible. Further, evidence of a collateral contract—one related to but not part of the integrated contract, and not inconsistent with it—is admissible even when the parties adopt a completely integrated writing.

4.   The parol evidence rule is subject to a number of exceptions. For example, parol evidence is always admissible (1) to resolve ambiguities in the writing, (2) to prove fraud, duress, undue influence, illegality, or otherwise attack the validity of the integrated writing, and (3) to prove oral conditions to the promises contained in the writing.

5.   The UCC retains the parol evidence rule for contracts involving goods but provides that the terms of the writing may be explained or supplemented by course of dealing, usage of trade, course of performance, and by evidence of consistent additional terms.

6.   For certain contracts—those subject to the Statute of Frauds—written evidence of the contract is required for enforceability. The original Statute of Frauds, enacted in England in 1677, requires some writing indicating that a contract has been made, stating certain minimum terms, and signed by the party to be bound for (1) contracts to answer for the debt or duty of another (suretyship contracts), (2) contracts for the sale of interests in land, (3) contracts that cannot be performed within one year, and (4) contracts made upon consideration of marriage.

7.   In addition to contracts subject to the English, or common law, statute, the UCC requires that a contract for the sale of goods with a price of $500 or more be evidenced by a writing to be enforceable. No writing is required, however, if the goods are to be specially manufactured for the buyer, or if the defendant admits the existence of the contract in court. Further, no writing is required to validate a contract within the statute to the extent the agreement has been partially performed. The UCC requirements for the sufficiency of the writing are much less rigorous than those imposed by the English statute.

8.   The UCC also requires a writing for contracts creating security interests in personal property. Further, various state statutes impose writing requirements for certain types of contracts in addition to those governed by the English statute or the UCC.

9.   If an oral contract subject to the Statute of Frauds is fully performed, the statute has no further legal effect; the contract is treated as if it had been originally enforceable. If the contract is still executory the parties may agree to rescind or modify it. An executory written contract subject to the statute may be rescinded orally. If the contract is modified but not rescinded, the statute's requirements must be satisfied if the contract as modified is within its provisions.

10.   Generally, if a contracting party fraudulently and materially alters a writing that determines the content or enforceability of the contract, then the duty of the other party to the contract is discharged.

Key Terms

interpretation
parol evidence
parol evidence rule
integrated agreement
complete integration
partial integration
collateral contract doctrine
merger (integration) clause
course of dealing

usage of trade
course of performance
Statute of Frauds
main purpose (leading object) rule
part performance doctrine
specially manufactured goods
writing
signature

Questions and Problems

12.1 Hutchinson, who owned several pieces of land, entered into a contract with Contractor to build houses on the land. After the houses had been built, the parties sought court construction of the following clause in the contract:

> The ultimate cost of the houses shall include the actual cost of construction plus Contractor's fixed fee of Four Hundred Thirty-Five Dollars ($435.00), plus Owner's price of Nine Hundred Fifty Dollars ($950.00) for the land upon which each house is to be constructed. Fifty percent (50%) of any amount obtained from the sale of any house exceeding the aforementioned ultimate cost, shall be paid Contractor as additional compensation for construction of said houses.

Contractor argued that he should be paid half of all money received from the sales of the houses in excess of the costs of construction, Contractor's fixed fee, and Hutchinson's cost of the land. Hutchinson argued that Contractor was entitled to half of the money received from the sales of the houses in excess of the costs of construction, the Contractor's fixed fee, Hutchinson's cost of the land, and costs incurred by him in selling the property. That is, Hutchinson argued that he was entitled to deduct selling expenses—for example, realtors' commissions, advertising expenses, and FHA closing fees— prior to dividing the profits with Contractor. Before entering into the contract, the parties had discussed the necessity of advertising the houses and using real estate agents to market the houses. Although the sale of the houses generated a net profit, Contractor's interpretation would give him a $38,000 profit on the transaction while imposing an $18,000 loss on Hutchinson. What arguments might Hutchinson raise in support of his interpretation of the contract? What arguments might Contractor raise? Who should prevail?

12.2 Would the oral evidence offered in the following situations violate the parol evidence rule?

(a) Jude contracted to remodel Belinda's kitchen. A written contract was executed and signed by both parties, although Belinda later asserted that she thought the writing was merely an estimate. The writing also contained an integration (merger) clause. The contract required Belinda to pay 50 percent of the remodeling costs in advance. Belinda later refused to make this payment and Jude sued. Belinda sought to admit evidence that the contract was subject to an oral condition precedent, providing that the contract, unconditional on its face, would not become binding unless she was able to obtain financing. Because Belinda was unable to obtain financing, she asserted that her duty to perform never arose. Should the court admit the evidence?

(b) Steve, a farmer, contracted to sell grain to Oscar, a grain buyer. Steve intended to grow the crops to satisfy the contract on his own land. A written contract was executed stating nothing about the source of the grain. Steve's crop failed due to adverse weather conditions and through no fault of Steve. When Steve failed to deliver, Oscar sued for breach. Should Steve be allowed to admit oral evidence that the parties understood that the crops were to be grown only from a specified source, and that performance would be excused if that source failed?

12.3 In 2002, Stone and Pacific Co. entered into a written contract for the sale of concrete for use in the construction of the building foundation of a power plant. The contract stipulated that Stone was to supply "approximately 70,000 cubic yards" of concrete from September 2002 to June 2003. The contract further stipulated that "No conditions which are not incorporated in this contract will be recognized." By June 2003, Pacific had ordered only 12,542 cubic yards of concrete, which was the total amount needed for the construction work. Stone brought suit for breach of contract.

At trial Pacific claimed that the contract should be interpreted in light of the custom of the trade and additional terms allegedly intended by the parties. Pacific sought to admit evidence that contractors in the trade generally did not insist upon literal compliance with quantity terms in such contracts, and that in any event the parties had orally agreed prior to signing the contract that the quantity term was not mandatory and was subject to renegotiation. In effect Pacific sought to prove that the term "70,000 cubic yards" should be interpreted to mean "up to 70,000 cubic yards." Should the court admit such evidence under §2–202 of the UCC? Explain.

12.4 Kemp Fisheries, Inc. (Kemp) agreed to charter a boat from Bumble Bee Seafoods Division (Bumble Bee) to fish for herring and salmon in Alaska. Following negotiations, Kemp and Bumble Bee signed a letter of intent that stated that it would serve as their agreement "pending preparation and execution of final documentation required for the bareboat charter." After Kemp's and Bumble Bee's attorneys had reviewed drafts of the documents, Bumble Bee sent the final charter agreement to Kemp. Kemp's president signed the agreement even though it did not include several provisions that he thought had been included in the negotiations. Specifically, he had understood that Bumble Bee warranted that the freezing system would meet Kemp's needs during the fishing season. The final agreement, however, did not include this provision but instead disclaimed all warranties.

While Kemp was fishing in Alaska two of the engines that powered the freezing system broke down. Because of inadequate freezing, Kemp was forced to sell its herring and salmon at lower prices than it would have realized for properly frozen fish. Kemp sued Bumble Bee for breach of contract. During the trial, the judge admitted evidence from Kemp that showed that Bumble Bee orally had warranted that the freezing system would meet Kemp's needs for fishing in Alaska. Based on this evidence, the trial court ruled in favor of Kemp, holding that Bumble Bee had breached its oral promises concerning the freezing system. Should the court have admitted this evidence? Discuss the legal principles that will guide the court in this case.

12.5   S entered into a contract with B for the sale of cotton. A writing exists sufficient to indicate a contract for sale signed by S, and specifying the quantity as "all the cotton to be produced on my 825 acres." Does the writing satisfy the UCC Statute of Frauds (§2–201) against S?

12.6   Yarbro, a printer, needed a photocopying machine for his shop. Because he was a poor credit risk, Xerxes Co. refused to sell Yarbro a copier. Yarbro then asked his friend Rosalie, who operated an advertising agency in an adjacent office, to purchase the copier. Xerxes agreed to sell the copier to Rosalie on credit for monthly payments of $300. After installation, Rosalie and Yarbro shared the use of the machine. Rosalie failed to make the first payment, so a Xerxes representative came to her office to repossess the copier. When Yarbro paid Xerxes the $300, Xerxes did not repossess the machine. In subsequent months, Yarbro made several other monthly payments to Xerxes. Yarbro also told the Xerxes representative, "If Rosalie ever fails to make a payment, see me immediately and I will pay you." After eight months both Yarbro and Rosalie went out of business. Rosalie left town.

Xerxes sued Yarbro for the full amount of the installment contract. Yarbro alleged that he could not be held liable because his promise to pay Rosalie's debt was not in writing. How should the court rule?

12.7   Consider whether the following oral agreements are unenforceable under the one-year provision of Statute of Frauds:
 (a) Andrew designed an advertisement for Beth, who paid him $42,500. Andrew alleges an oral "understanding" obligating Beth to pay Andrew $5,000 per year for every year Beth uses the ad. Beth is not obligated to use the advertisement in the future and can incur no liability for not using it. Further, Beth's failure to use the ad for any period of time, however long, does not terminate the contract.
 (b) Anwar alleged that Branch, a construction company, orally agreed to pay him a fee for arranging construction of a chemical plant in Saudi Arabia. Anwar negotiated with Saudi officials, resulting in Branch's removal from an Arab blacklist and the subsequent award of a contract to Branch to construct the plant. Anwar asserted that pursuant to the oral agreement he was entitled to a substantial fee for his services. Although neither party contended that the alleged contract contained any provision regulating the time of performance, Anwar admitted

that his negotiation efforts took three years, and completion of the plant took another six years.

12.8   To what extent, if at all, are the following contracts enforceable under the part performance exception to UCC §2–201?
 (a) Smigel owned a 1967 Rolls-Royce Silver Shadow. He orally offered to sell the car to Lockwood for $11,400, of which $100 was to be paid upon acceptance and the balance on delivery. Lockwood accepted the offer and paid $100 to Smigel. Smigel thereafter refused to deliver, asserting noncompliance with the Statute of Frauds.
 (b) Sage is a cattle dealer. Barry is a broker who buys cattle in quantity for resale to third parties. Barry telephoned Sage in December 2004 and allegedly agreed to purchase 2,000 head of cattle from Sage to be delivered by January 15, 2005. Barry made no payment at the time of the telephone conversation and no writings were exchanged by the parties. Subsequently, Sage delivered 222 head of cattle to Barry, but refused to deliver any more. Barry sued Sage for breach of its duty under the alleged contract to deliver 1,778 additional head. Sage asserted the Statute of Frauds as a defense. Determine on these facts whether the contract is enforceable for (1) no cattle, (2) the 222 head delivered, or (3) 2,000 head.

12.9   LTV Corporation, a manufacturer of all-terrain vehicles, needed shipping crates to export the vehicles. LTV therefore circulated a detailed invitation to bid to obtain a local supplier who could manufacture 8,000 crates according to specifications at a total cost exceeding $50,000. Bateman submitted a written bid, which LTV accepted. LTV never signed Bateman's bid and repudiated the contract after only 1,000 crates had been ordered. Bateman sued and LTV asserted the Statute of Frauds as a defense. What result?

12.10   Under the UCC (§2–201(3)(b)), a party may not admit the existence of an oral contract in court and still rely on the Statute of Frauds as a defense. This rule has been criticized because it encourages the defendant to perjure himself by denying the existence of the contract. Is this a valid criticism given the basic purposes of the Statute of Frauds?

12.11   Consider the application of the Statute of Frauds to the following contracts:
 (a) S conveyed land to B under a written contract. Subsequently, the parties agreed to rescind the transaction; S promised to return the money in exchange for B's promise to reconvey the land. Is the agreement to rescind required to be written under the Statute of Frauds?
 (b) A and B make an enforceable oral contract that A will work for 30 days at $20 a day. The next day, they orally contract to substitute employment for two years at $6,000 per year. The second contract is unenforceable because a writing is required by the one-year provision of the Statute. What effect does the unenforceable modification have on the original enforceable oral contract?

12.12 Trilco, a steel fabricator, telephoned Prebilt Corporation, a steel wholesaler, to discuss purchasing $5,000 worth of sheet steel. Trilco then sent a written purchase order signed by Trilco describing the various sizes and quantities of steel desired. The purchase order contained the typewritten word "Confirmation" as well as the printed language "This order not valid without return acknowledgment."

Prebilt never responded to Trilco's order and never delivered any steel. When sued by Trilco's for breach of contract, Prebilt asserted that the alleged agreements were unenforceable due to noncompliance with the relevant Statute of Frauds, UCC §2–201. Trilco, however, asserted that because both parties were merchants, §2–201(2) should apply. Trilco argued that its purchase orders were written confirmations of the oral agreements, sufficient to satisfy §2–201 against Trilco, and became binding upon Prebilt through its failure to object within ten days. Is Trilco correct? What particular language contained in §2–201(2) is particularly relevant in resolving this dispute?

CHAPTER 13

THIRD PARTIES

- **the role played by third parties in contracts**
- **the law of assignment and delegation, which determines when contract rights and duties may be transferred, the rights acquired upon transfer, and the liability of the parties after transfer**
- **third-party beneficiary law, which determines when a person who is not a party to a contract is entitled to enforce it**

To this point in the study of contracts, we have examined the various elements of an enforceable promise and the circumstances—such as lack of capacity, illegality, misrepresentation, or absence of a writing—rendering an otherwise binding promise either voidable or unenforceable. This chapter discusses the role played by third parties in contract law. The **parties** to a contract are simply the people who have made the agreement. If Sue and Bill have a contract for the sale of Sue's boat for $15,000, Sue and Bill are the contracting parties. Anyone else in the world who may be affected by or have rights in the contract is referred to as a **third party.** Third parties become important in contract study in primarily two contexts: (1) in the assignment and delegation of contract rights and duties and (2) in third-party beneficiary promises.

Contracts are merely a type of property. Like other property interests, contracts are often transferred from one person to another. The law of assignment and delegation is concerned with the transfer of contract rights and duties by a contracting party to a third party. The principles of assignment and delegation are important because they form the basis for understanding many important concepts in legal subjects outside general contract law, including property, negotiable instruments, partnership, and secured transactions.

In addition to assignment and delegation cases, third parties often become involved in contracts as third-party beneficiaries. Ordinarily, only the parties to contractual promises are entitled to enforce them. Occasionally, however, a beneficiary—a person who is not a party to a contract but benefits from its performance—may enforce a contract against the original parties. This chapter first discusses assignment and delegation concepts, followed by coverage of third-party beneficiary promises.

Assignment and Delegation

Assignment

In a bilateral contract, the parties have both rights and duties. Each party has the right to receive the other's performance as well as the duty to perform his promise.

Suppose Andrew and Barbara enter into a contract in which Andrew promises to paint Barbara's house in exchange for Barbara's promise to pay $500. Both rights and duties have been created by the contract. Andrew has the right to receive $500, and the duty to paint the house. Barbara has the right to have her house painted, and the duty to pay $500.

An **assignment** is simply the transfer of the rights under a contract to a third party. The parties to an assignment are as follows: (1) the **assignor,** the person who is transferring the rights; (2) the **assignee,** the person to whom the rights are transferred; and (3) the **obligor,** or nonassigning party, the person required to render performance. To illustrate using the previous example, assume Andrew assigns his right to receive $500 to Tom. The relationship of the parties is shown in Figure 13.1.

Prior to the assignment, the assignor, Andrew, is the **obligee** of Barbara's duty, that is, the person entitled to receive her performance. Conversely, Barbara is the obligee of Andrew's duty to paint the house, with Andrew the obligor.

The assignment of a right involves the manifestation of the assignor's intention to transfer it to the assignee. Generally, no particular formalities are necessary to make an assignment. The assignment may be made either orally or in writing.[1] By virtue of the assignment, the assignor's right to the obligor's performance is extinguished and the assignee acquires the right to that

performance. Thus, in the previous example, by assigning the right to Tom, Andrew's right to Barbara's performance is extinguished and Tom acquires the right to receive $500 from Barbara. Note that all or part of a right may be assigned. Therefore, although Andrew is contractually entitled to receive $500 from Barbara, he may assign any portion of it to Tom.

When Contract Rights May Be Assigned. All contract rights may be assigned without the obligor's consent unless the assignment would:

1. materially change the duty of the obligor (the most common case), or
2. materially increase the burden or risk imposed on the obligor by the contract, or
3. materially impair the obligor's chance of obtaining return performance or materially reduce the performance's value.[2]

All claims to receive money generally may be assigned, because a change in the person to whom payment is to be made (from the assignor to the assignee) does not materially affect the duty of the nonassigning party (obligor).

To illustrate situations in which rights may not be assigned without consent, assume Alice agrees to paint Craig's picture. Craig assigns his right to have his picture painted to Mona. Alice need not perform for Mona, because her duty has been materially changed. That is, painting Mona's portrait is a materially different duty than painting Craig's portrait. The same result would follow had Alice originally agreed to give Craig violin lessons or if she had agreed to take care of Craig for life. Or, assume that Continental Casualty, a fire insurance company, agrees to insure a building owned by Sheila against fire. Sheila sells the building to Barbara and assigns the policy to her. The assignment is ineffective without Continental's consent because its risk (not its duty) has been materially changed. This result is based upon the premise that a fire insurance policy protects the insured, not the property, against loss. Therefore, the company should not be required to accept a substitute without its consent, because the decision of the company to insure is, in part, based upon the character of the insured. Once a loss occurs, however, the right to receive the proceeds is freely assignable, because it is merely a claim for money.

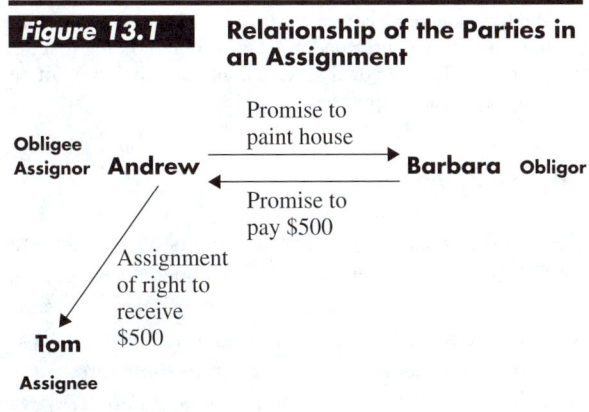

| **Figure 13.1** | **Relationship of the Parties in an Assignment** |

Obligee
Assignor **Andrew** ⟷ **Barbara** Obligor

Promise to paint house
Promise to pay $500

Assignment of right to receive $500

Tom
Assignee

---

[1]The Statute of Frauds may require a writing for certain types of assignments. For example, contracts for sale of accounts require a writing for enforceability (UCC §9–203(b)). This provision is discussed in Chapter 31.

[2]UCC §2–210(2); RESTATEMENT (SECOND) OF CONTRACTS §317(2).

Revocable and Irrevocable Assignments. An assignment may be revocable or irrevocable by the assignor. An assignment is generally irrevocable if it is supported by consideration unless the contract grants the assignor a right to revoke. Similarly, an assignment made as security for, or in satisfaction of, a preexisting debt or other obligation owed by the assignor to the assignee is irrevocable. On the other hand, a gratuitous assignment—one which is neither supported by consideration nor given as security for or in satisfaction of a debt—is generally revocable. Revocation may occur expressly, by the assignor's death, or by a subsequent assignment of the same right to another assignee. A gratuitous assignment, however, may be irrevocable if it meets the formal requirements of a valid gift. For example, a gratuitous assignment is irrevocable if the assignor delivers to the assignee a signed writing containing the assignment or any other writing that is customarily accepted as a symbol or evidence of the assigned right, such as a savings account passbook, a stock certificate, or a life insurance policy.

Delegation and Novation

A **delegation** is a transfer of the duties under a contract to a third party.

When Contract Duties May Be Delegated. Contract duties may be delegated without the nondelegating party's (obligee's) consent unless the obligee has a substantial interest in having his original promisor perform or control the acts required by the contract.[3] Therefore, generally, all contract duties may be delegated except those in contracts for personal services or others in which the promisor's personal skill, judgment, discretion, or supervision is required. Delegation is therefore permitted unless substantial reason can be shown why substitute performance will not be as satisfactory as personal performance.

Assume Mogul Studios hires Dustin Hoffman to act in a movie. Clearly, Dustin Hoffman could not delegate his duty to perform to his plumber, Joe Doaks, because the particular skill and reputation of Dustin Hoffman form the basis of the contract. The delegation would cause a substantial change in Mogul's expectations. However, had Mogul hired Dustin Hoffman to mow Mogul's lawn, performance could be delegated,

because substitute performance on these facts would be satisfactory. In either case, nothing prevents Dustin Hoffman's assignment of his right to receive payment under the contract. It is only delegation of performance in the first situation that is prohibited. Even in that situation, delegation would be permitted if Mogul consented. Other examples of duties that are nondelegable without consent include those owed by an attorney to a client or a doctor to a patient or, in general, any duty whose performance may be judged only by reference to subjective criteria. If there is an objective basis for judging performance—as when goods are manufactured to explicit specifications—the duties are ordinarily delegable.

In the following case, the court was required to determine whether the disputed contract involved personal services that could not be delegated.

Macke Company v. Pizza of Gaithersburg, Inc.
270 A.2d 645 (Md. 1970)

Appellee, Pizza of Gaithersburg, Inc. (PGI), operated six pizza parlors in Maryland. PGI entered into several contracts with Virginia Coffee Service, Inc. (Virginia) by which Virginia agreed to install and maintain cold drink vending machines in PGI's restaurants and to pay all necessary licenses and taxes on the machines. PGI agreed to provide electric power and water and was to receive a percentage of the profits on the machines.

Appellant, Macke Company, later purchased all of Virginia's assets and Virginia assigned the contracts with PGI to Macke. PGI refused to recognize the assignment and terminated the contract. Macke sued for breach of contract. The trial court ruled in favor of PGI, holding that the contract was a personal service contract that could not be assigned. Macke appealed.

Singley, Judge

. . . In the absence of a contrary provision—and there was none here—rights and duties under an executory bilateral contract may be assigned and delegated, subject to the exception that duties under a contract to provide personal services may never be delegated, nor rights be assigned under a contract where *delectus personage* [choice of the person] was an ingredient of the bargain. . . .

We cannot regard the agreements as contracts for personal services. They were either a license or concession granted Virginia by the appellees, or a lease of a portion

---

[3]UCC §2–210(1); Restatement (Second) of Contracts §318(2).

of the appellees' premises, with Virginia agreeing to pay a percentage of gross sales as a license or concession fee or as rent . . . and were assignable by Virginia unless they imposed on Virginia duties of a personal or unique character which could not be delegated. . . .

The appellees earnestly argue that they had dealt with Macke before and had chosen Virginia because they preferred the way it conducted its business. Specifically, they say that service was more personalized, since the president of Virginia kept the machines in working order, that commissions were paid in cash, and that Virginia permitted them to keep keys to the machines so that minor adjustments could be made when needed. Even if we assume all this to be true, the agreements with Virginia were silent as to the details of the working arrangements and contained only a provision requiring Virginia to "install . . . the above listed equipment and . . . maintain the equipment in good operating order and stocked with merchandise." We think the Supreme Court of California put the problem of personal service in proper focus a century ago when it upheld the assignment of a contract to grade a San Francisco street:

> All painters do not paint portraits like Sir Joshua Reynolds, nor landscapes like Claude Lorraine, nor do all writers write dramas like Shakespeare or fiction like Dickens. Rare genius and extraordinary skill are not transferable, and contracts for their employment are therefore personal, and cannot be assigned. But rare genius and extraordinary skill are not indispensable to the workmanlike digging down of a sand hill or the filling up of a depression to a given level, or the construction of brick sewers with manholes and covers, and contracts for such work are not personal, and may be assigned. [*Taylor v. Palmer,* 31 Cal. 240, 247–248 (1866).]

. . . Moreover, the difference between the service the Pizza Shops happened to be getting from Virginia and what they expected to get from Macke did not mount up to such a material change in the performance of obligations under the agreements as would justify the appellees' refusal to recognize the assignment. . . .

As we see it, the delegation of duty by Virginia to Macke was entirely permissible under the terms of the agreements. . . .

[Judgment reversed.]

Effect of General Assignment. In strict legal terms, contract rights are assigned, and contract duties are delegated. Despite this distinction, the parties, as well as lawyers and courts, frequently (and confusingly) use the word "assignment" to encompass both an assignment of rights and a delegation of duties. For example, the assignor may merely state that she is assigning "the contract" or "all of my rights under the contract" to the assignee without explicitly stating whether an assignment of rights only, a delegation of duties only, or a transfer of both rights and duties is intended. Both the UCC and the common law resolve this ambiguity by treating a general assignment as both an assignment of the rights and a delegation of the duties under the contract. Acceptance of the assignment by the assignee constitutes a promise by him to perform those duties, which is enforceable by either the assignor or the other party to the original contract.[4]

Liability After Delegation; Novation. When duties are delegated, it is important to remember that one cannot avoid liability under a contract simply by transferring the duty to perform to a third party. In other words, the obligee's rights against the delegating party cannot be jeopardized without his consent. Any other rule would allow a person to avoid a contractual obligation by simply delegating it. Therefore, the delegating party remains totally liable for performance of the contract despite the delegation. The UCC succinctly states the rule in §2–210(1): "No delegation of performance relieves the party delegating of any duty to perform or any liability for breach." After delegation the party delegating becomes a surety for the assignee's performance, liable if the assignee fails to perform as agreed.

The obligee—the person entitled to receive performance of the delegated duty—may, however, agree to release the original obligor and look only to the party to whom the duty has been delegated. In other words, one contracting party may be substituted for another. This arrangement is known as a **novation.** A novation is a special form of substituted contract,[5] which adds a new party to the contract, who was not a party to the original duty. An effective novation requires that the obligee

---

[4]UCC §2–210(5); Restatement (Second) of Contracts §328.

[5]A substituted contract is one accepted by a contracting party in full satisfaction of an existing duty owed her. Unlike an accord, discussed in the consideration material, a substituted contract immediately discharges the original duty. Thus, breach of the substituted contract does not revive any right to sue on the original duty.

agree to release the original obligor and that the new obligor agree to assume the delegated duty. The original obligor need not incur any additional detriment—that is, furnish additional consideration—to be discharged. By assuming the delegated duty, the new obligor satisfies the consideration requirement on his behalf. In other words, in exchange for the new obligor's promise to assume the duty, the obligee promises to discharge the original obligor's duty.[6]

For example, assume Steinberg and Brooks have a contract for the sale of goods. Steinberg assigns the entire contract to Adler including the right to receive payment as well as the duty to deliver the goods. If Adler fails to perform, Steinberg remains totally liable on the contract; she is a surety for Adler's performance. If, however, Brooks agrees to discharge Steinberg in exchange for Adler's promise to perform the delegated duty, a novation is created relieving Steinberg of liability on the contract. Note here that Adler's assumption of the delegated duty alone is insufficient to create a novation. Brooks's consent also is required. That is, Brooks's rights against Steinberg on the contract cannot be jeopardized without Brooks's consent.

The original contract may provide for a novation. Assume Price is acting as promoter for a corporation yet to be formed, Concert, Inc. Price enters into a contract with Sounds for purchase of equipment. The contract provides that if Concert, Inc. adopts the contract after organization, Price will be released. If Concert, Inc., once formed, agrees to be bound, Price is discharged.

The following case illustrates the principles of delegation and novation in contract law.

Brooks v. Hayes
395 N.W.2d 167 (Wis. 1986)

Under a construction contract with plaintiffs John and Judith Brooks, defendant Wayne Hayes agreed to "provide all necessary labor and materials and perform all work" required to build a house on a lot owned by the plaintiffs. Hayes retained Claude Marr, a mason, to construct the fireplace and install a "heatilator," a device designed to improve the efficiency of the fireplace. Two years after

completion of the house, it was damaged in a fire caused by improper installation of the heatilator. The plaintiffs sued Marr and Hayes for breach of contract. After dismissing the suit against Marr, who had declared bankruptcy, the trial court also dismissed the claim against Hayes finding that he was not responsible for Marr's negligent installation. The court of appeals affirmed and the Brookses appealed.

Abrahamson, Justice

. . . Although Hayes assumed a contractual duty to the plaintiff-owners to perform the construction contract with skill and due care, Hayes delegated the performance of the contract to others. The question then is whether the delegation of performance of the masonry work relieved Hayes of liability for breach of contract when the mason, an independent contractor, negligently performed that part of Hayes's contractual obligation.

The plaintiff-owners assert that Hayes may not avoid responsibility to them for his failure to perform his contractual duty of due care merely by hiring an independent contractor. We agree with this assertion. The hornbook principle of contract law is that the delegation of the performance of a contract does not, unless the obligee agrees otherwise, discharge the liability of the delegating obligor to the obligee for breach of contract. . . .

Hayes argues he is not liable for breach of contract for the mason's negligence because the plaintiff-owners knew about and acquiesced in his hiring the independent contractor.

We are not persuaded by Hayes's argument. Hayes has confused delegation of the performance of an obligation with delegation of responsibility for the performance of an obligation. The rule for delegation of the performance of a contractual obligation is that the obligor may delegate a contractual duty without the obligee's consent unless the duty is "personal." The rule for delegation of responsibility is that if the obligor delegates the performance of an obligation, the obligor is not relieved of responsibility for fulfilling that obligation or of liability in the event of a breach. The obligor under the contract is treated as having rendered the performance even when an independent contractor has rendered it, and the obligor remains the party liable for that performance if the performance proves to be in breach of the contract.

Where the obligee consents to the delegation, the consent itself does not release the obligor from liability for breach of contract. More than the obligee's consent

---

[6]As discussed in Chapter 9, consideration may be given to a person other than the promisor by a person other than the promisee.

to a delegation of performance is needed to release the obligor from liability for breach of contract. For the obligor to be released from liability, the obligee must agree to the release. If there is an agreement between the obligor, obligee and a third party by which the third party agrees to be substituted for the obligor and the obligee assents thereto, the obligor is released from liability and the third person takes the place of the obligor. Such an agreement is known as a novation.

If Hayes is asserting that he and the plaintiff-owners modified the contract to release Hayes from liability for the performance of the independent contractor or that there was a novation by which he, the plaintiff-owners and the mason agreed to substitute the mason as obligor in place of Hayes, the circuit court made no such findings. This court cannot make such findings on this record. . . .

[Judgment reversed and remanded.]

Contract Provisions Precluding Assignment and Delegation

Both the UCC and the common law recognize assignment and delegation as normal and permissible incidents of contracts.[7] That is, all contract rights may be assigned and all contract duties may be delegated unless the assignment or delegation would cause a substantial change in the obligation or expectation of the other contracting party. This rule applies whether or not the other party consents to the assignment or delegation. Any contract right or duty, even if it causes a substantial change, can be assigned or delegated with consent.

If the parties desire protection against an assignment or delegation, they may insert a clause in the contract prohibiting assignment without consent. Such clauses are enforceable, even if the contract would be otherwise assignable. Their effect, however, may be limited. For example, under both the UCC and the common law, a prohibition of assignment of "the contract" prevents only the delegation to the assignee of the assignor's performance. Thus, rights may be assigned despite the nonassignment clause.[8]

To illustrate, assume Seller and Buyer have a contract for the sale of auto parts. Because personal skill, judgment, or discretion is not involved, the duties can normally be delegated under the rules discussed above. However, the contract contains a provision prohibiting assignment of "the contract" by Seller. The clause prevents Seller from delegating its duty to perform, but does not prevent the assignment of its right to receive payment from Buyer.

Rights of the Assignee

To protect its interests, the assignee should notify the nonassigning party, or obligor, of the assignment. No particular formality is required; **notification** is effected when the assignee takes whatever steps are reasonably required to inform the obligor of the assignment. The obligor receives the notification when it comes to his attention, or is delivered at his place of business or at any other place utilized for receipt of such communications, such as an office, residence, or post office box.[9] Therefore, the obligor may have received the notification without having actual knowledge of it. The various legal issues governed by notification to the obligor are discussed below.

Duty of Obligor to Perform for Assignee. The obligor is free to perform for the assignor until she has notice of the assignment from the assignee. Obviously, the obligor cannot perform for the assignee until aware of the assignment. The assignment extinguishes the assignor's right to performance and transfers it to the assignee. Therefore, as soon as the obligor receives notice of the assignment, she must perform for the assignee, and performance for the assignor will not relieve her of her obligation to the assignee. To illustrate, assume that Sue and Beth have a contract for the sale of goods. Beth assigns her right to receive the goods to Alex. Once Alex notifies Sue of the assignment, she must perform for Alex. If Sue delivers the goods to Beth and Beth leaves town with them, Sue remains liable to Alex.[10]

The following case illustrates the unfortunate legal consequences of an assignee's failure to notify the obligor of an assignment.

---

[7]UCC §2–210, Official Comment 1.
[8]UCC §2–210(4); RESTATEMENT (SECOND) OF CONTRACTS §322(1).

[9]UCC §1–202; RESTATEMENT (SECOND) OF CONTRACTS §338 comment e.
[10]Note that if Sue does deliver to Beth, Beth is deemed to hold the goods for the benefit of Alex on equitable grounds. If, however, Sue performs for Beth after notification, she bears the risk of loss in the event Beth misappropriates the goods.

Equilease Corporation v. State Federal Savings and Loan Association

647 F.2d 1069 (10th Cir. 1981)

Equilease Corporation leased seven trucks to Henry Oil Company. As security for the lease Henry Oil assigned and delivered to Equilease six savings certificates that had been issued to Henry Oil by State Federal Savings and Loan Association. Equilease, however, did not notify State Federal that Henry Oil assigned the certificates to Equilease. Over a year later, after encountering financial difficulties, Henry Oil notified State Federal that the savings certificates had been lost and requested early withdrawal of the funds. State Federal allowed Henry Oil to withdraw the funds. Seven months later, after Henry Oil defaulted on one of its leases, Equilease discovered that Henry Oil had withdrawn the assigned funds. Equilease sued State Federal. The district court granted summary judgment in favor of State Federal and Equilease appealed.

Barrett, Circuit Judge

. . . It is generally agreed that prior to notification of an assignment, a debtor may pay the creditor the funds owing and such payment constitutes a complete defense against an action brought by the undisclosed assignee against the debtor. . . .

Oklahoma has followed the general rule that an assignee must notify the debtor prior to debtor's payment to the assignor in order to bind the debtor to the obligation asserted by the assignee. . . .

Equilease's fourth cause of action alleged a breach of contract theory. The predicate was that because Equilease became the owner of the savings certificates following their pledge from Henry Oil, Equilease was entitled to rely upon the express terms of the savings certificates that no withdrawals could be expected without presentation of the passbooks issued by State Federal. In light of its failure to give notice, we hold that Equilease is not entitled to invoke a contractual obligation against State Federal. . . .

[Judgment affirmed.]

Defenses and Claims Available Against the Assignee.
In an ordinary contract assignment, the assignee "steps into the shoes" of the assignor, which means that he receives rights no better or worse than the assignor had. Therefore, any claim or defense that the obligor has against the assignor also may be asserted against the assignee. As explained in comment b to Section 336 of *Restatement (Second) of Contracts:*

> [T]he assignment of a non-negotiable contractual right ordinarily transfers what the assignor has but only what he has. The assignee's right depends on the validity and enforceability of the contract creating the right, and is subject to limitations imposed by the terms of that contract and to defenses which would have been available against the obligee [assignor] had there been no assignment.

The assignee's right against the obligor also is subject to any claim or defense arising out of his own conduct.

To illustrate, assume that Aronson defrauds Barton. Aronson assigns his right to receive Barton's performance to Carlson. Carlson attempts to enforce the contract against Barton. Barton can assert Aronson's fraud as a defense against Carlson, just as he could have asserted it against Aronson. Or, assume Spencer and Becker have a contract for the sale of goods. Spencer assigns her right to receive payment to Casey. The goods shipped by Spencer to Becker are defective. If Casey seeks enforcement of the contract against Becker, Becker can assert the defective nature of the goods as a defense to Casey's action. In both cases, the assignee takes no better rights than the assignor has.

Despite the general rule outlined above, a buyer or lessee may contractually agree not to assert against a subsequent assignee any claim or defense he may have against the seller or lender. These terms commonly are known as **waiver of defense clauses.** They are enforceable only in limited circumstances because of their potential for unconscionable application, particularly in consumer transactions.

Variation of Assignee's Rights by Agreement of the Original Parties. Though the assignee "steps into the shoes" of the assignor and takes subject to defenses available against the assignor, she is not subject to defenses arising as a result of agreement between the assignor and obligor *after* the assignee has given notice of the assignment. In other words, once notice is received, the assignee's rights become vested and cannot be altered by later agreement between the original parties—assignor and obligor. Assume S contracts to sell auto parts to B for $15,000. B assigns the contract to X, who notifies S. X's rights are vested and may not be altered by subsequent modification of the original contract by S and B.

The rule previously discussed binding the obligor to perform for the assignee after notification is merely an application of this principle. That is, once notice is received, as against the assignee, it is no defense to the obligor that he performed for the assignor. Similarly, a binding release (one supported by consideration) of the obligor by the assignor after notice is ineffective against the assignee.

Successive Assignments of the Same Right. Notification also may become an issue if there have been successive assignments of the same right. Assume Stewart is contractually obligated to deliver goods to Beth. For consideration, Beth assigns the right to Stewart's performance to Austin. Beth assigns the same right to Ernest, who pays cash and has no knowledge of the prior assignment. Beth has acted wrongfully in making the second assignment, and leaves town with the money received from both Austin and Ernest. As between the two innocent assignees, who has the benefit of Stewart's performance?

Two conflicting common law rules govern this situation in the absence of statute. The majority rule is that the first assignee in time prevails (in this case, Austin). The conflicting rule, arising from the early English case *Dearle v. Hall*,[11] and adopted in a number of states, is that the first assignee to notify the obligor prevails, regardless of the order in which the assignments were made. Therefore, in the preceding example under the English rule, the first assignee to notify Stewart prevails.

Statutes, particularly Article 9 of the UCC, now govern most priority problems relating to successive assignees and claims of the assignor's creditors against the assignee. The application of Article 9 to successive assignments of accounts is discussed in Chapter 32.

Assignments of Accounts

An account is a contract representing the merchant's right to payment for goods sold or services rendered to its customers, known as account debtors. A merchant's accounts receivable often occupy an important position in commercial financing. For example, financial institutions often lend money secured by a merchant's accounts or purchase them outright.

Although transactions in accounts are effectively contract assignments (with the merchant as assignor and financial institution as assignee), all transactions in accounts are governed by Article 9 of the UCC, discussed in detail in Chapters 31 and 32. Accordingly, the rights and obligations of the parties to an account assignment are governed by Article 9, specifically §§9–404 to 9–406, not the common law of contracts. Although these provisions generally follow ordinary contract law principles, certain important differences, briefly discussed in the following section, do exist.

Assignability. An account, being a claim for money, is freely assignable. Section 9–406(d) reinforces that right by providing that contract terms prohibiting assignment of accounts, or requiring the account debtor's permission for an assignment, are unenforceable. This approach facilitates the use of accounts in commercial financing.

Notification. As previously noted, various legal issues depend on notification to the obligor that an assignment has been made. If the assigned right is an account, notification of the obligor (account debtor) is governed by UCC §9–406(a). Consistent with general contract principles, the account debtor may pay the assignor until notified that the account has been assigned and that payment is to be made *to the assignee.* When accounts are assigned, collection on them can be either direct or indirect. If collection is direct, the assignee notifies the account debtor to make payments to the assignee. In indirect collection, the assignee allows the assignor to collect the accounts and remit the payments to the assignee. Both methods commonly are used in commercial financing. Thus, the account debtor in an indirect collection situation may continue to pay the assignor even after notification. An assignee who wants to take over collections must notify the account debtor to make future payments to the assignee.

Variation of Assignee's Rights by Agreement of the Original Parties. Under general contract principles, once notice of an assignment is received, the assignee's rights become vested and cannot be altered by later agreement between the original parties (assignor and obligor). Article 9 alters this rule somewhat for assignments of accounts. Section 9–405 provides that a good faith modification of (or substitution for) an *executory* contract by the assignor and obligor (account debtor) is effective against the assignee without his consent even

---

[11]3 Russ. 1, 38 Eng. Rep. 475 (Ch. 1823).

after notification. The assignee automatically acquires corresponding rights under the modified or substituted contract. Once the services are performed or goods delivered (that is, the contract is executed), the basic vesting rule applies. That is, the parties may modify the contract until the account debtor is notified of the assignment.

Section 9–405 is designed to facilitate modification of large government procurement contracts:

> When for example it becomes necessary for a government agency to cut back or modify existing contracts, comparable arrangements must be made promptly in hundreds and even thousands of subcontracts lying in many tiers below the prime contract. Typically the right to payments under these subcontracts will have been assigned . . . [§9–405] gives the prime contractor (the account debtor) the right to make the required arrangements directly with his subcontractors without undertaking the task of procuring assents from the many banks to whom rights under the contracts may have been assigned.[12]

Third-Party Beneficiaries

In general, contracts may be enforced only by the contracting parties—the promisees of the respective broken promises. Under certain circumstances, however, a beneficiary, also known as a "third-party beneficiary," may be entitled to enforce a contract. A **beneficiary** is a person other than the promisee who will be benefited by performance of the promise. Generally, a beneficiary may enforce a contractual promise only if the promise was made with the *intent to benefit* him. The third party is then known as an **intended beneficiary.** A beneficiary who is not an intended beneficiary is an incidental beneficiary.

Intended beneficiaries commonly are of two types: (1) creditor beneficiaries and (2) donee beneficiaries. A promisor is under a duty to an intended beneficiary to perform and the beneficiary may enforce that duty. An incidental beneficiary, however, by virtue of a promise, acquires no rights upon the contract.

Intended Beneficiaries

Creditor Beneficiaries. A person is a **creditor beneficiary** if performance of the promise will satisfy a debt owed by the promisee to the beneficiary. For example, assume that B purchases a car from S on credit. With $1,000 still owing on the purchase price, B sells the car to C who promises B that he will pay the remaining installments to S. Figure 13.2 illustrates this example.

Note that C's promise to pay is made to B, not to S. Thus, C is the promisor, B is the promisee, and S is the beneficiary of the promise. In this case, S is an intended beneficiary because a promise was made with the intent to benefit S, that is, to satisfy a debt owing to S. S is a creditor beneficiary because performance by C will satisfy B's (the promisee's) obligation to S.

S can enforce the promise to pay the $1,000 against either B or C. First, as against C, the promisor, S is an intended beneficiary. Second, S may recover from B if C fails to pay, because, as previously discussed, a person cannot avoid a contractual duty simply by transferring it to a third party. B becomes a surety on C's promise. Unless B is expressly released by S under circumstances creating a novation, B remains liable in the event C fails to pay. Thus, a creditor beneficiary can enforce the promise to pay against both the promisor (on the third-party beneficiary promise) and against the promisee (as surety on the original debt).

As previously discussed, the promisor is under a duty to an intended beneficiary to perform the promise

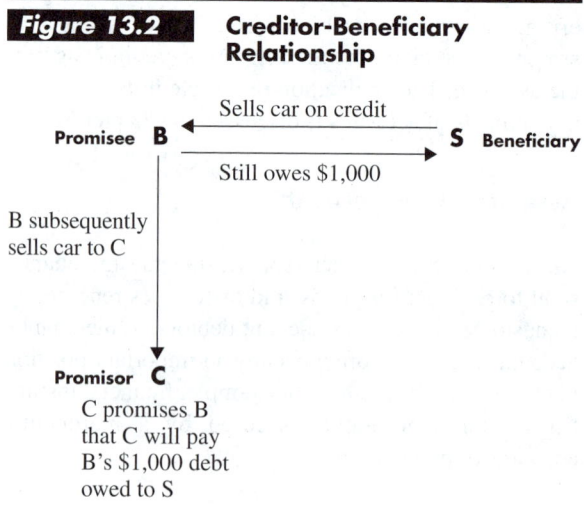

Figure 13.2   **Creditor-Beneficiary Relationship**

Promisee **B** ⟵ Sells car on credit ⟶ **S** Beneficiary

Still owes $1,000

B subsequently sells car to C

Promisor **C**

C promises B that C will pay B's $1,000 debt owed to S

---

[12]UCC §9–318, Official Comment 2 (1995 Official Text).

and the intended beneficiary may enforce that duty. The promisee, however, as in other contractual situations, also is entitled to enforce the promise. The contract to pay the creditor is an asset of the promisee. If the promisor breaches, and the promisee pays the beneficiary, the promisee is entitled to reimbursement of that amount from the promisor. The promisor is therefore under a duty to both the promisee and the beneficiary.

Donee Beneficiaries. The second type of intended beneficiary is referred to as a **donee beneficiary.** A person is a donee beneficiary if the promisee intends to make a gift of the promisor's performance to the beneficiary. Assume that A, in exchange for B's $200 payment, promises to manufacture an oak cabinet and deliver it to C as a birthday present from B. Figure 13.3 illustrates this example.

In this case, C is a donee beneficiary of A's promise to B to manufacture and deliver the cabinet. C can enforce the promise against the promisor, A, because the promise was made with the intent to benefit C—that is, make a gift to her. If A fails to perform, however, C may not recover against the promisee B, because B's conduct is equivalent to a promise to make a gift, which is not supported by consideration. Therefore, although the creditor beneficiary can enforce the promise against both the promisor and the promisee, the donee beneficiary may recover only against the promisor.

The most typical donee beneficiary promise is made in a life insurance contract. The promisor is the insurance company, the insured is the promisee, and the designated beneficiary under the contract is the intended beneficiary. The beneficiary, on the death of the promisee (insured), may enforce the insurance company's promise to pay the face of the policy.[13]

Other Intended Beneficiaries. Traditional creditor and donee beneficiaries are not the only beneficiaries entitled to enforce a promise. The basic test is intent to benefit the third party. Normally, only the promisee need express that intent. "If the beneficiary would be reasonable in relying on the promise as manifesting an intention to confer a right on him, he is an intended beneficiary," entitled to enforce the promise.[14] For example, lenders have been held to be third-party beneficiaries of contracts between auditors and borrowers. If the auditor knows the lender will rely upon the accuracy of the financial statements he prepares as a basis for making the loan, the lender may recover contractually as a third-party beneficiary if the auditor improperly performs the audit and fails to prepare accurate statements.[15]

An intended beneficiary need not be explicitly identified when the promise is made and the promise may extend to a class of persons. For example, assume B promises A that he will pay anyone to whom A becomes indebted for the purchase of an automobile. A buys a car from C. C is an intended beneficiary of B's promise.

The following case explains and applies third-party beneficiary principles.

Swann v. Hunter
630 So.2d 374 (Ala. 1993)

Bobby Wood, the developer of Chriswood subdivision, retained defendant William P. Hunter, a surveyor, to draw a plat of the subdivision and to perform percolation tests on each of the 18 lots. The percolation tests were required by regulations of the Alabama Department of Health to determine whether the ground absorption was suitable for sewage disposal systems. After Hunter performed the tests and found the lots suitable for septic systems, Wood hired defendant M. C. Mabry, a civil engineer, to verify the results and prepare the reports required by Alabama law.

Plaintiffs Tina and Tim Swann purchased a house in Chriswood subdivision and soon began to experience

---

Figure 13.3	**Donee-Beneficiary Relationship**

[13]Life insurance is discussed in Chapter 57.

[14]RESTATEMENT (SECOND) OF CONTRACTS §302 comment d.

[15]This issue is discussed in more detail in Chapter 56.

problems with their sewage system. New percolation tests conducted by a surveyor revealed that their lot was not suitable for a septic system. The Swanns sued Hunter and Mabry for breach of contract alleging that the Swanns— as third-party beneficiaries of the contracts between Wood and Hunter, and Wood and Mabry—were entitled to enforce those contracts. The trial court entered judgment in favor of Hunter and Mabry and the Swanns appealed.

Per Curiam

. . . To recover in a breach of contract action, as a third-party beneficiary, the plaintiff must prove the following: (1) that the contracting parties intended, when they entered the contract, to bestow a direct, as opposed to an incidental, benefit upon a third party, (2) that the plaintiff was the intended third-party beneficiary of the contract, and (3) that the contract was breached. . . . The intention of the contracting parties, as disclosed by the writing, if any, and the surrounding circumstances known to the parties, determines the rights of the alleged third-party beneficiary. . . .

The Swanns argue that purchasers of the lots in the Chriswood subdivision, such as they, directly benefited from the contracts between Wood and Hunter and Wood and Mabry. They contend that there was no reason to perform the percolation tests, other than to directly benefit purchasers of these lots by determining whether the lots were suitable for individual sewage disposal systems. . . .

Hunter and Mabry contracted with the developer of a residential subdivision to perform percolation tests for the purpose of obtaining approval of the subdivision from state and local health agencies. In the circumstances of this case, it was obvious that Wood intended to sell the lots, on which the percolation tests were performed, to individuals for the construction of residential dwellings, which would require a properly functioning sewage disposal system. . . . Hunter and Mabry could clearly envision that purchasers of lots in the Chriswood subdivision would be direct beneficiaries of their performance under the contract with Wood.

Hunter and Mabry argue that they entered into the contract with Wood solely for the purpose of complying with state and local regulations and obtaining approval of the Chriswood subdivision, not, they say, for the purpose of benefiting future purchasers of lots in the Chriswood subdivision. However, the state and local regulations, in accordance with which Wood had to obtain approval of the subdivision, were promulgated for the protection and benefit of the public, especially those members of the public purchasing real property for residential purposes. The most direct benefit of Hunter and Mabry's performance of the percolation tests under the contract to obtain approval of the Chriswood subdivision inured ultimately to the benefit of the purchasers of lots in the subdivision, such as the Swanns. Therefore, we hold that Tim and Tina Swann presented substantial evidence that they were intended beneficiaries of the contracts, between Wood and Hunter and Wood and Mabry, to perform percolation tests on the lot purchased by the Swanns. . . .

[Judgment reversed and remanded.]

Incidental Beneficiaries

Performance of a contract often benefits a third person. Unless the person is an "intended" beneficiary as discussed above, no duty to her is created. She is an **incidental beneficiary.** An incidental beneficiary of a promise acquires no right against either the promisor or the promisee. The following examples illustrate the incidental beneficiary concept.

1. Assume that Hughes and the State have a contract for construction of an interstate highway. Smith owns a piece of property adjoining an exit ramp on the proposed highway. The contract between the State and Hughes calls for completion by September 1. Smith therefore builds a restaurant, completed on September 1, so that she will be ready for business when the interstate opens. Hughes breaches the contract, and as a result the opening of the interstate is delayed six months. During that time, Smith's restaurant, with no ready market of interstate travelers, goes bankrupt. Clearly, Smith is a beneficiary of the promise made by Hughes to the State to complete construction by September 1. Nevertheless, on these facts, Smith cannot recover against Hughes for breach of that promise because no intent to benefit Smith was indicated by the promise.

2. Alan contracts with Bud to dig a drainage ditch across Bud's property. The ditch would also improve drainage on Chuck's property, which is adjacent to

Bud's. Alan breaches the contract. Chuck is an incidental beneficiary of Alan's promise.

Courts often resolve the intended-incidental beneficiary issue by examining to whom the promisor renders performance. If the promisor performs directly for the promisee, the third party is usually an incidental beneficiary. If the performance runs to the third party, he or she is generally an intended beneficiary. To briefly summarize, creditor beneficiaries have rights against both the promisor and promisee, donee beneficiaries against the promisor but not the promisee, and incidental beneficiaries against neither the promisor nor the promisee.

The following case explains and analyzes the distinction between intended and incidental beneficiaries.

BIS Computer Solutions, Incorporated v. City of Richmond, Virginia
122 Fed. Appx. 608 (4th Cir. 2004)

Defendant, the City of Richmond, Virginia (the City), and Halifax Corporation entered into a written contract under which Halifax agreed to create, install, and maintain a computerized records system for the Richmond Police Department. The contract stated that Halifax would hire plaintiff BIS Computer Solutions, Incorporated (BIS) as a subcontractor to perform specified computer work and prohibited Halifax from replacing BIS without the City's written approval. The contract divided Halifax's performance into two phases. At completion of the first phase, the City would determine whether the system was free of "Level 1 or Level 2 Bugs." If such bugs existed, the contract provided that the City could, "at its sole discretion," terminate the contract.

After Halifax completed the first phase of the contract, the City concluded that the new software contained unacceptable bugs and, after paying Halifax's invoices, terminated the contract. BIS sued the City for breach of contract asserting that it was an intended third-party beneficiary entitled to enforce the contract between the City and Halifax. Following a jury trial, the trial court found in favor of BIS and awarded damages of $1.6 million. The City appealed.

Niemeyer, Circuit Judge

. . . The facts relevant to whether BIS was an intended third party beneficiary are not disputed. BIS was not a party to the contract between the City and Halifax, although it was a designated subcontractor that could not be changed without the City's permission. The contract was a services contract entered into to provide the City with a computerized system to manage its police department records in exchange for compensation payable to Halifax. There is nothing in the record to indicate that the contract was entered into for any other purpose. . . .

It is well-settled that [Virginia third beneficiary law] "enables a third party to take an interest under an instrument, although not a party to it, if the promise is made for the third party's benefit and the evidence shows that the contracting parties clearly and definitely intended to confer a benefit upon such third party." *Ashmore v. Herbie Morewitz, Inc.,* [475 S.E.2d 271, 275 (Va. 1996)]. But "a person who benefits only incidentally from a contract between others cannot sue thereon." *Copenhaver v. Rogers,* [384 S.E.2d 593, 596 (Va. 1989)]. . . .

Section 302(1) of the *Restatement (Second) of Contracts* provides that:

> . . . a beneficiary of a promise is an intended beneficiary if recognition of a right to performance in the beneficiary is appropriate to effectuate the intention of the parties and . . . the circumstances indicate that the promisee intends to give the beneficiary the benefit of the promised performance.

Part (2) of §302 defines an "incidental beneficiary" as "a beneficiary who is not an intended beneficiary," and illustrations 17 and 19 of §302 make clear that BIS falls into this latter category:

17. B contracts with A to buy a new car manufactured by C. C is an incidental beneficiary, even though the promise can only be performed if money is paid to C.
19. A contracts to erect a building for C. B then contracts with A to supply lumber needed for the building. C is an incidental beneficiary of B's promise, and B is an incidental beneficiary of C's promise to pay A for the building.

In contrast, the classic situations of intended third-party beneficiaries involve creditor beneficiaries, where the promisee is surety for the promisor, . . . and donee beneficiaries. . . .

With these principles in mind, it is clear that, as a matter of law, BIS was merely an incidental third-party beneficiary of the contract. While the recognition of BIS as a subcontractor may have added to the City's comfort in being assured that performance of the contract would be satisfactorily completed, the City surely did not secure a records management system in order to benefit BIS or any other subcontractor. It did so solely to benefit itself and its police department, and any benefit to BIS and other subcontractors was incidental. For example, in *Valley Landscape Co., Inc. v. Rolland,* [237 S.E.2d 120,122 (Va. 1977)], the Supreme Court of Virginia explained that the primary purpose of a contract between a property owner and an architect was "to assure that the owner [would] get a finished product in accordance with the plans" he had approved. Therefore, the court held, a contractor of the owner could not bring suit as an intended third-party beneficiary against the architect. Similarly in this case, the primary purpose of the contract between the City and Halifax was to assure that the City would receive a working records management system for its police department in accordance with the contractual specifications, and BIS cannot bring suit as an intended third-party beneficiary.

The nature of the contract between the City and Halifax is essentially analogous to any standard construction contract in which a property owner retains a contractor to complete a project, and the contractor hires subcontractors to assist in performing the contractor's work. Unless the parties otherwise specify, the sole intended beneficiaries of any such contract are the property owner and the contractor. Any third party benefiting from the contract, such as a subcontractor, is only an incidental beneficiary. And under Virginia law and under contract law generally, such an incidental beneficiary of a contract who is not a party to the contract may not sue for breach of that contract. . . .

Were we to hold that BIS was an intended beneficiary of the contract between the City and Halifax, we would be broadening the third-party beneficiary doctrine inappropriately. This is especially clear in this case because the contracting parties apparently have no dispute. The City paid all invoices submitted by Halifax to the City, and Halifax made no objection to the City's termination of the contract. If Halifax has not paid BIS under their subcontract, that is a matter between them.

Because BIS was not an intended third-party beneficiary entitled to sue under a contract to which it was not a party, we vacate the judgment entered by the district court and remand with instructions to enter judgment in favor of the City.

[Judgment reversed and remanded.]

Defenses Against Beneficiary

Against an intended beneficiary, the promisor can assert any defense that she has against the promisee. Thus, the beneficiary is in a position similar to an assignee of a right; the assignee takes subject to defenses the obligor has against the assignor. The beneficiary's right is created by the contract. If no contract exists between the promisor and promisee, or if the contract is voidable or unenforceable when formed, the infirmity can be asserted against the beneficiary as well. Therefore, defenses such as fraud, lack of consideration, lack of capacity, and Statute of Frauds are available to the promisor. For example, assume B promises A that she will pay C $100. B's promise was procured through fraud on A's part. B may assert the defense of fraud against C.

The beneficiary also is subject to any limitations or conditions imposed by the terms of the contract. Assume Multiplan, a life insurance company, insures Jim's life. Jim names Betty as beneficiary. The policy reserves to Jim the power to change the beneficiary. Betty's right is terminated if Jim changes the beneficiary before the policy maturity. Additionally, failure by the promisee to perform her return promise discharges the promisor's duty to the beneficiary. For example, assume Belinda has promised Hoyt that she will pay Cathy $100. Hoyt, in return, promises to paint Belinda's house. Hoyt's failure to paint the house is a defense to Belinda when sued on her promise by Cathy.

The agreement may provide, however, that the right of the beneficiary is unaffected by defenses the promisor may have against the promisee. The "standard mortgagee clause" in fire insurance policies is an example of such a provision. These clauses provide that the insurance company (promisor) will pay the mortgagee (beneficiary) for a loss under the policy despite defenses it may have against the insured (mortgagor-promisee). This allows the mortgagee (lender holding a security interest in the property) to recover even though the insured may have violated the terms of the policy — by, for example, failure to pay the premium, storage of hazardous materials, or an intentionally set fire.[16]

Concerning other defenses that may be asserted by the promisor, the beneficiary occupies the same position as an assignee after notification has been given to

---

[16]Insurance is discussed in Chapter 57. Mortgages are discussed in Chapter 37.

the obligor. That is, the beneficiary is bound by the terms of the contract creating his right and any defenses arising from it, but is not subject to defenses that the promisor has against the promisee arising independently of that contract. Additionally, the promisor may not assert defenses that the promisee may have against the beneficiary. Assume A owes C $100 for goods purchased from C. A then fraudulently procures B's contractual promise to pay C $100. Figure 13.4 illustrates this example.

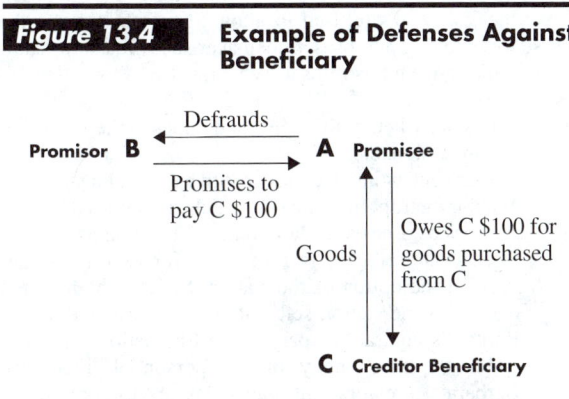

Figure 13.4 **Example of Defenses Against Beneficiary**

On these facts, B may assert A's fraud as a defense to paying C. B, however, cannot assert a defense that A may have against C—for example, the goods shipped to A were defective or not as warranted.

Variation of the Duty to Beneficiary

The contract may provide that any duty to an intended beneficiary cannot be modified or discharged without the beneficiary's consent; that is, the beneficiary's rights may become vested. The most common example of such a provision is an irrevocable designation of beneficiary in a life insurance policy. In the absence of a term creating an irrevocable duty, the parties retain the power to modify or discharge the duty to the beneficiary by subsequent agreement.

The power to alter the duty is also terminated if the beneficiary, before receiving notice of the discharge or modification, changes position in justifiable reliance on the promise, or brings suit on the promise, or assents to the promise at either the promisor's or promisee's request.[17] Note that the beneficiary's assent to or knowledge of the contract is not necessary to give her a right of action on it. The beneficiary's assent, however, terminates the power of the parties to alter the duty to her.

Summary

1. For contract purposes, the parties are simply the people who have made an agreement. Anyone else is a third party. Third parties become important in contract study primarily in two contexts: assignment and delegation and third-party beneficiary promises.

2. The law of assignment and delegation is concerned with the transfer of contract rights or duties by a contracting party to a third party. Literally, assignment is the transfer of contract rights. The assignor is the person transferring the rights and the assignee is the person to whom the rights are transferred. Delegation is transfer of contract duties. The terms assignment, assignor, and assignee are, however, often used to describe transfers of both rights and duties.

3. Generally all contract rights may be assigned and all contract duties may be delegated unless the assignment or delegation would cause a substantial change in the obligation or expectation of the other original party to the contract.

4. Although consent of the nonassigning party is not usually required, the contract may contain a provision prohibiting assignment without consent. Such a provision ordinarily pro-

hibits only the delegation to the assignee of the assignor's performance.

5. If duties are delegated, the delegating party is not relieved of any duty to perform or any liability for breach. The delegating party may, however, be relieved of liability if a substituted contract known as a novation is effected. In a novation, the obligee—the person entitled to performance of the delegated duty—agrees to release the original contracting party and look only to the party to whom the duty has been delegated. If the new party agrees to assume the delegated duty, the original party is discharged.

6. When contract rights are assigned, the assignee should notify the obligor—the person required to render performance—that the assignment has been made. Notification resolves many legal issues occurring in assignments including: (1) whether the duty of the obligor to perform for the assignee arises, (2) which defenses may be asserted against the assignee, (3) when the assignee's rights may be varied by agreement of

---

[17]Restatement (Second) of Contracts §311(3).

the original parties, and (4) the effect of successive assignments of the same right.

7.   When a contract is assigned, the assignee "steps into the shoes" of the assignor, meaning that the assignee acquires no better rights under the contract than the assignor has. Thus, any claim or defense that the obligor has against the assignor may also be asserted against the assignee.

8.   The law of third-party beneficiaries determines when a person who is not a party to a contract but benefits from its performance—a beneficiary—is entitled to enforce it against the original contracting parties. The law provides that a third-party beneficiary may enforce a promise made with the intent to benefit the beneficiary.

9.   Intended beneficiaries are most commonly creditor beneficiaries and donee beneficiaries. A creditor beneficiary is entitled to enforce a promise made to satisfy an obligation owed by the promisee to the beneficiary. A donee beneficiary is allowed to enforce a promise effecting a gift from the promise to the beneficiary.

10.   A person who benefits from performance of a contract but is not an intended beneficiary is an incidental beneficiary. An incidental beneficiary of a promise acquires no rights under the contract.

Key Terms

party	novation
third party	notification
assignment	waiver of defense clause
assignor	beneficiary
assignee	intended beneficiary
obligor	creditor beneficiary
obligee	donee beneficiary
delegation	incidental beneficiary

Questions and Problems

13.1   Buyer ordered 2,500 cases of light bulbs from Seller for delivery in 30 days. Seller had overestimated her inventory, and found herself unable to perform as agreed. Consequently, Seller assigned "the contract" to Crooks, who promised Seller he would perform. Crooks delivered defective merchandise to Buyer.
  (a) Is the duty in this case delegable?
  (b) Is Seller, as a result of the assignment, relieved of her duty to perform?
  (c) Who may Buyer sue for breach of contract?
  (d) Did Seller's assignment transfer the right to Buyer's payment to Crooks?
  (e) Did Seller's assignment transfer Seller's duty to perform to Crooks?

  (f) If the contract had included a provision prohibiting assignment, would the provision preclude a transfer of rights, a delegation of duties, or both, or neither?
  (g) Assume that the goods delivered under the contract conformed to the contract. Crooks had notified Buyer of the assignment. Buyer adamantly refused to pay Crooks, and instead paid Seller. Is Buyer's obligation to pay Crooks affected?

13.2   Shoemaker sold a registered stud quarterhorse to Breeder, who agreed in writing to allow Shoemaker to use the horse for two breedings per year for as long as the horse lived "regardless to whom the horse may be sold." Breeder sold the horse to Joe Doaks, who was aware of and understood the terms of the contract between Shoemaker and Breeder. Nevertheless, Doaks refused to allow Shoemaker to use the horse for breeding purposes. Shoemaker sued Doaks for damages resulting from this refusal. What result?

13.3   Consider whether the rights and duties in the following contracts are assignable.
  (a) Barbara enters into a contract with a television station in a major metropolitan area by which she agrees to render services as a news anchorwoman. The contract is for a three-year term but is renewable for two additional years at the option of the station. Six months later the owners of the station sell it to a third party and assign Barbara's contract as part of the transaction. The new owner replaces many of the personnel, including Barbara's directors, but wants Barbara to continue as anchorwoman. Barbara alleges that she is no longer obligated to perform because the contract was one for personal services which was nonassignable.
  (b) Eli, a cotton farmer, enters into a contract with the Alabama Cotton Company by which Eli agrees to sell all of the cotton grown on his 300-acre farm to Alabama Cotton for 30 cents per pound. Alabama Cotton assigns the contract to the Boll Weevil Corporation. Eli subsequently refuses to deliver the cotton to Boll Weevil alleging that the growing, harvesting, and ginning of cotton constitute personal services so that the contract may not be assigned.
  (c) Eli also alleged that he had entered into the contract with Alabama Cotton in reliance on the fact that Alabama Cotton was an established company of sound financial condition. He further alleged that Boll Weevil was not financially sound and, therefore, would have been unable to pay for Eli's cotton if the price of cotton had declined. In fact, however, the price of cotton increased substantially; at the time Eli was supposed to deliver the cotton, the market price of cotton was 80 cents per pound. Does the fact that Eli relied on Alabama Cotton's financial condition render the contract nonassignable?

13.4   Nails agreed to build a house for Brown for $30,000. Nails assigned the right to payment as well as the duty to perform to Carter. Nails then notified Brown he was leaving the construction business and would not be responsible for

Carter's performance. Brown made no objection and Carter proceeded with the work. Does Brown have any rights against Nails if Carter improperly performs the house construction contract? Why or why not?

13.5   As noted in Chapter 8, an offer may be accepted only by the person or persons to whom it has been directed. That is, offers are generally nonassignable. An option, which limits the offeror's power to revoke an offer, creates contract rights in the offeree (the holder of the option). Under what circumstances, if any, should rights under an option contract be assignable? In other words, should an option holder be allowed to transfer the offer represented by the option to a third party?

13.6   In August 2002, MonArk Boat Company agreed to custom build a houseboat for Roy. As part of a corporate merger, MonArk assigned the contract to AlumaShip, Inc. in July 2003. After AlumaShip notified Roy of the assignment, he paid the final $30,000 installment on the purchase price to AlumaShip and picked up the boat at the AlumaShip dock facilities. The boat immediately required repairs for a bent propeller. En route to a repair shop, a fire broke out on the boat, causing $37,000 damage. Roy sued MonArk alleging that it had breached the contract. In defense, MonArk argued that (1) it could not be held liable for breach because it assigned the contract to AlumaShip, and (2) if it is held liable on the contract, Roy must make the final payment under the contract to MonArk. Is MonArk correct in either of its assertions? Explain.

13.7   Nexxus Products Company, a manufacturer and marketer of hair care products, entered into a contract with Best Company appointing Best as the exclusive distributor of Nexxus products throughout most of Texas. Subsequently, Sally Beauty Company, a distributor of beauty and hair care products in Texas, purchased all of the stock of Best and received assignment of Best's contracts, including the agreement with Nexxus. Nexxus soon learned that Sally Beauty was a wholly owned subsidiary of Alberto-Culver, a manufacturer of hair care products and a direct competitor of Nexxus, and refused to allow Sally Beauty to act as distributor of Nexxus products. May Best's duty of performance under the exclusive distributorship be delegated to Sally Beauty without Nexxus's consent? Explain. See UCC §§2–210(1), 2–306(2).

13.8   Consider the following contracts:
(a) The State of Confusion enters into a contract with B to construct a state office building. The contract provides that B will pay damages to any person injured as a result of the construction. C is injured when she is struck by a brick falling from the partially completed building. Is C a party to the contract between B and the state? May C recover on the contract from B? On what theory?
(b) Shirley contracts to buy a new Corvette from Joe's Chevrolet, Inc. Is General Motors, the manufacturer of Corvettes, a beneficiary of either Joe's promise to deliver the car or Shirley's promise to pay for it? May General Motors recover against either Shirley or Joe if either fails to perform their respective promises? Why or why not?

(c) A promises B that A will pay B's $100 debt to C. B notifies C of the contract and C assents to it. A and B later agree to rescind the contract. Is the rescission effective against C? Explain.

13.9   In each of the following cases, consider whether the plaintiff is entitled to recover for breach of contract as a third-party beneficiary.
(a) Executive Airlines hired Tom Doe as a pilot. Executive then contracted with Avon & Co., an independent insurance agent, to obtain workers' compensation insurance, which was required by state law. After Avon notified Executive that the insurance had been obtained from Liberty Insurance Co., Executive assigned Doe to flight duties. Several weeks later, Doe was killed in a plane crash. When Tina Doe, the pilot's wife and beneficiary, contacted Liberty about the insurance, Liberty informed her that Avon had never obtained a workers' compensation insurance policy. Tina Doe has sued Avon for breach of contract alleging that she was a third-party beneficiary of the contract between Executive and Avon. How should the court rule?
(b) Davis, who operated a ranch in New Mexico, entered into a contract with the U.S. Department of Agriculture by which Davis agreed to provide data to the government on cows, calves, and steers. The contract provided in part, "To protect the contractor [Davis], he must carry workers' compensation insurance on all labor employed under this agreement." Davis employed Ben Cartwright, a cowboy, to perform the labor needed under the contract. Davis, however, failed to buy workers' compensation insurance. While performing his cowboy services, Ben was injured. Because he was not entitled to receive workers' compensation, Ben sued Davis alleging that Davis's failure to buy insurance constituted a breach of the contract between Davis and the government. Ben alleged that he was a third-party beneficiary under the contract thereby entitling him to damages for breach of the contract. What result?

13.10   Leroy Lear hired Phineas Phogg, an attorney, to draft a will. Because Lear's children never called or visited him, he asked Phogg to write the will leaving all of his property to Lear's friend Bill. After signing the will and paying Phogg, Lear told Bill that he would receive all of Lear's property. After Lear died, a court reviewed the will and found that it violated a state law. The will was ruled invalid and Lear's children received all of his property. Bill sued Phogg alleging that Phogg had breached the contract with Lear and that Bill was entitled to damages as an intended third-party beneficiary of the contract. How should the court rule?

13.11   The Washington Metropolitan Area Transit Authority (WMATA) entered into a contract with Massman Construction Company by which Massman agreed to construct a part of the subway system. Under the contract Massman agreed to "maintain, protect and restore those utilities affected by the construction, to perform the construction in such a manner as to keep existing utilities in operation and to repair at its expense all damage to utilities caused by its work." Among the utilities listed in the contract were "Telegraph Company Facilities." The contract also required Massman to submit its plans to Western Union Telegraph Company and other utilities for approval. During the construction, Western Union's underground equipment was damaged and Western Union submitted several bills to Massman for the costs of repairing the equipment. After Massman refused to pay, Western sued alleging that it was a third-party beneficiary of the contract between WMATA and Massman. Is Western correct? Explain.

13.12 Lake University entered into a contract with Carpenter Co. by which Carpenter agreed to complete construction of a new dormitory no later than March 1. Lake also entered into a contract with Plumber, Inc., which agreed to install all plumbing fixtures in the dormitory after the building was constructed. Because Carpenter did not finish the construction until December, the plumbing installation was delayed by more than eight months. Plumber sued Carpenter for breach of contract alleging that Carpenter's failure to complete the building by March 1 caused Plumber to incur damages of $10,000. Is Plumber entitled to sue Carpenter as a third-party beneficiary of the Lake-Carpenter contract? Explain.

PERFORMANCE OF THE CONTRACT

To this point the contracts coverage has focused on the creation and transfer of legally enforceable promises. Contracting parties do not, however, bargain merely for promises—they also bargain for performance of those promises. The law of contracts, therefore, also is concerned with the *performance* of contractual promises, including the standards by which performance is measured and the consequences of nonperformance or breach of a contractual duty.

Even though an enforceable contractual promise may exist, the duty to perform it may not arise because of the occurrence or nonoccurrence of an event known as a *condition*. The first step in performance analysis,

therefore, is to examine the contract to determine the existence and occurrence of any conditions to the promises contained in the contract. Once any conditions to a party's duty have occurred, failure to properly perform that duty results in liability for **breach of contract,** unless performance is excused. Breach may occur in one of two ways: either by nonperformance of a duty when performance is due or by repudiation of the duty prior to that time. If one party's conduct constitutes breach, the other is entitled to a contract remedy. This chapter defines and distinguishes the various types of contract conditions and discusses the important legal issues surrounding breach of contract.

Conditions

A **condition** is an event that must occur before the duty of performance under a contract becomes due.[1] A condition is therefore an event qualifying a contractual duty. Assume S contracts to sell his farm to B. B promises to pay $500,000 for the land, but only if B is able to obtain a mortgage loan from First Bank to cover the purchase price. Obtaining the loan is a condition to B's promise to pay $500,000.

---
[1] RESTATEMENT (SECOND) OF CONTRACTS §224.

Figure 14.1   **Effect of a Condition on a Contractual Promise**

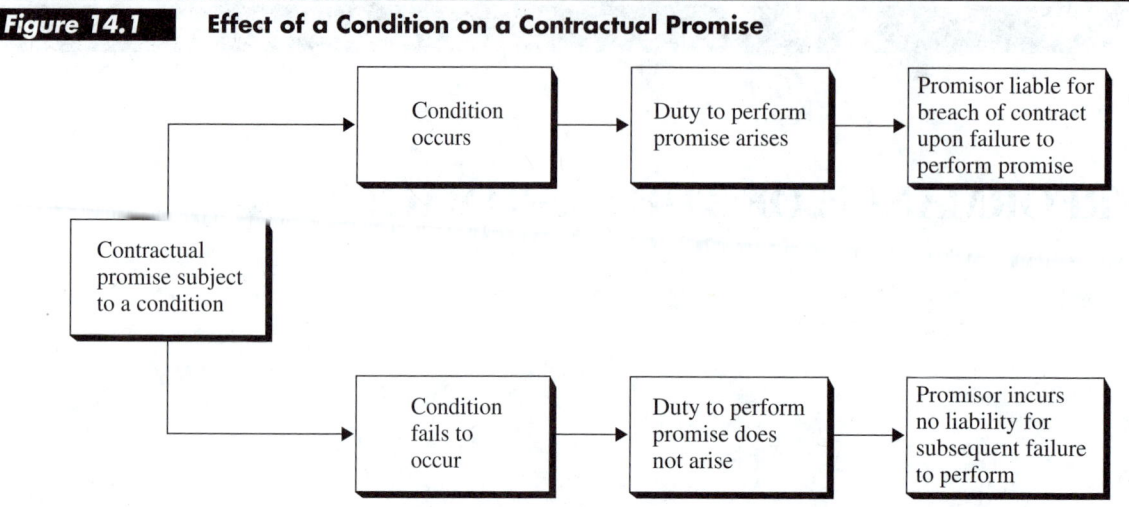

If a promise is subject to a condition, the promisor's duty to perform does not arise unless or until the condition occurs. If the condition occurs and the promisor later fails to perform as agreed, liability for breach of contract usually results. On the other hand, if the condition fails to occur, the promisor's duty to perform is discharged;[2] that is, she incurs no liability for a subsequent failure to perform. Figure 14.1 illustrates the effect of a condition on a contractual promise.

Time of Occurrence — Conditions Precedent, Concurrent, and Subsequent

Conditions frequently are classified according to their time of occurrence as conditions precedent, concurrent, or subsequent. Most conditions are **precedent;** that is, they must occur *before* a duty to perform arises. The financing condition in the above example is a condition precedent.

In some contracts, performances are rendered simultaneously and each party's performance is a condition to the other's duty to perform; that is, the parties' performances are **concurrent conditions.** For example, in contracts for the sale of land, the seller's delivery of the deed and the buyer's payment of the purchase price are usually concurrent conditions. Concurrent conditions may therefore be viewed as mutual conditions precedent. This concept is discussed in more detail below in the material relating to conditions implied in law or "constructive" conditions.

A **condition subsequent** is an event, the occurrence or existence of which, by the terms of the contract, extinguishes a duty to perform after the duty has arisen along with any claim for breach.[3] To illustrate a condition subsequent, assume General Casualty, an insurance company, agrees to insure Marian's property against fire. The policy provides that (1) in order to recover, Marian must notify General within 30 days after the loss, and (2) no recovery under the policy is allowed unless suit is brought within two years after the loss. On these facts, notification within 30 days is a condition precedent to General's duty to pay. Failure to bring suit against the company within two years after the loss (the "condition subsequent") extinguishes that duty after it has arisen, along with any claim against General for breach.

Express Conditions

Conditions provided for in the language (oral or written) of a promise or agreement are known as **express conditions.** The contract term creating an express condition precedent commonly begins with language such as "if," "provided that," "on condition that," or "subject

---

[2]The concept of "discharge" of contract is discussed in Chapter 7.

[3]RESTATEMENT (SECOND) OF CONTRACTS §224 comment e, §230(1).

to." A condition must be an event that is *not certain to occur.* Therefore, the mere passage of time is not a condition to a contractual duty. Thus, a party's duty to perform may depend both upon the passage of time and the occurrence of any conditions. Conditions commonly relate to events occurring after formation of the contract, although they may relate to a present or even a past event. The condition also may be based upon failure of an event to occur as well as occurrence of the event. Generally, exact compliance with the terms of an express condition is necessary before any duty of performance arises.

Purposes of Express Conditions. A promisor may condition his duty primarily for two reasons: (1) to shift the risk of nonoccurrence of the condition to the promisee, or (2) to induce the promisee to cause the event to occur.

The first reason is perhaps most common. Unconditioned contract liability is strict liability. Ordinarily a contracting party states, in effect, "I promise to perform as agreed, under all circumstances, no matter what happens. Period." Many contracting parties are unwilling to assume this rather harsh absolute responsibility for performance, and reduce their potential liability by conditioning the promise by stating in effect, "I promise to perform, if . . ." Assume Scott wishes to contract with Branch for sale of 500 widgets, delivery to be made on June 1. Scott, however, does not have sufficient raw materials to manufacture the goods. The raw materials have been ordered from Goldberg, but the time of their delivery is uncertain. Scott knows that unless she receives them by May 1, she will have insufficient time to perform by June 1. The parties therefore agree that unless Scott receives the raw materials by May 1, her duty to deliver on June 1 will not arise. Receipt of the raw materials by May 1 is an express condition precedent. If it fails to occur, Scott's duty to perform her promise (to manufacture and deliver 500 widgets) will not arise. That is, the risk of nonoccurrence of the condition (nonreceipt of the raw materials) is borne by the promisee, Branch, not the promisor, Scott. If the raw materials are received by May 1, the condition has been met and duty to perform arises. If Scott subsequently fails to manufacture and deliver the goods by June 1, she is liable for breach of contract.

Note that in the preceding example, the occurrence or nonoccurrence of the condition—Goldberg's delivery of raw materials by May 1—was not within the control of either party. Conditions often have the effect of allocating risk from promisor to promisee even if the occurrence or nonoccurrence of the condition is wholly or partially within the promisor's control. For example, real estate contracts often condition the buyer's duty to pay the purchase price upon his or her ability to obtain adequate mortgage financing. In these cases, the buyer makes an implied promise to use best efforts to bring about occurrence of the condition.[4]

In addition to allocating risk, a condition also may be used to induce the promisee to cause the condition to occur. Assume Seller contracts to specially manufacture and deliver goods to Buyer. Buyer intends to use the goods as part of a trade show display beginning at 1 P.M. on June 1. Because later delivery would substantially impair (if not totally defeat) the value of Seller's performance to Buyer, Seller promises to deliver the goods not later than 9 A.M. on June 1 and that delivery by that time is a condition to Buyer's duty to accept and pay for the goods. A term making time of performance a condition to the promisor's duty is commonly known as a **time of the essence** provision. On these facts, two consequences result if Seller fails to deliver by 9 A.M. First, because a condition has not occurred, Buyer's duty to perform does not arise and is discharged. Second, Seller becomes liable for breach of contract because he failed to perform his express promise.

The parties should always clearly express their intent to create conditional promises, because disputes often arise when ambiguous language is used. For example, a promisor may state, "I promise to pay for these goods when I get my Christmas bonus," or "I promise to pay my lawyer when he collects the debt." If a dispute over the duty to pay arises, the court must determine whether receiving the Christmas bonus or collecting the debt are express conditions to the promisor's duty.

In making this determination, courts usually state that an event is not a condition to the promisor's duty unless the promisee has control over occurrence of the event or the contract language or other circumstances clearly indicate that the promisee has assumed the risk of the event's nonoccurrence. This rule

---

[4]Conditional promises giving the promisor partial or total control over occurrence of the condition raise mutuality of consideration issues, discussed in Chapter 9.

of interpretation is designed to reduce the promisee's risk of **forfeiture**—the denial of compensation that results when the promisee loses the right to the agreed exchange after relying substantially, through preparation or performance, on the expectation of that exchange.[5]

In the following case, the court was required to determine whether the contract provisions created express conditions.

A. A. Conte, Inc. v. Campbell-Lowrie-Lautermilch Corporation
477 N.E.2d 30 (Ill. App. 1985)

Campbell-Lowrie-Lautermilch Corporation (Campbell-Lowrie), the general contractor for a construction project, entered into a contract with A. A. Conte, Inc. (Conte), a subcontractor who was to perform excavating work on the project. The contract provided in part:

> Article 5: Material invoices submitted before the 25th of the current month will be paid by the 28th of the following month, provided the material so delivered is acceptable, and if payment for invoiced material has been received by Campbell-Lowrie-Lautermilch Corporation under its general contract. . . .

> Article 18: . . . [I]f the work has been satisfactorily performed and invoice as rendered is approved and if payment for such labor and material so invoiced has been received by Campbell-Lowrie-Lautermilch Corporation under its general contract, the subcontractor will be paid 85% of invoice as approved, less any payments previously made on account for previous periods.

After completing the excavation, Conte submitted a bill for $83,956 to Campbell-Lowrie who submitted it with other bills to the property owners in accordance with the general contract. The owners failed to pay Campbell-Lowrie and subsequently became insolvent.

Conte sued Campbell-Lowrie, demanding payment of its bill. The trial court granted summary judgment in favor of Campbell-Lowrie, holding that payment to Conte was contingent upon Campbell-Lowrie's receiving payment from the owners. Conte appealed.

Johnson, Justice

. . . The gist of Campbell-Lowrie's affirmative defense was that Article 18 of its contract with Conte set forth a condition precedent to payment. The condition was that Campbell-Lowrie must first receive payment from the owners of the project under the general contract before it was obligated to pay its subcontractors. The owners had not paid Campbell-Lowrie; therefore, Conte was not entitled to payment from Campbell-Lowrie. . . .

Campbell-Lowrie points out that the plain meaning of the language in Articles 5 and 18 of the contract creates a condition precedent to payment and that there is no ambiguity in the language. . . .

A court may not rewrite a contract to suit one of the parties but must enforce the terms as written. . . . Thus, the rights of the parties are limited by the terms expressed in the contract. . . .

We do not believe that the record supports Conte's claim that its right to payment by Campbell-Lowrie was absolute and not in any way contingent upon Campbell-Lowrie's receiving payment from the owners under the general contract. Our analysis of paragraphs 5 and 18 of the contract in question convinces us that the language is clear and unambiguous and, thus, there is no need to resort to rules of construction . . . nor extrinsic evidence. . . . It is true, as pointed out by Conte, that conditions precedent are not generally favored and courts will not construe stipulations to be a condition precedent when such a construction would result in forfeiture. It is also true, as acknowledged by Conte, that plain, unambiguous language contained in the contract binds the parties to a condition precedent.

Since we have already determined that the language of the contract is plain and unambiguous, we must also conclude that the parties are bound by it. We note that the contract in question was between two entities engaged in business in the construction industry and presumably often entered into other contractual agreements of a similar nature in the course of their business. While it is clear that with the benefit of hindsight Conte may have chosen to exclude or draft differently the language of paragraphs 5 and 18, which gave rise to this dispute, this court cannot redraft the contract, and we must enforce the contract as written and agreed upon by the parties. . . .

[Judgment affirmed.]

---

[5]RESTATEMENT (SECOND) OF CONTRACTS §227 and comment b.

Conditions Implied in Fact

In addition to conditions created by the express language of the parties, conditions also may be implied from the language or other conduct of the parties. These are **conditions implied in fact.** For example, assume Todd is a tenant in a house owned by Larry. Upon renewal of the lease, Todd agrees to do the labor necessary to remodel the bathroom and the kitchen. In exchange, Larry agrees to reduce the rent and supply the necessary materials. In this case, Todd cannot perform unless Larry performs his promise. Therefore, Larry's supplying the building materials is a condition implied in fact to Todd's duty even though not expressly stated in the contract.

Implied (Constructive) Conditions

An important class of contract conditions arises neither from the language (express conditions) nor from the other conduct (conditions implied in fact) of the parties. These conditions are imposed as a matter of law and are referred to as conditions **implied in law,** or more commonly, **constructive conditions.**

Constructive Conditions of Exchange. The most important implied or constructive conditions are known as **constructive conditions of exchange.** This concept can be explained as follows: In a bilateral contract, the parties exchange promises with the expectation of a subsequent exchange of performances. That is, the parties bargain for performance, not the right to sue the other for breach. The constructive conditions doctrine is designed to protect the parties' expectation that the subsequent exchange of performances will occur. Under this approach, it is a condition to each party's duty to perform the remaining duties under a promise that there be no uncured material failure of the other party's performance due at an earlier time.[6] In other words, proper performance by each party is a constructive condition to the other's duty to render any subsequent performance.

For example, assume Bill contracts to landscape Mary's yard in exchange for Mary's promise to pay $1,000. By terms of the contract, Bill is to complete the work by May 1, with Mary's payment due ten days thereafter. Bill fails to do the work. Under the constructive conditions of exchange doctrine, Bill's proper performance is a condition to Mary's duty to pay. Because Bill did not perform, a condition to Mary's duty has not occurred; Mary is therefore not required to perform her promise (pay $1,000).

Courts and statutes frequently state that **failure of consideration** is a defense to enforcement of a contractual obligation. What this terminology actually means is "failure of performance," that is, failure of the other party to perform his promise—failure of a constructive condition of exchange. It *does not mean* lack or absence of consideration, because the consideration is provided by the exchange of promises, making them enforceable. It is the subsequent failure to perform the promises that gives rise to the defense.

As a result of constructive conditions of exchange, contractual promises are sometimes said to be **dependent** in nature, meaning that failure by one party to perform justifies the other's failure to perform. It should be noted, however, that covenants in leases and in other conveyances of land have traditionally been treated as **independent.** That is, nonperformance by one party generally does not excuse further performance by the other.[7]

Order of Performance. Frequently in contract disputes both parties fail to perform. Ascertaining the required order of performance is therefore important in determining whether a party's failure to perform constitutes a breach or is justified by the other's failure. In other words, in applying the constructive conditions of exchange doctrine, the threshold question is, who is required to perform *first?*

The order of performance may be determined by the express terms of the contract. Suppose S and B have a contract for sale of goods, calling for delivery in 30 days and payment within ten days after delivery. On these facts, it is apparent from the terms of the contract that S is to perform first. Additionally, if the performance of one party extends over a period of time, his performance is due first unless the contract provides otherwise. This rule generally applies in

---

[6]RESTATEMENT (SECOND) OF CONTRACTS §237.

[7]This concept is discussed in conjunction with the landlord-tenant material in Chapter 36.

contracts involving services, such as employment or construction contracts.[8]

Unless the contract or circumstances indicate otherwise, performances are due simultaneously. Simultaneous performance is possible under an agreement in the following circumstances: (1) if the same time (or period of time) is fixed for performance of each party, (2) if the time of performance is fixed for one party but not the other, or (3) if no time is fixed for the performance of either party. This approach is followed both for UCC and common law contracts.[9] As previously noted, a contract for the sale of land, for example, normally contemplates a simultaneous exchange of the deed (the conveyance of the property) and the purchase price. A contract for the sale of goods, unless otherwise agreed, requires simultaneous delivery of the goods and payment of the price.

Tender of Performance. If performance is to occur simultaneously, the concept of tender of performance becomes important. A **tender of performance** is either actual performance or an offer to perform, coupled with the manifested present ability to do so. When performances are to be exchanged simultaneously, each party's tender of performance is a condition to the other's duty. Thus, it is frequently stated that mutual tenders of performance are "concurrent conditions." A tender of performance need not be actual performance. One advantage of simultaneous performance is that one party is not required to perform without reasonable assurance that the other also will perform. Additionally, simultaneous performance avoids placing the burden on one party of financing the other's performance. In order to put the nonperforming party in breach, the injured party need not actually perform, but must make only a tender or offer to perform. Until a party has at least made an offer to perform, the other's duty does not arise. If both parties fail to make a tender, neither party is in breach.

To illustrate the operation of the preceding rules, assume Sandberg agrees to sell Bench a machine for $10,000, delivery to be made at Sandberg's warehouse on June 1. On June 1 both parties are present at the warehouse, but Sandberg neither delivers nor offers to deliver the machine and Bench neither pays nor offers to pay for the machine. Neither party can hold the other liable for breach. If Sandberg places the machine on his loading dock ready for delivery and Bench fails to pay, Sandberg has a claim for breach against Bench. Conversely, if Bench tenders the price to Sandberg at the agreed time and place and Sandberg fails to deliver, Sandberg is liable for breach.

Whether or not simultaneous performance is required under a contract, and unless the contract or other circumstances indicate otherwise, a party is required to render her entire performance at one time if it is possible to do so. In other words, a party is generally not entitled to perform part of her promise at a time, and the other party may not require her to do so.

Excuse of Condition

Occasionally, a duty to perform a promise will arise even though a condition to that duty has not occurred. Two common situations excusing occurrence of a condition, waiver and failure to act in good faith, are discussed in the following paragraphs.

Waiver. **Waiver** is a term used somewhat loosely in the law. It generally is defined as the voluntary surrender or relinquishment of a known right, usually unaccompanied by consideration. In particular, a party granting a waiver effectively promises to perform a duty despite the nonoccurrence of a condition to that duty. A waiver may occur either before or after nonoccurrence of the condition.

Because a waiver effectively operates as a contract modification, the issue of consideration for the modification may arise. Generally, a promise to perform a conditional duty, even though the condition has not occurred, is binding without consideration. If, however, the promise to disregard the nonoccurrence of the condition has a material effect upon what is received by the promisor or materially changes the burden or risk he has agreed to assume, consideration to support it is generally required.[10]

Therefore, the types of conditions subject to waiver without consideration under the preceding rule are those that may be viewed as merely technical or procedural in nature or conditions concerning comparatively

---

[8]In these cases, however, the contract generally provides for periodic or progress payments to the party rendering the longer performance. Further, most states have statutes requiring frequent periodic payment of wages in employment contracts.

[9]UCC §§2–507(1), 2–511(1); RESTATEMENT (SECOND) OF CONTRACTS §234(1) and comment b.

[10]RESTATEMENT (SECOND) OF CONTRACTS §84(1) and comment c.

minor matters. Examples include conditions relating to the time or manner of performance or requirements of notice.[11]

Notwithstanding lack of consideration, waivers frequently are enforceable on the basis of estoppel. That is, if one contracting party leads the other to believe that she will not insist upon occurrence of a condition to her duty, and the other changes position in reliance on that representation—for example, by failing to cause the condition to occur—enforcement of the waiver is frequently necessary to avoid injustice to the reliant party.

Failure to Act in Good Faith—Prevention and Hindrance. Both the UCC and the common law impose a duty of good faith and fair dealing upon the parties in the performance and enforcement of the contract.[12] For example, bad faith performance takes many forms, including evasion of the spirit of the contract, lack of diligence, intentionally rendering imperfect performance, abusing a power to specify terms, and interference with, or failure to cooperate in, the other party's performance.[13] Breach of the duty to act in good faith in contract performance is commonly discussed as **prevention** or **hindrance** by one party of the other's performance. Nonperformance of this duty has two effects.

1. Because each party is under a duty to act in good faith, nonperformance of that duty is a breach of the contract. Assume Standard Packaging, Inc. agrees to manufacture and sell 100,000 plastic containers to Bottle, Inc. for $25,000. Bottle is to select an assortment of sizes and colors from a list stated in the contract. Bottle fails to make the selection within a reasonable time, and as a result, the manufacture of the containers is delayed, causing Standard loss. Because the duty of good faith requires Bottle to make the selection within a reasonable time, its failure to do so is a breach.

2. If a party's failure to act in good faith substantially contributes to the nonoccurrence of a condition to his duty, the occurrence of that condition is excused. In other words, the party who prevents or hinders the occurrence of the condition becomes liable to perform despite its nonoccurrence. Thus, if a duty to cooperate is imposed (either by the terms of the contract or as part of the duty to act in good faith), lack of cooperation results in breach. For example, assume Sullivan contracts with Bancroft to sell a tract of land for $25,000. Bancroft's duty is conditional upon her procurement of mortgage financing at a specified interest rate and term in the amount of the purchase price. Bancroft fails to make reasonable efforts to obtain financing and subsequently refuses to perform when Sullivan tenders the deed. Sullivan has a claim for breach of contract against Bancroft. Bancroft's breach of her duty to act in good faith substantially contributed to the nonoccurrence of a condition to her duty to pay the purchase price (obtaining adequate mortgage financing), thereby excusing it. To illustrate further, assume Anderson, an auditor, contracts with Nationwide, a corporation, to prepare audited financial statements as of June 30, and to issue a report by August 1, the date of the annual stockholders' meeting. Anderson is subsequently unable to complete the report by August 1 because of delays and lack of cooperation by the company's staff. In this case, because Nationwide's lack of cooperation substantially contributed to nonoccurrence of a condition to Nationwide's duty to pay (completion by August 1), the condition is excused.

Performance and Breach

Contract duties are discharged—extinguished or terminated—in various ways. For example, a contractual obligation may be discharged by a mutual agreement to rescind or modify it, a novation or other substituted contract, an accord and satisfaction, or nonoccurrence of a condition. In addition, contracts may be discharged by a promisor's bankruptcy, expiration of the statute of limitations, or through material alteration of a written agreement.

Most contracts are discharged by full performance on both sides, while others are discharged by material breach of the promises contained in the agreement. The remainder of this chapter examines the various legal doctrines that distinguish proper performance of a contract from breach, the legal tools designed to protect each party's expectation of performance prior to the time of agreed performance, and the circumstances in

---

[11]It should be noted, however, that, under the UCC, contract modifications need no consideration to be binding if sought in good faith. A similar rule applies to common law contracts in certain circumstances. Thus, a waiver affecting even a material part of the exchange may be binding without consideration as a contract modification.

[12]UCC §1–304; RESTATEMENT (SECOND) OF CONTRACTS §205; good faith is discussed in Chapter 6.

[13]RESTATEMENT (SECOND) OF CONTRACTS §205 comment d.

which contract performance is excused without liability for breach.

The "Substantial Performance" Doctrine

It is one thing to say that nonperformance of a contractual duty constitutes breach of the contract. It is quite another to apply this principle to concrete fact situations. That is, a fundamental issue in any breach of contract case is to examine the nature of the nonperformance causing the dispute. For example, the promisor may utterly fail to perform or may render virtually full performance containing only minor defects or omissions. Courts must therefore determine the legal effect of these varying degrees of contract performance.

Although simultaneous performance of contract promises is preferred, the contract may either expressly or impliedly require one party to perform before the other. Sometimes the first party to perform will unintentionally and inadvertently render performance not literally in compliance with the contract. Contract disputes frequently arise when the party rendering such a performance asserts a right to payment on the basis of completed performance. The other party, however, refuses to perform asserting that, under the constructive conditions of exchange doctrine, she should be excused from performance because of a material defect in the first party's performance. Before one party's failure to perform causes the nonoccurrence of a constructive condition to the other's duty (thereby discharging that duty), the failure of performance must be judged **material.** The resolution of such disputes, therefore, turns upon which defects in performance are material and which are not.

The court may find that the defect in performance is immaterial or, alternatively, as is commonly stated, there has been *substantial* performance. In this situation, the constructive condition to the second party's duty has occurred, and she is required to perform her promise. This is known as the **substantial performance doctrine,** derived from the landmark case *Jacob & Youngs v. Kent* decided in 1921.[14] However, because substantial performance is not full performance, damages are recoverable for **partial breach;** damages are based only upon *part* of the right to performance under the contract. The benefit of the bargain is obtained partially through the award of damages and partially through the "substantial" performance.

The court, however, may find that the defect in performance is material. In this case, the constructive condition to the second party's duty has not occurred. Therefore, the second party's duty to perform does not arise and is discharged if the breach cannot be cured. The second party is entitled to damages for **total breach** of the contract; damages based upon *all* of his right to performance. The benefit of the bargain is obtained by completely substituting a judgment for money damages for the wrongdoer's duty to perform, and the breaching party is absolved from further duty to perform the contract. Nevertheless, the breaching party may have a claim in restitution for benefits conferred upon the other. In sum, if the failure to perform is a material breach, the injured party may sue for damages for total breach and is relieved of his corresponding duty to perform. If the breach is immaterial, the injured party must perform but is entitled to damages for partial breach.

The substantial performance doctrine must be viewed as a limited exception to the general rule that exact, literal performance of contractual promises is required for recovery. Contract law provides certainty and predictability; it is designed to protect the parties' reasonable expectations that contractual promises will be performed as agreed. To allow a party who has not literally fulfilled the terms of his promise to recover effectively binds the other to an agreement to which he has not assented. It also encourages the parties to deviate, however slightly, from the literal terms of the bargain. Both results are inconsistent with the basic purposes of contract law. Therefore, the substantial performance doctrine applies only if the departure from the agreed terms is unintentional and "immaterial."

The substantial performance doctrine is often used by the courts, in the interest of justice, when extreme forfeiture would otherwise result from the nonoccurrence of a condition. The risk of forfeiture is greatest when one party must partially or completely perform before the other party's duty to perform arises. For this reason, the substantial performance doctrine has been most frequently invoked in construction contracts to rescue a contractor rendering defective performance.

As noted earlier in this chapter, a risk of forfeiture follows failure of an express as well as a constructive condition. Express conditions must be literally fulfilled before a duty to perform arises, in contrast to constructive conditions, which need only be substantially performed. Nevertheless, even when the parties expressly condition their duties in unmistakable language upon

---

[14]129 N.E. 889 (N.Y. 1921).

the occurrence of an event, the court may, in order to do justice, excuse the occurrence of the condition if necessary to avoid an extreme forfeiture unless the occurrence was a material part of the agreed exchange. This rule may apply, for example, to a "time of the essence" provision when the court finds that time of performance was not, in fact, a material part of the agreed exchange.

The following case illustrates the application of the substantial performance doctrine.

Continental Dredging, Inc. v. De-Kaizered, Inc.

120 S.W.3d 380 (Tex. App. 2003)

Defendant De-Kaizered, Inc. owns and operates a dock at the port of Houston, Texas. To accommodate larger shipping vessels, De-Kaizered hired plaintiff Continental Dredging, Inc. to dredge the channel in front of its dock to a depth of thirty-six feet. Their contract provided that De-Kaizered would pay $4.00 per cubic yard of excavated material based on a before and after survey to be conducted by Survey Resources Inc. (SRI). After Continental completed the work, SRI determined that the channel had been dredged to at least 36 feet through removal of 27,882 cubic yards of material. During the next few months, several large ships were unable to dock at De-Kaizered's dock because the channel was not deep enough. The ship channel Pilots Association eventually ruled that De-Kaizered's dock should be used only by ships requiring 33 feet or less of depth. After De-Kaizered refused to pay, Continental sued De-Kaizered for breach of contract. A jury found that Continental had breached the contract but that De-Kaizered also was in breach for failure to pay Continental. Both parties appealed.

Ross, Justice

De-Kaizered contends Continental materially breached the contract as a matter of law because legally and factually sufficient evidence exists to support the jury's finding that Continental failed to dredge to a depth of thirty-six feet in front of the dock. Therefore, De-Kaizered claims it is excused from payment under the contract. . . . While there is no explicit finding on whether Continental dredged to thirty-six feet, the jury did find Continental breached the contract. Since the only theory proposed and argued for the breach of contract claim was failure to dredge to thirty-six feet, the jury implicitly held Continental failed to dredge to a depth of thirty-six feet.

Because the contract at issue involved a sale of services, the common law applies. In the context of construction contracts, the standard for whether a breach of contract excuses performance by the other party has long been whether there was "substantial performance." "Substantial performance" means:

> The contractor must have in good faith intended to comply with the contract, and shall have substantially done so in the sense that the defects are not pervasive, do not constitute a deviation from the general plan contemplated for the work, and are not so essential that the object of the parties in making the contract and its purpose cannot, without difficulty, be accomplished by remedying them.

[*Turner, Collie & Braden, Inc. v. Brookhollow, Inc.,* 642 S.W.2d 160, 164, (Tex. 1982).] The "substantial performance" test has also been expanded beyond construction contracts. . . . If there is a material breach of the contract, the contract has not been substantially performed. . . .

In *Hernandez v. Gulf Group Lloyds,* [875 S.W.2d 691, 693 (Tex. 1994)], the Texas Supreme Court quoted five factors from the Second Restatement of Contracts used by courts to determine materiality of the breach. These factors are: 1) the extent to which the non-breaching party will be deprived of the benefit that it could have reasonably anticipated from full performance; 2) the extent to which the injured party can be adequately compensated for the part of the benefit of which he or she will be deprived; 3) the extent to which the party failing to perform will suffer forfeiture; 4) the likelihood that the party failing to perform will cure his or her failure, taking into account all the circumstances, including reasonable assurances; and 5) the extent to which the behavior of the party failing to perform or to offer to perform comports with the standards of good faith and fair dealing. . . .

The first factor under *Hernandez* is the extent to which the nonbreaching party was deprived of the benefit expected under the contract. . . . De-Kaizered argues it "would have gotten what it bargained for only if Continental achieved the depth specified in the contract." However, the question is not whether De-Kaizered received exactly that for which it bargained, but rather the extent it was deprived of that for which it had bargained. The term substantial performance always means something less than full and exact performance of the contract. . . . The channel was deepened approximately ten feet, from around twenty-five feet to around thirty-five or thirty-six feet. The SRI survey and testimony concerning the leadline tests all indicate Continental dredged close to, if not actually, thirty-six feet. Further, the fact that the ship channel Pilots Association restricted access to De-Kaizered's dock to ships requiring thirty-three feet or less shows that, even though ships of thirty-six-foot draft could not dock, ships of considerably greater draft could dock than before Continental's dredging. Generally, "the ratio between what was left unperformed and the total performance promised will frequently be decisive." 8 *Corbin on Contracts* §36.6 (2003). While in this case the ratio is not easy to state in mathematical terms, it is clear Continental performed substantially close to the contract terms. Therefore, De-Kaizered received substantially close to that for which it had bargained.

An examination of the other factors also indicates there was factually sufficient evidence to support a conclusion there was no material breach. Because De-Kaizered could have collected under contract law for both the costs of completing the dredging to the contract specifications, and the damages incurred due to the alleged breach, De-Kaizered could have been adequately compensated for the benefit of which it was deprived. If De-Kaizered is excused from performance, Continental will suffer considerable forfeiture. Further, all circumstances indicate Continental acted in good faith in concluding it had completed the contract. . . .

The great weight and preponderance of the evidence does not indicate Continental failed to meet its burden of proving substantial performance. The evidence, therefore, is factually sufficient to support the jury's finding. . . .

[Judgment affirmed.]

Substantial Performance Under the UCC— The "Perfect Tender" Rule

In contracts for the sale of goods, courts have long held that the buyer is entitled to expect strict, literal performance of the contract by the seller. Under UCC §2–503(1), to make a valid tender of delivery the seller must "put and hold conforming goods at the buyer's disposition." Under §2–601, if the goods or the tender of delivery fail "in any respect to conform to the contract," the buyer may reject the entire shipment. Additionally, because goods may fluctuate rapidly in price, performance at the agreed time is generally essential; that is, time is of the essence. Therefore, in order to recover, the seller must tender goods conforming in every respect to the terms of the contract. This requirement is commonly known as the **perfect tender rule,** which, if interpreted literally, means that there is no "substantial performance" doctrine applicable to contracts for the sale of goods.

The Code, however, provides many exceptions to the perfect tender rule, outlined below, that create a special form of the substantial performance doctrine for sales contracts.

1. The perfect tender rule does not apply to installment contracts. An **installment contract** is one requiring or authorizing the seller to deliver the goods in separate lots to be separately accepted by the buyer. In such contracts, governed by §2–612, the buyer is entitled to reject an installment only if its nonconformity *substantially impairs* the value of that installment and cannot be corrected by the seller. Similarly, a default as to one or more installments is a breach of the whole contract only if it *substantially impairs* the value of the whole. The rationale for this approach is that "the fact of a continuing relationship normally justifies a less rigid standard for installment contracts than for contracts for a single delivery."[15]

2. Perfect tender is not required if the parties' contract allows a less strict standard of performance. The effect of UCC provisions may generally be varied by agreement of the parties under §1–302. As such, the parties are free to set by contract the standards by which performance is to be measured.[16]

3. Under certain circumstances, §2–508 gives a seller the opportunity to "cure" or correct a defective performance without liability for breach.

4. A buyer, entitled to reject a tender of delivery, may lose that right through failure to make an adequate rejection or failure to particularize the defects in the goods.

5. Under certain limited circumstances, a buyer may revoke a previous acceptance of goods under §2–608. The buyer may, however, revoke only if the nonconformity "substantially impairs" their value to him.

---

[15] Supplement Number 1 to the Uniform Commercial Code 1 (1955).
[16] See discussion in Chapter 6.

The perfect tender rule and the concepts of rejection, cure, acceptance, and revocation of acceptance are discussed in more detail in Chapter 18.

Part Performances as Agreed Equivalents — Divisibility

A contracting party may properly render part performance under a contract, but fail to properly perform her remaining obligations.[17] When a contract has been partially performed, the law must determine to what extent, if at all, the party in default is entitled to recover under the contract for the performance actually rendered. The answer to this question is determined by applying the **divisibility** doctrine. Under the original *Restatement of Contracts* definition, a contract is divisible if by its terms: "(1) performance of each party is divided into two or more parts, and (2) the number of parts due from each party is the same, and (3) the performance of each part by one party is the agreed exchange for a corresponding part by the other party."[18] If a contract is divisible, performance of a divisible part by one party entitles her to the agreed exchange for that part, despite her nonperformance of other parts of the contract. The *Restatement (Second) of Contracts*[19] finds a contract divisible if full performance under the contract can be apportioned into corresponding pairs of part performances so that the exchange of the part performances can be regarded as **agreed equivalents.**

The rationale for the principle of divisibility and agreed equivalents is the same as that supporting the substantial performance doctrine — to reduce the risk of forfeiture to the breaching party. If the doctrine of agreed equivalents applies, the party who renders part performance is entitled to recover its agreed equivalent as if the parties had made a separate contract concerning that pair of performances. Failure to perform some other part, though possibly constituting a breach of contract, does not affect the right to recover for the part performance. Assume Seller and Buyer have a contract for the sale of 600 watches for $30,000 to extend over a one-year period. Seller is to deliver 50 watches on the first of each month. Buyer is required to pay one-twelfth of the purchase price for each shipment upon delivery. On these facts, the court may find that each delivery and the corresponding payment are agreed equivalents, making the contract divisible. Therefore, if Seller properly makes the first delivery, but subsequently breaches by refusing to render further performance, she may enforce Buyer's corresponding duty to pay for that performance (one-twelfth of $30,000). Buyer, however, has a claim against Seller for breaching the remainder of the contract.

To apply the divisibility doctrine, the court must be able to calculate the amount due for the part performance. This calculation is possible, for example, if the prices for each performance are separately stated in the contract or can be ascertained from other sources, such as price lists. In addition to apportioning the price for the corresponding part performances, the court also must find that the corresponding pairs are agreed equivalents. That is, the injured party should not be required to pay for a part performance unless he can make full use of that portion without the rest of the performance.[20] If the court finds that the part performance is insufficient to meet this test, the contract is generally designated **entire.** Contracts are deemed entire, for example, if performance is divided into parts representing only periodic progress payments toward the completion of a single job.

To illustrate, assume Ace Construction Company agrees to build a house for Doaks for $40,000, who agrees to finance the construction by paying one-fourth of the purchase price when the foundation is completed, one-fourth upon completion of the basic frame, one-fourth when the exterior is finished, and the final one-fourth upon receipt of the architect's certificate. Ace unjustifiably stops work upon completion of the basic frame and sues to recover the second installment. Ace's partial performance (construction of the basic frame on the foundation) and Doak's promise to pay $10,000 are not agreed equivalents. Ace is entitled to recover nothing from Doaks under the contract for that performance. That is, the payments are not made in exchange for a specified fraction of the building (creating in essence four separate contracts), but are part payments on the total purchase price of the house. Doaks has a claim against Ace for damages for breach of the contract.[21]

---

[17]The failure to render complete performance may or may not constitute a breach of the contract; for example, the party's remaining duties may be excused on grounds of impracticability (discussed later in this chapter).

[18]RESTATEMENT OF CONTRACTS §266 comment e.

[19]RESTATEMENT (SECOND) OF CONTRACTS §240.

[20]RESTATEMENT (SECOND) OF CONTRACTS §240 comment e.

[21]Although Ace is able to recover nothing *under the contract* for its part performance, the court may, in order to avoid unjust enrichment, require Doaks to make restitution of the value of any benefit conferred upon him by Ace's performance; see the restitution discussion in Chapter 15.

Effect of Prospective Nonperformance

Each party to a contract involving an exchange of promises contemplates a subsequent exchange of performances. The preceding discussion concerns the effect of a party's failure to perform a promise when performance becomes due. Each party also expects that the other will do nothing to jeopardize the expectation of return performance *prior to* the time of agreed performance. The following two sections outline the legal tools designed to protect the *expectation* of performance. First, UCC §2–609 is discussed, which protects a party when "reasonable grounds for insecurity" arise concerning the other's ability to perform. Second, the more aggravated case, repudiation, is discussed. Here, one party, before performance is due, unequivocally indicates an intent not to perform.

Safeguarding the Expectation of Performance—UCC §2–609

The Uniform Commercial Code recognizes that the essential purpose of a contract for sale is actual performance. The parties "do not bargain merely for a promise, or for a promise plus the right to win a lawsuit. . . . [A] continuing sense of reliance and security that the promised performance will be forthcoming when due, is an important feature of the bargain."[22] Section 2–609(1) imposes an obligation on each party that the other's expectation of receiving due performance will not be impaired. To accomplish this purpose, the Code provides that whenever reasonable grounds for insecurity arise concerning the willingness or ability of either party to perform, the insecure party

1. may demand adequate assurance of due performance in writing, and
2. until he receives such assurance may, if commercially reasonable, suspend any performance for which he has not already received the agreed return.

Two legal questions must be answered to apply this provision: What are **reasonable grounds for insecurity,** and what constitutes **adequate assurance of due performance?**

Concerning the first question, note that the grounds for insecurity need not be *actual,* they need only be *reasonable.* To illustrate, assume S contracts to sell 500 printed circuit boards to B for future delivery. Prior to delivery, B hears a false rumor from an apparently trustworthy source that S is making defective deliveries to other buyers (or that S is on the verge of bankruptcy). The rumor would give B reasonable grounds for insecurity about S's ability to perform. To protect her expectation of performance, B may suspend her own performance. The rumor need not actually be true; the buyer must simply have *reasonable grounds* for believing it to be true. The same reasoning applies if a seller hears a false rumor concerning the financial condition of a buyer to whom he extends credit. The obligation of good faith is, of course, imposed upon any requests for assurance. Therefore, a party may not invoke §2–609 merely as a means to delay or avoid contractual obligations.

What constitutes adequate assurance of due performance is a question of fact, depending upon the circumstances of the case, including the reputation of the party receiving the demand, the relationship and any prior dealings of the parties, the nature of the reason for insecurity, and whether there have been past delinquencies or defective shipments.

The test of adequate assurance is objective, not subjective; that is, the issue is whether a reasonable person would be satisfied with the assurance, not whether the demanding party is, in fact, satisfied. Under §2–609(2), between merchants, the reasonableness of grounds for insecurity and the adequacy of any assurance offered are determined according to commercial standards.

Based upon these and any other relevant factors, adequate assurance may be provided (if the problem involves defective deliveries) by a reputable seller's statement that he is giving the matter his prompt attention and that the defects will not recur. Any assurance relative to defective delivery that interferes with the buyer's use of the goods must be accompanied by replacement, repair, credit against the purchase price, or other reasonable cure. In the case of a disreputable seller, more assurance may be required, such as posting a bond or immediate replacement of the defective shipment. On the other hand, if the buyer's ability to pay is in issue, adequate assurance may simply involve a satisfactory explanation by the buyer. In more serious cases, a credit report from the buyer's banker, or a surety, or collateral to secure the debt may be required.

Once a justified demand has been received, the party to whom it is directed has a reasonable time, not

---

[22]UCC §2–609, Official Comment 1.

exceeding 30 days, to provide adequate assurances. Failure to do so constitutes a repudiation of the contract, which is then governed by the principles discussed in the following section. Assume Jake and Mike contract on January 1 for delivery of goods on June 1. In February, Mike hears a rumor concerning Jake's impending bankruptcy and demands assurances on February 15. Jake has a reasonable time from February 15 not exceeding 30 days to provide assurance. His failure to do so is a repudiation of the contract governed by principles discussed in the following section.

Note finally that §2–609 is an innovation in the law. Though applicable only to UCC contracts (sales of goods), a similar rule, based upon §2–609, has been adopted for common law contracts in the *Restatement (Second) of Contracts.*[23] In the following case, the court discusses the policy behind §2–609 and adopts its principles for common law contracts in New York.

Norcon Power Partners, L.P. v. Niagara Mohawk Power Corp.
705 N.E.2d 656 (N.Y. 1998)

Niagara Mohawk Power Corp., a public utility that provides gas and electric power to upstate New York, entered into a 25-year contract with Norcon Power Partners, L.P., an independent power producer. The contract required Niagara Mohawk to purchase all electricity generated at Norcon's plant at a fixed rate. Norcon, however, was required to maintain an adjustment account of the difference between Niagara's fixed payments and Niagara Mohawk's "avoided cost"—the lesser of the cost for Niagara Mohawk to generate the electricity itself or its cost to purchase the electricity from other sources. If the balance of the adjustment account was positive, Norcon would have to repay Niagara Mohawk; if the adjustment account balance was negative, Niagara Mohawk would have to pay Norcon. Payments of the adjustment account balance were scheduled over the term of the contract. In 1994, Niagara Mohawk reviewed the cost estimates and calculated that Norcon would have to repay $610 million at the first scheduled payment date. Concerned by the size of the estimated credit, Niagara Mohawk threatened to terminate the contract unless Norcon provided adequate assurance that it would "duly perform all of its future repayment obligations."

Norcon sued Niagara Mohawk in federal District Court, seeking a declaratory judgment that Niagara

Mohawk had no right to demand adequate assurance and requested a permanent injunction to stop Niagara Mohawk from terminating the contract. The District Court ruled in favor of Norcon and Niagara Mohawk appealed to the Second Circuit Court of Appeals. Because the decision depended on New York common law, the Second Circuit Court of Appeals requested the Court of Appeals of New York to answer the following question of law: "Does a party have the right to demand adequate assurance of future performance when reasonable grounds arise to believe that the other party will commit a breach by nonperformance of a contract governed by New York law, where the other party is solvent and the contract is not governed by the UCC?" In the following opinion, the New York Court of Appeals answers that question.

Bellacosa, Judge

. . . Our analysis should reference a brief review of the evolution of the doctrine of demands for adequate assurance. Its roots spring from the doctrine of anticipatory repudiation. . . . [W]hen a party repudiates contractual duties "prior to the time designated for performance and before" all of the consideration has been fulfilled, the "repudiation entitles the nonrepudiating party to claim damages for total breach" [*Long Is. R. R. Co. v. Northville Indus. Corp.,* 362 N.E.2d 558, 563 (N.Y. 1977)]. A repudiation can be either "a statement by the obligor to the obligee indicating that the obligator will commit a breach that would of itself give the obligee a claim for damages for total breach" or "a voluntary affirmative act which renders the obligor unable or apparently unable to perform without such a breach" [*Restatement (Second) of Contracts* §250]. . . .

That switch in performance expectation and burden is readily available, applied and justified when a breaching party's words or deeds are unequivocal. Such a discernible line in the sand clears the way for the nonbreaching party to broach some responsive action. When, however, the apparently breaching party's actions are equivocal or less certain, then the nonbreaching party who senses an approaching storm cloud, affecting the contractual performance, is presented with a dilemma, and must weigh hard choices and serious consequences. One commentator has described the forecast options in this way:

> If the promisee regards the apparent repudiation as an anticipatory repudiation, terminates his or her own performance and sues for breach, the promisee is placed in jeopardy of being found to have breached if the court

---

[23]RESTATEMENT (SECOND) OF CONTRACTS §251.

determines that the apparent repudiation was not sufficiently clear and unequivocal to constitute an anticipatory repudiation justifying nonperformance. If, on the other hand, the promisee continues to perform after perceiving an apparent repudiation, and it is subsequently determined that an anticipatory repudiation took place, the promisee may be denied recovery for post-repudiation expenditures because of his or her failure to avoid those expenses as part of a reasonable effort to mitigate damages after the repudiation, [Crespi, *The Adequate Assurances Doctrine after U.C.C. §2–609: A Test of the Efficiency of the Common Law,* 38 Vill.L.Rev. 179, 183 (1993)]. . . .

The Uniform Commercial Code settled on a mechanism for relieving some of this uncertainty. It allows a party to a contract for the sale of goods to demand assurance of future performance from the other party when reasonable grounds for insecurity exist (see UCC §2–609). . . . When adequate assurance is not forthcoming, repudiation is deemed confirmed, and the nonbreaching party is allowed to take reasonable actions as though a repudiation had occurred. . . .

In theory, this UCC relief valve recognizes that "the essential purpose of a contract between commercial [parties] is actual performance . . . and that a continuing sense of reliance and security that the promised performance will be forthcoming when due, is an important feature of the bargain" (UCC §2–609, Comment 1). In application, section 2–609 successfully implements the laudatory objectives of quieting the doubt a party fearing repudiation may have, mitigating the dilemma flowing from that doubt, and offering the nonbreaching party the opportunity to interpose timely action to deal with the unusual development. . . .

Indeed, UCC §2–609 has been considered so effective . . . that some States have imported the complementary regimen of demand for adequate assurance to common-law categories of contract law. . . . Commentators have helped nudge this development along. They have noted that the problems redressed by UCC §2–609 are not unique to contracts for sale of goods, regulated under a purely statutory regime. Thus, they have cogently identified the need for the doctrine to be available in exceptional and qualifying common-law contractual settings and disputes because of similar practical, theoretical, and salutary objectives (*e.g.,* predictability, definiteness, and stability in commercial dealings and expectations). . . .

The American Law Institute through its *Restatement (Second) of Contracts* has also recognized and collected the authorities supporting this modern development. Its process and work settled upon this black letter language:

1. Where reasonable grounds arise to believe that the obligor will commit a breach by nonperformance that would of itself give the obligee a claim for damages for total breach under §243, the obligee may demand adequate assurance of due performance and may, if reasonable, suspend any performance for which he has not already received the agreed exchange until he receives such assurance.

2. The obligee may treat as a repudiation the obligor's failure to provide within a reasonable time such assurance of due performance as is adequate in the circumstances of the particular case [*Restatement (Second) of Contracts* §251].

. . . Some States have adopted *Restatement* §251 as their common law of contracts . . . New York, up to now, has refrained from expanding the right to demand adequate assurance of performance beyond the Uniform Commercial Code. . . .

This Court is now persuaded that the policies underlying the UCC §2–609 counterpart should apply with similar cogency for the resolution of this kind of controversy. A useful analogy can be drawn between the contract at issue and a contract for the sale of goods. If the contract here was in all respects the same, except that it was for the sale of oil or some other tangible commodity instead of the sale of electricity, the parties would unquestionably be governed by the demand for adequate assurance of performance factors in UCC §2–609. We are convinced to take this prudent step because it puts commercial parties in these kinds of disputes at relatively arm's length equilibrium in terms of reliability and uniformity of governing legal rubrics. The availability of the doctrine may even provide an incentive and tool for parties to resolve their own differences, perhaps without the necessity of judicial intervention. Open, serious renegotiation of dramatic developments and changes in unusual contractual expectations and qualifying circumstances would occur because of and with an eye to the doctrine's application.

The various authorities, factors and concerns, in sum, prompt the prudence and awareness of the usefulness of recognizing the extension of the doctrine of demand for adequate assurance, as a common-law analogue. It should apply to the type of long-term commercial contract between corporate entities entered into by Norcon and Niagara Mohawk here, which is complex and not reasonably susceptible of all security features being anticipated, bargained for and incorporated in the original contract. Norcon's performance, in terms of reimbursing Niagara Mohawk for credits, is still years away. In the meantime, potential quantifiable damages are accumulating and Niagara Mohawk must weigh the hard choices and serious consequences that the doctrine of demand for adequate assurance is designed to mitigate. . . .

[Certified question answered in the affirmative.]

Breach by Anticipatory Repudiation

A party's conduct may go well beyond merely creating reasonable grounds for insecurity and may constitute repudiation of the contract. **Repudiation** occurs when one contracting party, by words or conduct, unequivocally indicates its inability or unwillingness to perform without breach.[24]

To constitute a repudiation, a party's statement or conduct must be sufficiently definite and positive to be reasonably interpreted by the other as indicating an unwillingness or inability to perform. Mere expressions of doubt concerning one's ability or inclination to render performance are not enough. An indication of possible inability to perform would, however, create reasonable grounds for insecurity, allowing the insecure party to request assurance and suspend its own performance. As noted above, failure to provide assurances within a reasonable time (not exceeding 30 days for a Code contract) would then constitute a repudiation of the contract.

A party who repudiates a duty with respect to performance not yet due commits an **anticipatory repudiation.** This term simply means that the party repudiates the duty before committing a breach by nonperformance. The effect of an anticipatory repudiation is to give the other party an immediate claim against the repudiating party for damages for total breach of the contract even though the time agreed upon for performance has not yet arrived. Thus, anticipatory repudiation gives rise to what is commonly known as "anticipatory breach," or, more accurately stated, breach by anticipatory repudiation. In addition to giving rise to a claim for damages for total breach, one party's repudiation of his duty discharges the other's remaining duties to perform.

Assume that on April 1 Graves contracts to sell land to Brown. The contract calls for delivery of the deed and payment of the purchase price on July 30. On May 1, Graves informs Brown that she will not perform. Graves's statement is an anticipatory repudiation of the contract. Brown's duty to pay the purchase price is discharged and Brown has a claim against Graves for damages for total breach of the contract.

When faced with an anticipatory repudiation, the injured party need not elect to sue immediately for total breach, but may await the time agreed upon for performance and attempt to convince the repudiating party to retract the repudiation. During this time, the aggrieved party may elect to continue or suspend her own performance.

For UCC contracts, §2–610 follows the principles discussed above. It provides that if either party repudiates the contract with respect to a performance not yet due, the loss of which will *substantially impair* the value of the contract to the other, the aggrieved party may (1) for a commercially reasonable time await performance by the repudiating party or (2) resort to any Code remedy for breach even though he has notified the repudiating party that he is awaiting performance and has urged retraction. In either case, the aggrieved party may suspend his own performance.

Retraction of Repudiation. In both UCC and common law contracts, the repudiating party may retract her repudiation unless the aggrieved party has (1) materially changed her position in reliance on the repudiation (for example, by covering, that is, procuring substitute performance), or (2) canceled or otherwise indicated that she considers the repudiation final (for example, by bringing suit for total breach). Thus, the right to retract is entirely dependent upon action taken by the aggrieved party.[25] The retraction may be made in any manner clearly indicating the repudiating party's intention to perform. However, because the repudiation itself creates reasonable grounds for insecurity, the retraction must include any assurances justifiably demanded. An effective retraction then reinstates the repudiating party's rights under the contract.[26]

Limitation to Executory Contracts. Most courts have held that the breach by anticipatory repudiation doctrine

---

[24]RESTATEMENT (SECOND) OF CONTRACTS §250.

[25]UCC §2–611(1) and Official Comment 1; RESTATEMENT (SECOND) OF CONTRACTS §256.

[26]UCC §§2–611(2)–(3).

applies only to mutually executory contracts; that is, unperformed duties must remain on both sides. Thus, an immediate action for total breach is unavailable if the aggrieved party (the plaintiff) has fully performed his obligations under the contract (the contract is executed on his side), and the repudiator's duty is still executory (requiring either the payment of money in a lump sum or installments, or other performance).[27] In other words, a party who has fully performed cannot sue for breach of contract—even if the other party repudiates—until an actual breach by nonperformance occurs.

Assume, for example, that Smead contracts to sell a painting to Carter for $10,000 with delivery to be made on June 1 and payment to follow on July 1. Smead delivers the painting on June 1 and on June 5 Carter tells Smead that she will not make payment on July 1. Because the contract is not executory, Smead may not sue Carter for breach of contract until Carter fails to pay on July 1. This rule is especially important in installment contracts. Assume that in the preceding example, the contract provides for delivery of the painting and payment of $2,000 on June 1, with additional $2,000 payments due on July 1, August 1, September 1, and October 1. Carter makes the June and July payments and then repudiates on July 15 by indicating that she will not make any further payment. Because Smead has fully performed, she has no claim against Carter for total breach on July 15. Smead is required to sue for breach of each successive installment as it comes due.

Contracting parties often protect themselves against this result by including an **acceleration clause** in the contract. These clauses provide that upon the occurrence of a given contingency (normally a default in one or more installments), all future installments are accelerated and become immediately due and payable. In this manner the entire amount owed can be collected in a single action.

Limiting the anticipatory repudiation doctrine to wholly executory contracts has been criticized. It places a party who has already fully performed and faced with a repudiation at a disadvantage in remedy when compared with an injured party whose duties remain executory. In other words, the party whose duties are executory has an immediate action for total breach, whereas a party who has fully performed does not. Further, the aggrieved party may be unable to collect a judgment if required to wait until the time of agreed performance to sue. For example, the repudiating party may become

insolvent or leave the jurisdiction. Fortunately, this limitation is applied only infrequently because courts often protect the injured party by ordering restitution by the repudiator or other relief.

Excuses for Nonperformance

Contract liability is strict liability. A contracting party generally runs the risk that the contract will be more burdensome, more expensive to perform, or less desirable than anticipated, or that he paid too much or charged too little for the goods or services involved. A person can reduce these risks by incorporating special contract provisions that limit the extent of his undertaking. For example, a party may agree only to use "best efforts," or reserve a right to cancel, or limit his obligation to requirements or output, or use a "force majeure" clause, or adopt a flexible pricing arrangement, or limit liability for breach to a specified amount.

Under certain limited circumstances, however, a party who has undertaken an absolute duty is excused from performance of that duty under the doctrines of impracticability (impossibility) of performance or frustration of purpose. In these situations, generally, an extraordinary event occurs that so substantially alters the parties' reasonable expectations that the essential nature of the performance is changed. In some cases, the event rendering performance impracticable occurs before or at the time the contract is made (existing or original impracticability). Normally, however, the extraordinary event **supervenes,** meaning that it occurs after the contract is made but before performance. In such cases, the court, in the interests of justice, may discharge the obligor from his duty to perform without liability for breach. If one party's duty is discharged on impracticability or frustration grounds, the other's remaining duties are also discharged. The issue is generally considered to be a question of law, not fact, and is thus for the court rather than the jury to decide. The following material examines the law governing impracticability caused by supervening events. Note that the same basic principles also govern cases of existing impracticability.

Impracticability (Impossibility)

Introduction to Impracticability. Historically, contractual duties were discharged by supervening events only if performance was objectively **impossible.** That is,

---

[27]Restatement (Second) of Contracts §253 comment c.

relief under early common law required proof that no one could render the promised performance—the mere inability of the promisor to perform was insufficient. This statement simply means that a contracting party generally assumes the risk of his own inability to perform his duty. For example, a debtor's inability to pay a debt because of financial difficulties does not discharge the duty. Similarly, a manufacturer who contracts with the government to design and build a new computer system is not discharged if, due to its own lack of technical expertise, it is unable to produce a workable system.

Both the UCC and the *Restatement (Second) of Contracts* have abandoned the term "impossibility" in favor of the more expansive concept of **impracticability** (or **commercial impracticability**). Contract duties are discharged under the doctrine of impracticability not only if performance is objectively impossible, but also if it is rendered impracticable due to circumstances causing extreme or unreasonable difficulty or expense. The UCC impracticability doctrine is contained in §2–615, entitled "Excuse by Failure of Presupposed Conditions." Section §2–615(a) provides:

> Except so far as a seller may have assumed a greater obligation . . . delay in delivery or non-delivery in whole or in part by a seller . . . is not a breach of his duty under a contract for sale *if performance as agreed has been made impracticable by the occurrence of a contingency the non-occurrence of which was a basic assumption on which the contract was made.* . . . [28] (Emphasis added.)

The *Restatement (Second) of Contracts* follows this language in formulating the doctrine applicable to common law contracts. Section 261 provides:

> Where, after a contract is made, a party's performance is made impracticable without his fault by the occurrence of an event the non-occurrence of which was a basic assumption on which the contract was made, his duty to render that performance is discharged, unless the language or the circumstances indicate the contrary.

Thus, the test governing discharge of a duty on grounds of impracticability is whether nonoccurrence of the event was "a basic assumption on which the contract was made."[29] As one court succinctly noted, this test "seems a somewhat complicated way of putting [the] question of how much risk the promisor assumed."[30] Impracticability analysis therefore requires resolution of three issues: (1) Did an unexpected event occur after formation of the contract, (2) did that event render performance impossible or impracticable, and (3) did the promisor assume the risk that the event would occur? Impracticability relief is unavailable if the promisor is at fault in causing the occurence of the event. "Fault" includes willful wrongs and other conduct amounting to negligence or breach of contract. In addition, under both the Code and the common law, the explicit language or other circumstances of the contract may indicate that a party has assumed an obligation to perform despite impracticability.

For the nonoccurrence of an event to be a basic assumption the parties need not consciously address themselves to that possibility. For example, death of the obligor in a personal service contract is a circumstance, the nonoccurrence of which is a basic assumption on which the contract is made, even though the parties may never consciously consider its occurence. The fact that the event is unforeseeable strongly indicates that its nonoccurrence was a basic assumption, and therefore that the promisor did not assume the risk of its occurrence. Nevertheless, the fact that the event was foreseeable (or even foreseen) does not necessarily mean that the promisor assumed the risk because the parties may not have considered the contingency important enough to address in their agreement.

Events causing impracticability may be due either to Acts of God or acts of third parties. Both the common law and the Code deliberately refrain from any effort to list all possible contingencies. Several common fact situations to which the doctrine has been applied are discussed in the following sections.

Death or Incapacity of a Person Necessary for Performance. The most common basis for discharge on impracticability grounds is the death or incapacity of a person necessary for performance. Frequently, both parties

---

[28]Occasionally, the event causing impracticability will only partially prevent the seller from performing. In this situation, the seller is required to allocate production and deliveries among the customers in a fair and reasonable manner. UCC §2–615(b).

[29]By its terms, UCC §2–615 only operates to discharge an aggrieved *seller.* A buyer is apparently required to proceed under the common law principles supplementing the Code through §1–103. However, the new *Restatement*'s formulation of the doctrine for common law contracts makes it available to both parties. Additionally, cases decided under §2–615 have applied it to buyers.

[30]United States v. Wegematic Corporation, 360 F.2d 674, 676 (2d Cir. 1966).

understand that proper performance is dependent upon the continued existence or capacity of a particular person. The parties may provide that the services of a specific person are required. More frequently, however, they are silent on the point, and the court must then decide whether the duty so involves elements of personal service, expertise, judgment, or discretion that only personal performance is acceptable. If so, the duty to perform is discharged by supervening death or incapacity. Note that this approach corresponds directly to the rules relating to delegation of contract duties. That is, if the obligor could have delegated the duty, his death or incapacity does not excuse performance. In other words, upon the death of an obligor, his estate remains liable for performance of the contract unless the contract sufficiently involves elements of personal service or discretion.

Suppose Boggs hires Calhoun, a noted trial lawyer, to handle a major tort case. Calhoun dies prior to performance. Calhoun's duty is discharged by her death because performance required the exercise of Calhoun's personal skill and judgment; that is, she could not have delegated her duty to perform. Thus, Boggs has no claim against Calhoun's estate for breach of contract. On the other hand, assume Seller contracts to sell and deliver 500 bales of cotton to Buyer. Seller dies prior to performance. Seller's estate remains liable to Buyer for performance of the contract because Seller could have delegated his duty to perform because his personal skill, discretion, or supervision is not necessary for performance.

Destruction of Subject Matter Necessary for Performance.

Frequently, the existence of a specific subject matter is a basic assumption on which the contract is made. Therefore, its destruction, deterioration, or failure to come into existence discharges a duty relating to it. This principle is derived from the classic early English case *Taylor v. Caldwell,* decided in 1863.[31] In this case, the defendant promised to allow the plaintiff to use the defendant's music hall for an agreed fee to give a series of four concerns. Prior to the time of agreed performance, the music hall burned down through no fault of either party. The court held that the destruction discharged the defendant's duty to perform and he was therefore not liable to the plaintiff for breach.

Failure of Anticipated Source of Supply. Perhaps the most common modern situation concerning destruction of subject matter necessary for performance occurs

when the promisor's source of supply fails. For example, a seller of goods may assert impracticability if its only factory burns down. As a general rule, unless the parties make the source a basic assumption of the contract (an exclusive source agreed in the contract), its failure does not discharge the obligor's duty. Assume Swatch Textiles, Inc. contracts to sell a certain quantity of cloth to Birk. Swatch expects to manufacture the cloth in its factory. Prior to performance, however, the factory is destroyed through no fault of Swatch. Although cloth meeting the contract description is readily available on the market, Swatch refuses to purchase it in order to satisfy the contract with Birk. Swatch's duty to deliver the cloth is not discharged and it is liable to Birk for breach. Assume, however, on these same facts, that the original contract had stated that the cloth was to be manufactured at Swatch's factory. In this situation, if the factory is subsequently destroyed, Swatch's duty to perform is discharged and it is not liable to Birk for breach because the particular source of supply was "a basic assumption on which the contract was made." Even if the contract is silent concerning the source, the court may grant relief upon its failure, if it can be shown from the circumstances, such as prior negotiations or previous contracts, that the parties had a common understanding or assumption regarding the source of supply.

Casualty to Identified Goods. The UCC resolves a related problem arising when goods which have been *identified* to the contract are destroyed prior to performance. Identification occurs when the parties designate or specify the particular goods to which the contract refers.[32] Under §2–613, if (1) the contract involves the sale of goods identified when the contract is made, and (2) the goods suffer casualty through no fault (including both willful and negligent conduct) of either party, (3) before risk of loss passes to the buyer,[33] then:

1. If the loss is total, the contract is avoided (rescinded). In this case, the burden of the casualty loss falls on the seller, but the buyer may not sue for breach of contract.

2. If the loss is partial or if the goods have deteriorated so as no longer to conform to the contract, the buyer may demand inspection and elect either to avoid the contract or accept the goods with an allowance

---

[31]3 B. & S. 826, 122 Eng. Rep. 309 (K.B. 1863).

[32]The concept and effect of identification are discussed in conjunction with the definition of "goods" in Chapter 7 and in Chapter 17.

[33]Risk of loss is discussed in Chapter 17.

against the price for the deterioration or deficiency in quality. As in the case of total loss, the buyer has no action for breach against the seller.

To illustrate, S, on June 1, contracts to sell three specified machines located at S's warehouse to B for $5,000. Delivery is to be made on June 30. On June 10, S's warehouse is destroyed by fire after being struck by lightning. On these facts, S's duty to deliver the machines is discharged and S is not liable to B for breach.

The principles discussed above commonly are applied to contracts involving the sale by farmers of agricultural commodities. Here, the seller seeks to avoid his obligation on the basis of a crop failure resulting from drought, flood, or other adverse weather conditions, insects, disease, or the like. Note that crops being grown are goods, identified when planted.[34] Therefore, if they are specifically identified at the time the contract is made, excuse due to their destruction may be based either upon §2–615 (Impracticability) or §2–613 (Casualty to Identified Goods). Even if the source is not explicitly stated, courts often have relieved farmers from their obligations after a crop failure. To do so, the court, based on the circumstances, finds that the parties at the time of contracting contemplated or assumed a single source of supply (the farmer's land) with no recourse to the market in case of deficiency.[35]

Supervening Illegality, Government Regulation or Order.

Parties to a contract generally assume that, subsequent to formation of a contract, the government (foreign or domestic) will not (1) make acts required for performance illegal, or (2) otherwise intervene by regulation or order to make performance impracticable. Therefore, supervening illegality, government regulation or order generally will discharge a duty on grounds of impracticability. Note that if acts required for performance were illegal at the time the contract was made, the contract is unenforceable in any event on grounds of public policy.

To illustrate, assume Signal Corp. contracts to sell oil to Hughes. Prior to performance, the government adopts

an allocation plan requiring Signal to sell its entire output to Walters. Signal's duty to Hughes is discharged and Hughes has no claim against Signal for breach. Or assume Tilto, Inc. contracts to sell pinball machines to George in a state where it is legal to own them. Prior to performance, the state passes a statue making sale, possession, and ownership of all such machines illegal. The duties of both parties are discharged.

The UCC specifically addresses the issue of government intervention in §2–615(a) by providing for the seller's discharge if performance as agreed has been made impracticable "by compliance in good faith with any applicable foreign or domestic government regulation or order whether or not it later proves to be invalid." Thus, the Code affords equal significance to both foreign and domestic regulation.

Increased Cost.

Circumstances making performance more expensive or difficult than anticipated usually do not form a basis for impracticability. Contracting parties generally assume the risk that performance as agreed may become more burdensome than expected. Even when dramatic increases in costs are encountered, courts in both UCC and common law contracts generally have denied relief both because the increase was insufficiently onerous to render performance impracticable and because the rise in price was foreseeable. A contracting party can rarely prove that a price increase is an event "the nonoccurrence of which was a basic assumption on which the contract was made." For this reason, courts will likely continue to deny most impracticability claims based on increased cost, particularly because a major purpose of contract law is to protect one party against fluctuations in cost by allocating the risk of those fluctuations to the other.

In the following case, the court explicitly addresses the risk allocation issue.

Seaboard Lumber Company v. United States
308 F.3d 1283 (Fed. Cir. 2002)

In September 1980, plaintiff Seaboard Lumber Company entered into a contract with the Forest Service, an agency of the United States government. Under the contract Seaboard agreed to cut, remove, and pay for all of the timber on a parcel of Forest Service land known as the What parcel by March 1983. Seaboard then would be entitled to sell the timber. In 1980, timber prices were high because

---

[34]See discussion of identification in Chapter 17 and goods closely associated with land in Chapter 34.

[35]In addition to failure of an anticipated source of supply, occasionally the parties' intended manner of delivery or payment will fail. The Code rules dealing with this situation are contained in §2–614. Application of these rules ordinarily results in the continuation of the contract using a substitute means of delivery or payment.

of a national housing boom. In the next two years, however, timber prices dropped significantly because of a decline in housing construction due to increased interest rates. Because of the low timber prices, Seaboard decided not to harvest the timber on the What parcel and, therefore, did not pay the Forest Service. The Forest Service terminated the contract and demanded that Seaboard pay damages as outlined in the contract. Seaboard then sued the U.S. government in the Court of Federal Claims asserting that it was excused from performance of the contract because of impossibility and commercial impracticability. The Court of Federal Claims rejected Seaboard's argument and ruled in favor of the United States. Seaboard appealed.

Linn, Circuit Judge

Seaboard argues that the slump in the timber market made its performance impossible or in the alternative commercially impracticable, thus excusing its nonperformance. Performance is only excused under this doctrine when it is objectively impossible. . . . It is thus not enough for Seaboard to show that it was incapable of performing on the contract; it must show that no similarly-situated contractor could have performed. The market fluctuation did not make Seaboard's contract impossible to perform, only unprofitable. Other contractors performed on logging contracts during the same period. Therefore, Seaboard's performance was not objectively impossible and cannot be excused on that basis.

This court and its predecessor have long recognized that the doctrine of impossibility does not require a showing of actual or literal impossibility of performance but only a showing of commercial impracticability. . . . The Supreme Court has reformulated the common law doctrine of impossibility as follows:

> Where, after a contract is made, a party's performance is made impracticable without his fault by the occurrence of an event the non-occurrence of which was a basic assumption on which the contract was made, his duty to render that performance is discharged, unless the language or the circumstances indicate the contrary.

United States v. Winstar Corp., 116 S. Ct. 2432 (1996) (quoting *Restatement (Second) of Contracts* §261). This defense requires Seaboard to show that (i) a supervening event made performance impracticable; (ii) the non-occurrence of the event was a basic assumption upon which the contract was based; (iii) the occurrence of the event was not Seaboard's fault; and (iv) Seaboard did not assume the risk of occurrence. . . .

Even if we assume without deciding that Seaboard's performance is impracticable because it would bankrupt the company, Seaboard must show that the non-occurrence of a slump in the timber market was a basic assumption of the What contract. . . . "If [the risk] was foreseeable there should have been a provision for it in the contract, and the absence of such a provision gives rise to the inference that the risk was assumed." *Id.* . . .

The non-occurrence of a slump in the timber market was not a basic assumption of the What contract. Seaboard contracted to harvest timber at a fixed price. "The normal risk of a fixed price contract is that the market price will change." [*N. Ind. Pub. Serv. Co. v. Carbon County Coal Co.,* 799 F.2d 265, 275 (7th Cir. 1986).] Seaboard bet that the timber market would remain strong. The government, in contrast, insulated itself from the market's downward movement. Thus, the non-occurrence of market fluctuation was not a basic assumption of both parties in this case. See *Karl Wendt Farm Equip. Co. v. Int'l Harvester Co.,* 931 F.2d 1112, 1118 (6th Cir. 1991) ("Neither market shifts nor the financial inability of one of the parties changes the basic assumptions of the contract such that it may be excused under the doctrine of impracticability. To hold otherwise would not fulfill the likely understanding of the parties as to the apportionment of risk under the contract.")

Moreover, while the occurrence of a market slump cannot be Seaboard's fault, no impossibility defense will lie where the "language or the circumstances" indicate allocation of the risk to the party seeking discharge. [*Restatement (Second) of Contracts* §261.] Because Seaboard entered into a fixed-price contract, it carried the risk that the market would slump. . . . Therefore, because the non-occurrence of a market slump was not a basic assumption of both parties and Seaboard bore the risk, Seaboard's impossibility defense fails as a matter of law. The Court of Federal Claims' rejection of both the impossibility and commercial impracticability defenses was thus correct.

[Judgment affirmed.]

Frustration of Purpose

The **frustration of purpose** doctrine relieves a contracting party of her duty to perform when the underlying purpose of the contract is defeated. In such cases, due to a supervening event, the value of the other party's performance becomes virtually worthless to the obligor. Note the difference between the frustration cases and the situations discussed above. In those cases, performance becomes impracticable. In the frustration cases, neither party's ability to *perform* is affected; the *purpose* of the contract is frustrated. For UCC contracts, issues of impracticability and frustration both are governed by §2–615.

The doctrine was originally adopted in the 1903 English case *Krell v. Henry.*[36] In this case, the defendant agreed to rent an apartment from the plaintiff for two days for the purpose of viewing the coronation process of King Edward VII. The King became seriously ill, and, as a result, the procession was canceled. The defendant then refused to pay the balance on the rental agreement, resulting in the plaintiff's suit. On these facts, performance of the contract was certainly not impossible (as would be the case had the apartment burned down), but the underlying purpose for which the defendant had rented the premises (to view the coronation procession) had been defeated. On this basis, the court relieved the defendant of his duty to perform, thus creating the "frustration of purpose" doctrine.

To invoke the doctrine, the frustrated purpose must have been the principal or primary reason inducing the aggrieved party to make the contract. Both parties must understand that the transaction would make little sense in the absence of that purpose. It is not enough that the objective simply induces the making of the contract; that is, without it the party would not have made the contract. Additionally, the nonoccurrence of the frustrating event must be a basic assumption on which the contract is made. Once again, whether or not the event is foreseeable plays an important role in this determination.

At issue in the following case was whether a lessee should be excused from performance based on frustration of purpose.

Mel Frank Tool & Supply, Inc. v. Di-Chem Company
580 N.W.2d 802 (Iowa 1998)

In May 1994, Di-Chem Company signed a three-year lease to rent a building in Council Bluffs, Iowa from Mel Frank

---

[36][1903] 2 K.B. 740 (C.A.).

Tool & Supply, Inc. During the lease negotiations, Di-Chem's representatives told Mel Frank's owner that Di-Chem's business was distribution of chemicals. The lease included provisions limiting Di-Chem's use of the premises to "storage and distribution" and requiring Di-Chem to use the building in compliance with the law. In 1995, Council Bluffs adopted an ordinance regulating storage of hazardous materials. City officials notified Di-Chem that it was in violation of the ordinance and ordered Di-Chem to remove the hazardous materials. Di-Chem vacated the premises and stopped paying rent after written notification to Mel Frank that stated: "The city's position that we cannot legally store all of our inventory at this site prior to extensive alteration of the building makes the structure useless to us as a chemical warehouse."

Mel Frank sued Di-Chem for breach of contract. Di-Chem asserted that it was excused from performance of the lease contract because of impossibility. The trial court found that Di-Chem had breached the lease and ordered it to pay rent for the balance of the three-year lease term. Di-Chem appealed to the Iowa Supreme Court.

Lavorato, Justice

. . . A. The law. The introduction to the *Restatement (Second) of Contracts* covers impossibility of performance but with a different title: impracticability of performance and frustration of purpose. . . . The Restatement recognizes three distinct grounds for the discharge of the obligor's contractual duty:

> First, the obligor may claim that some circumstance has made his own performance impracticable. . . . Second, the obligor may claim that some circumstance has so destroyed the value to him of the other party's performance as to frustrate his own purpose in making the contract. . . . Third, the obligor may claim that he will not receive the agreed exchange for the obligee's duty to render that agreed exchange, on the ground of either impracticability or frustration.

[*Restatement (Second) of Contracts* ch. 11 at 310.]

The rationale behind the doctrines of impracticability and frustration is whether the nonoccurrence of the circumstance was a basic assumption on which the contract was made. . . . The parties need not have been conscious of alternatives for them to have had a "basic assumption." . . .

B. Discharge by supervening frustration. For reasons that follow, we think the facts of this case fall within the parameters of section 265 of the *Restatement.* Section 265 provides:

Where, after a contract is made, a party's principal purpose is substantially frustrated without his fault by the occurrence of an event the nonoccurrence of which was a basic assumption on which the contract was made, his remaining duties to render performance are discharged, *unless the language or the circumstances indicate the contrary.* (Emphasis added.) . . .

The rule deals with the problem that arises when a change in circumstances makes one party's performance virtually worthless to the other, frustrating the purpose in making the contract. . . . The obligor's contractual obligation is discharged only if three conditions are met:

First, the purpose that is frustrated must have been a principal purpose of that party in making the contract. It is not enough that he had in mind some specific object without which he would not have made the contract. The object must be so completely the basis of the contract that, as both parties understand, without it the transaction would make little sense. *Second, the frustration must be substantial. It is not enough that the transaction has become less profitable for the affected party or even that he will sustain a loss. The frustration must be so severe that it is not fairly to be regarded as within the risks that he assumed under the contract.* Third, the nonoccurrence of the frustrating event must have been a basic assumption on which the contract was made. . . . The foreseeability of the event is . . . a factor in that determination, but the mere fact that the event was foreseeable does not compel the conclusion that its non-occurrence was not such a basic assumption. (Emphasis added.)

[*Restatement (Second) of Contracts* §265, comment a.]. . . . Iowa case law is in accord with *Restatement* section 265. . . .

C. The merits. It is clear from the pleadings and testimony that Di-Chem was asserting a defense of frustration of purpose. Di-Chem had the burden of persuasion to prove that defense. . . . Di-Chem produced no evidence that *all* of its inventory of chemicals consisted of hazardous material. In fact, its own correspondence to Mel Frank indicates otherwise. For example, Di-Chem's October 23 letter to Mel Frank stated: "The city's position that we cannot legally store *all* of our inventory at this site prior to extensive alteration of the building makes the structure useless to us as a chemical warehouse." (Emphasis added.) A reasonable inference from this statement is that not all of Di-Chem's inventory consisted of hazardous material. Testimony from one of Di-Chem's representatives corroborates this inference:

Q. Were you involved at all in the discussions with the City of Council Bluffs relative to the various code deficiencies that existed at the building?
A. My involvement was that the city had pointed out that there was some deficiencies with the building and asked us to remove *what* chemicals they found [objectionable]. (Emphasis added.)

Another Di-Chem representative testified that Di-Chem's product line included industrial chemicals and *food additives.* Presumably, food additives are not hazardous materials.

. . . Di-Chem has to establish as a matter of law that its principal purpose for leasing the facility — storing and distributing chemicals — was substantially frustrated by the city's actions. Di-Chem presented no evidence as to the nature of its inventory and what percentage of the inventory consisted of hazardous chemicals. The company also failed to show what its lost profits, if any, would be without the hazardous chemicals. Thus, there is no evidence from which the district court could have found the city's actions substantially frustrated Di-Chem's principal purpose of storing and distributing chemicals. Put another way, there is insufficient evidence that the city's action deprived Di-Chem of the beneficial enjoyment of the property for other uses, i.e., storing and distributing nonhazardous chemicals. Simply put, Di-Chem failed to establish its affirmative defense of what it has termed impossibility.

[Judgment affirmed.]

Summary

1. Contracting parties do not bargain for promises alone, they bargain for performance of those promises. Generally speaking, nonperformance of a contractual promise when performance is due is breach of the contract. Before existence of breach can be determined, however, the existence and occurrence of any conditions must be determined.

2. A condition is an event qualifying a contractual promise, meaning that the duty to perform does not arise unless the condition occurs. Conditions may be classified as precedent, concurrent, or subsequent. Conditions are also designated as express or implied in fact (arising from the language or other conduct of the parties) or imposed by the law (conditions implied in law or constructive conditions).

3. Constructive conditions of exchange are the most important implied conditions. Under the constructive conditions of exchange doctrine, it is a condition to each party's duty to perform that there be no material failure of the other party's performance due at an earlier time. This doctrine prevents one party from having to perform after a material breach of duty by the other.

4. In applying the constructive conditions doctrine, the order of performance must be determined. Unless the contract or circumstances indicate otherwise, if performance can be rendered simultaneously, it is due simultaneously. Simultaneous performance assures each party that the other will perform and avoids requiring one party to finance the other's performance.

5. Nonoccurrence of a condition may be excused, due, for example, to a waiver of the condition or failure of one party to act in good faith and consistent with standards of fair dealing.

6. In contracts requiring one party to perform before the other, such as construction contracts, disputes often arise when the party rendering the first performance (for example, the contractor) asserts a right to payment on the basis that he has completed performance. The other party (for example, the owner) refuses to pay asserting that the first party's performance is defective, resulting in failure of the constructive condition of exchange. Under the "substantial performance" doctrine, if the failure to perform is a material breach, the other party may both sue for damages for total breach and is relieved of his obligation to perform. If the breach is not material, the other party must perform his part of the bargain but may recover damages for the partial breach.

7. In contracts for the sale of goods governed by the UCC, performance is measured by the "perfect tender rule," empowering the buyer to reject goods which fail *in any respect* to conform to the contract. The UCC contains a number of provisions relieving a breaching seller from the harsh effects of the perfect tender rule, resulting in a special form of substantial performance doctrine for sales contracts.

8. A contracting party may render part performance under a contract, but fail to properly perform his remaining obligations. The contract must then be analyzed to determine to what extent, if at all, the defaulting party is entitled to recover under the contract. The result depends upon whether the contract is divisible or entire. If a contract is divisible, performance of a divisible part by one party entitles him to the agreed exchange for that part, despite nonperformance of other parts of the contract. If a contract is deemed entire, the breaching party is not entitled to recover under the contract for part performance rendered.

9. Both actual and prospective nonperformance may constitute breach of contract. Prospective nonperformance involves insecurity and repudiation. Both the UCC and the common law impose an obligation upon each party that the other's expectation of receiving due performance will not be impaired. Whenever reasonable grounds for insecurity arise concerning the willingness or ability of either party to perform, the insecure party may demand adequate assurance of due performance from the other and until he receives such assurance may suspend his own performance.

10. Anticipatory repudiation occurs when one party prior to the time of agreed performance unequivocally indicates an intent not to perform when performance is due. The effect of anticipatory repudiation is to give the injured party an immediate claim for damages for total breach of the contract even though the time of agreed performance has not yet arrived.

11. Occasionally a party will be excused from performance without liability for breach if performance as agreed has been made impracticable by the occurrence of an event, the nonoccurrence of which was a basic assumption on which the contract was made. Examples of supervening events that may excuse nonperformance include death or incapacity of a party in a personal service contract, destruction of subject matter necessary for performance, failure of a specifically designated source of supply, and supervening illegality or government regulation. Even if performance is not impracticable, a promisor may be excused if the underlying purpose of the contract is frustrated.

Key Terms

breach of contract	condition subsequent
condition	express condition
condition precedent	time of the essence
condition concurrent	forfeiture

condition implied in fact
condition implied in law
  (constructive condition)
constructive conditions
  of exchange
failure of consideration
dependent promise
independent promise
tender of performance
waiver
prevention and hindrance
material breach
substantial performance
  doctrine
partial breach
total breach

perfect tender rule
installment contract
divisibility
agreed equivalents
entire contract
reasonable grounds for
  insecurity
adequate assurance of
  due performance
repudiation
anticipatory repudiation
acceleration clause
supervening event
impracticability (impossibility)
frustration of purpose

Questions and Problems

14.1   Bean agreed to purchase a tract of land from Snooker for $20,000. The contract was expressly conditioned upon Bean's ability to obtain a mortgage loan to cover the purchase price. Prior to the agreed date of performance. Bean informed Snooker that he would not obtain a mortgage loan to cover the price, but would instead generate the cash by selling certain shares of stock owned by Bean. When the date of performance arrived, Snooker refused to perform, asserting that Bean's failure to obtain a loan rendered the contract null and void. Bean tendered the full purchase price in cash on the required date, and upon Snooker's refusal to convey the land, sued Snooker for breach of contract. What result?

14.2   On June 1, 2004, Eiffel contracted in writing to sell a large quantity of scrap metal to Tinker. The contract did not specify a delivery date, but provided that delivery would occur no later than September 1, 2004. On July 1, Eiffel called Tinker concerning the delivery date. Tinker replied that he was not ready to take delivery and would call Eiffel when he was. The parties had no further contact concerning the contract between July 1 and September 1, 2004. In October, Eiffel sold the scrap to others, sustaining a loss because of a decline in market price. Eiffel sued Tinker to recover the difference between the contract price and the resale price, alleging that Tinker breached the contract by failing to take delivery by September 1 and by failing to pay the agreed price. Tinker responded that he had no liability because Eiffel had not tendered delivery of the scrap metal. What result? Explain.

14.3   Pope, the general contractor on a highway construction project, hired Rail to act as subcontractor for construction of the guardrails. The rails require 30 days to install and cannot be installed until all other construction is complete. The contract between Pope and Rail stated in part:

> Rail agrees to furnish all labor, materials, equipment, and services as may be necessary to complete items of work relating to installation of guardrails.
>
> Pope agrees to conduct the work for construction of the highway in such manner and with sufficient materials, equip-

ment, and labor as are necessary to insure its completion by October 31, 2004.

The highway project ran behind schedule and was not ready for installation of the guardrails until August 2005. When Pope requested Rail to perform, Rail refused saying its obligation of performance had been discharged for failure of conditions precedent. Do you agree? Explain.

14.4   Consider the application of the prevention or hindrance doctrine to the following facts:

(a) Kehm Corporation contracted to manufacture and deliver concrete practice bombs for the U.S. Navy. The completed bombs were to include tail assemblies to be furnished by the Navy. Delivery was to occur by November 1, 2000. However, Kehm failed to deliver until April 2001. Although the government paid the contract price, Kehm sued for an additional $22,000 for damages sustained resulting from delays caused by the government that retarded completion of the contract. The evidence established that the Navy had lost interest in the concrete bomb program, had shipped nonconforming tail assemblies for many of the bombs, thereby causing manufacturing delays, had shipped many of the tail assemblies late, and had failed to promptly accept delivery of many of the completed bombs. Has the government breached the contract?

(b) The National Rifle Association's management committee voted to move the NRA's headquarters from Washington, D.C., to Colorado. Accordingly, it engaged Shear, a real estate agent, to secure a buyer for its old headquarters building. Shear was to be paid a commission when a sale was "fully consummated." Shear obtained a buyer. A contract for sale was signed subject to approval by the management committee. Subsequently, however, a new NRA management committee was elected and voted not to move the headquarters after all. Because board approval was necessary to consummate the sale, the deal fell through and NRA then refused to pay Shear's commission. Shear sued. What result?

(c) The U.S. government contracted with Arborite, a lumber company, to supply one million board feet of lumber to be used in the construction of an Army base. As Arborite knew, it was only one of several suppliers for the entire project, which required over 20 million board feet. When Arborite attempted to acquire the lumber, it was unable to do so because the demand created by the Army construction had created a market shortage. Consequently, Arborite failed to deliver and was sued by the government for breach. May Arborite avoid liability on prevention grounds?

14.5   Contractor built a country home for Owner at a cost of approximately $77,000. One of the specifications for the plumbing work provided: "All wrought-iron pipe must be well galvanized, lap welded pipe of the grade known as 'standard pipe' of Reading manufacture." Approximately nine months after completion of the house, Owner learned that only 40 percent of the pipe used was manufactured by Reading, with the remainder produced by other factories. Owner then ordered Contractor to redo the work. At this point, the plumbing was encased within the walls, and compliance with the order would have required demolition of substantial parts of the completed structure. Contractor refused to comply and sued for the final installment on the purchase price ($3,500) that had not been paid. The evidence indicated that Contractor's failure to comply was neither fraudulent nor willful, but resulted from an oversight by one of its subcontractors. Should Contractor recover? How much, and if so on what grounds? Determine whether the use of Reading pipe is an express condition to Owner's duty to pay and explain the effect of your determination on Contractor's recovery.

14.6   Sheila contracted to sell sheet metal to Bill, delivery to be made in monthly installments over a two-year period beginning June 1, 2004. Payments for the goods were to be made within ten days after each delivery. Almost from the first installment, Bill was behind in his payments, and these arrearages were often quite substantial. Sheila repeatedly called these arrearages to Bill's attention, but continued to make all shipments called for by the contract.

   By March 2005, Bill became concerned about Sheila's ability to complete performance of the contract because of rumors that Sheila's plant might close and because the market price of the goods now significantly exceeded the contract price. Bill called Sheila who provided assurances of future performance even though at the time Bill still owed substantial amounts for goods already delivered. Despite Sheila's assurances Bill stopped payment on a $10,000 check given in partial payment of Bill's past due account. Bill's reason for stopping payment was that one of Sheila's truck drivers had told Bill that Sheila would make no further deliveries. Sheila's plant was forced to close in May 2005, primarily due to Bill's refusal to accept further deliveries or pay his outstanding bill.

   Sheila sued Bill for breach of contract for nonpayment of over $20,000 in accepted deliveries. Bill admitted his indebtedness but counterclaimed for damages resulting from Sheila's failure to perform the remaining installments under the contract. Should Bill prevail on his counterclaim?

14.7   In March 2004, Semo Grain Co. contracted to buy 75,000 bushels of soybeans from Oliver, Inc. at $3.10 per bushel, delivery to be made in January 2005. Nothing in the agreement required Oliver, a farming corporation, to grow the beans, and indeed, Oliver was not required to grow them. Oliver failed to deliver any soybeans to Semo, resulting in Semo's suit for breach of contract. Oliver asserted that adverse weather conditions excused his performance under UCC §§2–613 and 2–615. Oliver contended that although the various farms under its control planted over 3,500 acres, only 1,500 survived heavy rainfall, resulting in a harvest of less than 20,000 bushels. (a) Should Oliver be relieved of liability under §2–613? (b) Should Oliver be relieved of liability under §2–615? (c) Assuming Oliver is excused from performance under §2–615, has it complied with its obligations under that section? See §2–615(b).

14.8   Corbin, a 37-year-old college graduate, enrolled for dancing lessons at Williston Dance Studio. After the instructor told Corbin that he had exceptional potential, Corbin signed several contracts for additional lessons eventually paying over $20,000 for 2,700 hours of future dance lessons. Each contract included the following provision in boldface type:

> NONCANCELLABLE CONTRACT, I UNDERSTAND THAT NO REFUNDS WILL BE MADE UNDER THE TERMS OF THIS CONTRACT.

Corbin was seriously injured in an automobile accident that left him permanently disabled and unable to continue the dancing lessons. Corbin demanded refund of his payments asserting impracticability of performance. Williston refused arguing that, by signing the contract provision. Corbin had waived his right to claim impracticability. Is Williston correct? Explain.

14.9   Florida Power & Light Co. (Florida) agreed to purchase two nuclear reactors from Westinghouse Electric Corp. (Westinghouse). Because Florida had no experience with nuclear power generation, it insisted that Westinghouse agree to remove spent nuclear fuel. To secure the contract, Westinghouse agreed in writing "to remove the irradiated fuel from the plant site and dispose of it as Westinghouse sees fit," advising Florida that it intended to have the spent fuel reprocessed. Westinghouse required the contract to include a "force majeure clause" that excused it from losses resulting from various contingencies, including "restrictions of the U.S. government." Five years later the president of the United States issued an order prohibiting construction of nuclear fuel reprocessing plants. Thereafter, all spent nuclear fuel had to be stored in government-approved disposal sites. Westinghouse repudiated its duty to remove nuclear fuel from Florida's reactors. As a result, Florida was forced to develop a storage facility for its spent fuel at great expense. Florida sued Westinghouse for breach of contract.

   (a) Westinghouse defended the suit on the grounds of impracticability under §2–615 of the UCC. How should the court rule?

   (b) Westinghouse also alleged that the nonavailability of reprocessing facilities frustrated the purpose of the contract. What result?

   (c) Westinghouse further alleged that it was relieved of liability under the force majeure clause. How should the court rule?

   (d) Westinghouse asserted that both parties expected that the fuel would be reprocessed and that this expectation could no longer be fulfilled. Westinghouse, therefore, requested rescission on the ground of mutual mistake. What result?

14.10   Sunflower Electric Co-op, a public utility, entered into a written contract with Tomlinson Oil Co., providing that Tomlinson would provide 3 million cubic feet of natural gas per day for 15 years from the Stranger Creek gas field to Sunflower. The gas was to be piped to a storage facility from which Sunflower would pipe the gas to its customers. Tomlinson had already performed tests at Stranger Creek and its engineers concluded there was sufficient gas to meet the requirements of the contract. Sunflower immediately constructed a pipeline to the storage facility. Two years later Tomlinson provided notice that it would be unable to perform the contract. All gas wells at Stranger Creek had ceased operating because the field's gas reserves had been exhausted.

Sunflower sued Tomlinson for breach of contract. Tomlinson argued that it could not be held liable because of impracticability.

(a) Did Tomlinson assert original or supervening impracticability?

(b) The Tomlinson-Sunflower contract made no provision for the possibility that the gas at Stranger Creek would be exhausted. Who assumed the risk?

(c) How should the court rule on the case? Be sure to consider §2–615 of the UCC in resolving the case.

14.11 In July 1956, Egypt nationalized the Suez Canal creating tension throughout the Middle East. Under a contract made with the U.S. government on October 2, 1956, Transatlantic Corp. agreed to transport wheat by ship from Galveston, Texas, to Iran. The ship set sail on October 27 with a projected course requiring it to go through the Suez Canal. Two days later, Israel invaded Egypt, which closed the Suez Canal on November 2. Transatlantic's ship was forced to change course and sail around the Cape of Good Hope to deliver the wheat to Iran. Transatlantic sued the United States claiming that the government should pay the additional costs of shipping because performance of the contract by means of the Suez Canal was impracticable.

(a) Assume that the October 2 contract included a provision stating that delivery of the wheat would be made by ship on a route through the Suez Canal. Should the United States have to pay the additional costs? Explain.

(b) Assume instead that the October 2 contract included no provisions governing the route by which delivery would be made. Should the United States have to pay the additional costs? Explain.

CONTRACT REMEDIES

The vast majority of contracts are performed as agreed, thereby discharging the duties involved. If, however, a contractual promise is not performed, or is improperly performed, the law of **contract remedies** determines the type of judicial relief available to the injured promisee.

The Role of Contract Remedies

Remedies promote certainty and predictability in commercial transactions. A major reason a businessperson seeks another's contractual promise is to be assured that the promise will be performed, thus allowing planning in reliance upon the promise. The fact that contracting parties know (or should know) that legal consequences—liability for a contract remedy—follow a failure to perform a contractual obligation provides a strong incentive to contracting parties to perform their promises. The traditional goal of contract remedies is to fully *compensate* the injured promisee for actual loss resulting from the breach. Thus, the underlying premise of contract remedies is compensatory, not punitive.

Types of Contract Remedies

Contract remedies are divided into three general types: (1) legal remedies (or remedies at law), (2) equitable remedies, and (3) restitution.

The **remedy at law** is, in all cases, dollar damages; that is, a party injured by breach of contract is generally entitled to money damages from the breaching party. The amount of damages is a question of fact, determined either by the jury, or by the judge in cases heard without a jury.

Contract law, therefore, usually requires a breaching promisor to pay money, not perform the broken promise. Forcing the promisor to perform as agreed forms the basis of the **equitable remedies** of specific performance and injunction against breach. Equitable remedies are available only if, in the sole discretion of the court, the remedy at law is inadequate to compensate the injured party.[1]

Finally, restitution may be available as a contract remedy. Restitution is a broad remedial concept that is used when one person confers a benefit upon another, who retains it. If necessary to prevent unjust enrichment of the benefited party, the court may order restitution, requiring payment for the reasonable value of the benefit conferred. Restitution often is used in contract cases when other remedies are unavailable. For example, a person who has breached the contract may nevertheless be entitled to restitution.

The obligation of good faith discussed in Chapter 6 applies both to the performance and *enforcement* of a contract. Parties seeking judicial remedies for breach of contract therefore must act in good faith. Bad faith enforcement may involve fabricating a dispute where none exists, falsifying facts, or asserting an interpretation contrary to one's true belief. Bad faith also has been held to include harassing demands for adequate assurance of performance, rejecting performance for unstated reasons, and abusing a power to determine compliance with or to terminate the contract. No exhaustive catalog of the possible types of bad faith is possible and each case is decided on its own peculiar facts.

Interests Protected by Contract Remedies

Contract remedies are designed to protect one or more interests of the injured promisee, including an expectation interest, a reliance interest, and a restitution interest.

Expectation Interest. The **expectation interest** is the interest most commonly protected by both legal and equitable contract remedies. Simply stated, relief on this basis seeks to give the injured party the **benefit of the bargain** by placing her in as good a position as she would have obtained had the contract been performed as agreed. In other words, when the court is presented with a contract breach, it ordinarily enforces the broken promise by protecting the injured party's expectation that the contract would be performed, not breached. Normally, a party faced with breach of contract will attempt to satisfy her expectation interest by enforcing the other party's promise against her.

Assume a seller contracts to sell and deliver machinery to a buyer for $5,000 and fails to perform. The buyer then purchases substitute goods from an alternative source for $6,000. The basic measure of damages is $1,000. The amount that the buyer actually paid ($6,000) less the damages recovered ($1,000) equals $5,000. The buyer is thus placed in the same position he would have enjoyed upon full performance. He has received the benefit of the bargain — the contracted goods for $5,000. Alternatively, had equitable relief, specific performance, been awarded, the buyer's expectation interest is satisfied by the seller's actual performance of the promise.[2]

Reliance Interest. Contract remedies also may serve to protect a promisee's **reliance interest.** A promisee may change his position in reliance on a contract, for example, by incurring expenses in preparing for, or actual, performance. In such a case, the court may allow recovery based upon a reliance, rather than expectation, interest. In this case the court requires reimbursement of the injured party sufficient to return him to the position he enjoyed before the contract was made. The reliance interest ordinarily is smaller than the expectation interest because it does not include any profit lost by the injured party on the contract. For example, a party who is unable to prove profit with reasonable certainty or who would have lost money on the contract may sue to recover damages based upon reliance rather than expectation.

Restitution Interest. Finally, a contract remedy may be designed to protect a promisee's **restitution interest.** In this case, the court awards the promisee the value of any benefit she has conferred on the other party. The restitution interest is normally smaller than either the expectation or reliance interest because it does not include either profits or expenditures not benefiting the other party.

This chapter first examines principles governing the computation and award of money damages, the primary remedy in contracts cases. Second, equitable relief through specific performance and injunction against breach is covered. In either case, the goal is to give the

---

[1]The derivation of the law-equity distinction and the relationship between the two forms of judicial relief are discussed in Chapter 1.

[2]The expectation interest also is the basis of remedy under UCC. Section 1–305 provides: "The remedies provided by the Uniform Commercial Code must be liberally administered to the end that the aggrieved party may be put in as good a position as if the other party had fully performed. . . ."

injured party the benefit of his bargain or to reimburse him for loss caused by reliance on the promise. Finally, restitution is discussed both in general and as a contract remedy. The general remedies concepts discussed below are applicable to both UCC (sales of goods) and common law contracts. Additional specialized remedial rules concerning contracts for the sale of goods are discussed in Chapter 18.

Enforcement by an Award of Damages—The Remedy at Law

General Measure of Damages

Breach of contract ordinarily gives the promisee a claim for money damages to compensate for actual loss caused by the breach. In this case a dollar damages award generally is computed to include:

General compensatory damages (the loss in the value of the other party's performance caused by failure of, or deficiency in, that performance), *plus*

Any other loss caused by the breach, *less*

Expenses saved as a result of the breach (expenditures or other loss the promisee avoids by not having to perform).

The manner of computing general compensatory damages for breach of contract—the loss in value caused by the breach—varies somewhat depending upon a number of factors, including the type of contract, the extent and nature of the breach, and the difficulties in proving damages. In contracts involving the sale of real or personal property, damages generally are computed by comparing the contract price to the market price or to the cost incurred by the injured party in obtaining substitute performance. Thus, in contracts for the sale of land, an injured buyer or seller who seeks money damages is ordinarily entitled to the difference between the contract price and the market price of the land on the date of the breach. In contracts involving goods, after breach by the buyer, the seller generally recovers the difference between the contract price and the market price on the date of performance, or the difference between the contract price and the resale price if the seller resells the goods. In limited circumstances—as when goods are accepted by the buyer or when the seller is unable to resell—a seller may

recover the entire purchase price of goods from a breaching buyer. If the seller of goods breaches, the buyer also ordinarily recovers the difference between the contract price and the market price when the buyer learned of the breach. If, due to the breach, the buyer "covers" by acquiring substitute goods from another seller, damages equal the difference between the contract price and the cover price.

A damage award generally does not include attorneys' fees unless provided for by statute or in the agreement. **Court costs,** however, usually are assessed against the losing party. The term costs generally refers to statutory fees to which officers, jurors, witnesses, and others are entitled for their services in a lawsuit, and that are authorized by statute to be taxed and included in a judgment.[3]

Foreseeability as a Limitation on Damages—"Consequential" Damages

Most breaches of contract cause a direct or immediate loss, which would be suffered generally by any injured promisee. The general measure of damages discussed above is designed to compensate this type of loss. In some, but not all cases, however, the breach may trigger a chain of events causing additional loss as the ultimate result or consequence of the breach. In business contracts, courts often have been required to determine when a particular promisee should be entitled to recover such **consequential damages,** usually lost profits, in addition to its general damage claims.

The Rule of Hadley v. Baxendale. The test governing the issue originally was announced in *Hadley v. Baxendale,*[4] an English case decided in 1854 and subsequently generally followed in the United States. In this case, the operators of a mill (plaintiffs) delivered a broken shaft used in the mill to a carrier (defendant) for shipment to an engineering company, which manufactured a new shaft using the broken one as a model. Through the negligence of the carrier, the return of the shaft was delayed several days and, because the mill was totally inoperative without the shaft, the plaintiffs lost several days' profits. At issue in the case was whether the lost profits (consequential damages) should be recoverable from the defendants. Note that the

---

[3]BLACK'S LAW DICTIONARY 346 (6th ed. 1990).
[4]9 Ex. 341, 156 Eng. Rep. 145 (Ex. 1854).

general measure of damages for a delay in shipment of goods would be the loss of the value of the use of the goods during the delay, that is, their rental value. In establishing the governing standard, the court stated that damages are recoverable for loss that the breaching party had *reason to foresee* when the contract was made, occurring as the probable result of its breach. Two types of loss are foreseeable and therefore recoverable under this test:

1. Losses arising in the ordinary course of events— these are commonly known as "general" damages; and

2. Losses resulting from special circumstances, beyond the ordinary course of events, of which the breaching party has reason to know. These losses are commonly labeled "special" or "consequential" damages.

Thus, losses resulting from the *special* circumstances under which a contract is made are recoverable only if the defendant is made aware of the specific consequences of a failure to perform as agreed.

In applying the rule to the facts of the case, the *Hadley* court found that the plaintiffs had communicated to the defendants only that they were mill operators and the article to be carried was a broken shaft of the mill. The fact that the mill was inoperative without the shaft was not communicated. On these facts, the court reasoned that the defendants could have assumed that the mill was shut down for independent reasons, or that the shaft was a spare. In neither case would additional profits be lost as a result of defendant's delay in delivery. Because the special circumstances were not communicated to, or known by, the defendants, the court refused to award lost profits to the plaintiff.

Hadley was a special circumstances case. Losses arising in the ordinary course of events do not have to be communicated to the defendant to be recoverable. For example, a seller of a commodity to a wholesaler would ordinarily have reason to foresee that failure to deliver as agreed would probably cause the wholesaler to lose a reasonable profit upon resale. Similarly, a seller delivering defective or nonconforming merchandise to be used in a manufacturing process has reason to know that a disruption in production will occur and profits will be lost. In addition, the seller of a machine to a manufacturer usually has reason to foresee that a delay in delivery will cause the buyer to lose the profit

from its use during the period of the delay. In all such cases lost profits should be recoverable, even without explicit communication of circumstances to the defendant, because the loss involved occurs in the ordinary course of events.

Lost profits caused by a breach of contract often far exceed the amount of general damages resulting from the same breach. For this reason, the parties often include a term in their contract limiting or eliminating liability for consequential damages.

The following case illustrates a modern application of the principles of *Hadley v. Baxendale.*

Florafax International, Inc. v. GTE Market Resources, Inc.

933 P.2d 282 (Okla. 1997)

Florafax International, Inc. acts as a clearinghouse for flower orders in the United States and internationally. Through a network of retail florists who join Florafax's system, member florists can arrange sale and delivery of flowers in distant locations. In early October 1989, Bellerose Floral, Inc., a major floral marketer, contracted to have Florafax handle orders placed through Bellerose's toll free (1-800-FLOWERS) marketing system. The contract provided that Florafax would process consumer orders placed through the toll free number and would have the orders filled by florists in its network. About two weeks later, Florafax made a contract with GTE Market Resources, Inc. (GTE), a company specializing in telecommunications and telemarketing services. Under the contract, GTE agreed to operate a call answering center to handle Florafax's telecommunications, including incoming calls for floral orders and outgoing calls to fill those orders. In return, Florafax agreed to pay GTE a service fee for each order.

Following Valentine's Day in February 1990, GTE's performance began to deteriorate. In April, GTE requested an increase in the service fees paid by Florafax, but the parties were unable to agree on a contract modification. During the week before Mother's Day in May 1990, the highest volume day for the floral industry, GTE failed to provide a sufficient number of telephone representatives to handle the calls for Florafax. Due to GTE's understaffing, orders placed through Bellerose's toll free number were not properly handled and Bellerose terminated its contract with Florafax.

Florafax sued GTE for breach of contract. A jury found that GTE had breached the contract and awarded Florafax damages of $1.57 million, including $750,000 in lost profits that Florafax would have earned under its contract with Bellerose. The court of appeals reversed the award of damages for lost profits. The Oklahoma Supreme Court granted the parties' petitions for review.

Lavender, Justice

. . . The time-honored general rules on recovery of damages for breach of contract are found in *Hadley v. Baxendale,* 9 Ex. 341, 156 Eng. Rep. 145 (1854)— rules this Court has generally followed. . . . They are: 1) where no special circumstances distinguish the contract involved from the great mass of contracts of the same kind, the damages recoverable are those as would naturally and generally result from the breach according to the usual course of things, and 2) where there are special circumstances in the contract, damages which result in consequence of the special circumstances are recoverable, if, and only if, the special circumstances were communicated to or known by both parties to the contract at the time they entered the contract. . . . The lost profits involved here fall under the second branch of the *Hadley v. Baxendale* formulation.

Generally speaking, this Court has long espoused the view that loss of future or anticipated profit—i.e., loss of expected monetary gain—is recoverable in a breach of contract action: 1) if the loss is within the contemplation of the parties at the time the contract was made, 2) if the loss flows directly or proximately from the breach—i.e. if the loss can be said to have been caused by the breach—and 3) if the loss is capable of reasonably accurate measurement or estimate. . . . An award in the form of a loss of profits, in fact, is generally considered a common measure of damages for breach of contract; it frequently represents fulfillment of the non-breaching party's expectation interest, and it often closely approximates the goal of placing the innocent party in the same position as if the contract had been fully performed. . . .

Our cases also recognize that where there is sufficient evidence presented on the issue of the recovery of special damages—including lost profits—what was or was not in the contemplation of the parties at the time of contracting is a question of fact to be determined by the trier of fact. . . . Liability for lost profits arises where the loss of anticipated profits upon breach can reasonably be said to be in the contemplation of the parties at the time of contracting. . . .

Here, there is clearly sufficient competent evidence to show GTE had within its contemplation at the time of contracting the potential for profits from a Florafax

association with Bellerose. . . . GTE knew it would be providing services not only directly for Florafax, but for others on behalf of Florafax. It knew Florafax was soliciting other entities to use the services of a call answering center like GTE's and, in fact, GTE looked upon Florafax's solicitation of these other entities as a positive aspect of a contractual relationship with Florafax because of the potential for increased revenue.

Trial evidence also showed the Florafax/Bellerose contract was entered two weeks prior to the Florafax/ GTE agreement and that GTE officials knew either before or contemporaneously with signing the latter contract that Bellerose was considering turning over a portion of its inbound and outbound business via its 1-800-FLOWERS network to Florafax—business GTE also knew consisted of 100,000–200,000 orders annually. Further, . . . a clause in the Florafax/GTE contract itself expressly reflects the parties' contemplation of the recovery of lost profits by Florafax should GTE cease to perform its duties and obligations during the term of the contract: . . . "Termination. . . . In the event GTE ceases to perform. . . . its duties hereunder after a notice of termination is given or otherwise, Florafax may suffer tremendous damage to its business. GTE agrees to pay Florafax consequential damages and lost profits on the business lost." . . .

In our view then, contrary to the arguments of GTE, lost profits from a collateral contractual relationship may be recovered in a breach of contract action if such damages can be said to have been within the contemplation of the parties at the time of contracting. Here, there is evidence in the record—if believed by the jury— that plainly would support a finding special circumstances were communicated to or known by GTE at the time of contracting, so that a reasonable conclusion would be that the prospect of profits and, conversely, their loss upon breach, were in the contemplation of the parties at the time of contracting and would be suffered by Florafax should GTE cease to adequately perform under the Florafax/GTE agreement. . . .

The award of the jury of lost profit damages associated with the Florafax/Bellerose contract was an appropriate remedy for GTE's breach of its contract with Florafax. . . .

[Judgment of the court of appeals reversed; trial court judgment as to award of lost profits affirmed.]

Consequential Damages Under the UCC. Section 2–714(1) of the UCC adopts the rule of *Hadley* for contracts for the sale of goods by providing that a buyer may recover from a breaching seller for "loss resulting in the ordinary course of events from the seller's breach as determined in any manner which is reasonable." Section 2–715(2)(a) further authorizes buyer recovery for "any loss resulting from general or particular requirements and needs of which the seller *at the time of contracting had reason to know* and which could not reasonably be prevented by cover or otherwise." (Emphasis added.) Consistent with the preceding discussion, "particular needs of the buyer must generally be made known to the seller while general needs must rarely be made known to charge the seller with knowledge."[5]

Under the Code a buyer's recovery is limited to those damages not preventable by cover (obtaining substitute goods from another seller) or otherwise, and are available only to the buyer. Consistent with general UCC policy, consequential damages may be limited or excluded by agreement unless the provision is unconscionable.[6]

Avoidability as a Limitation on Damages — "Mitigation"

The concept of avoidability, embodied in the doctrine of **mitigation,** places an additional important limitation on damages awarded for breach of contract. Once a breach has occurred, the injured party must mitigate the damages — that is, take steps to keep damages to a minimum. The injured party may not sit idly by and allow damages to accumulate. The mitigation doctrine is designed to prevent economic waste and to assure that damages awarded do not exceed the amount necessary to compensate the injured party. Mitigation ordinarily requires suspending performance and taking affirmative steps to avoid further loss, such as making substitute arrangements. What constitutes suitable substitute performance depends upon an analysis of all circumstances including the similarity, time, and place of the alternative performance.[7]

Courts and commentators frequently assert that an injured party is under a "duty" to mitigate damages. This statement is incorrect, because the injured party incurs no liability for failure to mitigate. Upon failure to mitigate the injured party is simply unable to recover from the contract breacher for loss that could have been avoided by reasonable effort. The following examples illustrate this point.

1. S contracts to sell and deliver a machine to B. Prior to shipment, B repudiates the contract. Despite B's repudiation, S ships the machine to B, who refuses to receive it. S may not recover the cost of shipping the machine as part of the damages for breach.

2. Star Corp. contracts to sell production equipment to Black Mfg. Co. for $10,000, delivery to be made on June 1. Star breaches the contract by repudiating it on May 1. With reasonable effort, Black could have acquired suitable replacement equipment for $11,000 by June 1. Black fails to do so and as a result loses $15,000 in profits that would have resulted from the use of the machine. Black may not recover the $15,000 lost profit, but may recover $1,000 from Star. The $1,000 represents the general measure of a buyer's damage for nondelivery or repudiation by the seller under a contract for the sale of goods. Note that if Black, after reasonable effort, is unable to find a suitable replacement — that is, unable to cover — the $15,000 lost profits *may* be recoverable from Star as consequential damages if the test of foreseeability is met.

3. Albert hires Sally to manage Albert's business for one year for $20,000. Shortly after starting work, he fires her without cause, breaching the contract. Sally could obtain an equally good managerial job at $19,900. Sally fails to do so and remains unemployed. Her recoverable damages are $100, not the $20,000 lost earnings.[8]

Mitigation requires only that a reasonable effort to avoid loss be made. An injured party is not precluded from recovery simply because his efforts were unsuccessful in *actually* avoiding loss. Further, any incidental expenses such as commissions, storage charges, or employment agency fees incurred by the injured party in attempting to mitigate (whether successful or not) may be recovered from the breaching party. In addition, because efforts to mitigate need only be "reasonable," it

---

[5]UCC §2–715, Official Comment 3.

[6]UCC §2–719(3). Unconscionability is discussed in Chapter 10.

[7]Under the UCC, the interrelated doctrines of cover (buyer) and right to resell (seller) provide for mitigation by substitute performance in contracts for sale of goods. These concepts are discussed in Chapter 18.

[8]RESTATEMENT (SECOND) OF CONTRACTS §350, ills. 2, 5, and 8.

is not necessary that the *maximum* possible loss under the circumstances be avoided.

Frequently, the injured party is able to avoid certain expenses that would have been incurred had she performed. Thus, in computing damages, her recovery is reduced by costs saved as a result of the breach. For example, Jenny Corp. contracts to build a hotel for Bart to be completed by May 1. It fails to complete performance until June 1. The cost Bart avoids by not having to operate the hotel for the month is subtracted from income lost during May in computing his damages. This same principle governs computation of damages awarded to buyers and sellers for breach of Code contracts.

Other Money Damages

Liquidated Damages. The term "liquidated" means fixed or settled in amount. By use of a **liquidated damages provision,** the parties specify in the contract the amount of damages to be awarded in the event of a breach, rather than leaving that amount to the calculation of a court or jury. These provisions reduce litigation expense and save time for courts, juries, witnesses, and parties. They are particularly useful if the amount in controversy is small.

The theory of contract damages is compensatory, not punitive. Thus, damages may be liquidated in the agreement, but only at an amount that is *reasonable* in light of (1) the anticipated or actual harm caused by the breach, and (2) the difficulties in proving loss.[9] The provision must therefore represent a reasonable good faith effort by the parties at the date of the contract to forecast or pre-estimate the amount of probable loss to be sustained in the event of the breach. It must not be a "penalty," that is, a threat designed to prevent or punish breach. A term fixing unreasonably large liquidated damages is void as a penalty. Punishment of a promisor for breach has no justification on economic or other grounds and a penalty is therefore unenforceable for public policy reasons. The name attached to the provision by the parties—for example, when the contract provides for the award of a fixed sum "as liquidated damages and not as a penalty"—is irrelevant in making this determination. This point is particularly important in contracts of adhesion in which the drafting party often attempts to disguise a penalty by calling it a liquidated damages clause.

As noted above, courts judge the enforceability of a liquidated damages clause based on circumstances existing at contract formation. At issue in the following case is whether actual damages resulting from the breach also should be considered.

Kelly v. Marx
705 N.E.2d 1114 (Mass. 1999)

In May 1994, plaintiffs John and Pamela Kelly signed a contract agreeing to purchase a house owned by defendants Steven and Merrill Marx for $355,000. After the plaintiffs paid a deposit of $17,750, the parties agreed to close on September 1. Because the plaintiffs were unable to sell their current home, they asked the defendants to put the house back on the market. The defendants contracted to sell the house to another purchaser who paid them $360,000 on September 20. The defendants refused the plaintiffs' request for a refund of their deposit citing the following provision in the contract: "If the Buyer shall fail to fulfill the Buyer's agreements herein, all deposits made hereunder by the Buyer shall be retained by the Seller as liquidated damages." The plaintiffs sued defendants for return of the deposit. The trial court granted judgment for the defendants. On appeal by the plaintiffs, the court of appeals reversed. The Massachusetts Supreme Court agreed to review the case.

Ireland, Justice

. . . Liquidated damages clauses which provide for the seller of real estate to retain the buyer's deposit are recognized in Massachusetts, . . . and, as both parties concede here and the Appeals Court concluded, they are a common real estate practice. . . . The question before us is whether enforceability of a liquidated damages clause is to be tested by analyzing the circumstances at contract formation, the prospective or "single look" approach, or when the breach occurs, the retrospective or "second look" approach.

This question has created confusion in our courts. . . . Many decisions . . . have concluded that liquidated damages should be measured, first, by assessing the reasonableness of the liquidated damages in light of the parties' ability to anticipate damages at contract formation, and, second, against the actual damages resulting from the breach. . . .

We agree with the . . . decisions of many other States, that a judge, in determining the enforceability of

---

[9]RESTATEMENT (SECOND) OF CONTRACTS §356(1); UCC §2–718(1).

a liquidated damages clause, should examine only the circumstances at contract formation. Our position is that "[w]here actual damages are difficult to ascertain and where the sum agreed upon by the parties at the time of the execution of the contract represents a reasonable estimate of the actual damages, such a contract will be enforced." *A-Z Servicenter, Inc. v. Segall,* [138 N.E.2d 266, 268 (Mass. 1956)]. Liquidated damages will not be enforced if the sum is "grossly disproportionate to a reasonable estimate of actual damages" made at the time of contract formation. *Lynch v. Andrew,* [481 N.E.2d 1383, 1386 (Mass. App. 1985)].

This approach most accurately matches the expectations of the parties, who negotiated a liquidated damage amount that was fair to each side based on their unique concerns and circumstances surrounding the agreement, and their individual estimate of damages in event of a breach. . . .

In addition to meeting the parties' expectations, the "single look" approach helps resolve disputes efficiently by making it unnecessary to wait until actual damages from a breach are proved. By reducing challenges to a liquidated damages clause, the "single look" approach eliminates uncertainty and tends to prevent costly future litigation. The "second look," by contrast, undermines the "peace of mind and certainty of result," [*Kelly v. Marx,* 694 N.E.2d 869, 875 (Mass. App. 1998) (Spina, J., dissenting)] the parties sought when they contracted for liquidated damages. It increases the potential for litigation by inviting the aggrieved party to attempt to show evidence of damage when the contract is breached, or, more accurately, evidence of damage flowing from the breach but occurring sometime afterward. In other words, "the 'parties must fully litigate (at great expense and delay) that which they sought not to litigate.'" *Watson v. Ingram,* [881 P.2d 247 (Wash. 1994)], quoting Note, *Keep the Change!: A Critique of the No Actual Injury Defense to Liquidated Damages,* 65 Wash. L. Rev. 977, 991 (1990).

The plaintiffs argue that application of a "second look" approach would allow the court to guard against undue windfalls, such as the one the defendants would receive here if they were to keep the deposit, because the defendants suffered no loss from the breach of the sale. We disagree. In essence, the plaintiffs want to undo the agreement between the parties, who expect to receive stipulated damages, not damages resolved by a court examining postbreach circumstances. The parties agreed to the extent of their damages when they agreed on a liquidated damages clause. "[T]he proper course is to enforce contracts according to their plain meaning and not to undertake to be wiser than the parties, and therefore that in general when parties say that a sum is payable as liquidated damages they will be taken to mean what they say and will be held to their word." *Guerin v. Stacy,* [56 N.E. 892 (Mass. 1900)] (Holmes, C.J.).

Turning to the present case, we conclude the plaintiffs are not entitled to the return of the deposit they paid to the defendants. The potential damages were difficult to predict when the agreement was made. . . . Viewing the facts at the time of contract formation, the liquidated damages were a reasonable estimate of the damage to the defendants. The deposit, five percent of the purchase price, was a reasonable forecast of the defendants' losses that would result if the buyers were to breach the agreement. These costs could arise from a host of issues relating to finding another buyer and waiting for an uncertain period of time before selling their property, and in light of the risk of an undeterminable loss that is dependent on many factors (primarily the shape of the real estate market at the time of the breach). The sum is not grossly disproportionate to the expected damages arising from a breach of the sale agreement, nor is it "unconscionably excessive" so as to be defeated as a matter of public policy.

[Judgment of the Appeals Court reversed; judgment of the Superior Court affirmed.]

Punitive Damages. **Punitive,** or **exemplary damages,** are used to punish the conduct of the defendant. They usually are awarded in tort cases as a deterrent to similar future conduct by the defendant or others. Punitive damages are not awarded in contract actions unless the conduct constituting the breach is also a tort for which punitive damages may be recovered. As previously discussed, contract remedies seek to compensate the injured party, not punish the wrongdoer. A contract breach ordinarily does not involve conduct that justifies the extraordinary punitive damage remedy. If, however, the defendant has acted intentionally, maliciously, or fraudulently, or his conduct constituted gross negligence (that is, acting with reckless disregard for the consequences of his actions), punitive damages may be awarded in addition to compensatory damages.

Nominal Damages. Occasionally, the promisee of a broken contractual promise does not incur or is unable to prove loss or injury. Thus, though breach is established, damages are not. In these cases, the court may award the plaintiff **nominal damages,** such as $1, to acknowledge the existence of a breach. Court costs also may be awarded in such cases.

Equitable Remedies—Specific Performance, Injunction Against Breach, and Reformation

As previously discussed, equitable remedies are granted in the discretion of the court when the remedy at law, dollar damages, is inadequate. Specific performance and injunction against breach, discussed below, represent alternatives to an award of damages as a means of enforcing a contract. Although specific performance and injunction are extraordinary remedies, modern courts now grant them in a wide variety of situations both in UCC and common law contracts.

Specific Performance

Specific performance requires that the breaching party actually perform the contract as agreed. For example, if Seller contracts with Buyer to deliver 500 widgets and fails to do so, the remedy at law would allow compensatory damages (money) to the buyer for his loss. The remedy of specific performance, however, actually forces the seller to deliver the 500 units as promised. Specific performance is granted only if dollar damages are inadequate to compensate the injured party. Factors to be considered in determining the adequacy of legal relief include:

1. the difficulty of proving damages with reasonable certainty,
2. the difficulty of procuring a suitable substitute for the performance required by the contract, and
3. the likelihood that a damage award could not be collected, due, for example, to the defendant's insolvency.[10]

---

[10]RESTATEMENT (SECOND) OF CONTRACTS §360.

Personal Property. Under the traditional test, the legal remedy is inadequate only if the subject matter is unique. Because most personal property is not unique, and a market for substitute property exists, dollar damages for breach are generally adequate. Specific performance may, however, properly be granted if the item is one of a kind (such as a rare painting or antique), or when the item has personal significance to one of the contracting parties. For example, a contract to purchase a family heirloom may be specifically enforced by the buyer. Additionally, contracts for the sale of patents and copyrights, shares of stock in a corporation (if substitute shares are not readily obtainable or the stock is necessary for control of a corporation whose shares are publicly traded), and businesses have been specifically enforced because the subject matter is deemed "unique." In these situations, specific performance may be granted because of the difficulty (or impossibility) of finding a suitable substitute. Further, certain types of interests cannot be valued in money, making damages difficult to prove with reasonable certainty. For example, it is difficult to value sentimental attachment to a family heirloom or loss of control over a corporation.

Land. Contracts for the sale of real property (land) are always specifically enforceable because courts long have treated each piece of, and interest in, real property as unique. Assume Steve, on March 1, contracts to sell land to Cathy for $25,000, with the conveyance of the land and payment of the purchase price to occur on August 1. Steve fails to perform. Upon suit by Cathy requesting specific performance, the court will order Steve to convey the property to Cathy, who must pay the purchase price.

Note that specific performance is not available in land sale contracts if the seller, after the contract is made but before the time agreed upon to transfer the property, conveys the property to a bona fide purchaser, who takes without notice of the original buyer's interest. In these cases, the court will not order the purchaser to return the property. The original buyer's recovery is limited to the traditional measure of contract damages, that is, the difference between the fair market value and the contract price on the date of performance. To illustrate using the preceding example, assume that on June 1 Steve conveyed the land to Megan, who paid fair value for the property and took it in good faith without knowledge of Cathy's interest. If Cathy later sues Steve for breach of contract, the court will not disturb the title in Megan's hands, but will instead award Cathy the remedy at law, money damages.[11]

Personal Services. Specific performance will not be granted in contracts requiring personal services or supervision, such as employment contracts, for several reasons. First, forcing an unwilling party to perform may violate the Thirteenth Amendment to the U.S. Constitution, which provides "neither slavery nor *involuntary servitude . . .* shall exist within the United States. . . ." (Emphasis added.) Second, such decrees are difficult for the court to supervise because, although the court may order performance, it has no way of monitoring the quality of the performance, the fundamental basis of contracts for personal services. Third, it is undesirable to compel people to continue contractual personal associations that have become unworkable.

For example, assume A agrees to act in a play being produced by B. A breaches the contract because personal animosity develops between A and B. Although A is liable for damages for her breach, the court will not order specific performance.

Specific Performance Under the Uniform Commercial Code. The UCC retains but expands the common law rule of specific performance by providing in 2–716(1) that "specific performance may be decreed where the goods are *unique or in other proper circumstances.*" (Emphasis added.) The UCC initially expands the availability of specific performance by redefining "uniqueness," the traditional specific performance test, to emphasize the "commercial feasibility of replacement."[12] Under the Code, goods may be "unique" even though not specific or ascertained at the time of the contract, like a family heirloom or a work of art.

Further, uniqueness is not the sole basis of the specific performance remedy under the UCC. For example, inability of the buyer to "cover"—obtain substitute goods from an alternative source—is strong evidence of "other proper circumstances" supporting specific enforcement of the contract. The buyer's inability to cover may result either from a market shortage or a monopoly on the part of the breaching party. To illus-

trate, assume Stern Chemical Co. has agreed to sell and deliver a certain chemical to Blake Corp. for use in Blake's manufacturing process. If Stern breaches, and Blake is unable to acquire the chemical from an alternative source, the court properly may grant specific performance.

In Code contracts, therefore, the inquiry focuses on the buyer's reasonable ability to replace the performance of the breaching seller. If replacement is not commercially feasible, specific enforcement should be decreed. If the injured buyer is able to "cover," specific performance will seldom be granted. Because a market exists for most goods, damages will ordinarily be an adequate remedy. Further, arranging for substitute performance usually avoids loss more effectively than a suit for specific performance.

In the following case, decided under Article 2 of the UCC, the court was required to determine whether specific performance should be granted.

Klein v. PepsiCo, Inc.
845 F.2d 76 (4th Cir. 1988)

Defendant PepsiCo, Inc. owned a Gulfstream G-II corporate jet that plaintiff Eugene Klein was interested in purchasing. Following negotiations, PepsiCo agreed to sell the jet, but several days later PepsiCo's chairman decided that the jet should be withdrawn from the market. After PepsiCo refused to deliver the jet as agreed, Klein sued PepsiCo for breach of contract. The trial court ruled in favor of Klein and ordered specific performance of the contract. PepsiCo appealed.

Ervin, Circuit Judge

. . . [U.C.C. 2–716] permits a jilted buyer of goods to seek specific performance of the contract if the goods sought are unique, or in other proper circumstances. Judge Williams ruled that: 1) the G-II aircraft involved in this case is unique and 2) Klein's inability to cover with a comparable aircraft is strong evidence of "other proper circumstances." . . . These conclusions are not supported in the record.

We note first that Virginia's adoption of the Uniform Commercial Code does not abrogate the maxim that specific performance is inappropriate where damages are recoverable and adequate. . . . In this case Judge

---

[11]In this situation, the buyer under an executory contract for the sale of land may protect itself against subsequent purchasers by recording its interest, thereby giving constructive notice to would-be purchasers. The operation of the real property recording statute is discussed in Chapter 37.

[12]UCC §2–716, Official Comment 2.

Williams repeatedly stated that money damages would make Klein whole. . . . Klein argued that he wanted the plane to resell it for a profit. . . . An increase in the cost of a replacement does not merit the remedy of specific performance. . . . There is no room in this case for the equitable remedy of specific performance.

Turning now to the specific rulings of the court below, Judge Williams explained that the aircraft was unique because only three comparable aircraft existed on the market. Therefore, Klein would have to go through considerable expense to find a replacement. . . . Klein's expert testified that there were twenty-one other G-II's on the market, three of which were roughly comparable. . . . Klein's chief pilot said that other G-II's could be purchased. . . . Finally, we should note that two G-II's [were] offered to Klein after this deal fell through, . . . and Klein made bids on two other G-II's after PepsiCo withdrew its aircraft from the market. . . . Given these facts, we find it very difficult to support a ruling that the aircraft was so unique as to merit an order of specific performance.

Judge Williams ruled further that Klein's inability to cover his loss is an "other proper circumstance" favoring specific performance. Klein testified himself that he didn't purchase another G-II because prices had started to rise. . . . Because of the price increase, he decided to purchase a G-III aircraft. As noted earlier, price increases alone are no reason to order specific performance. Because money damages would clearly be adequate in this case, and because the aircraft is not unique within the meaning of the Virginia Commercial Code, we reverse the grant of specific performance and remand the case to the district court for a trial on damages.

[Judgment reversed and remanded.]

Injunction

An **injunction** is an order directed to a defendant by the court to do (a **mandatory injunction**) or to refrain from doing (a **prohibitory** or **negative injunction**) an act. The effect of a mandatory injunction is remedial. For example, if Bob's garage is built three feet over his property line onto Andy's property, the court may order Bob to remove the encroachment on Andy's land, a mandatory injunction. Note that in contracts, a specific performance decree is merely a mandatory injunction. That is, the court orders the defendant to perform the contract.

A negative injunction, on the other hand, is preventative in effect. For example, assume Ace Corporation's factory is polluting the air in the community. Beth, a homeowner, sues the factory in tort for the loss in value of her home and other damage to her property. If the court merely awards dollar damages to compensate for past injury, future pollution and deterioration of the property are not prevented. Payment of the money judgment is, in effect, a license to continue polluting. Therefore, if the court determines that the remedy at law is inadequate, it also may issue an injunction preventing future damage to the property. Thus, whereas dollar damage awards are generally retroactive in effect, a negative injunction has prospective application.

Injunction is a pervasive remedy used in many areas of the law including tort (the preceding example), property, contract, antitrust, and labor law. Injunctions frequently are used in the criminal or administrative context to prevent future violations of the law. For example, the Federal Trade Commission issues "cease and desist" orders to enjoin (prevent) antitrust law violations.

Injunction Against Breach. In contract law, injunction and specific performance are closely associated remedies. Like specific performance, **injunction against breach,** a court order not to breach a contract, is available only when money damages are an inadequate remedy. Generally, a court will order a person *not* to breach a contract duty in two situations:

1. if the duty is a forbearance—a promise that something will not happen in the future—or
2. the duty is to act (as opposed to forbear) and specific performance would be denied by the court only for reasons inapplicable to an injunction.[13]

If the duty is merely a forbearance, the only way to specifically enforce it is through an injunction against its breach. For example, assume Mel sells his bakery to Bob. The bakery has a reputation for excellence in the community. A substantial portion of the purchase price therefore represents goodwill. In order to protect this goodwill, Mel agrees that he will *not* open a bakery in

---

[13]Restatement (Second) of Contracts §357(2).

competition with Bob in the locality for five years.[14] Within one year, Mel opens a competing bakery. Bob sues for breach. Mel may properly be enjoined from opening a competing bakery.

In the second situation, the court enforces the promise indirectly by ordering forbearance from inconsistent action. For example, assume that Acme makes a contract with Fabro whereby Acme agrees to sell Fabro's appliances exclusively in Acme's stores for a period of five years. After one year, Acme breaches. Fabro sues Acme for specific performance of Acme's duty to sell Fabro's appliances and to enjoin Acme from selling appliances manufactured by others. Even if specific performance is denied on the grounds that supervision and enforcement of the order would impose an undue burden on the court, an injunction may properly be granted.

Reformation

Although oral contracts are generally enforceable, the parties often commit their agreement to writing. Occasionally, mistakes are made in the process of reducing the agreement to writing. To correct such mistakes, courts of equity have developed the remedy of **reformation.** Like other equitable remedies, reformation is granted in the discretion of the court. A party requesting reformation alleges that the parties have reached an agreement that they have reduced to a writing, but because of a mistake by both parties regarding the content or effect of the writing, it fails to correctly state their agreement.

The deviation between the writing and the original agreement has taken many forms. Common examples include typographical errors, computational mistakes, misdescription of the subject matter (for example, incorrect legal description of real property), omission of an agreed term, misstatement of an agreed term, or inclusion of a term not agreed upon. In these situations, the court may "reform" (rewrite) the contract to the actual agreement of the parties.

Courts are fairly hesitant to grant reformation. As illustrated by the parol evidence rule, contract law attaches great importance to integrated written contracts. Further, under the "duty to read" principle,[15] a person signing a contract is generally deemed to know

its contents and agree to its terms, and may not later assert ignorance of provisions stated in the writing. Additionally, by its very nature, reformation seeks to alter the terms of a signed written contract, which has very high probative value, by oral testimony or other evidence having significantly lower probative value. In general, then, the evidence in support of reformation must be "clear and convincing" to the court.

Restitution

Generally speaking, the term **restitution** refers to restoration, or the act of restoring something to its rightful owner, commonly to make good for some loss, damage, or injury. As a judicial remedy, all restitutionary relief is couched in terms of preventing **unjust enrichment** of one party at the expense of another. Simply stated, the law requires that "a person who has been unjustly enriched at the expense of another is required to make restitution to the other."[16]

A person is unjustly enriched if he has received a benefit from another, and it would be unjust to allow retention of the benefit without paying for it. A benefit is conferred if one party gives another possession or some other interest in real or personal property, tangible or intangible, performs services beneficial to or requested by the other, satisfies an obligation of the other, or otherwise adds to the other's security or advantage. Therefore, whereas a claim for damages seeks to *compensate* the injured plaintiff for his loss, restitution is designed to force the defendant to pay for those benefits it would be unjust for him to keep.

Restitution is a pervasive judicial remedy, available in contract or tort actions, based upon statutes or common law principles, and may be sought in law or in equity. Although the person receiving the benefit frequently acts wrongfully in acquiring it, restitution is available even from an honest or innocent defendant. That is, restitution seeks to deprive a person of benefits that in equity and good conscience he ought not be allowed to keep, though he may have acquired them honestly and with no demonstrable injury to the other party.

A person receives restitution when she is restored approximately to the position she originally occupied. In form, restitution is generally either substitutionary or *in specie.* In substitutionary restitution, the thing taken

---

[14]The validity of covenants not to compete in the sale of a business is discussed in Chapter 10.

[15]"Duty to read" is discussed in Chapter 10.

[16]RESTATEMENT OF RESTITUTION §1.

from the plaintiff is not restored. The defendant is instead required to provide some substitute, usually a payment of money. If money is awarded, measuring the appropriate amount frequently is difficult. On the other hand, if restitution is *in specie,* often called "specific restitution," certain specific property received by the defendant is restored to the plaintiff.

The distinction between substitutionary and specific restitution is of critical importance in understanding the development and application of the remedy. Restitution historically developed both in courts of law and in courts of equity, governed by the same general principles of fairness and justice. Restitution at law developed mainly through the "quasi-contract" remedy, which is generally substitutionary, requiring a payment of *money* by the defendant. Equitable restitution developed a number of remedies, most notably the "constructive trust" doctrine, which requires return of *specific property* to the plaintiff. Note, therefore, a basic dichotomy in the law of restitution. If money is sought to prevent unjust enrichment, the legal remedy, quasi-contract, is appropriate. If, however, return of specific property is desired, the equitable constructive trust remedy may be used.

Restitution at Law — Quasi-Contract

Contract law developed through the common law action of assumpsit. By the early 1600s, assumpsit was used to enforce both express promises and those inferred from the parties' conduct (the so-called implied-in-fact contract[17]). By the mid-1600s, the assumpsit action was used in cases in which no contract, express or implied in fact, existed between the parties. The purpose was restitution, achieved by the court's imposing a promise upon the defendant to pay the plaintiff for the value of the benefit conferred. So was born the **contract implied in law** or **quasi-contract.**

Early cases involved the plaintiff's payment of money by mistake to the wrong person, overpayments, and payment by a third party of money to the defendant that should have been paid to the plaintiff. For example, assume Tom owes Lew $100. He inadvertently mails a payment to Fred instead. Tom subsequently sues Fred to recover the money mistakenly paid. In this case, the court would order Fred to pay the $100 back to Tom, not on the basis of any actual contractual promise by Fred to pay $100, but on the basis of a promise "implied in law" to prevent Fred's unjust enrichment. That is, in

order to prevent a windfall to Fred, the court imposes a binding promise (a quasi-contract) to pay, even though no actual agreement, express or implied in fact, exists between Tom and Fred.

Note that, unlike a contract implied in fact, the implied in law contract is not a contract at all. No contractual relationship need exist between the parties and liability is imposed without regard to intent. The law simply requires that a benefit be conferred on the defendant which he has retained.[18] To the extent necessary to prevent a windfall, the court will imply a promise on the part of the defendant to pay the reasonable value of the benefit conferred. That is, in order to do justice, the court proceeds "as if" a contractual promise to pay exists.

At issue in the following case was whether the court should apply quasi-contract principles to require the defendant to pay for a benefit conferred by the plaintiff.

DCB Construction Co., Inc. v. The Central City Development Co.
965 P.2d 115 (Colo. 1998)

Central City Development Company (CCDC) owns a historic commercial building in Central City, Colorado that it leased to Santa Barbara Capital, Inc. (Tenant). The five-year lease, with monthly rental payments of $30,000, allowed Tenant to remodel the building subject to CCDC's approval of all plans and specifications. Tenant was required to pay all remodeling costs. Tenant hired DCB Construction Co., Inc. (DCB) to perform significant remodeling of the interior of the building. CCDC approved the remodeling plans and a CCDC representative visited the premises regularly while the work was being done. As required by the lease, Tenant posted the following notice on the building:

> [CCDC] shall not be liable for any erection, construction, alteration, removal, addition, repair, or other improvement, and the owner's interest in the above described property shall not be subject to a lien for any erection, construction, alteration, removal, addition, repair, or other improvement to [the leased premises].

After about five months, DCB had constructed a foundation retaining wall, steel frame with flooring, roof joists, stairs, fire sprinkler system, wiring, plumbing, heating, ventilation, and air conditioning. DCB stopped work,

---

[17]Contracts implied in fact are discussed in Chapter 7.

[18]Restitution is available not only when an expenditure made by one person adds to the property of another, but also when the expenditure saves the other from expense or loss.

however, because Tenant had paid only $76,515 on bills of $371,245 submitted by DCB. The following month, Tenant, which already had paid $427,500 in rent, defaulted on the lease agreement.

Plaintiff DCB sued defendant CCDC for unjust enrichment, seeking payment for the construction it had completed on the building. The trial court ruled in favor of DCB and awarded damages of $333,191. Following the court of appeals' reversal of the judgment, the Colorado Supreme Court granted DCB's petition for review.

Kourlis, Justice

. . . DCB's claim of unjust enrichment is a legal claim in quasi-contract for money damages based upon principles of restitution. . . . When restitution is the primary basis of a claim, as opposed to a remedy for bargains gone awry, it invokes what has been called a "contract implied in law." . . . The unjust enrichment claim in the context of a contract implied in law does not depend in any way upon a promise or privity between the parties. . . . Thus a "contract implied in law" is not really a contract at all, and may even be imposed in the face of a clearly expressed contrary intent if justice requires. . . .

The elements of the claim are based upon the principles stated in the *Restatement of Restitution §1,* [which require that:] (1) at plaintiff's expense (2) defendant received a benefit (3) under circumstances that would make it unjust for defendant to retain the benefit without paying. . . .

Considering the first prong of the test, in this case there is no question that any benefit CCDC received came at DCB's expense. DCB performed construction work on CCDC's building over a period of approximately six months, and Tenant paid DCB for only a fraction of the work.

The second prong examines whether defendant was benefited or enriched. The trial court specifically found, based on the expert evidence submitted, that the building is now worth more than it was before DCB's work. . . . The trial court's finding that the building is now worth more after the remodeling than before is sufficient to show that CCDC benefited. Accordingly, the first two elements of the test, benefit to CCDC at DCB's expense, have been established.

The third prong of the test requires consideration of whether it would be unjust to allow CCDC to retain the benefit conferred without paying its value. The notion

of what is or is not "unjust" is an inherently malleable and unpredictable standard. . . . [W]e think it is important to articulate a general rule, applicable in this context, that provides more stability and predictability than an ad hoc review. . . .

With this principle in mind, we begin our analysis with two basic propositions. First, there is the general rule that when an individual who is not the owner orders improvements on the owner's land and then fails to pay the contractor or supplier, "the owner is not liable to the contractor or supplier unless he agreed to pay them." 3 Dan B. Dobbs, *The Law of Remedies* §12.20(3) (2d ed. 1993). . . . The rule seeks to protect personal autonomy and rights of choice. . . . Ordinarily, an owner should not be forced into "legal relations with someone other than the contract partner he ha[s] chosen." [J. Dawson, *The Self-Serving Intermeddler,* 87 Harv. L. Rev. 1409, 1444 (1974).]

Second, the *Restatement of Restitution* §110 provides that "[a] person who has conferred a benefit upon another as the performance of a contract with a third person is not entitled to restitution from the other *merely* because of the failure of performance by the third person." *Restatement of Restitution* §110 (1937)(emphasis added).

Application of these principles to this case suggests that CCDC should not be held liable for the improvements ordered by Tenant. CCDC did not agree to pay for the improvements, and should not be forced into a quasi-contractual relationship with DCB. It is not enough that CCDC owns the improved building and that Tenant breached its contract to pay for those improvements. There must be more. It is unjust for a contractor to bear the loss of a debt unpaid. However, it is not necessarily just or right to impose that debt upon the owner of the property merely to rectify the first injustice. . . .

Hence, an injustice that warrants the court's imposition of the remedy of restitution must rest not only in the loss to the contractor, but also in the conduct of the owner. The *Restatement of Restitution* sets forth several general doctrines, such as fraud, mistake, coercion, and request, that are instructive in defining the notion of injustice. . . . In the instant case, we do not have allegations that fit neatly into the applicable "injustice" categories suggested by the *Restatement.* However, the general theme . . . that defines and connects these examples is that "injustice" involves some form of improper conduct by the party to be charged.

DCB . . . contends that the nature of CCDC's involvement in the enterprise is sufficient to render its retention of the benefit unjust. . . . A landlord will virtually always retain the right to give or withhold permission for work to be done on its premises. As owner of the premises, the landlord is generally required to apply for and execute building permits or other necessary documents. The landlord has a strong and legitimate interest in pre-approving and monitoring any significant construction. Similarly, the landlord's participation in creating and/or approving specifications is a natural product of its interest in the property and is a matter of concern solely between the landlord and the tenant. . . .

DCB also argues that it is important that CCDC knew of and acquiesced in the renovation and "never objected to anything that DCB was doing." As discussed above, CCDC's "acceptance" of the work carries no significance in this context where the work was an expected result of its lease with Tenant. CCDC could not be expected to object to or attempt to stop work which was clearly anticipated and bargained for with another. . . .

We do not find it unjust for a landlord to be closely involved in an enterprise for which it has contracted and given consideration to another. . . . If we were to approve this formula for evaluating injustice, we would adopt a rule that essentially makes the landlord an insurer of the risk assumed by contractors in extending credit to tenants. . . .

Rather, we hold that injustice in this context requires some type of improper, deceitful, or misleading conduct by the landlord. . . . Here, there is no evidence that CCDC improperly created the impression that either CCDC or Tenant would pay for the work being done. In fact, CCDC posted a notice that not only informed DCB that it would not be subject to mechanics' liens, but also explicitly disclaimed any type of liability for the work. A notice alone might not suffice to absolve a landlord from liability if the landlord had otherwise engaged in improper conduct that negated the effect of a notice. However, here CCDC did not engage in any type of improper, deceitful, or misleading conduct. Absent such conduct, we do not find that CCDC's retention of any benefit received is unjust.

[Judgment affirmed.]

Restitution in Equity — Constructive Trust

As discussed in Chapter 1, various substantive and procedural deficiencies in the early English common law courts drove many litigants to the chancellor whose jurisdiction, grounded on equitable principles, led to the creation of the independent court of chancery or equity. Various remedies developed in courts of equity are restitutionary in nature, including the constructive trust.[19] The constructive trust concept is grounded partially in the law of trusts, but primarily in the law of restitution. A **constructive trust** is an equitable restitutionary remedy that is used when a person who has obtained *title to property* would be unjustly enriched if permitted to retain it. In this situation, the court subjects the person holding title (the constructive trustee) to an equitable duty to convey the property to the person who should have it. The constructive trust, therefore, simply uses the trust concept (in which one person possesses title to property subject to an equitable duty to hold it for or convey it to another) as the tool to force conveyance of the property by the wrongdoer to the person who, in fairness, should have it. But for this basic similarity there is little resemblance between the constructive trust and trusts discussed in Chapter 39.

A constructive trust, therefore, bears the same relationship to an express trust that a quasi-contractual obligation bears to a contractual obligation. That is, like a quasi-contractual promise, a constructive trust is simply a fiction imposed by the court as a means of achieving justice. Constructive trusts are imposed in a variety of situations, including, for example, when property is acquired by fraud, mistake, duress, or undue influence.

Restitution as a Contract Remedy

Restitution is a common remedy in contract cases, available to a plaintiff (1) as an alternative to enforcing the contract between the parties, (2) when, for some reason, such as his own breach, the plaintiff is prevented from enforcing the contract, or (3) upon avoidance of a contract voidable on grounds of fraud, misrepresentation, mistake, infancy, or duress. A party is

---

[19]Other remedies developed were: (1) subrogation discussed in suretyship (Chapter 33), and in insurance (Chapter 57); (2) the accounting discussed in partnership (Chapter 42); and (3) rescission and reformation covered in this chapter.

entitled to restitution as a contract remedy to the extent she has conferred a benefit on the other party either through her part performance of or reliance upon the contract. Generally, a party seeking restitution of a benefit conferred is expected to return what she has received from the other party—such as land, goods, or other property. The objective, then, is to return the parties, as nearly as practicable, to their precontract positions.

Restitution as an Alternative to Enforcement. When faced with a breach of contract, the injured party ordinarily sues the breaching party on his promise to recover money damages, or in appropriate cases, specific performance or injunction against breach. As previously noted, these remedies seek to protect the expectation (benefit of the bargain) interest, or in some instances, the reliance interest of the injured party. Alternatively, the injured party may sue in restitution to prevent unjust enrichment by recovering the value of any benefit conferred on the defendant through part performance or reliance. Although an injured party who has partially performed will usually seek damages based on his expectation interest (because this includes his lost profit on the transaction), restitution may provide a larger recovery in some cases, for example, if the injured party would have lost money on the contract.

Restitution When Plaintiff Breaches. Restitution is commonly used in contract cases to protect a party who has either breached the contract or for some other reason cannot enforce it against the other party. For example, if a contract is partially performed but is later discharged or avoided because of impracticability of performance, or noncompliance with the Statute of Frauds, restitution may be granted. In these cases, it is often unjust to allow the other party to retain the benefit of the part performance without paying for it. A party who has breached is entitled to restitution to the extent that the benefit received by the injured party exceeds the loss resulting from the breach. For example, assume Susan contracts to sell land to Belinda for $100,000, payment to be made in ten equal monthly installments before transfer of title. Belinda pays $30,000, but fails to pay the remaining installments. Susan sells the land to Daniel for $95,000. Belinda can recover $25,000 from Susan: $30,000 in restitution less $5,000 damages for Belinda's breach of contract.

Restitution in Voidable Contracts. Perhaps the most common use of restitution in contract cases occurs when a party avoids a contract on grounds of infancy,

mistake, duress, undue influence, misrepresentation, or fraud. In these cases, restitution is available to the party avoiding the contract for any benefit conferred on the other party resulting from part performance or reliance. Generally, the term **rescission** is used to describe the act of avoiding a transaction, commonly one based upon the parties' agreement. Rescission generally is followed by restitution on both sides, thereby placing both parties in the position they occupied before the contract was made. For example, assume B, a minor, purchases a car from an adult, S, for $1,000. B subsequently avoids (rescinds) the contract on grounds of infancy. S is entitled to restitution of the car from B, and B may recover the $1,000 from S in restitution.

Election of Remedies

As the foregoing discussion indicates, a variety of remedies are available for breach of contract. Neither the UCC nor the *Restatement (Second) of Contracts* imposes any requirement that a party must elect one remedy to the exclusion of others—that is, make an **election of remedies.** The *Restatement* provides that if a party has more than one remedy, choosing one of them (for example, by bringing suit requesting a given remedy) does not bar another remedy unless (1) the remedies are inconsistent, and (2) the other party materially changes position in reliance on the initial choice of remedy.[20] The UCC adopts a similar policy by providing that Code remedies are cumulative not exclusive.[21]

For example, the remedy of specific performance and dollar damages for total breach are inconsistent. However, damages to compensate the buyer for the seller's delay in performance would not be inconsistent with the buyer's action for specific performance. To illustrate the reliance aspect of the above rule, assume Seller and Buyer have a contract for the sale of land, breached by Seller. Buyer brings an action for damages. While the suit is pending, Seller, believing that Buyer does not intend to request specific performance, makes valuable improvements to the property. Buyer then amends her complaint to ask for specific performance. Buyer may not obtain specific performance because both aspects of the above test are met.

Another problem of potentially inconsistent remedy exists between a claim for rescission and an action for

---

[20]Restatement (Second) of Contracts §378.
[21]UCC §2–703, Official Comment 1. §2–703 and Code remedies generally are discussed in detail in Chapter 18.

money damages. Rescission and dollar damages achieve different results. Dollar damages place the injured party in a position approximating proper performance of the contract. Rescission and restitution return the parties to their original positions and thus treat the contract as if it never existed. Therefore, an action for dollar damages appears inconsistent with a claim for, or after, rescission. The UCC avoids this result by providing that expressions of "cancellation" or "rescission" of the contract are not construed to extinguish any claim for damages.[22] This rule is intended to safeguard

the rights of an injured party, who, after a breach, ill-advisedly uses language indicating the contract is at an end. Therefore, unless the cancellation expressly states that it is "without reservation of rights," the injured party's right to recover damages is unimpaired. If the plaintiff's claim is based upon fraud or material misrepresentation, the Code reaches the same result by providing that neither rescission nor a claim for rescission is inconsistent with a claim for damages or any other Code remedy.[23]

Summary

1.   The law of contract remedies concerns the judicial relief available when one party breaches a contractual promise. Contract remedies are of three general types: legal remedies, equitable remedies, and restitution.

2.   The remedy at law is, in all cases, money damages. The traditional goal of contract remedies is to fully compensate the injured promisee for actual loss resulting from the breach. To this end, damages are generally computed to give the injured party the "benefit of the bargain." Under this test, the injured party is awarded a sum of money sufficient to place him in a position equivalent to full performance.

3.   Because the underlying goal of contract remedies is to compensate the injured party, punitive damages, those designed to punish the conduct of the defendant, are not generally awarded in contract cases. In addition to basic compensatory damages, consequential damages (usually lost profits in contract cases) are recoverable for loss that the breaching party had reason to foresee when the contract was made, occurring as the probable result of its breach.

4.   After breach of the contract, the injured party must take reasonable steps to mitigate damages—to keep damages to a minimum. An injured party who fails to mitigate may not recover for loss which could have been avoided by reasonable effort. The mitigation doctrine prevents economic waste by relieving the breaching party of liability for losses that the other party could have prevented.

5.   By using a liquidated damages provision the parties may specify in the contract the damages to be awarded in the event of a breach rather than leaving this determination to the court or jury. To be enforceable, damages must be liquidated at an amount that is reasonable in light of the anticipated or actual harm caused by the breach and the difficulties in proving actual loss. This limitation assures that the provision is not a "penalty"—a threat designed to prevent or punish breach.

6.   If dollar damages are not adequate to remedy a breach of contract, the injured party may seek equitable relief, awarded in the discretion of the court, in the form of specific performance or injunction against breach. Both remedies effectively require the breaching party to perform the contract as agreed, rather than pay money damages for failure to perform it. Traditionally, specific performance is awarded only when the subject matter is unique, such as a rare antique or work of art. The UCC adopts a more liberal test emphasizing the commercial feasibility of replacing the promisor's performance. Contracts involving real property are always specifically enforceable because courts have long treated each piece of real property as unique. On the other hand, for various policy reasons, courts refuse to specifically enforce contracts involving personal services, such as employment contracts.

7.   Another equitable remedy used in contracts cases is reformation. Reformation is used when the parties reduce their agreement to a writing, which due to a mistake fails to correctly state their agreement. If evidence of a mistake is clear and convincing, the court may reform, or rewrite, the contract to conform to the actual agreement of the parties.

8.   Restitution also may be available as a contract remedy. Restitution is a broad remedial concept designed to prevent unjust enrichment of one party at the expense of another. A person who is unjustly enriched is required to make restitution either by return of a specific thing or the payment of money. Restitution developed both in courts of law and in courts of equity. If a sum of money is sought, restitution at law, or quasi-contractual relief, is appropriate. If return of specific property is desired, the equitable constructive trust doctrine is

---

[22]UCC §2–720 and Official Comment. "Rescission" as used in the Code refers to a mutual agreement to discharge contractual duties. "Cancellation" occurs when either party puts an end to the contract because of a breach by the other. §2–106(4).

[23]UCC §2–721.

utilized. As a contract remedy, restitution may be used by a person who has breached the contract to recover the value of the benefit conferred upon the other party, and to restore the parties to their original positions after avoidance of the contract on grounds of infancy, mistake, duress, undue influence, misrepresentation, or fraud.

9.   Although a variety of remedies are available for breach of contract, the law generally rejects any notion that an injured party must elect one remedy to the exclusion of others.

Key Terms

contract remedies	injunction
remedy at law	mandatory injunction
equitable remedy	prohibitory (negative)
expectation interest	injunction
benefit of the bargain	injunction against breach
reliance interest	reformation
restitution interest	restitution
court costs	unjust enrichment
consequential damages	quasi-contract (contract
mitigation of damages	implied in law)
liquidated damages provision	constructive trust
punitive (exemplary) damages	rescission
nominal damages	election of remedies
specific performance	

Questions and Problems

15.1   Contract remedies seek to protect one or more interests of an injured promisee, including an expectation, reliance, and restitution interest. Explain and distinguish the relationship among these various interests.

15.2   Mayfield entered into a contract with Swafford by which Mayfield agreed to pay $7,000 for Swafford's construction of a swimming pool on Mayfield's property. Mayfield later sued alleging that the pool had not been constructed in a "good workmanlike manner" and requested damages equal to the cost of repair.

The evidence established that the pool was improperly constructed. Witnesses testified that substantial work was required to correct the construction—for example, removal of the concrete deck, replacement of the piping system, and realignment, replacement, and reinforcement of the walls. The trial court awarded damages of $11,381 to Mayfield, the cost to repair the defects in the pool. Is cost of repair the correct measure of damages in this case? Explain. What alternative method might the court have used?

15.3   Cricket Alley Corporation, which operates a chain of eight retail clothing stores, agreed to purchase a computerized cash register system from Data Terminal. As described by Data Terminal representatives, the system would connect the cash registers from each store to a centralized computer where records on inventory, sales, and payroll could be maintained

for all stores. Data Terminal installed the new system, but it failed to operate as described. Over a period of several months, Data Terminal unsuccessfully tried to correct the problem. Finally, Cricket Alley purchased another system from Business Machinery, Inc. and sued Data Terminal for breach of contract. Cricket Alley sought damages of $50,000 representing the cost of wages it paid to employees for manually performing the tasks that the Data Terminal computer system was intended to handle. Data Terminal argued that although it knew Cricket Alley operated retail stores, it did not know of the general or particular requirements of the business at the time the contract was made. Therefore, Data Terminal claimed it could not be held liable for consequential damages—the increased cost of wages. How should the court rule?

15.4   Gomer was a sales director for the Major Advertising Company located in Chicago. Major was to make an important presentation for a potential new client in New York. If the client accepted Major as its new agency, Major would earn over $1 million in the next two years. Due to unforeseen delays, the prints of the sample advertisements were not ready until the day before the presentation. Gomer rushed the prints to the Snail Express Company, an air express firm that advertised that it guaranteed overnight delivery. Gomer explained the situation to the Snail Express clerk concluding, "So if this doesn't get to New York by tomorrow, I will lose my job and my company will lose the account which is worth over $1 million." The clerk nodded his head and accepted the package for shipment. The package did not arrive in New York until three days later. Gomer lost his job (which paid $125,000 per year) and Major lost the account.

(a)   Gomer plans to sue Snail Express for breach of contract. Is Gomer entitled to damages? How much? Explain.

(b)   Major also is considering a breach of contract suit against Snail Express. Is Major entitled to damages? Explain.

(c)   Gomer's attorney notified Snail Express of the breach of contract suit. In response, Snail Express suggested that the attorney review the receipt given to Gomer at the time of shipment. The receipt included a long list of provisions under the heading "Terms and Conditions of Contract." Paragraph 23(c) stated, "Snail Express shall not be liable for any special, incidental, or consequential damages, including but not limited to loss of profits or income whether or not Snail Express had knowledge that such damages might be incurred." Would you recommend that Gomer continue with his plans to sue? Why or why not?

15.5   Riley, a 71-year-old man, lived in an area of the southern United States where the heat and humidity are extremely high during the summer. In May, Riley called Giles Appliance Store about purchasing a new air conditioner for his house. After visiting Riley's house, Giles recommended a suitable unit that Riley agreed to buy for $1,000. In May, Giles installed the unit and Riley soon began to use it. The unit, however, had a leak that allowed the refrigerant to seep out. By August, the blower continued to operate but the air conditioner no longer cooled the air. As a result, temperatures in the house exceeded 100 degrees causing Riley to suffer a heart attack. Riley was taken to the hospital and his medical expenses were $100,000. Riley sued Giles for breach of contract. The court has found that Giles breached the contract. Should the damages include Riley's medical expenses of $100,000? Explain.

15.6 Mr. and Mrs. Burns contracted with the Speedy Construction Company for the construction of a duplex apartment house. The Burnses intended to live in one apartment and to rent the second apartment. The contract required that the construction company would complete the building by April 1. The contract also contained the following provision:

> If the construction is not completed by April 1, Speedy Construction Company shall pay to Mr. and Mrs. Burns on an actual expense basis as established by receipts, not more than $1,000 for packing and storing of furnishings and $30 per day for temporary accommodations.

Mr. and Mrs. Burns sold their house; the purchasers were to take possession on April 1. Mr. and Mrs. Burns also found a tenant for the second apartment in the duplex and signed a one-year lease to receive $250 a month as rent. In late March, Speedy advised the Burnses that the duplex would not be completed until June 1. On April 1, the Burnses moved out of their house and into a motel that charged $50 per day. They put all of their furnishings in storage at a cost of $2,000. They advised the tenant that the apartment was not completed; the lease was terminated and the tenant moved into another apartment. By the time the Burnses finally were able to move into the new duplex, they had incurred expenses in excess of $6,000. Further, they calculated that termination of the lease cost $3,000 ($250 times twelve months).

Mr. and Mrs. Burns demanded that Speedy pay damages of $9,000 resulting from breach of the construction contract. Speedy offered to pay $1,000 plus $30 per day stating that this was the amount required under the terms of the liquidated damages clause in the contract.

(a) Mr. and Mrs. Burns sue Speedy. They allege that the clause is not a liquidated damages clause. Are they correct? Explain.

(b) If it is a liquidated damages clause, should it be enforced in light of the fact that the damages would be disproportionately low in relation to actual damages? Explain.

15.7 C & H operates several sugar plantations in Hawaii. In 1999, C & H decided to purchase a vessel to transport the sugar crop during the harvest. The vessel consisted of two parts, a tugboat and a barge, neither of which could be used without the other. C & H contracted to have Sun Ship construct the tug at a cost of $25 million with delivery to be made on June 30, 2001. The contract included a liquidated damages clause requiring Sun to pay $17,000 for each day that delivery was delayed past the delivery date. C & H contracted to purchase the barge from Halter at a cost of $20 million, delivery to made on June 30, 2001. A liquidated damage clause in that contract required Halter to pay $10,000 per day for late delivery. Both Sun and Halter failed to complete construction by June 30. Sun deliv-

ered the tug on March 1, 2002 (243 days late); Halter delivered the barge on July 1, 2002 (365 days late). C & H has sued both Sun and Halter for breach of contract.

(a) The court found that the liquidated damages clauses were valid and enforceable. What amount of damages should be assessed against each defendant? Explain.

(b) Assume that the contracts contained no liquidated damages provisions and that C & H suffered total damages of $370,000. How should the damages be apportioned between the defendants? Explain.

15.8 TRC and Puritan entered into a contract, by which Puritan agreed to lease a fleet of 25 new milk trucks from TRC for seven years and TRC agreed to supply and maintain the trucks. The contract included a liquidated damages clause requiring Puritan, if it breached the contract, to pay damages equal to one-half of all rentals that would have become due had the contract been fully performed. The contract also stated various factors that the parties had considered in calculating the liquidated damages—for example, the investment that TRC had made in purchasing and maintaining the trucks, the uncertainty of TRC's ability to sell or release the trucks upon breach, and Puritan's savings for gas, oil, and other service items.

Almost three years later, Puritan terminated the contract on the grounds that TRC had failed to repair and maintain the trucks. TRC sued for breach of contract alleging that it had fully maintained the trucks and that Puritan had terminated the contract because it had acquired other delivery trucks by purchasing the assets of several other dairies. The trial court held that TRC had substantially performed the contract but that Puritan had unjustifiably terminated. Should the court award damages in accordance with the liquidated damages clause or is the clause an unenforceable penalty? What factors should the court consider in making its determination? Explain.

15.9 On March 1, 2005, Archie contracted to sell his farm to Beulah for $200,000, closing to occur on June 1, 2005. On April 1, Archie received a $250,000 offer from Zack. Archie accepted and the parties agreed to a May 1 closing date. Archie conveyed the land to Zack on May 1. Zack was at all times unaware of Archie's prior contract with Beulah. Beulah subsequently sued Archie for breach of contract. Is Beulah entitled to specific performance?

15.10 Campbell Soup Company entered into a contract with Wentz for sale of carrots to be grown on the Wentz farm. The contract price was $30 per ton. By the date of this contract, however, the market price had risen to $90 per ton and Wentz refused to deliver. Carrots meeting the contract description were in short supply, and could not be obtained elsewhere by Campbell. The contract, contained on a form drafted by Campbell, included the following provisions:

(1) Campbell's judgment is conclusive concerning whether or not the carrots delivered conform to the contract.

(2) Campbell may refuse carrots in excess of 12 tons per acre.

(3) The grower may not sell carrots to anyone else except carrots rejected by Campbell.

(4) A liquidated damages clause of $50 per acre upon breach by the grower (no liquidated damages clause covers a breach by Campbell).

(5) If Campbell is unable to receive the grower's carrots (for example, because of a strike or any other circumstance beyond Campbell's control), "grower may with Campbell's written consent, dispose of his carrots elsewhere. Grower may not, however, sell or otherwise dispose of any carrots which he is unable to deliver to Campbell."

Campbell sues Wentz for specific performance (or an injunction against selling the carrots to others). Should the court grant it? Should the court enforce the contract at all? Explain.

15.11 Lorch, Inc. agreed to lease a store in a shopping mall from Bessemer, Inc. for a term of 15 years. Under the lease agreement, Lorch promised "continuously and uninterruptedly to use for retail sales purposes all of the Leased Premises," "to open for business and remain open during the entire Lease Term," and not to conduct any "going out of business" sales. For over five years, Lorch operated a combination jewelry, furniture, and appliance store on the leased premises, but the store always operated at a substantial loss. During the sixth year, Lorch began advertising and conducted a going out of business sale, and then notified Bessemer that it was closing the store and vacating the premises on October 1. On September 24, Bessemer sued Lorch and requested that the court issue an injunction requiring Lorch to continue operating its store at the mall. Should the court issue the injunction against Lorch's breach? What factors should the court consider in reaching its decision? Explain.

15.12 Strauss sold a racehorse to West. Upon delivery, the horse was discovered to be lame. West accordingly shipped the horse back to Strauss at Belmont Park Racetrack. Strauss refused to accept it, and the horse was shipped to Bailey's farm to be cared for. When Bailey received the horse he was aware that a dispute had arisen concerning the ownership of the horse. Two months later he sent a bill for boarding the horse to West, who replied immediately, "The horse doesn't belong to me and it was not sent to your farm at my request." Nevertheless, Bailey continued to care for the horse until he sold it to a third party four months later. In the contract dispute between Strauss and West, the court found that West was liable to Strauss for the purchase price of the horse. Bailey sued West to recover for the care, feeding, and maintenance of the horse during the six-month period. Should Bailey recover on a contract implied-in-fact theory? If not, should he recover on the basis of quasi-contract (a contract implied in law)?

15.13 Bill, a contractor, agreed to repair the porch on Stella's cabin, located on a remote lake in northern Wisconsin. Because the parties lived in Madison, Bill did not inspect the property at the time of the contract. Following Stella's written directions Bill located an unoccupied cabin with a dilapidated porch and spent several days repairing it. It was subsequently discovered that Bill had taken a wrong turn and had repaired Jones's cabin by mistake. Should Bill be entitled to recover the reasonable value of the improvements from Jones?

SALES

THE SALES CONTRACT— GENERAL OBLIGATIONS

The general law of contracts is of common law origin, developed primarily through a long series of decided cases. Indeed, many fundamental contract doctrines can be traced to early decisions of English courts. The common law of contracts is continuously developing, forming an ever-expanding framework for modern commercial law.

Contracts is not, however, exclusively a common law topic. Many statutes, both state and federal, modify or replace common law contract principles in certain transactions. Perhaps the most important of these statutes is Article 2 of the Uniform Commercial Code that governs contracts for the sale of goods, or "sales contracts." Goods generally include tangible personal property, such as automobiles, appliances, and other consumer goods, business inventory and equipment, clothing, books, food, and animals. Article 2 therefore governs a wide variety of contracts made by consumers and businesspersons.

This and the following four chapters focus primarily upon issues relating to contracts for the sale of goods that have not been covered in the preceding contracts material. Although most of the material is drawn from specific Article 2 sections, other statutory provisions and common law doctrines also are involved.

Introduction to the Sales Contract

Article 2 and General Contract Law

Before undertaking a detailed study of sales contracts, it may be helpful briefly to review Article 2's approach to the various contracts issues discussed in the previous nine chapters.

Contract Formation and Modification. Article 2 generally follows the common law principles regarding contract formation, with certain notable exceptions.

Offers. Under the common law, offers are freely revocable at any time prior to the effectiveness of an acceptance unless the parties have agreed to an "option" contract to keep the offer open. Under the UCC, "firm offers" made by a merchant in a signed writing are irrevocable for up to three months, even if the offers are not supported by consideration.

Acceptance. Under the common law, unless an attempted acceptance is the mirror image of the offer, no contract results. Under the UCC, a definite and seasonable expression of acceptance operates as an acceptance even if it contains terms in addition to, or different from, the offer. This rule creates a contract, even though the parties use forms to communicate offer and acceptance containing minor differences.

Consideration. Under the preexisting duty rule, modifications of existing common law contracts require consideration to be binding. Modifications of Code contracts, if sought in good faith, need no consideration to be binding.

Additional issues relating to formation and terms of a sales contract are discussed throughout the following sales material.

Capacity of Parties. Article 2 effects no change in the law of contractual capacity. State law regarding contractual capacity generally also governs under Article 2.

Illegality; Unenforceability on Public Policy Grounds. As with capacity of parties, Article 2 leaves most illegality and public policy questions to non-Code state law. One notable exception is the unconscionability doctrine, which allows a court to refuse to enforce unreasonably unfair contracts or terms. Unconscionability principles now are generally applied to common law contracts as well.

Reality of Assent. Like capacity and legality issues, Article 2 leaves resolution of disputes involving fraud, misrepresentation, mistake, duress, and undue influence to state law existing outside the Code.

Parol Evidence Rule. Article 2 retains the parol evidence rule for sales contracts but provides that an integrated writing may be explained or supplemented by course of dealing, course of performance, usage of trade, and evidence of consistent additional terms.

Statute of Frauds. Article 2 contains an elaborate Statute of Frauds provision applicable to contracts for the sale of goods. Generally, a contract for the sale of goods with a price of $500 or more is unenforceable unless some writing exists that indicates a contract for

sale has been made, is signed by the party to be charged, and specifies a quantity term.

Third Parties. Article 2 generally follows common law principles regarding assignment and delegation of contracts and third-party beneficiaries. It explicitly addresses the legal effect of contract provisions prohibiting assignment and the consequences of a general assignment of a sales contract.

Performance of the Contract. Two performance characteristics often distinguish sales contracts from their common law counterparts. First, unless otherwise agreed, performance by the parties occurs simultaneously. Second, the seller's performance is governed generally by the "perfect tender rule," which means that if the seller's performance fails in any respect to conform to the contract, the buyer may reject the goods. Thus, no "substantial performance" doctrine as it exists under the common law is applicable to sales contracts. Nevertheless, various Article 2 provisions, discussed in Chapter 18, relieve the seller somewhat from the harsh effects of the perfect tender rule.

Note that certain important performance doctrines, originally based upon Code provisions, now generally are applied to common law contracts as well. Examples include: (1) the obligation of good faith; (2) the right of a contracting party, insecure about the other's willingness or ability to perform, to demand adequate assurance of due performance and suspend its own performance; and (3) the impracticability doctrine. Additional issues relating to performance of sales contracts are covered throughout the following sales material.

Contract Remedies. Article 2 retains the common law distinction between legal (money damages) and equitable (specific performance and injunction against breach) remedies available for breach of contract. The Code generally follows common law principles governing mitigation and liquidation of damages. It adopts, with slight modification, the common law foreseeability test to determine when consequential damages should be awarded.

In determining when the equitable remedies of specific performance and injunction against breach are available, Article 2 follows but expands upon the common law uniqueness test. By emphasizing the commercial feasibility of replacement rather than "one of a kind" uniqueness, the Code enhances the availability of the equitable contract remedies. Table 16.1 lists

Table 16.1	Major Uniform Commercial Code Provisions Relating to Contracts Covered in Chapters 6–15	

Subject	Code Section	Principle
Coverage of UCC and Scope of Article 2	1–302	variation of Code provisions by agreement
	1–103(b)	supplementary principles of law applicable
	1–201	general definitions
	2–102	scope of Article 2
	2–104(1),(3)	"merchant" defined
	2–105(1)	"goods" defined
Contract Formation and Modification	2–204(3)	contract formation requirements
	2–205	firm offers
	2–206(1)	manner and medium of acceptance
	2–206(2)	notification of acceptance
	2–207	additional or different terms in acceptance
	2–209(1)	modification of sales contracts
General Obligations	2–306(2)	exclusive dealing contracts
	2–309(3)	notice of termination
Capacity of Parties	1–103(b)	supplementary principles of law applicable
Illegality; Unenforceability on Public Policy Grounds	1–103(b)	supplementary principles of law applicable
	2–302	unconscionability
Reality of Assent	1–103(b)	supplementary principles of law applicable
	2–721	remedies for fraud and material misrepresentation
Parol Evidence Rule and Contract Interpretation	2–202	parol evidence rule
	1–303	course of performance, course of dealing, usage of trade
Statute of Frauds and Formality	2–201	Statute of Frauds—goods
	9–203(b)	Statute of Frauds—security interests
	2–209(2),(3)	contract modification and the Statute of Frauds
Third Parties	2–210	assignment and delegation of sales contracts
Performance and Discharge of Contracts	1–304	obligation of good faith in performance
	1–201(20)	
	2–503(1)	seller's tender of delivery
	2–601	perfect tender rule
	2–609	adequate assurance of performance
	2–610	anticipatory repudiation
	2–611	retraction of repudiation
	2–612	breach in installment contracts
	2–613	casualty to identified goods
	2–615	impracticability
Contract Remedies	1–304	obligation of good faith in enforcement
	1–201(20)	
	1–305	Code remedies liberally administered
	2–715(2)(a)	buyer's consequential damages
	2–716(1)	specific performance
	2–718(1)	liquidated damages
	2–719(3)	limitation of consequential damages
	2–720	effect of cancellation or rescission—election of remedy

the major UCC provisions covered in the contracts material.

Scope of Article 2

As discussed in Chapter 7, Article 2 governs contracts for the sale of goods. Section 2–105 defines goods generally as "all things movable at the time of identification to the contract." "Identification" refers to the process by which the particular goods to which the contract refers are designated or specified. That is, once the parties have chosen, manufactured, or otherwise designated the specific goods to be sold, they are "identified" to the contract. Sales contracts therefore usually are easily recognizable; any contract that involves the sale of a tangible, movable object is governed by Article 2.

Determining applicable law when goods are involved, however, may be difficult. For example, goods that are closely associated with land (such as crops, timber, or minerals) may be severed and sold apart from the land. In this case, UCC §2–107 determines whether the contract is for the sale of goods (governed by Article 2) or for the sale of an interest in land (governed by common law contract principles). Section 2–107 is discussed in Chapter 34 in conjunction with the coverage of the law of fixtures.

Problems in determining applicable law also have arisen if the contract involves a mixture of goods and services—for example, a contract by an artist to paint a portrait or by a plumber to deliver and install a hot water heater. The following case illustrates the principles used to determine whether such contracts are within the scope of Article 2.

Design Data Corporation v. Maryland Casualty Company

503 N.W.2d 552 (Neb. 1993)

Plaintiff Design Data Corporation of Lincoln, Nebraska, contracted to sell and install a computer system and to provide training to HHB Drafting, Inc. of Pevely, Missouri. After shipping the system to HHB's office, Design Data began installation and discovered that the drafting plotter was damaged. Design Data filed a claim with its insurer, defendant Maryland Casualty Company, which denied coverage on the ground that Design Data did not own the

plotter when the damage occurred. Design Data sued Maryland Casualty. The trial court ruled in favor of Design Data and Maryland Casualty appealed. To determine whether ownership of the plotter had transferred to HHB, the court first had to decide whether the contract was governed by the common law or the UCC.

Hastings, Chief Justice

. . . The initial question to be resolved is whether the Nebraska Uniform Commercial Code is applicable to the transaction at issue. Design Data argues that the transaction was not governed by the provisions of the Uniform Commercial Code because it was primarily for the performance of services and not for the sale of goods.

The president of HHB [Howard Becker] testified that from his discussions with Design Data, he was under the impression that he was purchasing a complete system for the price of $73,495, which included the hardware and software that worked together, a license to use the software, a 3-day training seminar in Lincoln, and installation of the software and hardware at his office. Becker stated that he would not have purchased the hardware from Design Data apart from the system, because although he could have purchased the same hardware locally, a condition of the sale was the purchase of the hardware and software as a bundled unit, and the software was the most important part of the system. Both hardware and software would be considered "goods."

In *Mennonite Deaconess Home & Hosp. v. Gates Eng'g Co.,* [363 N.W.2d 155, 160 (Neb. 1985)], this court discussed the applicability of the Uniform Commercial Code when a contract calls for both the sale of goods and the rendition of services, noting:

The question of whether this is a contract for the sale of goods depends upon an examination of the entire contract. The cases are uniform in holding that the U.C.C. applies where the principal purpose of the contract is the sale of goods, even though in order for the goods to be utilized, some installation is required. On the other hand, if the contract is principally for services and the goods are merely incidental to the contract, the provisions of the U.C.C. do not apply.

The test for inclusion in or exclusion from the sales provisions is not whether the contracts are mixed but, granting that they are mixed, whether their predominant factor, their thrust, their purpose, reasonably stated, is the rendition of service, with goods incidentally involved, or whether they are transactions of sale, with labor incidentally involved.

While Becker stated that he would not have purchased the hardware apart from the system as a whole, it is evident from his testimony that the hardware and software, sold as a bundled unit, were the essential elements of the sale, and not the installation or other peripheral items, such as the 3 days of training, which were included in the purchase price. Becker also testified that "[w]e had made arrangements for Design Data's representative to be here [at HHB's plant] on a Sunday to install this so that we could productively start using it on a Monday." It would seem apparent that installation required no more than a relatively short time to hook up the $73,495 system and test it. Thus, the sale of goods was the predominant factor in the transaction, with labor incidentally involved, and the provisions of the Uniform Commercial Code therefore apply. . . .

[Judgment reversed.]

Formation and Terms of the Sales Contract

Though its formation is governed generally by traditional contract principles, a contract for the sale of goods is easily created under the UCC. Under §2–204(1), a sales contract may be made in any manner sufficient to show agreement, including conduct by the parties recognizing the existence of the contract. Even the exact time of contract formation may be indefinite. For example, the correspondence of the parties may not disclose the exact time at which the deal was closed. Additionally, §2–204(3) provides that if (1) the parties have intended to make a contract, and (2) there is a reasonably certain basis for awarding an appropriate remedy in the event of breach, the contract will not fail for indefiniteness even though one or more of its terms are left open. The missing terms are then supplied by Code provisions often referred to as **default rules** or **gap fillers.** As elaborated in the Official Comment to §2–204:

> If the parties intend to enter into a binding agreement, this subsection [§2–204(3)] recognizes that agreement as valid

in law, despite missing terms, if there is any reasonably certain basis for granting a remedy. . . . [C]ommercial standards on the point of "indefiniteness" are intended to be applied, *this Act making provision elsewhere for missing terms needed for performance, open price, remedies and the like.* (Emphasis added.)

The terms referred to above, supplied by the Code in the absence of express agreement, are discussed throughout this and the next three chapters. Examples include terms governing price, delivery, passage of title, risk of loss, remedies, and warranties.[1]

The Code additionally provides in §2–311(1) that as long as the formation requirements outlined above are met, a contract will not fail for indefiniteness simply because it leaves particular details of performance to be specified by one of the parties at a later date. In this situation, any such specification must be made in good faith and in a commercially reasonable manner.

Although Article 2 supplies numerous missing terms, the UCC Statute of Frauds requirement, §2–201, applying to contracts for the sale of goods with a price of $500 or more, requires that the memorandum include the *quantity* term. The quantity need not be accurately stated in the memorandum, but enforcement is limited to the amount stated. Thus, at least for contracts subject to the Statute of Frauds, the agreement must contain a quantity term[2] to be enforceable.

Finally, it is important to remember that the Code generally does not limit the parties' freedom to contract, but merely supplies those terms that the parties fail to include. This freedom is expressly provided in §1–302, which simply states that the effect of Code provisions may be varied by agreement whether or not the specific provision involved includes the language "unless otherwise agreed." Certain UCC provisions, however, explicitly provide that they may not be varied by agreement. For example, the obligations of good faith, diligence, reasonableness, and care may not be disclaimed by the parties. The standards measuring performance of these obligations, however, may be determined by agreement if the standards are

---

[1]In addition, a number of gap filling provisions (for example, §2–306(2) relating to exclusive dealing contracts) are discussed in the contracts material in Part II of the text.

[2]The quantity term may be either stated explicitly or measured by the requirements of the buyer or output of the seller.

not manifestly unreasonable.[3] Similarly, §2–302 (unconscionability) may not be varied by agreement.

In summary, Article 2 provisions taken collectively form a standardized statutory contract governing the rights, obligations, and remedies of the parties to contracts for the sale of goods. These provisions insure that bargains intended by the parties to be contracts are enforced, despite inexact expression and missing terms. Article 2's statutory contract does not, however, limit the parties' freedom of contract because its terms apply only in the absence of contrary agreement.

General Obligations of the Parties

Although sales contracts can become quite complex, the primary obligations of the parties are very straightforward. Under §2–301, the obligation of the seller is to transfer and deliver the goods to the buyer, who is obligated to accept and pay for the goods in accordance with the contract.

As in all contracts, the order of performance is a fundamental consideration. Under the Code, performances are to be exchanged simultaneously unless the agreement provides otherwise. Section 2–507(1) states:

> *Tender of delivery is a condition to the buyer's duty* to accept the goods and, unless otherwise agreed, to his duty to pay for them. (Emphasis added.)

With respect to the simultaneous obligation of the buyer, §2–511(1) provides:

> Unless otherwise agreed *tender of payment is a condition to the seller's duty* to tender and complete any delivery. (Emphasis added.)

From these primary obligations of delivery and payment a myriad of legal issues arise. The following material examines first the seller's responsibilities regarding delivery of the goods and second, the duty of the buyer to pay the price.

Seller's Duty of Delivery

The parties to a sale of goods usually expressly provide for the time, place, and manner of delivery. If they fail

to do so, the UCC contains several gap fillers relating to delivery. These provisions relate both to contracts requiring shipment by the seller as well as those involving parties residing in the same locality.

Time of Delivery. Under §2–309(1), if the parties fail to agree, the *time* for any shipment or delivery is a *reasonable* time. What is reasonable is a question of fact, considering all relevant factors such as the nature of the goods and market conditions. The parties may agree to leave the time of delivery open. Unless otherwise agreed, however, arrangements relating to shipment generally are within the seller's discretion.[4]

Place of Delivery. Under §2–308, unless otherwise agreed, the *place* for delivery is the *seller's* place of business, or, if he has none, then at his residence. If, however, the goods have been identified to the contract and both parties know where the goods are located, then that place is the place of delivery. For example, assume S contracts to sell B two specified spools of electrical cable. Due to lack of storage space, the spools are stored at X's warehouse, a fact known to B. Unless agreed to the contrary, X's warehouse is the place of delivery.

Manner of Delivery. The *manner* of the seller's tender of delivery is determined in §2–503. The seller must (1) put and hold conforming goods at the buyer's disposition and (2) give the buyer reasonable notification to take delivery. Note that if the contract requires payment on delivery, the seller may retain control of the goods until payment. The tender must be at a reasonable hour and the goods must be kept available for a period long enough to allow the buyer to take possession. However, unless otherwise agreed, the *buyer* must furnish facilities (for example, a truck) for receiving the goods.

If the goods are in the possession of a bailee (generally a carrier or warehouseman) and are to be delivered without being moved, tender of delivery requires that the seller either tender a negotiable document of title covering the goods, or procure acknowledgment by the bailee that the buyer is entitled to possession of

---

[3]UCC §§1–302(b)–(c).

[4]UCC §2–311.

the goods. In addition, tender of a nonnegotiable document of title *or* a written direction to the bailee to deliver is sufficient tender unless the buyer objects. Thus, when documents of title are involved, proper tender requires action by the seller or the bailee giving the buyer the right to complete control of the goods.

Delivery in Lots. Unless the contract explicitly provides that performance is to be made in installments, §2–307 requires the seller to tender all goods called for by the contract in a single delivery and the buyer's payment is due only upon that tender. Circumstances may, however, give either party the right to make (by the seller) or demand (by the buyer) delivery in lots. A **lot** is a parcel or single article that is the subject matter of a separate sale or delivery, whether or not it is, by itself, sufficient to perform the contract.[5] For example, a seller required to deliver ten carloads of coal could deliver in lots if only two cars were available at the time of delivery. Similarly, a buyer could receive delivery in lots if its storage facilities are inadequate to receive the entire shipment at once. In the case of a partial delivery, the price, if it can be apportioned, may be demanded for each lot. Therefore, in the above example, if the circumstances allow the seller to deliver two carloads of coal at a time, it could demand one-fifth of the price from the buyer for each delivery.

Delivery by Carrier

Frequently, the contract will require or authorize the seller to ship the goods to the buyer—for example, when the parties are at a distance. Such contracts generally are referred to either as shipment or destination contracts. In a **shipment contract,** the seller is authorized or required to ship the goods to the buyer, but is not required to deliver them at any particular destination. In a **destination contract,** the seller is required to transport the goods to a stated destination and there tender them to the buyer. Unless explicitly stated, a shipment contract is presumed. The distinction is important not only in determining the seller's obligation with respect to delivery, but also in determining who bears the risk of loss if the goods are damaged or destroyed in transit.

---

[5]UCC §2–105(5).

The seller's obligations in a *shipment* contract are stated in §2–504. In order to make a valid tender, the seller must, unless otherwise agreed,

1. put the goods in the possession of a carrier and make a contract for their transportation to the buyer,
2. obtain and promptly deliver or tender any document necessary to enable the buyer to obtain possession of the goods (or required by the agreement or trade usage), and
3. promptly notify the buyer of the shipment.

Note that the seller's failure to meet the foregoing requirements is not a grounds for rejection by the buyer unless material loss or delay ensues.

Shipping Terms Defined. In contracts requiring shipment, the parties frequently employ specialized terminology in defining their obligations. Terms defined by Article 2 include F.O.B., F.A.S., C.I.F., C. & F., "ex ship," and "no arrival, no sale" terms. In shipment contract cases (such as F.O.B. place of shipment, C.I.F., and C. & F.) the meaning of these terms is supplemented by §2–504, discussed above.

F.O.B. and F.A.S. Terms—§2–319. Unless otherwise agreed, the term **F.O.B.** (meaning "free on board") at a named place—shipping point or destination—is a *delivery* term, not a price term. Under §2–319, it imposes the following obligations on the seller. If the term is F.O.B. place of shipment, the seller is required, at that place, to ship the goods as outlined in §2–504, discussed above. In this situation, the seller bears the risk and expense of putting the goods into the carrier's possession. For example, assume S, a Chicago seller, contracts to sell and deliver steel girders to B, a New York buyer, "F.O.B. Chicago." This term creates a shipment contract. S completes its delivery obligations when it meets the three requirements for shipment imposed by §2–504.

In contrast, if the term is F.O.B. place of destination, the seller is required (at the seller's own expense and risk) *to transport the goods* to the named destination and there tender delivery to the buyer. This term thus creates a "destination" contract, requiring the seller to deliver at a particular destination. If the F.O.B. term (shipment or destination) is more specific, naming a vessel, car, or other vehicle, the seller is additionally obligated (at its expense and risk) to load the goods on board.

The contract may require the seller to deliver the goods to a freighter, tanker, or other vessel for further shipment. In this case, an **F.A.S.** (meaning "free along-side") term may be used. The term F.A.S. vessel at a named port (for example, F.A.S. *Jolly Roger,* New York Harbor), like an F.O.B. term, is a delivery term. It requires the seller to (1) deliver the goods (at the seller's expense and risk) alongside the vessel in the manner usual in that port or on a dock designated and provided by the buyer, and (2) obtain and tender to the buyer a receipt for the goods. Note that under both F.O.B. and F.A.S. terms, the buyer must promptly give the seller any instructions necessary to make delivery.

C.I.F. and C. & F. Terms—§2–320. Section 2–320 outlines the meaning and effect of C.I.F. and C. & F. terms in sales contracts. The term **C.I.F.** means that the price of the goods includes, in a lump sum, the cost of the goods, insurance, and freight to the named destination (for example, C.I.F. London). The term **C. & F.** (or **C.F.**) means that the price includes only the cost and freight to the named destination. A C.I.F. destination term requires the seller to (1) put the goods into the possession of the carrier and obtain a negotiable bill of lading covering the goods and a receipt from the carrier indicating payment of (or provision for) the freight charges, (2) obtain an insurance policy covering the goods providing for payment of any loss to the buyer, (3) prepare an invoice for the goods and procure any other necessary documents, and (4) promptly forward and tender all the required documents to the buyer. A C. & F. term imposes the same obligations upon the seller except that relating to insurance. Note that the language "landed" or "duty paid" added to a C.I.F. or C. & F. term requires the seller, in addition to its other obligations, to pay the import duties imposed by the buyer's country.

"Ex Ship" Term—§2–322. A term requiring delivery **"ex ship"** (from the carrying vessel), is a destination contract, requiring the seller to bear the expense and risk of the ocean voyage and of unloading the goods at the named port of destination. That is, an "ex ship" term is effectively the opposite of an F.A.S. term (though an "ex ship" term does not require delivery from any particular vessel), and imposes risk of loss on the seller until the goods leave the ship's tackle or are otherwise properly unloaded. Under an "ex ship" term, the seller also must discharge all liens arising out of the carriage and furnish the buyer with a direction obligating the carrier to deliver the goods.

"No Arrival, No Sale" Term—§2–324. A **"no arrival, no sale"** term is sometimes used in destination contracts (such as "ex ship," or "F.O.B. destination") to relieve the seller from liability for breach of contract if the goods fail to arrive. Because the "no arrival, no sale" term is used in a destination contract, the seller bears the risk of loss in transit, and therefore cannot recover the purchase price from the buyer if the goods fail to arrive. The seller, however, generally assumes no obligation that the goods will arrive. Such a term is particularly useful when the seller is reselling goods purchased from a third party, who is shipping them directly to the buyer.

A "no arrival, no sale" term is designed to protect the seller against transportation and other risks over which it has no control, not losses caused by the seller's fault. Accordingly, the provision protects the seller only if it timely ships conforming goods, properly tenders them on delivery if they arrive, and has not interfered with the arrival of the goods. If the goods are partially lost, damaged upon arrival, or arrive late through no fault of the seller, the seller must nevertheless tender them, and the rights and duties of the parties are governed by UCC §2–613 (casualty to identified goods) discussed in Chapter 14. Note that "no arrival, no sale" terms are not used in shipment contracts (such as C.I.F., C. & F., and F.O.B. shipping point) because risk of loss in transit in such contracts is borne by the buyer.

Incoterms. The foregoing definitions are default rules that will be used to resolve litigated cases if parties use these terms and do not otherwise define them. The parties are of course free to define their own delivery obligations and often incorporate the definitions stated in *Incoterms.* **Incoterms** (INternational COmmercial TERMS) were first published by the International Chamber of Commerce in 1936 to provide "international rules for the interpretation of trade terms."[6] To keep the rules up to date, they were amended in 1953, 1967, 1976, 1980, 1990, and 2000.

---

[6]INTERNATIONAL CHAMBER OF COMMERCE, Pub. No. 560, Incoterms 2000, at 5 (1999).

Incoterms 2000 contains 13 shipping terms divided into four categories:

E Term—Departure
    EXW Ex Works (. . . named place)
F Terms—Main Carriage Not Paid by the Seller
    FCA Free Carrier (. . . named place)
    FAS Free Alongside Ship (. . . named port of shipment)
    FOB Free On Board (. . . named port of shipment)
C Terms—Main Carriage Paid by the Seller
    CFR Cost and Freight (. . . named port of destination)
    CIF Cost, Insurance and Freight (. . . named port of destination)
    CPT Carriage Paid To (… named place of destination)
    CIP Carriage and Insurance Paid To (… named place of destination)
D Terms—Arrival
    DAF Delivered at Frontier (. . . named place)
    DES Delivered Ex Ship (. . . named port of destination)
    DEQ Delivered Ex Quay (. . . named port of destination)
    DDU Delivered Duty Unpaid (. . . named place of destination)
    DDP Delivered Duty Paid (. . . named place of destination)

As under Article 2, *Incoterms* characterize contracts involving carriage as either "shipment" or "destination" contracts, and provide that risk of loss passes to the buyer when the seller completes its delivery obligation. In a shipment contract, the seller is required or authorized to ship the goods but is not required to deliver them at any particular destination. The F and C terms, for example, are shipment contracts under which the seller's delivery obligation ends when it delivers the goods to the carrier. Thus, risk of loss in transit is on the buyer. This is true even if the seller is obligated to pay the freight and/or insurance to the named destination (the C terms). In contrast, under a destination contract, the seller is obligated to transport the goods to a stated destination and there tender them to the buyer. The D terms, for example, are destination contracts under which the seller's delivery obligation ends only upon proper tender at a named place or port of destination. Thus, under a D term, risk of loss in transit is on the seller.

If carriage is not involved, the seller's minimum delivery obligation under *Incoterms* is "Ex Works." This corresponds to the minimum delivery obligation imposed under UCC §2-503(1). Both simply obligate the seller to place the goods at the buyer's disposal at the named place of delivery, typically the seller's place of business.

The table appearing at the end of the book in Appendix B summarizes the 13 *Incoterms,* indicating for each: the appropriate mode of transport; when the seller completes its delivery obligation and risk of loss passes to the buyer; the seller's insurance obligation, if any; who pays for carriage; who is responsible for obtaining export and important clearance; and comments indicating the appropriate use of, pitfalls of, and relationship among various terms.[7]

Buyer's Duty of Payment

A proper tender of delivery requires the buyer to accept and pay for the goods according to the contract. Although the contract usually provides time, place, and manner of payment, the agreement may be silent regarding one or more aspects of the buyer's payment obligation. In this case, as with delivery, the UCC fills in the gaps in the parties' agreement.

Unless otherwise agreed, payment and delivery are exchanged simultaneously in sales contracts. That is, the seller is not required to extend credit to the buyer unless the parties have explicitly agreed to a credit term. If credit is extended, the credit period generally runs from the date of shipment, or from the date of the invoice which usually indicates the time of shipment. The buyer may tender payment by check or other customary method unless the seller demands cash and gives the buyer any extension of time reasonably necessary to procure it. This rule protects the buyer against breach if the seller unexpectedly demands cash when (as is normally the case) the buyer reasonably believes that payment by a check is acceptable.[8]

---

[7]This section is adapted with permission from Mark E. Roszkowski, *Shipping Terms Based on Incoterms 2000: A Statutory Proposal,* 34 U.C.C.L.J. 159, 171-72 (Fall 2001).

[8]UCC §§2–310(d), 2–511(2). The check is, however, only a conditional payment. The effect of payment by check on the obligation for which it is given is discussed in Chapter 25.

Right of Inspection. Unless otherwise agreed, the buyer must tender payment at the "time and place at which the buyer is to receive the goods."[9] This requirement allows the buyer to exercise his preliminary right of inspection stated in §2–513. As a general rule, the buyer has a right before payment or acceptance to inspect the goods tendered. The inspection may be at any reasonable place and time and in any reasonable manner. If the seller is required to ship the goods to the buyer, inspection may be made at the place of arrival. During the inspection, the seller is not required to relinquish physical possession of the goods to the buyer. The buyer acquires that right upon tender of payment, unless the seller has agreed to extend credit. Any expense of the inspection must be borne by the buyer, but may be recovered from the seller as incidental damage if the buyer rejects the goods because of nonconformity revealed by the inspection.

In certain types of contracts, the buyer is not entitled to inspect before payment. These include (1) C.I.F. and C.F. contracts, (2) other contracts requiring payment against documents of title unless the contract provides that payment is due only after the goods become available for inspection,[10] and (3) contracts providing the delivery "C.O.D." or on similar terms. Note that such contracts simply require payment before inspection. The payment neither constitutes an acceptance of the goods, nor impairs the buyer's subsequent right to inspect. The buyer retains all rights and remedies against the seller in the event the goods do not conform to the contract. The buyer is simply required to proceed *after* making payment because the essence of such a payment term is to shift to the buyer risks which would ordinarily rest upon the seller.

Open Price and Quantity Terms

Ordinarily, the parties explicitly agree upon the price to be charged and the exact quantity of goods to be delivered. Article 2, however, permits enforcement of contracts in which either the price or the quantity is left open. Sections 2–305 and 2–306 contain the principles by which price and quantity are determined in such contracts.

Open Price Term—§2–305

Under §2–305, the parties can conclude a contract for sale even though the price is not settled. For example, the parties may intend a binding contract even though they have not yet agreed to a price or have left the price to be fixed by a market standard or a third party. If the parties intend not to be bound unless the price is later determined, no contract results if, for some reason, the price is not subsequently agreed or fixed. The parties' intention in this regard ordinarily is a question of fact.

Perhaps the most common reason the parties may leave the price open is that neither wishes to assume the risk of market fluctuations prior to delivery by agreeing to a fixed price. If the market price rises after the date of the contract, the seller may want to charge the increased price. Conversely, if the market falls, the buyer may wish to purchase the goods at the reduced rate.

Assuming a binding contract has been made without a price term, Section 2–305(1) provides that the price is a *reasonable price at the time for delivery if:*

1. nothing is said as to price,
2. the price is left to later agreement of the parties and they fail to agree, or
3. the price is to be determined by some agreed market or other standard fixed by a third person who later fails to set the price.

The third situation listed occurs, for example, when the price is left to be fixed in a trade journal that subsequently ceases publication or is to be set by a third person who dies prior to fixing the price.

The obligation of good faith imposed upon every Code contract also is relevant when the price term is left open. For example, the contract may provide that the price is to be fixed by the buyer or seller. In this situation, the party empowered to set the price must act in good faith. Similarly, if the price fails to be fixed through the fault of one party—for example, interference with any agreed machinery for price fixing or other failure to cooperate—the other may either cancel the contract (that is, treat the conduct as a repudiation) or fix a reasonable price.

---

[9]UCC §2–310(a).

[10]In this and the C.I.F. case, the shipping documents may arrive and be tendered while the goods are still in transit.

Open Quantity Term: Requirements and Output Contracts — §2-306

In addition to price, the parties also may contract without fixing a quantity. The most common and important of such "open quantity" contracts are requirements and output contracts. A **requirements contract** is one in which a *buyer* promises to purchase its *requirements* of a given commodity from the seller. An **output contract** is one in which a *seller* agrees to sell its entire *output* to the buyer. A requirement or output promise protects the promisor against uncertainties in demand or production. That is, a business is required to purchase only its requirements or sell its output. It is not obligated to buy or sell a fixed quantity which it may not be able to use or produce.

At first glance, requirements and output promises appear illusory under principles discussed in Chapter 9. For example, a buyer could supposedly avoid obligation under a requirements contract by ceasing or changing its business; thus having no requirements. Similarly, a seller could cease production, generating no output. Actually, promises to purchase requirements or to sell output are not illusory. In both cases, the promisor incurs a detriment by surrendering the right to buy or sell elsewhere.

The UCC broadly validates requirements and output promises. Section 2-306(1) provides that a term that measures the quantity by the output of the seller, or the requirements of the buyer means such *actual output or requirements as may occur in good faith*. Additionally, because the quantity term is determined by actual output or requirements occurring in good faith, the contract will not fail on the basis that the quantity is too indefinite to afford an adequate remedy.

The party who determines the quantity must operate its plant or conduct its business in good faith and according to reasonable commercial standards of fair dealing in the trade. When business is conducted in this manner, the quantity purchased or produced under the contract will approximate a reasonably foreseeable figure. In other words, ceasing operations to avoid a requirements or output contract would violate the obligation of good faith imposed upon all Code contracts or duties and therefore incorporated into §2-306.

In addition to the good faith requirement, §2-306 provides that no quantity may be tendered (an output contract) or demanded (a requirements contract) that is unreasonably disproportionate (1) to any stated estimate, or (2) to any normal or otherwise comparable prior output or requirements in the absence of a stated estimate. This proviso sets reasonable limits (in addition to good faith) upon the actual quantity to be bought or sold under the contract; that is, it establishes the range within which the parties may expect the quantity to vary. Any minimum or maximum limits set in the contract clearly define intended elasticity. A stated estimate is treated as a midpoint around which the parties intend any variation to occur.

Effect of Increase in Quantity. The most common requirements contract dispute involves an unreasonable increase in quantity demanded by the buyer when the market price rises substantially above the contract price. The buyer then resells the excess at a profit. This conduct is bad faith. The buyer therefore breaches the contract and the seller need not supply the excess amount. If the buyer's increase in quantity demanded occurs in good faith, the seller must supply the increase unless the increase is unreasonably disproportionate to a stated estimate or prior requirements. For example, assume S, a gasoline distributor, agrees to supply B, a bakery, with B's requirements of gasoline for its delivery trucks for ten years. The contract contains a stated estimate. Two years into the contract, B's business improves dramatically because B's high quality breads and pastries become popular with restaurants, caterers, and grocery stores. As a result, B's delivery trucks require twice the amount of gasoline estimated in the contract. Although B's increase in quantity demanded was incurred in good faith, it is unreasonably disproportionate to the stated estimate. Thus, although S would be required to supply some increase (an amount the court determines is not unreasonably disproportionate to the stated estimate), B would have to look elsewhere for its remaining requirements.

Effect of Decrease in Quantity. An additional problem arising in requirements contracts is the legal effect of unreasonable *decreases* in quantity. Whereas the statute provides that no quantity unreasonably disproportionate to a stated estimate or prior output may be tendered or demanded, Official Comment 2 to §2-306 indicates that "good faith variations from prior requirements are permitted *even when the variation may be such as to result in discontinuance.*" (Emphasis added.) This discrepancy can be reconciled if the statutory language is interpreted to mean that a party acting in good faith may not *increase* demand or supply to an amount unreasonably disproportionate to a stated estimate, or prior consumption or production (see prior example). However, substantial *decreases* are permitted as long as the party who determines quantity is acting in good faith. In other words, an increase in quantity tendered or demanded is allowed if it (1) is made in good faith and (2) is not unreasonably disproportionate to a stated estimate or prior experience. A *decrease* is permitted subject only to the good faith test.

This approach has received considerable support from legal commentators and in decided cases. It allows a requirements buyer to reduce purchases drastically when justified by improved equipment or operating efficiency. Assume Ben operates a steel plant requiring large amounts of natural gas to fire the furnaces. Ben contracts to buy its requirements of gas, subject to a stated estimate, from People's Gas, Inc., a public utility. Ben subsequently installs new fuel-efficient furnaces, requiring only 20 percent as much gas as the old units. Even though Ben now requires drastically reduced quantities of gas, he does not breach the contract because the reduction was undertaken in good faith. If the second "unreasonably disproportionate" test is also applied, Ben could not improve his plant without breaching the contract.

The following case illustrates the principles governing requirements contracts discussed above.

Indiana-American Water Company, Inc. v. Town of Seelyville
698 N.E.2d 1255 (Ind. App. 1998)

A 25-year contract made by the town of Seelyville, Indiana (Town) and Indiana-American Water Company (Water Company) in 1983 provided in part: "Water Company agrees to sell to the Town, and Town agrees to purchase from Water Company, at the rates hereinafter mentioned, such quantities of water as the Town may hereafter from time to time need." The contract limited the quantity purchased by the Town to one million gallons per day. In 1997, the Town began development of a wellfield, on land that it had purchased in 1967, to supply water for the Town's residents. The Water Company filed a lawsuit asserting that the Town was required to purchase all of its water from the Water Company until expiration of the 1983 contract. The Water Company requested a declaratory judgment that the Town's development of its own water supply would constitute a breach of the contract. The trial court ruled in favor of the Town and the Water Company appealed.

Bailey, Judge

A requirements contract is one in which the purchaser agrees to buy all of its needs of a specified material exclusively from a particular supplier, and the supplier agrees, in turn, to fill all of the purchaser's needs during the period of the contract. . . . [W]e interpret the present contract as a valid and enforceable exclusive requirements contract which requires Town to use Water Company exclusively to supply all the water it must purchase to meet its needs up to the amount of one million gallons of water per day.

Good Faith Reduction or Curtailment of Requirements

The most common problem arising out of a requirements contract is the situation where the price of the commodity is advantageous to the buyer who then demands a quantity unreasonably in excess of his needs in order to resell the excess at a profit, placing himself in competition with the seller. . . . The provision in §2–306(1) forbidding the "demand" by a buyer under a requirements contract to a "quantity unreasonably disproportionate to any stated estimate" applies . . . where the buyer requests more, as opposed to less, of the commodity in question. [The court in *Empire Gas Corporation v. American Bakeries Co.,* 840 F.2d 1333, 1338 (7th Cir. 1988)] noted that there was no indication that the drafters of the UCC were equally, if at all, concerned about the case, such as the one at bar, where the buyer takes less than his estimated requirements, provided, of course, that he does not buy from anyone else. . . .

Generally, the buyer in a requirements contract governed by UCC §2–306(1) is required merely to exercise good faith in determining his requirements and the seller assumes the risk of all good faith variations in the buyer's requirements even to the extent of a determination to liquidate or discontinue the business. . . . However, the buyer is not free, on any whim, to quit buying from seller. . . . How exigent the buyer's change of circumstances must be to allow him to scale down his requirements is a difficult question. . . . The seller assumes the risk of a change in the buyer's business that results in a substantial reduction in the buyer's needs, but the buyer assumes the risk of a less urgent change in circumstances. The essential ingredient of the buyer's good faith under such circumstances is that he not merely have had second thoughts about the terms of the contract and want to get out of it. However, if the buyer has a legitimate business reason for eliminating its requirements, as opposed to a desire to avoid its contract, the buyer acts in good faith. . . .

It is well-settled that it is not bad faith to take advantage of a technological advance which reduces the buyer's requirements. . . . [In *Southwest Natural Gas Co. v. Oklahoma Portland Cement Co.,* 102 F.2d 630 (10th Cir. 1939)], the buyer agreed to buy all its gas from seller for fifteen years. Seven years later, the buyer replaced its boiler, which had worn out, with more modern equipment which reduced its requirements for gas by 80%. The court held that this was a good faith reduction in requirements because it would have been unreasonable to require the buyer to replace its boiler with an obsolete, inefficient unit. . . .

In the present case, Town had acquired a wellfield many years before the execution of the contract under scrutiny. Town's decision to develop its preexisting wellfield constitutes a legitimate, long-term business decision, and not merely a desire to avoid the terms of its contract with Water Company. Therefore, based on the above, we cannot conclude that . . . Town's development of its pre-existing wellfield to reduce its need to purchase water from Water Company constitutes bad faith. . . .

[Judgment affirmed.]

Assignability of Requirements Contracts. Section 2–306 also determines the assignability of rights under a requirements contract. Assume S agrees to sell B, a small intrastate trucking company, its requirements of gasoline for two years. B assigns the right to be supplied with gasoline to X, another trucking company (or sells the business, including the contract, to X). Under traditional common law principles of assignment discussed in Chapter 13, S need not supply X with its requirements because a substantial change in S's duty results.

Section 2–306, which now governs requirements contracts, adopts an apparently more liberal attitude than the common law, because it permits assignment if the assignee meets the section's guidelines. That is, after the assignment, the quantity continues to be measured by actual good faith requirements under normal operation of the business prior to the assignment. Further, the assignment does not justify a sudden or unreasonable increase or decrease in the quantity

demanded. In this manner, no material change in the seller's duty is effected.[11]

Auction Sales—§2–328

Most of the sales discussed in this and the contracts material are private in nature; that is, they are the result of bargaining between parties who are known to each other. An **auction,** on the other hand, is a public sale of property (either real or personal) to the highest bidder by an auctioneer, who is authorized or licensed by law to conduct such sales.[12] The auctioneer (who is an agent of the seller) solicits bids (offers) from prospective buyers present at the sale. The UCC provides rules governing the conduct of auction sales of goods in §2–328.

The auction is complete—that is, the highest bidder's offer is accepted—when the auctioneer so announces by the fall of the hammer or in another customary manner. If a bid is made while the hammer is falling (in acceptance of a prior bid), the auctioneer may either reopen the bidding, or declare the goods sold at the bid on which the hammer was falling. If the auctioneer elects to reopen the bidding, the prior bid is discharged and further bidding continues.

As a general rule, auction sales are made **with reserve.** This means that the auctioneer (seller) may withdraw the goods at any time prior to announcing completion of the sale as indicated above. The goods, however, in explicit terms may be put up "without reserve." In this case, the auctioneer, after the calls for bids, may not withdraw an article or lot, unless no bids are received within a reasonable time. Regardless of the character of the auction, any bidder may retract his bid (withdraw his offer) prior to the auctioneer's announcement of the completion of the sale. However, one bidder's retraction does not revive any prior bid.

The seller may bid at the auction provided notice is given that liberty for such bidding is reserved. If no notice is given, and the auctioneer knowingly receives a bid on the seller's behalf or the seller makes or procures such a bid, the buyer may, at his option, either (1) avoid the sale, or (2) take the goods at the last good faith bid prior to completion of the sale. This rule does not apply if the seller's bid is made at a "forced" sale, that is, one

---

[11]UCC §2–210, Official Comment 4; §2–306, Official Comment 4.
[12]Black's Law Dictionary 130 (6th ed. 1990).

not voluntarily made by the seller but prescribed by law to satisfy some obligation of the seller, such as a mortgage, debt, judgment, or tax lien.

A sale at auction, like other sales, may be subject to the Statute of Frauds. For example, the property sold may be land or goods with a price of $500 or more. In this situation the auctioneer is an agent of *both* parties for purposes of satisfying the statute. In other words, after accepting a bid on property subject to the Statute of Frauds, the auctioneer has an *irrevocable* power to sign the necessary memorandum for both the buyer and the seller. This power continues for a reasonable time during the day of the sale.

Personal Property Leases

Increasingly in recent years, consumers and businesses lease rather than buy goods they use, such as automobiles or manufacturing equipment. Despite the dramatic growth of the lease as a substitute for purchase, however, a comprehensive body of law governing personal property leasing transactions was slow to develop. For example, though a personal property lease is a bailment, the common law of bailments, discussed in Chapter 35, is limited in scope and does not address the myriad contract-related issues arising in the modern lease. General landlord-tenant law, discussed in detail in Chapter 36, governs real property, rather than personal property, leases. Article 2 of the UCC, though applying to "transactions in goods,"[13] focuses specifically on sales, rather than lease, transactions. Finally, Article 9 of the UCC governs only those personal property leases intended to create a security interest in the property leased (that is, the lease is in essence a credit sale secured by the property "leased").

To fill this gap in the law, the American Law Institute and National Conference of Commissioners on Uniform State Laws drafted and approved in 1987 a new Article 2A of the UCC, entitled "Leases." Article 2A applies to "any transaction, regardless of form, which creates a lease,"[14] and defines a lease as "a transfer of the right to possession and use of goods for a term in return for consideration."[15]

Article 2A, which is patterned generally after Article 2, divides the law governing such "true" personal property leases into five parts: (1) general provisions, (2) the formation and construction of lease contracts, (3) the effect of lease contracts, (4) the performance of lease contracts, and (5) default. Part 1 contains definitions and general provisions borrowed generally from Article 2, and an unconscionability provision. Part 2 adopts Article 2's liberal contract formation principles and contains a statute of frauds (with a $1,000 minimum), a parol evidence rule, a firm offer rule, and warranty and risk of loss provisions. Part 3 includes provisions governing assignability of the lease, a subsequent lease of the goods by the lessor, a sale or sublease by the lessee, and the consequences of the leased goods becoming fixtures. Part 4 includes familiar Article 2 performance principles such as anticipatory repudiation, adequate assurance, and impracticability. Part 5 is the longest part of Article 2A, governing the rights and obligations of the parties upon default by either the lessor or lessee. Part 5 borrows heavily from Article 2 (including, for example, the concepts of acceptance, revocation of acceptance, and rejection of goods; cure; and buyers' and sellers' remedies discussed in Chapter 18) and Article 9 (for example, the right of the lessor to take possession of the goods on default without judicial process).

Summary

1.   Contracts for the sale of goods, governed generally by Article 2 of the UCC, play an important role in modern business. The Code adopts a liberal attitude regarding formation of such contracts, enforcing them despite missing terms or inexact expression, if the parties have intended to make a contract and there is a reasonably certain basis for awarding a remedy in case of breach. Missing terms are then supplied in a variety of Article 2 "gap filling" provisions which govern generally only in the absence of contrary agreement by the parties.

---

[13]UCC §2–102.

[14]UCC §2A–102.
[15]UCC §2A–103(1)(j).

2. In a sales contract the obligation of the seller is to transfer and deliver the goods to the buyer who is obligated to pay for the goods in accordance with the contract. The Code contains provisions governing the time, place, and manner of delivery governing in absence of agreement, and provisions defining specialized delivery terms. The Code also contains corresponding provisions governing the time, place, and manner of the buyer's payment. In addition, the UCC outlines the legal effect of an open price and quantity term. Unless otherwise agreed, the performances of the parties are exchanged simultaneously.

3. Most sales contracts are privately negotiated. Goods may however, be sold at auction, which is a public sale. Article 2 has specific provisions governing the conduct of auction sales.

4. Increasingly in recent years, consumers and businesses lease rather than purchase goods they use. Despite this dramatic growth in personal property leasing, the law governing such transactions was slow to develop. To fill this gap in the law, the National Conference and American Law Institute approved in 1987 new UCC Article 2A, entitled "Leases," which is patterned closely after Article 2.

Key Terms

gap fillers (default rules)	"ex ship" term
lot	"no arrival, no sale" term
shipment contract	Incoterms
destination contract	requirements contract
F.O.B. term	output contract
F.A.S. term	auction
C.I.F. term	sale with reserve
C. & F. term	

Questions and Problems

16.1 Seller and Buyer have an oral agreement for the sale of 200 desk calendars. No other terms are included. Is the contract unenforceable for indefiniteness? If not, what is the price? When and where is the price to be paid? When is delivery to be made? Where is delivery to be made? What must Seller do to make an effective tender of delivery?

16.2 What are the advantages of a requirements contract to a buyer? Of an output contract to a seller?

16.3 Consider whether the following transactions are within the scope of Article 2 of the UCC.
(a) Brookhaven contracts to purchase a one million gallon water tank from Pittsburgh-Des Moines Steel Co. (PDM) for $175,000. Under the terms of the contract, PDM agrees to build the tank on Brookhaven's property and Brookhaven agrees to pay $175,000 after the tank has been tested and inspected.

(b) Zuma, who is remodeling her house, contracts for new flooring with Colorado Carpet Installation, Inc. The contract provides that CCII will sell and install ceramic tile in the bathrooms, vinyl flooring in the kitchen, and carpeting throughout the house, and Zuma will pay $12,000.

16.4 Gunn, a subcontractor for a construction project at the University of Texas, needed various paving tiles for the project. On August 31, 2003, Gunn telephoned Alamo, a tile manufacturer, to order two sizes of paving tiles: $4'' \times 8''$ and $8'' \times 12''$ tiles. During the conversation, neither party discussed price or time, place, or method of delivery. Alamo mailed Gunn a document called a "telephone confirmation purchase order" that described the tiles ordered by Gunn but did not specify a price or time, place, or method of delivery. Alamo delivered the $4'' \times 8''$ tiles and charged the prices effective on August 31, 2003. Because of production problems, Alamo was unable to furnish the $8'' \times 12''$ tiles. After a delay of several months, Alamo delivered $6'' \times 9''$ tiles which Gunn purchased "under protest." Gunn installed the tiles but incurred additional labor costs. Gunn sued Alamo for breach of contract alleging that the failure to deliver the $8'' \times 12''$ tiles was a breach of contract and requesting damages for the additional costs incurred by Gunn. Alamo alleged that the parties had not entered into a contract because they had not agreed to a price or date, method, or place of delivery.
(a) Have the parties made a contract?
(b) Assume the parties have made a contract. What are its terms? Has Alamo breached the contract?

16.5 Associated Hardware, Inc. sent an offer to Big Wheel Distributors to purchase hand tools for a price of "cost plus 10 percent." Big Wheel replied that it would sell-for "dealer catalog prices less 11 percent," assuring Associated that its price quotation was equivalent to cost plus 10 percent. Although acting in good faith, Big Wheel was mistaken and the two prices were not equivalent. Associated agreed and the goods were shipped and accepted by Associated. When Big Wheel sent its bill, Associated objected because the price was not equivalent to cost plus 10 percent. Do the parties have a contract? If so, what is the price?

16.6 Pumpernickel, Inc., a major producer of bread and bread products, decided to sell breadcrumbs in an effort to use leftover and stale bread. Each week, Pumpernickel ground up all leftover bread products, toasted the crumbs, and sold them to food processors. CTC Co., a food processor, needing a regular and large supply of breadcrumbs for its line of frozen casserole dishes, contracted to purchase breadcrumbs from Pumpernickel. The written contract provided that CTC would purchase "all breadcrumbs produced by Pumpernickel at its New York bakery at the price of 20 cents per pound." The contract was for an indefinite term but both parties had the right to cancel by giving six months' notice to the other party. After the contract had been in effect for a year, Pumpernickel's financial staff suggested that breadcrumb production terminate because the company was losing money on the operations. During several conversations with CTC personnel, Pumpernickel's sales officer indicated that breadcrumb production was likely to be terminated unless Pumpernickel could sell the crumbs for at least 25 cents per pound. Finally, without notice to CTC, Pumpernickel stopped producing breadcrumbs. The leftover bread products previ-ously used to make the crumbs were sold to animal food man-ufacturers. CTC sues Pumpernickel alleging that it breached the contract. Pumpernickel argues that the contract with CTC did not require Pumpernickel to manufacture breadcrumbs but only to sell to CTC any breadcrumbs it did manufacture. How should the court rule?

CHAPTER 17

THE SALES CONTRACT — TITLE AND RISK OF LOSS

Major Topics

- **an explanation of Code provisions governing passage of title and resolving title disputes**
- **the definition of "identification" and the legal consequences of identification**
- **Article 2 provisions regarding risk of loss in sales contracts**

The Uniform Commercial Code in §2–106(1) defines a "sale" of goods as the passage of title from the seller to the buyer for a price. A number of legal issues arise in connection with this transfer of **title** (generally meaning ownership). For example, the law must determine the nature of the interest that the buyer acquires, and whether that interest is subject to claims of third parties, such as the seller's creditors or prior owners of the goods. It also must ascertain when the risk of casualty to the goods is transferred to the buyer and when the buyer acquires a sufficient interest in the goods to insure against that risk. The UCC resolves these and related issues through principles of title, identification, and risk of loss.

Passage of Title

Even though title is used in the definition of sale, the importance of title and passage of title in Code con-

tracts is extremely limited. As stated in §2–401, containing the general rules relating to title:

> Each provision of this Article with regard to the rights, obligations and remedies of the seller, the buyer, purchasers or other third parties applies irrespective of title to the goods except where the provision refers to such title.[1]

One important issue resolved under the UCC without regard to title is risk of loss. **Risk of loss** rules determine the rights of the parties if the goods involved in the contract are lost, destroyed, or stolen. That is, risk of loss principles determine when the risk of such casualties passes from the seller to the buyer. If risk of loss is on the seller and the goods are destroyed, the seller bears the loss and cannot recover the price from the buyer. Additionally, the seller also may be liable for breach of contract unless the seller procures or manufactures substitute goods in time to perform the

---

[1]Code sections in which title *does* affect rights and duties of the parties include: (1) §2–106(1), the definition of a sale; (2) §2–312, the warranty of title discussed in Chapter 19; (3) §§2–326, 2–327, governing sale on approval and sale or return; (4) §2–403(1), the voidable title rule; (5) §2–501, relating to insurable interest of a seller who retains title; and (6) §2–722, under which a person who has title can sue third persons for damage to goods.

contract. On the other hand, if risk of loss has passed to the buyer, the buyer is liable for the price of the goods despite their destruction. Determining the precise point at which the risk passes to the buyer is therefore a fundamental issue in the sales contract.

Under the Uniform Sales Act (USA), the law that governed sales contracts prior to the UCC, the party who had title also had the risk of loss. Unfortunately, the USA rules governing passage of title were unclear and operated in many cases to transfer title (and therefore risk of loss) to the buyer while the goods were still in the seller's possession and covered by the seller's insurance. The Code drafters found that this approach caused substantial confusion, uncertainty, and litigation concerning risk of loss issues. Therefore, in order to make the rules clearer and more certain, the UCC completely divorces risk of loss (and the related issue, insurable interest) from title and instead addresses these issues in other specific Code sections. This approach has resulted in a marked reduction in litigation involving risk of loss questions. The specific rules covering insurable interest and risk of loss are discussed in detail later in this chapter.

When Title Passes

Although insurable interest and risk of loss are determined without regard to title, title is relevant in resolving a number of legal issues, both under the UCC and other state law. For example, title may be relevant in determining whether an owner's property can be attached by creditors or in assessing of property taxes. Therefore, if title becomes material, the Code contains a general provision, §2–401, governing passage of title. As a general rule, unless otherwise agreed, title passes to the buyer at the time and place at which the seller completes performance with respect to the physical delivery of the goods.

Shipment and Destination Contracts. If the contract requires or authorizes the seller to ship the goods to the buyer but does not require delivery at a particular destination—a "shipment" contract such as F.O.B. point of shipment, C.I.F., or C. & F.—title passes to the buyer at the time and place of shipment. If shipment is required or authorized but delivery at a destination is required—a "destination" contract such as F.O.B. point of destination—title passes on tender at the destination.

Delivery Without Moving Goods. In some cases, the goods sold never move; they may, for example, be stored in a warehouse. If the parties do not explicitly agree and the goods are to be delivered without being moved, passage of title depends upon whether a document of title is involved. If the seller is to deliver a document of title, title passes at the time and place the document is delivered. If no document of title is to be delivered and the goods are identified at the time of the contract, title passes at the time and place of contracting.

Transfer of Title and Third Parties

Section 2–403 governs the extent of title acquired by a purchaser of goods. Note that the rules discussed below relate to rights acquired by *purchasers* of goods. Although "purchaser" is usually synonymous with "buyer," the term **purchaser** is defined broadly in the Code to include any person taking "by sale, lease, discount, negotiation, mortgage, pledge, lien, security interest, issue or re-issue, gift or any other voluntary transaction creating an interest in property."[2]

The rule governing transfer of title to such "purchasers" is contained in §2–403(1) that states simply:

> A purchaser of goods *acquires all title which his transferor had or had power to transfer* except that a purchaser of a limited interest acquires rights only to the extent of the interest purchased. (Emphasis added.)

Thus, generally, a buyer gets whatever interest the seller had in the goods. If the seller has "good" title, the buyer gets good title. If the seller has no title—for example, she is a thief, or has acquired the goods from a thief, or an earlier transferor of the goods was a thief—the buyer gets no title. In such cases, the seller's title is referred to as "void" and, unless properly disclaimed, the seller breaches the warranty of title ordinarily given by a seller to a buyer.[3]

Voidable Title Rule. A special title rule, known as the **voidable title rule,** applies if a transferee of goods is a "good faith purchaser for value." Under §2–403(1):

> A person with *voidable title* has power to transfer a good title to a *good faith purchaser for value.* (Emphasis added.)

---

[2]UCC §§1–201(b)(29), (30).

[3]The warranty of title, contained in §2–312, is discussed in Chapter 19.

The term "voidable title" is not explicitly defined, but §2–403(1) lists four situations specifically covered by the rule. To illustrate these situations, assume that S sells goods to B and that (1) B represents herself as X in the transaction to induce S to sell; that is, B is an imposter, or (2) B pays for the goods with a check that later bounces, or (3) the parties agree that the transaction is to be a "cash sale," which means that S and B agree that title will not pass until the price is paid, or (4) the sale was procured through fraud on B's part. B subsequently sells the goods to X, a good faith purchaser for value. In all of these situations, under the voidable title rule, B has the power subsequently to transfer good title to X. Thus, S may not recover the goods from X, but could, of course, proceed against B for damages. Figure 17.1 illustrates the operation of the rule assuming B's fraud has rendered her title voidable.

This rule does not apply to a person holding "void" title; that is, a thief or a person acquiring from or through a thief. Here, any transferee, good faith or not, takes subject to the rights of the owner. In these cases, the loss ordinarily falls on the person buying from the thief (assuming the thief cannot be held accountable).

To acquire good title under the voidable title rule, the purchaser must act in good faith and give value. **Value** is expansively defined in the UCC §1–204 to include, generally, any consideration sufficient to support a simple contract, including satisfying or providing security for an antecedent debt. Therefore, almost any purchaser would satisfy the value requirement, though the amount of value given is, of course, relevant in determining whether the purchase is made in good faith or with knowledge of the original seller's claim.

| Figure 17.1 | Voidable Title Rule |

S — Sells diamond ring → B–Acquires voidable title to the ring

Perpetrates fraud, which induces S to sell

Pays cash without knowledge of B's fraud

Sells ring

X–Good faith purchaser for value who acquires good title free of S's claim to the goods

The following case illustrates the voidable title rule.

Mitchell Motors, Inc. v. Barnett
549 S.E.2d 445 (Ga. App. 2001)

In March 1998, Plaintiff David Barnett purchased a used Jeep Cherokee from Chris Auto Sales, Inc. and paid in full with a check for $16,743.69 that was cashed by Chris Auto. When Barnett did not receive the Jeep's certificate of title within six weeks, he called Chris Auto and learned that title to the Jeep was held by defendant Mitchell Motors, Inc. Mitchell Motors had sold the Jeep to Chris Auto in February 1998, but had refused to transfer the title because Chris Auto's check had been dishonored by the bank. Barnett contacted Mitchell Motors which refused to send the title to Barnett unless he paid $14,000. Barnett sued Mitchell Motors seeking title to the Jeep. The trial court granted Barnett's motion for summary judgment and ordered Mitchell Motors to deliver the certificate of title to Barnett. Mitchell Motors appealed.

Ruffin, Judge

Title to the Jeep passed to Chris Auto, despite the dishonored bank draft. Under [U.C.C. §2–401(2)], "unless otherwise explicitly agreed title passes to the buyer at the time and place at which the seller completes his performance with reference to the physical delivery of the goods, despite any reservation of a security interest and even though a document of title is to be delivered at a different time or place." Because the record reveals no explicit agreement to the contrary, Chris Auto obtained title to the Jeep Cherokee when it took possession of the vehicle on or about February 20, 1998. Mitchell Motors' refusal to deliver the certificate of title to Chris Auto does not alter this result. As we have noted, "ownership may change hands without the necessity of transferring a title certificate by the seller and obtaining a new one in the name of the purchaser." [*Right Touch of Class v. Superior Bank*, 536 S.E.2d 181, 183 (Ga. App. 2000).]

Given the dishonored bank draft, Chris Auto's title was likely voidable. A person with voidable title, however, can transfer good title to a good faith purchaser for value:

A purchaser of goods acquires all title which his transferor had or had power to transfer. . . . A person with voidable title has power to transfer a good title to a good faith purchaser for value. When goods have been delivered under a transaction of purchase the purchaser has such power even though . . . the delivery was in exchange for a check which is later dishonored. [U.C.C. §2–403(1).]

The record shows that Mitchell Motors delivered the Jeep to Chris Auto under a "transaction of purchase." Chris Auto subsequently sold the vehicle for over $16,000 to Barnett, who was not aware of the dispute between Mitchell Motors and Chris Auto until well after the sale. Nothing in the record raises a question about—and Mitchell Motors apparently does not dispute—Barnett's good faith; he simply purchased a used car from a dealer that he trusted. Furthermore, although it is unclear when Mitchell Motors learned that Chris Auto's bank draft had been dishonored, the record shows that Mitchell Motors did not void or rescind its purchase contract with Chris Auto before the sale to Barnett. At most, Mitchell Motors demanded that Chris Auto "immediately pay the amount of the dishonored draft or return the Jeep." Mitchell Motors thus gave Chris Auto the option of paying the purchase price by some other means; it did not cancel the sale.

Construing [U.C.C. §2–403(1)], an Ohio court has noted:

> The "voidable title" doctrine evolved to ameliorate the harshness of the basic rule that a seller can convey no greater title than that seller has to convey. The doctrine attempts to reconcile the rights of a "true owner" who was fraudulently induced to transfer title in goods to a "wrongdoer" with the rights of an innocent purchaser from the wrongdoer. Title in the wrongdoer is "voidable" because the true owner is entitled to rescind the transaction and recover the goods from that individual. The right of rescission is cut off, however, by a transaction to a "good faith purchaser."

[*Creggin Group v. Crown Diversified Indus. Corp.*, 682 N.E.2d 692, 696 (Ohio App. 1996).]

Mitchell Motors did not rescind the voidable contract or reclaim the Jeep, and its right of rescission was cut off by the subsequent sale to a good faith purchaser for value. Barnett received good title to the Jeep under [U.C.C.§2–403(1).] Accordingly, the trial court did not err in awarding summary judgment to Barnett and denying Mitchell Motors' motion for summary judgment.

[Judgment affirmed.]

"Shelter" or "Umbrella" Protection. It is important to note the relationship between the general rule governing transfer of title and the voidable title rule. Under the general rule, the seller can generally transfer *what he has*. Therefore, a transferor with good title can transfer good title, even though the transferee might otherwise be subject to the claims of a former owner.[4] This provision creates what is commonly known as "shelter" or "umbrella" protection for the transferee. The purpose of this protection is to assure the seller a free market for what he has.

To illustrate the operation of the rule in this context, assume Bob buys a car from Sam and pays for the car with a bad check. Before Sam discovers what has happened, Bob resells the car to Tom, who pays cash and is unaware of Bob's wrongdoing. In this situation, Tom acquires good title to the car free of Sam's claim to it under the voidable title rule. Tom then sells the car to Fred, who is fully aware of (though not a party to) Bob's conduct. Fred acquires good title. (Fred would not take free of Sam's claim had he acquired the car from Bob because he is not a "good faith purchaser.") By purchasing from Tom, Fred "acquires all title which his transferor had." Fred, therefore, acquires the *rights* of a good faith purchaser without being one himself. The shelter rule protects Tom's market by allowing him to sell what he has—the rights of a good faith purchaser.

The Entrusting Rule. Under §2–403(2), any entrusting of possession of goods to a merchant who deals in goods of that kind gives the merchant the power to transfer all rights of the entruster to a buyer in the ordinary course of business. Assuming this "entrusting rule" applies, the buyer cuts off the entruster's claim to the goods. The entruster is then limited to a claim against the merchant in tort or contract. The purpose of this provision is to protect a person who buys goods in the ordinary course out of a dealer's inventory from ownership claims of third parties.[5]

Before illustrating the operation of the rule, certain terms must be defined and explained:

---

[4]A similar rule applies under UCC §3–203(b) to transfers of negotiable instruments, such as notes and checks, in which the transferee of the paper acquires the transferor's rights. Section 3–203(b) is discussed in Chapter 24.

[5]UCC §9–320 provides similar protection to buyers against persons holding a security interest in the goods sold. Section 9–320 is discussed in Chapter 32.

1. Under §2–403(3), **entrusting** includes "any delivery and any acquiescence in retention of possession" without regard to (a) any conditions attached to the delivery or retention by agreement of the parties, or (b) whether the merchant's acquisition or disposition of the goods is punishable under the state criminal law.

2. The goods must be entrusted to a merchant "who deals in goods of that kind." Thus, not all persons who qualify as "merchants" for some Code provisions fall within the reach of this section.[6]

3. The merchant has the power to transfer "all rights of the entruster." Thus, if the entruster is a thief, the buyer in the ordinary course takes subject to the owner's rights.

4. The purchaser must be a "buyer in the ordinary course of business." Under §1–201(b)(9), a **buyer in the ordinary course of business** is:

> . . . a person that buys goods in good faith, without knowledge that the sale violates the rights of another person in the goods, and in the ordinary course from a person, other than a pawnbroker, in the business of selling goods of that kind.

Though not explicitly stated, implicit in the definition is that the goods sold are inventory in the merchant's hands.

To illustrate the operation of the rule, assume that Joe owns a TV set in need of repair. He therefore brings it to Red's Radio & TV, Inc. for repair. Red's both repairs electronic equipment and sells new and used equipment at retail. Red repairs the set and then places it in his used equipment showroom, where it is subsequently sold to Mary, one of Red's customers. Mary cuts off Joe's ownership rights to the television. Joe has the right to recover from Red. The same result follows if the entruster leaves the goods in the merchant's possession for any other purpose. For example, Joe buys a new TV from Red and pays cash. However, because the set is a large wide screen model, Joe leaves it in Red's possession while he gets a pickup truck. During the hour Joe is gone, Red sells the set to Lois, another retail customer. Lois cuts off Joe's rights in the set and once again Joe's recourse is against Red.

The Ostensible Ownership Rule. It is important to note the relationship between the entrusting rule and the ostensible ownership rule stated in §2–402. A buyer who leaves goods in the seller's possession after sale creates the misleading impression that the seller actually owns them. This impression may deceive both buyers from and creditors of the seller. As the preceding example indicates, §2–403(2) protects most buyers in this situation against claims of the original buyer. Similarly, the seller's creditors also may be protected under the doctrine of ostensible ownership, which treats the sale as void against creditors if the seller's retention is fraudulent under any rule of law of the state where the goods are situated. That is, unpaid creditors who seize the goods in the seller's possession (using state debt collection remedies discussed in Chapter 29) defeat the original buyer's claim to the goods.

If, however, as in the preceding example, the seller is a *merchant* dealing in goods of the kind, retention is not fraudulent as against creditors if the possession is (1) in good faith, (2) in the current course of trade, and (3) only for a commercially reasonable time. The reason for this exception is apparently that creditors of a merchant seller are less likely to be misled by his retention of the goods in a current transaction for a reasonable period of time after sale. In addition, this exception is consistent with the Code policy of protecting persons who buy in the ordinary course out of a merchant's inventory.

Identification

The preceding discussion explains the UCC principles regarding transfer of title in sales contracts. As previously noted, under the Code, title does not govern the important concepts of insurable interest and risk of loss. Rather, these issues are addressed in separate Code provisions discussed in the following material.

"Identification" Defined

Many Code issues, including insurable interest, turn upon whether (and when) goods have become "identified" to the contract. **Identification** is the process by which the particular existing goods referred to in the contract are designated and specified. Under UCC §2–105(2), goods must be both existing and identified before any interest in them, including title, can pass. Goods not both existing and identified are known as **future goods.** For example, goods to be manufactured

---

[6]See discussion of the definition of merchant in Chapter 7.

are not yet existing and are future goods. Ten dishwashers to be chosen out of a manufacturer's inventory of 1,000 are not yet identified and also are future goods. Article 2 governs both a present sale of goods and a sale of future goods.

Time and Manner of Identification

Section 2–501 provides that the parties may explicitly agree as to the time and manner of identification. In the absence of such agreement, the following rules apply.

1. If the goods are already existing and identified, identification occurs when the contract is made. For example, assume Sally offers to sell Ben her boat for $8,000. Ben comes over to Sally's house to examine the boat, which is in the driveway. After inspecting it, Ben accepts Sally's offer. The boat is identified to the contract at the time of Ben's acceptance.

2. If the goods are future goods (as defined above), identification occurs when the goods are shipped, marked, or otherwise designated by the seller as the goods to which the contract refers. For example, assume Buyer orders 100 dishwashers from Seller. Seller's warehouse contains 1,000 dishwashers (or it has no dishwashers in stock and has yet to manufacture them). Identification occurs when the seller segregates from its inventory (or manufactures and segregates) the specific 100 dishwashers to be delivered to Buyer under the contract.

3. Unborn young of animals are identified when they are conceived if the young are to be born within 12 months after contracting.

4. Growing crops are identified when they are planted if the crops are to be harvested within 12 months or the next normal harvesting season after contracting, whichever is longer.

Effect of Identification

Insurable Interest. Identification gives the buyer an *insurable interest* in the goods. Although insurable interest is discussed in more detail in the insurance material,[7] generally, in property insurance, a person has an **insurable interest** if she will be exposed to monetary injury in the event of loss, damage, destruction, or theft of the property. Insurable interest distinguishes an insurance policy from a gambling contract.

Obviously, the seller, being the owner of the goods, has an insurable interest in them. The Code designates the time of identification as the point at which the buyer obtains an insurable interest. Thus, both the buyer and the seller have an insurable interest from the point of identification. The buyer's interest continues after it acquires title. The seller retains an insurable interest as long as it has either title to, or a security interest in, the goods.

The risk of loss does not ordinarily pass to the buyer upon identification. Risk of loss rules are discussed later in this chapter. Identification merely gives the buyer the right to insure the goods to whatever extent he is exposed to the possibility of monetary loss in the event of the goods' destruction. For example, the buyer may make a down payment on the purchase price prior to the passage of title and risk of loss and would therefore have an insurable interest to that extent. Additionally, because identification and insurable interest precede transfer of risk of loss, the buyer can always be protected by insuring the goods before the risk of their loss, damage, or destruction passes to the buyer.

Identification and Third Parties. Section 2–722 provides that identification gives the buyer the right to sue third parties who tortiously damage or destroy the goods. Consistent with the rules stated above, the seller also has a right of action if it has either title to, or a security interest in, the goods. Thus, after identification, both parties may proceed against the third party. Prior to identification, only the seller has such a right.

Other Consequences of Identification. Identification has several other legal consequences, discussed in other parts of the contracts and sales material.

1. Under §2–716(3), a buyer has the right to replevy (recover possession of) *identified* goods from the seller in certain situations.

2. In certain limited circumstances, §2–502 allows a buyer may recover *identified* goods in the hands of an insolvent seller.

3. Special rules apply under §2–613 if goods *identified* when the contract is made are destroyed without fault of either party before risk of loss passes to the buyer.

---

[7]Insurance law is covered in Chapter 57.

4.   Section 2–510(3) provides a special risk of loss rule if a buyer breaches a contract as to conforming goods *identified* to the contract.

5.   Under §2–709, the seller has the right to recover the purchase price of *identified* goods after a buyer's breach if the seller is unable to resell them.

6.   Identification also is an integral part of the definition of "goods" in §2–105 and thus determines in part whether or not Article 2 of the UCC applies to a given transaction.[8]

Risk of Loss

Risk of loss rules determine whether the buyer or seller bears the risk of loss, damage, or destruction of the goods sold under the contract. The Code addresses risk of loss in two separate provisions, §§2–509 and 2–510,[9] which divide the issue into two parts: (1) risk of loss in the absence of breach, and (2) risk of loss when either party is in breach.

Risk of Loss in Absence of Breach — §2–509

Section 2–509, which governs risk of loss in the absence of breach, generally places the risk on the person controlling possession of the goods, who is more likely to be insured against their loss, theft, or destruction. Section 2–509 divides risk of loss into three situations: (1) when the seller is required or authorized to ship the goods to the buyer, (2) when the goods are in the hands of a bailee such as a warehouseman and are to be delivered without being moved, and (3) all other cases. As with most other Code provisions, the risk of loss rules discussed below may be changed by contrary agreement of the parties.

Risk of Loss in Shipment and Destination Contracts.
If the seller is required or authorized to ship the goods to the buyer, risk of loss depends upon whether a "shipment" or "destination" contract is involved. If the seller is not required to deliver the goods at a particular destination — for example, a shipment contract such as F.O.B. shipping point or C.I.F. — risk of loss passes to

the buyer when the goods are duly delivered to the carrier. Thus, risk of loss in transit in shipment contracts is borne by the buyer.[10]

If the seller is required to deliver at the destination — a destination contract, such as F.O.B. destination — the risk of loss passes to the buyer when the goods are tendered at the destination so as to enable the buyer to take delivery. Thus, risk of loss in transit in destination contracts remains on the seller.

At issue in the following case was whether the parties had contractually altered the Code rule governing risk of loss in an F.O.B. shipping point contract.

A. M. Knitwear Corp. v. All America Export-Import Corp.
359 N.E.2d 342 (N.Y. 1976)

Defendant All America Export-Import Corp. ("buyer") and plaintiff A. M. Knitwear Corp. ("seller") entered into a contract, by which the seller agreed to sell several thousand pounds of yarn to the buyer. The buyer placed the order by using its own purchase order form and filling in the information describing the goods, quantity, and the dollar amount of the order. In the column labeled "price" buyer typed: *FOB PLANT PER LB.* $1.35." In the space marked "Ship Via," buyer typed "Pick Up from your Plant to Moore-McCormak Pier for shipment to Santos, Brazil." The buyer left blank a space marked "F.O.B." where an F.O.B. term could have been added. Further shipment instructions subsequently discussed by the parties were explained by the buyer's vice president at deposition:

> I said, "As you know, most of the goods being shipped to South America is being containerized. I have to order a container or a trailer, whatever is the simplest expression. And then in turn you will have to put it into the container."
>   Mr. Lubliner [of A. M. Knitwear Corp.] said, "This is no problem. Just send down the container. I will try to help you."

The buyer had an empty trailer delivered to the seller's premises and seller loaded the yarn into the trailer. Seller then notified buyer that the load was complete and buyer advised its freight forwarder to pick up the loaded trailer.

---

[8]UCC §§2–716(3), 2–502, and 2–709 are discussed in Chapter 18. Section 2–613 is covered in Chapter 14, §2–105 is discussed in Chapter 7, and §2–510(3) is covered later in this chapter.

[9]Risk of loss in contracts for the sale of *land* is covered in Chapter 57.

[10]A C.I.F. term also creates a "shipment" contract. Thus, the risk of loss, theft, or destruction in transit in such a contract is on the buyer. Although the buyer has the benefit of the insurance in this case, it bears the risk of inability to collect from the insurance company (for example, due to insolvency) or the carrier.

Prior to the arrival of the freight forwarder, however, an unknown individual (apparently a thief) driving a tractor arrived at seller's premises, hooked up the trailer to his tractor, signed a bill of lading with an undecipherable signature, and removed the goods.

Seller sued buyer to recover payment for the goods, alleging that its contractual obligations were met when the yarn was loaded on the trailer. Buyer alleged that seller's obligations were not fulfilled until the yarn was delivered to a carrier. The trial court ruled in favor of the seller. The appellate court reversed. Seller appealed the appellate court decision.

Cooke, Judge

. . . Despite the provisions of the Code which place the risk of loss on the seller in the F.O.B. place of shipment contract until the goods are delivered to the carrier, here the seller contends that the parties "otherwise agreed" so that pursuant to its agreement, the risk of loss passed from the seller to the buyer at the time and place at which the seller completed physical delivery of the subject goods into the container supplied by the buyer for that purpose. In support of this contention, the seller alleges that the language of the purchase order "Pick Up from your Plant" is a specific delivery instruction and that the language *"FOB PLANT PER LB.* $1.35," which appears in the price column, is a price term and not a delivery term. Further support for the seller's contention is taken from the fact that the space provided in the buyer's own purchase order form for an F.O.B. delivery instruction was left blank by the buyer. Thus, the seller contends its agreement with the buyer imposed no obligation on it to make delivery of the loaded container to the carrier. . . .

The seller's contention, that the parties intended the F.O.B. term as a price term and not a delivery term, conflicts with the code provision that states that the F.O.B. term is a delivery term "even though used *only* in connection with the stated price" ([UCC §2−319(1)]; emphasis added). . . .

Since the term "FOB PLANT" was a delivery term, the risk of loss was on the seller until the goods were put into the possession of the carrier—unless the parties "otherwise agreed" or there was a "contrary agreement" with respect to the risk of loss. . . .

With respect to the agreement of the parties, the seller contends that the statements in the affidavits of the parties and a portion of an examination before trial of the buyer's vice-president manifest that the parties intended that the seller's performance would be com-

plete when the goods were loaded into the container and the buyer was notified thereof. . . .

The term "FOB PLANT" is well understood to require delivery to the carrier and does not imply any other meaning. If a contrary meaning was intended, an express statement varying the ordinary meaning is required. The statements made by an officer of the buyer and the other circumstances of this case are not enough to show that the term did not mean what it does in ordinary commercial transactions. One of the principal purposes of the code is to simplify, clarify and modernize the law governing commercial transactions. . . . To allow a commonly used term such as F.O.B. to be varied in meaning, without an express statement of the parties of an intent to do so, would not serve that purpose. . . .

[Judgment affirmed.]

Presumption of Shipment Contract. Under the UCC a shipment contract is presumed. Therefore, if no F.O.B. destination or equivalent term is used, risk of loss passes to the buyer on shipment, even if the seller has promised to pay the freight charges. That is, unless the contract specifies otherwise, the seller is not required to deliver goods at a named destination and bear the risk of loss in transit.[11]

The following case illustrates the application of this rule.

Wilson v. Brawn of California, Inc.
33 Cal Rptr. 3d 769 (Cal. App. 2005)

Plaintiff Jacq Wilson placed two orders for catalog purchases from defendant Brawn of California, Inc., a clothing retailer that sells through catalogs and over the Internet. Brawn's mail order form required customers to pay the price of the goods purchased plus a delivery fee and an insurance fee of $1.48. The form further stated: "INSURANCE: Items Lost or Damaged in Transit Replaced Free." Wilson sued asserting that Brawn's charging an insurance fee was a deceptive business practice in violation of California law. Wilson argued that customers did not need to purchase insurance because Brawn was

---

[11]UCC §2−503, Official Comment 5.

legally responsible for goods in transit. The trial court ruled in favor of Wilson based on its conclusion that the catalog purchase created a destination contract. Because the seller retains the risk of loss in transit under a destination contract, the court found that Brawn's practice of charging the customer for insurance was deceptive. Brawn appealed.

Stein, Judge

. . . Neither party has cited any significant source of law concerning mail order sales or the risk of loss in mail order consumer sales, resting their contentions on provisions of the California Uniform Commercial Code. As the California Uniform Commercial Code, and the cases cited there, typically involve arm's-length sales between fairly sophisticated parties, the fit is not perfect. Nonetheless, there appears to be little legislation or case law specifically concerned with mail order sales or risk of loss in consumer sales contracts, and we, too, turn to the California Uniform Commercial Code's provisions.

. . . [S]ection 2–509 sets forth the general rules for determining which party bears the risk of loss of goods in transit when there has been no breach of contract. Subdivision (1) provides, as relevant:

(1) Where the contract requires or authorizes the seller to ship the goods by carrier
    (a) If it does not require him to deliver them at a particular destination, the risk of loss passes to the buyer when the goods are duly delivered to the carrier . . . ; but
    (b) If it does require him to deliver them at a particular destination and the goods are there duly tendered while in the possession of the carrier, the risk of loss passes to the buyer when the goods are there duly so tendered as to enable the buyer to take delivery.

Official Comment 5 to U.C.C. §2-503, concerning the seller's manner of tendering delivery, explains:

[U]nder this Article the 'shipment' contract is regarded as the normal one and the 'destination' contract as the variant type. The seller is not obligated to deliver at a named destination and bear the concurrent risk of loss until arrival, unless he has specifically agreed so to deliver or the commercial understanding of the terms used by the parties contemplates such a delivery.

Of course, a seller will have to provide the carrier with shipping instructions. It follows that a contract is not a destination contract simply because the seller places an address label on the package, or directs the carrier to "ship to" a particular destination. "Thus a 'ship to' term has no significance in determining whether a contract is a shipment or destination contract for risk of loss purposes." (*Eberhard Manufacturing Company v. Brown,* [232 N.W.2d 378, 380 (Mich. App. 1975)].) The point is illustrated in *La Casse v. Blaustein,* [403 N.Y.S.2d 440 (N.Y. App. 1978)], where the plaintiff, a student in Massachusetts, purchased 23 pocket calculators by telephone from a New York manufacturer. The method of shipment was left to the seller, but the plaintiff wrote a check to cover postage, and directed the seller to ship the goods to the plaintiff's residence. The court held:

Under the Uniform Commercial Code, the sales contract which provides for delivery to a carrier is considered the usual one and delivery to a particular destination to a buyer the variant or unusual one. In view of the foregoing, the request of the plaintiff's letter to ship to his residence is insufficient to convert the contract into one requiring delivery to a destination rather than one to a carrier. The request was nothing more than a shipping instruction and not of sufficient weight and solemnity as to convert the agreement into a destination contract.

(*Id.,* at 442.) . . .

In addition, although the risk of loss does not necessarily pass at the same time title to the goods passes, [U.C.C. §2–401(2)(a)] provides that "[i]f the contract requires or authorizes the seller to send the goods to the buyer but does not require him to deliver them at [a] destination, title passes to the buyer at the time and place of shipment." This section, therefore, also distinguishes between the seller's obligation to deliver goods to a carrier, and the seller's obligation to deliver goods to the buyer.

It is not at all uncommon for a contract to shift the risk of loss to the buyer at the point at which the seller delivers the goods to a common carrier, while calling for the seller to pay for delivery and insurance. The California Uniform Commercial Code recognizes this type of contract in its provisions pertaining to the term "C.I.F." The parties often make their intent explicit by using terms such as "F.O.B.," "F.A.S.," "C.I.F." or "C. & F." [U.C.C. §§2–319 & 2"320.] The general rule is that a contract containing neither an F.O.B term nor any other term explicitly allocating loss is a shipment contract. "The term C.I.F. means that the price includes in a lump sum the cost of the goods and the insurance and freight to the named destination." [U.CC. §2–320(1).] Official Comment 1 to the section explains that "[t]he C.I.F. contract is not a destination but a shipment contract with risk of subsequent loss or damage to the goods passing to the buyer upon shipment if the seller has properly performed all his obligations with respect to the goods. Delivery to the carrier is delivery to the buyer for purposes of risk and title." Official Comment 5 to [U.C.C. §2–503], similarly, explains that a term requiring the seller to pay the freight or the cost of delivery is not to be interpreted as the equivalent of a term requiring the seller to deliver to the buyer or to an agreed destination. In a standard "C.I.F." contract, then, the buyer bears the risk of loss in transit even though the cost of insurance is rolled into the purchase price and is in fact paid by the seller. By breaking out the cost of insurance, and requiring the buyer to pay it, Brawn's mail order contracts even more clearly place the risk of loss in transit on the buyer.

Other evidence, while not determinative, is consistent with the conclusion that Brawn, at least, intended the contracts to be shipment contracts. Brawn's own insurance covers goods lost while in Brawn's possession, but does not cover goods destroyed or lost after the goods left Brawn's physical possession. Brawn pays California use tax, rather than sales tax, on the theory that the goods were "sold" when they left Brawn's place of business, located outside of California. Brawn records the revenue for the goods sold at the point of shipment, and removes the goods from its inventory at the time of shipment.

In sum, nothing in Brawn's conduct, and nothing in the delivery or insurance terms of Brawn's mail order forms, suggest that it was offering anything other than a standard, C.I.F.-type shipment contract, which the customers agreed to when they used Brawn's mail order form to purchase goods. . . . We reverse, concluding that Brawn did not bear the risk of loss of goods in transit under the appplicable California Uniform Commercial Code sections. . . .

[Judgment reversed and remanded.]

Risk of Loss When Goods Not Moved. In some instances, the goods may be held by a bailee (generally a warehouseman) and are to be delivered without being moved. For example, S may sell goods stored at X's warehouse to B. In this case, risk of loss passes to the buyer.

1. on the buyer's receipt of a negotiable document of title, such as a warehouse receipt or bill of lading, covering the goods,
2. on acknowledgement by the bailee of the buyer's right to possession of the goods, or
3. after receipt of a *nonnegotiable* document of title or other written direction to the bailee to deliver.

Even though risk of loss is tied to "receipt" of a nonnegotiable document or written direction in the third case above, the risk does not actually pass when the buyer acquires physical possession of the piece of paper, as it does when a negotiable document is used. Under §2–503(4)(b), risk of loss does not pass to the buyer until the buyer has had a reasonable time to present the document or direction to the bailee *and* the bailee has honored it. Refusal by the bailee to honor the document or to obey the direction defeats the tender.

Residual Risk of Loss Rule. In cases not governed by the rules outlined above, a residual risk of loss rule is contained in §2–509(3). Under this provision, if the seller is a *merchant*,[12] risk of loss passes when the buyer takes physical possession of the goods. If the seller is not a merchant, risk of loss passes on *tender* of delivery. Thus, in the case of a merchant seller, risk of loss may remain on the seller after a tender has been made and after title passes. Assume Bill buys a sofa from Slavin's, a furniture store. Bill pays the price and Slavin places the sofa on its loading dock. Bill, however, leaves the sofa with Slavin's while he gets a van necessary to remove it. The risk of loss remains on Slavin's until Bill returns and takes actual physical possession. This result is consistent with the premise of §2–509 to place the risk of loss on the person—the merchant seller in control and possession of the goods—most likely to be insured against it.

---

[12]"Merchant" is defined in §2–104 discussed in Chapter 7. §2–509(3) applies to persons who are merchants under either the "practices" or "goods" aspect of the merchant definition. §2–104, Official Comment 2.

Sale on Approval, Sale or Return — §§2–326 and 2–327

Sections 2–326 and 2–327 adopt special rules regarding title and risk of loss in specialized contracts allowing a buyer to return goods already delivered even though they conform to the contract. These contracts are the "sale on approval" and the "sale or return."

If goods delivered by the seller may be returned by the buyer even though conforming, the transaction is a **sale on approval** if the goods are delivered primarily for *use*. For example, sale of a vacuum cleaner to a *consumer* on "30-day free trial" or "on satisfaction" is a sale on approval. On the other hand, the transaction is a **sale or return** if the goods are delivered primarily for resale. Assume Electro, a manufacturer of appliances, wants Margret, an appliance dealer, to carry its line of products. Because Electro is not established in the trade, it overcomes Margret's reluctance to buy by promising to take back any goods remaining unsold in lieu of payment. The transaction is a sale or return. In short, if the goods can be returned even though they are wholly as warranted, delivery to a consumer for use is a sale on approval and delivery to a merchant for resale is a sale or return.

The *sale on approval* transaction has several legal consequences. First, unless otherwise agreed, risk of loss and title do not pass to the buyer until acceptance. "Acceptance" generally refers to conduct by the buyer indicating an intent to keep the goods. Thus, if goods on approval in the hands of the buyer are destroyed before the buyer accepts them, the seller bears the risk of loss. In this context, use of the goods for their intended purpose does not constitute acceptance, but failure to seasonably notify the seller of an election to return is an acceptance. If the goods are conforming, acceptance of any part is acceptance of the whole. If the buyer elects to return and duly notifies the seller, both the expense and risk of return are borne by the seller, but a merchant buyer must follow any reasonable instructions.

In a *sale or return,* the legal consequences are diametrically different. Even though the buyer has the right to return, risk of loss passes to the buyer upon delivery and remains with him until the goods are returned to the seller. Additionally, the return is at the buyer's expense. Also, unlike a sale on approval, acceptance of part of the goods is not acceptance of the whole. A primary purpose of a sale or return agreement is to allow the buyer to return goods remaining unsold. Therefore, the buyer, provided he acts seasonably, may return all or part of the delivery so long as the goods remain in substantially their original condition.

Rights of creditors of the buyer also differ in the two situations. Goods in the hands of a buyer on approval are not subject to the claims of his creditors until acceptance. While in the buyer's possession, however, goods delivered under a sale or return agreement are subject to the claims of the buyer's creditors. This aspect of the sale or return arrangement is discussed in more detail in the secured transactions material in Chapter 32.

Effect of Breach on Risk of Loss — §2–510

The foregoing rules apply in the absence of a breach by either party. If the seller breaches, risk of loss is governed by §§2–510(1) and (2). The effect of a buyer's breach or repudiation is stated in §2–510(3).

Seller in Breach. If the seller's tender or delivery so fails to conform to the contract as to give the buyer the right to reject the goods, risk of loss remains on the seller until cure by the seller or acceptance by the buyer. "Cure," in this context, refers to changes made in the goods already tendered such as repair or partial substitution. Risk of loss shifts when such a cure is completed. Cure by repossession and new delivery has no effect upon risk of loss for the goods originally tendered.

In the following case, the court was required to determine which party bore risk of loss after a nonconforming delivery by the seller.

Graybar Electric Company v. Shook
195 S.E.2d 514 (N.C. 1973)

Plaintiff Graybar Electric Company and defendant Harold Shook entered into a contract by which Graybar agreed to sell three reels of underground cable to Shook. The delivery was to be made at the Six Run Grocery Store in a rural community in North Carolina. On April 6, Graybar delivered one reel of underground cable and two reels of aerial cable. Because the aerial cable was unsuitable for Shook's use, he notified Graybar that he rejected the aerial cable. He further notified Graybar that the cable would be left in a well-lit storage space he had rented behind the Six Run Grocery Store. On July 20, a reel of the aerial cable was stolen from the storage space and the second reel was stolen within a few days. Shook notified Graybar of both thefts.

Graybar sued Shook for the cost of the aerial cable. The trial court dismissed the suit and the court of appeals affirmed. Graybar appealed.

Higgins, Justice

. . . The plaintiff, having made the error of delivering the nonconforming goods on a moving job in the country, was entitled to notice of the nonconformity sufficient to enable it to repossess the nonconforming goods. The plaintiff was given prompt notice but delayed action for more than three months. The cable was stolen from the defendant's regular storage space where the plaintiff had delivered it. Evidence is lacking that a safer storage space was available. The defendant's workmen moved on, leaving the cable and the responsibility for its safety to the owner.

The plaintiff, . . . contends that . . . [UCC §2–602(2)(b)] required the defendant to exercise reasonable care in holding the rejected goods pending the plaintiff's repossession and removal and that the defendant failed to exercise the required care in storage.

Actually, the plaintiff made an on the spot delivery at a store and dwelling in the country. The defendant's work force was stringing underground cable along the highway and the crew was in continual movement. Obviously the crew could not be expected to carry with it two thousand pounds of useless cable and was within its rights placing the cable in its regular storage space and notifying the plaintiff of the place of storage. Both parties realized that cable weighing almost a ton would require men and a truck to remove it. Also both parties assumed that the danger of theft from a well lighted store area was a minimal risk. The property itself was a poor candidate for larceny. The cable was permitted to remain where the plaintiff knew it was located for more than three months. The plaintiff, therefore, had ample opportunity to repossess its property.

The Uniform Commercial Code emphasizes promptness and good faith. The prospective purchaser may exercise a valid right to reject and even if he takes possession, responsibility expires after a reasonable time in which the owner has opportunity to repossess. "Where a tender or delivery of goods so fails to conform to the contract as to give a right of rejection the risk of their loss remains on the seller until cure or acceptance." . . . [UCC §2–510(1)]. The defendant did not accept the aerial cable. According to the evidence and the court's findings, the defendant acted in accordance with the request of the owner in attempting to facilitate the return of that which the defendant rejected. The plaintiff with full notice of the place of storage which was at the place of delivery did nothing but sleep on its rights for more than three months. . . .

[Judgment affirmed.]

Buyer in Breach. Under §2–510(3), if the buyer, with respect to conforming goods already identified to the contract, repudiates or otherwise breaches before risk of loss passes to it, risk of loss rests on the buyer for a commercially reasonable time to the extent the seller is not covered by insurance. Assume Seller contracts to sell identified goods for $5,000 to Buyer, delivery to be made on June 30. On June 15, Buyer repudiates the contract and on June 16 the goods are destroyed. The loss is covered by Seller's insurance to the extent of $4,000. Seller can recover $1,000 from Buyer. If the loss had been fully covered, Seller would have no claim against Buyer. If Seller is uninsured, the entire loss falls on Buyer.

A similar rule applies under §2–510(2) if the buyer accepts goods but then rightfully revokes the acceptance. (The requirements for revocation of acceptance are discussed in the next chapter.) In this case, risk of loss is deemed to rest on the seller from the beginning to the extent of any deficiency in the buyer's effective insurance coverage.

The purpose of both §§2–510(2) and 2–510(3) is to give an injured party who controls the goods the benefit of the breaching party's insurance coverage to the extent the loss or damage is not covered by the injured party's insurance. Thus, these provisions effectively place risk of loss on the injured party to the extent of its insurance.

Summary

1. Article 2 defines a sale as the passing of title from the buyer to the seller for a price. Despite its use in such a fundamental definition, title occupies a limited role under Article 2 because issues previously resolved by title, insurable interest, and risk of loss, are governed by separate Code provisions. Nevertheless, the Code contains a residual rule governing the passage of title and resolves ownership disputes arising when a person with voidable title—for example, one acquiring property through fraud—transfers the property to a good faith purchaser. Article 2 also resolves disputes between persons who entrust goods to a merchant dealing in goods of the kind and buyers of the goods in the ordinary course of the merchant's business.

2. Risk of loss rules determine the rights of the parties if the goods involved in the contract are lost, destroyed, or stolen. If the risk of loss falls on the seller when the goods are destroyed, the seller is liable in damages for nondelivery unless the seller can acquire or manufacture replacement goods. On the other hand, once the risk of loss passes to the buyer, the buyer is liable to the seller for the purchase price of the goods despite the destruction. The buyer should therefore be insured prior to passage of the risk of loss. The buyer acquires an insurable interest upon identification of the goods to the contract. Identification, which is the process by which the particular goods to which the contract refers are designated or specified, always occurs before the risk passes to the buyer.

3. Article 2 contains separate provisions governing risk of loss in the absence of breach and risk of loss when either party is in breach. In the most common case, the absence of breach, separate rules govern risk of loss when (1) the seller is required or authorized to ship the goods to the buyer, (2) the goods are in the hands of a bailee, such as a warehouseman, and are to be delivered without being moved, and (3) all other cases. The effect of these rules is to place the risk on the person in possession, who is most likely to be insured against their casualty. If either party breaches the contract, risk of loss is placed upon the breaching party, limited in some cases, however, to the extent of any deficiency in the other party's insurance coverage.

Key Terms

title	ostensible ownership
risk of loss	identification of goods
purchaser	future goods
voidable title rule	insurable interest
value	sale on approval
entrusting	sale or return
buyer in the ordinary course of business	

Questions and Problems

17.1   On January 1, Seller contracted to sell two photocopiers to Buyer, F.O.B. shipping point. Half of the purchase price was paid on January 1, the remainder was due on delivery. On January 2, Seller selected the two machines to be shipped to the Buyer. On January 3, Seller delivered the machines to the carrier and arranged for shipment to the Buyer. On January 4 the goods were delivered and tendered to Buyer by the carrier. Seller retains a security interest in the goods. Buyer paid final installment on January 5. On what day did title pass to the Buyer? On what day did risk of loss pass to the Buyer? On what day did the Buyer obtain an insurable interest? On what day did the Seller's insurable interest cease, if at all?

17.2   Lloyd Co., a catalog retailer, operates a plant and shipping facility in Grandview, Missouri. Lloyd contracted to purchase a conveyor system for its plant from Vendo, Inc., an Arkansas company. The contract, which was written on a purchase order prepared by Lloyd, included the following terms:

1. Shipment is to be made F.O.B., Vendo's plant, Truman, Arkansas.
2. Vendo shall install the conveyor system in Lloyd's plant in Grandview, Missouri.
3. Risk of loss shall pass to Lloyd at the time the conveyor system is actually tendered for delivery at Lloyd's office in Grandview, Missouri.
4. The contract shall be governed by the Uniform Commercial Code.

The state of Missouri imposes a sales tax on all personal property. The state sued Lloyd claiming it owed taxes on the conveyor system. Under Missouri law, personal property becomes taxable when title transfers to the new owner. In this case, if title passes after the conveyor system is installed, no tax is owed. If, however, title passes anytime prior to installation, the property is taxable. Because the contract is governed by the UCC, the court must apply the UCC to determine when title transferred. How should the court rule? Explain.

17.3   Hollow, who owned and operated a truck dealership in Decatur, Georgia, sold a truck to Moon on June 22, 2003, promising that the truck would be delivered from Chattanooga, Tennessee, where special equipment was being installed on it. Moon paid $8,800 for the truck and received an invoice and papers necessary to obtain a Georgia certificate of title. Although Moon made several inquiries to Hollow regarding date of delivery, the truck was not delivered.

On November 13, 2003, Hollow sold the same truck to Simson, who paid $8,700 for it. Hollow also told Simson the truck was in Chattanooga for installation of equipment. On November 16, Simson went to Chattanooga and took delivery of the truck.

On January 25, 2004, Moon discovered that Simson had possession of the truck. Moon then applied for a certificate of title. After learning that Hollow had absconded with all the money, Moon sued Simson to obtain possession of the truck.

How should the court rule? Cite the UCC provisions that support your answer.

17.4   We Try Harder, Inc. (WTHI) is an automobile leasing company. Although the management of WTHI is knowledgeable about car leasing, it is unfamiliar with many of the legal principles affecting its business. Consider the following events that recently occurred:

(a) WTHI leased an automobile to Al Newman. Al owned and operated Al's Auto Center, an automobile dealership. Al fraudulently obtained title to the automobile from the state in the name of Al's Auto Center. He then placed the vehicle on the dealership lot. Marvin purchased the car for cash, and Al transferred title to him. Al suddenly left town and WTHI wants its automobile returned. If WTHI sues Marvin, to whom should the court award title? Explain, citing appropriate UCC provisions.

(b) To make room for a new shipment of 2006 automobiles, WTHI decided to sell its 2005 cars. WTHI consigned the automobiles to American Auto Auction (AAA), an auto wholesaler. WTHI and AAA signed a five-page contract by which AAA agreed not to accept any bids on the cars without prior approval of WTHI. The contract further provided that upon WTHI's approving the acceptance of a bid, WTHI would provide the documents of title to the purchaser. AAA sold ten of the cars for cash to Sam, who owned and operated a used car lot, without providing certificates of title. AAA also sold one of the cars to Marylou for cash, again without providing a certificate of title. AAA failed to obtain WTHI's approval for the sale. AAA is in bankruptcy. If WTHI sues Sam and Marylou, to whom should the court award title? Explain, citing appropriate UCC provisions.

(c) A Cadillac was stolen from WTHI's lot. The car eventually came into the hands of a used automobile wholesaler who sold it to Silver Hill Motors. Silver Hill then sold the car to Betty Bonafide, a good faith purchaser for value. Silver Hill promised to obtain and deliver a certificate of title to Betty. Several days later, however, the police seized the Cadillac as stolen property. To whom should the court award title to the car? Explain, citing appropriate UCC provisions.

17.5   Mr. and Mrs. Kahr owned a valuable set of sterling silver flatware. While on vacation, they stored the silver and other valuables in their attic. Several weeks later, they decided to donate some old clothes to Goodwill Industries. Among the bags of clothes was a bag containing the silver, which Mr. Kahr inadvertently delivered to Goodwill with the old clothes. Unaware of the value of the silver, Goodwill sold it to a customer for $15. After the Kahrs realized their mistake, they demanded that the purchaser return the silver. She refused and the Kahrs sued her and Goodwill. Citing the entrusting rule of UCC §2–403(2), the purchaser argued that Goodwill had transferred good title to her. How should the court rule? Explain.

17.6   Section 2–510(1) of the UCC provides that risk of loss remains upon a seller who makes a nonconforming shipment of goods. Is this a wise rule given the policy underlying §2–509 (risk of loss in absence of breach)? Policy considerations aside, what problems might be encountered by courts in applying §2–510(1)?

17.7   John Farmer ordered a new tractor from Lykins Tractor Sales, which delivered the tractor to Farmer's residence on Friday. On Saturday, Farmer tried to use the tractor, but discovered that it was inoperable. The battery was dead, the water pump was missing, and various other parts were defective or improperly installed. On Monday, Farmer called Lykins to notify it that he wanted to return the tractor. Farmer stated that he would leave the tractor in his front yard and Lykins's manager agreed that an employee would pick up the tractor within a few days. On Wednesday, the tractor was stolen from Farmer's yard. Lykins asserts that Farmer is responsible to pay for the tractor, but Farmer insists that Lykins bears the risk of loss. Who is correct? Explain, citing the appropriate UCC provisions.

17.8   Seven Seas Shipbuilders, Inc. sold a mast for a yacht to Peter Posh. Seven Seas agreed to deliver the mast after installing some hardware on it. Peter made a $4,500 down payment. Prior to completion of the installation, however, a fire destroyed Seven Seas' premises including the mast. Seven Seas' insurance covered only the buildings of its business.

(a) Who bore the risk of loss at the time of the fire? Explain, citing the appropriate UCC provisions.

(b) Prior to the fire, Seven Seas had asked Peter whether his insurance would cover it. Peter had replied that the mast would be fully covered under his insurance. Do these additional facts change your answer in (a)? Explain, citing appropriate UCC provisions.

THE SALES CONTRACT—REMEDIES

- **the remedial philosophy of Article 2 of the Uniform Commercial Code**
- **the concepts of rejection, acceptance, revocation of acceptance, and cure**
- **the various remedies available to an injured buyer after breach by the seller**
- **the various remedies available to an injured seller after breach by the buyer**

Chapter 15 discussed the principles governing legal and equitable remedies that apply both to Code and common law contracts. This chapter examines additional specific obligations and remedies of the buyer and seller in contracts for the sale of goods.

Remedial Philosophy of the Code

Article 2 provides buyers and sellers injured by breach of contract with a wide variety of remedies. The UCC, however, explicitly rejects any doctrine of "election of remedy." That is, the remedies available under the Code are not exclusive; under §1–305, the injured party may resort to any combination of available relief in order

that "the aggrieved party[1] may be put in as good a position as if the other party had fully performed." With this goal in mind, whether pursuit of one remedy rules out another depends entirely on the facts of the case.

Contractual Modification or Limitation of Remedy

Freedom of contract is a fundamental policy of the Code. Consistent with this policy, §2–719 permits the parties to provide for remedies in their contract in addition to or in substitution for those outlined in the UCC and to limit or alter the measure of damages otherwise available. For example, the buyer's remedies may be limited to returning the goods and receiving a refund of the purchase price, or to repair or replacement of defective goods.

Although the parties may limit or modify remedies, minimum adequate remedies must be available to an injured buyer or seller. Inadequate contractual remedies often are present in adhesion contracts in which the

---

[1]"Aggrieved party" as used in the UCC means a party entitled to pursue a remedy. §1–201(b)(2).

drafting party dictates the relief available upon breach. If these remedies are unreasonably favorable to that party or unfairly limit available remedies, they may be deleted or modified as unconscionable under §2–302, as discussed in Chapter 10. This same approach applies to consequential damages, which may be limited or excluded under §2–719(3) by contract unless the effect is unconscionable.

Unless expressly agreed to the contrary, the contractually provided remedy is optional, not exclusive. Under §2–719(2), however, if the circumstances cause an exclusive or limited remedy to "fail of its essential purpose" or to deprive either party of the substantial value of the bargain, Code remedies are reinstated. In the following case, the court was required to determine whether a limited remedy failed of its essential purpose.

Phillips Petroleum Company v. Bucyrus-Erie Company
388 N.W.2d 584 (Wis. 1986)

In the early 1970s, plaintiff Phillips Petroleum Company solicited proposals from manufacturers to construct and sell cranes to be used on Phillips's offshore oil drilling platforms located near Norway in the North Sea. Information provided by Phillips described weather conditions and wind and wave stresses under which the cranes would have to perform. Phillips accepted a written proposal submitted by defendant Bucyrus-Erie Company and the parties agreed that adapters, used to place the cranes on the drilling rigs, would be made of a grade of steel specified in design drawings approved by Phillips. The cranes and adapters were installed in 1973. On February 28, 1974, a crane broke loose from a platform and fell into the sea. Subsequent analysis revealed that the adapter rings were not constructed of the steel specified in the drawings and that Bucyrus-Erie had substituted steel that was too brittle for the intended use.

Phillips sued for damages for breach of contract but Bucyrus-Erie claimed that the written proposal limited its liability to replacement of any defective part F.O.B. Erie, Pennsylvania. This provision appeared in the proposal under the heading "Warranty." The trial court ruled that the limitation of liability clause was ineffective because it failed of its essential purpose in violation of §2–719(2) of the UCC. The court found Bucyrus-Erie liable for breach of contract and awarded damages of $1.6 million. The appellate court reversed and Phillips appealed to the Wisconsin Supreme Court.

Heffernan, Chief Justice

. . . Although we do not disagree with the trial court's conclusion that a disclaimer of liability or a limitation on damages that is inappropriately masked under a heading captioned, "Warranty," is in itself a reason to disregard it, we look to the merits of the Phillips' argument that damages ought not be limited to replacement of the defective part F.O.B. Erie because, under [§2–719(2) of the UCC]:

> Where circumstances cause an exclusive or limited remedy to fail of its essential purpose, remedy may be had as provided in [this Act].

Here, the Phillips' argument is that to replace the adapters at Erie—a site thousands of miles from where the replacement was needed—is simply an unrealistic remedy. The adapter ring only failed on one crane, but the domino effect of that failure was that none of the Bucyrus-Erie cranes purchased by Phillips could be used until they were repaired and certified. Thus, the damage was not limited to the replacement value of a single part even on the 13 cranes. The defect resulted in the total failure of Phillips' ability to use expensive and complex equipment for a protracted period of time. This was damage caused for the "want of a horseshoe nail."

The circumstances here, the possibility of a physical failure because of wind and wave stresses of the North Sea, were those that should have been reasonably anticipated. Here the Bucyrus-Erie Company not only culpably, though perhaps inadvertently, used a type of steel that, in view of the express warranty agreed to by the seller and the buyer, was destined to fail with all the consequent, and to be anticipated, injury to the purchaser. The essential purpose of any damage award is to make the injured party whole. . . . The replacement or the supply of new conforming adapters at Erie, Pennsylvania, only minusculely compensated the purchaser. The circumstances here require that the compensation fulfill the essential purpose of all damage awards—to make the innocent party whole. It is understandable that the boilerplate limit on damages may be appropriate in most cases. In most cases, the timely supplying of the deficient part will make a party whole. Not so in this case. While both parties to this action are giants in their areas of enterprise, we do not feel that the Uniform Commercial Code makes giant corporations fair game for either intentional sharp practices or a skewed rule of law. Under our justice system, the persona of the corporation is entitled to be treated fairly in commercial transactions. While we see no willfulness or any evidence of subjective sharp practices in the performance of the contract, it is apparent that the remedy offered by Bucyrus-Erie's contract (concealed or masked in the warranty section) provides damages that are, in the circumstances, unconscionably low. The damage clause is unreasonably. . . . [I]t is our conclusion that the philosophy of damage awards expressed by this court . . . leads to . . . a conclusion consistent with the underlying philosophy of the Uniform Commercial Code that there be at least a fair quantum of remedy for breach of obligations. [UCC §2–719, Official Comment 1.]

Accordingly, in accordance with the code, the damage remedy is not that purportedly provided in the documents, but "remedy may be had as provided in [the UCC]" as applied by the trial court. . . .

[Judgment reversed.]

Buyers' Obligations

As noted in Chapter 14, the standard governing a seller's performance of a Code contract is the "perfect tender" rule of §2–601; that is, if the goods or the tender of delivery fail *in any respect* to conform[2] to the contract, the buyer is entitled to (1) *reject* the entire shipment, or (2) *accept* the entire shipment, or (3) accept any commercial unit[3] or units and reject the rest. The rights and obligations of the buyer after the seller's tender or delivery are discussed in the following material. First, the rights and obligations of the parties after a buyer's "rejection" are discussed. These include the manner of rejection, the buyer's duties with respect to rightfully rejected goods in its possession, and the limited right of the seller to cure or correct a nonconforming delivery. Second, the concept and effect of "acceptance" and the circumstances justifying the buyer's revocation of acceptance are discussed.

Rejection — Buyers' Obligations

After delivery, the buyer generally has the right to inspect the goods. If, after inspection, the goods are found to be nonconforming, the buyer is entitled to reject them. To be effective, §2–602(1) provides that the **rejection**

1. must be made within a reasonable time after tender or delivery of the goods, and
2. the buyer must seasonably[4] notify the seller of rejection.

To fully protect its rights, the buyer also should state the particular defect or defects justifying rejection, because a buyer, under §2–605(1), may not rely upon unstated defects to justify rejection or establish breach if

1. the seller could have corrected the defect had it been seasonably stated, or
2. as *between merchants,* the buyer, after written request by the seller, fails to provide a full and final written statement of all defects.

A buyer who rightfully rejects a delivery after taking possession of the goods must hold the goods with reasonable care for a time sufficient to allow the seller to remove them, but has no further obligation concerning them. If the seller fails to give instructions within a reasonable time after notification of rejection, the buyer (merchant or nonmerchant) may (1) store the rejected goods, *or* (2) reship them to the seller, *or* (3) resell them for the seller's account. In all cases, the buyer is entitled to reimbursement for expenses.[5]

Section 2–603 imposes certain additional responsibilities upon a *merchant* buyer who rightfully rejects goods. If the seller has no agent or place of business at the place of rejection, the buyer must follow any reasonable instructions from the seller concerning the disposition of the goods. The seller may instruct the buyer

---

[2]As used in the UCC, goods or conduct are "conforming" or "conform to the contract" when they are in accordance with the obligations under the contract. §2–106(2).

[3]A "commercial unit" is a unit of goods treated as a single whole for purposes of sale and whose value is significantly impaired by division. A commercial unit may be a single article (for example, a machine), a set of articles (for example, an assortment of sizes), or a quantity (for example, a bale or carload). UCC §2–105(6).

[4]The buyer acts "seasonably" by notifying the seller (1) at or within the time agreed in the contract, or (2) if no time is agreed, at or within a reasonable time. UCC §1–205(b).

[5]UCC §§2–602(2), 2–604.

to reship, store, or resell the goods, or deliver them to a third party. The seller must, however, reimburse the buyer for any expenses incurred, including a commission if the buyer resells. If the seller gives no instructions and the goods are perishable or threaten to decline quickly in value, the buyer must make a reasonable effort to resell them on the seller's behalf. The foregoing rules are designed to give both merchant and non-merchant buyers, who reject in good faith, reasonable leeway in disposing of the goods and to prevent the buyer's conduct from being interpreted as an "acceptance" of them.

Cure—§2–508

The remedy of **cure,** stated in §2–508, protects the seller in two specific situations against the effects of a rejection by the buyer resulting from the seller's nonconforming tender or delivery. Cure is perhaps the most important of the various Code provisions relieving a seller from the harsh effect of the "perfect tender rule" generally governing sales contracts. Cure severely limits the buyer's right to reject for minor, insubstantial defects.

The seller is given the right to cure (correct a defective performance) if the buyer rejects a nonconforming tender or delivery and the *time for performance agreed in the contract has not passed.* In this situation, the seller may cure by seasonably notifying the buyer of an intention to cure and making a conforming delivery within the time called for by the contract. Assume Charles contracts to sell and deliver 500 navy blue T-shirts to Amy for $2,000, delivery to be made "on or before June 1." On May 15, Charles inadvertently ships 500 royal blue shirts that Amy immediately rejects because they are the wrong color. Charles may cure by notifying Amy and delivering navy blue shirts by June 1.

A seller also is given an opportunity to cure when the buyer rejects a nonconforming tender that the seller *had reasonable grounds to believe would be acceptable.* In this situation, the seller may cure by seasonably notifying the buyer of an intention to cure, and substituting a conforming tender within "a further reasonable time." Note that the seller is always allowed to cure if a conforming delivery can be made within the time agreed upon for performance, but is allowed to cure after that time only if the original tender was made on the reasonable belief that it would be acceptable. In this second case, the seller is then granted a further reasonable time to cure.

The rationale for the second type of cure is to avoid injustice to the seller resulting from a surprise rejection by the buyer. The seller must, however, have "reasonable grounds to believe" that the tender would be acceptable. Thus, if a reasonable businessperson would know that the goods are unacceptable, either because of the nature of the goods themselves or the surrounding circumstances, the cure remedy is unavailable.

For example, the seller may reasonably believe that goods that are substantial equivalents of those called for, or that are a newer model, are acceptable. Or, the seller may believe that slight quantity or assortment variations will be tolerated. Or, a retailer selling manufactured goods of a reputable manufacturer in the original cartons has reasonable grounds to believe that the goods will be acceptable. Commonly the seller's belief is grounded on trade usage, the contract itself, or prior dealing of the parties.

If the seller successfully cures (corrects the defective performance), the buyer may no longer *reject.* The buyer may, however, be entitled to recover damages under §2–714 (discussed in Chapter 19) governing buyer's damages for breach with respect to accepted goods. Additionally, the buyer may recover for any incidental damages.

At issue in the following case was whether the breaching seller made a legally sufficient offer to cure.

Travelers Indemnity Co. v. MAHO Machine Tool Corporation
952 F.2d 26 (2d Cir. 1991)

Defendant MAHO Machine Tool Corporation contracted to sell an industrial machine to Windward International, Inc. The contract required MAHO to provide "seaworthy preparation and crating" of the machine, which was to be shipped to Singapore. Plaintiff Travelers Indemnity Company insured the machine for Windward. During shipment, the machine was seriously damaged by rust resulting from MAHO's improper crating. By letter dated June 13, 1988, MAHO offered to replace the damaged machine if Windward shipped it to MAHO's plant in Germany. Windward did not ship the machine to Germany but instead purchased a different machine. As a result, MAHO did not provide a replacement. In accordance with the insurance policy, Travelers paid the cost of the machine and then, based on Windward's rights, sued MAHO for breach of contract. The trial court dismissed the case ruling that Windward had rejected MAHO's offer to replace the damaged machine and, therefore, both Windward and Travelers had lost the right to obtain damages from MAHO. Travelers appealed.

Newman, Circuit Judge

. . . In substance, MAHO offered to cure the defect in performance of the contract by replacing the machine with a new one to be manufactured in a month. Conspicuously left open by the June 13 letter was the identification of which party would pay for shipping the damaged machine back to Germany and for shipping the replacement machine to Singapore. . . . [T]he evidence is undisputed that MAHO expected Windward or its insurer to pay these expenses. A June 27, 1988, letter from [MAHO] to Windward's office in Virginia stated. . . . "Transportation cost from Singapore to Phronton, West Germany would be the responsibility of Windward International." . . .

[Section 2–508 of the U.C.C. provides in part:]

Where the buyer rejects a non-conforming tender which the seller had reasonable grounds to believe would be acceptable with or without money allowance the seller may if he seasonably notifies the buyer have a further reasonable time to substitute a conforming tender.

. . . The plain import of this opportunity for cure is that both the opportunity to cure and the burden, *i.e.,* the cost, of doing so are lodged with the seller. The law of sales does not impose upon the buyer any obligation to assume the expenses of the seller in effecting a cure for the delivery of non-conforming goods. . . .

The issue is whether the breaching seller made a legally sufficient offer of cure that defeats the buyer's suit for damages for delivery of non-conforming goods. . . . The cure offer defeats the damage claim only if it is a legally sufficient cure offer, and MAHO's offer was deficient.

MAHO's replacement offer was legally deficient as an offer of cure because it sought to impose upon Windward the substantial cost of returning the damaged machine to Germany and the further cost of transporting the replacement machine to Singapore. Windward, having already become obligated for the cost of transporting the original machine to Singapore, had no duty whatever to spare MAHO any of the expenses of return-

ing the machine and delivering a new one. The option to cure a defect merely extends the time available for the seller to complete its obligations under the contract. . . . Having delivered non-conforming goods, it must either respond in damages or effect cure. Since its cure offer was deficient, it remains liable for damages.

[Judgment reversed and remanded.]

Acceptance of Goods — §§2–606 and 2–607

The buyer's alternative to rejecting delivered goods is to "accept" them. Several important legal consequences occur upon acceptance. Under §2–606, a buyer accepts goods in three situations. First, acceptance occurs if, after a reasonable opportunity to inspect, the buyer indicates to the seller that the goods are conforming or that he will take them despite their nonconformity. Acceptance also occurs if, after a reasonable opportunity to inspect, the buyer fails to make an effective rejection as discussed in the preceding subsection. Assume Tapeco contracts to sell 200 cases of cassette tapes to Billings, which Tapeco delivers on June 1. Billings performs an inspection and places the tapes in its warehouse. Six months later Billings attempts to reject the shipment. Billings has accepted the goods. Finally, a buyer accepts by any act inconsistent with an initial claim of rejection. For example, a buyer who first attempts to reject and then acts inconsistently — such as by making part payment on the price, or using the goods in the buyer's business or manufacturing process, or modifying or repairing the goods — has accepted the goods. Note that any use of the goods by the buyer *prior to* discovering their defective nature does not constitute an acceptance.

Once a buyer has accepted goods, several important legal consequences, stated in §2–607, follow:

1. The buyer must pay at the contract rate for any goods accepted.
2. After acceptance, the buyer may no longer *reject* the goods. Acceptance does not, however, impair any other remedy available to the buyer for nonconformity. For example, the buyer may recover dollar damages for any defects in the goods accepted. However, it is important to note that buyers' remedies under the UCC differ depending upon whether

or not the goods in question have been accepted or rejected.

3. If a tender has been accepted, the buyer must notify the seller within a reasonable time after discovery of any breach or is barred from *any* remedy.
4. After acceptance, the buyer has the burden of establishing any breach.

At issue in the following case was whether the buyer had accepted goods, thereby becoming liable for their purchase price.

Design Plus Store Fixtures, Inc. v. Citro Corporation

508 S.E.2d 825 (N.C.App. 1998)

Plaintiff Design Plus Store Fixtures, Inc. (Design) contracted with defendant Citro Corporation to custom build retail display tables for direct delivery to stores owned by Design's customer Springmaid. The tables, which were delivered late, failed to conform to Design's specifications. Because Springmaid needed the tables for scheduled store openings, Design sufficiently repaired the defects so that the tables could be used and agreed to replace them in the future. After securing replacements from another supplier, Design donated the defective tables to charity. Design sued Citro, seeking damages for the expenses incurred due to Citro's breach. The trial court found that Design had accepted the nonconforming tables and awarded Citro damages of $985 (the agreed price of $19,405 less $18,420 damages caused by Citro's breach). Design appealed.

Martin, Judge

. . . Design's transaction with Citro is governed by the Uniform Commercial Code. . . . Initially, Design properly rejected the tables by providing reasonable notice of the nonconformity to Citro. Rejection of an installment, under section [UCC §2–612(2)], is appropriate only if "the nonconformity substantially impairs the value of that installment. . . . A proper rejection also requires (1) rejection within a reasonable time after delivery or tender, and (2) seasonable notice to seller. . . . The trial court found that the nonconformities "made it impossible to properly assemble the table," and that this constituted a substantial impairment, justifying rejection of the installments. . . .

Design notified Citro of significant nonconformities on 10 November 1993; and after Citro made no offer to cure the defects, Design refused to pay for the defective tables on 21 November 1993. Thus, Design's actions after discovery of the non-conformities were consistent with a rightful rejection of the tables. . . .

"Acceptance of goods occurs when the buyer . . . does any act inconsistent with the seller's ownership; but if such act is wrongful against the seller, it is an acceptance only if ratified by him," [UCC §2–606(1)(c)]. "Acts inconsistent with the seller's ownership" can best be understood in light of the buyer's statutory options and duties with respect to rightfully rejected non-conforming goods. The buyer's options and duties upon rejection are described in [UCC §§2–602 to 2–604]. For most buyers, there is a general duty to hold goods with reasonable care "for a time sufficient to permit the seller to remove them," [UCC §2–602(2)(b)]. Merchant buyers have a more specific duty when the seller has no agent or place of business in the market of rejection:

[A] merchant buyer is under a duty after rejection of goods in his possession or control to follow any reasonable instructions received from the seller with respect to the goods and in the absence of such instructions to make reasonable efforts to sell them for the seller's account if they are perishable or threaten to decline in value speedily. [UCC §2–603(1).]

In this case, Design is a merchant dealing in tables . . . and Citro had no place of business or agent in the markets of rejection, Oregon and Kansas. In addition, the tables are not "perishables" such that "the value of the goods is threatened and the seller's instructions do not arrive in time to prevent serious loss," [UCC §2–603(1), Official Comment 1]. Thus, Design's duty, upon rejection, was to follow Citro's reasonable instructions with respect to Citro's tables. However, no instructions from Citro were forthcoming.

Absent such instructions, the statute presents three options for a buyer who has given reasonable notification rejecting non-conforming goods: (1) store the rejected goods on the seller's account, (2) re-ship them to seller, or (3) resell them on the seller's account with reimbursement for expenses incurred in caring for and selling them, [UCC §2–604]. These potential courses of action are "intended to be not exhaustive but merely illustrative," [UCC §2–604, Official Comment].

The basic purpose of this section is twofold: on the one hand it aims at reducing the stake in dispute and on the other at avoiding the pinning of a technical "acceptance" on a buyer who has taken steps towards realization on or preservation of the goods in good faith. . . . (*Id.*)

A merchant buyer in possession of rejected goods, and without instructions from the seller, is in the somewhat difficult position of having a choice of reasonable options, but no clear affirmative duties with respect to those goods . . . ; yet, the buyer must avoid acts "inconsistent with the seller's ownership" in order to avoid accepting the non-conforming goods, [UCC §2–606(1)(c)]. The issue is whether Design's actions constitute good faith steps toward "realization on or preservation of the goods," on the one hand, or "acts inconsistent with ownership" on the other. . . .

The repair and continued use of the non-conforming, rejected goods constitutes a reasonable good faith effort to preserve the goods while mitigating damages. . . . In this case, Citro entered into the contract with the understanding that manufacturing and delivering the tables in a timely manner was necessary to serve Design's primary customer, Springmaid. Citro delivered the tables late, and the tables were defective. According to the trial court's findings of fact, the plaintiff "performed corrective measures" on the tables, and provided them to Springmaid with the understanding they would be replaced and "replacement of the tables could not affect any of the scheduled store openings;" and, Citro "offered neither explanation nor solution." Design bore the expense of repairing the tables for temporary use by Springmaid. Citro offered no instructions as to the disposal or return of the tables. Under these circumstances, we hold that repairing the tables and allowing Springmaid the continued use of the tables were reasonable actions in good faith and did not constitute acceptance of the tables.

However, after allowing Springmaid the reasonable continued use of the repaired tables, Design gave the nonconforming tables away, contending they had no market value. The trial court concluded, *inter alia,* that "disposal of the tables after their replacement without notifying or attempting to obtain the consent of [Defendant] Corporation constituted acceptance of the goods under the code as acts inconsistent with Defendant's ownership." We agree.

As discussed above, reasonable repair and use of the tables to temporarily satisfy a contract contemplated at the time of the transaction is not inconsistent with ownership; thus those actions did not constitute an acceptance. However, discarding the tables without notifying Citro is an unreasonable act, inconsistent with ownership, where the tables had some salvageable value. Underlying the issue of acceptance, in this context, is the question of whether Design acted inconsistently, by rejecting the goods and then disposing of these goods as an owner. Giving the tables to charity without notifying Citro was such an act of ownership. There are some circumstances where it might be reasonable to discard rejected goods when there is no salvageable value. . . . In this case, however, the court found that the un-bored, un-edged, parts . . . had a salvage value of $15.60 per table; and its finding is supported by the evidence. . . . Discarding these goods constituted an act inconsistent with Citro's ownership, and so Design is deemed to have accepted the goods. . . .

[Judgment affirmed.]

Revocation of Acceptance—§2–608

In certain limited circumstances, the buyer may revoke a previous acceptance of goods. The requirements for **revocation of acceptance,** stated in §2–608, are more stringent than those imposed upon the buyer rejecting the goods initially. The rationale for this approach is that, in the revocation case, the buyer has been in possession of the goods long enough to constitute an acceptance. In this situation, it is more likely that the problem was caused or at least magnified by the buyer's use of the goods, rather than any initial defect in the goods themselves. Further, due to the passage of time or other factors, the market value of the goods may have substantially deteriorated resulting in greater loss to the seller. Additionally, the buyer may have benefited by using the goods prior to revocation.

Accordingly, §2–608(1) allows a buyer to revoke a previous acceptance in two situations only if the nonconformity of the goods "substantially impairs"[6] their value to him. First, the buyer may accept goods known to be nonconforming on the reasonable assumption that

---

[6]This is the same test governing breach of Code contracts performed in installments. See discussion of §2–612 in Chapter 14.

the nonconformity would be corrected, or cured, by the seller. If the seller fails to cure the defect within a reasonable time, the buyer may revoke acceptance. This situation is common in sales of automobiles or other complex machinery exhibiting defects that the seller promises, but is subsequently unable, to remedy.

In this case the buyer accepts with knowledge of the defect. A buyer who is unaware of the nonconformity at the time of acceptance may revoke acceptance if acceptance was induced either by the difficulty of discovering the nonconformity before acceptance or by the seller's assurances causing the buyer to delay discovery. Absent fraud or mistake, the buyer's right to return accepted goods under the Code is limited to the two situations outlined above. That is, the concept of "revocation of acceptance" generally replaces "rescission" for Code contracts.

Revocation of acceptance must be made within a reasonable time after the buyer discovers (or should have discovered) the defect and before any substantial change in the condition of the goods. Additionally, the revocation is not effective until the buyer notifies the seller of it. The revocation and notice to the seller must occur within a reasonable time. Whether the buyer has acted within a reasonable time is a frequently litigated issue in both rejection and revocation cases. An effective revocation gives the buyer the same rights and duties regarding the goods as if they had been rejected initially.[7]

At issue in the following case was whether a buyer who accepted without knowledge of the defect was entitled to revoke his acceptance.

Kesner v. Lancaster
378 S.E.2d 649 (W.Va. 1989)

In response to a newspaper advertisement, plaintiff Donald Kesner arranged to see a used John Deere tractor-loader offered for sale by defendant James Lancaster. Kesner inspected the vehicle and asked to operate it, but Lancaster dissuaded him because the attachments would have had to be changed. Lancaster, however, started the engine and assured Kesner that all of the equipment was in fine shape. Kesner agreed to purchase the loader and, after paying Lancaster $9,000, had it transported to a work site. Within minutes after beginning to use the tractor, it stopped. After removing the seats and floorboards, Kesner observed that

---

[7]UCC §§2–608(2), (3).

the transmission had pulled away from its housing, the bolts securing the transmission were rusted and stripped, several bolts were missing, and the transmission and frame rails were cracked and had been welded together. Kesner took the tractor to a mechanic who estimated that the repairs would cost at least $720 and that additional repairs might be needed after disassembling the transmission. Because Lancaster refused Kesner's demands to return the loader for a full refund, Kesner sued Lancaster. The trial court found that Kesner had justifiably revoked his acceptance and was therefore entitled to recover the purchase price. Lancaster appealed, arguing that §2–608 should not apply.

Miller, Justice

. . . In this case, the parties raise the issues of whether the loader was substantially impaired and whether the defects should have been reasonably discovered. . . .

[The seller] contends that since the cost of repairs was much less than the purchase price, the value of the loader was not substantially impaired by the defects. . . . Most commentators and courts agree that there are both subjective and objective aspects to the determination of whether a defect "substantially impairs" the value of goods so as to enable a buyer to revoke his acceptance of them. The subjective component of the test takes into consideration the particular buyer's needs and expectations. The objective element focuses on the actual defects, which must not be trivial or insubstantial. . . .

In the present case, there was sufficient evidence for the jury to find that the value of the loader had been substantially impaired within the meaning of the statute. The loader was inoperable and needed major repairs. The mechanic's estimate of $720 did not include the cost of disassembling the transmission nor the repair of any internal damage. From the time he purchased the loader, the buyer has been unable to use it. . . .

The seller also argues that the buyer accepted the goods when the nonconformity could reasonably have been discovered prior to acceptance. . . . [T]o be entitled to revocation under the UCC, the buyer must show that his acceptance of the goods without discovery of the nonconformity was either due to the difficulty of discovering the defect or induced by the assurances of the seller. . . . A buyer need only prove one of these factors. . . .

Courts have generally concluded that unless a defect is reasonably apparent or the buyer has some special expertise, a buyer who has made a reasonable inspection of goods and failed to find the defect has satisfied the "difficulty of discovery" test. . . . Here, both parties testified that the buyer visually inspected the equipment prior to purchasing it. The buyer noted that the machine had been freshly painted, the undercarriage was in good condition, and the engine ran well. It was not until the machine stopped running, and the buyer removed the seats, floorboard, and belly pan that the defects were discovered. We believe there was sufficient evidence to carry the question to the jury.

It is also clear that this is not a case where the buyer purchased the goods after disclosure by the seller of the defects. Where this occurs, or where the defects were sufficiently obvious that the buyer is charged with knowledge of them, he is foreclosed from revoking his prior acceptance of the goods. . . .

[Judgment affirmed.]

Buyers' Remedies

Buyers' Remedies in General

Section 2–711 lists the remedies available to an injured buyer in four situations: (1) when the buyer rightfully rejects the goods, (2) when the buyer justifiably revokes acceptance, (3) when the seller fails to deliver, and (4) when the seller repudiates the contract. Note that in all of these situations, the buyer either never received the goods or justifiably returned them to the seller. If nonconforming goods are delivered and the buyer elects to accept them anyway, damages are nevertheless recoverable for breach of warranty under §2–714, the type of breach covered in the next chapter. The manner of determining damages therefore differs depending upon whether the goods have been accepted (§2–714) or not (§2–711).

Assuming the case falls into one of the four situations listed above, the buyer has various rights, outlined below.

Cancellation and Recovery of Amount Paid. The buyer may cancel the contract. **Cancellation** occurs when either party puts an end to the contract because of breach by the other. Cancellation discharges all obliga-

tions still executory on both sides. However, the canceling party retains all remedies available for breach relating both to prior and future performance.[8] In addition to being relieved of any further obligation to pay the price, the buyer may recover whatever amounts it already has paid on the price.

Recovery of Damages. Whether or not the contract is canceled, the buyer is entitled to recover damages in addition to prior payments on the price. Section 2–712 is used to determine damages when the buyer covers, that is, acquires substitute goods from another seller. Section 2–713 governs cases when the buyer does not cover. Both of these provisions are discussed below.

Recovery of Identified Goods or Specific Performance. If the goods have been identified to the contract, and the seller fails to deliver or repudiates, the buyer may recover them from the seller in certain limited circumstances. Additionally, as discussed in Chapter 15 specific performance may be awarded if the goods are unique or in other proper circumstances.

Recovery of Damages

When the seller breaches, the buyer may elect to pursue the remedy at law: an award of money damages.

Cover. Under §2–712(1), after breach the buyer may cover by purchasing or contracting to purchase goods to substitute for those due from the seller, if the buyer acts in good faith and without unreasonable delay. Cover is a primary means used by buyers in sales contracts to mitigate damages after breach. Therefore, although the buyer is not required to cover,[9] failure to do so may prevent the buyer from recovering damages that could have been avoided by cover. Further, as stated in §2–715(2)(a), a buyer may only recover for consequential damage "which could not reasonably be prevented by cover or otherwise." Additionally, inability to cover is a strong factor to be considered in determining whether or not specific performance should be granted

---

[8]UCC §§2–106(3), (4).
[9]UCC §2–712(3). The buyer may choose to sue for damages for non-delivery under §2–713 discussed below.

to the buyer. In short, it is usually in the buyer's best interest to make a good faith attempt to cover.[10]

Under §2−712(2), a buyer who covers is entitled to recover from the seller

> the difference between the cover price and the contract price, *plus* incidental damages, *plus* consequential damages *minus* expenses saved as a consequence of the seller's breach.

Buyer's **incidental damages** stated in §2−715(1) include (1) expenses incurred in inspection, receipt, transportation, and care of rightfully rejected goods, (2) expenses and commissions incurred in effecting cover, and (3) any other reasonable expenses incident to the breach. Consequential damages are available under the *Hadley v. Baxendale* foreseeability test discussed in Chapter 15.[11] Assume Bates, Inc. contracts to purchase steel from Steelco for $10,000 to be used in Bates's manufacturing process. Steelco breaches the contract by failing to deliver and Bates immediately acquires substitute steel from MacGregor for $12,000. Because Bates was able to cover, it suffered no disruption in its manufacturing process and therefore lost no profits. Bates did, however, pay Smith a $200 commission for arranging the contract with MacGregor. Bates is entitled to recover $2,200 from Steelco in damages: the cover price ($12,000) less the contract price ($10,000) plus incidental damages ($200). Had Bates's production process been interrupted as a result of Steelco's breach, lost profits may be recoverable as consequential damages if they were foreseeable.

Damages in Absence of Cover. If the buyer does not cover, damages for nondelivery or repudiation are computed under §2−713(1), which awards the buyer

> the difference between the market price at the time the buyer learned of the breach and the contract price *plus* incidental damages *plus* consequential damages *minus* expenses saved as a consequence of the seller's breach.

Under §2−713(2), "market price" is determined at the *place for tender.* In cases of rejection after arrival or revocation of acceptance, however, market price is determined at the *place of arrival.* Thus, damages are measured according to the price prevailing at the time and in the place at which the buyer would have covered had it chosen to do so.

The UCC, in §§2−723 and 2−724, adopts a liberal approach to determine market price. For example, if evidence of the price at a given time is unavailable, the court may use the prevailing price existing within any reasonable time before or after that time. If the price at a certain place is unavailable, a commercially reasonable substitute place may be used allowing, however, for the cost of transportation between the two places. Additionally, the court may use market price quotations contained in official publications, trade journals, newspapers, or periodicals to show market price of goods traded in any established market.

The §2−713(1) formula protects the buyer who does not become aware of the seller's breach immediately upon tender. That is, the market price is measured on the date the buyer learned of the breach, which may be long after the seller's tender of nonconforming goods or outright failure to deliver. For example, the goods may be tendered to the distant buyer under an "F.O.B. shipping point" contract in which tender occurs on delivery to the carrier. In this case, the buyer is not jeopardized if the market price rises between the date of the breach and the date he learns of it, because damages are measured at the later date.

Under §2−713(1), market price is determined when the "buyer learned of the breach" both in nondelivery and anticipatory repudiation cases. In repudiation cases, courts generally interpret this language to mean that market price is to be computed at a reasonable time after the buyer learned of the repudiation, but not later than the time for tender of delivery under the contract. What is a "reasonable time" depends in part upon whether the buyer is able to mitigate damages by cover. Under this rule, if the buyer attempts, but is unable to cover, market price is measured at the contract's original delivery date. If the buyer is able to cover, but unreasonably fails to do so, damages are measured at the time the buyer should have covered.

Recovery of Identified Goods

Occasionally, the seller will breach by failing to deliver goods that have been *identified* to the contract. The Code allows the buyer to recover such goods from the seller in two situations.

---

[10]The buyer's right to replevy identified goods from the seller, discussed later in this chapter, also is dependent upon the buyer's inability to cover. Mitigation, consequential damages, and specific performance are covered in Chapter 15.

[11]UCC §2−715(2)(a).

Replevin. Under §2–716(3), if the goods are identified, the buyer may replevy (recover possession of) them from the seller if the buyer is unable to cover or circumstances indicate that an effort to cover will be unavailing. **Replevin** is a legal remedy whereby a person entitled to possession of goods recovers them from a person who has wrongfully either taken or detained them. Assume Birch is a maker of high quality custom furniture. Birch contracts with Sawyer, a sawmill operator, to purchase 25 oak logs that Birch personally selected from Sawyer's inventory. Before the delivery date, however, the market price of oak skyrocketed due to a severe shortage of the wood. As a result, Sawyer refused to deliver the logs at the contract price. In this case, because the goods are identified to the contract and efforts to cover would be futile, Birch may replevy the logs from Sawyer under §2–716(3). Note that replevin is the buyer's equivalent to the seller's action for the purchase price discussed later in this chapter.

When used as a contract remedy to recover *identified* goods, replevin under §2–716(3) effectively orders specific performance in favor of the injured buyer. If unable to cover when the goods have *not* been identified, the buyer has a very strong case for specific performance under §2–716(1), discussed in Chapter 15. Nevertheless, because specific performance is an equitable remedy, granted only in the discretion of the court, the buyer has no *right* to the goods under these circumstances. The replevin remedy (a legal remedy) gives the buyer a *right* to the goods. The buyer who is unable to cover therefore receives somewhat greater protection if the goods are identified.

Recovery from an Insolvent Seller. A buyer also may recover identified goods from an insolvent seller in certain limited circumstances. Under §2–502(1) if (1) identified goods are in the possession of the seller, and (2) the buyer has paid all or part of the purchase price, the buyer may recover the goods from the seller by tendering any unpaid portion of the price if: (1) the seller becomes insolvent within ten days after receipt of the first installment on the price, or (2) the contract involves consumer goods, and the seller repudiates or fails to deliver as required by the contract. Although §2–402(1) provides that unsecured creditors of the seller take subject to the buyer's rights to recover the goods under both §§2–716(3) and 2–502(1), neither section provides much protection to the buyer if the seller is bankrupt. In this case, the buyer's claim often is subordinated to the rights of the seller's other creditors.

Sellers' Remedies

A buyer may breach the contract (1) by repudiating it before the seller's performance is due, (2) by failing to pay the purchase price of goods delivered, (3) by wrongfully rejecting conforming goods, or (4) by wrongfully revoking a previous acceptance of conforming goods. In these cases, the UCC gives the seller a wide range of remedies (listed in §2–703) including the right to withhold further delivery of goods and cancel the contract. Note that these remedies often differ depending upon the existence and location of the goods. For example, a buyer may breach (1) before delivery while the seller still possesses the goods, or (2) after they have been delivered and are in the buyer's possession, or (3) before either party possesses the goods because they have not yet been procured or manufactured by the seller, or (4) while the goods are in transit (for example, in possession of a carrier such as a railroad or trucking company) from the seller to the buyer. Specific sellers' remedies in these various situations are discussed below.

Sellers' Damages with Resale—§2–706

Upon repudiation, breach, or insolvency of the buyer, the seller in possession of the goods has the right to resell them to another buyer. Resale is the seller's equivalent to the buyer's remedy of "cover." If the seller resells in the manner discussed below, the seller may recover, under §2–706(1),

> the difference between the resale price and the contract price *plus* incidental damages (§2–710) *minus* expenses saved as a consequence of the buyer's breach.

Seller's incidental damages include any commercially reasonable charges incurred in connection with (1) stopping delivery, (2) transportation, care, and custody of the goods after the buyer's breach, (3) return or resale of the goods or otherwise resulting from the breach. As discussed in Chapter 15, a seller is not entitled to recover consequential damages, because the buyer's breach almost always involved a failure to pay the price. A failure to pay money generally is recognized as insufficient grounds to support a consequential damage award even when injury to the creditor is foreseeable. For example, assume Simpson contracts to sell her living room furniture to Frost for $2,500. Frost repudiates the contract and Simpson resells the furniture to Green for $2,200, but only after spending $15 to place a classified advertisement offering the furniture for sale. Simpson's damages are $315—the difference between the resale price and the contract price ($300) plus incidental damages ($15).

Unidentified or Unfinished Goods—§2–704. When the buyer breaches, the seller may be in possession of conforming goods not yet identified to the contract. In this case, §2–704 authorizes the seller to identify them as the goods intended for the breached contract for the purposes of resale. If the goods are unfinished at the time of the breach, the seller may "in the exercise of reasonable commercial judgment for the purposes of avoiding loss" either (1) complete manufacture and wholly identify the goods to the contract, or (2) cease manufacture and resell for scrap or salvage value. Note that ordinarily mitigation principles require that an injured party suspend performance after breach to avoid further expenditure and thus further loss. Under the UCC, however, the seller is protected by acting reasonably in completing unfinished goods even if it later appears that it could better have avoided loss by stopping manufacture. The burden is upon the buyer to prove that the seller was acting in a commercially unreasonable manner in completing manufacture. By completing manufacture (or by identifying previously unidentified goods), the seller makes the goods available for resale, and if resold, damages are computed under the formula of §2–706 discussed above.

Manner of Resale. In reselling the goods, §2–706 requires the seller to act in good faith and in a commercially reasonable manner to realize as high a price as possible under the circumstances. The resale may be made in a public (auction) or private (by solicitation and negotiation either directly or through a broker) manner. The seller is not accountable to the buyer for any profit made on resale. If resale is made privately, the seller must simply give reasonable notification to the buyer of the intent to resell. If resale is by public auction, however, the seller must reasonably notify the buyer of the time and place of the public sale unless the goods are perishable or threaten to decline speedily in value. This notice enables the buyer to bid at the sale or secure the attendance of other bidders. The seller also may bid at the auction. This right benefits the buyer because it tends to increase the resale price, thus reducing the seller's damages.

The time and place of the resale is governed by standards of "commercial reasonableness." Generally, the time for resale is a reasonable time after the buyer's breach. What is reasonable depends upon all the circumstances of the case including the nature of the goods and the condition of the market. Similarly, the place of resale is flexible so that the seller can dispose of the goods to maximum advantage. A public sale must be made at a usual place or market for such sales if one is reasonably available. The place or market must be one that prospective bidders may reasonably be expected to attend. A market may be "reasonably available" even if the goods must be shipped a considerable distance. The cost of transporting the goods may be recovered from the buyer as part of the seller's incidental damage. The buyer may benefit, however, because the goods are sold where a market for them exists, possibly resulting in a higher resale price.

Sellers' Damages Without Resale—§2–708(1)

When the buyer breaches a sales contract, resale is not always an appropriate remedy. For example, if the breach is by repudiation (as opposed to wrongful rejection or revocation of acceptance), the seller may not yet have acquired or manufactured the goods. In this situation, damages are generally determined under §2–708(1). Under this provision, the seller is entitled to recover

> the difference between the market price at the time and place for tender and the unpaid contract price *plus* incidental damages *minus* expenses saved in consequence of the buyer's breach.

Market price may be proven according to the liberal evidentiary standards discussed in the buyers' remedies material.

Lost Profits—An Alternative Measure of Damages—§2–708(2)

Frequently, the measures of damages discussed above are inadequate to place the injured seller in the same position as full performance. In this case, the Code allows the seller, as an alternative measure, to recover under §2–708(2)

> the *profit* (including reasonable overhead) which the seller would have made from full performance by the buyer *plus*

incidental damages *plus* costs reasonably incurred by the seller in manufacture or procurement *minus* payments made by the buyer and proceeds of resale of the goods.

This formula is designed to compensate the seller primarily in two situations: (1) the so-called lost volume case, and (2) when the seller is to manufacture, assemble, or acquire goods for the buyer, but prior to their manufacture or acquisition the buyer breaches.

The Lost Volume Seller. Many businesses sell standardized products or products in essentially unlimited supply. The inadequacy of the basic measure of damages when the buyer breaches a contract for sale of these goods is illustrated by the following example. Silco, a seller of widgets, has an inventory of 1,000 widgets and the ability to produce more if justified by the demand. Silco contracts with Beta for the sale of ten widgets at a total price of $1,000. Silco's profit on the sale (including reasonable overhead) is 20 percent of the purchase price, or $200. Beta subsequently breaches the contract, and Silco immediately resells the widgets to Miller for $1,000. In this case, the seller's basic remedy after resale (§2–706) would leave the seller uncompensated because the difference between the contract price and the resale price is zero.[12] Similarly, the difference between the contract price and the market price (§2–708(1)) also is zero. In this situation, therefore, damages under §2–708(2) are appropriate.

Note that in this case Miller didn't buy the ten widgets because of Beta's breach. Miller would have purchased them whether or not Beta had breached. Thus, assume that Silco *actually* sold 500 widgets for the year, including the sale to Miller. But for Beta's breach, Silco *would have* sold 510 units, not 500. Silco is known as a **lost volume seller**—one who but for the buyer's breach would have had the benefit of *both* the original contract and the resale contract. As such, the proper measure of seller's damage in this case is the lost profit on the sale of ten units, $200.

Breach Before or During Manufacture. As indicated above, §2–708(2) allows lost profits to be recovered

together with any incidental damages provided in this article (§2–710), *due allowance for costs reasonably incurred and due credit for payments or proceeds of resale.* (Emphasis added.)

If interpreted literally, this language would deny recovery to the lost volume seller in exactly the situation §2–708(2) is designed to cover. That is, using the above example, Silco would recover lost profits, $200, plus "costs reasonably incurred," $800 (the cost of manufacture), minus "proceeds of resale," $1,000, or nothing. This result is avoided, however, because the cases, commentators, and legislative history of the UCC all indicate that the italicized language quoted earlier is not meant to apply to the volume seller situation; that is, damages as indicated in the preceding paragraph are appropriate. It is intended instead to apply to the situation discussed below in which the seller discovers the buyer's breach while in the process of manufacturing the goods. This language allows the injured seller to recoup expenditures made on the buyer's behalf (which now prove to be worthless to the seller and cannot be allocated to other contracts) and to realize by resale the junk or salvage value of the unfinished goods or their components, giving credit to the buyer for the proceeds of the salvage.

The application of §2–708(2) to this second situation is illustrated by the following example. Carol Corporation contracts to design and build a machine for Ezra Corporation for $20,000 to be used in Ezra's manufacturing process. Because it is specially designed, the machine when completed will have no resale value (other than for scrap) on the open market. Carol's price is calculated to include a $2,500 profit. After Carol expends $3,000 on engineering and $2,000 to acquire various component parts, Ezra repudiates the contract. Because resale of the finished machine would be impractical, Carol ceases manufacture. Neither the engineering expenses nor the acquired parts can be applied to any of Carol's other contracts. However, Carol realizes $1,000 upon resale of the component parts for scrap, but must pay Janet, a broker, a $50 commission to effect the salvage.

On these facts, damages under §§2–706 and 2–708(1) are inappropriate because Carol has no finished goods on hand to resell, or upon which to base a market price calculation. Additionally, unless it expends substantial additional sums to complete—certainly a risky alternative which a later court may intepret as a failure to mitigate damages—an action for the

---

[12]If it had been unable to resell, Silco may be entitled to the entire purchase price under §2–709 as discussed in the following subsection.

purchase price under §2–709, discussed in the following subsection, would be unavailable. Further, Carol has lost the profit it otherwise would have earned on the sale to Ezra. In this situation, therefore, damages computed under §2–708(2) are appropriate. Carol should therefore be entitled to lost profit ($2,500) plus incidental damage (the $50 sales commission) plus costs reasonably incurred on the buyer's behalf ($5,000) minus the proceeds of the sale of the components for scrap ($1,000), or $6,550.

Note that recovery under §2–708(2) is not limited to manufacturers or assemblers, but is also available to a so-called jobber, a middleman who acquires the goods from a third party and sells them to the buyer. Assume, for example, that the buyer breaches before the jobber acquires the goods, and, because of the breach, the jobber does not obtain them. Because neither the jobber nor the buyer has the goods, both resale and an action for the purchase price are inappropriate. In such cases, the jobber's lost profit on the sale is the most accurate measure of damages.

The following case illustrates the operation of §2–708(2) and its relationship to §§2–706 and 2–708(1).

National Controls, Inc. v. Commodore Business Machines, Inc.

209 Cal. Rptr. 636 (Cal. App. 1985)

Plaintiff National Controls, Inc. (NCI), a manufacturer of electronic weighing and measuring devices, manufactures and sells the model 3221 electronic microprocessor scale, which is designed to interface with cash registers for use at checkout stands. NCI does not maintain an inventory of the 3221 scales but builds them to order to meet specifications required by different cash registers. In 1981, defendant Commodore Business Machines ordered 900 of the 3221 scales with delivery to be made in four shipments over a four-month period. After accepting delivery of 50 scales, Commodore refused to accept or pay for the remaining 850. NCI then sold the 850 scales to another customer, National Semiconductor.

NCI sued Commodore for breach of contract and the trial court ruled in favor of NCI. The trial court found that NCI was a "lost volume seller" and awarded damages of $280,000, the net profit NCI would have realized had Commodore fully performed the contract. Commodore appealed.

Scott, Associate Justice

. . . Damages caused by a buyer's breach or repudiation of a sales contract are usually measured by the difference between the resale price of the goods and the contract price, as provided by Uniform Commercial Code section 2–706. When it is not appropriate to use this difference to measure the seller's loss (as when the goods have not been resold in a commercially reasonable manner), the seller's measure of damages is the difference between the market and the contract prices as provided in [UCC §2–708(1)]. Ordinarily, this measure will result in recovery equal to the value of the seller's bargain. However, under certain circumstances this formula is also not an adequate means to ascertain that value, and the seller may recover his loss of expected profits on the contract under [UCC §2–708(2)]. . . .

When buyers have repudiated a fixed price contract to purchase goods, several courts elsewhere have construed [UCC §2–708(2)] or its state counterpart to permit the award of lost profits under the contract to the seller who establishes that he is a "lost volume seller," i.e., one who proves that even though he resold the contract goods, that sale to the third party would have been made regardless of the buyer's breach. . . .

In this case, the evidence was undisputed that in 1980 and 1981, NCI's manufacturing plant was operating at approximately 40 percent capacity. The production of the 900 units did not tax that capacity, and the plant could have more than doubled its output of 3221s and still have stayed within its capacity. That evidence was sufficient to support the court's findings that NCI had the capacity to supply both Commodore and National Semiconductor, and that had there been no breach by Commodore, NCI would have had the benefit of both the original contract and the resale contract. Accordingly, the trial court correctly determined that NCI was a lost volume seller, that the usual "contract price minus market price" rule set forth in [UCC §2–708(1)] was inadequate to put NCI in as good a position as performance would have done, and that NCI was therefore entitled to its lost profits on the contract with Commodore. . . .

[Judgment affirmed.]

Sellers' Recovery of the Purchase Price—§2–709

The preceding sellers' remedies award damages based upon the difference between the contract price and the resale or market price, or upon the seller's lost profit. In three limited situations, stated in §2–709, the seller may recover the entire *purchase price* of the goods from the buyer. If the buyer fails to pay the price as it comes due, the seller is entitled to recover (together with incidental damages under §2–710) the price when

1. the goods have been accepted by the buyer, or
2. the goods have been identified to the contract and the seller cannot resell them, or
3. the goods have been damaged or destroyed after risk of loss has passed to the buyer.

These are the only situations in which an action for the price lies.

The thrust of the preceding rules is that the seller generally may recover the price of accepted goods (or when risk of loss has passed to the buyer) but may not recover the price of unaccepted goods unless resale is impracticable due, for example, to market conditions, obsolescence, or because the goods are specially manufactured for the buyer. Thus, unless accepted or destroyed, the burden of disposing of the goods rests on the seller, who is normally in a better position than the buyer to resell because it is in the business of selling goods of that kind. On resale the seller is then entitled to recover damages under §§2–706 or 2–708 as previously discussed.

Sellers' Remedies on Discovery of Buyer's Insolvency

A seller who discovers its buyer to be insolvent has several remedies under §§2–702 and 2–705 of the UCC.

Stopping Delivery. Assuming the buyer has not yet taken possession, §2–702(1) allows a seller who learns of the buyer's insolvency to

1. refuse delivery except for cash, including payment for prior deliveries, and

2. stop delivery of goods in the hands of a carrier or other bailee.[13]

Under §2–705, a seller is entitled to stop delivery of goods in the hands of a carrier or other bailee, such as a warehouseman, not only when the buyer is insolvent, but also when the buyer has repudiated or has failed to make a payment due before delivery. However, because stopping delivery is a burden on the carrier, the right to stop delivery for reasons *other than insolvency* is limited to large shipments (for example, carload, truckload, planeload, or larger). To stop delivery, the seller must notify the bailee in such a manner to enable it, in the exercise of reasonable diligence, to prevent delivery of the goods. After notification, the bailee must hold and dispose of the goods according to the seller's directions. If a negotiable document of title covers the goods, the bailee need not obey a notification to stop until surrender of the document. If the seller's action in stopping delivery is unjustified, the seller must indemnify the bailee for any ensuing charges or damages. The seller's right to stop delivery ends when the buyer takes physical possession of the goods, or a negotiable document of title covering the goods is negotiated to the buyer, or the bailee acknowledges to the buyer that it holds the goods for the buyer.

Reclamation from an Insolvent Buyer—§2–702(2). Once the buyer has taken possession of the goods, the seller may reclaim them only in the limited circumstances outlined in §2–702(2). Under this provision, a seller who discovers that the buyer has received goods on credit while insolvent may reclaim the goods by making a demand for their return within ten days after the goods are received by the buyer. The ten-day limit does not apply, however, if the buyer has made a written misrepresentation of solvency to the particular seller seeking to reclaim the goods within three months prior to the delivery. A successful reclamation under this rule bars the seller from recovering any other remedy with respect to them. The rationale for allowing recovery from the insolvent credit buyer is that "any receipt on credit by an insolvent buyer amounts to a tacit business misrepresentation of solvency and therefore is fraudulent as against the particular seller."[14]

---

[13]Section 252 of the *Restatement (Second) of Contracts* adopts a rule analogous to §2–702(1) that applies to common law contracts.

[14]UCC §2–702, Official Comment 2.

Because the buyer receives the goods while insolvent, the seller's right to reclaim often is challenged by the buyer's trustee in bankruptcy, who represents the buyer's general unsecured creditors and who may seek the goods to satisfy the claims of all creditors. The rights of the reclaiming seller as against the trustee in bankruptcy are governed by §546(c) of the Bankruptcy Code, under which the trustee must honor the seller's right to reclaim if the seller sold the goods in the ordinary course of its business to a buyer, who received them while insolvent within 45 days before the bankruptcy filing. To use this provision, the seller must make a written reclamation demand on the buyer (1) within 45 days after the buyer received the goods, or (2) within 20 days after the bankruptcy petition is filed, if the 45 day period expires after that filing. If the seller fails to meet this requirement, its claim for the purchase price is nevertheless entitled to priority as an administrative expense in the debtor's bankruptcy.

Statute of Limitations—§2–725

Section 2–725 is the statute of limitations applicable to contracts for the sale of goods. Generally, an action for breach of a sales contract must be commenced within four years after the cause of action arises. The parties may by agreement reduce the limitation period to not less than one year, but may not contractually extend it. By adopting a uniform statute of limitations, the UCC avoids possible conflicting limitation periods applicable to interstate transactions in goods. Further, because most business retain business records at least four years, the Code statute increases the likelihood that relevant documentary and other evidence will be available to resolve the claim.

Under §2–725(2) the statute of limitations begins to run when the breach occurs, whether or not the aggrieved party knows of its occurrence. In general, a breach of warranty (discussed in the next chapter) occurs upon the seller's tender of delivery, unless the warranty explicitly extends to future performance of the goods and discovery of any breach must await the time of that performance. For example, the seller may warrant its product "for life," or for "5 years or 50,000 miles, whichever comes first." In this situation, the statute begins to run when the breach is or should be discovered.

In the following case, the court was required to determine when "tender of delivery" occurred in a breach of warranty case.

Flagg Energy Development Corporation v. General Motors Corporation
709 A.2d 1075 (Conn. 1998)

Plaintiffs Flagg Energy Development Corporation and CCF-1, Inc. hired plaintiff Process Construction Services, Inc. (PCS), to construct a power plant in Hartford, Connecticut. As part of the project, PCS contracted to purchase two gas turbine generator assemblies from Sulzer Turbosystems, Inc. The assemblies included engines manufactured by defendant General Motors Corporation. The contract required Sulzer to deliver the engines to plaintiffs' construction site, to install the engines, and to perform "check-out, start-up, and preliminary acceptance testing." CCF-1 was required to pay Sulzer "30 days after satisfactory completion of the preliminary acceptance test, but not more than 60 days from date of delivery." Under the contract, Sulzer provided both express and implied warranties. After delivering the engines to the construction site on May 27 and June 23, 1988, Sulzer completed installation on July 26, 1988. The preliminary acceptance testing was performed on November 11, 1988. With plaintiffs' consent, Sulzer delegated its responsibilities under the contract to General Motors Corporation. Sometime before 1990, plaintiffs notified General Motors that the engines were not performing properly. Despite efforts to resolve the problems, the plaintiffs remained dissatisfied with the engines. On October 26, 1992, plaintiffs filed a lawsuit against defendant General Motors, alleging breach of warranties. The trial court ruled that the plaintiffs' breach of warranty claims were subject to a four-year statute of limitations that expired on June 23, 1992. The trial court granted summary judgment to the defendant and the plaintiffs appealed.

Peters, Associate Justice

. . . The principal issue in this case is the applicability of [UCC §2–725] to a contract for the sale of goods in which the seller agrees not only to deliver the goods but also to perform testing of the goods at the buyer's work site. . . .

[Plaintiffs] claim that, under the terms of their purchase agreement, their breach of warranty claims were filed properly within the four-year limitation period contained in [UCC §2–725]. . . . The parties agree that §2–725 contains the applicable statute of limitations. They disagree about the proper construction of subdivision (2) of that statute, which provides that a breach of warranty occurs when tender of delivery is made. . . .

The plaintiffs argue that, under article 2 of the Uniform Commercial Code, the testing obligations contained in the 1987 purchase agreement postponed the date of accrual of their cause of action, from the date of the physical delivery of the second engine in June, 1988, until the date of completion of the contemplated testing in November, 1988. . . .

It is indisputable that [UCC §2–503 (1) states that the time for tender is] "determined by the agreement and this article. . . . " Textually, that language does not address what constitutes a "tender of delivery." Nowhere else does the statutory text of article 2 of the Uniform Commercial Code contain an express definition of the phrase.

The closer statutory rule may be found in the definitions of "tender of delivery" contained in the official comment 1 to [UCC §2–503]. The language of the comment does not support the plaintiffs' position. One definition describes "tender" as "an offer coupled with a present ability to fulfill all the [contractual] conditions . . . [which] must be *followed* by actual performance. . . . " (Emphasis added.). . . . The other definition describes "tender" as "an offer of goods . . . under a contract *as if* in fulfillment of [contractual] conditions. . . . " (Emphasis added.) The meaning of this "as if" proposition is clarified in the immediately suc-ceeding sentence, which defines "tender," in all cases, as "such performance by the tendering party as puts the other party in default if he fails to proceed in some manner." Under the Uniform Commercial Code, the defendant's physical delivery of the engines required the plaintiffs, on pain of default [UCC §2–703] to take some action, either by rejecting their tender [UCC §2–602] or by paying the contract price to the defendant upon their acceptance. [UCC §2–607. Section 2–606(1)] expressly ties "a reasonable opportunity to inspect the goods" to "acceptance" rather than to "tender of delivery." Accordingly, the relevant statutory provisions in article 2 of the Uniform Commercial Code do not, by themselves, make performance of the defendant's on-site testing obligations a condition of a tender of delivery.

Our conclusion that there is a statutory distinction between preacceptance testing and tender of delivery is supported by holdings of courts in other jurisdictions. Many courts have held that contractual provisions for postdelivery testing or inspection do not delay the accrual of breach of warranty claims. . . .

[Judgment affirmed.]

Summary

1.   The UCC contains a variety of remedies available to both buyers and sellers for breach of sales contracts. These remedies are liberally administered to place the injured party in as good a position as if the other party had fully performed. Consistent with basic Code policy, the parties may contractually provide for remedies in addition to or in lieu of those contained in Article 2.

2.   Under the perfect tender rule, if the goods tendered by the seller fail in any respect to conform to the contract, the buyer may accept all of them, reject all of them, or accept some and reject the rest. An effective rejection requires that the buyer reject within a reasonable time and promptly notify the seller. After rejection by the buyer, the seller may be afforded an opportunity to cure or correct the defective performance, thus restricting the buyer's right to reject for minor defects, and often relieving the seller from the harsh effect of the perfect tender rule.

3.   A buyer who fails to make an adequate rejection, or indicates that it will take the goods, or does an act inconsistent with a claim of rejection, accepts the goods. Generally the buyer must pay at the contract rate for goods accepted, but is entitled to damages for defects in the goods. A buyer who has accepted may, however, revoke a previous acceptance under very limited circumstances if their nonconformity substantially impairs their value.

4.   Upon rejection or revocation of acceptance by the buyer, or upon the seller's repudiation or failure to deliver, the buyer is entitled to cancel the contract and recover amounts already paid on the price. The buyer also is entitled to recover damages based either upon the difference between the contract price and the market price, or the contract price and the "cover" price—the price at which the buyer acquires goods in substitution for those due from the seller. The buyer also may obtain specific performance in appropriate cases and may recover identified goods from a breaching seller under limited circumstances.

5.   Seller's remedies correspond to those available to the buyer. After nonacceptance or repudiation by the buyer, the

seller may recover the difference between the market price and the contract price, or if the seller resells, the difference between the resale price and the contract price. If the market price or resale remedy is inadequate to place the seller in as good a position as full performance, then the seller is entitled to recover the profit that it would have made from full performance. The lost profit remedy is primarily appropriate when the seller is a "lost volume" seller, and when a seller ceases manufacture of, or attempts to acquire, goods after repudiation by the buyer. In lieu of the foregoing remedies, the seller may recover the entire purchase price of goods accepted by the buyer, of goods destroyed after risk of loss has passed to the buyer, and of identified goods that the seller is unable to resell. Finally, the Code provides various remedies to a seller upon discovery of his buyer's insolvency.

6.   Article 2 generally requires that an action for breach of a sales contract be commenced within four years after the breach occurs.

Key Terms

rejection	cover
cure	incidental damages
acceptance	replevin
revocation of acceptance	lost volume seller
cancellation	

Questions and Problems

18.1   Under what circumstances does a buyer "accept" a tender of goods under Article 2 of the UCC? What are the legal consequences of "acceptance"?

18.2   Reliable Electronics has contracted to purchase 10,000 computer chips from Samson Electronics for use in Reliable's electronic calculators. The contract calls for delivery to Reliable's warehouse by June 1, 2004, with payment of the $20,000 purchase price to follow 30 days thereafter. The contract provides that defective chips may not exceed more than 0.001 of the total shipped. Because of the explicit provisions of the contract and past dealing of the parties, Samson knows that a higher defect percentage will not be tolerated, and that significant defects will cause a disruption of Reliable's assembly operation, which is currently running at full capacity.

(a) Assume the chips are delivered as agreed on June 1, 2004; what should Reliable do? If the goods are found to be nonconforming and Reliable decides to reject them, what should Reliable do? If the goods are nonconforming should Samson be given an opportunity to cure its defective performance? What obligations does Reliable have regarding the rightfully rejected goods in its possession?

(b) Assume that the chips are delivered as agreed and pass preliminary testing. Reliable places them in its raw materials inventory and pays the purchase price. Samson, however, had improperly engineered the chips, rendering them incapable of performing an important

calculating function called for by the contract. This defect could not be detected until the chip was incorporated into the calculator. As a result, the defect was not discovered until assembly of calculators utilizing the chips began August 1, 2004. What recourse, if any, does Reliable have against Samson?

(c) Assume the chips delivered do not conform to the contract or that Samson simply fails to deliver as agreed. List the basic remedial options available to Reliable under the UCC.

(d) Assume that Samson utterly fails to deliver the chips, citing increased cost. Reliable is notified of this fact shortly before June 1, 2004, the contract delivery date. As Samson knew, the 10,000 chips were to be incorporated into a shipment of calculators being specially manufactured for Sears, Roebuck & Co. The delivery date of the Sears contract is August 1, 2004. Time is of the essence under the Sears contract because the calculators are being offered as part of Sears "back to school" sale. Reliable expects to make a $20,000 profit on the Sears contract.

(1) Assume that substitute chips are available on the market for $4 each, which could be delivered in time to perform the Sears contract. Reliable must, however, incur a $500 brokerage fee and $1,000 in added shipping expenses. How much should Reliable recover from Samson for breach of contract if it buys the substitute chips? What should it recover if it elects not to cover and as a result breaches the contract with Sears?

(2) Assume that substitute chips are not otherwise available. Samson has the chips in its possession destined for the Reliable contract. What should Reliable do? Assume alternatively that Samson has not manufactured the chips but has the ability to do so in time to enable Reliable to perform the Sears contract? What should Reliable do? Assume alternatively that Samson neither has the goods nor can it manufacture them. As a result Reliable breaches its contract with Sears. How much should Reliable recover in its subsequent breach of contract action against Samson?

18.3   Sam owns a store that sells antique furniture, as well as custom-made and stock cabinets. Doaks enters the store and indicates his interest in an antique brass bed Sam has in stock. The piece is extremely rare and after some dickering the parties agree to a price of $2,000. The bed originally cost Sam $800. Prior to the date agreed upon for delivery, Doaks phoned Sam and indicated that he would not take the bed since he had found another one at a lower price. Sam sues Doaks for breach of contract.

How would Sam's damages be computed assuming alternatively:

(1) He resells the bed to Jones for $1,500, its fair market value.

(2) He resells to Jones for $2,500, its fair market value.

(3) He does not resell but instead uses the bed in his home. At the date agreed upon for delivery the bed was worth $1,500 on the market.

18.4 Beaumont contacted Sam concerning purchase of cabinets for an apartment complex Beaumont was building. Beaumont required 500 cabinets. Two hundred and fifty were standard bathroom cabinets, which Sam stocked and could be acquired in unlimited quantity from Standard Fixtures, Inc. Beaumont contracted to purchase these for $100 each. Sam paid Standard $75 for each cabinet. The remaining 250 cabinets were to be custom-made by Sam to fit the kitchens in the various apartments. Approximately 25 different sizes and styles of cabinets were involved. Sam quoted Beaumont a total price of $75,000 which included a $20,000 profit on the job. Sam acquired the raw materials for $20,000 and expended several months labor working on the cabinets. Two months before the delivery date, however, Beaumont called and indicated that financial problems had forced him to abandon the apartment project. Sam had not yet ordered the bathroom cabinets, but had completed one-third of the kitchen cabinets. They could not be resold because they had been custom built. Sam had not yet started to manufacture the remaining cabinets, and was able to resell the remaining raw lumber for $8,000. Sam sues Beaumont for breach of contract. How much should be recover? Cite relevant UCC provisions in formulating your answer.

18.5 S has sold iron rails to B for many years on open 30-day account. On June 15, S shipped $10,000 worth of rails to B (now located in B's warehouse); another $10,000 shipment was in transit via Red Ball Trucking Company on that date. B also owed an additional $5,000 for rails previously shipped, and already incorporated into B's products. B has had financial difficulty but provided a favorable financial statement to S on June 1, inducing S to make the last two $10,000 shipments. On June 21, while the second shipment was in transit, however, S discovered that the financial statement was false, and that B planned to declare bankruptcy on June 22. What should S do? Cite relevant UCC and Bankruptcy Code provisions.

18.6 Frank, a manufacturer of metal frames for motorcycles, ordered steel tubing from Karen. The tubing was delivered, accepted, and paid for by Frank. When Frank began to use the tubing, however, he discovered it was cracked and corroded. Frank wrote a letter to Karen revoking acceptance of the tubing and stating that he would hold it for 30 days, after which he would sell it applying the proceeds to offset the amount to be refunded by Karen. Karen refused to pick up the tubing or to refund Frank's money. Sixty days later, Frank removed the tubing from his warehouse because he needed the storage space, and because he feared the defective tubing might inadvertently enter his production process. Frank then scrapped the tubing because its resale value as steel scrap was minimal. Frank sued Karen seeking the purchase price of the tubing as damages. Karen argued that Frank's scrapping the tubing constituted acceptance of the goods. Should the court award the damages requested by Frank? Explain, citing any relevant Code provisions.

18.7 Robert Purdon sells Christmas trees at retail between Thanksgiving and Christmas. Sales usually build gradually and peak about one week before Christmas. According to standards of the U.S. Department of Agriculture (USDA), which are used in the trade, a "number one" tree is at least 66 inches tall and has three good sides without holes or gaps. Purdon ordered 3,000 number one grade trees from Martin Birkner, a grower of pine trees, with delivery to be made in five shipments beginning on November 24. When Purdon received the first shipment, he telephoned Birkner and questioned the quality of the trees. After Birkner provided assurances that the trees were number one quality, Purdon offered them and those received in later shipments for sale. Because Purdon was unable to sell many of the trees, he asked the USDA to inspect them and on December 20, the USDA reported that a large percentage of the trees failed to meet number one grade standards. The following day, after consulting with his attorney, Purdon sent Birkner a telegram revoking acceptance. Birkner sued for breach of contract and alleged that Purdon's revocation was not made within a reasonable time. How should the court rule? Explain.

18.8 Barb purchased a new automobile from Ed the Car Dealer. The car failed to operate properly and Barb revoked her acceptance of it. She then notified Ed that she would retain the automobile as security under UCC §2–711 and would store it until Ed returned the purchase price. Ed refused to return the purchase price so Barb sued him. The trial court ruled that the car was a "lemon" and that Barb was entitled to revoke acceptance. Barb testified that she incurred the following costs pursuant to the transaction:

Purchase price	$5,900
Storage costs (@ $30 per month)	780
Insurance on the stored automobile	250
Interest on loan (to finance the purchased car)	1,180
Cost to rent a replacement automobile (@ $150 per month)	3,900

Which of these costs is Barb entitled to recover as damages from Ed? Explain, citing appropriate Code provisions.

18.9 Acme Co. manufactures and sells "gadgets." Acme entered into a contract to sell 20,000 gadgets to Smith at $12 apiece. Because Acme's manufacturing plant was operating at full capacity Acme ordered the gadgets from Bento, a competitor, who agreed to sell the 20,000 gadgets to Acme at $8 each. After the cost of materials for gadgets suddenly increased, Bento notified Acme that it would be unable to supply the gadgets at the contract price. Acme solicited bids from other gadget manufacturers but concluded that it could manufacture the gadgets more cheaply than the current market price of $13. Therefore, Acme manufactured the gadgets at a cost of $11 each and thereby was able to fulfill its contractual obligations to Smith. Acme then sued Bento for breach of contract asserting that it had covered by buying the gadgets from itself rather than paying the market price. The court ruled in favor of Acme and awarded the following damages:

Actual damages (difference between the cover price of $11 and the contract price of $8 × 20,000 units)	$60,000
Potential profits (profits that Acme would have earned had it used its facilities to manufacture gadgets for other customers)	40,000
Lost profits on the Smith contract (difference between the profits of $4 apiece that Acme would have earned had Bento fulfilled the contract and the actual profits of $1 each × 20,000 units)	60,000
	$160,000

Bento has appealed.
  (a) Under the UCC, was Acme entitled to cover by manufacturing the gadgets itself? Explain.
  (b) Assuming that the trial court's ruling was correct, did the court properly compute the damages? Explain.

18.10 Malvern, Inc. needed two trailers to be used for shipping timber. After discussing its needs with Dane Trailer Sales Co., a trailer manufacturer, Malvern contracted to purchase two Dane trailers. The contract included a five-year warranty and the following provision: "Dane's sole obligation under this warranty shall be limited to repair or replacement, at its option, of the trailer." Dane delivered the trailers, but within several months, both trailers became unusable because a steel support broke. Dane welded the support but Malvern refused to use the repaired trailers because they did not meet safety standards. Dane then replaced both trailers but the steel supports in the new trailers also broke. Dane offered to repair the trailers by welding but Malvern refused and sued Dane seeking damages of $40,000. The damages included $15,000 to cover the difference between Dane's contract price and that of another manufacturer from whom Malvern bought new trailers and $25,000 in lost profits.
  (a) Dane asserts that Malvern's case should be dismissed because the contract limited its remedies to repair or replacement. Should the case be dismissed? Explain.
  (b) Assume the case was not dismissed and a jury found for Malvern. Is Malvern entitled to the damages it requested? Explain.

18.11 In 1968, Mr. and Mrs. Rosen purchased a painting for $15,000 from Ira Spanierman, the owner of an art gallery in New York. At the time of the sale, Spanierman told the Rosens that the work had been painted by John Singer Sargent, a well-known artist. Spanierman also provided an invoice that included the following warranty: "This picture is fully guaranteed by the Seller to be an original work by John Singer Sargent." In 2005, the Rosens decided to sell the painting and secured appraisals estimating the value to be about $200,000. After placing it for auction with an art dealer, however, the Rosens learned that the painting was a fake and had not been painted by Sargent. The Rosens sued Spanierman for breach of warranty. How should the court rule? Explain.

CHAPTER 19

THE SALES CONTRACT—WARRANTIES

Major Topics

- the definition of warranty
- how the various warranties contained in the Uniform Commercial Code are created, their content, and the methods by which they may be disclaimed
- the remedies available for breach of warranty
- the Magnuson-Moss Warranty Act, a federal statute governing written warranties in sales of consumer goods

The various buyers' remedies discussed in Chapter 18 impose liability upon a seller who fails to deliver the goods required by the contract, or who delivers defective goods that the buyer ultimately rejects. A buyer may, however, *accept* goods that do not conform to the contract. In this situation, the buyer may recover damages from the seller for breach of *warranty,* the subject of this chapter.

Introduction to Warranties

In its broadest sense, a **warranty** is a statement or other representation made by a seller of goods concerning the quality, character, or capabilities of the goods sold. If the goods fail to conform to the standards created by a warranty, the seller is liable in damages for breach of warranty. The warranty concept is therefore very expansive; it essentially defines the seller's obligation in a contract for the sale of goods.

Warranties may be created expressly by the language or other conduct of the seller, or may be implied—that is, imposed by law. Under the UCC, the implied warranties are merchantability and fitness for a particular purpose. In addition, the Code imposes a warranty of title and against infringement upon a seller.

Disclaimer of Warranty

Because freedom of contract is a fundamental principle of the UCC, the seller may, within certain limitations, undertake to contractually limit, modify, or exclude warranty liability. Although commonly used, such **warranty disclaimers** have great potential for unconscionable[1] application, particularly when the term is imposed upon a consumer buyer in a standardized form contract. The Code provisions allowing the seller to alter or eliminate warranty liability or to limit the buyer's remedy in the event of breach therefore also provide a significant amount of protection for the buyer.

---

[1]Unconscionability is discussed in detail in Chapter 10.

Additionally, at the federal level, the Magnuson-Moss Warranty Act imposes limitations on written warranty disclaimers in transactions involving consumer goods. Warranty disclaimers therefore invite close judicial scrutiny, regarding both compliance with relevant statutory provisions, and whether or not, in the circumstances of the case, enforcement of the disclaimer would be unconscionable.

The following material examines how the various warranties contained in the UCC are created and disclaimed, remedies for breach of warranty, and the Magnuson-Moss Warranty Act.

Express Warranties

Creation of Express Warranties—§2–313

Under §2–313 of the UCC, any *affirmation of fact or promise* made by the seller to the buyer that (1) relates to the goods, and (2) becomes part of the basis of the bargain, creates an **express warranty** that the goods will conform to the affirmation or promise. To create an express warranty, it is not necessary that the seller use the words "warrant," "warranty," or "guarantee." Nor is it necessary that the seller intend to create a warranty. Express warranties rest upon the dickered, or bargained-for, aspects of the bargain. The seller's affirmations of fact concerning the goods made during the bargaining process are part of the description of the goods. As stated in Official Comment 4 to §2–313, "[T]he whole purpose of the law of warranty is to determine what it is that the seller has in essence agreed to sell."

Express Warranty—Fact or Opinion. Ordinarily, express warranties are created by explicit oral or written statements made by the seller regarding the quality, character, or capabilities of the goods being sold. A major problem in this situation is to distinguish statements constituting mere "seller's talk" or "puffing" from those creating express warranties. The distinction is stated in §2–313(2):

> . . . [A]n affirmation merely of the value of the goods or a statement purporting to be merely the seller's opinion or commendation of the goods does not create a warranty.

Although the Code thus exempts a seller from warranty liability for "puffing," distinguishing such statements from those creating express warranties is extremely difficult. The line between "puffing" (for example, a used car dealer stating, "This car is a real honey") and an "affirmation of fact" (for example, the same salesman stating, "This car has just had an engine overhaul") is very fine. Generally, the more specific the seller's statements concerning the qualities of the goods, the more likely a court is to construe the statement as an express warranty. In addition to careful analysis of the seller's language, the court also considers whether the statement was in writing, the nature of the defect, and the parties' relative knowledge concerning the characteristics of the goods. The following case illustrates the principles governing creation of express warranties and the role of reliance under §2–313.

Weng v. Allison
678 N.E. 2d 1254 (Ill. App. 1997)

> The defendant Thomas Allison (seller) sold a ten-year-old used car that had been driven about 96,000 miles to the plaintiffs Michael and Karla Weng (buyers) for $800. The buyers did not test drive the car, but agreed to buy it after the seller told them that the car was "mechanically sound," "in good condition," "a good, reliable car," that had "no problems." When the car failed to operate properly, the buyers took it to a dealer who told them that it was not safe to drive and required $1,500 in repairs. Buyers sued the seller for breach of express and implied warranties. The trial court ruled in favor of the seller and the buyers appealed.

Holdridge, Justice

. . . Express warranties are enforceable if the statements at issue are . . . affirmations of fact or promises which relate to the goods and become part of the basis of the bargain. . . . [U.C.C. §2–313.] If the goods fail to conform to the affirmations or promises, the seller may be held accountable for breach of warranty.

In this matter, the seller's statements to the buyers that the car was "mechanically sound," "in good condition," and had "no problems" were affirmations of fact . . . that created an express warranty. . . . We find the trial court's ruling that the statements of the seller could not have been part of the basis of the bargain simply because no reasonable persons could have relied upon those statements was erroneous. The trial court misconstrued the role of reliance in determining whether an affirmation of fact . . . is part of the basis of the bargain. Affirmations of fact made during the bargain are presumed to be part of the basis of the bargain unless clear, affirmative proof otherwise is shown. . . . It is not necessary, therefore, for the buyer to show reasonable reliance upon the seller's affirmations in order to make the affirmations part of the basis of the bargain. [UCC §2–313, Official Comment 3.] . . . The burden is upon the seller to establish by clear, affirmative proof that the affirmations did not become part of the basis of the bargain. . . .

In this matter, the record shows no clear, affirmative proof that the seller's affirmations of fact were not part of the basis of the bargain. Instead, the trial court simply assumed that no one could have reasonably relied upon the seller's statements that the car was mechanically sound, in light of the age, price, and mileage of the car. We disagree. Any car of the age and mileage of the car sold to the plaintiffs can be "mechanically sound" and yet worth only $800; many other factors enter into the price of a car, i.e. the condition of the body, the condition of the paint, the presence or absence of rust, the condition of the tires, the condition of the interior of the car, the presence or absence of broken glass, etc. A "mechanically sound" car, in otherwise poor condition can reasonably be worth $800. . . . We hold that the buyers proved the seller breached an express warranty, and the seller failed to establish otherwise by clear affirmative proof.

[Judgment reversed and remanded.]

Express Warranty — Description. In addition to explicit verbal statements of fact or promises relating to the goods, express warranties also may be created by description. Under §2–313(1)(b), any description of the goods that is made part of the basis of the bargain creates an express warranty that the goods will conform to the description. The description may be contained in technical specifications, blueprints, or the like, or may simply arise from the seller's language. A problem arises concerning the scope of the warranty when the seller uses very general descriptive language that may consist of one word — for example, when the seller agrees to sell a "lawn mower," or an "automobile," or a "tractor" to the buyer. In this context, the court must decide what qualities or characteristics these descriptions embody. For example, does an "automobile" have to be in running condition, or, for that matter, is it required to have an engine at all? Evidence of the negotiations of the parties and the buyer's awareness of the subject matter's condition are relevant to determine the content of the warranty. At issue in the following case was whether an express warranty had been created by description.

Daughtrey v. Ashe
413 S.E.2d 336 (Va. 1992)

In October 1985, plaintiff W. Hayes Daughtrey visited Ashe Jewelers and contracted to purchase a diamond bracelet for $15,000. When Daughtrey came to close the sale, defendant Sidney Ashe gave him an appraisal form that had been completed as follows:

The following represents our estimate for insurance purposes only, of the present retail replacement cost of identical items, and not necessarily the amounts that might be obtained if the articles were offered for sale. . . .

Description	Appraised Value
platinum diamond bracelet, set with 28 brilliant full ct diamonds weighing a total of 10 carats. H color and v.v.s. quality.	$25,000.00

In February 1989, another jeweler examined the bracelet and informed Daughtrey that the diamonds were not of "v.v.s." quality (one of the highest quality classifications used by jewelers). After Ashe refused to replace the diamonds with ones of v.v.s. quality, Daughtrey sued alleging that Ashe had breached an express warranty. The trial court ruled in favor of Ashe and Daughtrey appealed.

Whiting, Justice

. . . First, we consider whether Ashe's statement of the grade of the diamonds was an express warranty. [UCC §2–313] provides in pertinent part:

(1) Express warranties by the seller are created as follows: . . .

> (b) any description of the goods which is made part of the basis of the bargain creates an express warranty that the goods shall conform to the description.

[Ashe argues] that the statement in the appraisal form is not an express warranty for two reasons.

First, [he argues that] the "appraisal on its face stated that it was 'for insurance purposes only.'" However, we think that the balance of the . . . language in the appraisal form demonstrates that the limiting language relates *only* to the statement of the *appraised value.* Therefore, Ashe's description of the grade of the diamonds should be treated as any other statement he may have made about them.

Second, [Ashe contends] that Ashe's statement of the grade of the diamonds is a mere opinion and, thus, cannot qualify as an express warranty under [§2−313(2) which] provides:

> It is not necessary to the creation of an express warranty that the seller use formal words such as "warrant" or "guarantee" or that he have a specific intention to make a warranty, but an affirmation merely of the value of the goods or a statement purporting to be merely the seller's opinion or commendation of the goods does not create a warranty.

. . . However, here, Ashe did more than give a mere opinion of the value of the goods; he specifically described them as diamonds of "H color and v.v.s. quality."

Ashe did not qualify his statement as a mere opinion. And, if one who has superior knowledge makes a statement about the goods sold and does not qualify the statement as his opinion, the statement will be treated as a statement of fact. . . . Nor does it matter that the opinions of other jewelers varied in minor respects. All of them said, and the trial judge found, that the diamonds were of a grade substantially less than v.v.s. Clearly, Ashe intended to sell Daughtrey v.v.s. diamonds. . . . Ashe testified that "I know when I sold the bracelet and I classified it as vvs, I knew it was vvs."

Given these considerations, we conclude that Ashe's description of the goods was more than his opinion; rather, he intended it to be a statement of a fact. Therefore, the court erred in holding that the description was not an express warranty under [§2−313(2)]. . . .

[Judgment reversed and remanded.]

Express Warranty—Sample or Model. Goods often are described through the use of a sample or model. Any sample or model which is made part of the basis of the bargain creates an express warranty that the goods will conform to a sample or model. A **sample** is actually drawn from the bulk of goods involved in the sale. In contrast, a **model** is not drawn from the bulk of the goods, but is offered for inspection when the goods themselves are not at hand.[2] Any item exhibited by the seller ordinarily is presumed to become part of the basis of the bargain; that is, the seller bears the burden of showing that it is not a sample or model.

Time of Express Warranty. The time when the seller's representations are made (by affirmation of fact, promise, description, sample, or model) is not material in determining whether or not they constitute express warranties. The sole test is whether they have become part of the contract. If the seller's affirmation or promise occurs after the deal is otherwise closed—for example, after the buyer has taken delivery—the warranty may be effective without additional consideration as a contract modification under §2−209(1).

Express Warranty and Fraud. The seller's affirmations of fact concerning the goods is the basis of both express warranty, and fraud and misrepresentation liability. Note, therefore, the relationship between fraud and express warranty.[3] A seller acting in the good faith belief in the accuracy of his statements concerning the goods may nevertheless be held liable for breach of express warranty if the goods subsequently fail to conform to the seller's statements. If the seller's representations were made with actual knowledge of their falsity, fraud liability also may ensue.[4]

Disclaimer of Express Warranties—§2−316(1)

Warranty liability is strict liability. It is imposed whether or not the seller knows of the defect or is at fault in causing it. To avoid this essentially absolute

---

[2]UCC §2−313(1)(c) and Official Comment 6.

[3]The common law of fraud and misrepresentation discussed in Chapter 11 supplements the UCC provisions through §1−103(b).

[4]Under UCC §2−721, remedies for fraud and material misrepresentation include all Code remedies available for nonfraudulent breach including those available for breach of warranty. This provision changes pre-Code law under which common law remedies for fraud were more restricted than those available for breach of warranty.

obligation, sellers often attempt to contractually limit or extinguish their warranty liability. Disclaimers of express warranties are governed by §2–316(1). It provides that an express warranty and words or conduct tending to negate or limit that warranty are to be construed, if possible, as consistent with each other. If such a construction is unreasonable, the negation or limitation is inoperative. This language affords a court wide latitude in striking down disclaimer language it finds inconsistent with an express warranty created under §2–313. Inconsistency between warranty and disclaimer occurs primarily in two situations: (1) when both the warranty and the disclaimer are contained in the parties' written contract, and (2) when the warranty is made orally before the parties reduce the contract to a writing which contains the disclaimer.

Written Warranty and Disclaimer. Section 2–316(1) is designed to prevent express warranties, resting upon the negotiated aspects of the bargain and incorporated into the written agreement, from being disclaimed by boiler-plate language in a form contract such as "the seller hereby disclaims all warranties, express or implied." For example, assume S sells a car to B, inducing her to buy by stating "the brakes on this car were overhauled last week." This provision is included in the parties' written contract. The sales contract also contains general language disclaiming all warranties. Section 2–316(1) prevents the general disclaimer from excluding the warranty that the brakes are new, and thus would not prevent the buyer from recovering when she discovers that the brakes actually have 50,000 miles on them. That is, §2–316(1) protects "a buyer from *unexpected and unbargained language of disclaimer* by denying effect to such language when inconsistent with language of express warranty."[5]

Oral Warranty and Written Disclaimer. A much more troublesome problem under §2–316(1) is the effect of a written disclaimer upon oral warranties made prior to the written agreement and not incorporated into that agreement. In this case, the disclaimer issue often is complicated by a merger clause contained in the contract. For example, the contract may contain a provision generally disclaiming all warranties and a merger clause stating that the written contract, absent the warranty, represents the entire agreement of the parties. In

this situation the seller may assert the Code parol evidence rule, §2–202 (discussed in Chapter 12) to prevent the buyer from introducing evidence concerning existence of the oral warranty. Assume Bob goes to Joe's Motor Sales to buy a used truck for use in his construction business. Bob examines a 1992 Chevrolet which Joe's salesman describes in glowing terms, some of which ("this is a one-owner truck," "it is in A–1 shape," "it has just had an engine overhaul") are express warranties under §2–313. Partly in reliance upon the salesman's statements, Bob buys the truck, which proves to be a lemon. Joe's written form contract, signed by Bob, does not incorporate any of the salesman's statements, but instead contains terms disclaiming all warranties and a merger clause. Bob later sues Joe's for breach of warranty. In defense, Joe's asserts that the written contract, which contains no warranties, is the final expression of the parties' agreement. Accordingly, the parol evidence rule should prevent Bob from attempting to prove existence of oral warranties contradicting the terms of the written contract.

On similar facts, a number of courts have accepted this argument and excluded the buyer's evidence of previously made oral warranties. The buyer may be protected, however, if the court finds either that the writing is not a final expression of the agreement or that enforcement of the disclaimer would be unconscionable. Nevertheless, to avoid loss of warranty protection, a buyer should always make sure that the seller's oral representations are incorporated into any subsequent written contract. Particular care must be taken when the seller uses a standardized form contract, because such contracts often contain preprinted disclaimer and merger clauses.

Implied Warranties

Unlike express warranties, which are contractual in nature, resting upon the "dickered" aspects of the bargain, **implied warranties** arise by operation of law. Two implied warranties recognized under the Code are discussed below: the warranty of merchantability and the warranty of fitness for a particular purpose. The warranty of merchantability, imposed upon a merchant seller, requires that the goods sold meet certain minimum quality standards. The warranty of fitness is given by a seller who has reason to know of a particular

---

[5]UCC §2–316, Official Comment 1 (emphasis added).

purpose for which the buyer requires the goods and that the buyer is relying upon the seller's skill and judgment to choose suitable goods.

Merchantability — §2–314

Elements of Merchantability. Under §2–314(1), a warranty that the goods will be **merchantable** is implied if the seller is a merchant with respect to goods of that kind. Section 2–314(2) lists six criteria to determine whether or not goods are merchantable. This list contains the minimum requirements of merchantability. Other attributes of merchantability may arise in specific instances through case law or usage of trade.

1. To be merchantable, the goods must pass without objection in the trade under the contract description. That is, the goods need not be perfect, but "must be of a quality comparable to that generally acceptable in that line of trade under the description or other designation of the goods used in the agreement."[6] Therefore, trade usage is an important factor to be considered in determining the content and scope of the warranty. In addition, price should be considered in ascertaining the extent of the seller's warranty. The warranty applies both to new and used goods, but the seller's obligation for used goods is somewhat more limited because that fact is part of their contract description.

2. If fungible goods are involved, §2–314(2)(b) provides that the goods must be "fair average quality within the description." This requirement is an extension of the first criterion above. Goods are fungible if one unit is identical to any other unit, such as grain or oil. The term "fair average," directly applicable to agricultural bulk products, means "goods centering around the middle belt of quality, not the least or the worst that can be understood in the particular trade by the designation, but such as can pass 'without objection.'"[7]

3. The goods must be fit for the ordinary purposes for which such goods are used. This is the most commonly quoted definition of merchantability, meaning that the goods must be capable of performing the tasks ordinarily required of like goods. For example, to be merchantable, a broom must be capable of sweeping; a car should be capable of providing basic transportation; food should be fit for eating.

4. The goods must run, within variations permitted by the agreement or trade usage, of even kind, quality, and quantity, within each unit and among all units involved.

5. The goods must be adequately contained, packaged, and labeled as the agreement may require.

6. If any promises or affirmations of fact are made on the container or label, the goods must conform to the affirmation or promise.

Normally, the warranty of merchantability is breached because, due to the defective nature of the goods, they either do not work as anticipated—for example, a car fails to operate properly because of a defective transmission—or are unexpectedly dangerous in normal use—for example, a piece of glass found in a soda bottle.

Merchants Covered. Not all persons who qualify as "merchants" for purposes of applying some of the Code's "merchants' exceptions"[8] are merchants under §2–314. The warranty of merchantability is imposed only upon a seller who, in a professional status, sells or deals in the particular kind of goods that are the subject matter of the sale. The warranty is not given by a person, even one otherwise in business, making an isolated sale of goods. Note that to be a merchant under §2–314 the seller must both deal in goods and those goods must be involved in the sale. For example, an appliance dealer selling a dishwasher, a jeweler selling a watch, a grocer selling a loaf of bread, a restaurant owner selling a hamburger or soft drink, and generally other businesses selling goods out of inventory are "merchants" under §2–314. On the other hand, a jeweler selling a used car is not a merchant in cars, and therefore gives no warranty of merchantability to his buyer.

At issue in the following case was whether the seller breached the warranty of merchantability.

Ford v. Starr Fireworks, Inc.
874 P.2d 230 (Wyo. 1994)

Plaintiff Starr Fireworks, Inc., a wholesaler, contracted to sell an assortment of fireworks to defendant Vince Ford, a

---

[6]UCC §2–314, Official Comment 2.
[7]UCC §2–314, Official Comment 7.

[8]"Merchant" is defined in UCC §2–104(1). See the discussion of this definition in Chapter 7.

retailer, for $6,748.86. Starr delivered the fireworks to Ford's warehouse in May 1991 and, without inspecting them, Ford distributed the fireworks to his retail outlets. About a week to ten days after the delivery, Ford notified Starr that some of the packages of fireworks were damaged. Although Ford told his retailers not to sell the fireworks, one of Ford's stores later sold several cases of Starr bottle rockets to another fireworks retailer. On July 1, 1991, Ford went to Starr's office in Denver to obtain replacements but Starr refused to replace the goods unless Ford either returned the fireworks or paid for them. On August 3, Starr's sales representative traveled to Ford's warehouse to pick up the goods but was able to collect only $1,476.87 worth of fireworks.

Starr sued Ford for breach of contract and Ford counter-sued alleging that the fireworks were unmerchantable. The trial court awarded Starr damages of $5,251.99 ruling that the fireworks returned on August 3 were unmerchantable but those that had not been returned were merchantable. Ford appealed.

Taylor, Justice

. . . Ford asserts that the district court erred when it concluded that only some of the fireworks received from Starr were unmerchantable. Ford contends that his inspection of some of the fireworks disclosed packages with torn wrappings, mold or mildew on some fireworks, and paper wrappings which fell apart exposing the fireworks. Ford argues from this sampling that it was reasonable to assume all the goods delivered by Starr were unmerchantable. . . .

Determining whether goods are merchantable depends upon the facts of each individual case. . . . Merchantable goods are not necessarily of the best or highest quality, but instead are "measured by the generally acceptable quality under the description used in the contract." *Dickerson v. Mountain View Equipment Co.,* [710 P.2d 621, 624 (Idaho 1985)]. Merchantability does not imply the best quality or perfection; instead, it requires goods which operate for their ordinary purpose. . . .

The evidence produced at trial established that at least some of the fireworks Ford claimed were unmerchantable passed without objection in the trade. After Ford rejected the fireworks, Ford sold two to three cases of the bottle rockets received from Starr to another fireworks retailer. This resale implies the merchantability of at least some of the fireworks. If the fireworks were unmerchantable within trade standards, another retailer would not have purchased the bottle rockets. Also, no customer complaints were ever received about the mer-

chantability of the fireworks sold by the second retailer from the lot delivered to Ford by Starr.

Furthermore, Starr indicated that it received no complaints from any other purchaser of the remaining fireworks from the same shipment Ford claimed was unmerchantable. If all the fireworks received by Ford from Starr were unmerchantable, then other retailers who received fireworks from that same shipment would have rejected those goods as unmerchantable. Also, Starr's sales representative testified that some of the merchandise which Ford claimed was unmerchantable was later sold to other retailers without complaint after Starr recovered it from Ford.

As used in [UCC §2–314(2)], "merchantable" is not synonymous with "perfect." . . . The fireworks received by Ford, while not perfect, were of an "acceptable quality" within the trade. . . . We hold that the fireworks which Ford did not inspect or return to Starr were merchantable. . . .

[Judgment affirmed.]

Fitness for a Particular Purpose—§2–315

Under §2–315, if the seller, merchant, or nonmerchant, at the time of contracting, has reason to know

1. of any particular purpose for which the buyer requires the goods, *and*
2. that the buyer is relying upon the seller's skill or judgment to select or furnish suitable goods

then, unless properly disclaimed, there is an implied warranty that the goods will be fit for the buyer's particular purpose. For the warranty of **fitness for a particular purpose** to arise, the seller need only have "reason to know" (not necessarily actual knowledge) of the buyer's purpose. The buyer, however, must *actually* rely upon the seller's skill or judgment in selecting the goods.

Although both the warranties of fitness and merchantability warranties may be included in the same contract, the warranty of fitness is much narrower and more precise. That is, a particular purpose is a use peculiar to the buyer's business or specific requirements, whereas the ordinary purposes for which goods are used are uses made of the goods by buyers generally. For this reason, the goods sold under the contract may very well be merchantable under §2–314, but not fit for a particular purpose under §2–315. Assume Bonfour, who is in the process of opening a cafeteria, contacts Skillet, a restaurant equipment supplier, to purchase kitchen equipment. Bonfour has some idea of her anticipated volume, but is otherwise unfamiliar with the restaurant business, a fact that is obvious to Skillet after conversing with her. Bonfour therefore asks Skillet to recommend a commercial dishwasher capable of handling her anticipated business. After inspecting Bonfour's facilities, Skillet recommends a model thereafter purchased by Bonfour in reliance upon the recommendation. Even though her subsequent volume is less than anticipated, the dishwasher proves to be inadequate to handle the load. On these facts, even though the dishwasher is merchantable under §2–314—fit for the ordinary purposes for which dishwashers are used—it is not fit for the buyer's particular purpose. Skillet, therefore, breaches the implied warranty of fitness, but not the warranty of merchantability.

As the preceding example indicates, the implied warranty of fitness most commonly arises between merchants, although it may also be created between a merchant and a consumer. Nevertheless, §2–315 imposes no explicit requirement that the seller be a *merchant*, as in the warranty of merchantability. Ordinarily, however, only a merchant will possess the necessary "skill or judgment" with respect to the goods to justify imposing the warranty.

Disclaimer of Implied Warranties— §§2–316(2) and 2–316(3)

The UCC, in §§2–316(2) and 2–316(3), protects the buyer from surprise by permitting exclusion or modification of implied warranties only by conspicuous language or other appropriate circumstances.

Disclaiming the Warranty of Merchantability. To exclude or modify the implied warranty of merchantability, two requirements must be met: (1) the language of disclaimer must mention the word "merchantability," and (2) if the disclaimer is in writing, it must be conspicuous. Under §1–201(b)(10), a term is **conspicuous** if

> it is so written that a reasonable person against which it is to operate ought to have noticed it. . . . Conspicuous terms include the following:
> (A)   a heading in capitals equal to or greater in size than the surrounding text, or in contrasting type, font, or

color to the surrounding text of the same or lesser size; and
> (B)   language in the body of a record or display in larger type than the surrounding text, or in contrasting type, font, or color to the surrounding text of the same size, or set off from surrounding text of the same size by symbols or other marks that call attention to the language.

The test is "whether attention can reasonably be expected to be called to"[9] the term or clause involved. As the following case illustrates, an objective test is applied (a "reasonable" person should have noticed it) and the issue is one for the court, not the jury to decide.

Cate v. Dover Corporation
790 S.W.2d 559 (Tex. 1990)

> Plaintiff Edward Cate, doing business as Cate's Transmission Service, purchased three "Rotary" brand lifts (designed to elevate vehicles for maintenance) from Beech Tire Mart. The lifts, which were manufactured by defendant Dover Corporation, never operated properly despite efforts by Beech and Dover to repair them. Cate sued Dover for breach of the implied warranty of merchantability. Dover argued that it had provided its own express written warranty that included a disclaimer of the warranty of merchantability. The trial court ruled that the disclaimer was enforceable and granted judgment for Dover. The court of appeals affirmed and Cate appealed to the Texas Supreme Court.

Doggett, Justice

. . . This warranty is set forth on a separate page headed in blue half inch block print, with the heading: "YOU CAN TAKE ROTARY's NEW 5-YEAR WARRANTY AND TEAR IT APART." The statement is followed by bold black type stating, "And, when you are through, it'll be just as solid as the No. 1 lift company in America. Rotary." The text of the warranty itself is in black type, contained within double blue lines, and appears under the blue three-eighths inch block print heading "WARRANTY." The disclaimer of implied warranties, although contained in a separate paragraph within the warranty text, is in the same typeface, size, and color as the remainder of the text.

---

[9]UCC §1–201, Official Comment 10.

An implied warranty of merchantability arises in a contract for the sale of goods unless expressly excluded or modified by conspicuous language. . . . Whether a particular disclaimer is conspicuous is a question of law to be determined by the following definition: [The court then quoted UCC §1–201(10).] Further explanation is provided by comment 10 thereto:

> This [section] is intended to indicate some of the methods of making a term attention-calling. But the test is whether attention can reasonably be expected to be called to it.

In interpreting this language, Dover argues that a lesser standard of conspicuousness should apply to a disclaimer made to a merchant, such as Cate. Admittedly, an ambiguity is created by the requirement that disclaimer language be conspicuous to "a reasonable person *against whom it is to operate.*" Comment 10, however, clearly contemplated an objective standard, stating the test as "whether attention can reasonably be expected to be called to it."

We then turn to an application of an objective standard of conspicuousness to Dover's warranty. The top forty percent of the written warranty is devoted to extolling its virtues. The warranty itself, contained within double blue lines, is then set out in five paragraphs in normal black type under the heading "WARRANTY." Nothing distinguishes the third paragraph, which contains the exclusionary language. It is printed in the same typeface, size, and color as the rest of the warranty text. Although the warranty in its entirety may be considered conspicuous, the disclaimer is hidden among attention-getting language purporting to grant the best warranty available. . . .

We hold that, to be enforceable, a written disclaimer of the implied warranty of merchantability made in connection with a sale of goods must be conspicuous to a reasonable person. We further hold that such a disclaimer contained in text undistinguished in typeface, size or color within a form purporting to grant a warranty is not conspicuous, and is unenforceable unless the buyer has actual knowledge of the disclaimer. . . .

[Judgment reversed and remanded.]

Disclaiming the Warranty of Fitness. Unlike the warranty of merchantability, the warranty of fitness for a particular purpose may be disclaimed by general language, that is, language not specifically using the term "fitness for a particular purpose." Any disclaimer of the warranty of fitness, however, must be both (1) in writing *and* (2) conspicuous. The following language from §2–316(2) is sufficient to exclude the warranty of fitness: "There are no warranties which extend beyond the description on the face hereof."

Disclaimer Through Surrounding Circumstances. Section 2–316(3) outlines three additional situations in which implied warranties may be disclaimed without regard to the requirements outlined above. These are "common factual situations in which the circumstances surrounding the transaction are in themselves sufficient to call the buyer's attention to the fact that no implied warranties are made or that a certain implied warranty is being excluded."[10] Under §2–316(3)(a), *all* implied warranties (both merchantability and fitness) are excluded by language such as "as is," "with all faults," "as they stand," or other language which in common understanding calls the buyer's attention to the exclusion of warranties and makes it plain that no implied warranty exists. Such language in ordinary commercial usage is understood to mean that the buyer bears the entire risk as to the quality of the goods sold.

Section 2–316(3)(b) makes it clear that if the buyer, prior to entering into the contract, has examined the goods (or a sample or model) as fully as it desires or has refused to examine them, there is no implied warranty regarding defects that an examination should, in the circumstances, have revealed. Note that "examination" as used here is not synonymous with "inspection before acceptance," because any examination that may exclude warranty liability under this provision occurs *before* the contract is made. This rule applies whether the buyer voluntarily examines the goods before contracting or does so after a demand by the seller.

Finally, under §2–316(3)(c), an implied warranty also may be excluded or modified by the parties' prior course of dealing or course of performance, and by usage of trade.[11] To illustrate, assume Ohm has been selling resistors, capacitors, and other electronic components in bulk to Bart for many years. The preprinted forms used by the parties to evidence their contract do not expressly disclaim implied warranties. Nevertheless, the price of the compo-

---

[10]UCC §2–316, Official Comment 6.

[11]These terms, defined in §1–303, are discussed in Chapter 12 in conjunction with the UCC parol evidence rule, §2–202.

nents has always been "bargain basement," and over the years, Bart has routinely accepted Ohm's entire shipment, even those containing a substantial number of defective components. On these facts a court may find that the parties' prior course of dealing indicates that no implied warranty exists with respect to components retained by Bart. Note additionally that the "as is" disclaimer discussed above is merely an application of this rule allowing exclusion of implied warranty by usage of trade.

Warranty of Title and Against Infringement

The warranties discussed to this point assure the buyer that the goods sold possess certain minimum qualities and characteristics. A buyer in a sales contract, however, has an additional and more fundamental concern—that the seller has good title to the goods and the right to transfer them. This assurance is provided by the warranty of title.

Creation of Warranty of Title—§2–312(1)

Under §2–312(1), unless properly disclaimed, the seller in a contract for sale warrants that

1. the title conveyed will be good and its transfer rightful, and
2. the goods will be delivered free of security interests or other liens, except those known to the buyer.[12]

The purpose of this **warranty of title** is simply to provide what any good faith buyer of goods expects to receive, "a good, clean title transferred to him also in a rightful manner so that he will not be exposed to a lawsuit in order to protect it."[13]

A seller gives the warranty of title whether or not the seller (1) is a merchant, (2) knew or was ignorant of the defect in title, or (3) was in possession of the goods at the time the sale or contract to sell was made. Assume Tom stole stereo equipment from Mark and later sold the equipment to Sharon, who was unaware of Tom's

wrongdoing. Sharon subsequently sold the equipment to Bill through a newspaper advertisement. Ultimately, Mark, the true owner, located and repossessed the equipment from Bill. Sharon breaches the title warranty given to Bill even though she is innocent of any wrongdoing and is not a merchant. Of course, Tom, the thief, also breaches the warranty of title given in his sale to Sharon.

If the seller is a merchant, the buyer often is protected even if the seller breaches the title warranty. For example, under the "voidable title" and "entrusting" rules discussed in Chapter 17, a good faith buyer usually defeats third-party ownership claims. Further, under §9–320(a), discussed in Chapter 32, a buyer in the ordinary course of business of inventory from a merchant takes free of perfected security interests in the goods even if he knows about them.

Creation of Warranty Against Infringement—§2–312(3)

A second warranty contained in §2–312 is the **warranty against infringement.** Under §2–312(3), a merchant seller dealing in goods of the kind warrants that the goods will be delivered free of any third-party claim of patent or trademark infringement. No such warranty arises by implication if the seller is not a merchant. It applies only when goods are sold as part of the seller's normal stock in the ordinary course of business.

Commercial buyers often have goods manufactured to their own particular specifications. For example, a hardware retailer may purchase its line of hand tools from a manufacturer who provides the tools according to specifications provided by the retailer. In this case, the buyer who furnishes specifications must indemnify the seller against any patent or trademark infringement claims arising out of the seller's compliance with them. That is, by providing specifications, the buyer makes a tacit representation that the seller will be safe in manufacturing according to them. The buyer is therefore required to reimburse the seller for any loss suffered if the goods infringe upon a third party's patent or trademark. Note that this provision, in essence, imposes warranty liability upon the buyer.

Disclaimer of Warranty of Title—§2–312(2)

Section 2–312(2) provides that the warranty of title may not be disclaimed by general language disclaiming all warranties, even if the buyer is aware of the general

---

[12]Note that with respect to liens or security interests in the goods, the buyer's *actual knowledge* is required to defeat the warranty. Therefore, the seller is not relieved if the buyer has constructive knowledge simply because a secured creditor in the goods has filed a financing statement.

[13]UCC §2–312, Official Comment 1.

disclaimer. To effectively eliminate the warranty of title, either the seller's *specific language* (for example, "I don't have the title") or the *circumstances* must give the buyer reason to know (an objective test) that the seller does not claim title. The type of "circumstances" envisioned in §2–312(2) are sales by sheriffs, executors, and foreclosing lien holders. These sales occur outside the ordinary course of business, thereby putting the buyer on notice that the seller possesses only an unknown or limited right.

The warranty of title, like merchantability and fitness, is in effect an implied warranty because it arises automatically by operation of law. That is, the warranty is given whether or not it is explicitly or expressly stated by the seller. The title warranty is not, however, treated as an "implied" warranty for purposes of §2–316(3). Accordingly, title may not be disclaimed by language such as "as is" or "with all faults." It may be excluded only by specific language or under the circumstances described above.

The following case illustrates the "specific language" requirement necessary to disclaim the warranty of title.

Sunseri v. RKO-Stanley Warner Theatres, Inc.

374 A.2d 1342 (Pa. Super. 1977)

Appellant RKO-Stanley Warner Theatres, Inc. (RKO) owned a theater building, part of which it leased to appellee Michael Sunseri and his partner for a recreational center. At the time the parties entered into the lease, RKO also sold some recreational equipment (bowling alleys, pool tables) to Sunseri. The equipment had been owned by Francis Zatalava, a previous lessee of the recreational center who had been forced to close his business for failure to pay taxes. After RKO's sale of the equipment to Sunseri, Zatalava sued RKO to regain possession of and title to the equipment. The court ruled that Zatalava retained title to the equipment. As a result, Sunseri lost possession of the equipment.

Sunseri then sued RKO, alleging that RKO had breached its warranty of title. RKO defended by alleging that it had disclaimed the warranty of title. The trial court ruled in favor of Sunseri and awarded him damages. RKO appealed.

Price, Judge

. . . The document which evidences the transaction between Pagano and Sunseri, as partners, and RKO is entitled "Bill of Sale" and provides, in pertinent part, as follows:

> [Seller] . . . does hereby sell, assign, convey, transfer and deliver to Buyer any right, title and interest Seller may have in the following goods and chattels. . . .
>
> It is expressly understood and agreed that the Seller shall in nowise be deemed or held to be obligated, liable, or accountable upon or under guaranties [sic] or warranties, in any manner or form including, but not limited to, the implied warranties of title, merchantability, fitness for use or of quality.

The lower court found that, as a matter of law, the above-quoted language was insufficient to disclaim the warranty of title. We agree. The statutory authority in this area is section 2–312 of the Uniform Commercial Code which states, in pertinent part, the following: [The court then quoted UCC §§2–312(1) and (2)]. . . .

In the instant case, the bill of sale did not disclaim warranty of title in the "specific" language required by U.C.C. §2–312. The provision for sale of "any right, title, and interest" is clearly not a positive warning or exclusion in regard to the status of title, and would be unlikely to offend or even catch the eye of an unsophisticated buyer. . . . The second relevant provision in the sale document, stating that "Seller shall in nowise be deemed or held to be obligated, liable or accountable upon or under any guaranties [sic] or warranties" is similarly ineffective. It is couched in negative terminology, expressing what the seller will not be liable for rather than what the buyer is or is not receiving. The inadequacy of such a caveat is best illustrated by juxtaposing it with title disclaimer provisions suggested by authorities in the subject area. For example, 18 *Am. Jur. Legal Forms 2d* §253:825 (1974), provides: "Seller makes no warranty as to the title to the goods, and buyer assumes all risks of nonownership of the goods by seller." Another illustration is contained in *Purdon's Pa. Forms,* 12A P.S. §2–312, Form 2 (1970), which recommends the following language: "The seller does not warrant that he has any right to convey the title to the goods." Appellant's attempt to disclaim the warranty of title in its transaction with appellee was ineffective in that it failed to comply with the requirement, under the Uniform Commercial Code, that such a disclaimer be made in "specific language. . . . "

[Judgment affirmed.]

Conflict of Warranties—§2–317

The preceding discussion concerns the effect of a conflict between the creation of a warranty and the seller's attempt to extinguish it. A similar conflict may arise, not between warranty and disclaimer, but between two or more warranties express or implied. This problem is resolved, in a manner similar to §2–316(1) governing disclaimer of express warranties, by §2–317. This section recognizes that a seller may make several warranties concerning the same goods. To the extent they can coexist, the buyer has the benefit of all of them. That is, the warranties Article are cumulative. For example, a seller may expressly warrant that fabric it sells is 100 percent wool. Such a warranty is not inconsistent with an implied warranty that the fabric is merchantable. Accordingly, the buyer has the benefit of both warranties.

A seller acting in good faith may, however, make inconsistent warranties. In this situation the *intent* of the parties determines which of the conflicting warranties applies. To aid the court in ascertaining intent, §2–317 states rules governing priority among conflicting warranties:

1. Exact or technical specifications displace an inconsistent (a) sample or model, or (b) general language of description.
2. A sample from an existing bulk, such as a storage bin of grain, displaces inconsistent general language of description.
3. Express warranties displace inconsistent implied warranties other than an implied warranty of fitness for a particular purpose.

The net effect of these rules is to enforce the more specific conflicting warranty. Note that for this section to apply, however, the seller must make warranties in good faith that later are shown to be irreconcilable. Under the principles of estoppel, a seller who leads the buyer to believe that all of the warranties can be performed may not thereafter assert any inconsistency as a defense.

Remedies for Breach of Warranty

The discussion of buyers' remedies in Chapter 18 illustrates how UCC Article 2 measures a buyer's damages when the buyer justifiably rejects or revokes acceptance of delivered goods, or when the seller repudiates or fails to deliver. These situations are governed generally by §§2–712 and 2–713. In warranty actions, the buyer has *accepted* the goods, but seeks to recover damages from the seller because the goods are not as warranted. Buyer's damages due to the nonconformity of accepted goods are computed under §2–714.

Whenever the buyer asserts breach after acceptance, §2–607(3)(a) requires that the buyer notify the seller within a reasonable time after he discovers (or should have discovered) the breach. Failure to do so bars the buyer from any remedy. The notice requirement serves three purposes: (1) it affords the seller an opportunity to correct any defect; (2) it gives the seller an opportunity to prepare for negotiation and litigation; and (3) it protects the seller against stale claims asserted by the buyer after it is too late to investigate them.

Basic Measure of Damages

Under §2–714(1), a buyer who has accepted nonconforming goods and properly notified the seller of breach may recover damages for nonconformity determined in any reasonable manner. The usual and most commonly applied formula for ascertaining damages for breach of warranty is stated in §2–714(2), which allows the buyer to recover

> the difference at the time and place of acceptance between the value of the goods accepted and the value they would have had if they had been as warranted.

The most common measure of the difference in value between the goods as accepted and as warranted is the cost of replacement or repair. However, to avoid a windfall to a buyer who has used the goods for a significant period of time before the breach of warranty becomes apparent, the court may reduce recovery by a reasonable allowance for depreciation. Note that the value of the goods as warranted is measured at the time and place of acceptance. This provides the most accurate measure of fair market value as warranted because the contract price may have been determined long before acceptance.

Consequential Damages

For breach of warranty actions, §2–714(3), like §§2–712 and 2–713, authorizes recovery of incidental and consequential damages in appropriate cases to supplement the basic measure of damages. As discussed in Chapter 15, consequential damages, usually lost profits, may be recoverable under the foreseeability test of *Hadley v. Baxendale,* codified for Code contracts in §2–715(2)(a). In addition, §2–715(2) (b) permits recovery as consequential damages, whether or not foreseeable, for "injury to person or property proximately resulting from any breach of warranty." Thus, in a warranty action, a seller may be liable not only for commercial injury (including in some cases lost profits), but also for personal injury and property damage caused by the defective product. Assume Buster pruchases a clothes dryer for use in his commercial laundry from a manufacturer, Sox. The dryer fails to work properly because of a defective motor, forcing Buster's business to close for several days. Buster may recover damages under §2–714(2) for breach of warranty (here the warranty of merchantability). Additionally, if the foreseeability test is met, Buster's lost profits may be recovered as consequential damages under §2–715(2)(a). Assume further, that the defective motor overheats and causes a fire which burns down Buster's business and seriously injures him. He may recover for his personal injury and property damage as consequential damages under §2–715(2)(b), whether or not such loss was foreseeable. The application of the law of warranty to cases involving personal injury and property damage is discussed in more detail in the next chapter.

Deducting Damages from Price — §2–717

An additional remedy available to the buyer for breach of warranty is contained in §2–717. Upon notification of his intention to do so, the buyer may deduct all or any part of damages for the seller's breach from any part of the price still owing under the same contract. This provision only applies if the breach involved is of the same contract for which the price is claimed. No particular formalities for the notice are required and no further action is necessary if the seller acquiesces in the deduction.

Magnuson-Moss Warranty Act

The **Magnuson-Moss Warranty Act,** a federal statute[14] enacted in 1975, regulates written warranties

---

[14]15 U.S.C. §§2301–2312.

that accompany the sale of consumer goods. The Act is designed to accomplish several purposes.

1.   It requires that the terms of written warranties be fully and conspicuously disclosed in simple and readily understood language.

2.   It requires that such warranties be conspicuously designated as "full" or "limited." To be designated as "full," the warranty must incorporate certain minimum federal standards.

3.   It prohibits the use of written warranties as a means to disclaim or modify the implied warranties of merchantability and fitness.

4.   It encourages warrantors to set up informal mechanisms to settle disputes, which the consumer must use before commencing court action.

5.   It allows actions for breach of warranty to be brought in federal court under limited circumstances.

Note that the Act applies *only if* the seller provides a written warranty. The law does not *require* that a consumer product or any of its components be warranted, or prescribe the duration of written warranties.

Content of Warranties

Section 2302 of the Act provides that:

> In order to improve the adequacy of information available to consumers, prevent deception, and improve competition in the marketing of consumer products, any warrantor warranting a consumer product to a consumer by means of a written warranty shall, to the extent of rules required by the [Federal Trade Commission], fully and conspicuously disclose in simple and readily understood language the terms and conditions of such warranty.

The Federal Trade Commission (FTC) has promulgated regulations requiring that written warranties covering consumer products contain the following information if the goods actually cost the consumer more than $15 exclusive of taxes:

1. the identity of the party or parties to whom the written warranty is extended;
2. a clear description and identification of products or parts covered by and excluded from the warranty;
3. a statement of what the warrantor will do in the event of a defect, malfunction, or failure to conform with the written warranty;

4. the point in time when the warranty term commences, if different from the purchase date, and the duration of the warranty;

5. a step-by-step explanation of the procedure that the consumer should follow in order to obtain performance of any warranty obligation;

6. information about any informal dispute settlement mechanism, if any, available to the consumer;

7. any limitations on the duration of the implied warranties of merchantability and fitness accompanied by the following statement:

> Some States do not allow limitations on how long an implied warranty lasts, so the above limitation may not apply to you.

8. any limitations on relief such as incidental or consequential damages, accompanied by the following statement:

> Some States do not allow the exclusion or limitation of incidental or consequential damages, so the above limitation or exclusion may not apply to you.

9. a statement in the following language:

> This warranty gives you specific legal rights, and you may also have other rights which vary from State to State.[15]

The information required to be disclosed must be made available to the consumer *prior to* the sale of the product. Additionally, to prevent deception, the FTC is empowered to determine the manner and form of presentation when the information is contained in advertising, labeling, point-of-sale material, or other written representation.

Designation of Warranties as "Full" or "Limited"

Under §2303 of the Act, any written warranty covering a consumer product actually costing more than $10 must clearly and conspicuously designate the warranty as either "full" (stating the duration), or "limited." A

full warranty is one that meets the federal minimum standards for warranty. A warranty not meeting these standards must be designated as **limited.**

In order to meet federal minimum standards for full warranty, four elements, stated in §2304, must be contained in the warranty. These include:

1.   In the event of a defect, malfunction, or failure to conform with the written warranty, the seller must, at a minimum, remedy the product within a reasonable time without charge. "Remedy" means that the seller may, at its option, repair or replace the item, or may refund the purchase price. However, the seller may not elect to refund the price unless it is impracticable to repair or replace, or the buyer is willing to accept a refund.

2.   No limitation may be imposed on the duration of any implied warranty.

3.   Consequential damages for breach of any written or implied warranty may not be limited or excluded unless the exclusion or limitation appears conspicuously on the face of the warranty.

4.   If the product (or a component part), continues to be defective after a reasonable number of attempts by the seller to resolve the problem, the seller must afford the buyer the option to elect either a refund of the purchase price or replacement. If replacement involves a component part, the seller must install the part in the product without charge.

In fulfilling the obligations previously outlined, the seller may not impose any duty upon the buyer, other than notification, as a condition to securing a remedy. The seller may, however, avoid warranty obligations by establishing that the failure to perform as warranted was caused by damage while in the consumer's possession or by the consumer's unreasonable use, including the failure to provide for maintenance. Note that a product may be sold with both "full" and "limited" warranties applicable to it, provided they are clearly and conspicuously designated. For example, a television set may contain a full two-year warranty on the picture tube and a limited warranty on other components—for example, restricted to parts only.

Limitation or Disclaimer of Implied Warranties

One of the most important provisions of the Act is §2308(a), which prohibits disclaimer or modification of

---

[15]16 C.F.R. §701.3.

implied warranties (merchantability and fitness) by a supplier who makes any written warranty to a consumer in connection with the sale of a consumer product. Additionally, the implied warranties may not be disclaimed if, at the time of the sale or within 90 days thereafter, the supplier enters into a contract with the consumer to maintain or repair the product for a specified period of time (a "service contract").

Although the seller may not *disclaim* implied warranties, it may *limit their duration* unless it is giving a "full" warranty. The duration of implied warranties may be limited to the duration of the written warranty if (1) the duration of the written warranty is *reasonable,* (2) the limitation is not unconscionable, and (3) it is contained in clear and unmistakable language, prominently displayed on the face of the warranty.

The prohibition against disclaimer of implied warranties is designed to prevent the unconscionable practice, widespread before passage of the Act, of using written warranties simply as a tool to disclaim implied warranties, primarily merchantability. That is, written warranties simply became a vehicle to comply with the requirements of UCC §2–316(2) concerning disclaimer of implied warranties. The written express warranty given would then be much less extensive than the disclaimed implied warranties—for example, 90 days' parts and labor on a toaster—leaving the consumer in a substantially worse position than if no written warranty had been provided. Further, the potential for unconscionability in this context was great, because by giving the warranty (generally on official-looking paper), the seller created the extremely deceptive impression that it was giving the buyer additional rights, when in fact it was taking away the buyer's existing rights.

Remedies

The stated policy of the Act is to encourage warrantors to establish informal dispute settlement mechanisms. The FTC has prescribed rules outlining the requirements for any such mechanism incorporated into a written warranty. These rules provide for participation by independent or governmental entities. If the warrantor establishes an informal dispute settlement procedure and incorporates it into the written warranty, then the consumer must first resort to the warrantor's procedure before commencing court action.

Assuming no such procedure is created, a consumer injured by a breach of warranty may bring a civil suit for damages or other relief in state court. The judgment may include court costs, attorneys' fees, and other expenses incurred in commencing and maintaining the lawsuit. The consumer may sue not only for the seller's failure to comply with Magnuson-Moss provisions, but also for breach of express or implied warranty under the UCC.

To provide a remedy in cases involving large numbers of relatively small claims, the Act allows some Magnuson-Moss Act suits to be brought in federal court. For example, in federal court suits (1) the overall amount in controversy must exceed $50,000, (2) individual claims must exceed $25, and (3) if the action is brought as a class action there must be at least 100 named plaintiffs.

Finally, the Act explicitly provides for governmental sanctions against violators. For example, the Act allows either the Attorney General or the FTC to bring an action in federal court to enjoin (1) any warrantor from making a deceptive warranty concerning a consumer product, or (2) any person from violating the Act.[16]

Summary

1.   A warranty is a seller's statement or other representation concerning the quality, character, or capabilities of the goods it sells. If the goods fail to conform to the standards created by a warranty, the seller is liable in damages for breach of warranty. The law of warranty, therefore, effectively defines the seller's obligation with respect to goods accepted by the buyer. Various types of warranties may be created under the UCC, including express warranties, implied warranties, and the warranties of title and against infringement.

2.   Under the Code, any affirmation of fact or promise that relates to the goods and becomes part of the basis of the bargain creates an express warranty that the goods will conform to the affirmation or promise. Express warranties also may be created by any description, sample, or model that becomes

---

[16]The Act also provides that Magnuson-Moss violations violate §5 of the FTC Act. 15 U.S.C. §2310(b). Section 5 and FTC enforcement power under it are discussed in Chapter 52.

part of the basis of the bargain. In short, express warranties rest upon the dickered, or bargained-for, aspects of the sales contract.

3.   The implied warranties under the Code, which arise by operation of law, are merchantability and fitness for a particular purpose. Merchantability imposes an obligation upon a merchant seller that its wares meet minimum standards of quality. Generally, to be merchantable, the goods must be fit for the *ordinary* purposes for which such goods are used. The warranty of fitness, requiring that the goods be suitable for the buyer's *particular* purpose, is imposed upon a seller who has reason to know of the particular purpose for which the buyer requires the goods and that the buyer is relying upon the seller's skill and judgment to choose suitable goods.

4.   The warranty of title simply requires the seller to provide the buyer with a good clean title free of security interests or other liens. The warranty against infringement obligates a merchant seller to deliver goods free of third-party claims of patent or trademark infringement.

5.   Consistent with Code policy, warranties may be excluded or modified by contract. Warranty disclaimers, however, offer great potential for unconscionable application. Therefore, the Code provisions allowing the seller to alter or eliminate warranty liability or to limit the buyer's remedies provide a significant amount of protection to the buyer. Similarly, if a seller gives more than one warranty concerning the same goods, the buyer has the benefit of all of them to the extent they can coexist.

6.   If goods accepted by the buyer are not as warranted, the buyer generally may recover as damages the difference between the value of the goods accepted and the value they would have had if they had been as warranted. The buyer also may recover incidental and consequential damages in appropriate cases. Consequential damages for breach of warranty include damages for personal injury and property damage caused by the breach.

7.   Although warranties largely are governed by state law (the UCC), a federal statute—the Magnuson-Moss Warranty Act—provides additional buyer protection when written warranties are given in connection with sales of consumer goods. The Act requires that the terms of a written warranty be fully and conspicuously disclosed in simple and readily understood language, and that the warranty be designated as "full" or "limited" to indicate whether it meets certain minimum federal standards. The Act also prohibits the use of written warranties to disclaim or modify the implied warranties of merchantability and fitness.

Key Terms

warranty	sample
warranty disclaimer	model
express warranty	implied warranty
merchantability	warranty against infringement
fitness for a particular purpose	Magnuson-Moss Warranty Act
conspicuous	full warranty
warranty of title	limited warranty

Questions and Problems

19.1   Section 2–313 of the UCC provides that an express warranty may be created whether or not the seller uses the words "warrant," "warranty," or "guarantee." Nor is it necessary that the seller intend to create a warranty. Why does the UCC adopt such a liberal standard governing creation of express warranties?

19.2   What is the distinction between express and implied warranties under the UCC? Compare and contrast the implied warranty of merchantability with the warranty of fitness for a particular purpose. What is the basic distinction between remedies available for breach of warranty and the buyer's remedies discussed in Chapter 18?

19.3   Explain why courts are hesitant to allow disclaimer of express warranties created under §2–313 by general language such as "seller hereby disclaims all warranties, express or implied."

19.4   Esther contracted Joe's Marina concerning purchase of a motorboat. Esther indicated that she needed the boat for use in a proposed water ski show, and that the boat therefore had to be capable of pulling ten skiers simultaneously at 35 miles per hour. Joe directed Esther to a used "Starcraft" boat with a 275-horsepower motor, indicating that "this baby has more power than you'll ever need. It can pull 20 skiers at 35 miles per hour." After further negotiation Esther purchased the boat. Trouble, however, soon developed. With the ten skiers in a "pyramid" formation the boat could never muster more than 20 miles per hour. In addition, after only two weeks' normal use, the boat began losing power. Inspection of the engine revealed a cracked block. Esther contacted Joe who stated, "Once that boat was off my property, it was yours, I never guarantee used equipment." Is Joe correct? More specifically, has Joe made any express warranties to Esther? Do any implied or other warranties run to Esther from Joe? Assuming a warranty or warranties exist, and have been breached, what remedy or remedies should Esther seek?

19.5   Jacques owned a saltwater aquarium housing many expensive tropical fish. Jacques visited the Verona Rock Shop where he selected several sea shells, pieces of coral, and driftwood for his aquarium. Prior to buying the pieces, Jacques asked the sales clerk if the items were suitable for use in a saltwater aquarium. The clerk said they would be suitable if they were rinsed.

Jacques rinsed the items and placed them in his aquarium. Within a week, 17 of his fish had died. Examination of the shells revealed the presence of toxic material from the decay of creatures inhabiting the shells. The toxic material had caused the death of the fish.

Jacques sued Verona Rock Shop alleging breach of express warranty, warranty of merchantability, and warranty of fitness. Should the shop be held liable for the cost of the fish?

19.6 Jones sold a motorcycle to Jefferson and provided a title certificate which Jones registered with the state. Two years later, a police officer stopped Jefferson and asked to see some proof of title to the motorcycle. Jefferson produced the title certificate, but the identification number on the certificate did not match the identification number on the motorcycle. The police therefore seized the motorcycle. After legal proceedings, Jefferson regained possession of the vehicle. Jefferson then sued Jones alleging that Jones had breached the warranty of title and requesting reimbursement of the expenses incurred in proving to the police that Jefferson owned the motorcycle. How should the court rule?

19.7 Challenger, a manufacturer of telecommunication equipment, wanted to buy a computer system for use in its accounting department. After consulting with several computer companies, Challenger bought a system from National for $120,000. The National salesman told Challenger that the system would provide various functions including accounts receivable, payroll, inventory, and state income tax. The contract signed by the parties provided in part:

1. National warrants that for 12 months the computer system will perform the enumerated functions in a skillful and workmanlike manner but in case of a failure to so perform National's sole obligation is limited to correcting any error in any program or routine within 60 days after notice of said failure.
2. In no event shall National be liable for special or consequential damages from any cause whatsoever.

The system delivered by National failed to perform the functions enumerated in the contract. Although National continuously attempted to repair the computer, only one program was operating two years after the signing of the contract.

(a) Challenger sued National for breach of the warranty of merchantability and fitness for a particular purpose and requested damages pursuant to UCC §2–714(2). National alleged that Challenger was not entitled to damages but that its sole remedy was to have National repair the computer. How should the court rule? Explain, citing appropriate UCC provisions.

(b) Challenger also sought damages of $8,500 representing salaries of employees who were unable to work because of the computer failure and lost profits. National denied that Challenger was entitled to such damages. How should the court rule? Explain.

19.8 Arnie, a young golfer, purchased a device called the Golfing Gizmo to help improve his game. The Gizmo is a simple device consisting of two metal pegs, two cords—one elastic, one cotton—and a regulation golf ball. After the pegs are driven into the ground approximately 25 inches apart, the elastic cord is looped over them. The cotton cord, measuring 21 feet in length, ties to the middle of the elastic cord. The ball is attached to the end of the cotton cord. When the cords are extended, the Gizmo resembles the shape of a large letter "T," with the ball resting at the base.

The instructions state that when hit correctly, the ball will fly out and spring back near the point of impact; if the ball returns to the left, it indicates a right-hander's "slice"; a shot returning to the right indicates a right-hander's "hook." If the ball is "topped," it does not return and must be retrieved by the player. The label on the shipping carton and the cover of the instruction booklet urge players to "drive the ball with full power" and further state. "COMPLETELY SAFE BALL WILL NOT HIT PLAYER."

After using the Gizmo a few times, Arnie hit the golf ball but his club became entangled in the cord. The ball struck Arnie in the head causing serious brain damage.

(a) Arnie sued the manufacturer for breach of express warranty alleging that the statement "COMPLETELY SAFE BALL WILL NOT HIT PLAYER" constituted an express warranty. The manufacturer denied that this was an express warranty. How should the court rule? Explain.

(b) Assume that no express warranty was made concerning the Golfing Gizmo. Has the manufacturer breached the warranty of merchantability? What characteristics would a merchantable "Golfing Gizmo" exhibit?

19.9 Color Carpet Co., a rug and carpet manufacturer, telephoned Acme Textile, Inc., a yarn manufacturer, to request information about Acme's yarn. After discussing its needs for yarn to be used to make home carpeting. Color Carpet ordered a large quantity of yarn. Acme then sent Color Carpet a written sales confirmation. The front of the confirmation included the following typed statement:

> THIS CONFIRMATION IS GIVEN SUBJECT TO ALL OF THE TERMS AND CONDITIONS ON THE FACE AND REVERSE SIDES HEREOF, including the provision for exclusion of warranties.

On the back of the confirmation was a series of typed paragraphs with headings in capital letters. Paragraph 4 read:

> WARRANTIES: Except as expressly stated on the face hereof, Seller makes no warranty express or implied, including without limitation as to: a) fitness of the yarn purchased hereunder for any specific purpose or end use; b) fastness of color or uniformity of shade from lot to lot; c) breaking strength; d) shrinkage; e) absence of minor contamination; f) physical or chemical qualities; and g) usual or ordinary variation in thickness or size. Seller shall not be liable for normal manufacturing defects nor for customary variations from specifications.

Color Carpet made no response after receiving the confirmation from Acme. Acme delivered the ordered yarn several weeks later and Color Carpet used it to manufacture carpets and rugs. After receiving numerous complaints from its customers about the quality of the yarn in these rugs and carpets. Color Carpet complained to Acme and refused to pay for the yarn. Acme responded by stating that the confirmation had effectively disclaimed all warranties. Is Acme correct? More specifically, did Acme disclaim the implied warranties of merchantability and fitness for a particular purpose? Explain, citing all relevant UCC provisions.

19.10 Paul Broke purchased a camera from Al's Pawnshop. As he was paying for the camera. Broke noticed a large neon sign over the cash register that read "All goods sold AS IS." The same statement was made in large (one-half inch), bright red type on the receipt. The agreement between Broke and the pawnshop was oral other than the receipt provided by Al's Pawnshop.

(a) Two days after purchasing the camera, Broke discovered that the camera did not work properly and could not be used to take pictures. Broke sued Al's Pawnshop for breach of the implied warranty of merchantability. How should the court rule? Explain.

(b) Two days after purchasing the camera, the police notified Broke that the camera was stolen property and confiscated it. Broke immediately notified Al's Pawnshop and demanded a refund. The store owner explained that he had not known the camera was stolen and refused to refund his money. Broke sued Al's Pawnshop for breach of the warranty of title. How should the court rule? Explain.

19.11 Smith visited the Fitz's Auto Sales Co. to buy a used automobile. After taking a car for a test drive, Smith offered to pay $8,000 for it if Fitz's would repaint the car and repair a rattle. The salesperson replied, "Our repair shop will put it in first-class shape. You've got a deal." After Fitz's repainted the car and repaired the rattle, Smith paid $8,000 and accepted delivery on November 3, 1989. Over the next eight months, Smith had numerous problems with the car and paid about $1,000 for repairs, including replacement of the intake gasket and installation of a new transmission and radiator. All repairs were performed by competent mechanics at a repair shop near Smith's house. Despite the repairs, the car stalled frequently in traffic. On August 1, Smith returned to Fitz's and demanded reimbursement of the purchase price. Fitz's refused. Smith then sued Fitz's.

(a) In his lawsuit, Smith alleged that the salesperson's statement "Our repair shop will put it in first-class shape" constituted an express warranty by Fitz's that the car would operate well. Was the statement an express warranty? Explain.

(b) Smith also alleged that Fitz's had breached the implied warranty of merchantability. Fitz's denied that the implied warranty of merchantability had been breached but further argued that, even if a breach had occurred, Fitz's should not be held liable because Smith had taken the car elsewhere for repairs. Assuming that the implied warranty of merchantability was breached, should Fitz's be held liable? Explain.

19.12 Between 1981 and 1985, General Motors Corporation (GM) manufactured several models of automobiles equipped with diesel engines. Because many of the cars had recurring mechanical problems, the diesel models acquired a poor reputation that reduced their demand in the used car market. A group of owners of GM cars with diesel engines brought a class action against GM alleging that it had breached the implied warranty of merchantability. Although the cars purchased by these owners were not mechanically defective, the resale value of the cars was low because of their poor reputation. The owners argued that because one of the ordinary purposes for which cars are used is resale, they were entitled to damages for the "lost resale value." Has GM violated the implied warranty of merchantability? Explain.

19.13 NSP, an electrical utility, was constructing new towers to carry electric transmission lines. The towers were to be supported by wires extending to the ground where they would be attached to buried screw anchors. NSP solicited proposals from manufacturers who wanted to supply the anchors, and provided detailed technical specifications for them. Meyer, after reading the specifications, submitted a proposal, which stated in part, "The material we propose to supply meets the design requirements as specified by NSP." NSP accepted Meyer's proposal and used the Meyer anchors. Between September 27 and September 30, 1988, four towers collapsed due to a defect in the anchors. NSP immediately notified Meyer and technical personnel from both companies inspected the anchors and discussed the problem. On October 15, NSP notified Meyer that it planned to remove all of the anchors. Although Meyer's technical staff believed that removal was unnecessary, Meyer did not object to NSP's plans. On February 28, 1989, NSP wrote Meyer asserting that Meyer had breached an express warranty by supplying defective anchors. A lawsuit followed.

(a) Did Meyer make an express warranty? Explain.

(b) Meyer argues that NSP failed to provide timely notice of the breach of warranty as required by UCC §2–607(3)(a). Is Meyer correct? Explain.

19.14 Section 2–314(1) provides that a "warranty that the goods shall be merchantable is implied in a contract for their sale if the seller is a *merchant with respect to goods of that kind.*" (Emphasis added.)

Assume the goods sold in the following transactions are not merchantable. Are the sellers involved "merchants" who give the implied warranty of merchantability? Explain.

(a) The city of Auburn, Washington, owned and operated the only aircraft fuel service at the city airport. The fuel service delivered contaminated fuel to its customers.

(b) City Hospital furnished and billed separately four units of blood to one of its patients during major surgery. The blood was contaminated, and as a result of the transfusion the patient contracted hepatitis. (Consider also in this case (a) whether any "sale" of goods is involved and (b) whether your answer would change had the supplier been a blood bank rather than a hospital.)

(c) Wilhelm, a commercial aerial and ground crop sprayer, was engaged by Doaks to spray his wheat crop to control wild oats. Wilhelm held himself out as an expert in aerial spraying, licensed by federal and state authorities and trained in use of crop sprays. Wilhelm had sole control over choice of the herbicide, mixing it, and applying it to Doaks's crops. After spraying Doaks's wheat became discolored and limp, ultimately yielding only six bushels per acre, compared with 16 per acre on his other fields.

(d) An association of mothers of high school band members organized a fund-raising luncheon. Turkey salad prepared and sold by the association proved to be contaminated with the bacteria salmonella. One of the persons purchasing the salad became seriously ill.

(e) The City National Bank loaned money to Jones to purchase a boat and took a security interest in the boat. When Jones failed to repay the loan. City repossessed the boat and sold it to Donald. The boat failed to operate properly.

(f) Would your answer in (e) above differ if the bank had sold five repossessed boats in the last year?

19.15 Northwest Auto Auction (NAA) acts as an auctioneer to sell cars for dealers who wish to sell the vehicles to other dealers. Gordo Vehicles purchased a car that was auctioned by NAA. NAA provided Gordo a bill of sale that described the car and listed the selling dealer as Archie's Auto Sales. The bill of sale also included the following:

THIS SALE IS SOLELY A TRANSACTION BETWEEN THE BUYING AND SELLING DEALERS.
Northwest Auto Auction guarantees title to the above car is free and clear of all liens. Northwest Auto Auction makes no warranty as to the mechanical condition of the car.

After purchasing the car, Gordo discovered that it was a stolen vehicle. Gordo sued NAA alleging that it had breached the warranty of title. How should the court rule? Explain.

19.16 Air Constructors, Inc. (ACI) was awarded a government contract to install a boiler room and underground piping system in a federal building. The government provided a list of specifications for the piping which included a requirement that all pipes be able to withstand temperatures of 240 degrees Fahrenheit. ACI provided the specifications to Howdy Co., a piping retailer, who recommended Copper-Gard pipe. Howdy sent ACI a product brochure for the Copper-Gard pipe that included the following statement: "Temperature Rating: Continuous working pressure through a temperature range of −40 degrees Fahrenheit to 250 degrees Fahrenheit." ACI submitted the product brochure to the government's supervising engineer who approved purchase of the pipe. ACI then ordered the pipe from Howdy. Included with the delivery of the pipe was an installation manual. Under the word "WARRANTY," which was printed in red capital letters on the front of manual, were six paragraphs of ordinary typed material. The first sentence read, "Seller expressly warrants that the pipe will be free from defects in material for one year after date of purchase." The final sentence of the last paragraph read, "This express warranty is in lieu of and excludes all other warranties expressed or implied including, without limitation, merchantability or fitness for a particular purpose." ACI properly installed the pipe but leaks soon developed because the piping could not withstand 240-degree water temperatures. ACI sued Howdy alleging that it had breached the warranty of fitness for a particular purpose.

(a) Howdy claimed that it had provided no warranty of fitness for a particular purpose but had provided only an express warranty that the pipe was free from defects in materials. Is Howdy correct? Explain fully.

(b) Assume that the court found that Howdy had provided a warranty of fitness for a particular purpose. Howdy then claimed that it had disclaimed the warranty. Was Howdy's disclaimer effective? Explain.

PRODUCTS LIABILITY

This chapter discusses **products liability,** the area of law imposing liability upon manufacturers and other suppliers of goods for personal injury and property damage caused by the products they sell. Assume, for example, that Home Appliances Co. manufactures hair dryers and sells them to a national distributor, Hair Product Wholesalers, which sells the dryers to various retailers, including Discount Mart, Inc. While Chris Consumer was using a home dryer purchased at the local Discount Mart, it overheated and caused a fire that injured Consumer and members of his family and damaged Consumer's house. The principles of products liability law determine whether Consumer and the other injured parties are entitled to recover damages and, if so, which of the sellers—the manufacturer, wholesaler, or retailer—should be liable for those damages.

Early American courts, applying seventeenth-century English precedents, followed the harsh *caveat*

emptor (let the buyer beware) doctrine. Under this theory a seller had no liability in tort or contract to anyone, including a purchaser, for injuries caused by its defective product. As a result, an injured party could recover only by proving fraud or that the seller had guaranteed some specific characteristic or quality of the product.

Overview of Modern Products Liability Law

During the twentieth century, in response to modern mass production and marketing of goods, courts and legislatures gradually have rejected the *caveat emptor* doctrine by imposing liability on sellers of defective products. Today, sellers of defective products may be held liable to third parties injured by the products under three theories: (1) negligence, (2) breach of warranty, and (3) strict liability in tort. Thus, modern product liability law is grounded partially in the law of contract (warranty) and partially in the law of torts (negligence and strict liability). Although all three theories are used to impose liability on manufacturers and suppliers, the strict liability in tort doctrine has, beginning in the early 1960s, emerged as the primary basis for recovery by injured plaintiffs in products liability cases.

This chapter discusses the three theories of products liability recovery by examining the elements of a plaintiff's claim and the defenses that insulate sellers from liability under each theory. Note that products liability law provides compensation to *individuals* for *personal* injury and property damage caused by defective products. Recovery for purely *economic* losses, including direct economic damages—for example, the cost of repairing or replacing a defective product—or indirect economic consequential damages—for example, lost profits—continue to be governed exclusively by the law of warranty discussed in Chapter 19.

Privity of Contract

A brief introduction to the "privity of contract" concept is needed to understand products liability law. Persons who have entered into a contractual relationship with each other are said to be in **privity of contract.** For example, if Seth sells a lawn mower to Linda, he and she are in privity of contract. An important issue in all products liability cases is to what extent injured persons not in privity with the seller may recover. Persons not in privity who are injured by the product stand in either a "horizontal" or "vertical" relationship to the manufacturer or other supplier from whom they seek to recover. A "vertical" party not in privity is a buyer of the goods who is one or more steps removed from the seller in the chain of distribution. For example, when a manufacturer sells a product to a wholesaler who sells it to a retailer who sells it to a consumer, the consumer is in privity only with the retailer. If, however, the product causes injury, the consumer may seek to recover from the wholesaler or manufacturer. The consumer's relationship to them is said to be "vertical."

"Horizontal" parties not in privity are those who are not buyers but others who by use, consumption, or other contact with the goods are injured by them. Assume Smith Corp. sells a car with defective brakes to Jones, who allows his son Art to use the car to take his girlfriend Beth to the senior prom. Art, Beth, and Carl, an innocent bystander, are injured when the car crashes because the brakes fail. Art, Beth, and Carl stand in a "horizontal" relationship to Smith but are not in privity with Smith (Jones is).

Privity issues under each theory (negligence, warranty, and strict liability) are discussed below. It is important to note at the outset, however, that in modern product liability law, lack of privity does *not* bar a plaintiff's recovery.

Negligence

The principles of the law of negligence are covered in Chapter 5. That material examined the law primarily as applied to cases not involving products liability, to compensate, for example, for injuries caused by negligently driven automobiles or dangerous conditions existing on land. The following material briefly reviews negligence law and then discusses how it has been applied to compensate persons injured by defective products.

Negligence in General

As discussed in Chapter 5, negligence law imposes liability for injuries proximately caused by a person's failure to use "reasonable" or "ordinary" care—the amount of care a reasonably careful and prudent person would use under similar circumstances. In other words, to avoid liability for negligence, a person must conform his or her conduct to that of a reasonable person under like circumstances. Negligence may result from doing an act a reasonable person would not do, or neglecting to do something a reasonable person would do. The hypothetical reasonable person is not an extraordinarily cautious or skillful individual, but one possessing merely ordinary prudence and judgment. Whether the defendant's conduct falls below the standard set by the reasonable person ordinarily is a question for the jury to decide. To recover on the basis of negligence, the plaintiff must show that (1) defendant owed plaintiff a duty not to be negligent, (2) defendant breached that duty by failing to exercise reasonable or ordinary care, and (3) defendant's breach of duty was the "proximate" or "legal" cause of (4) an actual loss or injury suffered by the plaintiff.

Manufacturer's or Supplier's Duty

Applied to products liability, the law of negligence imposes a duty upon the manufacturer or other supplier to exercise reasonable care in the design, production, and distribution of its products. Early cases, following *Winterbottom v. Wright* (1842),[1] held that the seller's

---

[1]10 Mees. & W. 109, 152 Eng. Rep. 402 (Ex. 1842).

duty extended to only those persons in privity of contract with the seller. The rule in *Winterbottom* was designed to protect the manufacturers that were developing during the Industrial Revolution. It was based on the assumption that "industry could not grow and prosper if it had to pay for any and all injuries its defective products caused. The assumption rested on the oft-disproved notion that wheels operate at peak efficiency when unattended by brakes."[2] The harshness of the rule was readily apparent; it left the injured party without a remedy unless in privity with the seller. Moreover, manufacturers who actually created the harmful product were insulated from liability. Courts quickly began to circumvent the rule by dispensing with privity when injuries were caused by "imminently or inherently dangerous" products.

The privity requirement in negligence actions for other products was first rejected in 1916 in *MacPherson v. Buick Motor Co.*[3] In this case, the defendant manufacturer sold a car to a dealer who then sold it to the plaintiff. Plaintiff was subsequently thrown out of the car and injured when a defective wheel collapsed. When sued, defendant asserted lack of privity as a defense. (Note that the plaintiff stood in a "vertical" relationship to defendant here, a buyer later in the distributive chain.) Judge Benjamin Cardozo (who later would sit on the U.S. Supreme Court) stated that abolition of privity should not be "limited to poisons, explosives, and things of like nature, to things which in their normal operation are implements of destruction." He went on to hold:

> If the nature of a thing is such that it is reasonably certain to place life and limb in peril when negligently made, it is then a thing of danger. Its nature gives warning of the consequences to be expected. If to the element of danger there is added knowledge that the thing *will be used by persons other than the purchaser, and used without new tests, then, irrespective of contract, the manufacturer of this thing of danger is under a duty to make it carefully.*[4]

Today, all states follow the rule adopted in *MacPherson* so that lack of privity is no longer a defense in products liability actions based on negligence. That is, a seller owes a duty to exercise reasonable care in the manufacture and distribution of its product not only to the seller's immediate purchaser, but also to all reasonably foreseeable persons who may be injured by the product.

Breach of Duty

After establishing that the defendant owed the duty to exercise reasonable care, the plaintiff must prove that defendant breached the duty by failing to exercise reasonable care in the design, production, or distribution of the product that injured the plaintiff. Typically, the defendant's breach of duty may result from the use of an unsafe design or improper materials, inadequate testing of the product, insufficient quality control during manufacture (for example, inspection), or failure to provide adequate instructions or warnings concerning proper use. In the following case, the court considers what evidence is appropriate to help a jury determine reasonable care in the design and manufacture of a product.

Hansen v. Abrasive Engineering and Manufacturing, Inc.
856 P.2d 625 (Or. 1993)

Plaintiff Timothy Hansen was employed at a millwork plant where he operated a six-head sanding machine made by the defendant, Abrasive Engineering and Manufacturing, Inc. The plaintiff was injured when his hand was pulled into the machine as he tried to remove wood buildup from the sanding belts while they were operating. The plaintiff sued for negligence claiming that the defendant had failed to exercise reasonable care in the design and manufacture of the sanding machine because it did not meet the safety standards established by the American National Standards Institute (ANSI) and did not include safety features required by the rules of the Oregon Occupational Safety and Health Code (OOSHC) and the federal Occupational Safety and Health Act (OSHA). The trial court allowed the plaintiff to present evidence of the ANSI standards but refused to admit the OOSHC or OSHA rules into evidence because they did not apply to the defendant. After the jury found in favor of the defendant, both parties appealed. The court of appeals reversed, holding that the rules of OOSHC and OSHA should have been admitted into evidence. The Oregon Supreme Court accepted the case for review.

---

[2]Traynor, *The Ways and Meanings of Defective Products and Strict Liability,* 32 TENN. L. REV. 363, 364 (1965).
[3]111 N.E. 1050 (N.Y. 1916).
[4]*Id.* at 1053 (emphasis added).

Van Hoomissen, Justice

. . . Defendant contends that the Court of Appeals erred in holding that the trial court properly allowed the jury to consider the ANSI advisory standards on the issue of whether defendant failed to meet the standard of care that defendant owed to plaintiff. Defendant argues that, because the ANSI standards are purely advisory and not binding on anyone, they are not relevant. . . .

In this case, both parties agree that the general "reasonable person" standard of care applies. Whether a defendant has met that standard of care is an issue of fact, to be determined by the jury. Thus, evidence pertaining to whether defendant's conduct was reasonable is relevant to the jury's determination of whether defendant met the reasonable person standard of care.

Because advisory safety standards that are adopted by nongovernmental entities such as ANSI may represent a consensus regarding what a reasonable person in a particular industry would do, they may be helpful to the trier of fact in deciding whether the defendant has met the standard of care due. . . . Although violation of an industry custom does not constitute negligence *per se,* it may be shown in order to establish whether a party has met a standard of care to which the party is required to conform. "It is a test of negligence, but not a conclusive or controlling test." *Mennis v. Cheffings,* [376 P.2d 672 (Or. 1962)].

The ANSI advisory standards provide some evidence of the custom in defendant's industry and, therefore, are relevant to the jury's consideration of whether defendant met the standard of care. We find no error in the admission of the ANSI standards into evidence.

Defendant next contends that the Court of Appeals erred in holding that evidence relating to the OOSHC and OSHA safety rules were improperly excluded at trial. Defendant argues that, because it is not an employer subject to the safety requirements contained in those two sets of rules, the court misapplied the rule of law . . . that allows for use of certain safety regulations in negligence cases. . . .

This court has held that a "manufacturer should have a duty of exercising due care to avoid foreseeable harm to the users of [its] product." *State ex rel Western Seed v. Campbell,* [442 P.2d 215 (Or. 1968)]. . . . In the present case, the jury was required to determine whether defendant's design and manufacture of its sanding machine fell below that standard of care. Defendant designed and manufactured its sanding machine for use

by customers such as plaintiff's employer for use in a workplace governed by the OOSHC and OSHA rules. Thus, the OOSHC and OSHA rules are relevant, even though not binding on defendant, for exactly the same reasons that the ANSI standards are relevant, *i.e.,* because they pertain to the issue of whether defendant met the standard of care. Those *non-binding* rules are properly to be considered as evidence, similar to evidence of industry custom or trade practice, and are admissible because they are relevant to the jury's asssessment of whether defendant complied with the standard of care. . . .

We conclude that the OOSHC and OSHA rules may be relevant to tort claims even when a defendant is not bound by those rules, depending on the circumstances of the case. Under circumstances such as these, where the defendant is not bound by the OOSHC and OSHA rules, those rules should be treated the same as the ANSI standards; they provide some relevant information for consideration by the jury about whether the defendant met the standard of care due and are, therefore, admissible as evidence. . . .

[Judgment affirmed.]

Plaintiff's Proof—*Res Ipsa Loquitur*

The plaintiff has the burden of proving by a preponderance of the evidence (meaning that it is more likely than not) defendant's negligence. In proving this issue, the plaintiff often is aided by the doctrine of **res ipsa loquitur,** literally meaning "the thing speaks for itself." Under this doctrine, it may be inferred that the harm suffered by the plaintiff has been caused by the defendant's negligence if:

1. the event is of a kind that ordinarily does not occur in the absence of negligence; and
2. other responsible causes, including the conduct of the plaintiff and third persons, are sufficiently eliminated by the evidence.[5]

The second element usually is established by plaintiff's proof that "a specific instrumentality which has caused the event, or all reasonably probable causes, were under the exclusive control of the defendant. Thus the

---

[5]RESTATEMENT (SECOND) OF TORTS §328D.

responsibility of the defendant is proved by eliminating that of any other person."[6]

If the plaintiff is able to establish the foregoing requirements, the jury is permitted to infer that the defect in the product was caused by the defendant's negligence. Thus, the plaintiff is allowed to recover even though unable to offer any direct evidence regarding the particular conduct of the defendant constituting negligence and even if the defendant introduces evidence that the event was not caused by its negligence. For example, the defendant may introduce evidence of quality control procedures in manufacture. In other words, the jury is entitled to weigh the fact that the event did occur against the defendant's evidence of due care tending to indicate that it could not have occurred. The doctrine most commonly is applied in the products liability context when products reaching the plaintiff in sealed containers cause injury. Examples include exploding beer or soda bottles; foreign objects found in bottled, canned, or baked goods; and tainted products, such as botulism in canned beans.

Defenses to Negligence

After a plaintiff proves the elements of negligence, the defendant may avoid or reduce its liability by proving one or more of the defenses to a negligence action. These defenses, which are based on the plaintiff's conduct, include assumption of the risk and comparative negligence. For example, the defendant may escape liability by proving that the plaintiff voluntarily assumed the risk of harm caused by the defendant's negligence. Under comparative negligence principles, the defendant's liability may be reduced by proof that the plaintiff's own negligence contributed to his or her injury. These defenses are discussed in more detail in Chapter 5.

The following case illustrates the application of negligence principles in a products liability case.

Nicholson v. American Safety Utility Corporation
476 S.E.2d 672 (N.C. App. 1996)

Plaintiff Tony Nicholson, an electrical lineman, suffered severe and permanent brain and nervous system injuries

---

[6]*Id.,* comment g.

when he was electrocuted by overhead power lines. Plaintiff, while working in an aerial utility bucket beneath lines carrying 7,200 volts of electricity, was wearing a protective helmet and rubber lineman's safety gloves that were marketed as safe for use with energized lines up to 17,000 volts. Just before the accident, the wind blew off his helmet. As plaintiff continued connecting a de-energized cable, electricity jumped from the overhead lines through his head and body and exited through his hands. The gloves failed to prevent completion of the electrical circuit. Plaintiff brought a products liability lawsuit against defendants Siebe North, the manufacturer of the gloves, and American Safety Utility Corporation (ASU), the company that had sold the gloves to the plaintiff's employer. Plaintiff's claims against the defendants included allegations that they failed "to exercise due care in the testing, inspection, marketing, promotion, sale and/or delivery" of the safety gloves. The trial court granted the defendants' motion for summary judgment and the plaintiff appealed.

John, Judge

. . . Summary judgment is generally inappropriate in a negligence action . . . "even when there is no dispute as to the facts, because the issue of whether a party acted in conformity with the reasonable person standard is ordinarily an issue to be determined by a jury." *Surrette v. Duke Power Co.,* [388 S.E.2d 129, 131 (N.C.App. 1986)]. . . . The essential elements of a products liability action predicated upon negligence are: "(1) evidence of a standard of care owed by the reasonably prudent person in similar circumstances; (2) breach of that standard of care; (3) injury caused directly or proximately by the breach, and; (4) loss because of the injury." *Ziglar v. Du Pont Co.,* [280 S.E.2d 510, 513 (N.C. App. 1981).] In addition, a plaintiff must present evidence the product was in a defective condition at the time it left the defendant's control. . . .

A *manufacturer* must use reasonable care in the design and manufacture of products, and this includes the duty to perform "reasonable tests and inspections to discover latent hazards." [*Cockerham v. Ward and Astrup Co.,* 262 S.E.2d 651, 654 (N.C. App. 1980).] Moreover, a manufacturer must exercise "the 'highest' or 'utmost' caution, commensurate with the risks of serious harm involved, in the production of a dangerous instrumentality or substance." [*Ziglar,* 280 S.E.2d at 515]. . . .

In addition, a manufacturer is under an obligation to provide warnings of any dangers associated with the product's use "sufficiently intelligible and prominent to reach and protect all those who may reasonably be expected to come into contact with [the product]." [*Ziglar,* 280 S.E.2d at 516.] Failure to warn adequately renders the product defective. . . .

A non-manufacturing *seller* acting as a "mere conduit" of the product, on the other hand, ordinarily has no affirmative duty to inspect and test a product made by a reputable manufacturer. . . . However, this rule does not stand where the seller knows or has reason to know of a product's dangerous propensity. Moreover, where the seller acts as more than a "mere conduit," such as in [this] case . . . where seller performed product tests and inspections, it must do so with reasonable care. . . .

Further, the exercise of due care requires a seller to warn of any hazard associated with use of a product if: (1) the seller has "actual or constructive knowledge of a particular threatening characteristic of the product;" and (2) the seller "has reason to know that the purchaser will not realize the product's menacing propensities for himself." [*Ziglar,* 280 S.E.2d at 513.]

Review of the record in light of the foregoing principles reveals the existence of a genuine issue of material fact as to the alleged failure of defendants Siebe and ASU to test and inspect the gloves properly and to convey adequate warning of potential deficiencies in the gloves.

At the summary judgment hearing, defendants presented evidence tending to show their compliance with industry inspection procedures for lineman safety gloves, including the subject gloves herein. Each defendant presented evidence it had conducted industry standard visual inspections and dielectric safety tests on the gloves used by plaintiff on 26 January 1990, the Siebe test taking place on or about 17 February 1989 and the ASU test on or about 12 January 1990.

Dielectric testing is a process of immersing and filling a glove in a vat of water, and then subjecting the inside and outside of the glove to increasing voltage. If the glove fails to insulate, a circuit is completed and the failure is recorded by the testing machine. Siebe's evidence indicated the gloves withstood dielectric testing of 20,000 volts for three minutes; ASU indicated it utilized a dielectric test of 20,000 volts for one and one-half minutes.

Defense counsel for ASU argued plaintiff had failed to present evidence of a discoverable defect, and Siebe's counsel contended there was no proof a defect existed when the gloves left Siebe's possession approximately 10 months prior to the accident. Ultimately, both defendants maintained the gloves must have been damaged by plaintiff in use or storage during the three days prior to the accident, and further argued that plaintiff's post-accident tests, which revealed defects in both gloves, had been improperly performed.

In contrast, plaintiff presented evidence . . . that (1) there were no signs plaintiff had abused or misused the gloves or that the gloves had been improperly stored subsequent to leaving defendants' possession, (2) that line workers, including plaintiff, were expected to rely on rubber safety gloves such as those at issue for protection from electrocution, and were permitted to do so by the National Electrical Safety Code and OSHA, and 3) that plaintiff had been electrocuted at approximately 7,200 volts—far less than the rated "use" voltage of 17,000 for the gloves.

Plaintiff also presented evidence that the right and left hand gloves each failed dielectric testing subsequent to the accident. According to statistical evidence developed from Siebe's own production reports and presented by plaintiff's expert, failure of this test by both gloves was a virtual impossibility if both Siebe and ASU had indeed properly tested the gloves as they asserted. In addition, the expert countered defendants' claims that plaintiff's test results were unreliable due to failure to wash the gloves prior to testing, and presented an explanation of why the right hand glove failed in the field at approximately 7,200 volts, but a failure did not register during subsequent testing until 10,000–15,000 volts were administered. Further, record evidence tended to show that despite defendant Siebe's knowledge that a certain percentage of gloves would fail in the field due to manufacturing defects, Siebe warned neither ASU nor line workers such as plaintiff of the potential for failure.

Finally, regarding the less-contested element of proximate cause, plaintiff presented evidence that burns on plaintiff's right hand correlated precisely with the area of the gloves which failed during post-accident testing.

Viewing the record in the light most favorable to plaintiff, . . . we conclude plaintiff produced a forecast of evidence sufficient to create a genuine issue of material fact in response to defendants' attempted showing of the non-existence of an essential element of plaintiff's negligence claim. . . . Most notably, evidence of the electrocution of plaintiff at 7,200 volts, far less than the "use" rating of the gloves, evidence of certain manufacturing defects in the gloves, and the testimony of plaintiff's expert calling into question defendants' assurances of testing and inspecting the gloves, work to offset defendants' showing. Questions of fact, therefore, remain regarding whether defendants "acted in conformity with the reasonable person standard," . . . in testing and inspecting the gloves and, particularly as to defendant Siebe, in providing adequate warnings. . . .

[Judgment on negligence claim reversed and remanded.]

Breach of Warranty

An alternative basis for products liability recovery is the law of warranty, a branch of contract law. As explained in Chapter 19, a contract for the sale of goods may include an express warranty, an implied warranty of merchantability, or an implied warranty of fitness for a particular purpose. As with contract liability generally, warranty liability is **strict**—liability is imposed without fault. Accordingly, liability for breach of warranty does not depend upon the seller's knowledge or reason to know of the product's defectiveness or upon negligence. If the seller makes an express or implied warranty and the goods fail to perform as warranted, liability follows. Although a breach of warranty often causes merely commercial or economic injury, UCC §2–715(2)(b) expressly authorizes recovery—as consequential damages—for "injury to person or property proximately resulting from any breach of warranty." To recover for personal injuries or property damage under this theory, a plaintiff must prove that the seller made an express or implied warranty, that the seller breached this warranty, and that the seller's breach was the proximate cause of the plaintiff's injuries. In the following case, the court was required to determine whether express and implied Code warranties had been created.

Sipes v. General Motors Corporation
946 S.W.2d 143 (Tex. App. 1997)

Plaintiffs Rick and Jamie Sipes filed a products liability lawsuit alleging that Jamie Sipes was injured in an automobile accident because the airbag in their Pontiac Firebird failed to deploy. The lawsuit claimed that defendants General Motors Corporation, Delco Electronics Corp., and J.O. Williams Motors, Inc. were liable for the injuries based on breach of warranty. The trial court granted the defendants' motion for summary judgment on breach of warranty and the Sipeses appealed.

Grant, Justice

. . . The overwhelming majority of products liability cases based on warranty are not only influenced but controlled by the Uniform Commercial Code. . . . The warranty remedies pertinent to products liability are express warranty, implied warranty of merchantability, and implied warranty of fitness for a particular purpose. . . .

An express warranty requires some affirmative representation by the seller. The Sipeses never said that any particular person made a statement to them about the airbag, but rather stated their general understanding of the functioning of the airbag. The material furnished by the manufacturer, however, suggested that the airbag would deploy upon a severe frontal impact. This amounted to a representation of the airbag's function. The fact finder could find in the present case that there was a severe frontal impact. Such a finding could be a basis for a breach of express warranty. Therefore, [defendants] are not entitled to a summary judgment on this theory of recovery.

In a products liability case, the implied warranty of merchantability is breached if the product was defective when it left the manufacturer's or seller's possession and was unfit for the ordinary purposes for which it is used because of a lack of something necessary for adequacy. . . . The defect in an implied warranty of merchantability case means the condition of the goods that, because of a lack of something necessary for adequacy, renders them unfit for the ordinary purpose for which they are used. . . . In strict products liability, "defect" means a condition of the product that renders it unreasonably dangerous. In [*Alvarado v. Hyundai*, 908 S.W.2d 243, 253 (Tex. App. 1995)], . . . the court made the following general statement involving the automobile restraint system: "The consumer's demand of the manufacturer is that the chosen option of a passive belt system should be reasonably effective for the intended use. A restraint system should restrain. If it does not, it is defective and liability attaches."

The contention in the present case is that the airbag system failed to restrain as it was designed to do and thus was not fit for the ordinary purpose for which such a product is to be used. The [defendants produced an affidavit by Bahling, an expert witness] to show that the ordinary purpose of the airbag was to deploy upon a frontal or near-frontal impact in which the driver could receive serious or life-threatening injuries. . . . [T]he Sipeses raised a fact question concerning whether the impact was one in which the airbag ordinarily was designed to deploy. Therefore, the [defendants] failed to conclusively establish this element against the Sipeses.

In a breach of implied warranty of merchantability, the consumer is not necessarily required to produce direct evidence of the cause of the defective condition or the improper function. . . . Rather, the consumer may satisfy this burden by showing that a product functioned improperly under normal use. . . . Circumstantial evidence can establish that an automobile component was defective when it left the automobile manufacturer's control. . . .

To show that the airbag was not defective when it left General Motor's possession, the [defendants] offered Bahling's affidavit saying that the airbag functioned as it was designed to function. As discussed above, the Sipeses raised a fact issue on this element. Therefore, the [defendants] have failed to conclusively negate breach of the implied warranty of merchantability. The [defendants] are not entitled to a summary judgment on the foregoing warranty contentions.

Warranty of fitness for a particular purpose arises if the seller has reason to know of a particular purpose for which the goods are acquired and that the buyer is relying on the seller's skill or expertise in selecting the goods. The "particular purpose must be a particular nonordinary purpose." *Miles v. Ford Motor Co.*, 922 S.W.2d 572, 587 (Tex. App. 1996). "The ordinary purposes for which goods are used are those included in the concept of merchantability and go to uses that are customarily made of the goods." *Id.* In the present case, the Sipeses were acquiring the airbags only for the general purpose for which they are designed. Therefore, they have not contended a situation in which a particular purpose would arise and this theory is not a part of this litigation.

[Judgment on warranty for a particular purpose affirmed; judgment on other warranties reversed and remanded.]

Defenses to Breach of Warranty

Because warranty is based on contract, the personal injury plaintiff suing for breach of warranty traditionally has encountered the seller's contract-based defenses blocking recovery. These defenses include, for example, (1) failure to give timely notice of the breach, (2) contractual limitation or disclaimer of warranty protection, and (3) lack of privity of contract between the warrantor-seller and the injured plaintiff. Although these defenses often were successful in early warranty cases, the UCC, which was widely adopted in the mid-1960s, and judicial decisions interpreting it, eliminate or reduce the effect of these defenses in modern products liability actions based on breach of warranty.

Notice of Breach. As a condition to recovery for a breach of warranty, UCC §2–607(3)(a) requires that the buyer notify the seller of breach within a reasonable time after its discovery. Though this is a sound rule in the commercial context (it protects the seller against unreasonably delayed damage claims by a buyer), in a personal injury case, the injured plaintiff is unlikely to give notice to a remote seller with whom he has not dealt. For this reason, the Code authorizes a more relaxed notice standard for consumers than for commercial purchasers. As noted in Official Comment 4 to §2–607:

> The time of notification is to be determined by applying commercial standards to a merchant buyer. "A reasonable time" for notification from a retail consumer is to be judged by different standards so that in his case it will be extended, for the rule of requiring notification is designed to defeat commercial bad faith, not to deprive a good faith consumer of his remedy.

In addition, courts often liberally construe the notice requirement when personal, as opposed to commercial, injury is involved. For example, in some cases, the plaintiff's filing a lawsuit has been held sufficient to provide notice to the defendant.

Disclaimer. Section 2–719, introduced in Chapter 18, generally allows the parties to contractually modify or limit remedies available for breach. Section 2–719(3), however, severely restricts a seller's ability to contractually disclaim warranty liability for personal as opposed to commercial, injury. Specifically, §2–719(3) provides that consequential damages may be limited or excluded unless the limitation or exclusion is unconscionable. Limitation of consequential damage for personal injury in cases involving consumer goods is unconscionable on its face, but limitation when the loss is commercial is not. That is, if a clause limiting consequential damages is used, the buyer has the burden of proving its unconscionable effect unless the clause attempts to limit damages for personal injury caused by a consumer good.

Privity. The UCC statutorily eliminates privity of contract as a defense to products liability cases based on breach of warranty in §2–318, which determines which third parties, not in privity with the seller, are entitled to recover for a breach of warranty. Recognizing that states may differ on this issue, §2–318 provides three separate alternatives defining the extent of the seller's liability for breach of express or implied warranty. Alternative A, adopted in a majority of states, is the most restrictive, allowing recovery to any natural person who is in the family or household of the buyer or who is a guest in the buyer's home if it is reasonable to expect that such person may use, consume, or be affected by the goods and who suffers personal injury because of the breach of warranty. Thus, under alternative A, liability extends horizontally beyond strict privity to the limited class of persons outlined above. In states adopting this alternative, the issue of liability to vertical parties not in privity is left to court determination through case law.[7]

Most of the remaining states use the more expansive Alternatives B and C. Alternative B extends the seller's warranty horizontally and vertically to any natural person who may reasonably be expected to use, consume, or be affected by the goods and who suffers personal injury as a result of the breach of warranty. Alternative C is identical to alternative B except that liability is extended for injury to both person and *property.* Under any alternative, the seller may not contractually reduce the class of persons to whom it would otherwise be liable for personal injury under §2–318.

Strict Liability in Tort

Development of the Doctrine

The law of warranty is designed and is well-suited to compensate the immediate parties to a contract for economic or commercial injury caused by breach of warranty. Warranty law, however, even since the adoption of the UCC, often proves cumbersome when applied to personal injuries sustained by parties remote to the contract. In the early 1960s, courts therefore began to develop a new doctrine, known as **strict liability in tort,** which uses a warranty concept (imposing liability without fault) but which imposes liability on the basis of tort law rather than contract law principles.

A major case in the development of the doctrine was *Henningsen v. Bloomfield Motors, Inc.* (1960),[8] in which plaintiffs sued for breach of the implied warranty of merchantability to recover for personal injuries caused by the crash of a new automobile. In finding for the plaintiffs, the court, in effect, interpreted the implied warranty of merchantability in products liability cases to mean that the product must be reasonably safe for its intended use—an implied warranty of safety. The court further found that this "warranty" was unencumbered by defenses traditionally available to the seller in contract warranty actions: lack of privity, lack of notice, and disclaimer. In the words of the court:

> . . . [U]nder modern marketing conditions, when a manufacturer puts a new automobile in the stream of trade and promotes its purchase by the public, an *implied warranty that it is reasonably suitable for use as such accompanies it into the hands of the ultimate purchaser.*[9]

This approach quickly evolved into the strict liability in tort doctrine, the dominant products liability theory today. The origin of the strict liability doctrine usually is traced to the following landmark case.

Greenman v. Yuba Power Products, Inc.
377 P.2d 897 (Cal. 1962)

> Plaintiff William Greenman was injured while using a combination power tool manufactured by defendant Yuba

---

[7]UCC §2–318, Official Comment 3.

[8]161 A.2d 69 (N.J. 1960).
[9]*Id.* at 84 (emphasis added).

Power Products, Inc. (Yuba). When using the tool as a lathe, Greenman was severely injured when the piece of wood he was working flew out of the machine and struck him. Because of defective design or construction, the set screws used to hold parts of the machine together were inadequate and, as a result, normal vibration during operation caused the tail stock of the lathe to move away from the wood being turned resulting in the injury.

Greenman sued on the basis of negligence and breach of express warranty contained in Yuba's brochure. Before purchase, he had studied the brochure that indicated that the product's ruggedness and positive locking aspects made it an accurate lathe. The trial court found in favor of Greenman, and awarded damages of $65,000. Yuba appealed.

Traynor, Justice

. . . The manufacturer contends, . . . that plaintiff did not give it notice of breach of warranty within a reasonable time and that therefore his cause of action for breach of warranty is barred. . . .

The notice requirement . . . however, is not an appropriate one for the court to adopt in actions by injured consumers against manufacturers with whom they have not dealt. . . . "As between the immediate parties to the sale [the notice requirement] is a sound commercial rule, designed to protect the seller against unduly delayed claims for damages. As applied to personal injuries, and notice to a remote seller, it becomes a booby-trap for the unwary. The injured consumer is seldom 'steeped in the business practice which justifies the rule,' [James, *Product Liability,* 34 TEX. L. REV. 44, 192, 197 (1955)] and at least until he has had legal advice it will not occur to him to give notice to one with whom he has had no dealings." [Prosser, *The Assault Upon the Citadel (Strict Liability to the Consumer)*, 69 YALE L.J. 1099, 1130 (1960)] . . . We conclude therefore that even if plaintiff did not give timely notice of breach of warranty to the manufacturer, his cause of action based on the representations contained in the brochure was not barred.

Moreover, to impose strict liability on the manufacturer under the circumstances of this case, it was not necessary for plaintiff to establish an express warranty. . . . A manufacturer is strictly liable in tort when an article he places on the market, knowing that it is to be used without inspection for defects, proves to have a defect that causes injury to a human being. Recognized first in the case of unwholesome food products, such liability has now been extended to a variety of other

products that create as great or greater hazards if defective. . . .

Although in these cases strict liability has usually been based on the theory of an express or implied warranty running from the manufacturer to the plaintiff, the abandonment of the requirement of a contract between them, the recognition that the liability is not assumed by agreement but imposed by law . . . and the refusal to permit the manufacturer to define the scope of its own responsibility for defective products . . . make clear that the liability is not one governed by the law of contract warranties but by the law of strict liability in tort. Accordingly, rules defining and governing warranties that were developed to meet the needs of commercial transactions cannot properly be invoked to govern the manufacturer's liability to those injured by their defective products unless those rules also serve the purposes for which such liability is imposed. . . .

The purpose of such liability is to insure that the costs of injuries resulting from defective products are borne by the manufacturers that put such products on the market rather than by the injured persons who are powerless to protect themselves. Sales warranties serve this purpose fitfully at best. . . . In the present case, for example, plaintiff was able to plead and prove an express warranty only because he read and relied on the representations of the Shopsmith's ruggedness contained in the manufacturer's brochure. Implicit in the machine's presence on the market, however, was a representation that it would safely do the jobs for which it was built. Under these circumstances, it should not be controlling whether plaintiff selected the machine because of the statements in the brochure, or because of the machine's own appearance of excellence that belied the defect lurking beneath the surface, or because he merely assumed that it would safely do the jobs it was built to do. It should not be controlling whether the details of the sales from manufacturer to retailer and from retailer to [plaintiff] were such that one or more of the implied warranties of the sales act arose. . . . "The remedies of injured consumers ought not to be made to depend upon the intricacies of the law of sales." [*Ketterer v. Armour & Co.,* 200 F. 322, 323, (S.D.N.Y. 1912); *Klein v. Duchess Sandwich Co.,* 93 P.2d 799, 804 (Cal. 1939)] To establish the manufacturer's liability it was sufficient that plaintiff proved that he was injured while using the Shopsmith in a way it was intended to be used as a result of a defect in design and manufacture of which plaintiff was not aware that made the Shopsmith unsafe for its intended use. . . .

[Judgment affirmed.]

Restatement (Second) of Torts §402A

Since the *Greenman* decision, the strict liability in tort doctrine has been adopted by judicial decision or statute in most states, and is today the primary basis of products liability recovery. The *Restatement (Second) of Torts* §402A, drafted shortly after the *Greenman* decision, serves as the basis for the cause of action in most states. Section 402A (entitled "Special Liability of Seller of Product for Physical Harm to User or Consumer") provides in full:

1. One who sells any product in a defective condition unreasonably dangerous to the user or consumer or to his property is subject to liability for physical harm thereby caused to the ultimate user or consumer, or to his property, if

   a. the seller is engaged in the business of selling such a product, and
   b. it is expected to and does reach the user or consumer without substantial change in the condition in which it is sold.

2. The rule stated in Subsection (1) applies although

   a. the seller has exercised all possible care in the preparation and sale of his product, and
   b. the user or consumer has not bought the product from or entered into any contractual relation with the seller.

Therefore, to recover against a seller under §402A the plaintiff generally must show that

1. the product was in an unreasonably dangerous condition—that is, the product was "defective";
2. the unreasonably dangerous condition existed at the time the product left the seller's control; and
3. the unreasonably dangerous condition caused the plaintiff's injury or damage.

Liability exists despite the seller's lack of negligence (the "strict" aspect of the liability) and without regard to whether any contractual relationship (privity of contract) exists between the seller and the injured party.

Strict liability may be viewed, therefore, as an implied warranty, imposed by law and grounded on considerations of public policy, that a seller's product will not be unreasonably dangerous when used for its intended purpose. In fact, the doctrine often has been explained as nothing more than the implied warranty of merchantability stripped of the contract defenses of notice of defect, privity, and disclaimer.

Public Policy Grounds for Strict Liability

Strict liability in tort shifts the cost of an injury caused by a defective product from the person injured to the product's sellers. Courts and legislatures have cited several important public policy considerations to support imposing this liability. Perhaps most important, the public interest in human life and health requires that the law provide maximum protection against unreasonably dangerous products. Sellers who know that they are strictly liable for injuries caused by defective products are more likely to take steps to assure that their products are safe. As a general rule, the seller is in a better position than the buyer to determine whether or not a product is unreasonably dangerous. Further, defective products are available in the marketplace through the efforts of sellers. By inducing the use of their products—through advertising, promotion, and sale—sellers impliedly represent that the products are safe. Losses caused by defective products should therefore be borne by the sellers who create the risk and collect the profits, rather than by the innocent injured parties. The seller can protect itself against these losses, generally by securing liability insurance, and treat the expense as a cost of doing business, thus distributing the cost of product injuries to the seller's owners (usually its shareholders) and to the public generally.

Defective Product Defined

Under strict liability in tort, sellers are not insurers against all injuries caused by their products. Instead, sellers are responsible only for injuries caused by **unreasonably dangerous** or **defective** products. Courts have used differing language to define what constitutes a defective product. A common definition, based on consumer expectations, is derived from language in the comments to §402A of the *Restatement (Second) of Torts*. Under this definition, a product is defective if it fails to perform in the manner reasonably to be expected in light of its nature and intended function. Therefore, a defective condition is one not contemplated by the user or consumer and that is unreasonably dangerous, that is, more dangerous than would be contemplated by the ordinary user or consumer. For example, an ax or power saw is not unreasonably dangerous because of the possibility of serious cuts, because ordinary users know the obvious dangers in using such products. If, however, the ax or saw is made of defective metal, which could break apart and cause injury during normal use, but is undetectable by prudent users, the product is defective. On the same theory, a soft drink bottler would be liable for injuries caused by chips of glass found in its bottles but would not be liable for damage caused to the consumer's teeth from the sugar in the beverage. Therefore, the condition of the product is "unreasonably dangerous" if the danger cannot reasonably be perceived and appreciated by the user or consumer.

Product defects commonly are classified in three categories: (1) manufacturing defects, (2) design defects, and (3) warning defects. A manufacturing defect exists when a product, as made, fails to meet the manufacturer's specifications. Assume, for example, that a ladder manufacturer intends that each rung of the ladder be secured with four bolts. If during the manufacturing process, an assembly worker attaches only two bolts, the ladder would have a manufacturing defect.

Products liability cases often involve alleged defects in the design of the product. Many courts have ruled that to determine whether a design defect exists, the jury should apply a risk-benefit (or risk-utility) analysis. Under this standard a product is defective only if the risks of the design outweigh its benefits. In the following case, the court considers whether to adopt the risk-benefit standard.

Dart v. Wiebe Manufacturing, Inc.
709 P.2d 876 (Ariz. 1985)

Defendant Wiebe Manufacturing, Inc. manufactured a paper shredder and belt conveyor system used in recycling waste paper. Plaintiff Donald Dart's arm was torn off as he attempted to remove some paper wedged in the conveyor. Dart sued Wiebe for strict liability in tort alleging that the machine was defectively designed because it did not include safety guards that would have prevented the injury. The trial court ruled in favor of the defendant. Dart appealed on the ground that the trial court had improperly instructed the jury on the law of strict liability in tort as applied to design defects. After the court of appeals affirmed, the Arizona Supreme Court granted Dart's petition for review.

Feldman, Justice

. . . [T]he central issue in a strict liability action is the definition to be given to the terms "defect" and "unreasonable danger." . . . Dean Wade, a leading commentator, calls this issue "the most vexing and pressing problem of products liability" law. Wade, *On Product "Design Defects" And Their Actionability,* 33 VAND.L.REV. 551 (1980).

The Restatement . . . defines a product in a "defective condition unreasonably dangerous" as one in a "condition not contemplated by the ultimate consumer, which will be unreasonably dangerous to him." . . . [T]his test provides a legal standard by which to measure the concept of "defect" and works well in manufacturing defect cases where, almost by definition, the product contains a danger which the manufacturer did not intend and the customer did not expect. . . . Despite its virtues in the manufacturing defect setting, the consumer expectation test fails to provide an adequate legal standard in design defect cases.

> Design defects present the most perplexing problems in the field of strict products liability because there is no readily ascertainable external measure of defectiveness. While manufacturing flaws can be evaluated against the intended design of the product, no such objective standard exists in the design defect context.

Caterpillar Tractor Co. v. Beck, 593 P.2d 871, 880 (Alaska 1979). . . . Further, in manufacturing defect cases consumer expectation can often be equated with the manufacturer's own expectations, but in design defect cases the problem of whether to measure consumer expectations by objective or subjective standards complicates the task of determining what is an "expectation." . . . Some courts have devised a two-prong test for use in those design defect cases in which consumer expectation fails to provide an adequate standard. The first case to formulate this approach, *Barker v. Lull Engineering Co.,* [573 P.2d 443 (Cal. 1978)], holds that "defective design" exists either:

1. if the product has failed to perform as safely as an ordinary consumer would expect when used in an intended or reasonable manner, or
2. if, in light of the relevant factors . . . , the benefits of the challenged design do not outweigh the risk of danger inherent in such design.

. . . We believe that the *Barker* analysis is a logical refinement of our previous reasoning. . . . Where the consumer expectation test is inappropriate, the question of defective and unreasonably dangerous condition may be determined by applying Wade's risk/benefit factors. . . . [Dean Wade's risk/benefit analysis requires consideration of the following factors:]

1. the usefulness and desirability of the product,
2. the availability of other and safer products to meet the same need,
3. the likelihood of injury and its probable seriousness,
4. the obviousness of the danger,
5. common knowledge and normal public expectation of the danger (particularly for established products),
6. the avoidability of injury by care in use of the product (including the effect of instructions or warnings), and
7. the ability to eliminate the danger without seriously impairing the usefulness of the product or making it unduly expensive.

Byrns v. Riddell, [550 P.2d 1065, 1068 (Ariz. 1976)]. . . . Use of these risk/benefit factors does not signal the abolition of strict liability in tort. It is, on the contrary, simply an alternative method of determining unreasonable danger. . . .

[Judgment reversed and remanded.]

In warning defect cases, the product is considered defective because it fails to include an adequate warning of its potential dangers. That is, although the product itself may not be flawed, it is unreasonably dangerous because it lacks adequate warnings or instructions regarding its use. Some granulated drain cleaners, for example, may explode if water gets inside the can and

the top is replaced. A drain cleaner marketed without a warning of that danger, therefore, would be defective. Warnings generally are required for dangers resulting not only from the intended use of a product but also from a reasonably foreseeable misuse.

Not all products lacking a warning are defective because, as noted by one authority, "If there was an obligation to warn against all injuries that conceivably might result from the use or misuse of a product, manufacturers would find it practically impossible to market their goods."[10] A warning is not required for dangers that are obvious or that can be appreciated by the reasonable user. As a result, a knife manufacturer need not warn that its knives can cut because this danger is obvious. Some courts require a warning only if the seller knew or should have known of the danger—essentially holding sellers to a negligence standard. Other courts, however, have held sellers liable for warning defects even if the danger posed by their product was not known.

Class of Permissible Plaintiffs and Defendants

Plaintiffs Protected. Section 402A of the *Restatement (Second) of Torts* extends liability for personal injury and property damage only to the "ultimate user or consumer." Subsequent cases, however, have extended liability to protect bystanders and others who are injured as well. The purpose of strict liability is to place the cost of product-related injuries upon those who place the defective products on the market. Given this purpose, no reason exists to distinguish between injuries caused to the user or consumer of the product and those caused to persons unfortunate enough to be in the vicinity when the product malfunctions. Thus, privity of contract is not required in strict liability cases. Liability mirrors that imposed for negligence: any reasonably foreseeable plaintiff injured by the defective product is entitled to sue.[11]

Defendants Liable. The injured plaintiff may sue any seller of the defective product who is engaged in the business of selling such products for use or consumption. Liability, therefore, may be imposed not only on the manufacturer, but also on the wholesaler, retail dealer, distributor, or restaurant operator who sold

---

[10]Noel, *Products Defective Because of Inadequate Directions or Warnings,* 23 S.W.L.J. 256, 264 (1969).
[11]The class of plaintiffs protected in negligence actions and the foreseeability issue are discussed in Chapter 5.

the defective product. Thus, anyone in the chain of distribution that enabled the product to reach the marketplace is a potential defendant in a strict liability suit. The term "seller" has been interpreted broadly to include all those responsible for placing the product in the stream of commerce even if an actual sale was not involved. As a result, businesses have been held liable for injuries caused by defective products that were leased or were distributed as free samples. The occasional or casual seller who is not engaged in the business of selling products, however, is excluded from liability. Thus, a consumer who sells a defective product at a garage sale would not be liable.

The rationale for imposing liability on all firms in the distribution chain is that without their efforts the injury would not have occurred; the defective product simply would not have been available. Further, the potential liability encourages distributors and retailers to exert pressure on manufacturers to make safe products and to spread the risk through insurance. Many courts, however, recognize that a seller who is held liable, but who did not cause or contribute to the defect, is entitled to indemnification (reimbursement) from the party actually responsible for creating the risk—generally the manufacturer. If, however, the party who created the risk is insolvent or beyond a court's jurisdiction, the indemnification remedy may be illusory.

The following case illustrates the indemnity remedy in light of the public policy considerations supporting strict products liability.

Promaulayko v. Johns Manville Sales Corporation
562 A.2d 202 (N.J. 1989)

Plaintiff Marie Promaulayko filed a products liability suit claiming that various distributors of asbestos should be held strictly liable for the death of her husband who had contracted asbestosis, a lung condition caused by exposure to asbestos particles. The plaintiff alleged that the asbestos was defective because it failed to include a warning of the health risks associated with asbestos. Promaulayko had been exposed to the asbestos while working for Ruberoid Corporation from 1934 to 1978. Ruberoid had purchased the asbestos from defendant Leonard J. Buck, Inc. (Buck) who had bought it from defendant Amtorg Trading Corporation (Amtorg), a New York corporation that brokered products from the Soviet Union. The asbestos had

been supplied by a Soviet producer who shipped the product directly to Ruberoid. Neither Buck nor Amtorg ever had possession of the asbestos. The trial court ruled that Buck and Amtorg were liable for Promaulayko's disease but that Buck was entitled to indemnification from Amtorg. On appeal, the appellate court ruled that Buck and Amtorg should share the liability and that Buck was not entitled to indemnification. The New Jersey Supreme Court then reviewed the case.

Pollock, Justice

. . . Two basic principles underlie the development of strict liability in tort. The first principle is the allocation of the risk of loss to the party best able to control it. . . . The second is the allocation of the risk to the party best able to distribute it. . . . Accordingly, the essence of a *prima facie* case of liability is proof that defendant placed a defective product in the stream of commerce. As a matter of law, the seller is presumed to know of the defect, . . . so the injured party need not prove that the manufacturer was negligent or knew of the defect. . . .

In a strict-liability action, liability extends beyond the manufacturer to all entities in the chain of distribution. . . . Although a distributor and a retailer may be innocent conduits in the sale of the defective product, they remain liable to the injured party. . . . The net result is that the absence of the original manufacturer or producer need not deprive the injured party of a cause of action. . . .

In the absence of an express agreement between them, allocation of the risk of loss between the parties in the chain of distribution is achieved through common-law indemnity, an equitable doctrine that allows a court to shift the cost from one tortfeasor to another. The right to common-law indemnity arises "without agreement, and by operation of law to prevent a result which is regarded as unjust or unsatisfactory." W. Keeton, D. Dobbs, R. Keeton, & D. Owens, *Prosser & Keeton on the Law of Torts* §51 at 341 (5th ed. 1984). . . . Consistent with this principle, actions by retailers against manufacturers have been recognized in this State for twenty years. . . .

In the present case, we consider the application of the principles underlying strict liability in tort to a claim for common-law indemnification by one distributor against a distributor higher in the chain. . . .

In allowing claims for common-law indemnification by one party in the chain of distribution against a party higher up the chain, ... courts have proceeded in a manner consistent with the principle of allocating the risk of loss to the party better able to control the risk and to distribute its costs. The approach is consistent also with the principle of focusing on the defective product as it proceeds down the chain of distribution. In general, the effect of requiring the party closest to the original producer to indemnify parties farther down the chain is to shift the risk of loss to the most efficient accident avoider. . . . Passing the cost of the risk up the distributive chain also fulfills, as a general rule, the goal of distributing the risk to the party best able to bear it. . . . The manufacturer to whom the cost is shifted can distribute that cost among all purchasers of its product. Similarly, a wholesale distributor can generally pass the risk among a greater number of potential users than a distributor farther down the chain. . . .

In the present case, Amtorg was closer than Buck to the producer of the asbestos in the Soviet Union. As between the two of them, Amtorg is better positioned "to put pressure on" the producer to make the product safe. . . . Here, the defect was the absence of a warning of the dangers of asbestosis when the bags were placed in the stream of commerce. Because of Amtorg's relationship to Soviet commerce in general and to the producer in particular, it is more likely that it, rather than Buck, will be able to persuade the producer to provide an adequate warning. Further, Amtorg is better able to shift the cost of the loss to the asbestos producer and to require that producer to reflect the cost of injury in the price of its product.

Conceivably, a set of facts might arise in which the party at the end of the distributive chain will be a better risk-bearer than a party higher in the chain. As a general rule, however, we expect indemnification to follow the chain of distribution. Finally, we recognize that parties in a distributive chain may contract for a different allocation of the risk of loss. For example, one distributor may expressly agree to disclaim or waive any right of indemnification against a distributor farther up the chain. In the present case, the parties did not make any such agreement, and we are satisfied that Buck is entitled to indemnification from Amtorg, the distributor that was interposed between Buck and the producer of the product. . . .

Here, the injured party sued two distributors, neither of which altered or even possessed the product as it proceeded from the producer to the ultimate purchaser. In this context, the appropriate vehicle for allocating responsibility between the distributors is indemnification. . . .

[Judgment reversed and remanded.]

Not all merchant sellers sell new products in the original chain of distribution. Many sell used goods, such as used cars. Courts are divided concerning whether the strict liability doctrine should apply to such sellers. Some courts refuse to extend strict liability to sellers of used goods, reasoning that (1) buyers understand that the seller, though in the business of selling used goods, makes no representation of quality, and (2) sellers of used goods generally have no direct relationship with the manufacturer, and therefore are not in a position to exert pressure on the manufacturer to make the product safe. Other courts have rejected these arguments to hold merchant sellers of used goods liable, based on basic public policy considerations supporting strict tort liability generally. These courts have noted that application of strict liability in tort to sellers of used products better assures the consumer and the public that all reasonable efforts will be taken by the seller to see that the used product is safe, both through a reasonable inspection to discover defects and repair of those defects, however caused.

Defenses to Strict Liability

The Restatement Approach. Section 402A of the *Restatement (Second) of Torts* and its comments announced both the criteria for imposing strict liability and the defenses available to the seller. Under the *Restatement* approach, the plaintiff's contributory negligence is generally not available to the seller as a defense, because strict liability is not based upon the seller's negligence. "Contributory negligence" as defined in the *Restatement* refers to the plaintiff's unobservant, inattentive, or ignorant failure to discover or guard against the defect causing injury. Most courts, however, define contributory negligence in this context in its ordinary tort law sense—negligence on the plaintiff's part that is a contributing cause of the plaintiff's harm.

On the other hand, the plaintiff's contributory conduct amounting to (1) an assumption of the risk or

(2) outright misuse of the product constitutes an absolute defense. As previously noted, assumption of the risk involves the plaintiff's express or implied consent to encounter a known unreasonable danger created by the defendant's conduct. **Misuse** involves use of the product for purposes neither intended nor foreseeable by the defendant. Note that the *Restatement* and many jurisdictions do not regard misuse as an affirmative defense in the true sense; rather, evidence of misuse merely rebuts proof of defective condition or causation, necessary elements of the plaintiff's strict liability case. That is, a product that causes an injury because it is used in an unforeseeable manner may very well not be defective. Similarly, if a defective product is misused, the misuse, rather than the defect, may cause the injury.

In sum, under the *Restatement* approach, the plaintiff who fails to exercise reasonable care in using the product may nevertheless recover for her injuries in strict liability. However, a plaintiff who continues to use the product *after becoming aware* of its unreasonably dangerous character, or who uses it for an unintended or unforeseeable purpose, is barred from recovery for subsequent injury caused by the product.

Comparative Fault in Strict Liability. Although the *Restatement* provides that contributory negligence does not bar recovery in strict liability, a growing number of courts have, in recent years, applied **comparative fault** principles in strict liability actions. As discussed in Chapter 5, most American jurisdictions have abandoned contributory negligence as a defense in negligence actions and replaced it with some form of comparative negligence, in which the relative degrees of fault are weighed by the jury and the plaintiff's total damages are reduced in proportion to his fault. In negligence cases, comparative negligence has the effect of providing some compensation (reduced in proportion to his fault) to a plaintiff who would be denied any recovery under the contributory negligence approach.

Although a substantial majority of jurisdictions now apply some form of comparison in strict liability cases, the precise method of comparison differs widely and is often affected by state statutes governing comparative negligence or strict liability. For example, under the form of strict liability adopted in *Restatement (Second) of Torts* §402A, ordinary contributory negligence is not a defense, but the plaintiff's misuse or assumption of the risk are *absolute bars* to recovery. Under some formulations of comparative fault, the plaintiff's contribu-

tory conduct, however categorized (as contributory negligence, misuse, or assumption of the risk) is compared, proportionately reducing the injured party's recovery. Some states apply comparative principles only to plaintiff conduct that would have barred recovery altogether under the original *Restatement* formulation (misuse and assumption of risk). Under this approach, the plaintiff's contributory negligence, however characterized, is not a defense and does not reduce recovery. Misuse and assumption of risk are, however, compared to proportionately reduce recovery. In contrast, still other courts apply comparative principles to any level of plaintiff culpability, including negligence, except when the plaintiff's negligence consists solely in the failure to discover or guard against the defect that caused the injury. Depending upon the form of comparison adopted, an injured plaintiff may receive more or less protection than is afforded by the original *Restatement* approach.

Products Liability Today

Following the development of strict liability in tort, the field of products liability grew rapidly during the 1960s and 1970s. To a large extent, the expanded scope of products liability achieved the policy objectives of strict liability. In general, the safety of products has improved. Although businesses, especially manufacturers, were exposed to increasing liability for defective products, they generally were able to cover their risk by securing insurance to cover potential legal fees and judgments. Insurance premiums became a cost of doing business incorporated into businesses' pricing policies and thereby distributed among consumers. The policies underlying products liability, however, have become increasingly controversial as insurance prices have risen significantly.

Both state and federal legislatures, with the encouragement of businesses, considered tort reform and, more specifically, products liability reform, to reduce the potential liability of defendants for injuries resulting from their products. Proponents of reform argued that a "litigation explosion" seriously jeopardized American commerce, depriving consumers of many products and weakening the position of American business in international markets. Insurers pressed for reform asserting that premiums would continue to rise and, in some cases, insurance would be unavailable not only because of the increase in products liability cases but also because of unduly large judgments in particular cases. Opponents of reform characterized the crisis as one caused by the insurance industry, noting that the cyclical nature of the insurance industry usually was aggravated by fluctuations in interest rates. They further asserted that the claims of an explosive rate of growth in the number of cases and size of judgments were based on anecdotal evidence unsupported by statistical data. As a result of reform efforts, many states statutorily revised their tort and products liability law. The most common types of reform include eliminating or limiting the use of joint and several liability, placing "caps" on the amount of noneconomic (pain and suffering) or punitive damages, and shortening the statute of limitations. Numerous bills to establish a federal products liability statute have been introduced in Congress to provide uniform rules for businesses that operate in interstate commerce. No bill, however, has been passed by Congress.

Summary

1.   The law of products liability governs the liability of manufacturers and other suppliers of goods for personal injury and property damage caused by the products they sell. Three legal theories are used to impose liability upon a seller: (1) negligence, (2) breach of warranty, and (3) strict liability in tort. Generally, under all theories, protection is extended to injured third parties, whether or not in privity of contract with the seller.

2.   Under the negligence approach, the manufacturer or supplier is under a duty to exercise reasonable care in the design, production, and distribution of its products. Failure to do so constitutes negligence. If the manufacturer's or supplier's negligence causes injury, the injured party may recover damages. The injured party attempting to prove negligence may be aided by the *res ipsa loquitur* doctrine, under which recovery is allowed even though no direct evidence regarding particular negligent conduct can be shown.

3.   Breach of warranty actions have been a popular ground for recovery because warranty liability, based on contract, is strict, meaning liability is imposed without a showing of fault. If the breach of warranty causes personal injury, liability follows. Because a warranty action is based on contract, contract defenses such as lack of privity, disclaimer of warranty, and failure to give timely notice of the breach traditionally have been available to the defendant. The UCC, however, eliminates or reduces the effect of these defenses in warranty actions involving personal injury.

4.   The dominant products liability theory today is the strict liability in tort doctrine, which imposes liability without fault for injuries caused by defective products. Under this theory, the plaintiff recovers if he or she can prove (1) the product was defective (unreasonably dangerous), (2) the defect existed when the product left the seller's control, and (3) the defect caused the injury. Traditionally, contributory negligence was no defense to a strict products liability action, although assumption of the risk and misuse of the product were absolute bars to recovery. The modern approach is to apply comparative principles in strict liability actions, similar to that now applied generally in negligence cases.

Key Terms

products liability	defective (unreasonably
privity of contract	dangerous) product
res ipsa loquitur	misuse
strict liability	comparative fault
strict liability in tort	

Questions and Problems

20.1   Compare and contrast the three primary bases of recovery in products liability cases. Specifically: (1) Who is entitled to sue under each theory? (2) What must the plaintiff prove under each theory? (3) Which particular sellers or suppliers may be held liable under each theory? (4) What defenses are available to a defendant seeking to avoid liability?

20.2   Shipbuilder, Inc. contracted with Transamerica, Inc. to design, manufacture, and install turbines that would be the main propulsion units for four oil tankers constructed by Shipbuilder. When the ships were chartered and put into service, the turbines on all four ships malfunctioned due to design and manufacturing defects. Only the turbines themselves were damaged. The charterers then sued Shipbuilder on products liability theories of negligence and strict liability. The court found for Shipbuilder, noting that claims regarding dissatisfaction with product quality are protected by warranty laws, rather than tort doctrines of negligence or strict liability. Is the court correct? Discuss.

20.3   Eleanor, while grocery shopping at Dom's Market, was using a shopping cart provided by the store. The cart tipped over and Eleanor was injured as she attempted to prevent the cart from overturning. A hidden design defect had caused the cart to overturn when loaded with groceries.

(a) Eleanor sues Dom's Market, Inc. for strict liability in tort. What result?

(b) Eleanor sues the cart manufacturer for strict liability in tort. What result?

20.4 Wren, Inc. manufactures and distributes a pain reliever sold in tablet form. The product is packaged in a glass bottle with a screw top that is then placed in a small cardboard box. On the box and the bottle is printed the following statement in boldface type: THESE TABLETS ARE STRONG DRUGS. DO NOT EXCEED DOSAGE OF 2 TABLETS IN A FOUR HOUR PERIOD. The product is sold as an over-the-counter drug. Mary purchased a bottle of the pain reliever from Oswald's Drug Store. The drug store is self-service and Mary selected her purchase from an open shelf. When she returned home, Mary placed the unopened bottle in her medicine cabinet. While Mary's friend Lulu was visiting, she developed a terrible headache so she took four of the pain relievers. Within hours Lulu was dead. Examination of the bottle of pain relief tablets revealed that ten of the tablets contained curare, a lethal poison even in small doses. A police investigation established that without a doubt, the poisoned tablets were added to the bottle after the package left the Wren plant. Lulu's family files suit against Wren and Oswald's.

(a) If the lawsuit is based on negligence, what elements will the plaintiff have to prove? Explain how the plaintiff may try to prove the case based on the preceding facts.

(b) If the lawsuit is based on strict liability in tort, what elements will the plaintiff have to prove? Explain how the plaintiff may try to prove the case based on the preceding facts.

(c) Would the defendants have any defenses available to them? Explain, specifying which defenses are likely to be asserted.

(d) If the lawsuit is based on breach of warranty, what must the plaintiff prove? What defenses might the defendant assert in a warranty action? Will the plaintiff recover? Explain.

20.5 Southland Chemicals, Inc. manufactures and markets "Drain Clean," a household chemical for cleaning drain stoppages in sinks and bathtubs. The main ingredient in Drain Clean is sodium hydroxide, which when combined with water produces intense heat and steam, resulting in an explosion if the mixture is contained. The mixture is strong enough to eat away aluminum, burns and kills human tissue on contact, and causes incurable blindness if it comes in contact with the eyes even for a short period. Of course, ingestion of even small quantities of the substance causes internal bleeding and usually death. You are Southland's marketing director. What steps would you recommend be taken in the manufacture, marketing, labeling, and packaging of Drain Clean to minimize the risk of liability in lawsuits filed by persons injured while using the product?

20.6 Reese worked as a foreman, supervising a track repair crew for Chicago, Burlington, and Quincy Railroad. One morning the crew was loading equipment onto a flatcar using a crane manufactured by Kelly Crane Co. The boom on the crane contained two cables, one being used to load equipment, and the other holding a 1,200-pound "clamshell" bucket suspended at the top of the boom. The bucket was not in use during the loading operation, and to secure the cable holding it, the crane operator had engaged both a hand and foot brake. Either brake was intended to be independently sufficient to hold the cable fast. Reese was standing beneath the clamshell bucket supervising loading operations when the foot brake pedal "jumped off the floor" and the bucket fell, killing Reese instantly. Reese's estate sued Kelly in strict liability and proved that the defective design of the braking mechanism had caused it to fail. Kelly defended on the ground that Reese's conduct (standing beneath the suspended bucket) constituted alternatively (1) contributory negligence, (2) assumption of the risk, or (3) misuse of the product. Under §402A of the *Restatement (Second) of Torts,* would Kelly escape liability on any of the foregoing theories? Would your answer change if the jurisdiction in question applies comparative fault principles in strict liability actions? Explain.

20.7 Consider whether plaintiff's alleged misuse of the product should bar recovery in the following cases:

(a) Dagwood was driving a motor home on the highway when he ran into a guardrail. The mobile home veered off the road and overturned. Because of a defective and negligent design, the gas tank was not properly protected and it exploded, seriously injuring the passengers. The defendant manufacturer argued that mobile homes are not intended to be used in accidents so that the product was being misused.

(b) Billy, a 7-year-old child, found an empty disposable beer bottle. Billy threw the bottle at a telephone pole. The bottle shattered and several pieces of glass injured Billy's eye. Defendant bottle manufacturer argued that Billy had misused the bottle.

20.8 The text discusses the pros and cons of applying the strict liability in tort doctrine to sellers of goods. Consider the application of the doctrine to *lessors* of goods. For example, should a person in the business of renting automobiles, trailers, power tools, or other goods be held strictly liable for injuries caused by those goods? Should such *lessors* of used goods be treated differently from *sellers* of such goods? Do the policy considerations supporting strict liability require a different approach to the two cases?

20.9 Most courts have extended protection in strict liability to bystanders and others injured by defective products who are not in privity with the seller. How would you argue that a bystander should be entitled to even *greater* protection than the original user or consumer of the product?

20.10 The strict liability doctrine does not apply to an occasional or casual sale by one not engaged in business—for example, the sale of a bicycle through a classified advertisement. Why not?

20.11 Marine Manufacturing Co. manufactures diesel engines for tugboats and other water craft. The engines are distributed exclusively through franchised Marine dealers. Marine began manufacturing a new type of engine, but later learned that the fuel filter recommended for the engine would occasionally crack and rupture under pressure. Marine developed a new filter and sent letters to its franchisees instructing them to use the new filters. The letter warned that in some cases the old filter had ruptured causing fuel to spray over the engine. Boat Sales, Inc. was a franchised retailer of Marine engines and received a copy of the Marine letter. Boat Sales subsequently sold a Marine engine to Marco but installed an old filter. Boat Sales did not advise Marco of the need to use the new filters. Marco installed the engine on his tugboat. During the first voyage, the filter exploded and fuel sprayed in the engine room where it ignited. The boat burned and sank.

(a) Marco sues both Marine Manufacturing Co. and Boat Sales, Inc. for negligence. What result? Explain.

(b) Marco also sues Marine and Boat Sales, Inc. under the strict liability in tort theory. What result? Explain.

(c) Assume that the court finds Marine strictly liable in tort for the personal injury and property damage caused by its defective engine. Further evidence shows, however, that Marco had been negligent for the following reasons: (1) Marco's engineer negligently left the engine room and negligently failed to observe the engine, (2) the crew was negligent for failure to take several actions to put out the fire, (3) Marco failed to provide a switch outside the engine room to turn off the engine, failed to train the crew in firefighting techniques, and failed to have enough fire extinguishers on board. Should Marco's conduct be considered as a basis to reduce or extinguish Marine's liability to Marco? Explain.

20.12 The plaintiffs in the following cases alleged that the sellers should be held strictly liable in tort because they failed to include a warning on the products. Do you agree? Explain.

(a) Officer Thomas Delahanty, a District of Columbia police officer, was injured by gunshots fired by John Hinckley in an attempt to assassinate President Ronald Reagan. The gun used by Hinckley was a "Saturday Night Special," a small, inexpensive handgun manufactured by R. G. Industries, Inc. Delahanty sued the manufacturer.

(b) Marie was an 18-year-old college freshman who had had little exposure to the use of alcohol. After Marie purchased a bottle of Pepe Lopez Tequila at University Liquor Store, she and some friends drank straight shots of tequila during the evening. The following morning Marie was found dead in her dormitory room as a result of acute alcohol intoxication. Her family sued Brown Forman Corp., the manufacturer of the tequila, and University Liquor Store.

PART FOUR

NEGOTIABLE INSTRUMENTS

INTRODUCTION TO NEGOTIABLE INSTRUMENTS

This chapter and Chapters 22–26 examine the law of negotiable instruments—promissory notes, certificates of deposit, drafts, and checks. For centuries these commercial documents have served as primary vehicles for extending credit and as substitutes for money in the payment of debts. Negotiable instruments are able to perform these functions because they are easy to create and transfer. The paper itself is valuable property that can be sold or used as collateral on a loan. The rights and obligations of all parties to the paper are easily ascertained, extremely predictable, and readily enforceable in court. Negotiable instruments possess these attributes because they are "negotiable," a legal characteristic that promotes the free transferability and enhances the marketability of the paper.

Many legal issues arise in connection with the use of negotiable instruments. To a large extent these issues are resolved by Articles 3 and 4 of the Uniform Commercial Code (UCC), which form the basis of the following material.

Introduction to Article 3

Derivation of Article 3

The term **law merchant** refers to the system of routine rules, customs, or practices used in the business community to regulate transactions and solve controversies.[1] Negotiable instruments law is derived from the law merchant, specifically the practices of Western European merchants who recognized centuries ago the commercial need for freely transferable substitutes for currency. The rules and principles governing these documents were absorbed into the English common law during the seventeenth and eighteenth centuries and were ultimately codified in England in 1882 by the Bills of Exchange Act.

In the United States, the law was first codified in the Uniform Negotiable Instruments Law (UNIL) originally promulgated in 1896, and subsequently adopted in

---

[1]BLACK'S LAW DICTIONARY 886, 986 (6th ed. 1990).

every American jurisdiction. The UNIL was reorganized and modernized by original Article 3 of the UCC (1962), entitled "Commercial Paper," which was replaced in 1990 by Revised Article 3, entitled "Negotiable Instruments." Most states have enacted Revised Article 3, which forms the basis of the following discussion. Note that although Article 3 is a complete revision and modernization of the law, it borrows heavily from the UNIL in formulating the substantive rules governing negotiable instrument transactions. Of all Code articles, Article 3 departs least from the major rules and concepts of prior law.

Types of Article 3 Paper Defined and Distinguished

Used in law generally, the term **instrument** refers to any written document, particularly legal documents such as contracts, wills, and deeds. In the following material, the term will be used to designate a negotiable instrument as defined in Article 3.[2]

Negotiable instruments governed by Article 3 contain a promise or order to pay *money*. This characteristic distinguishes them from other negotiable contracts such as documents of title (for example, bills of lading and warehouse receipts) and investment securities (for example, stocks and bonds) that are governed by UCC Articles 7 and 8 respectively. Although Article 3 governs negotiable instruments payable in money and makes instruments within its scope substantially equivalent to money, Article 3 does not apply to money itself. The negotiability of money is determined by common law principles and under separate statutes.

Four types of negotiable instruments are within the scope of Article 3: (1) notes, (2) certificates of deposit, (3) drafts, and (4) checks. Functionally, however, it is necessary to distinguish only notes and drafts, because a certificate of deposit is a specialized form of note and a check is a specialized type of draft.

Notes and Certificates of Deposit. A **note** is two-party paper involving a promise by the **maker** of the note to pay a fixed amount of money to the order of the payee or to bearer on demand or at a future date.[3] An instrument may be payable to the order of a specified person, the **payee.** If no payee is specified, the instrument is payable to **bearer,** meaning anyone who

lawfully possesses the instrument when it is presented to the maker for payment. If an instrument is an acknowledgment by a bank of the receipt of money with a promise to repay it, then it is known as a **certificate of deposit** (see Figure 21.1). That is, a certificate of deposit is essentially a note that the bank as the maker issues to a depositor in the bank as payee.[4]

The note's primary purpose is as a credit device; it is the usual means by which money is borrowed to be repaid at a future date or by which property or services are sold on credit. Banks, savings and loan associations, and other lenders use notes in a variety of consumer and commercial transactions. Assume Buyer desires to buy a house from Seller for $150,000, but has insufficient cash. Buyer therefore goes to First Federal Savings and Loan and arranges to borrow the purchase price. First Federal, after checking Buyer's credit, agrees to loan the money. To evidence her obligation, Buyer issues a note to the bank promising to repay the loan in monthly installments over a 25-year period. In this case, Buyer, the debtor, is the maker of the note, and First Federal is the payee. Although a note is commonly issued in exchange for a loan of money, the obligation evidenced by the note need not be a cash advance. For example, Seller may sell goods on credit to Buyer, and Buyer may issue a note to Seller for the purchase price.

"Promise" Defined. The major characteristic of a note is a promise by the maker to pay. A **promise** is defined as an undertaking to pay and must more than merely acknowledge the existence of an obligation.[5] This definition makes it clear that a mere IOU is not a negotiable instrument. For example, the writing "Due X, $500 for value received, (signed) Z" contains no promise and is therefore not a note governed by Article 3. The writing may, of course, provide evidence of the existence of the debt or satisfy the Statute of Frauds against Z, but it is simply not a note to which Article 3 applies.

Drafts and Checks. Unlike notes and certificates of deposit, a **draft** (also known as a **bill of exchange**) may be designated three-party paper. The three parties are the **drawer,** the **drawee,** and the **payee.** Drafts are used both as substitutes for money and as credit devices. In drafts, the drawee and drawer generally stand in a debtor-creditor relation: the drawee owes the drawer

---

[2]UCC §3–104(b).
[3]UCC §3–104(e).

[4]UCC §3–104(j).
[5]UCC §3–103(a)(9).

Figure 21.1   **Certificate of Deposit**

money. A draft involves an *order* by the drawer directed to the drawee to pay to the order of the payee or to bearer a fixed amount of money on demand or at a fixed or computable future date.[6] In essence, the drawer of a draft says to the drawee, "rather than paying me the money you owe, I order you instead to pay to the order of the payee."

Drafts are "drawn" on the drawee and may be used whenever a debtor-creditor relationship exists. One common type of draft is a **trade acceptance,** which is a draft drawn by a seller of goods on credit against his buyer. A trade acceptance is a substitute for selling goods on open account. Once the buyer assumes liability upon the trade acceptance by "accepting" it, the account becomes liquid, permitting the seller to raise money on the instrument (by selling it to a third party) before the account is due under the sales contract (see Figure 21.2).

If a draft is drawn on a bank and is payable on demand, then it is known as a **check,** certainly the most common negotiable instrument governed by Article 3.[7] In the case of a check, the drawer-depositor is a creditor of the drawee-bank because the amount on deposit in the drawer's checking account represents a debt of the bank owed to the depositor (see Figure 21.3).

Although a draft is three-party paper, three persons need not necessarily be involved because one person may fulfill two roles. In a trade acceptance, for example, the seller may make the instrument payable to himself, becoming both the drawer and the payee. Or, a person may draw a draft upon herself, becoming both the drawer and drawee.

For example, the drawer is also the drawee in a **cashier's check**—a check drawn by the issuing bank upon itself.[8] Such a check may be procured by the payee of the instrument or a remitter. A **remitter** is a person, not a party to the instrument (that is, not the drawer, drawee, or payee), who purchases it in order to pay his own debt to the payee named in the check.[9] Assume Bill owes Fred $5,000. Fred refuses to take Bill's personal check in payment, so Bill purchases a cashier's check from National Bank naming Fred as payee. In this case, National Bank is both drawer and drawee, Fred is the payee, and Bill is a remitter. Another form of check is a **teller's check,** which is a draft drawn by a bank either (1) on another bank, or (2) that is payable at or through a bank.[10]

"Order" Defined. Unlike a note, which is characterized by a promise, a draft is an order to pay directed to the drawee. To bring the instrument within Article 3, an **order** must be a direction or instruction to pay and must be more than a mere authorization or

---

[6]UCC §3–104(e).
[7]UCC §3–104(f).

[8]UCC §3–104(g).
[9]UCC §3–103(a)(11).
[10]UCC §3–104(h).

| **Figure 21.2** | **Trade Acceptance** |

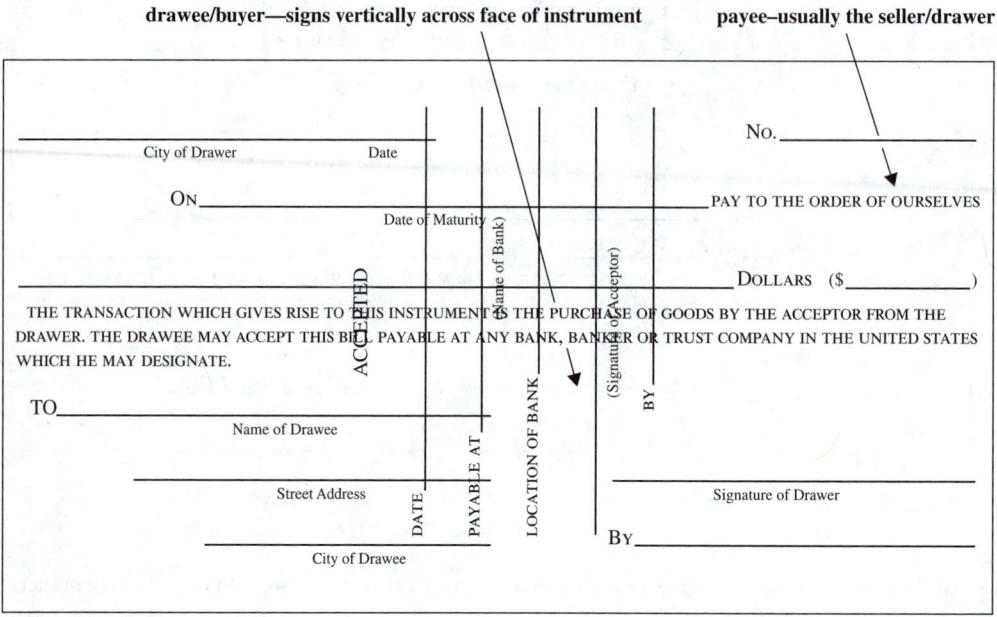

| **Figure 21.3** | **Check** |

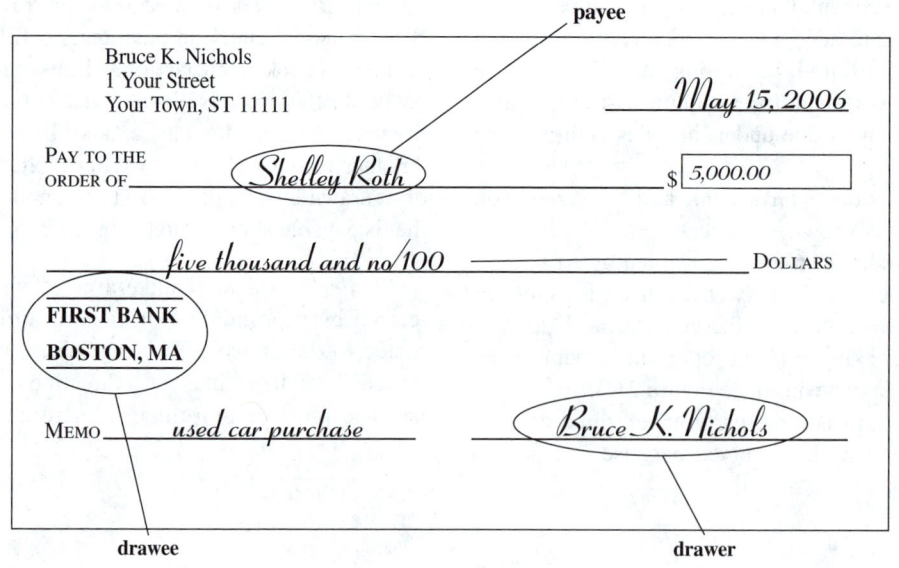

request.[11] The word "pay" generally satisfies the order requirement in drafts. Adding words of courtesy such as "please pay" or "kindly pay" does not reduce the order to a mere request. However, language such as "I wish you would pay" would not qualify as an order. The order must identify the drawee with reasonable certainty and may be addressed to the drawer itself (for example, a cashier's check) or to one or more drawees. The rule permitting alternative drawees allows, for example, a corporation, for commercial convenience, to draw its dividend checks upon a number of drawees (banks) usually located in different parts of the country.

Introduction to Negotiability

Advantages of Negotiability

Negotiability is a major characteristic of instruments governed by Article 3. **Negotiability** is a legal concept designed to promote the free transferability of the instrument from one owner to the next and to enhance its marketability. Marketability refers to salability or liquidity—the degree to which an asset can be converted to cash without causing serious decline in its value. Negotiable instruments are *contracts*. Much of their value and usefulness in commerce lies in the ability of the owner of the instrument (for example, the payee of a note) to transfer (negotiate) it freely, unencumbered by problems attending an ordinary contract assignment.

Assignment of an Ordinary Contract. As discussed in Chapter 13, rights under a contract may ordinarily be freely assigned or transferred by a contracting party. The party transferring the rights is the assignor and the person receiving them is the assignee. The major problem facing an ordinary contract assignee is that the assignee generally "steps into the shoes" of the assignor and acquires no better rights than the assignor had. Therefore, any defense, such as fraud, breach of warranty, or failure of consideration, that the other original contracting party (obligor) can assert against the assignor can also be asserted against the assignee. The assignee also runs the risk that some third party, such as a creditor of the assignor, may claim ownership of the rights assigned. In addition, the obligor remains

free to perform for the assignor until notified of the assignment. Thus, a prospective assignee of a contract is well advised to investigate the original transaction to determine its validity and whether it is subject to any claims or defenses. If no problems are found after making the investigation, the obligor must be notified of the assignment. Even then, however, the assignee is not completely protected because claims or defenses not uncovered by the investigation may still exist.

Assignment of a Negotiable Contract. If a negotiable contract is involved, many of the foregoing risks are eliminated because of the following characteristics of negotiable instruments.

Parol Evidence. In most cases, everything about a negotiable instrument, including liability of all parties, is determined by examining the instrument itself. Thus, a prospective assignee of a negotiable instrument need not "look behind" the instrument to any other document, or conduct an elaborate investigation of the original transaction giving rise to the instrument.

Transfer. Upon delivery of a negotiable instrument to the payee, the payee becomes the first "holder" of the instrument. Subsequent transferees become holders of the instrument by negotiation. Negotiation is effected simply and quickly either by mere delivery of the instrument to the transferee (assignee), or by delivery plus the signature (indorsement) of the original holder. After negotiation, the new holder of the instrument has no duty to give notice to the obligor that an assignment (negotiation) has been made. The obligor is under a duty to perform for the *holder* of a negotiable instrument, who may be someone other than the other original payee.

Freedom from Claims and Defenses. After the assignment (negotiation), an assignee (holder) who has purchased the instrument in good faith and for value takes the instrument free of all prior ownership claims and also free of most defenses asserted by other parties to the instrument. Note that the term **claim** refers to a claim of ownership of the instrument asserted either by a prior holder or by a third party not a holder. For example, a prior holder may assert that the instrument was stolen from him prior to its negotiation. Or a judgment creditor of a prior holder may claim ownership of the instrument by virtue of a judgment attaching all assets of the prior holder, including the instrument.

---

[11]UCC §3–103(a)(6).

A **defense,** on the other hand, is asserted by a party to the instrument to avoid all or part of her obligation to pay the instrument. Most commonly, the party asserting a defense is the maker of a note, or the drawer of a check or other draft.

Commercial Benefits of Negotiable Contracts. The net effect of the characteristics outlined above is that the major risk undertaken by an assignee (holder) of a negotiable instrument is the solvency and capacity of prior parties, and the genuineness of the instrument itself. Eliminating other risks enhances the value of a negotiable contract on the market thus benefiting all involved. Because of reduced risk and administrative cost (from not having to make an investigation of the original transaction), an assignee is willing to pay substantially more for a negotiable contract than a nonnegotiable one. That is, negotiable paper has a lower discount rate than nonnegotiable paper. The term **discount rate** refers to the percentage difference between the face value of an instrument at maturity and the amount an assignee, commonly a bank, is willing to pay for it prior to maturity. Although this discount, to a large extent, represents interest, it also reflects the risk of collection and costs of administering the transaction.

A lower discount rate facilitates, for example, the use by a merchant seller of his customer's promissory notes as a financing device. Assume Carter, Inc. sells manufacturing equipment to Brown on credit for $50,000. Brown issues a negotiable promissory note to Carter for the purchase price payable in one year. Carter, however, needs immediate cash to satisfy current obligations. He therefore sells the note to Regional Bank for $42,500 cash (reflecting a 15 percent discount rate). Because a negotiable instrument is involved, the discount rate reflects the fact that the bank will be paid even if Brown has a defense against Carter—for example, if the machinery delivered by Carter was defective. That is, because the instrument is negotiable, Brown will be required to pay the bank $50,000 at maturity even if Brown has a defense to paying Carter. Had the contract been nonnegotiable—for example, the assignment of an ordinary account receivable—the bank (the assignee) would be in no better position than Carter (the assignor) and would take subject to Brown's defense. In addition, it would incur costs in investigating the underlying transaction and notifying Brown of the assignment. As a result, the bank may be hesitant to take the paper at all, or would at least increase the discount rate to reflect the added risk and expense. Thus, if it cannot offer the bank a negotiable contract, Carter may be unable to obtain needed working capital. Brown also may be adversely affected because Carter now must charge more to realize the same amount of cash on his credit sales, or may not be able to sell on credit at all.

In addition to the benefits discussed above, various procedural rules make it easier to recover on a negotiable instrument after default than on a nonnegotiable instrument or a simple contract. When suing on a negotiable instrument, for example, the plaintiff (holder) need not plead or prove consideration, as is required in a suit on an ordinary contract. In addition, if the validity of the signatures is admitted or established, the holder is entitled to recover on the instrument merely by producing it, unless the defendant, such as the maker of a note, establishes a defense. Because signatures are generally presumed to be valid, the sole burden on the plaintiff in most cases is to produce the instrument and prove that he is a holder. The burden of proving any defense to payment rests upon the defendant.[12]

The "Holder in Due Course" Doctrine

In Article 3, negotiability is embodied in the **holder in due course doctrine** which states that if a negotiable instrument is negotiated to a holder in due course, the holder in due course takes free of all claims and most defenses to the instrument. The holder in due course is essentially the "good faith purchaser" of the instrument entitled to the benefits of negotiability previously outlined. Under §3–302(a), a holder in due course is a holder who takes an apparently valid instrument.

1. for value,
2. in good faith, and
3. without notice that it is overdue, has been dishonored, or of any defense against or claim to it on the part of any person.

To illustrate the general operation of the holder in due course doctrine, assume that Sara sells a used truck to Laura for use in Laura's construction business. Because Laura is unable to pay cash for the truck, she contractually agrees to pay the $10,000 purchase price in 24 monthly installments. Sara, however, breaches the contract because (1) she fails to deliver the truck, or (2) the truck is not as warranted (for example, it had not recently had an engine overhaul as represented

---

[12]UCC §3–308.

by Sara), or (3) she defrauds Laura by turning back the truck's odometer. Before Laura discovers the problem, Sara assigns her rights under the contract to Harry, who pays cash without knowledge of Laura's defense. In this case, because an ordinary contract assignment is involved, Harry steps into Sara's shoes and takes no better rights than she has. Therefore, Laura may assert any of the foregoing defenses against Harry when he brings an action to enforce the contract against her.

On the other hand, assume the same prior facts, except that instead of a mere contractual promise to pay, Laura issues a negotiable promissory note payable to the order of Sara. Sara immediately negotiates (assigns) the note to Harry, who pays cash without knowledge of Laura's defense; that is, Harry is a "holder in due course." In this case, Harry may compel Laura to pay the note despite Laura's defense against her original payee, Sara. Thus, the negotiability concept places the assignee of a negotiable instrument (the holder in due course, Harry) in a better position than his assignor (here, Sara). Although Sara cannot enforce the instrument against Laura, Harry (Sara's transferee) can. Simply stated, then, the net effect of the holder in due course doctrine is to negate the general principle of contract law that an assignee acquires no better rights than his assignor.

In order for an assignee to be placed in this preferred position, several requirements must be met:

1. The right assigned must be evidenced by a *negotiable instrument*. (The formal requisites of negotiability are covered in the next chapter.)

2. The instrument must be properly *negotiated* (assigned). (Negotiation is discussed in Chapter 23.)
3. The transferee of the instrument must be a *holder in due course*. (The holder in due course requirements listed above are discussed in Chapter 24.)

A person who qualifies as a holder in due course acquires various rights against other parties to the instrument and third parties. Namely, the holder in due course takes free of all claims to the instrument on the part of any person and certain defenses, commonly known as "personal" defenses, of other parties on the instrument. A holder in due course takes subject, however, to so-called real defenses. The rights of a holder in due course against persons asserting claims and defenses are covered in Chapter 24.

Parties to negotiable instruments, like parties to other contracts, have certain rights and duties. Generally, parties to negotiable instruments incur two types of liability: (1) liability for ultimate payment of the instrument (known as contract liability), and (2) liability for forgery and alteration of the instrument (known as warranty liability). Contract and warranty liability are discussed in Chapters 25 and 26 respectively. Chapter 27 concludes the negotiable instruments material with a discussion of special issues involving checks, including the bank collection process and the relationship between a bank and its checking account customer. Chapter 27 also discusses modern payment devices such as credit cards and electronic fund transfers.

Summary

1. Article 3 of the UCC governs notes, certificates of deposit, drafts, and checks, important tools by which credit is extended and debts are paid.

2. Although Article 3 governs four types of instruments, the basic distinction is between notes, designated as "two-party" paper, and drafts, which are "three-party" paper.

3. A note involves a promise by the maker to pay a sum certain in money to the order of the payee on demand or at a definite time. A certificate of deposit, a specialized form of note, is an acknowledgment by a bank of the receipt of money with a promise to repay it.

4. A draft, unlike a note, contains an order rather than a promise. In a draft, the drawer orders the drawee, who usually is a debtor of the drawer, to pay money to the order of the payee. A draft drawn on a bank and payable on demand is known as a "check," certainly the most common type of negotiable instrument.

5. The foregoing instruments are negotiable, a characteristic that aids them in performing their valuable commercial functions. Negotiability promotes free transferability and enhances the marketability of the paper by providing (1) that all relevant information about the instrument, including liability of parties thereto, be determined from the instrument itself,

(2) a simple and expeditious method of transferring the instrument, and (3) that good faith purchasers of the instrument take it free of ownership claims and free of most defenses that might be asserted by parties obligated on the paper.

Key Terms

law merchant	trade acceptance
instrument	check
note	cashier's check
maker	remitter
payee	teller's check
bearer	order
certificate of deposit	negotiability
promise	claim
draft (bill of exchange)	defense
drawer	discount rate
drawee	holder in due course doctrine

Questions and Problems

21.1   What are the characteristics of a negotiable, as opposed to a nonnegotiable, contract? Review the distinction between formal and informal (simple) contracts discussed in Chapter 7. Negotiable instruments governed by Article 3 are an important type of formal contract. Why are negotiable instruments formal contracts? What purposes do the formalities serve?

21.2   The law of negotiable instruments is primarily concerned with altering a basic principle of ordinary contract law. What is that principle? Why is it necessary to change it in negotiable instruments transactions?

NEGOTIABILITY

Because of the extraordinary legal consequences of negotiability, a negotiable instrument must be readily distinguishable from a nonnegotiable one. In addition, to reduce administrative expenses and encourage widespread use, negotiable instruments must be easily created. To achieve these ends, the Uniform Commercial Code requires that a negotiable instrument within Article 3 meet strict formal requirements. Negotiability under Article 3 is strictly a matter of *form.* If the instrument in question contains the necessary formal elements, it is negotiable. All other instruments are nonnegotiable.

Formal Requisites of Negotiability

The formal requisites of negotiability under Article 3 are stated in 3–104(a). To be negotiable,

1. the instrument must be in *writing signed* by the maker or drawer,[1]
2. the instrument must contain an *unconditional promise or order,*
3. the unconditional promise or order must be to pay a *fixed amount of money,*
4. the instrument must be payable on *demand* or at a *definite time,* and
5. the instrument must be payable to order or to bearer.

Any instrument that does not meet these requirements may nevertheless be a legally binding contract on the signer. It is simply not *negotiable.* No person may therefore become a holder in due course of such an instrument with the ability to cut off prior claims and defenses. Rather, the transfer of a nonnegotiable instrument is governed by the same principles applicable to contract assignments generally—an assignee of such an instrument acquires no better rights than the assignor.

In addition to conclusively identifying negotiable contracts, formal requisites serve an additional function critical to negotiability: they assure that all relevant information about the instrument can be determined

---

[1]UCC §§3–103(a)(6),(9).

from the instrument itself. Such terms include the amount payable, time of payment, and the liability of all parties.

The negotiability concept also requires that the information on the instrument not be subject to contradiction by evidence outside the instrument, such as oral testimony or other documents. For this reason, the UCC adopts a strict parol evidence rule applicable to negotiable instruments. *Everything* about Article 3 paper is determined by examining the face and back of the instrument itself. For example, all ambiguities are resolved by rules of construction provided in Article 3, and a party's liability is determined by the appearance and position of his or her signature on the paper. Further, with rare exceptions, no evidence other than what appears on the instrument itself (supplemented by UCC rules) is admissible in court to determine anything about the instrument.

A Writing Signed by the Maker or Drawer

"Writing" Defined. If a negotiable instrument is to adequately serve as a credit device or substitute for money, it must be in writing. This rule, recognized since the time of the law merchant, is necessary to promote certainty and prevent fraud. Although a writing is essential, UCC §1–201(b)(43) defines the term **writing** broadly to include printing, typewriting, and any other intentional reduction to tangible form. A negotiable instrument therefore may be handwritten in pen or pencil on ordinary paper, carved on the top of a desk, embossed on the back of a book or a briefcase, or, for that matter, inscribed on any surface. As a practical matter, of course, virtually all negotiable instruments are created on forms (such as an ordinary check) printed for the purpose. Additionally, by administrative regulation or contract, banks may refuse to process checks not written on the printed form.

"Signature" Defined. To be negotiable, a note must be signed by the maker and a draft must be signed by the drawer. Like the writing, no strict formalities are imposed in defining "signature." Instead, §1–201(b)(37) defines **signature** as "any symbol executed or adopted with present intention to adopt or accept a writing." A signature may be affixed by hand or by using a stamp or machine. Further, a signature may be made "by the use of any name, including a trade or assumed name, or by

a word, mark or symbol."[2] Thus, the signature may be handwritten, typewritten, printed, or indicated by thumbprint or other mark. Although the drawer's or maker's signature ordinarily appears at the end of the writing, it may appear in the body of the instrument (for example, "I, Janice Dean, promise to pay . . . ") without any further signature.

The signature requirement is important not only in determining negotiability, but also in ascertaining the contract liability of all parties to the instrument. Under §3–401(a), no person is liable on a negotiable instrument unless that person's *signature* appears on it. Signatures may be made in various capacities, which determine the nature and extent of the liability undertaken by the signer.

An Unconditional Promise or Order to Pay

A note involves a *promise* by the maker to pay money. In a draft, the drawer *orders* the drawee to pay. To be negotiable under Article 3, the note or draft must therefore contain language indicating that a promise or order has been made. Ordinarily the simple words "promise" in a note or "pay" in a draft satisfy this requirement.

The mere *existence* of a promise or order is not enough to make the instrument negotiable. The promise or order must be absolute and not conditioned upon the occurrence or nonoccurrence of any event. If paper is conditional, the holder must "look behind" the paper to see if the condition to payment has been met. The expense and delay inherent in investigating the condition defeats the purpose of negotiability. For this reason §3–104 requires that, to be negotiable, an instrument must contain an *unconditional* promise or order to pay a sum certain in money and *no other* promise or order except as explicitly authorized in Article 3.

What constitutes an unconditional promise or order is sometimes a difficult question. Negotiable instruments commonly are given in exchange for a loan of money, or a sale of property or services. These instruments often contain added language referring to the underlying contract, or indicating the source of payment. The mere *existence* of a separate agreement does not affect negotiability,[3] but certain references to it may. UCC §3–106, discussed below, aids the court in deter-

---

[2]UCC §3–401(b).
[3]UCC §3–106(a).

mining whether added language renders the promise or order conditional.

Express Versus Implied Conditions. The types of conditions affecting negotiability are *express,* not *implied* or *constructive.* Assume that on January 1 Barker issues a $1,000 promissory note to the order of Sullivan in exchange for goods sold by Sullivan to Barker to be delivered on June 1. The note is payable on December 1 "on condition that Sullivan properly delivers the goods for which this note is issued by June 1, and that they conform to the contract of sale." In this case, Barker's promise to pay is subject to an express condition: seasonable and conforming delivery by Sullivan. The instrument is therefore nonnegotiable, because any later holder must investigate the occurrence of the condition to determine whether he or she will be paid. Negotiability is defeated because the holder cannot ascertain all essential terms from the instrument itself.

In contrast, a promise is not made conditional simply because it is subject to "implied" or "constructive" conditions under general contract law discussed in Chapter 14. For example, assume that rather than expressly conditioning his duty, Barker merely stated in the instrument that "this note is given in exchange for my purchase of goods from Sullivan that are to be delivered on June 1." As a matter of general contract law under the theory of "constructive conditions of exchange," Sullivan's failure to deliver on June 1 would justify Barker's failure to pay on December 1. One may therefore argue that the implied condition to Barker's duty destroys negotiability. The Code explicitly rejects this argument in §3–106(a); implied or constructive conditions are not considered in determining negotiability.

Reference to a Separate Agreement. Negotiability is unaffected by a mere *reference to* a separate agreement to explain or provide information about the underlying transaction. In contrast, incorporation by reference[4] of the terms of a separate agreement into the instrument destroys negotiability because the holder must look to another document for terms of payment. The holder may not be required to look to other documents, even documents explicitly referred to in the instrument.

The difficulty lies in determining which statements about the separate agreement *incorporate* that agreement, destroying negotiability, and which are mere references.

To resolve this problem, §3–106(a) provides that a promise or order is rendered conditional if the instrument states (1) that it is "governed by" (or "conditioned by") or "subject to" any other agreement, or (2) that rights and obligations of the parties to the instrument are stated in another writing. On the other hand, negotiability is not destroyed by a simple statement that the promise or order is made, or the instrument matures, "in accordance with" or "as per" the transaction giving rise to the instrument. Without destroying negotiability, an instrument also may state its consideration or the transaction or agreement giving rise to the instrument, state that it is drawn under a letter of credit, or state that it is secured (for example, by a mortgage). Such language is clearly intended to indicate the origin of the instrument and to inform, not to condition payment according to the terms of another agreement.

Although requiring the holder to look to the separate agreement for essential terms ordinarily destroys negotiability, the Code does authorize certain limited incorporation by reference. For example, under §3–106(b), terms stating rights regarding collateral, giving the maker the right to prepay a note, or giving the holder the right to accelerate the due date may be contained in a separate agreement without destroying negotiability.

In the following case, the court was required to determine whether reference to another agreement rendered a note nonnegotiable.

Holly Hill Acres, Ltd. v. Charter Bank of Gainesville
314 So.2d 209 (Fla. App. 1975)

Appellant Holly Hill Acres, Ltd. purchased land from Rogers and Blythe and executed a promissory note secured by a mortgage on the property. The note contained the following provision:

> This note with interest is secured by a mortgage on real estate, of even date herewith, made by the maker hereof in favor of the said payee, and shall be construed and enforced according to the laws of the State of Florida. *The terms of said mortgage are by this reference made a part hereof.* (Emphasis supplied.)

---

[4]Incorporation by reference is a legal doctrine under which the terms of one identifiable writing are made part of another writing by referring to, identifying, and adopting the former as part of the latter.

Rogers and Blythe assigned the promissory note and mortgage to appellee, Charter Bank of Gainesville, to secure their own note to the bank. When Holly Hill Acres defaulted on the note, Charter Bank sued to foreclose the mortgage. Holly Hill Acres defended on the ground that it had been defrauded by Rogers and Blythe in the original sale. The trial court entered summary judgment in favor of Charter Bank, holding that the note was negotiable and that the bank was a holder in due course of the note. Holly Hill Acres appealed.

Scheb, Judge

. . . Appellee Bank relies upon *Scott v. Taylor,* [58 So. 30 (Fla. 1912)], as authority for the proposition that its note is negotiable. *Scott,* however, involved a note which stated: "this note secured by mortgage." Mere reference to a note being secured by mortgage is a common commercial practice and such reference in itself does not impede the negotiability of the note. There is, however, a significant difference in a note stating that it is "secured by a mortgage" from one which provides, "the terms of said mortgage are by this reference made a part hereof." In the former instance the note merely refers to a separate agreement which does not impede its negotiability, while in the latter instance the note is rendered nonnegotiable.

As a general rule the assignee of a mortgage securing a nonnegotiable note, even though a bona fide purchaser for value, takes subject to all defenses available as against the morgagee. . . . Appellant raised the issue of fraud as between himself and other parties to the note. . . .

The note having incorporated the terms of the purchase money mortgage was not negotiable. The appellee Bank was not a holder in due course, therefore, the appellant was entitled to raise against the appellee any defenses which could be raised between the appellant and Rogers and Blythe. . . .

[Judgment reversed and remanded.]

Note, finally, that persons obligated on a negotiable instrument need not put all of their assets behind the instrument. Under §3–106(b), a promise or order is not made conditional simply "because payment is limited to resort to a particular fund or source." Thus, Mike's promissory note "payable only out of the proceeds of the sale of my 2006 soybean crop" may be negotiable whether or not sufficient proceeds actually exist to pay the note. As explained in Official Comment 1 to §3–106:

> There is no cogent reason why the general credit of a legal entity must be pledged to have a negotiable instrument. Market forces determine the marketability of instruments of this kind. If potential buyers don't want promises or orders that are payable only from a particular source or fund, they won't take them, but Article 3 should apply.

Additional Terms Not Affecting Negotiability. A negotiable promise or order must be unconditional, and generally must be the *only* promise, order, power, or obligation given by the maker or drawer. For example, a note in which the maker promises to pay money and to perform services or deliver goods is nonnegotiable. Section 3–104(a)(3) recognizes certain limited exceptions to this rule by allowing an instrument to contain limited obligations or powers in addition to the bare promise or order to pay money. Specifically, the following terms included in the instrument do not destroy negotiability: (1) an authorization or power to give, maintain, or protect collateral; (2) an authorization or power given to the holder to confess judgment,[5] or realize on or dispose of collateral; or (3) a waiver of the benefit of any law intended to protect a person obligated on the instrument. Other than as authorized above, added promises, orders, powers, and obligations destroy negotiability.

A Fixed Amount of Money

Article 3 paper is payable in money. Section 3–104(a) states that the unconditional promise or order on the paper must be "to pay a fixed amount of money, with or without interest or other charges" described in the instrument. If all or part of an instrument is payable in goods or services, it cannot be negotiable under Article 3. Requiring payment in money promotes the marketability of the paper because it is easier to ascertain the present value of a promise to pay money than a promise to deliver goods or perform services. Further, the amount of money payable must be fixed or certain, generally computable from the instrument itself.

---

[5]Confession of judgment is discussed in Chapter 29.

Section 1–201(b)(24) defines the term **money** as "a medium of exchange currently authorized or adopted by a domestic or foreign government." Because "money" includes a medium of exchange authorized or adopted by a *foreign* as well as domestic government, an instrument may be negotiable under Article 3 even though payable in foreign currency. Provided it meets the other requirements, an instrument issued and to be paid in the United States, but payable in English pounds or French francs, is negotiable. Under §3–107, the instrument may be paid either in the foreign currency, or (unless foreign currency is explicitly required by the instrument) in the equivalent amount of U.S. dollars "calculated by using the current bank-offered spot rate at the place of payment for the purchase of dollars on the day on which the instrument is paid."

The amount payable on a negotiable instrument often includes both principal and interest. A provision for interest must be explicitly stated. That is, unless the instrument provides otherwise, it does not bear interest. If interest is to be paid, it runs from the date of the instrument, unless provided otherwise.[6]

Section 3–104(a) requires only that the principal be fixed in amount. Under §3–112(b), however, the amount of interest may be a fixed or variable amount of money, or may be expressed as a fixed or variable rate. The instrument may describe the interest rate or amount in any manner and may require reference to sources outside the instrument. Thus, a note requiring payment of interest at a rate of "3% over prime to be adjusted monthly" may be negotiable.

An instrument may be made payable "with interest" but with no interest rate stated. Section 3–112(b) provides that such an instrument is payable with interest "at the judgment rate in effect at the place of payment of the instrument and at the time interest first accrues." The **judgment rate** refers to the rate of interest required by state law to be paid on money judgments. This rate varies from state to state. For example, Illinois law provides "Judgments recovered in any court shall draw interest at the rate of 9% per annum from the date of the judgment until satisfied". . . .[7]

Payable on Demand or at a Definite Time

To be negotiable within Article 3 an instrument must be payable either on *demand* or at a *definite time*. This requirement assures that the holder can ascertain *when*

he will be paid, whereas the fixed amount rule determines the *amount* payable. Both are required to compute the present value of the instrument—a fundamental purpose of the formal requisites.

Instruments Payable on Demand. A demand instrument is payable whenever the holder chooses to present it for payment to the maker (of a note) or the drawee (of a draft). Under §3–108(a), instruments payable on demand or **demand instruments** include

1. those explicitly stated to be payable at the will of the holder (for example, instruments payable on "demand," "sight," or "presentation"), or
2. those in which no time for payment is stated.

The note in Figure 22.1 is a demand instrument of the first type.

The second type of demand instrument requires additional elaboration. Under §3–113, the negotiability of an instrument is unaffected by the fact that it is undated. Because the absence of a date has no effect on negotiability, an undated instrument—for example, when a blank for the date on a note or check form is not filled in—is one in which no time for payment is stated and is therefore payable on demand.

Negotiability of an instrument is similarly unaffected by the fact that it is antedated—for example, a note or check written on June 1 dated May 15—or postdated—for example, a note or check written on May 15 dated June 1. In either case, the time when the instrument is payable is determined by the stated date. For example, a note issued on June 1 dated May 15 and payable "30 days after date" is payable 30 days after May 15. Thus, an antedated instrument can be due before it is issued (for example, if the above instrument was payable "10 days after date"). Note also that any dated instrument not explicitly stating another time for payment is a demand instrument payable on the stated date. Checks ordinarily fall into this category.

Because the stated date determines the due date of an instrument, postdated demand instruments usually are not payable before the date stated on the instrument. Section 4–401(c), however, provides a major exception to this rule for the most common postdated demand instrument—the postdated check. Section 4–401(c) provides that a bank may pay a postdated check when presented and before the stated date unless the customer gives prior notice of the postdating that describes the check with reasonable certainty. The rules governing

---

[6]UCC §3–112(a).
[7]735 ILCS 5/2–1303.

Figure 22.1   **Demand Note**

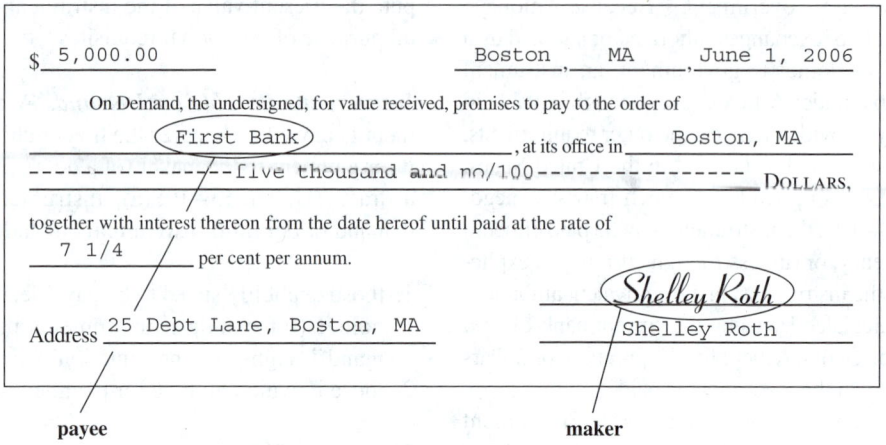

$ 5,000.00   Boston , MA , June 1, 2006

On Demand, the undersigned, for value received, promises to pay to the order of

_____First Bank_____ , at its office in ____Boston, MA____

--------------five thousand and no/100---------------- DOLLARS,

together with interest thereon from the date hereof until paid at the rate of

____7 1/4____ per cent per annum.

Shelley Roth

Address ___25 Debt Lane, Boston, MA___   Shelley Roth

payee   **maker**

the manner and effectiveness of postdating notices are identical to those applicable to stop payment orders, discussed in Chapter 27. The rationale for the notice rule is simply that "the automated check collection system cannot accommodate postdated checks. A check is usually paid upon presentment without respect to the date of the check."[8]

Instruments Payable at a Definite Time. Negotiable instruments are frequently used as credit devices, evidencing an obligation to pay money in the future in return for goods sold, services rendered, or money loaned. The party obligated (normally the maker of a note) is not able to pay the instrument on demand but desires to postpone payment to some future date. Instruments calling for future (other than demand) payment, or **time instruments,** must be payable at a *definite time.* This requirement assures that the instrument will ultimately be paid and aids in computing its value. As with other terms, the holder of such a time instrument must generally be able to compute the payment date from the instrument itself.

In §3–108(b), the UCC outlines typical situations in which an instrument is payable at a definite time for purposes of negotiability:

1.   An instrument is payable at a definite time if by its terms it is payable on or before a stated date, at a fixed period after a stated date, or at another time read-

ily ascertainable when the instrument is issued. For example, Mary may issue her $10,000 promissory note dated January 1, 2001, payable "on July 1, 2001," or alternatively "6 months after date." The note in Figure 22.2 illustrates this type of time instrument. Note that if the instrument is payable at a fixed period after a stated date, the inclusion of the date is important to negotiability. Without it, the maturity of the instrument cannot be determined.

2.   An instrument is payable at a definite time if by its terms it is payable at a fixed period after sight or acceptance. This is a time draft. "Sight" in this case refers to "acceptance," a concept discussed in detail in Chapter 25. For example, assume Sally draws a draft on Bob payable to Paul's order "60 days after sight." In this case Paul must first present the draft to Bob for acceptance. The date of acceptance fixes the ultimate maturity date. That is, 60 days after the date of acceptance, Paul or a later holder will again present the instrument to Bob, this time for payment.

3.   An instrument is payable at a definite time if by its terms it is payable at a definite time subject to any acceleration. Promissory notes often contain **acceleration clauses.** Such clauses generally make the note, originally payable at some fixed future date or in fixed future installments, either immediately due and payable or payable on a date sooner than originally agreed. To illustrate, assume Martin issues his $12,000 promissory note to Alice's order payable over two years in 24 equal monthly installments. The note contains a provision making the entire remaining balance immediately due

---

[8]UCC §4–401, Official Comment 3.

| Figure 22.2 | **Time Note** |

$ __5,000.00__   _____Boston__, __MA__, ___June 1, 2006__

___one year___ after date, the undersigned, for value received, promises to pay to the order of

_____First Bank_____, at its office in _____Boston, MA_____

----------------five thousand and no/100---------------- DOLLARS,

together with interest thereon from the date hereof until paid at the rate of

___7 1/4___ per cent per annum.

Shelley Roth

Address ___25 Debt Lane, Boston, MA___   Shelley Roth

---

and payable if Martin defaults on two consecutive monthly payments.

Because no one knows at the date of issue whether or not acceleration will be made, one may argue an instrument containing an acceleration clause is not payable at a definite time and should therefore be nonnegotiable. The Code decisively rejects this argument by broadly validating all acceleration clauses[9] provided the instrument is ultimately payable at a definite time if no acceleration is made.

4. An instrument is payable at a definite time if by its terms it is payable at a definite time subject to (a) *any* extension at the option of the holder, or (b) extension to a *further definite time* at the option of the maker or acceptor, or automatically upon or after occurrence of a specified act or event. An **extension clause** simply extends the maturity of an instrument (generally a note) from its original due date to a future time specified in the instrument. The Code broadly validates extension clauses but places a limitation upon them if the extension occurs by the terms of the instrument or at the maker's option. That is, such an extension must be to a *further definite time.* Any other rule would allow the maker to extend the instrument indefinitely, rendering the promise to pay illusory. On the other hand, any extension (even without a time limit) at the *holder's* option is permitted without affecting negotiability. The

formal requisite that an instrument be payable at a definite time is designed to benefit the holder. If the holder elects to extend the instrument past its original maturity, any uncertainty regarding time of payment is due to his own act.[10]

Payable to "Order" or to "Bearer"

Because of the consequences of negotiability, the formal requisites must clearly assure that the drawer or maker intends the instrument to be negotiable. Certainty concerning intention is provided by requiring that a negotiable instrument contain "words of negotiability." To be negotiable within Article 3, an instrument, in addition to the other formal requisites, must be payable to *order* or to *bearer.* By including one of these terms the maker or drawer provides conclusive evidence of an intention to issue a negotiable instrument. For example, a note in which Mary promises to pay $10,000 "to the order of Joan" is negotiable, whereas one simply payable "to Joan" is not.

This rule requiring words of negotiability is subject to an important exception. Under §3–104(c), a *check* meeting the other requirements of negotiability is negotiable even if it omits the words "order" or "bearer."

---

[9]The clause may operate at the option of the maker or holder, or automatically on occurrence of an event, and may be conditional or unrestricted. Acceleration clauses are discussed in more detail in Chapter 14.

[10]Note that a clause authorizing extension at the holder's option gives him no greater rights against the maker or acceptor than he would have without the clause. That is, assuming no clause and no tender of full payment by the maker of a note on the due date, the holder's mere inaction would operate to extend the instrument.

Official Comment 2 to §3–104 explains the rationale for both this exception and the general rule:

> Subsection (c) is based on the belief that it is good policy to treat checks, which are payment instruments, as negotiable instruments whether or not they contain the words "to the order of". These words are almost always preprinted on the check form. Occasionally the drawer of a check may strike out these words before issuing the check. . . . Absence of the quoted words can easily be overlooked and should not affect the rights of holders who may pay money or give credit for a check without being aware that it is not in the conventional form.
>
> Total exclusion from Article 3 of other promises or orders that are not payable to bearer or to order serves a useful purpose. It provides a simple device to clearly exclude a writing that does not fit the pattern of typical negotiable instruments and which is not intended to be a negotiable instrument.

The following case illustrates the critical importance of the "magic words" of negotiability.

First Investment Company v. Andersen
621 P.2d 683 (Utah 1980)

Defendants Robert and Donna Andersen executed two promissory notes, each of which stated:

> For value received, Robert Andersen of Nephi, Utah, promises to pay to Great Lakes Nursery Corp. at Waukesha, Wisconsin, six thousand four hundred twelve dollars [in installments over a period of five years at 7% interest].
>
> s/Robert Andersen
s/Donna Andersen

The promissory notes were executed when the Andersens entered into a franchise agreement with Great Lakes Nursery Corp. (Nursery), which by the terms of the agreement was to provide 65,000 trees, chemicals, fertilizers, and technical training to the Andersens. The Nursery assigned the Andersens' notes to plaintiff, First Investment Company. After paying several installments on the notes, the Andersens refused to make further payments on the grounds that the Nursery had failed to furnish the items and training required by the franchise agreement. First Investment sued the Andersens on the notes claiming to be a holder in due course. The trial court held that because the notes were not negotiable instruments, First Investment

was not a holder in due course and, therefore, took the notes subject to the defense of failure of consideration. First Investment appealed.

Maughan, Justice

. . . Under both the N.I.L. and the U.C.C. [§3–104], one of the requirements to qualify a writing as a negotiable instrument is that it contain the time-honored "words of negotiability," such as "pay to the order" or "pay to the bearer." The mere promise to pay, absent the magic words "payable to order or to bearer," renders the note non-negotiable, and the liability is determined as a matter of simple contract law.

In the instant case, the notes were payable simply to the payee, and were not payable to the order of the payee or to the payee or its order and were thus not negotiable instruments. Since the notes were not negotiable, the transfer by the Nursery to plaintiff must be deemed an assignment, and the assignee (plaintiff) stood in the shoes of the assignor and took subject to existing equities and defense. . . .

[Judgment affirmed.]

The major characteristic of an instrument payable to order (so-called **order paper**) is that the payee is specifically named or otherwise designated with reasonable certainty. Conversely, **bearer paper** is payable to whoever possesses the instrument and is therefore much like cash. The distinction between order and bearer instruments is extremely important in the law of negotiable instruments. As noted above, inclusion of the word "order" or "bearer" or its equivalent is essential to negotiability. In addition, the status of paper as order or bearer determines the means by which the paper is transferred (negotiated), and the liability of the parties on the instrument. The following material distinguishes instruments payable to order from those payable to bearer, and in the case of order paper, indicates to whose order the instrument is payable.

Instruments Payable to Order. Under §3–109(b), an instrument is payable to order if by its terms it is payable to the order of an identified person, or to an identified person or order. Thus, a note in which the maker promises to pay $10,000 "to the order of Joe

Doaks," or "to Joe Doaks or order," is payable to order. The payee of an order instrument is determined by the *intent* of the person, whether or not authorized, signing as, or on behalf of, the maker or drawer.[11]

The payee of an order instrument may be identified in any manner including by name, identifying number, office, or account number. If the instrument is payable to a single natural person—for example, "pay to the order of John Jones"—the person to whose order the instrument is payable is clearly identified.

Section 3–110(c) provides the following rules to determine the payee's identity for more difficult cases.

1. An instrument payable to a trust or estate is payable to the representative (the trustee, executor, or administrator) of the trust or estate, or the successor of such representative. For example, an instrument payable to "Jane Jones, trustee of City College Trust" or "Jane Jones, executor of the will of Joe Doaks" or "Jane Jones, administrator of the estate of Richard Wagner" is payable to Jane Jones. Although Jones is the proper party to negotiate or otherwise deal with the instrument, she is liable for breach of fiduciary duty if she uses the instrument for her own benefit rather than the benefit of the trust or estate.

2. An instrument payable to an agent of an identified person (for example, "John Jones, treasurer of XYZ Corporation" or "John Jones as agent for Joe Doaks") is payable either to the agent, the principal, or the agent's successor.

3. An instrument payable to a fund or organization that is not a legal entity (such as an unincorporated club) is payable to any representative of the members of the fund or organization.

4. An instrument payable to an office (the "Office of the County Recorder"), to an officer by his title as such (the "Treasurer of the City of Champaign" or the "Clerk of the Circuit Court"), or to a person described as holding an office ("Joe Doaks, City Manager") is payable either to the named person, the incumbent in the described office, or the incumbent's successor.

5. An instrument payable to an account identified only by number is payable to the owner of the account. If the instrument is payable to an account identified both by number and by the name of a person, the instru-

ment is payable to the named person, whether or not that person owns the numbered account. For example, an instrument payable to "XYZ Corporation's account No. 100–565 in Fifth National Bank of Chicago" is payable to XYZ Corporation and can be negotiated by XYZ Corporation whether or not it owns the numbered account.

Instruments Payable to Bearer. Unlike an order instrument, which is payable to a specific person, bearer paper is payable to the person possessing the instrument. Section 3–109(a) provides that an instrument is payable to bearer if (1) it is payable to "bearer," the "order of bearer," the order of a specified person or bearer ("pay to the order of John Doe or bearer"), or otherwise indicates that the person in possession of the instrument is entitled to payment; (2) no payee is stated; and (3) it is payable to "cash," the "order of cash," or otherwise indicates that it is not payable to an identified person. For example, all of the following instruments are payable to bearer: "pay cash," "pay to the order of cash," "pay to the order of a keg of nails," "pay to the order of one 1955 Chevrolet," "pay a copy of the 2000 Official Text of the Uniform Commercial Code."

Rules of Construction

The formal elements of negotiability permit the essential terms of the instrument to be determined accurately and quickly from the instrument. To provide even greater certainty concerning essential terms, the UCC adopts a fairly strict parol evidence rule applicable to negotiable instruments. That is, generally the only admissible evidence concerning the essential terms of a negotiable instrument, including the liability of all parties, is the instrument itself. Ambiguities are resolved or clarified not by outside evidence, but by rules of construction stated in Article 3. In most cases, no evidence, including oral testimony or other documents, is admissible to contradict what is stated on the instrument as supplemented by Code construction rules. Three important Article 3 construction rules are discussed below.

1. If an instrument qualifies as both a draft and a note, the holder may treat it as either. For example, a cashier's check (one drawn by a bank upon itself) may be treated by the holder as a check on the issuing bank or a demand promissory note.[12]

---

[11]UCC §3–110(a). If the maker's or drawer's signature is made by automated means, such as a check-writing machine, the payee is determined by the intent of the person (usually an employee of the drawer) supplying the payee's name or identification, whether or not that person was authorized to do so. UCC §3–110(b).

[12]UCC §3–104(e).

2.   Language on a negotiable instrument may be printed—for example, the language of a preprinted note or check form—typewritten, or handwritten. Anything typed or handwritten on a printed form controls an inconsistent printed term. If a conflict arises between what is typed and what is written, the handwritten term controls.[13]

3.   Notes and drafts commonly express the amount payable both in words ("one hundred dollars") and figures ($100.00). If a conflict arises between the figures and words, *words* control.[14] For example, assume Ann draws a check payable to Pat's order. Ann fills in the amount as "$10.00" in figures and "one thousand dollars" in words. The instrument is payable for $1,000. In the following case the court applied this rule of construction in resolving a dispute.

Yates v. Commercial Bank & Trust Company
432 So.2d 725 (Fla. App. 1983)

Emmett McDonald, while acting as personal representative of the estate of Marion Cahill, wrote a check drawn on the estate checking account at defendant Commercial Bank & Trust Company. The check read in pertinent part:

> Pay to the order of *Emmett E. McDonald $10075.00 Ten hundred seventy five* . . . . Dollars.

The italicized material was handwritten; the remainder was printed.

The bank paid $10,075 to McDonald, who absconded with the funds. Plaintiff William Yates, who was appointed as successor representative for the estate, sued the bank for $9,000 representing the difference between $10,075 and $1,075. The trial court dismissed the complaint. Yates appealed.

Schwartz, Chief Judge

. . . It is clear that the complaint stated a cognizable claim against the bank. [UCC §3–114 provides that words control figures.] Under this provision of the UCC, it was clearly improper for the bank to have paid the larger sum stated in numbers, rather than the smaller one unambiguously stated by McDonald's words. It is, therefore, prima facie liable to the estate for the excess. . . .

[Judgment reversed.]

Incomplete Instruments

An instrument is not negotiable unless it contains all of the formal requisites of negotiability. An instrument ultimately intended to be negotiable, which is *signed* by the maker or drawer but which omits some term or terms necessary to complete the instrument, is referred to as **incomplete.** An incomplete instrument contains blanks or spaces or otherwise indicates that additional terms are to be supplied. Usually, the omitted term or terms are some combination of the date, the payee, and the amount payable.

In some cases, an instrument is enforceable in incomplete form because Article 3 rules supply the missing terms. For example, an undated instrument is payable on demand.[15] An instrument that omits the payee is payable to bearer.[16] In other cases (for example, if the amount payable is omitted), the instrument cannot be enforced until completed. In these situations, under §3–115, if the instrument is completed as authorized, expressly or impliedly, by the maker or drawer, the instrument is enforceable as a negotiable instrument as completed. The instrument is treated as if completed personally by the maker or drawer. For example, assume that on June 1, Anne borrows $10,000 from John and issues a promissory note payable to John's order "90 days after date." The instrument is complete except Anne forgets to fill in the amount and the blank for the date. Anne mails the note to John. At this time the instrument is incomplete and nonnegotiable because it is not payable at a definite time, and the amount payable is not fixed. The next day, John discovers the omission and fills in the proper amount and date of issue on the note. The instrument is now complete and negotiable as completed.

Of course, not all completions are authorized. Assume Diane gives her roommate Joan a check signed by Diane with the date, payee, and amount blank. Diane

---

[13]UCC §3–114.
[14]*Id.*

[15]UCC §3–108(a).
[16]UCC §3–109(a)(2).

instructs Joan to take the check to the grocery store and buy groceries for the next week, not exceeding $75 in amount. Instead of buying groceries, Joan takes Diane's check to the stereo store, uses it to purchase $2,000 worth of stereo equipment, and promptly leaves town. This is an unauthorized completion. The rules governing unauthorized completion are covered in Chapter 24.

Summary

1.   Article 3 requires that negotiable instruments meet strict formal requisites. These formalities conclusively identify negotiable instruments and assure that all relevant information regarding the instrument can be determined from the instrument itself without recourse to any other document or individual. Further, all ambiguities are resolved by rules of construction provided in Article 3.

2.   To be negotiable under Article 3 (1) the instrument must be in *writing signed* by the maker or drawer; (2) the instrument must contain an *unconditional promise or order;* (3) the unconditional promise or order must be to pay a *fixed amount of money;* (4) the instrument must be payable on *demand* or at a *definite time;* and (5) the instrument must be payable to *order* or to *bearer.*

3.   The writing and signature requirement under the UCC are not rigorous. Though most negotiable instruments are preprinted forms such as checks, a "writing" is broadly defined to include any intentional reduction to tangible form. Similarly, a signature includes not only a formal signature, but also any other symbol adopted by a party with present intent to authenticate a writing.

4.   The signed writing must contain an unconditional promise (in a note) or order (in a draft). This requirement assures that the holder need not "look behind" the instrument to determine whether any condition to payment has been met. Negotiability is destroyed, for example, if the promise or order is subject to an express condition or incorporates the terms of a separate agreement into the instrument.

5.   To allow the holder to compute the amount payable, the unconditional promise or order must be to pay a fixed amount of money. Generally, no other promise or order may be included. Instruments payable in foreign currency are negotiable because "money" includes any medium of exchange adopted by a foreign or domestic government.

6.   To be negotiable, the instrument must be payable on demand or at a definite time. Instruments payable on demand include those expressly payable on demand, and those, such as checks, in which no time for payment is stated.

7.   An instrument is payable at a definite time if by its terms it is payable (1) on or before a stated date, at a fixed period after a stated date, or at another time readily ascertainable when the instrument is issued, or (2) at a fixed period after sight, or (3) at a definite time subject to any acceleration, or (4) at a definite time subject to any extension at the option of the holder or to extension to a further definite time at the option of the maker or by terms of the instrument.

8.   The final formal requirement is that the instrument be payable to "order" or to "bearer." Unlike order paper which is payable to a specific person, an instrument payable to bearer ("bearer paper") is payable to whoever possesses the instrument, and is therefore much like cash.

9.   Occasionally, an instrument ultimately intended to be negotiable will be signed, but will omit some term or terms (such as the date, payee, or amount payable) necessary to complete the instrument and make it negotiable. If the instrument is completed as authorized by the drawer or maker, the instrument becomes negotiable and is enforceable as completed.

Key Terms

writing	acceleration clause
signature	extension clause
money	order paper
judgment rate	bearer paper
demand instrument	incomplete instrument
time instrument	

Questions and Problems

22.1   Consider the following instrument:

> XYZ Co. hereby promises to pay Joe Doaks or bearer one hundred thousand (1,000) French Francs 30 days from date, for the purchase of goods delivered on July 15, 2004, governed by agreement dated July 1, 2004, with interest. We hereby acknowledge receipt of the goods and that Joe Doaks has a security interest in the goods.
>
> s/Sam Jones
> President, XYZ Co.

(a) Is the instrument a note or a draft?
(b) Is the instrument nonnegotiable *because* it is payable in foreign currency?
(c) Is the instrument nonnegotiable *because* the amount payable in words is different from the amount payable in figures?

(d) For what sum is the instrument payable?

(e) Is the instrument nonnegotiable *because* it is undated?

(f) Is the instrument nonnegotiable *because* it is not payable at a definite time? Could Joe Doaks complete the instrument by inserting the date? Would the instrument then be payable at a definite time?

(g) Is the instrument nonnegotiable *because* the interest rate is not stated? What is the interest rate of the instrument?

(h) Is the instrument nonnegotiable *because* it is stated to be governed by a separate agreement? Would your answer change if the instrument was stated to be payable "as per" the July 1, 2004, agreement?

(i) Is the instrument nonnegotiable *because* it states the consideration for which it was created?

(j) Is the instrument nonnegotiable *because* it states that it is secured?

(k) Assuming the instrument is negotiable, in what currency will the holder be paid?

(l) Is the instrument nonnegotiable *because* it is not payable to the "order" of Joe Doaks?

22.2   The Werner Co. agreed to perform construction work on a shopping mall owned by Stanley. After Werner finished the work, Stanley did not have sufficient cash to pay for the work; therefore, Stanley executed the following:

Promissory Note

Stanley acknowledges that a debt of $8,000 is owed to Werner Co. as a result of construction at Plaza Shopping Mall.

This note is payable at maturity on or before May 19, 2006, plus 10% interest.

s/ Stanley
April 4, 2005

Is the promissory note negotiable? Explain.

22.3   The *Liberty Advertiser,* a newspaper in need of capital, borrowed $15,000 and executed the following promissory note:

The undersigned promises to pay to the order of the Bank of Viola the sum of $15,000 payable in installments or payable $80 per week from the Jack & Jill contract.

s/ Liberty Advertiser
by Don Jackson,
President

Jack and Jill is a grocery store that contracted to advertise in the *Liberty Advertiser* for one year at $80 per week. Is the note negotiable? Explain.

22.4   M. S. Horne executed a promissory note by which he promised to pay $100,000 to the order of R. C. Clark in one year. On the note was a statement that the note could not be transferred, pledged, or assigned without the written consent of Home. In a separate letter, Home authorized Clark to pledge the note as collateral for a loan from First State Bank. Was the original note negotiable? If not, does Home's separate letter make it negotiable?

22.5   Peter Jones executes the following instrument:

June 15, 2004

Promissory Note

I promise to pay to the order of Max Allen the sum of $6,000.
s/ Peter Jones

(a) Is this instrument negotiable? When is it payable?

(b) Suppose the note stated:

At the earliest time possible after this date I promise to pay to the order of Max Allen the sum of $6,000.
s/ Peter Jones

Now is it negotiable? Explain.

(c) Suppose the note stated:

As soon as I am able I promise to pay to the order of Max Allen the sum of $6,000
s/ Peter Jones

Now is the instrument negotiable? Explain.

(d) Suppose the note stated:

I promise to pay to the order of Max Allen the sum of $6,000 within 10 years after June 15, 2004.
s/ Peter Jones

Is the instrument negotiable? If so, what is the earliest date Max could demand payment?

22.6   Steven Mudd served as president of Medical Interact Systems Corp. (MISC). After meeting with Mudd, Weatherford agreed to buy a computer system from MISC and mailed a $60,000 check as down payment to MISC's home office. The check was made payable to: "Stephen Mudd, President of MISC." When Mudd received the check, he indorsed it and deposited it in his personal checking account at Southeast Bank. Soon thereafter, Mudd withdrew the funds and disappeared. Weatherford sued Southeast Bank claiming that the bank wrongfully paid the check. How should the court rule?

22.7   A signed promissory note states in part:

June 1, 2006

Ninety days after date, I promise to pay to the order of *Three Thousand Four Hundred Ninety Eight and 45/100*—Dollars."

The italicized words and symbols are typed in; the remainder is printed. There are no blanks on the face of the instrument. All unused space has been filled in with hyphens. Is the instrument order or bearer paper? Is it negotiable?

22.8   Sam Sana, who operated Sana Travel Agency, wanted to purchase computing services on account from Albark Co. Because Sana had not previously done business with Albark, Albark was unwilling to extend credit to Sana. Sana then proposed that his company would provide a check in advance for the services on the condition that Albark would hold the check but would not cash it without Sana's permission. Albark agreed and Sana then wrote and signed a check dated March 15, 2005, payable to the order of Albark Co. in the amount of $10,000. In the lower left-hand corner of the check, Sana wrote, "Just to hold for the security of future business." Without notifying Sana, Albark indorsed the check on March 20, 2005, and negotiated it to Juan Carador in payment for goods that Carador had delivered to Albark. Carador indorsed the check and deposited it in his account at First World Bank. When Sana's bank dishonored the check, Carador sued Sana. Sana argued that it was not liable on the check because Albark had secured the check by fraud. Carador argued that because he was a holder in due course of the check, Sana could not assert the defense of fraud against him. The court held that Carador was not a holder in due course because the check was not negotiable. Is the court correct? What effect does the notation "Just to hold for the security of future business" have on the negotiability of the check?

NEGOTIATION

The negotiability or nonnegotiability of a particular note or draft is most important upon transfer of the instrument. Only negotiable paper may be transferred free of prior claims and defenses. In Article 3, the transferee enjoying this favored position is known as a holder in due course. The term "holder in due course" embodies two substantive requirements: that the transferee be a *holder* and that he or she hold in *due course.* Therefore, before studying the qualifications of a holder in due course and the preferred status such a transferee enjoys, the subject of Chapter 24, one must first understand how a person becomes a holder of an instrument and the rights of holders generally.

Introduction to Negotiation

"Holder" Defined

For Article 3 purposes, a **holder** is defined in §1–201(b)(21), as any person in possession of an instru-

ment payable to bearer. If the instrument is payable to order, the holder is the identified person to whom the instrument is payable, if that person is in possession of the instrument. Thus, to qualify as a holder, a person must have *possession* of the instrument. Without possession, a person cannot assert his or her status as a holder (or holder in due course) against those liable on the instrument. Every holder has the right to transfer the instrument, obtain payment of it, or sue upon it. A holder in due course, however, has rights superior to other holders if claims or defenses are asserted against the instrument.

The first holder of any instrument (note or draft) is the *payee.* The payee becomes a holder of an instrument through **issue**—when the maker or drawer, or in some cases a remitter,[1] transfers possession of the instrument to him. The instrument may be payable either to the payee's order or to bearer.

---

[1]UCC §3–105(a). A remitter is not a holder because the instrument, such as a cashier's check, is payable to a third party (for example, a creditor of the remitter), not the remitter. Upon delivery of the instrument from the remitter to the payee, the payee becomes a holder. To address this situation, §3–105(a) provides that "issue" means the first delivery of the instrument by the maker or drawer to a holder (the payee) or a nonholder (a remitter) "for the purpose of giving rights on the instrument to any person."

"Negotiation" Defined

Free transferability is the hallmark of a negotiable instrument. Some method must therefore be available to make transferees from or after the payee holders of the instrument. This method of transfer is known as **negotiation,** which is defined in §3–201(a) as a voluntary or involuntary transfer of possession of an instrument *by* a person other than the maker or drawer *to* a person who thereby becomes its holder.

Manner of Negotiation—Order Versus Bearer Paper

At this point the distinction between instruments payable to *order* and those payable to *bearer* is once again important. Under §3–201(b), if the instrument is payable to order, it is negotiated by transfer of possession and indorsement; if the instrument is payable to bearer, it is negotiated by transfer of possession alone. Thus, transfer of possession is *always* required for negotiation. An order instrument also requires an *indorsement*. The manner of indorsement and the legal effect of various types of indorsements are discussed below.

Indorsements

Indorsements in General

Under §3–204(a), an **indorsement** consists of at least the payee's or other holder's *signature* but may include additional language.[2] It must be made on the instrument and usually appears on the back. Indorsements also may be written on a separate piece of paper affixed to the instrument, known as an **allonge.** An allonge may be used, for example, when prior indorsements have exhausted the space on the back of the instrument itself.

Negotiation of bearer paper takes effect immediately upon delivery of the instrument. Negotiation of order paper, however, takes effect only when an indorsement is made, even if the instrument has been delivered previously. For example, if A transfers order paper to B without indorsement, B does not become a holder until the date she obtains A's indorsement.[3]

Partial Assignment. Under §3–203(d), to be effective as a negotiation, an indorsement must convey the entire instrument or any unpaid residue. An attempt to negotiate less operates as only a partial assignment of the transferor's interest in the instrument. Assume Mark issues a $1,000 promissory note payable to Paul's order. Paul sells the note to Christie, accomplishing the sale by signing his name on the back of the note and handing it to Christie. Christie is now the holder of the instrument. If, however, Paul had turned the note over and written "pay Christie $500, (signed) Paul," or "pay Christie one-half, (signed) Paul," or "pay Christie one-third and Jane two-thirds, (signed) Paul," neither Christie nor Jane becomes a holder of the instrument.

Although an indorsement purporting to convey less than the entire instrument is ineffective as a negotiation, it does operate as a partial assignment. Whether the partial assignee acquires any rights thereby is not addressed by Article 3 and is therefore left to the general contract law of the jurisdiction. Article 3 simply states that such an assignee does not become a holder.

Incorrect Spelling. The maker or drawer often incorrectly designates the payee or misspells the name. Suppose David, intending to make his check payable to Joe Doaks, writes "Joe Dokes" in the payee blank. In this case Joe Doaks may properly indorse and negotiate the instrument either in his own name ("Joe Doaks") or in the name as improperly designated ("Joe Dokes"), or by signing both names. A person who pays or gives value for the instrument, however, such as a bank cashing the check for Doaks, may require two signatures, the correct and incorrect spelling. Signing in both names is the most proper and desirable form. It leaves no doubt concerning either the state of the title or the signer's true identity.[4]

Multiple Payees. An instrument may be made payable to the order of two or more payees. For example, a check may be made payable to the order of "A and B" or "A or B" or "A and/or B." Section 3–110(d) governs the legal effect of such instruments. An instrument payable to "A and B" is held by the parties as tenants in common.[5] Because they have a common interest, the

---

[2]As developed later in this chapter, such additional language may restrict later payment of the instrument, or may negate the indorser's contract liability on the instrument.

[3]UCC §3–203(c).

[4]UCC §3–204(d).

[5]Tenancy in common is discussed in Chapter 36.

instrument is payable to all of them and may be negotiated, discharged, or enforced only by all. For example, negotiation of an instrument payable to the order of "A and B" requires the indorsement of both parties. If one signs and the other does not, or if one signature is a forgery, the negotiation is ineffective, meaning that the subsequent transferee does not become a holder of the instrument.

On the other hand, an instrument payable to "A or B" is payable to *either* A or B individually. That is, the instrument is payable to either of them and may be negotiated, discharged, or enforced by whoever has possession of it. For example, an instrument payable to the order of "A or B" could be further negotiated by A's (or B's) indorsement alone. The same rule applies if the instrument is ambiguous. Thus, an instrument payable to "A and/or B" may be negotiated either by A or B.

Types of Indorsements

As discussed above, both indorsement and delivery are required to negotiate an instrument payable to order. Indorsement is, however, much more than a mere formal requisite of negotiation. An indorsement also determines

1. the manner of future negotiation—this issue depends upon whether the indorsement is "blank" or "special";
2. the contract liability of the indorser on the instrument—this liability differs depending upon whether the indorsement is "qualified" or "unqualified"; and
3. the nature and extent of the interest transferred by the indorsement—the interest transferred depends upon whether the indorsement is "restrictive" or "nonrestrictive."

Every indorsement is either blank or special, either qualified or unqualified, and either restrictive or nonrestrictive. Thus, each indorsement has three terms modifying it. Assume D issues a check payable to P's order. P indorses the check on the back with her signature alone. P's indorsement is blank, unqualified, and nonrestrictive. The three classes of indorsement are discussed in the following subsections.

Blank Versus Special Indorsement. The distinction between blank and special indorsements, stated in §3–205, is important because it determines the manner of further negotiation. A **blank indorsement** is one that

specifies no particular indorsee and frequently consists of the indorser's signature alone. Suppose Dave draws his check payable to the order of Pat Jones. Pat indorses the instrument simply by signing her name "Pat Jones" on the back. The indorsement is in blank.

A **special indorsement** specifies the person to whom or to whose order the instrument is further payable. For example, using the same instrument as above, assume Pat Jones sold the instrument to Sam Sloan and indorsed the back as follows: "pay to Sam Sloan, (signed) Pat Jones" or "pay to the order of Sam Sloan, (signed) Pat Jones." These are special indorsements.

An instrument originally payable to order and indorsed in blank becomes payable to *bearer* and may be further negotiated by delivery alone unless it is later specially indorsed. An instrument that is specially indorsed becomes payable to the order of the **special indorsee** (Sam Sloan in the above example), and may be further negotiated only by his indorsement. Thus, whether an indorsement is required for negotiation depends not on whether the instrument was *originally* order or bearer paper, but on the character of the *last indorsement* on the instrument as either blank or special. For example, the above instrument is, on its face, payable to order ("pay to the order of Pat Jones"). It therefore requires Pat Jone's indorsement for further negotiation. If Pat Jones indorses in blank, the instrument becomes bearer paper and all further negotiation (to one or a hundred later holders) can be accomplished by delivery alone. If Pat Jones specially indorses the paper ("pay to Sam Sloan, (signed) Pat Jones") the instrument remains order paper, requiring Sam Sloan's signature for further negotiation. If Sam Sloan indorses in blank, the instrument becomes bearer paper and remains so unless and until some later holder specially indorses it. Note that the holder of an instrument payable to bearer (either originally or by virtue of a blank indorsement) may convert it into order paper by using a special indorsement. This is true even though no indorsement is required to negotiate the instrument prior to the addition of the special indorsement.[6]

One final point concerning the blank versus special distinction should be noted. Assume Louise issues a note payable to Don's order. As previously noted, Don may specially indorse the instrument to Worth by writ-

---

[6] For example, the holder of an instrument indorsed in blank may convert it to an order instrument by writing, above the indorser's signature, words identifying the person to whom the instrument is payable. UCC §3–205(c).

ing on the back "pay Worth, (signed) Don" or "pay to the order of Worth, (signed) Don." The use of the word "order" in an indorsement is not necessary, and it will not cure a defect in negotiability on the face of the instrument. For example, if Louise's note omits the word "order" or "bearer," it is nonnegotiable. This defect is not cured by use of the word "order" in an indorsement. Because the instrument is nonnegotiable, neither Worth nor Don is a holder. In short, negotiability is determined from the face of the instrument. Nothing in an indorsement can affect negotiability, either by making a nonnegotiable instrument negotiable or a negotiable instrument nonnegotiable.

Qualified Versus Unqualified Indorsement. Negotiable instruments are contracts. The extent of a person's contract liability on a negotiable instrument depends on the appearance and position of her *signature* thereon. By signing as an indorser, a person ordinarily undertakes "secondary contract liability" on the instrument. Under this contract, provided certain conditions are met, the indorser promises to pay the instrument if the party primarily liable, such as maker of a note or acceptor of a draft, fails to pay it.

Unless the indorsement specifically provides otherwise, the indorser undertakes secondary contract liability. Such an indorsement is **unqualified.** If, however, the indorsement contains the words "without recourse" added to the signature, it is qualified. A **qualified indorsement** negates secondary contract liability; a person indorsing "without recourse" does not undertake to pay the instrument if not paid by the primary party.

An indorser would, of course, prefer to sign "without recourse" because liability on the instrument is thereby substantially reduced. Section 3–203(c), however, prevents the widespread use of qualified indorsements by providing that unless otherwise agreed, a person who gives value for an instrument (as by cashing a check) that requires an indorsement for negotiation (one payable to order or specially indorsed) is entitled to an *unqualified* indorsement from the transferor. This right is enforceable against the transferor in an action for specific performance.

Restrictive Versus Nonrestrictive Indorsement. An indorsement may transfer the holder's entire interest in the instrument. Such an indorsement is **nonrestrictive.** Or language may be added to an indorsement making it **restrictive,** attempting to limit or restrict in some way the rights acquired by the indorsee. That is, a restrictive indorsee may acquire the instrument subject to an interest of the indorser or a third person.

Section 3–206 determines the legal effect of four types of restrictive indorsement:

1. conditional indorsements,
2. indorsements purporting to prohibit further transfer of the instrument,
3. indorsements for deposit or collection, and
4. indorsements for the benefit or use of the indorser or of another person.

A brief note regarding the bank collection process is required before analyzing the legal effect of restrictive indorsements. Assume Jones draws a check on his bank in Chicago payable to Pearl, who resides in New York, in payment for goods purchased by Jones from Pearl. Pearl will commonly deposit the check in her New York bank (the depositary bank) to be collected from Jones's bank (the drawee or payor bank) in Chicago. On the way the check may be transferred to one or more intermediary banks. In some cases the payor bank may also be the depositary bank. For example, the drawer and payee may have accounts in the same bank. With this introduction in mind, the four types of restrictive indorsements are distinguished in the following paragraphs.

Conditional Indorsements. Assume Mark issues a $1,000 promissory note payable to Paul's order on December 1. On May 1, Paul purchases a machine from Triad Company for $1,000, delivery to be made on June 1. Paul negotiates Mark's note to Triad on May 1 in payment for the machine, using the following indorsement: "Pay Triad Company if the machine is delivered by June 1 and conforms to the contract, (signed) Paul." This is a conditional indorsement. Note that although an indorsement may impose a condition to payment, such an indorsement does not make the instrument's promise or order conditional, thereby destroying negotiability. Negotiability is determined from the face of the instrument and is unaffected by the character of any later indorsement.

Section 3–206(b) provides simply that a conditional indorsement is ineffective to condition payment. It does not affect the indorsee's right to enforce the instrument, and a person who later pays the instrument or takes it for value or collection "may disregard the condition, and the rights and liabilities of that person are not affected by whether the condition has been fulfilled."

Thus, in the above example, the conditional indorsement does not affect Triad Company's rights on the instrument. When it is due Mark is obligated to pay Triad Company (or a later holder) without regard to the condition. Note that Paul may have rights against Triad Company (for example, for breach of contract) if it fails to deliver a conforming machine as agreed, but those rights exist whether or not Paul conditions his indorsement.

Indorsements Purporting to Restrict Further Transfer. Occasionally, an indorsement will attempt to prohibit further transfer of the instrument by the indorsee. Suppose Timmons draws a $100 check payable to Newman's order. Newman negotiates the instrument to Joe Doaks by an indorsement stating "pay Joe Doaks only, (signed) Newman." Regarding such indorsements, §3–206(a) states simply that "An indorsement limiting payment to a particular person or otherwise prohibiting further transfer or negotiation of the instrument is not effective to prevent further transfer or negotiation of the instrument." An instrument negotiable on its face cannot be rendered nonnegotiable by subsequent indorsement.

Indorsements for Deposit or Collection. Certainly the most common restrictive indorsement is one containing the language "for deposit only," "for deposit and collection only," "pay any bank," or similar terms that indicate the instrument has been negotiated solely for purposes of deposit or collection. Such indorsements often are used to protect a person depositing a check for collection against payment of the instrument to an unauthorized person. Section 3–206(c) provides such protection by stating that

1. a person other than a bank who purchases the instrument,
2. a depositary bank that purchases the instrument or takes it for collection, and
3. a payor bank that is also the depositary bank or that takes the instrument for immediate payment over the counter

converts the instrument unless the amount paid for the instrument is "received by the indorser or applied consistently with the indorsement." Note that (1) an intermediary bank and (2) a payor bank that takes the check from an intermediary bank or the depositary bank are not affected by the indorsement. Thus, liability for vio-

lating a "for deposit only" indorsement generally is imposed only on parties outside the bank collection process and on the first bank in the collection process. Banks later in the collection process usually are exempted because they handle instruments in bulk and usually have no opportunity to consider the effect of restrictive indorsements.

Official Comment 3 to §3–206 provides the following example to illustrate the operation of §3–206(c):

> A check is payable to X, who indorses in blank but writes above the signature the words "For deposit only." The check is stolen and is cashed at a grocery store by the thief. The grocery store indorses the check and deposits it in Depositary Bank. The account of the grocery store is credited and the check is forwarded to Payor Bank which pays the check. Under subsection (c), the grocery store and Depositary Bank are converters of the check because X did not receive the amount paid for the check. Payor Bank and any intermediary bank in the collection process are not liable to X.

Note finally that under §4–201(b), after a check in the collection process has been indorsed with the words "pay any bank," only a bank may acquire the rights of a holder until the check has been either returned to the depositor, or specially indorsed by a bank to a nonbank. Thus, a bank indorsement alone, without additional language, is a restrictive indorsement, which protects the depositor by effectively locking the instrument into bank collection channels.

Indorsements for the Benefit or Use of the Indorser or Another Person. An indorsement may expressly transfer the instrument to an indorsee for the use or benefit of the indorser or a third person. For example, an instrument payable to Paul's order may be indorsed "pay Brown in trust for Green, (signed) Paul" or "pay Brown for Green, (signed) Paul" or "pay Brown as agent for Green, (signed) Paul" or "pay Brown for account of Green, (signed) Paul." Under §3–206(d), the holder to whom Brown negotiates the instrument (including a bank that takes the instrument for deposit or collection) can pay Brown without liability to Paul unless that person has notice[7] that Brown is negotiating the instrument for his own benefit or otherwise in breach of a fiduciary duty. Similarly, subsequent transferees of the instrument from the holder or

---

[7]Notice of breach of fiduciary duty is defined in §3–307.

depositary bank are not affected by the indorsement unless they have actual knowledge that Brown negotiated the instrument in breach of his fiduciary duty.

Negotiation Subject to Rescission

Under §3–202, a negotiation, whether of order or bearer paper, is effective (the transferee becomes a holder) even though the negotiation is

1. made by an infant, a corporation exceeding its powers, or any other person lacking capacity,
2. obtained by fraud, duress, or mistake,
3. part of an illegal transaction, or
4. made in breach of duty.

As between the immediate parties to such a negotiation (or as against a later transferee not having the rights of a holder in due course), a court may allow rescission, impose a constructive trust, or afford other relief permitted by state law. For example, assume Megan issues a note payable to order of Stewart, a minor. Stewart indorses and delivers the note to Tim. Stewart's negotiation makes Tim a holder, but Stewart may rescind his negotiation and recover the instrument from Tim, because of the voidable nature of minors' contracts.

Although, as between Stewart and Tim, Stewart's negotiation can be rescinded, the fact that Tim nevertheless becomes a holder has important legal consequences. Because Tim is a holder, prior to recovery Tim may further negotiate the instrument—that is, make a transferee from Tim a holder. If this subsequent holder qualifies as a holder in due course, Stewart's right to recover the instrument is cut off. That is, the right to rescind may not be asserted against a holder in due course because a holder in due course takes an instrument free of all *claims* to it on the part of any person. Thus, a prior holder's claim to the instrument based upon lack of capacity to negotiate it or fraud inducing the negotiation may not be asserted against a holder in due course. Therefore, using the preceding example, assume that prior to any action by Stewart, Tim negotiates the note to Pat. Pat qualifies as a holder in due course because she takes in good faith, for value, and without notice of the voidable nature of Stewart's negotiation. In this situation Pat takes the note free of Stewart's claim to it. Stewart retains any rights he has against Tim under state law (for example, for the proceeds of Tim's sale of the note), but may not recover the paper from Pat.

Section 3–202 is fundamentally important in formulating the holder in due course doctrine. By making a negotiation subject to rescission effective, it enables a subsequent transferee to become a holder and, if the requirements are met, a holder in due course.

Summary

1. Negotiability, by permitting transfer of negotiable instruments free of claims and defenses, promotes its marketability. Transferees receiving this favored position are known as holders in due course. Thus, in studying the holder in due course doctrine, it is initially important to ascertain how one becomes a holder of an instrument.

2. A holder is defined as any person in possession of a bearer instrument. The holder of an order instrument is the identified person to whom the instrument is payable, if that person is in possession of the instrument. The first holder of any instrument is the payee. Thereafter, subsequent transferees of the instrument become holders by negotiation.

3. Negotiation is the voluntary or involuntary transfer of possession of an instrument by a person other than the maker or drawer to a person who thereby becomes its holder. If the instrument is order paper, negotiation is accomplished by the holder's indorsement, which may be his or her signature alone, and transfer of possession to the new holder. Bearer paper is negotiated by transfer of possession alone. A negotiation is effective to make the transferee a holder even though the negotiation is subject to rescission as a result, for example, of fraud upon or infancy of the transferor.

4. An indorsement is more than a mere formal requisite of negotiation. Indorsements are of various types and govern a number of legal issues arising in connection with the paper. An indorsement may be blank or special, which determines the manner of future negotiation. It may be qualified or unqualified, which ascertains the indorser's contract liability on the instrument. It may be either restrictive or nonrestrictive, which determines the nature and extent of the interest transferred by the indorsement.

Key Terms

holder	special indorsement
issue	special indorsee
negotiation	unqualified indorsement
indorsement	qualified indorsement
allonge	nonrestrictive indorsement
blank indorsement	restrictive indorsement

Questions and Problems

23.1 To what fundamental principle in contract law does negotiation correspond? What purposes are the negotiation concepts discussed in this chapter designed to achieve?

23.2 X issued a promissory note payable to the order of P. Z, the current holder, acquired the note from F. The note contains the following indorsements on the back:

1.	Pay to the order of A P
2.	A
3.	B, without recourse
4.	Pay C D
5.	Pay Joe Doaks if the deadbeat ever finishes painting my house C
6.	Pay E only Joe Doaks
7.	Pay F as trustee for my beloved nephew N E
8.	F

(a) If Z presents the instrument to X for payment, and the instrument is dishonored, is Z's only recourse to sue F?

(b) Was the instrument bearer paper in Z's hands?

(c) Was the instrument bearer paper in P's hands?

(d) Was C's signature necessary to negotiate the instrument?

(e) Does B have contract liability on the instrument?

(f) Does Joe Doaks's indorsement "Pay E only" prevent further negotiation?

(g) Could Z not qualify as a holder in due course because of B's indorsement?

(h) A's indorsement, consisting of his signature alone, caused the instrument to become bearer paper. Does it remain so despite the subsequent indorsements?

(i) Would Z be liable to E if F violated his trust—that is, applied the money for his own use, instead of N's?

(j) Would Z be liable to C if Joe Doaks never finished painting C's house?

23.3 On March 15, Sam Spender bought a new tennis racquet at A & J Sporting Goods. Sam paid for the racquet with a check dated March 15 payable to A & J Sporting Goods. On the back of the check, however, he wrote "Do not deposit until April 1," Is the statement on the back of the check a restrictive indorsement? Explain.

23.4 Olga Blair obtained a cashier's check to pay the balance due on a charter trip to China. The check was made payable to the order of Olga Blair. Olga indorsed the check to Simone Travel Bureau, Inc. and gave the check to S. Reiss, her travel consultant. Two weeks later, a Simone Travel Bureau representative called Olga requesting final payment on her trip. At that time, Olga learned that S. Reiss had failed to give the check to the travel agency. Olga obtained the negotiated check from her bank and found the following on the back of the check:

> S. Reiss to
>
> Pay to Simone Travel Bureau, Inc.
>
> Olga Blair
>
> July 28, 2005
>
> *S. Reiss*
>
> University Funding Corporation
> X22–058828

The italicized portions had been added to the check after Olga gave the check to S. Reiss. University Funding Corporation had cashed the check for Reiss, who left town with the money.

(a) Were any of the following holders of the instrument: Olga Blair, S. Reiss, Simone Travel Bureau, Inc., University Funding Corporation?

(b) List the names of all persons or corporations whose indorsement was necessary for negotiation.

23.5 Fred Klomann was payee of a promissory note issued by Sol Graff & Son. Fred Klomann then specially indorsed the note and handed it to his daughter, Candace. She examined the note and returned it to her father for collection. Subsequently Fred Klomann scratched out Candace's name in the special indorsement, inserted the name of his wife, Georgia Klomann, and delivered the note to Georgia. What interest did Fred have in the instrument when he transferred it to Georgia? What interest did Georgia acquire? Who is the holder of the instrument?

23.6 Dinah Wilson was bookkeeper for Palmer & Ray Dental Supply, Inc. of Abilene. She was expressly authorized to indorse checks received from customers with a rubber stamp and deposit the checks in the firm's account in First National Bank. The rubber stamp used by Palmer & Ray to indorse the checks stated:

> Palmer & Ray Dental Supply
> Inc. of Abilene
> Box 2894
> 3110 B N. 1st
> Abilene, Texas 79603

Auditors later discovered that Wilson had cashed at the bank 35 of the checks she was supposed to deposit. Palmer & Ray sued the bank to recover the losses on these checks. What type of indorsement does the stamp create? Should Palmer & Ray prevail? Explain.

23.7 One day a male customer, James Quick, handed a check and deposit slip to Bernard, a teller at State Bank. The check was made payable to Katherine Warner and the indorsement written on the back read "Katherine Warner For Deposit Only." Warner had no account at State Bank. The deposit slip instructed the bank to deposit the check in Quick's State Bank account.

(a) Should Bernard accept the check for deposit in Quick's account? Explain.

(b) Assume that Bernard refused to accept the check, but a subsequent investigation revealed that Quick had purchased the check from Warner, who negotiated it to Quick with a blank indorsement. Quick later added the "For Deposit Only" language before attempting to deposit the check in his State Bank account. Should Bernard now accept the check for deposit in Quick's account? Explain.

CHAPTER 24

HOLDERS IN DUE COURSE

Major Topics

- **the distinction between holders in due course and other holders of an instrument**
- **the general requirements for becoming a holder in due course or acquiring the rights of a holder in due course**
- **the rights of a holder in due course, including the distinction between real and personal defenses**

To this point, the discussion has focused on the formal requirements of a negotiable instrument and on negotiation—the manner in which a transferee of a negotiable instrument becomes a holder. This chapter examines the third element of negotiable instruments analysis, the qualifications and rights of a holder in due course, a holder of a negotiable instrument who stands in a better legal position than an ordinary contract assignee.

Under ordinary contract principles, an assignee "steps into the shoes" of the assignor and takes no better rights than the assignor had. In contrast, a holder in due course often acquires rights on the instrument superior to those of the transferor. Under UCC §§3–305 and 3–306, a holder in due course generally acquires the instrument free of

1. all claims of ownership or other claims to it on the part of any person, and

2. all defenses of any party to the instrument with whom the holder has not dealt, except a limited class of "real" defenses.

The defenses defeated by a holder in due course are usually referred to as "personal" defenses. A holder without holder in due course status acquires rights similar to an ordinary contract assignee, taking the instrument subject to all valid claims to it on the part of any person, and all defenses, real or personal. Thus, determining whether or not a transferee has the rights of a holder in due course becomes a critical issue in any negotiable instruments dispute.

Section 3–302(a) outlines the requirements for **holder in due course** status. Section 3–302(a)(1) initially provides that a holder cannot qualify as a holder in due course if the instrument, when issued or negotiated to the holder, bears "such apparent evidence of forgery or alteration" or is otherwise "so irregular or incomplete as to call into question its authenticity." Assuming this requirement is met, the holder qualifies as a holder in due course if he or she takes the instrument.

1. for value,
2. in good faith, and
3. without notice (a) that the instrument is overdue, or (b) that the instrument has been dishonored, or (c) of

any claim to or defense against it (including those based on forgery or alteration) on the part of any person.

These three elements are discussed in turn in the following three sections. Note that a holder in due course is, in essence, Article 3's "good faith purchaser for value." That is, the holder in due course receives preferred status because she gives something of value for the instrument while unaware of any legal problems affecting it.

General Requirements

Taking for Value

To qualify as a holder in due course, the holder must take the instrument "for value." Thus, one who acquires an instrument by gift is denied holder in due course status. Although the UCC generally defines **value** as the equivalent of "any consideration sufficient to support a simple contract,"[1] a specialized value definition, stated in §3–303, applies to negotiable instruments under Article 3. The concept of value in determining holder in due course status differs in important respects from ordinary principles of contract consideration discussed in Chapter 9.

Executory Promises Not Value. Under §3–303(a)(1) a holder takes an instrument for value only to the extent that the agreed consideration has been performed. Under this rule, a holder who is contractually bound to pay money or perform some other act in exchange for the instrument does not give value *until* the money is paid or the act is performed. In other words, an executory promise is not value for holder in due course purposes, even though it is sufficient consideration to support a simple contract. To illustrate, assume Mark issues a $1,000 note payable in one year to Paula's order. One month later, on June 1, Paula negotiates the note to Hank in exchange for goods sold by Hank to Paula to be delivered July 1. Even though Hank becomes a holder of the instrument on June 1, he does not give value for it until July 1, when the goods are delivered. Thus, if Hank learns of a defense to payment

prior to July 1—for example, that Paula had defrauded Mark—he would be denied holder in due course status.

At issue in the following case was whether a holder had given value sufficient to achieve holder in due course status.

Carter & Grimsley v. Omni Trading, Inc.
716 N.E.2d 320 (Ill. App. 1999)

In payment for grain purchases, Omni Trading, Inc. issued two checks to Country Grain Elevators, Inc. which endorsed the checks and delivered them to the law firm of Carter & Grimsley (Carter) as a retainer for legal services. After learning that Country Grain Elevators had become insolvent, Omni Trading stopped payment on the checks. Carter sued Omni Trading alleging that the law firm was a holder in due course entitled to payment of the checks. The trial court denied Carter's motion for summary judgment and Carter appealed.

Lytton, Justice

. . . Section 3–303(a) of the UCC . . . states that "An instrument is issued or transferred for value if: (1) the instrument is issued or transferred for a promise of performance, *to the extent that the promise has been performed.* . . . " (Emphasis added.)

Carter contends that in Illinois a contract for future legal services should be treated differently than other executory contracts. It contends that when the attorney-client relationship is created by payment of a fee or retainer, the contract is no longer executory. Thus, Carter would achieve holder in due course status. We are not persuaded.

A retainer is the act of a client employing an attorney; it also denotes the fee paid by the client when he retains the attorney to act for him. . . . We have found no Illinois cases construing section 3–303(a) as it relates to a promise to perform future legal services under a retainer. The general rule, however, is that "an executory promise is not value." *Crest Finance v. First State Bank of Westmont,* 226 N.E.2d 369, 373 (Ill. 1967). "The promise does not rise to the level of 'value' in the commercial paper market until it is actually performed." Quinn, *Uniform Commercial Code Commentary and Law Digest,* 2d Ed, Vol. 1, p. 3–135 (1991).

---

[1]UCC §1–204(4).

[Official Comment 1 to UCC §3–303] gives the following example: "X issues a check to Y in consideration of Y's promise to perform services in the future. Although the executory promise is consideration for issuance of the check it is value only to the extent the promise is performed." We have found no exceptions to these principles for retainers. Indeed, courts in other jurisdictions interpreting similar language under section 3–303 have held that attorneys may be holders in due course only to the extent that they have actually performed legal services prior to acquiring a negotiable instrument. . . . We agree.

This retainer was a contract for future legal services. Under section 3–303(a)(1), it was a "promise of performance," not yet performed. Thus, no value was received, and Carter is not a holder in due course.

Furthermore, in this case, no evidence was presented in the trial court that Carter performed any legal services for Country Grain prior to receiving the checks. Without an evidentiary basis for finding that Carter received the checks for services performed, the trial court correctly found that Carter failed to prove that it was a holder in due course. . . .

[Judgment affirmed.]

The purchaser of a negotiable instrument rarely pays face value for it. The buyer pays a discounted figure that represents interest and the risk of ultimate collection. For example, Wilcox might agree to purchase Molson's $1,000 note from Petty for $900. In this situation, Wilcox, after paying $900, may qualify as a holder in due course for the face amount of the instrument, $1,000. An excessive discount, however, may indicate lack of good faith defeating holder in due course status. Thus, if Wilcox pays $250 for the $1,000 note, the huge discount provides convincing circumstantial evidence that he knows of the legal problems affecting the instrument.

A special value rule, stated in §3–302(d), applies if the agreed consideration for an instrument has been partially performed. In this case, the holder provides value (and therefore may enjoy holder in due course rights) for "the fraction of the amount payable under the instrument equal to the value of the partial performance divided by the value of the promised performance." To illustrate, assume that on June 1 Hank agrees to purchase Mark's $1,000 promissory note from Paula for $900, payable $500 on June 1 and $400 on July 1. In this case, on June 1 Hank gives value and, if he meets the other requirements, qualifies as a holder in due course to the extent of $555.55 ($500 + $900 = .555 × $1,000 = $555.55). If Hank pays the remaining $400 on July 1 acting in good faith without notice of a claim or defense, he then qualifies as a holder in due course for the face amount of the instrument, $1,000. If Hank learns of a claim or defense, such as Paula's fraud, between June 1 and July 1, Hank qualifies as a holder in due course only to the extent of $555.55. That is, Hank could force Mark to pay $555.55 despite Paula's fraud, but takes subject to Mark's defense for the remainder. Thus, the other elements of holder in due course status — good faith and lack of notice — are measured each time value is given. A holder may therefore qualify as a holder in due course to the extent of value given on one date, but not a later date, after notice of a claim or defense is acquired.

The rationale for the rule that executory promises are not value is that a holder who has not yet performed does not need the protection afforded holders in due course. That is, if the holder learns of a claim or defense to the instrument, she may simply rescind the contract to purchase the instrument and refuse to perform the promise.[2] In contrast, a holder who has performed is "out of pocket" on the instrument and would be injured by a successfully asserted claim or defense. Accordingly, the UCC protects the holder by giving her holder in due course status to the extent of performance.

Exceptions to the Rule. The UCC recognizes two related exceptions to the executory promise rule. Under §§3–303(a)(4)–(5), a holder takes an instrument for value by giving another negotiable instrument for the instrument or by making an irrevocable commitment to a third party in exchange for the instrument. To illustrate the first exception, suppose Rick is the payee of Marcia's $1,000 note. Linda purchases the note from Rick with her personal check payable to Rick's order. Linda has given value for Marcia's note, even though her check is, in essence, an executory promise. The reason for this exception is that the check, a negotiable

---

[2]The basis of this right of rescission is breach of the §3–416(a)(4) warranty made by transferors of negotiable instruments that no defense of any party is good against the transferor. The transfer warranties are discussed in Chapter 26.

instrument, could itself be negotiated to a holder in due course, who could force Linda to pay despite any defense she may have against Rick.

For similar reasons, the Code provides that value is given when the holder makes an irrevocable commitment to a third party (for example, to loan money) in exchange for the instrument. In this case, after the instrument is taken the holder cannot refuse to perform for the third party. Rescission and loss avoidance is therefore unavailable to the holder, justifying holder in due course protection on the instrument.

Security Interest as Value. Under §3–303(a)(2), a holder also takes for value to the extent he or she acquires a security interest in or lien upon the instrument. In this situation, the holder takes possession of the instrument to secure payment of a debt owing to him. Such a security arrangement is known as a "pledge." Under §3–302(e), the secured creditor in this case gives value only to the extent of the secured debt, not necessarily the face amount of the instrument. Assume Miller issues a $1,000 promissory note payable in one year to Parker's order in exchange for goods sold by Parker to Miller. Parker then borrows $750 from Cox and indorses and delivers Miller's note to Cox to secure the loan. In this case, Cox has given value of $750, the extent of her security interest in the note. Assuming Cox meets the other holder in due course requirements, she could force Miller to pay $750 upon Parker's default even if Miller has a personal defense to payment such as Parker's fraud or shipment of defective goods. Cox then has no further interest in the instrument because her security interest is satisfied.

Antecedent Debt as Value. Under §3–303(a)(3), a holder takes for value when he takes the instrument in payment of or as security for an antecedent debt. The term **antecedent debt** refers simply to an old debt, one existing before the negotiation of the instrument. In this context, "value" for holder in due course purposes once again differs from general contract law consideration: payment of an antecedent debt, though value under Article 3, may, as "past consideration," be incapable of supporting an ordinary contract promise.

Assume that Stan sells goods to Betty on credit. Over a period of several years, Betty accumulates an open account balance of $10,000. Subsequently, Mary issues a $10,000 note to Betty in exchange for services performed. Betty then negotiates Mary's note to Stan in satisfaction of the $10,000 debt. Stan has given value for Mary's note for purposes of establishing Stan as a holder in due course.

Taking in Good Faith

To qualify as a holder in due course, the holder must, in addition to giving a value, take the instrument in good faith. For Article 3 purposes, §3–103(a)(4) defines good faith as "honesty in fact, and the observance of reasonable commercial standards of fair dealing."[3]

Taking Without Notice

In addition to value and good faith, holder in due course status requires that the holder take the instrument without notice (1) that it is overdue, (2) that it has been dishonored, or (3) of any defense against or claim to it on the part of any person. Before discussing these three elements, the term "notice" must be defined.

"Notice" Defined. Under §1–202, a person has **notice** of a fact in three situations. First, and most obviously, a person has notice upon acquiring actual knowledge of the fact. Second, notice is obtained upon receipt of a notice or notification of the fact. A person receives a notice or notification when it comes to her attention or is properly delivered at the "place of business through which the contract was made or at another location held out by that person as the place for receipt of such communications."[4] A person may therefore have notice of the contents of a communication delivered to her place of business, even without actual knowledge. Notice, knowledge, or notification received by an organization, such as a bank or corporation, is effective from the time it is brought to the attention of the individual conducting the transaction or, in any event, from the time it would have been brought to that person's attention had the organization exercised due diligence. Due diligence, in this context, requires that the organization maintain and comply with reasonable routines for communicating significant information within the organization. Further, to be effective a notice must be received in a

---

[3]See discussion of good faith in Chapter 7.
[4]UCC §1–202(e).

time and manner sufficient to give a reasonable opportunity to act upon it.[5]

Finally, a person also has notice of a fact when the surrounding facts and circumstances known at the time in question give the person reason to know that it exists. Generally, the term *"reason to know"* indicates an objective test (that is, what a reasonable person would know based on the facts presented). An important issue in many cases is the extent to which this "reason to know" standard imposes a duty on the holder to investigate the underlying transaction to discover possible claims or defenses. The following case examines the nature of a holder's duty of investigation under the "reason to know" requirement.

Money Mart Check Cashing Center, Inc. v. Epicycle Corporation
667 P.2d 1372 (Colo. 1983)

Plaintiff, Money Mart Check Cashing Center, Inc. (Money Mart), cashes payroll and government checks for a fee. On February 22, 1980, John Cronin cashed a payroll check issued to him by defendant, Epicycle Corporation, at Money Mart. Money Mart deposited the check but it was returned marked "Payment Stopped." Epicycle had stopped payment on the check because one of its employees had written the check in excess of the amount actually owed to Cronin.

Money Mart sued Epicycle for the face amount of the check. Money Mart claimed to be a holder in due course. The trial court ruled in favor of Money Mart but the appellate court reversed, holding that Money Mart was not a holder in due course because it had failed to verify that the check was good prior to cashing it. Money Mart appealed.

Rovira, Justice

. . . The question before us is whether Money Mart is a holder in due course. If it is, it takes the check free of any of Epicycle's claims to the check or defenses against Cronin. . . . That Money Mart took the check for value is undisputed, leaving the questions of "good faith" and "notice." . . . [The court found that Money Mart had cashed the check in good faith.] . . .

We now consider whether Money Mart had "notice" of the fact that payment had been stopped on the check or that Cronin had obtained the check improperly. [The court then quoted the Code definition of notice in §1–201.] As can be seen, tests other than "actual knowledge" may be used in determining whether a person is a holder in due course. . . . There is no allegation that Money Mart had received notification of the defenses, so we must now determine whether Money Mart had "reason to know" of them.

The County Court referee found that Money Mart had no reason to know of the defenses because there was nothing inherently suspicious in the transaction and Money Mart had no duty to inquire about any possible defenses or ensure that the check was good. The Superior Court held that Money Mart's failure to inquire about the validity of the check constituted negligence. However, there is nothing in the Uniform Commercial Code and nothing in the record to support such a conclusion.

A determination of whether a holder has "reason to know" is based upon "all the facts and circumstances known to him." A person "knows" of a fact when he has "actual knowledge" of it. . . . The question therefore is whether Money Mart had actual knowledge of facts giving it reason to know that a defense existed. There is nothing to distinguish the facts of this case from any other of the thousands of checks that Money Mart and others cash each year. A man came to Money Mart to cash his paycheck; Money Mart is in the business of cashing paychecks; the face of the check disclosed nothing to raise even a suspicion that there was something wrong with it.

It has often been held that where an instrument is regular on its face there is no duty to inquire as to possible defenses unless the circumstances of which the holder has knowledge are of such a nature that failure to inquire reveals a deliberate desire to evade knowledge because of a fear that investigation would disclose the existence of a defense. . . . There is nothing in using a check-cashing service instead of a bank that would lead to a rule imposing different standards on the two kinds of institutions. . . .

Accordingly, we hold that Money Mart is a holder in due course and, as such, is not subject to the defenses Epicycle may have against Cronin. . . .

[Judgment reversed.]

---

[5]UCC §§1–202(f), 3–302(f).

Note finally that under §3–302(b) the doctrine of "constructive notice" does not apply in determining notice for holder in due course purposes. That is, the public filing or recording of any document, such as a financing statement creating a security interest in the instrument under UCC Article 9, does not of itself constitute notice of a claim or defense to a person who otherwise qualifies as a holder in due course.

Notice That Instrument Is Overdue. To qualify as a holder in due course, the holder must take without notice that the instrument is overdue. Section 3–304 states the rules that determine when demand and time instruments become overdue.

Demand Instruments. Under §3–304(a), a demand instrument becomes overdue at the earliest of the following times:

1. on the day after a demand for payment is made;
2. if the instrument is a check, 90 days after the date on which it was issued; or
3. if the instrument is not a check, "when the instrument has been outstanding for a period of time after its date which is *unreasonably long* under the circumstances of the particular case in light of the nature of the instrument and usage of the trade."

Time Instruments. Under §3–304(b), time instruments (for example, instruments payable on a fixed future date or in installments) become overdue according to the following rules. In studying these rules, it is important to note that installment notes often provide that, upon default in payment of one or more installments, the holder may "accelerate" the instrument, making all future installments immediately due and payable.

1. If an installment note has not been accelerated, it becomes overdue upon default in payment of any installment and remains overdue until the default is cured.
2. If an installment note has been accelerated, the instrument becomes overdue on the day after the accelerated due date.
3. If the instrument is not payable in installments and has not been accelerated, it becomes overdue on the day after the due date.

Note that the preceding rules apply to defaults in payment of *principal.* Notice by the holder of nonpayment of *interest* due on the instrument does not constitute notice sufficient to defeat holder in due course status. Section 3–304(c) recognizes that interest payments are often delayed, without an accompanying nonpayment of principal. Accordingly, knowledge of interest payment defaults *alone* does not prevent holder in due course status.

Notice That Instrument Dishonored. To be a holder in due course, the purchaser must take the instrument without notice that it has been dishonored. Generally speaking, under §3–502 dishonor occurs when a draft is presented to the drawee for acceptance or payment and the drawee refuses to accept or pay it, or when a note is presented to the maker, who refuses to pay it. This fact is often noted on the instrument. Dishonor is important in determining the contract liability of parties to the instrument and is discussed more fully in Chapter 25.

Notice of Claim or Defense. A holder who takes the paper while aware of a claim or defense to it (including those based on forgery or alteration) cannot qualify for holder in due course protection. For example, the holder may be put on notice of a claim or defense if she takes with notice that the obligation of any party is voidable in whole or in part (such as for fraud or material misrepresentation), or subject to other defenses (such as breach of warranty or failure of consideration). Suppose that Pat induces Mike to buy a car by fraudulently misrepresenting its mileage. Mike issues a note to Pat in exchange for the car. Pat sells and negotiates the note to Harold. Harold is not a holder in due course if he takes the instrument with notice of Pat's fraud—that is, with notice that Mike's obligation is voidable.

A purchaser also may receive notice of a claim against the instrument if he has notice that a fiduciary, such as trustee of a trust, has previously negotiated the instrument in payment of or as security for his own debt or benefit, or otherwise in breach of duty. Mere knowledge that a prior holder is or was a fiduciary does not, by itself, give such notice.

The holder may receive notice of a claim or defense in various ways. The holder may receive information directly from the transferor or from the person obligated on the instrument disclosing the existence of a defense. The defense may appear in an accompanying document delivered to the holder with the instrument. Additionally, notice of a claim or defense or lack of good faith may be inferred if a close business relationship exists between the holder and the transferor.

At issue in the following case was whether the plaintiff qualified as a holder in due course under §3–302.

Cadle Company v. Ginsburg

721 A.2d 1246 (Conn. App. 1998)

In 1988, Great Country Bank loaned $2 million to Delco Development Company, Inc. Defendant Robert Ginsburg, who was a Delco shareholder, and two other shareholders contractually guaranteed the loan. In 1991, after Delco failed to repay the loan, Ginsburg arranged to settle his liability as guarantor by executing a $100,000 promissory note payable to the bank. The note provided for full payment by October, 1996 and required Ginsburg to make annual payments of interest at 9 percent. In 1992, Ginsburg learned that one of the other guarantors had arranged a more favorable settlement with Great Country. He then notified the bank that he would not pay the $100,000 promissory note, alleging that the bank's failure to disclose the prior settlement constituted fraud. In 1994, Great Country sold Ginsburg's note along with 105 other loans to plaintiff Cadle Company. Cadle sued Ginsburg demanding payment of the note and interest. The trial court granted judgment in favor of Cadle and Ginsburg appealed.

Lavery, Judge

. . . The defendant . . . claims that the trial court improperly determined that the plaintiff was a holder in due course of the promissory note that it purchased from Great Country on April 6, 1994. We disagree.

"Only a holder in due course may enforce a negotiable instrument without regard to a maker's assertion of a personal defense. . . . Evidence of the existence of a personal defense does, however, shift to the holder of the instrument the burden of proving his due course status." *Funding Consultants, Inc. v. Aetna Casualty & Surety, Co.,* 447 A.2d 1163 (Conn. 1982). The defendant offered evidence as to the existence of a personal defense and, therefore, the plaintiff was required to prove that it was a holder in due course.

[UCC §3–302 (a)(2)] provides that a holder in due course means the holder of an instrument if . . .

The holder took the instrument (i) for value, (ii) in good faith, (iii) without notice that the instrument is overdue or has been dishonored or that there is an uncured default with respect to payment of another instrument issued as part of

the same series, (iv) without notice that the instrument contains an unauthorized signature or has been altered, (v) without notice of any claim to the instrument described in [§3–306], and (vi) without notice that any party has a defense or claim in recoupment in [§3–305 (a)].

The defendant claims that the plaintiff failed to satisfy the first, second, [and] third . . . elements of [§3–302(a)(2)] and, therefore, the plaintiff is not a holder in due course. The trial court found that the plaintiff sustained its burden by adducing overwhelming evidence that it was a holder in due course. We will not disturb the trial court's finding of fact unless it was clearly erroneous. . . .

The defendant first claims that the trial court improperly determined that the plaintiff obtained the note from Great Country for value. Specifically, the defendant contends that the note was not transferred for value because the plaintiff "could not specify the amount [it] paid [for the note], since [the note] was purchased along with about 106 other notes." We disagree.

The plaintiff purchased the note from Great Country as part of a pool of 106 loans. . . . The defendant does not dispute that the plaintiff issued payment to Great Country for the pool of loans. Although the plaintiff could not specify the exact amount it paid for the note, the trial court properly determined that the note was taken for value because the plaintiff issued a single payment for the entire pool of 106 loans, which included the note in question. It is well established that "[a] single and undivided consideration may be bargained for and given as the agreed equivalent of one promise or two promises or of many promises. The consideration is not rendered invalid by the fact that it is exchanged for more than one promise." 2 A. Corbin, *Contracts* (Rev. Ed. 1995) §5.12, pp. 56–57. . . . We conclude, therefore, that the trial court properly determined that the note was taken for value.

The defendant next claims that the trial court improperly found that the plaintiff obtained the note in good faith. Specifically, the defendant alleges that the plaintiff acted in bad faith because (1) the plaintiff failed to make an inquiry so as to remain ignorant of facts that it feared would disclose a defect in the transaction and (2) it paid an amount far less than the note's face value. . . . We disagree.

"'Good faith' means honesty in fact and the observance of reasonable commercial standards of fair dealing." [UCC §3–103(a) (4).]

The definition [of good faith] requires not only honesty in fact but also 'observance of reasonable commercial standards of fair dealing.' Although fair dealing is a broad term that must be defined in context, it is clear that it is concerned with the fairness of conduct rather than the care with which an act is performed. Failure to exercise ordinary care in conducting a transaction is an entirely different concept than failure to deal fairly in conducting the transaction. . . . [F]air dealing . . . [is] to be judged in light of reasonable commercial standards but those standards in each case are directed to different aspects of commercial conduct. [UCC §3–103, Official Comment 4.]

The trial court found that the evidence overwhelmingly established that the plaintiff took the note in good faith. The court also found that the defendant did not provide any credible evidence to demonstrate that the plaintiff deliberately failed to make an inquiry into facts that would disclose a defect in the transaction. Additionally, there was no evidence of the exact amount the plaintiff paid for the note. . . . [T]he court's finding was not clearly erroneous.

The defendant next claims that the trial court improperly determined that the plaintiff purchased the note without notice that it was overdue and subject to an uncured default. We are not persuaded. The defendant claims that the plaintiff had notice that the note "was long overdue at the time of purchase" because the defendant had not made any interest payments when the plaintiff purchased the note on April 6, 1994. Although the note required the defendant to pay interest in the amount of 9 percent annually, commencing on October 11, 1992, the single payment of principal was not due until October 11, 1996.

[UCC §3–302 (a)(2)] provides in relevant part that a holder in due course must take an instrument without "notice that the instrument is overdue. . . . " [UCC §§3–304 (b) (2) and (c)] establish, however, that the note was not overdue when the plaintiff purchased it. "With respect to an instrument payable at a definite time . . . [i]f the principal is not payable in installments and the due date has not been accelerated, the instrument becomes overdue on the day after the due date." [UCC §3–304 (b) (2).] The note's principal was not payable in installments and neither Great Country nor the plaintiff accelerated the note until the plaintiff instituted this suit in April, 1995. Therefore, the note became overdue in April, 1995, approximately one year after the plaintiff purchased it from Great Country.

Although the defendant had defaulted on its payment of interest prior to the plaintiff's acquisition of the note, "[u]nless the due date of principal has been accelerated, an instrument does not become overdue if there is a default in payment of interest but no default in payment of principal." [UCC §3–304 (c).] When the plaintiff purchased the note, there was a default in the payment of interest, but the defendant had not defaulted in the payment of principal. Accordingly, the defendant's claim is without merit. . . .

We conclude, therefore, that the court properly found that because the plaintiff purchased the note for value, in good faith and without notice that it was overdue . . . the court properly determined that the plaintiff was a holder in due course.

[Judgment affirmed.]

Payee as Holder in Due Course

Ordinarily, a holder in due course is a holder who receives the instrument from the payee or a later holder. Although also a holder, the payee is usually unable to qualify as a holder in due course. As a party to the original transaction, the payee generally has notice of a claim or defense to the instrument. Assume Paula fraudulently induces Milt to issue a promissory note payable to Paula's order. Although Paula is a holder, she is not a holder in due course because she is aware of (and in fact responsible for) Milt's defense to paying the instrument.

Official Comment 4 to §3–302 makes it clear, however, that a payee may qualify as a holder in due course to the same extent and in the same manner as any other holder. The payee must simply meet the requirements for holder in due course status listed in §3–302. The payee who does not deal directly with the maker or drawer asserting the defense often is able to meet these requirements. Assume Smith and Jones are co-makers of a note. Smith has induced Jones to sign through fraud. Smith, without authority from Jones, delivers the note to Black, the payee, who gives value, and takes in good faith without notice of Smith's fraud. Black is a holder in due course.

Shelter Provision

The importance of the preferred status conferred upon a holder in due course is magnified when considered in conjunction with §3–203(b), which provides that "transfer of an instrument, whether or not the transfer is a negotiation, vests in the transferee any right of the transferor to enforce the instrument, including any right as a holder in due course.. . . " This so-called **shelter** or **umbrella provision** greatly expands the scope of the holder in due course doctrine by providing that transfer of an instrument by a holder in due course vests in the transferee the rights of a holder in due course even if the transferee does not qualify under §3–302. That is, with rare exceptions, *any transferee* (whether or not a holder) of an instrument from or after a holder in due course acquires the rights of a holder in due course and may enforce the instrument free of claims and personal defenses.

For example, Pam fraudulently induces Max to issue a note payable to her order. Pam specially indorses and delivers the instrument to Harold, a holder in due course. Harold transfers the note to Cheryl, who takes it, alternatively (1) without Harold's indorsement (that is, she is not a holder), (2) as a gift, (3) after it is over-due, or (4) with notice of (but not as a party to) Pam's fraud. In all four cases, Cheryl fails to qualify as a holder in due course under §3–302. Nevertheless, she acquires the *rights* of a holder in due course (her trans-feror, Harold) under §3–201, and could therefore force Max to pay the instrument despite his personal defense, fraud. Any subsequent transferee from Cheryl would acquire similar rights.

The shelter rule applies to transfer of a limited inter-est in an instrument to the extent of the interest trans-ferred. For example, transfer of a security interest in an instrument vests in the secured party (transferee) the rights of the transferor to the extent of the security inter-est. To illustrate, assume Sal is a holder in due course of Morey's $500 note. Sal transfers the note to Ken as security for a $250 loan from Ken to Sal. Ken acquires the rights of a holder in due course to the extent of $250.

The law generally favors free alienability (transfer-ability) of interests in property. The shelter rule pro-motes free transferability of negotiable instruments by enabling a holder in due course to transfer what he or she has—the rights of a holder in due course. If a holder in due course could transfer those rights only to transferees capable of satisfying §3–302 on their own, the market for negotiable instruments would be severely restricted, thus defeating a major purpose of negotiabil-ity. To prevent this result, §3–203(b) confers de facto holder in due course status on most transferees from or after a holder in due course. Such transferees, whether or not they qualify as holders in due course under §3–302, acquire the rights of a holder in due course under §3–203(b). The shelter provision might therefore be viewed as an application of ordinary rules of contract assignment. The transferee steps into the shoes of the transferor (the holder in due course or transferee from such a holder) and takes the same rights (the rights of a holder in due-course) that the transferor had.

Exception. Not all transferees from holders in due course receive the rights of a holder in due course. Any transferee who has been a party to any fraud or illegality affecting the instrument cannot improve her position by taking from a later holder in due course. That is, such a party cannot "launder" her position by transferring the instrument to a holder in due course and later reacquiring it. To allow such "laundering" would be an open invitation to fraud. Assume Phil fraudulently induces Mary to issue a note payable to Phil's order. Phil negotiates the note to Bob, a holder in due course. Phil (as a party to fraud affecting the instrument) could not later reacquire the instrument and assert Bob's rights (the rights of a holder in due course) against Mary.

The following case illustrates the application of the shelter rule.

Triffin v. Cigna Insurance Company
687 A.2d 1045 (N.J. Super. 1997)

Defendant Cigna Insurance Company issued a draft to James Mills in payment of workers' compensation bene-fits. Mills negotiated the draft to Sun Corp., a holder in due course, but falsely notified Cigna that he never received the draft. Cigna placed a stop order on the draft and issued a new draft to Mills. When Sun Corp. presented the draft for payment, Cigna's bank refused to honor it because of the stop order. The bank stamped "Stop Payment" on the draft and returned it to Sun Corp.'s bank. Plaintiff Robert Triffin, who subsequently purchased the draft from Sun Corp., sued Cigna demanding payment of the draft. The trial court ruled in favor of Cigna and Triffin appealed.

Dreier, Judge

. . . There is no question that had Sun Corp. . . . pressed its claim against the insurer as the issuer of the instrument, Sun Corp. would have been entitled to a judgment because of its status as a holder in due course.

Thereafter, plaintiff, who apparently is in the business of purchasing dishonored instruments, obtained an assignment of Sun Corp.'s interests in this instrument and proceeded with this lawsuit. Plaintiff does not contend that he is a holder in due course of the instrument by virtue of it being negotiated to him for value, in good faith, without notice of dishonor, under the [UCC §3–302].

Such negotiation is, of course, only one way for a holder to claim the status of a holder in due course. There exists a second method by which one may become a holder in due course. The shelter [provision of UCC §3–203(b) states:] "Transfer of an instrument, whether or not the transfer is a negotiation, vests in the transferee any right of the transferor to enforce the instrument, *including any right as a holder in due course. . . .*" (Emphasis added.)

The Uniform Commercial Code Comment 2 to this section . . . states:

> Under subsection (b) a holder in due course that transfers an instrument transfers those rights as a holder in due course to the purchaser. The policy is to assure the holder in due course a free market for the instrument.

. . . Uniform Commercial Code Comment 4, Case # 1, tracks the case before us.

> Payee, by fraud, induced Maker to issue a note to Payee. The fraud is a defense to the obligation of Maker to pay the note. . . . Payee negotiated the note to X who took as a holder in due course. After the instrument became overdue X negotiated the note to Y who had notice of the fraud. Y succeeds to X's rights as a holder in due course and takes free of Maker's defense of fraud.

These sections could not be clearer. Plaintiff received by assignment the right of a holder in due course to this instrument, which apparently had been presented and then dishonored because of defendant's stop payment order. . . .

[Judgment reversed and remanded with directions to enter judgment in favor of plaintiff.]

Rights of a Holder in Due Course

To this point we have examined how holders and transferees of a negotiable instrument achieve holder in due course status. A person enjoying this status takes the instrument free of all claims to the instrument and personal but not real defenses asserted by parties to the original transaction. These rights, embodied in UCC §3–305, are possessed by any person who qualifies as a holder in due course under §3–302, as well as any transferee acquiring the rights of a holder in due course under §3–203(b) discussed above.

Taking Free of Claims

Under §3–306, a holder in due course takes an instrument free of all claims to it on the part of any person. Claims defeated by a holder in due course include not only claims of legal title, but also all liens, equities, or claims of any other type, including a claim for rescission of a prior negotiation. Suppose Mark issues an instrument payable to Paul's order, and indorsed by Paul in blank, Paul negotiates the instrument to Andrew. Andrew's creditor, Jerry, obtains a lien upon all of Andrew's property, including the note, to satisfy an unpaid judgment. Andrew subsequently negotiates the instrument to Bart, a minor. Bart negotiates the instrument to Carl, who negotiates it to Dave, a holder in due course. Dave takes the instrument free of (1) Jerry's claim that he has a lien upon it to satisfy the unpaid judgment against Andrew, and (2) Bart's claim that, as a minor, he is entitled to rescind the transaction with Carl and recover the instrument.

Under §3–306, a person without the rights of a holder in due course takes the instrument subject to all valid claims to it on the part of any person. Thus, a person without holder in due course rights is defeated by all adverse claimants to the instrument, including those appearing in the preceding example.

Personal Defenses

Any person possessing the rights of a holder in due course takes the instrument free from "personal" but subject to "real" defenses asserted by a party to the instrument. Most commonly, the person asserting a defense is the drawer of a check or other draft or the maker of a note. A person without the rights of a holder in due course takes subject to all defenses, real or personal. Although the UCC text does not explicitly use the terms "real" and "personal" to describe the various defenses, it does retain the basic distinction between the two classes. Because the rights of a holder in due course are traditionally discussed in these terms, they will be used here.

The various **personal defenses** are divided into two categories: (1) any defense to a simple contract, including fraud and misrepresentation, and (2) unauthorized completion. These defenses, defeated by a holder in due course, are explained in the following paragraphs.

Any Defense to a Simple Contract. Section §3–305(a)(2) provides that a person without the rights of a holder in due course takes the instrument subject to all defenses of any party that would be available in an action on a simple contract. That is, ordinary contract defenses, which would be available in a contract action between the immediate parties to the instrument, may not be asserted against a holder in due course. The ability to avoid contract defenses lies at the heart of the negotiability concept and the holder in due course doctrine.

To illustrate, suppose that on March 1, Byrd issues a $15,000 promissory note payable in six months to Davenport's order to pay for 200 cameras to be delivered by Davenport to Byrd on April 1. Davenport immediately negotiates the note to a holder in due course, Harrison. In this case, Harrison could force Byrd to pay the note even though (1) Davenport never delivers the cameras (a so-called failure of consideration), or (2) the goods are delivered by Davenport but fail to conform to the contract (a breach of warranty), or (3) a condition to either party's duty to perform had failed to occur. All of the foregoing defenses are available to Byrd against one not having the rights of a holder in due course.[6]

As with other contract defenses, common law fraud and misrepresentation, which generally render a contract voidable, are personal defenses. Assume Len sells a car to Robert, inducing Robert to buy by fraudulently turning back the odometer and making other materially false representations regarding the vehicle. To pay for the automobile, Robert issues a $1,000 promissory note

payable to Len's order, which Len promptly negotiates to Steve, a holder in due course. Steve may require Robert to pay the instrument despite his fraud defense. Robert's recourse after payment is against Len.

Unauthorized Completion. As discussed in Chapter 22, an incomplete instrument is one that is *signed* while incomplete in some necessary respect, such as by omission of the payee, the amount, or in some cases, the date. Before examining the substantive rules governing incomplete instruments and holders in due course, it is important to distinguish unauthorized completion from forgery. In forgery, the *signature* of the maker or drawer is unauthorized. In **unauthorized completion,** the signature is genuine or authorized but other essential terms, such as the payee and amount, are completed in an unauthorized manner. The distinction is of fundamental importance because unauthorized completion is merely a personal defense, whereas, with rare exceptions, forgery is a real defense.

Sections 3–115(c) and 3–407(a)(ii) collectively provide that an unauthorized completion constitutes an alteration of the instrument. Under §3–407(c), when an incomplete instrument has been completed, either as authorized or in an unauthorized manner, a subsequent holder in due course may in all cases enforce the instrument *as completed*. In addition, §4–401(d)(2) provides that a drawee bank may charge its customer's account according to the terms of a completed check unless the bank has notice that the completion was improper. To illustrate, assume Diane gives her roommate Pam an otherwise blank check drawn on First Bank signed by Diane, with instructions to take the check to the grocery store and use it to purchase groceries for the following week, the amount not to exceed $75. Rather than obeying the instructions, Pam takes the check and Diane's identification to Red's Stereo, Inc. and uses the check to purchase $2,000 worth of stereo equipment from Red's by filling in the amount and payee blanks. Red's then presents the check to First Bank, which pays it. Pam leaves town with the equipment and is never seen again. In this situation, Red's, the payee, ordinarily qualifies as a holder in due course unless it takes with notice of Pam's wrongdoing. As a holder in due course, Red's may enforce the instrument as completed, despite the unauthorized completion, and First Bank may charge Diane's account for $2,000. Diane thus bears the loss unless she is able to find and collect from Pam.

This rule applies even if the instrument was not transferred voluntarily by the maker or drawer. Thus, an

---

[6]In addition to "failure of consideration" (actually meaning failure of *performance*), utter lack of consideration—for example, a note issued as a gift or in exchange for an illusory promise—is merely a personal defense, and may be asserted only against persons not possessing holder in due course rights.

incomplete instrument stolen by a thief and later completed is enforceable as completed by a later holder in due course. Assume that Diane, in the preceding illustration, signs a blank check and places it in her desk drawer for future use. Susan burglarizes Diane's house and steals the check and Diane's identification. Susan then takes the check to Red's, represents herself as Diane, and purchases $2,000 worth of stereo equipment. Red's is once again a holder in due course and may enforce the $2,000 check against Diane, who is relegated to chasing the thief, Susan. In short, the moral of the unauthorized completion story is: never *sign* a negotiable instrument with material terms, such as the amount or payee, left blank unless you are prepared to pay the instrument according to whatever is inserted in those blanks by any person. The law properly places the loss in such cases on the person "whose conduct in signing blank paper has made the fraud possible, rather than upon the innocent purchaser."[7]

The following case illustrates the principles governing unauthorized completion.

American Federal Bank, FSB v. Parker
392 S.E.2d 798 (S.C. App. 1990)

Timothy Kirkman, a horse dealer, arranged with American Federal Bank to provide financing for his horse buyers. The bank provided Kirkman with blank promissory notes and security agreements, which, when completed by Kirkman and his buyers, would be submitted to the bank for approval.

Kirkman subsequently agreed with Gene Parker, another horse dealer, to co-purchase a horse for $35,000. Parker signed a blank American Federal promissory note and security agreement. The security agreement authorized the bank to disburse the loan proceeds to the seller of the horse, which served as collateral on the loan. Kirkman told Parker that he would co-sign the note and complete the details with the bank. Kirkman, however, failed to co-sign the note, completed it for $85,000, and took the note to American Federal. In exchange for the note, the bank issued checks totaling $85,000 payable to Kirkman, who told the bank that he was the seller of the horse. Kirkman paid $35,000 to the actual seller, who delivered the horse to Parker. Kirkman then left town with the additional $50,000. After Parker refused to pay more than $35,000 on the note, the bank sued. Parker defended on the grounds

---

[7]Original 1962 UCC §3–115, Official Comment 5.

that he had authorized only a $35,000 loan, and that the bank failed to follow reasonable commercial practices in handling the loan. The trial court directed a verdict in favor of the bank and Parker appealed.

Cureton, Judge

. . . Parker executed a promissory note in blank. Under the Uniform Commercial Code the maker of a note agrees to pay the instrument according to its tenor at the time of engagement "or as completed pursuant to [UCC §3–115] on incomplete instruments." [UCC §3–413(1) (§3–412 under the 1990 Code)] Under Section [3–115(2) (§3–115(c) under the 1990 Code)] if the completion of an instrument is unauthorized the rules as to material alteration apply. Under Section [3–407(1)(b) (§3–407(a) under the 1990 Code)] the completion of an incomplete instrument otherwise than as authorized is considered an alteration. However, under Section [3–407(3) (§3–407(c) under the 1990 Code)] a subsequent holder in due course may enforce an incomplete instrument as completed. Official Comment 4 [to §3–407 of the 1962 Code] indicates that where blanks are filled or an incomplete instrument is otherwise completed, the loss is placed upon the party who left the instrument incomplete and the holder is permitted to enforce it according to its completed form.

We agree with the trial court that no jury issue is created and the bank was entitled to the directed verdicts. The responsibility for the situation rests with Parker. He and Kirkman negotiated their deal. Parker signed a blank promissory note. He relied upon Kirkman to co-sign the note and fill it in for $35,000. Parker's negligence substantially contributed to the material alteration as a matter of law. . . . Parker argues it was not reasonable commercial practice for American Federal to give Kirkman possession of blank promissory notes. After the fact, Parker argues the bank should have contacted him or checked to be sure everything was correct before disbursing the proceeds of the loan to Kirkman. There is no evidence in the record to establish the bank had any reason to inquire into the facial validity of the note. The note was complete when presented to the bank and there were no obvious alterations on it. The bank loan officer had known Kirkman for several years. He also had met Parker in the past and knew Parker was in the horse business. Further, there was testimony that banking practices do not prohibit execution of promissory notes outside of the bank in some cases although it is not a routine practice.

The record establishes American Federal took the note in good faith and without notice of any defense to it by Parker. American Federal gave value for the note when it disbursed the funds to Kirkman. As a holder in due course, American Federal may enforce the note against Parker as completed. . . .

[Judgment affirmed.]

Real Defenses

Although they acquire an instrument free of personal defenses, holders in due course are subject to a limited and extraordinary class of "real" defenses. Personal defenses are generally contractual in nature, asserted to avoid performance of an otherwise valid obligation. In contrast, most real defenses are based upon failure of the existence of an obligation initially. **Real defenses** include (1) forgery, (2) material alteration, (3) infancy, (4) other incapacity, duress, and illegality, (5) fraud in the execution, (6) discharge in bankruptcy, and (7) any other discharge known to the holder when he takes the instrument.

Forgery. Perhaps the most common real defense is **forgery.** A maker or drawer whose signature is forged has no liability on the instrument. Under §1–201(b)(41), a forgery is one type of **unauthorized signature,** which includes both outright forgeries and a signature affixed by an agent without actual, implied, or apparent authority. Under §3–403(a), an unauthorized signature is legally effective as the signature of the unauthorized signer in favor of any person who in good faith pays the instrument or takes it for value. It is wholly ineffective as the signature of the person whose name is signed. For example, if Tom steals Don's checkbook and forges Don's name to a check made payable to Peter, the signature by Tom in Don's name is wholly inoperative as Don's signature, but is totally effective as Tom's signature. The instrument in question is a valid check with Tom rather than Don assuming the liability of the drawer. Thus Peter or a later holder may enforce the instrument against Tom (assuming that he can be found and is solvent), but not against Don, who may assert Tom's forgery as a defense even against a holder in due course.

In many corporations and other organizations an authorized signature requires the signature of two or more persons. Under §3–403(b), the signature of the organization is "unauthorized," as discussed above, if one of the required signatures is missing.

Effect of Negligence. The availability of forgery as a defense is limited by §3–406, which provides that a person who by his negligence substantially contributes to making a forgery is precluded from asserting the signer's lack of authority against a later holder in due course. Negligence of a drawer or maker substantially contributing to a forgery therefore changes forgery from a real to a personal defense. The rationale for this result is that the loss should fall upon the drawer or maker whose conduct (negligence contributing to a forgery) makes the fraud possible rather than upon an innocent purchaser of the paper.

The Code makes no attempt to specify any particular negligent conduct that would change an unauthorized signing into a personal defense. Instead, the matter is left for the court or jury to decide, based on the facts of the particular case. Examples of negligence include failure to secure blank check forms, or a signature stamp or other automatic signing device, and negligent hiring or supervision of employees, such as bookkeepers, who write checks. Also included are cases in which a person learns that forgeries of her signature have been made, but subsequently fails to take steps to prevent further forgeries by the same person.

At issue in the following case was whether the drawer's conduct was negligent, converting a forgery into a mere personal defense.

Dubin v. Hudson County Probation Department
630 A.2d 1207 (N.J. Super. 1993)

Plaintiff Frank Dubin owned and operated a check-cashing business where three individuals presented checks dated March 13, 1992, drawn on an account of the defendant Hudson County Probation Department. After obtaining identification, an employee cashed the three checks, which totaled about $900. The drawee bank returned the checks indicating that the account had been closed. A police investigation disclosed that the defendant had closed the account in October 1991, and locked the unused checks in a storage room. Several months later, a mail clerk employed by the defendant was instructed to shred the checks. While shredding the checks, the mail clerk had left the mail room unlocked as he ran other errands required by his job. The police concluded that the checks had been stolen from the mail room during his absence. The plaintiff sued defendant seeking payment of the three checks. After concluding that plaintiff was a holder in due course, the court considered whether the defendant's negligence prevented it from asserting forgery as a real defense.

Fast, Judge

. . . I find the facts presented here to be . . . obvious in showing defendant's negligence, as it applies under [UCC §3–406] to bar defendant's assertions of unauthorized signatures and alterations of the checks. Defendant's actions, in not shredding the checks for several months and leaving the blank checks in a place where they were accessible to the public, are dispositive of defendant's negligence in contributing to the theft. Defendant could have (and should have) easily locked the door to the mail room when the room was unattended. Consequently, defendant's negligence "substantially contributed" to the theft, and thus, they are precluded from asserting the defense of forgery.

Defendant relies on the case of *Brogan Cadillac-Oldsmobile Corp. v. The Central Jersey Bank and Trust Company,* [443 A.2d 1108 (N.J. Super. 1981)]. The Court held in *Brogan* that where checks were stolen from a bank vault and there was no evidence of negligence on the part of defendant/bank, the statute [UCC §3–406] did not apply. I find the present case factually distinguishable from *Brogan.*

In *Brogan,* the checks were stored in a bank vault, which was not located in an area open to the public and where only a limited number of people were authorized to enter. The checks were drawn on a different bank, and were mainly used by defendant bank for the payment of certain obligations. Defendant bank learned that two checks had been cashed in another area of the state, and thereafter discovered that a total of 22 prenumbered checks were missing from the vault. Neither the bank nor the police were able to ascertain how the checks came to be missing. The Court based its holding on the belief that it would be unjust to require one to anticipate that a crime will be committed unless there has been a warning or previous criminal act on the premises. . . . *Brogan* found that the conduct of defendant bank was outside the law's conception of

fault. Since there was no clear evidence that the stolen check was ever in the hands of the bank officials, and that it was just as likely that the checks were stolen prior to being delivered to the defendant bank, the facts did not support a conclusion of negligence and the statute did not apply. . . .

Here, the conduct of defendant supports a conclusion of fault on the part of defendant. The facts show that the checks were in defendant's possession after the account had been closed, and support a finding that they were stolen from defendant. The testimony was uncontested that the checks were stolen from the unlocked mail room. . . . [T]he Uniform Commercial Code . . . support[s] the conclusion that plaintiff, as a holder in due course, is entitled to payment. . . .

[Judgment entered for plaintiff.]

Alteration. A negotiable instrument is "altered" when the holder changes its terms. Under §3–407(a), an **alteration** is an unauthorized change in an instrument that purports to modify the contract of any party to the instrument in any respect. As against a person other than a subsequent holder in due course, if a holder of an instrument fraudulently alters it, any party whose obligation is changed by the alteration is discharged. A subsequent holder in due course, however, may in all cases enforce the altered instrument according to its original terms.[8] Suppose Downs draws a $100 check payable to Parker's order. Parker expertly alters the amount payable to read $1,000 (a so-called raised check) and negotiates the check to Harris, a holder in due course. In this case, Downs may assert Parker's alteration as a defense to paying Harris, but only to the extent of the alteration, $900. Harris, as a holder in due course, may require Downs to honor the instrument according to its original amount, $100.

Effect of Negligence. As with unauthorized signatures, negligence of a drawer or maker that substantially contributes to a material alteration prevents its assertion against a later holder in due course. Negligence has been found, for example, when the drawer or maker leaves spaces in the body of the instrument allowing

---

[8]UCC §§3–407(b),(c).

additional figures or words to be inserted. Drafting an instrument in pencil also might be deemed negligence, reducing a subsequent alteration to a personal defense. If negligence is found, a later holder in due course may enforce the instrument as altered. Thus, in the preceding example, if Downs's negligence in drafting her check allowed Parker to alter it, Harris could enforce the instrument against Downs for the full $1,000.

Infancy. Under §3–305(a)(1)(i), infancy is a real defense to the extent that it is a defense to a simple contract under state law. Thus, infancy may be asserted against a holder in due course even though the infancy renders the instrument only voidable, not void. The rule is consistent with general contract policy protecting minors against their own immaturity, lack of judgment, and overreaching by adults. State law governing minors' contracts must be consulted to determine when infancy is available as a defense and the situations in which it may be asserted.

Although *defenses* based on infancy may be asserted against a holder in due course, *claims* may not, because holders in due course take free of all claims to the instrument. For example, assume Miller, a minor, issues a $1,000 promissory note payable to Palmer's order. Palmer negotiates the note to Foster, another minor, who negotiates it to Gregg, who negotiates it to Hatch, a holder in due course. Although Hatch takes the instrument free of any claim to the instrument asserted by Foster (attempting to rescind her negotiation to Gregg and recover the instrument), Hatch takes subject to Miller's minority defense.

Other Incapacity, Duress, and Illegality. In determining whether duress, illegality, or incapacity other than infancy constitutes a real defense, state law outside the UCC must once again be consulted. Section 3–305(a)(1)(ii) provides that such defects are real defenses *only* if their effect is to render the obligation totally *void* under state law. That is, if the incapacity, duress, or illegality renders the obligation merely *voidable,* it may not be asserted against a holder in due course. Examples of other incapacity, governed largely by statute, include mental incompetence and guardianship. Illegality typically involves gambling contracts or those violating usury laws. Whether duress constitutes a real defense is a matter of degree. For example, the fact that the maker was induced to sign through threats of legal action or suspension of future deliveries probably could not be asserted by the maker

against a later holder in due course. On the other hand, the defense that the note was signed at gunpoint should be available to the maker.

Fraud in the Execution. Although fraud generally is a personal defense, a special type of fraud, known as **fraud in the execution** (or **fraud in the essence, fraud in the factum, essential fraud,** or **real fraud**) is available even against a holder in due course. Under §3–305(a)(1)(iii), fraud in the execution occurs when a misrepresentation induces a party to sign an instrument "with neither knowledge nor reasonable opportunity to learn of its character or its essential terms." Examples of fraud in the execution include a baseball player signing an autograph that is transmitted through carbon paper to a promissory note underneath, or when a person is tricked into believing that what he or she is signing is merely an acknowledgment or receipt rather than a negotiable instrument.

Because, as a matter of general contract law, a person is deemed to know and assent to the contents of anything she signs, fraud in the execution is very difficult to establish. The signer must prove both lack of knowledge and a lack of reasonable opportunity to obtain knowledge. Because knowledge can usually be obtained by reading the instrument, the signer is unable in most cases to meet the test of the defense: excusable ignorance of the contents of the writing. Extraordinary circumstances are usually present, including deficiencies of the signer in intelligence, education, business experience, or knowledge of the English language.

Discharge in Bankruptcy. Under §3–305(1)(a)(iv), the maker's or drawer's discharge in bankruptcy may be asserted even against a holder in due course. Suppose that on June 1 Stevens issues a $1,000 promissory note payable in one year to Moore's order. Moore immediately negotiates the instrument to Hoskins, a holder in due course. Six months later, Stevens goes through bankruptcy and receives a discharge. Stevens may assert his discharge in bankruptcy as a defense to paying Hoskins.

Other Discharge. In addition to a discharge in bankruptcy, a holder in due course takes subject to the discharge of any party to the instrument of which the holder *has notice* when he takes the instrument.[9] No discharge of any party to the instrument is effective

---

[9]UCC §3–601(b).

against a later holder in due course unless the holder has notice of it when she takes the instrument. For example, the Code provides that a holder may discharge any party to an instrument in any manner apparent from the face of the instrument or an indorsement such as by striking out or canceling a party's signature.[10] If a signature is so canceled, a later holder in due course takes subject to the discharge of that party, because the cancellation provides notice of the discharge. Suppose Scott is a holder in due course of Martin's $1,000 promissory note payable to Paul's order and indorsed by Paul, Alan, Bob, Carl, and Don. Scott acquired the instrument from Don, who as a favor to Bob, had crossed out Bob's indorsement. Scott takes with notice of and subject to Bob's discharge. All other parties (Martin, Paul, Alan, Carl, and Don) remain liable on their contracts. This contract liability is discussed in detail in Chapter 25.

Effect of Payment. Although payment of an instrument normally discharges a party,[11] such a discharge, as noted above, is ineffective against a subsequent holder in due course without a notice of the discharge. Assume Burton issues a $1,000 demand promissory note payable to Fisher's order. One month later Fisher demands and receives payment from Burton, who does not require Fisher to surrender the instrument. Fisher subsequently negotiates the instrument to Holly, a holder in due course. Holly may require Burton to pay the note again because Holly took without notice of and therefore free from Burton's discharge based on his payment of the instrument. Any person paying an instrument should therefore require the holder to surrender it.

Federal Trade Commission Rule

The holder in due course doctrine has been restricted in consumer credit transactions because of the potential for abuse illustrated by the following example. Assume Perkins, a dealer in shoddy merchandise (or services), sells Masters a television set. Because Masters is unable to pay cash she buys under a "conditional sales contract" consisting of a promissory note for the purchase price payable in installments and a security agreement giving Perkins the right to repossess the television if Masters fails to pay the note. Immediately after the sale

to Masters, Perkins sells the contract for cash to a bank or finance company, which usually qualifies as a holder in due course under Article 3. Therefore, even if the television later proves defective, Masters, the consumer, is required to pay the purchase price to the bank or finance company. The consumer's most valuable remedy against a breaching seller, withholding the purchase price, is therefore extinguished under a strict application of the holder in due course doctrine.

Because of this perceived abuse, most states either by statute or judicial decision have imposed some restriction on the holder in due course doctrine in consumer transactions. Further, the Federal Trade Commission (FTC) promulgated rules and regulations effective since 1976 effectively abolishing the holder in due course doctrine in credit sales of goods or services to a consumer. Under these regulations,[12] the seller[13] must include the following notice (in at least ten-point boldface type) in any contract evidencing a sale or lease of goods or services to a consumer[14] on credit:

NOTICE

ANY HOLDER OF THIS CONSUMER CREDIT CONTRACT IS SUBJECT TO ALL CLAIMS AND DEFENSES WHICH THE DEBTOR COULD ASSERT AGAINST THE SELLER OF GOODS OR SERVICES OBTAINED PURSUANT HERETO OR WITH THE PROCEEDS HEREOF. RECOVERY HEREUNDER BY THE DEBTOR SHALL NOT EXCEED AMOUNTS PAID BY THE DEBTOR HEREUNDER.[15]

Failure to include this notice is deemed an unfair or deceptive trade practice, violating Section 5 of the Federal Trade Commission Act.[16]

The effect of including the above notice is that no transferee of the contract, such as a bank or finance company, acquires the rights of a holder in due course. Although Article 3 continues otherwise to govern the instrument,[17] the assignee of such consumer paper takes no better rights than its assignor, the seller, had.

---

[10]UCC §3–604.
[11]UCC §3–602(a).

[12]16 C.F.R. §§433.1–433.3.
[13]The regulations define "seller" as "a person who, in the ordinary course of business, sells or leases goods or services to consumers." 16 C.F.R. §433.1(j).
[14]The regulations define "consumer" as "a natural person who seeks or acquires goods or services for personal, family, or household use." 16 C.F.R. §433.1(b).
[15]16 C.F.R. §433.2.
[16]The Federal Trade Commission Act and the FTC's authority under §5 thereunder are discussed in Chapter 52.
[17]UCC §3–106(d).

Two points concerning the scope and operation of the FTC rule should be noted. First, it applies only to consumer, not business or commercial transactions. Second, it effects no change in Article 3 of the UCC or any other state law. It simply requires inclusion of the quoted notice to avoid violating the Federal Trade Commission Act. Note that a business transferee of consumer paper without the required notice may be unable to qualify as a holder in due course in any event, because it should know that the notice is required and therefore does not take the paper in good faith.

Summary

1.   A holder in due course is a specialized transferee of a negotiable instrument who stands in a better legal position than an ordinary contract assignee. A holder in due course takes the instrument free of all claims to it and personal, but not real, defenses asserted by a party to the instrument. A person without the rights of a holder in due course takes the instrument subject to all claims to it and all defenses, real or personal.

2.   To qualify as a holder in due course, the holder must take an apparently valid instrument (1) for value, (2) in good faith, and (3) without notice that the instrument is overdue, or has been dishonored, or of any defense against or claim to it on the part of any person.

3.   In general, any transferee who takes the instrument from or after a holder in due course acquires the rights of a holder in due course, whether or not the transferee meets the requirements listed above. This so-called shelter or umbrella rule assures marketability of the paper, and expands substantially the number of transferees afforded holder in due course status.

4.   Holders in due course take free of personal but not real defenses asserted by a party to the instrument, usually the maker of a note or drawer of a check or other draft. Personal defenses include (1) any defense to a simple contract, including fraud and misrepresentation, and (2) unauthorized completion.

5.   Real defenses include (1) forgery, (2) alteration, (3) infancy, (4) other incapacity, duress, and illegality, (5) fraud in the execution, (6) discharge in bankruptcy, and (7) any other discharge known to the holder when he takes the instrument.

6.   The holder in due course doctrine has been restricted in consumer credit transactions by Federal Trade Commission rule. Under this rule, any contract evidencing a sale or lease of goods to a consumer on credit must include a notice making the transferee subject to claims and defenses which the consumer could assert against the seller of the goods or services.

Key Terms

holder in due course	unauthorized completion
value	real defenses
antecedent debt	forgery
notice	unauthorized signature
shelter (umbrella) provision	alteration
personal defenses	fraud in the execution

Questions and Problems

24.1   To be a holder in due course, a person must take an instrument in good faith and without notice of various problems with the instrument. In their treatise on the Uniform Commercial Code, Professors White and Summers note that the good faith and notice requirements should be studied together because "they appear in the cases and in the flesh as first cousins." (WHITE & SUMMERS, UNIFORM COMMERCIAL CODE 627 (3d ed. 1988).) What does this statement mean?

24.2   Consider the following facts.
 (a) Samson sold goods to Baily for $500 on June 1. Baily gave Samson a check, which Samson promptly sold the same day to Lawson for $500, payable $150 on June 3, $150 on June 5, and $200 on June 7. Assume that the goods Samson sold to Baily were not as warranted. Lawson became aware of this fact on June 6. Assuming he meets the other requirements, for what amount could Lawson qualify as a holder in due course?
 (b) Miller issued a note payable to the order of Pierce in the amount of $1,000. Pierce sold the note to East for $980. East paid Pierce $300 cash, a $300 check made payable to East to Pierce, and canceled a prior loan of $380 that Pierce owed East. Assuming he meets all other requirements, for what amount could East qualify as a holder in due course?

24.3   Consider the following situations.
 (a) Alexander sues Benedict. After some negotiation, Alexander agrees to dismiss the lawsuit if Benedict will execute a promissory note for $1,000 payable in 60 days. Benedict executes the promissory note payable to Alexander who negotiates it to First Bank as collateral

for an $800 loan. On the due date, First Bank demands payment from Benedict. He refuses claiming that the promissory note is not supported by consideration because Alexander failed to dismiss the lawsuit.

(1) Is First Bank a holder in due course? To what extent? Explain.

(2) Is Benedict's defense legal grounds for refusing to pay the note? Explain.

(b) On July 1, Annette gave Frankie a $500 promissory note due on December 1 in exchange for a motorcycle sold by Frankie to Annette. On July 15 Frankie negotiated the note to Connie in payment for a used car that Connie promised to deliver on August 1. Annette has a defense to paying the note because Frankie fraudulently misrepresented the motorcycle's mechanical condition. Could Connie be a holder in due course on these facts? If so, when and under what circumstances would she achieve that status? If Connie qualifies as a holder in due course, would she take the instrument free of Annette's defense?

24.4   On August 1, Ralph sold real property located in Macon County to Mary Maker who in partial payment executed a promissory note for $15,000 payable to the order of Ralph. The note was secured by a mortgage on the real property. On August 15, Carl Creditor sued Ralph and took a judgment for $10,000, which Carl recorded on August 15 in the Macon County recorder's office, a place of public record. Recording the judgment gave Carl a lien on Ralph's property, including the note. On September 1, Ralph negotiated Mary Maker's promissory note to First State Bank as collateral for a loan.

(a) Has First State Bank taken the note for value? Explain.

(b) Ralph later defaulted on the loan. Both Carl and First State Bank assert a right to Mary's payment on the promissory note. First State Bank claims that it is a holder in due course. Carl alleges that the bank cannot be a holder in due course because it had constructive notice of Carl's lien because the lien was recorded. Who is correct? Explain.

24.5   Brown sold some property to Jones in exchange for a negotiable promissory note for $100,000. Brown, without indorsing the note, delivered it to his daughter Belle stating, "I want you to have this note as a gift." After Belle notified Jones of the gift, he began making payments to her. Brown died and his estate claimed that Brown owned the promissory note at his death.

(a) Assume that the promissory note was payable to bearer. Is Belle a holder? A holder in due course? Explain.

(b) Assume that the promissory note was payable to the order of Brown. Is Belle a holder? A holder in due course? Does Belle have any rights in the note? Explain.

(c) Assume that Belle refused to accept the note as a gift but instead paid her father the present value of the note. Is she a holder? A holder in due course? Does it matter whether the note is made payable to bearer or to the order of Brown? Explain.

24.6   On October 1, 2005, Hunt sold some cattle to Pierre who paid for them by check payable to Hunt in the amount of $30,000. When Pierre returned to his ranch, he discovered that the cattle had been miscounted and he had received more than he had paid for. Pierre called Hunt and told her he would send a new check in the proper amount of $35,000 and asked her to destroy the check. Approximately one year later in October 2006; Hunt was in financial difficulties and Creditor demanded that she make payments on a loan owed to Creditor. Hunt began searching through her files and discovered the two checks from Pierre. Hunt indorsed the checks and delivered them to Creditor. After noticing that the checks were almost a year old, Creditor called Pierre and told him that he would be depositing some "old checks" drawn on Pierre's account. Creditor then deposited the properly indorsed checks and Pierre's bank paid both. When reconciling his bank account the following month, Pierre realized that Creditor had cashed the check that Hunt should have destroyed. After the bank refused to recredit his account for $30,000, Pierre sued Creditor.

How should the court rule? In formulating your answer, consider whether Creditor is a holder in due course and discuss the effect of Creditor's telephone call notifying Pierre of the proposed deposit of the checks.

24.7   John bought a printing press from Leonard and paid for it with a check. Leonard indorsed the check to Virginia in payment of a preexisting debt. Virginia gave the check to Vanessa, her sister, and suggested she use it to buy herself a birthday present. Vanessa deposited the check in her account but it was returned marked "payment stopped." Vanessa telephoned John who said he had stopped payment on the check because the printing press was defective. When Vanessa threatened to sue, John told her she would lose the case because she had not given value for the check and, therefore, was not a holder in due course.

(a) Is Vanessa a holder in due course? Explain.

(b) If Vanessa sues, who will win? Explain.

24.8   On January 1, Smith executed a $1,000 negotiable promissory note payable on January 30 to the order of Jones for goods to be delivered by Jones to Smith. Jones breached the contract and the goods were never delivered. On January 2, Jones negotiated the note to Zimmer who had no knowledge of the breach. Zimmer agreed to pay $975, payment to be made on January 10. Zimmer, on January 3, negotiated the note to his nephew, Claypool, as a graduation present. Claypool then sold the note to Faust who paid $975 cash and had no knowledge of any defenses against the instrument. Faust then sold the note to Wilson for $959, who took it on January 29, with knowledge that Jones had breached the contract.

(a) Is Zimmer a holder in due course?

(b) Is Claypool a holder in due course?

(c) Is Faust a holder in due course?

(d) Is Wilson a holder in due course?

(e) Would Wilson take the note subject to Smith's defense against Jones?

24.9 Kroyden Industries, Inc. was enjoined by the court from committing specified unfair trade practices in connection with its sale of carpeting to consumers. In violation of the injunction, Kroyden obtained a $1,500 promissory note from Doaks for purchase of carpeting. Kroyden negotiated the note to Harris, a holder in due course. When Doaks refused to pay the note, Harris sued, Doaks asserted illegality as a real defense. He argued that because the transaction that resulted in the execution of his note was a violation of the injunctive order, the transaction was "illegal" and thus a nullity under UCC §3–305(a)(1)(ii). Is Doaks correct? Explain.

24.10 Following serious flooding in her home in Chicago, Illinois, Beulah Hogan called Fred Fender who was listed as a plumber in the telephone directory. Fender agreed to repair the pipes but requested advance payment of $500. After Hogan gave him a check, Fender left to purchase needed materials. When he failed to return, Hogan telephoned the Chicago Consumer Affairs office and learned that Fender was not a licensed plumber. Illinois law provides that only licensed plumbers can perform plumbing work in the state. Hogan notified her bank to stop payment on the check. Fender, however, already had cashed the check at A-1 Currency Exchange. A-1 sued Hogan alleging that it was a holder in due course entitled to payment. Hogan asserted that A-1 took the check subject to the real defense of illegality. She argued that because Fender's unlicensed performance of the plumbing would have been illegal under Illinois law, she should prevail. How should the court rule? Explain.

24.11 Louis Guerra entered into a retail installment contract agreeing to pay $10,000 to Modern Builders to install new siding on Guerra's home. After Modern Builders installed the siding, Guerra executed a negotiable promissory note in the amount of $10,000 payable to Modern Builders and requiring Guerra to pay $1,000 per year plus interest at 8 percent. Modern Builders assigned the note and contract to Home Savings and notified Guerra of the assignment. After Guerra had made the first annual payment of $1,800, the siding began to peel and fall from the house. Another siding dealer told Guerra that Modern Builders had improperly installed the siding and had used inappropriate materials. The dealer estimated that the cost of removing the old siding and installing new siding would be $12,000.

(a) Home Savings has sued Guerra for failing to make further payments on his promissory note. May Guerra assert Modern Builder's breach of contract as a defense to payment to Home Savings? Explain.

(b) Guerra has counterclaimed against Home Savings and Modern Builders. Assume that Guerra can prove damages of $12,000 for breach of the siding contract. Would Guerra be entitled to recover any damages from Home Savings? Explain.

CHAPTER 25

LIABILITY OF PARTIES — CONTRACT LIABILITY

Major Topics

- the distinction between primary and secondary contract liability on negotiable instruments
- the nature of primary liability and which parties assume that liability
- the nature of secondary liability and which parties assume that liability
- the conditions precedent to secondary liability
- the contract liability of accommodation parties and guarantors on negotiable instruments

Negotiable instruments, governed by Article 3, are formal contracts that require a payment of money. As in other contracts, the parties to negotiable instruments acquire certain rights and undertake certain duties. An important inquiry in negotiable instruments analysis is, therefore, to define and distinguish the various obligations of the maker of a note, the drawer and drawee of a draft, and an indorser or other transferee of either type of instrument.

Broadly speaking, parties to negotiable instruments incur two types of liability: contract and warranty. Whereas warranty liability generally imposes responsibility for forgery and alteration, contract liability concerns the obligation of the various parties for ultimate *payment* of the instrument.

This chapter explains and distinguishes the contractual undertakings of the parties and examines how those obligations are discharged or extinguished. Chapter 26 explains the circumstances under which the law imposes warranty liability for forgery and alteration.

Liability Based upon Signature

Signature in General

Although the nature and extent of negotiable instruments contract liability differs, all contract liability is imposed in the same manner. Under UCC §3–401(a) no person is liable on an instrument unless and until he or she signs it. As noted in Chapter 22, a signature includes any symbol used by the party to authenticate a writing, including, for example, a handwritten signature, an "X," and a signature stamp or other automatic device. The signature may be made using a trade or assumed name and, in appropriate cases, may be affixed by an authorized agent or other representative of the signer. Parties to negotiable instruments generally sign in one of four capacities: (1) the maker of a note, (2) the drawer of a check or other draft, (3) the acceptor of a check or other draft, or (4) an indorser of any instrument. Therefore, in order to determine the contract liability of a party, one must simply examine the instrument to ascertain the capacity in which the party signed.

Identifying Capacity of Signer. To aid in conclusively determining the capacity of a signature, §3–204(a) provides simply that "regardless of the intent of the signer, a signature and its accompanying words is an indorsement unless the accompanying words, terms of the instrument, place of the signature, or other circumstances *unambiguously indicate* that the signature was made for a purpose other than an indorsement." (Emphasis added.) Therefore, no person is liable on an instrument unless her signature appears thereon, and any signature in an ambiguous capacity is an indorsement. All ambiguities are resolved from the instrument alone, providing yet another example of the strict parol evidence rule applicable to negotiable instruments.

Because all ambiguous signatures are indorsements, it is necessary to identify those signatures that clearly indicate another capacity. Another capacity most commonly is indicated by the position of the signature on the instrument. For example, the drawer of a check or other draft and the maker of a note generally sign in the lower right-hand corner on the face of the instrument. A signature appearing in the lower right-hand corner is therefore presumed to be the signature of a drawer or maker. Similarly, a signature appearing on the back of an instrument is generally deemed an indorsement.

The capacity of the signer also is clearly indicated if words of description are used. For example, a signature appearing anywhere on an instrument stating "Joe Doaks, maker" imposes liability upon Joe Doaks as a maker, whereas a signature "Joe Doaks, witness" imposes no liability upon him. Similarly, a signature appearing in the body of an instrument often clearly indicates the signer's capacity. For example, if an instrument states "I, Jane Adams, promise to pay . . .," Jane Adams is obviously signing as the maker of a note.

Joint and Several Liability. Under §3–116(a), if two or more persons sign as maker, drawer, acceptor, or indorser and as part of the same transaction, they are jointly and severally liable.[1] The signers may be sued together (jointly) or individually (severally) on the obligation and the entire amount owing may be collected from any one of them. Assume A and B co-sign as makers of a $1,000 promissory note payable to P's order. P or a later holder may collect the entire $1,000 from either A or B, or from A and B together. Or, assume M issues a note payable to A and B. A and B both indorse the instrument and negotiate it to Z. A and B are jointly and severally liable as indorsers of the note.[2]

Signature by Authorized Representative

Individuals in business often act through agents. Corporations, which are artificial persons, act only through agents. Accordingly, a negotiable instrument may be signed by an authorized representative or agent, such as the treasurer, controller, or officer of a corporation. The representative's authority to sign is determined by principles of agency law, discussed in detail in Chapter 40. Under ordinary agency principles, if the agent is authorized to sign, the principal, such as the corporation, becomes liable on the instrument as signer, and the agent or representative has no liability upon it. Because the representative generally signs his or her own name to the instrument, however, care must be taken to disclose the representative capacity. Otherwise, later holders of the instrument may be misled concerning the extent of the signer's obligation. The Code resolves the problem by imposing *personal liability* on the instrument (as maker, drawer, acceptor, or indorser) upon an agent who fails properly to indicate his or her representative capacity. Because this issue has resulted in a substantial amount of litigation, persons in business must be familiar with the Code's approach to representative signatures.

Section 3–402(b)(1) states the general rule that if the signature "shows unambiguously" that it is made on behalf of an identified principal, then the principal is liable and the agent is not. For example, assume that Peter Pringle has appointed Arthur Adams as his agent with authority to sign negotiable instruments on Pringle's behalf. Adams signs an authorized instrument "Peter Pringle" or "Peter Pringle by Arthur Adams, Agent." In these cases Pringle is liable on the instrument and Adams is not.

The principal may be a corporation or other organization rather than an individual. In this case, the name of an organization preceded or followed by the name

---

[1] Joint and several liability is discussed in more detail in Chapter 7.

[2] As discussed later in this chapter, indorsers usually are not jointly and severally liable. Rather, they are liable in the order in which they indorse. The law recognizes two exceptions to this rule: (1) the joint payee case above, and (2) cases in which two or more anomalous indorsers sign the instrument. This situation is discussed in the material on liability of accommodation parties.

and office of an authorized individual is a signature unambiguously made in a representative capacity. For example, the signature "XYZ Corporation, by Arthur Adams, Treasurer" imposes no personal liability upon Adams. Section 3–402(c) further provides that if the instrument involved is a *check* that names the principal (for example, a typical preprinted business check naming "XYZ Corporation" as drawer), the agent (for example, the treasurer) who signs on the signature line need not indicate her representative capacity to escape personal liability.

In some cases the signature may not unambiguously indicate that it was made in a representative capacity (for example, Adams may sign "Peter Pringle, Arthur Adams") or the principal may not be named in the instrument (for example, Adams may sign "Arthur Adams" or "Arthur Adams, Agent"). In these cases, the principal (here, Peter Pringle) is still liable because the agent is authorized. Under §3–402(b)(2), the agent also is personally liable on the instrument, if the person seeking to enforce it is a later holder in due course who took the instrument without notice that the agent did not intend to be personally obligated. If, however, the person seeking to enforce the instrument is not a holder in due course, the agent may escape liability by proving that the original parties to the instrument (the agent-signer and the payee of the instrument) did not intend that the agent be personally obligated.

Note finally that §3–402(a) provides that the undisclosed or partially disclosed principal (for example, Peter Pringle when Adams signs simply "Arthur Adams" or "Arthur Adams, Agent") is liable on the instrument if the agent was authorized to sign. This result is therefore a limited exception to the general rule that no person is liable on an instrument unless his or her signature (affixed either personally or by an authorized agent) appears upon it.[3]

Primary Liability

Contract liability is either primary (incurred by primary parties) or secondary (incurred by secondary parties). A person having **primary liability** undertakes an absolute obligation to pay the instrument. The primary parties are the maker of a note (including the issuer of a

cashier's check or certificate of deposit) and the acceptor of a draft. An acceptor is simply a drawee who undertakes to pay a draft. Unlike primary liability, **secondary liability** is conditional; a secondary party agrees to pay only if the primary party does not and certain formal conditions are met. The secondary parties on negotiable instruments are the drawer of a draft or check and the indorser of any instrument. Whether liability is primary or secondary, subsequent events ultimately occur that discharge it. As in contracts generally, to "discharge" a duty means to extinguish or cancel it. The following material examines the contract liability of the various parties whose signatures appear upon a negotiable instrument. Primary liability is covered first followed by a discussion of secondary liability.

Maker of a Note

Section 3–412 provides that the maker of a note (which includes a bank issuing a cashier's check or certificate of deposit) undertakes to pay the instrument according to its terms at the time it was issued. Under §3–105(a), "issue" means the transfer of possession of the instrument by the maker to a holder or nonholder for the purpose of giving rights on the instrument to any person. If the instrument is not issued the maker is obliged to pay it according to its terms when the instrument first came into possession of a holder. The maker's liability is primary because the maker undertakes an absolute obligation to pay the note, and no conditions to that liability (such as a demand for payment) exist. Assume Matson issues a $1,000 promissory note on June 1, 2005, payable with interest to Peter's order on June 1, 2006. Matson is obligated to pay Peter (or a later holder) $1,000 plus interest as of June 1, 2006. The holder's failure to present the instrument to Matson on that date, however, has no effect on Matson's liability. Further, until a tender of payment by Matson or expiration of the statute of limitations, interest on the note continues to run after June 1, 2006.

Acceptor of a Draft

"Acceptance" Defined. Primary liability on a draft, including a check, requires an understanding of *acceptance,* a concept unique to drafts. Clearly, the drawee is the person who should pay a draft, because the essence of a draft is an order by the drawer to the drawee to pay. It is equally clear that drawer should not be able to

---

[3]The preceding discussion assumes that the agent's signature, however affixed, is authorized. The legal effect of an unauthorized signature is discussed in the next chapter.

impose primary liability upon the drawee without the drawee's consent. The drawee's consent to assume primary liability on a draft is known as **acceptance**—defined in §3–409(a) as the drawee's signed engagement to honor (pay) a draft as presented. Therefore, prior to acceptance, *no one* has primary liability on a draft. After acceptance the drawee has an absolute obligation to pay the draft when it is due to the payee or later holder.

An acceptance must be written on the draft and may consist of the drawee's signature alone. A drawee who accepts a draft is known as an **acceptor.** Although an acceptance usually is written vertically across the face of the instrument, the drawee's signature appearing anywhere on a draft is an acceptance. Because a drawee has no reason to sign a draft other than to accept it, the signature itself, regardless of its position, unambiguously indicates the capacity of the signer.

Demand and Time Drafts. Like notes, drafts may, by their terms, be payable on demand (a **demand draft**), or at some fixed or determinable future time (a **time draft**). The concept of acceptance is important only in a time draft. That is, a demand draft is given by the drawer to the payee and then presented to the drawee only once: for payment. Such drafts are commonly known as **sight drafts** because they are to be paid by the drawee on "sight." A demand draft is not presented to the drawee for acceptance (the drawee's *promise* to pay it); it is presented for *payment.* The drawee therefore never assumes primary liability on a demand draft; the drawee either pays the instrument or doesn't. If the drawee pays it, the transaction is at an end. If the drawee fails to pay (dishonors) it, the liability of the secondary party or parties (here, the drawer) ensues.

In time drafts, on the other hand, two presentments are required, the first for acceptance and the second for payment. Acceptance not only initiates the drawee's liability on the instrument, it also commonly fixes the date for payment. For example, time drafts are often stated to be payable a fixed period after "acceptance" or "sight."[4]

To illustrate, assume Bill Brown owes Susan Simon $1,000 for goods bought from Simon. In order to pay an obligation owed by Simon to Paul Potts, Simon draws a draft upon Bill Brown (see Figure 25.1). On June 2 Potts takes the instrument to Brown for accept-

---

[4]"Sight" in this context refers to acceptance.

Figure 25.1   Time Draft

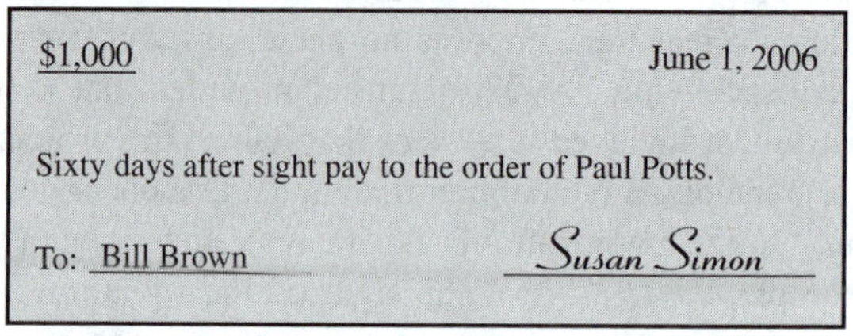

$1,000   June 1, 2006

Sixty days after sight pay to the order of Paul Potts.

To: Bill Brown   *Susan Simon*

ance. Brown accepts by signing "Bill Brown, accepted" across the face of the draft and dating his signature. By accepting, Brown has undertaken the absolute obligation to pay the instrument to Paul Potts (or to a later holder if Potts transfers the instrument) 60 days after June 2. Note that the instrument is ultimately presented twice to Brown, once for acceptance (in this case on June 2) and again for payment (60 days thereafter).

A drawee incurs no liability to the holder of an instrument for failure to accept because prior to acceptance the drawee's signature does not appear on the instrument. This rule applies even if the drawer and drawee stand in a contractual relationship that requires the drawee to accept drafts drawn by the drawer. After acceptance, however, the drawee is primarily liable to the holder of the instrument.

Certified Checks. Because a check is a demand draft, the drawee bank ordinarily has no obligation to the payee or to a later holder to pay the check. Because a check is presented for payment, not acceptance, the bank never undertakes primary liability upon it. If the bank refuses to pay, the holder simply proceeds against the drawer and any indorsers on their *secondary* contract liability.

Although under no obligation to do so, a bank may agree to accept or "certify" a check. **Certification** occurs when an authorized representative of a bank signs or stamps language on the face of the check indicating the bank's undertaking to pay. A certified check is therefore one that is *accepted* rather than *paid* by the bank. It is more valuable than an ordinary check because of the bank's undertaking to stand behind it. A certified check is similar in effect to a time draft because two presentments are made, one for acceptance (certification) and subsequently for payment. Unlike a time draft, however, a certified check is paid on demand by the bank at any time after certification.

Effect of Alteration Before Acceptance. Under §3–413(a), the acceptor of a draft is obligated to pay the instrument according to its terms at the time it was accepted. A maker is therefore primarily liable on the note as executed when it is issued, and an acceptor is liable on a draft as worded when he accepts it. Thus, a drawee who accepts an instrument that has been altered prior to acceptance is liable on the instrument as altered, not as originally drawn. Assume Donna draws a draft against Art ordering Art to pay $100 to Peter's order "30 days after acceptance." Peter takes the instrument from Donna and raises it to $1,000. Peter then negotiates it to Harry, who presents it to Art for acceptance. If Art accepts he is liable for the full $1,000.[5] If the instrument is altered after acceptance, §3–407(c) provides that the acceptor remains liable on the instrument according to its original tenor (as accepted) to a subsequent holder in due course.

Effect of Acceptance Varying Draft. Occasionally, a drawee will accept an instrument but attempt to vary the terms of the draft as presented. Suppose Denise draws a draft against Larry ordering him to pay $100 to Polly's order "30 days after acceptance." Polly indorses the instrument to Tony, who presents it to Larry for acceptance. Assume alternatively that Larry writes on the face of the instrument "accepted, Larry, but only if I receive the proceeds of the sale of my house within 30 days" or "accepted, Larry, payable in 60 days" or "accepted, Larry, for $75 because that is all I owe to Denise." In these situations, §3–410 gives the holder, Tony, two options. One option is to treat the drawee's variant acceptance as a dishonor and proceed immediately against Polly and Denise on their secondary contract liability. If the holder chooses this option, the drawee's acceptance is canceled. Alternatively, the holder may assent to the variance. In this case, each drawer and indorser who does not agree to the variance

is discharged. Thus, if Tony acquiesces in Larry's altered acceptance, Tony has no recourse against Polly or Denise if Larry fails to pay the instrument when due.

Secondary Liability

Nature of Secondary Contract Liability

Upon signing, the maker of a note or acceptor of a draft undertakes primary liability, an absolute obligation to pay the instrument. In contrast, the drawer of a check or other draft and the indorser of any instrument assume only secondary contract liability, promising to pay only if the drawee or maker does not.

Contract of Indorser. Section 3–415(a) provides that if the maker or drawee fails to pay or accept the instrument (that is, "dishonors" it), an indorser is obligated to pay the instrument according to its terms when indorsed. An indorser's liability is conditional, generally imposed only after three "conditions precedent" have been met:

1. *presentment* of the instrument to the drawee or maker for payment or acceptance,
2. *dishonor* by failure of the drawee or maker to pay or accept, and
3. *notice of dishonor* to the indorser.

In essence, indorsers, by virtue of their signatures, effectively make the following promise to every later holder of the instrument: "Present this instrument to the drawee or maker. If he or she doesn't pay (or accept) it, and you notify me of that fact, then I will pay the instrument." Note that compliance with the conditions precedent may be waived, usually through an express term on the face of the instrument itself. In addition, even without express waiver, the conditions precedent may differ depending upon the type of instrument or presence of special circumstances. These situations are explained in the detailed discussion of the conditions precedent later in this chapter.

Note finally that a person who indorses "without recourse" (a "qualified" indorsement) effectively negates his secondary contract obligation. A qualified indorser therefore assumes no liability to pay the instrument if the drawee or maker does not.

---

[5]As developed in the next chapter, however, Art has recourse against Harry and Peter based upon their "warranty" liability on the instrument.

Contract of Drawer. The contract liability of a drawer is similar to that of an indorser with several important exceptions:

1. Notice of dishonor is not required for unaccepted drafts, such as ordinary checks. Specifically, §3–414(b) provides that if the drawee dishonors an unaccepted draft, the drawer is obligated to pay the instrument according to its terms when the drawer issued it, or if not issued when the instrument first came into possession of a holder.

2. Like an indorser, the drawer of a draft other than a check may disclaim his or her contract liability by drawing "without recourse." Under §3–414(e), however, the drawer of a *check* may not eliminate contract liability in this manner. As noted in Official Comment 5 to §3–414: "There is no legitimate purpose served by issuing a check on which nobody is liable."

3. Under §3–414(c), if a check is certified the drawer is discharged, regardless of whether the drawer or a later holder procures the certification. Under §3–415(d), certification also discharges any indorser who has indorsed before certification. A person who indorses after certification assumes the ordinary contract liability of an indorser previously discussed.

4. If a draft that is not a check, such as a trade acceptance, is accepted, the drawer's liability is identical to that of an ordinary indorser. Thus, notice of dishonor would be required to impose contract liability on the drawer.

Order of Liability. Frequently, more than one person assumes secondary contract liability on an instrument.

For example, a check is signed by the drawer and is usually indorsed by the payee. Both notes and drafts often change hands before payment, requiring a number of indorsements. In such cases, the order of liability among those secondarily liable must be determined. Generally, indorsers are liable to each other in the order in which they indorse, which is presumed to be the order in which their names appear on the instrument. Assume Mark issues a $1,000 promissory note payable to Paul's order in one year. The note is subsequently negotiated several times resulting in the following indorsements on the back (see Figure 25.2). Ed, the last holder of the instrument, presents it on the due date to Mark, who refuses to pay it. In this situation, assuming Ed properly notifies them, Dave, Charles, Barbara, Alice, and Paul as indorsers all have secondary contract liability and are liable to Ed in the amount of the note. Ed is not, however, entitled to collect $5,000 ($1,000 each from Dave, Charles, Barbara, Alice, and Paul). The parties are liable successively in the order in which they sign. That is, if Ed collects $1,000 from Dave, Dave could collect $1,000 from Charles, who could collect $1,000 from Barbara, who could collect $1,000 from Alice, who would finally recover $1,000 from Paul. Thus, the ultimate loss from Mark's dishonor falls upon Paul, assuming he is solvent. If not, the loss falls upon Alice, and so on. Note that in the case of a check or other draft an additional secondary party, the drawer, is present. Thus, the payee of a draft has recourse against the drawer. In sum, assuming the solvency of all parties, the ultimate loss upon dishonor by the primary party falls upon the payee of a note and the drawer of a check or other draft.

Conditions Precedent

The Code rules governing the **conditions precedent** to secondary contract liability—presentment, dishonor, and notice of dishonor are stated in §§3–501 to 3–503.

Presentment—§3–501. A **presentment** is a demand for payment or acceptance made upon the maker, drawee, or acceptor by the person entitled to enforce the instrument (usually the holder). An instrument may be presented for payment (to the maker of a note or drawee of a draft) or for acceptance (to the drawee of a time draft).

Presentment may be made by any commercially reasonable means (including oral, written, or electronic

Figure 25.2	Order of Liability

Pay Alice Wood
Paul Bergman

Pay Barbara Mason
Alice Wood

Pay Charles Loo
Barbara Mason

Pay Dave Barnes
Charles Loo

Pay Ed Lopez
Dave Barnes

communication) at the place of payment of the instrument. Federal Reserve regulations specify that for ordinary checks the drawee bank must accept presentment of checks at (1) a location, including a check processing center, requested by the bank (the most common case), (2) a bank office associated with the encoded routing number on the check, (3) the address of any bank office printed on the check, or (4) any bank office, if the check states the drawee bank's name without address.[6] Presentment ordinarily is effective when received, unless the person to whom presentment is made has established a cutoff hour (not earlier than 2:00 P.M.) and presentment is made after the cutoff hour. In this case, presentment is treated as occurring on the next business day.

The person to whom a presentment is made may require exhibition of the instrument, reasonable, identification of the person making presentment a signed receipt on the instrument for any partial payment, and surrender of the instrument on full payment. In addition, without dishonoring the instrument, the person to whom presentment is made may return it for lack of a necessary indorsement, or refuse to pay or accept if the presentment fails to comply with the terms of the instrument, agreement of the parties, or other applicable law or rule. Note that the holder of a check should promptly present it for payment or give it to a depository bank for collection for two reasons. First, under §3–414(f), the *drawer* may be discharged if (1) the instrument is not presented for payment or collection within 30 days after issue, and (2) the drawee bank suspends payments (for example, due to insolvency) after the 30-day period expires without paying the check, and (3) the suspension of payments causes the drawer to lose funds on deposit that would have been available to pay the instrument had it been properly presented. Second, under §3–415(e), to hold *indorsers* liable on their secondary contracts, a check must be presented for payment or collection within 30 days after the indorser signs.

Dishonor—§3–502. Section 3–502 states separate principles governing **dishonor** of notes, unaccepted drafts, and accepted drafts.

Notes. Section 3–502(a) provides the following rules for dishonor of notes:

1. If the note is payable on demand, a presentment is required, and the note is dishonored if it is not paid on the day of presentment.

2. The note may be a time instrument either (a) payable at or through a bank, or (b) requiring presentment by its terms. In these cases, a valid presentment is required, and the note is dishonored if it is not paid on the due date or on the date of presentment if the instrument is presented after the due date.

3. For all other time instruments, no presentment is required, and the note is dishonored if not paid on its due date.

Most modern notes are in the third category, meaning that no formal presentment is required to hold the indorsers liable on their secondary contracts. In addition, most modern notes expressly waive compliance with the conditions precedent. Thus, as explained in Official Comment 2 to §3–502:

> In the great majority of cases presentment and notice of dishonor are waived with respect to notes. In most cases a formal demand for payment to the maker of the note is not contemplated. Rather, the maker is expected to send payment to the holder of the note on the date or dates on which payment is due. If payment is not made when due, the holder usually makes a demand for payment, but in the normal case in which presentment is waived, demand is irrelevant and the holder can proceed against indorsers when payment is not received.

Unaccepted Drafts. Section 3–502(b) provides the rules governing dishonor of unaccepted drafts.

1. If the draft is an ordinary check presented for payment to the drawee bank (other than a check presented for immediate payment over the counter), dishonor is governed by the principles of Article 4 discussed in Chapter 27. Generally, the drawee dishonors the check by returning it or giving notice of dishonor by the bank's midnight deadline—midnight of the next banking day following the banking day on which it receives the check.[7]

2. If the draft is a (1) check presented to the drawee bank for immediate payment over the counter, or (2) demand draft other than a check, the drawee dishonors it if the holder makes a proper presentment and the drawee fails to pay it on the day of presentment.

3. If the draft is a time draft payable on a stated date the drawee dishonors it if the holder properly presents it and the drawee fails to pay on the due date or on the date of presentment if presented after the due date. Because the

---

[6]12 C.F.R. §229.36(b).

[7]UCC §4–104(10).

drawee of such a draft may be unaware that it has been issued, the holder may desire to determine *before* the due date whether the drawee is willing to pay it. Accordingly, the Code permits the holder to present the instrument for acceptance before the due date. If the holder chooses this option, the drawee dishonors the instrument by refusing to accept it on the date of presentment.

4. If the draft is payable a fixed period after sight or acceptance (for example, the draft orders the drawee to pay $10,000 to the payee's order "30 days after acceptance"), the draft must be presented for acceptance to fix the ultimate payment date. In this instance, the drawee dishonors it by failing to accept on the date of presentment.[8]

Accepted Drafts. Section 3–502(d) provides the rules governing dishonor of accepted drafts, which are the equivalent of notes issued by the drawee-acceptor.

1. If the draft is payable on demand, a proper presentment is required, and the drawee-acceptor dishonors it by failing to pay the draft on the date of presentment. This rule is the same as that applied to demand notes.

2. If the accepted instrument is a time draft, a proper presentment is again required, and the drawee-acceptor dishonors by failing to pay on the due date or on the day of presentment if the draft is presented after the due date. This rule is the same as that applied to notes payable at a bank or explicitly requiring presentment.

Notice of Dishonor. Upon dishonor, the holder has an immediate right to sue any person primarily liable on the instrument (the maker of a note or the acceptor of a draft) and also has immediate recourse against all secondary parties (drawers and indorsers). The holder, therefore, need not pursue the primary party first, but may elect to proceed directly against the secondary parties. Indeed, in an ordinary check, no one has primary liability, meaning that the holder's only recourse is against secondary parties.

To hold certain secondary parties liable, however, they must be given timely notice that the instrument has been dishonored. **Notice of dishonor,** governed by §3–503, may be given to secondary parties by any per-

son including (1) the holder, (2) any party who has received notice, or (3) any other party who can be compelled to pay the instrument. A proper notice benefits all parties with rights on the instrument against the party notified. That is, anyone who may be required to pay the instrument may notify anyone who may be liable upon it.

As previously discussed, not all secondary parties are entitled to notice of dishonor. For example:

1. The drawer of an unaccepted draft, such as a check, is not entitled to notice of dishonor. Notice of dishonor is required for drawers only if the draft is accepted by a drawee other than a bank, who later dishonors. Note that the drawer of a draft accepted by a bank (a certified check) has no secondary contract liability.

2. By their terms most modern notes waive compliance with the conditions precedent. Thus, indorsers of notes generally are not entitled to notice of dishonor.

Because of these limitations, notice of dishonor is important primarily to hold check indorsers liable, who, as previously discussed, are automatically discharged if the holder fails to present the instrument for payment or transfer it to a depository bank for collection within 30 days after the indorsement is made. Assuming such a presentment is made and the instrument is dishonored, notice of dishonor is governed by the following rules:

1. If given by a bank, notice must be given by the bank's **midnight deadline,** meaning midnight of the next banking day following dishonor or receipt of notice of dishonor. For ordinary checks, however, Federal Reserve regulations discussed in Chapter 27 require the drawee and other banks in the collection process to notify the depository bank of dishonor within generally a much shorter period.

2. If given by a person other than a bank, notice must be given within 30 days following the day on which the person receives notice of dishonor.

Manner of Notice; Protest. Generally, notice of dishonor may be given in any reasonable manner. It may be an oral, written (including a stamp or other notation on the instrument), or electronic communication simply identifying the instrument and stating that it has been dishonored. Return of an instrument given to a bank for collection is a sufficient notice of dishonor.

Although informal notice is sufficient, occasionally a formal "protest" may be used. Under §3–505(b), a **protest** is a certificate of dishonor made by a U.S.

---

[8]Dishonor of an unaccepted documentary draft (such as those accompanying letters of credit discussed in Chapter 35) are governed by the principles outlined above, except that the time limit for dishonor is extended to the close of the drawee's third business day following presentment. UCC §3–502(c).

consul or vice consul, a notary public, or any other person authorized by local law to certify dishonor. Because a protest facilitates proof of dishonor in a subsequent lawsuit on the instrument, a protest may be advantageous to the holder of the instrument.

Accommodation Parties

The concept of "security" underlies much of the law governing debtor-creditor relations. In a typical security arrangement, a creditor loans money or sells goods on credit to a debtor. At the creditor's request, the debtor's promise to pay is backed by some form of security, providing the creditor an independent source of payment if the debtor defaults. One important type of security device is a suretyship arrangement, discussed in Chapter 33, under which a person known as a "surety" undertakes to satisfy the obligation if the debtor does not. The essence of suretyship is that although both the surety and principal debtor are liable to the creditor, the debtor, not the surety, should pay. Thus, under general suretyship principles, a surety who is required to pay the creditor is entitled to full reimbursement from the debtor.

Parties to negotiable instruments undertake a contractual obligation to pay money. That obligation, like any other, may be backed by a surety's promise. A surety on a negotiable instrument is referred to as an **accommodation party,** who is simply a person who signs an instrument in any capacity (maker, indorser, acceptor) for the purpose of lending his name or credit to another party to the instrument. Thus, an accommodation party is simply a surety whose obligation is on the instrument itself, guaranteeing the performance of another party to the paper, the accommodated party. The liability of the accommodation party is, therefore, determined by the capacity in which he signs the instrument. For example, an accommodation maker or acceptor assumes primary contract liability on the instrument. An accommodation indorser is secondarily liable. Further, the accommodation party's obligation is not subject to any Statute of Frauds provision generally applicable to suretyship promises and is enforceable whether or not the accommodation party receives consideration for signing. Section 3–419(e), however, follows general suretyship principles by providing that the accommodation party has no liability to the party accommodated, and if required to

Figure 25.3 **Accommodation Maker**

June 1, 2006

I promise to pay to the order of Rod Morris, one year from date $1,000.

Mary Greeley
Fred Greeley

pay, has a right of recourse on the instrument against that party.

To illustrate, assume Mary purchases a car from Rod and proposes to pay for it by issuing a promissory note. Because Mary's credit rating is not good, Rod refuses to take her note unless she obtains a surety. Mary convinces her father, Fred, to act as an accommodation party. Fred could sign as an accommodation maker, as shown in Figure 25.3. In this case Fred is liable as a maker. When the instrument is due, Rod may present it to either Mary or Fred for payment. If Fred pays, he may recover $1,000 from Mary (if she is solvent). If Mary pays, she is entitled to nothing from Fred. That is, Fred as an accommodation party is not liable to the party accommodated, Mary.[9]

Alternatively, Fred may sign as an accommodation indorser, as in Figure 25.4. In this case, Fred is liable as an indorser, and may be required to pay upon Mary's dishonor. Note that in this case, Fred's indorsement is said to be **irregular** or **anomalous,** meaning that it is made by a person who is not a holder of the instrument.[10] Section 3–419(c) provides that such an anomalous indorsement is notice to later holders of its accommodation status, even though it contains no additional words of description. Once again, if Fred is required to pay he may recover the amount paid from Mary.

[9]Note that ordinary co-makers are jointly and severally liable. A joint and several promisor is entitled to contribution from the others upon paying more than his proportionate share. Thus, if Mary and Fred were ordinary co-makers, not principal and surety, one who pays the entire amount is entitled to $500 in contribution from the other. Joint and several liability and its relationship to suretyship is discussed in Chapter 33.
[10]UCC §3–205(d).

| **Figure 25.4** | **Accommodation Indorser** |

Front of Note

June 1, 2006

I promise to pay to the order of
Rod Morris, one year from date $1,000.

Mary Greeley

Back of Note

Fred Greeley

Occasionally, a party will sign an instrument, usually as an indorser of a note, adding the words "collection guaranteed." Under §3–419(d), this language creates an obligation more limited than that assumed by an ordinary accommodation party. Specifically, the words **collection guaranteed** added to a signature mean that if the instrument is not paid when due, the signer will pay it but only if (1) the holder has reduced her claim against the maker or acceptor to judgment, and that execution on the judgment has been returned unsatisfied, or (2) the maker or acceptor is insolvent or cannot be served with process, or (3) it is otherwise apparent that it is useless to proceed against her. In sum, the guarantor of collection is liable only after the holder exhausts all legal remedies against the primary party.

Effect of Instrument on Underlying Obligation

Whether negotiable instruments liability is primary or secondary, subsequent events, usually proper payment of the instrument, discharge it. Other circumstances, discussed throughout this and the next chapter, that extinguish a party's liability include, for example, fraudulent and material alteration, certifica-

tion of a check, acceptance varying a draft, and unexcused delay in presentment or notice of dishonor. An additional discharge issue, relevant in lawsuits regarding negotiable instruments, concerns the effect of an instrument on the obligation for which it is given. Notes and checks are given, for example, in exchange for loans of money or sales of goods or services. The effect of the negotiable contract (the note or check) on the "underlying contract" (for example, the sale of goods or services) must therefore be carefully noted.

Under §3–310(b), a note or uncertified check is treated as **conditional payment.** This means that the payee-seller, by taking the instrument, surrenders the right to sue on the underlying obligation until the instrument is due. If the instrument is not paid when due, the right to sue on the underlying obligation is "revived," and the payee is given the option to sue either on the instrument (with the relaxed procedural requirements applicable to negotiable instruments) or on the underlying obligation. The payee prior to dishonor may sell and negotiate the note or check to a new holder. In this case, the new holder acquires the right to sue the drawer or maker on the instrument, and the payee's right to sue on the underlying obligation is extinguished. That right is represented by the instrument which is now owned by the new holder. Thus, if the payee sells the instrument to a holder and does not reacquire it after dishonor, the only surviving right is the new holder's right to enforce the instrument.[11]

The conditional payment rule does not apply if a certified check is used. As noted earlier in this chapter, the drawer is discharged on the instrument upon certification. Thus, under §3–310(a), upon certification of the check the original obligation is treated as paid and the holder's only recourse is against the bank, not the drawer. The same rule applies if a cashier's check or teller's check is taken for an obligation. To illustrate, suppose Dick draws a $1,000 check on First Bank payable to Art to pay for a car sold by Art to Dick. Art takes the check to First Bank, which certifies it. Dick is discharged on the instrument and upon the underlying obligation to pay for the car. Thus, if Art is subsequently unable to collect from the bank—for example, due to bank failure—Art has no recourse against Dick.

---

[11]UCC §3–310(b) and Official Comment 3.

Summary

1. Negotiable instruments under Article 3 are formal contracts requiring a payment of money. Contract liability is imposed when a person signs the instrument as (1) the maker of a note, (2) the drawer of a check or other draft, (3) the acceptor of a check or other draft, or (4) an indorser of any instrument. Any signature in an ambiguous capacity is an indorsement.

2. Contract liability on negotiable instruments is of two general types: primary and secondary. Primary liability is undertaken by the maker of a note and the acceptor of a draft. These parties undertake an absolute obligation to pay the instrument. The maker of a note promises to pay the instrument according to its terms when signed. The drawee of a draft assumes primary liability upon it by acceptance, making the drawee an acceptor. Prior to acceptance no one has primary liability on a draft. Because a check is a demand instrument, it is generally presented to the drawee bank only once—for payment. The bank may, however, accept the check, thereby undertaking an absolute obligation to pay. Such an acceptance is known as "certification."

3. Secondary contract liability is undertaken by the drawer of a check or other draft and the indorser of any instrument. These secondary parties agree to pay the instrument if the primary party does not, provided certain "conditions precedent" to that liability are met. The conditions precedent are presentment of the instrument to the primary party, dishonor of the instrument by that party, and notice of dishonor to the secondary parties. Secondary parties often waive compliance with the conditions precedent. Even without express waiver the specific conditions precedent may differ depending on the type of instrument or presence of special circumstances.

4. Occasionally, a person signs an instrument in order to lend his name or credit to another party to the instrument. Such an "accommodation party" is liable in the capacity in which he signs (for example, as a maker, acceptor, drawer, or indorser), but under general suretyship principles is not liable to the party accommodated. Thus, an accommodation party who is required to pay is entitled to reimbursement from the party accommodated.

5. A check or other negotiable instrument ordinarily operates as a conditional payment. This means that the payee, by taking the instrument, surrenders the right to sue on the underlying obligation until the instrument is due. If not paid when due, the holder may sue either on the instrument or on the underlying debt.

Key Terms

primary liability
secondary liability

acceptance
acceptor

demand draft
time draft
sight draft
certification
conditions precedent
presentment
dishonor
notice of dishonor

midnight deadline
protest
accommodation party
irregular (anomalous) indorsement
collection guaranteed
conditional payment

Questions and Problems

25.1 A signature on an instrument in an ambiguous capacity is always treated as an indorsement. What is the purpose of this rule?

25.2 Simpson Co. recently hired efficiency experts to help increase company profits. The experts discovered that Simpson was holding several overdue promissory notes. Management reported that it had never tried to collect the notes and had not even asked the makers for payment. One of the notes read:

> January 1, 2004
>
> I hereby promise to pay $50,000 to the order of Simpson Co. on December 1, 2004, with interest at 4% per annum.
>
> s/Peter Potts
> s/Willie Wilson

The efficiency experts are able to locate Willie Wilson and recommend that Simpson sue him.
   (a) Who is the maker of the note? In what capacity has Willie Wilson signed?
   (b) Willie argues that he is an indorser of the note but Simpson argues that he is a maker. What difference would it make whether Willie signed as maker or indorser?

25.3 Mr. Carl's Fashion, Inc. was a Texas corporation that operated beauty salons. Carl Nichols was the president of Mr. Carl's Fashion, Inc. Seale Enterprises loaned $10,000 for improvements to one of the beauty salons in return for a promissory note that was signed as follows:

   Carl V. Nichols (typewritten)
   s/Carl V. Nichols (handwritten)

No payments were made on the note so Seale sued Carl Nichols.
   (a) Carl alleges that he signed the note in his representative capacity as president of Mr. Carl's Fashion, Inc. so that he should not be held personally liable. How should the court rule? Explain, citing appropriate Code sections.
   (b) The court evidence establishes that Carl and the president of Seale Enterprises discussed the transaction and both believed that Carl was signing in his representative capacity

as president of Mr. Carl's Fashion, Inc. How should the court rule? Explain, citing appropriate Code sections.

(c) Assume instead that Seale transferred the note to First State Bank, a holder in due course, who sues Carl on the note. The evidence in (b) above was established but First State Bank proves that it was not aware that Carl had signed in his representative capacity. What result? Explain.

25.4   Norton and Keller sold $800 worth of farm equipment to Miles Knapp. Miles orally promised to pay the $800. Because Norton and Keller owed $800 to Exchange Bank, it prepared the following sight draft:

> $800   April 18, 2002
> At sight pay to the order of Exchange Bank $800, value received
> and charge to the account of Norton and Keller.
>
>   s/Norton and Keller
>
> To: Miles Knapp

Exchange Bank presented the draft to Miles Knapp who wrote on the back:

> Kiss my foot.
> s/Miles Knapp

When Miles Knapp refused to pay the draft, Norton and Keller sued him. Knapp argued that he could not be held liable on the instrument because he had not contracted to pay anything. Norton and Keller argued that by signing the back of the draft, Knapp had accepted it, thus assuming primary contract liability on the instrument. What result? Explain.

25.5   E. J. V. Drywall Co., Inc. (Drywall) issued a promissory note payable to the order of plaintiff Community National Bank in the amount of $9,082.50. A bank officer required Edward J. Varrichione, Drywall's president, to sign the back of the note under the words "Assenting to Terms and Waivers on the Face of this Note." After Drywall defaulted on the note, Community National Bank sued Varrichione alleging that he was an indorser on the note. Varrichione alleged that he had not signed as an indorser but as an accommodation to the bank merely indicating his assent to the terms of the note. Varrichione received none of the proceeds of the note, which were used solely by Drywall.

(a) In what capacity, if any, is Varrichione liable on the instrument? Explain.

(b) Assuming Varrichione is liable, what defenses might he assert?

25.6   Aloysius borrowed $20,000 from and executed a promissory note payable to Second National Bank. Bartholomew and Chauncey agreed to serve as accommodation indorsers. Bartholomew first signed his name to the back of the note, and Chauncey signed immediately thereafter. Aloysius defaulted on the note and Second National Bank sued Bartholomew and Chauncey. Bartholomew argued that the indorsers were jointly and severally liable while Chauncey argued that the indorsers were liable in the order in which they signed. Who is correct? Explain.

25.7   Joe Rad, who owns the Huntington Hotel, was looking for a partner to help operate the hotel. After Nick Tweet expressed an interest in the business, Rad and Tweet made an agreement by which Rad granted Tweet an option to purchase a 25 percent ownership interest. If Tweet failed to exercise the option, Rad agreed to pay Tweet a commission of $10,000 if Tweet secured a buyer willing and able to purchase a 25 percent interest in the hotel. Tweet was unable to raise enough money to exercise the option but he continued to try to find financing or to find a buyer to purchase the 25 percent interest. Because of cash flow problems, immediate funds were needed to keep the Huntington Hotel operating. Charleston Bank agreed to make a short term loan of $80,000 and prepared a promissory note with two signature lines. Joe Rad signed on one line; Nick Tweet signed on the other. Several weeks later, Tweet was discussing the note with his wife and Tweet stated, "I'm not too worried about that note. After all, I am only an accommodation maker and Rad has plenty of money to pay the note." After examining the note, however, his wife suggested that perhaps Tweet was a primary maker.

(a) What facts would be relevant in determining whether Tweet was an accommodation or primary maker?

(b) Assume that Charleston Bank demanded that Tweet repay the note when it was due. Would it be important to determine whether Tweet was an accommodation or primary maker?

(c) Assume instead that Rad paid the note when due and then sued Tweet to recover $40,000. Why would determination of Tweet's status as either an accommodation or primary maker be relevant?

LIABILITY OF PARTIES—FORGERY AND ALTERATION

To this point, the discussion of liability of parties has focused on contract liability. This liability, based on a party's signature, determines the responsibility for ultimate payment of the instrument and the relationship among the various parties liable. The material in this chapter addresses a significant problem in negotiable instruments analysis: the effects of forged or otherwise unauthorized signatures and of alteration of an instrument. In most cases, the party responsible for the forgery or alteration has disappeared, is insolvent, or is in jail, or otherwise cannot be held accountable for such actions. The law is therefore primarily concerned with resolving disputes among the various innocent parties affected by the wrongdoer's conduct.

Basic Concepts of Forgery and Alteration

To understand Article 3's approach to the forgery and alteration problem, one must be familiar with three concepts: (1) the definition and effect of an unauthorized signature, (2) the definition and effect of an alteration, and (3) the content and effect of the presentment and transfer "warranties."

Unauthorized Signatures

Effect of Unauthorized Signature. Signatures determine the contract liability of all parties to the instrument and also are often essential to transfer (negotiate) the instruments. Unfortunately, forged or otherwise unauthorized signatures are commonplace in negotiable instruments transactions, requiring the law to address specifically the effect of the "unauthorized" signature.

As discussed in Chapter 24, an "unauthorized signature" includes both an outright forgery and a signature affixed by an agent exceeding her authority. Any unauthorized signature is legally effective as the signature of the unauthorized signer in favor of any person who in good faith pays the instrument or takes it for value. It is wholly ineffective as the signature of the person whose name is signed. Suppose Faye forges Mary's signature as maker of a note payable to Paul. Mary has no liability on the instrument; Faye is liable on it as a maker.

Forged Drawer's or Maker's Signature and Forged Indorsement. It is important to distinguish between the legal effect of a forged drawer's or maker's signature

459

(illustrated above) and a forged indorsement. When a drawer's or maker's signature is forged, a valid negotiable instrument is created. The unauthorized signer, however, not the person whose name is signed, is the maker or drawer of the instrument. It therefore follows that the payee and subsequent transferees may be holders of the instrument, and if they qualify, holders in due course.

A forged indorsement, however, presents an entirely different situation. To illustrate, assume Dan draws a check payable to the order of Jean. The check is stolen by Sue who forges Jean's indorsement on the back and delivers the instrument to Cal who cashes it without knowledge of the forgery. Sue's signature in Jean's name is wholly inoperative as Jean's signature, but is wholly effective as Sue's signature. The instrument is, however, payable to Jean's order, requiring Jean's, not Sue's, signature (indorsement) for further negotiation. Thus, Sue's signature in Jean's name is ineffective to negotiate the instrument, and neither Cal nor any subsequent transferee from or after Cal becomes a holder of the instrument. Because there can be no holders after forgery of Jean's signature, there also can be no holders in due course.

In sum, although there may be holders and holders in due course of an instrument on which the *drawer's* or *maker's* signature is forged, there can be no holder or holder in due course after forgery of any *indorsement* necessary to negotiate the instrument. The liability of parties in both forgery situations is discussed later in this chapter.

Effect of Alteration

As noted in Chapter 24, under §3–407(a) an instrument is altered when the holder makes an unauthorized change in the instrument that purports to modify the contract of any party to the instrument in any respect. Alterations may change the number or relation of the parties, or add to or remove any part of the original signed writing. Examples include changing the name of the payee or the date or place the instrument is payable and, most often, raising the amount payable. Under §3–407(b), a fraudulent alteration by the holder of an instrument generally discharges any party whose contract is thereby changed. If, however, an altered instrument is negotiated to a holder in due course, the holder in due course may always enforce the instrument according to its original terms. Assume that June issues

a $100 note payable to Sam's order. Sam alters the instrument by raising the amount to $1,000 and negotiates it to Harold. If Harold is not a holder in due course, June is completely discharged on the instrument; that is, June has no liability either to Sam or Harold. If Harold is a holder in due course, June is liable to him for the original amount of the instrument, $100.[1]

Warranties on Presentment and Transfer

In addition to secondary *contract* liability, various holders of a negotiable instrument have *warranty* liability on the instrument. Whereas contract liability is based upon a party's signature, warranty liability is imposed (1) upon *presentment* of the instrument to the primary party for payment or acceptance, and (2) upon any *transfer* of the instrument for consideration. These warranties stated in UCC sections 3–416, 3–417, 4–207, and 4–208 are made (1) without regard to the holder's intent, (2) by banks transferring or presenting instruments in the bank collection process and holders who transfer or present an instrument outside that process, and (3) whether the holder transfers the instrument by indorsement and transfer of possession, or by transfer of possession alone. Thus, transferors of bearer paper without indorsement incur warranty liability, even though they have no contract liability.

Presentment Warranties. **Presentment warranties** are given *to* the party who is to pay or accept the instrument (including the maker of a note or the drawee or acceptor of a draft) *by* (1) any person presenting the instrument for payment or acceptance, and (2) any prior transferor of the instrument. Assume Molly issues a check payable to Joanne's order. Joanne indorses in blank and transfers the instrument to Walt, who transfers it to Sonia, who transfers it to Ken, who transfers it to Bill. Bill presents the instrument to the drawee bank for payment. Bill, Ken, Sonia, Walt, and Joanne all make presentment warranties to the bank.

The content of the presentment warranty differs depending upon the type of instrument involved. If the instrument is an uncertified check or other unaccepted

---

[1] An alteration made by a person not a holder (a spoliation) or a nonfraudulent alteration does not discharge any party to the instrument. In such cases a later holder, whether or not a holder in due course, may enforce the instrument according to its original terms. UCC §3–407(b).

draft, the following three warranties are given to the drawee:

1. that the warrantor has good title to the instrument, meaning that no indorsements on the instrument are forged or missing;
2. that the warrantor has *no knowledge* that the drawer's signature is forged or otherwise unauthorized; and
3. that the instrument has not been altered.

For all other types of instruments (for example, notes, dishonored drafts presented to the drawer or an indorser, and accepted drafts), only the first presentment warranty, that of good title, is given.

Transfer Warranties. Unlike the presentment warranties, which run to the primary party on the instrument, **transfer warranties** run *to* the various holders or other transferees of the instrument and are given *by* any person who transfers an instrument for consideration. Such a transferor warrants that

1. he or she has good title to the instrument, and
2. all signatures are genuine or authorized, and
3. the instrument has not been altered, and
4. no defense of any party is good against the transferor, and
5. he or she has no knowledge of any insolvency proceeding (for example, bankruptcy) pending against the maker or acceptor or the drawer of an unaccepted draft.

If the transfer is by indorsement, these warranties run from the transferor to all later holders of the instrument. If the transfer is made by transfer of possession alone — for example, when the instrument is in bearer form — the warranties run only to the immediate transferee. Therefore, even though a transferor of bearer paper has no contract liability, because his signature does not appear on the instrument, he does have warranty liability. This liability extends, however, only to an immediate transferee, not to all later holders of the instrument. For example, assume Marge issues a note payable to Pam's order. Pam indorses the note specially to Quincy, who indorses specially to Robert. Robert indorses the instrument in blank and transfers it to Sally, who transfers it to Ted, who transfers it to Una, who presents the

Figure 26.1   Transfer Warranty

Back of Instrument

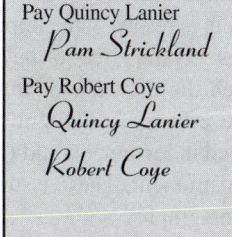

Pay Quincy Lanier
Pam Strickland
Pay Robert Coye
Quincy Lanier
Robert Coye

Robert then transfers it to Sally who transfers it to Ted who transfers it to Una who presents the note to Marge

note to Marge. These transactions are summarized in Figure 26.1.

In this situation, because Pam, Quincy, and Robert transferred by indorsement, their transfer warranties run to every subsequent holder of the instrument; Pam's run to Quincy, Robert, Sally, Ted, and Una; Quincy's run to Robert, Sally, Ted, and Una; and Robert's run to Sally, Ted, and Una. The warranties of the later holders, because transfer occurred by transfer of possession alone, run only to immediate transferees. Thus, Sally's warranties run only to Ted, and Ted's run only to Una. Thus, the final holder, Una, has the benefit of warranties running from Ted, Robert, Quincy, and Pam. Of course, Una is entitled to only one recovery, and assuming the warranties are breached (for example, Marge's signature is a forgery), the warrantors are liable in the order in which they transferred. For example, if Una recovered from Ted, Ted might proceed against Sally, who could proceed against Robert, who could recover from Quincy, who could recover from Pam.

If an indorser signs "without recourse," a qualified indorsement, all transfer warranties remain the same. Therefore, even though a "without recourse" indorsement negates secondary contract liability, it does not affect the indorser's transfer warranties.

The transferor does not warrant that the primary party is solvent. The buyer is required to determine the financial condition of the party to pay before taking the instrument. Nevertheless, a transferor who knows, but fails to disclose, that insolvency proceedings have been instituted against the party to pay, commits a fraud upon the buyer. The fifth transfer warranty accordingly protects the purchaser against such a knowing concealment.

Forgery and Alteration—Specific Problems

The principles governing unauthorized signature, alteration, and warranty liability help to resolve three important negotiable instruments issues: (1) the effect of payment of an instrument upon which the drawer's or maker's signature is forged, (2) the effect of payment of an instrument containing a forged indorsement, and (3) the effect of paying an altered instrument. These issues are discussed in the following paragraphs.

Effect of Payment on Forged Drawer's or Maker's Signature

The Rule of Price v. Neal. The legal effect of paying an instrument on which a drawer's or maker's signature is forged has confounded negotiable instruments students since 1762, when the classic English case, *Price v. Neal,*[2] was decided. Under the rule adopted in *Price v. Neal,* a drawee who pays or accepts an instrument for an innocent holder upon which the drawer's signature is forged is bound by the acceptance and cannot recover back the payment. The same rule applies if a maker pays a note upon which his or her signature is forged. The UCC codifies *Price v. Neal* in §3–418, which provides that a drawee that pays or accepts a draft on the mistaken belief that the drawer's signature is authorized may, under restitution principles, recover the payment from the person to whom it was made, or revoke an acceptance. This right of restitution may not, however, be asserted against a "person who took the instrument in good faith and for value or who in good faith changed position in reliance on the payment or acceptance."[3]

To illustrate the operation of the rule, assume that Thomas steals Dwyer's checkbook and forges Dwyer's name to a check made payable to Peters. Peters negotiates the instrument to Holt, a holder in due course.[4] Holt presents the instrument to First State Bank, the drawee. First State pays the instrument. On these facts, First State may not charge Dwyer's account for the amount of the check. It has not paid according to Dwyer's order, which is the basic contract between

Dwyer and the bank. That is, §4–401(a) permits a bank to charge its checking account customer's account only for checks that are "properly payable." A check bearing a forged drawer's signature is not properly payable. Further, under *Price v. Neal* as codified in UCC §3–418, the bank may not recover the amount it paid from Holt. Note that Holt does not breach her presentment warranty to the bank, because a presenting holder does not absolutely warrant the validity of the drawer's signature to the drawee. The holder merely warrants that she has *no knowledge* that the drawer's signature is forged. Therefore, the bank bears the loss unless it can find and recover from the forger, Thomas, (an unlikely prospect) or from a prior holder who obtained payment with knowledge of the forgery. For example, assume Peters knew of Thomas's forgery when he sold the instrument to Holt. In this case, Peters breaches his presentment warranty to First State that he had no knowledge that the signature of the drawer was unauthorized.

If the bank discovers the forgery, it is, of course, not required to pay the check. The bank may return the instrument to the holder who is then required to proceed against prior transferors for breach of the transfer warranties. Thus, in the preceding example, assume Holt presents the instrument to First State Bank, which discovers the forgery and refuses to pay. The bank returns the check to Holt, who is required to proceed against Peters for breach of Peters's transfer warranty that all signatures are genuine or authorized. Peters is then faced with the unenviable task of finding and recovering from Thomas.

Effect of Negligence. As noted in Chapter 24, a person whose negligence substantially contributes to a forgery may not assert the forgery as a defense against a holder in due course. Section §3–406 also prevents the negligence party from asserting the unauthorized signature against a drawee or other payor who pays the instrument in good faith. Thus, although a drawee bank that pays an instrument bearing a forged drawer's signature may not generally charge the drawer's account, it may do so if the drawer's negligence substantially contributed to the forgery. Such negligence may occur, for example, if the drawer uses a stamp or other automatic signature device and fails to adequately safeguard it. Note, however, that if the drawee bank or other payor *also* was negligent and that negligence also substantially contributed to the forgery, then the loss is allocated between the parties by

---

[2]3 Burr. 1354, 97 Eng. Rep. 871 (K.B. 1762).

[3]UCC §3–418(c).

[4]Note here that Holt may be a holder and therefore a holder in due course because the check is a valid negotiable instrument with Thomas, rather than Dwyer, as drawer.

applying comparative negligence principles discussed in Chapter 5.[5]

Effect of "Double Forgery." Check forgery schemes often involve the so-called double forgery. In this case the wrongdoer forges both the drawer's and the payee's signature. The payee is usually fictitious, but even if not, the forger intends the payee to have no interest in the instrument. In these cases, the bank paying the instrument attempts to characterize the case as one involving a forged indorsement (in which it can shift the loss to prior parties for breach of warranty of title under principles discussed below) rather than one involving a forged drawer's signature (in which it is bound by its payment under *Price v. Neal*). Courts considering this argument have generally held that the double forgery situation is treated as a forged drawer's signature case, leaving the loss on the drawee bank paying the check. The rationale for this result is that because the payee is not entitled to payment in any event, the drawee bank could never be required to pay the instrument twice. The bank's loss is not caused by paying the wrong person because of a forged indorsement. It results from paying the instrument at all because of the forged drawer's signature.[6]

Effect of Payment on a Forged Indorsement

The legal principles applied to forgery of an indorsement differ substantially from those governing forgery of the drawer's or maker's signature. This difference stems from the fact that there can be no holder or holder in due course of any instrument bearing a forgery of any indorsement *necessary to negotiate the instrument*. Further, any person who pays a note or draft bearing a forged necessary indorsement *converts* it,[7] meaning that any person paying is liable to the person whose name is forged for the face amount of the instrument.[8] Note

that in applying these rules, the law treats a *missing* necessary indorsement as the equivalent of a forged indorsement.

To illustrate the legal effect of payment on a forged indorsement, assume Diane draws a check on First Bank payable to Pam's order. The check is subsequently stolen by Tod who forges Pam's indorsement and cashes the check at Joe's Currency Exchange. Joe's presents the check to First Bank, which pays it. On these facts, note that although Tod's signature in Pam's name is effective as Tod's signature, it is wholly ineffective as Pam's signature. Because the check is an order instrument (payable to the order of Pam), Pam's signature is necessary to further negotiate it. Her signature, however, does not appear on the instrument. It therefore follows that no one possessing the check after Pam (Tod and Joe's) becomes a holder.

Because a forged indorsement is wholly inoperative and ineffective to negotiate the instrument, a check bearing a forged indorsement is not properly payable. That is, the drawee bank may apply funds from the drawer's account to paying an order instrument only upon receiving the payee's or special indorsee's authorized indorsement. Accordingly, as when the drawer's signature is forged, a drawee bank that pays an instrument bearing a forged indorsement may not charge its customer's account. Thus, in this case, First Bank may not charge Diane's account for the amount of the check.

In addition, Joe's and First Bank, who paid the instrument on a forged indorsement, are both liable in conversion to Pam. Joe's, however, is liable to First Bank for breach of the presentment warranty that it had good title to the instrument. That is, Joe's is not a holder and therefore has no title. In short, unlike the forged drawer's signature case in which the bank is bound by its payment, a bank that pays on a forged indorsement, though it may not charge its customer's account, may recover from prior transferors for breach of the presentment warranties. Therefore, the ultimate loss (assuming the forger cannot be found) falls upon the person who received the instrument from the forger, in this case, Joe's.[9] Note here that assuming Pam recovers from Joe's, First Bank may then charge the drawer's, Diane's, account for the amount of the check. The check has now

---

[5]UCC §3–406(b).

[6]O'Malley, *The Code and Double Forgeries,* 19 Syracuse L. Rev. 36, 43–44 (1967); Perini Corporation v. First National Bank of Habersham County, 553 F.2d 398, 414–416 (5th Cir. 1977).

[7]UCC §3–420(a). "Conversion" is a tort defined as "an intentional exercise of dominion or control over a chattel which so seriously interferes with the right or another to control it that the actor may justly be required to pay the other the full value of the chattel." Restatement (Second) of Torts §222A. See discussion of conversion in Chapter 5.

[8]UCC §3–420(b).

---

[9]If, after the forgery, the instrument is transferred several times before presentment, the same result follows. The person dealing with the forger is liable to the drawee for breach of the *presentment* warranty of title and to later transferees for breach of the *transfer* warranty of title.

been paid according to Diane's order; the intended payee, Pam, has been paid by Joe's.

The following case applies the principles governing forged indorsements.

The First National Bank of Chicago v. MidAmerica Federal Savings Bank
707 N.E.2d 673 (Ill. App. 1999)

Plaintiff The First National Bank of Chicago (First Chicago) sent a notice to the home address of its customer Muhamad Mustafa notifying him that his certificate of deposit was about to mature. The notice included a form allowing the customer to renew or redeem the certificate. First Chicago received a copy of the form, apparently signed by Muhamad Mustafa, with instructions to close the certificate. First Chicago issued a cashier's check payable to Muhamad Mustafa and mailed it to his home address. Muhamad Mustafa's nephew, Michael Mustafa, forged his uncle's signature on the check and deposited it in his account at defendant MidAmerica Federal Savings Bank (MidAmerica). About two months later, following an extended trip out of the country, Muhamad Mustafa notified First Chicago that he wanted to redeem his certificate of deposit. After discovering the forged indorsement on the original check, First Chicago issued a new check to Muhamad Mustafa and sued MidAmerica alleging that it had breached the presentment warranty. The trial court granted judgment in favor of First Chicago and MidAmerica appealed.

Quinn, Justice

. . . MidAmerica argues that the trial court erred in granting summary judgment in favor of First Chicago because First Chicago has not demonstrated that MidAmerica breached any presentment warranties. First Chicago responds that it clearly established a *prima facie* case of breach of warranty under [§3–417] . . . of the UCC. . . .

Under [§3–417(a)], a bank that accepts and pays a check with an unauthorized or forged indorsement warrants to subsequent transferees the validity of that indorsement and may be held liable on that warranty. . . . The purpose of the warranty is to place on the bank taking an instrument from a person making an unauthorized indorsement the responsibility of collecting from that person. As explained in *Federal Deposit Insurance Corp. v. Marine National Bank*, 303 F. Supp.

401, 403 (M.D. Fla. 1969), the reason for imposing the warranty is to:

> speed up the collection and transfer of checks and to take the burden off each bank to meticulously check the indorsements of each item transferred. Following that logic, the first bank taking in the item for collection is primarily responsible for checking the indorsements to make sure that they are proper. Each bank then warrants to each subsequent bank in the collection chain that the indorsements are good. Of course, the original bank has rights over against the person originally presenting the item.

> The rationale suggested puts the burden directly upon the first bank in the collection chain to make sure that the indorsements are valid. This is reasonable because the first bank is in a better position to insure that it is taking the item from someone with good title than are subsequent banks in the chain. If the rationale is to facilitate the speedy transfer and collection of items by removing the burden on each bank to inspect and verify each indorsement, subsequent banks are not negligent if they do not thoroughly inspect each item. In other words, the warranty feature of the statute is designed to remove the duty of each bank to check the indorsements, and, therefore, [the plaintiff bank] would not be negligent to fail to so inspect.

The rule recognizes that, while none of the parties may have had reason to suspect a fraud, the one who took from the forger was the closest to the person causing the loss and is presumed to have had the best opportunity to have prevented the loss. . . .

In the instant case, the record establishes that the indorsement on the cashier's check issued to Muhamad Mustafa was unauthorized and ineffective. MidAmerica, as the first bank in the collection chain, had a responsibility to ensure that the indorsement was valid, and through acceptance and payment of the check, MidAmerica warranted that the indorsement was valid. As this indorsement was in fact, invalid, we hold that MidAmerica breached it presentment warranty to First Chicago under section 3–417(a). . . .

[Judgment affirmed.]

The forged indorsement rules outlined above provide substantial protection to a payee or later holder whose indorsement is forged and highlight a recurring problem in negotiable instruments analysis: the danger of possessing an instrument indorsed in blank or otherwise payable to bearer. Because an instrument indorsed in blank is payable to bearer, the holder of such paper runs essentially the same risk of theft or loss as the possessor of cash. Suppose that Dawson draws a check payable to Patterson's order. Patterson indorses in blank and delivers to Hart in satisfaction of a debt owed to Hart by Patterson. Timms steals the check and takes it to Carver who cashes it without knowledge of the theft. In this case, Timms becomes a holder[10] and Timms's transfer of the instrument to Carver makes Carver a holder. Because the instrument is bearer paper, transfer of possession alone is sufficient to negotiate the instrument and make Carver a holder. If Carver additionally qualifies as a holder in due course (which the facts given indicate she does), she takes the instrument free of Hart's claim that it was stolen from him. That is, she will be paid out of Dawson's account, and Hart faces the unenviable task of trying to find and collect from Timms.

On the other hand, had the instrument been specially indorsed—for example, "pay Hart, (signed) Patterson"—it would be order paper when stolen by Timms. He must therefore forge Hart's indorsement to transfer the instrument. Assuming he does so, his transferee, Carver, does not become a holder and converts the instrument against Hart. A holder of a negotiable instrument is therefore well advised never to carry around an instrument indorsed in blank. If the instrument must remain in the holder's possession prior to further negotiation it should be in order form. If payable to order when stolen, a necessary indorsement must be forged, meaning there can be no further holder of the instrument.

Recognizing the risk inherent in possessing paper indorsed in blank, §3–205(c) allows the holder to protect herself by converting a blank indorsement into a special indorsement. The holder may do this by writing above the blank indorser's signature "words identifying the person to whom the instrument is made payable." Assume, as above, that Hart is the holder of Dawson's check originally payable to Patterson and indorsed in blank. Hart may convert the paper into an order instrument simply by writing "Pay Hart" above Patterson's signature. The paper is now specially indorsed, payable to Hart's order and cannot be further negotiated without his signature.

---

[10]UCC §3–201(a) and Official Comment 1.

Impostors and Fictitious Payees

The law recognizes an exception to the rules that generally govern forged indorsements in the cases described in the following three situations.

1. Smith, who bears a remarkable likeness to Joe Doaks, impersonates Doaks and induces Michelle to issue a check made payable to Doak's order. Smith indorses Doaks's name on the check. Alternatively, Smith may falsely represent that he is Doaks, an agent for XYZ Corporation. Michelle is thereby induced to issue a check to the order of Joe Doaks or XYZ Corporation. Smith indorses Doaks's or the corporation's name on the check. In all cases, First Bank cashes the check, knowing nothing of Smith's fraud.

2. Smith, treasurer of XYZ Corporation, makes a payroll check payable to Joe Doaks, a name picked at random out of the Chicago telephone directory (or a fictitious person). Smith has prepared phony documentation showing Joe Doaks as an employee of XYZ Corporation. Every week when payroll checks are distributed, Smith removes the check payable to Joe Doaks and indorses "Joe Doaks" on the back. First Bank cashes the check unaware of Smith's fraud.

3. Smith, a dishonest bookkeeper of XYZ Corporation, prepares a check payable to Supplier Corporation, to whom XYZ Corporation owes money. Smith gives the check to the treasurer of the corporation for signature. The treasurer signs and returns the check to Smith for mailing. Smith steals the check, forges Supplier Corporation's indorsement on the back, and deposits it in an account in First Bank which Smith has opened in Supplier Corporation's name. The check is ultimately paid by the drawee bank. Alternatively, assume Smith also is responsible for processing and posting checks received from customers for goods and services provided by the corporation. Smith takes a check made payable to the corporation, forges the corporation's indorsement, and deposits the check in an account Smith has opened in XYZ Corporation's name at First Bank. The check is ultimately honored by the drawee bank.

Sections 3–404 and 3–405 adopt a single rule to resolve the situations outlined above. Collectively, they provide that in these cases an indorsement by any person in the name of the named payee is effective as the payee's indorsement in favor of a person who, in good faith, pays the instrument or takes it for value or collection. Specifically, the rule applies:

1. If an imposter, by use of the mail or otherwise, induces the drawer or maker to issue the instrument to the imposter (or to a person acting in concert with the imposter), by impersonating the payee of the instrument or the payee's authorized agent (case 1).[11]

2. If a person whose intent determines the payee of the instrument intends that the named payee shall have no interest in the instrument, or if the named payee is a fictitious person (case 2).[12]

3. If an employee entrusted with responsibility for the instrument (or a person acting in concert with such an employee) makes a fraudulent indorsement of the instrument (case 3).[13] "Responsibility" for the instrument includes authority to sign, indorse, process, prepare, supply information for, or control disposition of, instruments received or issued by the employer. "Fraudulent indorsements" include forgeries of the employer's indorsement on checks issued to the employer, and of the payee's indorsement on checks issued by the employer.[14]

In these situations, an indorsement *by any person* in the name of the named payee is effective to negotiate the instrument. Thus, in the preceding examples, the indorsements affixed by Smith in the payees' names are not treated as forgeries. Therefore, in all cases, the person to whom Doaks transfers the instrument becomes a holder of the instrument and has not paid an instrument bearing a forged indorsement. This rule applies both when the payee actually exists, and when the payee is fictitious or nonexistent. The essence of the test applied in all cases is whether the person indorsing *intends that the payee shall have no interest in the instrument.*[15]

Assuming the dishonest party cannot be found or held accountable, this rule places the loss upon the drawer or maker of the instrument rather than upon an

innocent later holder or drawee who purchases or cashes it. The rationale for this result is that the loss should fall upon the party originally in the best position to protect itself. That party is clearly the maker or drawer of the instrument who is responsible for the defective instrument's appearance in the stream of commerce. That is, the drawer's or maker's failure to obtain adequate identification from the payee or to maintain adequate accounting controls enabled the fraud to occur. In addition, losses caused by dishonest employees can be insured against, and the cost of such insurance should be viewed as an expense of the drawer's rather than the holder's or drawee's business. Thus in the preceding examples, First Bank would be paid on the instrument and, if the drawee, could charge the drawer's account. The drawers, Michelle and XYZ Corporation, would bear the loss unless they could recover from the wrongdoer, Smith. If Smith's indorsements in the payee's names had been treated as forgeries, the loss would fall upon First Bank under the rules governing forged indorsements previously discussed.

Although the loss in the foregoing cases falls upon the drawer or maker of the instrument, the person who dealt with the wrongdoer may have been negligent in taking or paying the instrument, and that negligence may have substantially contributed to the loss. In this case, the loss is allocated between drawer or maker and the person taking or paying the instrument according to principles of comparative negligence discussed in Chapter 5.[16]

Although any person may effectively indorse an instrument procured under the circumstances outlined above, this rule has no effect on the civil or criminal liability of the indorser.[17] For example, the fact that Smith's signatures are effective indorsements of the checks has no effect upon Smith's probable criminal liability for embezzlement, or Smith's civil liability in tort to Michelle or XYZ Corporation. Additionally, Smith's signatures in the payees' names are effective to impose secondary contract liability upon him as an indorser on the instrument.

Effect of Payment of an Altered Instrument

This section examines the effect of alteration. As in forgery cases, the party altering the instrument is usually unavailable to answer for the wrongdoing. The law

---

[11]UCC §3–404(a).

[12]UCC §3–404(b).

[13]UCC §3–405(b).

[14]UCC §3–405(a).

[15]An indorsement is made in the name of the payee if (1) it is made in a name substantially similar to the payee's name, or (2) the instrument, whether or not indorsed, is deposited in a depositary bank to an account maintained in a name substantially similar to the payee's name. UCC §§3–404(c), 3–405(c). Under §4–205(a), a depositary bank may become the holder of a check deposited to a customer's account if the customer was a holder whether or not the customer indorses. Thus, the rules outlined above apply when the wrongdoer deposits the check in an account maintained in the payee's name, whether or not the wrongdoer indorses.

[16]UCC §§3–404(d), 3–405(b).

[17]UCC §3–403(c).

is, therefore, again primarily concerned with sorting out the rights of the various innocent parties injured by the alteration.

As a general rule, §4–401(d) allows a bank that pays an altered check to charge the drawer's account according to the original terms of the instrument. For example, a drawee bank that pays a check raised from $100 to $1,000 may generally charge the drawer's account for $100. In some alteration cases, however, the bank may not charge the account. For example, if the name of the payee is changed, the instrument bears a forged indorsement, and the rules discussed above apply. In any event, the drawee bank or other person paying an altered instrument may recover from prior parties for breach of the presentment warranty that the instrument has not been materially altered. Prior parties in turn may recover in the order of transfer for breach of the *transfer* warranty of no material alteration. Thus, as in the forged indorsement case, the ultimate loss usually falls upon the person who takes the instrument from the wrongdoer.

To illustrate, assume that Delbert draws a $100 check on Second Bank payable to Pauline's order. Pauline raises the check to $1,000 and cashes it at Joe's Currency Exchange, which deposits the check in its account in First Bank. First Bank ultimately presents the check to the drawee, Second Bank, which pays it. Pauline, of course, cannot be found when the alteration is discovered. In this case, Second Bank, the drawee, may charge Delbert's account for $100, the original amount of the instrument. Pauline, Joe's, and First Bank are all liable to Second Bank for $900 for breach of the *presentment* warranty against material alteration. Further, Pauline is liable to Joe's, who is liable to First Bank for breach of the *transfer* warranty against material alteration. Therefore, if Second Bank collects from First Bank, First Bank could collect from Joe's, who bears the task of collecting from Pauline.

As in the unauthorized signature case, §3–406 provides that a drawer whose negligence substantially contributes to an alteration of his instrument may not assert the alteration as a defense against a later holder in due course or a drawee or other person paying the instrument in good faith. Therefore, in the preceding example, if Delbert's carelessness in drafting the check—for example, by writing it in pencil or by leaving spaces where words or numbers could be inserted—provided the opportunity for Pauline to alter it, Delbert could not assert the alteration against later parties to the instrument. That is, Second Bank could charge Delbert's account for the full $1,000 and Delbert would be required to attempt to find and collect from Pauline.

Summary

1. The law often must resolve disputes involving forged or otherwise unauthorized signatures and alteration of a negotiable instrument. These problems generally are resolved through application of three fundamental concepts including (1) the legal effect of an unauthorized signature, (2) the legal effect of an alteration, and (3) the content and effect of the presentment and transfer warranties.

2. An unauthorized signature, which includes a forgery, is wholly ineffective as that of the person whose name is signed, but operates as the signature of the unauthorized signer. For this reason the forgery of a drawer's or maker's signature creates a valid negotiable instrument (with the unauthorized signer liable as drawer or maker). On the other hand, forgery of a necessary indorsement is ineffective to negotiate the instrument, meaning that no later transferee becomes a holder.

3. An instrument is altered when the holder makes an unauthorized change in the instrument that purports to modify the contract of any party to the instrument in any respect. Although a fraudulent alteration ordinarily discharges any party whose contract is thereby changed, a subsequent holder in due course may always enforce the instrument according to its original terms.

4. The UCC imposes liability for forgery and alteration generally through use of the presentment and transfer warranties. Presentment warranties are given by the party presenting an instrument for payment or acceptance and any prior transferor to the maker of a note or the drawee-acceptor of a draft. If the instrument is an uncertified check or other unaccepted draft, each person making a presentment warranty warrants that (1) he has good title to the instrument, (2) he has no knowledge that the signature of the maker or drawer is unauthorized, and (3) the instrument has not been materially altered. For all other types of instruments, only the first presentment warranty, that of good title, is given.

5. Transfer warranties are given by any person who transfers an instrument for consideration to later holders. Such a transferor warrants that (1) she has good title to the instrument, (2) all signatures are genuine or authorized, (3) the instrument has not been altered, (4) no defense of any party is good against her, and (5) she has no knowledge of any

insolvency proceeding pending against the party to pay the instrument.

6.   Application of the foregoing principles resolves common problems including the effect of payment of an instrument (1) upon which the drawer's or maker's signature is forged, (2) upon which a necessary indorsement is forged or missing, and (3) which has been altered. If the drawee or maker pays an instrument to a holder in due course upon which the drawer's or maker's signature is forged, the payment cannot be recovered from the holder paid, and the drawee or maker ordinarily bears the loss (assuming the wrongdoer cannot be found). If the drawee or maker discovers the forgery and refuses to pay, the loss usually falls upon the person who dealt with the forger.

7.   If an instrument is paid upon which a necessary indorsement is forged, any person paying does not become a holder of the instrument and converts it against the person whose name is forged. In these cases the loss ultimately falls upon the person dealing with the forger. An exception to this result is the "impostor" and "fictitious payee" case in which the loss falls not on the holder dealing with the wrongdoer but upon the drawer or maker of the instrument.

8.   General principles similar to those governing forged indorsements apply to alteration. That is, the loss generally falls upon the person who takes the instrument from the person altering it.

Key Terms

presentment warranties
transfer warranties

Questions and Problems

26.1   Greer stole an automobile that was the property of Brown. Brown's title to the automobile and other identification papers were in the automobile. Greer represented himself as Brown and sold the automobile to Alm Auto Co., which paid Greer with a check payable to the order of Brown. Greer indorsed the check with Brown's name and sold it to Clancy.
   (a) Is Greer's indorsement in Brown's name effective?
   (b) Does Clancy become a holder of the instrument?
   (c) Assuming Greer cannot be found, who will bear the ultimate loss on the instrument?
   (d) Does Greer's signature in Brown's name effectively bind Greer personally on the instrument as an indorser to Clancy? Explain.

26.2   Zack stole Sid's checkbook and forged Sid's signature to a check made payable to Terry. Terry indorsed the check to Hugh, a holder in due course. Hugh took the check to the drawee bank and the bank paid the check.
   (a) May the bank deduct the amount of the check from Sid's account? Explain.

   (b) May the bank recover the amount it paid from Hugh? Explain.

26.3   Dick drew a check on First Bank payable to the order of Paul. The check was stolen from Paul by John who forged Paul's signature and sold the check to Herb, who knew nothing of the theft. Herb then indorsed the instrument over to Mark in satisfaction of a debt owed by Herb to Mark. Mark presented the check to First Bank, and the bank paid it.
   (a) Could Mark be a holder in due course of the instrument?
   (b) Could Herb be a holder in due course of the instrument?
   (c) May the bank recover the amount of the check from Mark?
   (d) May Mark recover the amount of the check from Herb, if Mark is required to pay First Bank?
   (e) Do Herb, Mark, and the bank have any liability to Paul?
   (f) If the bank pays Paul, can it charge Dick's account?

26.4   Dykstra entered a written agreement to purchase a Cadillac purportedly owned by James and Peggy Bateman. Dykstra presented James Bateman with a personal check for $9,000 drawn upon National Bank of South Dakota payable to "James Bateman and Peggy Bateman." The bank knew that Dykstra, a customer of 20 years, had made a deal on a Cadillac because the bank had loaned Dykstra money to purchase the automobile. James Bateman appeared at bank's main office and, in the presence of bank officer James Murphy, endorsed "James Bateman and Peggy Bateman" on Dykstra's check. It was subsequently discovered that Peggy Bateman did not exist and James Bateman was not the owner of the Cadillac. Dykstra promptly informed the bank of the fraud. The true owner of the Cadillac subsequently repossessed the car. Dykstra sues the bank for wrongfully cashing the check. Should Dykstra prevail? Consider particularly the application of UCC §§3–404, 3–405 (impostor-fictitious payee rule) and 3–406 (negligence contributing to forgery or alteration).

26.5   Fred, while visiting Chicago, asked Lloyd, a local business associate, for assistance in cashing a check. Fred accompanied Lloyd to Lloyd's office, ABT, Inc., where the treasurer agreed to cash the check so long as Lloyd indorsed it. Fred handed Lloyd a check drawn on American Bank payable to Henry Sherman, Inc. The back of the check was indorsed Henry Sherman and Lloyd added his signature. The treasurer cashed the check and handed the money to Lloyd who immediately gave it to Fred. ABT deposited the check at Belmont Bank. Belmont presented the check to American, which dishonored it, because it had been notified that Sherman's indorsement was a forgery. Due to inadvertence, however, Lloyd was not notified of the dishonor until a month later. Fred has fled the country. ABT sued Lloyd to recover the amount of the check.
   (a) In what capacity is Lloyd liable on the instrument?
   (b) Does Lloyd have contract liability on the instrument to ABT? Explain.
   (c) Does Lloyd have any warranty liability on the instrument to ABT? Explain.

26.6   Levy, Inc. employed Michelle Veneto as accounts receivable supervisor. Over a period of five years, Veneto diverted 200 checks worth more than $2 million to her bank account at Fidelity Bank. Veneto diverted the funds by taking checks payable to Levy, Inc. and typing or printing the name Levy, Inc. followed by her personal account number in the endorsement space on the back of the check. She then deposited the checks to her account by delivering the checks to various Fidelity Bank branches throughout New York City. One time during the five-year period, a Fidelity Bank clerk questioned a transaction but Veneto merely took the check to a teller at another branch who accepted it for deposit. After discovering the diversions, Levy sued Fidelity alleging that the bank had paid the checks over unauthorized signatures. How should the court rule? Explain.

26.7   To assist in keeping the books of their auto repair business, Gordon and Mildred Neely hired Louise Bradshaw as a part-time bookkeeper. Although the business bank account was maintained at First Alabama Bank, the Neelys accepted Bradshaw's recommendation to open a second account for personal expenditures and corporate payroll at American National Bank. She explained that checks could be drawn on the First Alabama account to fund the second account at American National. Bradshaw also kept her personal account at American National. The Neelys signed the bank signature card authorizing them to draw checks on the account. They entrusted Bradshaw with the documents to return them to the bank. Without the knowledge or authorization of the Neelys, Bradshaw signed the signature card and added her name in a noticeably different type.

Subsequently, Bradshaw filled out checks drawn on the First Alabama account made payable to American National and with a large space to the left of the amount written on the designated lines. Mrs. Neely signed these checks being fully aware of these large gaps. Bradshaw altered the checks either by adding a digit or two to the left of the original amount, or by raising the first digit after using liquid erasure. She then deposited the original amount into Neely's American National payroll account, and depositing to her account or taking in cash the difference between the original and altered amounts.

When the bank statements were received, Bradshaw re-altered the checks using liquid erasure. Bradshaw and Mrs. Neely then reconciled the statements with Mrs. Neely calling out the information from her journal entry and with Bradshaw responding from the bank statements and items.

Consequently, Mrs. Neely never saw the altered checks or the statements. A new accountant later discovered the defalcations, which totaled over $17,000. Bradshaw has disappeared. The Neelys sued American National Bank to recover the amounts paid on the altered instruments. Who should prevail? Explain.

26.8   Nora Ray, an 80-year-old woman, gave a check to a man claiming to be Robert Freeman, an employee of the utility company. Mrs. Ray had admitted Freeman to her home when he stated he needed to check the electricity because of a power outage. After checking the outlets, Freeman told Mrs. Ray he would return but that she was required to pay a $1.50 service fee for which the utility company only accepted payment by check. Freeman wrote out the check in ink and Mrs. Ray signed it.

When Freeman failed to return, Mrs. Ray telephoned the bank to stop payment on the check because she believed that he had not earned the service fee. She then learned that Freeman had altered the check and had cashed it for $1,851.50 instead of $1.50. When Freeman had written out the check at Mrs. Ray's home, he had left enough room to allow his later alteration. The bank had cashed the check after Freeman produced two identification cards.

Nora Ray sued the bank to recover the $1,850 that it had paid on the altered check. The bank asserted that because Mrs. Ray's negligence had contributed to the alteration she should be denied recovery. What factors should the court consider in resolving the case? Who should prevail?

26.9   American Savings and Loan Association was a holder in due course of two Manville Corporation bearer notes due September 2, 2005, and payable at Morgan Guaranty Trust Company. On August 26, 2005, Manville filed a Chapter 11 bankruptcy petition. American, who was aware of the bankruptcy, did not anticipate payment on September 2. Nevertheless, Chase Manhattan, who held the notes for American, presented them on September 2 through the New York Clearing House. Although Morgan had instituted special procedures to process Manville notes and checks, it failed to dishonor the notes by the clearing house deadline. Morgan sought return of the money but American refused, arguing that Morgan's restitution claim was barred by §3–418, the UCC's codification of *Price v. Neal.* Is American correct? Explain.

CHAPTER 27

BANK DEPOSITS AND COLLECTIONS; CREDIT CARDS AND ELECTRONIC FUND TRANSFERS

Major Topics

- the operation and legal aspects of the check collection process
- the legal relationship between a bank and its checking account customer
- the law governing credit cards and electronic fund transfers

Checks are by far the most common type of negotiable instrument, used in millions of transactions every day and processed in large quantities by various banks and other financial institutions across the country. Although checks are governed by the same principles that apply to all negotiable instruments, the law provides special additional rules that govern the manner in which checks are processed through the banking system and the relationship between a bank and its checking account customers. These special principles are contained in federal statutes and administrative regulations, and in Article 4 of the UCC, "Bank Deposits and Collections."

This chapter summarizes the principles governing the check collection process and the bank-customer relationship, and then discusses modern alternatives to payment by check, such as credit cards and electronic fund transfers.

The Check Collection Process

Assume that Doaks, a Chicago retailer, owes Crenshaw, a Boston manufacturer, $1,000 for goods sold to Doaks. Doaks draws a check payable to Crenshaw upon his checking account in First State Bank of Chicago, and mails it to Crenshaw in Boston. Crenshaw then deposits the check in its account in the City Bank of Boston. Because it is not the drawee, City Bank does not pay the check. Rather, City Bank collects it from the drawee, First State. The process by which the check is transmitted and presented to the drawee, paid, and the proceeds transferred and credited to the depositor's account is known as the bank collection or **check collection process.**

UCC §§4–104 and 4–105 define a number of terms important to understanding the check collection process.[1] In the preceding example, both Doaks and Crenshaw are customers of their respective banks. A **customer** is any person having an account with a bank or for whom the bank has agreed to collect a check. City Bank is referred to as the **depositary bank,** meaning the first bank to take the check. First Bank, the drawee, is the **payor bank,** the bank by which the check is payable.

---

[1]Federal statutes and regulations governing the check collection process, discussed later in this chapter, use terminology generally corresponding to that appearing in Article 4.

Although the check may be presented directly by the depositary bank to the payor bank, it more commonly passes through one or more intermediary banks or a clearing house before reaching the payor bank. An **intermediary bank** is any bank to which a check is transferred in the course of collection other than the depositary or payor bank. Checks often pass through intermediary banks when the payor and depositary banks are in different cities or states. The Federal Reserve Banks located in major cities across the country serve as the major intermediary banks in a nationwide check collection and clearing system. If both the depositary and payor banks are located in the same city or region, a local or regional clearing house may be used to present the check. A **clearing house** is an association of banks or other payors regularly clearing checks. All banks handling checks for collection are designated **collecting banks** and the one ultimately presenting the check to the payor bank is the **presenting bank.** The process by which the various banks outlined above send checks to the payor-drawee bank for payment is known as "forward collection." Figure 27.1 illustrates the various stages of the forward check collection process.

The preceding discussion illustrates the most common check collection case, the "transit check"—a check deposited in one bank but payable by another. In some cases, the depositary bank will also be the payor bank. This occurs, for example, if both the drawer and payee maintain an account in the same bank or when the payee cashes the check at the payor bank. Such checks are referred to as "on us" checks.

The law governing bank deposits and collections focuses on two separate legal relationships. The first concerns checks *deposited* in the customer's account, and the second involves checks *drawn upon* the account. The following material, therefore, examines first the legal relationship among the customer, collecting banks, and the payor bank in the check collection process and then the relationship of the payor bank to its customer, the drawer of the check.

Legal Aspects of the Check Collection Process

A checking account deposit triggers a chain of legally significant events involving the customer (the payee or other holder of the check), the various collecting banks, and the bank upon which the check is drawn, the payor bank.

Collection, Payment, and Return of a Check

When depositing a check, the customer negotiates it to his bank for purposes of collection. If the instrument is order paper—for example, a check made payable "to

---

Figure 27.1   **The Check Collection Process**

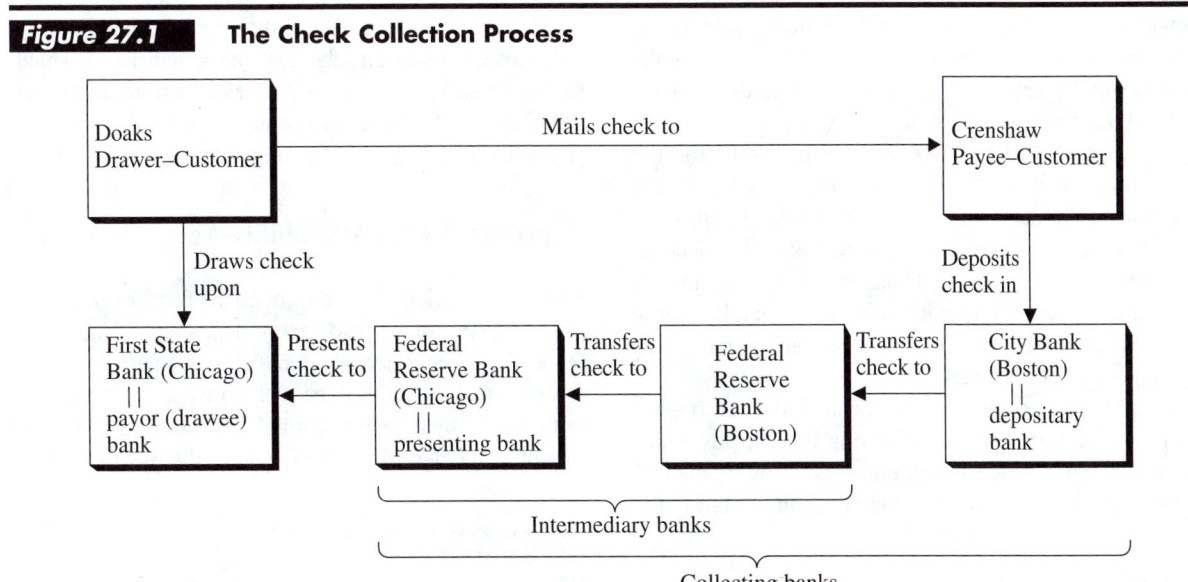

the order of Joe Doaks"—the customer must indorse the check upon deposit. This indorsement may be blank or special (payable to the bank's order), but should also contain restrictive language such as "for deposit only." As noted in Chapter 23, such a restrictive indorsement requires the depositary bank to make sure that the amount of the check gets into the depositor's account and effectively prevents a finder, thief, or anyone else outside the bank collection process from negotiating the check.

Upon deposit, the depositary bank becomes a holder, but not the owner of the check. The depositor is the owner. Under §4–201(a), the bank is merely an agent of the owner to collect the check from the drawee and to credit the proceeds of the check to the depositor-owner's account. The same agency relationship exists between the depositor and other collecting banks. Thus, in the example above, City Bank of Boston (the depositary bank) and the Federal Reserve Banks (intermediary banks) are all agents for the owner of the check (Crenshaw) to collect the check from the drawee, First State Bank of Chicago.

The check collection process is designed to secure final payment of the check from the drawee-payor bank. Upon final payment (1) the drawer's (the payor bank's customer) account is reduced by debiting or charging it in the amount of the instrument, (2) the contract liability of the drawer and prior indorsers on the instrument is discharged, and (3) the payor bank and other collecting banks become accountable for the amount of the check to its owner, the depositor. This result may be explained as follows. Before payment the drawee-payor bank has no liability on the check.[2] Under §3–602, however, when the bank pays the holder, the various other parties to the instrument are discharged. Thus, the payor bank by paying the check discharges the contract liability of prior parties to it including the drawer and any indorser. The bank is now accountable for the amount of the check to the holder who presented it, the presenting bank. The presenting bank is, in turn, accountable to the person or bank forwarding or depositing the check, and so on. Thus, accountability moves down the so-called remittance chain, ultimately ending with the depositary bank's liability to pay its customer, the depositor of the check.

Final payment is generally accomplished through a series of "settlements" made among the various banks in the collection process. Settlement is accomplished by paying the check in cash, by adjusting and offsetting the banks' clearing house balances, by debiting or crediting accounts between banks, or by forwarding various types of remittance instruments.

Although most checks are paid, the payor-drawee bank may refuse to honor a check upon presentment—due, for example, to insufficient funds in the drawer's account. If the check is dishonored when presented, the payor bank will return it (often through the same chain of intermediary banks, now known as "returning" banks, used for forward collection) to the depositary bank, which ultimately returns the check to its customer, the depositor; that is, the check "bounces." The payor and other returning banks then settle for the dishonored check with each other and the depositary bank, which in turn settles with the depositor.

Traditionally, the process of presenting and returning checks involved physically transporting the paper checks. Today, many checks are "truncated," with the paper check removed from circulation and an electronic copy instead forwarded to the appropriate bank. Check truncation is facilitated by statute,[3] effective in 2004, authorizing the use of "substitute checks" that are the legal equivalent of the original checks if they accurately represent all the information on the front and back of the original check, and contain the legend: "This is a legal copy of your check. You can use it the same way you would use the original check."[4] A reproduction of the original check qualifies as a substitute check if it contains an image of the front and back of the original check, bears a magnetic ink character recognition (MICR) line, conforms in paper stock and dimension to industry standards, and is suitable for automated processing in the same manner as the original check.[5] Thus, by removing the original check from circulation and creating a substitute check in its place, a bank (a "reconverting bank") can perform electronically check collection and return functions that formerly required physical transportation of the original paper check.

Expedited Funds Availability Act

Because a check presented through the forward collection process may not be paid, many depositary banks place "holds" on checks deposited in their customers' accounts, refusing to allow funds to be withdrawn pending payment of the check by the payor bank. These holds are designed to protect the depositary bank against the risk inherent in

---

[2] UCC §§3–401(a), 3–408.

[3] 12 U.S.C. §5001 *et seq.*
[4] 12 U.S.C. §5003.
[5] 12 U.S.C. §5002(16).

allowing its depositor to withdraw funds that the bank has not yet collected. Critics have long asserted that holds placed by many banks are unduly long and that bank customers have a right to prompter access to their deposits. Banks, however, have argued that the holds merely reflect the time needed for the attempted collection and return of unpaid checks.

In response to this problem, Congress in 1987 passed the **Expedited Funds Availability Act.**[6] The Act requires banks to make funds available to depositors within specified time frames, and to disclose their funds availability policies in writing to depositors. The Act also mandates that improvements be made in the check collection and return process to reduce the risk of loss to banks resulting from the expedited funds availability requirement. In addition, for interest-bearing accounts, the Act requires banks to begin accruing interest not later than the day the bank receives credit for the deposit (one or two days after deposit for most checks). The Act delegates broad authority to the Federal Reserve Board (Board) to implement its provisions, including the authority to regulate "any aspect of the payment system, including the receipt, payment, collection, or clearing of checks; and any related function of the payment system with respect to checks."[7] Pursuant to this authority, the Board adopted **Regulation CC,**[8] which became effective on September 1, 1988. Because the Act and Regulation CC are federal law, they preempt any inconsistent Uniform Commercial Code provisions but only to the extent of the inconsistency.[9]

Funds Availability Schedules. Under the Act as implemented by Regulation CC, funds availability depends on the type of deposit. For the following types of deposits, the funds can generally be withdrawn by cash or check on the first business day[10] following the banking day[11] of deposit: cash; electronic payments; checks withdrawn on the U.S. Treasury, a Federal Reserve Bank, or a Federal Home Loan Bank; checks drawn by a state or a unit of general local government; U.S. Postal Service money orders; cashier's or certified checks; "on us" checks (checks deposited in a branch of the depositary bank and drawn on the same or another branch of the same bank, if both branches are located in the same state or check-processing region); and the first $100 of any amount deposited by checks not subject to next-day availability.[12]

The availability of other checks deposited in an account depends upon whether they are "local" or "nonlocal." A "local" check is one deposited in a bank located in the same Federal Reserve processing region as the drawee-payor bank. (There are 46 Federal Reserve processing regions in the United States.) A "nonlocal" check is a check deposited in a bank located in a different check-processing region than the payor-drawee bank.[13]

Under the statute, local checks must be available for withdrawal by the second business day after the banking day of deposit, and nonlocal checks must be available no later than the fifth business day after the banking day of deposit.[14]

The law recognizes limited exceptions to the availability schedules for new accounts, deposits exceeding $5,000 on any one banking day, redeposited checks, accounts with repeated overdrafts, deposits that the depositary bank has reasonable cause to believe are uncollectible from the drawee-payor bank, and deposits made under emergency conditions, such as computer or communications equipment failure. The exceptions generally permit the bank to delay funds availability for a "reasonable period" after the day dictated by the applicable availability schedule.[15]

Duties of Collecting Banks

The UCC explicitly imposes a duty of ordinary care upon collecting banks. For example, under §4–202(a) a collecting bank must use ordinary care in (1) presenting a check or sending it for presentment, (2) sending a notice of dishonor or returning a dishonored check, (3) settling for a check when it receives settlement, and (4) notifying its transferor of any loss or delay of an instrument in transit within a reasonable time after the loss or delay is discovered. Regulation CC imposes a similar duty of good faith and ordinary care upon all banks in the collection process.[16]

---

[6]12 U.S.C. §§4001–4010.

[7]12 U.S.C. §4008(c).

[8]12 C.F.R. part 229.

[9]12 U.S.C. §4007(b).

[10]A "business day" is generally a calendar day other than Saturdays, Sundays, and holidays. 12 U.S.C. §4001(3).

[11]A "banking day" is that part of any business day on which an office of a bank is open to the public for carrying on substantially all of its banking functions. 12 C.F.R. §229.2(f); UCC §4–104(a)(3).

[12]12 U.S.C. §4002(a).

[13]12 U.S.C. §§4001(13), (15).

[14]12 U.S.C. §4002(b); 12 C.F.R. §229.12.

[15]12 U.S.C. §4003; 12 C.F.R. §229.13.

[16]12 C.F.R. §229.38(a).

In addition to the duty of care, §§4–207 and 4–208 impose transfer and presentment warranties upon collecting banks and upon the customer depositing the check for collection that are virtually identical to those discussed in the preceding chapter. Thus, the payor and the various collecting banks receive the protection against forgery and alteration these warranties provide. Despite warranty liability, a collecting bank is an agent of the owner of the check, not the other collecting banks. It is therefore not liable for the insolvency, negligence, or other misconduct of other banks or for the loss or destruction of a check in the possession of others.[17]

Collecting Banks as Holders in Due Course

Although banks in the collection process are holders, they qualify as holders in due course only under limited circumstances. To illustrate, assume Daniel draws a $500 check on State Bank payable to Nancy's order in exchange for goods purchased from Nancy. Nancy deposits the check in her account in National Bank, and the bank credits her account for $500. In this case, the bank has not yet given value for the instrument, a prerequisite to holder in due course status, because its deposit credit is a mere executory promise under §3–303(a)(1).

Under §4–210(a), however, a collecting bank acquires a *security interest* in a deposited check (and therefore gives value) to the extent it (1) allows the depositor to withdraw the deposit credit prior to collecting the check, (2) gives a deposit credit available for withdrawal as of right, whether or not the depositor actually withdraws it, or (3) makes an advance on or against the check—for example, loans money secured by the deposited check. In short, the bank gives value to the extent it extends credit on items in the course of collection.

To illustrate using the preceding example, assume National Bank allows Nancy to withdraw $400 from her account prior to collecting Daniel's check from State Bank. National Bank has a $400 security interest in (and has therefore given value for) the instrument. Under §4–211, if National Bank meets the other requirements, it therefore qualifies as a holder in due course of the check for $400. National Bank could therefore collect $400 on the instrument from Daniel even if he stops payment on the check and has a valid personal defense to paying Nancy—for example, if the goods delivered by Nancy to Daniel were defective.

Frequently, a number of checks are deposited either simultaneously or successively in the same account. If the bank permits the depositor to withdraw a part of the total of all checks prior to collection, the law must determine how the bank's security interest is allocated among the various checks deposited. Section 4–210(b) resolves the problem by providing that the bank's security interest is spread proportionally over all checks in a single deposit. If checks are deposited successively, credits first given are first withdrawn. That is, the Code adopts a "first-in, first-out rule" for successive deposits. Assume that on Monday Pam deposits five checks in her account in Security Bank, drawn by Albert, Bob, Carol, Don, and Ed respectively, each for $200. Security Bank permits Pam to withdraw $800 on Tuesday prior to collecting any of the checks. The bank gives value for each check to the extent of $160 (0.8 × $200). Assume alternatively that Albert's and Bob's checks are deposited on Monday, Carol's and Don's Tuesday, and Ed's on Wednesday. On Wednesday, the bank permits Pam to withdraw $800 prior to collecting any of the checks. Security Bank has given value for the first $800 worth of checks, those drawn by Albert, Bob, Carol, and Don.

Relationship Between Payor Bank and Its Customer

To this point the discussion has focused upon the legal principles governing the collection of a check *deposited* in a customer's account. This section examines the nature of the relationship existing between the customer and the bank regarding checks *drawn upon* the account.

Contract Between Payor Bank and Customer

When a person opens a checking account by depositing a sum of money with a local bank, a contract is created between the customer and the bank. The money becomes the property of the bank (cash) and the duty to repay it a general current liability (a demand deposit). The bank and its customer therefore stand in a simple creditor-debtor relation.

The contract between the customer and the bank is usually informal in nature. The depositor fills out an account application, submits identification, signs a signature card, and makes an initial deposit. By signing the signature card, the customer usually agrees to abide by the bank's rules governing checking accounts. These rules

---

[17]UCC §4–202(c); 12 C.F.R. §229.38(a).

usually are stated on the signature card, the deposit receipt, or some separate writing provided to the customer. The remaining terms of the contract are supplied by Articles 3 and 4 of the UCC, other statutes or common law doctrines, and banking custom.

Checks Properly Payable. Upon creation of the checking account, the bank acknowledges its indebtedness for the balance in the account and agrees to pay demand drafts (checks) within that balance to the customer's order upon presentment. In other words, the bank obligates itself to pay according to the customer's (drawer's) order. If the bank does so, it is entitled to charge (debit) the customer's account for the amount of the check. If the bank pays contrary to its customer's order, it has violated its contract and may not charge its customer's account. This contract is stated in §4–401(a), which provides that a bank may charge its customer's account only for checks that are "properly payable." A check is properly payable if "it is authorized by the customer and is in accordance with any agreement between the customer and bank."

For example, suppose Carr has a checking account in First Bank. A check bearing Carr's signature is presented to First Bank ordering it to pay $1,000 to Paul's order. In this case, First Bank can charge Carr's account for $1,000 if it pays $1,000 to Paul. If the check is not properly payable—for example, because it bears a forged drawer's signature or forged indorsement or has been materially altered—the bank has not paid according to its customer's order and may therefore charge the drawer's account only under circumstances outlined in Chapter 26.

The bank is not obligated to pay a check that results in an overdraft. If the bank does pay, however, it may charge the drawer's account for the full amount of the check. That is, a check creating an overdraft authorizes payment from the drawer's account and creates an implied promise to reimburse the drawee bank on demand.

In addition to checks properly payable under the preceding analysis, a bank may charge its customer's account in two other situations. Section 4–401(d) permits a bank paying a holder in good faith to charge the account according to (1) the original terms of an altered check, or (2) the terms of a completed check, even though the bank knows the check has been completed unless the bank has notice that completion was improper.

Order of Payment. Under §4–303(b), the bank may pay checks presented to it in any order. If the account balance is insufficient to pay all checks presented at any one time, the bank must honor checks in any order it chooses until the account balance is too small to pay any remaining check. The remaining checks may then be dishonored. Although the bank may pay checks in any order, it must continue to pay until the balance will not cover any remaining check. The bank may not dishonor all checks simply because the account balance is insufficient to cover all of them.

Liability for Wrongful Dishonor. If the bank refuses or neglects to honor a properly payable check, it is liable to its customer for damages proximately caused by its wrongful dishonor. Liability is limited to actual damages proved. Recovery may include damages for an arrest or prosecution of the customer—for example, for writing a bad check—or other consequential damages such as loss of credit rating. If the dishonor is intentional, punitive damages also may be available if permitted by state law outside the Code. The burden of proving the existence and amount of damages rests upon the customer.[18]

Stop Payment Orders

The bank is contractually obligated to pay checks according to the drawer's order. This order is communicated to the bank when the check is presented to it for payment. Occasionally, however, the drawer may issue a check but subsequently discover that the check should not be paid. For example, the drawer may issue a check in payment for goods, but later learn that the payee has defrauded him or that the goods involved are defective. In such cases, the Code, in §4–403, recognizes the right of the customer to countermand, or "stop," the order represented by a check. If payment is effectively stopped, the check will not be paid when presented to the payor-drawee bank. Rather, the check will be returned, and the bank will not charge the drawer's account.

Most **stop payment orders** are given to the bank by telephone and later confirmed in writing. The Code authorizes oral stop orders but provides that they are binding on the bank for only 14 days unless confirmed in writing during that time. A written order is binding for six months but may be renewed in writing. Because it is inconvenient and expensive to stop payment, most banks charge for the service.

Only the drawer may stop payment on a check; the payee or other holder of the check has no such right.

---

[18]UCC §§4–402, 1–305.

The customer, however, has no right to stop payment on a cashier's check, a teller's check, or a certified check, regardless of who procures certification. The certified check is the bank's own obligation, and the drawer has no right to require the bank to impair its own credit by dishonoring a certified check.

Effectiveness of Stop Order. Section §4–403(a) provides that to be effective, a stop order must be received by the bank at a *time* and in a *manner* sufficient to give the bank a reasonable opportunity to act upon it. Thus, a telephoned stop order is not effective immediately when the bank's switchboard operator answers the phone; it must be brought to the attention of the person responsible for processing such orders. Under §4–303 a stop order comes too late to bind the bank if, prior to receipt of the order, the bank has (1) accepted or certified the check, (2) paid it in cash, or (3) otherwise become accountable for the amount of the check. In these cases, the amount of the check may be charged to (deducted from) the drawer's account despite the stop order.

At issue in the following case was whether a stop order had been given in a proper manner.

FJS Electronics, Inc. v. Fidelity Bank
431 A.2d 326 (Pa. Super. 1981)

On February 27, 1976, plaintiff FJS Electronics, Inc. (FJS) drew a check in the amount of $1,844.98 on its account at defendant Fidelity Bank. On March 9, 1976, FJS telephoned a stop payment order on the check to Fidelity and later provided written confirmation of the stop order. Both the oral and written order indicated the amount of the check to be $1,844.48. All other information, including the number of the check and the payee, was correct. On March 15, 1976, Fidelity paid the check.

FJS sued Fidelity. The evidence at trial established that Fidelity used a computer to detect checks subject to stop payment orders. The computer was programmed to pull checks according to the dollar amount of the check. Thus, if the dollar amount was incorrect, the check would not be detected. The trial court ruled in favor of FJS; Fidelity appealed.

Brosky, Judge

. . . The central issue for our determination is whether a bank had a reasonable opportunity to stop payment on a check in the sum of $1,844.98 when the amount given by the customer was $1,844.48, hence, inaccurate. . . .

It is clear that the order here was timely received. The court below determined that even though it contained an error, the order was given in such manner as to give the bank a reasonable opportunity to act. Fidelity, in essence, asserts that [§4–403(1) (§4–403(a) under the 1990 Code)] should be read to require compliance with the procedures of a particular bank, regardless of what they are and regardless of whether the customer has been made aware of them. Fidelity argues that since its technique for ascertaining whether payment had been stopped required absolute accuracy as to the amount of a stopped check, this section would require absolute precision in order for the notice to be reasonable. Such a narrow view is not consistent with the intent [of] §4–403, expressed in Comment 2 [to the 1962 Code] following the section:

> . . . [S]topping payment is a service which depositors expect and are entitled to receive from banks notwithstanding its difficulty, inconvenience and expense. The inevitable occasional losses through failure to stop should be borne by the banks as a cost of the business of banking.

Fidelity does not contend that it could not have used a technique which required less precision in the stop payment order. It does not contend that it could not have found the check had it used a more thorough system. It merely asserts that since it chose a system which searched only by amount, notice is not reasonable unless it conforms to the requirements of this system.

Fidelity made a choice when it elected to employ a technique which searched for stopped checks by amount alone. It evidently found benefits to this technique which outweighed the risk that an item might be inaccurately described in a stop order. This is precisely the type of inevitable loss which was contemplated by the code drafters and addressed by the comment quoted above. The focus of §4–403 is the service which may be expected by the *customer,* and a customer may expect a check to be stopped after the bank is given reasonable notice. A bank's decision to reduce operating costs by using a system which increases the risk that checks as to which there is an outstanding stop payment order will be paid invites liability when such items are paid.

An error of fifty cents in the amount of a stop payment order does not deprive the bank of a reasonable opportunity to act on the order. . . .

[Judgment affirmed.]

Payment Over a Stop Order. A bank may receive a stop order, but due to inadvertence or neglect, pay the check anyway. In this case, the bank is liable to its customer because the bank has not paid according to the customer's order. Nevertheless, §4–403(c) imposes the burden of proving loss due to payment over the stop order upon the customer. If the customer is unable to prove loss, the bank may charge her account even though it failed to honor the stop order. Further, under §4–407, a bank that pays a check over a stop order is subrogated to (succeeds to) the rights of

1. the payee or other holder against the drawer,
2. the drawer against the payee or other holder of the check, and
3. any holder in due course against the drawer.

To illustrate the third subrogation case, assume that Dan draws a check upon First Bank payable to Pam for the purchase of a car. Pam defrauds Dan, who later discovers the fraud and stops payment on the check. Pam negotiates the check to Hal, a holder in due course, who presents the check to First Bank. First Bank inadvertently pays over Dan's stop order. In this case, First Bank may charge Dan's account because Dan can prove no loss due to the bank's improper payment. Hal, as a holder in due course, could have forced Dan to pay in any event because Dan's defense (fraud) is merely personal. First Bank, upon payment, succeeds to Hal's rights against Dan and could also therefore force Dan to pay.

In sum, the stop payment order provides somewhat limited protection to the drawer. The order, if honored, simply prevents the check from being paid initially out of the drawer's account. It does not prevent the payee or other holder from later suing the drawer on the underlying obligation for which the check was given. Further, even if the bank fails to honor the order, it is subrogated to the rights of the payee or later holder. If, as is commonly the case, the person presenting the check is a holder in due course—for example, a currency exchange that cashes the check in good faith for the fraudulent payee—the bank may pay over the order and charge the account unless the drawer has a real defense.

Effect of Customer's Death or Incompetence

A checking account customer may deposit checks in or draw checks upon an account shortly before death or, less frequently, before being adjudicated mentally incompetent. Section §4–405(a) provides that a payor or collecting bank's authority to pay, certify, or collect an item is not revoked by the death or incompetence of a customer until the bank knows of the death or adjudication of incompetence and has a reasonable opportunity to act upon it. Under this rule, banks need not verify the continuing vitality and competence of their customers before paying or collecting checks. Any other rule would be unworkable given the staggering volume of checks processed by modern banks.

Section 4–405(b) provides an additional rule governing checks drawn shortly before death. Even with knowledge of the death, the bank may continue to pay checks drawn against the account for a period of ten days after the date of death unless ordered to stop payment by some person claiming an interest in the account such as a creditor of the drawer, or the executor of the drawer's estate. This rule allows holders of checks issued shortly before death to cash them without having to file a claim against the deceased drawer's estate. Because these checks usually are given in immediate satisfaction of an obligation (for example, the grocery bill) and no defense to payment exists, filing a claim usually is a needless formality burdensome on the bank, the probate court, the executor of the estate, and the holder of the check.

Stale Checks

In banking and commercial practice a check more than six months old is considered a **stale check.** Under §4–404, a bank is under no obligation to pay a stale check and, therefore, its failure to pay is not a wrongful dishonor. The bank *may,* however, pay a stale check and charge its customer's account provided it acts in good faith. Thus, the bank has the option to pay the check and charge its customer's account or refuse to pay it with no liability for dishonor. Although not required to do so, many banks will consult the customer for instructions when presented with a stale check.

The preceding rule does not apply to a certified check. The drawer's account is charged when the check is certified and it thereafter becomes the bank's obligation. This obligation extends to the holder of the check until the local statute of limitations governing such instruments expires.

Customer's Duty to Discover Forgery and Alteration

As noted in Chapter 26, a drawee bank that pays an altered check may charge its customer's account only for the original terms of the check, and if it pays a check bearing a forged drawer's signature, it may not charge the account at all. Section 3–406 provides, however, that a drawer whose negligence "substantially contributes" to the forgery or alteration may not assert the alteration or lack of authority against the drawee bank who pays the instrument in good faith. A bank that pays a forged or altered instrument therefore may escape liability if its customer has failed to exercise reasonable care in preparing or safeguarding checks.

A checking account customer who is negligent in examining bank statements also may be prevented from asserting certain forgery and alteration against the bank under §4–406. In other words, a customer may be liable for negligent conduct both before and after the forgery or alteration has occurred. Under §4–406(c), when a bank sends its customer a statement of account,[19] the customer must exercise reasonable care and promptness to examine the statement to discover forgeries of his signature and alterations, and to notify the bank promptly if a forgery or alteration is discovered.

Under §4–406(d)(1), if the bank is able to prove loss caused by the customer's failure to perform these duties, the customer may not assert a forgery of his signature or an alteration against the bank. For example, the bank may be able to prove that with prompt notice it could have located and recovered from the wrongdoer but that it cannot now do so. In this case, the customer could not force the bank to recredit the account.

Effect of Successive Forgery or Alteration. Occasionally, a series of checks are forged or altered by the same wrong-doer, usually a relative or employee of the drawer. In this case, the relationship between the drawer and the bank is governed by §4–406(d)(2). Under this provision, the drawer-customer is liable upon any forged or altered instrument paid by the bank after the bank statement containing the first such instrument is made available to the customer for a reasonable time (not exceeding 30 days), and before the customer notifies

the bank of the problem. Losses resulting from successive forgeries or alterations by the same person can usually be traced to the customer's negligence in failing to examine bank statements and notify the bank of objections. Because this failure prevents the bank from avoiding payment of the later checks and allows the wrongdoer to continue his misdeeds, the law places the loss on the customer.

To illustrate, assume Don maintains a checking account at First Bank. On November 15, Nick, Don's dishonest nephew, steals three checks from Don's checkbook. Nick forges Don's signature to the first check, makes it payable to cash, and cashes it at a currency exchange. First Bank pays the check on November 17. On December 2, Don receives his monthly bank statement from First Bank containing the forged check. On December 12, First Bank pays a second check forged by Nick, and on January 5 pays the third. On January 7, Don notifies the bank of the forgeries. On these facts the bank may not charge Don's account for the first check it paid. Concerning the second check, paid within the 30-day period, the jury is required to decide as a matter of fact whether Don had the statement in his possession long enough (a "reasonable period") to allow him to examine it, discover the forgery, and notify the bank. On these facts Don had the statement for ten days (December 2 to December 12) before the second check was paid. If the jury finds that this was sufficient time to take action, the bank may charge his account despite the forgery. Finally, the third check was paid on January 5, beyond the 30-day period prescribed by the Code. Thus, First Bank may charge Don's account for the amount of the check.

Even if the customer is negligent under the principles previously outlined, the bank nevertheless remains liable under §4–406(e) if the customer proves that the bank was itself negligent in paying the forged or altered check, and such negligence "substantially contributed" to the loss. In this case, the loss is allocated between the customer and the bank by applying comparative negligence principles.

Regardless of the care or lack of care exercised by either the customer or the bank, §4–406(f) states that the customer must discover and report a forgery of her signature or an alteration to the bank within one year after the statement containing the offending instrument is made available. Failure to discover and report the problem to the bank within the prescribed time limit

---

[19]The account agreement between the customer and the bank determines whether the bank must return the customer's canceled checks with the statement. If the checks are not returned, the statement must contain sufficient information to permit the customer reasonably to identify the checks paid. Information that must be supplied includes the check number, the amount, and the date of payment. If the checks are not returned, the bank must either retain them (or the capacity to furnish copies) for seven years. UCC §§4–406(a)–(b).

prevents the customer from asserting the forgery or alteration against the bank.

In many §4–406 cases, the drawer fails to discover the forgery or alteration because he has entrusted examination of the bank statements to the dishonest employee responsible for the embezzlement. This fact does not relieve the drawer of his duty to examine bank statements and, as a result, the drawer is charged with knowledge of whatever information is contained in those statements. Thus, in applying §4–406, the depositor is deemed to know all facts that a reasonable and prudent examination of the bank statement would disclose if made by an honest employee.

The following case illustrates the general operation of §4–406.

Ossip-Harris Insurance, Inc. v. Barnett Bank of South Florida

428 So.2d 363 (Fla. App. 1983)

Plaintiff Ossip-Harris Insurance, Inc. (Ossip) maintained a checking account at defendant Barnett Bank. Between May 1980 and June 1981, Ossip's bookkeeper forged the signature of Edward Harris, Ossip's president, on 99 checks and wrongfully diverted almost $20,000. During the year-long period, Harris periodically reviewed the bank statements but did not detect the forgeries until June 1981.

Ossip sued Barnett Bank for wrongful payment of forged checks. Barnett alleged that Ossip should be denied recovery because it had been negligent in failing to detect and report the forgeries. The trial court ruled in favor of Barnett Bank. Ossip appealed.

Hendry, Judge

. . . Resolution of this dispute turns on the provisions of [§4–406 of the UCC]. . . .

We find that Barnett met its burden . . . of conclusively showing that Ossip failed to meet its initial burden under [§4–406(1) (§4–406(c) under 1990 Code)] in that it did not "exercise reasonable care and promptness to examine the statement and items to discover" the unauthorized signatures. The undisputed evidence demonstrates that Ossip received bank statements from Barnett each month from May 1980 to June 1981 and

that the statements contained the cancelled checks alleged to be forgeries. In response to a question posed by Ossip's own attorney, Edward Harris admitted that he did not actually review the signature on all of the company's cancelled checks and even admitted that he didn't pay attention to the signatures on the checks but was more concerned with the amounts and whether it was "the kind of check [Ossip-Harris] would normally pay." The checks were thus not scrutinized for unauthorized signatures as required by statute, nor was reasonable notice given to Barnett of any wrongdoing after the first statement and checks were made available to Ossip within the meaning of [UCC §4–406(2)(b) (§4–406(d)(2) under 1990 Code)]. Consequently, the evidence supports the conclusion, as a matter of law, that Ossip failed to exercise the degree of care required by statute . . . [and] is therefore precluded from recovering against Barnett unless it can establish lack of ordinary care by Barnett in paying the forgeries.

Under [UCC §4–406(3) (§4–406(e) under 1990 Code)], the burden of proving Barnett's lack of ordinary care falls squarely on Ossip-Harris. . . . Deposition testimony by Estella Brown, an employee of Barnett that handled the Ossip-Harris account, established that she had received six months of on-the-job training and that she examined each check against the signature card on file with the bank to determine the validity of the signature. When any problems arose with regard to signatures, she would bring the checks to the attention of her supervisor. Ossip presented no evidence of either the accepted standard of ordinary care in the banking world, or that Barnett's method of detecting forgeries did not meet this standard. Ossip's only argument in this regard, that the bank was negligent in not detecting the forgery, is particularly unavailing in light of the fact that Edward Harris failed to detect the forgery of *his own signature.* To require Barnett's employees to be handwriting experts as Ossip seems to imply, would establish a higher standard than that required by the statute, which is simply *ordinary* care. . . .

[Judgment affirmed.]

In the *Ossip-Harris* case, the bank examined each check to determine the validity of the drawer's signature. Most banks today, however, use forgery detection systems that examine only a representative sample of checks. For example, a bank might examine all signatures on checks over $1,000 and on those giving the bank reason to suspect a problem (for example, if the customer has warned the bank of a possible forgery or if the check is drawn against insufficient funds). The bank then examines a randomly selected one percent of all other checks. Note that §3–103(a)(7), makes it clear that the bank need not examine every check to avoid negligence liability under §4–406(e). That is, a bank exercises ordinary care "if the failure to examine does not violate the bank's prescribed procedures and the bank's procedures do not vary unreasonably from general banking usage. . . ." As explained in Official Comment 4 to §4–406. "A bank should not have to share that loss solely because it has adopted an automated collection or payment procedure in order to deal with the great volume of items at a lower cost to all customers."

Credit Cards

A **credit card** is simply a device, such as a card or plate, for obtaining money, property, or services on credit. As a money substitute and a credit device, credit cards perform commercial functions similar to those performed by notes and checks. For example, a person often uses a credit card to satisfy obligations that would otherwise be paid in cash or by check. Credit cards are also often used to borrow money or purchase goods or services on credit to be paid in future installments. This section examines the various types of credit cards and the legal principles governing them.

Types of Credit Cards

Credit cards are generally classified as single-party, dual-party, or multiparty. Through use of a **single-party credit card,** the oldest type, the issuer of the card sells goods or services on credit to its customer, the cardholder. This sale may be made by the card issuer directly or through an agent or franchised dealer. The cardholder is subsequently billed, commonly on a monthly basis, for the charges incurred on the card. Thus, a single-party transaction is a simple credit sale with the card used to identify persons to whom credit should be extended. Common examples of single-party cards are those issued by oil companies and department stores.

In a **dual-party credit card,** the card issuer does not sell goods or services but instead provides credit and collection services for those who do. The card issuer has two classes of customers, its cardholders and the merchants who honor its cards. Under a dual-party plan the cardholder uses the card to buy goods or services from a merchant belonging to the plan. The merchant is then reimbursed, less a discount, for charges incurred by cardholders. The issuer then undertakes to collect the outstanding balances from various cardholders. Examples of dual-party cards are American Express and Diner's Club cards.

Closely related to dual-party cards are **multiparty bank cards,** such as Visa and MasterCard. Under bank card plans, a participating bank enlists both cardholders and merchants. Like the dual-party cards, merchants are paid by the bank that enlisted them in the plan, and the bank bills its cardholders periodically for charges incurred against the card. In the multiparty card, however, merchants honor cards issued by any participating bank. Thus, when a bank pays its customer, the merchant, the bank may be required to collect the charge from another bank that issued the card. The collection process is similar to that used for ordinary checks.

Regardless of the type of card involved, two principal legal problems have arisen: (1) the effect of unauthorized use of the card, and (2) when a cardholder may assert defenses against the card issuer. Although initially matters of state law, these and other credit card issues are now primarily governed by federal legislation. The federal approach is embodied in portions of the Federal Truth-in-Lending Act,[20] discussed below.

Liability of Cardholder for Unauthorized Use

Perhaps the most common legal problem presented by credit cards is the effect of unauthorized use—the extent of a cardholder's liability when the card is used by a thief or a person acting without authority. The common law reached differing results on this issue depending upon the type of card involved.

The Truth-in-Lending Act provides for extremely limited liability for unauthorized use of a consumer's credit card, regardless of type. Under this statute,[21] the card-

---

[20]The "Truth-in-Lending Act" is the popular name for Subchapter I of the Consumer Credit Protection Act, 15 U.S.C. §1601 *et seq.*
[21]15 U.S.C. §1643, 12 C.F.R. §226.12.

holder is liable for unauthorized charges on the card occurring before notifying the card issuer up to the *lesser* of $50 or the amount of money, property, or services obtained by the unauthorized use of the card. This liability attaches only if the following three conditions are met:

1. The card involved must be an "accepted" credit card—one that the cardholder has requested or applied for and received, or has signed or used to obtain credit. Thus, a cardholder has no liability for unauthorized use of cards mailed on an unsolicited basis.

2. The issuer must provide adequate notice to the cardholder of the maximum potential liability outlined above and of means such as a telephone number or address by which the issuer may be notified orally or in writing of loss or theft of the card.

3. The issuer must provide a method whereby the user of the card can be identified as the person authorized to use it. Most commonly, the method of identification is the cardholder's signature appearing on the card.

Even if the foregoing conditions are met, the cardholder may nevertheless escape even the limited liability imposed by the statute if no liability would have been imposed upon him under state common law. For example, at common law, the holder of a single-party card is not responsible in most states for unauthorized use. Thus, the federal law does not expand the liability of the single-party cardholder up to the $50 maximum. Rather, it limits liability to $50 or less in cases in which state law would have imposed greater responsibility. For example, in dual-party or multiparty cards some states have held a cardholder liable for all unauthorized charges made before the cardholder notifies the issuer.

The limitations outlined above apply only to consumer credit transactions, not to transactions involving extensions of credit for business, commercial, or agricultural purposes, or to organizations, such as corporations or government agencies. Credit card transactions in these cases continue, therefore, to be governed by state law.[22]

Assertion of Defenses Against Issuer

Even when their use is authorized, credit cards are sometimes used to purchase defective goods or services. The law must, therefore, determine when a cardholder may assert against the card issuer defenses he or she may have against the merchant providing the defective goods or services. As with unauthorized use, the issue is governed primarily by federal law, and single-party cards are treated differently from other types.

In a single-party card transaction, the card issuer is also effectively the seller of the goods or services involved. The single-party cardholder may therefore assert any defective performance by the seller's company-owned outlet, agent, or franchised dealer against the parent company issuing the card. Suppose Sue Cohen uses her Amoco card to purchase a battery from Bill's Amoco of Chicago, Illinois. If the battery proves defective, Sue may assert the defect as a defense to paying the bill submitted by Amoco, provided she first makes an effort to settle the dispute with Bill's. That is, Sue's defense against Bill's may be asserted against Amoco.

Dual-party and multiparty cards present more difficult problems because the card issuer—for example, American Express or a bank issuing a Visa card—is not the seller of the defective goods or services, but instead merely provides a credit and collection service for the merchants. Because card issuers enlist participating merchants, however, they do have some ability to screen and police against troublesome merchants honoring their cards. For this reason, federal law[23] allows a cardholder to assert defenses against credit card issuers if

1. the cardholder first makes a good faith effort to resolve the dispute with the merchant honoring the card,
2. the amount of the initial transaction exceeds $50,
3. the merchant's place of business is located either in the same state as the cardholder's billing address or within 100 miles of that address.

Note that only the first limitation (good faith effort to resolve the dispute) applies (1) to single-party cards, and (2) when the issuer of a dual- or multiparty card induces its cardholder through a mail solicitation to use the card to purchase the goods which prove defective. For example, MasterCard and Visa bills commonly include promotional literature for products that can be

---

[22]15 U.S.C. §1603(1).

[23]15 U.S.C. §1666i(a).

purchased by mail and billed to the card. The card issuer is subject to defenses arising out of sales of these goods without regard to the dollar or geographic limitations outlined above. If the cardholder is able to assert a defense, the *amount* asserted may not exceed the amount of credit outstanding with respect to the transaction at the time the cardholder first notifies the card issuer or the offending merchant of the problem.[24]

Limitations on Credit Card Issuers

To protect cardholders and merchants against certain unfair or anticompetitive practices, the Truth-in-Lending Act imposes several limitations upon credit card issuers. For example, consumer holders of bank cards, such as Visa or MasterCard, often maintain checking accounts in the bank issuing the card. In such cases, the bank may not, either before or after credit card privileges are revoked, offset amounts owing on credit card transactions against funds held on deposit with the bank. The bank must instead resort to ordinary creditors' remedies, available under either federal or state law, to collect the amount due.[25]

The law also provides that no card issuer may prohibit a merchant from offering a discount to any consumer to pay by cash, check, or similar means other than the credit card.[26] Further, the merchant may not be required, as a condition to participating in a credit card plan, to open an account with (or procure any other service from) the card issuer not essential to the operation of the plan.[27]

Electronic Fund Transfers

Electronic Fund Transfer Act

In recent years, many banks have installed automated teller machines as part of their drive-up or walk-up facilities or in remote locations such as shopping centers. These machines enable bank customers, using a special card and identification number, to deposit or withdraw money from their accounts electronically.

In 1978, Congress enacted the **Electronic Fund Transfer Act (EFTA)**[28] to establish a framework for the rights, liabilities, and responsibilities of participants in electronic funds transfer systems such as automated tellers. The Act is limited in scope. It concerns only consumer transfers, not the substantial volume of transfers occurring among banks and other large business organizations. Further, the Act does not displace all state law on the subject; it supplants state law only if state law provides less protection to consumers than the federal statute.

As defined in the Act, an "electronic fund transfer" includes any transfer of funds other than one initiated by check, draft, or similar paper instrument that is initiated through an electronic terminal, telephone, computer, or magnetic tape, and that orders, authorizes, or instructs a financial institution to debit or credit an account. The term includes transfers through point of sale terminals and automated teller machines, preauthorized direct deposits and withdrawal of funds, and transfers initiated by telephone pursuant to a prearranged plan. The Act prescribes guidelines for the contract between a bank and its customer regarding electronic transfers, requires that the bank provide written documentation of such transfers including a periodic statement, and imposes limited consumer liability for unauthorized transfers involving the account.

As with credit cards, the consumer has no liability for unauthorized transfers unless the card or other means of access used for the transfer is accepted and the bank provides a means whereby the card user can be identified as the person authorized to use the card. This is commonly accomplished by a personal identification number, which the customer is supposed to keep secret and separate from the access card. If these two conditions are met and the card is lost, the customer is liable up to a maximum of $50 for unauthorized transfers occurring before he notifies the bank. The customer has no liability for unauthorized transfers occurring after the bank is notified.

Liability is expanded up to a $500 maximum if the bank is able to prove that the unauthorized transfer was caused by the customer's failure to report an unauthorized transfer within 60 days after transmittal of the bank

---

[24] 15 U.S.C. §1666i(b).

[25] 15 U.S.C. §1666h.

[26] 15 U.S.C. §1666f, 12 C.F.R. §226.12(f)(1).

[27] An account solely for clearing purposes may be used, but no finance charges or minimum balance requirements may be imposed. 15 U.S.C. §1666g, 12 C.F.R. §226.12(f)(2).

---

[28] 15 U.S.C. §§1693–1693r. Subchapter VI of the Consumer Credit Protection Act; 12 C.F.R. part 205.

statement disclosing the transfer. Liability also is increased if the unauthorized transfer is caused by the customer's failure to report any loss or theft of a card within two business days after learning of it.

UCC Article 4A—Funds Transfers

Checks, credit cards, and fund transfers governed by the EFTA provide alternative methods for paying debts through the banking system. Another method, used primarily by large business or financial institutions, is commonly known as the wholesale wire transfer. The daily volume of such payments, effected primarily over two major systems, the Federal Reserve wire transfer network (Fedwire), and the New York Clearing House Interbank Payments System (CHIPS), far exceeds the dollar volume of payments made by other means. To provide a comprehensive body of law to govern wholesale wire transfers, Article 4A, entitled "Funds Transfers," was added to the UCC in 1989, and has now been enacted in all states.

An Article 4A "funds transfer" refers to "the series of transactions, beginning with the originator's payment order, made for the purpose of making payment to the beneficiary of the order."[29] A "payment order" is an unconditional "instruction of a sender to a receiving bank; transmitted orally, electronically, or in writing, to pay, or to cause another bank to pay, a fixed or determinable amount of money to a beneficiary."[30] To illustrate the typical Article 4A transfer, assume Debtor owes Creditor $2 million. Instead of giving Creditor a check, Debtor instructs its bank (First Bank) to credit $2 million to Creditor's bank account in Second Bank. First Bank carries out Debtor's instruction by directing Second Bank to credit Creditor's account for $2 million. The instruction issued by Debtor to First Bank is a "payment order." Debtor is the "sender" of the order and First Bank is the "receiving bank" of that order. Creditor is the "beneficiary" of Debtor's order. First Bank "executes" Debtor's order by instructing Second Bank to credit Creditor's account. First Bank's instruction to Second Bank is also a "payment order" with First Bank as the "sender," Second Bank as the "receiving bank," and Creditor as the "beneficiary." The series of transac-

tions through which Debtor pays Creditor is the "funds transfer," in which Debtor is the "originator," First Bank is the "originator's bank," Creditor is the "beneficiary," and Second Bank is the "beneficiary's bank." In more complex transfers, there may be one or more "intermediary banks" between First Bank and Second Bank. Note that an Article 4A fund transfer is unlike a check or credit card payment (a debit transfer) in which the instruction to pay is given by the person receiving payment (for example, the payee of the check). Rather, under Article 4A (a credit transfer) the instruction to pay is given by the person making payment. Article 4A governs credit, not debit, transfers. Article 4A also is inapplicable to any transaction governed by the EFTA.

An Article 4A payment order, unlike a check, does not embody an independent obligation to pay money. Rather, a payment order is a request by its sender to the receiving bank to execute or pay the order, a request that the receiving bank can accept or reject. A bank has no duty to accept a payment order unless it has entered into a formal or informal agreement to do so. An originator's bank or intermediary bank that accepts a payment order is obliged to execute the sender's order by issuing a payment order to the beneficiary's bank or a later intermediary bank. The beneficiary's bank accepts the order when it pays the beneficiary, notifies the beneficiary that the order has been received, or receives payment of the order from the bank that issued it.[31] Note that when the originator's bank executes the order, it is entitled to receive payment from the originator, and a bank later in the chain is similarly entitled to reimbursement from its sender. The obligation of each sender (the originator, the originator's bank, and any intermediary bank) to pay the order is excused if, for any reason, the beneficiary's bank fails to accept the order.[32] If the beneficiary's bank accepts the order, the debt for which the originator issued the order generally is discharged.[33]

Perhaps the most important provisions of Article 4A are those allocating risk of loss between the originator and its bank for unauthorized or erroneous payment orders. For example, a dishonest employee, as part of an embezzlement scheme, may order payment to an account she controls, or an authorized order may be a duplicate of a previous order or may contain an error in amount or in the

---

[29]UCC §4A–104(a).

[30]UCC §4A–103(a)(1).

[31]UCC §4A–209.

[32]UCC §4A–402.

[33]UCC §4A–406.

name or account number of the beneficiary. Under Article 4A, these issues are resolved by examining the existence and use of "security procedures," which are simply procedures established by agreement of a customer and its bank to (1) verify the authenticity of a payment order, or (2) detect error in the transmission or content of the order.[34] Security procedures typically involve use of codes, identifying numbers or words, or callback procedures. Regarding unauthorized orders, Article 4A generally places the loss on the customer if a commercially reasonable security procedure was in place and the bank accepted the payment order after verifying it in good faith and in compliance with the security procedure.[35] Risk of loss is shifted to the bank, however, if the customer proves that the person initiating the unauthorized order was an interloper; that is, one who obtained the confidential security procedure information from a source other than (1) a current or former agent or employee of the customer, or (2) a source controlled by the customer.[36]

Regarding erroneous orders, risk of loss is similarly placed on the customer unless (1) the security procedure involved was designed to detect errors, and (2) the customer complied with it but the bank did not.[37] The purpose of the Article 4A rules governing unauthorized and erroneous orders is to minimize fraud and error by encouraging the parties to develop and use effective security procedures.

Summary

1.   Federal statutes and administrative regulations, and Article 4 of the UCC entitled "Bank Deposits and Collections," contain the rules governing the check collection process—the process by which a check is presented to the drawee bank, paid, and the proceeds transferred and credited to the depositor's account.

2.   To assure that checking account customers have prompt access to their funds, Congress, in 1987, enacted the Expedited Funds Availability Act. The Act requires banks to make funds available to depositors within specified time frames, and mandates that improvements be made in the check collection process, primarily to speed the return of unpaid checks. The Federal Reserve Board has adopted comprehensive Regulation CC to implement the Act's provisions.

3.   Article 4 of the UCC governs the legal relationship between a bank and its checking account customer. A checking account involves a contract requiring the bank to pay checks within the balance of the account according to the customer's (drawer's) order.

4.   The order to pay is communicated to the bank when the check is presented to it for payment. Prior to that time the drawer may countermand or stop the order to pay embodied in a check. If the bank, due to negligence or inadvertence, pays the check after receiving a stop order, it is liable to its customer for breach of its basic contract. Nevertheless, the burden of proving loss due to payment over a stop order rests upon the customer. Further, after payment the bank is subrogated to the rights of the payee or other holder against the drawer, the drawer against the payee or other holder, and any holder in due course against the drawer.

5.   In addition to governing the contract between the customer and the bank and the legal implication of stop payment orders, Article 4 also resolves additional issues arising in the bank-depositor relationship. These include, for example, the effect of the customer's death or incompetence, payment of stale checks, and the customer's duty to examine bank statements to discover forgery and alteration.

6.   In addition to checks and notes, credit cards often are used as a method to purchase goods or services. A credit card is simply a device, such as card or plate, utilized to obtain money, goods, or services on credit. Cards are often designated as single-party (for example, an oil company card), dual-party (for example, an American Express Card), or multiparty (for example, a Visa or MasterCard). Regardless of the type of card used, two principal legal problems have arisen: first, the effect of unauthorized use of the card, and second, when a cardholder may assert defenses against the card issuer arising out of the underlying transaction. Although initially matters of state law, these and other credit card issues now are governed primarily by the federal Truth-in-Lending Act.

7.   Electronic funds transfers provide an alternative to paper instruments or credit cards as a means of payment. Consumer

---

[34]UCC §4A–201.
[35]UCC §4A–202.

[36]UCC §4A–203(a)(2) and Official Comment 5.
[37]UCC §4A–205.

transfers are substantially governed by federal law, the Electronic Fund Transfer Act. UCC Article 4A, promulgated in 1989, is designed to govern the substantial volume of transfers occurring among banks and other large business organizations.

Key Terms

check collection process	Regulation CC
customer	stop payment order
depositary bank	stale check
payor bank	credit card
intermediary bank	single-party credit card
clearing house	dual-party credit card
collecting bank	multiparty credit card
presenting bank	Electronic Fund Transfer Act
Expedited Funds	
Availability Act	

Questions and Problems

27.1   Explain the general operation of the bank collection process, including the sequence of events occurring when the check is honored and when it is dishonored. Why are banks required to return dishonored checks promptly?

27.2   Michael drew a check upon his checking account in Gulfstream Bank payable to Paul's order. The check was signed but blank in amount. Paul was to fill in the amount at a future date for carpentry work to be performed by Paul. Before the check was presented Michael closed his account at Gulfstream Bank. After Paul performed the work, he filled in the check in the amount of $100 and presented it to the bank, which paid it, creating an overdraft on Michael's closed account. On these facts may Gulfstream recover the amount of the check from Michael? On what theory?

27.3   James, who maintained a checking account at Highland National Bank, died on June 1, 1985. Two days later, before the bank had notice of James's death, James's sister, Stella, appeared at the bank with checks signed in blank by James and informed bank officials that James had sent her to close out his account. She inquired as to the balance of the account and filled in the check payable to herself for the amount of that balance. The bank verified the authenticity of James's signature and Stella's identity. Stella subsequently cashed the check at a currency exchange and fled the country. In fact, Stella had no authority to make the withdrawal, and the executor of James's estate sued the bank to recover the amount paid. What result?

27.4   Tusso delivered a $600 check drawn on Security National Bank to Adamson Construction Co. in payment for work performed by Adamson. The payment was made by mistake, however, because Adamson had already been paid for the services as part of a previous bill. Realizing the mistake, Tusso went to the bank the next day at 9 A.M., stopped payment on the check, and paid the required fee. At 10:30 the same morning, Adamson presented the check to the bank, which paid it. On these facts, may Security charge Tusso's account for the amount of the check? If not, does Security have any rights against Adamson?

27.5   Azad maintains a bank account at Heritage Bank. In each of the following cases, Heritage Bank received notice of a stop order on a check deposited to Azad's account. Heritage claims to be a holder in due course that has given value for the check deposited to Azad's account. In each case, assume that no activity other than the described transactions occurred in Azad's account and determine whether the bank gave value for the check subject to the stop order.

(a) On June 1, Azad's account at Heritage Bank had a balance of $5,000. On June 2, Azad deposited a $1,000 check, issued by Dolan as drawer and drawn on an account at First Bank. On June 2, Heritage credited $1,000 to Azad's account. On June 4, First Bank notified Heritage that Dolan stopped payment on the check.

(b) On June 1, Azad's account at Heritage Bank had a balance of $1,000. On June 2, Azad deposited a $1,000 check, issued by Dolan as drawer and drawn on an account at First Bank. On June 2, Heritage credited $1,000 to Azad's account. On June 3, Azad withdrew $1,500 from his account at Heritage Bank. On June 4, First Bank notified Heritage that Dolan stopped payment on the check.

(c) On June 1, Azad's account at Heritage Bank was overdrawn in the amount of $5,000. On June 2, Azad deposited a $5,000 check, issued by Dolan as drawer and drawn on an account at First Bank. On June 2, Heritage credited $5,000 to Azad's account. On June 4, First Bank notified Heritage that Dolan stopped payment on the check.

27.6   Nu-Way Services, Inc. (Nu-Way), a truck repair company, maintained a checking account at Mercantile Trust Company. Over a period of approximately six months, James Ussery, Nu-Way's night manager, altered seven checks prepared by Nu-Way to pay for auto parts by substituting his name as payee. Additionally, Ussery stole 43 of Nu-Way's blank checks and forged the signature of Nu-Way's president, Mariano Costello. Although Nu-Way received the canceled and altered checks with its monthly bank statements, the clerk who reconciled the statements failed to detect the alterations or forgeries. When one of Nu-Way's vendors notified Costello of a check made payable to Ussery, Costello discovered Ussery's wrongdoing.

Costello notified Mercantile of the alterations and forgeries, but Mercantile refused to recredit Costello's account. Costello sued Mercantile to recover on the checks. The evidence established that the forgeries were expertly done and several bank employees were unable to distinguish between the forgeries and the genuine signatures. The alterations, however, were crudely done, accomplished by making obvious erasures on the instrument. How should the court rule in this case?

27.7   The use of credit cards and electronic fund transfers certainly eliminates the need for many checks. For example, a hotel bill formerly paid by check is now often paid by credit card. Automatic teller devices eliminate the need for many checks formerly written simply to obtain cash. Do you think these devices will ever eliminate the need for ordinary checks? What future role do you see for checks? What are the relative advantages and disadvantages of payment by check as opposed to credit card and electronic fund transactions?

27.8   A common practice among hotels, car rental companies, and other merchants is to utilize a so-called open credit card slip as a means of securing payment. Under this arrangement, the customer allows the merchant to take an impression of the credit card and the voucher is then signed by the customer. The amount is not filled in but the merchant retains the voucher as security for ultimate payment of the bill. Eventually, the merchant fills in the amount and gives the customer a copy of the voucher. The arrangement is therefore similar to giving the merchant a check, otherwise blank, signed by the drawer. The risks to the drawer of unauthorized completion of a check are outlined in Chapter 24. Does a credit card customer using the open credit card voucher run similar risks? Explain.

PART FIVE

DEBTOR-CREDITOR RELATIONS

CHAPTER 28

INTRODUCTION TO DEBTOR-CREDITOR RELATIONS

Major Topics

- an overview of credit transactions, including types of credit, the decision to extend credit, and the risks of extending credit
- an introduction to the law of debtors and creditors, including the source of the law, the concept of priority among creditors, and the definition of security
- discussion of federal and state laws affecting credit transactions

Millions of debtor-creditor relationships occur each day in a wide variety of situations. A consumer may buy a dishwasher on credit from a local appliance store, borrow money from a bank to buy a new car or house, contract with a local builder to remodel the kitchen, or simply become indebted to pay the phone or utility bills. In the commercial setting, businesses often borrow money to finance inventory, acquire equipment, construct buildings, or to provide working capital. Businesses also often purchase goods and services on credit.

In each of these transactions, one party — the **debtor** — has incurred an obligation or debt that is owed to a second party — the **creditor.** Although most debtor-creditor relationships are created voluntarily by contract or agreement of the parties, the relationship often arises by operation of law without the consent of the debtor. If,

for example, one person sues another and wins a judgment for damages, the judgment becomes a legally enforceable obligation owed by the losing party, the **judgment debtor,** to the person who has won the judgment, the **judgment creditor.** In addition, a person may involuntarily become a debtor of a local, state, or federal government after incurring liability to pay property or income taxes, penalties, or fines.

The Law of Debtors and Creditors

Most substantive law governing debtor-creditor relations is derived from state statutes including Articles 6 and 9 of the UCC. Superimposed upon this state law system is the federal law of bankruptcy. In addition, federal law regulates, particularly for consumer transactions, much of the process of extending credit and collecting debts from recalcitrant debtors. The foregoing statutes and regulations form the basis of this and the following chapters on debtor-creditor relations.

Types of Credit

Financial institutions, retailers, and other businesses provide many types of credit. Credit that is extended to businesses frequently is called **commercial** (or business)

credit, while credit to persons for personal, family, or household purposes usually is called **consumer credit.** In **closed-end credit,** the amount of the debt is fixed and a repayment date is specified. In closed-end credit transactions, the parties agree at the time the credit is extended to the number of payments, due date, and amount of each payment. The typical car loan is a closed-end credit transaction. The debtor borrows a fixed amount of money and agrees to repay the debt through fixed monthly payments over a specified period.

In contrast, **open-end credit** is credit extended on an account in which the debtor will incur obligations in a series of transactions. Although the terms of open-end credit, such as the billing period and interest rate, usually are established in advance, neither the amount of the debt nor the specific due date is set. The amount of the debt fluctuates as the debtor makes purchases and remits payment on the account, with an agreed interest rate charged on the outstanding balance. Credit card accounts offered by retailers and banks are examples of open-end credit.

Credit also may be secured or unsecured. For reasons developed later in this chapter, secured creditors enjoy substantial advantages over unsecured creditors when the debtor encounters financial difficulty.

The Credit Decision

To determine whether an applicant is worthy of credit, most creditors require a potential debtor to complete a credit application. Of course, the creditor's primary concern is whether the debtor will repay the debt. Creditors consider many factors in making this determination. For commercial credit, the creditor usually reviews the business's accounting records, especially items such as current assets, current liabilities, profitability, and asset and inventory turnover. For consumer credit, the creditor usually reviews the applicant's assets (such as real estate and checking and savings ac-counts), employment and other sources of income, outstanding debts, and credit history. Most creditors verify the information a credit applicant provides and often obtain further information from a consumer reporting agency or credit bureau. These organizations compile information on individuals from public records, such as the courts, the recorder of deeds, and other recording agencies, and regularly obtain reports from retailers and financial institutions on delinquent accounts.

To simplify the credit decision, many creditors use credit scoring systems, which list several factors as indicators of a debtor's creditworthiness. The creditor assigns each factor a number of points and establishes a minimum score for creditworthiness. Many creditors that use credit scoring systems supplement the information with subjective criteria.

The credit decision also includes the terms upon which credit will be extended. Financial institutions frequently set the amount of the credit, the interest rate, the payment schedule, and other terms according to the perceived risk of the obligation. Retailers and credit card issuers using open-end credit generally extend credit on the same terms to all debtors but establish individualized credit limits.

Risks of Extending Credit—Default and Bankruptcy

Creditors run two major risks in extending credit: that the debtor will default and that the debtor will become insolvent. Default is simply the debtor's failure to pay or perform the obligation. **Insolvency** occurs when a debtor has insufficient assets to meet his total obligations or is unable to pay debts as they come due. A debtor generally reveals insolvency by defaulting on one or more outstanding obligations.

A debtor who has become insolvent may commence a bankruptcy proceeding under federal law. Bankruptcy law is designed to relieve an honest debtor from overburdensome financial obligations by granting a discharge if certain legal requirements are met. This discharge gives the debtor a fresh start, free of claims of former creditors. That is, a creditor who is not paid in full in the bankruptcy proceeding may not thereafter assert a claim against the debtor. To protect creditors claiming against a debtor's limited assets, the law also provides an elaborate priority system to assure equitable treatment of competing creditors. Bankruptcy is discussed in detail in Chapter 30.

Liens, Priorities, and General Creditors

When a debtor is insolvent, bankrupt, or otherwise possesses limited financial ability, questions of priority arise. That is, because the debtor's assets are insufficient to pay all creditors in full, the law must determine the order in which competing creditors are paid. A creditor who is paid before another is said to have a "priority" over that creditor. Creditors may achieve priority in many ways. Perhaps the most common method of establishing priority is by creating a lien upon all or a specified portion of the debtor's property, real or personal.

Liens. A **lien** is an interest in property designed to secure the payment or other performance of an obligation. A lien gives the creditor recourse to the specific property in which the lien exists to satisfy the obligation secured by the lien. That is, if property is subject to a lien and the obligation secured by the lien is unpaid, the creditor may sell the property and apply the proceeds to the unpaid debt to the exclusion of other creditors. A lien, therefore, gives such a creditor priority over other creditors in the specific property subject to the lien. Frequently, two or more creditors will hold a lien upon the same property owned by the debtor. In these cases, debtor-creditor law also determines the priority among competing lien creditors.

Consensual Liens. Liens may be created with the debtor's consent, usually evidenced in a contract. Consensually created liens are introduced later in this chapter in the introduction to security.

Statutory Liens. Some liens are created by operation of law. Most of these are **statutory liens,** imposed or authorized solely by statute, that arise when specified circumstances or conditions occur. Many statutory liens are descendants of liens originally granted to certain creditors at common law. These **common law liens** generally allowed creditors such as landlords, bailees, and innkeepers to retain possession of the debtor's property until the debt was paid.

Some of the most common statutory liens are discussed below. As in other liens, if the debt secured by a statutory lien remains unpaid, the property may be sold and the proceeds applied to the debt.

An **artisan's lien** is the right of an artisan to retain possession of the object repaired or worked upon (such as an automobile) until receipt of payment for the work performed. An artisan is a skilled worker, such as a tailor, carpenter, or auto mechanic, in a trade requiring manual dexterity.

A **bailee's lien** is granted to carriers and warehousemen allowing them to retain possession of goods entrusted to them pending payment for the shipment or storage charges.

A **landlord's lien** secures payment of rent by giving the landlord a lien upon the tenant's personal property located on the leased premises and, in the case of farmland, crops grown thereon.

A **mechanic's lien** is given to persons who supply services, labor, or material in the construction or improvement of real property. For example, a mechanic's lien may be used to secure payment for labor and materials

of a contractor who remodels a property owner's kitchen. A mechanic's lien is recorded in the real estate records to provide constructive notice of its existence. If the debt secured by the lien is not paid, the lien is ultimately satisfied out of the proceeds of the next sale of the underlying real property.

A **tax lien** is held by the state or federal government or a governmental subdivision to secure payment of delinquent taxes. For example, a tax lien may be imposed in favor of a state or local government upon real property to secure unpaid real property taxes. Additionally, a federal tax lien may be imposed upon all property of a taxpayer who refuses or neglects to pay a tax for which she is liable.

Judicial Liens. A third type of lien is a **judicial lien,** created by judicial action. Judicial liens include those created by judgment, levy, garnishment, or other legal or equitable process or proceeding. Judicial liens are discussed in the following chapter.

Priorities. In some cases, a creditor without a lien is granted a priority in payment over certain other creditors. Unlike liens, which may be created by contract, these **priorities** are almost always created by statute, most notably federal bankruptcy law. For example, bankruptcy law provides that administrative expenses and employee claims for wages, among others, are given a priority in distribution of the bankrupt debtor's limited assets. This priority exists even though the creditors involved have no lien upon specific property of the debtor.

General Creditors. A **general creditor** is a creditor who has neither a lien nor a priority. General creditors of a consumer debtor often include the power or phone company, and sellers of goods or services on credit. General creditors stand in the worst possible position when financial difficulty arises because they are paid only after creditors with a lien or statutorily authorized priority are paid. For this reason, the bulk of debtor-creditor law concerns when and how creditors establish a priority in distribution of the debtor's assets, thereby avoiding the unenviable general creditor status.

In summary, in the distribution of a debtor's assets, creditors with a lien ordinarily are paid first out of the proceeds of the property subject to the lien. If more than one creditor holds a lien on the same property, the law provides rules to establish priority among the competing lienholders. If assets remain that are not subject to liens, their proceeds are distributed first to creditors given a priority by statute. Any remaining assets are then distributed to general creditors.

Introduction to Security

To protect themselves against other creditors upon bankruptcy and to provide for expeditious collection upon default, creditors often insist upon some form of **security.** Virtually all security issues are based on a common situation. One person (the creditor) loans money to, sells property to, or performs services for another (the debtor) who then becomes bound to repay the loan or pay for the property or services. Because of the debtor's credit history, financial position, or other reason, the creditor desires more than merely the debtor's personal promise to pay. The creditor wants some additional "security" to satisfy the obligation in whole or in part if the debtor defaults.

The most common form of security is a contractually created lien in the debtor's property. That is, the debtor and creditor enter into a contract creating a lien in specific property owned by the debtor, often known as the "collateral." The contract provides that if the obligation secured by the collateral is not paid, the creditor may take possession of and sell the collateral to satisfy the debt. This right is known as the secured party's **right of foreclosure.** If the collateral (security) is *real property,* the transaction is governed by the law of mortgages discussed in Chapter 37. If the security is *personal property,* the arrangement is known as a "secured transaction" and is governed by Article 9 of the UCC. Secured transactions under Article 9 are discussed in detail in Chapters 31 and 32.

A creditor who has a contractually created lien is usually known as a **secured creditor,** and has important advantages over unsecured creditors. Upon default a secured creditor has recourse to specific assets of the debtor, often without the necessity of a judicial proceeding. These assets may then be sold and the proceeds applied to reduce or extinguish the secured debt to the exclusion of unsecured claims. In contrast, an unpaid unsecured creditor must first obtain a judgment and then may have a court officer seize and sell the debtor's assets to satisfy the debt. The unsecured creditor, however, often finds that the assets have been dissipated, are statutorily exempt, or are subject to secured creditors' claims.

In addition to liens created in specific property, security also may be provided by the contractual promise of someone other than the debtor to satisfy the obligation

if the debtor does not. Such a security arrangement is known as "suretyship" and the third party guaranteeing the debt is a "surety." Suretyship is a common and important security device, and suretyship principles underlie many fundamental legal concepts. Suretyship is the subject of Chapter 33.

Lender Liability

A debtor's default or bankruptcy is not the only risk assumed by a creditor lending money or extending credit on a secured or unsecured basis. Increasingly, in recent years, debtors and others have sued lenders on a variety of common law and statutory theories for damages allegedly resulting from the creditor's conduct in extending or refusing to extend credit, revoking a line of credit or foreclosing on security, or administering a loan. Examples of various common law theories of recovery include:

1. *Breach of Contract.* For example, current or prospective debtors often sue banks for breach of an alleged agreement, usually oral, to extend credit or to renew existing credit.

2. *Fraud and Misrepresentation.* A lender may, for example, be held liable for misrepresenting its customer's financial condition to a third-party financing company, or for fraudulently inducing its customer to provide additional collateral on the false assurance that additional credit would be extended.

3. *Breach of Implied Duty of Good Faith and Fair Dealing.* Under this theory, creditors have been held liable for discontinuing a borrower's financing without prior notice, thus preventing the borrower from obtaining alternate financing; bad faith refusal to reimburse the debtor for funds negligently paid from the debtor's account on a stolen check; and accelerating a loan or demanding additional collateral without good cause.

4. *Liability for Excessive Control.* Creditors often demand significant management control over debtors, often as a condition to continuing credit or extending additional credit to a troubled borrower. If the creditor's control is excessive, courts may subordinate the controlling creditor's claim to those of other creditors, or hold the controlling creditor liable as a principal, and therefore responsible for all of the debtor's acts and transactions in connection with the business. Creditors attempting to exert excessive control also have been sued for intentional interference with the debtor's contractual relations.

5. *Economic Duress.* As discussed in Chapter 11, creditors in financial difficulty may avoid coerced

settlements of obligations owed them by proving economic duress or business compulsion. Debtors also may use the theory to impose liability on creditors who in bad faith enforce or threaten to enforce legal rights.

6. *Negligence.* On this theory, creditors have been held liable for failing to exercise reasonable care to service a loan properly, to post loan payments to the debtor's account, or to inform the debtors that their loan had been approved.

7. *Breach of Fiduciary Duty.* Many courts hold that a fiduciary duty (similar to that discussed in the text material on trusts and business organizations) may arise in certain situations in the lender-borrower context.

In addition to common law theories, creditors have been sued under a variety of statutes including federal bankruptcy, securities, environmental, racketeering, tax, and wage law; and state consumer fraud legislation. Perhaps the most important statutory basis for imposing liability is the Comprehensive Environmental Response, Compensation, and Liability Act (CERCLA), discussed in Chapter 55, which provides a federal system for cleanup of hazardous waste sites. In recent years, a number of lenders who have exercised actual control in the management of a contaminated site, or acquired it through foreclosure, have been held liable for CERCLA cleanup costs.

In an attempt to limit lender liability litigation, many states have enacted or are considering statutory reforms. Although the content of these statutes varies widely, many amend the Statute of Frauds to require that commitments to loan money or extend credit exceeding a minimum dollar amount be evidenced by a signed writing to be enforceable. These provisions are designed to reduce the most common form of lender liability litigation: suits by disappointed borrowers against banks, based on breach of contract or estoppel theories, seeking damages for failure to honor oral promises or commitments to lend.

Consumer Credit Protection

In most consumer credit transactions, the creditor possesses greater bargaining power than the debtor. Some creditors have abused this power by arbitrarily refusing credit to deserving consumers or by misrepresenting contractual credit terms. To help eliminate these abusive practices, the federal government has enacted the **Consumer Credit Protection Act (CCPA),**[1] which includes three major statutes relating to the extension of consumer credit: the Equal Credit Opportunity Act, the Fair Credit Reporting Act, and the Truth-in-Lending Act. These statutes are supplemented by state laws that further regulate credit transactions.

Equal Credit Opportunity Act

The **Equal Credit Opportunity Act (ECOA)**[2] prohibits discrimination in credit transactions on the basis of sex, marital status, religion, race, color, national origin, or age. The ECOA also prohibits discrimination because all or part of a credit applicant's income is derived from a public assistance program or because the applicant has in good faith exercised any right under the Consumer Credit Protection Act. The purpose of ECOA is to prevent creditors from denying a person access to credit because of factors unrelated to creditworthiness. The Federal Reserve Board has issued **Regulation B**[3] to implement the ECOA.

The Credit Application. The ECOA restricts the information that a creditor may request on a credit application and limits the use of that information. A credit application, which includes both oral and written requests for credit, cannot request the applicant's race, color, religion, or national origin. Although the creditor may sometimes ask the applicant's sex, marital status, or age, this information may be used only for limited purposes not related to determining creditworthiness. A creditor may not ask for data about the applicant's spouse unless both spouses are applying for use of the credit (for example, a joint credit card account). Some types of information, such as the applicant's title (Mr., Ms., Miss, Mrs.), may be requested only if the application states that responding is optional. Disclosure of alimony, maintenance, or child support may be required only if the applicant relies on these payments as an income source for credit purposes. To ensure that applicants are aware of their rights, the creditor must provide notice of the general provisions of the ECOA.

---

[1] 15 U.S.C. §§1601–1693r.
[2] 15 U.S.C. §§1691–1691f (Subchapter IV of the Consumer Credit Protection Act).
[3] 12 C.F.R. part 202.

Use of Information. The ECOA prohibits the creditor from using any information about the applicant to discriminate on the basis of sex, marital status, age, religion, race, color, or national origin. Acts of intentional discrimination are illegal. A creditor, therefore, cannot deny credit to an applicant because she is a married woman or because he is Moslem or Hispanic. Credit practices with discriminatory effect on persons protected by the ECOA also are illegal. A creditor, for example, cannot routinely disregard part-time employment, alimony, or child support as sources of income because statistics show that women are more likely to rely on these sources of income. By disregarding these resources, the creditor would commit sex-based discrimination, illegal under the ECOA. Compliance with the ECOA requires that creditors evaluate the reliability of income from part-time employment, alimony, or child support in the same manner as they evaluate other sources of income.

The ECOA also prohibits certain discriminatory practices based on race, color, national origin, age, sex, or marital status in the actual extension of credit. For example, a creditor cannot impose a $1,000 credit line for a woman applicant while setting a $2,500 credit limit for a man with similar qualifications. Similarly, a creditor may not use different standards in evaluating married and unmarried applicants.

Notification of Credit Decision. One of the most important provisions of the ECOA requires a creditor to notify the applicant of the creditor's decision to extend or not to extend credit within 30 days after receiving the application. A creditor who takes adverse action must state specific reasons for the action taken. Adverse action includes a denial or revocation of credit, changing the terms of an existing credit arrangement, or refusing to extend credit in the amount or on the terms requested. A creditor who uses a credit scoring system cannot merely indicate that the applicant failed to achieve the requisite number of points, but must state the factors that most significantly affected the adverse score.

Enforcement. Several federal administrative agencies, including the Federal Trade Commission (FTC), are charged with enforcing compliance with ECOA requirements. The ECOA also creates a statutory civil cause of action for violation of the statute. A successful plaintiff is entitled to actual damages and reasonable attorneys' fees and may recover up to $10,000 in punitive damages.

Fair Credit Reporting Act

The federal **Fair Credit Reporting Act (FCRA)**,[4] as amended by the Fair and Accurate Credit Transactions Act (FACTA) of 2003, is designed to promote accuracy and fairness in consumer credit information. The FCRA primarily regulates the activities of **consumer reporting agencies,** organizations that regularly assemble or evaluate consumer credit information and other consumer information for use by third parties. Consumer reporting agencies include three companies that operate nationwide in the U.S.—Equifax, Inc., Experian Information Solutions, Inc., and TransUnion LLC—as well as smaller credit bureaus that operate regionally or locally. Consumer reporting agencies generally maintain a **credit file,** a record of all information on each consumer, composed of data provided by furnishers of credit information such as creditors, insurers, banks, and landlords. Consumer reporting agencies then provide reports on the consumer to creditors, insurers, and employers. FCRA also establishes rights of consumers affected by these reports including protection of victims of identity theft.

Regulated Reports. The FCRA regulates two types of reports prepared by consumer reporting agencies: consumer reports and investigative consumer reports. As defined by the FCRA, a **consumer report** is a communication of information, including oral and written communications, from a consumer reporting agency that bears on "a consumer's creditworthiness, credit standing, credit capacity, character, general reputation, personal characteristics, or mode of living."[5] Consumer reports generally are used or intended to serve as a factor in deciding a consumer's eligibility for credit, insurance, or employment. Consumer reports typically contain information collected by the agency from public records and the consumer's creditors. An **investigative consumer report** contains personal data about a consumer (information on the consumer's character, reputation, personal characteristics, or mode of living) obtained not from creditors but from personal interviews with the consumer's neighbors, friends, acquaintances, or associates. A creditor may not request an investigative consumer report without disclosing to the consumer that such a report will be obtained as part of the credit decision.

---

[4]15 U.S.C. §§1681–1681x (Subchapter III of the Consumer Credit Protection Act).
[5]15 U.S.C. §1681a(d)(1).

Use of Reports. A consumer reporting agency may provide reports only to persons that the agency has reason to believe intend to use the information (1) in connection with the extension of credit or review of a credit account, (2) for employment or insurance purposes, (3) to determine the consumer's eligibility for a license or other governmental benefit, or (4) for legitimate business purposes connected with a business transaction involving the consumer. The agency also may release a consumer report to a court or grand jury, or to the consumer on whom the report is made.

An employer may request a report for employment purposes only after providing written notification to employees or applicants and securing their written authorization. FCRA also limits medical information that may be provided by consumer reporting agencies. Agencies are prohibited from furnishing a report that contains medical information without the consumer's consent. Employers and creditors must secure a more detailed consent than is required for insurers. Consumer reports may include information on *financial* transactions with a medical provider but only if the provider's identifying information and nature of the medical services are excluded. Those who secure medical information in a consumer report cannot disclose the information to others.

Before taking adverse action based upon the report, the employer must provide the employee or applicant with a copy of the report and a statement of the FCRA consumer rights. When obtaining the report, the employer must certify to the consumer reporting agency that it will comply with the preceding requirements and other applicable law.

Excluded Information. The FCRA prohibits consumer reporting agencies from disclosing obsolete adverse information in a consumer report. Such information includes bankruptcies that occurred more than ten years before the report and other negative information that antedates the report by more than seven years, such as civil lawsuits and judgments (although judgment records may be disclosed throughout the statute of limitations period if longer than seven years), paid tax liens, accounts placed for collection, and criminal records of arrest, indictment, or conviction. In addition, before releasing information from an investigative consumer report, the agency must reverify any adverse information that was obtained more than three months prior to the date of the report.

Consumer Rights. To help ensure accurate credit information, the FCRA grants a number of rights to consumers. Every consumer is entitled to receive a free credit file disclosure—commonly called a credit report—once every 12 months from each of the nationwide consumer credit reporting companies. Consumer also have the right to a free copy of the information in their credit file if adverse action, such as denial of credit, insurance, or employment, is taken based on a consumer report. The company or person who takes the adverse action is required to provide to the consumer the name and contact information of the consumer reporting agency that provided the report.

Consumers have the right to dispute incomplete or inaccurate information in their credit file by providing written notice to the credit reporting agency. The agency then must investigate and delete or correct any inaccurate, incomplete or unverifiable information within 30 days. If the agency finds that the information is accurate, the consumer is entitled to file a brief statement explaining the dispute. Upon request of the consumer, the consumer reporting agency must provide notice of a deletion or the consumer's statement explaining a dispute to creditors who received the re-port during the previous six months (two years if provided for employment purposes). In all subsequent reports, the agency must include the consumer's statement explaining the dispute or a summary of that statement.

FACTA grants additional consumers' rights with respect to furnishers of information to credit reporting agencies. A financial institution or other company that regularly extends credit must notify a consumer when initially providing negative information to a credit report agency. The consumer then has the right to dispute inaccurate or incomplete information and the furnisher of the information generally must investigate, correct any inaccurate information, and must provide correct information to all credit reporting agencies to which it provided the inaccurate information. Furnishers of information are prohibited from reporting information that they know or have reasonable cause to believe is inaccurate.

Identity Theft. Because credit information often contributes to identity theft, FACTA requires that credit card numbers on electronically printed receipts be truncated (abbreviated) no later than 2007. Consumers also may request that their social security number be truncated in credit reports. To help victims of identity theft, FACTA allows consumers to add to their credit file a fraud alert that requires any business to verify the consumer's identity prior to extending credit. A consumer may request an "initial fraud alert," which remains in the credit file for 90 days, by notifying, and providing proof of identity to, any one of the three nationwide consumer reporting agencies which then must convey the information to the other two agencies. To secure an "extended fraud alert," which stays in the credit file for seven years, the consumer must provide an identity theft report from a law enforcement agency. After filing a fraud alert, a consumer receives additional rights to free consumer reports. Consumers who go on active military have the option of adding the active duty military alert to their credit file.

Compliance Procedures and Enforcement. To assure compliance with its provisions, the FCRA requires that credit reporting agencies maintain and follow reasonable procedures designed to avoid violating the Act and to "assure maximum possible accuracy of the information"[6] in credit reports. To enforce its provisions, the FCRA provides for administrative enforcement by the FTC and other federal agencies, private civil remedies, and criminal penalties. If a credit reporting agency negligently violates any FCRA requirement, an injured consumer may sue in state or federal court and recover actual damages, court costs, and reasonable attorneys' fees. If the violation is willful, punitive damages also may be recovered. Obtaining information on a consumer from a credit reporting agency under false pretenses is punishable by fine or imprisonment for up to two years, or both. An employee or officer of the agency who knowingly or willfully provides information to an unauthorized person is subject to the same penalties.

In the following case, the court must determine whether a major nationwide consumer reporting agency used reasonable procedures in preparing a credit report.

Sarver v. Experian Information Solutions, Inc.
390 F.3d 969 (7th Cir. 2004)

In August 2002, Monogram Bank of Georgia rejected plaintiff Lloyd Sarver's application for credit based on a credit report sent to the bank by defendant Experian Information Solutions, Inc. (Experian). The report showed Sarver's accounts with Cross Country Bank as having been "involved in bankruptcy." Sarver, who never had been involved in bankruptcy, later discovered that a person named "Lloyd Sarver" had filed for bankruptcy in Pennsylvania in 1997. Sarver sued Experian asserting that it had violated the Fair Credit Reporting Act (FCRA) by providing an inaccurate credit report. The trial court granted summary judgment for Experian and Sarver appealed.

Evans, Circuit Judge

. . . Sarver's claim under [§1681e(b) of the FCRA] . . . requires that a credit reporting agency follow "reasonable procedures to assure maximum possible accuracy" when it prepares a credit report. . . . [T]o state a claim under the statute,

> a consumer must sufficiently allege that a credit reporting agency prepared a report containing 'inaccurate' information. However, the credit reporting agency is not automatically liable even if the consumer proves that it prepared an inaccurate credit report because the FCRA does not make reporting agencies strictly liable for all inaccuracies. A credit reporting agency is not liable under the FCRA if it followed reasonable procedures to assure maximum possible accuracy, but nonetheless reported inaccurate information in the consumer's credit report.

[*Henson v. CSC Credit Servs.,* 29 F.3d 280, 284 (7th Cir. 1994).]

The Commentary of the Federal Trade Commission to the FCRA, 16 C.F.R. pt. 600, app., section 607 at 3.A, states that the section does not hold a reporting agency responsible where an item of information, received from a source that it reasonably believes is reputable, turns out to be inaccurate unless the agency receives notice of systemic problems with its procedures.

Experian has provided an account of its procedures. The affidavit of David Browne, Experian's compliance manager, explains that the company gathers credit information originated by approximately 40,000 sources. The information is stored in a complex system of national databases, containing approximately 200 million names and addresses and some 2.6 billion trade lines, which include information about consumer accounts, judgments, etc. The company processes over 50 million updates to trade information each day.

---

[6]15 U.S.C. §1681e(b).

Lenders report millions of accounts to Experian daily; they provide identifying information, including address, social security number, and date of birth. The identifying information is used to link the credit items to the appropriate consumer. Mr. Browne also notes that Experian's computer system does not store complete credit reports, but rather stores the individual items of credit information linked to identifying information. The credit report is generated at the time an inquiry for it is received.

One can easily see how, even with safeguards in place, mistakes can happen. But given the complexity of the system and the volume of information involved, a mistake does not render the procedures unreasonable. In his attempt to show that Experian's procedures are unreasonable, Sarver argues that someone should have noticed that only the Cross Country accounts were shown to have been involved in bankruptcy. That anomaly should have alerted Experian, Sarver says, to the fact that the report was inaccurate. What Sarver is asking, then, is that each computer-generated report be examined for anomalous information and, if it is found, an investigation be launched. In the absence of notice of prevalent unreliable information from a reporting lender, which would put Experian on notice that problems exist, we cannot find that such a requirement to investigate would be reasonable given the enormous volume of information Experian processes daily.

We found in *Henson* that a consumer reporting agency was not liable, as a matter of law, for reporting information from a judgment docket unless there was prior notice from the consumer that the information might be inaccurate. We said that a

> contrary rule of law would require credit reporting agencies to go beyond the face of numerous court records to determine whether they correctly report the outcome of the underlying action. Such a rule would also require credit reporting agencies to engage in background research which would substantially increase the cost of their services. In turn, they would be forced to pass on the increased costs to their customers and ultimately to the individual consumer.

Henson, 29 F.3d at 285. The same could be said for records from financial institutions. . . . [L]enders report many millions of accounts to Experian daily. Sarver's report, dated August 26, 2002, contains entries from six different lenders. The increased cost to Experian to examine each of these entries individually would be

enormous. We find that as a matter of law there is nothing in this record to show that Experian's procedures are unreasonable.

[Judgment affirmed.]

Truth-in-Lending Act

The most comprehensive federal statute concerning consumer credit is the **Truth-in-Lending Act (TILA),**[7] which requires creditors to disclose to consumers specified contractual terms of credit transactions. **Regulation Z,**[8] issued by the Federal Reserve Board, implements the TILA.

Scope. The TILA governs only consumer credit transactions, those in which the debtor is a natural person seeking credit for personal, family, or household purposes. The TILA applies only to creditors who regularly extend credit and to whom the debt is initially payable. Accordingly, banks, savings and loan institutions, credit card companies, retailers, and professionals who make loans or sell goods or services on credit generally are subject to the provisions of the TILA. Under the TILA, a transaction involves the extension of credit if the creditor imposes a finance charge or if the debt is payable in more than four installments (even if no finance charge is imposed). Most credit transactions in excess of $25,000 are exempted. If, however, the transaction creates a security interest in the consumer's real property (for example, a loan to make improvements on a house), or if the creditor takes a security interest in personal property that is the consumer's primary dwelling (for example, a mobile home), the creditor must comply with the TILA regardless of the amount of credit.

Disclosure Requirements. Regulation Z specifies the credit terms that a creditor must disclose and requires the disclosures to be made "clearly and conspicuously" in a written form that the consumer may keep.[9] Two of the most important credit terms are the "finance charge"

---

[7]15 U.S.C. §§1601–1667e (Subchapter I of the Consumer Credit Protection Act).
[8]12 C.F.R. part 226.
[9]15 U.S.C. §1632(a); 12 C.F.R. §§226.5(a), 226.17(a).

and the "annual percentage rate," which must be disclosed more conspicuously than other information provided except the creditor's identity.

The **finance charge** is the cost of consumer credit expressed in a dollar amount. It includes all charges imposed by the creditor upon the consumer incident to or as a condition of extending credit. Under the TILA, therefore, a finance charge includes not only interest or a time-price differential but also other fees that the creditor requires the debtor to pay to obtain credit. Such fees include service or carrying charges, loan fees, finder's fees, fees for appraisals and credit reports, charges for insurance paid by the debtor to protect the creditor if the debtor defaults, and certain other insurance premiums.[10]

The **annual percentage rate (APR)** generally is the finance charge on an annual basis expressed as a percentage of the amount of credit. Thus, whereas the finance charge is the cost of credit expressed in a dollar amount, the APR is its cost expressed as a yearly percentage rate. The TILA and Regulation Z provide a detailed explanation of the method of calculating the APR. Regulation Z also includes tables to assist the creditor.[11]

The TILA establishes different disclosure requirements for open-end and closed-end credit plans.[12] A creditor entering into an open-end agreement must make certain disclosures in writing in a statement issued at the time the account is opened and in statements issued on a periodic basis according to the creditor's billing cycle for periods in which the account has a debit or credit balance or in which a finance charge is made. The opening statement must include the conditions under which a finance charge is made, the method of determining the finance charge, the method of determining the balance upon which the finance charge is based, the periodic rate (for example, $1^{1}/_{2}$ percent per month), and the APR. The periodic statement provides similar information applied to specific transactions that occurred during the billing period: the previous balance, identification of each transaction, credits and payments, the balance subject to the finance charge, the finance charge and the periodic rate, and the APR. The TILA also requires the creditor to make other disclosures when changes in credit terms or other changes occur.

Prior to entering into a closed-end credit transaction, the creditor must provide a written disclosure statement that includes the identity of the creditor, the finance charge, the APR, the amount financed, the total of payments (amount financed plus finance charge), and the number, amount, and due dates of payments, and late fees (expressed in a dollar amount or on a percentage basis). If the creditor is taking a security interest in the debtor's property, the security interest must be disclosed. If the creditor is also the seller of the property for which the credit transaction was arranged, the disclosure statement also must show the "total sales price," indicating the cash price plus additional charges plus the finance charge. Figure 28.1, taken from Regulation Z, is a model disclosure form for a closed-end credit sale.

Other Provisions. In addition to these disclosure requirements, the TILA includes other provisions regulating credit transactions. For example, if the consumer credit transaction creates a security interest in the debtor's principal residence, the law grants the debtor an unconditional right to rescind the transaction until midnight of the third business day after the transaction is closed. The law extends the debtor's right of rescission to three years after the closing (or until the property is sold, whichever occurs first) if the creditor fails to make all "material disclosures" required by TILA including disclosure of the debtor's right of rescission.[13]

The TILA also includes the **Fair Credit Billing Act,**[14] which regulates billing practices and disputes for open-end credit accounts. The Fair Credit Billing Act includes procedures that the debtor and creditor must follow when billing errors occur. Each year the creditor must furnish the debtor with a statement outlining the debtor's rights and creditor's responsibilities under the Act.

Enforcement. The FTC and several other federal administrative agencies are responsible for enforcing the TILA. The Act also creates a civil cause of action for failure to comply with its disclosure requirements. A consumer who successfully sues a creditor for violation of the TILA may be awarded actual damages, plus a penalty generally equal to twice the finance charge. The TILA, however, creates a minimum penalty

---

[10]15 U.S.C. §1605.

[11]15 U.S.C. §1606(a); 12 C.F.R. part 226, Appendices F, J.

[12]15 U.S.C. §§1637–1638.

[13]15 U.S.C. §1635.

[14]15 U.S.C. §§1666–1666j.

Figure 28.1 — Credit Sale Sample

Big Wheel Auto				Carmen Green
ANNUAL PERCENTAGE RATE The cost of your credit as a yearly rate.	**FINANCE CHARGE** The dollar amount the credit will cost you.	**Amount Financed** The amount of credit provided to you or on your behalf.	**Total of Payments** The amount you will have paid after you have made all payments as scheduled.	**Total Sale Price** The total cost of your purchase on credit, including your down payment of $ 1500-
14.84 %	$ 1496.80	$ 6107.50	$ 7604.30	$ 9129.30

You have the right to receive at this time an itemization of the Amount Financed.
☐ I want an itemization. ☒ I do not want an itemization.

Your payment schedule will be:

Number of Payments	Amount of Payments	When Payments Are Due
36	$211.23	Monthly beginning 6-1-06

Insurance
Credit life insurance and credit disability insurance are not required to obtain credit, and will not be provided unless you sign and agree to pay the additional cost.

Type	Premium	Signature
Credit Life	$120-	I want credit life insurance. _Carmen Green_ Signature
Credit Disability		I want credit disability insurance. Signature
Credit Life and Disability		I want credit life and disability insurance. Signature

Security: You are giving a security interest in:
☒ the goods being purchased.
☐ _____

Filing fees $ _12.50_   **Non-filing insurance** $_____

Late charge: If a payment is late, you will be charged $10.

Prepayment: If you pay off early, you
☐ may ☐ will not have to pay a penalty.
☒ may ☐ will not be entitled to a refund of part of the finance charge.

See your contract documents for any additional information about nonpayment, default, any required repayment in full before the scheduled date, and prepayment refunds and penalties.

I have received a copy of this statement.

Carmen Green   5-1-06
Signature   Date

e means an estimate

of $100 and a maximum penalty of $1,000 in an individual suit. The successful consumer also may recover court costs and a reasonable attorneys' fee. A creditor may avoid liability by proving that its failure to comply was unintentional and resulted from a bona fide error (for example, clerical, calculation, or printing errors, and errors resulting from computer malfunction and programming). A creditor's "error of legal judgment" concerning its obligations under TILA is not a bona fide error.[15] To encourage creditors to correct disclosure violations, the TILA exempts from civil liability a creditor who discovers an error, notifies the debtor, and makes any necessary adjustments within 60 days after discovering the error, provided that the debtor is notified of the correction before the debtor institutes

[15] 15 U.S.C. §1640(c).

a lawsuit or gives written notice of the error to the creditor.

Finally, a creditor may be subject to criminal penalties of a maximum fine of $5,000 and up to one year imprisonment, or both, for willfully and knowingly providing false or inaccurate information required by the Act or Regulation Z.[16]

State Regulation of Credit Transactions

Many states have adopted statutes similar to the ECOA, the FCRA, and the TILA that govern credit transactions within the individual state. In general, state statutes supplement the provisions of federal law, and creditors must comply with both federal and state law. State statutes vary considerably but many provide more stringent requirements or more severe penalties than the federal laws. Almost every state has adopted some form of disclosure law concerning certain types of consumer transactions. These statutes have a variety of names, including the "Retail Installment Act," "State Truth-in-Lending Act," and "Motor Vehicle Sales Act."

The **Uniform Consumer Credit Code (UCCC),** originally promulgated in 1968 and revised in 1974, has been enacted in some form in approximately one-fourth of the states. It is designed to replace piecemeal state consumer credit laws with a single comprehensive code. The UCCC regulates, for example, interest rates, garnishment, home solicitation and referral sales, credit insurance, contract terms and disclosure, and creditors' remedies.

Usury Laws. Every state has adopted some form of usury statute that establishes a maximum rate of interest that may be charged for credit transactions. **Usury** is the act of charging an interest rate in excess of that allowed by state law.

State law often establishes two maximum interest rates. The "legal rate" applies to transactions in which the parties did not agree on an interest rate. For example, if a person or business buys goods or services on an open account and fails to pay, the creditor generally may charge the legal rate of interest on the outstanding balance. In most states, this rate is between 6 percent and 9 percent.

The second maximum interest rate is the "contract rate," which applies to transactions in which the parties have agreed to a specified rate of interest. The maximum contract rate usually is higher than the legal rate. Frequently, commercial credit transactions are exempted from the laws concerning the contract rate. That is, in transactions between two businesses, the parties may be free to establish as high a level of interest as they desire. Many states establish different contract rates for open-end and closed-end credit transactions, allowing a higher interest rate for open-end transactions.

A creditor is well advised to review state usury laws prior to entering into a credit transaction. Some states provide that the penalty for violating the usury law is forfeiture of the interest in excess of the allowed rate while other states penalize usury by requiring forfeiture of all interest or even by voiding the contract.

Summary

1. The debtor-creditor relation is governed primarily by state statutes, including Articles 6 and 9 of the UCC, and the federal law of bankruptcy. In addition, federal law regulates, particularly for consumer transactions, much of the process of extending credit and collecting debts from recalcitrant debtors.

2. In many debtor-creditor disputes, two or more creditors hold claims that, taken collectively, exceed the debtor's total assets. In this case, the order on priority in which competing creditors are paid must be determined.

3. One method used by creditors to establish priority in distribution of a debtor's assets is to create a lien upon all or some of the debtor's property. A lien—an interest in property securing payment or other performance of an obligation—gives a creditor recourse to specific property in which the lien exists to the exclusion of other creditors. Liens may be created with the debtor's consent, by statute or common law doctrine, or by judicial action.

4. In some cases, a creditor without a lien is granted a priority by statute in payment over certain other creditors. For example, federal bankruptcy law grants a priority in the distribution of the debtor's limited assets to certain creditors, such as employees, who do not possess a lien upon the debtor's property. General creditors, who possess neither a lien nor a

[16]15 U.S.C. §1611.

priority, are paid only after creditors with a lien or statutorily authorized priority.

5. To protect themselves against other creditors and to expedite collection upon default, creditors often insist upon some form of security. A contractually created lien in the debtor's property is the most common form of security. If the debtor's real property forms the security, the transaction is governed by the law of mortgages; if the debtor's personal property provides the security, the transaction is governed by Article 9 of the UCC. Another form of security is suretyship, in which a third party, the surely, is obligated to satisfy the obligation if the debtor does not.

6. To help eliminate abusive practices by creditors, the federal government has adopted the Consumer Credit Protection Act, which includes three statutes governing the extension of consumer credit: the Equal Credit Opportunity Act, the Fair Credit Reporting Act, and the Truth-in-Lending Act.

7. The Equal Credit Opportunity Act (ECOA) prohibits discrimination in credit transactions on the basis of sex, marital status, religion, race, color, national origin, age, or the applicant's receiving public assistance.

8. The Fair Credit Reporting Act (FCRA), which regulates consumer reporting agencies, limits the use of inaccurate information in consumer credit reports, and provides a mechanism to facilitate consumers' correcting and supplementing information in those reports.

9. The Truth-in-Lending Act (TILA) requires disclosure of specified credit terms in consumer credit transactions.

10. Many states have adopted statutes regulating consumer credit transactions that supplement federal law. In addition, state usury laws establish a maximum interest rate that may be charged in credit transactions.

Key Terms

debtor	statutory lien
creditor	common law lien
judgment debtor	artisan's lien
judgment creditor	bailee's lien
commercial credit	landlord's lien
consumer credit	mechanic's lien
closed-end credit	tax lien
open-end credit	judicial lien
insolvency	priorities
lien	general creditor

security	credit file
right of foreclosure	consumer report
secured creditor	investigative consumer report
Consumer Credit Protection Act (CCPA)	Truth-in-Lending Act (TILA)
	Regulation Z
Equal Credit Opportunity Act (ECOA)	finance charge
	annual percentage rate (APR)
Regulation B	Fair Credit Billing Act
Fair Credit Reporting Act (FCRA)	Uniform Consumer Credit Code (UCCC)
consumer reporting agency	usury

Questions and Problems

28.1 As discussed in the text, general creditors are in the worst position when a debtor encounters financial difficulty. Why would a creditor extend credit without taking security — that is, does a creditor ever act reasonably by becoming a general creditor?

28.2 Major Department Store uses a credit scoring system to determine an applicant's creditworthiness. One of the factors used in the system is the zip code. If an applicant's residence is in zip code 12345, the applicant receives five points. If the applicant's residence is in zip code 67890, the applicant receives negative five points. Zip code 12345 is an upper-middle-class suburb with predominantly white residents. Zip code 67890 is an inner-city neighborhood with predominantly black residents. Does this system violate the ECOA?

28.3 Patsy Anderson, a married woman, has applied for a loan from United Finance Co. United verified Anderson's credit background and agreed to lend her the money provided she grants a security interest in her household goods. United has prepared a promissory note that requires both Anderson's and her husband's signature. United also has prepared a security agreement for both of their signatures. Anderson has explained to United that the loan is for her own use and she — not her husband — will repay it. Nevertheless, United has insisted that both parties sign because the household goods that will serve as collateral are jointly owned by Anderson and her husband. Has United violated the ECOA?

28.4 Mr. and Mrs. Freeman borrowed money from Southern Bank. Although the Freemans fully repaid the loan, Southern Bank has on several occasions sent reports to the local credit bureau and to other creditors stating that the Freemans have failed to repay the loan.
(a) The Freemans have filed a lawsuit alleging that Southern Bank has violated the Fair Credit Reporting Act. How should the court rule on their complaint?
(b) What other remedies are available to the Freemans?

CHAPTER 29

CREDITORS' REMEDIES

Major Topics

- **the remedies available under state law that assist creditors in collecting debts, and the laws protecting debtors against abusive or deceptive collection practices**
- **the law of fraudulent conveyances and bulk sales, which protect creditors when a debtor transfers property to a third party in an effort to hinder, delay, or defraud creditors**

Most debtors promptly pay their obligations as they come due. The law of debtors and creditors is concerned with those who do not. A debtor may be unwilling or unable to pay a legitimate debt for various reasons. The debtor may be overextended due to poor management of his business or finances, or because of illness or disability. Or the debtor may have fraudulently incurred the obligation, with no intent to repay it or at least with no qualms about leaving creditors unpaid at the first sign of financial difficulty. Whatever the reason for nonpayment, in debtor-creditor law the validity of the plaintiff-creditor's claim usually is not in question. Rather, the law generally addresses two fundamental issues: debt collection remedies and priority disputes.

This chapter examines the first of these issues, the various remedies available under state law to aid creditors in collecting debts from unwilling or dishonest debtors. These remedies, which may be available either before or after a judgment is obtained, are designed to locate and apply to the debt assets held (1) by the debtor, (2) by third parties indebted to the debtor, or (3) by third parties to whom the debtor has transferred the property with intent to frustrate or defraud creditors.

In addition to providing debt collection remedies, debtor-creditor law resolves so-called priority disputes among competing creditors all holding valid claims against the debtor. Disputes often arise among secured creditors, between secured creditors and creditors holding judicial or statutory liens upon the debtor's property, between secured creditors and buyers of the collateral from the debtor, and between secured creditors and general unsecured creditors of the debtor. Priority disputes among various creditors of the same debtor form the bulk of debtor-creditor law. They are the primary focus of the law of secured transactions (discussed in Chapters 31 and 32), mortgages (covered in Chapter 37), and bankruptcy (discussed in Chapter 30).

State Debt Collection Remedies

If an individual fails to pay a debt when due, the creditor usually first tries nonjudicial means of collection including phone calls, letters threatening legal action ("dunning letters"), or personal visits. If these efforts fail, the creditor may turn to the legal system.

Although judicial debt collection remedies are designed to reach the debtor's assets and apply them to the unpaid debt, every state, by statute or constitutional provision, exempts certain property from creditors' claims. These state **exemption statutes** protect the debtor or her family from total destitution. Although individual state statutes vary widely, all exempt certain personal property identified by type or value. Real property used as a residence may be exempt under a "homestead" exemption. State statutes also usually protect certain forms of income, such as income from trusts and wages.[1]

The following material discusses the state debt collection remedies used by creditors to reach a debtor's nonexempt assets.

The Judgment

Under the Fifth and Fourteenth Amendments to the Constitution, no person may be deprived of life, liberty, or property without due process of law. Due process generally includes notice to the defendant and a hearing relevant to the nature of the case. In the debtor-creditor context, therefore, a debtor generally may not be forced to part with property (money) without a judicial determination of the validity of the creditor's claim. This judicial determination is embodied in a judgment rendered by a court.

To obtain a judgment, the creditor files a lawsuit against the debtor alleging facts supporting the existence of the debt and the debtor's default. A copy of the complaint and summons are then served upon the debtor (service of process), which satisfies the notice aspect of the due process requirement. The debtor is then given the opportunity to appear in court to contest the existence or amount of the debt. If the debtor contests the claim, a trial is held (the hearing aspect of the due process requirement) after which the court may find for the debtor or may render judgment against the debtor for all or part of the creditor's claim. If the debtor fails to answer the complaint or appear in court, a **default judgment** will be entered for the creditor for the amount stated in the complaint. Collection lawsuits usually result in a default judgment in the creditor's favor.

A creditor desires to obtain a judgment as quickly and cheaply as possible after default to take advantage of the collection remedies available to a judgment creditor. One device traditionally used by creditors to expedite the process of obtaining judgment is the **cognovit or confession of judgment clause.** A cognovit clause is a term contained in the original contract creating the debt, such as a lease or promissory note, authorizing the creditor to obtain a judgment against the debtor upon default without notice to the debtor or a hearing. The clause generally authorizes the creditor to choose an attorney to appear in court and confess judgment against the debtor for the amount in default along with other charges, usually including attorneys' fees. Because their operation is diametrically at odds with the Due Process Clause, cognovit clauses have been harshly received by the courts. Although the Supreme Court has not declared cognovit clauses unconstitutional *per se*,[2] most states, by statute, either have abolished them or severely limited their use. The legal attitude toward cognovit clauses is particularly harsh if they are imposed in adhesion contracts governing consumer transactions such as residential leases or installment sales of consumer goods.

Both secured and unsecured creditors may obtain a judgment because both have a personal right against the debtor for the amount of the debt. The secured creditor, additionally, has rights in the collateral that may or may not require a judicial proceeding to enforce. If a secured creditor obtains a judgment and the value of the collateral is insufficient to discharge it, the balance due is known as a **deficiency judgment.** The creditor may then attempt to collect the deficiency from the debtor's remaining assets by using the various collection remedies outlined below.

Prejudgment (Provisional) Remedies

In certain limited situations, a creditor may have rights to the debtor's assets before judgment. For example, a secured creditor may, as part of the security agreement, be entitled to repossess the debtor's assets upon default without judicial authorization. Further, an unsecured creditor may acquire rights in the debtor's property before the validity of the creditor's claim is determined by using prejudgment or "provisional" remedies. Prejudgment remedies are extraordinary and provisional because the creditor's ultimate right to the assets is dependent upon its later

---

[1]The federal Bankruptcy Code, discussed in Chapter 30, also contains a provision exempting certain property from creditors' claims.

[2]D. H. Overmyer Co., Inc. v. Frick Co., 92 S. Ct. 775 (1972).

obtaining a judgment against the debtor. Prejudgment remedies also are subject to constitutional due process limitations outlined later in this chapter.

Attachment. **Attachment,** originally developed in early English common law, is a prejudgment remedy now generally governed by statute and is designed to reach assets in the hands of the debtor. Attachment is used most often by a creditor who fears that the debtor may dissipate, squander, fraudulently transfer, or conceal assets during the course of the lawsuit establishing the validity of the creditor's claim. To assure that assets are available when a judgment is obtained, state statutes authorize the use of a **writ of attachment.**

To use the attachment remedy, the creditor files a motion and supporting affidavit with the court. The affidavit must allege facts indicating the grounds for attachment and the validity of the creditor's underlying claim. Notice is served on the debtor, who then has an opportunity to contest the application. If the court finds the remedy appropriate, it authorizes issuance of a writ of attachment. The writ directs the sheriff to take custody of the debtor's personal or real property and hold the property during the trial of the case to assure its availability if and when the creditor obtains a judgment. If the creditor obtains a judgment, the seized assets then are used to satisfy it.

The sheriff's act in taking custody of the debtor's property is known as **levy.** For tangible personal property, the sheriff levies by physically seizing the property and taking it into custody. This method also is used for intangibles evidenced by an indispensable document, such as negotiable instruments or stock certificates. For other intangibles, levy requires serving notice on the person holding the property (the garnishee) using the garnishment process discussed below. For real property, the sheriff levies by filing an appropriate notice in the real estate records discussed in Chapter 37.

A creditor seeking attachment usually must post a bond to reimburse the debtor for losses if the debtor successfully defends the creditor's action on the underlying debt. All states allow the debtor to recover damages from the creditor for a wrongful attachment.

Attachment creates a lien upon the property levied. The lien is effective from the date the levy is made, or in some states, from the date the writ is delivered to the sheriff. If the creditor subsequently obtains a judgment, the attaching creditor generally has priority over other liens that took effect after the effective date of the attachment lien.

Prejudgment Garnishment. **Garnishment** (in some states known as "trustee process") is a collection remedy directed to a third party (the "garnishee") who holds property of, or is indebted to, the debtor. Garnishment is both a prejudgment and postjudgment remedy.

The procedure for prejudgment garnishment is similar to that used for attachment. Once authorized by the court, the writ directs the garnishee not to pay the debtor until the creditor's suit against the debtor has concluded and any judgment rendered therein paid. Most garnishees either are banks in which the debtor maintains an account or are employers owing wages to the debtor. Prejudgment garnishment is similar to attachment in that both remedies preserve assets which may be used to satisfy a later judgment. Additionally, both remedies create a lien upon the property involved. In garnishment the lien usually is effective from the date process is served on the garnishee.

Replevin and Self-Help. **Replevin** is a statutory prejudgment remedy enabling the plaintiff to recover possession of specific goods wrongfully taken or detained. Unlike attachment, which may be used to reach all nonexempt property of the debtor, replevin is available only to a creditor who has a lien upon the property involved or the right to possession. As such, replevin is used primarily by secured creditors to recover possession of (repossess) property in which they have a security interest after default by the debtor. For example, a replevin action might be used by a bank to repossess an automobile after default by a borrower on an auto loan. In most states, the plaintiff obtains a writ of replevin by filing an affidavit with the clerk of the court and posting a bond. Following notice to the debtor and a hearing, the sheriff then "replevies" (seizes) the property and turns it over to the plaintiff pending resolution of the suit over the right to possession.

Closely related to replevin is the ancient remedy of **self-help,** widely used in secured lending. Under self-help, upon default by the debtor, the creditor simply repossesses the collateral (such as an automobile) without resort to judicial process. The self-help remedy may be provided for in the contract between debtor and creditor, and Article 9 of the UCC explicitly authorizes its use. Self-help is quicker and cheaper than obtaining a writ of replevin, but replevin is more appropriate if the creditor fears that the debtor will resist attempts at self-help repossession.

Receivership. A **receiver** is a person appointed by the court to take possession of an administer, preserve, or manage the debtor's property under court direction. Receivership is an extraordinary equitable remedy, available only when the remedy at law, such as attachment, is inadequate. Like garnishment, receivership is both a prejudgment and postjudgment remedy.

A receiver is a neutral, disinterested party, possessing only those powers and duties conferred by the court. Usually those powers include taking possession of (but not title to) specified property and preserving it pending the outcome of the litigation. Additionally, limited management duties, such as collection of rent, may be imposed.

Unlike other provisional remedies, appointment of a receiver does not create a lien upon or affect title to the property. Existing liens on the property remain valid and subsequent judgment creditors, including the petitioning creditor, may obtain liens upon it. Receivership therefore benefits all creditors by preserving the property while conflicting creditors' claims to it are resolved.

Constitutional Limitations on Prejudgment Remedies.

Attachment, garnishment, replevin, and other prejudgment remedies deprive the debtor of property before the court determines validity of the creditor's claim. For this reason, debtors often have challenged state prejudgment remedies as a taking of property without due process of law, thereby violating the Fourteenth Amendment. Since the classic case of *Sniadach v. Family Finance Corporation of Bay View,*[3] decided in 1969, the Supreme Court has held in a series of cases that prejudgment remedies are subject to constitutional due process limitations generally requiring either notice to the debtor and an opportunity for a hearing before state governmental agents (such as a court officer, marshal, or sheriff) seize the debtor's property, or other procedural safeguards to provide debtor protection. In the following case, the Supreme Court considered the constitutionality of a statute authorizing prejudgment attachment.

Connecticut v. Doehr

111 S. Ct. 2105 (1991)

John DiGiovanni sued Brian Doehr for damages alleging that Doehr had committed an assault and battery injuring DiGiovanni. Under Connecticut law, a court may authorize

---

[3]89 S. Ct. 1820 (1969).

attachment of a defendant's real estate before a trial (that is, prejudgment) provided that the plaintiff in the lawsuit submits an affidavit establishing probable cause that the plaintiff's claim is valid. DiGiovanni requested the court to attach Doehr's home and filed a five-sentence affidavit. The trial court found that the affidavit established probable cause and ordered attachment of Doehr's house. After the sheriff attached the property, Doehr received a notice informing him that he could request a hearing to challenge the attachment. At that time he had not yet received service of the complaint in the assault and battery lawsuit. Doehr sued the state of Connecticut and DiGiovanni alleging that the Connecticut attachment statute violated the Due Process Clause of the Fourteenth Amendment. The District Court upheld the statute but the Court of Appeals reversed. The U.S. Supreme Court granted Connecticut's petition for review.

Justice White

. . . This case requires us to determine whether a state statute that authorizes prejudgment attachment of real estate without prior notice or hearing, without a showing of extraordinary circumstances, and without a requirement that the person seeking the attachment post a bond, satisfies the Due Process Clause of the Fourteenth Amendment. We hold that, as applied to this case, it does not. . . .

With this case we return to the question of what process must be afforded by a state statute enabling an individual to enlist the aid of the State to deprive another of his or her property by means of the prejudgment attachment or similar procedure. Our cases reflect the numerous variations this type of remedy can entail. In *Sniadach v. Family Finance Corp. of Bay View,* [89 S. Ct. 1820 (1969)], the Court struck down a Wisconsin statute that permitted a creditor to effect prejudgment garnishment of wages without notice and prior hearing to the wage earner. In *Fuentes v. Shevin,* [92 S. Ct. 1983 (1972)], the Court likewise found a Due Process violation in state replevin provisions that permitted vendors to have goods seized through an *ex parte* application to a court clerk and the posting of a bond. Conversely, the Court upheld a Louisiana *ex parte* procedure allowing a lienholder to have disputed goods sequestered in *Mitchell v. W. T. Grant Co.,* [94 S. Ct. 1895 (1974)]. . . . [Unlike the statute in *Fuentes,* the Louisiana statute provided for] an immediate postdeprivation hearing along with the option of damages; the requirement that a judge rather than a clerk determine that there is a clear showing of entitlement to the writ; the necessity for a detailed affidavit; and an emphasis on the lien-holder's interest in preventing waste or alienation of the encumbered property. . . .

In [*Mathews v. Eldridge,* 96 S. Ct. 893, 902 (1976),] we drew upon our prejudgment remedy decisions to determine what process is due when the government itself seeks to effect a deprivation on its own initiative. . . . That analysis resulted in the now familiar threefold inquiry requiring . . . first, consideration of the private interest that will be affected by the prejudgment measure; second, an examination of the risk of erroneous deprivation through the procedures under attack and the probable value of additional or alternative safeguards; and third, . . . the interest of the party seeking the prejudgment remedy. . . .

[1.] [T]he property interests that attachment affects are significant. For a property owner like Doehr, attachment ordinarily clouds title; impairs the ability to sell or otherwise alienate the property; taints any credit rating; [and] reduces the chance of obtaining a home equity loan or additional mortgage. . . . [E]ven the temporary or partial impairments to property rights that attachments, liens, and similar encumbrances entail are sufficient to merit due process protection. . . .

[2.] [T]he risk of erroneous deprivation that the State permits here is substantial. By definition, attachment statutes premise a deprivation of property on one ultimate factual contingency—the award of damages to the plaintiff which the defendant may not be able to satisfy. . . . As the record shows, . . . only a skeletal affidavit need be and was filed. . . . It is self-evident that the judge could make no realistic assessment concerning the likelihood of an action's success based upon these one-sided, self-serving, and conclusory submissions. . . . [I]n a case like this involving an alleged assault, even a detailed affidavit would give only the plaintiff's version of the confrontation. Unlike determining the existence of a debt or delinquent payments, the issue does not concern "ordinarily uncomplicated matters that lend themselves to documentary proof." [*Mitchell v. W. T. Grant Co.,* 94 S. Ct. 1895, 1901 (1974).] . . . What safeguards the State does afford do not adequately reduce this risk. . . .

[3.] Finally, we conclude that the interests in favor of an *ex parte* attachment, particularly the interests of the plaintiff, are too minimal . . . here. . . . His only interest in attaching the property was to ensure the availability of assets to satisfy his judgment if he prevailed on the merits of his action. Yet there was no allegation that Doehr was about to transfer or encumber his

real estate or take any other action during the pendency of the action that would render his real estate unavailable to satisfy a judgment. Our cases have recognized such a properly supported claim would be an exigent circumstance permitting postponing any notice or hearing until after the attachment is effected. . . . Absent such allegations, however, the plaintiff's interest in attaching the property does not justify the burdening of Doehr's ownership rights without a hearing to determine the likelihood of recovery. . . .

Historical and contemporary practice support our analysis. . . . Generally speaking, attachment measures in both England and this country had several limitations that reduced the risk of erroneous deprivation which Connecticut permits. Although attachments ordinarily did not require prior notice or a hearing, they were usually authorized only where the defendant had taken or threatened to take some action that would place the satisfaction of the plaintiff's potential award in jeopardy. . . . Attachments, moreover, were generally confined to claims by creditors. . . . [D]isputes between debtors and creditors more readily lend themselves to accurate *ex parte* assessments of the merits. Tort actions, like the assault and battery claim at issue here, do not. . . .

Connecticut's statute appears even more suspect in light of current practice. A survey of state attachment provisions reveals that nearly every State requires either a preattachment hearing, a showing of some exigent circumstance, or both, before permitting an attachment to take place. . . . [T]he procedures of almost all the States confirm our view that the Connecticut provision before us, by failing to provide a preattachment hearing without at least requiring a showing of some exigent circumstance, clearly falls short of the demands of due process. . . .

[Judgment affirmed.]

Postjudgment Collection Remedies

Because most collection lawsuits result in a default judgment for the creditor, obtaining a judgment against the debtor is frequently a simple task. Collecting the judgment usually is much more difficult. The law provides various remedies designed to assist the creditor in locating, seizing, and converting to cash, assets necessary to pay the judgment creditor.

Judgment Liens. In most states, a judgment creates a lien upon the judgment debtor's real property. In some states, the **judgment lien** is created the moment the judgment is rendered. In most states, the lien does not arise until the judgment is docketed or recorded with an appropriate public officer, such as the county recorder of deeds. Generally, the law determines priority between the judgment lienor and other competing interests in the property by the order of recording or docketing.

Execution. A judgment and judgment lien do not put money into the creditor's pocket. Creditors are paid through the judicial process of **execution,** which is similar in many ways to attachment. The creditor possessing an unpaid judgment petitions the clerk of the court to issue a **writ of execution** directed to the sheriff or other appropriate public official. The writ directs the sheriff to levy upon (seize) the debtor's real and personal property, sell the property at public sale (an **execution sale**), and apply the proceeds to the unpaid judgment.

The writ specifies a "return date" by which the sheriff must return it to the issuing clerk indicating which assets were seized and sold or that no assets could be found. If no leviable assets are found, the writ is returned unsatisfied. Note that unlike attachment (after which the sheriff holds the assets pending the outcome of the litigation), a levy in execution anticipates sale of the assets to satisfy the judgment.

The judgment creditor possesses a lien upon the debtor's *real property* due to his judgment lien. The judgment creditor obtains a lien upon *personal property* through the writ of execution. In most states, the lien does not attach until the sheriff actually levies upon the property involved. In a few states, however, the lien attaches when the writ is delivered to the sheriff. Priority among execution liens is therefore determined by the order of delivery of the writ or order of levy, depending on the state.

Postjudgment Garnishment. In postjudgment garnishment, the creditor files a complaint alleging that it holds an unpaid judgment against the debtor and that the garnishee holds property belonging to the debtor that may be used to satisfy the judgment. A copy of the complaint and summons is then served on the garnishee and in many states notice also is served upon the judgment debtor. The garnishee then has a stated period within which to file an answer to the complaint stating the property, wages, or other liability, if any, owing to the debtor. If the garnishee admits liability to the debtor, the garnishee must turn the property over to the court for disposition to the judgment creditor. If the garnishee contests the existence or amount of any obligation, the court holds a hearing to determine the garnishee's liability to the judgment debtor.

Certainly the most common garnishee is an employer owing wages to an employee-debtor. Wage garnishments, made either before or after judgment, are subject to important limitations imposed by federal law. Under Subchapter II of the Consumer Credit Protection Act,[4] creditors may garnish no more than 25 percent of the debtor's weekly disposable earnings,[5] *or* the amount by which his weekly disposable earnings exceed 30 times the federal minimum wage, whichever is less. The law authorizes a larger garnishment percentage (50 to 65 percent of disposable earnings) to satisfy orders for support of a spouse or child. Orders issued by a court to implement a rehabilitation plan under Chapter 13 of the federal Bankruptcy Code, and debts due for any state or federal tax, are not subject to the restrictions outlined above. In addition to limiting the amount of wages that may be garnished, the law also prohibits an employer from discharging any employee because the employee's earnings have been garnished for any one indebtedness.

Creditor's Bill and Supplementary Proceedings. In attempting to enforce a judgment by execution or garnishment, creditors often are frustrated by lack of knowledge concerning the existence or whereabouts of the debtor's assets. To aid the creditor in discovering assets and to prevent the debtor from conveying or encumbering them, the law provides two related remedies, the creditor's bill and supplementary proceedings.

At early common law, a writ of execution could not be used to reach equitable assets, such as a beneficiary's interest in a trust, or intangibles. To correct this deficiency in the legal remedy, courts of equity developed the **creditor's bill,** under which the creditor files a "bill" with the court requesting that the debtor be ordered to turn over his equitable and intangible assets for sale in satisfaction of the judgment. Commonly, part of the creditor's bill is a bill of discovery under which

[4]15 U.S.C. §§1671–1677.
[5]"Disposable earnings" means the employee's wages, salary, or commissions less deductions required by law, such as income and Social Security tax withholding.

the debtor and third parties can be examined in court in an effort to locate assets.

The importance of the creditor's bill has diminished somewhat in recent times. Most modern execution statutes now reach equitable and intangible assets in the debtor's hands and garnishment may be used to reach claims owed to the debtor by third parties. Further, simpler, more expeditious supplementary proceedings now commonly accomplish the discovery function of the creditor's bill.

Unlike the creditor's bill, which is a separate equitable action commenced by the creditor, **supplementary proceedings** are summary in nature and used as part of the original lawsuit. Supplementary proceedings generally may be used as soon as the judgment is rendered, and provide for discovery of assets, injunctions against transfer, and discretionary power to appoint receivers. Although supplementary proceedings are cheaper and quicker than a creditor's bill, they may provide less protection to the judgment creditor. Whereas the service of process upon the debtor under the creditor's bill generally creates a lien upon the debtor's assets, supplementary proceedings do not create a lien in some states.

Although largely supplanted by supplementary proceedings, the creditor's bill is, however, often used to recover property transferred by the debtor to third parties with intent to hinder, delay, or defraud creditors. The law of such "fraudulent conveyances" is discussed later in this chapter.

Debtor Protection

The Debt Collection Problem. If informal creditor efforts at debt collection fail, merchants often turn the collection effort over to a collection agency. Because a collection agency is called in only after polite request and persuasion have failed, some collection agencies, which often operate on a 50 percent commission, have resorted to questionable, extrajudicial tactics to collect. Examples include false or misleading representations, harassment or abuse, and unfair collection practices.

Individual states have taken steps to curb collection abuse. For example, harassed debtors have been allowed to recover damages under common law tort theories such as defamation, invasion of privacy, interference with contractual relations, and malicious prosecution. In addition, many states have enacted legisla-

tion requiring licensing and regulation of collection agencies. These state efforts were largely ineffective. General tort theories required the expense and delay of a lawsuit and were available only in aggravated cases. State legislation was piecemeal, often providing no civil damage remedy to injured debtors, and was unable to control debt collectors operating in interstate commerce.

The Fair Debt Collection Practices Act. In response to these inadequate state law remedies, Congress in 1977 enacted the **Fair Debt Collection Practices Act (FDCPA).**[6] The FDCPA applies to collection of debts contracted by consumers for personal, family, or household purposes. It imposes various restrictions and obligations upon independent "debt collectors," which generally include all third persons such as collection agencies regularly engaged in the business of collecting debts for others. Debt collectors also include attorneys who collect debts on behalf of their clients. Generally, the original creditor attempting to collect a debt in its own name is not a "debt collector" subject to the Act. The creditor loses this exemption, however, by using a name other than its own to falsely indicate that a third party (such as an attorney or collection agency) is involved in the collection effort.

The FDCPA preempts state law governing debt collection practices only to the extent that the state law is "inconsistent" with the Act's provisions. A state providing greater debtor protection than the FDCPA is not deemed to be inconsistent. The major substantive provisions of the FDCPA are discussed below.

Obtaining Location Information. Debt collectors may communicate with third parties only to determine the debtor's whereabouts, including the debtor's residence, telephone number, and place of employment. In these communications the debt collector may not state that the debtor owes any debt and may not use language, symbols, or mail indicating that the correspondence relates to debt collection. The debt collector generally may contact a third party only once unless further contact is necessary to obtain complete information. Additionally, once the debt collector learns that the debtor is represented by an attorney, all further communication with third parties must stop

---

[6]15 U.S.C. §§1692–1692o (Subchapter V of the Consumer Credit Protection Act).

unless the attorney fails to answer the debt collector's communications.

Communication with the Debtor. The debt collector may not communicate with the debtor (1) at an inconvenient time (between 9 P.M. and 8 A.M.) or place; (2) if the debt collector knows the debtor is represented by an attorney; or (3) at the debtor's place of employment if the debt collector knows that the debtor's employer prohibits such communications. Generally, all debtor contact must cease after the debtor notifies the debt collector in writing that the debtor refuses to pay the debt or desires further communication to cease.

Prohibited Practices. The Act prohibits debt collectors from using false, deceptive, or misleading representations in their efforts to collect debts. Examples include: false representations that the debt collector is a government official, including use of badges or uniforms; false representations that any individual is an attorney or that any communication is from an attorney; a statement that nonpayment of the debt will result in legal proceedings or other action unless such action is lawful and the debt collector or creditor intends to take it; using written communications that resemble legal process forms; using a name other than the debt collector's actual or company name; falsely stating that the debtor has committed fraud or a violation of criminal law; misrepresenting the character, amount, or legal status of any debt, or the legal consequences of the debtor's action or inaction.

The Act also prohibits conduct designed to harass, oppress, or abuse the debtor. Examples include: using obscene or profane language, threats of violence, harassing or anonymous telephone calls, and publishing "deadbeat" lists. Finally, the Act prohibits unfair or unconscionable collection practices, such as collecting more than is legally owed, misusing postdated checks, and using envelopes identifying the sender as a debt collector.

Validation of Debts. A debt collector, within five days of the first communication, must provide the debtor with written notice of the amount of the debt and the creditor to whom it is owed. The debtor then has 30 days to contest the validity of the debt. If the debtor does so, collection efforts must cease until the debt collector sends the debtor verification, such as a copy of a judgment rendered against the debtor. This require-

ment prevents collection efforts against the wrong person or concerning previously paid debts.

Forum Abuse. To prevent "forum abuse," debt collectors may not institute legal proceedings in courts distant from or inconvenient to the debtor. Collection proceedings must be brought in the judicial district where the debtor resides or the underlying contract was signed. If real property is involved, the action must be brought where the land is located.

Remedies. The FDCPA authorizes private civil damage actions maintained by injured debtors. Debt collectors who violate the Act are liable for actual damages sustained, additional damages (not exceeding $1,000) as the court may allow, court costs, and attorneys' fees. Actions may be maintained in either state or federal court, subject to a one-year statute of limitations.

The Act also provides for administrative enforcement by the Federal Trade Commission. Violations of the FDCPA are treated as violations of a FTC trade regulation rule for which civil penalties may be imposed, as discussed in Chapter 52.

Fraudulent Conveyances and Bulk Sales

Creditors attempting to locate and seize assets may find that the debtor has conveyed away his property to third parties, such as friends and relatives, in an effort to prevent creditors from reaching them. For over four centuries, the law has protected creditors against such **fraudulent conveyances** or transfers by allowing them to recover the property from the transferee. The remainder of this chapter discusses fraudulent conveyance law and its counterpart, the law of bulk sales.

Fraudulent Conveyances

Development of the Law. The origin of fraudulent conveyance law is generally traced to the **Statute of Elizabeth,** enacted in England in 1570.[7] This statute provides generally that any transfer of property made with the "end purpose and intent, to delay, hinder or defraud creditors" is "utterly void." Although the statute rendered such transfers void, subsequent judicial inter-

---

[7]13 Eliz., ch. 5 (1570).

pretation held the transfers merely *voidable* by the transferor's creditors. That is, a fraudulent conveyance is valid as between the transferor and transferee.

Because the statute required proof of an actual intent to defraud—a difficult issue to prove—courts soon developed various circumstantial criteria, known as **badges of fraud,** to distinguish fraudulent from non-fraudulent transfers. Typically, a transfer evidencing one or more of the following characteristics is treated by the court as a fraudulent conveyance, voidable by the transferor's creditors: (1) if the transfer is general—involving all or substantially all of the debtor's assets; (2) if the transferor retains possession or the beneficial use of the property after transfer; (3) if the transfer is made in secret; (4) if the transfer is made to a family member, such as a spouse or child, or other insider; (5) if the transfer is made without consideration or for less than full and adequate consideration; (6) if the transfer is made in anticipation of or during litigation, or in anticipation of financial difficulty; (7) the debtor absconds or removes or conceals assets; or (8) the debtor was insolvent or became insolvent shortly after the transfer.[8]

In some American states, the Statute of Elizabeth was recognized as part of the common law inherited from England. In other states, the statute or its equivalent was legislatively enacted. Despite its common origin, state fraudulent conveyance law varied widely among states. To provide uniformity of the law and to reach injurious transfers made without *actual* intent to defraud, the National Conference of Commissioners on Uniform State Laws drafted the **Uniform Fraudulent Conveyance Act (UFCA)** in 1918. In 1984, the National Conference adopted a revision of the UFCA, known as the **Uniform Fraudulent Transfer Act (UFTA),** which is designed to integrate fraudulent conveyance law with the UCC and the federal Bankruptcy Code. The following discussion is based upon the UFTA, which has been enacted in most states.

Types of Fraudulent Transfers. As under the Statute of Elizabeth, the UFTA provides that a transfer[9] made or

obligation incurred with *actual* intent to hinder, delay, or defraud any creditor is fraudulent against both present creditors (those whose claims arose before the transfer was made) and future creditors. Like the Statute of Elizabeth, the UFTA uses the badges of fraud concept to determine actual intent.[10] The UFTA also states that a transfer made or obligation incurred by a person who receives less than reasonably equivalent value in exchange is constructively fraudulent (that is, fraudulent without regard to the debtor's actual intent) in three cases:

1. if the debtor after the transfer or obligation is left with assets that are unreasonably small to conduct the business or transaction in which she is engaged (fraudulent as to present and future creditors);
2. if the debtor intended to incur, or believed that she would incur, debts beyond her ability to pay as they mature (fraudulent as to present and future creditors);
3. if the debtor was insolvent at the time of or as a result of the transfer (fraudulent as to present creditors only).[11]

Finally, the UFTA recognizes as fraudulent certain preferential transfers by the debtor to an insider such as a relative of or corporation controlled by an individual debtor, a director or officer of a corporate debtor, or a partner of a partnership debtor. Specifically, a transfer is fraudulent as to present creditors if (1) the transfer was made to an insider for an antecedent debt (that is, an old or preexisting debt), (2) the debtor was insolvent at the time of the transfer, and (3) the insider had reasonable cause to believe that the debtor was insolvent.[12]

Remedies. If the debtor makes a fraudulent conveyance, an injured creditor has a choice of remedies. The creditor may maintain an action to have the conveyance set aside. Alternatively, the creditor may disregard the conveyance and attach or levy execution directly upon the property conveyed in the hands of the transferee. Other remedies also may be available to the creditor. For example, the court may enjoin the debtor from making further disposition of property, and in

---

[8]The badges of fraud concept was originally announced in *Twyne's Case,* 3 Co. Rep. 80b, 76 Eng. Rep. 809 (K.B. 1601).

[9]The UFTA defines "transfer" as "every mode, direct or indirect, absolute or conditional, voluntary or involuntary, of disposing of or parting with an asset or an interest in an asset, and includes payment of money, release, lease, and creation of a lien or other encumbrance." UFTA §1(12).

[10]UFTA §§4(a)(1); 4(b).

[11]UFTA §§4(a)(2); 5(a).

[12]UFTA §5(b). The bankruptcy implications of preferential transfers to insiders are discussed in Chapter 30.

aggravated cases, may appoint a receiver to take charge of the debtor's property.

In the following case, the court was required to determine whether a transfer of real property was made with actual intent to defraud, and therefore a fraudulent conveyance.

Dime Savings Bank of New York, FSB v. Butler

1997 Conn. Super. LEXIS 491 (1997)

> Defendant Nancy Butler and her brother Lawrence Noel co-owned real estate located in West Haven, Connecticut. On December 5, 1991, Butler conveyed all of her interest in the property to Noel. At the time of the transfer, Butler was in default on three loans owed to plaintiff Dime Savings Bank of New York. The bank sued Butler alleging that the conveyance to her brother was fraudulent.

DeMayo, Judge Trial Referee

. . . At the time of the conveyance, December 5, 1991, the Uniform Fraudulent Transfer Act (hereafter UFTA) was in effect. . . . The UFTA . . . offers guidance to the courts for cases alleging an intentional fraudulent conveyance:

> (b) In determining actual intent under subdivision (1) of this section, consideration may be given, among other factors, to whether: (1) The transfer or obligation was to an insider, (2) the debtor retained possession or control of the property transferred after the transfer, (3) the transfer or obligation was disclosed or concealed, (4) before the transfer was made or obligation was incurred, the debtor had been sued or threatened with suit, (5) the transfer was of substantially all the debtor's assets, (6) the debtor absconded, (7) the debtor removed or concealed assets, (8) the value of the consideration received by the debtor was reasonably equivalent to the value of the asset transferred or the amount of the obligation incurred, (9) the debtor was insolvent or became insolvent shortly after the transfer was made or the obligation was incurred, [and] (10) the transfer occurred shortly before or shortly after a substantial debt incurred. . . . [UFTA §4(b).] . . .

The plaintiff claims to have proved nearly all 10 applicable criteria. The definition section of UFTA . . .

includes a relative of a debtor as an "insider." Consequently, the first factor listed in [§4(b)] has been resolved in favor of the plaintiff.

In support of its claim that the debtor retained possession or control over the property transferred after the transfer, the plaintiff introduced Exhibit SS. This exhibit is an agreement dated December 5, 1991 by and between the defendants, Nancy Butler and Lawrence Noel. Under its terms, Noel agreed not to sell, transfer, mortgage or encumber the one-half interest he had just acquired from Butler without her prior written consent, nor to sell it to anyone but Butler. Noel also agreed that if Butler predeceased the defendant's mother, he would transfer a one-half interest to their mother and if the mother died before Butler, he would transfer a one-half interest to the defendant's brother.

This agreement is significant in itself, but the circumstances of its appearance are startling. In discovery, these defendants responded to interrogatories posed by the plaintiff that there was no agreement between them covering this property. However, on the morning of trial, defendants' counsel provided plaintiff's counsel with what became Exhibit SS.

The existence of the agreement reflects unfavorably on the testimony of Noel who offered a totally different explanation of how the transfer came about.

Though the deed between these defendants was recorded, the terms embodied in Exhibit SS were not, and in fact its existence was denied until trial. Certainly, the true nature of the transaction was concealed.

Though the three foreclosures had not actually been commenced, Butler, a licensed real estate agent, knew what would follow her defaults of November 1, 1991. No payments were made on the three loans after that date and Butler is presumed to have known that she faced the prospects of deficiency judgments. One must conclude that she transferred her interest in the unencumbered Kelsey Avenue property in order to put it beyond the reach of creditors. The debtor was certainly "threatened" with suit.

The plaintiff has prepared a balance sheet, derived mainly from discovery disclosures as well as the foreclosure files, to show that on December 5, 1991, she had outstanding liabilities of almost $60,000. Her assets were bank accounts totalling about $5,000. . . . Thus, the conclusion is inescapable that "the transfer was substantially all of the debtor's assets." And, since the sum of her debts was greater than all of her assets, she was insolvent. . . .

By virtue of her failure to make payments on the three loans owed the plaintiff, the defendant Butler was not paying her debts as they were due. This is another definition of insolvency under [the UFTA]. . . . The defendant thus satisfied the indicia of [UFTA §4(b)(9)].

It is undisputed that the transfer was made without consideration, thus fitting another indicia of a fraudulent transfer. . . . Finally, the defendant Butler's actions corresponded to that in [UFTA §4(b)10] in that the transfer was made shortly after a substantial debt was incurred. On December 2, 1991, she placed a mortgage on her residence in the amount of $99,000. The transfer occurred on December 5, 1991. In view of this financial situation, $99,000 must be defined as a "substantial debt."

Once a creditor establishes that the indicia of fraud exist, the burden shifts to the debtor to present evidence, either that the conveyance was for consideration or that the debtor was not insolvent.

The defendant Nancy Butler offered no evidence and in fact did not appear for trial. The defendant Lawrence Noel offered an explanation for this transfer, but that explanation failed to stand up under cross examination and close scrutiny. The existence of Exhibit SS, revealed just prior to the commencement of trial, the financial dealings of Butler, and the lack of evidential support for the defendants' version of the event compel the conclusion that the defendants have not sustained their burden.

The court concludes that the plaintiff has proved by clear and convincing evidence that the transfer in question was fraudulently made with the intention to place the property in question beyond the reach of the plaintiff-creditor. . . .

[Judgment and costs for plaintiff.]

The law does not protect creditors against all fraudulent conveyances. For example, the UFTA[13] provides that a creditor may not recover a transfer from a good faith purchaser for value—one who pays reasonably equivalent value for the property and has no knowledge of the fraud at the time of the purchase. Thus, creditors generally are allowed to subject fraudulently transferred property to their claims only if the transferee has participated in the scheme to hinder or defraud creditors, has

taken with notice of the fraud, or is a donee or has taken for less than full and adequate consideration.

Bulk Sales—UCC Article 6

Development of the Law. The bulk sale is a common form of fraudulent conveyance, which is not voidable under ordinary fraudulent conveyance law. In the typical case, a merchant, owing debts, sells all or a major part of his inventory at once out of the ordinary course of business (the "bulk sale" or "bulk transfer") to an innocent purchaser, pockets the proceeds, and then disappears, leaving unsecured creditors unpaid. In the bulk sale case the transferee buys the merchant's stock in trade for adequate consideration with no knowledge of, or participation in, the seller's scheme to defraud his creditors. Thus, creditors generally may not avoid the transfer as a fraudulent conveyance, and may not levy upon or otherwise reach the assets in the purchaser's hands. Absent additional legal protection, therefore, the unpaid unsecured creditors have no recourse unless they can establish that the purchaser has assumed the merchant's existing debts.

Beginning in the late nineteenth century, the bulk transfer became a common method used by dishonest merchants to defeat their creditors' claims. To protect creditors in this case and to close the bulk transfer loophole in state fraudulent conveyance law, every state enacted "bulk sales" legislation. By the mid-twentieth century these statutes had become outdated, causing substantial uncertainty and litigation. Additionally, the lack of uniformity of the various enactments made it difficult for creditors involved in interstate transactions to protect themselves.

For these reasons, the drafters of the UCC prepared Article 6, "Bulk Transfers," to provide a uniform bulk transfer law, embodying the better rules of the prior statutes. Article 6 provides creditor protection primarily by requiring advance notice of the transfer so that creditors may take steps to protect themselves before the assets are transferred and before the purchase price is paid. Specifically, under Article 6 the buyer must give written notice of the transfer to all persons included on a list of creditors furnished by the seller, and all other persons known by the buyer to hold or assert claims against the seller. The notice must be given at least ten days before the buyer takes possession of the goods or pays for them, whichever occurs earlier. If the required notice is not given, the transfer is "ineffective" as

---

[13]UFTA §8(a).

against the seller's creditors. This means that the creditors can disregard the sale and reach the goods in the transferee's hands to satisfy their claims, even though the transferee is a good faith purchaser for adequate consideration.

Because it protects the seller's creditors at the expense of a good faith purchaser without notice of the seller's wrongdoing, Article 6 has long been criticized as impeding normal business transactions. The text of Article 6 also has been criticized for being loosely drafted and insufficiently specific. For these reasons, the Code drafters undertook an extensive study culminating in 1988 in the promulgation of two alternative recommendations. One alternative (Alternative A) is to repeal Article 6 outright. The rationale for this recommendation is that (1) modern credit reporting technology enables creditors quickly to determine the debtor's credit history and to discover liens against the debtor's assets, (2) fraudulent bulk sales are decreasing because advances in communication technology make it difficult for a debtor to defraud his creditors *en masse,* and (3) changes in the law of civil procedure make it easier for creditors to collect their debts.

Because the Code drafters recognized that some states will desire continued bulk sales regulation, they provided as "Alternative B" a revised Article 6, entitled "Bulk Sales," to replace original Article 6. This revision is designed to afford improved creditor protection while reducing the obstacles to good faith sales. Although most states have followed Alternative A and repealed Article 6, four states have enacted Revised Article 6.[14] For this reason the following material briefly summarizes the basic operation of Revised Article 6.

Overview of Revised Article 6.

Under Revised Article 6, a **bulk sale** is defined as

> a sale not in the ordinary course of the seller's business of more than half the seller's inventory, as measured by value on the date of the bulk sale agreement, if on that date the buyer has notice, or after reasonable inquiry would have had notice, that the seller will not continue to operate the same or a similar kind of business after the sale.[15]

Under Revised §6–103(1)(a), sellers subject to Article 6 are those whose "principal business is the sale of inven-

tory from stock." "Inventory" generally includes property held by a person for immediate or ultimate *sale* in the ordinary course of business. Businesses principally engaged in the sale of services, such as farming, professional services, cleaning shops, barber shops, hotels, and restaurants, are exempted. Because extremely small or large transactions impose little bulk sales risk, Revised Article 6 does not apply if the seller's equity in the transferred assets is less than $10,000 or greater than $25 million.[16]

Compliance Requirements.

If the transfer qualifies as a bulk sale, the buyer[17] must:

1. require the seller to furnish a list of creditors and make that list available to creditors;
2. obtain a list of all business names and addresses used by the seller within the preceding three years;
3. obtain from the seller, or prepare, a "schedule of distribution" outlining how the contract price is to be distributed;
4. give written notice to creditors on the seller's list and to any other creditor of whom the buyer has knowledge; and
5. distribute the contract price as outlined in the schedule of distribution.[18]

The written notice must be accompanied by a copy of the schedule of distribution and must be given not less than 45 days prior to the date of the bulk sale. If the seller has 200 or more creditors, the buyer need not notify all creditors individually, but may comply by filing a written notice of the sale with the state secretary of state's office. A buyer who gives notice in this manner is excused from complying with the requirements outlined in paragraph 1 above.

Revised Article 6 does not require that the sale proceeds be used to satisfy the seller's debts. Rather, the schedule of distribution required by Revised Article 6 simply notifies creditors of the proposed disposition, and objecting creditors can then proceed under state law

---

[14]Arizona, California, Indiana, and Virginia.

[15]Revised UCC §6–102(1)(c)(ii).

[16]Revised UCC §6–103(3)(l).

[17]In addition to privately negotiated transactions, Article 6 applies to bulk transfers made by sale at auction and by liquidators (persons who dispose of inventory to one or more buyers for businesses contemplating liquidation). In these cases, Revised Article 6 imposes upon the auctioneer or liquidator duties and liabilities similar to those of the buyer in a private sale.

[18]Revised UCC §6–104.

or federal bankruptcy law to prevent the sale or tie up the price. The parties must, therefore, carefully consider likely creditor reaction when drafting the schedule of distribution. That is, creditors are far more likely to block a sale providing for payment of the entire contract price to the seller than one making provision (such as an escrow account) for payment of the seller's debt.

Effect of Noncompliance. Under Article 6, a noncomplying bulk transfer rendered the sale ineffective, thereby permitting creditors to reach the assets in the buyer's hands. In contrast, under Revised Article 6, noncompliance with the foregoing requirements does not render the sale voidable or otherwise alter the buyer's rights in or title to the inventory. Rather, Revised §6–107 provides that a noncomplying buyer is simply liable for money damages to any creditor who is injured as a result of the buyer's failure to comply. Damages are equal to the creditor's claim against the seller reduced by any amount the creditor could not have collected even if the buyer had complied. Total aggregate liability to all creditors resulting from any one bulk sale may not exceed twice the net contract price paid by the buyer for inventory and equipment, less any portion of that price paid to the seller or his creditors. This double liability parallels the maximum recovery generally available under original Article 6. Under that Article, the noncomplying buyer pays twice: the purchase price to the seller and the goods to the seller's creditors.

A noncomplying buyer may escape liability completely under Revised §6–107(3) by proving that he or she made a good faith and commercially reasonable effort to comply with Article 6 or to exclude the transaction from its application, or held a good faith and commercially reasonable belief that Article 6 did not apply to the sale.

Under Revised §6–110, lawsuits by creditors against a noncomplying buyer must be commenced within one year[19] after the date of the bulk sale. Actions on concealed transfers may be brought within one year after the creditor discovered or should have discovered the transfer, but in no event later than two years after the sale. Complete noncompliance with Revised Article 6 does not, by itself, constitute concealment.

Summary

1. State debtor-creditor law provides the various remedies designed to aid a creditor in collecting an obligation from an unwilling or dishonest debtor, and resolves disputes among competing creditors all holding valid claims against the debtor.

2. Some state law remedies are available before a judgment is obtained against the debtor on the underlying debt. These prejudgment, or provisional, remedies include, for example, attachment, prejudgment garnishment, replevin and self-help, and receivership. Prejudgment remedies generally are subject to constitutional due process limitations.

3. After a judgment has been obtained, state laws provide various remedies that permit creditors to discover the debtor's assets, liquidate them, and apply them to the debt. These include, for example, foreclosing judgment liens, execution, postjudgment garnishment, creditor's bills, and supplementary proceedings.

4. To protect debtors against abusive and deceptive debt collection practices, both state and federal law regulate conduct of independent collection agencies. Because state remedies were perceived as inadequate, Congress in 1977 enacted the Fair Debt Collection Practices Act.

5. Creditors' remedies are generally designed to reach assets in the possession either of the debtor or of third parties indebted to the debtor. A debtor may, however, transfer his or her property to third parties with actual or implied intent to hinder, delay, or defraud creditors. Such "fraudulent conveyances" are generally voidable by creditors, under ancient legal principles embodied in most states today in the Uniform Fraudulent Transfer Act.

6. Traditional fraudulent conveyance law does not protect creditors against a "bulk sale" type of fraud, under which a fraudulent merchant sells its entire inventory to a good faith purchaser, pockets the proceeds, and disappears, leaving creditors unpaid. Bulk sales law, now codified in Article 6 and revised Article 6 of the UCC, protects creditors in some states by requiring that they be given advance notice of the sale.

Key Terms

exemption statute	cognovit (confession of
default judgment	judgment) clause

---

[19]Original Article 6 provides a six-month statute of limitations. UCC §6–111.

deficiency judgment
attachment
writ of attachment
levy
garnishment
replevin
self-help
receiver
judgment lien
execution
writ of execution
execution sale

creditor's bill
supplementary proceedings
Fair Debt Collection Practices
    Act (FDCPA)
fraudulent conveyance
Statute of Elizabeth
badges of fraud
Uniform Fraudulent
    Conveyance Act (UFCA)
Uniform Fraudulent Transfer
    Act (UFTA)
bulk sale

Questions and Problems

29.1 In 2003, Terry Hanson borrowed $10,000 from Interfirst Bank to purchase an automobile. Hanson promised to repay the loan in 36 monthly payments, and the bank retained a security interest in the car. The contract authorized self-help repossession by the bank upon default. In 1984, Hanson stopped making monthly car payments. Interfirst sent Hanson a notice demanding payment and later hired a company to repossess the car. On August 12, 2004, Interfirst filed a replevin action and the court set a hearing for a prejudgment writ of replevin on August 27. In the meantime, the repossession company located the car and repossessed it on August 21. Hanson challenged the repossession as a violation of the due process clause. Hanson argued that once the bank sought intervention of the court in the replevin action, the right to self-help repossession without a hearing was extinguished. Is Hanson correct?

29.2 Collection Accounts Terminal, Inc. is a debt collection agency that has been considering new procedures to make its debt collection operations more efficient. It has decided to send each debtor a series of three form letters described below. Do any of these procedures violate the FDCPA? Explain.

(a) The first letter will notify the debtor that his or her account has been placed with Collection Accounts Terminal, Inc. and will request the debtor to contact the agency. The letter will be written on stationery and mailed in envelopes with Collection Accounts Terminal's name and address written prominently so the debtor will know whom to contact.

(b) If the debtor fails to contact the agency, it will send a second letter stating the following: "Our field investigator has been instructed to make an investigation in your neighborhood and to personally call on your employer. The immediate payment of your account or a personal visit to our office will spare you this embarrassment." Nevertheless, the agency does not intend to visit neighbors or employers.

(c) If the debtor still fails to respond, the agency will send a third letter stating, "Unless you pay your account in full, it may be referred to an attorney with instructions to commence legal proceedings." Collection Accounts Terminal has retained an attorney and intends to refer most of its large accounts to her for filing lawsuits.

29.3 In 2004, Abraham borrowed $30,000 from Albuquerque Bank and signed a promissory note for that amount plus interest. At the time he signed the note, Abraham owned one large piece of real estate plus several smaller tracts, all located in New Mexico. Late in 2005, Abraham conveyed the large piece of real estate to his sister in exchange for a loan of $37,000. The real estate then held a fair market value of $177,000. At the time of the conveyance to his sister, Abraham owed various creditors a total of $71,000. Albuquerque Bank recently discovered that Abraham conveyed the property to his sister and is now considering filing a lawsuit to have the transfer set aside as a fraudulent conveyance. Would you recommend that the bank take this action? Explain.

CHAPTER 30

BANKRUPTCY

Major Topics

- an introduction to bankruptcy law including its source, purposes, the general structure of the statute, and the nature and function of bankruptcy courts
- operation of a straight bankruptcy (liquidation) proceeding from commencement through discharge
- analysis of the debtor rehabilitation provisions contained in bankruptcy law that provide an alternative to liquidation
- collective creditor's remedies outside bankruptcy including assignments for the benefit of creditors and composition and extension agreements

State law collection remedies generally reward the creditor or creditors who act first in proceeding against the debtor's assets. They generally are not designed to promote equal or equitable treatment of creditors when the debtor's assets are insufficient to pay all creditor claims. In addition, state remedies do not protect an honest, though hopelessly indebted, person from repeated and often harassing creditor attempts at collection.

Resolving these problems is the function of the law of bankruptcy. Bankruptcy is simultaneously a collective creditors' remedy and debtor relief provision embodied in a federal statute. It is designed to serve two

fundamental purposes: (1) to relieve an honest debtor from overburdensome financial obligations and give him or her a fresh start, free of claims of former creditors, and (2) to provide for equitable treatment of creditors who are competing for the debtor's limited assets.

Introduction to Bankruptcy

Bankruptcy is federal law. One of the powers granted to Congress in the Constitution is the power to establish "uniform Laws on the subject of Bankruptcies throughout the United States."[1] Congress first exercised this power in 1800 and subsequently enacted bankruptcy statutes in 1841, 1867, 1898, and 1978. This chapter is based upon the Bankruptcy Reform Act of 1978, as amended through 2005.

Note that the Bankruptcy Code provides that the dollar amounts or limitations stated in the various Code sections discussed in this chapter are to be automatically adjusted, beginning in 1998 and every three years thereafter, to reflect the change in the Consumer Price Index. This chapter reflects the dollar amounts in effect until April 1, 2007.

---

[1]U.S. CONST. art. I, §8, cl. 4.

General Organization and Operation of the Statute

The law of bankruptcy is contained in Title 11 of the United States Code, commonly referred to as the "Bankruptcy Code." Title 11 is divided into nine substantive "chapters," which are organized as follows:

Chapter 1	General Provisions
Chapter 3	Case Administration
Chapter 5	Creditors, Debtor, and the Estate
Chapter 7	Liquidation
Chapter 9	Adjustment of Debts of a Municipality
Chapter 11	Reorganization
Chapter 12	Adjustment of Debts of a Family Farmer with Regular Annual Income
Chapter 13	Adjustment of Debts of an Individual with Regular Income
Chapter 15	Ancillary and Other Cross-Border Cases

The relief afforded by the statute is of two general types: liquidation (governed by Chapter 7) and rehabilitation (the subject of Chapters 9, 11, 12, and 13). Chapters 1, 3, and 5, governing the operation of the bankruptcy proceeding, apply generally to both liquidation cases (under Chapter 7) and rehabilitation cases (under Chapters 11, 12, and 13).[2]

Most bankruptcies (70 to 80 percent) are liquidation cases involving nonbusiness debtors (80 to 90 percent). In a **liquidation case,** usually known as **straight bankruptcy,** the debtor surrenders all nonexempt assets, the bankruptcy "estate," to a "trustee in bankruptcy." The trustee in bankruptcy collects the estate's assets, converts them to cash, and distributes the proceeds to creditors who have filed claims against the estate according to a priority scheme provided in the Bankruptcy Code. Unless the debtor is guilty of certain specified conduct, he or she is "discharged" from liability upon any debts remaining unpaid, except those that may not be discharged under bankruptcy law.

In a **rehabilitation case** under Chapters 11, 12, and 13, the debtor's assets are not liquidated. Rather, the debtor retains them and pays creditors out of future earnings according to a plan filed with and approved by the court.

Chapter 11 addresses primarily business or corporate rehabilitation. Chapter 13 governs rehabilitation of individual or consumer debtors, plus some eligible businesses. Chapter 12 provides relief for certain persons engaged in farming operations whose debts do not exceed prescribed limits.

Bankruptcy Courts and Jurisdiction

Because bankruptcy is federal law, bankruptcy cases are tried in federal courts. The various federal district courts have original and exclusive jurisdiction of all cases under Title 11 and acquire exclusive jurisdiction over all property, wherever located, of the debtor as of the commencement of the case. The district courts also may hear civil cases arising in or related to a case commenced under Title 11. For example, the district court could (but is not required to) adjudicate a breach of contract case between a bankrupt debtor and one of its suppliers or customers.

Although the federal courts have jurisdiction, federal district judges do not ordinarily hear bankruptcy cases. Rather, the law provides for the creation in each judicial district of a **bankruptcy court,** a unit of the district court staffed by **bankruptcy judges.** Whereas federal district judges appointed under Article III of the Constitution enjoy life tenure (subject to impeachment), bankruptcy judges are appointed to 14-year terms by the Court of Appeals for the circuit in which the judge sits. Further, federal judges' compensation may not be reduced during their continuance in office.[3] Because bankruptcy judges are not appointed under Article III, their jurisdictional powers are limited.

Appeals from bankruptcy court decisions are taken to bankruptcy appellate panels established in each judicial circuit and consisting of sitting bankruptcy judges. Three members of the panel hear each appeal unless either party elects to have the appeal heard by the district court. Subsequent appeals are made to the appropriate U.S. Court of Appeals.[4]

To relieve bankruptcy judges of burdensome administrative and supervisory duties, Congress in 1978 created a pilot U.S. Trustee system, which became permanent and nationwide in 1986.[5] The system is under the

---

[2]11 U.S.C. §103(a). Chapter 9 is generally self-contained and is supplemented only by provisions of Chapter 1. 11 U.S.C. §103(e).

[3]U.S. CONST. art. III, §1.

[4]The provisions governing creation of bankruptcy courts, appointment of bankruptcy judges, and the relationship between the bankruptcy courts and the district courts are contained in 28 U.S.C. §§151–158.

[5]28 U.S.C. §§581–589a.

control of the Attorney General of the United States, who appoints for a five-year term a U.S. Trustee and one or more Assistant U.S. Trustees to each of 21 geographic regions. The U.S. Trustee establishes and supervises a panel of private trustees to serve in Chapter 7 cases, appoints or serves as standing trustee in Chapter 12 and 13 cases, and when necessary, convenes a meeting of creditors to elect a Chapter 11 trustee. The U.S. Trustee also generally supervises the administration of bankruptcy cases, including, for example, monitoring the progress of cases to prevent undue delay, monitoring rehabilitation plans, and ensuring that the debtor timely files all reports, schedules, and fees required by law.

Consumer and Business Bankruptcy

Though much of bankruptcy law applies both to business bankruptcies and those involving individual consumers, certain areas of the law are much more important in one type than the other. For example, in consumer bankruptcies, the debtor usually has few assets that are not exempt or already subject to secured creditors' claims. Accordingly, consumer bankruptcy usually generates little creditor interest. Legal disputes typically focus upon whether the debtor or a given debt should be discharged or whether certain property should be exempt from creditors' claims. In contrast, a business bankrupt is likely to have substantial assets, generating heated disputes among creditors over priority in distribution of those assets. Thus in business bankruptcy, the orderly collection and distribution of the estate is the primary issue, whereas in consumer bankruptcy, discharge is the focus. Indeed, in most consumer bankruptcies there are no assets to liquidate and distribute, and in most corporate bankruptcies, discharge is irrelevant. A bankrupt corporate shell with no assets has little need for a "fresh start."

Straight Bankruptcy—Chapter 7

Commencing a Chapter 7 Case

Under the Bankruptcy Code a liquidation (Chapter 7) proceeding may be either voluntary (debtor initiated) or involuntary (creditor initiated).[6]

Voluntary Cases; Limitations on Consumer Cases. In a **voluntary case,** the debtor files a petition with the bankruptcy court requesting the relief afforded by Chapter 7. Filing the petition constitutes an automatic "order for relief." Generally, any individual, partnership, or corporation may file a voluntary bankruptcy petition under Chapter 7. Railroads, banking institutions, and insurance companies, however, are ineligible.[7] Approximately 99 percent of liquidation cases are commenced voluntarily by the debtor.

To prevent consumer debtors with debt-paying ability from using Chapter 7 to avoid their obligations, the law imposes several limitations on consumer bankruptcy filings under Chapter 7. These provisions have the effect of channeling many consumer bankruptcies into Chapter 13 rehabilitation plans. Most importantly, under §707(b), the court may dismiss a case filed by an individual debtor whose debts are primarily consumer debts if it finds that granting a discharge would be an "abuse" of the provisions of Chapter 7. Abuse of Chapter 7 is presumed if the debtor's current monthly income reduced by (1) monthly expenses, (2) payments on account of secured debts, and (3) expenses for payment of priority claims, exceeds $100. The presumption may be rebutted by proof of special circumstances such as a serious medical condition. Note that even if the above presumption does not arise or is rebutted, the court may nevertheless find an abuse of Chapter 7 if it finds that the debtor filed the petition in bad faith or the entire circumstances surrounding the debtor's financial condition indicates abuse. A motion to dismiss a case under §707(b) generally may be made by the court, the United States trustee, other bankruptcy trustee or administrator, or creditors. The law may, however, limit or prohibit motions against a debtor whose income is equal to or below the median annual income in the debtor's state.

In addition to the "means testing" limitation outlined above, individual debtors may not file a petition under any Bankruptcy Code chapter until receiving credit counseling from an approved nonprofit budget and credit consulting agency. This counseling must occur during the 180 day period preceding the filing.[8] In addition, individual debtors may not receive a discharge under either Chapter 7 or 13 until completing, after filing the petition,

---

[6]U.S.C. §§301, 303.

[7]Railroad bankruptcies are governed by Subchapter IV of Chapter 11 of the Bankruptcy Code. 11 U.S.C. §§1161–1174. Bank and insurance company liquidations are governed by other state and federal regulatory statutes. 11 U.S.C. §109(b).

[8]11 U.S.C. §109(h)(1).

an instructional course concerning personal financial management.[9] Finally, the court may dismiss a voluntary case filed by an individual convicted of a crime of violence or drug trafficking crime if the court finds that dismissal "is in the best interest of the victim."[10]

Involuntary Cases. Creditors also may force a debtor involuntarily into a Chapter 7 bankruptcy proceeding by filing a petition with the bankruptcy court, provided (1) the aggregate claims of petitioning creditors are at least $12,300, and (2) if the debtor has twelve or more creditors, at least three join in the petition. If the debtor has fewer than twelve unsecured creditors, only one need file.

Unlike a voluntary case, the mere filing of an **involuntary case** petition does not constitute an "order for relief." The debtor may challenge the creditors' attempt to force him into bankruptcy. After the petition and summons are served, the debtor has 20 days to file defenses and objections.[11] If the debtor fails to object, the court enters an order for relief. If the debtor timely objects, a trial is held, which may be heard by the court sitting without a jury. After the trial, the court is required to order relief against the debtor if it finds either that the debtor is not paying undisputed debts as they become due *or* a general receiver, assignee, or custodian has been appointed for or has taken possession of substantially all of the debtor's property within 120 days preceding the filing of the petition.

The first test—failure to pay debts as they come due—is known as the "equity" or "accounting" definition of insolvency.[12] The second test—appointment of a custodian within 120 days before the petition—creates an irrefutable presumption that the debtor is unable to pay his debts as they mature. Creditors who fail to seek bankruptcy liquidation within 120 days after the appointment may nevertheless file an involuntary petition. They are, however, required to prove equity insolvency rather than the more easily provable custodian test. The custodian test is covered in more detail later in this chapter in conjunction with collective creditor remedies outside bankruptcy.

Certain debtors, such as railroads, banking institutions, and insurance companies, may not be forced into involuntary bankruptcy. In addition, creditors may not commence involuntary cases against farmers or non-profit corporations, such as churches, schools, and charitable organizations.

Because an involuntary petition adversely affects the debtor's business operation and reputation, the Bankruptcy Code includes provisions to discourage frivolous claims. For example, if the court finds that the petition was filed in bad faith, it may dismiss the case and may award the debtor court costs, attorneys' fees and punitive and other damages.

Automatic Stay. The **automatic stay**[13] is an important legal consequence of filing either a voluntary or involuntary bankruptcy petition. Simply stated, filing the petition "stays" or prevents further efforts by creditors to collect their debts. Efforts stayed by the bankruptcy include the judicial debt collection remedies discussed in Chapter 29 as well as informal collection efforts such as phone calls and letters. Also stayed is the creation, perfection, or enforcement of any lien upon the debtor's property.

The stay generally continues until the case is closed or dismissed, or the debtor is granted or denied a discharge. If the debtor receives a discharge, the debtor's liability to pay most of the debts stayed is permanently extinguished. Note that certain debts survive a bankruptcy proceeding and certain debtors are denied discharges. After the stay is lifted, therefore, collection efforts may continue against such debts or debtors.

Upon a creditor's request, the bankruptcy court may "for cause" terminate or otherwise modify the automatic stay. Relief from the stay primarily aids secured creditors, whose interest in specific property of the debtor may be jeopardized if the stay is continued. At issue in the following case was whether a creditor had violated the automatic stay.

In the Matter of Holland

21 B.R. 681 (Bkrtcy. N.D. Ind. 1982)

Wilbert Glenn Holland (debtor) borrowed money from the Dana Corporation Federal Credit Union (Credit Union) and authorized his employer to transfer $80 from his weekly paycheck to the Credit Union for repayment of the loan. Every week the Credit Union deposited the payroll deduction into

---

[9]11 U.S.C. §§727(a)(11), 1328(g)(1).

[10]11 U.S.C. §707(c).

[11]Bankr. R. 1011.

[12]This test differs from the insolvency definition used elsewhere in the Bankruptcy Code, requiring balance sheet insolvency, meaning that total liabilities exceed total assets at fair valuation. 11 U.S.C. §101(32).

[13]11 U.S.C. §362.

Holland's share draft account, and once a month the Credit Union transferred the deductions to its loan department where they were applied toward payment of the loan.

On November 21, 1980, Holland filed a petition for bankruptcy and the bankruptcy court sent a notice of the bankruptcy and automatic stay to the Credit Union. Shortly after November 21, 1980, Holland went to the Credit Union with copies of the bankruptcy petition to request termination of the payroll deduction. Credit Union procedures required that Holland complete a form to be delivered to his employer to terminate the payroll deductions. Despite Holland's visit and subsequent telephone calls to the Credit Union, none of the Credit Union's employees advised him of the procedure or provided the necessary forms. As a result, the payroll deductions continued and the Credit Union applied the deductions to repay the loan.

Holland filed a motion with the bankruptcy court seeking an order finding the Credit Union in violation of the automatic stay.

Rodibaugh, Bankruptcy Judge

. . . For the reasons stated below, the Court . . . finds that the Credit Union has violated the Automatic Stay of §362(a)(6) of the Bankruptcy Code. . . .

There is no doubt that the Credit Union had actual notice of the debtor's petition in bankruptcy and of the automatic stay before it continued to make transfers from the debtor's share draft account to the loan account with the Credit Union. There is no question that at the time the Credit Union made these transfers it had notice and actual knowledge that the debtor no longer wanted his post-petition earnings to be applied against his loan with the Credit Union. . . .

The Credit Union contends it did not violate the stay because it took *no act* to collect the debt. Rather it just received the debtor's voluntary payments of the debt through payroll deduction arrangement. . . .

[W]e do not hold that the Credit Union violated the stay by receiving money pursuant to the arrangement in this case and depositing it into the debtor's account. This alone would not be an act to collect a debt. However, when the credit union transfers the money to pay a pre-petition debt owed to itself it has then committed an act to collect a claim and thereby violates the stay unless . . . there is clear evidence that, post-petition, the debtor demonstrated willingness to voluntarily have these earnings applied to the debt. . . .

This result is consistent with the plain language of §362(a)(6), with the intent of Congress as demonstrated in the Legislative History, and with case law. . . .

Congressional intent seems clear. "The automatic stay is one of the fundamental debtor protections provided by the bankruptcy laws. It gives the debtor a breathing spell from his creditors. It stops *all collection efforts* (emphasis added), all harassment and all foreclosure actions." H. R. Rep. No. 595, 95 Cong. 1st Sess. 340 (1977). . . . "Paragraph (6) prevents creditors from attempting in *any way* (emphasis added) to collect a pre-petition debt." Id. at 342. . . . Section 362 was added to the bankruptcy laws to protect the inexperienced, frightened, or ill-counseled debtors who might succumb to attempts to evade the purpose of the bankruptcy laws by sophisticated creditors. Id. at 342.

Furthermore, courts have held that inactivity on the part of a creditor with notice of the bankruptcy which permits the forces of collection to go forward is as offensive to the automatic stay provision as is activity. . . .

Acts taken in violation of the automatic stay are void ab initio. . . . Consequently all transfers to the loan account made after the date of the petition (November 21, 1980) must be returned to the debtor plus the interest that would have been earned had that money remained in the debtor's share draft account. . . .

[So ordered.]

Trustee Election and Duties; Creditors' Meeting. Once the bankruptcy proceeding begins, the debtor's property is effectively held in trust for the benefit of her creditors. The trustee of the property, known as the **trustee in bankruptcy,** occupies a pivotal role in the bankruptcy proceeding. The trustee in bankruptcy is responsible for investigating the debtor's financial affairs; locating and collecting the debtor's property; invalidating certain transfers of property made by the debtor; reducing the assets to cash; determining the validity of creditor claims against the estate; distributing the money to creditors according to the priorities provided by the Bankruptcy Code; and, in some cases, operating the debtor's business and opposing the debtor's discharge. The trustee in bankruptcy is a private citizen, not a government employee or judicial officer.

Within a reasonable time after the order for relief is entered, the U.S. Trustee appoints, from a panel of private trustees, an interim trustee who convenes and presides over a meeting of creditors. The debtor must appear at this meeting and submit to examination under oath. Creditors and the trustee may question the debtor concerning his or her conduct, property, or any other matter affecting administration of the estate or the debtor's right to a discharge. This examination is designed to determine whether assets have been improperly transferred or concealed or if grounds exist to object to the debtor's discharge. At the meeting, the trustee must inform the debtor (1) of the legal effect and potential consequences of bankruptcy (for example, the effect of discharge and the automatic stay and the fact that the bankruptcy filing will be included in the debtor's credit history), (2) whether relief under another bankruptcy chapter (for example, Chapter 13) is available, and (3) of the effect of agreements reaffirming a debt discharged in bankruptcy (discussed later in this chapter).

In addition to examining the debtor, the meeting affords the debtor's general unsecured creditors an opportunity to elect the trustee in bankruptcy. If the creditors fail to elect a trustee, the interim trustee serves as permanent trustee in the case. The bankruptcy judge may not attend the meeting.

Property of the Estate

Filing a bankruptcy petition, either voluntarily or involuntarily, creates an **estate**.[14] In a liquidation case, the property of the estate passes to the trustee in bankruptcy and is distributed to the debtor's creditors. The estate contains all legal or equitable, tangible or intangible, property interests owned by the debtor wherever located and by whomever held.

Generally, property acquired after the filing of the petition does not become "property of the estate." If the debtor receives a discharge, such postpetition property may not therefore be subjected to most prepetition claims with the following exceptions: (1) property acquired by the debtor within 180 days after the filing of the petition acquired (a) as a bequest, devise, or inheritance (that is, by will or intestate succession), (b) as a result of a property settlement agreement with the debtor's spouse, and (c) as a beneficiary of a life insurance policy; (2) proceeds, products, offspring, rents, or profits received from property of the estate (such as interest on bonds, rent from an apartment building, or insurance proceeds); (3) property recovered by the trustee under the avoidance powers discussed

later in this chapter; and (4) property acquired by the *estate* after commencement of the case.

Exempt Property. The Bankruptcy Code allows the debtor to exempt various types of property of the estate from creditors' claims.[15] Additionally, as noted in Chapter 29, each state has enacted an exemption statute insulating certain property. The Bankruptcy Code provides the debtor with a choice between exemptions allowed under state law and under federal statutes other than the Bankruptcy Code,[16] or those provided by the Bankruptcy Code. Individual states may, by statute, require the debtor to use state exemptions. A majority of states have enacted such legislation.

Bankruptcy Code exemptions, if available, include the following:

1. Certain sources of income and compensation for losses—such as unemployment compensation; public assistance; social security, veterans's, disability, and crime victim reparation benefits; alimony, child support, and separate maintenance payments; certain pension, annuity, and profit-sharing benefits; payments resulting from the death of a person supporting the debtor (for example, a wrongful death award or proceeds of a life insurance policy); and payments to compensate for personal injury (up to $18,450) or lost income of the debtor or a person supporting the debtor.

2. Certain specific property without dollar limitation—such as professionally prescribed health aids and unmatured life insurance contracts.

3. Certain specific property with dollar limitation—such as the debtor's equity interest in real or personal property used as a residence, not exceeding $18,450 (homestead exemption); a motor vehicle not exceeding $2,950; household furnishings, clothes, appliances, and other goods held for consumer purposes not exceeding $475 per item or $9,850 in aggregate value; jewelry not exceeding $1,225; implements, books, or tools of the debtor's trade not exceeding $1,850; and the loan value of the debtor's life insurance policy not exceeding $9,850.

4. Unspecified property with dollar limitation—such as $975 in any property plus up to $9,250 in the unused amount of the homestead exemption.

---

[14]11 U.S.C. §541.

[15]11 U.S.C. §522.

[16]For example, federal law outside Title 11 exempts Social Security benefits, railroad retirement annuities, civil service retirement benefits, and veteran's benefits, among others.

Although debtors generally may elect to use state exemptions, the homestead exemption, which is unlimited in some states, may not be available to certain debtors electing to exempt property under state law. Specifically, such a debtor may not exempt any interest in a homestead that was acquired within 1215 days prior to the bankruptcy filing that exceeds $125,000.[17] Note finally that any waiver of exemptions, state or federal, executed by the debtor in favor of a creditor, made either before or after bankruptcy, is unenforceable.

Collecting Estate Property—General Trustee Powers

The trustee in bankruptcy is the representative of the estate, with the capacity to sue and be sued. As previously noted, the trustee's principal duty is to collect the property of the estate, convert it to cash, and pay competing creditors according to the priorities provided by law. A variety of Bankruptcy Code provisions aid the trustee in maximizing the value of the estate for distribution to creditors.

Initially, the law imposes various duties upon the debtor regarding the property of the estate. For example, the debtor must (1) appear and submit to examination under oath at the meeting of creditors concerning the nature, location, and extent of his property, (2) submit a list of creditors, a schedule of assets and liabilities, and a statement of the debtor's financial affairs, (3) cooperate with the trustee to enable the trustee to perform his or her duties, and (4) surrender to the trustee all property of the estate including books, documents, records, and papers relating to that property.

The law also requires that persons in possession of the debtor's property or those owing money to the debtor turn it over to the trustee. Additionally, the court may order third parties, such as attorneys and accountants possessing books, documents, or records regarding the debtor's property or financial affairs, to turn over or disclose that information. Because the trustee's duty is to maximize the value of the estate for the benefit of creditors, the court may authorize or order the trustee to abandon property that is burdensome to the estate or is of inconsequential value.

If the estate includes a business owned by the debtor, the court may authorize the trustee to operate the business for a limited period if the continued operation is in the best interest of the estate and is consistent with an orderly liquidation. Such an authorization might be made, for example, to convert work in process into finished goods that can be sold at a much higher price than the unfinished goods.

Executory Contracts and Unexpired Leases. In addition to buildings, equipment, inventory, and other tangible property, the estate also may contain intangible property, including any rights the debtor may have under executory contracts (contracts on which performance remains due to some extent on both sides) and unexpired leases. For example, assume D, a boat manufacturer, has filed for bankruptcy. Property of the estate would include the rights D possesses under an existing supply contract with S, a manufacturer of fiberglass, and the rights D has under a ten-year lease with L on the building housing D's manufacturing operation. Filing a bankruptcy petition does not terminate executory contracts and unexpired leases, even if the contract or lease contains a "bankruptcy clause" or "*ipso facto* clause" that purports to terminate the contract or lease upon bankruptcy. Such clauses are unenforceable in bankruptcy.

After commencement of the case, the lease or contract continues in force, and the trustee in bankruptcy is given the option, subject to court approval, to (1) assume and perform the lease or contract, (2) assume and assign the lease or contract to a third party, or (3) reject the lease or contract.[18] If the trustee fails to assume within time periods outlined in the Bankruptcy Code, the contract or lease is deemed rejected.

The options outlined above allow the trustee to retain leases or contracts beneficial to the estate, and to rid the estate of those that burden it. For example, a building leased by the debtor may be in a good business location at a reasonable rent. A new tenant might be willing to pay the trustee for an assignment of the lease. In this case, assumption and assignment of the lease by the trustee would be in the best interest of the estate. In a liquidation case, the trustee ordinarily rejects leases and contracts. In this case, the nonbankrupt party may file a claim against the estate as a general unsecured creditor for breach of the lease or contract.

---

[17]11 U.S.C. §522(p).

[18]11 U.S.C. §365.

Collecting Estate Property — Trustee's Avoidance Powers

Under bankruptcy law, the trustee possesses certain extraordinary "avoidance" powers to (1) defeat claims of certain creditors, and (2) recover property of the estate held by third parties. In most cases, the trustee may file lawsuits under these "avoidance powers" until the case is closed or dismissed, or within two years after the court enters the order for relief, whichever occurs first.[19]

Defenses of the Estate. Initially, the trustee "steps into the shoes" of the debtor and may assert any defense the debtor has against a creditor's claim. For example, suppose Carl fraudulently induces Donna to purchase a car on credit for $1,000 by misrepresenting its mechanical condition. Donna files for bankruptcy and Carl files a $1,000 claim against the estate. Donna's trustee in bankruptcy acquires her rights and therefore may assert Carl's fraud as a defense to paying Carl's claim. Had Donna already paid Carl, Donna's trustee could use the fraud as a basis to recover the money from Carl.[20]

Rights of Actual Creditors. In addition to assuming the debtor's position, the trustee acquires the rights of actual unsecured creditors who have valid claims against the debtor.[21] Therefore, the trustee may avoid any transfer of property by the debtor or any obligation incurred by the debtor that could be attacked under state or federal law by one of the debtor's actual unsecured creditors.[22] As discussed later in this chapter, trustees use this provision primarily to recover fraudulent conveyances made by the debtor more than two years before the bankruptcy filing.

Rights of Hypothetical Creditors—"Strong-Arm" Clause. The trustee is not limited to the rights possessed by the debtor's *actual* creditors. Under §544(a) of the Bankruptcy Code (the so-called strong-arm clause), the trustee also may assert the rights of "hypothetical" lien creditors or bona fide purchasers. Specifically, under this clause the trustee may avoid any transfer of property or any obligation incurred by the

debtor that could be avoided by (1) a creditor who extends credit to the debtor and obtains a judicial lien on the debtor's property (a lien creditor), (2) a creditor with an unsatisfied writ of execution against the debtor's property (a judgment creditor), and (3) a bona fide purchaser of the debtor's real property, *whether or not such a creditor or purchaser actually exists.* This power is particularly helpful to the trustee when no actual creditor of the estate possesses the power transferred to the trustee under the strong-arm clause.

As discussed in Chapter 28, creditors often protect themselves against a debtor's default by obtaining a consensual or contractual lien upon the debtor's personal property (a "security interest") or real property (a "mortgage"). The trustee uses the strong-arm clause primarily to avoid certain consensual liens on the debtor's property, including (1) "unperfected" security interests in personal property (as discussed in Chapter 32, a lien creditor — case 1 above — defeats an unperfected security interest), and (2) "unrecorded" real estate mortgages. To illustrate this second case, assume Crenshaw loans Doaks $25,000. Doaks gives Crenshaw a mortgage on real property owned by Doaks to secure repayment of the loan. Crenshaw, however, fails to record the mortgage. As discussed in Chapter 37, a bona fide purchaser of the property from Doaks would therefore take it free of Crenshaw's mortgage. Doaks subsequently files for bankruptcy, while still owning the real property. Doaks's trustee in bankruptcy takes the land free of Crenshaw's mortgage under the strong-arm clause. Note that the trustee acquires the rights of a bona fide purchaser of the land, even though no such purchaser actually exists; Doaks did not sell the land prior to bankruptcy.

Preferences. Shortly before bankruptcy, a debtor has insufficient assets to pay all creditors. With the limited assets remaining, however, the debtor may pay one or more creditors to the exclusion of others. Because a fundamental purpose of bankruptcy is to insure the equitable treatment of similarly situated creditors, bankruptcy law[23] allows the trustee to recover certain prebankruptcy transfers known as **preferences** that favor one creditor over another. Note that "transfers" include both (1) the debtor's voluntary outright conveyance of her money or property, and (2) the creation of liens, either voluntarily (for example, the debtor creates a mortgage or secured transaction on her

---

[19] 11 U.S.C. §546(a).

[20] 11 U.S.C. §558.

[21] 11 U.S.C. §544(b).

[22] The trustee may avoid the entire transfer and recover the property for the benefit of the estate. The trustee's recovery is not limited to the amount of the creditor's claim. Moore v. Bay, 52 S. Ct. 3 (1931).

---

[23] 11 U.S.C. §547.

property as security for a loan) or involuntarily (a creditor obtains a judicial lien on the debtor's property to satisfy an unpaid judgment).

Preferences are recoverable from a favored creditor if the trustee proves the following five conditions.

1. The transfer was made to or for the benefit of a creditor.
2. The transfer was made for or on account of an "antecedent debt," one owed by the debtor before the transfer was made.
3. The debtor was insolvent when the transfer was made. The debtor is presumed to be insolvent during the 90 days immediately preceding the filing of the petition.
4. The transfer was made (a) on or within 90 days immediately preceding the filing of the petition, or (b) between 90 days and one year before the petition was filed if the creditor was an **insider.** An insider is a person in a sufficiently close relationship to the debtor that his or her conduct is subject to closer scrutiny than creditors dealing with the debtor at arm's length. Examples include a relative of (or corporation controlled by) an individual debtor, a general partner of a partnership debtor, and a director, officer, or controlling shareholder of a corporate debtor.
5. The creditor, by virtue of the transfer, receives more than would have been received in a Chapter 7 bankruptcy proceeding if the transfer had not been made.

In short, a preference occurs when a debtor pays off an old debt shortly before bankruptcy to the detriment of other similarly situated creditors. A preference, unlike a fraudulent conveyance discussed in the next section, does not reduce the net worth of the estate. Assets and liabilities are reduced equally. Preferences involve payment of legitimate debts and do not constitute fraud on the debtor's part. Preferences are nevertheless avoidable because they treat competing creditors inequitably.

Preference Analysis. In analyzing preference cases, three dates are relevant: (1) the date of the debt, (2) the date of the transfer, and (3) the date of bankruptcy. The date of the debt must precede the date of the transfer. This requirement establishes the "antecedent" nature of the debt; it is not a preference to pay current debts as they come due. The 90-day (or in insider cases, up to one year) period within which the trustee may recover is measured between dates (2) and (3) above, that is, between the date of transfer and the date of bankruptcy.

To illustrate, assume that on January 1, Adams, Baxter, and Charles each ship $10,000 worth of goods to Dodd on open account for use in Dodd's business. Dodd makes no payment on these accounts during the next six months. On July 1, Dodd's financial position has deteriorated to the point where his only remaining assets are a building worth $10,000 and $10,000 cash. Dodd pays Adams $10,000.[24] On August 1, Dodd files a bankruptcy petition. The $10,000 payment to Adams is a preference recoverable by the trustee for the benefit of the estate. The relevant dates are as follows:

1. Date of Debt . . . . Jan. 1 $\left.\right\}$ Establishes
2. Date of Transfer . . . . July 1 antecedent debt

3. Date of Bankruptcy . . . . . Aug. 1   Occurs within 90 days of transfer

The adverse effect of the transfer to Adams upon Dodd's other creditors is clear. Assuming no other expenses or creditors, but for the transfer Adams, Baxter, and Charles would each receive $6,667. That is,

$$\frac{\text{assets}}{\text{claims}} \quad \frac{\$20,000}{\$30,000} = 66¢ \text{ on the dollar}$$

Because of the July 1 transfer, however, Adams receives $10,000, which is more than she would receive in the bankruptcy proceeding if the transfer had not been made. Adams will be required to return the $10,000 payment to the trustee, but will then be entitled to file a $10,000 claim in Dodd's bankruptcy proceeding.

In the following case, the court was required to determine whether a debtor's payment to an insider was voidable as a preference.

In re Perry
158 B.R. 694 (Bkrtcy. N.D. Ohio 1993)

After selling a piece of real estate, Fanchon Perry issued a check dated December 12, 1991 for $3,300 to her brother, Nick Nardolillo. The check was issued to repay money

---

[24]If the debtor pays the debt by check, the "transfer" for preference purposes occurs on the date the check is honored by the bank, not on the date it is delivered to the creditor. Barnhill v. Johnson, 112 S. Ct. 1386 (1992).

that Nardolillo had loaned Perry for a down payment on the real estate. On March 31, 1992, Perry filed a voluntary petition for relief under Chapter 7 of the Bankruptcy Code. The bankruptcy trustee filed a complaint against Nardolillo alleging that Perry's payment was a voidable preference under 11 U.S.C. §547(b) and sought judgment of $3,300. Following a hearing, the bankruptcy court issued the following opinion.

Speer, Bankruptcy Judge

. . . In order for the Court to hold that the transfer is avoidable . . . the particular elements of an action under 11 U.S.C. §547(b) must be established. The five (5) elements which must be shown are the following: (1) the transfer was made for the benefit of the Creditor; (2) the transfer was for or on the account of a debt owed before the Debtor made the transfer; (3) the Debtor was insolvent when the transfer was made; (4) the transfer was made [within 90 days before the filing of the petition or] between ninety (90) days and one (1) year before the filing of the petition [if] the Creditor was an insider; and (5) the transfer enabled the Creditor to receive more than he would otherwise have received if the transfer had not been made. Furthermore, it has been held that the Trustee bears the burden of proof. . . .

The first element is established by the transfer of the money from Perry to Nardolillo. The transfer was made specifically for the benefit of the Creditor. The check constituted a repayment of a previous loan made to Perry for a down payment on real property. . . . As the money at issue was repaid on account of an antecedent debt owed by the Debtor prior to the occurrence of the transfer, the second element necessary to show that a preferential transfer is avoidable is established. The loaning of the money undoubtedly was made before the transfer of money for repayment of the funds took place.

The next item which must be shown is Debtor's insolvency at the time the transfer took place. Section 101(32) of the Bankruptcy Code [provides] . . . a "balance sheet" test to determine insolvency [under which] a Debtor is . . . insolvent when its liabilities exceed its assets. . . .

When the "balance sheet" test is applied to this case, it is clear that at the time the preferential transfer took place, Perry was insolvent. . . . While the Debtor is presumed to have been insolvent on and during the ninety (90) days preceding the date of filing a

Bankruptcy Petition, . . . this presumption does not work in this case as transfer of funds took place more than ninety (90) days prior to filing and involves an insider. Thus, the Trustee has the burden of proving Perry's insolvency. . . . By examining Perry's Voluntary Petition for filing a Chapter 7 Bankruptcy Proceeding, it is evident that Perry's liabilities exceeded her assets at a fair valuation. The Debtor's total liabilities are listed as [$23,382.48] while her total assets are listed as [$3,443.58] . . . Upon viewing the lists of Creditors holding claims against Perry, the Debtor, it is revealed that the majority of these debts were incurred prior to December 12, 1991, the date of the transfer. . . . As such, it is clear that the Debtor was insolvent at the time the transfer was made.

Because the transfer took place outside of the ninety (90) day period but within one (1) year of the date of filing the Bankruptcy Petition, the Creditor must be an insider in order for the Trustee to succeed in its case against Nardolillo. . . . 11 U.S.C. §101(31) states that the term "insider" includes a relative of the debtor. Nardolillo falls within these specifications as he is the brother of the Debtor. . . . Thus, . . . the fourth element is established.

[Finally,] to establish an avoidable [preference, the transfer must] enable the Creditor to receive more than the Creditor would receive if "(a) the case were a case under chapter 7 of this title; (b) the transfer had not been made; and (c) such creditor received payment of such debt to the extent provided by the provisions of this title." Upon examining the entire record in this case, it is clear that Nardolillo's position was improved by the transfer that took place. Through the transfer that took place in December of 1991, Nardolillo was able to be repaid the money that he had loaned to Perry, his sister. This is more than he would have received had the transfer not taken place. If the transfer had not taken place and Perry's estate been liquidated under Chapter 7, Nardolillo, an unsecured creditor, would not have received the entire amount of the loan. Thus, the fifth and final element for avoidance of a preferential transfer is proven. Accordingly, the Court can conclude that all of the elements set forth in 11 U.S.C. §547(b) necessary for the avoidance of a preferential transfer are present. . . .

[Judgment in the amount of $3,300 entered for the bankruptcy trustee and against Nick Nardolillo.]

To stay in business, a financially troubled debtor must purchase, either for cash or on credit, goods and services needed for current operations. Two important provisions of the Bankruptcy Code insulate most payments made in satisfaction of current obligations from preference attack. Section 547(c)(1) provides that the trustee may not avoid a transfer intended by the parties to be a "contemporaneous exchange" for new value given to the debtor. Thus, using the previous example, assume that on July 1, Adams delivers an additional $10,000 worth of goods and Dodd pays for them in cash. No preference occurs because there is no antecedent debt. If the debtor buys goods or services on credit, §547(c)(2) prevents most of the debtor's *later* payments on account from being treated as voidable preferences. Under this provision the trustee may not avoid the transfer if (1) the debt involved was incurred in the ordinary course of business or financial affairs of both the debtor and the transferee, and (2) the transfer in satisfaction of the debt was made in the ordinary course of business or financial affairs of both parties, or according to ordinary business terms. The rationale for both §§547(c)(1) and 547(c)(2) is that such payments are made on account of current, not antecedent debts, and permit the debtor to stay in business.

Note finally that §§547(c)(8) and 547(c)(9) exempt small transfers from preference attack. For example, the trustee may not avoid a transfer if the debtor is an individual owing primarily consumer debts, and the total value of all property transferred is less than $600. If the debtor owes primarily business debts, the trustee may not avoid transfers less than $5,000.

Fraudulent Conveyances. The Bankruptcy Code[25] permits the trustee in bankruptcy to avoid fraudulent conveyances made or obligations incurred on or within two years prior to the date the bankruptcy petition is filed. Specifically, the trustee may avoid any transfer of property or obligation made with actual intent to hinder, delay, or defraud past or future creditors. Additionally, the trustee may avoid any transfer or obligation for which the debtor received less than a reasonably equivalent value if the debtor (1) was insolvent at the time of the transfer or was rendered insolvent by the transfer, or (2) was engaged (or about to engage) in business for which the debtor's remaining property was an unreasonably small capital, or (3) intended to incur or believed that he would incur debts beyond his ability to pay. These provisions are substantially similar to those contained in the Uniform Fraudulent Transfer Act. discussed in Chapter 29. As under state law, the Bankruptcy Code protects a transferee who receives the property from the debtor in good faith and for value.

In many cases, the debtor makes fraudulent conveyances more than two years prior to bankruptcy. To recover such transfers, the trustee uses the provision, previously discussed, allowing the trustee to recover any prebankruptcy transfer that could have been avoided by one of the debtor's actual unsecured creditors. Under this provision, any transfer that a creditor could avoid as a fraudulent conveyance under state law (such as the Uniform Fraudulent Transfer Act), also can be avoided by the trustee. This power to assume the position of actual creditors significantly benefits the trustee because state law commonly allows a much longer period (for example, three to ten years) to recover fraudulent conveyances.

Statutory, Judicial, and Consensual Liens. To assure equitable treatment of creditors, the trustee in bankruptcy has significant power to avoid various liens that attach to the debtor's property prior to bankruptcy. The trustee may avoid statutory liens, such as mechanics liens and various tax liens, if (1) the lien first becomes effective because of the debtor's financial difficulty or when a bankruptcy petition is filed, or (2) the lien is not perfected and enforceable at the time the case is commenced against a bona fide purchaser of the property subject to the lien. The trustee also may avoid any statutory lien possessed by a landlord for unpaid rent.[26]

Judicial liens (judgment liens and other liens obtained by legal or equitable proceedings) may be avoided if they arise within 90 days prior to filing of the bankruptcy petition. That is, judicial liens constitute transfers on account of an antecedent debt. If obtained within 90 days of bankruptcy, they simply are preferences that may be avoided by the trustee under principles previously discussed.

The trustee also may avoid consensual liens in certain cases. Generally, to defeat the trustee in bankruptcy, creditors holding a security interest in the debtor's *real* property (a mortgage) must properly record their interest prior to bankruptcy in an appropriate public office, usually the county recorder of deeds.

---

[25]11 U.S.C. §548.

[26]11 U.S.C. §545.

Similarly, creditors with security interests in personal property (a secured transaction), such as inventory and equipment, defeat the trustee in bankruptcy if their interests are "perfected" prior to bankruptcy. Perfection requires that the creditor either take possession of the collateral or file a "financing statement," commonly with the state secretary of state. As with judicial liens, consensual liens recorded or perfected within 90 days prior to bankruptcy often may be avoided by the trustee as preferences. Consensual liens in personal property are covered in detail in the next two chapters. Recording and mortgages are discussed in Chapter 37.

Postpetition Transfers. The trustee in bankruptcy does not take possession of the debtor's property immediately after the petition is filed. A period of time elapses before the property is turned over. During this "gap," the debtor may transfer property belonging to the estate to a third party. Generally, the trustee may avoid transfers of estate property made by the debtor after the case is commenced unless the transfer is authorized by the Bankruptcy Code or the bankruptcy court.[27] The proceeds of any postpetition transfer that is not avoided become property of the estate.

Distributing Property of the Estate

Claims. After the bankruptcy petition is filed and the debtor files a list of creditors, the court sends a notice of the bankruptcy proceeding to the listed creditors. To participate in the assets of the estate, creditors usually must file a proof of claim with the court within 90 days after the date set for the meeting of creditors.[28] **Claims** include any right to payment or to receive any equitable remedy, such as specific performance of a contract. Shareholders of a bankrupt corporation may file a proof of interest.

Once filed, a proof of claim is prima facie evidence of the creditor's claim. As such it is **allowed**—participates in the distribution of the estate's assets—unless another creditor or the bankruptcy trustee objects. In that event the court, after notice and a hearing, determines the validity and amount of the claim and then allows it, subject to the following exceptions and limitations.[29]

1. The claim is disallowed to the extent it is unenforceable against the debtor or his property.
2. A claim is disallowed to the extent it represents interest accruing on the debtor's obligations after the petition is filed.
3. Claims for property taxes are disallowed to the extent the tax claim exceeds the value of the debtor's interest in the land.
4. Claims for services rendered by the debtor's attorney or an "insider" are allowed only to the extent of the reasonable value of the services.
5. Claims for postpetition alimony, maintenance, or child support are disallowed.[30]
6. Claims of the debtor's landlord for future rent due on a lease terminated in bankruptcy (for example, if the trustee rejects the lease) are limited.
7. Claims of the debtor's employees for future compensation due under employment contracts are limited.
8. Federal tax claims resulting from the debtor's late payment of state unemployment taxes are disallowed.

Generally, only claims arising before the petition is filed are allowed. Certain claims arising thereafter, however, may be allowed. Such claims include (1) in an involuntary case, any claim arising in the ordinary course of the debtor's business after the filing, but before the order for relief or appointment of the trustee, whichever occurs first, (2) claims arising from the trustee's rejection of executory contracts or unexpired leases, (3) claims of a person from whom property was recovered by the trustee as a preference or fraudulent conveyance, and (4) certain tax claims entitled to priority in distribution of the estate.

Priorities. Once the trustee has collected the assets of the estate, the trustee sells them and distributes the proceeds to the various creditors with allowable claims. Distribution is made first to secured creditors and then to unsecured creditors according to Bankruptcy Code priority rules.

Secured Creditors. Assuming a creditor has obtained a lien upon the debtor's property that is valid against the trustee in bankruptcy, that creditor is paid out of the collateral to the exclusion of other creditors.[31] Various methods may be used to apply the collateral to the

---

[27]11 U.S.C. §549(a).

[28]Bankr. R. 3002(c).

[29]Rules relating to allowance of claims or interests are contained in 11 U.S.C. §502.

[30]These debts are not discharged in bankruptcy and may therefore be satisfied out of the debtor's postpetition assets.

[31]11 U.S.C. §725.

secured debt. The court may order the automatic stay imposed at the commencement of the case lifted, allowing the creditor to seize the property and sell it in satisfaction of the debt. Alternatively, the trustee may simply abandon the encumbered property to the creditor with the same result. If these alternatives are not used, the trustee ultimately will sell the property and distribute the proceeds to the secured creditors, less the costs the trustee incurs in preserving and selling the collateral.

If the collateral is insufficient to satisfy the underlying debt in full, the excess is treated as a general creditor's unsecured claim, and receives a percentage distribution equal to that received by other unsecured claims.[32]

Unsecured Creditors. After secured creditors are paid, the remaining nonexempt property of the estate is applied to pay the administrative expenses of the bankruptcy and unsecured creditors in the order outlined below.[33] All claims of one class are paid in full before the next class receives anything. If the assets are insufficient to pay all claims of a given class, the claimants share pro rata:

1. Claims for "domestic support obligations." These include, for example, debts owed to a spouse, former spouse, child, or governmental unit for alimony, maintenance, or child support.

2. administrative expenses of the bankruptcy such as the costs of maintaining and selling property of the estate, the trustee's compensation, and the debtor's and the trustee's attorneys' fee;

3. in an involuntary case, certain claims arising in the ordinary course of the debtor's business arising after the petition is filed but before the order for relief is entered or the trustee is appointed, whichever occurs first;

4. claims of employees and independent sales representatives against a bankrupt employer for wages, salaries, and commissions (including vacation, severance, and sick leave pay) up to $10,000 per employee earned within 180 days prior to the date the petition was filed or the date the debtor ceased business operations, whichever occurred first;

5. claims for contributions to employee benefit plans that arise from services rendered by the employee within 180 days prior to the filing of the petition (or cessation of the debtor's business, whichever is earlier) and that are limited in amount to $10,000 multiplied by the number of employees covered by the plan, *less* any amount paid to employees under the fourth priority listed above;

6. claims of farmers who stored grain in a bankrupt grain elevator and fishermen who sold or transferred fish to a bankrupt fish produce storage or processing facility up to $4,925 per individual;

7. claims of consumers who paid money to a bankrupt business for goods or services to be provided at a later date, which were not provided, up to $2,225 per individual;

8. tax claims including income or gross receipts taxes, property taxes, any tax required to be withheld or collected, employment taxes, excise taxes, and customs duties;

9. claims based on the debtor's commitment to a federal regulatory agency (such as the FDIC) to maintain the capital of an insured bank or other depository institution;

10. claims for death or personal injury resulting from the debtor's operation of a motor vehicle or vessel while intoxicated from using alcohol, a drug, or other substance; and

11. claims of general unsecured creditors whose claims are timely filed.

In computing total general creditor claims, deficiencies in secured creditor's claims and priority claims exceeding the time or amount limitations outlined above are included. Because assets usually are insufficient to pay general creditor claims in full, claimants share pro rata. For example, if $10,000 remains after payment of priority claims and allowed unsecured claims total $100,000, each creditor receives 10 percent of its claim

$$\frac{\$10,000 \text{ assets}}{\$100,000 \text{ claims}}$$

or ten cents on the dollar. The distribution to general creditors is called the **dividend** and the percentage of their claims general creditors are paid is the **dividend percentage.**

Discharge

Effect of Discharge. A fundamental purpose of bankruptcy, in addition to equitable treatment of creditors, is debtor relief. In bankruptcy law, debtor relief is embodied in the discharge, designed to give the debtor a "fresh start" free of claims of former creditors. A **discharge in bankruptcy** releases the debtor from any further liabil-

---

[32]11 U.S.C. §506(a).

[33]These priorities are contained in 11 U.S.C. §507.

ity for most debts that arose prior to the date the order for relief is entered. Discharge generally is granted whether or not a proof of claim was filed for the debt in question and whether or not the claim based on the debt was allowed.

A discharge voids any judgment against the debtor imposing personal liability for a prepetition debt and prevents creditors from commencing or continuing any legal proceeding or other act to collect a discharged debt. Thus, the discharge constitutes a total prohibition of debt collection efforts, including informal action such as telephone calls, letters, and personal contacts.

Not all debtors and not all debts are discharged in bankruptcy. A debtor who is denied a discharge occupies an unenviable position. All nonexempt assets are seized, liquidated, and distributed to satisfy creditors' claims. The remaining balances of all prepetition creditor claims survive and may be asserted against the debtor after bankruptcy. Even if the debtor is granted a discharge, some specific debts survive the proceeding and may be collected after bankruptcy. Note that if the debtor is denied a discharge, *all* creditor claims survive. If the debtor is discharged, only specifically enumerated debts survive; the remainder are discharged.

Debtors Not Discharged. The Bankruptcy Code provides that the court is to grant the debtor a discharge unless a creditor or the trustee in bankruptcy objects and establishes a ground for denying a discharge.[34] These grounds generally are based upon the debtor's dishonesty or lack of cooperation in the bankruptcy proceeding. When the court has determined whether to grant the debtor a discharge, the court may hold a hearing to inform the debtor that a discharge has been granted or the reason why a discharge has been denied. The court may deny the debtor a discharge if one of the following grounds is proven.

1. The debtor is not an individual. (Corporations and partnerships are ineligible for discharge under Chapter 7.)

2. The debtor made a fraudulent conveyance of property, either before or after the case was commenced.

3. The debtor concealed, destroyed, falsified, or failed to keep or preserve financial books and records

from which the debtor's financial condition or business transactions could be ascertained.

4. The debtor knowingly and fraudulently (a) made a false oath or account, (b) presented or used a false claim, (c) received consideration for acting or failing to act in connection with the bankruptcy, or (d) withheld financial books and records from the bankruptcy trustee.

5. The debtor failed satisfactorily to explain any loss or deficiency of assets necessary to meet liabilities.

6. The debtor (a) refused to obey any lawful order of the court, (b) failed to respond on the ground of the privilege against self-incrimination to a material question approved by the court after being granted immunity, or (c) when self-incrimination is not involved, failed to testify or to respond to a material question approved by the court.

7. The debtor committed any of the acts specified in paragraphs 2 through 6 above in connection with a separate bankruptcy case involving an "insider" within one year prior to the debtor's bankruptcy petition.

8. The debtor signs a written waiver of discharge approved by the court after the order for relief is entered.

A discharge previously granted may be revoked on the request of the trustee or a creditor, upon proof that the discharge was obtained through fraud, or that the debtor knowingly and fraudulently retained property belonging to the estate or failed to obey a court order. In addition, the Bankruptcy Code limits the frequency of a bankruptcy discharge. In a liquidation case, the debtor may receive a discharge only once every eight years, measured between the dates on which bankruptcy petitions are filed.

Debts Not Discharged. Even if the debtor receives a discharge, the Bankruptcy Code provides[35] that certain prepetition debts survive the proceeding and may be collected against the debtor's postbankruptcy assets. Examples of debts not discharged include

1. most taxes;
2. money, property, or services obtained through misrepresentation or fraud;
3. money, property, or services obtained through use of a materially false and fraudulent written financial statement;

---

[34]11 U.S.C. §727.

[35]11 U.S.C. §523.

4. liability for "luxury" consumer goods or services obtained by the debtor on or within 90 days prior to the order for relief from a single creditor with a total value exceeding $500;

5. cash advances obtained within 70 days prior to the order for relief totaling more than $750 that are extensions of consumer credit under an open end credit plan (such as a credit card);

6. debts that the debtor fails to include on his or her list of creditors if as a result the unlisted creditor is unable to file a timely claim in the proceeding;

7. debts resulting from the debtor's fraud or embezzlement while acting in a fiduciary capacity, such as a trustee or officer or director of a bank;

8. debts resulting from embezzlement or theft;

9. domestic support obligations;

10. debts resulting from the debtor's willful and malicious injury of another person or his property;

11. liability for fines, penalties, or forfeitures payable to governmental units;

12. student loans, unless excepting the loan from discharge would impose an undue hardship on the debtor and the debtor's dependents;

13. debts, such as a tort judgment, incurred by the debtor as a result of driving a motor vehicle while intoxicated from using alcohol, a drug, or other substance;

14. debts from a prior bankruptcy in which the debtor was denied a discharge;

15. liability for a malicious or reckless failure to fulfill any commitment to a federal regulatory agency to maintain the capital of an insured bank;

16. certain fees or assessments owed to a cooperative or condominium association relating to the debtor's dwelling unit;

17. debts arising from an order of restitution issued under the federal criminal code;

18. debts owed to a pension, profit-sharing, stock bonus, or other plan established under the Internal Revenue Code;

19. debts arising from violation of federal or state securities laws, or regulations adopted under those laws; and

20. debts resulting from common law fraud, deceit, or manipulation in connection with the purchase or sale of any security.

At issue in the following case was whether a debt was caused by the debtor's willful and malicious conduct, rendering the debt nondischargeable.

In re Posta
866 F.2d 364 (10th Cir. 1989)

Gregory and Mary Posta purchased a mobile travel trailer and granted a security interest in the trailer to C.I.T. Financial Services, Inc. (CIT), which had financed the purchase. The security agreement signed by the Postas provided that they could not sell, rent, or transfer the trailer, or move it from their home address without CIT's written permission. Within a year, because of financial difficulties, the Postas decided to sell or lease the trailer and moved it to a dealership. The Postas were contacted by Ronald Swartz who, after agreeing to buy the trailer, prepared a sales agreement. In compliance with the agreement, Swartz paid $962 in cash, provided a promissory note for $22,245—the balance owed to CIT—and granted the Postas a mortgage on a condominium. After Swartz disappeared with the trailer without making payments on the promissory note, the Postas discovered that he had no interest in the mortgaged condominium and reported the incident to the authorities and to CIT. The Postas defaulted on their loan payments to CIT and later filed for bankruptcy.

CIT objected to discharge of the debt alleging that the Postas had willfully and maliciously converted the trailer. The bankruptcy court ruled that the Postas' actions were not malicious and granted discharge of the debt. The district court affirmed and CIT appealed to the federal court of appeals.

Per Curiam

. . . Section 523(a)(6) of the Code excepts from discharge any debt "for willful and malicious injury by the debtor to another entity or the property of another entity." Such injury includes the conversion of property subject to a creditor's security interest. . . . For a debt to be nondischargeable under this section, however, the debtor's conversion of property must be both "willful" and "malicious." The creditor objecting to the discharge has the burden of proving both of these elements. . . .

The "willful" element is straightforward. It simply addresses whether the debtor intentionally performed the basic act complained of. . . . "Willful" conduct is conduct that is volitional and deliberate and over which the debtor exercises meaningful control, as opposed to unintentional or accidental conduct. . . .

In this case, there seems to be little question but that the Postas voluntarily and intentionally sold the trailer; so their conduct was "willful." The issue is, instead, whether in doing so, they acted maliciously. CIT asserts that when a debtor intends to do an act which results in harm to his creditor, such conduct is "malicious." Consequently, because the Postas intentionally sold the trailer, and because the sale was in violation of the security agreement and ultimately harmed CIT, CIT contends that the "malicious" element is satisfied. We disagree. Were we to accept CIT's argument, nearly any intentional conduct would fall within this exception to discharge, and the word "malicious" in this section would be rendered meaningless. . . . [T]he focus of the "malicious" inquiry is on the debtor's actual knowledge or the reasonable foreseeability that his conduct will result in injury to the creditor. . . .

Under §523(a)(6), the debtor's malicious intent can be shown in two ways. In the rare instances in which there is direct evidence that the debtor's conduct was taken with the specific intent to harm the creditor, the malice requirement is easily established. . . . More commonly, however, malicious intent must be demonstrated by evidence that the debtor had knowledge of the creditor's rights and that, with that knowledge, proceeded to take action in violation of those rights. . . . Such knowledge can be inferred from the debtor's experience in the business, his concealment of the sale, or by his admission that he has read and understood the security agreement. . . .

[The bankruptcy] court correctly looked to whether the Postas had willfully disregarded the rights of CIT in making the sale. The court noted that the Postas were relatively inexperienced in business matters, that they had difficulty in understanding business concepts, and that they had not read the security agreement. . . . The evidence shows that, at all times, the Postas intended to fulfill their loan obligations to CIT by applying the proceeds of Mr. Swartz' note to the loan. . . . They did not conceal the sale from CIT and, in fact, requested CIT's assistance when it appeared their arrangement with Mr. Swartz had gone sour. . . . We agree with the bankruptcy court that, in light of these facts, at most, all that occurred was a "technical conversion." Technical conversions do not fall within the §523(a)(6) exception to discharge. . . .

[Judgment affirmed.]

Reaffirmation Agreements. A debtor may promise in a **reaffirmation agreement** to pay a debt discharged in bankruptcy. To prevent erosion of the fresh start aspect

of bankruptcy, the Bankruptcy Code severely limits enforcement of such agreements. To be enforceable, a reaffirmation agreement must be made before the discharge is granted, and be filed with the court. The debtor also must receive (before signing the agreement) a written statement that clearly and conspicuously discloses to the debtor a variety of information, including, for example, the amount of debt reaffirmed, the annual percentage interest rate, that reaffirmation agreements are not required by law and may be rescinded by the debtor (at any time prior to discharge or within 60 days after being filed with the court, whichever occurs later), and information concerning the certification and approval process discussed below.

If the debtor is represented by an attorney, the attorney must file an affidavit certifying that (1) the attorney has advised the debtor of the legal effect of the agreement, (2) the debtor's assent to the agreement was voluntary and based on complete information, and (3) the agreement will not impose undue hardship on the debtor. If the debtor is not represented by an attorney during negotiation of the reaffirmation agreement, the court must hold a hearing to (1) inform the debtor that reaffirmation agreements are not required by law and explain the consequences of reaffirmation, and (2) approve the agreement (unless it reaffirms a consumer debt secured by real property). Note that the foregoing requirements do not prevent a debtor from voluntarily repaying any previously discharged debt.[36]

Dismissal. Once commenced, most liquidation cases run their intended course from collection and distribution of the debtors' assets to discharge of the debtor. As previously discussed, the court may dismiss a Chapter 7 case filed by an individual debtor whose debts are primarily consumer debts if it finds that granting relief would be an abuse of Chapter 7 provisions. The bankruptcy court also may dismiss or terminate a Chapter 7 case for "cause," including, for example, the debtor's unreasonable delay prejudicial to creditors; nonpayment of required fees or charges; and the debtor's failure to provide financial information (such as a list of creditors, balance sheet, and income statement) in a timely fashion.[37]

In addition to specific provisions, the Bankruptcy Code authorizes the court, on its own motion, to take

[36]11 U.S.C. §§524(c),(d),(f).
[37]11 U.S.C. §707(a).

any action "necessary or appropriate to enforce or implement court orders or rules, or to prevent an abuse of process."[38]

Rehabilitation—Chapters 11, 12, and 13

An alternative to liquidation, often more advantageous to all concerned, is to keep the financially troubled debtor in business, postponing, compromising, or altering creditor claims, and allowing the debtor to attempt to work out his problems. Such debtor "rehabilitation" arrangements often are preferable to general creditors who usually receive little or nothing upon liquidation. Four chapters of the Bankruptcy Code are concerned with debtor rehabilitation: Chapter 9 (Adjustment of Debts of a Municipality), Chapter 11 (Reorganization), Chapter 12 (Adjustment of Debts of a Family Farmer with Regular Annual Income), and Chapter 13 (Adjustment of Debts of an Individual with Regular Income). In all cases, rehabilitation "plans" are adopted under which creditor claims are reduced, converted into other forms of debt or equity, or the time of payment extended. In corporate reorganization, claims of equity security holders (shareholders) also may be affected.

A debtor, at any time during pendency of a Chapter 7 case (either voluntary or involuntary), has an absolute one-time right to convert the case to a proceeding under Chapter 11, 12, or 13.[39] This conversion privilege assures that the debtor has the opportunity, if desired, to repay debts. Cases filed under Chapters 11, 12, or 13 generally may be converted by the debtor to a Chapter 7 liquidation at any time. Chapters 12 and 13 debtors also usually possess the right to have the court dismiss their cases at any time. In addition, the court, at the request of a party in interest such as a creditor, may dismiss a Chapter 11, 12, or 13 case or convert it to a Chapter 7 liquidation for "cause," including, for example, unreasonable delay by the debtor prejudicial to creditors, nonpayment of required fees, failure to file a plan or commence payments, denial of confirmation of a plan, or material default in performing the terms of a confirmed plan.[40]

---

[38]11 U.S.C. §105(a).
[39]11 U.S.C. §706(a).
[40]11 U.S.C. §§1112, 1208, 1307.

Chapter 11—Reorganization

Commencement of the Case. Chapter 11 is the primary device used to rehabilitate corporate, as opposed to individual, debtors in financial difficulty. A Chapter 11 case may be commenced in various ways. The case may be commenced either voluntarily (by the debtor) or involuntarily (by creditors) using the same requirements discussed earlier in this chapter. Second, upon request of the trustee or creditor, the court may, after notice and a hearing, convert a Chapter 7 case into a Chapter 11 case. Finally, the debtor may commence the case through conversion from a Chapter 7 case.

In reorganization cases, unlike those under Chapter 7, the debtor usually retains possession of property of the estate and continues to manage and operate the business as a "debtor in possession." No trustee in bankruptcy is appointed; rather, the debtor in possession has the rights and powers, and performs the functions and duties, of the trustee. After commencement of the case, but before confirmation of the plan, however, any interested party may petition the court to appoint a trustee for cause, including fraud, dishonesty, incompetence, or gross mismanagement by the debtor's current management, or if the court finds the appointment to be in the best interest of creditors, shareholders, or others interested in the estate. If the court orders a trustee appointed, the U.S. Trustee convenes a meeting of creditors, who may elect the trustee using the same procedures applied in Chapter 7 cases. Even if the court finds it unnecessary to appoint a trustee, it may appoint an examiner to investigate any allegations of fraud, dishonesty, misconduct, or other irregularity.

Under Chapter 11, like Chapter 7, the debtor is required to file a list of creditors, a schedule of assets and liabilities, and a statement of the debtor's financial affairs. A creditor's proof of claim (or proof of interest in the case of a shareholder) is deemed to be filed if it appears in the above schedules, unless the claim or interest is disputed, contingent, or unliquidated. Chapter 11 therefore does not require that every creditor or shareholder file a proof of claim or interest in a reorganization case.

Because a Chapter 11 debtor often has hundreds or thousands of creditors, after the order for relief, the U.S. Trustee is required to appoint a committee of creditors holding unsecured claims. The court also may order the U.S. Trustee to appoint committees representing other classes of creditors or shareholders. A **creditors' committee** ordinarily consists of persons holding the seven largest claims against the debtor of the type represented by the committee. Creditors' committees perform various functions such as consulting with the trustee or debtor in possession regarding administration of the case, investigating the debtor's conduct, participating in the formulation of the reorganization plan, and requesting the appointment of a trustee or examiner.

Conversion or Dismissal. Under §1112(b), the court may dismiss a Chapter 11 petition (or convert it to a Chapter 7 liquidation) for "cause." The statute provides a nonexhaustive list of factors constituting cause including, for example: (1) continuing reduction in the value of the estate and absence of reasonable likelihood of rehabilitation; (2) gross mismanagement of the estate; (3) failure to comply with an order of the court, or any filing or reporting requirement imposed by law; (4) failure to attend a meeting of creditors or provide information; (5) failure to pay taxes owed or file tax returns due; (6) failure to file or confirm a plan within time limits fixed by law or the court; and (7) inability to perform or material default in performing a confirmed plan. Most courts also have held that Chapter 11 petitions may be dismissed for cause under §1112(b) if not filed in good faith. The following case discusses the rationale for this good faith requirement.

In re Integrated Telecom Express, Inc.
384 F.3d 108 (3d Cir. 2004)

In the summer of 2000, Integrated Telecom Express, Inc. (Integrated), a supplier of software and communications equipment, entered into a 10-year lease of property in Silicon Valley, California with NMSBPCSLDHB, L.P. (Landlord). The lease required Integrated to pay $200,000 per month with an automatic annual increase of 5 percent. In 2001, following a decline in demand for its products, Integrated suffered net losses of $36.2 million. In 2002, Integrated's Board of Directors decided to dissolve the company, but first needed to resolve its lease obligations. The Board learned that §502(b)(6) of the Bankruptcy Code limited a landlord's claims for future rent to the greater of (1) one year's rent; or (2) 15 percent of the rent owed for the remaining term (not to exceed three years) of the lease. Calculating the present discounted value of the future rent to be about $26 million, the Board directed the officers to negotiate with the landlord and authorized the firm to pay up to $8 million to be released from the lease. The Board further authorized Integrated to file for bankruptcy if the Landlord was unwilling to settle. Although Integrated informed the Landlord of its intent to go into bankruptcy unless a settlement was reached, the Landlord refused the

settlement offer. Integrated then filed a petition for Chapter 11 bankruptcy. The Landlord moved to dismiss the bankruptcy proceeding, asserting that Integrated's petition was not filed in good faith. The Bankruptcy Court denied the motion and the District Court affirmed. The Landlord filed an appeal with the federal Third Circuit Court of Appeals.

Smith, Circuit Judge

This appeal tests the limits of the good faith requirement applicable to petitions filed under Chapter 11 of the Bankruptcy Code. . . . The issue on appeal is whether, on the facts of this case, a Chapter 11 petition filed by a financially healthy debtor, with no intention of reorganizing or liquidating as a going concern, with no reasonable expectation that Chapter 11 proceedings will maximize the value of the debtor's estate for creditors, and solely to take advantage of a provision in the Bankruptcy Code that limits claims on long-term leases, complies with the requirements of the Bankruptcy Code. We conclude that such a petition is not filed in good faith. . . .

Chapter 11 bankruptcy petitions are subject to dismissal under 11 U.S.C. §1112(b) unless filed in good faith, and the burden is on the bankruptcy petitioner to establish that its petition has been filed in good faith. . . . Whether the good faith requirement has been satisfied is a "fact intensive inquiry" in which the court must examine "the totality of facts and circumstances" and determine where a "petition falls along the spectrum ranging from the clearly acceptable to the patently abusive." [*In re SGL Carbon Corp.*, 200 F.3d 154, 162 (3d Cir. 1999).] . . .

At its most fundamental level, the good faith requirement ensures that the Bankruptcy Code's careful balancing of interests is not undermined by petitioners whose aims are antithetical to the basic purposes of bankruptcy. . . . The Supreme Court has identified two of the basic purposes of Chapter 11 as (1) "preserving going concerns" and (2) "maximizing property available to satisfy creditors." *Bank of Am. Nat'l Trust & Sav. Ass'n v. 203 N. LaSalle St. P'ship*, [119 S. Ct. 1411, 1421 (1999).] . . . Our cases have accordingly focused on two inquiries that are particularly relevant to the question of good faith: (1) whether the petition serves a valid bankruptcy purpose, for example, by preserving a going concern or maximizing the value of the debtor's estate, and (2) whether the petition is filed merely to obtain a tactical litigation advantage.

It is easy to see why courts have required Chapter 11 petitioners to act within the scope of the bankruptcy laws to further a valid reorganizational purpose. Chapter 11 vests petitioners with considerable powers—the automatic stay, the exclusive right to propose a reorganization plan, the discharge of debts, etc.—that can impose significant hardship on particular creditors. When financially troubled petitioners seek a chance to remain in business, the exercise of those powers is justified. But this is not so when a petitioner's aims lie outside those of the Bankruptcy Code.

SGL Carbon, 206 F.3d at 165-66.

As the Bankruptcy Court recognized, Integrated is unquestionably "out of business," and therefore has no going concern value to preserve in Chapter 11 through reorganization or liquidation under the Bankruptcy Code. The question therefore becomes whether Integrated's petition might reasonably have maximized the value of the bankruptcy estate. For the reasons that follow, we conclude that it would not.

To say that liquidation under Chapter 11 maximizes the value of an entity is to say that there is some value that otherwise would be lost outside of bankruptcy. . . . As Integrated conceded at oral argument, good faith necessarily requires some degree of financial distress on the part of a debtor. . . . To be sure, a debtor need not be insolvent before filing for bankruptcy protection. . . . Saying that there is no insolvency requirement, however, does not mean that all solvent firms should have unfettered access to Chapter 11. . . . [T]he absence of a solvency requirement recognizes that even solvent firms can, at times, suffer from financial distress. . . . "It is not uncommon for debtors to be solvent under the balance sheet test, and yet to have severe financial problems. . . . The United States bankruptcy law is designed to provide relief from creditor pressures for debtors with cash flow difficulties, even where they are clearly solvent under a balance sheet test." [*In re Marshall*, 300 B.R. 507, 512-13 (Bankr. C.D. Cal. 2003).]

Both the Bankruptcy Court and the District Court concluded that Integrated faced financial distress because it "was losing a lot of money," and "was experiencing a dramatic downward spiral" in September 2001, and that, as a result, Integrated had gone "out of business." We do not see how bankruptcy offers Integrated any relief from this sort of distress, which has no relation to any debt owed by Integrated. That is, we can identify no value for Integrated's assets that was threatened outside of bankruptcy by the collapse of Integrated's business model, but that could be preserved or maximized in an orderly liquidation under Chapter 11. Because Integrated's "dramatic downward spiral" does not establish that Integrated was suffering from financial distress, it does not, standing alone, establish that Integrated's petition was filed in good faith.

Creditors that fear an impending default may seek to protect their claims, triggering "the chaotic mix of self-help repossession and judicial execution available at state law" to which the Bankruptcy Code provides an alternative. [E. Warren, *Bankruptcy Policymaking in an Imperfect World*, 92 Mich. L. Rev. 336, 350 (1993).] The absence of an insolvency requirement encourages companies to file for Chapter 11 before they face a financially hopeless situation. . . . Yet, this is decidedly not the case here.

Integrated had $105.4 million in cash and $ 1.5 million in other assets at the time that it filed for bankruptcy, and yet the Landlord's proof of claim lists the present discounted value of Integrated's lease obligations at approximately $26 million. Integrated's schedules also list miscellaneous liabilities of approximately $ 430,000. Thus Integrated was highly solvent and cash rich at the time of the bankruptcy filing. . . . In light of the foregoing, we conclude that the collapse of Integrated's business model does not support a finding of good faith. Integrated was not suffering financial distress when it filed its petition, and the rulings of the Bankruptcy Court and the District Court to the contrary constitute legal error. The failure of Integrated's business did not subject the company to any pressure on the value of its assets that could be reduced or avoided in an orderly liquidation under Chapter 11. Because Integrated's economic difficulties do not establish that Integrated was suffering from financial distress, they do not, standing alone, establish that Integrated's petition was filed in good faith. . . .

Having determined that Integrated was not in financial distress, . . . we turn to the . . . argument that Integrated's desire to take advantage of the cap on landlord claims provided by §502(b)(6) establishes good faith in and of itself. . . . The Bankruptcy Court did not hold that Integrated's desire to take advantage of the §502(b)(6) cap established *good* faith. Instead, the Bankruptcy Court held that "it does not establish *bad* faith for a debtor to file a Chapter 11 case for the purpose of taking advantage of provisions which alter prepetition rights, including altering the rights of a landlord under state law." (Emphasis added). We agree. Indeed, we believe it to be a truism that it is not bad faith to seek to avail oneself of a particular protection in the Bankruptcy Code—Congress enacted such protections with the expectation that they would be used. . . .

The far more relevant question is whether a desire to take advantage of a particular provision in the Bankruptcy Code, standing alone, establishes *good* faith. We hold that it does not. . . . Section §502(b)(6) and the legislative policy underlying that provision assume the existence of a valid bankruptcy, which, in turn, assumes a debtor in financial distress. The question of good faith is therefore antecedent to the operation of §502(b)(6).

Although the Bankruptcy Code contains many provisions that have the effect of redistributing value from one interest group to another, these redistributions are not the Code's *purpose*. Instead, the purposes of the Code are to preserve going concerns and to maximize the value of the debtor's estate. . . .

To be filed in good faith, a petition must do more than merely invoke some distributional mechanism in the Bankruptcy Code. It must seek to create or preserve some value that would otherwise be lost—not merely distributed to a different stakeholder—outside of bankruptcy. This threshold inquiry is particularly sensitive where, as here, the petition seeks to distribute value directly from a creditor to a company's shareholders. . . .

As we have explained above, in a smoking gun resolution approved by the Board, and notwithstanding its strong financial position, Integrated authorized a letter to the Landlord threatening that if it did not enter into a settlement of the lease in the amount of at least $8 million, Integrated would file for bankruptcy so as to take advantage of §502(b)(6), which sharply limits the amount that a landlord can recover in bankruptcy for damages resulting from the termination of a lease.

Taken to its logical conclusion, the . . . argument is that any entity willing to undergo Chapter 11 proceedings may cap the claims of its landlord. Nothing in the Bankruptcy Code or its legislative history suggests that §502(b)(6) was meant to allow tenants to avoid their leases whenever the landlord's state law remedy exceeds the cap under §502(b)(6) by an amount greater than the cost of proceeding through a Chapter 11 reorganization or liquidation. Such a rule would not only obviate the need for a good faith requirement, but would be antithetical to the structure and purposes of the Bankruptcy Code.

We hold that both the District Court and the Bankruptcy Court erred as a matter of law in concluding that Integrated suffered financial distress. Although Integrated's business model had failed, the company had no significant debt apart from the Landlord's claim. . . . Because Integrated was not in financial distress, its Chapter 11 petition was not filed in good faith

as it could not—and did not—preserve any value for Integrated's creditors that would have been lost outside of bankruptcy. . . .

[Judgment reversed and remanded to the Bankruptcy Court with instructions to dismiss Integrated's bankruptcy petition.]

Formulation of the Plan. The proposal and acceptance of a **reorganization plan** and its confirmation by the court make up the major part of a Chapter 11 proceeding. The debtor may file a reorganization plan at any time, with the exclusive right to do so during the first 120 days after the order for relief is entered. Any party may file a plan if (1) the debtor has not filed within 120 days, (2) a trustee has been appointed, or (3) the debtor's plan is not accepted by creditors or shareholders within 180 days after the order for relief.[41] The court may extend the 120 and 180 day periods up to a maximum of 18 months and 20 months respectively, after the date of the order for relief. Most plans are the result of intensive negotiations among the debtor, its creditors, and shareholders.

Because creditors and equity security holders in reorganization cases are so numerous, the plan generally divides the claimants into "classes," consisting of claims or interests that are substantially similar. Each secured creditor (for example, a bank holding a mortgage on the debtor's factory) generally constitutes a separate class. The plan then designates how creditors within each class are treated. Generally, the plan must provide the same treatment for each claim or interest of a particular class.

Confirmation of the Plan. Once formulated, plans are submitted to the various classes of creditors and shareholders for approval. In addition to the plan or a summary thereof, the holders of claims or interests receive a written disclosure statement approved by the court, containing information adequate to enable them to make an informed judgment about the plan.[42] To be accepted by a class of creditors, the plan must be approved by those holding at least two-thirds in dollar amount and more than one-half in number of allowed claims. To be accepted by a class of equity security holders, persons holding at least two-thirds in dollar amount of a given class of security must approve. No

---

[41]11 U.S.C. §1121.
[42]11 U.S.C. §1125.

vote is required of any class whose claims or interests are unimpaired by the plan (who are deemed to accept it) or of any class that receives nothing under the plan (who are deemed to reject it).[43]

After the vote, the court is required to hold a hearing on confirmation of the plan. The court may confirm the plan only if it meets the requirements outlined in §1129(a) of the Bankruptcy Code. Among the most important requirements are that (1) the plan has been proposed in good faith; (2) each *class* of creditors or shareholders has either accepted the plan or the class's interests are not impaired by the plan; (3) each *member* of an impaired class of claims or interests must either have (a) accepted the plan or (b) will receive an amount under the plan equal to what that person would have received in a Chapter 7 liquidation (the "best interests of creditors" test); (4) priority claims (discussed earlier in this chapter) are provided for; (5) the plan is "feasible" — that is, confirmation is not likely to be followed by liquidation or the need for further financial reorganization; and (6) the plan and its proponent comply with all applicable Bankruptcy Code provisions, including payment of fees.

Assuming the other requirements are met, the court may confirm a plan even if a class rejects it if (1) at least one impaired class accepts it, and (2) the court finds that the plan does not discriminate unfairly and is fair and equitable to the impaired class's interest. Confirmation of the plan over the objection of one or more classes of creditors or interests, stated in §1129(b) of the Bankruptcy Code, is appropriately known as a **cramdown.**

The Bankruptcy Code defines the circumstances under which a plan is "fair and equitable" thereby permitting a cramdown. Generally, objecting secured creditors may be bound by the plan if they are allowed to retain their security interest in the collateral and are to receive payments with a present value equal to the value of the collateral. For unsecured creditors, cramdown is allowed if the impaired class and all below it are treated according to a rule of "absolute priority," meaning that the dissenting class must be paid in full before any junior class receives anything. Thus, objecting unsecured creditors may be bound if under the plan either (1) their claims are to be paid in full or (2) no class junior to them is entitled to share under the plan. An analogous rule applies to various classes of shareholders. Under these rules, for example, a trade creditor owed $500 must be paid in full if the shareholders are to receive anything.

Implementation of the Plan. Once confirmed, the provisions of the plan are binding on the debtor and anyone issuing securities or acquiring property under the plan. The debtor's creditors or shareholders also are bound including those whose claims or interests were impaired and those who voted against the plan.[44] Title to estate property vests in the debtor free and clear of all liens or other interests except those provided in the plan. In short, after confirmation, creditor and shareholder rights and interests are determined by the terms of the plan and preconfirmation rights and interests are extinguished.

Note finally that Chapter 11 contains provisions, added in 1994, designed to expedite reorganization of small businesses (those with total debt of less than $2 million). These provisions permit small business reorganization without creditors' committees and simplify the requirements governing disclosure of, and solicitation of votes for, a proposed plan.

Chapter 13—Adjustment of Debts of an Individual with Regular Income

Chapter 13 governs rehabilitation of individual debtors. Chapter 13 relief is available to any individual with a "regular income" who owes, on the date the petition is filed, fixed unsecured debts of less than $307,675 and fixed secured debts of less than $922,975.[45] Thus, Chapter 13 is available to wage earners, sole proprietors, and other persons in business with a regular income, for whom a full-blown reorganization under Chapter 11 is too cumbersome.

Commencement of the Case. Like other bankruptcy proceedings, a Chapter 13 case commences with the filing of a petition. A Chapter 13 case may be commenced *only* by the debtor, who may convert a Chapter 13 case to a Chapter 7 case or may dismiss it at any time.[46] Thus, the law prohibits involuntary (creditor-initiated) Chapter 13 cases. The court may, however, convert a Chapter 13 case to Chapter 7 for "cause," including, for example, the debtor's unreasonable delay, failure to pay fees or file a plan, denial of confirmation of a plan, or material default in performing a confirmed plan.

Under Chapter 13, like Chapter 11, the debtor generally retains possession of all property of the estate, and

---

[43]11 U.S.C. §1126.

[44]11 U.S.C. §1141(a).
[45]11 U.S.C. §109(e).
[46]11 U.S.C. §1307.

a debtor engaged in business continues to operate the business unless the court orders otherwise. In a Chapter 13 case, however, after the case is commenced, a trustee is appointed to oversee performance of the debtor's rehabilitation plan. A Chapter 13 trustee has many of the same duties as the trustee in a liquidation case. Under Chapter 13, property of the estate includes all property acquired and earnings received by the debtor both before and after the case is commenced.

Formulation of the Plan. Chapter 13 is designed as a flexible tool for planned repayment of all or part of the debtor's obligations. Under Chapter 13 only the debtor may file a plan of repayment. The plan must be filed either with the petition or within 15 days after the petition is filed. The plan, at a minimum, must (1) provide for submission to the trustee of whatever portion of the debtor's future income is necessary to implement the plan, (2) provide for full payment of claims entitled to priority, and (3) provide identical treatment of all claims within a particular class.[47] For reasons discussed below, plans typically provide for payments over a period of three or five years.

Confirmation of the Plan. Once the plan is formulated, the court holds a hearing on confirmation. Unlike Chapter 11, creditors do not vote to accept or reject a Chapter 13 plan. The plan requires court approval only. To confirm the plan, the court must find that it meets the following criteria:

1. the plan contains terms required or authorized by Chapter 13 or other applicable provisions of the Bankruptcy Code;
2. the filing fee has been paid;
3. the plan was proposed in good faith;
4. unsecured creditors receive an amount under the plan at least equal to the amount that would be paid to them in a Chapter 7 liquidation (the "best interests of creditors" test);
5. interests of secured creditors are protected under the plan;
6. the debtor will be able to make all required payments and otherwise comply with the plan;
7. the debtor's action in filing the petition was in good faith;
8. the debtor has paid all amounts due under a domestic support obligation; and

9. the debtor has filed all applicable federal, state, and local tax returns.[48]

In addition to the previous requirements, if the trustee or an unsecured creditor objects to confirmation, the court may not approve the plan unless either

1. the amount to be distributed under the plan pays the objecting creditor's claim in full, or
2. the plan provides that all of the debtor's projected "disposable income" to be received for the "applicable commitment period" after payments commence is to be used to make payments to unsecured creditors under the plan.[49]

As used above, the "applicable commitment period" is either (1) three years, or (2) if the debtor's monthly income exceeds the median annual income for residents of the debtor's state, five years. A plan of a shorter period satisfies the statute only if it provides for payment in full of all allowed unsecured claims over the shorter period.[50] The provisions of a confirmed plan are binding upon both the debtor and creditors, and vest title to all property of the estate in the debtor.

After confirmation, the debtor makes payments to the trustee, who in turn pays the creditors as soon as practicable according to the terms of the plan. To expedite the plan's implementation, the debtor must start making payments proposed by the plan within 30 days after the plan is filed. Once payments under the plan are completed, the debtor receives a discharge of all debts provided for by the plan, except:

1. domestic support obligations;
2. money, property, or services obtained through misrepresentation or fraud;
3. money, property, or services obtained through use of a materially false and fraudulent written financial statement;
4. liability for "luxury" consumer goods or services obtained by the debtor on or within 90 days prior to the order for relief from a single creditor with a total value exceeding $500;
5. cash advances obtained within 70 days prior to the order for relief totaling more than $750 that are extensions of consumer credit under an open end credit plan (such as a credit card);

---

[47]Bankr. R. 3015(b); 11 U.S.C. §§1321, 1322.

[48]11 U.S.C. §1325(a).

[49]11 U.S.C. §1325(b).

[50]11 U.S.C. §1325(b)(4).

6. debts that the debtor fails to include on his or her list of creditors if as a result the unlisted creditor is unable to file a timely claim in the proceeding;

7. debts resulting from the debtor's fraud or embezzlement while acting in a fiduciary capacity, such as a trustee or officer or director of a bank;

8. debts resulting from embezzlement or theft;

9. student loans, unless excepting the loan from discharge would impose an undue hardship on the debtor and the debtor's dependents;

10. debts, such as a tort judgment, incurred by the debtor as a result of driving a motor vehicle while intoxicated from using alcohol, a drug, or other substance;

11. restitution obligations or damages awarded in a civil action against the debtor for personal injury or death caused by the debtor's willful or malicious conduct;

12. restitution obligations and fines imposed on the debtor as part of the sentence for commission of a crime;

13. certain long-term debts covered by the plan that require payments beyond the plan period;

14. a tax required to be collected or withheld and for which the debtor is liable; and

15. a tax or customs duty owed: for which a return was fraudulently filed, filed late, or not filed; or that the debtor willfully attempted to evade.

Even if all payments have not been made, the court may grant a "hardship" discharge to the debtor if the debtor's failure was due to circumstances beyond the debtor's control, creditors have already been paid at least what they would have received in a Chapter 7 proceeding, and modification of the plan is not practicable.

As previously noted, a Chapter 7 discharge prevents the debtor from receiving another Chapter 7 discharge for eight years. Under Chapter 13, the refiling limitation periods are shorter. For example, a debtor may receive a Chapter 13 discharge four years after a Chapter 7, 11, or 12 discharge; and two years after a previous Chapter 13 discharge.

Chapter 12—Adjustment of Debts of a Family Farmer with Regular Annual Income

In 1986, Congress added Chapter 12, entitled "Adjustment of Debts of a Family Farmer with Regular Annual Income," to the Bankruptcy Code. Relief under this rehabilitation chapter is available to a "family farmer," defined generally as an individual (or individual and spouse) engaged in farming operations who meets the following criteria: (1) total debts do not exceed $3,237,000; (2) at least 50 percent of the total fixed debt arises out of a farming operation owned or operated by the debtor; and (3) at least 50 percent of the debtor's gross income is derived from the farming operation. A partnership or corporation also may qualify as a debtor under Chapter 12 if (1) it meets the first two criteria outlined above, (2) more than 80 percent of its assets are related to the farming operation, and (3) more than half of its stock or equity is owned by members of the same family, who conduct the farming operation. To qualify under Chapter 12, the family farmer must generate a "regular annual income," meaning income that is "sufficiently stable and regular," to enable the debtor to make payments under the plan.[51]

Chapter 12 was enacted to provide an effective rehabilitation alternative to small farmers affected by low crop prices and dramatically dropping farmland values. As noted in the Conference Report accompanying the bill enacting Chapter 12:

> Under current law, family farmers in need of financial rehabilitation may proceed under either Chapter 11 or Chapter 13 of the Bankruptcy Code. Most family farmers have too much debt to qualify as debtors under Chapter 13 and are thus limited to relief under Chapter 11. Unfortunately, many family farmers have found Chapter 11 needlessly complicated, unduly time-consuming, inordinately expensive and, in too many cases, unworkable.[52]

Chapter 12 is modeled closely upon Chapter 13. The debtor files a plan of reorganization within 90 days after the petition is filed. At the confirmation hearing, which must be concluded within 45 days after the plan is filed, the court confirms the plan if it meets standards similar to those applied under Chapter 13, including the "disposable income" requirement. Although similar to Chapter 13, Chapter 12 alters certain provisions that Congress deemed inappropriate for family farm reorganization. For example, Chapter 12 raises the debt limits for qualification (to $3,237,000), extends the time limits for filing the plan (90 days versus 15 days under Chapter 13), and extends the time limits for commencing payments under a confirmed plan (no specific period versus 30 days under Chapter 13).

---

[51] 11 U.S.C. §§101(18), 101(19), 109(f).

[52] H.R. Rep. No. 99–958, 99th Cong., 2d Sess. 48 (1986).

Collective Creditors' Remedies Outside Bankruptcy

Unlike state law collection remedies, bankruptcy law is designed to achieve equitable treatment of competing creditors by requiring that creditors act together rather than individually. Bankruptcy, however, is expensive and time-consuming. As a result, the law has developed various collective remedies outside bankruptcy through which creditors, though not paid in full, often receive a larger percentage on their claims than would be available in bankruptcy. The primary remedies of this type are assignments for the benefit of creditors, and composition and extension agreements. These remedies usually are initiated by the debtor.

Assignments for the Benefit of Creditors

In an **assignment for the benefit of creditors,** a financially troubled debtor transfers all nonexempt assets to an assignee or trustee who liquidates the assets and distributes the proceeds to the debtor's creditors. An assignment for the benefit of creditors is therefore the common law or state statutory counterpart to a liquidation under Chapter 7, although significant differences exist between the two devices.

Creditor consent is not required for an assignment for benefit of creditors. Nevertheless, because the assignment transfers title to the debtor's property to the assignee, it may be challenged as a fraudulent conveyance. To avoid this result, the assignment must be "general," conveying all of the debtor's property without restriction to the assignee.

After the assignment, the assignee sells the assets and distributes the cash to creditors. Secured creditors satisfy their claims out of the collateral and the remaining creditors are treated equally, each receiving the same pro rata share of the proceeds. After an assignment, the debtor is not discharged from any debts remaining unpaid because bankruptcy law preempts the states' right to grant discharges. For this reason, assignments for the benefit of creditors are used primarily by corporate rather than individual debtors.

Although an assignment for the benefit of creditors is of common law origin, the device is regulated by statute in most states. Many of these statutes are permissive, allowing the debtor to choose between a common law or a statutory assignment. Statutes generally require recording of the assignment and provide procedures for notifying creditors and filing schedules of assets and liabilities.

It is important to note that an assignment for the benefit of creditors provides a basis for creditors to file an involuntary bankruptcy petition against the debtor. Because a custodian (the assignee) takes possession of substantially all of the debtor's property, one of the two alternative bases for involuntary bankruptcy has been met. Creditors dissatisfied with the assignment therefore have an absolute right to have the liquidation proceed in a bankruptcy court under bankruptcy law with the creditor protection that law provides.

Compositions and Extensions

A **composition** is a contract between the debtor and two or more creditors under which the creditors agree to accept a partial payment in full satisfaction of their claim. An **extension** is a similar agreement that extends the time of payment. Generally, debtor-creditor agreements of this type involve elements of both composition and extension; creditors accept a reduced amount, payable over a longer period.

Compositions and extensions are governed by ordinary contract law principles. Consideration supporting the agreement is the promise of other creditors to accept less or extend time of payment. Accordingly, a binding composition or extension agreement requires promises by the debtor and at least two creditors.

In contrast to an assignment for the benefit of creditors, a binding composition or extension agreement discharges the debts covered by the arrangement. This discharge is effected, however, not by the law of bankruptcy, but simply by the binding contractual promises of the debtor and his creditors. Therefore, the rights of creditors who are not parties to the agreement are unaffected.

Composition and extension agreements are primarily rehabilitation, not liquidation, devices. The debtor retains property except as provided in the agreement, and continues to operate its business. The agreement is not a basis for an involuntary bankruptcy proceeding. Although consent of all creditors is not required, effective rehabilitation will not be achieved unless most creditors participate. Accordingly, the agreement should be comprehensive and designed to secure wide creditor participation. To protect the agreement against later avoidance on fraud grounds, the debtor should fully and honestly disclose all relevant information to creditors and no creditor should receive secret consideration preferring him over others.

Summary

1.   Bankruptcy is a collective creditors' remedy and debtor relief provision, governed by the federal Bankruptcy Code. It serves two fundamental purposes: (1) to relieve an honest debtor from overburdensome financial obligations, giving him or her a fresh start free of former creditors' claims, and (2) to provide for equitable treatment of creditors competing for the limited assets of the debtor.

2.   Bankruptcy cases are heard in the bankruptcy court, a unit of the federal district court, that is staffed by bankruptcy judges.

3.   Bankruptcy relief is of two general types: liquidation, or "straight" bankruptcy, and rehabilitation. Liquidation is governed by Chapter 7 of the Bankruptcy Code and debtor rehabilitation is the subject of Chapters 9, 11, 12, and 13.

4.   All bankruptcy cases are commenced by filing a petition with the court. A liquidation case may be commenced upon the debtor's own petition (a voluntary case) or upon the petition of his creditors (an involuntary case). After the petition is filed, further creditor action against the debtor is "stayed" and the court enters an order for relief provided certain requirements are met.

5.   Upon entry of the order for relief, the debtor surrenders all nonexempt property to a trustee in bankruptcy who is appointed by the court or elected by creditors. The property transferred creates the bankruptcy estate.

6.   The trustee in bankruptcy represents the debtor's general unsecured creditors. The trustee's duties include collecting the debtor's assets, converting them to cash, and distributing the proceeds to creditors who file allowable claims against the estate according to priorities provided in the Bankruptcy Code.

7.   The trustee possesses significant "avoidance powers," which enable the trustee to defeat certain creditor claims. For example, the trustee may assert any defenses the debtor has against any creditor. The trustee also may avoid any transfer of property by the debtor or any obligation incurred by the debtor that could be attacked either by the debtor's actual unsecured creditors, or by a lien creditor, judgment creditor, or bona fide purchaser of real property, whether or not such a creditor or purchaser actually exists.

8.   The trustee also may recover, for the benefit of the estate, certain property transferred by the debtor to third parties, such as (1) preferences—transfers of property made shortly before bankruptcy by an insolvent debtor in payment of an antecedent debt that prefers one creditor over others; (2) fraudulent conveyances—generally transfers made with actual or implied intent to hinder, delay, or defraud creditors; and (3) postpetition transfers.

9.   Once the property is collected, it is distributed to creditors, who file allowable claims against the estate. Secured creditors are paid first to the extent of the value of their collateral. Unsecured creditors are paid next according to the priorities outlined in the Bankruptcy Code. After secured and priority claims are paid, any remaining assets are distributed to general creditors.

10.   After the bankruptcy proceedings, most debtors receive a discharge in bankruptcy, releasing the debtor from liability for most debts that arose prior to bankruptcy. Certain debtors, however, such as those who were dishonest or failed to cooperate in the bankruptcy, are denied a discharge. Further, even if the debtor receives a discharge, certain specific debts survive the proceeding and may be collected against the debtor's postbankruptcy assets.

11.   Chapter 7 liquidation is the harshest bankruptcy remedy. Bankruptcy law also provides for debtor rehabilitation, which pays creditors from future income while postponing, compromising, or altering creditor claims. Rehabilitation involves formulation and confirmation of a rehabilitation plan. Bankruptcy Code rehabilitation provisions are contained in Chapter 11 (Reorganization), Chapter 12 (Adjustment of Debts of a Family Farmer with Regular Annual Income), and Chapter 13 (Adjustment of Debts of an Individual with Regular Income).

12.   State law provides collective remedies that often are more advantageous to creditors than bankruptcy because they are quicker and less costly. Among these are the assignment for the benefit of creditors and composition and extension agreements.

Key Terms

liquidation (straight bankruptcy) case	allowed claim
	dividend
rehabilitation case	dividend percentage
bankruptcy court	discharge in bankruptcy
bankruptcy judge	reaffirmation agreement
voluntary case	creditors' committee
involuntary case	reorganization plan
automatic stay	cramdown
trustee in bankruptcy	assignment for the benefit
estate	of creditors
preference	composition
insider	extension
claim	

Questions and Problems

30.1 The purposes of bankruptcy are to provide the debtor with a fresh start free of claims of former creditors and to provide equitable treatment of the debtor's creditors. Summarize the specific Bankruptcy Code provisions that effectuate these purposes under Chapters 7, 11, 12, and 13.

30.2 As bankruptcy law has developed, it has provided increasingly greater debtor protection. For example, prior to the Bankruptcy Act of 1898, consent of a majority of creditors was required for discharge. Why has the law changed to provide for automatic discharge, subject to limited exceptions? Should debtors be discharged in bankruptcy? What are the arguments for and against a discharge in bankruptcy?

30.3 The automatic stay has sometimes been described as the most important provision in the Bankruptcy Code. Why is the automatic stay so valuable to debtors? Consider both individual and business debtors.

30.4 What policies justify bankruptcy law's failure to provide a discharge of certain debtors? Of certain debts? Consider each ground individually.

30.5 Loman has filed a petition for straight bankruptcy. The total value of his nonexempt assets is $6,000 and his total debts are $15,000. During the meeting of creditors, Loman testified that he owned an interest in a pension plan that he had not included in his list of assets. The creditors have discovered that XYZ Bank manages the pension plan and holds all the pension assets in trust. Loman has contributed $100 per month to the pension plan. When he reaches age 65 he will be entitled to receive $1,000 per month from the pension plan. Loman is now 47 years of age and the value of his contributions to the pension plan is $35,000. The creditors request that the bankruptcy judge order XYZ Bank to transfer the $35,000 to the trustee in bankruptcy for inclusion in the bankrupt's estate. Should the judge order the transfer? Explain the reasons for your answer.

30.6 In July 2005, CP & A Accounting Services prepared financial statements for Sharpe Construction Company. Sharpe used the statements in an effort to obtain a bank loan but failed to qualify for the loan. Sharpe paid CP & A $500 in July prior to preparation of the statements and the balance of $2,000 in October. In December Sharpe declared bankruptcy.
(a) Were the payments to CP & A avoidable preferences? Explain.
(b) CP & A has argued to the court that even if the payments were preferences, the court should grant the firm's expenses a priority as an administrative expense. CP & A has pointed out that the trustee used the financial statements thereby reducing the costs of administration of the estate. Should CP & A's expenses be granted priority as administrative expenses?

30.7 XYZ Corporation borrows money from First Bank, and John Jones, XYZ's president, personally guarantees payment of the debt. Between 90 days and one year prior to XYZ's bankruptcy, the corporation makes substantial preferential payments on First Bank's loan. Such payments, though made to an outsider creditor (First Bank), directly benefit an insider creditor (John Jones) by reducing his ultimate liability to the bank on his guaranty. Should such payments be recoverable by the trustee, even though made to an outside creditor beyond the 90-day preference period?

30.8 Prestige Manufacturing Co. began having financial problems in January 2000. Norman Noles, the sole shareholder of Prestige, attributed the problems to a general economic recession and was confident that the company would weather the bad period. To alleviate cash flow problems, Norman frequently advanced money to the company from his own savings account to meet the company payroll. Within a few months, Prestige generally repaid the advances to Norman. The recession lasted longer than Norman had anticipated, and in January 2003 Prestige filed a petition in bankruptcy under Chapter 7. A review of the company checking account revealed that Prestige had paid Norman $2,000 in October 2002, $3,500 in November 2002, and $4,000 in December 2002. Norman testified that these checks represented repayments of advances that Norman had made to pay the company payroll in the summer of 2002.
(a) The trustee in bankruptcy has requested that Norman repay $9,500 because the transfers were fraudulent. Norman has testified that he had no intent to hinder or delay creditors but rather that he was attempting to keep the company afloat to protect creditors. Were the transfers to Norman fraudulent conveyances? Explain.
(b) Discuss any other provisions of the Bankruptcy Code that might help the trustee to obtain turnover of the payments to Norman.

30.9 Parr Meadows Racing Association, Inc. borrowed approximately $14 million from Flushing Bank for construction of a racetrack. Because of financial difficulties, Parr Meadows defaulted in repaying the loan. On June 11, Parr Meadows transferred ownership of the racetrack to its president Ronald Parr. On June 12, Parr declared bankruptcy. Flushing Bank sued Parr Meadows and Parr seeking to have the transfer set aside as a fraudulent conveyance. At trial, Parr testified that the transfer was not made with the intent to hinder, delay, or defraud creditors. Parr explained that because of the automatic stay provisions of bankruptcy law, he believed that the transfer served to preserve the racetrack as an asset. He believed that if the racetrack was able to continue its operations, sufficient money would be earned to allow payment to Flushing Bank and other creditors. Thus, he argued that the transfer actually preserved assets for the creditors. Was the conveyance a fraudulent conveyance? Explain.

30.10 Under a reaffirmation agreement, a debtor may promise to pay a debt discharged in bankruptcy. Under what circumstances would a debtor want to enter into a reaffirmation agreement?

INTRODUCTION TO SECURED TRANSACTIONS

Because of the risks involved in making loans or extending credit, many debtor-creditor relationships involve some form of security. Secured creditors enjoy a substantial advantage in remedy over unsecured creditors in the event of a debtor's financial difficulty or bankruptcy. The secured creditor possesses a property interest—a security interest—in specific assets of the debtor. Upon the debtor's default the secured creditor may proceed against those assets and apply them to the unpaid debt to the exclusion of other creditors. If the security interest exists in real property, the arrangement is governed by the law of mortgages, discussed in Chapter 37. If the encumbered property is personal property, a "secured transaction" is involved, governed by Article 9 of the UCC. For example, assume Ann borrows $25,000 from First Bank. Ann gives First Bank a security interest in her house to satisfy the debt in event of Ann's default. This situation is governed by the law of mortgages. Had Ann instead given the bank a security interest in her inventory or equipment, which are personal property, a secured transaction is created, governed by UCC Article 9. The secured transactions material that follows is based upon Article 9 as amended in 1998 and 2000.

Introduction to Article 9 of the UCC

In a **secured transaction,** a borrower or buyer gives a lender or seller an interest in personal property or fixtures to secure performance of an obligation. Under §1–201(b)(35), the interest created in the property is known as a **security interest.** The secured obligation is virtually always a duty to pay money, either in repayment of a loan or for the purchase price of property sold on credit. The **secured party** is the lender, seller, or other party in whose favor a security interest exists. Property in which the secured party's security interest exists is known as the **collateral.** The **debtor** is the person who owns (or has a more limited interest in) the collateral. Typically, the debtor is also an **obligor,** the person who owes payment or other performance of the obligation that the collateral secures.

Article 9 covers generally any consensual or contractual security interest created in personal property. The contract creating the security interest is known as the **security agreement.**[1]

Types of Security Interests

Various types of security interest are recognized under Article 9. For example, a security interest may be possessory or nonpossessory. In a **possessory security interest,** the debtor delivers possession of the collateral to the secured party, who retains the property until the debt is paid. Such an arrangement is known as a **pledge,** the simplest form of secured transaction. A pledge is in essence a bailment[2] for security with the debtor-bailor the "pledgor" and the secured party-bailee the "pledgee."

In a **nonpossessory security interest,** the debtor retains possession of the collateral that is subject to the security interest. Nonpossessory interests are the most important modern security arrangements, as illustrated by the inventory financing devices discussed in the next chapter.

A security interest also may be purchase-money or non-purchase-money. Under §9–103, a security interest is a **purchase money security interest** to the extent that it is (1) taken or retained by a seller of the collateral to secure all or part of its price, or (2) taken by a person who makes an advance or incurs an obligation that enables the debtor to acquire rights in collateral. All other security interests are non-purchase-money.

In many instances, Article 9 provides special priority rules applicable to purchase money security interests. To recognize a purchase money security interest, ask two questions: (1) What is the collateral? and (2) What

is the debt? If the debt is all or part of the purchase price of the collateral, the interest is a purchase money security interest.

Assume Alice's TV sells a television set to Bill on credit, taking a security interest in the television set to secure payment. Alice's interest is a purchase money security interest. Or assume that First Bank loans Bill the money to buy the television set from Alice's for cash. First Bank takes a security interest in the set to secure payment of the debt. First Bank has a purchase money security interest. In both cases the secured debt is the purchase price of the collateral, the television set.

Types of Collateral

The study of personal property security is complicated by the fact that personal property takes many forms, and Article 9 priority rules differ in most cases depending upon the type of collateral involved. Three major types of personal property collateral are recognized: goods, semi-intangibles, and intangibles.

Goods. Under Article 9, as under Article 2, goods generally include *tangible personal property.*[3] Section 9–102 divides goods into four categories: consumer goods, farm products, inventory, and equipment.

Consumer Goods. **Consumer goods** are those used or bought for use primarily for personal, family, or household purposes.

Farm Products. **Farm products** include crops or livestock, products of crops or livestock in the unmanufactured state (for example, milk, eggs, and wool), and supplies used or produced in farming operations. To be classified as farm products, the debtor must be engaged in farming operations, and the goods must not have been subjected to a manufacturing process. If the farm products have been subjected to a manufacturing process, they then become inventory in the farmer's hands.

Inventory. Goods are **inventory** if they are held primarily for immediate or ultimate resale (or lease) in the ordinary course of the seller's business. Inventory also includes raw materials, work in process, and materials

---

[1]Article 9's definitions and an index of definitions are contained in UCC §9–102.

[2]Bailments are discussed in Chapter 35.

[3]UCC §9–102(a)(44).

used or consumed in a business, such as fuel consumed in operations and containers used to package goods.

Equipment. **Equipment** includes goods used or bought for use primarily in business, including a profession or farming. Trucks, rolling stock, tools, and machinery are examples of equipment.

The four classes of goods outlined above are exhaustive and mutually exclusive. Goods not within one of the other definitions are treated as equipment.

In order to determine the proper classification of the collateral, one must first identify the debtor, because the same piece of collateral may change classifications depending on the debtor's identity. Suppose Joe's Appliances purchases several television sets from Zenith Radio Corporation on credit, giving Zenith a security interest in the sets. Joe's sells one set to Connie on credit for Connie's home use, taking a security interest in the set. Joe's sells five other sets to Northern University for use in its audio-visual program. Northern University borrowed money to finance the purchase, using the sets as collateral on the loan. In these examples, the TV sets are (1) inventory—in Zenith's and Joe's hands, (2) consumer goods—in Connie's hands, and (3) equipment—in Northern University's hands.

Semi-intangible Collateral. Article 9 recognizes four types of semi-intangible collateral: documents of title, chattel paper, instruments, and investment property. This collateral, though intangible in the sense that it represents a valuable claim against a third party, is evidenced by an indispensable document showing the existence of the property.

Documents of Title. **Documents of title,** discussed in detail in Chapter 35, are documents issued by specialized bailees such as carriers or warehousemen evidencing the right to receive, hold, and dispose of goods in storage or transit. Examples include bills of lading and warehouse receipts. These documents, which may be negotiable or nonnegotiable, tangible or electronic, are governed in part by Article 7 of the UCC.

Chattel Paper. **Chattel paper,** often involved in inventory financing, is a writing or writings that evidence both an obligation to pay money and a security interest in or a lease of specific goods. To illustrate how chattel paper is created, assume that Dealer sells a photocopier to Customer on credit. Customer signs a promissory note for the price and gives Dealer a security interest in

the machine to secure the debt. This arrangement usually is known as a **conditional sales contract.** In this case, (1) Dealer is the secured party, (2) Customer is the debtor, (3) the conditional sales contract is the security agreement, and (4) the photocopier is collateral—equipment in Customer's hands.

Assume that Dealer needs additional cash to finance its business. Dealer therefore borrows money from First Bank using the conditional sales contract from Customer as collateral to secure its loan. In this case, (1) Dealer is the debtor; (2) First Bank is the secured party; (3) the conditional sales contract is the collateral—chattel paper, an obligation to pay money (from Customer to Dealer), and a security interest in specific goods (the photocopier); and (4) Customer is now an **account debtor,** a person obligated on an account, chattel paper, or general intangible.

Chattel paper also may be created through a lease of specific goods. Assume Dealer leased rather than sold the photocopier to Customer and then used the lease as collateral on the loan from First Bank. In this case, the lease is chattel paper in the transaction between Dealer and First Bank.

Note that the prior examples describe **tangible chattel paper,** in which the information is inscribed on a tangible medium (paper). If the information is stored in an electronic medium (for example, digital, electrical, magnetic, or optical), the chattel paper is called **electronic chattel paper.**

Instruments. **Instruments** include (1) negotiable instruments, such as notes, checks, and other drafts, and (2) any other writing that evidences a right to the payment of money (and is not itself a security agreement or lease) that is transferred in the ordinary course of business by transfer of possession with any necessary indorsement or assignment.

Investment Property. **Investment property** includes (1) securities, such as stocks and bonds, whether certificated (evidenced by a document such as a stock certificate) or uncertificated, and whether held directly by the debtor or indirectly by the debtor's broker (in the indirect holding situation, the debtor holds a "security entitlement" in a "security account"); and (2) "commodity contracts" (for example, a commodity futures contract or option traded on a board of trade) that may be held by the debtor's commodity broker in a "commodity account." In sum, investment property consists of securities (certificated or uncertificated), securities entitlements, securities accounts, commodity contracts, and commodity accounts.

Intangible Collateral. Article 9 recognizes four types of intangible collateral: accounts, commercial tort claims, deposit accounts, and general intangibles.

Accounts. An **account** is any right to payment for goods sold or leased (or to be sold or leased) or for services rendered (or to be rendered) that is not evidenced either by an instrument or chattel paper. An account is, therefore, the ordinary open account receivable. Such a right to payment is an account even though not "earned by performance," that is, even though the seller has not yet delivered the goods or rendered the services in question.

Accounts also include rights to receive payment: (1) for the sale of real property, (2) for a license of intellectual property, (3) for becoming a surety on another person's debt, (4) under a life, health, or other insurance policy, (5) for the lease or hire of a vessel, (6) arising out of the use of a credit card, or (7) for winning a government lottery. As with the traditional commercial accounts described above, these additional rights to payment are accounts, whether or not earned by performance.

Commercial Tort Claims. As discussed in Chapter 5, a tort is a civil wrong, other than breach of contract, for which the law provides a remedy, commonly in the form of an action for money damages. Under Article 9, a plaintiff's tort claim for business or commercial injury may be used as collateral. Specifically, a **commercial tort claim** is a tort claim in which the plaintiff is: (1) an organization, such as a corporation, or (2) an individual *if* the claim arose out of that person's business or profession and does not involve personal injury.

Deposit Accounts. **Deposit accounts** include demand, time, savings, or passbook accounts maintained with a bank. Note that if the bank's obligation is evidenced by an instrument (for example, a negotiable certificate of deposit), it is categorized as an instrument, not a deposit account.

General Intangibles. **General intangibles** include all personal property other than goods, documents of title, chattel paper, instruments, investment property, accounts, commercial tort claims, deposit accounts, and money. This catchall category includes any item of personal property not previously discussed, such as goodwill, trademarks, patents, literary rights, royalty rights, and copyrights. A general intangible is called a **payment intangible** if the account debtor's primary obligation is to pay money.

Scope of Article 9

Introduction; Transactions Intended for Security. Before Article 9 was enacted, personal property security was governed by a fragmented, nonuniform assortment of devices including chattel mortgages, pledges, conditional sales contracts, factors liens, trust receipts, and assignments of accounts receivable. Article 9 replaces these devices with a comprehensive scheme governing the creation, priority, and foreclosure of security interests in personal property. Section 9–109 creates a single security device applicable to any transaction, *regardless of its form,* that creates a security interest in personal property or fixtures by contract. Article 9 therefore governs all consensual or contractual security interests in personal property or fixtures. Article 9 does not expressly abolish pre-Code security devices, and indeed they continue to be used. Whatever form the transaction takes, however, the rights and obligations of the parties and third parties are determined by Article 9 if the transaction is intended to have effect as security.

To illustrate, suppose that Seller sells goods to Buyer on credit. To assure the right to reposses the property upon buyer's default, Seller reserves title in herself until Buyer pays purchase price. The reservation does not prevent title from passing to Buyer. It does, however, create a security interest in the goods sold in favor of Seller. That is, Seller intended to create a security interest in the goods sold by reserving title. The transaction is governed by Article 9.

Leases as Security Interests. As noted above, Article 9 applies to all security interests in goods created by contract including a lease of personal property that creates a security interest in that property. In contrast, Article 2A governs "true" leases, those involving the "transfer of the right to possession and use of goods for a term in return for consideration."[4] Whether a lease is true or is intended as security (that is, the arrangement is in fact a disguised secured installment sale of the goods "leased") has important legal consequences. In a true lease, the lessor's rights in the goods generally are superior

---

[4]UCC §2A – 103(1)(j). Article 2A is introduced in Chapter 16.

to those of (1) the lessee's other creditors (including the trustee in bankruptcy), and (2) buyers of the leased property from the lessee. If the lease is intended as security the lessor's (secured party's) rights are determined by Article 9, which generally protects such creditors and buyers absent the "lessor's" compliance with the perfection requirements of Article 9. For example, assume Lessor delivers a cash register to Lessee, who agrees to pay monthly rental for 24 months. At the end of the term, Lessee has the option to purchase the cash register for little or no additional consideration. The arrangement is not a true lease, but is in reality a secured installment sale of the cash register, using the cash register as collateral to secure payment of Lessee's obligation. The arrangement is designed to allow Lessor to repossess the cash register (by asserting that he is only leasing it) upon Lessee's default in payment of the monthly installments. It is therefore governed by Article 9.

Section 1–203 is designed to aid courts in distinguishing between true leases and those intended as security. As a general rule, whether a transaction creates a lease or security interest depends upon the facts of each case. Nevertheless, a lease transaction automatically creates a security interest if the lessee is obligated to make payments for the entire term of the lease and cannot cancel it, and one of the following tests is met:

1. the original lease term equals or exceeds the economic life of the goods, or
2. the lessee is bound to renew the lease for the remaining economic life of the goods or become the owner of the goods, or
3. upon expiration of the lease term, the lessee has the option to renew the lease for the remaining economic life of the goods (or become the owner of the goods) for no or nominal additional consideration.

In short, under §1–203, a lease transaction is a secured sale governed by Article 9 if the "lessor" at the end of the lease term has "surrendered any claim to the residual value of the leased goods."[5] Note that if the lease fails to meet this test (for example, the lessee has a right to cancel or the option price is not nominal), the court must then apply the general rule, requiring a full examination of the "facts of each case" to determine whether the transaction is a true lease or a security interest.

---

[5]*In re* Aspen Impressions, Inc., 94 B.R. 861, 866 (Bkrtcy. E.D. Pa. 1989).

In applying the general rule, §1–203 states explicitly that a lease transaction does not create a security interest merely because (1) the present value of the lease payments equal or exceed the initial fair market value of the goods (a "full payout" lease); (2) the lessee assumes the risk of loss of the goods and agrees to pay taxes, insurance, and maintenance costs applicable to them (a "net" lease); or (3) the lessee has an option to renew the lease or become the owner of the goods (other than for no or nominal consideration).

In the following case, the court uses §1–203 to determine whether a transaction created a true lease or a security interest.

In re Vital Products Company
210 B.R.109 (Bkrtcy. N.D. Ohio 1997)

On October 1, 1992, plaintiff Andrew Hanes, owner of H&B Leasing Company, and Debtor/defendant Vital Products Company signed a contract titled "Lease Agreement." The contract provided that the Debtor would pay plaintiff $1,600 per month for 24 months to lease a punch press. At the end of the lease period, Debtor had the option of paying $1,167 to purchase the press. The plaintiff did not file a financing statement. After making ten monthly payments, Debtor defaulted and subsequently filed a Chapter 11 bankruptcy petition. Plaintiff demanded return of the press, but the bankruptcy trustee contended that it was part of the bankruptcy estate.

Baxter, Bankruptcy Judge

. . . The principal dispositive issue for determination is whether the subject Lease is a true lease or one which should be construed as a disguised security agreement. In such matters the burden of proof is upon the party seeking the recovery as a true lease. . . . Under . . . U.C.C. [§1–203], as codified in Ohio, a transaction qualifies as a security interest and falls within the scope of Article 9 where the obligation to pay a stream of rent payments extends for the entire term of the lease and is not subject to termination by the lessee. Once this threshold requirement is satisfied, then the transaction will be treated as a secured loan if any one of the following four standards are met:

(1) The original term of the lease is equal to or greater than the remaining economic life of the goods;

(2) The lessee is bound to renew the lease for the remaining economic life of the goods or is bound to become the owner of the goods;

(3) The lessee has an option to renew the lease for the remaining economic life of the goods for no or minimal consideration;

(4) The lessee has an option to become the owner of the goods for no or nominal consideration.

. . . [T]he present version of U.C.C. [§1–203] has shifted the focus from "the intent of the parties" to the economic realities of a given transaction in determining whether the transaction is a true lease or a disguised security arrangement.

In view of the above statutory standards and factual findings herein, the threshold requirement is met which shows a disguised security interest: (1) the subject Lease requires monthly rental payments in the amount of $1,600.00 during the life of the 24 month lease and (2) the Plaintiff conceded during his testimony that the Debtor-lessee had no right to terminate the Lease prior to its agreed upon period of 24 months. Consequently, the presence of any one of the four remaining standards of U.C.C. [§1–203] is needed to conclusively establish whether the subject transaction is indeed a true lease or, rather, is a disguised security interest. Under the Lease, it is observed that the Debtor is afforded an option to "acquire complete and unencumbered ownership of said lease items" at the and of the lease term by making a single payment of $1,167.00 to H&B Leasing (the lessor). That specific provision completely satisfies one of the four remaining elements of U.C.C. [§1–203] to conclusively establish a security interest: (4) The lessee has an option to become the owner of the goods for no or nominal consideration.

The above-quoted language from the Lease clearly shows that the Debtor was provided an opportunity to become owner of the equipment at the end of the lease period by simply making a single payment of $1,167.00. Remarkably, not only was the modest option purchase price less than the agreed upon monthly rental, it was substantially less than the stipulated value of the Press which was at all relevant times in excess of $17,500.00. Thusly, the option price to acquire ownership was quite nominal in view of the stated value of the Press. Indeed, the unrefuted testimony of William Laufer [owner of Vital Products Company] revealed that as of October, 1992 when the Lease was executed the anticipated buyout value of the Press would be $40,000.00, and from 1992 when the

Debtor commenced operations the Press was carried as an asset on its books as a "long term debt" with a stated value of $70,000.00.

In its decision in *In re Celeryvale Transport, Inc.,* 822 F.2d 16 (6th Cir. 1987), the Sixth Circuit affirmed the existence of a true lease on grounds factually dissimilar from the facts herein. The Circuit correctly applied the standards of U.C.C. [§1–203] as codified in Tennessee law to show an instance when a lease was not found to be a secured transaction. In *Celeryvale:* (1) the lease's purchase option price was not nominal; (2) the debtor was expressly obligated to return the lease equipment; (3) there was no real evidence that the debtor would be "economically compelled" to invoke the purchase option. In the present case: (1) the option purchase price was extremely nominal in view of the stated and agreed upon valuations; (2) there was no express obligation addressed in the Lease requiring a return of the Press; and (3) the extremely low option price, when compared to the higher monthly rental rate and the stated valuation of the Press presented a most "economically compelling" reason for the Debtor-lessee to invoke the purchase option.

Collectively, the above findings fully satisfy U.C.C. [§1–203's] factors . . . for creation of a secured transaction, as opposed to a true lease. Accordingly, the Plaintiff failed to meet his burden of proof. . . .

[Judgment granted for Vital Products Company.]

Sales of Accounts, Chattel Paper, Payment Intangibles, and Promissory Notes. In addition to consensual security interests in personal property, Article 9 governs *any sale* of accounts, chattel paper, payment intangibles, and promissory notes, *whether or not intended for security.* In this case, Article 9's scope is expanded to avoid the often difficult problem of distinguishing between transactions in these assets that are intended for security and those that are not. In these transactions, the seller is the "debtor," the buyer is the "secured party," the buyer's interest is a "security interest," and the accounts, chattel paper, payment intangibles, or promissory notes are the "collateral."

Consignments. Like leases of personal property, consignments may either be "true" or "intended for security." To avoid confusion, Article 9 governs all consignments. Consignments are discussed in detail in Chapter 32.

Transactions Excluded from Article 9. Article 9 primarily is concerned with commercial financing, particularly involving inventory, arising by contract between a lender and borrower or buyer and seller. Article 9 therefore excludes from its scope, in §9–109(c), certain transactions, such as the following, that do not fit this mold:

1. liens arising under statute or common law by virtue of status, not by the consent or agreement of the parties. Examples include federal statutory liens to the extent they preempt Article 9, and liens given under state law to suppliers of services or materials (for example, artisan's and mechanic's liens).

2. any interest in or lien upon real estate, including a lease or a landlord's lien;

3. transactions not related to commercial financing, such as (a) a sale of accounts or chattel paper as part of a sale of the business out of which they arose, (b) assignments of accounts or chattel paper for purposes of collection, (c) transfer of a right to payment under a contract to an assignee who is to perform the duties under the contract, and (d) a transfer of a single account to an assignee in whole or partial satisfaction of a preexisting debt; and

4. security transactions using property that does not customarily serve as commercial collateral, such as noncommercial tort claims; judgments; and employees' claims to wages, salary, or other compensation.

Creation and Perfection of a Security Interest

Article 9 provides creditor protection by creating a security interest in the debtor's property as security for an obligation owed to the creditor. To provide this protection, Article 9 addresses two fundamental issues: (1) how a legally enforceable security interest is created between the debtor and the secured party, and (2) how a creditor holding a security interest is protected against claims of third parties to the collateral.

Under Article 9, a security interest is effective between the immediate parties upon **attachment.** That is, after attachment, if the debtor defaults, the secured party has the right to foreclose or otherwise use the collateral to satisfy the claim. Prior to attachment the secured party has no such right. Enforceability against the debtor alone provides little protection to a secured creditor, however. Upon default, other secured creditors may assert claims to the same collateral and unsecured creditors may attempt to levy upon it if they obtain judgments. Further, if the

security interest is non-possessory, the debtor may previously have sold the collateral. To be protected against such third-party claims, the secured party must "perfect" its interest in the collateral. In short, attachment governs the rights of the secured party against the debtor and **perfection** determines the secured party's rights against third-party claimants to the collateral.

Note that under §9–308(a), a security interest is perfected only after it has attached and all the applicable steps required for perfection have been met. The steps for attachment and perfection may occur in any order. If, however, the steps necessary to perfect are taken before the security interest attaches, the interest is not perfected until it attaches. That is, a security interest cannot be perfected until it has attached.

Attachment of a Security Interest

Under §9–203(b), a security interest is not enforceable against the debtor or third parties until it has attached to the collateral. Attachment requires the coexistence of three elements, which may occur in any order. That is, the interest attaches when the last of the following three events occurs:

1. the parties must enter into an enforceable security agreement,
2. the secured party must give value, and
3. the debtor must have rights in the collateral.

The Agreement

Attachment requires the existence of a valid security agreement, the agreement creating or providing for a security interest. To be enforceable, the security agreement must be in a record, be authenticated by the debtor, and contain a description of the collateral. These formalities are designed to provide reliable evidence concerning the existence and terms of the security agreement, including the property serving as collateral.

The Writing (Record) Requirement. The UCC provides that a security agreement must be in a record unless the secured party is in possession of the collateral pursuant to the agreement (a "pledge"). A "record" includes both traditional writings discussed in Chapter 12, and information stored in an electronic or other medium that can be retrieved in perceivable form. No record is required in a pledge because the secured party's possession already provides evidence of the security agreement and the identity of the collateral. Unless the secured party is in possession of the collateral, however, the security agreement, if not in a record, is unenforceable both against third parties (such as the debtor's other creditors or buyers of the collateral) *and* the debtor. That is, §9–203(b) operates as a statute of frauds, denying any enforcement of an oral nonpossessory security interest. Thus, the holder of such an interest has no right even to repossess the collateral from the debtor on default. Because the term "security interest" under §1–201(b)(35) includes a buyer's interest in accounts, chattel paper, payment intangibles, or promissory notes, an agreement for the sale (assignment) of such property also is a "security agreement," required to be in a record.

The Signature (Authentication) Requirement. The security agreement must be signed (or "authenticated" in the case of an electronic record) by the debtor.

Description of the Collateral. The security agreement must contain a description of the collateral sufficient to identify it. The test for sufficiency of the description is contained in §9–108, which provides that any description of collateral is sufficient "whether or not it is specific, if it reasonably identifies what is described." Thus, the description requirement under the Code is not rigorous. The identity of the collateral need simply be "objectively determinable." Generally, the types of collateral defined in Article 9 (for example, inventory, equipment) satisfy this test. For example, assume XYZ Corporation borrows money from First Bank, giving the bank a security interest in its inventory. A statement in the agreement that the loan is secured by "the inventory of XYZ Corporation" would be a sufficient description for Article 9 purposes. Serial numbers and detailed listing of the inventory are not required. Although general usually descriptions are sufficient, so-called "super-generic" descriptions are not. For example, describing the collateral as "all the debtor's assets" or "all the debtor's personal property" is insufficient. Figure 31.1 illustrates a simple security agreement form.

Value Given by Secured Party

The secured party must give value before a security interest can attach. Section 1–204 defines **value** generally to include any consideration sufficient to support a

simple contract. In most cases, the secured party gives value by loaning money to or selling goods on credit to the debtor. A creditor's binding contractual promise to extend credit or loan money in the future also constitutes value as of the time the promise is made. Further, a secured party who takes a security interest in the debtor's property to secure a preexisting debt owed by the debtor gives value.

Debtor's Rights in the Collateral

A debtor must have an interest in a specified piece of property to use it as collateral. Accordingly, attachment cannot occur until "the debtor has rights in the collateral." The debtor's rights may constitute full ownership or a lesser interest. For example, the debtor may own property as a tenant in common with another. A debtor with a limited interest, however, has only limited rights to use as collateral.

The debtor often has rights in the collateral at the time the secured party gives value. Article 9, however, also broadly validates so-called after-acquired property clauses allowing obligations covered by the security agreement to be secured both by the debtor's currently owned property and property acquired by the debtor in the future.[6]

Perfection of a Security Interest

The Secured Party and Third Parties

Once the security interest attaches, the security arrangement is enforceable against the debtor, thereby allowing the secured party to resort to the collateral upon default. Upon attachment, the secured party also defeats any claim to the collateral asserted by the debtor's general unsecured creditors. That is, a secured party, by virtue of attachment, possesses an enforceable lien upon the debtor's property; general creditors, by definition, do not. Perfection rules determine the rights of the secured party against third parties (other than general creditors) asserting an interest in the collateral, including:

1. lien creditors,
2. buyers of the collateral from the debtor, and
3. other secured parties claiming an interest in the same collateral.

---

[6]See discussion of UCC §9–204 in Chapter 32.

Figure 31.1   **Simple Security Agreement**

_____
Date

_____ ("Debtor") hereby grants to
Name   No. and Street   City   County   State   Zip

_____ ("Secured Party") a security
Name   No. and Street   City   County   State   Zip

interest in the following property ("Collateral"): _____

_____

_____

to secure payment and performance of obligations identified or set out as
follows ("Obligations"): _____

_____

_____

Default in payment or performance of any of the Obligations or default
under any agreement evidencing any of the Obligations is a default under
this agreement. Upon such default Secured Party may declare all Obligations immediately due and payable and shall have the remedies of a
secured party under the _____ Uniform Commercial Code.

Signed in (duplicate) triplicate.

_____   _____
Debtor   Secured Party

By_____   By_____

Examples illustrating how competing claims arise follow. As with other statutes involving debtors and creditors,
Article 9 perfection rules generate a system of priorities
determining the order in which creditors are paid out of
the debtor's limited assets.

Lien Creditors. Fundamentally, a secured party needs
protection against claims of the debtor's other creditors.
Although a security interest defeats general creditors
upon attachment, it does not defeat lien creditors. Under
§9–102(a)(52), a **lien creditor** is a creditor who has
acquired a lien upon the property involved by attachment,
levy, or other judicial process and includes an assignee
for the benefit of creditors (from the time of the
assignment), the trustee in bankruptcy (from the date
the petition is filed), and a receiver in equity (as of the
date the court appoints the receiver).

The most common lien creditors are judgment creditors
and the trustee in bankruptcy. For example, assume
Charles loans Dana $500. Dana gives Charles a security
interest in a painting she owns to satisfy the debt in event
of default. Dana negligently runs a stop sign and destroys a
car owned by Jim. Jim sues her for damages and the court
awards him a $5,000 judgment. Dana fails to pay the judg-
ment and also defaults on Charles's loan. Jim brings an
action to enforce the judgment, which results in issuance
of a writ of execution against Dana's property, including
the painting. Jim is a lien creditor, and the rules of perfection determine whether Charles or Jim will get the painting.

To illustrate further, assume the same facts as above,
except that after the loan, Dana files a bankruptcy petition. The trustee in bankruptcy is a lien creditor, who, as
discussed in Chapter 30, wishes to seize and sell the
painting for benefit of all creditors. The rules of perfec-

tion determine whether the trustee or Charles will have benefit of the painting. It is important to note that defeating the trustee in bankruptcy's claim is the fundamental purpose of any secured transaction. That is, the debtor's default, raising the need for recourse to the collateral, often is followed by bankruptcy. The secured party must therefore, at a minimum, take the steps necessary to assure a preferred claim to the collateral as against the debtor's bankruptcy trustee.

Buyer of the Collateral. Most modern secured transactions are nonpossessory; that is, the debtor retains possession of the collateral that secures the obligation. In this case, the debtor may sell the collateral to a third party, who may or may not be aware of the secured party's claim. The rules of perfection determine whether the buyer or the secured party is entitled to such collateral upon the debtor's default.

Conflicting Security Interests in the Same Collateral. A common priority problem arises when two or more *secured* creditors assert an interest in the same collateral. For example, assume that Dana borrows $500 from Charles and gives him a security interest in her painting. She retains possession of the painting. Dana then borrows $500 from Bob, giving him a security interest in the same painting. Dana leaves town, leaving both debts unpaid. The rules of perfection determine which creditor will have the benefit of the painting to satisfy the debt.

A secured party with a perfected security interest is not protected under *all* circumstances against *all* third-party claims. That is, "perfection" is not a synonym for "absolute protection." More accurately, a secured party with a perfected interest is protected against some, but not necessarily all, third-party claims, and in some cases only for a limited period. The extent of protection provided depends upon a combination of three interrelated factors: (1) the identity of the third-party claimant, (2) the type of collateral involved, and (3) the method of perfection. In analyzing any secured transaction dispute, therefore, each of these three factors must be carefully considered.

Purposes and Methods of Perfection

A creditor with a perfected security interest enjoys a preferred claim to the debtor's assets to the exclusion of other creditors and others claiming an interest in those assets. The rules of perfection are designed to insure that a creditor granted this preferred status has taken steps

necessary to put third parties on notice of the secured party's claim. These steps generally involve either taking possession or control of the collateral, or filing a document giving public notice of the interest. Once notified, other creditors and buyers will not be misled concerning the nature and extent of the debtor's interest in the property. Thus, perfection by possession or filing protects both the secured party—by preserving a preferred claim to the property—and others who, once notified, will not be induced to lend money secured by, or to purchase, previously encumbered property. In certain limited situations, however, the UCC authorizes "automatic" perfection, protecting a secured party who has neither filed nor taken possession or control. In these cases, the administrative costs of providing notice are deemed to outweight the benefits of public notice.

The following material discusses the three methods of perfecting a security interest recognized by Article 9:

1. perfection by taking possession or control of the collateral,
2. perfection by filing a "financing statement" in an appropriate public office, and
3. automatic perfection occurring upon attachment with no further action by the secured party.

The discussion that follows assumes that the security interest has attached. As previously noted, if the steps necessary for perfection occur first, the interest is perfected at the time it attaches.

Perfection by Possession

The simplest and oldest method of perfection, authorized by §9–313, is the pledge—perfection by the creditor's possession of the collateral. A security interest in most types of collateral—including goods, instruments, money, negotiable documents of title, and tangible chattel paper—may be perfected by possession. Possession is the only way to perfect a security interest in money.

The secured party's possession puts third parties on notice of the secured interest and no further notice or filing is required. A security interest is perfected by possession from the time the secured party takes possession and continues as long as possession is retained. Possession may be taken by the secured party or an agent on the secured party's behalf. The debtor or a person controlled by the debtor may not act as the secured party's agent for this purpose. As the following case illustrates, the debtor's possession, even on the secured party's behalf, will not put third parties on notice of the secured party's interest.

In re Stewart
74 B.R. 350 (Bkrtcy. M.D. Ga. 1987)

Plaintiff First American Bank & Trust Company lent the debtor Thomas Stewart money in exchange for a promissory note secured by a diamond ring owned by Stewart. At the time of the loan, the bank took possession of the ring but later released it to Stewart, who intended to sell it. Upon receipt of the ring, Stewart signed the following document prepared by the bank:

Athens, GA., September 14, 1984

RECEIVED from FIRST AMERICAN BANK & TRUST COMPANY, ATHENS, GEORGIA the following property, held by the Bank as collateral security: 1 ladies' Diamond Ring and in consideration thereof I HEREBY AGREE TO HOLD SAID PROPERTY IN TRUST for the following purposes, viz: give to Armonds Diamond Center for Sale and I will return the said property, or Cash Equivalent with due diligence to the Bank, the intention of this arrangement being to protect and preserve unimpaired the lien of FIRST AMERICAN BANK & TRUST COMPANY on said property.

s/Thomas Stewart

Stewart took the ring to Armond Parks Diamond Center, which sold the ring to a third party in exchange for another diamond ring and $4,917. Stewart did not return the cash or ring to the bank and several months later he filed for bankruptcy. American Bank & Trust Company sued the trustee in bankruptcy seeking delivery of the diamond ring and $4,917, which had been recovered by the trustee in bankruptcy from Armond Parks. The trustee argued that the bank did not have a perfected security interest in the diamond ring or its proceeds and, therefore, the bank was not entitled to the cash or ring.

Hershner, Bankruptcy Judge

. . . To perfect a security interest, a secured party must file a financing statement unless the secured party elects to take possession of the collateral as provided for under [§9–305, Revised §9–313, of the UCC]. . . .

Under Georgia law, the court concludes that Plaintiff had a perfected security interest in the diamond ring prior to the release of the diamond ring to Debtor under

the document executed on September 14, 1984. The security interest had attached because Plaintiff had possession of the diamond ring pursuant to the security agreement between Plaintiff and Debtor; value had been given; and Debtor had rights in the diamond ring. Plaintiff perfected its security interest in the diamond ring by taking possession of it. . . .

The real issue for the court to determine is what effect the September 14, 1984, document plaintiff and Debtor executed had upon plaintiff's security interest which it had perfected by possession. The court notes that the primary purpose behind requiring a secured party to comply with the perfecting provisions under Article 9 is to "put a diligent searcher on notice of the secured party's claim." J. White & R. Summers, Handbook of the Law Under the Uniform Commercial Code §23–5 (2d ed. 1980). Actual possession of the collateral in which the secured party claims a security interest "gives notice to the world that the debtor does not have full use of the collateral." 9 R. Anderson, Anderson on the Uniform Commercial Code §9–305:7 (3d ed. 1985). Subsequent lenders and creditors thus are adequately informed of the possible existence of a perfected security interest in the collateral, and they can inquire of the secured party the extent of the secured party's interest in the collateral. . . .

Plaintiff asserts that pursuant to the September 14, 1984, document, it did not release its perfected security interest in the diamond ring because under the terms of that document, Debtor held the diamond ring in trust for plaintiff. Official Comment 2 to §9–305 of the Uniform Commercial Code provides that "[p]ossession may be by the secured party himself or by an agent on his behalf; it is of course clear, however, that the debtor or a person controlled by him cannot qualify as such an agent for the secured party." Official Comment 2, U.C.C. §9–305. The argument that a debtor possesses collateral on behalf of a secured party for the purpose of perfection by possession has been uniformly rejected because possession by the debtor does not give adequate notice to other creditors of the secured party's interest in the collateral. . . .

By relinquishing possession of the diamond ring, Plaintiff lost its perfected security interest in the diamond ring because it failed to perfect its security interest by one of the other methods of perfection provided for by the Georgia commercial code. The September 14, 1984, document simply does not qualify as one of these methods. The court notes that potential lenders and creditors were not put on notice of plaintiff's security interest in the diamond ring even though Debtor possessed the diamond ring pursuant to a trust arrangement. This is evidenced by Mr. Parks' testimony. Mr. Parks testified that he thought Debtor owned the diamond ring and that he was completely unaware of any claim plaintiff had to the diamond ring. The court therefore concludes that as of the date Debtor filed his bankruptcy petition, plaintiff's security interest in the diamond ring was unperfected. . . .

[Judgment for defendant.]

Perfection by Control

"Control" is a method of perfection analogous to possession used for collateral that cannot be physically possessed. Collateral in which a security interest may be perfected by control includes investment property, deposit accounts, electronic documents of title, and electronic chattel paper. A security interest in deposit accounts may be perfected only by control. Security interests in investment property, electronic documents of title, and electronic chattel paper also may be perfected by filing, discussed in the next section.

Investment Property. Under §§9–106 and 8–106, a secured party may obtain control of investment property by taking possession of a certificated security (for example, a stock certificate) held by the debtor. For investment property held in uncertificated form or by brokers in securities or commodities accounts, the secured party obtains control by securing the broker's (or issuer's) agreement to dispose of the account (or securities) as directed by the secured party without further consent by the debtor. A secured party also obtains control if the securities, securities account, or commodity account is registered in the secured party's name. In short, the secured party has control if it can sell or order the sale of the collateral without further action or consent by the debtor. Note that if the secured party is a securities or commodities broker, a security interest in investment property is perfected automatically upon attachment.

Electronic Chattel Paper. Under §9–105, a secured party has control of electronic chattel paper if only one

authoritative copy of the chattel paper exists, which: identifies the secured party as assignee, is communicated to and maintained by the secured party, and can be transferred or changed only with the secured party's participation.

Electronic Documents of Title. Under §7–106, a person has control of an electronic document of title "if a system employed for evidencing the transfer of interests in the electronic document *reliably establishes* that person as *the* person to which the electronic document was issued or transferred." This test generally is met if, at any given time, a person can identify the single authoritative copy of the document that is unique, identifiable, and unalterable. Control of electronic documents is discussed in more detail in Chapter 35.

Deposit Accounts. Under §9–104, a secured party obtains control over a deposit account if: (1) the secured party is the bank in which the account is maintained, (2) the account is maintained in the secured party's name, or (3) the debtor, secured party, and bank have agreed that the bank will honor the secured party's instructions concerning disposition of the account without further consent by the debtor.

Perfection by Filing

For many types of collateral, a secured party may perfect a security interest by filing a **financing statement** in an appropriate public office. Filing a financing statement is by far the most common method of perfection because in most cases the debtor requires possession and use of the collateral, such as inventory or equipment, in order to repay the loan. Security interests in goods, tangible or electronic negotiable documents of title, tangible or electronic chattel paper, instruments, and investment property may be perfected by filing as an alternative to taking possession or, in some cases, control. Filing is the only method of perfection for accounts, commercial tort claims, and general intangibles. Filing may not be used to perfect an interest in money (possession is required) or deposit accounts (control is required).

If the collateral is goods covered by a non-negotiable document of title, §9–312(d) provides a special perfection rule. It states that the security interest is perfected when (1) the bailee issues a document of title in the name of the secured party, (2) the bailee is notified of the secured party's interest, or (3) the secured party files a financing statement covering the goods. If the goods are possessed by a bailee who has not issued a document of title (negotiable or nonnegotiable), under §9–313(c), perfection occurs when the bailee authenticates a record acknowledging that it holds the goods for the secured party's benefit.

Contents of Financing Statement. Like taking possession, filing is designed to put third parties on notice of an interest in the debtor's property. A third party who desires further information may then contact the debtor or secured party for details. Consistent with the basic notice function, under §9–502(a) a financing statement is sufficient if it (1) contains the names of the debtor and the secured party, and (2) indicates the collateral covered by the financing statement. Under §9–504, a statement that the financing statement covers "all of the debtor's assets," or "all of the debtor's personal property" is a sufficient *indication* of the collateral. Although these "supergeneric" descriptions are sufficient for use in a financing statement, they may not, as previously noted, be used to satisfy the *description* requirement in the security agreement. Finally, under §9–506, a financing statement that "substantially" complies with the above requirements is effective even though it contains minor errors that are not "seriously misleading."

Although not required, a copy of the security agreement may be used as a financing statement if it meets the above requirements. A filed financing statement is not, however, a substitute for the security agreement necessary for attachment.

Because financing statements are indexed under the debtor's name, a financing statement that fails properly to identify the debtor is ineffective. That is, if the debtor is named incorrectly, the financing statement will not be discovered by creditors searching the public record, and thus will not provide public notice of the secured party's interest. Under §9–503, proper identification requires the debtor's individual, partnership, corporate, or other organizational name. Generally, the individual names of the partners, members, associates, or other persons comprising an organizational debtor are not required unless the organization does not have a name. Note that any trade name used by the debtor is not required, and a financing statement using only a trade name is insufficient. For example, assume the debtor John Jones, a sole proprietor, conducts business as A-1 Television and Appliance. First

Bank loans money to Jones secured by his equipment and inventory. First Bank's financing statement should be filed under the debtor's individual name (John Jones) rather than the trade name, A-1 Television and Appliance.

At issue in the following case was whether the debtor was properly identified in the financing statement.

The First National Bank of Lacon v. Strong
663 N.E.2d 432 (Ill. App. 1996)

> Defendant E. Strong Oil Company, Inc., borrowed $75,000 from plaintiff, the First National Bank of Lacon (Bank) and granted the Bank a security interest in the company's inventory, equipment, accounts, and general intangibles. The Bank filed a financing statement in 1986 and a continuation statement in 1991 with the Secretary of State. Both documents listed the debtor as Strong Oil Co. In 1991, the Department of Revenue seized the corporate assets of E. Strong Oil Company, Inc. for failing to pay $228,640 of motor fuel taxes owed to the state. Public auction of the assets generated proceeds of $22,516. The Bank filed a lawsuit asserting that it held a perfected security interest in the assets and proceeds. The Department of Commerce, alleging that its interest had priority over the Bank's, claimed that the Bank's security interest was unperfected because the statements incorrectly identified the name of debtor. The trial court ruled in favor of the Bank and the Department of Commerce appealed.

Slater, Justice

. . . The general rule is that to perfect a security interest under the Code, a financing statement must be filed. . . . A financing statement sufficiently shows the name of the debtor if it gives the individual, partnership or corporate name of the debtor, whether or not it adds other trade names or names of partners. . . . To perfect a security interest in the type of collateral involved herein the proper place of filing is in the office of the Secretary of State. . . . The Secretary of State indexes filing statements according to the name of the debtor for public inspection. . . .

The Department of Revenue, after a demand and nonpayment, issued a warrant to levy upon the assets of E. Strong Oil Company in November of 1991. . . . This action on the part of the Department of Revenue placed it in the status of a "lien creditor" as defined in section [9–102(a)(52)] of the Code. . . . As a lien creditor, the Department of Revenue has priority over an unperfected security interest [UCC §9–317(a)]. Therefore, if the bank's financing statement and continuation statement listing the debtor as "Strong Oil Co." was insufficient to perfect its interest, that interest is subordinate to the Department's rights.

The bank claims that its filing under the name "Strong Oil Company," though an error, is not seriously misleading. Section [9–506] provides that a financing statement substantially complying with the requirements of section [9–502(a)] is effective even though it contains minor errors which are not seriously misleading. . . .

Under the notice filing system of the Code, a party seeking to perfect a security interest must provide enough information to alert an interested party of a possible prior security interest. . . . When a debtor's name is inaccurately listed on a financing statement, the critical inquiry is whether a reasonably prudent subsequent creditor would be likely to discover the prior security interest. . . . However, "resolution of the question cannot be made simply by comparing two names, but must be settled with an eye toward the intended operation of the UCC indexing system. . . . A reasonable searcher properly using the index is looking for the name of the debtor amid a host of similar names. The system may contain hundreds or millions of names, depending on the size of the index." *In re A.C. Ballard,* 100 B.R. 526, 531 (Bankr. D. Nev. 1989). Accordingly, "it has been held in a substantial number of cases that a financing statement is defective and insufficient to constitute perfection where the filing is under an entity's name that is legally different from the actual owner even if the names are virtually identical." [*In re Terry Pierson, Inc.,* 84 B.R.533, 535 (Bankr. S.D.Ill. 1988)]; see, e.g., *In re Wardcorp, Inc.,* 133 B.R. 210 (Bankr. S.D. Ind. 1990) (filing under "Ward Corporation, Inc." was seriously misleading where correct name was "Wardcorp, Inc."); *In re McGovern Auto Specialty, Inc.,* 51 B.R. 511 (Bankr. E.D. Pa. 1985) (discrepancy between debtor's true name "McGovern Auto Specialty, Inc." and erroneous name "McGovern Auto & Truck Parts, Inc." found to be seriously misleading); *In re Tyler,* 23 B.R. 806 (Bankr. S.D. Fla. 1982) (discrepancy between "Tri-State Moulded Plastics, Inc.", and "Tri-State Molded Plastics, Inc.", seriously misleading).

We find that omission of the letter "E" from the financing statement is seriously misleading. This is because the Secretary of State files financing statements alphabetically, by the debtor's name. A diligent search using the correct legal name of this corporation would not likely, in our opinion, disclose the bank's financing statement in this case. To hold otherwise would frustrate the underlying purpose of the Code's filing requirements. A rule that would burden a searcher with guessing at misspellings and various configurations of a legal name would not provide creditors with the certainty that is essential in commercial transactions. . . . Indeed, the public-notice aspect of Article 9 of the Code "rises and falls on the integrity of the debtor-name index" since "if the index does not lead the searcher to the filed financing statement, no real public notice is effected." *Ballard,* 100 B.R. at 532.

Because the bank did not properly perfect its security interest, the bank's rights to the proceeds of the sale are subordinate to the rights of the Department of Revenue, a lien creditor. . . .

[Judgment reversed.]

Effectiveness, Duration, and Termination of Financing Statement. The financing statement is deemed filed either when: (1) it is presented, with payment of the filing fee, to the recording officer, or (2) it is accepted by the filing officer. Upon filing, the filing officer marks each statement with a file number, the date, and the time of filing, indexes it under the debtor's name, and holds it for public inspection. A financing statement is effective for a period of five years from the date it is filed. It thereafter lapses unless the secured party files a **continuation statement** within six months prior to expiration of the five-year period. If a continuation statement is properly filed, the financing statement's effectiveness is extended for five years beyond its original expiration date. Thus, succeeding continuation statements may be filed to continue indefinitely the effectiveness of the original statement. In this way, Article 9 provides a self-clearing public filing system because filing older than five years, for which no continuation statement is filed, automatically become ineffective.[7]

A debtor who has satisfied the obligation for which the security interest was created may require the secured party to file a **termination statement** to publicly note that the financing arrangement has been terminated.

---

[7]UCC §§9–516(a), 9–519, 9–515.

Because most financing statements expire automatically in five years, under §9–513, the secured party generally is not required to file a termination statement unless one is explicitly demanded by the debtor. If, however, the collateral is consumer goods, the secured party must file a termination statement after the secured obligation is satisfied. Such termination statements are only infrequently required because many security interests in consumer goods are perfected without filing under the automatic perfection rules discussed later in this chapter.

Place of Filing. Under §9–501, most financing statements are filed centrally, usually in the office of the state secretary of state. Local filing is required when the collateral is (1) timber to be cut, (2) minerals in place, including oil and gas, (3) accounts arising from the sale of minerals including oil and gas at the minehead or well-head, and (4) when the financing statement is filed as a "fixture filing." In these cases, the filing is made in the local public office, usually the county recorder's office, where a mortgage on the underlying real estate would be recorded. Figure 31.2 is a facsimile of the general financing statement form used under Article 9.

Article 9 is not the only recording system governing security interests in personal property. Indeed, Article 9 explicitly exempts from its filing provisions transactions for which an adequate public notice filing system already exists under state or federal law. For example, alternative federal filing systems exist for security interests in ships, railroad equipment, copyrights, patents, and civil aircraft. At the state level, "certificate of title" statutes commonly require that security interests in motor vehicles be noted on the title document. If a filing system that supplants Article 9 exists, the secured party must comply with that system. Perfection under such an alternative system, however, has the same legal consequences as an Article 9 perfection.

Automatic Perfection

Article 9 provides a number of "automatic" perfection rules under which a security interest is perfected upon attachment without requiring that the secured party either file or take possession. Automatic perfection is provided for situations in which possession of the collateral is not feasible, but in which a filing requirement would impose an undue burden on Article 9's recording system. That is, automatic perfection rules are applied when the public notice benefits of filing are deemed outweighed by potential clogging of the recording system. Article 9's automatic perfection rules, most of which are discussed below,[8] generally are characterized by one or more limiting factors: (1) they apply only to certain types of collateral, (2) they do not protect the secured party against all third-party claimants, and (3) they often are limited in duration.

Purchase Money Security Interests in Consumer Goods.
Perhaps Article 9's most important automatic perfection rule is contained in 9–309(1), which provides that a purchase money security interest in consumer goods is perfected automatically upon attachment without filing. For this rule to apply, the security interest must be a purchase money security interest *and* the collateral must be consumer goods. Thus, a financing statement must be filed to perfect purchase money security interests in other types of collateral such as equipment or inventory. The rationale for the automatic perfection rule in consumer goods cases is that such goods are frequently financed on a purchase money basis and that filing a financing statement with respect to every purchase creates a costly burden on sellers. In addition, automatic perfection prevents burdening the filing system with thousands of financing statements covering very small amounts. Further, other creditors are unlikely to be injured by automatic perfection. Creditors other than the seller rarely lend against consumer goods due to their limited value and rapid depreciation.

Automatic perfection in consumer goods protects the seller against claims of the debtor's other creditors but does not protect the seller, under certain circumstances, against a sale of the collateral by the debtor. Under §9–320(b), a buyer of consumer goods takes free of a perfected security interest if she buys (1) without knowledge of the security interest, (2) for value, (3) for her own personal, family, or household purposes, and (4) before the secured party files a financing statement covering the goods. Thus, a secured party who desires protection against a sale of the collateral by the debtor to a bona fide purchaser for consumer purposes must file a financing statement. Because the risk presented by such sales is small in relation to the cost of filing financing statements, most sellers assume the risk and do not file.

---

[8]An additional automatic perfection rule, §§9–315(c)–(d), is discussed in Chapter 32.

Figure 31.2   **Financing Statement**

UCC FINANCING STATEMENT
FOLLOW INSTRUCTIONS (front and back) CAREFULLY

A. NAME & PHONE OF CONTACT AT FILER [optional]

B. SEND ACKNOWLEDGMENT TO: (Name and Address)

THE ABOVE SPACE IS FOR FILING OFFICE USE ONLY

1. DEBTOR'S EXACT FULL LEGAL NAME - Insert only <u>one</u> debtor name (1a or 1b) - do not abbreviate or combine names

1a. ORGANIZATION'S NAME			

OR

1b. INDIVIDUAL'S LAST NAME	FIRST NAME	MIDDLE NAME	SUFFIX
1c. MAILING ADDRESS	CITY	STATE / POSTAL CODE	COUNTRY

1d. TAX ID #; SSN OR EIN	ADD'L INFO RE ORGANIZATION DEBTOR	1e. TYPE OF ORGANIZATION	1f. JURISDICTION OF ORGANIZATION	1g. ORGANIZATIONAL ID #, if any ☐ NONE

2. ADDITIONAL DEBTOR'S EXACT FULL LEGAL NAME - Insert only <u>one</u> debtor name (2a or 2b) - do not abbreviate or combine names

2a. ORGANIZATION'S NAME			

OR

2b. INDIVIDUAL'S LAST NAME	FIRST NAME	MIDDLE NAME	SUFFIX
2c. MAILING ADDRESS	CITY	STATE / POSTAL CODE	COUNTRY

2d. TAX ID #; SSN OR EIN	ADD'L INFO RE ORGANIZATION DEBTOR	2e. TYPE OF ORGANIZATION	2f. JURISDICTION OF ORGANIZATION	2g. ORGANIZATIONAL ID #, if any ☐ NONE

3. SECURED PARTY'S NAME (or NAME of TOTAL ASSIGNEE of ASSIGNOR S/P) - Insert only <u>one</u> secured party name (3a or 3b)

3a. ORGANIZATION'S NAME			

OR

3b. INDIVIDUAL'S LAST NAME	FIRST NAME	MIDDLE NAME	SUFFIX
3c. MAILING ADDRESS	CITY	STATE / POSTAL CODE	COUNTRY

4 This FINANCING STATEMENT covers the following collateral:

5. ALTERNATIVE DESIGNATION If applicable: ☐ LESSEE/LESSOR ☐ CONSIGNEE/CONSIGNOR ☐ BAILEE/BAILOR ☐ SELLER/BUYER ☐ AG. LIEN ☐ NON-UCC FILING

6. ☐ This FINANCING STATEMENT is to be filed [for record] (or recorded) in the REAL ESTATE RECORDS   Attach Addendum   [if applicable]   7. Check to REQUEST SEARCH REPORT(S) on Debtor(s) (ADDITIONAL FEE)   [optional]   ☐ All Debtors ☐ Debtor 1 ☐ Debtor 2

8. OPTIONAL FILER REFERENCE DATA

NATIONAL UCC FINANCING STATEMENT (FORM UCC1) (REV. 07/29/98)

To illustrate the operation of these provisions, assume that Art's Appliances, a retailer, sells a television set on credit to Roe. Roe signs a security agreement promising to pay the purchase price and giving Art's a security interest in the set to secure payment—a conditional sales contract. Art's security interest is perfected automatically upon attachment. Thus, even without filing, Art's will have the benefit of the television to the exclusion of Roe's other creditors in the event of Roe's nonpayment or bankruptcy. Assume, however, that Roe subsequently sells the television for cash to Doaks, who buys it for use in his home with no knowledge of Art's security interest. In this case, unless Art's has filed a financing statement covering the set before its sale to Doaks, Doaks acquires the set free of Art's interest.

Sales of Certain Accounts. Assignments of a merchant's accounts, either as an outright sale or as security for a loan, often form an integral part of commercial financing. In these cases, the assignee must file a financing statement to perfect its interest in the accounts. Section 9–309(2) provides that a financing statement is not necessary to perfect an assignment of accounts or payment intangibles that does not (either alone or in conjunction with other assignments to the same assignee) transfer a *significant part* of the assignor's outstanding accounts or payment intangibles. This section is designed to exempt from filing casual or isolated assignments of a single account or small group of accounts under circumstances not related to business financing. Because all transactions in accounts are governed by Article 9, and accounts are so commonly involved in financing, §9–309(2) must be viewed as a limited exception to the filing requirement. As Official Comment 4 to §9–309 cautions, "Any person who regularly takes assignments of any debtor's accounts . . . should file."

20-Day Perfection in Instruments, Certificated Securities, or Documents. Section 9–312(e) provides that a security interest in instruments, certificated securities (such as stocks and bonds), or negotiable documents of title is perfected without filing or taking possession for a period of 20 days after attachment to the extent it arises (1) for new value given (2) under a written security agreement. Under §§9–312(f)–(g), a creditor who has perfected a security interest in instruments, certificated securities, or negotiable documents of title by taking possession retains a perfected interest for 20 days

after relinquishing possession of the collateral to the debtor if the transfer is made to permit the debtor (a) to sell or exchange the goods covered by the document, (b) to store, load, unload, ship, or process the goods to prepare them for sale or exchange, or (c) to sell, exchange, present, or collect the instrument. This rule also applies if a secured party perfects its security interest in goods held by a bailee who has not issued a negotiable document of title, and later permits the bailee to make the goods available to the debtor for purposes of sale or exchange. In this case, the security interest remains perfected for 20 days after the goods are delivered to the debtor. The rationale for both of the 20-day rules discussed above is explained in Official Comment 9 to §9–312, which states, "There are a variety of legitimate reasons . . . why certain types of collateral must be released temporarily to a debtor. No useful purpose would be served by cluttering the files with records of such exceedingly short term transactions."

Note that the protection afforded by these provisions is somewhat limited. For example, during the 20-day period, the debtor might transfer the instrument, security, or document to a good faith purchaser. As discussed in Chapter 32, such a purchaser would cut off the rights of the secured party under §9–331. Further, after the 20-day period has expired, the secured party has an unperfected interest and must take additional steps to protect itself against any third party. Table 31.1 summarizes the various methods of perfection discussed in this chapter.

Default

The secured party's rights in specific property owned by the debtor—the collateral—distinguish a secured from an unsecured obligation. These rights commonly are triggered by the debtor's **default,** which generally occurs upon the debtor's nonpayment of the secured obligation as it comes due. Part 6 of Article 9 governs the rights and obligations of the parties upon default. Article 9 does not define "default," instead allowing the parties to define it in their security agreement. Accordingly, security agreements often incorporate elaborate default provisions.

Assuming the secured party has created a security interest that is enforceable against the debtor (attachment) and defeats third-party claims (perfection), after default, the secured party generally has the right to take possession of the collateral and dispose of it in satisfaction of the debt.

Table 31.1	Methods of Perfection				
	Method of Perfection				
Type of Collateral	**Possession**	**Control**	**Filing**	**Automatic**	**Other**
Goods	•		•		
Negotiable Tangible Documents of Title	•		•		
Negotiable Electronic Documents of Title		•	•		
Goods Held by Bailee–Nonnegotiable Document					§9–312(d)
Goods Held by Bailee–No Document					§9–313(c)
Electronic Chattel Paper		•	•		
Tangible Chattel Paper	•		•		
Instruments	•		•		
Investment Property		•	•		
Accounts			•		
Commercial Tort Claims			•		
Deposit Accounts		•			
General Intangibles			•		
Money	•				
Consumer Goods (purchase money security interest)				•	
Accounts (certain sales)				•	
Instruments, Certificated Securities, or Documents (20 day perfection)				•	

Taking Possession of the Collateral

Under §9–609, unless otherwise agreed, a secured party has the right to take possession of the collateral upon the debtor's default. In taking possession, the secured party may proceed without judicial process and without the debtor's consent, if possession can be obtained without breach of the peace. The UCC therefore authorizes "self-help" repossession provided the creditor's action does not result in breach of the peace. "Breach of the peace" is not defined in Article 9, but its meaning has been at issue in many pre-Code and post-Code cases. Generally, a secured party may not use force, threats, intimidation, or harassment to repossess collateral. In addition, a creditor may not enter or break into the debtor's house or other buildings and may not repossess collateral located elsewhere over the debtor's unequivocal protest. However, clandestine repossessions of cars from driveways, parking lots, or public streets are generally upheld. Note that the secured party's entry upon the debtor's land to repossess collateral does not by itself constitute a criminal trespass.

As an alternative, or in addition to self help, the creditor may proceed by legal action, such as replevin, discussed in Chapter 29. The remedies may be pursued simultaneously. That is, filing a replevin action does not prevent the secured party from also attempting to recover the property through self-help repossession.

At issue in the following case was whether a secured party's conduct in repossessing collateral constituted a breach of the peace.

Davenport v. Chrysler Credit Corporation
818 S.W.2d 23 (Tenn. App. 1991)

> Plaintiffs Debbie and Larry Davenport purchased a new car and granted defendant Chrysler Credit Corporation, which had financed the purchase, a security interest in the

car. Because the car developed mechanical problems, the Davenports refused to make two monthly payments. Chrysler Credit hired American Lender Service Co. to repossess the automobile, but the Davenports refused to turn it over to American Lender employees who came to their home one evening. The following day, before leaving for work, Larry Davenport parked the car in their garage and chained its rear end to a post using a logging chain and two padlocks. When the Davenports returned from work that day, they discovered that someone had entered the garage, cut one of the padlocks and removed the automobile. The Davenports sued Chrysler Credit alleging that the repossession violated §9–609 of the UCC. The trial court ruled in favor of Chrysler Credit and the Davenports appealed.

Koch, Judge

. . . Tennessee has long recognized that secured parties have a legitimate interest in obtaining their collateral from a defaulting debtor. Prior to the Uniform Commercial Code, secured parties could repossess collateral either with or without the assistance of the courts. . . . The General Assembly preserved the secured parties' self-help remedies when it enacted the Uniform Commercial Code in 1963. It also preserved the requirement that repossessions must be accomplished without a breach of the peace. . . . Tennessee's version of the Uniform Commercial Code does not define "breach of the peace." Like the U.C.C.'s drafters, the General Assembly decided that this task should be left to the courts. . . .

The term "breach of the peace" is a generic term that includes all violations or potential violations of the public peace and order. . . . It includes all unlawful acts and acts of public indecorum that disturb or tend to disturb the public peace or good order. . . . While breaches of the peace frequently involve offenses against individuals, they also include offenses against the public at large or the State. . . . The term "peace" means

the tranquility enjoyed by citizens of a municipality or community where good order reigns among its members, or, that individual sense of security which every [person] feels so necessary to his [or her] comfort, and for which all governments are instituted.

[*State ex rel. Thompson v. Reichman,* 188 S.W. 597, 601 (Tenn. 1916).]

Offenses against individuals, generally criminal offenses, must be accompanied by violence or a threat of violence in order to be considered a breach of the

peace. However, conduct that is "incompatible with the tranquility and good order which governments are organized to maintain" need not involve violence, . . . the threat of violence, [or] personal confrontation . . . in order . . . to amount to a breach of the peace under [§9–609]. . . .

Secured parties may repossess their collateral at a reasonable time and in a reasonable manner. . . . Thus, determining whether a particular secured creditor's conduct amounts to a breach of the peace requires a review of the reasonableness of the secured party's conduct in light of the facts of the case. . . .

Public policy favors peaceful, non-trespassory repossessions when the secured party has a free right of entry. . . . However, forced entries onto the debtor's property or into the debtor's premises are viewed as seriously detrimental to the ordinary conduct of human affairs. . . . Accordingly, courts have consistently found that repossessions accomplished by breaking locks or cutting chains are inconsistent with the Uniform Commercial Code. . . .

The courts have also disapproved of repossessions in which the secured party or its agent entered the debtor's closed premises without permission. . . . These decisions, and others like them, have prompted Professors White and Summers to observe that "a breach of the peace is almost certain to be found if the repossession is accompanied by the unauthorized entry into a closed or locked garage." [*White & Summers, Uniform Commercial Code* 577 n. 11 (3d ed. 1988).]

Self-help procedures such as repossession are the product of a careful balancing of the interests of secured parties and debtors. On one hand, secured creditors have a legitimate interest in obtaining possession of collateral without resorting to expensive and sometimes cumbersome judicial procedures. On the other hand, debtors have a legitimate interest in being free from unwarranted invasions of their property and privacy interests. . . .

Repossession is a harsh procedure and is, essentially, a delegation of the State's exclusive prerogative to resolve disputes. Accordingly, the statutes governing the repossession of collateral should be construed in a way that prevents abuse and discourages illegal conduct which might otherwise go unchallenged because of the debtor's lack of knowledge of legally proper repossession techniques. . . .

American Lender Service's repossession of the Davenports' automobile was not accompanied by violence or the threat of violence because the Davenports were not at home at the time. However, Chrysler Credit and American Lender Service do not dispute that they obtained the automobile by entering a closed garage and by cutting a lock on a chain that would have prevented them from removing the automobile. Despite the absence of violence or physical confrontation, entering the closed garage and cutting the lock amounted to a breach of the peace. Thus, unlike the trial court, we find that the manner in which the Davenports' automobile was repossessed was inconsistent with requirements [§9–609] places on secured parties who are repossessing collateral from defaulting debtors. . . .

[Judgment reversed and remanded.]

Disposition of the Collateral

Once in possession of the collateral, the secured party has two alternatives: (1) accept and retain the collateral in satisfaction of the debt—a "strict foreclosure," or (2) sell the collateral and apply the proceeds to the unpaid obligation.

Strict Foreclosure. Under **strict foreclosure,** authorized in §9–620, after default, the secured party merely accepts and retains the collateral in satisfaction of the debt. A secured party who intends to use strict foreclosure must send authenticated notice to the debtor unless the debtor has, after default, waived or modified the right to notice. The secured party also must notify other secured parties known to have an interest in the collateral. If the secured party receives written objection from a person notified within 20 days after the notice was sent, the secured party generally will dispose of the collateral by resale. If no one objects, the secured party may accept and retain the collateral in satisfaction of the debt.

If the collateral is consumer goods and the debtor has already paid 60 percent or more of the price, the secured party must dispose of the collateral by resale unless the debtor, after default, signs an agreement renouncing or modifying her rights. The reason that strict foreclosure is unavailable in this case is that a debtor who has paid 60 percent of the price has probably built up equity in the goods, so that a resale would result in a surplus to be returned to the debtor.

Note that in a commercial setting, the secured party may accept and retain the collateral in full or *partial* satisfaction of the debt. If accepted in partial satisfaction, the debtor remains liable for the deficiency—the difference between the unpaid debt and the value of the collateral. In a consumer transaction, however, a secured party may accept collateral only in full, not partial, satisfaction of the obligation it secures.

Resale of the Collateral. Resale, rather than retention, of the collateral is the most common remedy used by secured creditors after default. It is authorized in §9–610, which provides that after default, a secured party "may sell, lease, license, or otherwise dispose" of the collateral either "in its present condition or following any commercially reasonable preparation or processing." Under §9–615, the proceeds of this disposition are applied in the following order:

1. reasonable expenses incurred by the secured party in disposing of the collateral—for example, expenses of retaking possession, preparation for sale, and if the security agreement provides, attorneys' fees;
2. the satisfaction of the indebtedness owed to the secured party; and, finally,
3. the satisfaction of any indebtedness owed to any subordinate secured party in the same collateral.

Any surplus is to be returned to the debtor and, unless otherwise agreed, the debtor is liable for any deficiency.

Under §9–610, the collateral may be sold either by public (auction) or private sale. Two major requirements govern the conduct of the sale. First, the secured party must notify the debtor of the time and place of any public sale, or of the time after which a private sale will be made. Second, "every aspect of a disposition of collateral including the method, manner, time, place, and other terms, must be commercially reasonable."

Courts are divided concerning the legal effect of a secured party's failure to satisfy one or both of these requirements. Some courts hold that noncompliance is an absolute bar to later recovery of any deficiency from the debtor; others hold that the secured party may recover a deficiency, reduced by damages that the *debtor* proves resulted from the improper sale. Still other courts adopt a middle ground, holding that no deficiency is available unless the *secured party* proves that the collateral was worth less than the outstanding debt upon default (the "rebuttable presumption" rule). The 1998 amendments to Article 9 partially resolve this conflict by adopting the rebuttable presumption rule for commercial transactions. If the collateral is consumer goods, however, courts will continue to use one of the three approaches outlined above.

Secured Party's Collection Rights. Problems of disposition inherent in a sale of goods, such as inventory or equipment, are not present if the collateral is accounts receivable, chattel paper, instruments, or general intangibles. These assets are very liquid and may be collected without interrupting the debtor's business. As a result, §9–607(a) provides that upon default, the secured party may notify the persons obligated on the collateral to make payments directly to the secured party. This right exists whether the method of collection contemplated by the security agreement before default was *direct* (account debtors making payments directly to the secured party, referred to as "notification" financing) or *indirect* (payment by the account debtors to the debtor, referred to as "non-notification" financing). The security agreement may grant the secured party the right to give notice and make collections before default. Section §9–607, however, automatically gives the secured party this right after default.

Summary

1. In a secured transaction, governed by Article 9 of the UCC, a borrower or buyer gives a lender or seller a security interest in personal property or fixtures to secure performance of an obligation. The debtor is the party who owes the obligation and is giving security. The secured party is the lender, seller, or other party in whose favor a security interest exists. The property providing the security is the collateral. Security interests may be possessory or nonpossessory, purchase-money or non-purchase-money.

2. The major types of personal property collateral are goods, semi-intangibles, and intangibles. Goods include consumer goods, farm products, equipment, and inventory. Semi-intangibles include documents of title, chattel paper, instruments, and investment property. Intangibles include accounts, commercial tort claims, deposit accounts, and general intangibles.

3. Article 9 governs any transaction that, regardless of its form, creates a security interest in personal property or fixtures by contract. Article 9 also governs any sale of accounts, chattel paper, payment intangibles, and promissory notes, whether or not intended for security. Article 9 excludes from its coverage security transactions that do not arise by agreement of the parties and transactions not related to commercial financing.

4. Before a security interest is effective between the debtor and secured party, it must attach to the collateral. Attachment requires that (1) an enforceable security agreement must exist, (2) the secured party must give value, and (3) the debtor must have rights in the collateral.

5. Perfection determines the secured party's rights against most third-party claimants to the collateral. These third parties include (1) lien creditors primarily the debtor's trustee in bankruptcy, (2) buyers of the collateral from the debtor, and (3) other secured parties claiming an interest in the collateral.

6. Article 9 recognizes three methods of perfecting a security interest:
    1. perfection by taking possession or control of the collateral,
    2. perfection by filing a "financing statement" in an appropriate public office, and
    3. automatic perfection occurring upon attachment with no further action by the secured party.

7. Security interests in money may be perfected only by taking possession. Security interests in accounts, commercial tort claims, and general intangibles may be perfected only by filing. Security interests in other types of collateral including goods, negotiable tangible documents of title, instruments, and tangible chattel paper may be perfected either by filing or taking possession. Security interests in investment property, electronic chattel paper, and electronic documents of title may be perfected by either filing or control. Security interests in deposit accounts may be perfected only by control.

8. Automatic perfection rules apply only to certain types of collateral, do not protect the secured party against all third parties, and often are limited in duration. Article 9's most important automatic perfection rule provides that a purchase money security interest in consumer goods is perfected automatically upon attachment without filing.

9. The secured party's rights in specific property owned by the debtor—the collateral—distinguish a secured from an unsecured obligation. These rights are triggered by the debtor's default, which usually involves the debtor's nonpayment of the secured obligation as it comes due. After

default the secured party generally has the right to take possession of the collateral and dispose of it in satisfaction of the debt.

10. In taking possession of the collateral the secured party may proceed without judicial process (self-help) if possession can be obtained without breach of the peace, or may proceed by judicial proceeding such as a replevin action.

11. Once in possession of the collateral, the secured party either may retain the collateral in full satisfaction of the debt—a strict foreclosure—or may sell the collateral at public or private sale and apply the proceeds to the debt. If the collateral involved is accounts receivable, chattel paper, instruments, or general intangibles, Article 9 permits the secured party upon default to notify account debtors to make payments directly to the secured party.

Key Terms

secured transaction	account debtor
security interest	tangible chattel paper
debtor	electronic chattel paper
obligor	instruments
secured party	investment property
collateral	account
security agreement	commercial tort claim
possessory security interest (pledge)	deposit account
nonpossessory security interest	general intangibles
	payment intangible
	attachment
purchase money security interest	perfection
	value
consumer goods	lien creditor
farm products	financing statement
inventory	continuation statement
equipment	termination statement
document of title	default
chattel paper	strict foreclosure
conditional sales contract	

Questions and Problems

31.1 Compare and contrast the concepts of attachment and perfection under Article 9 of the UCC. What are the requirements for attachment? What functions do these requirements serve? Indicate the possible method or methods of perfecting a security interest in the various types of collateral discussed in the text.

31.2 McCormick Dude Ranch is a tourist site that attracts paying guests who participate in various ranch activities. One of the ranch's most popular events is its monthly cattle drive that recreates the experience of an actual drive. McCormick maintains a herd of 1,000 head of cattle that it uses for the cattle drives. Because of financial difficulties, McCormick borrowed $100,000 from First Bank, secured by a perfected security interest in McCormick's inventory. Second Bank also loaned $100,000 to McCormick, secured by a perfected security interest on McCormick's equipment. If McCormick defaults on both loans, which bank is entitled to the cattle? Explain.

31.3 Consider whether each of the following descriptions of collateral is sufficient to identify a security interest (a) in the security agreement and (b) in the financing statement. See §§9–108 and 9–504 of the Code.
  (a) Consumer goods of the debtor.
  (b) All of the contents of Joe's Diner.
  (c) All farm equipment.
  (d) Inventory.
  (e) All personal property.

31.4 First State Bank has agreed to lend Mrs. Carraway $30,000 and to take a security interest in three certificates of deposit that she owns. The certificates are nonnegotiable and non-transferable. How should the bank perfect its security interest?

31.5 Richard Valway owned a restaurant named Ricardo's. Gregg Equipment Co. sold restaurant equipment to Valway pursuant to a written security agreement retaining a purchase money security interest in the equipment. Gregg filed a financing statement listing the debtor as "Ricardo's." Does Gregg hold a perfected security interest? Why or why not?

31.6 In December 2003, Silverline Building and Maintenance Company (Silverline) contracted to perform janitorial services for the District of Columbia (the District). Silverline then entered into a factoring arrangement under which Thomas Funding Corporation advanced working capital to Silverline in exchange for Silverline's assigning to Thomas Funding the contract payments due from the District. On January 4, 2004, Thomas Funding filed a financing statement with the District of Columbia Recorder of Deeds. The financing statement incorrectly listed the debtor's name as Silvermine Building and Maintenance Company. On October 5, 2004, the federal Internal Revenue Service (IRS) filed a tax lien against Silverline with the Recorder of Deeds. The District of Columbia subsequently paid $18,747 owed to Silverline to the IRS. Thomas Funding sued the District claiming that it was entitled to the money because it held a perfected security interest superior to that of the IRS, a lien creditor. Is Thomas Funding correct? Explain.

31.7 International Bank lent $11 million to Big Oak Company, which granted the bank a security interest in industrial equipment owned by the company. On October 12, 1998, International Bank filed a financing statement with the county clerk that perfected its security interest. On April 4, 2003, the bank filed a continuation statement. On November 1, 2003, Big Oak Company sold some of the equipment to Davis Construction Co. International Bank claimed that its interest in the equipment took priority over Davis's interest. Is the bank correct? See UCC §9–515(d).

31.8 Woofer and Tweeter, Inc. sold a stereo system on credit to Mr. and Mrs. Brown and retained a security interest in the stereo. After the Browns defaulted in making monthly payments, an employee of Woofer and Tweeter went to the Brown home to repossess the stereo. The employee was accompanied by a deputy sheriff in full uniform. The employee explained that he wanted the stereo and the Browns allowed him to take it with no argument. The deputy merely stood at the door while the repossession took place. The Browns then sued Woofer and Tweeter for unlawful repossession.

(a) Did a breach of the peace occur?

(b) Should the court uphold the repossession? Explain

31.9   The Money Bank loaned Daria money to purchase a mobile home. The parties signed a written agreement granting the bank a security interest in the mobile home. Darla defaulted in repaying the loan but refused to give the bank possession of the mobile home. Rinaldo, an employee of the bank, went to Darla's home while she was at work, used a crowbar to remove a lock from the door, released Darla's dog, and tied it to a nearby tree. Rinaldo then removed the mobile home from its concrete foundation and hauled the mobile home to the bank. Darla sued the bank alleging that the repossession constituted a breach of the peace. How should the court rule? Explain.

31.10 Rinaldo also repossessed a car subject to the Money Bank's security interest. He visited the debtor and asked for return of the automobile. The debtor asserted that he had made all the necessary loan payments, so Rinaldo suggested that the debtor go to the bank with Rinaldo to verify his payment record. While the debtor was reviewing his account with the loan officer, Rinaldo towed the car from the bank's parking lot to a nearby garage. Even though the bank records confirmed that the debtor was one payment in arrears, the debtor sued the bank alleging that the repossession violated §9–609 of the UCC. How should the court rule? Explain.

SECURED TRANSACTIONS—PRIORITIES

Like much of debtor-creditor law, Article 9 of the UCC is designed to resolve disputes among creditors competing for the limited assets of a defaulting debtor. The primary goal of any Article 9 secured creditor is to have a priority claim to the collateral. This chapter discusses whether a given security interest is effective in achieving that result.

General Rules of Priority

The value of perfected security interest is most easily illustrated by first examining the priority between an unperfected security interest and the various types of claimants discussed in the preceding chapter, and then comparing those results with the position enjoyed by a perfected secured party against the same claimants.

Unperfected Security Interests

Versus General Creditors. Under §9–201, a security agreement is effective according to its terms against the debtor's unsecured creditors. That is, an unsecured general creditor has no lien upon any specific property belonging to the debtor. In contrast, as noted in Chapter 31, a secured party whose interest has attached (but has not been perfected) has a lien upon the collateral. Accordingly, the unperfected secured party may repossess the collateral upon default and defeat an unsecured creditor's claim to the property.

Versus Lien Creditors. The most important priority contest is between the secured party and lien creditors, particularly the debtor's trustee in bankruptcy. Indeed, the acid test of any secured transaction is determining whether it will enjoy a priority in the debtor's bankruptcy. The trustee in bankruptcy, who represents the debtor's general creditors, often seeks to avoid the security interest and use the collateral to satisfy the general creditors' claims. Herein lies the weakness of an unperfected security interest. Under §9–317(a)(2)(A), the rights of a holder of an unperfected security interest are subordinate to the rights of a person who becomes a lien creditor before the security interest is perfected. For example, assume Roberts loans $1,000 to Simpson on June 1, taking a security interest in a stamp collection in the possession of Simpson pursuant to a written agreement. Roberts does not file a financing statement. On August 1, a petition in bankruptcy is filed against Simpson. Simpson's trustee in bankruptcy becomes a lien creditor on August 1. The trustee in bankruptcy prevails over Roberts with respect to the stamp collection, because the trustee became a lien creditor before Roberts's interest was perfected.

Under §9–317(e), if the security interest in question is a purchase money security interest that must be perfected by filing—that is, it is a purchase money security interest in inventory or equipment, not consumer goods—a secured party who files a financing statement within 20 days after the debtor receives possession of the collateral will take priority over the rights of a lien creditor arising between the time the security interest attaches and the time of filing.

The following case illustrates a priority dispute between a secured party and the trustee in bankruptcy in the context of a typical "certificate of title" statute.

In the Matter of Keidel
613 F.2d 172 (7th Cir. 1980)

On May 17, 1977, Esther Keidel borrowed $3,500 from the First National Bank of Wood River to purchase a mobile home. After Keidel signed a promissory note and security agreement giving the bank a security interest in the mobile home, the bank issued a check payable jointly to Keidel, the sellers, and Olin Employees' Credit Union, which held a lien on the mobile home. When Keidel delivered the check to the Credit Union, she was given a certificate of title indicating that the Credit Union had released its lien and had named First National Bank of Wood River as lienholder. A Credit Union employee advised Keidel to send the certificate of title to the secretary of state. Keidel failed to file the certificate.

On November 7, 1977, Keidel filed for bankruptcy. Soon thereafter, First National Bank of Wood River filed the certificate of title to the mobile home with the secretary of state, and on December 15, 1977, a new certificate showing the bank as lienholder was issued. The bank also repossessed the mobile home.

The trustee in bankruptcy filed a complaint with the bankruptcy court alleging that the mobile home was a part of Keidel's bankruptcy estate. The bankruptcy estate. The bankruptcy judge ordered First National Bank of Wood River to pay $3,500, representing the value of the mobile home, to the trustee. The district court affirmed and the bank appealed.

Cudahy, Circuit Judge

. . . Under Illinois law, security interests in personal property are, in general, governed by the Uniform Commercial Code as adopted in Illinois. . . . With respect to the means of perfection of security interests in motor vehicles (including mobile homes), however, the Illinois Vehicle Code exclusively controls. . . . Thus, the Illinois Vehicle Code provides that:

> A security interest is perfected by delivery to the Secretary of State of the existing certificate of title, if any, an application for a certificate of title containing the name and address of the lienholder and the date of his security agreement, and the required fee. It is perfected as of the time of its creation if the delivery is completed within 21 days thereafter, otherwise as of the time of the delivery. Ill. Rev. Stat. ch. 95 1/2, §3–202(b).

In the instant case the old certificate of title and an application for a new certificate were not delivered to the Secretary of State until shortly before December 15, 1977. But the security interest of the First National Bank of Wood River was created on May 17, 1977, when the security agreement and the promissory note were signed. [UCC §9–203]. . . . Therefore, since the security interest was not perfected within 21 days of its creation, it was not perfected until the application was delivered to the Secretary of State—well after the date of bankruptcy (Nov. 7, 1977). . . . On November 7, 1977, therefore, the security interest of the Bank was unperfected. . . .

Hence, as of the date of the bankruptcy, the rights of the Bank, as the holder of an unperfected security interest, were subordinate to those of the trustee in bankruptcy, who stood in the position of a lien creditor or lienholder. . . . This result illustrates the general rule that a lien creditor or lienholder (in whose shoes the trustee stands) prevails over the holder of an unperfected security interest but is defeated by the holder of a perfected security interest. . . .

The Bank contends that the result here produces a windfall for the bankrupt's estate at the expense of the secured creditor, which furnished the purchase price of the mobile home. This may indeed be the result this case, but the Bank has only itself to blame for failure to perform its statutory duty prescribing application for a new title. The Illinois law applicable to secured transactions in personal property, including motor vehicles, places strong emphasis on the need for diligence in perfection of the security interest in accordance with the statutory method. . . . The strong policy favoring diligence in perfection (and the consequent gain in certainty and regularity) outweighs the possibility here of "unjust enrichment" or a "windfall."

[Judgment affirmed.]

Versus Buyer of the Collateral. Under §9–317(b), a buyer of goods, instruments, documents of title, tangible chattel paper, and security certificates from the debtor prevails against an unperfected security interest in the collateral if the buyer (1) gives value and (2) receives delivery of the collateral without knowledge of the security interest and before the interest is perfected. For example, assume that on June 1, Carol loans Don $10,000, taking a security interest in Don's equipment. On June 2, Don contracts to sell a lathe (a piece of his equipment) to Janet, who pays $5,000. On June 3, Carol files a financing statement covering the equipment. On June 4, Janet picks up the lathe from Don without knowledge of Carol's interest. Carol will prevail, because, though Janet gave value before perfection, she did not take possession before perfection.

Section 9–317(d) applies a similar rule to accounts, general intangibles, electronic chattel paper, and investment property other than a certificated security. Because such property often has no physical existence or indispensable document by which it is customarily transferred, a buyer of the property prevails over an unperfected security interest in it simply by giving value for the property without knowledge of the security interest and before it is perfected.

Priority Among Unperfected Security Interests. Under §9–322(a)(3), if two or more unperfected secured parties claim an interest in the same collateral, the first to attach will prevail. To illustrate, on June 1, Roberts loans Simpson $1,000, taking an enforceable

security interest in Simpson's stamp collection. Roberts does not file. On July 1, Carter loans Simpson $1,000 and takes an enforceable security interest in the same collection. Carter does not file. As between Roberts and Carter, Roberts prevails, because her interest attached first; that is, on June 1.

Perfected Security Interests

A secured party with a perfected security interest fares much better than unperfected secured parties in the various priority contests with third parties claiming an interest in the collateral.

Versus General Creditors. As noted above, even an unperfected security interest defeats a general creditor's claim to the collateral. Perfected interests therefore also defeat a general creditor's claims.

Versus Lien Creditors. The ability to defeat a lien creditor is the hallmark of a perfected security interest. Under §§9–317(a)(2) and 9–323(b), a perfected security interest takes priority over the claims of a lien creditor to the extent that the security interest secures advances made before the person became a lien creditor or within 45 days thereafter. The primary value of these provisions to the secured party is that they protect the secured party against the most potent lien creditor—the debtor's trustee in bankruptcy. That is, a creditor who obtains a perfected security interest before the date the bankruptcy petition is filed (the date on which the trustee becomes a lien creditor) will have the benefit of the collateral free of the trustee's claim to it.[1]

Versus Buyer of Collateral. As a general rule, under §9–315(a)(1) the holder of a perfected security interest defeats subsequent buyers of the collateral from the debtor unless the secured party has authorized the disposition. This rule is subject to a number of important exceptions that substantially limit its effect. For example, as previously noted, a purchase money security interest in consumer goods is perfected automatically upon attachment. If, however, the secured party does not file, a consumer buyer of the collateral from the debtor defeats the secured party's claim to the

---

[1] The debtor's trustee in bankruptcy may avoid certain security interests perfected shortly before bankruptcy as preferences under principles discussed later in this chapter.

goods. Three additional important exceptions are discussed below.

Buyers in the Ordinary Course of Business. Under §1–201(b)(9), a **buyer in the ordinary course of business** is

> a person that buys goods in good faith, without knowledge that the sale violates the rights of another person in the goods, and in the ordinary course from a person, other than a pawnbroker, in the business of selling goods of that kind. . . .

Although not explicitly stated in the definition, a buyer in the ordinary course of business is primarily a purchaser of *inventory* from a person in the business of selling that inventory. For example, a person buying a diamond ring from a jeweler or a dishwasher from an appliance dealer is a buyer in the ordinary course of business.

Section §9–320(a) provides that such a buyer takes the goods "free of a security interest created by the buyer's seller, even if the security interest is perfected and the buyer knows of its existence." To illustrate, assume that First Bank loans money to Red's Television and to secure repayment takes a security interest in Red's inventory. First Bank files a financing statement covering the transaction in an appropriate public office. James, a customer, walks into Red's store and buys a television set. In this case, James is a buyer in the ordinary course of business. James takes the set free of First Bank's security interest, even though the interest is perfected (by filing) and even if he knows of the bank's security interest, unless he knows that the sale is in violation of the security agreement. Note that §9–320(a) protects the buyer when the debtor's sale of the collateral is unauthorized. If the secured party has authorized the sale in the security agreement or otherwise, the buyer, under §9–315(a)(1), takes the property free of the security interest.

Two important reasons justify the rule protecting buyers in the ordinary course of business against preexisting security interests in the inventory. First, a buyer of inventory should not be required in every transaction with a merchant to determine whether a security interest exists in the goods or whether they might later be repossessed by a secured party. Second, and perhaps more important, any other rule would permit merchants who purchase inventory without creating a security interest to offer their goods for sale free and clear of creditors'

interests, while those who finance their inventory on a secured basis could not. This result would place the merchants who finance inventory at a definite competitive disadvantage, making it difficult for them to generate cash through the sale of inventory to repay their loans.

A buyer in the ordinary course of business does not take free of all preexisting security interests in the goods; rather, §9–320(a) protects the buyer only against a security interest "created by the buyer's seller." This point is well illustrated by the well-known case, *National Shawmut Bank of Boston v. Jones.*[2] In this case, Robert Wever purchased an automobile from Wentworth Motor Company under a conditional sales contract by which Wentworth retained a security interest in the car. Wentworth assigned the contract to National Shawmut Bank of Boston, which perfected the security interest by filing a financing statement. Wever, without the permission of the bank, sold the car to Hanson-Rock, Inc., another automobile dealer, which later sold the car to Victor Jones. Hanson-Rock and Jones had no knowledge of the bank's security interest and neither examined the public records to search for prior security interests. In a lawsuit by National Shawmut Bank against Jones for return of the car, the Court noted that although Jones qualified as a buyer in the ordinary course of business under §1–201(b)(9), National Shawmut Bank's security interest was not created by Jones's seller, Hanson-Rock, Inc., but by Wever in favor of Wentworth Motor Company. Because the security interest was not created by the buyer's seller, Jones could not purchase the automobile free of National Shawmut Bank's perfected security interest.

Repeal of Farm Products Exception. By its terms, the rule of §9–320(a) does not apply to a person who is buying farm products from a person engaged in farming operations. Under this so-called farm products exception, the purchaser of farm products is not protected against liens created by his seller and thus effectively becomes a guarantor of the loan made to the agricultural borrower secured by the farm products.

Federal law, however, largely preempts Article 9 on this issue. In 1985, Congress enacted §1324 of the Food Security Act of 1985, which repeals the farm products exception on a nationwide basis. Under the statute, "notwithstanding any other provision of Federal, State,

---

[2]236 A.2d 484 (N.H. 1967).

or local law," a buyer in the ordinary course of business who buys farm products from a seller engaged in farming operations takes the goods free of a security interest in them created by the seller, even though the security interest is perfected and the buyer knows of its existence.[3] A similar rule protects commission merchants or selling agents who sell farm products for others in the ordinary course of business. Under the law the secured party may, however, protect itself by giving advance notice to the purchaser, commission merchant, or selling agent of the security interest. Notice may be given directly by the secured party. Alternatively, the statute authorizes the states to establish an optional central filing system, which generates statewide lists of security interests that are furnished to prospective purchasers, commission merchants, or selling agents.

Purchasers of Instruments, Documents, and Securities. Section 9–331 provides that Article 9 does not limit the rights of (1) a holder in due course of a negotiable instrument (such as a note or check), (2) a holder to whom a negotiable document of title (such as a warehouse receipt or bill of lading) has been duly negotiated, or (3) a protected purchaser of a security (such as a stock or bond). For example, a holder in due course of a negotiable instrument would take priority over an earlier nonpossessory security interest in the instrument. In addition, a holder to whom a negotiable document of title has been duly negotiated takes priority over an earlier security interest in the document that is perfected by filing. Note that filing a financing statement, which provides constructive notice to most third parties, is not notice to the holders or purchasers listed in §9–331. For example, assume Canfield, Inc. loans Delbert $10,000 secured by negotiable warehouse receipts belonging to Delbert. Delbert retains possession of the receipts and Canfield perfects its interest in the receipts by filing a financing statement. Subsequently, Delbert duly negotiates[4] the receipts to Holbrook. Holbrook cuts off Canfield's rights to the receipts, even though Canfield's interest is perfected. To be protected against holders such as Holbrook, therefore, a secured party must take possession.

Purchasers of Chattel Paper. When chattel paper is used as collateral, the secured party may take possession of the paper, notify the account debtors, and make collections. This approach is a "notification" or "direct collection" arrangement. Alternatively, the secured party may perfect by filing and leave the debtor in possession of the paper to make collections and remit the proceeds to the secured party. This method is known as a "nonnotification" or "indirect collection" arrangement. Because both methods are widely used, and because chattel paper is not negotiable, Article 9 permits perfection of security interests in chattel paper either by filing or taking possession.

Perfection by filing may, however, provide more limited protection to the secured party. Under §9–330(b), a purchaser of chattel paper who (1) gives new value and (2) takes possession or obtains control of it in the ordinary course of the purchaser's business has priority over a security interest in the chattel paper even though perfected, if the purchaser buys the paper in good faith and without knowledge that the purchase violates the rights of the secured party. Note that this rule applies only if the paper is purchased in the ordinary course of the *purchaser's* business. As such, only purchasers in the business of buying such paper, such as banks or finance companies, qualify for protection under this provision.

For example, Dealer, an appliance retailer, sells goods on credit to customers under conditional sales contracts giving Dealer a security interest in the goods sold. Dealer then borrows money from First Bank, giving the bank a security interest in the contracts to secure repayment. The bank files but leaves Dealer in possession of the paper in order to make collections. Dealer subsequently sells the paper to Finance Company, which pays cash and takes possession of the paper in the ordinary course of its business without knowledge of the bank's security interest. Dealer subsequently defaults on the loan and First Bank seeks to use the paper purchased by Finance to satisfy the unpaid debt. In this case, Finance will take the paper free of the bank's claim even though that claim is perfected.

First Bank can easily protect itself from the effect of §9–330(b) by stamping (with a rubber stamp) or noting on the paper itself that it is subject to a security interest in favor of the bank. In this manner, the bank can allow the debtor to retain possession of the paper to collect on it from the account debtors but is protected from purchasers such as Finance who can no longer meet the requirement that they take without knowledge that the purchase violates the secured party's rights.

---

[3]7 U.S.C. §1631(d).

[4]The due negotiation doctrine applicable to negotiable documents of title under Article 7 is discussed in Chapter 35.

Priority Among Perfected Security Interests. The most important priority rule in Article 9 is §9–322(a)(1), which governs priority between two or more secured parties, all of whom have perfected their interests. Section 9–322(a)(1) is a catchall rule, governing situations not otherwise specifically addressed. It adopts a "first in time, first in right" rule with the "time" computed as the *earlier* of (1) the date on which a financing statement is filed, or (2) the date of perfection. That is, each secured party gets its "better date" (the earlier date) in determining priority in relation to other perfected secured creditors. Note that if one security interest is perfected and another is not, the perfected secured party has priority under §9–322(a)(2).

Security Interests Versus Liens Arising by Operation of Law. Under state common law or statute, persons who regularly repair or improve goods obtain a possessory lien upon the goods (an "artisan's lien") to secure payment for labor or material charges. The priority between such a possessory lien and a prior security interest in the goods is governed by §9–333. The operation of §9–333 is explained and illustrated in the following case.

National Bank of Joliet v. Bergeron Cadillac, Inc.
361 N.E.2d 1116 (Ill. 1977)

In February 1973, plaintiff National Bank of Joliet loaned Gladys Schmidt $4,120 to purchase an automobile. The bank took and perfected a security interest in the automobile. In August 1973, defendant Bergeron Cadillac, Inc. (Bergeron) performed repairs costing approximately $2,000 on the automobile. When Schmidt failed to pay for the repairs, Bergeron retained possession of the car. Under Illinois law, a common law lien is created when a repairman retains possession of a vehicle to secure payment for repairs performed on the vehicle.

When Schmidt defaulted in paying the loan, the bank sued Bergeron demanding delivery of the car. Bergeron alleged that its common law lien had priority over the bank's security interest. Both the trial and appellate courts ruled in favor of Bergeron. The bank appealed.

Ward, Chief Justice

. . . The plain language of [§9–310, Revised §9–333] gives the lien of persons furnishing services or materi-als upon goods in their possession priority over a perfected security interest unless the lien is created by statute and the statute expressly provides otherwise.

The comment of Anderson (Anderson, Uniform Commercial Code) is:

Such a lien is, basically, the artisan's lien of the common law. Whether such a lien is based upon decision or statute law, Code [§9–310, Revised §9–333] gives it priority, with one exception, over a pre-existing security interest in the goods. . . .

The single exception relates to a lien created by statute; such a lien does not have such priority if the statute expressly provides otherwise. Accordingly, the lien has priority when it is based upon the common law or deci-sion, or when it is based upon a statute which is silent as to priorities or which gives the lien priority. The lien is subor-dinated to the security interest only when the lien statute expressly so declares. 4 Anderson, Uniform Commercial Code sec. 9–310, at 341–42 (2d ed. 1971). . . .

The artisan's possessory lien of the common law is recognized in Illinois. . . .

As the defendant had a common law possessory lien for services and materials in connection with the repairs it made, its lien takes priority over the plaintiff's earlier perfected security interest under the provisions of [§9–310, Revised §9–333]. . . .

[Judgment affirmed.]

The Floating Lien Priority Rules

Commercial financing arrangements (whereby a mer-chant uses its business assets—such as inventory, equip-ment, accounts receivable, or chattel paper—as collateral on a loan or other obligation) are the primary concern of Article 9. If the business debtor encounters financial diffi-culty or bankruptcy, these arrangements present a myriad of priority problems. These problems are complicated by the "floating lien" often used in inventory and accounts financing and the need for determining priority not only in the original collateral, but also in the "proceeds" of its sale or exchange. The following material explains how Article 9 resolves the problems presented by common commer-cial financing arrangements.

After-Acquired Property Clauses

Although inventory often serves as collateral in business financing arrangements, its use presents an obvious problem: inventory is sold to third parties in the ordinary course of the debtor's business to generate funds to repay the loan secured by the inventory, and to purchase additional inventory. Because a merchant's inventory is constantly changing, an inventory financier usually desires a security interest not only in the original inventory, but also in additional inventory later acquired by the debtor. To accomplish this result, the parties include an **after-acquired property clause** in the security agreement. Such clauses are expressly validated in §9–204(a), which states that "a security agreement may create or provide for a security interest in after-acquired collateral." The after-acquired property clause creates a **floating lien**, or a **floating charge.** That is, the lien "floats" over the debtor's ever-changing stock, covering whatever inventory is found there. Inventory financing secured by after-acquired inventory is often referred to as **floor planning.**

Under §9–204(c), a security agreement also may provide that existing collateral will secure additional advances of money from the secured party. In addition, although the UCC generally[5] validates the floating lien in commercial financing arrangements, the lien's use in consumer lending is severely restricted. Under §9–204(b)(1), after-acquired consumer goods may be used to provide additional security only if the debtor acquires them within ten days after the secured party gives value. Of course, in the commercial lending context, collateral subject to the floating lien is commonly acquired months or even years after the original agreement.

Most Article 9 priority provisions are designed to resolve systematically the various conflicts created by the inventory floating lien. The following material examines the major Code provisions that resolve the priority disputes created when a bank or other lender loans money to a debtor to finance the debtor's inventory and takes a security interest in that inventory, both currently existing and after-acquired.

At issue in the following case was whether a security agreement created a security interest in after-acquired collateral.

---

[5]A security interest may not be created in after-acquired commercial tort claims. UCC §9–204(b)(2).

In re Filtercorp, Inc.
163 F.3d 570 (9th Cir. 1998)

On June 30, 1992, Filtercorp, Inc., a Washington corporation, signed a promissory note payable to Henry Paulman that stated in part: "This note is secured by . . . the accounts receivable and inventory of Filtercorp. (See UCC-1 filing and attached inventory listing.)" No inventory list was attached to the note. Paulman perfected his security interest by filing a UCC-1 financing statement that identified the collateral as "(1) accounts receivable and (2) materials inventory." In February 1995, Gateway Venture Lenders loaned Filtercorp $355,000 and Filtercorp granted it a security interest in all of Filtercorp's assets, including after-acquired property. In November 1995, Filtercorp filed for Chapter 11 bankruptcy. Both Paulman and Gateway Venture Lenders claimed a priority interest in Filtercorp's accounts receivable and inventory. The bankruptcy court ruled that Gateway Venture Lenders' security interest took priority because Filtercorp had not expressly granted Paulman a security interest in accounts receivable and inventory acquired by Filtercorp after Paulman's loan. The Ninth Circuit Bankruptcy Appellate Panel affirmed and Paulman appealed.

Schwarzer, Senior District Judge

. . . Whether a security agreement creates a lien on particular assets is a question of state law. . . . Because no reported decisions of Washington courts or federal courts interpreting Washington law have answered the question whether a security agreement that grants an interest in "inventory" or "accounts receivable," without more, extends to after-acquired property, we must determine how Washington's highest court would resolve the issue. . . .

Courts disagree over what terms are required in a security agreement to cover after-acquired inventory and accounts receivable. A minority of jurisdictions require express language evidencing the parties' intent to cover after-acquired inventory or accounts receivable. . . . These courts view the Uniform Commercial Code . . . as contemplating express after-acquired property clauses. They reason that it is "neither onerous nor unreasonable to require a security agreement to make clear its intended collateral." [*In re Middle Atlantic Stud Welding Co.*, 503 F.2d 1133, 1136 (3d. Cir. 1974).] To do so simplifies the interpretation of security agreements and provides more precise notice to third parties of the extent of a perfected security interest in the debtor's property. . . . In these jurisdictions, a grant of a security interest in "inventory" or "accounts receivable," without more, is insufficient to include after-acquired property. . . .

However, we find more persuasive the contrary position, adopted by the majority of jurisdictions, that a security interest in inventory or accounts receivable presumptively includes an interest in after-acquired inventory or accounts receivable, respectively. . . . The rationale for this position rests on the unique nature of inventory and accounts receivable as "cyclically depleted and replenished assets." [*Stoumbos v. Kilimnik,* 988 F.2d 949, 956 (9th Cir. 1993).] . . . Because inventory and accounts receivable are constantly turning over, "no creditor could reasonably agree to be secured by an asset that would vanish in a short time in the normal course of business." *Stoumbos,* 988 F.2d at 955. . . . Essentially, a floating lien on inventory and accounts receivable is presumed because the collateral is viewed in aggregate as a shifting body of assets. . . .

[T]he majority of courts and commentators reason that the presumption of a floating lien on inventory and accounts receivable is not created by particular language but rather springs from an appreciation of the cyclical nature of the collateral itself. . . . The presumption that a grant of a security interest in inventory or accounts receivable includes after-acquired property is of course rebuttable. For example, the presumption would be overcome where the security agreement language itself manifests an intent to limit the collateral to specific identified property, where a party presents clear evidence of contemporaneous intent to limit the collateral, or where the debtor can demonstrate that it was engaged in a type of business where the named collateral, whether inventory or receivables, does not regularly turn over so that the rationale for the presumption does not apply. . . .

We conclude that were the issue to come before the Washington Supreme Court, it would hold that after-acquired collateral is presumptively covered by a security agreement referencing "inventory" or "accounts receivable." . . .

Applying the foregoing analysis to the security agreement between Paulman and Filtercorp, we reach different results with respect to accounts receivable and inventory. The note (which serves as the security agreement) states that it was secured by "the accounts receivable and inventory of Filtercorp (see UCC-1 filing and attached inventory listing.)." While the presumption that after-acquired property is included stands unrebutted as to accounts receivable, it is rebutted for inventory by the reference to the attached inventory listing.

Under the approach we adopt, the reference to "accounts receivable" presumptively includes after-acquired accounts receivable. . . . That security interest was perfected when Paulman filed a UCC-1 financing statement before other creditors and before Filtercorp filed for bankruptcy.

With respect to the security interest in inventory, the note referenced an "attached inventory listing" which, however, was never attached to either the note or the financing statement. . . . When, as in this case, a security interest in inventory is described by reference to a list, it suggests an intent to limit the collateral rather than cover inventory as a floating mass including after-acquired inventory. . . . Here, the Paulman-Filtercorp note referenced an inventory listing, which rebuts the presumption that after-acquired inventory is attached, and failed to demonstrate any particular intent to cover after-acquired inventory. The note's ambiguity regarding the security interest in inventory must be construed against Paulman, the drafter of the note. . . . We conclude that Paulman does not have a security interest in after-acquired inventory of Filtercorp. . . . Because Paulman has no interest in after-acquired inventory and the bankruptcy estate does not include any original inventory or assets traceable to original inventory, he cannot recover from the bankruptcy estate by reason of his security interest in Filtercorp's inventory. . . .

Accordingly, we reverse the summary judgment with respect to Paulman's lien on accounts receivable, including after-acquired accounts receivable, of Filtercorp, and affirm with respect to his lien on inventory. . . .

[Judgment affirmed in part, reversed in part, and remanded.]

Introduction to Proceeds

Under §9–102(a)(64), **proceeds** generally include whatever is acquired upon the sale, lease, license, exchange, collection or other disposition of collateral or proceeds. Money, checks, and deposit accounts are "cash proceeds." All others are "noncash proceeds." Under §9–315(a), a security interest continues in (1) collateral notwithstanding a sale, exchange, or other disposition (unless otherwise provided in Article 9 or unless the disposition of the collateral was authorized by the secured party), and (2) any identifiable proceeds of the collateral.

In the inventory financing case, under §§9–320(a) or 9–315(a), the buyer in the ordinary course of business defeats the secured party's right in the collateral—the inventory. Therefore, after the sale, the secured party's interest extends only to the *proceeds* of the sale of the inventory. Under §9–203(f), the secured party automatically obtains a right to proceeds whether or not the parties include a specific provision covering proceeds in the security agreement.

Section 9–315(c) states that the secured party has a *continuously perfected* security interest in the proceeds if the interest in the original collateral was perfected. That is, the secured party need take no additional action to perfect this interest. Nevertheless, the secured party's perfected interest in proceeds often is limited in duration. Under §9–315(d), a security interest in proceeds becomes unperfected 20 days after receipt of the proceeds by the debtor unless (1) a filed financing statement covers the original collateral (here inventory) and the proceeds are collateral in which a security interest may be perfected by filing in the office or offices where the financing statement covering the inventory has been filed, or (2) the proceeds are identifiable cash proceeds, or (3) the security interest in the proceeds is separately perfected within the 20 day period.

Although a security interest in inventory is cut off when the debtor sells it to a buyer in the ordinary course of business and, as discussed below, a perfected interest in the proceeds often provides limited protection, a floating lien is nevertheless valuable to a secured party. The debtor ultimately converts the proceeds of the sale of the inventory to cash, which it then uses to purchase more *inventory* subject to the secured party's floating lien. This process is known as the recoupment cycle. At some point in the **recoupment cycle,** the debtor uses some of the money to pay its salary, overhead, and other fixed expenses. This process is called **extraction.** What remains of the money is used to purchase additional inventory, which then becomes subject to the secured party's security interest. The secured party protects its security interest by making periodic surprise counts of the inventory. If the inventory level remains at an acceptable level, the secured party is assured that there has not been excessive extraction, either by fraudulent conduct or by the debtor's poor business practices. A significant reduction in the inventory level alerts the

secured party to potentially excessive extraction of cash from the proceeds. The secured party can then take steps to determine the reason for the excessive extraction, enforce its security interest against the collateral, or accelerate the debt. In most cases, the various remedies available to the secured party are stated explicitly in the security agreement.

The following material examines the common priority problems arising when a debtor whose property is subject to a floating lien encounters financial difficulty. The rules are most easily understood by assuming that the debtor is in bankruptcy, possessing on the date of bankruptcy specific assets including inventory and proceeds of the sale of inventory in various forms. Various creditors, including the trustee in bankruptcy, seek to use these limited assets to satisfy their unpaid claims. The secured party holding a floating lien is protected against such claims in two ways. First, the normal operation of the recoupment cycle provides a continuing stock of inventory subject to the security interest. Second, some protection is provided in the proceeds themselves. Proceeds generated by the sale of inventory fall into six general categories: (1) cash, (2) instruments, (3) accounts receivable, (4) chattel paper, (5) trade-ins, and (6) barter.

Figure 32.1 illustrates the floating lien situation, the recoupment cycle, and the types of proceeds that may be generated by the sale of inventory. The extent of the secured party's protection in these proceeds is covered below.

Specific Proceeds Priority Rules

Cash. If a buyer in the ordinary course of business pays cash for the inventory, the security interest in cash proceeds is automatically perfected, but only for 20 days. Unless the cash is identifiable, as discussed below, the interest becomes unperfected thereafter. The reason is that filing, which is the means of perfection for the inventory, is an inappropriate means of perfection for cash, for which the only means of perfection is possession. While the proceeds remain in a cash state, the secured party enjoys very limited protection in them. Taking possession of cash is not normally a viable alternative because cash is necessary for the continued operation of the business. Further, even during the 20 day automatic perfection period, the security interest is cut off if the cash proceeds are transferred to a third party or commingled with other cash generated by the business.

Figure 32.1   The Inventory Floating Lien

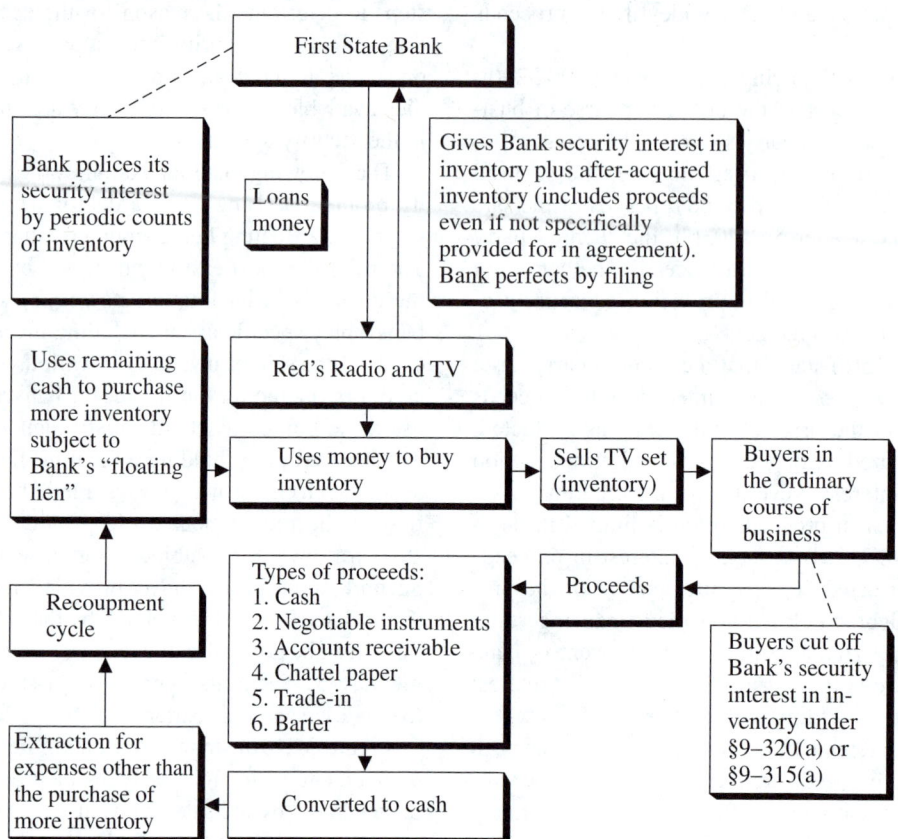

A prudent secured lender may obtain significant protection by including a term in the security agreement requiring the debtor promptly to deposit all cash proceeds from the sale of the collateral in a separate bank account clearly identified as containing only proceeds. As previously noted, if the security interest in the original inventory was perfected, a security interest in identifiable cash proceeds remains perfected indefinitely.

Instruments. Frequently buyers give negotiable instruments, usually checks, in exchange for the inventory. Even though the secured party's interest is continuously perfected by filing, the secured party has somewhat limited protection in the instruments. For example, the secured party is *not* protected against the transfer of the instrument to a holder in due course (under §9–331), and once the instrument is converted

to cash or deposited, the problems of commingling and identification discussed above arise.

Accounts Receivable. Merchants often extend credit to their customers by selling goods on open account. A secured party holding a floating lien in the inventory sold enjoys substantial protection in such accounts receivable proceeds, because filing a financing statement is the only means of perfection with respect to accounts. Therefore, the bank's original financing statement relating to the inventory gives the bank a continuously perfected security interest in the accounts receivable that are proceeds. As a result, the bank defeats a claim to the accounts asserted by the debtor's trustee in bankruptcy. Other priority disputes in the accounts may, however, arise. For example, assume that First Bank loans money to Carl's Appliances. To secure repayment, First Bank takes a security interest in Carl's present and after-acquired inventory including proceeds and files a financing statement covering the transaction on June 1. Subsequently, Carl's finds itself short of cash and approaches Second Bank for a loan. Second Bank loans the money, taking a security interest in Carl's accounts receivable generated by the sale of its inventory. Second Bank files a financing statement on October 1 to perfect its interest in the accounts. Subsequently, Carl's defaults on both loans and both First Bank and Second Bank claim an interest in the accounts. Because this situation is not explicitly addressed in other Article 9 provisions, §9–322(a)(1), the general rule governing priority between two perfected secured parties, applies. In determining priority, this rule gives each secured party the earlier of two dates: its date of filing or the date it perfected its security interest. Note that §9–322(b)(1) provides that in applying §9–322(a)(1), the date of filing or perfection as to the collateral is also the date of filing or perfection as to the proceeds. In the above example, First Bank both perfected and filed on June 1; Second Bank both perfected and filed on October 1. First Bank therefore prevails in the contest over the accounts receivable. Second Bank has little room to complain in this case because a simple check of the public records before loaning money to Carl's would have uncovered First Bank's financing statement indicating a security interest in the accounts.

This rule appears to favor the inventory financier, who often has been financing the debtor's inventory over a long period of time resulting in a much earlier filing date. Note, however, that the debtor often undertakes accounts and inventory financing separately. Thus, the earlier filing may very well belong to a financial institution that has been financing the merchant solely on the basis of accounts claiming no interest in the underlying inventory. In this case, the original accounts financier would have priority in the accounts over a subsequent inventory financier claiming the accounts as proceeds.

Chattel Paper. Section §9–330(a) resolves a common priority problem relating to chattel paper as proceeds of the sale of inventory subject to a security interest. The rule provides that a purchaser of chattel paper, who in good faith gives new value and takes possession of it in the ordinary course of the purchaser's business, has priority over a security interest in the chattel paper that is claimed merely as *proceeds of the sale of inventory* subject to a security interest, unless the paper indicates that it has been assigned to a person other than the purchaser. As explained in Official Comment 5 to §9–330:

> Subsection (a) recognizes the common practice of placing a "legend" on chattel paper to indicate that it has been assigned. This approach, under which the chattel paper purchaser who gives new value in ordinary course can rely on possession of unlegended, tangible chattel paper without any concern for other facts that it may know, comports with the expectations of both inventory and chattel paper financers.

To illustrate the operation of this rule, assume as before that First Bank loans money to Carl's Appliances and acquires a floating lien including proceeds in Carl's inventory, perfected by filing. Carl's sells microwave ovens on credit to customers using a conditional sales contract giving Carl's a security interest in the goods sold. Carl's, in need of cash, then sells the conditional sales contracts to Discounters, a finance company. Discounters pays cash (gives value) and takes possession of the paper.

If Carl's subsequently defaults upon its loan, First Bank may attempt to claim an interest in the chattel paper in Discounter's hands as proceeds of the sale of inventory subject to its security interest. In this case, Discounters' claim to the paper as a purchaser will prevail over the bank's claim to the paper as proceeds, unless the paper contains a legend indicating that it has been assigned to First Bank. Therefore, persons in the business of buying chattel paper are protected without examining the public record, a result consistent with ordinary business expectations. This rule gives the debtor a ready market for its paper, and therefore indirectly benefits a secured party holding a floating lien. That is, §9–330(a) makes it easier for the debtor (Carl's) to convert the proceeds to cash that can be used to pay off the loan or buy more inventory subject to the bank's interest.

It is important to note the distinction between §9–330(a) and §9–330(b). The secured party enjoys greater protection in §9–330(b)—the purchaser prevails only if it takes without knowledge that the purchase violates the rights of the secured party—because in that situation, the chattel paper in question *is* the underlying collateral securing the debt. The paper is left in the debtor's possession primarily to facilitate collection. In §9–330(a), however, the chattel paper is claimed merely as proceeds of the sale of inventory subject to a security interest. The inventory, not the paper, provides the primary security in this case.

Trade-In. Frequently, part of the consideration for the sale of inventory will be a trade-in. For example, a buyer in the ordinary course of business may purchase a new television set and pay for it partly in cash and partly with a trade-in of the old set. The old set is proceeds of the sale of inventory subject to a security interest. The trade-in item then becomes inventory in the debtor's hands subject to the bank's security interest.

Barter. Occasionally, part of the consideration for the sale of inventory is a bartered item. For example, assume Fred's Video sells a television camera to a buyer, and the buyer pays for the item by transferring a used car to Fred's Video, which Fred's plans to use in its business. In this case, the secured party must assure itself that its filing with respect to the inventory is a proper means of perfection with respect to the bartered item. In the above example, the car is now equipment in the hands of Fred's. Filing is an appropriate means of perfecting an interest in equipment. In this example, however, because the bartered item has a title document, the proper means of perfection is to note the security interest on the title document, which the secured party should do. Further, the secured party should assure itself that it has filed its financing statement in the proper office for the type of property that the bartered item represents.

Conflicting Security Interests in the Same Collateral

The following material discusses two important rules governing priority between the holder of the floating lien in inventory or equipment and other creditors holding a conflicting security interest in the same collateral.

Purchase Money Security Interests in Inventory— §9–324(b). The secured party polices the floating lien arrangement by periodically counting the debtor's inventory. This policing effort can be defeated by a dishonest debtor who purchases additional inventory, not for cash, but on credit from a supplier, giving the supplier a purchase money security interest in the inventory sold. In this manner, when the original secured party counts the inventory, the level is high. Unknown to the

secured party, however, some or all of the inventory is subject to a security interest of the purchase money supplier. If the debtor subsequently goes bankrupt or absconds, a priority contest arises between the bank's floating lien on after-acquired inventory and the supplier's purchase money security interest in that inventory.

Section §9–324(b) resolves this conflict as follows. The purchase money supplier of the inventory will prevail over the bank's after-acquired clause if the supplier (1) perfects its interest by filing a financing statement covering the inventory, *and* (2) gives written notice to the prior secured party that it has or expects to acquire a purchase money security interest in the debtor's inventory. Both the perfection and the notice must occur *before* the debtor receives possession of the inventory from the supplier. Note that the notice to the prior party is, like a financing statement, valid for five years. Thus, once notice is given, the supplier can continue to sell on a purchase money basis for five years and defeat any claim to the inventory under the prior secured party's after-acquired property clause.

To illustrate, assume that First Bank loans money to Red's Radio and acquires a floating lien in Red's inventory, which is perfected by filing. Rather than pumping the proceeds of the sale of inventory back into the business, Red instead pockets the money. To keep the inventory level high and avoid alerting First Bank of any problem, Red approaches Ace Electronics, a manufacturer of radios, and purchases radios on credit, giving Ace a purchase money security interest in the radios to secure the payment of the purchase price. As a result, when First Bank counts the inventory, the level remains high, in spite of Red's excessive extraction.

When the underlying loans to Ace and First Bank are not repaid, both parties claim an interest in Red's inventory (Ace on the basis of its purchase money security interest and First Bank on the basis of its after-acquired clause). In this context First Bank will win unless Ace both perfects its interest by filing (note that the bank's interest is already perfected) and notifies the bank in writing before it delivers the inventory to Red's.

The foregoing rule benefits all parties to the transaction. The bank holding the floating lien enjoys a priority in the inventory shipped on a purchase money basis unless the supplier meets the requirements outlined above. Once notified of its debtor's attempt to buy inventory on credit, it can proceed to ascertain the reason for excessive extraction. The purchase money inventory supplier who meets the §9–324(b) requirements obtains a priority over a *prior perfected* security interest in inventory. Section 9–324(b) also allows the debtor to give a purchase money supplier a security interest in the inventory, which enjoys a priority over a prior secured lender. Without such a rule an honest debtor may be unable to obtain additional credit if a prior secured lender insists upon retaining a floating lien on the debtor's inventory but refuses to advance additional money.

A purchase money supplier of inventory who complies with §9–324(b) achieves priority only in the inventory and identifiable cash proceeds of its sale. Thus, a prior secured party with a perfected security interest in accounts (whether or not related to inventory financing) would defeat the purchase money inventory supplier's claim to the accounts as proceeds of the sale of the inventory it delivered.

Consignments. The consignment is a device often used in inventory financing, and which has important secured transactions implications. A **consignment** may be defined succinctly as a bailment[6] for sale. In a consignment, the owner of the goods (the "consignor"), who retains title, delivers possession of them to the "consignee." The consignee, who commonly is a merchant dealing in goods of the kind, then attempts to sell the consigned goods. Consignments may be either (1) "intended as security" or (2) "true." In a **consignment intended as security,** the bailee-consignee assumes initial responsibility for the purchase price of the goods, whether or not he or she sells or otherwise disposes of them. This type of consignment is functionally equivalent to the conditional sale discussed above. That is, a debtor-creditor relationship exists between the parties with a reservation of title in the seller to secure payment of the purchase price of goods in the consignee's possession. Because the transaction is intended to create a security interest in personal property, it is, of course, governed by Article 9.

In contrast, a **true consignment** is a principal-agent relationship. The consignee is merely the consignor's agent for the purpose of selling the consigned goods to third parties. In a true consignment, the title remains in the consignor, but the consignee does not undertake an absolute obligation to pay for them upon receipt of the goods. That is, the true consignee is not a buyer, but merely an agent, who may return unsold goods. Upon a sale of consigned goods, title moves from the consignor

to the purchaser. The consignee becomes liable to pay for them only upon a sale, appropriation to his own use, or violation of the agency contract.

Either type of consignment creates a "secret lien" against other creditors of the consignee. In other words, consigned goods in the possession of and apparently owned by the consignee are likely to mislead other creditors concerning the consignee's financial position. For this reason, many disputes have arisen between consignors and the consignee's creditors upon insolvency of the consignee.

The Code effectively abolishes the "secret lien" aspect of a consignment by treating virtually[7] all consignments, whether intended for security or not, as secured transactions governed by Article 9. For example, §9–109(a)(4) provides that Article 9 applies to consignments, and §1–201(b)(35) defines "security interest" to include "any interest of a consignor" in the goods. Further, §9–103(d) provides that the "security interest of a consignor in goods that are the subject of a consignment is a purchase money security interest in inventory." Thus, if the consignee is financing its inventory under a perfected floating lien prior to the consignment, the consignor prevails over the bank's after-acquired inventory clause only by complying with the notice and filing requirements of §9–324(b), discussed above.

Noninventory Purchase Money Security Interests— §9–324(a). Section 9–324(a) provides a rule governing purchase money security interests in collateral other than inventory. In this situation, a purchase money supplier—usually of equipment—has priority over a prior secured party's after-acquired clause if the purchase money security interest is perfected at the time the debtor receives possession of the collateral, or within 20 days thereafter. This provision differs in three important respects from the inventory rule previously discussed. First, a 20-day grace period for perfection is provided. This approach is consistent with the 20-day period generally applicable to purchase money security interests. Second, no notice to the prior secured party is required. Third, a purchase money equipment supplier who complies with §9–324(a) enjoys a priority over prior secured parties both in the equipment and all proceeds of its sale, including accounts. The reason for this result is that equipment, unlike inventory, is not ordinarily resold resulting in proceeds.

---

[6]Bailments are discussed in detail in Chapter 35.

[7]Section 9–102(a)(20)(B) excludes deliveries on consignment valued at less than $1,000.

To illustrate the operation of §9–324(a), assume Rachel's Discount store borrows money from First Bank, giving the bank a security interest in its equipment (for example, counters, repair equipment, delivery, and service trucks) plus after-acquired equipment. First Bank perfects its interest by filing. Rachel's buys a photocopier on credit for use in its business from Alpha Business Supply, which takes a purchase money security interest to secure the price. If Rachel's defaults on all loans, Alpha will have priority in the photocopier over the bank proceeding under its after-acquired equipment clause if Alpha's interest is perfected (by filing) at the time Rachel's receives possession of the equipment *or* within 20 days thereafter. Alpha is not required to notify First Bank.

Priorities in Fixtures — §9–334

Security interests in real property (mortgages) are governed by state law outside the UCC. A public "recording" system similar to, but separate from, Article 9's filing system exists for real property interests including mortgages. That is, persons holding security interests in real property (mortgagees) provide public notice of their interest by recording it in a public office, usually the County Recorder of Deeds.[8]

Although non-Code law generally determines real estate priorities, Article 9 does address one important security issue affecting real property—the priority between personal property security interests in fixtures and persons holding an interest in the land to which the fixture is attached. A fixture is an item of personal property that has become so closely related to particular real estate that it is treated in law as part of the land. The following discussion assumes that the disputed property has become a fixture under the state property law principles discussed in Chapter 34.

Fixture priorities, governed by §9–334, require an initial understanding of the "fixture filing" concept. A fixture filing may be required to provide protection against certain real estate interests. A secured party makes a **fixture filing** by filing a financing statement in the office where a mortgage on the underlying real estate would be recorded covering goods that are or are to become fixtures. Under §9–502(b), the financing statement in this case must state that it covers fixtures,

recite that it is to be filed for record in the real estate records, and contain a description of the real estate. If the debtor is not the owner of the land (for example, a lessee), the record owner's name also must be included.

Note that a fixture filing, when required, protects the secured party against claims of persons who hold an interest in the *real property* and claim the fixture as part of that property. An ordinary filing that complies with §9–301 protects the secured party against everyone else. Because a fixture filing is filed for record and indexed, it assures that any person examining the real estate records will discover the secured party's interest.

Given this background, three common priority disputes governed by §9–334 are illustrated below using the following example. Assume Tom owns a house. The house needs a new furnace, but Tom is short of cash. Accordingly, he approaches Joe's Plumbing and Heating, which agrees to install a new furnace on credit, taking a security interest in the furnace to secure payment of the purchase price. In the following discussion Joe's will be referred to as the "fixture financier."

Fixture Financier Versus Lien Creditor. Assume Tom fails to pay off the loan and subsequently goes bankrupt. Tom's trustee in bankruptcy (a lien creditor) claims the furnace for the benefit of all creditors. Under §9–334(e)(3), a fixture financier prevails over any person becoming a lien creditor after the security interest is perfected by any method permitted by Article 9—for example, an ordinary filing or automatic perfection of a purchase money security interest in consumer goods. Fixture filing is not required to defeat a lien creditor, because lien creditors, such as judgment creditors and the trustee in bankruptcy, do not extend credit in reliance upon the real estate records. Thus, Joe's would prevail over Tom's bankruptcy trustee if his interest is perfected by any method before the bankruptcy petition is filed.

Fixture Financier Versus Mortgagee. Assume that prior to Joe's installation of the furnace Tom had borrowed money to buy the house from First Bank. Tom gave First Bank a mortgage on the house to secure repayment, which First Bank properly recorded. After installation of the furnace, Tom borrowed additional funds from Second Bank, giving Second Bank a mortgage on the house, which the bank recorded. If Tom later defaults on all three loans, Section 9–334 determines who has the benefit of the furnace. It adopts

---

[8]Mortgages and the operation of the real property recording system are discussed in Chapter 37.

two different rules, one applicable to prior real estate interests (here First Bank) and the other applicable to subsequent real estate interests (here Second Bank). To defeat a preexisting real estate interest, four requirements, stated in §9–334(d), must be met: (1) the security interest in fixtures must be a purchase money security interest, (2) the interest must be perfected by fixture filing, (3) the filing must be made before the goods become fixtures or within 20 days thereafter, and (4) the debtor must have a record interest in or be in possession of the real estate. In the above example, therefore, Joe's will prevail over First Bank if it made a fixture filing covering the furnace within 20 days after it was installed in Tom's house. This rule, which gives the fixture financier priority over a prior real estate interest, promotes the availability of short-term credit for modernization and improvement of the real estate. These improvements, once paid for, ultimately benefit the long-term real estate lenders.

Concerning subsequent real estate interests, §9–334(e)(1) provides that the first secured party to file or record prevails. The fixture financier must perfect by fixture filing. In the above example, therefore, Joe's will prevail against Second Bank if it perfects by fixture filing before Second Bank records its mortgage.[9]

Fixture Financier Versus Buyer of Real Estate. The priority between the fixture financier and a subsequent buyer of the real estate from the debtor is governed by the general "first to file or record" rule explained above. Thus, Joe's would prevail against a buyer of the house in which the furnace is installed if its security interest is perfected by fixture filing before the buyer recorded his deed.

Special Topics

Field Warehousing

A field warehouse is a security device commonly used in inventory financing. Field warehousing uses warehouse receipts covering inventory to provide a secured lender with effective control over disposition of the debtor's inventory.

---

[9]The law does not provide a 20-day grace period for filing in this case. Whoever records or files first wins. The 20-day period provides protection only against *prior* real estate interests.

To illustrate warehouse receipts financing, assume that Doaks Novelties, Inc., a manufacturer of Christmas decorations, needs working capital to finance its operations during the off-season summer months. Doaks therefore approaches First Bank for a loan, proposing to use its large inventory of Christmas lights as collateral. First Bank agrees, but desires complete control over the inventory but does not, of course, want to take possession. Doaks therefore transports the inventory to Gray's Terminal Storage, Inc., a commercial warehouse. Gray's issues a negotiable warehouse receipt to Doaks covering the inventory, which Doaks then pledges to the bank as collateral on the loan. First Bank is protected because it now possesses the warehouse receipt and Gray's will not surrender the inventory without it.

Although this arrangement provides significant protection to the secured party, it has distinct disadvantages for the debtor. For example, the debtor incurs substantial time and expense in transporting inventory to and from the warehouse and must pay storage charges. Additionally, the inventory is not immediately available to the debtor when needed for sale or to finish work on it. These problems are resolved by using a field warehouse arrangement. Simply stated, **field warehousing** involves the creation of a warehouse on the debtor's premises—the "field" warehouse—into which inventory is placed. Warehouse receipts are issued from this warehouse, which are then used by the debtor as collateral on the loan.

To create a field warehouse the debtor must first obtain a warehouseman, who must be independent of the debtor. Several commercial warehouse companies specialize in field warehouse arrangements. Space on the debtor's property is then selected as the site for the warehouse, and leased to the warehouse company, usually at a nominal rent. The warehouse company then segregates the leased area by setting up fences, locks, and gates to establish control over the property within the field warehouse, and hires a warehouse manager. The manager, who is covered by a fidelity bond and is usually an employee of the debtor, is authorized to issue warehouse receipts and is instructed when to allow inventory out of the warehouse.

Once established, the debtor stores inventory in the field warehouse and receives warehouse receipts, which are used as collateral to secure a loan. The bank may police the stored inventory loosely or strictly depending upon its arrangement with the debtor. Although the warehouse receipts may be negotiable, the parties commonly use nonnegotiable receipts because they do not have to be obtained from the bank and surrendered to the warehouseman each time inventory is removed from the warehouse. Rather, the lender gives the warehouse company written instructions outlining the circumstances under which inventory is to be released.

Courts often have invalidated field warehousing arrangements either because the warehouseman was not independent of the debtor or had not established actual and exclusive control over the stored inventory. In many of these cases, the field warehouse lender had perfected its security interest only in the now invalid documents (for example, by taking possession of negotiable warehouse receipts). As a result, the lender was left with an unperfected security interest in the underlying inventory. For this reason, a field warehouse should be used as a policing device, not an independent method of creating and perfecting a security interest in the stored inventory. To be protected against other creditors claiming an interest in the stored inventory if the field warehouse is ruled invalid, the secured party always should obtain a written security agreement covering the inventory and perfect its interest in that inventory by filing a financing statement.

Security Interests as Preferences in Bankruptcy

Because a perfected secured party enjoys a preferred position in collateral upon the debtor's bankruptcy, a security interest perfected shortly before bankruptcy to secure an old debt may effectively prefer the secured creditor over other creditors of the debtor. That is, if the interest is recognized in bankruptcy, the secured creditor is preferred in the same manner as if the debtor had sold the underlying property and then paid the creditor directly.

To prevent this result, the federal Bankruptcy Code provides that the creation of a security interest in the debtor's property, like an outright transfer of that property, may constitute a voidable preference. Specifically, the trustee in bankruptcy may avoid security interests that secure antecedent debts and that are perfected or recorded within 90 days (or between 90 days and one year if the secured creditor is an insider) prior to bankruptcy. That is, for security interests, the date of the transfer (date 2 in basic preference analysis) is generally the date on which a mortgagee records its mortgage (if the security interest is a real property mortgage) or the date on which the secured party files a financing

statement (if the security interest is created in personal property governed by Article 9 of the UCC)[10]

Assume that on January 1, Alan, Bob, and Chris each ships $10,000 worth of goods to Donna on open account for use in her business. Donna makes no payment on these accounts during the next six months. On July 1, when Donna's only remaining assets are equipment worth $10,000 and $10,000 cash, she gives Alan a security interest in the equipment to secure his $10,000 debt. Alan promptly files a financing statement. On August 1, Donna declares bankruptcy. On these facts, Alan's security interest constitutes a preference. The date of the transfer (date 2) is July 1, the date of filing. The date of transfer (July 1) follows the date of the debt it secures (January 1) creating the essence of a preference—transfer to a creditor on account of an antecedent debt. The date of bankruptcy (August 1) follows the transfer (occurring on July 1) by less than 90 days resulting in a voidable preference.

To protect bona fide secured parties who delay, through inadvertence or otherwise, in perfecting their security interests, the Bankruptcy Code provides a thirty-day[11] "grace period" after the debt is created in which to file or record the security interest. If the interest is perfected by filing or recording within the thirty-day period, the date of transfer "relates back" to the date of the debt; thus, there is no transfer on account of an antecedent debt, and therefore no preference.[12] Assume that on June 1, Cathy loans $10,000 to Donald, secured by Donald's equipment. If Cathy files a financing statement within thirty days after June 1, her security interest may not be avoided as a preference. If, however, Cathy delays filing her financing statement until July 15, and Donald goes bankrupt within 90 days after July 15, the trustee in bankruptcy will be able to avoid Cathy's security interest as a preference. A prudent secured lender, therefore, whether in real or personal property, should always take steps to perfect its interest within thirty days after the debt is created to avoid potential preference attack.

When the trustee avoids an outright transfer as a preference, the property is recovered from the transferee and becomes property of the estate. When the trustee avoids a preferential security interest, the property simply enters the estate free of any lien. The

---

[10]11 U.S.C. §547(e)(1).

[11]A thirty-day grace period also applies to a purchase money security interest. 11 U.S.C. §547(c)(3).

[12]11 U.S.C. §547(e)(2).

preferred creditor, as in absolute transfers, then files a claim against the estate for the amount of the debt and receives the same distribution from the estate as other creditors of his class.

The "Floating Lien" as a Preference. Though it is an extremely useful financing tool, the "floating lien" in inventory discussed earlier in this chapter may operate unfairly to prefer its holder over other creditors if the debtor is allowed to build up its inventory shortly before bankruptcy. To prevent this result, the Bankruptcy Code provides[13] that a creditor holding a floating lien is subject to preference attack to the extent that it improves its position during the 90-day period preceding bankruptcy. This "improvement in position" test requires a determination of the creditor's position 90 days before the petition (up to one year in the case of an insider) and on the date the petition is filed. The creditor's "position" is computed by subtracting the value of the collateral from the amount of the debt, yielding the amount of unsecured debt. A creditor improves its position to the extent the amount of unsecured debt is reduced. Assume Dan, an appliance dealer, files for bankruptcy on June 1. On that date, Dan owes First Bank $85,000 secured by a perfected floating lien in his inventory, which is worth $70,000. Ninety days prior to bankruptcy, the outstanding loan was $100,000 secured by $50,000 in inventory. First Bank has improved its position during the 90 days preceding bankruptcy and has therefore received a voidable preference of $35,000 computed as follows:

	90 days prior to bankruptcy	Date of bankruptcy
Amount of debt	$100,000	$85,000
Amount of collateral	<50,000>	<70,000>
Amount of unsecured debt	$50,000	$15,000 = $35,000

In this case, therefore, the trustee in bankruptcy is able to avoid $35,000 of First Bank's $70,000 security interest in Don's inventory. Thus, the bank will file an $85,000 claim against the estate, $35,000 of which is secured by Don's inventory. Regarding the remaining $50,000, First Bank is a general creditor and will receive the same percentage on the dollar as other general creditors. Note that the bank is relegated to the same position it occupied 90 days before bankruptcy — $50,000 of its loan is not secured.

Summary

1.   Like much of debtor-creditor law, Article 9 is primarily concerned with resolving priority disputes among creditors competing for the limited assets of debtors who default. Analysis of the general rules of priority reveals that unperfected security interests have priority over general creditors, but are subordinate to most other third-party claimants to the collateral, including the debtor's trustee in bankruptcy. Perfected interests, on the other hand, defeat most third-party claims.

2.   The parties often conduct inventory financing by using a "floating lien," under which the secured party loans money, and to secure repayment takes a security interest in all the debtor's inventory, both currently existing and after-acquired. The UCC broadly validates such after-acquired property clauses and then systematically resolves the various priority disputes they create.

3.   When a merchant finances its inventory using a floating lien, the merchant's customers who buy the inventory, "buyers in the ordinary course of business," take the inventory free of the secured party's claim to it even though the security interest is perfected and the buyer knows of its existence. Although the secured party's claim to the inventory is thus extinguished upon sale, the security interest continues in the proceeds of sale, including cash, instruments, accounts receivable, chattel paper, trade-ins, or bartered items. Article 9 contains several provisions resolving disputes between the secured party and various third-party purchasers and creditors claiming an interest in these proceeds.

4.   Suppliers of inventory and equipment often sell on credit, taking a purchase money security interest in the goods sold. Article 9 allows the purchase money supplier of inventory to prevail in this case over a prior perfected floating lien in inventory provided it perfects its interest and notifies the prior secured party before delivering the inventory to the debtor. A similar rule applies to suppliers of inventory on consignment. The purchase money supplier of equipment prevails over a prior secured party merely by perfecting its interest within 20 days after the debtor receives possession of the collateral.

5.   Article 9 contains specialized provisions governing priority in fixtures. These provisions generally allow a creditor

---

[13]11 U.S.C. §547(c)(5).

holding a security interest in fixtures attached to real property to protect its interest against third-party purchasers or creditors asserting a claim to the collateral.

6. Field warehousing is a device using warehouse receipts to provide a secured lender with effective control over disposition of the debtor's inventory. In field warehousing, the debtor places inventory in a warehouse created on the debtor's premises—the "field" warehouse. Warehouse receipts issued from this warehouse are then used by the debtor as collateral on the loan.

7. Under bankruptcy law, a secured transaction may not be used as an indirect method to give one creditor a preference. The law allows the trustee in bankruptcy to avoid security interests in real or personal property that secure antecedent debts if those interests are perfected or recorded within the preference period. The law also prevents the holder of a "floating lien" from improving its position (reducing the amount of unsecured debt) within the preference period.

Key Terms

buyer in the ordinary course
  of business
after-acquired property clause
floating lien (floating charge)
floor planning
proceeds
recoupment cycle

extraction
consignment
consignment intended as
  security
true consignment
fixture filing
field warehousing

Questions and Problems

32.1 Shepler borrowed money for plant expansion from Myertown Bank and executed a security agreement. The bank filed a financing statement that covered all "present and future inventory." Shepler was a dealer in farm machinery. Moline entered into a contract with Shepler whereby Moline appointed Shepler its franchise dealer for Moline farm machinery. The franchise provided that title to the farm machinery would remain in Moline until the purchase price was paid in full. The agreement was not filed or recorded. Shepler is now bankrupt. At the time of the adjudication of bankruptcy, Shepler had $15,000 worth of inventory delivered to him by Moline in his possession.
(a) Did the bank's security interest attach to the inventory?
(b) Was the description of the collateral insufficient?
(c) Was the bank's security interest valid only insofar as it was limited to Shepler's currently existing inventory?
(d) Was the bank's security interest unperfected because only the financing statement was filed, rather than the security agreement?
(e) Did Moline's security interest attach to the inventory shipped by Moline?
(f) Does Moline have a purchase money security interest?
(g) Does the bank have a purchase money security interest?
(h) Does Moline have a perfected security interest?
(i) As between Moline and the bank, who will have the benefit of the $15,000 of inventory?

32.2 Franklin Novelties borrowed $25,000 from Commercial Bank secured by certain chattel paper in the possession of Franklin. The paper in question was purchased by Franklin from various retailers and was treated by Franklin as a short-term investment. The bank filed a financing statement covering the transaction. Franklin finances its inventory through First State Bank. Because its products are expensive, Franklin routinely accepts conditional installment sales contracts for the sale of inventory evidencing both an obligation to pay the purchase price and creating a security interest in the item sold. First State Bank has filed a financing statement covering the inventory. Franklin is now in financial difficulty. In an effort to generate cash, Franklin sold all of the paper in its possession (that is, both held for investment and arising from the sale of inventory) to Money, Inc., a finance company. Money paid cash and took possession of the paper with full knowledge of Commercial Bank's and First State Bank's security interest.
(a) Does First State's security interest extend to the contracts that were generated by sale of the inventory?
(b) May Commercial Bank recover the paper from Money, Inc. to satisfy its debt?
(c) May First State Bank recover the paper from Money, Inc. to satisfy its debt?

32.3 Shady Characters, Inc. is a dealer in masks and magic supplies. Shady borrowed $90,000 from Regional Bank on June 1 to finance a purchase of inventory. Regional Bank took a security interest in inventory plus after-acquired inventory as well as Shady's equipment, both current and after-acquired. Regional Bank immediately filed a financing statement covering the transaction. Shady maintains open accounts with many of its large customers. In an effort to generate more working capital, Shady borrowed $10,000 from Downstate Bank, using the accounts receivable as collateral to secure the loan. Downstate Bank immediately filed a financing statement on July 1. Shortly thereafter, Sam, owner of Shady, approached Monsters, Inc. and purchased $10,000 worth of masks on credit, giving Monsters a security interest in the masks to secure payment of the purchase price. Monsters made delivery on August 15 and filed a financing statement on August 16. On August 17, Sam then approached City Office Supply and purchased $10,000 worth of office equipment on credit giving City a security interest in the equipment to secure payment of the purchase price. City delivered on August 18 and filed a financing statement on August 30 covering the transaction. Shady, on October 1, was adjudicated a bankrupt. The trustee in bankruptcy now claims all inventory, accounts, and equipment to satisfy claims of general unsecured creditors, a sum in excess of $100,000. Assume Regional Bank's claim remains totally unpaid. Regional Bank asserts a security interest in all inventory and equipment on hand as well as the accounts receivable being used to secure the loan from Downstate Bank.
(a) As between Regional Bank and Downstate Bank, who has priority in the accounts? Explain, citing relevant Code sections.
(b) As between Regional Bank and Monsters, Inc., who has priority in the masks? Explain, citing relevant Code sections.

(c) As between Regional Bank and City Office Supply, who has priority in the equipment? Explain, citing relevant Code sections.

(d) Is Regional Bank's security interest valid against the trustee in bankruptcy? If so, in what collateral?

32.4 Donald purchased a 2.5-carat diamond ring from Mayor Jewelry Co. as an anniversary present for his wife, Lorraine. Donald signed a written contract, agreeing to pay for the ring in 48 monthly installments and granted Mayor a security interest in the ring. Donald took possession of the ring. The owner of Mayor Jewelry Co. advised the store manager to be certain that she perfected the security interest immediately. The store manager did not file a financing statement.

(a) The owner of Mayor Jewelry Co. hears a rumor that Donald is about to go bankrupt. Mayor's owner asks the store manager if she has perfected the security interest and she replies "Of course—there's nothing to worry about." Is she correct? Explain.

(b) Instead of giving the ring to his wife, Donald sells the ring for $10,000 to his friend Ronald, who retains it for his own use. Prior to purchasing the ring, Ronald asks Donald if the ring is free and clear of all liens and Donald replies, "Yes." One year later Donald declares bankruptcy still owing $7,500 to Mayor Jewelry Co. After Ronald refuses to give the ring to Mayor, Mayor sues Ronald. To whom should the court award possession of the ring? Explain. Would your answer be different if Mayor had filed a financing statement? Explain. (See UCC §9–320.)

(c) Instead of selling the ring to Ronald, Donald sells the ring to Acme Jewelers, a jewelry retailer. Donald declares bankruptcy still owing Mayor Jewelry Co. $7,500. Mayor sues Acme. To whom should the court award the ring? Explain. (See UCC §§9–315 and 9–320.)

(d) Instead of selling the ring, Donald gives it to his wife, Lorraine, as he had intended. Donald declares bankruptcy still owing Mayor $7,500. Mayor sues Lorraine. To whom should the court award possession of the ring?

(e) Instead of selling the ring or giving it to his wife, Donald uses the ring as collateral to borrow $10,000 from First National Bank. He signs a security agreement giving the bank a security interest in the ring. For safekeeping, the bank stores the ring in its vault. Donald declares bankruptcy. To whom should the court award the ring, Mayor Jewelry Co. or First National Bank? Would your answer be different if Mayor Jewelry Co. or First National Bank had filed a financing statement? (See UCC §9–322.)

32.5 A-1 Auto Sales, a retailer of new and used automobiles, has requested American State Bank to act as inventory financier. You are the bank's loan officer who has been assigned to handle the transaction. You have agreed to lend up to $100,000 to A-1 each month to purchase inventory and you also have agreed to allow A-1 to sell the inventory to its customers. To secure the loan, you require A-1 to grant American a security interest in all inventory it purchases with money obtained from American.

(a) How would you perfect the security interest? Explain and include in your explanation the exact description of the collateral that should be used in the financing statement.

(b) Describe the procedures you would use after making the loan to ensure that A-1 complies with the terms of your agreement.

(c) Assume that A-1 sells to Carla one of the cars in the inventory purchased with the loan from American. Carla pays for the car with funds borrowed from Federal Bank pursuant to a written loan and security agreement. To secure the loan, Federal takes and perfects a security interest in the car. Federal then transfer $10,000, the cost of the car, to A-1 but A-1 fails to pay any of that amount to American. Carla defaults in paying Federal and Federal takes possession of the car. Meanwhile American learns of the sale to Carla and demands payment from A-1 who no longer has the money. You call an officer of Federal claiming a prior security interest in the car. Federal asserts that its security interest takes priority. Who is correct? Explain. (See UCC §§9–320 and 9–330.)

(d) A-1 has encountered financial difficulties and needs cash quickly. Jones, an officer of A-1, develops a scheme to obtain the money. He completes a purchase and security agreement showing a sale of a car to John Smith by which Smith promises to pay $10,000 to A-1 and grants a security interest in a car as security. Jones takes the agreement to Fidelity Loan Co., a company to which A-1 frequently sells chattel paper, which pays A-1 $7,500 for the contract. Fidelity perfects a security interest in the car. By the time Fidelity discovers that the transaction was a sham, Jones has left town and A-1 is bankrupt. During the bankruptcy proceeding, Fidelity discovers that the car described in the contract purchased from A-1 is listed among A-1's inventory. Fidelity requests that it be awarded possession of the car but American claims a prior security interest. To whom should the car be awarded? Explain, citing pertinent Code provisions and discussing any relevant policy issues.

(e) Although Fidelity wants to continue purchasing chattel paper from auto retailers, it also wants to avoid sham transactions such as the one by Jones. What procedures might Fidelity adopt to protect itself in the future?

32.6 On February 1, 2004, Herman purchased a computer from Computers Galore, a retailer. Herman paid the purchase price in full and requested delivery to his office on February 15. Computers Galore's inventory was financed by Second Bank and Trust, which retained a security interest perfected in 2003 in all inventory and proceeds. The security agreement between the bank and Computers Galore allowed the retailer to sell the inventory. On February 12, 2004, Computers Galore defaulted in its payments to the bank and the bank took possession of all of the inventory of Computers Galore. Included in the inventory was the computer that Herman had purchased. Herman sued Second Bank and Trust demanding delivery of his computer. How should the court rule? Explain.

32.7 Nelson Company, a sporting goods manufacturer, is considering selling inventory to Haggett's Sport Shop on credit, retaining a security interest in the inventory. Nelson has searched the UCC filing system records and discovered a financing statement dated two years earlier showing that Haggett owed money to First State Bank. The financing statement states that the bank holds a security interest in "all accounts receivable and/or inventory in connection with a retail sporting goods shop."

(a) Nelson must determine whether to make the sale to Haggett. If nelson takes a security interest in the items of inventory it sells to Haggett, will First State Bank's interest conflict with Nelson's?

(b) Suggest steps that Nelson might take to protect itself if it makes the sale.

32.8 Marina Boat Co. is a retailer of boats and sailing equipment. On June 1, 2002, Warner Bank agreed to act as Marina's primary inventory financier and took a security interest in all of Marina's inventory, including after-acquired inventory. Warner properly filed a financing statement the same day. On April 1, 2005, Crestliner Boat Builders sold Marina seven boats for its inventory pursuant to a written credit agreement by which Crestliner retained a purchase money security interest in the seven boats. Crestliner properly perfected its security interest on April 1 and delivered the boats to Marina on April 5. Prior to selling the boats to Marina, Crestliner had requested a search of the UCC records.

(a) The search of the UCC records had revealed Warner's security interest in inventory. On April 2, Crestliner provided a written notice to Warner notifying it that Crestliner was selling seven boats to Marina and was retaining a purchase money security in the boats. The notification included a description and serial number for each boat. On September 1, 2005, Marina declared bankruptcy. Both Warner and Crestliner claimed a perfected security interest in the seven boats. Whose interest takes priority? Explain. See UCC §9–324.

(b) Disregard the facts stated in the preceding paragraph. Assume instead that Crestliner's search of the UCC records revealed no prior security interests. On May 1, Warner extended further credit to Marina, relying on its previously filed financing statement. On September 1, Marina declared bankruptcy. Both Warner and Crestliner claim a security interest in the seven boats. The evidence at trial reveals that the secretary of state had filed Warner's financing statement under "Warner Bank" instead of "Marina Boat Co." thus explaining why Crestliner's search had not revealed Warner's prior interest. To whom should the court award possession of the boats? Explain, including a discussion of the policy issues.

32.9 COF, Inc. sells several items of inventory to Sullivan, a retailer, retaining a security interest in the specified items of inventory and their proceeds. COF perfects its security interest and opens a special bank account into which Sullivan agrees to deposit the proceeds. Sullivan sells the inventory over a period of six months but deposits the proceeds in his own bank account rather than in the special account. Thus the proceeds become intermingled with money from other sales. Sullivan also pays other creditors from his bank account. COF sues Sullivan demanding payment of $20,000, the value of the inventory that it had sold to Sullivan. Sullivan's only assets are his inventory, which is subject to perfected security interests of other creditors, and $20,000 that is deposited in his bank account. In addition to his debt to COF, Sullivan owes approximately $30,000 to general creditors, who also have sued Sullivan. The court is attempting to determine to whom it should award the money in Sullivan's bank account.

(a) Consider §9–315 of the UCC. Explain how COF could identify and trace the proceeds of the sale of the inventory it sold to Sullivan.

(b) Assume that in the period following Sullivan's sale of the inventory purchased from COF, Sullivan's bank account has always had a balance of at least $20,000. To whom should the court award the bank account?

(c) Assume instead that during the period following Sullivan's sale of the inventory purchased from COF, Sullivan's bank balance has fluctuated. At one time the balance was as low as $2,500. To whom should the court award the bank account?

32.10 On October 17, 2004, First Security Bank lent Elliot $10,000 to be used for renovating and redecorating a business he operated called "Elliot's Paint and Supply." Elliot executed a promissory note and security agreement granting First Security a security interest in all inventory, including after-acquired inventory. First Security perfected the security interest. Most of Elliot's inventory consisted of paint that he sold at retail. He purchased his paint inventory on open account from Absco, Inc. On the date of the bank loan Elliot's inventory was valued at $17,000. During the following year, the value of the inventory fluctuated between $15,000 and $20,000. In late November 2005, a bank officer paid a routine visit to Elliot's Paint and Supply and discovered the store was closed and vacant. The bank later discovered that in early November, Elliot had returned paints valued at $12,000 to Absco for credit on his open account. First Security Bank sued Absco alleging that Absco had converted the bank's property. Absco alleged that the bank's security agreement with Elliot permitted him to "sell and dispose of the collateral in the ordinary course of business." Absco provided evidence showing that Elliot regularly returned slow-moving inventory to Absco for credit.

(a) Was Elliot's return of his paint inventory to Absco "in the ordinary course of business"?

(b) How should the court decide the case?

32.11 On June 30, 1998, Cudmore-Neiber Shoe Company sold a business known as The Bootery to Merlyn Pugh. Cudmore-Neiber financed the sale through an installment contract and retained a security interest in the business including inventory, accounts receivable, fixtures, and all after-acquired property. Cudmore-Neiber filed a financing statement in the county recorder's office on May 29, 2003, and in the secretary of state's office on June 17, 2005.

While Pugh was operating The Bootery, he purchased inventory from United States Shoe Company. Pugh defaulted in paying the purchase contract and Cudmore-Neiber repossessed the business on May 29, 2003. At that time, Pugh owed United States Shoe Company over $10,000.

United States Shoe Company sued Cudmore-Neiber alleging that its repossession of The Bootery was unlawful because Cudmore-Neiber had not perfected its security interest prior to the repossession. Is United States Shoe Company correct? Explain.

32.12 In 2001, Union State Bank loaned Cockrum a large sum of money to finance his farm and hog confinement operation. To secure repayment Union obtained and perfected a security interest in Cockrum's currently existing and after-acquired equipment and farm products, including livestock. In 2003, Farmers Cooperative Elevator Company sold Cockrum livestock feed on credit, taking a purchase money security interest in the feed. Farmers perfected its interest by filing a financing statement when the feed was delivered to Cockrum. After Cockrum defaulted on both loans, Farmers claimed priority over Union Bank in Cockrum's remaining feed. Farmers also asserted that it was entitled to priority in Cockrum's hogs, which had eaten much of the feed, alleging that the hogs were "proceeds" of Farmers' collateral, the feed, and were automatically subject to Farmers' security interest under §9–203. Farmers argued that §9–102(a)(64) defines proceeds to include whatever is received upon the sale, exchange, collection, or "other disposition" of the collateral, a definition broad enough to include hogs as proceeds of feed.

  (a) Does Farmers have a priority over Union Bank in the feed remaining in Cockrum's possession? Explain.
  (b) Does Farmers have a priority over Union Bank in the hogs that ate the feed supplied by Farmers? Explain.

32.13 Mr. and Mrs. Gerayne Poole operated Greenway Elevator Co., a grain elevator, in Clay County, Arkansas. On March 17, 2005, Corming Bank loaned money to the Pooles for the purchase of grain bins. Corning Bank took a security interest in the grain bins and filed a financing statement in the Clay County circuit clerk's office on March 19, 2005. The financing statement described the grain bins as "goods" to be retained at the place of business of Greenway Elevator Co., Post Office Box 94, Greenway, Arkansas. The financing statement contained no description of any real estate and no indi-cation that the property described was attached to, or to become attached to, land. Accordingly, the clerk filed the financing statement under the Pooles' name in the UCC records for security interests in goods; the instrument was not recorded or noted in the real estate records.

On May 17, 2005, Bank of Rector loaned money to the Pooles and recorded a mortgage showing that it held a security interest in the real estate on which Greenway Elevator Co. was located. The mortgage was filed in the county real estate records.

The Pooles subsequently defaulted in their loan payments to both banks and a dispute arose between Bank of Rector and Corning Bank as to who had a priority security interest in the grain bins. Bank of Rector argued that the bins constituted fixtures for which no proper financing statement had been filed and, therefore, the Bank of Rector was entitled to foreclose on the grain bins as a part of the real estate. Corning Bank argued that the grain bins were goods subject to its perfected security interest so that Corning Bank was entitled to the bins. Who is correct? Explain.

32.14 Assume you are a loan officer of First State Bank, which is considering lending money to Chips, Inc., a manufacturer of integrated circuits and other electronic components. Chips has proposed and the bank has accepted a field warehousing arrangement to provide security for a $500,000 loan. What steps would you take in the creation and operation of the field warehouse to provide maximum security to the bank in the event of Chips, Inc.'s default or bankruptcy?

32.15 On June 1, Barry borrowed $10,000 from Lois giving her a security interest in a valuable painting owned by Barry. Lois did not file a financing statement covering the transaction at that time. On August 1, she discovered that Barry was insolvent and immediately filed a financing statement. Barry filed a voluntary bankruptcy petition on September 1. Who will have the benefit of the painting, Lois or the trustee in bankruptcy? Explain. Would the trustee have the benefit of the painting if Barry's bankruptcy petition had been filed on December 15? Would the trustee have the benefit of the painting if Lois had filed her financing statement on June 9? Explain.

CHAPTER 33

SURETYSHIP

- an introduction to the law of suretyship, including the definition and purposes of suretyship, how suretyship relationships are created, and the distinction among the various types of sureties and suretyship contracts
- the relationship between a surety and the principal, the person whose obligation a surety guarantees
- the relationship between the surety and creditor, including defenses available to the surety when sued by the creditor
- the definition of and relationship among cosureties

In the secured transactions discussed in the preceding two chapters, the secured party has recourse to specific property belonging to the debtor if the debtor defaults upon the secured obligation. Instead of (or in addition to) a security interest in the debtor's property, a creditor may obtain security by the promise of a third party (a surety) to perform the obligation if the debtor does not. Many legal issues arise in this situation that are resolved by the law of *suretyship,* the subject of this chapter.

The common law is the primary source of suretyship principles, which are summarized in the *Restatement of Security* (1941) and its recent revision, the *Restatement of Suretyship* (1995). In many states, common law sure-

tyship doctrines are codified or modified by statute. If a surety becomes bound upon a negotiable instrument (for example, a promissory note or check), the rights and duties of the surety (known as an "accommodation party") are governed by Revised Article 3 of the UCC and by the common law of suretyship that supplements Article 3 through UCC §1–103(b).[1] Accommodation parties are introduced in Chapter 25 and additional issues affecting them are discussed later in this chapter.

Introduction to Suretyship

Suretyship is the legal relationship existing when

1. one party, the *principal,* is legally bound to a *creditor* who is entitled to but one satisfaction,
2. another party, the *surety,* has become bound by contract to the creditor to perform the same acts for which the principal is liable, and
3. as between the two who are bound (principal and surety), the principal rather than the surety should perform.[2]

---

[1]Section 1–103(b) is discussed in Chapter 6.
[2]RESTATEMENT OF SECURITY §82; RESTATEMENT OF SURETYSHIP §1.

Thus, suretyship always involves at least three parties: the **principal,** the person for whose debt or default the surety is liable; the **creditor,** the person to whom both the surety and principal owe their duties; and the **surety,** the person liable on the debt or obligation of another, the principal. Although both the principal and surety are liable on the same obligation to the creditor, as between the two, the principal rather than the surety should perform. In other words, in suretyship the creditor has rights against both the principal and surety, but the surety may shift the ultimate loss to the principal. This latter characteristic marks the arrangement as a suretyship. The relationship may therefore be characterized as shown in Figure 33.1. The principal's duty to the creditor is commonly called the "principal" or "underlying" obligation, suggesting that its performance is secured by another promise, the surety's, known as a "collateral" or "accessorial" obligation.

To illustrate the typical case, assume Paula needs $10,000 to open a business. She, therefore, approaches Chris for a loan. Because of Paula's somewhat precarious financial condition, Chris agrees to loan the money only if Paula provides collateral or obtains a surety who will guarantee repayment of the loan. Because Paula has no (or insufficient) collateral, Paula convinces her rich aunt, Stella, to act as a surety. Stella promises Chris that if he will loan money to Paula, Stella will repay the loan if Paula fails to do so. Chris then loans the money to Paula. In Chris's eyes, both Paula and Stella are liable on the $10,000 debt, though Chris is entitled to only one recovery—that is, $10,000, not $20,000. As between Paula and Stella, however, Paula should pay.

Creation of Suretyship

Suretyship relationships usually are created by an express contract between the surety and creditor in which the surety intends at the time of contracting to become a surety. The surety's promise may be made either in the same instrument evidencing the principal's

contract or in a separate instrument. The surety may agree to guarantee all or merely a specified portion of the principal's obligation.

Ordinarily, the surety is obtained with the consent of, or at the request of, the principal. Suretyship is not, however, dependent upon any agreement between the surety and principal that the principal should perform. The surety may have undertaken his obligation by dealing directly with the creditor without the consent or even knowledge of the principal.

In addition to express contract, suretyship also may arise by operation of law, as a consequence of new contractual relations with third parties. For example, a suretyship by operation of law usually is created after assignment of a contract. That is, in the absence of a novation, after an assignment that delegates a duty to perform, the assignee becomes the principal and the assignor becomes a surety guaranteeing the assignee's performance of the contract. A suretyship is created because two people, assignor and assignee, are liable on the same debt to a creditor, the other original party to the contract, who is entitled to but one performance. As between the two who are liable, however, one, the assignee, rather than the other, the assignor, should perform.[3]

Compensated and Uncompensated Sureties

Sureties are generally described as either **compensated** or **corporate** sureties, or **accommodation, uncompensated,** or **gratuitous** sureties. A compensated surety, normally a corporation, is one engaged in the business of executing surety contracts for compensation known as a "premium." The surety determines the premium by computing risk on an actuarial basis. Contracts executed by compensated sureties are called **bonds.** Common types of bonds are the **fidelity bond,** securing an employer against embezzlement or defalcation by an employee, and a **performance bond,** securing an owner (commonly a governmental body) for the proper performance of a building construction contract by a contractor.

Most other sureties are not principally engaged in entering into suretyship contracts for a fee. Their contracts are occasional and incidental to other business. Such sureties may act gratuitously—for example, a father guaranteeing his son's credit purchase of an automobile—or

---

[3]Assignment, delegation, and novation are discussed in detail in Chapter 13. Another common example of suretyship created by operation of law occurs when real property burdened by a mortgage is transferred, and the transferee assumes the mortgage. This situation is explained in Chapter 37.

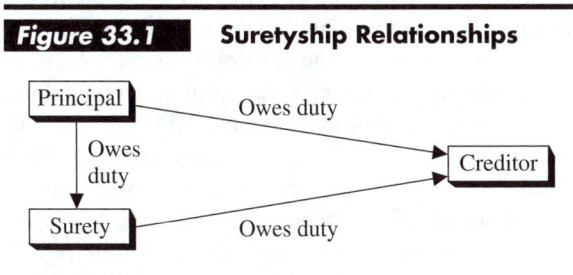

Figure 33.1   **Suretyship Relationships**

may receive some pecuniary advantage—for example, a shareholder guaranteeing a loan to her corporation.

Under traditional suretyship law, compensated sureties are governed, in certain cases, by legal principles that differ from those applied to other sureties. Modern suretyship law, however, embodied in the *Restatement of Suretyship,* applies the same rules in most cases to both types of surety.

Sureties and Guarantors

Suretyship law distinguishes between persons answering for the debt of another, based upon whether the promise is "primary" or "secondary." An undertaking involving the promisor's direct and absolute promise to perform, one not conditioned upon another's failure to perform, is a "primary" obligation. On the other hand, the term "secondary obligation" means that the promisor has undertaken to perform only if another person fails to perform. A "surety," pursuant to a contract of *suretyship,* makes a primary promise, whereas a "guarantor," pursuant to a contract of **guaranty,** makes a secondary promise.

A special type of guaranty contract is the **guaranty of collection** (sometimes known as a **conditional guaranty** or **guaranty of collectibility**). In the ordinary or "absolute" guaranty, the creditor may proceed against the guarantor *immediately* upon the principal's default. In the guaranty of collection, however, the creditor must put the principal in default and *additionally* exhaust all legal remedies against the principal before suing the guarantor. These remedies might include, for example, obtaining a judgment against the defaulting debtor and applying any collateral possessed by the creditor to reduce the guaranteed debt. The following case illustrates the importance of the distinction between a surety and a guarantor.

General Motors Acceptance Corporation v. Daniels

492 A.2d 1306 (Md. 1985)

In June 1981, John Daniels agreed to buy a used car from Lindsay Cadillac Company (Lindsay). Because John had a poor credit rating, his brother, defendant Seymoure Daniels, agreed to co-sign the installment sales contract. Both John and Seymoure signed the contract at the same time on lines designated "buyer" and "co-buyer." Lindsay

assigned the contract to plaintiff General Motors Acceptance Corporation (GMAC). In May 1982, GMAC declared the contract in default and sued Seymoure for the unpaid balance because John could not be located. The trial and appellate courts found that Seymoure was a guarantor of the contract between John and GMAC, and as a result GMAC was required to bring suit first against John before it could sue Seymoure. GMAC appealed to the Court of Appeals of Maryland.

Cole, Judge

We shall decide in this case whether a person who signs an installment sales contract for the sole purpose of lending his credit to the purchaser makes the contract of a surety or the contract of a guarantor. . . .

A contract of suretyship is a tripartite agreement among a principal obligor, his obligee, and a surety. This contract is a direct and original undertaking under which the surety is primarily or jointly liable with the principal obligor, . . . and therefore is responsible at once if the principal obligor fails to perform. A surety is usually bound with his principal by the same instrument, executed at the same time, and on the same consideration. . . .

Ultimate liability rests upon the principal obligor rather than the surety, but the obligee has remedy against both. . . . With respect to notice of default, the surety is ordinarily held to know every default of his principal because he is under a duty to make inquiry and ascertain whether the principal obligor is discharging the obligation resting on him. . . . Consequently, the surety is ordinarily liable without notice.

A contract of guaranty, similar to a contract of suretyship, is an accessory contract. . . . Despite this similarity, a contract of guaranty has several distinguishing characteristics. First, this particular contract is collateral to and independent of the principal contract that is guaranteed and, as a result, the guarantor is not a party to the principal obligation. A guarantor is therefore secondarily liable to the creditor on his contract and his promise to answer for the debt, default, or miscarriage of another becomes absolute upon default of the principal debtor and the satisfaction of the conditions precedent to liability. . . . Second, the original contract of the principal is not the guarantor's contract, and the guarantor is not bound to take notice of its nonperformance. Rather, the guarantor agrees that the principal is able to and will perform a contract that he has made or is about to make, and that if he defaults the guarantor will pay the resulting damages provided the guarantor is notified of the principal's default. As such, the guarantor insures the ability or solvency of the principal. Third, the contract of guaranty is often founded upon a separate consideration from that supporting the contract of the principal and, consequently, the consideration for the guarantor's promise moves wholly or in part to him. Fourth, and in sum, the guarantor promises to perform if the principal does not. By contrast, a surety promises to do the same thing that the principal undertakes. . . .

Our review of the evidence in this case convinces us that the District Court erred in finding that Seymoure was a guarantor rather than a surety with respect to the installment sales contract. . . .

Seymoure agreed to purchase the subject automobile by affixing his signature to the installment sales contract on the line designated "Buyer." The contract clearly stated that all buyers agreed to be jointly and severally liable for the purchase of that vehicle. . . .

Seymoure executed the same contract as his brother, thereby making himself a party to the original contract. There is no evidence that Seymoure executed an agreement collateral to and independent of this contract. This fact, standing alone, ordinarily negates the existence of a guaranty. . . .

Both Seymoure and John signed the contract at the same time. . . . Furthermore, there are no competent facts indicating that Seymoure expressly agreed to pay for the automobile only upon the default of John. Seymoure also did not qualify his signature in any manner. Thus, by the terms of the contract Seymoure agreed to be primarily and jointly liable with John for the purchase of the automobile. GMAC was therefore not required to proceed against John in the first instance, and the failure of GMAC promptly to notify Seymoure of the default in payments and of the lapse in physical damage insurance coverage does not constitute a discharge.

Finally, on the facts of this case it is immaterial that the contract did not expressly designate Seymoure as a "surety." Whether a party has entered into a contract of suretyship or guaranty is to be determined by the substance of the agreement and not by its nomenclature. . . .

[Judgment reversed.]

Despite the distinction between sureties and guarantors outlined previously, courts generally use the term "surety" in a broad sense to include not only strict sureties (primary promisors) but also guarantors. This approach is consistent with the emphasis in suretyship upon the principal-surety relationship and has the support of most courts and commentators.[4] Because most of the legal consequences of suretyship and guaranty are the same, and to avoid needless duplication of terms, in the material that follows the term "surety" includes both a surety and guarantor, unless otherwise noted.

The Suretyship Contract

Rights and duties of the parties in suretyship are governed almost exclusively by agreement. Therefore, fundamental contract principles, discussed in Part II of this book, govern many problems raised in suretyship cases. The following material focuses upon a few important contracts issues as they apply to suretyship.

Interpreting Suretyship Contracts

Courts and commentators often state that the uncompensated surety is a "favorite of the law," subjecting her contracts to a special standard requiring an interpretation strictly in favor of the surety (a rule of *strictissimi juris*). The rationale for this statement is that the uncompensated surety commonly binds herself as a favor to another, without receiving any personal benefit or direct compensation. In contrast, the compensated surety is said not to be a favorite of the law, requiring ambiguous language to be strictly construed against the surety (its own language because the compensated surety virtually always drafts the contract). In fact, no special standard of interpretation applies to suretyship contracts. The judicial attitude apparently favoring the accommodation surety is often no more than an application of general contract interpretation rules (for example, ambiguous language is construed most strongly against its user), and substantive suretyship law rules designed to protect sureties. As with all contracts, careful drafting that anticipates and resolves potential contingencies prevents many disputes.

---

[4]This approach also is consistent with the definition of the term "surety" in UCC §1–201(b)(39).

Formation of the Contract

A suretyship contract must meet the same general requirements for enforceability as other contracts. There must be an agreement supported by consideration, which may not be rendered unenforceable or voidable by defects such as fraud, misrepresentation, illegal purpose, lack of contractual capacity, or noncompliance with the Statute of Frauds.

Offer and Acceptance. In suretyship, the initial element, the agreement (or mutual manifestation of assent) is satisfied when an offer made by the surety is accepted by the creditor. Like other offers, the surety's offer may be accepted only by or for the benefit of the person to whom it is made. If the offer is made to a particular individual (an offer for a **special guaranty**), only that individual can accept it. On the other hand, an offer for a **general guaranty** is limited by its terms to no particular individual and may be accepted by any person to whom the principal communicates the offer and who accepts it by extending the credit contemplated by the offer. A suretyship offer frequently is continuing in nature, that is, a **continuing guaranty,** rather than for a single extension of credit.

A surety usually offers to guarantee the principal's performance of a *contractual* obligation, such as repayment of a debt or proper performance of a construction contract (a performance bond). In a fidelity bond, however, the surety may guarantee performance of a public duty owed by the principal, such as faithful performance of the principal's function as a public fiscal officer.

Consideration. The consideration supporting the uncompensated, or accommodation, surety's promise is the creditor's extension of (or promise to extend) credit to the principal. If the surety is obtained after credit is extended, the prior extension of credit is "past consideration" and will not support the surety's promise. Unlike most contracts, in which the benefit of each promise runs to the promisee, in suretyship the benefit of the creditor's promise or performance runs to the principal, not the surety (promisee).

The compensated surety, of course, receives direct consideration in the form of the premium paid by the creditor, such as the principal's employer, to the surety. The compensated surety is therefore bound whether it is obtained before or after the principal obligation arises.[5]

Capacity and Formality

A natural person having general contractual capacity also has capacity to become a surety. A business corporation also generally has the power to act as a surety.[6] Indeed, most modern sureties, such as bonding companies, are corporations.

The promise of the surety to answer for the duty of another is within the common law Statute of Frauds. Therefore, the law usually requires a signed writing to make the surety's promise enforceable.

Relationship Between Surety and Principal

The primary characteristic of a suretyship relation is that although both the surety and the principal are liable to the creditor, as between the two, the principal should perform. The surety's rights against the principal are equitable in nature and origin and are embodied in three doctrines: reimbursement, exoneration, and subrogation.

Reimbursement

Reimbursement is the surety's right to be reimbursed by the principal *after* paying or otherwise performing the principal obligation. The principal is under a duty to reimburse the surety if either (1) the surety's undertaking was consensual—obtained at the request of the principal or with the principal's acquiescence or consent,[7] or (2) the principal has assumed a duty, once the

---

[5]As discussed in Chapter 9, suretyship promises also may be enforceable if contained in a signed writing that states a recited or nominal consideration.

[6]The Revised Model Business Corporation Act provides that corporations have the power "to make contracts and guarantees" and incur liabilities. RMBCA §3.02(7). Further, suretyship contracts fall within broadly drafted corporate purposes clauses in the corporate charter, now in widespread use.

[7]The duty to reimburse is commonly based on an express or implied contract (a contract "implied in fact") between the principal and surety. If the surety becomes bound without the principal's knowledge or consent and later satisfies the principal's obligation, many courts recognize the surety's right to recover in restitution (quasi-contract—a contract "implied in law") in order to prevent the principal's unjust enrichment.

primary obligation of the surety—for example, a contract assignment.

The right of reimbursement does not permit the surety to profit at the principal's expense. If the surety satisfies his or her own obligation and discharges the principal's duty by paying less than the amount nominally due (for example, through a negotiated settlement with the creditor), reimbursement is limited to the amount paid. Similarly, if the surety transfers property or performs services to settle the principal obligation, reimbursement is limited to the reasonable value of the property or services.

Exoneration

Exoneration is the surety's right, *before* paying the creditor, to compel the principal to perform. Thus, whereas reimbursement forces the principal to pay the *surety,* exoneration forces the principal to pay the *creditor.*

Exoneration, which is equitable in nature, is based on the premise that the principal owes the surety a duty to perform the principal obligation, thereby "exonerating" the surety from suit by the creditor. The law therefore refuses to subject the surety to the inconvenience and temporary loss involved in performing the obligation if the principal is able to do so. To achieve exoneration, the court may order the principal to perform for the creditor, or pay money due the creditor to the court for the creditor's benefit, or provide collateral to the surety to secure the surety's right of reimbursement.

Subrogation

A surety who satisfies the principal obligation succeeds to the position ("steps into the shoes") of the creditor for purposes of proceeding against the principal. This is known as the surety's right of **subrogation.** Subrogation is grounded in restitution and is designed to prevent unjust enrichment of the principal (whose obligation has been paid in full) at the surety's expense. Subrogation operates as an equitable assignment (or assignment by operation of law) of the creditor's rights to the surety after the obligation to the creditor has been satisfied. Note that reimbursement and exoneration give the surety direct rights against the principal, whereas in subrogation, the surety proceeds indirectly by asserting the creditor's rights against the principal.

Subrogation therefore entitles the surety, after payment, to use any remedy against the principal that the creditor could have used and to succeed to any other advantage enjoyed by the creditor including (1) a mortgage or other lien on the principal's property, (2) the right to proceed against any third party who has promised or is otherwise liable to either the creditor or principal to pay the debt, and (3) any priority (for example, in the principal's bankruptcy proceeding) that the creditor possesses. To illustrate the first situation above, assume Sam is a surety on Paul's $100,000 obligation to Cathy. The debt is secured by a mortgage on Paul's real property and by Paul's coin collection in Cathy's possession. Upon Paul's default, Sam satisfies the obligation. He is now entitled by subrogation to the benefit of the mortgage and the coin collection limited by the amount that he has paid.

Relationship Between Surety and Creditor—In General

The following material is divided into two parts and examines the various aspects of the relationship between the creditor and surety. The first part surveys the mutual rights and duties of the surety and creditor. The second part discusses the defenses available to the surety to avoid paying the creditor after the principal's default.

Enforcement of Creditor's Claim Against Principal

Surety's Right to Compel Creditor to Proceed Against Principal. A suretyship promise provides both assurance of payment to the creditor and protects the creditor against the burden and delay required to collect the debt from the principal through judicial proceeding. Thus, as a general rule, the surety has no right to compel the creditor to enforce its claim against the principal, and is not discharged by the creditor's failure to attempt to collect the debt from the principal. A surety who intends to be bound only after exhaustion of remedies against the principal should contract as a guarantor of collection.

A number of states that follow the doctrine of *Pain v. Packard* (1816)[8] alter this rule by statutes that enable the surety to compel the creditor to sue the principal. Under these statutes, if the creditor after receiving

---

[8]13 Johns. 174 (N.Y. 1816).

written notice fails or refuses to sue the principal, the surety is discharged to the extent of the loss caused by the creditor's failure or refusal to proceed.

Application of Collateral Held by Creditor. The principal obligation may be secured both by the surety's promise and by a security interest in specific property owned by the debtor. As a general rule, a creditor having a security interest in the principal's property may, on default, compel the surety to pay without first resorting to the collateral. This rule implements a primary purpose of suretyship: to assure the creditor's immediate payment, without the expense and delay inherent in proceeding against the principal (or in this case, the principal's collateral). That expense and delay is borne by the surety as part of the suretyship undertaking.[9] A surety who pays the creditor is, of course, subrogated to the creditor's position, and may use the collateral to obtain reimbursement.

A court of equity may protect the surety from the operation of this rule, forcing the creditor to proceed first against the collateral if the creditor's failure to do so will cause severe hardship to the surety, and applying the collateral will not significantly burden the creditor. That is, the court applies a balancing test, weighing the relative hardship on the surety against the burden that enforcing the security would impose on the creditor.

Application of Payments to Creditors

Frequently, the principal owes several separate obligations to the same creditor. Some of these obligations may be totally unsecured, while others may be secured by collateral or a surety's promise, or both. In this situation, a dispute may arise over proper allocation of part payments by the principal debtor to the various obligations. For example, assume Sally is surety on Pam's $1,000 obligation to Carla. Pam also owes Carla $2,000 on a separate unsecured debt. Pam pays Carla $1,000. How is the $1,000 part payment to be applied to the outstanding obligations?

As a general rule, the creditor is bound to follow the principal's directions regarding the application of a payment. If the principal fails to direct application of a part payment between two or more matured debts, the

payment is applied at the *creditor's* discretion. Therefore, in the preceding example, if Pam pays Carla $1,000 without instructions, Carla may apply the payment as she sees fit. In this case, Carla would most likely apply the payment to the unsecured obligation, leaving the $1,000 debt on which Sally is a surety outstanding.

Similar rules apply to application of the proceeds of collateral held by the creditor. If the creditor holds security for performance of the obligation guaranteed by the surety, proceeds of the sale of that security must be applied to reduce the surety's ultimate liability. If, however, the creditor holds security from the principal to secure all debts, including those not secured by the surety, the creditor is under no obligation to apply any of the proceeds of the security for the surety's benefit. Therefore, the original agreement between creditor and principal fixes the subsequent rights of the parties concerning application of the collateral.

Relationship Between Surety and Creditor — Surety's Defenses

Certain events, occurring either during the formation of the principal's or surety's contract or subsequently, may extinguish or reduce the surety's duty to the creditor. The events collectively composing the surety's defenses are usually (though not necessarily) caused by the conduct of either the creditor or the principal, or both. Most of the defenses are applications of one or more of the following general concepts.

1. As a general rule, the surety is not liable to the creditor unless the principal is liable. Accordingly, defenses available to the principal against the creditor (allowing the principal to avoid performance of the obligation to the creditor) also may be asserted by the surety. The incapacity or bankruptcy of the principal are notable exceptions to this rule.

2. Generally, defenses arising between the surety and principal, such as fraud perpetrated by the principal on the surety, are not available to the surety as a defense to paying the creditor.

3. Conduct by the creditor (or by the creditor and principal) that releases the principal, impairs the surety's right of subrogation, or modifies the principal obligation, discharges the surety, but only to the extent that the release, impairment, or modification causes actual loss to the surety.

---

[9]This rule does not apply if the surety is merely a guarantor of collection, because such a guarantor is obligated to pay only after the creditor has exhausted all legal remedies against the principal, including the enforcement of any collateral.

4. The creditor must act reasonably, and therefore a surety is liable only for losses that could not have been prevented through the creditor's exercise of reasonable diligence.

5. Sureties may agree to forgo the protection afforded by suretyship defenses. That is, a surety may consent to an act that would otherwise provide a basis for discharge; or more commonly, may waive suretyship defenses in the original contract creating the surety's obligation. It is important to note that in many suretyship contracts, suretyship defenses are routinely waived.

Defenses Arising During Contract Formation

Infancy or Other Incapacity of the Principal. The principal's lack of capacity to contract, due to mental incompetence or more commonly, infancy, is not a defense available to the surety against the creditor. One of the major reasons a creditor obtains a surety is to be protected against the principal's incapacity to contract that insulates the principal from suit by the creditor.

Fraud or Duress upon the Principal or Surety. If the principal has been induced to contract as a result of the fraud or duress of the creditor, the surety is not liable to the creditor. In this case, the creditor has concealed facts (the duress or fraudulent misrepresentations) that make performance by the principal less likely and thus increase the surety's risk beyond that originally contemplated. Thus, two separate defenses are involved, one available to the principal, the other to the surety.

A related problem arises when the *surety* is induced to become bound due to fraud or duress upon him by the principal. As a general rule, the principal's fraud or duress gives the surety no defense against the creditor unless the creditor has knowingly accepted the advantages of the fraud.

Fraud by Creditor upon Surety. Fraud by the creditor upon the surety is a defense to the surety. Fraud may result from the creditor's express misrepresentations, concealment, or nondisclosure of material facts. For example, if the surety requests information from the creditor, the creditor must fully disclose all material facts. Disclosure is required when the creditor knows facts unknown to the surety that materially increase the surety's risk. Material facts include the principal's financial condition, his past conduct (for example, performance of prior contracts or dishonesty as an employee), or secret agreements between creditor and principal (for example, that the actual contract between principal and creditor differs from the one upon which the surety is relying).

Effect of Discharge of Principal Obligation

Nonperformance by Creditor. The suretyship contract is collateral or ancillary to the principal obligation. Therefore, as a general rule, the surety is not liable unless the principal is liable. The surety may plead most defenses available to the principal when sued by the creditor. Possibly the most basic defense available to any contracting party is that the other party failed to perform as agreed. For example, the creditor may fail to lend money, sell goods, or perform services as provided in the contract with the principal. In this case, the principal has a defense to performance that may be asserted by the surety.

Performance by Principal. Because the creditor is entitled to only one performance, performance by the principal or by another on the principal's behalf discharges the surety to the extent of the performance.

Tender of Performance by Principal. As indicated in Chapter 14, a tender is an offer of performance coupled with the present ability to perform. If accepted, the tender becomes performance, discharging both principal and surety. The suretyship undertaking is not intended to protect against loss resulting from the creditor's refusal to accept the principal's payment or performance. Thus, if the creditor refuses to accept the principal's tender of performance involving a payment of money (or unreasonably refuses any other tender) the surety is discharged. The principal is not fully discharged by the refusal but is generally discharged to the extent of all subsequent liability for interest.[10]

Under the traditional rule, a tender of performance by the *surety* that is refused discharges the surety. The *Restatement of Suretyship,* however, adopts the rule of more recent cases which discharge the surety only to the extent that the creditor's refusal to accept tender causes the surety actual loss. Under either rule, the principal nevertheless remains liable after the surety's tender.

---

[10]See, for example, Revised UCC §3–603(c).

Impracticability of Performance. As discussed in Chapter 14, events occuring subsequent to formation of the contract may render performance by one or both parties impracticable, excusing performance of the duties involved. If performance of the principal obligation becomes impracticable, giving the principal a defense to its enforcement, the defense may be asserted by the surety unless the surety has contracted otherwise with the creditor.

Release of the Principal Debtor. A surety protects the creditor against the principal's unwillingness or inability to perform. The creditor may assure that nonperformance by releasing the principal, thereby extinguishing the underlying obligation. In this case, the surety also is discharged because the surety's rights of exoneration, reimbursement, and subrogation have been destroyed by the creditor's conduct.

Modern suretyship law, as summarized in the *Restatement of Suretyship,* recognizes a number of exceptions to this rule. First, if the principal is insolvent at the time of the release, the surety's rights against the principal are likely to be worthless. The release causes no loss to, and therefore does not discharge, the surety. Second, assuming the principal is solvent, the surety is not discharged if the creditor in the instrument containing the release expressly preserves the surety's recourse against the debtor. To achieve such a "preservation of recourse" the instrument must provide that (1) the creditor retains its right to seek collection from the surety of any unpaid portion of the underlying debt, and (2) the surety retains its rights of exoneration, reimbursement, and subrogation against the principal. Because the surety's rights are unaffected by the release with preservation of recourse, the surety is not discharged except to the extent that the release causes actual loss to the surety. The release with preservation of recourse also subjects the principal to the risk (and puts him or her on notice) that the protection afforded by the release may be illusory. Note that the above exceptions apply only if, as is usually the case, the underlying obligation is a duty to pay money. If the creditor releases the principal from a duty other than the payment of money, the surety is discharged automatically without proof of loss.

The law also recognizes an exception to the rule if the surety consents to remain bound despite the release. By assenting to become the principal debtor, the surety waives the normal incidents of the principal's release, and is not discharged, as the following case illustrates.

Hickory Springs Manufacturing Company, Inc. v. Evans

541 S.W.2d 97 (Tenn. 1976)

In 1970, Hickory Springs Manufacturing Company, Inc. agreed to extend credit to Star-Line Manufacturing Company. Glenn Evans and Howard Gose, the only shareholders of Star-Line, personally guaranteed Star-Line's indebtedness to a maximum of $10,000. In 1972, Gose sold his stock in Star-Line to Evans but remained liable upon the guaranty. By late 1973, Star-Line had encountered financial difficulties and owed Hickory Springs almost $35,000. Evans began to negotiate the sale of his stock to Mr. Jarnagin. Jarnagin contacted Hickory Springs and negotiated a deal by which Hickory Springs would accept payment of $17,433.45 from Star-Line in full settlement of the debt it owed to Hickory Springs. Hickory Springs agreed to this compromise because it realized that if Jamagin did not purchase Star-Line, the company would file for bankruptcy. Jarnagin purchased all of the stock in Star-Line and paid $17,433.45 to Hickory Springs, and Hickory Springs released Star-Line from further liability on the debt. Hickory Springs then sued Evans and Gose for $10,000 pursuant to the guaranty they had signed in 1970. The trial court dismissed the case holding that Hickory Springs' release of the principal Star-Line discharged the sureties. After the appellate court affirmed the judgment, Hickory Springs appealed to the Tennessee Supreme Court.

Fones, Chief Justice

. . . The applicable provisions of the guaranty agreement are as follows:

> The liability of the undersigned shall not exceed the sum of Ten Thousand Dollars ($10,000.00) but such liability shall extend to all present and future indebtedness from time to time of said debtor [Star-Line Manufacturing Co.] to creditor and shall not be affected by said debtor's insolvency, at any time . . . or by creditor's acceptance of any composition, plan of reorganization, settlement, compromise, dividend, composition, payment of distribution. . . .

Under the general principles of suretyship law, a release of the principal also releases the surety to the extent that the principal is released. . . . The surety is not released, however, . . . if the surety consents to remain liable notwithstanding release of the principal. . . .

In the guaranty agreement quoted above, respondents clearly consented to remain liable notwithstanding any "settlement" or "compromise." By the terms of the agreement, the guaranty is not expressly limited to involuntary situations, nor do we think the parties intended the agreement to be so limited. As the terms of a commercial guaranty agreement are to be construed as strongly against the guarantor as the sense will admit, . . . we hold that the agreement contemplated voluntary as well as involuntary settlements and compromises, and that respondents remain liable on their guaranty. . . .

[Judgment reversed and remanded.]

Principal's Discharge in Bankruptcy. Various provisions of the federal Bankruptcy Code are concerned with the rights of sureties in the principal's bankruptcy proceeding. The Bankruptcy Code expressly provides[11] that a surety's liability is not affected by the principal's discharge in bankruptcy. That is, although the discharge destroys the rights of both the surety and creditor against the principal, it does not alter the surety's obligation to the creditor. This result is consistent with the intention of the parties, because protecting the creditor against the principal's discharge in bankruptcy is a fundamental purpose of suretyship.

Modification of Principal's Duty

The surety contracts to be bound for the principal's performance of a particular duty or set of duties. If, without the surety's consent, the principal and creditor modify the principal's contract, the new obligation differs from the one originally guaranteed. In this case the law must determine the effect of the modification on the surety's liability. Under the modern approach taken by the *Restatement of Suretyship,* a surety is completely discharged by a modification only if it (1) creates a substituted contract (a new contract accepted by the creditor in full satisfaction of the original contract guaranteed by the surety), or (2) imposes risks on the surety that differ

fundamentally from those imposed by the original contract. In all other cases the surety is bound to guarantee the contract as modified, but is discharged to the extent that the modification later causes the surety actual loss.

Extension of Time for Payment. In many cases, the principal and creditor will modify the principal obligation by agreeing to extend the time for payment or other performance by the principal. In such cases, under the *Restatement of Suretyship,* the extension also extends the time for performance of the principal's duties to the surety, unless the extension agreement preserves the surety's recourse against the principal. If the agreement preserves the surety's recourse (1) the creditor retains the right to obtain payment from the surety on the original due date, and (2) the surety's rights against the principal (based on exoneration, reimbursement, and subrogation) are unaffected by the extension. In any event, the surety is discharged only to the extent that the extension causes a loss. For example, if the principal's financial position deteriorates during the extension period, the surety is discharged to the extent of the reduction in value of its right of reimbursement against the principal. Note that the surety is less likely to suffer loss if the extension contains a preservation of recourse. In this case, for example, the surety could ignore the extension, pay the debt on its original due date, and sue the principal immediately for reimbursement.

Modification and Extension—Negotiable Instruments. Revised Article 3 of the UCC adopts rules similar to those previously outlined above applicable to indorsers or accommodation parties (discussed in Chapter 25) on promissory notes and other negotiable instruments. Under §§3–605(c)–(d), if, with or without consideration, the holder and the party obligated on the instrument (usually the maker of a note) agree to extend the due date or to other material modification, an accommodation party or indorser is discharged only to the extent that the extension or modification causes loss by reducing the value of the indorser's or accommodation party's right of recourse against the party whose obligation was extended or otherwise modified.

Impairment of Collateral

After paying the creditor, the surety succeeds by subrogation to the creditor's rights in any collateral held by the creditor. Because of the surety's inherent interest in

---

[11]11 U.S.C. §524(e).

the collateral, the creditor is under a duty not to destroy or reduce its value, and thereby lessen the surety's potential recovery through subrogation. Therefore, *if* a creditor who has collateral from the principal and knows of the surety's obligation

1. fails to obtain or maintain a perfected security interest in the collateral (for example, by failing to file a financing statement or record a mortgage), or
2. surrenders or releases the collateral to the principal, or
3. willfully or negligently harms it, or
4. fails to take reasonable steps to preserve its value, or
5. fails to comply with applicable law (for example, Part 5 of UCC Article 9) in selling or otherwise disposing of the collateral,

then the surety's obligation is reduced to the extent of the value of the lost security.

Revised Article 3 applies the same rule to discharge indorsers and accommodation parties on negotiable instruments. Under Revised §3–605(e), if the obligation to pay the instrument is secured by collateral and the holder impairs its value (as outlined above), the indorsers and accommodation parties are "discharged to the extent of the impairment."

The following case illustrates the general principles governing impairment of collateral.

Farmer's Loan & Trust Co. v. Letsinger
652 N.E.2d 63 (Ind. 1995)

In 1982, Farmer's Loan & Trust Co. (Farmer's Loan) loaned money to T-C Crop Care, Inc., (T-C). As security, T-C granted Farmer's Loan a first lien and security interest in T-C's accounts receivable and inventory then owned or acquired thereafter and in all proceeds. Farmer's Loan perfected its interest by filing a financing statement. Robert and Hulda Letsinger (the Letsingers), two of T-C's shareholders, also personally guaranteed the loan. Over the next seven years, the loan and guaranty were renewed several times. In 1985, T-C granted a second lien and security interest in T-C's accounts receivable and inventory to Erny's Fertilizer Service, Inc. (Erny's), which also perfected its security interest by filing a financing statement. In 1988, Farmer's Loan's security interest in T-C's property expired because it failed to file a continuation statement. As a result, Erny's lien, which previously had been subordinate to that of Farmer's Loan, gained priority. In

March 1989, T-C filed a petition for bankruptcy and all of its assets were liquidated to pay its debts. Most of the proceeds were paid to Erny's. After receiving only $34,163 from the proceeds, Farmer's Loan sued the Letsingers, as guarantors of T-C's debt, for $115,554. The trial court found that Farmer's Loan's failure to maintain its security interest in T-C's property constituted an unjustifiable impairment of the collateral that released the Letsingers from liability. The Court of Appeals affirmed and the Indiana Supreme Court granted Farmers Loan's petition for review.

Sullivan, Justice

. . . [I]n *Weed Sewing Machine Co. v. Winchel,* [7 N.E. 881 (Ind. 1886)], we said, "Guarantors and sureties are exonerated if the creditor by any act, done without their consent, alters the obligation of the principal in any respect, or impairs or suspends the remedy for its enforcement."

That a guarantor may interpose the defense that the creditor impaired the collateral makes sense for two reasons. First, the guarantor at the time of making a guaranty may make the judgment that the collateral for the loan to the guarantor's principal will be sufficient to cover the debt. If the creditor impairs the collateral, and the guarantor has not consented to release or other impairment of the collateral, the guarantor may become exposed to liability beyond the guarantor's expectation at the time the parties entered into the contract.

In this case, it is undisputed that T-C's corporate property would have covered T-C's debt to Farmer's Loan had the bank not failed to refile its financing statement at or before the five-year mark on the loan. Because the Letsingers did not consent to impairment of the collateral in its guaranty, Farmer's Loan exposed the Letsingers to personal liability to which they did not contract.

Second, a guarantor who satisfies the principal debtor's obligation to the creditor generally steps into the shoes of the creditor, becoming subrogated to the creditor's claim and assuming both the creditor's rights and duties. . . . Thus, when a creditor unjustifiably impairs the collateral securing a guaranteed loan, it impairs the guarantor's recourse against the guarantor's principal, which recourse the guarantor would have understood itself to have at the time of contracting to guaranty the principal's debt. . . .

[Judgment affirmed.]

In most suretyship arrangements, the creditor performs first and the surety guarantees the principal's obligation to pay money (for example, the creditor loans money or extends credit to the principal to be repaid in future installments). The underlying contract may, however, require the principal to provide goods or services to the creditor, who is required to pay for them either after the principal performs or in periodic installments as performance progresses. In these cases, the creditor's return performance (usually, as indicated above, the payment of money) acts as security for the principal obligation. Therefore, the creditor's premature payment to the principal is a release of collateral that constitutes an impairment of collateral. For example, construction contracts frequently provide that a certain percentage of the contract price is to be withheld from amounts paid by the owner to the contractor, as security for the latter's proper performance of the contract. If, despite the contractor's default, the owner nevertheless pays the amount to be withheld, a surety for the contractor's performance is discharged to the extent of actual loss due to the payment. Thus, in this case the surety would be discharged to the extent the contractor does not use the payment to perform the contract guaranteed by the surety.

Surety's Duty of Good Faith

The preceding discussion outlines the various circumstances under which a surety may reduce or avoid liability to the creditor upon the principal's default. A surety with no valid defense, who nevertheless refuses or delays payment, may be held liable for breach of contract. At issue in the following case was whether such a surety also should be liable in tort for breach of its duty to act in good faith.

Dodge v. Fidelity and Deposit Company of Maryland
778 P.2d 1240 (Ariz. 1989)

In March 1978, Homes & Son Construction Company, Inc. (Homes) contracted to build a residence for the plaintiffs, David and Anneliese Dodge. The contract required Homes to obtain a performance bond for $205,903, the amount of the contract. Defendant Fidelity and Deposit Company of Maryland (Fidelity), as surety, issued the bond which provided in part:

> Whenever Contractor [Homes] shall be, and declared by Owner [the Dodges] to be in default under the Contract, the Owner having performed Owner's obligations thereunder, the Surety [Fidelity] may promptly remedy the default, or shall promptly
> 1. Complete the Contract in accordance with its terms and conditions, or
> 2. Obtain a bid or bids for completing the Contract. . . .

The Dodges claimed that Homes failed to complete the construction project and to correct defective workmanship and declared Homes to be in default. Although the Dodges demanded that Fidelity remedy the default, they claimed that the surety refused to investigate or remedy the default. An arbitrator found that Homes had breached the construction agreement and awarded the Dodges $9,714, which was paid by Homes. The Dodges sued Fidelity for the tort of bad faith, alleging that they were entitled to damages because of Fidelity's failure to investigate or remedy the construction contract default. The trial court dismissed the complaint and the court of appeals affirmed. The Arizona Supreme Court granted the Dodge's petition for review.

Corcoran, Justice

. . . In *Noble v. National American Life Ins. Co.,* [624 P.2d 866 (Ariz. 1981)], we recognized as a tort an insurer's bad faith refusal to pay a valid claim submitted by its insured. . . .

[S]ureties have the same duty to act in good faith that we recognized in *Noble* and *Rawlings v. Apodaca,* [726 P.2d 565 (Ariz. 1986)]. In those cases, we identified the factors that create a "relationship in which the law implies special duties not imposed on other contractual relationships," and for which we would recognize a tort action for breach of those duties. *Rawlings,* . . . 726 P.2d at 574. The two most important factors are (1) whether the plaintiff contracted for security or protection rather than for profit or commercial advantage, and (2) whether permitting tort damages will "provide a substantial deterrence against breach by the party who derives a commercial benefit from the relationship." *Rawlings,* . . . 726 P.2d at 575.

The purpose of the construction performance bond required by plaintiffs' contract with Homes was not for plaintiffs' commercial advantage, but to protect plaintiffs from calamity—Homes' default on the contract. A contractor's default has the potential for creating great financial and personal hardship to a homeowner. [A construction performance bond] is obtained with the hope of avoiding such hardships. Imposing tort damages on a surety who in bad faith refuses to pay a valid claim will deter such conduct. . . . In *Noble* we noted that "[t]he whole purpose of insurance is defeated if an insurance company can refuse or fail, without justification, to pay a valid claim." . . . 624 P.2d at 868. The same is true with construction performance bonds and other types of [suretyship contracts]. Permitting a surety to withhold performance of its obligations without reason would defeat the purpose for which [suretyship contracts are] intended. . . .

Defendant does not dispute that a surety owes a duty to the obligee on a performance bond. However, defendant contends that a surety agreement requires the surety to divide its loyalty between the principal and the obligee. For example, a surety may lose its right to reimbursement from the principal if the surety knowingly prejudices any defenses the principal may have against the obligee. . . .

We do not dispute that a surety has an enforceable obligation of good faith toward its principal. . . . However, the duty imposed on a surety to deal in good faith with its obligee does not require it to act in bad faith with its principal. . . .

So long as a surety acts reasonably in response to a claim made by its obligee, the surety does not risk bad faith tort liability. . . . In *Noble,* we [stated]:

> The tort of bad faith can be alleged only if the facts pleaded would, on the basis of an objective standard, show the absence of a reasonable basis for denying the claim, i.e., would a reasonable insurer under the circumstances have denied or delayed payment of the claim under the facts and circumstances. [624 P.2d at 868.] . . .

We hold that a surety has a [similar] duty to act in good faith in responding to its obligee's claims that the principal has defaulted. Breach of this duty entitles the obligee to maintain a tort action and recover tort damages. . . .

Plaintiffs in our case alleged that defendant breached its duty of good faith and fair dealing by refusing even to investigate plaintiffs' claim, "even though Defendant . . . knew or had reason to know that defaults existed under the construction agreement." This allegation states a claim sufficient to withstand defendant's motion to dismiss. The trial court erred by granting the motion.

[Judgment reversed and remanded.]

Multiple Sureties

Frequently two or more persons become sureties on the same underlying obligation. In this case, the sureties become cosureties unless they, by contract, create a subsuretyship relation. The following material discusses the general principles governing cosuretyship and subsuretyship.

Cosuretyship Defined

When two or more sureties guarantee the same debt, their relationship is **cosuretyship** if, as among themselves, they are required to *share* the loss caused by the principal's default. Apportioning the loss caused by the principal's default may be required by an express contract between the parties, but more commonly results from the application of equitable principles. Cosureties may be bound upon the same or different instruments. Their obligations may be in differing amounts and may arise at different times. Cosureties need not know of each other's existence when undertaking their obligations.

Contribution

The chief characteristic of cosuretyship is the proportionate sharing of the loss caused by the principal's default, a process known as **contribution.** Contribution is equitable in nature, required because of the benefit conferred upon one cosurety by another's performance. The right may be modified by contract between the sureties.

Computation of Contribution. Because the right to contribution depends upon the proportionate shares of the various cosureties, the law has developed rules to determine how those shares are computed.

Equal Shares. In many cases, each surety is liable for an equal portion of the principal's default. This result occurs, for example, if all sureties guarantee performance of the principal's duty generally or stipulate equal amounts, or fail to contract among themselves for other than equal shares. In this situation, the proportionate share is determined by dividing the loss by the number of *solvent* sureties within the jurisdiction. In computing the loss, a surety's contributive share is reduced by any part performance by the principal.

For example, assume Jack, Kelly, Laura, and Mark are cosureties for Pam's $150,000 debt to Calvin. All sureties have agreed to guarantee the entire debt. Pam pays $30,000 and then defaults. The proportionate share of each surety for purposes of contribution is $30,000 [($150,000 − $30,000) ÷ 4]. If one or more of the sureties is insolvent or outside the jurisdiction of the court, the remaining sureties must contribute a proportionate amount of the loss so caused. Thus, if Mark is insolvent, the contributive share of Jack, Kelly, and Laura is $40,000. These rules apply only in determining the amount of contribution one cosurety may obtain from another. They have no effect on each surety's liability to the *creditor*. Thus, if Laura, Kelly, and Mark are all insolvent upon Pam's default, Jack can be held liable for the full $120,000 loss, because he did not limit his liability to Calvin. That is, the extent of a surety's liability is dependent upon her agreement with the creditor. That liability is unaffected by the surety's inability to obtain contribution from cosureties.

A surety is entitled to contribution from a cosurety only after discharging *more* than his proportionate share of the principal's obligation. For example, assume Alice and Betty are cosureties on Patty's $10,000 debt to Cindy. Patty defaults and Alice pays Cindy $5,000 (her proportionate share—one-half of the loss). Alice is not entitled to contribution from Betty. If Alice had paid $6,000, she would be entitled to $1,000 contribution from Betty.

Unequal Shares—All Obligations Specified. Because cosureties enter into separate contracts with the creditor, the individual suretyship obligations may be restricted to specific amounts that vary among the sureties. In this situation, if the amounts guaranteed are unequal, the surety's shares are determined in proportion to the risk assumed by each. For example, assume Jack, Kelly, and Laura are cosureties on Pam's $50,000 debt to Calvin.

Jack has agreed to guarantee $35,000, Kelly, $15,000, and Laura, $10,000. Pam pays $20,000 and then defaults. The sureties' contributive shares toward the $30,000 loss are as follows:

Surety	Liability Assumed	Fraction	Loss	Contributive Share
Jack	$35,000	35/60	× $30,000	$17,500
Kelly	15,000	15/60	× 30,000	7,500
Laura	10,000	10/60	× 30,000	5,000
				$30,000

If Laura becomes insolvent, the shares would be computed as follows:

Surety	Liability Assumed	Fraction	Loss	Contributive Share
Jack	$35,000	35/50	× $30,000	$21,000
Kelly	15,000	15/50	× 30,000	9,000
				$30,000

If Jack becomes insolvent, the shares would be computed as follows:

Surety	Liability Assumed	Fraction	Loss	Contributive Share
Kelly	15,000	15/25	× $30,000	$18,000
Laura	10,000	10/25	× 30,000	12,000
				$30,000*

*Total liability only $25,000.

Note in this last case that because Kelly and Laura have limited their total liability to $25,000 ($15,000 and $10,000 respectively), they cannot be compelled to pay the entire $30,000 loss. In this case, Calvin will not be able to collect the $5,000 deficiency from any surety because Jack is insolvent and Kelly and Laura have fully performed their suretyship obligations.

Unequal Shares—All Obligations Not Specified. Occasionally, one surety assumes liability without limit and the remaining sureties limit their obligations to stated amounts. In this case, contributive shares are determined by comparing the loss with the amount guaranteed by the surety who assumes the largest *stipulated* obligation. If the loss is *less than or equal to* the amount guaranteed by the largest stipulated surety, then contributive shares are computed as if the surety without limit guaranteed the same amount as the largest stipulated surety. If the loss is *more than* the amount guaranteed by the largest stipulated surety, then the surety without limit is required to contribute as if he had guaranteed the amount of the *default*.

Assume Jack, Kelly, and Laura are sureties on Pam's debt to Calvin, an open line of credit. Jack has agreed to guarantee payment up to the full amount of the obligation as it finally accrues. Kelly has limited her liability to $15,000 and Laura to $10,000. Assuming Pam's ultimate default is $8,000, Jack's contributive share is computed as if he had guaranteed $15,000. In this case, the amount of the loss ($8,000) is less than the amount guaranteed by the largest stipulated surety (Kelly—$15,000) and therefore the first rule above applies. The contributive shares are as follows:

Surety	Liability Assumed	Fraction	Loss	Contributive Share
Jack	$15,000	15/40 ×	$8,000	$3,000
Kelly	15,000	15/40 ×	8,000	3,000
Laura	10,000	10/40 ×	8,000	2,000
				$8,000

If, however, the loss is $25,000, Jack's contributive share is computed as if he had guaranteed the amount of the default because the default ($25,000) is greater than the amount guaranteed by the largest stipulated surety (Kelly—$15,000). In this case, the respective shares are therefore computed as follows:

Surety	Liability Assumed	Fraction	Loss	Contributive Share
Jack	$25,000	25/50 ×	$25,000	$12,500
Kelly	15,000	15/50 ×	25,000	7,500
Laura	10,000	10/50 ×	25,000	5,000
				$25,000

Effect of Settlement and Existence of Security. If the principal defaults, and one cosurety settles with the creditor at less than the amount nominally due from the principal, cosureties are entitled to the benefit of the settlement. For example, assume Frank, Gayle, and Harry are cosureties on Peter's $30,000 obligation to Cameron. Peter defaults and Cameron agrees with Frank to accept a stamp collection fairly valued at $24,000 in full satisfaction of the debt. Frank can recover $8,000 each from Gayle and Harry.

A surety may receive security from the principal to secure the surety's right of reimbursement. Although the existence of the security does not affect the duty of other sureties to contribute, the surety receiving the security must share it with cosureties. That is, in settling the sureties' ultimate liability, each cosurety is entitled to an interest in the security in proportion to his or her liability for the principal's default. Because of this duty to account, a surety's right of contribution is reduced by a

pro rata share of the security if he or she loses, destroys, or releases it to the principal. Assume Frank and Gayle are cosureties on Peter's $10,000 obligation to Cameron. Frank has received rare coins worth $5,000 from Peter as security for Frank's reimbursement. Peter defaults, and Frank pays Cameron $10,000. Frank has a right of contribution from Gayle for $5,000 but must share the security with her. Thus, ultimately both Frank and Gayle will contribute $2,500. The same result follows had Frank sold the coins for $5,000, negligently lost them, failed to realize their fair value on sale, or released them to Peter.

Effect of Release of Cosurety. Occasionally, the creditor will release one cosurety from his obligation. Although such a release does not discharge the remaining cosureties, it does extinguish their ability to obtain contribution from the released cosurety. Therefore, when the creditor releases one of several cosureties, the obligation of the remaining cosureties is reduced by the amount the released cosurety could have been compelled to make contribution.[12] That is, the ultimate liability of each cosurety is computed as if the released surety had contributed. For example, assume Smith and Thompson are cosureties on Palmer's $10,000 obligation to Clark. Clark releases Thompson, and Palmer defaults. Clark can collect no more than $5,000 from Smith, because Thompson could have been compelled to contribute one-half of the loss.

If, as part of the release of one surety, the creditor *preserves his recourse* against cosureties, the obligations of the remaining sureties are not discharged or reduced. In this case, the preservation of recourse puts the released surety on notice that the release is effective only between that surety and the creditor and does not affect the rights of other sureties. Thus, if the remaining sureties pay more than their proportionate share, they are entitled to contribution from the released surety.

Contribution Among Co-promisors. As discussed in Chapter 7, several people may promise to render the same performance making their contractual liability joint or joint and several. When multiple promises of the same performance are made, a suretyship relation necessarily exists between the promisors. That is, whenever two people promise the same performance, either (1) one is the principal obligor and the other a

---

[12]If the creditor can show that the released cosurety is insolvent, the release has no effect on the remaining cosureties' shares, because they could not have obtained contribution from the released cosurety.

surety, or (2) each is *both* a principal obligor *and* a surety. Assume that Art agrees to act as a surety on Ben's $10,000 debt to Corrine. In this case, only Ben (the principal) has assumed ultimate liability. If Art is required to pay, he as a surety may obtain reimbursement from Ben for the full amount. Thus, assuming Ben is solvent, Art, in the final analysis, should pay nothing to Corrine.

Assume, alternatively, that Art and Ben are jointly liable on the $10,000 obligation to Corrine. In this case, both Art and Ben have ultimate liability to pay Corrine $10,000. In addition, Art is a surety for Ben's performance and Ben is a surety for Art's performance. That is, Art and Ben are cosureties. Therefore, if Ben defaults and Art pays Corrine $10,000, Art is entitled to $5,000 in contribution from Ben, under the general principles discussed above.

Exoneration

In the principal-surety context, exoneration is the surety's equitable right to compel the principal to pay the *creditor.* A similar right exists among cosureties. Because each cosurety is liable only for part of the loss, exoneration is limited to the amount that the suing surety would be entitled to receive as contribution had she paid the entire debt. Assume Redman and Story are cosureties on Pendleton's $10,000 obligation to Coffin. Pendleton defaults. If Redman sues Story in exoneration, Story will be required to pay Coffin $5,000.

Subrogation

A surety who satisfies the creditor's claim is subrogated to the creditor's rights against the principal. Such a surety also succeeds to the creditor's position as against *cosureties,* but may receive only her *contributive share* from any cosurety, because as among the cosureties, the subrogated surety should bear a portion of the loss. This

principle is most commonly applied upon bankruptcy of a cosurety.

Suppose Ruth and Sarah are cosureties on Phil's $10,000 debt to Cindy. Phil defaults and Sarah is petitioned into bankruptcy. Ruth pays Cindy $10,000. Ruth may file a $10,000 claim (as subrogee of Cindy's rights) in Sarah's bankruptcy proceeding. Ruth is then entitled to dividends from Sarah's bankrupt estate, but not exceeding $5,000, the extent of Ruth's right of contribution against Sarah. Thus, even if Sarah's estate pays a 60 percent dividend to creditors, Ruth receives only $5,000 on her $10,000 claim.

A surety, after paying the creditor, is similarly subrogated to the creditor's rights in any collateral received from cosureties. Once again, the surety may use such collateral only to the extent necessary to satisfy her right of contribution from the other cosureties.

Subsuretyship

In cosuretyship, the sureties share the ultimate liability. In contrast, in subsuretyship, although there are multiple sureties, at least one surety is entitled to have the other or others bear the *entire* burden. **Subsuretyship** exists when two sureties are bound to answer for the same duty of the principal, but as between the sureties, one bears the whole duty of performance. That is, as between the sureties one is a principal (the "principal surety") and the other (the "subsurety") is a surety. In general, the rules governing the relationship between principal and surety also apply to the principal surety-subsurety relation. The most important characteristic of subsuretyship is that the subsurety, after performance, is entitled to reimbursement from the principal surety. However, if the principal surety performs, he is not entitled to contribution from the subsurety. As previously noted, when multiple sureties are present, they are presumed to be cosureties unless they have agreed to a subsuretyship relation.

Summary

1.   Suretyship provides security to a creditor by the promise of a third party (the surety) to perform the obligation if the debtor does not. Suretyship is a contractual arrangement created when two parties, principal and surety, become legally bound to a creditor for the same performance. Though both principal and surety are liable, as between the two, the principal rather than the surety should perform. Sureties often are described as either compensated (or corporate) or uncompensated (accommodation or gratuitous).

2.   A surety's liability may be primary (a contract of suretyship) or secondary (a contract of guaranty). In the former the

surety's liability is coextensive with the principal's; in the latter, the surety is liable only after the principal's default. In a specialized guaranty contract, a "guaranty of collection," the creditor must both put the principal in default and exhaust all legal remedies against the principal before proceeding against the surety.

3. An offer for a suretyship contract usually is made by the surety to the creditor, and may be made to one creditor (a special guaranty) or to a group of creditors (a general guaranty), and may guarantee a single obligation or successive extensions of credit (a continuing guaranty). The consideration supporting the compensated surety's promise is the premium. An uncompensated surety's promise usually is supported by the creditor's extending credit to the principal.

4. The surety has three rights against the principal: (1) reimbursement—the surety's right to be reimbursed by the debtor *after* paying or otherwise performing the principal obligation, (2) exoneration—the surety's right, *before* paying the creditor, to compel the principal to perform, and (3) subrogation—the right of the surety to succeed to the rights of ("step into the shoes of") the creditor against the principal, after satisfying the principal's duty to the creditor.

5. Suretyship protects the creditor against the burden and delay required to collect the debt from the principal. Accordingly, the surety generally has no right to compel the creditor to attempt collection of the debt from the principal before proceeding against the surety. Similarly, the surety generally may not require the creditor to apply any collateral received from the principal to the debt before proceeding against the surety.

6. Various defenses are available to a surety to reduce or extinguish his obligation to the creditor. These defenses arise from (1) events, such as fraud, occurring during formation of the principal or suretyship contract, (2) events discharging the principal obligation, (3) modification of the principal's duty without the surety's consent, and (4) impairment of collateral by the creditor. A surety with no valid defense, who nevertheless refuses or delays payment, may be held liable for breach of contract or liable in tort for breach of its duty to act in good faith.

7. If two or more sureties are bound to answer for the same duty of the principal, they generally are cosureties who share the loss caused by the principal's default. The process of sharing the ultimate burden among cosureties is known as "contribution." The law has developed detailed rules governing computation of cosureties' shares. In addition to the right of contribution, a surety also possesses rights against cosureties based on exoneration and subrogation. Although cosuretyship is presumed, the sureties may agree to a subsuretyship relation. In this case, as between the sureties one bears the whole duty of performance, that is, one is a principal (the "principal surety") and the other (the "subsurety") is a surety.

Key Terms

suretyship	guaranty of collection
principal	(conditional guaranty,
creditor	guaranty of collectibility)
surety	special guaranty
compensated (corporate)	general guaranty
surety	continuing guaranty
uncompensated (gratuitous or	reimbursement
accommodation) surety	exoneration
bond	subrogation
fidelity bond	cosuretyship
performance bond	contribution
guaranty	subsuretyship

Questions and Problems

33.1 Creditors often obtain security by contractually creating an interest, a lien, in specific real or personal property belonging to the debtor. Obtaining a surety is an alternative or additional method of providing security. What are the advantages to a creditor of suretyship over other types of security? What advantages do contractually created liens have over suretyship?

33.2 Courts and commentators frequently state that an accommodation surety is a "favorite of the law." Why? Should accommodation sureties be treated any differently from corporate sureties? Explain.

33.3 Farmers Produce Co. purchased goods on account from Acme Feed and Supplies, Inc. By March 2005, Farmers owed over $8,000 on account. Acme refused to make further sales on credit unless Farmers obtained a surety. National Insurance Co. agreed to act as surety for debts incurred after March 2005 and Acme extended an additional $5,000 worth of supplies on credit. In July, Farmers advised National that it was in default on the payments to Acme but that Farmers would be able to pay the bills after the fall harvest. National provided $1,000 to Farmers to make a payment on its bill to Acme. Farmers made the payment without giving instructions regarding the application of the payment.
   (a) Acme applied the payment to Farmers' oldest bill dating back to March 2004. Does Acme have the right to apply the payment in this manner? Explain.
   (b) Assume you work for National Insurance Co. You are the officer who decided to advance $1,000 for the payment to Acme. Would you have handled the transaction differently? Explain.

33.4 Watkins Co. is a wholesale supplier of beauty salon products. Pierre, a beauty salon operator, has purchased supplies on credit from Watkins for over ten years. During the last year, however, Pierre had written four checks to Watkins that were returned for insufficient funds. Pierre later covered the checks with cash payments. Watkins called several of Pierre's other creditors and learned that they too had received bad checks from Pierre.

Pierre placed an order for $5,000 worth of supplies from Watkins. Watkins advised Pierre that it would sell the goods on credit only if Pierre obtained a surety. Pierre asked his friend Ruth to act as surety.

(a) Ruth asked Pierre if he had ever had financial problems or trouble paying his bills. Pierre denied having had such problems even though during the last six months his business had suffered severe cash flow problems. Ruth then agreed to become Pierre's surety. Pierre filed for bankruptcy and Watkins sued Ruth for the $5,000 debt. Ruth alleged that Pierre had defrauded her by misrepresenting his financial problems. Assuming that the misrepresentation constituted fraud, would Pierre's fraudulent misrepresentation be grounds for relieving Ruth from liability as a surety to Watkins? Explain.

(b) Assume that the discussion between Pierre and Ruth had occurred while a representative of Watkins was present. The representative knew that Pierre had had financial problems but was unsure whether to mention the problems. Would you recommend that the representative advise Ruth of Pierre's recent financial difficulties? Explain.

(c) Disregard the facts in (a) and (b) above. Assume that after Pierre asked Ruth to serve as surety, Ruth immediately visited Watkins Co.'s office to sign the necessary papers. Does Watkins Co. have any obligation to advise Ruth that Pierre had recently written several bad checks? Explain.

33.5   Wally agreed to purchase a house from Stanley and on March 30, 2004, signed a promissory note by which he agreed to pay $50,000 on March 30, 2005. Wally's wife Rebecca signed the promissory note as an accommodation maker. On March 1, 1985, Wally and Stanley entered into a second agreement by which Stanley agreed to accept five monthly installments of $10,000 (with the first payment due in March) in lieu of $50,000 on March 30. Rebecca was not advised of the second agreement. One provision of the agreement stated "Wally and Stanley agree that Stanley's forbearance on the full payment due on March 30, 2005, does not waive any of the terms of the original note and that all rights and obligations set forth therein are binding in all respects."

Wally defaulted in making the monthly payments. Stanley demanded that Rebecca, as surety, make the $50,000 payment. Rebecca refused saying that Stanley's extension of the time to make payments without her consent discharged her from liability. Is she correct? Explain.

33.6   Third State Bank loaned $10,000 to Dewey to purchase a car. The bank took a security interest in the car and also required Dewey to obtain a surety. Dewey's uncle Jack agreed to serve as surety. Dewey later filed for bankruptcy. At the bankruptcy hearing, Jack discovered that the bank had failed to perfect its security interest in the car. When the bank sued Jack as surety, Jack alleged that he could not be held liable because the bank's failure to perfect its security interest constituted an impairment of collateral. How should the court rule? Explain.

33.7   First State Bank agreed to lend $65,000 to Floyd Dunn for operation of his retail business. The loan agreement, which was signed on August 1, 2003, required Floyd to repay the loan in annual installments with the first installment due on August 1, 2004. The interest rate for the first year was set at 8 percent and was to be adjusted each year after that to a rate equal to 1/2 percent below First State Bank's prime rate. Floyd's mother, Minnie, agreed to act as surety and she signed the loan papers as guarantor. On February 1, 2004, the bank, at Floyd's request, agreed to extend the due date for the first installment to February 1, 2005. As part of the extension agreement, the interest rate was increased to 9.5 percent, which was 1/2 percent below First State Bank's prime rate on February 1, 2004. Despite the extension, Floyd failed to repay any of the debt and First State Bank sued Floyd and his mother, Minnie. Minnie argued that she should be discharged as surety because, without her consent, the bank had extended the due date of the first installment and had increased the interest rate on February 1, 2004. Is Minnie correct? Explain.

PART SIX

PROPERTY

PERSONAL PROPERTY OWNERSHIP AND TRANSFER

Property acquisition, ownership, use, possession, and disposition pervade both personal and commercial life. Individuals and businesses own vast quantities of land devoted to agriculture, manufacturing, product distribution, and retailing. They buy and sell equipment, inventory, and other businesses, enter into contracts, issue stocks and bonds, and secure patents and copyrights. Individuals acquire and dispose of goods (such as appliances, household furnishings, and clothing) for personal use, invest or borrow money, buy and sell homes, and provide for disposition of property on death.

As discussed in Chapter 6, property is defined as the totality of legal relations among persons with respect to a thing, tangible or intangible. Specifically, the law of property addresses the legal relationships existing between a person or persons possessing a legally protected interest in the thing, the owner, and other members of society. Legally protected interests in land are called "real property." Personal property includes everything else capable of ownership. Personal property may be tangible (such as an automobile, stereo equipment, a cat, or any other object that can be moved) or intangible (such as patents, copyrights, negotiable instruments, stocks and bonds, accounts receivable, or other contract rights).

The law of property governs the creation of, transfer of, and limitations on the various ownership interests in the property. This and the following five chapters expand on the property introduction in Chapter 6 by examining these issues for both personal and real property.

Introduction to Property Ownership and Transfer

Character of Property Ownership

The totality of rights constituting full ownership of property may be held by one person or may be divided in a variety of ways, resulting in multiple interests in the same property. The permissible ownership interests existing in property known as "estates" differ in several major respects:

1. *Duration.* A property interest may be created to last infinitely or indefinitely, or to terminate at a given time or upon the occurrence of an event.

2. *Extent of interest held by the owner.* A property owner may have full ownership or may have a more limited interest such as merely a right to possess the property or to receive the income from it.

3. *Time of possession.* Property interests may be split successively with the present right to possession held by one person and the future right to possession (a "future interest") resting in another.

4. *Number of persons concurrently holding a possessory interest.* Two or more persons may simultaneously have the right to possess the same property.

As each property issue is discussed in the following chapters, note how the bundle of rights representing full ownership has been divided. In this manner, the various property subjects can more easily be contrasted and distinguished.

Property Transfer

The holder of an interest in either real or personal property usually acquires it by transfer from a prior owner. The law ordinarily favors the free transferability (alienability) of interests in both real and personal property. In general, interests in property may be transferred either voluntarily or involuntarily during the life of the owner (designated *inter vivos* transfers) or upon the death of the owner.

Voluntary Transfers. Voluntary transfers—those intentionally made without coercion during the life of the transferor—are made either by sale or by gift. An *inter vivos* transfer of an interest in real property is known as a **conveyance** or a **grant** and is accomplished by using a formal document known as a deed. The party making the transfer is known as the grantor and the party to whom the transfer is made is the grantee.

Unlike real property, interests in personal property generally may be transferred *inter vivos* without formality. For example, title to most tangible personal property may be acquired by sale or gift simply by transferring possession from one owner to the next. This general rule is subject to a number of exceptions. For example, statutes commonly provide that certain types of property, such as automobiles, may be transferred only through a formal title certificate. In addition, intangibles, such as accounts, notes, checks, stocks, and bonds, require formalities for transfer dictated by statute.

A person may voluntarily transfer her entire interest in property or may create a more limited interest in the transferee. For example, the owner may transfer the right to possession of the property for a period of time without surrendering ownership. If real property is involved, such a transfer creates a landlord-tenant relationship. If the owner transfers the right to use but not possess the land, an easement is created. Transfer of possession but not ownership of personal property creates a bailment.[1]

Involuntary Transfers. Under certain circumstances, property interests may be transferred involuntarily—without the owner's consent. For example, in real property, under the doctrine of adverse possession, an involuntary transfer occurs when the statute of limitations expires. Further, the eminent domain power allows governmental bodies to take private property for public use if the owner receives just compensation.[2] In addition, both real and personal property transfers may occur upon the bankruptcy of the owner, enforcement of a security interest in the property, or a judicial sale to satisfy an unpaid judgment.

Transfers on Death and in Trust. A person also may transfer property at death, a power recognized by law as one of the bundle of rights constituting private property ownership. Property is transferred on death either by a will or by state "intestate succession" statutes if a person fails to leave a valid will. A transfer of property by will is commonly known as a devise and the transferees known as devisees. Takers of property through intestate succession statutes are known as heirs. Property transfers by will or intestate succession are in essence gifts, but differ from ordinary gifts in that they take effect after the transferor's death.

A property owner also may transfer property by a "trust" created either during her lifetime or upon death. The essence of a trust is a "splitting" of ownership between the trustee who takes and holds legal title to the property and the beneficiaries who hold the equitable or beneficial title.

The property issues previously outlined are covered in the following five chapters and Chapter 59. This chapter examines the various methods of acquiring title

---

[1]Landlord-tenant, easements, and bailments are discussed in Chapters 36, 38, and 35.
[2]Adverse possession and eminent domain are discussed in Chapters 37 and 38.

to or an interest in personal property during life other than by sale or trust, and the law of fixtures. Chapter 35 continues the personal property material with coverage of the law of bailments and documents of title. Finally, Chapter 59 covers intellectual property, such as patents, copyrights, and trademarks.

Chapters 36 through 38 comprise the real property coverage, addressing the fundamental principles of land ownership and transfer and land use regulation. Chapter 39 discusses transfers of both real and personal property on death and in trust.

Acquiring Title to, or an Interest in, Personal Property

Gifts

A **gift** is a voluntary transfer of an interest in property by the owner (the **donor**) to another (the **donee**) without any consideration or compensation. This lack of consideration distinguishes a gift from a transfer by contract or sale. To be legally effective to transfer title to the donee, a gift must meet three requirements, designed generally to prevent fraud:

1. delivery of the subject matter to the donee,
2. present intent by a competent donor to make the gift, and
3. acceptance of the gift by the donee.

The burden of proving these requirements rests with the donee. If they are proven, the gift is said to be "valid" and is generally irrevocable by the donor or those who would otherwise take the property by will or intestate succession upon the donor's death. Note that a gift is an inter vivos transfer of property. Any purported gift that is to take effect only upon the donor's death is invalid. Transfers on death are legally effective only if made in compliance with state statutes governing the validity of wills.

Although both real and personal property may be transferred by gift, most gift cases involve personal property. Real property transfers, whether by sale or gift, require substantial formality—for example, the execution and delivery of a deed to the transferee. Compliance with these formalities generally leaves little doubt regarding the existence of the gift. Most personal property, however, is easily transferable without

particular formality, and the owner often has no formal evidence of title. In this context, the alleged donee's possession of the subject matter may be the only hard evidence that a gift has been made. For this reason, most gift disputes arise after the donor's death. Typically, the parties to the dispute are the alleged donee and the donor's heirs or devisees who assert that they are entitled to the property because no valid gift had been made during the donor's life. The person best qualified to resolve the dispute, the donor, is obviously unavailable to testify concerning how the alleged donee acquired possession.

Delivery. **Delivery** occurs when the donor transfers possession of the subject matter to the donee. Delivery requires that the donor relinquish absolutely the power to use, manage, or otherwise control the property. If the alleged donor fails to do so, no valid gift is made. For example, if the donor states her intent to make a gift of an antique gold watch, but retains it in a safe deposit box to which only she has access, the gift fails for lack of delivery.[3]

The delivery requirement accomplishes several purposes. First, the formal act of delivery serves a cautionary function, protecting the donor against ill-advised or impulsive gifts. Second, delivery is important in establishing the second element of a valid gift—whether the owner actually *intended* to make a gift. By surrendering control over the property to the donee the donor provides strong evidence of intent to make a gift and thus helps resolve cases in which other evidence of intent is ambiguous or sketchy. Third, the delivery requirement protects the donor against fraudulent assertions by others that a gift has been made.

Symbolic or Constructive Delivery. The manner of delivery varies depending on the nature of the subject matter, its location, and the location and physical condition of the parties. As a general rule, if the property can be transferred manually—for example, a watch, jewelry, or a television set—physical delivery of the object itself is required. The donee need not actually take physical possession as long as the object is placed within her control and out of the control of the donor.

---

[3]A valid delivery may be made before, at the same time as, or after the words of gift or other expression of intent. Thus, redelivery is not required if the owner decides to make a gift of property already in the donee's possession.

For example, the property may be placed in a bank account, trunk, or other receptacle owned by the donee.

Frequently, manual delivery is impossible or impractical because of the size or location of the subject matter. To address this situation, the doctrines of symbolic and constructive delivery have been developed. A **symbolic delivery** occurs when the donor delivers another object in place of the actual subject matter. In a **constructive delivery** the donor transfers to the donee the means to obtain possession and control of the property involved.[4]

The most common type of constructive delivery is the transfer of a key to a safe deposit box, trunk, or other locked receptacle in order to make a gift of the contents. Courts generally sustain constructive deliveries when physical transfer of the contents is inconvenient or impractical (for example, when the donor is bedridden), or the subject matter is large or bulky or located at a site remote to the parties.

Constructive deliveries have been sustained, however, even if the property can be manually transferred. For example, delivery of keys to a locked box located in the bedridden donor's room may be an effective delivery of the contents. Most cases appear to turn on whether, after considering all facts and circumstances of the individual case, the court is convinced that the alleged donor in fact intended to make a gift of the property in dispute.

Not all gifts involve tangible personal property ("goods" or "choses in possession") that can be transferred manually. In many cases, the property is intangible (a "chose in action"), consisting of a claim by one person against another for the performance or transfer of something valuable. Examples include ordinary debts and contract rights, bank accounts, checks and notes, bonds, shares of stock, and life insurance policies. As a general rule, a gift of such assets may be accomplished by delivering either the writing customarily accepted as evidence of the obligation (such as shares of stock, an insurance policy, or a savings account passbook) or a writing signed by the donor.

In the following case, the court considered whether the donor had made delivery of a gift of stock.

---

[4]As used in law, the term "constructive" means that a given legal result is implied, inferred, or deduced by law when certain facts are present. The term is used as a modifier to mean, in essence, "as if."

Estate of Ross v. Ross
626 P.2d 489 (Utah 1981)

David Ross was a corporate officer and director in five family-owned corporations. In 1972, David's son Rod began working for one of the corporations, Equitable Life and Casualty Insurance. Between 1974 and 1978 David told several persons that he wanted to reward Rod for his work with Equitable Life by giving him company stock. David exchanged some of his stock in Equitable for new shares issued in Rod's name. Both the corporate records and the stock certificates listed Rod as owner. David, however, kept the certificates in an envelope in a bank safety deposit box with certificates of other family members. The stock later was moved to a safe in the company office to which only David and his brother had access. When stock dividends were issued, David placed the new certificates in Rod's envelope in the safe. All cash dividends were paid to Rod, who attended and voted at shareholders' meetings.

David died in 1978 after having transferred 25 percent of his stock in the family businesses to Rod. David's will divided his estate equally among his three children. Thus, in combination with the lifetime transfers, Rod would have owned 50 percent of his father's stock while his brother and sister each would have received 25 percent.

The brother and sister filed a claim in probate court alleging that the lifetime transfers were not valid gifts because David had failed to deliver the stock certificates to Rod. The trial court ruled that David had made a valid lifetime gift of 25 percent of his stock to Rod. Appellants, Rod's brother and sister, appealed.

Howe, Justice

. . . Appellants assert that three elements must be proven for a person to claim valid title to property by inter vivos gift: a clear and unmistakable intention on the part of the donor to pass immediate ownership, an irrevocable delivery, and acceptance. . . . They contend . . . that the court's decision was erroneous in that the element of irrevocable delivery was not established by clear and convincing evidence.

An important purpose of the delivery requirement is to avoid the hedging of a would-be donor who wishes to retain certain benefits of ownership, including the control of the gift property, while designating another as the recipient of the property during the donor's lifetime. If a gift is not completed before one's death, of course, it is subject to the formalities of testamentary disposition. In the instant case, therefore, the finding of a gift must be based on the decedent's voluntary parting with the control of the stock during his lifetime.

It is appellants' position that decedent should have parted with his dominion over the certificates by physically delivering them to Rod and that the transfer of ownership on the corporate records was insufficient to meet the requirements of delivery. . . .

Viewing the facts of this case in light of the requirements of inter vivos gifts, we find the gifts of stock to Rod were complete and valid. Evidence of decedent's intention that Rod be made the owner of the stock in question during his lifetime was uncontroverted. Appellants do not challenge the sufficiency of the evidence as to donative intent nor the finding of the trial court that the change in ownership was recorded on the corporate books. New certificates were issued in Rod's name. The decedent did not thereafter exercise control over the stocks. On the contrary, Rod voted the stock as its legal owner and received cash and stock dividends.

The fact that the stock certificates were kept in a safe to which decedent, but not Rod, had access is not fatal to the finding of a completed gift. The decedent had physical possession of stock certificates belonging to a number of other Ross family members. There was no assertion or evidence that he exerted control or possessory rights over any of that stock. His custody of Rod's stock was simply consistent with the practice within the family businesses of keeping the stock certificates in a central location clearly identified as to the owners of the shares. Individual envelopes carried owners' names, stock certificate numbers, and the number of shares represented by the certificates.

We find no error in the trial court's . . . conclusion that the inter vivos gifts to Rod were valid. . . .

[Judgment affirmed.]

Intent. A valid gift requires proof that the donor intended to transfer title gratuitously. The person to whom the property is delivered must become the new owner rather than a custodian of the property, or an agent for the original owner. Evidence of the donor's express statements, the relationship of the parties, the size of the gift, and the donor's financial situation may be used to show intent to pass title gratuitously. The donor also must possess sufficient mental capacity to appreciate the nature of his or her action. A gift induced by fraud, undue influence, or duress may be avoided by the donor or the donor's estate.

Even if intention can be shown, the gift fails without a proper delivery. That is, a gift that is to take effect in the future is simply a promise to make a gift and is unenforceable for lack of consideration. Suppose that at a family reunion rich uncle Arthur says to his favorite nephew John, "I promise to give you my antique gold watch at your college graduation ceremony next Saturday." Arthur incurs no liability for a subsequent failure to make the gift.

Acceptance. Acceptance of the gift by the donee is the final element of a valid gift. It is required because a person cannot, in an *inter vivos* transaction, have property forced upon her against her will. If, however, the gift is beneficial, the donee's acceptance is presumed. This presumption is used to sustain gifts made to a third party on the donee's behalf unknown to the donee until after the donor's death, and gifts to minors and mental incompetents.

Gifts Causa Mortis. Two types of gifts are recognized: *inter vivos* gifts (the subject of the preceding discussion) and gifts *causa mortis*. Both require the elements of intent, delivery, and acceptance. The **gift *causa mortis*** differs from an *inter vivos* gift in two respects. First, it is made in anticipation or contemplation of the donor's imminent death. Second, it is revocable by the donor at any time prior to his death and is automatically revoked upon the donor's recovery or delivery from the illness, injury, or peril inducing the gift, or if the donee fails to outlive the donor.

A gift *causa mortis* is similar to a testamentary (by will) transfer because it is not finally and irrevocably effective until the donor's death. Nevertheless, in order to fulfill the donor's intention, courts do not treat a gift *causa mortis* as an invalid attempt to circumvent the formalities of a will. Instead, the deathbed gift is deemed a present transfer, subject to revocation as previously indicated. To prevent fraud courts usually validate such deathbed gifts only if evidence of their existence is clear and convincing.

Original Acquisition

At any given time, certain tangible objects may not be owned by anyone. Two primary examples of unowned property are (1) wild animals, birds, and fish in their natural state, and (2) abandoned property. Title to unowned goods may be acquired by **original acquisition** by taking possession.

Title acquired by capturing or killing wild animals is subject to applicable game laws and the rights of the owner of the land on which the animal is captured. Although a landowner does not own the wildlife on her property until reducing it to possession, the landowner has superior rights to game killed or caught on the land by a trespasser. In addition, mere pursuit of a wild animal does not constitute possession, allowing an intervening party to acquire title. Nevertheless, animals or fish caught in a trap or net are in the "constructive possession," and therefore owned, by the person owning the trap or net. If the animal escapes, possession and ownership cease, meaning that any person subsequently capturing the animal becomes the owner.[5]

Title to abandoned property also may be acquired by taking possession. To establish **abandonment** the owner must have *intended* to relinquish permanently and absolutely all interest in the property. Most disputes arise when no positive evidence of abandonment exists—for example, the owner's express statements or conduct—and intent must be inferred from the owner's failure after a lapse of time to make an effort to reclaim the property. A common form of abandoned property is marine wreckage, which is governed by special principles of admiralty law.

Accession

Accession (literally meaning "something added") occurs when value in the form of labor or property, or both, is added to tangible personal property. The doctrine, in one form, supports the right of an owner to all that her property produces. For example, the off-spring of an animal belongs to its owner. These are "natural" accessions in contrast to "artificial" accessions in which value is added to one person's property by the labor or materials or both of another. Most disputes involve artificial accessions and arise after either the property improved or property added has been "converted"[6]; that is, after the owner has been *wrongfully* deprived of the property either by the person making the improvements or another. The law must then determine the state of the title to the new article created and the rights of the respective parties.

To resolve accession disputes, the court must determine whether labor, materials, or both are added by the converter. If labor alone is added—for example, the owner's lumber is converted into a cabinet—the result appears to turn on a combination of two factors:

1. *The increase in the value of the property caused by the addition of labor.* As the disparity in value, before and after, increases, the court is more likely to hold that the converter has acquired title to the finished product. In this case, the original owner is entitled to money damages for the value of the property before conversion.

2. *Whether the conversion was innocent or willful.* As a general rule, a willful converter may not acquire title to a chattel because of added value caused by his labor. That is, the finished product remains the property of the original owner, regardless of the increase in value.

If *goods* of one owner are added to those of another, the resulting product generally belongs to the owner of the principal goods. This result follows even if the owner of the principal goods acts wrongfully in acquiring and incorporating the accessions into the property. Assume Joan fraudulently acquires fabric from Bob and uses it to reupholster the interior of her car. Both the fabric and the car belong to Joan. Bob, of course, is entitled to recover money damages. This principle has been applied in some cases even if the accessions can be removed without substantial damage to the principal good.

Confusion

Like accession, confusion disputes arise when property of two or more persons is combined causing conflicting claims to the resulting whole. In **confusion,** however, the combination involves mere *commingling* of similar goods rather than a change in the nature of the goods (by adding labor or combining them with other goods) characteristic of accession. The goods involved in confusion disputes usually are **fungible,** meaning that one unit of the combined mass is indistinguishable from another. Fungible goods, which are usually sold by weight or measure, include oil, sand, gravel, other minerals, timber, and grain. Confusion does not arise if the specific property of the individual owners remains segregated or can be identified. Disputes arise when goods, though physically unchanged, have become so

---

[5]These rules apply only to wild animals. Domestic animals are governed generally by the same rules of law applicable to inanimate tangible personal property, such as a car or television set.

[6]Conversion is discussed in Chapter 5.

commingled that it is impossible to ascertain and return specific property.

If the confused goods are similar in grade and quality, and the proportion contributed by each owner can be established, each owner may take her proportionate share. This approach achieves an equitable result even when the commingling is fraudulent or intentional, because the innocent party receives goods similar in grade, quality, and amount to those confused.

If the proportions contributed by each owner cannot be ascertained, either because the respective quantities are unknown or because the goods are not of like grade and quality, some courts award the entire mass to the innocent party if the confusion is fraudulent or willful. Some courts have applied this harsh forfeiture remedy even to a careless or negligent commingling. Other courts have adopted a more equitable approach to both the willful and the negligent case by allocating the burden of proof. Once the innocent party has established the commingling, the burden shifts to the wrongdoer to prove what portion of the combined property he owns. If the wrongdoer is unable to do so, the entire mass belongs to the innocent party. Thus, the innocent party is protected to the full value of his contribution in either case, but the law prevents a forfeiture of any excess if the wrongdoer can prove his share.

If the commingling is not negligent or willful but instead occurs (1) with the consent of the parties, (2) by an act of a third party, or (3) by an Act of God, the parties are treated as tenants in common[7] of the resulting mass in proportion to their contributed share. If the amounts contributed cannot be ascertained, courts often achieve rough justice by treating the owners as holding equal shares.

Finding Lost Property

Personal property is **lost** when its owner casually and involuntarily parts with it without recalling either the circumstances or place of the loss. A **finder** is a person who discovers and takes possession of the lost property. The finder does not obtain title to lost goods against the owner, but has superior rights in the goods against all persons but the true owner. Assume Andrew finds a watch belonging to Oscar. Before Oscar is located, Andrew loses the watch, which is subsequently found by Bart. Andrew may recover the watch from Bart. The

same result follows if Bart had stolen the watch from Andrew.

After taking possession, the finder must make a reasonable effort to locate the owner and return the property to her. In many states, appropriate procedures are stated in **estray statutes,** which commonly provide for advertisement of the goods found followed by a stated period after which the property belongs absolutely to the finder, to the state, or partly to each. A finder who knows or learns the identity of the owner, but fails to take reasonable measures to return the property to the owner, is guilty of theft.

The finder's title and right to possession are not affected by the ownership of the property in or on which it is found. This rule is subject to a number of exceptions, the most important of which is based upon the distinction between "lost" and "mislaid" property.

Property is "lost" casually and involuntarily. In contrast, the owner may intentionally and voluntarily lay down an article and then depart, forgetting to take the property. Such property is deemed **misplaced** or **mislaid,** not lost. Under the traditional rule, mislaid property belongs to the owner of the property where it is found, not to the finder. This rule is designed to facilitate return of the item to its true owner. That is, once the owner discovers the property missing, the owner may remember where she left it and return there. Distinguishing lost from mislaid property is often a difficult issue resolved after considering a number of factors including the nature of the property, the place where it is found, and the circumstances of the original parting.

Fixtures

A **fixture** is an item of personal property that, because of its attachment to, or close association with, land, is regarded as part of the land. The essence of a fixture is that what was once tangible movable personal property (hereafter called a "chattel") subsequently becomes part of the real estate with which it is associated. Although treated as part of the real estate, a fixture such as a furnace, hot water heater, or chandelier does not lose its identity. Personal property integrated into the structure of a building such as boards, nails, bricks, and plaster is governed by the law of accession.

Fixture disputes generally arise between a person (or persons) claiming an interest in the chattel as *personal*

---

[7]Tenancy in common is discussed in Chapter 36.

property and another (or others) holding an interest in the *land* on which the article is located, asserting that it has become a fixture and therefore part of the real estate. The question for judicial determination is whether the chattel, by definition originally personal property, has become so closely related to real estate that it should now be legally treated as real property. Typical fixture disputes, usually classified as involving either "common stem" or "divided" ownership, are discussed below.

Common Stem Ownership

The **common stem ownership** situation is the simplest and most frequently encountered case. In these cases the **annexor** (person placing the chattel on the real estate) owns *both* the chattel and the land to which it is annexed. To illustrate, assume Vicky, a property owner, makes an improvement to her property by installing a furnace, central air conditioning, a chandelier, kitchen cabinets, or a hot water heater. Subsequently she sells the house to Walter. Nothing is said about the improvement in the contract for sale. After moving in, Walter discovers that Vicky has taken the article with her. Was Vicky entitled to do so, or did the chattel pass to Walter with the ownership of the real estate? The answer to this question depends upon whether the property in question is a fixture. A fixture, as part of the land, passes with ownership of the real estate. Thus, if the article is deemed a fixture Walter prevails; if not, Vicky prevails. Fixtures also pass as real property under a will, are part of any security covered by a mortgage, and are subject to a real property tax.

Whether or not a chattel has become a fixture is a legal conclusion, usually a question of fact for the jury to decide. To guide the jury, various tests for distinguishing a fixture have been developed by statute and judicial decision. Certainly the most commonly recited test is the three-part standard originally adopted by the Ohio Supreme Court in 1853 in *Teaff v. Hewitt.*[8] In that case, the court stated that a fixture is characterized by (1) actual annexation of the chattel to the realty, (2) *appropriation* or adaptation to the use or purpose of the realty to which the chattel is connected, and (3) *intention* by the annexor to make the chattel a permanent part of the land.[9]

The *Teaff* standard places primary emphasis on the third aspect, the *intent* of the annexor at the time of annexation to permanently improve the property. All other fac-

tors are merely circumstantial evidence of that intent. Circumstantial evidence is necessary because the annexor has not expressly indicated intent. Further, relevant intent is not subjective (what the annexor intended in his or her own mind) but objective (what impression the annexor's conduct created in others, such as creditors or purchasers).

Determining Intent. In resolving the issue of intent, important factors that should be considered suggested by the foregoing discussion include the following.

Mode and Degree of Annexation. This factor often, although not necessarily, provides the strongest guidance toward resolving the issue. The inquiry generally focuses on whether the chattel may be removed without substantial damage either to it or to the premises to which it is attached. For example, a central air conditioning system is more likely to be held a fixture than a window air conditioner.

Extent to Which the Article Is Specially Adapted to the Premises. This factor may be used, for example, to find keys, storm windows, screens, gas stoves, refrigerators, and rollaway beds to be fixtures even though the degree of annexation is slight or nonexistent.

Time and Place the Case Arises. Storm windows may more likely be held fixtures in northern climates, whereas an air conditioner may more often be designated a fixture in the south.

No one factor is determinative. All the surrounding circumstances are considered together to resolve the ultimate issue: *intent* as objectively manifested by the annexor. The following case illustrates the application of the *Teaff* standard to determine whether certain chattels were fixtures, and therefore subject to a real property tax.

Crocker National Bank v. City and County of San Francisco
782 P.2d 278 (Cal. 1989)

The defendants, the city and county of San Francisco, determined that electronic data processing and computer equipment owned by plaintiff Crocker National Bank constituted fixtures and imposed real property taxes on the equipment. Crocker sued the city and county alleging that

---

[8]1 Ohio St. 511 (1853).

[9] *Id.* at 529–530.

the equipment was personal property and, therefore, not subject to the taxes. The trial court held that the equipment was a fixture and ruled in favor of the city and county. After the intermediate appellate court affirmed, Crocker appealed to the California Supreme Court.

Mosk, Justice

. . . [I]n California "It is well settled that in determining whether an article constitutes a fixture, three criteria must be taken into consideration: (1) the manner of its annexation to the realty; (2) its adaptability to the use and purpose for which the realty is used; and (3) the intention with which the annexation is made. . . . It is also settled that for tax purposes the "intention" must be determined by the physical facts or reasonably manifested outward appearances. . . . In resolving whether an article placed on the premises constitutes a fixture or personal property, the aforelisted three elements do not play equal parts. In making the determination in a particular case the element of intent is regarded as a crucial and overriding factor, with the other two criteria being considered only as subsidiary ingredients relevant to the determination of the intent." [*Seatrain Terminals of California, Inc. v. County of Alameda,* 147 Cal. Rptr. 578 (Cal. App. 1978).] . . .

[T]he test reduces itself to whether a reasonable person would consider the item to be a permanent part of the property, taking into account annexation, adaptation, and other objective manifestations of permanence. . . .

The record establishes a number of facts beyond dispute. The equipment at issue comprises scores of separate items, including central processing units and various kinds of so-called "peripheral" devices. The superior court expressly found that "most of the . . . equipment herein can be characterized as 'general purpose,' 'off-the-shelf,' and 'fungible'. . . ." The evidence shows that the rest cannot reasonably be characterized otherwise.

As for annexation, the equipment was not physically attached to the building through permanent connections, as by means of cement, plaster, nails, bolts, or screws. Rather, it was attached merely through standardized "quick-disconnect" plugs that were inserted into the power source. Also, the items were readily movable without damage to themselves or to the building, and were in fact readily moved into, around, and out of, the structure. This was true of large central processing units, which weighed several thousand pounds

and were rolled about on built-in casters; it was also true of small peripheral devices, which weighed only a few pounds and were carried by hand. Although certain pieces were connected to each other in "systems" or "groupings," they were joined not by permanent links but by standardized "quick-disconnect" cables.

As for adaptation, the equipment was not designed or modified for the building and the building was not designed or modified for the equipment. It is true that the building was planned and constructed as an operations or data processing center, and that safety, security, cooling, power, and fire-suppression systems were designed into, or added onto, the structure at least in part to accommodate electronic data processing equipment. Such facts, however, are not dispositive of the question of permanence. If they were, modern office buildings would automatically transform modern office equipment, such as telecommunication and reproduction systems, into fixtures. Obviously, they do not.

Finally, there are no other objective manifestations of permanence that are sufficient to outweigh the manifestations revealed by the evidence bearing on annexation and adaptation—viz., that the equipment did *not* constitute a permanent part of the building. . . . Here, those facts compel a determination that the equipment did not constitute a permanent part of the building. . . .

Accordingly, we conclude that a reasonable person, taking into account annexation, adaptation, and other objective manifestations of permanence, would not consider the equipment at issue to constitute a permanent part of the building. . . .

[Judgment reversed and remanded.]

Divided Ownership

A second type of fixture dispute, the **divided ownership** case, arises when the owner of a chattel annexes it to the land of another, requiring a determination of whether the attached article now belongs to the landowner. Although this divided ownership may arise with respect to chattels annexed by a life tenant, or even a trespasser, it usually occurs when a tenant makes improvements on the landlord's property and then seeks to remove them at the expiration of the lease. Although the primary issue is again intent, tenants are not as likely as owners to intend to permanently improve the real estate. Accordingly, courts have generally allowed removal of chattels affixed by tenants.

If the chattels are attached for use in the tenant's trade or business (for example, counters, machinery, shelves, or light fixtures), the tenant's right to remove them is well settled. Such articles are somewhat confusingly known as **trade fixtures,** which are not fixtures at all because they do not pass to the owner of the underlying real property interest, the landlord. This right of removal has generally been liberally construed in the tenant's favor to include chattels affixed either for particular business or agricultural needs, and the right commonly extends even to substantial structures on the land, such as a barn or shed. In fact, tenants have been allowed to remove structures, even if the structure is thereby reduced to its raw materials.

Despite this broad policy favoring the tenant in these cases, limitations on the right of removal exist that arise either expressly or from the surrounding circumstances:

1. Because the lease is a contract, the parties may explicitly provide for disposition of the chattels, making items otherwise removable nonremovable, and vice versa.

2. Courts commonly draw a distinction between those articles affixed to further the tenant's particular needs (allowing removal) and those that amount to a permanent improvement of the lessor's premises (more hesitant to allow removal).

3. The tenant must generally remove the chattels during the term of the lease. This approach prevents the disturbance of the succeeding possessory interest (landlord or subsequent tenant) caused by the former tenant's entry to remove the chattel.

Sale of Goods Apart from Land — Applicable Law

A property owner may desire to sever an item that is a fixture or otherwise part of the land and sell, use, or otherwise dispose of it *apart* from the land. When goods closely associated with real estate are sold, the law must determine whether a sale of real or personal property is involved. If the item is real property, the transaction is governed by common law contract and property principles. If the item is personal property, the transaction is a sale of goods governed by Article 2 of the UCC.

The rules determining the law applicable to sales of goods apart from the land are stated in §2–107, summarized below.

1. A contract for the sale of (1) minerals (including oil and gas) to be extracted or (2) a structure or its materials to be removed from the land (for example, an old barn to be torn down and its lumber salvaged) is a contract for the sale of *goods* subject to Article 2 if the seller is required to sever. If the buyer is to sever, the transaction is considered one affecting *land* and is subject to the law governing real estate transfers. Assume Seller contracts to sell to Buyer an old barn that is to be torn down and removed from the land. The contract is governed by Article 2 if Seller is to sever, but is a sale of an interest in land (and thus outside the scope of Article 2) if Buyer is to sever.

2. A contract for the sale apart from the underlying real estate of growing crops, timber to be cut, or fixtures is a sale of goods governed by Article 2 regardless of who severs even though they form part of the land at the time of the contract. Assume Seller owns a house containing an ornate chandelier. Seller sells the chandelier to Buyer under a contract requiring Buyer (or Seller) to remove it from the house. The chandelier is a good and its sale is therefore governed by Article 2. Note that Article 2 governs only the contract for sale. It does not resolve the various disputes arising concerning ownership of such property. These are left primarily to the common law of fixtures.

Summary

1. The law of both real and personal property is concerned with the creation and transfer of various ownership interests in the property. Property ownership may be held by one person or by a number of persons who may hold widely varying interests in the same property. Whatever their nature or extent, ownership interests usually are acquired by transfer from a prior owner. Property may be transferred either voluntarily or involuntarily during the owner's life or on the owner's death.

2. In addition to transfers by contract or in trust, an interest in personal property may be acquired during the owner's life by gift, original acquisition, accession, confusion, and by finding lost property.

3. A gift is a voluntary transfer of an interest in property by the donor to the donee without consideration or compensation. To be valid, and thus irrevocable by the donor, the gift must meet three requirements: (1) delivery of the subject matter to the donee, (2) present intention by a competent donor to make the gift, and (3) acceptance by the donee. Even if these three elements are met, a gift made in anticipation of death (a gift "causa mortis") is revocable by the donor at any time prior to death and is automatically revoked if the donor recovers.

4. Title to personal property may be acquired by original acquisition by reducing previously unowned property to possession. Two primary examples of property that may be acquired by original acquisition are wild animals, birds, and fish in their natural state and abandoned property.

5. The law of accession has been developed to resolve disputes arising when the labor and materials of one person are added to the property of another. The law determines the state of the title to the new article created and the rights of the respective parties.

6. Confusion occurs when similar property of two or more persons becomes so commingled that the specific property of each can no longer be ascertained. The law of confusion determines the proportionate share of the commingled goods owned by each party.

7. Property is lost when the owner involuntarily parts with it without recalling the circumstances or the place of the loss. In this case, a finder who subsequently takes possession of the property has superior rights in it against all but the true owner. The finder's title and right to possession are not generally affected by the ownership of the land in or on which property is found. This rule is subject to a number of exceptions, the most important of which is based on the distinction between "lost" and "mislaid" property.

8. Disputes may arise when items of personal property become closely affixed or adapted to a particular tract of real property. In this case, two competing parties, one holding an interest in the chattel as personal property and another holding an interest in the land to which the property is attached, may claim an interest in the chattel. These disputes are resolved by the law of fixtures. The UCC resolves a related question determining whether goods severed and sold apart from land, such as crops, timber, or minerals, are treated as real or personal property.

Key Terms

conveyance (grant)
gift
donor
donee
delivery
symbolic delivery
constructive delivery
gift *causa mortis*
original acquisition
abandonment
accession
confusion
fungible goods
lost property
finder
estray statute
misplaced (mislaid) property
fixture
common stem ownership
annexor
divided ownership
trade fixtures

Questions and Problems

34.1 Assume Dave transfers a diamond ring to Carl with instructions to deliver the ring to Dave's daughter Sue as a gift. Under what circumstances would Dave's transfer of the ring to Carl constitute a valid delivery of the ring to Sue? When would such a transfer not be a valid delivery? Would a valid gift be made if Dave had directed Carl to deliver the ring only after Dave's death?

34.2 William and Beth were engaged to be married in June. In January, William purchased a diamond engagement ring and gave it to Beth. In May, Beth broke the engagement. William sued Beth demanding return of the engagement ring. Beth alleged that the ring was a gift. What result? Explain.

34.3 Father opened a joint savings account with his adult Son. Both Father and Son provided specimen signatures and Father told Son, "This account is to be for your benefit." For the next ten years, Father kept the account passbook, made deposits and withdrawals, and declared the interest as his income for tax purposes. Assume that Son obtains the passbook and withdraws all of the funds in the account. Father demands return of the funds and Son refuses saying Father had made a gift of the account to Son. Father explains that it was his intention that Son have the account only after Father's death. Did Father make a valid gift? Explain.

34.4 Henry suffered a severe heart attack and was admitted to the hospital in critical condition. When his good friend Theresa came to visit him, Henry told her to go to his house and to take the envelope on the top of his desk saying, "The envelope is for you." With another friend, Theresa picked up the envelope and found that it contained several certificates of deposit. Henry died the following day. The heirs claim that the certificates of deposit were estate assets. Theresa claimed the certificates of deposit were a gift *causa mortis* to her.
(a) What arguments should the heirs raise to prove that the gift was invalid?
(b) What arguments should Theresa raise to prove the gift was valid?

34.5 Old Orchard Bank provides a vault where customers may rent safety deposit boxes to keep valuables and documents. In the vault are private booths with tables accessible to customers who are using their safety deposit boxes. Bernice Pace, who rented a safety deposit box at Old Orchard Bank, found $10,000 on a chair in one of the private booths. She turned the money over to the bank, which notified customers that a large sum of money had been found in a booth. No one claimed the money. After one year, Pace asserted that the money was rightfully hers. The bank refused to return the money to her. Who owns the money? Explain.

34.6   A state has enacted a statute imposing a tax on "real property and improvements thereon and fixtures attached thereto." The state tax assessor has decided the following property may be taxed under the statute. Is the assessor correct?

(a)   A storage shed located on Fred's farm. Fred purchased the prefabricated shed at a hardware store and placed it on his property, using a concrete foundation.

(b)   A specially constructed bank vault door (fair market value of $100,000). First National Bank installed the door when it created a vault room on its premises to provide safety deposit storage for its customers.

(c)   A crystal chandelier recently installed in Nelson's palatial mansion. Nelson purchased the chandelier in Europe where it had been hanging in the castle of a German baron. The chandelier was installed in Nelson's mansion by bolting it to an electrical socket in the ceiling.

34.7   Clarence purchased a radio transmission tower on an installment contract from Motorola Communications. Clarence then leased a parcel of land from the Industrial Corporation. Clarence installed the tower on the land. The tower was 400 feet tall and was anchored to the ground by a concrete slab measuring ten feet square and extending eight feet into the ground. Additionally, guy wires secured the tower and were attached to rods sunk six feet in the ground. Two years after installing the tower, Clarence defaulted in making payments to both Motorola and Industrial. Motorola attempted to repossess the tower but Industrial asserted that the tower had become a fixture. Who owns the tower? Explain.

34.8   T-V Transmission, Inc. (T-V) furnishes cable television service to subscribers in Pawnee County, Nebraska. The company operates an antenna that feeds signals to a cable that T-V has constructed and attached to utility poles throughout the area. When a person subscribes to the cable television service, T-V runs an additional cable and support wire (known as an "aerial housedrop") from the utility pole to the subscriber's house. If a subscriber discontinues cable television service, service is cut off at the utility pole by installation of a terminator, but the aerial housedrop remains in place.

Pawnee County Board of Equalization assesses taxes on personal property in the county. The board assessed taxes against T-V for all aerial housedrops it had installed in the county. T-V appealed, alleging that upon installation, the aerial housedrops became fixtures. Under the three-part standard governing fixtures discussed in the text, is T-V correct? Explain.

34.9   Bear Bluff Farms operates a farm on which it grows cranberries. Cranberry vines generally do not produce a marketable crop of fruit until at least four years after planting, but after the first crop the vines will produce fruit indefinitely. Some vines have produced cranberries for more than 100 years. Bear Bluff Farms borrowed $2 million from the Federal Land Bank to purchase 5,000 acres of land and granted Federal Land Bank a mortgage on the land to secure the loan. Federal Land Bank recorded the mortgage on May 4. Bear Bluff Farms then borrowed $500,000 from First Wisconsin Bank to purchase cranberry vines that it planted on the 5,000 acres of land. First Wisconsin Bank retained a security interest in "all cranberry vines, growing vines, and cranberry produce." First Wisconsin Bank recorded its security interest on May 12. A year later Bear Bluff Farms went bankrupt. The bankruptcy court must determine which of the two banks is entitled to the cranberry vines. Federal Land Bank argues that the cranberry vines are fixtures and, therefore, are part of the real estate to which it is entitled. First Wisconsin Bank argues that the cranberry vines are personal property to which it is entitled. How should the court rule? Explain.

CHAPTER 35

BAILMENTS, DOCUMENTS OF TITLE, AND LETTERS OF CREDIT

Bailments are pervasive in modern life. Whenever you loan a book to a friend, borrow your neighbor's lawn mower, drop your car off for repairs, ship goods by air express, or store goods in a warehouse, a bailment exists. In its broadest sense a **bailment** is simply the rightful possession of goods by someone not the owner. A bailment typically is created by delivery of tangible personal property from a person in possession (the **bailor**) to another (the **bailee**) for a specified purpose without transfer of title. The bailor retains ownership and expects that the property will be returned upon completion of the bailment.

Bailments are fundamentally different from sales or gifts. In a sale or gift, title to the property and the unlimited right to possess and use it pass to the buyer or donee. In a bailment, title remains in the bailor and the bailee's use of the property is limited by the terms of the bailment. In addition, a sale or gift does not envision a return of the property to the owner present in a bailment.

Introduction to Bailments

Types of Bailments

Most bailments arise out of contract between the bailor and bailee, such as leases of personal property and bailments for repair, shipment, or storage. Thus, the rental of a car or the shipment of goods by rail, truck, or air creates a bailment. Bailments also may be created gratuitously. For example, a person may lend her binoculars to a friend to use at a football game.

Although most bailments result from an agreement between the parties, occasionally a person obtains possession of another's goods without that person's knowledge or consent. Most courts classify this arrangement as an **involuntary, constructive,** or **quasi-bailment.**

Examples include the finder of lost articles, a person in possession of goods delivered by mistake or deposited on her land by accident or force of nature, and a landlord in possession of goods left by a tenant upon termination of a lease.

The law of bailments determines the bailee's liability for (1) the loss, theft, damage, or destruction of goods in the bailee's possession and (2) misdelivery—delivery of the goods to a person other than the bailor or otherwise contrary to the terms of the bailment. Bailment law is derived from several sources: the common law, state statutes (most notably Article 7 of the UCC), and federal law. This chapter divides the substantive law of bailments into two general parts: bailee's liability in general and the specialized liability of professional bailees (warehousemen and carriers).

Possession in Bailments

The bailee's possession of the property is the essence of a bailment. Without possession, no bailment exists, and the legal consequences discussed later in this chapter do not arise. Possession generally requires that the bailee obtain physical control over the property involved and intend to exercise that control.

Physical Control. "Parking lot" cases illustrate the concept of possession in bailments. Ann, a car owner, parks her auto for a fee in a parking lot or garage owned by Ben. While still on the lot, the car is damaged or stolen. In determining Ben's liability (if any) for the theft or damage, the nature of the relationship between Ann and Ben must be ascertained. If Ann merely rents a reserved space from Ben, but parks the car herself and keeps the key, the relationship may be characterized as a lease of land or in some cases a license (a revocable privilege to use another person's land). No bailment has been created because Ann did not transfer possession of the car to Ben. Parking garage receipts commonly state explicitly that no bailment results from parking the car (for reasons that will become apparent below). On the other hand, if Ben directs Ann to leave the keys in the car, issues a claim check, and then has the car parked by an attendant, a bailment is created because possession has been transferred from Ann to Ben.

Intent to Exert Control. Because the bailee not only must have physical control, but also must intend to exercise control, a bailment may not be forced upon the bailee without consent. The intent requirement helps determine

the identity of the property subject to bailment. Suppose Art delivers a coat to Beth for safekeeping. Unknown to Beth, a valuable diamond has been sewn into the coat's lining. Beth is a bailee of the coat, but not necessarily the diamond. A bailee is therefore not responsible for items the existence or value of which she is unaware. Bailees may, however, be held liable for the contents of bailed articles, if the presence and value of the contents can reasonably be anticipated by the bailee—for example, gloves in the pocket of a coat or a tire in the trunk of a car.

General Liability of the Bailee

Liability for Theft, Damage, or Destruction of the Bailed Goods

Article 2 of the UCC determines risk of loss in contracts for the *sale* of goods without regard to whether title has passed from seller to buyer.[1] In bailments, however, risk of loss is tied to title. Because a bailment involves only a transfer of *possession,* and not title, the risk of loss, theft, damage, or destruction of the goods in the bailee's possession is ordinarily borne by the bailor.

In some cases, however, a bailee may be liable for casualty to the bailed goods. Since the classic case of *Coggs v. Bernard,*[2] the law is well settled that a bailee, although not an *insurer* of goods under its control, is liable for loss or damage for which it is at *fault.* In determining the degree of fault necessary to impose liability upon the bailee, courts traditionally have employed a three-part test based on whether the bailment is (1) for the benefit of the bailor, (2) for the benefit of the bailee, or (3) for the mutual benefit of the parties.

Bailor's Benefit. A bailment may be created for the sole benefit of the bailor. In this case, the bailee performs a service without compensation concerning the bailed property. Under the traditional rule, such a "gratuitous bailee" is responsible only if casualty to the goods is caused by its "gross negligence." In other words, the gratuitous bailee is required to exercise only "slight care."

Suppose Alan, an auto mechanic, as a favor agrees to tune up his friend Nancy's car for free. Nancy delivers the car to Alan's house. In this case, a bailment is created for

---

[1] Risk of loss in contracts for sale of goods is governed by UCC §§2–509 and 2–510, which are discussed in Chapter 17.
[2] 2 Ld. Raym. 909, 92 Eng. Rep. 107 (K. B. 1703).

the benefit of Nancy, the bailor. The car is subsequently destroyed by fire while parked in Alan's garage. The fire started after Alan inadvertently kicked over a gasoline can. Nancy sues him for the loss. On these facts Alan escapes liability for the destruction of Nancy's car unless the trier of fact, usually the jury, finds that his conduct was grossly negligent.

Bailee's Benefit. A bailment also may be created solely for the bailee's benefit—for example, when a friend or neighbor borrows your car, lawn mower, or power tool. In this case, the bailee is traditionally required to use "extraordinary care" in preserving the goods against loss or injury. In other words, the bailee is liable for damage or destruction caused by her "slight negligence."

Mutual Benefit. Bailments also are commonly created for the benefit of both parties. Mutual benefit bailments include rentals of motor vehicles and other property and bailments in which the bailee performs services to the bailed article for a price. For example, delivering a car to a mechanic for repair creates a mutual benefit bailment. In these cases, the bailee is required to exercise "ordinary care" in handling the goods. Ordinary care, in this context, means the amount of care a reasonably prudent person would exercise in the preservation of her own goods under similar circumstances. Therefore, in the mutual benefit bailment, the bailee is liable for simple negligence.

In the following case, the proper classification of the bailment under the three-part test was in issue.

American Enka Company v. Wicaco Machine Corp.
686 F.2d 1050 (3rd Cir. 1982)

Plaintiff American Enka Company (Enka) planned to construct a rayon manufacturing plant in Tennessee. Defendant Wicaco Machine Corp. (Wicaco) was employed as a subcontractor to manufacture machinery for the plant. In preparing to make the machinery (spinnerettes), Wicaco purchased 6,000 pounds of hastelloy (a special alloy of nickel, chromium, molybdenum, and carbon) in October 1974. Enka paid for the hastelloy but it was stored at Wicaco's plant. In April 1977, Enka canceled construction of the new plant due to declining demand for rayon. Wicaco agreed to hold the hastelloy until Enka was able to find a use for it. In January 1979, Enka requested return of the hastelloy, at which time Wicaco discovered that the metal had disappeared.

Enka sued Wicaco for damages. The trial court ruled that Wicaco was a bailee for the mutual benefit of Enka and Wicaco. The trial court held that Wicaco had breached its duty to exercise reasonable care and awarded damages to Enka Wicaco appealed alleging that it had acted as a gratuitous bailee.

Aldisert, Circuit Judge

. . . The dispute in this case is whether the facts establish a bailment for mutual benefit or one for the sole benefit of Enka. Wicaco argues that although the bailment began as one for mutual benefit because of its expectation of profit in making the spinnerettes, once Enka notified it that the Tennessee project was canceled, Wicaco's agreement to continue holding the ingots without charge converted the bailment to one for the sole benefit of the bailor. Accordingly, it contends that it can be held liable only for gross neglect.

Classification of a bailment as one for mutual benefit does not require the bailor to demonstrate a specific, tangible benefit or compensation running to the bailee. Pennsylvania's appellate courts have said that "a possibility or chance of expected profit to accrue" from the bailment is sufficient to make the relationship one for mutual benefit. . . . The specific question presented for review is whether, as the district court found, Wicaco retained a realistic expectation of profit from the bailment relationship after the Tennessee project was canceled. . . .

We conclude that the district court's findings were supported by the evidence and we reject Wicaco's argument because it ignores the business realities of Wicaco's relationship with Enka. As evidenced by the testimony of Wicaco president Donald F. Palmer, Wicaco expected either that the Tennessee project would be revived or that it would receive future orders from Enka . . . allowing use of the bailed hastelloy. Indeed, in June 1977 Enka solicited a Wicaco bid for the manufacture of spinnerettes for use in existing Enka plants. Because Wicaco is in the business of manufacturing mill equipment, not the storage of metal alloys, an expectation of future orders would be sufficient to make the bailment one for mutual benefit. We therefore conclude that the district court's finding that the bailment was for mutual benefit was not clearly erroneous. . . .

[Affirmed as to the issue of liability.]

Modern Approach. The traditional three-part test, in which a bailee's liability turns upon the benefit accruing to each party, has been widely criticized for various reasons. The standards of care (slight, ordinary, extraordinary) are difficult to apply to specific fact situations, and as the preceding case indicates, it is often unclear which type of bailment is involved. For these reasons, modern decisions in many states impose liability, *in all cases,* for failure to exercise ordinary care under the circumstances. The relative benefits conferred on the parties—for example, a compensated versus a gratuitous bailment—are still relevant, but are only one factor considered by the court in determining whether the bailee exercised ordinary care. Other factors include the nature and value of the property, the business or specialized skill, if any, of the bailee, and the place where the goods are delivered.

Burden of Proof

The bailor seeking to recover for loss or damage to the bailed goods must prove (under the modern approach) that the bailee failed to exercise ordinary care in handling the goods. Proving the bailee's negligence often is difficult because the bailee's acts of negligence occur while the goods are in the bailee's possession and are known only to the bailee. In other words, on the issue of negligence, the bailor can prove that the bailee failed to return the property or returned it in a damaged condition but little else. For this reason, courts generally hold that the bailor establishes a "prima facie" case for recovery once the bailor proves both

1. the existence of the bailment (delivery of the property to the bailee) and
2. that the bailee failed to return the goods or returned them in a damaged condition.

If these two requirements are proven, the burden of proof shifts to the bailee; that is, negligence of the bailee is presumed. In order to rebut the presumption and avoid liability, the bailee must then introduce some evidence to prove that he was not at fault in causing the damage or loss.

Contractual Limitation or Exclusion of Liability

Bailments often are created by contract between the bailor and bailee—for example, for repair, storage, or use of the bailed article. As part of that contract, the parties generally may limit the bailee's potential liability for casualty to the bailed goods. Thus, a contractual liability limitation reached after arm's length bargaining between the parties is enforceable. For example, a commercial bailee such as a warehouseman may agree to accept a reduced fee in exchange for reduced liability.

Disputes often arise, however, when a warehouseman, coat-check room operator, or parking lot operator seeks to limit liability for damage or loss of goods by posting a sign noting the limitation and also by placing the limitation on the claim check or ticket. Because any attempted liability limitation is legally effective only if the parties mutually agree to it, a bailee cannot limit the liability otherwise imposed by law unless the bailor knew and accepted the terms of the bailment. Thus, a bailor who does not read the sign is not bound to a limitation stated on it. In addition, customers (bailors) ordinarily view a claim check or parking lot ticket as merely an identification token, *not* a writing containing the terms of the contract between the parties. Therefore, if the bailor is unaware that the bailee intends the token to be a contract, the bailor should not be bound by terms printed on it.

In contrast, a limitation in a sign or claim check made known to the bailor, who subsequently enters into the bailment, is generally enforceable. In this case, however, the bailor may be protected by the unconscionability doctrine, discussed in Chapter 10. That is, the typical liability limitation is imposed in an "adhesion" contract, a standardized contract drafted by the bailee and presented on a "take it or leave it" basis. The bailor's freedom of choice often is limited because the bailee possesses a virtual monopoly—for example, the only parking garage at an airport—or because similar terms are used by all bailees. On similar facts, courts have refused to enforce an *unreasonable* limitation on grounds of unconscionability—absence of meaningful choice coupled with contract terms that are unreasonably favorable to one party.

The preceding discussion examines the enforceability of liability *limitations.* The bailee may attempt, through an **exculpatory clause,** to *exempt* itself completely from liability for negligence. Clearly, a contract term relieving a party from tort liability for reckless or intentional conduct is unenforceable on grounds of public policy. As the following case indicates, modern courts also tend to deny enforcement of disclaimers of liability for negligence.

Brockwell v. Lake Gaston Sales and Service

412 S.E.2d 104 (N.C.App. 1992)

When plaintiff R. W. Brockwell took his boat to defendant Lake Gaston Sales and Service for repair work, he signed a repair order that included the following provision:

> It is understood and agreed that [defendant] assumes no responsibility whatsoever for loss or damage by theft, fire, vandalism, water or weather related damages, nor for any items of personal property left with the unit placed with [defendant] for repair, storage or sale.

About ten days later, the defendant delivered the repaired boat to the plaintiff, who paid $706 for the services. At the time of delivery, numerous items of personal property—including fishing gear, navigation and electronic equipment, and a radio that had been installed in the boat—were missing. The plaintiff sued the defendant alleging that the defendant's negligence during the bailment had caused the loss of plaintiff's property from the boat. The trial court awarded the plaintiff $2,424 in damages and the defendant appealed.

Hedrick, Chief Judge

The sole question raised by this appeal is whether the trial court erred by failing to find that defendant's bailment liability to plaintiff had been expressly relieved by contract. . . . Essentially, defendant argues that "liability disclaimer" signed by the plaintiff, bailor, is an insurmountable bar to plaintiff's claim for relief. We disagree.

As a general rule, in an ordinary mutual benefit bailment, where there is no great disparity of bargaining power, the bailee may relieve himself from the liability imposed on him by the common law so long as the provisions of the contract do not run counter to the public interest. . . . Where the public has no interest in the subject matter of the contract and the contract involves only private concerns of the parties, a liability disclaimer will be enforced. . . .

However, some contractual provisions which attempt to avoid liability for a party's negligence which are contrary to law and against public policy are void and unenforceable. [As stated in *Insurance Assoc. v. Parker,* 65 S.E.2d 341, 344 (N.C. 1951):]

> Many courts hold that where the bailee makes it his business to act as bailee for hire, on a uniform and not an individual basis, it is against the public interest to permit him to exculpate himself from his own negligence. And the decided trend of modern decisions is against the validity of such exculpatory clauses or provisions in behalf of proprietors of parking lots, garages, parcel check rooms, and warehouses, who undertake to protect themselves against their own negligence by posting signs or printing limitations on the receipts or identification tokens delivered to the bailor-owner at the time of bailment. . . .

In the present case, defendant, bailee, attempted to exculpate itself from liability for its own negligence where it "was [its] business to act as a bailee for hire on a uniform . . . basis." Defendant, bailee, took plaintiff's boat, its contents, equipment and attachments into its sole possession in order to perform repairs on the boat in the regular course of its business, and we hold it was against public policy for defendant, bailee, to attempt to exculpate itself from the duty of ordinary care it owned to plaintiff, bailor. We therefore hold the liability disclaimer in the present case is void and unenforceable as a matter of law. . . .

[Judgment affirmed.]

Effect of Misdelivery

Once the purposes of the bailment have been accomplished, the bailee has a duty to redeliver the bailed goods to the bailor on demand. Unlike the standard applied to the bailee's conduct while in possession of the goods (reasonable care), the bailee's duty to redeliver is absolute. For example, a bailee who refuses to redeliver the property upon completion of the bailment is liable to the bailor for the tort of conversion. A bailee who delivers the property to an unauthorized person or one who has no rightful claim to the goods against the bailor is liable for conversion of the goods or for damages for breach of contract, even if the bailee is acting in good faith and without negligence. For example, the bailee may be held liable for delivery to an imposter who has cleverly forged an order to deliver. Bailees protect themselves in some cases by requiring presentation of a ticket or claim check as a condition to redelivery. The bailee then must redeliver the goods in good faith to the person who possesses the ticket.

Although ordinary bailees generally incur absolute liability for misdelivery, involuntary bailees such as finders of lost articles are liable for misdelivery only if negligent. The basis of this rule is that an involuntary bailee, who does not willingly assume a bailee's obligations, should be held liable only to a general duty to exercise reasonable care.

Third-Party Claims. The bailee faces a dilemma if a third party, such as a creditor or person alleging ownership, asserts a claim to the goods adverse to the bailor. A bailee delivering to such a third party incurs absolute liability to the bailor for misdelivery if the claim is later found invalid. The bailee is excused from liability if delivery is made under valid legal process, such as a writ of attachment or execution,[3] or if the third-party claim is later determined to be valid. For example, the bailee has no liability if the bailor is a thief.

Absent compulsory legal process, however, the bailee initially must determine the validity of the adverse claim. To make this determination, the bailee may use an *interpleader* action, in which the bailee surrenders the property to the court (and is relieved of further liability) leaving the bailor and third party to litigate their conflict concerning the property. In other words, the bailee faced with conflicting claims may compel the claimants to litigate their claims with each other rather than with the bailee.

Effect of Use Contrary to Terms of the Bailment

In addition to misdelivery, the bailee also may incur expanded liability for using the bailed property in an unauthorized manner. In general, the bailee's right to possess and use the bailed property is determined by the terms of the bailment. These terms may be expressly stated in the bailment contract or may be implied based on the circumstances of the case. For example, the use may be necessary to maintain the property or may be a method of compensating the bailee for her services concerning the property. To determine the implied limits of permitted use courts ask whether a reasonable person, after considering all circumstances, would regard the use as one that would have been included in the agreement if the parties had anticipated the occasion for the use.

The bailee may, however, go beyond the scope of the bailment by (1) selling the bailed property,

(2) using it as collateral on a loan, or (3) using it for purposes not contemplated or authorized by the bailment. For example, an auto mechanic may accept a car for storage or repair but subsequently use the property for personal or business purposes. Most unpermitted uses constitute a conversion of the property, rendering the bailee liable to pay the bailor the full value of the property. Nevertheless, a minor, temporary deviation that does not damage the property or inconvenience the bailor and that is not intended as a defiance or repudiation of the bailor's rights does not constitute a conversion.

Bailment disputes over unauthorized use normally arise because the bailed property is damaged or destroyed while in the bailee's possession. A bailee who departs from the terms of the bailment effectively becomes an insurer of the goods. That is, the bailee becomes responsible for all injury to the goods whether or not caused by negligence and whether or not the bailee's conduct constitutes a conversion. Assume Joan takes her car to Sam, an auto dealer, with instructions to sell it. In violation of this agreement, Sam drives the car 5,000 miles on personal business. While so using the car, it is destroyed by lightning. Because Sam has converted the car, he is liable to Joan for its full value even though he was not at fault in causing the loss. Assume alternatively that Sam does not regularly use the car on personal business, but on one occasion drives the car five miles on a personal errand. During this trip the auto is destroyed by lightening. Even though the use is not a conversion and the destruction is not due to Sam's negligence, Sam is liable to Joan for the value of the property. Of course, if the car is destroyed by lightning on Sam's lot, while being displayed for sale, Joan bears the loss because Sam was not negligent and did not depart from the scope of the bailment.

Innkeepers' Liability

The law imposes a special form of bailee liability upon hotels and innkeepers for theft or destruction of goods of their guests. The liability extends to (1) goods within the actual physical control of the innkeeper (for example, valuables stored in the hotel safe), and (2) the guest's property located in her room. Although the second situation arguably involves no transfer of possession, courts have treated it as a bailment for purposes of imposing liability.

Under the majority common law rule, an innkeeper is a qualified insurer of the goods of guests, relieved of liability only by proving that the loss resulted from an Act of God or an act of a public enemy, the inherent nature

---

[3]State debt collection remedies, including writs of attachment and execution, are covered in Chapter 29.

of the goods, or the contributory fault of the guest. The common law subjects the innkeeper to a strict liability standard similar to that governing common carriers discussed below. This extraordinary liability developed centuries ago when travelers were easy prey for bandits and thieves, and innkeepers were expected to provide protection as well as lodging and food for guests.

In most states, the common law rule has been modified by statute. These statutes vary significantly, but generally repudiate the common law doctrine, strictly limiting the dollar amount of an innkeeper's liability for loss of, or damage to, a guest's property. A copy of the innkeeper's statute usually is posted in each guest room. A guest carrying valuable articles should therefore read and comply with its terms. If the statutory liability limitation does not cover the value of the articles, the guest should make special arrangements with the hotel or others for their safekeeping.

Bailments for Shipment or Storage

Documents of Title Under UCC Article 7

The law of bailments provides specialized rules to govern the rights, duties, and liabilities of bailees known as "carriers" and "warehouses" who perform two fundamental commercial functions: the shipment and the storage of goods. To perform these functions, these bailees use instruments known as "documents of title." For example, a person wishing to store goods may deliver them to a commercial warehouse (a bailee), which issues a document of title known as a "warehouse receipt" to the storer (bailor). Or, a person desiring to ship goods may deliver them to a carrier (a bailee), which issues a document of title known as a "bill of lading" to the shipper (bailor).

"Document of Title" Defined. Article 7 of the UCC governs documents of title and the rights and obligations of persons issuing them. The following material is based upon Article 7 as amended in 2003. A **document of title** is defined in §1–201(b)(16) as any document accepted in business or financing transactions:

1. as adequately evidencing that the person in possession or control of the record is entitled to receive, control, hold, and dispose of the record and the goods it covers; and
2. that purports to be issued by or addressed to a bailee and to cover goods in the bailee's possession.

A record is defined in §7–102(a)(10) as "information that is inscribed on a tangible medium or that is stored in an electronic or other medium and is retrievable in perceivable form."

Documents of title, which cover goods in the bailee's possession, include a bill of lading, dock warrant, dock receipt, warehouse receipt, or order for the delivery of goods. Although the bailee ordinarily issues documents of title, an order for delivery of goods (a **delivery order**) is issued by a shipper or storer addressed to a carrier or warehouse ordering it to deliver goods in its possession to a specified person.[4]

Under §1–201(b)(16), documents of title are either tangible or electronic. A tangible document is one "evidenced by a record consisting of information that is inscribed on a tangible medium" (for example, a piece of paper). An electronic document is one "evidenced by a record consisting of information stored in an electronic medium."

"Bill of Lading" Defined. Section 1–201(b)(6) defines a **bill of lading** as a "document of title evidencing the receipt of goods for shipment issued by a person engaged in the business of directly or indirectly transporting or forwarding goods." The term includes an "airbill"—a document that serves the same functions for air transportation that a bill of lading does for marine, truck, or rail transportation. The definition also includes bills issued by **freight forwarders**—those in the business of consolidating less than carload shipments to obtain the benefit of lower rail and truck rates—in addition to carriers such as railroads and trucking companies.

The person named in a bill of lading as the person "from which the goods have been received for shipment" is known as the **consignor.** The person named in the bill "to which or to whose order the bill promises delivery" is the **consignee.**[5] A **through bill of lading** is one issued by the first of two or more carriers when the carriage is to be performed in part by connecting carriers other than the issuer.

Generally, a bill of lading is issued by the carrier to the consignor at the place of shipment. The carrier may, however, at the request of the consignor, issue a **destination bill.** Such bills are issued at the destination or at any other place designated in the request. A destination bill assures that the bill of lading will be available before the goods arrive to the person taking delivery at the destination.

---

[4] UCC §7–102(a)(5).
[5] UCC §§7–102(a)(3)–(4).

"Warehouse Receipt" Defined. Section 1–201(b)(42) defines a **warehouse receipt** as "a document of title issued by a person engaged in the business of storing goods for hire."[6] A person engaged in the business of storing goods for hire is a **warehouse.**[7] Under §7–207, a warehouseman must generally keep the goods covered by each receipt separate to permit identification and delivery of the particular goods stored. Different lots of fung-ible goods, such as oil or grain, may, however, be commingled. In this case the owners become tenants in common of the resulting mass.

Negotiable and Nonnegotiable Documents of Title. A warehouse receipt, bill of lading, or other document of title may be either negotiable or nonnegotiable. Under §7–104(a), a document of title is **negotiable** if by its terms the goods are to be delivered to *bearer* or to the *order* of a named person. Any other document is nonnegotiable or "straight." A nonnegotiable document generally requires delivery of the goods to the consignee, and usually includes the words "nonnegotiable" or "not negotiable" on the document. Note that nonnegotiable documents are more common than negotiable documents. For example, most bills of lading covering interstate railroad shipments and airbills issued by air express companies are nonnegotiable.

The distinction between negotiability and nonnego-tiability is important for several reasons. For example, the person entitled to delivery differs depending on the type of document involved, and a negotiable document provides much more effective control of the goods because it must be surrendered to obtain delivery. In addition, a transferee of a negotiable document may acquire ore rights than the transferor had. These issues are discussed in more detail later in this chapter. Finally, as outlined in Chapters 16 and 17, the negotiable-nonnegotiable distinction is important in determining risk of loss, passage of title, and manner of seller's deliv-ery when goods covered by a document of title are sold.

Scope of Article 7. Article 7 represents a consolidation and revision of two prior uniform state laws, the Uniform Bills of Lading Act and the Uniform Warehouse Receipts Act. In 1916, Congress enacted the Federal Bills of Lading Act (FBLA), which was reorganized and revised in 1994.[8] Thus, warehouse receipts are governed by Article 7, but bills of lading are governed by both state (UCC Article 7) and federal law.

Generally, the FBLA governs any bill of lading issued by a common carrier (defined below) for the transporta-tion of goods in interstate or foreign commerce.[9] Article 7 governs bills issued for intrastate shipments and for shipment from a foreign country into a state.

The bailee issuing a document of title acknowledges possession of the goods and contracts to deliver them. From this obligation, three fundamental issues arise: (1) liability for loss, damage, or destruction of the goods while in the bailee's possession, (2) contractual limitation or exclusion of that liability, and (3) the bailee's duty to deliver the goods upon termination of the carriage or storage.

Liability for Loss, Damage, or Destruction of Bailed Goods—Warehouses

Under Article 7, a warehouse's liability for damage to, or destruction of, stored goods is governed by the same standard as that applied to ordinary bailees at common law. Section 7–204(a) provides that a warehouse is liable for casualty to stored goods "caused by its failure to exer-cise care with regard to the goods that a reasonably care-ful person would exercise under similar circumstances." Thus, the warehouse, like most other bailees, is liable only for damage or destruction caused by negligence— failure to exercise reasonable care.

Liability for Loss, Damage, or Destruction of the Bailed Goods—Common Carriers

The extent of a carrier's liability for loss or destruction of goods in its possession depends upon whether it is a "common" as opposed to a "private" or "special" carrier. Whereas a private carrier is subject to the same standard imposed on other bailees—liability for loss or destruc-tion caused by negligence—a common carrier is a quali-fied insurer of goods entrusted to it by the shipper. Thus, a carrier's status as common or private is an initial and fundamental determination in ascertaining liability.

The common law definition of common carrier, articulated in many decisions, involves three elements. To be a **common carrier,** a person must undertake or

---

[6]Because the definition applies to storing goods "for hire," not "for profit," state-operated and cooperative warehouses are included. UCC §7–102, Official Comment 2.

[7]UCC §7–102(a)(13).

[8]49 U.S.C. §80101 *et seq.*

[9]49 U.S.C. §80102.

hold out to perform (1) carriage, (2) for hire, (3) for all those who apply. The essence of this definition is the public holding out.

Rule of Liability. A person classified as a common carrier is, subject to five limited exceptions, absolutely liable for loss, damage, or destruction of goods in transit. Although the early common law justified the rule as necessary to prevent collusion with robbers and thieves, modern authorities recognize broader grounds for imposing a qualified insurer's liability upon a common carrier, including (1) stimulating care and fidelity on the carrier's part, (2) the carrier's exclusive possession of evidence concerning circumstances of the loss, (3) the difficulties in discovering and proving the carrier's fault, and (4) the carrier's ability to adjust its rates to cover hazards. Whatever the justification, the principle of absolute liability prevailing under the common law is adopted and applied to common carriers issuing bills of lading under both federal law[10] and Article 7.[11]

Exceptions to Liability. The law has long recognized five exceptions to the general rule of absolute liability. The carrier may escape liability by proving that the loss was caused by

1. an Act of God,
2. an act of a public enemy,
3. an act of public authority,
4. an act of the shipper, or
5. the inherent nature of the goods.

Even if the loss is caused by one of the recognized exceptions, the carrier nevertheless remains liable unless it also establishes that it used *reasonable care* to prevent losses from the excepted causes. A discussion of the five exceptions to absolute liability follows.

Act of God. Damage or destruction generally occurs by Act of God if it results from the operation solely of natural forces without human intervention. Sudden and violent disturbances such as lightning, earthquakes, wind, tornadoes, hurricanes, or other violent storms are considered Acts of God.

Act of a Public Enemy. A carrier is not liable for destruction caused by an act of an organized military or naval force with which the carrier's country is at war. This exception does not apply to acts of robbers or thieves such as hijackers, nor generally to civil disturbances. Perhaps because of improved communications and intelligence, allowing carriers to avoid potential trouble spots, this exception is seldom applied.

Act of Public Authority. The carrier is excused from its absolute duty to deliver if the goods involved have been taken by valid legal process—for example, replevin, execution, or attachment to satisfy an unpaid judgment against the owner—or under the state's police power—for example, a seizure of stolen goods, drugs, liquor, or other contraband. If the goods are taken by public authority, the carrier is under a duty promptly to notify the shipper of the seizure so that it may appear in the proceedings and defend its interest.

Act of the Shipper. The carrier is not liable for loss caused solely by the shipper's act or default. In this context, the loss typically results from the shipper's improper loading or packaging of the shipped goods. If, however, the defect in packaging or loading is apparent or "patent"—for example, the carrier knew or should have known that the shipper's packing or loading was defective—the carrier that accepts the goods remains an insurer of their safety in transit.

Inherent Nature of the Goods. A common carrier is not liable for losses resulting from the inherent nature of the goods shipped. Examples include perishable items such as fruits, vegetables, and livestock. To escape liability, however, the carrier must prove that the loss was due solely to the inherent nature of the goods and that the carrier's negligence did not contribute to the loss. For example, the carrier is liable if perishable goods spoil because of the carrier's negligent delay in transporting them.

In summary, to recover from the carrier for damage or destruction of a shipment, the shipper must prove delivery of the goods to the carrier in good condition, the carrier's subsequent nondelivery or delivery in a damaged condition, and the amount of damages. The burden of proof then shifts to the carrier, who escapes liability only by proving both that the damage or destruction was caused by an excepted peril and that the carrier's negligence did not contribute to the loss. The following case illustrates the principles governing carrier liability.

---

[10]The so-called Carmack Amendment (49 U.S.C. §14706(a)(1)) provides that a common carrier issuing a receipt or bill of lading and any other common carrier delivering the goods are liable to the full extent of common law liability to the person entitled to recover under the receipt or bill.

[11]UCC §7–309(a).

Martin Imports v. Courier-Newsom Express, Inc.

580 F.2d 240 (7th Cir. 1978)

Martin Imports hired the Courier-Newsom Express, Inc., a motor common carrier, to ship 250 cases of wine from Chicago to Rockford, Illinois. The usual transit time for the trip was one day. A driver picked up the shipment from Martin Imports at 4:30 P.M. on December 23. The driver delivered the wine in an unheated tractor-trailer to Courier-Newsom's terminal in Rockford at 5:00 A.M. on December 24. The terminal, however, was closed because Courier-Newsom's employees' collective bargaining agreement required that December 24 and 25 were nonwork days. No attempt was made to notify the consignee of the arrival of the shipment. The trailer remained at Courier-Newsom's terminal until the morning of December 26. During that period, the temperature in Rockford was below freezing. When Courier-Newsom tendered delivery to the consignee on December 26, the consignee refused to accept the shipment because the wine had frozen and many of the bottles had exploded.

Martin Imports sued Courier-Newsom to recover the value of the wine. The trial court held in favor of Courier-Newsom, the appellee; Martin Imports, the appellant, appealed.

Jameson, Senior District Judge

. . . [The trial] court concluded that appellee had not been negligent in its handling of the wine shipment [and] that the damage was due to one of the excepted causes relieving a carrier of liability, namely the inherent vice or nature of the commodity shipped. . . .

Appellee's manager testified . . . that appellee knew when it accepted the shipment that it contained wine and knew that due to the collective bargaining agreement it would not be delivered the next day, as shipments tendered on Mondays normally would be. He said appellee also knew that the shipment would remain in the trailer and the trailer would be left outside until its employees returned to work on the 26th. And, after the shipment arrived in Rockford, there was no attempt to communicate with or notify the consignee of its arrival until the 26th. Under these circumstances we can only conclude that appellee was negligent in failing to advise the appellant that its shipment would not be delivered according to appellee's normal schedule, due to the fact that under the collective bargaining agreement not only was Christmas day a holiday, but the preceding day as well. While the delay in delivery of the wine arguably may have been reasonable, the failure to advise the shipper in advance of the abnormally long delivery time was not.

We find nothing in the record that would impute knowledge of the collective bargaining agreement to appellant. In appellant's business the day preceding Christmas is apparently among its busiest of the year. It was not unreasonable for it to assume that the carrier would also be open for business that day. It is reasonable to infer that if appellant had any reason to believe that the wine would not be delivered on the 24th according to the normal transit schedule, it would not have tendered the shipment in the first place. . . .

Appellee accepted the shipment knowing that it was wine, that sub-freezing temperatures would be encountered, and that there would be a delay in delivery of 48 hours in excess of the normal transit schedule. Appellee was negligent in failing to advise appellant that the wine would not be delivered until December 26—two full days after the normal time of delivery. . . .

[Judgment reversed.]

Commencement and Termination of Liability. Because a carrier bears an extraordinary liability, the law must determine precisely when that liability begins and ends. Ordinarily, absolute liability commences when the goods are delivered into the carrier's possession and accepted for immediate shipment. Thus, a carrier who possesses goods while awaiting shipping instructions incurs the liability of a warehouse—for negligence only. Once the goods have been transported to the destination, the carrier's strict liability ceases when the carrier tenders delivery to the consignee at a suitable time and place giving the consignee a reasonable opportunity to receive the goods. If the goods remain in the carrier's possession after that time, liability is reduced to that of an ordinary bailee or warehouse.

Contractual Limitation of Liability

Like ordinary bailees, carriers and warehouses often contractually limit their liability for loss, damage, or destruction of goods received for shipment or storage. If the bailee is a warehouse, §7–204(b) provides that liability for loss or destruction of stored goods may be limited by a term in the warehouse receipt or storage agreement. The bailor may, however, request that the warehouse's liability be increased on all or part of the stored goods. In this situation, the warehouse may charge an increased rate, but must assume the added liability. Note that §7–204(b) authorizes liability limitation, not a total exclusion or disclaimer of liability for negligence.

A common carrier, like the warehouse and ordinary bailee, is permitted to limit the amount of liability (except for conversion) in a written contract with the shipper. Both federal law and Article 7 adopt a rule consistent with that applied to warehouse receipts, allowing rates to be varied depending on the value of the goods shipped.[12] In addition, carriers often disclaim responsibility for undeclared hidden articles of extraordinary value. Thus, although the common carrier's liability at common law is nearly absolute, the carrier and shipper frequently limit that liability by contract, exchanging a reduced rate for reduced liability.

Note that under Article 7, a carrier or warehouse may not contractually limit liability for conversion of the goods to its own use.

The Duty of Delivery

Consistent with the common law approach, Article 7 imposes absolute liability upon carriers and warehouses for misdelivery. Under §7–403(a), absent a valid excuse, carriers and warehouse must deliver to "a person entitled under a document of title."[13] The person entitled to delivery may or may not be the original storer (in a warehouse receipt) or consignee (in a bill of lading). That is, documents of title often are used to transfer title to (or a security interest in) the goods from the person originally entitled to delivery under the document to another. The bailee's delivery obligation differs depending on whether the document of title covering the goods is negotiable or nonnegotiable.

Negotiable Tangible Documents. If a negotiable document is involved, §7–102(a)(9) provides that delivery of the goods must be made to the **holder** of the document. The first holder is usually the storer or consignee to whom the document is originally issued.

Holders also include any person to whom the document has been *negotiated* by the storer or consignee or a later holder. **Negotiation** is made by transferring possession of the document to the transferee if the document is in bearer form, or by indorsement and transfer of possession if the document is in order form.[14] Note that documents in bearer form include (1) those that initially require delivery of the goods to bearer and have not been indorsed, and (2) any document indorsed in blank (the holder's signature alone) by the original or a later holder. Documents in order form include (1) those that initially require delivery of the goods to the order of a named person and have not been indorsed, and (2) any document specially indorsed (the holder's signature plus language designating the person to whom delivery is to be made) by the original or a later holder. These rules are virtually identical to those governing negotiation of notes and checks, discussed in Chapter 23.

A negotiable document of title represents the goods and provides effective control over them. Under §7–403(3), a bailee (carrier or warehouse) who delivers goods covered by a negotiable document without requiring surrender of the document for cancellation (or notation for partial deliveries) is liable for misdelivery to any person to whom the document is later negotiated. Because of this liability, a bailee will not deliver goods governed by a negotiable document without the document. The person controlling the document therefore controls the goods.

Negotiable Electronic Documents. Determining the delivery duty and method of transfer for an electronic document of title requires an understanding of the concept of "control" outlined in §7–106. "Control of an electronic document of title substitutes for the concept of indorsement and possession in the tangible document of title context."[15] That is, tangible documents are negotiated by physically transferring the document and, in some cases, indorsing it. Electronic documents are negotiated by transfer of control, with no requirement of indorsement.[16]

As defined in §7–106(a), a person has control of an electronic document of title if a

> system employed for evidencing the transfer of interests in the electronic document *reliably establishes* that person as

---

[12]49 U.S.C. §14706(c); UCC §7–309(b). Rates are fixed in published "tariffs." The tariff, a public document, also sets forth the services offered by a common carrier and the rules, regulations, and procedures relating to those services.

[13]A similar standard is imposed for federal bills of lading under the Revised FBLA. 49 U.S.C. §80110.

[14]UCC §7–501. The Revised FBLA contains substantially identical provisions governing interstate bills of lading. 49 U.S.C. §80104.

[15]UCC §7–106, Official Comment 2

[16]UCC §7–501(b)(1).

the person to which the electronic document was issued or transferred.[17]

As noted in Official Comment 3 to §7–106:

> For example, a carrier may issue an electronic bill of lading by having the required information in a database that is encrypted and accessible by virtue of a password. If the computer system in which the required information is maintained identifies the person as *the* person to which the electronic bill of lading was issued or transferred, that person has control of the electronic document of title. That identification may be by virtue of passwords or other encryption methods.

Under §7–106(b), a system meets the control test outlined above and "a person is deemed to have control . . . if the document is created, stored, and assigned in such a manner that . . . a single authoritative copy . . . exists which is unique, identifiable, and . . . unalterable."

Nonnegotiable Documents. If a nonnegotiable document is used, §7–102(a)(9) requires the bailee to deliver according to its specific promise made in the document. In a bill of lading the bailee usually promises to deliver to the consignee and in a warehouse receipt to the storer. The bailee also may deliver according to written instructions from a person authorized in the document to give them.

Under negotiable and nonnegotiable documents, as a prerequisite to delivery, the person obtaining the goods must pay the charges for storage or shipment[18] and must be ready and willing to sign, if requested, an acknowledgment that the goods have been delivered.

At issue in the following case involving a nonnegotiable bill of lading was whether the carrier should be held liable for misdelivery.

Refrigerated Transport Co., Inc. v. Hernando Packing Co., Inc.

544 S.W.2d 613 (Tenn. 1976)

Plaintiff, Hernando Packing Co., Inc. (Hernando) of Memphis, Tennessee, received a telephone order from Al Hark of J&A Trading Company (J&A) requesting delivery of a truckload of meat to Fort Lauderdale, Florida. Hernando shipped the meat via defendant Refrigerated Transport Co., Inc. (Refrigerated) for delivery to Broward Cold Storage, a public warehouse in Fort Lauderdale. Hernando completed the bill of lading as follows:

> To BROWARD COLD STORAGE
> (acct. of J&A Trading Co.)
> 3220 S.W. 2nd Avenue
> Fort Lauderdale, Florida.

When Refrigerated's truck arrived at Fort Lauderdale, a person identifying himself as Al Hark of J&A Trading Co. met the truck across the street from Broward. Hark requested delivery of part of the meat to another location to which the truck driver agreed. The following morning, Hark met the truck at the Broward loading dock and transferred some of the meat to another truck. The remainder of the load was stored at Broward. When Hernando telephoned J&A to notify it of the pending delivery, Hernando learned that J&A had gone out of business. Hernando then telephoned Broward and learned of the delivery to Al Hark, who had disappeared.

Hernando sued Refrigerated alleging that the trucker had failed to deliver the meat to Broward as required by the bill of lading. The trial court ruled in favor of Hernando and Refrigerated appealed.

Henry, Justice

. . . This controversy pivots upon the precise provisions of the bill of lading, viz: the consignment to "Broward Cold Storage (account of J&A Trading Co.)." Refrigerated earnestly insists that this, in effect, was a consignment to "J&A Trading Co., care of Broward Cold Storage." While this position is plausible, when consideration is given to the nature and purpose of bills of lading, the duties and obligations arising thereunder, and to the plain terms of the consignment, we cannot embrace this theory of the case.

At the very outset we point out that we are dealing with a "straight" bill of lading . . . which is not negotiable. . . .

Delivery under a straight bill of lading may only be made to "[a] person lawfully entitled to the possession of the goods, or (b) the consignee named" therein. [FBLA, 49 U.S.C. §89; now Revised FBLA, 49 U.S.C. §§80110(b)(1)-(2)(1994).]

While there are various areas of potential disagreement in this controversy they all boil down to a single question: Who was the consignee under the bill of lading?

In our view, there is no ambiguity. The consignment was to Broward. The parenthetical matter inserted

---

.[17]UCC §7–106(a). Emphasis added.

[18]Article 7 gives warehouses (under §§7–209, 7–210) and carriers (under §§7–307, 7–308) a lien upon goods received for shipment or storage to secure payment of charges incident to the bailment. A similar lien is imposed for federal bills of lading under the Revised FBLA. 49 U.S.C. §80109.

simply advised the warehouse as to the identity of the ultimate receiver of the goods upon Broward's reconsignment. The only address inserted was that of Broward. Al Hark's name does not appear on the bill. It is fairly inferable that the consignment was to Broward as a precautionary measure against an unknown purchaser. Such would have been reasonable and prudent. But we need not speculate since the language was clear. There is no way that this delivery could have been properly made except to Broward and at Broward's address. Most assuredly a street corner delivery to a stranger not named in the bill and not shown by the record to have presented any credentials or authority cannot constitute valid delivery. All the driver ever had to do was to present his bill of lading to an authorized representative of Broward. The failure to do so was a breach of the contract of carriage.

To constitute a valid delivery, absent special circumstances, it is imperative that delivery be made to the right person, at the proper time and place and in a proper manner. This is implicit in the Contract of Carriage. . . .

We hold that Refrigerated breached its duty to deliver the cargo to Broward, the party designated in the bill of lading; that delivery to Al Hark was at Refrigerated's peril; that the burden of validating this delivery by establishing Al Hark's ownership and right to possession was upon Refrigerated and that it failed to carry that burden.

While we make this holding within the context of our view that Broward was the consignee, had we adopted Refrigerated's view that J&A Trading Company was the consignee, with the goods being shipped "in care of" Broward, the result would be the same. This necessarily follows from the facts that J&A was not in existence; that Al Hark had no connection with J&A; and that delivery was made to him without proper inquiry and without notice to Broward, or J&A. Had such inquiry been made and such notice given the driver would have discovered that he was dealing with an imposter. . . .

[Judgment affirmed.]

Excuse and Delay. A bailee may escape liability for misdelivery if it establishes the existence of a lawful excuse, including delivery to a person with paramount title, destruction or damage to the goods for which it is not liable, sale of the property in lawful enforcement of the carrier's lien, stoppage of delivery in transit by the seller under UCC §2–705, delivery of goods under court order, destruction of hazardous goods, refusal to deliver pending interpleader, and compliance with authorized changes in delivery instructions.[19] Although a carrier is responsible for unexcused nondelivery or misdelivery, a carrier who merely delays delivery is liable only if the carrier's negligence caused the delay.

The "Due Negotiation" Doctrine

Huge quantities of goods in storage or transit are bought and sold every day simply by transferring the documents of title that cover them. After a document is issued and transferred, disputes often arise when two or more persons claim ownership of either the document or the goods it covers.

As previously noted, a carrier or warehouse is obligated to deliver to the holder of a *negotiable* document. As against the bailee, therefore, any holder is entitled to the goods. As against third parties claiming superior rights in the goods or the documents, the holder's rights depend on whether the document was acquired by due negotiation. To constitute **due negotiation,** §7–501 states that a negotiable document of title must be negotiated to a holder who purchases it (1) in good faith, (2) without notice of any defense against or claim to it on the part of any person, (3) for value, (4) in the regular course of business or financing, and (5) in a transaction not involving mere settlement or payment of a money obligation. Under §7–502(a), a holder to whom a negotiable document of title has been duly negotiated acquires title to both the document and the goods it covers, because transfer of the document is the exclusive method of transferring title to both the document and the goods.

A holder by due negotiation of a negotiable document acquires the same rights against the carrier or warehouse as any other holder (the duties of delivery and care) and in addition defeats virtually all outstanding prior equities and claims both to the document and the goods. Assume Olsen stores goods with White, who issues a negotiable warehouse receipt requiring delivery to Olsen's order. Olsen duly negotiates the receipt to Henry. Subsequently, White sells the stored goods to Zimmer, an innocent purchaser. Henry cuts off Zimmer's claim to the goods. Or, assume Pam directs Art to take goods to White for storage and obtain a negotiable warehouse receipt to Pam's order. Art delivers the goods to White, obtains a negotiable

---

[19]UCC §7–403(a).

bearer receipt, duly negotiates it to Henry, and disappears with the money. Henry defeats Pam's claim to the goods and the document.

Not all third-party claims are cut off by good faith purchasers of negotiable documents. For example, if a necessary indorsement on a tangible document is forged, the transferee does not become a holder and therefore does not defeat the claim of the person whose name is forged. A good faith purchaser also is not protected if the original bailor was a thief. A thief cannot acquire the power to transfer a good title simply by storing or shipping the stolen goods.

The due negotiation doctrine, the Article 7 counterpart of the holder in due course doctrine applied to negotiable instruments (notes and drafts),[20] applies only to negotiable documents. Under §7–504(a), transferees of nonnegotiable documents (and holders of negotiable documents who do not take by due negotiation) acquire "the title and rights that its transferor had or had actual authority to convey." Thus, the transferee "steps into the shoes" of the transferor and is subject to any defects in the transferor's title. For example, assume Doaks acquires goods from Olsen by fraud or with a bad check, and delivers the goods to White who issues a nonnegotiable warehouse receipt. Doaks subsequently transfers the receipt to Barnett. Olsen may recover the goods from Barnett.

Carriers' Liability—Ocean Carriage

In international trade, goods often are transported by oceangoing vessels. The liability of an ocean carrier for loss or destruction of goods in its possession is governed by the **Carriage of Goods by Sea Act (COGSA).**[21] This statute applies to all contracts for carriage of goods by sea to or from United States ports and ports of foreign countries. Carriers generally are liable for losses (up to $500 "per package") caused by their negligence, and may not contractually eliminate or reduce their negligence liability. Under the statute, for example, a carrier is liable for loss or damage caused by a vessel's unseaworthiness if the carrier fails to exercise due diligence to (1) make the ship seaworthy; (2) assure that the ship is properly manned, equipped, and supplied; and (3) make the cargo holds fit and safe for the reception, carriage, and preservation of the goods. The carrier also must "properly and carefully" load, handle, stow, and

discharge the goods being shipped. Assuming these duties are met, the statute also insulates the carrier from liability for losses caused by: errors in navigation or management of the ship; fire, unless caused by actual fault of the carrier; perils of the sea; act of God; act of war; act of public enemies; seizure of the ship under legal process; quarantine restrictions; act or omission of the shipper; strikes or lockouts; riots and civil commotions; saving life or property at sea; inherent defects in the goods; insufficient packing or labeling of the goods; latent defects in the ship not discoverable by due diligence; and any other cause arising without the actual fault of the carrier or its servants. The burden of proof in COGSA cases is similar to that applied in general bailment law. The shipper establishes a prima facie case by proving that cargo delivered to the carrier in good condition was either lost or unloaded in a damaged condition. The burden then shifts to the carrier to prove freedom from negligence.

Letters of Credit

A letter of credit is an important financing, payment, and security device widely used both in international and domestic trade. The principles governing letters of credit developed as part of the law merchant—the system of routine rules, customs, and practices used in the business community to regulate transactions and resolve disputes.[22] Today, these principles are summarized in the *Uniform Customs and Practice for Documentary Credits* (UCP), a trade code published by the International Chamber of Commerce. The UCP was first published in 1933 and revised versions were adopted in 1951, 1962, 1974, 1983, and 1993. Though the UCP, which is used in over 140 countries, is not a law, it often governs because most banks incorporate UCP provisions by reference into letters of credit they issue. In the United States, letters of credit not subject to the UCP are governed by Article 5 of the Uniform Commercial Code, which was revised in 1995. Though the UCP and Article 5 impose the same general obligations on the parties, Article 5 contains general rules, derived primarily from case law, to resolve disputes. These litigation rules generally may be varied by agreement of the parties. In contrast, the UCP, drafted by bankers, provides detailed rules governing the day-to-day mechanics of letter of credit transactions.

---

[20]The holder in due course doctrine is discussed in Chapters 22–24.
[21]46 U.S.C. Appx. §§1300–1315.

[22]BLACK'S LAW DICTIONARY 886, 896 (6th ed. 1990).

A **letter of credit** is an undertaking made by a bank or other person (the "issuer") to a "beneficiary" at the request of the issuer's "customer." The letter obligates the issuer to honor a draft or other demand for payment presented by the beneficiary if the draft or de-mand is accompanied by documents that strictly comply with any conditions specified in the letter.[23] Letters of credit are of two major types, the traditional or "commercial" letter of credit, and the standby letter of credit.

Commercial Letters of Credit

Buyers and sellers of goods, particularly in international sales, often use documents of title and letters of credit to reduce the risk of nondelivery of the goods by the seller and nonpayment of the price by the buyer. To illustrate, assume Barker, a New York buyer, wishes to purchase $500,000 worth of perfume from Sylvan, a Paris manufacturer. Neither party has previously dealt with the other. Several methods of financing the transaction may be used. First, the buyer could send cash or a check with the order. This approach, of course, presents substantial risks to the buyer because the seller might abscond with the money without shipping the goods or may ship inferior goods. If nonconforming goods are shipped, Barker probably would have to sue Sylvan for breach of contract in France. Further, even if Sylvan properly performs, Barker is out-of-pocket the purchase price until the goods arrive and are sold. Conversely, if Sylvan ships the goods and awaits Barker's remittance, it runs similar risks: Barker's dishonesty, rejection of the goods at the destination, and delay in receiving payment.

A better, though not ideal alternative, is the **shipment under reservation,** or documentary sale. Under this approach, Sylvan draws a draft for the purchase price against Barker and forwards it, together with a bill of lading covering the goods, to a New York bank with instructions not to surrender the bill of lading (which allows Barker to obtain the goods on arrival) until Barker accepts or pays the draft. Shipment under reservation assures that Barker cannot obtain the goods until paying for them but does not guard against its possible insolvency or refusal to pay for the goods when they arrive. If Barker defaults, Sylvan must dispose of the goods at a distant port or pay freight charges back to France. In addition, Sylvan would probably have to file its lawsuit for breach of contract against Barker in New York.

A commercial letter of credit solves most of the problems inherent in the foregoing financing methods, by effectively substituting a bank's credit for that of the buyer. Under this approach, Barker (the customer) requests First Bank (the issuer) to issue a letter of credit directed to Sylvan (or Sylvan's bank) providing that First Bank will honor a draft drawn against it for the purchase price, if the draft is accompanied by certain documents relating to the goods. These documents typically include a bill of lading, an invoice, and an insurance policy covering the goods. If Sylvan (the beneficiary) strictly complies with the terms of the letter, it is assured of payment by First Bank. Barker promises to reimburse First Bank and pays a small commission.

Thus, the letter of credit is a three-part relationship: (1) the underlying contract between the beneficiary and the customer—here the sale of goods from Sylvan to Barker; (2) the reimbursement agreement between the customer and the issuer—here Barker and First Bank; and (3) the letter of credit between the issuer and the beneficiary—here First Bank and Sylvan. These three relationships create obligations that are completely independent of one another, a characteristic that gives letters of credit their great commercial utility. Under this *independence principle,* "the issuer must pay on a proper demand from the beneficiary even though the beneficiary may have breached the underlying contract with the customer."[24]

All parties benefit from this form of financing. The buyer is assured that goods have been shipped that (at least on the face of the documents) conform to the contract. After paying the beneficiary, the seller, the issuing bank possesses the shipping documents and therefore can control the goods until it is reimbursed by its customer, the buyer. Alternatively, the bank may turn the shipping documents over to the buyer and take a perfected security interest in the goods, allowing the buyer to obtain the goods and then repay the bank out of the proceeds of their resale. On the other hand, the seller is virtually assured of payment upon compliance with the letter, because a bank's credit is substituted for the buyer's. Further, the letter of credit creates an absolute, independent obligation to pay upon presentation of conforming documents without regard to any dispute existing between the buyer and seller on the underlying sales contract. In addition, the draft backed by the letter of credit may be readily discounted, often allowing the seller to obtain payment as soon as the goods are shipped.

---

[23]UCC §5–102(a)(10); UCP, Art. 2, ICC Pub. No. 500 (1993).

[24]White & Summers, Uniform Commercial Code 813 (3d ed. 1988).

Standby Letters of Credit

Although letters of credit were developed and are still primarily used to finance international sales transactions, they also are widely used, both domestically and internationally, outside the sale of goods field. One of the most common modern applications is the **standby letter of credit** in which the customer's *default* in performance of a financial or other obligation (such as repayment of a loan or proper completion of a construction contract) triggers the issuer's duty to pay the beneficiary. Thus, whereas the traditional or commercial letter of credit contemplates payment upon proper *performance* of an obligation (the beneficiary-seller's delivery of documents indicating shipment of goods), a standby letter of credit is paid upon *nonperformance*. For example, assume Lender contracts to loan Borrower $1 million to be repaid in periodic installments. To secure repayment, Lender requires Borrower to obtain a standby letter of credit from First Bank. Borrower (the customer) then fills out an application requesting First Bank (the issuer) to issue a letter of credit obligating the bank to honor Lender's (the beneficiary) draft for payment upon Lender's presentation of a statement specifying default by Borrower on the loan repayment obligation. If the bank agrees to issue the letter of credit, Borrower will be required by contract to reimburse the bank for sums expended under the letter.

Although it often serves the same function as the suretyship or guaranty contract discussed in Chapter 33, the standby letter of credit differs from a guaranty in two important respects. First, because the guarantor's obligation is secondary, the guarantor generally may assert contract defenses that the principal debtor has against the creditor. In contrast, the issuer's obligation to pay the beneficiary under a letter of credit is primary and independent of other contracts or relationships involved in the transaction. Thus, the issuer may not assert either (1) a defense the customer (Borrower) has against the beneficiary (Lender) or (2) a defense the issuer has against the customer, to avoid paying the beneficiary upon default. Second, a guarantor is liable upon the debtor's actual default. In contrast, letters of credit require payment upon presentation of conforming documents. Thus, the issuer under a standby letter of credit is obligated to pay when the beneficiary presents it with a draft and statement certifying default that conforms to the terms of the letter, whether or not the customer has in fact defaulted.[25]

---

[25]WHITE & SUMMERS, UNIFORM COMMERCIAL CODE 814 (3d ed. 1988).

A bank issuing a commercial letter of credit has recourse to the goods purchased to secure its right of reimbursement from the customer. In contrast, the standby letter provides no security of its own. For this reason banks typically analyze applications for standby letters in the same manner as ordinary business loans or lines of credit, and often require that customers provide collateral to secure their reimbursement obligations.

Under the independence principle, the issuer's obligation is very limited—to pay only if the documents submitted strictly comply with the terms of the letter of credit. At issue in the following case was whether a bank properly dishonored a request for payment under a standby letter of credit.

Mueller Company v. South Shore Bank
991 F.2d 14 (1st Cir. 1993)

George A. Caldwell Company (Caldwell) regularly purchased supplies on credit from plaintiff Mueller Company. In early 1990, after Caldwell became delinquent in making payments, Mueller rejected new orders from Caldwell and agreed to resume shipments only if Caldwell would provide an irrevocable standby letter of credit in favor of Mueller. On May 24, 1990, defendant South Shore Bank issued the standby letter of credit naming Mueller as beneficiary. The letter, which stated that it was to be governed by the 1983 Uniform Customs and Practice for Documentary Credits (UCP), was to expire on December 31, 1990. The letter provided that Mueller, upon Caldwell's failure to pay, should present to South Shore a sight draft accompanied by invoices "clearly evidencing that the goods described in said invoice(s) represent goods ordered and shipped after May 24, 1990."

In October 1990, Caldwell again defaulted in making payments and Mueller notified the bank that it planned to draw on the letter of credit. On December 31, 1990, Mueller presented to South Shore a sight draft in the amount of $221,996 accompanied by 163 invoices. Because many of the invoices listed order dates prior to May 24, 1990, South Shore refused to honor the draft. Mueller sued South Shore for wrongful dishonor of the standby letter of credit. Mueller characterized the improper invoice dates as "technical inconsistencies" and asserted that South Shore knew or should have known that the invoices were for goods that Caldwell had reordered after issuance of the letter of credit. The trial court ruled in favor of South Shore and Mueller appealed.

Stahl, Circuit Judge

. . . Under the provisions of the UCP, "[b]anks must examine all documents with reasonable care to ascertain that they appear, on their face, to be in accordance with the terms and conditions of the credit." UCP, Art. 15. Moreover, letters of credit "by their nature, are transactions separate from the sales or other contract(s) on which they may be based, and banks are in no way concerned with or bound by such contract(s)." UCP, Art. 3. . . . Thus, in determining their rights and obligations under a letter of credit, "parties are *not* required to look beyond the face of the documents presented." *Auto Servicio San Ignacio, S.R.L. v. Compania Anonima Venezolana de Navegacion,* 765 F.2d 1306, 1310 (5th Cir. 1985) (emphasis in original). *See also* UCP, Art. 4 ("[A]ll parties concerned deal in documents, not in goods, services and/or other performances to which the documents may relate.").

In this case, the letter of credit required that the sight draft be accompanied by invoices "clearly evidencing" that the goods were "ordered and shipped after May 24, 1990." Surely, an invoice with an order date *prior* prior to May 24, 1990 does not "clearly evidence" an order placed after that date. Rather, such an invoice directly contradicts the terms of the letter of credit. In contending that South Shore knew or should have known that these invoices represented goods that had been

reordered and shipped subsequent to May 24, 1990, Mueller is essentially urging that South Shore should have looked beyond the face of invoices to the underlying transaction. As we have stated, however, South Shore was under no such obligation. . . . Because the invoices failed to meet the requirements of the letter of credit, we find that dishonor was proper. . . .

We reject Mueller's contention that the invoices with valid order dates constituted separate or partial drawings on the letter of credit. While the letter of credit did allow partial drawings, Mueller chose to draw upon the letter of credit only once with a single sight draft presented on the letter's expiration date. Mueller directs us to no authority, nor have we located any, which stands for the proposition that an issuing bank must pay a *portion* of a documentary sight draft on the grounds that *some* of the documents comply. Because the "valid" invoices presented did not meet the amount of the sight draft, the bank properly declined to honor the entire draft. . . .

[Judgment affirmed.]

Summary

1.   A bailment is created by a transfer of possession of tangible personal property from its owner or other person in possession (the bailor) to another (the bailee) for a specified purpose. In its broadest sense, a bailment is simply the rightful possession of goods by someone not the owner. The law of bailments primarily concerns the bailee's liability for loss, theft, damage, or destruction of the bailed goods in its possession, and for misdelivery.

2.   A bailee is generally liable for loss of or damage to the bailed goods for which it is at fault. Traditionally, the degree of fault necessary to impose liability depends on whether the bailment is for the bailor's benefit, the bailee's benefit, or for the mutual benefit of the parties. The modern approach, however, requires the bailee simply to exercise reasonable care under the circumstances. Under appropriate circumstances, this liability may be altered by contract.

3.   Unlike the reasonable care standard applied to the bailee's possession, the bailee's duty to deliver is absolute. Thus, a bailee who delivers the property to an unauthorized person is liable to the bailor even though acting in good faith and free from negligence. Similarly, if the bailee uses the property in an unautho-

rized manner, the bailee is absolutely liable for loss or destruction of the property whether or not caused by negligence.

4.   At common law, an innkeeper was a qualified insurer of its guests' goods. This standard, similar to that imposed upon common carriers, has been modified in most states by statutes that strictly limit the dollar amount of an innkeeper's liability.

5.   The most important modern bailments are those for carriage and storage of goods undertaken by professional bailees—known as "carriers" and "warehouses." In exchange for goods received for shipment or storage, these bailees issue documents of title to the bailors. Warehouses issue warehouse receipts and carriers issue bills of lading.

6.   Although warehouses are ordinarily subject only to the same negligence standard applied to other bailees, common carriers (those who perform carriage for hire for all who apply) are qualified insurers of goods they carry. That is, a common carrier is absolutely liable for loss, damage, or destruction of goods in transit unless it proves both its freedom from negligence and that the loss was caused by an Act of God, an act of a public enemy, public authority, or the

shipper, or the inherent nature of the goods. As in ordinary bailments, this liability may be altered by contract.

7.   Carriers and warehouses are obligated to deliver the goods to the person entitled under the document of title. The person entitled to delivery is the holder of a negotiable document and the person to whom the bailee promises delivery in a nonnegotiable document.

8.   The rights of the parties upon transfer of a document of title also depend upon negotiability. If a negotiable document is "duly negotiated" the holder obtains title both to the document and to the goods it covers. A holder by due negotiation therefore defeats virtually all outstanding claims and equities both to the document and the goods. A holder of a negotiable document who does not take by due negotiation or the transferee of a nonnegotiable document acquires only the rights that his or her transferor had.

9.   The liability of an ocean carrier for loss or destruction of goods in its possession is governed by the Carriage of Goods by Sea Act.

10.   The letter of credit is a useful financing, payment, and security device widely used in a variety of domestic and international transactions. Letters of credit are of two types, the traditional or commercial letter of credit, and the standby letter of credit.

Key Terms

bailment	destination bill of lading
bailor	warehouse receipt
bailee	warehouseman
involuntary (constructive) (quasi) bailment	negotiable document of title common carrier
exculpatory clause	holder
document of title	negotiation
delivery order	due negotiation
bill of lading	Carriage of Goods by Sea
freight forwarder	Act (COGSA)
consignor	letter of credit
consignee	shipment under reservation
through bill of lading	standby letter of credit

Questions and Problems

35.1   In each of the following cases, determine whether a bailment has been created and if so, identify the bailee and the bailor. Determine the standard of care to which the bailee should be held in determining liability for the loss or destruction of the bailed property.

(a)   Great Dane Trailers, a manufacturer of trailers for tractor-trailer trucks, manufactures a trailer in Detroit that must be delivered to Houston. Central Transport, Inc., a trucking company, agrees to haul the trailer to Houston at no charge if it may use the trailer to haul freight on the trip. The trailer is stolen by an unknown party during the trip.

(b)   While at a party, Fred finds an unusual and valuable bracelet that he recognizes as one owned by Marsha. Fred telephones Marsha to tell her he has found her bracelet. Several days later Marsha comes to Fred's house to pick up the bracelet. Fred cannot find the bracelet.

(c)   Leo borrows Louise's computer to help prepare his tax returns. While using the computer, he notices a small mechanical problem. When Leo tries to fix the computer, it explodes and is totally destroyed.

35.2   Evelyn delivered two rings to Gem Jewelers, Inc. to have the stones reset. Gem stored the rings in its walk-in fireproof vault that was reinforced with steel and concrete. One night a burglar broke into the store, gained access to the vault by ripping the door off, and stole the contents including Evelyn's rings. The store had not previously been burglarized. Evelyn sues Gem for the value of her rings. Should Gem be held liable? Explain.

35.3   Consider whether bailments have been created in the following situations.

(a)   Seth drives his car to a municipal airport parking lot. Although he parks the car himself, the lot management requires presentation of a claim check to retrieve it. Further, the municipal lot is the only available parking at the airport. Is the city a bailee of Seth's car?

(b)   Seth rents a safe-deposit box at First State Bank. Two keys are needed to open the box, one of which is retained by Seth. Is the bank a bailee of the contents of the box?

35.4   Marlene, a jewelry designer, sent a package of jewelry to one of her salesmen who was staying at the Baltimore Hotel. Marlene insured the package and put her return address on the outside of the package. It was sent by United Parcel Service, a private delivery company. Although the salesman checked at the hotel desk several times a day, the package did not arrive before he had to check out of the hotel. Before leaving, the salesman gave the hotel desk clerk written instructions not to accept the package and to have it returned to the sender. Despite the instructions the hotel accepted the package when it was delivered. The hotel held the package for 30 days and when no one claimed it, the hotel turned the package over to the local post office marked return to sender. The hotel did not check its records to see if the addressee had ever been registered there. The post office lost the package. Marlene sues United Parcel Service, the Baltimore Hotel, and the post office. Who should be held liable? Why?

35.5   At the end of each day, First American Bank sent a car to pick up checks and cash from its branch banks. During the rush hour, the driver of the car locked it and parked it in a "No Parking" zone outside one of the branch banks. A police officer ticketed the vehicle and had Transportation Management, Inc. (TMI), a company employed by the city, tow the vehicle to the city's impound lot. When a bank employee arrived two hours later, he discovered that the car was unlocked and a dispatch bag containing $50,000 was missing from the car. The bank sued TMI alleging that the towing company had acted negligently and should be liable for the bank's loss. TMI asserted that it was a gratuitous bailee and, therefore, could be held liable only for gross negligence. How should the court rule?

35.6　Assume that goods being shipped by Red Ball Express, a common carrier, are destroyed. Red Ball is liable for their destruction under the principles discussed in the text. The goods were being shipped by Seller (located in New York) to Buyer (located in Chicago) pursuant to a contract for sale of the goods. To whom is Red Ball liable? Explain.

35.7　Assume Malloy acquires goods from Olson by fraud. Malloy delivers the goods to William, who issues a negotiable warehouse receipt. Malloy duly negotiates the document to Briggs. May Olson recover the goods from Briggs? Assume the document was nonnegotiable. May Olson recover the goods from Briggs? Assume no document of title was issued. After acquiring the goods from Olson, Malloy sold them to Briggs, who paid fair value and was unaware of Malloy's wrongdoing. May Olson recover the goods from Briggs?

35.8　In anticipation of moving out of state, Mr. and Mrs. Turner stored all of their household goods with Pilgrim Co., a moving and storage company. Pilgrim issued a nonnegotiable bill of lading to Mr. and Mrs. Turner. Mrs. Turner writes to the Pilgrim office explaining that the Turners' plans have changed and they have decided to get a divorce. She requests that Pilgrim hold the goods until further notice.
　(a) Mr. Turner appears at the Pilgrim office requesting delivery of the goods. What should Pilgrim do? Explain.
　(b) Assume instead that Mr. Turner forges a letter over Mrs. Turner's signature requesting delivery of the goods to 123 Oak Street. Pilgrim delivers the goods. The house is owned by a woman friend of Mr. Turner who accepts the goods. Pilgrim asks for the bill of lading but the woman says it has been lost. Mrs. Turner sues Pilgrim for its misdelivery of the goods. What result? Explain.

35.9　El Paso Coin Co. delivered four boxes of valuable coins to Panhandle Airways, an air common carrier, to ship to New York's LaGuardia Airport. Panhandle issued a bill of lading and flew the coins to Dallas where it transferred the four boxes of coins to World Airlines because Panhandle did not fly to New York. A consignee picked up the coins in New York; however, only three boxes arrived. The fourth disappeared and was never found. El Paso sued Panhandle. Should Panhandle be held responsible for the loss? Explain.

35.10　Norfolk & Western Railway, a common carrier, agreed to transport 16 shipments of lumber for Masonite Corp.

During one of the early shipments, some of the lumber shifted and almost fell from the railroad car. Norfolk & Western notified Masonite of the problem and requested that Masonite pack the subsequent shipments in a safer manner and directed Masonite to have the packing checked thoroughly by the Norfolk & Western safety inspector prior to shipping. Masonite failed to follow Norfolk and Western's request. The final shipments were placed on the railroad car and were subjected only to the railway's external inspection. En route, the lumber shifted because of the poor packing and fell from the train causing a derailment that destroyed all of the lumber.
　Masonite sued Norfolk & Western claiming the railway company should be held strictly liable as a common carrier. Norfolk & Western defended by alleging that it could not be held responsible for latent defects in packing. How should the court rule? Explain.

35.11　Armour Co. hired Rush Delivery Service, a licensed common carrier, to transport a shipment of meat from the stockyards to Wiener Corp. Rush picked up the shipment and drove to Wiener's plant where the driver attempted delivery but the plant manager refused, explaining that it was too late in the day to accept deliveries. Rush called Armour for instructions and Armour told Rush to deliver the shipment the following morning. Armour further advised Rush that the truck could be parked in a nearby yard owned by Armour. After securing the vehicle, Rush's driver took the keys with him and left the truck in Armour's yard. When he returned the following morning, the truck was missing. Armour sued Rush for the value of the lost shipment alleging that Rush was strictly liable as a common carrier. Rush asserted that its status as common carrier had terminated when it left the truck in Armour's yard and, at most, Rush was a warehouseman at the time the goods were lost. How should the court rule? Explain.

35.12　Under the Carriage of Goods by Sea Act (COGSA), a shipper's liability for goods damaged during shipment is limited to $500 per package. Monica Textile Corp. (MTC) hired the *S.S. Tana* to ship 76 bales of cotton from Africa to the United States. MTC packed all of the cotton in a 20-foot shipping container. An agent of the *S.S. Tana* prepared the bill of lading form. Under the column titled "Number of Units Shipped," the agent wrote "One" and in the column labeled "Description of Goods," he wrote "76 bales of cotton." The goods were damaged in transit and MTC sought damages. The *S.S. Tana* asserted that MTC had shipped only one package so that the maximum amount for which it could be held liable was $500. MTC argued that it had shipped 76 packages so that the *S.S. Tana* could be held liable for $38,000. Who is correct? Explain.

REAL PROPERTY OWNERSHIP

American property law, like much of our legal system, is derived from English common law. Originally grounded in feudal society, the concept of estates has developed as the basic scheme of land ownership in the United States. Simply stated, an **estate** is an ownership interest in property. This ownership interest may be absolute (subject only to governmental control for the needs of society generally) or may be limited as to its nature, quality, quantity, duration, or time or extent of possession.

Traditionally, estates are classified as either **freehold** or **nonfreehold.** This distinction, also derived from the English feudal system, provides a convenient basis for organizing our discussion of the various property interests. Freehold estates are characterized by their uncertain or potentially unlimited duration. In contrast, non-freehold estates have a fixed or determinate duration and are considered lesser interests in property than freeholds. The various freehold estates are covered below followed by a discussion of co-ownership, in which two or more persons simultaneously have the right to possess the same property. The chapter concludes with coverage of nonfreehold estates, the basis of the law of landlord and tenant.

Freehold Estates in Property

Introduction to Future Interests

Before discussing the various freehold estates, one must distinguish present possessory estates from future interests in property. A **present possessory estate** is one in which the owner has the present right to *possession* of the property. As discussed below, full property ownership may be split into lesser estates, which take effect in possession and enjoyment *successively.* In other words, the owner or group of owners of an estate may not have the present right to possess the property; rather, they must await the termination of the preceding estate, or estates, in the property. In this situation the owner possesses a **future interest,** one that takes effect in possession and enjoyment, if at all, at some future time. Note that the owner of a future interest may never acquire the right to possess the property or, on the other hand, may be assured of that right. Resolution of this issue depends upon the nature of the future interest in relation to the preceding estates, or upon the occurrence or nonoccurrence of uncertain events. Thus, future interests are in fact present interests in property. "Future" simply refers to the *time* of possession (whether or not the right to possession is assured), not the *existence* of the interest. Because a future interest takes effect in the future, its owner may be dead when the interest becomes possessory. In this situation, the property passes to the owner's estate and is distributed according to the owner's will or by the state intestate succession statute if the owner fails to leave a will. In other words, unless explicitly stated in the instrument creating the interest, the holder of a future interest need not outlive the preceding estates in order to take.

The Fee Simple

The Fee Simple Absolute. The law recognizes two types of fee simple estates: the fee simple absolute and the defeasible, or qualified, fee simple. The fee simple absolute is the most common of all estates and comports closely with the layman's understanding of ownership. The **fee simple absolute** (commonly shortened to "fee simple" or "fee") is the entire bundle of rights a person may possess in property—the largest quantity of ownership interest recognized by the law.

The fee simple is potentially unlimited in duration and is freely transferable by sale or gift during the owner's lifetime; it passes by will or intestate succession after death. In such cases, the transferee then receives a fee simple that continues indefinitely until transferred as outlined above. The owner need not convey her entire fee simple interest but may transfer only a part. Further, whether or not the entire interest is transferred, the owner may create lesser estates in any number of transferees.

At common law, a fee simple could be transferred inter vivos only by using the language "to (the grantee) and his heirs" in the deed. Today, by statute in most states, this formal language is no longer required, and unless it appears from the instrument (deed or will) that a lesser estate is intended, a fee simple absolute is presumed.

Therefore, a simple grant of property "to B" would now vest fee simple title in B.

Defeasible Fees and Related Future Interests. The **defeasible fee** (sometimes called a "qualified," "determinable," or "base" fee) contains all of the incidents of the fee simple absolute except that it is subject to a condition: it can be terminated by the occurrence or nonoccurrence of an event stated in the instrument, such as a will or deed, creating the estate. The three major types of defeasible fee simple estates are

1. the fee simple determinable,
2. the fee simple subject to a condition subsequent, and
3. the fee simple subject to an executory limitation.

Fee Simple Determinable. The **fee simple determinable** (known also as a "fee on common law limitation" or "modified fee") is commonly characterized by use of the words "so long as," "until," "during," or "while" preceding the language qualifying the interest. Assume Smith sells a building to Jones using the following language in the deed: "To Jones and his heirs so long as the premises are not used for the sale of alcoholic liquor." This language creates a fee simple determinable in Jones. In this situation, Jones has all of the incidents of absolute ownership subject, however, to *automatic* termination if the property is used for the sale of liquor. This same limitation also is imposed upon a buyer of the property from Jones, a taker through Jones's will or by intestate succession, and other persons later in the chain of ownership. Upon termination, the property passes in fee simple absolute back to Smith, or her heirs or devisees if Smith is deceased. After creating the fee simple determinable, Smith, or her successors in interest, possess a future interest in the property known as a **possibility of reverter.**

Fee Simple Subject to a Condition Subsequent. The **fee simple subject to a condition subsequent** is similar to the fee simple determinable but differs in one important respect. Whereas a fee simple determinable ends automatically and the property reverts to the grantor on occurrence or nonoccurrence of the stated event, the fee simple subject to a condition subsequent continues until the grantor or his successors in interest take some affirmative steps (such as entering the premises or commencing a lawsuit to enter) to terminate the estate. The fee simple subject to a condition subsequent usually is created by the language "upon condition that" or "provided that" preceding the condition, coupled with language allowing termination upon failure of the condition. A fee simple subject to a condition subsequent would, for example, be created by Smith's conveyance to "Jones and his heirs on condition that the premises are never used for the sale of alcoholic liquor, and if they are so used then Smith or her heirs may enter and terminate the estate hereby conveyed." The future interest possessed by Smith or her successors in interest in this case is known as a **right of entry for condition broken** or more commonly, a **power of termination.**

Because the possibility of reverter and power of termination can exist for a potentially indefinite period, they often cloud land titles. For example, as time passes and conditions change, a remote buyer may wish to use the property for purposes prohibited by terms of the defeasible estate. In this case, the buyer must acquire the defeasible fee from its current owner, and must extinguish the future interest. Because the original grantor and immediate heirs are long dead, the buyer must track down remote heirs and purchase their interests. To reduce this problem, many states have enacted statutes (1) requiring that action be taken within a limited time (for example, seven years) after occurrence of the prohibited event, or (2) limiting the overall duration of the interest (for example, to 40 years), or (3) restricting the transferability of the interest.

Fee Simple Subject to an Executory Limitation. The third type of defeasible interest is the **fee simple subject to an executory limitation.** It differs from the interests previously discussed in that, upon termination of the fee simple estate, the property passes to a *third party,* someone other than the grantor or her heirs. Transfer of the interest to the third party, as in a fee simple determinable, occurs *automatically* upon occurrence or nonoccurrence of the stated event. For example, assume White conveys property "to Brown and his heirs, but if Brown dies without leaving children surviving him, then to Cox and her heirs." Brown, in this case, has a fee simple subject to an executory limitation and Cox has a future interest in the property known as an **executory interest** or **executory limitation,** which cuts off and divests Brown's fee simple estate if Brown dies without children surviving him. Note that Cox's interest in the property is known as a "shifting" use or interest because it destroys an estate vested in a grantee and "shifts" it to the holder of the executory interest—in this case, Cox.

Executory interests also may be designated as "springing" uses or interests, which destroy an existing estate held by the *grantor.* For example, Nelson by deed may convey property to "Black and her heirs, Black's interest to begin one year from the date of this deed." In this situation, Nelson has a fee simple subject to an executory limitation. Black has a "springing" executory interest because it "springs" into existence in one year, destroying the estate of the grantor, Nelson. In most states, executory interests are freely transferable *inter vivos* by deed, and pass on death by will or intestate succession.

Life Estates

A **life estate** is an interest in property limited in duration to the life or lives of one or more persons. After the fee simple absolute, life estates represent the most common type of freehold interest. Life estates are created primarily in connection with family settlements or estate planning. For example, a person with a family may wish to leave property to a surviving spouse to provide for him or her until death and then ultimately transfer the property to the children.

Life estates generally are created by explicit language contained in a deed or will. If a deed is used, the estate may be created in the grantor by reservation—for example, when the grantor conveys a fee simple in the property but reserves to herself a present life estate—or in a person other than the grantor. The holder of a life estate is known as the **life tenant** and it is most frequently her life that determines the duration of the estate. For example, a conveyance of property "to Ann for life" creates a life estate in Ann terminating on Ann's death. The life tenant need not, however, be the measuring life. The duration of the estate may be determined by the life of another. This is known as a life estate *pur autre vie.* The person whose life is used as the measuring stick, the *cestui que vie,* takes nothing as a result of the grant. For example, property conveyed "to Ann for the life of Bob" creates a life estate *pur autre vie.* Ann is the "life tenant" and Bob is the *cestui que vie.*[1]

Life estates, like most other property interests, are freely transferable. Of course, the estate normally ends at the owner's death. Therefore, if James owns a life estate and sells it to Ron, Ron's interest ordinarily terminates on James's death. (That is, Ron's life estate is

---

[1]There may be more than one measuring life. In this case, the estate continues until the death of the last surviving *cestui que vie.*

an estate *pur autre vie*.) Further, because the life estate terminates on death, no interest ordinarily passes to the life tenant's heirs or persons taking under a will. In the estate pur autre vie, however, the life tenant may predecease the measuring life. For example, if property is conveyed "to James for the life of Ron," James may die before Ron. In this situation, the life estate passes by will or intestate succession, like other property interests, and ultimately terminates on the death of the cestui que vie, in this case, Ron.

Life estates, like fee simple estates, may be defeasible. Assume Alan, in his will, leaves a house "to my wife, Beth, for life, so long as she continues to occupy it as her residence." In this case, the life estate is defeasible (or determinable) subject to termination before Beth's death if she ceases to occupy the premises.

The life tenant is in essence treated as the owner of the property for the duration of the estate. As such, he is entitled to the use and possession of the property, including any rents or profits the property generates. Because other interests in the property follow the life estate, however, the law protects these interests against unreasonable reduction in value by imposing a duty on the life tenant not to commit waste. **Waste** is conduct by the life tenant in the use of the land resulting in a substantial and unreasonable reduction in the value of the property passing to the following estates. If the life tenant is committing waste, the holder of the subsequent injured estate may bring an action for damages or an injunction.

Other Future Interests

Reversions. A **reversion** is a future interest remaining in a *grantor* of property who transfers away less than her entire interest in the property. No reversion may, therefore, be created when the grantor conveys a fee simple absolute to the grantee.[2] Reversions arise automatically by operation of law; they need not be expressly created. Assume Sarah, by deed or will, transfers land "to Bob for life." Because Sarah has not transferred her entire interest in the property—she has not stated what happens to the property on Bob's death—a reversion is created in Sarah. Therefore, on Bob's death, fee simple title "reverts" to Sarah. More accurately stated, the right to possession reverts to Sarah. The reversion itself essen-

tially *remains in* the grantor since she has transferred less than her entire interest. Sarah is free, during her lifetime, to convey her reversionary interest by deed. On Sarah's death, it passes to the person entitled to her property under her will or by intestate succession.

The grantor need not possess fee simple title to create a reversion. For example, the owner of a life estate may convey an estate for years (that is, a leasehold interest) to a grantee. On termination of the leasehold, the right to possession of the property reverts to the life tenant for the duration of the life estate.

Remainders. In contrast to a reversion, which arises in a *grantor,* a **remainder** is a future interest that arises in a third party (someone other than the grantor) that takes effect in possession and enjoyment on the natural termination of the preceding estate. Assume Carol conveys property "to Alice for life, then to Ted in fee simple absolute." In this case, Alice has a life estate, and Ted has a remainder, taking effect on the natural termination of Alice's estate, Alice's death. Ted, the owner of the remainder, is known as the "remainderman." In this case, no reversion is created in Carol because she has transferred her entire interest in the property. Like most other future interests, remainders are freely transferable during life, and pass by will or intestate succession on death.

A remainder need not confer a fee simple interest. Suppose Carol conveys property "to Alice for life, remainder to Ted for life." In this case, Ted owns a remainder—a future interest created in someone other than the grantor becoming possessory upon the natural termination of the preceding estate, Alice's death. Carol, in this case, retains a reversion that takes effect on Ted's death.

Vested and Contingent Remainders. Remainders are classified as either vested or contingent. A remainder is vested when the remainderman is unconditionally entitled to possession immediately upon termination of the prior possessory estate (normally a life estate). Assume Mark conveys property "to Greg for life, remainder to Dan." Dan's remainder is absolutely vested.

If the identity of the remainderman is uncertain or if his interest depends on occurrence or nonoccurrence of an event, the remainder is contingent. In other words, a contingent remainder is a remainder subject to a condition precedent. Suppose Larry conveys property "to Darrell for life, remainder to Darrell's first-born child in fee simple absolute." At the time of the grant, Darrell has

---

[2]Other future interests, such as a possibility of reverter or power of termination, may arise in a grantor in conjunction with transfer of a fee simple interest.

no children. In this case, Darrell has a life estate, Darrell's first-born child has a "contingent" remainder, contingent upon being born alive. If a child is born alive, the remainder becomes vested. The child need not then outlive Darrell in order to take. The remainder would then simply pass to the child's estate. The original grant could, however, have required that the child survive Darrell or attain a certain age. In that case, a second contingency would be imposed upon the remainder; the child must be both born and survive Darrell or attain a minimum age.

If the contingencies governing the remainder fail to occur and the grantor has not provided for disposition of the property in that event, a reversion is created in the grantor. Thus, using the preceding example, if Darrell dies childless, the grant becomes simply "to Darrell for life" and the property reverts to Larry or those taking through his will or by descent. Therefore unless the grantor provides for alternative disposition of the property, a reversion always accompanies a contingent remainder.[3]

Because a contingent remainder creates only an expectancy or possibility of an interest, the early common law refused to recognize it as an estate in land. As such, the interest could not be transferred either inter vivos or on death. In most states today, however, contingent remainders are freely alienable like other future interests.

Co-ownership of Property

Two or more persons often simultaneously hold an interest in the same property. The nature of these interests varies greatly. For example, a life tenant and remainderman hold interests representing a successive right to posession of or income from property. The material that follows addresses a particular type of simultaneous interest, **co-ownership** or **concurrent ownership,** in which two or more persons, known as "co-owners" or, more commonly, "co-tenants," have a concurrent right to *possession* of the same property. In concurrent ownership, each co-tenant holds an "undivided" interest in the property. This means that each co-tenant has a simultaneous, proportionate share of the entire property, but no separate interest in any particular or identifiable portion of it. For example, assume Ann, Barbara, Carol, and Dawn are co-owners of a farm, each holding an undivided one-fourth interest. In this situation, Ann owns one-fourth of the entire property and has equal right to possession and enjoyment of the farm subject to the rights of the other co-tenants. This is the unity of possession common to all forms of co-ownership. The interest is undivided because there is no designation regarding which particular one-fourth of the farm each co-tenant owns—for example, that Ann owns the northeast quarter, Barbara the northwest quarter, and so on. Although co-ownership originally developed in the real property context, personal property such as bank accounts, government bonds, or other securities also may be jointly owned.

Joint Tenancy and Tenancy in Common Distinguished

The law recognizes three major forms of co-ownership: **joint tenancy,** tenancy by the entirety (a specialized form of joint tenancy recognized in some states between husband and wife), and tenancy in common.[4] The fundamental difference among these forms of ownership is the **right of survivorship** existing in joint tenancies and tenancies by the entirety but not tenancies in common. Under the right of survivorship, if one of two joint tenants or tenants by the entirety dies, the deceased's share is owned by the other, who becomes sole owner. If the property is owned by more than two joint tenants, the deceased's share belongs to the survivors jointly.

Assume Hart, Sloan, and Davis own real estate in fee simple as joint tenants each owning an undivided one-third interest. Assume Hart leaves a will leaving all of his property to Rogers. On Hart's death, his one-third interest remains in the surviving joint tenants, Sloan and Davis, equally; that is, after Hart's death, Sloan and Davis each own an undivided one-half interest in the property in joint tenancy. On Sloan's death, the survivor, Davis, owns the entire property in fee simple. Thus, if property is held in joint tenancy and the joint tenancy is not severed prior to the death of any joint tenant, the joint tenant who lives the longest ultimately becomes sole owner of the property.

When a person dies, an "estate" is created. This estate is distributed, after paying creditors' claims, by the terms of the decedent's will or by state "intestate succession" statutes if the decedent does not leave a valid will. Because a joint tenant's interest does not pass to his or her

---

[3]Even though the reversion itself is contingent (that is, on failure of the condition attached to the remainder), the grantor's interest is still known as a reversion, not a "contingent" reversion.

---

[4]A fourth type, community property, is discussed in Chapter 39.

estate on death, Rogers, the taker under Hart's will, has no claim to Hart's one-third joint tenancy interest. That interest automatically resides in the survivors, Sloan and Davis.

If **tenancy in common,** on the other hand, has no right of survivorship. On death of a tenant in common, the tenant's interest passes, like any other property (such as a car, television set, or house) to the tenant's estate. Thus, whoever is designated to take the property by will or intestate succession is entitled to the decedent's interest. To illustrate using the preceding example, assume Hart, Sloan, and Davis own the farm as tenants in common. In this case, on Hart's death, his interest passes by the will to Rogers.

Creditors' Claims. Because joint tenancy property never gets into the decedent's estate, it is not generally subject to claims of the deceased joint tenant's creditors. Assume, for example, on the above facts, that Carl is Hart's creditor, holding a valid $10,000 claim. On Hart's death, Carl may not reach Hart's one-third interest in the farm in the hands of Sloan and Davis to satisfy the debt. If, however, Hart, Sloan, and Davis hold the farm as tenants in common, Hart's one-third interest passes to his estate and, like most other property in his estate, is subject to claims of his creditors. A creditor of a person owning joint tenancy property may be protected by forcing a severance of the joint tenancy prior to death, under principles outlined later in this chapter.

Effect of Simultaneous Death. Because rights in a joint tenancy or tenancy by the entirety depend on survivorship, disputes have arisen when the co-tenants die in a common disaster. The **Uniform Simultaneous Death Act,** adopted in most states, partially resolves this problem by providing that joint tenants or tenants by the entirety who die simultaneously are treated as having died as tenants in common holding equal shares.[5]

Creation and Termination of Co-ownership

Presumption of Tenancy in Common. At early common law, a conveyance of property to two or more persons, if ambiguous, was presumed to create a joint tenancy. Because this presumption often results in transfer of the property on death contrary to the decedent's intent, the modern presumption, often imposed by statute, is that a

---

[5]Uniform Simultaneous Death Act §3. Problems of simultaneous death in wills and intestate succession are discussed in Chapter 39.

grant of property to two or more persons creates a tenancy in common unless the intent to form a joint tenancy is clearly indicated in the instrument creating the interest. Thus, today a conveyance of property "to Andrew and Robert," or "to Andrew and Robert equally," or "to Andrew and Robert jointly" should create a tenancy in common. To create a joint tenancy, the grantor should make his intent clear by using language such as "to A and B, as joint tenants, and not as tenants in common, with right of survivorship."

Creation of Co-ownership. To create a joint tenancy, four elements, commonly known as the **four unities,** must be present. These unities are

1. *Time*—all joint tenancy interests must vest at the same time.
2. *Title*—all joint tenants must acquire their interests in the same instrument, such as a deed or will.
3. *Interest*—the interest of each co-owner must be identical. This means that fractional shares must be equal—for example, three joint tenants each must have a one-third interest—and the type and duration of the estate must be the same—for example, all must be life estates or fee simples.
4. *Possession*—all joint tenants have an undivided interest in the property and an equal right to possess the entire property subject to the rights of the other co-tenants.

In a tenancy in common, only the unity of possession need be present. Therefore, a tenancy in common may be created with unequal fractional shares. For example, A, B, and C may be tenants in common holding one-half, one-third, and one-sixth interests. Tenants in common also may have differing interests acquired at different times. For example, Rose may, during her lifetime, convey a one-half interest in her farm to Sally in fee simple, and leave a life estate in the remaining one-half to Tom in her will. Sally and Tom are tenants in common.

Termination of Joint Tenancy. Once created, a joint tenancy may be terminated or severed whenever one of the four unities ceases to be present. Thus, if one joint tenant, during her lifetime, transfers her interest to a third party, the unities of time and title are destroyed and a tenancy in common is created.

For example, assume Art and Bob are joint tenants. Bob sells his interest to Joan. Because the four unities are not present between Art and Joan, they hold the property as tenants in common. Assume further that

Ann, Betty, and Carol are joint tenants. Carol sells her interest to Mark. As between Ann and Betty, the unities are still present and therefore Ann and Betty hold an undivided two-thirds of the property as joint tenants. Mark, however, holds his one-third as a tenant in common with Ann and Betty. Therefore, on Mark's death, his one-third passes to his estate, but on Betty's death her one-third interest goes to Ann by right of survivorship. Similarly, if Carol sells her interest to Ann, Ann (now owning two-thirds) holds one-third of the property as a joint tenant with Betty, and one-third as a tenant in common. Thus, if Ann predeceases Betty, one-third of the property goes to Betty by right of survivorship and one-third passes to Ann's estate. If Betty predeceases Ann, Ann then owns the entire property.

A joint tenancy may be severed either voluntarily or involuntarily. For example, a person's creditors may force a sale of property held in joint tenancy to satisfy an unpaid judgment. The consent of the remaining joint tenants is not necessary to sever the joint tenancy in this manner. At issue in the following case was whether a joint tenancy had been created, and if so, whether it had been severed, resulting in a tenancy in common.

Downing v. Downing
606 A.2d 208 (Md. 1992)

Helen Downing owned a farm in Maryland that, by written agreement, was leased to John Myers. On August 7, 1972, Helen Downing conveyed her farm to Stanford Hoff, who immediately reconveyed the property to "Helen S. Downing and John Robert Downing, Junior [Helen's son], as joint tenants, their heirs and assigns, forever in fee simple." The deeds did not mention the written lease agreement and Myers continued to pay rent only to Helen Downing. In 1985, Helen Downing and John Downing, Jr. (John Jr.) granted a mortgage on the farm to Union National Bank. Helen died in 1987. Under her will, which made no mention of the farm, half of her estate was left to John Jr. and the other half was left to her daughter, Bonnie Downing. Plaintiff Bonnie Downing filed a claim requesting the court to rule that Helen and John Jr. had held the farm as tenants in common. John Jr. argued that he and his mother had held the property as joint tenants with right of survivorship thereby entitling him to sole ownership of the farm. The trial court ruled that the farm had been owned by John Jr. and Helen as tenants in common. John Jr. appealed.

Chasanow, Judge

. . . In this case we must resolve two questions: (1) Is a conveyance using the language "as joint tenants, their heirs and assigns, forever in fee simple" sufficient to create a joint tenancy? (2) If so, did either the farming agreement with Myers or the execution of a subsequent mortgage by both Helen and John Jr. sever this joint tenancy? . . .

Joint tenancy means that each joint tenant owns an undivided share in the whole estate, has an equal right to possess, use, and enjoy the property, and has the right of survivorship. . . . For the purposes of this case, the crucial distinction between a joint tenancy and a tenancy in common is the right of survivorship identified with a joint tenancy. . . . Therefore, if we determine that a joint tenancy was created, the family farm passes to John Jr. as surviving joint tenant. If we find that a joint tenancy was not created, the deed establishes merely a tenancy in common and Helen's interest in the family farm will become part of her estate.

"At common law it was presumed that a conveyance to two or more persons created a joint tenancy." [*Alexander v. Boyer,* 253 A.2d 359, 363 (Md. 1969).] Chapter 162 of the Acts of 1822 reversed the common law and declared joint tenancy to be disfavored in Maryland. . . . Chapter 162's embodiment in effect at the time of the August 7, 1972 deed . . . provided, "No deed, devise or other instrument of writing shall be construed to create an estate in joint tenancy, unless in such deed, devise or other instrument of writing it is expressly provided that the property hereby conveyed is to be held in joint tenancy." [Maryland Code, Art. 50, §9.]

Bonnie [argues that] no Maryland decision . . . "flatly states that the term, 'joint tenants,' standing alone, is sufficient to overcome the disfavor with which joint tenancies are viewed in Maryland." This Court has held that in the case of a joint tenancy, it must be so clearly expressed as to leave no doubt about the parties' intention. . . . However, we believe that when a deed uses the words "joint tenants," as does the instrument in the instant case, this language can be sufficient to establish that the property granted is to be held in joint tenancy. . . .

In *McManus v. Summers,* [430 A.2d 80 (Md. 1981).], we held that although joint tenancies are disfavored, a clear manifestation of intent to create a joint tenancy will be effectuated. . . . We reasoned that . . . "as to the formula for creation of joint tenancies . . . [the statutory] requirement is only one of clear manifestation of intention, not one of particular words . . ." [*Id.* at 82–83.] . . .

McManus concluded that a right of survivorship existed even when no right of survivorship was mentioned in the deed because the parties' intent was clear.

Helen and John Jr., in the instrument now before this Court, indicated that they intended to hold the property as joint tenants. . . . By using the words, "as joint tenants," they satisfied the requirements of the Real Property Article. The Court need look no further than the deed itself to conclude that a valid joint tenancy came into being. . . . Had the author of the deed employed such language as, "as joint tenants with the right of survivorship" or "as joint tenants and not as tenants in common," the intent to create a joint tenancy would have been more readily apparent. . . .

We now turn to the unities of time, title, interest, and possession required for the existence of a valid joint tenancy. Bonnie, in her brief, concedes that the unities of time and title are satisfied, but she argues that letting Myers farm the land destroyed the unities of interest and possession. Bonnie contends that because of the pre-existing farming agreement with Myers, the unity of interest was never met, and if met, was destroyed by the next annual renewal of the "lease" to Myers. Bonnie also argues that because the farming rights had been assigned to Myers, John Jr.'s right to possession was frustrated, and the unity of possession was destroyed.

The simple answer to Bonnie's contention with respect to the unity of interest is that the mere fact that Helen might have given Myers the right to farm the land does not preclude a joint tenancy. What Helen conveyed to Hoff and Hoff reconveyed to Helen and John Jr. was the fee simple estate subject to Myers' right to farm. Regardless of whether we categorize this farming right as a lease, license, or profit, it would not preclude a joint tenancy. A joint tenancy can be created in an estate less than an unencumbered fee simple estate. . . . Nor does Helen's receipt of the rents, with John Jr.'s consent, destroy the unities of interest or possession. . . .

The circuit court was wrong in concluding that the mortgage on the property by Helen and John Jr. destroyed the joint tenancy. A mortgage by a *single* joint tenant does destroy the unities of interest and title and this destroys the joint tenancy. . . . However, where all joint tenants join in the mortgage, none of the unities are destroyed, and there is no reason why the joint tenancy should not continue. We hold that a mortgage executed by all joint tenants does not sever the joint tenancy. . . .

For the above reasons we conclude that a joint tenancy was formed by the deed of August 7, 1972.

Furthermore, we conclude that the acts of the joint tenants—including the granting of farming rights to Myers and the subsequent execution of a mortgage by both joint tenants—did not sever this relationship. . . .

[Judgment reversed and remanded.]

Termination of Co-ownership. If a joint tenancy is severed, a tenancy in common generally results. The parties to either a joint tenancy or a tenancy in common may, however, desire to terminate concurrent ownership altogether. This result is accomplished by **partition**—physically dividing the property into distinct portions resulting in individual ownership by the former co-tenants of each portion. Partition destroys the undivided nature of co-ownership and may be accomplished either by agreement of the parties or by order of the court. Generally, any co-tenant has an absolute right to judicial partition under statutory procedures that vary among the states. The property may be physically divided, or "partitioned in kind," if such a division is possible. More commonly, however, the property is sold at judicial sale and the proceeds apportioned among the co-tenants.

Tenancy by the Entirety

A **tenancy by the entirety** is a specialized form of joint tenancy with right of survivorship existing between co-tenants who are husband and wife. The estate is based on the common law concept of "spousal unity"—that husband and wife are one person. At common law, therefore, a transfer of property to husband and wife resulted in only one estate, an entirety. In this estate, the spouses own the whole interest collectively but no undivided individual share. In contrast, in a joint tenancy the tenants own both the whole and an undivided share.

The legal effect of this distinction is as follows. First, the tenancy by the entirety may not be partitioned except with the consent of both parties or by divorce. A joint tenancy may be partitioned at the request of one joint tenant. Second, a tenancy by the entirety may not be severed by the act of a single spouse. A joint tenancy, on the other hand, is severed when one joint tenant voluntarily or involuntarily conveys his or her interest.

With the modern erosion of the fiction that husband and wife are one, most states have abolished the tenancy by the entirety, with the result that a conveyance of property to husband and wife creates either a joint tenancy or tenancy in common, depending upon the language used. In states that still retain the interest (limited in many states to real property), the spouses usually possess equal rights in the control and enjoyment of the property. At common law, these rights were possessed solely by the husband.

Cooperatives and Condominiums

Two additional forms of joint property ownership, the cooperative and the condominium, provide a method for co-ownership of multiple-unit dwellings. The **cooperative** is a form of real estate ownership by which residents in a multiple-unit building own shares in a corporation that owns the building. Ownership of shares in the corporation entitles each resident to lease a unit in the building and to use common areas of the building. As part of a shareholder agreement, each resident makes a monthly payment that represents a prorated share of the cost of repaying the loan that the corporation has secured to purchase the building and a share of the building maintenance costs. Generally, each tenant is jointly and severally liable on the loan. Therefore, if any resident fails to make a monthly payment, the other tenants must arrange to pay the tenant's share of the loan to avoid default.

Because of the risk imposed by the cooperative's joint and several liability, the condominium has evolved as a more popular form of ownership for multiple-dwelling buildings. In a **condominium** system, each resident purchases a living unit in the building and all residents own common areas, such as hallways, basement storage areas, roads, and recreation facilities, as tenants in common. Although a resident may secure a loan to finance the purchase of an individual unit, the other residents assume no liability for that loan. Condominiums maintain a condominium association of which each resident is a member and that is responsible for operating the building. Residents pay a monthly fee to the condominium association to cover the costs of maintaining common areas. Most states regulate condominium ownership by statutes that require condominium developers to adopt a master deed and condominium association bylaws. These documents describe the interests held by each condominium owner and the methods of maintaining and paying the expenses for the common areas. Under most statutes, a purchaser of a condominium unit is entitled to receive copies of these documents prior to transfer of ownership.

Introduction to Landlord and Tenant

Leases of real property are among the most common legal relationships entered into by both consumers and businesspersons. Individuals often rent rather than buy their homes or apartments. Businesses routinely rent the land and buildings used to conduct their retail, wholesale, manufacturing, and service operations. A **lease** creates a **landlord-tenant relationship,** which arises upon a transfer of the right to possession of real property from the owner—the **lessor** or **landlord**—to another—the **lessee** or **tenant**—for consideration known as "rent." Thus, in a lease a real property owner, the lessor, relinquishes possession of the property but retains ownership. A lease creates a possessory "non-freehold" estate in the property in the tenant—a "leasehold." The landlord, who conveys away less than her entire interest in the land, retains a reversion that takes effect upon termination of the agreed lease term. The landlord also has the right to receive rents for the duration of the lease. The landlord's reversion plus her right to receive rent is collectively known as the "leased fee."

Elements of a Valid Lease

A lease is a conveyance of the property for a given period of time during which rights and obligations of the parties are governed by their express agreement. The promises made by the landlord and tenant to each other in the lease are known as "covenants." A lease, therefore, contains elements of two major substantive legal areas: property and contracts. In recent years, the law has moved away from the older property-oriented approach, placing more emphasis on the contract aspects of a lease in determining rights and duties of the parties.

Statute of Frauds. A lease, like an agreement to transfer a fee simple interest in land, generally is enforceable only if it is evidenced by a writing signed by the party to be charged. This requirement was first imposed by the English (or "common law") Statute of

Frauds,[6] which has been adopted, with modifications, in virtually all states. Most state enactments, however, exempt leases with a term of one year or less from the operation of the Statute of Frauds, rendering such leases enforceable even if oral.

Essential Terms. The legal requirements for an enforceable lease are not rigorous. The parties need not use formal words of leasing. They simply must indicate an intent to transfer possession and create the relationship. The minimum terms necessary to create an enforceable lease are (1) the names of the parties, (2) a description of the property, (3) the term of the lease, (4) the amount of the rent, and (5) the time of payment. Many of the minimum terms are supplied by law if not explicitly stated. For example, if not stated, the amount of rent is assumed to be the reasonable value of the premises, with payment due at the end of the term.

Even though a writing is not always required for enforceability, a written lease that outlines the rights and obligations of the parties and resolves as many contingencies as possible is always desirable. An integrated written lease provides maximum protection to the parties in the event of a dispute, and the act of reducing the agreement to writing frequently uncovers misunderstandings that can then be resolved. In addition to the provisions outlined above, other terms commonly appearing in a lease include restrictions on use of the property; rights of inspection; disposition of fixtures; liability for repairs, maintenance, taxes, utilities, and insurance; effect of destruction of premises, or taking by eminent domain; default and remedies for default; rights of tenant to assign or sublease premises; security for payment of rent or damage to property and application of security; and termination or renewal of lease including the effect of tenant's holding over.

Effect of Recording. Most states have statutes providing that leases exceeding a statutorily specified duration are recordable interests in land. The statutory period varies substantially from state to state. Thus, the lessee often records a long-term lease with the local recorder of deeds to give constructive notice to third parties of the lessee's interest in the property. The importance and effect of recording is discussed in detail in Chapter 37.

---

[6]29 Car. 2, ch. 3, §1 (1677). The common law statute is discussed in detail in Chapter 12.

Duration of the Lease — "Nonfreehold" Estates

A lease creates an interest in the land in the tenant known as a "nonfreehold" estate. Unlike the freehold estates (which are created by deed or will and have unlimited or indeterminate duration), nonfreehold estates are created by contract and are terminated upon expiration of the lease term, by acts of the parties, or upon occurrence of an agreed condition. Even though the nonfreehold is an estate in land and immovable, it is personal property, a so-called chattel-real. This anomaly is a historical remnant of early judicial hostility toward nonfreehold estates.

The duration of a lease depends on the type of nonfreehold estate created. The law classifies these estates (or "tenancies") as one of four types: the estate for years, the estate from period to period, the estate at will, and the estate at sufferance.

The Estate for Years. The **estate for years** is the most prevalent form of nonfreehold estate, characterized by a fixed beginning and ending date. Assume that on June 1, 2005, L agrees to lease real property to T, beginning July 1, 2005, and running for five years, ending June 30, 2010. The parties have created an estate for years. Note that the duration of the estate is unimportant. Any lease for a fixed period, however long or short, is designated an estate for years. For example, an estate for years is created if L leases the premises for one day or 99 years.

The estate expires automatically at the conclusion of the stated period. Unless the lease provides otherwise, no notice of termination is required by either party. The estate may, however, be terminated before expiration of the period upon occurrence of an agreed event, such as tenant's nonpayment of rent.

Estate from Period to Period. An **estate from period to period** or **periodic tenancy** continues indefinitely for successive periods (week to week, month to month, year to year) until notice of termination is given by either party. Periodic tenancies may be created expressly. For example, L may lease property to T from year to year. More commonly, however, periodic tenancies arise by implication when the parties fail to specify the duration of the lease. In this case, if the tenant pays rent periodically — by the week or month — a period to period lease is created for successive one-week or one-month periods that continue indefinitely until terminated by proper advance notice of either party.

Unless explicitly agreed upon, the required notice period is governed by statute in most states, and therefore individual state law must be consulted. For year to year tenancies, for example, the statutory periods range between 30 days and six months, whereas tenancies for shorter periods generally require 30 days advance notice.

A periodic tenancy also may arise when a tenant continues in possession, or "holds over," after expiration of an estate for years. In this case, the landlord may elect to treat the tenant as a trespasser and evict her, or may choose to continue to recognize her as a tenant, generally by accepting further rental payments. If the landlord elects the latter alternative, a periodic tenancy is created by implication and the tenant's lack of intent to renew is irrelevant. This new lease is governed generally by the provisions of the old lease with the exception of the term.

The Estate at Will. A landlord who leases property "to T at the will of L," creates an **estate (tenancy) at will** which may be terminated at the will of either T or L. The tenancy at will is the lowest form of leasehold interest but is recognized as an estate because it confers the right of exclusive possession upon the tenant. This characteristic distinguishes a tenant at will from a mere "licensee"[7] or lodger. At common law, no notice by either party was necessary to terminate the tenancy. Many states today, however, have statutes requiring minimum advance notice, such as 30 days.

Ordinarily, tenancies at will arise by implication. For example, if a tenant takes possession with no explicit agreement regarding payment of rent, a tenancy at will arises. In most states, however, this tenancy at will is quickly converted into a period to period tenancy upon payment of rent based upon the period for which rent is paid. Similarly, a tenant in possession under an invalid lease—for example, due to noncompliance with the Statute of Frauds—is, in most states, a tenant at will until periodic rental payments are made, thereby creating a period to period lease. Tenants at will also include purchasers of property who take possession either (1) before receiving legal title, or (2) when the underlying contract for sale is unenforceable.

The Estate at Sufferance. The **estate at sufferance** is not an estate at all. It arises when a holdover tenant wrongfully remains in possession upon expiration of the lease term. The landlord may elect to treat the holdover tenant either as a trespasser or as a tenant under a new periodic tenancy. If the landlord elects the first alternative, the former tenant possesses merely at the "sufferance" of the landlord, pending the landlord's efforts to evict. A tenant at sufferance differs from an ordinary trespasser only in that his original possession was rightful.

Effect of Death of Either Party. Unless provided otherwise in the lease, an estate for years or a periodic tenancy is not terminated by the death of either party. The interest passes as part of the decedent's estate by will or intestate succession and the rights and duties under the lease are enforceable by or against the estate. The lease continues until expiration of the term (in an estate for years), or until termination by proper notice (in a periodic tenancy).

A tenancy at will depends upon the continuing will of both landlord and tenant that the tenancy continue. The death of either extinguishes the will of the deceased and therefore terminates the tenancy on the date the survivor becomes aware of the death.

Rights and Obligations of Landlord and Tenant

The rights and obligations of landlord and tenant to each other arise both from the express terms of the lease and from the law governing the landlord-tenant relation generally. The primary obligations on the lease are implicit in its definition—the landlord transfers exclusive possession of the property for the agreed term to the tenant who becomes obligated to pay rent.

Possession and Use of the Property

Because a lease involves a transfer of the exclusive right to possession, the landlord has no right to enter the premises to inspect, maintain, or repair unless she has reserved the right to do so. In other words, the landlord who enters the premises during the lease term without authorization in the lease or consent of the tenant is liable as a trespasser.[8]

---

[7]Licenses are discussed in Chapter 38.

[8]The landlord may, however, show the premises to prospective tenants after receiving notice of termination.

Unless the lease provides otherwise, the tenant may use the premises for any reasonable, legal purpose. For this reason, landlords often insert a provision in the lease restricting the use of the property—for example, to residential purposes only—or by prohibiting certain uses. Because the law does not favor restrictions on land use, courts often construe such terms strictly against the landlord.

When using the property, the tenant owes the landlord a duty not to commit waste. This duty requires that the tenant cause no permanent or lasting injury to the property—the landlord's reversion. In other words, the tenant ordinarily must return the property in its original condition, excepting ordinary wear and tear.

Duty to Pay Rent and Events Terminating the Duty

Corresponding to the landlord's duty to deliver possession is the tenant's duty to pay rent. Rent usually is payable in money but the lease may provide payment in services or property. The lease generally states the time of payment, but rent is due at the end of the term (or each period) if not stated. Most leases explicitly provide that rent is payable in advance periodically over the term of the lease.

The amount of rent may be fixed or variable depending on whether a gross, net, or percentage lease is used. In a gross lease, the tenant pays a flat sum out of which the landlord is required to pay expenses such as taxes, utilities, and insurance. A net lease requires the tenant to pay, in addition to rent, expenses such as those listed above. The parties often use a percentage lease when the business location of the property is an important part of its value. The amount of rent is computed as a percentage of gross sales, gross profits, or net profits of a business conducted by the lessee on the premises, usually in addition to a minimum stipulated rent.

Effect of Destruction of the Property. The duty to pay rent ordinarily continues until the normal termination of the lease term. As a general rule, this duty continues even if the leased premises are accidentally destroyed by fire or other casualty during the term. That is, under the traditional majority view, unless the lease provides otherwise, the tenant assumes the risk of loss and must continue to pay rent even though improvements on the land are damaged or destroyed. The reasoning for this

result is that the tenant still possesses the *land* and could have protected any interest in the improvements by insurance.[9]

Many tenants are, however, protected from the operation of this rule. For example, a lease is terminated if fire or casualty destroys the entire subject matter of the lease, leaving nothing for the tenant to occupy (a lease of an apartment or single room in a building). In addition, most leases expressly provide that the tenant's duty to pay rent is altered or extinguished if the building is damaged or destroyed without fault of the tenant.

Effect of Surrender and Abandonment. The tenant's duty to pay rent also may be extinguished by surrender. A **surrender** is a contract involving either the transfer of the landlord's reversion to the tenant or of the tenant's nonfreehold estate to the landlord. In either case, one party acquires fee simple title through the merger of the reversion and the nonfreehold estate. A surrender requires *mutual agreement,* express or implied, between landlord and tenant to terminate the lease. A tenant's surrender extinguishes both his interest in the property and any further duty to pay rent.

In contrast, **abandonment** is the tenant's wrongful *unilateral* act in vacating the premises without further intent to perform the terms of the lease. After abandonment, the tenant's duty to pay rent continues unaffected. The law, however, treats abandonment as an offer for surrender, and later conduct by the landlord, such as leasing the premises to another, may be construed as acceptance of the offer, thereby creating an implied surrender that extinguishes the tenant's further duty to pay rent.

Breach of Covenant of Quiet Enjoyment—Eviction and Constructive Eviction. After the tenant has taken possession, the landlord may not interfere with the tenant's possession and enjoyment of the property. This duty is imposed through an implied **covenant of quiet enjoyment,** generally arising independent of the lease by operation of law. The covenant is breached by an **eviction.** Acts constituting an eviction may be taken by the landlord, someone acting under the landlord's authority, or a person having title to the property superior (paramount) to the landlord's.

---

[9]Although both parties have an insurable interest, neither the landlord nor the tenant is under any obligation to insure, unless the duty is imposed by the lease.

Evictions are of two types, actual and constructive. In either case, an eviction terminates the tenant's further liability for rent and gives the tenant an action for damages against the landlord for breach of the covenant of quiet enjoyment. An actual eviction occurs when the tenant is physically removed from all or part of the premises. More commonly, however, eviction is **constructive.** In constructive eviction the landlord does not actually deprive the tenant of possession. Instead, the landlord, by conduct or neglect, so substantially disturbs or interferes with the tenant's right of possession and enjoyment that the premises are rendered uninhabitable. For example, constructive eviction may be shown by the landlord's failure to provide heat, running water, or other essential services; or to perform a covenant to repair necessary to make the property fit for occupancy.

To assert constructive eviction as a defense to paying rent, the tenant must *vacate* the premises within a reasonable time after the event constituting eviction occurs. The vacating tenant must prove both that the landlord's conduct constitutes an eviction and that she moved out within a reasonable time thereafter. If eviction is proven, the tenant's duty to pay rent is suspended from the time she abandoned possession.

At issue in the following case was whether the landlord's conduct caused a constructive eviction.

GMS Management Co., Inc. v. Datillo
2000 Ohio App. LEXIS 2626 (Ohio App. 2000)

Plaintiff/Appellant GMS Management Co., Inc., owner of Shaker Moreland Shopping Center, leased space in the shopping center to defendants/appellees James and Sabrina Baker for a five-year term starting January 1, 1994. The Bakers used the space to operate a restaurant, Bubba's Q, through December, 1995. In May 1996, they assigned the lease to defendant/appellee Albert Datillo who also planned to operate a restaurant on the premises. Three months later, Datillo vacated the space because of serious water leakage problems. GMS sued Datillo and the Bakers seeking unpaid rent through the end of the lease. Evidence presented at trial showed that the ceiling in the shopping center had leaked regularly since 1992, that the Bakers and Datillo had requested GMS to repair the ceiling, that GMS had hired people to repair the ceiling, but that the leaking had never stopped. The evidence included a videotape, made by Datillo shortly after he vacated, showing standing water on the floor of the restaurant and water dripping through the ceiling.

McMonagle, Judge

. . . In Ohio, a covenant of quiet enjoyment is implied into every lease contract for realty and protects the tenant's right to a peaceful and undisturbed enjoyment of its leasehold. . . . Appellant contends that a covenant of quiet enjoyment means only that the landlord will not permit anyone with a paramount title to interfere with the tenant's possession of the leasehold during the lease term. Contrary to appellant's assertion, however, neither this court nor the Ohio Supreme Court has limited the covenant of quiet enjoyment in this way. Rather, the covenant is breached when the landlord "obstructs, interferes with, or takes away from the tenant in a substantial degree the beneficial use of the leasehold." *Howard v. Simon,* [480 N.E.2d 99 (Ohio App. 1984).] . . . [T]o constitute a breach of the covenant, "the interference with the tenant's quiet enjoyment must be so substantial as to be tantamount to an eviction, actual or constructive." *Endress v. Equitable Life Assurance,* [1987 Ohio App. LEXIS 9433 (1987)]. A constructive eviction occurs when "the acts of interference by the landlord compel the tenant to leave, and . . . he is thus in effect dispossessed, though not forcibly deprived of possession." *Sciascia v. Riverpark Apts.,* [444 N.E.2d 40 (Ohio App. 1981)]. . . .

Here, there is no question that appellant's failure to fix the roof interfered so substantially with Dattilo's possession of the premises that he was forced to leave. Dattilo testified that in January 1996, when he met Steven Eisenberg [the real estate agent] at the space formerly occupied by Bubba's Q, "the whole place looked like it was raining inside." Eisenberg testified that when he took Dattilo through the space, there was standing water on the floor, the ceiling was "noticeably leaking" and it would have been impossible for Dattilo to open a restaurant under those conditions. The videotape taken by Dattilo in September 1996 after he vacated the space showed that the leak was still not fixed. There was standing water on the floor of the space and water dripping through the ceiling around the ventilation ducts. On this evidence, it is apparent that appellant's refusal to fix the roof made it impossible for Dattilo to operate a restaurant on the premises and so interfered with his use of the premises that he was constructively evicted. Therefore, the trial court properly found that appellant breached the covenant of quiet enjoyment. . . .

Appellant also argues that the covenants in the lease are independent of each other and, therefore, even if appellant breached its contractual obligation to repair the roof or the covenant of quiet enjoyment, appellees were still obligated to pay rent. The Ohio Supreme Court has stated, "Covenants in leases . . . are generally independent, in the absence of clear indications to the contrary, and *the lessee is relieved from performance of his covenants only by actual or constructive eviction.*" (Emphasis added.) *Liberal Savings & Loan Co. v. Frankel Realty Co.,* [30 N.E.2d 1012 (Ohio 1940)]. Because Dattilo was constructively evicted by appellant, even if the clauses in the lease agreement are independent, neither he, nor the Bakers, were obligated to pay rent. . . .

[Judgment affirmed.]

Condition of the Leased Property

Common Law Approach. Under the traditional common law rule, the landlord makes no implied covenant that the premises are suitable for any particular purpose including habitation and is not liable for dangerous conditions existing on the property. The tenant, therefore, is responsible for determining the safety, fitness, and suitability of the property. In addition, under traditional common law principles, the landlord has no duty to repair the leased premises, unless the lease contains an express provision requiring repair. The landlord is, however, bound to repair portions of the property not transferred to the lessee, such as the common areas of an apartment building such as elevators, stairs, hallways, sidewalks, fire escapes, and porches.

These principles were developed in an agrarian society and are based on the assumption that (1) the land (commonly unimproved farmland) was the most important feature of the leasehold, (2) the tenant could be expected personally to ascertain the quality and characteristics of the property and make most necessary repairs, and (3) the lease was a result of arm's length bargaining between parties with relatively equal bargaining power. These assumptions are no longer true when applied to the modern urban residential lease.

Modern urban tenants, most of whom live in multiunit apartment buildings, are interested not in land, but in a dwelling suitable for habitation. These tenants usually are unskilled in maintenance and repair work, may not have the financial resources to contract for repairs, and have little incentive to undertake repairs because they have no long-term interest in the property. Further, the modern residential lease is commonly an adhesion contract (a standardized form contract) given to the tenant on a "take it or leave it" basis.[10] It usually deals almost exclusively with landlord's rights and tenant's duties and imposes no express obligations on the landlord to repair or deliver and maintain the property in a habitable condition.

Even if the lease contains covenants of suitability or fitness or imposes a duty to repair, the common law tenant is subject to the "independent covenants" doctrine. Under this doctrine, grounded upon the common law emphasis on the lease as a conveyance of an interest in land, covenants between landlord and tenant are deemed "independent." Promises are independent if the failure by one party to perform a promise does not excuse the other's duty to perform a corresponding promise. Assume the landlord has promised to repair the premises. Under traditional doctrine, the landlord's failure to do so does not excuse the tenant's duty to pay rent. The tenant is relegated to an action for damages for breach of covenant against the landlord but still must pay rent. Because of the time and expense of a lawsuit, recovery on this basis often is not feasible. In addition, the tenant may not use her most valuable weapon against the breaching landlord: withholding rent. This result differs substantially from the constructive conditions of exchange doctrine discussed in Chapter 14 normally applicable to *contracts,* which makes promises between contracting parties dependent. Briefly stated, in contract law, failure by one party to perform justifies the other's subsequent failure to perform.

The constructive eviction doctrine also provides little help to the residential tenant. The doctrine can be applied only in fairly aggravated cases, and even then the tenant must vacate promptly to extinguish the liability for rent. Further, a tenant who moves out does so at his peril because a court may later find the landlord's conduct insufficient to constitute a constructive eviction. In addition, constructive eviction is an inherently inadequate tenant's remedy because it does nothing to assure the tenant a habitable place to live after moving out and does not provide compensation for any moving expenses.

---

[10]Adhesion contracts are discussed in Chapter 10.

Implied Warranty of Habitability. Because of the harsh results imposed on modern residential tenants by traditional common law principles, courts developed the **implied warranty of habitability.** This warranty changes traditional common law doctrine in two major respects.

First, it imposes an implied covenant or warranty in the lease that the premises will meet certain minimum standards of habitability. The warranty is breached if the premises are unsuitable for residential use. Generally, the minimum standards of fitness for human habitation imposed by law are determined by reference to the objective legislative standard stated in local housing, safety, sanitary, or health codes, or similar public regulation. Many jurisdictions use substantial code violations as the primary test, while others require additional evidence of unsuitability.

Second, the implied warranty of habitability makes the residential landlord and tenant relation governed by contract rather than property principles. As such, the tenant's duty to pay rent and the landlord's duty to deliver and maintain the premises in a habitable condition are mutually dependent. The landlord's failure to maintain the property in a habitable condition extinguishes the tenant's duty to pay rent. After breach, the tenant may elect to terminate the lease and vacate the premises or affirm the lease and remain in possession, and may assert the landlord's breach either as a "sword" (tenant as plaintiff to recover damages) or a "shield" (tenant as defendant in landlord's suit for nonpayment of rent).

Today, the vast majority of states impose a warranty of habitability in residential leases. Though initially created by judicial decision, the issue is now governed by statute in many states. For example, the **Uniform Residential Landlord and Tenant Act (URLTA),** governing residential leases in 20 states, imposes explicit duties upon landlords regarding habitability of residential property.

Commercial Leases. The implied warranty of habitability was developed to protect urban residential tenants. Courts traditionally have been reluctant to extend implied warranty principles to leases of commercial or industrial property for several reasons. First, the parties are likely to possess relatively equal bargaining power. Second, the commercial tenant frequently occupies an entire building under a long-term lease. The business tenant is therefore much closer to being the owner of the property than the

apartment dweller, and as a businessperson can be expected to make, or contract for, needed repairs. Third, commercial leases often contemplate substantial renovation or adaptation of the property to the tenant's use—for example, conversion of a warehouse into a restaurant. Despite these differences a number of courts recently have extended implied warranty principles to commercial leases. The reasons for this approach are explained in the following case.

Davidow v. Inwood North Professional Group—Phase I
747 S.W.2d 373 (Tex. 1988)

Defendant Joseph Davidow, a physician, entered into a written five-year lease with plaintiff Inwood North Professional Group—Phase I (Inwood) for medical office space. The lease required Inwood to provide air conditioning, electricity, hot water, janitorial and maintenance services, light fixtures, and security services. Davidow encountered numerous problems with the leased premises. Because the air conditioning did not work properly, office temperatures often exceeded 85 degrees. The roof leaked whenever it rained preventing use of part of the waiting room and causing stained tiles and rotting, mildewed carpet. Inwood did not provide cleaning and maintenance so that pests and rodents often infested the office, and the parking lot was constantly littered with trash. Hot water was not provided and the electricity was turned off for several days after Inwood failed to pay the electric bill. Several burglaries and incidents of vandalism also occurred. Fourteen months prior to the lease expiration, Davidow moved to a new office and refused to continue paying the rent.

Inwood sued Davidow for the unpaid rent and Davidow counterclaimed, alleging breach of an implied warranty that the premises were suitable for use as a medical office. The trial court ruled in favor of Davidow, but the court of appeals reversed and rendered judgment for Inwood for the unpaid rent. Davidow appealed to the Texas Supreme Court.

Spears, Justice

This case presents the question of whether there is an implied warranty by a commercial landlord that the leased premises are suitable for their intended commercial purpose. . . .

At common law, the lease was traditionally regarded as a conveyance of an interest in land, subject to the doctrine of *caveat emptor.* The landlord was required only to deliver the right of possession to the tenant; the tenant, in return, was required to pay rent to the landlord. Once the landlord delivered the right of possession, his part of the agreement was completed. The tenant's duty to pay rent continued as long as he retained possession, even if the buildings on the leasehold were destroyed or became uninhabitable. The landlord's breach of a lease covenant did not relieve the tenant of his duty to pay rent for the remainder of the term because the tenant still retained everything he was entitled to under the lease—the right of possession. All lease covenants were therefore considered independent. . . .

In the past, this court has attempted to provide a more equitable and contemporary solution to landlord-tenant problems by easing the burden placed on tenants as a result of the independence of lease covenants and the doctrine of *caveat emptor.* . . . The land is of minimal importance to the modern tenant; rather, the primary subject of most leases is the structure located on the land and the services which are to be provided to the tenant. The modern residential tenant seeks to lease a dwelling suitable for living purposes. The landlord usually has knowledge of any defects in the premises that may render it uninhabitable. In addition, the landlord, as permanent owner of the premises, should rightfully bear the cost of any necessary repairs. In most instances the landlord is in a much better bargaining position than the tenant. Accordingly, we [previously have held] that the landlord impliedly warrants that the premises are habitable and fit for living. We further implicitly recognized that the residential tenant's obligation to pay rent is dependent upon the landlord's performance under his warranty of habitability. . . .

When a commercial tenant such as Dr. Davidow leases office space, many of the same considerations are involved. . . . It cannot be assumed that a commercial tenant is more knowledgeable about the quality of the structure than a residential tenant. A businessman cannot be expected to possess the expertise necessary to adequately inspect and repair the premises, and many commercial tenants lack the financial resources to hire inspectors and repairmen to assure the suitability of the premises. . . . Additionally, because commercial tenants often enter into short-term leases, the tenants have limited economic incentive to make any extensive repairs to their premises. . . . Consequently, commercial tenants generally rely on their landlord's greater abilities to inspect and repair the premises. . . .

In light of the many similarities between residential and commercial tenants and the modern trend towards increased consumer protection, . . . here is no valid reason to imply a warranty of habitability in residential leases and not in commercial leases. . . . Therefore, we hold there is an implied warranty of suitability by the landlord in a commercial lease that the premises are suitable for their intended commercial purpose. This warranty means that at the inception of the lease there are no latent defects in the facilities that are vital to the use of the premises for their intended commercial purpose and that these essential facilities will remain in a suitable condition. . . . The tenant's obligation to pay rent and the landlord's implied warranty of suitability are . . . mutually dependent.

The existence of a breach of the implied warranty of suitability in commercial leases is usually a fact question to be determined from the particular circumstances of each case. Among the factors to be considered when determining whether there has been a breach of this warranty are: the nature of the defect; its effect on the tenant's use of the premises; the length of time the defect persisted; the age of the structure; the amount of the rent; the area in which the premises are located; whether the tenant waived the defects; and whether the defect resulted from any unusual or abnormal use by the tenant. . . .

The jury found that Inwood leased the space to Dr. Davidow for use as a medical office and that Inwood knew of the intended use. The evidence and jury findings further indicate that Dr. Davidow was unable to use the space for the intended purpose because acts and omissions by Inwood rendered the space unsuitable for use as a medical office. The jury findings establish that Inwood breached the implied warranty of suitability. Dr. Davidow was therefore justified in abandoning the premises and discontinuing his rent payments. . . .

[Judgment reversed.]

Transferring Interests in Leased Property

The interests of both the landlord and tenant in the leased property are freely assignable or transferable without consent unless the lease (1) provides otherwise, or (2) creates a tenancy at will, or (3) requires significant personal services from either party and transfer of one party's interest would substantially impair the other's ability to obtain those services. An interest in leased property may be transferred in any manner that complies with the formalities dictated by governing law. For example, the interest of both landlord and tenant may generally be transferred by will or intestate succession on death. During life, the landlord's interest is transferred by deed. Some states require a writing to transfer the tenant's interest in leased property, generally when the term of the original lease is greater than one year.

If none of the exceptions outlined above apply (or if applicable, consent is obtained), the interest of either party may be transferred. The following material explains the legal effect of a transfer of the tenant's and the landlord's interest.

Transfer of the Tenant's Interest

Assignment and Sublease Defined. A tenant may transfer her interest either by an "assignment" or a "sublease." An **assignment** occurs when the tenant transfers away her entire interest under the lease. In a **sublease,** the tenant transfers all or part of her interest in the property for a period less than the entire term. Further, a transfer, originally for the entire term, is a sublease if the tenant may reacquire the right to possession upon occurrence of an event. In other words, the tenant who wishes to create an assignment may not retain any reversionary interest in the leased property. If the transfer is an assignment, the original tenant is the "assignor" and the transferee is the "assignee." In a sublease, the original tenant is the "sublessor" and the transferee is the "sublessee."

For example, assume Lang leases property to Turner for ten years. With eight years remaining on the lease, Turner transfers the entire property to McGrath for the balance of the term. The transfer is an assignment. McGrath holds the property under Lang. If Turner transfers the entire property to McGrath for five years, the transfer is a sublease. McGrath holds the property under Turner for the five years that he is entitled to possession. During the five-year period, Turner continues to hold under Lang. Similarly, assume Turner transfers the entire property to McGrath for the balance of the term but reserves the right to take possession of the leased property if McGrath uses the property for other than residential purposes. The transfer is a sublease.

In distinguishing an assignment from a sublease, most courts continue to apply the foregoing traditional test, which is based upon the transferor's retention of a reversion. Some courts, however, resolve the issue by examining the parties' intent, determined from all surrounding circumstances including the name the parties attach to the transfer.

Liability of Parties After Transfer. Classifying the transfer as an assignment or a sublease has important legal consequences for both the transferor and the transferee. The major issue presented is the liability of the parties after the transfer for performance of "covenants running with the land." Common examples of covenants running with the land include promises to repair, to pay rent, to build on the land, to renew or extend the lease, to pay taxes, to supply heat and hot water, or restricting use of the property—for example, to residential purposes.

Consistent with the general principles of assignment discussed in Chapter 13, the tenant is not relieved of liability on the lease simply by transferring an interest in the property, whether by assignment or sublease. In other words, the original tenant's liability to the landlord is based on contract. To be relieved of this liability, the tenant must obtain a release from the person entitled to the benefit of the tenant's promise, the landlord. This release is accomplished through a novation, which occurs if the transferee promises to perform the tenant's promises and the landlord in return agrees to release the original tenant from any further liability on the lease.

Effect of Assignment. If the transfer is an assignment, the liability of the assignee to the landlord for performance of covenants running with the land depends upon whether the assignee assumes or does not assume the lease. The assignee assumes the lease if he promises either the landlord or the tenant[11] that he will assume and agree to perform the lease during the balance of the term. An assignee who assumes the lease may be held liable for performance of covenants running with the land both during the period of his occupancy *and after reassignment.* By assuming the lease, the assignee incurs contract liability to the landlord which, like the liability of the original tenant, is not extinguished by a later transfer of the property, absent a novation. The assignee's liability extends to the landlord, the original tenant, and any intermediate assignee, who, being obligated to do so, has performed the lease.

On the other hand, an assignment may be made in which the assignee does *not* agree to perform the lease during the balance of the term. In this case, the assignee may be held liable by the assignor or by the landlord for performance of covenants running with the land but only during the *period of the assignee's occupancy.* An

---

[11]If the promise is made to the tenant, the landlord is a third-party beneficiary of the assignee's promise to perform the lease. Third-party beneficiary promises are discussed in detail in Chapter 13.

assignee who does not assume, therefore, has no liability if a subsequent assignee defaults on the lease.

After an assignment, in the absence of a novation, both the assignor and the assignee are liable to the landlord. As between the assignor and the assignee, ordinary principles of suretyship (discussed in Chapter 33) apply to determine who ultimately pays. After an assignment, the assignee becomes primarily liable on the lease and the assignor becomes secondarily liable; that is, the assignor is a surety for the assignee's performance. If the assignee defaults and the assignor-surety is required to pay the landlord, the assignor-surety is entitled to reimbursement from the assignee.

Effect of Sublease. The rules discussed above determine the rights and liabilities of the parties after an *assignment.* If the tenant *subleases* the premises by retaining a reversionary interest, however small, in the leased property, no legal relationship is created between the sublessee and the landlord. As a result, the landlord has no right to sue a sublessee for breach of covenants contained in the lease. The sublessee is merely a tenant of the original tenant, who continues to be primarily liable on the lease. The rights and duties of the parties on the sublease are determined by the agreement between the sublessor (original tenant) and sublessee. A sublessee, though not liable on the lease, may be evicted by the landlord if covenants contained in the lease are not performed. For example, assume Larson leases property to Taylor for ten years. After two years, Taylor subleases the property for six years to Smith. Smith, as a sublessee, has no obligation on the original lease between Larson and Taylor. Smith holds under Taylor and Smith's rights and duties are determined by the sublease agreement with Taylor. If, however, the terms of the original lease are not performed, Smith, or anyone else possessing the property, could be evicted by Larson.

Effect of Provision Prohibiting Assignment. The lease may provide that the interest of either party may not be transferred without consent. Provisions prohibiting transfer by the tenant without the landlord's consent are by far the most common type, because the landlord usually has a substantial interest in the personal qualities of a tenant, particularly the tenant's reputation for meeting financial obligations. In contrast, the tenant's use and enjoyment of the property rarely depends significantly on the landlord's continued ownership.

Despite their general validity, restraints on alienation (transfer) are strictly construed because of the funda-

mental public policy favoring free transferability of property interests. For example, it is well settled that a provision in a lease prohibiting assignment is not breached by a sublease. Conversely, a prohibition against subleasing is not violated by an assignment. If the lease contains a prohibition against assignment by the tenant without the landlord's consent, most courts hold that consent to one assignment does not extinguish the landlord's right to approve future assignments, unless the lease provides otherwise.

Under the traditional majority rule, the party whose consent is required (generally the landlord) may withhold consent for any reason or arbitrarily. The minority view, however, provides that consent cannot be unreasonably withheld, unless a freely negotiated provision in the lease confers an absolute right to withhold consent. This latter approach, which has been adopted by §15.2 of the *Restatement (Second) of Property (Landlord and Tenant),* is more consistent with (1) the public policy favoring free alienability of property interests, and (2) modern contract law, which imposes an obligation upon the parties to act in good faith and consistent with standards of fair dealing.

Effect of Sale or Mortgage of Leased Property by the Landlord

Generally, the landlord's reversion and right to receive periodic rental payments (the "leased fee") are freely transferable. After the transfer, the tenant's rights and liabilities on the lease remain the same; that is, the buyer takes subject to valid existing leases on the property. The buyer has constructive notice of the leasehold interest because the tenant is in possession of the property, or the lease is recorded.

The buyer generally is entitled to receive rental payments accruing after the transfer as part of the transfer of the underlying property (the reversion). The seller may, however, expressly reserve the right to receive future rents. If the seller does so, the buyer receives only the bare reversion.

After the transfer, the landlord remains liable to the tenant on covenants contained in the lease. The buyer, in addition to receiving the benefits, becomes liable for all obligations under the lease arising after the transfer. The buyer is not liable for obligations arising under the lease prior to the transfer unless he expressly assumes them.

Leased property often is subject to a mortgage in favor of a lending institution. If the landlord defaults on the underlying loan secured by the mortgage, the law must determine whether the tenant can be evicted if the mortgagee subsequently forecloses the mortgage. Courts resolve the issue by determining which came first, the mortgage or the lease. If the mortgage precedes the lease, the tenant takes the property with notice of the mortgage, if it is recorded. The tenant's rights may therefore be extinguished by foreclosure of the mortgage. If, however, the lease is made before the mortgage, the mortgagee takes subject to the tenant's rights. In this situation, the later mortgagee (like the buyer discussed above) is put on notice of the lessee's interest because of her possession of the mortgaged property or because the lessee has recorded the lease. Thus, despite foreclosure, the tenant cannot be evicted before the lease expires. For example, assume that in 1995 Lawrence borrows $50,000 from First Bank secured by a mortgage on Lawrence's warehouse, which is promptly recorded by the bank. In 2000, Lawrence leases the warehouse to Trent for five years. In 2002, Lawrence defaults on the loan and First Bank forecloses the mortgage. Trent may be evicted by the foreclosure. If, however, Lawrence had mortgaged the property in 2001, the bank, after Lawrence's default, is required to honor the remaining term of Trent's lease.

Summary

1.   Ownership interests in land, known as "estates," differ in several major respects including the duration of the interest, the extent of the interest held by the owner, the time of possession, and the number of persons simultaneously holding an interest. Estates are classified as either "freehold" or "nonfreehold." Freehold estates are characterized by indefinite or indeterminate duration. Nonfreeholds form the basis of the law of landlord and tenant. Estates also are classified as either present or future interests according to the time when the owner becomes entitled to possession.

2.   The freehold estates include the fee simple absolute, the defeasible or qualified fees simple, and the life estate. The fee simple absolute is the largest ownership interest recognized by law.

3.   The defeasible fees simple include the fee simple determinable, the fee simple subject to a condition subsequent, and the fee simple subject to an executory limitation. If a defeasible estate is terminated, the property is transferred to the holder of a future interest in the property known respectively as a "possibility of reverter," a "power of termination," and an "executory interest."

4.   A life estate is an interest in property limited in duration to the life or lives of one or more persons. After a life estate, the holder of either a reversion or remainder interest acquires the property.

5.   Co-ownership occurs when two or more persons simultaneously have the right to possess the same property. The major forms of co-ownership are the joint tenancy and the tenancy in common. A third type, the tenancy by the entirety, is a specialized form of joint tenancy recognized in some states existing between husband and wife. In addition, the cooperative and condominium provide a method for co-ownership of multiple-unit dwellings.

6.   A lease creates a landlord-tenant relationship arising upon a transfer of the right to possession of real property from the owner, the lessor or landlord, to another, the tenant or lessee, in consideration of rent. A lease creates an interest in the property in the tenant known as a "nonfreehold estate" or "leasehold." The landlord's interest in the property is known as the "leased fee."

7.   The duration of the lease depends upon the type of estate created in the tenant. Nonfreehold estates include an estate for years, an estate from period to period, and an estate at will. The estate at sufferance is not an estate at all, but describes the possession of a tenant who wrongfully holds over upon termination of a lease.

8.   The primary obligations of the parties to a lease are implicit in its definition: the landlord transfers exclusive possession of the property to the tenant who becomes obligated to pay rent. The parties also frequently agree to assume other obligations such as duties to insure, repair, or pay taxes.

9.   The tenant's duty to pay rent ordinarily continues until expiration of a fixed lease term or proper notice in a periodic tenancy. The duty may be terminated before that time by events such as (1) the destruction of the leased property, (2) a surrender involving a mutual agreement by the parties to terminate the lease, and (3) breach by the landlord of the implied covenant of quiet enjoyment involving an actual or constructive eviction of the tenant.

10.   Under traditional common law rules, the landlord makes no implied covenant that the leased premises are safe or fit for any particular purpose, including habitation. The landlord also has no duty to repair unless the lease provides otherwise, and covenants between landlord and tenant are independent. Because these rules cause substantial hardship to urban resi-

dential tenants, the law developed a "warranty of habitability" for residential leases. This warranty imposes an implied covenant in the lease that the premises will meet certain minimum standards of habitability. It also makes covenants between landlord and tenant mutually dependent, thereby allowing the tenant to withhold rent as a remedy for the landlord's failure to deliver and maintain the premises in a habitable condition. Some jurisdictions have extended implied warranty principles to commercial leases.

11. Like other property interests, the interest of both landlord and tenant in the leased property usually are freely transferable. The liability of parties upon a tenant's transfer depends upon whether the tenant assigns or subleases his interest.

12. The landlord's reversion and right to receive periodic rental payments also may be transferred or mortgaged. The buyer or mortgagee, however, takes subject to valid existing leases on the property.

Key Terms

estate	Uniform Simultaneous
freehold estate	Death Act
nonfreehold estate	four unities
present possessory estate	partition
future interest	tenancy by the entirety
fee simple absolute	cooperative
defeasible fee	condominium
fee simple determinable	lease
possibility of reverter	landlord-tenant relationship
fee simple subject to a	landlord (lessor)
condition subsequent	tenant (lessee)
power of termination (right	estate for years
of entry for condition	estate from period to period
broken)	(periodic tenancy)
fee simple subject to an	estate (tenancy) at will
executory limitation	estate at sufferance
executory interest	surrender
(executory limitation)	abandonment
life estate	covenant of quiet enjoyment
life tenant	eviction
waste	constructive eviction
reversion	implied warranty of
remainder	habitability
concurrent ownership	Uniform Residential Landlord
(co-ownership)	and Tenant Act (URLTA)
joint tenancy	assignment of lease
right of survivorship	sublease
tenancy in common	

Questions and Problems

36.1 Courts frequently are required to construe deeds and wills in which the parties have not clearly stated what type of estate is being conveyed. American courts frequently state that they will presume a fee simple absolute was granted unless the grantor's intention clearly is otherwise. Similarly, the courts will presume that a conveyance to more than one person creates a tenancy in common rather than a joint tenancy. Why have the courts adopted these presumptions? Explain.

36.2 Donovan devised his farm to the Boy Scouts by his will that provided:

> I give, devise and bequeath to the Boy Scouts of America my farm located in Madison County to be retained and used by the Boy Scouts for the purposes of that organization.

The Boy Scouts accepted the devise but later entered into a contract to sell the farm with the intention of using the proceeds of sale to support scouting programs.

Donovan's heirs sued the Boy Scouts alleging that the Boy Scouts did not have the power to sell the farm. The heirs sought to have the farm transferred to them.

(a) On what grounds could the heirs allege that they were entitled to the property? Explain.
(b) How should the court rule? Explain.

36.3 Marie died and left a will that stated:

> I give all of my property to my husband Melvin for and during his lifetime with the power to use, consume or sell the property as he sees fit. All of my property remaining at the death of my husband I give to my daughter Dixie.

(a) What interest does Melvin own in the property?
(b) During his lifetime, Melvin gave all of Marie's valuable antique furniture to his second wife. Dixie sued to prevent the gift to the second wife. What result?
(c) Melvin died. His will provided that the house which had been owned by Marie was to be given to his son Howard. Dixie sues alleging that the house is her property. What result?

36.4 Pearl owned a life estate in a tract of land covered by woods. From time to time, Pearl cut and sold timber from the woods. Bobby, who owned the remainder interest in the property, sued Pearl alleging that cutting timber from the property constituted waste. Should the court enjoin Pearl from cutting timber? Explain.

36.5 Edith, a widow, wanted to buy a house. Because she did not have enough money to pay for the house, her son Mike and his wife Gloria helped finance the purchase. The seller deeded the property as follows:

> To Mike and Gloria, husband and wife, and Edith, a single woman, as joint tenants and not as tenants in common. It is seller's intention to convey to Mike and Gloria, husband and wife, an undivided one-half interest and to Edith, a single woman, an undivided one-half interest.

(a) A state statute provides that any conveyance to a husband and wife creates a tenancy by the entirety. What interest in the property is held by each of the parties? Assume that Mike dies, what interest would Gloria and Edith hold?

(b) Assume instead that Mike and Gloria obtained a divorce. The following year Edith died. What interest would Mike and Gloria own in the property?

36.6 In 1990, Grandfather Miller conveyed the family farm by a deed which included the following language:

> . . . to Harry Miller and Bertha Miller, his wife, as tenants by the entireties and Ford Miller and Helen Miller, his wife, as tenants by the entireties, with right of survivorship.

Harry died in 2005. Bertha died in 2006, leaving her interest in the farm to her son Robert. After Bertha's death, who owns the Miller family farm? Explain.

36.7 Consider the following cases to determine whether the lease has been renewed.

(a) Tenant and Landlord signed a ten-year lease that provided that "Tenant has the option to re-lease the premises for an additional term provided that if Tenant exercises the option, Landlord may increase the rental payments by 10 percent." At the end of the ten-year term, Tenant provided no notice to Landlord but the Tenant held over and pays the rent.

(b) Lessor and Lessee entered into a four-year commercial lease for which Lessee agreed to pay 40 cents per square foot. The lease provided that "Lessee has a two-year option under the same conditions except rental will increase to 43 cents per square foot." The lease also provides, "In the event Lessee holds over after the expiration of the term, such holding over shall not be deemed to extend or renew the term of this lease but such tenancy thereafter shall continue on a month to month basis upon all terms and conditions of this lease." At the end of four years, Lessee sent his rental payment calculated at 40 cents per square foot. Lessor provided a notice that the lease was to terminate in 30 days. Lessee then sent a notice of his exercise of the option and enclosed a check for the additional rent under the option.

(c) Tenant and Landlord enter into a lease for a term of five years that includes the following provision: "Tenant shall have the option to take a renewal lease for a further term of three years at a monthly rate to be negotiated by the parties." Tenant provides notice of exercise of the option but Tenant and Landlord are unable to agree on the rental amount. The parties ask the court to set the rent.

36.8 On August 1, 2005, Tenant and Landlord enter into a written lease for office space. The lease provides that Tenant is entitled to possession of the premises on September 1.

(a) On September 1, Landlord informs Tenant that the construction of the office building is not complete so the office will not be ready for occupancy until October 1. Tenant refuses to pay the rent and moves his office to another building. Landlord sues Tenant for breach of the lease. What result?

(b) Instead, on September 1, Tenant discovers that the current occupant of the office space whose lease expired on

August 31 has not vacated the office. Tenant refuses to pay the rent and moves his office to another building. Landlord sues Tenant for breach of the lease. What result?

36.9 Fast Foods Co. leases a vacant lot on Main Street from Leasehold, Inc. for a term of 20 years. The lease requires Fast Foods to construct a drive-in restaurant building, parking lot, and driveways on the property and to obtain all necessary permits to operate the restaurant. After preparing architectural plans for the restaurant, Fast Foods applies to the city for a permit to construct a driveway to provide access to Main Street. The city refuses to grant the driveway permit because increased traffic would create unsafe traffic conditions. As a result, the restaurant would be inaccessible to automobiles. Fast Foods notifies Leasehold that it is terminating the lease. Should Leasehold try to enforce the lease? Explain.

36.10 Nathan leased an apartment in his eight-unit apartment building to Florence. Although the back entrance to the building was locked, the front entrance had no lock. One afternoon while Florence was returning to her apartment, an assailant attacked her in the hallway and stole her purse. She suffered serious injuries requiring hospitalization.

Florence sued Nathan alleging that his failure to provide security for the building, specifically a lock on the front door, constituted a breach of the implied warranty of habitability. State law provides that a warranty of habitability extends to all "facilities vital to the use of the premises for residential purposes." Evidence introduced at trial established that in the three years preceding the attack on Florence, numerous burglaries and street muggings had occurred in the neighborhood. Has Nathan breached the implied warranty of habitability by failing to provide adequate security in the building? Explain.

36.11 On January 1, Anchor Inn entered into a ten-year lease of a building from Lessor to be used as a restaurant. The lease provided that "Lessor will be responsible for maintaining the heating and air conditioning system, including the replacement thereof if necessary." Anchor Inn spent substantial amounts remodeling the building and operated the restaurant successfully for several months. When the weather became warm, however, the air conditioning system began to malfunction. Lessor sent in numerous repairmen, all of whom told Lessor that the air conditioning system was not large enough to cool the premises. Lessor refused to install a new system. Anchor Inn was uncertain what action to take. It could not afford to move to a new building. Nevertheless, it also was losing customers because of the heat in the restaurant. What should Anchor Inn do? Explain.

36.12 Shirley Yee owned a strip mall, part of which was leased to Howard Weiss, who operated a repair shop for cars and recreational vehicles. The lease provided that Weiss and the other tenants in the mall had the nonexclusive right to use the parking areas surrounding the mall. On several occasions, Weiss complained to Yee that his customers were having difficulty finding parking places and that his customers with recreational vehicles were unable to maneuver them in the crowded parking lot. After

Yee failed to do anything about the parking problems, Weiss vacated the premises telling Yee that the lack of parking had substantially hurt his business. Yee sued Weiss for breach of the lease and Weiss claimed that he had been constructively evicted as a result of the inadequate parking. How should the court rule?

36.13 In anticipation of his upcoming marriage, Sonny entered into a one-year lease for an apartment in Newtown, a city to which he and his new wife planned to move on July 1. A few weeks before the wedding, his fiance broke the engagement. On May 15, Sonny wrote to the landlord and asked to break the lease and explained the circumstances. The landlord did not reply. A year later, however, the landlord sued Sonny requesting as damages the rental payments for the year term of the lease. The evidence at trial established that the landlord had made no attempt to re-lease the apartment after receiving Sonny's letter. How should the court rule? Why? Would your answer be different if the evidence also showed that the landlord had received inquiries about renting the apartment but that she had told all persons that the apartment already was rented? Explain.

36.14 United Industries Co. leased a building from Landowner for a term of ten years. After two years, United subleased the building to Maplewood Furniture Co. Maplewood occupied the building for the remaining eight years and paid the rent to Landlord in a timely fashion. After Maplewood vacated the premises, Landlord discovered that the building had suffered excessive damage. Landlord sued United for waste. United established that all damage had occurred during Maplewood's occupation of the premises. Should the court hold United liable for the waste?

36.15 E & S Realty leased a building for $3,000 per month to Healthco, which operated a dental laboratory known as Denthetics in the building. The lease restricted use of the building to medical or dental facilities. The lease also stated that the tenant could not assign the lease "without the written consent of the Landlord, which consent the Landlord shall not unreasonably withhold." Five years later, Healthco sold Denthetics to H & M Laboratory Services, which continued to operate a dental laboratory with no change in personnel or services. H & M Laboratory Services was a well-known dental laboratory in excellent financial condition. As part of the sale, Healthco assigned its interest in the lease and later notified E & S of the assignment. Upon receipt of the notice, E & S advised H & M that it was a tenant at will responsible to pay $5,500 per month, and notified Healthco that it had breached the lease. Is E & S correct?

REAL PROPERTY TRANSFER

In the study of business law, transfers of both real and personal property by sale occupy an especially important position. The purpose of many contracts is to transfer land, or tangible or intangible personal property, for consideration. The law of sales and negotiable instruments is concerned with bargained-for transfers of special types of personal property: goods, promissory notes, and drafts. This chapter expands the coverage of property transfers by discussing **conveyancing,** the performance of the various functions, including financing, necessary to transfer real property interests.

Voluntary Transfer of Real Property by Sale — Conveyancing

The land sale contract contains the seller's legally enforceable promise to convey title to the property to the buyer in exchange for the buyer's promise to pay the purchase price. In the absence of an express contrary provision, the contract contains an *implied* term that the seller will convey a marketable title in fee simple absolute. A title is **marketable** (or **merchantable**) if it would be acceptable to a reasonably prudent and legally well-informed buyer. Generally, a title is marketable if the court finds that no reasonable doubt exists concerning its validity and that the buyer will likely not be exposed to a lawsuit in order to defend it.

The Real Estate Contract

Although not absolutely required, the parties almost always use a formal written contract to convey real property for several reasons. First, the Statute of Frauds requires that contracts for the sale of interests in land be evidenced by a written memorandum to be enforceable. The minimum terms necessary for enforcement are the identity of the parties, a sufficient identification of the property, and the purchase price.

Second, a real estate transfer is a complicated transaction. For example, the buyer must be sure before conveyance that title to the property is marketable and must make arrangements for financing. In addition, the parties should agree upon risk of loss, payment of taxes, rights on default, the condition of the premises (including the plumbing, heating, air conditioning, and electrical systems), and the effect of the discovery of termites or other structural defects. These issues are best handled in a comprehensive written contract outlining the rights and duties of both parties.

In the typical real estate transaction, the parties make contracts in addition to the contract to convey the real property interest. For example, the seller may employ a real estate agent using a listing agreement to aid in procuring a buyer. Further, because financing usually is required, the buyer often contracts with a lending institution for a loan to be secured by the property purchased. This security interest, known as a "mortgage," is discussed later in this chapter.

The contract usually fixes a date for performance, known as the "law day," commonly three to five weeks after the contract is made. Unless otherwise agreed, real estate contracts require simultaneous performance by the parties. Thus, on the law day the seller usually conveys the property by delivering a formal document known as a "deed" to the buyer and the buyer pays the purchase price. This performance is known as **title closing, closing,** or **settlement.** In addition to the duties of conveyance and payment of the price, the parties pay other expenses incident to the transfer at the closing, including, for example, the costs of financing and establishing a merchantable title. For residential property, the **Real Estate Settlement Procedures Act (RESPA),** a federal statute, requires advance itemized disclosure of closing costs to the buyer. If either party fails to perform (breaches the contract), the other is entitled to an appropriate contract remedy, either money damages or, as is always available in land sale contracts, specific performance.[1]

The Deed

A **deed** is a written instrument used to transfer (convey) an interest in real property. The parties to a deed are the **grantor** (the person transferring the interest), and the **grantee** (the person to whom the interest is transferred). A deed is used to convey any interest in real property (a fee simple or a lesser estate), by sale or by gift.

Formalities of a Valid Deed. To be valid and effective to transfer the interest, a deed must comply with certain formalities, generally prescribed by statute. Although the requirements vary somewhat among states, generally a deed must (1) be in writing, (2) identify both the grantor and grantee, (3) contain words of conveyance (such as "convey," "grant," or "bargain and sell") to indicate the grantor's intent to transfer an interest to the grantee, (4) indicate the nature of the estate taken by the grantee (for example, fee simple absolute or life estate), and (5) contain a sufficient legal description of the property.

Legal Description. A deed fails because of an insufficient description if it is possible that more than one tract of land could be identified by the language used. No particular method of description is required by law. Courts often sustain informal or imprecise descriptions because the parties, merely by drafting the deed, indicate an obvious intent to transfer some interest. Nevertheless, a precise, formal description is always advisable to avoid confusion and litigation, and to protect marketability of the title. Well-drafted deeds commonly describe the property by metes and bounds, the rectangular survey system, or reference to a subdivision plat or map.

Under a "metes and bounds" description, the oldest method, the deed uses distances (metes) and directions (bounds) to trace the perimeter of the described property by starting from a fixed point, then moving either clockwise or counterclockwise, and ultimately returning to the starting point. Most of the eastern United States uses this method. The rectangular survey system adopted by the Continental Congress in 1785 is the dominant form of legal description used in 30 states.[2] This system describes property based on a government survey conducted to facilitate development and settlement of areas west of the original 13 colonies. The survey divides the country into a grid formed by 35 north-south lines, known as "principal meridians," and east-west lines known as "principal base lines." The grid further is subdivided into a series of "townships," the primary unit of measurement, each six miles square. The township is further divided into 36 "sections," each one mile square containing 640 acres. The rectangular survey system primarily is used to describe large agricultural areas. Finally, subdivided land in urban areas usually is described by reference to a plat or map prepared by a

---

[1]Specific performance is discussed in Chapter 15.

[2]These include all states north of the Ohio River, those west of the Mississippi (except Texas), and Alabama, Florida, and Mississippi.

surveyor or engineer and recorded in the local county recorder of deeds office. Lots within the plat are numbered or lettered and the property is subsequently described by that number or letter, the subdivision name, and reference by page to the book in the county recorder's office containing the map. The plat frequently contains additional information about easements, setback and sidelot restrictions, and lot measurements. These become part of the description and are incorporated into the deed by reference.

In the following case, the sufficiency of the legal description was in issue.

Overton v. Boyce
221 S.E.2d 347 (N.C. 1976)

Plaintiffs Penelope Badham Overton and Alexander Badham and defendant A. C. Boyce claimed title to a tract of land located in North Carolina. The deed under which the plaintiffs based their claim described the land in dispute as follows:

> [T]he following real estate in Chowan County, to wit: A certain tract of Pocosin Land adjoining the lands of the late Henderson Luton & others, containing, by estimation, Three Hundred and Nineteen Acres.

Plaintiffs filed suit against Boyce in an effort to quiet title to the land. The trial court granted summary judgment to Boyce holding that the description of the land in the plaintiffs' deed did not describe the property sufficiently to identify it. Plaintiffs appealed and the appellate court reversed, holding that the plaintiffs should have been allowed to offer extrinsic evidence that allegedly identified the land. Boyce appealed.

Lake, Justice

. . . When it is apparent upon the face of the deed, itself, that there is uncertainty as to the land intended to be conveyed and the deed, itself, refers to nothing extrinsic by which such uncertainty can be resolved, the description is said to be patently ambiguous. . . . Parol evidence may not be introduced to remove a patent ambiguity since to do so would not be a use of such evidence to fit the description to the land but a use of such evidence to create a description by adding to the words of the instrument. . . .

The description in the deed under which the plaintiffs claim title is patently ambiguous. It refers to nothing extrinsic to which one may turn in order to identify with certainty the land intended to be conveyed. All that the deed tells us about the land is that it is "pocosin land," i.e., swamp land, in Chowan County, it adjoins the lands of the late Henderson Luton and contains, *by estimation,* 319 acres. It is a matter of common knowledge that there are numerous, extensive tracts of pocosin land in Chowan County. The deed leaves the reader of it in doubt as to each of the following things: (1) The exact area of the tract intended to be conveyed, (2) whether the tract intended to be conveyed is all or only part of a single pocosin area, (3) assuming the "Henderson Luton" tract can be located with certainty, on which side of it lies the land here intended to be conveyed, and (4) the length of the common boundary between the "Henderson Luton" tract and the land here intended to be conveyed. Furthermore, the record shows, and the Superior Court found, there were recorded in the office of the Register of Deeds of Chowan County three separate deeds conveying large tracts of land in Chowan County to Henderson Luton and another deed conveying a smaller tract to Henderson Luton and another. The descriptions of the three larger tracts conveyed to Henderson Luton alone show that each of these tracts had one or more boundary lines running along or through a swamp or along the Chowan River.

Since the description in the deed under which the plaintiffs claim is patently ambiguous, the deed is void and cannot be the basis for a valid claim of title in the plaintiffs to the land now claimed by them. . . .

[Judgment reversed.]

Execution of a Deed. In addition to the formal requirements, the deed must be properly executed before it is effective to convey the interest to the grantee. The requirements for a valid execution are sometimes summarized by the expression "signed, sealed, and delivered." In addition, the law may require attestation or acknowledgment of the instrument.

Signature. The deed must be signed by the grantor. Although the grantee must be identified in the deed, the grantee need not (and rarely will) sign. A deed signed only by the grantor is known as a deed "poll." Almost all deeds are of this type. A deed signed by both parties is known as an indenture.

Seal. The seal, used to authenticate an instrument in an era when few could write, has little modern significance. Most states no longer require a seal on deeds or other written instruments. Nevertheless, seals still are used as a matter of custom in many cases. At common law, the seal was a wax impression, but in modern deeds the seal is simply the word "Seal" or "L.S." printed on the standard form.

Delivery and Acceptance. To be effective the deed must be delivered to and accepted by the grantee. By accepting the deed, the grantee is bound by its terms, thus eliminating the need for his signature. The deed is effective to transfer title on the date it is delivered to the grantee.

Attestation and Acknowledgment. Approximately one-fifth of the states require that deeds be attested to be effective to transfer title. Attestation refers to the act of witnessing the execution of a written instrument, at the request of the person making it, and subscribing it as a witness.[3] Other states, as proof of authenticity, require attestation as a prerequisite to recording the deed in the recorder of deeds office. Many states require acknowledgment as a condition to recording. Acknowledgment is a more formal witnessing by a public officer, such as a notary public or justice of the peace, of the grantor's declaration that the execution is her free and voluntary act.

Consideration. A deed simply transfers an interest in land and is not itself a contract. The conveyance is therefore valid even if no consideration is paid or stated. Because a consideration clause was required in certain early common law deeds, modern deeds customarily contain a clause reciting a purported or nominal consideration such as one dollar. The nominal recital of consideration in the deed is purely a matter of form and bears no relationship to the amount paid by the grantee for the property.

Warranty Deeds. Two types of deeds commonly are used to convey real property interests, the warranty deed and the quitclaim deed. The **warranty deed** contains

---

[3]Black's Law Dictionary 128 (6th ed. 1990).

a number of promises, known as **covenants for title,** concerning the status of the grantor's title. The common or usual covenants contained in a general or full warranty deed are the covenants of seisin and right to convey, the covenant against encumbrances, and the covenant of quiet enjoyment.

Covenants of Seisin and Right to Convey. These two covenants in effect mean that the grantor owns the estate she purports to convey, usually a fee simple absolute, and has the right and power to transfer it.

Covenant Against Encumbrances. This covenant means that the property is transferred free of encumbrances not specifically stated in the deed. An **encumbrance** is a right or interest in land, which diminishes its value, but does not prevent transfer of a fee simple. Encumbrances are of three types: (1) liens against the property to satisfy monetary obligations such as mortgages, taxes, special assessments, or judgments, (2) interests less than a fee simple such as leaseholds and life estates, and (3) restrictions on the use of the property, such as easements or restrictive covenants. To avoid breaching this warranty, deeds generally state that the property is subject to real estate taxes, covenants, conditions, restrictions, and easements apparent or disclosed by the public record and all applicable zoning laws and ordinances.

Covenant of Quiet Enjoyment. This covenant promises that the grantee will enjoy the quiet and peaceable possession of the property and will not be evicted by a person holding a better title.

Although the foregoing warranties may be stated in full in the deed, many states authorize a statutory "short-form" deed. If the form dictated by statute is used—for example, if the grantor "conveys and warrants" the property to the grantee—the warranties are included even though not expressly stated in the deed.

Limited Warranty Deeds. The covenants contained in the "full" or "general" warranty deed are discussed above. Fewer warranties are given if a "special" or "limited" warranty deed is used. In a special warranty deed, the grantor warrants only against defects arising since he acquired title, but not against defects or third-party claims arising prior to that time. Statutes generally prescribe the language necessary to create a special warranty deed. For example, in Illinois, a deed using the language of conveyance, "grant," "bargain," or "sell," or a combination thereof, is deemed to include the following covenants: (1) that the grantor owns an indefeasible fee simple estate, (2) that the property is free from encumbrances created by the grantor, and (3) that the grantee will have quiet enjoyment of the property against the grantor and those taking through the grantor.[4]

Breach of Covenant. If a covenant for title is breached, the injured party generally may recover money damages. The buyer may receive the entire purchase price plus interest for a total failure of title, or a proportionate reduction in price for a partial failure. If the grantor conveys a lesser estate than warranted (for example, a life estate when a fee simple is warranted), damages equal the price paid less the value of the estate received. If the breach involves an encumbrance, the buyer may recover the amount paid to remove it and clear the title, not exceeding the purchase price. If the easement or other encroachment cannot be removed, damages are measured by the reduction in value of the burdened property.

Merger. The seller's obligations are discharged by delivering a deed of a type required by the contract. Under the doctrine of merger, the purchaser's acceptance of the deed extinguishes many of her rights under the contract. Therefore, if title later proves defective, the buyer's recourse is for breach of the covenants in the deed, not the contract provisions. Generally, however, merger applies only to matters of title, and not to collateral promises, such as the seller's promise to build or to make improvements or repairs. These promises survive the deed and may form the basis of a subsequent suit by the buyer.

Quitclaim Deeds. The **quitclaim deed,** unlike a warranty deed, makes no warranties or promises regarding title to the grantee. The grantor of a quitclaim deed states in effect, "Whatever interest I may have in the property (and I may have none), I convey to you." Thus, the grantee may obtain a fee simple title or no title upon acceptance of a quitclaim deed and has no recourse against the grantor for any failure of title. Examples of operative language used in quitclaim deeds include "Grantor hereby releases, surrenders, and relinquishes any right, title, or interest that he may have . . ." or "The grantor

---

[4]765 ILCS 5/8.

does remise, release, and quitclaim . . ." or simply "Grantor conveys and quitclaims. . . ." Quitclaim deeds are used when the grantor is uncertain of his interest, to clear up defects in the chain of title, to transfer an interest from one co-tenant to another, and to transfer an interest from one spouse to the other as part of a divorce settlement.

Recording Statutes

Even though the seller may be obligated by the contract or deed to transfer fee simple title, any deed, regardless of type, transfers only the seller's interest in the property. Thus, the seller's representations regarding title are only valuable to the buyer if the seller either possesses the promised interest or is solvent and available to be sued when a problem arises. Because title assurance based upon the seller's representations provides such limited protection to the buyer, the buyer must, before delivery of the deed, independently determine whether the seller in fact possesses the interest she purports to convey. This task is accomplished by professional examination of the public record of land titles generated by state **recording statutes.**

Each state has enacted a recording statute designed to provide reliable public information regarding the status of real estate titles. By examining this public record, a prospective purchaser or lender can determine whether the seller or debtor possesses the interest he contracts to convey or use as security for payment of an obligation, and whether any liens or encumbrances exist against the property.

As a general rule, any document concerning the creation or transfer of an interest in real property, including deeds, wills, contracts, mortgages, leases, assessments, tax liens, and mechanic's liens, are recordable. The documents evidencing the interest are recorded in a local office known as the **recorder of deeds, county recorder,** or **registry** (or **registrar**) **of deeds.** Because these typically are county offices, the proper place of recording usually is the recorder's office in the county where the land is located. Ordinarily, documents accepted for recording must meet certain statutory formalities to insure authenticity, such as attestation or acknowledgment.

Effect of Recording. Recording is not required to make the instrument effective between the *immediate parties* to the transaction. For example, a deed is effective to transfer an interest from the grantor to the grantee upon delivery even though never recorded. A deed of mortgage given by a debtor (mortgagor) to a lender (mortgagee) is effective to create a security interest in the debtor's property even if not recorded by the mortgagee.[5] The recording statute is designed to protect the purchaser or mortgagee against conflicting claims to, or interests in, the same property by *third parties*—persons other than the original grantor or mortgagor. Simply stated, the recording statute protects purchasers and mortgagees acting in good faith against prior unrecorded recordable interests in the property. Recording is constructive notice to third parties of the recording party's interest.[6]

Constructive notice means that later third parties are deemed to know of a prior recorded interest, and therefore take subject to it, even if they have no *actual* knowledge of its existence. Therefore, a transferee who fails to record her interest is protected only against her transferor and those who have *actual* knowledge of the transfer. Recording provides protection against everyone else. A purchaser or mortgagee is thus protected by the recording statute in two ways: (1) she takes free of prior unrecorded interests in the property, and (2) recording is constructive notice to all third parties of her interest.

Generally, recording statutes protect only those purchasers or lenders who act in good faith and give value or consideration for their interest in the property. To meet the good faith standard, the purchaser or lender must take without either actual subjective knowledge or constructive notice via the recording statute. Further, a purchaser or lender who has knowledge of facts that would induce a reasonable person to investigate further is charged with notice of facts that would be disclosed by a reasonable inquiry. This inquiry notice commonly arises when someone other than the grantor occupies the property at the time of the conveyance. Donees of property and persons taking under a will or by intestate succession receive property gratuitously. Because these transferees do not give value, they are not protected by the recording statute and therefore take the property subject to prior unrecorded interests.

The recording statute serves two closely related functions in protecting land titles. First, it provides a public record that prospective purchasers and lenders can examine to verify the truth and completeness of the owner's representations concerning the property. Second, it determines priority among *successive* purchasers and mortgagees of the same property. These functions are discussed in more detail below.

The Title Search. Because each document affecting ownership of property is recorded, the recording statute creates a chronological public record of transactions concerning the property. By means of a **title search**—systematic examination of this record—a prospective purchaser or lender ascertains whether the seller actually owns the interest she purports to convey and what interest others, including creditors, may hold in the property.

To facilitate locating documents affecting the particular property under examination, all recording statutes mandate that instruments accepted for recording be indexed. In most states, instruments are indexed alphabetically under the name of both the grantor and the grantee (a grantor-grantee index). In other states, instruments are indexed according to the legal description of the land involved (a tract index).

A prospective purchaser or lender has constructive notice of all instruments recorded within the chain of title of the particular tract in question. The **chain of title** refers to the succession of deeds, wills, and other instruments by which a person can trace the ownership of the property and other interests in it from the present owner back to the original patent or deed from a governmental authority to the first private owner. All land titles originate in a grant from a sovereign including the United States, Spain, France, Mexico, England, or the original 13 states, depending upon the area of the country involved.

In some states, the title search extends back to the original grant from a sovereign. In others, the search is limited to a shorter period—for example, 30 to 100 years. Several states have adopted **Marketable Title Acts** that reduce the period of title search by extinguishing all claims and title defects automatically after a fixed period, such as 30 to 40 years, unless preserved by filing a statutory notice.

Even if a title search establishes an unbroken chain of ownership or good "record title," the prospective purchaser may not receive a clear, unencumbered title due to events not disclosed by the recording statute.

---

[5]As discussed later in this chapter, a mortgage is an interest in real property created by a "mortgagor" in favor of a "mortgagee" as security for performance of an obligation.

[6]Just as failure to record does not affect the validity of an instrument between parties, recording does not validate an otherwise invalid instrument. Recording simply provides constructive notice of the *existence,* not necessarily the legal effectiveness, of the instrument.

Examples include defects in a conveyance in the chain, such as forgery of a grantor's signature; fraud or duress inducing a grantor to execute the instrument; minority or other incapacity of a grantor; failure of delivery of a deed in the chain; misrepresentation of marital status by a grantor (leaving the possibility of a claim by the spouse or spouse's heirs); or failure of all persons holding an interest in property to join in a conveyance (leaving the possibility of a claim by an omitted person or his heirs). In addition, errors may exist in the record itself, such as an incorrectly filed document.

The county recorder's office is not the only source of public information concerning land titles. For example, court records may indicate an outstanding judgment against the record owner affecting his or her title. In addition, probate, tax, and assessment records contain important information. A thorough title search therefore requires examination of all relevant public records.

In addition to searching the public record, the title searcher should always physically inspect the premises to determine the rights of parties in possession and other information that may not be disclosed by the public record. This physical inspection should, in all cases, include a precise determination of lot boundary lines. Unless the property lines are known (by locating surveyor's stakes or from a prior survey), a survey may be required. The physical inspection and survey are of particular importance because neither an attorney's opinion nor title insurance (discussed below) protects the buyer against defects an inspection or survey would uncover.

In virtually all states private abstract or title companies maintain a private duplicate set of real estate records. These records are kept up to date on a daily basis by information obtained from the recorder's office. The information obtained by the abstract company over time is used to prepare an **abstract of title,** which is a chronological summary of the contents of all recorded instruments pertaining to a particular tract of land. The abstract is then rented to persons desiring to examine the title. Thus, although the buyer, lender, seller, or their attorneys could conduct the title search, the parties ordinarily engage a professional abstracter to perform this task. Unless otherwise agreed, a seller or borrower has no duty to furnish an abstract to the buyer or lender. The parties often provide by contract, however, that the seller or borrower furnish the abstract.

The Attorney's Opinion and Title Insurance. Once an abstract of title has been prepared, an attorney examines it and renders a professional opinion concerning the status of the title through either an attorney's opinion or title insurance. In an **attorney's opinion,** an attorney examines the title as disclosed by the abstract and renders a formal written opinion regarding its marketability. The opinion will note any areas for concern and list any liens or encumbrances burdening the property. The attorney does not insure the title, but is liable for injury caused by negligent errors or omissions.

Title insurance provides an alternative form of title protection. **Title insurance** is a contract between the insurer—a title insurance company—and an insured—a property owner or person lending money secured by real property. The insurer agrees to indemnify or reimburse the insured against losses resulting from certain specified defects in the title to the covered property. Note that the *title* is not really insured; the owner or lender is merely indemnified against loss resulting from failure of the title.

Title insurance is, like the attorney's opinion, based upon a search of the public record. Usually, attorneys employed by the title insurance company render the opinion after examining the private land records maintained by the insurance or abstract company. Title insurance provides somewhat more protection than an attorney's opinion because the owner need not show negligence in order to recover, defects not of record may be covered, and the insurance company bears the expense of defending any suit necessary to protect the title.

The "Torrens" System. Under the recording statute, the instruments constituting evidence of various interests in or claims to property such as deeds, mortgages, and easements are recorded. From this ever-expanding body of information, the prospective buyer or lender must draw a conclusion concerning the status of the seller's or borrower's title. This is an expensive, cumbersome process, requiring multiple searches and examinations of the same title as the property is transferred from one owner to the next.

The **Torrens system** is an alternative method involving registration of title to property, instead of recording evidence of that title. Under the Torrens system, the title is registered in a judicial proceeding in which all parties claiming an interest in the property are notified and given the opportunity to assert their claims. After a hearing, a certificate of title, similar to an automobile title, is issued to the person found to be the owner. The certificate indicates the nature of the owner's title (usually a fee simple) and any liens or encumbrances against the property. Once the title is registered, the owner, as well as subsequent buyers or lien holders, takes free of all claims or interests, except those noted on the certificate. To transfer the property, the owner simply executes a deed to the grantee. The deed and the owner's certificate are filed with the registrar of titles (the Torrens equivalent of the recorder of deeds), who simply cancels the grantor's certificate and issues a new one to the grantee. Any liens or encumbrances surviving against the grantee are noted on the new certificate. Thus, after registration, title can be transferred quickly and without a costly title search.

Despite its apparent advantages, the Torrens system has not achieved widespread acceptance in the United States. Today, fewer than one-fourth of the states have enabling statutes providing for land title registration under the Torrens system. Even in those states, registration is optional with the owner and may exist only in certain geographic areas.

Priority Among Successive Purchasers. Recording statutes protect purchasers or mortgagees by providing a public record that discloses the condition of title to land they are about to purchase or lend against. To achieve this protection, the recording statute effectively gives a property owner the *power* to make successive conveyances of the same property, even though she may have no *right* to do so. The problem is simply illustrated by the following example. Ann, the fee simple owner of a tract of land, sells it by warranty deed to Bob, who pays fair market value. One week later, Ann conveys the same property by warranty deed to Carl, who also pays fair value. Ann pockets the proceeds of both sales and disappears. As between Bob and Carl, the innocent purchasers left behind, who is entitled to the land? In the absence of any recording statute, the common law rule, known as "first in time, first in right," provides that the first purchaser *in time* (in this case, Bob) prevails. That is, after the conveyance to Bob, Ann has no interest remaining to transfer to Carl.

With a recording statute in effect, however, the law determines priority by the terms of the recording statute, not by chronological order of conveyance. This approach protects the integrity of the recording system and enables a prospective purchaser to rely upon the public record as indicating the state of the title. Statutes are classified as one of three types according to the manner of resolving the priority issue: (1) pure race,

(2) pure notice, and (3) race-notice. For real property interests, most states use either a pure notice or race-notice statute. Pure race statutes are in effect in a few states, but do not apply to all recorded instruments.[7] The characteristics of each type are discussed below.

Pure Race Statute. Under a **pure race statute,** the first purchaser to record prevails; that is, the purchaser who wins the "race" to the county recorder's office prevails. This result follows even if the first person to record takes with actual knowledge of a prior unrecorded conveyance.

Pure Notice Statute. Under a **pure notice statute,** a subsequent purchaser who takes without actual knowledge of a prior unrecorded conveyance prevails, regardless of who later records first. To illustrate using the preceding example, assume Bob fails to record before Ann's conveyance to Carl. Carl wins if at the time of the conveyance to him, he has no *actual* knowledge of Bob's interest regardless of whether Bob or Carl later records first. If Bob had recorded prior to Ann's conveyance to Carl, Bob prevails because Carl takes the property with constructive notice of Bob's interest.

Race-Notice Statute. Under a **race-notice statute,** a combination of the first two, the subsequent purchaser prevails if he *both* (1) takes without actual knowledge of the prior conveyance and (2) records first. Thus, under a race-notice statute, even if Carl takes without actual knowledge of Bob's interest, Bob prevails if he records first.

In addition to purchasers of and lenders against the real estate, real property recording statutes also may affect the rights of purchasers of goods closely associated with the land but sold apart from it, such as minerals, structures, crops, timber, or fixtures. Under §2–107(3) of the Uniform Commercial Code, the buyer of such goods takes subject to rights of a *prior* purchaser or mortgagee of the underlying real estate who records her interest. The buyer of the goods also may be jeopardized by *subsequently* created interests in the land. For example, a purchaser of real estate commonly receives crops growing on it, raising the possibility of conflicting claims between the buyer of the growing crops and a person who later purchases the underlying land before

---

[7]Note that the recording statute created by Article 9 of the Uniform Commercial Code, governing priority of security interests in *personal* property, is a pure race statute. Article 9 is discussed in Chapters 31 and 32.

the crops are harvested. To protect the crop buyer in this situation, §2–107(3) provides that the crop sale contract may be recorded in the real estate records where it provides constructive notice to third parties of the buyer's rights under the contract. Some courts protect the crop buyer in this situation even if he fails to record by holding that the crops are personalty to which the recording act does not apply or that the crops are "constructively severed" at the time the crops are sold.

Financing Real Property

A real estate buyer seldom has the financial resources to pay cash for the property. Normally, the buyer makes a down payment and must borrow the remainder of the purchase price. Creditors financing real property usually require security, generally provided by a mortgage, or in some cases an installment contract.

Introduction to Mortgages

A **mortgage** is an interest in real property that is created to secure performance of an obligation, normally repayment of a debt. The person creating the mortgage and giving the security is known as the **mortgagor.** The person receiving the benefit of the security afforded by the mortgage is known as the **mortgagee.** The mortgage gives the mortgagee a security interest in specific real property owned by the mortgagor. If the obligation secured by the mortgage is not performed, the mortgagee has recourse against the property to satisfy the obligation. In other words, in a mortgage, real property serves as collateral for a loan or other obligation.

The mortgage is not the debt; the debt usually is evidenced by a promissory note signed by the mortgagor. This note, usually payable in installments over an extended period, evidences what is known as the "underlying debt." Most mortgage notes are of the "direct reduction" or "amortizing" type, in which each equal installment payment is part principal and part interest. Thus, the principal amount is gradually reduced (amortized) over the term of the loan and interest is charged on the unpaid balance. An increasing proportion of each payment is allocated to principal as the debtor builds equity in the property.[8]

To illustrate, assume Burns contracts to buy a house from Smith for $50,000. To finance the purchase, Burns borrows $50,000 from First Federal Savings and Loan and executes a promissory note payable to the order of First Federal for $50,000. Burns then pays the $50,000 to Smith, who conveys the property to Burns. In addition, Burns gives First Federal a mortgage on the property purchased to secure repayment of the promissory note. If Burns defaults, First Federal is entitled to the mortgaged property to satisfy any unpaid portion of the debt.

Under the traditional definition, a "purchase money" mortgage is created if the *seller,* rather than a third party, finances the buyer. The buyer pays the seller an agreed down payment and the seller conveys the property to the buyer. The remainder of the purchase price is then paid in installments to the seller, who takes a mortgage on the property to secure the unpaid balance. Today, in a majority of states, any mortgage given on property to secure its purchase price is known as a "purchase money" mortgage no matter who (the seller or a third party) provides the financing.[9]

Creation of a Mortgage. A mortgage, like other interests in real property, is created by a deed, a mortgage deed, in which the mortgagor conveys the property to be used as security to the mortgagee. The mortgage deed, like the general warranty deed, contains the names of the parties, a legal description of the property, covenants for title, and language of conveyance, and is signed by the grantor (mortgagor). In addition, the deed describes the underlying loan secured by the mortgage. It also contains additional covenants designed to protect the mortgagee's interest in the property, such as the mortgagor's promise to keep the premises insured and in good repair, and to pay taxes, other liens, and assessments against the property.

In approximately one-third of the states, a security device known as a **deed of trust** or **trust deed** may be used as the functional equivalent of a mortgage. A deed of trust, like other trusts, uses three parties instead of the two (mortgagor-mortgagee) present in the ordinary mortgage. The borrower (settlor or trustor) transfers the property to the trustee, who holds it in trust for the benefit of the lender (beneficiary) as security for payment of the debt. The rights of the parties are determined by

---

[8]Equity refers to the difference between the market value of the property (evidenced by the purchase price) and the outstanding indebtedness.

[9]This approach is consistent with the "purchase money security interest" definition applicable to personal property under Article 9 of the UCC. See discussion of UCC §9–103 in Chapter 31.

the trust instrument, including the borrower's right to reconveyance upon repayment of the debt and the lender's rights on default.

"Title" Versus "Lien" Theory of Mortgages. The law has developed two theories to describe the nature of the property interest created by a mortgage. Traditionally, under the "title theory" of mortgages, a mortgage is an outright conveyance of the property to the mortgagee (who at early common law took possession of the property) subject to reconveyance upon satisfaction of the secured obligation.[10] Under this theory, if the mortgagor defaults, the mortgagee retains the property even if the value of the property exceeds the amount owing on the secured debt at the time of default.

Because strict application of the title theory may result in a windfall to the mortgagee (the difference between the outstanding debt and the value of the property), the law generally applies a "lien theory" to characterize a mortgage. Under this approach, because the mortgage is created only as security for a debt, the mortgagee's interest in the property is limited to the amount of the outstanding debt. If upon default the value of the property exceeds the unpaid balance, any surplus is returned to the mortgagor. Many states reach this "lien theory" result even though they treat a mortgage technically as an outright conveyance of the property. In other words, these states use a hybrid "title-lien" approach.

Liability on the Underlying Debt. In most cases, the mortgagor is personally liable for payment of the debt secured by the mortgage because she also has signed the underlying promissory note. This liability is important if after default, the mortgaged property is worth less than the outstanding debt; that is, a "deficiency" occurs. Because the mortgage is given as security for payment of the debt, not as a substitute for it, a mortgagor who also signs the note is generally liable for any deficiency upon default. Conversely, a property owner may be liable on the mortgage but not on the secured debt. In this case, the mortgagor loses her interest in the property, but has no liability for any deficiency.

Priority Among Successive Mortgagees

A property owner may borrow money from two or more lenders and give each a mortgage on the same property. In this case, legal disputes commonly arise when the mortgagor defaults and the value of the mortgaged property is less than the total of the outstanding obligations it secures—for example, two $50,000 loans secured by a mortgage on property worth $75,000. The law must then determine the priority of the various mortgagees in distribution of this limited fund.

Priority among successive mortgagees, like priority among successive purchasers, is determined by the recording statute regardless of which mortgage occurred first in time. A mortgage is an interest in land, and the mortgage deed, like other deeds, is a recordable instrument. Recording protects the mortgagee against a subsequent sale or mortgage of the same property to another. If the mortgagee fails to record, subsequent buyers or mortgagees without actual knowledge of the mortgage take free of the unrecorded mortgagee's claim.

Therefore, if a dispute arises, generally the first mortgage to record is paid first (a "first mortgage"), the second to record is paid second (a "second mortgage"), and so on until the sum generated on sale of the property is exhausted. For this reason, a first mortgage is often termed a "senior" mortgage and second and subsequent mortgages are referred to as "junior" mortgages. Although the recording statute usually determines the rights of successive mortgagees, a mortgagee may, by "subordination" agreement, contractually relinquish a right to priority it would otherwise possess.

Although no rule theoretically limits the number of mortgages, seldom do more than two mortgages burden a given parcel of land. Many lenders, by statute or as a matter of policy, will loan only upon first mortgage security. Additionally, loans secured by second and subsequent mortgages usually have shorter terms and higher interest rates than first mortgage loans.

A mortgagor who satisfies the secured obligation is entitled to have the encumbrance indicated by the mortgage removed from the public record. To achieve this result, the mortgagee executes a written release in a form necessary for recording. The release is then recorded, clearing the mortgagor's title.

Sale of Mortgaged Property

As a general rule, and in the absence of contrary agreement, the mortgagor is free to sell the mortgaged prop-

---

[10]Under the title theory, a mortgage is similar to the fee simple subject to a condition subsequent (discussed in Chapter 36). That is, title to the property remains in the mortgagee until repayment of the underlying debt—occurrence of the condition subsequent.

erty without consent of the mortgagee. The sale, however, has no effect upon either the mortgage itself or the mortgagor's liability on the underlying debt. In other words, the mortgagee's rights against both the mortgagor and the property are unaffected by the sale. The sale may be made with or without retiring the existing mortgage.

Refinancing. In most cases, the existing mortgage will be retired as part of the sale; that is, the buyer will "refinance." The buyer pays the purchase price in cash, part of which is paid to the mortgagee to extinguish the mortgage debt (and the mortgage) and the remainder is paid to the seller. Both the seller and the original mortgagee are thus paid in full. Because the buyer usually cannot finance the purchase himself, he generally borrows the necessary funds from a lending institution securing the loan with a new mortgage on the property purchased.

Taking "Subject to" or "Assuming" Mortgage. The property also may be sold without retiring the existing mortgage. The buyer simply pays the seller for the seller's equity in the property, continues to make payments on the mortgage, and takes either "subject to" the existing mortgage or agrees to "assume" the mortgage debt. A buyer who takes "subject to" the mortgage incurs no personal liability for payment of the debt that the mortgage secures. Thus, if the buyer fails to repay the debt, she will lose the property if the mortgagee subsequently forecloses. The buyer is not, however, liable if the amount realized when the property is sold is insufficient to satisfy the outstanding debt. If the foreclosure sale realizes more than the remaining debt, the buyer receives the excess because the seller has already been paid for her equity in the property. Note that even if the deed or contract fails to mention that the conveyance is "subject to the mortgage," the result is effectively the same as outlined above if the mortgage is recorded. In other words, a seller cannot transfer property free of an existing recorded mortgage.

Alternatively, the buyer may agree to "assume" the underlying mortgage indebtedness. Although it is frequently stated that the buyer "assumes the mortgage," the buyer actually assumes, and thereby becomes personally obligated to pay, the underlying loan that the mortgage secures.[11] Under traditional contract principles, the

seller remains totally liable for repayment of the debt despite the buyer's assumption. That is, a suretyship relation is created between the seller and buyer upon assumption of the mortgage. If the buyer defaults, the seller may be compelled to satisfy the unpaid obligation. The seller may, however, escape liability if the mortgagee agrees to release her and look only to the buyer for payment. In this case, a novation is created in which one contracting party, the buyer, is substituted for another, the seller, whose liability is extinguished.[12]

The following case illustrates the effect of default after a mortgage assumption on the original mortgagor's liability.

Swanson v. Krenik
868 P.2d 297 (Alaska 1994)

In 1977, Thomas and Leila Krenik executed a promissory note secured by a deed of trust (the functional equivalent of a mortgage under Alaska law) on their property in favor of Alaska Federal Savings and Loan Association (Alaska Federal). In 1981, the Kreniks sold the property to Keith and Marie Swanson who assumed the Alaska Federal note and deed of trust. Alaska Federal consented to the assumption but did not release the Kreniks. In August 1983, following her husband's death, Marie Swanson sold the property to Ray Rush and Howard Luther, Jr. With the consent of the Kreniks and Alaska Federal, Rush and Luther assumed the Alaska Federal note and deed of trust but neither the Kreniks nor Swanson was released. In 1986, Rush and Luther defaulted in paying Alaska Federal, which began a foreclosure action. After Rush and Luther filed for bankruptcy, Swanson filed a claim seeking a ruling that she and the Kreniks were "joint codebtors" who were jointly liable for any deficiency remaining after the foreclosure sale. The Kreniks argued that they were merely sureties for Swanson and asserted, therefore, that Swanson was not entitled to any contribution from them. The trial court ruled in favor of the Kreniks. A deficiency of $1,173,992 remained after the foreclosure sale. Swanson paid the deficiency and appealed the trial court's ruling.

Moore, Chief Justice

. . . As both parties in this case recognize, when an original mortgagor transfers mortgaged land to a

---

[11]The buyer's promise to assume the mortgage debt may be made either to the seller or the bank. In either case, it is enforceable by the bank. That is, the bank, as a third-party creditor beneficiary, may enforce the promise against the buyer, even if the promise is not made to the bank directly. Third-party beneficiary promises are discussed in Chapter 13.

[12]The elements of a novation are discussed in Chapter 13 in conjunction with the law of assignment and delegation, and in Chapter 36 in conjunction with coverage of landlord-tenant law.

grantee who assumes the mortgage, the assuming grantee becomes the principal mortgage obligor and the mortgagor becomes a surety. . . .

The parties agree that in 1981 the Swansons expressly assumed the Kreniks' mortgage obligation under the Alaska Federal note and deed of trust. . . . In 1981, therefore, the Swansons became the principal obligors on the debt. The Kreniks, who were not released from their obligation to Alaska Federal, became sureties. In the event of a default by the Swansons, Alaska Federal retained its right of recourse against both the Swansons and the Kreniks for any amount outstanding on the loan. If the Kreniks satisfied any amount due, their status as sureties would entitle them to indemnification from the Swansons. . . . Conversely, the Swansons would not be entitled to indemnification or contribution from the Kreniks for any deficiency satisfied by the Swansons.

Swanson's contention is that, upon Rush and Luther's assumption of the deed of trust in 1983, she and the Kreniks became cosureties. Her claim is based largely on Paragraph 10 of the 1983 Rush and Luther assumption agreement, which states:

> Rush and Luther, [the Kreniks] and Marie O. Swanson, whether principal, surety, grantor, endorser or other party hereto, *agree to be jointly and severally bound . . .* and expressly agree that the Note or any payment thereunder may be extended from time to time and consent to the acceptance of further security including other types of security all without in any way affecting the liability of said parties.

(Emphasis added). Swanson argues that this paragraph demonstrates the Kreniks' express consent to become joint debtors with her on the Alaska Federal deed of trust.

Swanson misinterprets this provision. Indeed, the fact that Paragraph 10 also binds Rush and Luther as jointly and severally liable with Swanson and the Kreniks would defeat Swanson's interpretation of the clause. We conclude that the language of Paragraph 10 establishes the Kreniks' agreement to be jointly and severally bound with all assuming grantees *as to the mortgagee,* Alaska Federal, in the case of a default on the loan. It does not, however, establish any relationship or hierarchy among the successive grantors regarding contribution or indemnity.

The relationship between Swanson and the Kreniks is clarified in Paragraph 13 of the 1983 Rush and Luther assumption agreement, which states:

> [The Kreniks] and Marie O. Swanson agree that their present liability under the Note and Deed of Trust *shall not be impaired, prejudiced or affected in any way whatsoever by this Agreement. . . .*

(Emphasis added).

The unambiguous terms of this provision indicate that the 1983 assumption agreement did not alter Swanson's obligations to the Kreniks under the previous assumption agreement. Accordingly, Swanson and the Kreniks did not become cosureties in 1983 as Swanson maintains. As between themselves, they remained principal obligor and surety, respectively. Therefore, with respect to Rush and Luther, who became the principal obligors, Swanson and the Kreniks became surety and subsurety, respectively. In this relationship, the Kreniks' liability on the deed of trust remains one step removed from that of Swanson, as it was under their original agreement. Therefore, Swanson is liable for the deficiency resulting from Rush and Luther's default on the deed of trust, and she is not entitled to contribution from the Kreniks. We find that, absent some express agreement to the contrary, a second grantee's purchase of property and assumption of a mortgage obligation does not modify the surety-principal obligor relationship created between the mortgagor and the first grantee in their previous transaction. . . .

Lastly, we are unpersuaded by Swanson's argument that the equities of this case mandate a finding of cosuretyship. . . . In our view, the equities in the present situation fall on the side of the Kreniks. As original mortgagors, they had no real influence over their grantee's decision to convey the property to a second grantee, or over the selection of that grantee. They did not stand to directly benefit from the transfer. Their only real involvement in the transaction consisted of a reacknowledgement of their underlying obligation to Alaska Federal, so that the transfer could be accomplished. While it is unfortunate that Swanson is faced with a substantial obligation in this case, it would seem patently unfair to actually enlarge the Kreniks' original liability under the 1981 assumption agreement simply because Swanson transferred the property to a second grantee. . . .

[Judgment affirmed.]

Effect of Due-on-Sale Clause. A **due-on-sale clause** is a contractual provision contained in the promissory note or mortgage, permitting the mortgagee, at its option, to declare the entire balance of the mortgage immediately due and payable if the property secured is sold or otherwise transferred without the prior consent of the mortgagee. Due-on-sale clauses are designed (1) to protect the mortgagee against impairment of its security or increased risk of default caused by a sale, and (2) to retire old, unprofitable mortgages when the encumbered property is sold, thereby enabling the mortgagee to maintain its long-term portfolio at current interest rates. Although prior to 1982 many state courts refused to enforce due-on-sale clauses as unreasonable restraints on alienation, federal law[13] now makes them generally enforceable.

Regulations issued by the Federal Home Loan Bank Board provide that if a mortgage contains a due-on-sale clause, the lender is not required to exercise it upon sale, but may instead waive it and allow the buyer to assume the existing mortgage. The assumption agreement must be in writing and executed before the transfer is made. In this case, the buyer becomes contractually obligated on the original loan and the lender is allowed to adjust the interest rate upward. After the assumption, however, the lender must release the original borrower (seller) from all obligations under the loan.[14] This result differs from the traditional contract approach discussed above under which the original mortgagor remains liable after assumption.

Transfer of Mortgagee's Interest. The mortgagor's promissory note secured by the mortgage is freely transferable by the mortgagee. Because the mortgage merely secures the note, they must be transferred together. Sale of the mortgage without the debt is ineffective, and sale of the note automatically carries with it the security provided by the mortgage; that is, the mortgage "follows" the debt.

Rights on Default; Foreclosure

After default, the mortgagee may always proceed upon the underlying note, obtain a judgment, and seek to enforce it against the debtor's general assets. Because these assets often are insufficient or subject to other creditors' claims, however, the mortgagee usually desires to enforce its interest in the security. **Foreclosure** is the method by which the mortgaged property, or proceeds of its sale, is applied in satisfaction of the debt.

Literally, the term "foreclosure" refers to barring or terminating the mortgagor's "equity of redemption." The **equity of redemption** concept was developed to allow the mortgagor to "redeem" his property by satisfying the debt plus interest within a reasonable time after default. Because the mortgagee could not sell or otherwise dispose of the property while a possibility of redemption remained, the law required a method of fixing the duration of the mortgagor's equity of redemption. The method developed was the mortgagee's suit to foreclose or extinguish the mortgagor's equity of redemption.

In early foreclosure actions, the mortgagee filed a petition with the court alleging default by the mortgagor and obtained a court decree ordering payment within a fixed time. Failure to pay within that time, such as six months to a year, forever extinguished the equity of redemption and vested title absolutely in the mortgagee without any sale of the property. This is known as "strict" foreclosure.

In modern times foreclosure by sale has supplanted strict foreclosure as the primary method of enforcing the mortgagee's security. Two types of foreclosure involve sale of the mortgaged property: (1) foreclosure by judicial sale, and (2) foreclosure by power of sale. The procedure for foreclosure by judicial sale varies somewhat among the states. Generally, the mortgagee files a complaint alleging default by the mortgagor. If the court finds in the mortgagee's favor after a hearing, it renders a decree or judgment of foreclosure giving the mortgagor a specified period of time (the equity of redemption) to pay the obligation, after which the property is sold at public auction. Some states also give the mortgagor an additional "statutory" right of redemption, allowing the mortgagor to reclaim the property even after sale. Ultimately the proceeds of the sale are used first to pay the mortgagee's debt and then any junior lenders in the order of their priority. Any surplus remaining after all secured parties are paid is returned to the mortgagor.

Although judicial foreclosure is available in all states, it is expensive and time-consuming. A cheaper, more expeditious method, authorized in more than two-thirds of the states, is foreclosure by power of sale. Under this method, a foreclosure sale may be conducted without recourse to the courts if the mortgage instrument itself gives the mortgagee the power to sell the property upon default. Conduct of the sale, by public auction, is strictly regulated by statute to protect the mortgagor.

If the proceeds of the sale are insufficient to satisfy the costs of the proceeding and secured debts, the mort-

---

[13]12 U.S.C. §1701j–3; 12 C.F.R. §§591.1–591.6.
[14]12 C.F.R. §591.5(b)(4).

gagee may, in most states, obtain a deficiency judgment, which may be satisfied out of the debtor's other assets. Some states have enacted "antideficiency" statutes preventing the mortgagee from obtaining a deficiency judgment after foreclosure of a purchase money mortgage. Other states limit any deficiency judgment to the difference between the fair market value of the mortgaged property and the debt. This approach reduces the amount of the deficiency because the amount realized on public sale frequently is less than would be realized through arm's length bargaining.

Installment Sales Contracts

In mortgage financing, as discussed above, the buyer makes a down payment, borrows the remainder of the purchase price from the seller or a third party, and receives a deed from the seller. The contract remains executory (yet to be performed) only for a relatively short period—that is, the time between the date of the contract and the seller's delivery of the deed at closing. If mortgage financing is unavailable because of a tight money market or because the buyer is unable to make a sufficient down payment, the parties may use an **installment sales contract** (also known as a "contract for deed," "agreement for deed," or "land contract").

In an installment contract, the seller finances the buyer who generally takes possession of the property, makes periodic installment payments against the price, and is usually responsible for payment of taxes, assessments, insurance, and repairs on the property. The seller retains title as security for performance of the contract and delivers the deed only after the purchase price is paid. Thus, unlike the ordinary real estate contract, the installment contract remains executory for an extended period, commonly several years. Because the purchaser has no deed during the executory period, a memorandum of the contract should be recorded when the contract is made to provide constructive notice to third parties of the purchaser's interest in the property. Recording, for example, protects the buyer against a subsequent sale or mortgage of the property by the seller.

Escrow Agreements

An escrow is a convenient and flexible device for closing many types of real estate transactions including installment contracts. In an **escrow,** one party to the contract deposits a deed, other instrument, or money with a

third party (known as an "escrowee," "escrow agent," or "escrow holder"), who holds the deposited instrument or funds until the performance of a condition or happening of an event outlined in the "escrow agreement." Upon occurrence of the agreed condition or conditions, the escrow agent is authorized to deliver the deposited instrument or funds to another party to the arrangement.

To illustrate the operation of an escrow arrangement, assume that Smith contracts to sell her apartment building to Black for $100,000. Although both Black and the building are located in Illinois, Smith currently resides in California. Because the parties are dealing at a distance, neither wants to risk performing without assurance that the other also will perform. This assurance is provided by an escrow arrangement, involving an Illinois bank or trust company where Black resides acting as escrow agent. Smith simply sends a deed to the property, executed naming Black as grantee, to the bank with instructions to deliver the deed to Black when he deposits the purchase price to Smith's account. In this manner, Black is assured that he will receive the deed upon payment of the price, and Smith is assured that the property will not be conveyed to Black unless and until Smith receives the purchase price.

Escrows also are used in installment sales contracts. Because the seller retains title in such contracts until the purchaser performs, the purchaser runs the risk that the seller will be unwilling or unable to convey the property at the time contractually agreed. For example, the seller may be dead, incompetent, or absent from the jurisdiction when the duty to convey arises. To prevent this result, installment contracts often require the seller to deposit a deed to the property with an escrow agent to be delivered to the buyer upon payment of the purchase price.

An escrow is an agency relationship resulting from the agreement between the parties and the escrow agent. As an agent of both buyer and seller, the escrowee stands in a fiduciary relationship to both parties concerning both the deposited property and performance of the escrow agreement.[15] Once created, the escrow agent's authority is not terminated or otherwise affected by the death or incapacity of either party prior to performance of the conditions.[16]

---

[15]The nature of the fiduciary duty owed by an agent to a principal is discussed in Chapter 40.

[16]The escrow arrangement discussed above should be distinguished from an "escrow account." An escrow account is a bank account usually maintained in the name of a mortgagor and mortgagee into which the mortgagor makes periodic payments to satisfy recurring charges such as property taxes and insurance premiums.

Transfer of Real Property by Adverse Possession

The preceding discussion concerns voluntary transfer of real property by sale. The following material examines adverse possession, which transfers real property involuntarily, without the owner's consent.

Introduction to Adverse Possession

Adverse possession is a method of acquiring title to real property through operation of the statute of limitations.[17] Legislatures have enacted statutes of limitation to avoid prejudice to the defendant and to encourage prompt resolution of a dispute by requiring that a prospective plaintiff file a lawsuit within a specified period of time after the cause of action arises or be barred from recovery. Statutes of limitation vary depending upon the nature of the claim.

The adverse possession doctrine is based upon the statute of limitations applicable to an action by an owner of real property against a person wrongfully possessing it. Although the limitation period varies between five and 30 years among the states, approximately one-fourth of states use a 20-year limitation and the vast majority (approximately 80 percent) provide for periods between ten and 20 years. If the owner fails to file suit for recovery of possession from the **adverse possessor** within the statutory period, two legal results follow: (1) the owner's claim against the possessor is extinguished, and (2) the adverse possessor acquires title to the property.

For example, assume Sam and Bob own adjoining lots in a residential subdivision. Sam constructs a fence in his backyard six feet over the property line resulting in Sam's wrongful possession of a strip of Bob's land. The possession continues for the statutory period and the other elements of adverse possession outlined below are met. In this case, Bob may no longer sue Sam to recover possession of the disputed strip of land, and Sam, the adverse possessor, acquires title to it.

The principal purpose of the adverse possession doctrine is neither to punish the negligent owner for sleeping on her rights nor to reward the adverse possessor for her wrong. It is instead to strengthen the title of the possessor of land, thereby quieting titles through the passage of time and correcting technical errors in conveyancing.

The adverse possessor's title is a new or original[18] title, destroying the record owner's title and vesting automatically by operation of law when the legal requirements are met. A person may therefore have acquired title by adverse possession, even though the public record discloses record title in another. The adverse possessor need not publicly announce the interest by recording it to be protected against purchasers from the original owner. For this reason, a prospective buyer of real property always should conduct a physical inspection or survey of the property to determine boundary lines. In this manner, adverse possession claims, not disclosed by an ordinary title examination, may be discovered.

Title to property owned by the federal or state government or governmental entity generally may not be acquired by adverse possession. This result may be dictated either by statute or by the general common law rule that the statute of limitations does not run against the government. Similarly, persons may not acquire title by adverse possession against land registered under the Torrens system.

Elements of Adverse Possession

Adverse possession cases usually arise when the original owner discovers the possession and files suit to recover the property. The possessor then defends by asserting that she has acquired title to the property by adverse possession. To prevail, the adverse possessor generally must prove that the possession was (1) in an open and notorious manner, (2) hostile, exclusive, and adverse to the original owner's interest and under a claim of right, and (3) continuous over the period of the statute of limitations.

Open, Visible, and Notorious Possession. To establish title by adverse possession, the occupation of the property must be sufficiently obvious to put the owner on notice of the possession. The owner need not actually know of the possession, but is deemed to know facts that would have been discovered if he had conducted a reasonable inspection of the property. For example, an adverse possession interest may run against an absentee landowner who is not physically present and therefore unaware of the possession. The "open and notorious" requirement provides the landowner an opportunity to protect his interest.

---

[17]Statutes of limitation are introduced in Chapter 1.

[18]The title is "original" as opposed to "derivative." Title is derivative if acquired through the original owner by sale, gift, will, or intestate succession.

Hostile, Exclusive, and Adverse Possession Under a Claim of Right. The term "hostile," as used in the law of adverse possession, does not mean that the possessor's conduct is antagonistic, belligerent, or threatening. It simply means that the possession is without the permission, express or implied, of the owner, that is, the possession must be wrongful on the possessor's part. The possession also must generally be under a "claim of right," meaning that the adverse possessor must indicate an intent to possess the land as against the whole world, including the true owner. In other words, mere trespass or simple possession is not enough. The possessor must intend to claim the title as the owner.

Some question exists concerning whether hostile possession requires an intentional usurpation of another's land, or whether mistaken or innocent possession also is sufficient. For example, assume Ann and Beth are adjoining property owners. Ann plants a hedge or builds a fence on what she mistakenly believes to be the property line. In fact, the fence or hedge is several feet over the property line, resulting in Ann's wrongful possession of a strip of Beth's land.

On these facts, most courts hold that the possessor's subjective intention is irrelevant. Mere physical possession over the property line whether intentional or mistaken is sufficient to make the possession hostile and adverse under a claim of right. That is, the only intent required is the intent to possess.

The person claiming title by adverse possession also must prove that her possession was exclusive over the statutory period. Thus, mere shared or common possession with the record owner generally defeats any adverse possession claim. Further, exclusive possession of land by one co-tenant (a joint tenant or tenant in common) generally is not deemed hostile to the interests of the other co-tenants. Nevertheless, if actual "ouster" can be shown (conduct by the co-tenant in possession excluding the others and indicating that he or she holds adversely to their interests), the statute of limitations begins to run against the ousted co-tenants.

Continuous and Uninterrupted Possession Over the Statutory Period. Generally, the statute of limitations begins to run when the possessor commences hostile and adverse, open and notorious possession. Once commenced, possession must be continuous and uninterrupted for the statutory period. Continuous does not mean constant, but instead depends upon the nature of the land involved. For example, possession of farming or grazing land is continuous if used in an open and notorious manner for its intended purpose during appropriate times of the year. Possession may therefore be continuous even though the adverse possessor is not physically present every day of the year. A break in this continuity of possession places constructive possession back in the legal owner. The statute of limitations then stops running and a new statutory period commences upon retaking possession.

Because of the length of the limitation period in adverse possession cases, the law has been required to determine the legal effect of successive adverse possessors of the same property, none of whom individually holds the property for the required period. In this case, the successive adverse possessors may add, or "tack," their respective holding periods to establish possession for the period required by the statute of limitations if they are in "privity," or as is frequently stated, "in privity of blood or contract." This simply means that tacking of holding periods is permitted if there is some connection between the successive possessors—for example, by deed, will, intestate succession, contract, or even oral permission or consent. Note that transfer of the adversely possessed property by the record owner does not interrupt the running of the statute.

Adverse Possession Under Color of Title

The adverse possessor usually occupies the property wrongfully without any semblance of actual title prior to expiration of the statutory period. The original possession may, however, occur under **color of title.** In this situation, the possessor claims the land under an instrument purporting to pass title but which is ineffective to operate as a conveyance. Examples include a deed to which the grantor's signature is forged, or a deed executed by a grantor with defective or nonexistent title. Some but not all states require that the instrument constituting color of title be recorded.

The effect of possession under a color of title differs from possession under a claim of right. Many states shorten the statutory period of possession if possession is under a color of title provided the possessor pays the annual property taxes assessed against the property.[19]

---

[19]In most states, when occupancy is not based upon color of title, the adverse possessor need not pay taxes to obtain title. Thus, the legal owner may pay the taxes and still lose the property.

The extent of the property acquired also differs when property is held under color of title. Ordinarily, the adverse possessor may claim only that portion of the land actually possessed and occupied during the statu- tory period. A person holding under color of title may acquire title to the entire tract, if adequately described in the instrument, even though actual possession is lim- ited to a portion of the property.

Summary

1.   A transfer of an interest in real property is known as a "conveyance" and, collectively, the performance of the vari- ous functions necessary to make the transfer is known as "conveyancing." A conveyancing contract generally requires the seller to convey marketable title to the property to the buyer in exchange for some consideration, usually the pay- ment of money. The parties perform the contract at the title closing, when the seller delivers a deed to the property to the buyer, who pays the purchase price.

2.   The deed is simply an instrument used to transfer an inter- est in real property. To be effective the deed must meet formal requirements prescribed by state law. Generally the deed must be in writing, identify the grantor and the grantee, contain words of conveyance, and give a legal description of the prop- erty. The deed generally is effective to transfer the property once it is signed by the grantor and delivered to the grantee.

3.   Deeds are of two general types: the warranty deed and the quitclaim deed. A warranty deed contains a number of promises ("covenants for title") concerning the status of the grantor's title. If a covenant for title is breached, the injured grantee may recover damages from the grantor. In contrast, the quitclaim deed simply transfer whatever interest, if any, the grantor possesses.

4.   Before delivery of the deed, the real estate buyer must be assured that the seller possesses the interest he or she has con- tracted to convey. Such title assurance is provided primarily by professional examination of public land records generated by state recording statutes.

5.   Each state has a recording statute, designed to provide reliable public information concerning the ownership of and other interests in real property. Recording statutes permit recordation of various instruments affecting land ownership, and a purchaser of property generally takes it free of a prior unrecorded instrument. The ownership of a particular tract and other interests in it can be ascertained by searching the public record created by the recording statute. Recording statutes also resolve priority disputes among persons succes- sively acquiring an interest in a given piece of property.

6.   Once the various interests in the land have been deter- mined from the public record, the record is examined by an attorney, who renders an opinion concerning the marketability of the title. This opinion may be embodied in a formal attor- ney's opinion or may be backed by a title insurance policy.

7.   Under the Torrens system, an alternative to title assur- ance based upon examining the instruments evidencing title, a legal proceeding is held in which the title itself is registered and a certificate of title is issued to the owner. Once regis- tered, the land may be transferred merely by issuing a new certificate of title to the buyer, avoiding the necessity of a title search before each transfer.

8.   Creditors financing real estate purchases usually require security. In most cases, this security is provided by a mort- gage, an interest in real property that is created to secure per- formance of an obligation, usually repayment of a debt. Like other real property interests, a mortgage is created by deed, a mortgage deed, in which the mortgagor conveys an interest in the property to be used as security to the mortgagee.

9.   A property owner may borrow money from two or more lenders and give each a mortgage on the same property. If the value of the mortgaged property is less than the total of the outstanding obligations it secures, the real property recording statute determines priority of the various mortgagees.

10. The mortgagor generally may sell or otherwise transfer the mortgaged property without the mortgagee's consent. If the property is sold without paying off the underlying debt and retiring the mortgage, the buyer takes the property either "sub- ject to" the existing mortgage or "assumes" the mortgage debt. A buyer who takes "subject to" the mortgage incurs no personal liability for payment of the debt which the mortgage secures, whereas one who "assumes" does undertake such liability.

11. "Foreclosure" is the method by which the mortgaged property, or its proceeds, is applied in satisfaction of the debt. Foreclosure by sale is the most common method used in the United States.

12. An alternative to conventional mortgage financing is the "installment sales contract" or "contract for deed." In this case, the seller finances the buyer, who takes possession of the property and makes periodic installment payments against the price. The seller retains title as security for the buyer's perfor- mance and delivers the deed only after the purchase price is paid in full.

13. The parties often use an "escrow" agreement as a convenient and flexible tool for closing real estate transactions including installment sales contracts.

14. Although most real property transfers are voluntary, a transfer may be made without the owner's consent by adverse possession. Under this doctrine a person wrongfully possessing another's property, the adverse possessor, acquires title to it if the possession is (1) in an open and notorious manner, (2) hostile, exclusive, and adverse to the original owner's interest under a claim of right, and (3) continuous over the period of the statute of limitations. The adverse possession doctrine stabilizes land titles by recognizing longstanding possession of property.

Key Terms

conveyancing	abstract of title
marketable (merchantable) title	attorney's opinion
	title insurance
title closing (settlement)	Torrens system
Real Estate Settlement Procedures Act (RESPA)	pure race statute
	pure notice statute
deed	race-notice statute
grantor	mortgage
grantee	mortgagor
warranty deed	mortgagee
covenants for title	deed of trust (trust deed)
encumbrance	due-on-sale clause
quitclaim deed	foreclosure
recording statute	equity of redemption
recorder of deeds	installment sales contract
constructive notice	escrow
title search	adverse possession
chain of title	adverse possessor
Marketable Title Acts	color of title

Questions and Problems

37.1 You are considering purchasing a home in Shady Acres, a residential subdivision. You have begun preliminary negotiations with the seller of the property. What issues should be addressed in the contract for sale? Assuming you decide to purchase the property, what steps should be taken prior to conveyance to assure that you receive a good title?

37.2 Most real estate contracts require that the seller convey the property by warranty deed. What protection does a warranty deed provide the purchaser? Under what circumstances might the buyer be willing to accept a quitclaim deed?

37.3 Fred and Ethel, residents of New Jersey, applied to First National Bank for a loan. As collateral for the loan, they offered to pledge a house in Missouri. Fred and Ethel explained that they owned the house; however, Ethel's retired parents had rented the property and were living there.

A junior loan officer had a title search performed and all records indicated that Fred and Ethel owned the property. A bank representative also drove by the house and noticed an elderly couple working in the garden.

You are the senior loan officer at the bank. The junior loan officer states that the value of the house is more than the requested loan and recommends that the loan be approved without further investigation. Missouri has adopted a race-notice recording statute. Would you approve the loan? Explain.

37.4 Russell fraudulently obtained title to 75 acres of land in Florida owned by Mrs. Elliott, an elderly, uneducated woman. Mrs. Elliott had agreed to sell Russell 15 acres but Russell prepared a deed conveying 75 acres. Because Mrs. Elliott could not read well, she relied on Russell's statement that the deed conveyed only 15 acres and signed the deed. Russell recorded the deed.

(a) Russell enlisted the aid of a shady friend, Boris. Russell explained how he had fooled Mrs. Elliott and offered to sell the property to Boris for $25,000, the fair market value of the property. Boris paid $25,000 and Russell deeded the property to Boris, who recorded the deed. Mrs. Elliott sues Boris claiming that she owns the property. Who owns the property? Explain.

(b) Assume instead that Boris immediately offers to sell the property to an acquaintance, Rocky. Rocky performed a title search and traced the chain of title to Boris. Rocky paid $25,000 and Boris deeded the property to Rocky. Mrs. Elliott sues Rocky. Who owns the property? Explain.

37.5 (a) By warranty deed, Adam conveys Blackacre to Eve. Eve records the deed at the recorder's office. The recorder inadvertently misfiles the deed. Adam later conveys the same property to Joseph by quitclaim deed. Joseph searches the title at the recorder's office and, because of Eve's misfiled deed, finds that Adam is shown as the title holder. Joseph records his deed. Who owns Blackacre? Explain.

(b) Ernest signed an agreement to sell a piece of land to Ricardo and agreed to provide an abstract of title. At Ernest's request, First Title Service prepared an abstract but negligently failed to find a prior deed by which Ernest had conveyed the property to Sam. Ernest paid First Title's abstract fee and provided a copy of the abstract to Ricardo. Ricardo took the abstract to Sun City Bank and, relying on the abstract, the bank loaned Ricardo $100,000 secured by a mortgage on the land. Ricardo defaulted on the loan and the bank began foreclosure proceedings. Sun City then discovered that Sam owned the property. Sun City sued First Title Service Company alleging that its negligence in failing to find Sam's deed had caused Sun City to lose $100,000. How should the court rule? Explain.

37.6 In exchange for a loan from Liberty Bank, the Bergs executed a promissory note and granted the bank a mortgage on their real estate to secure the loan. In 1990, the Bergs sold the real estate to the Howards, who agreed to assume the loan and mortgage. Following the sale, the Howards made payments directly to Liberty Bank and discussed the loan a number of times with loan officers from the bank. In 1994, the Howards defaulted in making loan payments to the bank. Liberty Bank sued the Bergs.

(a) The Bergs argued that they were no longer liable on the loan because Liberty Bank had dealt and corresponded with the Howards. How should the court rule? Explain.

(b) The Bergs also argued that Liberty Bank should be required to foreclose on the real estate before suing on the promissory note. Do you agree? Explain.

37.7   Installment land contracts sometimes are used to make a "silent sale." In the silent sale the contract is used to transfer the property without notifying the seller's mortgagee of the sale, thereby preventing it from exercising its due-on-sale clause. The buyer is therefore effectively able to assume the seller's low interest rate mortgage. To prevent the mortgagee from learning of the sale the parties do not record a memorandum of the contract in the recorder's office. In addition, the seller continues making payments on the mortgage, and taxes, utilities, and insurance continue to be carried in the seller's name. What risks do silent sales pose to the parties involved: the buyer, the seller, their attorneys, title companies, and real estate brokers?

37.8   Because adverse possession constitutes an involuntary transfer of property, the interest of an owner by adverse possession usually will not show up in a title search. How is a person who purchases property protected from the claims of an adverse possessor? Explain.

37.9   In 1958, Katy and Adolph conveyed by warranty deed a portion of their real property to Adam, an adjoining landowner. For almost 50 years, Adam did not develop the property. Katy and Adolph, however, continued to use the property. They stored farm equipment on it and planted and maintained a garden there. In 2005, Adam died and devised the property to his son, who began construction of a house on the property. Katy and Adolph sue to enjoin the con-

struction, alleging that they had acquired title to the property by adverse possession.

(a) Should the court grant or allow Katy and Adolph's claim of adverse possession? Explain.

(b) Would your answer be different if the 1958 deed to Adam had been a quitclaim deed? Explain.

37.10 As noted in the text, most courts hold that in adverse possession cases, mistaken or innocent possession is sufficient to constitute hostile possession. A minority of courts hold that if a person possesses property up to the boundary without knowledge of the actual property line, but intending only to possess up to the true property line, his possession does not meet the hostility requirement. Thus, under the minority rule, the subjective intention of the adverse possessor is determinative. Do you agree with this approach? What problems might a court encounter in applying it?

37.11 In 1963, Ben purchased a piece of land suitable for cattle grazing and took title by warranty deed. Adam owned a ranch that adjoined the piece of land. In 1964 Adam erected a fence around his ranch and fenced in approximately 100 acres of Ben's land. During the next 40 years, Adam allowed his cattle to graze on the land three or four weeks each year. Although Ben did not use the land, he paid the real estate taxes on it every year. Adam claims title to the land by adverse possession. Who owns the land? Explain.

37.12 Vincent conveyed a parcel of land by warranty deed to Wanda. Wanda later learned that Lee claimed title to the land by adverse possession. Wanda sued Lee to clear title to the land.

(a) Assume that Lee fails to prove title by adverse possession because he has had possession of the land for only three years. Has Vincent breached any of the warranties of the warranty deed?

(b) Assume instead that Lee's claim to title by adverse possession is valid because he possessed the land for over 20 years. Has Vincent breached any of the warranties of the warranty deed? Explain.

REGULATING LAND USE

Many property rights protect the owner's possession and use of the property after acquisition. Ownership rights are not, however, absolute; they are subject to rights of neighboring property owners and other members of the community. This chapter examines various limitations on the use of land imposed either by private agreement or by act of public authority including federal, state, or local government.

Private individuals may regulate land use either by creating easements and profits, which are limited inter- ests in the use of the property itself, or by contract. Public regulation is of two general types: zoning, through which the government regulates or restricts the use and physical configuration of property, and eminent domain, under which the government takes private property from its owner and applies the property to a public use.

Private Regulation of Land Use

Easements and Profits

An **easement** is an interest in land that gives its owner the right (1) to use another person's land for a limited and specified purpose, or (2) to prevent another person from using his land in a specified way. The most common easements are "rights of way" that give a person the right to pass over or under another's land. Examples include driveways, roads, sidewalks, footpaths, and easements granted to public utilities to run power or telephone lines, underground cables, pipelines, and sewer lines. The par- ties may create easements for a wide variety of uses, limited only by the specific needs of the parties.

An easement is a *nonpossessory interest* in land. Thus, the owner of the property burdened by the easement has the full right to possess and use the property subject only to the easement. Assume Ann and Beth are adjoining property owners. Ann grants Beth an easement across a 16-foot strip of her property for driveway and sidewalk purposes. In this case, Beth has an interest in Ann's land, the easement, allowing her to *use* Ann's property for a specified purpose—as a driveway and sidewalk. Beth has no right to use the strip of land for any other purpose—for example, to run a drainage tile or to use portions of Ann's property not covered by the easement for the stated purpose. Ann retains the right to possess and use the property, subject only to Beth's right of way. If Beth desires the unrestricted possession and use of the property to plant a garden or build a garage, she should purchase fee simple title or lease the premises from Ann. The nonpossessory aspect of an easement is, therefore, an important factor distinguishing it from other property interests.

If the right to use another's property includes the right to *remove* part of the land or products of the land, it is known as a **profit,** or more fully, a **profit à prendre.** Through a profit, a landowner may transfer the right to remove from the land (1) sand, dirt, or gravel; (2) other minerals such as coal; or (3) grass or timber. A profit includes the right to enter the property, to make use of the property necessary to sever the minerals or products, and to remove them from the property. The right to take from the property (the profit) distinguishes the profit from an ordinary easement. Generally, the same legal principles govern both interests.

Because an easement is a nonpossessory estate, the law generally permits the owner of the land to share in the use authorized by the easement. This rule is particularly important if the easement includes a profit, because it allows the landowner to join the easement holder in extracting minerals or other natural resources.

Affirmative and Negative Easements. The easements illustrated above are "affirmative" easements. An affirmative easement allows its holder to use or do some act on another's land that would be unlawful without the easement. In contrast, a "negative" easement does not permit the holder to use another's land. Instead, it prevents the owner of the burdened property from doing something otherwise lawful upon her own land. Assume Ann and Beth are adjoining property owners. In order to preserve the free flow of light or air across her property, or to preserve an unobstructed view, Beth purchases an easement from Ann preventing Ann from building on her property or limiting the height of any

structures erected on Ann's land. Beth has no right to use Ann's property for any purpose. The easement in this case limits Ann's use of her own land.

Easements Appurtenant and Easements in Gross. Easements also are classified as appurtenant or in gross. An **easement appurtenant** involves two tracts of land, one benefited by the easement (the "dominant tenement" or "dominant estate") and one burdened by the easement (the "servient tenement" or "servient estate"). An easement appurtenant benefits land owned by the holder of the easement—the dominant tenement. The preceding examples are easements appurtenant. In both cases, Beth's land, the dominant tenement, is benefited by the easement, either because of the right to use a driveway across Ann's land, or the right to have an unrestricted view or flow of light or air across Ann's land. Ann's land, the servient estate, is burdened because her use of the property is restricted by the easement. Easements appurtenant typically, although not necessarily, involve adjoining tracts of land.

An **easement in gross,** in contrast, is not obtained for the benefit of land owned by the holder of the easement. In other words, in an easement in gross, there is no dominant tenement. The most common example of an easement in gross is a right of way obtained by a public utility to run lines, poles, or underground cables. Profits also are usually in gross, because the right to enter the land to remove minerals, timber, or other resources frequently exists independently of the holder's ownership of land.

Creation of Easements

Easements are created by an express act of the parties, by implication, by prescription, or by eminent domain.

By Express Act of the Parties. Like other interests in land, most easements are created upon delivery of a deed describing the nature and extent of the interest conveyed. A deed may create the easement in either the grantor or the grantee. Assume Sally and Bob own adjoining tracts of land. In exchange for an agreed sum, Sally, the grantor, conveys an easement to Bob, granting him the right to run a drainage tile across Sally's land. Bob, the grantee, has obtained an easement by "express grant."

An easement may be created in the grantor by "exception" or "reservation." Assume Sally owns a tract of land that has a highway running along its southern border, but no other access to a public street. Sally conveys the southern one-half of the tract to Bob. To assure continued access to the highway, Sally, as part of the conveyance to Bob, creates or retains an easement in herself across the property transferred for driveway and sidewalk purposes. Sally, the grantor, has created an easement by reservation or exception.

By Implication. Easements also may be created in favor of either the grantor or grantee by implication. These easements, which are based upon the inferred or presumed intention of the parties, arise when an owner of a tract of land divides it into two or more parts and conveys one or more of the parts to others. Implied easements are of two types: easements implied from quasieasements and easements implied from necessity.

Frequently, a property owner uses one part of her land to benefit another part. Assume Susan owns a tract of land that abuts a highway running along its southern boundary. She resides in a farmhouse located on the northern one-half of the land, and constructs a driveway across the southern one-half providing access to the road. Because a person cannot possess an easement in her own land, the tract's southern one-half is said to be burdened by a "quasi-easement" (the driveway running across it). Susan subsequently sells the northern one-half of the tract to Betty. The deed of conveyance makes no mention of any easement for driveway purposes across the tract's southern one-half. On these facts, an easement may be implied in favor of the grantee, Betty, resulting from the quasi-easement originally existing on the land. If Susan had sold the southern one-half of the tract, an easement across it may be implied (an implied reservation) in favor of Susan, the grantor.

An easement also may be implied because of *necessity,* without regard to any prior use of the property. An "easement by necessity" (or "way by necessity") arises when an owner of a single tract conveys part of it, and thereby "landlocks" the portion retained or conveyed, leaving no way to enter or exit the land without trespassing upon neighboring property. In this case, an easement by necessity is created in favor of the grantor if the landlocked land is retained, or the grantee if the landlocked land is conveyed. Unlike an easement implied from a quasi-easement, which continues indefinitely, an easement created by necessity continues only so long as the need for the use continues.

By Prescription. As discussed in Chapter 37, fee simple title, a possessory interest in property, may be acquired through a person's adverse *possession* of another's property for the period of the statute of limitations. Similarly, an easement, a nonpossessory interest, may be obtained through adverse *use* for the statutory period. In this case, an easement (known as a "prescriptive easement") is created by **prescription.** The requirements necessary to create an easement by prescription are similar to those needed to acquire title by adverse possession. Thus, an easement by prescription may be created by *use* of another's land (such as for a footpath or driveway) if the use is hostile, open, and notorious, and is continuous and uninterrupted for the period of the statute of limitations.

By Eminent Domain. Unlike easements created by express grant or reservation, prescriptive easements are created involuntarily. An easement also may arise involuntarily when the sovereign exercises its eminent domain power, the power of the government to take private property for public use. In many eminent domain cases, the interest acquired is merely an easement, not a fee simple. For example, easements often are taken by eminent domain for highways, streets, railroads, utility lines, subterranean pipes or cables, flowage (the right to overflow, flood, and submerge the servient land), and for overflight and clearance near airports.

Transfer of Easements

Like most other property interests, both easements appurtenant and easements in gross are freely transferable. As a general rule, the easement follows the ownership or possession of the dominant estate in an easement appurtenant. Similarly, a transferee of the servient estate takes subject to the easement. This rule applies to all easements appurtenant whether created by grant, reservation, implication, or prescription. Assume Bob and Carol own adjoining tracts of land. Bob also holds an easement across Carol's land for driveway and sidewalk purposes to reach a public street. Bob sells his land to Ted. Ted has the benefit of the easement across Carol's land even if the instrument of conveyance makes no mention of the easement. If Carol sells or leases her land to Alice, Alice takes subject to the burdens imposed by the easement. In other words, an easement appurtenant is unaffected by a transfer of possession of either the dominant or servient estate.[1]

In contrast, under the "English Rule," an easement in gross created only individual or personal rights, which could not be transferred. American courts have, however, generally rejected this approach. As a result, in the United States, easements in gross, except those clearly intended to benefit only the original easement holder, are freely transferable during life or at death.

Termination of Easements

Easements may terminate by expiration or extinguishment. Termination by either method removes the burden imposed upon the servient estate by the easement.

By Expiration. Although the duration of easements usually is indefinite, easements may be created to last for a specified period of time or to accomplish a given purpose, after which they terminate by expiration. Assume that Alan grants Bob a right of way across his land for the term of a lease of adjoining property by Alan to Bob. Here, the easement terminates upon expiration of the lease. Or assume XYZ Corporation is constructing a factory on its property. To provide access for construction equipment during the period of construction, XYZ purchases a right of way across Joe Doaks's land to continue until XYZ finishes construction. Upon completion of the factory, XYZ's easement terminates.

By Extinguishment. An easement may be terminated by events not contemplated by the parties when they created the easement. In this case, the easement terminates by extinguishment. Extinguishment may be complete or partial, depending upon the nature of the easement and the manner of termination. An easement usually is extinguished by conduct of the dominant owner, conduct of the servient owner, or conduct of both parties.

Conduct of the Dominant Owner. The dominant owner may extinguish the easement by release or abandonment. Release is the transfer of the easement back to the owner of the servient estate. A release by sale

or gift is made by deed (normally a quitclaim), and a release on death must be contained in a valid will. Extinguishment by abandonment occurs if the dominant owner's conduct indicates an intent to relinquish the right to use the easement further. The court determines intent to abandon from all surrounding circumstances including the dominant owner's nonuse of the easement, verbal statements of an intention to abandon, or other conduct inconsistent with further use of the easement. For example, a railroad may abandon a right of way by tearing up and removing rails and ties.

Conduct of the Servient Owner. Extinguishment also may result from acts of the servient owner. For example, as previously discussed, an easement may be created by prescription. It also may be terminated in the same manner by the servient owner's adverse use of the easement (for example, by building a fence across a right of way) over the period of the statute of limitations.

Conduct of Both Parties. The conduct of both parties may extinguish the easement by merger. A merger occurs when the holder of an easement in gross becomes the owner of the servient estate, or the same person acquires both the dominant and servient estates in an easement appurtenant. These events permanently terminate the easement because the lesser estate (the easement) is merged into the greater (the fee simple).

"Licenses" Distinguished

Not every privilege to use the land of another is an easement. A privilege to enter upon or perform acts on another's land that lacks one or more of the elements essential to create an easement is known as a **license.** The person in possession of the land who grants the right of use is the "licensor" and the person empowered to use the land is the "licensee." A license, which arises when the licensor consents to allow the use, simply gives the licensee the right to use another's land without incurring liability as a trespasser.

Unlike an easement, which continues until it expires by its terms or is extinguished, a license is always revocable at the will of the property owner, the licensor. The licensor may indicate an intent to revoke expressly or by using the property inconsistently with the license. A license also ends upon the death of either party, a con-

---

[1] An easement appurtenant cannot be transferred apart from the dominant estate to which it is attached, unless the transfer is made to the owner of the servient estate to extinguish the easement.

veyance of the property by the licensor, or upon the licensee's attempt to transfer the license.

Although a license is an interest in land, it is created without the formalities (for example, a deed) necessary to create other interests in land. A license therefore arises whether the initial consent is express or implied, oral or written. Further, an ineffective attempt to create an easement creates a license. Assume Sam attempts to grant to his neighbor, Bill, an easement across Sam's yard for use as a footpath. However, Sam grants the right orally or in a deed that Sam does not sign. On these facts, Bill acquires a license rather than an easement to use Sam's land. Sam may revoke the license at any time by indicating his intent to end it.

Covenants

An easement alters the normal incidents of land ownership and possession by creating a limited property interest in the servient estate. In addition, subject to public policy limitations, all conceivable land uses may be regulated privately by contract.

Covenants are contractual promises concerning land use. An **affirmative covenant** requires the promisor (covenantor) to do something on the covenantor's land, such as building or maintaining a party wall,[2] irrigation or drainage ditch, or structure such as a dam or bridge. A **negative,** or **restrictive, covenant** restricts or limits the permissible uses of the land or the acts that may be performed upon it. Like a negative easement, a restrictive covenant limits the property owner in the use of his own land. A landowner who breaches a restrictive covenant may be liable to neighboring property owners for money damages and may be enjoined by the court against further breach of the covenant. Most covenants affecting land use are restrictive.

Frequently, restrictive covenants are used in residential subdivisions to achieve a coordinated, consistent pattern of land use within the subdivision. When so used, the covenants are known as "building restrictions" and are intended to maintain property values and to preserve the residential character of the area. Common building restrictions include those (1) restricting the use of all lots or certain lots to residential purposes only (or

prohibiting certain uses), (2) imposing minimum cost or square footage requirements on any building constructed in the subdivision, and (3) requiring that any building constructed on a lot must be located a minimum distance from streets (a setback restriction), or from an adjoining lot (a sidelot restriction), or from the rear lot line. As with easements, the list of possible restrictions is potentially infinite, limited only by the needs of the property owners.

Although courts uphold most restrictions as beneficial and essential tools of private land use control, they refuse to enforce covenants that are illegal, unconstitutional, or otherwise contrary to public policy. For example, in the famous case *Shelley v. Kraemer,*[3] the Supreme Court refused to enforce on constitutional grounds a restrictive covenant prohibiting "any person not of the Caucasian race" from residing on a specified street. If the court refuses to enforce a covenant, neither the deed containing it nor other permissible restrictions are affected; the offending covenant is simply void.

Creation of Covenants

Covenants governing land use may be imposed with or without the conveyance of any land. Assume Adams and Branch are adjoining owners of large tracts of scenic rural land. To assure a continued unobstructed view, Adams and Branch, by contract, agree that no structures may be built within 500 feet of either side of their mutual boundary line. Adams and Branch have created a restrictive covenant by contract without conveyance.

Usually, however, restrictive covenants are created by the grantor upon a conveyance of land, and limit the grantee's use of the land. The grantor may include the covenant in the deed. Alternatively, a grantor who is subdividing land into a residential or other development may include land use restrictions in the plat or map of the subdivision filed in the county recorder's office when the land is subdivided. As discussed in Chapter 37, this map provides the basis for the legal description of property located in the subdivision. The restrictions are then incorporated by reference into the individual deeds to lots within the subdivision, even though they are not set out in full in each deed. The person performing a title search on property in a subdivision must therefore read the plat restrictions to determine whether

---

[2]A party wall is a wall built next to, or upon, a boundary line, which serves as a common wall of two adjoining structures.

[3]68 S. Ct. 836 (1948).

the property under examination complies with limitations imposed on its use.

The Statute of Frauds, discussed in Chapter 12, generally requires that promises concerning land use be evidenced by a writing to be enforceable. Further, the Statute ordinarily requires that the writing be signed by the person against whom enforcement is sought. Although covenants often are contained in or incorporated into the deed, and modern deeds usually are signed only by the grantor, most courts hold that the grantee, by accepting the deed, is bound by covenants contained in the deed, even without signing it.

Effect Upon Subsequent Transferees

When property subject to restrictive covenants is transferred, the law must determine the extent to which the covenant runs with the land. A covenant **runs with the land** if either the liability to perform it or the right to take advantage of it passes to a transferee of the property.

Either the benefit or the burden, or both, of the covenant may run. Assume Art and Bob own adjoining tracts of land. In order to preserve his view of the ocean, Art secures Bob's covenant not to build any structure more than one story tall on Bob's land. Art subsequently sells his land to Carol and Bob sells his tract to Diane. If the covenant runs with the land, Carol may enforce the restriction against Diane. That is, the benefit of the covenant runs to Carol with the sale of Art's tract, and the burden runs to Diane upon transfer of Bob's land.

Originally, covenants running with the land were enforced in courts of law. Because the stringent requirements for covenants running with the land at law prevented judicial enforcement of many beneficial covenants, nineteenth-century courts of equity began to enforce promises governing land use by imposing an **equitable servitude** upon the burdened land.[4] An equitable servitude, which is treated as an interest in land, runs with the land if four elements are present.

1. The restriction must be contained in a *writing* that satisfies the Statute of Frauds.

2. The original parties must *intend* that the restriction run with the land. Intent is easily established if the covenant, by terms of the creating instrument, expressly

binds "assigns" or "successors." Express language is not, however, required. Rather, the court considers all surrounding circumstances.

3. The restriction must *touch and concern* the land. The burden of a covenant touches and concerns land if it decreases the utility or value of the land in the hands of its owner, the covenantor (promisor). Conversely, the benefit of a covenant touches and concerns the land if it increases the utility or value of the affected land in the hands of its owner, the covenantee (promisee). The subdivision restrictions previously listed illustrate covenants that touch and concern the land.

4. The subsequent purchaser must take with actual or constructive *notice* of the restriction. Notice usually is provided by recording a document containing the restriction in the county recorder's office. If the covenant is not properly recorded, a bona fide purchaser of the property without actual knowledge of it takes free of the restriction.

At issue in the following case was whether a covenant touched and concerned the land.

Regency Homes Association v. Egermayer
498 N.W.2d 783 (Neb. 1993)

The Regency subdivision, which includes residential, commercial, and recreational areas, was developed in Omaha, Nebraska, during the late 1960s. The subdivision declaration, which was recorded with the county recorder of deeds, requires all property owners to be members of the Regency Homes Association (RHA) and authorizes the RHA to impose and collect annual dues to finance its operations. The subdivision declaration further stated, "[E]very lot will be automatically included in membership in [RHA] as a benefit or burden running with and charge upon the ownership of each such lot." The RHA was formed in 1968 and by 1978 the annual dues were $225. The RHA paid for maintenance of the entrance to the subdivision and a park within the subdivision, reviewed architectural plans for proposed new buildings, and paid for a security patrol. In 1980, the RHA began operating the Regency Lake and Tennis Club (RLTC), which included a park, tennis courts, and swimming pool. As part of their membership in the RHA, all subdivision residents were members of the RLTC; nonresidents could become members by paying special membership dues to the RHA.

In 1978, George and Jean Egermayer bought a house and lot in the Regency subdivision. The deed to their prop-

---

[4]The equitable servitude doctrine is derived from the English case, *Tulk v. Moxhay,* 2 Ph. 774, 41 Eng. Rep. 1143 (Ch. 1848).

erty stated that it was "subject to easements, reservations, restrictions, and protective covenants of record." The Egermayers refused to pay annual dues to the RHA arguing that the covenant requiring membership in the RHA was not a valid covenant running with the land because it required them to join and pay dues to a social club open to the public. The RHA sued the Egermayers seeking payment of the dues. The trial court ruled in favor of the RHA and the Egermayers appealed.

Fahrnbruch, Justice

. . . The nature of the covenant to pay dues to the RHA, that is, whether the covenant runs with the land, is central to the determination of the issue before the court. . . . [T]he Egermayers argue that the covenant in question does not "touch and concern" the land. Therefore, we limit our analysis to that issue.

The "touch and concern" requirement . . . is one with which many jurisdictions have struggled. . . . [W]e adopt the New York Court of Appeals' rule [announced in *Neponsit Property Owners Association v. Emigrant Independent Savings Bank,* 15 N.E.2d 793, 796 (N.Y. 1938)] that the touch and concern requirement . . . is met when the covenant affects the legal relations—the advantages and the burdens—of the parties to the covenant, as owners of particular parcels of land and not merely as members of the community in general, such as taxpayers or owners of other land. The covenant must impose, on the one hand, a burden upon an interest in land, which on the other hand increases the value of a different interest in the same or related land. . . . In [*Neponsit*], the court held that purchasers of individual lots in a residential community also obtained the right of enjoyment of the roads, streets, beaches, and other improvements, and thus were liable for paying the costs of such improvements as required by covenant. . . .

[The Egermayers'] position is that because Regency property owners are not the *exclusive* users of RLTC, the covenant requiring payment of dues to RHA does not touch and concern the land. The Egermayers assert that the existence of a special membership class for those who live outside the Regency subdivision makes RLTC a public facility which has no particular value to property owners in Regency. . . .

This brings us to the ultimate question of whether RLTC enhances the value of individual properties in the Regency subdivision. George Egermayer testified

that in his opinion, RLTC adds no value whatsoever to his property because the facility is located across four lanes of traffic from the residential area, it is not centrally located, it is next to a commercial area, and it is open to the public. . . . [Other witnesses] testified that . . . mandatory membership in the RHA definitely enhanced the property values in the area and that property values would be adversely affected if membership in RHA were to be voluntary rather than mandatory. . . .

The only evidence that membership in RHA does not benefit individual property owners was offered by the party seeking to avoid payment of the mandatory dues. After considering all the testimony on this issue, we agree with the California Court of Appeals that "the maintenance of a well-kept club-house, recreational area and swimming pool . . . enhance[s] the value of each home therein. . . . [T]he so-called 'burden' of maintaining membership in this association would in reality be an asset to each and every property owner in the use of his land." [*Anthony v. Brea Glenbrook Club,* 130 Cal.Rptr. 32, 34 (Cal. App. 1976).]

Apart from the social amenities offered by RLTC, we find that membership in RHA provides numerous other benefits to property owners. There was testimony that RHA dues pay for maintenance of a 1-acre park within the subdivision, as well as the green areas at the 96th Street entrance to the subdivision. George Egermayer concedes that maintenance of the common areas of the subdivisions, parks, drives, and trees adds value to his property. We can only conclude that maintenance of the green areas owned by RHA and paid for through part of the annual $225 assessment contributes some of this added value.

Dues also paid for the services of a private security patrol for the residential neighborhood until sometime after the subdivision was annexed by the city of Omaha. . . . Private security service is an asset which enhances the value of individual properties.

The bylaws of RHA provide for an architectural control committee and authorize the expenditure of funds by that committee. The architectural review committee reviews and approves all new construction, as well as additions or modifications to existing structures. . . . Again, this is a function of RHA which benefits all property owners in Regency by protecting against unsightly or inappropriate building in the subdivision. . . .

[W]e conclude that the covenant requiring membership in the RHA enhances the value of individual properties in the Regency subdivision so as to meet the "touch and concern" requirement of a . . . covenant running with the land. . . .

[Judgment affirmed.]

Termination of Covenants

Assuming a covenant runs with the land, its duration depends upon a number of factors, such as the intent of the original parties, statutory restrictions, and subsequent events. Because covenants impose a limitation on the free use of land, courts do not favor their unlimited duration. The parties may explicitly provide for termination by fixing a definite period—for example, 20 to 50 years—after which the limitation expires. In addition, covenants often include explicit provisions allowing termination by the original grantor or by a vote of all (or a portion of) the affected landowners.[5] Many states, either by statute or judicial decision, limit the permissible duration of covenants regulating land use.

Subsequent events may extinguish an existing covenant prior to the time it would otherwise terminate. For example, covenants may be terminated if neighborhood conditions have so changed since the creation of the covenants that it is impossible to achieve the intended purposes or benefits of the restrictions. The change of condition may result from acts of one or both parties or their successors or from a change in the character of the area—for example, from residential to commercial use.

Public Regulation of Land Use

Easements and restrictive covenants govern land use by private agreement. Land use also may be regulated by governmental action. For example, the sovereign may impose limitations on land use through zoning. In addition, the sovereign may take private property involuntarily for a public use under the power of eminent domain.

Introduction to Zoning

Zoning is the process by which a municipality regulates the use of property and the physical configuration of the development of land within its jurisdiction. The power to zone is derived from the state's police power that authorizes legislation for the protection of the public health, safety, welfare, and morals.[6] Although local governments ordinarily implement zoning, the power to zone is derived from the various state legislatures that have passed enabling statutes delegating the power to local government, or from state constitutional provisions giving localities the specific authority to zone. In most states, this authorization is patterned, in whole or in part, upon the provisions of the **Standard State Zoning Enabling Act,** which was originally drafted in 1924.

Under traditional zoning, the land affected by the ordinance is divided into zones or districts, with only certain uses permitted within each zone. Zoning restrictions are of three general types: limitations on the use of property within each zone; height, bulk, and area restrictions; and architectural limitations on the exterior design of buildings. Use districts are frequently of four major types: residential, commercial, industrial, and special.

Constitutional Limitations on Zoning Power

The police power, the basis of zoning, is certainly the most extensive and pervasive power of state government. To be valid, however, an exercise of police power (including zoning) must bear a substantial relation to public health, safety, morals, or general welfare. In essence, this means that a zoning restriction must be reasonable both by its terms and in its application. Thus, zoning restrictions that impose an arbitrary, unreasonable, oppressive, or unduly discriminatory interference with the rights of property owners are prohibited by the U.S. Constitution, specifically the Due Process and Equal Protection Clauses of the Fourteenth Amendment.[7]

Although some early state cases struck down comprehensive zoning ordinances, two landmark U.S. Supreme Court cases firmly established the constitutional validity of and limitations upon the zoning power. In *Village of*

---

[5]Even without an explicit provision, covenants may be extinguished or amended by agreement of all affected owners.

[6]The state police power is discussed in more detail in Chapter 4.

[7]In relevant part, the Fourteenth Amendment provides that "No state shall . . . deprive any person of life, liberty, or property, without due process of law; nor deny to any person within its jurisdiction the equal protection of the laws."

Euclid, Ohio v. Ambler Realty Co., decided in 1926,[8] the Court upheld comprehensive zoning regulation as a valid exercise of the state's police power that did not involve an unconstitutional deprivation of property.

In the case that follows, the Court determined whether a zoning ordinance may be unconstitutional as applied to a particular piece of property.

Nectow v. City of Cambridge

48 S. Ct. 447 (1928)

Saul Nectow owned a tract of land in the city of Cambridge, Massachusetts. The city enacted a zoning ordinance fixing a boundary that placed approximately 20 percent of Nectow's land within a residential zone, with the remainder unrestricted. Because adjacent property was used for railroad and industrial purposes, the tract in question had no practical value for residential use. Nectow sued the city alleging that, as applied to his land, the zoning ordinance deprived him of property without due process of law in violation of the Fourteenth Amendment. The Massachusetts state courts sustained the ordinance as applied to Nectow and he appealed to the U.S. Supreme Court.

Justice Sutherland

. . . A zoning ordinance of the city of Cambridge divides the city into three kinds of districts, residential, business, and unrestricted. . . . The ordinance is an elaborate one, and of the same general character as that considered by this court in *Euclid v. Ambler Co.* . . . In its general scope it is conceded to be constitutional within that decision. [Nectow's land] was put in district R-3, in which are permitted only dwellings, hotels, clubs, churches, schools, philanthropic institutions, greenhouses and gardening, with customary incidental accessories. . . .

[B]ecause of the industrial and railroad purposes to which the immediately adjoining lands to the south and east have been devoted and for which they are zoned, the locus is of comparatively little value for the limited uses permitted by the ordinance. . . .

An inspection of a plat of the city upon which the zoning districts are outlined, taken in connection with the [trial court's] findings, shows with reasonable cer-

tainty that the inclusion of the locus in question is not indispensable to the general plan. The boundary line of the residential district before reaching the locus runs for some distance along the streets, and to exclude the locus from the residential district requires only that such line shall be continued 100 feet further. . . . There does not appear to be any reason why this should not be done. Nevertheless, if that were all, we should not be warranted in substituting our judgment for that of the zoning authorities primarily charged with the duty and responsibility of determining the question. . . . But that is not all. The governmental power to interfere by zoning regulations with the general rights of the land owner by restricting the character of his use, is not unlimited, and, other questions aside, such restriction cannot be imposed if it does not bear a substantial relation to the public health, safety, morals, or general welfare. . . . Here, the express finding of the . . . court below, is that the health, safety, convenience, and general welfare of the inhabitants of the part of the city affected will not be promoted by the disposition made by the ordinance of the locus in question. This finding . . . after a hearing and an inspection of the entire area affected, supported, as we think it is, by other findings of fact, is determinative of the case. That the invasion of . . . [Nectow's] property . . . was serious and highly injurious is clearly established; and, since a necessary basis for the support of that invasion is wanting, the action of the zoning authorities comes within the ban of the Fourteenth Amendment and cannot be sustained.

[Judgment reversed.]

State courts, following *Nectow,* continue to test the validity of zoning regulations as applied to particular parcels of land on a case-by-case basis. This approach allows the court to relieve landowners from excessively burdensome restrictions without striking down an entire ordinance. Nevertheless, a zoning ordinance, like all exercises of the police power, usually is given a strong presumption of validity. That is, courts ordinarily defer to the legislative judgment that the particular regulation bears a substantial relationship to the public health, morals, safety, or welfare.

Objectives of Zoning

To avoid constitutional objections, all zoning regulation must be based upon a comprehensive plan. The

_____
[8]47 S. Ct. 114 (1926).

comprehensive plan is an overall program for the future physical development of an area, including furnishing city services, such as streets, mass transit, sewers, and police and fire protection. Responsibility for the comprehensive plan ordinarily rests with the city zoning or planning commission. In addition to formulating the plan, zoning commissions study and determine the community's zoning needs and necessary changes, give notice and hold hearings, and make recommendations to the municipal legislative body.

The comprehensive plan must be consistent with the objectives for which zoning ordinances may be enacted—protecting public health, safety, welfare, and morals. For example, regulations that insure adequate light and air and limit the density of land use (such as building height and lot size restrictions) are designed to protect public health. Regulations aimed at reducing the risk of fire (by restricting the location or existence of gasoline stations or refineries) or street congestion (by regulating the existence of multifamily dwellings in single-family residential districts and the location of shopping centers, hospitals, and public facilities) are justified on grounds of public safety. Aesthetic zoning, or zoning to enhance community appearance, is justified as promoting the general welfare. Included under this heading are regulation of junkyards and mobile homes, and zoning to preserve open spaces and historical districts and buildings. Ordinances regulating the location of adult bookstores and theaters by dispersing them throughout allowable districts or concentrating them into one district are attempts to protect public morals and property values of nearby residences and businesses.

Altering the Zoning Plan

Zoning enabling statutes require that zoning regulations be uniform for each class or kind of building throughout each district. The uniform operation of zoning classifications may be reduced by various devices, including nonconforming uses, amendments, variances, and special permits. These devices, if frequently used, can defeat the essential purpose of comprehensive land use planning.

Nonconforming Uses. When a zoning ordinance is enacted, it affects both previously developed land and undeveloped land. Invariably, certain developed property is used for purposes prohibited by the new ordinance, such as a drugstore in a newly established residential zone. In this case, the affected property is known as a **nonconforming use,** meaning that it does not conform to the current restrictions on the zoned area, but lawfully existed when the ordinance went into effect and has continued in existence since that time.

Zoning ordinances usually permit nonconforming uses to continue, thereby reducing both political opposition to the passage of the ordinance and the likelihood that a court will find the ordinance unconstitutional as a deprivation of property without due process of law. The ordinance may permit the nonconforming use to continue indefinitely or may require that it be amortized and gradually eliminated within a specified period of time.

Amendments. The local legislative body, which enacted the zoning ordinance, may alter the plan by amendment. Amendments commonly take one of two forms: reclassification of property to a different zone known as **rezoning,** or changes made in the uses allowed in a particular zone. Amendments must be enacted in accordance with the comprehensive plan. If not, they may be challenged in court as invalid spot zoning. **Spot zoning** occurs when a zoning amendment classifies a single property or group of properties within a district to a use that is inconsistent with the general zoning pattern of the surrounding area, and is designed primarily for the economic benefit of the owner.

Variances. Zoning amendments involve a legislative change in the ordinance. In addition, zoning ordinances usually provide for administrative relief—for example, from a zoning board of appeals, zoning board of review, or board of adjustment—by allowing an adversely affected landowner to apply for a variance or special permit under certain circumstances. **Variances,** which are designed to prevent rigidity, are of two general types: use variances, which permit a different use than that authorized by ordinance, and area variances, which permit modification of area, yard, height, setback, or similar restrictions. An area variance is less disruptive of the zoning plan because it does not threaten neighboring property with an incompatible use, and is therefore more often granted.

Special Permits. Another type of administrative remedy that adds flexibility to the zoning ordinance is the **special permit,** also known as a "special use permit," "special exception," or "conditional use." Unlike the variance, which authorizes a use prohibited by the ordinance, special permits allow a landowner to use her land in a manner expressly *permitted* by the ordinance, provided that the owner meets certain conditions and standards set forth in the zoning regulations. A major function of the administrative zoning board is to hear and act on applications for special permits. Special permits are used, for example, to control: uses posing safety, traffic, or noise problems to neighboring property; uses that are necessary but incompatible within a specific zone; and facilities customarily located in residential zones that attract large numbers of people. Uses commonly allowed by special permit include gas stations, parking lots, churches, schools, parks, utility substations, funeral homes, and certain recreational uses such as bowling alleys or golf courses.

Introduction to Eminent Domain

Increasingly in recent years, private property has been required by local, state, and federal government for public purposes such as community facilities, housing, highways, airports, schools, public utilities, and a host of other public needs. The power, inherent in a sovereign, to take, or authorize the taking of, private property for public use without the owner's consent upon making just compensation is known as **eminent domain.**[9] Use of eminent domain power is authorized by act of the legislature. The power may be exercised by the federal or state legislature itself or may be delegated to a municipal corporation or other governmental subdivision or public corporation, or in some cases, to a private corporation or individual, such as a railroad or utility.

The eminent domain power is inherent in the power of the sovereign to enact laws affecting persons or property within its jurisdiction. Like all governmental action, however, the eminent domain power is subject to restrictions imposed by the U.S. Constitution. State governments also are bound by individual state constitutions. The federal Constitution contains two provisions limiting the eminent domain power. The last clause of the Fifth Amendment states:

> . . . nor shall private property be taken for public use, without just compensation.

The various state constitutions contain similar language. For example, the constitution of Illinois (1970) provides:

> Private property shall not be taken or damaged for public use without just compensation as provided by law.

Both the Fifth Amendment (applicable by its terms to action of the federal government) and the Fourteenth Amendment (applicable by its terms to the states) also contain a "due process" clause providing that no person shall be deprived of

> . . . life, liberty, or *property,* without due process of law . . . (Emphasis added.)

The term "due process" means that before a person may be deprived of life, liberty, or property, he must be afforded notice of the potential deprivation and a hearing relevant to the nature of the case.

By placing the Eminent Domain and Due Process clauses together, the procedure and issues in eminent domain are highlighted. If the government or governmental agency desires property for a public use, such as an interstate highway, it will offer to buy the property for a stated price from the owner. If the owner refuses to sell at the price offered and subsequent negotiations do not result in agreement, the government initiates a legal action, known as a **condemnation proceeding,** to exercise its eminent domain power. The government or governmental agency seeking condemnation is the "condemnor," and the person whose property is to be taken, or condemned, is the "condemnee." The condemnation proceeding is necessary to satisfy the requirements of due process that the owner be afforded notice and a hearing before his property is taken. The issues decided in that hearing are dictated by the Eminent Domain Clause of the Constitution: (1) is there a *taking,* (2) is the taking for a *public use,* and (3) if the taking is for a public use, how much money is necessary to provide *just compensation* to the owner whose property is taken? The answers to these questions form the major issues in eminent domain cases.

A condemnation proceeding is unlike an ordinary lawsuit because the government, the party initiating the suit (the plaintiff), is required to pay damages (just compensation). Ordinarily the plaintiff seeks to recover damages from the defendant. In an **inverse condemnation** proceeding, however, the property owner initiates the suit. The premise in inverse condemnation is that, although the sovereign has in fact taken private property

---

[9]The term "eminent domain" apparently originated in 1625 with the Dutch statesman, Hugo Grotius, who commented that the property of individual citizens is under the "eminent domain" of the state so that the state or its representative may transfer or destroy it. Although the power to take private property for public use is now generally considered to be based upon the sovereignty of the state, the term "eminent domain" has been accepted in this country to describe the power.

for public use, it has done so without resort to a formal condemnation procedure and without compensation. Inverse condemnation therefore represents an alternative method to recover compensation in the absence of the usual formal procedure initiated by the government.

A Taking

The heart of the eminent domain power is a taking of private property by the sovereign for public use. Compensation is required whether the taking is total or partial, and whether a fee simple or lesser interest, such as an easement, is appropriated. The existence of a taking is apparent when the owner is actually deprived of possession. For example, the state may condemn a portion of privately owned farmland in order to construct a highway or public building. A taking also may occur without formally divesting the owner of title to or possession of the property. For example, the construction of a ditch, drain, fence, or elevated railway over property is a taking because the usefulness, though not necessarily possession, of the property is impaired. Furthermore, a law that limits the height of buildings near a public park in order to preserve its beauty appropriates for public use an interest in the adjoining property (an easement) requiring compensation.

Examples of takings are endless and ever-expanding. Therefore, courts cannot determine whether compensation is constitutionally required under the Eminent Domain Clause by applying mechanical rules that are readily applicable to all cases. Each case must be decided on its own merits until the courts, by the gradual process of inclusion and exclusion, determine which injuries to private property rights must be compensated. A substantial body of case law at both the federal and state levels already exists to aid the property owner or her attorney in making this determination.

Exercise of "Police Power" Compared. Not every governmental interference with the possession, use, or enjoyment of private property is compensable under the Eminent Domain Clause. In fact, most governmental restriction concerning private property, such as zoning, is constitutionally valid *without compensation* as an exercise of the sovereign's police power. The fundamental distinction between the eminent domain and the police power is that in eminent domain, an interest in the property is *taken* from the owner and applied to a use beneficial to the public. In contrast, the police power does not appro-

priate private property for public use, but simply *regulates* its use and enjoyment by the owner to prevent use in a manner detrimental to the public interest.

The following case outlines the principles governing the distinction between regulation and taking.

Lingle v. Chevron U.S.A. Inc.
125 S.Ct. 2074 (2005)

Plaintiff Chevron U.S.A. Inc. (Chevron) refines and markets gasoline in Hawaii. Chevron sells most of its products through service stations that it owns but rents to independent dealers (called lessee-dealer stations). Typically, Chevron buys or leases land from a third party, builds the service station and then leases it to a dealer charging a monthly rent based on a percentage of the dealer's sales. In 1997, in an effort to control the effect of market concentration in the retail gasoline industry on gasoline prices, Hawaii enacted a statute regulating lessee-dealer stations. The statute, which protects independent dealers in several ways, limits the amount of rent that an oil company may charge lessee-dealers. After calculating that the rent cap would reduce the amount of rent that it charged eleven of its dealers by about $207,000, Chevron sued Linda Lingle, the Governor of Hawaii, claiming that the statute violated the U.S. Constitution. Chevron argued that the rent cap was a taking of its property in violation of the Fifth and Fourteenth Amendments. The trial court ruled in favor of Chevron holding that the statute was an unconstitutional taking of property because it did not substantially advance Hawaii's goal of controlling retail gas prices. After the Ninth Circuit Court of Appeals affirmed, the U.S. Supreme Court granted certiorari.

Justice O'Connor

. . . The Takings Clause of the Fifth Amendment, made applicable to the States through the Fourteenth . . . provides that private property shall not "be taken for public use, without just compensation." As its text makes plain, the Takings Clause "does not prohibit the taking of private property, but instead places a condition on the exercise of that power." *First English Evangelical Lutheran Church of Glendale v. County of Los Angeles,* [107 S. Ct. 2378, 2385 (1987)]. In other words, it "is designed not to limit the governmental interference with property rights *per se,* but rather to secure *compensation* in the event of otherwise proper interference amounting to a taking."

[Id. at 2385-85] (emphasis in original). While scholars have offered various justifications for this regime, we have emphasized its role in "barring Government from forcing some people alone to bear public burdens which, in all fairness and justice, should be borne by the public as a whole." *Armstrong v. United States,* [80 S. Ct. 1563, 1569 (1960).]. . . .

The paradigmatic taking requiring just compensation is a direct government appropriation or physical invasion of private property. . . . Indeed, until the Court's watershed decision in *Pennsylvania Coal Co. v. Mahon,* [43 S. Ct. 158 (1922)], "it was generally thought that the Takings Clause reached only a direct appropriation of property, or the functional equivalent of a practical ouster of [the owner's] possession." *Lucas v. South Carolina Coastal Council,* [112 S. Ct. 2886, 2892 (1992)]. "[E]arly constitutional theorists did not believe the Takings Clause embraced regulations of property at all." [*Id.* at 2900, n.15.]

Beginning with Mahon, however, the Court recognized that government regulation of private property may, in some instances, be so onerous that its effect is tantamount to a direct appropriation or ouster—and that such "regulatory takings" may be compensable under the Fifth Amendment. In Justice Holmes' storied but cryptic formulation, "while property may be regulated to a certain extent, if regulation goes too far it will be recognized as a taking." [43 S. Ct. 158, 160.] The rub, of course, has been—and remains—how to discern how far is "too far." In answering that question, we must remain cognizant that "government regulation—by definition—involves the adjustment of rights for the public good," *Andrus v. Allard,* [100 S. Ct. 318, 326 (1979)], and that "Government hardly could go on if to some extent values incident to property could not be diminished without paying for every such change in the general law," [*Pennsylvania Coal Co. v. Mahon,* 43 S. Ct. 158, 159 (1922)].

Our precedents stake out two categories of regulatory action that generally will be deemed per se takings for Fifth Amendment purposes. First, where government requires an owner to suffer a permanent physical invasion of her property—however minor—it must provide just compensation. See *Loretto v. Teleprompter Manhattan CATV Corp.,* [102 S. Ct. 3164 (1982)] (state law requiring landlords to permit cable companies to install cable facilities in apartment buildings effected a taking). A second categorical rule applies to regulations that completely deprive an owner of "*all* economically

beneficial use" of her property. [*Lucas v. South Carolina Coastal Council,* [112 S. Ct. 2886, 2895 (1992)] (emphasis in original). . . .

Outside these two relatively narrow categories . . . regulatory takings challenges are governed by the standards set forth in *Penn Central Transp. Co. v. New York City,* [98 S. Ct. 2646 (1978)]. The Court in *Penn Central* acknowledged that it had hitherto been "unable to develop any 'set formula'" for evaluating regulatory takings claims, but identified "several factors that have particular significance." [*Id.* at 2659.] Primary among those factors are "the economic impact of the regulation on the claimant and, particularly, the extent to which the regulation has interfered with distinct investment-backed expectations." *Id.* In addition, the "character of the governmental action"— for instance whether it amounts to a physical invasion or instead merely affects property interests through "some public program adjusting the benefits and burdens of economic life to promote the common good"—may be relevant in discerning whether a taking has occurred. *Id.* The *Penn Central* factors . . . have served as the principal guidelines for resolving regulatory takings claims that do not fall within the physical takings or *Lucas* rules. . . .

[T]hese three inquiries (reflected in *Loretto, Lucas,* and *Penn Central*) share a common touch-stone. Each aims to identify regulatory actions that are functionally equivalent to the classic taking in which government directly appropriates private property or ousts the owner from his domain. Accordingly, each of these tests focuses directly upon the severity of the burden that government imposes upon private property rights. The Court has held that physical takings require compensation because of the unique burden they impose: A permanent physical invasion, however minimal the economic cost it entails, eviscerates the owner's right to exclude others from entering and using her property—perhaps the most fundamental of all property interests. . . . In the *Lucas* context, of course, the complete elimination of a property's value is the determinative factor. . . . And the *Penn Central* inquiry turns in large part, albeit not exclusively, upon the magnitude of a regulation's economic impact and the degree to which it interferes with legitimate property interests. . . .

A quarter century ago, in *Agins v. City of Tiburon,* [100 S. Ct. 2138, 2141 (1980)], the Court declared that government regulation of private property "effects a taking if [such regulation] does not substantially advance legitimate state interests . . . ." Through reiteration in a half dozen or so decision since *Agins,* this language has been ensconced in our Fifth Amendment takings jurisprudence. . . .

In the case before us, the lower courts applied *Agins'* "substantially advances" formula to strike down a Hawaii statute that limits the rent that oil companies may charge to dealers who lease service stations owned by the companies. The lower courts held that the rent cap effects an uncompensated taking of private property in violation of the Fifth and Fourteenth Amendments because it does not substantially advance Hawaii's asserted interest in controlling retail gasoline prices. This case requires us to decide whether the "substantially advances" formula announced in *Agins* is an appropriate test for determining whether a regulation effects a Fifth Amendment taking. We conclude that it is not.

. . . Although a number of our takings precedents have recited the "substantially advances" formula minted in *Agins,* this is our first opportunity to consider its validity as a freestanding takings test. We conclude that this formula prescribes an inquiry in the nature of a due process, not a takings, test, and that it has no proper place in our takings jurisprudence. . . . Although *Agins'* reliance on due process precedents is understandable, the language the Court selected was regrettably imprecise. The "substantially advances" formula suggests a means-ends test: It asks, in essence, whether a regulation of private property is *effective* in achieving some legitimate public purpose. An inquiry of this nature has some logic in the context of a due process challenge, for a regulation that fails to serve any legitimate governmental objective may be so arbitrary or irrational that it runs afoul of the Due Process Clause. . . . But such a test is not a valid method of discerning whether private property has been "taken" for purposes of the Fifth Amendment.

In stark contrast to the three regulatory takings tests discussed above, the "substantially advances" inquiry reveals nothing about the *magnitude or character of the burden* a particular regulation imposes upon private property rights. Nor does it provide any information about how any regulatory burden is *distributed* among property owners. In consequence, this test does not help to identify those regulations whose effects are functionally comparable to government appropriation or invasion of private property; it is tethered neither to the text of the Takings Clause nor to the basic justification for

allowing regulatory actions to be challenged under the Clause. . . .

We hold that the "substantially advances" formula is not a valid takings test, and indeed conclude that it has no proper place in our takings jurisprudence. In so doing, we reaffirm that a plaintiff seeking to challenge a government regulation as an uncompensated taking of private property may proceed under one of the other theories discussed above—by alleging a "physical" taking, a *Lucas*-type "total regulatory taking," [or] a *Penn Central* taking. . . .

[Judgment reversed and remanded.]

Public Use

Private property may be taken by eminent domain only for public uses. That is, the Constitution forbids a governmental appropriation of private property for purely or predominantly private purposes. As with the term "taking," a comprehensive definition of "public use" necessarily evolves on a case-by-case basis through judicial inclusion and exclusion. In addition, the character, commercial development of land in the region, and local conditions frequently determine which uses are public. In other words, the various states, by judicial decision and constitutional provision, define "public" differently based upon the history and the particular needs and problems of the region.

Although no comprehensive definition covers all cases, three general classes of uses emerge as public. The first class includes government buildings, libraries, schools, museums, highways, airports, parks, bridges, subways, public parking lots, sewage treatment plants, public housing, and urban redevelopment. The second class includes private property taken for the benefit of a railroad for its roadbed or for a utility, such as a telephone or power company, to run lines or cables. The third class includes uses that, though essentially private, are recognized as public on historical grounds or because of abnormal local conditions. For example, in some states mining, logging, or irrigation is vital to the economic welfare of the state, and is treated as public for eminent domain purposes; in other states, eminent domain power could not be used for these purposes because of the private use involved.

Just Compensation

An owner whose property is taken by eminent domain is entitled, under both the federal and state constitutions, to receive just compensation.[10] The constitutional prohibition against uncompensated taking serves as a limitation on the exercise of eminent domain power and is designed to prevent the injustice that results if benefits are conferred upon the public at the expense of an individual property owner. The condemnor satisfies the compensation requirement by paying to the condemnee a sum of money equivalent to the loss sustained.

Just compensation generally equals the fair market value[11] of the property taken on the date of the taking. In the case of a partial taking, just compensation equals the depreciation in value of the land remaining. The amount of compensation is a judicial, not a legislative question. The trier of fact, which in most states is the court (judge) sitting without a jury, determines just compensation based upon the testimony presented.[12]

Evidence of value usually is provided by testimony of professional appraisers. These experts are hired by the respective parties and often give widely varying opinions concerning the value of the property. Generally, neither the property owner's attorneys' fees nor payments to appraisers acting as expert witnesses are taken into account in computing the award.

The owner is compensated for the land and not for the loss of its particular use. Under the general common law rule, therefore, the owner generally is not entitled to recover for the value of any business conducted on the property or loss of goodwill. This approach, though failing to compensate an important element of the owner's damage, is justified on the grounds that the owner's property, not the right to conduct a business, is taken by the sovereign. Some states have statutes specifically authorizing recovery for the going concern value of a business in eminent domain cases. Other states, which follow the common law rule, recognize exceptions to its application.

Federal Relocation Assistance and Land Acquisition Policy

In recent years, the federal government, acting on its own behalf or by providing funds to various state governments, has become increasingly involved in major public works projects requiring exercise of eminent domain power. Projects such as the interstate highway program, public housing, and urban renewal have required an unprecedented taking of private property, displacing vast numbers of people, often in densely populated urban areas. In order to provide for uniform and equitable treatment of persons displaced from their homes, businesses, and farms by federal and federally assisted programs, and to establish uniform and equitable land acquisition policies for these programs, Congress passed the **Uniform Relocation Assistance and Real Property Acquisition Policies Act** in 1970.[13]

The Act provides relocation assistance to persons who are forced to move from real property because the property is acquired for a program or project undertaken by a federal agency or with federal financial assistance. The assistance takes one of three general forms: (1) moving expenses for persons occupying the property as a dwelling, (2) compensation for moving or other expenses relating to a business or farming operation conducted on the property taken, and (3) payments for replacement housing for owners and tenants. The Act also establishes a uniform land acquisition policy to guide federal agencies (and state agencies acting with federal assistance) in acquiring land for public projects. The policy provisions are designed to encourage real property acquisition by agreement rather than litigation, to assure consistent treatment of property owners affected by the many federal programs, and to promote public confidence in federal land acquisition practices.[14]

---

[10]Even in the absence of an explicit eminent domain clause, just compensation for public taking would undoubtedly be required as an essential element of due process.

[11]Though "fair market value" is defined in various ways, the term generally means the amount of money that a willing purchaser would pay to a willing owner considering all uses for which the land is suited or might be applied.

[12]Many states, however, require by constitutional provision that the value of property taken by eminent domain be ascertained by a jury in all or certain types of cases.

---

[13]42 U.S.C. §§4601–4655.

[14]42 U.S.C. §4651.

Summary

1.   An owner's right to possess, use, and enjoy land may be limited by private agreement or by act of public authority. Land use may be regulated privately either by creating a limited interest of use (an easement) in the property itself or by contract. The government also may impose land use restrictions through exercise of its police power and its eminent domain power.

2.   An easement is an interest in land giving its owner the right either to use the land of another for a limited and specified purpose, or to prevent the other from doing something otherwise lawful upon his or her land. Easements may be obtained for the benefit of land owned by the easement holder (an easement appurtenant) or the right of use may exist independently of the holder's ownership of any land (an easement in gross). Easements may be created by express act of the parties, implication, prescription, and eminent domain. Like most other property interests, easements are freely transferable. Although the duration of an easement is often indefinite, easements may terminate by their terms (expiration) or may be extinguished by events, such as an abandonment, occurring after creation.

3.   Not every privilege to use another's land is an easement. Privileges of use that lack the formalities necessary to create an interest in land result in a license. A license, unlike an easement, is freely revocable by the property owner granting it.

4.   Land use may be regulated privately by contract as well as conveyance. Promises concerning land use, usually known as "covenants," may require a landowner to do something on his or her land, such as maintain a fence. More commonly, covenants are negative or restrictive, limiting the permissible uses of the land or the acts that may be performed upon it. Restrictive covenants often are used in residential subdivisions to maintain property values and preserve residential character.

5.   Covenants governing land use usually are created upon conveyance of the land and are generally imposed by the grantor to limit the grantee's use of the land. If the property is transferred later, the liability to perform the covenant or the right to take advantage of it passes to the transferee of the property (the covenant "runs with the land") if certain criteria are met. Once created, a covenant may terminate according to its own terms, by vote of all or a portion of the affected landowners, or by subsequent events such as changed neighborhood conditions.

6.   The law of zoning is perhaps the most common exercise of the state police power affecting rights in real property. Zoning is the process by which a municipality regulates the permissible uses of property and the physical configuration of land within its jurisdiction. Zoning ordinances usually divide land into zones or districts, permitting only certain uses within each zone. The ordinance must be adopted pursuant to a comprehensive plan of development. The plan may be altered thereafter by permitting nonconforming uses, rezoning partic-

ular parcels, and allowing variances. In addition, uses may be authorized by special permit.

7.   Through its eminent domain power, the sovereign may take private property for a public use, such as a road, park, or public building. If the parties are unable to agree to a voluntary sale, the government may initiate a condemnation proceeding to force a conveyance of the property. To satisfy constitutional requirements, however, the owner must be paid just compensation for the property that is involuntarily transferred. In addition, federal law provides for relocation expenses for persons displaced by federal or federally funded projects.

Key Terms

easement
profit (profit à prendre)
easement appurtenant
easement in gross
prescription
license
affirmative covenant
negative (restrictive) covenant
covenants running with
   the land
equitable servitude
zoning
Standard State Zoning
   Enabling Act

nonconforming use
rezoning
spot zoning
variance
special permit
eminent domain
condemnation proceeding
inverse condemnation
Uniform Relocation
   Assistance and Real
   Property Acquisition
   Policies Act

Questions and Problems

38.1   This chapter discusses various methods of regulating or restricting land use. Should the law generally favor restrictions on land use? For what purposes are private restrictions, such as easements and restrictive covenants, imposed? For what purposes are public restrictions, such as zoning ordinances and takings by eminent domain, imposed? What criteria do courts employ in determining the validity of private restrictions? Do these differ from those used to judge public restrictions?

38.2   Efficient Company, Inc. constructed a new office building heated only by solar energy. Ten years later, an adjoining landowner began construction of a new high-rise office building. Efficient realized that the new building would block the sun and make the solar heating system inoperable. Efficient sues to enjoin construction of the building.
   (a) Efficient argues that it has obtained a prescriptive easement in the area over the neighbor's land. Should the court grant the injunction?
   (b) What steps might Efficient have taken to better protect itself?

38.3 The ABC Shipping Co. owns a large tract of land near the riverfront in St. Louis. The city has proposed to create several new, wide streets in the area to relieve traffic congestion. A city official meets with the president of ABC concerning acquiring part of ABC's land for a new street. Because the street will benefit ABC's property, the president has no objection to relinquishing some of the land to the city for street purposes. The land to be sold, however, would be useful in any future expansion of ABC's businesses at the site. The president, therefore, desires assurance that if the proposed streets are not built, ABC may reacquire the property for use in its business. Offer some suggestions concerning how the assurance could be accomplished.

38.4 Rock Promotions, Inc. owns a large theater that it uses for rock concerts. Fred Stone buys a ticket from Rock Promotions and attends a concert. Soon after the performance begins, several members of the audience sitting near Fred become rowdy and unruly. Two employees of Rock Promotions eject not only the unruly people but also Fred. When Fred complains, a Rock Promotions employee says that the company has the right to revoke Fred's ticket at will. Is the employee correct? What type of legal relationship is created between the owner of a theater or arena and the holder of a ticket to an event held on the property?

38.5 In each of the following cases, the court must decide whether the restrictive covenant should be enforced. How should the court rule? Explain.
(a) Plaintiffs own a lot in the Myers Park subdivision, an area developed pursuant to a common plan in 1950. The deeds to all of the lots provide that each lot shall be used only for residential purposes. In 1954, all of the property owners signed an agreement allowing construction of a library on one lot. In 1970, an apartment building was built on one lot. In 1975, a bank branch office was opened in a house located on one lot. The remaining 30 lots are improved with single-family dwellings. Much of the surrounding neighborhood is commercial property. Plaintiffs want to build an office building and allege that the restrictive covenant should not be enforced.
(b) Defendants own property in the Sun and Fun Subdivision, a residential community in Florida developed pursuant to a common plan. The deeds to all of the lots in the subdivision contain a covenant that provides that all homeowners agree that no child under the age of 21 shall be a permanent resident. Bob and Marylou, a married couple, bought a house in the subdivision and five years later, Marylou unexpectedly became pregnant. The day that she arrived home from the hospital with the baby, the other homeowners delivered a letter requesting that Bob, Marylou, and the baby vacate the premises to comply with the covenant. Bob and Marylou sue to have the covenant lifted.
(c) At the time that Valley Subdivision was created, a Subdivision Declaration, including several restrictive covenants, was recorded. The Declaration provided that each lot must include a single-family residence and that all structures on the lots must be at least 25 feet from the

lot lines. The Declaration further stated, "These covenants are an obligation and benefit for each and every lot and shall run with the land." Under the Declaration, the lot owners in the subdivision elected a Control Committee that was responsible for approving construction within the subdivision. Lindsey purchased lot 23 in Valley Subdivision and submitted plans to build only a garage and workshop that would extend within ten feet of the lot lines. The Control Committee approved Lindsey's plans and he began building the structure. Morris, who owns lot 24, sued Lindsey seeking an injunction that would require Lindsey to comply with the restrictive covenants. Lindsey argues that because the Control Committee approved the plans, compliance with the restrictive covenants is unnecessary.

38.6 Peaceville is a city that prides itself on being a quiet and safe place to live. Donald purchased two acres of land in Peaceville, where he planned to construct a low-income housing project. Because the land was zoned for single-family residences only, Donald applied to the Peaceville zoning commission to have the property rezoned for multifamily dwellings. The city refused to rezone and Donald sued.
(a) At the trial Donald offers in evidence the minutes of the zoning commission meeting containing several statements from commission members that they were opposed to the rezoning because it would lead to an influx of "minorities and other undesirables." How should the court rule?
(b) Assume instead that there are no minutes of the zoning commission meeting. Nevertheless, Donald offers evidence to show that many potential residents of the housing project are minority members. Donald argues that the refusal has the effect of discriminating on the basis of race. How should the court rule? Explain.

38.7 The city of Detroit sought to obtain 465 acres of land within a residential area of the city known as Poletown. After obtaining the property, the city intended to sell it to General Motors Corporation as the site for a new automobile assembly plant. Although the city was willing to pay the fair market value for the property, many Poletown residents opposed the project because they would lose their homes. The city, however, believed the project would help to alleviate the 18 percent unemployment rate in Detroit. A group of Poletown residents sued the city alleging that it had misused its powers of eminent domain by taking property for a private rather than public use. How should the court decide the case? Explain.

38.8 In 1990, Buck Construction Co. purchased 60 acres of farmland with the intention of developing a subdivision. Buck subdivided the property into numbered lots and began preparing the lots for construction. After workers found some human bones on lot 15, the state archaeologist determined that the lot contained Native American burial mounds and ordered that no construction be allowed on the lot. A state statute, adopted in 1978, provides for protection and preservation of ancient burial grounds and allows the state archaeologist to prohibit any construction or land use that would destroy burial grounds. Buck sued the state demanding just compensation on the grounds that the state statute, as implemented by the state archaeologist, constituted a taking of its property. How should the court rule? Explain.

38.9 Betty Potter bought a lot on Spring Road where she built a franchised Burger King restaurant. The franchise contract with Burger King, which specified the size of the parking lot and required construction of a drive-through facility, allowed the restaurant to be moved to a new location if these requirements could not be met. Several years later, the city decided to widen Spring Road and, using its eminent domain power, condemned a 20-foot-wide strip of land parallel to the road that included part of Potter's lot. Because of the reduction in the size of the lot, Potter had inadequate space to meet the parking lot and drive-through requirements of the franchise contract. The city offered to pay Potter $400,000 (the value of the property before the taking minus the value of the property after the taking) as compensation for the taking of the property. According to the city's valuation experts, the best use of the lot continued to be a fast-food restaurant and the property was suitable for restaurants other than Burger King franchises. Potter asserted that she was entitled to compensation of $1 million, which included the full value of the land and the "going concern value" of the restaurant. She argued that because she no longer could operate the Burger King restaurant on the property, she was entitled to payment for the goodwill or going concern value. How should the court rule? Explain.

DECEDENTS' ESTATES AND TRUSTS

Property law is primarily the study of the ownership and transfer of legally recognized property interests. Earlier chapters have focused upon transfers by an owner through sale or gift. This chapter examines two additional methods of transferring either real or personal property interests: wills and intestate succession statutes, which transfer property upon an owner's death; and trusts, which may be used to transfer property either during or after the owner's life.

Introduction to Transfers on Death

Methods of Transfer

For purposes of transfers made on death, a person (the "decedent") may die in one of two ways, testate or intestate. A person who leaves a valid will directing the disposition of her property dies **testate.** A **will** is simply a formal instrument by which a person makes a disposition of her property to take effect after death. A person making the will is known as a **testator.** A transfer of property through a will is known as a **testamentary disposition.** A person who (1) fails to leave a will, (2) fails to leave a "valid" will (the requirements of which are discussed later in this chapter), or (3) leaves a valid will that does not dispose of all of the testator's property dies intestate. If a valid will fails to dispose of all the testator's property, the decedent dies partially testate and partially **intestate.** If a person dies intestate, her property is distributed to persons known as "heirs" according to rules provided in state **intestate succession statutes.**

Estates and Estate Administration

On a person's death, an **estate** is created, which includes all property, real and personal, tangible and intangible, owned by the decedent. The administration of a decedent's estate is within the jurisdiction of the **probate court.** A probate court has two major functions. First, assuming the decedent leaves a will, the court must determine whether it complies with the statutory requirements. Second, the court supervises the administration of the estate. Estate administration includes locating and collecting the decedent's assets; ascertaining and paying taxes, funeral expenses, and other creditors' claims against the estate; and distributing the remaining assets according to the terms of the will or intestate succession statute. Though literally referring only to the first function (to probate or prove the will), the term **probate** generally is used to refer to any matter or proceeding pertaining to the administration of a decedent's estate. A decedent's estate is probated in the state in which the decedent was domiciled at the time of death. **Domicile** generally refers to a person's permanent residence to which he intends to return.

Although the court supervises the administration of the estate, the **executor** (female, **executrix**) has actual responsibility for discovery, collection, and distribution of the decedent's assets and payment of lawful claims and taxes against the estate. The executor often is named by the testator in the will. Nevertheless, the named executor must be appointed or authorized by the probate court to serve in that capacity. If the testator leaves a will that does not name an executor, or if the named executor is deceased, incompetent, or refuses to serve, the court appoints an administrator "c.t.a." (short for *cum testamento annexo* meaning "with the will annexed"). In an intestate estate, the court appoints an **administrator** (female, **administratrix**) to perform the functions outlined previously. The formal instruments issued by the court appointing and authorizing the executor or administrator to act are known as "letters testamentary" or "letters of administration" respectively. Executors and administrators are known as "personal representatives" of the estate.

The executor is entitled to compensation for his duties and may be a beneficiary (even a principal beneficiary) under the will. The executor is, however, a *fiduciary* with respect to the estate and, in dealing with its assets, must observe the same standards that would be followed by a prudent person dealing with the property of another.[1]

Each state has enacted a "probate act" or "probate code." These statutes contain, for example, the requirements of a valid will and a plan of intestate succession.

They also prescribe rules of estate administration, relating to the duties, qualifications, and appointment of executors and administrators, notification of creditors, time limits within which creditors' claims must be filed, the priority for payment of claims against the estate, and the manner of ultimate distribution of the remaining assets and closing the estate.

Probate statutes vary widely from state to state. In an effort to modernize probate law and provide greater uniformity among the states, the National Conference of Commissioners on Uniform State Laws has drafted a **Uniform Probate Code (UPC).** Completed in 1969 and later substantially revised, the UPC has now been enacted in approximately one-third of the states.

In the following case, the U.S. Supreme Court discusses administration of a probate estate and notification of creditors with claims against the estate.

Tulsa Professional Collection Services, Inc. v. Pope
108 S. Ct. 1340 (1988)

> Following five months of hospitalization at St. John Medical Center, H. Everett Pope, Jr. died testate on April 2, 1979. At the time of his death, Pope owed St. John Medical Center for the costs of his medical care. Pope's wife, appellee JoAnne Pope, initiated probate proceedings and was appointed executrix of the estate. As required by Oklahoma statute, the executrix published a notice beginning on July 17, 1979, and continuing for two consecutive weeks in the *Tulsa Daily Legal News* that advised creditors that they must file any claims against the estate within two months. St. John Medical Center did not file a claim against the estate within the two-month period, but in 1983 appellant Tulsa Professional Collection Services, Inc., a subsidiary of the hospital responsible for collecting overdue bills, filed a claim with the probate court. The court rejected the claim on the ground that it had not been filed within the statutory claim period. Both the appellate court and state supreme court affirmed. On appeal to the U.S. Supreme Court, Tulsa Professional Collection Services, Inc. argued that the Oklahoma statute violated due process because it failed to require actual notice of probate proceedings to known creditors of a deceased debtor.

Justice O'Connor

. . . Oklahoma's probate code requires creditors to file claims against an estate within a specified time period,

---

[1]The fiduciary concept is discussed in more detail later in this chapter in the material on trusts, and appears in various other contexts throughout this text.

and generally bars untimely claims. . . . Such "nonclaim statutes" are almost universally included in state probate codes. . . . Giving creditors a limited time in which to file claims against the estate serves the State's interest in facilitating the administration and expeditious closing of estates. . . . Most States also provide that creditors are to be notified of the requirement to file claims imposed by the nonclaim statutes solely by publication [in a newspaper]. Indeed, in most jurisdictions it is the publication of notice that triggers the nonclaim statute. The Uniform Probate Code, for example, provides that creditors have 4 months from publication in which to file claims. . . .

Under Oklahoma's probate code, any party interested in the estate may initiate probate proceedings by petitioning the court to have the will proved. . . . The court is then required to set a hearing date on the petition, . . . and to mail notice of the hearing "to all heirs, legatees and devisees, at their places of residence," [Okla. Stat. Title 58, §§25, 26.] If no person appears at the hearing to contest the will, the court may admit the will to probate on the testimony of one of the subscribing witnesses to the will. . . . After the will is admitted to probate, the court must order appointment of an executor or executrix, issuing letters testamentary to the named executor or executrix if that person appears, is competent and qualified, and no objections are made. . . .

Immediately after appointment, the executor or executrix is required to "give notice to the creditors of the deceased." [Okla. Stat. Title 58, §331.] Proof of compliance with this requirement must be filed with the court. . . . This notice is to advise creditors that they must present their claims to the executor or executrix within 2 months of the date of the first publication. As for the method of notice, the statute requires only publication: "[S]uch notice must be published in some newspaper in [the] county once each week for two (2) consecutive weeks." [Okla. Stat. Title 58, §331.] A creditor's failure to file a claim within the 2-month period generally bars it forever. . . .

Appellant's interest is an unsecured claim, a cause of action against the estate for an unpaid bill. Little doubt remains that such an intangible interest is property protected by the Fourteenth Amendment. . . . Appellant's claim, therefore, is properly considered a protected property interest.

The Fourteenth Amendment protects this interest, however, only from a deprivation by state action. Private use of state sanctioned private remedies or procedures does not rise to the level of state action. . . . But when private parties make use of state procedures with the overt, significant assistance of state officials, state action may be found. . . . The question here is whether the State's involvement with the nonclaim statute is substantial enough to implicate the Due Process Clause. . . .

Here . . . there is significant state action. The probate court is intimately involved throughout, and without that involvement the time bar is never activated. The nonclaim statute becomes operative only after probate proceedings have been commenced in state court. The court must appoint the executor or executrix before notice, which triggers the time bar, can be given. Only after this court appointment is made does the statute provide for any notice; §331 directs the executor or executrix to publish notice "immediately" after appointment. . . . Finally, copies of the notice and an affidavit of publication must be filed with the court. . . . It is only after all of these actions take place that the time period begins to run, and in every one of these actions, the court is intimately involved. This involvement is so pervasive and substantial that it must be considered state action subject to the restrictions of the Fourteenth Amendment.

Where the legal proceedings themselves trigger the time bar, . . . due process is directly implicated and actual notice generally is required. . . .

Creditors, who have a strong interest in maintaining the integrity of their relationship with their debtors, are particularly unlikely to benefit from publication notice. As a class, creditors may not be aware of a debtor's death or of the institution of probate proceedings. Moreover, the executor or executrix will often be, as is the case here, a party with a beneficial interest in the estate. This could diminish an executor's or executrix's inclination to call attention to the potential expiration of a creditor's claim. There is thus a substantial practical need for actual notice in this setting.

At the same time, the State undeniably has a legitimate interest in the expeditious resolution of probate proceedings. Death transforms the decedent's legal relationships and a State could reasonably conclude that swift settlement of estates is so important that it calls for very short time deadlines for filing claims. . . . Providing actual notice to known or reasonably ascertainable creditors, however, is not inconsistent with the goals reflected in nonclaim statutes. Actual notice need not be inefficient or burdensome. We have repeatedly recognized that mail service is an inexpensive and efficient mechanism that is reasonably calculated to provide actual notice. . . .

On balance then, a requirement of actual notice to known or reasonably ascertainable creditors is not so cumbersome as to unduly hinder the dispatch with which probate proceedings are conducted. . . .

Whether appellant's identity as a creditor was known or reasonably ascertainable by appellee cannot be answered on this record. . . . If appellant's identity was known or "reasonably ascertainable," then termination of appellant's claim without actual notice violated due process. . . .

[Judgment reversed and remanded.]

Wills and Intestate Succession

Since ancient times, the law has allowed persons to dispose of personal property by will. The ability to transfer real property, however, is a more recent development, derived primarily from the English Statute of Wills,[2] enacted in 1540.

A transfer of real property by will is known as a **devise.** A person receiving a devise is a "devisee." A gift of money by will is known as a **legacy,** received by a "legatee." The term **bequest** describes any form of personal property passing by will and is hence a broader term than "legacy." The UPC abolishes the distinction and treats any disposition by will of either real or personal property as a "devise" and any person designated in the will to receive a devise as a "devisee." For the sake of simplicity, the UPC approach is used in the following material.

Devises of property are commonly classified as specific, general, or demonstrative. A **specific devise** is one of particularly designated property—for example, the testator may leave "my 1955 Chevrolet" or "my house at 203 Elm Street" to X. A **general devise** is a gift payable out of the general assets of the testator's

estate—for example, "I leave $2,000 to Z." A **demonstrative devise** is one payable out of specific property or a specific fund—for example, the testator may leave $1,000 payable "from my savings account at First Federal Savings."

The "Valid" Will

Formalities of Execution. In order to control the disposition of his property after death, a person must leave a valid will. The term "valid" means that the will satisfies all formalities prescribed by state statute. These formalities are designed to prevent fraud, and, as previously indicated, compliance with them is determined by the probate court. The modern trend, evidenced by the UPC provisions, is to simplify the requirements for execution of a valid will, and to validate the will whenever possible, so that more people may use wills to transfer property on death. A few states even have statutory will forms that the testator completes simply by filling in appropriate blanks. Despite these developments, a majority of persons owning property die intestate.

Modern state will statutes are based upon early English statutes, but vary somewhat among the states. Generally, a valid will must be in writing, signed by the testator, and witnessed. Under the UPC, the witnesses must witness either the signing of the will by the testator, an acknowledgment by the testator that the signature is his, or an acknowledgment by the testator that the document is his will. Though only the signature of the witnesses is *required,* wills often contain an **attestation clause** signed by the witnesses, simply reciting that the statutory formalities necessary for proper execution have been observed. An attestation clause aids in subsequently establishing the validity of the will in probate or if contested.

Although the UPC and most other statutes require the signature of only two witnesses, a few states require three. To assure the validity of the will wherever the testator is domiciled on death, the testator should have three witnesses in all cases. Nevertheless, the UPC and many other statutes provide that a will is deemed validly executed if it complies with the law in the state of its execution.

As illustrated in the following case, courts strictly enforce the statutory formalities even if the result may defeat the testator's clear intentions.

---

[2]32 Hen. 8, ch. 1 (1540). Traditionally, a "will" referred only to an instrument transferring real property, whereas a "testament" transferred personal property—hence the term "last will and testament." The term "will," however, now designates a document disposing of both real and personal property interests.

Matter of Will of Daly
402 N.Y.S.2d 747 (N.Y. Surrogate Ct. 1978)

Robert M. Daly, a resident of New York, died leaving an estate of approximately $175,000. Although Daly was married and had three children, he devised most of his property to friends in a will that Daly had prepared without the advice of an attorney.

The evidence established that two of Daly's employees had signed the will as witnesses. Daly's children requested summary judgment denying probate of the will because it had not been executed in accordance with the New York statute that provided:

> The signature of the testator shall be affixed to the will in the presence of each of the attesting witnesses, or shall be acknowledged by the testator to each of them to have been affixed by him or by his direction. The testator may either sign in the presence of, or acknowledge his signature to each attesting witness separately.

In the following opinion, the surrogate court ruled on the admissibility of the will.

Kahn, Surrogate

. . . The pertinent subdivision mandates that the testator's signature be made in the presence of each of the subscribing witnesses, or be acknowledged by him to have been so made. The testator may either sign in their presence or acknowledge his signature to each attesting witness separately. Two facts are essential—that the testator sign his name, and that the witnesses see him sign or that he acknowledges his signature to them. It is not required that the signing or acknowledgment be in the presence of both witnesses at the same time. . . .

It is clear from reading the statute that the procedural formalities called for have not been complied with in the factual setting hereinabove described. What is not clear, however, is how far the courts have gone in allowing deviations from those prescribed procedural formalities, particularly where the instrument in question has not been executed under the auspices of an attorney. Not surprisingly there are numerous precedents which have addressed themselves to just that issue now before the Court. . . .

In summarizing the . . . precedents, it can be stated that where the witnesses cannot recollect the circumstances surrounding the execution of the instru-

ment, the document may be admitted to probate. . . . Given considerable weight in such cases is the length of time elapsing between the execution of the document and its being offered for probate.

Where however there is no question that the testator did not sign his name in the presence of the witness and further failed to acknowledge his signature, then in such a case a motion for Summary Judgment would indeed be appropriate. . . .

The instrument before the Court is dated December 29, 1976. The witnesses' testimony was taken only four (4) months thereafter on May 2, 1977. The first witness has testified that he was not told what he was signing; that the testator did not sign his name in the witness' presence; that the document was so folded that he could not tell whether the testator's signature was on the document and that the testator never acknowledged any signature to him. The testimony of the second witness is equivocal and covers the widest range of possibilities. Alternatively, he testified that the testator's signature was on the document, was not on the document, or that he did not recall whether it was or was not upon the document. In any event, said "signature," was in no way or manner acknowledged by decedent to this witness.

Based on the testimony adduced, as well as the precedents examined, the Court finds that the testator's signature was not acknowledged to either witness as required by statute. . . .

Finally, this Court must note how this proceeding once again points up the disastrous results which can occur when a lay person takes it upon himself to do his own will. In this case, decedent was a young and intelligent person who was knowledgeable in death and estate matters due to his professional status as a funeral director. Nevertheless, his do-it-yourself will did not meet the requirements of law, with the unfortunate result that his intentions as expressed in the purported will were thwarted. The Court cannot ignore this opportunity to warn others to seek professional legal advice and guidance before they execute such a vitally important document as their Last Will and Testament.

A common problem regarding execution arises if a witness is "interested," that is, a beneficiary under the will. Some statutes provide that although an interested witness does not affect the validity of the will, the interested witness's share under the will is limited to whatever she would have received if there had been no will. Other statutes provide that the right of an interested witness to take under the will is unaffected if a sufficient number of disinterested witnesses have signed to satisfy statutory requirements. The UPC provides that neither the will nor any provision is invalidated because it is signed by an interested witness. Thus, under the UPC, the interested witness takes the share outlined in the will.

Age and Capacity Requirements. In addition to formalities of execution, probate statutes impose certain minimum age and capacity requirements. For example, the UPC provides that any person 18 years of age or older who is of sound mind may make a will. The 18-year age requirement, now effective in most states, represents a reduction from the traditional requirement, 21 years.

That the testator be of "sound mind" generally requires that, at the time of execution of the will, she can understand in a general way (1) the nature and extent of her property, (2) the persons who are the natural objects of her bounty, and (3) the disposition that she is making of her property. In addition, the testator must be capable of appreciating these elements in relation to each other and forming an orderly plan regarding the disposition of the property.[3] A person does not lack testamentary capacity merely because she disposes of her property unfairly or excludes persons who are the natural objects of her bounty. The will, however, may be invalidated by proof of fraud or undue influence on the testator.

Nuncupative and Holographic Wills. In some states, the nuncupative will and the holographic will are valid, even though they fail to meet the formalities outlined above. A **nuncupative will** is an *oral* will dictated by the testator during his last illness before a sufficient number of witnesses and later reduced to a writing. Not all states recognize such wills and those that do impose restrictions upon their use. For example, statutes generally limit the amount or type of property that may be transferred and require that the will be reduced to writing within a specified number of days. The nuncupative

will therefore represents a limited exception to the general rule that wills be in writing.

Holographic wills constitute an exception to the requirement that wills be witnessed. **Holographic wills** are those, according to most statutes, written entirely in the handwriting of the testator. Holographic wills are validated without witnesses because the fact that the will is entirely in the testator's handwriting reduces the risk of fraud that the formalities are designed to prevent. Although many states do not recognize the validity of holographic wills, the UPC expressly authorizes their use.

Revocation of Wills

A will is "ambulatory," which means that it takes effect only upon the testator's death and until that time she is free to alter or revoke it. A will may be revoked by physical act, a subsequent writing, or by operation of law.

Revocation by Physical Act. State statutes prescribe specific physical acts that constitute revocation. Under the UPC, a will is revoked by physical act if the will is burned, torn, canceled, obliterated, or destroyed, "with the intent and for the purpose of revoking" it. The UPC also permits *partial* revocation by physical act—the obliteration of a devise by crossing it out. Many states prohibit such partial revocations and instead require a subsequent document complying with the state wills statute to accomplish this result.

Revocation by Subsequent Writing. A will also may be revoked in whole or in part by a written instrument that is itself given testamentary effect because of statutory compliance. This subsequent instrument may be (1) a will, (2) an instrument that revokes the prior will but does not itself dispose of any property, or (3) a codicil. A **codicil** is an addition or supplement to the will that may add to, subtract from, modify, or revoke provisions of an existing will. Ordinarily, it leaves the will intact except for the changes indicated; that is, a codicil generally does not dispose of all of the testator's property or completely revoke the existing will. All of the foregoing instruments are given effect because they comply with the formalities necessary for creation of a valid will generally.

At issue in the following case was whether a will had been revoked.

---

[3]These criteria govern only a person's mental capacity to make a will. A person may have testamentary capacity even though she is under guardianship or has no contractual capacity.

Goode v. Estate of Hoover

828 S.W.2d 558 (Tex. App. 1992)

In 1982, Ivan Hoover retained an attorney to prepare a will for him. The will drafted by the attorney consisted of three pages and was executed by Ivan at the attorney's office on February 2, 1982. The provisions on the first page directed that, after payment of his debts, 25 percent of Ivan's estate should be paid to his wife, Vera Hoover, and that the balance of the estate should be paid to Ivan's surviving sisters. The second and third pages of the will contained the signatures of Ivan and three witnesses. The attorney retained a copy of the will. Ivan died in 1988 and his sister filed a copy of the February 2, 1982, will with the probate court. Ivan's widow, Vera Hoover, challenged the will and provided a copy of a will that Ivan had given to her nephew prior to his death. The second and third pages of this will, containing the signatures of Ivan and witnesses, were from the will signed on February 2, 1982. The first page, however, had been replaced with a new page that left all of Ivan's estate to Vera or, if she predeceased him, then to her daughter, Betty. Vera asserted that Ivan, by substituting a page in the will without properly executing it, effectively had revoked the February 2, 1982, will. She argued that he therefore had died intestate leaving his widow as his surviving heir. The probate court, after finding that the February 2, 1982, will had been properly executed and never revoked, accepted the original will for probate. After Vera died, her executor appealed the probate court's decision.

Osborn, Chief Justice

The issue presented to the Court in this case is whether the substitution of the single page of a will, which provided entirely for the disposition of the deceased's estate, constituted a revocation of the will so that the deceased died intestate. We conclude that a will may not be revoked by one page being substituted for a page of the original will, and that under the facts in this case, the original will was entitled to be admitted to probate. . . .

The Texas Probate Code Section 63 provides:

No will in writing, and no clause thereof or devise therein, shall be revoked, except by a subsequent will, codicil, or declaration in writing, executed with like formalities, or by the testator destroying or canceling the same, or causing it to be done in his presence.

. . . A will can only be revoked in a manner prescribed by statute. . . . Since only the testator could change, amend or revoke his will, we begin by assuming that he changed the first page of the will which he executed in his attorney's office. Did that legally alter or revoke the will as executed? Certainly, there was no subsequent will, codicil or declaration in writing executed with like formalities as the original will.

The question is then limited to whether the change of the first page resulted from the testator destroying or canceling the will. . . . [I]n *Pullen v. Russ,* 209 S.W.2d 630 (Tex.Civ.App. 1948), a will was offered for probate that had both erasures and interlineations to reflect changes made on at least two separate occasions by the testator to change the beneficiaries. In holding that the will should have been admitted to probate as originally written, the Court said:

It is the law in this state that changes in the original will properly executed by the testator are ineffective, and that the will must be probated as originally written unless such changes were made with the formalities required in the making of a will. A will cannot be changed or revoked except in a manner provided by law. . . .

We conclude that a testator cannot remove some parts of a valid will by obliterations. In this case, an attempt was made by someone to change all of the dispositive clauses in the will while leaving the execution . . . provisions intact. If in fact the testator did make the substitution of one page of the will for the original first page, he never intended to revoke his will and die intestate because clearly the execution pages remained intact and fully operative on any disposition clauses that were valid. The changes which were made by the substitution of another page were not ones made in accordance with the statute which permits revocation of the original will which was executed in the attorney's office.

The original will was valid. The changes, by whomever made, were not valid. . . .

[Judgment affirmed.]

Revocation by Operation of Law. A will, or part thereof, also may be revoked by operation of law due to changes in the testator's circumstances. For example, some states provide that marriage or marriage plus the birth of a child after the execution of a will revokes it automatically. Many state statutes also provide that a divorce, subsequent to execution of a will, revokes any disposition of property to the former spouse. Under the UPC, however, only a divorce revokes a will by operation of law.

Dependent Relative Revocation. Occasionally, the testator will revoke a will while under a mistaken assumption of law or fact. In order to best carry out the testator's intent—the primary issue in all will construction—courts often apply the **dependent relative revocation doctrine.** Under this doctrine, if the court finds that the testator's revocation is dependent, or conditional, upon the truth of her assumption, then the revocation is ineffective if the assumption is, *in fact,* false. For example, the doctrine commonly is applied when the testator destroys the will on the mistaken assumption that a subsequently executed will is valid. If the later will proves invalid—for example, due to noncompliance with the will formalities—the court may apply the doctrine to reinstate the prior will by treating the revocation as conditional on the validity of the second will.

Effect of Subsequent Events

Even if the will has not been revoked, persons named in the will nevertheless may be prevented from receiving property because of events occurring after the execution of the will.

Lapse. Generally, to take property under a will, devisees or legatees must survive (outlive) the testator. If a beneficiary predeceases the testator, the beneficiary's gift is said to **lapse.** The effect of a lapse is dependent on a number of factors. Ordinarily, a will contains a "residuary" clause disposing of all property not otherwise provided for in the will. For example, Todd may leave a valid will devising his farm to Carol and leaving the "rest, residue, and remainder" of his estate to Michael. If Carol predeceases Todd, her gift then passes under the residuary clause to Michael. If Michael predeceases Todd, the property in the residuary is distributed as if Todd died intestate. Similarly, if Todd had not included a residuary clause, the property would pass by intestacy.

Most states have enacted anti-lapse statutes, which vary significantly from state to state, to prevent this result in certain situations. For example, under the typical approach, if the deceased devisee is a grandparent (or lineal descendent of a grandparent) of the testator, who leaves "issue" surviving the testator, then the surviving issue of the deceased devisee take the gift in his place. **Issue** generally means lineal descendants, for example, a father's sons and daughters, grandsons and granddaughters, and so on. Lineal descendants are distinguished from "collateral" descendants, such as nieces and nephews.

Ademption. A second doctrine that may prevent a beneficiary from receiving property provided for in the will is ademption. **Ademption by extinction** occurs when the subject matter of the gift is not in the testator's estate at the time of death. For example, the testator may execute a will devising her farm to John, but subsequently sell the property prior to her death. In this situation, the gift fails and John gets nothing; John usually is not entitled to the proceeds of the sale. The doctrine of ademption by extinction applies only to *specific* bequests and devises—for example, when the testator leaves "my house at 203 Elm Street" to John.

Note that the UPC finds ademption by extinction only if the "facts and circumstances indicate that ademption of the devise was intended by the testator or . . . is consistent with the testator's manifested plan of distribution."[4] Unless this "intent" test is met, the beneficiary receives the proceeds of the property (for example, sales or insurance proceeds) or the property acquired by the testator as a replacement for the specifically devised property.

The testator may, after execution of the will but during his lifetime, make a gift of property to a beneficiary under the will. If the testator intends the gift to be in lieu of the bequest or devise, the lifetime gift operates as a partial or total **ademption by satisfaction** of the testamentary disposition. Ademption by satisfaction occurs only when the decedent leaves a valid will. If he dies intestate, the analogous doctrine of **advancement** may operate to reduce the amount of property that otherwise would pass to an heir. Under the UPC, lifetime gifts do not operate to reduce the share of a person who would otherwise take, absent some clear indication that the gift is in satisfaction or is an advancement.

Abatement. A beneficiary's share under a will also may be reduced or extinguished by **abatement.**

---

[4]UPC §2–606(a)(6).

Abatement—or reduction—must occur when insufficient property remains in the estate to satisfy all gifts provided in the will after creditors' claims, taxes, and administration expenses have been paid. An abatement statute determines the order in which the testator's property is applied to satisfy his obligations. The UPC, which is similar to the law applied in most states, provides first that the testator's intention, either as expressed in the will or implied by the testamentary plan, controls. If intention cannot be proven, shares abate without any preference between real or personal property in the following order: (1) property not disposed of by the will (intestate property), (2) residuary devises, (3) general devises, and (4) specific devises. If the assets of the estate are insufficient to pay all devises within a given classification, the beneficiaries share those assets pro rata. For example, assume Tom leaves $6,000 to Pam and $4,000 to Sarah. After payment of claims, only $5,000 remains to be distributed for general devises. Pam receives $3,000 and Sarah receives $2,000.

Protection of the Testator's Family

Although a person generally may dispose of her property on death as she sees fit, the law imposes certain limitations on the ability to disinherit a surviving spouse. At common law, a surviving widow was entitled to **dower,** a life estate[5] in one-third of all real estate owned by the husband at any time during the marriage. A widower, under the comparable right of **curtesy,** was entitled to a life estate in all of his wife's real estate if a child was born alive during the marriage. Dower and curtesy encumber land titles and provide inadequate protection for surviving spouses because most wealth today is held in the form of personal property. As a result, common law dower and curtesy have been abolished in most jurisdictions.

Most states now protect the spouse through "forced share" or "elective share" statutes. These statutes give the surviving spouse the option either to take under the testator's will or to reject the provisions of the will and receive a share prescribed by statute. This share is commonly either one-third to one-half of the estate, or the portion of the estate that would have passed to the spouse if the decedent had died intestate. The UPC approach awards the surviving spouse an increasing percentage of the estate based upon the number of years that the decedent and the surviving spouse were married to each other, up to a maximum of one-half of the estate for marriages lasting fifteen years or more.[6]

If the surviving spouse elects to take the forced share, the estate is not thereby rendered intestate. The shares of other beneficiaries must, however, be reduced because by electing, the surviving spouse generally receives more than is provided in the will.

A minority of states provide for spousal protection through the **community property doctrine,** derived from the French and Spanish civil law. In the majority of states (designated "common law" states) each spouse owns whatever he or she has earned. In community property states, husband and wife are treated as equal co-owners of property (community property) acquired with the earnings of either during marriage without regard to which spouse actually supports the family. Community property also includes the income from, or proceeds of, the sale of community property. Separate property includes property owned by either spouse before marriage, or acquired by gift, inheritance, or devise after marriage and the income from such property. Therefore, on death, either spouse can dispose of only one-half of the community property. The other one-half belongs to the surviving spouse. Thus, the decedent may transfer by will or intestate succession only his or her separate property and one-half of the community property.

The law also provides some degree of protection to the family by statutes, varying considerably from state to state, that give the surviving spouse and children a preference in certain property over unsecured creditors of the estate and persons to whom the property has been devised by will. These exemptions or allowances generally include the homestead exemption, personal property exemptions, and the family allowance. The homestead exemption, available in most states, protects the family unit by exempting a certain portion of the family residence from creditors' claims. The exemption continues after the death of the head of the family for the benefit of the surviving spouse and minor or dependent children.

In addition to the homestead exemption, the decedent's family generally is entitled to retain certain items of personal property (such as household furniture, automobiles, appliances, and personal effects) free of general creditors' claims. Finally, most states provide a

---

[5]Life estates are discussed in Chapter 36.

[6]UPC §2–202.

family allowance during administration of the estate. The allowance entitles the surviving spouse and children to a specified sum of money or property for the support and maintenance of the family while the estate is being administered. Generally, the homestead exemption, personal property exemption, and family allowance are provided in addition to any property otherwise passing to the spouse or children.

Intestate Succession

A person who fails to leave a valid will dies intestate. A person who dies leaving a will that does not dispose of his or her entire estate, whether by the terms of the will or by partial revocation or lapse, dies partially intestate. Intestate property is transferred as provided in state intestate succession statutes, frequently designated "statutes of descent and distribution." "Descent" refers to the transfer of real property and "distribution" to the transfer of personal property. Some states provide that real and personal property are distributed differently. Under the UPC, and many other state statutes, all of the decedent's intestate property passes in the same manner.

Persons entitled to an intestate decedent's property are known as **heirs.** A person has heirs, determined at death, whether or not she leaves a valid will. If the decedent leaves a valid will, the heirs take nothing, unless (as is commonly the case) the decedent provides for one or more of them in the will. If, however, the decedent is wholly or partially intestate, intestate property passes to the heirs. Thus, if the validity of a will is contested, the parties are usually the beneficiaries under the will on one side and the heirs on the other.

Operation of a Typical Statute. Statutes of descent and distribution vary substantially from state to state. Typically, property is first distributed to any surviving spouse or children of the decedent. If both survive, they share the estate—for example, one-half goes to the spouse and one-half to the children. If the decedent leaves no surviving spouse or children, the property is distributed to the decedent's parents and their descendants (the brothers, sisters, nieces, and nephews of the decedent). If no persons survive in this class, distribution is made to the decedent's grandparents and their descendants (the uncles, aunts, and cousins of the decedent), great-grandparents and their descendants, and so on. If there are no takers

alive in any of the classes listed above, the intestate estate then passes or "escheats" to the state.

Note that the UPC, unlike many other state intestate succession statutes, prohibits inheritance by persons more remote than grandparents and their descendants. This approach simplifies proof of heirship and eliminates will contests by remote relatives (so-called laughing heirs) who are outside the class of persons the decedent probably intended to benefit.

Degree of Kinship and Representation. As noted previously, the portion of the intestate estate not passing to the surviving spouse (or the entire estate if there is no surviving spouse) is distributed first to any surviving descendants (children, grandchildren, etc.) of the decedent. If all descendants are of the same degree of kinship to the decedent, they take equally. If they are of unequal degree, those of more remote degree take by representation.

In the United States, the degree of kinship (blood relationship) is determined according to the civil law method. This method determines the degree of relationship between the decedent and collateral relatives by counting the number of generations from the decedent to the common ancestor and from that ancestor down to the relative. In the lineal line (grandparent, parent, child, grandchild), it is simply necessary to count the number of generations, up or down. By applying these rules, the degrees of kinship for common relatives are as follows:

1st degree—the decedent's children and his parents;
2d degree—the decedent's brothers, sisters, grandparents, and grandchildren;
3d degree—the decedent's aunts, uncles, nieces, nephews, great-grandparents, and great-grandchildren;
4th degree—the decedent's great uncles and great aunts (sons and daughters of great-grandparents), first cousins (sons and daughters of uncles and aunts), grandnephews and grandnieces (sons and daughters of nephews and nieces), great-great-grandparents, and great-great-grandchildren.

Assume that Donald dies intestate, survived only by his three children: Alan, Bonnie, and Charles (no surviving spouse). Because they are all of equal degree (first), they share equally; each takes one-third of the estate. Assume, however, that Alan has predeceased Donald, leaving two children surviving, Robert and Sally. Because Robert and Sally are of more remote degree than Bonnie and Charles—Robert and Sally are of second degree (grandchildren), whereas Bonnie and Charles are of first degree (children)—they take by "representation."

Taking by **representation,** commonly known as taking *per stirpes* or **by stocks,** means that the lineal descendants or "issue" of a deceased heir inherit the share of an estate (the intestate's) that their immediate ancestor would have inherited had he survived (outlived) the intestate. To illustrate, because Alan has predeceased Donald, his share passes by representation to his children Robert and Sally equally; each takes one-sixth of Donald's estate. Note that Robert and Sally are not entitled to inherit from Donald if Alan is still alive. If both Alan and Sally predecease Donald, but Sally leaves three children surviving (Donald's great-grandchildren), Ed, Frank, and Gail, they share Sally's one-sixth equally (that is, one-eighteenth each). Donald's estate is thus divided as shown in Figure 39.1.

In contrast to *per stirpes* distribution, a will or intestate succession statute may provide that property is to be distributed *per capita*. Under this method, the estate is simply divided by the number of surviving descendants, regardless of degree. Thus, in the preceding example, under a per capita distribution, Bonnie, Charles, Robert, Ed, Frank, and Gail each take one-sixth of Donald's estate.

Simultaneous Death. In inheritance cases, the rights of heirs depend upon surviving (outliving) the intestate. This survivorship requirement creates a problem in estate administration when several family members are involved in a common disaster and die simultaneously or within a few days of each other. To resolve one aspect of this issue, most states have adopted the **Uniform Simultaneous Death Act.** Section 1 of the Act provides that if the disposition of property by will or intestate succession depends upon priority of death *and* there is no sufficient evidence that persons have died otherwise than simultaneously, each person's property is distributed as if she had survived. This rule only partially solves the problem, however, because if evidence can be obtained to prove who survived, even if only for a second, the survivor is entitled to inherit. As a result, courts often have been required to resolve the grisly issue of who lived longest after a common tragedy, necessitating multiple administrations of the same property. The UPC, borrowing a tool long used in wills and trusts, resolves the problem for most cases by requiring an heir to survive the intestate by five days (120 hours) in order to inherit from him. In other words, a person who fails to outlive the decedent by 120 hours is deemed to have predeceased him for purposes of intestate succession. The UPC applies the same rule to those taking under a will. The law recognizes an exception to this requirement if its application would cause the estate to escheat to the state. In other words, no minimum survivorship requirement is imposed upon the last eligible relative of the intestate.

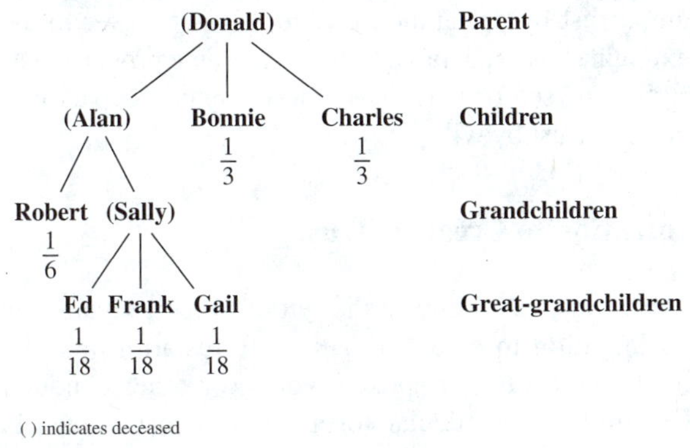

Introduction to Trusts

A trust is an extremely useful tool for family settlement, as well as for tax and estate planning. It is simply one of the methods by which property may be transferred. Other methods include sale or gift during life and will or intestate succession on death.

A **trust,** in essence, *splits* title to property between the **trustee,** who holds legal title, and the **beneficiary** or beneficiaries who hold beneficial or equitable title. The trustee is required by law or the terms of the trust to possess and manage the property for the benefit of the beneficiaries. The person creating the trust is known as the **settlor** or **trustor.** The property subject to the trust is known as the **trust property, trust res, corpus,** or simply "subject matter of the trust." The benefit may be conferred by a trust created during the settlor's lifetime—an *inter vivos* **trust**—or in his will on death—a **testamentary trust.** The settlor's *intention*

Figure 39.1   Inheritance by Representation

(Donald) — Parent

(Alan)   Bonnie $\frac{1}{3}$ Charles $\frac{1}{3}$ — Children

Robert   (Sally) $\frac{1}{6}$ — Grandchildren

Ed $\frac{1}{18}$ Frank $\frac{1}{18}$ Gail $\frac{1}{18}$ — Great-grandchildren

( ) indicates deceased

is paramount in construing the terms of the trust to determine the duties and powers of the trustee and rights of the beneficiaries.

Types of Trusts

Express Trusts. Trusts are classified as either "express" or "implied." An **express trust** arises as a result of the settlor's *language* indicating her intent to create it. Express trusts are either private or charitable. In a **private trust,** the most common type, the trust property is devoted to the use of specified persons designated as beneficiaries. In a **charitable trust,** the property is devoted to charitable purposes beneficial to the community in favor of a class of beneficiaries who are not specifically designated.

Purposes of Express Trusts. The primary motivation for creation of a trust is donative: the settlor wishes to confer the benefit of the property upon the beneficiary. The settlor usually transfers the property in trust, rather than by outright gift or devise, to provide for the management and possession of the property by someone other than the person or persons who are to enjoy the benefits of the property. The settlor may desire this separation of management and enjoyment for many reasons. For example, the beneficiaries may be children or others who through mental infirmity, senility, illness, drug or alcohol addiction, or mere immaturity or improvidence, are unable, in the settlor's estimation, to adequately manage the property. The settlor also may wish to limit the permissible uses of the property—for example, to the support, maintenance, or education of the beneficiary or for charitable purposes. The trust also may be used to provide for successive beneficiaries. For example, the settlor may, in a will, leave an apartment building in trust to pay the income to her ailing mother for life for her support and care, with the remainder in fee simple passing to her children.

Implied Trusts. **Implied trusts** arise by operation of law, not by the express language of the settlor. They are of two types: resulting trusts and constructive trusts. A resulting trust, like an express trust, is based on the intent of the person creating it. In a resulting trust, however, intent is presumed when the surrounding circumstances indicate that the settlor does not intend that the person taking or holding the property should have the beneficial interest in it. Resulting trusts are discussed later in this chapter.

A constructive trust, unlike any of the foregoing trusts, is not based upon intent but is imposed to redress wrong or prevent unjust enrichment and is therefore remedial in nature. Because a constructive trust is merely one form of restitution, constructive trusts are covered in the restitution discussion in Chapter 15.

Creation, Modification, and Termination of Trusts

The private express trust results from the settlor's indication of intent to create it. In addition to intent, a trust requires trust property, a trustee, and a beneficiary.

Methods of Creating a Trust

The settlor must own or control the property that is to become the trust corpus. Either real—for example, an apartment building—or personal—for example, stocks and bonds—property may be used. A trust usually is created by a *transfer* of the property from the settlor to another person as trustee for the beneficiary or beneficiaries. This transfer may be accomplished during the settlor's life creating an inter vivos trust or upon her death by will forming a testamentary trust. Creation of a trust, therefore, ordinarily involves at least three people (the settlor, trustee, and beneficiary), requiring a transfer of the property from the settlor to the trustee.

A trust also may be created by the settlor's *declaration* that he holds the property as trustee for another person. In this case, the trust arises without any transfer of title to the property. Assume Andrew, the owner of a bond, declares himself as its trustee for specified beneficiaries. Andrew, the settlor, also is trustee of the bond for the beneficiaries. The settlor has the capacity to create a trust by declaration or inter vivos transfer to the extent he has capacity to transfer the same property outright. The settlor must have a testamentary capacity to create a trust by will.

Intention to Create a Trust

A trust is created only if the settlor properly manifests an intention to create it. This manifestation may be made by written or spoken words, or other conduct. Generally, no particular form of words or conduct is required. Courts are, however, often required to determine whether the settlor's language indicates an intent to create a trust or is merely "precatory." Precatory words are those stating the transferor's suggestion or hope that the transferee will use or dispose of the property in a given way, but allowing the transferee full discretion in deciding whether or not to follow the suggestion or comply with the wish. For example, rather than transferring property "to Carol in trust for Bob," the language used may instead be "to Carol hoping (wishing, desiring, recommending, relying, requesting, on confidence) that she will use the income from the property to care for Bob." In these situations, the court must interpret the language used, often contained in a decedent's will, to determine whether a trust is created under which Carol is trustee of the property for Bob's benefit, or whether she is entitled to the property beneficially, subject at most to a moral or ethical obligation.

In the case that follows, the court considers whether a valid trust has been created.

Cabaniss v. Cabaniss
464 A.2d 87 (D.C. App. 1983)

Charles Cabaniss committed suicide on September 16, 1979, leaving a will naming his wife (appellant) as executrix. Two days before his suicide, Cabaniss telephoned his daughter Stephanie (appellee) and asked her to keep some checks that he had set aside for another daughter, Carla, who was incompetent. The following day Cabaniss took the checks to Stephanie's home and told her to set up a joint checking account for Carla's benefit. Cabaniss also wrote a letter to his attorney giving him power of attorney to provide Stephanie the authority to open a bank account for the benefit of Carla with some checks endorsed by Cabaniss. A postscript to the letter stated that Stephanie was "to act as trustee and withdrawals are to be used only for the benefit of Carla." Cabaniss then told Stephanie he would "check out" the letter with his attorney and implied that he would accompany her to the bank at a later time. Cabaniss indorsed the checks, which he left with the letter in a file cabinet at Stephanie's house. Stephanie then left town for the day. When she returned, she found that Cabaniss had left his key to her house inside the house. The following day Cabaniss committed suicide in his office.

The issue before the trial court was whether the checks in Stephanie's possession constituted part of Cabaniss's estate or whether the checks were trust property that passed outside the probate estate. The trial court ruled that Cabaniss had created a trust funded with the checks of which Stephanie was trustee and Carla was beneficiary. Appellant appealed.

Belson, Associate Judge

. . . The elements of a trust, including an *inter vivos* trust created for the benefit of a third person, are the following: (1) a trustee, who holds the trust property and is subject to equitable duties to deal with it for the benefit of another; (2) a beneficiary, to whom the trustee owes equitable duties to deal with the trust property for his benefit; (3) trust property, which is held by the trustee for the beneficiary. . . .

Unless otherwise provided by statute, such as the Statute of Frauds or Statute of Wills, an enforceable trust can be created without a writing. . . . Essential to the creation of a trust is the settlor's manifestation or external expression of his intention to create a trust. . . . Such manifestation may be by written or spoken language or by conduct, in light of all surrounding circumstances. . . .

Appellant contends that decedent failed to demonstrate sufficiently his intention to create a trust by his incomplete testamentary transfer of the endorsed checks to Stephanie. . . . She also contends that decedent simply designated Stephanie as his agent to hold the checks for safekeeping pending his further instructions regarding their disposition, and that such agency authority terminated with his death. Alternatively appellant asserts that decedent failed to manifest an unambiguous firm intention to create a present trust. . . . In support of this contention appellant maintains that decedent specifically conditioned any trust arrangement upon his accompanying Stephanie to the bank to open up the trust account following a disposition of the trust funds with attorney Dolphin. Appellant also asserts that decedent, at most, delivered possession of the endorsed checks to Stephanie, and not title, because he retained access to and subsequent control over them. . . .

We agree with the trial court that decedent adequately manifested his intention to create a trust and subsequently complied with the formalities necessary to bring about that result. In his oral declarations to Stephanie and in his letters executed in Stephanie's presence, decedent imperatively and unambiguously designated his daughter Carla as beneficiary, appointed Stephanie trustee, and identified the endorsed checks as the trust property. Simultaneously, decedent unconditionally negotiated the checks to Stephanie by [i]ndorsing them in blank and by delivering them to, and leaving them in, Stephanie's exclusive possession. . . . Moreover, decedent's later surrender of his key to Stephanie's house confirms that he relinquished all control of the trust property to Stephanie. . . . Such definitive acts negate any inference that Stephanie held the checks as decedent's agent, subject to his further instructions regarding disposition of the checks. . . .

We also conclude that the record does not support appellant's contention that decedent manifested his intention to create a trust only when, but not until, he initiated a trip to the bank with Stephanie or discussed the trust arrangements with Dolphin. It was Stephanie who raised the possibility that decedent's cooperation might be needed to open a savings account. Decedent had already made clear that he was creating the trust, and his agreement to comply with any requirements of a savings institution did not alter that fact. Nor did the agreement to review the matter with attorney Dolphin have that effect. We are satisfied that Dr. Cabaniss went to his unfortunate death in the belief that he had taken additional steps to assure the well-being of his incompetent daughter.

We conclude that the trial court correctly ruled that decedent had unconditionally manifested his intention to create a trust, that the trust was created for the benefit of Carla. . . .

[Judgment affirmed.]

Formalities of Creation

Requirement of a Writing. Unless otherwise required by statute, no writing is required to create an enforceable *inter vivos* trust. Thus, oral trusts in personal property are recognized as valid and enforceable. Almost all jurisdictions, however, require that express trusts of real property be evidenced by a writing.

Testamentary Trusts. A valid will is necessary to create a testamentary trust. In order to create a valid trust by will, the will must indicate an intention to create a trust, the identity of the beneficiaries, the identity of the trust property, and the purposes of the trust.

Frequently, the testator desires, not to create a trust in a will, but, by testamentary disposition, to add property to a trust created *inter vivos.* Such a trust is commonly known as a **pour over trust** because on death property is "poured over," or into, the living trust.

Pour over trusts are advantageous because they eliminate the need to repeat the terms of the trust, which may be long and involved, in the will, and remove prop-

erty transferred from involvement in probate proceedings. As a result, courts generally have held that pour over trusts are valid and do not constitute invalid testamentary dispositions. Today, the problem is resolved in most states by the **Uniform Testamentary Additions to Trusts Act,** which also is included as part of the Uniform Probate Code. Under §1 of the Act, if the trust is identified in the testator's will,[7] and its terms are set forth in a written instrument (other than a will), and it is executed before or concurrently with execution of the testator's will, then a devise or bequest to the trust is valid even if the trust is amendable or revocable, or both, and even if the trust is in fact amended after execution of the will.

The Trustee

The trustee holds title to trust property subject to equitable duties to deal with it for the benefit of another, the beneficiary. Unless the trust provides otherwise, a trust is created even though no trustee is named in the instrument creating the trust, or the named trustee is dead or otherwise incapable of taking title to the property, or the named trustee refuses to serve. This rule applies to inter vivos and testamentary trusts and in both cases the court appoints a trustee to administer the trust.

The settlor may appoint a single trustee or may name two or more co-trustees, whose functions, powers, and duties may differ. Co-trustees hold legal title to the property as joint tenants.

As a general rule, any natural person may hold property in trust to the extent that he may do so for his own benefit. Private corporations (artificial persons), such as trust companies or banks, are capable of holding and administering property in trust subject to statutes governing corporate existence, and if the purposes of the trust are consistent with those for which the corporation is created. Similarly, a sovereign, such as the United States, a state, or municipality, may hold and administer property in trust.

Because a trust may be created by declaration, the settlor may act as trustee. A beneficiary also may be a trustee unless she is both the sole beneficiary and sole trustee. In that situation, the legal and equitable interests in the property "merge" and the beneficiary owns the property free of any trust.

---

[7]The testator need not be the settlor of the trust, which could therefore be created in another person's will.

The trustee is entitled to compensation out of the trust property for his services, but may waive this right. The amount of compensation (usually a percentage of income or principal) may be fixed by statute, the terms of the trust, or by the court.

The Beneficiary

Because a trust is a method of disposing of property, the person receiving the beneficial interest, the beneficiary, must be definitely ascertained. The description is sufficiently definite if (1) the beneficiary is specifically named in the trust instrument, or (2) the beneficiary's identity may either be ascertained from facts existing when the trust is created or, in most circumstances, facts occurring thereafter.

The trust may designate one or several beneficiaries. If there is more than one beneficiary, the beneficial interest may be held simultaneously (as joint tenants or tenants in common) or successively (one beneficiary may be a life tenant and another a remainderman). Any natural person or corporation having capacity to take and hold legal title to property has capacity to be a beneficiary of a trust of that property.

The trust may designate a definite class of persons as beneficiaries. A class is definite as long as the identity of its members is ascertainable, even though it consists of a changing or shifting group, which may increase or decrease in size. For example, the class may be affected by births, deaths, or other events. The settlor may specifically name the members of the class or may use more general language, transferring property in trust, for example, for the benefit of "children," "grandchildren," "nephews," or "issue."

A settlor may transfer the property in trust for the erection or maintenance of tombstones or monuments, the care of graves, or the care of specific animals. Because there is no beneficiary to enforce the trust, such a distribution is not a trust at all, but is commonly known as an **honorary trust.** Legal recognition of honorary trusts varies from state to state, though many jurisdictions, by statute, validate provisions for the maintenance of graves and monuments. In any event, the purported trustee is not allowed to keep the property. He must either apply it for the stated purpose or return it to the settlor.

Nature, Extent, and Transfer of the Beneficiary's Interest. Modern trust law treats the beneficiary as owning an equitable interest in the underlying trust property. The extent of the beneficiary's interest in that property depends upon the settlor's intent. For example, the beneficiary may have an absolute right to the property, or may merely have a contingent interest. The beneficiary's share of trust property may be explicitly stated or may, by the terms of the trust, be subject to the trustee's uncontrolled discretion (a "discretionary" trust). The trustee may have the power to exclude the beneficiary altogether. The beneficiary's interest may begin or end only upon occurrence of a designated event such as marriage, starting college, or reaching a stated age. The duration of the interest may be fixed or indefinite. The trust may provide that the trustee will pay or apply only so much of the trust property and income therefrom as is necessary for the education or support of the beneficiary (a "support" trust). In short, the trust instrument determines the extent of the beneficiary's interest.

Unless the beneficiary's interest is one that terminates on death, such as a life estate, it passes, like other property, by will or intestate succession at the death of the beneficiary. The interest also may be transferred inter vivos (by sale, gift, or through attachment by creditors), unless the interest is subject to a spendthrift clause. In a **spendthrift trust** the beneficiary may not voluntarily transfer the interest, and creditors of the beneficiary may not reach it to satisfy their claims. In other words, the beneficiary may not transfer the interest either voluntarily or involuntarily. The spendthrift aspect of the trust may be imposed either by the terms of the trust, or, in some states, by statute.

Spendthrift trusts are designed to protect the beneficiary against her own wastefulness, incompetence, inexperience, or improvidence. A settlor may not create a spendthrift trust for herself, because this would be a simple way to frustrate creditors. Spendthrift clauses are upheld in most U.S. jurisdictions on the ground that the settlor, as owner of property, should be able to limit or qualify the interest transferred to the beneficiary unless the limitation violates public policy.

Modification and Termination of Trusts

As a general rule, the settlor has no power to revoke or modify a properly created trust *unless* he has reserved such a power by the terms of the trust. Even if the settlor fails to reserve a power of revocation or fails to exercise a reserved power, the trust may terminate when the time period for which the trust was created expires or upon the happening of a certain event, such as the completion of the beneficiary's college education. The trust also may be terminated by consent of the parties in certain situations. For example, if all beneficiaries consent, the trust will be terminated if all beneficiaries have capacity and the material purposes of the trust have been accomplished.

Even if trust purposes have not been accomplished *and* the settlor has not reserved a power of revocation or modification, the trust may be modified or revoked with the consent of all of the beneficiaries and the settlor. This rule applies only if the trust is created inter vivos and the settlor is still living. This method could, for example, be used to terminate a spendthrift trust, which could not be terminated by consent of the beneficiaries alone.

In the course of administering a private trust, it may become impossible or illegal to follow the settlor's directions, or due to circumstances unknown to or not anticipated by the settlor, following them will defeat or substantially impair accomplishment of the trust purposes. In such cases, the court may permit or direct the trustee not to comply with the direction in the trust, to perform an act not authorized, or even to do an act forbidden by terms of the trust.[8]

Trust Administration

The trustee has a duty to administer the trust. In an *inter vivos* trust, the trustee derives authority from the trust instrument and administers the trust without court supervision. A testamentary trustee, like an executor or administrator, is appointed by the court and usually is accountable to it.

Powers of the Trustee

The trustee may exercise those powers conferred upon him by the terms of the trust (express powers), or those necessary and appropriate to carry out the purposes of the trust (implied powers), which are not forbidden by terms of the trust. Modern trusts generally grant the trustee very broad powers in accomplishing trust purposes. These powers allow the trustee to act quickly in an emergency and to adapt the trust to changing circumstances without obtaining court authorization. In many states, statutes such as the Uniform Trustee's Powers

Act confer a large number of customary powers upon the trustee. Express powers may be "mandatory," requiring the trustee to do an act such as invest in a certain type of property, or "discretionary," giving the trustee the privilege but not the duty to perform. The trustee incurs no liability for exercising or failing to exercise a discretionary power, unless he has abused his discretion. Generally, the court will not interfere and substitute its judgment for that of the trustee even if the court would act differently in the situation.

Duties of the Trustee

The "Fiduciary" Relationship. The most important duty imposed upon the trustee is "loyalty," requiring the trustee to administer the trust solely in the interest of the beneficiary. This duty embodies the fiduciary relationship existing between the trustee and beneficiary. A **fiduciary relationship** is simply one in which one person is under a duty to act solely for the benefit of another concerning matters within the scope of the relation. In addition to trustee and beneficiary, other fiduciary relationships exist, for example, between guardian and ward, attorney and client, agent and principal, and partners. The extent of the obligations imposed differs somewhat among the various fiduciary relations. The duties of the trustee are the most intensive of any fiduciary.

The fiduciary duty of loyalty imposes a duty upon the trustee

1. not to profit at the expense of the beneficiary, or use trust property for the trustee's personal benefit;
2. not to enter into competition with the beneficiary without the beneficiary's consent, unless authorized to do so by the terms of the trust or the court;
3. not to sell property to or buy property from the trust, without court approval, regardless of the trustee's good faith, the fairness of the transaction, or whether the trustee makes a profit;[9]
4. not to disclose to third persons information acquired as trustee, if the effect of the disclosure would be detrimental to the beneficiary's interest; and
5. not to delegate the administration of the trust to a third party.

---

[8]A similar, though distinguishable, problem arising in charitable trusts is governed by the *cy pres* doctrine, discussed later in this chapter.

[9]Additionally, a trustee may not purchase for personal benefit property that he is under a duty to purchase for the trust. The court may allow the trustee to buy trust property only if it finds the purchase to be in the best interests of the beneficiary.

Other duties owed by the trustee to the beneficiary include the duty to

1. keep and render clear and accurate accounts concerning trust administration;
2. give, on request, complete and accurate information regarding the nature and amount of trust property, and to permit inspection of trust property and records;
3. take, keep control of, and preserve the trust property;
4. take reasonable steps to enforce claims that the trustee holds against third parties concerning the trust, and to defend actions that may result in a loss of the trust estate;
5. prevent commingling of trust property with the trustee's own property or that held by the trustee upon other trusts, and to earmark the property as belonging to the trust; and
6. deal impartially with the beneficiaries, if there are two or more, and if the trust is created to pay income to the beneficiary, to pay the net income at reasonable intervals, or according to terms of the trust.

The "Prudent Investor" Rule. The trust estate ordinarily contains income producing property, such as cash, stocks, bonds, rental real property, a farm, or a business. The trustee usually is required to make periodic payments of the income from the property to the beneficiaries. In managing the property, the trustee must use reasonable care and skill to preserve it and make it productive. These duties require the trustee to invest the property or periodically to sell a trust asset and reinvest the proceeds. The settlor often specifies permissible types of trust investments, which are binding upon the trustee.

In the absence of the settlor's express direction, most states have statutes governing investments by trustees. Older statutes used either a "legal list" or "prudent person" approach. A legal list statute limited the trustee to certain specified types of investment. The prudent person approach required the trustee to make only those investments that a prudent person would make of his own property taking into consideration both the preservation of the estate and the amount and regularity of the income to be generated.

These approaches have been supplanted in most states by the **prudent investor rule,** as codified in the **Uniform Prudent Investor Act.** This approach, based upon modern portfolio theory, provides that the trustee must manage and invest trust assets "as a prudent investor would,

by considering the purposes, terms, distribution requirements, and other circumstances of the trust," using "reasonable care, skill, and caution."[10] The most important characteristic of this rule is that the "trustee's investment and management decisions respecting individual assets must be evaluated not in isolation but in the context of the trust portfolio as a whole and as part of an overall investment strategy having risk and return objectives reasonably suited to the trust."[11] Thus, under the Act, an investment that might be deemed too risky standing alone under the older tests can nevertheless be prudent when considered in the context of the trust portfolio as a whole. The Act generally requires that the trustee diversify the trust portfolio, and requires the trustee to consider various factors in investing and managing trust assets, including tax considerations.

Regardless of the rule generally applied, the terms of the trust determine proper trust investments. That is, an investment permitted by the prudent investor rule may be prohibited in the trust instrument. Conversely, a speculative investment, not otherwise permissible, may be authorized. Therefore, as in almost all trust issues, the terms of the trust must be carefully consulted.

Liability of the Trustee

A trustee who violates the duty of loyalty, or any other duty owed to the beneficiary, commits a "breach of trust." A breach of trust renders the trustee liable to the beneficiary for any loss in value of the trust property resulting from the breach, any profit resulting from the breach, and any profit that would have been made by the trust if there had been no breach. For example, the trustee is liable if she is directed by terms of the trust to purchase IBM stock and fails to do so, resulting in loss when the price of the stock rises. The trustee also would be liable for profits made by using trust property for personal business.

The trustee is not liable for loss or depreciation of the property or for failure to make a profit in the absence of a breach of trust. For example, the trustee incurs no liability if through no fault of the trustee trust property is lost or stolen, or if the trustee fails to buy profitable securities that he is authorized but under no duty to purchase.

---

[10]Uniform Prudent Investor Act §2(a).
[11]Uniform Prudent Investor Act §2(b).

As a general rule, only the beneficiary can sue the trustee to enforce the trust or for breach of trust. In an action by the beneficiary, the court may compel the trustee to perform duties under the trust, issue an order preventing the trustee from committing a breach of trust, compel the trustee to redress a prior breach of trust, or remove the trustee. The settlor may not sue to enforce the trust or for breach of trust unless the settlor has retained some interest, such as a power of revocation, in the trust property.

The trustee is entitled to reimbursement from the trust estate for expenses properly incurred in trust administration. The trustee also is entitled to be reimbursed for liability incurred in contract or tort arising in the proper course of trust administration.

In the following case, the court was required to determine whether the trustee committed a breach of trust.

Ramsey v. Boatmen's First National Bank of Kansas City

914 S.W.2d 384 (Mo. App. 1996)

Defendant Boatmen's Bank served as co-trustee of a trust established in 1951 for the benefit of plaintiff Imogene Ramsey. Ramsey's husband had been co-trustee until his death; Hoit Campbell, Ramsey's son, subsequently became co-trustee. Under the terms of the trust, the trustees were authorized to "purchase investments of any kind or character" and to sell or exchange investment assets after securing Ramsey's written approval. Throughout her life, Ramsey relied on others to help conduct her financial affairs. Before his death, Ramsey's husband had managed her affairs. In 1976, when Ramsey was 72 years of age, Campbell became her financial advisor. Based on Campbell's advice, Ramsey approved investing trust assets in twelve real estate limited partnerships in which Campbell had financial interests. She also authorized the trust to make unsecured loans totaling $155,000 to Campbell. Boatmen's did not communicate with Ramsey about these investments. Instead, Campbell communicated with the bank on Ramsey's behalf and transferred her written authorizations to the bank. In 1976, the trust's portfolio was composed primarily of blue chip stocks, bonds, and government securities. By 1990, the limited partnerships and Campbell's promissory notes were a substantial proportion of the trust's investments. When Campbell declared bankruptcy, the promissory notes became worthless. Ramsey sued the Boatmen's for breach of trust and negligence in its management of the trust. The trial court granted judgment for Ramsey and the bank appealed.

Ulrich, Judge

. . . Boatmen's claims as its first point on appeal that the trial court erred in entering judgment against Boatmen's for breach of trust and common law negligence. Boatmen's claim of error is premised on the contention that Ms. Ramsey consented to, directed, or ratified the challenged trust transactions and, therefore, is precluded from holding Boatmen's liable as trustee. A trustee is a fiduciary of the highest order and is required to exercise a high standard of conduct and loyalty in administration of the trust. . . . Although the trustee has many duties emanating from the fiduciary relationship, the most fundamental is the duty of loyalty. As part of this duty the trustee is to administer the trust solely in the interest of the beneficiary. . . . Part of this duty precludes self dealing, which under most circumstances is a breach of the fiduciary duty.

An exception to this rule exists when a competent beneficiary who has full knowledge of the facts and his legal rights consents to a transaction and cannot thereafter seek redress against the trustee even though the transaction would otherwise be a breach of trust. . . . Section 216 *Restatement (Second) of Trusts* provides that:

> [t]he consent of the beneficiary does not preclude him holding the trustee liable for a breach of trust, if . . . (b) the beneficiary, when he gave his consent, did not know of his rights and of the material facts which the trustee knew or should have known and which the trustee did not reasonably believe that the beneficiary knew; or (c) the consent of the beneficiary was induced by improper conduct of the trustee.

The key factor in precluding the beneficiary from holding the trustee liable is the beneficiary's full knowledge of his legal rights and all material facts.

In this situation Boatmen's never discussed with Ms. Ramsey the various investments and loans that were being made to Hoit Campbell, although her son was a co-trustee. When a transaction involves a trustee, it must be fair and open, and consent must be informed with all parties holding equal knowledge of material facts and rights and otherwise free of influence. . . .

"It is the duty of a trustee to fully inform the cestui que trust [trust beneficiary] of all facts relating to the subject matter of the trust which come to the knowledge of the trustee and which are material for the cestui que trust to know for the protection of his interests." *In re Dryden's Estate,* [52 N.W.2d 737 (Neb. 1952)] . . . The trustee, even if not dealing with the beneficiary on the trustee's own account, is under a duty to communicate to the beneficiary material facts affecting the interest of the beneficiary which the trustee knows the beneficiary does not know and which the beneficiary needs to know for his protection in dealing with another person with respect to his interest. . . .

In this case Boatmen's had at the minimum a duty as a trustee to advise Ms. Ramsey of the conflict of interest created by investing in a co-trustee's ventures and in making the loans to Hoit Campbell. Boatmen's also should have ensured that Ms. Ramsey was deciding to make these investments with adequate knowledge of the facts and surrounding circumstances. Boatmen's had a policy of not investing in limited partnerships of this kind because Boatmen's considered such investments nonquality investments for trusts. This policy should have been directly communicated to Ms. Ramsey by co-trustee Boatmen's. Boatmen's could not rely solely on Hoit Campbell as co-trustee to properly administer the trust. A co-trustee cannot delegate the administration of the trust to a single trustee. . . . A co-trustee does not escape liability by failure to participate in the administration of the trust. . . .

When the trust was first created, the grantor chose Boatmen's predecessor as trustee. As a corporate trustee, a bank is generally chosen for objectivity and expertise. A bank cannot take a passive role in the administration of the trust for which it accepted a fiduciary responsibility as a trustee. If the trustee were obligated to merely do as instructed by a co-trustee, the role of trustee would be diminished to conduct less than that expected of a fiduciary. Ms. Ramsey was relying on Boatmen's expertise and objectivity to care for her interest in the trust. The ultimate beneficiary, not a co-trustee, of a revocable trust directs the actions of the trustee, who must comply. . . . Boatmen's was obligated to inquire of Ms. Ramsey whether she desired to make transactions that involved co-trustee Hoit Campbell after Boatmen's communicated to her its expert opinion of the nature of the proposed investments and their potential ramifications. This is especially true because the investments at the co-trustee's directions to Boatmen's in behalf of the trust beneficiary benefited the co-trustee. In acquiescing to Mr. Campbell's actions without first communicating with Ms. Ramsey to determine that she understood the nature of the investments, Boatmen's opinion on the advisability of the investments, the conflict of interest created by her son/co-trustee benefiting from the investments, and the risks involved with these type of investments, Boatmen's did not fulfill its fiduciary responsibility. . . .

[Judgment affirmed.]

Principal and Income Allocation

In many trusts, the interests of the beneficiaries are successive. In this situation, one beneficiary, the income beneficiary, is entitled to income from the trust property, commonly for life. A later beneficiary is then to receive the trust property, or principal, outright on the termination of the income beneficiary's interest. For example, assume Oliver, in his will, leaves an apartment building and stocks and bonds to First National Bank in trust, to pay the income annually to Oliver's wife, Wanda, for her life. On Wanda's death, the property is to be conveyed to Oliver's son, Fred, in fee simple; Wanda has a life estate and Fred a remainder. Because Wanda and Fred have separate and distinct interests in the property, during Wanda's life the trustee must allocate receipts and expenditures relating to the property between the two beneficiaries. That is, in administering the trust, the trustee must determine how much to pay the income beneficiary each year or, stated conversely, how much to retain for the remainderman. The net income payable currently to the income beneficiary is computed by subtracting expenditures allocable to income from receipts allocable to income. This process of apportionment is commonly known as **principal and income allocation.**

As always, the trust instrument may dictate how various receipts and expenditures are to be allocated. In the absence of such express provision, the issue is resolved in most states by the **Uniform Principal and Income Act,** originally promulgated in 1931 and revised in 1962 and 1997. The following general allocation rules are derived from the 1997 Act.

General Allocation Rules

Income is the return in money or property derived from the use of, or as profit produced by, the principal. Thus ordinary current receipts, such as interest or rental income, are credited to income. Against these gross receipts, ordinary current expenses incurred in managing or preserving trust property are deducted. Examples include: (1) interest expense, (2) ordinary repairs, (3) regularly recurring taxes assessed against principal, (4) recurring insurance premiums covering loss of a principal asset or its income or use, (5) income taxes, and (6) expenses of a legal proceeding concerning the income interest. The trustee may, but is not required to, deduct a reasonable amount for depreciation of the trust's fixed assets.

In contrast, principal is the property set aside by the settlor to be held in trust and delivered to the remainderman upon termination of the income beneficiary's interest. Principal also includes property received in substitution for, or as a change in form of, the original principal. Therefore, proceeds from the sale or exchange of the trust property are principal. Any gain or loss resulting from such a disposition is allocated to principal. Conversely, losses incurred in the sale, exchange, destruction, or casualty of the trust property are charged against principal, but any insurance proceeds received upon loss, damage, theft, or destruction of trust property are added to principal. Additionally, proceeds of property taken through condemnation (eminent domain) proceedings are principal.

Deducted from amounts allocated to principal are (1) payments on the principal of a trust debt, (2) disbursements made to prepare the principal for rental or sale, (3) title insurance premiums, (4) estate, inheritance, and transfer taxes apportioned to the trust, (5) environmental expenses (for example, costs to remedy or remove environmental contamination), and (6) expenses incurred in maintaining or defending any lawsuit to construe the trust, to protect it or the property, or to assure the title of any trust property. In addition, the cost of extraordinary repairs, or expenditures incurred in making a capital improvement to the property, are payable out of principal. Similarly, the cost of special assessments levied against the trust property for improvements also are charged to principal.

Finally, the cost of periodic judicial accounting, the trustee's regular compensation, and the trust's current management expenses are divided equally between principal and income. In order to equalize income distributions from year to year, the trustee may estimate expenditures out of income in advance, and withhold sufficient income from distribution to build up a reserve to meet them. Similarly, a trustee who incurs unanticipated, large expenses out of income may spread the payment over several years.

Unproductive and Wasting Property

When a trust is created for successive beneficiaries, the trustee owes a duty to the income beneficiary both to preserve the property and to make it productive in order to produce a reasonable income. The trustee owes the beneficiary entitled to the principal the duty to preserve the trust estate. Because these interests are competing and trust law requires the trustee to deal impartially with the beneficiaries, the trustee may risk a breach of duty if some of the trust property is unproductive (injuring the income beneficiary) or wasting (injuring the beneficiary entitled to principal). To provide guidance to the trustee, the UPIA provides a number of simply applied rules to resolve these problems.

Unproductive Property. Trust property is or may become unproductive or underproductive. That is, property may be valuable but yield no income, or income substantially lower than the current rate of return on trust investments. Under the UPIA, this issue is governed by the prudent investor rule, previously discussed, under which the trustee's duty to make the trust property productive applies to the trust portfolio as a whole, not to any individual asset. Thus, the trustee has no duty to sell unproductive property, and the proceeds of the property, if sold, are allocated to principal. The trustee breaches his duty to the income beneficiary only if the trust property as a whole produces insufficient income.

Wasting Property. Wasting property includes interests that terminate or necessarily depreciate over time either because of the nature of the interest or because of the character of the property involved. Examples of such property include (1) liquidating assets (for example, leaseholds, patent rights, copyrights, and royalty rights); (2) minerals, water, and other natural resources; and (3) timber. Unless the trustee has established a reserve for depreciation, the trustee is required to allocate 10 percent of the receipts from a liquidating asset to income and the balance to principal. A similar allocation is required for royalty payments received on minerals, other natural resources, and nonrenewable water interests. Receipts from timber harvested from trust property are allocated according to the rate of growth of the timber during the accounting period; that is, receipts reflecting the current period's growth rate are income, the balance is principal. Note that proceeds of the sale of standing timber, as a replacement of principal, is allocated to principal.

Deferred Compensation and Annuity Payments. Trust property may include an annuity; an individual retirement account; or a pension, profit sharing, or stock ownership plan. For example, the settlor may transfer to the trust a commercial annuity she purchased providing payments for a fixed number of years. Receipts under such plans are income if they are characterized as interest or a dividend. If they are not so characterized, and the payer (for example, an insurance company or state retirement fund) is required to make the payment, 10 percent of the payment is income and the balance is principal. If the payer is not required to make the payment, or if the payment is the entire amount owed to the trustee, the entire payment is principal.

Securities as Trust Property

Dividends. Frequently, the trustee will receive dividends or other distributions on stock owned by the trust. As a general rule, cash dividends are income, and dividends in property other than money are principal. A cash distribution is, however, principal if it is received: (1) in exchange for part or all of the trust's interest in the corporation, or (2) in partial or total liquidation of the corporation. To distinguish partial liquidations from ordinary cash dividends, the UPIA provides that a payment is in partial liquidation if: (1) the corporation so states, or (2) the distribution exceeds 20 percent of the corporation's total assets. Note that when classifying a distribution, the trustee generally may rely upon any statement by the corporation concerning the source or character of any dividend or other distribution.

Discount Obligations. The trust assets may include certain monetary obligations purchased at a discount. Examples include short-term obligations, such as U.S. Treasury Bills, and long-term instruments such as U.S. Savings Bonds or zero-coupon bonds. If the obligation is sold or redeemed more than one year after it is acquired by the trustee, the entire amount received is allocated to principal. If the obligation matures within one year after acquisition, the amount received in excess of its original value or purchase price is allocated to income.

Charitable Trusts

In a private trust the property is used to benefit certain specified persons designated as beneficiaries. In a charitable trust, the property is devoted to purposes beneficial to the public. Charitable purposes include, for example, the relief of poverty, the advancement of education, the promotion of health, governmental or municipal purposes, and other purposes beneficial to the community. Although private and charitable trusts have much in common, significant differences exist regarding the validity, enforcement, and modification of the trust.

Because a charitable trust is designed to accomplish public purposes and not to give a beneficial interest to individual beneficiaries, the persons who are to receive benefits from a charitable trust need not be designated. In other words, the individuals to whom the benefits accrue are not the beneficiaries. Rather, by aiding them, the interests of the real beneficiary, the public, are served.

In a private trust, the named beneficiary is entitled to enforce it. Because the public generally is the beneficiary of a charitable trust, it is enforced by the attorney general of the state in which the trust is to be administered, who acts as a representative of the public. A person with a special interest in performance of the trust—such as a specific charity or agency, which, by terms of the trust, is to be benefited—also may enforce it. Neither the settlor nor members of the public generally may maintain an enforcement action.

Alteration of Charitable Trusts—The *Cy Pres* Doctrine

As previously discussed, the court, in both private and charitable trusts, may permit the trustee to deviate from a trust term if compliance becomes impossible, illegal, or would, due to circumstances unforeseen by the settlor, defeat or substantially impair trust purposes. The **cy pres doctrine,** which is applicable only to charitable trusts, is an analogous but more extensive principle, under which the court directs that the trust property be used for a charitable purpose different from that designated by the settlor.

The doctrine applies if the designated charitable purpose becomes impossible, impracticable, or illegal, *and* the settlor has manifested a more general intention to devote the property to charitable purposes. In this situation, the trust will not fail. Instead, upon application by the trustee, attorney general, or other interested party, the court will direct that the property be used for some other charitable purpose falling within the settlor's general charitable intention. In other words, the property is applied to charitable purposes "as near as possible" (from the French phrase *"cy pres comme possible"*) to those intended by the settlor.

The settlor's intended purpose may fail for a variety of reasons. For example, if the settlor leaves property in trust to establish a hospital and the amount proves insufficient for that purpose, the court may order the property used to benefit an existing hospital or otherwise for the promotion of health, if the settlor has indicated a general charitable intent to aid the sick. Although *cy pres* literally requires application of the property to a purpose "as near as possible" to that envisioned by the settlor, courts, in choosing among possible alternatives, do not necessarily select the one closest to the settlor's plan. Rather, courts attempt to identify and select an approach that seems best suited to accomplish the settlor's general charitable purpose.

Resulting Trusts

A **resulting trust** is created when a person disposes of property under circumstances indicating that he does not intend that the person taking or holding the property should have the beneficial interest in it. A resulting trust, like an express trust, is based upon the settlor's intent, but intent is *presumed* or *implied,* rather than explicitly stated. Because the person holding the property (the trustee of the resulting trust) is not entitled to it, the beneficial interest springs back or "results" to the transferor or his estate. A resulting trust is "passive"; that is, the only duty of the trustee is to convey the property to the beneficiary (the original transferor) or according to his direction.

A resulting trust arises if an express private or charitable trust fails, or is fully performed without exhausting the trust property. In these cases, the trustee, who generally has no beneficial interest, should not be entitled to keep the trust property but rather should be compelled to return it to the settlor or his estate. For example, assume that Gene transfers $10,000 to First State Bank in trust to pay the income to Chris for life. On Chris's death, First State Bank holds the $10,000 upon a resulting trust for Gene or his estate. Or, assume Gene transfers $50,000 to First State Bank in trust to build a hospital. If the amount proves insufficient to accomplish the charitable purpose, and Gene has not indicated a general charitable intent, the trust fails. The bank then holds the money upon a resulting trust for Gene or his estate.

In the preceding examples, the settlor could have created an express (as opposed to resulting) trust by stating as a trust term what disposition should be made of the property upon termination or failure of the trust. If the settlor fails to include such a term, however, the resulting trust is used to achieve the settlor's probable or presumed intent.

Summary

1.   Upon death, an estate is created containing all of the property formerly owned by the decedent. This property is distributed under the supervision of a state probate court according to the terms of a will or the state "intestate succession" statute.

2.   A will is a formal instrument by which a person, known as a "testator," makes a disposition of property to take effect after death. If the will meets the formal requirements prescribed by state law, the decedent's property will be distributed, after payment of lawful claims against the estate, according to the terms of the will. If the decedent fails to leave a valid will, the estate is distributed according to state intestate succession statutes.

3.   A will has no legal effect before death and until that time may be altered or revoked by the testator. A will may be revoked by physical act, a subsequent writing complying with the formalities of a will revoking the former will, or by certain changes in the testator's circumstances, such as divorce. Even if the will meets the statutory formalities and is not revoked, persons named in the will may be prevented from receiving their designated share of the estate through the doctrines of lapse, ademption, and abatement.

4.   Although the testator generally is allowed to dispose of property on death as he or she desires, the law imposes certain limitations, such as forced share statutes, on the ability to disinherit a surviving spouse. The testator's family also is

protected by statutes creating a homestead exemption, exempt property, and a family allowance. These statutes give the surviving spouse and children a preference in certain property over unsecured creditors and other persons named in the will.

5. A trust splits the ownership of property between the trustee, who holds legal title, and the beneficiary, who holds equitable or beneficial title. Most trusts are created expressly, arising as a result of a property owner's language, indicating an intention to create it. The owner, or settlor, usually creates the trust by transferring the property to the trustee either during life (an inter vivos trust) or in the settlor's will on death (a testamentary trust). Trusts also are created during life by the settlor's declaration that he holds the property as trustee for another.

6. The powers and duties of the trustee and the nature and extent of the beneficiary's interest are determined by the instrument creating the trust. The settlor has no power to modify or terminate the trust unless such a power has been reserved in the terms of the trust. Even in the absence of a power to revoke, the trust may terminate for various reasons, such as completion of the purpose for which the trust was created.

7. The trustee has a duty to administer the trust. The law imposes various duties upon the trustee during trust administration, such as the fiduciary duty of loyalty, and the duty to make only those investments of trust property that a prudent investor would make. A trustee who fails properly to perform any duty imposed by law or the terms of the trust is liable to the beneficiary for damages for breach of trust.

8. If the interests of the trust beneficiaries are successive, the trustee must allocate receipts and expenditures arising from managing the trust property between the income beneficiary and remainderman. This process of apportionment, known as "principal and income allocation," may be governed by the trust instrument. In the absence of an express provision, trustees are guided by statutes such as the Uniform Principal and Income Act.

9. Express trusts may be either private or charitable. Although the two have much in common, significant differences exist between the two regarding the validity, modification, and enforcement of the trust.

10. A resulting trust, like an express trust, is based upon the settlor's intent, but intent is presumed or implied, rather than explicitly stated. Resulting trusts arise when a person transfers property under circumstances indicating that he or she does not intend that the person possessing the property should have the beneficial interest in it.

Key Terms

testate
will
testator
testamentary disposition
intestate
intestate succession statute
estate
probate court
probate
domicile
executor (executrix)
administrator (administratrix)
Uniform Probate Code (UPC)
devise
legacy
bequest
specific devise
general devise
demonstrative devise
attestation clause
nuncupative will
holographic will
codicil
dependent relative revocation doctrine
lapse
issue
ademption by extinction
ademption by satisfaction
advancement
abatement
dower
curtesy
community property doctrine
heirs
per stirpes distribution (taking by representation)
per capita distribution
Uniform Simultaneous Death Act
trust
trustee
beneficiary
settlor (trustor)
trust property (res, corpus)
inter vivos trust
testamentary trust
express trust
private trust
charitable trust
implied trust
pour over trust
Uniform Testamentary Additions to Trusts Act
honorary trust
spendthrift trust
fiduciary relationship
prudent investor rule
Uniform Prudent Investor Act
principal and income allocation
Uniform Principal and Income Act
cy pres doctrine
resulting trust

Questions and Problems

39.1 The requirements for a valid will often have been criticized as a trap for the unwary. This criticism seems especially valid in cases such as *Matter of Will of Daly.* Why do states continue to adhere strictly to the will formalities?

39.2 Why do most people in the United States die intestate? Given this fact, what factors should the legislature consider in enacting an intestate succession statute?

39.3 In September, Theresa gave her friend Jean a check in the amount of $5,000 with a note stating, "Jean, I'm leaving you this check rather than putting you in my will. I hope I will have enough money to cover the check in my account after I die." Theresa died two months later. When Jean tried to cash the check, the bank refused to honor it because of Theresa's death. Jean petitioned the probate court requesting a distribution of $5,000 from Theresa's estate. How should the court rule? Explain.

39.4 Leonard died in an automobile accident in which his automobile was destroyed totally. Leonard's insurance company paid $3,500, the value of the car, to his estate. Leonard's will provided:

> To my brother, David, I will any automobile which I may own at my death. The rest, residue and remainder of my property, I devise to my daughter Carol.

Is David entitled to any distribution from Leonard's estate? Explain.

39.5 In 2000, Harry executed a will leaving his farm, a savings account at ABC Bank, and some personal property to his daughter, Emily. The will further provided that if Harry sold the farm during his lifetime, he bequeathed an additional $20,000 to Emily. In June 2003, Harry sold the farm for $25,000. In August 2003, Harry deposited $20,000 in the savings account at ABC Bank. Harry died in September 2003. The executor of his estate petitioned to allow distribution of the savings account, the personal property, and $20,000 to Emily. The residuary legatees objected to this distribution arguing that Harry's transfer of the $20,000 to the savings account during his lifetime was an ademption by satisfaction. How should the court rule?

39.6 June Cleaver died leaving the following will:

LAST WILL AND TESTAMENT

I, June Cleaver, being of sound mind make this my last will and testament and revoke all prior wills.

1. I give all of my real property to my husband, Ward, if he survives me.
2. I give my diamond ring to my sister, May Reed.
3. I give $50,000 to my son, Wallace, and $100,000 to my son, Theodore.
4. I give my car to my son's friend, Eddy Haskell.
5. All of the rest, residue and remainder of my property I give, devise, and bequeath to my brother, Herbert.
6. I appoint Eddy Haskell to be executor of this my last will and testament.

IN WITNESS WHEREOF, I hereunto have signed my name this 2d day of July 1963.

s/June Cleaver
WITNESSED   s/May Reed

At the time of her death, June resided in the state of Michigan, which has enacted the Uniform Probate Code. Answer each of the following questions concerning her will.

(a) At the time she executed the will, June lived in a state that required only one witness to a will. Michigan law, however, requires two witnesses. Is the will valid? Explain.
(b) May Reed is an interested witness. Is she entitled to receive the diamond ring? Explain.
(c) June had executed a will in 1961 and in a codicil in 1962 she bequeathed her diamond ring to another sister, April. Who is entitled to receive the ring? Explain.
(d) At the time she executed the will, June owned a 1960 Chevrolet. At her death, the only car that she owned was a Mercedes Benz. Has the bequest to Eddy been adeemed?
(e) June's son Wallace, predeceased her. Wallace's wife and daughter were living at the time of June's death; however, the daughter died the day after June died. Who is entitled to receive the $50,000 left to Wallace? Explain.

39.7 Alex, during his lifetime, gave Barb a paper signed by Alex which stated, "I hereby give to Barb such shares of IBM stock as I may own at my death. Barb shall hold these shares in trust for Charles." Alex died intestate one year later leaving his wife as his sole heir. At his death Alex owned 1,000 shares of IBM stock.

(a) Did the instrument that Alex gave to Barb create a trust?
(b) Was a trust created when Alex died?
(c) Who should receive the IBM stock after Alex dies?

39.8 Christie deposits $10,000 in a savings account in First Federal Savings and Loan. The deposit was made in Christie's name "as trustee for my beloved daughter, Kay." Is a trust created? If a trust is created, is it revocable or irrevocable? Assume Christie dies without withdrawing any part of the deposit. Christie left a will leaving her entire estate to Sam. Should Kay be entitled to the $10,000 in the account? Why or why not?

39.9 Oliver died leaving the following will:

I hereby devise that all of my property be placed in trust and that the income be paid in equal shares to my wife so long as she shall not remarry and to my sister for her life.

Oliver was survived by both his wife and sister as well as by his son.

(a) Oliver's son files suit alleging that the will did not create a valid trust. Do you agree? Explain.
(b) Assume that the court determines that the trust is valid. For five years, Oliver's wife and sister share the income. Then Oliver's wife remarries. How should the income be paid?
(c) Three years after Oliver's wife remarries, his sister dies. Now how should the income be paid?

39.10 Pearl died leaving a will with a residuary clause that provided:

All the rest and residue of my estate, I give, devise and bequeath to my nephew Kenneth to distribute among my relatives as he sees fit.

The executor of Pearl's estate determines that Pearl intended to establish a trust and notifies the probate court that he intends to transfer the residuary assets to Kenneth in trust. Pearl's husband files a complaint with the court objecting to the trust. He asserts that Pearl failed to create a trust so that the property should be distributed to him in accordance with the intestacy laws. Kenneth argues that if the court should find that no trust was created then the residuary assets should be distributed to Kenneth outright.

How should the court rule? Explain.

39.11 Calvin established an inter vivos trust naming First National Bank as trustee. The trust instrument provided that all income should be paid to Calvin during his life. It also provided:

At the death of the Settlor, the net income of the trust property in the discretion of the trustee may be used for the following:

a) an annual donation to St. Phillip's Church to assist in the maintenance and upkeep of the church or for the operation of the recreational center owned by the church;

b) scholarships for boys or girls attending St. Phillip's Church who desire to go to college; and

c) annual donations to local or national civil rights organizations for work in voter registration and political education of minorities.

At Calvin's death, Calvin's sole heir, his sister, sued the trustee for the trust assets. She alleged that the trust should fail because Calvin used only precatory language and because the trust beneficiaries were indefinite. What result? Explain.

39.12 When Mary was 21, her father died leaving her a large amount of money. Upon the recommendation of her attorney, Mary established an irrevocable spendthrift trust and transferred all of the money to First State Bank as trustee. The trust provided that the trustee should pay all income to Mary during her life, remainder to be distributed as Mary provided in her will. Three years later, Mary requested that the trustee terminate the trust and transfer the trust corpus to Mary. The bank refused to terminate the trust and Mary sued.

At trial, a representative of the bank testified that Mary had had no experience with financial matters. He also testified that Mary had become a member of a religious cult to which she had donated almost all of the income paid to her. How should the court rule? Explain.

39.13 Consider the following facts and determine whether the trustee has committed a breach of trust.

(a) The trust holds a farm appraised at $100,000. Because the trust is not generating sufficient income, the trustee decides to sell the farm. After receiving several offers of less than $100,000, the trustee purchases the farm for his own use for $105,000.

(b) Trustee is an insurance agent. The trust assets include several buildings that must be insured. The trustee takes out insurance and pays himself the usual commission for such a sale.

(c) Trustee is a bank. As part of the securities portfolio of the trust, trustee invests in its own bank stock.

(d) Trustee is a bank. The trust maintains a checking and savings account at the bank.

39.14 Charles Xavier died leaving a will that named Central National Bank as trustee of a trust for the benefit of two beneficiaries. The trust estate included 4,300 shares of Sears Roebuck & Co. common stock that had a value of $117 per share on the date of Xavier's death. The Sears stock comprised 70 percent of the trust estate and 97 percent of the stock of the trust estate. The trustee retained the Sears stock and in less than 18 months its value had dropped to $88 per share. The beneficiaries sued Central National alleging that it had breached its fiduciary duties by mismanaging the trust assets. Specifically, the beneficiaries claimed that the trustee should have diversified the stock holdings within three months after the trust was established. How should the court rule?

39.15 Josie established a testamentary trust from which all income was to be paid to the Cancer Research Fund. The trustee determines that there is not and has never been any organization known as the "Cancer Research Fund." In another provision of the will, Josie stated her intention to disinherit her heirs. The trustee petitions the court for instructions as to whether the trust should be dissolved. How should the court rule?

PART SEVEN

BUSINESS ORGANIZATIONS

CHAPTER 40

INTRODUCTION TO AGENCY

Major Topics

- **the definition of agency and the general principles governing agency relationships**
- **the circumstances under which a principal is liable upon contracts made by an agent**
- **the liability of a principal for notice given to or knowledge acquired by an agent**
- **the methods by which agency powers are terminated**

The law of agency governs the legal rights and duties that arise when one person acts on behalf of another. Agency relationships are a fundamental institution in a capitalist economy, enabling employers to conduct many business activities in many places simultaneously. Even the smallest business owned by a single individual proprietor usually must hire employees, and even completely self-employed and self-sufficient individuals conduct business with others through their agents. As a business grows in size and adopts a formal structure, agency becomes increasingly important. For example, the partnership is largely a mutual agency relationship existing among the co-owners of the business, the partners. The corporation, the dominant organizational form for modern business, is an artificial person that acts only through agents.

Agency is a consensual fiduciary relationship in which one party, an **agent,** agrees to act on behalf of and under the control of another, known as the **principal.**[1] The principal is the person for whom an action is to be taken and the agent is the person who is to act. Either of the parties to the relation may be a natural person, a partnership, or a corporation.

Agency is based upon the premise that a person who acts through another, acts himself. That is, the acts of the agent are treated in law as the acts of the principal. Accordingly, the benefits, as well as the liabilities, derived from the agent's conduct accrue to the principal.

The law of agency encompasses the legal relationship existing between principal and agent and the legal relationship of principal and agent to third parties. The first category involves such issues as the creation of the relationship, the capacity of parties, and the duties of principal and agent to each other. The second category comprises the bulk of agency law and governs the liability of the principal and the agent to a third party (1) upon a *contract* made by the agent with the third party, and (2) for a *tort* committed by the agent against the third party. Separate and distinct rules apply to contract and tort liability. Therefore, in analyzing a third-party agency question, one must first determine whether the agent has committed a tort against a third party or has entered into a contract with a third party. One can

---

[1]RESTATEMENT (SECOND) OF AGENCY §1.

then apply the relevant legal principles to the issues raised by the question.

In addition to determining the liability for contracts made and for injuries caused *by* agents, the law of agency addresses the liability for accidental injuries or death inflicted *upon* agents acting within the scope of their employment. Traditionally governed by the common law of agency, this issue now is governed largely by state "workers' compensation" statutes.

This chapter examines the relationship between principal and agent, and the law of agency and contract, including the legal effect of notice or knowledge acquired by an agent and the principles governing termination of agency powers. Chapter 41 addresses agency and torts, including a discussion of workers' compensation statutes.

General Principles of Agency

Creation and Formality

According to the *Restatement (Second) of Agency,* an agency relationship results from "the manifestation of consent by one person to another that the other shall act on his behalf and subject to his control, and consent by the other so to act."[2] Although agency relationships often are created by contract, no contractual relationship is required. Assume Jane Doaks asks her friend Moe to purchase an antique lamp at an auction Moe plans to attend. If Moe consents to act, an agency relationship exists between the parties even though they have not entered into a contract. Agencies also may be created by **power of attorney,** a written instrument by which one person authorizes another to act as her agent.[3]

Agents often are empowered to enter into contracts on behalf of their principals. The Statute of Frauds may apply to these contracts, requiring a writing for enforceability. Assume Paul appoints Alice as agent to purchase a machine for Paul for $1,000. Alice subsequently contracts to purchase the machine from Ted. Because the contract involves a sale of goods with a price exceeding $500, a writing is required for enforceability under §2–201 of the Uniform Commercial Code. As Paul's authorized, agent, however, Alice may sign the writing on Paul's behalf, thereby satisfying the Statute of Frauds against Paul.

As a general rule, an agent need not be authorized in writing to act as an agent even if the agent is authorized to enter into written contracts and even if those contracts must be evidenced by a writing under the Statute of Frauds. Many states, however, alter this rule by statutes that require written authorization if the contract to be negotiated by the agent is within the Statute of Frauds.[4] These statutes are the modern versions of the **equal dignity rule** existing at common law requiring written agents' authorization. For example, if Paul appoints Alice as agent to purchase land on his behalf in a state that has adopted a statutory equal dignity rule, Alice's authorization also must be in writing.

Types of Agents

Agents may perform a wide variety of tasks for their principals. They may buy or sell property, pay or collect money, drive motor vehicles or operate machinery, manage people and assets, and more generally, perform any task a person could do without an agent. A number of terms, defined below, have developed to describe the functions and characteristics of certain agents.

General and Special Agents. A **general agent** is one "authorized to conduct a series of transactions involving a continuity of service."[5] General agents are characterized by continuous service, not the degree of skill or discretion exercised. Thus, managers, clerks, and sales and purchasing agents all are general agents. They are an integral part of a business enterprise, not requiring additional authorization for each transaction conducted on the principal's behalf.

A **special agent,** in contrast, is one who conducts "a single transaction or a series of transactions not involving continuity of service."[6] Thus, a real estate broker or auctioneer employed to sell the principal's house or other property, a stockbroker empowered to buy certain securities, or an attorney hired to negotiate a contract are special agents. The distinction between general and special agents is important in determining the extent and termination of the agent's authority to bind the principal to contracts made by the agent with third parties.

Masters and Servants. A **master** is a principal who has the control of (or the right to control) an agent's *physical conduct.* A **servant** is an agent whose physical conduct in the performance of his duties is subject to

---

[2]Restatement (Second) of Agency §1.
[3]A person designated an agent under a power of attorney need not be an attorney.

[4]Some states impose this requirement for all contracts within the Statute; others impose it for land sale contracts only.
[5]Restatement (Second) of Agency §3(1).
[6]Restatement (Second) of Agency §3(2).

the principal's control or right of control. Most employees, such as managers, clerks, truck drivers, salespersons, or factory workers, are servants, and their employers are masters. A servant should be distinguished from an **independent contractor,** a person who contracts to do something for another but whose physical conduct in the performance of the undertaking is not subject to the other's control or right of control. An independent contractor may be, but is not necessarily, an agent.[7] The master-servant relationship, discussed in detail in Chapter 41, is a prerequisite to imposing liability upon a principal for torts committed by agents against third parties.

Brokers, Factors, and Del Credere Agents. A **broker** is simply an agent empowered to make or procure contracts on her principal's behalf for compensation, usually called a "commission." Perhaps the most common brokers are real estate brokers (those empowered to procure the purchase or sale of land) and stockbrokers (those employed to buy or sell stocks, bonds, or other securities).

A **factor,** or **commission merchant,** on the other hand, is an agent entrusted with possession and control of the principal's goods for purposes of sale, compensated by a commission or "factorage." A factor, unlike a broker, is commonly in possession and control of the property involved and sells in her own, rather than her principal's name.

A **del credere agent** is simply a factor who sells goods on credit and then guarantees to the principal the purchaser's solvency and the purchaser's performance of the contract. In other words, the del credere agent acts as a surety, liable to the principal if the purchaser defaults. Normally, the agent is compensated for this suretyship promise by an additional commission (a del credere commission) on the sale. Because the main purpose of the agent's promise is to benefit the agent, not to accommodate the principal, the promise of a del credere agent need not be in writing under the Statute of Frauds like other suretyship promises.

Capacity of Parties

Because agency is not necessarily a contractual relationship, a person need not have contractual capacity to be a principal. Agency is based upon consent, and therefore the parties need only possess the capacity to give legally operative consent. Most natural persons and corporations meet this test. In fact, without capacity to appoint agents, a corporation could not act. In addition, persons with limited capacity, such as minors, may be principals. Nevertheless, the creation of the agency and the transactions made under it are affected by the principal's limited capacity. For example, assume Mel, a minor, appoints Alan as his agent to purchase a car from Tom. Alan later purchases the car from Tom. Both the appointment of Alan as agent and the subsequent contract with Tom are voidable by Mel.[8]

On the other hand, a person has capacity to be an agent even though she has no capacity to be a principal. Capacity to have rights or be subject to duties is not required. To illustrate, suppose Joe tells his daughter Mary, a minor, to go to the hardware store, purchase an electric drill, and charge the purchase to Joe's account. In this case, Mary has capacity to be an agent, and is thereby able to bind Joe to the contract, even though Mary could not have been bound to the same contract herself because she has limited contractual capacity.

Duties of Agent to Principal

The rights and obligations of principal and agent often are determined by an express contract. Failure of either party to perform results in liability for breach. Thus, in determining the scope of an agency relation, the explicit terms of any contract existing between the parties first must be examined.

Unless the parties otherwise agree, agency law imposes various duties upon both principal and agent. Among these duties are the duties of loyalty and obedience owed by an agent to a principal, and the correlative duties of compensation, indemnity, and protection owed by a principal to an agent. A party injured by breach of these duties may sue for damages or other appropriate judicial relief.

Duties of Service and Obedience. A fundamental characteristic of agency is that the agent acts under the direction and control of the principal. The following specific duties imposed upon the agent achieve this result.

Duty of Obedience. The agent has a duty to obey all reasonable instructions from the principal regarding the manner of performing the agency. The extent of obedience

---

[7]RESTATEMENT (SECOND) OF AGENCY §2.

[8]Alan may incur liability to Tom in this situation for breach of the agent's warranty of authority discussed later in this chapter.

required and the manner of the agent's performance are determined by the agency contract or by the character of the agency. In master-servant relationships, for example, the master usually closely controls and supervises the servant's activities. In other agencies, however, certain customary aspects of the agent's performance are left to the agent's discretion. Clients, for example, usually may not interfere in the specific details of their attorney's performance, including the conduct of court proceedings.[9]

Duty to Act as Authorized. Principles of "authority," discussed in detail later in this chapter, determine when principal and agent are liable on contracts made by the agent with third parties. An agent has a duty to act only as authorized by the principal, and not to act on the principal's behalf after her authority is terminated. An agent breaches this duty, for example, by making an unauthorized contract for which the principal is liable or by improperly delegating her authority.

Duty to Keep and Render Accounts. The agent must keep and render accurate accounts of money or property received or disbursed on the principal's behalf. The duty extends to the amounts of receipts or payments and other relevant information such as the persons involved and the dates of transactions. The extent of the duty to account varies with the nature of the agency and business custom. For example, a traveling salesperson has more extensive accounting duties than a store clerk.

Duty to Give Information. The agent is required to keep the principal informed of important facts acquired during the course of the agency that may affect the principal's interests. The duty to disclose such information is particularly important because notice or knowledge acquired by an agent during the course of his employment may be imputed to the principal, whether or not actually communicated.

Duty of Care and Skill. The agent also has a duty to exercise reasonable care and skill in the performance of her work, and in addition, to exercise any special skill she may have. Under this duty, for example, the principal may recover for an agent's negligent destruction of the principal's goods. A client may recover from an attorney whose negligent failure to file a lawsuit in a timely fashion, or to be aware of changes in the law, causes loss to the client. The principal also may sue the agent for conduct that subjects the principal to tort liability to third parties under principles outlined in Chapter 41.

Duties of Loyalty. Agency is a fiduciary relationship imposing duties of utmost trust and confidence upon an agent. That is, an agent acts on behalf of and subject to the control of the principal, and is a fiduciary in the performance of those acts. The fiduciary nature of an agent's obligation is embodied in the **duty of loyalty**, under which the agent is required to act solely for the benefit of the principal regarding all matters within the scope of the agency. Thus, in dealing with the principal, the agent must not act for his personal benefit or for the benefit of a third party, and must fully disclose all information material to the agency relation. An agent's fiduciary obligation closely parallels that owed by a trustee to the beneficiaries of a trust.

The duty of loyalty requires the agent to account for all profits arising out of the agency, including incidental or unusual profits, whether or not received in a breach of the agent's duty. Assume Art is a salesperson in Penny's store. Thelma purchases goods from Art, but inadvertently overpays her bill by ten dollars. Thelma disappears before the mistake can be corrected. Art must account to Penny for the overpayment. In addition to the duty to account, the agent also is required to have title to property obtained on the principal's behalf held in the principal's name and not to commingle the principal's property with his own.

The duty of loyalty also prevents the agent from competing with the principal concerning matters within the scope of the agency. Assume Ann is an agent to buy and sell antiques for Paul. Unknown to Paul, Ann maintains a personal stock of antiques that she sells to Paul's customers and periodically replenishes with purchases from Paul's customers. Ann has committed a breach of her duty of loyalty to Paul. Note that competition by the agent is permitted with the principal's consent and in areas outside the scope of the agency. For example, an agent employed to buy and sell land may compete with the principal in the sale of goods.

The duty of loyalty also prevents an agent from disclosing or otherwise using confidential information acquired during the course of the agency to the principal's detriment. The agent may not use the information for his own benefit or disclose it to a competitor of the principal. Protected information includes specialized business practices or trade secrets, customer lists, and

---

[9]Restatement (Recond) of Agency §385 and comment a.

other matters peculiar to the principal's business, such as the principal's intention to buy or sell property, issue securities, declare dividends, or merge with another business. The agent is accountable for any profits made by the use or disclosure of confidential information whether or not the principal has been harmed thereby. This rule is designed to foster the free flow of sensitive business information between principal and agent.

At issue in the following case was whether an agent had breached his fiduciary duty of loyalty.

Insurance Company of North America v. Miller
765 A.2d 587 (Md. 2001)

Defendant William Miller, a licensed insurance agent, was an employee and officer of Hickman & Company, Inc. (Hickman), a firm that sold insurance policies to businesses and individuals. In 1995, Miller, on behalf of Hickman, signed a contract with Insurance Company of North America (INA), in which Hickman agreed to sell INA insurance policies, collect the premiums for those policies, and pay the premiums less Hickman's commissions to INA. The Hickman agency, however, failed to forward premium payments to INA as agreed. Hickman, after receiving full payment of a premium (either from the insured or a company financing the insured), would notify INA that the customer was paying the premium in installments. Hickman would retain the full premium payment in its own bank account and send payments to INA in periodic installments. Hickman used the excess premiums to pay various expenses. Miller was fully aware of this scheme. He managed several of the bank accounts and signed checks for those accounts. In one instance, when a customer's premium had to be reimbursed, Miller borrowed the funds needed for repayment because Hickman had spent the money. In 1997, Hickman became insolvent. INA sued Miller, alleging that he had breached his fiduciary duty to INA and, therefore, should be liable for INA's losses. The trial evidence established that under the contract with INA, Miller was an agent of INA. The trial court ruled, however, that Miller was an agent only for purposes of selling insurance policies and that he owed no duties to INA. After the trial court ruled in favor of Miller, INA filed an appeal and the Maryland Court of Appeals agreed to review the case.

Cathell, Judge

. . . The duties an agent owes to his or her principal are well established. . . . As Professor Mechem has observed:

It is the duty of the agent to conduct himself with the utmost loyalty and fidelity to the interests of his principal, and not to place himself or voluntarily permit himself to be placed in a position where his own interests or those of any other person whom he has undertaken to represent may conflict with the interests of his principal.

Philip Mechem, *Mechem Outlines Agency* §500, at 345 (4th ed. 1952).

One of the primary obligations of an agent to his or her principal is to disclose any information the principal may reasonably want to know. . . . The obligation to disclose is strongest when a principal has a conflicting interest in a transaction connected with the agency. See *Restatement (Second) Of Agency* §389 (1958) ("Unless otherwise agreed, an agent is subject to a duty not to deal with his principal as an adverse party in a transaction connected with his agency *without the principal's knowledge*.") (emphasis added). An agent's failure to disclose information material to the agency thus constitutes a breach of the principal-agent relationship. Where an agent breaches a duty to the principal and profits from the breach, the principal may maintain an action to recover those profits for her or himself. . . .

In [this] case . . . , [Miller] stipulated that he was an agent of INA from 1995 until May 1997. The evidence is clear that he had knowledge of what was occurring and participated in part of the scheme. As an agent, he had a fiduciary duty to INA, which he breached.

Among the agent's fiduciary duties to the principal is the duty to account for profits arising out of the employment, the duty not to act as, or on account of, an adverse party without the principal's consent, the duty to not compete with the principal on his own account or for another in matters relating to the subject matter of the agency, and the duty to deal fairly with the principal in all transactions between them. [*Restatement (Second) Of Agency* §13.] The federal courts and courts of our sister states are generally in accord. . . .

As an agent and a fiduciary, Mr. Miller had the duty to act with the utmost loyalty and fidelity towards his principal, INA, and was required by this fiduciary relationship to give the fullest measure of service in all matters pertaining to the agency. Instead of acting with loyalty and fidelity towards INA, Mr. Miller breached his fiduciary duty in numerous ways. First, he knew that premiums were not being remitted to INA, but failed to inform INA, and did not cause the remittance of premium (payments) to the insurer. Second, he participated in a double financing scheme where the Hickman agency withheld premiums from INA based on the representation to INA that the premiums were to be paid in installments, when the Agency was already in possession of the entire premium amount either from insureds or from premium financing companies on behalf of insureds. He signed company checks to INA for installments due when in fact he had obtained the entire premiums from premium financing companies (or from insureds) and kept this plan concealed from INA — actions, which clearly demonstrate his awareness and participation in this scheme. Third, when . . . premium funds [had to be paid] back from the Hickman Agency, and there was no money to pay the premiums because the money was out-of-trust, Mr. Miller directed the premium financing of another account . . . expressly for the purpose of repaying the premium due. . . . Fourth, consistently throughout this relationship, Mr. Miller, who had knowledge of what was occurring, failed to disclose his, and Hickman's, conflicting actions to INA. . . . Mr. Miller placed himself in a position where INA's interests and his interests conflicted. . . . [O]ne of the primary obligations of an agent to a principal is to disclose any information the principal may reasonably want to know. It is safe to say that Mr. Miller's actions were not made with INA's best interests in mind and that INA would reasonably want to have known of his actions while he was acting as its agent.

We therefore hold that the trial court erred when it ruled that [Miller] was not an agent of INA for the purpose of collecting and forwarding premiums, and as a result did not breach any fiduciary duties by failing to do so. To the contrary, Miller had knowledge of what was happening and actively participated in a significant portion of the improper actions. In failing to share his knowledge with INA, and by participating in the scheme, he breached his fiduciary duty to [INA]. . . .

[Judgment reversed and remanded.]

Duties of Principal to Agent

Although an agency is a fiduciary relationship, imposing a duty of loyalty upon the agent in dealing with the principal, no such fiduciary duty is imposed upon the principal. That is, the principal generally has no duty to act solely for the agent's interest in matters within the scope of the agency. The principal does, however, owe various duties to the agent, most notably the duties of compensation, indemnity, and protection.

Unless the agent agrees to serve gratuitously, the agent is entitled to compensation for work performed on the principal's behalf. If no specific amount is stated in the agency agreement, the agent is entitled to the fair value of the services performed. In the ordinary employment (master-servant) relationship, the employer generally must maintain and render accurate accounts of amounts due the employees. Other agents, such as factors, brokers, and auctioneers, maintain an independent business and usually keep their own accounts of amounts due from the principal.

In addition to the duty to compensate, the principal is required to indemnify, or reimburse, the agent for expenses reasonably and properly incurred on the principal's behalf in the conduct of the agency. These include, for example, authorized or necessary payments made in conducting the principal's business, payments made in performing authorized contracts, and payments arising from the ownership or possession of property that the agent is authorized to hold for the principal. The principal also must reimburse the agent for losses incurred through no fault of the agent in transactions the principal authorizes. This duty often arises either expressly or by implication from the agency contract between the parties. It also may be restitutionary,[10] imposed to prevent unjust enrichment of the principal after the agent personally satisfies an obligation of the principal, or suffers a loss that, in fairness, the principal should bear.

The principal also owes a general duty to use reasonable care to prevent agents from being injured during their performance of the agency. In master-servant relationships, for example, breach of this duty of care provides a basis for employees to recover from their employers for job-related injuries. The common law governing employer liability for injuries to employees and the impact of state workers' compensation statutes on that liability are discussed in Chapter 41.

Agency and Contracts

Perhaps the most pervasive agency issue concerns the liability of the principal and agent for *contracts* made by the agent with third parties on the principal's behalf. The law addresses two questions. First, when is an agent

---

[10]Restitution is discussed in Chapter 15.

personally liable upon a contract made on the principal's behalf, and second, when is the principal liable upon a contract made by an agent? Both questions are answered by applying fairly straightforward rules that require an initial understanding of the concept of "authority."

General Principles of Contract Liability

The Concept of Authority. Every day agents enter into contracts that may be enforced by or against their principals. An agent's power to bind the principal to a contract is derived from the principal's directions or instructions to the agent concerning the extent of the agent's power. This power is referred to as the agent's **authority** (sometimes called the agent's **actual authority**).[11] The extent of the agent's authority is determined by examining the principal's words (oral or written) or other conduct indicating the principal's consent that the agent act on the principal's behalf. Thus, authority is based upon a manifestation of consent running from the principal to the agent. The existence and extent of authority is important because a principal generally is liable upon contracts he has authorized the agent to make, but not for an agent's unauthorized contracts. To illustrate, assume Parker authorizes Andrews in writing to sell Parker's car at a price not less than $25,000. Andrews contracts to sell the car to Thomas for $26,000. Andrews also contracts with Sax to sell Parker's house for $500,000. Parker is bound to the contract with Thomas, but not with Sax. Andrews has authority to sell the car but not the house.

Express and Implied Authority. An agent's authority may be either express or implied. **Express authority** is based upon explicit oral or written statements defining the agent's power. Thus, in the preceding example, Andrews is expressly authorized to transfer title to Parker's car in exchange for money. Most authority is not express but arises by implication. Authority is often **implied** because the express language is very general in nature. For example, Carol may appoint Jean to "manage" Carol's grocery store or apartment building. In this case, much of Jean's authority is implied from the general express grant; that is, it flows as a natural or logical consequence of the express authority granted.

For example, a person hired to manage a business possesses implied authority to (1) make contracts reasonably necessary to conduct the business, (2) procure equipment and supplies and make necessary repairs, (3) hire, supervise, and fire employees, (4) sell goods or services in the ordinary course of business, (5) receive money and pay debts arising from the operation of the business, and (6) otherwise direct the ordinary operation of the business.[12]

Implied authority extends only to those acts incident and necessary to exercise the express authority granted. That is, implied authority may not contradict the express grant in any way. To determine the extent of implied authority, therefore, one must carefully examine the express authority granted. To illustrate, assume P hires A to manage P's business, but reserves the sole power to hire and fire employees. A has no implied authority to hire and fire employees.

Agent's Warranty of Authority. A person who purports to make a contract for a principal impliedly represents that he has the power to bind the principal. An agent who has no such authority breaches this **implied warranty of authority** and is liable in damages to the third party. The agent breaches this warranty even if the agent is reasonably mistaken concerning the existence or extent of her authority. For example, assume Price hires Acheson as a sales representative with authority only to solicit orders for Price's products, fabrics and carpeting. Acheson, representing herself as Price's purchasing agent, contracts to purchase carpeting from Tilton, a carpet manufacturer. Price has no liability on the contract, and Acheson is liable to Tilton for breach of the implied warranty of authority. Note that Acheson is liable even if she reasonably believed that she had authority to make the purchase.

An agent also may be liable if the principal lacks contractual capacity. For example, an agent acting on behalf of a totally incompetent principal breaches the warranty of authority. The agent does not automatically breach the warranty, however, if the principal's contracts are merely *voidable*. For example, an agent acting on behalf of a minor principal is liable to the third party if the minor later disaffirms the contract only if the agent either (1) represents to the third party that the principal has full capacity or (2) knows of the principal's incapacity and the third party's ignorance of that

---

[11]Restatement (Second) of Agency §7.

[12]Restatement (Second) of Agency §73.

fact. An agent representing a principal with limited capacity should, therefore, disclose that fact to the third party to avoid potential liability.

Contract Liability—Undisclosed Principals

A principal is **disclosed** if the third party knows both that the agent is acting for a principal and the principal's identity. In this the most common agency arrangement, if the agent is authorized the principal is liable on the contract—that is, becomes a party to the contract—and the agent is not. An agent acting on behalf of a disclosed principal does not intend to become personally liable on the contract. Rather, the intent of all concerned is that the principal and the third party are to be the contracting parties.

Agents may, however, act on behalf of partially disclosed or undisclosed principals. A principal is **partially disclosed** if the principal's existence, but not identity, is known to the third party. For example, assume Allison is acting as agent for Peter to purchase land. She communicates with Thomas, a prospective seller, and states, "I am acting as an agent in this transaction but I am not at liberty to disclose my principal's name." Peter is a partially disclosed principal. A principal is **undisclosed** if neither the existence nor identity of the principal is known to the third party at the time of the contract. Suppose Peter wants to acquire a large block of land from several sellers for a shopping center. To avoid provoking a drastic increase in price, Peter appoints Allison as an agent to purchase the necessary parcels of land. Allison is instructed not to tell prospective sellers that she is acting for Peter. A number of landowners later enter into contracts with Allison to sell, unaware that she is acting as Peter's agent. As far as the individual sellers are concerned, they are dealing only with Allison. In this case, Peter is an undisclosed principal.[13]

A principal is always liable if the agent is authorized. Thus, a principal's liability is the same whether the principal is disclosed, partially disclosed, or undisclosed. An agent's liability, however, differs. Unlike the agent acting for a disclosed principal, the agent acting for a partially disclosed or undisclosed principal becomes a party to, and therefore personally liable upon, the contract. Thus, when an authorized agent acts on behalf of a partially

disclosed or undisclosed principal, *both* principal and agent are liable to the third party on the contract. That is, the law recognizes the existence of two contracts.

Although both principal and agent are liable when the principal is partially disclosed or undisclosed, the nature of that liability differs. If the principal is *partially disclosed,* the principal and agent are jointly and severally liable[14] on the contract. Thus, the third party may proceed against either or both parties and may collect any portion of the debt from either of them until the total contract obligation is satisfied. This rule fulfills the normal expectation of the parties, because third parties seldom rely solely on the credit of an unidentified person, and an agent who refuses to reveal the principal's identity usually expects to be held liable as a guarantor of the principal's performance.

If the principal is wholly *undisclosed,* the traditional common law rule holds that principal and agent are not jointly and severally liable. Rather, the liability is essentially in the *alternative,* governed by the doctrine of **election.** Under this doctrine, after discovering the existence and identity of the principal, the third party may elect to hold either the principal or the agent liable on the contract. For example, assume Allen is appointed by Potter, an undisclosed principal, to purchase land for a shopping center. Thompson contracts with Allen to sell a tract of land. In this case Thompson will initially look to Allen for performance of the contract because Thompson is unaware of the agency. Once Thompson discovers Potter's existence and identity, however, Thompson may elect to hold Allen liable on the contract, thereby releasing Potter, or may elect to hold Potter liable, thereby releasing Allen. No election can be made unless and until the third party discovers the principal's existence and identity.

The election rule has been criticized as outdated and unjust, and a minority of states have rejected it in favor of joint and several liability, the rule long applied to the partially disclosed principal case. Under this approach, once the third party discovers the principal's existence and identity, the third party may "recover judgments against both the principal and the agent, may attempt to collect its judgment against either party, and, to the extent that the judgment remains unsatisfied, may subsequently pursue collection from the other party."[15]

---

[13]RESTATEMENT (SECOND) OF AGENCY §4.

[14]Joint and several liability is discussed in Chapter 7.

[15]Crown Controls, Inc. v. Smiley, 756 P.2d 717, 722 (Wash. 1988).

At issue in the following case was whether a person should be held personally liable on contracts allegedly made on behalf of a corporate principal.

Estate of Saliba v. Dunning
682 A.2d 224 (Me. 1996)

Plaintiffs Samuel and Ruth Saliba (the Salibas) purchased a warehouse in Bangor, Maine in January 1988. The sole tenant of the building was the R.B. Dunning Company, an industrial supply wholesaler that had rented the warehouse since 1985. When the Salibas met with defendant John Dunning, the company's sole officer and manager of the business, to discuss the lease, he informed them that he had rented the building from the prior owner at $1,500 per month under an oral lease agreement. The Salibas agreed to continue the arrangement. In September 1992, the R.B. Dunning Company encountered financial difficulties and eventually terminated the business. The Salibas sued Dunning for breach of contract seeking damages of $15,600 including unpaid rent and cleaning charges. The trial court ruled in favor of the Salibas. Following an unsuccessful appeal to the Superior Court, Dunning appealed to the Maine Supreme Court.

Lipez, Judge

. . . An agent who makes a contract for an undisclosed principal or a partially disclosed principal will be liable as a party to the contract. *Restatement (Second) of Agency* §§321, 322 (1958). Hence, "[i]n order for an agent to avoid personal liability on a contract negotiated in his principal's behalf, he must disclose not only that he is an agent but also the identity of the principal. . . . [W]ithout that, the party dealing with the agent may understand that [the agent] intends to pledge his personal liability and responsibility in support of the contract and for its performance." *3 Am. Jur. 2d Agency* §327 (1986). A third party with whom the agent deals is not required to inquire whether the agent is acting for another. . . . Finally, neither the use of a corporate name . . . nor the use of corporate checks . . . is necessarily sufficient to notify a third person of a corporate principal.

The record supports the trial court's conclusion that Dunning did not make clear the fact of his agency to the Salibas at the time he entered into a contract with them to continue his tenancy in their building, and he thereby led the Salibas reasonably to believe that he was personally promising to pay the rent. Dunning testified that the company had been a family-run business since its founding and that he had been almost entirely responsible for its continued operation since 1989 or 1990. Ruth Saliba testified that "*Mr. Dunning* had rented [the building] from [the previous owner] for years . . . " (emphasis added). Both Saliba and Dunning testified that Dunning informed the Salibas during their initial meeting that he had never had a written lease with the previous owner, that he did not have any problems with this arrangement, and that he paid his rent on time. None of these assurances revealed that Dunning was acting as an agent of the company. In fact, there is no testimony from Saliba or Dunning that Dunning informed the Salibas at any time during this initial meeting, or at any other point in their relationship, including those instances when he reaffirmed his promise to pay the rent, that he was acting solely in his capacity as an officer of The R.B. Dunning Company. In light of this testimony, we cannot say that the court clearly erred in finding that Dunning did not provide the Salibas with notice of his agency relationship at the outset of the parties' contractual relationship, and that he therefore incurred personal liability for the rental amounts. . . .

[Judgment affirmed.]

The preceding discussion generates two simple rules governing most agency contract situations:

1. An agent is liable on a contract made in an agency capacity unless both (a) the agent is authorized, and (b) the principal is disclosed.
2. The principal (disclosed, partially disclosed, or undisclosed) is liable upon contracts made on his behalf if the agent is authorized to act.

The doctrines of ratification and apparent authority, discussed below, may be viewed as exceptions to the general rule that the principal is liable only if the agent is authorized.

Ratification

Ratification involves words or other conduct by the principal indicating an intent to be bound upon (to treat as authorized) a previously unauthorized contract made on her behalf. Ratification may be inferred from various types of conduct including express statements to the third party of a willingness to be bound, silence indicating consent, accepting the benefits of the contract, or bringing suit to enforce the contract. If disputed, the ratification issue is a question of fact for the jury to decide.

A ratification automatically "relates back" to the date of the unauthorized contract, which is then treated as originally authorized. After ratification, therefore, the agent's liability to the third party for breach of the warranty of authority is terminated, and no notice of the ratification need be given to the third party to bind him. Nevertheless, the third party may withdraw from the unauthorized contract at any time *prior to* ratification. Similarly, the death or incapacity of the third party extinguishes the principal's power to ratify. The principal also may not ratify if circumstances have so materially changed since the contract was made that it would be inequitable to hold the third party liable.

To illustrate, assume that Page is the owner of a stable and several thoroughbreds. Page hires Archer to manage the stable, but gives Archer no authority to buy or sell any horse. Nevertheless, on June 1, Archer represents himself to Tudor as Page's authorized agent and contracts to sell one of Page's horses to Tudor. At this point, Page is not liable on the contract because Archer is unauthorized. Archer is liable to Tudor for breach of the warranty of authority. Although unauthorized, Archer has exacted a good price for the horse, and Page decides to go through with the sale. On June 10, the day Tudor is to pick up the horse, Page assists in readying the horse for transport and prepares the papers necessary to complete the sale. When Tudor arrives, the transfer is made with no mention of Archer's lack of authority. Page's conduct constitutes ratification of Archer's contract. Although Tudor could have withdrawn drawn from the contract prior to ratification (between June 1 and June 10), once ratified, Tudor is bound as if the contract had been originally authorized. Tudor may not now avoid the contract on the grounds that it was unauthorized when made, and Archer has no liability to Tudor for breach of the warranty of authority. If the horse (or Tudor) had died on June 5, however, Page could not ratify the contract.

Prerequisites to Ratification. Agency law imposes two important prerequisites to an effective ratification. First, the principal must have capacity both at the time of the unauthorized act and at the time of ratification. A person who has no capacity to authorize an act may not later ratify it. For example, persons organizing a corporation (corporate promoters) often purport to contract on its behalf before the corporation is formed. Because the corporation is not a legal entity when the contracts are made, the corporation may not ratify them when it comes into existence.[16]

A second requirement for effective ratification is that the person making the contract must purport to be acting for, and on behalf of, the person subsequently ratifying the contract. No preexisting agency relationship need exist between the parties. The person acting must simply purport to act as an agent for another, who need not be identified. Thus, a wholly undisclosed principal may not ratify an unauthorized contract. The rationale for this requirement is that "one reason for allowing ratification to be effective as prior authorization is to give to the other party what the other expected to get in dealing with the agent. This reason does not exist if the other party does not intend to deal with the principal."[17]

In the following case, the court was required to determine whether a principal's silence constituted ratification.

Sea Lion Corporation v. Air Logistics of Alaska, Inc.
787 P.2d 109 (Alaska 1990)

Myron Naneng was president and chairman of the board of directors of defendant Sea Lion Corporation, a company that provided air taxi services. In 1984, Naneng, on behalf of Sea Lion, and Larry Gillespie, who operated an air cargo service, began efforts to set up a joint venture in which they planned to use aircraft owned by plaintiff Air Logistics of Alaska, Inc. (Air Log). In mid-1984, however, Air Log decided to transfer those aircraft out of state and to close its Alaska operations. In response to inquiries from Gillespie, Air Log said that it would keep its aircraft in Alaska only if Sea Lion contractually agreed to pay all expenses of the aircraft. Following further discussion, Air Log prepared a written flight service agreement (FSA) that Naneng signed on behalf of Sea Lion. After learning of the agreement, James Joseph, who served as general manager, secretary/treasurer, and director of Sea Lion, and Sea Lion's attorney reprimanded Naneng for signing the FSA. When the agreement expired, Air Log again threatened to remove its aircraft from Alaska and Naneng signed another agreement—the 1985 FSA—on behalf of Sea

---

[16]Promoters' liability is discussed in Chapter 45.

[17]RESTATEMENT (SECOND) OF AGENCY §85 comment a.

Lion. After failing to receive payment for the expenses of its aircraft, Air Log sued Sea Lion for breach of the 1985 FSA. The trial court ruled that Sea Lion was liable on the contract and Sea Lion appealed.

Compton, Justice

. . . Air Log contends . . . that Sea Lion by its silence ratified Naneng's signature on the 1985 FSA. . . . Ratification is an agency doctrine, created by common law courts to deal with a situation where, after a transaction is entered into by a second party purporting to act for a principal, the principal manifests an intent to be bound by the acts of the second party. . . . [F]or an otherwise unauthorized act to be ratified by the principal's silence, . . . the principal must . . . have failed to act in response under circumstances which "according to the ordinary experience and habits of men, one would naturally be expected to speak if he did not consent." . . . Restatement (Second) of Agency §94, comment a (1957). . . . Moreover, the Restatement notes:

A principal's silence is usually more significant if an agent has exceeded his powers in the particular transaction, especially if the agent acted from an excess of zeal. If such an agent reports the matter to the principal at a time or in a manner calculated to call for dissent if the principal were unwilling to affirm, the latter's failure to dissent, if unexplained, furnishes sufficient evidence of affirmance.

Restatement (Second) of Agency §94, comment b (1957).

Cases adopting and interpreting this section of the Restatement have often held that this . . . requirement is met as to a third party where the principal has actual knowledge of the material facts surrounding a transaction entered into by an agent with some authority to act for the principal and takes no action to repudiate it. . . . Thus it appears that the Sea Lion board would have to have known of Naneng's execution of the 1985 FSA, and therefore done nothing to repudiate that act, in order for Naneng to have bound the corporation. . . . [L]iability is not predicated upon some act of the board, but upon its failure to act. The lack of evidence that Sea Lion's board did not hear of or discuss Naneng's signature at a formal board meeting is thus not fatal.

The relevant facts, taken in the light most favorable to Sea Lion, show that Naneng was its president and chairman of its Board, with some authority to act on its behalf. Naneng admits that he signed the 1985 FSA on behalf of Sea Lion. Naneng and Joseph, another board member, were both aware that the reason Air Log insisted that Naneng sign the 1985 FSA was to make Sea Lion liable on it, and that Air Log would not have entered the 1985 FSA if he did not. Naneng admits that he signed the contract so that Air Log would not withdraw from negotiations.

When confronted with the fact that Naneng signed the 1985 FSA, Joseph read the document and exclaimed, "Myron, come on, you shouldn't have signed this." Joseph knew that the document exposed Sea Lion to a risk of liability, having earlier testified that Sea Lion knew in connection with the analogous 1984 FSA that "we had to get out of this contract because we're [Sea Lion] not supposed to be in this kind of contract at all." More importantly, Joseph, testifying as Sea Lion's designated representative, admitted that Sea Lion knew it. . . . Joseph also testified that he had "told Myron not to sign, but apparently Gillespie needed the aircraft, so it was" and that "we were forced into this." "We" obviously refers to Sea Lion. Joseph characterized Air Log's insistence that Naneng sign in his corporate capacity as "blackmail." Despite being "blackmailed," . . . Sea Lion said nothing tending to disavow the effect of Naneng's signature to Air Log. . . .

This fact pattern is indistinguishable from the Restatement (Second) of Agency §94, comment b, quoted [above]. An admitted agent exceeded his authority in a moment of zeal to avoid the loss of an investment opportunity for his principal. . . . [T]he secretary/treasurer of the principal chastised the agent, realizing the risk created. The principal then said nothing to the third party (Air Log) to disavow the agent's signature until it was sued about a year later. This is "sufficient evidence of affirmance" absent an adequate explanation. . . . There is no adequate explanation on the record. In fact, the obvious explanation for Sea Lion's conduct was concern that disavowal would both jeopardize the deal with Air Log as well as subject its president to individual liability on a large contract.

To summarize: Air Log has shown (1) an agency relationship, (2) actual knowledge of the purportedly unauthorized act by the principal, and (3) no act of subsequent disavowal by Sea Lion communicated to Air Log until litigation arose over a year later. . . .

[Judgment affirmed.]

Apparent Authority

As previously outlined, a principal is personally liable for the authorized acts of an agent and for those unauthorized acts that he ratifies. The principal also may be bound because of the agent's apparent authority. Unlike *actual authority,* which is based upon the principal's conduct toward the *agent,* **apparent authority** (sometimes called "ostensible" authority) is based upon the principal's conduct toward *third parties* who deal with the agent or purported agent. To illustrate:

Principal ⟶ Agent
Actual Authority

Principal ⟶ Third Party
Apparent Authority

Apparent authority is based on estoppel principles, which were discussed in the contracts material.[18] Apparent authority is created when a principal, by words or conduct, leads a third party to believe that another person is an agent, vested with certain authority. In fact, the person possesses no actual authority or less authority than the third parties are led to believe. In reliance upon the principal's representations, and while unaware of the agent's lack of actual authority, the third party contracts with the agent on the principal's behalf. In this case, the principal is liable on the contract, not because the agent is authorized, but because the principal has created "apparent authority" in the agent. After creating apparent authority by inducing reliance upon the apparent agency, the principal is estopped, or prevented, from asserting the agent's lack of actual authority as a defense to enforcement of the contract.

A contract made by an apparent agent may be enforced both against and by the principal. That is, an apparent agent may confer both contractual rights and liabilities upon the principal. Suppose Ashe, without actual authority, represents herself to Trotter as Park's agent to purchase supplies for Park's business. Park is present while Ashe makes the representation and says nothing. Trotter enters into a contract with Ashe. Park is bound because his conduct—in this case silence in the face of Ashe's false statements—indicates to Trotter that Ashe is authorized to contract for Park. Ashe has apparent authority with no actual authority.

---

[18]Estoppel principles are introduced in Chapter 9 as part of the promissory estoppel coverage.

Although no preexisting agency relationship is required, apparent authority is most commonly used to expand the authority of an existing agent. For example, Austen, acting as agent for Parish, is expressly authorized to enter into contracts on Parish's behalf for the purchase of goods not exceeding $500. Austen and Trevor negotiate a contract in the amount of $600. Trevor is aware of Austen's limitation and informs Parish of the proposed purchase. Parish says to Trevor, "Don't worry about it." Austen then enters into a contract with Trevor for $600. In this case, Parish's conduct toward Trevor has created apparent authority in Austen to enter into a contract for $600, thereby expanding Austen's authority. Note that Austen has no actual or implied authority to enter into a contract for $600 because actual authority runs from the principal to the agent. In this case, Parish's representation of authority to Trevor creates apparent authority in Austen.

Apparent authority is similarly created in an agent when a principal repeatedly ratifies the agent's unauthorized conduct. Using the preceding example, assume that Austen enters into several $600 contracts with Trevor over a period of time. Parish consistently ratifies Austen's conduct by remaining silent and performing the contracts. Parish's repeated ratification has created apparent authority in Austen to enter into contracts for that amount. Once again, the apparent authority is created by Parish's conduct toward Trevor, leading Trevor to believe that Austen possesses the requisite authority.

Apparent authority also may expand the authority of an existing agent when the agent's actual authorization is narrow or is limited in some respect by the principal, but the agent is appointed to a position, such as manager or treasurer, that involves certain generally recognized powers and duties. The very title "manager," for example, is a representation that the agent has certain powers normally incident to that position. Therefore, any limitation placed upon these normal and ordinary incidents by the principal, known as a **secret limitation,** is not binding upon third parties who have no notice of the limitation. The agent, by virtue of his position, possesses apparent authority. For example, assume A is hired to manage P's apartment building, but is given no authority to collect rent checks. This limitation is not binding upon tenants without notice of the limitation, because a normal incident of an apartment building manager's duties is to collect the rent.

The following case illustrates the general principles of apparent authority.

Cartinez v. Reliable Amusement Co., Inc.
746 So.2d 246 (La. App. 1999)

Defendant Reliable Amusement Company, Inc. (Reliable) installs and maintains video poker games in Louisiana. Reliable contracts with eligible commercial establishments (such as restaurants and bars) to provide and service the poker games in exchange for 50 percent of the net revenues generated by the games. In early 1992, Reliable hired Gorman Avery (doing business as G & G Enterprises) as a router/operator for western Louisiana. Avery's duties included installing and servicing the poker machines and collecting the revenues. Reliable compensated Avery by paying him 30 percent of Reliable's share of the profits at any location he acquired and serviced. On May 8, 1992, Avery hired plaintiff Pam Cartinez to make sales presentations and provide follow-up services for businesses in Sabine Parish, Louisiana. Identifying himself as a representative of Reliable, Avery prepared a written contract that he and Cartinez signed. The contract provided that Cartinez would receive 30 percent of net revenues for each video poker game that she placed. Avery provided business cards for Cartinez and form contracts for the businesses to sign. Cartinez negotiated four contracts on Reliable's behalf and assisted in acquiring 14 other contracts. Although Reliable began operating video poker games in the establishments, Cartinez never received any payment. Cartinez sued Reliable for breach of contract. The trial court found that Reliable, through its agent Avery, had entered into a valid contract with Cartinez. The court awarded her over $300,000 in damages and ordered Reliable to pay her 30 percent of the net profits from 12 of the contracts. Reliable appealed.

Peters, Judge

. . . Reliable asserts that . . . Avery was not its agent and had no express or apparent authority to enter into contracts on its behalf. . . . An excellent summary of the law relative to agency relationships . . . is found in *Barrilleaux v. Franklin Foundation Hospital,* [683 So.2d 348, 353–54 (La. App. 1996)], which we quote with approval:

An agent is one who acts for or in place of another by authority from the latter. . . . An agency relationship may be created by express appointment . . . or by implied appointment arising from apparent authority. . . . Therefore, an agent's authority is composed of his actual authority, express or implied, together with the apparent authority which the principal has vested in him by his con-

duct. . . . As between principal and agent, the limit of an agent's authority to bind the principal is governed by the agent's actual authority. However, as between principals and third parties, the limit of an agent's authority to bind the principal is governed by the agent's apparent authority. . . . Apparent agency arises when the principal has acted so as to give an innocent third party a reasonable belief that the agent had the authority to act for the principal, . . . and the third party reasonably relies on the manifested authority of the agent. . . . Apparent agency is established by the words and conduct of the parties and the circumstances of the case. An agency relationship may be created even though there is no intent to do so. . . .

The distinction between actual and apparent authority of an agent to bind a principal in a business transaction has been further clarified by the supreme court as follows:

Apparent authority is a doctrine by which an agent is empowered to bind his principal in a transaction with a third person when the principal has made a manifestation to the third person, or to the community of which the third person is a member, that the agent is authorized to engage in the particular transaction, although the principal has not actually delegated this authority to the agent. In an actual authority situation the principal makes the manifestation first to the agent; in an apparent authority situation the principal makes this manifestation to a third person. However, the third person has the same rights in relation to the principal under either actual or apparent authority. Further, apparent authority operates only when it is reasonable for the third person to believe the agent is authorized and the third person actually believes this.

Tedesco v. Gentry Dev., Inc., 540 So.2d 960, 963 (La. 1989). . . .

Further, as stated in *Barrilleaux,* 683 So.2d at 354:

An agency relationship is never presumed; it must be clearly established. . . . The burden of proving apparent authority is on the party seeking to bind the principal. A third party may not blindly rely on the assertions of an agent, but has a duty to determine, at his peril, whether the agency purportedly granted by the principal permits the proposed act by the agent. . . . One must look from the viewpoint of the third party to determine whether an apparent agency has been created. . . .

We find that the trial court was clearly wrong in finding that Mrs. Cartinez established Avery to be the express or apparent agent of Reliable. There is no evidence that Reliable gave Avery actual authority to contract with Mrs. Cartinez. Additionally, at the time the contract was executed, Reliable had made no manifestation to her or her community that Avery was authorized "to engage in the particular transaction" involved herein. *Tedesco,* 540 So.2d at 963. Furthermore, Reliable had done nothing prior to May 8, 1992, to give Mrs. Cartinez a reasonable belief that Avery functioned as its agent and had authority to enter into this contract.

These conclusions are supported by the contract itself, which provides that it is between G & G Enterprises and Mrs. Cartinez and that G & G Enterprises, and not Reliable, would provide all materials, supplies, assistance, and training. Mrs. Cartinez did not rely on the clear and unambiguous language of the contract but relied entirely on Avery's assertions. Mrs. Cartinez specifically testified that before meeting Avery, she had never heard of Reliable and that her whole belief in the nature of the contractual relationship was based on what Avery told her. As stated in *Barrilleaux,* 683 So.2d at 354, "[a] third party may not blindly rely on the assertions of an agent" to establish an apparent agency relationship. In fact, "it is a well-established rule that the declarations and representations of an alleged or reputed agent are not admissible evidence to prove the fact of his agency against the principal." *Lou-Ark Equip. Rentals Co. v. Hong Ah Fong,* 355 So.2d 1019, 1021 (La. App. 1978). . . . Thus, we find that the trial court was clearly wrong in concluding that Avery was the agent of Reliable and that the May 8, 1992 contract constituted a contract between Reliable and Mrs. Cartinez.

[Judgment reversed.]

Partially Disclosed and Undisclosed Principals. An agent whose principal is partially disclosed also may possess apparent authority if the principal provides the agent with a writing or other manifestation of the agent's authority to act. For example, assume P entrusts A with possession of a painting and a document shown to prospective buyers stating that "the owner of this painting has authorized A to sell it." A has apparent authority to bind P.

An agent acting on behalf of an undisclosed principal generally possesses no apparent authority to bind the principal. That is, because the third party is unaware of the principal's existence, the principal makes no representations or manifestations to the third party concerning the agent's authority. Thus, the undisclosed principal usually is bound only for acts within the scope of the agent's actual authority. As noted previously, however, courts have held that placing a person in a position, such as manager, involving generally recognized powers and duties, is a sufficient representation to create apparent authority in the agent even without direct communication between the principal and third party. Under this theory, an undisclosed principal may be held liable for an agent's unauthorized acts if the agent is placed in a position in which the agent appears to be the owner or manager of a business or property. As noted by one court:

> The typical application of this rule is to a going concern with an established place of business and obvious assets operated by one who ostensibly is the proprietor but secretly is agent for an undisclosed principal. . . . In such cases liability is imposed upon the undisclosed principal because he has placed the agent in such apparent relationship to an observable enterprise as is likely to induce reliance upon him as a responsible proprietor.[19]

Finally, creation of apparent authority must be carefully distinguished from an agent's attempt to "bootstrap" authority. To illustrate, assume Anson, with intent to perpetrate a fraud, represents himself to Teller as Palmer's purchasing agent. In fact, Palmer has never even seen Anson. Anson then purchases goods from Teller for Palmer's account and leaves town with the merchandise. In this case Palmer has no liability on the contract to Teller. Anson has neither actual nor apparent authority, but has attempted to bootstrap authority. That is, authority capable of binding the principal runs from the principal to agent or principal to third party, *not* from the agent to the third party.

Liability of Principal for Notice of Agent

In the course of performing their duties, agents often receive notice of facts having actual or potential legal significance to the principal. The law of agency determines when notice to an agent is legally effective as

---

[19]Senor v. Bangor Mills, Inc., 211 F.2d 685, 688 (3d Cir. 1954).

notice to the principal. A person has **notice** of a fact if: (1) he has actual knowledge of it; (2) from all facts and circumstances known to him at the time he has reason to know that it exists; or (3) he has received notification of it.[20] **Knowledge** refers to a person's subjective conscious belief in the truth of a fact or condition.[21] **Notification** is a formal act intended to affect the legal relations between the notifier and the person notified.

Note that notice is a much broader concept than knowledge, and a person therefore may have notice of a fact without actual knowledge. For example, a person generally "receives" a notification when it either comes to his attention or is delivered at a place (for example, an office or post office box) held out by him as the place for receiving such communications.[22] In the law governing real property transfers, discussed in Chapter 37, recording a deed or mortgage in the country recorder's office provides "constructive notice" to the entire world of the recording party's interest, even though most persons have no actual knowledge of the recording.

Agent's Notification

As a general rule, a notification given to an agent is notice to the principal if the agent is actually or apparently authorized to receive it. Conversely, notification given by an authorized agent are notifications by the principal.[23] The agent's notice is often said to be "imputed" to the principal, based upon the legal fiction that principal and authorized agent are one person.

For example, assume Price appoints Allen to manage a number of commercial buildings leased by Price to various businesses. Allen is authorized to lease the buildings, contract for their repair, settle disputes with tenants, hire and fire employees, and give and receive notifications in connection with the property. Tate is a tenant in one of the buildings. A provision in the lease provides that it may be terminated by either party upon 90 days advance notification. Tate notifies Allen of her intent to terminate the lease and move out in 90 days. Tate's notification to Allen is notice to Price, whether or not Allen communicates it to Price. Note that the same result follows even if Price fires Allen before notice is given, if Tate is unaware of the firing. That is, Allen still possesses apparent though not actual authority. If Tate

had instead notified a janitor employed by Price, the notification would not be imputed to Price. The janitor, unlike Allen, is not actually or apparently authorized to receive such notification.

Agent's Knowledge

An agent's knowledge also may be imputed to the principal. Generally, the principal is deemed to have knowledge of facts known to an agent if that knowledge is important in the transaction the agent is authorized to conduct.[24] Suppose Amy is Paula's agent to buy and sell antiques. Amy defrauds Terry into buying a worthless vase by knowingly representing it as a valuable antique. Paula is liable to Terry for fraud, because Amy's knowledge of falsity is imputed to Paula. Similarly, Paula could not retain property acquired for her through Amy's fraud or other wrongdoing.

At issue in the following case was whether an agent's knowledge should be imputed to the principal.

E. Udolf, Inc. v. Aetna Casualty and Surety Company
573 A.2d 1211 (Conn. 1990)

Leonard Udolf was the sole shareholder, director, and officer of plaintiff E. Udolf, Inc., a corporation that operated a retail clothing store in Hartford, Connecticut. Udolf frequently was away from the store and in his absence, Kenneth Auer served as store manager. In 1981, Anna Shukis, the bookkeeper, discovered that Lynn Bjork, a store employee, had embezzled $6,000 from the store. Shukis reported the wrongdoing to Auer but they decided not to tell Udolf and instead allowed Bjork to repay the funds. After repaying the $6,000, Bjork again began stealing money from the store and by 1983 had taken $48,715. In 1983, Udolf learned of Bjork's embezzlement and she was fired. Udolf filed a claim under an employee dishonesty insurance policy that the corporation had purchased from defendant Aetna Casualty and Surety Company. Aetna refused to pay the claim based on the following provision:

> The coverage . . . shall not apply to any Employee from and after the time that the Insured or any partner or officer thereof not in collusion with such Employee shall have knowledge or information that such Employee has committed any fraudulent or dishonest act in the service of the Insured or otherwise,

---

[20]UCC §1–202(a); RESTATEMENT (SECOND) OF AGENCY §9(1).

[21]RESTATEMENT (SECOND) OF AGENCY §9 comment c.

[22]See, for example, UCC §1–202(e).

[23]RESTATEMENT (SECOND) OF AGENCY §268.

[24]RESTATEMENT (SECOND) OF AGENCY §272 comment a.

whether such act be committed before or after the date of employment by the Insured.

E. Udolf, Inc. sued Aetna seeking payment for its losses. The trial court ruled in favor of Aetna and E. Udolf, Inc. appealed.

Hull, Associate Justice

. . . The trial court concluded that . . . the plaintiff was not entitled to recovery of the losses it had incurred as a result of Bjork's actions. The basis of the court's conclusion was its determination that the knowledge of Auer and Shukis concerning misappropriations committed by the plaintiff's employees was imputed to the plaintiff. The court thus reasoned that because the 1980–81 misappropriations by Bjork constituted "fraudulent or dishonest act[s]" within the scope of Section 7 of Aetna's policy, . . . and because the plaintiff, by imputation of Auer's and Shukis' knowledge, became aware of those misappropriations no later than the summer of 1981, any subsequent losses caused by a "fraudulent or dishonest act" on the part of Bjork were excluded from coverage under the policies. In so concluding, the court rejected the plaintiff's claim that, because Auer and Shukis did not inform Leonard Udolf of Bjork's 1980–81 misappropriations, they were in collusion with Bjork. The court stated that while the failure of Auer and Shukis to notify Leonard Udolf may have been an act of poor judgment, it was not a fraudulent act and therefore was not collusive. . . .

As stated in the Restatement (Second) of Agency §272, "a principal is affected by the knowledge of an agent concerning a matter as to which he acts within his power to bind the principal or upon which it is his duty to give the principal information." The plaintiff argues, however, that this agency principle should not apply in the context of employee dishonesty insurance. . . . We conclude that the knowledge of an employee may be imputed to an employer under an employee dishonesty insurance policy if the employee holds a position of management or control in the exercise of which a duty to report known dishonesty of a fellow employee can be found to exist either explicitly or by fair inference from a course of conduct. . . .

Auer was principally in charge of operations during Leonard Udolf's absences from the store and . . . one of his responsibilities in that capacity was to report matters such as misappropriations to Leonard Udolf. The court further determined that Anna Shukis, the plaintiff's bookkeeper, was responsible for running the book-keeping operation and that she likewise had a responsibility to report to Leonard Udolf any misappropriations that occurred in that department. . . . Bjork testified at trial that in 1980–81, Auer's position was that of "store manager." . . . Further, while Auer stated that he did not have the authority to hire and fire employees in 1980–81, he did arrange with Bjork, without first consulting with Leonard Udolf, for repayment of the $6000 and then fired Bjork upon learning of the 1983 misappropriations. Auer's testimony also revealed that he was expected to report to Leonard Udolf everything that happened in the store. Finally, Leonard Udolf was present in the store only 10 to 20 percent of the time. Although Leonard Udolf claimed at trial that he was always in charge of the store, even while absent, this claim conflicted with his deposition testimony in which, in response to the question of "who was in charge of the operations in your absence," he answered: "Well I felt I had them in capable hands with Ken Auer . . . on the floor . . . and in the office with Anna Shukis. . . ."

We conclude that the trial court's factual findings concerning the responsibilities and consequent duties of Auer and Shukis were supported by the evidence. . . . Therefore, since the court found that the positions held by Auer and Shukis gave rise to a duty to report misappropriations to Leonard Udolf, the court's imputation to the plaintiff of Auer's and Shukis' knowledge concerning Bjork's 1980–81 actions was not error. . . .

[Judgment affirmed.]

Termination of Agency Powers

At some point, the agent's authority terminates, and the agent no longer has the power to bind the principal to contracts with third parties. The following material examines the methods by which an agent's actual and apparent authority are extinguished.

Termination of Actual Authority

The principal's manifestation of consent to an agent creates the agent's actual authority. Similarly, the agent's actual authority is terminated when the principal, by words or other conduct, leads the agent to believe that the principal no longer desires the agency to continue. Typically, actual authority is terminated either upon occurrence of subsequent events, or by acts of the parties.

Effect of Subsequent Events. The principal's intent to terminate the agency may be inferred from the original authorization in light of subsequent events. For example, agencies often terminate according to the terms of the agency contract, the occurrence of a given event, or on completion of the purpose for which the agency was initially created. To illustrate, assume A agrees to work for P for a period of three years. At the end of three years the agency terminates according to the terms of the contract. Or, assume P appoints A as agent to sell his car. After A sells the car, the agency terminates because the act authorized by the agency has been accomplished. In these cases, the agency is terminated by events clearly indicated in the original authorization.

An agent's authority also may terminate due to a substantial change in circumstances from which the agent reasonably should infer termination. Under this rule, for example, an agent's authority terminates upon the loss, destruction, or substantial change in value of the subject matter; a substantial change in business conditions; a loss of (or failure to acquire) a license or other qualification by either principal or agent; a change in law that makes it illegal to carry out an authorized act; or a serious breach of the duty of loyalty by the agent. For example, assume A is appointed P's agent to sell P's antique Rolls-Royce. Prior to the sale, the car is destroyed by fire as A knows. A's authority is terminated. Or assume P hires A, an attorney, to represent him in a divorce suit. A is subsequently disbarred. A's authority is terminated.

The law applies a similar analysis to the bankruptcy of either principal or agent. Generally, bankruptcy terminates the agency only if the agency depends upon the continued solvency or credit rating of the bankrupt party. For example, assume P appoints A as agent to purchase raw materials on credit for use in P's business ventures. P subsequently declares bankruptcy and A learns of that fact. A's authority to make further contracts for P is terminated. Note that on these same facts, A's bankruptcy would not necessarily terminate the agency.

Effect of Death or Incapacity. An agency terminates automatically by operation of law upon the death or incapacity of either the principal or agent. Because no notice to the other party is required, an agent may be held liable for breach of the warranty of authority on contracts made after the principal's death, but without knowledge of it. Some courts protect the agent in this case by providing that the warranty of authority is breached only if the agent contracts with actual knowledge of the principal's death. Under this approach, if the agent contracts with a third party after the principal's death but before learning of the death, neither the agent nor the principal's estate is liable on the contract.

Termination by Act of the Parties. Because agency is a consensual relationship, it is terminated when either or both parties withdraw their consent. Thus, either the principal or agent can unilaterally terminate the agency at any time or they can mutually agree to termination. Generally, the agent's actual authority is extinguished when the intent to terminate is communicated to the other party.

Agency for Agreed Term. In many cases, the principal and agent contractually agree that the agency will continue for a fixed term. P, for example, might contract to hire A as her purchasing agent for a term of three years. Even if the parties are contractually obligated to continue the agency, either party may nevertheless unilaterally terminate the agency at any time. A party who wrongfully terminates the agency in violation of a contract, however, is liable to the other for breach of contract. In short, both the principal and agent have the power—but not necessarily the right—to terminate their relationship at any time.

Agency for Indefinite Term—Employment at Will Doctrine. If the parties have not agreed to a specific term, their relationship is described as an "agency at will." Generally, either party may terminate an agency at will by providing notice of the termination to the other.[25] Traditionally, this rule also applied to employment relationships so that, in the absence of a contract for a definite term, either an employee or employer was free to end their relationship at any time. From this rule evolved the common law **employment at will doctrine** that allows an employer to fire an at will employee for any reason. Today, however, the employment at will doctrine is subject to numerous statutory exceptions. All states also have created common law exceptions, based primarily on implied in fact contract principles and public policy. These exceptions are discussed below.

Statutory Exceptions. Under state and federal equal employment opportunity statutes, employers cannot use certain criteria—including an employee's race, religion, sex, age (over the age of 40), or disability—as a basis

[25]RESTATEMENT (SECOND) OF AGENCY §442.

for terminating employees. Federal law also prohibits an employer from firing an employee for engaging in union activities. Other federal and state statutes further limit employers' rights to terminate employees.[26]

Implied in Fact Contract Exception. A majority of states recognize that the employer through its conduct can create implied in fact contract provisions that limit the employer's right to terminate an employee.[27] For example, if an employer orally assures its employees that they will be discharged only for "just cause," those oral assurances may be considered part of the employment contract. Termination of the employee arbitrarily without just cause, therefore, would constitute breach of contract.

Similarly, many states have ruled that provisions in personnel manuals, employee handbooks, and other policies disseminated by the employer are implied in fact contract terms that are binding on the employer. XYZ Co., for example, distributes an employee handbook that explains its policies on working hours, vacation and sick leave, benefits, appropriate dress and conduct, and similar matters. Assume that this handbook states that employees will be discharged only for just cause or that XYZ Co. will provide two written warnings before terminating an employee. In most states, these provisions are interpreted as limitations on the employer's right to terminate an employee at will so that dismissal of an employee without just cause or without providing two written warnings constitutes breach of contract.

If the parties expressly agree that the employment relationship is at will, courts generally refuse to recognize contradictory implied in fact contract terms. Many employers, therefore, include a written provision in employment contracts explicitly stating that the employment is at will, or include a disclaimer or other provision in personnel manuals and employee handbooks clearly indicating that they do not constitute terms of employment. Courts generally enforce such provisions if they are clear and conspicuous.

Public Policy Exception. A substantial majority of states also recognize the public policy exception to the employment at will doctrine. Under this rule, it is unlawful to dismiss an employee in violation of clearly mandated public policy. In applying this exception to the employment at will doctrine, courts first must determine what

constitutes public policy. One court succinctly summarized the issue as follows:

> In determining whether a clear mandate of public policy is violated, courts should inquire whether the employer's conduct contravenes the letter or purpose of a constitutional, statutory, or regulatory provision or scheme. Prior judicial decisions may also establish the relevant public policy. However, courts should proceed cautiously if called upon to declare public policy absent some prior legislative or judicial expression on the subject.[28]

Under the public policy exception, courts have found dismissal to be unlawful if the employee was discharged for reporting the employer's illegal acts to authorities (whistleblowing) or for refusing to engage in illegal acts such as committing perjury, falsifying company records, or participating in price-fixing schemes. Courts also have found a violation of public policy when an employee was discharged for exercising legal rights or complying with a statutory duty, for example, by filing a workers' compensation claim, for serving jury duty, or for obeying a subpoena and appearing at a hearing.

States recognize different types of claims for employee terminations in violation of public policy. In some states, the discharge is considered a breach of contract. Other states allow the former employee to bring suit for a tort claim called unlawful discharge, wrongful discharge, or retaliatory discharge. The following case discusses the public policy exception to the employment at will doctrine.

Rocky Mountain Hospital and Medical Service v. Mariani
916 P.2d 519 (Colo. 1996)

Defendant Rocky Mountain Hospital and Medical Service d/b/a Blue Cross and Blue Shield of Colorado (BCBS) hired plaintiff Diana Mariani, a licensed certified public accountant, as manager of general accounting for the human resources department in November 1987. Mariani, an employee at will, was reassigned to the position of manager of special projects in April 1990 and was fired in February 1991. She sued BCBS for wrongful discharge, alleging that her termination violated public policy. At trial, she testified that BCBS discharged her because she

---

[26]Some of the federal statutes limiting employers' power to discharge employees are discussed in Chapters 53 and 54.

[27]Contracts implied in fact are discussed in Chapter 7.

[28]Parnar v. Americana Hotels, Inc., 652 P.2d 625, 631 (Hawaii 1982).

had reported improper accounting practices to her supervisors, had questioned the classification of some information on financial statements, and had objected to inappropriate omissions and representations in merger documents. Her testimony included specific examples such as BCBS's allowing an affiliate to report a $3.5 million computer purchased by BCBS as an asset of the affiliated company; another affiliate's failure to refund $1.5 million received as overpayments; and BCBS's not fully disclosing the nature of a $13.5 million note listed as an asset. Mariani asserted that she was fired for refusing to violate Colorado State Board of Accountancy Rule 7.3 that provides in part: "A [certified public accountant] shall not in the performance of professional services knowingly misrepresent facts, nor subordinate his judgment to others." The trial court ruled that Mariani had failed to prove that her discharge violated a specific public policy and directed a verdict for BCBS. After the court of appeals reversed, the Colorado Supreme Court agreed to review the decision.

Kourlis, Justice

. . . In general, employment contracts are at-will and either the employer or the employee may terminate the relationship at any time. . . . In *Martin Marietta Corp. v. Lorenz,* 823 P.2d 100 (Colo. 1992), we recognized an exception to this general rule in situations where the employer terminated the employment contract in violation of public policy. The rationale underlying this exception was the long-standing rule that a contract violative of public policy is unenforceable. . . . We concluded that it is the manifest public policy of this state that "an employee whether at will or otherwise, should not be put to the choice of either obeying an employer's order to violate the law or losing his or her job." [*Id.* at 109.]

. . . Mariani claims that BCBS terminated her for refusing to violate the Colorado State Board of Accountancy Rules of Professional Conduct. . . . At issue in this appeal is whether the Colorado State Board of Accountancy Rules of Professional Conduct and in particular Rule 7.3 may constitute a clear mandate of public policy for the purpose of a wrongful discharge cause of action.

BCBS argues that we should limit the sources of public policy for a wrongful discharge claim to constitutional or statutory provisions. BCBS claims that ethical codes, such as the one upon which Mariani relies, are too variable and ill-defined to provide employers and employees with fair notice as to what comprises public policy. We disagree.

We have never conclusively defined the sources of public policy for purposes of the public policy exception

to employment at-will. In *Martin Marietta v. Lorenz,* 823 P.2d 100, 109, (Colo. 1992), we stated that in order to establish a prima facie case for wrongful discharge in violation of public policy, the employee must prove that ". . . the action directed by the employer would violate a *specific statute* relating to the public health, safety, or welfare, or would undermine a *clearly expressed public policy* relating to the employee's basic responsibility as a citizen or the employee's rights as a worker. . . ." (Emphasis added.) Although we suggested that public policy would generally be limited to specific statutory mandates, we left open the question of whether clearly expressed public policy might be manifested elsewhere.

Jurisdictions are split as to whether to recognize nonlegislative sources of public policy. Some jurisdictions limit the sources of public policy to statutory or constitutional sources. This limitation stems from concerns that an expansive definition of public policy would be both unwieldy and unpredictable, leaving employers and employees alike without direction as to the contours of the public policy exception. However, even courts that limit the public policy exception to statutory and constitutional sources cannot escape that concern. The identification of the statutory or constitutional provisions that qualify as clear expressions of public policy is a matter for judicial determination. . . .

Other jurisdictions have recognized that nonlegislative sources, including professional ethical codes, may provide the basis for a public policy claim. Courts that have recognized ethical codes as a potential source of public policy have noted that employees who are professionals have a duty to abide not only by federal and state law but also by the recognized codes of ethics of their professions. . . . As these ethical codes are central to a professional employee's activities, there may be a conflict at times between the demands of an employer and the employee's professional ethics.

A professional employee forced to choose between violating his or her ethical obligations or being terminated is placed in an intolerable position. . . . It is just such a situation that the public policy exception was meant to prevent. . . .

As is clear from the above discussion, the term public policy is not subject to precise definition. . . . A common requirement in cases discussing the issue is that public policy must concern behavior that truly impacts the public in order to justify interference into an employer's business decisions. In addition, public policy must be clearly mandated such that the acceptable behavior is concrete and discernible as opposed to a broad hortatory statement of policy that gives little direction as to the bounds of proper behavior.

Statutes by their nature are the most reasonable and common sources for defining public policy. In limited circumstances, however, we agree with the jurisdictions that hold there may be other sources of public policy such as administrative regulations and professional ethical codes. However, we quickly note that even those courts that have adopted ethical codes as a source of public policy have not done so without limitation. . . . In particular, in order to qualify as public policy, the ethical provision must be designed to serve the interests of the public rather than the interests of the profession. The provision may not concern merely technical matters or administrative regulations. In addition, the provision must provide a clear mandate to act or not to act in a particular way. Finally, the viability of ethical codes as a source of public policy must depend on a balancing between the public interest served by the professional code and the need of an employer to make legitimate business decisions. We also adopt these limitations as a prudent check on the public policy exception to employment at-will.

Thus, we hold that professional ethical codes may in certain circumstances be a source of public policy. However, we emphasize that any public policy must serve the public interest and be sufficiently concrete to notify employers and employees of the behavior it requires. We now turn to the issue of whether Rule 7.3 of the Colorado State Board of Accountancy Rules of Professional Conduct is of sufficient clarity and public value to qualify as an expression of public policy.

BCBS argues that the Colorado State Board of Accountancy Rules of Professional Conduct are not clear mandates of public policy but rather broad aspirational statements that cannot support a public policy claim. We disagree.

The Colorado State Board of Accountancy . . . has responsibility for making appropriate rules of professional conduct, in order to establish and maintain a high standard of integrity in the profession of public accounting. . . . These rules of professional conduct govern every person practicing as a certified public accountant [in Colorado]. Failure to abide by these rules may result in professional discipline. . . .

The rules of professional conduct for accountants have an important public purpose. They ensure the accurate reporting of financial information to the public. They allow the public and the business community to rely with confidence on financial reporting. . . . In addition, they ensure that financial information will be reported consistently across many businesses. The legislature has endorsed these goals in section 12–2–101, 5A [of the Colorado Revised Statutes] (1991), which includes the legislative declaration for establishing the Board of Accountancy. Section 12–2–101 states in pertinent part:

> It is declared to be in the interest of the citizens of the state of Colorado and a proper exercise of the police power of the state of Colorado to provide for the licensing and registration of certified public accountants, . . . to provide for the maintenance of high standards of professional conduct by those so licensed and registered as certified public accountants.

Given this legislative declaration and the purposes of the rules of professional conduct for accountants, we hold that the rules have a sufficient public purpose to constitute public policy.

Further, we conclude that Rule 7.3 of the Colorado State Board of Accountancy Rules of Professional Conduct is a sufficiently clear mandate of public policy to sustain a wrongful discharge cause of action. . . . This rule mandates accuracy in financial reporting and furthers the laudable goal of establishing public confidence in financial reporting. The rule specifically directs an accountant to refrain from knowingly misrepresenting facts. The clear purpose of this rule is to prohibit accountants from falsifying information when completing tasks. The rule also directs accountants not to subordinate their judgment to others, such that an accountant may not succumb to pressure from his or her employer to misrepresent facts or deviate from generally accepted accounting principles. Both of these proscriptions provide clear direction to an accountant as to the scope of duty, and clear notice to an employer that accountants have a duty to report financial information fairly and accurately.

Thus, we hold that Rule 7.3 represents a clear mandate of public policy for purposes of establishing a claim for wrongful discharge in violation of public policy. Mariani was entitled to rely on this rule for purposes of her suit against BCBS. We affirm the court of appeals in its holding that the Colorado State Board of Accountancy Rules of Professional Conduct and Rule 7.3 in particular can be an adequate source of public policy for a wrongful discharge claim.

[Judgment affirmed.]

Termination of Apparent Authority

Agents often possess both actual and apparent authority. Termination of actual authority does not terminate apparent authority, because apparent authority is based upon the principal's representations to third persons, not to the agent. If an agent possesses apparent authority, therefore, the principal desiring to terminate the agency must extinguish both types of authority.

Actual authority is terminated in the same manner as it is created—by the principal's manifestation to the agent. Apparent authority is also extinguished as it is created—by the principal's manifestations to third parties. That is, the principal extinguishes apparent authority by giving notice to third parties that the agent no longer has authority to bind the principal. This notice is accomplished in one of two ways depending upon the relationship of the particular third party to the agent. Persons who have previously extended credit to, or received credit from, the principal through the agent are entitled to actual oral or written notice of the agent's lack of continuing authority. Other third parties entitled to actual notice include persons who have been specially invited by the principal to deal with the agent (the specially accredited agent), persons with whom the principal knows the agent has begun to deal, and persons who rely upon a writing, such as a power of attorney, indicating the agent's authority entrusted to the agent by the principal. All other persons, including those who have not previously dealt with the agent or who have dealt with him on a cash basis, are entitled to notice by publication. The principal gives **notice by publication** by advertising the termination in a newspaper of general circulation in the area where the agent operates or publicizing the termination by another effective means.[29]

The rules outlined above apply only to general agents. Generally, if the principal represents to a third party that an agent is employed as a special agent, the agent's apparent authority is extinguished upon termination of his actual authority. That is, no notice is required to terminate the apparent authority of a special agent, unless the principal leads the third party to believe that he will receive notice of termination. Further, any agent's apparent authority terminates automatically without notice upon the death or incapacity of the principal.[30]

Termination of a Power Given as Security

In an ordinary agency relationship, the agent acts on behalf of and subject to the control of the principal. The agency device may, however, be used to create powers in the agent to be used for the agent's rather than the principal's benefit, usually used to secure performance of an obligation owing from the principal to the agent. In this case, the parties create in the "agent" a **power given as security** (sometimes known as an **agency coupled with an interest**). For example, assume A agrees to loan money to P, but only if P provides some collateral to secure the loan. P therefore delivers a valuable stamp collection to A, and gives A the power to sell the stamp collection in the event P defaults. A has a power given as security.

A power given as security is not a true agency, because the agent (creditor) does not act subject to the principal's (debtor's) control, or for his benefit. As such it may not be terminated in the same manner as authority or apparent authority. As a general rule, a power given as security is irrevocable by the person granting it and is not extinguished by the death or incapacity of either party. In other words, a power given as security generally may be terminated only with the consent of the holder of the power or upon satisfaction of the obligation secured by the power. Thus, in the preceding example, if P repays the loan, A's power to sell is terminated. Assuming, however, that the loan remains unpaid, the power may not be revoked unilaterally by P and is unaffected by the death or incapacity of either A or P.

Summary

1.   Agency is a fiduciary relationship in which one party, an agent, agrees to act on behalf of and under the control of another, the principal. An agency is created by the manifestation of consent by both parties. Although agency relationships often are created by contract, no contractual relationship is required, and the parties need not have contractual capacity. The law of agency

---

[29]Restatement (Second) of Agency §136.

[30]Restatement (Second) of Agency §§132–133.

primarily addresses (1) the relationship between principal and agent, and (2) the liability of principal and agent to third parties for contracts made and torts committed by the agent.

2.   An agency is a fiduciary relationship imposing several duties upon the parties. Most important is the duty of loyalty owed by the agent to the principal. This duty requires the agent to act solely for the benefit of the principal regarding matters within the scope of the agency. The agent also owes the principal duties of service and obedience. Although the principal owes no duty of loyalty to the agent, the principal must compensate the agent, reimburse him for expenses and losses incurred during the course of the agency, and use reasonable care to prevent injury to the agent during performance of the agency.

3.   The legal effect of contracts made by the agent on the principal's behalf depends upon whether the agent is authorized and whether the principal's existence and identity are disclosed to the third party contracting with the agent. The extent of an agent's authority, which may be express or implied, is determined by examining the principal's words or other conduct toward the agent indicating the principal's consent that the agent act on the principal's behalf.

4.   Two rules govern most agency and contracts cases: (1) an agent is liable on a contract made in an agency capacity unless both the agent is authorized and the principal is disclosed, and (2) the principal (disclosed, partially disclosed, or undisclosed) is liable upon contracts made on his behalf if the agent is authorized to act. In the partially disclosed and undisclosed principal cases both principal and agent are liable. If the principal is partially disclosed, the principal and agent are jointly and severally liable on the contract. In contrast, if the principal is undisclosed, the traditional common law rule requires the third party, after discovering the existence and identity of the principal, to elect to hold either the principal or the agent liable. A minority of jurisdictions reject this approach and hold the principal and agent jointly and severally liable.

5.   Two important doctrines provide exceptions to the general rule that the principal is liable if the agent is authorized—ratification and apparent authority. Ratification is conduct by the principal indicating an intent to be bound upon a previously unauthorized contract made on his behalf. After ratification, the principal is bound as if the contract had been originally authorized. An effective ratification requires that the principal have capacity both at the time of the unauthorized act and at the time of ratification, and that the person making the contract purport to be acting on behalf of the person subsequently ratifying.

6.   Unlike actual authority, which is based upon the principal's conduct toward the agent, apparent authority is based upon the principal's conduct toward *third parties* who deal with the agent or purported agent. Apparent authority, based upon estoppel principles, is created when a principal, by words or conduct, leads a third party to believe that another person is an agent, vested with certain authority. After creat-ing apparent authority by inducing reliance upon the apparent agency, the principal is estopped, or prevented, from asserting the agent's lack of actual authority as a defense to enforcement of a contract made by the apparent agent.

7.   In addition to liability upon contracts made by agents, a principal's legal relations also may be affected by notification to or knowledge acquired by an agent. As a general rule, a notification given to an agent is notice to the principal if the agent is actually or apparently authorized to receive it. An agent's knowledge is imputed to the principal if that knowledge is important to the transaction the agent is authorized to conduct.

8.   Agency relationships generally are terminated in the same manner in which they were created. For example, an agent's actual authority ceases when the agent, based upon the principal's words or conduct, is led to believe that the principal no longer desires the agency to continue. An agency also is terminated automatically by operation of law upon death or incapacity of either party. Apparent authority is terminated by giving notice to third parties that the agent no longer has authority to bind the principal. A power given as security, or "agency coupled with an interest," is not a true agency and therefore may not be terminated in the same manner as actual or apparent authority. Such a power is generally irrevocable by the person granting it and is not extinguished by the death or incapacity of either party.

Key Terms

agency	implied warranty of authority
agent	disclosed principal
principal	partially disclosed principal
power of attorney	undisclosed principal
equal dignity rule	election
general agent	ratification
special agent	apparent authority
master	secret limitation
servant	notice
independent contractor	knowledge
broker	notification
factor (commission merchant)	employment at will doctrine
del credere agent	notice by publication
duty of loyalty	power given as security
authority (actual authority)	(agency coupled with an
express authority	interest)
implied authority	

Questions and Problems

40.1   What business functions are served by allowing agents to bind their principals to contracts? Consider both corporate and individual principals. Summarize the various methods by which a principal can be held liable upon contracts made by an agent.

40.2   Laverne was manager of a store operated by Hartford Co. Over a period of several months Laverne embezzled funds belonging to Hartford.

(a) Has Laverne violated any of her fiduciary obligations to Hartford? Explain.

(b) Hartford sued Laverne for repayment of the misappropriated funds. Hartford also demanded repayment of all wages that it had paid to Laverne during the period that the embezzlement occurred. Should Laverne be required to repay the wages? Explain.

40.3   Lewis University and Canel Management Co. entered into an agreement by which Canel agreed to provide all maintenance services for the university campus. The agreement provided that Canel had the power to "contract on behalf of Lewis for the purchase of any items necessary and incidental to Canel's performing its duties." The agreement was signed by the president of Lewis University and the president of Canel. Canel appointed its employee Don Boyd to supervise the maintenance at the university. Boyd signed a contract with Roscoe Co., which agreed to provide 1,000 cases of soap and cleansers at a cost of $50 per case. Boyd signed the agreement "Lewis University by Don Boyd, its agent." Lewis University refused to pay for the soap and cleanser claiming that Boyd lacked the authority to enter into the contract. Roscoe has sued both Lewis University and Don Boyd. Who is liable on the contract? Explain.

40.4   Peter Novera was a gardener who worked for Phillip Lederle. Novera advised Lederle that a tree on Lederle's property had died and Lederle asked Novera to find someone to remove the tree. Novera called Jacob Wing, a tree surgeon, and they met on the grounds near the dead tree. After discussing removal of the tree, Wing pointed out some other trees that needed special care. Novera authorized Wing to remove the tree and to spray and trim the other trees. Wing sent a bill to Novera who then advised Wing that the property belonged to Lederle. Wing then sent the bill to Lederle. Lederle paid for the removal of the dead tree but refused to pay for the other services. Wing has sued Lederle. Is Lederle liable for payment of the bill? Explain.

40.5   Gloria operates a store and gas station that allows customers to charge purchases on an open account. Ronald Abare opened an account in the name of "Abare Wells" and periodically purchased on credit gasoline that was pumped into trucks bearing the name Abare & Sons Artesian Well Drilling Co. Monthly bills were paid by checks with the name Abare & Sons Artesian Well Drilling Co. on them. After several bills were left unpaid, Gloria sued Ronald Abare for the amounts due on the account. Abare claimed that the account was for a corporation, Abare & Sons Artesian Well Drilling Co., and that he should not be held personally liable. How should the court rule?

40.6   Under bylaws adopted by First Parish Church in 1950, the Business Committee is responsible for making contracts on behalf of the church. The Business Committee hired P. J. Rich as pastor of the church. In an effort to raise revenues for the church, Rich decided to create an amusement park adjacent to the church. Rich borrowed money from Bay State Bank and signed the loan documents "First Parish Church by P. J. Rich, Pastor." Using the money, he hired contractors to begin construction of two swimming pools, several buildings, and a large parking lot. After construction of the amusement park was about 75 percent complete the church defaulted in repayment of the bank loans and failed to pay the building contractors. The bank and building contractors then sued First Parish for breaches of contract. The church asserted that it could not be held responsible because Rich did not have actual authority to make the contracts. How should the court rule? Explain.

40.7   Liberty Loan Co. operated a branch office in a building that it leased from Joseph Ripani. Although Michael Anderson, who was employed as branch manager of the Liberty Loan office, had negotiated the lease with Ripani, Liberty Loan's president and vice president had signed the lease. Anderson made the monthly rental payments to Ripani by checks drawn on a Liberty Loan account and signed by Anderson. Whenever maintenance problems arose, Anderson notified Ripani. In October, Ripani reminded Anderson that the building lease would expire in two months unless it was renewed. Anderson then signed a contract on behalf of Liberty Loan renewing the lease for three years. Several weeks later, the president of Liberty Loan advised Ripani that it did not intend to renew the lease. When Ripani showed the president the renewal with Anderson's signature, the president stated that it was unenforceable against Liberty Loan because Anderson did not have actual authority to sign the contract. Ripani sued Anderson and Liberty Loan. How should the court rule? Explain.

40.8   Crystal Computers planned to have a sales show of its new products at the Brandywine Hilton Hotel. Crystal and Brandywine entered into a contract by which Crystal agreed to rent six of the hotel's meeting rooms for a three-day period. Several days before the show, Brandywine notified Crystal that construction of the meeting rooms was not complete and the sales show would have to be canceled. Crystal filed a lawsuit for breach of contract naming both Brandywine and the Hilton Corporation as defendants. Hilton Corporation denied that Brandywine was its agent. Crystal, however, provided evidence to support its allegation that Brandywine had the apparent authority to act as Hilton's agent. The evidence showed that Brandywine was owned by a group of businessmen pursuant to a franchise agreement with Hilton. Hilton required Brandywine to display the Hilton logo and sign. The architectural style of the hotel, its furnishings and color schemes all were subject to approval of Hilton. Linens, matches, and ashtrays of the hotel bore the Hilton logo. The president of Crystal testified that at all times he believed he was dealing with the Hilton Corporation even though the rental contract listed Brandywine Hilton Hotel as the renting party. Did Brandywine have the apparent authority to act as Hilton's agent? Explain.

40.9   (a) Emard, quality control director at Frosted Foods, Inc., wrote a memo to his supervisor advising him that substandard ingredients were being used in the company's products. Emard noted that the use of these ingredients was inconsistent with the products' labels, thereby violating the state Food, Drug, and Cosmetic Act. Shortly thereafter, Frosted Foods, Inc. fired Emard. Emard sued Frosted Foods alleging that he was discharged in retaliation for attempting to correct the labeling of the company's products. Assuming that Emard can prove his allegations, how should the court rule?

(b) Murphy was assistant treasurer of AHP Corp. While reviewing financial statements he discovered that the accounts had been illegally manipulated to show $50 million growth in income that enabled several officers to receive bonuses. Murphy notified top management of the improprieties and was fired several weeks later. Was Murphy's dismissal unlawful? Explain.

40.10 Valley View Hospital hired Clara as operating room supervisor in 1992 but no employment agreement was signed. After starting work she received a copy of the Valley View Policy Manual, a 20-page pamphlet summarizing various general matters such as holidays, sick leave, insurance, dress code, wages and hours, termination procedure, and grievance proceedings. In 1998, following several promotions, Clara was fired. The Policy Manual included the following provision: "The discharged employee who feels himself aggrieved by the terms of the discharge may appeal to Administration and will be granted hearing." Clara requested a hearing but it was denied.

(a) Clara has sued Valley view for breach of contract. Valley View alleges that Clara's employment was terminable at will. How should the court rule?

(b) Would your answer to (a) be different if Valley View could prove that Clara did not read the Policy Manual until after she had been fired? Why or why not?

(c) Assume that you have been hired by Valley View as personnel administrator. Suggest provisions that might be included in the Policy Manual to minimize the likelihood that the manual would be considered part of an employment contract.

AGENCY AND TORTS

Chapter 40 examines the liability of principal and agent for *contracts* made on the principal's behalf. In contrast, this chapter covers the tort aspects of the agency relationship. It focuses first upon the tort liability of the parties when the agent injures a third party while acting for the principal. Second, this chapter discusses the law of workers' compensation, which provides compensation to employees for accidental injuries that occur during the course of employment.

Introduction to Agency and Torts

As a general principle of tort law a person always is liable for her own torts. The fact that a person may be acting in an agency capacity does not excuse the agent from responsibility for her wrongs. Assume, for example, that Amber, while working as a truck driver for

Pennington, drives negligently and causes an accident that injures Terry. Amber is personally liable for Terry's injuries even though she was working for Pennington. Thus, agents always can be held liable for their torts.

In some circumstances, the principal also can be held liable for injuries caused by an agent. Generally, this liability is based on one of two theories. First, the principal may be liable if its own intentional or negligent conduct was a cause of the injury. Second, the principal may be held liable "vicariously" for an agent's tortious conduct under the *respondeat superior* doctrine.

Liability of Principal for Principal's Torts

A person is always liable for an intentional wrong he directs another to do. A principal is therefore liable for harm caused to a third person by an agent acing on the principal's express direction. Assume Peterson, with intent to disrupt Todd's business, directs Archer to cut the electrical and telephone lines to Todd's store. Archer cuts the lines. Peterson is liable in tort to Todd.

In addition to express direction, a principal may be liable for his own negligence in conducting the agency that results in harm to a third person. The principal's liability usually results from negligence in hiring, training, or supervising the agent (for example, by giving improper or ambiguous orders or failing to establish proper working rules and regulations). Assume, for example, that Pennington, when it hired Amber as its truck driver, knew that Amber had a history of erratic driving behavior including several accidents and traffic citations. If Amber later causes a traffic accident injuring Terry, Pennington probably would be liable because of its own negligence in selecting Amber as its agent. Similarly, Pennington could be held liable for injuries caused by its failure adequately to train or supervise Amber during the agency relationship.

Liability of Principal for Agent's Torts—*Respondeat Superior*

A principal also may be held liable for an agent's torts under the doctrine of *respondeat superior* (Latin: "let the master respond"). Under this doctrine, a master (employer) is liable for torts of his servants (employees) committed while acting within the scope of their employment.[1] Liability under the *respondeat superior* doctrine is **vicarious** (or **derivative**); in other words, it derives from the wrong of another—the employee's tortious conduct. *Respondeat superior,* therefore, imposes liability even if the employer was not negligent or otherwise at fault in causing the injury.

Rationale for Respondeat Superior

Respondeat superior liability is imposed upon employers for a variety of reasons. One rationale for holding an employer liable for an employee's torts is that the employer both selects and controls the employee and should therefore be responsible for his conduct. Another rationale for the doctrine is that the employer reaps the benefit of the employee's labor and places the employee in a position where the employee may injure third parties. The employer should therefore also bear the responsibility for the employee's actions, treating them as an ordinary cost of doing business, rather than imposing the loss upon the innocent third parties who have been injured. The employer can insure against this liability and pass the cost of insurance along to all of its customers, thereby spreading the loss among those who benefit from the employer's business. *Respondeat supe-*

rior liability also induces employers to be more careful in choosing, training, instructing, and supervising their employees. Whatever the justification, the *respondeat superior* doctrine is firmly entrenched in the law, with precedents dating back nearly three centuries.[2]

As a general rule, unless authorized to act in the manner causing the injury, an employee who subjects the employer to liability under *respondeat superior* for a negligent or other wrongful act in the course of employment is liable to the employer for the loss incurred. This result has been criticized as inconsistent with the basic policy of the *respondeat superior* doctrine outlined above. As noted by one court:

> [R]espondeat superior rests upon a public policy that the employer bear the burden as an expense of the operation he expands through the employment of others. . . . The theoretical liability of an employee to reimburse the employer is quite anachronistic. The rule would surprise the modern employer no less than his employee. Both expect the employer to save the harmless employee rather than the other way round, the employer routinely purchasing insurance which protects the employee as well.[3]

Despite this criticism, many courts continue to permit the employer's suit against the negligent employee for indemnity. Such suits, though uncommon, may be valuable if the employee, such as a corporate officer or manager, has substantial personal assets or separate insurance coverage.

Liability is imposed under the *respondeat superior* doctrine if two elements are present:

1. a *master-servant relationship* exists between principal and agent, and
2. the agent (servant) was acting in the *scope of employment* when the tort was committed.

The Master-Servant Relationship

As noted in Chapter 40, master and servant are specialized forms of principal and agent. A master is a principal who employs an agent and who has the right to control the physical conduct of the agent's activities. A servant is the agent who performs continuous service for another and whose physical conduct is subject to control

---

[1] Restatement (Second) of Agency §219(1).

[2] Jones v. Hart, Holt, K.B. 642, 90 Eng. Rep. 1255 (K.B. 1698).
[3] Eule v. Eule Motor Sales, 170 A.2d 241, 242 (N.J. 1961).

by the other. Thus all masters are principals, but not all principals are masters because not all principals possess the right to control the physical conduct of their agents. Similarly, all servants are agents, but not all agents are servants because certain agents are not subject to the principal's physical control in the performance of their duties. Most employment arrangements create a master-servant relationship between the employer (master) and employee (servant). For this reason the term "employer-employee" often is used as a substitute or synonym for "master-servant."

Servant or employee status is characterized by continuous service, not by the character or quality of the service rendered. Thus, servants include not only manual laborers but also ship captains and corporate managers. In addition, although control or right of control by the master or employer is essential, this requirement is easily established. For example, corporate managers and cooks are servants even though it is often understood, if not explicitly stated, that they have wide latitude and discretion in performing their duties.

A servant must be carefully distinguished from an independent contractor. An independent contractor is a person who contracts with another to do something but who is not subject to the other's control or right of control in the performance of the undertaking. That is, an independent contractor contracts with another to render a service, but retains control over the manner in which the acts constituting performance are performed. An independent contractor may or may not be an agent.[4] Assume P appoints A, a real estate broker, as agent to sell P's land. A is an agent, but is an independent contractor, not a servant. Or, assume P contracts with A, a building contractor, to build an office building for P at an agreed price. A is an independent contractor, but is neither an agent nor a servant.

The distinction between a servant and an independent contractor is an important one. A master controls the physical conduct of servants and is therefore liable for torts committed by servants against third persons. On the other hand, with certain exceptions, a person using an independent contractor is not responsible for the physical conduct, and therefore the torts, of the independent contractor. Because tort liability turns upon the distinction, courts often have been required to determine whether a person committing a tort is a servant or independent contractor. The major factors to be examined by the court in

making this determination are listed in §220 of the *Restatement (Second) of Agency*. No one factor alone is determinative; all relevant factors are considered. The following case explains and applies the *Restatement* test.

Santiago v. Phoenix Newspapers, Inc.
794 P.2d 138 (Ariz. 1990)

Defendant Frank Frausto delivered newspapers for defendant Phoenix Newspapers, Inc. (PNI) in accordance with a written contract prepared by PNI. The contract, which designated Frausto as an "independent contractor," allowed him to pursue other business activities that did not interfere with his delivery services and required him to carry liability insurance. The agreement included detailed instructions concerning delivery of PNI's papers and allowed PNI to terminate the agreement on 28 days advance notice, or immediately if Frausto failed to provide satisfactory service or if PNI ceased publishing. PNI paid Frausto a set amount each week regardless of the number of papers delivered and also provided health and disability insurance. While delivering newspapers for PNI, Frausto's car collided with a motorcycle driven by plaintiff William Santiago. Santiago sued Frausto and PNI alleging that Frausto had acted negligently and that PNI was vicariously liable for Frausto's negligence under the doctrine of *respondeat superior*. The trial court found that Frausto was an independent contractor and granted summary judgment in favor of PNI. The court of appeals affirmed and Santiago appealed to the Arizona Supreme Court.

Grant, Chief Judge

. . . The court may grant summary judgment only if no dispute exists as to any material facts, if only one inference can be drawn from those facts, and if the moving party is entitled to judgment as a matter of law. . . . We apply the rule in this case by asking whether the courts below correctly decided that no inferences could be drawn from the material facts suggesting Frausto was acting as PNI's employee when the accident occurred. . . .

Section 220 of the *Restatement (Second) of Agency,* adopted by Arizona . . . defines a servant as "a person employed to perform services in the affairs of another and who with respect to the physical conduct in the performance of the services is subject to the other's control or right to control." The *Restatement* lists several additional

---

[4]Restatement (Second) of Agency §2(3).

factors, none of which is dispositive, in determining whether one acting for another is a servant or an independent contractor. We now review those factors . . . for evidence of an employer-employee relationship which could preclude the entry of summary judgment. . . .

1. *The extent of control exercised by the master over the details of the work.* . . . The fundamental criterion is the extent of control the principal exercises or may exercise over the agent. . . . Such control may be manifested in a variety of ways. A worker who must comply with another's instructions about when, where, and how to work is an employee. . . . A strong indication of control is an employer's power to give specific instructions with the expectation that they will be followed. . . . In this case, PNI designated the time for pick-up and delivery, the area covered, the manner in which the papers were delivered, *i.e.*, bagged and banded, and the persons to whom delivery was made. Although PNI did little actual supervising, it had the authority under the contract to send a supervisor with Frausto on his route. Frausto claimed he did the job as he was told, without renegotiating the contract terms, adding customers and following specific customer requests relayed by PNI.

2. *The distinct nature of the workers' business.* Whether the worker's tasks are efforts to promote his own independent enterprise or to further his employer's business will aid the fact finder in ascertaining the existence of an employer-employee relationship. . . . A concomitant inquiry to this factor also considers whether the worker's job performance results in a profit or loss for the worker. Thus, where the worker purchases the product and then sells it at a profit or loss, the worker is more likely to be found an independent contractor. . . .

As far as the nature of the worker's business, Frausto had no delivery business distinct from that of his responsibilities to PNI. . . . Frausto had an individual relationship and contract with the newspaper company. Furthermore, he did not purchase the papers and then sell them at a profit or loss. Payments were made directly to PNI and any complaints of requests for delivery changes went through PNI. If Frausto missed a customer, a PNI employee would deliver a paper.

3. *Specialization or skilled occupation.* The jury is more likely to find a master-servant relationship where the work does not require the services of one highly educated or skilled. . . . PNI argues that its agents must drive, follow directions, and be diligent in order to perform the job for which they are paid. However, these skills are required in differing degrees for virtually any

job. Frausto's services were not specialized and required no particular training. In addition, an agreement that work cannot be delegated indicates a master-servant relationship. . . . In this case, Frausto could delegate work but only up to twenty-five percent of the days.

4. *Materials and place of work.* If an employer supplies tools, and employment is over a specific area or over a fixed route, a master-servant relationship is indicated. . . . In this case, PNI supplied the product but did not supply the bags, rubber bands, or transportation necessary to complete the deliveries satisfactorily. However, PNI did designate the route to be covered.

5. *Duration of employment.* Whether the employer seeks a worker's services as a one-time, discrete job or as part of a continuous working relationship may indicate that the employer-employee relationship exists. The shorter in time the relationship, the less likely the worker will subject himself to control over job details. . . . In addition, the employer's right to terminate may indicate control and therefore an employer-employee relationship. . . . In this case, . . . [a] jury could reasonably infer that an employer-employee relationship existed since PNI retained significant latitude to fire Frausto. . . . In addition, the jury could also infer that PNI provided health insurance to encourage a long-term relationship and disability insurance to protect itself in case of injury to the carrier, both of which support the existence of an employer-employee relationship.

6. *Method of payment.* PNI paid Frausto each week, but argues that because Frausto was not paid by the hour, he was an independent contractor. Santiago responds that payment was not made by the "job" because Frausto's responsibilities changed without any adjustment to his pay or contract. . . .

7. *Relation of work done to the employer's regular business.* A court is more likely to find a worker an employee if the work is part of the employer's regular business. . . . Home delivery is critical to the survival of a local daily paper; it may be its essential core. . . . PNI is hard-pressed to detach the business of delivering news from that of reporting and printing it, especially when it retains an individual relationship with each carrier. . . .

8. *Belief of the parties.* As stated above, Frausto believed that he was an employee, despite contract language to the contrary. Even if he believed he was an independent contractor, that would not preclude a finding of vicarious liability. . . . In addition to the parties' belief, the finder of fact should look to the community's belief. . . . The fact that the community regards those

Table 41.1	Characteristics of Independent Contractor and Servant	
Characteristic	**Independent Contractor**	**Servant (Employee)**
Nature of work	Is engaged in distinct enterprise often involving a specialized or skilled occupation	Performs work that is a part of the employer's regular business
Method of payment	Is paid for a completed job	Is paid on regular basis by salary or hourly wage
Duration of employment	Works long enough to complete a particular job	Works regular hours as part of continuous working relationship
Materials/place of work	Provides own tools, equipment, and materials; often works at own place of business	Uses tools, equipment, and materials supplied by employer; often works at employer's workplace
Right of control	Works without supervision; not subject to control of employer; generally determines time, place, and manner of performing the job	Works under supervision of employer who has power to control, including setting time, place, and manner of performing work

doing such work as servants indicates the relation of master and servant. The newspaper's customers did not have individual contact or contracts with Frausto. All payments, complaints, and changes were made directly to PNI. From these facts, a jury could infer that the community regarded Frausto as PNI's employee. . . .

Whether an employer-employee relationship exists may not be determined as a matter of law in either side's favor, because reasonable minds may disagree on the nature of the employment relationship. A jury could infer from these facts that Frausto was an employee because PNI involved itself with the details of delivery, received directly all customer complaints and changes so as to remove much of Frausto's independence, retained broad discretion to terminate, and relied heavily on Frausto's services for the survival of its business. The jury could also infer that Frausto was an independent contractor because he used his own car, was subject to little supervision, provided some of his own supplies, and could have someone else deliver for him within limits. Therefore, the trial court erred in finding as a matter of law that Frausto was an independent contractor. . . .

[Judgment reversed and remanded.]

Table 41.1 summarizes some of the important differences between a servant and an independent contractor.

Respondeat Superior Liability Standards

Respondeat superior liability may be imposed upon an employer in three situations: (1) injuries caused by the employee's *negligent* conduct deemed within the scope of employment; (2) injuries caused by the employee's *intentional use of force* deemed within the scope of employment; and (3) injuries caused by the employee's intentional misconduct clearly outside the scope of employment if the employee "was aided in accomplishing the tort by the existence of the agency relation."[5]

Liability for Negligence. The first two grounds of liability, negligence and use of force, require that the tort be committed within the scope of the employee's employment. Scope of employment is a broad concept that includes not only those acts authorized by the master, but also many acts expressly forbidden by the master. Thus, an employer cannot avoid respondeat superior liability simply by stating to employees that they are not authorized to commit torts in the course of their work. Scope of employment, therefore, is not tied to principles of authority and authorization, governing the imposition of *contract* liability, discussed in Chapter 40. Rather, the basic question for judicial determination in tort cases is whether the employee's deviation from his employment either in time, place, act, or motive is so

---

[5]RESTATEMENT (SECOND) OF AGENCY §219(2)(d).

great that the employer should no longer be held accountable for the employee's actions.

In the vast majority of *respondeat superior* cases, the issue is whether an employee's *negligent* act causing injury occurred within the scope of employment. Most courts use the test stated in §228(1) of the *Restatement (Second) of Agency,* which finds an employee's conduct within the **scope of employment** if "(a) it is of a kind he is employed to perform; (b) it occurs substantially within the authorized time and space limits; and (c) it is actuated, at least in part, by a purpose to serve the master." Courts generally use the terms "frolic" and "detour" to describe the character of an employee's deviation in *respondeat superior* cases.[6] A servant who embarks upon a **frolic** departs from the scope of employment, relieving the master of liability for the servant's torts. A mere **detour,** however, is a less severe deviation, insufficient to remove the servant from the scope of employment. If an act is clearly outside the scope of employment, the court (judge) resolves the issue as a matter of law. In most cases, however, the scope of employment issue is a close factual question and is decided by the jury.

A related question concerns when an employee, who has clearly departed from the scope of employment (embarked on a "frolic"), sufficiently returns to the scope of employment to reimpose tort liability upon the master. To reenter the scope of employment the servant must again be reasonably near the authorized geographic and time limitations of employment and must be acting with an intent to perform assigned duties.[7] This issue, like scope of employment, often presents a close factual question and is usually left to the jury in difficult cases.

In the following case, the court was required to decide whether an employee's negligent conduct occurred within the scope of employment.

Clover v. Snowbird Ski Resort
808 P.2d 1037 (Utah 1991)

Defendant Snowbird Ski Resort operates a ski area on a mountain in Utah and also operates the Plaza Restaurant,

located at the base of the mountain, and Mid-Gad Restaurant, located halfway up the mountain. Snowbird employed defendant Chris Zulliger as a chef at the Plaza but regularly required him to make trips to Mid-Gad to monitor operations. On December 5, 1985, Zulliger was scheduled to begin work at the Plaza at 3:00 P.M. That morning, the manager of the restaurants requested Zulliger to inspect operations at Mid-Gad before reporting to work at the Plaza. In the morning, Zulliger decided to ski with a friend who also worked for the restaurants. During their first run, they stopped at Mid-Gad where Zulliger performed the inspection. They then skied three more runs. On his fifth and final run, Zulliger took a route that Snowbird employees often used to travel from the top of the mountain to the Plaza. During this run, Zulliger collided with and seriously injured the plaintiff, Margaret Clover. Clover sued Zulliger and Snowbird alleging that Zulliger had acted negligently and that Snowbird should be held vicariously liable under the doctrine of *respondeat superior*. The trial court ruled as a matter of law that Zulliger was not within the scope of employment at the time of the accident. Clover appealed arguing that the issue should have been submitted to the jury.

Hall, Chief Justice

. . . In [*Birkner v. Salt Lake County,* 771 P.2d 1053 (Utah 1989)], we observed that . . . the issue of whether an employee's actions . . . are within or without the scope of employment have focused on three criteria. "First, an employee's conduct must be of the general kind the employee is employed to perform. . . . In other words, the employee must be about the employer's business and the duties assigned by the employer, as opposed to being wholly involved in a personal endeavor." Second, the employee's conduct must occur substantially within the hours and ordinary spatial boundaries of the employment. "Third, the employee's conduct must be motivated at least in part, by the purpose of serving the employer's interest.". . .

In applying the *Birkner* criteria to the facts in the instant case, it is important to note that if Zulliger had returned to the Plaza Restaurant immediately after he inspected the operations at the Mid-Gad Restaurant, there would be ample evidence to support the conclusion that on his return trip Zulliger's actions were within the scope of his employment. There is evidence that it was part of Zulliger's job to monitor the operations at the Mid-Gad and that he was directed to monitor the operations on the day of the accident. There is also evidence that Snowbird intended Zulliger to use the ski lifts and the ski runs on his trips to the Mid-Gad. It is clear, therefore, that Zulliger's actions could be consid-

---

[6]These terms were originally used in the English case, *Joel v. Morison,* 6 Car. & P. 501, 172 Eng. Rep. 1338 (N.P. 1834).

[7]RESTATEMENT (SECOND) OF AGENCY §237.

ered to "be of the general kind that the employee is employed to perform." It is also clear that there would be evidence that Zulliger's actions occurred within the hours and normal spatial boundaries of his employment. Zulliger was expected to monitor the operations at the Mid-Gad during the time the lifts were operating and when he was not working as a chef at the Plaza. Furthermore, throughout the trip he would have been on his employer's premises. Finally, it is clear that Zulliger's actions in monitoring the operations at the Mid-Gad, per his employer's instructions, could be considered "motivated, at least in part, by the purpose of serving the employer's interest."

The difficulty, of course, arises from the fact that Zulliger did not return to the Plaza after he finished inspecting the facilities at the Mid-Gad. Rather, he skied four more runs and rode the lift to the top of the mountain before he began his return to the base. Snowbird claims that this fact shows that Zulliger's primary purpose for skiing on the day of the accident was for his own pleasure and that therefore, as a matter of law, he was not acting within the scope of his employment. In support of this proposition, Snowbird cites . . . the dual purpose doctrine. Under this doctrine, if an employee's actions are motivated by the dual purpose of benefiting the employer and serving some personal interest, the actions will usually be considered within the scope of employment. However, [the employee is outside the scope of employment] if the primary motivation for the activity is personal. . . . In situations where the scope of employment issue concerns an employee's trip, a useful test in determining if the transaction of business is purely incidental to a personal motive is "whether the trip is one which would have required the employer to send another employee over the same route or to perform the same function if the trip had not been made." [*Whitehead v. Variable Annuity Life Insurance,* 801 P.2d 934, 937 (Utah 1989).]

In [this case,] . . . the activity of inspecting the Mid-Gad necessitates travel to the restaurant. Furthermore, there is evidence that the manager of both the Mid-Gad and the Plaza wanted an employee to inspect the restaurant and report back by 3 P.M. If Zulliger had not inspected the restaurant, it would have been necessary to send a second employee to accomplish the same purpose. Furthermore, the second employee would have most likely used the ski lifts and ski runs in traveling to and from the restaurant.

There is ample evidence that there was a predominant business purpose for Zulliger's trip to the Mid-Gad.

Therefore, this case is better analyzed under our decisions dealing with situations where an employee has taken a personal detour in the process of carrying out his duties. This court has decided several cases in which employees deviated from their duties for wholly personal reasons and then, after resuming their duties, were involved in accidents. In situations where the detour was such a substantial diversion from the employee's duties that it constituted an abandonment of employment, we held that the employee, as a matter of law, was acting outside the scope of employment. However, in situations where reasonable minds could differ on whether the detour constituted a slight deviation from the employee's duties or an abandonment of employment, we have left the question for the jury.

Under the circumstances of the instant case, it is entirely possible for a jury to reasonably believe that at the time of the accident, Zulliger had resumed his employment and that Zulliger's deviation was not substantial enough to constitute a total abandonment of employment. First, a jury could reasonably believe that by beginning his return to the base of the mountain to begin his duties as a chef and to report . . . his observations at the Mid-Gad, Zulliger had resumed his employment. . . . This is an important factor because if the employee had resumed the duties of employment, the employee is then "about the employer's business" and the employee's actions will be "motivated, at least in part, by the purpose of serving the employer's interest." . . . Second, a jury could reasonably believe that Zulliger's actions in taking four ski runs and returning to the top of the mountain do not constitute a complete abandonment of employment. It is important to note that by taking these ski runs, Zulliger was not disregarding his employer's directions. . . . In the instant case, far from directing its employees not to ski at the resort, Snowbird issued its employees season ski passes as part of their compensation.

These two factors, along with other circumstances—such as, throughout the day Zulliger was on Snowbird's property, there was no specific time set for inspecting the restaurant, and the act of skiing was the method used by Snowbird employees to travel among the different locations of the resort—constitute sufficient evidence for a jury to conclude that Zulliger, at the time of the accident, was acting within the scope of his employment. . . .

[Judgment reversed and remanded.]

The *Restatement* test, as the above case indicates, is often difficult to apply in the context of a litigated case. For this reason, a number of courts use the test applied in California under which an employee's negligent conduct is within the scope of employment if "in the context of the particular enterprise an employee's conduct is not so unusual or startling that it would seem unfair to include the loss resulting from it among other costs of the employer's business."[8] This is an application of the "hindsight foreseeability" test governing proximate causation discussed in Chapter 5, and the use of force cases discussed below. That is, whether the employee's conduct was "unusual or startling" is determined from the jury's point of view looking back on events that have already occurred. Factors relevant to applying the *Restatement* test also are relevant to the hindsight foreseeability inquiry. Also relevant is evidence of whether the employee would, in fact, have been reprimanded or discharged for the conduct if the employer had learned of it and no tort had occurred. Evidence that the employer had tolerated employee deviations of a similar type in the past is strong evidence that the deviation resulting in the tort was not "unusual or startling" and that the employer already had judged such deviations as one of the normal risks of the business.

Borrowed Servants. Occasionally, one employer may permit or direct its employee to perform services for another employer. For example, ABC Construction may rent a dump truck and driver to XYZ Construction for temporary use in a construction project undertaken by XYZ. If the employee loaned or rented then negligently injures a third party, the law must determine which of the two employers should bear the loss. To make this choice, courts traditionally analyze the factors previously discussed to determine whether a master-servant relationship exists, emphasizing particularly the factor of control. The court then imposes liability upon the employer with the right to control or direct the elements of the specific act that caused the injury. That employer is deemed to be in the best position to prevent the injury. Under this approach, although the employee is employed by two employers, only one of them is held responsible for the employee's torts.

This approach to the "borrowed servant" problem has been criticized for reaching inconsistent results within and among the various jurisdictions and because no convincing policy reasons exist for placing the loss on one employer rather than the other. That is, the employee is subject to a significant degree of control by both employers and is furthering the business interests of both employers. For this reason, an increasing number of jurisdictions reject the borrowed servant rule and apportion the loss between the two employers.

Liability for Use of Force. In most *respondeat superior* cases, the employee's negligence (failure to exercise reasonable care) is the cause of the injury to the third party. Intentional torts frequently are viewed as outside the scope of employment. Liability may, however, be imposed for intentional torts involving use of force if the particular use of force "was not unexpectable in view of the duties of the servant."[9] This test is another application of the "hindsight foreseeability" standard discussed above and in Chapter 5, and is usually satisfied if the dispute resulting in the assault arose out of the performance of the employee's duties. The following examples illustrate the application of this standard.

1. If the use of force is expressly ordered or authorized by the employer, liability clearly follows. A principal is always liable for his directed acts.

2. In certain employment relationships, use of force is an integral part of the job. An employer is therefore liable for intentional harm inflicted by such employees as bouncers, bodyguards, or persons employed to repossess goods from defaulting debtors.

3. Employers often are held liable for intentional torts committed by an employee who is acting to protect or recover the employer's property or otherwise to further the employer's business. In these cases, the conduct involved is not expressly or impliedly authorized by the employer and may not actually benefit or protect the employer's business or property. For example, suppose Adelman is hired by Perez to manage a jewelry store. One Sunday, while the store is closed, Adelman drives by and observes Toomey walk out of the rear entrance, get into a car, and drive away. Believing Toomey to be a burglar, Adelman gives chase and ultimately drives Toomey off the road, severely injuring him. Toomey is in fact an employee of the gas company who had been called out on an emergency basis to investigate a reported gas leak in the building. Perez may be liable to Toomey because Adelman's tort, though intentional, was committed in Adelman's good faith, though mistaken, belief that he was protecting Perez's property.

---

[8]Rodgers v. Kemper Construction Co., 124 Cal. Rptr. 143, 148-49 (Cal. App. 1975).

[9]RESTATEMENT (SECOND) OF AGENCY §245.

4. An employer may be held liable for intentional torts that are caused by friction inherent in the employment situation. That is, an employer who places an employee "in a position which requires contacts with third persons under circumstances likely to lead to disputes"[10] may be held liable for injuries inflicted by the employee. For example, assume Ahem is hired by Peake to drive a delivery truck. Ahern works long hours in heavy traffic and frequently must carry heavy parcels in extreme weather conditions. Near the end of a long day, Ahern backs into a car owned by Tully, causing minor damage. Tully proceeds to yell at Ahern and in the ensuing argument Ahern punches Tully, breaking his jaw. Peake may be held liable for the intentional tort committed by Ahern, because such a situation is likely to arise in the performance of Ahern's job.

Liability for Torts Aided by the Agency Relation. Although a master generally has no liability for torts committed by servants who are acting outside the scope of their employment, the law recognizes an exception if the servant acting outside the scope of employment "was aided in accomplishing the tort by the existence of the agency relation."[11] This rule may be used, for example, to impose liability on employers for sexual or other assaults committed by police officers, medical personnel, counselors, teachers, clergy members, or managers of businesses, such as hotels or storage facilities. It also may be used if an employee uses his employment-based access to computers or files wrongfully to obtain, use, or disclose information about the plaintiff, such as medical records or credit reports.

Note that this rule does not impose liability simply because the servants' responsibilities provided proximity to and contact with the plaintiff. Such a rule would impose liability for virtually all intentional torts committed outside the scope of employment. Rather, the employer is liable only if the tort "was accomplished by an instrumentality, or through conduct associated with the agency status."[12] It is important to note that the aided-by-agency principles discussed above provide the basis for the rules governing employer liability under federal equal employment opportunity laws for sexual harassment of employees by supervisors. These rules are discussed in Chapter 54.

Liability for Agent's Fraud. In addition to liability for use of force, a principal may be legally responsible for an agent's intentional torts not involving physical conduct, most commonly fraud. The principal's liability for the agent's fraud is governed by a rule similar to that applied to agency and contracts. That is, a principal is liable for an agent's fraudulent misrepresentation if the agent is actually or apparently authorized to make the representation. For example, assume Paula appoints Ann as agent with full authority to negotiate the sale of Paula's house. Ann defrauds Tina by fraudulently representing that the house is free of termites. In reliance upon Ann's statement, Tina purchases the house. Paula is liable for fraud to Tina. Note that although liability for most torts is based upon *respondeat superior* and requires a master-servant relation, the rule governing nonphysical conduct torts is based upon contract principles. Thus, liability may be imposed upon any principal, whether or not a master.

Workers' Compensation

The doctrine of *respondeat superior* imposes liability on employers for injuries to *third parties*—that is, non-employees—caused by an employee acting within the scope of employment. Liability for work-related injuries sustained by *employees* is governed primarily by state "workers' compensation" statutes.

History

Under the common law, developed in the early days of the industrial revolution, an employee who was injured on the job could recover damages from the employer only by proving that the injury was caused by the negligence or other fault of the employer. Thus, although the employer was liable without fault for injuries caused to third parties *by* employees under respondeat superior, injuries *to* employees were compensated only if the employer was at fault, making employee recovery difficult. This difficulty was magnified by three defenses available to the employer in a negligence suit by an injured employee: (1) the fellow-servant doctrine, (2) assumption of the risk, and (3) contributory negligence.

Under the **fellow-servant doctrine,** created by the English courts in 1837[13] an employer was not liable for injury to an employee caused by the negligent conduct of

---

[10]Restatement (Second) of Agency §24 comment i.
[11]Restatement (Second) of Agency §219(2)(d).
[12]Gary v. Long, 59 F.3d 1391, 1397 (D.C. Cir. 1995).

[13]Priestley v. Fowler, 3 M. & W. 1, 150 Eng. Rep. 1030 (Ex. 1837).

another employee. Although some courts later held employers responsible for injuries caused by supervisory employees, such as foremen, the fellow servant doctrine effectively protected employers from many lawsuits. The *assumption of the risk* defense further denied recovery if the employee, after learning of dangerous conditions in the workplace, voluntarily continued to work. Thus, even if an employer negligently created a condition that caused injury—for example, by failing to maintain machinery—an employee who was aware of that condition assumed the risk of injury. The *contributory negligence* defense had a similar effect by denying recovery to injured employees whose own negligence contributed to their injury even if their negligence was slight when compared to that of the employer.

The net effect of the common law fault approach, bolstered by these three defenses, was to insulate employers from responsibility for job-related injuries in the vast majority of cases, or to allow recovery only after a lengthy court battle. Alarmingly, this contraction in employee protection coincided with a sharp increase in industrial accidents resulting from the vast expansion of manufacturing and transportation industries in the late nineteenth century. By the beginning of the twentieth century, it had become apparent that a radical change in employee compensation law was necessary.

In response to this problem the various states began to enact workers' compensation statutes, modeled upon systems first adopted in Germany and England. By 1920 all but eight states had workers' compensation statutes and by 1949 a statute had been enacted in every state. Because workers' compensation laws are state statutes, the employers and employees covered, and the benefits paid, vary greatly among the states. For example, agricultural workers, domestic servants, and casual laborers are excluded under the laws of many states, as are nonprofit organizations and employers having a small number of employees. Although individual statutes are far from uniform, the following material outlines the operation of a typical workers' compensation act.

Requirements for Compensation

In contrast to the common law approach based upon fault, **workers' compensation statutes** typically provide that an injured employee is automatically entitled to benefits prescribed by statute if the injury (1) was accidental and (2) arose out of and in the course of employment. Negligence or fault of either the employer or employee are generally irrelevant. That is, an employee whose own neg-

ligence caused or contributed to the injury is nevertheless entitled to recover, and an employer who is completely free from fault is not excused from liability. Workers' compensation laws thus are based on a policy that the cost of job-related accidents should be borne by employers as a cost of doing business, which is factored into the price of the goods or services sold by the employer.

Workers' compensation statutes cover work-related injuries to employees, not independent contractors. Both courts and legislatures have, however, expanded "employee" status in borderline workers' compensation cases to cover individuals who would not be servants under traditional tort analysis. Generally, a person is an employee if her work is done as an integral part of the employer's business and she has no independent business or profession of her own. After determining that the injured person is an employee, the fundamental issues in all workers' compensation cases are whether the employee suffered (1) a personal injury by accident, (2) arising out of and in the course of employment.

Personal Injury by Accident. An accidental injury is an unexpected mishap or event, which usually can be traced to a specific time, place, and cause. The most common industrial accidents are caused by motor vehicle collisions, explosions, slips and falls, and contact with factory machinery. In these cases both the cause and the result of the accident are unexpected. An employee also may be compensated for an accidental result alone—that is, when the injury is an unexpected consequence of the routine performance of the employee's job. Under this test most states provide compensation for heart attacks, hernias, strokes, or back injuries resulting from the normal exertion or exposure of the employee's duties.

Compensation also may be awarded for injuries caused by employment-related diseases. For example, in many states, preexisting diseases, such as heart disease, aggravated by the employment are compensable. Diseases of exposure (such as pneumonia) and infectious or contagious diseases acquired during employment are covered. Further, all states provide compensation for occupational diseases, which are caused by prolonged exposure to the normal, but harmful, conditions of a particular employment.

Arising out of and in the Course of Employment. To be compensable, the accidental injury must both "arise out of" and occur "in the course of" the employment. The requirement that the injury "arise out of" the employment establishes the causal connection between the employment and the injury. Under the traditional approach, causality requires proof that the injury resulted from risks distinctly associated with the employment. Under the more modern positional risk test, used in a growing number of jurisdictions, an injury arises out of the employment if the conditions of employment placed the employee in the position (time and place) where he was injured. This approach provides compensation for injuries caused by so-called neutral risks such as stray bullets, random acts of violence, or Acts of God. These risks are termed "neutral" because they are neither clearly employment-related nor personal to the employee.

An injury arises in the course of employment if it occurs (1) during the time of the employment, (2) at a place where the employee should or may be expected to be, and (3) while the employee is performing her duties or acts incidental to those duties. This test, which judges the connection between the employment and the time, place, and circumstances of the accident, is generally similar to the "scope of employment" test used in *respondeat superior* cases. In many cases, however, courts have allowed workers' compensation to an injured worker who would probably be deemed outside the scope of employment for tort purposes. In the following case, the court was required to determine whether an employee was entitled to workers' compensation benefits.

Johannesen v. New York City Department of Housing Preservation and Development

638 N.E. 2d 981 (N.Y. 1994)

In 1981, Veronica Johannesen, an office assistant for the city of New York, was assigned to work at the Department of Housing Preservation and Development. The job required her to work in a large room with approximately 50 employees, at least half of whom smoked cigarettes. Although the office ventilation system did not function properly, the windows were kept closed to keep out smoke from the kitchen of a restaurant below the office. Within two years, Johannesen began wheezing and coughing at work and in January 1985, she was diagnosed as suffering from bronchial asthma aggravated by exposure to tobacco smoke and dust in the workplace. In 1986, Johannesen twice underwent emergency medical treatment for asthma attacks at work. After her requests for transfer were denied, she filed a claim for workers' compensation benefits. The New York Workers' Compensation Board found that Johannesen had sustained an accidental injury from exposure to passive cigarette smoke and the appellate court affirmed. The New York Court of Appeals agreed to review the case.

Bellacosa, Judge

. . . The Workers' Compensation Law was enacted for socioeconomic remediation purposes "as a means of protecting work[ers] and their dependents from want in case of injury" on the job (*Matter of Post v. Burger & Gohlke*, . . . [111 N.E. 351 (N.Y. 1916)]). An employee is entitled to receive compensation on a "no fault" basis for all injuries "arising out of and in the course of the employment" (Workers' Compensation Law §10[1]). . . . Under Workers' Compensation Law §2(7), "injury" and "personal injury" means only "accidental injuries arising out of and in the course of employment and such disease or infection as may naturally and unavoidably result therefrom". . . .

On this appeal, the causal relationship between claimant's inhalation of the secondhand tobacco smoke and the aggravation of her bronchial asthma is not disputed. In addition to claimant's proof, the employer's own medical expert confirmed the existence of claimant's obstructive lung disease and concluded that her work environment aggravated her asthma condition. Thus, the sole focus of this Court's law question inquiry is whether claimant sustained an accidental injury within the meaning of the Workers' Compensation Law. . . .

The term of art, accidental injury, lacks a statutory definition and, thus, requires a distinctive analysis and tracking of pertinent precedents. An accidental injury need not result suddenly or from the immediate application of some external force but may accrue gradually over a reasonably definite period of time. . . . [In *Matter of Middleton v. Coxsackie Correctional Facility*, 341 N.E.2d 527 (N.Y. App. 1975)], a correction officer contracted tuberculosis through exposure, over a period of three or four months for two or three hours a day, to an infected, coughing inmate. In holding that the claimant's tuberculosis was an accidental injury, the Court in *Middleton* relied on *Matter of Pessel v. Macy & Co.*, [304 N.E.2d 565 (N.Y. 1973)], where we held that a claimant's exposure to repeated bursts of cold air over a period of three months, which activated an underlying arthritic condition, was an accidental injury. . . . Gradual injury was also recognized as a compensable disability accident . . . where a garage mechanic, while in the course of his employment, routinely inhaled carbon monoxide gas from which he developed bronchitis. . . .

In the present case, claimant's bronchial condition progressively worsened from 1981 to 1986. The injury may have been gradual, but the record substantiates that her working environment was highly dangerous for her and aggravated her asthma. . . .

Appellant . . . interjects, however, that the absence of a "catastrophic or extraordinary" event disqualifies these events from the accidental injury category. While exposure to cigarette smoke in our society and in workplaces may have been and still is relatively endemic, the facts surrounding this claimant's exposure . . . demonstrate an exacerbative and excessive quality. Claimant was required to work in an unventilated office and forced to share the polluted atmosphere with numerous smokers, who were all around her. She was allowed no alternative but to inhale the dense, dangerous and debilitative smoke-filled air. Graphically, she suffered two bronchial breakdowns at work requiring emergency medical attention. Claimant worked in an office where the tools of her trade are papers, pens, files, computers and telephones. Cigarette smoke is surely not a natural by-product of the Department of Housing Preservation and Development's activities and her employment role. Thus, . . . this risk was not a commonly understood, ordinary incident to the environmental workplace. . . .

We are also satisfied that the severe bronchial aggravation, reflected among other facets of this case, by two on-the-job asthma episodes, requiring immediate emergency medical attention, met the time-definite component of the accidental injury rule. . . . We perceive no legally cognizable distinction between this claimant's "attack" following years of exposure to excessive levels of secondhand cigarette smoke in her workplace and the now quintessential cardiac collapse cases ensuing from extended periods of strain for which awards are customarily upheld. . . .

Claimant's predisposition with an asthma condition does not change the analysis or result. It is well settled that where causally related injuries from a claimant's employment precipitate, aggravate or accelerate a preexisting infirmity or disease, the resulting disability is compensable. . . .

Finally, in a policy-based argument, appellant suggests that recovery here will open floodgates and make every allergic reaction, common cold or ordinary ailment compensable. This argument is often advanced when precedent and analysis are unpersuasive. It is unavailing in this case. . . . The holding in this case does not change existing criteria and legal principles for determining whether a work-related and work-site injury is accidental. Claimants are still required to make showings of unusual environmental conditions or events assignable to something extraordinary that caused an accidental injury. This claimant did so to the satisfaction of the Board and each court that has

reviewed the matter. Standard preexisting legal tests were met in this case and substantial evidence supports the Board's determination that claimant's disabling and aggravated asthmatic condition, caused by prolonged exposure to secondhand cigarette smoke in her confined employment workplace, constituted an accidental injury within the meaning and intent of the Workers' Compensation Law. The award should be upheld. . . .

[Judgment affirmed.]

Operation of Workers' Compensation Statutes

To expedite the processing of claims, most workers' compensation statutes are administered by a state agency, often called a commission or board, rather than by the courts. Through rule-making powers, the agency then may establish procedures for filing claims.

Claims Procedure. State laws generally require the employee to give notice of the injury to the employer within a period of time specified by statute. This period varies among the states from a few days to as long as six months. Because liability is not contested in a substantial majority of cases, many states allow the employee and employer to agree to the appropriate payments, and then file reports with the state agency.

If the employer does contest the claim, the employee must file a formal claim with the state agency within a stated period, usually one or two years. Commonly, a single hearing officer or examiner makes initial findings that are later affirmed, modified, or rejected by the full board or commission. Rules of procedure and evidence generally are relaxed before these administrative tribunals.

Final decisions of the workers' compensation board are then reviewable, like other administrative agency decisions, by the courts. Judicial review is, however, limited to questions of law. The reviewing court generally accepts the commission's findings of fact if supported by any evidence, even if the court would have ruled differently on the same facts.

Benefits. Each state's statute specifies the types of benefits to which the injured employee is entitled. In a contested claim, the hearing officer must determine the benefits to be awarded. The statutes generally require payment of "medical and rehabilitation benefits" including, for example, payment for physicians and hospitals, medical appliances, supplies, therapy, and, if the employee can no longer perform the work for which he was trained, the costs of vocational retraining and job placement.

Additionally, an employee who becomes disabled because of the injury is entitled to disability benefits to compensate for lost earnings. A disability may be total — meaning the employee is completely unable to work — or partial — indicating that employee is capable of performing some work. Disability benefits generally are calculated as a percentage of the employee's average weekly wage. In many states, for example, a person who suffers total disability receives compensation equal to two-thirds of her average weekly wage. Workers with a partial disability generally receive a specified percentage of the difference between their average weekly wage at the time of the injury and their average weekly wage after the injury.

Disabilities also may be classified as either permanent or temporary. In many states, those with permanent disabilities are entitled to disability benefits for life while other states allow payment only for a specified period, for example, 500 weeks. A worker with a temporary disability is entitled to benefits only for the duration of the disability. Some states impose a maximum dollar limitation on payment of benefits.

Most states also provide additional specified benefits (often called scheduled benefits) for certain types of dismemberment or loss of a body part. The statute might provide, for example, that a worker will receive payment of 100 weeks of her average weekly wage for loss of an arm. Finally, workers' compensation statutes typically provide death benefits, again based on the average weekly wage, to the employee's surviving spouse and dependents.

Exclusive Remedy. Generally, workers' compensation benefits do not fully compensate the employee for the injury. This modest recovery usually is justified by the reasoning that the employee, through workers' compensation, receives a reasonably certain, expedited recovery, without regard to the fault of either the employer or employee. In exchange for the benefits guaranteed under workers' compensation, the employee also surrenders the common law right to sue the employer for negligence in causing the injury. That is, workers' compensation benefits generally are the injured employee's sole remedy against the employer.

A workers' compensation recovery does not, however, prevent an employee from suing any other third party responsible for the accident. For example, if an employee is injured while using a defectively manufactured machine, a workers' compensation award would not prevent a suit against the manufacturer of the machine. If the employee recovers from the third party, however, the proceeds are first applied to reimburse the employer for the compensation award, with any balance paid to the employee.

Funding. Employers unilaterally fund workers' compensation systems. Statutes generally require the employer to secure this liability through a private insurance policy, a state insurance fund, or in some cases by self-insurance. Premiums commonly are based upon an employer's or industry's injury-experience rating, increased or decreased on the basis of prior accident and liability record. In this manner, employment-related injuries are treated as a business expense with the cost distributed among the consumers of the employer's product. Workers' compensation and respondeat superior therefore both rest upon the policy that employment-related injuries are a cost of doing business and should therefore be borne by business enterprise, not the individuals injured as a result.

In most jurisdictions, workers' compensation coverage is compulsory. In the minority of states providing for "elective" or "optional" workers' compensation coverage, the employer may elect either to be covered under workers' compensation or be subject to a common law negligence action by injured employees, without the benefit of the common law defenses previously discussed.

Summary

1. The law of agency addresses the tort liability of the parties when the agent injures a third party while acting for the principal. Because a person is always liable for his own torts, the fact that a person is acting as an agent does not excuse the agent from responsibility for his wrongs. Similarly, the principal is liable for tortious acts he directs an agent to do and for negligence in the selection, training, or supervision of agents. The law of agency also imposes "vicarious" or "derivative" liability upon completely innocent principals for torts of agents under the doctrine of *respondeat superior.*

2. Liability is imposed under the *respondeat superior* doctrine if (1) a master-servant (employer-employee) relationship exists between principal and agent (a principal has no liability for torts of independent contractors), and (2) the agent (servant, employee) was acting within the scope of employment when the tort was committed. An employee's conduct is within the scope of employment if it is of the kind he is employed to perform, occurs substantially within authorized time and space limitations, and is motivated, at least in part, by a purpose to serve the employer.

3.   Although vicarious liability generally is imposed for an employee's negligent rather than intentional torts, an employer may be held liable for an employee's use of force if the use of force is (1) expressly ordered or authorized by the employer, (2) an integral part of the job, (3) used to protect or recover the employer's property or otherwise further the employer's business, or (4) caused by friction inherent in the employment situation. An employer also may be held liable for intentional torts by a servant acting outside the scope of employment if the servant was aided in accomplishing the tort by the existence of the agency relation. A principal is liable for intentional torts not involving physical conduct, such as fraud, if the agent is actually or apparently authorized to act.

4.   In addition to liability for torts committed by employees, the law of agency also addresses job-related injuries to employees. Traditionally, the law imposed liability upon an employer whose negligence caused the employee's injury. Three defenses available to the employer—the fellow-servant doctrine, contributory negligence, and assumption of risk—made employee recovery difficult.

5.   To provide greater employee protection in the face of increasing industrial accidents, states have replaced the common law negligence approach with workers' compensation statutes that typically provide that an injured employee is entitled to specified benefits if the injury was (1) accidental and (2) arose out of and in the course of employment. Under these statutes, which are funded unilaterally by the employer, the negligence or fault of either the employer or employee are generally irrelevant. Like the respondeat superior doctrine, workers' compensation is designed to treat employment-related injuries as a cost of doing business, borne by business enterprise, not the injured individuals.

Key Terms

respondeat superior doctrine	detour
vicarious liability	fellow-servant doctrine
scope of employment	workers' compensation
frolic	statute

Questions and Problems

41.1   Which of the various policy reasons supporting the *respondeat superior* doctrine is most important? Should employers be held vicariously liable for the torts of their employees?

41.2   Workers' compensation statutes are designed to remedy the deficiencies in the traditional common law approach to employee compensation for work-related injuries. Given the relatively modest benefits paid under workers' compensation, what are its advantages to the employee over even a liberal common law recovery? What are the advantages to the employer of workers' compensation over common law tort recovery?

41.3   Western Company owned an office building in which Adams Box Co. rented an office. Western hired STOP Corp. to remove and replace some pipes and valves located in the basement of the office building. STOP agreed to complete the work within a two-week period and to provide all specialized equipment necessary for the job. An employee of STOP was using a blowtorch to cut through a pipe when a small explosion occurred followed by a fire. The offices of Adams Box Co. were destroyed. An inspection revealed that the blowtorch had been used improperly and negligently.
   (a) If Adams Box Co. sues STOP Corp. for negligence, should the court hold STOP liable? Explain.
   (b) If Adams Box Co. sues Western Company for negligence, should the court hold Western liable? Explain.

41.4   Clearwater Drilling Company was drilling a well and setting a water line for a restaurant under construction. Kastner had been hired by Clearwater to lay pipe for the water line. As was its custom, Clearwater leased a backhoe and driver on an hourly basis from Toombs Construction Co. to dig the water line ditch. The backhoe driver, Malcolm, was instructed by Clearwater to dig the ditch to a depth of six feet. Malcolm warned Clearwater that the soil was soft and might cave in, but was instructed to dig the six-foot trench anyway. Although Malcolm knew that a six-foot trench was unsafe without reinforcement, Malcolm followed Clearwater's instructions and dug the ditch. Subsequently, Kastner was seriously injured when the ditch caved in. Kastner sued Malcolm, Toombs, and Clearwater to recover for his injuries. Which, if any, of the defendants should be held liable to Kastner and on what theory?

41.5   T & G Realtors, Inc. agreed to serve as real estate brokers for Mr. and Mrs. Feldman, who were trying to sell their home. While answering questions in preparing the listing agreement, the Feldmans said they had never had problems with leakage or water in the basement. Mr. and Mrs. Thurston were interested in purchasing a house and Lois, a T & G real estate agent, took them on a tour of the Feldmans' home. The Thurstons asked if the owners had had problems with water in the basement. After consulting the information sheet prepared by the Feldmans, Lois replied in the negative. The Thurstons purchased the house and subsequently learned that while the Feldmans owned the home, the basement had flooded every spring. The Thurstons sued the Feldmans, T & G Realtors, Inc., and Lois for fraud and misrepresentation. Who among the defendants should be held liable? Explain.

41.6   In each of the following cases, the employee was involved in an automobile accident. Consider whether at the time of the accident the employee was acting in the scope of employment, so that the employer should be held liable for the damages caused by the employee.
   (a) Elliott worked as a clerk at Stop and Save, a 24-hour convenience store, located on Green Street. Elliott also lived on Green Street approximately two miles from the Stop and Save. Every day Elliott drove his car down Green Street to the Stop and Save. One day Elliott negligently failed to stop at the stop sign on First Street and collided

with a car driven by Mrs. Sanchez. Mrs. Sanchez sued both Elliott and Stop and Save. Should Stop and Save be held vicariously liable for Elliott's negligence?

(b) Elliott's supervisor asked him to drive to the office of Stop and Save's accountant to pick up some papers. The accountant's office also was located on Green Street. Elliott drove to the office, picked up the papers, and decided to drop off his laundry at the cleaners on First Street. Elliott then drove down First Street and was making the turn on Green Street to return to the Stop and Save. While making the turn, Elliott negligently drove his car onto the sidewalk injuring Mr. Smith. Mr. Smith sued Elliott and Stop and Save. Should Stop and Save be held liable?

(c) Elliott's supervisor requested Elliott to drop off some papers at the accountant's office on Green Street. While driving down Green Street, Elliott engaged in a "drag race" with another driver and collided with a car driven by Ms. Jay. She sued Elliott and Stop and Save. Is Stop and Save liable?

(d) Assume that in each of the previous situations, Elliott also was injured and filed a worker's compensation claim against Stop and Save. Did Elliott's injuries "arise out of and in the course of employment"? Should the court consider the same factors it does when determining whether a tort occurred "in the scope of employment"? Explain.

41.7 A. J. Gatzke, a district manager for Walgreen Co., supervises the opening of new Walgreen's stores within his district. Walgreen pays Gatzke's hotel bills and living and entertainment expenses during his business trips. To obtain reimbursement of these expenses, Gatzke must submit expense account information to Walgreen. For a two-week period, Gatzke stayed at the Edgewater Motel while supervising the opening of a new store nearby. During this period, Gatzke worked in the store at least 12 hours a day and was on call 24 hours. One night after working 17 hours, Gatzke went to a bar where he had several drinks. He then returned to his hotel room where he smoked several cigarettes while working on his expense account. That night a fire broke out in his hotel room and officials later determined that it had been caused by Gatzke's negligent failure to extinguish a cigarette. Edgewater Motel sued Gatzke and Walgreen Co. seeking to hold both liable for Gatzke's negligence. Should the court hold Gatzke liable? Should the court hold Walgreen Co. liable? Explain.

41.8 Ronnell was a salesman employed by National Biscuit Co. While visiting Jerome's Grocery Store, Ronnell and Jerome became involved in an argument stemming from Jerome's complaint that Ronnell was using too much shelf space for display of National Biscuit products. Ronnell assaulted Jerome, who was seriously injured by the attack.

(a) Jerome sued National Biscuit Co. seeking damages under the doctrine of *respondeat superior.* How should the court rule?

(b) Assume that National Biscuit Co. had received complaints about Ronnell's aggressive conduct from other grocers prior to the incident at Jerome's Grocery Store. Would your answer to part (a) differ based on this information? Suggest another basis for suing National Biscuit Co., assuming that it was aware of Ronnell's violent tendencies.

41.9 Fred Jones worked as a brakeman for Penn Central. After completing 24 hours on duty, Jones left the train and flagged a taxicab. The taxi driver requested that Jones wait a few minutes while the driver used the restroom facilities in the train station. Jones became angry and kicked the taxi driver, breaking his leg. The taxi driver sued Penn Central seeking damages resulting from the injuries caused by its employee, Jones.

(a) Assume that Jones had intended to take the cab to another train station to continue his work for Penn Central. How should the court rule?

(b) If Jones had intended to take the cab home, how should the court rule?

41.10 Edmund was a sales agent for Family Insurance, a job requiring him to visit customers and potential customers at their homes or offices to discuss insurance coverage. On May 22, Edmund visited the Greens at their home to complete an insurance transaction requiring the legal description of their home. While Edmund was present, the Greens produced their lockbox containing the deed to their home as well as jewelry and other valuables. Five weeks later, the Greens' house was burglarized and the lockbox and contents were stolen. Later police investigations revealed that Edmund had hired two convicts to commit the burglary. The Greens have sued Edmund and Family Insurance seeking damages for the tort of conversion, alleging that Family Insurance should be held liable under the doctrine of *respondeat superior.* How should the court rule?

41.11 In each of the following cases, determine whether the employee suffered an accident or injury that should be compensated under workers' compensation.

(a) Osgood, an electrician, spent the morning installing wiring in a factory. The work included carrying and lifting fixtures weighing about 20 pounds. In the early afternoon while Osgood was taking a coffee break in the cafeteria, he suddenly slumped over and fell from his chair. A doctor found that Osgood suffered a heart attack.

(b) Would your answer in part (a) be different if the evidence showed that Osgood had suffered from heart disease for several years?

(c) Carlos worked as a bookbinder, a job that required him to lift paper bundles weighing 100 pounds each from the floor to his work bench. In January he began to experience back pain and by February 1, Carlos could no longer lift the bundles and entered a hospital for back surgery. Carlos could not remember a specific day or incident when his back pains had begun.

(d) Due to severe job stress, Deather suffered a mental breakdown and attempted to commit suicide. Deather later filed a claim for workers' compensation for the mental breakdown.

CHAPTER 42

INTRODUCTION TO PARTNERSHIP

- **an overview of the principal forms of business organization**
- **an introduction to partnership, including the sources of partnership law**
- **a discussion of the legal criteria used to determine the existence of a partnership and the legal characteristics of a partnership**
- **coverage of the legal relationship existing among partners**
- **a discussion of partnership property and partner's property rights**

This chapter begins the text's coverage of business organizations, the various forms in which capital, labor, and management are combined in an undertaking for profit. The principal forms of business organization used in the United States are the sole proprietorship, the general partnership, the limited partnership, the limited liability company, and the corporation. The following material provides a brief overview of the major characteristics of these organizational forms.

Forms of Business Organizations

Sole Proprietorship

The simplest and most common form of business organization, in absolute numbers, is the sole proprietorship, a business owned and controlled exclusively by one person.

The proprietor reaps all profits, bears all losses, and exercises sole management responsibility. He or she has unlimited personal liability for all obligations incurred in operating the business, whether created by tort or contract. The proprietorship's profits and losses are reported on the proprietor's individual federal income tax return. Although commanding a substantial edge in absolute numbers, the sole proprietorship accounts for a relatively small percentage of total business receipts in the United States.

General Partnership

A general partnership is the simplest form of business organization involving two or more owners. It is a common and useful form for small business of almost any type and often is used to combine services of some partners with property or money of others. A partnership is like a proprietorship except that there are two or more owners who generally have equal right to participate in management and deal with third parties, and who have unlimited personal liability for all debts incurred by the business. Profits and losses of the firm are shared according to the agreement of the partners. Like a proprietorship, a partnership is not a taxable entity. Rather, each partner reports his proportionate share of the firm's profit or loss on his individual income tax return. The business may be altered or even destroyed by the death or withdrawal of a partner, or the transfer of a partner's interest. Most partnerships are created without formality, and are often as simple as an oral understanding to pool assets and talents and split the profits. A general partnership might therefore be viewed as a residual organizational form, used when two or more people combine in a business venture, but fail to adopt one of the more formal structures discussed below. The law governing general partnership is discussed in this and the following chapter.

Corporation

The corporation is the most sophisticated and formalized type of business organization, and may be created only by complying with state statutes allowing the corporate form. The corporation becomes a separate legal entity apart from its owners, who transfer assets to it in exchange for evidence of ownership, shares of stock. The owners, the shareholders, do not manage the business directly, but instead periodically elect directors who are required by statute to manage the enterprise. The directors, in turn, select officers to manage the daily operation of the firm.

Because the corporation is a separate legal entity, shareholders, directors, and officers generally have no personal liability for corporate obligations, and the corporation is unaffected by death or withdrawal of its shareholders, directors, or officers, or by transfer of its shares. Losses are borne by the corporation to the extent of its assets. Profits are either distributed to the shareholders as dividends or are retained in the business at the directors' discretion.

A corporation is an entity for federal tax purposes, meaning that the income of most corporations (so-called C corporations) is subjected to "double taxation," first to the corporation on its tax return, and then to the shareholders on their individual returns when the income is distributed as dividends. If certain requirements are met, however, the corporation may elect to be taxed under Subchapter S of the Internal Revenue Code. The income of such an "S corporation" is not subject to tax at the corporate level. Rather, the income is passed through the corporation and taxed on the shareholders' individual returns in a manner somewhat similar to a partnership. The law of corporations is covered in Chapters 45 through 48.

Limited Partnership and Limited Liability Companies

The limited partnership and limited liability company are organizational forms that combine the characteristics of a corporation and a general partnership. For example, like a corporation, these organizations are created only by complying with formalities dictated by state enabling statutes and provide limited liability for firm debts for some or all owners. In contrast, these organizations are generally taxed, managed, transferred, and terminated much like general partnerships. The purpose of these forms, discussed in detail in Chapter 44, is to combine the limited liability of a corporation with the income tax advantages of a general partnership.

Appendix C, appearing at the end of the text, provides a brief comparison of the forms of business organization listed above.

Introduction to Partnership Law

General and Limited Partners

Partners are characterized as general or limited. A **general partner** is one who is personally liable to partnership creditors for the full amount of all debts and obligations incurred by the partnership. Most partnerships are composed wholly of general partners, and are, as noted above, known as "general partnerships." A **limited partner,** on the other hand, is a person whose liability to creditors of the partnership is limited to the amount of capital he or she has contributed to the partnership. A partnership composed of one or more general partners and one or more limited partners is known as a "limited partnership."

Sources of Partnership Law

In early English law, legal disputes among merchants were resolved primarily by distinct and varied mercantile courts, which existed apart from the English common law courts. These courts recognized two forms of partnership already used in continental Europe, the *societas* (the general partnership) and the *commendam* or *société en commandité* (the limited partnership). In the eighteenth century, merchants' cases, including partnership cases, began to appear more frequently in the regular English courts as the common law developed its principles of commercial law. The nineteenth century saw the rise of the partnership as a popular organizational form and the development of the common law of partnership. The law generated so much confusion and uncertainty, however, that statutory relief became necessary, resulting in the enactment of the Partnership Act of 1890[1] in England.

---

[1]53–54 Vict., ch. 39 (1890).

During the late nineteenth century, the United States was experiencing similar difficulties with its common law of partnership, which lacked uniformity among the states, lacked a consistent legal theory, and failed to address many recurring problems. To resolve this situation, in 1902 the National Conference of Commissioners on Uniform State Laws[2] commissioned the drafting of a uniform law on partnership. The result, completed in 1914, was the **Uniform Partnership Act (UPA),** which was enacted in 49 states and the District of Columbia.[3] The UPA was revised in 1994 in the **Revised Uniform Partnership Act (RUPA),** which is the basis of the following general partnership discussion.

To govern limited partnership, the National Conference drafted the Uniform Limited Partnership Act (ULPA), completed in 1916, revised in 1976 and 1985, and redrafted in 2001. The 2001 ULPA forms the basis of the limited partnership discussion in Chapter 44.

The RUPA and ULPA are not the sole sources of law governing partnership. They are supplemented by basic principles of law and equity,[4] including, most importantly, the law of contracts, estoppel, property and agency. Indeed, a partnership is often described as a mutual agency relation, with each partner acting as both principal and agent. In addition to common law doctrines, state and federal statutes supplement partnership law. Examples include the Statute of Frauds, statutes relating to capacity of persons to become partners, and, most importantly, federal bankruptcy law.

This chapter discusses the legal principles governing the creation of a general partnership and the relation of partners among themselves.

Nature and Formation of Partnership

Partnership Defined

A substantial portion of partnership case law concerns whether two or more persons are, in fact, partners. In these cases, courts usually must determine whether the disadvantages of partnership status (usually personal liability for a partnership debt) should be imposed upon a person who denies he is a partner. In most disputes, a creditor who has loaned money or sold goods or services on credit to one person (who is now insolvent or otherwise unwill-

ing or unable to pay) seeks to hold another liable for payment, asserting that the two are partners. If the creditor succeeds in proving that the parties are partners, the creditor can collect from either. If the parties are not partners but are, for example, buyer and seller, landlord and tenant, lender and borrower, employer and employee, or co-tenants, one party cannot be held vicariously responsible for the other's obligations. The law must therefore distinguish those joint business arrangements that are partnerships from those that are not.

To make this distinction, the RUPA defines a **partnership** as "an association of two or more persons to carry on as co-owners a business for profit."[5]

"An Association." A partnership requires an association, a voluntary collection, uniting, or a coming together of two or more persons for a certain purpose. The term connotes both voluntariness and intent to be a member of the association. Thus, a person cannot become a partner without his or her consent and "a person may become a partner only with the consent of all of the partners."[6] A partner's right to exercise choice and preference regarding admission of new members to the firm is known as *delectus personae* (Latin: "choice of the person"). Consent to become a partner is ordinarily expressed in a formal or informal agreement or contract between the parties, the partnership agreement. The partnership agreement is discussed in more detail later in this chapter.

Although a partnership is a voluntary, intentional relationship, the parties need not intend to create a partnership or call themselves "partners." They must simply intend to create a relationship that includes the essential elements of a partnership outlined below. Indeed, the issue in many partnership disputes is whether partnership status should be imposed upon a person who denies she intended to be a partner.

"Of Two or More Persons." A partnership requires an association of two or more "persons." The RUPA defines persons to include individuals, partnerships, corporations, and other associations.[7] Most partners are natural persons. Any natural person with general contractual capacity has capacity to become a partner. A minor may also become a partner. Because a minor's contracts are voidable, however, he or she may disaffirm both the partnership agreement and personal liability to creditors

---

[2]See discussion of the National Conference in Chapter 1.
[3]All states except Louisiana enacted the UPA.
[4]RUPA §104(a).

[5]RUPA §§101(6), 202(a).
[6]RUPA §401(i).
[7]RUPA §101(10).

on partnership debts. Nevertheless, the minor's capital contribution is subject to the claims of firm creditors.

Under the RUPA definition, a corporation may become a partner. A corporation's capacity to become a partner, however, has generally been governed by state corporation law and the articles of incorporation, rather than partnership law. Early cases held that becoming a member of a partnership was beyond the scope of corporate power because membership required an excessive delegation of management power by the board of directors. Modern corporation statutes, however, reject this view and permit a corporation to become a partner. For example, the Revised Model Business Corporation Act provides that each corporation has the power "to be a promoter, partner, member, associate, or manager of any partnership, joint venture, trust, or other entity."[8]

"To Carry on . . . a Business." To be a partnership, the association of two or more persons must be formed "to carry on . . . a business." The RUPA defines a business to include "every trade, occupation, and profession."[9] The term "business" implies continuity, a series of acts directed toward a profit-making end rather than a single or isolated undertaking. An association of two or more persons to carry out a single enterprise, specific transaction, or single series of transactions for profit is known as a **joint venture.** Generally, the same legal principles govern both partnerships and joint ventures.[10]

Even though a partnership is formed to carry on a business, partnership status does not require that any business actually be transacted. For example, assume Art and Bob agree to pool their resources to buy souvenirs to sell at football games. After each has contributed money to a common fund, Art refuses to carry on the business as agreed. A partnership has nevertheless been created.

"As Co-owners." Co-ownership of the business is a hallmark of partnership. Nevertheless, the RUPA makes it clear that mere co-ownership of income-producing property, such as in joint tenancy or tenancy in common, does not of itself establish a partnership, whether or not the co-owners share profits made by the use of the property.[11] These co-ownership arrangements often are not commercial in nature and may not even involve a voluntary association. For example, two sisters, Pam and Sally, may inherit income-producing farmland as joint tenants from their deceased grandmother. Pam and Sally are not partners. In addition, the concept of "business" generally contemplates more than mere passive co-ownership or investment. The greater the degree of activity, the more likely a business, and therefore a partnership, exists. Thus, if Pam and Sally in the preceding example agree to subdivide the property inherited into lots, build homes, and split the profits, they are partners. Two major components characterize co-ownership arrangements recognized as partnerships: profit sharing and control sharing.

Profit Sharing. Profit (and loss) sharing is the most critical attribute of partnership. Indeed, except for the specific situations outlined below, the RUPA provides that "a person who receives a share of the profits of a business is presumed to be a partner in the business."[12] Note that partners share profits (receipts minus expenses); sharing gross receipts, a much more limited participation in a business, does not of itself establish a partnership.[13] For example, an author receiving royalties is not thereby a partner with her publisher. An insurance company charging a premium based upon the insured's gross receipts is not thereby a partner of the insured.

Although sharing profits is usually evidence of partnership, §202(c)(3) of the RUPA provides that profit sharing *alone* is insufficient to establish partnership status if the profits were received in payment:

1. Of a debt by installments or otherwise, or as interest on a loan, even if the amount of payment varies with the profits of the business. For example, assume Carl loans Diane $10,000 for use in Diane's clothing store and Diane agrees to make monthly payments to Carl equal to one-half of Diane's montly profits. Sharing profits in this manner, alone, does not make Carl a partner in Diane's business.

2. As wages of an employee. For example, assume Ed, a manager of Joe's store, is paid a fixed salary plus a percentage of monthly profits. Ed, because of this fact alone, does not become a partner.

3. As rent to a landlord. For example, assume Laura leases her commercial building for five years to Tim, who intends to open a restaurant on the premises. Rent is computed as a percentage of Tim's net profits from the restaurant. Laura, by this fact alone, does not become a partner in Tim's restaurant.

---

[8]RMBCA §3.02(9).
[9]RUPA §101(1).
[10]One difference that has been noted between a joint venture and a partnership is that each partner is a general agent of the partnership, but each joint venturer is not an agent for other joint venturers.
[11]RUPA §202(c)(1).

[12]RUPA §202(c)(3).
[13]RUPA §202(c)(2).

4.   As an annuity to a widow, widower, or other representative of a deceased partner. When a partner dies, the partner's widow or widower or estate often desires to keep the business going and participate in the profits of the business, rather than accept a lump sum settlement for the deceased partner's interest. Sharing profits in this manner, alone, does not make the widow or widower or other representative a partner.

5.   As consideration for the sale of business goodwill or other property. When a business or other income-producing property is sold, the purchase price may be computed as a percentage of income generated by the asset after sale. For example, Sam may sell his business to Beth in exchange for Beth's promise to pay Sam 25 percent of the profits derived by Beth from the business. This fact alone does not make Sam a partner in Beth's business.

Note that the situations described above, standing alone, do not create partnerships. Additional facts, such as participation in management and control of the business, may make the creditor, employee, landlord, widow, or seller a partner.

Control Sharing.   A common interest in management and control of the business is also essential to partnership. That is, "to state that partners are co-owners of a business is to state that they each have the power of ultimate control."[14] Control sharing is what distinguishes a partnership from an agency relation. An agent, unlike a partner, is not a co-principal with equal right to participate in management and control of the business.

The power of control is affirmative, involving, for example, the power to set prices, control costs, hire and fire employees, and make other business decisions. Negative control, such as veto power over a certain transaction or prior consulation rights, is often used by lenders to protect their investment. This indirect or incidental control generally indicates a debtor-creditor, not a partnership relation.

"For Profit."   A partnership is a business association organized "for profit." Accordingly, noncommercial, nonprofit associations, organized, for example, for civic, religious, fraternal, or charitable purposes, are not partnerships. In addition, labor unions and trade associations are not partnerships. To be a partnership, an association need only be organized with the *expectation* of profit. Failure to make a profit does not defeat partnership status.

In the following case, decided under the UPA, the court was required to determine whether partnership

---

[14]UPA §6, Official Comment.

liability should be imposed upon a person insisting that he was merely a co-owner of property, not a partner.

Allied Steel Corporation v. Cooper
607 So.2d 113 (Miss. 1992)

Defendant Carl Cooper, a real estate developer and contractor, and defendant Bernard Heaps, the owner of an interior construction company known as House of Interiors, purchased a commercial building intending to resell it. Their sales efforts were unsuccessful, however, so Cooper and Heaps decided to renovate the building for use as a retail mall named Chimney Square and they obtained a bank loan to finance the project. Cooper and his crew performed exterior construction while Heaps and his employees refurbished the interior. Materials were purchased from several companies, including plaintiff Allied Steel Corporation, and billed to House of Interiors. After Cooper and Heaps failed to pay these bills, the suppliers brought suit seeking to foreclose on liens they held on the building, and to hold Cooper and Heaps liable as partners for any deficiency. The trial court found that no partnership existed and ruled that only Heaps, as owner of House of Interiors, was personally liable for the debts. The suppliers appealed.

McRae, Justice

. . . In 1976, this state adopted the "Mississippi Uniform Partnership Law". . . . These provisions, a codification of the common law, define and govern the operation of businesses explicitly and implicitly run as partnerships. Pursuant to §79–12–29, all partners are jointly and severally liable for all debts and obligations of the partnership. Thus, our finding that Cooper and Heaps developed Chimney Square as a partnership renders them both personally liable for the debts owed to the [plaintiffs] for payment of materials they supplied for the project.

The statutory provisions of the Uniform Partnership Law are also applicable to joint ventures. . . . [A joint venture] is a business relationship used for a specific undertaking for profit as opposed to a general, ongoing business. . . . Thus, whether the development of a single project such as the Chimney Square Mall is characterized as a partnership or a joint venture is immaterial; the same principles are used to determine the existence of each relationship and Uniform Partnership Law applies if either is found.

Miss. Code Ann. §79–12–11 defines a partnership as "an association of two (2) or more persons to carry on as co-owners a business for profit." . . . Miss. Code Ann. §79–12–13(4) provides that "the receipt by a person of a share of the profits of a business is prima facie evidence that he is a partner in the business," unless those profits were received as payment for a debt, wages, interest on a loan or consideration for the sale of the goodwill on a business. Cooper's argument that his business relationship with Heaps falls outside the statutory definition because there was no profit is not persuasive. Further, we find no meaningful distinction between the concept of "profit" and the "decent financial return" Cooper sought to achieve.

A small but thorough body of case law serves to articulate further the factors determinative of a partnership, supplementing the parameters set forth in The Uniform Partnership Act. That Cooper and Heaps each [owned] an undivided one-half interest in the Chimney Square property does not, in and of itself, make them partners. . . . For their relationship to be more than a mere co-tenancy, there must be an intent to form a partnership or joint venture. . . . "What is essential to any intent to form a joint venture is the idea that the parties are engaging in the undertaking with both parties owning the venture, with a right of mutual control, and joint obligations and liabilities." [*Hults v. Tillman,* 480 So.2d 1134, 1146 (Miss. 1988).]

Although Heaps testified that the two were partners in the Chimney Square venture, Cooper vehemently denied the existence of a partnership relationship. The record before us indicates that Cooper and Heaps entered into no express agreement defining their business relationship. However, absent an express agreement defining the nature of an association, the intent of the parties may be inferred from their actions or conduct. . . . The record clearly indicates that both Cooper and Heaps conducted themselves [as partners]. . . . Although the existence of the co-tenancy is not in and of itself, indicative of the intent to form a partnership or joint venture, once the decision was made to develop the property as a shopping mall rather than to just resell it without improvements, Cooper and Heaps, in turn, acted to assume joint obligations and liabilities. Despite the fact that Heaps provided most of the initial capital for the purchase of the building, ownership of the property was recorded in both men's names, with each possessing an undivided one-half interest. To finance the rehabilitation of the building, they signed as co-obligors a note for $410,000 with the First National Bank of St. Tammany Parish. The proceeds of the loan were deposited in a joint checking account. Checks from this account, bearing both men's names and requiring the signatures of both, were used to pay construction workers as well as materialmen. Indicative of his recognition of the potential liability, Cooper acquired on their behalf both a builder's risk insurance policy as well as a loss of earnings policy from Thigpen Insurance Agency.

The record further contains substantial evidence of mutual control over the Chimney Square development by the manner in which Cooper and Heaps carried out the project. . . . [T]he record indicates that Cooper was deeply involved in the project on a daily basis. Heaps testified that the project was not developed according to an overall plan; rather, he and Cooper met on an almost daily basis to make decisions about design and construction details. Cooper, by his own admission, spent a considerable amount of time actually at the Chimney Square site. Further, the site foreman purchased materials for the project under Cooper's authority and received paychecks signed by both Cooper and Heaps. . . .

From the testimony given by William Bligh, president of Allied Steel and David Travis, vice-president of Quick & Grice, it is apparent that when supplying materials for Chimney Square, they believed that they were dealing with both Heaps and Cooper, acting as partners. Likewise, Glenda Wilson, credit and office manager for Park Supply Company testified that she only spoke with Cooper after the accounts for materials delivered to Chimney Square became past due. She stated, as did the others, that the accounts were billed under the name "House of Interiors."

Finding that the evidence in the record does not support the lower court's decision and that there is substantial evidence showing that Cooper and Heaps acted as partners or joint venturers in the development of Chimney Square Mall, . . . we reverse the decision of the Pearl River County Circuit Court. . . .

[Judgment reversed and remanded.]

Partnership Name and Registration Requirements

Although not required, most partnerships use a firm name. The partnership may do business in the name of one or more partners—for example, Joe Doaks and Millie Hobbs may transact business under the name

"Doaks and Hobbs"—or may use a fictitious, assumed, or trade name, such as "Star Bar & Grill," or "The Record Service," or "A-1 Tire & Battery," or "ABC Home Remodelers." The firm name of a successful business often acquires substantial value.

Most states have fictitious or **assumed business name statutes** requiring that a certificate listing the names and addresses of persons conducting business under an assumed or trade name be filed in the public records (for example, the country clerk's office). Some states also require that a notice of the filing be published in a newspaper of general circulation for a stated period (for example, once a week for three consecutive weeks). These statutes provide public information of business ownership to interested persons such as creditors. In some states, no filing is required if the partnership name consists solely of the owners' surnames.

Sanctions for noncompliance vary among the states, and range from a fine to, occasionally, imprisonment. Early statutes rendered the noncomplying firm's contracts unenforceable. Many modern statutes, however, simply deny the firm access to the state court system to sue on its contracts or other transactions until it complies.

Note that assumed business name statutes apply primarily to partnerships and sole proprietorships. The more formal organizational forms, the limited partnership, limited liability company, and corporation, often operate in the name stated in the formal documents filed for public record when the entity is created. This name generally must include words or abbreviations indicating the status of the entity.

Entity and Aggregate Characteristics of Partnership

An issue that has long troubled partnership law is whether a partnership is merely an aggregate of the individual partners, or is a legal entity or legal person, like a corporation, existing apart from its owners. Many legal issues are resolved differently, depending upon the theory chosen. Under an aggregate theory, for example, a partnership cannot be sued in the firm name; rather, each individual partner must be named as a defendant in the lawsuit. An entity approach, in contrast, would permit suits in the firm name.

Under the traditional aggregate, or common law, theory, the rights and obligations created by partnership activities are those of the partners; the partnership is not recognized as a legal person. Section 201 of the RUPA

rejects this approach, providing simply that "a partnership is an entity distinct from its partners." Thus, although the partners are personally liable for firm debts, the partnership is an entity for purposes of acquiring, holding, and transferring property, and each partner is considered an agent of the partnership. Further, partnership assets, liabilities, and transactions are separate and distinct from those of the partners.

Like the RUPA, other modern statutes often treat a partnership as an entity. For example, both federal bankruptcy law and the Uniform Commercial Code define "person" to include a partnership.[15] Modern procedural statutes generally permit a partnership to sue and be sued in the firm name. On the other hand, as previously noted, federal tax law treats the partnership as an aggregate, attributing income or losses incurred by the partnership to the individual partners. The partnership is not viewed as a taxpaying entity.

Relationship Among Partners

Assuming a partnership exists, a number of important legal issues arise during the course of carrying on the partnership business. The law must initially determine the nature of the partners' interest in the partnership and partnership property, and the legal relationship among partners. These issues are discussed below.

The Partnership Agreement

Existence and Formality. The primary and most important source of "law" governing the legal relationship among partners is a private contract, known as the **partnership agreement** (or sometimes **articles of partnership**). This contract governs the rights and obligations of the various partners and the internal structure of the partnership. As one court long ago noted, the agreement is "the law of [the] partnership, made by the parties, . . . which a court of equity ought to regard as the rule in all questions arising between them."[16] This principle is carefully followed by the RUPA, which precisely regulates the rights of partners as against *third parties* but allows the partners great flexibility to govern relations among themselves by contract. The RUPA does, however, include a number of provisions governing the relation of partners to one another which apply in the absence of agreement among them.

---

[15]11 U.S.C. §101; UCC §§1–201(25),(27).
[16]Jacob C. Slemmer's Appeal, 58 Pa. 168, 176 (1868); RUPA §103(a).

Although governed essentially by contract, the law usually does not require a written agreement to create or maintain a partnership. The common law Statute of Frauds, however, does require a writing if the partnership is, by terms of the agreement, to continue for more than one year.[17] Nevertheless, unwritten partnership agreements without fixed terms generally are deemed to continue "at will" and are terminated upon death or at the will of any partner. Accordingly, such oral agreements are capable of performance within one year and are enforceable without a writing.

Even though a formal written contract is not generally required, a comprehensive, attorney drafted, carefully negotiated, written partnership agreement is always advisable. Casually created business relations, including partnerships, are a fruitful source of litigation. A comprehensive written contract prevents many disputes, because potential problems are anticipated and ambiguities resolved while reducing the agreement to writing. Additionally, the writing can be used by the court to resolve any later dispute between the parties, eliminating the need to prove the existence and terms of a disputed oral contract.

Terms of the Agreement. The partnership agreement should include all terms necessary to the orderly operation and liquidation of the partnership. Although specific provisions vary based upon such factors as the type of business and number of partners, the following issues should be addressed explicitly in the agreement. The operation of many of these terms is covered in more detail throughout the partnership material.

General Provisions. Included in this category, for example, are terms stating the names of the partners, and the name, purpose, term, and place of business of the partnership.

Capitalization. The agreement should contain provisions indicating the initial and subsequent capital contributions of each partner, whether separate capital, income, and drawing accounts are to be maintained, and limitations or restrictions on withdrawals.

Other Financial and Accounting Matters. The agreement should include provisions determining the accounting method, fiscal year, profit-and-loss-sharing ratio, com-

pensation of partners, and the right of partners to be reimbursed for business expenses. Provision for firm bank accounts and maintenance and inspection of partnership books should also be made.

Property. The agreement should clearly state what property is partnership property, what property, if any, belonging to individual partners is to be made available for partnership use, and how title to partnership property is to be held.

Management. The agreement should outline the rights of each partner in the management of the business, the voting requirements for taking partnership action, the powers, limitations, and authority of each partner, and the amount of time each partner is expected to spend on firm business.

Dissolution. The agreement should state which events dissolve the partnership, whether the business is to be continued after dissolution, how the value of a withdrawing or deceased partner's interest is computed, and the procedure for liquidating and distributing partnership assets.

Partners' Compensation

Profit sharing, the hallmark of partnership, is the primary method of compensating partners. The partnership agreement often provides for unequal shares among the partners (for example, A, B, and C may agree to share profit 50, 30, and 20 percent, respectively) and may provide loss-sharing ratios that differ from those governing profit sharing. Unless otherwise agreed, however, the RUPA provides that profits and losses are shared equally, even if the partners have unequal capital contributions. If a profit-sharing ratio is agreed upon (for example, 5:3:2) but nothing is provided regarding losses, losses are shared in the same percentage as profits.[18]

Each partner is generally required to render services to the partnership in the conduct of its business. Absent contrary agreement, however, a partner is not entitled to compensation for services rendered to the firm, to rent upon property she permits the partnership to use, or to interest on her capital contribution.[19] Partners are compensated by a share of profits; other forms of compensation, such as

---

[17]The common law Statute of Frauds and the "one year" provision are discussed in detail in Chapter 12.

[18]RUPA §401(b).
[19]RUPA §401(h).

salaries, rents, and interest, must be explicitly agreed upon. In many partnerships one or more partners manage the day-to-day affairs of the partnership and receive salaries, while others are inactive. The rule denying compensation in addition to profits is subject to one notable exception. Upon dissolution of a partnership, a partner is entitled to reasonable compensation for her services in winding up the partnership affairs.[20] In addition to any basic compensation, the partnership is required to reimburse a partner who makes payments from her own funds or reasonably incurs personal liabilities in the ordinary and proper conduct of the firm's business or for the preservation of its business or property.[21]

Participation in Management

Unless otherwise agreed, all partners have equal rights in the management and control of the partnership business.[22] In many partnerships, however, the partnership agreement vests management authority in a small group of partners or, in some cases, one partner. Among partners entitled to vote, any disagreement arising out of ordinary partnership affairs may be decided by a majority vote of the partners.[23] For example, a majority vote could authorize ordinary business transactions such as borrowing money, approving accounts, and hiring and firing employees. In many cases, a partner's authority to act for the partnership is explicitly stated in the partnership agreement. For example, the agreement may give one partner exclusive authority to buy raw materials for use in the business. No further vote of the partners is required to authorize that partner to purchase raw materials.

Certain extraordinary business matters require a unanimous vote of the partners. For example, a unanimous vote is required

1. to admit a new partner[24];
2. to change or do any act that violates the partnership agreement[25];
3. to change the capital of the firm;
4. to change the scope of the partnership business; or
5. to change the place of the firm business.

The voting requirements outlined above often are changed by agreement of the partners. For example, less than or greater than a majority of votes may be required for certain actions. Some partners may receive more than one vote based upon capital contribution, profit-and-loss-sharing ratio, or seniority.

Whatever voting requirements a partnership adopts determines a partner's actual authority to deal with third parties on behalf of the firm. Accordingly, the preceding discussion is an important prerequisite to understanding the relationship between partners and third parties discussed in Chapter 43.

Duty to Furnish Information

Adequate accounting records are particularly important in a partnership, which requires accurate computation of the ever-changing interests of multiple owners. Thus, although the RUPA imposes no liability upon partners for failure to keep partnership books, prudent business practice dictates that books should be kept. At a minimum the books should permit computation of each partner's share of profits and losses, and rights upon withdrawal. Unless otherwise agreed, the books, if any, are to be maintained at the partnership's chief executive office.[26] Wherever the books are kept, each partner shall have access to and may inspect and copy them during ordinary business hours.[27]

The partnership books provide important information to each partner concerning partnership affairs. To supplement this information, the RUPA also requires each partner and the partnership to furnish to a partner (1) "without demand, any information concerning the partnership's business and affairs reasonably required for the proper exercise of the partner's rights and duties" under either the RUPA or the partnership agreement, and (2) "on demand, any other information concerning the partnership's business and affairs" unless the demand is unreasonable or improper under the circumstances.[28] The same information must be provided to the legal representative of any partner who is deceased or under a legal disability.

Collectively, the firm's books and each partner's duty to furnish information provide each partner with the tools to discover and investigate breaches of perhaps the most important duty existing among partners—the fiduciary duty of loyalty.

---

[20]*Id.*
[21]RUPA §401(c).
[22]RUPA §401(f).
[23]RUPA §401(j).
[24]RUPA §401(i).
[25]RUPA §401(j).

[26]RUPA §403(a).
[27]RUPA §403(b).
[28]RUPA §403(c).

The Partner as Fiduciary

A partnership is a fiduciary relationship similar to that existing between trustee and beneficiary, principal and agent, and director and corporation. The fiduciary duty of loyalty imposes an obligation upon each partner to act solely for the benefit of the other partners or the partnership in matters within the scope of the partner-ship relation. The relationship is one of strict trust and confidence, requiring the partner generally to subordinate personal interests to those of fellow partners. The RUPA holds a partner liable as a fiduciary by requiring every partner

1. to account to the partnership and hold as trustee for it any property, profit, or benefit derived by the partner in the conduct and winding up of the partnership business or derived from a use by the partner of partnership property, including the appropriation of a partnership opportunity;
2. to refrain from dealing with the partnership in the conduct or winding up of the partnership business as or on behalf of a party having an interest adverse to the partnership; and
3. to refrain from competing with the partnership in the conduct of the partnership business before the dissolution of the partnership.[29]

Many litigated cases involve breach of a partner's fiduciary duties. Prohibited conduct includes, for example:

1. A partner may not divert a partnership opportunity for personal benefit. A partnership opportunity includes any business transaction (1) necessary or related to partnership business, (2) offered to or learned about through the partnership, and (3) developed with partnership funds or facilities.

2. A partner may not secretly use or deal in the partnership assets for personal benefit, personally acquire a partnership asset, or otherwise use the partnership or its property in ways not contemplated by the partnership agreement.

3. A partner may not compete with the partnership in transactions within the scope of partnership business, and must account to co-partners for all "secret" profits realized in transactions injurious to partnership interests.

4. "A partner may lend money to and transact other business with the partnership."[30] In so doing, however,

the partner must disclose all material facts to co-partners concerning his ownership of property, business dealings, future plans, potential conflicts of interest, and any other matter indicating an actual or potential interest adverse to the partnership. Disclosure is required under these circumstances, whether or not information is specifically requested by other partners. A partner who is purchasing another partner's interest in the firm owes a similar duty of full and honest disclosure.

The following classic case explains the nature of the fiduciary relationship among partners.

Clement v. Clement
260 A.2d 728 (Pa. 1970)

In 1923, L. W. Clement and his brother Charles formed a partnership engaged in the plumbing business and operated under the name "Clement Brothers." L. W. assumed complete control over the business finances for over 40 years. In 1964, the two partners entered into negotiations for L. W. to purchase Charles's interest in the partnership.

Charles filed a suit in equity requesting dissolution of the partnership and an accounting. The chancellor found that L. W. had diverted partnership funds to purchase real estate and insurance policies. The chancellor awarded Charles a one-half interest in the real estate and insurance. L. W. appealed and the appellate court en banc reversed, holding that Charles had failed to prove that L. W. had committed fraud and that under the doctrine of laches Charles's delay in bringing suit precluded his recovery. Charles Clement appealed to the Supreme Court of Pennsylvania.

Roberts, Justice

. . . [P]artners owe a fiduciary duty one to another. . . . One should not have to deal with his partner as though he were the opposite party in an arm's length transaction. One should be allowed to trust his partner, to expect that he is pursuing a common goal and not working at cross-purposes. This concept of the partnership entity was expressed most ably by Mr. Justice, then Judge, Cardozo in *Meinhard v. Salmon,* [164 N.E. 545, 546 (N.Y. 1928)]:

Joint adventurers, like co-partners, owe to one another, while the enterprise continues, the duty of the finest loyalty. Many forms of conduct permissible in a workaday world for those acting at arm's length, are forbidden to those bound by fiduciary ties. A trustee is held to something stricter than the morals of the marketplace. Not honesty

---

[29]RUPA §404(b).
[30]RUPA §404(f).

alone, but the punctilio of an honor the most sensitive, is then the standard of behavior. As to this there has developed a tradition that is unbending and inveterate. Uncompromising rigidity has been the attitude of courts of equity when petitioned to undermine the rule of undivided loyalty by the "disintegrating erosion" of particular exceptions. . . . Only thus has the level of conduct for fiduciaries been kept at a level higher than that trodden by the crowd. It will not consciously be lowered by any judgment of this court. . . .

It would be unduly harsh to require that one must prove actual fraud before he can recover for a partner's derelictions. Where one partner has so dealt with the partnership as to raise the probability of wrongdoing it ought to be his responsibility to negate that inference. It has been held that "where a partner fails to keep a record of partnership transactions, and is unable to account for them, every presumption will be made against him." *Bracht v. Connell,* [170 A. 297, 301 (Pa. 1933)]. Likewise, where a partner commingles partnership funds with his own and generally deals loosely with partnership assets he ought to have to shoulder the task of demonstrating the probity of his conduct.

In the instant case L. W. dealt loosely with partnership funds. At various times he made substantial investments in his own name. He was totally unable to explain where he got the funds to make these investments. The court en banc held that Charles had no claim on the fruits of these investments because he could not trace the money that was invested therein dollar for dollar from the partnership. Charles should not have had this burden. He did show that his brother diverted substantial sums from the partnership funds under his control. The inference that these funds provided L. W. with the wherewithall to make his investments was a perfectly reasonable one for the chancellor to make and his decision should have been allowed to stand.

The doctrine of laches has no role to play in the decision of this case. It is true that the transactions complained of cover a period of many years. However, we do not think that it can be said that Charles negligently slept on his rights to the detriment of his brother. L. W. actively concealed much of his wrongdoing. He cannot now rely upon the doctrine of laches — that defense was not intended to reward the successful wrongdoer. . . .

[Judgment vacated and remanded.]

In addition to the duty of loyalty, the RUPA also imposes the duties of care and good faith upon partners. Under the duty of care, a partner may be held liable to co-partners for injuries caused by "grossly negligent or reckless conduct, intentional misconduct, or a knowing violation of law."[31] The duty of good faith and fair dealing, drawn from the law of contracts, is discussed in Chapter 7.[32]

Actions by Partnership and Partners

As an entity, the partnership may sue a partner for breach of the partnership agreement or for breach of a duty to the partnership imposed by law (for example, the duties of loyalty, care, and good faith discussed above).[33] Conversely, a partner may sue the partnership or another partner for legal or equitable relief to enforce rights granted by the partnership agreement and the RUPA, and rights arising independently of the partnership relation.[34]

Certainly the most valuable remedy in the partnership setting is an **accounting,** an equitable proceeding in which the court directs[35] a comprehensive investigation of the partners' and partnership transactions in order to adjudicate the rights of the various partners. The accounting determines, for example, the amount of cash or other assets invested by each partner, actual profit (or loss) from operations, the extent of partnership property, and ultimately the status of the various partners' capital accounts. Once it is completed, the court then renders a money judgment for or against each partner in the amounts determined by the accounting. Traditionally, an accounting was available only upon dissolution of the firm. The RUPA, as noted above, expands the availability of the remedy.

Partnership Property

Partnership business usually commences after the partners have made their capital contributions to the firm. The partners may contribute money, property, or services. Property contributed may be of any type, real or personal, tangible or intangible, and often includes

---

[31]RUPA §404(c).
[32]RUPA §404(d).
[33]RUPA §405(a).
[34]RUPA §405(b).
[35]Ordinarily, the accounting is conducted by an auditor, referee, or master, subject to court review.

money. This property is then used to generate or purchase other property in the course of the firm's business. Property transferred to or otherwise acquired by the partnership belongs to the partnership, not to the partners individually.[36] As a legal entity, the partnership may buy, sell, and hold title to property (real or personal, tangible or intangible) in the firm name.

Distinguishing Partnership from Individual Property. Distinguishing between partnership property and property that, though used in the business, belongs to an individual partner is important in resolving a number of legal issues. Examples include (1) how the property is disposed of upon the death of a partner or dissolution of the firm, (2) whether firm creditors have the right to reach the property, (3) whether income or loss from use or disposition of the property is to be shared by the partners, and (4) who is entitled to transfer the property.

In general, the partners' intention, as outlined in the partnership agreement, determines whether specific property belongs to an individual partner or the partnership. If the agreement fails to address the issue, the status of the property may be ambiguous, and ultimately lead to a dispute that the court must resolve by inferring the parties' intent from their conduct.

To resolve such disputes courts generally hold that property acquired with partnership funds is partnership property. Property with a record title, such as automobiles, real estate, or stock certificates, is presumed to be partnership property if title is held in the firm name. Firm ownership also is indicated if the partnership pays for taxes, repairs, and insurance on the property, or if the property is entered and carried on the partnership books. On the other hand, mere partnership use, possession, or occupancy of property owned by one or more partners raises no presumption of firm ownership.[37] Partners often mix personal and partnership affairs, especially in family partnerships.

Rights in Specific Partnership Property. Partnership property takes many forms including, for example, cash, equipment, inventory, accounts receivable, land, and buildings. Because the partnership owns the property, an individual partner may use or possess it only for partnership purposes.[38] Further, "a partner is not a co-owner of

partnership property and has no interest in partnership property which can be transferred, either voluntarily or involuntarily."[39]

To illustrate, assume A and B are partners in a printing shop, operating as Reliable Printing. Partnership property includes the building (contributed by A) in which the shop is located and various printing presses and other equipment (contributed by B). Reliable Printing, the partnership, owns the property, meaning that A and B may possess it for partnership purposes, but neither has the right to possess it for personal use without the consent of the other. Neither A nor B can independently sell or otherwise assign any interest in specific partnership property (for example, a printing press) to a third party. A and B acting together, however, could transfer title to specific property. Personal creditors of A or B may not, by judicial process, seize specific partnership property to satisfy an unpaid personal debt. Creditors of the partnership could, however, force a seizure and sale of the specific property to satisfy a partnership debt. On A's death, A's estate receives no interest in any specific partnership property.

Partner's Interest in the Partnership

Even though the partnership is the owner of the partnership property, the partners collectively own the partnership. An individual partner's ownership interest is embodied in his or her **partnership interest,** which is the partner's share of the profits and surplus of the business. That is, the partnership interest is essentially each partner's share of the difference between the firm's assets and liabilities. For example, if A and B are equal partners with equal capital contributions in a partnership with assets of $150,000 and liabilities of $100,000, each partner has a $25,000 interest in the firm. Like a share of corporate stock, a partnership interest is intangible personal property.

A partner, through the partnership interest, possesses most of the incidents of individual ownership not existing in specific partnership property. For example, a partner's interest may be individually transferred, personal creditors may reach it, and it may be transferred to the partner's estate on death.

Transfer of Partnership Interest. An individual partner may sell or otherwise transfer his interest in the partnership. The transfer does not extinguish the partnership

---

[36]RUPA §203.
[37]See generally RUPA §204.
[38]RUPA §401(g).

[39]RUPA §501.

and, unless otherwise agreed, the transferee is not entitled (1) to participate in the management or administration of the business, (2) to require any information or account of partnership transactions, or (3) to inspect partnership books. In short, the transferee does not become a partner—that requires unanimous consent of the other partners. Rather, the transferee is entitled to receive, according to his contract, the profits to which the transferring partner would otherwise be entitled. If the partnership is liquidated, the transferee also is entitled to any surplus—share of undistributed profits and return of capital contribution—to which the transfering partner would have been entitled.[40]

Creditors' Rights. Although a partner's personal creditors may not reach specific partnership property to satisfy their claims, they may reach the partner's interest in the partnership either voluntarily, through an assignment by the partner, or involuntarily through a **charging order**. To use this device, the creditor first reduces its claim against the debtor partner to judgment, and then petitions the court to "charge" that partner's partnership interest with payment of the unsatisfied debt. The court may then order that payments, including distributions of profits and withdrawals of capital, to which the partner becomes entitled are to be made to the creditor. A charging order is a judgment creditor's sole remedy to reach a debtor partner's interest in the partnership. The creditor, like the transferee, does not become a partner, has no right in specific partnership property, and has no right to participate in management. The debtor partner continues as a partner, except that distributions otherwise payable to the partner are paid to the creditor.

The charging order creates a lien on the partner's interest and continues until the judgment debt is repaid. The creditor's claim may, however, be so large that the partner's periodic income from the firm will not satisfy the debt within a reasonable time. In this case, the court may order "foreclosure"—a sale of the debtor's partnership interest, with the proceeds to be paid to the creditor. The purchaser at the foreclosure sale acquires the rights of a transferee, discussed above. At any time before foreclosure, the debtor-partner (or one or more of the other partners) may redeem the interest charged by paying the balance of the judgment debt. A redemption with partnership assets requires the consent of all nondebtor partners.[41]

Inheritability. Upon death of a partner, the partnership interest generally passes as personal property according to the terms of his or her will, or by intestate succession. The partner's devisee or heir (for example, a surviving spouse) is then paid for the value of the deceased partner's interest in the firm through, for example, an accounting action involving liquidation of the firm and distribution of the proceeds. Alternatively, the partnership agreement may provide for continuation of the firm after death of a partner by stating that a deceased partner's interest passes to the surviving partner or partners who are required to purchase it from the partner's estate. To prevent liquidation of the firm to pay for a deceased partner's interest, these buy-out arrangements often are funded by life insurance policies maintained on the life of each partner. The effect of death of a partner and the method of computing his interest should be clearly outlined in the partnership agreement.

Summary

1. The primary forms of business organization used in the United States are the sole proprietorship, the general partnership, the limited partnership, the limited liability company, and the corporation.

2. A general partnership is the simplest organizational form involving two or more owners. It consists entirely of general partners, who possess unlimited liability for firm debts. In contrast, a limited partnership is one composed of one or more general partners and one or more limited partners, who are liable only to the extent of their investment in the business.

3. Partnership law is based upon the Revised Uniform Partnership Act (RUPA) and the Revised Uniform Limited Partnership Act (RULPA), which are liberally supplemented by common law principles of contracts, estoppel, property, and agency.

---

[40]RUPA §503.

[41]RUPA §504.

4. A general partnership is defined in the RUPA as "an association of two or more persons to carry on as co-owners a business for profit." Although each element of the definition must be met, sharing profits and losses is the most important attribute of partnership. A partnership is a legal entity or legal person, like a corporation, existing apart from its owners. It therefore may own property and sue or be sued in the partnership name. For some purposes, however, such as taxation and legal liability, a partnership is merely an aggregate of the individual partners.

5. Rights and obligations of the partners and internal structure are generally determined by contract among them, the partnership agreement. This agreement commonly contains detailed provisions governing capitalization, other financial and accounting matters, partnership property, management, and dissolution. In the absence of contrary agreement, partners are compensated by a share of profits generated by the business, and each partner has an equal voice in the management and control of the business.

6. The RUPA requires that each partner furnish information to co-partners regarding partnership affairs. Each partner also owes a fiduciary duty of loyalty to the other partners and the partnership, which prevents a partner from diverting a partnership opportunity for personal benefit or from competing with the partnership. Partners also owe co-partners duties of care and good faith. Partnership disputes, including those involving breaches of duty, often are resolved in an equitable proceeding known as an accounting.

7. Partnership property includes all property originally contributed to the partnership and subsequently acquired by the partnership. Because the partnership is an entity, partnership property is owned by the partnership, not the partners. A partner's ownership of the partnership is embodied in his or her interest in the partnership—a share of the profits and surplus of the business. Unlike specific partnership property, a partnership interest may be transferred by an individual partner, reached by creditors of an individual partner, and transferred on death by a partner.

Key Terms

general partner	assumed business name
limited partner	statutes
Uniform Partnership Act (UPA)	partnership agreement (articles of partnership)
Revised Uniform Partnership Act (RUPA)	accounting
partnership	partnership interest
joint venture	charging order

Questions and Problems

42.1 After reading the text and cases regarding the definition of partnership, what steps would you take to avoid being treated as a partner

(a) of a debtor (if you are a creditor)?
(b) of a tenant (if you are a landlord)?
(c) of an employer (if you are an employee)?
(d) of a buyer of a business (if you are the seller)?

42.2 In each of the following questions, determine whether the parties are partners.

(a) In 2000, Dale entered into a long-term lease of a building. For three years, he subleased the building to a business that operated a bar on the premises. In 2003, the subtenant moved and Dale made an oral agreement with Frances for operation of the bar. Frances agreed to manage the bar by purchasing supplies, paying bills, keeping the records, and hiring and firing employees. Frances and Dale agreed that each would receive $200 per week plus one-half of the profits. Frances agreed to provide a monthly accounting to Dale. Dale claims that he owns the business and Frances is an employee. Frances believes she and Dale are partners. Are Frances and Dale partners? Explain.

(b) Elwood, a bachelor, inherited a farm from his father in 1980. Soon thereafter, he and his sister Nora moved into the farmhouse and began farming operations. Elwood raised the crops and livestock while Nora handled the cooking and housework and kept the books. A sign on the land read "The Elwood and Nora Farms." Elwood and Nora discussed all major purchases such as equipment and livestock. Nora wrote all checks but the checks were drawn on account solely in Elwood's name. All property was registered in Elwood's name. Elwood annually filed an individual tax return and Nora filed no tax returns. All profits were reinvested in the farming operation. On several occasions in discussion with friends, Elwood referred to Nora as his partner. Are Elwood and Nora partners? Explain.

42.3 Joe and Tony were partners who operated a grocery store for over 20 years. They both worked full time in the store until 2000 when they decided they could no longer work together because of irreconcilable differences. Joe advised Tony that he wanted to terminate the partnership and requested that Tony make available all of the accounting records. Although Tony had kept complete records during the term of the partnership, most of the records had been inadvert-ently destroyed when Tony's son had cleaned the basement of their house. After Joe's request to terminate the business, Tony changed the sign on the store to read "Tony's Supermarket" but continued to operate the store. Despite Joe's frequent requests for his assets in the business, Tony refused to pay any money to Joe. In 2004, Joe sued Tony requesting $750,000 as his half of the profits. Tony countersued claiming that he was entitled to wages for the three years he had solely operated the business. Tony also claimed that $750,000 was greater than half of the profit but could not provide a more accurate figure because of destruction of the records. How should the court rule? Explain.

42.4 In *Clement v. Clement,* one of the justices filed a dissent stating in part:

> In 1923, L. W. Clement and his younger brother, Charles, formed a partnership for the purpose of engaging in the plumbing business under the name of Clement Brothers. They agreed to share the profits of the business equally after payment of the debts. L. W. was the more alert and aggressive of the two. He attended special training schools to upgrade his plumbing skills, and became a master plumber. He alone conducted the business here involved, and had complete control of its finances. He frequently worked nights, Sundays and holidays. Charles, on the other hand, refused to be "bothered" with the administration of the business or its finances. He insisted also on limiting his work to a regular eight-hour shift and confining his contribution to the business to the performance of various plumbing jobs assigned to him.

(a) Should these facts affect the outcome of the case? Explain.

(b) The dissenting justice further stated:

> > Over the years, L. W. accumulated assets which eventually became quite valuable. For instance, in 1945 he purchased two lots of land for $5,500, and subsequently constructed a commercial building thereon. This construction was financed in most part by money secured through placing a mortgage on the property.

> Assume that the original $5,500 used to purchase the land had been diverted from the partnership. Do you think Charles was entitled to one-half of the value of the property? Explain.

(c) In explaining the importance of partners' fiduciary duties, one text states: "Without the protection of fiduciary duties, each [partner] is at the other's mercy." Crane & Bromberg, *Law of Partnership* 389 (1968). What does this statement mean?

(d) If you had been advising L. W. Clement, what suggestions would you have made to ensure that L. W.'s investments did not become partnership property?

42.5 Heloise applied to First State Bank for a personal loan of $10,000. When Bart, the lending officer, inquired about her assets, Heloise explained that she was the owner of Heloise's Antique Shop and provided an appraisal showing the value of the inventory to be $100,000. Bart verified that the inventory was not subject to a security interest. Bart then recommended to his supervisor that the bank grant the loan. The supervisor suggested that Bart check the county clerk's records where he discovered that Heloise's Antique Shop was operated as a partnership by Heloise and Abelard.

(a) Bart still recommended that the loan be granted explaining that one-half of the inventory would be valued at $50,000, more than enough to cover the value of the loan. Is Bart's explanation correct? Explain.

(b) What further information would you request prior to determining whether to grant the loan?

42.6 In many partnership agreements, the partners agree to purchase life insurance on the life of each partner naming the partnership (or the partners) as the beneficiaries. The face amount of each policy usually is an amount approximately equal to the value of the partner's interest in the partnership. Why would such a policy be advisable for the partnership and for the insured partner?

42.7 In 1990, David purchased a piece of real estate for $10,000 on which he constructed an automobile repair shop. In 1992, David and Jonathan formed a partnership to operate the repair shop. David contributed the land and shop and Jonathan contributed $15,000 in cash. In 2000, Jonathan died leaving his entire estate to his daughter, Esther. Later that year, David agreed to sell the land and repair shop to Peter. After Peter checked the real estate records and found that the property was registered in David's name, Peter paid $50,000 to David. After Esther learned of the sale, she filed a lawsuit against Peter, claiming that one-half of the real estate belonged to her, and demanding that Peter convey one-half of the property to her.

(a) Does Esther own a one-half interest in the real estate? Explain.

(b) Should the court award anything to Esther? Explain.

42.8 Judith Held was one of six partners in a partnership. Bill Bauer loaned $800,000 to Held and she pledged her partnership interest as collateral. At the time of the loan Held received about $5,000 per month as her share of the profits. Held defaulted on her loan and, with the consent of the partnership, she assigned her partnership interest to Bauer. For several months, the partnership paid Held's share of the income to Bauer. Following a special partnership meeting, however, the partners voted to pay a monthly bonus to Jones and Day, two partners who had been instrumental in attracting an important new customer, for two years. Neither Bauer nor Held participated in this partnership meeting. The partnership profits were just adequate to pay the monthly bonus to Jones and Day so no funds were available for payments to Bauer.

(a) Bauer sued the partnership claiming that he should have been allowed to vote at the special partnership meeting or, at least, that his consent to the bonus should have been required. Is he correct? Explain.

(b) Do the partners or the partnership owe any duty to Bauer that might protect him from this type of arrangement? Explain.

OPERATION AND TERMINATION OF PARTNERSHIP

In the course of its business, a general partnership frequently enters into contracts with third parties, such as lenders, customers, and suppliers of goods or services. These contractual obligations often are incurred by one or more, but fewer than all, partners acting or purporting to act on behalf of the partnership. In addition to making contracts, an individual partner, in the course of partnership business, may tortiously injure a third party through negligent or intentional conduct. The first part of this chapter examines the law determining when co-partners should be held liable for contracts made or torts committed by other partners. The second part discusses the legal principles governing termination of the partnership, including the legal relationship among partners, and the liability of the partners to partnership creditors.

General Partners and Third Parties

Nature of Partners' Liability

Under the Revised Uniform Partnership Act, partners are jointly and severally liable for all partnership obligations.[1] Thus, partners are bound upon partnership contracts and for partnership torts both individually (severally) and as a unit (jointly). Procedurally, this means that the third party plaintiff may sue one or more partners separately or all of them together at her option.

The net effect of such liability is that each partner has unlimited liability to pay all debts and obligations of the firm. That is, the partners usually agree *among themselves* to share losses. Creditors are not bound by this arrangement and may collect the entire amount of a partnership debt from any one partner. The paying partner must then attempt to recover a proportionate share of the loss from co-partners. To illustrate, assume Smith, Jones, and White are equal partners. White enters into a contract with (or tortiously injures) Brown. Brown sues Smith, Jones, and White as partners for damages. Jones, White, and the partnership are all insolvent. Smith is independently wealthy. Despite Smith's inability to

---

[1]RUPA §306. Joint and several promises are discussed in Chapters 7 and 33.

obtain any reimbursement from Jones or White, partnership law may hold Smith personally liable for the entire debt owing to Brown and other partnership creditors. The principles determining when that liability is to be imposed are discussed below.

Contract Liability — In General

The law of agency supplements the RUPA and the Act explicitly provides that "each partner is an agent of the partnership for the purpose of its business."[2] Accordingly, the power of a partner to bind the partnership to contracts with third parties is governed by the same principles that enable an ordinary agent to bind her principal. In short, the partnership is bound on contracts made by a partner acting within the scope of her (1) express actual authority, (2) implied actual authority, and (3) apparent authority. In addition the partnership is bound on contracts outside the scope of the partner's actual or apparent authority if it ratifies them.[3]

Partners' Authority—Actual. The methods of conferring actual authority upon a partner have already been discussed. For example, the partnership agreement often expressly authorizes one or more partners to contract for purchases of inventory and supplies, to hire employees, to purchase equipment, and to make other contracts normally incident to the partnership business. A contract made pursuant to such an authorization binds the partnership without further action by the partners. Actions not expressly authorized by the partnership agreement may be authorized by vote of the partners. If the voting percentages required for a given action are not outlined in the partnership agreement, the voting rules outlined in the RUPA apply.

Partners' Authority—Apparent. A partner possesses perhaps the greatest apparent authority of any agent. That is, "partner," like "manager," is itself an implied representation to third parties that the person bearing the title possesses certain generally recognized powers. Thus, §301(1) of the RUPA provides that the act of every partner "for apparently carrying on in the ordinary course the partnership business or business of the kind carried on by the partnership" binds the

partnership, unless the acting partner has no actual authority to act for the partnership in the transaction, and the person with whom he is dealing has knowledge or has received a notification[4] of that fact. Courts ordinarily interpret this language to mean that a partner has apparent authority to perform acts "usual" for the particular partnership and those usual for similar partnerships in the locality. Partners generally have apparent authority to buy and sell goods, borrow money, execute negotiable instruments, make representations to customers, hire and fire employees, make contracts for compensation, and receive delivery of property or payments from third parties.

Acts not within the apparent scope of partnership business do not bind the partnership unless actually authorized by the other partners.[5] Traditional examples of such acts include contracts for guaranty or suretyship, using firm assets to pay individual debts, and giving away partnership property.

Contract Liability — Partnership by Estoppel

Liability of Nonpartners. As a general rule, persons who are not partners among themselves are not partners as to third parties.[6] A notable exception to this rule is **partnership by estoppel,** under which equitable estoppel principles are used to impose partnership liability upon a person who is not, in fact, a partner. Such a person is known as a "partner by estoppel," "ostensible partner," "apparent partner," or "purported partner."

As noted in Chapter 9, estoppel[7] is the legal principle under which a person is estopped, or prevented, from asserting a position inconsistent with her prior conduct if injustice would thereby result to a person who changes position in justifiable reliance on that conduct. The RUPA uses estoppel principles to establish partnership liability in §308(a), which provides in part that

> If a person, by words or conduct, purports to be a partner, or consents to being represented by another as a partner, in a partnership or with one or more persons not partners, the

---

[2]RUPA §§104(a), 301(1).

[3]See discussion of these issues in the agency material in Chapter 40.

[4]Under RUPA §102(d), a person receives a notification when it comes to his attention or is delivered at his place of business or other place (such as a post office box) established by him as the place to receive communications.

[5]RUPA §301(2).

[6]RUPA §308(e).

[7]The law of estoppel applies to partnership law through RUPA §104(a).

purported partner is liable to a person to whom the representation is made, if that person, relying on the representation, enters into a transaction with the actual or purported partnership.

A nonpartner may be represented as a partner in various ways. For example, the representation may be made in a private manner, such as a face-to-face conversation in which the person directly represents himself, or permits others to represent him, as a partner. In this case, only the person to whom the representation is made may hold the apparent partner liable. A person also may be held out as a partner in a public manner. For example, the person's name may appear in a public document such as an assumed name certificate or license application, or may be used in the firm name, letterhead, or advertising. A person who makes or consents to a public representation is liable to any person extending credit to whom the representation is communicated in any manner. That is, liability is imposed even if the form of representation upon which the creditor relies in extending credit (for example, a printed circular or word of mouth) is not the form of representation to which the apparent partner has consented (for example, a newspaper advertisement). Note that in both the public and private cases, the creditor must in fact rely upon the representation of partnership in extending credit.

The following case illustrates the operation of partnership by estoppel principles.

Cheesecake Factory, Inc. v. Baines
964 P.2d 183 (N.M. App. 1998)

> Plaintiff Cheesecake Factory, Inc. extended credit on an open account to Triples American Grill, a sports bar and restaurant located in Albuquerque, New Mexico. When Triples American Grill failed to pay the account, Cheesecake Factory sued defendant John Baines alleging that he was a partner in a partnership that owned Triples American Grill and, therefore, liable on the account. Baines denied liability. Evidence at trial demonstrated that Baines was not a partner and that Triples American Grill was owned by Triple Threat, Inc., a corporation. Cheesecake Factory, however, asserted that Baines should be held liable on the theory of partnership by estoppel based on evidence that Baines had held himself out as a partner in a partnership that owned Triples American Grill. The trial court entered judgment for Cheesecake Factory and Baines appealed.

Hartz, Chief Judge

. . . Cheesecake Factory . . . contended that it did not know that the entity to which it was advancing credit was a corporation. It claimed that representations by Frank Kolk, the manager of the business, caused it to believe that the sports bar was owned by a partnership. Its theory of liability in the district court was that Baines was a partner by estoppel and therefore liable for the debt incurred by the sports bar . . .

Consent to Being Represented as a Partner

Steve Mager, the president of Cheesecake Factory, testified that before Cheesecake Factory advanced credit to the sports bar, Kolk told him that Kolk and Baines were in a partnership of three persons that owned the bar. Although there was no direct evidence that Baines authorized Kolk to tell Cheesecake Factory that Baines was a partner in the business, there was ample evidence to support an inference that Baines consented to Kolk's making such a representation. Among that evidence was the following: Cheesecake Factory first extended credit to the business on February 10, 1993. On February 23, 1993, an account was opened at Western Bank of Albuquerque in the name of "Baines: Bob DBA Triples American Grill." (Baines was generally known in the community as "Bob" Baines.) The signature card contains two signatures, those of "Bob Baines, owner" and "Frank Kolk, owner." On March 3, 1993, a payroll account was opened at Western Bank in the same name. The signatures on the signature card were "Bob Baines" and "Frank Kolk." Baines was frequently present at the sports bar and freely entered the business office. As a result, employees believed that Baines was a partner. In addition, there was testimony that Baines himself had told others that "he had a sports bar" and "was a partner" in the business. Although these statements by Baines may have been as much as nine months after Kolk first told Mager that Baines was a partner, they are probative of a consistent pattern of behavior over the course of several months indicating Baines' consent, indeed desire, to be perceived as a partner in the business. Viewing the evidence in the light most favorable to the judgment, . . . we believe that the district court could reasonably infer that Baines consented to Kolk's representing Baines' partnership status to Cheesecake Factory.

Reliance

Finally, we address the claim that Cheesecake Factory did not prove that it relied on the purported partnership. In one respect the evidence of reliance by Cheesecake Factory is clearly supported by the evidence. Mager and his sales manager, Don Grosso, testified that Cheesecake Factory was willing to extend credit to the new business only because it was a partnership. In particular, they testified that credit would not have been extended to a new restaurant organized as a corporation because the restaurant business is risky and it may be impossible to collect a debt from a failed corporation. Mager testified that he had "never gotten burnt" by a partnership and "I'm more likely to go in looking at it from the bright side because there are partners involved and liability runs to the individual partners."

Cheesecake Factory contends that reliance on the existence of a partnership sufficed for creation of a partner by estoppel. It relies on *Hunter v. Croysdill,* [337 P.2d 174,179 (Cal. App. 1959), in which the court stated]. . . .

> Defendant takes the position that as plaintiffs did not make exhaustive inquiries into his financial status, they could not have relied thereon. There is no requirement that credit be given in reliance upon the financial status of the apparent partner, but only that the party claiming the benefit of [partnership by estoppel] relied on the existence of the partnership.

The rule in *Hunter* is an attractive one for Cheesecake Factory, because the evidence of reliance on Baines' credit is slim. Cheesecake Factory sought no financial statement from Baines and made no credit inquiry or, apparently, any inquiry whatsoever about Baines. Mager said simply that he was familiar with the name Baines and associated it with the construction or automobile business. Also, Mager said that he was told by Kolk that the partners owned the extensive sports memorabilia on display, that one of the partners was going to arrange for display of a pace car, and that Baines was helping to remodel the restaurant.

Mager's failure to obtain a credit check on Baines limits the extent to which Cheesecake Factory could reasonably rely on Baines to cover debts incurred by the sports bar. But that does not mean that Cheesecake Factory could not reasonably rely at all on the fact that Baines was a partner. As indicated by Mager's testimony, the very fact of a person's being a partner provides some comfort for creditors. One whose personal assets are at risk in a business venture can be expected to take a particular interest in having the enterprise run properly and paying its bills out of business revenue.

Moreover, the evidence at trial, although marginal, would support the inference that Mager reasonably believed Baines to be the proprietor of an established business. At least two rational inferences can be drawn from that fact. First, as proprietor of an established business, Baines would have expertise that could be helpful in the financial affairs of the sports bar. Second, even if Mager could not be confident that Baines could pay very large debts, he could expect Baines to be financially responsible. Cheesecake Factory's dealings with the sports bar would not be likely to lead to huge debts. We note that the principal amount owed on open account in this case was slightly more than $20,000. Although this is not an insignificant amount, even one without great wealth—and probably most owners of established businesses—could be expected to pay off a substantial portion of the sum. Thus, the evidence at trial would support a rational inference that Cheesecake Factory reasonably relied on Baines' being a partner. . . .

By the above reasoning the trier of fact could almost always find reasonable reliance. . . . In our view, however, faithfulness to the statutory language requires us to leave open the possibility in any particular case that there was no reliance on a particular person's being a member of the partnership. We find the words of Professor Painter to be persuasive. In discussing whether a plaintiff should be required to prove that it would not have extended credit but for the representation of partnership, he wrote as follows:

> . . . [I]n most instances where the plaintiff is aware of the holding out and, being so aware, extends credit to what he supposes is a partnership, he will be motivated at least in part by an assumption, albeit a vague one, that the defendant is financially responsible and that his credit stands back of that of the firm. Hence there should be at least a presumption of reliance on the defendant's financial responsibility, subject to possible rebuttal by a showing of complete indifference on the part of the plaintiff to the representation. [William H. Painter, *Partnership by Estoppel,* 16 VAND. L.REV. 327, 335 (1963).]. . . .

In sum, the test for reliance is not whether it would have been good business practice to advance credit relying solely on Baines' being a partner. Many factors may go into the decision whether to advance credit. The only question is whether it was reasonable for one of the factors to be that Baines was a partner. Although it may be tempting to rule against a creditor who apparently has not engaged in the wisest business practices, it must be realized that the partner by estoppel is the "victim" only of misrepresentations that he himself authorized. This is a close case, but we hold that the evidence of reliance is sufficient to sustain the judgment. . . .

[Judgment affirmed.]

Liability of Partners and Partnership. The doctrine of partnership by estoppel is used to impose contractual liability upon the purported partner. Under ordinary principles of apparent authority, acts of the purported partner also may contractually bind his supposed partners. A person who has been represented as a partner in an existing partnership (or with one or more persons not actual partners) is an agent of the persons consenting to the representations. Thus, the purported partner may contractually bind those consenting to the same extent and in the same manner as an actual partner to third persons who rely upon the representation. If all members of an existing partnership consent to the representation, a partnership obligation results; otherwise, the liability is the joint and several obligation of the person acting and those consenting to the representation.[8] For example, Addison, Burke, and Crabbe (ABC) are partners in the business of buying and selling used cars. Dunne, a car dealer, but not a partner, represents himself to Thacker as a partner in ABC partnership. Addison and Burke are present when the representation is made, but say nothing. Thacker, believing that he is dealing with the partnership, contracts to sell cars to Dunne. On these facts, Dunne, Addison, and Burke are jointly and severally liable on the contract to Thacker; that is, by their silence, Addison and Burke created apparent authority in Dunne to bind them. Neither Crabbe nor the partnership is liable on the contract.

Transfer of Partnership Property

Although the RUPA allows title to real or personal property to be acquired and conveyed in the firm name, property owned by the firm often is held or transferred in the names of one or more of the partners. Section 302 of the RUPA states the rules governing how title to property is conveyed in various situations and the legal effect of such conveyances on the rights of the partners and third parties.

If title to property is held in the partnership name, any partner may convey the property by an instrument executed in the partnership name. If title to property is held in the name of one or more partners or other persons, the partnership interest may be transferred by an instrument signed by the persons in whose name the property is held. Once a transfer has been made, the partnership may recover the property only if it proves (1) that the partner or partners making the transfer had no actual or apparent authority to do so, and (2) that the transferee knew or had received notification that the property was partnership property and that the partners lacked authority to transfer it.

If the partnership owns real property, it can protect itself against unauthorized transfers by (1) holding title in the partnership name, and (2) filing a "statement of partnership authority" with the state secretary of state and recording a certified copy in the appropriate local real property recorder's office.[9] In this case, third parties are deemed to know of any limitation on the authority of a partner to transfer the land contained in the statement.[10]

Partnership Tort Liability

Partnership tort liability, like contract liability, is based upon general agency principles. Accordingly, the partnership is liable to third parties injured by tortious acts or omissions of partners acting in the ordinary course of the partnership business. Partners also are liable for tortious acts of other partners that they have expressly authorized or ratified.[11]

As in ordinary agency, tort liability most commonly is imposed for a partner's negligent conduct causing injury. For example, assume A, a partner in ABC Partnership, is driving a firm vehicle (or her own vehicle) to make a call on a prospective customer. En route, A negligently runs a stop sign and collides with T, another motorist. The partnership is liable to T for A's tort. Whether a partner has deviated sufficiently from the ordinary course of partnership business to relieve the partnership from liability is determined by the principles governing scope of employment that were previously discussed in the agency material.

---

[8]RUPA §308(b).

[9]Real property recording statutes are covered in detail in Chapter 37.
[10]RUPA §303(e).
[11]RUPA §305(a).

Liability for negligence also may be imposed in professional partnerships. For example, a law firm is liable for damages caused by incorrect advice negligently furnished by a partner to a client. Similarly, a partnership of physicians is liable for one partner's negligent treatment of a patient.

Not all partnership tort liability is based upon negligence. A partnership may be liable for intentional torts committed by a partner in the scope of partnership business, such as fraud, misrepresentation, defamation, trespass, or conversion. Suppose A is a partner in ABC Partnership, which buys and sells used cars. A fraudulently induces T to buy a car by turning back the odometer and falsely represents that the car has never been involved in an accident. The partnership is liable to T for A's fraud because the representations were made in the ordinary course of the partnership business.

In addition to tort liability, a partnership also is bound by any partner's breach of trust. For example, partners in an investment firm may be actually or apparently authorized to receive, hold, and invest money or property of others. In this case, the partnership is liable if any partner misapplies the money or property received (for example, uses it to pay personal debts).[12]

Partnership Criminal Liability

The preceding discussion concerns partnership civil liability for an individual partner's tort or breach of trust. Responsibility for a partner's criminal acts generally is not imposed upon co-partners unless they participate in the crime, authorize it, or assent to it. All partners may, however, be held liable for crimes committed by one of them in the course of business for which no criminal intent is required. These so-called strict liability crimes include, for example, violations of pure food and drug laws and illegal sales of liquor. In addition, the partnership (rather than the individual partners) may be held criminally responsible and punished, for example, by a fine levied against partnership assets.

Notice or Knowledge of Partner

In the course of their duties, partners often acquire knowledge or receive notice or notification of facts having actual or potential legal significance to the partnership.

Consistent with general agency principles, "a partner's knowledge, notice, or receipt of a notification of a fact relating to the partnership is effective immediately as knowledge by, notice to, or receipt of a notification by the partnership."[13] For example, notice of a license revocation hearing given to one partner is notice to the partnership, whether or not communicated to the other partners. The rule that knowledge of a partner is knowledge of the partnership is subject to an important exception. The partnership is not charged with knowledge of a fraud on the partnership committed by or with the consent of a partner.

Limited Liability Partnership

The rules governing partners' liability outlined above may be significantly altered if the partnership elects to become a **limited liability partnership (LLP).** Virtually all states today have statutes authorizing LLP status, many based upon the 1996 Limited Liability Partnership Amendments to the RUPA. Generally, to qualify, the partners first vote to approve the change to LLP status. Typically, the vote required is the same as that necessary to amend the partnership agreement (usually unanimous). Once the vote is taken, the partnership files a statement of qualification with and pays a fee to the state secretary of state, and adds "registered limited liability partnership," "limited liability partnership," "R.L.L.P.," or "L.L.P." to its name. Once qualified, the partnership must file an annual report with the secretary of state.[14] Note that an LLP remains a general partnership; it is not a completely new entity like a limited partnership, limited liability company, or corporation.

Under the RUPA and most state statutes, LLP status insulates the partners from personal liability for firm debts. The RUPA, for example, provides that:

> [A]n obligation of a partnership incurred while the partnership is a limited liability partnership, whether arising in contract, tort, or otherwise, is solely the obligation of the partnership. A partner is not personally liable, directly or indirectly, by way of contribution or otherwise, for such an obligation solely by reason of being or so acting as a partner.[15]

---

[12]RUPA §305(b).

[13]RUPA §102(f). The liability of a principal for notice to or knowledge of an agent is discussed in the agency material in Chapter 40.
[14]RUPA §§1001–1003.
[15]RUPA §306(c).

Note that under the RUPA, a partner remains personally liable for obligations caused by that partner's negligence, wrongful acts, errors, and omissions. In many states, a partner also is personally liable for wrongful acts of persons under that partner's direct supervision and control.

Dissociation, Dissolution, and Liquidation

A general partnership does not continue indefinitely. Partners may die or withdraw, or the partnership business may become unprofitable. The legal and financial consequences of a partnership breakup are important and should be addressed explicitly in the partnership agreement. In the absence of such agreement, the RUPA applies the following principles.

The process of extinguishing a partnership begins with **dissociation,** which occurs when any partner ceases to be associated in conducting the partnership business. Upon dissociation, either (1) the partnership, a legal entity, continues and the dissociated partner's interest is purchased, or (2) the partnership is "dissolved" and must be "wound up."[16] **Winding up,** often referred to as **liquidation,** is the series of transactions necessary to settle partnership affairs after dissolution. During winding up, the partnership's uncompleted transactions are finished, assets are converted to cash, debts are paid, and the excess, if any, is distributed to partners.

To apply the RUPA rules, the student must therefore know (1) the cause of dissociation, and (2) when the business is continued, rather than liquidated, after a dissociation.

Causes of Dissociation

Under §601 of the RUPA, a partner is dissociated from the partnership under the following circumstances.

1.   A partner has the power to dissociate by notifying the partnership that he or she intends to withdraw from the partnership. Such a dissociation by "express will" is effective either upon notice to the partnership or upon any later date specified by the partner. Note that a partnership is a mutual agency relation with each partner acting both as a principal and as agent for the other partners. Like other agencies, a partnership is a personal relationship, resting on mutual consent. This consent may be withdrawn by any partner at any time even if the acting partner is contractually obligated to continue the partnership. That is, all partners have the *power,* but not necessarily the *right,* to dissolve the partnership at any time.[17] For example, assume A, B, and C are partners in an auto repair business. Their partnership agreement provides that the partnership will continue for three years. Though the business is profitable, B becomes dissatisfied with the arrangement after one year. B may dissociate from the partnership even though his act violates the partnership agreement, rendering him liable for damages to the partnership and to the other partners.

2.   Partners are dissociated upon occurrence of an event provided in the partnership agreement as causing a partner's or partners' dissociation.

3.   The partnership agreement may confer a power upon partners to expel another partner under certain circumstances. Expulsion of a partner in accordance with the agreement dissociates the expelled partner.

4.   Even in the absence of express provision, a partner may be expelled (and therefore dissociated) by unanimous vote of the other partners if (1) it becomes unlawful to carry on partnership business with that partner, (2) the partner has transferred all or substantially all of her partnership interest, (3) the partner's interest has been subjected to a charging order, or (4) the partner is a corporation or partnership that has been dissolved.

5.   Conduct by a partner that prejudicially interferes with (or makes it impracticable to conduct) partnership business and willful or persistent breaches of the partnership agreement are grounds for dissociation by court decree at the request of the injured partners. On this basis, for example, the court may order dissociation for irreconcilable differences or deadlock between partners, misappropriation of partnership assets, neglect of business responsibilities, or exclusion of one or more partners from management.

6.   A partner is dissociated by becoming a debtor in bankruptcy or by taking other action indicating insolvency or financial irresponsibility.[18]

7.   A partner may become physically or mentally incapacitated. In this case, the partner is dissociated if

---

[16]RUPA §603, comment 1.

[17]RUPA §602.

[18]Bankruptcy law generally invalidates *ipso facto* laws, which cause a forfeiture of a debtor's property or contract rights upon a bankruptcy filing. As a result, dissociation by bankruptcy may be held invalid under the Supremacy Clause in the partner's bankruptcy.

the court appoints a guardian or conservator for that partner or otherwise determines that the partner is no longer capable of performing her duties under the partnership agreement.

8. Dissociation occurs upon the death of a partner who is a natural person. If a partner is a trust or estate, dissociation occurs upon distribution of its entire transferable interest in the partnership.

Consequences of Dissociation—Liquidation or Continuation

Upon dissociation, the partnership has two alternatives: dissolution and liquidation, or continuation of the business. Liquidation involves a sale of all assets, payment of creditors, and distribution of any excess to the partners. Alternatively, the partnership entity and business may be continued by the remaining partners and a financial settlement paid to the outgoing partner or partners.

Which alternative is followed depends upon the cause of dissociation. Under RUPA §801, occurrence of one of the following events triggers dissolution and liquidation of the business. All other dissociations result in a buyout of the departing partner and continuation of the business.

1. If the partnership is "at will," a partner's notice to the partnership of his intent to withdraw.

2. In a partnership for a definite term (for example, five years) or a particular undertaking (for example, to build an apartment building), expiration of the term or completion of the undertaking, or consent of all partners.

3. Occurrence of an event stated in the partnership agreement as causing dissolution and liquidation.

4. Occurrence of an event making it unlawful to continue the business.

5. A judicial determination (after a request by any partner) that (a) the "economic purpose of the partnership is likely to be unreasonably frustrated," (b) another partner's conduct has made it impracticable to continue business in partnership with her, or (c) it is "not otherwise reasonably practicable" to continue the business in conformity with the partnership agreement.

6. A judicial determination (after a request by a transferee of a partner's interest) that it is equitable to liquidate the business either after its term expires or its particular undertaking is completed, or at any time if the partnership is "at will."

If an event listed above occurs, the partnership dissolves, and unless otherwise agreed, continues only for the purpose of liquidation.[19] The liquidation generally is conducted by the partners or the legal representative of the last surviving partner. A partner who has wrongfully caused the dissolution has no right to participate in the liquidation. As an alternative to liquidation by the partners, any partner may, for good cause shown (for example, fraud by co-partners), obtain court-supervised liquidation. In this case, the court usually appoints a receiver to conduct the liquidation.[20]

Under RUPA §701, if a partner's dissociation does not trigger dissolution and liquidation, the partnership will continue in business with the remaining partners and purchase the dissociated partner's interest. The buyout price is the amount that would have been distributable to the partner if, on the date of dissociation, the partnership assets were sold "at a price equal to the greater of the liquidation value or the value based on a sale of the entire business as a going concern."[21] Damages for wrongful dissociation and any other amounts owed by the partner to the partnership are then offset against the buyout price.

In many cases, liquidation causes substantial injury to the partners. That is, the partnership often possesses substantially more value as a viable, going concern than it does upon a forced sale of its assets. In addition, the partnership often represents an employment opportunity for the partners not available elsewhere.

Though the RUPA rules operate to continue the business in many cases, their application often will trigger an unexpected dissolution and liquidation of the business. Fortunately, these rules apply only if the partners fail to agree otherwise in their partnership agreement.[22] Thus, by a **continuation agreement,** the partners can explicitly anticipate and control the circumstances causing liquidation. Because dissociation and its consequences are so fundamental, and the effects of liquidation so potentially ruinous, a comprehensive continuation provision usually should be incorporated into the basic partnership agreement. Issues that should be addressed by the continuation provision include, for example, the causes of dissociation and dissolution, the method of

---

[19]RUPA §802(a).
[20]RUPA §803.
[21]RUPA §701(b). The partner also is entitled to interest on this amount measured from the date of dissociation to the date of payment.
[22]RUPA §103(a).

computing the value of the departing partner's interest, the method and medium of payment for that interest, the method of funding the buyout (such as insurance owned by the firm or partners, or firm assets, or the partners' individual assets), and the method of protecting outgoing interests against firm debts.

Consequences of Dissociation—Partners' Authority

Rights and Duties Among Partners. Under RUPA §603, upon dissociation a partner's right to participate in management and control terminates unless the dissociation causes a dissolution. In that event, all partners who have not wrongfully dissociated may participate in liquidating the business.[23] Though the duty not to compete with the partnership terminates upon dissociation, the partner's remaining duties of care and loyalty continue to apply (1) to events or transactions occurring before dissociation, and (2) to the partner's participation in liquidating the business. To illustrate the first case, "a partner who leaves a brokerage firm may immediately compete with the firm for new clients, but must exercise care in completing ongoing client transactions and must account to the firm for any fees received from the old clients on account of those transactions."[24]

Partners and Third Parties—Liquidation. If a dissociation causes dissolution of the partnership, the partners' actual authority terminates except for transactions appropriate to winding up partnership affairs, and to complete transactions unfinished at dissolution.[25] Although dissolution terminates the actual authority of the partners, persons who previously have dealt with the firm and others who know of its existence may be unaware of the firm's dissolution. The partners still possess apparent authority to bind the partnership to such persons. Under the RUPA, a partnership is bound by a partner's act after dissolution that would have bound the partnership before dissolution (because it was within the pre-dissolution actual or apparent authority of the partner), if the third party did not have notice of the dissolution.[26] Therefore, to prevent one partner from creating new partnership obligations (those not necessary to wind up the business) after dissolution, the partners must take affirmative steps to terminate each partner's apparent authority.

As with other agents, a partner's apparent authority is terminated by giving appropriate notice to third parties of the partner's lack of authority. Until proper notice is given, any partner has continuing authority to bind the others after dissolution to contracts with third parties. Partners of a dissolved partnership also may protect themselves against liability on post-dissolution contracts by filing a "statement of dissolution" with the state secretary of state.[27] Under RUPA §805(c), third parties are deemed to have notice of the dissolution and consequent limitation of the partner's authority 90 days after it is filed.

Partners and Third Parties—Continuation. If the partnership business continues after dissociation, a dissociated partner may nevertheless contract with third parties on the partnership's behalf. As in the liquidation case, the partner has continuing apparent authority to bind the partnership if at the time of the contract the third party (1) reasonably believed that the person was still a partner, and (2) did not have notice of the partner's dissociation.[28] To protect itself the partnership should therefore give prompt notice of the partner's dissociation to third parties, such as the firm's customers, suppliers, and bankers. Even without notice, under §702(a) of the RUPA, a partner's apparent authority continues only for two years after dissociation and the partnership can reduce that period to 90 days by filing a "statement of dissociation" with the state secretary of state. As with the "statement of dissolution" discussed above, third parties are deemed to have notice of the partner's lack of authority 90 days after the statement is filed.[29] In any event, the dissociated partner is liable to the partnership for damages if he or she binds the partnership to a contract with a third party after dissociation.[30]

Consequences of Dissociation—Partners' Liability

Dissociation does not affect the existing liability of any partner or the partnership to firm creditors.[31] Any other rule would allow a partner to avoid liability for partnership

---

[23]RUPA §803.
[24]RUPA §603, comment 2.
[25]RUPA §804(1).
[26]RUPA §804(2).

[27]RUPA §§805(a), 105(a).
[28]RUPA §702(a).
[29]RUPA §704.
[30]RUPA §702(b).
[31]RUPA §703(a).

obligations simply by withdrawing. Consistent with the preceding discussion, a former partner is liable for firm debts *after* dissociation if the third party contracted with the partnership reasonably believing that the former partner was still a partner and without notice of her dissociation. To avoid liability the former partner should therefore give notice of dissociation to third parties. A partner's liability is, in any event, limited to transactions made within two years after dissociation, which she can reduce to 90 days by filing a "statement of dissociation."[32]

Upon retirement or withdrawal of a partner, remaining partners who continue the business often assume the burden of paying firm creditors as part of the settlement of the departing partner's interest. Although such an agreement is binding among the partners, it has no effect upon the creditors; the retiring partner remains liable for all debts incurred while a partner,[33] becoming a surety for the assuming partners' performance. The retiring partner is, however, discharged from partnership debts if the creditors consent to a novation, under which the continuing partners assume the duty to perform existing obligations and the retiring partner is released.[34]

A person who is admitted as a partner in an existing partnership is liable for partnership debts incurred before she became a partner, as if she had been a partner when the obligations were incurred. This liability may, however, be satisfied only out of partnership property; that is, the incoming partner is generally liable for pre-existing firm debts only to the extent of her capital contribution.[35] The new partner is, of course, personally liable for all debts incurred after becoming a partner.

Distribution Priorities

Solvent Partnership. If, upon dissociation, the business is dissolved and liquidated, partnership assets are reduced to cash and distributed to partnership creditors and partners. Property subject to distribution upon liquidation includes both the partnership property and any additional contributions collected from the partners necessary to pay partnership obligations.[36] This principle simply recognizes that the part-

ners are personally liable for firm obligations and may therefore be required to contribute additional funds to cover any deficiency between firm assets and liabilities. The duty to contribute to firm losses may be enforced against living partners and the estate of a deceased partner. The duty may be enforced by any partner or his legal representative, or by representatives of creditors.[37]

The RUPA outlines generally the order in which assets are distributed.[38] First, claims of partnership creditors (including partners) are paid. Note that because partners are personally liable to firm creditors for all firm obligations, as a practical matter debts owing to partners (for example, a loan made by a partner to the partnership) are paid only after debts owed to outside creditors are satisfied. Second, the remaining assets are distributed to the partners as a liquidating distribution. Each partner's distribution consists of the partner's capital contribution (the amount of money plus the value of other property contributed to the partnership) increased by the partner's share of profits that have not previously been distributed, and reduced by the partner's share of partnership losses. In computing the liquidating distribution, first the partner's capital contributions are returned and then any amount remaining is distributed to the partners as profits.

For example, suppose A, B, and C are equal partners who have each contributed $25,000 to the business. In addition, B has loaned the partnership $25,000. Upon liquidation, firm assets are sold for $200,000 and creditors' claims total $50,000. The $200,000 would be distributed $50,000 to creditors, then $25,000 to B to repay his loan, then $75,000 to the partners in repayment of their capital contributions. The remaining $50,000 would be divided equally among the partners as profits.

If firm assets are insufficient to repay in full partnership creditors, advances or loans made by partners, or capital contributions, the loss is shared (subject to contrary agreement) in the same proportion as the partners share profits. If, in the example above, firm assets are sold for $135,000, A, B, and C would each receive $20,000 as a return on their capital contributions; that is, after paying creditors (including B), $60,000 remains to cover the partners' $75,000 in capital contri-

---

[32]RUPA §§703(b), 704.

[33]As noted above, such a partner may be liable for obligations incurred thereafter unless third party creditors are properly notified.

[34]RUPA §703(c). Novation is discussed in detail in Chapter 13.

[35]RUPA §306(b).

[36]RUPA §807(b).

---

[37]RUPA §§807(c),(e),(f).

[38]RUPA §§807(a),(b).

butions. This results in a $15,000 loss shared equally by the partners.

To illustrate the distribution rules further, assume that A, B, and C are partners. A contributed $20,000, B, $15,000, and C, $10,000. On liquidation, after all creditors are paid, $12,000 remains to be distributed to the partners. They have agreed to share profits and losses equally. The $33,000 loss ($45,000 − $12,000) is allocated equally to the partners as follows:

	A	B	C
Capital	$ 20,000	$ 15,000	$ 10,000
Loss	(11,000)	(11,000)	(11,000)
	$ 9,000	$ 4,000	$ (1,000)

When finally settled, C must contribute an additional $1,000 from his personal assets. This $1,000 plus the $12,000 will be used to pay A $9,000 and B $4,000. If C is insolvent and unable to contribute additionally, A and B share this loss equally ($500 each) and of the $12,000, A is entitled to $8,500 and B, $3,500.

In the following case, the court was required to determine the proper allocation of assets among partners on liquidation. Note the special rule applicable to a partner who contributes services but not money or property to the partnership.

Langness v. The "O" Street Carpet Shop, Inc.
353 N.W.2d 709 (Neb. 1984)

Herbert J. Friedman, Strelsa Langness, and The "O" Street Carpet Shop, Inc. formed a general partnership in 1973. Langness contributed $14,000 in cash, and Friedman contributed his legal services, upon which no value was placed in the articles of partnership. "O" Street Carpet contributed a real estate contract entitling it to purchase for $56,000 a piece of rental property valued at $65,000. The partnership used $6,000 of the cash as a down payment on the real estate and $8,000 was given to "O" Street Carpet for its operations. The articles provided that the partnership would pay $116.66 per month to Langness, and Gerald Neva, president of "O" Street Carpet, personally guaranteed the payments.

In 1978, the partnership sold the rental property and the partners agreed to dissolve the partnership. Following payments of its debts, the partnership's net assets were $48,824.41, which were distributed as follows:

Langness	$16,792.01
"O" Street Carpet	26,808.58
Friedman	5,223.82

Langness sued "O" Street Carpet and Friedman alleging that she was entitled to a greater share of the assets. The trial court held that Friedman and "O" Street Carpet were jointly and severally liable to Langness for $7,290.42. Friedman appealed.

Per Curiam

. . . Friedman's first three assignments of error are best analyzed by reviewing the capital contributions made by the parties, the nature of the payments made to Langness, and the distributions made to each of the three partners upon the winding up of the partnership.

. . . [A]t the time the partnership was formed, "O" Street Carpet contributed a $56,000 purchase agreement on property with a fair market value of $65,000, for a contribution of property worth $9,000. However, $8,000 of the $14,000 contributed by Langness went to "O" Street Carpet, thereby reducing its capital contribution at that time to $1,000. During the life of the partnership, "O" Street Carpet contributed an additional $4,005 in capital. Thus, "O" Street Carpet's total capital contribution is $5,005.

Friedman contributed no money or property. It is the general rule that a partner who contributes only services to the partnership is not deemed to have made a capital contribution to the partnership such as to require capital repayment upon dissolution unless the parties have agreed to the contrary. . . .

Friedman argues that since, by the agreement, he was given 10 percent of the partnership, he was entitled to be credited with a like amount of the partnership capital upon dissolution. While the agreement specifically states that Friedman is entitled to 10 percent of the partnership profits, it mentions nothing concerning his rights to partnership capital upon dissolution. We see nothing in the agreement which indicates the general rule is not to apply. Therefore, Friedman made no capital contribution to the venture.

We next address the nature of the payments made to Langness. The articles of partnership called for the partnership to pay to Langness $116.66 per month for the life of the partnership. While this provision of the articles is found under a section labeled *"Distribution of Profits and Losses,"* the agreement does not state whether it is to be treated as an advance on profits or a capital withdrawal. The personal guarantee executed by Neva labeled it a "return on the $14,000.00 investment."

Both accountants who testified at the trial stated that the payments were treated as capital withdrawals. Langness treated the payments as such when preparing her tax returns. The tax returns of the partnership did not treat them as expenses. Although Friedman argues that they should be treated as advances against Langness' future profits, we do not see any reason to do so when the partnership itself treated them otherwise.

From our review of . . . a ledger of the payments made by checks issued by NFL Associates, we find that Langness was issued 47 checks for $116.66, 3 checks for $233.32, and 1 check for $117.32. We calculate her total capital withdrawals as $6,300.30, a figure different than that urged upon us by the parties or found by the district court. This $6,300.30 reduced her capital in the partnership to $7,699.70.

We now reach the question of the appropriate amounts of the distribution to each of the partners. The partnership agreement provides: "Upon the dissolution of the partnership after settlement of all of it's [sic] debts, liabilities, and other obligations, the partners are entitled to all remaining assets of the partnership in equal proportions in liquidation of all of their respective interests in the partnership." Amounts owing to partners to reimburse them for capital contributions are liabilities of the partnership and take priority over amounts owing to partners in respect to profits. . . .

Of the $48,824.41 in assets remaining after payment of the partnership's debts, $7,699.70 is to be paid to Langness for her capital contribution and $5,005 to "O" Street Carpet for its capital contribution. The remaining $36,119.71 is to be divided according to the partners' share in the profits, which is on a 45-45-10 basis. This calculation requires $16,253.87 to be paid to Langness for profit, the same amount to "O" Street Carpet, and $3,611.97 to Friedman. At the time of the winding up of the partnership, the distributions should have been as follows:

	Return of Capital	+	Share of Profits	=	Total
Langness	$7,699.70		$16,253.87		$23,953.57
"O" Street Carpet	5,005.00		16,253.87		21,258.87
Friedman	0.00		3,611.97		3,611.97
	$12,704.70		$36,119.71		$48,824.41

Since Langness was paid only $16,792.01, she is entitled to an additional $7,161.56. . . .

Therefore, the judgment of the district court is modified as follows: Langness shall have judgment against and recover from Friedman the sum of $1,611.85, the difference between the amount he received, $5,223.82, and the amount he should have received, $3,611.97. Further, Langness shall have judgment against and recover from "O" Street Carpet the amount of $5,549.71, the difference between the amount it received, $26,808.58, and the amount it should have received, $21,258.87. . . .

[Judgment affirmed as modified.]

Insolvent Partnerships. In the preceding examples, the partnership assets were sufficient to pay outside creditors' claims in full; that is, the partnerships were solvent. Because individual partners may be compelled to contribute toward firm losses, any partnership is solvent as long as any partner is solvent.[39] Both the partnership and the partners may, however, be insolvent with the assets of each being administered in a bankruptcy proceeding. In this situation, a dispute may arise between creditors of the partnership and creditors of the individual partners concerning distribution of partnership and individual assets. Traditionally, this problem was resolved both under federal bankruptcy law and the UPA[40] by the rule of "dual priorities," often known as the "jingle rule." This rule gave partnership creditors priority in the distribution of partnership assets, and creditors of individual partners priority in distribution of a partner's individual assets. The rule permitted partnership creditors to proceed against a partner's individual assets only after individual creditors had been paid. Conversely, individual creditors could attach an individual partner's interest in the partnership only after firm creditors had been paid.

The jingle rule was harshly criticized for many years for destroying or diminishing partnership creditors' rights against the partners' separate property. That is, the rule that paid partners' individual creditors first

---

[39]Under federal bankruptcy law, a partnership is insolvent if firm debts exceed the sum of partnership assets and each individual partner's net worth (nonpartnership assets less nonpartnership debts). 11 U.S.C. §101.

[40]Bankruptcy Act §5g; 11 U.S.C. §23(g) (repealed 1978); UPA §§40(b),(h),(i); 36(4).

from individual assets undermined the principle that partners are personally liable for firm debts. For this reason, the Bankruptcy Reform Act of 1978 repealed the jingle rule insofar as it insulates a partners' separate property from claims of partnership creditors until the partner's individual creditors are paid in full. Under the Bankruptcy Code and the RUPA, partnership creditors retain their priority in partnership assets, but share equally with individual creditors in individual assets.[41]

Summary

1.   Partnership law determines when partners are held liable for contracts made or torts committed by other partners. Partners are generally jointly and severally liable for partnership torts, breaches of trust, and contracts. Each partner, therefore, has unlimited liability for all debts and obligations of the firm.

2.   Every partner is an agent of the partnership for the purpose of its business. Accordingly, the power of a partner to bind the partnership to contracts with third parties is determined by general agency principles. The partnership is therefore bound on contracts made by a partner acting within the scope of his (1) express actual authority, (2) implied actual authority, and (3) apparent authority. In addition, the partnership is bound upon contracts outside the scope of the partner's actual or apparent authority if it ratifies them.

3.   Persons who are not partners among themselves generally are not partners as to third parties. An exception to this rule is partnership by estoppel, under which equitable estoppel principles are used to impose partnership liability upon a person who is not, in fact, a partner.

4.   Although the RUPA allows title to property to be acquired and conveyed in the firm name, property owned by the firm often is held or transferred in the names of one or more of the partners. The RUPA governs how title to property is conveyed in various situations and the legal effect of such conveyances on the rights of the partners and third parties.

5.   Partnership tort liability, like contract liability, is based on general agency principles. Thus, the partnership is liable to third parties injured by a negligent act or omission of any partner acting in the ordinary course of the partnership business. A partnership also may be liable for intentional torts committed by a partner in the scope of partnership business, such as fraud, misrepresentation, defamation, trespass, or conversion. A partnership also is bound by an individual partner's breach of trust and, in certain limited cases, for a partner's criminal act.

6.   Notice to, or knowledge of, any partner concerning any fact relating to partnership affairs operates as notice or notification to, or knowledge of, the partnership.

7.   Dissociation occurs when any partner ceases to be associated in conducting the partnership business. Upon dissociation, either (1) the partnership continues and the dissociated partner's interest is purchased, or (2) the partnership is "dissolved" and must be liquidated or "wound up." Which alternative if followed depends upon the cause of dissociation. Occurrence of events listed in RUPA §801 triggers dissolution and liquidation of the business. All other dissociations result in a buyout of the departing partner and continuation of the business.

8.   Dissociation terminates a partner's authority and right to participate in management and control, except for transactions necessary to liquidate the business. A partnership may, however, be bound by a partner's act within her pre-dissociation actual or apparent authority if the third party did not have notice of the dissociation.

9.   Partners may withdraw or retire and others may be admitted. Generally, withdrawal of a partner does not affect the existing liability of any partner. In addition, a dissociated partner may be held liable on post-dissociation firm debts until third parties are notified of her dissociation. A newly admitted partner is liable for preexisting firm debts but only to the extent of her capital contribution.

10. If, upon dissociation, the partnership is liquidated rather than continued, partnership assets are reduced to cash and distributed to partnership creditors and partners. The RUPA specifies how assets are distributed. If the business is continued, the dissociated partner's interest is bought out at a price determined either by the partnership agreement or the RUPA. If the partnership is insolvent, a dispute may arise between creditors of the partnership and creditors of the individual partners over distribution of partnership and individual assets. This situation is governed by the federal Bankruptcy Code.

Key Terms

partnership by estoppel	dissociation
limited liability partnership (LLP)	winding up (liquidation)
	continuation agreement

---

[41]11 U.S.C. §723; RUPA §807, comment 2.

Questions and Problems

43.1   Courts and commentators often state that a partnership is a mutual agency relationship. What are the similarities and differences between the rights and obligations of a partner and an ordinary agent?

43.2   For many years J. T. Katz and A. Z. Downs operated the Food Town grocery store as partners. Although their partnership agreement placed no restrictions on either partner's powers, Katz handled the bookkeeping and Downs operated the grocery store. Katz and Downs purchased their inventory from Ace Food Suppliers on open account and always paid their bills from a partnership bank account.

(a) One day, Katz telephoned Ace and notified the company that he no longer would be responsible for purchases made from Ace. Ace's president asked if Katz and Downs were dissolving their partnership, and Katz replied in the negative, explaining that he believed inventory could be purchased elsewhere at cheaper prices. The following day, Downs placed a $5,000 order with Ace. Ace delivered the goods but never received payment. Ace sued Katz and Downs. Can Katz be held liable on the bill? Explain.

(b) Disregard the facts in part (a). Assume instead that Downs placed an order with Ace and asked for delivery at Food Town. When Ace's salesclerk began to write the order to the account of Katz and Downs, Downs asked that it be charged only in his name. After Ace failed to receive payment, it sued Katz and Downs. Can Katz be held liable? Explain.

43.3   Environmental Services (ES) is a partnership with five general partners. According to the written partnership agreement, the purpose of the business is "to collect and sell recyclable waste products including newspapers, glass, and cans." The agreement lists Ann Ely and Dexter Bain as the managing partners and authorizes either of the managing partners to sign checks on behalf of the partnership. When ES opened a checking account at Pioneer Bank, the bank requested a copy of the partnership agreement to document who was authorized to sign checks on the account. ES provided a complete copy of the partnership agreement. One year later, after regularly signing ES's checks, Ann Ely requested that Pioneer Bank lend ES $35,000 to finance the purchase of a new truck to be used to collect recyclable materials. The bank agreed to the loan and Ely signed the loan contract: "Environmental Services by Ann Ely, partner." No payments were made on the loan and Pioneer Bank sued ES and the partners.

(a) Based only on this information, do you think that ES is liable on the loan taken out by Ely? Explain.

(b) ES argued that it should not be held liable on the loan because Ely did not have actual authority for the loan. In support of its argument, ES pointed to the following provision in the partnership agreement: "No partner shall borrow money on behalf of the partnership except with the written consent of all partners." None of the partners had provided written consent for the loan. Do you that ES is liable on the loan taken out by Ely? Explain.

43.4   Charlie McLain and his brother, Lance, formed a partnership to operate C & L Farms. They signed a short agreement which provided that Charlie would manage the farm on a full-time basis and receive 75 percent of the profits while Lance would be a nonworking partner and receive 25 percent of the profits. The only other provision of the agreement stated that all losses would be split 50–50. Charlie and Lance borrowed $20,000 from First National Bank to finance the purchase of hogs. Both brothers signed a promissory note. When the note came due, the bank agreed to renew it, and Charlie and Lance signed a renewal promissory note. When the renewal note matured, it was again renewed, but because Lance was out of town, only Charlie signed the renewal note as follows: "C & L Farms by Charlie McLain and Lance McLain." When the note came due, First National wrote a letter to both Charlie and Lance requesting payment. Lance responded that he was not responsible for payment of the note because he had not authorized Charlie to sign his name. Is Lance liable on the note? What other information is necessary to determine Lance's liability? Explain.

43.5   In the fall of 2003, Frank Burger, a traveling salesman of restaurant supplies, visited Roberts Town and Country Restaurant in an effort to sell supplies to Mr. Roberts, the owner of the restaurant. Roberts declined to purchase any supplies. In the spring of 2004, Burger again visited Roberts Town and Country Restaurant and talked to Hank Hanna. Hanna agreed to buy supplies costing $5,000. They signed a sales agreement listing Burger as seller and Town and Country Restaurant as buyer. Burger delivered the supplies but Hanna failed to pay for them. Burger sued Mr. Roberts and Hank Hanna, a partnership, doing business as Roberts Town and Country Restaurant. The evidence at trial established that during January 2004, Mr. Roberts had leased the restaurant to Hanna. Roberts had not participated in the operation of the restaurant since that time. Roberts, however, had left a neon sign reading "Roberts Town and Country Restaurant" on the building. Should the court hold Mr. Roberts liable on the contract as a partner by estoppel? Explain.

43.6   Harry Owens, Ray Chavez, and Alan Hunt formed a corporation called Crosswind Enterprises, Inc. to develop a new fastfood restaurant chain. Owens contacted Betty Blueprint, an architect, to discuss her designing a prototype building for the restaurants. While describing the firm's business plans to Blueprint, Owens referred to Chavez and Hunt as his "partners." Blueprint agreed to perform the architectural services and requested a retainer of $1,000. Several days later she received the retainer check, which had the name Crosswind Enterprises printed at the top and was signed by Ray Chavez and Alan Hunt. Blueprint completed the building design but never received payment for her services. She filed a breach of contract suit against Owens, Chavez, and Hunt, who asserted that they were not personally liable because their business was operated as a corporation. Blueprint argued that

Owens, Chavez, and Hunt should be held liable as partners by estoppel. How should the court rule? Explain.

43.7 A federal statute provides that any person who knowingly transports explosive and dangerous articles in interstate commerce is guilty of a misdemeanor. A & P Trucking Co., a partnership operating in Missouri and Illinois, was charged with violation of the statute. A & P Trucking Co. has moved for dismissal of the indictment.

(a) How should the court rule? Explain.

(b) Assume that an employee who was not a partner was the only person who knew that the truck was carrying explosives. Can the individual partners be convicted and sentenced to prison? Explain.

43.8 Will Wong, Tom Tune, and Sue Sharp formed a partnership called Longview Estates on January 15, 1994, for the purpose of developing real estate. Each contributed $25,000 to the partnership. On May 1, 1994, National Bank loaned the partnership $1 million, which was to be repaid on May 1, 1996. On June 1, 1994, the partnership signed a five-year lease to rent office space at the rate of $2,500 per month. On July 10, 1994, Vera Verde became a new partner and made a capital contribution of $25,000. On March 20, 1995, Tune, with the consent of his partners, withdrew from the partnership and the partnership bought out his interest. The buyout agreement, signed by all partners, included the following provision: "The partners hereby agree that Tune shall not be responsible for any debts of the partnership."

(a) Assume that on May 1, 1996, the partnership failed to repay the $1 million loan to National Bank. What is the maximum amount for which each partner (Wong, Tune, Sharp, and Verde) could be held liable? Explain.

(b) Assume that Longview Estates also failed to pay its rent on a regular basis and eventually vacated the premises. The landlord had difficulty finding a new tenant and, on June 15, 1997, sued the partnership for the unpaid rent. The landlord proved that the partnership had failed to pay the monthly rent of $2,500 for 20 months. Is Vera Verde liable for this rent? Explain.

43.9 Lewis and Collins formed a partnership to construct and operate a restaurant. Lewis was to construct and equip the restaurant while Collins was to operate the restaurant. Due to unexpected expenses, the cost of constructing the restaurant greatly exceeded estimates. As a result, Lewis was forced to obtain a loan that was due in two years. Because of the need to repay the loan, Lewis was quite anxious to see the restaurant show a profit. In the first few months of operation, the business broke even, but Lewis demanded that Collins manage the business in a different manner. Lewis regularly interfered with operations. Finally, Lewis demanded that the partnership be dissolved. When Collins refused, Lewis filed suit requesting the court to dissolve the business. Following presentation of evidence, the jury found that the restaurant could reasonably be expected to operate at a profit and that Lewis's interference had caused the restaurant to operate at a loss. How should the court resolve the dispute? Explain.

43.10 Harry and Jeff formed a partnership for the operation of a retail furniture store. The partnership agreement provided:

> If either partner dies, the surviving partner agrees to pay to the estate of the deceased partner an amount equal to the value of the deceased partner's interest in the partnership property as of the date of death.

Harry died on June 1, 2005. As of that date, the partnership property consisted entirely of inventory—that is, furniture located in the store's showroom. The furniture had been purchased from a wholesaler for $100,000. Retail markup on the furniture was approximately 150 percent. The firm's liabilities were $10,000.

(a) If you were the surviving partner, what amount would you think was the proper amount to pay to the deceased partner's estate? Explain your calculations.

(b) If you were the administrator of the deceased partner's estate, what amount would you expect the estate to receive? Explain your calculations.

(c) What is the correct amount to be paid to the estate?

CHAPTER 44

LIMITED PARTNERSHIP AND LIMITED LIABILITY COMPANIES

- a discussion of the law governing creation, operation, and termination of limited partnerships
- coverage of the law governing creation, operation, and termination of limited liability companies

Unlimited personal liability for firm debts and obligations is a distinct disadvantage of a general partnership. The law has, therefore, long recognized the need for a form of business organization that allows persons to invest in the firm and share in profits with no liability for firm obligations beyond the amount invested in the business. Although the corporation, discussed in Chapters 45–48, fulfills this need, the limited partnership and limited liability company, discussed in this chapter, are additional organizational forms that combine profit sharing with limited liability for losses.

Limited Partnership

Introduction to Limited Partnership

During the Middle Ages, an arrangement known as the *commendam* allowed a financier to share in the profits of another's trade without personal liability for losses. This device was ultimately incorporated into the French Commercial Code of 1807, which formed the basis of early American limited partnership acts first enacted in New York (1822), Connecticut (1822), and Pennsylvania (1836). In 1916, the National Conference of Commissioners on Uniform State Laws adopted the **Uniform Limited Partnership Act (ULPA),** which was rewritten in 1976 and 2001. The following discussion is based upon the 2001 version of the ULPA.

Limited Partnership Defined. A **limited partnership** is a partnership formed by two or more persons under a limited partnership statute having as members one or more general partners and one or more limited partners.[1] As developed below, the general partner or partners may or may not have unlimited liability for firm debts and obligations characteristic of partners generally. In contrast, the limited partner or partners are not personally liable for partnership obligations and therefore have no liability for partnership losses beyond the amount invested in the firm. A person may simultaneously be both a general and limited partner in the same partnership possessing the rights and obligations of both.[2]

---

[1]ULPA §102(11).
[2]ULPA §113.

Formation of Limited Partnership

Formal Requirements. To create a limited partnership, §201 of the ULPA provides that its members must sign a certificate that states basic information about the business, including the name of the limited partnership, the address of its office, the name and address of each general partner and of an agent for service of process on the limited partnership. It also must state whether the limited partnership is to be a "limited liability limited partnership" (LLLP). Once executed, the certificate is filed in the state secretary of state's office where it is available for continuous public inspection. Technical defects in the certificate do not prevent formation of a limited partnership if there has been substantial compliance with the filing requirements. A limited partnership is formed either at the time that the certificate of limited partnership is filed with the secretary of state, or at any later time specified in the certificate.

During the term of the partnership, a certificate of amendment must be filed to reflect important changes in partnership structure. These include, for example, admission or withdrawal of a general partner, appointment of a person to wind up a limited partnership lacking a general partner, and acquiring or relinquishing LLLP status. The certificate, with amendments, provides accurate information about the partnership on a continuing basis.

The certificate of limited partnership is a formal document filed to provide basic information about the partnership to interested third parties. It is not an exhaustive statement of the partners' rights and obligations. As in a general partnership, the partners usually execute a separate private partnership agreement governing the affairs of the partnership and the conduct of its business.

Type of Business Conducted.

Type of Business Conducted. A limited partnership may be organized for "any lawful purpose."[3] The recognition of additional organizational forms that limit liability has reduced the traditional role served by limited partnerships. As explained in the Prefatory Note to the 2001 ULPA

> The new Act has been drafted for a world in which limited liability partnerships and limited liability companies can meet many of the needs formerly met by limited partnerships. This Act therefore targets two types of enterprises

that seem largely beyond the scope of LLPs and LLCs: (i) sophisticated, manager-entrenched commercial deals whose participants commit for the long term, and (ii) estate planning arrangements (family limited partnerships). This Act accordingly assumes that, more often than not, people utilizing it will want strong centralized management, strongly entrenched, and passive investors with little control over or right to exit the entity. This Act's rules, and particularly its default rules, have been designed to reflect these assumptions.

Many limited partnerships of the first type are organized to finance and manage commercial real estate such as apartment complexes, office buildings, and shopping centers.

Partnership Name. The partnership name may include the name of any partner, general or limited. The name must include "limited partnership," "L.P.," or "LP." If the partnership elects limited liability limited partnership status, the name must include "limited liability limited partnership," "L.L.L.P.," or "LLLP." Finally, the name also must be distinguishable in the secretary of state's records from the name of any corporation or other entity incorporated, organized, or authorized to transact business in the state.[4]

Partnership Office, Agent, and Records. The ULPA requires a limited partnership continuously to maintain an office, which need not be its place of business, in the state. At this office, the partnership is required to keep (1) a current list of the names and addresses of all partners, (2) a copy of the certificate of limited partnership and any amendments, (3) a copy of all financial statements, tax returns, and annual reports to the secretary of state for the three most recent years, and (4) a copy of any written partnership agreement binding on the partners. The ULPA also requires that certain additional information (such as the partners' contributions and events causing dissolution) be kept at the office unless already contained in a written partnership agreement. In addition to an office, the partnership must maintain an agent in the state for service of process on the limited partnership.[5]

The office, record keeping, and agent requirements assure that the limited partnership has certain minimum

---

[3]ULPA §104(b).

[4]ULPA §108.
[5]ULPA §§111, 114, 304.

contacts with its state of organization. They also assure that the limited partners, whose participation is passive in nature, will have access to the basic documents affecting the partnership.

Foreign Limited Partnership. A "foreign" limited partnership is one doing business in a state other than that of its formation. The ULPA requires foreign limited partnerships to apply for and obtain a certificate of authority from states in which it seeks to do business. The application, filed with the secretary of state, requires disclosure of certain basic information regarding the partnership. A foreign limited partnership also must maintain an agent for service of process in the state. Until it registers, a foreign limited partnership may not sue in the foreign state. Further, the state may bring an action to restrain an unregistered partnership from doing business in the state. Failure to register does not, however, impair the validity of any contract or act of the foreign limited partnership, or prevent it from defending a lawsuit in the state.[6] The requirements for registration of foreign limited partnerships are similar to those discussed in Chapter 45 imposed upon foreign corporations.

Relationship Among Partners

Capital Contribution. A partner's capital contribution may consist of cash or property (including a promissory note or other obligation to contribute cash or property in the future), services rendered, or an obligation to perform services in the future. A partner's obligation to contribute "is not excused by the partner's death, diability, or other inability to perform personally."[7]

Distributions. The distributions of cash or property of a limited partnership are allocated among the partners as outlined in the partnership agreement. If the partnership agreement is silent, profits, losses, and distributions are allocated "on the basis of the value, as stated in the required records . . . , of the contributions the limited partnership has received from each partner.[8]

Management and Control. In a limited partnership, the general partner or partners manage the business. Limited partners are passive investors who do not participate in management. In a limited partnership, the general partners enjoy all the rights and powers and are subject to the same duties and liabilities (to other partners, the partnership, and third parties) as exist in a general partnership. Management powers and authority of general partners generally are stated in the agreement and actions not explicitly authorized are taken by appropriate vote of the general partners. Although "a limited partner does not have the right or the power . . . to act for or bind" the partnership[9] unanimous consent of all partners, general and limited, is required for a variety of actions including for example: (1) admission of a new limited or general partner, (2) amendment of the partnership agreement, (3) election or relinquishment of LLLP status, (4) sale of limited partnership assets outside the ordinary course of business, and (5) various issues relating to expulsion of a partner, and dissolution and winding up the business.[10] Note that, unlike general partners, limited partners owe no fiduciary duty of loyalty to the partnership or other partners. Limited partners do, however, owe a duty of good faith and fair dealing in performing duties or exercising rights under the partnership agreement or ULPA.[11]

Information. A limited partner is entitled to information on important matters affecting the partnership business. A limited partner has an absolute right, by giving ten days advance written notice, to inspect and copy the information required to be kept at the partnership office. Limited partners also have the right to obtain upon reasonable demand from general partners true and full information regarding the business and financial condition of the partnership, and other information concerning partnership affairs as is "just and reasonable."[12] In addition, for matters on which the limited partners are entitled to vote "the limited partnership shall, *without demand,* provide the limited partner with all information material to the limited partner's decision that the limited partnership knows."[13]

---

[6]ULPA Article 9.
[7]ULPA §§501, 502(a).
[8]ULPA §503; note that this rule differs from that applied to general partnerships in which profits and losses are shared equally in the absence of agreement. RUPA §401(b).

[9]ULPA §302.
[10]ULPA §302, Comment.
[11]ULPA §305.
[12]ULPA §304(b).
[13]ULPA §304(i), emphasis added.

Partners and Third Parties

Liability for Firm Debts. A limited partner has no personal liability for any obligation of the limited partnership, whether arising in tort, contract, or otherwise. Thus, a limited partner's liability is limited to her investment in the business, even if the limited partner participates in the management and control of the limited partnership.[14]

General partners, in contrast, are jointly and severally liable for all obligations of the limited partnership.[15] This liability may be limited or extinguished in two ways. First, the general partner may be a corporation, which creates an independent liability shield. Second, as previously discussed, the partnership may elect **Limited Liability Limited Partnership (LLLP)** status in its certificate of limited partnership. If this election is made, the general partners enjoy the same limited liability as the limited partners.[16]

Liability for False Statements in Filed Record. Any person who signs the certificate of limited partnership (or other document filed with the secretary of state) knowing that it contains a false statement is liable to any person who subsequently suffers loss by relying on the statement. Moreover, after formation of the partnership, circumstances may change and render a statement in the initial certificate or other filing inaccurate. In this case, the general partners are liable to persons who rely upon the original, now misleading, certificate after sufficient time has passed to enable the partners to amend or cancel the certificate.[17]

Mistaken Belief of Limited Partner Status. A person may contribute capital to a business, erroneously, but in good faith, believing that she has become a limited partner. Under the ULPA, the person escapes liability as a general partner if she (1) causes an appropriate certificate or amendment of limited partnership to be executed and filed, or (2) withdraws from future equity participation in the enterprise. No renunciation, withdrawal, or filing is effective, however, to avoid liability to a third person who had previously transacted business with the enterprise believing the mistaken contributor to be a general partner.[18]

Transfer of Partnership Interest. Like a general partner's interest, a limited partner's interest is personal property and is freely transferable in whole or in part. A limited partner's interest includes the right to receive a share of profits or other compensation as stipulated in the partnership agreement and a return of capital contribution. The transfer does not cause the partner's dissociation or trigger a dissolution and winding up of the business. Nor does a transfer entitle the transferee to exercise any of the rights of a limited partner (for example, to inspect books and records and to be kept informed of firm business matters). The transfer merely entitles the transferee to receive, to the extent transferred, any distribution to which the transferring partner would otherwise be entitled.[19]

A transferee of a partnership interest may become a limited partner if the transferor gives the transferee that right according to authority granted in the partnership agreement, or if all other partners consent. A transferee who becomes a limited partner succeeds to the rights and liabilities of the old limited partner, but is not obligated for unknown liabilities.[20]

If a partner dies, his executor, administrator, or other legal representative may exercise all of that partner's rights in order to settle his estate. The estate of a deceased limited partner remains liable for obligations incurred by the partner.[21]

A limited partner's interest, like that of a general partner, may be transferred involuntarily through a charging order to satisfy a debt owed to a creditor of the partner. To the extent charged, the creditor has only the rights of a transferee of the partner's interest; that is, the creditor does not become a limited partner by virtue of the charging order.[22]

Dissociation, Dissolution, and Liquidation — Limited Partnership

Dissociation. As in a general partnership, dissociation occurs when a partner ceases to be associated in conducting the partnership business. A limited partner has no right to dissociate before the termination of the limited partnership.[23] A limited partner, however, has the

---

[14]ULPA §303.
[15]ULPA §404(a).
[16]ULPA §404(c).
[17]ULPA §208.
[18]ULPA §306.

[19]ULPA §§701, 702.
[20]ULPA §702(g).
[21]ULPA §704, 502(a).
[22]ULPA §703.
[23]ULPA §601(a).

power to dissociate (or to be involuntarily dissociated) under the same circumstances outlined in §601 of the Revised Uniform Partnership Act (RUPA), discussed in Chapter 43.[24] A dissociated limited partner remains liable for any obligation to the partnership incurred while a limited partner.[25]

A general partner may dissociate by notifying the partnership of the partner's intent to withdraw. Such a dissociation by "express will" is wrongful, and subjects the partner to liability for damages, if, for example, it violates an express provision of the partnership agreement. Like a limited partner, a general partner is also dissociated by the circumstances stated in §601 of the RUPA.[26] A dissociated general partner remains liable for any partnership obligation incurred before dissociation.[27]

Upon dissociation of either a general or limited partner, partner status ceases and the dissociated partner has only the rights of a transferee of his former limited partnership interest.[28] As previously noted, dissociation does not by itself trigger a dissolution and winding up of the partnership.[29]

Dissolution and Liquidation. A limited partnership is dissolved primarily (1) upon occurrence of an event stated in the partnership agreement; or (2) the consent of all general partners and those limited partners owning a majority of rights to receive distributions.[30] Judicial dissolution also may be ordered if the court finds it "not reasonably practicable to carry on the activities of the limited partnership in conformity with the partnership agreement."[31]

In winding up the partnership, its assets are first applied to pay creditors, including debts owed to partners. The remainder is paid in cash to the partners as a distribution according to the terms of the partnership agreement.[32] As previously noted, if the partnership agreement is silent, distributions are allocated "on the basis of the value . . . of the contributions the limited partnership has received from each partner."[33]

Limited Liability Companies

A **limited liability company** is a relatively new form of business organization possessing characteristics of both partnerships and corporations. Like a partnership, a limited liability company may have a decentralized management structure, limited transferability of interest, and limited continuity of existence. Most importantly, for federal income tax purposes, it may be treated as a partnership, meaning that a proportionate share of the firm's profits and losses are allocated to each partner, who reports it on his or her individual tax return.[34] Like a corporation, owners of a limited liability company have limited liability for firm debts even if they participate in management. This characteristic distinguishes a limited liability company from a limited partnership, in which limited partners who participate in management become personally liable as general partners to firm creditors. In essence, a limited liability company combines the management flexibility and tax advantages of a partnership with the limited liability of a corporation.

Like a limited partnership and corporation, a limited liability company may be formed only by complying with a state enabling statute. The limited liability company form originated in German law in 1892 and has been commonly used in Europe and Latin America. The first American statutes were passed in Wyoming in 1977 and Florida in 1982. Other states, however, showed little interest because the Internal Revenue Service treated limited liability companies as corporations for tax purposes. The IRS's attitude changed in 1988, when it issued a revenue ruling interpreting the Wyoming statute that permitted a limited liability company lacking certain corporate characteristics to be taxed as a partnership. This approach was replaced in 1997 by IRS regulations that allow any unincorporated business association to elect to be taxed as either a corporation or a partnership.[35] With this favorable tax treatment, the limited liability company has become a viable alternative organizational form, and all states now have limited liability company enabling statutes. Though the various state statutes are not identical, they are similar, and may become uniform if the **Uniform Limited Liability**

---

[24]ULPA §601(b).
[25]ULPA §602(b).
[26]ULPA §603, 604.
[27]ULPA §607(a).
[28]ULPA §§602(a)(3), 605(a)(5).
[29]ULPA §702(a)(2).
[30]ULPA §801.
[31]ULPA §802.
[32]ULPA §812(a)(6).
[33]ULPA §503.

---

[34]As discussed in Chapter 42, a corporation is an entity for tax purposes, meaning that corporate income may be taxed both at the corporate level and later when distributed to the shareholders as dividends. Also, corporate losses cannot immediately be used by shareholders to reduce their taxable income from other sources.
[35]26 C.F.R. §301.7701–3.

Company Act (ULLCA), completed in 1995, is widely adopted. For illustrative purposes, the following material is based upon the ULLCA, as amended in 1996.

Formation of a Limited Liability Company

Under the ULLCA, one or more persons may form a limited liability company by delivering "articles of organization" to the state secretary of state. The limited liability company may be organized with one or more "members," but is a legal entity distinct from its members, and may sue or be sued in its own name.[36] A limited liability company may be managed by its members like a general partnership. Alternatively, the members may relinquish management authority to managers, who may or may not also be members. In this case, management structure resembles a corporation. Unless a later date is specified, company existence begins when the articles are filed by the secretary of state, and the filing is conclusive proof that the organization has been properly created.[37] Like a limited partnership and corporation, a limited liability company must designate and continuously maintain in the state (1) an office and (2) a registered agent to receive service of process for lawsuits filed against the company.[38]

The articles of organization are required to contain minimal information about the company including: (1) its name (which must include the words "limited liability company," "limited company," or an abbreviation such as L.L.C. or L.C.); (2) the address of its office and name and address of its registered agent; (3) the name and address of each organizer; (4) whether the company is to continue in existence for a specified period, and if so, the duration of the period; (5) whether the company is to be managed by its members or by managers; and (6) whether any members of the company are to be liable for its debts. If the company is manager-managed, the name and address of each manager also must be included. The organizers may, but are not required to, include other information in the articles, and may subsequently amend the articles if filed information changes or was initially erroneous.[39]

Article 10 of the ULLCA contains provisions governing a foreign limited liability company, one transacting business in one state, but organized under the limited liability company law of another state. Generally, the law of the state of organization governs the formation of the company and the relationship among its members. The foreign limited liability company must, however, obtain a "certificate of authority" to lawfully transact business in states other than its state of organization. The procedure for obtaining (and the consequences of failure to obtain) a certificate of authority are similar to those governing foreign corporations, discussed in Chapter 45.

Relationship Among Members

Like a partnership and limited partnership, the relationship among members of a limited liability company is governed by contract, the "operating agreement." In the absence of explicit agreement, the ULLCA supplies important "default" or "gap filling" rules[40] discussed below.

Capital Contribution and Compensation. A member's capital contribution may consist of any tangible or intangible property including money, promissory notes, and services performed or to be performed. A member or his estate is legally obligated to make any required contribution, and is conversely entitled to be reimbursed by the company for payments made or liabilities incurred in the ordinary course of company business. Profits and losses are shared equally; a member is not entitled to further compensation except for services rendered in liquidating the business.[41]

Management Responsibilities. Management responsibilities vary depending upon whether the company is managed by members or managers. Note that a limited liability company is member-managed unless it is designated as manager-managed in its articles of organization. In a member-managed company, rules analogous to a general partnership apply. Each member has an equal voice in management and control and, except as discussed below, business decisions are made by majority vote. In a manager-managed company, the managers have exclusive right to manage and conduct the business. Ordinary business decisions are made by the manager or a majority of the managers (if there is more than one).[42]

Although most business decisions are made by majority vote of members or managers, the ULLCA requires the consent of all members for certain extraordinary

---

[36]ULLCA §§201, 202.
[37]ULLCA §§202(b), (c).
[38]ULLCA §108.
[39]ULLCA §§105, 203, 204, 207.

[40]ULLCA §103(a).
[41]ULLCA §§401, 402, 403, 405(a).
[42]ULLCA §§404(a),(b).

actions including, for example (1) amendment of the operating agreement, (2) amendment of the articles of organization, (3) compromising a member's obligation to make a contribution to the company, (4) admitting a new member, (5) using company property to redeem a member's interest subject to a charging order, (6) dissolution or merger of the company, and (7) transfer of all or substantially all of the company's property.[43]

Duties of Members and Managers. Members (of a member-managed company) and managers (of a manager-managed company) owe the company and its other members duties of care, loyalty, and good faith virtually identical to those existing in a general partnership.[44] Note that in a manager-managed company, members who are not also managers have no duties to the company or its members.[45] In all cases, as in a partnership, members have rights to inspect books and records and to be kept informed of the company's business and affairs.[46]

Members and Third Parties

A member of a member-managed limited liability company, and a manager of a manager-managed company are, like general partners, agents of the company for the purpose of its business. Therefore, the act of a member or manager "for apparently carrying on in the ordinary course the company's business or business of the kind carried on by the company" binds the company unless the member or manager "had no authority to act for the company in the particular matter" and the third party knew or had received a notification of the member's or manager's lack of authority.[47] Note that in a manager-managed company, a member is not an agent of the company solely because she is a member.[48] In addition to contract liability, the company is liable for injuries caused to third parties by the negligence or other tort of a member or manager acting with authority or in the ordinary course of company business.[49]

As noted above, the methods used to impose liability on a limited liability company are similar to those used

in a general partnership. The extent of that liability, however, is different. All debts or obligations of the limited liability company, whether arising in contract, tort, or otherwise, are solely those of the company. A member or manager is not personally liable on a company debt solely because he is a member or manager.[50] This is the primary characteristic distinguishing a limited liability company from a general or limited partnership, in which some or all owners have unlimited personal liability for firm debts.

At issue in the following case was whether the members of a limited liability company should be held personally liable for a company debt.

Water, Waste & Land, Inc. v. Lanham
955 P.2d 997 (Colo. 1998)

Donald Lanham and Larry Clark were managers and members of Preferred Income Investors, L.L.C. (P.I.I. or the Company), a limited liability company organized under Colorado law. Water, Waste & Land, Inc. is a corporation, doing business under the name "Westec," that provides land development and engineering services. Clark contacted Westec about performing engineering work for a restaurant project planned by P.I.I. During a meeting on the project, Clark gave his business card to a Westec representative. The card listed Clark's name, Lanham's address, and the initials "P.I.I." above the address. The company's name was not on the card, and there was no indication what "P.I.I." meant, or that it was a limited liability company. During several months of negotiations, Westec communicated with Clark and sent written correspondence, including draft contracts, to Lanham at the address on Clark's business card. Based on Clark's oral authorization, Westec performed the engineering work and sent the bill to Lanham. After receiving no payment, Westec sued Clark, Lanham, and P.I.I. The trial court, after finding that Clark was Lanham's agent, ruled that Lanham and P.I.I. were liable for Westec's bill. On appeal, the district court reversed the judgment against Lanham. The district court held that Westec was on notice that it was dealing with a limited liability company because of the letters "P.I.I." on Clark's card and because P.I.I. had filed its articles of organization with the secretary of state as required by Colorado statute. The court ruled that only P.I.I. was liable for Westec's bill. The Colorado Supreme Court granted Westec's petition for review.

---

[43]ULLCA §404(c).
[44]Compare ULLCA §409 with RUPA §404, discussed in Chapter 42.
[45]ULLCA §409(h)(1).
[46]Compare ULLCA §408 with RUPA §403, discussed in Chapter 42.
[47]ULLCA §301. This is the same rule applied to general partnerships under RUPA §301 discussed in Chapter 43.
[48]ULLCA §301(b)(1).
[49]ULLCA §302.

[50]ULLCA §303(a). As previously discussed, members may be held personally liable for all or specified company debts if a provision to that effect is included in the articles of organization. ULLCA §§203(a)(7), 303(c).

Scott, Justice

. . . In 1990, our General Assembly adopted the Limited Liability Company [LLC] Act. . . . [It] includes the same basic features of limited liability, single-tier tax treatment, and planning flexibility shared by the Uniform Limited Liability Company Act and LLC legislation adopted by other states. . . . This case requires us to decide whether the members or managers of a limited liability company are excused from personal liability on a contract where the other party to the contract did not have notice that the members or managers were negotiating on behalf of a limited liability company at the time the contract was made. . . . Resolution of the controversy between Westec and Lanham requires us to analyze the relationship between the common law of agency and the reach of our statutes governing managers and members of a limited liability company. . . .

Under the common law of agency, an agent is liable on a contract entered on behalf of a principal if the principal is not fully disclosed. In other words, an agent who negotiates a contract with a third party can be sued for any breach of the contract unless the agent discloses both the fact that he or she is acting on behalf of a principal *and* the identity of the principal. . . .

> It is not sufficient that the third party has knowledge of facts and circumstances which would, if reasonably followed by inquiry, disclose the identity of the principal. The duty of disclosure clearly lies with the agent alone; the third party with whom the agent deals has no duty to discover the existence of an agency or . . . the identity of the principal.

3A James Solheim and Kenneth Elkins, *Fletcher Cyclopedia of the Law of Private Corporations* §1120 (1994 revised volume). Thus, an agent is liable on contracts negotiated on behalf of a "partially disclosed" principal; that is, a principal whose existence — but not identity — is known to the other party.

Whether a principal is partially or completely disclosed is a question of fact. . . . [T]he district court erred in substituting its own factual determinations for the findings of the county court . . . [by concluding] that the initials "P.I.I." on Clark's business card sufficiently alerted Westec's representatives to the fact of Clark's agency relationship with the Company and to the Company's identity. . . .

In light of the partially disclosed principal doctrine, the county court's determination that Clark and Lanham failed to disclose the existence as well as the identity of the limited liability company they represented is dispositive under the common law of agency. Still, if the General Assembly has altered the common law rules applicable to this case by adopting the LLC Act, then these rules must yield in favor of the statute. We conclude, however, that the LLC Act's notice provision was not intended to alter the partially disclosed principal doctrine.

Section 7–80–208, C.R.S. (1997) states:

> The fact that the articles of organization are on file in the office of the secretary of state is notice that the limited liability company is a limited liability company and is notice of all other facts set forth therein which are required to be set forth in the articles of organization.

In order to relieve Lanham of liability, this provision would have to be read to establish a conclusive presumption that a third party who deals with the agent of a limited liability company always has constructive notice of the existence of the agent's principal. We are not persuaded that the statute can bear such an interpretation.

Such a construction exaggerates the plain meaning of the language in the statute. Section 7–80–208 could be read to state that third parties who deal with a limited liability company are always on constructive notice of the company's limited liability status, without regard to whether any part of the company's name or even the fact of its existence has been disclosed. However, an equally plausible interpretation of the words used in the statute is that once the limited liability company's name is known to the third party, constructive notice of the company's limited liability status has been given, as well as the fact that managers and members will not be liable simply due to their status as managers or members.

Moreover, the broad interpretation urged by Lanham would be an invitation to fraud, because it would leave the agent of a limited liability company free to mislead third parties into the belief that the agent would bear personal financial responsibility under any contract, when in fact, recovery would be limited to the assets of a limited liability company not known to the third party at the time the contract was made. . . .

In sum, then, section 7–80–208 places third parties on constructive notice that a fully identified company — that is, identified by a name such as "Preferred Income Investors, LLC," or the like — is a limited liability company provided that its articles of organization have been filed with the secretary of state. Section 7–80–208 is of little force, however, in determining whether a limited liability company's agent is personally liable on the theory that the agent has failed to disclose the identity of the company. . . .

For these reasons, we conclude that where an agent fails to disclose either the fact that he is acting on behalf of a principal or the identity of the principal, the notice provision of our LLC Act, section 7–80–208, cannot relieve the agent of liability to a third party. When a third party deals with an agent acting on behalf of a limited liability company, the existence and identity of which has been disclosed, the third party is conclusively presumed to know that the entity is a limited liability company and not a partnership or some other type of business organization. Where the third party does not know the identity of the principal entity, however, the situation is fundamentally different because the third party is without notice and the law does not contemplate that he has any way of finding the relevant records.

If Clark or Lanham had told Westec's representatives that they were acting on behalf of an entity known as "Preferred Income Investors, LLC" the failure to disclose the fact that the entity was a limited liability company would be irrelevant by virtue of the statute, which provides that the articles of organization operate as constructive notice of the company's limited liability form. The county court, however, found that Lanham and Clark did not identify Preferred Income Investors, LLC, as the principal in the transaction. The "missing link" between the limited disclosure made by Clark and the protection of the notice statute was the failure to state that "P.I.I.," the Company, stood for "Preferred Income Investors, LLC."

[Judgment reversed and remanded.]

Transfer of Limited Liability Company Interest

A member of a limited liability company is not a co-owner of company property, and has no interest in it that can be transferred either voluntarily or involuntarily. The limited liability company, a legal entity, owns company property. Like a general or limited partner, a member of a limited liability company may transfer only his or her "distributional interest," consisting generally of the member's share of the difference between the firm's assets and liabilities.[51] Like

a partnership interest, a distributional interest may be transferred voluntarily, involuntarily (through a charging order to a creditor to satisfy an unpaid personal debt of the member),[52] or upon death. In any case, the transferee does not become a member unless authorized in the operating agreement or all remaining members consent. The transferee therefore has no right to participate in management, to require access to information concerning the business, or to inspect books and records. Rather, the transferee simply becomes entitled to the money or property that the transferor would otherwise receive from the company.[53]

Limited Liability Companies—Dissociation, Dissolution, and Liquidation

Under the ULLCA, the events causing a member's dissociation are virtually identical to those applied to a general partnership under the RUPA.[54] The rules governing termination of the dissociated member's duties to the firm and authority also correspond to those applicable to general partnerships under the RUPA.[55]

Upon dissociation of a member, the company may dissolve and liquidate or may continue with the remaining members. Under ULLCA §801, the company is dissolved and must be liquidated if any of the following events occur:

1. an event stated in the operating agreement;
2. consent of a number or percentage of members provided in the operating agreement;
3. an event making it unlawful to continue the business;
4. a judicial determination (upon petition by an existing or dissociated member) that (a) the "economic purpose of the company is likely to be unreasonably frustrated," (b) another member's conduct has made it impracticable to continue company business with him, (c) it is "not otherwise reasonably practicable" to continue business under the articles of organization and operating agreement, (d) the company has failed to purchase the petitioning

---

[51]ULLCA §501.

[52]ULLCA §504.
[53]ULLCA §§502, 503.
[54]Compare ULLCA §601 with RUPA §601.
[55]Compare ULLCA §§603(b), 804 with RUPA §§603(b), 804.

member's interest under principles outlined below, or (e) the managers or members controlling the business are acting in an illegal, fraudulent, or oppressive manner;

5. a judicial determination (after request by a transferee of a member's interest) that it is equitable to liquidate the company either after its term expires, or at any time if the company is at will.

Upon liquidation of company assets, the proceeds are applied first to pay outside creditors, second to repay loans from members, and third to return members' cap-ital contributions. Any amount remaining is distributed equally among the members.[56]

If a member's dissociation does not trigger a dissolution and liquidation, the company is required to purchase that member's interest at its "fair value."[57] If the member's dissociation was wrongful (for example, the member withdraws in violation of an express term in the operating agreement),[58] the company's damages are offset against the purchase price. As noted above, if the company improperly fails to purchase the interest, the dissociated member may petition the court for dissolution and liquidation of the company.

Summary

1. The limited partnership, limited liability company, and the corporation are organizational forms that couple profit sharing with limited liability for losses. Limited partnerships are governed by the Uniform Limited Partnership Act (ULPA). Limited liability companies are governed by similar, but nonuniform, state enabling statutes.

2. A limited partnership is a partnership formed by two or more persons under a limited partnership statute (the ULPA) having as members one or more general partners and one or more limited partners. The general partners manage the business and have unlimited liability for firm debts unless the partnership elects Limited Liability Limited Partnership (LLLP) status. The limited partners are passive investors whose liability is generally limited to the extent of their investment. The relationship among limited and general partners is governed by the partnership agreement, supplemented by the ULPA. Unlike a general partnership which may be created informally, a limited partnership may be formed only by complying with formalities provided in the ULPA.

3. Like a limited partnership, a limited liability company may be created only by complying with the formalities provided in the relevant state enabling statute. A limited liability company may be managed either by its members (like a general partnership) or by managers (like a corporation or limited partnership, which is managed by the general partners). Unlike a limited partnership, all members of a limited liability company have limited liability for firm debts. The company is generally taxed as a partnership, and the relationship among members, and between members and third parties, is governed by principles similar to those applied in general partnership.

4. The ULPA lists the various events causing dissociation of a partner, and dissolution and liquidation of the firm. Distribution priorities upon liquidation of a limited partner-ship are determined by the ULPA, unless otherwise provided in the partnership agreement. In general, the rules governing dissociation, dissolution, and liquidation of a limited liability company are similar to those applied to general partnerships under the RUPA.

Key Terms

Uniform Limited Partnership Act (ULPA)
limited partnership
Limited Liability Limited Partnership (LLLP)

limited liability company
Uniform Limited Liability Company Act (ULLCA)

Questions and Problems

44.1 Through limited partnerships and limited liability companies, as well as corporations, the law provides an opportunity for owners of a business to avoid personal liability for business debts. Although the advantages of limited liability to the owner are obvious, it is less clear why the law allows limited liability. Discuss the policy reasons that justify allowing business owners to escape personal liability for debts of their businesses.

44.2 Discuss the advantages and disadvantages of operating a business as
(a) a limited partnership.
(b) a limited liability company.

---

[56]ULLCA §806.

[57]ULLCA §701.

[58]ULLCA §602.

44.3 Glen purchased Apple Square, a commercial office building. Three years later, he formed a limited partnership and sold the building to the limited partnership. Glen became the general partner and 25 investors purchased limited partnership interests. Two years later, the partnership offered the limited partners the opportunity to purchase additional limited partnership interests. Lou, a limited partner, wrote to Glen and asked for any additional information that he could provide that would be helpful in determining whether to buy additional interests. Glen replied, "I really do not know your investment situation and, therefore, suggest that you inspect the building and records to see if this investment is appropriate for you." Glen then told him where he could inspect the records. After purchasing an additional limited partnership interest, Lou learned that Apple Square contained hazardous asbestos and that Glen had known about the asbestos for more than two years. Lou sued Glen.

(a) Glen argued he had fulfilled his duty to Lou under the ULPA by making the building and records available for Lou's inspection. Do you agree? Explain.

(b) Has Glen violated any other duties that he owed to Lou? Explain.

44.4 Ralph purchased Mac's Restaurant for $50,000. Because he needed additional capital, he entered into a limited partnership agreement, with Arnold serving as limited partner and Ralph serving as general partner. Ralph contributed the restaurant, and Arnold contributed $50,000 cash to the limited partnership. Arnold also took a security interest in the restaurant and equipment to secure his $50,000 investment. The restaurant failed to show a profit and eventually closed owing general creditors $75,000. The general creditors have won a judgment and have requested that the court order a judicial sale of the restaurant to pay the judgment. Arnold, however, claims that he now is entitled to foreclose on the restaurant, and that the general creditors may receive the proceeds in excess of $50,000. How should the court rule? Explain.

CHAPTER 45

INTRODUCTION TO CORPORATIONS

Major Topics

- the nature and types of corporations and the development of American corporation law
- how a corporation is formed and is qualified to do business outside its state of incorporation
- the law governing transactions by persons who organize and plan the creation of a corporation
- the situations in which a defectively organized corporation will be legally recognized, and in which the existence of a duly formed corporation will be disregarded

Although the partnership provides a flexible and easily created organizational form for many businesses, it has a number of disadvantages. Partners have unlimited personal liability for firm debts and obligations. Partnerships often are of limited duration and ownership interests are difficult to transfer. As the number of investors increases, lack of centralized management may make operating the partnership unwieldy. In addition, new partners participate in management, making it difficult to raise large amounts of equity capital without diluting control. To remedy these and other problems, the law has developed additional organizational forms, the limited partnership, the limited liability company, and the business corporation. The first two of these forms are discussed in Chapter 44. The business corporation, the dominant form of organization for modern business, is discussed in this and the following three chapters.

The Law of Corporations

Nature of a Corporation

A **corporation** is recognized as a legal entity, existing apart from, and independent of, its owners or investors. That is, provided certain statutory formalities are met, the law recognizes a corporation as a fictitious being or artificial person. The corporate person is owned by shareholders, or stockholders, who transfer assets to it in exchange for shares of stock. The shareholders do not manage the corporation directly, but rather elect directors who have a statutory responsibility to manage or direct its business and affairs. The directors, in turn, appoint officers who handle the day-to-day operation of the business.

The corporation has unlimited liability for corporate obligations. Its owners, the shareholders, are generally liable only to the extent of their investment. They enjoy limited liability because corporate debts are obligations of the artificial person, the corporation, not the shareholders. The corporation is not affected by changes in ownership. Existing shareholders may die, file for bankruptcy, or transfer their shares, and new investors may be added by the sale of additional stock without affecting the corporation. Like a natural person, the corporation can own property, enter into contracts, sue, and be sued. Similarly, corporations may be subject to criminal liability and are entitled to many of the protections accorded natural persons in the federal and state constitutions.

Types of Corporations

Corporations commonly are classified as either "public" or "private." A **public corporation** (sometimes called a "municipal" or "political" corporation) is one created by the government for political purposes to administer civil government, often vested with local legislative powers. Examples include cities, counties, towns, and school districts. The federal government also has created public corporations, such as the Federal Deposit Insurance Corporation, to administer specific federal programs. **Private corporations** are those formed by private individuals for private purposes and include generally nonprofit and business corporations. **Nonprofit corporations** include, for example, those organized for religious, educational, or philanthropic purposes. Income from such corporations is applied to the specific purpose or purposes for which the organization is created (such as to provide scholarships), rather than the personal enrichment of the persons who own or operate it. In contrast, **business corporations** generally include those organized to carry on a definite business for profit.

Closely-Held and Publicly-Held Corporations. Business corporations are often described as either "closely-held" or "publicly-held." A **closely-held corporation** (sometimes called a "close corporation," "closed corporation," or "incorporated partnership") is one whose shares are owned by one shareholder or a closely knit group of shareholders. The vast majority of business corporations are closely held and they usually, though not necessarily, are relatively small business enterprises. In the typical closely-held corporation, all or most of the shareholders are also directors or officers, no public market exists for the corporation's shares, and the parties may impose restrictions on transfer of shares. In short, most closely-held

corporations operate internally like proprietorships or partnerships, but use the corporate form for limited liability or tax advantages.

A **publicly-held corporation** is one whose shares are owned by many people. Examples of publicly-held corporations are those that have shares traded on established securities exchanges, or for which public share price quotations exist. Unlike shareholders in closely-held corporations, those in publicly-held corporations have little voice in management. Their participation is limited to electing corporate directors and voting upon major corporate changes. In addition, shares are freely transferable, with a public market for the shares.

Despite significant differences between closely- and publicly-held corporations, both are generally organized and operate under the same state corporation statutes governing all corporations. Some states, however, provide special provisions addressing specific problems of closely-held corporations.

Professional Corporations. The **professional corporation** or association is a closely-held corporation formed by professionals such as doctors, lawyers, accountants, and engineers. All states and the District of Columbia have passed enabling statutes allowing professionals to incorporate. These statutes normally require that all shareholders of the corporation be licensed in the particular profession involved.

C and S Corporations. As noted in Chapter 42, a corporation, unlike a partnership, limited partnership, and limited liability company, is an entity for federal income tax purposes. As a result, the income of most corporations (known as "C" corporations) is subject to "double taxation," first to the corporation on its tax return, and then to the shareholders on their individual returns when the income is distributed as dividends. To avoid this result, certain corporations may elect to be taxed under Subchapter S of the Internal Revenue Code. Such an "S" corporation pays no income tax at the corporate level; rather, the income is passed through the corporation and taxed directly to the shareholders on their individual returns in a manner somewhat similar to a partnership. To qualify for the Subchapter S election, the corporation may have no more than 100 shareholders and one class of stock and must meet other requirements of the federal tax code.

Development of American Corporation Law

Unlike a partnership, which may be created by informal agreement of the parties, a corporation is created only by complying with a statute authorizing or enabling business organization in the corporate form. The federal government has no express power to authorize incorporation and has not generally sought to regulate incorporation through its enumerated powers, such as the Commerce Clause. As a result, virtually all modern business corporations are organized under state corporate enabling statutes, often known as "business corporation acts."

In the late 1700s, incorporation was an infrequently used and closely guarded legislative function granted only with specific legislative approval, that is, by "special incorporation." Spurred by the industrial revolution, however, in the early 1800s the states began enacting general incorporation statutes, which allowed persons to form corporations by complying with certain formalities without specific legislative consent.

Early general incorporation statutes often imposed limitations and restrictions regarding corporate size and duration, invested capital, and corporate powers and purposes. These restrictions were effective as long as businesses remained local. With the rise of the railroads and other interstate operations, however, businesses could shop among the various states to find the least restrictive incorporation statute. In the early twentieth century, many states began to "liberalize" their incorporation statutes to attract incorporation business. Liberalization involved, for example, provisions weakening shareholder control, abolishing maximum capitalization and indebtedness requirements, and expanding permissible corporate purposes and powers. To avoid losing incorporation business, states with restrictive statutes also were forced to relax their statutes.

The state of Delaware is the clear winner of this competition for corporate charters. Since 1899, it has had the most flexible incorporation statute, particularly attractive to large corporations and corporate management. The Delaware bar and legislature also have made a concerted and continuous effort to maintain a well-settled and predictable body of corporate law. Their efforts have been very successful in attracting large corporations, and many states have modeled their business corporation acts upon the Delaware statute.

Sources of Corporation Law

Although Delaware law has distinct advantages for incorporation of large, publicly-held, interstate businesses, most small businesses are incorporated under the law of the jurisdiction in which their property and principal place of business are located. In many jurisdictions, corporation law is heavily influenced by the **Model Business Corporation Act (MBCA),** which was drafted by a committee of the American Bar Association. The MBCA was first published as a complete statute in 1950 and is today the basis of, or influenced the drafting of, incorporation statutes in many states. The Act has been amended many times since its first publication and was completely overhauled and renumbered in 1984 in the **Revised Model Business Corporation Act (RMBCA).** These model acts are designed to balance the interests of management, the shareholders, corporations, and the public.

Although state competition to attract local incorporation business and the MBCA have tended to promote uniformity in corporate law, substantial differences remain among the various jurisdictions. Even among MBCA jurisdictions, significant differences are found because the Act has been frequently amended and is intended merely as a drafting guide, not a uniform statute. For this reason, this text discusses generally applied corporate law principles, with specific statutory provisions from the RMBCA used for illustrative purposes.[1]

The law of corporations is derived not only from state corporate enabling statutes, but also from other important statutory and common law sources. For example, publicly-held corporations must comply with many federal and state statutes that regulate the conduct and operation of larger corporations. For example, major regulatory statutes govern the law of securities regulation, antitrust, employment, labor relations, and pollution control. These statutes are discussed in detail in Chapters 49–55 of the text. In addition to statutes, corporation law is based heavily on general common law agency principles discussed in Chapters 40 and 41. A corporation is an artificial person, which acts only through agents.

---

[1]Examples are based on the RMBCA as amended through 2005.

Incorporation and Admission

Persons desiring to create a corporation must comply with the formation procedures stated in the business corporation statute of the state chosen for incorporation. Once the corporation is created, the parties also must take steps to qualify it to do business in states outside the jurisdiction in which it is incorporated.

Procedures for Incorporation

Although the details vary among the states, the procedure for incorporation is similar. One or more persons (who may be corporations themselves), known as incorporators, prepare a document usually known as the articles of incorporation.[2] The articles of incorporation are then delivered, together with any necessary fee, to an appropriate state official, usually the secretary of state, who reviews the application. If the articles conform to legal requirements, the secretary will issue a certificate of incorporation. Typically, corporate existence begins either when the secretary of state issues the certificate or on the date the articles are filed by the secretary of state. In some states, additional requirements must be met, such as filing or recording in a local office or publishing the articles in a newspaper.

Contents of Articles. The articles of incorporation must contain certain information prescribed by statute. In many states, official forms for the articles are used. Although the contents of the articles vary among the states, modern corporate statutes tend to minimize the mandatory requirements of the articles. For example, under the RMBCA, the articles need only state (1) the name of the corporation, (2) the number of shares of stock that the corporation is authorized to issue, (3) the address of the registered office and the name of the corporation's registered agent, and (4) the name and address of each incorporator.[3] In addition to mandatory information, the articles may contain provisions concerning regulation of the internal affairs of the corporation. The following material elaborates upon certain typical provisions of the articles.

Corporate Name. Generally, the corporate name must include language indicating corporate form such as "corporation," "company," "incorporated," or "limited,"

and may not be the same as or deceptively similar to any other corporate name. Secretaries of state generally maintain lists of existing corporate names against which new corporate applications are checked. The prohibition against deceptively similar names is designed to prevent unfair competition.

Corporate names generally are allocated on a first-come, first-served basis. Many corporation statutes, however, permit reservation of available corporate names for a limited period. For example, the RMBCA allows names to be reserved, upon application to the secretary of state, for a nonrenewable 120-day period.[4]

Corporate Duration. Some older corporation statutes limited corporate duration. Virtually all modern statutes permit perpetual corporate existence, which often is presumed unless a limited period of duration is stated in the articles.

Corporate Purposes. Although many statutes require that corporate purposes be fully stated, the modern trend is to authorize extremely broad corporate purposes clauses, or to dispense with them entirely. For example, the RMBCA does not require that the articles contain a purposes clause, but simply presumes that every corporation is organized to conduct any lawful business unless a narrower purpose is outlined in the articles of incorporation. Certain purposes, however, are beyond the scope of even a broadly drafted purposes clause. For example, banks and insurance companies are regulated under separate statutes and may therefore not be incorporated under the state's general business corporation act.[5]

Registered Office and Agent. A corporation is required to maintain a registered office with a registered agent in the state of incorporation. The registered office need not be the corporation's place of business. The registered agent is the corporation's agent to receive service of process on the corporation, other notices or demands, and official communications from the state. A corporation that fails to maintain a registered agent may, under the RMBCA, be served by registered or certified mail, addressed to the secretary of the corporation at its principal office. Changes in the registered office or agent may be made by filing a statement outlining the change with the secretary of state.[6]

---

[2]See, for example, RMBCA §2.01.
[3]RMBCA §2.02(a).

[4]RMBCA §4.02.
[5]RMBCA §§2.02(b), 3.01.
[6]RMBCA §§5.01–5.04.

Organization of the Corporation. After the certificate of incorporation is issued, the directors named in the articles hold a meeting to complete the organization of the corporation. If directors are not named in the articles, the incorporators hold the meeting.[7] This meeting often is orchestrated by the parties' attorney, with minutes prepared in advance to assure that all necessary legal formalities have been met. At the meeting, typically, directors are formally elected, officers are appointed to manage the corporation, preincorporation contracts are adopted or rejected, shares of stock are issued and consideration for shares is established, a resolution is made to open a corporate bank account that designates the persons authorized to sign checks, and a corporate seal is adopted. In addition, corporate bylaws, if desired, are adopted.

Bylaws are a set of rules governing the corporation's internal affairs. Bylaws may contain any provision for the management of corporate affairs not inconsistent with law or the articles of incorporation. Unlike the articles of incorporation, the bylaws are not filed with the secretary of state. Under the RMBCA, both the shareholders and the board of directors may make, amend, or repeal the corporation's bylaws, unless that power is reserved exclusively to the shareholders in the articles of incorporation.[8] Bylaws generally may be amended much more easily than the articles of incorporation.

Corporate Powers

Statutory Powers. To implement the corporate purposes stated in the articles of incorporation, every state corporation statute includes an extensive list of powers possessed by businesses incorporated in the jurisdiction. For example, §3.02 of the RMBCA provides that each corporation has the power

1. to have perpetual existence, unless limited in the articles of incorporation;
2. to sue, be sued, and defend in the corporate name;
3. to acquire, own, hold, improve, and use any interest in either real or personal property including stocks or bonds;
4. to sell, convey, mortgage, pledge, lease, or otherwise transfer any or all of its property;
5. to lend money and take a security interest in either real or personal property to secure its repayment;
6. to make contracts and guarantees (that is, act as a surety), to borrow money and issue notes, bonds, or other obligations that may be secured by corporate assets;
7. to make charitable contributions;
8. to be the member of any partnership or joint venture;
9. to exercise other powers necessary and convenient to effect its purposes including the power to conduct its business, maintain offices, elect officers and directors, adopt bylaws regulating its internal affairs, and establish pensions, profit-sharing, and other incentive plans for its officers, directors, and employees.

This enumeration gives a corporation virtually the same powers as a natural person. Although not always legally required,[9] articles of incorporation often include powers clauses which restate or expand upon the statutory list, or provide more limited corporate powers.

"Ultra Vires" Acts. A corporation that acts beyond the scope of its powers or stated purposes acts ***ultra vires.*** *Ultra vires* acts include both those expressly prohibited and those in excess of granted powers or purposes. Because modern corporation statutes authorize extremely general purposes clauses (for example, "the transaction of any or all lawful business"), few corporate activities are *ultra vires.* In addition, even if corporate purposes or powers are restricted, the RMBCA and many state statutes provide that no corporate act or conveyance is invalid because the corporation lacked the power to act, except in three limited circumstances: (1) a suit by a shareholder against the corporation to enjoin it from doing an act, (2) a proceeding by the corporation against incumbent or former officers or directors for their unauthorized acts, and (3) a suit by the state attorney general to dissolve the corporation or to enjoin it from transacting unauthorized business.[10]

Admission of Foreign Corporations

A corporation organized under the laws of a given state is referred to as a **domestic corporation** in that state.

---

[7]RMBCA §2.05.
[8]See, for example, RMBCA §§2.06, 10.20.

[9]See, for example, RMBCA §2.02(c).
[10]RMBCA §3.04.

For example, in Illinois, a corporation incorporated under the laws of Illinois is a domestic corporation. If such a corporation does business in another state, it is referred to as a **foreign corporation** in that state. Thus, an Illinois corporation doing business in Indiana is a foreign corporation in Indiana.

Because corporate status is a privilege granted by state law, foreign corporations must qualify to do business in states outside the state of incorporation. In order to qualify, the corporation must obtain a "certificate of authority" from the secretary of state of each state in which it is a foreign corporation. To obtain a certificate of authority, the foreign corporation must generally file an application with the secretary of state. The foreign corporation also must file a verified copy of its articles of incorporation and pay all required fees or taxes. If the application is in order, the secretary of state will issue the certificate that authorizes the corporation to transact business in the state for the purposes set forth in the application.[11]

Once authorized to do business, the foreign corporation must continuously maintain both a registered office and a registered agent in the state.[12] Under the RMBCA, if the foreign corporation fails to maintain a registered agent in the state or if its certificate of authority has been suspended or revoked, the corporation may be served by registered or certified mail, addressed to the secretary of the corporation at its principal office.[13]

Until it obtains a certificate of authority, a foreign corporation is denied the use of the courts of the state; it is not permitted to maintain any action or suit in the state with respect to its business. Failure to obtain the certificate, however, neither prevents the corporation from defending a suit in the state, nor impairs the validity of any contract the corporation makes. A foreign corporation, that transacts business without a certificate of authority is liable for all fees or franchise taxes that would have been imposed if the corporation had obtained the certificate, and for all penalties imposed for failure to pay the fees or taxes. Proceedings to recover these amounts are brought by the state attorney general.[14]

---

[11]See, for example, RMBCA §§15.01, 15.03, 15.05.
[12]See, for example, RMBCA §15.07.
[13]RMBCA §15.10.
[14]See, for example, RMBCA §15.02.

Promoter and Shareholder Liability

After a corporation has been properly formed, the corporation, now a legal entity, is liable for its debts, and the shareholders have only limited liability. That is, a shareholder's liability for corporate debts is limited to the amount he or she has invested in the business. Occasionally, however, courts impose personal liability for corporate debts on shareholders (and in some cases nonshareholders acting on behalf of the corporation) if a properly formed corporation is not in existence. Alternatively, a court may "pierce the corporate veil" to impose personal liability on shareholders of a duly formed corporation if the shareholders have abused the corporate form. The principles governing these issues are discussed below.

Liability for Preincorporation Transactions

As discussed earlier in this chapter, a corporation comes into existence only upon compliance with the procedures outlined in the appropriate state business corporation statute. Before these steps are taken and, therefore, before corporate existence begins, the person or persons organizing and planning the corporation, known as **promoters,** often enter into contracts or other transactions on behalf of the corporation yet to be formed. Promoters' activities include, for example, discovering and developing the business opportunity, arranging the necessary capital, obtaining the property and personnel required to conduct the business, and complying with the statutory formalities for forming the corporation.

The corporation may be formed before activities on its behalf are taken. In this case, authorized contracts made in the corporate name are binding upon the corporation but not the promoter under ordinary principles of agency. Frequently, however, the corporation is not yet in existence during the promotional stage. In this case, the law must determine (1) to what extent the promoters are personally liable upon contracts made with third parties on behalf of the corporation, and (2) to what extent the corporation, upon coming into existence, is liable upon contracts made by the promoters. Basic principles, borrowed generally from the law of agency and contracts, govern these issues.

Liability of the Promoter. A promoter who contracts on behalf of a corporation not yet formed, without disclosing that fact, is personally liable on the contract. In addition, a promoter who represents that the corporation is in existence, when in fact it is not, incurs personal liability to the third party for breach of the warranty of competent principal made by agents generally, or upon misrepresentation grounds. More commonly, however, a promoter contracts for the corporation and discloses to the third party that the corporation is not yet formed. In this case, the result depends upon how the parties characterize the transaction. For example, the promoter might escape personal liability if the arrangement is framed as a revocable or irrevocable offer running to the corporation, to be accepted or rejected after formation. Or the arrangement may provide that the promoter is initially bound but will be released if the corporation is later formed and assumes liability on the contract. That is, the promoter and third party may contract in advance for a novation, releasing the promoter and substituting the corporation. Alternatively, the parties may provide that the promoter remains liable, even if the corporation is formed and assumes liability on the contract. To avoid litigation, the extent of the promoter's undertaking should be carefully drafted into the agreement between the promoter and third party.

Liability of the Corporation. The corporation, upon coming into existence, is not immediately liable upon promoters' contracts. That is, the promoter cannot bind the corporation as its agent because the corporation (the principal) was not in existence when the contract was made. For the same reason, the corporation does not generally incur liability by "ratifying" promoters' contracts, as that term is used in agency law. Rather, the corporation becomes liable by "accepting" the third party's offer, or "adopting" or "assuming" the contract, or by taking an "assignment" of the contract from the promoter. However characterized, corporate liability requires some affirmative act by the corporation indicating its assent to the preincorporation transaction.

The following case illustrates promoters' liability principles.

Coopers & Lybrand v. Fox
758 P.2d 683 (Colo.App. 1988)

In November 1981, defendant Garry Fox met with a representative of plaintiff Coopers & Lybrand (Coopers), a national accounting firm, to request tax and accounting services for G. Fox and Partners, Inc., a new corporation

that Fox was forming. With knowledge that the corporation was not yet in existence, Coopers agreed to perform the services. G. Fox and Partners, Inc. was incorporated on December 4, 1981, and Coopers completed its services later that month. After rendering a bill that was not paid, Coopers sued Fox for breach of contract. The trial court found that Coopers failed to prove that Fox individually had agreed to pay the firm's bill and ruled in favor of Fox. Coopers appealed.

Kelly, Chief Judge

. . . As a preliminary matter, we reject Fox's argument that he was acting only as an agent for the future corporation. One cannot act as the agent of a nonexistent principal. . . .

On the contrary, the uncontroverted facts place Fox squarely within the definition of a promoter. A promoter is one who, alone or with others, undertakes to form a corporation and to procure for it the rights, instrumentalities, and capital to enable it to conduct business. . . .

When Fox first approached Coopers, he was in the process of forming G. Fox and Partners, Inc. He engaged Coopers' services for the future corporation's benefit. In addition, though not dispositive on the issue of his status as a promoter, Fox became the president, a director, and the principal shareholder of the corporation, which he funded, only nominally, with a $100 contribution. Under these circumstances, Fox cannot deny his role as a promoter. . . .

As a general rule, promoters are personally liable for the contracts they make, though made on behalf of a corporation to be formed. . . . The well recognized exception to the general rule of promoter liability is that if the contracting party knows the corporation is not in existence but nevertheless agrees to look solely to the corporation and not to the promoter for payment, then the promoter incurs no personal liability. . . . In the absence of an express agreement, the existence of an agreement to release the promoter from liability may be shown by circumstances making it reasonably certain that the parties intended to and did enter into the agreement. . . .

Here, the trial court found there was no agreement, either express or implied, regarding Fox's liability. Thus, in the absence of an agreement releasing him from liability, Fox is liable. . . .

It is undisputed that the defendant, Garry J. Fox, engaged Coopers' services, that G. Fox and Partners, Inc., was not in existence at that time, that Coopers performed the work, and that the fee was reasonable. The only dispute, as the trial court found, is whether Garry Fox is liable for payment of the fee. We conclude that Fox is liable, as a matter of law, under the doctrine of promoter liability. . . .

[Judgment reversed and remanded.]

Promoters' Fiduciary Duties. Frequently, two or more persons are actively involved in promoting a corporation. During the promotional stage, co-promoters are treated as joint venturers or partners, and therefore owe each other the strict fiduciary duties of fair dealing and disclosure generally existing among partners. Promoters also owe similar fiduciary duties to the corporation and its shareholders after incorporation. For example, a promoter who sells property to the corporation in exchange for stock or cash owes duties of good faith, fair dealing, and full disclosure to the corporation's board of directors and shareholders. Secret profits obtained by the promoter in violation of these duties may be recovered by the corporation.

Defective Incorporation

A ***de jure*** **corporation** is one formed in compliance with all mandatory state requirements. A *de jure* corporation is recognized as a corporation for all purposes and its existence is not subject to attack either by the state or by creditors.

The incorporators may, however, attempt to comply with the provisions authorizing corporate status but fail in some respect, resulting either in delay in or failure of corporate formation. For example, the secretary of state may return the initial application to correct a technical defect, or the parties may prepare but inadvertently fail to file the articles. Despite the problem, the parties conduct business as a corporation. Subsequently, firm creditors seek to hold the shareholders personally liable as partners for business debts, citing the defective incorporation. In this situation the common law has recognized two doctrines to protect shareholders of the defectively organized corporation: the "*de facto* incorporation doctrine" and "corporation by estoppel."

Under the traditional test, a ***de facto* corpora-tion** is created if (1) an enabling statute exists permitting corporate form, (2) the parties have made a good faith effort to comply with the statute, and (3) the parties subsequently conduct business as a corporation. If these requirements are met, only the state can challenge corporate existence. Third parties, such as creditors, may not assert lack of corporate status as a basis to impose personal liability on the owners.

Another common law doctrine used to insulate owners of defectively organized corporations is **corporation by estoppel.** This doctrine has been applied, for example, when a third party transacts business with a corporation, unaware of its defective organization and relying solely upon the corporation's credit. Subsequently, after discovering that a corporation has not been formed, the third party seeks to hold the promoters or shareholders personally liable on the obligation as partners. On these facts, courts often estop, or prevent, the third party from holding the owners personally liable. Courts have reasoned that it is unjust to allow a person who has relied only upon corporate credit to impose personal liability upon shareholders and promoters, especially when the failure of incorporation was not caused by negligence or willful failure to comply with statutory requirements.

The problem of defective incorporation often is addressed explicitly by statute. For example, under §2.03 of the RMBCA, the secretary of state's filing of the articles of incorporation begins corporate existence and is conclusive evidence that all conditions precedent to proper incorporation have been met. Subsequently, corporate existence may be attacked only by the state in a proceeding to cancel or revoke the certificate of incorporation or for involuntary dissolution of the corporation. Under this approach, if the secretary of state accepts and files the articles, a de jure corporation is created, despite technical defects in the filing. Because any steps short of obtaining filing by the secretary of state do not constitute substantial or apparent compliance, a number of courts have concluded that the RMBCA and similar statutes have abolished both the *de facto* incorporation doctrine and corporation by estoppel principles.

Disregarding Corporate Existence — "Piercing the Corporate Veil"

Because the primary purpose of corporate form is limited personal liability for its shareholders, courts generally recognize the separate legal existence of a corporation formed in full compliance with state law. Accordingly, if a corporation incurs debts in excess of its assets, unpaid corporate creditors have no recourse against the corporation's shareholders. To prevent fraud or injustice, however, courts in certain limited circumstances disregard the corporate entity, or "pierce the corporate veil," to impose personal liability upon shareholders for corporate obligations.

Cases that impose shareholder responsibility for corporate debt often include some or all of the following characteristics: (1) insufficient capital contributed to the business in relation to the nature of the business and its risks, (2) failure to observe corporate formalities, such as meetings and issuance of stock, (3) failure to separate corporate from shareholder affairs, such as failure to keep separate corporate records, commingling shareholder and corporate assets, or paying personal debts with corporate assets (or vice versa), or (4) evidence of affirmative wrongdoing or fraud such as creating the corporation to avoid an existing obligation or siphoning off corporate funds by a dominant shareholder. Cases on piercing the corporate veil most commonly arise in one-person, family, or other closely-held corporations (for example, when the corporation is used merely as a facade for the shareholders' personal dealings) and in subsidiary or other affiliated corporations (for example, when a corporation uses an undercapitalized subsidiary to undertake a particularly risky venture, or divides a single business into a number of separate, undercapitalized corporations).

The corporate claim asserted against the shareholders may result either from a contract between the creditor and the corporation, or from a tort committed by a corporate agent for which the corporation is liable. For example, a person injured in an auto accident by the negligent driving of a corporate agent may seek to recover from the corporation under the theory of *respondeat superior,* discussed in Chapter 41.

In the following contract case, the court was required to decide whether shareholders should be held personally liable on a corporate obligation.

Kvassay v. Murray

808 P.2d 896 (Kan. App. 1991)

In 1984, Michael Kvassay contracted to sell 24,000 cases of the pastry baklava to defendant Great American Foods, Inc. (Great American), a corporation owned by defendants Albert and Deana Murray. The Murrays frequently wrote personal checks to Kvassay for payments due under the contract because checks issued by Great American were dishonored for insufficient funds. After Great American failed to complete performance of the contract, Kvassay sued for breach of contract and a jury awarded him $35,674 in damages. Kvassay further requested the trial court to pierce the corporate veil to hold the Murrays personally liable for the judgment. The evidence established that the Murrays also owned a corporation named Great American Subs, Inc., which operated fast-food restaurants and controlled another business known as Murray Investments. The Murrays additionally used a bank account held in the name of Great American Distributors, Inc. although no incorporation papers had been filed under that name. All of their businesses were operated from one address in Wichita, Kansas. After the trial court ruled that the Murrays were personally liable for Great American's debts, the Murrays appealed.

Walker, Judge

. . . Each case involving disregard of the corporate entity must rest upon its special facts. . . . Before examining the record to determine if there is sufficient competent evidence to support the trial court's decision, it is helpful to understand when Kansas courts have determined that piercing the corporate veil is appropriate.

We start with the basic premise that a corporation and its stockholders are presumed separate and distinct, whether the corporation has many stockholders or only one. Debts of a corporation are not the individual indebtedness of its stockholders. However, in an appropriate case the corporate form will be disregarded and the corporation and its stockholders may be treated as identical. . . . Power to pierce the corporate veil is to be exercised reluctantly and cautiously. . . . *Amoco Chemicals Corporation v. Bach,* [567 P.2d 1337 (Kan. 1977)]. . . .

In determining whether disregarding the corporate entity is appropriate, eight factors have been considered:

"(1) undercapitalization of a . . . corporation, (2) failure to observe corporate formalities, (3) nonpayment of dividends, (4) siphoning of corporate funds by the dominant stockholder, (5) nonfunctioning of other officers or directors, (6) absence of corporate records, (7) the use of the corporation as a facade for operations of the dominant stockholder or stockholders, and (8) the use of the corporate entity in promoting injustice or fraud." [*Sampson v. Hunt*, 665 P.2d 743 (Kan. 1983).]

The trial court made several factual findings which, when considered in light of the eight factors, provide sufficient foundation for disregarding the corporate entity.

1. *Undercapitalization of the corporation.* The trial court found that, while the Murrays loaned approximately $250,000 to Great American from mild-1983 until the end of 1984, the infusions of cash were made on an "as needed" basis. Further, sometimes the loans were deposits in corporate accounts while at other times the Murrays simply paid corporate debts from their personal accounts. The record is filled with evidence to support these findings. An audit completed at the end of 1984 showed Great American's total corporate funding included $15,000 in common stock and $21,728 in "[c]ontributed capital in excess of par value." In addition, the corporation held inventory valued at $160,371 and property and equipment valued at approximately $38,000. When $37,000 in original capital investment in Great American is viewed in light of the fact that Kvassay's contract required that Great American pay $456,000 in one year and the Murrays only loaned the company funds when shortages occurred, it is clear there is substantial evidence in the record to support the conclusion that the corporation was "never capitalized, except on a haphazard and as needed basis."

2. *Failure to observe corporate formalities.* The trial court concluded the Murrays failed to observe corporate formalities, basing its decision in part on the absence of a number of required corporate records, as well as a complete failure to record most of the financial transactions between the Murrays and their various entities. Further, the court noted Great American failed to file annual corporate reports for 1983 and 1984 with the Secretary of State until October 1985. The court also noted that, while the Murrays started Great American Distributors to conduct the business of Great American Foods, there was never any effort to change Great American Foods' corporate name or to register Great American Distributors. . . . [T]here is substantial competent evidence to show Great American Foods and the Murrays failed to abide by general corporate formalities.

3. *Nonpayment of dividends.* There is no evidence in the record that dividends were ever paid by Great American.

4. *Siphoning of corporate funds by the dominant stockholder.* The trial court noted that no ledgers or journals of expenses paid or income received were maintained by Great American Foods or by Great American Subs and that accounting records for the firm were reconstructed on the basis of checks issued, without any accompanying invoices or receipts, making it impossible to determine what the corporate payments covered. The court did note that Great American paid health club dues for the Murrays. The Murrays received a number of payments from Great American but the court noted that, since no employment contracts existed between the Murrays and Great American, it was impossible to determine the reasonableness or basis of such payments. In addition, the trial court found that Deana Murray withdrew $6,000 on September 2, 1983, from Great American Foods, and Albert Murray withdrew $1,500 on September 24, 1984, from Great American Distributors. Albert testified that he and his wife frequently paid the bills of their various corporations with personal checks and often wrote themselves checks on corporate accounts. In addition, there were times when the corporations would pay the Murrays' personal expenses or expenses of other Murray corporations. The trial court also noted that, on August 31, 1984, Great American Distributors obtained a line of credit, of which $25,000 was deposited in Great American Subs' account. The same day, Great American Subs deposited $26,000 in a Great American Distributors' account.

5. *Nonfunctioning of other officers or directors.* This factor is not at issue here since there were no directors other than the Murrays.

6. *Absence of corporate records.* The complete absence of a number of corporate records has already been discussed.

7. *Use of corporation as facade for operations of dominant stockholders.* The trial court specifically found the Murrays used their various corporations as a facade to conduct their personal business. A number of factors already discussed, including the Murrays' complete failure to keep corporate records or to abide by corporate formalities, combined with the history of unexplained transfers of funds, provide ample evidence on which the court could base its conclusion. In addition, it was undisputed at trial that the Murrays conducted business for all of their entities and personal business from one street address in Wichita.

8. *Use of corporate entity in promoting injustice or fraud.* The trial court found the Murrays used the corporation as a facade for their own interests and, in doing so,

"worked to the injustice of the plaintiff by inducing him to enter into the contract." Great American focuses most of its argument that the corporate veil should not be pierced on this point, arguing specifically there must be proof that control of the corporation was used to commit fraud or to perpetrate a wrong and that there is no such proof.

Great American's emphasis is misplaced. Injustice alone will support a disregard of the corporate entity. . . . [T]he Murrays operated their corporations as alter egos, putting cash in when convenient and removing it when equally convenient. The Murrays conducted business with such unity of interest and ownership that the separate personalities of the corporations and themselves no longer existed. . . .

In effect, it was the Murrays together with Great American who breached the contract with Kvassay. If that breach was considered an act of Great American alone, "an inequitable result would follow" because Kvassay would be unable to collect damages to which he is entitled. . . . While the power to pierce the corporate veil is to be exercised reluctantly and cautiously, the corporate entity can be disregarded if it is used to cover fraud or to work injustice, or if necessary to achieve equity. . . .

[Judgment affirmed.]

Summary

1. The most dominant form of organization for modern business is the business corporation. A corporation is recognized as a legal entity, an artificial person existing apart from, and independent of, its owners, the shareholders, who enjoy limited liability for corporate obligations.

2. Business corporations often are classified as either publicly-held or closely-held. Whereas a publicly-held company has many shareholders whose shares are traded in a public market, a closely-held company has shares owned by one or a closely knit group of shareholders.

3. A corporation is created only by complying with state business corporation acts, which authorize or enable business organization in the corporate form. Corporation law has been heavily influenced by the flexible Delaware statute and the Revised Model Business Corporation Act.

4. A corporation is formed by complying with formalities outlined in the business corporation act of the state chosen for incorporation. Typically, one or more persons, known as "incorporators," prepare the "articles of incorporation," which then are delivered to the secretary of state. The articles contain information on the corporation's business and capital structure, its registered office, and agent. If the articles conform to law, the secretary of state files the articles or issues a certificate of incorporation, and the directors named in the articles hold a meeting to complete the organization of the corporation. Once legally created, the corporation has most of the same legal powers as a natural person.

5. If the corporation does business in states outside its state of incorporation, it must qualify to do business in those states as a foreign corporation. In order to qualify, the corporation must obtain a "certificate of authority" from the secretary of state of each state in which it is a foreign corporation. Various legal sanctions are imposed against foreign corporations that fail to obtain certificates of authority.

6. The persons organizing and planning the corporation, known as "promoters," often enter into contracts on behalf of the corporation yet to be formed. General principles of the law of agency and contracts determine (1) the liability of the promoters on contracts made with third parties on behalf of the corporation, and (2) the liability of the corporation, after coming into existence, on contracts made by the promoters. In addition to contract liability, promoters also may owe fiduciary duties to the corporation and its shareholders.

7. One purpose of incorporating is to insulate the shareholders from unlimited personal liability for corporate obligations. Corporation law, however, through the doctrines of "de facto incorporation" and "corporation by estoppel" occasionally provides limited liability to persons who do business as a corporation with out complying with corporate formalities. Conversely, in some instances, courts "pierce the corporate veil" to impose personal liability on shareholders of a duly formed corporation.

Key Terms

corporation
public corporation
private corporation
nonprofit corporation
business corporation
closely-held corporation
publicly-held corporation
professional corporation
Model Business Corporation Act (MBCA)

Revised Model Business Corporation Act (RMBCA)
bylaws
ultra vires
domestic corporation
foreign corporation
promoter
de jure corporation
de facto corporation
corporation by estoppel

Questions and Problems

45.1   Bob and Cara wanted to open a retail clothing store but needed $100,000 capital to do so. Their life savings amounted to $3,000. Nevertheless, they formed a corporation named "Craig Place Ltd." and found four investors who were willing to invest $12,000 each. Craig Place Ltd. issued 12,000 shares of stock to each of the investors. Bob and Cara promised to provide the remaining $52,000. They requested a loan from First State Bank, which refused to lend the money to Bob and Cara but agreed to lend $50,000 to Craig Place Ltd. Bob and Cara personally guaranteed the loan. They took the money, added $2,000 from their savings, and deposited it in Craig Place Ltd.'s bank account. In exchange they received 52,000 shares of stock. The retail clothing store failed. Following payment of all creditors except the bank the corporation's total assets were $40,000. First State Bank has filed a lawsuit claiming that it is entitled to the money because it is a creditor of the corporation. The four investors claim that they should receive the money.

(a) Do Bob and Cara have any liability to the corporation or minority shareholders for using a bank loan to the corporation to pay for stock issued to them? On what theory?

(b) Assuming Bob and Cara are insolvent, how should the court distribute the $40,000 remaining upon liquidation of the corporation?

(c) Would your answer in (b) be different if the investors were able to prove that the bank knew Bob and Cara were using the money to purchase their shares in Craig Place Ltd.? Explain.

45.2   On April 1, How and Associates, an architectural firm, and Ed Boss signed a written contract by which How agreed to develop an architectural plan for a hotel and restaurant complex for payment of $50,000. Ed Boss signed the contract as follows: "Ed Boss, as agent for a corporation to be formed which will be the obligor." On May 15, the Hunter Hotel Co. was incorporated. On July 1, How received a check for $10,000 from the Hunter Hotel Co. as partial payment for "architectural plans for hotel complex per contract dated April 1." The check was signed by "Ed Boss, President Hunter Hotel Corp."

(a) Assume that How completed the architectural plans but received no further payments. Is Hunter Hotel Co. liable for the $40,000 owed to How? Explain.

(b) Assume that How completed the architectural plans and then learned that Hunter Hotel Co. was insolvent. Is Ed Boss liable for the $40,000 owed to How? Explain.

(c) Assume that Ed Boss formed a new corporation called Boss Corp. on August 1 and submitted $50,000 to How "in full payment per contract dated April 1." Hunter Hotel Co. notifies How that although Ed Boss has resigned from Hunter, Hunter intends to honor its April 1 contract with How. Both Boss Corp. and Hunter request delivery of the architectural plans. With which party does How have a contract? Explain.

45.3   On October 15, 2002, Arnold personally borrowed $10,000 from First City Bank. First City required that Arnold obtain a guarantor for his promissory note. Westover, Inc., a real estate corporation of which Arnold was a director, agreed to guarantee payment of the note. On November 15, 2002, Morton and Edith purchased all of the shares of Westover. On October 15, 2003, Arnold failed to repay the note and First City sued Westover. Morton, who is now president of Westover, requests that the court refuse to enforce the guaranty on the ground that Westover acted ultra vires by guaranteeing the note. Westover's bylaws provide that it was formed for the purpose of "transacting business relating to real estate." Has the corporation acted *ultra vires*?

45.4   In January, Bennett and Davenport agreed to form a corporation called "Aero-Fabb Co." They submitted articles of incorporation to the state on January 22 in which both were named as corporate directors. Both parties actively participated in the policy and operational decisions of the organization. On February 15, Davenport, on behalf of Aero-Fabb Co., signed two contracts by which the company agreed to rent equipment from Timberline Equipment, Inc. Davenport signed one contract "Kenneth L. Davenport d/b/a Aero-Fabb Co." and the other contract "Kenneth L. Davenport d/b/a Aero-Fabb Corp." On March 1, the secretary of state notified Bennett and Davenport that the articles of incorporation that they had submitted were incomplete. They provided the additional requested information and on April 1, the state issued a certificate of incorporation to Aero-Fabb Co. The corporation was not successful and defaulted in payments on the contracts with Timberline. Timberline filed suit naming Aero-Fabb Co., Bennett, and Davenport as defendants.

(a) Bennett and Davenport alleged that the contracts were with Aero-Fabb Co., a de facto corporation. Explain what is meant by de facto corporation and why Bennett and Davenport would raise it as a defense. Assuming the doctrine is recognized in the state, can Bennett and Davenport establish it?

(b) Bennett and Davenport allege that the doctrine of corporation by estoppel precludes their being held personally liable on the contract. Explain the applicability of corporation by estoppel to these facts.

(c) The state Business Corporation Act contains the following provision:

> All persons who assume to act as a corporation without the authority of a certificate of incorporation issued by the Corporation Commissioner, shall be jointly and severally liable for all debts and liabilities incurred or arising as a result thereof.

Bennett asserts that he cannot be held personally liable on the Timberline contracts because he did not sign them. Should Bennett be held liable under the above provision? Would your answer change if Bennett was merely an investor who did not participate in management?

45.5   Trucking Brothers, Inc. is a corporation formed by Ray and Ed who each contributed $2,500 to the corporation.

Trucking Brothers is engaged in the business of selling produce on a commission basis. The growers of the produce deliver it to Trucking Brothers, which then arranges a sale to a wholesaler or retailer and delivers the produce to the purchaser. Trucking Brothers requires payment on delivery, and after deducting 25 percent as its commission, pays the grower the proceeds of sale. Trucking Brothers uses Ray's truck to deliver the produce. Frank delivered a shipment of artichokes to Trucking Brothers, which sold them to a grocery store. Trucking Brothers failed to pay Frank for the artichokes.

   (a) Frank sues Ray and Ed seeking to hold them personally liable on the contract. He alleges that the corporate veil should be disregarded because Trucking Brothers was inadequately capitalized. What factors should the court consider in determining inadequate capitalization?

   (b) Other than capitalization, what other factors might affect the court's determination? Suggest further general information that would be helpful to the court.

45.6 Archie was a cab driver in New York City. State law required that every cab carry liability insurance of at least $10,000. Archie formed five corporations; he was the sole shareholder of each corporation. Each corporation owned only one asset—a taxicab which carried $10,000 liability insurance. Archie maintained separate records for each corporation and did not intermingle corporate funds with his own funds. While riding in a taxicab owned by one of Archie's corporations, Gloria suffered serious injuries. She sued not only the corporation that owned the taxi in which she had been riding, but also the four other corporations and Archie. Gloria alleged that the court should "pierce the corporate veil" and hold Archie personally liable for her injuries. How should the court rule? Explain.

45.7 Plaintiff was injured while using fireworks distributed by Oriental Fireworks Co. Because Oriental Fireworks carried no liability insurance and had assets less than $12,000, plaintiff requested the court to pierce the corporate veil and hold J. C. Chou liable for the injuries. Evidence at trial revealed that Oriental Fireworks had never carried insurance and that its assets never exceeded $13,000. J. C. Chou owned one-half of the shares of Oriental Fireworks and his wife owned the other half. They were the only officers of the corporation. The Chous were unable to provide evidence that they had paid consideration for their shares or that the corporation had ever held meetings. No corporate records could be found. How should the court rule?

45.8 Courts must often decide whether to disregard the corporate entity to hold the shareholders liable for a corporate obligation. Should the courts apply different criteria to claims based upon contracts between the plaintiff and the corporation from those based upon a tort committed by the corporation?

CORPORATE FINANCIAL STRUCTURE

Major Topics

- an introduction to corporate financial structure
- the legal requirements governing issuance of, and payment for, shares of stock
- the law relating to ownership and transfer of corporate securities, governed by Article 8 of the Uniform Commercial Code
- a discussion of corporate dividends and other distributions of corporate assets to shareholders

Like an individual or unincorporated association, a corporation must have a source of funds to acquire assets and finance its business operations. In ongoing corporations, most funds are generated by reinvesting all or part of corporate earnings into the business. An additional, and usually the initial, method of raising corporate funds is the issuance of corporate "securities" in exchange for transfer of cash, property, or services to the corporation.

Introduction to Corporate Financial Structure

Sources of Corporate Funds

A **security** is a share, participation, or other interest in the property of the issuing corporation (an equity security),

or an obligation of the issuer (a debt security).[1] **Equity securities,** such as shares of stock, are those that create an ownership interest in the business. The owners of the equity securities, and therefore the corporation, are the shareholders or stockholders. In contrast to equity securities, which represent an investment in the business, **debt securities** represent obligations that must ultimately be repaid and create a debtor-creditor relationship between their holders and the corporation. Common debt securities include notes, debentures, and bonds. Many corporations use both debt and equity securities to finance the business, and the combination of the two for a particular corporation is known as its "capital structure."

Types of Equity Securities

A corporation's equity securities, its shares of stock, are the "units into which the proprietary interests in a corporation are divided."[2] They represent the underlying ownership interest of the corporation and confer three rights upon shareholders: (1) the right to share in distributions of corporate income (dividends) when declared by the board of directors, (2) the right to vote on important

---

[1]UCC §8–102(a)(15).
[2]RMBCA §1.40(21).

corporate matters and thereby participate in control, and (3) the right to a proportionate share of net assets upon liquidation of the firm.

Preferred and Common Shares. Not all shares are created equal with respect to these rights. The articles of incorporation may divide shares into classes. If classes are authorized, the articles must describe the designations, preferences, limitations, and relative rights of each class. Voting rights of any class of shares may be limited or denied, or special voting rights may be provided. In addition, a corporation may issue stock in preferred or special classes that have preference over other classes in the payment of dividends or in the assets of the corporation upon liquidation, or both.[3] Classes of shares that have such preferential rights are known as **preferred shares.** Preferred shares generally are non-voting.

In contrast, **common shares** are the residual ownership interest in the corporation. Common shares are entitled to dividends only after shares with a dividend preference are paid. They are entitled to distributions on liquidation only after creditors (including holders of debt securities) and equity securities with a liquidation preference are paid. If a corporation has only one class of shares, they are, in effect, common shares. A corporation need not, however, have only one class of common shares. State corporation statutes generally authorize creation of various classes of common shares with each possessing different rights and privileges.

Redeemable and Convertible Shares. The articles of incorporation may make certain classes of stock subject to reacquisition, or redemption, by the corporation at a fixed price.[4] Although such redemption or "call" provisions generally apply only to preferred shares, some states permit redeemable common shares if there is at least one class of voting common shares not subject to redemption. Redemption of a class of shares may be mandatory or optional, as well as total or partial.

The articles of incorporation also may provide that shares of a given class may be convertible into shares of another class on some predetermined ratio. Some state statutes prohibit conversion of one class of stock into a class having prior or superior rights to dividends or to corporate assets upon liquidation. Under these provi-sions, for example, preferred stock may be convertible into common, but not vice versa.

A given class of security often possesses both redemption and conversion privileges. In this situation, after the call for redemption, the shareholder usually has a limited period within which to exercise the conversion right. Note that redemption and conversion provisions also are common in debt securities.

Options, Warrants, and Rights. A corporation may create and issue rights or options that entitle their holders to purchase a specified number of shares of a given class of stock from the corporation at a specified price usually within a limited period of time. Rights or options may be issued in conjunction with, or independently of, the corporation's issue of other securities, and may be issued as incentives to corporate directors, officers, or employees.[5]

Share options usually are evidenced by certificates known as "warrants," which generally are long-term in nature. In contrast, short-term share options are known as "rights," which are often issued in lieu of dividends or in conjunction with the issuance of debt securities or preferred stock. Both warrants and rights of publicly-held companies are freely transferable and publicly traded. Their value depends upon the difference between the stock's market price and the option price.

Issuance of Shares

A corporation has the power to create and issue the number of shares stated or authorized in its articles of incorporation.[6] The law generally places no limit on the number of shares of various classes that may be authorized and does not require that all authorized shares be issued. Some states, however, impose an organization tax based on authorized shares, which creates a practical limit on the number of such shares. Nevertheless, sufficient shares should be authorized to meet both present and future financing needs to avoid the need later to amend the articles of incorporation.

Some or all of the authorized shares will be issued to shareholders in exchange for consideration and are then said to be "outstanding." Shares are outstanding until they are later reacquired by the corporation through redemption, exercise of conversion privilege, or purchase. Such

---

[3]See, for example, RMBCA §6.01.
[4]See, for example, RMBCA §6.01(c)(2).

[5]See, for example, RMBCA §6.24.
[6]See, for example, RMBCA §6.03(a).

shares often are known as "treasury shares" or "treasury stock."

Shares may generally be issued with a "par" or "stated" value or may be "no par" shares. **Par value** of a share is simply the amount designated as par value for the share in the articles of incorporation. In contrast, "no par" shares are simply those that are stated in the articles to have no par value.

Consideration for Shares. Both par and no par shares are issued for consideration, determined by the board of directors, unless that right is reserved to the shareholders in the articles of incorporation. Historically, if par value stock was used, the par value was the selling price of the stock. Today, par value usually bears no relation to the issue price. Stock may not, however, be sold for less than par value. For this reason, among others, modern corporate par value stock usually bears a nominal par value, such as one dollar. In the absence of fraud in the transaction the judgment of the board of directors regarding the value of the consideration received for stock, or for stock rights or options, is generally conclusive.[7] Note that treasury stock may be sold for any price fixed by the board of directors without regard to any par value stated on the stock.

Minimum Capital Requirements. Many older corporate statutes prohibit a corporation from commencing business until a certain minimum capital has been received in exchange for issuance of shares. Because minimum capital provisions take no account of the actual capital needs of the business and generally involve nominal amounts, they provide no real creditor protection. For this reason, the RMBCA and many modern state statutes have eliminated any minimum capitalization requirement.

Stated Capital and Capital Surplus. The par–no par distinction not only affects the consideration requirements for the issue of shares, but also determines the composition of the corporation's stated capital and capital surplus accounts. If the corporation issues par value stock, the par value of the shares is credited to the "stated capital" account and the difference between the selling price and par value is credited to a "capital surplus" account. "Surplus" of a corporation is the amount by which the net assets (assets minus liabilities) exceed its stated capital. Surplus of the corporation is of two types,

---

[7]See, for example, RMBCA §§6.21, 6.24.

capital surplus and earned surplus (retained earnings). In a newly formed corporation with no accumulated earnings, the entire surplus, if any, of the corporation will be capital surplus.

Assume ABC Corporation issues 10,000 shares of stock sold for $10 per share with a par value of $1 per share. Stated capital is $10,000 (10,000 × $1) and capital surplus is $90,000 (10,000 × ($10 − $1)). The balance sheet of the corporation after issuing the stock is therefore

Assets		Liabilities	
Cash	$100,000		-0-
		Capital Accounts	
		Stated Capital	$ 10,000
		Capital Surplus	90,000
		Earned Surplus	-0-
	$100,000		$100,000

If the corporation issues no par stock, the entire consideration received for the shares is allocated to stated capital. The board of directors may, however, allocate some or all of the consideration to capital surplus within a specified time after the stock is issued. For example, assume DEF Corporation issues 10,000 shares of no par stock, selling for $20 per share. Stated capital is $200,000 (10,000 × $20). If the board of directors later votes to transfer $19 per share to capital surplus, stated capital would be $10,000 ($200,000 − (10,000 × $19)) and capital surplus $190,000.

How a corporation divides its capital contribution between capital surplus and stated capital may have important legal consequences. Older corporate statutes provide that corporate funds may be expanded to pay dividends or to repurchase or redeem outstanding shares to the extent of amounts in the corporation's earned surplus (retained earnings) account and in some cases, its capital surplus account. Stated capital, in contrast, is effectively locked into the corporation and may usually be distributed only upon liquidation of the firm. Accordingly, allocating a substantial portion of the consideration for stock to capital surplus gives the corporation more future flexibility to pay dividends or reacquire its stock, and accounts in part for the common use of nominal par value stock.

Allocating a corporation's capital contribution between stated capital and capital surplus is artificial and provides no real protection to creditors against excessive distribution of corporate assets to shareholders. For this reason the RMBCA and many modern state statutes eliminate the concept of par value and any legal consequences attached to the distinction between stated capital and capital surplus. Under this approach, the validity of corporate distributions is determined solely by the insolvency test discussed later in this chapter.

Payment for Shares

Stock Subscriptions. A corporation has no need to issue and set the consideration for stock unless it has investors willing and able to buy it. A stock subscription is one method used to acquire investment capital or the assurance of such capital. A **stock subscription** is an offer or agreement by a "subscriber" to purchase and pay for a specified number of previously unissued shares of the corporation. Stock subscriptions may be postincorporation or preincorporation. Postincorporation stock subscriptions are ordinary bilateral contracts between the subscriber and the corporation. Preincorporation subscriptions are, however, complicated by the fact that the corporation is not a legal entity at the time of the subscription. Accordingly, under the traditional approach, a preincorporation subscription was a mere offer, revocable by the subscriber until accepted by the corporation after its formation. This result created uncertainty regarding corporate capitalization until after incorporation.

To prevent this result, state corporation statutes make preincorporation subscriptions enforceable for a limited period. For example, the RMBCA provides that a subscription for shares of a corporation to be organized is irrevocable for six months unless the subscription agreement provides otherwise or all other subscribers agree to revocation.[8] Modern statutes also frequently provide for automatic acceptance of the subscription upon incorporation and require that the subscription be in writing signed by the subscriber.

The payment terms of a stock subscription, unless specified in the subscription itself, are determined by the board of directors. Generally, the stock certificate is issued when the subscription price is fully paid. If a subscriber defaults in payment under the agreement, the corporation may proceed to collect it in the same manner as any other debt owed to the corporation.

Note that modern distribution techniques and securities registration requirements generally prevent the use of stock subscriptions in connection with securities issued by publicly-held corporations.

Shareholder Liability for Watered Shares. In exchange for the issuance of shares, shareholders and subscribers are legally obligated to pay to the corporation the consideration fixed by the board of directors. Older statutes provide that consideration for the issuance of shares may be paid in money, property, or services actually performed for the corporation. Under this approach, neither promissory notes nor the promise of future services constitute payment or part payment for issuance of shares. The RMBCA, however, permits stock to be issued for promissory notes or contracts for future services.[9]

Shares issued for the full eligible consideration are deemed validly issued, fully paid, and nonassessable.[10] Shares issued to persons who pay less than the law requires are called "bonus," "discount," or "watered" shares. Bonus shares are those for which no lawful consideration is received by the corporation. Discount shares are shares issued for cash less than the fixed consideration. Watered shares are those issued for property or services worth less than the required consideration. The term **watered shares** usually is used to describe all three types.

Watered shares in a corporation's capital structure may injure both the corporation's creditors and its shareholders. Creditors may be injured because watered shares artificially inflate the corporation's capitalization. If creditors are involved, the shareholder may be compelled to contribute additional consideration to make up the difference between the consideration fixed by the board of directors and the amount of valid consideration paid. If a holder of watered shares later sells them, a good faith purchaser incurs no liability to the corporation or its creditors for any unpaid consideration. Similarly, a creditor to whom the holder transfers the shares as collateral is not personally liable as a shareholder. In both cases, however, the transferor remains liable despite the transfer.[11]

Creditor claims involving watered shares are rare today primarily because of federal and state securities regulation statutes. In modern cases, the complaining parties usually are other shareholders of the corporation whose equity in the corporate assets is unfairly diluted by issuance of new shares without lawful consideration. In these cases, the appropriate remedy is to cancel the offending shares.

---

[8]RMBCA §6.20.

[9]RMBCA §6.21(b).
[10]See, for example, RMBCA §6.21(d).
[11]See, for example, RMBCA §6.22.

Debt Securities

Debt securities are issued in exchange for loans made to the corporation. Like other loans, debt securities require periodic interest payments and ultimately must be repaid. Thus, unlike the holder of an equity security, who is an owner of the corporation, the holder of a debt security is a creditor. Holders of debt securities, as creditors, enjoy a claim on corporate assets prior to shareholders.

Publicly-held corporations issue debt securities known as "bonds" and "debentures." Technically, a **debenture** is an unsecured obligation rendering debenture holders general creditors of the corporation. In contrast, a **bond** is an obligation secured by a lien or mortgage upon specific corporate property. Despite this difference, the term "bond" often is used to describe both bonds and debentures. Bonds and debentures are usually long-term obligations issued in $1,000 denominations (or multiples thereof) with a fixed interest rate, often known as the "coupon" rate.

Both bonds and debentures typically are issued and administered under an **indenture** (sometimes called a "trust agreement" or "deed of trust") between the corporation issuing the securities and a trustee, usually a financial institution. The indenture contains the terms of the issuance, including any redemption or conversion provisions, and a description of the nature and extent of any security. It also includes protective provisions such as minimum ratios of assets to liabilities, restrictions on dividends or share redemption, and limitations on additional issues of securities. The trustee generally represents the interests of the various security holders.[12]

Bonds and debentures are not the only source of corporate debt financing. For example, the corporation may borrow money from commercial banks and insurance companies in exchange for long-term or short-term notes. In addition, suppliers of goods or services often extend credit to corporations on a secured or unsecured basis.

Selection of Capital Structure

Although every corporation issues some stock, corporate management enjoys considerable flexibility in determining the corporation's particular mix of debt

and equity securities, its capital structure. Management considers various factors including market conditions, stability of corporate earnings, interest rates, the nature and extent of corporate assets, and the amount of capital required. In addition, tax considerations also weigh heavily in the decision.

Shareholder Debt. Shareholders often lend a portion of their investment to the corporation, rather than contributing it outright for shares of stock. Because interest payments on the debt are deductible by the corporation and dividend payments are not, such debt reduces the problem of corporate "double taxation." In addition, the ultimate repayment of the debt may receive more favorable tax treatment than a repurchase or redemption of equity securities.

Because of the tax advantages of corporate debt payable to shareholders, a substantial body of tax law has evolved from Internal Revenue Service attempts to reclassify corporate debt as stock in corporations with excessive debt capitalization. A corporation with a high debt to equity ratio (for example, four to one or higher) is commonly known as a "thin" corporation. The Internal Revenue Code and IRS regulations provide guidelines distinguishing debt from share interests.

In addition to tax advantages, shareholders who loan money to the corporation may, as creditors, enjoy greater rights upon bankruptcy or insolvency of the corporation than ordinary shareholders. Shareholder debt is often, however, subordinated to the claims of outside general creditors in a bankruptcy proceeding.

The following tax case illustrates the principles distinguishing debt from equity interests.

AMW Investments, Inc. v. Commissioner of Internal Revenue
71 Tax Court Memorandum Decisions (CCH) 3047 (1996)

Harry Mohney, the owner and operator of several businesses, created AMW Investments, Inc. (AMW or petitioner) in 1977 to hold and lease real estate to his other businesses. Mohney was president and owned all voting stock of AMW. By deed recorded in 1978, Mohney transferred to AMW a drive-in theater located in Clarksville, Indiana in exchange for AMW's $120,000 promissory note payable to Mohney plus interest at 10% on or before November 3, 1982. By deed recorded in 1980, Mohney

---

[12]The issuance of debt securities to the public may be subject to the federal Trust Indenture Act of 1939, discussed in Chapter 49.

also transferred a movie theater he owned in Mishawaka, Indiana to AMW for a $45,000 promissory note. Between 1977 and 1988, AMW made no payments on the promissory notes. During 1989 and 1990, AMW paid Mohney the face amounts of the notes plus accrued interest of $160,000. The Internal Revenue Service (IRS) disallowed AMW's interest deduction of $160,000 on its federal tax returns. Finding that the properties Mohney had transferred to AMW should have been classified as his equity in AMW, the IRS ruled that AMW's payments to Mohney in 1989 and 1990 were return of capital rather than payments of debt. AMW petitioned the Tax Court, asserting that the payments to Mohney were repayment of debts entitling it to deduct $160,000 as interest payments.

Laro, Judge

. . . The term "debt" connotes an existing, unconditional, and legally enforceable obligation for the payment of money. . . . Courts refer to numerous factors to determine whether a payment is for debt or equity. . . . These factors are: (1) the names given to the instruments evidencing the indebtedness; (2) the presence or absence of a fixed maturity date and schedule of payments; (3) the presence or absence of a fixed interest rate and interest payments; (4) the source of repayments; (5) the adequacy or inadequacy of capitalization; (6) the identity of interest between the creditor and stockholder; (7) the security for the advances; (8) the corporation's ability to obtain financing from outside lending institutions; (9) the extent to which the advances were subordinated to the claims of outside creditors; (10) the extent to which the advances were used to acquire capital assets; and (11) the presence or absence of a sinking fund to provide repayment. [*Roth Steel Tube Co. v. Commissioner,* 800 F.2d 625, 630 (6th Cir. 1986).] . . .

We now analyze and weigh all relevant facts to determine whether petitioner and Mr. Mohney intended to create a debt, and whether their intention comported with the economic reality of a debtor-creditor relationship. Petitioner carries the burden of establishing that the subject transfers generated debt rather than equity.

1. *Name of Certificate.* We look to the name of the certificate evidencing purported debt to determine the "debt's" true label. The issuance of a note weighs toward debt. . . . The mere fact that a taxpayer issues a note, however, is not dispositive of debt. An unsecured note, with no payments made thereon until long after the due date, weighs toward equity. . . .

Although petitioner issued the . . . Clarksville note to Mr. Mohney, we give this fact little weight. The record shows that the transfer of the subject properties to petitioner occurred in 1977, yet the related deeds were not recorded until sometime thereafter. We also find that Mr. Mohney's 1977 individual income tax return did not report a sale of either of the properties, and petitioner did not make any payments on either of the properties until 1989. Petitioner focuses on the fact that it recorded debt on its books in connection with the transfer. We are not impressed. Under the facts at hand, petitioner's accounting entry lends little (if any) support for a finding of debt. . . . This is particularly true, given the fact that the parties did not deal at arm's length. This factor is neutral.

2. *Fixed Maturity Date.* The presence of a fixed maturity date weighs toward debt, but is not dispositive of a debtor-creditor relationship. . . . The presence of a fixed maturity date may be offset by other facts in the record.

Although the . . . Clarksville note bore a maturity date of November 3, 1982, petitioner made no payments on this note until 1989. Petitioner also made no payments for the Mishawaka property until 1989. The timing of these payments indicates that a debtor-creditor relationship was not contemplated by petitioner and Mr. Mohney. The presence of the fixed maturity date on the . . . Clarksville note is further downplayed by the fact that Mr. Mohney did not pursue collection or inquire as to payment. Mr. Mohney testified that he simply forgot about the transaction and the debt owed to him. We find this testimony unbelievable, and, even assuming arguendo that it was credible (which it was not), we find this testimony to be uncharacteristic of a bona fide creditor. This factor weighs toward equity.

3. *Interest Rate and Payments.* The presence of a fixed rate of interest and actual interest payments weigh toward debt. The absence of payments in accordance with the terms of a debt instrument weighs toward equity. . . . Although the Clarksville note bore an interest rate of 10 percent, petitioner made no principal or interest payments to Mr. Mohney until 12 years after the transfer. Petitioner also made no principal or interest payments to Mr. Mohney on the Mishawaka transfer until 12 years after the transfer. This factor weighs toward equity.

4. *Repayment.* Repayment that is dependent upon corporate earnings weighs toward equity. Repayment that is not dependent on earnings weighs toward debt. . . .

Petitioner's ability to make payments on the subject properties depended primarily (if not solely) on the rental income from the properties. Immediate payment of the purported debt also does not seem to have been available from petitioner's existing assets which consisted primarily (if not entirely) of the subject properties. This factor weighs toward equity.

5. *Capitalization.* Thin or inadequate capitalization weighs toward equity. . . . The record indicates that petitioner did not have meaningful equity either before or at the time Mr. Mohney transferred the subject properties to it. This factor weighs toward equity.

6. *Identity of Interest.* Advances made by stockholders in proportion to their respective stock ownership weigh toward equity. A sharply disproportionate ratio between a stockholder's ownership percentage in the corporation and the debt owing to the stockholder by the corporation generally weighs toward debt. . . . Mr. Mohney owned the subject properties immediately before their transfer, and he effectively owned 100 percent of petitioner's equity at the time of the transfer. This factor weighs toward equity.

7. *Presence or Absence of Security.* The absence of security for purported debt weighs toward equity. . . . Mr. Mohney did not receive security for his transfer of the subject properties to petitioner. This factor weighs toward equity.

8. *Inability to Obtain Financing.* The question of whether a transferee could have obtained comparable financing is relevant in measuring the economic reality of a transfer. . . . Evidence that the taxpayer could not obtain loans from independent sources weighs toward equity. . . . Petitioner presented no evidence on whether it could have obtained financing from an unrelated party at the time of the transfer, or on the order of priority of its debts. Given the fact, however, that the purported debts were completely unsecured and that the subject properties were petitioner's main asset, we are left unpersuaded that an unrelated third party would have entered into financing with petitioner under the terms that it alleges were entered into between it and Mr. Mohney. This factor weighs toward equity.

9. *Subordination.* Subordination of purported debt to the claims of other creditors weighs towards equity. . . . Petitioner presented no evidence on the order of priority of its debts. This factor weighs toward equity.

10. *Use of Funds.* The transfer of funds from a shareholder to a corporation in order to meet the corporation's daily business needs weighs toward debt. The transfer of funds from a shareholder to a corporation in order to purchase capital assets weighs toward equity. . . . The subject properties were petitioner's initial and primary assets, and the purported notes represented a long-term commitment that was payable mainly from the future rental income from the properties. We also find relevant that Mr. Mohney was willing to go unpaid for many years so that petitioner could continue to enjoy the advantage of uninterrupted ownership of the properties. This factor weighs toward equity.

11. *Presence or Absence of a Sinking Fund.* The failure to establish a sinking fund for repayment weighs toward equity. . . . The record does not indicate that petitioner established a sinking fund for the repayment of the purported notes. To the contrary, it appears that repayment was to come solely from petitioner's earnings. This factor weighs toward equity.

Based on the above, we conclude that petitioner may not deduct the $160,000 that it claimed as an interest expense paid to Mr. Mohney. . . .

Leverage. If money can be borrowed from outside creditors, another possible advantage of debt financing is "leverage" or "trading on equity." Leverage occurs if the total investment in the business (debt and equity) yields a higher rate of return than the interest cost of borrowing money. For example, a business with a $500,000 total investment may generate $75,000 per year in earnings (a 15 percent rate of return) when the interest rate on borrowed funds is 12 percent. Under these circumstances, the business should borrow as much of the $500,000 investment as possible. The entire difference between the rate of return on total investment and the interest payments on the borrowed portion of that investment is profit which magnifies the rate of return on the equity securities. If earnings are poor and insufficient to cover the fixed interest payments, however, losses on equity capital also are magnified.

Ownership and Transfer of Securities

Corporate debt and equity securities may be evidenced by a document—for example, a stock certificate—and are known as **certificated securities.** State corporation statutes generally also authorize corporations to issue securities in **uncertificated** form, not represented by an instrument. Most securities, including virtually all those issued by publicly-held corporations, are issued in certificated form. Article 8 of the Uniform Commercial Code, entitled "Investment Securities," as revised in 1994, states rules governing the transfer of the rights constituting certificated and uncertificated securities and how those rights are established against the issuer and third parties.

Note initially that state corporation statutes require that corporations maintain a record of their shareholders, showing the class and number of shares held by each shareholder.[13] These records are sometimes known as "share books" or "share ledgers" and in small corporations the stubs in the share certificate book serve as the record of shareholders. In larger corporations, transfers of shares are recorded by a "stock transfer" agent, but in smaller corporations this task may be handled by the corporate secretary or other officer. Statutes generally allow the corporation to rely upon record ownership to determine which shareholders are entitled to vote, to be sent notices, to receive dividends, and otherwise to exercise the rights and powers of a shareholder.[14]

Transfer of Securities

Certificated securities may be issued in registered or bearer form. A certificated security is in "registered" form if (1) it specifies the person entitled to the security, and (2) its transfer may be registered upon books maintained for that purpose by or on behalf of the issuer. A certificated security is in "bearer" form if it is payable to the bearer of the certificate according to its terms.[15] A certificated security in bearer form is transferred simply by delivery of the certificate to the transferee or to a securities intermediary, such as a stockbroker, bank, clearing corporation, or other entity that ordinarily maintains security accounts for its customers. If in registered form, the transfer requires both delivery and a proper indorsement. The transferor

indorses by signing an assignment or transfer of the instrument on the instrument or on a separate document, or by affixing his or her signature to the back of the security. As in negotiable instruments under UCC Article 3,[16] the indorsement may be blank (the holder's signature alone) or special (specifying to whom the security is to be transferred). If indorsed in blank the security becomes a bearer instrument and may subsequently be transferred by delivery alone. If specially indorsed, the special indorsee's indorsement is required for further transfer. After the transfer, the security may be presented to the issuer for registration, who will register the transfer to designate the transferee as the new registered owner.

Debt securities, such as bonds and debentures, usually are freely transferable bearer instruments. Interest payments are made to bearers of interest "coupons" that are periodically clipped from the instrument and submitted for payment. If the instrument is registered with the issuer, the periodic interest payments, and the principal at maturity, are paid to the registered owner. Coupon securities also may be registered as to principal ("registered coupon" form). In this case, principal is payable to the registered owner upon maturity, but interest is payable to the bearers of the individual interest coupons.

Certificated shares of stock, like debt securities, are generally freely transferable. Restrictions on transfer may, however, be imposed by appropriate provisions in the articles of incorporation or bylaws. Share transfer restrictions commonly are used in closely-held corporations as a control device and are sometimes required for securities issued under securities regulation exemptions discussed in Chapter 49. Under UCC §8–204, any share transfer restriction imposed by the issuer is effective against any person without knowledge of the restriction only if it is conspicuously noted on the share certificate. For uncertificated securities, the restriction is effective only if the registered owner has been notified of the restriction.

Note finally that an uncertificated security is recorded on the books of the issuer, though there is no instrument evidencing the holder's interest in or claim against the corporation. Because there are no certificates to indorse or deliver, uncertificated debt or equity securities usually are transferred by registering the

---

[13]See, for example, RMBCA §16.01(c).
[14]See, for example, UCC §8–207(a).
[15]UCC §§8–102(a)(2),(13).

[16]Negotiable instruments law is discussed in Chapters 21–27.

transfer with the issuer, according to the transferor's instructions.

Rights of Purchasers

The buyer of a security expects to receive a good title, rightfully transferred, free of liens or claims. Section 8–108 of the Uniform Commercial Code provides for the buyer's basic title need by imposing warranty liability upon sellers who transfer certificated securities or originate instructions to transfer uncertificated securities. A person transferring a certificated security warrants to any subsequent purchaser that the security is genuine and has not been materially altered, that the transfer does not violate any restriction on transfer, that she knows of no fact that might impair the security's validity, and that the transfer is otherwise effective and rightful. The seller who originates instructions to transfer an uncertificated security undertakes a similar obligation.

Under §8–302, upon transfer of a security, the purchaser acquires whatever rights in the instrument the transferor had or had authority to convey. This provision creates a "shelter rule" for investment securities identical to the one applicable to sales of goods (§2–403(1)) and negotiable instruments (§3–203(b)). In addition to acquiring the rights of his transferor, under §8–303, a "protected purchaser" acquires the security free of any adverse claim. Adverse claims include, for example, an assertion by a third party that the transfer is wrongful or that he or she is the owner of or has an interest in the security. A protected purchaser is one who pays value for and obtains control of the security without notice of any adverse claim to it. Thus, a protected purchaser is the Article 8 equivalent of the holder in due course of a negotiable instrument.

Lost, Destroyed, or Stolen Certificated Securities

A certificated security may be lost, destroyed, or stolen. The issuer who issues a replacement security runs the risk that the original certificate will later appear in the hands of a protected purchaser. Accordingly, §8–405(a) requires the issuer to issue a replacement security only if the owner (1) makes a request for a new security before the issuer has notice that the security has been acquired by a protected purchaser, (2) furnishes an adequate bond to indemnify the corporation if the original security is later presented for registration, and (3) satisfies any other reasonable requirements imposed by the issuer. Under §8–406, an owner who fails to notify the issuer promptly that a security has been lost, destroyed, or stolen may not assert any claim against the issuer either for improperly registering a subsequent transfer or for a replacement security.

After the corporation issues a new certificate, a bona fide purchaser of the original certificate may present it for registration. In this situation, under §8–405(b), the corporation must register the transfer, but may then recover on the indemnity bond and also may recover the new certificate unless it has been transferred to a protected purchaser.

Indirect Securities Holding

The foregoing material describes what is known as the "direct" holding system for securities, in which the shares are registered in the name of the beneficial owner, who receives dividends, proxies, and other corporate communications directly from the issuer. This system is used for most corporations, whose shares are not publicly traded. In contrast, most securities issued by publicly-held corporations are held "indirectly" through a chain of "securities intermediaries." For example, the certificates are registered in the name of, and held by, a depository (the Depository Trust Company in most cases), which holds them on behalf of various banks and brokers, which in turn hold them for the beneficial owners. Under this indirect holding system, the owner holds a "securities entitlement" against the securities intermediaries, which pass the incidents of ownership, such as dividends and voting rights, through to the beneficial owner. Virtually all active individual and institutional investors hold their securities through brokers or banks in this manner. The securities certificates do not move and transfers are not registered on the issuer's share book; rather, each day's trading is reflected in bookkeeping entries on the books of the various securities intermediaries. To accommodate this system, which facilitates the huge trading volume in modern securities markets, UCC Article 8 was completely revised in 1994. This revision states, in Part 5, rules specifically designed for the indirect holding system.

Dividends, Distributions, and Redemptions

Corporate **distributions** are transfers of money or other property by the corporation to its shareholders. A distribution out of a corporation's current or past earnings is a **dividend.** Corporate distributions, whether of earnings or capital, may be proportionate or disproportionate to share ownership. For example, preferred shares may have preferential rights either to dividends or distributions in liquidation or both over other shares. In addition, a corporation's redemption, repurchase, or other acquisition of some of its shares may result in a disproportionate distribution. Because any corporate distribution may affect the rights of various classes of shareholders and, most importantly, corporate creditors, the law imposes limitations and restrictions on distributions of corporate assets to shareholders.

Kinds of Dividends

Dividends are divided into three types: (1) cash, (2) property, and (3) share or stock. A cash dividend, the most common type, is a distribution of legally available funds to the shareholders. The amount of the dividend is usually stated on a cents or dollars per share basis, or as a percentage of the stated or par value of the shares. Property dividends, or dividends-in-kind, are those consisting of property other than cash or the corporation's own shares. Shares of a subsidiary or other corporation or other securities often are used for such dividends.

Unlike cash or property dividends, share dividends do not distribute corporate assets to the shareholders. Rather, a share dividend distributes to shareholders additional shares of the declaring corporation, or fractions thereof, for each share owned. For example, in a 10 percent share dividend, each shareholder receives an additional one share for each ten shares owned. A share dividend increases the total number of shares representing the corporation's equity, and proportionately reduces the percentage ownership each share represents. Usually, but not necessarily, the additional shares are of the same class as the original shares.

Shareholders owning fewer than the minimum number of shares or an amount not divisible by the minimum may receive fractional shares. Alternatively, **scrip,** a certificate representing the right to receive a portion of a share, may be used. Scrip, unlike fractional shares, does not confer voting, dividend, or liquidation rights upon its holder. Scrip may, however, be bought and sold, and when combined with sufficient additional scrip, is surrendered to the corporation in exchange for a full share.

Closely related to a share dividend is a share split, because both increase the number of outstanding shares but do not distribute assets. They differ, however, in their effect on the corporate capital accounts. In a share dividend, the par value, or in some cases the fair market value, of the dividend shares is capitalized, transferred from the earned surplus to the stated capital or capital surplus account. In a share split, there is no transfer of earnings to capital.

Dividend Preferences

As a general rule, shareholders participate in dividends declared by the corporation in proportion to share ownership. The articles of incorporation may grant one or more classes of shares — preferred shares — the right to receive dividends or distributions in liquidation of the corporation, before the common shares. Dividend preferences usually are fixed in the articles in an amount expressed in dollars or as a percentage of the par value of the stock and may be cumulative, noncumulative, or cumulative-to-the-extent-earned. A **cumulative dividend preference** entitles a shareholder to receive a prescribed dividend for the current year and all prior years in which the preferred dividend was not paid, before any dividend may be paid on the common shares. If a dividend preference is **noncumulative,** preferred dividends not paid in prior years do not accumulate and need not be satisfied before dividends are subsequently paid to shares with subordinate dividend rights. Only the current year's preference need be satisfied.

A dividend preference that is **cumulative-to-the-extent-earned** entitles preferred shareholders to carry forward and accumulate unpaid dividends to the extent that the corporation had earnings available to pay the dividend in the year or years that the dividend was omitted. For example, assume a corporation had no earnings in 2003, but substantial earnings in 2004 and 2005. If the preferred is cumulative-to-the-extent-earned and dividends are to be paid in 2005, the preferred dividends for 2004 and 2005 must be satisfied before any dividend is paid to the common.

Preferred shares, whether cumulative, noncumulative, or cumulative-to-the-extent-earned, may or may not be entitled to additional dividends beyond their fixed dividend preference. Shares that are entitled to receive the amount of the stated dividend preference and no more are **nonparticipating.** In contrast, **participating** preferred are entitled to share in dividends with other classes of shares in addition to the dividend preference. The articles of incorporation outline whether preferred shares are participating or not and the nature of that participation—for example, equally with other shares, in a fixed ratio, after other classes have been paid, or upon occurrence of a condition.

The Dividend Decision

A corporation pays dividends if, when, and as declared by the board of directors. Once declared, a dividend becomes a legally enforceable obligation of the corporation and cannot be repealed or retracted by the board. Dividend policy is influenced by factors such as corporate earnings, future capital needs of the business, and shareholder expectations. In closely-held corporations, federal income tax consequences of distribution or retention to major shareholders often is determinative.

The decision to pay dividends, even upon shares with a dividend preference, is within the business judgment and therefore the discretion of the board. Courts generally will not intervene to compel payment of dividends unless a complaining shareholder proves an abuse of that discretion. Abuse of discretion may be found, for example, if the directors' conduct is fraudulent, dishonest, or clearly unreasonable. Although relief has been granted in very few cases, such as the following, preferred shareholders and shareholders in closely-held corporations have been the most successful in suits to compel dividend distributions.

Dodge v. Ford Motor Co.

170 N.W. 668 (Mich. 1919)

Defendant Ford Motor Company (Ford) was organized and incorporated in 1903. In 1916, plaintiffs John and Horace Dodge, who owned 10 percent of the stock of Ford, sued the corporation demanding that it pay dividends to the shareholders.

The evidence at trial established that Ford had paid regular annual dividends of $1.2 million and from 1911 through 1915 had paid additional "special dividends" totaling $41 million. After the board of directors adopted a plan to expand the company by increasing the plant and equipment, Ford began to accumulate a large surplus to finance the expansion.

The trial court ruled in favor of the Dodges and ordered Ford Motor Company to pay a dividend of $10 million. Ford appealed.

Ostrander, Chief Justice

. . . When plaintiffs made their complaint and demand for further dividends, the Ford Motor Company had concluded its most prosperous year of business. The demand for its cars at the price of the preceding year continued. It could make and could market in the year beginning August 1, 1916, more than 500,000 cars. Sales of parts and repairs would necessarily increase. The cost of materials was likely to advance, and perhaps the price of labor, but it reasonably might have expected a profit for the year of upwards of $60,000,000. It had assets of more than $132,000,000, a surplus of almost $112,000,000, and its cash on hand and municipal bonds were nearly $54,000,000. Its total liabilities including capital stock, was a little over $20,000,000. It had declared no special dividend during the business year except the October, 1915, dividend. It had been the practice, under similar circumstances, to declare larger dividends. Considering only these facts, a refusal to declare and pay further dividends appears to be not an exercise of discretion on the part of the directors, but an arbitrary refusal to do what the circumstances required to be done. These facts and others call upon the directors to justify their action, or failure or refusal to act. . . .

A business corporation is organized and carried on primarily for the profit of the stockholders. The powers of the directors are to be employed for that end. The discretion of directors is to be exercised in the choice of means to attain that end, and does not extend to a change in the end itself, to the reduction of profits, or to the nondistribution of profits among stockholders in order to devote them to other purposes. . . .

We are not, however, persuaded that we should interfere with the proposed expansion of the business of the Ford Motor Company. . . .

Assuming . . . that the plan and policy and the details agreed upon were for the best ultimate interest of the company and therefore of its shareholders, what does it amount to in justification of a refusal to declare and pay a special dividend or dividends? The Ford Motor Company was able to estimate with nicety its income and profit. It could sell more cars than it could make. . . . [T]he yearly income and profit was determinable, and, within slight variations, was certain. . . .

The company was continuing business, at a profit—a cash business. If the total cost of proposed expenditures had been immediately withdrawn in cash from the cash surplus (money and bonds) on hand August 1, 1916, there would have remained nearly $30,000,000.

Defendants say, and it is true, that a considerable cash balance must be at all times carried by such a concern. But, as has been stated, there was a large daily, weekly, monthly, receipt of cash. The output was practically continuous and was continuously, and within a few days, turned into cash. Moreover, the contemplated expenditures were not to be immediately made. The large sum appropriated for the smelter plant was payable over a considerable period of time. So that, without going further, it would appear that, accepting and approving the plan of the directors, it was their duty to distribute on or near the 1st of August, 1916, a very large sum of money to stockholders. . . .

The decree of the court below fixing and determining the specific amount to be distributed to stockholders is affirmed. . . .

Funds Legally Available for Dividends

To protect corporate creditors and, in some instances, preferred shareholders, the law limits distributions of corporate assets to shareholders. State business corporation acts determine which funds are legally available for dividends. In all states, a dividend payment is prohibited if the corporation is insolvent or would be rendered insolvent by the distribution. Insolvency is commonly defined as inability to pay debts as they come due in the ordinary course of business (equity insolvency) or an excess of total liabilities over total assets (bankruptcy insolvency).

Assuming solvency, many older corporate statutes permit dividends to be paid to the extent of the corporation's unrestricted and unreserved earned surplus (retained earnings). Earned surplus consists of accumulated profits earned by the corporation since its formation reduced primarily by prior dividend distributions. Other statutes permit corporate distributions to be made out of any surplus, capital, earned, or both. These statutes are commonly said to prohibit an "impairment" of stated capital by a dividend. Still other statutes permit dividends to be paid from current profits even if a deficit exists in the earned surplus account from losses incurred in prior periods. These are known as "nimble" dividends.

The dividend tests tied to surplus, previously outlined, are confusing and provide little creditor protection. For this reason, the RMBCA and modern statutes eliminate the concept of par value, surplus, and stated capital, and make validity of corporate distributions turn solely upon whether the corporation is insolvent in either the equity or bankruptcy sense immediately after the distribution.[17]

State corporate statutes generally impose liability upon directors for unlawful dividends or other distributions. For example, under the RMBCA, a director who votes for or assents to the declaration of any dividend or other distribution in violation of statutory limitations or the articles of incorporation is liable to the corporation for the amount by which the dividend or distribution exceeds that legally permissible.[18]

Repurchase or Redemption

A corporation has the power to acquire its own shares. It may also issue stock, generally preferred, that may be redeemed by the corporation. The shares (sometimes called "treasury shares") acquired by the corporation are functionally equivalent to authorized but unissued shares.[19] Accordingly, after the repurchase or redemption, the remaining outstanding shares each represent a proportionately larger interest in a reduced pool of assets.

A repurchase or redemption is similar in effect to a dividend; in both cases, the corporation distributes

---

[17]RMBCA §6.40(c).
[18]RMBCA §8.33.
[19]See, for example, RMBCA §6.31(a). Under RMBCA §6.31(b), the articles of incorporation may prohibit reissue of reacquired shares. In this case, the acquired shares are canceled and the number of authorized shares is reduced by the number of shares acquired.

corporate assets to its shareholders without consideration. Unlike a dividend, however, a redemption or repurchase involves an element of exchange—shares of stock for corporate assets. It also results in a disproportionate distribution of corporate assets to the selling shareholders. Dividends usually are paid to all shareholders in proportion to their holdings.

A corporation may repurchase its own shares for a variety of reasons. In a closely-held corporation, for example, the repurchase may be used to buy out one or more shareholders. In a publicly-held corporation, repurchased shares

may be used for employee compensation plans or to purchase other corporations. Additionally, substantial repurchases may drive up the price of remaining shares and may thus be used as a defensive measure to defeat a hostile takeover bid.

To protect creditors, reacquisitions and redemptions are subject to legal restrictions similar to those applicable to dividends. Indeed, the RMBCA applies the same insolvency standard previously described to all corporate distributions including dividends and repurchase and redemption of shares.

Summary

1. In ongoing corporations, most funds are generated by reinvesting some portion of corporate earnings into the business. An initial, and often continuing, method of raising corporate funds is to issue corporate "securities" in exchange for cash, property, or services. Securities are of two basic types: equity and debt. Equity securities, such as shares of common and preferred stock, create an ownership interest in the business. In contrast, debt securities, such as notes, bonds, and debentures, are issued in exchange for loans made to the corporation. Corporate management usually has flexibility in determining the corporation's mix of debt and equity securities, its capital structure.

2. A corporation has the power to create and issue as many shares of stock as are authorized in its articles of incorporation. These shares may be preferred (enjoying a preference over other shares for dividends or for amounts distributed on liquidation, or both) or common, and may be redeemable by the corporation or convertible into another class of shares.

3. In exchange for shares issued, shareholders and subscribers are legally obligated to pay to the corporation the amount determined by the board of directors. If a purchaser fails to pay full consideration for shares, the shares may be canceled, or alternatively, the shareholder may be compelled to contribute additional consideration.

4. Publicly-held corporations commonly issue debt securities known as bonds and debentures. These securities are often issued and administered under an indenture between the issuing corporation and a trustee, usually a financial institution.

5. Corporate debt and equity securities are generally evidenced by a document—for example, a stock certificate—and are known as "certificated securities." Certificated securities may be issued in registered or bearer form. A certificated security may be transferred by delivery of a bearer security or indorsement and delivery of a registered security. After the

transfer, the security may be presented to the issuer for registration of the transferee as the new registered owner. An uncertificated security is recorded on the books of the issuer though there is no instrument evidencing the holder's interest in or claim against the corporation. Uncertificated debt or equity securities may be transferred by registering the transfer with the issuer according to the transferor's instructions.

6. Rights of purchasers of investment securities are governed by principles similar to those applied to transferees of negotiable instruments. Article 8 of the Uniform Commercial Code imposes warranty liability upon transferors for title and other defects, and transferees have the benefit of a "shelter" rule. Further, a "protected purchaser," the Article 8 equivalent of a holder in due course, acquires the security free of any adverse claim.

7. A certificated security may be lost, destroyed, or stolen. The issuer is required to issue a new security only if the owner meets specific legal requirements designed to protect the issuer.

8. Most securities issued by publicly-held corporations are not held "directly" in the name of the owner, but are instead held "indirectly" through a chain of securities intermediaries, including banks and brokers. Under this indirect holding system, the owner holds a "securities entitlement" against the securities intermediaries, which pass the incidents of ownership, such as dividends and voting rights, through to the beneficial owner. To accommodate this system, which facilitates the huge trading volume in modern securities markets, UCC Article 8 was completely revised in 1994.

9. Corporate distributions are transfers of money or other property by the corporation to its shareholders. A distribution out of a corporation's current or past earnings is a dividend. Other distributions include repurchases and redemptions of outstanding shares.

10. Dividends are of three types: cash, property, and share. Although shareholders generally participate in dividends declared by the corporation in proportion to share ownership, the articles of incorporation may grant one or more classes of shares—preferred shares—the right to receive dividends or distributions in liquidation of the corporation, before the common shares. Dividend preferences may be cumulative, cumulative-to-the-extent-earned, or noncumulative, and may be participating or nonparticipating. A corporation pays dividends if, when, and as declared by the board of directors.

11. To protect corporate creditors and in some instances, preferred shareholders, the law limits the extent to which a corporation may distribute dividends to shareholders. Funds legally available for dividends traditionally have been determined by various tests tied to insolvency, earned or other surplus, or existence of net profits. The RMBCA and many modern statutes adopt insolvency as the sole test; that is, a dividend payment is prohibited if the corporation is insolvent or would be rendered insolvent by the distribution.

12. A corporation has the power to acquire its own shares and may issue stock that may be redeemed by the corporation. Legal restrictions, similar to those governing dividends, are imposed to protect creditors in reacquisitions and redemptions.

Key Terms

security	uncertificated securities
equity securities	distribution
debt securities	dividend
preferred shares	scrip
common shares	cumulative dividend
par value	preference
stock subscription	noncumulative dividend
watered shares	preference
debenture	cumulative-to-the-extent-
bond	earned dividend preference
indenture	nonparticipating
certificated securities	participating

Questions and Problems

46.1 State statutes traditionally have allowed issuance of corporate shares only in exchange for cash, property, or services previously performed for the corporation. The Revised Model Business Corporation Act, however, allows shares to be issued for future services, promissory notes, or any tangible or intangible property or benefit to the corporation. (See RMBCA §6.21(b).)

(a) What is the purpose of the traditional requirement that stock be issued only for money, property, or services previously performed?

(b) Suggest reasons warranting the relaxed standards contained in the Revised Model Business Corporation Act.

46.2 A partnership known as "Leonard Plumbing and Heating Supply Co." was organized in October 2000. The three partners, Fazio, Ambrose, and B. T. Leonard, had capital contributions as of September 2002 totaling $51,620.78, distributed as follows: Fazio, $43,169.61; Ambrose, $6,451.17; and Leonard, $2,000.

In the fall of that year, it was decided to incorporate the business. In contemplation of this step, Fazio and Ambrose, on September 15, 2002, withdrew all but $2,000 apiece of their capital contributions to the business. This was accomplished by the issuance to them, on that date, of partnership promissory notes in the sum of $41,169.61 and $4,451.17, respectively. These were demand notes, no interest being specified. The capital contribution to the partnership business then stood at $6,000—$2,000 for each partner.

During 2002 the corporation lost $22,000 on sales of $400,000. The firm's ratio of current assets to current liabilities was 1:1. In June 2004, after suffering additional losses, the corporation filed a voluntary bankruptcy petition. Fazio and Ambrose filed claims against the estate for the promissory notes given to them upon incorporation. Over the objection of the trustee in bankruptcy, the bankruptcy court allowed their claims finding that the paid-in capital at the time of incorporation was adequate, and that Fazio and Ambrose had not mismanaged the business, or practiced fraud or deception.

(a) Do you agree with this conclusion or should the claims of Fazio and Ambrose be subordinated to the claims of the corporation's other unsecured creditors?

(b) The issue of undercapitalization of a corporation usually arises, as in this case, only after the corporation has become insolvent or bankrupt. How can a business person know whether an ongoing business is undercapitalized?

46.3 Glenn owned 100 shares of Moonlight Co. common stock. After Glenn died on September 23, his brother Roy was appointed executor and began to collect the assets of Glenn's estate. The task was difficult because Glenn had been in the habit of hiding important papers in his house. Roy thoroughly searched Glenn's house four times between October 1 and November 1 but could not find the certificates for the Moonlight stock. On November 15, Roy wrote to the Moonlight Co. transfer agent requesting information on replacing the stock certificates. Roy's letter stated, "Although we continue to search for the certificates, we now assume they have been lost."

(a) What procedure should the transfer agent recommend?

(b) Pursuant to instructions from his attorney, on December 28, Roy sent a "stop order" to the transfer agent requesting that it not transfer Glenn's shares of Moonlight Co. because the certificates had been lost. The transfer agent replied by notifying Roy that his stop order had arrived too late: the stock had been sold on October 29 and Glenn's signature had been forged. The purchaser had bought the shares through a broker and had paid market price for the shares. The transfer agent claims that it owes nothing to Glenn's estate. Is the transfer agent correct? Explain.

46.4 Park Corporation has issued 50,000 shares of cumulative, preferred stock. Park's bylaws provide: "The holders of the preferred stock shall be entitled to receive, and the Corporation shall be bound to pay thereon, but only out of the net profits of the Corporation, a fixed yearly dividend of one dollar ($1.00) per share."

(a) In 2003, Park operated at a loss and had no net profit. Are the preferred shareholders entitled to receive a dividend? Explain.

(b) In 2004, Park had net profits of $35,000. Are the preferred shareholders entitled to a dividend? Explain.

(c) In 2005, Park Corporation's net profits exceeded $200,000. Are the preferred shareholders entitled to a dividend? Explain.

46.5 Explain the similarities and differences between a dividend and a redemption or repurchase of shares. Summarize the various types of legal restrictions on corporate distributions. What purpose are these restrictions designed to serve?

46.6 The decision to pay corporate dividends is within the discretion of the board of directors. Why are courts hesitant to disturb the board's decision regarding the timing and amount of dividends?

CHAPTER 47

CORPORATE MANAGEMENT — STRUCTURE AND DUTIES

Major Topics

- a discussion of the management structure of a corporation, including the functions and powers of the shareholders, directors, and officers
- coverage of the various duties owed by corporate management to the corporation and its shareholders, including the primary duties of care and loyalty

Once created, a corporation must be managed by natural persons, whose functions, rights, powers, and duties are determined by constitutions, statutes, administrative rules and regulations, and a variety of intracorporate sources such as the articles of incorporation, bylaws, resolutions, and private contracts. Corporate management powers are divided among the shareholders, the board of directors, and corporate officers. The shareholders, the owners of the corporation, periodically elect the board of directors, who have ultimate responsibility to manage the corporation. The board of directors, in turn, appoints corporate officers and delegates to them the authority to operate the corporation consistent with management policy determined by the board. The officers often appoint additional executive officers and employees to manage day-to-day business activities. Collectively, the officers and directors of a corporation are known as its "management." In closely-held corporations the same persons are often simultaneously shareholders, directors, and officers.

Shareholders

Shareholder Meetings

Although the shareholders are the owners of the corporation, their participation in management is generally limited to voting on the election of directors and upon extraordinary corporate matters such as amendments to the articles of incorporation, dissolution, merger or consolidation, or sale of corporate assets outside the ordinary course of business. In addition, the power to amend, adopt, or repeal bylaws may be reserved to the shareholders in the articles of incorporation, and shareholders may generally repeal or change bylaws adopted by the directors.[1]

Shareholder votes are normally taken at either annual or special meetings. Corporations usually are required to hold an annual shareholders' meeting at a time stated in, or fixed by, the bylaws.[2] Although the primary purpose of the annual meeting is to elect some or all of the directors, other business also may be conducted. For example, management reports may be made, bylaws may be amended or repealed, and shareholder or

---

[1]See, for example, RMBCA §10.20.
[2]See, for example, RMBCA §7.01(a).

management resolutions may be considered and submitted for a vote. In addition to the annual meeting, special meetings addressing specific issues may be called by the board of directors, the holders of a specified number of shares, or other persons specified in the articles of incorporation or bylaws. Written advance notice of the time, place, and the date of both annual and special meetings must be given to each shareholder entitled to vote. Notice of a special meeting must include a description of its purpose, and only business within that purpose may be conducted at the meeting.[3]

At annual and special meetings, shareholders may vote in person or may authorize other persons to vote their shares by proxy. To conduct business, a quorum must be present—usually a majority of shares entitled to vote, represented either in person or by proxy.[4] Although the articles of incorporation may provide a different quorum percentage, many state statutes provide that a quorum may not be less than one-third of shares entitled to vote. Unless otherwise stated in the articles or bylaws, a majority vote of a quorum constitutes the act of the shareholders.

The RMBCA and many state statutes permit shareholders to take action without a meeting if written consent to the action is signed by all shareholders entitled to vote on the issue. The consent device eliminates unnecessary formal meetings and is particularly useful in closely-held corporations in which many decisions are unanimous.[5]

To determine which shareholders are entitled to notice of a meeting, to demand a special meeting, to vote, or to take other shareholder action, the bylaws or board of directors may fix a "record date." Persons listed on the corporate books as the registered owners of shares on the record date are entitled to vote. Statutes generally require that the record date be fixed within a limited period preceding the meeting, for example, under the RMBCA not more than 70 days before the meeting.[6] Once the record date is established, the officer or agent in charge of the stock transfer books prepares a complete "voting list" or "voting record" of shareholders entitled to vote. This list must be made available to shareholders for inspection and copying at the meeting and under some statutes, in advance of the meeting.[7]

Shareholder Voting

Unless otherwise provided in the articles of incorporation, each outstanding share, regardless of class, is entitled to one vote on each matter presented at the meeting. The articles may provide for more than one vote for any share. Treasury shares and shares held by other corporations controlled by the issuing corporation are not entitled to vote and are not counted in determining the number of outstanding shares. Redeemable shares are not entitled to vote after notice of redemption is mailed and money sufficient to redeem the shares has been deposited with a financial institution.[8]

Voting rights of any class of shares may be limited or denied in the articles of incorporation. The RMBCA provides, however, that shareholders are entitled to vote as a class, even if otherwise denied voting rights, if an amendment to the articles of incorporation is proposed that would alter the rights of that class (for example, a change in number of authorized shares, preferences, or preemptive rights).[9] A similar rule applies to votes concerning merger or voluntary dissolution of the corporation.

Election of Directors—Straight and Cumulative Voting. Voting to elect the board of directors may be either straight or cumulative. **Straight voting** is the usual method of shareholder voting. Under this approach, each share is entitled to one vote on each matter, including one vote for each vacant directorship. Because directors are elected by a plurality of votes, the shareholder with the largest block of shares elects all the directors.

To assure minority representation on the board of directors, many states require cumulative voting. In other states, cumulative voting may be provided for or excluded in the articles of incorporation.

Under **cumulative voting,** which applies only to the election of directors, the number of votes each shareholder receives is equal to the number of his or her shares multiplied by the number of directorships to be filled. Therefore, if seven directors are to be elected, a shareholder owning 300 shares receives 2,100 votes, all of which may be cast for one director or may be distributed as the shareholder sees fit.

As the number of directors to be elected decreases, an increasingly greater number of minority shares is required to elect one director. Thus, the value of cumulative voting decreases with the size of the board

---

[3] See RMBCA §§7.01, 7.02, 7.05.
[4] See, for example, RMBCA §7.25.
[5] RMBCA §7.04.
[6] RMBCA §7.07(b).
[7] See, for example, RMBCA §7.20.

[8] See, for example, RMBCA §7.21.
[9] RMBCA §10.04.

of directors. In addition, as discussed later in this chapter, the RMBCA and most other state statutes authorize classification of directors, which further minimizes the effect of cumulative voting as a means of assuring minority representation.

Proxies and Proxy Voting. The grant of authority by a shareholder to another to vote his or her shares is a **proxy.** In large publicly-held corporations, management usually must solicit proxies to obtain a quorum at a meeting, because few shareholders personally attend.[10] Many statutes require that the proxy be in a writing signed by the shareholder.[11] The proxy holder, the agent appointed to vote the shares, need not be a shareholder but must have capacity to act as an agent. A general proxy authorizes the proxy holder to vote on all issues presented at the meeting. The duration of the proxy varies among the states. The RMBCA provides that a proxy is valid for 11 months, unless a longer period is provided in the proxy.[12]

Like other agencies, appointment of a proxy is generally revocable by the shareholder. A proxy also may be revoked by operation of law upon the shareholder's death or incapacity. Some statutes, however, provide that revocation by operation of law is ineffective, unless notice of the death or incapacity is communicated to the corporation before the proxy is exercised.[13] A proxy may, however, be irrevocable if it is "coupled with an interest" or "given as security." For example, a shareholder may pledge her shares to a creditor as collateral on a loan, appointing the creditor irrevocably as proxy holder.[14] Such a proxy is, however, revoked when the interest with which it is coupled is extinguished—for example, when the debt secured by the shares is paid.[15]

Voting Trusts and Voting Agreements. A person who accumulates sufficient proxies from shareholders can obtain control of the corporation or at least assure representation on the board of directors. Voting trusts and voting agreements also may be used to control large blocks of stock. A **voting trust** is created when a group of shareholders transfer legal title to their shares to a trustee in exchange for "voting trust certificates." The trustee has the power to vote the shares subject to any limitations in the trust agreement. Corporate dividends and other distributions usually are passed through the trust to the equitable owners of the shares, the holders of the voting trust certificates. The voting trust certificates often are freely transferable, like the shares they represent.

Early cases refused to enforce voting trusts, holding that separating the right to vote from other incidents of share ownership was contrary to public policy. Modern corporation statutes, however, uniformly authorize voting trusts subject to certain restrictions. For example, under the RMBCA, to be enforceable, a voting trust must be in writing signed by the participating shareholders, and is not valid for more than ten years unless the parties extend it.[16]

The voting trust may concentrate control of a large block of shares in one or a few persons, who can thereby elect directors and control the corporation. Voting trusts often are used in corporate reorganizations to give control to former creditors whose debt has been reclassified as stock as part of the reorganization plan.

The shareholder **voting agreement** (or **pooling agreement**) is a less formal control device. Unlike the voting trust, which involves a transfer of title to the shares to a third party, a shareholder voting agreement is simply a contract between two or more shareholders providing how their shares will be voted on certain matters, usually the election of directors. Shareholder agreements are enforceable under basic contract principles and generally are expressly authorized by statute.[17] Shareholder agreements often are used to allocate and maintain control in closely-held corporations. Their use in that context is discussed in more detail in Chapter 48.

Preemptive Rights. Frequently, an existing corporation issues additional shares of stock to finance corporate operations or expansion. Existing shareholders may enjoy "preemptive rights" in such new shares issued by an ongoing corporate concern. A **preemptive right** allows an existing shareholder to purchase a new issue of shares in proportion to his present interest in the corporation, before the shares are sold to others. A preemptive right,

---

[10]Important securities regulation laws govern solicitation of proxies from shareholders of publicly-held corporations by management and nonmanagement groups.

[11]See, for example, RMBCA §7.22(b).

[12]RMBCA §7.22(c).

[13]See, for example, RMBCA §7.22(e). Revocation of agency is discussed in Chapter 40.

[14]Other types of irrevocable proxies are listed in RMBCA §7.22(d).

[15]See RMBCA §7.22(f).

[16]RMBCA §7.30.

[17]See, for example, RMBCA §§7.31, 7.32.

if exercised, prevents dilution of a shareholder's financial or voting interest in the corporation. Though initially recognized by judicial decision, preemptive rights now generally are governed by statute. For example, the RMBCA and many state statutes provide that shareholders have no preemptive right to acquire the corporation's unissued shares unless a provision creating such a right is included in the articles of incorporation.[18]

Even if preemptive rights are permitted, both the common law and statutes recognize a number of exceptions. For example, preemptive rights generally apply only to new issues, not to shares that were previously authorized but unissued, or to a reissue of treasury shares. In addition, shareholders may have no preemptive right to acquire shares issued: for property or services rather than cash; in connection with a merger, consolidation, or reorganization; to satisfy conversion or option rights; or to officers, directors, or employees under incentive or compensation plans.

Preemptive rights are likely to be valuable to shareholders of a closely-held corporation to protect proportionate interests in control, dividends, and surplus. In contrast, most shareholders in publicly-held corporations own an insignificant percentage of its stock and possess a minimal voice in control of the business. In publicly-held corporations, therefore, denial of preemptive rights has little effect upon shareholders, who can maintain proportionate ownership, if desired, by purchasing shares on the market.

Shareholders' Right to Information

Corporate Records. Each corporation is required by law to keep appropriate accounting books and records minutes of its shareholders' and board of directors' meetings, and a detailed record of its shareholders. These records must be maintained in written form or in another form that can be reduced to writing within a reasonable time.[19]

Shareholder Inspection of Records. Shareholders have a right to be kept informed of corporate affairs. To achieve this purpose, both common law and statute give shareholders a qualified right to inspect corporate books and records. Under the common law, for example,

shareholders have the right to inspect books and records for "proper purposes."

State business corporation acts generally supplement the common law right with a statutory inspection right. This right is exercised by written demand on the corporation stating the purpose of the demand. Penalties for failure to honor a statutory demand for inspection vary among the states.

Under the RMBCA, a shareholder's right to inspect certain records, such as the articles of incorporation or bylaws, is absolute. Inspection of other records, however, such as accounting records or the list of shareholders, requires that the demand be made in good faith and for a proper purpose.[20] A proper purpose is one designed to obtain information to protect the shareholder's interest in the corporation. Proper purposes include, for example: ascertaining the financial condition of the corporation, the value of shares, or the propriety of dividend payments; discovering the existence of dishonesty or mismanagement by corporate officers or directors; and communicating with other shareholders to solicit proxies or publicize mismanagement. Improper purposes include harassment or extortion, acquiring trade secrets for personal benefit or a corporate competitor, and obtaining the shareholder list to sell for profit.

Corporate Management

Directors

All corporate powers are exercised by, or under the authority of, the board of directors. In addition, the business and affairs of the corporation are managed under the direction, and subject to the oversight, of the board.[21]

As part of its management function the board (1) makes basic policy decisions concerning, for example, products, services, prices, or labor relations, (2) selects, supervises, and removes corporate officers and other executive personnel and delegates authority to them, (3) determines executive compensation including pension and retirement plans, (4) determines if, when, and in what form or amount dividends will be paid, (5) determines financing and capital changes, (6) adopts, amends, and repeals bylaws, (7) participates with shareholders in effecting major corporate changes such as merger or dissolution, and (8) supervises the overall operation of

---

[18]RMBCA §6.30(a).
[19]See, for example, RMBCA §§16.01 (a)–(d).

[20]RMBCA §16.02.
[21]See RMBCA §8.01(b).

the enterprise.[22] Directors may be insiders—persons who also are officers or employees of the corporation or its affiliates. The board also may include "outside" directors, persons not affiliated with management. Boards of large publicly-held companies typically include a mixture of inside and outside directors.

Election, Constitution, and Tenure of Board of Directors. Although older corporation statutes required that the board consist of at least three directors, modern statutes commonly permit one-person or two-person boards. The number and qualifications of directors must be specified in the articles of incorporation or bylaws.[23]

The initial board of directors, named in the articles of incorporation or elected by the incorporators, serves until the first annual meeting of shareholders, which is usually held shortly after incorporation. Permanent directors are elected at that meeting and at each annual meeting thereafter. Under the RMBCA, the articles of incorporation may provide for two or three classes of directors. If there are two classes, each class comes up for election every other year; that is, each serves a two-year term. Because the terms are staggered, only one class's term expires in any given year. In the absence of classification, all directors are elected each year. After incorporation, the number of directors may be increased or decreased by appropriate amendment of the articles of incorporation or bylaws. A reduction in the number of directors does not shorten any incumbent director's term.[24]

A director whose term has expired continues to serve until a successor is elected and qualified. Under this rule, corporate power to transact business is unaffected by failure to hold an annual meeting because existing directors continue in office. Vacancies on the board are filled as provided by statute or the bylaws. Under modern statutes, vacancies caused by death or resignation usually are filled by the board of directors. Vacancies caused by an increase in the number of board members also are often filled by the board, although some states require shareholder action. A director elected to fill a vacancy generally serves until the next meeting of shareholders at which directors are elected.[25]

During their terms of office, directors may be removed by the shareholders for cause, such as fraud or breach of duty, usually by majority vote. Modern statutes, such as the RMBCA, also permit removal without cause by shareholder vote, unless the articles of incorporation provide otherwise.[26]

Formalities of Board Action. Corporate management authority is vested in the board of directors as a body, not in individual directors. Accordingly, directors usually must act in properly constituted meetings, affording opportunity for discussion, deliberation, and collective judgment. The timing and other aspects of board of directors' meetings usually are governed by detailed bylaw provisions. Meetings are either regular or special and may be held either within or outside the state of incorporation. Although all types of business may be conducted at both regular and special meetings, directors generally are entitled to advance written notice of special, but not regular, meetings.[27]

Unless the articles or bylaws provide otherwise, a majority of the number of directors fixed in the bylaws or articles of incorporation constitutes a quorum for transaction of business. The articles or bylaws may provide greater quorum requirements, and some states permit less than a majority of the board—for example, one-third—to constitute a quorum. Many states also permit board members to participate in meetings by telephone. If a quorum is present, the vote of a majority of directors present is the act of the board unless the articles or bylaws prescribe a greater number. Each director is entitled to one vote and may generally not vote by proxy.[28] Although the board usually acts in a meeting, the RMBCA and most state statutes permit directors to act without a meeting if a written consent, stating the action taken, is signed by all directors. Such a consent has the same legal effect as a unanimous vote.[29]

A director who objects to an action authorized by a majority of the board must either request that a dissent be entered in the minutes of the meeting or give written notice of dissent. Either action eliminates the dissenting director's potential personal liability for the action taken.[30]

Committees of Directors. Typically, the board of directors of a large corporation delegates much of its

---

[22]Henn & Alexander, Laws of Corporations 564 (3d ed. 1983).
[23]See, for example, RMBCA §§8.02, 8.03(a).
[24]RMBCA §§8.03, 8.05, 8.06.
[25]See generally RMBCA §§8.05, 8.10.

[26]RMBCA §8.08(a).
[27]See, for example, RMBCA §§8.20, 8.22.
[28]See RMBCA §§8.20, 8.24. Although a quorum usually is required for director action, vacancies on the board of directors generally may be filled by majority vote of the directors remaining in office, even if this number is less than a quorum. See RMBCA §8.10.
[29]See, for example, RMBCA §8.21.
[30]See RMBCA §8.24(d).

management authority to corporate officers and to executive and other committees of the board. Unless prohibited by the articles of incorporation or bylaws, the board of directors may establish one or more committees and appoint board members to serve on them.[31] Once created, a committee may exercise the board's authority to the extent specified by the board or provided in the articles or bylaws.

The executive committee, which performs board functions between meetings of the full board, is the most common committee. Other committees may include, for example, an audit, a nominating, a compensation, and a finance committee. To prevent excessive delegation of board authority to committees, their powers are limited by statute. For example, the RMBCA provides that a committee may not (1) authorize distributions, (2) approve actions requiring shareholder vote, (3) fill vacancies on the board, or (4) adopt, amend, or repeal bylaws. These important matters must be undertaken by vote of the full board.[32]

Officers

Functions of Officers. Corporate officers who conduct the day-to-day affairs of the business are appointed and removed by the board of directors. Officers are agents of the corporation to whom the board delegates authority to execute and administer board policy decisions. Although corporate management is legally under direction of the board, in many large corporations the officers effectively manage the corporation.

State corporation statutes require or authorize a corporation to have certain officers. Typically, a corporation will have a president, who is the principal executive officer of the corporation, one or more vice presidents in charge of various aspects of the business (for example, marketing, sales, or finance), a treasurer, and a secretary. In addition, numerous junior officers may be appointed such as assistant treasurer, assistant secretary, assistant vice president, comptroller, cashier, or loan officer. The duties of the various corporate officers generally are outlined in the bylaws.

Officers usually are appointed by the board of directors and serve at the pleasure of the board, subject to removal at any time. If a valid employment contract exists between the officer and the corporation, however, premature termination constitutes a breach of contract.

Officers' Authority. Because officers, unlike directors, are agents of the corporation, their authority to bind the corporation is governed by general principles of agency law, discussed in Chapters 40 and 41. Indeed, much of modern agency law concerns the liability of a corporation (the principal) for the acts of corporate officers (agents) on its behalf.[33] Like other agents, a corporate officer's authority to act for the corporation is derived from (1) actual authority—express or implied, (2) apparent authority, or (3) corporate ratification of a previously unauthorized act. An officer's express authority is derived primarily from four sources: the state corporation statute, the articles of incorporation, the bylaws, and resolutions of the board of directors. The most common and reliable of these sources is a resolution adopted by the board of directors authorizing the transaction in question.

Like other agents, corporate officers may possess a degree of implied authority that flows from their express authority. Most corporate officers, such as secretaries, treasurers, or vice presidents, possess little, if any, implied authority by virtue of their offices. Although many older cases held that a corporation's principal executive officer also had no implied authority to bind the corporation, many modern courts have expanded the implied authority of corporate presidents to include transactions within the corporation's ordinary or everyday course of business. Other courts give a president implied authority to bind the corporation to any contract that the board of directors could authorize or ratify. Despite this modern trend, prudent third parties always should require a board of directors' authorizing resolution to insure corporate liability upon important transactions negotiated by the officers. This approach provides maximum third-party protection by recognizing that the directors, not the officers, are the ultimate source of corporate authority.

Even if a corporate officer possesses no express or implied actual authority, the corporation may be bound by the officer's apparent authority or on grounds of ratification. As discussed in Chapter 40, apparent authority arises when a person (here the corporation) leads third parties to believe that another (here the corporate officer) has authority to act on its behalf. Third parties who

---

[31]See RMBCA §8.25(a).
[32]RMBCA §8.25(e).

[33]In addition, the principles governing the liability of persons signing negotiable instruments and other contracts in a representative capacity, discussed in Chapter 25, often are applied in the corporate context.

reasonably rely upon the officer's apparent authority may bind the corporation despite the officer's lack of actual authority. Even if the officer's conduct is beyond the scope of her actual or apparent authority, the corporation may be bound if it ratifies the previously unauthorized act of the officer.

Duties of Management

Corporate management, including directors, officers, and, in some cases, controlling shareholders, owes various legal duties to the corporation, and in certain instances, its shareholders and creditors. These duties, which have generated a substantial amount of litigation, are derived from a variety of sources including both state and federal law. Management duties existing under state law are discussed in the material that follows. Liability imposed under federal law, specifically federal securities law, is covered in Chapter 49.

The most important duties imposed upon management under state law are derived from the common law, and include primarily (1) the duty to exercise reasonable care in managing the corporation and (2) the fiduciary duty of loyalty to the corporation. In some jurisdictions, one or both of these duties are codified by statute. For example, under the RMBCA, an officer must discharge his duties "(1) in good faith; (2) with the care a person in a like position would reasonably exercise under similar circumstances; and (3) in a manner the officer reasonably believes to be in the best interests of the corporation."[34] A director must act "(1) in good faith, and (2) in a manner the director reasonably believes to be in the best interests of the corporation." In addition, directors "when becoming informed in connection with their decision-making function or devoting attention to their oversight function, shall discharge their duties with the care that a person in a like position would reasonably believe appropriate under similar circumstances."[35]

In addition to the duties of care and loyalty, state business corporation acts commonly impose liability upon officers and directors for violations of specific statutory directives. For example, directors may be held liable for improper dividends or repurchase of the corporation's shares, improper distribution of assets to shareholders upon liquidation of the corporation, and unlawful loans to corporate directors, officers, or shareholders.

Duty of Care

The duty of care is perhaps the most basic duty imposed upon corporate management. For example, as noted above, the RMBCA requires officers and directors to exercise the degree of care a person in a like position would reasonably exercise under similar circumstances. Although other formulations abound, this duty simply renders directors and officers liable to the corporation for negligence in the performance of their responsibilities. The duty of care does not, however, render management liable for every mistake or error in judgment. Under the **business judgment rule,** officers and directors have no liability for honest, unbiased transactions undertaken with reasonable care, even if it later appears that the act was ill-advised or mistaken.

Negligent management may take many forms, including negligent selection or supervision of employees, inadequate consideration or research of major decisions, or authorizing unnecessarily risky or unusual transactions. Directors and officers also must keep reasonably informed of corporate affairs. To help them accomplish this duty, the RMBCA and many state statutes permit officers and directors who act in good faith to rely upon information prepared by other corporate officers or employees, legal counsel, public accountants, or a committee of the board of directors.[36]

Although the business judgment rule insulates most management decisions from attack, courts will impose liability in appropriate circumstances, as the following case demonstrates.

Smith v. Van Gorkom
488 A.2d 858 (Del. 1985)

Trans Union Corporation was a publicly-held Delaware corporation. Although Trans Union had an annual cash flow of hundreds of millions of dollars, the corporation was unable to use all of its available investment tax credits. In 1980, company management began considering strategic alternatives, including the possibility of selling Trans

---

[34]RMBCA §8.42(a).
[35]RMBCA §§8.30(a)–(b).

[36]RMBCA §§8.30(d)–(f), 8.42(c).

Union to a company that could take advantage of the tax credits. Trans Union's chief financial officer suggested a leveraged buyout by management and calculated the feasibility of a buyout if Trans Union's shares were sold at $50 and $60 per share. The officer selected these figures merely for purposes of illustration; they did not reflect the officer's valuation of Trans Union stock.

Jerome Van Gorkom, Trans Union's chairman and chief executive officer, vetoed the suggestion of a leveraged buyout by management but, without the knowledge of other officers, approached Jay Pritzker to discuss his purchasing Trans Union. On September 18, after several meetings with Van Gorkom, Pritzker offered to purchase Trans Union at $55 per share, a figure that Van Gorkom had suggested because a leveraged buyout would be feasible at that price. Pritzker advised Van Gorkom that the board of directors must act on the offer no later than September 21. Van Gorkom called a board meeting for September 20 at which he explained Pritzker's proposal in a 20-minute presentation. Following the two-hour meeting, the board of directors approved Pritzker's offer on the condition that Trans Union could accept any better offer. That evening Van Gorkom signed a merger agreement while attending a social event. On February 10, Trans Union's shareholders approved the merger with 70 percent of the shareholders voting in favor, 7 percent opposed, and 23 percent not voting.

Plaintiffs, shareholders of Trans Union, brought a class action suit against the board of directors alleging that the board had violated its fiduciary duty by approving the merger at the meeting on September 20. The trial court ruled in favor of the board of directors. Plaintiffs appealed.

Horsey, Justice

. . . A director's duty to inform himself in preparation for a decision derives from the fiduciary capacity in which he serves the corporation and its stockholders. . . . Since a director is vested with the responsibility for the management of the affairs of the corporation, he must execute that duty with the recognition that he acts on behalf of others. Such obligation does not tolerate faithlessness or self dealing. But fulfillment of the fiduciary function requires more than the mere absence of bad faith or fraud. Representation of the financial interests of others imposes on a director an affirmative duty to protect those interests and to proceed with a critical eye in assessing information of the type and under the circumstances present here. . . .

Thus, a director's duty to exercise an informed business judgment is in the nature of a duty of care, as distinguished from a duty of loyalty. . . .

In the specific context of a proposed merger of domestic corporations, a director has a duty . . . , along with his fellow directors, to act in an informed and deliberate manner in determining whether to approve an agreement of merger before submitting the proposal to the stockholders. . . .

On the record before us, we must conclude that the Board of Directors did not reach an informed business judgment on September 20, 1980 in voting to "sell" the Company for $55 per share pursuant to the Pritzker cash-out merger proposal. Our reasons, in summary, are as follows:

The directors (1) did not adequately inform themselves as to Van Gorkom's role in forcing the "sale" of the Company and in establishing the per share purchase price; (2) were uninformed as to the intrinsic value of the Company; and (3) given these circumstances, at a minimum, were grossly negligent in approving the "sale" of the Company upon two hours' consideration, without prior notice, and without the exigency of a crisis or emergency.

. . . [T]he Board based its September 20 decision to approve the cash-out merger primarily on Van Gorkom's representations. None of the directors, other than Van Gorkom and Chelberg, had any prior knowledge that the purpose of the meeting was to propose a cash-out merger of Trans Union. . . .

Without any documents before them concerning the proposed transaction, the members of the Board were required to rely entirely upon Van Gorkom's 20-minute oral presentation of the proposal. No written summary of the terms of the merger was presented; the directors were given no documentation to support the adequacy of the $55 price per share for sale of the Company; and the Board had before it nothing more than Van Gorkom's statement of his understanding of the substance of an agreement which he admittedly had never read, nor which any member of the Board had ever seen. . . .

As of September 20, the Board had made no evaluation of the Company designed to value the entire enterprise, nor had the Board ever previously considered selling the Company or consenting to a buy-out merger. . . .

Despite the foregoing facts and circumstances, there was no call by the Board, either on September 20 or thereafter, for any valuation study or documentation of the $55 price per share as a measure of the fair value of the Company in a cash-out context. . . .

The record also establishes that the Board accepted without scrutiny Van Gorkom's representation as to the fairness of the $55 price per share for sale of the Company—a subject that the Board had never previously considered. The Board thereby failed to discover that Van Gorkom had suggested the $55 price to Pritzker and, most crucially, that Van Gorkom had arrived at the $55 figure based on calculations designed solely to determine the feasibility of a leveraged buy-out. . . .

None of the directors, Management or outside, were investment bankers or financial analysts. Yet the Board did not consider recessing the meeting until a later hour that day (or requesting an extension of Pritzker's Sunday evening deadline) to give it time to elicit more information as to the sufficiency of the offer, either from inside Management . . . or from Trans Union's own investment banker, Salomon Brothers, whose Chicago specialist in merger and acquisitions was known to the Board and familiar with Trans Union's affairs.

Thus, the record compels the conclusion that on September 20 the Board lacked valuation information adequate to reach an informed business judgment as to the fairness of $55 per share for sale of the Company. . . .

[W]e hold that the directors of Trans Union breached their fiduciary duty to their stockholders . . . by their failure to inform themselves of all information reasonably available to them and relevant to their decision to recommend the Pritzker merger. . . .

[Judgment reversed and remanded for determination of damages.]

Following *Smith v. Van Gorkom,* many outside directors of publicly-held corporations, concerned about increased financial risk and rising director and officer liability insurance costs,[37] resigned, declined to stand for reelection, or refused nomination. In response, most state legislatures have enacted statutes limiting the personal liability of corporate directors for money damages. These statutes are of three basic types: (1) "charter option" statutes, which permit the articles of incorporation to include a provision eliminating or limiting a director's personal liability for damages, subject to stated exceptions; (2) "self-executing" statutes, which automatically limit a director's liability, subject to stated exceptions; and (3) statutes limiting the amount of money damages, with stated exceptions. Most director liability statutes are of the charter option variety, pioneered by Delaware in 1986. The RMBCA also incorporates a charter option provision, which permits the articles of

incorporation to include a provision limiting or eliminating director liability to the corporation or its shareholders for money damages for any action or omission, except liability for (1) the amount of any financial benefit received by the director to which she is not entitled (for example, money received as a result of breach of the duty of loyalty discussed below); (2) intentional infliction of harm on the corporation or its shareholders; (3) improper corporate distributions (dividends or repurchase of shares); or (4) intentional violation of criminal law.[38] Note that the RMBCA, like virtually all state charter option statutes, is applicable only to actions for money damages (not equitable relief) maintained by the corporation or its shareholders (not third parties).

Duty of Loyalty

Officers and directors owe a fiduciary duty of loyalty to the corporation. Like other fiduciaries discussed in this text—trustees, agents, and partners—corporate directors and officers are under a strict duty to act honestly, and in good faith, and solely in the interest of another, here the corporation, regarding matters within the scope of the relation. As noted by one court, a director or officer

> owes loyalty and allegiance to the company—a loyalty that is undivided and an allegiance that is influenced in action by no consideration other than the welfare of the corporation. Any adverse interest of a director will be subjected to a scrutiny rigid and uncompromising.[39]

Cases alleging breach of the duty of loyalty are often litigated, and occur in a wide variety of fact situations, including those discussed below.

Conflict of Interest. The duty of loyalty may be breached when an officer or director has an interest actually or potentially in conflict with the interest of the corporation. Conflict of interest may arise, for example, in transactions between the fiduciary and the corporation—such as a sale of corporate property to a director, a sale of property by the director to the corporation, or other contracts between the director and the corporation. Conflict may also arise in transactions between two corporations having common directors.

---

[37]Director and officer liability insurance is discussed in Chapter 48.

[38]RMBCA §2.02(b)(4).
[39]Litwin v. Allen, 25 N.Y.S. 2d 667, 677 (N.Y. Sup. Ct. 1940).

Fiduciary transactions involving outright fraud or bad faith are voidable by the corporation. Further, under the modern approach, other transactions in which an officer or director has an interest are voidable by the corporation unless the contract or transaction is fair to the corporation, or is approved, ratified, or authorized by a vote of the disinterested members of the board or of the shareholders after full disclosure of all relevant facts.[40] "Fairness" in this context is determined by deciding whether "the transaction as a whole was beneficial to the corporation" taking into account both the fairness of the director's dealings with the corporation, and whether an independent corporate fiduciary dealing at arm's length would have entered into the transaction.[41] The officer or director asserting the validity of the transaction usually has the burden of proving fairness. These principles, which are derived from the common law and statutory provisions, apply to contracts or transactions between the corporation and the fiduciary individually, or another entity in which the fiduciary is an officer, director, partner, or is otherwise financially interested.

Competing with the Corporation. Officers and directors may not compete with the corporation in business transactions within the scope of their corporate responsibilities. The rule prevents fiduciaries from using the corporate position to unfairly or inequitably favor personal over corporate interests. For example, an officer or director may not use corporate assets or personnel to conduct personal business, use corporate trade secrets or customer lists for personal benefit or sell them to others, solicit corporate customers or employees for personal ventures, receive secret profits, kickbacks, or commissions on corporate transactions, or breach reasonable and enforceable covenants not to compete after leaving corporate employment.[42] A fiduciary who wrongfully competes is liable to the corporation for money damages and may hold any property acquired in breach of duty on a constructive trust for the benefit of the corporation.

Many wrongful competition cases involve the **corporate opportunity doctrine,** which prevents corporate officers and directors from usurping and diverting to themselves a business opportunity in which the corporation has an expectancy, property interest or right, or that in fairness should belong to the corporation.[43] In determining what constitutes a corporate opportunity, courts have developed a number of tests, including whether the opportunity was:

1. the same, as, or similar to, the corporation's current or planned business activities ("line of business" test);
2. one that the corporation had already formulated plans or taken steps to acquire for its own use ("expectancy" test);
3. developed by the director through the use of the corporation's property, personnel or proprietary information ("appropriation" test); or
4. presented to the director with the explicit or implicit expectation that the director would present it to the corporation for its consideration—or—in contrast, one that initially came to the director's attention in the director's individual capacity unrelated to the director's corporate role ("capacity" test).[44]

Although these tests provide guidance, they are not the sole test of liability. In each case, the court's perception of permissible business ethics and of the fairness of the transaction to the corporation often is determinative.

The standards governing liability for improper diversion of a corporate opportunity are similar to those applied to conflicting interest transactions discussed above. That is, a corporate opportunity may be pursued by a director only after approval by a vote of disinterested directors after full disclosure. Note that the Revised Model Business Corporation Act, as amended in 2004, provides identical standards for both cases.[45]

In some cases, corporate fiduciaries have been permitted to divert opportunities that the corporation is unwilling or unable to pursue because, for example, the corporation lacked the financial ability to undertake the transaction or because the persons offering the opportunity refused to deal with the corporation. Recognizing corporate inability as a defense to diversion, however, reduces management incentive to use best efforts to obtain corporate financing and resolve other problems. The following case illustrates the modern judicial approach to the defense of financial inability in corporate opportunity cases.

---

[40]See, for example, RMBCA §§8.60–8.63.
[41]RMBCA §8.60(6).
[42]Henn & Alexander, Laws of Corporations 629 (3d ed. 1983).

[43]*Id.* at 632.
[44]RMBCA §8.70, Official Comment.
[45]RMBCA §8.70.

Klinicki v. Lundgren
695 P.2d 906 (Or. 1985)

Plaintiff F. R. Klinicki was a shareholder, director, and vice president of Berlinair, Inc., a closely-held corporation that provided air taxi service. Defendant Kim Lundgren was a shareholder, director, and president of Berlinair. In 1977, Klinicki and Lundgren met with representatives of Berliner Flug Ring (BFR), a group of travel agents who chartered flights for German tourists, to discuss a contract by which Berlinair would provide charter flights for BFR. No agreement was reached but in June 1978 Lundgren learned that BFR might be willing to enter into a charter contract. On July 7, 1978, Lundgren incorporated Air Berlin Charter Company (ABC) and became its sole shareholder. On August 20, 1978, ABC presented BFR a charter contract proposal. After a series of discussions BFR entered into a contract with ABC on September 1, 1978.

Klinicki filed a shareholder derivative suit on behalf of Berlinair against Lundgren alleging that he had breached his fiduciary obligations as president and director of Berlinair by diverting a corporate opportunity to ABC. Lundgren argued that Berlinair had lacked the financial resources to handle the BFR contract and, therefore, the contract could not have been a corporate opportunity for Berlinair. The trial court held Lundgren liable for diversion of corporate opportunity and the Oregon court of appeals affirmed. Lundgren appealed to the Oregon Supreme Court.

Jones, Justice

. . . While courts universally stress the high standard of fiduciary duty owed by directors and officers to their corporation, there are distinct schools of thought on the circumstances in which business opportunities may be taken for personal advantage. One group of jurisdictions severely restricts the corporate official's freedom to take advantage of opportunities by saying that the ability to undertake the opportunity is irrelevant and usurpation is essentially prohibited; other jurisdictions use a test which gives relatively wide latitude to the corporate official on the theory that financial ability to undertake a corporate opportunity is a prerequisite to the existence of a corporate opportunity. . . .

Counsel for defendant . . . contends there is no corporate opportunity if there is no capacity to take advantage of the corporate opportunity. We reject this argument. By the same token, we reject plaintiff's contention . . . that financial ability is totally irrelevant in an unlawful taking of a corporate opportunity. . . .

Where a director or principal senior executive of a close corporation wishes to take personal advantage of a "corporate opportunity," . . . the director or principal senior executive must comply strictly with the following procedure:

1. The director or principal senior executive must promptly offer the opportunity and disclose all material facts known regarding the opportunity to the disinterested directors or, if there is no disinterested director, to the disinterested shareholders. If the director or principal senior executive learns of other material facts after such disclosure, the director or principal senior executive must disclose these additional facts in a like manner before personally taking the opportunity.

2. The director or principal senior executive may take advantage of the corporate opportunity only after full disclosure and only if the opportunity is rejected by a majority of the disinterested directors or, if there are no disinterested directors, by a majority of the disinterested shareholders. If, after full disclosure, the disinterested directors or shareholders unreasonably fail to reject the offer, the interested director or principal senior executive may proceed to take the opportunity if he can prove the taking was otherwise "fair" to the corporation. Full disclosure to the appropriate corporate body is, however, an absolute condition precedent to the validity of any forthcoming rejection as well as to the availability to the director or principal senior executive of the defense of fairness.

3. An appropriation of a corporate opportunity may be ratified by rejection of the opportunity by a majority of disinterested directors or a majority of disinterested shareholders, after full disclosure subject to the same rules as set out above for prior offer, disclosure and rejection. Where a director or principal senior executive of a close corporation appropriates a corporate opportunity without first fully disclosing the opportunity and offering it to the corporation, absent ratification, that director or principal senior executive holds the opportunity in trust for the corporation.

Applying these rules to the facts in this case, we conclude:

1. Lundgren, as director and principal executive officer of Berlinair, owed a fiduciary duty to Berlinair.
2. The BFR contract was a "corporate opportunity" of Berlinair.

3. Lundgren formed ABC for the purpose of usurping the opportunity presented to Berlinair by the BFR contract.

4. Lundgren did not offer Berlinair the BFR contract.

5. Lundgren did not attempt to obtain the consent of Berlinair to his taking of the BFR corporate opportunity.

6. Lundgren did not fully disclose to Berlinair his intent to appropriate the opportunity for himself and ABC.

7. Berlinair never rejected the opportunity presented by the BFR contract.

8. Berlinair never ratified the appropriation of the BFR contract.

9. Lundgren, acting for ABC, misappropriated the BFR contract. Because of the above, the defendant may not now contend that Berlinair did not have the financial ability to successfully pursue the BFR contract. . . .

[Judgment affirmed.]

Management Duties in Public Companies. In response to a series of massive failures of publicly-held companies, Congress passed the Sarbanes-Oxley Act of 2002. This statute, discussed in detail in Chapter 49, is designed to improve, for companies whose stock is publicly traded: audit quality and auditor independence; corporate governance; and the accuracy, reliability, and timeliness of corporate disclosures. In 2004 and 2005, the Model Business Corporation Act adopted a number of provisions also designed to improve governance of "public corporations," defined as those having "shares listed on a national securities exchange or regularly traded in a market maintained by one or more members of a national or affiliated securities association."[46]

As previously discussed, the "business and affairs of the corporation shall be managed by or under the direction, and subject to the oversight, of its board of directors."[47] Although the nature of the board's oversight will vary by corporation, new §8.01(c) makes clear that the oversight responsibilities of directors of public corporations include attention to:

1. business performance and plans;

2. major risks to which the corporation is or may be exposed;

3. the performance and compensation of senior officers;

4. policies and practices to foster the corporation's compliance with law and ethical conduct;

5. preparation of the corporation's financial statements;

6. the effectiveness of the corporation's internal controls;

7. arrangements for providing adequate and timely information to directors; and

8. the composition of the board and its committees, taking into account the important role of independent directors.

As fiduciaries, corporate officers and directors have always owed duties of full disclosure to the corporation. New §8.30(c) of the RMBCA reinforces this duty for directors by providing that "[i]n discharging board or committee duties a director shall disclose, or cause to be disclosed, to the other board or committee members information not already known by them but known by the director to be material to the discharge of their decision-making or oversight functions. . . ." A similar duty to disclose material information to superiors or the board is imposed on officers, who also must report "any actual or probable material violation of law involving the corporation or material breach of duty to the corporation by an officer, employee, or agent of the corporation, that the officer believes has occurred or is about to occur."[48]

Duties to Minority Shareholders. A number of cases have considered the nature of the duty owed by corporate directors and controlling shareholders to shareholders owning a minority of the corporation's stock. Directors are under a statutory duty to manage in the best interests of the corporation as a whole, and are subject to fiduciary duties when undertaking corporate actions such as issuance or redemption of shares, amending the articles of incorporation, or authorizing a plan of merger or dissolution. These duties require the directors to treat each class of shareholders fairly in taking corporation action and preclude attempts to favor

---

[46]RMBCA §1.40(18A).
[47]RMBCA §8.01(b).

[48]RMBCA §8.42(b).

one intracorporate group at the expense of another. For example, directors who authorize issuance of additional shares in an attempt to unfairly dilute the voting power of minority shareholders (freeze them out) violate their fiduciary duties.

The ordinary shareholder has no fiduciary duty to the corporation and is entitled to vote her shares for directors or other corporate actions as desired. Courts have, however, subjected a shareholder who possesses a controlling block of stock to fiduciary duties. Thus, controlling shareholders, through their ability to elect directors or approve extraordinary corporate matters, may not cause the corporation to take action that unfairly and adversely affects the rights of minority shareholders.

Summary

1. Corporate management powers are divided among the shareholders, the board of directors, and corporate officers. The shareholders, who are the owners of the corporation, periodically elect the board of directors, who have ultimate management responsibility. The board of directors, in turn, appoints corporate officers and delegates to them the authority to operate the corporation consistent with board policy.

2. Shareholders generally are entitled to elect directors and approve certain extraordinary corporate matters. Shareholder votes normally are taken at annual or special meetings, at which a shareholder may vote either in person or by proxy. To assure minority representation on the board of directors, many states require cumulative voting. In addition to accumulating proxies, large blocks of stock may be controlled through voting trusts and voting agreements.

3. To prevent dilution of a shareholder's proportionate financial or voting interest upon issuance of new shares, the articles of incorporation may provide for preemptive rights. A preemptive right allows an existing shareholder to purchase a new issue of shares in proportion to his or her present interest in the corporation, before the shares are sold to others.

4. Both common law and statute confer upon shareholders a qualified right to inspect corporate books and records.

5. All corporate powers are exercised by, or under the authority of, the board of directors. In addition, the business and affairs of the corporation are managed under the direction of the board. The number and qualifications of directors are specified in the articles of incorporation or bylaws. Unless the board is divided into classes with staggered terms, all directors are elected annually.

6. Corporate management authority is vested in the board of directors as a body, not in individual directors. Accordingly, directors must usually act in properly constituted meetings. The timing, quorum requirements, and other aspects of directors' meetings are usually governed by detailed bylaw provisions. Further, if allowed by the articles of incorporation or bylaws, the board of directors may establish committees of board members.

7. The officers conduct the day-to-day business of a corporation and are appointed and removed by the board of directors. Officers are agents of the corporation to whom the board delegates authority. As an agent, an officer's authority to bind the corporation is governed by general principles of agency law.

8. Corporate management, including directors, officers, and in some cases controlling shareholders, owe various legal duties to the corporation and in certain instances its shareholders and creditors. The primary duties of management under state law are (1) a duty to exercise reasonable or due care in managing the corporation and (2) the fiduciary duty of loyalty to the corporation.

Key Terms

straight voting	preemptive right
cumulative voting	business judgment rule
proxy	corporate opportunity
voting trust	doctrine
voting (pooling) agreement	

Questions and Problems

47.1 Melvin, a shareholder of Peoples State Bank, requested to inspect all of the bank's books and records to determine whether the bank directors had abused their fiduciary duties by diverting corporate assets to directors or by providing favorable treatment to certain bank customers who were friends and relatives of directors.
(a) Should the bank allow Melvin to inspect the books and records? Explain.
(b) The bank president is willing to allow Melvin access to some of the books and records. The president maintains, however, that allowing access to certain records would breach the bank's confidential relationship with its customers and would constitute an invasion of the customers' privacy. Melvin sues the bank to obtain all books and records. How should the court rule? Explain.

47.2 The bylaws of most corporations include a provision that allows the officers or directors to call special meetings of the board of directors. These provisions generally require that a notice of the special meeting be mailed to all directors within a given number of days prior to the meeting and that the notice specify the purpose of the meeting. In the absence of proper notice, any action of the board is invalid unless later ratified by the absent directors. Assume that Doaks, a director of Davidson Company, sent a notice of a special meeting to other directors for the purpose of "analyzing and discussing financial and legal problems facing the corporation and for the purpose of authorizing any action necessary for resolving such financial and legal matters." Jones, another director of the company, received the notice but decided to attend an important golf match rather than the special meeting. At the meeting, the other directors voted to dissolve the corporation. Jones, who strongly opposed dissolution, challenged the decision reached at the special meeting. Should the decision be enforced by a court? Why or why not?

47.3 Florence Barth owned the common shares of Barth, Inc. Its principal asset was an apartment complex managed by Florence. In addition to the common shares, preferred shares had been issued to the Federal Housing Administration, which had guaranteed corporate indebtedness for the purchase price of the apartment complex. To protect the FHA's interest, the articles of incorporation, which were duly filed and a matter of public record, provided that the corporation could not take the following actions without prior consent of the preferred shareholders: (1) pay for repairs from a reserve fund, (2) remodel, reconstruct, or demolish the apartment house, (3) rent apartments below a fixed rate, (4) carry out any basic change in corporate structure such as consolidation, merger, or voluntary liquidation, (5) amend the articles of incorporation, or (6) assign, transfer, dispose of, or encumber any real or personal property. Despite this limitation, Florence, without the knowledge or consent of the FHA, contracted to sell the apartment building to Newberry, who was unaware of the corporation's existence. When the FHA learned of the sale, it sought to avoid the contract on the basis of Florence's lack of authority. Newberry asserted that he believed that Florence was the owner of the property, or that in any event Florence had actual or apparent authority to sell because of her position as secretary-treasurer of the corporation, sole common shareholder, and apartment manager. Who should prevail? Explain.

47.4 Major Equipment Co. and four of its employees were convicted in federal court of illegal price-fixing. The company paid a $1 million fine. Several shareholders brought a derivative suit against the directors of Major Equipment Co. alleging that they had breached their duty of care by failing to discover the employees' illegal acts. Although the shareholders could not prove that the directors had actual knowledge of the price-fixing, the shareholders alleged that the failure to detect the price-fixing was evidence of negligence by the directors.
  (a) Do you agree with the shareholders' reasoning? Explain.
  (b) Would your answer differ if Major Equipment Co. was a large corporation with tens of thousands of employees or if it was a small corporation with only a few employees?

47.5 Reconsider the facts of *Smith v. Van Gorkom*. On appeal, the directors argued that even if they had breached their duty of care, they should not be held liable because the shareholders had ultimately approved the transaction. Under what circumstances, if any, should shareholder ratification of the actions of officers or directors relieve them of their liability for breach of duty?

47.6 By January 1, 2005, Lunken Corp., a Delaware corporation, had issued approximately 100,000 shares of common stock and was authorized to issue an additional 75,000 shares. During early 2005, Condec, Inc. acquired approximately one-half of Lunken's outstanding stock through tender offers to the shareholders. On May 1, 2005, Lunken's board approved sale of all of its assets to U.S. Industries on the condition that the sale be approved by Lunken's shareholders. On May 2, 2005, Lunken sold its 75,000 unissued shares to a subsidiary of U.S. Industries for 75,000 shares of U.S. Industries preferred stock. Lunken agreed to repurchase the 75,000 shares if Lunken's shareholders failed to approve sale of the entire company to U.S. Industries.

Condec sued Lunken and its board of directors alleging that the issuance of the 75,000 shares of its stock served no legitimate corporate purpose and had been designed merely to prevent control of Lunken by Condec. Testimony at trial established that if Condec obtained control of Lunken, Condec intended to replace the officers and directors.
  (a) Delaware law provides that shares of a corporation cannot be issued for an improper purpose. What do you think was the purpose of issuing the 75,000 to U.S. Industries' subsidiary? Is this a proper purpose?
  (b) Have the officers and directors of Lunken violated their fiduciary duty? Why or why not?

47.7 SAC is a corporation that manufactures and sells computer graphic equipment. Albert and Stanley were employees of SAC who managed the research and development of the corporation. Dr. Brennan, a university professor, invented a new type of computer graphic equipment and asked Albert and Stanley if they would like to form a business with him to market the machine. Albert suggested that Dr. Brennan allow SAC to market his invention, but Brennan stated that he was unwilling to allow his concept to be disclosed to or used by SAC. Further, due to poor financial condition, SAC was at the time neither inclined nor able to develop new products.

For six months Albert and Stanley worked with Brennan to establish a new company. During this time, they continued their employment with SAC. Finally, they quit SAC and devoted their full efforts to operating the new business.
  (a) Have Albert and Stanley violated their fiduciary duties as agents of SAC?
  (b) If Albert and Stanley had been officers or directors of SAC, would their conduct have violated their fiduciary duties?

CORPORATE MANAGEMENT — SPECIAL TOPICS

Chapter 47 examined the basic corporate management structure, including the roles, powers, and duties of shareholders, directors, and officers. This chapter examines important specialized topics in corporate management, including the principles governing litigation by or against the corporation, its officers, or directors; how major corporate changes are accomplished; and the problems of operating a closely-held corporation under traditional principles of corporate governance.

Corporate Litigation

As a legal entity, a corporation has the capacity to sue and be sued in the corporate name. Lawsuits for injury to the corporation may be maintained by corporate management directly, by shareholders "derivatively," or by others on behalf of the corporation. Claims against the corporation may be asserted by a variety of third parties such as creditors, federal or state governments, or shareholders (for example, to recover dividends or to examine corporate records). As previously discussed, notice of a lawsuit against a corporation is provided by serving process on the corporation's registered agent.

Important issues peculiar to corporate litigation include shareholder derivative suits and indemnification for litigation expenses of officers and directors.

Shareholder Derivative Suits

A corporation may sustain serious injury from a breach of duty, negligence, or other wrongdoing of corporate officers or directors. For example, officers or directors may have converted a corporate opportunity for personal profit. Although the corporation is a legal entity, capable of suing in its own name to recover for such an injury, corporate management has no interest in maintaining suit because it is allegedly involved in the wrongdoing. To provide a remedy in this case and others in which corporate management refuses to act, the law allows one or more shareholders to bring a **derivative suit** in the corporate name to enforce a corporate cause of action. That is, in a derivative suit, shareholders sue not in their individual capacities, but as representatives of the corporation. The corporation is the plaintiff in the case, though it is often a nominal defendant for procedural purposes. Any judgment in a derivative action is paid to the corporation, not the shareholders. The judgment nevertheless benefits both corporate creditors and shareholders indirectly by protecting the value of their investment in the corporation. If the suit is successful, however, the plaintiff-shareholder is entitled to reimbursement by the corporation for reasonable expenses, including attorneys' fees.

Prerequisites for Derivative Suits. Although derivative actions are a valuable tool for policing management conduct, they have been used as abusive "strike suits," suits brought not to redress a corporate wrong, but to secure a favorable private settlement for the shareholders and their attorneys. To prevent abuse, the law imposes a number of restrictions upon shareholder derivative actions that are discussed below. These restrictions are derived from the Federal Rules of Civil Procedure,[1] state civil procedure statutes, state business corporation acts,[2] and case law. Note that most modern shareholder derivative suits are brought in federal court under the federal securities laws or on diversity of citizenship grounds.

The following material explains the various legal and procedural requirements that must be met to maintain a derivative action.

Exhaustion of Intracorporate Remedies. Before commencing a derivative action, the shareholder must first make a demand upon the board of directors (or in some cases other shareholders) to enforce the claim, or prove that such an appeal would be futile — for example, because the wrongdoers control the corporation. That is, before proceeding derivatively, the shareholder must exhaust remedies available within the corporation.

Note that under the RMBCA, a written demand is required in all cases, whether or not it would be futile. Further, the derivative suit cannot be commenced until 90 days have expired from the date of demand unless (1) the demand is rejected by the corporation within the 90-day period, or (2) the 90-day delay would cause "irreparable injury" to the corporation.[3] This provision

is designed to eliminate the huge volume of litigation that now is maintained in many states concerning when and whether demand is required.

Contemporaneous Share Ownership. Under the "contemporaneous share ownership" requirement, the plaintiff must have been a shareholder at the time when the alleged wrong took place. Persons acquiring shares after that time by operation of law (for example, by will or intestate succession) also are eligible plaintiffs. The plaintiff also must own shares when the action is commenced, during its pendency, and through entry of final judgment. In addition, the plaintiff must "fairly and adequately" represent the interests of the corporation in enforcing its rights. These requirements assure that the plaintiff has a financial stake in a corporate recovery, prevents the plaintiff from "buying a lawsuit," and, in federal cases, prevents collusion in establishing diversity of citizenship.

Security for Expenses. In approximately one-fifth of the states, plaintiffs who own less than a minimum amount of the corporation's stock may be required, upon application by the corporation, to provide security (usually a bond) for reasonable expenses including attorneys' fees that may be incurred by the corporation or others in defending the suit. These "security for expenses" statutes are designed to prevent strike suits and have been upheld as constitutional even though they affect only small shareholders. Courts sometimes permit the plaintiff to bring additional shareholders into the suit in order to meet the minimum shareholding requirement, thereby eliminating the need to provide security.

Settlement and Dismissal of Derivative Suits. To discourage "strike suits" and unfair settlements, the Federal Rules of Civil Procedure[4] and a number of state statutes, including the RMBCA,[5] require court approval for dismissal or compromise of derivative suits, and notice to other shareholders of the terms of the dismissal or compromise. In approving the settlement, the court considers various factors, including the size of the settlement in relation to the value of the claim and the difficulty in proving it, the solvency of the defendants, and objections or proposals of other shareholders. Note that any settlement secretly paid to an individual

---

[1] Fed. R. Civ. P. 23.1.
[2] See, for example, RMBCA §§7.40–7.47.
[3] RMBCA §7.42.

[4] Fed. R. Civ. P. 23.1.
[5] RMBCA §7.45.

plaintiff-shareholder generally may be recovered for the benefit of the corporation in another derivative action.

The RMBCA and a number of modern state statutes expressly require the dismissal of a derivative suit if an independent group of directors determine in good faith and after reasonable inquiry that maintaining the derivative proceeding is not in the best interests of the corporation.[6] This provision "confirms the basic principle that a derivative suit is an action on behalf of the corporation and therefore should be controlled by those directors who can exercise an independent business judgment with respect to its continuance."[7] To protect the corporation, however, the court is required to assess the good faith and independence of the directors and the reasonableness of their inquiry.

Indemnification for Litigation Expenses

Directors, officers, and other corporate personnel often must defend lawsuits brought against them based upon the conduct of their corporate responsibilities. These suits may be civil, criminal, administrative, or investigatory in nature and maintained by either private or governmental plaintiffs. A question that has long concerned the law of corporations is the extent to which corporate personnel are entitled to be indemnified or reimbursed by the corporation for expenses of litigation brought against them in their corporate capacities. These expenses include primarily attorneys' fees and amounts paid in settlement of a suit or satisfaction of a judgment.

Although originally addressed by common law, indemnification is now governed by statute in all states.[8] Under the RMBCA, as amended in 1994, indemnification is allowed generally if the defendant acted in good faith and in a manner reasonably believed to be in the best interests of the corporation. If the action was criminal in nature, the defendant must additionally have had no reasonable cause to believe that his conduct was unlawful. The corporation, in its articles of incorporation, may permit or require broader indemnification than that outlined above, except for liability for (1) receipt of a financial benefit to which the director

was not entitled, (2) an intentional infliction of harm on the corporation or its shareholders, (3) an unlawful distribution, or (4) an intentional violation of criminal law.[9]

Unless the court determines that indemnification of some or all expenses is "fair and reasonable" in light of the circumstances of the case, the corporation may not indemnify a director

1. in an action maintained by or on behalf of the corporation (for example, a shareholder derivative suit) unless the director has met the appropriate standard of conduct outlined above; or
2. in any other proceeding, if the director was held liable for receiving "a financial benefit to which he was not entitled."[10]

A defendant who is successful on the merits or otherwise in defense of any suit described above is entitled to indemnification for expenses actually and reasonably incurred. Any other indemnification (unless ordered by the court) is made only as authorized in the specific case upon a determination that the person seeking reimbursement has met the standards of conduct discussed above. The determination is made by vote of the board of directors, or in some cases, by independent legal counsel or the shareholders. Note that indemnification of corporate officers is governed by principles similar to those governing directors.[11]

Directors' and Officers' Liability Insurance

A corporation may purchase and maintain insurance on behalf of officers, directors, employees, or agents against any liability incurred by them in their corporate capacities whether or not the corporation has the power to indemnify the loss.[12] Such insurance usually is called "D & O liability insurance." The policy usually covers both the corporation for amounts paid to indemnify corporate personnel, and officers and directors for amounts not indemnifiable by the corporation (for example, liability for negligence). The corporation and the person covered, therefore, often

---

[6]RMBCA §7.44.
[7]Report, *Changes in the Model Business Corporation Act—Amendments Pertaining to Derivative Proceedings,* 45 Bus. Law. 1241, 1242 (1990).
[8]See, for example, RMBCA §§8.50–8.59.

[9]RMBCA §§2.02(b)(5), 8.51(a), 8.58.
[10]RMBCA §8.51(d).
[11]RMBCA §§8.52–8.56.
[12]See, for example, RMBCA §8.57.

share the cost of the premium. Although the insurance protects against negligence, it does not cover liabilities incurred through self-dealing, dishonesty, knowing violation of securities law, or other intentional misconduct.

Extraordinary Corporate Matters

Although voting for directors is the usual extent of shareholder management participation, shareholder approval also is required to authorize certain extraordinary corporate transactions deemed beyond the scope of ordinary powers delegated to the board. These matters generally include amendments to the articles of incorporation, merger and consolidation, sale of substantially all corporate assets, and voluntary dissolution.

The procedure for effecting extraordinary corporate transactions is governed by statute. Generally, the board of directors adopts a resolution setting forth the proposed transaction. Written notice of the proposal is given to shareholders, who then vote upon it at either an annual or special shareholders' meeting. Unless a greater percentage is required by the articles of incorporation, a majority vote of all shares entitled to vote on the proposal usually is required for approval. For some transactions, approval of specific classes of shareholders also may be required. Once approved, documents reflecting the change are filed with the secretary of state of the state of incorporation. To protect minority shareholders who dissent from major corporate changes, the law provides a statutory "appraisal" remedy, through which dissenting shareholders are paid in cash for their shares. In addition, even if statutory procedures are met, courts may intervene on equitable grounds to prevent oppression of minority shareholders.

Amendment of Articles of Incorporation

A corporation has the power to amend its articles of incorporation. The amended articles may contain any provision that could have been included in original articles filed at the time of amendment.[13] Although changes may be made in any of the articles' provisions, amendments most commonly involve the corporate capital structure. If the amendment involves a change in shares or rights of shareholders, the procedures necessary to make the change should be included in the articles.

Although certain minor changes in the articles may be made by the directors alone, most amendments require approval by shareholder vote. Because many article amendments adversely affect the rights of one or more classes of shareholders, specific approval by vote (generally either a majority or two-thirds) of the adversely affected class may also be required.[14] Dissenting minority members of the class generally are bound by the majority vote but may assert the statutory appraisal rights discussed later in this chapter.

Combinations

Corporate combinations are extraordinary corporate transactions that often require shareholder approval. Combination occurs by merger or consolidation, or acquisition by one corporation of the assets or stock of another corporation.

Statutory Merger. Any two or more corporations may be merged into one of them (referred to as the "surviving" corporation) or may consolidate into a "new" corporation. In a merger, one survives and the other dissolves. In contrast, in a consolidation, both constituent corporations dissolve upon the creation of the new corporation. Shareholders of the disappearing corporations typically receive shares of the surviving or new corporation in exchange for their shares. The surviving or new corporation succeeds to all rights and property of the dissolved corporation, as well as all liabilities of the constituent corporations, by operation of law. Therefore, no creditors' rights are adversely affected by the combination.

To achieve the combination, a plan of merger or consolidation is approved by resolution of the respective boards of directors and is submitted for approval by vote of shareholders of both corporations. An appraisal remedy generally is available to dissenting shareholders of either corporation. Corporate combination using the method described above is commonly known as "statutory merger."

Before combining, corporations may be wholly independent or may stand in a parent-subsidiary relationship. Many states have adopted "short-form" merger statutes to provide a summary procedure for merger of parents and wholly owned or substantially wholly owned subsidiaries.

---

[13]See, for example, RMBCA §10.01(a).

[14]See, for example, RMBCA §§10.03, 10.04.

Under the RMBCA, for example, a parent owning 90 percent or more of the outstanding subsidiary shares may, by resolution of the parent board, merge the subsidiary into the parent without a vote by the shareholders of either corporation.[15] Short-form merger statutes generally create an appraisal remedy for dissenting shareholders of the subsidiary, but not for the parent's minority shareholders.

Asset or Stock Purchase. Corporate combination also may occur if one corporation buys all, or substantially all, of the assets of another corporation. In this case, although the corporate existence of both corporations is unaffected, the form of corporate assets is changed. For example, the selling corporation's assets now may consist solely of cash or securities rather than the inventory, equipment, land, or buildings that were sold. After the sale, the selling corporation may liquidate and distribute its assets to shareholders or may remain in existence as a holding or investment company.

The sale or lease of all, or substantially all, corporate assets outside the ordinary course of business is an extraordinary transaction, requiring board resolution and shareholder approval. Dissenting shareholders generally are entitled to an appraisal remedy. In contrast, a vote by the acquiring corporation's shareholders is not required, and shareholders of the acquiring corporation who object to the purchase have no appraisal remedy.

Corporate combination also may be achieved if one corporation purchases all, or a controlling block, of another corporation's stock. The purchase may be accomplished by negotiated sale with a major stockholder or stockholders, by purchases on the open market, or by tender offer to existing shareholders. No overall shareholder approval is required; rather, individual shareholders of the target company decide whether or not to sell their shares. If the buyer accumulates enough shares to control the corporation, it may be operated as a subsidiary, liquidated, or merged into the acquiring corporation. Because the sale involves no action by the acquired company's board and no formal shareholder approval, appraisal remedies are not available.

An issue that often arises when one company is purchased by another is whether the acquiring corporation is liable for the debts and liabilities of the selling company. The following case discusses the legal principles governing this issue.

---

[15]RMBCA §11.05.

Savage Arms, Inc. v. Western Auto Supply Co.
18 P.3d 49 (Alaska 2001)

Sixteen months after filing a voluntary petition in bankruptcy, Savage Industries, Inc., a firearms manufacturer, submitted a proposal to sell its assets to Savage Arms, Inc. The bankruptcy court approved the sale which was completed in November 1989. One year later Kevin Taylor filed a product liability suit seeking damages for injuries he incurred in May 1989 from a defective rifle manufactured by Savage Industries. Taylor's suit named Savage Industries and Western Auto Supply, a retailer of the rifle, as defendants. Western Auto settled its suit with Taylor and then sued Savage Arms seeking reimbursement of the settlement costs. The trial court granted summary judgment in favor of Western Auto ruling that Savage Arms was liable as "the legal successor to Savage Industries, Inc." The Alaska Supreme Court granted Savage Arms' petition for review.

Eastaugh, Justice

. . . Generally, when one company sells all its assets to another, the acquiring corporation is not liable for the debts and liabilities of the selling company. Courts have traditionally recognized four exceptions to this rule of nonliability, where (1) the purchaser expressly or implicitly agrees to assume liability, (2) the asset purchase amounts to a consolidation or merger, (3) the purchasing corporation is a "mere continuation" of the selling corporation, or (4) the transfer amounts to little more than a "sham" transaction to avoid liabilities. More recently, some courts have recognized . . . additional "modern" exceptions to the rule of nonliability: the "continuity of enterprise," [and "product line" exceptions]. . . .

1. *The traditional "mere continuation" exception.* Courts have traditionally imposed liability on successor corporations where the successor corporation is "merely a continuation" of the selling corporation. The primary elements of the "mere continuation" exception include use by the buyer of the seller's name, location, and employees, and a common identity of stockholders and directors. This well-established exception stems from judicial refusal to honor a transaction which is "little more than a shuffling of corporate forms, lacking any fundamental change with independent significance." [P. Blumberg, *The Continuity of the Enterprise Doctrine: Corporate Successorship in United States*

Law, 10 FLA. J. INT'L L. 365, 371 (1996).] The "mere continuation" exception is available to claimants seeking to impose liability on a successor corporation for products manufactured by a predecessor. Although Savage Arms argues that we should not adopt this exception, we disagree, because this is a well-recognized exception, and we see no reason to reject its application here. We therefore hold that it is available under Alaska law.

2. *The modern "continuity of enterprise" exception.* Western Auto also asks us to adopt the modern "continuity of enterprise" and "product line" exceptions. . . . Under the "product line" exception, a successor will be liable if it acquires substantially all of the predecessor's assets and undertakes essentially the same manufacturing operation of the same or similar products. . . . We conclude that the facts in this case are ill-suited to the "product line" exception, and we therefore decline to consider it at this time. . . .

The "continuity of enterprise" exception is an outgrowth of the traditional "mere continuation" theory of liability. Under this exception, a successor corporation may be held liable for injuries caused by its predecessor's products where the totality of the transaction between the successor and the predecessor demonstrates a basic continuity of the predecessor enterprise. The successor may be held liable even though the sale of assets is for cash and there is no continuity of shareholders.

Thus, whereas the traditional "mere continuation" exception depends on the existence of identical shareholders, the "continuity of enterprise" looks beyond that formal requirement and considers the substance of the underlying transaction. The key factors under the "continuity of enterprise" exception . . . are: (1) continuity of key personnel, assets, and business operations; (2) speedy dissolution of the predecessor corporation; (3) assumption by the successor of those predecessor liabilities and obligations necessary for continuation of normal business operations; and (4) continuation of corporate identity. This is a limited exception that looks past the identity of shareholders and directors, and focuses on whether the business itself has been transferred as an ongoing concern.

Only a minority of courts have thus far adopted the "continuity of enterprise" exception. . . . Critics of the modern exceptions (such as "continuity of enterprise") argue primarily that expanding liability harms the overall economy by making it more difficult for companies to reorganize or sell their assets without destroying the value of the ongoing business enterprise. For example, they assert that a buyer interested in purchasing substantially all of the assets of a corporation will, in some cases, decline to make the purchase if it will be forced to assume liability for past product defects as well. As a result, some corporations will be unable to find purchasers, and will instead be forced to sell off the corporate assets on a piecemeal basis, squandering any accumulated goodwill. Such a piecemeal sale would give a corporation certain economic advantages: the seller's shareholders would be able to receive full value for the remaining assets, and successor liability would not flow to the purchasers under any of the traditional or modern theories. But a piecemeal sale would cause an ongoing business to be lost to society, and potential claimants would be no better off.

This argument, although compelling in theory, seems to paint an incomplete picture of the economic realities. If successor liability is expanded to include the "continuity of enterprise" exception, some companies indeed might be unable to find buyers for their ongoing businesses. But we have not been referred to any evidence that adopting this modern "continuity of enterprise" exception (or the marginally more popular "product line" exception) has in fact increased the number of corporate liquidations or piecemeal breakups, or that rejecting the modern exceptions has in fact decreased liquidations or piecemeal sales. And our research has not disclosed studies that have so concluded.

We also note that permitting successor liability under the "continuity of enterprise" exception will not discourage large-scale transfers so long as anticipated successor liabilities do not exceed the value of the corporation's accumulated goodwill. Presumably, many corporations will continue to engage in efficient and productive transfers, with the purchasing firm merely factoring into the purchase price the cost of those successor liabilities. When firms contract for an asset transfer where the basic enterprise is to be continued, they negotiate to a price that reflects the fair market value of the transfer, taking heed of the risk of future claims. The purchasing firm will value any potential successor liability claims at least at the incremental cost of obtaining insurance coverage against successor liability for them. Where that insurance is too expensive or is unavailable, negotiations could collapse, and the firm will either continue to exist (and be subject to liability claims) or liquidate (and future victims will receive no recovery). But in many cases, we would expect selling and purchasing firms simply to negotiate to a rational price that takes account of these potential claims. The posited negative effects on the overall economy are too indeterminate and speculative to outweigh the policy of compensating persons injured by product defects.

[Critics also suggest that the continuity of enterprise theory will create a potential windfall to those injured by defective products.] In many cases, a predecessor manufacturing company will be purchased by a larger, more financially-sound corporation. The rule we adopt here does not limit injured plaintiffs' recovery to the value of the assets purchased by the successor corporation, so there could conceivably be situations in which product defect victims would receive a larger recovery than they conceivably could have received had the predecessor company remained an ongoing concern, and been bankrupted by the total claims. [Some critics] view the added recovery potential as an "injustice" to the successor corporation. . . . We assume that meritorious claims will be paid; that they are sometimes not paid due to insolvency does not change that underlying assumption. To characterize as a "windfall" full recovery for losses caused by product defects unjustly challenges the legitimacy of the injuries suffered. And once again, purchasing corporations can attempt to account for this risk of loss in the purchase price.

The other objections to expanded successor liability rules are also not dispositive. . . . [S]ome courts have argued that the modern exceptions impose liability on entities having no causal relationship with the harm. But basic to the "continuity of enterprise" exception is the preservation of a substantial portion of the goodwill of the predecessor corporation; the successor is fundamentally the same enterprise as the predecessor. When a firm negotiates to purchase another corporation, keeping the "enterprise" intact, it must anticipate any potential successor liabilities and negotiate an appropriate price. To permit the successor, which presumably negotiated a discount for potential successor liabilities when dickering over the purchase price, to avoid liability based on lack of causation would give the successor an unwarranted windfall.

Finally, this new rule will also have the effect of encouraging existing corporations to produce safer products, in keeping with the public policy goals that underlie product liability law generally. Corporations are currently motivated to correct defects to reduce their own exposure to liability, but the traditional successor liability regime undermines that incentive by giving the manufacturing corporation another option: offering itself for sale to a new investor. Without successor liability, the original shareholders can receive full compensation for the current value of the firm, without sharing the burden caused by any defective products manufactured before the sale. The rule we announce today will give manufacturing corporations additional incentives to market non-defective products, in order to maximize the corporations' market value in event of sale. We therefore adopt the "continuity of enterprise" exception to the general rule of nonliability for corporate successors. . . .

[Judgment reversed and remanded for consideration of the "mere continuation" and "continuity of enterprise" exceptions in the context of this case.]

Dissolution and Liquidation

Unless its duration is limited in the articles of incorporation, a corporation enjoys indefinite or perpetual existence. Therefore, once created, some formal action must be taken by the corporation or others to terminate it. Corporation statutes include procedures for voluntary or nonjudicial dissolution. In addition, both statutes and the common law permit involuntary, or judicial, dissolution by court decree in certain circumstances.

Voluntary Dissolution. The procedure for voluntary dissolution is similar to that for other major corporate changes. The board of directors adopts a resolution that must be approved by shareholder vote. Appraisal remedies are not available to dissenting shareholders. The decision to dissolve is then reflected in documents filed with the secretary of state.[16] A dissolved corporation continues its corporate existence, but solely for the purpose of winding up the business. Thus, upon dissolution, corporate assets are collected and liquidated, creditors are paid, and what remains is distributed, subject to any liquidation preference, proportionately to the shareholders.[17]

---

[16]See, for example, RMBCA §§14.02–14.03.
[17]See, for example, RMBCA §14.05(a).

Involuntary Dissolution. State corporation statutes also provide for involuntary dissolution by judicial decree in some cases. Proceedings for involuntary dissolution may be maintained by the secretary of state, the state attorney general, shareholders, or creditors. For example, under the RMBCA, a corporation may be dissolved in an action filed by the secretary of state if the corporation has failed to file its annual report, to pay its franchise tax, to maintain or appoint a registered agent, or to notify the state of a change in registered agent. The attorney general may seek judicial dissolution if the corporation procured its articles of incorporation through fraud, or exceeded or abused its legal authority.[18]

The court may order liquidation of the corporation in an action maintained by shareholders if they prove that (1) the directors are deadlocked in the management of the corporation and the shareholders are unable to break the deadlock, which threatens irreparable injury to the corporation; (2) the acts of the directors or those controlling the corporation are illegal, oppressive, or fraudulent; (3) corporate assets are being misapplied or wasted; or (4) the shareholders are deadlocked in voting power and have failed for at least two consecutive annual meetings to elect successors to directors whose terms have expired.[19] Note that even without statutory authorization, courts often have ordered dissolution upon proof of mismanagement or deadlock.

A creditor may obtain judicial dissolution by proving (1) that it has obtained a judgment against the corporation, the judgment is unsatisfied, and the corporation is insolvent, or (2) that the corporation has admitted in writing that the creditor's claim is due and owing and that the corporation is insolvent.[20]

Appraisal Remedies

State statutes afford shareholders a right to dissent from certain extraordinary corporate transactions and obtain payment in cash for their shares. This statutory "appraisal" remedy generally awards the dissenting shareholder the "fair value" of her shares. Under the RMBCA, fair value is defined as the value of the shares immediately before the action to which the dissenter objects is taken. Value is determined using "customary

and current valuation concepts and techniques generally employed for similar businesses," and with no discount for "lack of marketability or minority status."[21] Fair value must be determined by judicial proceeding—the "appraisal" aspect of the remedy—only if the corporation and the shareholder cannot voluntarily agree upon a fair price for the shares.

The appraisal remedy generally is available to shareholders who dissent from major corporate action requiring shareholder approval, including mergers and consolidations (subsidiary shareholders only in short-form mergers), sales of substantially all corporate assets outside the ordinary course of business, and amendments of the articles of incorporation that materially and adversely affect the rights of shares owned by the dissenting shareholder.[22]

Approximately one-half of the states and the RMBCA eliminate appraisal remedies for publicly traded shares (for example, those traded on a national stock exchange).[23] The rationale for this exception is that when "an efficient market exists, the market price will be an adequate proxy for the fair value of the corporation's shares, thus making appraisal unnecessary." In addition, "the uncertainty, costs, and time commitment involved in any appraisal proceeding are not warranted where shareholders can sell their shares in an efficient, fair, and liquid market."[24]

The statutory procedures for dissenting are complex and vary among the states. Strict time limits apply to virtually every action taken by either party. If statutory procedures are not literally followed, the shareholder loses the right to dissent and must accept the objectionable transaction.

Typically, if a proposed corporate action is one that creates dissenters' rights, shareholders must be notified of their right to dissent in the notice of the shareholders' meeting at which the vote will be taken. Before the vote, an objecting shareholder must file with the corporation a written notice of intention to demand that she be paid fair compensation for her shares and refrain from voting the shares in approval of the action. After the shareholder demands payment, the corporation offers or pays each dissenter the amount the corporation estimates to be the value

---

[18]RMBCA §§14.20, 14.30(1).
[19]RMBCA §14.30(2).
[20]RMBCA §14.30(3).

[21]RMBCA §13.01(4).
[22]Note that the RMBCA generally eliminates appraisal remedies in connection with amendments to the articles of incorporation. RMBCA §13.02(a)(4).
[23]RMBCA §13.02(b)(1).
[24]RMBCA §13.02, Official Comment 2.

of the shares. A shareholder who is dissatisfied with the payment or offer files another demand for payment with the corporation indicating her own estimate of the fair value of the shares. If the parties do not agree upon a fair value of the shares within a specific time, the corporation files suit to judicially determine their value. Based upon the evidence, usually including the testimony of one or more appraisers, the court determines the value of the shares and renders judgment for the shareholder in that amount with interest.[25]

The Closely-Held Corporation— Special Problems

State business corporation statutes are designed to govern creation and operation of all corporations, regardless of size or number of shareholders. Typically, however, these statutes envision a fairly large business with numerous stockholders who exercise little management control beyond their ability to elect directors. Shares are freely transferable and a public market often exists for the shares. The board of directors, which consists of at least three, and usually more, persons, exercises broad discretion in management of corporate affairs and appoints additional persons as officers to run the business. Board action is taken by majority vote with each director entitled to one vote. Formal meetings of directors and shareholders at which votes are taken are held periodically.

Most corporations, however, do not fit this statutory mold. They are closely-held corporations in which the few stockholders participate substantially in management, simultaneously serving as officers and directors. Corporate management is conducted on an informal basis, usually by unanimous shareholder consent. In addition, no public market exists for the shares. In this context, special problems are created not addressed by general corporation statutes. Although some state statutes have subchapters or groups of sections applicable, by election or otherwise, to closely-held corporations, many do not. In any event, these statutes have proven to be of limited utility. The shareholders of a closely-held corporation must, therefore, by careful drafting of the articles of incorporation and other corporate documents, antici-

pate and resolve in advance the problems peculiar to such a corporation within the confines of the state's general business corporation act. Some of those problems are discussed below.

Distribution of Management Power

Business corporation acts adopt a three-part management scheme involving shareholders, directors, and officers, each with specific responsibilities and rights in corporate management. In a closely-held corporation, in which shareholders are involved in daily management as both officers and directors, a realistic separation of powers is not attainable and corporate formalities such as votes and meetings may be ignored. Rather, the business may operate by unanimous or majority shareholder consent, indistinguishable from a partnership.

Ignoring corporate formality and blurring management functions in a closely-held corporation causes various problems. For example, disregard of corporate formality is one factor often considered in a court's decision to "pierce the corporate veil" to impose personal liability upon shareholders for corporate obligations.[26] Another issue is the extent to which management functions may be governed by private agreements that vary the statutory scheme of corporate control. Note that agreements among shareholders to exercise their functions as shareholders—for example, to vote for certain persons as directors—are perfectly valid and enforceable. Such agreements, together with share transfer restrictions, help assure that control will remain in the hands of specified individuals, preventing a transfer of ownership or management power to potentially undesirable outsiders.

In contrast, however, shareholders may, by agreement among them, attempt to dictate the decisions they will make in their capacities *as directors*. These agreements may relate, for example, to directors' decisions to pay dividends, or to employ a shareholder as an officer of the corporation. Such agreements often have been successfully attacked as limiting or extinguishing the *discretionary* power of the board, conferred by statute, to manage the corporation in the best interests of the

---

[25]See generally RMBCA §§13.20–13.31.

[26]Disregard of corporate form, or "piercing the corporate veil," is discussed in Chapter 45.

corporation. The agreements are said to "fetter" or in some cases "sterilize" the board of directors.

The modern legal trend, however, permits enforcement of shareholder agreements governing director functions in closely-held corporations. For example, modern judicial decisions have upheld such agreements as necessary to effective, flexible, management of closely-held corporations. As noted in the classic Illinois Supreme Court case, *Galler v. Galler* (1964).

> [S]hareholder agreements . . . are often, as a practical consideration, quite necessary for the protection of those financially interested in the close corporation. While the shareholder of a public-issue corporation may readily sell his shares on the open market should management fail to use, in his opinion, sound business judgment, his counterpart of the close corporation often has a large total of his entire capital invested in the business and has no ready market for his shares should he desire to sell. He feels, understandably, that he is more than a mere investor and that his voice should be heard concerning all corporate activity. Without a shareholder agreement, specifically enforceable by the courts, insuring him a modicum of control, a large minority shareholder might find himself at the mercy of an oppressive or unknowledgeable majority. Moreover, . . . the shareholders of a close corporation are often also the directors and officers thereof. With substantial shareholding interests abiding in each member of the board of directors, it is often quite impossible to secure, as in the large public-issue corporation, independent board judgment free from personal motivations concerning corporate policy. For these and other reasons . . . , often the only sound basis for protection is afforded by a lengthy, detailed shareholder agreement securing the rights and obligations of all concerned. . . .
>
> This court has recognized . . . the significant conceptual differences between the close corporation and its public-issue counterpart. . . . [Where] no complaining minority interest appears, no fraud or apparent injury to the public or creditors is present, and no clearly prohibitory statutory language is violated, we can see no valid reason for precluding the parties [in a closely-held corporation] from reaching any arrangements concerning the management of the corporation which are agreeable to all.[27]

In addition to judicial decisions, statutes in a growing number of states expressly authorize shareholder agreements in closely-held corporations that alter the generally applicable principles of corporate governance. For example, §7.32 of the RMBCA, adopted in 1991 and enacted in several states, provides that if the corporation's shares are not publicly traded, a shareholder agreement may

1. eliminate the board of directors, or restrict the board's discretion;
2. authorize dividends or other distributions of corporate assets in a manner not in proportion to share ownership;
3. establish who shall be officers and directors, their terms of office, and the manner of their selection or removal;
4. govern, in general or regarding specific matters, the exercise or division of voting power by or between shareholders and directors;
5. establish the terms of any contract for goods or services between the corporation and any officer, shareholder, or director;
6. transfer to one or more shareholders or other persons the authority to exercise corporate powers or manage the corporation, including the power to resolve a deadlock among directors or shareholders;
7. require dissolution of the corporation upon request of one or more shareholders or upon occurrence of a stated event; or
8. otherwise govern the exercise of corporate powers, corporate management, or the relationship among shareholders, directors, and the corporation in a manner that is not contrary to public policy.[28]

To be enforceable under §7.32, the shareholder agreement must be (1) set forth in the articles of incorporation, bylaws, or in a separate written agreement, and (2) approved by all persons who are shareholders at the time of the agreement.

Duties to Minority Shareholders

As in other corporations, officers and directors of a closely-held corporation (usually its majority shareholders) owe a fiduciary duty of loyalty to the corporation and its remaining (minority) shareholders. The

---

[27]203 N.E.2d 577, 583–585 (Ill. 1964).

[28]RMBCA §7.32(a). Examples of terms that would be unenforceable as contrary to public policy include those that eliminate appraisal rights, rights to inspect books and records, or rights to file derivative suits.

nature and extent of this duty is a frequently litigated issue in closely-held corporations because majority shareholders often have used their control of management and superior access to corporate information to treat minority shareholders unfairly. The following case examines the unique nature of the fiduciary duty of loyalty in closely-held corporations. The remainder of this chapter focuses on additional problems minority shareholders encounter and how those problems are resolved, either by the parties or the courts.

Van Schaack Holdings, Ltd. v. Van Schaack
867 P.2d 892 (Colo. 1994)

Van Schaack Corporation (VSC), a closely-held corporation, was established in 1951 by H. C. Van Schaack, Sr. In 1974, Beth Ellen Van Schaack (Van Schaack) became owner of 750 of VSC's 4,750 shares. VSC's principal asset was a one-half interest in Box Elder Farms Co. (Box Elder) that owned 29,000 acres of farmland located north of Denver, Colorado. The value of VSC shares depended almost exclusively on the value of the Box Elder land. During the early 1980s, plans were being made for construction of a new airport in the Denver area. In January 1981, Henry Van Schaack (Henry), who was a VSC director, informed VSC's board of directors that he had information that the new airport would be built on the Box Elder land. The directors obtained tax advice from VSC's accountant concerning the effect of the planned airport expansion and formed a special committee of VSC directors to monitor the airport project.

Van Schaack, who had not been informed of the directors' activities, met with Henry in 1982 to discuss the possible sale of her shares. In response to her questions about the value of the Box Elder land, Henry told her that he had no information and stated that in his opinion there was "no way" that the airport would be built on the land. At the VSC shareholders' meeting in May 1982, Henry, in the presence of the other directors, again indicated that VSC had no information about the land's value. Immediately after the shareholders' meeting, VSC's board of directors met and discussed Box Elder's recently completed sale of 155 acres of Box Elder land for about $8,000 per acre. In February 1983, Box Elder purchased 40 acres of nearby land at about $2,750 per acre. In August 1983, after over a year of negotiations, Van Schaack sold all of her shares to VSC for $2,000 per share. In January 1985, Denver authorities announced that the new airport and a new highway would be built on a portion of the Box Elder land.

Van Schaack sued defendants, VSC's directors, alleging that they had violated their fiduciary duties by failing to disclose material facts relating to the value of the Box

Elder land that affected the value of her stock. The jury found in favor of Van Schaack and awarded damages of $750,000. The court of appeals affirmed and defendants appealed to the Colorado Supreme Court.

Rovira, Chief Justice

. . . The question of what, if any, fiduciary duty is owed by directors or officers of a closed corporation to minority shareholders when purchasing that shareholder's stock is one of first impression for this court. . . . We have previously recognized that corporate directors owe a fiduciary duty to shareholders in exercising their responsibilities. . . . This duty encompasses the requirement that directors of a corporation and its controlling shareholders act with an extreme measure of candor, unselfishness, and good faith in relation to remaining shareholders. . . . In addition, it is widely recognized that the fiduciary duty imposed on corporate directors and officers dealing with minority shareholders is enhanced in the context of closed corporations. . . .

The duties previously recognized in this jurisdiction applicable to corporate directors dealing with shareholders include exercise of complete candor with minority shareholders in the negotiation of stock transactions. In our view, this duty encompasses the obligation to fully disclose all material facts and circumstances surrounding or affecting a proposed transaction. . . .

Imposition of such a duty is particularly justified in the context of closed corporations because shares of closed corporations are not publicly traded and information affecting the value of such shares is not generally known. While the value of publicly traded securities presumably reflects the marshalling and analysis of all information known by "the market," including information which is required to be disclosed under state and federal securities laws, a liquid and efficient market for shares of a closed corporation is, generally speaking, not available. . . .

Because there is no established market for a closed corporation's stock, little or no trading takes place in the shares and thus, "the valuation of [those] shares is a difficult task." [*O'Neal's Close Corporations* §1.02, at 33 (3d ed. 1992)]. Holding corporate "insiders" to a duty to fully disclose all material facts and circumstances surrounding or affecting the value of shares is warranted, therefore, because much of the information bearing on the value of a closed corporation's stock is not publicly available, and because no market exists in which the shares of such a corporation can be valued through the interplay of market forces.

As a result of this unique aspect of closed corporations, there arises the "necessity of preventing a corporate insider from utilizing his position to take unfair advantage of the uninformed minority shareholders," and the imposition of a duty of disclosure is warranted as "an attempt to provide some degree of equalization of bargaining position in order that the minority may exercise an informed judgment in any such transaction." *Sherman v. Baker,* [472 P.2d 589, 593–594 (Wash. App. 1970).] . . .

We hold, therefore, that it is a violation of a fiduciary duty for an officer or director of a closed corporation to purchase the stock of minority shareholders without disclosing material facts affecting the value of the stock, known to the purchasing officer or director by virtue of his position but not known to the selling shareholder. . . .

We . . . reject defendants' argument that . . . the undisclosed facts here were not material and thus, no duty of disclosure existed as a matter of law. . . .

First, we note that Van Schaack contended that defendants had failed to disclose the value of Box Elder land based on, among other things, the undisclosed prices of two land sales. The occurrence of the land sales, and the per-acre price of those sales, were not speculative or the subject of defendants' opinion. Furthermore, considerable evidence was presented at trial bearing on defendants' knowledge regarding the relocation of Denver's international airport. While it would be accurate to characterize that knowledge as being based, in part, on speculation and opinion, the fact remains that defendants took concrete, tangible actions, including committee formation and tax advice, in response to that knowledge. Given the conduct of defendants in preparation for the airport relocation, and the nonspeculative fact of that conduct, reasonable minds could differ regarding the importance of defendants' assessment of the likelihood of the airport relocation and the conduct taken as a result of that assessment.

Thus, we conclude that the undisclosed information cannot be said to be immaterial as a matter of law. . . .

[Judgment affirmed.]

Oppression of Minority Shareholders. As noted by the court in *Galler,* a major reason for shareholder agreements regarding shareholder and director functions is to maintain control of the corporation and to prevent oppression of minority shareholders. Oppression of the minority is a distinct risk in closely-held corporations. Because corporate statutes provide that corporate action is taken by majority vote of directors, a faction within the corporation with the power to elect a majority of directors may consistently outvote the minority and, therefore, exclude them from corporate management. The majority may "freeze out" the minority by refusing to pay dividends, and may drain off corporate earnings in the form of salaries, bonuses, or rents payable to majority shareholders. The majority also may deprive minority shareholders of corporate offices or employment and may purchase corporate assets at inadequate prices.

Because no outside market exists for shares of the corporation, which also may be subject to share transfer restrictions, a disgruntled minority shareholder may be locked into the corporation, excluded from management, employment, or dividends, but unable to sell out or force liquidation of the business (which would require 50 percent share ownership). These problems are exacerbated by the fact that all or most shareholders are involved in day-to-day management, increasing the likelihood of disputes and acrimony.

A number of devices have been developed to protect minority interests in closely-held corporations, devices that should be negotiated during corporate formation and may be included in the articles of incorporation, by-laws, or shareholder agreements. One device is to provide for greater than majority (commonly unanimous) voting requirements for shareholder or director action. This approach gives the minority an effective veto power over unfair or high-handed majority action. Another method is to create separate classes of stock for the majority and minority shareholder, with the majority shares entitled to superior dividend rights but with both classes entitled to elect an equal number of directors. Another protection device is a mandatory agreement among shareholders requiring the majority shareholders or the corporation to buy out the minority at a price fixed by a predetermined formula.

The following case illustrates one form of oppression in a closely-held corporation.

Wilkes v. Springside Nursing Home, Inc.
353 N.E.2d 657 (Mass. 1976)

In 1951, plaintiff Stanley Wilkes, T. Edward Quinn, Leon Riche, and Hubert Pipkin formed Springside Nursing Home, Inc., a Massachusetts corporation. Each of the men invested $1,000 and received ten shares of stock. They agreed that each shareholder would serve as a director and they divided the duties of operating the nursing home among themselves. In 1952, the corporation began paying each of the shareholders a weekly salary. In 1959, Pipkin sold all of his stock to Lawrence O'Connor but, otherwise, the corporation continued to operate as originally planned. Following a disagreement between Quinn and Wilkes in 1965, the relationship among all shareholders began to deteriorate. In 1967, Wilkes announced his intention to sell his shares but refused an offer from the other three shareholders because the price was too low. In February 1967, the corporation terminated Wilkes's salary. At the annual meeting in March, the three other shareholders failed to reelect Wilkes as a director or officer and he was advised that his services were no longer needed.

Wilkes sued Springside, Quinn, Riche, and O'Connor alleging that they had breached their fiduciary duties. The trial court ruled in favor of the majority shareholders. Wilkes appealed.

Hennessey, Chief Justice

. . . [W]e do not consider it vital to our approach to this case whether the claim is governed by partnership law or the law applicable to business corporations. This is so because, as all the parties agree, Springside was at all times relevant to this action, a close corporation. . . .

"[S]tockholders in the close corporation owe one another substantially the same fiduciary duty in the operation of the enterprise that partners owe to one another." [*Donahue v. Rodd Electrotype Co. of New England, Inc.*, 328 N.E.2d 505 (Mass. 1975)]. As determined in previous decisions of this court, the standard of duty owed by partners to one another is one of "utmost good faith and loyalty." [*Cardullo v. Landau*, 105 N.E.2d 843 (Mass. 1952)]. . . .

In the *Donahue* case we recognized that one peculiar aspect of close corporations was the opportunity afforded to majority stockholders to oppress, disadvantage or "freeze out" minority shareholders. In *Donahue* itself, for example, the majority refused the minority an equal opportunity to sell a ratable number of shares to the corporation at the same price available to the majority. The net result of this refusal, we said, was that the minority could be forced to "sell out at less than fair value," . . . 328 N.E.2d at 515, since there is by definition no ready market for minority stock in a close corporation.

"Freeze outs," however, may be accomplished by the use of other devices. One such device which has proved to be particularly effective in accomplishing the purpose of the majority is to deprive minority stockholders of corporate offices and of employment with the corporation. . . . This "freeze-out" technique has been successful because courts fairly consistently have been disinclined to interfere in those facets of internal corporate operations, such as the selection and retention or dismissal of officers, directors and employees, which essentially involve management decisions subject to the principle of majority control. . . .

The denial of employment to the minority at the hands of the majority is especially pernicious in some instances. A guaranty of employment with the corporation may have been one of the "basic reason[s] why a minority owner has invested capital in the firm." Symposium—The Close Corporation, 52 Nw.U.L.Rev. 345, 392 (1957). . . . The minority stockholder typically depends on his salary as the principal return on his investment. . . . Other noneconomic interests of the minority stockholder are likewise injuriously affected by barring him from corporate office. . . . Such action severely restricts his participation in the management of the enterprise, and he is relegated to enjoying those benefits incident to his status as a stockholder. . . . In sum, by terminating a minority stockholder's employment or by severing him from a position as an officer or director, the majority effectively frustrate the minority stockholder's purpose in entering on the corporate venture and also deny him an equal return on his investment.

. . . [A] strict obligation [is imposed] on the part of majority stockholders in a close corporation to deal with the minority with the utmost good faith and loyalty. On its face, this strict standard is applicable in the instant case. . . . Nevertheless, we are concerned that untempered application of the strict good faith standard . . . to cases such as the one before us will result in the imposition of limitations on legitimate action by the controlling group in a close corporation which will unduly hamper its effectiveness in managing the corporation in the best interests of all concerned. The majority, concededly, have certain rights to what has been termed "selfish ownership" in the corporation which should be balanced against the concept of their fiduciary obligation to the minority. . . .

Therefore, when minority stockholders in a close corporation bring suit against the majority alleging a breach of the strict good faith duty owed to them by the majority, we must carefully analyze the action taken by the controlling stockholders in the individual case. It must be asked whether the controlling group can demonstrate a legitimate business purpose for its action. . . . In asking this question, we acknowledge the fact that the controlling group in a close corporation must have some room to maneuver in establishing the business policy of the corporation. It must have a large measure of discretion, for example, in declaring or withholding dividends, deciding whether to merge or consolidate, establishing the salaries of corporate officers, dismissing directors with or without cause, and hiring and firing corporate employees. . . .

If called on to settle a dispute, our courts must weigh the legitimate business purpose, if any, against the practicability of a less harmful alternative.

Applying this approach to the instant case it is apparent that the majority stockholders in Springside have not shown a legitimate business purpose for severing Wilkes from the payroll of the corporation or for refusing to reelect him as a salaried officer and director. . . . There was no showing of misconduct on Wilkes's part as a director, officer or employee of the corporation which would lead us to approve the majority action as a legitimate response to the disruptive nature of an undesirable individual bent on injuring or destroying the corporation. On the contrary, it appears that Wilkes had always accomplished his assigned share of the duties competently, and that he had never indicated an unwillingness to continue to do so.

It is an inescapable conclusion from all the evidence that the action of the majority stockholders here was a designed "freeze out" for which no legitimate business purpose has been suggested. Furthermore, we may infer that a design to pressure Wilkes into selling his shares to the corporation at a price below their value well may have been at the heart of the majority's plan.

In the context of this case, several factors bear directly on the duty owed to Wilkes by his associates. At a minimum, the duty of utmost good faith and loyalty would demand that the majority consider that their action was in disregard of a long-standing policy of the stockholders that each would be a director of the

corporation and that employment with the corporation would go hand in hand with stock ownership; that Wilkes was one of the four originators of the nursing home venture; and that Wilkes, like the others, had invested his capital and time for more than fifteen years with the expectation that he would continue to participate in corporate decisions. Most important is the plain fact that the cutting off of Wilkes's salary, together with the fact that the corporation never declared a dividend . . . assured that Wilkes would receive no return at all from the corporation.

[Judgment reversed and remanded for determination of damages.]

Deadlock. Control devices designed to protect the minority create serious risk of deadlock at either the shareholder or director level. That is, with unanimous voting requirements, one dissenting vote can cripple corporate action. If the majority and minority each have the power to elect, for example, two directors, a 2–2 vote is not an unlikely possibility.

Various devices can be built into the corporate structure to control deadlock, such as providing that if the board is unable to agree for a specified time, then the dispute will be submitted to an arbitrator for a binding decision. Provisions concerning how the arbitrator is to be chosen and the extent of the arbitrator's power must be carefully drafted. Another device is to require one competing faction to buy out the other. Determining which faction buys and which sells, and at what price, is often a difficult issue.

The most drastic deadlock remedy is voluntary or involuntary liquidation of the corporation. In some cases, the parties, through a shareholder agreement, prescribe in advance the circumstances and procedures for corporate liquidation. More commonly, the minority shareholders will petition the court for involuntary dissolution, a remedy increasingly used by courts and legislatures in recent years in both deadlock and oppression cases. Because of the harsh consequences of involuntary liquidation, however, the RMBCA permits the corporation or any shareholder to avoid dissolution by electing to purchase at fair value the shares owned by the complaining minority shareholder or shareholders.[29]

---

[29]RMBCA §14.34.

Summary

1.   As a legal entity, a corporation has capacity to sue and be sued. Lawsuits for injury to the corporation may be maintained by corporate management directly. Alternatively, shareholders may sue "derivatively" as representatives of the corporation to recover for injury to the corporation caused by the negligence, breach of duty, or other wrongdoing of corporate officers or directors. To prevent abuse, derivative suits are subject to strict procedural limitations.

2.   Subject to a number of limitations, state corporation statutes, and in some cases the articles of incorporation or bylaws, allow indemnification of directors, officers, and other corporate personnel for expenses of litigation brought against them in their corporate capacities. Indemnification often is funded by insurance that protects both the corporation and corporate personnel.

3.   Although shareholder management participation is usually limited to voting for directors, shareholder approval also is required for certain extraordinary corporate transactions deemed beyond the ordinary powers of the board. These matters generally include amendments to the articles of incorporation, merger and consolidation, sale of substantially all corporate assets, and voluntary dissolution. State statutes afford shareholders a right to dissent from certain extraordinary corporate transactions and obtain payment in cash for their shares. This statutory "appraisal" remedy generally awards the dissenting shareholder the "fair value" of his shares.

4.   State business corporation statutes are designed to govern creation and operation of all corporations, regardless of size or the number of shareholders. Closely-held corporations, however, create management problems not addressed by general corporation statutes. For this reason, shareholders in a closely-held corporation should by careful negotiation and drafting anticipate and resolve in advance problems relating to distribution of management power and control, oppression of minority shareholders, and deadlock in corporate management.

Key Term

shareholder derivative suit

Questions and Problems

48.1   A plaintiff who wishes to initiate a shareholder derivative suit must meet a variety of requirements (for example, demand on directors, ownership of stock at the time the wrongdoing occurred) not generally imposed on plaintiffs. Why have courts adopted these requirements?

48.2   On September 1, Harris purchased 50 shares of Raygo Co. In October, Raygo purchased a small company owned by Raygo's president's sister for a price of $100 million. Harris immediately wrote to the president of Raygo demanding that the sale be rescinded because the purchase price far exceeded the value of the small company. Because Harris received no reply, she sold all of her shares of Raygo Co. on November 15. On December 1, Harris brought a shareholder derivative suit alleging that the president of Raygo had breached his fiduciary duties. The state statute concerning derivative suits provides in part:

> In a derivative action brought by one or more shareholders to enforce a right which may properly be enforced by the corporation, the plaintiff shareholder shall have been a shareholder at the time of the transaction of which he complains.

(a)   Assume that Harris did not own any stock at the time she filed the derivative suit. Under the statute, is she entitled to bring the suit? Explain.

(b)   Assume instead that on November 31, Harris purchased one share of Raygo. Would she legally be entitled to bring the derivative suit under the statute? Explain.

48.3   In 1984, General Motors Corporation (GM) acquired 100 percent of the stock of EDS, a corporation founded by H. Ross Perot. The sales agreement provided that Perot would exchange his shares of EDS stock for shares of GM stock and would remain as chairman of EDS. Perot also was elected to GM's board of directors. Within two years, major disagreements arose between Perot and GM and Perot repeatedly criticized GM management in public. In 1986, Perot offered to sell his GM stock to GM and after negotiations Perot and GM officers agreed to the terms of a repurchase agreement, which then was submitted to a committee of three GM outside directors who unanimously recommended board approval. The following day GM's board of directors approved the agreement that required Perot to transfer all of his GM stock to GM, to resign from GM's board, and to resign as chairman of EDS. Under the agreement, Perot also agreed to stop criticizing GM management, not to purchase GM stock or engage in a proxy contest against GM's board of directors for five years, and not to compete with EDS for three years or recruit EDS executives for 18 months. In exchange, GM agreed to pay Perot approximately $740 million, which was about twice the market value of Perot's stock. A group of GM shareholders filed a shareholder derivative suit against GM, Perot, and GM's board of directors alleging that they had violated their fiduciary duties by paying a grossly excessive price to Perot and by wasting company assets by paying "hushmail" to Perot. The defendants moved to dismiss the suit on the ground that plaintiffs had failed to make a written demand to GM's board of directors seeking corrective action prior to filing the suit. The plaintiffs contended that such a written demand would have been futile. How should the court rule?

48.4   The bylaws of Elmira Corporation provide in part:

> Every person who is or was a director, officer or employee of Elmira Corporation shall be indemnified by the Corporation against any and all liability and reasonable expense that may be incurred by him in connection with or resulting from any claim, action, suit or proceeding, civil or criminal, or in connection with an appeal relating thereto, in which he may be involved as a party or otherwise, by reason of his being or having been a director, officer or employee of the Corporation.

(a)   While Annabelle Jones was serving as a director of Elmira Corporation, she became involved in a struggle for control of the corporation. Jones and three other directors sued the remaining directors alleging that they had violated state law in a recent board of directors' election. The case later was dismissed by the court. Jones sought indemnification of her attorneys' fees and court costs from Elmira. Under the by-laws, is she entitled to indemnification? Explain.

(b)   Leon Lynch, treasurer of Elmira, embezzled several million dollars from the corporation. Elmira sued Leon and won a judgment against him. Is Leon entitled to indemnification of his legal expenses? Explain.

(c)   Many state statutes provide that a corporation may not indemnify an officer or director for defending a suit in which the officer or director is found liable for negligence or misconduct. Other statutes allow indemnification of an officer or director who has been found liable for negligence or misconduct only if the court approves the indemnification. Still other statutes allow indemnification regardless of the officer's or director's liability. Explain the advantages and disadvantages of each type of statute.

48.5   Big Bank shareholders approved a merger with First Bank Corp. Hanson, who owned 200 shares of Big Bank, voted against the merger and elected to exercise a statutory right to appraisal. After the appraisers valued the stock, Big Bank offered to pay Hanson the appraised price for his shares but he refused stating that he wished to withdraw from the appraisal process. Big Bank sued Hanson demanding that he tender his shares for the appraised price. Should the court allow Hanson to withdraw from the appraisal process? Why or why not?

48.6   Assume that you, your father, your brother, and a close family friend desire to create a corporation with equal shares to build and operate a restaurant. The family friend has the expertise in restaurant management, your brother will do the accounting, and you and your father are providing most of the capital, but will stay out of the day-to-day operations. What provisions should be included in the articles of incorporation, bylaws, or shareholder agreements to provide harmonious management, prompt resolution of disputes, prevent deadlock, prevent oppression of a dissenting shareholder, and provide orderly liquidation of the business, if necessary?

48.7   In 1998, five members of the Gray family formed a corporation to operate its farming and ranching operations. The family members also entered into a written agreement that provided in part: "So long as all of the original stockholders are alive, they shall not sell, trade, encumber or otherwise dispose of the stock which they now own or later may acquire without the written consent of the remaining stockholders." In 2005, Robert, one of the shareholders, notified the corporation of his desire to sell his stock. The other four shareholders refused to consent to the sale. Robert filed suit requesting the court to hold that the consent provision was unenforceable. He argued that the provision in effect permanently prohibited his right to sell his property. How should the court rule?

PART EIGHT

GOVERNMENT REGULATION OF BUSINESS

SECURITIES REGULATION

Corporate securities, such as stocks and bonds, represent claims against and ownership interests in a corporation, and are therefore only as valuable as the assets and the ongoing business that underlie them. Because corporate securities have no intrinsic value, but are a popular medium for investment, they often have been used in schemes intended to mislead or defraud investors. To prevent fraud and to assure the orderly functioning of the securities markets, the states and the federal government have enacted comprehensive securities regulation statutes. These statutes require full and honest disclosure of relevant business information by persons who offer or sell securities to the public. To promote public confidence, these laws also regulate the operation of the securities markets and the qualifications of the people who operate them.

Introduction to Securities Regulation

Development of the Law — State Regulation

The rapid industrial growth of the late nineteenth century was fueled to a great extent by the sale of corporate securities. Though most of these sales represented legitimate investments, many did not, and state legislatures were soon pressured to enact remedial legislation. In 1911, Kansas passed the first state statute regulating the distribution and sale of securities. Other states soon followed and all states now have such legislation. To this day, these statutes are known as **blue sky laws,** because their basic purpose is to prevent fraud perpetrated through "speculative schemes which have no more basis than so many feet of 'blue sky.' "[1]

State blue sky legislation typically requires registration of securities brokers and dealers, registration of securities offered or traded in the state, and proscribes certain fraudulent conduct. State statutes commonly require both disclosure of relevant information and qualification of the security. Under the qualification procedure, the state securities commissioner evaluates the merits of the proposed investment before the securities can be

---

[1]Hall v. Geiger-Jones Company, 37 S. Ct. 217, 220–221 (1917).

offered for sale. Although most blue sky statutes are based in whole or in part upon the Uniform Securities Act, promulgated in 1956 and revised in 1985 and 2001, significant differences in language and interpretation exist among the states.

State securities regulation proved inadequate in policing securities frauds, however, especially those operating on a national scale. After the stock market crash of 1929, which was precipitated in large part by vast quantities of fraudulent securities, Congress acted. Federal securities law, the subject of the remainder of this chapter, is based upon six statutes enacted between 1933 and 1940 pursuant to Congress's power to regulate interstate commerce.[2]

Federal Securities Regulation Statutes

Congress initiated federal securities regulation with the **Securities Act of 1933** (the 1933 Act),[3] which governs the public distribution of securities. With certain exceptions, it prohibits the offer or sale of securities to the public unless the offering is properly registered. Rejecting the state "qualification" or "merit" approach, the 1933 Act requires broad disclosure of relevant corporate information to prospective investors, provides civil remedies for violations, and prohibits fraudulent or deceptive practices in the sale of securities.

To complement the 1933 Act, Congress enacted the **Securities Exchange Act of 1934** (the 1934 Act).[4] The 1934 Act created the **Securities and Exchange Commission (SEC)** to administer federal securities law and created a comprehensive plan regulating public "trading" in securities. Thus, whereas the 1933 Act governs distributions by an issuer to the public for the first time, the 1934 Act governs subsequent trading in those securities among private investors on the various securities exchanges or in the more informal over-the-counter markets. The 1934 Act also requires comprehensive periodic disclosure of business information by companies with publicly traded securities, and imposes significant federal regulation on the securities markets.

Collectively, the 1933 and 1934 Acts are the heart of federal securities regulation. To supplement these statutes, Congress enacted four regulatory statutes of more limited scope between 1935 and 1940. These are

(1) the **Public Utility Holding Company Act of 1935,**[5] correcting abuses in the financing and operation of electric and gas utilities owned by holding companies, (2) the **Trust Indenture Act of 1939,**[6] protecting bond holders by regulating the terms of bond indentures under which large issues of corporate debt securities are administered, (3) the **Investment Company Act of 1940,**[7] regulating publicly owned companies, such as mutual funds, which are engaged in the business of investing and trading in securities, and (4) the **Investment Advisers Act of 1940,**[8] regulating persons who are in the business of rendering investment advice but are not securities brokers or dealers.

The Securities and Exchange Commission

The Securities and Exchange Commission (SEC) is composed of five commissioners, appointed by the president, each serving five-year terms. The terms are staggered so that one commissioner's term expires each year, and no more than three commissioners may be members of the same political party. Although the SEC itself has responsibility for SEC action and decisions, its staff is responsible for the day-to-day operations. The SEC operates from a head office in Washington, D.C., and various regional and branch offices. It is divided into five major divisions governing enforcement, corporation finance, market regulation, investment management, and corporate regulation. Like other major federal agencies, the SEC possesses quasi-legislative (rule-making) power, the power to investigate violations of the statutes it administers, and the power to adjudicate those violations and impose penalties.

The SEC has exercised its rule-making power extensively to promulgate rules governing procedural and technical matters, defining terms used in the various acts, and stating substantive principles of law. These rules are published in Volume 17 of the Code of Federal Regulations. The SEC also has adopted detailed forms that are used to comply with the disclosure and filing requirements of the securities laws. The SEC also periodically publishes "releases," which include guidelines for statutory or rule interpretation and outline the commission's position on current issues, and responds to

---

[2]The power of Congress to regulate interstate commerce under the Commerce Clause of the Constitution is discussed in detail in Chapter 4.
[3]15 U.S.C. §77a *et seq.*
[4]15 U.S.C. §78a *et seq.*

[5]Repealed and reenacted in 2005 at 42 U.S.C. §§16451–16463.
[6]15 U.S.C. §77aaa *et seq.*
[7]15 U.S.C. §80a-1 *et seq.*
[8]15 U.S.C. §80b-1 *et seq.*

individual inquiries regarding compliance with the law through its "no action" letters.

As part of its enforcement and adjudicatory powers, the SEC has supervisory and disciplinary power over persons registered with it including brokers, dealers, investment companies, investment advisers, securities exchanges, and attorneys and accountants who practice before the SEC. The commission also may proceed against persons who distribute securities in violation of the 1933 Act registration requirements, or who violate other securities law provisions, such as the "antifraud" provisions contained in both the 1933 and 1934 Acts. Many violations, such as disciplinary actions against persons registered with the SEC, are punished through administrative sanctions imposed after a hearing before the SEC. In addition, the SEC may maintain administrative proceedings to issue cease and desist orders against actual or potential violations of the securities laws or SEC rules. The SEC also may proceed in federal court against violators to obtain injunctions, civil penalties, and other relief. Finally, the SEC may refer serious violations to the Justice Department for criminal prosecution.

Definition of "Security"

An important securities law issue is whether a particular investment transaction constitutes a **security.** Resolving the issue determines whether securities law registration requirements or antifraud provisions, or both, apply to the transaction. Both federal and state securities laws broadly define "security" to cover a wide range of investment instruments. For example, the definitions include traditional securities, such as stocks and bonds, and catchall categories, such as "investment contracts" and "any interest or instrument commonly known as a security."[9]

Courts often must decide whether an unconventional investment transaction is a security, usually as an "investment contract." The leading case formulating the judicial definition of investment contract is *Securities and Exchange Commission v. W. J. Howey Co.,* decided by the Supreme Court in 1946.[10] In this case, W. J. Howey Co. offered for sale to the public individual rows of trees in a citrus grove, conveying the land by deed to the purchasers. In conjunction with the sale,

a service company affiliated with Howey offered the purchasers a service contract under which the company would cultivate, harvest, and market the fruit and distribute the net profit to the owner. In holding that the sale-service contract promotion was an "investment contract" and therefore a "security" requiring registration under the 1933 Act, the Court announced the now famous *Howey* test:

> [A]n investment contract for purposes of the Securities Act means a contract, transaction or scheme whereby a person invests his money in a common enterprise and is led to expect profits solely from the efforts of the promoter or a third party. . . .[11]

The Court noted that a security may be found under the test even if no formal stock or other certificate is used and even if, as in *Howey,* the investors have nominal interests in the physical assets of the enterprise. The test "embodies a flexible rather than a static principle, one that is capable of adaptation to meet the countless and variable schemes devised by those who seek the use of the money of others on the promise of profits."[12]

The *Howey* test has been applied to hold a wide variety of investment schemes "securities" including, for example, sales of limited partnership interests, interests in oil and gas leases, withdrawable capital shares in a savings and loan association, variable annuities, and interests in whiskey warehouse receipts. The guiding principle in all cases is whether the investors need the protection of the securities laws. Indeed, in several cases, courts have refused to apply the securities laws when other federal regulations adequately protect the parties.

At issue in the following case was whether a transaction constituted an "investment contract" under the *Howey* test.

Securities and Exchange Commission v. Edwards
124 S. Ct. 892 (2004)

Respondent Charles Edwards, chief executive officer and sole shareholder of ETS Payphones, Inc. sold pay telephones to the public. Through a package deal costing

---

[9]Securities Act §2(a)(1).
[10]66 S. Ct. 1100 (1946).

[11]*Id.* at 1103.
[12]*Id.*

about $7,000, a purchaser received a pay phone, site lease, a 5-year leaseback and management agreement and a buyback agreement. Under the leaseback and management agreement, the purchaser was supposed to receive $82 per month, a 14% annual return. ETS handled all day to day operations for the purchasers including selecting the site for the phone, installing the phone, arranging connection and service, maintaining and repairing the phone, and collecting the coin revenues. ETS' marketing materials and website described the arrangement as "an exciting business opportunity" that had become available because deregulation had "opened the door for profits for individual pay phone owners." The materials further noted that very few "business opportunities can offer the potential for ongoing revenue generation that is available in today's pay telephone industry."

The Securities and Exchange Commission filed an enforcement action against Edwards and ETS alleging violations of both the Securities Act of 1933 and the Securities Exchange Act of 1934. Edwards argued that he and his company were not subject to the federal securities laws because the pay telephone packages were not "investment contracts." The trial court ruled that the payphone sale and leaseback arrangement was an investment contract subject to federal securities regulation. After the federal Court of Appeals reversed, the U.S. Supreme Court granted review of the case.

Justice O'Connor

. . . "Congress' purpose in enacting the securities laws was to regulate investments, in whatever form they are made and by whatever name they are called." *Reves v. Ernst & Young,* [110 S. Ct. 945, 949 (1990)]. To that end, it enacted a broad definition of "security," sufficient "to encompass virtually any instrument that might be sold as an investment." *Id..* Section 2(a)(1) of the 1933 Act, [15 USCS §77b(a)(1)], and §3(a)(10) of the 1934 Act, [15 USCS §78c(a)(10)], in slightly different formulations which we have treated as essentially identical in meaning, . . . define "security" to include "any note, stock, treasury stock, security future, bond, debenture, . . . investment contract, . . . [or any] instrument commonly known as a 'security'." "Investment contract" is not itself defined.

The test for whether a particular scheme is an investment contract was established in our decision in *SEC v. W. J. Howey Co.,* [66 S. Ct. 1100 (1946)]. We look to

"whether the scheme involves an investment of money in a common enterprise with profits to come solely from the efforts of others." [*Id.* at 1104.] This definition "embodies a flexible rather than a static principle, one that is capable of adaptation to meet the countless and variable schemes devised by those who seek the use of the money of others on the promise of profits." [*Id.* at 1103.]

In reaching that result, we first observed that when Congress included "investment contract" in the definition of security, it "was using a term the meaning of which had been crystallized" by the state courts' interpretation of their "blue sky" laws. [*Id.*] . . . The state courts had defined an investment contract as "a contract or scheme for the placing of capital or laying out of money in a way intended to secure income or profit from its employment," and had "uniformly applied" that definition to "a variety of situations where individuals were led to invest money in a common enterprise with the expectation that they would earn a profit solely through the efforts of the promoter or [a third party]." [*Id.*] Thus, when we held that "profits" must "come solely from the efforts of others," we were speaking of the profits that investors seek on their investment, not the profits of the scheme in which they invest. We used "profits" in the sense of income or return, to include, for example, dividends, other periodic payments, or the increased value of the investment.

There is no reason to distinguish between promises of fixed returns and promises of variable returns for purposes of the test, so understood. In both cases, the investing public is attracted by representations of investment income, as purchasers were in this case by ETS' invitation to "watch the profits add up." . . . Moreover, investments pitched as low-risk (such as those offering a "guaranteed" fixed return) are particularly attractive to individuals more vulnerable to investment fraud, including older and less sophisticated investors. . . . Under the reading respondent advances, unscrupulous marketers of investments could evade the securities laws by picking a rate of return to promise. We will not read into the securities laws a limitation not compelled by the language that would so undermine the laws' purposes.

Respondent protests that including investment schemes promising a fixed return among investment contracts conflicts with our precedent. We disagree. No distinction between fixed and variable returns was drawn in the blue sky law cases that the *Howey* Court used, in formulating the test, as its evidence of

Congress' understanding of the term. . . . Indeed, two of those cases involved an investment contract in which a fixed return was promised. *People v. White,* [12 P.2d 1078, 1079 (Cal. App. 1932)] (agreement between defendant and investors stated that investor would give defendant $5,000, and would receive $7,500 from defendant one year later); *Stevens v. Liberty Packing Corp.,* [161 A. 193, 193-194 (N.J. Eq. 1932)] ("ironclad contract" offered by defendant to investors entitled investors to $56 per year for 10 years on initial investment of $175, ostensibly in sale-and-leaseback of breeding rabbits).

None of our post-Howey decisions is to the contrary. In *United Housing Foundation, Inc. v. Forman,* [95 S. Ct. 2051 (1975)], we considered whether "shares" in a nonprofit housing cooperative were investment contracts under the securities laws. We identified the "touchstone" of an investment contract as "the presence of an investment in a common venture premised on a reasonable expectation of profits to be derived from the entrepreneurial or managerial efforts of others," and then laid out two examples of investor interests that we had previously found to be "profits." [*Id.* at 2060.] Those were "capital appreciation resulting from the development of the initial investment" and "participation in earnings resulting from the use of investors' funds." We contrasted those examples, in which "the investor is 'attracted solely by the prospects of a return'" on the investment, with housing cooperative shares, regarding which the purchaser "is motivated by a desire to use or consume the item purchased." [*Id.*] Thus, *Forman* supports the commonsense understanding of "profits" in the *Howey* test as simply "financial returns on . . . investments." [*Id.* at 2061.] . . .

Given that respondent's position is supported neither by the purposes of the securities laws nor by our precedents, it is no surprise that the SEC has consistently taken the opposite position, and maintained that a promise of a fixed return does not preclude a scheme from being an investment contract. It has done so in formal adjudications, e.g., *In re Abbett, Sommer & Co.,* 44 S.E.C. 104 (1969) (holding that mortgage notes, sold with a package of management services and a promise to repurchase the notes in the event of default, were investment contracts) . . ., and in enforcement actions, *e.g., SEC v. Universal Service Asso.,* 106 F.2d 232, 234, 237 (7th Cir. 1939) (accepting SEC's position that an investment scheme promising "assured profit of 30% per annum with no

chance of risk or loss to the contributor" was a security. . .); see also *SEC v. American Trailer Rentals Co.,* [85 S. Ct. 513 (1965)] (noting that "the SEC advised" the respondent that its "sale and lease-back arrangements," in which investors received "a set 2% of their investment per month for 10 years," "were investment contracts and therefore securities" under the 1933 Act).

The Eleventh Circuit's perfunctory alternative holding, that respondent's scheme falls outside the definition because purchasers had a contractual entitlement to a return, is incorrect and inconsistent with our precedent. We are considering investment *contracts*. The fact that investors have bargained for a return on their investment does not mean that the return is not also expected to come solely from the efforts of others. Any other conclusion would conflict with our holding that an investment contract was offered in *Howey* itself.

We hold that an investment scheme promising a fixed rate of return can be an "investment contract" and thus a "security" subject to the federal securities laws.

[Judgment reversed and remanded.]

The Securities Act of 1933— Registration

The Securities Act of 1933 is concerned with distributions of securities—the process by which a corporation or other issuer offers and sells its securities to the public. It protects investors by requiring full and fair disclosure of relevant information regarding the securities offered and the issuer. The heart of the 1933 Act is §5, which provides that no security may be offered or sold to the public unless a "registration statement" has been filed with the SEC. Major 1933 Act provisions are discussed in the following.

Public Distribution of Securities

A corporation may be able to finance its operations or expansion out of its earnings or from private sources such as bank loans. Alternatively, it may raise necessary funds through a transaction exempt from securities law registration. If large sums of money are required, however, or if the company desires additional equity rather than debt financing, it may undertake a registered public offering (an initial public offering or IPO) of securities.

A public offering is not without its hazards. Registration is an extremely expensive and time-consuming process requiring extensive public disclosure of corporate affairs. Periodic reporting requirements under the 1934 Act impose additional expense. The offering may fall upon an unreceptive market. Dividend policy and control of the business will be affected.

If the corporation chooses public financing, it must devise some method to offer and sell the securities to members of the public. Although the corporation may undertake the task itself, most issuers have neither the expertise nor the personnel to make a public offering. Rather, the issuer enlists a network of underwriters and dealers registered with the SEC and appropriate state agencies. Under §2(a)(11) of the 1933 Act, an **underwriter** is a person who (1) offers or sells for an issuer in connection with a distribution of securities (that is, acts as an agent for the issuer), or (2) purchases securities from an issuer with a view toward distribution to the public. Under §2(a)(12), a **dealer** is any person who engages in the business of offering, buying or selling, or otherwise trading in securities issued by others.

Typically, securities in an underwritten offering are sold by the issuer to the underwriters, who sell them to dealers, who in turn sell them to the public. In a "firm commitment" underwriting, the underwriters purchase an allotment of securities outright from the issuer and resell them at a markup to the dealers. In this case, the underwriters bear the expense of any unsold securities. In a "best-efforts" underwriting, commonly used by less established issuers, underwriters attempt to sell what they can on a commission basis, with no liability for unsold shares.

1933 Act Disclosure Requirements

Superimposed upon this distribution scheme is the Securities Act of 1933 that requires that issuers file a **registration statement** with the SEC before securities are offered or sold to the public. The first part of the registration statement is the **prospectus,** a copy of which must be delivered to persons to whom the security is offered or sold. The contents of this "statutory" prospectus are outlined in §10 of the Act and SEC rules. The remainder of the registration statement (Part II) contains information that, though not distributed to all investors, is available for public inspection in the SEC files.

The prospectus states the price and nature of the securities offered, the amount and intended use of the proceeds, the plan of distribution, information concerning underwriters and counsel, current financial statements and other financial information, and management's discussion and analysis of the issuer's financial condition. It also contains detailed information about the issuer (for example, a description of its business and property), its officers and directors (for example, their compensation, ownership of the issuer's securities, and business relationships or transactions with the issuer), and its stock (for example, market price, dividend record, and other shareholder matters). Finally, the prospectus discusses material legal proceedings pending by or against the issuer. The second part of the registration statement contains copies of agreements with underwriters, opinions of counsel, certain major contracts, the articles of incorporation, and agreements or indentures affecting the security offered.

Various registration statement forms are available, depending upon the nature of the issuer, the surrounding circumstances, the type of security, and size of the offering. To ease the burden imposed upon issuers by federal securities regulation, in 1982 the SEC adopted a system integrating the disclosure requirements of the 1933 and 1934 Acts. This system permits issuers who are already registered and periodically reporting substantial corporate information under the 1934 Act to use special forms that require less detailed disclosure than the basic long-form registration statement. These forms incorporate by reference much of the information already on file with the SEC under the 1934 Act reporting requirements, discussed later in this chapter.

In 1992, the SEC continued its efforts to simplify the registration and reporting process by adopting Regulation S-B, which may be used by small business issuers. A "small business issuer" generally includes a domestic or Canadian company with revenues of less than $25 million. Regulation S-B, however, may not be used by investment companies, subsidiaries of companies that do not qualify as small business issuers, and companies with a public float (the aggregate market value of the issuer's securities held by nonaffiliates) of $25 million or more. Generally, Regulation S-B reduces the financial and nonfinancial information that a small business issuer must disclose both when registering a public offering of securities under the 1933 Act, and when reporting quarterly and annual information under the 1934 Act.

The Registration Process—Introduction

Section 5 of the 1933 Act divides the registration process into three periods: the pre-filing period (the period before the registration statement has been completed and filed with the SEC), the waiting period (the period between the filing date and the date the registration statement becomes "effective"), and the post-effective period. The registration process may be illustrated as follows:

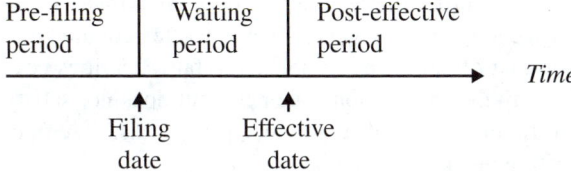

Permissible selling efforts differ depending on how far the registration process has progressed, reflecting the level of public information about the offering, and whether the issuer is registered and filing periodic reports under the 1934 Act. Violation of the provisions discussed below generally is referred to as "gun jumping." Before discussing these "gun jumping" provisions, several preliminary points should be noted.

Oral v. Written Communication. Under the 1933 Act, communications are either oral or written. Written communications include those that are: written or printed, broadcast by radio or television, or graphic. Graphic communications include virtually all electronic communications including, for example, audio tapes, video tapes, facsimiles, CD-ROMs, electronic mail, Internet websites, computers, computer networks, and other forms of computer data compilation. Communications that fall outside the above definition are oral, a term that includes telephone calls and live, real-time communications to a live audience.

Safe Harbors for Ongoing Business Communications. Two "safe harbor" provisions insulate most routine business communications from gun jumping liability. First, all issuers reporting under the 1934 Act may, during the registration process, continue to disseminate or publish: (1) regularly-released factual business information, and (2) forward-looking information, such as earnings and other financial projections, and management statements concerning its plans and objectives for future operations, products, or services.

Non-reporting issuers may publish only regularly-released factual business information that is intended for use by persons other than in their capacity as investors or prospective investors.[13]

Prefiling Communications. Communications made by issuers more than 30 days prior to filing a registration statement do not constitute offers to sell prohibited by Section 5 unless they refer to a securities offering that is or will be registered under the 1933 Act.[14]

The Registration Process—Permissible Selling Efforts

The following material outlines the selling efforts permitted by Section 5 during the various stages of the registration process for non-reporting companies. Some of the more liberal requirements for companies already reporting information are then discussed.

The Pre-filing Period. Before a registration statement is filed, both sales of securities and oral or written offers to buy or sell securities are prohibited. The term "offer" is broadly defined to include any activity reasonably calculated to solicit or create buying interest.[15] Although preliminary negotiations between the issuer and underwriters and among underwriters are exempted from the definition of "offer," virtually any other selling effort during the pre-filing period, including offers to or by dealers, is a violation of the Act.

The Waiting Period—Duration. Section 8(a) of the Act provides that the registration statement becomes "effective" 20 days after it is filed with the SEC, but that a new 20-day period begins to run upon the filing of any subsequent amendment to the registration statement. Although the statutory waiting period is 20 days, the period usually is in fact much longer, often several months. Section 8 empowers the SEC to issue a "refusal" or "stop" order to suspend the effectiveness of an inaccurate or incomplete registration statement or one that contains a material misrepresentation or omission. Rather than using the refusal or stop order procedures, however, the SEC usually proceeds through a more informal process that prevents a deficient registration from becoming effective. Specifically,

---

[13]Securities Act Rules 168–169.
[14]Securities Act Rule 163A.
[15]Securities Act §2(a)(3).

registrants typically stipulate to a "delaying amendment," authorized under Rule 473, which creates the fiction that the issuer is continuously amending the registration statement and thus continuously restarting the 20-day waiting period. The SEC works with the issuer to correct deficiencies through a "deficiency letter" or "letter of comment" procedure through which the SEC informs the issuer of problems in the registration statement. The issuer then amends the registration statement to address the SEC's concerns and, when the SEC finally becomes satisfied that all of the deficiencies have been corrected, the SEC uses its power under §8(a) to accelerate the effective date of the registration statement.

Common deficiencies in the registration statement include inadequate disclosure of specific sources of corporate income or loss; inadequate explanation of the use of the proceeds of the offering; inadequate disclosure of transactions between the issuer and insiders, such as officers, directors, or major shareholders; and failure to make the prospectus readable.

The Waiting Period—Permissible Selling Efforts. As in the pre-filing period, no sales of securities are permitted during the waiting period. Offers to buy or sell are, however, allowed. Although the Act imposes no restrictions upon oral offers during the waiting period, written offers are closely regulated. As a general rule, three types of written offering materials are permitted: the preliminary or "red herring" prospectus, the "tombstone" advertisement, and the "free-writing prospectus."

Preliminary Prospectus. The 1933 Act makes it unlawful to transmit any prospectus (defined in §2(a)(10) to include all written offers to sell a security) after the registration statement is filed that does not disclose all relevant information about the issuer outlined in §10. Because the offering price (and information dependent upon the offering price) generally is unavailable during the waiting period, the 1933 Act authorizes the use of a preliminary prospectus during the waiting period. Such a prospectus must contain a legend in red ink (hence the term "red herring") that a registration statement has been filed but has not yet become effective, that information in the prospectus is subject to completion or amendment, and that sales may be made only after the registration statement becomes effective.

Tombstone Advertisement. The 1933 Act excludes from the definition of prospectus any written com-munication that merely identifies the security and its price, states by whom orders will be executed and from whom a prospectus may be obtained, and contains other information which may be authorized or required by SEC rules and regulations.[16] Communications of this type are known as "tombstone advertisements" because they are customarily framed by a black border. Most financial publications contain a number of these notices in each issue.

Free-Writing Prospectus. A third permitted communication during the waiting period is the "free-writing prospectus," defined generally as a written communication that offers to sell or solicits to buy securities covered by the registration statement, but does not satisfy the requirements of a statutory prospectus.[17] A free-writing prospectus may be used if:

1. a statutory prospectus has been delivered or (for certain large issuers) is available;
2. its information does not conflict with that contained in the registration statement;
3. it contains a legend indicating that: it relates to a registered public offering; the registration statement is available on the SEC website; and that a prospectus can be obtained from the issuer, any underwriter, or dealer, by calling a toll-free number; and
4. it is filed with the SEC.[18]

The Post-effective Period. Once the registration statement becomes effective, the underwriters and dealers are free to make offers and sales of the registered securities. The Act provides, however, that a registered security delivered for sale must be accompanied or preceded by a copy of the final prospectus. By SEC rule,[19] this requirement is deemed satisfied when the final prospectus is filed with the SEC. At that point the prospectus will be publicly available on the SEC website. A prospectus used more than nine months after

---

[16]Securities Act §2(a)(10). Pursuant to this authority, the SEC has adopted Rule 134, which specifically outlines the various categories of information that may be included.

[17]Securities Act Rule 405.

[18]Securities Act Rule 433. Free-writing prospectuses prepared, used, or referenced by persons other than the issuer (such as underwriters or dealers) need not be filed. They must, however, be retained for three years.

[19]Securities Act Rule 172.

the registration statement becomes effective must be updated so that its information is no more than 16 months old.[20] In addition, whether or not the nine-month period has expired, the prospectus must be updated to reflect any development occurring after the effective date, such as a change in earnings, that would make the original prospectus materially misleading.

Offerings by Reporting Companies

The preceding discussion outlines the procedure used by non-reporting companies. The SEC permits many companies filing periodic reports under the 1934 Act to use much less rigorous procedures for securities offerings. The reason for this approach is that much of the information contained in a registration statement already is publicly available for these companies through their periodic filings under the 1934 Act, discussed later in this chapter. In addition, the activities of these companies are widely reported in the popular and business press, and analyzed by market professionals and institutional investors. Depending upon their size, market following, and reporting history, reporting companies are classified as either "unseasoned," "seasoned," or "well-known seasoned" issuers.

One device used by seasoned companies is shelf registration, authorized by 1933 Act Rule 415. Under shelf registration a company files a "base" prospectus, and then may issue securities as needed under it (a "takedown" of securities from the shelf) for up to three years. An issuer who files a new shelf registration statement within three years after the effective date of the original can continue to offer and sell securities under the original until the earlier of: (1) six months after the new registration statement is filed; or (2) the new registration statement's effective date. Once the new registration statement is effective, securities remaining unsold under the original are then included for sale under the new statement. In this manner, issuers using shelf registration can offer and sell securities on a continuous basis with no "blackout" period every three years between the expiration of the old and effectiveness of the new registration statement.

The offering requirements are further liberalized for "well-known seasoned issuers," defined as 1934 Act reporting companies that have equity securities with a market value of at least $700 million, or at least $1 bil-

lion in debt issued in the last three years.[21] Such issuers, which include approximately 30 percent of listed issuers, enjoy almost complete exemption from §5's gun jumping provisions. For example, unlike other issuers, they are allowed to make oral or written offers and may use free-writing prospectuses before filing a registration statement.[22] In addition, they qualify for "automatic shelf registration," under which the registration statement is effective immediately upon filing and permits the issuer freely to add additional information including new classes of securities, or majority-owned subsidiaries as registrants, to the registration statement.

Exemption from 1933 Act Registration

Sections 3 and 4 of the 1933 Act exempt certain securities and security transactions from the registration requirements outlined above. These provisions are heavily supplemented by various SEC rules and releases. Although the exemptions excuse registration or impose alternative requirements, they do not alter liability under the Act's antifraud provisions (discussed later in the chapter). In addition, exemptions generally are strictly construed and the person claiming an exemption has the burden of proving its availability. Table 49.1 provides an overview of the various security and transaction exemptions in the 1933 Act, which are discussed in detail below.

Exempt Securities and Transactions

Section 3(a) of the 1933 Act exempts various securities from registration based upon the nature of the security or its issuer. These include (1) qualified securities issued or guaranteed by state, local, and federal governments and governmental organizations, banks, and certain insurance companies, (2) a negotiable instrument, such as a promissory note, if the instrument has a maturity date not exceeding nine months, (3) securities issued by a not-for-profit organization organized and operated solely for religious, educational, benevolent, fraternal, charitable, or reformatory purposes, (4) securities issued by savings and loan associations or similar institutions supervised or

---

[20]Securities Act §10(a)(3).

[21]Securities Act Rule 405.
[22]Securities Act Rule 163.

Table 49.1	**Overview of Securities and Transaction Exemptions— Securities Act of 1933**

Exemptions	Applicable Law
Exempt Securities	
• Government, bank, and certain insurance company securities	§3(a)(2)
• Short-term negotiable instruments	§3(a)(3)
• Securities issued by certain not-for-profit organizations	§3(a)(4)
• Savings and loan, and farmers' cooperative securities	§3(a)(5)
• Certain securities issued by federally regulated common carriers	§3(a)(6)
• Insurance policies and annuity contracts	§3(a)(8)
Exempt Distributions by Issuers	
• Small or limited offerings	§§4(2), 3(b), 4(6), and 28
	Regulation A (Rules 251–263)
	Regulation D (Rules 501–508)
• Intrastate offerings	§3(a)(11), Rule 147
• Securities exchanged by issuer with existing security holders or in corporate reorganization	§§3(a)(9), 3(a)(10)
• Certificates issued in bankruptcy proceedings	§3(a)(7)
Secondary Trading Exemptions	
• Transactions by persons other than issuers, underwriters, or dealers	§4(1), Rule 144
• Most transactions by dealers	§§4(3), 4(4)

examined by state or federal authorities, and by farmers' cooperatives exempt from federal taxation, (5) certain securities issued by federally regulated common carriers, and (6) insurance policies and annuity contracts issued by companies supervised by a state insurance commissioner or similar officer.[23]

In addition to specific securities, the Act exempts from registration securities distributed in certain types of transactions. Unlike exempt securities, those sold under a transaction exemption may not, in many cases, be resold without registration or compliance with another transaction exemption. A transaction exemption is available, for example, for securities exchanged by the issuer exclusively with existing security holders; securities issued in exchange for securities, claims, or property interests in a judicially or administratively approved corporate reorganization plan; and certificates issued by a receiver, trustee, or debtor in possession with court approval in a federal bankruptcy proceeding.[24] The Act also exempts from registration (1) certain transactions involving small or limited

offerings, (2) purely intrastate offerings, and (3) transactions by persons other than issuers, underwriters, or dealers. The following sections discuss these important transaction exemptions.

Small or Limited Offering Exemptions

The exhaustive disclosures required in a 1933 Act registration impose an onerous and expensive burden upon issuers. Because of this expense, public financing often is not a viable alternative for smaller businesses or small issues of securities. To resolve this problem, the 1933 Act and SEC rules provide a number of exemptions for small issues, which provide less burdensome disclosure requirements than those imposed in a full-blown 1933 Act registration.

The limited issue exemptions are derived primarily from four separate sections of the 1933 Act.

1.   Section 4(2) of the Act exempts from registration "transactions by an issuer not involving any public offering." Significant amounts of securities are sold pursuant to this "private placement" exemption, which

---

[23]Securities Act §§3(a)(2)–(6), (8).
[24]Securities Act §§3(a)(7), (9), (10).

may be used to sell a large block of securities to an institutional investor, such as an insurance company, or to a small group of private individuals. In both cases, the exemption is based on the fact that the purchasers are sophisticated and possess the bargaining power necessary to require the disclosures that registration would provide. If the class of persons to whom the securities are offered is shown to need the protection of the Act, the exemption is lost. General solicitation of purchasers is not permitted and resale of the securities is restricted.

2. Section 3(b) authorizes the SEC, through its rules and regulations, to exempt offerings not exceeding $5 million if it finds that registration "is not necessary in the public interest and for the protection of investors by reason of the small amount involved or the limited character of the public offering."

3. Section 4(6), added in 1980, exempts sales not exceeding $5 million made exclusively to any number of "accredited investors." Accredited investors include virtually all types of institutional investors (such as banks, insurance companies, registered investment companies, savings and loan associations, credit unions, and securities brokers or dealers); directors, executive officers, or general partners of the issuer; certain partnerships, corporations, trusts, and employee benefit plans with total assets exceeding $5 million; and individuals meeting certain minimum net worth or income requirements. Though no specific information need be furnished, general solicitation of purchasers is not permitted and resale is restricted.

4. Section 28, added in 1996, authorizes the SEC, through its rules and regulations, to exempt any person, security, or transaction from any 1933 Act requirement without dollar limitation if the SEC finds that "such exemption is necessary or appropriate in the public interest, and is consistent with the protection of investors."

Pursuant to its statutory authority under these provisions, the SEC has adopted various rules governing limited offerings. The most important of these rules are contained in Regulation A (Securities Act Rules 251–263) and Regulation D (Securities Act Rules 501–508). Regulation A provides a somewhat simplified form of registration for small issues, while Regulation D simplifies and coordinates the various limited offering exemptions.[25]

---

[25]In addition to these regulations, the SEC has adopted Regulation E, under §3(c) of the Act, which provides an exemption for offerings by certain investment companies.

Regulation A. Adopted under §3(b) of the Act, Regulation A imposes registration and disclosure requirements similar to, but much less expensive and burdensome than, a full-blown 1933 Act registration. Regulation A may be used by a domestic or Canadian issuer that is not subject to the reporting requirements of the 1934 Act, except (1) an investment company, (2) a blank-check company (one raising capital for an unidentified business opportunity), or (3) a company issuing interests in oil, gas, or mineral rights. Note that under Rule 262, an otherwise eligible company may be disqualified from using Regulation A if the company (or any director, officer, or major shareholder) has, within specific time periods, been convicted of securities offenses or subject to SEC disciplinary proceedings. If the issuer qualifies for the exemption, Regulation A may be used to issue not more than $5 million in securities during any 12-month period. Securities can be offered or sold to any person under Regulation A and once issued they can be resold without restriction.

To use Regulation A, the issuer files an "offering statement" with the SEC's nearest regional office, containing a "notification" and "offering circular." The information required in the offering statement is less detailed than a 1933 Act registration statement, and the financial statements need not be audited. Generally, no offers to sell securities may be made until the offering statement has been filed. Once filed, offers may be made orally, by "preliminary offering circulars," or by tombstone advertisements. Unless extended by the SEC letter of comment procedure previously discussed, the offering statement is "qualified" on the twentieth calendar day after its filing. Once the offering statement is qualified, other types of written offers may be made and selling may commence, but offerees and purchasers must be furnished with a copy of the final offering circular.

A unique aspect of Regulation A is Rule 254, which authorizes an issuer, before filing an offering statement, to "test the waters" by contacting prospective purchasers through written or broadcast advertisements "to determine whether there is any interest in a contemplated securities offering." After the issuer submits the document or script to the SEC, oral communication with prospective investors and other broadcasts are permitted, but no money or commitments to purchase may be accepted. Sales may not be made until an offering statement has been filed and qualified.

Regulation D. Regulation D provides a comprehensive framework governing many small issues and issuers. It consists of SEC Rules 501 through 508. Rules 501–503 and 507–508 contain the definitions, conditions, and filing and disclosure requirements applicable to the three specific exemptions contained in Rules 504, 505, and 506. Although Regulation D provides an exemption from *federal* registration, it does not excuse compliance with any applicable state "blue sky" law.

Rule 501. Rule 501 defines certain important terms used in Regulation D.

Rule 502. Rule 502 specifies the type of information that must be furnished to purchasers in offerings exempted by Regulation D. If the sales are made under Rule 504 or to accredited investors only, no specific information need be furnished. If, however, sales are made to nonaccredited purchasers under Rules 505 or 506, specific financial and other information must be supplied to such purchasers. The amount and format of this information differ depending upon whether the issuer is registered under the 1934 Act. The rule also provides that securities exempted under Regulation D may not be offered or sold by any form of general solicitation or advertising, including newspaper, radio, or television advertisements. Finally, Rule 502 provides that securities sold under Regulation D cannot be resold by the purchasers without registration or an independent exemption. The issuer must place a legend on the certificates stating that the securities are not registered and that their transfer is restricted.

Rule 503. Rule 503 states that notice of exempt sales made under Regulation D must be filed with the SEC within 15 days after the first sale of securities.

Rule 504. Exemption for issues not exceeding $1 million. Rule 504 permits an issuer to sell a total of up to $1 million of securities to an unlimited number of investors in any 12-month period. The exemption is not available to investment companies, blank-check companies, or to companies subject to the registration and reporting requirements of the 1934 Act. If the offering is conducted in compliance with a state blue sky law requiring delivery of a disclosure document before sale, the manner of offering and resale restrictions imposed by Regulation D do not apply. Rule 504 imposes no requirement that any specific information be furnished to purchasers.

Rule 505. Exemption for limited offerings not exceeding $5 million. Rule 505 permits an issuer to sell up to $5 million in securities in any 12-month period to any number of accredited investors and up to 35 other purchasers. Any purchaser who is not an accredited investor must be furnished with the disclosures required by Rule 502. The exemption may be used by all issuers except investment companies and issuers who are disqualified under Rule 262 because they have been convicted of securities offenses or subject to SEC disciplinary proceedings within specified time periods.

Rule 506. Private placement safe harbor. Federal case law provides general guidelines for availability of the private placement exemption under §4(2). To provide greater certainty in corporate planning, Rule 506 provides a safe harbor for the exemption. That is, compliance with Rule 506 assures availability of the private placement exemption, but failure to satisfy its provisions does not necessarily mean that the exemption is unavailable. Rule 506, which is available to all issuers, permits issuers to sell an unlimited amount of securities to an unlimited number of accredited investors and up to 35 other purchasers. If sales are made to nonaccredited purchasers, the issuer must reasonably believe that the purchaser, either alone or with a representative, "has such knowledge and experience in financial and business matters that he is capable of evaluating the merits and risks of the prospective investment."[26] That is, the issuer must reasonably believe that any nonaccredited purchaser is a sophisticated investor. As under Rule 505, the disclosures required by Rule 502 must be furnished to all nonaccredited purchasers.

Rule 507. Rule 507 states that no Regulation D exemption is available to any issuer who has been subject to court injunction for failure to comply with the notice requirements of Rule 503.

Rule 508. Substantial Compliance Defense. Rule 508 provides that noncompliance with a term or condition stated in Rules 504, 505, or 506 will not destroy the Regulation D exemption for any offer or sale to a particular person if (1) the failure to comply did not relate to a term directly intended to protect that person (for example, Regulation D terms requiring the issuer to furnish information or to assure that an individual is sophisticated are designed to protect particular persons), (2) the failure to comply was insignificant in relation to the offering as a whole, and (3) the issuer made a good

---

[26]Securities Act Rule 506(b)(2)(ii).

faith and reasonable attempt to comply. Note, however, that violations of the ban on general solicitations in Rule 502(c), the dollar limitations of Rules 504 and 505, and the limits on the number of nonaccredited purchasers in Rules 505 and 506 are always deemed to be "significant" violations, and thus will destroy the substantial compliance defense.

Intrastate Offering Exemption

Section 3(a)(11) of the 1933 Act exempts from federal registration "any security which is a part of an issue offered and sold only to persons resident within a single State . . . , where the issuer of such security is . . . a corporation, incorporated by and doing business within, such State. . . ." State blue sky laws continue to apply, however, if the offer is made to the public. Both the courts and the SEC have interpreted this "intrastate offering" exemption very narrowly. It exempts only those issues that "represent local financing by local industries, carried out through local investment."[27]

Rule 147. To provide greater certainty to corporate planners intending to use the intrastate exemption, the SEC in 1974 adopted Rule 147, which defines certain terms of the statute. Rule 147, like Rule 506 discussed above provides a "safe harbor."

The statute itself provides that the exemption is available only if all purchasers *and* offerees are residents of a single state and the issuer is incorporated by and doing business in that state. Thus, a corporation operating solely in Illinois, but incorporated in Delaware to take advantage of Delaware's liberal corporation law, could not qualify for the exemption. Rule 147 provides that an issuer is presumed to be "doing business" in the state if (1) it derives at least 80 percent of its annual gross revenues from activities in the state, (2) at least 80 percent of its assets are located in the state, (3) at least 80 percent of the proceeds of the offering are to be used in the state, and (4) the issuer's principal office is located in the state.

Even if the foregoing requirements are met, the exemption is lost for the entire offering if securities sold under the exemption are subsequently resold to nonresidents. This approach applies both to intrastate transfers

intended merely as a first step in an interstate distribution and to inadvertent later sales to nonresidents. Rule 147 provides, however, that the exemption is preserved if no resales are made to nonresidents within nine months after the initial sale by the issuer is completed. To protect against interstate offers and sales, Rule 147 requires the issuer to (1) place a legend on the stock certificate indicating that the securities are unregistered and cannot be resold interstate, (2) issue stop transfer instructions to the issuer's transfer agent, and (3) obtain a written statement from each purchaser regarding his or her residence. Table 49.2 summarizes the major 1933 Act transaction exemptions discussed above.

Secondary Trading Exemptions

Unless specifically exempted, the 1933 Act requires registration of all security transactions. To this point the discussion has examined the transaction exemptions used by issuers to avoid registering an initial distribution of securities. Most security transactions, however, are not part of the original distribution but involve secondary trading—for example, on a stock exchange—of securities already issued and outstanding.

Section 4(1) of the 1933 Act provides that the Act's registration provisions apply only to issuers, underwriters, and dealers, thus exempting transactions by nonprofessionals. Section 4(3) then exempts all transactions by securities dealers, except for sales that are part of the original distribution and resales made within a limited time after the registration statement becomes effective. Section 4(4) further exempts unsolicited "brokers transactions" executed upon customers' orders upon a securities exchange or in the over-the-counter market.[28] Collectively, these provisions exempt most day-to-day secondary trading occurring on securities exchanges and in the over-the-counter markets from the Act's registration requirements.

Liability of Underwriters. Despite the exclusion of most brokers' and dealers' transactions, underwriters, like issuers, remain subject to the Act's registration requirements. As previously noted, underwriters generally include persons who purchase securities from the issuer for public distribution. For purposes of defining "underwriter," however, the term "issuer" includes both

---

[27]Securities Act Release 4434, 26 Fed. Reg. 11896, 11897 (Dec. 6, 1961).

[28]A broker is simply a person engaged in the business of executing securities transactions as agent for others.

Table 49.2   Summary of Major Distributions Exemptions—Securities Act of 1933

Exemption and Eligible Issuers	Total Offering Price	Limitations on the Offering			Disclosures Required
		Number/Qualifications of Investors	Manner of Offering	Resale of the Securities	
Regulation A Domestic or Canadian issuers not subject to reporting requirements of Securities Act of 1934*	$5.0 million in any 12-month period	No limitations	Testing the waters permitted before offering statement filed; limited offers permitted thereafter, and sales permitted after offering statement qualified	No restrictions	Offering circular must be furnished to offerees and purchasers
Rule 504 (Regulation D) All issuers not subject to reporting requirements of Securities Exchange Act of 1934**	$1 million in any 12-month period	No limitations	General solicitation not permitted unless conducted in compliance with state blue sky law requiring delivery of disclosure document before sale	Restricted unless offering conducted in compliance with state blue sky law requiring delivery of disclosure document before sale	None
Rule 505 (Regulation D) All issuers***	$5.0 million in any 12-month period	Unlimited number of accredited investors, and up to 35 other purchasers	General solicitation and advertising not permitted	Restricted	None for accredited investors; Rule 502 disclosures required for non-accredited investors
§4(2), Rule 506 (Regulation D) All issuers	Unlimited	Unlimited number of accredited investors, and up to 35 other purchasers; sophisticated investors only; accredited investors presumed qualified	General solicitation and advertising not permitted	Restricted	None for accredited investors; Rule 502 disclosures required for non-accredited investors
§4(6) All issuers	$5.0 million	Accredited investors only (unlimited number)	General solicitation and advertising not permitted	Restricted	None
§3(a)(11), Rule 147 Intrastate issuers—all issuers organized and doing business within one state in which securities are offered and sold	Unlimited	All offerees and purchasers must be residents of same state in which issuer is incorporated and doing business	Offering may be public or private	Unlimited resales to residents; resales to nonresidents permitted after nine months	None; state blue sky laws may apply if offering is public

* except investment companies; blank check companies; issuers of oil, gas, or mineral rights; and companies disqualified under Rule 262

** except investment companies and blank check companies

*** except investment companies and companies disqualified under Rule 262 the corporation and any person (an "affiliate") who controls or is controlled by the corporation.[29] Because "underwriters" therefore include those who sell securities for a person who controls a corporation, underwriter liability is imposed upon persons not otherwise engaged in the investment banking business in two important situations:

1. A controlling person may sell all or a portion of his or her stock in stock exchange or over-the-counter transactions effected through securities brokers or dealers. In this case, the broker or dealer is not insulated by the "brokers" transaction exemption and may be held liable as an "underwriter" for selling unregistered securities to the public. The selling controlling person is liable as an "issuer."

2. A person may purchase securities from an issuer in a transaction exempt from registration as a private placement or under Regulation D. Subsequently, the purchaser may wish to resell these "restricted" securities. If the purchaser is deemed to have purchased the securities from an issuer with a view to distribution, resale will render the purchaser liable as an underwriter for selling unregistered securities.

Rules 144 and 144A. To provide practical guidance in determining when a registration statement must be filed for these secondary distributions, the SEC in 1972 adopted Rule 144. If the sale is made in compliance with the rule, a person selling restricted or other securities on behalf of an affiliate (case 1) and a person reselling restricted securities (case 2) are deemed not to be engaged in the distribution of securities, and therefore not underwriters. The rule imposes the following "safe harbor" requirements:

1. sufficient current public information must be available about the issuer;
2. securities acquired in a nonpublic transaction must be held by the purchaser for one year before resale;
3. once the one-year period has expired, the amount of any securities resold during any three-month period may not exceed the greater of (a) one percent of the shares of that class currently outstanding, or (b) the average weekly trading volume in the securities for the previous four weeks;

4. sales must be made through brokers' transactions or in transactions directly with a "market maker"—a dealer who maintains a trading market for over-the-counter securities; and
5. notice of the sales must be filed with the SEC.

Note that a person who is not an affiliate may resell restricted securities without complying with the above requirements after owning them for at least two years. Affiliates may resell their securities only by complying with Rule 144, regardless of how long they have owned the securities.

Rule 144A, adopted in 1990, provides an important safe harbor for specified resales of restricted securities to a "qualified institutional buyer." Qualified institutional buyers include banks and savings and loan associations (which have more than $100 million invested in securities of nonaffiliated issuers, and an audited net worth of at least $25 million), registered broker-dealers (with at least $10 million invested in securities), and any other entity (such as an insurance company, investment company, trust fund, or employee benefit plan) that meets the $100 million in securities threshold.

Under the rule, resale of a security originally issued under a 1933 Act exemption is permitted without violating §5's registration requirements if the buyer is a qualified institutional buyer, and

1. the securities, when issued, were not of the same class as those listed on a stock exchange or traded through an automated inter-dealer quotation system;
2. the seller takes reasonable steps to inform the buyer that the seller may rely upon the registration exemption provided by Rule 144A; and
3. if the issuer is not a reporting company under the 1934 Act, a foreign government, or exempt foreign private issuer, the buyer receives "reasonably current" information, including financial statements, about the issuer.

Relationship Between State and Federal Securities Regulation

State securities regulation is in part preempted by federal law. Section 18 of the 1933 Act, as revised in 1996, provides that states may not regulate offerings of "covered securities." These include, for example, securities listed on a national securities exchange; securities issued by an investment company registered under the Investment Company Act of 1940; securities exempt under §3(a) (except securities issued by charitable organizations and

---

[29]Securities Act §2(a)(11). "Control" is a question of fact, defined in Securities Act Rule 405 to include "the power to direct or cause the direction of the management and policies of a person, whether through the ownership of voting securities, by contract, or otherwise."

under the intrastate offering exemption); and securities sold in a transaction exempt under §4. States, however, retain authority to collect fees, require notice filings, and investigate fraud relating to covered securities.

As a result of §18, state regulation now primarily governs: securities traded on regional securities exchanges and in the over-the-counter market; debt securities of nonlisted issuers; securities issued in private placements under §4(2) that do not meet the requirements of Rule 506 of Regulation D; securities issued under Rules 504 and 505 of Regulation D; and securities issued under Regulation A.

Liability Under the 1933 Act

The 1933 Act contains specific remedies to prevent the sale of unregistered securities and to assure the accuracy of the registration materials. These remedies may be enforced by SEC administrative proceedings, court injunctions, and, in some cases, criminal prosecution. In addition, various civil remedies are available to private individuals injured by violations of the Act.

Liability for Failure to Register—§12(a)(1)

Section 12(a)(1) of the Act provides that any person who offers or sells a security in violation of §5 is liable for damages to the person purchasing the security. For purposes of §12(a)(1), a "seller" includes not only the owner of the security who passes title, but also any nonowner, such as a broker, who successfully solicits the purchase and who is motivated at least partially by a desire to serve his own financial interests or those of the security's owner. The purchaser may sue either in state or federal court to rescind the sale and recover the purchase price of the security plus interest in exchange for the security. A purchaser who no longer owns the security may recover money damages equal to the difference between the original purchase price and subsequent selling price. A §12(a)(1) action must be brought within one year after the violation upon which it is based, but may not be maintained more than three years after the security was offered to the public.

Liability for False Registration Statement—§11

Section 11 of the 1933 Act imposes liability for misstatements and omissions in the registration statement.

Under §11(a), if the registration statement, when it becomes effective, contains an untrue statement of material fact or omits to state a material fact, any person acquiring the security (either as part of the original distribution or in subsequent secondary trading) may maintain a civil suit against specified persons either in state or federal court. The injured purchaser may recover damages equal to the difference between the purchase price of the security and its value at the time of suit, or its selling price if the plaintiff no longer owns it. Persons liable, jointly and severally, to injured purchasers include:

1. every person who signed the registration statement;[30]
2. every director;
3. every person who consents to being named in the registration statement as being or about to become a director;
4. every accountant, engineer, appraiser, or other expert who has, with his or her consent, been named as having prepared or certified any part of the registration statement; and
5. every underwriter.

To recover under §11, the purchaser simply must prove loss and the existence of an untruth or omission in the registration statement. Proof of reliance on the registration statement is not required unless the buyer acquires the security after the issuer has published an earnings statement covering at least 12 months beginning after the effective date of the registration statement. A §11 action must be filed within one year after the purchaser discovers or should have discovered the untrue statement or omission, but may not be brought more than three years after the security is offered to the public.

Defenses. Persons charged with violating §11 may assert a number of affirmative defenses. For example, defendants may escape liability by proving either that the purchaser knew of the untruth or omission in the registration statement when acquiring the security, or that the decline in the security's value had been caused by factors other than the material falsities and omissions. An additional, and the most important, defense to

---

[30]Section 6 of the Act requires that the registration statement be signed by the issuer, its principal executive officer or officers, its principal financial and accounting officer, and the majority of its board of directors.

§11 liability is the "due diligence" defense contained in §11(b)(3). This defense is available to all defendants except the issuer, who is strictly liable for all errors or omissions in the registration statement.

The due diligence defense imposes differing standards of conduct upon the various parties to the registration statement and absolves them from liability if they meet that standard. The standards of conduct, discussed below, are based upon: (1) the location in the registration statement of the untruth or omission; and (2) the status of the defendant.

Regarding material untruths or omissions in parts of the registration statement prepared by an expert (for example, audited financial statements prepared by a certified public accountant):

1. the expert (for example, the accountant who prepared the erroneous financial statements) escapes liability only by proving (a) that it made a reasonable investigation (b) that provided a reasonable grounds for the expert's actual belief that the information was true and not misleading;
2. a nonexpert (for example, a corporate director) escapes liability simply by proving that she had no reasonable grounds to believe that there were any material untruths or omissions.

Regarding material untruths or omissions in a portion of the registration statement not prepared by an expert (the so-called "nonexpertised" portion):

1. an expert has no liability for errors in the unexpertised portion of the registration statement and thus does not need the protection of the due diligence defense;
2. a nonexpert escapes liability only by proving (a) that it made a reasonable investigation (b) that provided a reasonable grounds for the nonexpert's actual belief that the information was true and not misleading.

The standard of reasonableness for "reasonable investigation" and "reasonable grounds to believe" is "that required of a prudent man in the management of his own property."[31]

Although potential §11 liability is a fundamental concern of all persons involved in preparing the registration statement, it has generated surprisingly little litigation. Indeed, the most definitive interpretation of §11 is *Escott v. BarChris Construction Corporation,* a classic federal district court decision decided 35 years after the Act was passed. (The facts of the case and the portion of the opinion concerning the liability of an independent public accountant under §11 are included in Chapter 56.) *Escott* and subsequent cases indicate that the standard of care required to avoid §11 liability differs depending upon the nature of the defendant, the issuer, and the defendant's participation in the registration process. In 1982, the SEC adopted Rule 176, which attempts to codify the relevant factors to be considered.

Antifraud Provisions — §§12(a)(2) and 17(a)

The 1933 Act contains two provisions imposing liability for fraud and misrepresentation in securities sales, §§12(a)(2) and 17(a). Section 12(a)(2) permits a purchaser to recover from a person who offers or sells a security by oral or written communication that contains material misstatements or omissions. The Supreme Court has held, however, that §12(a)(2) applies only to widely disseminated sales materials used in a public offering.[32] As under §12(a)(1), under §12(a)(2) the purchaser may sue only his seller, the remedy is either rescission or money damages, and suit may be maintained either in state or federal court. An affirmative defense is available to a seller who can prove that: (1) she neither knew, nor could have known, of the un-truth or omission; or (2) the decline in the security's value was caused by factors other than the seller's untrue statements or omissions. Suit must be filed within one year after the untruth or omission was discovered or should have been discovered, but not more than three years after the security was sold.

Section 17(a) is the 1933 Act's general antifraud provision providing a remedy for fraud, material misrepresentations, and omissions in the sale of securities. The remedy governs activities of offerors and sellers, not purchasers, but applies to all securities whether registered or exempt from registration. It supplements the express civil liability provisions (§§11 and 12) and may be enforced in state or federal court through SEC civil suit or criminal proceedings. Virtually all courts have held that no private remedy for injured purchasers should be implied under §17(a). Section 17(a)'s counterparts in the 1934 Act, §10(b) and Rule 10b-5, are discussed later in this chapter. Table 49.3 summarizes the civil remedies available under the 1933 Act.

---

[31]Securities Act §11(c).

[32]Gustafson v. Alloyd Co., Inc., 115 S. Ct. 1061 (1995).

Table 49.3   Summary of 1933 Act Remedies

Section	Conduct Proscribed	Permissible Plaintiffs	Permissible Defendants	Securities Covered
12(a)(1)	Offer or sale of security in violation of §5	Purchaser	Seller	Securities required to be registered
11	Misrepresentations or omissions in registration statement	Purchaser	Persons signing registration statement, directors, experts, and underwriters	Securities covered by registration statement
12(a)(2)	Offer or sale of security by written or oral communications containing material misstatements or omissions	Purchaser	Seller	Any security, whether or not requiring registration
17(a)	Fraud, material misrepresentations, and omissions in sale of securities	SEC civil suit or government criminal suit; no implied private remedy for purchaser	Offerors and sellers	Any security, whether or not requiring registration

1933 Act Criminal Liability

Under §24 of the Securities Act of 1933 any person who willfully violates any provision of the Act, its rules and regulations, or willfully makes a material misstatement in a registration statement, is guilty of a crime. Offenders may be punished by fines of up to $10,000, or imprisonment not exceeding five years, or both.

Introduction to the Securities Exchange Act of 1934

The Securities Exchange Act of 1934 regulates secondary trading in securities, the securities markets, and persons conducting securities transactions. The 1934 Act imposes registration and disclosure requirements upon many issuers, the securities exchanges, self-regulatory organizations, and securities brokers and dealers. It also regulates insider trading, and fraud and manipulative practices in securities trading.

Registration and Reporting Requirements

The 1934 Act requires the following companies to register with the SEC: (1) issuers that have securities traded on a national securities exchange, (2) issuers that have both a class of equity securities held by at least 500 shareholders and total assets exceeding $10 million,[33] and (3) all issuers with outstanding securities sold under a 1933 Act registration. Note that 1934 Act registration is in addition to any registration of a specific securities offering required by the 1933 Act.

Initial registration under the 1934 Act requires detailed disclosure of information regarding the issuer's organization, capital structure, officers and directors, financial condition, and major contracts. In addition, under §13 of the Act, registered companies are required to file annual and other periodic reports with the SEC. These reports include the Form 10-K annual report, the Form 10-Q quarterly report, and a Form 8-K current report, which must be filed when certain specified changes in the issuer's condition or operations occur. In addition, issuers are required to supplement their periodic reports with "real time" disclosures ("on a rapid and current basis") of "information concerning material changes in the financial condition or operations of the

[33]Securities Exchange Act §12(g)(1). Note that the statute requires registration of issuers with assets exceeding $1 million, but Securities Exchange Act Rule 12g-1 exempts issuers with less than $10 million in assets.

issuer."[34] These reports assure continuing public availability of current information about companies whose securities are publicly traded. Note that small business issuers registered under Regulation S-B provide more limited periodic information on Form 10-KSB (annual report) and Form 10-QSB (quarterly report).

In addition to periodic reporting requirements, 1934 Act registration triggers a number of other disclosure and remedial provisions relating to insider short-swing profits, and fraud and manipulative practices in connection with the purchase or sale of a security. These provisions are discussed in more detail later in this chapter.

Financial and Accounting Requirements

The 1934 Act imposes a number of financial reporting and accounting requirements. The SEC generally adheres to generally accepted accounting principles (GAAP) and generally accepted auditing standards (GAAS) used by the private sector, but closely guides the form and substance of financial disclosure. The Act also imposes, as part of the **Foreign Corrupt Practices Act of 1977,** substantial internal control requirements upon reporting companies. Under the Act, reporting issuers must maintain books and accounts that accurately and fairly reflect "in reasonable detail" the issuer's transactions and disposition of its assets. In addition, the issuer must devise and maintain a system of internal accounting control sufficient to assure that (1) transactions are executed according to management's general or specific authorization, (2) all transactions are accounted for according to generally accepted accounting principles, (3) access to corporate assets is permitted only with management's general or specific authorization, and (4) the recorded accountability for assets is periodically compared with existing assets, and appropriate action is taken to reconcile any difference.[35]

Liability for Misleading Statements in Filed Documents — §18(a)

To assure accurate disclosure, §18(a) of the 1934 Act imposes liability upon any person who is responsible for any false or misleading statement in any application,

document, or report filed with the SEC under the terms of the 1934 Act or its rules and regulations. Liability extends to the issuer and its officers and directors, particularly those who sign the filed documents. Relief is available to any investor who reads the filed document, relies upon it, and is injured by purchasing or selling a security at a price affected by the statement.

A defendant may escape liability under §18(a) by proving that "he acted in good faith and had no knowledge that such statement was false or misleading." This defense is similar to, but somewhat less rigorous than, the due diligence defense of §11 of the 1933 Act for misrepresentations in a registration statement. Suit under §18(a) must be commenced within one year after discovery of the violation, and in any event within three years after the facts constituting the cause of action occurred.

1934 Act Criminal Liability

In General. Section 32(a) of the Securities Exchange Act of 1934 provides that any person who willfully violates any provision of the 1934 Act, its rules and regulations, or who willfully and knowingly makes materially false or misleading statements in any document filed with the SEC is guilty of a crime. Punishment may include a fine of up to $10 million, or imprisonment not exceeding twenty years, or both. Corporate defendants may be fined up to $25 million.

Foreign Corrupt Practices Act of 1977. SEC investigations conducted in the 1970s revealed corporate bribery of foreign officials by over 300 U.S. companies involving hundreds of millions of dollars. In many cases, the bribery had been facilitated and concealed by falsification of corporate records. In order to deter corporate bribery of foreign government officials, Congress, in 1977, added the Foreign Corrupt Practices Act to the Securities Exchange Act of 1934.[36] The Act which was amended in 1988 and 1998, adopts a two-fold approach. First, as previously noted, it requires companies to maintain strict accounting standards and management control over their assets. Second, the Act makes it a crime for most companies and individuals to bribe foreign officials for specific corrupt purposes.

The Act's criminal provisions apply both to individuals (United States and foreign citizens) and to organizations such as corporations and partnerships (organized

---

[34]Sarbanes-Oxley Act §409; Securities Exchange Act §13(l).
[35]Securities Exchange Act §13(b)(2).

[36]Securities Exchange Act §§13(b)(2), 30A, 32(c); 15 U.S.C. §78dd-2.

under the laws of either the United States or of a foreign nation). In the case of an organization, liability extends to: (1) its officers, directors, employees, or agents; and (2) any shareholder acting on behalf of a corporation. United States citizens and organizations are liable for acts committed anywhere in the world. Foreign citizens and organizations are liable for acts committed while in the territory of the United States.

The Act prohibits persons covered from corruptly offering or transferring anything of value to a foreign official, or foreign political party or party official (or to any other person while knowing that it will be offered or transferred to such an official or political party). To be illegal the purpose of the payment must be

1. to influence any action or decision of the official or political party in his or its official capacity, or
2. to induce the foreign official or party to do (or omit to do) any act in violation of his or its lawful duty, or to use his or its influence to affect an act or decision of the government, or
3. to secure any improper advantage

in order to assist persons making payment in obtaining, retaining, or directing business to any person.

The Act excepts payments made to expedite or facilitate routine government actions, such as issuing permits or licenses, processing government papers, providing inspections associated with contract performance or transit of goods, and providing utility service. Routine govbernment action does not include an official's decision to award new business or continue business with a particular party. The Act also excepts payments made that are legal under the written laws or regulations of the foreign country. To aid in compliance, the Justice Department will issue, upon request, its written opinion regarding the legality of any proposed payment.

Corporate violators are subject to a fine of up to $2 million. Individuals who willfully violate the Act may be fined up to $100,000, imprisoned for up to five years, or both. Fines imposed upon individuals may not be paid, directly or indirectly, by the corporation.

For many years, the FCPA was the only international antibribery law. Beginning in the mid 1990s, however, many other countries began to adopt antibribery legislation pursuant to multilateral treaties. The most important of these treaties is the OECD (Organization for Economic Cooperation and Development) Convention, which went into force in 1999. It requires member states to criminalize foreign official bribery in a manner similar to the FCPA. The OECD Convention has been ratified by many of the world's largest exporting countries, including the United States, Canada, Germany, Japan, and the United Kingdom.

1934 Act Insider Trading and Antifraud Regulation

Insider Reporting and Trading Regulation—§16

Section 16 of the 1934 Act prevents short-term trading and other transactions in a corporation's securities by corporate insiders. Its purpose is to prevent "the unfair use of information which may have been obtained"[37] by the insider as a result of his or her relationship to the issuer.

To monitor insider transactions, §16(a) imposes reporting requirements upon all persons who beneficially own, directly or indirectly, more than 10 percent of a class of equity securities registered under §12 of the 1934 Act, and every officer and director of an issuer of such a security. These persons are required to file an ownership statement with the SEC within ten days after becoming an officer, director, or 10 percent beneficial owner, and before the end of the second business day following the day on which the insider buys or sells the corporation's equity securities. Note that purchases and sales subject to the two-day limit must be filed electronically.

An annual statement also must be filed within 45 days after the end of the corporation's fiscal year to report transactions that should have been, but were not, reported during the year. Although no private remedy is available for violation of §16(a)'s reporting requirements, SEC administrative and criminal sanctions may be imposed. In addition, the corporation must disclose any delinquent §16(a) filings in its proxy statements and in its annual 1934 Act report.

Section 16(b) restricts short-term trading in the issuer's stock by persons subject to §16(a)'s reporting requirements. Under this provision the issuer (or a shareholder suing on behalf of the issuer) may recover any profit realized by the insider from any purchase and sale, or any sale and purchase, of the issuer's stock within any six-month period. For purposes of §16(b), "profit" is computed by comparing the highest sales price against the lowest purchase price within any six-month period. This approach

---

[37]Securities Exchange Act §16(b).

can result in a recoverable "profit" even though the insider may have incurred an out-of-pocket loss from a series of transactions during the six-month period.

Section 16 authorizes recovery of so-called short-swing profits to prevent unfair use of inside information. The law does not, however, require proof that the insider actually used inside information in deciding whether to buy or sell. That is, §16 imposes strict liability, requiring that short-swing profits be returned even if the insider obtaining them engaged in no wrongdoing.

A §16(b) suit must be maintained in federal court subject to a two-year statute of limitations running from the date of the transaction that creates §16(b) profits. As noted above, suit may be maintained by the corporation or a shareholder suing derivatively, and recovery is paid to the corporation. The SEC has no enforcement authority under §16(b).

1934 Act Antifraud Provision—§10(b) and Rule 10b-5—Introduction

In federal securities law, general "antifraud" provisions often supplement the specific statutory requirements and express remedies.[38] The general antifraud provision under the 1934 Act is §10(b), which provides that it is unlawful

To use or employ, in connection with the purchase or sale of any security . . . , any manipulative or deceptive device or contrivance in contravention of such rules and regulations as the Commission may prescribe as necessary or appropriate in the public interest or for the protection of investors.

Pursuant to this authority the SEC has adopted rules[39] prohibiting a variety of specific manipulative or deceptive conduct. In addition to these specific prohibitions, the SEC in 1942 adopted Rule 10b-5, a general antifraud provision, which states in full:

It shall be unlawful for any person, directly or indirectly, by the use of any means or instrumentality of interstate commerce, or of the mails or of any facility of any national securities exchange,

(a) To employ any device, scheme, or artifice to defraud,

(b) To make any untrue statement of a material fact or to omit to state a material fact necessary in order to make the statements made, in the light of the circumstances under which they were made, not misleading, or

(c) To engage in any act, practice, or course of business which operates or would operate as a fraud or deceit upon any person, in connection with the purchase or sale of any security.

in connection with the purchase or sale of any security.

Implied Private Remedy. Although Rule 10b-5 creates no express private remedy for violations, lower federal courts starting in 1946[40] began to imply a private remedy for injured investors, a remedy formally recognized by the Supreme Court in 1971.[41] Such lawsuits must be filed within 2 years after the plaintiff discovers the facts constituting the violation, and within 5 years after the violation occurred.[42]

During its early years, the Rule 10b-5 implied remedy received an expansive judicial interpretation. Supreme Court decisions since 1975 have, however, limited its availability in two important respects discussed below.

Purchaser or Seller Requirement. Rule 10b-5, by its terms, prohibits fraud or deception in the purchase or sale of any security by any person. All securities are covered, whether registered or exempted from registration under the 1933 or 1934 Acts, and whether issued by publicly-held or closely-held corporations. Despite this expansive coverage, the Supreme Court has held that to maintain a private action under Rule 10b-5, the plaintiff (but not the defendant) must be either a purchaser or seller of the securities involved.[43]

Scienter Requirement. The Supreme Court held in *Ernst & Ernst v. Hochfelder*[44] that a private cause of action for damages under Rule 10b-5 requires proof of scienter—an intent to deceive, manipulate, or defraud. The defendant's negligent conduct alone is insufficient to invoke Rule 10b-5 liability. Although not yet resolved by the Supreme Court, most lower federal court decisions have held that statements made in reckless disregard of the truth also meet the scienter requirement and are therefore actionable under Rule 10b-5.

Rule 10b-5's broad antifraud proscription has been applied to a wide variety of fact situations generally divided into three broad areas: corporate mismanagement, corporate misstatements, and insider trading.

---

[38]For example, §17(a) is the 1933 Act's general antifraud provision.
[39]Securities Exchange Act Rule §10b-1 *et seq.*

[40]Kardon v. National Gypsum Co., 69 F.Supp. 512 (E.D. Pa. 1946).
[41]Superintendent of Insurance v. Bankers Life and Casualty Company, 92 S. Ct. 165 (1971).
[42]28 U.S.C. §1658(b).
[43]Blue Chip Stamps v. Manor Drug Stores, 95 S. Ct. 1917 (1975).
[44]96 S. Ct. 1375 (1976).

Application of Rule 10b-5—Corporate Mismanagement.

In a number of early cases, minority shareholders used Rule 10b-5 as a remedy to redress abuses by corporate management or controlling shareholders involving transactions in stock. Examples include sales of controlling stock interests at a premium and mergers that freeze out the minority shareholders. Although these abuses also often violate fiduciary obligations imposed by state law, a Rule 10b-5 claim, if available, may present fewer substantive or procedural obstacles. In 1977, however, the Supreme Court decided *Santa Fe Industries, Inc. v. Green,*[45] which substantially limited the use of Rule 10b-5 as a remedy for corporate mismanagement. In this case, the Court reaffirmed its *Hochfelder* holding that Rule 10b-5 reaches only manipulative or deceptive conduct. Although a number of lower courts have given *Santa Fe* a narrow reading, the law is clear that claims based solely on breach of fiduciary duty or internal corporate mismanagement under state law do not involve manipulation or deception sufficient to support a Rule 10b-5 action.

Application of Rule 10b-5—Corporate Misstatements.

Various securities law provisions are designed to assure the accuracy of specific documents such as registration statements and proxy solicitation materials. Rule 10b-5 provides an additional remedy for misstatements in these and other corporate documents such as press releases and reports.

In the following case involving alleged corporate misstatements, the Supreme Court addressed two important elements of a Rule 10b-5 claim, materiality and reliance.

Basic, Incorporated v. Levinson

108 S. Ct. 978 (1988)

Beginning in September 1976, representatives of Combustion Engineering, Inc. held a series of meetings and telephone conversations with officers and directors of Basic, Incorporated concerning the possibility of a merger. During 1977 and 1978, addressing the issue of increased trading in Basic stock, Basic made three public statements denying that it was engaged in merger negotiations. On October 21, 1977, an article in the *Cleveland Plain Dealer*

---

[45]97 S. Ct. 1292 (1977).

stated that Basic's president had said that "no negotiations were under way with any company for a merger." On September 25, 1978, Basic issued a release stating that "management is unaware of any present or pending company development that would result in the abnormally heavy trading activity and price fluctuations in company shares." Basic reiterated this statement in a report to shareholders on November 6, 1978. On December 18, 1978, Basic requested the New York Stock Exchange to suspend trading in its shares because Basic had been approached by another company concerning a merger. Two days later, Basic publicly announced its approval of Combustion's tender offer of $46 per share for all outstanding shares.

Plaintiff Max Levinson, a former Basic shareholder, brought a class action against the defendants, Basic and its directors, on behalf of all shareholders who had sold their stock after Basic's statement on October 21, 1977 and before suspension of trading on December 18, 1978. Plaintiffs alleged that the defendants had violated §10(b) of the Securities Exchange Act and Rule 10b-5 by issuing three false or misleading statements in 1977 and 1978, thereby causing injury to plaintiffs who had sold their stock at artificially depressed prices. The trial court ruled that plaintiffs' reliance on the statements could be presumed based on the fraud-on-the-market theory. Nevertheless, the trial court held that any mistatements were immaterial and granted summary judgment in favor of the defendants. The Sixth Circuit Court of Appeals reversed. The Supreme Court granted certiorari.

Justice Blackmun

. . . The Court previously . . . has defined a standard of materiality under the securities laws, . . . concluding in the proxy-solicitation context that "[a]n omitted fact is material if there is a substantial likelihood that a reasonable shareholder would consider it important in deciding how to vote." [*TSC Industries, Inc. v. Northway, Inc.,* 96 S. Ct. 2126, 2132 (1976)]. . . . It further explained that to fulfill the materiality requirement "there must be a substantial likelihood that the disclosure of the omitted fact would have been viewed by the reasonable investor as having significantly altered the 'total mix' of information made available." [*Id.*]. We now expressly adopt the *TSC Industries* standard of materiality for the §10(b) and Rule 10b-5 context.

. . . The application of this materiality standard to preliminary merger discussions is not self-evident. Where the impact of the corporate development on the target's fortune is certain and clear, the *TSC Industries* materiality definition admits straightforward application. Where, on the other hand, the event is contingent or speculative in nature, it is difficult to ascertain whether the "reasonable investor" would considered the omitted information significant at the time. Merger negotiations, because of the ever-present possibility that the contemplated transaction will not be effectuated, fall into the latter category. . . .

Even before this Court's decision in *TSC Industries,* the Second Circuit had explained the role of the materiality requirement of Rule 10b-5, with respect to contingent or speculative information or events, in a manner that gave that term meaning that is independent of the other provisions of the Rule. Under such circumstances, materiality "will depend at any given time upon a balancing of both the indicated probability that the event will occur and the anticipated magnitude of the event in light of the totality of the company activity." *SEC v. Texas Gulf Sulphur Co.,* [401 F.2d 833, 849 (2d Cir. 1968)]. . . .

Whether merger discussions in any particular case are material therefore depends on the facts. Generally, in order to assess the probability that the event will occur, a factfinder will need to look to indicia of interest in the transaction at the highest corporate levels. Without attempting to catalog all such possible factors, we note by way of example that board resolutions, instructions to investment bankers, and actual negotiations between principals or their intermediaries may serve as indicia of interest. To assess the magnitude of the transaction to the issuer of the securities allegedly manipulated, a factfinder will need to consider such facts as the size of the two corporate entities and of the potential premiums over market value. No particular event or factor short of closing the transaction need be either necessary or sufficient by itself to render merger discussions material.

As we clarify today, materiality depends on the significance the reasonable investor would place on the withheld or misrepresented information. . . .

We turn to the question of reliance and the fraud-on-the-market theory. Succinctly put:

> The fraud on the market theory is based on the hypothesis that, in an open and developed securities market, the price of a company's stock is determined by the available material information regarding the company and its business. . . . Misleading statements will therefore defraud purchasers of stock even if the purchasers do not directly rely on the misstatements. . . . The causal connection between the defendants' fraud and the plaintiffs' purchase of stock in such a case is no less significant than in a case of direct reliance on misrepresentations. *Peil v. Speiser,* 806 F.2d 1154, 1160–1161 (3d Cir. 1986).

Our task, of course, is not to assess the general validity of the theory, but to consider whether it was proper for the courts below to apply a rebuttable presumption of reliance, supported in part by the fraud-on-the-market theory. . . .

Petitioners . . . complain that the fraud-on-the-market theory effectively eliminates the requirement that a plaintiff asserting a claim under Rule 10b-5 prove reliance. . . .

We agree that reliance is an element of a Rule 10b-5 cause of action. . . . Reliance provides the requisite causal connection between a defendant's misrepresentation and a plaintiff's injury. . . . There is, however, more than one way to demonstrate the causal connection. . . .

The modern securities markets, literally involving millions of shares changing hands daily, differ from the face-to-face transactions contemplated by early fraud cases, and our understanding of Rule 10b-5's reliance requirement must encompass these differences.

> In face-to-face transactions, the inquiry into an investor's reliance upon information is into the subjective pricing of that information by that investor. With the presence of a market, the market is interposed between seller and buyer and, ideally, transmits information to the investor in the processed form of a market price. Thus the market is performing a substantial part of the valuation process performed by the investor in a face-to-face transaction. The market is acting as the unpaid agent of the investor, informing him that given all the information available to it, the value of the stock is worth the market price. *In re LTV Securities Litigation,* 88 F. R. D. 134, 143 (N. D. Tex. 1980). . . .

Presumptions typically serve to assist courts in managing circumstances in which direct proof, for one reason or another, is rendered difficult. . . . The courts below accepted a presumption, created by the fraud-on-the-market theory and subject to rebuttal by petitioners, that persons who had traded Basic shares had done so in reliance on the integrity of the price set by the market, but because of petitioners' material misrepresentations that price had been fraudulently depressed. Requiring a plaintiff to show a speculative state of facts, *i.e.,* how he would have acted if omitted material information had been disclosed . . . or if the misrepresentation had not been made, . . . would place an unnecessarily unrealistic evidentiary burden on the Rule 10b-5 plaintiff who has traded on an impersonal market. . . .

Arising out of considerations of fairness, public policy, and probability, as well as judicial economy, presumptions are also useful devices for allocating the burdens of proof between parties. . . .

An investor who buys or sells stock at the price set by the market does so in reliance on the integrity of that price. Because most publicly available information is reflected in market price, an investor's reliance on any public material misrepresentations, therefore, may be presumed for purposes of a Rule 10b-5 action. . . .

Any showing that severs the link between the alleged misrepresentation and either the price received (or paid) by the plaintiff, or his decision to trade at a fair market price, will be sufficient to rebut the presumption of reliance. For example, if petitioners could show that the "market makers" were privy to the truth about the merger discussions here with Combustion, and thus that the market price would not have been affected by their misrepresentations, the causal connection could be broken: the basis for finding that the fraud had been transmitted through market price would be gone. Similarly, if, despite petitioners' allegedly fraudulent attempt to manipulate market price, news of the merger discussions credibly entered the market and dissipated the effects of the misstatements, those who traded Basic shares after the corrective statements would have no direct or indirect connection with the fraud. Petitioners also could rebut the presumption of reliance as to plaintiffs who would have divested themselves of their Basic shares without relying on the integrity of the market. . . .

[Judgment vacated and remanded.]

The fact-specific approach to materiality announced in *Basic* prevents the creation of an exhaustive list of information or events that are material. The SEC, however, has suggested that the following information or events often are material, necessitating a careful review before disclosure:

> (1) earnings information; (2) mergers, acquisitions, tender offers, joint ventures, or changes in assets; (3) new products or discoveries, or developments regarding customers or suppliers (for example, the acquisition or loss of a contract); (4) changes in control or in management; (5) change in auditors or auditor notification that the issuer may no longer rely on an auditor's audit report; (6) events regarding the issuer's securities—for example, defaults on senior securities, calls of securities for redemption, repurchase plans, stock splits or changes in dividends, changes to the rights of

security holders, public or private sales of additional securities; and (7) bankruptcies or receiverships.[46]

In some cases, a corporation may issue inaccurate "forward looking" statements, such as: projections of income, dividends, or future economic performance; and statements regarding management plans and objectives for future operations. Under §§27A of the 1933 Act, and 21E of the 1934 Act, added in 1995, if such forward looking statements made by a 1934 Act reporting company are identified as such and include "meaningful cautionary statements identifying important factors that could cause actual results to differ materially from those in the forward looking statement," then private plaintiffs may recover under the securities laws only if the defendant has actual knowledge that the statements were false or misleading.

The Supreme Court recently summarized the elements of a private damages action under Rule 10b-5 as follows:

1. a material misrepresentation (or omission);
2. scienter, i.e., a wrongful state of mind;
3. a connection with the purchase or sale of a security;
4. reliance, often referred to in cases involving public securities markets (fraud-on-the-market cases) as "transaction causation," (nonconclusively presuming that the price of a publicly traded share reflects a material misrepresentation and that plaintiffs have relied upon that misrepresentation as long as they would not have bought the share in its absence);
5. economic loss; and
6. "loss causation," i.e., a causal connection between the material misrepresentation and the loss.[47]

Insider Trading

Rule 10b-5's most important function is to police against **insider trading**—buying and selling securities based upon access to confidential or proprietary information not available to the public. Insider trading destroys the integrity of the securities markets and undermines the basic "full disclosure" philosophy of federal securities law. Its abolition is one of the SEC's top enforcement priorities. In most cases, insider trading is attacked under Rule 10b-5(c), which prohibits acts or practices that operate as a fraud on any person.

---

[46]Securities and Exchange Commission, Final Rule: Selective Disclosure and Insider Trading.
[47]Dura Pharmaceuticals v. Broudo, 125 S. Ct. 1627, 1631 (2005) (citations omitted).

In 1961, the SEC decided the landmark case, *In the Matter of Cady, Roberts & Co.*,[48] which established the basic standards governing insider trading under Rule 10b-5. In *Cady, Roberts,* a corporate director called his broker during a break in the board of directors meeting to report that the board had decided to cut the corporation's quarterly dividend. Before news of the board's decision became public, the broker entered orders to sell several thousand shares of the corporation's stock for his various customers at $40. When news of the dividend cut became public, the stock price dropped to under $35. The SEC instituted proceedings against the broker and found a violation of Rule 10b-5 noting

Rule 10b-5 [applies] to securities transactions by "any person." Misrepresentations will lie within [its] ambit, no matter who the speaker may be. An affirmative duty to disclose material information has been traditionally imposed on corporate "insiders," particularly officers, directors, or controlling stockholders. We, and the courts have consistently held that insiders must disclose material facts which are known to them by virtue of their position but which are not known to persons with whom they deal and which, if known, would affect their investment judgment. Failure to make disclosure in these circumstances constitutes a violation of the anti-fraud provisions. If, on the other hand, disclosure prior to effecting a purchase or sale would be improper or unrealistic under the circumstances, we believe the alternative is to forgo the transaction. . . .

[O]fficers, directors and controlling stockholders . . . do not exhaust the classes of persons upon whom there is such an obligation. Analytically, the obligation rests on two principal elements; first, the existence of a relationship giving access, directly or indirectly, to information intended to be available only for a corporate purpose and not for the personal benefit of anyone, and second, the inherent unfairness involved where a party takes advantage of such information knowing it is unavailable to those with whom he is dealing. In considering these elements under the broad language of the anti-fraud provisions we are not to be circumscribed by fine distinctions and rigid classifications. Thus our task here is to identify those persons who are in a special relationship with a company and privy to its internal affairs, and thereby suffer correlative duties in trading in its securities. Intimacy demands restraint lest the uninformed be exploited.

The facts here impose on [the broker] the responsibilities of those commonly referred to as "insiders." He received the

information prior to its public release from a director . . . [whose] relationship to the company clearly prohibited him from selling the securities affected by the information without disclosure. By logical sequence, it should prohibit [the broker]. This prohibition extends not only over his own account, but to selling for discretionary accounts and soliciting and executing other orders. . . .[49]

Cady, Roberts and subsequent cases make it clear that insiders possessing material, nonpublic information have a duty either to disclose it or abstain from trading. This duty is based upon the "special relationship" of trust or confidence existing between the insiders and the corporation. In virtually all cases, this relationship is based upon the fiduciary duty of loyalty owed by corporate officers and directors to the corporation and its shareholders. As discussed in Chapters 40 and 47, the duty of loyalty requires one person (here corporate officers, other agents, and directors) to act solely for the benefit of another (here, the corporation and its shareholders) as to matters within the scope of the relation. Among many other obligations, this "fiduciary" duty prevents the officer, other employee, or director from disclosing or otherwise using confidential information acquired in the course of the relationship for personal benefit. All insider trading liability is based upon breach of this duty. As developed below, a person may be held liable for breaching the duty himself or may "inherit" the liability created by someone else's breach. In addition, a person may be held liable for violating the duty of loyalty either to the corporation whose stock is traded, or to anyone else who lawfully possesses the material nonpublic information.

Classical Insider Trading—Insider Liability

The *Cady, Roberts* disclose-or-abstain rule applies most clearly to: (1) corporate insiders, such as officers, directors, and controlling shareholders; and (2) to other employees, such as engineers, who acquire material information from a corporate source. These insiders breach their fiduciary duty of loyalty to the corporation by using their advance knowledge of material nonpublic corporate information to trade in the corporation's stock for personal benefit.

Note that insiders may be held liable either (1) by trading in the stock themselves; or (2) as a "tipper" by

---

[48]40 S.E.C. 907 (1961).

[49]*Id.* at 911–912.

passing the information onto others, "tippees" (typically, a spouse, relative, friend, or business associate), who trade based on the information. That is, Rule 10b-5 liability extends to tippers whether or not they also trade in the stock. The standards governing tipper and tippee liability are more fully developed in the next section.

Certainly the most famous of such "classical" insider trading cases is *Securities and Exchange Commission v. Texas Gulf Sulphur Company* (1968).[50] In this case, Texas Gulf Sulphur insiders and their tippees purchased Texas Gulf Sulphur stock based upon their advance knowledge of a significant mineral ore discovery in eastern Canada. In holding the insiders liable for violating Rule 10b-5 by trading on this material nonpublic information, the court noted:

> The core of Rule 10b-5 is the implementation of the Congressional purpose that all investors should have equal access to the rewards of participation in securities transactions. It was the intent of Congress that all members of the investing public should be subject to identical market risks,—which market risks include, of course the risk that one's evaluative capacity or one's capital available to put at risk may exceed another's capacity or capital. The insiders here were not trading on an equal footing with the outside investors. They alone were in a position to evaluate the probability and magnitude of what seemed from the outset to be a major ore strike; they alone could invest safely, secure in the expectation that the price of TGS stock would rise substantially in the event such a major strike should materialize, but would decline little, if at all, in the event of failure. . . . Such inequities based upon unequal access to knowledge should not be shrugged off as inevitable in our way of life, or, in view of the congressional concern in the area, remain uncorrected.[51]

Insider Trading—Outsider Liability

The *Cady, Roberts* disclose-or-abstain rule applies to insiders as defined above, and certain others, known collectively as "outsiders." Outsiders fall into three categories, discussed below: (1) tippees, (2) temporary insiders, and (3) misappropriators.

Tippee Liability. Tippee liability is based on a number of Supreme Court cases, most importantly *Dirks v. Securities and Exchange Commission* (1983).[52] Under

Dirks, a tipper who passes along material nonpublic information is liable under Rule 10b-5 for breaching his fiduciary duty if the tipper obtains some personal gain (direct or indirect) or reputational benefit by doing so. Virtually all tippers meet this test. Tippees "inherit" the tipper's disclose-or-abstain duty under the following test:

> a tippee assumes a fiduciary duty to the shareholders of a corporation not to trade on material nonpublic information only when the insider has breached his fiduciary duty to the shareholders by disclosing the information to the tippee and the tippee knows or should know that there has been a breach.[53]

Most tippees meet this test. For example, the tippees in *Cady, Roberts* and *Texas Gulf Sulphur* were liable because (1) the insiders clearly breached their fiduciary duty by disclosing the information, and (2) the tippees were fully aware of the breach when they traded in the stock.

Dirks provides the rare example of a case in which a tippee would not be held liable under the above test. The tippee in *Dirks* was a securities analyst who received information from corporate insiders that the corporation's assets were vastly overstated because of fraudulent corporate practices. On these facts, the Court found no liability because the insiders did not breach any fiduciary duty to the corporation by disclosing the fraud to the analyst. That is, they were motivated not by a desire to exploit undisclosed corporate information for personal gain, but by a desire to expose the fraud.

Temporary Insiders. Outsider liability also may be imposed on "temporary insiders." Under this theory, when corporate information is revealed legitimately to an underwriter, accountant, lawyer, or consultant working for the corporation, these outsiders (the "temporary insiders") may become fiduciaries of the shareholders. In this case, a duty to disclose or abstain is imposed, if the corporation expects the outsider to keep the disclosed nonpublic information confidential, and the relationship between the parties at least implies a duty of confidentiality. The fiduciary duty in this case is based upon the existence of a special confidential relationship giving the outsider access to information solely for corporate purposes.[54]

Misappropriation Theory. An additional theory of outsider liability is the "misappropriation" theory

---

[50]401 F.2d 833 (2d Cir. 1968).
[51]*Id.* at 851-52.
[52]103 S. Ct. 3255 (1983).

[53]*Id.* at 3264.
[54]103 S. Ct. 3262 n. 14.

announced by the Second Circuit Court of Appeals in *United States v. Newman,*[55] under which

> one who misappropriates nonpublic information in breach of a fiduciary duty and trades on that information to his own advantage violates §10(b) and Rule 10b-5.[56]

The distinction between classical insider trading and misappropriation liability is simple. In classical insider trading, the fiduciary duty is owed by the insider (and tippees) to the corporation whose stock is traded. In misappropriation cases, the defendant owes no duty to and has no relationship with the corporation whose stock is traded. Rather, the defendant is breaching a duty to someone else (usually the defendant's employer) who lawfully possesses the material nonpublic information.

This theory has been used, for example, to support criminal prosecutions and SEC injunctive proceedings against employees who breach an employer-imposed duty of confidentiality by stealing and subsequently trading upon material nonpublic information entrusted to the employers (such as investment and commercial banks, financial printers, or law firms) by their clients. In the following case, the Supreme Court adopts and applies the theory.

United States v. O'Hagan
117 S. Ct. 2199 (1997)

In July 1988, the British corporation Grand Metropolitan PLC (Grand Met) retained Dorsey and Whitney, a Minneapolis law firm, as local counsel in a potential tender offer for the common stock of Pillsbury Company. James O'Hagan, a partner in Dorsey and Whitney, was not involved in the firm's work for Grand Met but allegedly learned of Grand Met's plans through other partners in the firm. Beginning on August 18, 1988, O'Hagan purchased call options entitling him to buy Pillsbury stock at a set price. By the end of September, O'Hagan owned 2,500 Pillsbury options. He also purchased about 5,000 shares of Pillsbury stock during September for under $39 per share. When Grand Met announced its tender offer in October, Pillsbury stock rose to almost $60 per share. O'Hagan then

sold his Pillsbury options and stock making a profit of more than $4.3 million.

The United States government indicted O'Hagan, charging that he had violated §10(b) of the Securities Exchange Act of 1934 and SEC Rule 10b-5. The indictment alleged that O'Hagan had defrauded Grand Met and Dorsey and Whitney by misappropriating nonpublic information about the tender offer and using it for his own profit. The jury convicted O'Hagan and he was sentenced to prison for 41 months. O'Hagan appealed and the federal Eighth Circuit Court of Appeals reversed the conviction ruling that liability under §10(b) and Rule 10b-5 could not be based on the misappropriation theory. The United States Supreme Court granted certiorari to review the case.

Justice Ginsburg

. . . [Section] 10(b) of the Exchange Act . . . proscribes (1) using any deceptive device (2) in connection with the purchase or sale of securities, in contravention of rules prescribed by the [Securities and Exchange] Commission. The provision, as written, does not confine its coverage to deception of a purchaser or seller of securities . . . ; rather, the statute reaches any deceptive device used "in connection with the purchase or sale of any security."

Pursuant to its §10(b) rulemaking authority, the Commission has adopted Rule 10b-5. . . . Under the "traditional" or "classical theory" of insider trading liability, §10(b) and Rule 10b-5 are violated when a corporate insider trades in the securities of his corporation on the basis of material, nonpublic information. Trading on such information qualifies as a "deceptive device" under §10(b), we have affirmed, because "a relationship of trust and confidence [exists] between the shareholders of a corporation and those insiders who have obtained confidential information by reason of their position with that corporation." [*Chiarella v. United States,* 100 S. Ct. 1108, 1114 (1980).] That relationship, we recognized, "gives rise to a duty to disclose [or to abstain from trading] because of the 'necessity of preventing a corporate insider from . . . tak[ing] unfair advantage of . . . uninformed . . . stockholders.'" [*Id.* at 1115.] The classical theory applies not only to officers, directors, and other permanent insiders of a corporation, but also to attorneys, accountants, consultants, and others who temporarily become fiduciaries of a corporation. . . .

The "misappropriation theory" holds that a person commits fraud "in connection with" a securities transaction, and thereby violates §10(b) and Rule 10b-5, when

---

[55]664 F.2d 12 (2d Cir. 1981).
[56]Securities and Exchange Commission v. Materia, 745 F.2d 197, 203 (2d Cir. 1984).

he misappropriates confidential information for securities trading purposes, in breach of a duty owed to the source of the information. . . . Under this theory, a fiduciary's undisclosed, self-serving use of a principal's information to purchase or sell securities, in breach of a duty of loyalty and confidentiality, defrauds the principal of the exclusive use of that information. In lieu of premising liability on a fiduciary relationship between company insider and purchaser or seller of the company's stock, the misappropriation theory premises liability on a fiduciary-turned-trader's deception of those who entrusted him with access to confidential information.

The two theories are complementary, each addressing efforts to capitalize on nonpublic information through the purchase or sale of securities. The classical theory targets a corporate insider's breach of duty to shareholders with whom the insider transacts; the misappropriation theory outlaws trading on the basis of nonpublic information by a corporate "outsider" in breach of a duty owed not to a trading party, but to the source of the information. The misappropriation theory is thus designed to "protect the integrity of the securities markets against abuses by 'outsiders' to a corporation who have access to confidential information that will affect the corporation's security price when revealed, but who owe no fiduciary or other duty to that corporation's shareholders." [*Brief for the United States* 14.]

In this case, the indictment alleged that O'Hagan, in breach of a duty of trust and confidence he owed to his law firm, Dorsey & Whitney, and to its client, Grand Met, traded on the basis of nonpublic information regarding Grand Met's planned tender offer for Pillsbury common stock. This conduct, the Government charged, constituted a fraudulent device in connection with the purchase and sale of securities.

We agree with the Government that misappropriation, as just defined, satisfies §10(b)'s requirement that chargeable conduct involve a "deceptive device or contrivance" used "in connection with" the purchase or sale of securities. We observe, first, that misappropriators, as the Government describes them, deal in deception. A fiduciary who "[pretends] loyalty to the principal while secretly converting the principal's information for personal gain" . . . "dupes" or defrauds the principal. . . . Deception through nondisclosure is central to the theory of liability for which the Government seeks recognition. . . .

We turn next to the §10(b) requirement that the misappropriator's deceptive use of information be "in connection with the purchase or sale of [a] security." This element is satisfied because the fiduciary's fraud is consummated, not when the fiduciary gains the confidential information, but when, without disclosure to his principal, he uses the information to purchase or sell securities. The securities transaction and the breach of duty thus coincide. This is so even though the person or entity defrauded is not the other party to the trade, but is, instead, the source of the nonpublic information. . . . A misappropriator who trades on the basis of material, nonpublic information, in short, gains his advantageous market position through deception; he deceives the source of the information and simultaneously harms members of the investing public. . . .

The misappropriation theory comports with §10(b)'s language, which requires deception "in connection with the purchase or sale of any security," not deception of an identifiable purchaser or seller. The theory is also well-tuned to an animating purpose of the Exchange Act: to insure honest securities markets and thereby promote investor confidence. . . . Although informational disparity is inevitable in the securities markets, investors likely would hesitate to venture their capital in a market where trading based on misappropriated nonpublic information is unchecked by law. An investor's informational disadvantage vis-à-vis a misappropriator with material, nonpublic information stems from contrivance, not luck; it is a disadvantage that cannot be overcome with research or skill. . . .

In sum, considering the inhibiting impact on market participation of trading on misappropriated information, and the congressional purposes underlying §10(b), it makes scant sense to hold a lawyer like O'Hagan a §10(b) violator if he works for a law firm representing the target of a tender offer, but not if he works for a law firm representing the bidder. The text of the statute requires no such result. The misappropriation at issue here was properly made the subject of a §10(b) charge because it meets the statutory requirement that there be "deceptive" conduct "in connection with" securities transactions. . . .

[Judgment reversed and remanded.]

Rules 10b5-1 and 10b5-2. As discussed above, insider trading law is developed by judicial decisions interpreting Rule 10b-5 on a case-by-case basis. To resolve two issues on which courts have disagreed, the SEC adopted Rules 10b5-1 and 10b5-2 in 2000.

Insider trading law prohibits trading on the basis of material nonpublic information. Under Rule 10b5-1, a trade is made "on the basis of" such information if the trader was aware of that information when making the purchase or sale. "Awareness" is used in its ordinary sense to mean "having knowledge; conscious; cognizant." Rule 10b5-1 recognizes an affirmative defense for knowing purchases in which the information clearly was not a factor in making the trade, such as a purchase made under a preexisting stock purchase plan.

Rule 10b5-2 defines when a fiduciary duty (duty of trust or confidence) exists for purposes of applying the misappropriation theory outside the traditional employment relationship—for example, when the trader is a spouse or family member of the source of the information. Under Rule 10b5-2, personal or family relationships create a duty of trust or confidence if: (1) the person agrees to keep the information confidential; (2) the parties have a "history, pattern, or practice" of sharing confidences, such that the recipient should know that the source expects the information to remain confidential; or (3) the recipient is the source's spouse, parent, child, or sibling.

Additional Federal Insider Trading Statutes. To supplement Rule 10b-5, Congress enacted the **Insider Trading Sanctions Act of 1984** and the **Insider Trading and Securities Fraud Enforcement Act of 1988**[57] to control insider trading. Collectively, these statutes (1) require brokers, dealers, and investment advisors to establish systems to prevent insider trading, and to enforce policies designed to prevent misuse of material nonpublic information by the firm, its employees, or associated persons, and (2) permit the SEC to recover a civil penalty from anyone violating the 1934 Act or rules by "purchasing or selling a security while in possession of material nonpublic information." Liability extends both to violators and persons who directly or indirectly control them. Such controlling persons include employers and others with the power to control the violator's management, policies, or other activities. A violator's penalty may not exceed three times the profit gained or loss avoided as a result of the unlawful purchase or sale. The violator also may be required to disgorge any illegal profit and may be subject to criminal penalties under §32(a) of the 1934 Act discussed earlier in this chapter. Controlling persons are subject to a similar penalty not exceeding the greater of $1 million or three times the violator's profit gained or loss avoided.

Controlling persons are not liable merely for employing a violator, rather, the SEC may impose a penalty only if it establishes that the controlling person knew of or recklessly disregarded the likelihood of a controlled person's violation and failed to take appropriate steps to prevent the violation. A controlling person who is a registered broker, dealer, or investment adviser also may be held liable for knowingly or recklessly failing to establish, maintain, or enforce the policies or procedures required by law to prevent insider trading, if such failure substantially contributed to the violation. To aid the SEC in uncovering violations, the law authorizes the Commission to award bounties to persons who provide information leading to imposition of a penalty.

In addition to civil penalties, the law also authorizes an express private right of action for contemporaneous traders against violators. Total damages in such actions, however, may not exceed the profit gained or loss avoided by the defendant in the illegal transaction or transactions, less any amounts recovered by the SEC as a civil penalty for the same conduct. In private actions, a controlling person may escape liability by showing that it acted in good faith and did not induce the acts constituting the violation. Note that both civil penalty and private actions are subject to a five-year statute of limitations.

Regulation FD. An issuer may selectively disclose material nonpublic information to market insiders, such as securities analysts or institutional investors, before disclosing the same information to the general public. As noted by the SEC, this practice:

> bears a close resemblance . . . to ordinary "tipping" and insider trading. In both cases, a privileged few gain an informational edge—and the ability to use that edge to profit—from their superior access to corporate insiders, rather than from their skill, acumen, or diligence. Likewise, selective disclosure has an adverse impact on market integrity that is similar to the adverse impact from illegal insider trading: investors lose confidence in the fairness of the markets when they know that other participants may exploit 'unerodable informational advantages' derived not from hard work or insights, but from their access to corporate insiders.[58]

To prevent selective disclosure, which had become widespread by the late 1990s, the SEC adopted Regulation FD[59] in 2000. Under Regulation FD, if an issuer dis-

---

[57]Securities Exchange Act §§15(f), 20A, 21A; Investment Advisers Act §204A.

[58]Securities and Exchange Commission, Final Rule: Selective Disclosure and Insider Trading.
[59]17 C.F.R. §§243.100–243.103.

Table 49.4	Summary of 1934 Act Remedies		
Provision	**Conduct Proscribed**	**Permissible Plaintiffs**	**Permissible Defendants**
§18(a)	False or misleading statement in any document filed under 1934 Act or Rules	Investors who purchase or sell in reliance upon document	Issuer, its officers, and directors
§16(a)	Insiders' failure to report ownership of or transactions in corporation's stock	SEC administrative and civil proceedings	Officers, directors, and shareholders owning more than 10 percent of company's stock
§16(b)	Profit realized by insiders who buy or sell corporation's stock within any six-month period	Issuer (or shareholder acting on issuer's behalf)	Officers, directors, and shareholders owning more than 10 percent of company's stock
Rule 10b-5	Fraud in connection with purchase or sale of any security	SEC enforcement; purchaser or seller of security	Any person who commits fraud or deception in sale of any security; proof of scienter required
Foreign Corrupt Practices Act	Bribery of foreign officials	Government enforcement	Individuals and organizations (including officers, directors, employees, agents, and certain shareholders of organizations)

closes material nonpublic information about the issuer or its securities to certain market professionals[60] or to shareholders who are likely to trade on the basis of that information, then the issuer must make public disclosure of the same information simultaneously (for intentional disclosures) or promptly (for unintentional disclosures). "Public disclosure" may be made by filing a Form 8K with the SEC, or alternatively, any other method "reasonably designed to provide broad, non-exclusionary distribution of the information to the public." "Promptly" in the case of unintentional disclosure means as soon as reasonably practicable (but in no event after the later of 24 hours or the commencement of the next day's trading on the New York Stock Exchange) after a senior official of the issuer learns of the unintentional disclosure. Regulation FD excludes from coverage advance disclosures made: (1) to persons who owe the issuer a duty of trust and confidence (such as the issuer's attorneys, accountants, or investment bankers) and others who expressly agree to keep the information confidential; (2) to credit rating agencies;

and (3) in connection with securities offered under a 1933 Act registration.

Table 49.4 summarizes the various 1934 Act remedies discussed in this chapter.

Sarbanes-Oxley Act of 2002

To protect investors, securities laws require that the financial statements of publicly traded companies be independently audited. Independence refers to an auditor's objectivity and lack of bias. In the 1990s, the SEC became increasingly concerned that consulting and other nonaudit services provided by accounting firms to audit clients substantially compromised auditor independence. Accordingly, in 2001, the SEC adopted revised rules governing auditor independence. [61]

The SEC's concern proved well-founded, when in 2002, a series of massive corporate failures cost investors billions of dollars. In most cases, the public accountants had certified materially fraudulent financial statements, exposing serious deficiencies in audit qual-

---

[60]These include securities brokers or dealers, investment advisers, and investment companies.

[61]17 C.F.R. §§210.2-01; 240.14a-101.

ity and auditor independence. To address the problem, Congress passed the **Sarbanes-Oxley Act of 2002,**[62] (the Act), a wide ranging statute designed not only to improve auditing standards and auditor independence, but also to improve corporate governance; and the accuracy, reliability, and timeliness of corporate disclosures. Most of the Act's provisions are additions or amendments to the Securities Exchange Act of 1934. In addition, important amendments were made to the bankruptcy code and the federal criminal code. The following material discusses the obligations imposed by the Act upon public accountants, issuers, corporate officers and directors, attorneys, and securities analysts.

Public Accountants

Public Company Accounting Oversight Board. To oversee the auditing of public companies subject to the securities laws ("Issuers"), the Act establishes the Public Company Accounting Oversight Board (PCAOB or Board) and requires accounting firms auditing public companies to register with the Board. The Board, which operates as a not for profit corporation, not a federal government agency, has the following duties:

1. register public accounting firms that prepare audit reports for issuers. . . . ;
2. establish by rule, auditing, quality control, ethics, independence, and other standards relating to the preparation of audit reports for issuers;
3. conduct inspections of registered public accounting firms . . . ;
4. conduct investigations and disciplinary proceedings concerning, and impose appropriate sanctions where justified upon, registered public accounting firms;
5. perform such other duties or functions as the Board (or the SEC, by rule or order) determines are necessary or appropriate to promote high professional standards among . . . registered public accounting firms . . . in order to protect investors, or to further the public interest;
6. enforce compliance with this Act, the rules of the Board, professional standards, and the securities laws relating to the preparation and issuance of audit reports . . . ; and
7. set the budget and manage the operations of the Board and the staff of the Board.[63]

The Board is composed of five members, who serve five year terms. Two, but only two, of the members are required to be certified public accountants. The inspections noted above are conducted annually for accountants who audit more than 100 issuers, and at least every three years for other accountants.[64]

Auditing Standards. As noted above, a major function of the Board is to adopt auditing, quality control and independence standards for registered public accounting firms (hereafter, Accountants).[65] Under the auditing standards, Accountants are required to prepare, and maintain for at least seven years, audit work papers; and provide a concurring or second partner review and approval of audit reports. Accountants also must describe in each audit report the scope and findings of the auditor's testing of the issuer's internal control structure and procedures, and a description of material weaknesses in, and noncompliance with, internal controls.

Finally, the Accountant's audit report must contain an evaluation of whether the issuer's internal control structure and procedures: 1) generate records that accurately and fairly reflect the issuers transactions and dispositions of assets; and 2) provide reasonable assurance that a) transactions are recorded as necessary to permit financial statements to be prepared in accordance with GAAP, and b) receipts and expenditures are made only as authorized by management.

Quality Control Standards. The quality control standards include requirements for every Accountant relating to: (1) monitoring professional ethics and independence from audit clients; (2) consultation within the firm on accounting and auditing questions; (3) supervision of audit work; (4) hiring, professional development, and promotion of personnel; (5) the acceptance and continuation of engagements; and (6) internal inspection.

Independence Standards. As noted in the introduction, revised auditor independence standards were adopted by the SEC in 2001. These standards were amended and supplemented by the Sarbanes-Oxley Act.

Under the Act and revised rules, an auditor is not independent of an audit client if "the accountant is not, or a reasonable investor with knowledge of all relevant facts and circumstances would conclude that the accountant is not, capable of exercising objective and impartial judgment on all issues encompassed within

---

[62]P.L. 107-204.
[63]S-O Act §101(c).

[64]S-O Act §104.
[65] S-O Act §103.

the accountant's engagement."[66] This standard is designed to assure that an auditor is independent of its audit client both in fact and in appearance. In applying this standard, the SEC examines

> whether a relationship or the provision of a service: (a) creates a mutual or conflicting interest between the accountant and the audit client; (b) places the accountant in the position of auditing his or her own work; (c) results in the accountant acting as management or an employee of the audit client; or (d) places the accountant in a position of being an advocate for the audit client.[67]

Although auditor independence generally is judged by considering "all relevant circumstances,"[68] an auditor is specifically prohibited from: (1) having a financial interest in, or an employment or other business relationship with, the audit client; (2) providing services or products on a contingent fee or commission basis; and (3) providing the following nonaudit services to the client:

1. bookkeeping or other services related to the client's accounting records or financial statements;
2. financial information systems design and implementation;
3. appraisal or valuation services, or fairness opinions or contribution-in-kind reports;
4. actuarial services;
5. internal audit outsourcing services;
6. management and human resource functions;
7. broker-dealer, investment adviser, or investment banking services; and
8. legal services and expert services unrelated to the audit.[69]

Non-audit services other than those listed above are permitted only if (1) approved in advance by the issuer's audit committee, or (2) authorized by pre-approval policies and procedures established by the audit committee.[70]

In 2005, the PCAOB adopted regulations clarifying the nonaudit services rules as applied to tax services. Under these regulations, auditors may provide routine tax return preparation, general tax planning and advice, and employee personal tax services, but may not provide tax services: (1) compensated on a contingent fee basis, (2) involving aggressive tax shelter products, or (3) to corporate officers who oversee the client's financial reporting.

The independence rules also require public disclosure by the issuer in its annual proxy statement of the total fees paid to its principal accountant for (1) audit fees; (2) audit-related fees; (3) tax fees, and (4) all other fees. The proxy statement also must disclose the audit committee's pre-approval policies and procedures for non-audit services not prohibited above.[71]

To further assure auditor independence, the Act requires that lead and concurring audit partners rotate at least every five years.[72] After rotation, these two partners are prohibited from acting as the issuer's lead or concurring partners for five years. The Act also prohibits an Accountant from auditing any issuer whose chief executive, financial or accounting officer was employed by the Accountant and participated in the issuer's audit during the one-year period preceding the date on which the current audit was begun.[73] The Act also requires Accountants to report to the issuers audit committee:

1. all critical accounting policies and practices to be used;
2. all alternative treatments of financial information within [GAAP] that have been discussed with the issuer's management officials, ramifications of [the alternatives], and the treatment preferred by the Accountant; and
3. other material written communications between the Accountant and the issuer's management. . . .[74]

Issuers

The Act imposes a number of important obligations on "issuers", generally defined as those companies required to register and report under the Securities Exchange Act of 1934. Many of the Act's provisions relating to issuers require enhanced disclosures in periodic reports filed under the 1934 Act. To assure compliance, the SEC is required to review the issuer's reports, including financial statements, at least once every three years.[75]

Audit Committee Independence. Under the Act,[76] the issuer's audit committee (a committee of the Board of Directors) is directly responsible for the appointment,

---

[66]17 C.F.R. §210.2-01(b).

[67]17 C.F.R. §210.2-01, Preliminary Note.

[68]17 C.F.R. §210.2-01(b).

[69]S-O Act §201(a); Securities Exchange Act §10A(g); 17 C.F.R. §210.2-01(c).

[70]S-O Act §201(a); Securities Exchange Act §10A(h).

[71]17 C.F.R. §240.14a-101.

[72]S-O Act §203; Securities Exchange Act §10A(j).

[73]S-O Act §206; Securities Exchange Act §10A(l).

[74]S-O Act §204; Securities Exchange Act §10A(k).

[75]S-O Act §408.

[76]S-O Act §301; Securities Exchange Act §10A(m).

compensation, and oversight of the Accountants auditing the company's books, and the Accountants are required to report directly to the audit committee. The members of the audit committee must be independent of the issuer and may not receive any consulting or advisory fee, other than for acting as a board, or audit or other board committee, member. Although members of the audit committee need not generally possess special qualifications, the issuer must disclose in its annual report whether or not at least one member of the audit committee is a "financial expert," and if not, why not.[77]

The Act requires the audit committee to establish procedures for "the receipt, retention, and treatment of complaints received by the issuer regarding accounting, internal accounting controls, or auditing matters; and the confidential, anonymous submission by employees of the issuer of concerns regarding questionable accounting or auditing matters."[78] The audit committee has the authority to engage independent counsel and other advisors, and the issuer is required to provide appropriate funding to compensate these advisers and the Accountants auditing the company's books.

To aid in compliance, the Act prohibits national securities exchanges and national securities associations from listing any company that fails to comply with the audit committee independence requirements discussed above.

Enhanced Financial Disclosures. To improve financial disclosures in reports filed by issuers under the 1934 Act, the Act requires:[79]

1. that all financial statements required to be prepared in accordance with (or reconciled to) GAAP must reflect all material correcting adjustments identified by the Accountant necessary to comply with GAAP or SEC rules;
2. disclosure of all material off-balance-sheet transactions that may have a material effect on financial condition; and
3. that any "pro-forma" financial information used by the issuer in 1934 Act reports, press releases, or other public disclosures be (a) free of material misstatements or omissions, and (b) reconciled with the same information computed under GAAP.

Loans to Executives. The Act[80] generally prohibits issuers from extending credit in the form of personal loans to its officers and directors. Excepted from this prohibition are certain home improvement loans, consumer credit transactions, and loans by securities firms to employees to purchase stock.

Financial Officers Code of Ethics. The Act[81] requires an issuer to state in its annual report whether it has adopted a code of ethics (and if not, why not) for its senior financial officers (principal financial officer, and comptroller or chief accounting officer). The Act also requires "immediate disclosure" of any change to, or waiver from, its code of ethics. The code must include standards as are reasonably necessary to promote:

1. honest and ethical conduct, including the ethical handling of actual or apparent conflicts of interest between personal and professional relationships;
2. full, fair, accurate, timely, and understandable disclosure in the periodic reports required to be filed by the issuer; and
3. compliance with applicable governmental rules and regulations.

Officers

Certification of Reports. Under the Act,[82] the issuer's principal executive officer and principal financial officer are required to certify each quarterly and annual report filed under the 1934 Act. Specifically, each signing officer certifies that: (1) the signing officer has reviewed the report; (2) based on the officer's knowledge, the report does not contain any material misstatements or omissions; and (3) the financial statements fairly present the issuer's financial condition and results of operations.

As previously noted, the Foreign Corrupt Practices Act of 1977 imposes significant internal control requirements upon reporting companies. To bolster this requirement, the Sarbanes-Oxley Act requires the signing officers listed above to certify that they

1. (a) are responsible for establishing and maintaining internal controls; (b) have designed internal controls to assure that material information relating to the issuer is made known to the officers by others within the issuer; (c) have evaluated the issuer's internal controls within 90 days prior to the report; and (d) have presented in the report their conclusions about the effectiveness of internal controls.

---

[77]S-O Act §407.
[78]S-O Act §301; Securities Exchange Act §10A(m)(4).
[79]S-O Act §401; Securities Exchange Act §§13(i)-(j).
[80]S-O Act §402; Securities Exchange Act §13(k).

[81]S-O Act §406.
[82]S-O Act §302.

2. have disclosed to the issuer's auditors and the audit committee all significant deficiencies in the design or operation of internal controls and any fraud involving employees who have a significant role in the issuer's internal controls; and

3. have indicated in the report whether or not there were significant changes in internal controls subsequent to the date of their evaluation, including any corrective actions relating to significant deficiencies and material weaknesses.

To further assure adequate internal control, in its annual report, an issuer must provide an internal control report:

1. stating the responsibility of management for establishing and maintaining an adequate internal control structure and procedures for financial reporting; and

2. providing an assessment, as of the end of the most recent fiscal year, of the effectiveness of such structure and procedures.[83]

The report must disclose the framework used to assess the effectiveness of the company's internal control over financial reporting and any material weaknesses in that internal control identified by management. Any material weakness prevents management from concluding that its internal control is effective. Note finally that the issuer's Accountant is required to attest to, and report upon, management's internal control report.

Improper Influence on Conduct of Audits. The Act prohibits any officer or director of an issuer (or person acting under their direction) from taking any action to coerce, manipulate, mislead, or fraudulently influence any accountant auditing the issuer's financial statements, in order to render the financial statements materially misleading.[84]

Forfeiture of Bonuses and Profits. Due to misconduct, an issuer's financial statements may materially violate a financial reporting requirement imposed by the securities laws. If the violation requires that the issuer's financial statements be restated, the issuer's chief executive officer and chief financial officer must reimburse the issuer for:

1. any bonus or other incentive-based or equity-based compensation received within 12 months following the issuance of the offending financial statement; and

2. any profit realized from the sale of the issuer's securities during that 12 month period.[85]

Attorneys and Analysts

Attorneys. The Act[86] authorizes the SEC to issue rules providing minimum standards for attorneys representing issuers who appear or practice before the SEC. The rules include a requirement that:

1. the attorney must report to the issuer's chief legal counsel or chief executive officer any material violation of the securities laws or breach of fiduciary duty by the company or any of its agents; and

2. if the legal counsel or CEO does not respond by adopting appropriate remedial measures or sanctions, then the attorney must report the evidence to the company's audit, or other independent board committee, or to the board of directors.

Note that this is essentially the same obligation imposed upon public accountants in 1995, discussed in text Chapter 56.

Securities Analysts. The huge frauds and subsequent corporate failures leading to the passage of the Act were caused only in part by deficiencies in audit quality, auditor independence, and corporate governance. Also contributing was a lack of objectivity and conflicts of interest among securities analysts, who failed to inform the investing public of the true financial health of companies they covered.

Accordingly, the Act[87] requires the SEC to adopt rules (1) "to foster greater public confidence in securities research, and to protect the objectivity and independence of securities analysts"; (2) to define periods during which persons who participate in a public offering of securities as underwriters or dealers are prohibited from publishing research reports relating to the securities or the issuer; and (3) "to establish structural and institutional safeguards within registered brokers or dealers to assure that securities analysts are separated by appropriate informational partitions within the firm from the review, pressure, or oversight of those whose involvement in investment banking activities might potentially bias their judgment or supervision."

The rules adopted under (1) above (a) restrict prepublication clearance of analyst reports by persons within the analyst's employer who are not directly responsible for investment research; (b) prohibit supervision and compensatory evaluation of analysts by persons within

---

[83]S-O Act §404.
[84]S-O Act §303.
[85]S-O Act §304.

[86]S-O Act §307.
[87]S-O Act §501; Securities Exchange Act §15D.

the employer who are involved in investment banking; and (c) prohibit the employer or investment banking employees within the employer from retaliating against an analyst who renders an adverse, negative, or otherwise unfavorable research report concerning an investment banking client of the employer.

The Act also mandates rules requiring enhanced disclosures of conflicts of interest by analysts and broker-dealers in public appearances and research reports including

1. the extent to which the securities analyst has debt or equity investments in the issuer . . . ;
2. whether any compensation has been received by the registered broker or dealer, or . . . the securities analyst, from the issuer . . . ;
3. whether [the] issuer . . . currently is, or during the one-year period preceding the date of the appearance or . . . report has been a client of the registered broker or dealer . . . ; and
4. whether the securities analyst received compensation with respect to a research report, based upon (among any other factors) the investment banking revenues (either generally or specifically earned from the issuer being analyzed) of the registered broker or dealer. . . .

Criminal Sanctions

The Act creates a number of new criminal offenses and enhances the penalties for many existing crimes. Perhaps most importantly, the Act increases the penalties for violation of §32(a) of the 1934 Act.[88]

Individuals now are subject to fines of up to $5 million, and imprisonment of up to 20 years, or both (up from $1 million and 10 years). Corporate defendants now are subject to a maximum $25 million fine (up from $2.5 million). The Act also substantially increases the criminal penalties for mail and wire fraud, and for violation of the Employee Retirement Income Security Act (ERISA), regulating private pension funds.[89]

The Act also includes criminal provisions designed to preserve corporate and audit documents relevant to investigation of securities law violations. For example, under the Act it is a crime:

1. for any person knowingly to alter, destroy, or falsify any document, record, or tangible object with intent to impede, obstruct, or influence an investigation by any federal department or agency;[90] and
2. for any accountant who audits a company subject to the 1934 Act to fail to retain all audit or review work papers for five years following the end of the fiscal period for which the audit or review was conducted.[91]

Finally, the Act protects employees of public companies who provide evidence of securities fraud to the government or to the employee's supervisor. An employer who retaliates against such a whistle-blower (for example, by discharging, demoting, threatening, or harassing the employee) is subject to a civil action for money damages by the injured employee, and a criminal action by the government.[92]

Summary

1. Because corporate securities often have been used in schemes intended to mislead or defraud investors, the states have regulated distribution and sale of securities through "blue sky" laws since the early 1900s. State securities regulation proved inadequate in policing securities frauds, however, especially those operating on a national scale. The stock market crash of 1929 provided the impetus for federal regulation embodied in the Securities Act of 1933, the Securities Exchange Act of 1934, the Public Utility Holding Company Act of 1935, the Trust Indenture Act of 1939, the Investment Company Act of 1940, and the Investment Advisers Act of 1940. These statutes are administered by the Securities and Exchange Commission.

2. A major issue in securities law is to determine whether a particular investment transaction constitutes a security. Although the definition includes prototypical securities such as stocks and bonds, the law is broadly drafted to bring a wide range of investment instruments within the securities laws.

3. The Securities Act of 1933 governs the process by which a corporation or other issuer offers and sells its securities to the public for the first time. It provides generally that no security may be offered or sold to the public unless a registration statement has been filed with the SEC and become effective.

---

[88]The 1934 Act's general criminal provision discussed earlier in this chapter.

[89]ERISA is discussed in text Chapter 53.
[90]S-O Act §§802, 1102; 18 U.S.C. §§1512(c); 1519.
[91]S-O Act §802; 18 U.S.C. §1520.
[92] S-O Act §§806, 1107; 18 U.S.C. §§1513(e), 1514A.

Through a prospectus, certain information in the registration statement is provided to investors. The 1933 Act protects investors by providing full and fair disclosure of relevant information regarding the securities offered and the issuer.

4. The registration process under the 1933 Act is divided into three periods: the pre-filing period (the period before the registration statement has been completed and filed with the SEC), the waiting period (the period between the filing date and the date the registration statement becomes "effective"), and the post-effective period. Permissible selling efforts differ depending on how far the registration process has progressed, reflecting the level of public information about the offering.

5. Certain securities and security transactions are exempt from the 1933 Act's registration requirement. Major exempt transactions include (1) certain transactions involving small or limited offerings, (2) purely intrastate offerings, and (3) transactions by persons other than issuers, underwriters, or dealers.

6. The 1933 Act contains a variety of specific remedies designed to prevent the sale of unregistered securities and to assure the accuracy of the registration materials. These include §§12(1) and 11, which impose liability for selling unregistered securities and for deficiencies in registration statements, and §§12(2) and 17(a), which provide remedies for fraudulent conduct in the sale of securities.

7. The Securities Exchange Act of 1934 regulates secondary trading in securities, the securities markets, and persons conducting securities transactions. The 1934 Act, for example, imposes registration and disclosure requirements upon many issuers, the securities exchanges, self-regulatory organizations, and securities brokers and dealers. It also regulates insider trading, fraud and manipulative practices in securities trading, and corporate bribery of foreign officials.

8. One of the most important 1934 Act provisions is Rule 10b-5 adopted by the SEC, which prohibits fraud in the purchase or sale of any security. Courts have long recognized an implied private remedy under Rule 10b-5 for injured investors. The plaintiff must be a purchaser or seller of the securities involved and the defendant must have acted with scienter or intent to deceive.

9. Rule 10b-5's broad antifraud proscription has been applied to a wide variety of fact situations generally divided into three general areas: (1) corporate mismanagement, (2) corporate misstatements, and (3) insider trading. Rule 10b-5's most important function is its use in policing against insider trading—buying and selling securities based on access to information not available to the public.

10. Under insider trading law, certain persons possessing material, nonpublic information must either disclose it or refrain from trading. Liability extends to classic corporate insiders (such as officers, directors, and major shareholders) and three classes of outsiders: (1) certain tippees, (2) temporary insiders, and (3) misappropriators.

11. In 2002, Congress passed the Sarbanes-Oxley Act, a wide-ranging statute designed to improve: auditing standards and auditor independence; corporate governance; and the accuracy, reliability, and timeliness of corporate disclosures.

Key Terms

blue sky laws	security
Securities Act of 1933	underwriter
Securities Exchange Act of 1934	dealer
	registration statement
Securities and Exchange Commission (SEC)	prospectus
Public Utility Holding Company Act of 1935	Foreign Corrupt Practices Act of 1977
Trust Indenture Act of 1939	insider trading
Investment Company Act of 1940	Insider Trading Sanctions Act of 1984
Investment Advisers Act of 1940	Insider Trading and Securities Fraud Enforcement Act of 1988
	Sarbanes-Oxley Act of 2002

Questions and Problems

49.1 Federal securities laws provide investor protection by requiring full disclosure of accurate and timely information to investors, who can then make an informed choice concerning a securities transaction. Is this approach sufficient to protect investors? Should the SEC impose substantive requirements on issuers and "insiders" beyond full disclosure? Should federal law adopt a "merit" system to monitor which securities may be publicly offered?

49.2 Koscot Interplanetary, Inc. provides the opportunity for participation in the distribution and sale of cosmetics. A person may become a "beauty advisor" by purchasing Koscot cosmetics at a discount of 45 percent off the retail price. The beauty advisor then may sell the cosmetics at the retail price. A person may become a "supervisor" or "retail manager" by paying $1,000 to Koscot in return for the right to purchase Koscot cosmetics for a 55 percent discount. The supervisor then may sell the cosmetics directly to the public or may sell them to beauty advisors. A person who wishes to become a distributor pays $5,000 to Koscot and is entitled to receive cosmetics at a 65 percent discount which then may be sold to beauty advisors or supervisors. A supervisor or distributor who enlists another person to become part of the organization receives $600 for enlisting a supervisor or $3,000 for enlisting a distributor. Supervisors and distributors are encouraged to enlist others to join the organization by inviting them to "Opportunity Meetings" where Koscot employees attempt to recruit them to become beauty advisors, supervisors, or distributors.

(a) Mary White has paid $1,000 to Koscot to become a supervisor. How is she likely to make a profit from this investment? Explain.

(b) Harry Smith has paid $5,000 to become a distributor. How would he anticipate making a profit? Explain.

(c) Would either White's or Smith's investments be considered the purchase of a security under the federal securities laws? Explain.

49.3 As part of a collective bargaining agreement, various trucking companies employing Teamsters Union members agreed to pay $20 per week to the Teamsters Union Pension Trust Fund for each union member who was employed at one of the companies. A union member who worked in the union for at least 20 years would be entitled to receive a monthly pension of approximately $500 from the Trust Fund upon retirement. Each employee is required to participate in the pension plan so that employees do not have the option to receive direct payment from the employer in lieu of a contribution to the pension plan. Is the employer's contribution to the pension fund an investment on behalf of the employee? Would the contribution be considered a security under federal securities law? Explain.

49.4 Manor Nursing Centers, Inc. submitted a registration statement to the SEC in conjunction with the issuance of new securities. The effective date was December 8, 1989. Manor then issued the securities, which were accompanied by a prospectus containing the information set forth in the registration statement. Although the registration statement was accurate and correct on December 8, subsequent business developments rendered the information false and misleading. Was Manor required to correct this information? Explain. What, if any, statutes were violated?

49.5 Alphonse made the following transactions in Aladdin Lamp Co. stock:

Date	Transaction	Number of Shares	Price Per Share
2/1/2005	Bought	15,000	$24
4/3/2005	Sold	15,000	40
5/5/2005	Bought	5,000	35
9/1/2005	Sold	5,000	30
10/15/2005	Bought	5,000	25

(a) Determine whether Alphonse would be subject to the provisions of §16(b) of the Securities Exchange Act of 1934 if:
1. Alphonse was president of Aladdin and on 1/3/05 owned 2.2 percent of Aladdin stock;
2. Alphonse was a director of Aladdin;
3. Alphonse's wife was president of Aladdin;
4. Alphonse was not an officer or director of Aladdin. On 1/31/05, Alphonse owned 15,000 shares (all of which he had purchased in 1995) of a total of 200,000 shares of outstanding Aladdin stock.

(b) Assume that Alphonse was subject to the provisions of §16(b) and that prior to 2/1/05 he owned 10 percent of Aladdin stock. Aladdin has demanded that he turn over the profits he has realized in 2005. What amount does Alphonse owe to Aladdin?

49.6 Reports and predictions published in influential business publications can affect the prices of stocks and bonds. In the following cases, consider whether any violations of the federal securities laws have occurred.

(a) Foster writes a column for the *Wall Street Journal* entitled "Heard on the Street" that discusses market developments affecting stocks. Information in the column is obtained from security analysts and traders but not from corporations or corporate insiders. On February 13, Foster reported rumors of a takeover of Beatrice Corporation. Within two days, Beatrice stock had risen by $10 per share. On February 12, before publication of his story, Foster told a friend of the upcoming story. The friend purchased 5,000 shares of Beatrice stock on February 13.

(b) *Business Week,* a weekly magazine owned by McGraw-Hill, Inc., is printed by R. R. Donnelley Company. The magazine, which includes news and investigative stories about businesses and executives, and market reports and projections, is officially issued every Thursday at 5:00 P.M. Printing begins at Donnelley each Wednesday afternoon. Cobb, who operates a printing press at Donnelley, agrees to provide a copy of the new *Business Week* to Sue Sharp every Thursday morning at 7:00 A.M. Is this arrangement illegal? Explain.

49.7 Annabelle Stephens appeared on the nationally broadcast television show *Investigative Report* on April 6, 2004, to report on her findings that a new drug, Espadril, was unsafe and possibly carcinogenic. Espadril is manufactured by Drugco. On April 1, 2004, Dr. Stephens had purchased "put" options on Drugco stock. The put options entitled Dr. Stephens to sell the stock at a price of $50 during the following 90-day period. On April 1, the market price of Drugco's stock was $55 per share.

(a) Immediately following the broadcast of *Investigative Report,* the market price of Drugco stock dropped to $40 and Dr. Stephens exercised her put options. Has she violated any securities laws? Explain.

(b) The April 6 edition of *Investigative Report* was broadcast opposite a special showing of *Flames of Passion,* an immensely popular soap opera. During the following week, the market price of Drugco stock climbed to $60 per share and Dr. Stephens lost a great deal of money. Has Dr. Stephens violated any securities laws? Explain.

49.8 As the text discusses, insider trading is not defined in federal securities statutes but instead is considered a form of securities fraud in violation of §10(b) of the Securities Exchange Act of 1934.

(a) Do you think that insider trading should be illegal? Why or why not?

(b) Some people argue that insider trading is beneficial to the securities markets and to businesses. What are the benefits of insider trading to the markets and to businesses?

(c) Write a definition of insider trading. Suggest reasons why no statutory definition has been developed.

CHAPTER 50

INTRODUCTION TO ANTITRUST LAW

■ **an introduction to antitrust law, including its historical background, major statutory provisions, enforcement tools, and its scope and exemptions**

Antitrust law is concerned primarily with three federal statutes: the Sherman Antitrust Act, passed in 1890, and the Clayton Act and Federal Trade Commission Act, both enacted in 1914. These statutes, supplemented by state legislation, are designed to promote and preserve competition in a free and open market, and to prevent a firm or group of firms from acquiring or maintaining monopoly power—the power to establish prices above competitive equilibrium. The strong public policy favoring preservation of competition and prevention of monopoly is at the heart of our free enterprise system.

This and the following two chapters examine the antitrust laws, detailing the conduct they proscribe, the remedies they make available, and the analysis used by the courts in determining violations.

Historical Background

Early Business Regulation

The drafters of the Constitution incorporated several devices into our political system designed to prevent concentration of political power. A similar decentralization policy prevailed in the development of the American economic system. A major cause of the colonists' hostil-

ity toward England was dissatisfaction with the mercantilist system, which was characterized by government regulation of industry and commerce, and restrictions upon individual economic effort. Early Americans, self-sufficient and free of the rigid class system prevailing in Europe, readily embraced a policy of economic individualism with minimal government interference in economic affairs. Thus, free enterprise and *laissez-faire* capitalism, like political liberty, were cornerstones of the new American system.

By the mid-nineteenth century, the development of the telegraph and improvements in transportation, most notably the railroad, made large, centralized businesses feasible. A new form of business organization, the corporation, emerged to manage the vast amounts of capital and economic power aggregated by rapid industrialization. Increasing business concentration threatened the continued vitality of the free enterprise system by vesting excessive economic and political power in the hands of a few.

The trend toward economic concentration and its consequent abuses began with the railroads. To counter the effects of previous, often bitter, rate wars, individual railroads began to act in concert by forming "pools," first implemented in the early 1870s. The pools were used to divide traffic, earnings, and geographic markets, discriminate in price among various shippers and localities, and grant secret rebates to preferred shippers and buyers.

In response to the abusive railraod practices, inadequate state regulation, and widespread public concern,

Congress passed the Interstate Commerce Act in 1887. It proscribed the "pool" arrangement, assured just and reasonable rates, and prohibited rate discrimination. The Act also created the Interstate Commerce Commission (ICC) to enforce its provisions. Thus began what has become a recurring theme in government regulation of business: a pervasive federal regulatory statute coupled with enforcement by a strong federal administrative agency.

The Movement Toward "Antitrust"

The railroad "pools" were not the only combinations threatening the free enterprise system in the late nineteenth century. Depending upon voluntary adherence, the pool was a less than ideal method of expeditious, consistent, concerted action. To achieve a more effective business organization, attorneys for the Standard Oil Company devised an arrangement patterned after a shareholders' voting trust.[1] The trust agreement provided that the owners of stock in several companies would transfer their securities to a board of trustees who had full management control. In exchange, the stockholders received trust certificates that entitled them to a percentage of the earnings of the jointly controlled companies.

By 1887, the trust device had been used to monopolize entire industries, including fuel oil, cotton, linseed oil, sugar, lead, and whiskey. The trusts destroyed competition and their conduct in acquiring and maintaining power was frequently ruthless. For example, trusts often would enter a market selling at well below cost to drive competitors out of business or force them to sell (predatory pricing). Once competition was eliminated, the trust would raise the price far above that obtained under competitive conditions. Other unscrupulous trust practices included stock fraud and other financial scandals, political bribery, and labor oppression. By the presidential election of 1888, a strong bipartisan movement, including small business, labor, and agrarian interests, was calling for strong remedial "antitrust" legislation. The result was the **Sherman Antitrust Act,**[2] introduced by Senator John Sherman of Ohio and signed into law by President Benjamin Harrison on July 2, 1890. Although the holding company soon superseded the trust as the primary device for effecting business combination, the term **antitrust** has survived and today designates both the state and federal laws designed to promote competition and prevent monopoly.

---

[1] Shareholders' voting trusts are covered in Chapter 47.
[2] 15 U.S.C. §§1–7.

The Sherman Act

Backed by criminal, civil, and equitable sanctions, the Sherman Antitrust Act is the primary tool of antitrust enforcement in the United States. The Sherman Act contains only two substantive provisions. Section 1 provides that

> Every contract, combination in the form of trust or otherwise, or conspiracy, in restraint of trade or commerce among the several States, or with foreign nations, is declared to be illegal.

Section 2 states that

> Every person who shall monopolize, or attempt to monopolize, or combine or conspire with any other person or persons, to monopolize any part of the trade or commerce among the several States, or with foreign nations, shall be deemed guilty of a felony. . . .

The Act is not specific concerning the particular conduct it seeks to prevent and makes no effort even to define its fundamental concepts of "restraint of trade" or "monopolization." Rather, the Sherman Act serves as a broad and general "charter of freedom," allowing the federal courts (and most importantly, the Supreme Court) to develop a common law of antitrust to preserve and promote competition and prevent monopoly. This statutory charter is general enough to allow the court flexibility in determining whether, on the unique facts of a specific case, the policy objectives of antitrust are violated.

Sections 1 and 2 of the Sherman Act exhibit both fundamental differences and fundamental similarities. Section 1 is concerned with *contracts, combinations, and conspiracies* in restraint of trade. Thus, §1 violations require *two or more persons* banding together (for example, to fix prices or divide markets) to achieve the anticompetitive result. The existence of a combination is therefore always at the heart of any §1 violation. In contrast, although §2 speaks of conspiracies to monopolize (which also would be §1 violations), it is primarily concerned with single-firm conduct (such as predatory pricing) or a structural condition likely to create or maintain a monopoly in a particular market. Despite this difference, both sections may be viewed as complementary methods of achieving the same goal: to prevent monopoly. Both aim at acts or practices that tend to control markets or reduce competition.

Within 20 years after its enactment in 1890, the courts had interpreted the Sherman Act to prohibit price-fixing by combining railroads, a massive merger of two western railroads, and to declare the trusts controlling the meat, tobacco, and oil industries to be illegal monopolies. Despite these successes and the widespread public support for antitrust, early enforcement of the Sherman Act was characterized by judicial hostility and government indifference. Critics assailed both the judicial interpretation of the Act and the law itself, which appeared to reach only anticompetitive conduct in fruition, not trade restraints in their incipiency or simply unfair trade practices or methods of competition. Critics also believed new enforcement techniques were required, given the somewhat inconsistent performance by the Department of Justice.

By the presidential election of 1912, bipartisan support again existed for antitrust reform. Upon his election in 1912, Woodrow Wilson promptly urged the passage of new legislation both to strengthen the antitrust laws and to create a federal administrative agency entrusted with enforcement responsibilities. Consequently, Congress, in 1914, passed the Clayton Act and the Federal Trade Commission Act. Since 1914 there have been no further major antitrust enactments.

The Clayton Act

The **Clayton Act**[3] was designed to strengthen the Sherman Act by bringing certain specific monopolistic or restrictive practices within the reach of the antitrust laws. It contains four substantive provisions discussed more fully in later material:

1. Section 2, as amended in 1936 by the Robinson-Patman Act, prohibits certain types of price discrimination.
2. Section 3 prohibits certain sales made on condition that the buyer not deal with the seller's competitors.
3. Section 7 prohibits certain corporate mergers.
4. Section 8 prohibits a person from serving on the board of directors of two competing companies (an "interlocking directorate") in certain circumstances.

Unlike the Sherman Act, which generally requires proof of actual and substantial anticompetitive effect, the Clayton Act is designed to reach anticompetitive acts or practices in their *incipiency*. Thus, the Clayton Act §§2, 3,

and 7[4] all are appended by language that finds a violation if the effect of the price discrimination, exclusive contract, or merger "*may* be to substantially lessen competition or *tend* to create a monopoly in any line of commerce."[5]

Thus, a showing of probable, rather than actual, adverse competitive effect is sufficient to establish a Clayton Act violation. In other words, the Clayton Act is, at least in theory, more sensitive to anticompetitive conduct than the Sherman Act.

The Federal Trade Commission Act

Due to public dissatisfaction with both the adequacy of antitrust law and the zeal of the Justice Department, Congress determined that a strong federal administrative agency was needed to aid in antitrust enforcement, monitor business conduct, and advise business, the courts, and Congress on antitrust matters. Consequently, in 1914, Congress enacted the **Federal Trade Commission Act,**[6] which created the **Federal Trade Commission (FTC).** The commission is composed of five commissioners, appointed by the president to seven-year terms, and approved by the Senate. No more than three of the commissioners may be members of the same political party. The FTC is empowered to enforce both the Clayton and Federal Trade Commission Acts, but not the Sherman Act. The FTC Act's sole substantive provision is §5, which authorizes the FTC to issue "cease and desist" orders prohibiting "unfair methods of competition" and "unfair or deceptive acts or practices." Note that §5 not only is a tool of antitrust enforcement, but also is the basis of the FTC's consumer protection activities.

The legal principles governing violations of the Sherman, Clayton, and FTC Acts are covered in the next two chapters. The following material provides an overview of the legal remedies available for antitrust violations, and the persons and conduct covered.

Enforcing the Antitrust Laws

The remedies available for antitrust violations include (1) criminal sanctions, (2) equitable proceedings by either government or private plaintiffs, (3) private actions for money damages, and (4) forfeiture.

---

[3]15 U.S.C. §§12–27.

[4]Section 8 imposes a fixed dollar limitation for violation.
[5]Language of §3 Clayton Act (emphasis added).
[6]15 U.S.C. §§41–58.

Criminal Sanctions

Violations of both §§1 and 2 of the Sherman Act are felonies. For individuals, violations are punishable by imprisonment of up to ten years and fines up to the largest of the following three alternatives: (1) $1 million, (2) twice the monetary gain the individual derived from the offense, or (3) twice the monetary loss suffered by victims of the offense. Corporate violators may be punished by fines of up to the largest of the following three alternatives: (1) $100 million, (2) twice the monetary gain the corporation derived from the offense, or (3) twice the monetary loss suffered by victims of the offense.[7]

The Antitrust Division of the Department of Justice or a local United States attorney under the direction of the attorney general can initiate criminal prosecution. Like other federal felonies, prosecution commences after indictment returned by a grand jury. Criminal prosecution under the Sherman Act generally has been used only when the challenged conduct is particularly aggravated and of unquestioned illegality. With one rarely invoked exception, no criminal sanctions are imposed for violations of the Clayton Act or the FTC Act.[8]

Equitable Remedies

Civil equitable actions maintained either by the government or private plaintiffs are far more common than criminal proceedings as a method of antitrust enforcement. Both the Sherman Act and the Clayton Act[9] confer jurisdiction upon the federal courts to "prevent and restrain" violations and impose a duty upon the attorney general to institute proceedings in equity for that purpose. Similarly, §16 of the Clayton Act authorizes private plaintiffs to maintain actions to enjoin actual or threatened injury resulting from violation of either the Sherman Act or the Clayton Act.

The relief afforded in a civil equitable action is remedial rather than punitive. As in all cases of equity, the court has broad discretion in fashioning an appropriate remedy. As a result, antitrust decrees have, for example, (1) restrained certain acts or conduct, (2) ordered divestiture of subsidiary companies, (3) created new companies, (4) ordered patents, trade secrets, or technology made available to competitors, and (5) canceled or modified contracts. After entry of the judgment, the court often retains jurisdiction in order to modify or supervise performance of the decree.

Consent Decrees. When the government commences a civil antitrust action, both parties often have a strong incentive to settle rather than litigate the dispute. Suits often take years to resolve and legal fees commonly are measured in the millions of dollars. The business disruption and adverse publicity resulting from major antitrust litigation are detrimental to a company. An adjudication of liability in a government antitrust suit also opens the door for subsequent private suits for damages. From the Justice Department's point of view, settlement frees limited resources to pursue other cases.

For these reasons, most civil suits instituted by the government are settled through **consent decrees.** Under this procedure, a compromise agreement between the government and the defendant is filed with the federal court, and, if the court approves of the settlement, it is incorporated into a judicial order known as a consent decree. Once entered, the consent decree has the same effect as any other judicial order and may be subsequently modified only upon court approval. Even though the defendant is bound by its terms once entered, the consent decree generally is neither an adjudication nor admission of liability for antitrust violations. Accordingly, private plaintiffs may not use it to establish the defendant's liability in subsequent civil suits for damages.

Section 5 of the Clayton Act imposes detailed requirements designed to provide public information and solicit public comment concerning proposed consent decrees. For example, the proposed decree and a "competitive impact statement" must be published at least 60 days before the decree's effective date. Further, written public comments must be solicited and considered.

Although a proposed decree may be approved by the court without change, the judge is not bound by the settlement reached by the parties. Rather, the court, before entering the consent decree "shall determine that the entry of such judgment is in the public interest." In making this determination, the court may consider the impact of the judgment upon competition, the public generally, and individuals alleging specific injury from the challenged conduct. Under §5, therefore, the judge takes an active role in framing the decree.

Cease and Desist Orders. The FTC possesses significant antitrust enforcement powers because it is able to

---

[7]15 U.S.C. §§1, 2; 18 U.S.C. §3571(d).

[8]Violations of §3 of the Robinson-Patman Act (15 U.S.C. §13a) are punishable by imprisonment of up to one year and a $5,000 fine or both.

[9]Sherman Act §4 (15 U.S.C. §4); Clayton Act §15 (15 U.S.C. §25).

issue **cease and desist orders.** These orders provide injunctive relief by preventing or restraining unlawful conduct. A cease and desist order is thus prospective in effect, imposing neither criminal nor other civil penalties for past conduct. Like Justice Department civil proceedings, most FTC investigations are settled by a consent order procedure. If negotiations are unsuccessful, the FTC initiates the formal adjudication process by filing a complaint outlining the alleged antitrust violation.[10] After an opportunity for preparation, a hearing is held before an administrative law judge appointed by the FTC. The findings and orders of the judge may then be appealed to the full Commission, allowed as a matter of right. The Commission's decision (for example, to issue a cease and desist order) may then be appealed to the court of appeals. Note that reviewing courts seldom overturn FTC decisions, commonly deferring to the Commission's expertise and findings of fact. Although no criminal sanctions or private damage remedies are imposed for FTC Act violations, violation of a final cease and desist order carries an $10,000 per day civil penalty. In addition, the federal district courts are empowered to grant mandatory injunctions and other appropriate equitable relief to enforce final FTC orders.[11]

Private Action for Damages

"Treble" Damages. Because of the limited resources of the Justice Department and FTC, public antitrust enforcement is necessarily selective, focusing on major industries or flagrant violations. Private enforcement, by individuals or businesses injured by antitrust violations, is therefore necessary to supplement government efforts. To this end, the Clayton Act includes private remedies, legal and equitable in nature, for violations of both the Sherman and Clayton Acts. Equitable relief, under §16 of the Clayton Act, was discussed above. Legal relief, a private action for money damages, is authorized by §4 of the Clayton Act, which provides:

[A]ny person who shall be injured in his business or property by reason of anything forbidden in the antitrust laws[12] may sue therefor [in a federal district court of competent

jurisdiction], and shall recover threefold the damages by him sustained, and the cost of suit, including a reasonable attorney's fee.[13]

A private plaintiff proceeding under this provision recovers *three* times its actual damages. That is, damages sustained are tripled or "trebled" in computing the ultimate recovery. The prospect of a treble damage award provides a strong incentive for private antitrust enforcement, increasing the likelihood that antitrust violations will be discovered. This increased risk, coupled with the severe treble damage penalty, helps deter illegal conduct. Suits under §4 must be commenced within four years after the cause of action accrues. Note finally that §4A of the Clayton Act[14] provides a similar treble damage action for the government when it is injured by conduct that violates the antitrust laws.

Class of Permissible Plaintiffs—Standing to Sue. Though Clayton Act §4 literally allows *any* person to recover damages for injury caused by antitrust violations, it requires that a prospective plaintiff be injured "in his *business or property*." Read restrictively, this language applies only to injury to commercial (business) interests or enterprises. Courts have not, however, strictly adhered to this definition, and have allowed recovery by nonprofit or professional groups and ultimate consumers. For example, in *Reiter v. Sonotone Corporation* (1979),[15] the Supreme Court held that consumers who because of antitrust violations, pay a higher price for goods purchased for personal use, sustain an injury to their "property" within the meaning of §4.

Consumer recovery is limited, however, by the judicially imposed requirement that purchasers entitled to sue under §4 must be "direct" or immediate.[16] For example, C, a consumer who purchases directly from M, a manufacturer involved in a price-fixing conspiracy, is allowed to recover. If the manufacturer first sells to W, an innocent wholesaler, from whom the consumer purchases, W is a "direct" purchaser entitled to recover treble damages, whereas C is said to be an "indirect" purchaser,

---

[10]That is, of §§2, 3, 7, or 8 of the Clayton Act, or §5 of the FTC Act.
[11]Federal Trade Commission Act §5(1) (15 U.S.C. §45(1)).
[12]Under §1(a) of the Clayton Act (15 U.S.C. §12(a)), the term "antitrust laws" includes the Sherman Act, the Clayton Act, and the Wilson Tariff Act (15 U.S.C. §§8–11).

[13]Note that §16 (15 U.S.C. §26) differs from §4 (15 U.S.C. §15) in that §16 requires merely threatened rather than actual injury, and injunctive relief is not necessarily limited to injuries to business or property interests.
[14]15 U.S.C. §15a.
[15]99 S. Ct. 2326 (1979).
[16]Hanover Shoe, Inc. v. United Shoe Machinery Corp., 88 S. Ct. 2224 (1968); Illinois Brick Co. v. Illinois, 97 S. Ct. 2061 (1977).

prevented from recovery. Although treble damage recovery is limited to direct purchasers under federal law, many *state* antitrust statutes permit indirect purchaser recovery. Further, even under federal law, indirect purchasers are not prevented from seeking equitable relief under §16.

Relationship to Government Suits. Under Clayton Act §5(a), a final judgment or decree rendered in any civil or criminal proceeding brought by the United States finding that the defendant has violated the antitrust laws is prima facie evidence against that defendant in an action maintained by any other party concerning matters determined in the government suit. This provision greatly benefits subsequent private plaintiffs seeking treble damages. In a private action under §4, the plaintiff must ordinarily prove both the existence of an antitrust violation, and damages resulting from that violation. If the *existence* of the violation is already established in the prior government suit (by a plea of guilty or a conviction after trial in a criminal case or a finding of liability in a civil case), the private plaintiff may recover merely by proving damages.

Because private plaintiffs may number in the thousands and damages are trebled, an adverse determination in a government suit may have disastrous financial consequences. As a result, antitrust defendants often have a strong incentive to settle the government's suit in a manner that is not conclusive in subsequent cases. If the government action is civil, a consent decree frequently is sought because it is ordinarily neither an adjudication on the merits nor an admission of liability by the defendant. In a criminal case, the court may allow the defendant to plead "nolo contendere" or "no contest" to the charge. Through such a plea the defendant accepts the punishment for the crime charged but does not admit guilt. Because, under §5(a), neither a consent decree nor a "nolo" plea involves a finding of antitrust violation, subsequent private plaintiffs must prove both the existence of the violation and damages in order to recover.

Forfeiture

Section 6 of the Sherman Act contains the seldom used forfeiture remedy. It provides for the forfeiture to the United States of any property being transported interstate (or to a foreign country) if the property is owned under, and the subject of, a contract, combination, or conspiracy in restraint of trade violating §1 of the Sherman Act. The property may be seized in proceedings similar to those used for property illegally imported into the country.

The Reach of the Antitrust Laws— Scope and Exemptions

Although the policy underlying the antitrust laws is the preservation of competition and prevention of monopoly, the antitrust laws do not enjoy universal application. For example, wholly intrastate activity is outside the reach of federal antitrust law, and certain anticompetitive conduct enjoys limited antitrust immunity. The remainder of this chapter examines the various limitations on antitrust application.

The Interstate Commerce Requirement

The Sherman Act prohibits both restraints (§1) and monopolization (§2) of "trade or commerce among the several States." This interstate commerce requirement is imposed because the antitrust laws, like other federal regulatory statutes, were enacted pursuant to the Commerce Clause, giving Congress the power "to regulate Commerce . . . among the several States."[17]

Congressional authority to regulate under the Commerce Clause has long been interpreted to extend beyond activities actually in interstate commerce to reach other activities, even wholly local in character, that nevertheless substantially *affect* interstate commerce.[18] The Supreme Court has adopted a correspondingly broad interpretation in applying the Sherman Act, as *McLain v. Real Estate Board of New Orleans, Inc.,* excerpted in Chapter 4, indicates.

In contrast to the Sherman Act, the Clayton Act generally imposes a stricter jurisdictional requirement under the Commerce Clause. Although §7 reaches mergers of firms engaged "in any activity affecting commerce," §2 (as amended by the Robinson-Patman Act) and §3 (exclusive dealings) both apply only to persons engaged in "commerce" and conduct occurring "in the course of such commerce." Section 8 (interlocking

---

[17]U.S. CONST. art. I, §8, cl. 3. The Commerce Clause is discussed in Chapter 4.

[18]Wickard v. Filburn, 63 S. Ct. 82 (1942).

directorates) applies to corporations "engaged in whole or in part in commerce."

The Federal Trade Commission Act (§5) allows the FTC to enjoin unfair methods of competition and unfair or deceptive trade practices "in or affecting commerce." No satisfactory explanation exists for the differing jurisdictional reach of the various antitrust provisions.

State law may govern conduct arguably beyond the reach of federal antitrust law. For example, virtually all states have antitrust statutes similar to federal law, applicable to intrastate activity. State tort law also often provides a private remedy for certain unfair competitive acts or practices.

Exemptions

Certain types of conduct receive a limited exemption from the antitrust laws. For example, labor unions, agricultural cooperatives, and export associations, which are in effect combinations in restraint of trade, are exempt. Certain industries that are regulated by state or federal administrative agencies are exempt. Further, action taken by state governments or governmental entities and private conduct intended to influence government action may be beyond the reach of antitrust law. The scope of and rationale for these exemptions vary widely. Some are expressly stated in the antitrust laws, some are express or implied in other statutes, and some are judicially created through statutory interpretation.[19]

Labor Unions and Agricultural Cooperatives. Labor unions are essentially labor monopolies that collectively determine wages and other conditions of employment. Without antitrust exemption, therefore, labor unions could be attacked as illegal combinations in restraint of trade. In response to several early Sherman Act cases questioning the legality of unions, Congress enacted §6 of the Clayton Act in 1914, which provides that the antitrust laws shall not be construed to (1) forbid the existence and operation of labor organizations, (2) forbid or restrain individual members of such organizations from lawfully carrying out their legitimate ends, or (3) find a labor organization, or its members, to be an illegal combination or conspiracy in restraint of trade.

Clayton Act §20[20] restricts the power of federal courts to grant injunctions in labor disputes, and exempts from antitrust scrutiny employee conduct, such as strikes and boycotts, arising during the course of disputes concerning terms and conditions of employment. The Norris-LaGuardia Act of 1932[21] also generally prohibits injunctions in labor disputes. Collectively, these statutes and subsequent cases exempt most union activity and collective bargaining agreements from the antitrust laws.

The scope of the labor antitrust exemption is, however, limited. Conduct that would violate the Sherman Act in the absence of union involvement is not immunized by the participation of the union. For example, a union may not band together with a nonlabor party, such as a contractor or manufacturer, to achieve a result forbidden by the antitrust laws.

Agricultural cooperatives and fishermen's organizations also enjoy a limited antitrust exemption.[22] In these cases, persons who would otherwise be in competition (farmers, fishermen) are allowed to form associations to collectively prepare and market their products, including fixing prices at which the association will sell. As with labor unions, however, the exemption extends to the existence and operation of such organizations, not to combinations or conspiracies in restraint of trade with persons not so exempted.

Export Trade Associations; Joint Ventures. Congress has long sought to encourage U.S. businesses to become aggressive exporters of goods and services. A joint venture among two or more companies involving a pooling of capital, labor, technology, and other resources has become an increasingly popular device to enter international markets, in part because it often spreads the increased financial and political risk inherent in international transactions. In 1918, Congress sought to facilitate joint export activities by enacting the **Webb-Pomerene Act,**[23] which provided limited antitrust immunity to exporters of goods who registered as Webb-Pomerene Associations with the Federal Trade Commission. Few associations, however, remain registered under the act, because it is not available to exporters of services,

---

[19]Patent law (discussed in Chapter 59) also effectively provides a limited exemption from antitrust in order to promote innovation and invention. That is, an inventor is granted a limited monopoly—the exclusive right to make, use, or sell his invention for a specified period.

[20]29 U.S.C. §52.

[21]29 U.S.C. §§101–115.

[22]The agricultural exemption is contained in §6 of the Clayton Act and the Capper-Volstead Act of 1922 (7 U.S.C. §§291–292). The fisherman's exemption is stated in the Fisherman's Cooperative Marketing Act (15 U.S.C. §§521–522). Export trade associations, discussed in the next section, may enjoy a similar exemption.

[23]15 U.S.C. §§61–66.

currently a strong U.S. export sector, and because many firms believe that it provides insufficient antitrust immunity.

To remedy these deficiencies, Congress enacted the **Export Trading Company Act of 1982.**[24] This statute authorizes the creation of the Office of Export Trading Company Affairs within the U.S. Department of Commerce to promote and encourage the formation of export trade associations and export trading companies, and to issue antitrust Certificates of Review to those export ventures that apply and qualify. Under the certification procedure, the applicant discloses a variety of information, including the types of goods and services it intends to export, and the scope of its activities and methods of operation. Each application is analyzed by both the Justice and Commerce Departments and a Certificate of Review is issued if the applicant has established that its activities will

1. result in neither a substantial lessening of competition or restraint of trade within the United States nor a substantial restraint of the export trade of any competitor of the applicant,
2. not unreasonably enhance, stabilize, or depress prices within the United States of the goods, wares, merchandise, or services of the class exported by the applicant,
3. not constitute unfair methods of competition against competitors engaged in the export of goods, wares, merchandise, or services of the class exported by the applicant, and
4. not include any act that may reasonably be expected to result in the sale for consumption or resale within the United States of the goods, wares, merchandise, or services exported by the applicant.[25]

If the certificate is issued, the applicant and its members are immune from most state and federal criminal and civil antitrust actions, including private actions for treble damages. Immunity extends, however, only to conduct specified in and complying with the certificate.

Congress also has sought to enhance international competitiveness by enacting the **National Cooperative Research Act of 1984 (NCRA),**[26] which is designed to promote creation of research and development joint ventures. The Act provides that the legality of joint research activities under antitrust law is to be judged by a "rule of reason," rather than the more stringent *per se* standard. The Act also reduces the antitrust exposure of research and development joint ventures that notify the Federal Trade Commission and Justice Department of their activities. After notification, private plaintiffs suing the venture participants are limited to recovering actual, rather than the usual treble, damages for claims resulting from conduct within the scope of the notification. In 1993, Congress amended the NCRA, renaming it the **National Cooperative Research and Production Act of 1993.** This amendment extends the protections of the NCRA to joint production ventures—collaborations of firms to produce or manufacture products, processes, or services. The Act was further amended in 2004 to extend its protections to the activities of "standards development organizations," domestic or international organizations that develop and establish industry standards based upon voluntary consensus among industry members involved.

Antitrust Immunity of State Governmental Entities: The "State Action" Exemption. The Sherman Act does not apply to actions of the federal government. It also is generally inapplicable to actions of state legislatures and state administrative agencies. The landmark case establishing this so-called state action exemption is *Parker v. Brown* (1943).[27] In this case, the Court stated that neither the language nor the legislative history of the Sherman Act suggests that it was intended to restrain state action or official action directed by a state. Rather, the Act must be taken as a prohibition solely on individual or corporate action. Although *Parker* involved the acts of a state official, the Court subsequently has recognized that certain anticompetitive acts of private parties enjoy state action immunity if those acts are, in fact, the product of state regulation. The following case explains the rationale for the *Parker* doctrine, and outlines the two-part standard governing the state action immunity of private parties.

California Retail Liquor Dealers Association v. Midcal Aluminum, Inc.
100 S. Ct. 937 (1980)

A California statute required wine producers and wholesalers to file fair trade contracts or price schedules with the state. The fair trade contracts established the sales price at

---

[24]15 U.S.C. §4001 *et seq.*
[25]15 U.S.C. §4013(a).
[26]15 U.S.C. §4301 *et seq.*

[27]63 S. Ct. 307 (1943).

which wines were to be sold to retailers and consumers. If a producer did not use a fair trade contract, the wholesaler was required to file and post a schedule of the sales prices for the wines. The law prohibited state licensed wine merchants from selling wines except at the price set in a fair trade contract or price schedule.

The California Department of Alcoholic Beverage Control charged that Midcal Aluminum, Inc., a wholesale wine distributor, sold Gallo wine for prices less than those established by E. & J. Gallo Winery's price schedule. Midcal admitted the charges but requested the California court of appeal to enjoin the state's wine pricing system alleging that it violated the federal Sherman Act. The court of appeal granted the injunction. The California Retail Liquor Dealers Association sought review by the U.S. Supreme Court, which granted a writ of certiorari.

Justice Powell

. . . The threshold question is whether California's plan for wine pricing violates the Sherman Act. . . .

California's system for wine pricing plainly constitutes resale price maintenance in violation of the Sherman Act. . . . The wine producer holds the power to prevent price competition by dictating the prices charged by wholesalers. . . .

Thus, we must consider whether the State's involvement in the price-setting program is sufficient to establish antitrust immunity under *Parker v. Brown* [63 S. Ct. 307 (1943)]. That immunity for state regulatory programs is grounded in our federal structure. "In a dual system of government in which, under the Constitution, the states are sovereign, save only as Congress may constitutionally subtract from their authority, an unexpressed purpose to nullify a state's control over its officers and agents is not lightly to be attributed to Congress." [*Id.,* at 313.] In *Parker v. Brown,* this Court found in the Sherman Act no purpose to nullify state powers. Because the Act is directed against "individual and not state action," the Court concluded that state regulatory programs could not violate it. [*Id.,* at 314.]

Under the program challenged in *Parker,* the State Agricultural Prorate Advisory Commission authorized the organization of local cooperatives to develop marketing policies for the raisin crop. The Court emphasized that the Advisory Commission, which was appointed by the Governor, had to approve cooperative policies following public hearings: "It is the state which has created the machinery for establishing the prorate program. . . . [I]t is the state, acting through the Commission, which adopts the program and enforces

it. . . ." *Ibid.* In view of this extensive official oversight, the Court wrote, the Sherman Act did not apply. Without such oversight, the result could have been different. The Court expressly noted that "a state does not give immunity to those who violate the Sherman Act by authorizing them to violate it, or by declaring that their action is lawful. . . ." [*Id.,* at 314.]

Several recent decisions have applied *Parker's* analysis. In *Goldfarb v. Virginia State Bar* [95 S. Ct. 2004 (1975)], the Court concluded that [attorneys'] fee schedules enforced by a state bar association were not mandated by ethical standards established by the State Supreme Court. The fee schedules therefore were not immune from antitrust attack. "It is not enough that . . . anticompetitive conduct is 'prompted' by state action; rather, anticompetitive activities must be compelled by direction of the State acting as a sovereign." [*Id.,* at 2015.] Similarly, in *Cantor v. Detroit Edison Co.* [96 S. Ct. 3110 (1976)], a majority of the Court found that no antitrust immunity was conferred when a state agency passively accepted a public utility's tariff. In contrast, Arizona rules against lawyer advertising were held immune from Sherman Act challenge because they "reflect[ed] a clear articulation of the State's policy with regard to professional behavior" and were "subject to pointed reexamination by the policymaker—the Arizona Supreme Court—in enforcement proceedings." *Bates v. State Bar of Arizona* [97 S. Ct. 2691, 2698 (1977)].

Only last Term, this Court found antitrust immunity for a California program requiring state approval of the location of new automobile dealerships. *New Motor Vehicle Bd. of Cal. v. Orrin W. Fox Co.* [99 S. Ct. 403 (1978)]. That program provided that the State would hold a hearing if an automobile franchisee protested the establishment or relocation of a competing dealership. [*Id.,* at 408.] In view of the State's active role, the Court held, the program was not subject to the Sherman Act. The "clearly articulated and affirmatively expressed" goal of the state policy was to "displace unfettered business freedom in the matter of the establishment and relocation of automobile dealerships." [*Id.,* at 412.]

These decisions establish two standards for antitrust immunity under *Parker v. Brown.* First, the challenged restraint must be "one clearly articulated and affirmatively expressed as state policy"; second, the policy must be "actively supervised" by the State itself. *City of Lafayette v. Louisiana Power & Light Co.* [98 S. Ct. 1123, 1135 (1978)] (opinion of Brennan, J.). The California system for wine pricing satisfies the first standard. The legislative policy is forthrightly stated and clear in its purpose to permit resale price maintenance. The program, however, does not meet the second requirement for *Parker* immunity. The State simply authorizes price setting and enforces the prices established by private parties. The State neither establishes prices nor reviews the reasonableness of the price schedules; nor does it regulate the terms of fair trade contracts. The State does not monitor market conditions or engage in any "pointed reexamination" of the program. The national policy in favor of competition cannot be thwarted by casting such a gauzy cloak of state involvement over what is essentially a private price-fixing arrangement.

[Judgment affirmed.]

Attempts to Influence Government Action: The Noerr-Pennington Doctrine. A problem related to state action immunity concerns the antitrust implications of private efforts to influence government action. Simply stated, may a competitor or group of competitors petition the government or a government agency to take an action that would injure the petitioners' competitors? The landmark case addressing this issue is *Eastern Railroads Presidents Conference v. Noerr Motor Freight, Inc.*[28] In this case, the Supreme Court reasoned that the whole concept of representative government depends upon the ability of people to make their wishes, however selfish, known to their representatives and that the Sherman Act was designed to reach business, not political, conduct. The Court also stated that the right to petition the government is a freedom protected by the Bill of Rights. The Court therefore held that no violation of the Sherman Act can be based upon mere attempts to influence the passage or enforcement of laws. The Court further held that the Act does not prohibit two or more persons from associating together (that is, a combination) in an effort to persuade the legislature or executive to take particular action concerning a law that would produce a trade restraint or a monopoly.

In a later case, *United Mine Workers of America v. Pennington,*[29] the Supreme Court made it clear that

Noerr shields from the Sherman Act a concerted effort to influence public officials regardless of intent [or] pur-

pose. . . . Joint efforts to influence public officials do not violate the antitrust laws even though intended to eliminate competition. Such conduct is not illegal, either standing alone or as part of a broader scheme itself violative of the Sherman Act.[30]

Despite the apparent broad antitrust exemption for lobbying activities embodied in this *Noerr-Pennington* doctrine, *Noerr* itself stated that there may be instances in which the alleged conspiracy

. . . ostensibly directed toward influencing governmental action, is a mere sham to cover what is actually nothing more than an attempt to interfere directly with the business relationships of a competitor. . . .[31]

In such a case, the Court indicated that Sherman Act liability would indeed be appropriate.

Both *Noerr* and *Pennington* involved allegedly illegal attempts to influence legislative and executive action. The Supreme Court has held that the *Noerr-Pennington* doctrine and its "sham" exception quoted above also apply to attempts to influence adjudicative bodies, such as administrative agencies and courts.[32] The sham exception may be applied in this context, for example, if the defendant files a series of objectively baseless, repetitive lawsuits designed not to obtain a judicial remedy but rather to prevent a competitor from entering the market or obtaining necessary administrative permits or approvals.

Economics and Antitrust

The policy underpinnings of antitrust, preserving competition and preventing monopoly, are rooted in history, experience, and economic theory. Any basic economics text will ably illustrate the evils of monopoly. These include, for example, restricted output at higher prices resulting in inefficient resource allocation, lack of incentive to improve or innovate, and concentration of economic power with attendant undue political influence. Conversely, competition is said to result in efficient pricing and resource allocation, provide an incentive for innovation and efficiency, give purchasers a wider range of choice, improve quality, and result in

---

[28]81 S. Ct. 523 (1961).
[29]85 S. Ct. 1585 (1965).

[30]*Id.* at 1593.
[31]81 S. Ct. at 533.
[32]California Motor Transport Co. v. Trucking Unlimited, 92 S. Ct. 609 (1972).

diversification of economic power more consistent with a democratic society.

In recent years, economic analysis has assumed an increasingly larger role both in the development of substantive antitrust rules and in the resolution of individual cases. For example, many antitrust scholars argue that economic efficiency should be the exclusive goal of the antitrust laws. This approach has greatly influenced the development of many antitrust principles, such as the law governing vertical restraints of trade discussed in the next chapter. In addition, many antitrust cases, particularly those involving mergers or monopolization, require a determination of relevant market, market structure, and the effect of certain conduct on competition. In making these determinations, courts usually are guided, in part, by the testimony of witnesses expert in economics.

The importance of economics in antitrust should not, however, be overestimated. Economics is a theoretical social science. Conflicting theories and approaches abound. Antitrust is law. Like all areas of law, antitrust must be used to resolve specific, concrete disputes, requiring application of relevant legal rules to the facts of a particular case. The rules governing antitrust cases come not from economic theory, but from relevant statutes (the Sherman, Clayton, and Federal Trade

Commission Acts) and federal (most notably Supreme Court) cases interpreting them. In short, whereas economic theory currently plays an increasingly important role in the *development* of antitrust rules, it is no substitute for a detailed study of relevant precedent. As Supreme Court Justice Stephen Breyer once succinctly stated, "Economics informs the law. . . . It is not the case that economics is the law."[33]

In addition, many antitrust theorists believe that efficient resource allocation and prevention of enhanced prices are not the sole objects of antitrust policy. Antitrust law is grounded in a populist tradition. As noted by one commentator, the law recognizes various additional policy objectives of antitrust including for example, a preference for (1) decentralization of economic power, (2) reduction of the range within which private choice may be exercised in matters materially affecting others, (3) enhancement of opportunity for independent entrepreneurship, and (4) small over large.[34] These factors are recurrent themes in antitrust legislation and judicial decisions. Antitrust policy also is affected by the prevailing political and social climate.

In sum, although economics provides a useful tool in formulating antitrust policy, it is for the courts and legislatures to balance economic and other goals of antitrust, and to develop a comprehensive body of law.

Summary

1. Antitrust law is designed to promote and preserve competition in a free and open market, and to prevent the acquisition or maintenance of monopoly power. The law is based primarily upon three federal statutes: the Sherman Act, passed in 1890, and the Clayton Act and Federal Trade Commission Act, both enacted in 1914.

2. The Sherman Act contains only two substantive provisions. Section 1 declares contracts, combinations, and conspiracies in restraint of trade to be illegal. Section 2 proscribes monopolization, and attempts and conspiracies to monopolize.

3. The Clayton Act was designed to strengthen the basic Sherman Act prohibitions by bringing certain specific monopolistic or restrictive practices within the reach of the antitrust laws. It contains four basic substantive provisions: (1) §2, as amended in 1936 by the Robinson-Patman Act, prohibits certain types of price discrimination; (2) §3 prohibits certain sales made on condition that the buyer not deal with the seller's competitors; (3) §7 prohibits certain corporate mergers; (4) §8 prohibits a person from serving on the board of

directors of two competing companies (an "interlocking directorate") in certain circumstances.

4. The Federal Trade Commission Act created the Federal Trade Commission and prohibits unfair methods of competition and unfair or deceptive trade practices.

5. Four remedies are available for antitrust violations: (1) criminal sanctions, (2) equitable proceedings by both government and private plaintiffs, (3) private actions for money damages, and (4) forfeiture.

6. The antitrust laws do not enjoy universal application. Wholly intrastate activity is outside the reach of federal antitrust law. In addition, certain combinations in restraint of trade, such as labor unions, agricultural cooperatives, export

---

[33]Quoted in T. Lewin, *Antitrust Ideas: Three Problems,* N.Y. Times (March 8, 1983) at D2.

[34]Sullivan, Handbook of the Law of Antitrust 11 (1977).

associations, and research development, and production joint ventures, enjoy limited antitrust immunity. Finally, action taken by state governments or governmental entities and private conduct intended to influence government action may be beyond the reach of antitrust law.

Key Terms

Sherman Antitrust Act	Webb-Pomerene Act
antitrust	Export Trading Company
Clayton Act	Act of 1982
Federal Trade	National Cooperative
Commission Act	Research Act of 1984
Federal Trade Commission	(NCRA)
(FTC)	National Cooperative
consent decrees	Research and Production
cease and desist order	Act of 1993

Questions and Problems

50.1 Under the common law of contracts, discussed in Part II of the text, a promise is in restraint of trade if its performance would (1) limit competition in any business, or (2) restrict the promisor in the exercise of any gainful occupation. A promise in restraint of trade is generally unenforceable as contrary to public policy unless it is both (1) reasonable and (2) ancillary to an otherwise valid transaction or relationship. The railroad pools and trusts discussed above were certainly effective restraints of trade of the first type, limiting or eliminating competition in the industry involved. They were also patently unreasonable "naked" restraints with no purpose other than the suppression of competition. Why then was the common law of restraint of trade an ineffective method of antitrust enforcement necessitating enactment of major federal remedial legislation?

50.2 In what respect is antitrust law similar to constitutional law?

50.3 What are the advantages and disadvantages of awarding treble damages to private plaintiffs injured through violation of the antitrust laws?

50.4 Union electrical workers in New York City exacted an agreement from local contractors to purchase electrical equipment only from local manufacturers who had closed-shop agreements with the union. The union also agreed with several local manufacturers to confine local sales to contractors employing union members. The combination between the union, contractors, and manufacturers was successful for all concerned. Electrical equipment manufactured outside New York was effectively excluded from the market. Prices of New York electrical equipment soared, to the great profit of local manufacturers and contractors. Wages went up, hours were shortened, and union employment multiplied. Is the union in this case immune from antitrust liability under the labor exemption?

50.5 Hahn and Codding develop and operate shopping centers. Both Hahn and Codding submitted offers to develop a proposed shopping center in downtown Santa Rosa, California. In 2002, the Urban Renewal Agency (Agency) selected Hahn as the exclusive developer of the center. To finance purchase of the land for the project, the Agency decided to issue municipal bonds. Beginning in 2003, Codding filed a series of nine lawsuits challenging various aspects of the shopping center development and Codding financed four lawsuits filed by other parties. Although each of the lawsuits was dismissed, the development of the shopping center was delayed because the bonds could not be issued until all litigation had been resolved.

Hahn sued Codding alleging that he had violated §1 of the Sherman Act. Hahn asserted that by filing "a series of overlapping, repetitive and baseless lawsuits," Codding had conspired to eliminate potential competition from the new shopping center. The trial court held that Codding's involvement in the lawsuits was protected conduct under the *Noerr-Pennington* doctrine. Is the court correct? Explain.

50.6 The National Fire Protection Association (Association)—a private organization with more than 31,500 members representing industry, labor, academia, insurers, organized medicine, firefighters, and government—publishes product standards and codes relating to fire protection. In its National Electric Code (Code), the Association establishes product and performance requirements for the design and installation of electric wiring systems. A substantial number of states and local governments routinely adopt the Code into law and many private certification laboratories, insurance underwriters, electrical inspectors, and contractors accept and adopt the standards listed in the Code. For many years, the Code had approved the use of steel electrical conduit (the tubing used to carry electrical wires through the walls and floors of buildings) and steel was the primary material used for conduit. After Indian Head, Inc., began manufacturing plastic conduit made of polyvinyl chloride, the Association placed on the agenda of its annual meeting a proposal to include plastic conduit as an approved material in the Code. Allied Tube & Conduit Corporation, the nation's largest producer of steel conduit, met with its independent sales agents, other steel conduit manufacturers, and members of the steel industry to plan strategy to prevent the Association's approval of plastic conduit. They agreed to pack the annual meeting with new members whose sole function was to vote against the polyvinyl chloride proposal. The steel interests recruited 230 persons to join the Association and paid over $100,000 for their membership, registration, and attendance expenses. At the Association's annual meeting, the proposal to approve polyvinyl chloride conduit was rejected by a vote of 394 to 390.

Indian Head sued Allied Tube & Conduit, alleging that it had violated federal antitrust laws by conspiring with other steel interests to restrain trade in the electrical conduit market. The trial court ruled in favor of Allied Tube & Conduit, reasoning that its conduct was protected under the *Noerr-Pennington* doctrine because the Association was the equivalent of a legislature, and Allied Tube & Conduit's activities were protected political activity intended to influence state and local government. Is the court correct? Explain.

THE SHERMAN ACT

- **an introduction to legal analysis under §1 of the Sherman Act**
- **discussion of horizontal restraints of trade under §1, including price-fixing, division of markets, concerted refusals to deal, and exchange of market information**
- **discussion of vertical restraints of trade governed by §1, including resale price maintenance; territory, customer, and location restrictions; dealer terminations; and tying and other exclusive dealing contracts**
- **discussion of the law governing monopolization, attempt to monopolize, and conspiracy to monopolize under §2 of the Sherman Act**

Although the Sherman Act is over a century old, it remains the primary tool of antitrust enforcement in the United States. The Sherman Act's two substantive provisions have been applied in hundreds of federal cases to proscribe a wide variety of anticompetitive conduct. This chapter examines the principles developed by the Supreme Court governing trade restraints and monopolization under §§1 and 2 of the Sherman Act.

Introduction to §1

Section 1 of the Sherman Act declares *contracts, combinations,* and *conspiracies* in restraint of trade to be illegal. Section 1 therefore reaches concerted action by separate firms; it does not reach unilateral conduct. In §1 violations, the parties involved remain under separate ownership and control, but they combine or conspire together to obtain or exercise market power. Occasionally, proof of conspiracy is the pivotal issue in the case. The first part of this chapter explores the various types of loose-knit combinations that violate the Sherman Act. Unlike monopolization, which requires elaborate analysis of market structure, Section 1 violations more often are conduct oriented.

Development of the Legal Standard for §1 Violations

By its terms, §1 of the Sherman Act condemns "every" contract combination or conspiracy in restraint of trade. Early in Sherman Act history, however, it became apparent that such a literal interpretation was unworkable.

In a sense, every contract restrains trade. For example, if Seller contracts to sell 50 bicycles to Buyer for $5,000, trade is thereby restrained because Buyer forgoes the opportunity to buy from other sellers and Seller surrenders the opportunity to sell to other buyers. In short, a literal interpretation of the Sherman Act condemns contract law generally, a result certainly not intended by the statute. Some standard therefore had to be established to separate those contracts or combinations that violate the statute from those that do not.

The Rule of Reason. In 1711, the common law of contracts adopted the standard of *reasonableness* in *Mitchel v. Reynolds,*[1] a standard it continues to apply in judging the enforceability of promises in restraint of trade. In the landmark case *Standard Oil Company v. United States,*[2] decided in 1911, Chief Justice White adopted a similar standard to judge Sherman Act violations. Under this **rule of reason** the Sherman Act does not condemn all restraints of trade, but only those restraints whose character or effect is unreasonably anticompetitive. In applying the rule of reason the court may hear evidence concerning three issues: (1) what harm to competition results from the challenged restraint, (2) what is the purpose of the restraint and is it legitimate and important, and (3) are there alternative means, less restrictive to competition, to achieve the same result? For most Sherman Act cases, the rule of reason continues to be the standard by which violations of the Act are judged.[3]

Under the rule of reason, the plaintiff bears the initial burden of proving that the restraints involved have had, or are likely to have, a substantial adverse effect on competition. In some cases, the plaintiff is able to prove actual anticompetitive effects, such as higher prices or lower output. Generally, however, the plaintiff attempts to predict the restraint's effect by proving the relevant product and geographic market and that the defendants have sufficient market power in that market (usually because of large market share) to be able to produce an anticompetitive effect.

If the plaintiff establishes harm to competition, the burden shifts to the defendant to show that the restraint produces benefits to competition that offset the harms identified by the plaintiff. If benefits are proven, the burden then shifts back to the plaintiff to show that these benefits can be achieved by alternative means having fewer anticompetitive effects.

Note that the standard dictated by the Sherman Act is *competition.* As the following case indicates, courts generally will not balance the anticompetitive effect of the restraint against social goals other than the maintenance of competition.

National Society of Professional Engineers v. United States
98 S. Ct. 1355 (1978)

> The National Society of Professional Engineers (Society) was organized to govern the nontechnical aspects of engineering practice, including promotion of professional, social, and economic interests of its members. Its canon of ethics prohibited engineers from discussing the fee to be charged until after the client had selected the engineer for a particular project. The United States filed a civil antitrust action against the Society, alleging that the canon prohibiting submission of competitive bids for engineering services suppressed price competition and deprived customers of the benefits of free and open competition in violation of §1 of the Sherman Act. The Society defended on grounds that awarding engineering services to the lowest bidder would produce inferior engineering work, endangering the public safety. For this reason, it argued that the canons were not an unreasonable restraint of trade in violation of the Sherman Act. The District Court granted an injunction against the canon and the Court of Appeals affirmed. Both courts found the canon unlawful on its face and therefore illegal without regard to claimed or possible benefits. The Supreme Court granted certiorari.

Justice Stevens

. . . This is a civil antitrust case brought by the United States to nullify an association's canon of ethics prohibiting competitive bidding by its members. The question is whether the canon may be justified under the Sherman Act . . . , because it was adopted by members of a learned profession for the purpose of minimizing

---

[1] P. Wms. 181, 24 Eng. Rep. 347 (Ch. 1711). See Chapter 10.
[2] 31 S. Ct. 502 (1911).
[3] By announcing the rule of reason in the *Standard Oil* case, the Supreme Court pleased neither antitrust reformers nor business interests. The reformers thought the rule rendered the Act vague and general and delegated too much power in antitrust policy to the judicial branch. Business complained that the rule provided no specific guidelines, making it difficult to predict the legality of any proposed business conduct. This dissatisfaction was a major reason for passage of the Clayton Act and Federal Trade Commission Act in 1914.

the risk that competition would produce inferior engineering work endangering the public safety. . . .

To evaluate this argument it is necessary to identify the contours of the Rule of Reason and to discuss its application to the kind of justification asserted by petitioner. . . .

The test prescribed in *Standard Oil* is whether the challenged tracts or acts "were unreasonably restrictive of competitive conditions." Unreasonableness under that test could be based either (1) on the nature or character of the contracts, or (2) on surrounding circumstances giving rise to the inference or presumption that they were intended to restrain trade and enhance prices. Under either branch of the test, the inquiry is confined to a consideration of impact on competitive conditions. . . .

[T]he purpose of the analysis is to form a judgment about the competitive significance of the restraint; it is not to decide whether a policy favoring competition is in the public interest, or in the interest of the members of an industry. Subject to exceptions defined by statute, that policy decision has been made by the Congress. . . .

Price is the "central nervous system of the economy," *United States v. Socony-Vacuum Oil Co.,* [60 S. Ct. 811, 845 (1940)], and an agreement that "interfere[s] with the setting of price by free market forces" is illegal on its face. . . . In this case we are presented with an agreement among competitors to refuse to discuss prices with potential customers until after negotiations have resulted in the initial selection of an engineer. While this is not price fixing as such, no elaborate industry analysis is required to demonstrate the anticompetitive character of such an agreement. It operates as an absolute ban on competitive bidding, applying with equal force to both complicated and simple projects and to both inexperienced and sophisticated customers. . . .

The Sherman Act does not require competitive bidding; it prohibits unreasonable restraints on competition. Petitioner's ban on competitive bidding prevents all customers from making price comparisons in the initial selection of an engineer, and imposes the Society's views of the costs and benefits of competition on the entire marketplace. It is this restraint that must be justified under the Rule of Reason, and petitioner's attempt to do so on the basis of the potential threat that competition poses to the public safety and the ethics of its profession is nothing less than a frontal assault on the basic policy of the Sherman Act.

The Sherman Act reflects a legislative judgment that ultimately competition will produce not only lower prices, but also better goods and services. . . . The assumption that competition is the best method of allocating resources in a free market recognizes that all elements of a bargain—quality, service, safety, and durability—and not just the immediate cost, are favorably affected by the free opportunity to select among alternative offers. Even assuming occasional exceptions to the presumed consequences of competition, the statutory policy precludes inquiry into the question whether competition is good or bad. . . .

[B]y their nature, professional services may differ significantly from other business services, and, accordingly, the nature of the competition in such services may vary. Ethical norms may serve to regulate and promote this competition, and thus fall within the Rule of Reason. But the Society's argument in this case is a far cry from such a position. We are faced with a contention that a total ban on competitive bidding is necessary because otherwise engineers will be tempted to submit deceptively low bids. Certainly, the problem of professional deception is a proper subject of an ethical canon. But, once again, the equation of competition with deception, like the similar equation with safety hazards, is simply too broad; we may assume that competition is not entirely conducive to ethical behavior, but that is not a reason, cognizable under the Sherman Act, for doing away with competition.

In sum, the Rule of Reason does not support a defense based on the assumption that competition itself is unreasonable. . . .

[Judgment affirmed.]

Although *reasonableness* is the sole standard governing Sherman Act violations, courts use primarily two approaches to determine reasonableness. In most cases the rule of reason requires proof of competitive injury and allows the defendant to introduce evidence of the reasonableness of the restraint to avoid a violation. The Supreme Court has, however, declared that certain specific practices or business relationships are so inherently destructive of competition that they are unreasonable *per se*, that is, "conclusively presumed to be unreasonable and therefore illegal without elaborate inquiry as to the precise harm they have caused or the business excuse for their use."[4] *Per se* illegality has been

---

[4]Northern Pacific Railway Company v. United States, 78 S. Ct. 514, 518 (1958).

imposed, on a case-by-case basis, on a variety of conduct including price-fixing, division of markets, group boycotts, and certain tying arrangements.

The defendant is not permitted to justify conduct in the *per se* category because the Court has already determined, through considerable experience with the practice or device, that it has no purpose other than to destroy or stifle competition. *Per se* rules simplify enforcement of the Act, and reduce the length of litigation because the plaintiff is not required to prove injury to competition or refute the defendant's justification. *Per se* rules also provide greater predictability and therefore greater deterrence against conduct the law finds particularly offensive.

Types of Trade Restraints

In analyzing §1 cases, one must initially characterize the nature of the restraint. Restraints of trade are of two types: "horizontal" and "vertical." A **horizontal restraint** is an agreement among competitors, persons at the same functional level. For example, an agreement among competing manufacturers to fix prices of commodities they sell imposes a horizontal restraint. A similar agreement among wholesalers or among retailers also is horizontal. In contrast, a **vertical restraint** is an agreement between persons standing in a buyer-seller or supplier-supplied relationship. For example, assume a manufacturer sells loudspeakers to a retailer on condition that the retailer resell the speakers to its customers only at prices set by the manufacturer. Such a "resale price maintenance" arrangement imposes a vertical restraint.

Horizontal and vertical restraints tested under §1 are discussed below. Horizontal restraints covered include price-fixing, division of markets, and concerted refusals to deal (group boycotts). Vertical restraints discussed include resale price maintenance; location, territory, and customer restrictions; and tying and exclusive dealing contracts.

Horizontal Restraints

Introduction to Cartels

Agreements among competitors to restrain trade are a major concern under §1, reaching full-blown **cartels** (agreements among competitors to restrict output and raise prices) as well as other types of concerted conduct having some cartel effects.

The anticompetitive impact of cartels can readily be illustrated. Microeconomic theory teaches that the monopolist will maximize its return at a lower output and therefore a higher price than would prevail in a competitive industry. This restricted output and higher price is antitrust law's basic concern. Monopoly effects may, however, be achieved without a monopolist if firms in an industry who would otherwise compete instead agree to cooperate on matters of price and output. This is the classic cartel, through which the parties, acting collectively rather than independently, reduce output and reap and share the extraordinary profit characteristic of a monopolist. Section 1 of the Sherman Act is the primary legal tool used to attack such combinations.

Despite their promise of shared monopoly profit, cartels do not pervade American industry for various reasons. Initially, a cartel is plagued by problems of administration. The parties must devise some mechanism to restrict and divide output or fix prices among participating firms, and to police the arrangement to assure compliance. This mechanism must be sophisticated because the decisions involved are complex. For example, an agreement on optimum price and output is difficult, because the profit-maximizing price for the industry as a whole will be too high for some firms and too low for others.[5] The cartel also must be geared to operate in secret because the entire arrangement is, of course, illegal. These administrative difficulties commonly prevent cartelization if the number of firms in the industry is large, but may be overcome if the market structure is oligopolistic, in which a few large firms dominate the industry.

Once a cartel is in operation and a price is successfully set, cartel members have a strong incentive to cheat. Because the cartel price is higher than that prevailing under competitive conditions, each cartel member could lower its price and still make a profit. Thus, as long as other firms can be relied upon to honor the cartel price, and undercutting that price can be done without alerting them, a firm can substantially increase sales and profits by cheating. This is the ideal situation for a cartel member: competing while the others do not. Once discovered, cheating causes the cartel to break down.

Despite these problems, cartels do exist and their operation, even for a limited period, exacts a great social and economic cost. The following material discusses

---

[5]This assumes that the conspirators actually know what output will maximize profit in the short run, an amount that is difficult if not impossible to determine accurately.

various types of horizontal arrangements, from classic cartels involving blatant price-fixing or market division to more subtle devices used to control or affect output or price.

Price-Fixing

Price-fixing is the cooperative setting of price levels or ranges by competing firms.[6] In its various forms, price-fixing is the most onerous conduct reached by the antitrust laws, and has been treated accordingly by the courts.

The classic case outlining the judicial approach to price-fixing is *United States v. Socony-Vacuum Oil Co.,*[7] decided in 1940. In this case, a group of major oil-refining companies were indicted and convicted for conspiring to raise prices of gasoline sold in the mid-western area. Through a concerted program of bidding for and buying gasoline and then storing it when necessary, the defendants were able to affect the quantity and therefore the price of gasoline sold in the market. The case reached the Supreme Court, and the opinion, rendered by Justice Douglas, remains the definitive statement regarding the application of the Sherman Act to price-fixing.

The Court initially reaffirmed that the standard dictated by the Sherman Act is *competition,* and upheld the defendants' conviction concluding that

> [u]nder the Sherman Act a combination formed for the purpose and with the effect of raising, depressing, fixing, pegging, or stabilizing the price of a commodity in interstate or foreign commerce is illegal *per se*.[8]

Socony-Vacuum was the first case to use the now familiar *per se* language to characterize certain §1 violations.

In addition to announcing a *per se* rule for horizontal price-fixing, the court indicated that the definition of price-fixing is expansive: any agreement between competitors that affects or is intended to affect price, however accomplished, is price-fixing. As noted by the court:

> [P]rices are fixed . . . if the range within which purchases or sales will be made is agreed upon, if the prices

paid or charged are to be at a certain level or on ascending or descending scales, if they are to be uniform, or if by various formulae they are related to the market prices. They are fixed because they are *agreed upon*.[9]

Applying this test to the facts, the Court labeled the concerted buying program of the oil companies price-fixing, because its effect was to establish a floor price in the spot market, effectively manipulating that market, and resulting in higher prices than would otherwise have prevailed.

Under the test announced by the Court, a wide variety of business conduct constitutes price-fixing. Agreements to pay or charge a fixed price or a minimum or maximum price, to confine prices within a given range, or to tie price to some external standard all are *per se* illegal. Similarly, fixing trade-in allowances, markups, discounts, or the spread between premium and nonpremium products is illegal. These arrangements might be termed direct price-fixing. As *Socony-Vacuum* indicates, however, indirect arrangements affecting price are equally suspect. For example, the defendants in that case manipulated price by reducing supply (by purchasing and storing gasoline). A similar agreement among buyers to limit purchases, thereby driving price down, or by sellers to limit output, driving prices up, is *per se* illegal. Another form of price-fixing is "bid rigging," which is common in the construction industry. Government contracts usually are awarded by competitive bidding. Contractors can manipulate the bidding process by collusively submitting bids higher than would exist under competitive conditions, frequently taking turns submitting the "low" bid. In this case, the conspirators fix prices by concertedly tampering with the *offers* they make. In short, any agreement between competitors that has or may have an effect on the price the competitors charge or offer is suspect under the Sherman Act, including agreements that alter the mechanisms by which price is determined (for example, agreements restricting output), and agreements that affect merely part of the price. For example, competitors may jointly agree to fix discounts or credit terms offered to customers. At issue in the following case was whether such an agreement should be *per se* illegal.

---

[6]BLACK'S LAW DICTIONARY 1189 (6th ed. 1990).
[7]60 S. Ct. 811 (1940).
[8]*Id*. at 844.

[9]*Id*. (Emphasis added).

Catalano, Inc. v. Target Sales, Inc.
100 S. Ct. 1925 (1980)

Prior to 1967, beer wholesalers in Fresno, California, extended short-term, interest-free credit to their retailers. During this time, the wholesalers competed with each other regarding trade credit, and credit terms for individual retailers varied substantially. Beginning in early 1967, the wholesalers allegedly agreed that as of December 1967, they would sell to retailers only if payment was made in advance or on delivery. Plaintiffs, a group of retailers, sued, alleging that the agreement to eliminate short-term trade credit constituted price-fixing in violation of §1 of the Sherman Act. The district court certified the case to the Court of Appeals to determine whether the alleged agreement among competitors to fix credit terms, if proven, was a *per se* violation of the Sherman Act. The Court of Appeals held that the agreement should not be characterized as a form of price-fixing, noting that such an agreement might actually be procompetitive by (1) removing entry barriers to the market, and (2) making the price term more visible. The Supreme Court granted certiorari.

Per Curiam

. . . It has long been settled that an agreement to fix prices is unlawful *per se*. It is no excuse that the prices fixed are themselves reasonable. . . . In *United States v. Socony-Vacuum Oil Co.,* [60 S. Ct. 811 (1940)], we held that an agreement among competitors to engage in a program of buying surplus gasoline on the spot market in order to prevent prices from falling sharply was unlawful without any inquiry into the reasonableness of the program, even though there was no direct agreement on the actual prices to be maintained. In the course of the opinion, the Court made clear that

the machinery employed by a combination for price-fixing is immaterial.

Under the Sherman Act a combination formed for the purpose and with the effect of raising, depressing, fixing, pegging, or stabilizing the price of a commodity in interstate or foreign commerce is illegal *per se*. [*Id.* at 844.]

Thus, we have held agreements to be unlawful *per se* that had substantially less direct impact on price than the agreement alleged in this case. For example, in *Sugar Institute v. United States,* [56 S. Ct. 629, 643 (1936)], the Court held unlawful an agreement to adhere to previously announced prices and terms of sale, even though advance price announcements are perfectly lawful and even though the particular prices and terms were not themselves fixed by private agreement. Similarly, an agreement among competing firms of professional engineers to refuse to discuss prices with potential customers until after negotiations have resulted in the initial selection of an engineer was held unlawful without requiring further inquiry. [*National Society of Professional Engineers v. United States,* 98 S. Ct. 1355, 1365–66 (1978).] Indeed, a horizontal agreement among competitors to use a specific method of quoting prices may be unlawful. [*FTC v. Cement Institute,* 68 S. Ct. 793, 798–799 (1948).]

It is virtually self-evident that extending interest-free credit for a period of time is equivalent to giving a discount equal to the value of the use of the purchase price for that period of time. Thus, credit terms must be characterized as an inseparable part of the price. An agreement to terminate the practice of giving credit is thus tantamount to an agreement to eliminate discounts, and thus falls squarely within the traditional *per se* rule against price fixing. While it may be that the elimination of a practice of giving variable discounts will ultimately lead in a competitive market to corresponding decreases in the invoice price, that is surely not necessarily to be anticipated. It is more realistic to view an agreement to eliminate credit sales as extinguishing one form of competition among the sellers. In any event, when a particular concerted activity entails an obvious risk of anticompetitive impact with no apparent potentially redeeming value, the fact that a practice may turn out to be harmless in a particular set of circumstances will not prevent its being declared unlawful *per se*.

The . . . Court of Appeals suggested, however, that a horizontal agreement to eliminate credit sales may remove a barrier to other sellers who may wish to enter the market. But in any case in which competitors are able to increase the price level or to curtail production by agreement, it could be argued that the agreement has the effect of making the market more attractive to potential new entrants. If that potential justifies horizontal agreements among competitors imposing one kind of voluntary restraint or another on their competitive freedom, it would seem to follow that the more successful an agreement is in raising the price level, the safer it is from antitrust attack. Nothing could be more inconsistent with our cases.

Nor can the informing function of agreement, the increased price visibility, justify its restraint on the individual wholesaler's freedom to select his own prices and terms of sale. For, again, it is obvious that any industry-wide agreement on prices will result in a more accurate understanding of the terms offered by all parties to the agreement. As the *Sugar Institute* case demonstrates, however, there is a plain distinction between the lawful right to publish prices and terms of sale, on the one hand, and an agreement among competitors limiting action with respect to the published prices, on the other.

Thus, under the reasoning of our cases, an agreement among competing wholesalers to refuse to sell unless the retailers make payment in cash either in advance or upon delivery is "plainly anticompetitive." Since it is merely one form of price fixing, and since price-fixing agreements have been adjudged to lack any "redeeming virtue," it is conclusively presumed illegal without further examination under the rule of reason. . . .

[Judgment reversed and remanded.]

In addition to accepting an expansive definition of price-fixing, the Court in *Socony-Vacuum* stated that the power to fix prices is not necessary to establish an illegal conspiracy under §1. The plaintiff need prove only an act of conspiring, not that the conspirators had the means available to accomplish their objective.

Socony-Vacuum and other cases also address the applicability of two defenses commonly raised by persons charged with illegal price-fixing: (1) that price-fixing was necessary to prevent ruinous or cutthroat competition destructive of the industry, and (2) that in any event the prices fixed were reasonable. Regarding the first defense, early §1 cases clearly establish that competition is the standard mandated by the Sherman Act. Conduct that destroys competition is prohibited, even if in the opinion of the defendants or others some other arrangement (for example, a cartel) would be more beneficial to the industry or the public. The reasonable price defense has suffered a similar fate. Price, under competition, is determined by market and cost conditions. Therefore, a reasonable price is one determined in response to those conditions, which are ever changing. Thus, any price set by collusive behavior manipulates and distorts normal price-setting mechanisms and is inherently unreasonable.

Horizontal Market Division

Agreements among competitors to divide the market in which they would otherwise compete inherently destroy competition. Market division schemes come in many forms. Competing firms may agree to divide a market geographically by allocating a specific territory to each firm. For example, Anson and Barber, competing manufacturers, may agree to divide the country in half, with Anson selling in the East and Barber selling only in the West. Or, firms may divide a market by customers. For example, Anson may agree to sell only to wholesalers, and Barber to retailers. Or, the conspirators may divide a product market. For example, if Anson and Barber manufacture products X and Y, Anson may agree to sell only X in the future and Barber only Y.

The problem of any market division is that the firms involved agree not to compete with one another in the divided market. By removing competitors or potential competitors from the market, supply is reduced and price is raised. Further, if no independent firms (that is, those not a party to the conspiracy) compete, the division may award its members a monopoly of their respective shares. For these reasons, courts have long condemned horizontal market division, regardless of form, as inherently anticompetitive.

In *United States v. Topco Associates, Inc.,*[10] decided in 1972, the Supreme Court announced explicitly what had been implicit in a number of earlier decisions: horizontal market division is a *per se* violation of §1. The Court went on to hold that horizontal market division is per se illegal whether or not accompanied by other antitrust violations. In the following case, the Court reaffirms its long-standing principles governing horizontal price-fixing and market division.

Palmer v. BRG of Georgia, Inc.
111 S. Ct. 401 (1990)

In 1976, Harcourt Brace Jovanovich (HBJ) began offering a review course to prepare law school graduates to take the Georgia Bar Examination. From 1977 to 1979, HBJ competed directly with a bar review course offered by BRG of

---

[10]92 S. Ct. 1126 (1972).

Georgia, Inc. (BRG). During this period, HBJ and BRG were the main providers of bar review courses in Georgia. In early 1980, they entered into an agreement that gave BRG an exclusive license to market HBJ's material in Georgia and to use its trade name "Bar/Bri." Under the licensing agreement HBJ received $100 for every student enrolled by BRG and 40 percent of all revenues over $350. The parties further agreed that HBJ would not compete with BRG in Georgia, and that BRG would refrain from competing with HBJ in the rest of the country. Immediately after the agreement, the price of BRG's course increased from $150 to $400.

In 1985, plaintiffs Jay Palmer and other law graduates who had contracted to take BRG's review course sued BRG and HBJ alleging that the defendants' market division agreement artificially inflated the price of BRG's course and violated §1 of the Sherman Act. The district court granted summary judgment for the defendants, and the Court of Appeals affirmed, holding that (1) horizontal price-fixing is *per se* unlawful only if the parties reach explicit agreement on prices to be charged or if one party has the right to be consulted regarding the other's prices, and (2) horizontal geographic market division is per se illegal only if the defendants subdivide some market in which they previously had competed. The Supreme Court granted certiorari.

Per Curiam

. . . In *United States v. Socony-Vacuum Oil Co.,* [60 S. Ct. 811 (1940)], we held that an agreement among competitors to engage in a program of buying surplus gasoline on the spot market in order to prevent prices from falling sharply was unlawful, even though there was no direct agreement on the actual prices to be maintained. We explained that "[u]nder the Sherman Act a combination formed for the purpose and with the effect of raising, depressing, fixing, pegging, or stabilizing the price of a commodity in interstate or foreign commerce is illegal *per se.*" [*Id.* at 844]. . . .

The revenue-sharing formula in the 1980 agreement between BRG and HBJ, coupled with the price increase that took place immediately after the parties agreed to cease competing with each other in 1980, indicates that this agreement was "formed for the purpose and with the effect of raising" the price of the bar review course. It was, therefore, plainly incorrect for the District Court to enter summary judgment in [defendants'] favor. Moreover, it is equally clear that the District Court and the Court of Appeals erred when they assumed that an allocation of markets or submarkets by competitors is not unlawful unless the market in which the two previously competed is divided between them.

In *United States v. Topco Associates, Inc.,* [92 S. Ct. 1126 (1972)], we held that agreements between competitors to allocate territories to minimize competition are illegal. . . . The defendants in *Topco* had never competed in the same market, but had simply agreed to allocate markets. Here, HBJ and BRG had previously competed in the Georgia market; under their allocation agreement, BRG received that market, while HBJ received the remainder of the United States. Each agreed not to compete in the other's territories. Such agreements are anticompetitive regardless of whether the parties split a market within which both do business or whether they merely reserve one market for one and another for the other. Thus, the 1980 agreement between HBJ and BRG was unlawful on its face.

[Judgment reversed and remanded.]

Group Boycotts—Concerted Refusals to Deal

Purpose and Effect of Boycotts. A **group boycott,** or **concerted refusal to deal,** is a horizontal combination intended to eliminate (or prevent the entry of) a competitor of the parties to the combination. Group boycotts usually span more than one functional level (that is, manufacturer, wholesaler, retailer). In the classic case, a group of competitors at one level desires, for whatever reason, to eliminate a competitor at its level. For example, assume Adams, Bowman, Cox, and Davis are wholesalers. Davis is troublesome to the others because she engages in rigorous price competition, which Adams, Bowman, and Cox wish to avoid. To eliminate Davis from the market, the other three approach Martin a major supplier of all four wholesalers and indicate that they will refuse to buy from Martin unless he stops selling to Davis. If Martin fears the loss of the conspirators' business he may be persuaded to go along and cease selling to Davis. If this happens, Davis is cut off from a trade relationship she needs to compete effectively and the conspirators may achieve their intended result. Note that this case, like virtually all boycotts, involves an element of coercion to achieve cooperation.

Although boycotts usually involve two functional levels and some concerted refusal to deal, neither is absolutely required to achieve the anticompetitive result of a boycott. For example, assume Adams, Bowman, Cox, and Davis are all brokers. To be effective, a broker requires the cooperation of fellow brokers. Adams,

Bowman, and Cox could effectively eliminate Davis by refusing to deal with him. In this case the concerted refusal to deal is aimed at the intended victim, Davis (rather than against a person above or below the victim in the distribution chain) and includes only one functional level. Or, assume Adams, Bowman, and Cox, retailers, persuade Martin, a manufacturer, not to deal with their competitor, Davis, by circulating false rumors concerning her financial position. The three have not refused to deal with anyone, and Martin's refusal to sell to Davis is unilateral, not concerted. Nevertheless, the effect is the same: elimination of a competitor of the conspirators.

Thus, neither "concerted refusal to deal" nor "boycott" fully describes the conduct subject to antitrust scrutiny in this context. The law merely requires that, regardless of the means used, a group of competitors concertedly act to deprive an actual or potential competitor of suppliers, customers, or other essential trade relationships needed to compete with those conspiring.

Legal Test Governing Group Boycotts. Classic group boycotts have been declared in a number of Supreme Court cases to be per se violations of §1 of the Sherman Act. As noted in the following landmark case, these arrangements clearly injure competition and exhibit no countervailing procompetitive effects.

Fashion Originators' Guild of America, Inc. v. Federal Trade Commission
61 S. Ct. 703 (1941)

> Fashion Originators' Guild of America (FOGA) was an association of designers and manufacturers of textiles and women's clothing. Although FOGA members claimed that their fabric and fashion designs were original and unique, they were not patented or copyrighted. As a result, soon after FOGA designs reached the market, other manufacturers routinely made and sold copies, usually at lower prices. Claiming that such "style piracy" was unethical and immoral, FOGA members in combination agreed to refuse to sell clothing to retailers who also bought from the "style pirates." About 12,000 retailers signed agreements promising to cooperate with FOGA's boycott. FOGA further developed an elaborate system to police the retailers and enforce the agreements. The Federal Trade Commission found that FOGA's boycott arrangement was an unfair method of competition in violation of §5 of the FTC Act and issued a cease and desist order. The Court of Appeals affirmed and the Supreme Court granted certiorari.

Justice Black

. . . If the purpose and practice of the combination of garment manufacturers and their affiliates runs counter to the public policy declared in the Sherman [Act], . . . the Federal Trade Commission has the power to suppress it as an unfair method of competition. . . .

[T]he findings of the Commission bring [FOGA's] combination in its entirety well within the inhibition of the policies declared by the Sherman Act. . . . [A]mong the many respects in which the Guild's plan runs contrary to the policy of the Sherman Act are these: it narrows the outlets to which garment and textile manufacturers can sell and the sources from which retailers can buy . . . ; subjects all retailers and manufacturers who decline to comply with the Guild's program to an organized boycott . . . ; takes away the freedom of action of members by requiring each to reveal to the Guild the intimate details of their individual affairs . . . ; and has both as its necessary tendency and as its purpose and effect the direct suppression of competition from the sale of unregistered textiles and copied designs. . . .

In this case, the Commission found that the combination exercised sufficient control and power in the women's garments and textile businesses "to exclude from the industry those manufacturers and distributors who do not conform to the rules and regulations of [FOGA], and thus tend to create in themselves a monopoly in the said industries." . . .

But [FOGA] further argue[s] that their boycott and restraint of interstate trade is not within the ban of the policies of the Sherman [Act] because "the practices of FOGA were reasonable and necessary to protect the manufacturer, laborer, retailer and consumer against the devastating evils growing from the pirating of original designs and had in fact benefited all four." The Commission declined to hear much of the evidence that [FOGA] desired to offer on this subject. As we have pointed out, however, the aim of [FOGA's] combination was the intentional destruction of one type of manufacture and sale which competed with guild members. The purpose and object of this combination, its potential power, its tendency to monopoly, the coercion it could and did practice upon a rival method of competition, all brought it within the policy of the prohibition declared by the Sherman [Act]. . . . Under these circumstances it was not error to refuse to hear the evidence offered, for the reasonableness of the methods pursued by the combination to accomplish its unlawful object is no more material than would be the reasonableness of the prices fixed by unlawful combination. . . . Nor can the unlawful combination be justified upon the argument that systematic copying of dress designs is itself tortious, or should now be declared so by us. In the first place, whether or not given conduct is tortious is a question of state law. . . . In the second place, even if copying were an acknowledged tort under the law of every state, that situation would not justify [the members of FOGA] in combining together to regulate and restrain interstate commerce in violation of federal law. . . .

[Judgment affirmed.]

Though classic group boycotts are *per se* illegal, not all concerted activity that excludes a competitor is treated as harshly under §1. Many exclusionary devices have purposes not solely related to the self-interest of the challenged combination and are tested under a less harsh rule of reason standard. For example, industry self-regulation plans designed to prevent fraud or establish safety standards frequently have boycott effects, yet are not categorically declared illegal. Such plans are nevertheless subject to close antitrust scrutiny.

Vertical Restraints

Vertical trade restraints exist between parties standing in a buyer-seller or customer-supplier relation. In other words, whereas horizontal combinations exist among parties at one function level, vertical combinations include parties at two or more levels. Unlike horizontal restraints, which usually are informal aggregations, vertical restraints often are imposed by express contract between the parties. This agreement supplies the "contract, combination, or conspiracy" necessary to establish jurisdiction under §1 of the Sherman Act.

Although firms at different functional levels are not in competition, vertically imposed restraints do significantly affect competition in the markets occupied by the parties to the restraint. Many vertical restraints are imposed in the chain of a product's distribution, as for example, a contractual restriction imposed by a manufacturer upon a retailer dictating the price at which the retailer resells or dictating where or to whom he may sell. Such "distributional" restraints compose the first two sections of the following material. Following the treatment of distributional restraints, tying and other exclusive dealing contracts are discussed.

Resale Price Maintenance

Per Se Illegality of Vertical Price Restrictions. An agreement between a seller and a buyer fixing the price at which the buyer may resell the goods purchased (a **resale price maintenance** or "vertical price-fixing" agreement) constitutes a *per se* violation of §1 of the Sherman Act. For example, assume M, a manufacturer sells a television to R, a retailer, for $250. As part of the contract, R agrees that he will not resell the set to a retail customer for less than $500. The contract constitutes a *per se* §1 violation. In the landmark case, *Dr. Miles Medical Company v. John D. Park & Sons Company,*[11] decided in 1911, the Court held that resale price maintenance is both an unreasonable restraint on a buyer's right to transfer the item sold, and unreasonably forecloses price competition among traders competing in reselling the restricted article. Further, the seller has no legitimate countervailing interest to justify such a restraint.

Motives for Resale Price Maintenance. In resale price maintenance, a manufacturer commonly fixes its retailers' resale price at a level higher than would prevail under competitive conditions. Because the quantity demanded falls as price rises, resale price maintenance generally results in fewer sales by manufacturers to retailers than would be made had the retailers competed. Ordinarily, however, a manufacturer maximizes profits by selling to retailers at a price satisfactory to itself and then stimulating competition at the retail level. Competition among retailers reduces the price to consumers, and increases the number of units sold. Competition also reduces dealer profits, thereby minimizing the cost to the manufacturer of having the retail function performed. Why, then, would a manufacturer want to contractually fix its dealers' resale prices at a level that may reduce the number of units sold and increase dealer profits?

One purpose of resale price maintenance is to facilitate or disguise a cartel among retailers. Pressure to impose resale price restrictions often comes from *retailers,* not manufacturers. Retailer cartelization through

---

[11]31 S. Ct. 376 (1911).

resale price maintenance is possible if the manufacturer sells a branded or differentiated product and retailers are sufficiently powerful to induce the manufacturer to "impose" resale price restrictions at prices exceeding those prevailing under competitive conditions.

Even without a push from below, a substantial number of manufacturers have, over the years, formulated and maintained complicated resale price maintenance plans because of perceived benefits to the manufacturer. For example, the Supreme Court has noted that when total consumer demand

> is affected less by price than by the number of retail outlets for the product, the availability of dealer services, or the impact of advertising and promotion, it will be in the interest of manufacturers to squelch price competition through a scheme of resale price maintenance in order to concentrate on nonprice competition.[12]

Manufacturers also sometimes assert that fixing resale prices allows them to achieve more efficient distribution of their products. For example, resale price maintenance is sometimes justified on grounds that (1) it provides a larger profit margin for retailers, inducing them to carry the product, to promote it effectively, and to provide necessary ancillary services, (2) it cultivates a "prestige" image accompanying a high price, and (3) the manufacturer is better able than retailers to determine the optimum price at which its products should be sold.

These and other distributional justifications are open to criticism, either on theoretical grounds, or because the same result can be achieved in less anticompetitive ways. For example, competing independent retailers, each acting in response to changing costs and market conditions, should be better able to identify the optimum price than a manufacturer who is removed from the retail market. Additionally, a high resale price can be maintained by charging an appropriately high price to retailers. Promotion can be done directly by the manufacturer, or a high wholesale price may be coupled with an allowance to dealers who provide promotional services, or the manufacturer can require promotional expenditures as a condition of sale.

Attempts to Circumvent the Prohibition Against Resale Price Maintenance. Despite long-standing

judicial hostility, both buyers and sellers frequently have sought to legalize resale price maintenance arrangements, either through statutory authorization or by characterizing the arrangement as outside the scope of §1. On one hand, between 1937 and 1975, federal law provided an exemption for certain price maintenance agreements authorized under state "fair trade" laws. Such legislation was enacted in response to intense lobbying by retail trade associations. On the other, parties often have attempted to avoid an antitrust violation by characterizing the arrangement as (1) an agency or consignment (resulting in no "sale" of the restricted product to the nominal agent or consignee) or (2) a unilateral refusal by a seller to deal with buyers who fail to observe its resale price restrictions (resulting in no "combination" triggering operation of §1).

Agency and Consignment Arrangements. A consignment is, in essence, a bailment for sale. The owner of personal property (the consignor) transfers its possession to the consignee, who acts as the owner-consignor's agent to sell the item. The consignor retains title and sets the price at which he is willing to sell. After sale, the consignee pays the consignor the purchase price less a commission. Because the seller retains title to the merchandise and can therefore dictate the selling price, consignment arrangements often have been used to implement resale price maintenance arrangements.

Although early cases validated resale price maintenance effected through consignment arrangements, the Supreme Court has more recently taken a harsher approach. For example, in the 1964 landmark decision, *Simpson v. Union Oil Company,*[13] Union Oil Company "consigned" rather than sold gasoline to over 4,000 retail stations in the eight western states in order to fix the resale prices charged by the independent dealers. In holding that Union's "consignment" arrangement violated §1, the Supreme Court stated:

> One who sends a rug or a painting or other work of art to a merchant or a gallery for sale at a minimum price can, of course, hold the consignee to the bargain. . . . When, however, a "consignment" device is used to cover a vast gasoline distribution system, fixing prices through many retail outlets, the antitrust laws prevent calling the "consignment" an agency, for then the end result of *United States v. Socony-Vacuum Oil Co.* . . . would be avoided

---

[12]Albrecht v. The Herald Company, 88 S. Ct. 869, 872 n.7 (1968).

[13]84 S. Ct. 1051 (1964).

merely by clever manipulation of words, not by differences in substance. The present, coercive "consignment" device, if successful against challenge under the antitrust laws, furnishes a wooden formula for administering prices on a vast scale.[14]

Under the rationale of *Simpson,* consignments used to comprehensively and coercively administer resale prices among independent businesspersons on a large scale are unlikely to survive judicial scrutiny under the Sherman Act.

Unilateral Refusals to Deal—The Colgate Doctrine. Sellers often have attempted to legalize resale price restrictions by simply refusing to deal with buyers who fail to observe a resale price maintenance policy. Legal support for such a "unilateral refusal to deal" is found in the Supreme Court's early decision, *United States v. Colgate & Co.* (1919),[15] in which the Supreme Court stated:

> In the absence of any purpose to create or maintain a monopoly, the [Sherman Act] does not restrict the long recognized right of trader or manufacturer engaged in an entirely private business, freely to exercise his own independent discretion as to parties with whom he will deal; and, of course, he may announce in advance the circumstances under which he will refuse to sell.[16]

Thus, under the "*Colgate* doctrine," as it has come to be known, a seller may avoid antitrust liability if it does nothing more than announce a resale price maintenance policy and refuse to deal with buyers (wholesalers, retailers, or both) who fail to observe it. The doctrine considers the seller to be acting unilaterally, not in combination with its wholesalers and retailers, and therefore outside the scope of the Sherman Act.[17]

Nonprice Vertical Restraints

Territorial, Customer, and Location Restrictions.
Resale price maintenance is not the only form of vertical distribution restraint. Sellers also may impose *nonprice* vertical restraints including location, territorial, and customer restrictions. Under a "location" restriction, the seller contractually requires the buyer to resell only from a stated location, such as the buyer's existing retail store. A "territorial" restriction requires a buyer to confine its sales to a given geographic area, such as a city or country or portion thereof. A "customer" restriction requires, for example, a retailer to sell goods purchased only to consumers and not to other retailers.

Nonprice vertical restraints most commonly arise in franchising arrangements. In one sense, a **franchise** is simply a license from the owner of a trademark or trade name (the franchisor) permitting another (the franchisee) to sell a product or service under that name or mark.[18] The term today has, however, developed a broader meaning encompassing the "elaborate agreement under which the franchisee undertakes to conduct a business or sell a product or service in accordance with methods and procedures prescribed by the franchisor and the franchisor undertakes to assist the franchisee through advertising, promotion and other advisory services."[19] This "elaborate agreement" usually is the source of the vertical restrictions subject to antitrust scrutiny.

Franchise arrangements vary in many ways. For example, the relationship between franchisor and franchisee may simply be one of buyer and seller; or the franchisee may be designated an "authorized dealer" with certain additional manufacturer control over the franchisee's business operation; or the franchisor may have almost total control over all aspects of the business, as in a fast-food restaurant. The franchisee may carry only the franchisor's products or it may carry competing lines; it may be large or small, well financed or short of funds, experienced in the business or a novice. Each of these factors may be relevant in ruling on the legality of vertical restraints imposed by the franchisor.

All franchise arrangements, however, have one thing in common: the franchisees are independent businesspersons. In all cases, the manufacturer has determined, for whatever reason, that it can more efficiently distribute its product or service through independent wholesale or retail outlets rather than through a company-owned (vertically integrated) distribution system. If the manufacturer declines to make the substantial investment required for vertical integration, the antitrust question presented is: to what extent should

---

[14]*Id.* at 1055, 1057.
[15]39 S. Ct. 465 (1919).
[16]*Id.* at 468.
[17]The preceding discussion concerns a manufacturer's setting price *floors,* a minimum resale price. The Supreme Court has held that maximum resale price maintenance is governed by the rule of reason, not the *per se* standard governing minimum resale price maintenance. State Oil Co. v. Khan, 118 S. Ct. 275 (1997).

[18]BLACK'S LAW DICTIONARY 658 (6th ed. 1990).
[19]H & R Block, Inc. v. Lovelace, 493 P.2d 205, 212 (Kan. 1972).

the law permit a manufacturer to interfere with the decisions of its buyers concerning how they compete in reselling the goods? As to resale price maintenance, the Supreme Court has long prohibited such interference. We turn now to its treatment of nonprice vertical restraints.

Legal Standard Governing Nonprice Vertical Restraints. The current legal standard for vertical nonprice restraints was announced in *Continental T.V., Inc. v. GTE Sylvania, Incorporated,*[20] decided in 1977. In this case, Sylvania, a manufacturer of television sets, sold directly to franchised retail dealers. The franchise agreement contained a location clause, allowing the franchisee to sell only from a designated location or locations. The agreement did not grant territorial exclusivity to franchisees (that is, Sylvania was free to license new dealers in competition with an existing franchisee), but did not preclude franchisees from selling competing brands. The case arose when Sylvania franchised Young Brothers, an established San Francisco television retailer, as an additional retail outlet one mile from Continental T.V., Inc., one of Sylvania's most successful franchised dealers. In displeasure over Sylvania's decision, Continental canceled a large order, and indicated an intent to begin selling Sylvania televisions in Sacramento, in violation of the location restriction. Upon termination of the franchise,[21] Continental sued Sylvania challenging the legality of Sylvania's location clause under §1 of the Sherman Act. The trial court held that Sylvania's location restriction constituted a *per se* §1 violation. The Supreme Court granted certiorari and held that the legality of nonprice vertical restraints should be governed by a rule of reason rather than the harsh *per se* standard applicable to vertical *price* restraints (resale price maintenance). In authorizing rule of reason analysis, the Court stated that:

> The market impact of vertical restrictions is complex because of their potential for a simultaneous reduction of intrabrand competition and stimulation of interbrand competition. . . .
>
> Vertical restrictions promote interbrand competition by allowing the manufacturer to achieve certain efficiencies in the distribution of his products. . . . For example, new manufacturers and manufacturers entering new markets can

use the restrictions in order to induce competent and aggressive retailers to make the kind of investment of capital and labor that is often required in the distribution of products unknown to the consumer. Established manufacturers can use them to induce retailers to engage in promotional activities or to provide service and repair facilities necessary to the efficient marketing of their products. Service and repair are vital for many products, such as automobiles and major household appliances. The availability and quality of such services affect a manufacturer's goodwill and the competitiveness of his product. Because of market imperfections such as the so-called "free rider" effect, these services might not be provided by retailers in a purely competitive situation, despite the fact that each retailer's benefit would be greater if all provided the services than if none did.[22]

Although these justifications for nonprice vertical restraints enjoy a wide following, their validity is questionable. Initially, any argument made in favor of nonprice vertical restrictions can also be used to justify resale price maintenance, long a *per se* Sherman Act violation. Further, although vertical nonprice restrictions do not fix resale prices, they eliminate or significantly reduce competition, including *price* competition, between dealers governed by the restrictions. That is, by insulating dealers who might otherwise compete in the sale of a product, thereby reducing intrabrand competition, vertical nonprice restraints are likely to cause higher prices and reduced consumer choice concerning dealer services and other amenities.

Because they obviously restrict intrabrand competition, any argument against treating territorial, customer, or location restrictions as *per se* violations must be based on some offsetting benefit to competition. The asserted benefit in this case is that intrabrand insulation encourages greater selling effort by dealers, stimulating interbrand competition. But, as noted by one commentator:

> We may assume, in general, that the more competition a dealer faces, the more vigorous will that dealer be obliged to be; and this holds true whether the competition is interbrand or intrabrand. A dealer worried about losing even those buyers with some pre-commitment to its brand will hustle more earnestly than a dealer free of intrabrand competition and which must worry about losing only those prospective customers who lack a clear preference for the brand. "Effort" is encouraged not by freeing a dealer from important competi-

---

[20]97 S. Ct. 2549 (1977).

[21]Note that many, if not most, antitrust cases testing vertical restrictions arise out of franchise terminations.

[22]97 S. Ct. at 2558, 2560.

tive pressures, but by subjecting each dealer to whatever competitive pressure the market generates.[23]

Other antitrust commentary supports the view that intrabrand restraints do not promote interbrand competition. In fact, vigorous intrabrand competition, rather than restraint, may better promote interbrand competition: "it is the onset of intrabrand competition that *first* forces down the margins and prices of well-known brands. *Then,* interbrand competition—primarily within stores rather than between them—depresses the price of competing goods."[24]

In sum, the current and more lenient "rule of reason" standard for vertical nonprice restraints may not be justified. The approach undercuts the long-standing prohibition against resale price maintenance and the arguments supporting it are controversial.

Termination of One Dealer at the Request of Another

Among the most frequently litigated modern antitrust cases are those in which one retail or wholesale dealer is terminated by the manufacturer at the request of another dealer or group of dealers. To illustrate the typical case, assume that Manufacturer A has four franchised wholesale distributors W, X, Y, and Z serving a given geographic area. Z is a low overhead, aggressive price-cutter, who is luring customers away from W, X, and Y, who complain to A about Z's price-cutting. Shortly thereafter, A terminates Z's franchise. Determining the appropriate legal standard to resolve cases of this type has proven to be perhaps the single most controversial modern antitrust issue.

The Supreme Court traditionally treated such a case as a classic horizontal group boycott. In the 1984 case, *Monsanto Company v. Spray-Rite Service Corporation,*[25] however, the Supreme Court focused on the vertical rather than horizontal aspects of dealer terminations, and adopted a strict evidentiary standard regarding proof of conspiracy to be applied in such cases. Monsanto terminated the distributorship of Spray-Rite after receiving numerous complaints from competing Monsanto distributors about Spray-Rite's price-cutting practices. The

Court initially discussed the distinction between independent and concerted activity, and the differing standards applicable to price and nonprice vertical restraints. It then rejected the Court of Appeals' holding that an antitrust plaintiff can survive a motion for a directed verdict (that is, the Court will permit the jury to decide whether an unlawful agreement or conspiracy exists) if the plaintiff proves that a manufacturer terminated a price-cutting distributor in response to or following complaints by other distributors. The Court stated:

> Permitting an agreement to be inferred merely from the existence of complaints, or even from the fact that termination came about 'in response to' complaints, could deter or penalize perfectly legitimate conduct. As Monsanto points out, complaints about price cutters are 'natural—and from the manufacturer's perspective, unavoidable—reactions by distributors to the activities of their rivals.' . . .
>
> Thus, *something more than evidence of complaints is needed. There must be evidence that tends to exclude the possibility that the manufacturer and nonterminated distributors were acting independently.* . . . [T]he antitrust plaintiff should present direct or circumstantial evidence that reasonably tends to prove that the manufacturer and others 'had a conscious commitment to a common scheme designed to achieve an unlawful objective.'[26]

Applying this standard to the facts, the Court found sufficient evidence to support the jury finding of unlawful conspiracy.

In 1988, the Court decided another important dealer termination case, *Business Electronics Corporation v. Sharp Electronics Corporation,*[27] in which the Court held that an agreement between a manufacturer and dealer to terminate another dealer is a per se violation of §1 of the Sherman Act only if the agreement requires the surviving dealer to set prices at a particular level.

The clear consequence of cases such as *Monsanto* and *Business Electronics* is to insulate most manufacturers from Sherman Act suits by terminated dealers, even if the motive for termination was partially, or even largely, the dealer's price-cutting activities. Many in the legal community are critical of this result, and bills periodically have been introduced in Congress to statutorily overrule *Monsanto* and *Business Electronics*. These bills have, however, encountered stiff opposition, and are unlikely to be enacted.

---

[23]SULLIVAN, HANDBOOK OF THE LAW OF ANTITRUST 419 (1977).

[24]Steiner, *Sylvania Economics, A Critique,* 60 ANTITRUST L.J. 41, 45 (1991) (emphasis in original).

[25]104 S. Ct. 1464 (1984).

[26]*Id.* at 1470–1471. (Emphasis added).

[27]108 S. Ct. 1515. (1988).

Tying Arrangements

A **tying contract** is one in which a seller agrees to sell one product (the so-called tying product) only if the buyer also purchases a second product (the tied product) from the seller. For example, a manufacturer might sell its photocopier only to buyers who also agree to buy paper from the manufacturer. In this case, the photocopier is the tying product, and the paper is the tied product. In a tying agreement, the buyer, in order to get something it wants, is required to buy something it either doesn't want or can obtain on more favorable terms from another supplier. The basis of antitrust concern over tying arrangements is that the buyer should be able to obtain the tied products or services separately if it so desires.

Applicable Statutory Provisions. Tying and other exclusive dealing contracts are governed both by §1 of the Sherman Act (as contracts in restraint of trade) and by §3 of the Clayton Act. Section 3 provides in relevant part:

> It shall be unlawful for any person engaged in commerce, in the course of such commerce, to lease or make a sale or contract for sale of goods, . . . whether patented or unpatented, . . . on the condition, agreement, or understanding that the lessee or purchaser thereof shall not use or deal in the goods . . . of a competitor or competitors of the lessor or seller, where the effect . . . may be to substantially lessen competition or tend to create a monopoly in any line of commerce.

Although §3 is theoretically more sensitive to a violation than §1 of the Sherman Act (it reaches conduct that "may" substantially lessen competition or "tend" to create a monopoly), it is more limited in scope. That is, §3 applies only to sales or leases of "goods, wares, merchandise, machinery, supplies, or other commodities"—in short, tangible personal property. It does not apply to tying or other exclusive arrangements involving services, intangible property, or land. Because §1 must be used in cases not involving goods, the judicial criteria for establishing a violation have tended to merge, whether the court is applying §1 or §3.

Purposes of Tying Arrangements. Tying arrangements often constitute a seller's attempt to use power over one product (the tying product) to obtain power over another, or otherwise distort or foreclose freedom of trade in the

second (tied) product. To effect a tying arrangement, therefore, the seller must have some market power in the tying product. That is, the seller cannot use a generic product as the tying device because buyers will simply buy substitute goods from other sellers. For example, a grocer who tells his patrons "I will sell you apples only if you also buy oranges" is not likely to foreclose competition in oranges, because buyers desiring only apples will go to another grocer. If, however, the tying product is unique, the seller may attempt to parlay its preferred position in that product into a similar position in the tied product, over which it would otherwise hold no particular competitive advantage. Buyers of the tied product are thereby injured because their preference for the seller's tying product artificially forces them to make a less than optimal choice for the tied product. Antitrust concern over tying is based on the fact that a single seller should not be able to restrict competition in a product the seller does not lawfully monopolize.

Legal Standard Governing Tying Arrangements. The legal standard governing tying arrangements under the Sherman and Clayton Acts was developed in a line of cases beginning in the mid-1930s and culminating in the 1958 landmark, *Northern Pacific Railway Company v. United States.*[28] During the 1860s Congress had granted Northern Pacific approximately 40 million acres of land in several northwestern states to facilitate railroad construction from Lake Superior to Puget Sound. By 1949, the railroad had sold over 90 percent of the land, but retained mineral rights to much of it. Most of the unsold land was leased for one purpose or another.

The suit arose out of Northern Pacific's "preferential routing" clauses contained in both its contracts leasing or selling the land. These clauses compelled the buyer or lessee to ship all commodities produced or manufactured on the land over Northern Pacific's lines provided that its rates were equal to those of competing carriers. Alternative means of transportation existed for many of the covered shipments, including two major rail carriers. The government challenged the preferential routing clause as an unlawful tying device under §1 of the Sherman Act, tying freight service (the tied product) to the sale or lease of the land (the tying product).[29]

After noting the difference between agreements or practices governed by the rule of reason and those

---

[28]78 S. Ct. 514 (1958).

[29]Note that §3 of the Clayton Act is not involved here because land and services, not goods, were the subject of the arrangement.

relegated to *per se* illegality, the Supreme Court placed tying arrangements into the *per se* category stating that tying contracts

> serve hardly any purpose beyond the suppression of competition. . . . They deny competitors free access to the market for the tied product, not because the party imposing the tying requirements has a better product or a lower price but because of his power or leverage in another market. At the same time buyers are forced to forego their free choice between competing products. For these reasons . . . tying agreements fare harshly under the laws forbidding restraints of trade. . . . They are unreasonable in and of themselves whenever a party has sufficient economic power with respect to the tying product to appreciably restrain free competition in the market for the tied product and a "not insubstantial" amount of interstate commerce is affected.[30]

As the language quoted above indicates, the Court applies a two-fold test in determining the legality of tying arrangements under antitrust law. A violation is established upon proof that (1) the defendant possesses sufficient economic power in the market for the "tying" product and (2) a substantial volume of commerce in the market for the "tied" product is restrained by the tie. Applying this test, the court found that Northern Pacific possessed substantial economic power by virtue of its extensive landholdings, using these as leverage to induce large numbers of purchasers and lessees to give it preferential treatment, thereby excluding competing carriers. Thus finding both power and foreclosure of substantial competition, the Court held Northern Pacific guilty of a *per se* Sherman Act violation.

In the following case, the Supreme Court was required to determine the legality of a tying arrangement.

Eastman Kodak Company v. Image Technical Services
112 S. Ct. 2072 (1992)

> Eastman Kodak Co. (Kodak) manufactures and sells business copying equipment, and also sells replacement parts and services the machines. In the early 1980s, a number of independent service organizations (ISOs) began to repair and ser-

---
[30]78 S. Ct. at 518.

vice Kodak equipment at prices substantially lower than Kodak's. In response, Kodak implemented a new policy of selling replacement parts only to Kodak equipment owners who used Kodak's repair and maintenance services or who serviced their own machines. Manufacturers and distributors of Kodak parts also promised not to sell them to ISOs. As parts became unavailable, some of the ISOs went out of business and others lost substantial revenues because their customers switched to Kodak for service.

Eighteen ISOs (respondents) sued Kodak alleging that it had violated §1 of the Sherman Act by unlawfully tying the sale of service for Kodak machines to the sale of parts. The federal district court entered summary judgment for Kodak but the Ninth Circuit Court of Appeals reversed. The U.S. Supreme Court granted Kodak's petition for review. The Supreme Court initially ruled that service and parts are two distinct products and that Kodak tied the sale of the two products. The Court then discussed whether Kodak's tying arrangement violated §1.

Justice Blackmun

. . . A tying arrangement is "an agreement by a party to sell one product but only on the condition that the buyer also purchases a different (or tied) product, or at least agrees that he will not purchase that product from any other supplier." [*Northern Pacific R. Co. v. United States,* 78 S. Ct. 514, 518 (1958).] Such an arrangement violates §1 of the Sherman Act if the seller has "appreciable economic power" in the tying product market and if the arrangement affects a substantial volume of commerce in the tied market. [*Fortner Enterprises, Inc. v. United States Steel Corp.,* 89 S. Ct. 1252, 1258 (1969).] Kodak did not dispute that its arrangement affects a substantial volume of interstate commerce. [Kodak], however, did challenge whether [it] . . . exercised "appreciable economic power" in the tying market. . . .

Market power is the power "to force a purchaser to do something that he would not do in a competitive market." [*Jefferson Parish Hospital Dist. No. 2 v. Hyde,* 104 S. Ct. 1551, 1559 (1984).] It has been defined as "the ability of a single seller to raise price and restrict output." [*Fortner* at 1259.] . . . The existence of such power ordinarily is inferred from the seller's possession of a predominant share of the market. . . .

Respondents contend that Kodak has more than sufficient power in the parts market to force unwanted purchases of the tied market, service. Respondents provide evidence that certain parts are available exclusively through Kodak. Respondents also assert that Kodak has control over the availability of parts it does not manufacture. According to respondents' evidence, Kodak has prohibited independent manufacturers from selling Kodak parts to ISOs, pressured Kodak equipment owners and independent parts distributors to deny ISOs the purchase of Kodak parts, and taken steps to restrict the availability of used machines.

Respondents also allege that Kodak's control over the parts market has excluded service competition, boosted service prices, and forced unwilling consumption of Kodak service. Respondents offer evidence that consumers have switched to Kodak service even though they preferred ISO service, that Kodak service was of higher price and lower quality than the preferred ISO service, and that ISOs were driven out of business by Kodak's policies. Under our prior precedents, this evidence would be sufficient to entitle respondents to a trial on their claim of market power.

Kodak counters that even if it concedes monopoly *share* of the relevant parts market, it cannot actually exercise the necessary market *power* for a Sherman Act violation. This is so, according to Kodak, because competition exists in the equipment market. Kodak argues that it could not have the ability to raise prices of service and parts above the level that would be charged in a competitive market because any increase in profits from a higher price in the aftermarkets at least would be offset by a corresponding loss in profits from lower equipment sales as consumers began purchasing equipment with more attractive service costs. . . .

[Kodak] contends that higher service prices will lead to a disastrous drop in equipment sales. Presumably, the theory's corollary is to the effect that low service prices lead to a dramatic increase in equipment sales. According to the theory, one would have expected Kodak to take advantage of lower-priced ISO service as an opportunity to expand equipment sales. Instead, Kodak adopted a restrictive sales policy consciously designed to eliminate the lower-priced ISO service, an act that would be expected to devastate either Kodak's equipment sales or Kodak's faith in its theory. Yet, according to the record, it has done neither. Service prices have risen for Kodak customers, but there is no evidence or assertion that Kodak equipment sales have dropped. . . .

Respondents offer a forceful reason why Kodak's theory, although perhaps intuitively appealing, may not accurately explain the behavior of the primary and derivative markets for complex durable goods: the existence of significant information and switching costs. These costs could create a less responsive connection between service and parts prices and equipment sales.

For the service-market price to affect equipment demand, consumers must inform themselves of the total cost of the "package"—equipment, service and parts— at the time of purchase; that is, consumers must engage in accurate lifecycle pricing. Lifecycle pricing of complex, durable equipment is difficult and costly. In order to arrive at an accurate price, a consumer must acquire a substantial amount of raw data and undertake sophisticated analysis. . . .

Given the potentially high cost of information . . . it makes little sense to assume, in the absence of any evidentiary support, that equipment-purchasing decisions are based on an accurate assessment of the total cost of equipment, service, and parts over the lifetime of the machine. . . .

A second factor undermining Kodak's claim that supracompetitive prices in the service market lead to ruinous losses in equipment sales is the cost to current owners of switching to a different product. If the cost of switching is high, consumers who already have purchased the equipment, and are thus "locked-in," will tolerate some level of service-price increases before changing equipment brands. . . . Respondents have offered evidence that the heavy initial outlay for Kodak equipment, combined with the required support material that works only with Kodak equipment, makes switching costs very high for existing Kodak customers. . . .

We conclude, then, that Kodak has failed to demonstrate that respondents' inference of market power in the service and parts markets is unreasonable, and that, consequently, Kodak is entitled to summary judgment. It is clearly reasonable to infer that Kodak has market power to raise prices and drive out competition in the aftermarkets, since respondents offer direct evidence that Kodak did so. It is also plausible, as discussed above, to infer that Kodak chose to gain immediate profits by exerting that market power where locked-in customers [and] high information costs . . . limited and perhaps eliminated any long-term loss. . . .

We need not decide whether Kodak's behavior has any procompetitive effects and, if so, whether they outweigh the anticompetitive effects. We note only that Kodak's service and parts policy is simply not one that appears always or almost always to enhance competition, and therefore to warrant a legal presumption without any evidence of its actual economic impact. In this case, when we weigh the risk of deterring procompetitive behavior by proceeding to trial against the risk that illegal behavior go unpunished, the balance tips against summary judgment. . . .

[Judgment affirmed.]

Exclusive Dealing

In an **exclusive dealing contract** a buyer agrees to deal only with a particular seller, or alternatively, not to deal in the goods of the seller's competitors. Tying arrangements are one form of exclusive dealing. In requirements contracts[31] another form of exclusive dealing, a buyer agrees to purchase all of its requirements of a given commodity from the seller. For example, P, a publisher, might contract to purchase its "requirements" (rather than a fixed quantity) of paper from a particular paper company. This arrangement involves exclusive dealing, not tied to any other product sold by the paper company.

Antitrust law is concerned with requirements contracts because they effectively prevent the seller's competitors from competing for the buyer's business. They also restrict the buyer's freedom of choice to deal with a number of suppliers. For these reasons, requirements contracts and other exclusive dealings (such as a franchise under which a retailer agrees to carry only one manufacturer's line) are, like tying contracts, subject to antitrust scrutiny under both §1 of the Sherman Act and §3 of the Clayton Act.

Requirements contracts have fared better under judicial examination than have tying arrangements. As noted by Justice Frankfurter in *Standard Oil Co. of California and Standard Stations, Inc. v. United States* (1949):

Requirements contracts . . . may well be of economic advantage to buyers as well as to sellers, and thus indirectly of advantage to the consuming public. In the case of the buyer, they may assure supply, afford protection against rises in price, enable long-term planning on the basis of known costs, and obviate the expense and risk of storage in the quantity necessary for a commodity having a fluctuating demand. From the seller's point of view, requirements contracts may make possible the substantial

reduction of selling expenses, give protection against price fluctuations, and—of particular advantage to a newcomer to the field to whom it is important to know what capital expenditures are justified—offer the possibility of a predictable market. . . . They may be useful, moreover, to a seller trying to establish a foothold against the counterattacks of entrenched competitors.[32]

Because of the significant economic advantages of requirements contracts, the judicial approach to determining their legality differs substantially from that used for tying arrangements. Tying devices may be declared illegal merely upon a showing of some market power in the tying product and foreclosure of substantial dollar amount of commerce in the tied product. In contrast, for requirements contracts, the Court has rejected simple "quantitative substantiality." An exclusive dealing arrangement does not violate §3 unless "the court believes it probable that performance of the contract will foreclose competition in a substantial share of the line of commerce affected."[33] In applying this test a court first determines the line of commerce (the type of goods or services involved), and the geographic market (the market area in which the seller operates and to which the purchaser can practically turn for suppliers). The court then determines whether the competition foreclosed by the contract constitutes a substantial share of the relevant market.

Monopolization

Section 2 of the Sherman Act specifies that it is a crime to (1) monopolize, (2) attempt to monopolize, or (3) conspire to monopolize any part of interstate or foreign commerce.

Whereas §1 of the Sherman Act is concerned with concerted or joint conduct in restraint of trade, §2 is violated when a single firm obtains or seeks to obtain a position of such size and power that it is able to assert an extreme degree of market power known as "monopoly power." Simply defined, a seller has market power if it has the power to affect the price prevailing in the market for its goods or services. Most sellers possess little or no market power because there are adequate substitutes for their products. Therefore,

---

[31]Requirements and output contracts are discussed in Chapter 16. A brief review of that material is helpful in understanding this section.

[32]69 S. Ct. 1051, 1058–1059 (1949).
[33]Tampa Electric Company v. Nashville Coal Company, 81 S. Ct. 623, 628 (1961).

although a seller without market power can sell all it wants at the prevailing market price, buyers will acquire substitute goods from other sellers if the seller attempts to charge more.

If, however, the market is dominated by a single seller, there are few, if any, adequate substitutes. Such a seller faces essentially a downward sloping demand curve for its products, similar to that representing total market demand for products produced by many sellers. Such a seller has market power. It can sell a relatively small quantity, exacting a high price for each item sold or it can sell a large quantity at a somewhat lower price. If the degree of market power has ripened into monopoly, basic microeconomic theory teaches that prices will be higher and output lower than under competitive conditions. In addition to exacting this so-called monopoly profit, which distorts allocation of resources, the monopolist may use its size and power to consolidate or expand its position by practices which operate to exclude or eliminate actual or potential competitors from the market.

The Supreme Court articulated the elements of monopolization in *United States v. Grinnell* (1966): "(1) the possession of monopoly power in a relevant market, and (2) the willful acquisition or maintenance of that power as distinguished from growth or development as a consequence of a superior product, business acumen, or historical accident."[34] The initial element in the offense of monopolization under §2 is the possession of monopoly power. "Monopoly power" is the power to fix or otherwise control price in, or exclude competition from, the relevant market. Possession of monopoly power *alone* is not, however, sufficient to establish a violation. That is, being a monopoly is not necessarily illegal. For example, monopoly may be "thrust upon" a firm because of superior business skill or efficiency, or a superior product, or because the local economy is capable of supporting only one enterprise of that type, such as a newspaper. What is forbidden is the act of monopolization, which, as noted above, requires not only proof of monopoly power in the relevant market but also that the challenged firm has deliberately followed a course of market conduct through which it has acquired or maintained that power. The plaintiff (often the government) bears the burden of proving both of the elements of the §2 offense, which are discussed later.

Possession of Monopoly Power

To determine whether the defendant possesses monopoly power, the courts use a "structural" approach first announced in 1945 by Judge Learned Hand in the celebrated case, *United States v. Aluminum Co. of America (Alcoa)*.[35] Market structure refers to a market's basic characteristics and organization. The following factors, among others, are relevant in the analysis of market structure: (1) the degree of concentration in the market — the number and size of competing firms, (2) barriers to entry — barriers may be created, for example, by patents, huge capital requirements, or exclusionary practices of existing firms, (3) the degree of product differentiation — whether consumers perceive one firm's product as a substitute for another and the manner in which differentiation is achieved, (4) the degree of product diversity, (5) the degree of vertical integration — that is, the extent to which a single firm controls successive stages of production and distribution (for example, supply of raw materials or retail outlets), and (6) industry cost structure — the relationship of fixed to variable costs.[36]

In *Alcoa*, Judge Hand used a structural analysis of the aluminum industry to determine the existence and extent of Alcoa's market power, the threshold inquiry in monopolization cases. The analysis proceeds in two steps. First, the court determines the relevant product and geographic market. Second, it computes the defendant's share of that market and uses that share as a basis for judging the extent of the defendant's market power. That is, monopoly power is inferred if the defendant controls an undue percentage of transactions occurring in the market. In addition to market share, the court also may consider a host of structural and other factors indicating the firm's power in the relevant market, such as barriers to entry; number and size of other competitors; degree of competition present in the market; actual ability of the firm to affect market prices or exclude competitors; ability of the firm to implement price discrimination; excessive profits, margins, or prices of the firm; and the firm's absolute size. Because of these other factors, no exact market share necessary to constitute monopoly power has been established, either legislatively or judicially. Cases have, for example, held 50 percent or less insufficient but 70 to 80 percent sufficient. Although the threshold percentage necessarily varies with the type and characteristics of

---

[34]86 S. Ct. 1698, 1703–1704 (1966).

[35]148 F.2d 416 (2d Cir. 1945).

[36]SULLIVAN, HANDBOOK OF THE LAW OF ANTITRUST 24–25 (1977).

a particular market, control in the 50 to 70 percent range is likely to invite antitrust scrutiny.

A significant problem with this structural approach is defining the relevant market. The defendant will attempt to expansively define the market, so that its overall percentage is low. The government will attempt to define the market narrowly so that the defendant's share is large. For example, assume Coca-Cola Company is the sole manufacturer and licensor of Coca-Cola and that the relevant geographic market is the entire world. If the product market is defined as Coca-Cola, the manufacturer controls 100 percent of the market. If it is defined as all cola drinks, the percentage drops. If defined as all soft drinks, it falls even further. If it is defined as all beverages, including, for example, coffee, tea, milk, and beer, the percentage becomes minuscule. This process of inclusion and exclusion frequently dominates monopolization cases.

Purpose and Intent to Monopolize

Determining the relevant market and the defendant's share does not end the inquiry; it is simply a standard against which the existence of monopoly power may be inferred. The second element of the monopolization offense also must be proved: a deliberate course of market conduct evidencing a purpose and intent to monopolize. Unlike the early cases, which inferred illegal intent to monopolize from predatory conduct violating §1 of the Sherman Act, under the structural approach, acts "honestly industrial" and legal in themselves also are sufficient if their effect is to exclude competitors or erect barriers to entry. For example, courts have found the following practices sufficient to constitute monopolization when practiced by a firm with monopoly power: (1) espionage or sabotage; (2) mergers; (3) reduction of output; (4) expansion of capacity or output; (5) price discrimination; (6) vertical integration; (7) tying arrangements; (8) refusals to deal; (9) supply or price "squeezes"; (10) predatory or "manipulative" research and development; (11) failure to predisclose research and development; (12) patent abuses, including fraud, patent "accumulation," and refusal to license; (13) predatory pricing; and (14) vexatious or repetitive litigation.[37]

---

[37]HOVENKAMP, ECONOMICS AND FEDERAL ANTITRUST LAW 146 (1985); For coverage of the legal standard governing predatory pricing claims, see discussion of the Robinson-Patman Act in Chapter 52.

At issue in the following case was whether the defendant's conduct evidenced a purpose and intent to monopolize.

Bonjorno v. Kaiser Aluminum and Chemical Corporation
752 F.2d 802 (3d Cir. 1984)

Columbia Metal Culvert Co., Inc. fabricated aluminum drainage pipe from corrugated aluminum sheet and aluminum coil. Between 1962 and 1972, Columbia purchased these raw materials from defendant Kaiser Aluminum and Chemical Corporation (Kaiser) through its distributor Kaiser Aluminum and Chemical Sales, Inc. (KACSI). Following a falling out with Kaiser, Columbia began purchasing its raw materials from Alcoa and Reynolds. In 1973, Kaiser opened a pipe fabrication plant a few miles from Columbia's plant and Robert Kennedy, Columbia's best salesman, left Columbia to become an independent distributor of Kaiser's aluminum pipe. In 1974, Kaiser and other major aluminum producers raised the price of aluminum sheet and coil to approximately the same price that Kaiser charged for finished aluminum pipe. Following a period of financial difficulty, Columbia stopped producing aluminum pipe in 1975. In 1978, Columbia sold its assets to a third party who then sold the remaining Columbia assets to Kaiser in 1981.

In 1974, the plaintiffs, the sole shareholders of Columbia, sued Kaiser alleging that it had violated §2 of the Sherman Act by monopolizing the aluminum drainage pipe market in the Mid-Atlantic region of the United States. The case was tried by a jury that found that Kaiser had violated §2. Kaiser appealed on the ground that the evidence was insufficient to send to the jury.

Seitz, Circuit Judge

. . . There are two main elements in monopolization: "(1) the possession of monopoly power in a relevant market, and (2) the willfull acquisition or maintenance of that power as distinguished from growth or development as a consequence of a superior product, business acumen, or historical accident." [*United States v. Grinnell,* 86 S. Ct. 1698, 1703–1704 (1966)]. . . .

Kaiser's contentions on liability in this appeal go to the question of whether there is insufficient evidence that its alleged conduct demonstrates the willful acquisition or maintenance of monopoly power. . . .

1.   *Kaiser Attempted to Control Its Competition.* There was evidence that Kaiser attempted to control

the independent fabricators by requiring them to purchase all of their raw materials from Kaiser. Mr. Bonjorno of Columbia, and Mr. Arvay of U.S. Aluminum, a South Carolina fabricator, both testified that Kaiser attempted to coerce the fabricators into purchasing only from Kaiser. There was testimony that Holmes Collins, the Kaiser manager of the division that manufactured and marketed the aluminum pipe, threatened to open a pipe fabrication plant "across the street" from Columbia if it purchased its raw materials from other sources. There were threats that if Kaiser saw so much as one pound of metal from another producer that it would terminate its relationship with Columbia. When Columbia did purchase aluminum from another company, Kaiser carried through with its threats by locating a pipe plant only 40 miles from Columbia's and by refusing to sell any more coil to Columbia. Finally, there was evidence that Holmes Collins told Columbia's owners that Kaiser would control Columbia's growth and market. . . .

2. *Kaiser's Actions to Destroy Columbia.* In addition to locating a plant near Columbia's, the plaintiffs allege that Kaiser engaged in a series of deliberate acts to drive Columbia out of the pipe market. The most serious claim is that Kaiser deliberately raised the price of the raw materials to the same level as the price that it charged for the finished pipe, thus making it impossible for Columbia to operate at a profit if it sold pipe competitively with Kaiser. The plaintiffs term this price condition a "price squeeze."

The evidence and the record show that for a significant period of time in 1974, the distributor list price of Kaiser's aluminum pipe, per pound, was just above, or even below, the market price for aluminum coil. The mere existence, however, of a "price squeeze" is not necessarily an antitrust violation. The plaintiff must present evidence that the defendants deliberately produced the effect, sufficient to provide a reasonable basis for the jury to conclude that the "squeeze" was not the result of natural market forces such as supply and demand or legitimate competition. . . .

To show that the price squeeze was a deliberate act on the part of Kaiser, the plaintiffs produced evidence that Kaiser controlled both the price of the raw material and the price of the finished pipe, and that Kaiser exercised that power. That Kaiser could control the price of the finished pipe is evident. By setting the price at which it sold to distributors, Kaiser effectively controlled the prices at which the distributors bid to contractors. Further, because of Kaiser's large market

share, it was likely that it or one of its distributors would be bidding on nearly every job. In this fashion, Kaiser, if it desired, could keep the prices of the pipe low. . . .

Kaiser was not the largest supplier of aluminum coil or sheet to independent fabricators, although if the aluminum used by its own pipe plants were included, it produced over 80 percent of the aluminum used for making pipe. Kaiser contends that since it was not the dominant force in the commodity price market for aluminum coil and sheet, it did not control the prices of the raw materials. The plaintiff's theory, however, was that Kaiser was a price leader, and that Reynolds and Alcoa, the other major aluminum producers, usually followed Kaiser's pricing strategy. Thus, Kaiser's prices would determine the market prices.

The principal evidence in support of this theory was the testimony of Professor Oliver Williamson, an economist and expert in antitrust. He testified that the aluminum industry was an oligopoly limited to a few major producers of aluminum, and that in particular lines of aluminum products, one of the producers became dominant and set the pricing strategy for the rest of the industry. He indicated that the other aluminum producers usually followed the price leader because if an aluminum producer did not comply, he would not be followed in the areas where it was dominant. He further indicated that there were economic studies that tended to show that the price leadership phenomenon was especially noticeable during the early to mid-1970s and that aluminum prices were kept high by the producers during the relevant period. Further, Dr. Williamson testified that he believed that Kaiser was the dominant firm in setting the prices for aluminum coil and sheet used in making pipe. . . . Given that Dr. Williamson's opinion was well supported by the evidence, we cannot say that the question of price leadership should not have gone to the jury.

The next question is whether the evidence shows that Kaiser deliberately manipulated the coil and pipe prices to create a squeeze. There was evidence that the squeeze was not caused by natural market forces. The most significant evidence of deliberate manipulation of the coil prices was Kaiser's withdrawal of the commodity price for coil in January of 1974. This caused a steep rise in the price of coil from about 38 cents per pound to about 44 cents per pound. . . . Kaiser's manager, Holmes Collins, testified that the commodity price was withdrawn because Kaiser no longer wished to sell to independent fabricators. Thus, Collins' testimony supported an inference that the price change was not related to costs but was intended to affect the independent competition.

Perhaps some of the strongest evidence that the price squeeze was deliberate lies in the relationship of the price of coil charged by Kaiser and its distributor price for pipe. If the coil prices charged by KACSI truly reflected the cost of the coil plus a fair return, then the price of the finished pipe should be higher by at least the fabrication cost of the pipe. However, the price of the pipe was often below the price of the coil during the first six months of 1974. Alternatively, if the price of the pipe reflected Kaiser's true costs plus a fair return, then the price of the raw material should be less by at least the cost of the fabrication. Thus, either the pipe prices were too low, or the raw material prices too high. . . .

Given these facts, there was sufficient evidence for the jury to conclude that Kaiser not only possessed the power to create the price squeeze, but that it exercised that power to destroy its competition. . . .

There is additional evidence that Kaiser sought to destroy Columbia by setting up Robert Kennedy as a distributor. There is evidence that Kaiser extended credit to Kennedy even though its credit department concluded that Kennedy's operation was an "unacceptable credit risk." . . . The jury could infer that by going against the very strong recommendation of its credit department, Kaiser displayed its intent to drive Columbia out of business. . . .

When a monopolist competes by denying a source of supply to his competitors, raises his competitor's price for raw materials without affecting his own costs, lowers his price for the finished goods, and threatens his competitors with sustained competition if they do not accede to his anticompetitive designs, then his actions have crossed the shadowy barrier of the Sherman Act . . . . Given the evidence of Kaiser's anticompetitive behavior, we hold that there was sufficient evidence to permit the monopolization claim to go to the jury.

[Judgment affirmed.]

Attempt and Conspiracy to Monopolize

Section §2 of the Sherman Act prohibits not only monopolization, but also *attempts* and *conspiracies* to monopolize. The Supreme Court has recognized each as an independent offense, distinct from monopolization.[38]

The attempted monopolization offense is based upon *Swift & Company v. United States* (1905), which has been interpreted by the Supreme Court to require proof of three elements: (1) specific intent to attain monopoly power, (2) anticompetitive or exclusionary acts directed toward accomplishing that intent, and (3) a dangerous probability of success in achieving monopoly power.[39]

Unlike monopolization, which requires only proof of general intent (intent to do the acts that are ultimately analyzed as creating or maintaining a monopoly), the attempt offense requires a *specific* intent. The defendant must exhibit an intent to destroy competition or obtain a monopoly.[40] Because the defendant will seldom announce such a design publicly, intent generally is inferred from proof of conduct that is clearly destructive of competition, and that has no social, commercial, or economic justification. Thus, predatory price-cutting or coercive refusals to deal would certainly establish the requisite intent although less aggravated conduct by an already dominant firm may suffice if the effect is to exclude competition.

The defendant's illegitimate conduct evidencing a specific intent to monopolize must create a dangerous probability of successful monopolization, which is usually established by proof that the defendant possesses a significant amount of market power. As in monopolization cases, courts determine market power by examining the defendant's market share, the structure of the industry, and other relevant factors. Generally, minimum market shares of 30 to 50 percent are required to establish dangerous probability of successful monopolization.

Conspiracy to monopolize involves an agreement by two or more firms or individuals to commit the prohibited act. Monopolization, in contrast, is concerned primarily with single-firm conduct. Conspiracy to monopolize further differs from monopolization in that (1) specific intent is required as in attempt and (2) no showing of monopoly power is required. Because it involves concerted conduct, a conspiracy to monopolize also may violate §1 of the Sherman Act as a conspiracy in restraint of trade.

---

[38]Attempt to monopolize was recognized as a separate offense in *Swift & Company v. United States,* 25 S. Ct. 276 (1905), and conspiracy to monopolize was so recognized in *American Tobacco Co. v. United States,* 66 S. Ct. 1125 (1946).

[39]Spectrum Sports, Inc. v. McQuillan, 113 S. Ct. 884 (1993).

[40]Times-Picayune Pub. Co. v. United States, 73 S. Ct. 872, 890 (1953).

Summary

1.   Section 1 of the Sherman Act declares contracts, combinations, and conspiracies in restraint of trade to be illegal. It prohibits only unreasonable restraints of trade, and violations are generally analyzed under the rule of reason. Inherently anticompetitive and unreasonable conduct, however, may be condemned under §1 without any elaborate inquiry into its reasonableness or business justification. That is, the Supreme Court has held that certain specific practices or business relationships are so inherently anticompetitive that they are unreasonable *per se*.

2.   Trade restraints governed by §1 are of two types: horizontal and vertical. A horizontal restraint is an agreement among competitors or persons at the same functional level. A vertical restraint exists between persons in a buyer-seller or supplier-supplied relationship.

3.   Horizontal restraints governed by §1 include price-fixing, division of markets, and concerted refusals to deal. Price-fixing and division of markets have long been treated as *per se* violations of the Act. Although some concerted refusals to deal are *per se* illegal, others are governed by rule of reason analysis.

4.   Vertical restraints judged under §1 include resale price maintenance, nonprice vertical restraints (such as territory, location, and customer restrictions), and tying and other exclusive dealing contracts. Although resale price maintenance has long been a *per se* Sherman Act violation, nonprice vertical restraints now are judged by the rule of reason. Although certain tying arrangements also have been ruled *per se* illegal, not every refusal to sell two products separately has automatically been condemned. Unlike tying contracts, other exclusive dealing arrangements, such as requirements contracts, receive a more considered judicial treatment involving market definition and analysis of competitive impact. Tying and other exclusive dealing contracts are judged both under §1 of the Sherman Act and §3 of the Clayton Act.

5.   The offense of monopolization under §2 of the Sherman Act has two elements: (1) the possession of monopoly power in the relevant market and (2) the willful acquisition or maintenance of that power as distinguished from growth or development as a consequence of a superior product, business acumen, or historic accident. Although early cases used a "conduct" approach for violation, modern cases analyze market structure.

6.   Section 2 of the Sherman Act prohibits not only monopolization, but also attempts and conspiracies to monopolize.

Key Terms

rule of reason
per se violation
horizontal restraint
vertical restraint
cartel
price-fixing
group boycott (concerted
   refusal to deal)

conscious parallelism
resale price maintenance
franchise
tying contract
exclusive dealing contract

Questions and Problems

51.1   A group of independent grocery store chains desired to sell "house brand" or "private label" products to enable them to better compete with national and regional supermarket chains. Because none of the independent operations was large enough to market a house brand alone, they formed Topco to act as purchasing agent for goods to bear the Topco brand and to license the individual members to sell those products. Topco purchased products bearing the brand from packers and distributed them to participating stores. Ultimately, over 1,000 different items bearing the Topco name were marketed through member supermarket chains. The members completely controlled Topco's operations. Topco's by-laws provided for exclusive or in fact exclusive territorial licenses. Members were authorized to sell Topco products in a specific geographic territory and were precluded from selling outside that territory. Existing licensees also had an effective veto power over admission of a new member into their area. Thus, the members effectively divided up the geographic market for Topco products and had the ability to prevent another licensee from competing in their respective territories. Does this arrangement violate the Sherman Act as a division of markets because it effectively prohibits competition in Topco-brand products among member retail grocery chains?

51.2   Radiant Burners, Inc. manufactured and sold the "Radiant Burner," a ceramic gas burner for use in heating houses and other buildings. American Gas Association (a trade association including public utilities, gas pipeline companies, and manufacturers of gas burners) maintained laboratories in which it tested the safety, utility, and durability of gas burners. After successful testing, the Association affixed a "seal of approval" that was important to burner manufacturers since utilities would not supply gas to unapproved burners. The Association failed to approve the plaintiff's "Radiant Burner." Does American Gas Association's refusal to approve the "Radiant Burner" violate §1 of the Sherman Act? What additional facts regarding the "seal of approval" process would be important in making this determination?

51.3 A basketball player was suspended indefinitely by the National Basketball Association for betting on league games. He sued, alleging that the league and its members had engaged in an illegal boycott. Is the player correct?

51.4 The American Medical Association (AMA), a professional organization whose members comprise the majority of medical physicians in the United States, issues a code of ethics that is binding on its members. Principle 3 of the AMA's Principles of Medical Ethics provided: "A physician should practice a method of healing found on a scientific basis; and he should not voluntarily associate with anyone who violates this principle." In 1963, the AMA established its Committee on Quackery, a group that worked to eliminate chiropractic, a system of treating disease through manipulation and adjustment of body structures such as the spinal column. Although evidence existed supporting the belief that chiropractic was unscientific, countervailing evidence also showed that chiropractic was effective, and perhaps even more effective than the medical profession, in treating certain kinds of medical problems, such as back injuries. In 1966, the AMA House of Delegates passed a resolution labeling chiropractic an unscientific cult. Thus, under Principle 3, AMA physicians were prohibited from voluntarily associating with chiropractors by: referring patients to chiropractors; accepting referrals from chiropractors; providing diagnostic, laboratory, or radiology services to chiropractors; teaching chiropractors; or practicing with chiropractors. During the following years, the AMA encouraged medical boards and associations not to associate with chiropractors. A widely distributed article published in the AMA Journal warned hospitals that they might lose AMA accreditation if the hospitals dealt with chiropractors. Despite the AMA's efforts, chiropractic eventually became licensed in all 50 states. In addition, although medical physicians acted in conformity with Principle 3, the AMA never sanctioned or disciplined a member for violating it.

In 1976, four licensed chiropractors sued the AMA and its members alleging that they had conspired to eliminate the chiropractic profession in violation of §1 of the Sherman Act. The plaintiffs claimed that the AMA's use of Principle 3 constituted a group boycott of chiropractors.

Discuss the legal principles that will govern resolution of the case. Who should prevail? Is the AMA's conduct per se illegal? Apply the rule of reason to the AMA's conduct. Is the AMA's conduct illegal under the rule of reason? Explain.

51.5 General Electric "consigned" electric lamps to independent retail dealers, thereby fixing the price at which the dealers sold to consumers. The dealers assumed all expenses of storage, cartage, transportation, handling, sale, and distribution of the lamps. General Electric, on the other hand, paid the cost of shipment to the dealer and assumed the risk of loss (for example, due to fire, flood, obsolescence, or price decline), insured the goods, and paid all taxes assessed upon them. Does General Electric's consignment arrangement violate §1 of the Sherman Act? Explain.

51.6 Philips Corp. introduced Norelco brand rotary shavers in 1948 and has an estimated market share of 90 percent. In 1984, Windmere entered the market by selling rotary shavers made in Japan and sold under the Ronson trademark at a price lower than Philips shavers. Windmere sold one model for $34.99 and another for $22.

After Windmere's market entry, Philips introduced its model 1320 at a distributor price of $27.08, about 31 percent less than the $39 price at which the same razor had been sold as the model 1312 four years earlier and about 23 percent less than the comparable Ronson model. Philips also dropped the price of its model 1615 about 35 percent to a distributor price of $18.03, which was almost $4 less than the distributor price for Ronson's comparable corded rotary shaver. In December 1985, Windmere announced its withdrawal from the rotary shaver market, but continued to make other electric shavers. Shortly thereafter, Philips discontinued the sale of its model 1320 and 1615 rotary shavers.

Windmere sued, alleging that Philips had monopolized and attempted to monopolize the electric rotary shaver market in violation of Sherman Act §2 through predatory pricing. Discuss the legal principles that will govern Windmere's (1) monopolization and (2) attempted monopolization claim.

CHAPTER 52

THE CLAYTON ACT AND FEDERAL TRADE COMMISSION ACT

As outlined in Chapter 50, the Clayton Act contains four substantive provisions including §2, as amended by the Robinson-Patman Act, prohibiting price discrimination by a seller among various buyers in certain circumstances; §3, testing the legality of tying and other exclusive dealing arrangements; §7, prohibiting certain corporate mergers; and §8, prohibiting a person from simultaneously serving on the board of directors of two or more competing corporations in certain circumstances. With the exception of §3 (which was discussed in Chapter 51 in conjunction with vertical restraints of trade), each of these provisions is covered in the material that follows. The chapter concludes with a discussion of the role of §5 of the Federal Trade Commission Act in antitrust enforcement and consumer protection.

Price Discrimination — The Robinson-Patman Act

Section 2 of the Clayton Act, as amended in 1936 by the Robinson-Patman Act, prohibits price discrimination under certain circumstances. Price discrimination occurs when a seller charges one buyer more than another for the same commodity. Discrimination by a seller among its buyers, like the vertical restraints discussed in the previous chapter, may have anticompetitive impact at both the seller and buyer levels. For example, a seller operating in a number of markets may cut its price in one market in order to drive out local competition, while maintaining a higher price elsewhere. Such "predatory" pricing affects competitors of the discriminating seller (that is, injury occurs at the functional level horizontal to the seller) and causes **primary line competitive injury,** or injury at the same functional level as the discriminating seller.

On the other hand, discrimination may affect competition at the buyer's level. For example, assume a manufacturer ordinarily sells its widgets to retailers for $10. A large retailer that purchases in huge quantity is able to coerce the manufacturer into selling to it for $8. The manufacturer continues to sell to small retailers for $10. As a result of the discrimination the large buyer is able to undercut its competition in the market for resale of the goods. In this case, competitive injury occurs at the **secondary line,** among buyers at a functional level below (or vertical to) the discriminating seller. If the buyer receiving the discrimination itself resells (for example, a wholesaler receiving a discrimination passes the lower price onto its retail buyers), competition may be affected two functional levels below the discriminating seller. In this case, injury occurs to competitors of the buyer's customers and is known as **third line** or **tertiary line** injury.

As originally drafted in 1914, §2 was intended to reach only primary line discrimination—predatory, geographic price-cutting. After the First World War, however, mass buyers, including mail-order houses and chain stores, began to appear in the American marketplace. Aided partially by discriminatory price concessions from suppliers that were beyond the reach of §2, these large buyers were able to undercut independent retailers, jeopardizing their existence. Following a Federal Trade Commission inquiry, in 1936 Congress passed the **Robinson-Patman Act,**[1] which amended original §2 of the Clayton Act to reach secondary competitive effects and to outlaw certain of the more flagrant devices used by the chains to exact price concessions. Note that unlike other antitrust laws, the Robinson-Patman Act is primarily concerned with protection of small competitors, not competitive structure or process. The vast majority of Robinson-Patman Act cases decided since 1936 involve claims of secondary line injury.

The principal government enforcement body for the Act is the FTC, which proceeds against violators either informally or through the formal complaint procedure that may result in issuance of a cease and desist order. Robinson-Patman enforcement also may be undertaken by the Department of Justice. Neither government agency has actively enforced the Act for many years. As a result, virtually all modern Robinson-Patman Act cases are brought by private plaintiffs injured by price discrimination who maintain treble damage actions authorized under §4 of the Clayton Act.

As amended by the Robinson-Patman Act, Clayton Act §2 contains six subsections, §§2(a) through 2(f).[2] These provisions are discussed later beginning with the elements of the "*prima facie*" case.

---

[1] 15 U.S.C. §§13(a)–13(f).

[2] The Act contains an additional provision, §3, which makes certain price discrimination a criminal offense. 15 U.S.C. §13a.

The *Prima Facie* Case—§2(a)

Section 2(a) is the heart of the Robinson-Patman Act, stating the elements, which if proven, and in the absence of a defense, establish a violation (the "*prima facie*" case). Section 2(a) states in part:

> It shall be unlawful for any person engaged in commerce, in the course of such commerce, either directly or indirectly, to discriminate in price between different purchasers of commodities of like grade and quality, where either or any of the purchases involved in such discrimination are in commerce . . . , and where the effect of such discrimination may be substantially to lessen competition or tend to create a monopoly in any line of commerce, or to injure, destroy, or prevent competition with any person who either grants or knowingly receives the benefit of such discrimination, or with customers of either of them.

To facilitate discussion of §2(a), the text that follows divides the statutory language into a series of shorter, more manageable phrases, and examines each separately.

The "In Commerce" Requirement. The Robinson-Patman Act imposes a stringent in commerce requirement. The person charged with price discrimination (normally the seller) must be "engaged in commerce," the discrimination must occur "in the course of such commerce," and "either or any of the purchases involved in such discrimination" must be in commerce. Taken collectively, these three commerce-related requirements mean that at least one of the sales challenged as part of a pattern of price discrimination must cross a state boundary. Thus, a defendant with strictly intrastate sales is beyond the reach of the statute.

Discrimination in Price. The Act makes it illegal "either directly or indirectly, to discriminate in price." Indirect price discrimination comes in many forms. For example, a seller, although selling the same goods to different buyers at the same price, may give one purchaser more favorable credit or delivery terms, return privileges, or product-related services. Certain indirect forms of price discrimination effectuated through preferential brokerage, advertising, or promotional allowances are addressed explicitly in §§2(c) through 2(e) of the Act, discussed later. Even without these sections, however, the conduct involved would be subject to attack under §2(a) as an indirect form of price discrimination.

The Robinson-Patman Act specifically reaches the quantity discount, a major form of price discrimination. Quantity discounts are lower prices charged to buyers of large quantities of the seller's product. A stated purpose of the Robinson-Patman Act was to limit

the use of quantity price differentials to the sphere of actual cost differences, Otherwise, such differentials would become instruments of favor and privilege and weapons of competitive oppression.[3]

To violate the statute, the discrimination in price must be "between different purchasers." Thus, the Act applies only to sales,[4] not to leases, agency or consignment arrangements, licenses, or refusals to deal (that is, selling to one firm while refusing to deal with another).[5]

Commodities of Like Grade and Quality. The Act requires that the discriminatory sales be "of commodities of like grade and quality." Because Robinson-Patman applies only to sales of "commodities" (tangible personal property), it does not reach price discrimination in the sale of services or of intangibles such as advertising.

The "like grade and quality" requirement has generated many interpretation problems. Though sales of goods with "actual and genuine physical differentiations" at different prices are clearly beyond the reach of the Act,[6] how should the law treat physically identical goods that are differentiated solely because one carries a popular brand name and the other does not? The Supreme Court addressed this question directly in 1966 in *Federal Trade Commission v. Borden Company.*[7]

In this case, Borden produced and sold its evaporated milk under the "Borden" name, a nationally advertised brand. It also sold evaporated milk under private brand names owned by certain of its customers. Although all milk distributed under the Borden name was physically and chemically identical, the private label milk regularly sold at lower prices than the Borden brand milk. The FTC found the milk sold under the Borden and private labels to be of "like grade and quality," held the price differential discriminatory in violation of the Robinson-Patman Act, and issued a cease and desist order. The Court of Appeals reversed, holding that, as a matter of law, the customer label milk was not of the same grade and quality as Borden's brand. The Supreme Court reversed and remanded, holding that when physical differences between products are trivial or nonexistent, they are of "like grade and quality," even though sold under different brand names or labels with varying consumer acceptance. As noted by the Court:

If two products, physically identical but differently branded, are to be deemed of different grade because the seller regularly and successfully markets some quantity of both at different prices, the seller could, as far as §2(a) is concerned, make either product available to some customers and deny it to others, however discriminatory this might be and however damaging to competition. Those who were offered only one of the two products would be barred from competing for those customers who want or might buy the other. The retailer who was permitted to buy and sell only the more expensive brand would have no chance to sell to those who always buy the cheaper product or to convince others, by experience or otherwise, of the fact which he and all other dealers already know—that the cheaper product is actually identical with that carrying the more expensive label.[8]

Thus, under *Borden,* "the economic factors inherent in brand names and national advertising should not be considered in the jurisdictional inquiry under the statutory 'like grade and quality' test."[9] In other words, physically identical goods are of like grade and quality, regardless of market acceptance. As such, sales of these goods at different prices are within the reach of Robinson-Patman Act §2(a), and further inquiry is then made to determine whether the arrangement is discriminatory, having an adverse effect on competition.

Anticompetitive Effect. As the final element of the prima facie case, the Robinson-Patman Act requires examination of the competitive impact of the challenged conduct. A price discrimination meeting the foregoing requirements is illegal if its effect "may be substantially to lessen

---

[3]H. R. Rep. No. 2287, 74th Cong., 2d Sess. 9 (1936).

[4]Sales to certain purchasers, such as governmental bodies or nonprofit institutions, are exempt. A seller may therefore charge such buyers a lower price than its other customers without violating the Act.

[5]A proviso to §2(a) provides that "nothing herein contained shall prevent persons engaged in selling goods . . . from selecting their own customers in bona fide transactions and not in restraint of trade."

[6]Report of the Attorney General's National Committee to Study the Antitrust Laws 158 (1955).

[7]86 S. Ct. 1092 (1966).

[8]*Id.* at 1097.

[9]*Id.* at 1098, quoting Report of the Attorney General's National Committee to Study the Antitrust Laws 158 (1955).

competition or tend to create a monopoly in any line of commerce." This test parallels that contained in Clayton Act §§3 and 7, and original §2, and requires analysis of adverse competitive effect in the overall relevant market. Additionally, in language unique to the Robinson-Patman Act, violation also results if the effect of the discrimination may be to injure, prevent, or destroy competition (1) with the discriminating seller (primary line injury), or (2) among customers of the discriminating seller (secondary line injury), or (3) among customers of customers of the discriminating seller (third or tertiary line injury). The Act thus explicitly addresses secondary line injury as well as primary line injury. Further, by focusing upon the impact of discrimination on competitors, rather than competition, the new test eliminates the need for exhaustive market analysis in every case. For this reason, many Robinson-Patman cases use this test in establishing a violation.

In primary line cases, the plaintiff typically alleges injury resulting from the defendant's predatory pricing. The essence of the claim is that the defendant "has priced its products in an unfair manner with an object to eliminate or retard competition and thereby gain and exercise control over prices in the relevant market."[10] Predatory pricing may be challenged either under the Robinson-Patman Act or under §2 of the Sherman Act (for example, as an attempt to monopolize). To recover under either statute, the plaintiff must prove (1) that the prices charged are below the defendant's cost, and (2) that once competition is eliminated, the defendant has a reasonable prospect of recouping (in the form of later monopoly profits) its investment in below-cost prices.[11] Because these elements are extremely difficult to prove, plaintiffs rarely recover in primary line cases.

In secondary line cases, the court examines the effect of price differentials on competition among customers of the discriminating seller. In sharp contrast to the difficult proof problems encountered in primary-line cases, both the FTC and the courts have generally assumed that in a secondary line case *any* price discrimination has the requisite anticompetitive effect. That is, the mere showing that competing buyers were charged different prices generally is sufficient to establish a *prima facie* Robinson-Patman violation in a secondary-line case. Despite this almost *per se* standard, price discriminations

found illegal tend to be substantial in amount, systematic and continuing, and involve items for which resale profit margins are low and competition keen. Additionally, there must be proof that the buyers involved are in competition both at the functional level (manufacturer, wholesaler, or retailer) and in the geographic area.

In the following case, the court was required to determine whether there was sufficient proof of competitive injury to establish a Robinson-Patman Act violation.

Falls City Industries, Inc. v. Vanco Beverage, Inc.
103 S. Ct. 1282 (1983)

> Between 1972 and 1978, Falls City Industries, Inc. (Falls City) sold its beer to Vanco Beverage, Inc. (Vanco), the sole wholesale distributor for Falls City Beer in Evansville, Indiana, at a higher price than it charged its wholesale distributor, Dawson Springs, Inc. (Dawson Springs) in Henderson, Kentucky. The two cities form a single metropolitan area across a state line. The two distributors did not compete for sales to the same retailers because Indiana law prohibited Indiana wholesalers from selling to out-of-state retailers and Indiana retailers were prohibited from buying from out-of-state wholesalers. Indiana law also required brewers to sell to all Indiana wholesalers at a single price. Because Dawson Springs passed its cost savings on to retailers, Falls City's pricing policy resulted in lower retail beer prices in Henderson than in Evansville. Accordingly, many Indiana consumers crossed the border to purchase cheaper beer in Kentucky. As a result, Vanco sold less beer to Indiana retailers than would have been sold had Vanco been able to charge a competitive price.
>
> Vanco sued Falls City alleging that its pricing policy violated the Robinson-Patman Act. Both the trial court and the Court of Appeals found that Vanco had established a *prima facie* case of illegal price discrimination. The Supreme Court granted certiorari.

Justice Blackmun

. . . To establish a *prima facie* violation of §2(a), one of the elements a plaintiff must show is a reasonable possibility that a price difference may harm competition. . . . This reasonable possibility of harm is often referred to as competitive injury. . . .

Falls City contends that the Court of Appeals erred in relying on *FTC v. Morton Salt Co.,* [68 S. Ct. 822 (1948)], to uphold the District Court's finding of competitive injury. In *Morton Salt* this Court held that, for the

---

[10]Brooke Group Ltd. v. Brown & Williamson Tobacco Corp., 113 S. Ct. 2578, 2587 (1993).

[11]*Id.* at 2587–2588.

purposes of §2(a), injury to competition is established *prima facie* by proof of a substantial price discrimination between competing purchasers over time. . . . In the absence of direct evidence of displaced sales, this inference may be overcome by evidence breaking the causal connection between a price differential and lost sales or profits. . . .

According to Falls City, the *Morton Salt* rule should be applied only in cases involving "large buyer preference or seller predation." . . . Falls City does not, however, suggest any economic reason why *Morton Salt's* . . . inference should not apply when the favored competitor is not extraordinarily large. Although concerns about the excessive market power of large purchasers were primarily responsible for passage of the Robinson-Patman Act, . . . the Act "is of general applicability and prohibits discriminations generally." *FTC v. Sun Oil Co.,* [83 S. Ct. 358, 368 (1963)]. . . .

The *Morton Salt* rule was not misapplied in this case. In a strictly literal sense, this case differs from *Morton Salt* because Vanco and Dawson Springs did not compete with each other at the wholesale level; Vanco sold only to Indiana retailers and Dawson Springs sold only to Kentucky retailers. But the competitive injury component of a Robinson-Patman Act violation is not limited to the injury to competition between the favored and the disfavored purchaser; it also encompasses the injury to competition between their customers—in this case the competition between Kentucky retailers and Indiana retailers who, under a District Court finding not challenged in this Court, were selling in a single, interstate retail market.

After observing that Falls City had maintained a substantial price difference between Vanco and Dawson Springs over a significant period of time, the Court of Appeals, like the District Court, considered the evidence that Vanco's loss of Falls City beer sales was attributable to factors other than the price difference, particularly the marketwide decline of Falls City beer. Both courts found it likely that this overall decline accounted for some—or even most—of Vanco's lost sales. Nevertheless, if some of Vanco's injury was attributable to the price discrimination, Falls City is responsible to that extent. . . .

The Court of Appeals agreed with the District Court's findings that "the major reason for the higher Indiana retail beer prices was the higher prices charged Indiana distributors," and "the lower retail prices in Henderson County attracted Indiana customers away from Indiana retailers, thereby causing the retailers to

curtail purchases from Vanco." 654 F.2d, at 1229. These findings were supported by direct evidence of diverted sales, and more than established the competitive injury required for a *prima facie* case under §2(a). . . .

[Although the Court affirmed the Court of Appeals' holding that Vanco had established a *prima facie* case, it vacated and remanded the judgment on other grounds.]

Brokerage and Promotional Allowances

Before the Robinson-Patman Act was passed, large buyers obtained competitive advantages over smaller purchasers in several ways other than through direct reductions in price. One method commonly used was to set up a "dummy" broker, employed by the buyer who, in many cases, rendered no services. The buyer then demanded that the seller pay "brokerage" to these fictitious brokers who then turned it over to the buyer. Another method of disguising price discrimination was to provide large buyers with more favorable promotional allowances or services (such as advertising, instore displays, and special packaging) than those provided to other customers. To curb these specific abuses, Congress enacted §§2(c), 2(d), and 2(e), supplementing the basic price discrimination prohibitions of §2(a). The scope and operation of these provisions are discussed below.

Brokerage Under §2(c). Section 2(c) makes it unlawful for a buyer to exact price concessions through brokerage commissions paid to itself or its agents. More specifically, the statute makes it unlawful for any person either to pay or to receive anything of value as a commission, brokerage, or other compensation, except for services rendered in connection with the purchase or sale of goods.

Section 2(c) is self-contained and effectively imposes a rule of *per se* illegality on conduct within its scope. For example, the defenses available to a §2(a) charge do not apply to §2(c) actions, and no showing of anticompetitive effect is required under §2(c). Also, unlike §2(a), §2(c) requires only one transaction (commonly a payment by the seller to the buyer's broker) to establish violation. In short, the seller may generally legally make payments only to an independent broker retained and controlled by the seller. Most cases have held that only the seller's broker renders any real services within the meaning of the statute.[12]

Promotional Allowances and Services Under §§2(d) and 2(e). In addition to prohibiting price discrimination disguised as brokerage, the Robinson-Patman Act also prevents indirect price discrimination through discriminatory promotional allowances under §2(d), and services under §2(e). Allowances or services covered by the Act take many forms including advertising, catalogues, demonstrations, in-store displays and demonstrations, special packaging, warehouse facilities, accepting returns for credit, prizes, or merchandise used in promotional contests, or any other service designed to promote resale of the product.

Sections 2(d) and 2(e) are similar in operation to §2(a) in that they prohibit discriminatory treatment of purchasers who compete in the resale of the goods for which the promotional allowances or services are provided. To avoid Robinson-Patman liability, any promotional allowances or services granted by the seller must be made "available on proportionally equal terms" to all competing purchasers.

The concept of "availability" involves two elements. First, the seller must take affirmative steps to notify all competing buyers of the various types of promotional assistance offered by the seller. Second, the type of program offered by the seller must be usable by all competing customers. It is of little use to a buyer to be notified of a program that, though nominally available to all, is in fact limited only to large buyers. For example, a seller may offer to reimburse customers for a portion of television advertising expenses. If some customers are too small to use television advertising and no comparable benefits are provided these purchasers, the seller violates §2(d). Similarly, a seller would violate the Act by providing in-store demonstrators, who because of sales volume are practically available only to large department stores.

Assuming promotional allowances and services are "available," they must be furnished on "proportionally equal terms." Although no single method is prescribed by law, this requirement can generally be satisfied by "basing the payments made or the services furnished on the dollar volume or on the quantity of the product purchased during a specified period."[13] For example,

assume during a given year S sells $10,000 worth of goods for resale to B, and $20,000 to B1. If S provides promotional services or allowances with a cost of $500 to B, it should provide $1,000 to B1.

Defenses to a Robinson-Patman Act Violation

Proof of a *prima facie* case of price discrimination under §2(a) does not necessarily result in liability. The seller may avoid the consequences of the discrimination by proving one of three defenses: the "cost justification" defense, the "meeting competition" defense, or the "changing conditions" defense. The burden of proving a defense is on the discriminating seller. That is, they are "affirmative" defenses.

The "Cost Justification" Defense. The Robinson-Patman Act does not prohibit price discrimination that is cost justified or that reflects differences in the cost of selling to different purchasers. Specifically, the Act contains a proviso[14] to §2(a) that

> [n]othing herein contained shall prevent [price] differentials which make only due allowance for differences in the cost of manufacture, sale, or delivery, resulting from the differing methods or quantities in which such commodities are to such purchasers sold or delivered.[15]

Although the Act broadly authorizes a seller to pass on cost savings whether occurring in the manufacture or distribution of the goods, in most cases the alleged savings result from lower distribution or direct-selling costs. Some of the distribution costs that may vary among customers include transportation, warehousing and storage, sales promotion and advertising, administrative salaries and expenses, and special services to the customer.

Although, when comparing customers, the *existence* of savings in cost is evident, the *amount* of savings frequently is very difficult to prove because cost accounting

---

[12]Most cases have held that a buyer's broker does not render services to the seller, even if it performs some function, such as warehousing or breaking bulk.

[13]FTC Guides, 16 C.F.R. §240.9.

[14]A "proviso" is a clause or part of a clause contained in a statute that either excepts something from the enacting clause, qualifies, modifies, or restrains its generality, or excludes some possible ground of misinterpretation concerning its extent. BLACK'S LAW DICTIONARY 1225 (6th ed. 1990). Provisos usually are preceded by the words "provided," "provided that," or "provided, however." In the Robinson-Patman Act, provisos are used to introduce the defenses.

[15]Note that cost justification is a defense only to violations of §2(a) and §2(f) (relating to buyer liability). It does not provide a shield against discriminatory brokerage payments or disproportionate promotional allowances and services under §§2(c), 2(d), and 2(e).

in distribution is expensive and inexact. Many costs must be allocated in any attempt to prove the cost of serving a particular customer, and the FTC has not been content with accounting estimates based on ordinary business records. A detailed cost study is required, involving perhaps stopwatch studies of time spent by personnel such as salesmen or truck drivers, and other quantitative measurement of the business operation. These problems led the Supreme Court to lament, "Proof of a cost justification being what it is, too often no one can ascertain whether a price is cost-justified."[16]

The problem of proof, coupled with the fact that Robinson-Patman coverage may be avoided altogether by relatively minor changes in "grade and quality," explain why the cost justification defense has been rarely invoked as a defense.

Functional Discounts. Frequently, manufacturers distribute their products through both wholesalers and retailers, and charge the wholesalers less as compensation for the distribution function they perform. Although such "functional discounts" would appear to be governed by the cost justification defense, the Supreme Court has not imposed such a rigorous standard in judging their legality. Rather, the Court has held that legitimate functional discounts, involving a reasonable reimbursement for actual marketing functions, do not cause the substantial lessening of competition between the wholesaler's customers and the supplier's direct customers necessary to establish a prima facie violation of the Act. A violation may be established, however, if the alleged functional discount is not reasonably related either to the supplier's savings or the wholesaler's costs.[17]

The "Meeting Competition" Defense. The "meeting competition" defense, contained in §2(b), provides that a seller may escape liability by showing that

> his lower price or the furnishing of services or facilities to any purchaser or purchasers was made in good faith to meet an equally low price of a competitor, or the services or facilities furnished by a competitor.

The "meeting competition" defense is available in an action for price discrimination under §2(a) or for disproportionate promotional allowances and services under §§2(d) and 2(e) respectively. Meeting competition is not a defense to discriminatory brokerage payments violating §2(c). Like cost justification, meeting competition is an affirmative defense, difficult to prove, and made more difficult by a restrictive FTC view of its application.

The effect of the meeting competition defense is to allow the seller to lower its price to one customer to meet the competition without lowering its price to all customers. Because of the difficulty in drawing a workable line between "new" and "old" customers, courts have held that if a reduction is made in good faith to match a competitor's price, the meeting competition defense is available either to retain an existing customer or to acquire new customers. To establish the defense the seller must show that the lower price in issue is its competitor's price, not the lower price of its buyer's competitor. For example, assume S sells goods for resale to B, X, Y, and Z. B2, a competitor of B but not a customer of S, substantially undercuts B's price. S may not, consistent with the meeting competition defense, lower its price to B alone (that is, to B but not to X, Y, and Z) to meet B2's competition. The defense, if applicable, would allow S to lower its price to B to meet a price offered to B by a seller in competition with S.

The "Changing Conditions" Defense.   The last proviso to §2(a) provides that the Act is not designed to prohibit price differentials made in response to changing conditions affecting either the market for, or the marketability of, the goods concerned. The proviso gives examples of such changing conditions including actual or imminent deterioration of perishable goods, obsolescence of seasonal goods, distress sales under court process, and sales discontinuing business in the goods concerned.

The defense envisions two separate situations justifying price differentials. First, changing market conditions, and second, an alteration in the marketability of the product. Defendants have been much more successful using the defense in the second case, when the desirability of the product itself is diminished. Examples include reducing prices on 2002 automobiles once the 2003 models are introduced, or on fruits and vegetables in danger of spoiling.

The marketability of most products varies over time, or depends upon the time of year in which the goods (for example, Christmas ornaments) are sold. As a result, a seller charging different prices on sales widely separated in time may not be engaged in price discrimination prohibited by the Robinson-Patman Act. That is, an implied element of the prima facie case under §2(a) is that the different prices creating the discrimination must be charged in transactions reasonably contemporaneous in time.

---

[16]Automatic Canteen Co. v. Federal Trade Commission, 73 S. Ct. 1017, 1027 (1953).

[17]Texaco, Inc. v. Hasbrouck, 110 S. Ct. 2535 (1990).

Buyer Liability Under the Robinson-Patman Act

To this point the discussion has concerned statutory liability of sellers engaged in discriminatory pricing practices. The following material discusses the provisions penalizing buyers for their involvement in such discrimination: §§2(f) and 2(c) of the Robinson-Patman Act, and §5 of the FTC Act.

Buyer Liability for Inducing or Receiving Price Discrimination—§2(f). Section 2(f) of the Act provides:

> It shall be unlawful for any person engaged in commerce, in the course of such commerce, knowingly to induce or receive a discrimination in price which is prohibited by this section.

Thus, liability for illegal price discrimination under §2(a) extends both to the seller granting the discrimination and to any buyer knowingly receiving it.

Section 2(f) is, in essence, a corollary to §2(a), and liability is derivative. That is, a buyer cannot be held liable under §2(f) if a *prima facie* case under §2(a) could not be established against the seller or if the seller has an affirmative defense, such as cost justification or meeting competition. In either case, there is no price discrimination "prohibited by this section" triggering §2(f) liability.

Buyer Liability Under §§2(c), 2(d), and 2(e). Buyer liability also is imposed for receiving brokerage on promotional allowances and services in violation of §§2(c), 2(d), or 2(e) respectively.

Section 2(c), as previously noted, is self-contained and explicitly provides that it is unlawful either "to pay or grant, or to receive or accept" an unlawful brokerage. Thus, the prohibition applies both to buyers and sellers.

Sections 2(d) and 2(e) are explicitly aimed at sellers and make no mention of buyer liability. Early decisions nevertheless held §2(f) applicable to discriminatory promotional allowances and services even though §2(f) explicitly reaches only "discrimination in price." More recently the FTC has attacked buyers receiving discriminatory promotional allowances and services under §5 of the FTC Act as an unfair method of competition.

Mergers — Clayton Act §7

The antitrust movement grew in the late 1800s out of widespread concern over the competitive abuses of the early consolidations of industrial power, the trusts. Thus, antitrust is concerned not only with anticompetitive activities of competitors or buyers and sellers, but also with the permanent consolidation of previously separate enterprises into a single economic entity.

Antitrust analysis commonly uses the term "merger" to describe such a union. For antitrust purposes, "merger" is broadly defined. It generally makes no difference whether either or both corporations survive as a matter of state corporation law. The terms "merger," "consolidation," "acquisition," and "amalgamation" may generally be used interchangeably. The characteristic of antitrust concern is the imposition of unified control upon previously independent business entities.

Introduction to Merger Law

Mergers Classified. Mergers usually are classified and analyzed according to the business or market relationship of the parties. These classifications are useful in analyzing the competitive impact of a merger and will be used throughout the following discussion. A **horizontal merger** is one between former competitors. A **vertical merger** occurs when a firm acquires a supplier or customer. If a business acquires a supplier, it is said to vertically integrate "backward" or "upstream." Conversely, when a firm acquires a customer (for example, a manufacturer acquiring a chain of retail outlets), "forward" or "downstream" vertical integration occurs. A **conglomerate merger** involves parties who were neither former competitors nor in the same supply chain. Each type of merger outlined above may be subject to antitrust attack. Although mergers may be scrutinized under §1 of the Sherman Act, §7 of the Clayton Act is the most important provision testing the legality of a merger.

Statutory Basis of Merger Law. Originally, §7 of the Clayton Act was directed primarily at the development of holding companies,[18] and at the secret acquisition of *competitors* through purchase of all or part of a competitor's *stock*. Subsequent amendments have extended the Act's coverage to include both asset and stock acquisitions. The Act now also covers both mergers between actual competitors and vertical and conglomerate mergers having the

---

[18]A holding company confines its activities to owning stock in, and supervising management of, other companies. BLACK'S LAW DICTIONARY 731 (6th ed. 1990).

requisite anticompetitive effect. Section 7 of the Clayton Act[19] now states in relevant part:

> No person engaged in commerce or in any activity affecting commerce shall acquire, directly or indirectly, the whole or any part of the stock or other share capital and no person subject to the jurisdiction of the Federal Trade Commission shall acquire the whole or any part of the assets of another person engaged also in commerce or in any activity affecting commerce, where in any line of commerce or in any activity affecting commerce in any section of the country, the effect of such acquisition may be substantially to lessen competition, or to tend to create a monopoly.

The statutory language highlights the elements of a §7 proceeding. First, the relevant product (the "line of commerce") and geographic market (the "section of the country") must be defined. Then, the competitive impact of the merger is analyzed within that market. If the merger's "effect may be substantially to lessen competition, or to tend to create a monopoly," it is prohibited.

Remedies; Merger Guidelines; Premerger Notification. Private plaintiffs, the FTC, and the Justice Department may maintain proceedings under §7. Because of the prohibitive expense and complexity of merger litigation, however, the Antitrust Division of the Justice Department maintains most suits. If the court finds a violation, the usual remedy is divestiture. Preliminary injunction also may be decreed pending determination of the merger's legality.

Because the Department of Justice is the primary enforcement body of §7, and because §7 uses general language, the Department periodically issues merger guidelines that detail the general principles and specific standards used to determine which mergers are likely to be challenged. To aid in enforcement of §7, Clayton Act §7A, enacted in 1976, requires that advance notice be given the FTC and the Justice Department of certain large mergers.

Market Definition in Merger Cases. Section 7 proscribes only those mergers whose effect "may be substantially to lessen competition, or to tend to create a monopoly." To resolve this issue the relevant *market* within which competitive impact is to be analyzed must first be determined. Because §7 indicates that competitive effect may occur "in any line of commerce . . . in any section of the country,"

both a product and geographic market must be defined. The product market may consist of one or more products or services offered by either company. The geographic market includes the area within which either firm, or both combined, conducts business. The market definition process under §7 is similar to that undertaken in monopolization cases under §2 of the Sherman Act. Under that statute, monopoly power is in issue. Market definition establishes the boundaries within which a firm's power is measured. Merger involves a change in market structure. Market definition in this context establishes the framework to analyze probable anticompetitive consequences of that change.

In determining which products or services to include in the relevant "line of commerce" for §7 purposes, the Supreme Court in *Brown Shoe Co. v. United States* (1962) stated, "The outer boundaries of a product market are determined by the reasonable interchangeability of use or the cross-elasticity of demand between the product itself and substitutes for it."[20] Thus, product substitutability defines the outer limits of the relevant product market.

The criteria used to determine the appropriate geographic market are the same as those used for the product market. Geographic substitutability defines the market. Depending on the facts, the relevant market may range in size from a part of a single metropolitan area to the entire nation.

Once the relevant market is defined, the competitive effect of the merger within that market is analyzed. The following material examines the potential competitive impact of horizontal, vertical, and conglomerate mergers.

Horizontal Merger

The majority of mergers posing competitive problems are horizontal—between existing competitors. A horizontal merger, like a price-fixing agreement, eliminates competition among the parties, but does so permanently. For example, whereas A and B as individual competitors may not legally agree on prices to charge their customers, A and B as merger partners, now members of a single integrated economic entity, may. The parties may thus accomplish by merger what they are prohibited from doing by ordinary agreement. Further, by successive merger, a firm capable of exerting monopoly power may result.

---

[19]15 U.S.C. §18.

[20]82 S. Ct. 1502, 1523–1524 (1962).

Nevertheless, antitrust law has always been more hospitable to mergers than to cartels. The reasons for this approach are varied, including that (1) merger may achieve economies of scale or permit other genuine economic efficiencies, such as integration of production, (2) merger promotes free alienability (transferability) of assets, allowing owners of the acquired corporation to sell out, (3) merger may be an expeditious method of diversification, entry into a new market, or acquisition of a needed asset (for example, a patent) or technology, (4) merger allows productive assets to be quickly diverted to more beneficial purposes, (5) merger may expedite installation of more efficient management, and penalize inefficient operation, and (6) merger may occur for competitively neutral reasons, such as tax advantage. In short, the reasons for merger are widely varied, some beneficial to competition, others neutral, and still others injurious. Although the law is more tolerant of merger than loose-knit cartelization, it must still identify and proscribe mergers detrimental to competition.

The primary danger of horizontal merger is market concentration. Market concentration is a function of the number of firms in a market and their respective market shares. Markets can range from atomistic (in which very large numbers of firms compete, each small relative to the overall size of the market) to monopolistic (in which one firm controls the entire market). Of great antitrust concern is a market in which a relatively small number of firms account for most market sales. A market dominated by a small number of large firms is said to be "highly concentrated." High concentration increases the likelihood that one firm, or a small number of firms, can successfully exercise market power.

A horizontal merger eliminates one competitor and concentrates the power of two firms into one. Depending upon market structure, this result may or may not be of antitrust concern. If a large number of competitors still remain in the market and the resulting firm is small, the competitive impact may be negligible. But if the merger partners are large and the market concentrated, the anticompetitive potential is magnified. In *United States v. Philadelphia National Bank,*[21] the Court announced a two-part market concentration test establishing a violation of §7. Absent proof by the defendants that the merger is not likely to injure competition, a horizontal merger violates §7 if it (1) produces a firm controlling an undue percentage of the relevant market, and (2) results in a significant increase in concentration in that market.

Interlocking Directorates—Clayton Act §8. Although it does not directly address the horizontal merger problem, §8 of the Clayton Act[22] concerns a closely related issue: interlocking directorates. An interlocking directorate occurs when one person simultaneously serves on the board of directors of two or more competing corporations. As amended in 1990, §8 forbids a person from serving as a director or officer of two or more corporations (other than banks and trust companies[23]) if

1. the corporations involved are engaged in whole or in part in interstate commerce; and
2. each of the corporations has combined capital, surplus, and undivided profits exceeding $10 million; and
3. the corporations are competitors "so that the elimination of competition by agreement between them" would violate "any of the antitrust laws."

Even if these conditions are met, simultaneous service is not prohibited if

1. competitive sales (revenues from products and services sold by one corporation in competition with the other) of either corporation are less than $1 million; or
2. competitive sales of either corporation are less than 2 percent of that corporation's total sales; or
3. the competitive sales of each corporation are less than 4 percent of that corporation's total sales.

The foregoing "safe harbors" are designed to permit interlocks if the corporations do not compete to a significant degree or if they compete in a line of business that is not significant when compared to overall operations. Note that the $1 million and $10 million thresholds are automatically increased (or decreased) annually by an amount equal to the percentage increase (or decrease) in the gross national product. The primary remedy for a Section 8 violation is to require the offending director to resign one of the posts.

---

[21] 83 S. Ct. 1715 (1963).

[22] 15 U.S.C. §19.

[23] Bank and trust company interlocks are governed largely by the Depository Institution Management Interlocks Act, 12 U.S.C. §§3201–3208.

Unlike the other substantive Clayton Act provisions (§§2, 3, and 7), Section 8 requires no showing of probable anticompetitive effect. Liability follows upon proof of the elements outlined above.

Vertical Merger

Vertical merger combines firms formerly in a supplier customer relationship. The most commonly noted anticompetitive consequence of vertical merger is foreclosure. To illustrate, assume that a given industry consists of three equal-size manufacturers A, B, and C, which sell to three equal-size retailers X, Y, and Z. All retailers buy from all manufacturers. C subsequently integrates vertically by merging with Z. If C now acts as Z's sole supplier, A and B are "foreclosed" from selling to one-third of the retail market. Conversely, if C now sells only to Z, X and Y are "foreclosed" from buying from one-third of the supply market. The degree of foreclosure caused by a merger is an important factor in testing its legality.

Vertical integration by merger also may create competitively objectionable barriers to entry. A firm seeking to enter the market might find that, because of substantial vertical integration, it has too few potential customers (in case of entry at the supplier level) or suppliers (in case of entry at the customer level) to enter either market alone. Though entering both markets simultaneously may be possible, the incremental cost of entering two markets rather than one may be sufficient to deter entry at all. If existing market structure is conducive to monopolization or collusion (for example, highly concentrated), such a barrier may adversely affect future market performance.

Vertical merger also may facilitate collusion among competitors in violation of the Sherman Act. Because retail prices are generally more visible than prices in upstream markets, substantial vertical integration to the retail level may facilitate a price-fixing arrangement among manufacturers by making it easier to monitor price and police violations. Further, even without collusion, substantial vertical integration into the retail market reduces the number of independent firms competing at that level.

To judge the legality of a vertical merger, the relevant market is defined, usually to include the product that the acquired customer or supplier bought from or sold to the acquiring firm. Then, probable anticompetitive effect is estimated by determining what percentage of the unintegrated portion of the customer or supply market is being foreclosed by the merger. The larger the percentage, the greater likelihood of a §7 violation. Thus, as in horizontal mergers, the degree of concentration (in this case in either the upstream or downstream market) is an important factor in judging legality.

Conglomerate Merger

A conglomerate merger combines firms that neither compete nor stand in a buyer-seller relationship. Three types of corporate combination are generally categorized as "conglomerate." First, a "pure" conglomerate merger involves firms engaged in unrelated businesses (for example, an oil company acquiring a movie studio). Second, a market extension merger joins firms selling the same product, but operating in different geographic markets. A market extension merger, though closely related to a horizontal merger, differs in that it does not eliminate existing direct competition between the parties. Third, a product extension merger combines firms producing related, though not identical, products. In this manner, the acquiring firm adds a product to its line. The acquired firm's product may generally be produced by similar facilities, marketed through the same channels, and advertised in the same media.

Although the dangers of concentration and foreclosure inherent in horizontal and vertical mergers are not present in conglomerate mergers, such mergers may injure "potential" competition and create the danger of reciprocal buying and entrenchment.

In "market extension" and "product extension" mergers, the acquiring firm expands by merger to sell the same product in a different geographic market or to add a related product to its line. In this case, injury may occur to "potential" rather than actual competition, because prior to the merger the acquiring company is a "potential entrant" into the geographic or product market in which the acquired firm operates. Depending upon the characteristics of the merging firms and the structure of the target market, the loss of the potential competition occasioned by the merger may have sufficient anticompetitive effect to condemn the merger under §7.

Creating a market structure conducive to "reciprocity" or "reciprocal dealing" is another possible anticompetitive consequence of conglomerate merger. A reciprocal dealing arrangement arises when two parties are related as buyer to seller in one or more markets and seller to buyer in another or others. In this situation the parties may agree, in effect, "I'll buy from you, if you buy from me." The goods purchased under reciprocal buying arrangements are frequently dissimilar in kind, which could ordinarily be purchased from other sources on similar or even more advantageous terms. If the arrangement is well established, it prevents com-petitors of each company from selling to the other, and awards each party with the added size and strength attributable to its position as an assured supplier of the other.

In addition to reciprocity, conglomerate merger may cause competitive problems resulting from disparity in size of the acquiring firm relative to firms in the target market. If a company already dominant in a market is acquired by a large powerful firm, the dominant firm might become entrenched. That is, the "deep pockets" of the acquiring firm might discourage entry into the market as well as competitive challenges from existing competitors, who might fear retaliation by the dominant firm.

Federal Trade Commission Act

Section 5 of the Federal Trade Commission Act, which is enforced exclusively by the FTC through administrative proceedings, states:

> Unfair methods of competition in or affecting commerce, and unfair or deceptive acts or practices in or affecting commerce, are declared unlawful.[24]

Section 5 as originally drafted proscribed only "unfair methods of competition" occurring in interstate commerce. The Wheeler-Lea Act of 1938 added the prohibition of "unfair or deceptive acts or practices." In addition, §5 was amended in 1975 to extend the FTC's jurisdiction to matters merely "affecting" interstate commerce.

Under §5, as amended, the FTC has a dual role. First, through its power to prohibit "unfair methods of competition," the FTC protects the competitive system by prohibiting anticompetitive practices. In this context, §5 is a tool of antitrust enforcement, supplementing the Sherman and Clayton Acts. Second, by exercising its power to proscribe "unfair or deceptive acts or practices," the FTC protects consumers who are injured by practices such as deceptive advertising or labeling without regard to any effect on competitors. The Act does not define the

specific conduct prohibited as unfair, but allows the FTC to develop a flexible standard on a case-by-case basis.

Consumer Protection Under §5

Deceptive Advertising. A major purpose of the Wheeler-Lea Amendment to §5 was to protect consumers against deceptive advertising claims. Accordingly, much of the FTC's consumer protection activity has focused on false or misleading claims relating to product quality, quantity, and price, and deceptive endorsements and testimonials.

To determine whether an advertisement or other promotional activity is deceptive in violation of §5, the FTC applies the following standard:

1. there must be a representation, omission, or practice that is likely to mislead a reasonable consumer; and
2. the representation, omission, or practice must be "material."[25]

Typically, deceptive acts or practices include express or implied misrepresentations, half-truths, or significant nondisclosures. A deceptive act or practice is material if it "is likely to affect a consumer's choice of or conduct regarding" a product or service.[26] Note that the FTC may find an action or practice deceptive even if it caused no actual injury to consumers, and even though the defendant had no intent to deceive (scienter). In the following case, the court reviewed an FTC finding that an advertisement was materially deceptive.

Kraft, Inc. v. Federal Trade Commission
970 F.2d 311 (7th Cir. 1992)

> Between 1985 and 1987, Kraft, Inc. ran a national advertising campaign promoting Kraft Singles, a processed cheese food. One television commercial—the "Skimp" ad—first showed a child and then visual images of milk pouring into a glass accompanied by the following copy:
>
>> Could you look into those big blue eyes and skimp on her? So I buy Kraft Singles. Imitation slices use hardly any milk. But Kraft has five ounces per slice. Five ounces. So her little bones get calcium they need to grow. . . . Kraft Singles. More milk makes 'em . . . more milk makes 'em good.

---

[24]15 U.S.C. §45(a).

[25]FTC Policy Statement on Deception, 103 F.T.C. 174 (1984).
[26]*Id.* at 182.

Another commercial—the "Class Picture" ad—included an announcer reading the following as a group of children had its class picture taken:

> Well, a government study says that half the school kids in America don't get all the calcium recommended for growing kids. That's why Kraft Singles are important. Kraft is made from five ounces of milk per slice. So they're concentrated with calcium. Calcium the government recommends for strong bones and healthy teeth. . . . Say Kraft Singles. 'Cause kids love Kraft singles, right down to their bones.

Following an administrative hearing, the Federal Trade Commission (FTC) found that the advertising campaign violated §5 of the FTC Act by misrepresenting the amount of calcium in Kraft Singles. The FTC found that the ads implied that Kraft Singles contain the same amount of calcium as five ounces of milk (the "milk equivalency" claim) when, in fact, about 30 percent of the calcium contained in the milk is lost during processing. The FTC ordered Kraft to cease and desist from making the claims in the ads or nutritional claims about any of its cheese products unless supported by reliable scientific evidence. Kraft filed a petition in the federal circuit court of appeals requesting that the court set aside the FTC order.

Flaum, Circuit Judge

. . . The FTC Act makes it unlawful to engage in unfair or deceptive commercial practices, . . . or to induce consumers to purchase certain products through advertising that is misleading in a material respect. . . . [A]n advertisement is deceptive under the Act if it is likely to mislead consumers, acting reasonably under the circumstances, in a material respect. . . .

We find substantial evidence in the record to support the FTC's finding [that the advertisements were misleading]. [T]he ads emphasize visually and verbally that five ounces of milk go into a slice of Kraft Singles; this image is linked to calcium content, strongly implying that the consumer gets the calcium found in five ounces of milk. . . . [T]he average consumer is not likely to know that much of the calcium in five ounces of milk (30%) is lost in processing, which leaves consumers with a misleading impression about calcium content. . . .

[Kraft asserts, however, that the milk equivalency claim], even if made, [is] not material to consumers. A claim is considered material if it "involves information that is important to consumers and, hence, likely to affect their choice of, or conduct regarding a product." *Cliffdale Assocs.*, [103 F.T.C. 110, 165 (1984)]. . . .

In determining that the milk equivalency claim was material to consumers, the FTC cited Kraft surveys showing that 71% of respondents rated calcium content an extremely or very important factor in their decision to buy Kraft Singles, and that 52% of female, and 40% of all respondents, reported significant personal concerns about adequate calcium consumption. . . . Finally, the FTC found evidence in the record that Kraft designed the ads with the intent to capitalize on consumer calcium deficiency concerns.

Significantly, the FTC found further evidence of materiality in Kraft's conduct: despite repeated warnings, Kraft persisted in running the challenged ads. Before the ads even ran, ABC television raised a red flag when it asked Kraft to substantiate the milk and calcium claims in the ads. Kraft's ad agency also warned Kraft in a legal memorandum to substantiate the claims before running the ads. . . . Nonetheless, a high-level Kraft executive recommended that the ad copy remain unaltered because the "Singles business is growing for the first time in four years due in large part to the copy." . . . Finally, the FTC and the California Attorney General's Office independently notified the company in early 1986 that investigations had been initiated to determine whether the ads conveyed the milk equivalency claims. Notwithstanding these warnings, Kraft continued to run the ads and even rejected proposed alternatives that would have allayed concerns over their deceptive nature. From this, the FTC inferred—we believe, reasonably—that Kraft thought the challenged milk equivalency claim induced consumers to purchase Singles and hence that the claim was material to consumers. . . .

[Petition denied and FTC order enforced.]

Consumer Unfairness Rule-making Authority. The FTC is authorized to restrain both deceptive and unfair trade practices injuring consumers. Although Commission actions often have been based on alternate theories of deception and unfairness, more recently the FTC has used consumer unfairness as an independent basis for its actions. Congress facilitated the development of a consumer unfairness doctrine by adding §18 to the FTC Act in 1975,[27] in response to con-

---

[27]15 U.S.C. §57a, part of the Magnuson-Moss Warranty–Federal Trade Commission Improvement Act.

cern that the FTC cease and desist order procedure was ineffective in safeguarding the consumer public against unfair trade practices. Section 18 empowers the FTC to promulgate trade regulation rules that define specifically which acts or practices are unfair under §5. FTC rulemaking authority under §18 is, however, limited to unfair acts or practices that are "prevalent." To establish prevalence the FTC must prove either that it (1) previously has issued cease and desist orders regarding the challenged conduct, or (2) has other information indicating a "widespread pattern" of such conduct.

Before promulgating a rule, the FTC must publish notice of the proposed rule-making, allow interested parties to submit written comments, and provide opportunity for an informal hearing. After the rule (including a statement of its basis and purpose) is promulgated, persons objecting to the rule may obtain judicial review from a federal court of appeals. Violation of a trade regulation rule, which may be designed to prevent future conduct, is a §5 violation.

Section 18 does not provide standards to be used in identifying unfair practices. To remedy this problem, Congress in 1994 added a provision to §5 stating that the FTC has authority to declare an act or practice unfair only if

the act or practice causes or is likely to cause substantial injury to consumers which is not reasonably avoidable by consumers themselves and not outweighed by countervailing benefits to consumers or to competition.[28]

Note that this statute, emphasizing the prevention of unjustified consumer injury, codifies the informal standard used by the FTC since 1980.

Remedies. After finding a violation of §5 or trade regulation rule, the FTC issues a cease and desist order. The Commission has wide latitude in determining the type of order necessary to alleviate the particular unfair or deceptive practice, and courts usually defer to Commission discretion in framing remedies. For example, in antitrust cases cease and desist orders have required patent licensing and divestiture of corporations acquired in violation of §7 of the Clayton Act.

The FTC Act also provides for civil penalties against persons who violate a cease and desist order or a trade regulation rule. These penalties are imposed in lawsuits brought by the FTC or the Attorney General in federal district court. Violators are subject to a civil penalty of up to $10,000 for each violation (or $10,000 per day for continuing violations).[29]

Summary

1.   Section 2 of the Clayton Act, as amended in 1936 by the Robinson-Patman Act, prohibits price discrimination under certain circumstances. The Act covers primarily primary line discrimination (causing injury at the same functional level as the seller) and secondary line discrimination (causing injury to buyers from the discriminating seller who must compete in the resale of the commodities sold).

2.   A *prima facie* case of price discrimination violating the Robinson-Patman Act requires that a seller engaged in interstate commerce discriminate in price between different purchasers. The discriminatory sales must be of commodities of like grade and quality and must cause competitive injury. Liability for illegal price discrimination under §2(a) extends both to the seller who grants the discrimination and to any buyer who knowingly receives it.

3.   The Robinson-Patman Act was enacted primarily to curb and prohibit all devices by which large buyers use their purchasing power to exact discriminatory preferences from sellers. To curb specific abuses, the Robinson-Patman Act supplements its general price discrimination prohibition by explicitly prohibiting discriminatory brokerage and promotional allowances and services.

4.   The Robinson-Patman Act recognizes three major defenses to a violation: the cost justification defense, the meeting competition defense, and the changing conditions defense.

5.   Antitrust law addresses the permanent consolidation of previously separate enterprises through merger in §7 of the Clayton Act. Section 7 applies to horizontal, vertical, and conglomerate mergers, and prohibits those mergers that substantially lessen competition or tend to create a monopoly in

---

[28] 15 U.S.C. §45(n).
[29] 15 U.S.C. §§45(1)-(m).

any line of commerce in any section of the country. Section 7 cases require that the relevant product and geographic markets be established followed by analysis of the competitive impact of the merger in that market.

6. Horizontal mergers may adversely affect competition by creating excessive market concentration. Vertical mergers pose the risk of foreclosure. Conglomerate mergers may eliminate a potential competitor from the market, and create risk of reciprocal dealing and entrenchment. The courts have established tests to govern the legality of each type of merger, and the Justice Department has published "merger guidelines" indicating which mergers are likely to be challenged by the government.

7. Under §5 of the Federal Trade Commission Act, the FTC enforces the antitrust laws (through its power to restrain "unfair methods of competition") and protects consumers (by proscribing "unfair or deceptive acts or practices"). In antitrust enforcement, §5 may be used to reach incipient violations of the Sherman and Clayton Acts. In protecting consumers against unfair trade practices, the FTC may promulgate trade regulation rules outlawing specific practices that are unfair to consumers.

Key Terms

primary line competitive injury

secondary line competitive injury

third line (tertiary line) competitive injury

Robinson-Patman Act

horizontal merger

vertical merger

conglomerate merger

Questions and Problems

52.1 The Robinson-Patman Act is often criticized for not being effectively integrated with the rest of antitrust law. Is the Robinson-Patman Act a beneficial statute or should it be repealed?

52.2 Morton Salt sold its Blue Label salt to wholesalers and large retailers under a standard quantity discount system available to all customers. Under this system, the per case price decreased as the quantity purchased increased, as follows:

Quantity Purchased	Per Case
Less than one (rail) carload	$1.60
Carload	1.50
5,000 cases within any 12 months	1.40
50,000 cases within any 12 months	1.35

Only five companies, operators of large chains of retail grocery stores, purchased in sufficient quantity to obtain the $1.35 per case price. As a result of this low price, the chains were able to sell salt at retail cheaper than wholesale purchasers from Morton could resell to independent retailers, many of whom competed with local outlets of the five chain stores. Morton was charged with violating the Robinson-Patman Act and defended on the ground that its quantity discount was not discriminatory because it was available to all on equal terms. Is Morton correct? Explain. Morton also contended that because salt is a small item in most wholesale and retail businesses, and in consumer's budgets, the competitive effect of its program was insufficient to violate the Act. Is Morton correct? Explain.

52.3 A seller may sell to two wholesalers at different prices. The favored wholesaler (the one receiving the lower price) may pass the savings along to his retail customers, giving them a competitive advantage over customers of the disfavored wholesaler. Injury here occurs at the third line, among customers (retailers) of customers (wholesalers) of the seller granting the discrimination. Although tertiary (third) line injury is covered under the Robinson-Patman Act, very few cases have considered injury beyond secondary line. Why?

52.4 Consider whether the following advertising techniques are false or deceptive in violation of §5 of the FTC Act.

(a) In a newspaper advertisement, MC Paint Company advertised a gallon of paint for $10 and stated that the purchaser would receive a free can of paint of equal quality with each can purchased. Prior to the advertising campaign MC had sold the advertised paint for $5 per can.

(b) Would your answer to question (a) change if MC could prove that paint of comparable quality sold for $10 per can in other stores?

(c) Guten Tag, Inc. ran a television advertisement for its vanilla ice cream showing happy children eating the ice cream. Because ice cream rapidly melts under lights used to film the ads, Guten Tag used mashed potatoes in place of the ice cream.

(d) Yummy Soups Company ran a magazine advertisement showing a picture of a bowl of Yummy's vegetable soup. Yummy placed clear marbles in the bottom of the bowl causing all of the vegetables to rise to the surface of the soup, thus giving the soup the appearance of being thicker than it really was.

52.5 Sears, Roebuck and Co. began an advertising campaign as part of a new marketing program for its Lady Kenmore brand dishwasher. The advertisements claimed that the dishwasher cleaned all dishes without prerinsing or scraping and washed dishes on the top rack as clean as those on the bottom rack. These claims were false and tests conducted by Sears established their falsity. During the first three years of the advertising program, sales of Lady Kenmore dishwashers rose 300 percent.

Following an investigation, the Federal Trade Commission charged Sears with disseminating deceptive and unfair advertisements in violation of §5 of the FTC Act. After a hearing, an administrative law judge found that

Sears' advertising claims were false and ordered Sears to cease and desist from making the false claims. The judge also ordered Sears not to make any performance claims for its major home appliances without "competent and reliable tests" or other evidence that substantiated the claims. Sears appealed the order to the court of appeals on the ground that the order was overly broad because it extended to appliances other than the Lady Kenmore dishwasher. Sears argued that because the FTC complaint alleged a §5 violation only with respect to Sears' dishwasher advertising, the FTC lacked the power to issue an order covering any product except dishwashers. Is Sears correct? Why would the FTC want to issue an order covering all of Sears' major home appliances in this case?

EMPLOYEE PROTECTION AND LABOR LAW

- overview of federal employee protection statutes
- federal statutes governing labor and management relations
- election of collective bargaining agent and the collective bargaining process
- unfair labor practices

The employer-employee relationship, a form of the principal-agent relationship described in Chapters 40 and 41, is critical to businesses and the U.S. economy. Traditionally, employment issues were considered matters of local interest and, therefore, like agency, were governed by state common law. As a result of nineteenth-century industrialization, accompanied by the dramatic growth of businesses operating in interstate commerce, however, national economic and social interests increasingly were affected by employment matters such as employee compensation, child labor, worker safety, and labor strife between unions and management. Although the states attempted to resolve some of these problems — for example, by adopting workers' compensation statutes discussed in Chapter 41 — others were ignored as the states tried to encourage local business and economic growth.

When the Depression created a national labor crisis in the 1930s, the federal Congress, exercising its consti-tutional power to regulate interstate commerce, abandoned the policy of leaving employment regulation to the states and enacted a series of statutes designed to alleviate the crisis. As part of the New Deal, Congress enacted legislation that established a federal minimum wage, protected children in the labor force, created a retirement income system, and guaranteed workers the right to form unions. These employee protection laws, as later amended and supplemented with other federal statutes designed to protect employees' safety and welfare, are the subject of this chapter. Another major area of federal regulation — equal employment opportunity law — is discussed in the Chapter 54.

Employee Protection Statutes

Fair Labor Standards Act

The Fair Labor Standards Act (FLSA),[1] enacted in 1938, regulates minimum wages, overtime compensation, and child labor. Most employers and employees engaged in interstate commerce or in the production of goods for interstate commerce are subject to the Act, though numerous exemptions apply.

---

[1] 29 U.S.C. §201 *et seq.*

The FLSA requires employers to pay employees a federally established minimum wage, currently $5.15 per hour. Employees under age 20 may be paid $4.25 per hour during the first 90 days. States are permitted to set a higher minimum wage applicable to employers within the state. The FLSA does not limit the number of hours that an employee may work. An employer who requires employees to work more than 40 hours per week, however, must pay them time and one-half their regular rate for hours worked in excess of 40 hours. Special rules allow an employer to pay less than the minimum wage to students, apprentices, and handicapped workers if the employer obtains authorization from the secretary of labor.

Some "white collar" employees, as defined in Department of Labor regulations, are exempt from the overtime provisions of the FLSA. An executive employee, who earns a salary of at least $455 per week, is exempt from the overtime provisions if:

1. The employee's primary duty is managing the enterprise, or managing a customarily recognized department or subdivision of the enterprise;
2. The employee customarily and regularly directs the work of at least two or more other full-time employees or their equivalent; and
3. The employee has the authority to hire or fire other employees, or the employee's suggestions and recommendations as to the hiring, firing, advancement, promotion are given particular weight by the employer.[2]

An employee, who earns a salary of at least $455 per week, is considered to be exempt from overtime as an administrative employee if:

1. The employee's primary duty is performing office or non-manual work directly related to the management or general business operations of the employer or the employer's customers; and
2. The employee's primary duty includes the exercise of discretion and independent judgment with respect to matters of significance.[3]

Other exempt employees include some computer employees as well as certain professionals and outside salespersons.[4]

The FLSA also prohibits "oppressive child labor." The secretary of labor issues regulations defining the types of jobs that children may hold and the maximum number of hours they may work. Generally, minors who are age 16 or 17 may work unlimited hours in nonhazardous jobs. Children who are age 14 and 15 may work only limited hours in nonhazardous jobs and may not work in manufacturing or mining. Special rules apply to children employed in agriculture, generally allowing them to work longer hours at a younger age.

The Wage and Hour Division of the Department of Labor administers the FLSA. It investigates possible violations of the Act and may issue subpoenas compelling attendance of witnesses and production of employment records. Civil and criminal penalties may be imposed for violations of the Act. Workers who have received subminimum wages may file a civil suit under the Act for twice the amount of back pay plus attorneys' fees and costs.

Social Security Act

Congress enacted the **Social Security Act**[5] in 1935 to provide income to retired workers but later amended the Act to allow benefits to others including disabled workers and dependents of deceased workers. The Social Security Act also provides hospitalization and medical benefits for the elderly. Social Security programs are funded by taxes imposed on employers, employees, and self-employed persons.

Contributions. The Federal Insurance Contributions Act (FICA),[6] requires both employers and employees to make annual contributions of Social Security taxes. Determination of whether an employer-employee relationship exists is made using the common law standard.[7] Generally, any person who has the right to control and direct the result and means by which an individual's services are rendered is considered an employer. The FICA tax, which is calculated as a percentage of an employee's gross annual wages, is composed of two parts: one part for hospitalization or Medicare insurance (currently equal to 1.45 percent of the employee's gross annual wages) and the other for old-age, survivors, and disability insurance—OASDI—(currently equal to 6.20

---

[2]29 C.F.R. §§541.100–106
[3]29 C.F.R. §§541.200–203
[4]29 C.F.R. §§541.300–304, 541.400–402, 541.500–504.

[5]42 U.S.C. §301 *et seq.*
[6]26 U.S.C. §§3101–3127.
[7]See discussion in Chapter 41 of the text.

percent of the employee's gross annual wages). Employees, therefore, contribute 7.65 percent of their gross annual wages as their share of the FICA tax (subject to the cap discussed below). The employer must contribute an equal amount so that the total FICA tax for each employee currently is equal to 15.3 percent of the employee's gross annual wages, subject to the following cap. Federal law establishes a cap on the amount of an employee's wages that are subject to the OASDI portion of the FICA tax. The cap, which is adjusted annually using an escalator clause, was set at $94,200 in 2006. An employee's wages in excess of $94,200, therefore, were exempt from the 6.2 percent OASDI tax rate payable by both the employee and employer. No ceiling is set for the hospitalization portion of the tax. All wages, therefore, are subject to the 1.45 percent tax rate.

The employer must withhold the employee's share of the tax from wages, submit payment of both the employee's and employer's contributions, and maintain records of the employee's earnings. The employer is primarily liable for payment of the employee's share of the tax even if the employer fails to withhold the tax from the employee's wages. An employer who fails to submit taxes to the federal government when due must pay a penalty and interest and may be subject to criminal sanctions.

Self-employed persons who receive earnings from carrying on a trade or business also must pay Social Security taxes under the Self-Employment Contributions Act.[8] A self-employed person must contribute taxes equal to the combined employer-employee rate of 15.3 percent of net self-employment earnings, subject to the same ceiling applied to wages of an employed person. An individual who receives wages from an employer, as well as self-employment earnings, can offset the gross wages against this ceiling in determining the amount of self-employment earnings subject to the tax. A self-employed person who fails to pay the taxes when due must pay a penalty and interest and may be subject to criminal liability.

Benefits. The Social Security Administration, which administers the benefits programs, determines who is entitled to benefits and their amount. Individuals who have accumulated sufficient credits while employed qualify for full retirement benefits at age 65, but may retire at age 62 and receive reduced benefits. A person who qualifies for retirement benefits generally is entitled to them regardless of other retirement income such as

private pensions. A worker who becomes totally disabled prior to age 65 may qualify for disability benefits. In some cases, even persons who made no contributions to Social Security, such as the spouse or minor children of a deceased or disabled worker, may qualify for benefits under survivors' or dependents' programs.

Unemployment Compensation. The federal unemployment compensation program, embodied in the Federal Unemployment Tax Act (FUTA)[9], also is administered as a part of the Social Security programs. Unemployment compensation, which is designed to provide security to temporarily unemployed workers, is coordinated jointly through state and federal programs. Under state laws, employers may be required to pay a tax or contribution to state unemployment compensation programs. FUTA also requires that employers pay a tax, based on a percentage of each employee's earnings, to the federal government. Employers are then entitled to a credit against this tax for contributions paid to qualified state programs. Generally, benefits paid to unemployed workers are administered by the states in accordance with federal guidelines.

Family and Medical Leave Act of 1993

Federal law generally does not require employers to provide benefits such as paid vacations, holidays, sick leave, or maternity leave. Instead, these matters traditionally are privately negotiated by the employer and employee (or a union representing the employee). Congress, however, adopted the federal **Family and Medical Leave Act of 1993 (FMLA)**[10] based on its findings that existing employment policies failed to accommodate working parents' need to care for family members or provide adequate job security to employees suffering from temporary serious medical problems.[11] This statute requires many employers to provide limited unpaid family and medical leave to eligible employees. The FMLA does not preempt state law. In states with leave statutes, employers must comply with the more favorable law.

The FMLA requires employers with 50 or more employees to provide up to 12 weeks of leave during a 12-month period to eligible employees for the following purposes: (1) birth of the employee's child or placement of a child with the employee by adoption or foster

---

[8]26 U.S.C. §§1401–1403.

[9]26 U.S.C. §§3301–3311.
[10]29 U.S.C. §2601 *et seq.*
[11]29 U.S.C. §2601(a).

care; (2) care of the employee's spouse, child, or parent with a serious health condition; or (3) the employee's inability to perform his or her job functions because of the employee's serious health condition.[12] Illnesses or conditions requiring continuing care from a doctor, or inpatient care at a hospital or other residential facility, are considered serious health conditions.

Only employees who have worked for the employer for a total of at least 12 months, including a minimum of 1,250 hours of service during the preceding 12 months, are eligible for leave privileges. Employees at a work site employing fewer than 50 people are ineligible, but only if the total number of persons employed by the employer within a 75-mile radius of that work site is fewer than 50. With limited exceptions, eligible employees have a right to be restored to their prior position or an equivalent position after returning from a family or medical leave.

Employees who take a leave because of the birth, adoption, or foster placement of their child generally must take their full leave—up to the maximum 12 weeks—at one time within one year of the child's birth or placement. Leaves for medical conditions, however, may be taken on an "intermittent" basis—that is, in smaller blocks over an extended period—if medically necessary. An employee undergoing surgery, for example, may require an initial leave of four weeks followed by intermittent leaves of a day or even a few hours for subsequent doctor's visits. In cases of personal or family member's medical conditions, an employee also may use a "reduced leave schedule" in which the employee works only part of a workday or workweek.

The employer is not required to pay the employee during the leave. An employee may choose, or the employer may require the employee, to substitute accrued paid vacation, personal leave, or sick leave—if those benefits are provided by the employer—for the unpaid leave. During the leave, the employer must maintain any group health care insurance coverage benefits to which the employee would have been entitled.

The secretary of labor, who is responsible for administering and enforcing the FMLA, may bring civil actions seeking damages and equitable relief (such as an injunction or reinstatement or promotion of an employee) for violations. Alternatively, an employee may bring a civil action for damages, which may be doubled if the employer did not act in good faith, and equitable relief. Injured employees who prove a violation are entitled to reasonable attorneys' and expert witness fees.

Employee Retirement Income Security Act

To attract and retain qualified employees, many businesses voluntarily provide fringe benefits to employees. In 1974, in response to abuses and mishandling of private pension funds, Congress adopted the **Employee Retirement Income Security Act (ERISA).**[13] Although not requiring employers to provide benefits, ERISA establishes standards that must be followed by employers that voluntarily extend benefits to their employees. ERISA also preempts state regulation of many of the benefits covered by the federal law.

Employee Benefit Plans. ERISA regulates employee benefit plans—plans established by employers to provide benefits to employees. ERISA recognizes two general types of benefit plans: "employee welfare benefit plans" and "employee pension benefit plans." Employee welfare benefit plans provide fringe benefits such as medical and hospital benefits—including those covered by insurance and health maintenance organizations (HMOs)—benefits covering sickness, accidents, and disability; and vacation benefits. Employee pension benefit plans include programs that provide retirement income or severance pay to employees.

ERISA requires administrators of employee benefit plans to provide summary descriptions of the plans and notice of plan changes to participants and to file annual reports with the Department of Labor. ERISA designates an individual or organization that manages a benefit plan as a "fiduciary." Fiduciaries include those who exercise "discretionary authority or discretionary control" with respect to management of the plan or in management or disposition of plan assets.[14] As fiduciaries, they owe a duty of loyalty requiring them to act prudently and solely in the interest of plan participants and beneficiaries.

Pension Plans. Pension plans may be contributory or noncontributory. Under a "contributory" plan both the employee and employer make contributions to the plan while only the employer contributes to a "noncontributory" plan. "Qualified" pension plans are those that comply with Internal Revenue Service requirements entitling the employer to deduct its contributions for federal tax purposes and allow earnings on contributions to accumulate without tax recognition.

---

[12]29 U.S.C. §2612(a).

[13]29 U.S.C. §1001 *et seq.*
[14]29 U.S.C. §1002(21)(A).

ERISA requires all pension plans to be in writing and to name a plan manager. All assets (other than insurance) must be held in trust. Plan managers and advisors are fiduciaries. ERISA restricts the plan's investments by prohibiting certain transactions (such as loans and leases) with the sponsoring employer or certain employees, officers, directors, and major shareholders of the employer. A pension plan may invest in securities issued by the employer although such investments are subject to limitations. As further protection, ERISA created the Pension Benefit Guaranty Corporation to insure pension benefits if a plan fails or terminates. All plans must maintain such insurance.

ERISA provided important reforms of pension plan vesting requirements. **Vesting** occurs when the employees' rights to their interests in the pension plan cannot be forfeited or taken away. Prior to ERISA, many employers postponed vesting until immediately prior to the employee's retirement age. An employee who changed jobs or was discharged forfeited all rights to pension benefits and the employer recouped its contributions. Under contributory plans, ERISA requires that employees' rights to their own contributions vest immediately. Thus, the employees never forfeit their contributions. ERISA establishes minimum vesting requirements for employer contributions under both contributory and noncontributory plans. In general, employees' rights to employer contributions must fully vest within five or seven years in accordance with formulas set forth in ERISA.

Health Care Plans. Congress has added two amendments to ERISA that are designed to help workers maintain health care benefits. Under the **Consolidated Omnibus Budget Reconciliation Act (COBRA),** some employees, spouses, and dependents are entitled to continue health care coverage that otherwise would be lost due to termination of employment. COBRA requires employers with 20 or more employees that maintain a group health plan to allow some former employees to continue their coverage under the plan for a limited time. The former employee, however, must pay the premium for the coverage. Because group health plan premiums are less expensive than individual coverage, COBRA helps former employees maintain health care coverage. COBRA applies only to former employees who voluntarily resigned or who were terminated involuntarily for any reason other than "gross misconduct." Spouses or former spouses as well as dependent children may qualify under COBRA. Generally, COBRA allows the continued coverage for no more than 18 months although, under some circumstances, spouses and dependents may continue the coverage for 36 months.

In 1996, the **Health Insurance Portability and Accountability Act (HIPAA)** was added to ERISA to increase the availability of group health care coverage. Because most health plans exclude coverage for certain preexisting conditions, individuals with certain health conditions often are unable to secure health coverage if they change jobs. HIPAA requires a group health plan to provide coverage to new employees who previously had been covered for at least 12 months by an employer's health plan; the plan cannot impose a preexisting condition exclusion. HIPAA also requires health insurers and HMOs to guarantee coverage to small employers (employers with fewer than 50 employees). The law generally requires the insurer or HMO to accept all small employers that apply for coverage, as well as every employee in the employer's groups.

Enforcement. The Department of Labor and the Department of the Treasury are responsible for enforcing ERISA. Criminal penalties may be imposed for failure to comply with disclosure requirements. The statute also allows civil suits, including those for breach of fiduciary duties, for violations of the Act.

Occupational Safety and Health Act

In 1970, Congress adopted the federal **Occupational Safety and Health Act (OSHA)**[15] to ensure "safe and healthful working conditions and to preserve our human resources."[16] In contrast to state workers' compensation laws, which compensate an employee after an injury, OSHA was designed to prevent job injuries. Almost every private employer whose business affects interstate commerce is subject to the provisions of the Act although some special accommodations are made for small businesses. The **Occupational Safety and Health Administration** (also called "OSHA") of the Department of Labor has primary responsibility for administration and enforcement of the Act. If, however, a state law meets requirements set by OSHA, the state regulates safety and health standards within its borders.

OSHA imposes a general duty on the employer to provide "employment and a place of employment which are free from recognized hazards that are causing or are likely to cause death or serious physical harm to his

---

[15]29 U.S.C. §§651–678.
[16]29 U.S.C. §651(b).

employees."[17] A "recognized hazard" is a dangerous condition or activity of which the employer has actual knowledge or of which the employer should have known based on the standard of knowledge in the industry. An employer is obligated to eliminate recognized hazards if feasible.

The secretary of labor also issues regulations setting standards for specific industries and the employer must comply with the standards set for its industry. These regulations are adopted through a notice and hearing procedure that allows input from interested parties including employers and employees.

OSHA standards vary considerably from industry to industry and cover a variety of conditions in the workplace. They include, for example, maximum noise levels, air quality standards in the workplace, permissible locations for equipment and machinery, and safety procedures for employees. In response to criticism of OSHA's overly-detailed regulations, unnecessarily strict enforcement, and attention to safety rather than health hazards, OSHA has simplified some of its rules. Nevertheless, the cost of compliance with OSHA standards is a frequent subject of litigation as illustrated in the following case.

American Textile Manufacturers Institute, Inc. v. Donovan
101 S. Ct. 2478 (1981)

Byssinosis, a respiratory disease that may resemble chronic bronchitis or emphysema, is primarily caused by inhalation of cotton dust released during the handling and processing of cotton. Studies estimate that over 25 percent of all active cotton mill workers suffer from some form of the disease and that approximately one in twelve cotton mill workers suffer from the most disabling form of byssinosis.

In 1978, the secretary of labor and OSHA promulgated standards establishing maximum limits of cotton dust permissible in the air in workplaces maintained by the cotton industry. OSHA mandated installation of ventilation systems and special floor-sweeping procedures to reduce cotton dust and required employers to monitor cotton dust exposure and to provide medical surveillance including annual employee medical examinations. Prior to adopting the regulations, OSHA held public hearings and received comments from interested parties.

Petitioners, American Textile Manufacturers Institute and others representing the cotton industry, sued the secre-

tary of labor alleging that the standards were invalid because OSHA had failed to demonstrate a reasonable relationship between the costs and benefits of the cotton dust standard. The court of appeals (the court of original jurisdiction) upheld the validity of the standard. The Supreme Court granted certiorari to the petitioners.

Justice Brennan

. . . The principal question presented in these cases is whether the Occupational Safety and Health Act requires the Secretary, in promulgating a standard pursuant to §6(b)(5) of the Act . . . to determine that the costs of the standard bear a reasonable relationship to its benefits. . . . [P]etitioners urge not only that OSHA must show that a standard addresses a significant risk of material health impairment . . . but also that OSHA must demonstrate that the reduction in risk of material health impairment is significant in light of the costs of attaining that reduction. . . . Respondents on the other hand contend that the Act requires OSHA to promulgate standards that eliminate or reduce such risks "to the extent such protection is technologically and economically feasible." . . .

Section 6(b)(5) of the Act . . . (emphasis added), provides:

> The Secretary, in promulgating standards dealing with toxic materials or harmful physical agents under this subsection, shall set the standard which most adequately assures, *to the extent feasible,* on the basis of the best available evidence, that no employee will suffer material impairment of health or functional capacity even if such employee has regular exposure to the hazard dealt with by such standard for the period of his working life. . . .

The plain meaning of the word "feasible" supports respondents' interpretation of the statute. According to Webster's Third New International Dictionary of the English Language 831 (1976), "feasible" means "capable of being done, executed, or effected." . . . Thus, §6(b)(5) directs the Secretary to issue the standard that "most adequately assures . . . that no employee will suffer material impairment of health," limited only by the extent to which this is "capable of being done." In effect then, as the Court of Appeals held, Congress itself defined the basic relationship between costs and benefits, by placing the "benefit" of worker health above all other considerations save those making

---

[17]29 U.S.C. §654(a)(1).

attainment of this "benefit" unachievable. Any standard based on a balancing of costs and benefits by the Secretary that strikes a different balance than that struck by Congress would be inconsistent with the command set forth in §6(b)(5). Thus, cost-benefit analysis by OSHA is not required by the statute because feasibility analysis is. . . .

When Congress has intended that an agency engage in cost-benefit analysis, it has clearly indicated such intent on the face of the statute. . . . Certainly in light of its ordinary meaning, the word "feasible" cannot be construed to articulate such congressional intent. We therefore reject the argument that Congress required cost-benefit analysis in §6(b)(5). . . .

[Judgment affirmed.]

OSHA also requires businesses to maintain records documenting employee accidents and illnesses and records concerning particular hazards, including exposure to toxic substances. Employees and their unions have a right to inspect some records concerning hazards.

To ensure compliance with its safety and health standards, OSHA conducts workplace inspections. Such inspections are subject to the constitutional requirements of administrative searches discussed in Chapter 4. Employees and unions also may report hazards to OSHA. Upon discovering violations, OSHA issues a written citation to the employer providing a time limit for correction. The employer may challenge the citation through an administrative hearing process and the decision ultimately may be appealed to federal court. Employers who violate the Act or OSHA standards are subject to both civil and criminal penalties.

Employee Polygraph Protection Act

The federal **Employee Polygraph Protection Act** of 1988[18] limits private employers' use of lie detectors and other mechanisms designed to determine a person's honesty. The statute, which generally prohibits most uses of lie detectors by employers in industries operating in or affecting interstate commerce, bars employers from discharging, disciplining, discriminating, or denying employment or promotion to employees or prospective employees on the basis of the results of a lie detector test. Under the Act, however, employers may request current employees to submit to polygraph examinations while investigating incidents causing economic loss, such as theft, embezzlement, or industrial espionage or sabotage, if the employer has reasonable suspicion that the employee was involved in the incident and had access to the property subject to the investigation.

The statute exempts the federal and state government and also allows limited use of lie detectors in matters dealing with national defense and security. Other exemptions allow the use of lie detectors by security services in hiring employees who will protect facilities or materials with significant impact on the health and safety of the state or national security of the United States (including electric, nuclear power, or public water facilities, public transportation, and toxic waste), or by employers who manufacture or distribute certain drugs in hiring employees who will have access to those drugs. Even those employers who are exempt may not use lie detector results (or refusal to submit to a lie detector test) as the sole basis for discharging an employee or refusing to hire an applicant. The Act further establishes testing procedures for private employers who are allowed to use polygraph examinations. The employer must provide written notice to the employee, must use licensed examiners, and must not ask questions about certain subjects (such as questions about sexual behavior or those relating to religious, racial, or political beliefs or affiliations).

The secretary of labor, who is responsible for administering the Act and adopting regulations, may assess a $10,000 civil penalty against employers who violate the Act and may seek legal or injunctive relief against violators in federal district courts. An employer who violates the Act also may be liable for damages and attorneys' fees of an employee or prospective employee injured by the violation.

Worker Adjustment and Retraining Notification Act

Following a period of massive restructuring and permanent workforce reduction in manufacturing industries, Congress enacted the **Worker Adjustment and Retraining Notification (WARN) Act**[19] in 1988. This statute requires businesses with 100 or more employees

---

[18]29 U.S.C. §§2001–2009.

[19]29 U.S.C. §§2101–2109.

to provide advance notification of certain plant closings or mass layoffs of employees. The notification is required if an employer permanently or temporarily closes a plant causing employment loss to 50 or more full-time employees during a 30-day period or reduces the labor force causing employment loss to (1) at least 500 full-time employees at the site, or (2) at least 50 full-time employees that comprise at least one-third of the employees at the site. Under the Act, "employment loss" is considered to be termination (other than discharge for cause or voluntary departure or retirement), a layoff exceeding six months, or a reduction in working hours of more than 50 percent during each month of a six-month period.

Sixty days prior to a plant closing or layoff that creates such an employment loss, the employer must provide written notice to each affected employee (or if the employees are unionized, to the union representative), to the chief elected official of the community in which the plant is located, and to certain other state officials. A plant closing or layoff is allowed without the 60-day notice if, at the time the notice was due, the employer was attempting to obtain capital or business that would have prevented or postponed the closing or layoff and the employer reasonably and in good faith believed that the notice would have prevented its obtaining the capital or business. Further, the 60-day notice is not required if the closing or layoff was caused by natural disaster or by business circumstances that could not be reasonably foreseen. An employer that orders a plant closing or mass layoff without providing the 60-day notice may be held civilly liable to pay 60 days' compensation and benefits to the affected employees.

Labor Law

The federal statutes described in the preceding sections establish minimum standards for employee protection. Employees generally are free to negotiate more favorable employment terms and conditions; however, individual employees often lack sufficient bargaining power to secure such benefits. During the late 1800s and early 1900s, employees attempted to improve their bargaining position by forming unions to negotiate collectively with employers. These efforts were met with strong resistance by businesses. In addition, state and federal courts, many of which were hostile to collective action by workers or biased toward employers, routinely enjoined union activities including strikes, pick-eting, and boycotts. Following years of labor strife, often accompanied by violence, the federal Congress enacted a number of statutes to govern the formation and operation of labor organizations. The remainder of this chapter discusses these federal labor laws.

Introduction to Labor Law

Governing Statutes. Federal regulation of labor-management relations began in 1932 when Congress adopted the **Norris-LaGuardia Act**[20] that restricted the federal courts' power to issue injunctions in labor disputes. Three years later, Congress enacted the **National Labor Relations Act**[21] (the **NLRA,** commonly called the **Wagner Act**) that established employees' basic rights to engage in collective action: (1) the right to form, join, or assist unions, (2) the right to bargain collectively through a union chosen by the employees, and (3) the right to engage in concerted activities for the purpose of collective bargaining or other mutual aid or protection.[22]

Union membership increased dramatically after adoption of the Wagner Act but a series of major strikes following World War II brought renewed opposition to unions. Congress responded by amending the NLRA with the **Labor-Management Relations Act**[23] (usually called the **Taft-Hartley Act**) in 1947 in an effort to assume a more neutral federal policy toward labor-management relations. Following well-publicized reports of corruption and abuse of power within unions, Congress again amended the NLRA in 1959 with the **Labor-Management Reporting and Disclosure Act**[24] (the **Landrum-Grifflin Act**). This statute created a bill of rights to protect union members from improper treatment by unions and required unions to adopt constitutions and bylaws and to submit periodic financial reports to the secretary of labor.

The NLRA as amended is the most comprehensive statute regulating labor-management relations. Its coverage extends to employees of most businesses affecting interstate commerce except agricultural laborers, employees of federal and state governments, and workers subject to the Railway Labor Act. Supervisors and managerial employees also are not covered by the statute.

---

[20]29 U.S.C. §§101–115.
[21]29 U.S.C. §151 *et seq.*
[22]29 U.S.C. §157.
[23]29 U.S.C. §141 *et seq.*
[24]29 U.S.C. §§153, 158–160, 164, 186, 187, 401 *et seq.*

National Labor Relations Board. The Wagner Act established the **National Labor Relations Board (NLRB),** a federal administrative agency, to administer the NLRA. The NLRB is composed of five members and the general counsel, all of whom are appointed by the president with the advice and consent of the Senate. Board mem-bers serve five-year, staggered terms while the general counsel serves a four-year term. The NLRB possesses broad administrative authority, including the powers to investigate and prosecute alleged unfair labor practices, to issue regulations, and to hold administrative hearings. The NLRB also supervises the election process through which employees determine whether to be represented by a union.

Unfair Labor Practices. Section 8 of the NLRA lists a series of **unfair labor practices** that are prohibited by the statute. As originally adopted in the Wagner Act, unfair labor practices referred only to illegal conduct committed by employers. Through subsequent amendments, however, certain unlawful union activities were added to the list of unfair labor practices. In general, employers have a duty not to interfere with employees' rights to form or join unions or to engage in concerted activities; unions are obligated not to coerce or restrain employees who are exercising those rights. Violation of any of these duties is an unfair labor practice. More specific ·unfair labor practices are discussed in the material that follows.

The NLRB is responsible for investigating and prose-cuting unfair labor practices. An employee, union, or employer initiates an unfair labor practice case by filing a charge with the NLRB. A regional office of the NLRB investigates the charge and, if it has merit, issues a com-plaint and notifies the alleged wrongdoer. If the com-plaint is not settled, the case is scheduled for hearing before an administrative law judge (ALJ) who, after tak-ing evidence, recommends an order. If an unfair labor practice is found, the ALJ recommends an appropriate administrative remedy such as a cease and desist order or reinstatement. Unless one of the parties requests review by the NLRB, the ALJ's order becomes final as an order issued by the NLRB. Upon timely request of a party, the NLRB provides appellate-type review of the ALJ's order and issues a written decision and order. The U.S. Circuit Courts of Appeals are authorized to review NLRB orders and to enforce orders if the parties fail to comply.

The Campaign and Election Process

A primary goal of the NLRA is to enable employees to choose whether they will be represented by a union. If a union is selected, it has the exclusive power to engage in **collective bargaining**—negotiating on behalf of the employees—with the employer in an effort to reach a **collective bargaining agreement,** a formal contract covering wages, hours, and terms and conditions of employment. Most union elections are preceded by contentious campaigns between the employer and the union. As a result, one of the NLRB's most important roles has been to assure a fair election process.

Efforts to organize may be initiated by the employ-ees or by a union that tries to persuade employees of the benefits of electing a collecting bargaining repre-sentative. After obtaining sufficient support, docu-mented by authorization cards signed by employees, a union may demand that the employer recognize the union as the bargaining representative. The employer may voluntarily recognize the union and proceed to collective bargaining, but in such a case the union is not officially certified as the collective bargaining rep-resentative by the NLRB. If the employer refuses to grant recognition, the union, an employee, or the employer may file a petition with the NLRB requesting a representation election.

After investigating the petition, the NLRB must determine the appropriate bargaining unit for the elec-tion. The bargaining unit consists of the employees who will be entitled to vote in the election and who will be represented by the union if it is elected. The unit may consist of the entire business, or one or more depart-ments, plants, stores, or offices within the business. If an adequate number of employees in the bargaining unit (generally 30 percent of the employees as documented by authorization cards) demonstrate support for the union, the NLRB notifies the parties of the election, resolving any related issues through a hearing if neces-sary. With limited exceptions, all nonsupervisory and nonmanagerial employees within the unit are entitled to vote. The election is conducted by secret ballot under the supervision of an NLRB representative. Following the election the NLRB certifies the union as the collec-tive bargaining representative if a majority of employees voted for the union, or certifies the election results if no union received a majority.

Unlawful Activities. During the campaign and election, employers can engage in only limited activities to oppose unionization. The employer is entitled to express its opinion of a union or unionization through speeches, literature, or other means provided that the employer does not interfere with, restrain, or coerce employees who are exercising their rights to organize. For example, an employer who threatens reprisals for organizational activitities or grants benefits to induce employees to reject the union commits an unfair labor practice. Withholding existing benefits or revoking planned increased benefits during the election campaign also may be unlawful.

The employer also is prohibited from unduly interfering with the union's and employees' rights to distribute information to employees and to solicit employees' votes. In general, the employer may prevent or limit dissemination of literature or solicitation of votes by employees during working time. The employer, however, may not restrict these activities by employees in nonworking areas during nonworking time—such as lunch hours or breaks—without a showing of special circumstances. A retail business, for example, may prohibit employee solicitation activities on the sales floor during employees' nonworking time if the activities would disrupt business.

In the following case, the Supreme Court discusses the extent of cooperation required of an employer during a union campaign.

Lechmere, Inc. v. National Labor Relations Board
112 S. Ct. 841 (1992)

> Lechmere Shopping Plaza in Newington, Connecticut, is located adjacent to a four-lane public highway that is separated from the plaza's parking lot by a 46-foot-wide grass strip. Lechmere, Inc. owns and operates a retail store in the plaza and jointly owns the parking lot with the developer of the shopping area. Most of the grass strip is public property. In June 1987, Local 919 of the United Food and Commercial Workers Union, AFL-CIO (the union) began a campaign to organize the 200 employees of Lechmere, Inc. After running an advertisement in the local paper, the union organizers tried several times to place pamphlets on the windshields of cars in the shopping plaza's parking lot but Lechmere's manager denied them access to the lot. Union organizers then picketed and handed out pamphlets from the grassy strip near the entrance to the parking lot. The union also contacted about 20 percent of the store's employees through mailings, telephone calls, and home visits. Following seven months of efforts, only one employee had signed a union authorization card. The union filed a charge with the National Labor Relations Board (the Board) claiming that Lechmere's refusal to allow nonemployee organizers on its property was an unfair labor practice. The Board ruled in favor of the union and the court of appeals affirmed. The U.S. Supreme Court granted Lechmere's petition for review.

Justice Thomas

. . . This case requires us to clarify the relationship between the rights of employees under §7 of the National Labor Relations Act, . . . and the property rights of their employers. . . .

Section 7 of the NLRA provides in relevant part that "[e]mployees shall have the right to self-organization, to form, join, or assist labor organizations." . . . Section 8(a)(1) of the Act, in turn, makes it an unfair labor practice for an employer "to interfere with, restrain, or coerce employees in the exercise of rights guaranteed in [7]." . . . By its plain terms, thus, the NLRA confers rights only on *employees,* not on unions or their nonemployee organizers. . . . Thus, while "[n]o restriction may be placed on the employees' right to discuss self-organization *among themselves,* unless the employer can demonstrate that a restriction is necessary to maintain production or discipline, . . . no such obligation is owed nonemployee organizers. [*NLRB v. Babcock & Wilcox Co.,* 76 S. Ct. 679, 684 (1956).] . . . As a rule, then, an employer cannot be compelled to allow distribution of union literature by nonemployee organizers on his property. As with many other rules, however, we recognized an exception. Where "the location of a plant and the living quarters of the employees place the employees beyond the reach of reasonable union efforts to communicate with them," . . . employers' property rights may be "required to yield to the extent needed to permit communication of information on the right to organize." [*Id.*] . . .

The threshold inquiry in this case, then, is whether the facts here justify application of *Babcock's* inaccessibility exception. . . . [T]he Board [ruled] that "there was no reasonable, effective alternative means available for the Union to communicate its message to [Lechmere's] employees." 295 N.L.R.B. No. 15, Board slip op., at 4–5.

We cannot accept the Board's conclusion. . . . [T]he exception to *Babcock's* rule is a narrow one. It does not apply wherever nontrespassory access to employees may be cumbersome or less-than-ideally effective, but only where "*the location of a plant and the living quarters of the employees* place the employees *beyond the reach* of reasonable union efforts to communicate with them," . . . 76 S. Ct., at 684 (emphasis added). Classic examples include logging camps, . . . mining camps, . . . and mountain resort hotels. . . . *Babcock's* exception was crafted precisely to protect the §7 rights of those employees who, by virtue of their employment, are isolated from the ordinary flow of information that characterizes our society. . . .

The Board's conclusion in this case that the union had no reasonable means short of trespass to make Lechmere's employees aware of its organizational efforts is based on a misunderstanding of the limited scope of this exception. . . . Although the employees live in a large metropolitan area (Greater Hartford), that fact does not in itself render them "inaccessible" in the sense contemplated by *Babcock.* . . . Their accessibility is suggested by the union's success in contacting a substantial percentage of them directly, via mailings, phone calls, and home visits. Such direct contact, of course, is not a necessary element of "reasonably effective" communication; signs or advertising also may suffice. In this case, the union tried advertising in local newspapers; the Board said that this was not reasonably effective because it was expensive and might not reach the employees. . . . Whatever the merits of that conclusion, other alternative means of communication were readily available. Thus, signs (displayed, for example, from the public grassy strip adjoining Lechmere's parking lot) would have informed the employees about the union's organizational efforts. (Indeed, union organizers picketed the shopping center's main entrance for months as employees came and went every day.) *Access* to employees, not *success* in winning them over, is the critical issue—although success, or lack thereof, may be relevant in determining whether reasonable access exists. Because the union in this case failed to establish the existence of any "unique obstacles," . . . that frustrated access to Lechmere's employees, the Board erred in concluding that Lechmere committed an unfair labor practice by barring the nonemployee organizers from its property. . . .

[Judgment reversed.]

Unions also are prohibited from interfering with employees' organizational rights. Threatening employees who refuse to join the union, or granting special benefits or privileges—such as waiver of membership fees—to employees who vote in favor of the union, are unfair labor practices.

The Collective Bargaining Process

After certification or recognition as the collective bargaining representative, the union is the exclusive representative for all employees in the unit. The union and the employer then must negotiate in an effort to reach a collective bargaining agreement.

Duty to Bargain in Good Faith. The NLRA imposes on both the employer and the union a duty to bargain in good faith on wages, rates of pay, hours of employment, or other conditions of employment. Failure or refusal to bargain in good faith is an unfair labor practice. At a minimum, this duty requires both parties to meet at reasonable times and places and attempt to reach an agreement by offering and considering proposals. The duty to bargain in good faith requires neither the union nor the employer to make concessions or to reach an agreement. Offering proposals, counterproposals, and concessions, however, may demonstrate that a party has fulfilled its duty to bargain in good faith. In determining whether the duty to bargain has been violated, the courts and NLRB examine the parties' conduct during the entire course of negotiations.

Mandatory Subjects of Bargaining. The duty to bargain in good faith applies only to mandatory subjects of bargaining—those within the category of "wages, hours and other terms and conditions of employment," including, for example, discharge of employees, seniority work schedules, retirement and pension plans, insurance plans, and grievances. The parties are prohibited from negotiating illegal subjects of bargaining, which are proposals that violate the labor statutes. For example, "featherbedding" (paying employees for services that are not performed or not intended to be performed) is illegal under the NLRA and, therefore, may not be the subject of bargaining and may not be required under the collective bargaining agreement. All topics other than mandatory or illegal subjects of bargaining are considered voluntary or permissive subjects of bargaining which, if both parties agree, may be negotiated and included in the collective bargaining agreement.

In the case that follows, the Supreme Court considers collective bargaining and mandatory subjects of bargaining.

Ford Motor Company v. National Labor Relations Board
99 S. Ct. 1842 (1979)

Petitioner Ford Motor Company operates a parts-stamping plant employing 3,600 employees who are represented by the International Union, United Automobile, Aerospace, and Agricultural Implement Workers of America (the Union). Because no restaurants are located near the plant, Ford provides in-plant cafeterias and vending machines managed by ARA Services, Inc., an independent caterer. By contract with Ford, ARA furnishes food, management, machines, and personnel in exchange for reimbursement of all direct costs plus 9 percent of net receipts. If receipts exceed costs plus the 9 percent surcharge, Ford retains the excess but if the receipts are less than the costs and surcharge, Ford is obligated to pay ARA the deficit up to $52,000 per year. Ford has the right to review and approve the quality, quantity, and price of the food served by ARA.

In 1976, Ford notified the Union that cafeteria and vending machine prices were to be increased. The Union requested that Ford bargain over the prices and services but Ford refused maintaining that these matters were not mandatory subjects of bargaining. The Union filed an unfair labor practice charge with the National Labor Relations Board (the Board) alleging that Ford had refused to bargain over a mandatory bargaining subject.

The Board ruled that Ford had violated its duty to bargain in good faith. Ford appealed to the Seventh Circuit Court of Appeals, which held that the cafeteria and vending machine food prices and services were mandatory subjects of bargaining. The Supreme Court granted Ford's petition for review.

Justice White

. . . The principal question in this case is whether prices for in-plant cafeteria and vending machine food and beverages are "terms and conditions of employment" subject to mandatory collective bargaining. . . .

The Board has consistently held that in-plant food prices are among those terms and conditions of employment defined in §8(d) [of the National Labor Relations Act] and about which the employer and union must bargain. . . .

Construing and applying the duty to bargain and the language of §8(d), "other terms and conditions of employment," are tasks lying at the heart of the Board's function. . . . [W]e conclude that the Board's consistent view that in-plant food prices and services are mandatory bargaining subjects is not an unreasonable or unprincipled construction of the statute and that it should be accepted and enforced.

It is not suggested by petitioner that an employee should work a full 8-hour shift without stopping to eat. It reasonably follows that the availability of food during working hours and the conditions under which it is to be consumed are matters of deep concern to workers, and one need not strain to consider them to be among those "conditions" of employment that should be subject to the mutual duty to bargain. By the same token, where the employer has

chosen, apparently in his own interest, to make available a system of in-plant feeding facilities for his employees, the prices at which food is offered and other aspects of this service may reasonably be considered among those subjects about which management and union must bargain. The terms and conditions under which food is available on the job are plainly germane to the "working environment." *Fibreboard Paper Products Corp. v. NLRB,* [85 S. Ct. 398,409 (1964)] (Stewart, J., concurring). Furthermore, the company is not in the business of selling food to its employees, and the establishment of in-plant food prices is not among those "managerial decisions, which lie at the core of entrepreneurial control." [*Id.* at 409] (Stewart, J., concurring). The Board is in no sense attempting to permit the Union to usurp managerial decision-making; nor is it seeking to regulate an area from which Congress intended to exclude it.

Including within §8(d) the prices of in-plant supplied food and beverages would also serve the ends of the National Labor Relations Act. . . . As illustrated by the facts of this case, substantial disputes can arise over the pricing of in-plant-supplied food and beverages. National labor policy contemplates that areas of common dispute between employers and employees be funneled into collective bargaining. The assumption is that this is preferable to allowing recurring disputes to fester outside the negotiation process until strikes or other forms of economic warfare occur.

The trend of industrial practice supports this conclusion. In response to increasing employee concern over the issue, many contracts are now being negotiated that contain provisions concerning in-plant food services. . . . Although not conclusive, current industrial practice is highly relevant in construing the phrase "terms and conditions of employment." . . .

We affirm, therefore, the Court of Appeals' judgment upholding the Board's determination in this case that inplant food services and prices are "terms and conditions of employment" subject to mandatory bargaining under §§8(a)(5) and 8(d) of the National Labor Relations Act.

[Judgment affirmed.]

If the union and employer are unable to reach a collective bargaining agreement or to resolve mandatory bargaining subjects, the federal government provides mediation services through the Federal Mediation and Conciliation Service. Although mediation is not binding, effective mediators often succeed in bringing opposing parties to agreement.

Sometimes, however, after bargaining in good faith, the union and employer reach impasse, a point of irreconcilable differences on a mandatory bargaining subject or subjects. If the parties reach an impasse, they need not continue futile negotiations. Furthermore, after reaching impasse, the employer may act unilaterally on issues that caused the impasse provided that it does not implement a change more favorable than it offered during bargaining. If, for example, the parties reach impasse on the subject of wages, the employer generally may impose any wage rate equal to or less than the rate it offered during the bargaining.

Collective Bargaining Agreement

The goal of the collective bargaining process is to secure a collective bargaining agreement to govern the relationship between the employer and employees, and the employer and the union. The agreement, however, is not an employment contract; the employer hires employees individually. The collective bargaining agreement usually is a complex document covering a variety of issues such as job classifications, pay scales and increases for each classification, working hours, overtime pay, vacations, holidays, promotions, insurance and retirement benefits, and seniority. Most collective bargaining agreements extend for a term of three or more years.

Almost all collective bargaining agreements also include a provision in which the employees agree not to strike during the term of the contract. In exchange for such no-strike clauses, the employer usually agrees to binding arbitration of disputes that arise during the term of the contract. Arbitration is used both for general interpretation of contract provisions and as the final step of a grievance procedure available to employees who believe that their rights under the agreement have been violated. Many grievances concern discharge or discipline of an employee. The procedure usually requires an employee to file a written grievance specifying the alleged wrong. The grievance then may be reviewed at one or more levels of management and, if not resolved by negotiation, must be submitted to arbitration. Most collective bargaining agreements also include a method for selecting the arbitrator. Generally, the decision of the arbitrator is binding on both parties.

Even after a collective bargaining agreement is made, the employer and union remain subject to the duty to bargain in good faith. As a result, proposed modifications of the bargaining agreement or resolution of issues not covered in the agreement may require further negotiations by the parties.

Unfair Labor Practices in Labor-Management Relations

Prohibited unfair labor practices may occur not only during the election process or collective bargaining, but also at other times when unions and management interact. The material that follows discusses the legality of various practices that commonly arise from labor-management relations.

Hiring and Employment Practices. Under the NLRA, an employer commits an unfair labor practice "by discrimination in regard to hire or tenure of employment or any term or condition of employment to encourage or discourage membership in any labor organization."[25] A business, therefore, may not discharge or refuse to hire a person because of involvement in union activities. The **yellow dog contract**—an employee's agreement as a condition of employment not to join or retain membership in a union—also is illegal. Similarly, the employer cannot fire or discriminate against employees because they have filed charges against an employer under the NLRA or have testified at a hearing or trial brought under the Act.

Unions also are prohibited from causing employers to discriminate against employees because of their union membership. The **closed shop**—an employer's agreement to hire only members of a union—is illegal, but some union shop and agency shop agreements are legal. A **union shop** agreement requires newly hired employees to join the union within a specified period after beginning employment. Union shop agreements are legal only if union membership is required no sooner than 30 days after employment begins. An **agency shop** agreement allows employees not to join the union but requires nonmembers to pay a fee to cover the union's services. Agency shop agreements that require employees to pay fees no earlier than 30 days after beginning employment are legal.

The NLRA, however, allows states to enact **right-to-work laws** that prohibit union and agency shops. Almost half of the states, located primarily in the South

---

[25] 29 U.S.C. §158(a)(3).

and Southwest, have adopted right-to-work laws. In those states, union and agency shops are illegal.

Strikes and Picketing. The ultimate negotiating weapon of a union is a **strike,** a concerted work stoppage by the employees. During a labor dispute or collective bargaining, the threat of a strike strengthens the union's bargaining power. Because strikes generally are legal, labor law protects striking employees from discharge or other discipline. Employers, however, are not required to pay striking employees and may hire replacements to perform the strikers' work.

When employees strike for illegal purposes or participate in illegal strike activities, they lose the protection of the labor statutes and are subject to dismissal and discipline. Illegal strikes include, for example, a strike to compel an employer to commit an unfair labor practice, a strike in breach of a no-strike clause in a collective bargaining agreement, and a **wildcat strike,** a strike by a minority of employees without authorization of the union. Strikes during a statutory "cooling-off" period also are illegal. A 60-day cooling-off period is created, for example, after a union or employer notifies the other party of an intention to modify or terminate a contract. Further, if a strike would create a national emergency, a federal court, upon request of the president, may enjoin a strike during an 80-day cooling-off period.

The extent of protection afforded to employees engaged in lawful strikes depends on the type of strike in which they participate. An **unfair labor practice strike** is caused in whole or in part by the employer's commission of an unfair labor practice. Employees who engage in unfair labor practice strikes are entitled to reinstatement in their jobs upon request, even if the employer has hired replacements. All strikes other than unfair labor practice strikes are considered **economic strikes** because they frequently arise from employees' demands for economic benefits. Following an economic strike, strikers are entitled to reinstatement in their former jobs only if permanent replacement workers were not hired. The employer, therefore, need not reinstate economic strikers whose jobs were filled by permanent replacements. Nevertheless, economic strikers who have not secured comparable employment elsewhere are entitled to preferential treatment if their former job or a job for which they are qualified becomes vacant at a later date.

Unions and employees often use picketing to publicize strikes and other disputes with the employer. **Primary picketing**—picketing the business with which the union has a genuine dispute—generally is legal and protected under the labor laws. Primary picketing, which often has been recognized as an exercise of the right of free speech, may be illegal, however, if it is accompanied by violence or is likely to lead to violence. Further, employees and unions generally have no right to picket on the private property of the employer.

Secondary Boycotts. Federal protection of strikes and picketing generally extends only to activities directed at the primary employer; that is, the business with which the union has a genuine dispute. A **secondary boycott** is a union tactic of pressuring the primary employer by striking, picketing, or otherwise boycotting a business with which the primary employer does business. Inducing or engaging in a secondary boycott is an unfair labor practice under the NLRA.

Assume, for example, that the employees of Manufacturer Co. are striking their employer for higher wages and that Supplier, Inc. and Retailer Corp. both do business with Manufacturer Co. The striking employees may picket Manufacturer and may appeal to the employees of Supplier and Retailer not to cross the picket line. Manufacturer's employees also may request that Supplier and Retailer discontinue doing business with Manufacturer. All of such activities are considered to be primary activities directed at Manufacturer, the primary employer. Manufacturer's employees, however, cannot apply pressure to the secondary parties by trying to induce Supplier's or Retailer's employees to strike their own employer or even to engage in a concerted refusal to handle Manufacturer's products. Such conduct is an illegal secondary boycott. Similarly, Manufacturer's employees cannot picket Supplier or Retailer in an effort to discourage their employees or customers from dealing with them because such secondary picketing also is an unfair labor practice.

A hot cargo clause also is an unfair labor practice under federal labor law. A **hot cargo clause** is a provision in a collective bargaining agreement by which an employer agrees not to do business with a nonunion company or a company involved in a labor dispute. By prohibiting hot cargo agreements, the NLRA effectively eliminates voluntary secondary boycotts.

Certain secondary activities do not violate the NLRA. Under the ally doctrine, for example, a union may strike, picket, or boycott a second business that is an ally of the primary company. An ally, however, is narrowly defined as a business with which the primary employer has common ownership of capital plus either common management or interrelated and dependent activities.

Another exception to the secondary boycott rules allows employees to engage in informational picketing that is directed at the public to encourage boycott of a particular product at a secondary site. For example, striking employees of Manufacturer Co. may picket Retailer Co. to inform the public that Retailer sells a specific product of Manufacturer. Such picketing is legal if the public could boycott purchasing just one product without boycotting the secondary employer's entire business.

Employer Lockouts. A **lockout**—the temporary closing of all or part of a business by refusal to allow employees to work—is an employer tactic analogous to a strike. Some lockouts are defensive in nature. An employer, for example, may close a plant in anticipation of a strike to prevent work stoppage at an inopportune time, such as in the middle of the food manufacturing process when spoilage would be very costly. Other lockouts are taken for offensive purposes to put economic pressure on employees to accept bargaining proposals.

The legality of a lockout depends on the employer's intent. If the employer locks out employees to avoid its bargaining duties, to destroy the union, or to penalize employees for engaging in union activities, the lockout constitutes an unfair labor practice. If, however, the lockout is motivated by legitimate business or economic reasons, the lockout usually does not violate the law.

Employer Reorganization of Business. Rather than merely temporarily locking out employees, an employer may try to permanently close all or part of its unionized operations. The Supreme Court considered the legality of permanent closings in *Textile Workers Union of America v. Darlington Manufacturing Company* (1965)[26] and held:

> . . . [W]hen an employer closes his entire business, even if the liquidation is motivated by vindictiveness toward the union, such action is not an unfair labor practice. . . . [A] partial closing is an unfair labor practice . . . if motivated by a purpose to chill unionism in any of the remaining plants of the single employer and if the employer may reasonably have foreseen that such closing would likely have that effect.[27]

Thus, terminating a business is allowed for any reason, but a partial closing—for example, eliminating one plant or facility—is illegal if the employer does so to discourage union activities at other facilities. The **runaway shop,** which is closing one facility or moving its operations to another facility to avoid having to bargain with a union, also is an unfair labor practice. In some cases, however, a plant closing motivated by economic reasons, such as high labor costs that may be attributable to union bargaining, may be legal.

Economic problems also can cause an employer to seek reorganization under the bankruptcy laws. As part of the reorganization, the employer may want to reject or modify an existing collective bargaining agreement. The Bankruptcy Code[28] requires that, before filing an application with the court to reject the agreement, the trustee in bankruptcy or debtor in possession (the employer) make a proposal to the bargaining representative that outlines all modifications to the agreement that may be necessary for reorganization and that assures that all affected parties are treated "fairly and equitably." The union is entitled to receive all relevant information, such as financial statements, necessary to evaluate the proposal. Often the union and employees will cooperate with the trustee or employer to reach acceptable modifications in an effort to preserve their jobs for the long term. The law explicitly requires the parties to meet and confer in good faith in an attempt to reach mutually satisfactory modifications to the agreement.

If the union does not agree to the proposed modifications, the Bankruptcy Court determines whether to reject the collective bargaining agreement. Following a hearing at which all interested parties may testify, the court may approve rejection of the agreement if it finds that the union refused the proposed modification without good cause and that the balance of equities clearly favors rejection. While the proposed rejection is under consideration by the court, the judge may authorize a temporary change in the terms of the collective bargaining agreement.

---

[26]85 S. Ct. 994 (1965).
[27]*Id.* at 1001–1002.

[28]11 U.S.C. §1113.

Summary

1. Since the labor crisis created by the Great Depression, the federal government has increased regulation of the employer-employee relationship.

2. Various federal statutes govern employee compensation and safety. The Fair Labor Standards Act establishes a national minimum wage and regulates child labor. The Social Security Act provides benefits to retired workers funded by a tax on employers, employees, and self-employed persons, while the Employee Retirement Income Security Act regulates private pensions. The Occupational Safety and Health Act requires employers to provide a workplace free from recognized hazards.

3. Other federal employee protection statutes include the Family and Medical Leave Act of 1993, which requires employers to provide unpaid leave for certain family and health reasons; the Employee Polygraph Protection Act of 1988, which restricts private employers' use of lie detectors; and the Worker Adjustment and Retraining Notification Act, which requires advance notification of some plant closings and mass layoffs.

4. The National Labor Relations Act (composed of the Wagner Act, the Taft-Hartley Act, and the Landrum-Griffin Act), as interpreted through administrative rulings and case law, regulates relationships among labor organizations and unions, employers, and employees.

5. Under federal labor law, employees are entitled to organize and elect a collective bargaining representative to negotiate a collective bargaining agreement on behalf of the employees. The collective bargaining representative and the employer have a duty to bargain in good faith concerning wages, hours, and other terms and conditions of employment.

6. By prohibiting certain unfair labor practices, federal labor law attempts to prevent employers from interfering with employees' rights to form and join unions and to engage in concerted activities, and to prevent unions from restraining or coercing employees.

Key Terms

Fair Labor Standards Act (FLSA)
Social Security Act
Family and Medical Leave Act of 1993 (FMLA)
Employee Retirement Income Security Act (ERISA)
Consolidated Omnibus Budget Reconciliation Act (COBRA)
Health Insurance Portability and Accountability Act (HIPAA)
vesting
Occupational Safety and Health Act (OSHA)
Occupational Safety and Health Administration
Employee Polygraph Protection Act
Worker Adjustment and Retraining Notification Act
Norris-LaGuardia Act
National Labor Relations Act (NLRA) (Wagner Act)

Labor-Management Relations Act (Taft-Hartley Act)
Labor-Management Reporting and Disclosure Act (Landrum-Griffin Act)
National Labor Relations Board (NLRB)
unfair labor practices
collective bargaining
collective bargaining agreement
yellow dog contract
closed shop
union shop
agency shop
right-to-work laws
strike
wildcat strike
unfair labor practice strike
economic strike
primary picketing
secondary boycott
hot cargo clause
lockout
runaway shop

Questions and Problems

53.1 The unemployment rate for young workers, especially unskilled workers less than 20 years of age, tends to be higher than the unemployment rate for other workers. Some politicians have suggested that these workers be exempted from the provisions of the FLSA. Would such an exemption resolve the unemployment problem? Explain. Does the FLSA create unemployment? Explain.

53.2 Suggest reasons why administrative and executive employees are exempt from the overtime provisions of the FLSA.

53.3 In recent years, Congress has considered, but never passed, a number of proposed statutes to prohibit employers from hiring permanent replacement workers to replace striking employees during an economic strike. Do you think that such a statute would be beneficial to the American economy? Explain.

53.4 A hospital has adopted a rule prohibiting union solicitation in all patient-access areas of the hospital. As a result, union solicitation was restricted to several employee-only restrooms and locker areas that served approximately one-third of the employees. An employee decided to distribute a union newsletter in the hospital cafeteria. Prior to giving the newsletter to any person, she first asked if the person was an employee. The hospital reprimanded the employee for violation of the solicitation rule and the employee filed unfair labor practice charges. Is the hospital's solicitation rule an unfair labor practice? Explain.

53.5 During an organization campaign at Sinclair Co., Sinclair's president made an effort to talk to all employees about unionization. The president reminded the employees that a strike 15 years earlier had "almost put our company out of business" and stated that the company was on "thin ice" financially. The president also pointed out that many unionized companies in the area had gone out of business at a loss of 3,500 jobs. Has the president committed an unfair labor practice? Explain.

53.6 During an organization campaign, a union requested employees to sign "recognition slips." Any employee who signed a slip prior to the representation election would be entitled to a waiver of the initiation fee required to join the union. The employer charged that use of the recognition slips was an unfair labor practice. How should the court rule? Explain.

53.7 American Space Co. manufacturers jets, rockets, and other products used in the aerospace industry. The company has a collective bargaining agreement with the Space Industry Workers Union. During the last year, American has noticed a substantial decline in the quality of the construction of its products and is concerned that the poor quality may affect the safety of the products and ultimately may lead to a decline in sales. Attributing the poor quality to increased use of drugs and alcohol by its employees, American unilaterally announced that all employees would be subject to random testing for drugs and alcohol. The union files an unfair labor claim alleging that the testing program is a mandatory bargaining subject. How should the court rule? Explain.

53.8 DeBartolo Corp. owns East Lake Mall and leases shops in the mall to various retailers. Wilson's Department Store, which leases space in the mall, decided to rebuild its store and hired High Co., a nonunion company, to perform the construction work. Under the terms of its lease, Wilson's may hire any construction company it wishes without obtaining approval of DeBartolo or other mall tenants. Members of a local construction workers union began distributing handbills at the mall entrances. The leaflets stated:

> PLEASE DO NOT SHOP AT EAST LAKE MALL. WILSON'S DEPARTMENT STORE, NOW UNDER CONSTRUCTION AT EAST LAKE PAYS SUBSTANDARD WAGES AND FRINGE BENEFITS. WE ASK THAT YOU SHOW YOUR OPPOSITION TO SUBSTANDARD WAGES AND FRINGE BENEFITS BY REFUSING TO PATRONIZE THE TENANTS OF EAST LAKE MALL.

The handbill distribution was peaceful and caused no disruption at the mall. DeBartolo Corp. filed unfair labor practice charges with the NLRB alleging that the union's activities constituted an illegal secondary boycott. How should the Board rule?

FEDERAL EQUAL EMPLOYMENT OPPORTUNITY LAWS

Since 1960, Congress has enacted a number of additional statutes, generally described as equal employment opportunity laws, designed to eliminate discrimination that previously had limited the opportunities of certain groups in the workplace. The purpose of these laws is to encourage employers to base employment decisions—such as hiring, firing, promotion, and compensation—on a person's abilities and qualifications to perform the job rather than on considerations unrelated to job performance. This chapter focuses on three major federal equal employment opportunity statutes: Title VII of the Civil Rights Act of 1964, the Age Discrimination in Employment Act (ADEA), and Title I of the Americans with Disabilities Act (ADA). Statutes with more limited effect, including the Equal Pay Act, the Civil Rights Act of 1866, and the Immigration Reform and Control Act, also are discussed.

The **Equal Employment Opportunity Commission (EEOC)** is the federal agency primarily responsible for enforcement of Title VII, the ADEA, and Title I. As part of its executive functions, the EEOC is authorized to investigate complaints and to file lawsuits on behalf of groups or individuals who allegedly have suffered illegal employment discrimination. The agency also issues official guidelines explaining its interpretation of the statutes it administers. Although these guidelines do not have the force of law, courts generally give deference to the EEOC's interpretations.

Title VII of the Civil Rights Act of 1964

In response to the civil rights movements that culminated during the 1960s, Congress adopted the Civil Rights Act of 1964, a comprehensive federal statute intended to eliminate many forms of unfair discrimination against women and members of minority groups, particularly African-Americans. Workplace discrimination is addressed in **Title VII of the Civil Rights Acts of 1964,**[1] as amended, which generally prohibits employers, unions, and employment agencies from

---

[1] 42 U.S.C. §2000e *et seq.*

discriminating against employees and applicants on the basis of race, color, national origin, sex (gender), or religion. In 1978, Congress amended Title VII with the Pregnancy Discrimination Act that clarified that discrimination on the basis of pregnancy, childbirth, or related medical conditions is a form of illegal sex discrimination. Private employers with 15 or more employees, labor unions with 15 or more members, government employers, and employment agencies are required to comply with the provisions of Title VII.

Illegal Discrimination

Title VII prohibits all types of employment practices that discriminate on the basis of race, color, national origin, sex, or religion. An employment agency, therefore, cannot base referrals on any of these factors. Similarly, an employer is prohibited from using these illegal classifications—race, color, national origin, sex, or religion—as a basis for hiring, discharging, promoting, or compensating employees. Other conditions and privileges of employment, such as leave benefits, insurance programs, pension plans, and training opportunities, also must be administered without discrimination based on the prohibited characteristics. Any other classification of employees or applicants on the basis of race, color, national origin, sex, or religion that adversely affects employment opportunities also is illegal.

Two general types of conduct violate Title VII: (1) disparate treatment based on any of the illegal classifications, and (2) employment practices that have a disparate impact on those of a certain race, color, national origin, sex, or religion. The following material discusses each of these types of conduct as well as defenses that protect the employer from liability.

Disparate Treatment. **Disparate treatment,** which also is described as overt or intentional discrimination, occurs when an employer directly uses race, color, national origin, sex, or religion as a criterion for making an employment decision. An employer that refuses to hire blacks, for example, commits disparate treatment because it uses race or color as the basis for its hiring decision. A business employer that provides educational benefits only to male employees engages in disparate treatment based on sex or gender.

A claim of disparate treatment may be proven by direct or circumstantial evidence. Direct evidence might include, for example, a statement in a hiring notice restricting a job to men or records from an employer's files indicating the intent not to hire minority group members. Because such clear evidence rarely is available, most cases of disparate treatment involve circumstantial evidence. In a "pattern and practice" case, for instance, the EEOC uses statistical evidence to establish that a business systematically discriminates against a certain group such as women, African-Americans, Hispanic-Americans, or Moslems. These cases generally require expert witnesses to prove that the underrepresentation of members of a particular group is statistically unlikely in the absence of discrimination.

An individual plaintiff who alleges disparate treatment must initially establish a "prima facie" case that requires proof of the following: (1) the plaintiff belongs to a protected class (for example, the plaintiff is a minority group member or woman); (2) the plaintiff applied for a job for which the employer was seeking applicants; (3) the plaintiff was qualified for the job; (4) the plaintiff was denied the job; and (5) the job remained open and the employer continued to accept applications.[2] In such cases, the employer's discriminatory intent may be inferred. This inference, however, is overcome if the employer offers evidence showing a legitimate business reason (for example, the applicant was not qualified) for rejecting the plaintiff. To win the lawsuit, the plaintiff must prove that the reason offered by the employer was merely a pretext and that illegal discrimination was the real basis for the employment decision.

Defenses to Disparate Treatment Claims. An employer who has been sued for disparate treatment may contest the plaintiff's allegations. Often, the employer will try to establish that its employment decision was based not on illegal discrimination but on a legitimate business reason, such as the plaintiff's qualifications for the job. In cases based on statistical evidence, the defendant usually employs its own expert witness in an effort to prove that the evidence does not prove intentional systematic exclusion of members of a particular group.

Alternatively, the defendant may avoid liability by proving that the disparate treatment was permissible under Title VII's **bona fide occupational qualification (BFOQ)** defense. The BFOQ defense allows an employer to restrict a job to individuals of a particular sex, religion, or national origin if reasonably necessary to the normal operation of its business. Title VII thus recognizes that in limited circumstances, a person's sex, religion, or national

---

[2]McDonnell Douglas Corporation v. Green, 93 S. Ct. 1817, 1824 (1973).

origin may be a legitimate job qualification. Race or color, however, never is a valid BFOQ.

The BFOQ defense has been raised most frequently in cases involving sex discrimination. In discussing sex as a BFOQ, the U.S. Supreme Court has ruled that defense should be interpreted very narrowly:

> The wording of the BFOQ defense contains several terms of restriction that indicate that the exception reaches only special situations. The statute thus limits the situations in which discrimination is permissible to "certain instances" where sex discrimination is "reasonably necessary" to the "normal operation" of the "particular" business. Each one of these terms—certain, normal, particular—prevents the use of general subjective standards and favors an objective, verifiable requirement. But the most telling term is "occupational"; this indicates that these objective, verifiable requirements must concern job-related skills and aptitudes.[3]

Few jobs, therefore, legally can be restricted to men or to women. Instead, employment decisions should be based on the ability to perform the job.

Some employers, for example, have argued that jobs requiring strenuous manual labor or heavy lifting should be limited to men. Courts have ruled that such restrictions generally violate Title VII because the legitimate job qualification is not the employee's sex but the ability to perform the tasks of the job. In one case, involving unusual facts, the U.S. Supreme Court upheld restricting a prison guard position to males. The job was at a maximum security penitentiary that was understaffed, had a history of violence, and housed only male inmates—including many sex offenders—in a dormitory setting. The Supreme Court's ruling that sex was a BFOQ for the job was based primarily on safety and privacy concerns.[4] In subsequent decisions, courts have held that excluding women from prison jobs under less hostile conditions violates Title VII. For other types of jobs involving privacy concerns—employment positions, for example, in prisons, schools, hospitals, and nursing homes—courts have ruled that only particular tasks or duties, not entire jobs, may be restricted on the basis of sex.

Title VII explicitly allows religious organizations to restrict almost all jobs to members of their religion. The courts, therefore, broadly interpret religion as a BFOQ in cases in which the employer is a religious institution. The Supreme Court held, for example, that membership in the Mormon Church was a legal criterion for the job of maintenance engineer at a nonprofit gymnasium operated by the church.[5] For employment positions outside religious organizations, however, religion as a BFOQ is narrowly construed.

Disparate Impact. A second type of discriminatory conduct that may violate Title VII involves employment practices that cause **disparate impact** or discriminatory effect. Disparate impact occurs when an employment decision based on a neutral criterion (that is, some factor other than race, color, national origin, sex, or religion) has the *effect* of discriminating on the basis of race, color, national origin, sex, or religion.

Assume, for example, that a manufacturing company hires only factory workers who are at least six feet tall. The hiring decision is based on a neutral criterion— a minimum height requirement. Because race, color, national origin, sex, or religion is not the basis for the decision, no violation of Title VII is apparent. The *effect* or *impact* of using this criterion, however, is to exclude a higher proportion of women than men because, as a group, men tend to be taller than women. This minimum height requirement then would be described as having a disparate impact on women and could be considered discrimination on the basis of sex because of its adverse effect on women. Such a height requirement also might have a disparate impact on other groups, such as Asians, who generally are shorter than those of other races. Thus, the height requirement also might be considered a form of discrimination based on race or national origin.

To establish a disparate impact claim under Title VII, the plaintiff must: (1) identify the specific employment practice or job criterion (for example, a test, height, or weight requirement, or a particular skill); (2) prove through statistical evidence that this practice or criterion disproportionately affects individuals of a particular sex, race, color, national origin, or religion; and (3) prove through statistical evidence that the disparity is not due to chance; in other words that the identified practice or job criterion caused the discrimination. The plaintiff's case generally depends on expert witnesses who have conducted statistical analyses of the employer's job force and hiring practices.

---

[3]International Union, UAW v. Johnson Controls, Inc., 111 S. Ct. 1196, 1204 (1991).
[4]Dothard v. Rawlinson, 97 S. Ct. 2720 (1977).

[5]Corporation of the Presiding Bishop v. Amos, 107 S. Ct. 2862 (1987).

Defenses to Disparate Impact Claims. The defendant in a disparate impact case often challenges the methodology or conclusions drawn from statistical information through testimony of its own expert witness. As a result, disparate impact cases generally require interpretation of sophisticated analyses of complex data. The defendant may avoid liability by proving the **business necessity defense,** which is similar to the BFOQ defense in disparate treatment cases. The business necessity defense allows employment practices that are "job related for the position in question and consistent with business necessity"[6] even if the practice causes disparate impact. Thus, employers are allowed to use job criteria that are legitimately related to job performance.

Consider, for example, an employer who requires all applicants for a particular job to pass a strength test demonstrating the ability to lift 100-pound cartons. This requirement probably would have the effect of disproportionately excluding women from the job. Despite this disparate impact, the employer would not violate Title VII if the tasks associated with the job actually required lifting 100-pound cartons. In other words, use of the strength test would be permissible if legitimately related to the job. If the employer failed to show that the test actually was job-related, however, then its use would be illegal because of disparate impact. A strength test, for example, for a job of furniture mover probably is consistent with job necessity while use of the same test for a computer programmer would not be.

Many disparate impact cases concern height and weight restrictions, or the use of tests. The following case, however, challenges an employer's grooming policy.

Bradley v. Pizzaco of Nebraska, Inc.
7 F.3d 795 (8th Cir. 1993)

Domino's Pizza, Inc. (Domino's) has a grooming policy that prohibits employees of Domino's restaurants from wearing beards. Pizzaco of Nebraska, Inc. (Pizzaco), which operates a Domino's restaurant, hired Langston Bradley to deliver pizzas but later fired him when he refused to shave. Plaintiff Bradley sued defendants Domino's and Pizzaco claiming that the no-beard policy

---

[6]42 U.S.C. §2000e-2(k)(1)(A)(i).

violated Title VII because it discriminated against black males. Evidence offered by Bradley and the EEOC, including testimony from dermatologists and military studies, established that he and as many as 45 percent of black males suffer from the skin disorder pseudofolliculitis barbae (PFB). PFB causes skin irritation and scarring that are brought on by shaving. About 25 percent of PFB sufferers have severe cases requiring that they abstain from shaving. The trial court ruled that Domino's no-beard policy did not violate Title VII but on appeal, the Eighth Circuit Court of Appeals held:

> Title VII forbids employment policies with a disparate impact unless the policy is justified by legitimate employment goals. . . . The EEOC's evidence makes clear that Domino's strictly-enforced no-beard policy has a discriminatory impact on black males. PFB prevents a sizable segment of the black male population from appearing clean-shaven, but does not similarly affect white males. Domino's policy—which makes no exceptions for black males who medically are unable to shave because of a skin disorder peculiar to their race—effectively operates to exclude these black males from employment with Domino's.
> *Bradley v. Pizzaco of Nebraska, Inc. (Pizzaco 1),* 939 F.2d 610, 612–613 (8th Cir. 1991).

The court then remanded the case to determine whether Domino's no-beard policy had a legitimate business justification. The trial court ruled in favor of Domino's, and Bradley and the EEOC appealed.

Bowman, Circuit Judge

. . . [T]he burden is on Domino's to show a substantial business justification for its strict no-beard policy. This burden is a heavy one. . . . Domino's offered the testimony of Paul D. Black, Domino's vice president for operations. Black said it was "common sense" that "the better our people look, the better our sales will be." . . . Black also cited a public opinion survey indicating that up to twenty percent of customers would "have a negative reaction" to a delivery person wearing a beard. . . . Further, Black speculated that Domino's would encounter difficulty enforcing any exceptions to their dress and grooming code. . . . Black did not offer evidence of any particular exception that was tried without success; rather, he merely stated that monitoring the hair length and moustaches of employees at five thousand Domino's locations is difficult. . . .

Black's testimony was largely speculative and conclusory. Such testimony, without more, does not prove the business necessity of maintaining the strict no-beard policy. . . .

[O]nce the EEOC made out a prima facie case of disparate impact created by the strict no-beard policy (which, as we held in *Pizzaco I,* the EEOC clearly did here), the burden shifted to Domino's to establish a business justification defense. Domino's has not met this burden. It has failed to prove a compelling need for the strict no-beard policy as applied to those afflicted with PFB and has failed to present any evidence suggesting that the current policy is without workable alternatives or that it has a manifest relationship to the employment in question. . . . Domino's is free to establish any grooming and dress standards it wishes; we hold only that reasonable accommodation must be made for members of the protected class who suffer from PFB. We note that the burden of a narrow medical exception for African American males who cannot shave because of PFB appears minimal. The employer, of course, should not be precluded from requiring that any beards permitted under this narrow medical exception be neatly trimmed, clean, and not in excess of a specified length. . . .

[Judgment reversed and remanded.]

Mixed Motive Cases. In some instances, an employer's (or potential employer's) employment decision may be based on both a legal and an illegal factor. Assume, for example, that an employer fires a female construction worker and offers the following as the reason for termination: "Her skills were not good enough plus working on a construction site is no job for a woman." Such a case is known as a mixed motive case because the employer's decision was motivated by both a legitimate reason (poor skills) and an illegal reason (women should not work on a construction site). Under Title VII, basing an employment decision on mixed motives is illegal. If, however, the employer can prove that the same decision would have been made even without the illegal discriminatory reason, the plaintiff has only limited legal remedies.

Seniority Systems. Businesses and unions frequently use seniority systems that rank employees according to their length of employment as a basis for determining compensation, vacations, pensions, promotions, job security, and other employment benefits. In some occupations, women and minority group members tend to have low seniority because of limited employment

opportunities in the past. Basing employment decisions in seniority, therefore, can have a disparate impact on women and minority group members. For example, they may have fewer job benefits and may be the first to be laid off in business recessions. Seniority systems thus may have the effect of perpetuating past discrimination.

Despite this effect, Title VII allows the use of *bona fide* seniority systems that were adopted without the intent to discriminate on the basis of race, color, national origin, sex, or religion. As a result, seniority systems that merely have a disparate impact on certain minority group members or women generally do not violate Title VII. Individuals who prove that they were the actual victims of disparate treatment, however, may be awarded seniority privileges to which they would have been entitled had the discrimination not occurred.

Discrimination on the Basis of Religion. For many purposes under Title VII, claims of religious discrimination are evaluated in the same manner as cases involving other types of discrimination. Illegal discrimination on the basis of religion thus may include intentional disparate treatment of those of a particular religion, or employment practices that have a disparate impact on certain religious groups. As noted earlier, however, Title VII's BFOQ defense accords special treatment to religious organizations that are employers by allowing them to discriminate on the basis of religion even for secular jobs.

Additionally, Title VII effectively imposes on employers the duty to reasonably accommodate an employee's or prospective employee's religious observances and practices. The statute, however, excuses an employer from reasonable accommodation that creates undue hardship on the conduct of the business. Cases under these provisions commonly concern the extent to which an employer must accommodate an employee's requests for leave for occasional religious holidays or for regular observance of the Sabbath on a day that is an ordinary working day for the business. Reasonableness is determined on a case-by-case basis.

Sexual Harassment

Generally, the law does not protect employees from a supervisor or co-worker who harasses—that is, persistently bothers or disturbs—employees. Harassment in the workplace based on sex, race, color, national origin, or religion, however, is a form of discrimination that can violate Title VII. **Sexual harassment** includes "unwelcome sexual advances, requests for sexual favors, and other verbal or physical conduct of a sexual nature."[7] Harassment in violation of Title VII frequently involves a male supervisor or co-worker who sexually harasses a female employee. Illegal sexual harassment, however, can be committed by a woman or by a third party, such as a customer. Illegal sexual harassment can occur even if the victim and harasser are the same sex.[8] Federal law recognizes two general types of illegal sexual harassment: *quid pro quo* harassment and hostile environment harassment.

Quid Pro Quo Sexual Harassment. Quid pro quo (from the Latin meaning "this for that") **sexual harassment** occurs when an employer grants or withholds employment privileges or opportunities based on whether an employee submits to unwelcome sexual advances or provides sexual favors. A supervisor who hires only women employees who have sexual relations with him commits *quid pro quo* sexual harassment. Similarly, *quid pro quo* sexual harassment occurs when a woman manager grants raises to male employees only if they engage in a sexual relationship with her. *Quid pro quo* sexual harassment clearly is a form of disparate treatment based on sex that violates Title VII.

Hostile Environment Sexual Harassment. More recently, courts also have recognized that **hostile environment sexual harassment**—which includes unwelcome conduct of a sexual nature that has "the purpose or effect of unreasonably interfering with an individual's work performance or creating an intimidating, hostile, or offensive working environment"[9]—can violate Title VII. Hostile environment sexual harassment can be caused by a wide variety of conduct such as telling lewd jokes or displaying sexually graphic pictures in the workplace, persistently asking a co-worker for dates, commenting on the dress or physical appearance of an employee of the opposite sex, or sexual assault. At times, employers, employees, and even courts have had difficulty in distinguishing conduct that constitutes hostile environment sexual harassment from ordinary social interaction in the workplace. The Supreme Court has described the boundary of illegal sexual harassment:

When the workplace is permeated with 'discriminatory intimidation, ridicule, and insult,' . . . that is 'sufficiently severe or pervasive to alter the conditions of the victim's employment and create an abusive working environment,' . . . Title VII is violated.[10]

The Court has identified several factors that are relevant in making this determination:

This is not, and by its nature cannot be, a mathematically precise test. . . . But we can say that whether an environment is "hostile" or "abusive" can be determined only by looking at all the circumstances. These may include the frequency of the discriminatory conduct; its severity; whether it is physically threatening or humiliating, or a mere offensive utterance; and whether it unreasonably interferes with an employee's work performance.[11]

Employer's Responsibility for Sexual Harassment. Under the framework of Title VII, *employers* are prohibited from engaging in sexual discrimination. Often, however, sexual harassment is not committed by the employer, but by a supervisor or another employee. In such cases, Title VII imposes liability only on employers who are somehow responsible for the harassment. Based on the statute's legislative history, the Supreme Court has ruled that basic agency law principles (discussed in Chapters 40 and 41) should be used to determine an employer's liability for sexual harassment committed by employees. In the following case, the Supreme Court clarified how agency law principles apply when a supervisor harasses an employee.

Faragher v. City of Boca Raton
118 S.Ct. 2275 (1998)

After resigning from her job as a lifeguard with the City of Boca Raton, Beth Ann Faragher filed a lawsuit against her immediate supervisors, Bill Terry and David Silverman, and the City. Faragher alleged that the supervisors had created a sexually hostile atmosphere at work by

---

[7]29 C.F.R. §1604.
[8]Oncale v. Sundowner Offshore Services Incorporated, 118 S. Ct. 998 (1998).
[9]29 C.F.R. §1604.

[10]Harris v. Forklift Systems, Inc., 114 S.Ct. 367, 370 (1993), quoting Meritor Savings Bank v. Vinson, 106 S.Ct. 2399, 2405 (1986).
[11]*Id.* at 371.

repeatedly subjecting her and other female lifeguards to "uninvited and offensive touching," by making lewd remarks and comments about sexual matters, and by speaking of women in vulgar terms. Although the City had adopted a policy against sexual harassment, it had never distributed the policy to the lifeguards. Before quitting her job, Faragher never notified the City of her supervisors' conduct. After finding that the supervisors' conduct created an abusive working environment, the federal District Court ruled that the City was liable for Terry's and Silverman's harassment. The Eleventh Circuit Court of Appeals reversed, holding that the City should not be held liable because the supervisors were not acting within the scope of their employment when they engaged in the harassing conduct. The U.S. Supreme Court granted Faragher's petition for review.

Justice Souter

This case calls for identification of the circumstances under which an employer may be held liable under Title VII of the Civil Rights Act of 1964 . . . for the acts of a supervisory employee whose sexual harassment of subordinates has created a hostile work environment amounting to employment discrimination. We hold that an employer is vicariously liable for actionable discrimination caused by a supervisor, but subject to an affirmative defense looking to the reasonableness of the employer's conduct as well as that of a plaintiff victim. . . .

We . . . agree with Faragher that in implementing Title VII it makes sense to hold an employer vicariously liable for some tortious conduct of a supervisor made possible by abuse of his supervisory authority, and that the aided-by-agency-relation principle embodied in §219(2)(d) of the [*Restatement (Second) of Agency*] provides an appropriate starting point for determining liability for the kind of harassment presented here. Several courts, indeed, have noted what Faragher has argued, that there is a sense in which a harassing supervisor is always assisted in his misconduct by the supervisory relationship. . . . The agency relationship affords contact with an employee subjected to a supervisor's sexual harassment, and the victim may well be reluctant to accept the risks of blowing the whistle on a superior. When a person with supervisory authority discriminates in the terms and conditions of subordinates' employment, his actions necessarily draw upon his superior position over the people who report to him, or those under them, whereas an employee generally cannot check a supervisor's abusive conduct the same way that she might deal with abuse from a co-worker. When a fellow employee harasses, the victim can walk away or tell the offender where to go, but it may be difficult to offer such

responses to a supervisor, whose "power to supervise—[which may be] to hire and fire, and to set work schedules and pay rates—does not disappear . . . when he chooses to harass through insults and offensive gestures rather than directly with threats of firing or promises of promotion." Estrich, *Sex at Work,* 43 STAN. L. REV. 813, 854 (1991). Recognition of employer liability when discriminatory misuse of supervisory authority alters the terms and conditions of a victim's employment is underscored by the fact that the employer has a greater opportunity to guard against misconduct by supervisors than by common workers; employers have greater opportunity and incentive to screen them, train them, and monitor their performance. In sum, there are good reasons for vicarious liability for misuse of supervisory authority. . . .

Although Title VII seeks "to make persons whole for injuries suffered on account of unlawful employment discrimination," *Albemarle Paper Co. v. Moody,* [95 S. Ct. 2362, 2372 (1975)], its "primary objective," like that of any statute meant to influence primary conduct, is not to provide redress but to avoid harm. . . . As long ago as 1980, the Equal Employment Opportunity Commission (EEOC) . . . adopted regulations advising employers to "take all steps necessary to prevent sexual harassment from occurring, such as . . . informing employees of their right to raise and how to raise the issue of harassment." *29 CFR §1604.11(f)* (1997), and in 1990 the Commission issued a policy statement enjoining employers to establish a complaint procedure "designed to encourage victims of harassment to come forward [without requiring] a victim to complain first to the offending supervisor." EEOC Policy Guidance on Sexual Harassment, 8 FEP Manual 405:6699 (Mar. 19, 1990). It would therefore implement clear statutory policy and complement the Government's Title VII enforcement efforts to recognize the employer's affirmative obligation to prevent violations and give credit here to employers who make reasonable efforts to discharge their duty. Indeed, a theory of vicarious liability for misuse of supervisory power would be at odds with the statutory policy if it failed to provide employers with some such incentive.

The requirement to show that the employee has failed in a coordinate duty to avoid or mitigate harm reflects an equally obvious policy imported from the general theory of damages, that a victim has a duty "to use such means as are reasonable under the circumstances to avoid or minimize the damages" that result from violations of the statute. *Ford Motor Co. v. EEOC,* [102 S. Ct. 3057, 3065 (1982)]. . . . An employer may, for example, have provided a proven, effective mechanism for reporting and resolving complaints of sexual harassment, available to the employee without undue risk or expense. If the plaintiff unreasonably failed to avail herself of the employer's preventive or remedial apparatus, she should not recover damages that could have been avoided if she had done so. If the victim could have avoided harm, no liability should be found against the employer who had taken reasonable care, and if damages could reasonably have been mitigated no award against a liable employer should reward a plaintiff for what her own efforts could have avoided.

In order to accommodate the principle of vicarious liability for harm caused by misuse of supervisory authority, as well as Title VII's equally basic policies of encouraging forethought by employers and saving action by objecting employees, we adopt the following holding. . . . An employer is subject to vicarious liability to a victimized employee for an actionable hostile environment created by a supervisor with immediate (or successively higher) authority over the employee. When no tangible employment action is taken, a defending employer may raise an affirmative defense to liability or damages, subject to proof by a preponderance of the evidence. . . . The defense comprises two necessary elements: (a) that the employer exercised reasonable care to prevent and correct promptly any sexually harassing behavior, and (b) that the plaintiff employee unreasonably failed to take advantage of any preventive or corrective opportunities provided by the employer or to avoid harm otherwise. While proof that an employer had promulgated an antiharassment policy with complaint procedure is not necessary in every instance as a matter of law, the need for a stated policy suitable to the employment circumstances may appropriately be addressed in any case when litigating the first element of the defense. And while proof that an employee failed to fulfill the corresponding obligation of reasonable care to avoid harm is not limited to showing an unreasonable failure to use any complaint procedure provided by the employer, a demonstration of such failure will normally suffice to satisfy the employer's burden under the second element of the defense. No affirmative defense is available, however, when the supervisor's harassment culminates in a tangible employment action, such as discharge, demotion, or undesirable reassignment. . . .

Applying these rules here, we believe that the judgment of the Court of Appeals must be reversed. The District Court found that the degree of hostility in the work environment rose to the actionable level and was attributable to Silverman and Terry. It is undisputed that these supervisors "were granted virtually unchecked authority" over their subordinates, "directly control[ing] and supervis[ing] all aspects of [Faragher's] day-to-day activities," 111 F.3d at 1544 (Barkett, J., dissenting in part and concurring in part). It is also clear that Faragher and her colleagues were "completely isolated from the City's higher management." Id. The City did not seek review of these findings.

While the City would have an opportunity to raise an affirmative defense if there were any serious prospect of its presenting one, it appears from the record that any such avenue is closed. The District Court found that the City had entirely failed to disseminate its policy against sexual harassment among the beach employees and that its officials made no attempt to keep track of the conduct of supervisors like Terry and Silverman. The record also makes clear that the City's policy did not include any assurance that the harassing supervisors could be bypassed in registering complaints. Under such circumstances, we hold as a matter of law that the City could not be found to have exercised reasonable care to prevent the supervisors' harassing conduct. Unlike the employer of a small workforce, who might expect that sufficient care to prevent tortious behavior could be exercised informally, those responsible for city operations could not reasonably have thought that precautions against hostile environments in any one of many departments in far-flung locations could be effective without communicating some formal policy against harassment, with a sensible complaint procedure. . . .

[Judgment reversed and remanded for reinstatement of District Court's judgment.]

In *Faragher*, supervisory employees committed the harassment. Often, however, the hostile environment is created by co-workers. EEOC guidelines indicate the employer's liability should be determined using a standard similar to that adopted in *Faragher:*

> With respect to conduct between fellow employees, an employer is responsible for acts of sexual harassment in the workplace where the employer (or its agents or supervisory employees) knows or should have known of the conduct, unless it can show that it took immediate and appropriate corrective action.[12]

---

[12] 29 C.F.R. §1604.11(d).

Even if the harassment is conducted by a non-employee (such as a customer), the employer who knows or should have known of the conduct may be held liable if it fails to prevent or correct the harassment. The EEOC has suggested that courts consider the extent of an employer's power to control non-employees in determining appropriate remedial action.[13]

Other Forms of Discriminatory Harassment. A hostile work environment can be created not only by comments and conduct of a sexual nature, but also by harassment on the basis of race, religion, or national origin. In recent years, employers have been held liable under Title VII for racial and ethnic harassment that adversely affected the workplace environment. Moreover, the EEOC has reported an increasing number of hostile work environment claims based on racial and ethnic epithets, slurs, threats, and jokes.

Affirmative Action and Reverse Discrimination

One of the most controversial aspects of Title VII law concerns affirmative action. One reason for this controversy is that the term "affirmative action" often is used without clear definition. As discussed below, affirmative action and affirmative action plans are subject to a variety of meanings.

Court Ordered Affirmative Action. Title VII provides that a court may "order such affirmative action as may be appropriate"[14] in cases in which intentional illegal discrimination has been proved. The term **affirmative action,** which is not defined in the statute, generally is used to describe positive steps that an employer who had engaged in systematic discrimination against women or minority groups must take to increase their employment opportunities. Affirmative action includes a broad variety of activities ranging, for example, from encouraging women or minority groups to apply for positions, to giving employment preference to qualified members of those groups.

The type of affirmative action that is appropriate in a case depends on the extent and effect of the past discrimination. The U.S. Supreme Court has been sharply divided on whether establishing preferences or a quota (a set percentage or number of members of a particular group) is an appropriate form of affirmative action. The Court, however, has upheld imposing hiring quotas as part of the affirmative action remedy in cases involving overt and pervasive racial discrimination.

Other Forms of Affirmative Action. A court can mandate affirmative action only for employers or unions who illegally discriminated in violation of Title VII. Some businesses and unions, however, have established voluntary affirmative action plans in an effort to increase the diversity of their workforce. Further, many private contractors and state and local governments have adopted affirmative action plans to qualify to do business with the federal government. Federal Executive Order 11246, as supplemented by regulations of the Department of Labor, requires private contractors with 50 or more employees who have a federal contract of $50,000 or more, as well as state and local governments that receive federal revenue sharing, to develop written affirmative action plans. As part of the plan, the employer must conduct a detailed analysis of the composition of its workforce in comparison to the qualified labor market. If that comparison demonstrates that women or minority groups are underrepresented, the employer must develop goals and plans to eliminate the disparity.

The Supreme Court has upheld the legality of these affirmative action plans but only as temporary measures designed to correct a conspicuous imbalance of women or minority groups in the workforce due to past discrimination. Further, the Court has ruled that these affirmative action plans cannot use quotas and cannot exclude any groups from consideration for a particular position.

Criticisms of Affirmative Action. Affirmative action has been subject to considerable criticism. Some critics assert that affirmative action unfairly causes **reverse discrimination**—discrimination against white males in favor of women and minority group members—that undermines Title VII's purpose of encouraging hiring based solely on qualifications and abilities. Other critics assert that affirmative action merely perpetuates unfairness because it often benefits individuals who were not the actual victims of past discrimination while harming others who did not engage in discrimination. Finally, some critics suggest that affirmative action has stigmatized women or minority group members because

---

[13]29 C.F.R. §1604.11(e).
[14]42 U.S.C. §2000e-5(g)(1).

others often assume that they were hired because of their sex or race rather than their qualifications. Because affirmative action currently is being re-evaluated and scrutinized by the federal executive branch, Congress, and the judiciary, the legal principles may change during the next few years.

Retaliation Claims

Title VII also prohibits employers from engaging in certain retaliatory conduct. A claim for illegal retaliation requires a plaintiff to prove that the employer took an adverse employment action against the plaintiff because he or she engaged in an activity protected under Title VII. Protected activities include:

1. Filing a claim of illegal discrimination;
2. Complaining about allegedly illegal discrimination;
3. Participating in an investigation of allegedly illegal discrimination; and
4. Serving as a witness in an EEOC investigation or a discrimination trial.

An employer takes adverse action by unfavorably treating an employee (or potential employee) by, for example, firing, refusing to hire, denying a promotion, or otherwise engaging in negative treatment. Title VII thus prevents an employer from penalizing those who exercise their rights to oppose illegal discriminatory conduct.

Age Discrimination in Employment Act

After considering making age discrimination illegal under Title VII, Congress instead directed the secretary of labor to prepare a report and recommendations that became the basis of the **Age Discrimination in Employment Act (ADEA),**[15] enacted in 1967. The ADEA, which subsequently has been amended several times, is designed to protect older workers by prohibiting employment discrimination on the basis of age against individuals over the age of 40. Employers with 20 or more employees, employment agencies, and unions are subject to the statute.

Illegal Age Discrimination

Under the ADEA, an employer is prohibited from firing or refusing to hire or promote employees or applicants because they are over the age of 40. Discriminating against those individuals in granting compensation or other conditions or privileges of employment also is illegal. Because the costs of some benefits (such as insurance) are more expensive for older workers, employers have some flexibility in administering benefit plans. In general, the ADEA allows an employer with a bona fide benefit plan to offer employees either benefits of equal value or benefits that cost the employer equal amounts. The ADEA generally does not allow employers to establish a compulsory retirement age. Businesses, however, can mandate a retirement age of 65 or older for bona fide executives or other policy-making employees who are entitled to receive annual nonforfeitable retirement benefits of at least $44,000.

ADEA cases are very similar to Title VII claims. Under a disparate treatment claim, the plaintiff must prove that the employer illegally used age as a basis for making an employment decision. Typical cases include, for example, an applicant over the age of 40 who alleges that she was not hired because of age, or an employee over age 40 who charges that he was discharged because of age. In many cases, proof of illegal discrimination depends on circumstantial evidence. Although age discrimination can be proved by statistical evidence, this form of proof is used less commonly than in Title VII cases.

Claims under the ADEA also may be based on disparate impact. Disparate impact occurs under the ADEA if an employment decision based on a neutral factor—that is, some reason or reasons other than age—disproportionately affects individuals over the age of 40. If, however, the decision is based on "*reasonable* factors other than age," it does not violate the ADEA.[16] Retaliatory conduct by the employer against employees who exercise their rights under the ADEA also is illegal.

The federal courts also have adapted the model of a *prima facie* case, approved by the Supreme Court for Title VII cases, to ADEA claims. Thus, a plaintiff without direct evidence of age discrimination may prevail by first establishing the following: (1) the plaintiff was age 40 or over; (2) the plaintiff applied for a job for which

---

[15]29 U.S.C. §621 *et seq.*

[16]29 U.S.C. §623(f)(1).

the employer was seeking applicants; (3) the plaintiff was qualified for the job; (4) the plaintiff was denied the job; and (5) the employer continued to seek applications or filled the position with a younger person. If, after the plaintiff proves these elements, the employer provides evidence of a legitimate business reason for the decision, the plaintiff then must prove that age was the motivating factor for the employer's decision.

In the following case, the *prima facie* framework is modified to determine whether a manager was discharged in violation of the ADEA.

Gaworski v. ITT Commercial Finance Corporation
17 F.3d 1104 (8th Cir. 1994)

Plaintiff Richard Gaworski worked for defendant ITT Commercial Finance Corporation (ITT) from 1976 until he was fired in 1986. At the time of his discharge, Gaworski, age 55, was manager of credit and operations of ITT's Capital Resources Group (CRG) and was the oldest and highest paid person in that division. The day after Gaworski's termination, John Olker, age 46, was promoted to the newly created position of manager of credit and administration, moved into Gaworski's office, and assumed substantially all of Gaworski's former duties. During a performance review seven months prior to his discharge, Gaworski had been evaluated "above standard" while Olker had been rated "standard." Gaworski sued ITT alleging that he had been discharged based on his age in violation of the Age Discrimination in Employment Act. ITT claimed that it had discharged Gaworski and three other employees as part of a reduction in work force. Michael Guimbarda, director of the CRG division, testified that he had retained Olker rather than Gaworski because Olker had greater knowledge of the computer system and more experience in performing credit analyses. The jury found that age had been a determining factor in ITT's discharge of Gaworski and the court awarded back pay of $265,892. ITT appealed.

Lay, Judge

. . . It is axiomatic that employment discrimination need not be proved by direct evidence, and indeed, that doing so is often impossible, because as the Supreme Court has said, "[t]here will seldom be 'eyewitness' testimony as to the employer's mental processes." *United States Postal Serv. Bd. of Governors v. Aikens,* [103 S. Ct. 1478, 1482

(1983)]. In disparate treatment cases based on circumstantial evidence, courts apply the analytical framework of shifting burdens developed in *McDonnell Douglas Corp. v. Green,* [93 S. Ct. 1817 (1973)], and its progeny. Under this framework, the plaintiff has the burden of establishing a prima facie case of discrimination. . . . Once established, the prima facie case raises a legal presumption of discrimination in the plaintiff's favor, requiring the defendant to produce legitimate, non-discriminatory reasons for its actions. If such reasons are put forth, the plaintiff, who at all times retains the burden of proving discrimination, may attempt to demonstrate that the proffered reasons are pretextual. . . .

[The Supreme Court has] described the sufficiency of the evidence required to support a factfinder's determination of discrimination:

> The factfinder's disbelief of the reasons put forward by the defendant (particularly if disbelief is accompanied by a suspicion of mendacity) may, together with the elements of the prima facie case, suffice to show intentional discrimination. Thus, rejection of the defendant's proffered reasons, will *permit* the trier of fact to infer the ultimate fact of intentional discrimination. . . . [*St. Mary's Honor Center v. Hicks,* 113 S. Ct. 2742, 2749 (1993).]

In this case, it is clear that the elements of a prima facie case of age discrimination are present. . . . A plaintiff establishes a prima facie case of age discrimination if she can show that she is a member of the protected age class, that she was performing adequately in her job, that she was fired, and that she was replaced by a younger person after her dismissal. . . . Here, plaintiff Gaworski clearly was within the ADEA's "protected class" of those over forty years old. . . . His performance reviews and Guimbarda's admission that he was a good worker indicate that he was performing more than adequately. He was terminated from his employment. And contrary to ITT's claims, the evidence supports a finding that he was replaced by a younger employee.

Defendants argue that Gaworski was terminated as part of a reduction in force. . . . We agree with the district court, however, that the evidence supports a finding that Gaworski's position was filled by a younger employee rather than eliminated after Gaworski was laid off. Viewed in the light most favorable to Gaworski, the evidence shows that the younger Olker was given Gaworski's office, substantially all of Gaworski's former duties, a job description that Olker admits was "fairly comparable" to Gaworski's, and a title almost identical to the one

Gaworski had had. . . . Gaworski presented evidence that at the time ITT sought to cut its workforce, business was increasing—of the $30 million of new loans booked in the year preceding the [reduction in force], $20 million were booked in the final four months before the [reduction in force] took place. On this basis, reasonable minds could conclude that Gaworski had, in fact, been replaced and that ITT's purported [reduction in force] was a pretextual explanation for his discharge. . . .

ITT also claimed that Olker was more valuable to the company than Gaworski because of his greater computer skills. Guimbarda testified that the "computer experience to me was critical." . . . Again, Gaworski presented evidence to the contrary. He demonstrated that the need for computer skills was not mentioned in Olker's new job description, that the personnel director had never been informed of this need, and that Olker was in fact applying his computer skills much less in the new position than he had before. Moreover, Gaworski elicited testimony from Guimbarda that Guimbarda had never considered teaching Gaworski about the workings of the computer system, even though Gaworski's performance review spoke highly of his ability to grasp new concepts. . . .

The elements of the plaintiff's prima facie case are thus present and the evidence is sufficient to allow a reasonable jury to reject the defendant's non-discriminatory explanations. . . . The jury in this case could reasonably have accepted or rejected the defendant's proffered explanations. By its verdict, it presumably rejected them. . . .

The jury's finding that ITT intentionally discriminated against Gaworski on the basis of age was within its purview as the finder of fact. . . .

[Judgment affirmed.]

BFOQ Defense to Age Discrimination. The ADEA recognizes that for some jobs, age is a bona fide occupational qualification (BFOQ). An employer who used age as a basis for an employment decision for an employee over age 40 thus still may avoid liability if age was a BFOQ reasonably necessary to the normal operations of the business.

The BFOQ defense usually is raised in cases in which an employer establishes a maximum age limit for some position. In *Western Air Lines, Inc. v. Criswell,*[17] for

---

[17]105 S. Ct. 2743 (1985).

example, an airline that required all flight engineers to retire at age 60 argued that age was a BFOQ for the position because of safety reasons. The Supreme Court rejected this argument and held that a mandatory retirement age was a valid BFOQ for safety reasons only if the employer proved that it had reasonable cause to believe that all or substantially all persons over the retirement age could not perform the job duties safely, or that it was highly impractical to test employees' abilities on an individual basis. Under the ADEA, then, the BFOQ defense is very narrowly interpreted.

Early Retirement Incentives

When corporations and other large businesses reorganize or restructure, jobs often are eliminated to increase profitability. A common practice used by companies is to offer termination or early retirement incentives to upper-level employees who generally earn higher salaries and benefits than other employees. Often implicit in these arrangements is the threat that layoffs will occur if insufficient numbers of employees voluntarily retire. Because incentive packages usually are offered to employees over age 40, their retirement could constitute illegal age discrimination. As part of the termination package, therefore, companies frequently request employees to waive their legal rights, including the right to file an ADEA claim. In many cases, employees are given only a limited time in which to decide whether to accept early retirement benefits and waive their rights.

Following a series of cases in which former employees filed age discrimination claims despite waiver of their rights, Congress amended the ADEA in 1990. The amendment attempts to balance the interests of employers and employees by allowing businesses to require waiver of ADEA rights as a condition to receiving early retirement incentives, but provides that the waiver is valid and enforceable only if the employee's consent to the waiver was made knowingly and voluntarily. The statute lists a number of minimum elements necessary for a valid waiver including, for example: the waiver must be in writing; it must specifically refer to the ADEA if age discrimination claims are waived; the employee must be advised in writing to consult an attorney; and the employee is entitled to a specified number of days to consider and revoke the agreement. An employee who knowingly and voluntarily makes a valid waiver cannot subsequently sue for violations of the ADEA.

Title I of the Americans with Disabilities Act

The **Americans with Disabilities Act (ADA)** is a comprehensive federal statute adopted by Congress in 1990 to eliminate discrimination against individuals with disabilities. Titles II, III, and IV of the ADA are designed to make public services, public accommodations, and telecommunications more accessible to the disabled. **Title I of the ADA,**[18] which applies to employers with 15 or more employees and to employment agencies and unions, addresses employment discrimination. In drafting Title I, however, Congress created an enforcement framework similar to that of Title VII and drew much of the operative language from the **Rehabilitation Act of 1973,**[19] a federal statute that prohibits government employers, federal contractors, and employers receiving federal financial assistance from discriminating against the handicapped.

Qualified Individual with a Disability

Title I prohibits employment discrimination against qualified individuals with a disability. The statute defines a disability as a "physical or mental impairment that substantially limits one or more of the major life activities."[20] Individuals with a disability also include those who have a record of such a physical or mental impairment or who are regarded as having such an impairment. Title I then is designed to prevent discrimination not only against people with actual physical or mental limitations but also against those who only are perceived as having impairments. Major life activities include walking, seeing, hearing, learning, working, standing, and lifting. Impairments, therefore, cover a broad spectrum of conditions such as blindness, hearing limitations, dyslexia, mental retardation, loss of the use of a limb, as well as some contagious diseases like tuberculosis, hepatitis, or AIDS.

Individuals with a disability are considered qualified for a particular job if they can perform the essential functions of the job, with or without reasonable accommodation. Essential job functions are the primary duties of the job. The statute does not require an employer to restructure a job by reassigning essential functions to another person but accommodating an individual with a disability might require reassignment of marginal job duties. Title I

provides that in determining which job functions are "essential," consideration will be given to the employer's judgment, particularly if the employer has developed a written job description prior to advertising the position or interviewing applicants. Although courts generally will not require an employer to change the criteria or standards of a job, an employer may have to prove that functions described as essential truly are required in performing the job. In the following case, the Supreme Court analyzes the meaning of the term "individual with a disability."

Sutton v. United Air Lines, Inc.
119 S. Ct. 2139 (1999)

> Petitioners Karen Sutton and Kimberly Hinton are twin sisters who applied for jobs as commercial airline pilots with respondent United Air Lines, Inc. Both were invited for interviews but later were told that they did not meet United's requirement that commercial pilots have uncorrected vision of at least 20/100. Each petitioner's uncorrected vision was at best 20/200 in the right eye and 20/400 in the left eye. With corrective lenses, however, both had 20/20 vision. Petitioners filed a charge with the EEOC claiming disability discrimination in violation of Title I of ADA. After receiving a right to sue letter, they filed suit in federal district court. The trial court dismissed the suit on the ground that petitioners were not disabled within the meaning of the ADA. The Tenth Circuit Court of Appeals affirmed and petitioners were granted certiorari by the U.S. Supreme Court.

Justice O'Connor

. . . [W]e turn first to the question whether petitioners have stated a claim under subsection (A) of the disability definition, that is, whether they have alleged that they possess a physical impairment that substantially limits them in one or more major life activities. . . . Because petitioners allege that with corrective measures their vision "is 20/20 or better," . . . they are not actually disabled within the meaning of the Act if the "disability" determination is made with reference to these measures. Consequently, with respect to subsection (A) of the disability definition, our decision turns on whether disability is to be determined with or without reference to corrective measures.

Petitioners maintain that whether an impairment is substantially limiting should be determined without regard to corrective measures. They argue that, because the ADA does not directly address the question at hand, the Court should defer to the agency interpretations of the statute,

---

[18]42 U.S.C. §12111 *et seq.*
[19]29 U.S.C. §701 *et seq.*
[20]42 U.S.C. §12102(2)(A).

which are embodied in the agency guidelines issued by the EEOC and the Department of Justice. These guidelines specifically direct that the determination of whether an individual is substantially limited in a major life activity be made without regard to mitigating measures. . . .

Respondent, in turn, maintains that an impairment does not substantially limit a major life activity if it is corrected. It argues that the Court should not defer to the agency guidelines cited by petitioners because the guidelines conflict with the plain meaning of the ADA. . . .

We conclude that respondent is correct that the approach adopted by the agency guidelines—that persons are to be evaluated in their hypothetical uncorrected state—is an impermissible interpretation of the ADA. Looking at the Act as a whole, it is apparent that if a person is taking measures to correct for, or mitigate, a physical or mental impairment, the effects of those measures—both positive and negative—must be taken into account when judging whether that person is "substantially limited" in a major life activity and thus "disabled" under the Act. . . .

Three separate provisions of the ADA, read in concert, lead us to this conclusion. The Act defines a "disability" as "a physical or mental impairment that *substantially limits* one or more of the major life activities" of an individual. §12102(2)(A) (emphasis added). Because the phrase "substantially limits" appears in the Act in the present indicative verb form, we think the language is properly read as requiring that a person be presently—not potentially or hypothetically—substantially limited in order to demonstrate a disability. A "disability" exists only where an impairment "substantially limits" a major life activity, not where it "might," "could," or "would" be substantially limiting if mitigating measures were not taken. A person whose physical or mental impairment is corrected by medication or other measures does not have an impairment that presently "substantially limits" a major life activity. To be sure, a person whose physical or mental impairment is corrected by mitigating measures still has an impairment, but if the impairment is corrected it does not "substantially limit" a major life activity.

The definition of disability also requires that disabilities be evaluated "with respect to an individual" and be determined based on whether an impairment substantially limits the "major life activities of such individual." §12102(2). Thus, whether a person has a disability under the ADA is an individualized inquiry. . . .

The agency guidelines' directive that persons be judged in their uncorrected or unmitigated state runs directly counter to the individualized inquiry mandated by the ADA. The agency approach would often require

courts and employers to speculate about a person's condition and would, in many cases, force them to make a disability determination based on general information about how an uncorrected impairment usually affects individuals, rather than on the individual's actual condition. For instance, under this view, courts would almost certainly find all diabetics to be disabled, because if they failed to monitor their blood sugar levels and administer insulin, they would almost certainly be substantially limited in one or more major life activities. A diabetic whose illness does not impair his or her daily activities would therefore be considered disabled simply because he or she has diabetes. Thus, the guidelines approach would create a system in which persons often must be treated as members of a group of people with similar impairments, rather than as individuals. This is contrary to both the letter and the spirit of the ADA. . . .

Finally, and critically, findings enacted as part of the ADA require the conclusion that Congress did not intend to bring under the statute's protection all those whose uncorrected conditions amount to disabilities. Congress found that "some 43,000,000 Americans have one or more physical or mental disabilities, and this number is increasing as the population as a whole is growing older," §12101(a)(1). This figure is inconsistent with the definition of disability pressed by petitioners. . . . Indeed, the number of people with vision impairments alone is 100 million. . . .

Because it is included in the ADA's text, the finding that 43 million individuals are disabled gives content to the ADA's terms, specifically the term "disability." Had Congress intended to include all persons with corrected physical limitations among those covered by the Act, it undoubtedly would have cited a much higher number of disabled persons in the findings. That it did not is evidence that the ADA's coverage is restricted to only those whose impairments are not mitigated by corrective measures. . . .

Our conclusion that petitioners have failed to state a claim that they are actually disabled under subsection (A) of the disability definition does not end our inquiry. Under subsection (C), individuals who are "regarded as" having a disability are disabled within the meaning of the ADA. . . . Subsection (C) provides that having a disability includes "being regarded as having," §12102(2)(C), "a physical or mental impairment that substantially limits one or more of the major life activities of such individual," §12102(2)(A). There are two apparent ways in which individuals may fall within this statutory definition: (1) a covered entity mistakenly believes that a person has a physical impairment that substantially limits one or more major life activities, or (2) a covered entity mistakenly believes that an actual, nonlimiting impairment substantially limits one or more major life activities. In both cases, it is necessary that a covered entity entertain misperceptions about the individual—it must believe either that one has a substantially limiting impairment that one does not have or that one has a substantially limiting impairment when, in fact, the impairment is not so limiting. These misperceptions often "result from stereotypic assumptions not truly indicative of . . . individual ability." See 42 U.S.C. §12101(7). . . .

There is no dispute that petitioners are physically impaired. Petitioners do not make the obvious argument that they are regarded due to their impairments as substantially limited in the major life activity of seeing. They contend only that respondent mistakenly believes their physical impairments substantially limit them in the major life activity of working. To support this claim, petitioners allege that respondent has a vision requirement, which is allegedly based on myth and stereotype. Further, this requirement substantially limits their ability to engage in the major life activity of working by precluding them from obtaining the job of global airline pilot. . . .

Assuming without deciding that working is a major life activity and that the EEOC regulations interpreting the term "substantially limits" are reasonable, petitioners have failed to allege adequately that their poor eyesight is regarded as an impairment that substantially limits them in the major life activity of working. They allege only that respondent regards their poor vision as precluding them from holding positions as a "global airline pilot." . . . . Because the position of global airline pilot is a single job, this allegation does not support the claim that respondent regards petitioners as having a *substantially limiting* impairment. See 29 CFR §1630.2(j)(3)(i) ("The inability to perform a single, particular job does not constitute a substantial limitation in the major life activity of working"). Indeed, there are a number of other positions utilizing petitioners' skills, such as regional pilot and pilot instructor to name a few, that are available to them. . . .

[Judgment affirmed.]

Illegal Dicrimination Under Title I

Both disparate treatment of qualified individuals with a disability and employment practices that have a disparate impact on those individuals are illegal forms of discrimination under Title I. Additionally, an employer's failure to make reasonable accommodation to known limitations of a qualified disabled person also is considered to be illegal discrimination. Retaliation against individuals for exercising rights protected by the ADA also is illegal.

Disparate Treatment. Disparate treatment in violation of Title I occurs when an employer discriminates against individuals because they are disabled. Intentional discrimination, such as discharging a qualified employee or refusing to hire a qualified person due to a disability, is illegal under Title I. Other forms of disparate treatment include paying lower wages or providing fewer benefits to disabled individuals. Disparate treatment can be proved by direct evidence; for example, the employer informed an applicant that she was not hired because of her disability. In the absence of direct evidence, courts may allow a plaintiff to establish a *prima facie* case using the framework of *McDonnell Douglas Corporation v. Green*.[21] This approach requires the plaintiff to prove: (1) the plaintiff is an individual with a disability; (2) the plaintiff is qualified—with or without accommodation—for the job; (3) the plaintiff suffered an adverse employment decision (for example, was rejected, terminated, or denied a benefit); and (4) the employer continued to seek applicants (or filled the position with a person or granted benefits to another) without plaintiff's disability. If the plaintiff succeeds in establishing a *prima facie* case, to avoid liability the employer must offer evidence showing a legitimate business reason for the decision that adversely affected the plaintiff. The plaintiff then bears the burden of proving that the employer's reason is merely a pretext for unlawful discrimination.

An employer can be relieved of liability for disparate treatment in hiring, promotion, or discharge cases by proving that the disabled individual would pose a direct threat to health and safety in the workplace and that risk cannot be eliminated by reasonable accommodation. A person poses a direct threat only by creating a substantial risk of harm.

Disparate Impact. Title I also prohibits the use of employment standards or selection criteria that have the effect of screening out qualified individuals with disabilities. Although Title I thus prohibits practices causing disparate impact, it does recognize the business necessity defense used in Title VII cases. An employer's use of selection criteria that have disparate impact on disabled individuals, therefore, may be legal if the criteria are job-related and consistent with business necessity.

---

[21]93 S. Ct. 1817 (1973).

Reasonable Accommodation. A disabled person who can perform the essential functions of a job with "reasonable accommodation" is considered to be qualified for the job. Evaluation of an individual's qualifications for a job, therefore, must be made in light of reasonable accommodation. Further, failure to provide reasonable accommodation may be a violation of the statute. Title I thus effectively imposes on employers an affirmative duty to make reasonable accommodation to known limitations of qualified disabled persons. In other words, employers may be required to recognize disabilities and remove barriers that limit the employment opportunities of disabled persons.

Title I lists the following examples of reasonable accommodations:

(A) making existing facilities used by employees readily accessible to and usable by qualified individuals with disabilities; and . . .

(B) job restructuring, part time or modified work schedules, reassignment to a vacant position, acquisition or modification of equipment or devices, appropriate adjustment or modifications of examinations, training materials or policies, the provision of qualified readers or interpreters, and other similar accommodations for individuals with disabilities.[22]

The employer is prohibited from asking potential employees about disabilities or accommodations during the interview process. After extending an offer to a candidate, the employer may ask whether a reasonable accommodation is needed so long as the same question is asked of all others in the same job category. An employer may make an offer conditional upon the applicant's "passing" a medical examination. The employer may require a medical examination, but only if the same requirement applies to all others in the job category. A conditional offer may be withdrawn if the medical examination reveals that the employee is not qualified for the job—for example, he cannot perform the essential job functions.

Generally, it is the employee's responsibility to request reasonable accommodation. Once an employee makes a request, the employer and employee have a duty to engage in an "interactive process" to determine whether accommodation is needed and what accommodation is appropriate.[23] The employer is not obligated to provide what is requested by the employee. Failure to provide reasonable accommodation, however, constitutes illegal discrimination.

A business may be excused from providing reasonable accommodation, however, if it can establish that the accommodation would create undue hardship on the operation of the business. Undue hardship—defined as "an action requiring significant difficulty or expense"[24]—is evaluated on a case-by-case basis taking into consideration the effect both on the specific facility affected and the entire business. Title I lists a number of factors to be considered in determining undue hardship including the nature and cost of the accommodation, the financial resources and size of the business, and the impact of the accommodation on operations.

Enforcement of Title VII, the ADEA, and Title I

Enforcement Procedure

The EEOC is primarily responsible for administering Title VII, the ADEA, and Title I of the ADA. Congress has established an unusual procedure for enforcement of these statutes. Any person who wishes to file a claim for violation of Title VII, the ADEA, or Title I of the ADA first must file a written charge with the EEOC within 180 days of the allegedly illegal act. After notifying the employer, the EEOC is required to investigate the charge and determine whether there is reasonable cause for the allegation. If no reasonable cause is found, the EEOC dismisses the charge; however, a complaining party who wants to pursue the claim then may file a lawsuit in court. If the EEOC finds reasonable cause for the allegation, the agency must attempt to negotiate a conciliation or settlement agreement with the parties. As part of its settlement efforts, the EEOC may conduct hearings and require production of relevant evidence and attendance of witnesses. If the EEOC fails to negotiate a settlement, it may file a lawsuit on behalf of the complaining party against the employer. If the EEOC chooses not to file suit, it will issue a right-to-sue notice and the complaining party may file suit within 90 days.

The EEOC recognizes some state and local agencies, responsible for enforcing state antidiscrimination statutes, as Fair Employment Practices Agencies (FEPA). FEPAs work with the EEOC to perform functions such as processing and investigating discrimination charges that may violate both state and federal law.

---

[22]42 U.S.C. §§12111(9)(A)–(B).
[23]29 C.F.R. §1630.2(o)(3).

---

[24]42 U.S.C. §12111(10)(A).

Remedies for Violations

Title VII, the ADEA, and Title I of the ADA include a variety of remedies that are similar but also vary from statute to statute.

Equitable Remedies. In most discrimination cases, the court uses its equitable powers to fashion an appropriate remedy. An injunction can be used to order reinstatement, hiring, or promotion of individuals who were fired or denied employment opportunities because of illegal discrimination. A court that issues such an injunction usually requires the defendant also to provide **back pay:** wages and benefits that the plaintiff would have received if the discrimination had not occurred reduced by earnings during the period. Another form of equitable relief is **front pay,** the defendant's payment of wages and benefits that will be lost after the judgment date. If, for example, the court has ordered reinstatement or hiring of the plaintiff but a position is not immediately available, front pay will be awarded until the employer places the individual in a position. In some cases, a court will not order reinstatement or hiring if extreme antagonism or conflict that would interefere with job performance would result. Instead, the court may award front pay for a reasonable time or until the plaintiff secures substantially equivalent employment.

Damages. Equitable relief was the only remedy available under Title VII as originally enacted. The Civil Rights Act of 1991, however, expanded the remedies for intentional violations of Title VII and Title I of the ADA to include compensatory damages and, in some cases, punitive damages. The ADEA provides for an alternative form of damages.

Damages Under Title VII and Title I. Individuals who prove illegal intentional discrimination in violation of Title VII or Title I are entitled to recover compensatory damages for "future pecuniary losses, emotional pain, suffering, inconvenience, mental anguish, loss of enjoyment of life, and other nonpecuniary losses."[25] A court also may award punitive damages if the defendant acted "with malice or with reckless indifference"[26] to an individual's rights under Title VII or Title I.

Several limitations apply to the awarding of damages. Damages may be awarded only in cases proving disparate *treatment.* Equitable relief remains the sole remedy in cases involving disparate *impact.* Punitive damages may not be recovered from a governmental employer. Moreover, the total amount of compensatory and punitive damages is subject to a cap depending on the size of the defendant's work force. For example, the maximum amount of damages recoverable from an employer with 100 or fewer employees is $50,000; this cap increases to $300,000 for employers with more than 500 employees. Finally, in cases under the ADA, neither compensatory nor punitive damages may be awarded if the employer proves that it made good faith efforts to accommodate the individual's disability.

Damages Under the ADEA. While equitable remedies available under the ADEA are similar to those under Title VII and Title I, the ADEA uses a different approach to awarding damages. Plaintiffs who prove age discrimination are entitled to back pay and, if the violation of the ADEA was willful, to liquidated damages equal to the amount of back pay. The plaintiff's maximum recovery then is twice the amount of the lost wages. An employer's conduct is considered "willful" if the age discrimination was made with knowledge, or in reckless disregard, that the conduct was prohibited by the ADEA.

Attorneys' Fees. Title VII, Title I of the ADA, and the ADEA allow a court to award reasonable attorneys' fees and costs to a plaintiff who succeeds in proving illegal discrimination. Generally, attorneys' fees are not available to the defendant.

Other Statutes Limiting Employment Discrimination

Discrimination on the Basis of Sex

The **Equal Pay Act,**[27] adopted by Congress in 1963 as an amendment to the Fair Labor Standards Act, commonly is considered the first modern equal employment opportunity law. The Equal Pay Act is limited in scope and prohibits compensation differences based on the sex of the employee. Under the statute, an employer must provide equal pay to men and women for equal work on jobs requiring equal skill, effort, and responsibility under similar working conditions. Pay differences based on factors other than the employee's sex, such as merit or seniority, are permissible.

---

[25]42 U.S.C. §1981a(b)(3).
[26]42 U.S.C. §1981a(b)(1).

[27]29 U.S.C. §206(d).

A violation of the Equal Pay Act generally is a form of discrimination on the basis of sex that also is a violation of Title VII. Employees seeking damages under the Equal Pay Act, however, are not required to initiate their claim by filing a complaint with the EEOC. Damages recoverable under the Equal Pay Act are calculated in the same way as are damages under the ADEA. Thus, employees who prove a violation of the Equal Pay Act are entitled to back pay for the period during which they were underpaid and to liquidated damages in the same amount if the violation was willful.

Discrimination on the Basis of Race or National Origin

Civil Rights Act of 1866. Following the Civil War, Congress adopted the **Civil Rights Act of 1866** to extend basic civil rights to the newly freed slaves. This statute, which remains a part of the federal law, commonly is called "Section 1981," referring to its current statutory citation. Section 1981 provides that "All persons within the jurisdiction of the United States shall have the same right in every State . . . to make and enforce contracts . . . as is enjoyed by white citizens."[28] For almost 100 years, this statute was interpreted as being inapplicable to private contracts.

During the 1970s, however, the U.S. Supreme Court ruled that this statute applied to private employment contracts. The Supreme Court later held that §1981 prohibits contractual discrimination based not only on race but also on "ancestry or ethnic characteristics."[29] In a later decision, the Court ruled that the rights guaranteed by §1981 applied only to the formation of contracts. As part of the Civil Rights Act of 1991, Congress overruled this decision by adding statutory language indicating that §1981 applies to the "making" of contracts as well as to "the performance, modification, and termination of contracts, and the enjoyment of all benefits, privileges, terms, and conditions of the contractual relationship."[30]

Under §1981, therefore, employers are prohibited from discriminating on the basis of race, ancestry, or ethnic characteristics in all aspects of employment contracts. As a practical matter, the prohibitions of §1981 largely overlap those of Title VII based on race, color, and national origin. The coverage of Title VII, however, is limited to employers with at least 15 employees.

Thus, more employers are subject to the provisions of §1981, which applies to all employment contracts. Under Title VII, damages for international discrimination are capped at various levels depending on the size of the employer's business. Because §1981 includes no caps, victims of particularly outrageous racial or ethnic discrimination, for which punitive damages would be appropriate, may recover higher damages by bringing a claim under §1981. Finally, unlike Title VII, §1981 does not require claimants to initiate legal action by filing a complaint with the EEOC.

Immigration Reform and Control Act. In 1986, Congress enacted the **Immigration Reform and Control Act (IRCA)** in an effort to reduce the number of illegal aliens entering the United States. Before this statute was enacted, aliens without proper work authorization were prohibited from working in the United States, but employers were not prohibited from hiring these illegal aliens. The IRCA of 1986 prohibits employers from hiring or recruiting unauthorized aliens and further requires employers to verify each employee's eligibility for employment.[31]

To alleviate concern that this new statute might increase discrimination against individuals who appeared to be from foreign countries, Congress included an antidiscrimination provision in the statute. The IRCA prohibits discrimination in hiring, recruitment, or discharge based on national origin or citizenship status for persons who are citizens or "protected individuals." Protected individuals include aliens who are lawfully admitted for permanent or temporary residence, and certain aliens who are refugees or have been granted asylum. Generally, aliens lose protected status if they fail to apply for citizenship within six months after becoming eligible, or fail to be naturalized within two years after applying.[32] Discrimination against noncitizens otherwise is permitted under the act.

Charges of violations of IRCA must be filed with the Special Counsel of the federal Department of Justice, who investigates the charge and decides whether to file a complaint before an administrative law judge. If: (1) the charge alleges "knowing and intentional discriminatory activity" or "a pattern or practice of discriminatory activity," and (2) the Special Counsel fails to file a complaint within 120 days after receiving the charge, then the complaining party may

---

[28]42 U.S.C. §1981.
[29]St. Francis College v. Al-Khazraji, 107 S. Ct. 2022, 2028 (1987).
[30]42 U.S.C. §1981(b).

[31]8 U.S.C. §1324a.
[32]8 U.S.C. §1324b(a).

file a complaint directly before the administrative law judge. Remedies for violation include injunctions and civil penalties. In addition, the violator may be required to hire adversely affected individuals, and implement educational programs.[33]

The provisions of the IRCA prohibiting discrimination on the basis of national origin overlap somewhat with those of Title VII. Because the IRCA applies to all employers with four or more employees, however, the IRCA covers some businesses that are not covered by Title VII. Note that proceedings arising out of the same facts may not simultaneously be maintained under Title VII and IRCA.[34]

Summary

1. Since 1960, Congress has adopted various statutes designed to guarantee equal employment opportunity and created the Equal Employment Opportunity Commission to administer those statutes.

2. Title VII of the Civil Rights Act of 1964 prohibits most employment practices that discriminate on the basis of race, color, national origin, religion, or sex. Illegal conduct includes employment practices that intentionally discriminate as well as those that have a discriminatory impact.

3. The Age Discrimination in Employment Act protects individuals over the age of 40 from most forms of employment discrimination based on age.

4. Limiting jobs to individuals of a particular national origin, religion, sex, or age sometimes is permissible if the characteristic is a bona fide occupational qualification for a specific job. Employment practices that are job-related and consistent with business necessity are legal even if they have discriminatory impact.

5. Under Title I of the Americans with Disabilities Act, employment discrimination against qualified individuals with a disability is illegal. A person with a disability who can perform the essential functions of a particular job with or without reasonable accommodation is considered to be qualified for the job.

6. Title I imposes an affirmative duty on employers to make reasonable accommodation to known limitations of qualified disabled individuals unless the accommodation would create undue hardship on the business.

7. Under the Equal Pay Act, discrimination on the basis of sex in compensating employees is illegal.

8. The Civil Rights Act of 1866, commonly referred to as Section 1981, prohibits discrimination on the basis of race, ancestry, or ethnic characteristics in all aspects of employment contracts. The Immigration Reform and Control Act protects U.S. citizens and "protected individuals" from discrimination based on national origin or citizenship in hiring, recruitment, or discharge.

Key Terms

Equal Employment Opportunity Commission (EEOC)
Title VII of the Civil Rights Act of 1964
disparate treatment
bona fide occupational qualification (BFOQ) defense
disparate impact
business necessity defense
sexual harassment
quid pro quo sexual harassment
hostile environment sexual harassment

affirmative action
reverse discrimination
Age Discrimination in Employment Act (ADEA)
Americans with Disabilities Act (ADA)
Title I of the ADA
Rehabilitation Act of 1973
back pay
front pay
Equal Pay Act
Civil Rights Act of 1866
Immigration Reform and Control Act (IRCA)

Questions and Problems

54.1 Because the bona fide occupational qualification (BFOQ) defense is narrowly construed, it seldom is recognized as a valid defense in Title VII cases. Can you think of any jobs for which being of a particular sex or national origin is a valid BFOQ? Explain.

54.2 Actuarial data establish that, in general, women live longer than men. As a result, the cost of pensions for the average woman are higher than those for the average man. May an employer legally require a female employee participating in a contributory pension plan to make larger contributions than male employees? May the employer legally pay a smaller monthly pension to a retired woman than to a retired man? Explain.

---

[33]8 U.S.C. §1324b(b)-(g).

[34]8 U.S.C. §1324b(b)(2).

54.3 Ann Hopkins worked as an accountant at Price Waterhouse, a national accounting partnership. The firm annually nominates accountants as candidates for partnership. All of the firm's partners then have the opportunity to submit written comments on the candidates. When Hopkins was nominated for partnership, a number of partners submitted comments. The comments indicated that she possessed good accounting skills and had been successful in winning a large government contract for the firm. Several of the partners, however, noted that Hopkins lacked "interpersonal skills." She was described as being "overly aggressive, unduly harsh, difficult to work with, and impatient with staff." Other comments from partners included a description of Hopkins as "macho," a suggestion that "she overcompensated for being a woman," a recommendation that she take "a course at charm school," and several criticisms of her use of profanity. Hopkins was denied partnership with Price Waterhouse but the firm agreed to reconsider her as a candidate at a later date. In explaining the decision, a partner advised Hopkins to "walk more femininely, talk more femininely, dress more femininely, wear make-up, have her hair styled, and wear jewelry." Hopkins sued Price Waterhouse alleging that it had illegally discriminated against her on the basis of sex. How should the court rule? Explain.

54.4 Mechelle Vinson filed a lawsuit under Title VII alleging that she had been sexually harassed by her supervisor, Sidney Taylor. Vinson testified that shortly after she was hired as a teller trainee at Meritor Bank, Taylor had invited her to dinner where he suggested that they go to a motel. She testified that after first refusing, she subsequently agreed out of fear of losing her job. She admitted that over several years she had sexual relations with Taylor between 40 and 50 times. Vinson further testified that, against her will, Taylor fondled her in front of other employees, exposed himself to her, followed her into the women's restroom, and forcibly raped her on several occasions. Vinson continued her employment at the bank for four years during which she received several promotions. After Meritor Bank fired Vinson for excessive use of sick leave, she filed suit against the bank claiming that she had been subject to sexual harassment throughout her employment.

(a) Based on Vinson's testimony, has either *quid pro quo* or hostile environment sexual harassment occured? Explain.

(b) Assume that the court found that Taylor had committed sexual harassment. During the trial, Vinson admitted that she never had notified any bank officials of the alleged sexual harassment. Should the bank be held liable for Taylor's conduct? Why or why not?

(c) Meritor Bank had established a grievance procedure for resolving work-related complaints and problems. The first step in the grievance procedure required employees to file a complaint with their supervisor. If the supervisor's resolution was unsatisfactory, the employee then could appeal the decision to higher level supervisors. To use the grievance procedure, Vinson would have had to file her complaint with Taylor. In light of this information, do you believe that the bank should be held liable for Taylor's conduct? Explain.

(d) Assume that you are human resources manager for Meritor Bank. What would you have done if Vinson had notified you of Taylor's alleged sexual harassment? What procedures would you adopt to minimize the sexual or racial harassment among employees? Explain.

54.5 Johnson Controls Inc. manufactures batteries using lead as a primary ingredient. Exposure to lead creates health risks for workers and, if an employee is pregnant, also may cause harm to the fetus or unborn child. Johnson Controls adopted a policy that provided, "No women who are pregnant or who are capable of bearing children will be placed in jobs involving exposure to lead."

(a) Does Johnson Controls' policy cause disparate treatment or disparate impact on the basis of sex? Explain.

(b) What defense(s) could Johnson Controls raise to justify its policy? Explain.

54.6 Cove Packing Co. operates a business in Alaska that cans salmon during the summer. The business hires employees for two general types of jobs: cannery jobs and noncannery jobs. Cannery jobs are unskilled positions on an assembly line that cans the salmon. Noncannery jobs include a variety of support positions for the cannery, including machinists, engineers, carpenters, inspectors, bookkeepers, and cooks. Almost all noncannery jobs pay more than cannery jobs. A group of minority cannery workers sued Cove Packing Co. alleging that their employer had violated Title VII by discriminating against minority group members. As proof of discrimination, plaintiffs established that 90 percent of all cannery jobs were held by nonwhite minorities, including Native Americans and Filipinos, while only 5 percent of the noncannery jobs were held by nonwhites. Has Cove Packing Co. violated Title VII? Explain.

54.7 Raul Lopez, who was born and raised in Spain, emigrated to the United States and applied for several jobs. Lopez reads and understands English well but speaks with a pronounced accent. Following an interview at Mighty Big Company, Lopez was rejected for the job because his accent made him difficult to understand.

(a) Explain why Mighty Big's refusal to hire Lopez may violate Title VII.

(b) Suggest reasons why Mighty Big's refusal to hire Lopez may not violate Title VII.

54.8 A casino located in Reno, Nevada adopted the following grooming standards for employees who served beverages:

1. All beverage servers must be well groomed, appealing to the eye, and be firm and body toned; and
2. Female beverage servers must wear stockings, nail polish and makeup (foundation, blush, and mascara).

Male beverage servers may not wear nail polish, eye makeup, or facial makeup. Do the casino's grooming standards violate federal law? Explain.

54.9 After several years of financial problems, Transit Mix, Inc. decided to discharge several employees. Transit Mix fired Wayne Metz, a 54-year-old manager who had worked for the company for 27 years, and replaced him with another manager who was 43 years old. At the time of his discharge, Metz's salary was about twice that of his replacement.

(a) Metz sued Transit Mix alleging that it had violated the ADEA. Transit Mix argued that its decision to discharge Metz was based on his salary, not on his age. Metz argued that the higher level of his salary was due, at least in part, to his age. How should the court rule? Why?

(b) Assume that Transit Mix did not fire Metz but instead hired a younger employee to replace Metz and two other managers. Transit Mix offered Metz a new position as assistant sales manager of a different office. The new position would be a demotion for Metz. Further, he would be required to work irregular hours and his earnings would be based on a commission that probably would result in lower earnings. Metz rejected the offer, resigned, and sued Transit Mix for violation of the ADEA. How should the court rule? Explain.

54.10 Dexler, who is four feet five inches tall, suffers from achondroplastic dwarfism, a growth disorder that results in short limbs and short stature. Dexler applied for a job as distribution clerk at World Parts, Inc. The job includes a number of tasks including unloading mail and packages in large containers from trucks, sorting the mail into trays, and placing mail into slots and boxes. Dexler's physician has advised him not to unload the mail from trucks. Further, his limited vertical and horizontal reach affect his ability to sort and distribute the mail; he cannot reach the top rows of sorting slots and boxes and he must move back and forth more frequently than others to reach the full width of the sorting slots. is Dexler a "qualified individual with a disability" as defined in Title I of the ADA? Explain.

54.11 Bee Cook applied to Hope Hospital for a job as an attendant, a position that Cook had held at other institutions. She was able to perform all of the tasks required for the job. Hope Hospital rejected her for the job based on the fact that Cook was five feet two inches tall and weighed over 300 pounds. Cook sued Hope Hospital for violation of Title I of the ADA. Is Cook a "qualified individual with a disability"? Explain.

54.12 After working on the assembly line at a Toyota automobile plant for several years, Ella Williams developed carpal tunnel syndrome and tendnitis in her hands. Her physician recommended that she be restricted from work requiring her to repeatedly extend or flex her arms upward or to lift more than 10 pounds. For more than three years, Toyota assigned her to a position in the body paint inspection department that required no reaching or lifting. The company then added new duties to the position including wiping down cars with a wooden handled sponge. The new duties caused the carpal tunnel syndrome and tendinitis to return. After Toyota refused to excuse her from the new duties, Williams began missing work because of her condition. Toyota fired her for poor attendance. Williams has sued Toyota for violating Title I of the Americans with Disabilities Act. How should the court rule?

ENVIRONMENTAL LAW

Technology and industrialization, while improving the quality of life for many people, also have adversely affected the global environment. Industrial activities have consumed limited resources and seriously polluted air and water. Human health and safety, as well as other animal and plant life, are threatened by pesticides, chemicals, and the toxic byproducts of consumer and industrial goods. Businesses and governments face increasing difficulty in finding appropriate systems and sites for the safe disposal of waste, particularly hazardous substances.

In response to a broadly based political movement demanding improved environmental quality, Congress first began comprehensive regulation of environmental matters during the late 1960s and early 1970s. Since that time, local, state, and national governments have adopted laws that try to improve environmental quality while maintaining the benefits of economic and technological development. This chapter discusses environmental law first by reviewing common law remedies and then by examining federal statutes regulating air and water pollution, toxic and hazardous substances, and federal environmental policy.

Introduction to Environmental Law

Common Law Remedies

Many issues that today are considered to be environmental law problems first were addressed through common law principles of tort and property law. The law of trespass, for example, enables landowners to recover damages or obtain injunctive relief for harm caused by industrial smoke and dirt. Riparian rights long have limited the use of waters that pass through a person's property. Virtually all types of industrial pollution—including gases, smoke, odors, noise, and toxic substances in air and water—have been found to be public and private nuisances. Some businesses have been held liable for environmental damages under negligence law while other industrial operations have been held to be abnormally dangerous or ultrahazardous activities creating strict tort liability for resulting injuries to persons and property.

Although the common law has provided a flexible approach to resolving environmental issues, equitable resolution of individual cases can be hindered by underlying economic, social, and political concerns. In the following landmark case, the court tries to balance public and private needs in fashioning an appropriate remedy.

Boomer v. Atlantic Cement Company
257 N.E.2d 870 (N. Y. 1970)

The defendant Atlantic Cement Company had invested more than $45 million in a New York cement manufacturing plant that employed over 300 people. The plaintiffs, a group of landowners who lived near the plant, sued Atlantic seeking an injunction to restrain operation of the plant and damages for injuries to their property caused by dirt, smoke, and vibrations from Atlantic's operations. The trial and appellate courts denied the injunction but held that plaintiffs were entitled to damages incurred to the date of the trial. The courts also noted that plaintiffs could bring successive lawsuits as further damages were incurred. Plaintiffs appealed to the New York Court of Appeals.

Bergan, Judge

. . . The threshold question . . . on this appeal is whether the court should resolve the litigation between the parties now before it as equitably as seems possible; or whether, seeking promotion of the general public welfare, it should channel private litigation into broad public objectives. . . .

Effective control of air pollution is a problem presently far from solution even with the full public and financial powers of government. In large measure adequate technical procedures are yet to be developed and some that appear possible may be economically impracticable.

It seems apparent that the amelioration of air pollution will depend on technical research in great depth; on a carefully balanced consideration of the economic impact of close regulation; and of the actual effect on public health. It is likely to require massive public expenditure and to demand more than any local community can accomplish and to depend on regional and interstate controls.

A court should not try to do this on its own as a by-product of private litigation and it seems manifest that the judicial establishment is neither equipped in the limited nature of any judgment it can pronounce nor prepared to lay down and implement an effective policy for the elimination of air pollution. This is an area beyond the circumference of one private lawsuit. It is a direct responsibility for government and should not thus be undertaken as an incident to solving a dispute between property owners and a single cement plant—one of many—in the Hudson River valley. . . .

The ground for the denial of injunction, notwithstanding the finding both that there is a nuisance and that plaintiffs have been damaged substantially, is the large disparity in economic consequences of the nuisance and of the injunction. . . .

The rule in New York has been that such a nuisance will be enjoined although marked disparity be shown in economic consequence between the effect of the injunction and the effect of the nuisance. . . .

. . . [T]o follow the rule literally in these cases would be to close down the plant at once. This court is fully agreed to avoid that immediately drastic remedy; the difference in view is how best to avoid it.

One alternative is to grant the injunction but postpone its effect to a specified future date to give opportunity for technical advances to permit defendant to eliminate the nuisance; another is to grant the injunction conditioned on the payment of permanent damages to plaintiffs which would compensate them for the total economic loss to their property present and future caused by defendant's operations. . . .

[T]echniques to eliminate dust and other annoying by-products of cement making are unlikely to be developed by any research the defendant can undertake within any short period, but will depend on the total resources of the cement industry nationwide and throughout the world. The problem is universal whenever cement is made.

For obvious reasons the rate of the research is beyond control of defendant. If at the end of 18 months the whole industry has not found a technical solution a court would be hard put to close down this one cement plant if due regard be given to equitable principles.

On the other hand, to grant the injunction unless defendant pays plaintiffs such permanent damages as may be fixed by the court seems to do justice between the contending parties. All of the attributions of economic loss to the properties on which plaintiffs' complaints are based will have been redressed. . . .

Thus it seems fair to both sides to grant permanent damages to plaintiffs which will terminate this private litigation. The theory of damage is the "servitude on land" of plaintiffs imposed by defendant's nuisance. . . .

[Reversed and remanded to trial court for determination of permanent damages.]

Public and private plaintiffs continue to use the common law as a basis for obtaining damages and injunctive relief for injuries from industrial pollution. As a clearer public environmental policy has emerged, courts increasingly have applied tort principles in combination with federal statutory law to resolve difficult environmental problems.

Federal Regulation

Because private tort and property claims were not well suited to resolve or prevent widespread harms caused by powerful business and governmental organizations, public demand for comprehensive regulation of environmental matters grew during the 1960s. The National Environmental Policy Act, adopted in 1969, articulated a federal policy to "create and maintain conditions under which man and nature can exist in productive harmony."[1] The Act also created the Council on Environmental Quality (CEQ) to advise the president on environmental matters. In 1970, by executive order, President Richard Nixon created the **Environmental Protection Agency (EPA)** to centralize federal environmental regulation.

Subsequently, Congress has enacted a variety of laws designed to protect and improve the nation's environment. The EPA, now one of the largest federal administrative agencies, has been assigned primary responsibility for administering these laws. Authority for regulating more limited environmental matters is shared by over a dozen other federal agencies and departments, including, for example, the Department of the Interior, the Department of Defense, the Department of Labor, and the Food and Drug Administration.

Federal statutes form the core of environmental law today. Although over 20 federal statutes specifically address environmental concerns, only those statutes that substantially affect business and industry are discussed in this chapter.

---

[1]42 U.S.C. §4331(a).

Technology and Environmental Law

The effectiveness of all federal environmental statutes depends significantly on science and technology. Although some technological advances have improved environmental quality, implementation of some environmental laws has been hindered by technological limitations.

Many federal environmental statutes, after articulating broad policy goals, establish a general framework for regulation. The statutes then delegate to administrative agencies, most commonly the EPA, the responsibility for adopting specific rules and procedures to protect the environment and human health and safety. The scientific community, however, often has been unable to provide the EPA with definite and clear information necessary to set these standards. Because the EPA has had to evaluate vast numbers of reports and conflicting data, federal statutes have been implemented more slowly than initially anticipated by Congress. Due to technological lags, many statutes and regulations have been amended and substantially revised several times. In many instances, the EPA has had to establish environmental standards based on risk analysis evaluating the probability of harm, rather than on precise, quantitative information. Enforcement has been delayed while regulated businesses and industries have challenged in court the reliability of the data supporting EPA standards.

Even when the EPA has established clear standards and procedures, technology has limited implementation of environmental programs in other ways. In some cases, control equipment has not been available to achieve these standards. Some statutes and regulations are intended to be "technology-forcing"; that is, they require industry to invent and adopt new technology. In 1970, for example, Congress established auto emission standards that were beyond the technological capabilities of the automakers. Although new inventions have significantly reduced emissions, Congress has routinely extended compliance deadlines because of technological delays.

Other environmental laws are "technology-based" or "technology-limited"; that is, they take into consideration the limits of technology. For example, some regulations require industry to use the best available technology. State of the art equipment, however, often is extremely expensive for businesses. Although most federal statutes incorporate some form of cost-benefit balancing test, businesses frequently have challenged federal statutes and EPA regulations that impose high costs on industry. In considering the material that follows, give special attention to ascertaining the extent to which costs should be considered in achieving the environmental benefits of the federal statutes.

Clean Air Act

Air Pollution

Air pollution consists of airborne particles and gases that endanger human health, damage property, or destroy or interfere with plant and animal life. Although air pollution occurs naturally (for example, volcanoes emit pollutants), major pollution usually is the byproduct of industrial activities. Some of these industrial byproducts are harmful when produced while others become hazardous when they combine with one another or with other substances in the air. Air pollution is created by both stationary sources, including factories, power plants, or other industrial sites, and mobile sources, such as cars, trucks, aircraft, and other movable objects.

Regulatory Framework

Air pollution is regulated by the federal **Clean Air Act,**[2] as amended by the Clean Air Act Amendments of 1970, 1977, and 1990. Under the Clean Air Act, the federal government and the states share responsibility for improving air quality in the United States. The basic framework of the Act requires the federal EPA to establish air quality standards while the states develop and implement plans to achieve those standards. The EPA, which reviews and monitors the plans, has the power to perform a state's functions if not properly undertaken by the state.

Smog Control

The Clean Air Act directs the EPA to identify and set air quality standards for specific pollutants that "cause and contribute to air pollution which may reasonably be anticipated to endanger public health or welfare."[3] The EPA has identified six harmful pollutants that it designates as criteria air pollutants: sulfur dioxide, nitrogen dioxide, carbon monoxide, particulate matter (soot,

dust, smoke), ozone (ground level ozone), and lead. Most of these criteria air pollutants are released directly from burning fuel such as gasoline, oil, wood, coal, and natural gas. Ozone, however, is created by a chemical reaction of volatile organic compounds (VOCs) and nitrogen oxides in the presence of heat and sunlight. Vehicle emissions are a major source of VOCs. Metal refineries and lead batteries release lead. Other sources of lead, such as leaded gasoline and lead-based paints, that formerly contributed to lead pollution, have been phased out or significantly reduced.

For each of the criteria air pollutants, the EPA has established maximum air concentration levels called **national ambient air quality standards (NAAQS)**. The EPA has developed two levels of standards: primary standards are intended to protect health, and secondary standards are set to prevent environmental or property damage. The Clean Air Act requires each state to develop a **state implementation plan (SIP)** that specifies the methods and programs by which the state will attain and maintain the federally established NAAQS. After holding public hearings on their plans, the states submit the SIPs to the EPA for approval. If the SIP is in compliance with federal law and regulations, the EPA approves it, making the provisions of the SIP enforceable by both the state and federal governments. If the state's SIP is not in compliance, the state must correct all deficiencies or the EPA will develop a plan for the state.

A geographic area that meets or exceeds the primary standard for a specific pollutant is called an attainment area; in other words, that area has attained the standard set by EPA. Geographic regions that do not meet the primary standard are designated nonattainment areas. A city, for example, might be an attainment area with respect to lead but a nonattainment area for ozone. Construction of new pollution sources generally is restricted in nonattainment areas. As a result, failing to meet one or more of the NAAQS may limit economic and industrial development in an area.

The Clean Air Act requires major stationary sources of air pollutants to secure operating permits. Each state, subject to the approval of the EPA, creates and administers its own permit program financed by annual fees paid by the permit holders. Permits establish permissible emission limits for the facility and the state programs include procedures for reporting and monitoring compliance. The permit system is designed to improve pollution control by allowing direct regulation of individual facilities.

---

[2]42 U.S.C. §7401 *et seq.*
[3]42 U.S.C. §7408(a)(1)(A).

Mobile sources of pollution—including cars, trucks, and buses—are responsible for significant air pollution. Since 1970, the federal government has established precise and detailed vehicle emission standards for specific pollutants by model year. Subject to limited exceptions, vehicles that fail to meet these standards cannot be sold in the United States. Despite resistance from the automobile industry and technological delays, vehicle emissions of major pollutants have been reduced substantially.

Although as much as 90 percent of pollution from individual cars has been eliminated since enactment of the Clean Air Act, increased vehicle usage has offset these gains. Air pollution caused by vehicle emissions continues to be a serious problem in the United States, especially in large metropolitan areas. In recent years, alternative fuels and vehicles (including reformulated gasoline and electric and hybrid vehicles) have been promoted in an effort to reduce pollution from vehicles.

The NAAQS set by the EPA have been controversial because of the costs of compliance. Many businesses filed briefs in the following case urging the Supreme Court to order the EPA to consider implementation costs when setting air pollution standards.

Whitman v. American Trucking Associations, Inc.

121 S. Ct. 903 (2001)

In 1997, petitioner, the Administrator of the Environmental Protection Agency (EPA), issued revised NAAQs for ozone and particulate matter. Respondents American Trucking Associations, Inc. sued the Administrator, challenging the agency's authority to issue the regulations. The District of Columbia Court of Appeals ruled that the Clean Air Act, as interpreted by the EPA, delegated lawmaking authority to the agency in violation of the Constitution and remanded the NAAQS to the EPA. In response to petitions filed by both the EPA and the respondents, the U.S. Supreme Court agreed to review the case.

Justice Scalia

These cases present the following questions: (1) Whether §109(b)(1) of the Clean Air Act (CAA) delegates legislative power to the Administrator of the Environmental Protection Agency (EPA), (2) Whether the Administrator

may consider the costs of implementation in setting national ambient air quality standards (NAAQS) under §109(b)(1).

. . . [T]he Court of Appeals . . . unanimously rejected respondents' argument that the court should depart from the rule of *Lead Industries Assn., Inc. v. EPA,* [647 F.2d 1130, 1148 (D.C.Cir. 1980)], that the EPA may not consider the cost of implementing a NAAQS in setting the initial standard. . . .

In *Lead Industries Assn., Inc. v. EPA,* the District of Columbia Circuit held that "economic considerations [may] play no part in the promulgation of ambient air quality standards under Section 109" of the CAA. In the present cases, the court adhered to that holding, . . . as it had done on many other occasions. . . . Respondents argue that these decisions are incorrect. We disagree; and since the first step in assessing whether a statute delegates legislative power is to determine what authority the statute confers, we address that issue of interpretation first. . . .

Section 109(b)(1) instructs the EPA to set primary ambient air quality standards "the attainment and maintenance of which . . . are requisite to protect the public health" with "an adequate margin of safety." 42 U.S.C. §7409(b)(l). . . . The language, as one scholar has noted, "is absolute." D. Currie, *Air Pollution: Federal Law and Analysis* 4-15 (1981). The EPA, "based on" the information about health effects contained in the technical "criteria" documents, . . . is to identify the maximum airborne concentration of a pollutant that the public health can tolerate, decrease the concentration to provide an "adequate" margin of safety, and set the standard at that level. Nowhere are the costs of achieving such a standard made part of that initial calculation.

Against this most natural of readings, respondents make a lengthy, spirited, but ultimately unsuccessful attack. They begin with the object of §109(b)(1)'s focus, the "public health." . . .

[R]espondents argue many more factors than air pollution affect public health. In particular, the economic cost of implementing a very stringent standard might produce health losses sufficient to offset the health gains achieved in cleaning the air—for example, by closing down whole industries and thereby impoverishing the workers and consumers dependent upon those industries. That is unquestionably true, and Congress was unquestionably aware of it. Thus, Congress had commissioned in the Air Quality Act of 1967 (1967 Act) "a detailed estimate of the cost of carrying out the provisions of this Act; a comprehensive study of the cost of program implementation by affected units of government; and a comprehensive study of the economic impact of air quality standards on the Nation's industries, communities, and other contributing sources of pollution." §2, 81 Stat. 505. The 1970 Congress, armed with the results of this study, . . . not only anticipated that compliance costs could injure the public health, but provided for that precise exigency. Section 110(f)(1) of the CAA permitted the Administrator to waive the compliance deadline for stationary sources if . . . sufficient control measures were simply unavailable and "the continued operation of such sources is *essential . . . to the public health* or welfare." 84 Stat. 1683 (emphasis added). Other provisions explicitly permitted or required economic costs to be taken into account in implementing the air quality standards. . . . Subsequent amendments to the CAA have added many more provisions directing, in explicit language, that the Administrator consider costs in performing various duties. . . . We have therefore refused to find implicit in ambiguous sections of the CAA an authorization to consider costs that has elsewhere, and so often, been expressly granted. . . . The text of §109(b), interpreted in its statutory and historical context and with appreciation for its importance to the CAA as a whole, unambiguously bars cost considerations from the NAAQS-setting process, and thus ends the matter for us as well as the EPA. We therefore affirm the judgment of the Court of Appeals on this point. . . .

The Court of Appeals held that [§109(b)(1)] as interpreted by the Administrator did not provide an "intelligible principle" to guide the EPA's exercise of authority in setting NAAQS. "[The] EPA," it said, "lacked any determinate criteria for drawing lines. It has failed to state intelligibly how much is too much." The court hence found that the EPA's interpretation (but not the statute itself) violated the nondelegation doctrine. We disagree.

In a delegation challenge, the constitutional question is whether the statute has delegated legislative power to the agency. Article I, §1, of the Constitution vests "all legislative Powers herein granted . . . in a Congress of the United States." This text permits no delegation of those powers, . . . and so we repeatedly have said that when Congress confers decision-making authority upon agencies *Congress* must "lay down by legislative act an intelligible principle to which the person or body authorized to [act] is directed to conform." *J. W. Hampton, Jr., & Co. v. United States,* [48 S. Ct. 348 (1928)]. . . .

Whether the statute delegates legislative power is a question for the courts, and an agency's voluntary self-denial has no bearing upon the answer.

We agree with the Solicitor General that the text of §109(b)(1) of the CAA at a minimum requires that "for a discrete set of pollutants and based on published air quality criteria that reflect the latest scientific knowledge, [the] EPA must establish uniform national standards at a level that is requisite to protect public health from the adverse effects of the pollutant in the ambient air." [Transcript of Oral Argument, p. 5.] Requisite, in turn, "means sufficient, but not more than necessary." Id. at 7. These limits on the EPA's discretion are strikingly similar to the ones we approved in *Touby v. United States,* [111 S. Ct. 1752 (1991)], which permitted the Attorney General to designate a drug as a controlled substance for purposes of criminal drug enforcement if doing so was "'necessary to avoid an imminent hazard to the public safety.'" . . . They also resemble the Occupational Safety and Health Act provision requiring the agency to "'set the standard which most adequately assures, to the extent feasible, on the basis of the best available evidence, that no employee will suffer any impairment of health'" — which the Court upheld in *Industrial Union Dept., AFL-CIO v. American Petroleum Institute,* [100 S. Ct. 2844 (1980)]. . . .

The scope of discretion §109(b)(1) allows is in fact well within the outer limits of our nondelegation precedents. In the history of the Court we have found the requisite "intelligible principle" lacking in only two statutes, one of which provided literally no guidance for the exercise of discretion, and the other of which conferred authority to regulate the entire economy on the basis of no more precise a standard than stimulating the economy by assuring "fair competition." . . .

It is true enough that the degree of agency discretion that is acceptable varies according to the scope of the power congressionally conferred. . . . But even in sweeping regulatory schemes we have never demanded, as the Court of Appeals did here, that statutes provide a "determinate criterion" for saying "how much [of the regulated harm] is too much." In *Touby,* for example, we did not require the statute to decree how "imminent" was too imminent, or how "necessary" was necessary enough, or even — most relevant here — how "hazardous" was too hazardous. . . . Section 109(b)(1) of the CAA, which to repeat we interpret as requiring the EPA to set air quality standards at the level that is "requisite" — that is, not lower or higher than is necessary — to protect the public health with an adequate margin of safety, fits comfortably within the scope of discretion permitted by our precedent.

We therefore reverse the judgment of the Court of Appeals remanding for reinterpretation that would avoid a supposed delegation of legislative power. . . .

[Judgment affirmed in part, reversed in part and remanded.]

Hazardous Air Pollutants and Acid Rain

The Clean Air Act includes a different method for regulating hazardous air pollutants. The Clean Air Act designates 188 chemical substances as hazardous air pollutants and directs the EPA to review this list periodically to add other substances that threaten human health or the environment. The statute directs the EPA to set national emission standards for hazardous air pollutants (NESHAPs) based on maximum achievable control technology that may require, for example, changes in manufacturing processes or substitution of materials for some substances. By late 2000, the EPA had set standards for 45 hazardous air pollutants. Industrial sources—such as chemical plants, oil refineries, steel mills, dry cleaners, lead smelters, and chromium electroplating facilities—have had to change their methods of operation to meet these standards.

The Clean Air Act also includes provisions designed to reduce acid rain. For many years, scientists have maintained that the burning of fossil fuels (such as coal) increases the levels of acidic compounds in the atmosphere, creating acid rain that damages plant and animal life. The most harmful pollutants that contribute to acid rain are sulfur dioxide and nitrogen oxides that are emitted primarily by utilities that generate electricity. The 1990 Amendments set allowable emission levels that were to be phased in gradually. The first phase began in 1995 and primarily affected large coal-burning plants. The second phase, started in 2000, affects smaller plants as well as those burning other fuels.

The acid rain provisions of the CAA adopted a new approach to reducing sulfur dioxide based on free market principles. Based on historical data, utilities are allocated an annual allowance to discharge a specified amount of sulfur dioxide. Companies that use less than their allocated amount may save the excess or sell it to other companies. A company that exceeds its allocation is fined. Companies that anticipate excess sulfur dioxide emissions, therefore, can avoid legal action by purchasing allowances. The EPA and federal General Accounting Office have reported that the allowance trading system has been effective in reducing sulfur dioxide at lower costs than traditional control programs.

Enforcement

Both civil and criminal remedies are available for enforcement of the Clean Air Act. A maximum civil penalty of $25,000 per day may be imposed against those who violate emission standards. In determining the appropriate civil penalty, courts and the EPA must consider certain factors, such as the size of the business, the economic impact of the penalty, the violator's past compliance history, and the seriousness of the violation. Additionally, courts may issue injunctions to enforce the Act. Private citizens may bring civil suits against those who have violated the Act or against the EPA if the agency fails to perform its duties under the Act.

Criminal penalties also are available for enforcement of the Clean Air Act. Individuals may be fined up to $250,000 and corporations may be fined up to $500,000 for knowingly violating certain provisions or for negligently or knowingly releasing a hazardous pollutant. Some violations of the Act also carry a penalty of imprisonment ranging, for example, from a maximum one year of imprisonment for negligently releasing a hazardous pollutant to maximum imprisonment of 15 years for knowingly releasing a hazardous pollutant. All criminal penalties may be doubled for a second conviction for violation of the Clean Air Act.

Clean Water Act

Water Pollution

The primary cause of water pollution is effluent, the discharge of waste substances into rivers, lakes, and oceans. Industrial, agricultural, and municipal waste accounts for almost all water pollution. Manufacturing industries dispose of waste byproducts in lakes and rivers. Electric power plants and heavy industrial plants, which use water for cooling, discharge heated water into lakes and rivers. Agriculture creates animal waste and chemical fertilizers that add to water pollution. Finally, municipal waste treatment plants discharge large amounts of organic waste and chemicals.

Some chemical and toxic pollutants produce almost immediate harmful effects by contaminating the water, plants, and animals, rendering them unfit for human use or consumption. Other pollutants interfere with biological and chemical processes. Heavy water pollution, for example, may slow the decomposition of organic waste, and heated water interferes with fish reproduction. Chemicals, organic waste, or heated water also can accelerate plant growth, causing eutrophication—the dying of lakes.

Regulatory Framework

Federal regulation of water pollution began with the Federal Water Pollution Control Act that placed the primary burden of reducing water pollution on state and local government. The 1972 Amendments to the Act adopted a new federally oriented approach to regulation. In 1977, the Act was again amended and reorganized as the **Clean Water Act,**[4] which was further amended by the Water Quality Act of 1987. The objective of the Clean Water Act is to restore and maintain the chemical, physical, and biological integrity of the waters of the United States through a variety of federally supervised programs.

The Clean Water Act generally allows the discharge of pollutants into U.S. waters only by those who have been issued a valid permit. The National Pollutant Discharge Elimination System governs "point source" pollution—discharges into a body of water through a discrete conveyance such as a pipe, ditch, or conduit. The dredged and fill discharge permit program governs the discharge of dredged or fill material into U.S. waters. The Clean Water Act has left control of "nonpoint source" pollution—such as runoff from farmland and mines—primarily to the states, which are required to develop management programs subject to approval by the EPA. The Clean Water Act, as amended by the Oil Pollution Act of 1990, also regulates discharge of oil or hazardous substances into U.S. waters.

---

[4]33 U.S.C. §1251 *et seq.*

National Pollutant Discharge Elimination System

The **National Pollutant Discharge Elimination System (NPDES),** created by the Clean Water Act, authorizes the EPA and EPA-approved state programs to issue permits allowing discharge of pollutants into U.S. waters. The statute defines pollutants to include a wide variety of materials such as solid waste, sewage, garbage, sludge, chemical waste, biological materials, and industrial and agricultural waste. Permits are granted to publicly owned waste treatment works and to manufacturing businesses that directly discharge substances through point sources. Businesses that make indirect discharges of pollutants into a publicly owned waste treatment work are not required to obtain a permit but must pretreat their waste in compliance with EPA regulations.

NPDES permit holders are required to comply with effluent limitations set by the EPA. These limitations are established on an industry-specific basis using technology standards defined in the statute. For conventional pollutants, including biochemical oxygen-demanding substances, oil and grease, pH, total suspended solids, and fecal coliform, the EPA sets the effluent limitations based on a general cost-benefit analysis in the statute. In setting limitations for toxic and nonconventional pollutants, the EPA uses a more stringent standard, known as "best available technology economically achievable" (BAT), in which cost plays a lesser role. In issuing a particular permit, the EPA may establish stricter limitations if necessary to meet state-established water quality standards. NPDES permit holders further are required to monitor, report, and maintain records of pollutant discharges.

Dredged and Fill Material Discharge Permit Program

A second program under the Clean Water Act requires permits for the discharge of dredged materials (those excavated from water) and fill materials (which replace an aquatic area with dry land) in U.S. waters and adjacent wetlands. Permits under this program are issued by the Army Corps of Engineers (Corps) based on regulations issued by the EPA and the Corps. The permit program requires the Corps to consider a number of factors—such as the impact on fish and wildlife, including migratory birds, flood damage prevention, and general environmental concerns—and to consult with other appropriate government agencies prior to granting a permit. Violators of the permit program are subject to the Clean Water Act's administrative, civil, and criminal penalties described below. Additionally, courts can order those who engaged in illegal dredge or fill activities to restore the area to its previous condition.

The dredged and fill material discharge permit program is often criticized by property owners who argue that denial of permits constitutes a "taking" of property by the government without compensation.[5] Part of the controversy stems from the broad definition of "wetlands" to include swamps, marshes, bogs, and other areas that are saturated by water. As a result, permits are required to engage in many activities that appear to be ordinary construction and development in these areas.

Oil and Hazardous Substances

The Clean Water Act also governs prevention and cleanup of accidental spills of oil and hazardous substances. These provisions were substantially amended by enactment of the Oil Pollution Act of 1990 following the massive *Exxon Valdez* oil spill in the coastal waters of Alaska in 1989. To prevent and expedite responses to accidental discharges, the Clean Water Act requires tank vessels and facilities that handle oil and hazardous substances to develop Spill Prevention, Control, and Countermeasure (SPCC) plans. The plans, which are subject to approval and periodic review by the EPA, must ensure that sufficient trained personnel and equipment are available to respond to spills. Facilities or vessels are required to immediately notify the federal government of the discharge of oil or hazardous substances into U.S. navigable waters. If the spill creates an imminent or substantial threat to human health, welfare, or the environment, the federal government is responsible for directing removal and other responses to the discharge. The statute established the Oil Spill Liability Trust Fund to pay for the costs of cleaning up oil spills. The Superfund, discussed later in this chapter, is available for cleanup of hazardous substances.

Owners and operators of vessels and facilities are subject to the Clean Water Act's administrative, civil, and criminal penalties (described below) for illegal discharges and for failure to comply with notification or SPCC plan provisions. Additionally, they may be held liable for actual costs incurred for removal and damages resulting from spills.

Enforcement

The Clean Water Act provides for administrative, civil, and criminal enforcement. The EPA is authorized to assess two classes of administrative penalties: Class I penalties may not exceed $10,000 per day up to a maximum of $25,000 per violation, and Class II penalties may not exceed $10,000 per day up to a maximum of $125,000 per violation. Class II penalties may be assessed only after a full hearing on the record while Class I penalties require only written notice to the violator, who may request a less formal hearing. Those who commit statutory violations or fail to comply with an administrative order also may be subject to a judicial civil penalty of up to $25,000 per day. The Water Quality Act of 1987 requires the EPA and courts in determining appropriate administrative or civil penalties to consider specific factors, such as the seriousness of the violation, the violator's compliance history, the violator's ability to pay, and the economic benefit or savings resulting from the violation.

Violators also may be criminally prosecuted. Negligent violations by first offenders are punishable by fines of between $2,500 and $25,000 per day, and imprisonment up to one year, or both. For subsequent offenders, the potential maximum penalty may be increased to $50,000 per day and imprisonment up to two years, or both. Anyone who knowingly commits violations is subject to more severe criminal penalties including fines of between $5,000 and $50,000 per day, and imprisonment of up to three years, or both. The maximum penalties also may be doubled for subsequent knowing violations. Finally, very severe penalties of up to 15 years' imprisonment and a fine up to $250,000 may be imposed against individuals who commit a violation with knowledge that it places another person in imminent danger of death or serious bodily injury. An organization that commits such a violtaion is subject to a criminal fine of up to $1 million.

Regulation of Toxic and Hazardous Substances

In recent years, scientific evidence has revealed the potential toxicity of many synthetic chemicals that have

---

[5]The taking issue is discussed in more detail in Chapter 38.

been produced and used for decades. These chemicals have significantly benefited society, for example, by increasing agricultural production with fertilizers and pesticides, and by enabling development of new building materials, plastics, fibers, paper products, food preservatives, and drugs. Many of the synthetic substances that are the products and byproducts of commercial and industrial activities, however, are hazardous to human beings, even in minute quantities. Some chemicals accumulate in plants and animals thereby multiplying their dangerous effects, while other chemicals fail to break down for long periods and, thus, retain their toxic potential. The toxic effects of many of these substances do not appear until many years after exposure.

Federal law regulates toxic substances in a variety of ways. As previously discussed, hazardous substances in the air and water are governed by the Clean Air Act and the Clean Water Act. The material that follows examines two federal statutes that regulate commercial distribution of chemicals: the Federal Insecticide, Fungicide, and Rodenticide Act, and the Toxic Substances Control Act. Also discussed are the Resource Conservation and Recovery Act and the Comprehensive Environmental Response, Compensation, and Liability Act, two other federal statutes adopted to prevent and remedy unsafe disposal of hazardous waste.

Federal Insecticide, Fungicide, and Rodenticide Act

The **Federal Insecticide, Fungicide, and Rodenticide Act (FIFRA)**[6] regulates the sale and distribution of pesticides within the United States. FIFRA requires pesticide manufacturers to register their products with the EPA and to meet labeling requirements on proper use and safety precautions. To initiate registration of a pesticide, the manufacturer must submit the chemical formula, the proposed label, and comprehensive data about its probable effects on human beings based on animal studies. If the information provided by the manufacturer complies with federal standards, the EPA generally must register any pesticide that is effective as claimed and will not cause "unreasonable adverse effects on the environment" when used in accordance with EPA-imposed restrictions and "with widespread and commonly recognized practice."[7] In making this determination, the statute requires the EPA to employ a

cost-benefit analysis that considers the economic, social, and environmental costs and benefits of the product. As part of the registration, the EPA classifies the pesticide for general use or, if the product is especially hazardous, for restricted use by certified applicators.

FIFRA generally prohibits the sale, distribution, or use of unregistered pesticides. The EPA is required to establish procedures for periodic review of registrations with a goal of reviewing every 15 years. The EPA may cancel a registration if it determines that the pesticide causes unreasonable adverse effects on the environment. Upon the manufacturer's request, however, the EPA must hold an adjudicatory hearing prior to cancellation. If the pesticide creates an imminent hazard or emergency, the EPA may suspend the registration, thus banning production and distribution of the pesticide until completion of the hearing process.

At the cancellation hearing the manufacturer effectively bears the burden of proving that the pesticide poses only a minimal risk or that its benefits outweigh the risk. If the manufacturer is unable to establish the necessary proof, the registration may be canceled and further manufacture or sale of the pesticide is illegal. Alternatively, the registration may be canceled only in part by restricting use of the product or requiring labels that set forth precautions for its use. The EPA may require the registrant to recall a pesticide if the registration is suspended or canceled and to assume responsibility for disposal of the product after cancellation of registration.

Toxic Substances Control Act

In 1976, Congress enacted the **Toxic Substances Control Act (TSCA)**,[8] a statute that was intended to provide comprehensive regulation of toxic substances. TSCA requires EPA to develop and maintain an inventory of all chemicals manufactured in the United States. The TSCA inventory includes over 75,000 existing chemicals. At least 90 days prior to beginning commercial production of a new chemical—one that is not included in the EPA inventory—the manufacturer must provide a pre-manufacturing notice (PMN) to the EPA. A similar notice must be provided if the manufacturer intends to apply an existing chemical to a significant new use. If the EPA does not act upon the notice within ninety days, the manufacturer may commence production. After the chemical is manufactured, the EPA adds it to the TSCA inventory.

---

[6] 7 U.S.C. §136 *et seq.*
[7] 7 U.S.C. §136a(c)(5).

[8] 15 U.S.C. §2601 *et seq.*

Under TSCA generally a chemical is presumed to be marketable; the EPA does not license or affirmatively approve manufacture of a chemical. Nevertheless, the EPA has the power to limit use of a chemical if the EPA finds that it presents an unreasonable risk to health or the environment. If, for example, the PMN does not include sufficient data for the EPA to determine the risks of the chemical, the EPA can delay manufacture or distribution until the data are available. If the EPA finds that any chemical (whether new or on the existing inventory) presents, or will present, an unreasonable risk to health or the environment, the EPA may restrict marketing of the chemical. The EPA can prohibit use of the product, establish production quotas, limit its use, or require special labeling. The EPA's decision to restrict the use is subject to review through a hearing process. The manufacturer, however, bears the burden of proving that the chemical does not present an unreasonable risk to health or to the environment.

One objective of the TSCA was to enable the government to collect comprehensive data on potentially hazardous chemical substances. TSCA, for example, requires manufacturers to notify the EPA of any information that reasonably shows that a chemical presents a substantial risk of injury to health or to the environment. Manufacturers also must maintain records of significant adverse reactions allegedly caused by a chemical. TSCA further allows the EPA to request companies to conduct tests and to submit test data on chemicals suspected of being hazardous. To encourage the cooperation of businesses, TSCA prohibits the EPA from releasing to the public certain confidential information such as trade secrets and commercial information. As illustrated by the following case, TSCA has been subject to some criticism from businesses.

Dow Chemical Company v. United States Environmental Protection Agency
605 F.2d 673 (3d Cir. 1979)

Under authority of TSCA, the EPA issued regulations requiring manufacturers, processors, and distributors of ten chemicals suspected of being hazardous to submit to the EPA lists of studies initiated or conducted by the company. The regulation required such lists even from companies that were manufacturing or using the chemicals only for research purposes. Dow Chemical Company filed a petition in the Third Circuit Court of Appeals challenging the EPA's authority to require the tests from those using the chemicals for research purposes.

After analyzing the statute and regulations and reviewing the statutory history, the court held that the EPA had acted within the scope of its authority. The court then addressed Dow's arguments that the statute and regulations would discourage product research and development.

Adams, Circuit Judge

. . . The result we reach today may understandably cause concern to those troubled about the relative decline of technological innovation in the United States. If companies are required to submit to a federal administrative agency the results of tests they perform in the process of developing new products their chances of realizing a substantial competitive advantage may be measurably reduced. With the opportunity for [competitive advantage] diminished in this fashion, corporate research may concentrate on substances that are not presently subject to the agency's scrutiny. The result may be a net reduction of general research on the very substances—hazardous chemicals—on which research is greatly needed. Were this to come about, it would presumably conflict with one of Congress' purposes in passing the Act. Alternatively, companies may simply reduce their research and development spending altogether, particularly since the Toxic Substances Control Act is not the only current disincentive to innovation.

Of course, in the present case good arguments may be made for the Act as drafted. It is fair to doubt whether the primary commitment of large corporations is to the health of our citizenry—and reasonable for the government to seek to learn about and more carefully control toxic substances. The drafting of legislation often entails difficult policy choices, and the statute at issue here is no exception. But the issue for this Court cannot be whether we would have drafted [the statute] so as to provide greater protection for product research and development. Nor is the question whether the regulation actually promulgated is a desirable one. We recognize the potentially unfortunate consequences of the EPA's regulation and of our reading of the Act. Our role, however, is confined to construing the statute so as to give effect to the legislation as written and to the intent of Congress in enacting such legislation. In so doing we have determined that Congress delegated to the EPA the authority to promulgate the regulation that is under challenge here. Perhaps the public may have reason to regret this result, but the possibility that the Act as drafted may inhibit technological innovation may not be relied upon as a justification for ignoring the apparent congressional decision in the drafting of the statute. Rather, any change in this regard is for the Congress to consider. . . .

[Petition for review denied.]

Resource Conservation and Recovery Act

TSCA monitors and controls chemicals as they enter the stream of commerce. Another federal statute, the **Resource Conservation and Recovery Act (RCRA),**[9] regulates disposal of hazardous materials. These waste materials include commercial products, such as paint, cleaning fluids, and pesticides, discarded by businesses and consumers as well as byproducts of manufacturing processes. The regulatory process established by RCRA controls hazardous waste from the point that it is created until its final disposal. RCRA defines hazardous waste as:

> solid waste, or combination of solid wastes, which because of its quantity, concentration, or physical, chemical, or infectious characteristics may—(A) cause, or significantly contribute to an increase in mortality or an increase in serious irreversible, or incapacitating reversible, illness; or (B) pose a substantial present or potential hazard to human health or the environment when improperly treated, stored, transported, or disposed of, or otherwise managed.[10]

The EPA has identified over 500 specific waste products that are considered to be hazardous. Additionally, the EPA considers waste to be hazardous if it exhibits one of the following characteristics: ignitability, corrosivity, reactivity, or toxicity.

The RCRA requires generators—producers—of hazardous waste to maintain records on the quantity and composition of their waste products and to comply with EPA standards for labeling, storage, and transportation of the waste. A generator who disposes of the hazardous waste off-site must comply with a transport procedure established under the RCRA. A manifest, a written document describing the hazardous waste and designating the facility to which it is being transported, must accompany all shipments of hazardous waste to disposal sites. The manifest must be returned to the generator after delivery. The generator must notify the EPA if the manifest is not returned within 35 days.

The RCRA also requires facilities that treat, store, or dispose of hazardous waste—including the generator if it uses on-site disposal—to obtain an operating permit from the EPA. Permit holders must provide monitoring, employee training, emergency procedures, and fencing and warning signs. Permit holders also must carry insurance to cover potential liability for injuries from hazardous waste. The EPA has established disposal techniques for hazardous waste including, for example, incineration, deep-well injection, discharge into waters or oceans, and land disposal. Permit holders must comply with standards set by the EPA in disposing of the hazardous waste. Because of leakage problems with land disposal techniques, Congress amended the RCRA in 1984 to require phase-out of land disposal unless more permanent containment can be attained. At present such technology is not available.

The RCRA provides criminal penalties for knowingly or willfully violating the Act. Violation of the transportation, treatment, storage, or disposal provisions may be punished by a fine of $50,000 per day, or imprisonment up to five years, or both. Those who knowingly cause endangerment of death or serious injury may be imprisoned for 15 years, and/or fined up to $250,000 ($1 million for an organization). Violations of recordkeeping provisions are punishable by fines of $25,000 per day and imprisonment up to one year or both for a first conviction and $50,000 per day and imprisonment up to two years or both for subsequent convictions. Civil penalties up to $25,000 per day may be imposed for failure to comply with a state or EPA compliance order.

Comprehensive Environmental Response, Compensation, and Liability Act

The **Comprehensive Environmental Response, Compensation, and Liability Act (CERCLA),**[11] adopted in 1980, establishes a national system for the cleanup of hazardous waste sites and accidental spills and leakage of toxic substances. The statute also requires businesses to notify state and local governments of emergency releases of hazardous substances, and to publicly disclose annual emission of specified chemical

---

[9]42 U.S.C. §6901 *et seq.*
[10]42 U.S.C. §6903(5).

[11]42 U.S.C. §9601 *et seq..*

substances. CERCLA established the **Hazardous Substance Superfund**—the **Superfund**—to help finance the cleanup of hazardous waste sites. The Superfund was created with federal funds supplemented by revenues from special taxes on corporations and oil and chemical companies; the taxes were eliminated in 1995.

CERCLA requires the EPA to prepare a National Contingency Plan describing the procedures and standards to be used in cleaning up sites where hazardous waste has been spilled or improperly stored. CERCLA further requires the EPA to investigate, monitor, and inventory these sites and to establish a National Priorities List that ranks the most dangerous sites. CERCLA authorizes the EPA to undertake its own cleanup of these sites or to order the responsible parties to perform the cleanup. The Superfund is used to defray the costs of cleanups conducted by the EPA. A state or private party that cleans up a site for which it is not responsible also may seek funding from the Superfund.

Potentially Responsible Parties. The EPA may sue any or all of the potentially responsible parties (PRPs) for reimbursement of expenses—called response costs—paid from the Superfund. CERCLA broadly defines those who may be held liable to include generators of the hazardous substances (including anyone who arranged for disposal or transportation), transporters of the substances, and the owners and operators of the site (including current owners and operators as well as those who owned or operated the site at the time of the disposal). In interpreting the statute, courts have imposed liability not only on corporations that operated the site but also on corporate officers who were directly responsible for disposal of hazardous waste. Even secured creditors can be held liable if they participate in the management of a facility. For example, a bank or other financial institution holding a mortgage on the waste site may be held liable if it assumes some managerial responsibilities for the site after the owner has gone bankrupt or defaulted on a loan.

Liability Under CERCLA. The liability rules under CERCLA are severe, imposing strict liability—that is, liability without fault—on the PRPs. Thus, a PRP may be held responsible for cleanup costs even if it did not know that the waste was hazardous. Further, CERCLA applies retroactively. Parties, therefore, may be held liable for response costs incurred to clean up waste sites that were created before CERCLA was enacted. Liability of the PRPs is joint and several; all responsible

parties are jointly liable for the response costs and any party can be held individually liable for all of the costs. As a result, a financially sound business that contributed only a small amount of waste to a site could be held liable for all response costs.

At issue in the following case was the liability under CERCLA of a parent corporation for pollution caused by a subsidiary.

United States v. Bestfoods
118 S. Ct. 1876 (1998)

> Defendant CPC International, Inc. (now named Bestfoods) purchased Ott Chemical Co. (Ott I) in 1965 and operated it as a wholly owned subsidiary also called Ott Chemical Co. (Ott II). After the purchase, CPC appointed Ott I's managers to serve as officers of Ott II. CPC also appointed several of its own executives to serve as officers and directors of Ott II. In 1972, CPC sold Ott II. While operating as CPC's subsidiary, OTT II manufactured chemicals at a plant near Muskegon, Michigan that polluted the soil and ground water with hazardous waste. In 1981, the federal EPA began clean-up of the site under a plan with estimated costs of tens of millions of dollars. The U.S. government sued CPC and four other potentially responsible parties under CERCLA seeking to recover the clean-up costs. The trial court, after finding that CPC had participated in and exercised control over Ott II's functions and decision-making, ruled that CPC had acted as an "operator" and was liable for the clean-up costs. The court of appeals reversed, holding that CPC had not controlled Ott II's actions. The U.S. Supreme Court agreed to review the case.

Justice Souter

. . . The issue before us, under the Comprehensive Environmental Response, Compensation, and Liability Act of 1980 (CERCLA) is whether a parent corporation that actively participated in, and exercised control over, the operations of a subsidiary may, without more, be held liable as an operator of a polluting facility owned or operated by the subsidiary. We answer no, unless the corporate veil may be pierced. But a corporate parent that actively participated in, and exercised control over, the operations of the facility itself may be held directly liable in its own right as an operator of the facility. . . .

It is a general principle of corporate law deeply "ingrained in our economic and legal systems" that a parent corporation (so-called because of control through ownership of another corporation's stock) is not liable for the acts of its subsidiaries. Douglas & Shanks, *Insulation from Liability Through Subsidiary Corporations,* 39 YALE L. J. 193 (1929). . . . Thus it is hornbook law that "the exercise of the 'control' which stock ownership gives to the stockholders . . . will not create liability beyond the assets of the subsidiary. That 'control' includes the election of directors, the making of by-laws . . . and the doing of all other acts incident to the legal status of stockholders. Nor will a duplication of some or all of the directors or executive officers be fatal." [*Id.* at 196.] Although this respect for corporate distinctions when the subsidiary is a polluter has been severely criticized in the literature, . . . nothing in CERCLA purports to reject this bedrock principle, and against this venerable common-law backdrop, the congressional silence is audible. . . . The Government has indeed made no claim that a corporate parent is liable as an owner or an operator under §107 simply because its subsidiary is subject to liability for owning or operating a polluting facility.

But there is an equally fundamental principle of corporate law, applicable to the parent-subsidiary relationship as well as generally, that the corporate veil may be pierced and the shareholder held liable for the corporation's conduct when, *inter alia,* the corporate form would otherwise be misused to accomplish certain wrongful purposes, most notably fraud, on the shareholder's behalf. . . . Nothing in CERCLA purports to rewrite this well-settled rule, either. . . . The Court of Appeals was accordingly correct in holding that when (but only when) the corporate veil may be pierced, may a parent corporation be charged with derivative CERCLA liability for its subsidiary's actions. . . .

If the act rested liability entirely on ownership of a polluting facility, this opinion might end here; but CERCLA liability may turn on operation as well as ownership, and nothing in the statute's terms bars a parent corporation from direct liability for its own actions in operating a facility owned by its subsidiary. . . . The fact that a corporate subsidiary happens to own a polluting facility operated by its parent does nothing, then, to displace the rule that the parent "corporation is [itself] responsible for the wrongs committed by its agents in the course of its business," *Mine Workers v. Coronado Coal Co.,* [42 S. Ct. 570, 577 (1922)], and whereas the rules of veil-piercing limit derivative liability for the actions of another corporation, CERCLA's "operator" provision is concerned primarily with direct liability for one's own actions. . . .

Under the plain language of the statute, any person who operates a polluting facility is directly liable for the costs of cleaning up the pollution. . . . This is so regardless of whether that person is the facility's owner, the owner's parent corporation or business partner, or even a saboteur who sneaks into the facility at night to discharge its poisons out of malice. If any such act of operating a corporate subsidiary's facility is done on behalf of a parent corporation, the existence of the parent-subsidiary relationship under state corporate law is simply irrelevant to the issue of direct liability. . . .

This much is easy to say; the difficulty comes in defining actions sufficient to constitute direct parental "operation." . . . [U]nder CERCLA, an operator is simply someone who directs the workings of, manages, or conducts the affairs of a facility. To sharpen the definition for purposes of CERCLA's concern with environmental contamination, an operator must manage, direct, or conduct operations specifically related to pollution, that is, operations having to do with the leakage or disposal of hazardous waste, or decisions about compliance with environmental regulations. . . .

By emphasizing that "CPC is directly liable under section 107(a)(2) as an operator because CPC actively participated in and exerted significant control over Ott II's business and decision-making," the District Court applied the "actual control" test of whether the parent "actually operated the business of its subsidiary." . . .

The well-taken objection to the actual control test, however, is its fusion of direct and indirect liability; the test is administered by asking a question about the relationship between the two corporations (an issue going to indirect liability) instead of a question about the parent's interaction with the subsidiary's facility (the source of any direct liability). If, however, direct liability for the parent's operation of the facility is to be kept distinct from derivative liability for the subsidiary's own operation, the focus of the enquiry must necessarily be different under the two tests. "The question is not whether the parent operates the subsidiary, but rather whether it operates the facility, and that operation is evidenced by participation in the activities of the facility, not the subsidiary. Control of the subsidiary, if extensive enough, gives rise to indirect liability under piercing doctrine, not direct liability under the statutory language." Oswald, *Bifurcation of the Owner and Operator Analysis under CERCLA,* 72 WASH. U.L.Q. 223, 269 (1994). . . . The District Court was therefore mistaken to rest its analysis on CPC's relationship with Ott II, premising liability on little more than "CPC's 100-percent ownership of Ott II" and "CPC's active participation in, and at times majority control over, Ott II's board of directors." The analysis should instead have rested on the relationship between CPC and the Muskegon facility itself. . . .

In imposing direct liability on these grounds, the District Court failed to recognize that "it is entirely appropriate for directors of a parent corporation to serve as directors of its subsidiary, and that fact alone may not serve to expose the parent corporation to liability for its subsidiary's acts." *American Protein Corp. v. AB Volvo,* 844 F.2d 56, 57 (2d Cir. 1988).

This recognition that the corporate personalities remain distinct has its corollary in the "well established principle [of corporate law] that directors and officers holding positions with a parent and its subsidiary can and do 'change hats' to represent the two corporations separately, despite their common ownership." *Lusk v. Foxmeyer Health Corp.,* 129 F.3d 773, 779 (5th Cir. 1997). . . . Since courts generally presume "that the directors are wearing their 'subsidiary hats' and not their 'parent hats' when acting for the subsidiary," P. Blumberg, *Law of Corporate Groups: Procedural Problems in the Law of Parent and Subsidiary Corporations* §1.02.1, at 12 (1983), . . . it cannot be enough to establish liability here that dual officers and directors made policy decisions and supervised activities at the facility. The Government would have to show that, despite the general presumption to the contrary, the officers and directors were acting in their capacities as CPC officers and directors, and not as Ott II officers and directors, when they committed those acts. The District Court made no such enquiry here, however, disregarding entirely this time-honored common law rule. . . .

In sum, the District Court's focus on the relationship between parent and subsidiary (rather than parent and facility), combined with its automatic attribution of the actions of dual officers and directors to the corporate parent, erroneously, even if unintentionally, treated CERCLA as though it displaced or fundamentally altered common law standards of limited liability. Indeed, if the evidence of common corporate personnel acting at management and directorial levels were enough to support a finding of a parent corporation's direct operator liability under CERCLA, then the possibility of resort to veil piercing to establish indirect, derivative liability for the subsidiary's violations would be academic. There would in essence be a relaxed, CERCLA-specific rule of derivative liability that would banish traditional standards and expectations from the law of CERCLA liability. But, as we have said, such a rule does not arise from congressional silence, and CERCLA's silence is dispositive. . . .

[Judgment reversed and remanded.]

CERCLA has proved to be one of the most controversial environmental statutes. Many who criticize the high costs expended for cleanup suggest that the EPA should focus its efforts on containment and risk reduction. Clean-up of hazardous sites initially was complicated and often delayed by numerous lawsuits. Insurance companies sought clarification of their legal responsibility for claims filed under insurance policies that predated CERCLA. Many PRPs vigorously contested their liability for response costs, particularly in cases where they had contributed relatively small amounts of hazardous waste. After judicial resolution of issues fundamental to CERCLA enforcement, the EPA and businesses increasingly have settled liability issues through consent decrees.

CERCLA authorizes EPA to enter into *de minimis* settlements with PRPs that contributed waste of minimal volume or minimal toxicity to a hazardous waste site. Under these settlements, the PRP agrees to pay a specified sum or perform some cleanup in exchange for release from further liability. The EPA has significantly increased the use of *de minimis* settlements and expressed its commitment to their continued use to resolve the liability of minor parties.

As of September 2004, the EPA reported that it had completed cleanup of more than 900 National Priority List sites. Because of potential liability under CERCLA, developers often were hesitant to reuse "brownfields"—abandoned or idled property with actual or perceived environmental contamination from prior industrial or commercial activity. The federal Brownfields Revitalization and Environmental Restoration Act of 2001,[12] was designed to encourage reclamation of brownfields by providing funding and protecting bona fide prospective purchasers, contiguous property owners and innocent landowners from liability if they redevelop these properties. Since enactment of the law, the EPA has worked with many states to reclaim and redevelop brownfields.

---

[12]The statute amended 42 U.S.C. §§9601, 9604, 9605, and 9607, and added § 9628.

National Environmental Policy Act

One of the first federal statutes concerning the environment was the **National Environmental Policy Act (NEPA).**[13] Unlike the other statutes discussed in this chapter, NEPA is not a pollution control statute. Instead, NEPA imposes a duty on federal agencies to consider environmental matters in administering their programs. As a result, NEPA affects private business and industry only indirectly.

NEPA requires all federal agencies to include an **environmental impact statement (EIS)** with every proposal for legislation or major federal action that will significantly affect the environment. The Council on Environmental Quality has developed regulations governing the EIS process. In general, an agency must prepare an environmental assessment for any project subject to federal control. These projects include not only direct federal actions, such as construction of a federal highway or dam, but also private projects requiring a federal license or financed by federal funds. The environmental assessment addresses the issue of whether an EIS is necessary. If the agency determines that the project will not have a significant impact on the environment, it will not prepare an EIS. If it does prepare an EIS, the agency seeks input from the public and other agencies. It then prepares a report detailing the environmental impact of the project, unavoidable adverse environmental effects, and alternatives to the proposed action.

The provisions of NEPA are enforceable by judicial review. Many cases arise when an interested party or environmental interest group challenges an agency's decision to proceed with a project despite its adverse environmental impact. In such cases, the courts generally review the case to determine that the agency has followed the proper procedure. In the following case, the U.S. Supreme Court reviews a federal administrative agency's decision to grant permission for commercial development of national forest land despite potential injury to the environment.

Robertson v. Methow Valley Citizens Council
109 S. Ct. 1835 (1989)

The federal Forest Service is authorized to manage national forests for recreational purposes. Prior to the Forest

---

[13]42 U.S.C. §4321 *et seq.*

Service's issuing recreational special use permits, however, the National Environmental Policy Act (NEPA) requires that an environmental impact statement (EIS) be prepared. In 1978, Methow Recreation, Inc. (MRI), which owned 1,165 acres adjacent to Sandy Butte, a mountain located in the Okanogan National Forest that overlooks the Methow Valley in the state of Washington, applied to the Forest Service for a special use permit to develop and operate a ski resort at Sandy Butte. In response to the application, the Forest Service, working with local officials, prepared an EIS known as the Early Winters Alpine Winter Sports Study (Early Winters Study). As required by regulations of the Council on Environmental Quality, the study considered the environmental impact of a ski resort not only on Sandy Butte but also on the adjacent Methow Valley area. The study concluded that the ski area itself would not adversely affect air quality but that development of nearby land would reduce air quality as a result of increased automobile exhaust and fireplace and woodstove use. The EIS further found that the development would adversely affect the population of mule deer that used the Methow Valley as a winter range and migratory route. The Early Winters Study described various measures that could mitigate these adverse environmental impacts and recommended that the Forest Service require any development plan to include procedures to control the air pollution. The Forest Service issued MRI a special use permit to develop a ski resort. Noting the potential reduction of air quality and mule deer, the permit directed the supervisor of Okanogan National Forest and local officials to identify and implement certain mitigation measures. Plaintiffs Methow Valley Citizens Council and three other citizens groups filed a lawsuit claiming that the Early Winters Study did not satisfy the requirements of NEPA. The trial court found that the study was adequate, but the Circuit Court of Appeals reversed, holding that the EIS was inadequate because it did not include a fully developed plan to mitigate the harmful environmental consequences. The U.S. Supreme Court granted the Forest Service's petition for review.

Justice Stevens

We granted certiorari to decide: . . .

Whether the National Environmental Policy Act requires federal agencies to include in each environmental impact statement . . . a fully developed plan to mitigate environmental harm. . . .

Concluding that the Court of Appeals for the Ninth Circuit misapplied the National Environmental Policy Act of 1969 (NEPA), . . . we reverse and remand for further proceedings. . . .

Section 101 of NEPA declares a broad national commitment to protecting and promoting environmental quality. . . .

The statutory requirement that a federal agency contemplating a major action prepare . . . an environmental impact statement serves NEPA's "action-forcing" purpose in two important respects. . . . It ensures that the agency, in reaching its decision, will have available and will carefully consider detailed information concerning significant environmental impacts; it also guarantees that the relevant information will be made available to the larger audience that may also play a role in both the decisionmaking process and the implementation of that decision.

Simply by focusing the agency's attention on the environmental consequences of a proposed project, NEPA ensures that important effects will not be overlooked or underestimated only to be discovered after resources have been committed or the die otherwise cast. . . .

Publication of an EIS, both in draft and final form, also serves a larger informational role. It gives the public the assurance that the agency "has indeed considered environmental concerns in its decisionmaking process," [*Baltimore Gas & Electric Co. v. Natural Resources Defense Council, Inc.,* 103 S. Ct. 2246, 2252 (1983)], and, perhaps more significantly, provides a springboard for public comment. . . . Thus, in this case the final draft of the Early Winters Study reflects not only the work of the Forest Service itself, but also the critical views of the Washington State Department of Game, the Methow Valley Citizens Council, and Friends of the Earth, as well as many others, to whom copies of the draft Study were circulated. . . . Moreover, with respect to a development such as Sandy Butte, where the adverse effects on air quality and the mule deer herd are primarily attributable to predicted off-site development that will be subject to regulation by other governmental bodies, the EIS serves the function of offering those bodies adequate notice of the expected consequences and the opportunity to plan and implement corrective measures in a timely manner.

The sweeping policy goals announced in §101 of NEPA are thus realized through a set of "action-forcing" procedures that require that agencies take a "'hard look' at environmental consequences," [*Kleppe v. Sierra Club,* 96 S. Ct. 2718, 2730 (1976)], and that provide for broad dissemination of relevant environmental information. Although these procedures are almost certain to affect the agency's substan-tive decision, it is now well settled that NEPA itself does not mandate particular results, but simply prescribes the necessary process. . . . If the adverse environmental effects of the proposed action are adequately identified and evaluated, the agency is not constrained by NEPA from deciding that other values outweigh the environmental costs. . . . In this case, for example, it would not have violated NEPA if the Forest Service, after complying with the Act's procedural prerequisites, had decided that the benefits to be derived from downhill skiing at Sandy Butte justified the issuance of a special use permit, notwithstanding the loss of 15 percent, 50 percent, or even 100 percent of the mule deer herd. Other statutes may impose substantive environmental obligations on federal agencies, but NEPA merely prohibits uninformed—rather than unwise—agency action.

To be sure, one important ingredient of an EIS is the discussion of steps that can be taken to mitigate adverse environmental consequences. . . . Without such a discussion, neither the agency nor other interested groups and individuals can properly evaluate the severity of the adverse effects. . . .

There is a fundamental distinction, however, between a requirement that mitigation be discussed in sufficient detail to ensure that environmental consequences have been fairly evaluated, on the one hand, and a substantive requirement that a complete mitigation plan be actually formulated and adopted, on the other. In this case, the off-site effects on air quality and on the mule deer herd cannot be mitigated unless nonfederal government agencies take appropriate action. Since it is those state and local governmental bodies that have jurisdiction over the area in which the adverse effects need be addressed and since they have the authority to mitigate them, it would be incongruous to conclude that the Forest Service has no power to act until the local agencies have reached a final conclusion on what mitigating measures they consider necessary. Even more significantly, it would be inconsistent with NEPA's reliance on procedural mechanisms—as opposed to substantive, result-based standards—to demand the presence of a fully developed plan that will mitigate environmental harm before an agency can act. . . .

[Judgment reversed and remanded.]

Summary

1. Common law principles of tort and property law, which provide some remedies for pollution, can be used in combination with federal statutory law to resolve environmental problems.

2. Comprehensive federal regulation of the environment began with legislative enactments in the 1960s and creation of the Environmental Protection Agency, the agency primarily responsible for administering federal environmental laws.

3. Limited and conflicting scientific data, technological lags, and the costs of adopting expensive technology have delayed implementation of federal environmental law.

4. Under the Clean Air Act, the EPA establishes national ambient air quality standards (NAAQS) that are implemented by state implementation plans (SIPs) adopted by the states. The Clean Air Act further regulates air pollution by establishing vehicle emission standards, requiring the EPA to establish standards for hazardous air pollutants, and controlling substances that cause acid rain.

5. The Clean Water Act authorizes discharge of pollutants into U.S. waters only by those who hold valid permits that comply with EPA effluent limitations, and allows dredged and fill materials discharge only under permits issued by the Army Corps of Engineers. The Clean Water Act, as amended by the Oil Pollution Act of 1990, also governs prevention and cleanup of accidental spills of oil and hazardous substances.

6. Toxic and hazardous substances are subject to federal control under various statutes. FIFRA provides a registration system for pesticides and TSCA provides a similar system for registration of other chemicals. The EPA may cancel registration and restrict production and distribution of pesticides and chemicals that present a risk to the environment.

7. RCRA and CERCLA regulate hazardous waste. Under RCRA, the transportation, storage, and disposal of hazardous waste must comply with EPA regulations. CERCLA provides funding to clean up hazardous waste sites and establishes a procedure for recovering cleanup costs from responsible parties.

8. NEPA requires federal administrative agencies to consider the environmental impact of proposed major federal actions in an EIS.

Key Terms

Environmental Protection
    Agency (EPA)
Clean Air Act

national ambient air quality
    standards (NAAQS)
state implementation plan (SIP)

Clean Water Act
National Pollutant
    Discharge Elimination
    System (NPDES)
Federal Insecticide,
    Fungicide, and
    Rodenticide Act (FIFRA)
Toxic Substances Control
    Act (TSCA)
Resource Conservation and
    Recovery Act (RCRA)

Comprehensive Environ-
    mental Response,
    Compensation, and
    Liability Act (CERCLA)
Hazardous Substance
    Superfund (Superfund)
National Environmental
    Policy Act (NEPA)
environmental impact
    statement (EIS)

Questions and Problems

55.1 Various alternatives to the current statutes regulating air and water pollution have been suggested. Discuss the advantages and disadvantages of the following alternatives.
    (a) All sources of pollution in a given area should be required to reduce their emissions by a uniform percentage.
    (b) All sources of pollution in a given area should be required to limit their air or water pollution to a certain number of pounds per day.

55.2 In recent years, the federal government has increased its use of criminal prosecutions to enforce environmental laws. In 2000, for example, a total of $122 million in fines and 146 years of imprisonment were imposed as penalties; in 1993, fines totaled only $29.7 million and only 74 years of imprisonment were imposed.
    (a) Why do you think criminal penalties are being imposed more frequently? Explain.
    (b) Do you think criminal sanctions are appropriate for violations of the environmental laws? Explain.

55.3 Many of the federal environmental statutes are based on a "command and control" strategy by which the government dictates to businesses the exact methods by which they must reduce pollution to a specified level. In contrast, the acid rain provisions of the Clean Air Act Amendments of 1990 create "pollution rights."
    (a) Suggest reasons why the pollution control strategy of the 1990 Amendments might be more successful in achieving pollution control than the command and control strategy.
    (b) Do you think the concept of pollution rights should be used to control other types of pollution? Are there any types of pollution for which a pollution rights approach would be inappropriate? Explain.

55.4 Are the provisions of the Clean Water Act technology-forcing or technology-based? Explain.

55.5 When the EPA canceled registration under FIFRA of the pesticide DDT, the manufacturer challenged the EPA cancelation. The producers of DDT argued that the EPA had failed to prove that DDT use was harmful to human beings.

(a) The EPA based its conclusion that DDT posed an imminent hazard by relying on test data showing that DDT probably was carcinogenic (cancer causing) to mice and rats. Should the EPA be required to prove conclusively that a substance is hazardous to human beings before being allowed to cancel registration? Explain.

(b) Producers of DDT argued that the EPA should be required to prove that the benefits of canceling registration and use of a pesticide outweigh the benefits derived from the pesticide. Do you agree with the DDT producers? Explain.

(c) In the DDT cases, the court effectively held that in a registration cancellation hearing the producers of the pesticide must bear the burden of proving that the product causes only minimal risk and that the benefits of its use outweigh the costs. How would a producer of a pesticide prove these elements? Do you believe the allocation of the burden of proof in such cases is proper? Explain.

55.6   The Resource Conservation and Recovery Act has been described as a system for regulating hazardous wastes from "cradle to grave." What is meant by this description? Is it accurate? Explain.

55.7   Lee and Michael formed Chemical Company, a corporation that manufactures chemicals. Michael is the president and majority shareholder and Lee is vice president and also a shareholder. Both knew that manufacturing processes used by Chemical Company produced toxic byproducts, including dioxin. Lee approved the company's disposing of waste that contained toxic chemicals on a nearby farm. The EPA discovered the waste site and, after cleaning it up, sued both Lee and Michael alleging that they should be held responsible for the cleanup costs. How should the court rule? Explain.

55.8   Under CERCLA, the EPA may clean up a hazardous waste site and then sue some or all of the potentially responsible parties to recover the costs. The EPA, however, has entered into many settlement agreement in which the PRPs perform and pay for the cleanup. Both the EPA and private industry have suggested that cleanup by the polluters is less expensive and more efficient. Many members of Congress, however, do not favor cleanup by private industry.

(a) Why would members of Congress be opposed to settlements in which industry performs the cleanup?

(b) What incentives can the EPA offer to encourage industries to cooperate in cleanup of hazardous waste sites?

55.9   An environmental impact statement (EIS) prepared under the National Environmental Policy Act generally considers the impact of federal projects on the natural environment, for example, the quality of air and loss of resources such as plant and wildlife. An EIS, however, is required for all "major Federal actions significantly affecting the quality of the human environment." (42 U.S.C. §4332(2)(C).) Consider the requirements of an EIS in light of the following facts.

(a) The federal government proposes to construct a prison in New York City. What environmental factors should be considered in the EIS?

(b) Metropolitan Edison Co. requests the NRC's permission to restart one of the undamaged nuclear reactors at Three Mile Island. A local citizens group asserts that the NRC must prepare an EIS that considers the severe psychological damage that might be caused to local residents. Is this potential psychological damage an environmental impact? Explain.

55.10 Review the cases excerpted in this chapter. Does the judiciary appear willing to assume an active role in establishing substantive rules for environmental regulation? Explain. Suggest reasons for this judicial attitude toward environmental law.

SPECIAL TOPICS

ACCOUNTANTS' LIABILITY

In periodic audits, independent certified public accountants (CPAs) review, examine, and test a company's financial statements. The accountant's objective is to express an opinion regarding whether the financial statements present fairly, in all material respects, the client's financial position, results of operation, and cash flows. The independent CPA communicates this opinion in an audit report, which usually states that the audit was conducted in conformity with generally accepted auditing standards (GAAS), and that the financial statements are fairly presented in conformity with generally accepted accounting principles (GAAP). The client then often distributes the audit report and financial statements to interested third par-

ties, including shareholders, creditors, lenders, and potential investors. The audit report assists these people in evaluating the company's financial health before making a business decision.

Independent auditors render important services to their clients including evaluating and suggesting improvements in internal control procedures and, in some cases, detecting fraud or embezzlement by the client's employees. The auditor's undertaking also serves an important public function in our economic system. As noted by one commentator, "The functioning and, indeed, the perpetuation of our private enterprise system depends on the continuing confidence of investors and creditors in the reliability of financial statements. To provide this confidence is precisely the role that the auditor assumes."[1]

Occasionally, auditors have failed to meet their public responsibility by certifying as accurate financial statements that are materially inaccurate or misleading. In such cases, third parties who rely on the audit report and suffer damages often look to the auditor for compensation. To illustrate a typical case, assume Blake Company hires auditing firm Arthur Ross to perform an audit. Blake needs the audit report to obtain a loan

---

[1]Savoie, *Why Accountants Need to Tell a Fuller Story,* BUSINESS WEEK (February 6, 1971) at 87.

from First National Bank, which intends to use the audit information to evaluate Blake's loan application. Relying on Arthur Ross's report, the bank makes the loan. A short time later Blake Company files for bankruptcy and defaults on the loan. First National later learns that Arthur Ross failed to discover an irregularity—for example, that the treasurer had been embezzling large sums of money—that rendered the audited statements materially misleading. The bank sues Arthur Ross for damages, alleging that it would not have made the loan if the irregularity had been detected.

Accountants may be held liable to their clients and to third parties such as First National Bank on a variety of legal theories. Under the common law, liability may be based upon breach of contract, negligence, or fraud. Statutory liability usually is based upon the federal securities laws that are discussed in detail in Chapter 49. This chapter examines the major legal theories underlying accountant's liability, beginning with common law liability.

Common Law Liability

Contract Liability

The client's employment of an accountant is a contractual undertaking. Because the rights and obligations of the parties are controlled by private agreement, the auditor must properly perform the agreed undertaking to be entitled to compensation. The accountant's primary duties usually are expressed in the engagement letter, a contract between the auditor and the client. The letter normally specifies the nature of the auditor's examination, the responsibilities assumed, and limitations on the scope of the audit. In addition, implied in every contract for work or services is the duty to perform it skillfully, carefully, diligently, and in a workmanlike manner. The auditor may be liable to the client for breach of contract, for example, if the auditor issues a standard audit report without making an examination in accordance with GAAS, fails to deliver the audit report on time, violates the client's confidential relationship, or otherwise fails to perform.

An accountant's contract liability also may extend to third-party beneficiaries of the contract. As discussed in Chapter 13, a beneficiary (a person who benefits from performance of a contract but is not a party to it) may enforce a contract made with the intent to benefit the beneficiary. In the accountants' liability context, for

example, an audit may be undertaken for the express purpose of providing financial statements to a specific lender as part of a loan application. In this case, the bank or other lender may be an intended beneficiary of the contract between the auditor and client, entitled to recover damages for the auditor's breach.

Negligence Liability—Clients

As discussed in Chapter 5, negligence occurs when a person does something that a reasonable person would not do, or fails to do something that a reasonable person would do, under the circumstances. A client seeking to recover against an accountant in an action based on negligence must satisfy four requirements. First, the plaintiff must show that the accountant had a duty not to be negligent. Second, the accountant must have breached that duty by failing to exercise reasonable care. Third, the plaintiff must establish a causal connection between the negligence and the injury. Finally, the plaintiff must prove damage or actual loss. Many suits brought against an accountant for negligence involve failure to discover defalcations involving, for example, check kiting, concealment of inventory shortages, and embezzlement. The material that follows briefly outlines the elements of a negligence action in the accountants' liability context.

Duty. In most circumstances the auditor is engaged to issue a standard audit report, which states that the audit was conducted according to generally accepted auditing standards and that, in the auditor's opinion, the financial statements present fairly the client's financial position under generally accepted accounting principles. Auditing standards concern how the work of the particular audit is performed. For example, auditing standards determine what books, records, and assets are examined; how accounts such as cash and accounts receivable are verified; and how internal control is evaluated. In contrast, accounting principles determine how the completed work is presented in the financial statements. Accounting principles, for example, determine when a contingency reserve is required and how to account for a decline in the value of inventory.

Consistent with general negligence principles, the auditor owes a duty to the client to exercise reasonable care in conducting the audit. In determining whether this duty has been breached (that is, whether the auditor has been negligent), the court examines the auditor's compliance with both appropriate auditing standards and accounting principles. That is, liability may be imposed for lack of reasonable care either in planning and performing the audit or in presenting its results in the audit report.

As a professional, an accountant is held to possess the degree of skill, knowledge, and judgment commonly possessed by other members of the profession in the locality. Accordingly, the accountant is held to a higher standard of care than the ordinary "reasonable person." Generally to avoid liability, an accountant must act as a reasonably prudent accountant would act under similar circumstances. For this reason, negligence often must be proven or disproven by expert accounting testimony.

Note that failure to follow GAAS and GAAP, the custom of the profession, generally indicates negligence in the conduct of the audit. Literal adherence to customary practice, however, does not necessarily indicate lack of negligence. Compliance with GAAS and GAAP is merely one factor to be considered in evaluating the accountant's reasonable care.

Although under a duty to search for errors and irregularities, an auditor is not a guarantor of the accuracy of the financial statements. That is, an audit cannot be relied upon to disclose defalcations or management fraud. Nevertheless, failure to uncover certain frauds may be negligence. For example, GAAS are designed in part to uncover deliberate misrepresentations by management, but are less effective at detecting frauds involving collusion, forgery, or unrecorded transactions. Thus, an auditor who fails to follow GAAS may be liable in negligence for failure to uncover a fraud that would have been found if those standards had been properly applied.

Breach of Duty. An auditor may breach the duty to exercise reasonable care by using inadequate procedures and methods to ascertain the information on which the audit report is based. For example, an engagement to perform an audit implies the duties to verify cash, confirm accounts receivable, observe physical inventories, and generally adhere to professional standards. Failure to perform these tasks properly may constitute negligence. In addition, the accountant may be negligent in communicating the information to the client.

Causation and Damages. Once negligence is established, the plaintiff must prove the amount of his damage with reasonable certainty, and demonstrate that the accountant's acts or omissions were the cause of the loss. Causation is apparent if the client sues for losses caused by an employee's embezzlement that the accountant should have detected. More difficult cases arise if the plaintiff seeks recovery for losses resulting from bad business investments or decisions made in reliance on the audit report.

Negligence Liability — Third Parties

Although an audit is designed to inform management of inefficiencies and irregularities in the business, audited financial statements also are used by third parties who have no contractual relation with the accountant. Third parties such as banks, potential investors, and shareholders who are injured by relying upon negligently certified financial statements may sue the auditor. The following material examines the conflicting legal theories governing accountants' liability to third parties for negligence.

The Ultramares Rule. The landmark case concerning accountants' liability to third parties for negligence is *Ultramares Corporation v. Touche, Niven, & Company,* decided by the New York Court of Appeals in 1931.[2] In this case, Fred Stern & Company, a firm engaged in the importation and sale of rubber, required extensive use of credit to finance its operations. The defendant, Touche, Niven, & Company, was hired by Stern to prepare and certify a December 31, 1923, balance sheet. The defendants certified 32 copies of the financial statements knowing that the balance sheet would be used by Stern to obtain credit. The defendants certified the balance sheet even though Stern was insolvent with $706,000 in fictitious receivables on the books. On the faith of the certified financial statements, Ultramares Corporation loaned money to Stern. Shortly thereafter, Stern went bankrupt and Ultramares sued the accountant alleging that the accountant's misrepresentations were both negligent and fraudulent.

Judge Benjamin Cardozo, writing for a unanimous court, found negligence on the part of the accountant. Nevertheless, he held that the accountant had no liability to third parties for ordinary negligence even though liability to third parties could be imposed for fraud or

---

[2]174 N.E. 441 (N.Y. 1931).

gross negligence. Judge Cardozo, concerned with expansive accountants' liability to third parties, stated:

> If liability for negligence exists [between the accountant and unknown third party], a thoughtless slip or blunder, the failure to detect a theft or forgery beneath the cover of deceptive entries, may expose accountants to a liability in an indeterminate amount for an indeterminate time to an indeterminate class. . . . Our holding does not emancipate accountants from the consequences of fraud. It does not relieve them if their audit has been so negligent as to justify a finding that they had no genuine belief in its adequacy, for this again is fraud. It does no more than say that, if less than this is proved, if there has been neither reckless misstatement nor insincere profession of an opinion, but only honest blunder, the ensuing liability for negligence is one that is bounded by the contract, and is to be enforced between the parties by whom the contract has been made.[3]

The *Ultramares* case therefore takes a very restrictive view of an accountant's liability to third parties for negligence, allowing recovery only by persons in privity of contract with the accountant. Applying this test, the court refused to hold the negligent accountants liable to Ultramares, a lender with whom they had no contractual privity.

The New York Court of Appeals reaffirmed its support for the *Ultramares* privity rule and refined it in *Credit Alliance Corporation v. Arthur Andersen & Company* (1985), in which the court stated:

> [T]his court [has since] reiterated the requirement for a "contractual relationship or its equivalent." . . . Before accountants may be held liable in negligence to noncontractual parties who rely to their detriment on inaccurate financial reports, certain prerequisites must be satisfied: (1) the accountants must have been aware that the financial reports were to be used for a particular purpose or purposes; (2) in the furtherance of which a known party or parties was intended to rely; and (3) there must have been some conduct on the part of the accountants linking them to that party or parties, which evinces the accountants' understanding of that party or parties' reliance. While these criteria permit some flexibility in the application of the doctrine of privity to accountants' liability, they do not represent a departure from the principles articulated in

Ultramares, . . . but, rather, they are intended to preserve the wisdom and policy set forth therein.[4]

Alternatives to Ultramares. Both courts and commentators have criticized the *Ultramares* doctrine for unreasonably insulating negligent CPAs from third-party liability. Although many courts continue to follow the *Ultramares* rule of privity (and a few states have adopted it by statute), a majority of courts are rejecting it and extending accountants' liability for negligence to third parties. One alternative to the *Ultramares* privity doctrine is the rule stated in §552 of the *Restatement (Second) of Torts,* which has received considerable support. Section 552, entitled "Information Negligently Supplied for the Guidance of Others," provides in relevant part:

> (1) One who, in the course of his business, profession or employment, or in any other transaction in which he has a pecuniary interest, supplies false information for the guidance of others in their business transactions, is subject to liability for pecuniary loss caused to them by their justifiable reliance upon the information, if he fails to exercise reasonable care or competence in obtaining or communicating the information.
>
> (2) . . . [T]he liability stated in Subsection (1) is limited to loss suffered
>
> (a) by the person or one of a limited group of persons for whose benefit and guidance he intends to supply the information or knows that the recipient intends to supply it; and
>
> (b) through reliance upon it in a transaction that he intends the information to influence or knows that the recipient so intends or in a substantially similar transaction.

Under §552 an auditor owes a duty (1) to his client, (2) to intended or known third-party users of financial statements, and (3) to any individually unknown third parties who are members of a known or intended class of third-party users of financial statements. The *Restatement* extends liability beyond *Ultramares* in that the auditor need not know the plaintiff's identity, if the plaintiff belongs to an identifiable group to whom the information was intended to be furnished. For example, an auditor who knows that a report is to be prepared for bank borrowing would be liable to the particular bank to whom the client delivers the opinion.

Under either the *Ultramares* or *Restatement* approach, almost all third-party users of financial statements are pre-

---

[3] 174 N.E. at 444, 448.

[4] 483 N.E.2d 110, 117–118 (N.Y. 1985).

vented from suing negligent accountants at common law. That is, shareholders, creditors, and other third parties are in most cases merely "reasonably foreseeable" third parties; they are not known or intended ones. Accordingly, they are denied recovery under both the *Restatement* and *Ultramares*. For this reason, a few courts have adopted a third approach that extends an auditor's duty of reasonable care to reasonably foreseeable plaintiffs who are neither known nor a member of an intended class.

In the following case, the court weighs the advantages and disadvantages of the various approaches to accountants' liability to third parties for negligence.

Nycal Corporation v. KPMG Peat Marwick LLP

688 N.E.2d 1368 (Mass. 1998)

Gulf Resources & Chemical Corporation (Gulf) retained defendant KPMG Peat Marwick LLP to audit its 1990 financial statements. During 1990, two companies considered acquiring Gulf: in February, D.S. Kennedy & Co. identified Gulf as the target of a takeover and in September, Gulf's board considered selling the firm to Aviva Petroleum, Inc. In the course of its audit, the defendant learned of these negotiations but no takeover occurred in 1990. The defendant completed the audit and copies of its auditors' report were included in Gulf's 1990 annual report, which was issued in February 1991. In March 1991, plaintiff Nycal Corporation began discussions with Gulf concerning purchase of a large block of Gulf shares. During the negotiations, Gulf provided copies of its 1990 annual report to plaintiff. On July 12, 1991, Gulf and plaintiff closed a deal in which plaintiff purchased 35 percent of Gulf's outstanding shares. Defendant learned of the sale just a few days before the closing. Plaintiff's investment became worthless in October 1993 when Gulf filed a petition for bankruptcy. Plaintiff filed a lawsuit alleging that defendant had negligently prepared the 1990 auditor's report and that the report materially misrepresented Gulf's financial condition. Plaintiff claimed that it had relied on the report in purchasing the Gulf stock. The trial court granted summary judgment for the defendant. The Massachusetts Supreme Court granted a petition for review.

Greaney, Justice

. . . We have not addressed the scope of liability of an accountant to persons with whom the accountant is not in privity. Three tests have generally been applied in other jurisdictions, either by common law or by statute, to determine the duty of care owed by accountants to nonclients. These include the foreseeability test, the near-privity test, and the test contained in §552 of the *Restatement (Second) of Torts.*

The plaintiff urges our adoption of the broad standard of liability encompassed in the foreseeability test. Pursuant to this test, which is derived from traditional tort law concepts, . . . an accountant may be held liable to any person whom the accountant could reasonably have foreseen would obtain and rely on the accountant's opinion, including known and unknown investors. . . .

Our cases draw a distinction between the duty owed by a professional to a third party for personal injuries and that owed to a third party for pecuniary loss due to a professional's negligence. While we apply traditional tort law principles in cases involving the former, we have not done so in cases concerning the latter. Such principles are particularly unsuitable for application to accountants where, "regardless of the efforts of the auditor, the client retains effective primary control of the financial reporting process." *Bily v. Arthur Young & Co.,* [834 P.2d 745 (Cal. 1992)]. The auditor prepares its report from statements and information supplied by the client, and once the report is completed and provided to the client, the client controls its dissemination. If we were to apply a foreseeability standard in these circumstances, "a thoughtless slip or blunder, the failure to detect a theft or forgery beneath the cover of deceptive entries, may expose accountants to a liability in an indeterminate amount for an indeterminate time to an indeterminate class." *Ultramares Corp. v. Touche,* [174 N.E. 441 (N.Y. 1931)]. We refuse to hold accountants susceptible to such expansive liability, and conclude that Massachusetts law does not protect every reasonably foreseeable user of an inaccurate audit report.

The near-privity test, which originated in Chief Judge Cardozo's decision in *Ultramares Corp. v. Touche, supra,* and was modified by *Credit Alliance Corp v. Arthur Andersen & Co.,* [483 N.E.2d 110 (N.Y. 1985)], limits an accountant's liability exposure to those with whom the accountant is in privity or in a relationship "sufficiently approaching privity." Under this test, an accountant may be held liable to noncontractual third parties who rely to their detriment on an inaccurate financial report if the accountant was aware that the report was to be used for a particular purpose, in the furtherance of which a known party (or parties) was intended to rely, and if there was some conduct on the part of the accountant creating a link to that party, which evinces the accountant's understanding of the party's reliance. . . .

The defendant professes that the near-privity test is consistent with the standard we have previously applied to other professionals in the absence of privity. We disagree. A review of the relevant cases demonstrates that the first two elements of the near-privity test—reliance by the third party and knowledge that the party intended to rely—have analogs in our case law, but the third element—conduct by the accountant providing a direct linkage to the third party—does not.

The leading case in Massachusetts on the duty owed by a professional to persons with whom the professional is not in privity is *Craig v. Everett M. Brooks Co.,* [222 N.E.2d 752 (Mass. 1967)]. In *Craig,* the plaintiff, a general contractor, and the defendant, a civil engineer and surveyor, each had a contract with the same real estate developer. The defendant placed stakes on the developer's real estate to enable the plaintiff to build roads. The defendant knew that the plaintiff was the contractor, and that the work which the plaintiff was contracted to perform would be in accordance with the defendant's stakes. Because the defendant knew the plaintiff's identity, and the precise purpose for which the work was to be performed, as well as that the plaintiff would be relying on the work, we held that there would be recovery despite the lack of a contractual relation. . . . [S]ubsequent cases rely on *Craig* for the proposition that recovery for negligent misrepresentation is limited to situations where the defendant knew that a particular plaintiff would rely on the defendant's services. . . .

We believe that the third test, taken from §552 of the *Restatement (Second) of Torts* (1977), comports most closely with the liability standard we have applied in other professional contexts. Section 552 describes the tort of negligent misrepresentation committed in the process of supplying information for the guidance of others as follows. [The court then quotes §552.] . . . The attendant comments explain the policy behind §552 as follows:

> [T]he duty of care to be observed in supplying information for use in commercial transactions implies an undertaking to observe a relative standard, which may be defined only in terms of the use to which the information will be put, weighed against the magnitude and probability of loss that might attend that use if the information proves to be incorrect. A user of commercial information cannot reasonably expect its maker to have undertaken to satisfy this obligation unless the terms of the obligation were known to him. Rather, one who relies upon information in connection with a commercial transaction may reasonably expect to hold the

maker to a duty of care only in circumstances in which the maker was manifestly aware of the use to which the information was to be put and intended to supply it for that purpose.

[*Restatement (Second) of Torts* §552, comment a, at 128.]

The comments explain with regard to the requirement that the plaintiff be a member of a "limited group of persons for whose benefit and guidance" the information is supplied as follows.

> [I]t is not required that the person who is to become the plaintiff be identified or known to the defendant as an individual when the information is supplied. It is enough that the maker of the representation intends it to reach and influence either a particular person or persons, known to him, or a group or class of persons, distinct from the much larger class who might reasonably be expected sooner or later to have access to the information and foreseeably to take some action in reliance upon it. . . .

Id. comment h, at 132–133.

We concur with the California Supreme Court's conclusion in *Bily v. Arthur Young & Co.,* [834 P.2d 745 (Cal. 1992)] that the *Restatement* test properly balances the indeterminate liability of the foreseeability test and the restrictiveness of the near-privity rule. Section 552 "recognizes commercial realities by avoiding both unlimited and uncertain liability for economic losses in cases of professional mistake and exoneration of the auditor in situations where it clearly intended to undertake the responsibility of influencing particular business transactions involving third persons." *Id.* at 768.

Although the *Restatement* standard has been widely adopted by other jurisdictions, courts differ in their interpretations of the standard. The better reasoned decisions interpret §552 as limiting the potential liability of an accountant to noncontractual third parties who can demonstrate "actual knowledge on the part of accountants of the limited—though unnamed—group of potential [third parties] that will rely upon the [report], as well as actual knowledge of the particular financial transaction that such information is designed to influence." *First Nat'l Bank of Commerce v. Monco Agency Inc.,* 911 F.2d 1053, 1062 (5th Cir. 1990). . . . The accountant's knowledge is to be measured "at the moment the audit [report] is published, not by the foreseeable path of harm envisioned by [litigants] years following an unfortunate business decision." [*Id.,* at 1059.]

The plaintiff argues that, by limiting §552 to allow recovery only by those persons, or limited group of persons, that an accountant actually knows will receive and rely on an audit report, we will be rewarding an accountant's efforts to "remain blissfully unaware" of the report's proposed distribution and uses. We are unpersuaded by this argument. The axiom we have applied in other contexts applies to accountants as well: the *Restatement* standard will not excuse an accountant's "wilful ignorance" of information of which the accountant would have been aware had the accountant not consciously disregarded that information. . . .

The judge correctly concluded under §552, that the undisputed facts failed to show that the defendant knew (or intended) that the plaintiff, or any limited group of which the plaintiff was a member, would rely on the audit report in connection with an investment in Gulf. To the contrary, the record suggests that the defendant did not prepare the audit report for the plaintiff's benefit and that the plaintiff was not a member of any "limited group of persons" for whose benefit the report was prepared. At the time the audit was being prepared, the plaintiff was an unknown, unidentified potential future investor in Gulf. The defendant was not aware of the existence of the transaction between the plaintiff and Gulf until after the stock purchase agreement had been signed and only a few days before the sale was completed.

The summary judgment record further indicates that the defendant neither intended to influence the transaction entered into by the plaintiff and Gulf nor knew that Gulf intended to influence the transaction by use of the audit report. While the defendant was aware of the circumstances surrounding the Kennedy and Aviva transactions, which had occurred prior to the completion of the audit report, the plaintiff's purchase of Gulf stock did not resemble either of those transactions, and it occurred subsequent to the issuance of the defendant's report. Furthermore, contrary to the plaintiff's contention, the Kennedy and Aviva transactions did not indicate to the defendant that Gulf's controlling shareholders intended to use the audit report to locate a purchaser for their stock. In fact, the record reveals that at the time the report was being prepared, Gulf's controlling shareholders were responding to expressions of interest in acquiring their stock by aggressively rejecting those advances and taking actions to defend against a hostile takeover.

Moreover, the record suggests that the defendant's audit report was prepared for inclusion in Gulf's annual report and not for the purpose of assisting Gulf's controlling shareholders in any particular transaction. The record does not exhibit that the defendant knew of any particular use that would be made of its audit report. . . .

"Under the *Restatement* rule, an auditor retained to conduct an annual audit and to furnish an opinion for no particular purpose generally undertakes no duty to third parties." *Bily v. Arthur Young & Co., supra* at 758.

The rule we adopt today will preclude accountants from having to ensure the commercial decisions of non-clients where, as here, the accountants did not know that their work product would be relied on by the plaintiff in making its investment decision.

[Judgment affirmed.]

Fraud Liability

Under the *Ultramares* rule, privity is required in negligence cases, but not in suits brought by injured third parties on the basis of fraud. That is, an accountant may be held liable to reliant third parties whom the accountant intended to deceive by his reports. Consequently, in a jurisdiction following the *Ultramares* rule of privity, third-party plaintiffs often base their claim on fraud to avoid the privity requirement applicable to negligence actions. A fraud action also might be used by persons who fall outside the class of plaintiffs protected under the *Restatement* rule.

To be liable for fraud (1) the defendant must make a misrepresentation with knowledge of its falsity (scienter) and with the intent to induce the plaintiff to act in reliance upon it, (2) the misrepresentation must relate to a material fact, (3) the plaintiff must justifiably rely upon and act upon the misrepresentation, and (4) the plaintiff must suffer injury as a result of the reliance. Proving scienter is the major hurdle in an accountants' liability case based on fraud. The plaintiff must establish that the defendant lacked a genuine belief that the information disclosed was accurate and complete in all material respects. Scienter may be proven by either direct or circumstantial evidence of the defendant's state of mind.

In a number of cases, courts have recognized that acts constituting gross negligence raise an inference of fraud sufficient to support third-party recovery against an accountant. For example, one court stated:

Accountants . . . may be liable to third parties, even where there is lacking deliberate or active fraud. A representation certified as true to the knowledge of the accountants when knowledge there is none, a reckless misstatement, or an opinion based on grounds so flimsy as to lead to the conclusion that there was no genuine belief in its truth, are all sufficient upon which to base liability. A refusal to see the obvious, a failure to investigate the doubtful, if sufficiently gross, may furnish evidence leading to an inference of fraud so as to impose liability for losses suffered by those who rely on the balance sheet. In other words, heedlessness and reckless disregard of consequence may take the place of deliberate intention.[5]

Statutory Liability

Liability Under Federal Securities Law

The federal securities laws discussed in Chapter 49 provide investor protection by requiring full and accurate public disclosure of relevant information. Many of the required disclosures are accomplished through examinations and reports prepared by independent accountants. The securities laws impose substantial responsibilities and potential liabilities upon accountants who evaluate the fairness and accuracy of financial statements issued by publicly-held companies.

Initially, the SEC, through various rules and releases, regulates accounting practices and the form of financial statements used in SEC filings. The SEC also has the power to discipline accountants who prepare documents filed with the commission who are unqualified, have engaged in unethical or improper professional conduct, or have willfully violated (or aided and abetted others to violate) any provision of the federal securities laws.[6] In addition to administrative sanctions, accountants may be held liable to third parties for damages under the various civil liability provisions of the Securities Act of 1933 and the Securities Exchange Act of 1934, which are discussed in detail in Chapter 49. The material that follows highlights the civil liability provisions of particular concern to accountants.

Liability Under §11 of the 1933 Act. Section 11 of the Securities Act of 1933, which imposes liability for misstatements or omissions in a registration statement filed under the 1933 Act, applies to accountants, engineers, or other experts who prepare or certify parts

of the registration statement. Note that §11 measures the accuracy of the registration statement at the time it becomes effective. Thus, the auditor must undertake a review covering the period between the date of the audit report and the date of public sale of the securities to assure that the financial statements are accurate on the registration statement's effective date.

A number of defenses are available to defeat liability under §11. The most important of these is the "due diligence" defense, discussed as applied to an accountant in the following landmark case.

Escott v. BarChris Construction Corporation
283 F. Supp. 643 (S.D.N.Y. 1968)

BarChris Construction Corporation was engaged in the construction of bowling alleys. Generally, BarChris entered into a contract with a customer, receiving only a small down payment on the purchase price. When the building was finished, the customer paid the balance of the contract price in notes, payable in installments over a period of years. Because BarChris was compelled to expend considerable sums in construction before receiving reimbursement, it was in constant need of cash to finance operations. Accordingly, it made a public offering of debentures in early 1961, pursuant to a registration statement filed with the SEC on March 30, 1961, and which became effective May 16, 1961. By that time BarChris was experiencing difficulty collecting amounts due from some of its customers. Because of overbuilding in the industry, bowling alley operations had begun to fail. After an abortive attempt to obtain additional financing, BarChris filed for bankruptcy reorganization in October 1962 and defaulted upon the debentures.

The buyers of the debentures maintained a class action under §11 of the Securities Act of 1933 against the persons who signed the registration statement, the underwriters, and Peat, Marwick, Mitchell & Co., BarChris's auditors. Plaintiffs alleged that the registration statement contained a number of material false statements and omissions. The court found that the 1960 sales figures in the financial statements prepared by Peat, Marwick included the contract price of completed alleys, which in fact had not been sold by BarChris. For example, BarChris originally contracted to build Heavenly Lanes (also known as Capitol Lanes) for an outside purchaser. When the contract fell through, BarChris built the alley and leased it to its wholly owned subsidiary, Capitol Lanes, Inc., which operated the alley beginning in December 1960. By listing Heavenly Lanes in the 1960 sales figures as a completed contract, though it was never sold to any outside interest, 1960 sales were inflated by $330,000, and liabilities were understated by a similar amount. The court also found that the prospectus contained other misstatements and omissions including a failure to disclose unpaid

---

[5]State Street Trust Co. v. Ernst, 15 N.E.2d 416, 418–419 (N.Y. 1938).
[6]SEC Rule of Practice 2(e); 17 C.F.R. §102.2(e).

officers' loans, failure to disclose that most of the debenture proceeds would be used to pay preexisting debts rather than to provide additional working capital for the expansion of alley construction, failure to disclose substantial customer delinquencies, and failure to disclose that BarChris was already engaged in the operation of bowling alleys and would soon be engaged in operating alleys repossessed from defaulting customers.

To avoid liability for the false statements and omissions, each defendant asserted the "due diligence" defense contained in Section 11(b) of the 1993 Act. In the following portion of the opinion, the court considered whether Peat, Marwick had established the defense.

McLean, District Judge

. . . The part of the registration statement purporting to be made upon the authority of Peat, Marwick as an expert was . . . the 1960 figures. But because the statute requires the court to determine Peat, Marwick's belief, and the grounds thereof, "at the time such part of the registration statement became effective," for the purposes of this affirmative defense, the matter must be viewed as of May 16, 1961, and the question is whether at that time Peat, Marwick, after reasonable investigation, had reasonable ground to believe and did believe that the 1960 figures were true and that no material fact had been omitted from the registration statement which should have been included in order to make the 1960 figures not misleading. In deciding this issue, the court must consider not only what Peat, Marwick did in its 1960 audit, but also what it did in its subsequent "S-1 review." The proper scope of that review must also be determined. . . .

The 1960 Audit

Peat, Marwick's work was in general charge of a member of the firm, Cummings, and more immediately in charge of Peat, Marwick's manager, Logan. Most of the actual work was performed by a senior accountant, Berardi, who had junior assistants, one of whom was Kennedy.

Berardi was then about thirty years old. He was not yet a C.P.A. He had had no previous experience with the bowling industry. This was his first job as a senior accountant. He could hardly have been given a more difficult assignment. . . .

It is unnecessary to recount everything that Berardi did in the course of the audit. We are concerned only with the evidence relating to what Berardi did or did not do with respect to those items which I have found to have been incorrectly reported in the 1960 figures in the prospectus.

More narrowly, we are directly concerned only with such of those items as I have found to be material.

Capitol Lanes

First and foremost is Berardi's failure to discover that Capitol Lanes had not been sold. This error affected both the sales figure and the liability side of the balance sheet. Fundamentally, the error stemmed from the fact that Berardi never realized that Heavenly Lanes and Capitol were two different names for the same alley. . . .

Berardi assumed that Heavenly was to be treated like any other completed job. He included it in all his computations.

The evidence is conflicting as to whether BarChris's officers expressly informed Berardi that Heavenly and Capitol were the same thing and that BarChris was operating Capitol and had not sold it. I find that they did not so inform him.

Berardi did become aware that there were references here and there in BarChris's records to something called Capitol Lanes. He also knew that there were indications that at some time BarChris might operate an alley of that name. . . .

Berardi testified that he inquired of Russo [BarChris's chief executive officer] about Capitol Lanes and that Russo told him that Capitol Lanes, Inc. was going to operate an alley some day but as yet it had no alley. Berardi testified that he understood that the alley had not been built. . . .

I am not satisfied with this testimony. If Berardi did hold this belief, he should not have held it. The entries [in Peat, Marwick's work papers] as to insurance and as to "operation of alley" should have alerted him to the fact that an alley existed. He should have made further inquiry on the subject. It is apparent that Berardi did not understand this transaction. . . .

The burden of proof on this issue is on Peat, Marwick. . . . Peat, Marwick has not proved that Berardi made a reasonable investigation as far as Capitol Lanes was concerned and that his ignorance of the true facts was justified. . . .

The S-1 Review

The purpose of reviewing events subsequent to the date of a certified balance sheet (referred to as an S-1 review when made with reference to a registration statement) is to ascertain whether any material change has occurred in the company's financial position which should be disclosed in order to prevent the balance sheet figures from being misleading. The scope of such a review, under generally accepted auditing standards, is limited. It does not amount to a complete audit.

Peat, Marwick prepared a written program for such a review. I find that this program conformed to generally accepted auditing standards. . . .

Berardi made the S-1 review in May 1961. He devoted a little over two days to it, a total of $20^1/_2$ hours. He did not discover any of the errors or omissions pertaining to the state of affairs in 1961 which I have previously discussed at length, all of which were material. The question is whether, despite his failure to find out anything, his investigation was reasonable within the meaning of the statute.

What Berardi did was to look at a consolidating trial balance as of March 31, 1961 which had been prepared by BarChris, compare it with the audited December 31, 1960 figures, discuss with Trilling [BarChris's controller] certain unfavorable developments which the comparison disclosed, and read certain minutes. He did not examine any "important financial records" other than the trial balance. . . .

In substance . . . Berardi . . . asked questions, he got answers which he considered satisfactory, and he did nothing to verify them. . . .

There had been a material change for the worse in BarChris's financial position. That change was sufficiently serious so that the failure to disclose it made the 1960 figures misleading. Berardi did not discover it. As far as results were concerned, his S-1 review was useless.

Accountants should not be held to a standard higher than that recognized in their profession. I do not do so here. Berardi's review did not come up to that standard. He did not take some of the steps which Peat, Marwick's written program prescribed. He did not spend an adequate amount of time on a task of this magnitude. Most important of all, he was too easily satisfied with glib answers to his inquiries.

This is not to say that he should have made a complete audit. But there were enough danger signals in the materials which he did examine to require some further investigation on his part. Generally accepted accounting standards required such further investigation under these circumstances. It is not always sufficient merely to ask questions.

Here again, the burden of proof is on Peat, Marwick. I find that . . . Peat, Marwick has not established its due diligence defense. . . .

1934 Act Liability. Under §18(a) of the Securities Exchange Act of 1934, accountants may be held liable for material misstatements or omissions in documents they prepare that are filed with the SEC. Accountants also have been found civilly liable under §14 for their role in preparing false or misleading proxy solicitation material. In addition, an accountant may be held liable under §10(b) and Rule 10b-5 for fraud in the purchase or sale of any security.

Section 10A of the 1934 Act, added in 1995, requires that audits for 1934 Act filings must include procedures designed to detect illegal acts that materially affect the financial statements. If, in the course of the audit, illegal acts are discovered, the accountant must promptly inform management. If, after notification, management fails to remedy the problem, the accountant must notify the board of directors that the failure will warrant either a departure from the auditor's standard report or resignation from the engagement. The corporation must then report the accountant's notification to the SEC within one business day. If the corporation fails to do so, the accountant must itself notify the SEC, whether or not it also resigns from the engagement. An accountant who wilfully fails to notify the SEC is subject to civil penalties in cease-and-desist proceedings maintained by the SEC.

Finally, the Sarbanes-Oxley Act of 2002, discussed in detail in Chapter 49, imposes significant duties and responsibilities on auditors of public companies.

Criminal Liability

In addition to civil liability to injured third parties, accountants may be subject to criminal liability under various federal statutes. For example, as discussed in Chapter 49, it is a crime willfully to violate any provision of the federal securities laws (including rules and regulations adopted under those laws), or to make material misstatements in registration statements or other documents filed with the SEC.[7] In addition, the Federal False Statements Statute[8] makes it a crime knowingly and willfully to make false statements in matters within the jurisdiction of the executive, legislative, or judicial branch of the federal government. Violations of the statute, which include false SEC filings, carry fines and imprisonment of up to five years, or both. Collectively, these statutes have been used to impose liability on

---

[7]Securities Act §24; Securities Exchange Act §32.
[8]18 U.S.C. §1001.

accountants for their role in preparing false or misleading proxy materials or financial statements, commonly that conceal misconduct by management insiders. Note that because a number of people often are involved and the mails are used to distribute the misleading documents, federal conspiracy and mail fraud also may be charged.[9]

Accountant–Client Privilege

Generally, ethics standards prohibit an accountant from disclosing confidential client information without the client's consent. Although accountant–client communications are confidential and should not be disclosed to third parties unless the courts require it, they generally are not "privileged."

A **rule of privilege** enables a person to prevent certain information from being introduced into evidence in court. Examples include the Fifth Amendment privilege that protects a witness against self-incrimination and privileges that protect communications between parties to confidential relationships such as physician and patient, priest and penitent, attorney and client, and husband and wife. Under privileged communication rules, for example, a physician, priest, attorney, or spouse may not be compelled to disclose information in court over the objection of the patient, penitent, client, or other spouse. Rules of privileged communication are designed to preserve the confidentiality of, and to protect, certain socially important relationships.[10]

Although no accountant–client privilege is recognized at common law, some states have created such a privilege by statute. These statutes vary widely concerning the persons, accounting services, and legal proceedings covered by the privilege. Federal law does not recognize an accountant–client privilege. For this reason, a state-created privilege is inapplicable in federal tax cases, federal criminal cases, and federal administrative proceedings.

The law's refusal to recognize an accountant–client privilege is based upon important policy reasons. In *United States v. Arthur Young & Company* (1984),[11] the Supreme Court reaffirmed the general federal rule by holding that no confidential accountant–client privilege exists for the client for tax accrual work papers held by an accountant and sought by the IRS as part of a criminal investigation of the client's tax returns. In explaining its holding, the Court noted the difference between the attorney–client relationship (in which a privilege is recognized) and the accountant–client relation:

> [T]he private attorney's role [is] as the client's confidential advisor and adfvocate, a loyal representative whose duty it is to present the client's case in the most favorable possible light. An independent certified public accountant performs a different role. By certifying the public reports that collectively depict a corporation's financial status, the independent auditor assumes a public responsibility transcending any employment relationship with the client. The independent public accountant performing this special function owes ultimate allegiance to the corporation's creditors and stockholders, as well as to investing public. This "public watchdog" function demands that the accountant maintain total independence from the client at all times and requires complete fidelity to the public trust. To insulate from disclosure a certified public accountant's interpretations of the client's financial statements would be to ignore the significance of the accountant's role as a disinterested analyst charged with public obligations.[12]

Tax Return Preparation Liability

In recent years, the number of persons preparing tax returns for compensation has increased significantly, leading to a corresponding increase in the number of improperly prepared returns. To address this problem, the Internal Revenue Code includes several provisions regulating the conduct of paid income tax preparers. The law defines an income tax return preparer as any person who prepares for compensation (or who employs one or more persons to prepare for compensation) all or a substantial portion of any income tax return or claim for refund.[13] The bases of liability under the law are understatement of a taxpayer's liability and failure to meet certain disclosure, ministerial, or record-keeping requirements. The rules are enforced by a series of sanctions against tax preparers who violate the rules, including monetary penalties and injunctive relief.

An understatement of liability occurs if the net amount of taxes payable are understated *or* if the

---

[9]The federal conspiracy and mail fraud statutes are discussed in Chapter 3.
[10]McCormick, Law of Evidence 171 (3d ed. 1984).
[11]104 S. Ct. 1495 (1984).

[12]*Id.* at 1503.
[13]26 U.S.C. §7701(a)(36).

amount of a refund or credit is overstated. A tax return preparer may take a position that she knows (or should know) has no "realistic possibility of being sustained on its merits." If taking such a position results in an understatement of liability, the preparer is liable for a $250 penalty absent proof that there is reasonable cause for the understatement and that the preparer has acted in good faith. If an understatement of liability is willful or caused by reckless or intentional disregard of IRS rules and regulations, the preparer is subject to a $1,000 penalty.[14]

The tax preparer also may be subject to various penalties for failure to meet a number of technical requirements. For example, a $50 penalty may be imposed upon a preparer for each failure to furnish the taxpayer with a completed copy of the tax return, sign the return, furnish an identifying number on the return, keep copies or lists of returns prepared, or retain and make available a list of return preparers employed during the return period. Each type of technical violation is subject to $25,000 annual maximum, and preparers may avoid penalties by proving that any failure to comply was due to "reasonable cause," not willful neglect. Finally, a $500 penalty is imposed upon any preparer who negotiates or indorses a refund check issued to a taxpayer regarding a return or claim for refund prepared by the preparer.[15]

In addition to liability under the Internal Revenue Code, tax return preparers may be held liable to their clients if they are negligent in preparing the return. Negligence takes many forms including erroneous advice, failure to file the return in a timely fashion, or computational errors. Damages commonly are measured by the tax losses including penalties incurred by the client.

Summary

1.   Through periodic audits, independent public accountants render an important service to their clients and third parties. The audit assists the client in discovering inefficiencies and irregularities in its business, and third parties such as shareholders, creditors, and potential investors in evaluating the financial health of the client before making a business decision. Recipients of inaccurate audit reports who suffer injury often seek compensation from the accountants. Accountants may be held liable to their clients and, in some cases, third parties on various theories, based both upon the common law and statute.

2.   Common law theories of recovery include breach of contract, negligence, and fraud. In contract, liability is limited to the client, and third parties may recover only if they qualify as third-party beneficiaries of the contract. In negligence actions, courts are split. Under the restrictive *Ultramares* rule, liability extends only to persons in privity of contract with the accountant. Under the conflicting approaches, liability extends to certain third parties who are injured by the accountant's negligence. The identity of third parties protected varies somewhat among the states recognizing third-party liability. In contrast to negligence, fraud liability extends to all reliant third parties whom the accountant intends to deceive by his reports.

3.   Statutory accountants' liability is based primarily upon the civil liability provisions of the federal securities laws. In addition, various federal statutes may impose criminal liability upon accountants for intentionally preparing false or misleading financial statements or other documents.

4.   Although full disclosure between client and accountant is in the public interest, no accountant–client privilege is recognized at common law or under federal law. Some states, however, confer such a privilege by statute.

5.   The Internal Revenue Code includes several provisions regulating the conduct of paid income tax return preparers. Liability is based upon understatement of the taxpayer's liability and failure to meet certain disclosure requirements. In addition, an accountant who negligently prepares a tax return may be held liable to the client.

Key Term

rule of privilege

Questions and Problems

56.1   Compare the various approaches to accountants' liability to third parties for negligence discussed in the text. Review the policy reasons justifying each theory of liability. Which approach is preferable?

---

[14]26 U.S.C. §6694.

[15]26 U.S.C. §6695.

56.2 A public accountant was under contract to prepare a corporate tax return on or before March 15. The accountant failed to file on time. The corporation brought suit to recover for penalties paid due to the accountant's negligence in failing to file on time. Assume that no negligence is proven. Is the corporation without a remedy?

56.3 Jones, Inc. is negotiating for a loan from First Bank. The bank requests audited financial statements. Jones engages Doaks & Company CPAs to perform the audit, telling Doaks that the statements will be used to negotiate a loan from First Bank. Doaks issues an unqualified opinion, negligently failing to discover material overstatements of assets. Jones delivers the statements to First Bank, which denies the loan. Without communicating with Doaks, Jones then uses the statements to obtain a loan from Second Bank. In addition, Jones shows the statements to his friend, Fred, who buys stock in Jones, Inc. in reliance on the statements. When the errors are discovered, Jones, Inc. declares bankruptcy and both Second Bank and Fred lose their entire investments. Would Doaks be liable to Second Bank under *Ultramares?* The *Restatement?* The rule of reasonable foreseeability? Assuming negligence recovery is unavailable, could Second Bank proceed on any other theory? Would any of your answers change if Jones had originally told Doaks that he needed the audited statement "to negotiate a bank loan"? Would Doaks be liable to Fred under *Ultramares?* The *Restatement?* The rule of reasonable foreseeability?

56.4 An auditor certified its client's balance sheet, which listed accounts receivable at $2,000,000, without disclosing that $768,000 of the accounts were probably uncollectible. The auditor also failed to physically inspect the inventory, relying instead upon the client's balance sheet figure of $4,000,000. The auditor had been made aware that the financial statements were to be used for the purpose of obtaining credit. The client subsequently declared bankruptcy. On what theory or theories might a creditor who loaned money to the client on the basis of the financial statements recover from the auditor?

56.5 Assuming third-party negligence actions are allowed against accountants, should the client's negligence (for example, in permitting an embezzlement scheme to continue) contributing to the loss be a total or partial bar to recovery under principles of contributory or comparative negligence?

56.6 Ernst & Ernst performed periodic audits of First Securities Company, a small securities brokerage firm, and prepared annual reports for filing with the SEC under the 1934 Act. Nay, the president of the firm, fraudulently induced various customers to invest in "escrow" accounts that he represented would yield a high rate of return. In fact, no escrow accounts existed and Nay converted his customer's funds to personal use immediately upon receipt. The accounts were not reflected on First Securities' books. Ernst & Ernst did not uncover the fraud because it failed to use appropriate auditing procedures to discover certain internal practices that prevented an effective audit. One such practice was Nay's rule that only he could open mail addressed to him at First Securities, even if it arrived in his absence. If the audit had been properly performed, the "mail rule" would have been discovered and reported to the SEC as an irregular procedure, leading to an investigation that would have revealed the fraud. The fraud was finally discovered only after Nay committed suicide leaving a note describing the escrow accounts as "spurious" and First Securities as bankrupt.

(a) Customers who lost money subsequently sued Ernst & Ernst alleging that it had "aided and abetted" Nay's violation of Rule 10b-5. Has Ernst & Ernst violated Rule 10b-5? Explain.

(b) Could Ernst & Ernst be held liable under any other civil liability provision of the securities laws?

(c) Could Ernst & Ernst be held liable to the customers for negligence under any of the theories of third-party liability discussed in the text?

56.7 Summarize the policy reasons for and against recognition of an accountant–client privilege. Should such a privilege be recognized?

56.8 In *United States v. Arthur Young & Company,* the IRS sought Arthur Young's tax accrual workpapers for use in a criminal tax investigation. These workpapers pinpoint "soft spots" on the corporation's tax returns, highlighting those areas in which the taxpayer has taken a position that may at some later date require payment of additional taxes. The court of appeals recognized a privilege as necessary to promote full disclosure to public accountants and insure the integrity of the securities markets. The court of appeals feared that were the IRS to have access to tax accrual workpapers, a corporation might be tempted to withhold from its auditor certain information relevant and material to a proper evaluation of its financial statements. The Supreme Court rejected this argument. Why?

CHAPTER 57

INSURANCE LAW

- ■ an introduction to the law of insurance, including the regulation of insurance and the types and interpretation of insurance contracts
- ■ the concept of insurable interest and the principle of indemnity
- ■ the persons and interests protected by insurance and the nature of the risk transferred to the insurer
- ■ the obligations of an insured following a loss and the measure of recovery for various types of insurance
- ■ defenses available to an insurer and the rights an insurer acquires through subrogation

Insurance is a contractual arrangement used to transfer and distribute risk. Through an insurance contract, an insurer—an entity engaged primarily in the business of insurance—promises to pay another, the insured, a sum of money or provide other value upon the occurrence of some harmful event.[1] The insurer distributes the risk among a substantial number of persons who pay premiums to the insurer based upon the total estimated losses to be incurred by members of the insured class. In insurance, therefore, the insured

in effect exchanges a fixed, certain loss—the cost of the premium—to avoid a catastrophic loss caused by a risk insured against. Risk sharing among the insured class, under which all members contribute to pay the losses of a few, is a fundamental characteristic of insurance.[2]

Although insurance law is a branch of contract law, a number of characteristics distinguish it from ordinary contract law. For example, although insurance is an important tool of business and estate planning, insurance contracts are not individually negotiated. Rather, they are complex adhesion contracts, which often are neither read nor understood by insureds. Accordingly, both courts and legislatures have actively policed insurance contracts and companies to protect the reasonable expectations of the insured. This policing includes extensive government regulation of the insurance industry, strict construction of contract terms against the insurance company, and in some cases, statutorily mandated contracts. Insurance contracts also present a "moral risk." The presence of insurance often has motivated

---

[1] KEETON & WIDISS, INSURANCE LAW 3–4 (1988).

[2] In some cases, the insurer will spread the loss even farther through reinsurance. Under this arrangement, another insurance company contracts with the original insurer to reimburse it for liability under its own policies. Thus, in reinsurance, the original insurer becomes an insured (or reinsured) and another company becomes an insurer (or reinsurer).

schemes to defraud and even to murder. In addition, absent "insurable interest," insurance contracts can be used as a gambling device. Thus, the law of insurance must police abuses by both insurers and insureds while preserving the fundamental business and personal protection afforded by insurance.

Introduction to Insurance

Regulation of Insurance

Insurance companies engage in the sale and drafting of insurance contracts (policies), collecting information necessary to compute premiums; investigating, paying, and defending claims for insured losses; and managing vast amounts of cash collected from policyholders. Regulating insurance company activities has traditionally been a state, rather than federal, activity.

In 1944, however, the Supreme Court held that the business of insurance involved interstate commerce and was therefore subject to federal regulation under the Commerce Clause of the Constitution.[3] Lobbying by the insurance industry, however, led to passage in 1945 of the McCarran-Ferguson Act.[4] It authorized continued state insurance regulation, and exempted the business of insurance from federal antitrust law (except for Sherman Act violations involving agreements to boycott, coerce, or intimidate) in states enacting statutes regulating the insurance industry. To prevent federal regulation, the National Association of Insurance Commissioners (NAIC) and an "All-Industry Committee" promptly drafted comprehensive model legislation, which has been widely adopted by the states. State statutes, administered through a state "commissioner of insurance," commonly require licensing of insurance companies (local and out-of-state), insurance agents, and brokers. Statutes also regulate insurance rates to prevent inadequate, excessive, or discriminatory rates, prevent unfair trade practices, monitor the financial condition of insurers, provide for service of process upon out-of-state insurers, and monitor the terms of insurance policies.

---

[3]United States v. South-Eastern Underwriters Association, 64 S. Ct. 1162 (1944). Federal regulation under the Commerce Clause is discussed in Chapter 4.
[4]15 U.S.C. §§1011–1015.

Types of Insurance

Insurance contracts commonly are classified according to the nature of the risk covered as (1) life insurance, (2) fire and marine insurance, and (3) casualty insurance.[5] Although a number of insurers write all lines of insurance, many specialize in one or more types of coverage.

Life Insurance. **Life insurance** is a contract to make designated payments upon the death of the person whose life is insured. In a life insurance policy the insurer contracts with the "owner" of the policy to pay a specified amount—the proceeds—to a beneficiary upon the death of a named person—the *cestui que vie.* The owner of the policy pays the premiums, may in certain cases assign the policy or borrow against it, may elect among various options concerning distribution of proceeds, and has the power to name and in most cases change the beneficiary. The three roles (owner, *cestui que vie,* beneficiary) may be fulfilled by separate individuals or by one person. For example, a person may purchase a life insurance policy on her own life naming her estate as beneficiary.

Life insurance is commonly designated whole-life, endowment, or term. A whole-life policy provides coverage for the entire life of the insured. Premiums generally are paid for life or until the insured reaches a prescribed advanced age. The policy matures for payment only upon the death of the person insured. An endowment policy provides for payment of the proceeds upon the death of the insured within the endowment period (for example, 20 years) or at the end of that period if the insured survives. A term policy pays a specified amount only if death occurs within a term or period specified in the policy.

Both whole-life and endowment policies involve an element of savings or investment because it is certain that if the policy is kept in force, proceeds ultimately will be paid. Both types accumulate a cash surrender value after the policy has been in force for a given period such as two or three years. Generally, the insured may borrow from the insurance company against the cash surrender value, or may use the policy as collateral on a loan from another creditor. If the policy is terminated before the death of the person whose life is insured, the cash surrender value may be returned to the insured, or used to fund some other option offered by the insurance company (for example, to purchase a lesser face amount of fully paid-up insurance).

---

[5]KEETON & WIDISS, INSURANCE LAW 18–27 (1988).

In contrast to whole-life and endowment, payment under a term policy occurs only if the insured dies within the stated period. A term policy accumulates no cash surrender value and involves no certainty of payment. Accordingly, a term policy does not incorporate elements of saving or investment characteristic of the other forms.[6]

Fire and Marine Insurance. **Fire insurance** covers losses to specifically listed property (such as a building or its contents) caused by fire or lightning. Fire insurance does not cover fires intentionally set by the insured, and coverage usually is limited to losses caused by a hostile fire (one not occurring or contained in a place intended for a fire, such as a stove or fireplace). Fire insurance policies also commonly cover damage from wind, rain, collision, explosion, and water damage.

Marine insurance developed in the 1600s to protect ships and their cargos from "perils of the sea." Modern marine policies are similar to the one adopted in 1779 by the Society of Underwriters operating from Lloyd's Coffee House in London. Because marine policies did not cover ships or cargo transported on inland waterways, **inland marine insurance** was developed. Inland marine insurance has been extended in modern times to cover transportation risks generally; bridges, tunnels, and other devices of transportation and communication; and goods that may be affected by movement. A common type of inland marine policy is a personal property "floater" that protects, for example, the inventory or equipment of a business.

Casualty Insurance. **Casualty insurance** is designed to cover a variety of risks including burglary and theft, accident and illness, collision, workers' compensation, property damage, and legal liability. Liability insurance protects the insured against losses caused by the insured's legal (usually tort) liability to a third person.[7] Liability insurance policies may be issued separately or included as part of a policy providing other coverages. For example, automobile and homeowner's insurance policies protect against damage to the insured's vehicle or dwelling caused by events such as collision or fire. They also provide liability insurance, paying damages (up to specified policy limits) for which the insured be-comes liable as a result of her use of the vehicle or dwelling. For example, liability insurance would pay for injuries sustained by another motorist in an auto accident caused by the insured's negligence.

The Insurance Contract

Formation and Terms. Most insurance contracts are contained on standardized written forms drafted by the insurer. Typically, the insured makes the offer through an application to the company, which can accept the offer by issuing, or in some cases, delivering the policy to the insured. During the interim between application and issuance, the insurer may provide temporary coverage through "binding receipts" or "conditional binding receipts" in life insurance, or "binders" in other types of insurance.

In exchange for the premium, the insurer agrees to pay specified benefits upon occurrence of stated contingencies. Pecuniary liability limits are included, which in the case of liability insurance may be stated on a per person or per accident basis. The duration of the coverage is explicitly stated in the policy and may indicate that coverage begins on a specified date (for example, "April 15, 2006, 12:01 A.M. standard time at the address of the named insured"). Coverage in a life insurance policy usually commences upon delivery of the policy to the insured in good health and payment of the first premium. Constructive delivery of the policy (for example, to the insurance agent) may be sufficient for this purpose.

Although insurance contracts commonly cover a single insured, many standard forms of insurance such as life, health, accident, and hospitalization are marketed under group insurance plans. In group insurance, a master policy is issued to the person, such as an employer, who negotiates the contract with the insurer. Certificates of participation are then furnished to group members covered by the plan. The premium may be paid entirely by the employer (a noncontributory plan) or in whole or in part by the employees (a contributory plan). Premium costs in a group policy commonly are lower because of the insurer's reduced administrative expense.

Interpretation of Insurance Contracts. Courts often protect an insured by construing language of insurance contracts in favor of coverage. Perhaps because insurance is a fundamental tool of personal, business, and estate planning, courts believe that the public

---

[6]In contrast to ordinary life insurance, which protects against hardship caused by the insured's premature death, an annuity contract protects against economic problems of the insured's long life. Under an annuity, payments begin on a specified date and continue for the life of the insured.

[7]KEETON & WIDISS, INSURANCE LAW 376–377 (1988).

interest is best served by compensating insureds, even if the literal language of the contract could be interpreted to deny coverage. Another factor influencing judicial treatment of insurance contracts is the nature of the contract itself. An insurance contract is the classic adhesion contract—a standardized form contract, drafted by the insurance company, loaded with fine print, and given to the insured on a take-it-or-leave-it basis. In this context, courts construe ambiguous language against the drafter, and may refuse to enforce certain provisions by applying one of the legal theories discussed in Chapter 10 (for example, the unconscionability doctrine) designed to protect the party "adhering" to the standardized form.

In the following case, the court discusses and applies the legal principles governing interpretation of insurance contracts.

Outboard Marine Corporation v. Liberty Mutual Insurance Company

607 N.E.2d 1204 (Ill. 1992)

Plaintiff Outboard Marine Corporation (OMC) operates a manufacturing plant in Waukegan, Illinois. From 1959 to 1972, OMC used Pydraul, a hydraulic fluid that contained toxic polychlorinated byphenyls (PCBs) at the facility and discharged spills and leaks of Pydraul through a wastewater system that emptied into Lake Michigan. The federal Environmental Protection Agency and the state of Illinois sued OMC alleging violations of the environmental laws and seeking damages and injunctive relief for cleanup of the water pollution. OMC carried liability insurance issued by defendants Liberty Mutual Insurance Company and four other insurance companies. When OMC notified its insurers of the suits, they refused to defend OMC asserting that coverage was barred under the "pollution exclusion" provisions of the policies. OMC sued the insurers alleging that they had breached their duty to defend OMC. The trial and appellate courts ruled in favor of the insurers and OMC appealed.

Bilandic, Justice

. . . [T]he insurers' policies which contained pollution exclusion clauses provide in part:

This insurance does not apply . . . to bodily injury or property damage arising out of the discharge, dispersal, release or escape of smoke, vapors, soot, fumes, acids, alkalis, toxic chemicals, liquids or gases, waste materials or other irritants, contaminants or pollutants into or upon land, the atmosphere or any watercourse or body of water; but this exclusion does not apply if such discharge, dispersal, release or escape is *sudden and accidental.* (Emphasis added.)

This standard pollution exclusion provision contains two parts: (1) the insurer excludes coverage for the release of environmentally toxic materials into any part of our natural environment and (2) the insurer makes an exception from this broad exclusion for toxic releases which are *sudden and accidental.* . . . In other words, the pollution exclusion exception reinstates coverage for toxic releases which are *sudden and accidental.* In the instant case, OMC has allegedly released PCBs into Waukegan Harbor and Lake Michigan. Therefore, it appears that the first part of the exclusion applies. The issue before this court is whether, under the facts of this case, OMC's releases of PCBs were "sudden and accidental," thereby triggering the pollution exclusion exception and recreating coverage for OMC. . . .

[I]n construing the terms in an insurance policy, the court must ascertain the intent of the parties. . . . If the terms in the policy are clear and unambiguous, the court must give them their plain, ordinary, popular meaning. . . . If a term in the policy is subject to more than one reasonable interpretation within the context in which it appears, it is ambiguous. . . . Ambiguous terms are construed strictly against the drafter of the policy and in favor of coverage. . . . This is especially true with respect to exclusionary clauses. . . . This is so because there is little or no bargaining involved in the insurance contracting process . . . , the insurer has control in the drafting process, and the policy's overall purpose is to provide coverage to the insured. . . .

[T]he appellate court found that "sudden" was an unambiguous term, construing it to mean "abrupt" with a quick, temporal element in its connotation. . . . Before this court, OMC argues that the appellate court erred in its construction of the term "sudden." OMC contends that "sudden" is an ambiguous term and should be construed in its favor. OMC . . . urge[s] this court to construe "sudden" to mean unexpected or unintended. We find that the term "sudden" as used in the pollution exclusion exception contained in these . . .

policies is ambiguous and that the appellate court erred in this regard.

Numerous dictionaries define "sudden" as happening unexpectedly, without notice or warning, or unforeseen. These same dictionaries also define "sudden" as abrupt, rapid, or swift. (See, *e.g.,* Webster's Third New International Dictionary 2284 (1986); American Heritage Dictionary of the English Language 1286 (10th ed. 1981); Black's Law Dictionary 1432 (6th ed. 1990).) Courts throughout the country are divided on the meaning of "sudden" within the instant context. . . . Even panels of the Illinois appellate court are divided on this issue. . . . We conclude that the two definitions of "sudden" set forth above are both reasonable interpretations of this term in the context in which it appears. Therefore, "sudden" is, at a minimum, ambiguous as used in these policies. In Illinois, ambiguities and doubts in insurance policies are resolved in favor of the insured, especially those that appear in exclusionary clauses. . . . Consequently, in this particular context, we construe "sudden" in favor of OMC and find it to mean unexpected or unintended.

The insurers . . . argue that the rule of construction which directs the court to construe ambiguities in favor of the insured should not apply in the instant case. They assert that this rule of construction was developed to aid the unwary insured who was unsophisticated in insurance matters. The insurers argue that it should not apply here because OMC is a large corporation, sophisticated and counseled in insurance matters. We disagree with this contention. The insurance industry is powerful and closely knit. As evidenced by the . . . policies in the instant case, most policies are standard-form, are worded very similarly . . . , and are offered on a take-it-or-leave-it basis. . . . Any insured, whether large and sophisticated or not, must enter into a contract with the insurer which is written according to the insurer's pleasure by the insurer. . . . Generally, since little or no negotiation occurs in this process, the insurer has total control of the terms and the drafting of the contract. . . . This rule of construction recognizes . . . these facets of the insurance contracting process. . . . Like any insured, OMC is entitled to its application where the court has determined that the policy is ambiguous. . . . After all, the insurer chose the words used in the policy. . . .

[Judgment reversed and remanded.]

Insurable Interest

The Principle of Indemnity

Contracts of insurance, other than life insurance, generally are characterized as indemnity contracts. An **indemnity contract** is one in which the promisor (indemnitor) agrees to save the promisee (indemnitee) harmless from ("indemnify" or "reimburse" him for) the legal consequences of the promisee's conduct or that of some other person. Assume General Casualty, an insurance company, agrees to insure Mary against any liability she may incur as a result of harm to others caused by Mary's operation of her automobile—a contract of indemnity. Mary, while driving negligently, injures Tom, who sustains $10,000 damages. Under the contract, General Casualty is required to reimburse or indemnify Mary for the $10,000 obligation she owes to Tom. In addition, the contract requires General Casualty to indemnify Mary for any loss caused by the collision of her automobile with another object. Mary's automobile, worth $5,000, is destroyed in the accident. General Casualty's $5,000 payment to Mary protects her from the liability for the collision loss.[8]

Insurance, therefore, transfers the loss from the insured to the insurer. Under the indemnity concept, the benefit conferred by the insurer may not exceed the loss suffered by the insured. That is, an insured should not be able to realize a net profit through insurance. The law recognizes two reasons for this approach. First, the possibility of profit through insurance is an inducement to use insurance as a wagering or gambling device. Second, the prospect of profit may provide inducement to destroy intentionally the insured life or property. The legal principles designed to prevent net profit from occurrence of insured events are embodied in the concept of **insurable interest.** That is, to prevent use of the policy as a wagering contract and to minimize any inducement to cause the event insured against, the person who recovers under the

---

[8]An indemnity contract often is confused with a suretyship contract, discussed in Chapter 33. Though both types of contracts protect the promisee against loss, in suretyship, the promisee is a *creditor* who has or is about to extend credit to a third party, the principal. The surety's (promisor's) promise is made to the creditor to protect him against the principal's failure to perform. In contrast, in indemnity, the promisee is a *debtor or obligor,* present or prospective. Thus, a basic indemnity contract involves two parties (indemnitor, indemnitee), whereas suretyship always involves three parties (surety, principal, creditor).

policy must have an insurable interest in the property or person insured. Although the law of insurable interest is primarily common law or judge-made in nature, many states have statutes on the subject.

Though the purposes of the doctrine are the same for both forms of insurance, property and life insurance are governed by substantially different insurable interest rules. Differences exist primarily because the indemnity principle is much less pervasive in life insurance than in property insurance. These differing approaches to insurable interest are outlined below.

Insurable Interest in Property

Because property insurance is based on indemnity, a person possesses an insurable interest in property to the extent he may be subjected to economic injury if the property is lost, destroyed, or damaged. Generally, in property insurance, insurable interest need exist only at the time of the loss, not necessarily when the policy is acquired.

Persons Having Insurable Interest. Persons holding a legal interest in the property have an insurable interest to the extent of the value of the interest. Such persons include the outright owner of property, a life tenant, a remainderman or holder of other future interest in property, and a lessor, lessee, or sublessee of the same property. Persons having legal title in a representative capacity, such as trustees and executors, also have an insurable interest in property under their control. Proceeds of any insurance would then be held for the benefit of the person or persons (for example, beneficiaries of a trust) for whom the representative acts. In addition, a shareholder has an insurable interest in corporate property to the extent of the shareholder's proportionate share of corporate assets on liquidation.

Persons holding equitable interests also qualify. For example, the beneficiary of a trust has an insurable interest in the trust property. Even in the absence of a legal or equitable interest, a mere possessor of property has an insurable interest to the extent of the property's value. This category includes, for example, a bailee who may be liable to the bailor if the property is destroyed.

Although an unsecured creditor has no insurable interest in the debtor's property, a secured creditor does have an insurable interest in property subject to the security interest. The security interest may arise by contract (such as a mortgage of real property or secured transaction of personal property) or otherwise (for example,

a mechanic's or artisan's lien). The creditor's insurable interest is limited to the amount of the secured obligation, not necessarily the full value of the property.

Buyers and Sellers of Property. As noted in Chapter 17, in a contract for the sale of goods, once risk of loss passes to the buyer, the buyer is obligated to pay the purchase price of the goods even if they have been lost or destroyed. To protect against this risk, the Uniform Commercial Code gives the buyer an insurable interest in the goods at the time they are identified to the contract. Identification occurs before risk of loss passes, specifically, when the particular existing goods referred to in the contract are designated and specified.

The UCC risk of loss rules generally place the loss in contracts involving *goods* upon the party who controls possession of the goods. In contrast, in contracts for the sale of *land,* some courts, following the English "equitable conversion" doctrine,[9] have held that risk of loss passes to the buyer upon creation of an enforceable contract. Under this approach, based on the theory that the buyer under an enforceable contract is the equitable owner of the property, risk of loss passes before the buyer has either possession or title. Although the buyer as equitable owner has an insurable interest upon signing the contract, she is unlikely to be aware that the casualty risk has passed. For this reason, a number of states have enacted the **Uniform Vendor and Purchaser Risk Act,** which provides generally that risk of loss does not pass until the buyer acquires either legal title (for example, receives delivery of the deed) or possession of the property. A number of states have adopted a similar approach by judicial decision. To avoid disputes, the buyer and seller should always explicitly address the risk of loss issue in the contract, and alter or acquire insurance coverage to comply with their agreement.

Insurable Interest in Life

Insurable interest in life insurance arises in two contexts: obtaining insurance on one's own life and obtaining insurance on the life of another. A person always has an unlimited insurable interest in his own life. Inherent safeguards against the dangers of gambling or murder generally eliminate the need to inquire into insurable interest. A person who takes out a policy on his own life and pays the premiums may designate his

---

[9]Paine v. Meller, 6 Ves. Jun. 349, 31 Eng. Rep. 1088 (Ch. 1801).

estate or another person as beneficiary. The beneficiary need not have an insurable interest in the insured's life.

In contrast, to have an insurable interest in *another's* life, a person must have some pecuniary interest in the continued vitality of the *cestui que vie.* In addition, the consent of the person whose death triggers payment generally is required. In certain cases, pecuniary interest or benefit is presumed because the individuals are closely related by blood or law. For example, spouses and parents and minor children automatically have insurable interests in each other's lives. In addition, most courts considering the issue have held that a person has an insurable interest in the life of a brother or sister. Other relationships more remote, however, such as aunts, uncles, and cousins, commonly require some additional proof of economic interest (for example, that the insured supports the beneficiary). If insurable interest in life is based upon a familial relationship, the law usually places no limit upon the dollar amount of insurance that may be obtained.

Insurable interest in another's life also may be based upon a business relationship. For example, a creditor has an insurable interest in her debtor's life. Partners have insurable interests in each other's lives. Indeed, life insurance policies frequently are used to fund a buyout by the partnership of a deceased partner's interest. If insurable interest in life is based upon a commercial relationship, the insurance obtained may not greatly exceed the value of that interest.

In cases involving insurable interest in life, courts often have been required to determine (1) who may challenge the beneficiary's lack of insurable interest, and (2) when insurable interest must exist. The following case explains the general principles governing these two issues.

Secor v. Pioneer Foundry Company

173 N.W.2d 780 (Mich. App. 1970)

Defendant, Pioneer Foundry Company (Pioneer), employed Jack Secor from 1954 to 1963. In 1960, Pioneer obtained a $50,000 "keyman" insurance policy on Secor's life. Pioneer was the applicant, owner, and beneficiary of the policy, and paid the premiums. After the employment relationship terminated in July 1963, Pioneer paid the March 1964 annual premium, raising the total premiums paid to over $28,000. Secor died in April 1964, and the insurer paid the proceeds of the policy to Pioneer.

Plaintiff, Secor's widow and administratrix of his estate, sued Pioneer to recover the proceeds, arguing that after the termination of Secor's employment Pioneer Foundry lost whatever insurable interest it had in Secor's life. The trial court ruled that the plaintiff had no cause of action against Pioneer and she appealed to the appellate court.

Levin, Judge

. . . A preliminary issue—whether the plaintiff has standing to complain—is dispositive of plaintiff's contention that Pioneer Foundry no longer had an insurable interest after Secor left its employ. In *Hicks v. Cary,* [52 N.W.2d 351 (Mich. 1952)], on facts similar to those before us, the Michigan Supreme Court declared that the insurer alone may assert that the beneficiary of a life policy does not have an insurable interest. . . . The rule that only the insurer can raise the question of lack of insurable interest appears to be well supported in other jurisdictions.

In the present case, the insurer . . . paid the proceeds of the policy to Pioneer Foundry in May, 1964, without asserting this possible defense.

The plaintiff argues that, apart from whether she has standing to raise the insurable interest defense, the underlying premise of the insurable interest requirement—the public policy against speculation on the life of another—is so pervasive that Pioneer Foundry could not lawfully retain insurance on Secor's life after the termination of his employment. . . .

The purchaser of ordinary life insurance, as distinguished from casualty or property insurance, buys not only indemnification in a specific amount against a particular peril or potential loss but also makes an investment. To terminate the rights of the owner or beneficiary of ordinary life insurance because the relationship to the life insured has changed, perhaps after many years of making premium payments, at a time when death is bound to be more imminent than it was at the time the policy was issued, would not only adversely affect this investment quality of life insurance but would also confer an unanticipated and unwarranted windfall on the insurer.

In recognition of these considerations the almost universal rule of law in this country is that if the insurable interest requirement is satisfied at the time the policy is issued, the proceeds of the policy must be paid upon the death of the life insured without regard to whether the beneficiary has an insurable interest at the time of death. It has, accordingly, been held that an employer who is the beneficiary of a policy insuring the life of one of his employees may collect proceeds which become payable under the policy even though the employee's death occurs after the termination of his employment.

The ordinary life insurance policy issued to the defendant corporation is referred to in the insurance industry as "keyman" life insurance. The plaintiff emphasizes that the typical life insurance policy is purchased to provide for loss by family members who may be expected to suffer a personal as well as a financial loss upon the death of the life insured. From this she argues that keyman life insurance should not be governed by the same rules as apply to life insurance generally. The proffered distinction is not, in our opinion meaningful. Life insurance is not meant to assuage grief; its primary function is monetary. It serves fundamentally the same purpose whether the beneficiary is a widow or a business; it seeks to replace with a sum of money the earning capacity of the life insured.

The plaintiff's analogy to the public policy against a murderer collecting insurance on the life of the victim is inapposite. Pioneer Foundry's act of paying the yearly premium after Secor left its employ is not (contrary to plaintiff's argument) at all analogous to murdering him. Given the general rule that the beneficiary of a life policy may collect its proceeds although the insurable interest which existed when the policy was issued subsequently terminates, it would make no sense to hold that the act of paying the premium (necessary to the full preservation of the owner's rights under the policy) somehow or other brings about a termination of the owner-beneficiary's rights.

We also decline to limit Pioneer Foundry's recovery to the amount of its investment in the policy and its financial loss (probably nil) upon Secor's death. Pioneer Foundry's investment in the policy was large both quantitatively and relatively. It chose to make the premium payment due eight months after Secor's employment terminated to preserve recovery of its prior expenditures. It did this in its own interest; it has not been suggested that it was acting for, or because of any obligation it had assumed to, Secor or his family. . . .

[Judgment affirmed.]

Persons and Interests Protected; Risk Transferred

Like other contracts, an insurance contract outlines the legally enforceable rights and obligations of the parties. Important provisions in insurance policies include those identifying the person or persons who are entitled to benefits under the policy, the interests of those persons that are protected, and the extent and nature of the risk transferred to the insurer.

Property and Casualty Insurance

Persons Insured. In property and casualty insurance, the "insured" generally refers to the person or persons whose loss triggers the insurer's liability to pay benefits. The insured is designated in the policy, and additional insureds may subsequently be added by indorsements to the policy.

The interest of the insured or insureds in the property may or may not be designated. For example, two insureds might be designated "owner" and "mortgagee," or "life tenant" and "remainderman." Insurable interest principles define and limit an insured's potential recovery under the policy. Thus, if more than one insured is listed, proceeds commonly are payable "as their interests may appear," meaning that proceeds are paid "in proportion to the damage to their respective interests in the insured property."[10]

In addition to the insureds stated in the policy and added by indorsement, insureds may be added by explicit policy provisions. Important provisions of this type include the "omnibus" and "standard mortgage" clause. An **omnibus clause** defines additional insureds as a class bearing a specified relationship to the named insured. For example, an automobile policy often contains an omnibus clause that extends policy protection to the insured, members of the insured's household, and other persons using the insured's car. These clauses are designed to protect both the named insured and potential accident victims.

A **standard mortgage clause,** generally appearing in fire insurance or homeowner's policies, is designed to protect the lender holding a mortgage on the insured property. Under the clause, the mortgagee becomes an insured and loss is payable to the mortgagor and

---

[10]Keeton & Widiss, Insurance Law 288 (1988).

mortgagee "as interests appear." The clause further provides that the mortgagee may collect for losses under the policy even if the mortgagor would be denied recovery. For example, the mortgagor might be denied recovery for breaching a condition in the policy, such as by storing hazardous materials on the property. Or, the mortgagor may have previously sold the property, thereby extinguishing insurable interest. To recover, the mortgagee generally must pay any premium left unpaid by the mortgagor. The standard mortgage clause places the mortgagee in a better position than a mere assignee of the policy proceeds from the mortgagor. Under ordinary contract principles, the lender as mere assignee would take subject to any defenses the insurer has against the mortgagor.

Effect of Assignment. When an insured loss occurs, the proceeds of the insurance ordinarily are paid to the insured—for example, a homeowner covered by a fire insurance policy whose home is destroyed by fire. An insured may, however, designate a third party (such as a creditor) to receive the proceeds of the policy. Such an assignment may be made in the policy or in a separate contract, and may occur before or after the loss. The right transferred, merely a claim for money due from the insurance company, is freely assignable without the insurer's consent.

In an assignment of proceeds, the designation of insureds in the policy is not affected and the property insured is not transferred. In contrast, the insured may sell the insured property and attempt to transfer his entire interest in the policy to the buyer, who then becomes a new substituted insured. In this case, the insurer's consent is required, because an insurer bases its decision to insure in part upon the character of the individual insured. That is, a property insurance contract does not run with the land; rather, a novation must be created among the parties substituting the buyer for the seller with the insurer's consent.

Life Insurance

Designation of Beneficiary. In life insurance, the owner of the policy (who usually also is the *cestui que vie*) commonly designates a beneficiary to receive the proceeds, and retains the other rights of ownership. The beneficiary of a life insurance policy may be named irrevocably or revocably. In an irrevocable designation,

the owner has no power to change the beneficiary. More commonly, the policy expressly permits the owner to change the beneficiary at any time prior to the death of the *cestui que vie*. Policies also usually provide for contingent or secondary beneficiaries who receive the proceeds if the primary beneficiary predeceases the *cestui que vie*. The policy owner's estate usually is designated as final contingent beneficiary.

Effect of Assignment. The owner of a life insurance policy may assign the entire policy, including the various incidents of ownership, such as the right to borrow money from the insurer secured by the policy and the duty to pay premiums. The person whose death triggers payment of the proceeds remains the same after the assignment. A life insurance policy generally may be freely assigned without the insurer's consent, even to a person without an insurable interest in the *cestui que vie*. If the beneficiary has been irrevocably designated, however, the beneficiary's right to proceeds cannot be impaired without his consent. If the beneficiary designation is revocable, the assignee will simply change the beneficiary after the assignment.

An assignment of a life insurance policy may be made to a creditor other than the insurer to provide collateral on a loan from the creditor to the owner-assignor. On the owner's death, if the policy proceeds exceed the amount of the debt, other persons may assert a claim to the excess. Although the intent of the parties is controlling, most decisions have permitted the creditor to retain no more than the amount of the debt plus interest and charges, reasoning that the assignment or designation was intended merely as security for payment of the debt and no more.

Risk Transferred

The scope of an insurer's obligation regarding both the risk covered and the duration of coverage is determined by the express language of the insurance contract. In defining the risk insured against, policies commonly are designated either all-risk or specified-risk policies. An all-risk policy covers damage to the insured subject matter from any cause except those explicitly stated in the policy through exception, exclusion, or condition. A specified-risk policy, in contrast, covers injury caused only by the risks listed.

Marine and inland marine insurance are typical all-risk policies, whereas fire and automobile insurance are specified-risk contracts. Life insurance also may be viewed as an all-risk policy because it pays upon the death of the insured from any cause, except those specifically excepted (for example, suicide during the first year of the policy). Characterizing a policy as all-risk or specified-risk has important legal consequences. For example, in a specified-risk policy the insured has the burden of proving that the loss resulted from one of the specified causes. In an all-risk policy, once existence of the loss is proven, the insurer must prove that the loss fell within some exception or exclusion to the policy coverage to escape liability. This allocation of the burden of proof substantially aids the insured if the precise cause of the loss cannot be determined. In addition, an all-risk policy reduces gaps in coverage and therefore the likelihood that a court will find a given loss outside the protection of the policy.

Claims and Recovery

Parties' Duties After Loss

Both life and property insurance policies explicitly outline appropriate procedures for filing a claim to recover for a covered loss. In a life insurance policy, due proof of death of the insured and surrender of the policy are common prerequisites to payment of insurance proceeds. Property and liability insurance policies usually require that the insured give prompt notice of any loss to the insurer or its agent. The insured also may be required to furnish the names of persons injured and of any witnesses and to prevent further damage to the property. Within a stated period after the loss or after the insurer's request (for example, 60 days), the insured also generally must provide a "proof of loss." The proof of loss provides details of the accident, other insurance that may cover the loss, the interest of the insured and others in the property, receipts for repairs, detailed repair or replacement estimates, and inventories of lost or damaged personal property. The insured also usually is required to cooperate with the insurer regarding any investigation, settlement, or defense of any claim; forward copies of legal documents received; and submit to physical examinations or to questions under oath.

As illustrated by the following case, the insured's duty to comply with a policy's claim procedures can be of critical importance.

Commercial Union Insurance Company v. International Flavors & Fragrances, Inc.
822 F.2d 267 (2d Cir. 1987)

Under a comprehensive liability insurance policy issued to defendant International Flavors & Fragrances, Inc. (IFF) in 1976 and renewed through 1979, plaintiff Commercial Union Insurance Company (CU) agreed to indemnify IFF and to provide a defense in lawsuits within the policy's coverage. As a condition of coverage, IFF was required to give written notice of any "occurrence" to CU "as soon as practicable." This notice of occurrence provision became the subject of litigation after CU refused to defend or indemnify IFF in conjunction with a lawsuit brought by Plough, Inc.

The action arose from a contract by which IFF, between 1975 and 1977, had supplied 62,000 pounds of banana-coconut fragrance used in Plough's Tropical Blend suntan lotion. In 1976, Plough notified IFF and the Food and Drug Administration (FDA) that 15 persons had reported skin reactions after using Tropical Blend. During the next year, Plough and IFF employees consulted in an attempt to identify the cause of the skin reactions. By July 1977, after 50 cases had been reported, dermatologists conducting clinical tests concluded that the skin reactions were caused by a photoallergenic reaction to 6-methyl coumarin (6-MC), a chemical agent that IFF used in the banana-coconut fragrance. In September 1977, Plough notified IFF officers of these results. In December 1978, the FDA notified IFF that 6-MC was being banned from use in suncare products and IFF informed its insurance broker of the FDA's action. In March 1979, Plough sued IFF, which shortly thereafter notified CU of the suit.

CU filed suit seeking a declaratory judgment that it had no duty to defend or indemnify IFF because of its failure to give timely notice of the occurrence. Although the jury found in favor of CU, the trial judge granted in part a motion for judgment notwithstanding the verdict and ruled that CU had no duty to indemnify IFF but had a duty to defend the suit. CU and IFF appealed to the Second Circuit Court of Appeals.

Winter, Circuit Judge

. . . Notice-of-occurrence provisions have several purposes. . . . They enable insurers to make a timely investigation of relevant events and exercise early control over a claim. Early control may lead to a settlement before litigation and enable insurers to take steps to eliminate the risk of similar occurrences in the future. When insurers have timely notice of relevant occurrences, they can establish more accurate renewal premiums and maintain adequate reserves. . . .

[T]he photoallergenic nature of 6-MC was totally unknown and unexpected prior to the events giving rise to the instant action. . . . Plough did its best in 1977 and 1978 to avoid any public disclosure that its Tropical Blend products might be harmful. However, we cannot agree with the suggestion that these facts excuse IFF from complying with the notice-of-occurrence provision as a matter of law. As noted above, a principal purpose of such a provision is to enable insurers to reduce future risks to the public by preventing the continued use of known harmful substances by their insureds. Had IFF given timely notice, CU could have taken steps to protect the public from further exposure to 6-MC. Indeed, Plough's attempts to avoid publicity were feasible *only* because IFF, which also had a financial interest in concealment, did not give notice to CU. We believe that a rule of law that would inhibit insurance companies from eliminating risks known to manufacturers and sellers but concealed for purposes of commercial advantage is undesirable.

Under New York law, compliance with a notice-of-occurrence provision in an insurance policy is a condition precedent to an insurer's liability under the policy. . . . An insured's failure to give timely notice to its insurer may be excused, however, by proof that the insured either lacked knowledge of the occurrence or had a reasonable belief of nonliability. . . . Viewing the evidence, as we must, in the light most favorable to CU, . . . we conclude that it was more than sufficient to support the . . . jury's finding of an unexcused breach of the notice-of-occurrence provision.

The test for determining whether the notice provision has been triggered is whether the circumstances known to the insured at that time would have suggested to a reasonable person the possibility of a claim. . . . By September 1977, some eighteen months before Plough began its litigation, IFF executives knew, *inter alia,* that: (1) 6-MC was photoallergenic; (2) Plough had contracted to pay IFF over $700,000 for a fragrance containing 6-MC; (3) Plough had spent thousands of dollars to determine the cause of the Tropical Blend problem; (4) millions of units of Tropical Blend could not be sold and would have to be destroyed; and (5) many individuals had suffered personal injuries, some severe, because of the fragrance. Subsequent events merely confirmed 6-MC's photoallergenicity. The fact that this harmful property was unknown prior to September 1977 is of no aid to IFF in view of its failure to give the required notice until March 1979. A jury might thus easily have concluded that a reasonable person, knowing in September 1977 that IFF's product had

caused and was causing great losses to Plough, would have realized that there had been an occurrence possibly giving rise to a claim covered by the policy. . . .

Judge Pollack correctly held that IFF's breach of the notice-of-occurrence clause would relieve CU of its duty to indemnify IFF for Plough's recovery. He also concluded that this breach would not justify CU's refusal to defend the Plough lawsuit, however, because an insurer's duty to defend is broader than its duty to indemnify. . . . That was error. While an insurer's obligation to furnish a defense is indeed separate from and broader than its obligation to indemnify, . . . the added breadth arises out of the duty to provide a defense against even wholly frivolous, and thus nonindemnifiable, claims so long as the allegations fall within the policy's coverage. IFF's compliance with the notice requirement, however, was a condition precedent to all of CU's duties under the policy, including the duty to defend. . . . The . . . jury's finding that IFF had not complied with the notice provision thus excused CU's refusal to defend without reservation as well as its refusal to indemnify. . . .

[Judgment reversed and remanded.]

Duty of Good Faith and Fair Dealing. Once a claim is properly filed, the insurer evaluates, processes, and pays or denies it. A growing number of courts recognize that, in handling a claim, the insurer is under a duty to act in good faith and consistent with standards of fair dealing. This duty is breached, for example, if the insurer denies a claim or delays its payment, and (1) has no reasonable basis for the denial or the delay, or (2) has failed properly to investigate the claim to determine whether such a reasonable basis exists. An insurer who breaches the duty of good faith and fair dealing may be held liable for damages in a tort action filed by the insured.

Measure of Recovery

In a life insurance policy, the company pays to the beneficiary of record the amount fixed in the policy less the amount of any policy loans outstanding at the insured's death. Other policies, such as accident insurance, also may provide for fixed benefits.

In liability insurance, the insurer agrees to pay damages for personal injury and property damage that the insured becomes legally responsible to pay. Liability usually is limited to a specified maximum for each injured person and a total maximum for each accident or occurrence. The insurer also undertakes to provide a legal defense or settle at its expense any lawsuit or claim brought against the insured requesting damages.

In property insurance, recovery generally is based upon "actual cash value" at the time of the loss. For replaceable commodities with a fixed market price, that price usually is the measure of actual cash value. In many cases, however, actual cash value is determined only after the court has considered a combination of relevant factors including replacement cost, depreciation, and the effect of obsolescence of the insured property.

If the insured property is residential real estate, indemnity based upon replacement cost less depreciation usually is insufficient to allow the homeowner to rebuild. For this reason, modern comprehensive home-owner's policies often provide replacement cost insurance. Typically, such a provision states that if, at the time of the loss, the amount of insurance on the damaged building is 80 percent or more of the full replacement cost of the building immediately before the loss, then coverage is extended to include the full cost of repair or replacement without deduction for depreciation. Note that, for reasons developed below, replacement cost insurance induces the owner to insure the property for close to its full replacement cost.

Coinsurance. Nonmarine property insurance rates are fixed as a percentage of the total amount of insurance under the policy. Thus, the insured pays the same amount for the first and last thousand dollars' worth of coverage. Most property losses are, however, partial, meaning that the lower levels of coverage cost more to provide. In addition, because most losses are partial, insureds are induced to underinsure their property.

Coinsurance is one device developed by insurers to induce owners to insure their property for an amount close to its full value. Under a coinsurance clause, recovery for a partial loss is limited (that is, the insured becomes a coinsurer) unless the owner insures the property for at least a specified percentage (usually 80 percent) of its full value. Recovery under a coinsurance clause is computed using the following formula:

$$\text{loss} \times \left(\frac{\text{amount of insurance carried}}{\substack{\text{coinsurance} \\ \text{percentage}} \times \substack{\text{actual value of} \\ \text{property at time} \\ \text{of the loss}}} \right) = \text{recovery}$$

For example, assume property worth $200,000 sustains an $80,000 fire loss. The owner has insured the property for $100,000 under a policy containing an 80 percent coinsurance clause. The owner's recovery would be $50,000 computed as follows:

$$\$80,000 \times \left(\frac{\$100,000}{0.8 \times \$200,000} \right) = \$50,000$$

On these facts, therefore, the owner bears $30,000 of the $80,000 loss.

If the owner had insured the property for $160,000, recovery would be $80,000. That is:

$$\$80,000 \times \left(\frac{\$160,000}{0.8 \times \$200,000} \right) = \$80,000$$

Thus, by insuring the property consistently with the coinsurance percentage, the owner recovers in full for any partial loss up to the policy limit, $160,000.

Note that coinsurance applies to partial, not total losses; after a total loss, the owner may recover the face amount of the policy. In the first example, therefore, if the building had been completely destroyed, the owner could recover $100,000.

Other Insurance. An insured may take out more than one policy of insurance upon her life or property. The face amount of all life insurance policies will be paid on death. In contrast, to prevent the moral risk of net profit from overinsurance, property insurers use **other insurance clauses** to limit effective coverage if the insured obtains additional insurance on the same property. These clauses typically provide that each insurer pays the proportion of the loss that the face amount of each policy bears to the total amount of insurance carried. For example, if an owner insures property for its full value with two insurers and suffers a total loss, each insurer would be required to pay one-half of the loss.

Rights and Defenses of Insurer

Defenses of Insurer

An insured possesses information not known to the insurer, such as the state of his health, medical history, or the condition, type, or use of property owned. Such information is, of course, important to the insurer in evaluating the risk to determine whether to insure and at what premium. Insurers elicit the information from the insured through representations or warranties. A representation is a statement regarding the subject of insurance that forms part of the basis of the insurer's decision to insure. Generally, a material misrepresentation, whether or not intentionally (fraudulently) made, relied upon by the insurer is grounds for avoiding the policy. The insurer generally has the burden of proving that the misrepresentation was material.

In contrast to representations, certain statements or promises made by the insured may be expressly incorporated into the contract. Such "warranties" or "conditions" are affirmative—a statement asserting that certain facts are true when the contract is made—or promissory—that the facts will continue to be true throughout the life of the policy. Unlike representations, warranties are presumed to be material, and generally must be strictly observed to prevent avoidance by the insurer. For example, if the insured warrants that no flammable liquids will be stored on the insured property during the life of the policy, recovery for any fire loss may be denied if gasoline is stored on the premises. Because of its harsh effect upon the rights of the insured, a warranty must be expressly and conspicuously included in the policy and must clearly indicate that the insured's rights depend upon compliance.

To protect insureds, courts construe ambiguous language as representations rather than warranties, and ambiguous warranties as affirmative rather than promissory. In addition, various statutes prevent denial of recovery under a life insurance policy based upon immaterial technicalities. For example, to avoid upsetting the estate and financial planning of an insured, many states require that life insurance policies contain a clause making the policy incontestable (except for nonpayment of premiums) after the policy has been in effect for a given period, such as one or two years. If the insured survives the stated period, an **incontestable clause** prevents the insurer from asserting a misrepresentation or breach of warranty as a basis to avoid the contract. The law usually takes a similar approach to suicide; that is, the insured's suicide is not grounds for denial of recovery unless it occurs within a stated period after inception of the policy. The insurer has a limited defense, however, if the insured misrepresents his age. In this case, the amount payable on the insured's death is the amount of insurance the premiums actually paid would have purchased if the age had been correctly stated.

Subrogation

As noted in Chapter 33 (Suretyship), **subrogation** is an equitable remedy grounded in restitution designed to prevent unjust enrichment. In insurance law, the insurance company after paying the insured succeeds to, or is subrogated to, the insured's rights in contract or tort against any third party causing the loss. An insurer has no right of subrogation against its own insured. Subrogation is designed to prevent a double recovery by the insured (one from the insurer and another from the person causing the loss) and to place the ultimate loss upon the party responsible for the injury. For example, assume Tim negligently destroys John's car. Continental Casualty, John's insurer, indemnifies him for the loss. Continental is subrogated to John's tort claim against Tim to the extent of Continental's payments to John. Subrogation rights arise by operation of law and therefore need not be expressly provided for in the insurance contract.

Although the law recognizes a right of subrogation for amounts paid under property and liability insurance policies, subrogation generally has been denied in life insurance. In life insurance, the insurer is obligated to pay a fixed sum on death. Because indemnity for determinable economic loss is not the basis of recovery, there is no possibility of double recovery by the beneficiary. Thus, the beneficiary or other family member (not the insurer) also may recover in tort against any third party wrongfully causing the death of the insured.

Summary

1.   Insurance is a contractual arrangement for transferring and distributing risk. In an insurance contract, an insurer, an entity engaged in the business of insurance, promises to pay another, the insured, a sum of money or provide other value upon occurrence of some harmful event during a specified period. In exchange for this promise, the insured pays a premium. Insurance contracts and insurance company activities are regulated by the states.

2. Insurance contracts are of three basic types: (1) life insurance, (2) fire and marine insurance, and (3) casualty insurance. Insurance contracts are standardized form contracts tendered to the insured on a take-it-or-leave-it basis. To protect insureds, courts often construe insurance contracts to provide coverage for a given loss, and use contract doctrines, such as unconscionability, to police against unreasonably unfair terms.

3. Most insurance contracts are contracts of indemnity under which the insurance company promises to indemnify or reimburse the insured for some accrued or anticipated liability. Under the indemnity concept, the benefit conferred by the insurer may not exceed the loss suffered by the insured. This approach, prohibiting net profit from insurance, prevents use of an insurance contract as a gambling device and eliminates any inducement for the insured to cause the event insured against. The legal principles designed to prevent net profit from insurance are embodied in the concept of insurable interest.

4. In property and casualty insurance the insured generally is the person or persons whose loss triggers the insurer's liability to pay benefits. Persons insured may be explicitly named in the policy, subsequently added by indorsement, or included by operation of policy provisions such as an "omnibus" or "standard mortgage" clause. Although the insured usually receives the proceeds, the right may be assigned to a party not named as an insured under the policy.

5. A life insurance policy creates various rights in favor of its owner that generally may be assigned. The rights of the beneficiary of the policy depend upon whether the beneficiary is named revocably or irrevocably.

6. The scope of the insurer's obligation regarding both the risk covered and the duration of coverage are determined by express terms of the insurance contract. In defining the insured risk, policies are commonly designated either "all-risk" or "specified-risk."

7. Life and property insurance policies explicitly outline appropriate procedures for filing a claim to recover for an insured loss. In life insurance, proceeds are fixed in the policy, but in property insurance, recovery is based upon the actual cash value of the insured property at the time of the loss. The amount of recovery also may be affected by the operation of a coinsurance or other insurance clause.

8. An insurer relies upon information provided by the insured in evaluating risk and computing the premium. Certain misrepresentations by the insured or the insured's failure to comply with written warranties incorporated into the contract may provide a basis to avoid the contract. To protect insureds, courts and legislatures have devised various devices such as "incontestable clauses" to prevent denial of recovery based upon immaterial technicalities.

9. In insurance law, the insurer after paying the insured is subrogated to the insured's rights against any third party causing the loss. The right of subrogation, which prevents double recovery by the insured, is not recognized in some forms of insurance.

Key Terms

insurance	Uniform Vendor and
life insurance	Purchaser Risk Act
fire insurance	omnibus clause
marine insurance	standard mortgage clause
inland marine insurance	coinsurance
casualty insurance	other insurance clause
indemnity contract	incontestable clause
insurable interest	subrogation

Questions and Problems

57.1 Insurance is a method of transferring and distributing risk. What is risk? What benefits does a life insurance policy provide for an insured and the beneficiaries? What benefits do fire and casualty insurance provide to a business?

57.2 Life insurance often is characterized as a contract of investment rather than indemnity. How does life insurance differ from other forms of insurance? How is it similar? Is it accurate to say that life insurance is not a contract of indemnity? Explain.

57.3 A homeowner's policy provides that "we do not insure . . . any loss arising out of any act committed: (1) by or at the direction of the insured; and (2) with the intent to cause a loss." Why? Should an employer's insurance provide protection for deliberate acts of employees? Should recovery be denied for losses caused by the negligent (rather than intentional) conduct of an insured? Explain.

57.4 Leslie Owens, who operated a retail store, requested information concerning burglary insurance from an insurance agent. At the agent's recommendation, Owens purchased a policy issued by Allied Insurance. Owens looked over the policy and examined the coverage and amounts but did not read the definitions listed in small print on page three of the policy. The policy defined "burglary" as

> the felonious abstraction of insured property from within the premises by a person making felonious entry therein by actual force and violence, of which force and violence are visible marks made by tools, explosives, electricity or chemicals upon, or physical damage to, the exterior of the premises at the place of entry.

Two years later, the store was burglarized at night. Two employees testified that they had locked the store before leaving. When they reported for work the following day, the outside doors were locked. Interior doors to storage areas within the store, however, had been damaged and carried visible marks of tools. Police investigating the burglary demonstrated that an outside locked door could be removed without damage.

Allied Insurance refused to pay the claim filed by Owens because there were no visible marks or damage to the exterior of the store. Owens sued. How should the court rule? Explain.

57.5 What factors might the court take into account in determining the amount of insured's recovery for a fire loss to (1) income-producing property, such as an apartment or office building, (2) a residence, (3) personal property, such as household furnishing, (4) an automobile, and (5) inventory?

57.6 Bailey owned a fraternity house on the University of Oklahoma campus that he insured against fire with Gulf Insurance Company. The house fell into disrepair and was declared a public nuisance by the city. The city condemned the building and ordered it torn down. Subsequently, the building was severely damaged by an accidental fire. Should Bailey be entitled to recover anything under the policy? If so, how should recovery be computed?

57.7 A fire destroyed a storage building owned by Doelger, Inc., a company that has manufactured industrial equipment for almost 100 years. The property insurance policy covering the building provided that National Fire Insurance Company would pay Doelger the "actual cash value of the property." Doelger had used the building to store patterns for old equipment that was no longer in demand. After National Fire refused to pay Doelger for the patterns, Doelger sued. Doelger established that the cost of reproducing the patterns was $50,000. The insurer offered evidence proving that Doelger had not used the patterns for more than 15 years. National Fire asserted that because no demand existed for the equipment made from the patterns, they had no cash value. How should the court rule? Explain.

57.8 James Butler purchased a used sports car and acquired an auto insurance policy covering the car from Farmers Insurance Company. Two years later, it was discovered that, unknown to Butler, the car previously had been stolen. The police seized the car and returned it to its rightful owner. Butler sought to recover under a provision in the policy under which Farmers agreed to pay "for loss to the described automobile caused by accidental means." Farmers denied liability on the grounds (1) that Butler had no insurable interest in the automobile, and (2) that, in any event, repossession of the auto by the rightful owner was not a loss covered by the policy. Is Farmers correct? Explain.

57.9 To recover under a property insurance policy, the insured must show that an insured event caused the loss. In determining causation, some courts use a proximate cause test analogous to that used in tort cases discussed in Chapter 5. Other courts use a "contemplated damages" test and hold the insurer liable only for losses within the contemplation of the parties when the policy was issued. In the following fact situations, determine whether the insured should recover under either test.

(a) The policy covered "direct loss by windstorm." The insured livestock, exposed to a cold wind, took shelter on a frozen pond and drowned when the ice broke.

(b) The policy covered "loss by windstorm." A high wind blew down power lines, cutting off power to the insured's freezer, causing its contents to spoil.

(c) The policy covered "direct loss by vandalism and malicious mischief." Vandals threw cans onto the roof of insured's bowling alley. The cans clogged the downspouts, causing rainwater to accumulate on the roof, which collapsed.

57.10 In his will, Joe Doaks left his house to his daughter Gertrude for life, with the remainder in fee simple absolute passing to John Jones. Gertrude occupied the house and insured it against fire loss under a policy issued by Home Insurance Company, naming Gertrude as sole insured. While the policy was in force, a fire destroyed the house. Gertrude died in the fire approximately 20 minutes after it began. Gertrude's estate filed a claim against Home for the fire loss. Home denied liability, asserting that because Gertrude had only a life estate in the house, her insurable interest terminated by operation of law on her death and accordingly neither she nor her estate suffered any pecuniary loss from the fire. Is Home Insurance correct? Explain.

INTERNATIONAL LEGAL PROBLEMS

To this point, the text has examined the organization and operation of the American legal system, the legal principles governing rights and duties of private parties in commercial transactions, and the role of the government in regulating business activity. The U.S. legal system is, of course, only one among many. This chapter provides an overview of the legal concepts governing the legal relationship among sovereign states, the role of the state and federal government in international affairs, and the power of U.S. courts to adjudicate matters affecting foreign nations and their citizens.

International Law and Organizations

International law, often known as "public international law" or the "law of nations," is the system of law that governs relationships among states (nations). All states exhibit three basic characteristics: each has a fixed territory, a permanent population, and a sovereign government capable of controlling affairs within its territory and conducting international relations with other states.[1] States possess sovereignty, which is the supreme political authority from which the state derives other specific political powers such as the power to make and enforce laws, to impose and collect taxes, and to form treaties and alliances with other nations. Sovereignty provides the international independence of a state and the right and power to regulate its internal affairs free of foreign interference. Through international law, sovereign states regulate their relations with each other.

In the United States and other countries, a legislature enacts law. The executive, among other functions, enforces it, and the judiciary tries violations of criminal

---

[1] AKEHURST, A MODERN INTRODUCTION TO INTERNATIONAL LAW 1, 53 (6th ed. 1987).

law and resolves civil disputes. Violations of law are backed by sanctions that are enforceable by the government, including money damages, injunctions, fines, and imprisonment.

Among the sovereign states no centralized legislature exists, no court possesses mandatory jurisdiction, and no executive body imposes legally enforceable sanctions. For example, although the sovereign nations have established international legal tribunals, most notably the International Court of Justice (discussed below), these courts have no enforcement powers. This lack of sanctions—lack of an obligatory judicial forum whose judgments are enforceable by executive authority—has led some observers to conclude that international law is not "law" in the traditional sense of the term at all. Nevertheless, states normally obey principles of international law, which are derived from consensus or formal agreement, because it is in their individual self-interest to do so. States are few in number and cannot move; economic and other needs force most states to cooperate with their neighbors and to be reasonably reliable in international dealing. Violation of a rule may lead to economic or diplomatic sanctions by other states, an unacceptable result in light of increasing interdependence among nations.

Sources of International Law

Article 38(1) of the Statute of the International Court of Justice provides the most widely accepted list of the sources of international law. It states:

> The Court, whose function is to decide in accordance with international law such disputes as are submitted to it, shall apply:
> (a) international conventions, whether general or particular, establishing rules expressly recognized by the contesting states;
> (b) international custom, as evidence of a general practice accepted as law;
> (c) the general principles of law recognized by civilized nations;
> (d) . . . judicial decisions and the teachings of the most highly qualified publicists of the various nations, as subsidiary means for the determination of rules of law.

Treaties. The first source, "international conventions," refers to treaties. A **treaty** is an agreement or contract between two or more nations or sovereigns, formally signed by an authorized representative and ratified by the sovereign or supreme power of each state. Treaties may be bilateral (between two nations) or multilateral (among several nations). Because modern technology, communication, and trade have made states increasingly interdependent and willing to cooperate on a variety of common problems, treaties occupy an ever-expanding role in the orderly conduct of international relations. Some address critical national interests of a political character, such as alliances, peace settlements, and bans on atomic testing. Others involve less politically charged relationships between governments and government agencies, such as agreements on foreign aid or cooperation in provision of government services such as weather forecasting. Still others, such as tariff treaties, tax conventions, and treaties of friendship, commerce, and navigation, regulate business relationships between nationals or residents of the participating countries.

Custom. Custom is the original source of international law. A practice is recognized as part of international custom if it involves a consistent course of conduct by a number of states over a considerable period, a recognition that the practice is consistent with or required by international law, and general acquiescence in the practice by other states.[2] Many international customs have been codified in treaties in recent years, providing more precision and predictability in the law.

General Principles of Law. "General principles of law" provide the third source of international law. These principles, derived primarily from the internal or national law of the developed countries, supplement and fill in the gaps in treaties and customary law, the primary sources of international law. Examples of general legal principles used by international tribunals include estoppel, laches, and *res judicata.*

Judicial Decisions and Learned Writers. Although international courts are not required to follow previous decisions (that is, to observe the principle of *stare decisis* applicable under American law), they commonly do, particularly as the body of decided case law in international tribunals increases. Judgments of national courts also play a subsidiary role in developing rules of international law; for example, rules of law on subjects

---

[2]STEINER & VAGTS, TRANSNATIONAL LEGAL PROBLEMS 298 (3d ed. 1986).

such as diplomatic immunity have been developed by national courts. Writings of legal commentators, like judicial decisions, also can provide evidence of customary law and play a role in developing new international rules.

International Organizations

Primarily since the end of World War II, treaties have been used to create international organizations using a permanent staff, buildings, and other assets to maintain continuous activity. These organizations play an important role in addressing international legal problems not easily resolved through customary international law, or noninstitutional bilateral or multilateral treaties. The organizations are formed for various purposes including peace-keeping and world order, and regulating, facilitating, and developing commercial or economic activities among member states. Some of the more important organizations are briefly introduced below.

United Nations. The United Nations was created at the end of World War II to promote peaceful resolution of international disputes and provide for collective action to stop aggression. The United Nations also is concerned with economic development, social welfare, and human rights.

The United Nations Charter divides the organization into constituent parts. The Security Council is vested with primary responsibility for the maintenance of international peace and security. The Council's nonprocedural decisions are subject to veto by its permanent members: China, France, the Russian Federation, the United Kingdom, and the United States. The General Assembly is composed of representatives from all member states. The Secretariat, headed by the secretary general, administers the day-to-day affairs of the United Nations and occasionally takes initiative in political matters.

International Court of Justice. Perhaps the most important United Nations body from a legal standpoint is its judicial branch, the International Court of Justice (ICJ). The ICJ issues advisory opinions and decides actual disputes. Its jurisdiction is limited by two principles. First, only states may be parties to litigation before the ICJ. Second, jurisdiction is not compulsory but is based upon the states' consent. The Court consists of 15 judges, no more than two of whom may be from the same country. Judges are elected by the General Assembly

and the Security Council to nine-year terms with one-third of the Court being reelected or replaced every three years.

The ICJ is not the only international tribunal. Other international courts have been created, for example, under regional treaties of economic or political cooperation.

World Trade Organization. The World Trade Organization (WTO) was established in 1995 to serve as a forum for international trade negotiations and for resolution of trade disputes. The WTO is the successor to an organization created by the General Agreement on Tariffs and Trade (GATT), a multilateral trade treaty initially adopted in 1947. As explained in the preamble, the objectives of GATT were "the substantial reduction of tariffs and other barriers to trade and . . . the elimination of discriminatory treatment in international commerce." The WTO continues GATT's mission of fostering free and open trade.

As of November 2005, 148 nations, including the United States, were members of WTO. Countries become WTO members through a process called "accession" that requires agreement of all other members. The WTO is governed by a secretariat headed by a director general and a Ministerial Conference that meets at least every two years. The General Council supervises the general work of the WTO and also meets as the WTO's Dispute Settlement Body and Trade Policy Review Body.

The WTO charter includes three principal documents:

1. GATT 1994 (the original 1947 GATT as well as revisions and amendments adopted through 1994), which governs trade of goods;
2. the General Agreement on Trade in Services (GATS); and
3. the Agreement on Trade-Related Aspects of Intellectual Property Rights (TRIPS)

The fundamental principle of these agreements is eliminating discrimination in international trade. The Most Favored Nation Clause generally requires WTO members to treat other members equally. A nation that grants a reduced tariff for a product to one member country, for example, generally must grant the reduction to all WTO members. In other words, WTO members are supposed to treat each other as "most favored" trading partners. Some exceptions to most favored nation status are allowed including, for example, regional free trade associations that do not apply to goods from other countries. The "national treatment rule" also helps eliminate trade discrimination. This rule requires equal treatment of imported products after they have entered a market. In other words, a WTO member must treat products of other member countries the same as its own domestic products. Because the national treatment rule applies only after a product has entered a market, countries may impose duties on imports before they enter the market.

The WTO includes rules for tariff negotiations, tariff schedules, standards for conducting international trade, and principles for eliminating restrictive trade measures. Under GATT, the primary method for reducing tariff and trade barriers has been periodic, multinational, trade negotiations called "rounds." The "Uruguay Round," which was conducted between 1986 and 1994, was the eighth negotiating round completed under the auspices of GATT and ended with the creation of the WTO. In 2001, at a meeting in Doha, Qatar, WTO members agreed to launch a new round of trade talks. The Doha Round was initiated in early 2002 and was still in progress in 2005.

International Monetary Fund. The same concern over protectionist trade measures that led to GATT also motivated the Bretton Woods Conference of 1944 that created the International Monetary Fund (IMF). Most members of the United Nations, including the United States, belong to the IMF, which seeks to promote international monetary cooperation, stabilize currency exchange rates, and resolve balance of payments problems. Through a complex lending system, the IMF permits a country to borrow money necessary to maintain the stability of the currency relative to other currencies.

Free Trade Associations. Many nations have formed regional associations, commonly called free trade areas or customs unions, that eliminate duties and tariffs for imports from member countries. These associations are permitted under the WTO as an exception to the Most Favored Nation Clause. These regional associations include, for example, the European Union, the North American Free Trade Agreement, the Association of Southeast Asian Nations (ASEAN), and the Andean Community. Because of their importance to U.S. trade, the European Union and the North American Free Trade Agreement are discussed in more detail.

European Union. Political and economic instability in western European countries following World War II inspired various movements for western European unity to prevent another war among them and to accelerate economic revival. In 1952, a treaty among Belgium, the Federal Republic of Germany, France, Italy, Luxembourg, and the Netherlands created the European Coal and Steel Community (ECSC), which created a common market in these commodities. This action was followed in 1957 by the Treaty of Rome that created the European Economic Community (EEC) and the European Atomic Energy Community (Euratom). Collectively, these three agreements created the European Economic Community (also called the European Community (EC) or the European Common Market) composed of the original six members, Denmark, Greece, Ireland, Portugal, Spain, and the United Kingdom. In 1992, the EC countries signed the Treaty of European Union, or Maastricht Treaty, which created the European Union (EU) to unite the member nations politically and economically. When the treaty went into effect in November 1993, the EC became known as the EU. With the accession of ten countries in 2004, the European Union has expanded to 25 member states. Four other countries have applied for membership; two are expected to become members in 2007.

The EU has been very successful in eliminating trade barriers among its members. The markets for goods and services among member states are virtually free and open. The Treaty of European Union provides the groundwork for common foreign and defense policies and for an economic union. The European Central Bank, a central banking system similar to the U.S. Federal Reserve, is responsible for maintaining price stability and supporting the economic policies of the EU. The Euro, a common EU currency, was introduced in 1999 and has been the official currency in twelve EU countries since 2002. New member states are eligible to adopt the Euro only after meeting economic and financial criteria established by the EU.

The EU is structured according to the separation of powers. The European Commission, headed by a president, is the executive branch. The Council of the European Union, composed of one representative from each member state, is the principal legislative body. The Council shares legislative power with the European Parliament, elected directly by citizens of the member countries. The European Court of Justice serves as the judicial branch.

North American Free Trade Agreement. In 1992, the United States, Canada, and Mexico completed the North American Free Trade Agreement (NAFTA) which, following ratification by each nation's legislature, became effective in 1994. NAFTA establishes a plan to create a free trade area among its three members by eliminating tariffs and other trade restrictions over a 15-year period. The agreement further includes provisions designed to remove trade barriers for services and investments and to strengthen intellectual property protection.

In August 2005, the federal government approved the Central American–Dominican Republic Free Trade Agreement (CAFTA-DR). This free trade agreement, modeled on NAFTA, provides for elimination of trade barriers among the United States, five Central American countries (Costa Rica, El Salvador, Guatemala, Honduras, and Nicaragua), and the Dominican Republic.

Distribution of National Powers Over Foreign Affairs

Public international law governs the relationship among sovereign states. The following material examines how the power to address foreign affairs issues is distributed among the various branches of the U.S. government, and between the federal government and the states.

Regulation of Foreign Affairs

In the United States, a federal form of government, power to regulate internal affairs is divided by the Constitution between the federal government and the states. International law and U.S. constitutional law, however, regard the federal state rather than member states as the sovereign for purposes of conducting international relations.

Various constitutional provisions and Supreme Court opinions establish the primacy of the federal over the state governments in foreign affairs. For example, Article I, Section 8, Clause 3 of the Constitution vests in Congress the power "to regulate Commerce with foreign Nations." Both state and federal courts often have used this "Foreign Commerce Clause" to declare unconstitutional state and local laws that unduly burden international commerce or impermissibly interfere with congressional power to regulate foreign commerce.

The Supreme Court has noted that the Constitution in literal terms does not vest exclusive power over for-

eign affairs in the national government. Nevertheless, the Court has indicated that the power is inherently vested in the federal government as a necessary incident of nationality. As summarized by the Court in *United States v. Belmont* (1937):[3]

> [T]he external powers of the United States are to be exercised without regard to state laws or policies. . . . [C]omplete power over international affairs is in the national government and is not and cannot be subject to any curtailment or interference on the part of the several states.

In the external sphere occupied by the federal government, the president, the chief of the executive branch, is the constitutional representative of the United States. That is, the president generally is viewed as the sole agent of the nation regarding external relations and its sole representative with foreign nations.

The Treaty Power

In exercising power over foreign relations, the president commonly acts through treaties or executive agreements. Article 2, Section 2, Clause 2 of the U.S. Constitution (the Treaty Clause) provides that the president "shall have Power, by and with the Advice and Consent of the Senate to make Treaties, provided two-thirds of the Senators present concur." Some treaties, such as those requiring appropriation of money, require passage by both houses of Congress like ordinary federal legislation before they become effective. Most treaties are, however, "self-executing." That is, they require only approval by two-thirds of the Senate and presidential ratification to become part of judicially enforceable federal domestic law. Thus, in the United States, most treaties become part of national law and international law simultaneously.

International accords also are made by executive agreement. Executive agreements require no approval of either house of Congress to become law. Although executive agreements are not explicitly mentioned in the Constitution, courts have upheld them as authorized either by an implied delegation of congressional authority over foreign commerce or as an inherent executive power. Because it is simpler and quicker, the executive agreement has become an increasingly popular tool of international

---

[3]57 S. Ct. 758, 761 (1937).

accord. For example, between 1946 and 1972, executive agreements outnumbered treaties by 5,590 to 368.[4]

Relationship of Treaties to Other National Law. Under the Supremacy Clause, contained in Article VI of the Constitution, the federal Constitution, federal statutes, and treaties are the supreme law of the land, and therefore supercede any inconsistent state law.[5] The relationship between a treaty and other federal law is more trouble-some. Although a treaty supercedes a prior inconsistent federal statute, Congress may effectively repeal or modify a treaty commitment by a statute enacted after the treaty. As noted by one court, "Under our constitutional scheme, Congress can denounce treaties if it sees fit to do so, and there is nothing the other branches of government can do about it."[6] Such a treaty termination or modification may, of course, be a violation of international law.

Although federal statutes and treaties enjoy relatively equal status in the hierarchy of federal law, it is clear that treaties, like federal statutes, may not violate the Constitution. As noted by the Supreme Court:

> The United States is entirely a creature of the Constitution. Its power and authority have no other source. It can only act in accordance with all the limitations imposed by the Constitution. . . . [N]o agreement with a foreign nation can confer power on the Congress, or on any other branch of Government, which is free from the restraints of the Constitution. . . .[7]

National Courts in the International Setting

International law should be distinguished from an individual state's internal law, also known as its "national," "municipal," or "local" law. A country's national law may affect various aspects of international relations, though the extraterritorial effect of one country's law is necessarily limited by the sovereignty of other countries. For example, almost every country has developed a system of **private international law,** a branch of conflicts of law that determines (1) when a domestic court should exercise jurisdiction over a case involving foreign persons or territories, (2) when foreign rather than

domestic law should apply to a case, and (3) when judgments rendered by foreign courts should be recognized and enforced in a domestic court.

To this point, this chapter has examined the nature and sources of international law, the law governing relations among states, and the distribution of government power within the United States over foreign affairs. The following material examines some of the legal issues presented when a municipal or national court tries a case involving a foreign country or its agencies, foreign citizens, or events occurring beyond national boundaries.

Jurisdiction of National Courts

As noted in Chapter 1, the term "jurisdiction" refers to the power of a court to hear and render a binding judgment in a case. In the international context, the term refers to the capacity of a state to prescribe or to enforce a rule of law.[8] If the persons, property, or events involved touch more than one country, the appropriate jurisdiction of a given nation's courts must be determined. Generally, jurisdiction of a national court is determined by national law, subject to a few restrictions imposed by international law. That is, international law seldom requires a court to hear a case, but instead is concerned with the limits upon individual state discretion.

Criminal Cases. In determining national court jurisdiction, criminal and civil cases must be distinguished. A number of international law theories have been developed to define the criminal jurisdiction of a country's courts. In criminal cases, every country enjoys jurisdiction over crimes committed within its territory (a territorial principle) and over crimes committed by its own citizens anywhere in the world (a nationality principle). Other, less widely accepted bases of criminal jurisdiction include the "protective" principle (allowing a state to punish acts injurious to its security, even when committed by foreigners abroad), the "passive personality" principle (allowing jurisdiction based upon the nationality of the persons injured), and the "universality" principle (allowing jurisdiction over all crimes, even crimes committed by foreigners abroad if the wrong-doer is arrested within the prosecuting state).

Whatever the basis of jurisdiction, the criminal defendant must be brought before the courts of the country asserting jurisdiction. A defendant who has

---

[4]STEINER & VAGTS, TRANSNATIONAL LEGAL PROBLEMS 611 (3d ed. 1986).

[5]The Supremacy Clause is introduced in Chapter 1.

[6]Diggs v. Schultz, 470 F.2d 461, 466 (D.C. Cir. 1972).

[7]Reid v. Covert, 77 S. Ct. 1222, 1225, 1230 (1957).

[8]RESTATEMENT (SECOND) OF FOREIGN RELATIONS LAW OF THE UNITED STATES §6.

taken refuge in another country must be extradited. Generally, a country has no duty to extradite criminal defendants to other countries in absence of treaty. Though many extradition treaties are in force, deportation has become a common substitute for extradition.

Civil Cases. Unlike criminal law, international law imposes few restrictions upon jurisdiction of national courts in civil cases. Various theories of national law, however, limit the reach of a country's courts in civil litigation. For example, the doctrines of sovereign immunity and act of state discussed later in this chapter, are national law theories that limit the civil jurisdiction of a nation's courts. In addition, courts often are hesitant to take jurisdiction and impose local law upon conduct occurring at least in part outside the territorial limits of their country. Attempts by a nation to apply its law outside its borders create resentment in other countries, which regard the attempt as an unwarranted and illegal intrusion into their sovereignty.

Perhaps the most controversy in this area has arisen regarding judicial attempts to apply U.S. antitrust law extraterritorially. Although courts have long held that the place or location of anticompetitive *effects* (as opposed to the conduct) determines whether U.S. antitrust law applies to a given transaction,[9] they have articulated different formulations of the nature and amount of effects needed. To eliminate this uncertainty, Congress enacted the Foreign Trade Antitrust Improvements Act[10] in 1982, which provides that U.S. antitrust law applies to foreign business transactions only when the conduct giving rise to the claim has a "direct, substantial, and reasonably foreseeable" anticompetitive effect on the domestic, import, or export commerce of the United States. Anticompetitive conduct lacking the required domestic effect is exempt even if it originates in the United States or involves American-owned businesses operating abroad.

International Civil Dispute Resolution

Unlike criminal law, which is designed to punish socially harmful conduct, the civil law is remedial in nature, designed to resolve disputes between private individuals, corporations, or other entities. If all parties are located within a single country, the problems presented are matters of national law (state or federal) resolved in national courts. If, however, one or more parties is a foreign citizen, property is located in a foreign country, or events occur abroad, a myriad of additional problems arise. For example, assume B, a New York retailer, wishes to buy $500,000 worth of perfume from S, a manufacturer located in Paris, France. Even if no dispute arises, factors not present in domestic transactions must be considered. For example, the parties must consider the tariff, import-export, and currency regulations of both countries to arrange for payment for the goods. If a dispute arises (for example, the goods shipped are defective), other issues arise including what country's law applies, how the dispute will be resolved, and the location of the forum. In international transactions, the parties often resolve these issues expressly in their original contract.

International Arbitration. Because of uncertainty regarding substantive and procedural laws of the various nations, arbitration provisions are a popular method of dispute resolution in international business transactions. A contractual arbitration provision may provide for the creation of a panel of members representing each party concerned or may refer the dispute to a neutral international organization such as the International Chamber of Commerce. Enforcement of contractual arbitration clauses is facilitated by provisions of individual treaties of friendship, commerce, and navigation, and by the United Nations Convention on the Recognition and Enforcement of Foreign Arbitral Awards, which has been implemented in over 50 countries, including the United States.[11]

If the contract contains no arbitration provision, disputes are likely to result in litigation. To eliminate uncertainty regarding the proper court for resolution of the dispute and the law to be applied in that court, the contract may include a "choice of forum" or "choice of law" clause. A choice of forum clause enables the parties to specify in advance which country's courts shall hear disputes. Such clauses, if reasonable, generally are enforceable in most countries. A choice of law clause specifies which country's law is to be applied to a prospective dispute. Most nations enforce a choice of law clause if the body of law specified bears a substantial relationship to the parties and the transaction.

Note that each country's body of law generally includes choice of law rules determining which country's

---

[9]United States v. Aluminum Co. of America, 148 F.2d 416, 443–444 (2d Cir. 1945).

[10]15 U.S.C. §§6a, 45(a)(3).

[11]9 U.S.C. §201 *et seq.*

substantive law is to apply to an international dispute. That is, the forum country may be directed by its own law to apply another country's law to a particular transaction. Thus, in the absence of choice of forum and choice of law provisions in the contract, legal proceedings in two or more countries may result, with each court applying its own choice of law rules to determine the applicable body of substantive law.

Recognition and Enforcement of Foreign Judgments. Assume Seller, a citizen of France, sues Buyer, a citizen of the United States, in a French court for breach of contract. If the court renders a judgment in favor of Seller, Seller may attempt to enforce the judgment in the United States to reach assets owned by Buyer there. In the United States, courts generally enforce foreign judgments based on comity (courtesy or deference to the foreign court), provided no strong public policy is violated. The fairness of the trial, the voluntary appearance of the defendant, and lack of prejudice or fraud are factors favoring enforcement of foreign judgments.[12] Other legal systems enforce foreign judgments in varying circumstances, but generally are not as accommodating as the United States. Various bilateral and multilateral treaties and regional conventions now address the issue and have somewhat increased the enforceability of foreign judgments.[13]

United Nations Convention for International Sales. In October 1986, the U.S. Senate unanimously ratified the 1980 United Nations Convention on Contracts for the International Sale of Goods (CISG), which became effective among the initial contracting states on January 1, 1988. The CISG, which applies in the absence of contrary agreement by the parties, states substantive rules governing formation of international sales contracts, and the rights and duties of the buyer and seller. It is designed to minimize conflicts of law problems in international sales transactions and to provide a basis for settling issues that the parties have not resolved by contract. As of 2001, the CISG, which more closely resembles Article 2 of the Uniform Commercial Code than any foreign sales law, had been ratified in 58 countries.

---

[12]Hilton v. Guyot, 16 S. Ct. 139 (1895).

[13]Note that enforcement of sister-state judgments within the United States is guaranteed by the Full Faith and Credit Clause of the Constitution, discussed in Chapter 2.

Treatment of Foreign Nationals and Their Property

Potential civil disputes with foreign citizens are not the only risk of international transactions. Individuals or business entities living, investing, or transacting business in a foreign country may be injured by acts of the foreign sovereign itself. Nationalistic trends in developing countries resulting from colonialism and perceived economic imperialism have long created concern among western governments over the security of the person and property of nationals operating abroad. Not surprisingly, the western view regarding treatment of aliens and their property differs somewhat from that embraced by the developing countries. Note that the host state's duties are owed not to the injured alien but to the alien's sovereign, which makes a claim through diplomatic channels for compensation or other remedy. Disputes that cannot be settled by negotiation may, if the parties consent, be referred to arbitration or to an international tribunal.

Protection of the Person

A person who resides or acquires property in a foreign country is subject to the laws or customs of that country. The United States and western European countries have long asserted, however, that a claim against the host country may be justified if the foreign state's laws or conduct falls below a "minimum international standard." Although the elements of such a standard are disputed, it might include a prohibition against torturing or wrongfully killing or imprisoning the alien, looting or destroying his property, or maintaining excessively severe or unfair procedures or punishments.

In contrast, other states—including a number of Latin American, South American, Asian, and African countries—reject any minimum international standard, opting instead for a "national standard." Under this theory, aliens who establish themselves in a foreign country are entitled to the same rights of protection as nationals, but no more. Aliens are thus entitled to nondiscriminatory treatment, but otherwise consent to be treated as nationals.

Expropriation

In addition to protecting its citizens abroad, a country also has a significant stake in safeguarding the property and investments of its nationals in foreign countries. Although foreign investment takes many forms, foreign direct investment has had the greatest impact. Direct investment creates a sufficient ownership interest in a foreign asset or enterprise (usually 25 percent or more) to provide a significant degree of control.

The most important vehicle for foreign direct investment is the multinational corporation. Such enterprises engage in business activities that traverse national borders and take a variety of forms. A multinational corporation may initially export goods to markets abroad, then establish foreign sales organizations, and finally create foreign manufacturing facilities. Wholly owned subsidiaries of the multinational parent often are used to oversee foreign operations.

Foreign direct investment poses significant risks, the most important of which is the risk of **nationalization,** the forced taking of the foreign assets by the host government. This power has been exercised more than 260 times in the last 30 years. Nationalism and resentment against foreign exploitation have, among other factors, prompted these actions. Although investment nationalizations primarily have occurred in underdeveloped countries whose economies are dominated by foreign corporations, western nations such as Canada and England also have nationalized commercial enterprises.

Legal Standard Governing Nationalization. International law generally recognizes a sovereign's right to nationalize foreign investments to promote the national welfare. The power generally is recognized as an incident of a state's sovereignty over its national resources and economic activities.[14] A taking in accordance with national law is known as an **expropriation;** an unlawful taking is a **confiscation.**

Western countries have long asserted the existence of a two-fold minimum international standard governing expropriation based upon customary international law. Under this standard, a lawful taking (1) must be for a "public purpose," and (2) must be accompanied by payment of "just compensation" or "prompt, adequate and effective compensation" for the investor's loss.[15] In contrast, some countries take the position that international law imposes no legal obligation to pay compensation upon taking of a foreign investor's property.

Other countries take a middle position asserting that existence of a public purpose is an issue decided solely by the taking state and that any compensation payable is determined by all surrounding circumstances including the economic and political priorities of the taking state.

Disputes between states over expropriated property generally are settled by compromise, with the expropriating state paying part of the value of the property taken. The compromise payment usually covers all claims made by one state arising out of another's nationalization program. Customary international law generally imposes no duty upon a state to pursue expropriation claims of its nationals or to remit any recovery to the injured investors. Nevertheless, money received under such a blanket settlement, which usually represents only a fraction of the taken property's value, usually is distributed to former owners through an administrative tribunal, known in the United States as the Foreign Claims Settlement Commission.

Investment Protection. In order to attract new investment to developing countries, both developed and developing countries have taken steps to protect foreign investment. For example, many developing countries have constitutional provisions or statutes prohibiting expropriation for a stated period or guaranteeing a right to compensation. More important, a number of developing countries have entered into treaties with western nations including similar guarantees, which provide much greater certainty than customary international principles.

The United States, the United Kingdom, and other western countries also encourage foreign investment by insuring their nationals, for a premium, against certain political and other risks. In the United States, for example, insurance is available through the Overseas Private Investment Corporation (OPIC),[16] an agency of the United States under the policy guidance of the secretary of state. OPIC insures citizens of the United States and business entities substantially owned by United States citizens against losses and business interruption caused by (1) a foreign government prohibiting conversion of foreign earnings into dollars or prohibiting repatriation of investor capital, (2) expropriation or confiscation of assets including wrongful repudiation by the host government of its own contracts with the

---

[14]United Nations General Assembly Resolution 3201 (1974).

[15]This standard is similar to that governing exercise of eminent domain power in the United States, discussed in Chapter 38.

[16]22 U.S.C. §2191 *et seq.*

investor, and (3) war, revolution, insurrection, and civil strife.[17] An investor is charged an annual premium for OPIC insurance based upon the value of the investment and the type of risk (inconvertibility, expropriation, or war) covered. In addition to government insurance agencies such as OPIC, private insurers substantially are engaged in insuring a wide variety of international investment risks.

National Courts and Foreign Sovereignty

An investor who suffers an investment loss because of the act of a host state may attempt to recover through private civil litigation maintained in another country. Two legal theories, the doctrines of "sovereign immunity" and "act of state," may prevent or limit such litigation.

Sovereign Immunity

Sovereign immunity is a doctrine of international law under which domestic courts, in certain circumstances, will not exercise jurisdiction over a foreign state or its instrumentalities. The doctrine in the United States and elsewhere developed as a matter of grace or comity to promote good international relations. Traditionally, foreign sovereigns enjoyed complete immunity from suits in U.S. courts. This rule of "absolute immunity" is still followed by many countries. In 1952, however, the State Department in the so-called Tate Letter adopted the "restrictive" or "qualified" theory of foreign sovereign immunity that also is accepted by a majority of western European states. Under this theory, "immunity is confined to suits involving the foreign sovereign's public acts, and does not extend to cases arising out of a foreign state's strictly commercial acts."[18]

This theory is now codified as a matter of federal law in the **Foreign Sovereign Immunities Act of 1976 (FSIA).**[19] The Act contains the legal standards governing claims of immunity in civil actions against a foreign state or its political subdivisions, agencies, or instrumentalities. The Act provides that a foreign state normally is immune from the jurisdiction of

state and federal courts, subject to specified exceptions. These exceptions include, for example, (1) actions in which the foreign state has waived its immunity, (2) actions based upon the commercial activities of the foreign sovereign carried on in the United States, and (3) actions based upon the commercial activities of the foreign sovereign carried on outside the United States that cause a direct effect in the United States. If an exception applies, the foreign state may be sued in U.S. courts in the same manner and to the same extent as a private individual in the circumstances. Although cases may be maintained either in federal or state court, the sovereign defendant has the right to remove any civil action from a state to a federal court.

The governmental-commercial distinction embraced by the restrictive immunity approach is based upon the appropriateness of local court involvement in the dispute. Acts that can be performed only by states, such as expropriating property, involve sensitive international political issues, which should not be relegated to local courts for determination. In contrast, commercial activity, such as making contracts to purchase building materials, can and are performed both by states and individuals. In this context, the state is no different from any private litigant, and local courts are fully suited to resolve such disputes. In addition, refusal by local courts to hear such cases would impose needless hardship on the other party, who would be left without an effective remedy.

In determining which acts are commercial and which are governmental, the Act states that "commercial activity" means either a regular course of commercial conduct or a particular commercial transaction or act. A commercial activity is one that an individual might carry on for profit, and is determined by the nature of the transaction or course of conduct rather than its purpose.[20]

At issue in the following case was whether a foreign sovereign should be subject to suit in the United States under the commercial activity exception of the FSIA.

Republic of Argentina v. Weltover, Inc.
112 S. Ct. 2160 (1992)

The petitioners, the Republic of Argentina and its central bank Banco Central, issued bonds called "Bonods" in an

---

[17]22 U.S.C. §2194.

[18]Verlinden B.V. v. Central Bank of Nigeria, 103 S. Ct. 1962, 1968 (1983).

[19]28 U.S.C. §§1602–1611.

[20]28 U.S.C. §1603(d).

effort to stabilize the Argentinean currency. The Bonods were designed to refinance debts owed to foreign creditors that Argentina had incurred as part of a previous effort to stabilize its currency. The bonds provided for payment of principal and interest in U.S. dollars at institutions in Frankfurt, Zurich, or New York as selected by the creditor on the maturity date. When the Bonods began to mature, however, Argentina lacked the funds to retire them and unilaterally extended the time for payment. Respondents, two Panamanian corporations and a Swiss bank, refused to accept the time extension and demanded payment of their debts in New York. When Argentina failed to pay, the respondents brought suit for breach of contract in a New York federal district court. Argentina claimed that, as a sovereign nation, it was immune from suit in the United States but respondents asserted jurisdiction under §1605(a)(2) of the Foreign Sovereign Immunities Act. That statute provides, in part, that a foreign state is not immune from suit in the United States in any case based on "an act outside the territory of the United States in connection with a commercial activity of the foreign state elsewhere and that act causes a direct effect in the United States." After both the trial court and court of appeals ruled that Argentina was subject to suit in the United States, Argentina appealed to the Supreme Court.

Justice Scalia

. . . The Foreign Sovereign Immunities Act of 1976 . . . (FSIA) establishes a comprehensive framework for determining whether a court in this country, state or federal, may exercise jurisdiction over a foreign state. Under the Act, a "foreign state *shall* be immune from the jurisdiction of the courts of the United States and of the States" unless one of several statutorily defined exceptions applies. §1604 (emphasis added). The FSIA thus provides the "sole basis" for obtaining jurisdiction over a foreign sovereign in the United States. . . . The most significant of the FSIA's exceptions—and the one at issue in this case—is the "commercial" exception of §1605(a)(2). . . .

[O]ur analysis is . . . limited to considering whether this lawsuit is (1) "based . . . upon an act outside the territory of the United States"; (2) that was taken "in connection with a commercial activity" of Argentina outside this country; and (3) that "cause[d] a direct effect in the United States." . . . The fact that the cause of action is in compliance with the first of the three requirements—that it is "based upon an act outside the territory of the United States" (presumably Argentina's unilateral extension)—is uncontested. The dispute pertains to whether the unilateral refinancing of the Bonods was taken "in connection with a commercial activity" of

Argentina, and whether it had a "direct effect in the United States." We address these issues in turn. . . .

[W]e conclude that when a foreign government acts, not as regulator of a market, but in the manner of a private player within it, the foreign sovereign's actions are "commercial" within the meaning of the FSIA. Moreover, because the Act provides that the commercial character of an act is to be determined by reference to its "nature" rather than its "purpose," . . . the question is not whether the foreign government is acting with a profit motive or instead with the aim of fulfilling uniquely sovereign objectives. Rather, the issue is whether the particular actions that the foreign state performs (whatever the motive behind them) are the *type* of actions by which a private party engages in "trade and traffic or commerce. . . ." Thus, a foreign government's issuance of regulations limiting foreign currency exchange is a sovereign activity, because such authoritative control of commerce cannot be exercised by a private party; whereas a contract to buy army boots or even bullets is a "commercial" activity, because private companies can similarly use sales contracts to acquire goods. . . .

The commercial character of the Bonods is confirmed by the fact that they are in almost all respects garden-variety debt instruments: they may be held by private parties; they are negotiable and may be traded on the international market (except in Argentina); and they promise a future stream of cash income. . . . Argentina argues that the Bonods differ from ordinary debt instruments in that they "were created by the Argentine Government to fulfill its obligations under a foreign exchange program, designed to address a domestic credit crisis, and as a component of a program designed to control that nation's critical shortage of foreign exchange." . . . We agree with the Court of Appeals . . . that it is irrelevant *why* Argentina participated in the bond market in the manner of a private actor; it matters only that it did so. We conclude that Argentina's issuance of the Bonods was a "commercial activity" under the FSIA.

The remaining question is whether Argentina's unilateral rescheduling of the Bonods had a "direct effect" in the United States. . . . We . . . have little difficulty concluding that Argentina's unilateral rescheduling of the maturity dates on the Bonods had a "direct effect" in the United States. Respondents had designated their accounts in New York as the place of payment, and Argentina made some interest payments into those accounts before announcing that it was rescheduling the payments. Because New York was thus the place of performance for Argentina's ultimate contractual obligations, the rescheduling of those obligations necessarily had a "direct effect" in the United States: Money that was supposed to have been delivered to a New York bank for deposit was not forthcoming. . . .

We conclude that Argentina's issuance of the Bonods was a "commercial activity" under the FSIA; that its rescheduling of the maturity dates on those instruments was taken in connection with that commercial activity and had a "direct effect" in the United States; and that the District Court therefore properly asserted jurisdiction, under the FSIA, over the breach-of-contract claims based on that rescheduling. . . .

[Judgment affirmed.]

The Act of State Doctrine

The **act of state doctrine,** like sovereign immunity, is a principle of judicial restraint designed in part to prevent the judiciary from embarrassing and interfering with the executive in the conduct of foreign affairs. The doctrine prevents the courts of one state from challenging the validity of public acts that a recognized foreign sovereign commits within its own territory. Unlike sovereign immunity (which applies when a person seeks to make the state a *party* to the litigation), the act of state doctrine often applies in suits between two private litigants in which action taken by a state is relevant. If applicable, it prevents a court from finding state action invalid, thus protecting a party who bases a claim or defense upon actions of a foreign state. For example, assume State X expropriates without compensation property belonging to Doaks, a citizen of State Y. The expropriation is the act of state. Subsequently, State X sells the expropriated property to Jones, a citizen of State Y. Doaks sues Jones and State X in State Y to recover the property or its value. If applicable, the act of state doctrine would provide a defense to Jones and State X to Doaks's claim. State X, of course, also may assert the doctrine of sovereign immunity.

At issue in the following case was whether a private lawsuit should be barred by the act of state doctrine.

W. S. Kirkpatrick & Co., Inc. v. Environmental Tectonics Corporation, International
110 S. Ct. 701 (1990)

Petitioner W. S. Kirkpatrick & Co., Inc. (Kirkpatrick) and respondent Environmental Tectonics Corporation, International (ETC) competed to secure a contract with the government of Nigeria for a construction project at a Nigerian air force base. After paying bribes to Nigerian government officials, Kirkpatrick was awarded the contract. Payment and receipt of the bribes were illegal under Nigerian law. Following an investigation by the Federal Bureau of Investigation, Kirkpatrick and its chief executive officer were charged with and pleaded guilty to violations of the Foreign Corrupt Practices Act. ETC then sued Kirkpatrick and its chief executive officer seeking damages under U.S. antitrust and racketeering statutes. The trial court dismissed the suit on the ground that it was barred by the act of state doctrine because the suit "would result in embarrassment to the sovereign [Nigeria] or constitute interference in the conduct of foreign policy of the United States." The court noted that to win the suit, ETC would have to prove that the Nigerian government or its officials received bribes that influenced their decision to award the contract to Kirkpatrick. The Court of Appeals reversed, holding that the act of state doctrine did not bar the suit. The U.S. Supreme Court granted Kirkpatrick's petition for review.

Justice Scalia

In this case we must decide whether the act of state doctrine bars a court in the United States from entertaining a cause of action that does not rest upon the asserted invalidity of an official act of a foreign sovereign, but that does require imputing to foreign officials an unlawful motivation (the obtaining of bribes) in the performance of such an official act. . . .

This Court's description of the jurisprudential foundation for the act of state doctrine has undergone some evolution over the years. We once viewed the doctrine as an expression of international law, resting upon "the highest considerations of international comity and expediency," *Oetjen v. Central Leather Co.,* [38 S. Ct. 309, 311 (1918)]. We have more recently described it, however, as a consequence of domestic separation of powers, reflecting "the strong sense of the Judicial Branch that its engagement in the task of passing on the validity of foreign acts of state may hinder" the conduct of foreign affairs, *Banco Nacional de Cuba v. Sabbatino,* [84 S. Ct. 923, 937 (1964)]. . . .

The parties have argued at length . . . about whether the purpose of the act of state doctrine would be furthered by its application in this case. We find it unnecessary, however, to pursue those inquiries, since the factual predicate for application of the act of state doctrine does not exist. Nothing in the present suit requires the Court to declare invalid, and thus ineffective . . . the official act of a foreign sovereign.

In every case in which we have held the act of state doctrine applicable, the relief sought or the defense interposed would have required a court in the United States to declare invalid the official act of a foreign sovereign performed within its own territory. In *Underhill v. Hernandez,* [18 S. Ct. 83, 85 (1897)], holding the defendant's detention of the plaintiff to be tortious would have required denying legal effect to "acts of a military commander representing the authority of the revolutionary party as government, which afterwards succeeded and was recognized by the United States." In *Oetjen,* . . . denying title to the party who claimed through purchase from Mexico would have required declaring that government's prior seizure of the property, within its own territory, legally ineffective. . . . In *Sabbatino,* upholding the defendant's claim to the funds would have required a holding that Cuba's expropriation of goods located in Havana was null and void. In the present case, by contrast, neither the claim nor any asserted defense requires a determination that Nigeria's contract with Kirkpatrick International was, or was not, effective.

Petitioners point out, however, that the facts necessary to establish respondent's claim will also establish that the contract was unlawful. Specifically, they note that in order to prevail respondent must prove that petitioner Kirkpatrick made, and Nigerian officials received, payments that violate Nigerian law, which would, they assert, support a finding that the contract is invalid under Nigerian law. Assuming that to be true, it still does not suffice. . . . Act of state issues only arise when a court *must decide* — that is, when the outcome of the case turns upon — the effect of official action by a foreign sovereign. When that question is not in the case, neither is the act of state doctrine. That is the situation here. Regardless of what the court's factual findings may suggest as to the legality of the Nigerian contract, its legality is simply not a question to be decided in the present suit, and there is thus no occasion to apply the rule of decision that the act of state doctrine requires. . . .

Petitioners insist, however, that the policies underlying our act of state cases — international comity, respect for the sovereignty of foreign nations on their own territory, and the avoidance of embarrassment to the Executive Branch in its conduct of foreign relations — are implicated in the present case because, as the District Court found, a determination that Nigerian officials demanded and accepted a bribe "would impugn or question the nobility of a foreign nation's motivations," and would "result in embarrassment to the sovereign or constitute interference in the conduct of foreign policy of the United States." . . . The United States, as *amicus curiae,* favors the same approach to the act of state doctrine, though disagreeing with petitioners as to the outcome it produces in the present case. We should not, the United States urges, "attach dispositive significance to the fact that this suit involves only the 'motivation' for, rather than the 'validity' of, a foreign sovereign act," . . . and should eschew "any rigid formula for the resolution of act of state cases generally." . . . In some future case, perhaps, "litigation . . . based on alleged corruption in the award of contracts or other commercially oriented activities of foreign governments could sufficiently touch on 'national nerves' that the act of state doctrine or related principles of abstention would appropriately be found to bar the suit." . . .

These urgings are deceptively similar to what we said in *Sabbatino,* where we observed that sometimes, even though the validity of the act of a foreign sovereign within its own territory is called into question, the policies underlying the act of state doctrine may not justify its application. . . . But what is appropriate in order to avoid unquestioning judicial acceptance of the acts of foreign sovereigns is not similarly appropriate for the quite opposite purpose of expanding judicial incapacities where such acts are not directly (or even indirectly) involved. . . .

The short of the matter is this: Courts in the United States have the power, and ordinarily the obligation, to decide cases and controversies properly presented to them. The act of state doctrine does not establish an exception for cases and controversies that may embarrass foreign governments, but merely requires that, in the process of deciding, the acts of foreign sovereigns taken within their own jurisdictions shall be deemed valid. That doctrine has no application to the present case because the validity of no foreign sovereign act is at issue. . . .

[Judgment affirmed.]

Summary

1. International law is the system of law governing the relationship among states. Unlike a state's internal or national law, which may be enforced in an obligatory judicial forum whose judgments are enforceable by executive authority, international law is characterized by lack of binding sanctions.

2. International law is derived primarily from (1) treaties, (2) custom, (3) general principles of law, and (4) judicial decisions and writing of legal commentators.

3. International organizations created by treaty serve important functions in international affairs, including peacekeeping and regulation and development of economic and commercial activities. Some important international organizations include the United Nations (including its judicial arm, the International Court of Justice), the World Trade Organization, and free trade associations such as the European Union and the North American Free Trade Agreement.

4. In the United States, power to regulate foreign commerce and conduct foreign affairs rests exclusively with the federal government, not the states. In this external sphere the president, the chief of the executive branch, is the representative of the United States.

5. In conducting foreign affairs, the president commonly acts through treaties or executive agreements. Although treaties must be approved by a two-thirds vote of the Senate, executive agreements require no Senate approval. Although treaties enjoy a status equal to federal statutes (and thus take priority over inconsistent state legislation), treaties must comply with the provisions of the U.S. Constitution.

6. A national court may be presented with a case involving foreign citizens or property or events occurring in a foreign country. Various theories of international and national law operate to limit the jurisdiction of national courts in criminal and civil cases.

7. Because of uncertainty regarding the substantive and procedural laws of various countries and doubt regarding enforceability of foreign judgments, parties to international business transactions often use contractual provisions to govern any disputes arising out of their agreement. Common examples are arbitration, choice of forum, and choice of law clauses.

8. Individuals or business entities living or investing abroad may be harmed by acts of the foreign government. Although a foreign national living abroad is subject to foreign law, western states have long asserted that treatment of aliens must

meet a "minimum international standard." In contrast, other countries assert that a "national" standard is appropriate under which aliens are entitled to the same rights of protection as nationals, but no more.

9. In addition to protecting its citizens abroad, a country also has a stake in safeguarding property and investments of its nationals in foreign countries. Nevertheless, international law generally recognizes a sovereign's right to nationalize or expropriate foreign investment to promote the national welfare. Western countries assert that international law requires that any taking (1) must be for a public purpose, and (2) must be accompanied by prompt and just compensation of the owner. Other countries impose a more limited legal obligation upon the expropriating country. The expropriation risk may be reduced by treaty or by private or public insurance.

10. A private litigant may attempt to sue a foreign state or question an act of a foreign state in a national court. The national court may refuse to exercise jurisdiction in such a case under the doctrines of "sovereign immunity" or "act of state." These doctrines are designed in part to prevent the judiciary from embarrassing and interfering with the executive in the conduct of foreign affairs.

Key Terms

international law	sovereign immunity
treaty	Foreign Sovereign
private international law	Immunities Act of 1976
nationalization	(FSIA)
expropriation	act of state doctrine
confiscation	

Questions and Problems

58.1 The California Buy American Act requires that contracts for the construction of public works or the purchase of materials for public use be awarded only to persons who will agree to use or supply materials that have been manufactured in the United States. Ducommun, Inc. submitted a bid to the city of Los Angeles for steel beams to be used in constructing a bridge. Though Ducommun's bid was lowest, the city rejected it because it was based upon steel to be manufactured in Japan. Ducommun sued the city alleging that the statute is unconstitutional. What is the basis of Ducommun's claim? Should Ducommun prevail?

58.2 Asakura, a Japanese citizen, resides in Seattle, Washington, and has been engaged in business there as a pawnbroker since 1985. In 1995, the city passed an ordinance requiring licensing of pawnbrokers and providing that "no license shall be granted unless the applicant is a citizen of the United States." A treaty between the United States and Japan provides that "The citizens or subjects of each of the high contracting parties shall have liberty to enter, travel and reside in the territories of the other to carry on trade, . . . and generally to do anything incident to or necessary for trade upon the same terms as native citizens or subjects, submitting themselves to the laws and regulations there established." Does the statute violate the treaty? If so, should it be invalidated? On what grounds?

58.3 Sumitomo Shoji America, Inc., is a New York corporation and a wholly owned subsidiary of a Japanese general trading company. Lisa Avagliano, a secretarial employee of Sumitomo and a U.S. citizen, sued Sumitomo in federal district court, claiming that its alleged practice of hiring only male Japanese citizens to fill executive, managerial, and sales positions violated Title VII of the Civil Rights Act of 1964. Sumitomo moved to dismiss the complaint on the ground that its practices were protected under Article VIII(1) of the Friendship, Commerce and Navigation Treaty between the United States and Japan. Article VIII(1) provides that the "companies of either Party shall be permitted to engage, within the territories of the other Party, accountants and other technical experts, executive personnel, attorneys, agents and other specialists of their choice." The primary purpose of the provision was to give corporations of each signatory legal status in the territory of the other party and to allow them to conduct business in the other country on a comparable basis with domestic firms. Should the district court dismiss the complaint? Explain.

58.4 A French merchant ship collided with a Turkish merchant ship on the high seas. The Turkish ship sank and several Turkish citizens were drowned. The accident was caused by criminal negligence of Lieutenant Demons, an officer on the French ship. When the French ship docked in Turkey, Turkish police arrested him. Does France have jurisdiction to try Lieutenant Demons? On what basis? Does Turkey have jurisdiction to try Lieutenant Demons? On what basis? Does the United States have jurisdiction to try Lieutenant Demons? On what basis?

58.5 Nigeria and Ipitrade International entered into a written commercial contract for the purchase and sale of cement. By entering into the contract, Nigeria expressly agreed that the construction, validity, and performance of the contract would be governed by the laws of Switzerland and that any disputes arising under the contract would be submitted to arbitration by the International Chamber of Commerce, Paris, France. Subsequently, various disputes arose with respect to the contract and Ipitrade filed a demand for arbitration with the Secretariat of the Court of Arbitration of the International Chamber of Commerce. Thereafter, an arbitration proceeding was conducted in which the Federal Republic of Nigeria refused to participate, relying on the legal defense of sovereign immunity. Is Nigeria correct? Explain.

58.6 The Shanghai-Nanking Railway Administration, an official agency of the Republic of China, established a $200,000 bank account in National City Bank of New York. Subsequently, China sought to withdraw the funds but National refused to pay. China sued National in U.S. federal district court to recover the money. National asserted a counterclaim against China seeking a judgment for $1.6 million on defaulted treasury notes issued by China owned by the bank. China asserted that it was immune from suit on the counterclaim under principles of sovereign immunity. Is China correct?

58.7 During the early 1900s, American corporations acquired interests in copper properties in Chile. By the early 1970s, two companies—the Anaconda Company and Kennecott Copper Corporation—held vast stakes in these properties. In 1971, the Chilean government expropriated the mining assets of both companies. In computing the compensation due Kennecott, Chile contended that compensation need be paid only for plant and equipment taken, not for the vast mineral deposits in place. President Salvadore Allende, however, subsequently determined that "excess profits" previously withdrawn by Kennecott offset any compensation that might otherwise have been paid to Kennecott on account of the nationalization. Kennecott then filed suit in five European countries against various buyers of Chilean copper, requesting that the court order the buyers to pay amounts owed for the copper to Kennecott rather than the Chilean government. What factors should the European courts consider in determining whether to grant Kennecott's request? Should Kennecott prevail?

TECHNOLOGY LAW

This chapter explores the role of American law in regulating technological development. Businesses depend on technology to create and improve the products and processes needed for success. The pervasive influence of computer and information technology has heightened awareness of technology's importance to commercial growth, but technology has been an integral part of American business since the nineteenth century when technological developments fueled tremendous industrial growth. The law governing technology today, therefore, is built on a foundation of legal principles developed over the last 200 years.

Most of the law governing technology is federal. The drafters of the Constitution, recognizing the importance of invention and commerce to national growth, granted broad powers to Congress in these areas. As technology has become increasingly significant in the international marketplace, the federal government also has exercised its treaty power to ratify numerous treaties affecting regulation of technology.

This chapter discusses the legal regulation of patents, trade secrets, copyrights, and trademarks traditionally described as intellectual property law. The chapter then examines legal issues specific to information and computer technology, including regulation of the Internet and e-commerce.

Intellectual Property

Article I, Section 8, Clause 8 of the Constitution grants Congress the power "to promote the Progress of Science and Useful Arts, by securing for limited Times to Authors and Inventors the exclusive Right to their respective Writings and Discoveries." Using this power, Congress has enacted the Patent Act[1] and the Copyright Act.[2] Under its power to regulate interstate commerce, Congress also has adopted the Trademark Act, commonly

---

[1] 35 U.S.C. §1 et seq.
[2] 17 U.S.C. §101 et seq.

known as the Lanham Act.[3] These three areas of federal law—patents, copyrights, and trademarks—as well as state law of trade secrets, regulate **intellectual property,** a form of intangible property that results from creativity and invention.

The law of intellectual property demonstrates a continuing struggle to reconcile two sometimes conflicting objectives: (1) to encourage innovation by rewarding those who develop valuable inventions and creative works, and (2) to facilitate exploitation of new ideas that will lead to continued innovation and creativity. Achieving those objectives is further complicated by the increasing importance of the international marketplace where the concept and value of property vary significantly among nations.

This chapter focuses on law in the United States. Although international intellectual property law is beyond the scope of this chapter, students should be aware of major international organizations and agreements that significantly affect technology law. The World Trade Organization (WTO)—which is discussed in more detail in Chapter 58—is an international association that administers trade agreements with a goal of reducing international trade barriers. The World Intellectual Property Organization (WIPO), a specialized agency of the United Nations that works to promote and protect intellectual property, administers a number of treaties designed to promote and protect intellectual property. The WTO and WIPO have been working together to achieve their goals. A recurring problem has been accommodating the differing needs and demands of developing countries and industrialized nations. The United States, which is a member of both WTO and WIPO, has ratified a variety of treaties affecting intellectual property. Most of these treaties attempt to harmonize the laws of different nations, focusing on the procedures needed to secure protection of intellectual property although some substantive changes in U.S. law have occurred because of treaty ratification. Key treaties are identified at relevant points throughout the materials that follow.

Patents

A **patent** is a grant of the exclusive right to make, use, and sell an invention for a term of years. Patents, which are regulated by the federal Patent Act, are granted by the U.S. Patent and Trademark Office (PTO). After a patent expires, the invention becomes part of the public domain and may be used freely by anyone. By granting the inventor a limited monopoly of the invention, federal patent law is intended not only to reward innovation but also to encourage full disclosure of inventions so that they eventually will become available for public use.

The United States is a member of the Paris Convention for the Protection of Industrial Property (usually called the Paris Convention), a multinational treaty governing patents. The United States also is a party to the Patent Cooperation Treaty. Both of these treaties facilitate the international filing of patent applications. Because countries have different laws concerning what is patentable, however, inventors seeking global protection of their inventions are well-advised to retain attorneys who specialize in this area of law.

Patentability. Not all inventions are patentable. The Patent Act empowers the federal government to grant three general types of patents: utility patents, design patents, and plant patents.

A **utility patent,** the most common type, is granted to a person who invents or discovers "any new and useful process, machine, manufacture, or composition of matter, or any new and useful improvement thereof."[4] A "process" is a method of transforming something into another state or thing, such as a method of making a metal alloy, chemical, or drug. Even if the end product of a process is not patentable, the process itself may be patented. A "machine" is an apparatus or mechanical device that performs a function. A "manufacture" is "the production of articles for use from raw or prepared materials by giving to these materials new forms, qualities, properties, or combinations, whether by hand-labor or by machinery."[5] A "composition of matter" includes "all compositions of two or more substances . . . whether they be results of chemical union, or of mechanical mixture, or whether they be gases, fluids, powders, or solids."[6] An improvement of a process, machine, manufacture, or composition of matter also may be patentable.

In addition to utility patents, the Patent Act authorizes two other types of patents. A **plant patent** may be issued to anyone who "invents or discovers and asexually reproduces"[7] a new plant variety. Plant patents are

---

[3]15 U.S.C. §1051 *et seq.*

[4]35 U.S.C. §101.

[5]American Fruit Growers, Inc. v. Brogdex Co., 51 S. Ct. 328, 330 (1931).

[6]Shell Development Company v. Watson, 149 F. Supp. 279, 280 (D.D.C. 1957).

[7]35 U.S.C. §161.

granted only for plants, such as hybrid flowers and vegetables, that are developed by human beings and that do not occur naturally. The federal government also may grant a **design patent** for "any new, original and ornamental design for an article of manufacture."[8] Design patents concern the appearance of a manufactured article rather than its use or operation.

To qualify for any of these types of patents, an invention must meet two requirements: novelty and nonobviousness. Under the novelty requirement, only new inventions are patentable. Novelty is lacking if the invention was known or used by others in the United States or if it was patented or described in a printed publication in the United States or a foreign country prior to its invention by the applicant. The invention also must be nonobvious; that is, the differences between the invention and prior inventions must not be obvious to someone skilled in the art to which it pertains. A third element also must be proved prior to the granting of a patent. To qualify for a utility patent, an invention must have utility or usefulness. In place of the utility requirement, design patents require that the invention demonstrate ornamentality while a plant patent requires that the plant be distinctive.

Securing a Patent. To secure a patent, the inventor must submit an application to the PTO. The patent application requires a complete description of the invention in sufficient detail to enable someone skilled in the technical area of the invention to duplicate it. The application also must include one or more *claims* clearly defining the invention and explaining how it advances the useful arts. Finally, the application must be signed by the inventor. Each application is assigned to a patent examiner who not only reviews the application but also independently searches the technical literature to verify the inventor's claims. If the examiner finds that the invention meets the statutory requirements, the PTO will issue a patent to the applicant. If the patent application is rejected, the applicant may request review by the PTO and, ultimately, may appeal the decision to the Court of Appeals for the Federal Circuit.

To provide notice of the patent, the word "patent" (or the abbreviation "pat.") and the patent number should be placed on all copies of the invention or, if that is not possible, on the package containing the article. Failure to include the patent notice limits the remedies in an infringement suit.

---

[8]35 U.S.C. §171.

Conflicts sometimes arise when more than one inventor applies for a patent on the same invention. In such conflicts, U.S. law provides that the first to invent is entitled to the patent. Almost all other countries, however, issue the patent to the person who first files the patent application. Under the U.S. system, therefore, an inventor who can prove that he or she created an invention may be entitled to a patent even if another person first applied for the patent. As a result, anyone seeking a U.S. patent should keep detailed, dated records of the invention process as evidence of the time of invention. The "first-to-invent" rule has been strongly criticized because it has generated litigation and has inhibited the development of uniform international patent procedures. These criticisms ultimately may lead the United States to change to a "first-to-file" system.

Rights of the Patent Holder. The owner of a utility or design patent has the exclusive right to make, use, sell, and offer to sell the invention in the United States during the term of the patent. A plant patent holder has the exclusive right to reproduce the plant during the patent term. Prior to 1995, most patents extended for a term of 17 years from the date that the patent was granted. Since 1995, however, the term of a utility or plant patent begins on the date that the patent was granted by the PTO and ends 20 years from the date on which the patent application was filed. (Design patents extend for 14 years from the date the patent was issued.) In limited circumstances, the patent term may be extended if issuance of the patent was delayed during the application process.

A patent holder who produces or uses a patented invention is said to "work the invention." In some countries, patent holders must work the invention, but under U.S. law, a patent holder is not obligated to work the invention. Nevertheless, because the invention will enter the public domain after the patent term expires, a patent holder who is seeking financial benefit will work the invention.

The owner may assign all or part of the right, title, and interest in the patent to another. An assignment is a conveyance of title to the patent entitling the assignee full right to work the invention. Assignments of patents should be recorded in the PTO to protect the assignee from conflicting claims of subsequent assignees.

Instead of assigning the patent, the owner may retain legal title and grant a "license" of all or some of the rights to another. A license entitles the licensee to use the patent for the purposes and for the period of time specified in the licensing agreement. In exchange for the license, the licensee usually pays a royalty to the inventor. The royalty may be a lump sum payment or may be based on a percentage of sales or production. A license may be exclusive, thereby preventing the patent holder from granting other licenses. Some agreements create "cross-licenses" by which one patent holder grants a license in one invention in exchange for a license in a different patent from another patent holder. Although assignment and licensing of patent rights are legal, misuse of these rights, for example to restrain trade in violation of antitrust laws, may be illegal.

Today, many inventions are created in the course of an employment relationship. Although the individual who created the invention is considered the inventor under the patent laws, an employer may have property rights in the invention. The employer is considered the owner of the invention if the inventor (1) was hired specifically to create such inventions or (2) signed a valid agreement assigning the invention to the employer. Under all other circumstances, the inventor is considered to be the owner of the invention. If, however, the inventor developed the invention during working hours or using the employer's resources, the employer is entitled to "shop rights" to the invention. Shop rights entitle the employer to a nonexclusive, nontransferable license to make, use, and sell the invention without paying royalties to the inventor.

Infringement. Patent infringement occurs if someone makes, uses, or sells a patented invention in the United States without permission from the patent holder. Generally, infringement cases must be brought in federal district court. A court may award damages, injunctive relief, or both to a patent holder who proves infringement. At a minimum, damages will include an award of a reasonable royalty for use of the patent. The Patent Act also authorizes courts to increase the damages up to three times the actual damages, but this remedy usually is used only in cases involving willful infringement or bad faith. Attorneys' fees also may be awarded in exceptional cases.

To encourage inventors to promptly apply for a patent, the Patent Act includes several statutory "bars" to obtaining a patent. As a result, an inventor is not entitled to obtain a patent if any of the following occurs more than one year before filing a U.S. patent application:

1. The invention was patented in the United States or another country;

2. The invention was described in a printed publication in the United States or another country;

3. The invention was in public use in the United States; or

4. The invention was on sale in the United States.

In the following case, the U.S. Supreme Court discusses the policies underlying these statutory bars while determining whether an inventor was entitled to a patent.

Pfaff v. Wells Electronics, Inc.
119 S.Ct. 304 (1998)

In November 1980, at the request of Texas Instruments, Inc. (TI), petitioner Wayne Pfaff began developing a computer chip socket for use in the company's computers. In early 1981, Pfaff completed detailed engineering drawings that described the design, dimensions, and materials to be used in manufacturing the socket. He sent the drawings to a manufacturing company that began plans to manufacture the socket. Around the same time, Pfaff showed a sketch of the socket to TI representatives. On April 8, 1981, TI gave Pfaff a written confirmation of an order for 30,100 of the sockets. After creating new tooling to make the sockets, the manufacturing company began manufacture of Pfaff's sockets. TI's order was filled in July, 1981. Initial sales of the socket were very successful totaling more that $7.5 million through 1984.

On April 19, 1982, Pfaff filed an application for a patent on the computer chip socket. The Patent and Trademark Office issued him Patent Number 4,491,377 (the '377 patent) on January 1, 1985. After receiving the patent, Pfaff sued respondent Wells Electronics, Inc. alleging that it had infringed the '377 patent. The federal district court ruled in favor of Pfaff but the court of appeals reversed. The appellate court ruled that the one-year sales bar began to run on April 8, 1981 because Pfaff's invention had been "substantially complete" on that date. Because Pfaff had failed to apply for the patent prior to April 8, 1982, the '377 patent was invalid. The court of appeals ruled, therefore, that no infringement had occurred. The U.S. Supreme Court granted Pfaff's petition for review.

Justice Stevens

Section 102(b) of the Patent Act of 1952 provides that no person is entitled to patent an "invention" that has been "on sale" more than one year before filing a patent application. We granted certiorari to determine whether the commercial marketing of a newly invented product may mark the beginning of the one-year period even though the invention has not yet been reduced to practice. . . .

The primary meaning of the word "invention" in the Patent Act unquestionably refers to the inventor's conception rather than to a physical embodiment of that idea. The statute does not contain any express requirement that an invention must be reduced to practice before it can be patented, . . . The statute's only specific reference to that term is found in §102(g), which sets forth the standard for resolving priority contests between two competing claimants to a patent. That subsection provides:

> In determining priority of invention there shall be considered not only the respective dates of conception and reduction to practice of the invention, but also the reasonable diligence of one who was first to conceive and last to reduce to practice, from a time prior to conception by the other.

Thus, assuming diligence on the part of the applicant, it is normally the first inventor to conceive, rather than the first to reduce to practice, who establishes the right to the patent.

It is well settled that an invention may be patented before it is reduced to practice. In 1888, this Court upheld a patent issued to Alexander Graham Bell even though he had filed his application before constructing a working telephone. Chief Justice Waite's reasoning in that case merits quoting at length:

> It is quite true that when Bell applied for his patent he had never actually transmitted telegraphically spoken words so that they could be distinctly heard and understood at the receiving end of his line, but in his specification he did describe accurately and with admirable clearness his process, that is to say, the exact electrical condition that must be created to accomplish his purpose, and he also described, with sufficient precision to enable one of ordinary skill in such matters to make it, a form of apparatus which, if used in the way pointed out, would produce the required effect, receive the words, and carry them to and deliver them at the appointed place. . . . The law does not require that a discoverer or inventor, in order to get a patent for a process, must have succeeded in bringing his art to the highest degree of perfection. It is enough if he describes his method with sufficient clearness and precision to enable those skilled in the matter to understand what the process is, and if he points out some practicable way of putting it into operation. *The Telephone Cases,* [8 S. Ct. 778 (1888)].

When we apply the reasoning of *The Telephone Cases* to the facts of the case before us today, it is evident that Pfaff could have obtained a patent on his novel socket when he accepted the purchase order from Texas Instruments for 30,100 units. At that time he provided the manufacturer with a description and drawings that had "sufficient clearness and precision to enable those skilled in the matter" to produce the device. The parties agree that the sockets manufactured to fill that order embody Pfaff's conception as set forth in claims 1, 6, 7, and 10 of the '377 patent. . . .

As we have often explained, . . .the patent system represents a carefully crafted bargain that encourages both the creation and the public disclosure of new and useful advances in technology, in return for an exclusive monopoly for a limited period of time. The balance between the interest in motivating innovation and enlightenment by rewarding invention with patent protection on the one hand, and the interest in avoiding monopolies that unnecessarily stifle competition on the other, has been a feature of the federal patent laws since their inception. As this Court explained in 1871:

> Letters patent are not to be regarded as monopolies . . . but as public franchises granted to the inventors of new and useful improvements for the purpose of securing to them, as such inventors, for the limited term therein mentioned, the exclusive right and liberty to make and use and vend to others to be used their own inventions, as tending to promote the progress of science and the useful arts, and as matter of compensation to the inventors for their labor, toil, and expense in making the inventions, and reducing the same to practice for the public benefit, as contemplated by the Constitution and sanctioned by the laws of Congress." *Seymour v. Osborne,* 78 U.S. (11 Wall) 516, 533-534 (1871).

. . . [A]n inventor loses his right to a patent if he puts his invention into public use before filing a patent application. . . . A similar reluctance to allow an inventor to remove existing knowledge from public use undergirds the on-sale bar.

Nevertheless, an inventor who seeks to perfect his discovery may conduct extensive testing without losing his right to obtain a patent for his invention—even if such testing occurs in the public eye. The law has long recognized the distinction between inventions put to experimental use and products sold commercially. In 1878, we explained why patentability may turn on an inventor's use of his product.

It is sometimes said that an inventor acquires an undue advantage over the public by delaying to take out a patent, inasmuch as he thereby preserves the monopoly to himself for a longer period than is allowed by the policy of the law; but this cannot be said with justice when the delay is occasioned by a *bona fide* effort to bring his invention to perfection, or to ascertain whether it will answer the purpose intended. His monopoly only continues for the allotted period, in any event; and it is the interest of the public, as well as himself, that the invention should be perfect and properly tested, before a patent is granted for it. *Any attempt to use it for a profit, and not by way of experiment, for a longer period than two years [now one year] before the application, would deprive the inventor of his right to a patent. Elizabeth v. Pavement Co.,* 97 U.S. (7 Otto) 126, 137 (1878) (emphasis added).

The patent laws therefore seek both to protect the public's right to retain knowledge already in the public domain and the inventor's right to control whether and when he may patent his invention. . . . Petitioner correctly argues that these provisions identify an interest in providing inventors with a definite standard for determining when a patent application must be filed. A rule that makes the timeliness of an application depend on the date when an invention is "substantially complete" seriously undermines the interest in certainty. Moreover, such a rule finds no support in the text of the statute. . . .

The word "invention" must refer to a concept that is complete, rather than merely one that is "substantially complete." It is true that reduction to practice ordinarily provides the best evidence that an invention is complete. But just because reduction to practice is sufficient evidence of completion, it does not follow that proof of reduction to practice is necessary in every case. Indeed, both the facts of the *Telephone Cases* and the facts of this case demonstrate that one can prove that an invention is complete and ready for patenting before it has actually been reduced to practice.

We conclude, therefore, that the on-sale bar applies when two conditions are satisfied before the critical date. First, the product must be the subject of a commercial offer for sale. An inventor can both understand and control the timing of the first commercial marketing of his invention. . . . In this case the acceptance of the purchase order prior to April 8, 1981, makes it clear that such an offer had been made, and there is no question that the sale was commercial rather than experimental in character.

Second, the invention must be ready for patenting. That condition may be satisfied in at least two ways: by proof of reduction to practice before the critical date; or by proof that prior to the critical date the inventor had prepared drawings or other descriptions of the invention that were sufficiently specific to enable a person skilled in the art to practice the invention. In this case the second condition of the on-sale bar is satisfied because the drawings Pfaff sent to the manufacturer before the critical date fully disclosed the invention.

The evidence in this case thus fulfills the two essential conditions of the on-sale bar. As succinctly stated by Learned Hand: "It is a condition upon an inventor's right to a patent that he shall not exploit his discovery competitively after it is ready for patenting; he must content himself with either secrecy, or legal monopoly." *Metallizing Engineering Co. v. Kenyon Bearing & Auto Parts Co.,* 153 F.2d 516, 520 (2d Cir. 1946).

. . . When Pfaff accepted the purchase order for his new sockets prior to April 8, 1981, his invention was ready for patenting. The fact that the manufacturer was able to produce the socket using his detailed drawings and specifications demonstrates this fact. Furthermore, those sockets contained all the elements of the invention claimed in the '377 patent. Therefore, Pfaff's '377 patent is invalid because the invention had been on sale for more than one year in this country before he filed his patent application. . . .

[Judgment affirmed.]

Trade Secrets

Many important ideas, processes, mechanisms, and data used by businesses are not patented. In some cases, these inventions cannot be patented because they do not meet the strict requirements of the Patent Act. In other cases, however, businesses elect not to seek a patent because they do not want to publicly disclose ideas that have given them a competitive advantage. Even without a patent, "know-how" will be recognized and protected as property if it qualifies as a "trade secret."

Unlike other forms of intellectual property, trade secrets are regulated almost completely by state law. Trade secrets law developed through the common law, but more recently most states have enacted statutes to regulate trade secrets. Over 40 states have adopted the **Uniform Trade Secrets Act;** most also have adopted the 1985 amendments to the Act. The following discussion is based on the Uniform Trade Secrets Act with the 1985 amendments.

Elements of a Trade Secret. A precise definition of a trade secret has proved difficult both for courts and legislatures. The Uniform Trade Secrets Act defines a **trade secret** as

> information, including a formula, pattern, compilation, program, device, method, technique, or process that:
>
> (i) derives independent economic value, actual or potential, from not being generally known to, and not being readily ascertainable by proper means by, other persons who can obtain economic value from its disclosure or use, and
>
> (ii) is the subject of efforts that are reasonable under the circumstances to maintain its secrecy.[9]

Trade secrets, therefore, include a wide variety of information including formulas for consumer and commercial products, manufacturing and production processes and techniques, data bases, computer programs, customer and supplier lists, and even internal operating information such as marketing strategies or price lists.

To qualify for protection, however, the information must have commercial value because it is secret—that is, because the general public and those in the industry do not know the information and cannot easily ascertain it. In determining whether information is a trade secret, courts sometimes consider the amount of effort and money expended to develop or acquire the information as well as the difficulty others would have to acquire or duplicate it.

A trade secret is protected by law only if its owner makes reasonable efforts to preserve its secrecy. Because disclosure of a trade secret—for example, to employees, partners, or contractors—often is necessary to exploit its value, absolute concealment is not necessary. If the trade secret owner fails to take reasonable measures to control disclosure, the trade secret will no longer be entitled to protection as a property interest. Measures that are considered reasonable vary from case to case but may include keeping secret information in a locked area, restricting access to employees and others on a "need to know basis," or securing confidentiality agreements from those to whom the trade secret is revealed.

Rights of the Trade Secret Owner. The owner of a trade secret may use the secret, transfer full ownership by assignment, or license the secret. These property rights may last indefinitely so long as the information continues to meet the elements of a trade secret. Thus, unlike a patent, a trade secret does not expire after a term of years. But, while a patent holder's rights include exclusive use of the patent during its term, a trade secret owner is not entitled to exclusive use of a trade secret.

Misappropriation. The Uniform Trade Secrets Act only protects the trade secret owner from **misappropriation,** which is the wrongful acquisition, disclosure, or use of a trade secret. A person misappropriates a trade secret by knowingly acquiring it by improper means. Misappropriation also includes unauthorized use or disclosure of a trade secret by a person who acquired it by improper means or who knew that it was acquired by improper means. Under the Act, "improper means" include: "theft, bribery, misrepresentation, breach or inducement of a breach of a duty to maintain secrecy, or espionage through electronic or other means." The trade secret owner is not protected, however, from others' discovery of the secret by proper means, such as independent invention or reverse engineering (analyzing the product embodying the secret to determine how it was developed or manufactured). A person who learns a trade secret through proper means, therefore, is entitled to use the information.[10]

A trade secret owner is entitled to damages for misappropriation. Damages can be based either on the actual loss, including unjust enrichment, or on a reasonable royalty for use of the trade secret. The Uniform Trade Secrets Act authorizes attorneys' fees and punitive damages up to twice the amount of actual damages if the misappropriation was willful and malicious. Courts also may enjoin actual or threatened misappropriation of a trade secret. In addition to civil remedies, some states impose criminal penalties for misappropriation of trade secrets.

In the case that follows, the court applies the principles of the Uniform Trade Secrets Act to determine whether certain information learned by an employee on the job was a trade secret of his employer.

Allen v. Johar, Inc.
823 S.W.2d 824 (Ark. 1992)

> Appellee Johar, Inc. manufactures handgrips for sporting equipment, motorcycles, and tools. After working for Johar

---

[9]Uniform Trade Secrets Act §1 (4).

[10]At issue in *E. I. du Pont de Nemours & Company, Inc. v. Christopher,* excerpted in the Guide to Reading Legal Case Excerpts, was whether the defendant had used "improper means" to obtain another's trade secret.

for about nine years, primarily as sales manager, appellant Jerry Allen was fired. Allen then started his own business producing handgrips to compete with those made by Johar. Johar sued Allen alleging that he had used Johar's trade secrets in designing his production machines and in contacting Johar's customers. The chancery court found that Johar's machines and customer lists were protected under the Arkansas Trade Secret Law, the Arkansas version of the Uniform Trade Secrets Act. The court therefore granted Johar's request for an injunction that prohibited Allen from using his production machines or Johar's customer lists. Allen appealed to the Arkansas Supreme Court.

Glaze, Justice

. . . Under the Arkansas Trade Secret Law, a trade secret is defined as the following:

> "Trade secret" means information, including a formula, pattern, compilation, program, device, method, technique, or process that: (A) Derives independent economic value, actual or potential, from not being generally known to, and not being readily ascertainable by proper means by, other persons who can obtain economic value for its disclosure or use: and (B) Is the subject of efforts that are reasonable under the circumstances to maintain its secrecy.

Under [the Arkansas Trade Secret Law], actual or threatened misappropriation of a trade secret may be enjoined, which in pertinent part is defined as the following:

> (B) Disclosure or use of a trade secret of another without express or implied consent of a person who: . . .
>
> (ii) At the time of the disclosure or use, knew or had reason to know that his knowledge of the trade secret was: . . .
>
> (b) Acquired under circumstances giving rise to a duty to maintain its secrecy or limit its use: or
>
> (c) Derived from or through a person who owed a duty to the person seeking relief to maintain its secrecy or limit its use . . .

In ruling that the Johar's machines were protected under . . . the Arkansas Trade Secret Law, the chancellor made detailed findings comparing Johar's and the appellant's machines based upon the testimony and the chancellor's own viewing of the machines. Johar had entered the handgrip business by purchasing two production machines from a company in California. While these machines in their present form were capable of producing the rubber handgrips, Terry Vienna, the president and owner of Johar, decided to redesign the machines to make them more productive, and therefore more competitive. Dave Archer, an employee of Johar knowledgeable in industrial engineering, was in charge of the redesigning process. In this process, the main components were relocated—the grinding stone was placed in the middle with a mandrel and table on each side. The location of a mandrel and table on each side of the grinding stone gave Johar's production machines dual capacity and the ability to produce twice as many handgrips. Archer also made other refinements to the machines for Johar including eliminating dust build-up, easing the raw material loading process, and ensuring accuracy in the sizing procedure. According to Terry Vienna, Johar developed the "dual capacity" production technology in the late 1970's. . . .

The chancellor found that the appellant's new production machines were very similar to the Johar's machines—same size, same cutting apparatus and sliding tables, and same double-sided process. In sum, while the Allen machine has larger electrical motors and several new safety features that were not on the Johar machines, the Allen machine was the same in design, mode and method of operation for cutting the finished product, for loading and holding raw material for processing, and for sizing the product. Further, the Allen machine was built by Mr. Flowers, who previously worked for Johar with Dave Archer servicing Johar's machines. . . . Thus, the evidence in the record clearly establishes that Johar's machines fit under the definition of trade secret in [the Arkansas Trade Secret Law].

We also find support in the record for the chancellor's finding that Terry Vienna met the secrecy requirement under the trade secret law. Vienna testified that like his other competitors, he did not allow tours of the building. Further, evidence showed that this is a very competitive business because there are a limited number of companies involved, three or four major companies and only two minor companies. In short, we cannot say that the chancellor was clearly erroneous in finding that Johar's production machines are protected under the Arkansas Trade Secret Law.

In the second issue, the appellant argues that the chancellor erred in protecting Johar's customer lists under the Arkansas Trade Secret Law. We do not agree. . . . The Arkansas Trade Secret Law was enacted in 1981 and is a uniform law. There are a host of cases from other jurisdictions that hold that customer lists are trade secrets. . . . Generally, customer lists obtained through use of a business effort, and the expenditure of time and money that are not readily ascertainable and are kept confidential are given protection as a trade secret. . . . In the present case, Vienna testified that it has taken Johar since 1974 to accumulate its customers, and that Johar's customer lists and files contain detailed information about its customers—personality traits, hobbies and likes, credit history, buying habits and pricing agreements. Vienna testified that it would take two to three years of work for a company to obtain this kind of information. . . .

As previously discussed, an important factor in determining whether a customer list is a trade secret is whether the employer took actions to guard the secrecy or preserve the confidentiality of the list. . . . In this respect, the record supports the trial court's finding that Johar kept its customer lists and files confidential. Vienna testified that the information was kept confidential and was not to leave the premises. Further, he testified that he ordered old customer printouts destroyed. The evidence, we conclude, clearly supports the chancellor's holding that Johar's customer lists meet the requirements of protection as a trade secret. . . .

[Judgment affirmed.]

Economic Espionage Act. Although many states' laws allow criminal sanctions for trade secret misappropriation, they rarely have been imposed. Concerned that state civil remedies did not sufficiently deter trade secret misappropriation, Congress enacted the federal **Economic Espionage Act**[11] in 1996. Under the statute, theft of a trade secret related to a product in or produced for interstate commerce is a federal crime. Individuals convicted of trade secret theft may be sentenced to up to 10 years in prison (15 years if the individual knowingly acts in concert with a foreign government) and fined up to $500,000. Corporations and other organizations may be fined up to $5 million ($10 million if the organization knowingly acts to benefit a foreign government) for trade secret theft.

Copyrights

A **copyright** is the exclusive right to reproduce and distribute a creative work. Prior to 1976, copyrights were governed by both state common law and federal statute. Copyrights are now regulated solely by a comprehensive federal statute, the Copyright Act. Since 1989, the United States has been a member of the Berne Convention for the Protection of Literary and Artistic Works, and the Copyright Act has been amended to comply with the international standards of that treaty.

Copyrightable Works. The Copyright Act protects only "original works of authorship fixed in any tangible medium of expression."[12] The Copyright Act lists eight categories of creative works to illustrate the types of material that qualify for copyrights: literary works; musical works; dramatic works; pantomime and choreographic works; pictorial, graphic, and sculptural works; motion pictures and other audiovisual works; sound recordings; and architectural works. A 1980 amendment to the Act clarified that computer programs are considered literary works and, therefore, may be copyrighted. The creator of any type of copyrightable work is called the "author."

Originality is the critical criterion in determining whether a particular work may be copyrighted.

> The *sine qua non* of copyright is originality. To qualify for copyright protection, a work must be original to the author. . . . Original, as the term is used in copyright, means only that the work was independently created by the author (as opposed to copied from other works), and that it possesses at least some minimal degree of creativity.[13]

In other words, copyrightable works need not demonstrate novelty or artistic merit. So long as the work originated with the author, it is copyrightable.

To qualify for copyright protection, the Copyright Act further requires that a work be fixed in a tangible medium of expression such as, for example, paper, cloth, stone, marble, film, tape, record, disk, or chip. This fixation element highlights the long-established principle that copyright law does not protect *ideas;* rather, it protects the particular way in which an idea is expressed. The Copyright Act emphasizes this distinction by providing:

> In no case does copyright protection for an original work of authorship extend to any idea, procedure, process, system, method of operation, concept, principle, or discovery, regardless of the form in which it is described, explained, illustrated, or embodied in such work.[14]

---

[11]18 U.S.C. §§1831–1839.

[12]17 U.S.C. §102(a).

[13]Feist Publications, Inc. v. Rural Telephone Service Co., 111 S. Ct. 1282, 1287 (1992).

[14]17 U.S.C. §102(b).

Securing Copyright Protection. The author of a copyrightable work automatically secures a copyright when the work is fixed in a tangible medium. In other words, copyrights are not granted by the government. Only the author—and those who derive rights through the author—can claim the copyright. For most works the person who creates the work is considered the author. If more than one person created the work, the authors are co-owners of the copyright. Special rules apply to "works for hire," such as works made by an employee acting within the scope of employment. Certain specially commissioned works also are considered works for hire if the parties sign an instrument agreeing that the work was made for hire.

The federal Copyright Act establishes procedures for registering copyrighted works and for providing notice of a copyright. Neither registration nor notice is required, but these procedures ensure greater protection if the copyright is infringed. The federal registration process is relatively simple and inexpensive: the author (or holder of the copyright if the author has transferred ownership) must complete an application form and submit two copies of the work plus a filing fee to the Copyright Office. Although not required to secure the copyright, registration is required before a copyright holder may bring an action for infringement if the work originated in the United States or in a country that has not ratified the Berne Convention.

The Copyright Act also established three elements to provide notice of a copyright: (1) the word "copyright," or the abbreviation "Copr.," or the symbol © (℗ if the work is a sound recording); (2) the date of first publication; and (3) the name of the copyright owner. So, for example, a copyright notice might read:

© 2001 Mary Evans or Copyright 2001 Mary Evans

The copyright notice should be affixed to copies of the work in a way that provides reasonable notice of the copyright claim.

Rights of the Copyright Holder. The Copyright Act extends six exclusive rights to copyright owners:

1. the right to reproduce the work,
2. the right to prepare derivative works based on the copyrighted work,
3. the right to public distribution of copies of the work,
4. the right to public performance of the work,
5. the right to public display of the work, and
6. the right to perform copyrighted sound recordings publicly by means of a digital audio transmission.[15]

The sixth right was added to the Copyright Act in 1995 in direct response to changes in digital technology that threatened sales of audio compact disks (CDs), a major source of income for recording artists and producers. Some of this technology, which allows computer users to make high quality, inexpensive copies of CDs, is discussed in the next case, *A&M Records, Inc. v. Napster, Inc.* This new right is limited by highly technical provisions in the Copyright Act.[16]

The Act also imposes special rules on the owner of a copyright in a nondramatic musical work, such as a song. After the copyright holder (for example, the composer of a song) allows a recording of the work to be distributed in the United States, other performers have a right to record the work, provided that they pay a royalty to the copyright owner. The royalty for this "compulsory license" is set periodically by federal regulation. Thus, by allowing recording of a musical work, the copyright holder effectively loses the exclusive right to make or distribute recordings of that work.

Copyrights generally exist for the life of the author plus 70 years. If the work was created for hire, however, the copyright expires 95 years after publication or 120 years after creation, whichever occurs first.

Infringement. Copyright infringement is the violation of any of the exclusive rights granted to the copyright owner. If the owner proves infringement, a court may enjoin further infringement and may order impoundment and destruction of the infringing copies as well as articles (such as plates, tapes, film negatives, masters) used to produce them. The copyright owner also is entitled to actual damages and profits earned by the infringer. Statutory damages and attorneys fees are available to a copyright owner only if the copyright was registered with the Copyright Office prior to the infringement or within three months of publication. Statutory damages, which are awarded instead of actual damages, may be awarded in an amount from $750 to $30,000 ($150,000 if the infringement is willful) as determined by the judge.

Under the Copyright Act, willful infringement is a criminal offense if done for commercial advantage or financial gain. Following an incident in which a college student posted copyrighted software on an Internet Web site for others to download for free, a second type of criminal offense was added to the Copyright Act. The

---

[15]17 U.S.C. §106.

[16]17 U.S.C. §512.

No Electronic Theft Act imposes criminal penalties for willful infringement in which a person during any 180-day period reproduces or distributes one or more copies of copyrighted works with a total retail value of more than $1,000.[17] Depending on the number of copies reproduced or distributed, the penalties may range from a fine of $100,000 and imprisonment up to one year to a fine of $250,000 and imprisonment for three years.

Fair Use. An exception to the rights of a copyright owner is "fair use" of copyrighted works. Fair use of a copyrighted work without the owner's permission is not considered infringement. The statute does not define fair use but provides examples including "criticism, comment, news reporting, teaching, . . . scholarship, or research."[18] The fair use doctrine is designed to achieve the Constitutional goal of copyrights—the promotion of learning—by allowing limited use of copyrighted works. Traditionally, fair use has allowed limited copying of a work for educational purposes (teaching and research, for example) and for personal purposes (such as an individual's personal learning or entertainment). As technological advancements have created new and cheaper ways to duplicate copyrighted works, the courts have had to interpret the fair use doctrine in a variety of situations. The Supreme Court, for example, has held that a consumer's recording a copyrighted television program on a videocassette recorder (VCR) for later viewing constitutes personal fair use. In contrast, courts have held that duplication of copyrighted materials by copy shops for sale to university students as a customized pack of class materials is not a fair use.[19]

The following case involves copying of audio CDs using a technology known as MP3, a digital file format that compresses and stores audio information on computer disks. Because stored data is compressed, large files (such as audio files) can be transferred quickly by e-mail or other electronic means. In this part of the opinion, the court considers whether "sharing" these copyrighted recordings constitutes fair use.

---

[17]17 U.S.C. §506(a)(1).
[18]17 U.S.C. §107.
[19]Princeton University Press v. Michigan Document Services, Inc., 99 F.3d 1381 (6th Cir. 1996); Basic Books, Inc. v. Kinko's Graphics Corp., 758 F. Supp. 1522 (S.D.N.Y. 1991).

A&M Records, Inc. v. Napster, Inc.
239 F.3d 1004 (9th Cir. 2001)

The plaintiffs, A&M Records, Inc. and other businesses and individuals who record, distribute, or sell copyrighted compositions and sound recordings, sued defendant Napster, Inc. for copyright infringement. Napster operates an Internet site that allows users to share and copy MP3 audio files. With software provided by Napster, the Web site users can upload the names of their audio files to a server where Napster stores and indexes all users' file names in a directory. Napster's software then allows users to search the directory by artist or song and download selected files to their computer hard drive. The plaintiffs presented evidence through three studies—the Jay Report, the Fine Report, and the Teece Report—to establish that Napster's continued operation of its Web site would cause irreparable harm. Based on the evidence, the trial court issued a preliminary injunction enjoining Napster from "engaging in or facilitating others in copying, downloading, uploading, transmitting, or distributing" plaintiffs' copyrighted works. Napster appealed to the federal Ninth Circuit Court of Appeals.

Beezer, Circuit Judge

. . . [P]laintiffs have shown that Napster users infringe at least two of the copyright holders' exclusive rights: the rights of reproduction . . . and distribution. . . . Napster users who upload file names to the search index for others to copy violate plaintiffs' distribution rights. Napster users who download files containing copyrighted music violate plaintiffs' reproduction rights. . . .

Napster contends that its users do not directly infringe plaintiffs' copyrights because the users are engaged in fair use of the material. Napster identifies three specific alleged fair uses: sampling, where users make temporary copies of a work before purchasing; space-shifting, where users access a sound recording through the Napster system that they already own in audio CD format; and permissive distribution of recordings by both new and established artists.

The district court considered factors listed in 17 U.S.C. §107, which guide a court's fair use determination. These factors are: (1) the purpose and character of the use; (2) the nature of the copyrighted work; (3) the "amount and substantiality of the portion used" in relation to the work as a whole; and (4) the effect of the use upon the potential market for the work or the value of the work. . . . [T]he record supports the district court's conclusion that Napster users do not engage in fair use of the copyrighted materials. . . .

1. Purpose and Character of the Use. This factor focuses on whether the new work merely replaces the object of the original creation or instead adds a further purpose or different character. In other words, this factor asks "whether and to what extent the new work is 'transformative.' " [*Campbell v. Acuff-Rose Music, Inc.,* 114 S. Ct. 1164, 1171 (1994).] The district court first concluded that downloading MP3 files does not transform the copyrighted work. . . . Courts have been reluctant to find fair use when an original work is merely retransmitted in a different medium. . . .

This "purpose and character" element also requires the district court to determine whether the allegedly infringing use is commercial or noncommercial. . . . A commercial use weighs against a finding of fair use but is not conclusive on the issue. The district court determined that Napster users engage in commercial use of the copyrighted materials largely because (1) "a host user sending a file cannot be said to engage in a personal use when distributing that file to an anonymous requester" and (2) "Napster users get for free something they would ordinarily have to buy." . . . The district court's findings are not clearly erroneous.

Direct economic benefit is not required to demonstrate a commercial use. Rather, repeated and exploitative copying of copyrighted works, even if the copies are not offered for sale, may constitute a commercial use. . . .

2. The Nature of the Use. Works that are creative in nature are "closer to the core of intended copyright protection" than are more fact-based works. . . . The district court determined that plaintiffs' "copyrighted musical compositions and sound recordings are creative in nature . . . which cuts against a finding of fair use under the second factor." . . . We find no error in the district court's conclusion.

3. The Portion Used. "While 'wholesale copying does not preclude fair use per se,' copying an entire work 'militates against a finding of fair use.'" *Worldwide Church of God v. Philadelphia Church of God,* 227 F.3d 1110, 1118 (9th Cir. 2000). The district court determined that Napster users engage in "wholesale copying" of copyrighted work because file transfer necessarily "involves copying the entirety of the copyrighted work." . . . We agree. . . .

4. Effect of Use on Market. "Fair use, when properly applied, is limited to copying by others which does not materially impair the marketability of the work which is copied." *Harper & Row Publishers, Inc. v. Nation*

Enters., [105 S. Ct. 2218, 2234 (1985)]. Addressing this factor, the district court concluded that Napster harms the market in "at least" two ways: it reduces audio CD sales among college students and it "raises barriers to plaintiffs' entry into the market for the digital downloading of music." . . . The district court relied on evidence plaintiffs submitted to show that Napster use harms the market for their copyrighted musical compositions and sound recordings. . . . The district court cited both the Jay and Fine Reports in support of its finding that Napster use harms the market for plaintiffs' copyrighted musical compositions and sound recordings by reducing CD sales among college students. The district court cited the Teece Report to show the harm Napster use caused in raising barriers to plaintiffs' entry into the market for digital downloading of music. . . . The district court's careful consideration of defendant's objections to these reports and decision to rely on the reports for specific issues demonstrates a proper exercise of discretion in addition to a correct application of the fair use doctrine. Defendant has failed to show any basis for disturbing the district court's findings. . . .

We find no error in the district court's determination that plaintiffs will likely succeed in establishing that Napster users do not have a fair use defense. . . .

[Judgment on the issue of fair use affirmed.]

Four years after the Napster case, the U.S. Supreme Court ruled that distributors of products that allow users to engage in copyright infringement (such as the software distributed by Napster) also may be held liable for infringement under certain circumstances: "[O]ne who distributes a device with the object of promoting its use to infringe copyright, as shown by the clear expression or other affirmative steps taken to foster infringement, is liable for the resulting acts of infringement by third parties."[20]

Trademarks

Trademarks are words or symbols used in marketing to distinguish and identify the source of a product. The modern law of trademarks developed through the common law. The federal Lanham Act, which codifies much

---

[20]MGM Studios, Inc. v. Grokster, Ltd., 125 S. Ct. 2764, 2770 (2005).

of this common law, regulates the interstate use of trademarks and other similar marks. The statute is supplemented by state statutory and common law. The United States is a member of two treaties that facilitate international registration of trademarks: the Protocol Relating to the Madrid Agreement Concerning the International Registration of Marks (Madrid Protocol) and the Paris Convention for the Protection of Industrial Property.

Types of Marks. Trademarks and service marks comprise most of the marks protected under state and federal law. A **trademark** is identified by the Lanham Act as "any word, name, symbol, or device or any combination thereof" used by a manufacturer or merchant "to identify and distinguish his or her goods, including a unique product, from those manufactured or sold by others and to indicate the source of the goods, even if that source is unknown."[21] Examples of trademarks include the word "Nike" and the slogan "Just Do It" when used in conjunction with selling athletic shoes and equipment. The red flag displaying the word French's on mustard and condiments, the Coca-Cola bottle, and the stylized striped letters IBM used in marketing computer products: all are trademarks that distinguish specific goods from those of their competitors. **Service marks** are similar to trademarks but are used in the sale and advertising of services, rather than goods. The word "Mastercard" and the logo composed of overlapping red and gold circles are service marks that identify credit card services. Sprint and Verizon are service marks that distinguish telecommunication services. Service marks have proved to be especially effective for franchising. The service marks "McDonald's" and the golden arches, for example, clearly distinguish McDonald Corporation's fast food franchise restaurants from those of other food providers.

The Lanham Act also recognizes collective marks and certification marks. A **collective mark** is a trademark or service mark used by members of a collective group, such as a union or trade association, to identify that its goods or services are produced by members of the group. Many realtors, for example, display a symbol reading "MLS" indicating that they are members of Multiple Listing Service, a real estate cooperative. A **certification mark** is a mark that attests to a specified quality, material, or origin from a certain region. The symbol "UL," for example, certifies that a product is in compliance with the standards of Underwriters'

Laboratories, Inc. Textile and clothing manufacturers often use a symbol that certifies their goods are made, for example, of 100 percent cotton or wool.

Federal Registration. Ownership of a mark is created by use of the mark in marketing a product. The Lanham Act, however, provides a system for national registration of marks with the federal Patent and Trademark Office (PTO). Marks that meet the requirements for full protection under the Lanham Act are registered on the PTO's Principal Register; other marks may be registered on the PTO's Supplemental Register. Federal registration requires the owner to submit an application to the PTO establishing that the mark has been used in interstate commerce or that the owner has a bona fide intention to use the mark in interstate commerce.

Registration on the Principal Register also requires the owner to provide evidence that the mark is "distinctive." The PTO, therefore, will not register generic names—words that describe an entire class of products. So, for example, registration of the term "sweetener" for a product used to sweeten foods would not be allowed because the term describes an entire product class. Similarly, generic terms such as "computer" or "lawn mower" are not valid trademarks. Owners of distinctive trademarks must avoid "genericide," the process by which a trademark becomes a generic term. "Zipper," "aspirin," and "yo-yo," for example, were once valid trademarks but now are considered generic.

Federal law affords the greatest protection to distinctive marks including those that are suggestive, arbitrary, or fanciful as well as marks that have attained "secondary meaning." A suggestive mark is one that has some association with the product with which it is used. "Sweet'N Low," for example, is a trademark that hints at the product's characteristics: it sweetens food and is low in calories. Marks are described as arbitrary if they are ordinary words or pictures that have no natural association with the product. The mark "Domino," for example, is arbitrary when used to market sugar products. Similarly, the word "Apple" or a drawing of an apple used in marketing computers is arbitrary. Fanciful marks are those that are invented for use with a product. The word "Kodak" used for cameras and a red and white checkerboard for marketing pet foods would be considered fanciful marks.

Descriptive marks that distinguish a product may be registered on the PTO's Supplemental Register, but they receive little legal protection unless they have attained "secondary meaning." Descriptive marks

---

[21] 15 U.S.C. §1127.

include the name of the producer or seller (Moroni's Spaghetti) or its geographic location (Midwest Foods). When a descriptive term is associated with and distinguishes a particular product, it gains secondary meaning. At one time, for example, McDonald's was merely a surname of a business owner. When it became recognized as distinguishing a certain fast food restaurant or franchise, the term gained secondary meaning. Similarly, "American Airlines" once described a company that provided air transport in the western hemisphere. Now the term has secondary meaning distinguishing a specific air carrier. Once a mark achieves secondary meaning, it is considered distinctive and can be registered on the Principal Register, thereby receiving full federal protection. Registration on the Supplemental Register for five years creates a presumption that the mark has attained secondary meaning.

A mark that is likely to create confusion with a prior mark generally cannot be registered on either the Principal Register or Supplemental Register. There is a likelihood of confusion if a reasonable consumer might confuse the source of the product. For example, assume that Candle King is a valid, registered trademark for light bulbs made by World Electric Co. If an applicant sought to register Candel King for its own light bulbs, it is likely that a reasonable consumer might mistakenly believe that World Electric Co. is the source of the Candel King bulbs. As part of the federal registration process, the applicant must categorize its products using a product classification system. Products that are in different and unrelated categories generally will not create a likelihood of confusion. So, for example, "Explorer" might be a registrable trademark both for a vehicle and for an Internet Web browser.

Finally, the Lanham Act specifically prohibits registration of certain types of marks, including those that are scandalous, immoral, or deceptive. Flags, coats of arms, or other insignias of the United States, a state, a municipality, or another country cannot be registered.

The Patent and Trademark Office examines applications and those that are in compliance with the Lanham Act are published in the Official Gazette to allow the public the opportunity to oppose registration of the mark. If no successful opposition is raised, the Patent and Trademark Office registers the mark on the Principal Register for a term of ten years. Registration can be renewed indefinitely so long as use of the mark continues in compliance with the statute. The owner of the mark is entitled to use the ® to indicate that the mark is registered. Adverse decisions of the Patent and Trademark Office may be appealed to the Trademark Trial and Appeal Board and, ultimately, to the Court of Appeals for the Federal Circuit.

Rights of the Owner of the Mark. The owner of a mark is entitled to use the mark and to exclude others from using it or marks that would create a likelihood of confusion. The owner of a federally registered mark has nationwide priority in the mark against any subsequent users. Registration, whether on the Principal Register or the Supplemental Register, provides constructive notice of the ownership of the mark. Anyone who uses the mark—or a confusingly similar one—is presumed to have been aware of the owner's prior use. This priority is a major benefit of federal registration.

Determining rights in nonregistered marks, however, is more complicated. In general, the first to use the mark in a market is entitled to rights in the mark. Assume, for example, that in 1998, Anna began marketing yogurt products in Georgia using the mark Yodel Yogurt and that she was the first to use that mark. Under the general rule, Anna would have priority over anyone else's use of the mark in Georgia. Now assume that in 1999, Anna expanded her market and began selling products with the Yodel Yogurt mark in Florida. In 2000, Anna discovered that Brent also was using the Yodel Yogurt mark in Florida. In general, the first to use the mark in a market (here, Florida) is entitled to the rights in the mark. Therefore, if Anna can prove that she used the mark in Florida before Brent, she is entitled to the mark and Brent cannot use it. One exception to the first to use rule is that an owner takes priority over someone who used the mark with knowledge of the prior use. So, for example, even if Brent first used the mark Yodel Yogurt in Florida, Anna would have priority in Florida if she could prove that Brent had known of her use of the Yodel Yogurt mark in Georgia before he began using it.

Assume instead that in 1998 Anna federally registered the mark Yodel Yogurt when she began using it to market yogurt products in Georgia. In 1999, Brent began to use Yodel Yogurt as a mark for yogurt products in Florida. In 2000, Anna expanded her market to Florida. Because Anna federally registered the mark before Brent's first use, she is entitled to priority in the mark in Florida.

The owner of a mark also has the right to license the mark for use in marketing specified goods and services. Soft drink companies, for example, generally license the use of their trademarks to bottlers for use in selling beverages made according to the company's formulas. Many other businesses, including restaurants and motels, have successfully licensed their service marks as a part of franchise arrangements.

Trademarks and service marks also may be completely assigned to other persons and businesses. An assignment of a mark, however, must be made in conjunction with the assignment of the goodwill of the business in which the mark is used. In other words, an assignment of a mark "in gross" is ineffective. This rule naturally arises from the fact that marks are protected only when used in the marketing of a good or service. Assignments of registered marks should be recorded at the Patent and Trademark Office.

Infringement and Dilution.   Infringement of a mark is use of another's mark or use of a mark so similar that purchasers are likely to be confused as to the source of the product or service. A variety of remedies for infringement are available under state and federal laws. In an infringement suit brought under the Lanham Act, the court may grant an injunction prohibiting use of the mark and may award the plaintiff actual damages as well as the defendant's profits. The Act also authorizes the court to increase actual damages up to three times and to award attorneys' fees. The court further may order impoundment and destruction of infringing articles. The Lanham Act also prohibits counterfeiting of trademarks. Intentional use of a counterfeit trademark requires the court to award treble damages unless extenuating circumstances are shown.

In 1995, Congress adopted the **Federal Trademark Dilution Act (FTDA)**[22] to strengthen protection of some marks. The statute provides that the owner of a distinctive and famous mark can obtain a court injunction to prevent use that "causes dilution of the distinctive quality of the mark." The Lanham Act defines "dilution" as "the lessening of the capacity of a famous mark to identify and distinguish goods or services."[23] Unlike infringement, dilution may occur even if there is no likelihood of confusion or mistake. In other words, dilution occurs when a famous mark loses strength because of use with other products. Protection against dilution is designed to help businesses who have significant investment in their marks. Ordinarily, for example, the famous trademark "Microsoft," could be used to market products unrelated to computers and software. A consumer would be unlikely to confuse the source of

Microsoft deodorant with the maker of Windows software. Under the FTDA, however, Microsoft Corporation probably would be able to stop the use of the name Microsoft in conjunction with deodorant by proving that the Microsoft mark is famous and that use on other unrelated products would reduce its distinguishing ability.

The FTDA lists eight factors that courts should use in determining whether a mark is distinctive and famous:

> (1) the degree of inherent or acquired distinctiveness of the mark; (2) the duration and extent of use of the mark; (3) the duration and extent of advertising and publicity of the mark; (4) the geographical extent of the trading area in which the mark is used; (5) the channels of trade for the goods or services with which the mark is used; (6) the degree of recognition of the mark in the trading areas and channels of trade used by the mark's owner and the person against whom the injunction is sought; (7) the nature and extent of use of the same or similar marks by third parties; and (8) whether the mark is federally registered.[24]

In a dilution case, the owner of the mark generally is entitled only to an injunction ordering the defendant to cease using the mark. If, however, the mark's owner can prove that the defendant willfully intended to trade on the owner's reputation or to cause dilution, the owner is entitled to the other remedies available for infringement. Table 59.1 summarizes the basic intellectual property principles discussed previously.

Computer Law and Cyberlaw

The growth of the computer industry and the development of the Internet have created challenging new legal issues. The materials that follow discuss those issues, focusing first on computer technology and then on legal aspects of the Internet.

Protection of Computer Technology

Traditional areas of intellectual property—patents, copyrights, and trade secrets—have been used for the protection of computer technology. As discussed in the sections that follow, however, the scope of protection afforded by these laws has not yet been fully resolved by the courts or government.

---

[22]15 U.S.C. §1125(c).
[23]15 U.S.C. §1127.

[24]15 U.S.C. §1125(c)(1)(A)–(H).

Table 59.1	**Intellectual Property**		
Form of Protection	**Property Protected**	**Criteria for Protection**	**Maximum Length of Protection**
Patent	Inventions	Is novel, nonobvious, and	
1) utility patent	1) processes, machines, compositions of matter	1) useful	1) 20 years after date of filing
2) plant patent	2) hybrid plants	2) distinctive	2) 20 years after date of filing
3) design patent	3) designs	3) ornamental	3) 14 years after date of issue
Trade secret	Information	Has economic value, is secret, and is subject to reasonable efforts to maintain secrecy	Unlimited
Copyright	Creative works	Is original and is fixed in a tangible medium	Life of author plus 70 years
Trademark	Symbols, words, devices	Distinctive; distinguishes source of goods or services	Unlimited

Patent Law. The inventor of a computer or of improvements may be granted a utility patent provided that the basic requirements of novelty, nonobviousness, and usefulness are met. Determining whether computer programs and software may be patented has been a more difficult problem. Throughout the 1970s, both the PTO and the courts appeared reluctant to extend patent protection to computer programs. The rationale for this policy stemmed from a long-standing rule that considered mathematical algorithms to be unpatentable "ideas." Because computer programs used mathematical algorithms to perform various tasks, it was argued that the programs should not be patentable.

In a 1981 decision, however, the Supreme Court indicated that such a broad generalization was inappropriate. In *Diamond v. Diehr*,[25] the Court held that an industrial process that used a mathematical formula and calculations performed by a computer could be patented. The Court focused on the fact that the claimed invention was a "process" that should not be denied a patent "simply because it uses a mathematical formula, computer program, or digital computer."[26] More recently, the influential Federal Circuit Court of Appeals (which has jurisdiction to hear patent appeals from the federal district courts and appeals of decisions of the PTO) has decided a number of cases upholding patents that include computer programs. In the following case, the court directly addresses the issue.

State Street Bank & Trust Co. v. Signature Financial Group, Inc.
149 F.3d 1368 (Fed. Cir. 1998)

Signature Financial Group, Inc. (Signature) owns U.S. Patent Number 5,193,056 ('056 patent). Signature acts as administrator and accounting agent for investment portfolios composed of assets pooled by numerous mutual funds. The patent covers a data processing system for managing a pooled portfolio including a computer processor, disks for storing data, and programs to retrieve data and calculate information needed for managing the portfolio. These calculations include, for example, each mutual fund's additions to and withdrawals from the portfolio; the percentage of the portfolio owned by each mutual fund; allocation of income, expenses, gains, and losses to each mutual fund; and calculation of the share price for each of the funds. The system performs these calculations on a daily basis and aggregates the information for annual reporting for tax and accounting purposes. Signature and State Street Bank & Trust Co., a firm that also manages pooled portfolios for investment clients, began negotiations for a licensing agreement that would allow State Street to use Signature's patented system. After negotiations broke down, State Street filed a lawsuit alleging that Claim 1, as listed in the patent application for patent '056, did not meet the statutory requirements for a patent. The trial court ruled that patent '056 was invalid and granted judgment in State Street's favor. Signature appealed.

---

[25] 101 S. Ct. 1048 (1981).
[26] *Id.* at 1057.

Rich, Circuit Judge

. . . [C]laim 1, properly construed, claims a machine, namely, a data processing system for managing a financial services configuration of a portfolio. . . . A "machine" is proper statutory subject matter under §101 [of the Patent Act]. We note that, for the purposes of a §101 analysis, it is of little relevance whether claim 1 is directed to a "machine" or a "process," as long as it falls within at least one of the four enumerated categories of patentable subject matter, "machine" and "process" being such categories.

This does not end our analysis, however, because the court concluded that the claimed subject matter fell into . . . the "mathematical algorithm" exception. . . . Section 101 reads:

> Whoever invents or discovers any new and useful process, machine, manufacture, or composition of matter, or any new and useful improvement thereof, may obtain a patent therefor, subject to the conditions and requirements of this title.

The plain and unambiguous meaning of §101 is that any invention falling within one of the four stated categories of statutory subject matter may be patented, provided it meets the other requirements for patentability set forth in Title 35. . . .

The repetitive use of the expansive term "any" in §101 shows Congress's intent not to place any restrictions on the subject matter for which a patent may be obtained beyond those specifically recited in §101. Indeed, the Supreme Court has acknowledged that Congress intended §101 to extend to "anything under the sun that is made by man." *Diamond v. Chakrabarty,* [100 S. Ct. 2204 (1980)]. . . . Thus, it is improper to read limitations into §101 on the subject matter that may be patented where the legislative history indicates that Congress clearly did not intend such limitations. . . .

The Supreme Court has identified three categories of subject matter that are unpatentable, namely "laws of nature, natural phenomena, and abstract ideas." [*Diamond v. Diehr,* 101 S. Ct. 1048 (1981)]. Of particular relevance to this case, the Court has held that mathematical algorithms are not patentable subject matter to the extent that they are merely abstract ideas. . . . In *Diehr,* the Court explained that certain types of mathematical subject matter, standing alone, represent nothing more than abstract ideas until reduced to some type of practical application, *i.e.,* "a useful, concrete and tangible result." . . . This has come to be known as the

mathematical algorithm exception. This designation has led to some confusion. . . . By keeping in mind that the mathematical algorithm is unpatentable only to the extent that it represents an abstract idea, this confusion may be ameliorated. . . .

Unpatentable mathematical algorithms are identifiable by showing they are merely abstract ideas constituting disembodied concepts or truths that are not "useful." From a practical standpoint, this means that to be patentable an algorithm must be applied in a "useful" way. . . .

Today, we hold that the transformation of data, representing discrete dollar amounts, by a machine through a series of mathematical calculations into a final share price, constitutes a practical application of a mathematical algorithm, formula, or calculation, because it produces "a useful, concrete and tangible result"—a final share price momentarily fixed for recording and reporting purposes and even accepted and relied upon by regulatory authorities and in subsequent trades.

The district court erred by [ruling] that the claimed subject matter was an unpatentable abstract idea. . . . As we pointed out in *In re Alappat,* [33 F.3d 1526, 1543 (Fed. Cir. 1994)], . . . a process, machine, manufacture, or composition of matter employing a law of nature, natural phenomenon, or abstract idea is patentable subject matter even though a law of nature, natural phenomenon, or abstract idea would not, by itself, be entitled to such protection. . . . [T]he mere fact that a claimed invention involves inputting numbers, calculating numbers, outputting numbers, and storing numbers, in and of itself, would not render it nonstatutory subject matter, unless, of course, its operation does not produce a "useful, concrete and tangible result." *Alappat,* 33 F.3d at 1544. . . . After all, as we have repeatedly stated,

> every step-by-step process, be it electronic or chemical or mechanical, involves an algorithm in the broad sense of the term. Since §101 expressly includes processes as a category of inventions which may be patented and §100(b) further defines the word "process" as meaning "process, art or method, and includes a new use of a known process, machine, manufacture, composition of matter, or material," it follows that it is no ground for holding a claim is directed to nonstatutory subject matter to say it includes or is directed to an algorithm. This is why the proscription against patenting has been limited to mathematical algorithms. . . .

In re Iwahashi, 888 F.2d 1370, 1374 (Fed. Cir. 1989). . . . See, e.g., *Parker v. Flook,* [98 S. Ct. 2522 (1978)] ("[A] process is not unpatentable simply because it contains a law of nature or a mathematical algorithm."); *Funk Bros. Seed Co. v. Kalo Inoculant Co.,* [68 S. Ct. 440 (1948)] ("He who discovers a hitherto unknown phenomenon of nature has no claim to a monopoly of it which the law recognizes. If there is to be invention from such a discovery, it must come from the application of the law to a new and useful end."); *Mackay Radio & Tel. Co. v. Radio Corp. of Am.,* 59 S. Ct. 427 (1939) ("While a scientific truth, or the mathematical expression of it, is not a patentable invention, a novel and useful structure created with the aid of knowledge of scientific truth may be."). . . .

When a claim containing a mathematical formula implements or applies that formula in a structure or process which, when considered as a whole, is performing a function which the patent laws were designed to protect (e.g., transforming or reducing an article to a different state or thing), then the claim satisfies the requirements of §101. . . .

The question of whether a claim encompasses statutory subject matter should not focus on which of the four categories of subject matter a claim is directed to — process, machine, manufacture, or composition of matter — but rather on the essential characteristics of the subject matter, in particular, its practical utility. . . . [C]laim 1 is directed to a machine programmed with . . . software and admittedly produces a "useful, concrete, and tangible result." This renders it statutory subject matter. . . .

[Judgment reversed and remanded.]

The PTO and courts occasionally have indicated that business methods are not patentable. Because of this rule, many computer program developers and other inventors made no effort to secure patents on processes that they considered methods of doing business. In 1996, the PTO created some uncertainty about the patentability of business methods when it issued a regulation that stated: "Claims should not be categorized as methods of doing business. Instead, such claims should be treated like any other process claims."[27] In *State Street,* the Federal Circuit Court of Appeals directly addressed this issue by ruling: "Since the 1952 Patent Act, business methods have been, and should have

been, subject to the same legal requirements for patentability as applied to any other process or method."[28]

The *State Street* decision and its implementation by the PTO have created controversy in the business world, especially in the computer industry. The number of applications for business method patents has increased substantially since the *State Street* decision. Many business people have criticized business method patents approved by the PTO asserting that the agency lacks the expertise to evaluate whether a business method is novel or nonobvious. Much of the criticism suggests that patent examiners are not knowledgeable about the "prior art" — methods that long have been used by businesses. In 1999, Congress amended the Patent Act to protect inventors who had not applied for a patent on what they perceived as an unpatentable business method.[29] Under traditional rules of patent law, an inventor who intentionally conceals a patentable process as a trade secret generally is not considered the first inventor. The PTO, therefore, may grant a patent to another person who subsequently discovers the process. The "first inventor defense," however, protects a defendant from liability in an infringement suit if the defendant proves that it reduced the business method to practice at least one year before the plaintiff applied for the patent and commercially used the method before the filing date for the patent.

Copyright Law. Copyright protection of software offers advantages to its creator: copyright registration is inexpensive and continues far longer than a patent. Since a 1980 amendment to the Copyright Act clarified that programs could be copyrighted, copyrights for software have been routinely recognized. The extent of protection afforded by copyright law, however, has not yet been clearly defined, in part because traditional copyright principles are not easily applied to computer programs. Copyright law is intended to protect expression. Although software includes elements of expression, it is designed to operate as a system. Distinguishing which parts of a computer program constitute protectible expression from those elements that are merely part of the system (and, therefore, not subject to copyright) has proved to be difficult. In *Whelan Associates, Inc. v. Jaslow Dental Laboratory, Inc,*[30] a federal appellate court ruled that copyright protected the structure, sequence, and organization of

---

[27]U.S. Patent and Trademark 1996 Examination Guidelines for Computer Related Inventions, 61 Fed. Reg. 7478, 7479 (1996).

[28]State Street Bank & Trust Co. v. Signature Financial Group, Inc., 149 F.3d 1368, 1375 (Fed. Cir. 1998).

[29]35 U.S.C. §273.

[30]797 F.2d 1222 (3d Cir. 1986).

a program as well as the code. Some interpreted this case to mean that the "look and feel" of a computer program were protectible by copyright. More recent cases have denied such broad copyright protection to software. In *Lotus Development Corporation v. Borland International, Inc.*,[31] for example, the court ruled that a computer menu command hierarchy (the menu structure that allows the user to select and use functions such as "open file," "copy," or "print") was a method of operation, rather than an expression of an idea, that should not be protected by copyright law.

Current case law suggests that there may be a trend toward seeking protection of computer software through patents rather than copyrights. This controversy is likely to continue until Congress or the Supreme Court addresses the issue.

Semiconductor Chip Protection Act. In 1984, Congress enacted legislation to protect computer chip technology. The **Semiconductor Chip Protection Act (SCPA)**[32] was adopted at a time of rapid growth in the computer industry in response to manufacturers' concerns about piracy of chips in which they had invested substantial research and development resources. Because neither patent nor copyright law clearly protected chip designs, the SCPA effectively created a new form of intellectual property protection unique to the semiconductor industry. Under the SCPA, the creator of an original chip design may register the "mask work" with the federal Copyright Office. A mask work is a sort of topology map or blueprint that defines the chip's design in three dimensions. The owner is entitled to exclusive rights in the mask work, including the rights to reproduce, assign, or license it, for ten years. In a civil action for infringement of the owner's rights, a court may award actual damages (including the infringer's profits) or statutory damages of up to $250,000, injunctive relief, and attorneys' fees and may impound the infringing chips. To avoid stifling further innovation, the statute does allow copying of the mask work for reverse engineering. New designs developed as a result of that reverse engineering do not constitute infringement.

Digital Millennium Copyright Act. In 1998, Congress enacted the **Digital Millennium Copyright Act (DMCA)** to implement two WIPO treaties: the WIPO Copyright Treaty and the WIPO Performances and Phonograms Treaty. The DMCA added a new chapter, titled Copyright Protection and Management Systems, to the Copyright Act.[33] Computer technology has enabled copyright owners to reduce piracy by restricting access to copyrighted works through scrambling, encrypting, and other security measures. Section 1201 of the Act prohibits anyone from circumventing technological measures that control access to a copyrighted work. Also prohibited are devices or services that are designed to circumvent technological measures, that have limited commercially significant purposes other than circumvention, or that are marketed for circumvention. The statute lists a number exceptions that allow circumvention of protective technological measures including, for example, law enforcement and government activities, encryption research, and security testing.

Section 1202 of the Act is intended to preserve the integrity of "copyright management information," such as the copyright notice, copyright symbols, or information about the owner of the copyright. To do so, the DMCA prohibits knowingly providing or distributing false copyright management information to induce, enable, facilitate, or conceal copyright infringement. Unauthorized removal or alteration of the copyright information also is illegal.

The statute provides civil remedies, including injunctions, actual or statutory damages, similar to those generally available under the Copyright Act to copyright owners who are injured by violations of §1201 or §1202. Triple damages may be awarded in some cases of repeat violations. Violation of §1201 or §1202 also is a criminal offense punishable by a fine up to $500,000 and/or imprisonment for up to five years for the first offense and a fine up to $1 million and/or imprisonment up to 10 years for subsequent offenses.

Computer Fraud and Abuse Act. The **Computer Fraud and Abuse Act (CFAA)**,[34] first enacted in 1984 and amended most recently by the National Information Infrastructure Protection Act of 1996, is the major federal computer crime statute. The CFAA, which originally was intended to protect government computers and classified information, now criminalizes various types of conduct involving accessing "protected computers." Protected computers include any computer that (1) is exclusively for use by the U.S. government or a financial institution; (2) is used by the federal government or a

---

[31]49 F.3d 807 (1st Cir. 1995).
[32]17 U.S.C. §§901–914.

[33]17 U.S.C. §§1201–1205.
[34]18 U.S.C. §1030.

financial institution and the unauthorized access affects that use; or (3) is used in interstate or international commerce. Illegal conduct includes:

1. accessing files without or in excess of authorization and subsequently transmitting classified information;
2. obtaining information from certain protected computers without or in excess of authorization;
3. accessing a protected computer, without or beyond authorization, with the intent to defraud and obtain something of value;
4. knowingly trafficking in a password or information by which a computer may be accessed without authorization with intent to defraud; and
5. transmitting in interstate or foreign commerce any communication threatening to cause damage to a protected computer.

The CFAA also prohibits computer "hacking"—knowingly causing "transmission of a program, information, code, or command" and, as a result, intentionally causing damage to a protected computer.[35] Causing damage as a result of intentionally accessing a protected computer without authorization also is illegal. The penalties for violation of the CFAA, which vary depending on the specific offense, range from a fine and 5 years imprisonment for most violations to a fine and 10 years imprisonment for transmitting classified information (20 years for repeat offenders).

The Internet and E-Commerce

The Internet has evolved from a modest project funded by the U.S. Department of Defense to a global information and marketing network used daily by millions of people. During its early development, the Internet was subject to virtually no legal regulation because scientists and academics were able to agree on rules and protocols. As the commercial potential of the Internet has been realized, however, a variety of legal issues have arisen. Many of these issues involve little more than application of existing legal rules to a new medium. For example, contracts frequently are negotiated on-line. The basic principles of contract law—such as the requirement of offer, acceptance, and consideration—apply to these on-line contracts. In some instances, however, new laws and rules have developed because of issues that are new or unique to the Internet. This part of the chapter examines some of those new laws and rules.

---

[35]18 U.S.C. §1030(a)(5).

Domain Names. The Internet's domain name system creates the "addresses" by which computer users access Web sites. With the phenomenal growth of on-line businesses, the domain name system has become of critical importance. A domain name generally is composed of a second-level domain followed by a "dot," which is followed by a top-level domain. In the domain name Amazon.com, for example, "Amazon" is the second-level domain and "com" is the top-level domain. Top-level domain names available for general use by businesses include *com* (the most frequently used), *biz, net,* and *info.* Other top-level domain names may be used by businesses that meet certain criteria; *pro,* for example, is available for licensed professionals (accountants, attorneys, and physicians); and *mobi* may be used by mobile services providers.

Within each top-level domain, every second-level domain name must be unique. Thus, only one site may be assigned the name Microsoft.com although the domain name Microsoft could be used in another top-level domain, for example Microsoft.net. In the 1980s, a centralized registry was developed to record ownership of domain names.

ICANN. Since 1998, the Internet Corporation for Assigned Names and Numbers (ICANN), an internationally organized, non-profit corporation, has been responsible for managing the top-level domain name system. By accrediting various companies to act as domain name registrars, ICANN has been successful in simplifying and reducing the cost of obtaining a domain name.

ICANN also was instrumental in resolving "cybersquatting" and "cyberpiracy" problems that occurred when someone registered or used famous names or trademarks to capitalize on their fame or goodwill. Since inception of the domain name system, domain names had been assigned on a first come-first served basis without regard to others' rights in the name. Some cybersquatters would hold the name for "ransom" and eventually assign the name to the celebrity or trademark holder in exchange for a large amount of money. Other cybersquatters would use the name for their own Web sites to steal business or confuse consumers as to the site's operator. For many years, the domain name registration system ignored these problems because of the complexity of trademark law.

In 1999, ICANN adopted a Uniform Domain Name Dispute Resolution Policy based on a proposal of the World Intellectual Property Organization. The policy establishes a mandatory administrative proceeding to resolve disputes concerning the use of trademarks or service marks. Under the policy an owner of the mark may request a proceeding if a domain name is identical or confusingly similar to the owner's mark or if a domain name holder registered the mark in bad faith. The dispute resolution proceeding, which is similar to arbitration, generally is completed on-line by dispute resolution providers approved by ICANN. The only remedy is transfer of the domain name if the challenging party is successful. The process is intended to provide a relatively quick and inexpensive way to handle domain name disputes. Parties may use legal proceedings or arbitration as alternative forums or to resolve more complex issues relating to ownership of a mark. In the first five years after the dispute policy took effect, over 8,500 disputes have been resolved through the dispute resolution proceedings.[36]

Anticybersquatting Consumer Protection Act. In 1999, the U.S. government also addressed cybersquatting in the **Anticybersquatting Consumer Protection Act.**[37] The statute, which amends the Lanham Act, imposes civil liability for registering, trafficking in, or using a domain name that, at the time of registration of the domain name, is identical or confusingly similar to a trademark or service mark or that causes dilution of a famous mark. To recover under the statute, the owner of the mark must prove that the defendant had "bad faith intent to profit from the mark." The statute lists a number of factors that may indicate bad faith intent including, for example, the defendant's intent to divert customers to a Web site that could harm the goodwill of the mark's owner, the defendant's offering to sell the domain name to the mark's owner for financial gain without having used the name, or the defendant's having registered multiple domain names identical or confusingly similar to others' trademarks. The owner of a mark who successfully proves cybersquatting in violation of the statute is entitled to the remedies available under the Lanham Act. Instead of actual damages and profits, the owner may elect to receive statutory damages in an amount, determined by the court, not less than $1,000 but not more than $100,000 per domain name.[38]

Internet Service Providers. Widespread consumer access to the Internet has been achieved through private Internet Service Providers (ISPs), companies that provide technology that allows subscribers to log on to the Internet. ISPs, which generate profits from fees paid by subscribers, generally do not create the information and material on the Internet. Instead they merely store and transmit materials provided by others. During the 1990s, a number of lawsuits were filed seeking to hold ISPs liable for torts such as defamation and negligence and for copyright infringement resulting from information on the Internet. The federal government, however, has enacted two statutes that limit ISPs' liability for on-line materials.

Copyright Infringement. The Digital Millennium Copyright Act (described in the previous section of this chapter) extends protection from copyright infringement to ISPs that merely act as data conduits. The statute defines a service provider as "an entity offering the transmission, routing, or providing of connections for digital on-line communications, between or among points specified by a user, of material of the user's choosing, without modification to the content of the material as sent or received."[39] In general, the statute provides that an ISP cannot be held liable for copyright infringement based on copyrighted materials transmitted or temporarily stored (for example, by systems caching) by the ISP. The statute lists detailed conditions that the ISP must meet to qualify for protection. These conditions essentially require the ISP to serve in a passive capacity; that is, not to modify content or determine recipients of the information. Additionally, the service provider must implement and inform its subscribers of a policy that it will terminate services to those who repeatedly commit copyright infringement. ISPs that store infringing material long term (for example, by hosting a Web site that includes infringing copyrighted material) also are protected from liability if the provider does not have actual knowledge of the material, does not receive direct financial benefit, and promptly removes or disables access to the material after learning of the infringement.

Tort Liability. In 1996, Congress enacted the Communications Decency Act in an effort to protect children from offensive and indecent material on the Internet. The following year, the Supreme Court ruled that much of the statute was unconstitutional because it violated the First Amendment guarantee of free speech. Parts of the statute survived the constitutional challenge, including the following provision: "No provider or user of an interactive computer service shall be treated as the publisher or

---

[36]ICANN, Statistical Summary of Proceedings Under Uniform Domain Name Dispute Resolution Policy, May 10, 2004.
[37]15 U.S.C. §1125(d).
[38]15 U.S.C. §1117(d).
[39]17 U.S.C. §512(k)(1)(A).

speaker of any information provided by another information content provider."[40] Federal courts have construed this provision as a broad protection of ISPs.

In *Zeran v. America Online, Inc.,*[41] the court held that the statute protected ISP America Online (AOL) from liability for defamatory statements posted on its Web site bulletin board by a subscriber. The court ruled that AOL was not liable even though it had been notified of the statements and had failed to monitor and remove them. Similarly, in *Ben Ezra, Weinstein, and Company, Inc. v. America Online, Inc.,*[42] the court held that AOL was immune from liability for negligence and defamation based on inaccurate stock information on AOL's Web site. Although the information was created and posted by two companies under contract with AOL, the ISP previously had deleted allegedly inaccurate information from the site and had notified the companies of alleged errors. In both of these cases, the courts supported their decisions by referring to the statute's explicit policy statements including:

> It is the policy of the United States—
>
> (1) to promote the continued development of the Internet and other interactive computer services and other interactive media;
>
> (2) to preserve the vibrant and competitive free market that presently exists for the Internet and other interactive computer services, unfettered by Federal or State regulation.[43]

The New York Court of Appeals also ruled in favor of an ISP, but based on common law rules rather than the federal statute. In *Lunney v. Prodigy Services Company,*[44] the court held that an ISP was not liable for negligence or defamation for libelous statements posted on its Internet bulletin board and sent in e-mail messages. The court held that the ISP was entitled to a qualified privilege previously granted to telephone and telegraph companies that merely transmit communications. In reaching this conclusion, the court noted: "Although they were fashioned long before the advent of e-mail, these settled doctrines accommodate the technology comfortably, and with apt analogies."[45]

Electronic Transactions. In 1999, the National Conference of Commissioners on Uniform State Laws adopted the **Uniform Electronic Transactions Act (UETA).** Its Prefatory Note states:

> With the advent of electronic means of communication and information transfer, business models and methods for doing business have evolved to take advantage of the speed, efficiencies, and cost benefits of electronic technologies. These developments have occurred in the face of existing legal barriers to the legal efficacy of records and documents which exist solely in electronic media.

The Act's basic purpose is to eliminate these barriers by providing generally that "the medium in which a record, signature, or contract is created, presented or retained does not affect its legal significance."[46] UETA is a procedural statute; it defers to existing substantive law, but removes any biases or barriers in that law based upon the medium used in the transaction.

In 2000, Congress enacted the **Electronic Signatures in Global and National Commerce Act**[47] to address many of the issues covered by UETA. The Act provides, however, that it does not preempt the law in states adopting the uniform version of UETA.[48] Because UETA has now been adopted in almost all states, UETA, rather than the federal law, provides the governing rule in most cases.

Two important UETA definitions[49] are "electronic" and "record." The term **electronic** means "relating to technology having electrical, digital, magnetic, wireless, optical, electromagnetic, or similar capabilities." Electronic technologies include, for example, "information processing systems, computer equipment and programs, electronic data interchange, electronic mail, voice mail, facsimile, telecopying, [and] scanning."[50] A **record** is information that is "inscribed on a tangible medium or that is stored in an electronic or other medium and is retrievable in perceivable form." This definition includes "all means of communicating or storing information except human memory."[51]

Scope. UETA applies to electronic signatures and electronic records in "transactions," those interactions

---

[40]47 U.S.C. §230(c)(1).

[41]129 F.3d 327 (4th Cir. 1997).

[42]206 F.3d 980 (10th Cir. 2000).

[43]47 U.S.C. §§230(b)(1), (2).

[44]723 N.E.2d 539 (N.Y. 1999).

[43]*Id.* at 541.

[46]UETA §7, comment 1.

[47]15 U.S.C. §7001 *et seq.*

[48]15 U.S.C. §7002(a).

[49]Definitions are stated in §2 of the UETA.

[50]UETA §2, comment 6.

[51]UETA §2, comment 10.

between people relating to business, commercial, or government affairs.[52] An **electronic signature** includes any electronic sound, symbol, or process associated with a record that is "executed or adopted by a person with intent to sign the record." The Act does not define signature (leaving that to law outside UETA), and does not dictate required technology. The Act makes it clear, however, that the following taken with proper intent may suffice in appropriate cases: a person's voice on an answering machine, using one's name as part of an electronic mail communication, a digital signature, and using the standard Web page "click through" process. The Act "establishes, to the greatest extent possible, the equivalency of electronic signatures and manual signatures."[53]

An **electronic record** is a record "created, used, or stored in a medium other than paper." Examples include information stored on a computer hard drive or disk, facsimiles, voice mails, telephone answering machine messages, and audio and video tape recordings.[54]

The UETA does not apply to certain transactions governed by other law. Most important among these are laws governing the creation of wills and testamentary trusts, and Articles 3 through 9 of the Uniform Commercial Code. Thus, although the UETA applies to sales and leases of goods (UCC Articles 2 and 2A), it does not apply, for example, to the check collection and electronic fund transfer systems governed by UCC Articles 3, 4, and 4A.

Coverage. The UETA does not mandate the use of electronic records or signatures, and applies only if the parties agree to conduct transactions by electronic means.[55] If applicable, however, §7 of the Act broadly validates the parties' electronic transaction by providing:

1. a record or signature may not be denied legal effect or enforceability solely because it is in electronic form;
2. a contract may not be denied legal effect or enforceability solely because an electronic record was used in its formation;
3. if a law requires a record to be in writing, an electronic record satisfies the law; and
4. if a law requires a signature, an electronic signature satisfies the law.

In addition, UETA provides that, in a legal proceeding, evidence of a record or signature may not be excluded solely because it is in electronic form.[56]

UETA also permits notary publics to act electronically, thus eliminating stamp or seal requirements. For example:

> Buyer wishes to send a notarized Real Estate Purchase Agreement to Seller by e-mail. The notary must appear in the room with the Buyer, satisfy himself/herself as to the identity of the Buyer, and swear to that identification. All that activity must be reflected as part of the electronic Purchase Agreement and the notary's electronic signature must appear as a part of the electronic real estate purchase contract.[57]

Finally, if a law outside UETA requires a person to provide, send, or deliver information in writing to another, that information may be communicated in an electronic record that the recipient is able to retain. To be effective, the electronic record must follow any formating, type-size, or other requirements imposed by the law requiring the information. If, however, the law explicitly requires that the information be communicated by a specific method (for example, registered U.S. mail), that method must be used.[58]

Jurisdiction. As discussed in Chapters 1 and 2, to render a binding judgment in a civil case, a court must have both subject matter and personal jurisdiction. Subject matter jurisdiction refers to the type of case the court is empowered to hear by statute or constitutional provision. Personal jurisdiction is the court's power to render a judgment that is binding on the parties, the plaintiff and defendant. The plaintiff consents to the court's jurisdiction by filing the lawsuit. The court obtains jurisdiction over the defendant when "process" (a copy of the complaint and a summons) is served on the defendant.

The territorial reach of a court's process, however, is limited. Generally, due process requires that an out-of-state defendant must defend a lawsuit in a state only if he has "minimum contacts" with the state that are the basis of the lawsuit. Increasingly in recent years, the defendant's contact with a state has been through an Internet Web site that is accessible to residents of the state. The following case articulates the standards developed by the courts to determine when an Internet Web site creates minimum contacts sufficient to establish personal jurisdiction over the defendant.

---

[52]UETA §§2(16), 3(a).

[53]UETA §2, comment 7.

[54]UETA §2(7) and comment 6.

[55]UETA §§5(a)–(b).

[56]UETA §13.

[57]UETA §11, comment.

[58]UETA §8.

Zippo Manufacturing Company v. Zippo Dot Com, Inc.

952 F.Supp. 1119 (W.D. Pa. 1997)

Defendant Zippo Dot Com, Inc. (Dot Com), a California corporation with its principal place of business in Sunnyvale, California, operates a news service from an Internet Web site. Dot Com's customers subscribe to the service by completing an on-line application and making payment by credit card on-line. Dot Com then assigns the customer a password that provides access to various newsgroup messages stored on Dot Com's server in California. When a customer views or downloads newsgroup messages, the word "Zippo" appears on the screen preceding the message. Of Dot Com's 140,000 subscribers, about 2,000 are Pennsylvania residents. Dot Com also has contracted with seven Internet service providers in Pennsylvania to allow their subscribers to use Dot Com's news services. Plaintiff Zippo Manufacturing Company (Manufacturing), a Pennsylvania corporation with its principal place of business in Bradford, Pennsylvania, makes accessories including its most well-known product, Zippo lighters. Manufacturing sued Dot Com in federal district court in Pennsylvania alleging infringement and dilution of Manufacturing's Zippo trademark and other violations of the Lanham Act and state laws. Dot Com filed a motion to dismiss the suit alleging that the Pennsylvania court did not have personal jurisdiction over Dot Com.

McLaughlin, District Judge

. . . A three-pronged test has emerged for determining whether the exercise of specific personal jurisdiction over a non-resident defendant is appropriate: (1) the defendant must have sufficient "minimum contacts" with the forum state, (2) the claim asserted against the defendant must arise out of those contacts, and (3) the exercise of jurisdiction must be reasonable. . . . The "Constitutional touchstone" of the minimum contacts analysis is embodied in the first prong, "whether the defendant purposefully established" contacts with the forum state. *Burger King Corp. v. Rudzewicz,* [105 S. Ct. 2174, 2183–2184 (1985)]. . . .

The Internet makes it possible to conduct business throughout the world entirely from a desktop. With this global revolution looming on the horizon, the development of the law concerning the permissible scope of personal jurisdiction based on Internet use is in its infant stages. The cases are scant. Nevertheless, our review of the available cases and materials reveals that the likelihood that personal jurisdiction can be constitutionally exercised is directly proportionate to the nature and quality of commercial activity that an entity conducts over the Internet. This sliding scale is consistent with well developed personal jurisdiction principles. At one end of the spectrum are situations where a defendant clearly does business over the Internet. If the defendant enters into contracts with residents of a foreign jurisdiction that involve the knowing and repeated transmission of computer files over the Internet, personal jurisdiction is proper. . . . At the opposite end are situations where a defendant has simply posted information on an Internet Web site which is accessible to users in foreign jurisdictions. A passive Web site that does little more than make information available to those who are interested in it is not grounds for the exercise of personal jurisdiction. . . . The middle ground is occupied by interactive Web sites where a user can exchange information with the host computer. In these cases, the exercise of jurisdiction is determined by examining the level of interactivity and commercial nature of the exchange of information that occurs on the Web site. . . .

Traditionally, when an entity intentionally reaches beyond its boundaries to conduct business with foreign residents, the exercise of specific jurisdiction is proper. . . . Different results should not be reached simply because business is conducted over the Internet. . . . First, we note that this is not an Internet advertising case. . . . Dot Com has not just posted information on a Web site that is accessible to Pennsylvania residents who are connected to the Internet. This is not even an interactivity case. . . . Dot Com has done more than create an interactive Web site through which it exchanges information with Pennsylvania residents in hopes of using that information for commercial gain later. We are not being asked to determine whether Dot Com's Web site alone constitutes the purposeful availment of doing business in Pennsylvania. This is a "doing business over the Internet" case. . . . We are being asked to determine whether Dot Com's conducting of electronic commerce with Pennsylvania residents constitutes the purposeful availment of doing business in Pennsylvania. We conclude that it does. Dot Com has contracted with approximately 3,000 individuals and seven Internet access providers in Pennsylvania. The intended object of these transactions has been the downloading of the electronic messages that form the basis of this suit in Pennsylvania.

We find Dot Com's efforts to characterize its conduct as falling short of purposeful availment of doing business in Pennsylvania wholly unpersuasive. At oral argument, Defendant repeatedly characterized its actions as merely "operating a Web site" or "advertising." Dot Com also cites to a number of cases from this Circuit which, it claims, stand for the proposition that merely advertising in a forum, without more, is not a sufficient minimal contact. This argument is misplaced. Dot Com has done more than advertise on the Internet in Pennsylvania. Defendant has sold passwords to approximately 3,000 subscribers in Pennsylvania and entered into seven contracts with Internet access providers to furnish its services to their customers in Pennsylvania. . . .

When a defendant makes a conscious choice to conduct business with the residents of a forum state, "it has clear notice that it is subject to suit there." [*World Wide Volkswagen v. Woodson,* 100 S. Ct. 559, 567 (1980)]. Dot Com was under no obligation to sell its services to Pennsylvania residents. It freely chose to do so, presumably in order to profit from those transactions. If a corporation determines that the risk of being subject to personal jurisdiction in a particular forum is too great, it can choose to sever its connection to the state. If Dot Com had not wanted to be amenable to jurisdiction in Pennsylvania, the solution would have been simple—it could have chosen not to sell its services to Pennsylvania residents.

We also conclude that the cause of action arises out of Dot Com's forum-related conduct in this case. . . . In the instant case, both a significant amount of the alleged infringement and dilution, and resulting injury have occurred in Pennsylvania. The object of Dot Com's contracts with Pennsylvania residents is the transmission of the messages that Plaintiff claims dilute and infringe upon its trademark. When these messages are transmitted into Pennsylvania and viewed by Pennsylvania residents on their computers, there can be no question that the alleged infringement and dilution occur in Pennsylvania. Moreover, since Manufacturing is a Pennsylvania corporation, a substantial amount of the injury from the alleged wrongdoing is likely to occur in Pennsylvania. . . .

Finally, Dot Com argues that the exercise of jurisdiction would be unreasonable in this case. We disagree. There can be no question that Pennsylvania has a strong interest in adjudicating disputes involving the alleged infringement of trademarks owned by resident corporations. . . . These concerns outweigh the burden created by forcing the Defendant to defend the suit in Pennsylvania, especially when Dot Com consciously chose to conduct business in Pennsylvania, pursuing profits from the actions that are now in question. . . .

We conclude that this Court may appropriately exercise personal jurisdiction over the Defendant. . . .

[Motion denied.]

FTC Internet Regulation. The Federal Trade Commission (FTC), as part of its consumer protection activities, is responsible for some Internet regulation.

Internet Advertising. Chapter 52 discusses the Federal Trade Commission's (FTC) enforcement of §5 of the FTC Act, which prohibits "unfair or deceptive acts or practices." Through regulations and administrative proceedings, the FTC uses this authority to protect consumers against false or misleading advertising claims, promotional activities, and other sales practices.

The Internet provides an alternative medium for sales and advertising claims. The FTC has indicated:

> The same consumer protection laws that apply to commercial activities in other media apply online. The FTC Act's prohibition on "unfair or deceptive acts or practices" encompasses Internet advertising, marketing, and sales. In addition, many Commission rules and guides are not limited to any particular medium used to disseminate claims or advertising, and therefore apply to online activities.[59]

In addition, the terms "written," "writing," "printed," or "direct mail" used in FTC rules and guides generally also apply to Internet activities such as visual text, advertising displays, on-line catalogs, and e-mail solicitations.

Commercial Electronic Mail. Based on findings that unsolicited commercial email (spam) threatened the efficiency and convenience of electronic mail, the federal government enacted the Controlling the Assault of Non-Solicited Pornography and Marketing Act of 2003 (CAN-SPAM Act).[60] The statute regulates only "commercial electronic mail messages" defined as

---

[59]Dot Com Disclosures, Information About On-line Advertising, (2000) (available at FTC website http://www.ftc.gov).
[60]15 U.S.C §§7701-7713.

email messages "the primary purpose of which is commercial advertising or promotion of a commercial product or service."[61] The statute does not prohibit spam but instead requires senders of unsolicited commercial email messages to meet certain standards including:

1. Clearly identifying the email as a solicitation or advertisement and not creating a deceptive subject line;
2. Including a legitimate return email address as well as the sender's postal address; and

3. Providing an easily accessible means for the recipient to "opt-out" of receiving future messages.

The FTC has the power to enforce violations of CAN-SPAM Act as unfair or deceptive acts. Internet service providers, as well as the attorneys general of states also have the power to file civil lawsuits under the Act. Criminal penalties may be imposed in lawsuits initiated by the federal Department of Justice for predatory and abusive practices.

Summary

1.   Intellectual property law has two sometimes conflicting purposes: (1) to encourage innovation by rewarding those who develop inventions and creative works; and (2) to facilitate exploitation of new inventions and ideas that will further innovation and creativity.

2.   A patent is the exclusive right to make, use, and sell an invention for a term of years. In the U.S., the federal government grants patents through the Patent and Trademark Office. Patent infringement occurs when someone makes, uses, or sells a patented invention without permission from the patent holder.

3.   A trade secret is information that derives economic value from not being generally known to or ascertainable by others who could obtain economic value from its disclosure or use. Trade secrets are protected from misappropriation only if the owner exercises reasonable efforts to maintain its secrecy.

4.   A copyright is the exclusive right to reproduce and distribute a creative work for a term of years. In the U.S., the federal government extends copyright protection only to original works that are fixed in a tangible medium. Copyright infringement occurs when someone violates the exclusive rights of the copyright owner.

5.   Trademarks are symbols, words, and other devices used in marketing to identify and distinguish the source of goods. Service marks are symbols, words, and other devices that identify and distinguish the source of services. In the U.S., trademarks and service marks that are distinctive and that are not likely to cause confusion with a prior mark may be registered with the Patent and Trademark Office. Trademark infringement occurs when someone uses a mark that be-

longs to another or that is confusingly similar to the mark of another. Trademark dilution occurs when a famous mark loses its distinguishing capacity because it is used with other products.

6.   Computer programs and software that are novel, nonobvious, and useful may be patented under the U.S. Patent Act. Computer programs and software that are original and fixed in a tangible medium can be copyrighted. Judicial interpretation and application of these rules have caused some uncertainty about the extent of patent and copyright protection afforded to computer programs and software.

7.   Computer Fraud and Abuse Act, the major federal computer crime statute, prohibits computer hacking and other unauthorized access or use of information from protected computers including computers used in interstate and international commerce.

8.   The commercial importance of Internet domain names has led to an international registration system managed by the Internet Corporation for Assigned Names and Numbers (ICANN). ICANN provides a resolution system for domain name disputes and the U.S. government prohibits cybersquatting, the registration of a trademark or service mark that belongs to another with the bad faith intent to profit from the mark.

9.   The Digital Millennium Copyright Act protects Internet service providers that act in a passive capacity from copyright infringement. The Communications Decency Act further protects Internet service providers from liability for information provided by another.

10.   The Uniform Electronic Transactions Act is designed to eliminate barriers to the legal efficacy of electronic records and documents. If parties have agreed to conduct electronic transactions, the Act validates those transactions and will not deny the legal effect or enforceability of electronic records and signatures merely because they are in electronic form.

---

[61]15 U.S.C. §7702 (2)(A).

Key Terms

intellectual property
patent
utility patent
plant patent
design patent
Uniform Trade Secrets Act
trade secret
misappropriation
Economic Espionage Act
copyright
No Electronic Theft Act
trademark
service mark
collective mark
certification mark
Federal Trademark Dilution
  Act (FTDA)

Semiconductor Chip
  Protection Act (SCPA)
Digital Millennium
  Copyright Act (DMCA)
Computer Fraud and Abuse
  Act (CFAA)
Anticybersquatting
  Consumer Protection Act
Uniform Electronic
  Transactions Act (UETA)
Electronic Signatures in
  Global and National
  Commerce Act
electronic
record
electronic signature
electronic record

Questions and Problems

59.1 Jeff Bezos, founder of Amazon.com, has applied for a patent claiming that he invented a "method and system for placing purchase orders via a communications network." The invention refers to the system on the Amazon Web site in which a purchaser clicks a button labeled "1-Click." That action starts a process in which the purchased item is collected from the warehouse, packaged, sent, and delivered to the customer and the customer's account is billed for the item. Do you think that the PTO should grant the patent in 1-Click? Why or why not?

59.2 Jason was fired from his job as information systems network administrator at Ball Manufacturing Co. Before Ball deactivated his password, Jason used it to obtain passwords of several other employees. Using those passwords, he accessed Ball's computer system from his home computer and deleted all of the company's billing files and deleted several databases. Does Ball have any legal recourse? Explain.

59.3 Ralph Lauren designs, manufactures, and sells several very popular lines of clothing using the trademark "Polo." The mark has been registered for over 30 years with the PTO. Acme Publishing Company publishes leisure activity magazines on a variety of subjects including boating, skiing, and golf. Acme has started publication of a new magazine named *Polo* devoted to news about the sport of polo. Identify and discuss the legal grounds, including the remedies, for which Lauren might sue Acme.

59.4 A television company that broadcasts defamatory statements can be held liable for damages. Internet service providers (ISPs), however, generally are not liable for damages for defamatory statements that they transmit over the Internet even though the information is available to many more people. Discuss the reasons for this differing treatment. Do you think that the protection granted to ISPs is fair? Why or why not?

59.5 Carrie and Ben formed Virtual Works Inc., a company that provides web design services. Ben contacted an accredited Web site registration service that told him the following domain names were available: virtualworks.com, vwi.com, virtualworks.net, vwi.net, and vw.net. They chose vw.net noting that customers might find it easy to remember because VW was a familiar nickname for Volkswagen. Virtual Works Inc. operated for three years using the vw.net address. After receiving several calls from Volkswagen dealers interested in using the vw.net domain name, Carrie contacted Volkswagen of America, Inc. (VOA). Explaining that several parties were interested in the domain name, Carrie offered to sell it to VOA for $100,000. When the company rejected the offer, Carrie stated: "We are going to sell this address to the highest bidder regardless of what kind of business it operates." VOA is concerned that Virtual Works will sell the domain name to a disreputable business. Does VOA have any legal recourse? Explain.

59.6 Min, a resident of Texas, has developed and patented a software package for tracking inventory. At a trade show in Colorado, Allen, a resident of Vermont, contacted Min about marketing Min's software. They discussed the possibility over several months during which Min shared information about his product with Allen. Eventually they stopped negotiations because they were unable to reach an agreement. Min learned that AAA Co., a Vermont corporation with its principal place of business in Vermont, is selling software that is an almost exact copy of Min's package. Min visited AAA Co.'s Web site where AAA advertised its inventory program. The Web site provided a toll free number for interested customers. Min believes that Allen gave AAA information about Min's software. Min has filed suit in Texas against AAA Co. claiming violations of patent and trade secret law. Does the court have personal jurisdiction over AAA Co.? Explain.

59.7 Citigroup is an international financial company incorporated in New York with its principal place of business in New York. Citigroup sued CitiBank alleging that it had infringed on Citigroup's trademark. CitiBank is a West Virginia corporation located only in West Virginia. Citigroup sued CitiBank in New York. CitiBank argued that it was not subject to the personal jurisdiction of the New York courts. Evidence presented in a hearing showed that CitiBank conducts much of its business over the Internet. CitiBank's Web sites allow customers to apply for loans on-line and to click on a hyperlink that allows them to "chat" on-line with a Citibank lending officer. How should the court rule?

59.8 Lola Zerhold manufactures and markets xylophones in Zion, Ohio. She wants to use a trademark that can be registered with the federal PTO. Which of the following marks qualifies for registration? Explain.
  (a) Zion Xylophones
  (b) Zany Xylophones
  (c) Zerhold Xylophones
  (d) World's Best Xylophones
  (e) Zenith Xylophones

59.9 The Japanese government issues patents under a system similar to that used by the United States. Under the Japanese system, the government may order a patent holder to grant a nonexclusive license if the invention has not been worked sufficiently three years or more after the patent was granted.

(a) Suggest reasons for this compulsory licensing.

(b) In light of the stated U.S. policy on patents, should the U.S. adopt a compulsory licensing requirement? Why or why not?

59.10 A microbiologist applied for a patent of a human-made, genetically engineered bacterium capable of breaking down components of crude oil. No natural bacteria have this characteristic. Scientists plan to use the bacteria to treat oil spills. The PTO denied the patent asserting that living things are not patentable under the Patent Act. Does this bacterium qualify for a patent under the four classes of inventions that qualify for utility patents? Explain.

59.11 Rural Telephone Services (RTS), which provides telephone service in a small town in Kansas, issues a telephone directory that it distributes annually to its customers. The white pages section of the directory lists subscribers' names, addresses, and telephone numbers; the yellow pages section lists similar information about local businesses. RTS generates revenues by selling business advertisements that are published in the yellow pages. Feist Publications publishes regional telephone directories covering much larger areas than those covered by the local telephone directories. To gain access to subscribers' information, Feist generally pays a fee to the local telephone company. After RTS refused to sell Feist its subscribers' information, Feist copied the listings from the RTS directory and printed them in Feist's directory. RTS sued Feist for copyright infringement. How should the court rule? Explain.

59.12 A team of geologists employed by Amoco Production Co. conducted a study to locate new sources of oil. After reviewing maps published by the federal government and Amoco records, the team interviewed Amoco employees who had conducted prior explorations. Based on a statistical analysis, the team selected four sites. Amoco paid Data Co. $150,000 to conduct microwave radar surveys of the sites. All Data Co. employees were required to sign confidentiality agreements promising not to disclose any information learned in doing the work for Amoco. After completion of the surveys, Amoco decided to postpone further development. John Rock, an Amoco geologist, was disappointed with the postponement and told his friend, Bill Wildcatter, an independent oil explorer, about the studies. Rock gave Wildcatter a map with the promising sites circled. Wildcatter inspected the four sites and decided that one showed significant potential for oil reserves. Wildcatter bought or leased all real estate in the surrounding area. Several months later, Amoco decided to begin development of the four oil sites. Amoco then discovered Wildcatter's interests in the property.

(a) Identify all information that would qualify as a trade secret, explaining the reasons for your conclusions.

(b) Identify any conduct that would be considered misappropriation and explain the reasons for your conclusions.

(c) Assuming that Amoco could prove all information previously described, who could be held liable for trade secret misappropriation? Explain.

abandonment 1. in landlord-tenant law, the wrongful unilateral act of the tenant in vacating the premises without further intent to abide by terms of the lease. See *landlord-tenant relationship, lease;* 2. the intentional, permanent, and absolute relinquishment of all interest in an item of personal property by the owner. See *personal property, property.*

abatement doctrine of decedents' estates law that operates to reduce or extinguish a beneficiary's share when there is insufficient property in a decedent's estate to satisfy all gifts provided in the will after creditor's claims, taxes, and administrative expenses have been paid. See *will.*

abstract of title a chronological summary of the contents of all recorded instruments pertaining to a particular tract of land.

abuse of process the use of a legal process to accomplish a purpose for which it was neither designed nor intended.

acceleration clause contractual clause providing that upon occurrence of a given contingency (such as default in one or more installments in a promissory note), all future installments are accelerated and become immediately due and payable, or payable on a date sooner than originally agreed.

acceptance 1. in negotiable instruments law, the drawee's signed engagement to honor (pay) a draft as presented. See UCC §3–409(a); 2. in general contract law, the act by which an offeree manifests assent to the terms of an offer in the manner prescribed by the offeror; 3. in sales law, the buyer's indication of an intent to retain (rather than reject and return) goods delivered by a seller. See UCC §2–606.

acceptor a drawee who accepts a draft.

accession process by which value in the form of labor or property, or both, is added to tangible personal property.

accommodation (uncompensated or gratuitous) surety a surety that is not principally engaged in entering into suretyship contracts for a fee. An accommodation surety's contracts are occasional and incidental to other business. See *suretyship, compensated (corporate) surety.*

accommodation party in negotiable instruments law, a person who signs an instrument in any capacity (maker, indorser, acceptor) for the purpose of lending his or her name or credit to another party to the instrument. See *suretyship,* UCC §3–419(a).

accord and satisfaction the creation and performance of a compromise agreement used to settle a preexisting, usually disputed or unliquidated, obligation. Specifically, an accord is a contract in which a party entitled to a performance promises to accept an alternative stated performance in full satisfaction of the original duty owed. Satisfaction is the performance of the accord agreement.

account any right to payment for goods sold (or to be sold) or for services rendered (or to be rendered) that is not evidenced by either an instrument or chattel paper. Accounts also include rights to receive payment: (1) for the sale of real property; (2) for a license of intellectual property; (3) for becoming a surety on another person's debt; (4) under a life, health, or other insurance policy; (5) for the lease or hire of a vessel; (6) arising out of the use of a credit card; (7) for winning a government lottery. As with the traditional or commercial accounts described above, these additional rights to payment are accounts, whether or not earned by performance. See UCC §9–102(a)(2).

account debtor a person obligated on an account, chattel paper, or general intangible. See UCC §9–102(a)(3).

accounting in partnership law, an equitable proceeding in which the court directs a comprehensive investigation of the partners' and partnership transactions in order to adjudicate the rights of various partners.

acknowledgment formal witnessing of the signing of an instrument, such as a deed, by a public officer such as a notary public or justice of the peace of the signer's declaration that the execution is his or her voluntary act.

act of state doctrine doctrine of judicial restraint designed in part to prevent the judiciary from embarrassing and interfering with the executive in the conduct of foreign affairs. The doctrine prevents the courts of one state from challenging the validity of public acts that a recognized foreign sovereign state commits within its own territory.

ademption by extinction a doctrine of the law of wills that may prevent a beneficiary from receiving property provided for him or her in the will. Ademption by extinction occurs when the subject matter of the gift is not in the testator's estate at the time of death. See *ademption by satisfaction.*

ademption by satisfaction a doctrine of the law of wills that may prevent a beneficiary from receiving property provided for him or her in the will. Ademption by satisfaction occurs when the testator, after execution of the will but during his or her lifetime, makes a gift of property to a beneficiary under the will, that serves in lieu of the bequest or devise. See *advancement.*

adequate assurance of due performance in contract and sales law, when "reasonable grounds for insecurity" arise with respect to the performance of either party, the other party may demand adequate assurance of due performance and, until he or she receives such assurance, may suspend any performance for which he or she has not already received the agreed return. What constitutes adequate assurance is a question of fact, depending upon the circumstances of the case. The grounds for insecurity need only be "reasonable," not actual. See UCC §2–609.

adhesion contract a standardized form contract in which one party dictates many of the contract terms to the other (the adhering party).

administrative order judgment that terminates an administrative hearing.

Administrative Procedure Act comprehensive federal statute that sets forth procedures federal administrative agencies must follow when engaging in rule-making or adjudication and that regulates dissemination of information gathered by agencies.

administrative search usually a governmental civil inspection of a residential or commercial building to determine compliance with fire, health, and other safety codes.

administrator (administratrix) a person appointed by a probate court to fulfill an executor's functions in an intestate estate.

advancement doctrine of decedents' estates law that operates to reduce the amount of property that otherwise would pass to an heir if a person dies intestate. It is analogous to the doctrine of ademption by satisfaction applied when the decedent leaves a 7ill. See *intestate, ademption by satisfaction.*

adverse possession a method of acquiring title to real property through operation of the statute of limitations. See *statute of limitations.*

adverse possessor a person wrongfully possessing real property who may acquire title through the operation of the adverse possession doctrine. See *adverse possession.*

affirm action of an appellate court that confirms the judgment of a lower court.

affirmative action programs programs adopted to encourage hiring women or members of minority groups that are underrepresented in the company or institution.

affirmative covenant the promisor (covenantor) to do something on his or her land, such as building or maintaining a party wall, irrigation or drainage ditch, or structure such as a dam or bridge. See *covenant.*

affirmative defense facts that the law recognizes as a bar to the plaintiff's claim if proven by the defendant. Examples include expiration of the statute of limitations, discharge of the claim in bankruptcy, or prior adjudication of the claim.

after-acquired property clause clause that can be included in a security agreement, which provides that any or all obligations covered by the security agreement are to be secured by after-acquired collateral. See *floating lien (floating charge),* UCC §9–204(a).

Age Discrimination in Employment Act federal statute enacted in 1967 prohibiting employment discrimination against persons over 40 years of age.

agency a consensual fiduciary relationship in which one party, or agent, agrees to act on behalf of and under the control of another, known as the principal.

agency coupled with an interest See *power as given security.*

agency shop agreement requiring employees who do not join the union to pay for the union's services through fees that usually are equivalent to members' dues and fees.

agent See *agency.*

agreed equivalents See *divisibility.*

airbill a document of title serving for air transportation as a bill of lading does for marine or rail transportation. See *bill of lading, document of title.*

aleatory promise a contractual promise made conditional upon the occurrence or nonoccurrence of an uncertain or fortuitous event.

alteration in negotiable instruments law; (1) an unauthorized change in the terms of an instrument that purports to modify in any respect the obligation of a party, or; (2) an unauthorized addition (usually of words or numbers) to an incomplete instrument relating to a party's obligation. See UCC §3–407(a). In contract law generally, a change in terms of, or addition to, a writing that varies the legal relations of any party either with the maker of the alteration or with third parties.

allonge in negotiable instruments law, a separate paper used for indorsements, usually when prior indorsements have exhausted the space on the back of an instrument. An allonge must be affixed to the instrument. See *indorsement,* UCC §3–204(a).

allowed claim in a bankruptcy case, a claim that participates in the distribution of the estate's assets.

Americans with Disabilities Act federal statute, enacted in 1990, to eliminate discrimination against individuals with disabilities. It is designed to make public services, public accommodations, and telecommunications more accessible to individuals with disabilities, and to prevent employment discrimination against them. It is based upon the Rehabilitation Act of 1973. See *Title I of the Americans with Disabilities Act, Rehabilitation Act of 1973.*

ancillary restraint a promise in restraint of trade made as part of an otherwise valid transaction, such as a sale of a business. See *restraint of trade, naked restraint.*

annexor in the law of fixtures, the person who places the chattel on real estate. See *fixture.*

annual percentage rate (APR) under the Truth-in-Lending Act, the finance charge on an annual basis expressed as a percentage of the amount of credit. See *Truth-in-Lending Act.*

answer the pleading in a civil case in which a defendant replies to each allegation of a complaint. See *complaint, pleadings.*

antecedent debt an old debt, one existing before the negotiation of an instrument, or transfer of money or other property to satisfy it.

anticipatory repudiation a repudiation of a contractual duty that occurs before the repudiating party commits a breach by nonperformance. See *repudiation.*

Anticybersquatting Consumer Protection Act federal statute, enacted in 1999, imposing civil liability upon person who "with bad faith intent to profit from the mark," registers, traffics in, or uses a domain name that, at the time of registration, is confusingly similar to a trademark or service mark, or that dilutes a famous mark.

antitrust laws state and federal laws designed to promote competition and prevent monopoly. See *Sherman Antitrust Act, Clayton Act, Federal Trade Commission Act.*

apparent authority in agency law, conduct of the principal toward third parties who deal with the agent or purported agent, creating authority in the agent to bind the principal. See *agency.*

appellant party to a lawsuit seeking an appeal. See *appellee.*

appellate jurisdiction jurisdiction possessed by courts that are empowered to review cases that have been tried by a court of original jurisdiction. See *jurisdiction, original jurisdiction.*

appellee in an appeal, the party against whom an appeal is taken. See *appellant.*

arbitration method of resolving disputes in which an objective third party proposes a resolution that the two parties are bound by law to accept. See *mediation.*

arraignment in criminal law, a hearing before the court at which the indictment or information is read to the defendant.

artificial person entity such as a corporation that is treated in law as a person. See *natural person.*

artisan a skilled worker, such as a tailor, carpenter, or auto mechanic, in a trade requiring manual dexterity.

artisan's lien the right of an artisan to retain possession of an object repaired or worked upon until receipt of payment for the work performed. See *lien, artisan.*

assignee in a contract assignment, the person to whom rights are transferred. See *assignor.*

assignment the transfer of the rights under a contract to a third party. The term is sometimes used to designate both a transfer of rights and a delegation of duties under the contract.

assignment for the benefit of creditors the transfer of all nonexempt assets by a debtor to an assignee or trustee, who liquidates the assets and distributes the proceeds to the debtor's creditors.

assignment of lease the transfer by the tenant of his or her entire remaining interest under the lease.

assignor in a contract assignment, the person transferring rights under the contract. See *assignee.*

association a voluntary collection, uniting, or coming together of two or more persons for a certain purpose. The term connotes both voluntariness and intent to be a member of an association. See *partnership.*

assumed business name statute a state law requiring that a certificate listing the names and addresses of persons conducting business under an assumed name or trade name be filed in the public records.

assumption of the risk in tort law, a defense to liability based on the plaintiff's consent (express or implied) to encounter a known unreasonable danger created by the defendant's conduct.

attachment 1. in secured transactions law, the process making the security interest effective between the immediate parties: the debtor and secured party. See UCC §9–203; 2. in debtor-creditor law, a prejudgment remedy, generally governed by statute, designed to reach assets in the hands of the debtor and hold them to assure their availability if and when the creditor obtains a judgment.

attempt in criminal law, act or acts committed by the defendant with the intent to commit a crime, constituting a substantial step toward the commission of that crime. See *inchoate crimes.*

attestation the act of witnessing the execution of a written instrument, at the request of the person making it, and subscribing it as a witness.

attestation clause a clause in a will, signed by the witnesses, stating that the statutory formalities necessary for proper execution have been observed.

attorney a person who has been authorized by one or more states to practice law on behalf of clients.

attorney's opinion a formal written opinion regarding the marketability of title to real property that is rendered by an attorney after examining the title as disclosed by an abstract of title. See *abstract of title, marketable title.*

attractive nuisance doctrine rule of tort law stating the conditions under which a possessor of land is liable for injury to trespassing children. Also called the "turntable" doctrine. See *trespasser.*

auction a public sale of property (either real or personal) to the highest bidder by an auctioneer who is authorized or licensed by law to conduct such sales.

authenticate 1. to sign; 2. to execute or otherwise adopt a symbol, or encrypt or similarly process a record, with the present intent of the authenticating person to identify the person and adopt or accept a record. See UCC §9–102(a)(7). Authentication is the method of "signing" an electronic, as opposed to a paper, record. See *record, sign.*

authority in agency law, the power of an agent to bind the principal to a contract, derived from the principal's directions or instructions to the agent about the extent of the agent's power.

automatic stay a legal consequence of filing a bankruptcy petition that prevents further efforts by creditors to collect their debts.

back pay equitable remedy used in employment discrimination cases under which the employer pays the injured employee wages and benefits that she would have received if the discrimination had not occurred reduced by earnings during the period. See *front pay.*

badges of fraud in the law of fraudulent conveyances, circumstantial criteria used to distinguish fraudulent from nonfraudulent transfers of assets.

bail a security or obligation given by an accused person or another to obtain the accused's release from custody.

bailee in a bailment, a person in rightful possession of goods of another. See *bailor, bailment.*

bailee's lien a lien granted to carriers and warehousemen allowing them to retain possession of goods entrusted to them pending payment for the shipment or storage charges. See UCC §§7–209, 7–210, 7–307, 7–308.

bailment the rightful possession of goods by someone who is not the owner.

bailor in a bailment, a person originally in possession of goods who delivers them to another (the bailee) for a specified purpose without transfer of title.

banking day the part of a day on which a bank is open to the public to perform substantially all of its banking functions. See UCC §4–104(a)(3).

bankruptcy court a unit of the federal district court created to hear bankruptcy cases.

bankruptcy judge a judge appointed to a bankruptcy court to hear bankruptcy cases. Jurisdictional powers of bankruptcy judges are limited and their decisions are subject to review by the federal district court.

bargain an agreement to exchange a promise for a promise or a promise for a performance. Most agreements recognized as contracts are bargains. See *contract.*

bargained-for exchange in contract law, a performance or return promise is "bargained for" if it is sought by the promisor in exchange for his promise, and is given by the promise in exchange for that promise.

battery a harmful or offensive contact with a person that is intended by the actor to cause such a contact.

bearer a person in possession of an instrument, document of title, or certificated security payable to bearer or indorsed in blank. See UCC §1–201(b)(5).

bearer paper in negotiable instruments law, an instrument payable to bearer or indorsed in blank. See *order paper,* UCC §3–109.

beneficiary in contract law, a person other than the promisee who benefits from performance of a promise. See *trust.*

benefit of the bargain in contract law, after breach, the injured promisee receives the "benefit of the bargain" if the judicial relief awarded places him or her in as good a position as he or she would have obtained if the contract had been performed as agreed. See *expectation interest.*

bequest   a term generally describing any form of personal property passing by will. See *will, personal property.*

bilateral contract   contract involving a promise in exchange for a return promise. A bilateral contract therefore involves at least two promises in which each party is both simultaneously a promisor and a promisee. See *unilateral contract.*

bill of lading   a document evidencing receipt of goods for shipment issued by a person engaged in the business of transporting or forwarding goods. See *document of title,* UCC §1–201(b)(6).

blank indorsement   in negotiable instruments law, an indorsement that specifies no particular indorsee and frequently consists of the indorser's signature alone. See *indorsement.*

blue-sky laws   state laws regulating the distribution and sale of securities designed primarily to prevent fraud.

bona fide occupational qualification (BFOQ)   defense to claim alleging disparate treatment in violation of Title VII of the Civil Rights Act of 1964. Title VII prohibits certain forms of employment discrimination, including discrimination based on religion, sex, or national origin. If, however, religion, sex, or national origin is a bona fide occupational qualification reasonably necessary to the normal operation of a particular business, the employer may use these criteria for hiring, training, or promotion. See *Title VII of the Civil Rights Act of 1964, disparate treatment.*

bond   1. in corporation law, an obligation secured by a lien or mortgage upon specific corporate property; 2. in suretyship law, a contract executed by a compensated surety.

booking   in criminal law, an administrative procedure carried out after the arrest of a suspect in which the suspect's name, time of arrest, and alleged crime are recorded in police records.

breach of contract   generally, failure to perform a contract once any conditions to a party's duty have occurred. Breach may occur either by nonperformance of a duty when performance is due, or by repudiation of the duty prior to that time.

breach of trust   occurs when a trustee violates the duty of loyalty or any other duty owed to the beneficiary. A breach of trust renders the trustee liable to the beneficiary for any loss or depreciation in value of the trust property and for any profit resulting from the breach. See *fiduciary relationship, trust, duty of loyalty.*

brief   written document summarizing the legal errors that the appellant alleges occurred at trial and for which he or she requests review by the appellate court.

broker   an agent empowered to make or procure contracts on his or her principal's behalf for compensation, usually called a commission.

bulk sale   under Revised Article 6, a bulk sale is "a sale not in the ordinary course of the seller's business of more than half the seller's inventory, as measured by value on the date of the bulk-sale agreement, if on that date the buyer has notice, or after reasonable inquiry would have had notice, that the seller will not continue to operate the same or a similar kind of business after the sale." See UCC §6–102(1)(c)(ii).

burden of proof   the duty or obligation to prove the disputed fact or facts constituting a cause of action or affirmative defense.

business corporation   corporation organized to carry on a definite business for profit. See *corporation.*

business invitee   a person invited to enter or remain on another's land for purposes connected with business dealings with the possessor of the land. See *invitee, public invitee.*

business judgment rule   rule of corporation law under which officers and directors have no liability for honest, unbiased transactions undertaken with reasonable care, even if it later appears that the act was ill-advised or mistaken.

business necessity defense   defense to employment discrimination in violation of Title VII of the Civil Rights Act of 1964. This defense allows employment practices that are "job related for the position in question and consistent with business necessity" even if the practice causes disparate impact. See *Title VII of the Civil Rights Act of 1964, disparate impact.*

buyer in the ordinary course of business   a person who, in good faith and without knowledge that the sale to him or her is in violation of the ownership rights or security interest of a third party in the goods, buys in ordinary course from a person (not including a pawnbroker) in the business of selling goods of that kind. See UCC §1–201(9).

bylaws   a set of rules governing a corporation's internal affairs. See *corporation.*

C. & F. term   term in a sales contract indicating that the price of goods includes the cost of the goods and freight to the named destination. See UCC §2–320.

C.I.F. term   term in a sales contract indicating that the price of goods includes, in a lump sum, the cost of the goods, the insurance, and the freight to the named destination. See UCC §2–320.

cancellation   occurs when either party puts an end to a sales contract because of breach by the other party. See UCC §2–106(4).

capacity   the ability of a person to create or enter into a legal relationship.

Carriage of Goods by Sea Act (COGSA)   federal statute, enacted in 1936, governing the liability of ocean carriers for loss or damage to goods they carry.

cartel   an agreement among competitors to restrict output and raise prices.

cashier's check   a check drawn by the issuing bank upon itself. See *check,* UCC §3–104(g).

cause of action   a fact or set of facts that, if proven, entitle a plaintiff to judicial relief. Statutory law and the common law establish the elements of a cause of action.

cease and desist order   order issued by an administrative law judge or administrative agency that commands a wrongdoer to stop an illegal practice. A cease and desist order provides injunctive relief by preventing or restraining unlawful conduct. See *injunction.*

certificate of deposit   an instrument that is an acknowledgment by a bank of the receipt of money with a promise to repay it. A certificate of deposit is a note of the bank. See *note,* UCC §3–104(j).

certificated securities   corporate debt or equity securities evidenced by a document, such as a stock certificate. See *security, uncertificated securities,* UCC §8–102(a)(4).

certification   in negotiable instruments law, acceptance of a check by the drawee bank. Certification occurs when an authorized representative of a bank signs or stamps language on the face of a check to indicate the bank's undertaking to pay. See *acceptance,* UCC §3–409.

certification mark   a mark attesting to a specified quality, material, or origin from a certain region.

chain of title   the succession of deeds, wills, and other instruments by which the ownership of real property can be traced back to the original patent or deed from a governmental authority to the first private owner.

charging order device through which a judgment creditor can reach a debtor partner's interest in the partnership involuntarily to satisfy an unpaid debt.

charitable trust trust in which the property is devoted in charitable purposes beneficial to the community in favor of a class of beneficiaries who are not specifically designated. See *trust.*

chattel an article of personal property. The term is usually used to describe tangible, movable objects, such as automobiles.

chattel paper a record or records that evidence both an obligation to pay money and a security interest in or a lease of specific goods. Chattel paper is "tangible" if it is evidenced by a record consisting of information inscribed on a tangible medium (for example, a piece of paper). It is "electronic" if it is evidenced by a record consisting of information stored in an electronic medium. See *record*, UCC §§9–102(a)(31), (78).

check a draft drawn on a bank and payable on demand. See *draft,* UCC §3–104(f).

check collection process the process by which a check is transmitted and presented to the drawee, paid, and the proceeds transferred and credited to the depositor's account.

choice of forum clause contract term often used in international business transactions specifying which country's courts will be used to resolve disputes arising under the contract.

choice of law clause contract term often used in international business transactions specifying which country's law will be used to resolve disputes arising under the contract.

chose thing.

choses in action property rights for intangible things that can be claimed or enforced by action, not by taking physical possession; intangible personal property. See *choses in possession.*

choses in possession property rights in tangible physical objects; goods. See *choses in action.*

civil law law that establishes standards of conduct for relations between individuals and provides compensation to injured parties; areas of law other than criminal law. See *criminal law.*

Civil Rights Act of 1866 federal statute extending basic civil rights to the newly freed slaves. It provides that "all persons . . . shall have the same right in every state . . . to make and enforce contracts . . . as is enjoyed by white citizens." Now interpreted to prevent employment discrimination based on race, ancestry, or ethnic characteristics in all aspects of employment contracts.

claim 1. in bankruptcy and other debtor-creditor law, any right to payment or to receive any equitable remedy, such as specific performance of a contract; 2. in negotiable instruments law, a term referring to a claim of ownership of the instrument asserted against a holder either by a prior holder or a third party not a holder.

class action lawsuit involving numerous plaintiffs in which one or more persons file suit on their own behalf and on behalf of all persons (the class) having claims based on common issues of fact and law.

Clayton Act federal antitrust law, enacted in 1914, prohibiting certain types of price discrimination, certain sales made on condition that the buyer not deal with seller's competitors, certain corporate mergers, and certain interlocking directorates. See *Sherman Antitrust Act, Federal Trade Commission Act.*

Clean Air Act federal statute establishing the current framework for regulating air pollution.

Clean Water Act federal statute establishing the regulatory framework for water pollution control.

clearing house an association of banks or other payors regularly clearing items. See UCC §4–104(a)(4).

closed-end credit credit arrangement involving a fixed amount of debt and a specified repayment date.

closed shop illegal agreement under federal labor law by which an employer agrees to hire only members of a union.

closely-held corporation corporation whose shares are owned by one shareholder or a closely knit group of shareholders. See *corporation, publicly-held corporation.*

codicil an addition or supplement to a will that may add to, subtract from, modify, or revoke provisions of an existing will. See *will.*

cognovit (confession of judgment) clause a term in a contract creating a debt, such as a lease or promissory note, which authorizes the creditor to obtain a judgment against the debtor upon default without notice to the debtor or a hearing.

collateral in a secured transaction, property in which the secured party's security interest exists. The term includes: (a) proceeds to which a security interest attaches; (b) accounts, chattel paper, payment intangibles, and promissory notes that have been sold; and (c) goods that are the subject of a consignment. See UCC §9–102(a)(12), *secured transaction, security interest.*

collateral contract doctrine doctrine providing that the parol evidence rule does not bar admission of evidence of an agreement not within the scope of a completely integrated writing. In other words, the parol evidence rule does not bar proof of a related agreement that is neither inconsistent with nor part of the integrated contract. See *parol evidence rule, integrated agreement.*

collateral estoppel doctrine providing that issues actually decided in one lawsuit are conclusively determined for later lawsuits between the same parties involving different causes of action.

collecting bank any bank handling checks for collection except the payor bank. See UCC §4–105(5).

collection guaranteed words added to a signature on a negotiable instrument meaning that if the instrument is not paid when due, the signer will pay, but only if the holder exhausts legal remedies against the primary party, or circumstances indicate that proceeding against the primary party would be useless. See UCC §3–419(d).

collective bargaining negotiations between the employer and a union representing the employees.

collective-bargaining agreement a formal agreement between an employer and labor union covering wages, hours, and conditions of employment secured by collective bargaining.

collective mark a trademark or service mark used by members of a collective group to identify that its goods or services are produced by members of the group.

color of title a person who possesses land under an instrument that purports to pass title but which is ineffective to operate as a conveyance is said to possess under color of title.

Commerce Clause clause of the Constitution granting Congress the power to regulate commerce with foreign nations, among the states, and with the Indian tribes.

commercial credit credit that is extended for business purposes.

commercial speech expression for business purposes, such as an advertisement for a product or service.

commercial tort claim a tort claim in which 1. the plaintiff is an organization; 2. the plaintiff is an individual, and the claim (a) arose in the course of the plaintiff's business or profession, and (b) does not include damages arising out of personal injury to or the death of an individual. See *tort,* UCC §9–102(a)(13).

common carrier   a person who undertakes or holds out to perform carriage, for hire, for all those who apply.

common law   rules and principles of law embodied in cases previously decided by the courts.

common law liens   liens created by judicial decision that allow creditors such as landlords, bailees, and innkeepers to retain possession of a debtor's property until the debt is paid. See *lien.*

common shares   shares representing the residual ownership interest in a corporation. See *preferred shares.*

common stem ownership   fixture dispute in which the annexor (person placing the chattel on the real estate) owns both the chattel and the land to which it is annexed. See *fixture, divided ownership.*

community property doctrine   doctrine in which husband and wife are treated as equal co-owners of property acquired with the earnings of either during the marriage without regard to which spouse actually supports the family.

comparative fault   in products liability cases based on strict liability, the assignment of responsibility and liability for damage in direct proportion to the degree of fault of each of the parties. See *products liability.*

comparative fault (negligence)   rule of negligence law in which a negligent plaintiff is awarded damages reduced in proportion to his or her fault (negligence) in causing the injury. See *negligence.*

compensated (corporate) surety   a surety, normally a corporation, which is engaged in the business of executing surety contracts for compensation known as a premium. See *suretyship, accommodation surety.*

complaint   the initial pleading filed by the plaintiff that initiates a civil lawsuit. See *pleadings.*

complete integration   in contract law, a writing intended by the parties to be a complete and exclusive statement of the terms of the agreement. See *integrated agreement, partial integration.*

composition   a contract between a debtor and two or more creditors under which the creditors agree to accept partial payment in full satisfaction of their claim.

Comprehensive Environmental Response, Compensation, and Liability Act (CERCLA)   federal statute that provides a system for cleaning up abandoned hazardous waste sites and accidental spills and leakage of hazardous waste.

Computer Fraud and Abuse Act   federal computer crime statute, enacted in 1984 and amended in 1996, prohibiting, for example, computer "hacking," unauthorized accessing of files, and fraudulent trafficking in password information.

computer program   a set of statements or instructions to be used directly or indirectly in an information processing system in order to bring about a certain result. UETA §2(3). See *Uniform Electronic Transactions Act.*

concealment   misrepresentation by conduct other than express statements; that is, action by one person that is intended or likely to prevent another from learning of a fact.

concurrent conditions   in contract law, when performances of the parties are due simultaneously, each party's tender of performance is a condition to the other's duty. These mutual tenders of performance are often known as concurrent conditions. See *tender.*

concurrent ownership (co-ownership)   type of simultaneous ownership interest in which two or more persons have a concurrent right to possession of the same property. See *undivided property interest, tenancy in common, joint tenancy, tenancy by the entirety.*

condemnation proceeding   a legal action initiated by the government to exercise its eminent domain power. See *eminent domain.*

condition   an event that must occur before the duty of performance under a contract becomes due.

condition implied in fact   a condition implied from the language or other conduct of the parties. See *express condition.*

condition implied in law (constructive condition)   a condition imposed by law, arising from neither the language nor other conduct of the parties. See *express condition, condition implied in fact, constructive conditions of exchange.*

condition precedent   a condition that must occur before a duty to perform arises. See *condition.*

conditional check   a method of creating an accord and satisfaction in which a check is tendered in full satisfaction of a disputed claim. Cashing a check is deemed acceptance of an offer for an accord and satisfaction of the accord, thereby discharging the disputed claim.

conditional payment   effect of a check or other instrument on the obligation for which it is given. This means that the payee, by taking the instrument, surrenders the right to sue on the underlying debt until the instrument is due. If the instrument is not paid when due, the holder may sue either on the debt or the instrument. See UCC §3–310.

conditional sales contract   security transaction in which a seller sells goods on credit to a buyer and takes a security interest in the goods sold to secure payment.

conditions precedent   in negotiable instruments law, the conditions to secondary contract liability: presentment to the primary party, dishonor by the primary party, and notice of dishonor to the secondary parties. See *secondary contract liability.*

condition subsequent   an event, the occurrence of which, by the terms of the contract, extinguishes a duty to perform after the duty has arisen along with any claim for breach. See *condition.*

condominium   form of ownership for multiple-dwelling buildings in which each resident purchases a living unit in the building and all residents own common areas as tenants in common.

confiscation   an unlawful taking of foreign assets by a host government. See *nationalization, expropriation.*

conflict of laws   rules of law adopted by a state to determine when and how its courts will apply another state's law.

confusion   commingling of fungible goods (such as grain) of two or more owners in such a manner that the specific property of individual owners cannot be identified.

conglomerate merger   a merger between firms who were neither former competitors nor in the same supply chain. See *product extension merger, market extension merger.*

conscious parallelism   doctrine of antitrust law under which conspiracy in violation of §1 of the Sherman Act may be proven by evidence that two or more firms acted in the same way, each with knowledge of the other's actions. See *Sherman Antitrust Act.*

consent decrees   judicial orders that incorporate a compromise agreement between the government and the defendant in settlement of antitrust suits.

consent order order issued by an administrative law judge in which a party, without admitting guilt, agrees to stop an allegedly illegal practice.

consequential damages damages caused by the consequences or results of a breach of contract. That is, certain losses flow directly and immediately from a breach, and are common to all breaches. In some cases, however, a contract breach triggers a chain of events that cause losses in addition to those normally suffered by promisees after breach of similar contracts. Such additional losses are known as consequential or special damages and include, for example, lost profits, and personal injury and property damage. See *damages.*

consideration a promise or performance each contracting party bargains for and gives in exchange for the return promise or performance of the other party.

consignee in the law of documents of title, the person named in a bill of lading as the person to whom or to whose order the bill promises delivery. See UCC §7–102(1)(b).

consignment a bailment for sale. In a consignment, the owner of the goods (the consignor) retains title and delivers possession of them to the consignee, who then attempts to sell them. See *bailment.*

consignment intended as security type of consignment creating a debtor-creditor relationship in which the bailee-consignee assumes initial responsibility for the purchase price of goods, whether or not she sells or otherwise disposes of them. The consignor retains title to the goods to secure payment for the goods in the consignee's possession. See *consignment, true consignment.*

consignor in the law of documents of title, the person named in a bill of lading as the one from whom the goods have been received for shipment. See UCC §7–102(1)(c).

Consolidated Omnibus Budget Reconciliation Act (COBRA) federal statute, amending the Employee Retirement Income Security Act (ERISA), permitting some employees to continue health care coverage that otherwise would be lost due to termination of employment. See *Employee Retirement Income Security Act.*

conspicuous contract term or clause so written that a reasonable person against whom it is to operate ought to have noticed it. See UCC §1–201(b)(10).

conspiracy an inchoate crime committed when a person, with intent that a crime be committed, agrees with another or others to the commission of that offense. See *inchoate crimes.*

constitution document that establishes the basic principles, governmental structure, and law of a state or nation. The Constitution of the United States is reprinted in Appendix A.

constructive a term used as a modifier (for example, constructive delivery, notice, or eviction) meaning that the given legal result (for example, delivery, notice, or eviction) is implied, inferred, or deduced, by law, when certain facts are present. The term as so used means in essence "as if."

constructive conditions of exchange a doctrine of contract law providing that it is a condition to each party's duty to perform the remaining duties under a promise that there be no uncured material failure of the other party's performance due at an earlier time. See *condition, condition implied in law (constructive condition).*

constructive delivery in the law of gifts, a transfer to the donee of the means to obtain possession and control of the subject matter. See *delivery.*

constructive eviction form of eviction in which the landlord, by conduct or neglect, so substantially interferes with the tenant's right of possession and enjoyment that the premises are rendered uninhabitable. See *eviction.*

constructive notice effect of filing or recording certain documents, such as deeds and financing statements, in an appropriate public office. After filing or recording, third parties are deemed to know (they have constructive notice) of the filed or recorded interest, even if they have no actual knowledge of its existence.

constructive trust an equitable restitutionary remedy that is used to restore property to its rightful owner when a person who has obtained title to the property would be unjustly enriched if permitted to retain it. See *restitution, quasi-contract.*

consumer credit credit that is extended to persons for personal, family, or household purposes.

Consumer Credit Protection Act (CCPA) federal statute regulating consumer credit transactions that includes the Electronic Fund Transfer Act, the Equal Credit Opportunity Act, the Fair Credit Reporting Act, the Truth-in-Lending Act, and the Fair Debt Collection Practices Act, and imposes restrictions on wage garnishments.

consumer goods goods used or bought primarily for personal, family, or household purposes. See UCC §9–102(a)(23).

consumer report an oral or written communication of information from a consumer reporting agency relating to a consumer's creditworthiness, credit standing, credit capacity, character, general reputation, personal characteristics, or mode of living. See *consumer reporting agency.*

consumer reporting agency a person or organization that for a fee or on a cooperative nonprofit basis regularly assembles or evaluates credit or other information on consumers for use by third parties.

continuation agreement in partnership law, agreement through which partners may restrict or deny the liquidation right generally arising upon a partner's dissociation. See *dissociation.*

continuation statement in the law of secured transactions, a statement filed in an appropriate public office that extends the effectiveness of a financing statement.

continuing guaranty in suretyship law, a guaranty that is of an ongoing nature, rather than for a single extension of credit. See *suretyship.*

contract a promise or a set of promises for the breach of which the law gives a remedy, or the performance of which the law in some way recognizes as a duty.

Contract Clause clause of the Constitution prohibiting the states from passing any law impairing the obligation of contracts.

contract remedies judicial relief available to an injured promisee when a contractual promise is not performed or is improperly performed. See *damages, specific performance, equitable remedy.*

contractual capacity the ability of a person to create or enter into a contract, that is, to incur contractual duties.

contribution in cosuretyship, the process of proportionately sharing the loss among cosureties caused by the principal's default.

contributory negligence negligence on the plaintiff's part that, combining with the defendant's negligence, causes the plaintiff harm.

conversion a tort occurring when one person intentionally exercises control over a chattel belonging to another, which so seriously interferes with the other's right to control it, that the possessor is required to pay the full value of the chattel. See *trespass to chattels.*

conveyance (grant) a transfer of an interest in real property made during the life of the transferor, accomplished by using a formal document known as a deed.

conveyancing the performance of the various functions, including financing, necessary to transfer real property interests.

cooperative   a form of real estate ownership by which residents in a multiple-unit building own shares in a corporation that owns the building.

copyright   the exclusive right to reproduce and distribute a creative work.

corporate opportunity doctrine   doctrine of corporation law that prevents corporate officers and directors from usurping and diverting to themselves a business opportunity in which the corporation has an expectancy, property interest, or right, or which in fairness should belong to the corporation.

corporation   an artificial person or a legal entity created by compliance with laws authorizing the corporate form. A corporation exists apart from and independent of its owners or investors, possesses powers similar to those of natural persons, and generally enjoys continuous existence despite changes in ownership.

corporation by estoppel   common law doctrine used to insulate owners of defectively organized corporations from personal liability for corporate debts.

cosuretyship   the relation between two or more sureties who are bound to answer for the same duty of the principal, and who as between themselves should share the loss caused by the principal's default. See *suretyship, subsuretyship.*

Council on Environmental Quality (CEQ)   council created by the National Environmental Policy Act to advise the president on environmental matters.

counterclaim   a complaint filed by the defendant against the plaintiff in a civil case. See *complaint.*

course of dealing   a sequence of conduct between parties prior to an agreement establishing a common basis of understanding for interpreting their expressions and other conduct. See UCC §1–303(b).

course of performance   action taken by the parties under a contract involving repeated occasions for performance, such as an installment contract. See UCC §1–303(a).

court costs   statutory fees to which officers, jurors, witnesses, and others are entitled for their services in a lawsuit, and that are authorized by statute to be taxed and included in a judgment.

courts of chancery (equity)   courts that were developed to provide appropriate relief when no satisfactory remedy was available in the common law courts.

courts of equity   See *courts of chancery.*

covenant   promise; term is used primarily in the real property context (for example, conveyancing and landlord-tenant law) to describe promises made by the parties in leases, deeds, and contracts.

covenant of quiet enjoyment   in landlord-tenant law, an implied covenant between landlord and tenant that after the tenant has taken possession, the landlord may not interfere with the tenant's possession and enjoyment of the property. The covenant is breached by eviction. See *eviction.*

covenants for title   in a warranty deed, promises concerning the status of the grantor's title. They include generally the covenants of seisin and right to convey, the covenant against encumbrances, and the covenant of quiet enjoyment.

covenant running with the land   in real property law, a covenant under which either the liability to perform it, or the right to take advantage of it, passes to a transferee of the property.

cover   a buyer's remedy in a sales contract by which the buyer purchases or contracts to purchase goods to substitute for those due from the breaching seller. See UCC §2–712.

cramdown   in a bankruptcy case, the confirmation of a reorganization plan over the objection of one or more classes of creditors or interests.

credit card   a device, such as a card or plate, used to obtain money, property, or services on credit. See *single-party credit card, dual-party credit card, multiparty credit card.*

credit file   file maintained by a consumer reporting agency containing credit information on a consumer from furnishers of credit information such as creditors, insurers, banks, and landlords. See *consumer reporting agency.*

creditor   a person to whom a debt is owed by a person known as a debtor. See UCC §1–201(b)(13).

creditor beneficiary   in contract law, a type of intended beneficiary. A person is a creditor beneficiary if performance of the promise will satisfy a debt owed by the promisee to the beneficiary. See *beneficiary, intended beneficiary, donee beneficiary.*

creditor's bill   historically, a document filed by a creditor with the court requesting that a debtor be ordered to turn over her equitable and intangible assets for sale in satisfaction of a judgment. It often contained a bill of discovery permitting examination of the debtor and third parties in order to locate assets. The creditor's bill now is used primarily to recover fraudulent conveyances.

creditor's committee   in bankruptcy reorganization, a committee of persons holding large unsecured claims against the debtor of a particular type. Creditors' committees perform various functions in the reorganization, including participation in formulation of the reorganization plan.

crime   an act or failure to act, which is injurious to the public welfare, that violates a law prohibiting or commanding the act, and subjects the offender to punishment prescribed by law. See *offenses, felonies, misdemeanors.*

criminal law   principles and rules of law that protect society by establishing minimum standards of socially acceptable conduct and punishing those who fail to meet these standards. See *civil law.*

criminal procedure   the law that governs the various steps of a criminal proceeding from preliminary investigation to arrest to trial through termination of punishment.

crossclaims   in a civil lawsuit, complaints by a named defendant against other parties listed as defendants in the lawsuit. See *complaint.*

cross-examination   examination of a witness in a trial or hearing by the party opposed to the one who produced the witness, concerning the witness's testimony elicited on direct examination.

cumulative dividend preference   in corporation law, dividend preference that entitles a shareholder to receive a prescribed dividend for the current year and all prior years in which the preferred dividend was not paid, before any dividend may be paid on the common shares. See *preferred shares, dividend, noncumulative dividend preference.*

cumulative-to-the-extent-earned preference   in corporation law, dividend preference that entitles preferred shareholders to carry forward and accumulate unpaid dividends to the extent that the corporation had earnings available to pay the dividends in the year or years in which the dividends were omitted. See *preferred shares, dividend, cumulative dividend preference.*

cumulative voting   in corporation law, method of shareholder voting, which applies only to the election of directors, in which the number of votes each shareholder receives is equal to the number of his or her shares multiplied by the number of directorships to be filled. See *straight voting.*

cure   a seller's remedy under Article 2 of the Uniform Commercial Code, which permits a seller, in limited situations, to cure (correct a defective performance) without liability for breach. See UCC §2–508.

curtesy   the common law right of a widower to a life estate in all of his wife's real estate if a child was born alive during the marriage. See *dower, life estate.*

custom   one source of international law. A practice is recognized as part of international custom if it involves a consistent course of conduct over a considerable period, a recognition that the practice is consistent with or required by international law, and general acquiescence in the practice by other countries. See *international law, treaty.*

customer   in the law of bank deposits and collections, a person having an account with a bank or for whom a bank has agreed to collect an item. See UCC §4–104(a)(5).

cy pres doctrine   doctrine, applicable only to charitable trusts, under which the court permits or directs that trust property be applied to a charitable purpose different from that designated by the settlor. The doctrine applies if the designated charitable purpose fails, and the settlor has manifested a more general intention to devote the property to charitable purposes. See *trust, charitable trust.*

damages   a monetary award recovered in court by a person who has suffered injury through the wrongful conduct, such as tort or breach of contract, of another. Referred to as the "remedy at law" in civil cases. See *civil law, equitable remedy.*

de facto incorporation doctrine   common law doctrine used to insulate shareholders of a defectively organized corporation from personal liability for corporate debts. It applies if an enabling statute exists permitting corporate formation, the parties having made a good-faith effort to comply with the statute, and the parties subsequently conduct business as a corporation. See *corporation.*

de jure corporation   corporation formed in compliance with all mandatory state requirements whose existence is not subject to attack either by the state or by creditors.

dealer   person who engages in the business of offering, buying, selling, or otherwise trading in securities issued by others.

debenture   a type of corporate debt security, specifically an unsecured obligation rendering debenture holders general creditors of the corporation.

debt securities   corporate securities representing obligations that ultimately must be repaid and create a debtor-creditor relationship between their holders and the corporation. Examples include notes, debentures, and bonds. See *security, equity securities.*

debtor   1. a party who has incurred an obligation or debt that is owed to another, the creditor; 2. in a secured transaction, the party who has an interest in the collateral and is giving security. It includes a seller of accounts, chattel paper, payment intangibles, or promissory notes; and a consignee. See UCC §9–102(a)(28). The debtor typically also is the obligor, the person who is obligated to pay the debt the collateral secures. See *obligor.*

deed   a written instrument used to transfer (convey) an interest in real property.

deed of trust (trust deed)   a security device used in s/me states as the functional equivalent of a mortgage. A deed of trust, like other trusts, uses three parties (settlor, trustee, beneficiary) instead of two (mortgagor, mortgage) present in the ordinary mortgage. See *mortgage.*

deed poll   deed signed only by the grantor.

defamation   a tort action that protects a person's interest in her reputation and good name. Liability is imposed if a false and defamatory statement is made and communicated to a third party, and the defendant was at fault in disseminating the statement. See *libel, slander.*

defamatory communication   one that tends to so harm the reputation of another as to lower him in the estimation of the community or to deter third persons from dealing with him.

default judgment   judgment that is entered for the plaintiff in a civil case if the defendant fails to answer the complaint or file a motion to dismiss within the time specified in the summons.

defeasible (qualified) fee   a fee simple ownership interest in property that is subject to a condition; that is, it can be terminated by the occurrence or nonoccurrence of an event stated in the instrument creating the estate. See *fee simple determinable, fee simple subject to a condition subsequent, fee simple subject to an executory limitation.*

defective (unreasonably dangerous) product   in products liability law, a product that fails to perform in the manner reasonably to be expected in light of its nature and intended function (the consumer expectation test). That is, a defective product is in a condition that (1) is not contemplated by the user or consumer, and (2) is unreasonably dangerous (more dangerous than would be contemplated by the ordinary user or consumer). Product defects commonly are classified in three categories: (1) manufacturing defects (the product fails to meet the manufacturer's specifications), (2) warning defects, and (3) design defects. Some courts apply a risk-utility test to determine whether a product design is defective. Under this test, the product is defective only if the risks of the design outweigh its benefits. See *products liability, strict liability in tort.*

defendant   party from whom a plaintiff seeks some form of judicial relief or recovery in a legal proceeding.

defense   as used in the law of negotiable instruments, facts (such as fraud) asserted by a party to a negotiable instrument (usually the maker of a note or the drawer of a draft) to avoid his or her obligation to pay the instrument.

deficiency judgment   the balance due to a secured creditor who obtains a judgment and the value of the collateral is insufficient to discharge it.

definiteness   in contract law, a requirement that an offer be sufficiently definite and explicit so that if accepted, a court in a subsequent dispute has a reasonably certain basis upon which to determine the existence of a breach and to award an appropriate remedy. See UCC §2–204(3).

del credere agent   a factor who sells goods on credit and then guarantees to the principal the purchaser's solvency and the purchaser's performance of the contract. See *factor.*

delegation   the transfer of the duties under a contract to a third party.

delivery   1. in the law of gifts, the transfer of possession of the subject matter of the gift from the donor to the donee. Proper delivery requires that the donor absolutely relinquish the right to use, manage, or control the property. See *gift;* 2. with respect to instruments, documents of title, or chattel paper, delivery means a voluntary transfer of possession, see UCC §1–201(b)(15); 3. with respect to certificated and uncertificated securities, see UCC §8–301.

delivery order   an order for delivery of goods that is issued by a shipper or storer, and addressed to a carrier or warehouseman, ordering it to deliver goods in its possession to a specified person. See UCC §7–102(1)(d).

demand draft   a draft that is payable on demand. See *demand instrument.*

demand instrument in negotiable instruments law, instrument payable whenever the holder chooses to present it for payment to the maker (of a note) or the drawee (of a draft). See *instrument, time instrument.*

demonstrative devise devise payable out of specific property or a specific fund in a testator's estate. See *devise.*

dependent promises in contract law, a term used to mean that failure by one party to perform justifies the other's later failure to perform. It essentially describes the constructive conditions of exchange doctrine generally applicable to contracts. See *constructive conditions of exchange.*

dependent relative revocation doctrine principle of the law of wills stating that if a court finds a testator's revocation of a will is dependent, or conditional, upon the truth of an assumption of law or fact, then the revocation is ineffective if the assumption is, in fact, false.

deposition the testimony under oath of a person (the deponent) who is examined (deposed) out of court by a party to a lawsuit.

deposit account a demand, time, savings, passbook, or similar account maintained with a bank. See UCC §9–102(a)(29).

depositary bank the first bank to which a check is transferred for collection. See UCC §4–105(2).

design patent a patent that may be issued for any new, original, and ornamental design for an article of manufacture.

destination bill of lading bill of lading that is issued at the destination (rather than the place of shipment) or at any other designated place to ensure that the bill of lading will be available at the destination in advance of actual arrival of the goods.

destination contract a sales contract in which the seller is required to transport goods to a stated destination and there tender them to a buyer.

detour deviation by a servant from the scope of employment that is insufficient to remove the servant from the scope of employment. A detour, therefore, does not relieve the master of liability for the servant's torts. See *master, servant, frolic, scope of employment, respondeat superior doctrine.*

devise traditionally, a transfer of real property by will. Modern statutes, such as the Uniform Probate Code, treat any transfer of property by will, real or personal, as a devise.

Digital Millennium Copyright Act federal statute, enacted in 1998, prohibiting circumvention of technological measures, such as scrambling or encryption, designed to prevent piracy of a copyrighted work.

direct examination the first examination or interrogation of a witness by the party on whose behalf the witness is called.

disability See *immunity.*

discharge in contract law, to extinguish or terminate a contractual obligation.

discharge in bankruptcy in a bankruptcy case, a discharge that releases the debtor from any further liability for most debts that arose prior to bankruptcy.

disclosed principal in agency law, a principal whose identity and existence are known to the third party. See *partially disclosed principal, undisclosed principal.*

discount rate term referring to the percentage difference between the face value of an instrument at maturity and the amount an assignee, commonly a bank, is willing to pay for it prior to maturity.

discovery process that allows each party in a lawsuit to discover all relevant facts prior to trial.

dishonor in negotiable instruments law, dishonor occurs if, after proper presentment, the drawee or maker refuses to pay an instrument presented for payment, or the drawee refuses to accept an instrument presented for acceptance.

disparate impact condition occurring when an employment decision based on a neutral criterion (some factor other than race, color, national origin, sex, or religion) has the *effect* of discriminating on the basis of race, color, national origin, sex, or religion. Employment practices causing disparate impact generally are illegal under Title VII of the Civil Rights Act of 1964. See *Title VII of the Civil Rights Act of 1964.*

disparate treatment intentional employment discrimination based on race, color, national origin, religion, or sex. Employment practices involving disparate treatment generally are illegal under Title VII of the Civil Rights Act of 1964. See *Title VII of the Civil Rights Act of 1964.*

disputed claim claim, the existence of which is contested by the party allegedly obligated upon it. See *liquidated claim, unliquidated claim, claim.*

dissociation in partnership law, legal consequence occurring when any partner ceases to be associated in conducting the partnership business. Upon dissociation either (1) the partnership, a legal entity, continues, and the dissociated partner's interest is purchased, or (2) the partnership is "dissolved" and must be "wound up" or liquidated. See *winding up (liquidation).*

dissolution in partnership law, the commencement of the winding up process. See *dissociation, winding up (liquidation).*

distribution transfer of money or other property by the corporation to its shareholders.

diversity jurisdiction one type of subject matter jurisdiction that may be exercised by the federal courts. Generally, federal courts have subject matter jurisdiction over cases in which the plaintiff and defendant are citizens of different states and the amount in controversy exceeds $75,000. See *jurisdiction, subject matter jurisdiction, federal question jurisdiction.*

divided ownership type of fixture dispute that arises when the owner of a chattel (for example, a tenant) annexes it to the land of another (for example, a landlord), requiring a determination of whether the attached article now belongs to the landowner. See *chattel, fixture, common stem ownership.*

dividend 1. a distribution out of a corporation's current or past earnings; 2. in a bankruptcy case, the amount of money distributed to general creditors. See *distribution, general creditor.*

dividend percentage in a bankruptcy case, the percentage of their claims that general creditors are paid. See *general creditor.*

divisibility a contract doctrine used to determine when a party who has partially performed, but has failed to render complete performance, is entitled to recover for the part performance. If a contract is divisible, performance of a divisible part entitles a party to the agreed exchange for that part, despite nonperformance of other parts of the contract. Generally, a contract is divisible if full performance can be divided into corresponding pairs of part performances, so that the exchange of part performances can be regarded as agreed equivalents.

doctrine of judicial review doctrine that gives federal courts the power to determine whether the acts of the legislative and executive branches of government comply with the Constitution and to refuse to enforce those acts that violate it.

document of title any document accepted in business or financing transactions: 1) as adequately evidencing that the person who possesses it is entitled to receive, hold, and dispose of the document and the goods it covers; and 2) that purports to be issued by or addressed to a bailee and to cover goods in the bailee's possession. Examples include bills of lading and warehouse receipts. See *bill of lading, warehouse receipt,* UCC §1–201(b)(16).

documentary draft a draft the honor of which is conditioned upon the presentation of a document or documents. The drafts used in shipments under reservation and letters of credit are documentary drafts. See *letter of credit, shipment under reservation.*

domicile a person's permanent residence, to which he or she intends to return.

donee the person to whom a gift is made. See *gift, donor.*

donee beneficiary in contract law, one type of intended beneficiary. A person is a donee beneficiary if the promisee intends to make a gift of the promisor's performance to the beneficiary. See *beneficiary, intended beneficiary, creditor beneficiary.*

donor one who makes a gift. See *gift, donee.*

Double Jeopardy Clause a provision of the Fifth Amendment to the Constitution prohibiting a criminal defendant from being tried twice for the same offense in most circumstances.

dower common law right of a surviving widow to a life estate in one-third of the real estate owned by her husband at any time during the marriage. See *curtesy, life estate.*

draft (bill of exchange) a writing signed by the drawer containing an unconditional order by the drawer directed to the drawee to pay to the order of the payee or to bearer a fixed amount of money on demand or at a definite time. See UCC §3–104.

drawee the person to whom a draft is directed and who is ordered to pay the amount of the draft. See *draft.*

drawer the person drawing a draft and addressing it to the drawee. See *draft.*

dual-party credit card credit card issued by a card issuer who does not sell goods or services but instead provides credit and collection services for those who do. The card issuer has two classes of customers, its cardholders and the merchants who honor its cards. See *credit card, single-party credit card, multiparty credit card.*

due negotiation negotiation of a negotiable document of title to a holder (1) who purchases it in good faith without notice of any defense against or claim to it on the part of any person, (2) for value, (3) in the regular course of business or financing, and (4) in a transaction not involving mere settlement or payment of a money obligation. See UCC 7–501(4).

due-on-sale clause a contract provision contained in a promissory note or mortgage, permitting the mortgagee, at its option, to declare the entire balance of the mortgage note immediately due and payable if the property secured is sold or otherwise transferred without the mortgagee's consent. See *mortgage.*

Due Process Clause a clause in the Fifth and Fourteenth Amendments to the Constitution, which provides that no person shall be deprived of life, liberty, or property without due process of law. The clause generally requires that parties to civil and criminal cases receive procedural due process—notice and a hearing—before a deprivation of life, liberty, or property.

duress an element of compulsion or coercion in the bargaining process, resulting from either physical coercion or improper threat, which renders a contract voidable. See *voidable contract.*

duty See *right.*

duty of loyalty duty imposed upon agents, partners, corporate directors, and trustees. It requires these parties to act solely for the benefit of others (for example, the principal, other partners, the corporation, or beneficiaries of a trust) regarding all matters within the scope of the relation. See *fiduciary relationship.*

duty to read rule of contract law stating that a person who signs her name to a contract manifests her assent to its terms and may not later assert that she had not read or did not understand its contents.

easement an interest in land that gives its owner the right either to use another person's land for a limited and specified purpose, or to prevent another person from using his or her land in a specified way.

easement appurtenant an easement involving two tracts of land, one benefited by the easement and (known as the "dominant tenement" or "dominant estate"), and one burdened by the easement (known as the "servient tenement" or "servient estate"). An easement appurtenant benefits land—the dominant tenement—owned by the holder of the easement. See *easement, easement in gross.*

easement in gross an easement obtained other than for the benefit of land owned by the holder of the easement. In an easement in gross, there is no dominant tenement. See *easement, easement appurtenant.*

Electronic Espionage Act federal criminal statute, enacted in 1996, prohibiting theft of a trade secret related to a product in or produced for interstate commerce.

economic strike strike based on employees' demands for economic benefits. See *strike, unfair labor practice strike.*

effluent the discharge of waste substances into rivers, lakes, and oceans.

effluent limitations limitations set by the Environmental Protection Agency for those who discharge pollutants into lakes, rivers, or oceans.

election doctrine of the law of agency and contracts, applied when the principal is undisclosed. Under this doctrine, after discovering the existence and identity of the principal, the third party must elect to hold either the principal or the agent liable on the contract.

election of remedies choice by a party of one contract remedy to the exclusion of others. Contract law generally does not require that an injured promisee make an election of remedies.

electronic relating to technology having electrical, digital, magnetic, wireless, optical, electromagnetic, or similar capabilities. UETA §2(5). See *Uniform Electronic Transactions Act.*

electronic fund transfer under the Electronic Fund Transfer Act, any transfer of funds other than one initiated by check, draft, or similar paper instrument that is initiated through an electronic terminal, telephone, computer, or magnetic tape, and which orders, authorizes, or instructs a financial institution to debit or credit an account. See *Electronic Fund Transfer Act.*

Electronic Fund Transfer Act (EFTA) federal statute, enacted in 1978, establishing rights and duties of parties to consumer electronic funds transfer systems, such as automated tellers. See *electronic fund transfer.*

electronic record a record created, generated, sent, communicated, received, or stored by electronic means. UETA §2(7). See *record, Uniform Electronic Transactions Act.*

electronic signature an electronic sound, symbol, or process attached to or logically associated with a record and executed or adopted by a person with the intent to sign the record. UETA§2(8). See *electronic, record, signature, Uniform Electronic Transactions Act.*

Electronic Signatures in Global and National Commerce Act federal statute, enacted in 2000, providing that a signature, contract, or record shall not be denied legal validity solely because it is in electronic form. See *Uniform Electronic Transactions Act.*

emancipation legal result that occurs when a parent surrenders the right to control a minor (including the right to the care, custody, services, and earnings of the child), and renounces parental duties. See *minor.*

eminent domain the power, inherent in a sovereign, to take or authorize the taking of private property for public use without the owner's consent upon making just compensation.

Employee Retirement Income Security Act (ERISA) federal statute, enacted in 1974, to regulate most private pension programs that provide retirement income to employees or that allow employee deferral of income to termination of employment.

employment at will doctrine traditional doctrine of agency law permitting an employer to fire an employee for any reason ("at will") if the employee is hired for an indefinite term without an employment contract. Most states now recognize a number of exceptions to the doctrine.

encumbrance a right or interest in land that diminishes its value but does not prevent transfer of a fee simple absolute. See *fee simple absolute.*

enforceable contract term describing a contract in which the promisee is entitled to a contract remedy if the promisor fails to perform. See *contract remedies.*

entire contract a contract that is not divisible; that is, a contract in which corresponding part performances are not agreed equivalents. See *divisibility.*

entrenchment competitive or market condition that may occur if a company already dominant in a market is acquired by a larger, powerful firm.

entrusting any delivery of goods to (and any acquiescence in retention of possession of goods by) a merchant who deals in goods of the kind. See UCC §2-403(3).

environmental impact statement (EIS) a report required by the National Environmental Policy Act that federal agencies must include in every proposal for legislation or major federal action that will significantly affect the environment. See *National Environmental Policy Act.*

Environmental Protection Agency (EPA) agency created to centralize federal environmental regulation.

Equal Credit Opportunity Act (ECOA) federal statute prohibiting discrimination in credit transactions on the basis of sex, martial status, religion, race, color, national origin, or age.

equal dignity rule common law principle providing that if the contract to be negotiated by an agent is within the Statute of Frauds, the agent's authorization also must be written.

Equal Employment Opportunity Commission (EEOC) commission responsible for enforcing Title VII of the Civil Rights Act of 1964. See *Title VII of the Civil Rights Act of 1964.*

Equal Pay Act federal statute, enacted in 1963, requiring employers to pay equivalent wages to employees of both sexes who perform equal work on jobs requiring equal skill, effort, and responsibility under similar working conditions.

Equal Protection Clause provision of the Fourteenth Amendment to the Constitution stating that no state shall deny to any person within its jurisdiction the equal protection of the laws.

equipment goods used or bought for use primarily in business, including a profession or farming. Goods other than inventory, farm products, or consumer goods. See UCC §9-102(a)(33).

equitable estoppel (estoppel "in pais") estoppel that results when a person relies upon another's statement of *fact* (which may be made expressly, or inferred from silence or other conduct) resulting in injury. See *estoppel, promissory estoppel.*

equitable remedy judicial remedy available if, in the discretion of the court, the remedy at law (money damages) is inadequate to compensate the injured party. Examples include specific performance, reformation, and injunction. See *damages, civil law, specific performance, injunction, injunction against breach, reformation.*

equitable servitude legal theory developed in courts of equity to enforce promises respecting land use. See *courts of chancery (equity).*

equity in real property law, term referring to the difference between the market value of property and the outstanding indebtedness it secures.

equity of redemption concept developed in the law of mortgages that allows a mortgagor to redeem his or her property by satisfying the debt plus interest within a reasonable time after default. See *mortgage.*

equity securities securities, such as shares of stock, that create an ownership interest in the business. See *security, debt securities.*

escrow a flexible device for closing many types of real estate transactions, including installment sales contracts. In an escrow, one party to the contract deposits a deed, other instrument, or money with an escrow agent, who holds the deposited instrument or funds until occurrence of an event outlined in the escrow agreement. See *installment sales contract.*

escrow account a bank account commonly maintained in the name of a mortgagor and mortgage into which the mortgagor makes periodic payments to satisfy recurring charges such as property taxes and insurance premiums.

essential fraud See *fraud in the execution.*

estate 1. all legal or equitable, tangible or intangible property interests owned by the debtor in a bankruptcy case; 2. an ownership interest in property; 3. the combination of all property, real and personal, tangible and intangible, owned by a decedent.

estate at sufferance in landlord-tenant law, term used to describe the possession of a holdover tenant who wrongfully remains in possession of property upon expiration of the lease term.

estate for years in landlord-tenant law, a form of nonfreehold estate characterized by a fixed beginning and ending date. See *nonfreehold estate.*

estate from period to period (periodic tenancy) in landlord-tenant law, a form of nonfreehold estate characterized by its continuance for successive periods until notice of termination is given by either party. See *nonfreehold estate.*

estate (tenancy) at will in landlord-tenant law, an estate (a nonfreehold estate) that may be terminated at the will of either party. See *nonfreehold estate.*

estoppel the legal principle by which a person is prevented (estopped) from asserting a position that is inconsistent with his or her prior conduct, if injustice would thereby result to a person who has changed position in justifiable reliance upon that conduct. See *equitable estoppel, promissory estoppel.*

estray statute a statute that provides procedures by which a finder attempts to restore lost property to its true owner. These statutes commonly provide for advertising the goods followed by a stated period after which the finder acquires title to all or part of the property. See *lost property.*

ethics   systems of moral standards and beliefs; discipline involving study of right and wrong, good and bad, and moral rights and obligations.

Ethics in Government Act   federal statute that restricts some former government officials from lobbying their former agencies after leaving office.

European Union   free trade area including most European nations. See *free trade area.*

eviction   in landlord-tenant law, physical removal of a tenant from all or part of the leased premises by the landlord or person acting under the landlord's authority, or by a person having title to the property superior to the landlord. See *constructive eviction, covenant of quiet enjoyment.*

evidence   legally admissible testimony of witnesses, and documents or other pertinent items offered to prove the facts alleged in a case.

exclusionary rule   rule stating that evidence obtained in violation of the Fourth, Fifth, and Sixth Amendments to the Constitution must be excluded in a criminal prosecution of the person whose rights were violated.

exclusive dealing contract   contract in which a buyer agrees to deal only with a particular seller, or not to deal in the goods of the seller's competitors.

exculpatory clause   contract term that exempts a person from liability for his or her own torts.

executed contract   a promise or contract that has been completed or performed.

execution   judicial process by which a judgment is enforced, involving seizure of the debtor's assets, their public sale, and application of the proceeds to the unpaid judgment.

execution sale   public sale of a debtor's real and personal property to satisfy a judgment. See *execution.*

executor (executrix)   the person appointed or authorized by a probate court to discover, collect, and distribute a decedent's assets and pay lawful claims and taxes against the estate. See *estate, probate court.*

executory contract   a promise or contract that is yet to be performed.

executory interest (executory limitation)   a future interest that exists in property when the property is conveyed in fee simple subject to an executory limitation. See *future interest, fee simple subject to an executory limitation.*

exemption statute   a statute or constitutional provision that exempts certain property of a debtor from creditors' claims.

exhibits   tangible items that have been established as part of the evidence in a lawsuit.

exoneration   in suretyship law, the surety's right, before paying the creditor, to compel the principal to perform. See *suretyship.*

ex parte **proceeding**   legal proceeding in which only one party to a controversy presents testimony or other evidence to the court. The other party is not notified of the proceeding and has no opportunity to be heard.

expectation interest   the interest of the injured promisee most commonly protected by both legal and equitable contract remedies, designed to give the promisee the benefit of the bargain; that is, the court protects the injured party's expectation that the contract will be performed, not breached. See *contract remedies, benefit of the bargain, reliance interest, restitution interest.*

Expedited Funds Availability Act   federal statute, enacted in 1987, designed to ensure that checking account customers have prompt access to funds they deposit and to expedite the return of dishonored checks. See *Regulation CC.*

Export Trading Company Act   federal statute, enacted in 1982, providing antitrust immunity to export trade association for conduct specified in an antitrust Certificate of Review issued by the Department of Commerce.

express authority   in agency law, authority based on explicit oral or written statements of the principal defining the agent's power. See *authority, implied authority.*

express condition   a condition provided for in the language (oral or written) of a promise or agreement. See *condition.*

express contract   a contract that arises from the language, either oral or written, of the parties. See *contract.*

express trust   trust that arises as a result of the settlor's language indicating his or her intent to create it. See *trust.*

express warranty   in a sales contract, any affirmation of fact or promise made by the seller to the buyer that relates to the goods and becomes part of the basis of the bargain creates an express warranty that the goods will conform to the affirmation or promise. See *warranty,* UCC §2−313.

expropriation   nationalization in accordance with international law. See *nationalization, confiscation.*

"ex ship" term   in sales law, a term creating a destination contract requiring the seller to bear the expense and risk of an ocean voyage and of unloading the goods at the named port of destination. See *destination contract,* UCC §2−322.

extension   an agreement between a debtor and at least two creditors that extends the time for payment. See *composition.*

extension clause   clause extending the maturity of an instrument (generally a note) from its original due date to a future time specified in the instrument.

extraction   process by which a debtor uses the proceeds of the sale of inventory to pay his or her salary, overhead, and other fixed expenses.

extradition   the surrender by one state (or country) of an individual accused of a crime to another state or country having jurisdiction to try the offender.

F.A.S. term   a delivery term used in a sales contract requiring the seller to deliver goods (at the seller's expense !nd risk) alongside a named freighter, tanker, or other vessel and obtain and tender to the buyer a receipt for the goods. See UCC §2−319.

F.O.B. term   a delivery term in a sales contract requiring or authorizing the seller to ship the goods to the buyer. If the term is F.O.B. place of shipment, the seller bears the expense and risk of putting the goods in the carrier's possession. If the term is F.O.B. destination, the seller bears the expense and risk of transporting the goods to the named destination and there tendering delivery to the buyer. See UCC §2−319.

factor (commission merchant)   agent entrusted with possession and control of the principal's goods for purposes of sale, compensated by a commission or "factorage."

failure of consideration in contract law, the failure of the other contracting party to perform his or her promise; failure of a constructive conditions of exchange. See *constructive conditions of exchange.*

Fair Credit Billing Act federal statute that regulates billing practices and disputes for open-end credit accounts. See *open-end credit.*

Fair Credit Reporting Act (FCRA) federal statute protecting consumers from inaccurate and obsolete information in reports by consumer reporting agencies.

Fair Debt Collection Practices Act (FDCPA) federal statute imposing restrictions and obligations upon all third persons (such as collection agencies) who are engaged in the business of collecting debts for others.

Fair Labor Standards Act (FLSA) federal statute, enacted in 1938, that regulates minimum wages, hours of employment, and child labor.

fair market value in real property law, the amount of money that a willing purchaser would pay to a willing property owner considering all uses for which the land is suited or might be applied.

false imprisonment (false arrest) an intentional tort in which liability is imposed upon a person who intentionally confines another within fixed boundaries.

Family and Medical Leave Act of 1993 federal statute that requires many employers to provide limited, unpaid, family and medical leave to eligible employees.

farm products crops or livestock, products of crops or livestock in the unmanufactured state, and supplies used or produced in farming operations. See UCC §9–102(a)(34).

Federal Arbitration Act federal statute, enacted in 1925, stating that arbitration agreements are enforceable under the same standards governing other contracts.

Federal Bills of Lading Act (FBLA) federal statute, enacted in 1916 and revised in 1994, that governs any bill of lading issued by a common carrier for the transportation of goods in interstate or foreign commerce. See *document of title, bill of lading, common carrier.*

Federal Insecticide, Fungicide, and Rodenticide Act (FIFRA) federal statute regulating sale and distribution of pesticides within the United States. FIFRA requires manufacturers of pesticides to register their products with the EPA and to meet labeling requirements on proper use and safety precautions.

Federal Insurance Contributions Act (FICA) federal statute that requires employers and employees to make annual contributions of social security taxes. Self-employed persons who receive earnings from carrying on a trade or business also must pay social security taxes under the Self-Employment Contributions Act. See *Social Security Act.*

federal question jurisdiction one type of subject matter jurisdiction possessed by federal courts. It empowers federal courts to hear cases in which the Constitution or a federal statute or treaty is at issue. See *jurisdiction, subject matter jurisdiction, diversity jurisdiction.*

Federal Trade Commission administrative agency established in 1914 by the Federal Trade Commission Act empowered to enforce both the Clayton and Federal Trade Commission Acts, but not the Sherman Act. See *Federal Trade Commission Act, Sherman Antitrust Act, Clayton Act.*

Federal Trade Commission Act federal statute, enacted in 1914, which created the Federal Trade Commission and authorizes the FTC to issue cease and desist orders prohibiting unfair methods of competition and unfair or deceptive trade practices. The FTC Act, the Sherman Antitrust Act, and the Clayton Act comprise federal antitrust law. See *Sherman Antitrust Act, Clayton Act.*

Federal Trademark Dilution Act federal statute, enacted in 1995, designed to prevent dilution of distinctive and famous trademarks. "Dilution" refers to the lessening of the mark's capacity to identify and distinguish goods and services because of its use with other unrelated products.

fee simple absolute all the rights a person may possess in real property; the largest quantity of ownership interest in land recognized by the law.

fee simple determinable a defeasible fee simple interest in land that is automatically terminated (with the property reverting to the grantor) upon occurrence or nonoccurrence of an event stated in the instrument creating the interest. See *grantor, defeasible (qualified) fee, possibility of reverter.*

fee simple subject to a condition subsequent a defeasible fee simple interest in land that terminates upon occurrence or nonoccurrence of an event stated in the instrument, provided that the grantor takes some affirmative step to terminate the estate. See *grantor, defeasible (qualified) fee, power of termination.*

fee simple subject to an executory limitation a defeasible fee simple interest in land that passes to a third party (other than the grantor or her heirs) upon occurrence or nonoccurrence of an event stated in the instrument creating the interest. See *grantor, defeasible (qualified) fee, executory interest.*

felonies serious crimes, generally those punishable by death or imprisonment in a penitentiary. See *misdemeanors, offenses, crime.*

fellow servant doctrine common law defense to employer liability under which an employer is not liable for negligent injury to an employee caused by the conduct of a fellow employee.

fidelity bond a suretyship contract that secures an employer against embezzlement or defalcation by an employee. See *suretyship, performance bond, bond.*

fiduciary relationship relationship in which one person is under a duty to act solely for the benefit of another concerning matters within the scope of the relation. See *duty of loyalty.*

field warehousing a security device commonly used in inventory financing in which a warehouse is created on the debtor's premises. Inventory then is stored in the warehouse in exchange for warehouse receipts that are used by the debtor as collateral on a loan. See *security.*

finance charge under the federal Truth-in-Lending Act, the cost of consumer credit expressed in a dollar amount. See *Truth-in-Lending Act.*

financing statement in secured transactions, statement filed by a secured party in an appropriate public office to perfect a security interest in personal property or fixtures. See *perfection.*

finder a person who discovers lost property and reduces it to possession. See *lost property.*

firm offer rule rule of sales law, under which a written, signed offer to buy or sell goods made by a merchant stating that it will be held open is binding without consideration for the period stated, not exceeding three months. See UCC §2–205.

fitness for a particular purpose See *warranty of fitness for a particular purpose.*

fixture an item of personal property that, by virtue of its attachment to or close association with land, is regarded as part of the land.

fixture filing in secured transactions law, a type of public filing used when the collateral is fixtures. It requires filing a financing statement covering the goods that are or are to become fixtures in the office where a mortgage on the underlying real estate would be recorded. See UCC §§9–102(a)(40), 9–501(a).

floating lien (floating charge) in secured transactions law, lien created by an after-acquired property clause that "floats" over the debtor's ever-changing property (usually inventory) and covers whatever property is found there. See *after-acquired property clause.*

floor planning inventory financing secured by after-acquired inventory. See *floating lien.*

foreclosure 1. in mortgage and secured transactions law, the method by which mortgaged real property or the collateral, or proceeds of its sale, is applied in satisfaction of the debt secured by the mortgage or secured transaction; 2. in antitrust law, an anticompetitive consequence of vertical merger referring to the reduced ability of former suppliers or customers to sell to or buy from the merged firm. See *vertical merger.*

foreign corporation a corporation organized under the laws of a given state that does business in another state is a "foreign" corporation in the latter state. See *corporation, domestic corporation.*

Foreign Corrupt Practices Act federal statute, enacted in 1977, that imposes substantial internal control requirements upon companies reporting under the Securities Exchange Act of 1934 and makes it a crime for U.S. companies and individuals to bribe foreign officials for certain corrupt purposes.

Foreign Sovereign Immunities Act of 1976 (FSIA) federal statute governing claims of immunity in civil actions against a foreign state. The Act provides that a foreign state normally is immune from the jurisdiction of U.S. courts, subject to specified exceptions.

forfeiture in contract law, the denial of compensation that results when the promisee loses the right to the agreed exchange after relying substantially, through preparation or performance, on the expectation of that exchange.

forgery under the Uniform Commercial Code, one form of "unauthorized signature"—a signature or indorsement made without actual, implied, or apparent authority. See UCC §1–201(b)(41).

formal contract contract governed by special rules that result from the contract's formal characteristics. Includes a contract under seal, a recognizance, and most importantly, a negotiable contract. See *informal (simple) contract, negotiability.*

four unities traditional formalities that must be present to create a joint tenancy: the unities of time, title, interest, and possession. See *joint tenancy.*

franchise a license from the owner of a trademark or trade name (the franchisor) permitting another (the franchisee) to sell a product or service under that name or mark. See *trademark.*

fraud (deceit) an intentional tort under which the plaintiff may recover by proving that the defendant made a fraudulent misrepresentation of material existing fact with the intent to induce the plaintiff to rely upon it, and that the plaintiff justifiably relied upon the misrepresentation to his injury. See *fraudulent misrepresentation, misrepresentation.*

fraud in the essence See *fraud in the execution.*

fraud in the execution in negotiable instruments law, type of fraud that occurs when a misrepresentation induces a party to sign an instrument with neither knowledge nor reasonable opportunity to learn of its character or its essential terms. See UCC §3–305(a)(1)(iii).

fraud in the factum See *fraud in the execution.*

fraudulent conveyance the conveyance of property by a debtor to a third party with intent to hinder, delay, or defraud creditors.

fraudulent misrepresentation a misrepresentation made with knowledge of its untrue character or in reckless disregard of the truth. See *misrepresentation, scienter.*

Freedom of Information Act (FOIA) federal statute, which is part of the Administrative Procedure Act, that requires federal agencies to make most agency records available for examination or copying to any person who requests the records. See *Administrative Procedure Act.*

freedom of speech freedom of expression guaranteed by the First Amendment to the Constitution including oral and written communications and nonverbal actions with symbolic value.

freehold estate an estate in land that is characterized by its uncertain or potentially unlimited duration, including the fee simple absolute, the defeasible fees, and the life estate. See *nonfreehold estate.*

free trade area (customs union) regional association formed among nations that eliminates duties and tariffs for imports from member countries.

freight forwarder a person in the business of consolidating less than carload shipments to obtain the benefit of lower rail and truck rates.

frolic servant's departure from the scope of employment that relieves the master of liability for the servant's torts. See *master, servant, detour, scope of employment, respondent superior doctrine.*

front pay equitable remedy used in employment discrimination cases under which the employer pays the injured employee wages and benefits that the employee will lose after the judgment date. See *back pay.*

frustration of purpose contract law doctrine developed to relieve a contracting party of his or her duty to perform when the underlying purpose of the contract is defeated.

Full Faith and Credit Clause clause of the Constitution providing that full faith and credit shall be given in each state to the judicial proceedings of every other state. The clause prevents relitigation of cases previously decided in other states, and enables a plaintiff who obtains a judgment in one state to enforce it in other states.

full warranty under the Magnuson-Moss Warranty Act, a written warranty covering consumer goods that meets the federal minimum standards for warranty. See *Magnuson-Moss Warranty Act.*

functional discount the difference between the price charged for goods by a manufacturer to its wholesalers and retailers. The discount reflects compensation to the wholesalers for distribution services they perform, such as assuming risk of loss, warehousing, transportation, and administration. The legality of functional discounts is governed by the Robinson-Patman Act. See *Robinson-Patman Act.*

fund transfer under UCC Article 4A, the "series of transactions, beginning with the originator's payment order, made for the purpose of making payment to the beneficiary of the order." See UCC §4A–104(a).

fungible goods goods, such as grain or oil, any unit or part of which is indistinguishable from another. See *goods.*

future goods in sales law, goods not both existing and identified. See *goods, identification of goods,* UCC §2–105(2).

future interest an interest in property that takes effect in possession and enjoyment, if at all, at some future time. See *present possessory interest.*

gap fillers term used to describe provisions of UCC Article 2 that supply missing terms in the parties' agreement.

garnishment a debt collection remedy directed to a third party who holds property of, or is indebted to, the debtor.

general agent agent authorized to conduct a series of transactions involving continuity of service. See *agency*.

General Agreement on Tariffs and Trade (GATT) multilateral trade treaty, first drafted in 1947, designed to reduce substantially tariffs and other barriers to trade, and to assure that imported goods are treated no differently than domestic goods within a nation.

general creditor a creditor who has neither a lien upon the debtor's assets nor a priority in distribution of the debtor's assets. See *lien, priorities*.

general devise a transfer by will payable out of the general assets of a testator's estate. See *estate, will, devise*.

general guaranty (offer for) an offer for a suretyship contract that may be accepted by any person to whom the principal communicates the offer and who accepts it by extending the credit contemplated by the offer. See *suretyship, special guaranty*.

general intangibles any personal property other than accounts, chattel paper, commercial tort claims, deposit accounts, documents, goods, instruments, investment property, letter-of-credit rights, letters of credit, money, and oil, gas, or other minerals before extraction. The term includes payment intangibles and software. UCC §9–102(a)(42). See *payment intangible, software*.

general partner partner who is personally liable to partnership creditors for the full amount of all debts and obligations incurred by the partnership. See *limited partner*.

Generally Accepted Accounting Principles (GAAP) principles that determine how accounting information is presented in financial statements.

Generally Accepted Auditing Standards (GAAS) standards that determine how the work of a particular audit is performed.

gift a voluntary transfer of an interest in property by the owner (the donor) to another (the donee) without consideration or compensation.

gift *causa mortis* a gift made in anticipation or contemplation of the donor's imminent death. See *gift*.

good faith honesty in fact in the conduct or transaction concerned. In the case of a merchant, it also includes observance of reasonable commercial standards of fair dealing in the trade. See UCC §1–201(b)(20).

goods in general, all things (including specially manufactured goods) that are movable at the time of identification to the contract for sale; tangible personal property. See *identification of goods*, UCC §§2–105(1), 2–107.

grand jury a group of citizens who consider evidence of criminal conduct presented by the prosecutor and determine whether the accused should be required to stand trial for a criminal offense. See *criminal law*.

grantee the person to whom an interest in real property is transferred by deed. See *deed*.

grantor the person transferring interest in real property by deed. See *deed*.

group boycott (concerted refusal to deal) a horizontal combination intended to eliminate (or prevent the entry of) a competitor of the parties to the combination. See *restraint of trade, horizontal restraint*.

guaranty in suretyship law, a contract that creates a secondary obligation; that is, the promisor (guarantor) undertakes to perform only if another person fails to perform. See *suretyship*.

guaranty of collection (conditional guaranty, guaranty of collectibility) type of guaranty in which the creditor must put the principal in default and also exhaust all legal remedies against the principal before suing the guarantor. See *suretyship, guaranty*.

guardian a person appointed by a court to manage, subject to court supervision, the affairs and properties of a person (ward) considered incapable of administering his or her own affairs.

Hazardous Substance Superfund (Superfund) fund established under the Comprehensive Environmental Response, Compensation, and Liability Act (CERCLA) to help finance cleanup of hazardous waste sites. The Superfund is funded by general revenues, a special tax included in the corporate alternative minimum tax, and excise taxes on oil, chemical feedstocks, and motor fuel. See *Comprehensive Environmental Response, Compensation, and Liability Act*.

Health Insurance Portability and Accountability Act (HIPAA) federal statute, enacted in 1996, amending the Employee Retirement Income Security Act (ERISA), allowing employees with pre-existing medical conditions covered under their original employer's group health insurance plan, to continue coverage when they change jobs.

heirs people who are entitled to the decedent's property if he or she dies intestate. See *intestate*.

Herfindahl-Hirschman Index (HHI) an aid to interpreting market concentration data that is computed by summing the squares of the individual market shares of all firms included in the market. See *market concentration*.

holder with respect to a negotiable instrument, the person in possession of the instrument if the instrument is payable to bearer. If the instrument is payable to an identified person, that person is the holder if he or she is in possession of the instrument. With respect to a document of title, the holder is the person in possession of the document if the goods are deliverable to bearer or to the order of the person in possession. See *bearer, order, negotiation*, UCC §1–201(b)(21).

holder in due course holder of negotiable instrument who takes an instrument for value, in good faith, and without notice (1) that the instrument is overdue, (2) that the instrument has been dishonored, or (3) of any defense against or claim to it on the part of any person. See *holder*, UCC §3–302.

holder in due course doctrine doctrine of negotiable instruments law stating that if a negotiable instrument is negotiated to a holder in due course, the holder in due course takes free of all claims and most defenses to the instrument. See *holder in due course, negotiability, negotiation, claim, defense*.

holding rule of law used to resolve the issues in a court case.

holding company a company that confines its activities to owning stock in, and supervising management of, other companies.

holographic will generally, a will entirely in the handwriting of the testator. See *will, testator*.

honorary trust term used to describe a transfer of property in trust for the erection or maintenance of monuments, the care of graves, or the care of specific animals. Such an arrangement is not a trust under the definition of trust because it lacks a beneficiary. See *trust*.

horizontal merger a merger between former competitors. See *vertical merger*.

horizontal restraint of trade a restraint of trade involving an agreement among competitors—persons at the same functional level. See *restraint of trade, vertical restraint of trade*.

hostile environment sexual harassment sexual harassment involving unwelcome conduct of a sexual nature that has the purpose or effect of unreasonably interfering with an individual's work performance or creating an intimidating, hostile, or offensive working environment. See *sexual harassment.*

hot cargo clause   a provision in a collective bargaining agreement by which an employer voluntarily agrees not to do business with a nonunion company or a company involved in a labor dispute. See *collective bargaining agreement.*

identification of goods   the process by which the particular existing goods referred to in a contract for sale are designated and specified. See *goods.*

illegal bargain   traditional term used to describe a contract that is unenforceable because it violates an applicable criminal or civil statute, constitutes the commission of or inducement to commit a tort, or is otherwise contrary to public policy.

illusory promise   promissory language in a contract that makes one party's performance entirely optional. An illusory promise is not a promise at all and therefore does not furnish consideration for a return promise. See *promise, consideration.*

Immigration Reform and Control Act (IRCA)   federal statute, enacted in 1986, to reduce the number of illegal aliens entering the United States. Prohibits discrimination in hiring, recruitment, or discharge based on national origin or citizenship status for persons who are citizens or "protected individuals."

immunity   a person's freedom against having a given legal relation altered by the act or omission of another. The person who has no ability to alter the given legal relation is operating under a disability.

implied authority   in agency law, authority that is implied from a general express grant of authority; that is, it flows as a natural and logical consequence of the express authority granted and cannot contradict that authority. See *authority, express authority.*

implied in fact contract   a promise or contract that is inferred from conduct other than language.

implied trust   trust that arises by operation of law, not by the express language of the settlor. Implied trusts include resulting trusts and constructive trusts. See *resulting trust, constructive trust.*

implied warranty   a warranty that arises by operation of the law under Article 2 of the Uniform Commercial Code, including the warranty of merchantability and fitness for a particular purpose. See *warranty, express warranty,* UCC §§2–314, 2–315.

implied warranty of authority   principle of agency law by which a person who purports to make a contract for a principal impliedly represents that he or she has the power to bind the principal.

implied warranty of habitability   warranty applicable primarily to residential leases imposing an implied covenant in the lease that the premises will meet certain minimum standards of habitability, and making the landlord-tenant relation governed by contract rather than property principles.

import-export clause   clause of the Constitution that prohibits a state from imposing a direct tax on imports or exports solely because the goods have been received from or are bound for a foreign country.

impracticability (impossibility)   a contract doctrine relieving a contracting party from a duty to perform if performance as agreed has been made impracticable by the occurrence of a contingency, the nonoccurrence of which was a basic assumption on which the contract was made. See UCC §2–615.

inchoate crimes   crimes that are designed to culminate in the commission of another crime but fail to do so. See *attempt, conspiracy, solicitation.*

incidental beneficiary   in contract law, a beneficiary who is not an intended beneficiary. See *beneficiary, intended beneficiary.*

incidental damages   damages recoverable by an injured buyer or seller for breach of a sales contract in addition to the basic measure of damages, designed to provide reimbursement for reasonable expenses incurred by the injured party as a result of the breach. For specific examples, see UCC §§2–710, 2–715(1).

incomplete instrument   an instrument, ultimately intended to be negotiable, that is signed by the maker or drawer but which omits some term or terms necessary to complete the instrument. See UCC §3–115.

incontestable clause   clause in a life insurance policy that prevents the insurer from asserting a misrepresentation or breach of warranty as a basis for avoiding the contract after the policy has been in effect for a given period, such as one or two years.

incorporation by reference   a legal doctrine under which the terms of one identifiable writing are made part of another writing by referring to, identifying, and adopting the former as part of the latter.

Incoterms   shipping terms adopted by the International Chamber of Commerce to provide "international rules for the interpretation of trade terms."

indemnification   See *indemnity contract.*

indemnity contract   contract in which the promisor (indemnitor) agrees to save the promisee (indemnitee) harmless from (indemnify or reimburse him for) the legal consequences of the promisee's, or some other person's conduct.

indenture   1. trust agreement between a corporation issuing bonds or debentures and a trustee, usually a financial institution, under which the securities are issued and administered; 2. deed signed by both grantor and grantee.

independent contractor   a person who contracts to do something for another but whose physical conduct in the performance of the undertaking is not subject to the other's control or right of control. An independent contractor may or may not be an agent. See *servant.*

independent promises   a term traditionally used to describe promises in leases and other conveyances of land, meaning that nonperformance of one promise by one party does not excuse further performance of another promise by the other.

indictment   a written accusation issued by a grand jury setting forth the facts and charging the accused with violation of specific criminal statutes. See *grand jury.*

indorsement   in negotiable instruments law, term referring to the payee's or other holder's signature (and in some cases additional language) appearing on the instrument. An indorsement usually appears on the back of the instrument.

informal (simple) contracts   contracts that are enforceable without regard to form; basically, any contract other than a contract under seal, a recognizance, or a negotiable contract. See *formal contract.*

information   a written accusation prepared by the prosecutor that sets forth the facts and charges the accused of violating criminal statutes. An alternative to grand jury indictment as a means of initiating criminal prosecution. See *criminal law.*

infringement   unauthorized use of intellectual property. See *intellectual property.*

injunction   an equitable judicial remedy involving an order directed to a defendant by a court to do (mandatory injunction) or to refrain from doing (prohibitory or negative injunction) an act. See *equitable remedy.*

injunction against breach an equitable contract remedy closely related to specific performance involving a court order not to breach a contract. See *specific performance, equitable remedy, injunction.*

insider in bankruptcy law, a creditor, such as a relative of an individual debtor, who has a particularly close relationship to the debtor.

insider trading buying or selling securities based upon access to confidential or proprietary information not available to the public.

Insider Trading Sanctions Act of 1984; Insider Trading and Securities Fraud Enforcement Act of 1988 federal statutes designed to control insider trading by requiring brokers, dealers, and investment advisers to establish systems and enforce policies to prevent insider trading; and by permitting the SEC to recover a civil penalty from persons who violate the Securities Exchange Act of 1934 or rules by purchasing or selling a security while in possession of material nonpublic information. See *insider trading, Securities Exchange Act of 1934.*

insolvency state of a debtor who has insufficient assets to meet his or her total obligations (balance sheet insolvency) or who is unable to pay debts as they come due (equity insolvency).

installment contract in sales law, a contract requiring or authorizing the seller to deliver the goods in separate lots to be separately accepted by the buyer. See UCC §2–612(1).

installment sales contract (contract for deed) real estate contract in which the seller finances the buyer who takes possession of the property and makes periodic installment payments against the price. The seller retains title as security for performance of the contract and delivers the deed only after the purchase price is paid. See *escrow.*

instrument 1. in general, term referring to any written document, particularly legal documents such as contracts, wills, and deeds; 2. under UCC Article 3, a negotiable instrument as defined in §3–104 (See §3–104(b)); 3. under UCC Article 9, a negotiable instrument as defined in §3–104, and any other writing that evidences a right to the payment of money and is not itself a security agreement or lease. UCC §9–102(a)(47).

insurable interest the legal principles designed to prevent net profit from occurrence of insured events; that is, to prevent use of an insurance policy as a gambling device and to minimize any inducement to cause the event insured against, the person who recovers under the policy must have an insurable interest in the property or person insured.

insurance a contractual arrangement used to transfer and distribute risk.

integrated agreement (integration) in contract law, a writing that constitutes the final written expression of one or more terms of an agreement, either complete (exclusive statement of all terms of the agreement) or partial (conclusive on some but not all issues).

intellectual property the bundle of property rights associated with ideas and creative thoughts.

intended beneficiary if a contractual promise is made with intent to benefit a beneficiary, that person is an intended beneficiary. See *beneficiary, donee beneficiary, creditor beneficiary.*

intent in tort law, a person's conduct is intentional if she desires to cause the consequences of her act or believes that the consequences are substantially certain to result from it. See *negligence, strict liability.*

inter alia among other things.

inter vivos **trust** trust created during the settlor's lifetime.

intermediary bank in bank deposits and collections, any bank to which a check is transferred in the course of collection other than the depositary or payor bank. See UCC §4–105(4).

International Court of Justice (ICJ) judicial branch of United Nations that issues advisory opinions and resolves disputes among states (nations). Only states may be parties to litigation before the ICJ, and jurisdiction is not compulsory but is based upon the states' consent. See *United Nations.*

international law (public international law, law of nations) system of law that governs relationships among states.

interpleader a legal proceeding used when one person possesses property or a fund in which he claims no interest, but which is claimed by two or more other persons. In this case, the stakeholder may file an equitable interpleader action, requiring the rival claimants to litigate their claims to the property with each other rather than with the stakeholder. The interpleader therefore relieves the stakeholder from potential liability for paying the wrong claimant.

interpretation the process by which a court ascertains the meaning of a contract or contract term.

intestate a person who (1) fails to leave a will, (2) fails to leave a valid will, or (3) leaves a valid will that does not dispose of all of his or her property. See *will.*

intestate succession statutes state statutes governing the distribution of property of an intestate, a person who dies without a will, without a valid will, or with a will that does not dispose of the decedent's entire estate. See *heirs, intestate.*

intrastate offering exemption exemption from registration under the Securities Act of 1933 for securities offered and sold only to persons within a single state by a corporation incorporated by and doing business within the state. See *Securities Act of 1933.*

inventory goods that are held primarily for immediate or ultimate resale in the ordinary course of the seller's business. See UCC §9–102(a)(48).

inverse condemnation a condemnation action initiated by a property owner to recover compensation for property taken by the government for public use; used when the government takes private property for public use, but does so without a formal condemnation procedure and without compensation. See *condemnation, eminent domain.*

investigative consumer report consumer report containing personal data about a consumer from personal interviews with the consumer's neighbors, friends, acquaintances, or associates. See *consumer report.*

Investment Advisers Act of 1940 federal statute regulating persons who are in the business of rendering investment advice but are not securities brokers or dealers.

investment property term used in secured transactions law, including securities, such as stocks and bonds, whether certificated (evidenced by a document such as a stock certificate) or uncertificated, and whether held directly by the debtor or indirectly by the debtor's broker. In the indirect holding situation, the debtor holds a "security entitlement" in a "security account." Investment property also includes "commodity contracts" (for example, a commodity futures contract or option traded on a board of trade) that may be held by the debtor's commodity broker in a "commodity account." UCC §9–102(a)(49).

invitee a person invited to enter or remain on the land of another for purposes connected with business dealings (a business invitee) or for a purpose for which the land is held open to the public (a public invitee). See *licensee, trespasser.*

involuntary (constructive) (quasi) bailment bailment in which a person obtains possession of another's goods without either the latter's knowledge or consent. See *bailment.*

involuntary case bankruptcy case in which the creditor attempts to force the debtor into bankruptcy. See *voluntary case.*

ipso facto **law** rule of law that causes a forfeiture of a debtor's property or contract rights upon a bankruptcy filing. Such laws generally are invalid in a bankruptcy proceeding.

irregular (anomalous) indorsement an indorsement that is not in the chain of title (not necessary to negotiate the instrument); in other words, an indorsement by a person who is not a holder. Such an indorsement gives notice to later holders of the indorser's accommodation status. See *accommodation party,* UCC §§3–205(d), 3–419(c).

issue 1. in negotiable instruments law, manner in which payee becomes a holder of a negotiable instruments; occurs when the maker or drawer, or in some cases a remitter, transfers possession of the instrument to him. See *holder, remitter,* UCC §3–105(a); 2. in the law of decedents' estates, lineal descendants.

joint and several promises promises of the same performance made by two or more parties in which the promisors bind themselves jointly as one party and also severally as separate parties. See *joint liability, several liability.*

joint liability term describing contract liability when two or more promisors undertake the duty to render the same performance. In joint liability, all co-promisors are liable for the entire performance. Thus, a joint promisor is liable for the performance of each co-promisor. See *joint and several promises, several liability.*

joint tenancy form of concurrent ownership characterized by the right of survivorship; for example, if one of two joint tenants dies, the deceased's share is owned by the other, who becomes sole owner. See *right of survivorship, concurrent ownership.*

joint venture an association of two or more persons to carry out one enterprise, a specific transaction, or one series of transactions for profit. See *partnership.*

judgment creditor a person who has obtained a judgment against another, the judgment debtor, which has not been satisfied.

judgment debtor a person against whom a judgment has been recovered, which the debtor has not satisfied.

judgment lien generally, a lien upon the judgment debtor's real property. See *lien.*

judgment notwithstanding the verdict (judgment *non obstante veredicto,* or judgment *n.o.v.*), motion for motion filed by a party against whom the jury has decided a case that requests the court to find as a matter of law that the jury's verdict was incorrect and to enter judgment in favor of the moving party.

judgment rate term referring to the rate of interest required by state law to be paid on money judgments.

judicial lien lien created by judicial action, including judgment, levy, garnishment, or other legal or equitable process or proceeding. See *lien.*

jurisdiction the power and authority of a court to render a binding decision of law. See *original jurisdiction, appellate jurisdiction, subject matter jurisdiction, personal jurisdiction.*

jury instructions or charges instructions by the court to the jury which explain the rules of law pertinent to a case.

knowledge a person's subjective conscious belief in the truth of a fact or condition. See *notice.*

Labor-Management Relations Act (Taft-Hartley Act) federal statute that amended the National Labor Relations Act in 1947, mak-ing illegal certain unfair labor practices committed by unions. See *National Labor Relations Act.*

Labor Management Reporting and Disclosure Act (Landrum-Griffin Act) federal statute that amended the National Labor Relations Act in 1959 and that regulates internal union activities. See *National Labor Relations Act.*

landlord's lien statutory lien that secures payment of rent by giving the landlord a lien upon the tenant's personal property located on the premises. See *statutory lien.*

landlord-tenant relationship legal relationship created by the transfer of the right of possession of real property from its owner (the landlord or lessor) to another (the tenant or lessee) in consideration of rent. The tenant obtains a nonfreehold estate in the land. See *lease, nonfreehold estate.*

lapse in decedents' estates law, an event occurring if a beneficiary under a will predeceases the testator. See *will, testator.*

last clear chance doctrine doctrine of negligence law that allows a plaintiff to recover despite his or her own contributory negligence, if the defendant had the "last clear chance" to avoid the accident and negligently failed to do so.

law the body of rules and principles of conduct that are enforceable through sanctions.

law merchant term referring to the system of routine rules, customs, or practices used in the business community to regulate transactions and solve controversies.

lease an agreement that creates a landlord-tenant relationship. See *landlord-tenant relationship.*

legacy a gift of money by will. See *will.*

legal detriment an element of consideration requiring that the promisee of a contractual promise either (1) refrain (or promise to refrain) from doing something that he or she has a legal right to do, or (2) do (or promise to do) something that he or she is not legally obligated to do, in exchange for the promise. See *consideration.*

legal system institutions and processes for enforcing the law.

letter of credit an undertaking made by a bank or other person (the "issuer") to a "beneficiary" at the request of the issuer's "customer." The letter obligates the issuer to honor a draft or other demand for payment presented by the beneficiary if the draft or demand is accompanied by documents that comply strictly with any conditions specified in the letter. See *standby letter of credit.*

levy a sheriff's act in taking custody of a debtor's property pursuant to creditors' remedies available under state law.

liability See *power.*

libel the publication of a defamatory statement by written or printed words, by its embodiment in other physical form, or by radio or television communication. See *defamation, slander.*

license a revocable privilege to enter upon or perform acts on another's land.

licensee a person privileged to enter or remain upon another's land only by virtue of the possessor's consent. See *invitee, trespasser.*

lien an interest in property created to secure the payment or other performance of an obligation.

lien creditor in secured transactions law, a creditor who has acquired a lien upon the property involved by attachment, levy, or other judicial process, and includes an assignee for the benefit of creditors, a trustee in bankruptcy, and a receiver in equity. See UCC §9–102(a)(52).

life estate   an interest in property limited in duration to the life or lives of one or more persons.

life insurance   a contract to make designated payments upon the death of the person whose life is insured.

life tenant   the owner of a life estate.

limited liability company   form of business organization owned by members, who may participate in management and whose liability for company debts generally is limited to the amount they have invested in the business. Like a limited partnership and corporation, it may be formed only by complying with formalities outlined by state statute. In essence, a limited liability company combines the management flexibility and tax advantages of a partnership with the limited liability of a corporation. See *Uniform Limited Liability Company Act.*

limited liability limited partnership   limited partnership in which both the general and limited partners have limited liability for firm debts. See *limited partnership.*

limited partner   partner whose liability to creditors of the partnership is limited to the amount of capital he or she has contributed to the partnership. See *general partner.*

limited partnership   a partnership formed by two or more persons under a limited partnership statute having as members one or more general partners and one or more limited partners. See *general partner, limited partner.*

limited warranty   under the Magnuson-Moss Warranty Act, a written warranty covering consumer goods that does not meet the federal minimum standards for warranty. See *full warranty, Magnuson-Moss Warranty Act.*

liquidated claim   a claim that is fixed in amount. See *unliquidated claim, disputed claim, claim.*

liquidated damages clause   a contract term specifying the amount of damages to be awarded in the event of a breach.

liquidation (straight bankruptcy) case   bankruptcy case under Chapter 7 of the Bankruptcy Code in which the debtor surrenders all nonexempt assets to a trustee in bankruptcy, who converts the assets to cash and distributes the proceeds to creditors who have filed claims against the estate, according to priorities prescribed by law. The debtor then is generally discharged from liability on most debts remaining unpaid. See *rehabilitation case.*

litigation   contesting a disputed claim in court.

lockout   temporary closing of all or part of a business by refusal to allow employees to work.

long arm statutes   state statutes codifying the minimum contacts that subject a nonresident defendant to a state court's jurisdiction in a civil case.

lost property   legal status of property when its owner has casually and involuntarily parted with it without recalling either the circumstances or the place of the loss.

lost-volume seller   in sales law, a seller injured by a buyer's breach of contract who sells a standardized product or one in unlimited supply. Specifically, a lost-volume seller is one who, but for the buyer's breach, would have had the benefit of both the original contract and the resale contract. See UCC §2–708(2).

lot   a parcel or single article that is the subject matter of a separate sale or delivery, whether or not it is sufficient to perform the contract. See UCC §2–105(5).

Magnuson-Moss Warranty Act   federal statute regulating written warranties that accompany the sale of consumer goods.

mailbox acceptance rule (deposited acceptance rule)   rule of contract law stating that an acceptance is normally effective when sent or dispatched, that is, when the offeree relinquishes control over his or her acceptance.

main-purpose (leading-object) rule   exception to the Statute of Frauds writing requirement for suretyship promises providing that a surety's oral promise is enforceable if it is made to benefit the surety's personal economic interest, rather than to aid the debtor. See *suretyship, Statute of Frauds.*

majority   the age at which a person attains full contractual capacity. See *capacity, contractual capacity.*

maker   in negotiable instruments law, the person who makes or executes a note and promises to pay money. See *note.*

malicious prosecution   an intentional tort imposing liability for the initiation of a criminal case by a private person against another for any purpose other than to bring an offender to justice, if the case is initiated without cause to believe that the accused has committed a crime, and the case is terminated in favor of the accused.

mandatory injunction   See *injunction.*

market concentration   a function of the number of firms in a market and their respective market shares.

market extension merger   a merger that joins firms selling the same product, but operating in different geographic markets. See *product extension merger, conglomerate merger.*

marketable title   a title to real property that a reasonably prudent and legally well-informed buyer is willing to take and pay for; that is, title is marketable if no reasonable doubt exists concerning its validity and it is unlikely that the buyer will be exposed to a lawsuit in order to defend it.

Marketable Title Acts   in real property law, state statutes that reduce the period of title search by extinguishing all claims and title defects automatically after a fixed period, unless preserved by filing a statutory notice. See *title search.*

master   a principal who has control of, or the right to control, an agent's (servant's) physical conduct. See *servant.*

master of the offer rule   principle of contract law allowing the offeror to dictate the terms under which the offer may be accepted, including the time, place, and manner of acceptance. See *offer.*

material breach   in contract law, a breach of contract that causes the nonoccurrence of a constructive condition of exchange to the other party's duty (thereby discharging that duty). See *substantial performance doctrine, total breach, partial breach.*

material misrepresentation   a misrepresentation is material if either (1) a reasonable person would attach importance to the existence or nonexistence of the fact represented, or (2) the person making the misrepresentation knows or should know that the other person is likely to regard the fact as important.

mechanic's lien   statutory lien given to persons who supply services, labor, or material in the construction or improvement of real property. See *lien, statutory lien.*

mediation   tactic used to aid in resolving disputes in which an unbiased third party assists in negotiations and recommends a solution that the parties are free to accept or reject. See *arbitration.*

merchant   in sales law, a person who deals in goods of the kind or who otherwise by her occupation holds herself out as having knowledge or skill peculiar to the business practices or goods involved in a particular transaction. See UCC §2–104(1).

merchantability   See *warranty of merchantability.*

merger (integration) clause a clause contained in a written contract expressly stating that the writing is the entire agreement of the parties, and that there are no understandings, promises, or representations except those contained therein. See *integrated agreement.*

merger guidelines guidelines issued by the Justice Department detailing the general principles and specific standards used to determine which mergers are likely to be challenged by the government under §7 of the Clayton Act. See *Clayton Act.*

midnight deadline term used in negotiable instruments and bank deposits and collections, meaning, with respect to a bank, midnight of the next banking day following the banking day on which the bank receives a relevant item or notice. See *banking day,* UCC §4–104(a)(10).

minor (infant) a person who has not yet reached the age of contractual capacity. See *capacity, contractual capacity, majority.*

mirror-image rule principle of contract law stating that to create a contract the acceptance must exactly conform to (be the "mirror image" of) the terms of the offer.

misappropriation the wrongful acquisition, disclosure, or use of a trade secret. See *trade secret.*

misdemeanors crimes less serious than felonies, usually crimes punishable by fine or imprisonment in a local jail or for a term of less than one year. See *crime, felonies, offenses.*

mislaid (misplaced) property property that is intentionally and voluntarily placed in a given location by its owner and subsequently left behind when the owner departs, forgetting to take the property. See *lost property.*

misrepresentation an assertion that is not in accord with existing facts.

mistake a belief that does not accord with existing facts. See *unilateral mistake, mutual mistake.*

misuse in products liability cases, the use of a product by the plaintiff for purposes neither intended nor foreseeable by the defendant seller. See *products liability.*

mitigation of damages steps taken by an injured party to keep damages to a minimum.

model in sales contracts, goods exhibited by the seller to the buyer for inspection during precontract negotiation to describe goods to be sold when the goods themselves are not at hand. See UCC §2–313(1)(c).

model acts statutes that serve as guidelines to state legislatures in drafting legislation, such as the Model Business Corporation Act or the Model Penal Code.

Model Business Corporation Act (MBCA) model statute drafted by a committee of the American Bar Association that is the basis of incorporation statutes in many states. See *Revised Model Business Corporation Act.*

money a medium of exchange authorized or adopted by a domestic or foreign government. See UCC §1–201(b)(24).

moral consideration a common form of past consideration resting at most upon a moral but not legal obligation. See *past consideration, consideration.*

mortgage an interest in real property that is created to secure performance of an obligation, normally repayment of a debt.

mortgagee the person receiving the benefit of the security afforded by a mortgage; the grantee of the mortgage deed.

mortgagor the person creating a mortgage and giving the security to a mortgagee; the grantor of the mortgage deed.

motion an application to the court to issue an order on a matter of law.

motion for directed verdict motion requesting the court to direct a verdict in favor of the moving party, because, for example, the other party has not presented a prima facie case. See *prima facie case.*

motion for summary judgment motion made during the discovery stage of a civil case alleging that no relevant facts are in dispute, thereby allowing the judge to decide the case as a matter of law.

motion to dismiss the complaint motion filed by a defendant in a civil case, usually in lieu of answering the complaint, asking the court to dismiss the lawsuit for lack of jurisdiction, or because the complaint fails to state a claim on which judicial relief can be granted.

motion for judgment on the pleadings motion in a civil case made after all pleadings have been filed that allows the court to rule as a matter of law that one of the parties in a lawsuit is entitled to judgment. See *pleadings.*

multiparty credit card credit card issued by a bank that enlists both cardholders and merchants who honor its cards. Unlike a dual property card, however, merchants honor cards issued by any participating bank. See *credit card, single-party credit card, dual-party credit card.*

mutual mistake as used in contract law, mistake occurring when both parties, at the time of the contract, are mistaken about a basic assumption upon which the contract was made. See *mistake, unilateral mistake.*

mutuality of consideration requirement for enforceability of contracts that both parties to the contract must provide consideration. See *consideration.*

naked restraint promise in restraint of trade that has no purpose other than to suppress or eliminate competition. See *restraint of trade, ancillary restraint.*

National Ambient Air Quality Standards (NAAQS) air quality standards adopted by the EPA under the Clean Air Act for various identified pollutants. See *Clean Air Act.*

National Cooperative Research and Production Act federal statute, enacted in 1984 and amended in 1993, providing limited antitrust immunity for certain research and development joint ventures, and certain production joint ventures, that notify the Federal Trade Commission and Justice Department of their actions.

National Environmental Policy Act (NEPA) federal statute that imposes a duty on federal agencies to consider environmental matters in administering their programs. See *Environmental Impact Statement.*

National Labor Relations Act (NRLA, Wagner Act) federal statute, enacted in 1935, establishing employees' basic rights to engage in collective action and defining various unfair labor practices by employers.

National Labor Relations Board federal agency responsible for administering the NLRA and issuing rules and regulations.

National Pollutant Discharge Elimination System (NPDES) system created by the Clean Water Act for controlling "point-source" pollution, which consists of discharges into a body of water through a confined and discrete conveyance such as a pipe, ditch, or conduit. See *Clean Water Act.*

nationalization   forced taking of foreign assets by a host government. See *expropriation, confiscation*.

natural persons   human beings.

necessaries   in the context of minors' contracts, such articles of property and such services as are reasonably necessary to enable a minor to earn the money required to provide the necessities of life for herself and those who are legally dependent upon her. See *minor*.

negative (restrictive) covenant   in real property law, a covenant restricting or limiting the permissible uses of the land or the acts that may be performed upon it. See *affirmative covenant*.

negative (prohibitory) injunction   See *injunction*.

negligence   conduct that falls below the standard established by law for the protection of others against unreasonable risk of harm. Generally, the standard to which a person must conform to avoid being negligent is that of a reasonable person under like circumstances. Thus, negligence occurs when a person does something that a reasonable person would not do, or fails to do something that a reasonable person would do, under the circumstances. See *reasonable person*.

negotiable document of title   a document of title is negotiable if by its terms the goods are to be delivered to bearer or to the order of a named person, or, where recognized in overseas trade, it runs to a named person or assigns. See *document of title*, UCC §7–104(1).

negotiability   a legal concept characteristic of negotiable instruments, documents of title, and certificated investment securities that is designed to promote the free transferability of the paper from one owner to the next and to enhance its marketability, by permitting transfer free of claims and defenses.

negotiation   1. process of dispute resolution by which parties with differing demands reach an agreement through compromise and concession; 2. in the law of negotiable instruments, a voluntary or involuntary transfer of possession of an instrument by a person other than the maker or drawer to a person who thereby becomes its holder. See *holder*, UCC 3–201(a).

"no arrival, no sale" term   in sales law, term used in destination contracts that excuses the seller from liability for damages if the goods shipped fail to arrive, but continues (as in all destination contracts) to place the risk of loss in transit upon the seller. See *destination contract*, UCC §2–324.

No Electronic Theft Act   federal statute imposing criminal penalties for willful copyright infringement in which a person during any 180 day period reproduces or distributes one or more copies of copyrighted works with a total retail value of more than $1000.

nolo contendere plea   a form of plea in a criminal case. By pleading *nolo contendere* (no contest), the defendant may be sentenced as if he or she had been found guilty. The plea may not, however, be used as an admission of guilt in other court proceedings.

nominal consideration (recited consideration)   a statement in a contract that property or services are to be exchanged for "$1.00 and other valuable consideration," or similar language.

nominal damages   minimal damages awarded to acknowledge the existence of a contract breach or other injury when the plaintiff cannot prove or does not incur loss or injury. See *damages*.

nonconforming use   in the law of zoning, a property that does not conform to a new restriction on a zoned area, but which lawfully existed when the zoning ordinance went into effect and has continued in existence since that time. See *zoning*.

noncumulative dividend preferences   dividend preference in which preferred dividends not paid in prior years do not accumulate and need not be satisfied before dividends subsequently are paid to shareholders with subordinate dividend rights. That is, only the current year's preference need be satisfied before dividends are paid on shares with subordinate dividend rights. See *dividend, preferred shares, cumulative dividend preferences*.

nonfreehold estate   an estate in land that has a fixed or determinate duration. See *freehold estate*.

nonparticipating shares   preferred shares that are entitled to receive the amount of the stated dividend preference and no more. See *dividend, preferred shares, participating shares*.

nonpossessory security interest   a security interest in personal property in which the debtor retains possession of the collateral that is subject to the security interest. See *possessory security interest (pledge)*.

nonprofit corporation   corporation organized for religious, educational, or philanthropic purposes whose income is applied to the specific purpose for which the organization is created rather than the personal enrichment of the persons who own or operate it. See *corporation, business corporation*.

nonrestrictive indorsement   in negotiable instruments law, an indorsement that transfers the holder's entire interest in the instrument. See *indorsement, restrictive indorsement*.

Norris-LaGuardia Act   federal statute enacted in 1932 that restricts the federal courts' power to issue injunctions in labor disputes.

North American Free Trade Agreement (NAFTA)   treaty among Canada, the United States, and Mexico that became effective in 1994. It creates a free trade area among its three members by eliminating tariffs and other trade restrictions. See *free trade area*.

note   a writing signed by the maker containing an unconditional promise by the maker to pay a fixed amount of money to the order of the payee or to bearer on demand or at a definite time. See UCC §3–104.

notice   a person has notice of a fact when he or she has actual knowledge of the fact, receives notification of the fact, or when surrounding facts give the person reason to know that it exists. See *knowledge, notification*.

notice by publication   notice accomplished by advertising or publicizing a fact in a newspaper or other publication. See *notification*.

notice of dishonor   in negotiable instruments law, notice required to be given to secondary parties liable on an instrument that the instrument has been dishonored, as a condition precedent to secondary contract liability. See *secondary contract liability*.

notification   formal act intended to affect legal relations between the notifier and the person notified. How a person "notifies" or "gives" a notice or notification to another and when a person "receives" a notice or notification are outlined in UCC §1–202. See *notice, knowledge*.

novation   a special form of substituted contract that adds a new party to a contract, who was not a party to the original duty. See *substituted contract*.

Nuclear Regulatory Commission (NRC)   (formerly Atomic Energy Commission) federal agency responsible for civilian nuclear regulation.

Nuclear Waste Policy Act   federal statute, enacted in 1982, that requires the federal government to select and develop a site for permanent disposal of high-level radioactive waste.

nuisance   human activity conducted on land or physical condition of land that is harmful or annoying to neighboring landowners or members of the public generally.

nuncupative will an oral will dictated by a testator during his or her last illness before a sufficient number of witnesses and later reduced to writing. See *will, testator.*

objective theory of contract principle of contract law designed to protect the stability of contractual relationships, which provides that a contracting party is generally held to the impression his conduct or communication creates in a reasonable person in the position of the other party, and may not later assert that his subjective intention differs from his outward manifestation.

obligee the person entitled to receive a performance under a contract; promisee. See *obligor.*

obligor 1. a person required to render a performance under a contract; promisor; 2. in secured transactions, the person that, with respect to an obligation secured by a security interest: (i) owes payment or other performance of the obligation, (ii) has provided property other than the collateral to secure payment or other performance of the obligation, or (iii) is otherwise accountable in whole or in part for payment or other performance of the obligation. UCC §9–102(a)(59). See *debtor, obligee.*

Occupational Safety and Health Act (OSHA) federal statute, enacted in 1970, that generally requires employers to provide safe and healthful working conditions free from recognized hazards likely to cause death or serious physical harm to employees.

Occupational Safety and Health Administration division of the Department of Labor that has primary responsibility for the administration and enforcement of the Occupational Safety and Health Act.

offenses general term for crimes, including felonies and misdemeanors. See *crime, felonies, misdemeanors.*

offer a conditional promise made by the offeror to the offeree, giving the offeree the power of acceptance, or the power to create a contract. As defined in the *Restatement (Second) of Contracts,* "a manifestation of willingness to enter into a bargain so made as to justify another person in understanding that his assent to that bargain is invited and will conclude it." See *bargain.*

offeree person to whom an offer is directed who has power to create a contract by acceptance. See *offer.*

offeror person making an offer. See *offer.*

Oil Pollution Act of 1990 federal statute amending the Clean Water Act and governing prevention and cleanup of accidental spills of oil and hazardous substances. See *Clean Water Act.*

omnibus clause in an insurance contract, a clause defining additional insureds as a class bearing a specified relationship to the named insured.

on us check a check that is deposited in a bank that is also the payor bank. See *transit check.*

open-end credit credit extended on an account in which the debtor will incur obligations in a series of transactions. See *closed-end credit.*

operation of law general legal concept used to describe the manner in which a party's rights or duties are determined automatically by the application of a rule of law to a given set of facts, without the act or cooperation of the party.

option contract a contract to keep an offer open for a specified time. See *contract, offer.*

order in negotiable instruments law, a direction or instruction to pay, but more than an authorization or request. See UCC §3–103(a)(6).

order paper in negotiable instruments law, an instrument payable to the order of an identified person, or to an identified person or order. See UCC §3–109(b). Also includes an instrument bearing a special indorsement. See *bearer paper.*

original acquisition method of acquiring title to unowned goods, such as wild animals and abandoned property, by reducing them to possession.

original jurisdiction term referring to the jurisdiction of a court that has the power to render the initial decision in a case. See *jurisdiction, appellate jurisdiction.*

ostensible ownership doctrine of sales law applied when a seller retains sold goods. It provides that the sale is void against the seller's creditors if the seller's retention is fraudulent under any rule of law of the state where the goods are situated. See UCC §2–402.

output contract a sales contract in which a seller promises to sell its entire output of a given commodity to a buyer. See *requirements contract.*

Overseas Private Investment Corporation (OPIC) agency of the United States that insures U.S. citizens and business entities against certain political and other risks of operating in a foreign country. For example, OPIC insures against losses caused by expropriation, inability to convert foreign earnings into dollars, and war, revolution, or civil strife.

ownership the entire bundle of rights recognized in property possessed by a person or persons called the owner; title. See *property.*

parol evidence as used in applying the parol evidence rule, parol evidence includes oral or written evidence of prior or contemporaneous agreements or negotiations and more generally anything not contained in the integrated writing. See *parol evidence rule.*

parol evidence rule principle of contract law stating that if parties to a contract adopt a writing intended to be a final expression of some or all terms of the agreement (an integrated agreement), then all prior or contemporaneous, oral or written, agreements are discharged to the extent that they are within the scope of, or are inconsistent with, the writing. Because, under the rule, the writing effectively becomes the agreement, parol evidence is inadmissible in court to vary or contradict the terms of the writing. See *integrated agreement, parol evidence.*

part performance doctrine an exception to the Statute of Frauds writing requirement for land sale contracts recognized when the party seeking enforcement has changed position in reasonable reliance upon the oral contract. See *Statute of Frauds.*

partial integration in contract law, a writing intended by the parties to be a complete and exclusive statement of some but not all terms of the agreement. See *integrated agreement, complete integration.*

partial breach breach of contract occurring when a party renders substantial but not full performance. The injured promise achieves the benefit of the bargain partially through an award of damages and partially through the promisor's substantial performance. See *substantial performance doctrine, total breach, material breach.*

partially disclosed principal in agency law, a principal whose existence, but not identity, is known by the third party. See *disclosed principal, undisclosed principal.*

participating shares type of preferred shares that are entitled to share in dividends with other classes of shares in addition to the dividend preference. See *dividend, preferred shares, nonparticipating shares.*

parties 1. in contract law, the promisors and promisees of the various contractual promises; the persons who have engaged in a transaction or made an agreement. See UCC §1–201(b)(26); 2. the plaintiffs and defendants in a lawsuit.

partition   method of terminating concurrent ownership by dividing the property into distinct portions, resulting in individual ownership by the former cotenants of each portion. See *concurrent ownership (co-ownership).*

partnership   an association of two or more persons to carry on as co-owners a business for profit. See RUPA §202(a).

partnership agreement (articles of partnership)   contract governing the rights and obligations of the various partners and the internal structure of the partnership. See *partnership.*

partnership by estoppel   principle of partnership law under which equitable estoppel principles are used to impose partnership liability upon a person who is not, in fact, a partner. See *estoppel, equitable estoppel.*

partnership interest   a partner's share of the profits and surplus of the partnership. See *partnership, RUPA §502.*

party wall   in real property, a wall built next to, or upon, a boundary line that serves simultaneously as a common wall of two adjoining structures.

par value   as applied to shares of stock, the amount designated as par value for the shares in the articles of incorporation.

past consideration   a promise made or performance rendered before a return promise is made. The return promise is not binding upon the promisor because it has not been bargained for. See *consideration, bargained-for exchange, moral consideration.*

patent   a grant of the exclusive right to make, use, and sell an invention for a term of years.

payee   in negotiable instruments law, specified person to whom or to whose order an instrument, such as a note or draft, is made payable.

payment intangible   a general intangible under which the account debtor's principal obligation is to pay money. UCC §9–102(a)(61). See *account debtor, general intangible.*

payor bank   the bank by which a check is payable as drawn or accepted, that is, the bank that is the drawee of a draft. See UCC §4–105(3).

per capita **distribution**   distribution of a decedent's estate under which the estate is divided by the number of surviving descendants, regardless of degree. See *per stirpes distribution.*

per stirpes **distribution (taking by representation)**   distribution of a decedent's estate under which the lineal descendant's or "issue" of a deceased heir or devisee inherit the share of an estate that their immediate ancestor would have inherited if he had survived (outlived) the intestate or testator. See *per capita distribution.*

perfect tender rule   principle of sales law requiring the seller, in order to recover, to tender goods conforming in every respect to the terms of the contract. See UCC §2–601.

perfection   in secured transactions, the process by which a secured party achieves protection against third-party claimants to the collateral, including the debtor's other creditors, buyers of the collateral from the debtor, and other persons holding a security interest in the same collateral.

performance bond   a suretyship contract that secures an owner (commonly a governmental body) for the proper performance of a building construction contract by a contractor. See *suretyship, fidelity bond, bond.*

per se **violation**   violations of §1 of the Sherman Act that are so inherently destructive of competition that they are conclusively presumed to be unreasonable and therefore illegal without elaborate inquiry concerning the precise harm they have caused or the business excuse for their use. See *Sherman Antitrust Act.*

personal defenses   in negotiable instruments law, defenses that are defeated by a holder in due course. They include any defense to a simple contract (including fraud and misrepresentation), and unauthorized completion. See *holder in due course, holder in due course doctrine.*

personal jurisdiction   a court's power and authority to issue a judgment that is binding on the parties. See *jurisdiction, subject matter jurisdiction.*

personal property   all things capable of ownership except real property. See *ownership, property, real property.*

petit **jury**   body of disinterested persons selected to determine all issues of fact in a court case.

plaintiff   party who initiates a civil or criminal case seeking some form of judicial relief from another, the defendant.

plant patent   a patent that may be issued to anyone who invents or discovers and asexually reproduces any distinct and new variety of plant.

pleadings   written documents that summarize the facts and establish the legal issues of a civil lawsuit.

pledge   in secured transactions, a method of perfection established by the creditor's taking possession of the collateral; a possessory security interest. See *perfection, possessory security interest.*

police power   a state's inherent authority to establish laws protecting the health, safety, morals, and general welfare of its citizens.

positive law   law that is specifically enacted or adopted by an authority such as the government or the monarch.

possession   physical control of a tangible thing, coupled with an intent to exert control.

possessory security interest (pledge)   type of security interest in which the debtor delivers possession of the collateral to the secured party, who retains the property until the debt is paid. See *nonpossessory security interest.*

possibility of reverter   a future interest in property existing in the grantor or his successors in interest after creation of a fee simple determinable. See *future interest, fee simple determinable.*

potential competition doctrine   antitrust doctrine used to challenge market extension and product extension mergers under §7 of the Clayton Act that have the effect of eliminating a potential competitor (the acquiring firm) from the market in which the acquired firm operates. See *Clayton Act, market extension merger, product extension merger.*

pour-over trust   an *inter vivos* trust to which property is added by testamentary disposition; that is, on death, property is "poured over" or into the trust created during life. See *trust,* inter vivos *trust, testamentary disposition.*

power   the ability on the part of a person to produce a change in a given legal relation by doing or failing to do a given act. The person whose legal relation is liable to be changed through exercise of another's power is subject to a liability.

power given as security (agency coupled with an interest)   a power to affect another's legal relations, created in the form of an agency authority, but for the benefit of the power holder or a third person, and given to secure performance of a duty or to protect a title, such power being given when the duty or title is created or given for consideration. See *Restatement (Second) of Agency* §138.

power of attorney   a written instrument by which one person authorizes another to act as his or her agent.

power of termination (right of entry for condition broken)   future interest existing in property in the grantor or his successors in interest after creation of a fee simple subject to a condition subsequent. See *future interest, fee simple subject to a condition subsequent.*

power to tax   an inherent power of the states giving them the authority to require financial contributions to state government.

prayer for relief   statement in the complaint in a civil suit in which the plaintiff requests that the court provide a remedy for the alleged wrong, usually an award of damages. See *plaintiff, civil law.*

precedent   the holding of a prior case that serves as authority for resolution of the issues of subsequent cases that involve the same or similar facts.

preemptive right   in corporation law, the right of an existing shareholder to purchase a new issue of shares, in proportion to his or her present interest in the corporation, before the shares are sold to others.

preexisting duty rule   common law contract principle stating that a promise to perform (or the performance of) a preexisting legal or public duty does not furnish consideration to support a return promise. See *consideration.*

preference   in bankruptcy law, a transfer of property by an insolvent debtor to a creditor shortly before bankruptcy on account of an antecedent debt, by means of which the creditor receives more than he or she would have received in the bankruptcy proceeding if the transfer had not been made. See *antecedent debt.*

preferred shares   in corporation law, class of shares of stock that have preference over other classes in the payment of dividends or in the assets of the corporation upon liquidation, or both. See *common shares.*

Pregnancy Discrimination Act   federal statute enacted in 1978 (as an amendment to Title VII of the Civil Rights Act of 1964) that prohibits employment discrimination based on pregnancy, childbirth, or related medical conditions. See *Title VII of the Civil Rights Act of 1964.*

preliminary hearing   in criminal prosecutions, a proceeding held before the magistrate to protect an accused individual from unwarranted prosecution, and in which the prosecution must establish that probable cause exists to believe that a crime has been committed and that the accused committed it.

prescription   a method of obtaining an easement by the adverse use of another's land, if the use is hostile, open, and notorious, and is continuous and uninterrupted for the period of the statute of limitations. See *easement.*

present possessory interest   an interest in property in which the owner has the present right to possession of the property. See *future interest.*

presenting bank   any bank presenting a check except a payor bank. See UCC §4–105(6).

presentment   in negotiable instruments law, a demand for payment or acceptance of an instrument made by the holder upon the maker, acceptor, or drawee. See UCC §3–501(a).

presentment warranties   in negotiable instruments law, warranties regarding forgery and alteration given to the party who is to pay or accept an instrument by any person presenting the instrument for payment or acceptance and any prior transferor of the instrument. See *transfer warranties,* UCC §§3–417, 4–208.

prevention and hindrance   term sometimes used to describe a breach of the duty to act in good faith in contract performance.

price discrimination   practice by a seller of charging one buyer more than another for the same commodity. See *Robinson-Patman Act.*

price-fixing   cooperative setting of price levels or ranges by competing firms. Includes generally any agreement between competitors that affects or is intended to affect price, however accomplished.

prima facie case   in a civil case, some evidence supporting each allegation of the complaint that, unless contradicted or rebutted by other evidence, entitles the plaintiff to recover. That is, the defendant automatically prevails without producing any evidence unless the plaintiff proves a prima facie case. See *civil law.*

primary contract liability   in negotiable instruments law, the form of contract liability undertaken by the maker of a note and the acceptor of a draft. It involves an absolute obligation or promise to pay an instrument. See *secondary contract liability.*

primary line competitive injury   in price discrimination cases, injury occurring at the same functional level as the discriminating seller, that is, competitors of the discriminating seller are injured. See *secondary line competitive injury, Robinson-Patman Act.*

primary picketing   in labor law, picketing the business with which the union has a genuine dispute. See *secondary boycott.*

principal   1. in suretyship law, the person for whose debt or default the surety is liable. See *suretyship;* 2. In agency law, the person for whom the agent acts. See *agency.*

principal and income allocation   the process of apportioning receipts and expenditures in the administration of a trust between the income beneficiary and the remainderman. See *trust.*

priorities   rules of law, usually created by statute such as federal bankruptcy law, granting a creditor who does not possess a lien upon a debtor's property a priority in distribution of the debtor's assets over certain other creditors. See *lien.*

private corporation   corporation formed by private individuals for private purposes and including, generally, nonprofit and business corporations. See *public corporation.*

private international law   a branch of conflicts of law that determines when a domestic court should exercise jurisdiction over a case involving foreign persons or territories, when foreign rather than domestic law should apply to a case, and when judgments rendered by foreign courts should be recognized and enforced in a domestic court.

private law   rules and principles that involve persons (whether artificial or natural) as private individuals. See *public law.*

private nuisance   an intentional tort providing a remedy for invasions of the private interest in the use and enjoyment of land. See *public nuisance.*

private trust   an express trust in which the trust property is devoted to the use of specified persons designated as beneficiaries. See *express trust, charitable trust.*

privilege   1. the legal freedom on the part of one person as against another to do or refrain from doing an act. There is no right on the part of the person against whom the privilege exists that the person possessing the privilege should not engage in the particular course of action or nonaction in question; 2. rule of law that enables a person to prevent certain information from being introduced into evidence in court.

Privileges and Immunities Clause provision of the Constitution that prohibits states from unreasonably discriminating against out-of-state citizens, including out-of-state businesses.

privity of contract term used to refer to the relationship among persons who have entered into a contractual relationship.

probable cause in criminal law, facts and circumstances that would lead a reasonable person to believe: (1) for an arrest or indictment—that an offense has been committed and that the accused committed it; (2) for a search warrant—that the items are located in the place to be searched and that the items are connected with illegal activities. See *criminal law.*

probate any matter or proceeding pertaining to the administration of a decedent's estate.

probate court a state court having jurisdiction over the administration of a decedent's estate.

procedural law law that establishes the mechanisms with which to enforce the rights and duties created by substantive law. See *substantive law.*

procedural unconscionability a form of unconscionability occurring when a person signs a standardized-form contract containing a provision, commonly in fine print, that substantially alters his or her reasonable expectations under the agreement; unfair surprise. See *unconscionability, substantive unconscionability.*

proceeds in secured transactions, whatever is acquired upon the sale, lease, license, exchange, collection, or other disposition of collateral or proceeds. See UCC §9–102(a)(64).

product extension merger merger that combines firms producing related though not identical products. See *conglomerate merger, market extension merger.*

products liability the area of law imposing liability upon manufacturers and other suppliers of goods for personal injury and property damage caused by the products they sell.

professional corporation a closely-held corporation formed by professionals such as doctors, lawyers, accountants, and engineers. See *closely-held corporation, corporation.*

profit (*profit à prendre*) a right of use in another's property that involves the right to remove part of the land or products of the land. See *easement.*

promise 1. in general, a commitment or undertaking that something will or will not happen in the future; 2. in negotiable instruments law, an undertaking to pay that must more than merely acknowledge the existence of an obligation. See UCC §3–103(a)(9).

promisee person to whom a promise is made.

promisor person making a promise.

promissory estoppel doctrine of contract law making otherwise unenforceable promises enforceable if relied upon. Specifically, a promise that the promisor should reasonably expect to induce action or forbearance on the part of the promisee or a third person and that does induce such action or forbearance is binding if injustice can be avoided only by enforcement of the promise. See *estoppel, equitable estoppel.*

promoters persons organizing and planning a corporation. See *corporation.*

promulgate to publish; to announce officially.

property sum of the various legal relationships between identifiable persons with respect to a thing, tangible or intangible.

proprietorship (sole proprietorship) a business owned and controlled exclusively by one person.

prosecution a legal proceeding in which a person is charged with a crime and guilt or innocence is determined. See *criminal law, crime.*

prospectus the first part of a registration statement filed under the Securities Act of 1933, which must be delivered to persons to whom a security is offered or sold. See *registration statement, Securities Act of 1933.*

protest in negotiable instruments law, a certificate of dishonor made by a U.S. consul or vice consul, a notary public, or any other person authorized by local law to certify dishonor. See UCC §3–505(b).

proviso clause or part of a clause contained in a statute that either excepts something from the enacting clause; qualifies, modifies, or restrains its generality; or excludes some possible ground of misinterpretation concerning its extent. Provisos usually are preceded by the words "provided," "provided that," or "provided, however."

proximate cause in negligence law, the various legal issues that collectively limit the defendant's liability for the consequences of his or her negligent acts. Generally, to recover the plaintiff must prove that the defendant's negligent conduct was a substantial factor in producing the plaintiff's injury (causation in fact), and that the defendant owed a duty to the particular injured plaintiff to protect him or her against the event that in fact caused the injury (foreseeability of harm). See *negligence.*

proxy grant of authority by a shareholder to another to vote his or her shares.

prudent investor rule rule of trust law requiring the trustee to manage trust and investment assets as a "prudent investor" would. The rule, based upon modern portfolio theory, requires management and investment decisions concerning individual assets to be evaluated in the context of the trust portfolio as a whole. Thus, a risky investment prohibited by the "prudent person" rule might be permitted by the prudent investor rule when considered in the context of the trust portfolio as a whole. See *prudent person rule, Uniform Prudent Investor Act.*

prudent-person rule principle governing trust investments under which the trustee owes a duty to the beneficiary to make only those investments of trust property that a prudent person would make of her or his own property, taking into consideration both the preservation of the estate and the amount and regularity of the income to be generated. See *trust.*

public corporation (municipal, political corporation) corporation created by the government for political purposes to administer civil government, often vested with local legislative powers. See *corporation, private corporation.*

public invitee a member of the public invited to enter or remain upon another's land for a purpose for which the land is held open to the public. See *invitee, business invitee.*

public law principles and rules that involve the government in its capacity of representing society. See *private law.*

publicly-held corporation corporation whose shares are owned by many people, such as a corporation that has shares traded on a securities exchange, or for which public share price quotations exist. See *corporation, closely-held corporation.*

public nuisance criminal offense proscribing various activities or physical conditions as offensive to the public health, safety, morals, peace, or comfort. See *private nuisance.*

Public Utility Holding Company Act of 1935 federal statute designed to correct abuses in the financing and operation of electric and gas utilities owned by holding companies.

punitive (exemplary) damages damages that are designed to punish the conduct of the defendant and to deter similar future conduct by the defendant or others. See *damages.*

purchase money mortgage traditionally, a mortgage taken by a seller of real property to secure payment of its purchase price. Now generally used to describe any mortgage given on real property to secure its purchase price no matter who provides financing. See *mortgage.*

purchase money security interest a security interest that is taken or retained by a seller of the collateral to secure all or part of its price, or taken by a person who makes an advance or incurs an obligation that enables the debtor to acquire rights in collateral. See UCC §9–103.

purchaser person who takes property by sale, discount, negotiation, mortgage, pledge, lien, issue or reissue, gift, or any other voluntary transaction creating an interest in property. See UCC §§1–201(b)(29), (30).

pure notice recording statute recording statute under which a subsequent purchaser who takes without actual knowledge of a prior unrecorded conveyance prevails, regardless of who later records first. See *recording statute, pure race recording statute, race-notice recording statute.*

pure race recording statute statute under which the first purchaser to record an interest in property prevails even if he or she takes with actual knowledge of a prior unrecorded conveyance. See *recording statute, pure notice recording statute, race-notice recording statute.*

qualified indorsement in negotiable instruments law, an indorsement that contains the words "without recourse" added to the signature. A qualified indorsement negates secondary contract liability. See *unqualified indorsement, secondary contract liability.*

quasi-contract (implied-in-law contract) a form of restitution that provides a remedy when a benefit is conferred by one party upon another, who retains the benefit. If necessary to prevent unjust enrichment of the benefited party, the law implies or imposes a promise (the quasi-contract) to pay the reasonable value of the benefit conferred. See *restitution, constructive trust.*

quid pro quo **sexual harassment** sexual harassment that occurs when an employer grants or withholds employment privileges or opportunities based on whether an employee submits to unwelcome sexual advances or provides sexual favors. See *sexual harassment.*

quitclaim deed deed that conveys whatever interest the grantor has in property, but makes no warranties or promises regarding title to the grantee. See *deed, warranty deed.*

race-notice recording statute recording statute under which a subsequent purchaser prevails over a prior unrecorded conveyance if he or she both (1) takes without actual knowledge of the prior conveyance, and (2) records first. See *recording statute, pure notice recording statute, pure race recording statute.*

ratification 1. in contracts generally, an election to be bound upon a previously voidable obligation. See *voidable contract;* 2. in agency law, an indication by the principal through words or conduct of an intent to be bound upon (to treat as authorized) a previously unauthorized contract made on her behalf.

reaffirmation agreement an agreement in which a debtor promises to pay a debt discharged in bankruptcy.

real defenses in negotiable instruments law, defenses that may be successfully asserted against a holder in due course, including forgery; alteration; infancy, other incapacity, duress, and illegality; fraud in the execution; discharge in bankruptcy; and any other discharge known to the holder when he or she takes the instrument. See *holder in due course, holder in due course doctrine.*

Real Estate Settlement Procedures Act (RESPA) federal statute requiring advance itemized disclosure of real estate closing costs to the buyer.

real fraud See *fraud in the execution.*

real property property interests recognized in land and structures, objects, or other interests attached to or closely associated with land. See *property, personal property.*

reasonable (ordinary) care the amount of care a reasonably careful and prudent person would use under similar circumstances. See *negligence, reasonable person.*

reasonable grounds for insecurity See *adequate assurance of due performance,* UCC §2–609.

reasonable person a hypothetical, fictitious person who possesses the characteristics, attentiveness, knowledge, intelligence, and judgment required by society for the protection of others. See *negligence, reasonable care.*

receiver a person appointed by a court to take possession of and administer, preserve, or manage a debtor's property under court direction.

reciprocal dealing anticompetitive arrangement that arises when two parties are related as buyer to seller in one or more markets and seller to buyer in another or others. One party then agrees to buy from the other in one market, if the other agrees to buy from it in another market.

record information that is inscribed on a tangible medium or that is stored in an electronic or other medium and is retrievable in perceivable form. See UCC §9–102(a)(69). Record is the equivalent of "writing" for information contained in electronic, as opposed to paper, form. See *authenticate, writing, sign.*

recorder of deeds office public office in which documents evidencing an interest in real property are recorded.

recording statute state statute designed to provide reliable public information on the status of real estate titles. Recording statutes protect purchasers and mortgagees by allowing them to defeat prior unrecorded recordable interests in property. See *pure race recording statute, pure notice recording statute, race-notice recording statute.*

recoupment in general, action by which a defendant reduces an amount owing to the plaintiff by asserting claims or defenses arising out of the same contract or transaction on which the plaintiff's action is founded; action by which the obligor of an assigned right asserts against the assignee defenses that he or she has against the assignor arising out of the contract creating the assigned right. See *set-off.*

recoupment cycle in secured transactions involving inventory, the process of converting the proceeds of the sale of inventory to cash, which is then used to purchase more inventory.

reformation an equitable remedy used to rewrite or reform a written contract that, because of a mistake by both parties regarding the content or effect of the writing, fails to correctly state the parties' agreement. See *equitable remedy.*

registered limited liability partnership (RLLP) general partnership registered with the state under a RLLP statute. Upon registration, the partners remain personally liable for ordinary contract obligations of the partnership but escape personal liability for the other partners' torts or other misconduct. See *partnership, general partner.*

registration statement statement that must be filed with the SEC before securities are offered or sold to the public. See *prospectus.*

Regulation A Securities and Exchange Commission regulation governing limited offerings under the Securities Act of 1933, providing a simplified form of registration for small issues (not more than $5 million). Securities Act Rules 251–263. See *Securities Act of 1933.*

Regulation B   regulation issued by the Federal Reserve Board to implement the Equal Credit Opportunity Act. See *Equal Credit Opportunity Act.*

Regulation D   Securities and Exchange Commission regulation governing limited offerings under the Securities Act of 1933, which simplifies and coordinates the various limited offering exemptions. Securities Act Rules 501–508. See *Securities Act of 1933.*

Regulation Z   regulation issued by the Federal Reserve Board to implement the Truth-in-Lending Act. See *Truth-in-Lending Act.*

Regulation CC   regulation issued by the Federal Reserve Board to implement the Expedited Funds Availability Act. See *Expedited Funds Availability Act.*

Rehabilitation Act of 1973   federal statute that prohibits government employers, federal contractors, and employers receiving federal financial assistance, from discriminating against persons with disabilities. The Americans with Disabilities Act is based upon this statute. See *Americans with Disabilities Act.*

rehabilitation case   bankruptcy case in which the debtor retains its assets and pays creditors out of future earnings pursuant to a plan filed with and approved by the court. See *liquidation case.*

reimbursement   in suretyship law, the surety's right to be reimbursed by the principal after paying or otherwise performing the principal obligation. See *suretyship.*

rejection   1. in contract formation, the offeree's statement or other conduct indicating an intention not to accept an offer; 2. in sales law, an action taken by the buyer after delivery of nonconforming goods, indicating an intention to reject and return (rather than retain) the goods. See *acceptance.*

reliance interest   an interest of an injured promisee that may be protected by contract remedies, designed to reimburse the promise for expenses incurred in reliance upon the contract. See *expectation interest, restitution interest.*

remand   action of an appellate court that sends the case back to a lower court.

remedy at law   damages. See *damages, equitable remedy.*

remainder   a future interest arising in a third party (someone other than the grantor), which takes effect in possession and enjoyment on the natural termination of the preceding estate. See *future interest.*

remittance chain   the chain of banks in the check collection process that become accountable for the amount of a check, beginning with the payor bank and ultimately ending with the depositary bank's liability to pay its customer, the depositor of the check. See *check collection process.*

remitter   in negotiable instruments law, a person, not a party to the instrument, who purchases an instrument in order to pay his or her own debt to the payee named in the instrument.

reorganization plan   in a bankruptcy case, a rehabilitation plan filed with and approved by the court that divides creditors and shareholders into classes, and then designates how claimants within each class are to be treated. See *rehabilitation case.*

replevin   a statutory prejudgment creditor's remedy enabling the plaintiff to recover possession of specific goods wrongfully taken or detained. See *self-help.*

repudiation   in contract law, words or conduct of one contracting party that unequivocally indicate his or her inability or unwillingness to perform without breach.

requirements contract   a sales contract in which a buyer promises to purchase its requirements of a given commodity from a seller. See *output contract.*

res ipsa loquitur   doctrine of negligence law under which the jury may infer that the plaintiff's harm was caused by the defendant's negligence if (1) the event is one that does not ordinarily occur in the absence of negligence, (2) other responsible causes are eliminated by the evidence, and (3) the indicated negligence is within the scope of the defendant's duty to the plaintiff. See *negligence.*

res judicata   doctrine providing that final judgment by a court of competent jurisdiction is conclusive on the parties and prevents relitigation of the cause of action.

resale price maintenance   an agreement between a seller and a buyer fixing the price at which the buyer may resell the goods purchased.

rescission   a contract remedy in which the contract is avoided and each party receives restitution for the value of any benefit conferred on the other, thereby restoring both parties to the position they occupied before the contract was made.

respondeat superior doctrine   doctrine of agency law imposing liability without fault upon masters for the torts of servants committed while acting within the scope of their employment. See *master, servant.*

Resource Conservation and Recovery Act (RCRA)   federal statute that established a plan for transporting and disposing of hazardous waste.

Restatement of the Law   major civil law treatise published by the American Law Institute (ALI), the stated purpose of which is to define the principles of the common law as they would be decided today by the great majority of the courts. See *civil law, common law.*

restitution   generally, the act of restoring something to its rightful owner, commonly to make good for some loss, damage, or injury. As a judicial remedy, a person who has been unjustly enriched at the expense of another is required to make restitution to the other for the value of the benefit conferred. See *unjust enrichment, quasi-contract, constructive trust.*

restitution interest   an interest of a promise that may be protected by contract remedies. The interest is measured by the value of the benefit conferred by the promisee on the other party. See *expectation interest, reliance interest.*

restraint of trade   a promise is in restraint of trade if its performance limits competition in any business or restricts the promisor in the exercise of any gainful occupation. See *naked restraint, ancillary restraint.*

restrictive indorsement   an indorsement limiting or restricting in some way the rights acquired by the indorsee. See *indorsement, non-restrictive indorsement.*

resulting trust   an implied trust arising when a person makes a disposition of property under circumstances indicating that he or she does intend that the person taking or holding the property should have a beneficial interest in it. See *trust, implied trust, constructive trust.*

reverse   action of an appellate court that sets aside the judgment entered by a lower court.

reverse discrimination   employment discrimination in favor of minorities and women.

reversion   a future interest remaining in a grantor of property who transfers away less than his or her entire interest in the property. See *future interest.*

Revised Model Business Corporation Act (RMBCA)   Model Business Corporation Act, as revised and renumbered in 1984. See *Model Business Corporation Act.*

Revised Uniform Limited Partnership Act (RULPA) revision of the Uniform Limited Partnership Act promulgated by the National Conference of Commissioners on Uniform State Laws in 1976 and amended in 1985. It was superceded by the Uniform Limited Partnership Act in 2001. See *limited partnership, Uniform Limited Partnership Act.*

Revised Uniform Partnership Act (RUPA) revision of Uniform Partnership Act promulgated by the National Conference of Commissioners on Uniform State Laws in 1994. See *partnership, Uniform Partnership Act.*

revocation in contract formation, the offeror's statement or other conduct after the offer is made, indicating that he or she no longer intends to enter into the proposed contract. See *offer.*

revocation of acceptance in sales law, action taken by a buyer to revoke a previous acceptance of goods in limited circumstances in which the nonconformity of goods substantially impairs their value to the buyer. See *acceptance,* UCC §2–608.

rezoning an amendment to a zoning ordinance that reclassifies property into a new zone. See *zoning.*

right a legally enforceable claim of one person against another that the other shall do or not do a given act. The person against whom the right exists has a "duty"; that is, he or she is under a legally enforceable obligation to do or refrain from doing an act.

right of foreclosure the right of a secured creditor to take possession of and sell the collateral to satisfy a debt. See *secured creditor.*

right of survivorship characteristic of the joint tenancy and tenancy by the entirety form of concurrent ownership (co-ownership). Under the right of survivorship, if one of the joint tenants or tenants by the entirety dies, the deceased's share is owned by the other, who becomes the sole owner. If the property is owned by more than two joint tenants, the deceased's share belongs to the survivors jointly. See *joint tenancy, tenancy by the entirety, concurrent ownership (co-ownership).*

right to privacy the right to be left alone. Interference with this right is compensable in a tort action.

right-to-work laws state laws that prohibit union and agency shops. See *union shop, agency shop.*

risk of loss contract rules determining the rights of the parties if the property to be sold under the contract (such as goods) is lost, destroyed, or stolen. Risk of loss rules define when the risk of such casualties passes from the seller to the buyer.

Robinson-Patman Act amendment to §2 of the Clayton Act, enacted in 1936, to reach secondary line anticompetitive effects of price discrimination and to outlaw certain devices used to exact price concessions. See *price discrimination, secondary line competitive injury, Clayton Act.*

rule of reason basic standard by which violations of §1 of the Sherman Act are measured. Under the rule of reason, the Sherman Act does not condemn all restraints of trade, but only those restraints the character or effect of which is unreasonably anticompetitive. See *Sherman Antitrust Act, restraint of trade.*

runaway shop unfair labor practice in which an employer closes a facility or moves its operation to another facility to avoid having to bargain with a union.

sale the passing of title to goods from the seller to the buyer for a price. See UCC §2–106(1).

sale on approval sale in which goods are delivered to a consumer primarily for use and may be returned by the buyer even though they conform to the contract. See *sale or return,* UCC §§2–326, 2–327.

sale or return sale in which goods are delivered to a merchant for resale and may be returned even though they conform to the contract. See *sale on approval,* UCC §§2–326, 2–327.

sale with reserve auction sale in which the auctioneer (seller) may withdraw the goods at any time prior to announcing completion of the sale. See UCC §2–328.

sales contract contract for the sale of goods. See *goods, sale, contract.*

sample in sales contracts, goods drawn from the bulk of goods involved in the sale and exhibited by the seller to the buyer for inspection during precontract negotiation to describe goods to be sold. See *model,* UCC §2–313(1)(c).

Sarbanes-Oxley Act of 2002 federal statute designed to improve: auditing standards and auditor independence; corporate governance; and the accuracy, reliability, and timeliness of corporate disclosures.

scienter in fraud cases, a term used by the courts to refer to a defendant's knowledge of the falsity of his misrepresentation. See *fraud, fraudulent misrepresentation.*

scope of employment conduct of a servant that is of the kind he or she is employed to perform, that occurs substantially within authorized time and space limitations, and that is motivated, at least in part, by a purpose to serve the master. See *respondeat superior doctrine, master, servant, vicarious liability.*

scrip a certificate representing the right to receive a portion of a share used as an alternative to fractional shares in distributing share dividends.

search warrant a document issued by a judge or magistrate, upon a showing of probable cause, authorizing governmental officials to search a specific place and seize specific items connected with illegal activities. See *probable cause.*

secondary boycott an unfair labor practice by a union in a labor dispute involving pressuring the primary employer by striking, picketing, or otherwise boycotting a business with which the primary employer does business. See *primary picketing.*

secondary contract liability in negotiable instruments law, the form of contract liability undertaken by the drawer of a draft and the indorser of any instrument. It includes an obligation to pay the instrument only if the primary party does not pay and certain conditions are met. See *primary contract liability, conditions precedent.*

secondary line competitive injury in price discrimination cases, injury that occurs among buyers from the discriminating seller who later compete in the resale of the goods; that is, injury occurs at a functional level below (or vertical to) the discriminating seller. If the buyer receiving the discrimination itself resells, competition may be affected two functional levels below the discriminating seller. Injury at this level (among competitors of the buyer's customers) is "third line" or "tertiary line" injury. See *primary line competitive injury, Robinson-Patman Act, price discrimination.*

secret limitation in agency law, a limitation placed by the principal upon the normal incidents of an agent's authority and which is not known to third parties dealing with the agent.

secured creditor generally, a creditor who has a contractually created lien in a debtor's property. See *lien.*

secured party in a secured transaction, the lender, seller, or other party in whose favor a security interest exists. The term also includes a consignor, and a buyer of accounts, chattel paper, payment intangibles, or promissory notes. UCC §9–102(a)(72). See *security interest, secured transaction.*

secured transaction   a transaction in which a borrower or buyer gives a lender or seller an interest in personal property or fixtures to secure performance of an obligation. See *mortgage.*

Securities Act of 1933   federal statute governing the public distribution of securities. With certain exceptions it prohibits the offer or sale of securities to the public unless the offering is properly registered. The Act requires broad disclosure of relevant corporate information to prospective investors, provides civil remedies for violations, and prohibits fraudulent or deceptive practices in the sale of securities.

Securities and Exchange Commission   federal administrative agency established by the Securities Exchange Act of 1934 to administer federal securities law.

Securities Exchange Act of 1934   federal statute that created the Securities and Exchange Commission and regulates secondary trading in securities, the securities markets, and persons conducting securities transactions. The Act imposes registration and reporting requirements on many issuers and others, and regulates proxy solicitation, tender offers, insider trading, and fraud and manipulative practices in securities trading.

security   1. under securities law, a wide variety of investment instruments such as stocks, bonds, and investment contracts; 2. under UCC Article 8, a share, participation, or other interest in the property of the issuing corporation, or an obligation of the issuer. See UCC §8–102(a)(15); 3. in debtor-creditor law, devices used by creditors to protect themselves against other creditors in the event of the debtor's bankruptcy and to provide for expeditious collection upon default. Usually provided by a contractually created lien in the debtor's real or personal property (a mortgage or secured transaction), or the promise of a surety to pay the debt if the debtor does not. See *lien, suretyship.*

security agreement   in a secured transaction, the contract creating or providing for a security interest. UCC §9–102(a)(73). See *secured transaction, security interest.*

security interest   in a secured transaction, an interest in personal property or fixtures that secures payment or performance of an obligation. See *secured transaction,* UCC §1–201(b)(35).

Self-Employment Contributions Act   See *Federal Insurance Contributions Act.*

self-help   secured creditors' remedy under which, upon default by the debtor, the creditor simply repossesses the collateral without resort to judicial process. See *secured creditor, replevin.*

Semiconductor Chip Protection Act   federal statute, enacted in 1984, to prevent piracy of computer chip designs. The Act permits the creator of an original chip design to register the "mask work" (which defines the chip's design in three dimensions) with the federal Copyright Office.

servant   agent whose physical conduct in the performance of his or her duties is subject to the control or right of control of the principal (master). See *master.*

service mark   any word, name, symbol, or device used to identify and distinguish a particular service for sales and advertising purposes. See *trademark.*

service of process   formal delivery of a complaint and a summons to the defendant. See *complaint, summons.*

set-off   in general, action by which a defendant subtracts (sets off) against amounts owing to the plaintiff, amounts owed by the plaintiff to the defendant arising out of a contract or transaction other than the one upon which the plaintiff's claim is based; action by which the obligor of an assigned right asserts against the assignee defenses that he or she has against the assignor arising independently of the contract creating the assigned right. See *recoupment.*

settlement   as used in bank deposits and collections, a term referring to payment of an item in cash, through adjustment and offsetting balances through clearing houses, debit or credit entries in accounts between banks, or the forwarding of various types of remittance instruments.

settlor (trustor)   person who creates a trust. See *trust.*

several liability   in contract law, term describing liability of copromisors if each promises a separate performance to be rendered respectively by each of them, or each makes a separate promise that the same performance will be rendered. See *joint and several promises, joint liability.*

sexual harassment   unwelcome sexual advances, requests for sexual favors, and other verbal or physical conduct of a sexual nature. Sexual harassment is a form of employment discrimination based on sex that violates Title VII of the Civil Rights Act of 1964. See *Title VII of the Civil Rights Act of 1964.*

shareholder derivative suit   lawsuit in which shareholders sue not in their individual capacities, but as representatives of the corporation, in order to enforce a corporate cause of action.

shelter (umbrella) rule   in negotiable instruments law, doctrine providing that the transfer of an instrument by a holder in due course vests in the transferee the rights of a holder in due course even if the transferee cannot himself qualify under UCC §3–302. See *holder in due course, holder in due course doctrine,* UCC §3–203(b).

Sherman Antitrust Act   federal antitrust statute, enacted in 1890, that makes illegal: contracts, combinations, or conspiracies in restraint of trade; monopolization; attempts to monopolize; and conspiracies to monopolize. See *Clayton Act, Federal Trade Commission Act.*

shipment contract   sales contract in which the seller is authorized or required to ship goods to the buyer, but is not required to deliver them at any particular destination. See *destination contract.*

shipment under reservation (documentary sale)   sales contract in which the seller draws a draft against the buyer for the purchase price and forwards it, together with a bill of lading covering the goods, to the buyer's bank with instructions not to surrender the bill of lading to the buyer until the buyer accepts or pays the draft.

sight draft   a demand draft. See *draft, demand draft.*

signature   any symbol adopted or executed by a party with present intention to authenticate a writing. See *authenticate,* UCC §1–201(b)(37).

simple contracts   See *informal contracts.*

single-party credit card   credit card issued by a business to sell goods or services on credit to its customers, the cardholders; that is, a single-party card is a simple credit sale with the card used to identify persons to whom credit should be extended. See *credit card, dual-party credit card, multiparty credit card.*

slander   communication of a defamatory statement by spoken words or gestures. See *defamation, libel.*

Social Security Act   federal statute enacted in 1935 to provide income to retired workers and later amended to include benefits to disabled workers and to dependents of deceased workers.

software   a computer program and any supporting information provided in connection with a transaction relating to the program. UCC §9–102(a)(75). See *general intangible.*

solicitation   an inchoate crime committed when a person, with intent that a crime be committed, asks, orders, or otherwise encourages another to commit that crime. See *inchoate crimes.*

sovereign immunity   a doctrine of international law under which domestic courts, in certain circumstances, will not exercise jurisdiction over a foreign state or its instrumentalities. See *international law.*

special agent agent who conducts a transaction or series of transactions not involving continuity of service. See *general agent.*

special guaranty (offer for) an offer for a suretyship contract made to a particular creditor that can be accepted only by that creditor. See *suretyship, general guaranty.*

special indorsee the person to whom a specially indorsed instrument becomes payable. The instrument may be further negotiated only by the special indorsee's indorsement. See *indorsement, special indorsement.*

special indorsement in negotiable instruments law, an indorsement that specifies the person to whom or to whose order the instrument is further payable. See *indorsement, blank indorsement.*

special permit an administrative remedy provided for in zoning ordinances that allows a landowner to use his or her land in a manner expressly permitted by the ordinance, provided conditions and standards set forth in the zoning regulations are met. See *zoning.*

specially manufactured goods goods that are to be manufactured or acquired for a particular buyer, and that are not suitable for sale to others in the ordinary course of the seller's business. See *goods.*

specific devise a devise of particularly designated property. See *devise.*

specific performance an equitable contract remedy requiring that the breaching party actually perform the contract as agreed. See *equitable remedy, injunction against breach.*

spendthrift trust trust in which the beneficiary may not voluntarily transfer his or her interest, and creditors of the beneficiary may not reach it to satisfy their claims. See *trust.*

spot zoning a zoning amendment classifying a property or group of properties within a district to a use that is inconsistent with the general zoning pattern of the surrounding area, and is designed primarily for the economic benefit of the owner. See *zoning.*

stale check a check that is more than six months old. See *check.*

standard mortgage clause clause usually found in fire insurance or homeowner's policies that is designed to protect the lender holding a mortgage on the insured property. Under the clause, the mortgagee becomes an insured, and any loss is payable to the mortgagor and mortgagee as their interests appear. In addition, the clause provides that the mortgagee may collect for losses under the policy even if the mortgagor would be denied recovery. See *mortgage.*

Standard State Zoning Enabling Act statute drafted in 1924 that is the basis of many state statutes authorizing local governments to enact zoning ordinances. See *zoning.*

standby letter of credit a letter of credit that represents an obligation to the beneficiary on the part of the issuer (1) to repay money borrowed by or advanced to or for the account of the customer, or (2) to make payment on account of any evidence of indebtedness undertaken by the customer, or (3) to make payment on account of any default by the customer in the performance of an obligation. See *letter of credit.*

stare decisis doctrine forming the basis of the common law that provides that courts will adhere to and apply basic principles of law decided in prior cases to later cases involving substantially the same or similar facts and issues. See *common law.*

state implementation plan (SIP) under the Clean Air Act, state plan designed to attain the air quality established by the National Ambient Air Quality Standards (NAAQS). See *Clean Air Act, National Ambient Air Quality Standards.*

Statute of Elizabeth English statute, enacted in 1570, providing that any transfer of property made with the end purpose and intent of delaying, hindering, or defrauding creditors is void. The Statute of Elizabeth is the basis of modern fraudulent conveyances law. See *fraudulent conveyance, Uniform Fraudulent Conveyance Act, Uniform Fraudulent Transfer Act.*

Statute of Frauds English statute, enacted in 1677, requiring that certain types of contracts be evidenced by a writing to be enforceable; more generally, the term refers to any statute requiring that a contract be evidenced by a writing to be enforceable. See, for example, UCC §§2–201, 9–203.

statute of limitations statute that requires the plaintiff to file a lawsuit within a specified period of time after a cause of action arises, or be barred from recovery. See, for example, UCC §2–725.

statute of repose a statute requiring a plaintiff to file a lawsuit within a fixed time period without regard to when the cause of action arises or the plaintiff's awareness that a cause of action exists. See *statute of limitations.*

statutes written laws enacted by the legislature.

statutory lien a lien imposed or authorized solely by statute, which arises by operation of law when specified circumstances or conditions occur. See *lien.*

stock subscription an offer or agreement by a subscriber to purchase and pay for a specified number of previously unissued shares of the corporation.

stop-payment order oral or written order directed by the drawer to the drawee bank to countermand, or stop, an order to pay contained in a check. See *check.*

straight voting method of shareholder voting in which each share is entitled to one vote on each matter, including one vote for each vacant directorship. See *cumulative voting.*

strict foreclosure method of foreclosure in secured transactions in which, after default and repossession, the secured party merely retains the collateral in full satisfaction of the debt. It is used as an alternative to selling the collateral and applying the proceeds to the unpaid obligation. See *foreclosure.*

strict liability liability that is imposed without fault; liability that is imposed upon a defendant in the absence of both negligence and an intent to interfere with the plaintiff's legally protected interests. See *negligence, intent.*

strict liability in tort theory of recovery in products liability under which the plaintiff recovers by proving that an injury resulted from a condition of a product, that the condition was an unreasonably dangerous one (that is, the product was defective), and that the condition existed when the product left the seller's control. See *products liability, defective product.*

strike a concerted work stoppage by the employees. See *economic strike, unfair labor practice strike.*

substantial performance doctrine a doctrine of contract law under which a person is entitled to recover under a contract despite immaterial defects in performance. Because such "substantial performance" is not full performance, however, the other contracting party may recover damages for partial breach. See *partial breach, material breach, total breach.*

subject-matter jurisdiction the types or categories of cases that a court is empowered to hear. See *jurisdiction, personal jurisdiction.*

sublease in landlord-tenant law, transfer by the tenant of all or part of his or her interest in the property for a period less than the entire term; or a transfer, originally for the entire term, if the tenant may reacquire the right to possession upon occurrence of an event.

subpoena a legal process commanding a witness to appear and give testimony.

subrogation   an equitable remedy involving an equitable assignment grounded in restitution and designed to prevent unjust enrichment. In suretyship law, it refers to the surety's right to succeed to the position of the creditor, once the surety has satisfied the principal obligation, for purposes of proceeding against the principal. In insurance law, it refers to the insurance company's right, after paying the insured, to succeed the insured's rights in contract or tort against any third party causing the loss. See *equitable remedy, restitution, suretyship, insurance.*

substantive criminal law   the law defining which acts or omissions are crimes and describing the punishment to be imposed for that conduct. See *crime, criminal procedure.*

substantive law   law defining the rights to which a person is entitled and the duties a person is obligated to perform. See *procedural law.*

substantive unconscionability   unconscionability involving contractual oppression, occurring when a contract or provision is unreasonably harsh or unfair, generally exacted by a party with vastly superior bargaining power. See *unconscionability, procedural unconscionability.*

substituted contract   a contract accepted by a contracting party in full satisfaction of a duty owed, which immediately discharges the original duty.

subsuretyship   legal relationship existing when two sureties are bound to answer for the same duty of the principal, but as between the sureties, one bears the whole duty of performance; that is, as between the sureties, one is a principal (the principal surety) and the other (the subsurety) is a surety. See *suretyship, cosuretyship.*

summons   in a civil case, document delivered to the defendant with the complaint ordering the defendant to appear in court on a certain date or to answer the complaint within a specified number of days. See *complaint.*

Superfund   See *Hazardous Substance Superfund.*

supervening event   in contract law, an extraordinary event occurring after a contract is made but before performance.

supplementary proceedings   proceedings provided as part of a creditor's lawsuit that may be used to discover assets in the debtor's hands, and provide for injunctions against transfers and appointment of receivers.

Supremacy Clause   constitutional provision stating that the federal Constitution, federal statutes, and federal treaties are the supreme law of the land.

surety   in suretyship, the person liable on the debt or obligation of another, the principal. See *suretyship.*

suretyship   legal relationship existing when two parties (principal and surety) are liable for the same performance to a creditor who is entitled to but one satisfaction, and as between the two who are liable, the principal rather than the surety should perform.

surrender   in landlord-tenant law, a contract involving either the transfer of the landlord's reversion to the tenant or of the tenant's non-freehold estate to the landlord.

symbolic delivery   method of delivery of a gift that involves the delivery of another object in place of the actual subject matter. See *gift, delivery, constructive delivery.*

tariff   1. a schedule, scheme, or system of duties imposed by a government on imported or exported goods; 2. a public document filed by a common carrier setting forth its rates and services, and the rules, regulations, and procedures relating to those services.

tax lien   statutory lien held by the state or federal government or a government subdivision to secure payment of delinquent taxes. See *lien, statutory lien.*

teller's check   a draft drawn by a bank (1) on another bank, or (2) payable at or through a bank. See *draft,* UCC §3–104(h).

tenancy by the entirety   a specialized form of joint tenancy with right of survivorship existing between cotenants who are husband and wife. See *concurrent ownership, joint tenancy.*

tenancy in common   form of concurrent ownership having no right of survivorship; on death of a tenant in common, the deceased tenant's interest passes to the tenant's estate, rather than to the surviving cotenants. See *right of survivorship, joint tenancy, tenancy by the entirety, concurrent ownership.*

tenant (lessee)   one to whom the right of possession of real property is transferred in a landlord-tenant relationship. See *landlord-tenant relationship.*

tender of performance   in contract law, actual performance of the contract or an offer of performance coupled with the manifested present ability to do so.

termination   in sales contracts, an event occurring when either party pursuant to a power created by agreement or law puts an end to the contract otherwise than for its breach. See UCC §2–106(3).

termination statement   in secured transactions, a statement filed in an appropriate public office indicating that a financing arrangement has been terminated. See *secured transaction.*

testamentary disposition   a transfer of property through a will. See *will.*

testamentary trust   trust created in the settlor's will. See *will.*

testate   a person who dies leaving a valid will directing the disposition of his or her property is said to die "testate." See *will, intestate.*

testator   a person making a will. See *will.*

third line (tertiary line) competitive injury   See *secondary line competitive injury.*

third party   in contract law, anyone other than the contracting parties who may be affected by or have rights under the contract; generally, anyone other than the parties. See *party.*

time draft   a draft that is payable at some fixed or determinable future time. See *draft, demand draft.*

third-party complaint   in a civil case, pleading filed by a defendant to sue other persons not named as parties in the original suit. See *civil law, pleadings.*

through bill of lading   a bill of lading issued by the first of two or more carriers when the carriage is to be performed in part by connecting carriers other than the issuer. See *bill of lading.*

time instrument   in negotiable instruments law, an instrument calling for future (other than demand) payment. See *instrument, demand instrument.*

time of the essence clause   a contract term making time of performance a condition to the promisor's duty. See *condition.*

title   ownership.

title closing (settlement)   performance of a real estate contract in which the seller of property conveys the property by delivering a deed to the buyer and the buyer pays the purchase price.

title insurance   a form of real estate title protection under which a title insurance company agrees to indemnify or reimburse the insured property owner or lender against losses resulting from certain specified defects in the title to the covered property.

title search systematic examination of the chronological public record of transactions concerning a particular tract of real property.

Title I of the Americans with Disabilities Act (ADA) federal statute, enacted in 1990, designed to eliminate employment discrimination against persons with disabilities.

Title VII of the Civil Rights Act of 1964 federal statute that generally prohibits employers, unions, and employment agencies from discriminating against employees and applicants on the basis of race, color, national origin, sex (gender), or religion.

Torrens system a method of assuring real estate titles that involves registration of title to property, instead of recording evidence of that title.

tort a private or civil wrong or injury, other than breach of contract, for which the court will provide a remedy in the form of an action for damages.

tort-feasor person who commits a tort.

total breach breach of contract involving a material defect in performance. In this case, the constructive condition to the other party's duty does not occur and his duty to perform does not arise. The injured party is then entitled to damages for total breach—damages based upon all of his right to performance. See *substantial performance doctrine, partial breach, material breach, constructive conditions of exchange.*

Toxic Substances Control Act (TSCA) federal statute that provides comprehensive regulation of toxic substances.

trade acceptance draft drawn by a seller of goods on credit against his or her buyer. See *draft.*

trade fixtures chattels that are attached for use in a tenant's trade or business (for example, counters, machinery, shelves, or light fixtures). See *chattel, fixture.*

trademark any word, name, symbol, or device adopted and used by a manufacturer or merchant to identify and distinguish its goods from those manufactured or sold by others.

trade secret information, including a formula, pattern, compilation, program, device, method, technique, or process, that (1) derives independent economic value, actual or potential, from not being generally known to, and not being readily ascertainable by proper means by, other persons who can obtain economic value from its disclosure or use, and (2) is the subject of efforts that are reasonable under the circumstances to maintain its secrecy. Uniform Trade Secrets Act §1(4). See *Uniform Trade Secrets Act.*

transfer warranties in negotiable instruments law, warranties regarding forgery and alteration that run to the various holders or other transferees of an instrument and that are given by any person who transfers an instrument for consideration. See *presentment warranties,* UCC §§3–416, 4–207.

transit check in bank deposits and collections, a check deposited in one bank but payable by another. See *on us check.*

traveler's check an instrument that (1) is payable on demand, (2) is drawn on or payable at or through a bank, (3) is designated as a traveler's check, and (4) requires, as a condition to payment, a countersignature by a person whose specimen signature appears on the instrument. See UCC §3–104(i).

treason an attempt by overt acts to overthrow the government of the sovereign to which the offender owes allegiance, or to betray the sovereign into the hands of a foreign power.

treaty an agreement or contract between two or more nations or sovereigns, formally signed by an authorized representative, and ratified by the sovereign or supreme power of each state.

trespass intentional interference with another's right to exclusive possession of real property, for which the trespasser may be held liable in tort to the property owner. See *trespasser.*

trespass to chattels intentional interference with possession or use of another's personal property, or impairment of its physical condition, value, or quality, under circumstances not constituting an outright conversion of the property, but for which tort liability may be imposed. See *conversion.*

trespasser a person who enters or remains upon another's land without a privilege to do so created by the possessor's consent or otherwise. See *invitee, licensee.*

trial formal proceeding in court in which the issues of fact of a lawsuit are determined and the pertinent law is applied to the facts to resolve the dispute or criminal proceeding.

true consignment type of consignment in which the consignee acts as the consignor's agent for the purpose of selling goods to a third party. Title remains in the consignor but the consignee does not undertake an absolute obligation to pay for the goods. See *consignment, consignment intended as security.*

trust method of transferring property that splits title to property between the trustee, who holds legal title, and the beneficiary or beneficiaries, who hold beneficial or equitable title. The trustee is subject to a fiduciary duty to deal with the property for the benefit of the beneficiaries. See *fiduciary relationship, duty of loyalty.*

Trust Indenture Act of 1939 federal statute that protects bondholders by regulating the terms of bond indentures under which large issues of corporate debt securities are administered.

trust property (*res, corpus*) the property held by the trustee in trust. See *trust.*

trustee See *trust.*

trustee in bankruptcy the trustee of a debtor's property in a bankruptcy liquidation who locates and collects the debtor's property, converts the assets to cash, and distributes the proceeds to creditors who have filed claims against the estate. The trustee represents the debtor's general unsecured creditors.

Truth-in-Lending Act (TILA) federal statute that requires creditors to disclose to consumers specified contractual terms of credit transactions.

turntable doctrine rule of tort law stating the conditions under which a possessor of land is liable for injury to trespassing children. Also called the "attractive nuisance doctrine." See *trespasser.*

tying contract contract in which a seller agrees to sell one product (the so-called tying product) only if the buyer also purchases a second product (the tied product) from the seller.

***ultra vires* acts** acts beyond the scope of a corporation's powers or stated purposes.

unauthorized completion in negotiable instruments law, term describing completion of an instrument on which the signature of the maker or drawer is genuine or authorized, but on which other essential terms, such as the payee and amount, are completed in an unauthorized manner. See UCC §§3–115, 3–407.

unauthorized signature a signature made without actual, implied, or apparent authority and includes a forgery. See UCC §1–201(b)(41).

uncertificated securities   securities not represented by an instrument. See *security, certificated securities,* UCC §8–102(a)(18).

unconscionability   doctrine of contract law allowing a court to refuse to enforce unconscionable contracts or terms. Unconscionability generally is recognized to include an absence of meaningful choice on the part of one of the parties, together with contract terms that are unreasonably favorable to the other party. See *procedural unconscionability, substantive unconscionability,* UCC §2–302.

underwriter   person who purchases securities from an issuer with a view toward distribution to the public, and any person who participates in the underwriting effort. See *security.*

undisclosed principal   in agency law, a principal whose existence and identity are unknown to the third party. See *disclosed principal, partially disclosed principal.*

undivided property interest   characteristic of concurrent ownership arrangements (such as joint tenancy and tenancy in common) meaning that each co-tenant has a simultaneous, proportionate share of the entire property, but no separate interest in any particular or identifiable portion of it. See *concurrent ownership.*

undue influence   facts or circumstances rendering a contract voidable because of unfair persuasion in the bargaining process.

unenforceable contract   a contract for breach of which a court will not award a contract remedy (either damages or specific performance). See *voidable contract.*

unfair labor practices   conduct by employers and unions that is illegal under federal labor law.

unfair labor practice strike   strike caused in whole or in part by the employer's commission of an unfair labor practice. See *strike, economic strike.*

uniform codes, acts, or laws   legislation drafted by the National Conference of Commissioners on Uniform State Laws for areas of the law requiring uniformity among the states. After a uniform act is drafted, it is submitted to the various state legislatures, which consider it for enactment like other legislative bills.

Uniform Commercial Code (UCC)   uniform state law enacted in virtually all states governing a wide variety of commercial transactions including sales of goods, personal property leases, negotiable instruments, bank deposits and collections, commercial funds transfers, letters of credit, bulk transfers, documents of title, investment securities, secured transactions, and sales of accounts and chattel paper.

Uniform Consumer Credit Code (UCCC)   uniform state law designed to replace piecemeal state consumer credit laws with one comprehensive code.

Uniform Customs and Practice for Documentary Credits (UCP)   trade code, published by the International Chamber of Commerce, providing rules to govern letter of credit transactions. Though the UCP, which is used in over 140 countries, is not a law, it often governs because most banks incorporate UCP provisions by reference into letters of credit they issue. See *letter of credit.*

Uniform Electronic Transactions Act   uniform state law adopted in 1999, providing that a signature, contract, or record shall not be denied legal validity solely because it is in electronic form. See *Electronic Signatures in Global and National Commerce Act.*

Uniform Fraudulent Conveyance Act (UFCA)   uniform state law drafted in 1918 to provide uniformity in state fraudulent conveyance law and to reach transfers made without actual intent to defraud. See *fraudulent conveyance, Statute of Elizabeth, Uniform Fraudulent Transfer Act.*

Uniform Fraudulent Transfer Act (UFTA)   revision of Uniform Fraudulent Conveyance Act drafted in 1984 to integrate fraudulent conveyance law with the Uniform Commercial Code and the federal Bankruptcy Code. See *Uniform Fraudulent Conveyance Act.*

Uniform Limited Liability Company Act (ULLCA)   uniform state law adopted in 1995 to govern the creation, operation, and termination of limited liability companies. See *limited liability company.*

Uniform Limited Partnership Act (ULPA)   uniform state law adopted in 1916 to govern limited partnership. It was rewritten in 1976 and 2001.

Uniform Partnership Act (UPA)   uniform state law governing partnership, adopted in 1914 and subsequently enacted in virtually all states. See *Revised Uniform Partnership Act.*

Uniform Principal and Income Act   uniform state law adopted in 1931 and revised in 1962 and 1997 that resolves in the absence of express provision how various receipts and expenditures are to be allocated in a trust between the income beneficiary and the remainderman. See *trust.*

Uniform Probate Code   uniform state law adopted in 1969 designed to modernize probate law and provide greater uniformity among the states.

Uniform Prudent Investor Act   uniform state law codifying the "prudent investor rule" governing the duty of the trustee in managing and investing trust assets. See *prudent investor rule.*

Uniform Relocation Assistance and Real Property Acquisition Policies Act   federal statute passed in 1970 to provide for uniform and equitable treatment of persons displaced from their homes, businesses, and farms by federal and federally assisted programs, and to establish uniform and equitable land-acquisition policies for these programs.

Uniform Residential Landlord Tenant Act (URLTA)   uniform state law drafted to govern the residential landlord-tenant relationship.

Uniform Simultaneous Death Act   uniform state law adopted in most states that determines how property is distributed when persons whose rights depend upon survivorship (for example, joint tenants) die in a common disaster.

Uniform Testamentary Additions to Trusts Act   uniform state law stating requirements under which property may be transferred by will to a trust created during the testator's life. See *pour-over trust.*

Uniform Trade Secrets Act   uniform state law adopted in most states that governs the law of trade secrets. See *trade secret.*

Uniform Trustee's Powers Act   uniform state law outlining the powers that a trustee may exercise in administering a trust. See *trust.*

Uniform Vendor and Purchaser Risk Act   uniform state law governing risk of loss in land sale contracts. See *risk of loss.*

unilateral contract   a contract involving a promise in exchange for performance of an act. See *bilateral contract.*

unilateral mistake   in contract law, a situation in which one but not both parties are mistaken about a basic assumption upon which the contract is made. See *mistake, mutual mistake.*

union shop   agreement between an employer and a union requiring newly hired employees to join the union within a specified period after beginning employment.

United Nations   international organization created at the end of World War II to promote peaceful resolution of international disputes and provide for collective action to stop aggression. The United Nations also is concerned with economic development, social welfare, and human rights.

United Nations Convention on Contracts for the International Sale of Goods (CISG)   multilateral treaty drafted in 1980 that states substantive rules governing formation of international sales contracts, and the rights and duties of the buyer and seller. It applies only in the absence of contrary agreement by the parties. See *sales contract, goods.*

United States Code (U.S.C.)   compilation or codification of all federal statutes.

unjust enrichment   a person is unjustly enriched if he has received a benefit from another, and it would be unjust to allow retention of the benefit without paying for it. See *restitution.*

unliquidated claim   a claim that is not fixed in amount. See *liquidated claim, disputed claim, claim.*

unqualified indorsement   in negotiable instruments law, an indorsement under which the indorser undertakes secondary contract liability. See *indorsement, qualified indorsement, secondary contract liability.*

usage of trade   any regularly observed practice or method of dealing in a trade, place, or location. See UCC §1–303(c).

usurious contract   contract in which interest rates greater than the maximum legal rate are charged.

usury   the act of charging an interest rate in excess of that allowed by state law.

utility patent   a patent granted to a person who invents or discovers any new and useful process, machine, manufacture, or composition of matter, or any new and useful improvement thereof. See *patent.*

value   generally, any consideration sufficient to support a simple contract, including satisfaction of or security for an antecedent debt. See UCC §1–204. For negotiable instruments, see UCC §3–303.

variances   administrative relief provided for in zoning ordinances that permits either a different use of land than that provided for in the ordinance, or modification of area, setback, or similar restrictions. See *zoning.*

venue   place of trial; the particular court, among those having subject matter and personal jurisdiction, that should hear a case.

verdict   a formal decision on the issues of a case.

vertical merger   a merger between firms standing in a buyer-seller or supplier-supplied relation. See *horizontal merger.*

vertical restraint   a restraint of trade between persons standing in a buyer-seller or supplier-supplied relationship. See *restraint of trade, horizontal restraint.*

vesting   event occurring when the employees' rights to their interests in a pension plan cannot be forfeited or taken away.

vicarious liability   term describing liability of the master for the servant's tortious conduct without regard to the negligence or other fault of the master. See *respondent superior doctrine.*

void promise   a promise that is totally without legal force or effect.

voidable contract   contract in which one or more parties have the power, by electing to do so, to avoid the legal relations created by the contract, or by ratification of the contract to extinguish the power of avoidance. See *unenforceable contract.*

voidable title rule   rule of sales law that allows a person with voidable title to transfer a good title to a good-faith purchaser for value. See UCC §2–403(1).

voir dire examination   a procedure by which potential jurors are questioned under oath to determine their suitability to serve on a petit jury for a particular case. See *petit jury.*

voluntary case   bankruptcy case in which the debtor files a petition with the court requesting the relief afforded by the Bankruptcy Code. See *involuntary case.*

voting (pooling) agreement   a contract between two or more shareholders stating how their shares will be voted on certain matters, usually the election of directors.

voting trust   a trust created when corporate shareholders transfer legal title to their shares to a trustee in exchange for "voting trust certificates." The trustee then votes the shares subject to any limitations in the trust agreement. See *trust.*

waiver   the voluntary surrender or relinquishment of a known right, usually without consideration.

waiver-of-defense clause   contractual term indicating that a buyer or lessee will not assert against a subsequent assignee any claim or defense he or she may have against the seller or lender.

ward   See *guardian.*

warehouse   a person engaged in the business of storing goods for hire. See UCC §7–102(1)(h).

warehouse receipt   a receipt issued by a person engaged in the business of storing goods for hire. See *document of title,* UCC §1–201(b)(42).

warranty   generally, a statement or other representation made by a seller of goods about the quality, character, or capabilities of the good sold. See *express warranty, implied warranty.*

warranty against infringement   warranty made by merchant seller that goods will be delivered free of any third-party claim of patent or trademark infringement. See UCC §2–312(3).

warranty deed   type of deed containing a number of promises or warranties, known as covenants of title, concerning the status of the grantor's title. See *deed, quitclaim deed.*

warranty disclaimer   contract term that limits, modifies, or excludes warranty liability.

warranty of fitness for a particular purpose   an implied warranty arising under UCC Article 2 providing that goods will be fit for the buyer's particular purpose when the seller has reason to know of a particular purpose for which the buyer requires goods and when the buyer relies on the seller's skill or judgment to select suitable goods. See UCC §2–315.

warranty of merchantability   an implied warranty under UCC Article 2 generally requiring that goods sold by a merchant dealing in goods of the kind be fit for the ordinary purposes for which such goods are used. See UCC §2–314.

warranty of title   sales warranty that the title conveyed will be good and its transfer rightful, and that the goods will be delivered free of security interests or other liens, except those known to the buyer. See UCC §2–312(1).

waste   conduct of a life tenant resulting in a substantial and unreasonable reduction in the value of the property passing to the following estates. See *life estate.*

watered shares   shares issued without consideration, or for cash, property, or services worth less than the required consideration.

Webb-Pomerene Act   federal statute, enacted in 1918, designed to facilitate joint export activities by providing limited antitrust immunity for exporters of goods who register as Webb-Pomerene Associations with the Federal Trade Commission. See *Export Trading Company Act.*

wildcat strike   strike by a minority of employees without authorization by the union.

will   a formal instrument by which a person makes a disposition of his or her property to take effect after death.

winding up (liquidation)   the series of transactions necessary to settle the affairs of a business upon its termination. It includes completing unfinished transactions, converting assets to cash, paying debts, and distributing any excess to the owner or owners.

workers' compensation statute   state statute providing compensation for an injured employee if the injury was accidental and arose out of and in the course of employment.

writ of attachment   writ issued under the prejudgment creditor's remedy of attachment directing a sheriff to take custody of a debtor's personal or real property and hold it during the trial of the case to assure its availability if and when a creditor obtains a judgment. See *attachment.*

writ of certiorari   writ issued by the Supreme Court granting a petitioning party the right to Supreme Court review.

writ of execution   writ issued pursuant to the judicial process of execution, which directs the sheriff to levy upon the debtor's real and personal property, sell the property at public sale, and apply the proceeds to the unpaid judgment. See *execution.*

writ of *habeas corpus*   a post-conviction remedy in criminal cases involving a judicial order to a government official (such as a warden) requiring him or her to produce the prisoner in order to test the legality of the imprisonment.

writing   printing, typewriting, or any other intentional reduction to tangible form. See UCC §1–201(b)(43).

yellow dog contract   illegal agreement by which an employee, as a condition of employment, agrees not to join or retain membership in a union.

zoning   the process by which a municipality regulates the use that may be made of property and the physical configuration of the development of land within its jurisdiction.

THE CONSTITUTION OF THE UNITED STATES

PREAMBLE

We the People of the United States, in Order to form a more perfect Union, establish Justice, insure domestic Tranquility, provide for the common defence, promote the general Welfare, and secure the Blessings of Liberty to ourselves and our Posterity, do ordain and establish this Constitution for the United States of America.

ARTICLE I

Section 1. All legislative Powers herein granted shall be vested in a Congress of the United States, which shall consist of a Senate and a House of Representatives.

Section 2. [1] The House of Representatives shall be composed of Members chosen every second Year by the People of the several States, and the Electors in each State shall have the Qualifications requisite for Electors of the most numerous Branch of the State Legislature.

[2] No Person shall be a Representative who shall not have attained to the Age of twenty five Years, and been seven Years a Citizen of the United States, and who shall not, when elected, be an Inhabitant of that State in which he shall be chosen.

[3] Representatives and direct Taxes shall be apportioned among the several States which may be included within this Union, according to their respective Numbers, which shall be determined by adding to the whole Number of free Persons, including those bound to Service for a Term of Years, and excluding Indians not taxed, three fifths of all other Persons. The actual Enumeration shall be made within three Years after the first Meeting of the Congress of the United States, and within every subsequent Term of ten Years, in such Manner as they shall by Law direct. The Number of Representatives shall not exceed one for every thirty Thousand, but each State shall have at Least one Representative; and until such enumeration shall be made, the State of New Hampshire shall be entitled to chuse three, Massachusetts eight, Rhode Island and Providence Plantations one, Connecticut five, New York six, New Jersey four, Pennsylvania eight, Delaware one, Maryland six, Virginia ten, North Carolina five, South Carolina five, and Georgia three.

[4] When vacancies happen in the Representation from any State, the Executive Authority thereof shall issue Writs of Election to fill such Vacancies.

[5] The House of Representatives shall chuse their Speaker and other Officers and shall have the sole Power of Impeachment.

Section 3. [1] The Senate of the United States shall be composed of two Senators from each State, chosen by the Legislature thereof, for six Years; and each Senator shall have one vote.

[2] Immediately after they shall be assembled in Consequence of the first Election, they shall be divided as equally as may be into three Classes. The Seats of the Senators of the first Class shall be vacated at the Expiration of the Second Year, of the second Class at the Expiration of the fourth Year, and of the third Class at the Expiration of the sixth Year, so that one third may be chosen every second Year; and if Vacancies happen by Resignation, or otherwise, during the Recess of the Legislature of any State, the Executive thereof may make temporary Appointments until the next Meeting of the Legislature, which shall then fill such Vacancies.

[3] No Person shall be a Senator who shall not have attained to the Age of thirty Years, and been nine Years a Citizen of the United States, and who shall not, when elected, be an Inhabitant of that State for which he shall be chosen.

[4] The Vice President of the United States shall be President of the Senate, but shall have no Vote, unless they be equally divided.

[5] The Senate shall chuse their other Officers, and also a President pro tempore, in the Absence of the Vice President, or when he shall exercise the Office of President of the United States.

[6] The Senate shall have the sole Power to try all Impeachments. When sitting for that Purpose, they shall be on Oath or Affirmation. When the President of the United States is tried, the Chief Justice shall preside: And no Person shall be convicted without the Concurrence of two thirds of the Members present.

[7] Judgment in Cases of Impeachment shall not extend further than to removal from Office, and disqualification to hold and enjoy any Office of honor, Trust, or Profit under the United States: but the Party convicted shall nevertheless be liable and subject to Indictment, Trial, Judgment, and Punishment, according to Law.

Section 4. [1] The Times, Places and Manner of holding Elections for Senators and Representatives, shall be prescribed in each State by the Legislature thereof; but the Congress may at any time by Law make or alter such Regulations, except as to the Places of chusing Senators.

[2] The Congress shall assemble at least once in every Year, and such Meeting shall be on the first Monday in December, unless they shall by Law appoint a different Day.

Section 5. [1] Each House shall be the Judge of the Elections, Returns, and Qualifications of its own Members, and a Majority of each shall constitute a Quorum to do Business, but a smaller Number may adjourn from day to day, and may be authorized to compel the

Attendance of absent Members, in such Manner, and under such Penalties as each House may provide.

[2] Each House may determine the Rules of its Proceedings, punish its Members for Disorderly Behavior, and, with the Concurrence of two thirds, expel a Member.

[3] Each House shall keep a Journal of its Proceedings, and from time to time publish the same, excepting such Parts as may in their Judgment require Secrecy; and the Yeas and Nays of the Members of either House on any question shall, at the Desire of one fifth of those Present, be entered on the Journal.

[4] Neither House, during the Session of Congress, shall, without the Consent of the other, adjourn for more than three days, nor to any other Place than that in which the two Houses shall be sitting.

Section 6. [1] The Senators and Representatives shall receive a Compensation for their Services, to be ascertained by Law, and paid out of the Treasury of the United States. They shall in all Cases, except Treason, Felony and Breach of the Peace, be privileged from Arrest during their Attendance at the Session of their respective Houses, and in going to and returning from the same; and for any speech or Debate in either House, they shall not be questioned in any other Place.

[2] No Senator or Representative shall, during the Time for which he was elected, be appointed to any civil Office under the Authority of the United States, which shall have been created, or the Emoluments whereof shall have been increased during such time and no Person holding any Office under the United States, shall be a Member of either House during his Continuance in Office.

Section 7. [1] All Bills for raising Revenue shall originate in the House of Representatives; but the Senate may propose or concur with Amendments as on other Bills.

[2] Every Bill which shall have passed the House of Representatives and the Senate, shall, before it become a Law, be presented to the President of the United States; If he approve he shall sign it, but if not he shall return it, with his Objections to the House in which it shall have originated, who shall enter the Objections at large on their Journal, and proceed to reconsider it. If after such Reconsideration two thirds of that House shall agree to pass the Bill, it shall be sent together with the Objections, to the other House, by which it shall likewise be reconsidered, and if approved by two thirds of that House, it shall become a Law. But in all such Cases the Votes of both Houses shall be determined by Yeas and Nays, and the Names of the Persons voting for and against the Bill shall be entered on the Journal of each House respectively. If any Bill shall not be returned by the President within ten Days (Sundays excepted) after it shall have been presented to him, the Same shall be a Law, in like Manner as if he had signed it, unless the Congress by their Adjournment prevent its Return in which Case it shall not be a Law.

[3] Every Order, Resolution, or Vote, to Which the Concurrence of the Senate and House of Representatives may be necessary (except on a question of Adjournment) shall be presented to the President of the United States; and before the Same shall take Effect, shall be approved by him, or being disapproved by him, shall be repassed by two thirds of the Senate and House of Representatives, according to the Rules and Limitations prescribed in the Case of a Bill.

Section 8. [1] The Congress shall have Power To lay and collect Taxes, Duties, Imposts and Excises, to pay the Debts and provide for the common Defence and general Welfare of the United States; but all Duties, Imposts and Excises shall be uniform throughout the United States;

[2] To borrow money on the credit of the United States;

[3] To regulate Commerce with foreign Nations, and among the several States, and with the Indian Tribes;

[4] To establish an uniform Rule of Naturalization, and uniform Laws on the subject of Bankruptcies throughout the United States;

[5] To coin Money, regulate the Value thereof, and of foreign Coin, and fix the Standard of Weights and Measures;

[6] To provide for the Punishment of counterfeiting the Securities and current Coin of the United States;

[7] To Establish Post Offices and Post Roads;

[8] To promote the Progress of Science and useful Arts, by securing for limited Times to Authors and Inventors the exclusive Right to their respective Writings and Discoveries;

[9] To constitute Tribunals inferior to the supreme Court;

[10] To define and punish Piracies and Felonies committed on the high Seas, and Offenses against the Law of Nations;

[11] To declare War, grant Letters of Marque and Reprisal, and make Rules concerning Captures on Land and Water;

[12] To raise and support Armies, but no Appropriation of Money to that Use shall be for a longer Term than two Years;

[13] To provide and maintain a Navy;

[14] To make Rules for the Government and Regulation of the land and naval Forces;

[15] To provide for calling forth the Militia to execute the Laws of the Union, suppress Insurrections and repel Invasions;

[16] To provide for organizing, arming, and disciplining, the Militia, and for governing such Part of them as may be employed in the Service of the United States, reserving to the States respectively, the Appointment of the Officers, and the Authority of training the Militia according to the discipline prescribed by Congress;

[17] To exercise exclusive Legislation in all Cases whatsoever, over such District (not exceeding ten Miles square) as may, by Cession of particular States, and the Acceptance of Congress, become the Seat of the Government of the United States, and to exercise like Authority over all Places purchased by the consent of the Legislature of the State in which the Same shall be, for the Erection of Forts, Magazines, Arsenals, dock-Yards, and other needful Buildings;— And

[18] To make all Laws which shall be necessary and proper for carrying into Execution the foregoing Powers, and all other Powers vested by this Constitution in the Government of the United States, or in any department or Officer thereof.

Section 9. [1] The Migration or Importation of Such Persons as any of the States now existing shall think proper to admit, shall not be prohibited by the Congress prior to the Year one thousand eight hundred and eight, but a Tax or duty may be imposed on such Importation, not exceeding ten dollars for each Person.

[2] The privilege of the Writ of Habeas Corpus shall not be suspended, unless when in Cases of Rebellion or Invasion the public Safety may require it.

[3] No Bill of Attainder or ex post facto law shall be passed.

[4] No Capitation, or other direct, Tax shall be laid, unless in Proportion to the Census or Enumeration herein before directed to be taken.

[5] No Tax or Duty shall be laid on articles exported from any State.

[6] No Preference shall be given by any Regulation of Commerce or Revenue to the Ports of one State over those of another: nor shall Vessels bound to, or from, one State be obliged to enter, clear, or pay Duties in another.

[7] No money shall be drawn from the Treasury, but in Consequence of Appropriations made by Law; and a regular Statement and Account of the Receipts and Expenditures of all public Money shall be published from time to time.

[8] No Title of Nobility shall be granted by the United States: And no Person holding any Office of Profit or Trust under them, shall, without the Consent of the Congress, accept of any present, Emolument, Office, or Title, of any kind whatever, from any King, Prince, or foreign State.

Section 10. [1] No State shall enter into any Treaty, Alliance, or Confederation; grant Letters of Marque and Reprisal; coin Money; emit Bills of Credit; make any Thing but gold and silver Coin a Tender in Payment of Debts; pass any Bill of Attainder, ex post facto

Law, or Law impairing the Obligation of Contracts, or grant any Title of Nobility.

[2] No State shall, without the Consent of the Congress, lay any Imposts or Duties on Imports or Exports, except what may be absolutely necesarry for executing its inspection Laws: and the net Produce of all Duties and Imposts, laid by any States on Imports or Exports, shall be for the Use of the Treasury of the United States; and all such Laws shall be subject to the Revision and Control of the Congress.

[3] No State shall, without the Consent of Congress, lay any Duty of Tonnage, keep Troops, or Ships of War in time of Peace, enter into any Agreement or Compact with another State, or with a foreign Power, or engage in War, unless actually invaded, or in such imminent Danger as will not admit of delay.

ARTICLE II

Section 1.   [1] The executive Power shall be vested in a President of the United States of America. He shall hold his Office during the Term of four Years, and, together with the Vice President, chosen for the same Term, be elected, as follows:

[2] Each State shall appoint, in such Manner as the Legislature thereof may direct, a Number of Electors, equal to the whole Number of Senators and Representative to which the State may be entitled in the Congress; but no Senator or Representative, or Person holding an Office of Trust or Profit under the United States, shall be appointed as Elector.

[3] The Electors shall meet in their respective States, and vote by Ballot for two Persons, of whom one at least shall not be an Inhabitant of the same State with themselves. And they shall make a List of all the Persons voted for, and of the Number of Votes for each; which List they shall sign and certify, and transmit sealed to the Seat of the Government of the United States, directed to the President of the Senate. The President of the Senate shall, in the Presence of the Senate and House of Representatives, open all the Certificates, and the Votes shall then be counted. The Person having the greatest Number of Votes shall be the President, if such Number be a Majority of the whole Number of Electors appointed; and if there be more than one who have such Majority, and have an equal Number of Votes, then the House of Representatives shall immediately chuse by Ballot one of them for President; and if no Person have a Majority, then from the five highest on the List the said House shall in like Manner chuse the President. But in chusing the President, the Votes shall be taken by States the Representation from each State having one Vote; A quorum for this Purpose shall consist of a Member or Members from two thirds of the States, and a Majority of all the States shall be necessary to a Choice. In every Case, after the Choice of the President, the Person having the greater Number of Votes of the Electors shall be the Vice President. But if there should remain two or more who have equal Votes, the Senate shall chuse from them by Ballot the Vice President.

[4] The Congress may determine the Time of chusing the Electors, and the Day on which they shall give their Votes; which Day shall be the same throughout the United States.

[5] No person except a natural born Citizen, or a Citizen of the United States, at the time of the Adoption of this constitution, shall be eligible to the Office of President; neither shall any Person be eligible to that Office who shall not have attained to the Age of thirty five Years, and been fourteen Years a Resident within the United States.

[6] In case of the removal of the President from Office, or of his Death, Resignation or Inability to discharge the Powers and Duties of the said Office, the Same shall devolve on the Vice President, and the Congress may by Law provide for the Case of Removal, Death, Resignation or Inability, both of the President and Vice President, declaring what Officer shall then act as President, and such Officer

shall act accordingly, until the disability be removed, or a President shall be elected.

[7] The President shall, at stated Times, receive for his Services, a Compensation, which shall neither be increased nor diminished during the Period for which he shall have been elected, and he shall not receive within that Period any other Emolument from the United States, or any of them.

[8] Before he enter on the Execution of his Office, he shall take the following Oath or Affirmation: "I do solemnly swear (or affirm) that I will faithfully execute the Office of President of the United States, and will to the best of my Ability, preserve, protect and defend the Constitution of the United States."

Section 2.   [1] The President shall be Commander in Chief of the Army and Navy of the United States, and of the militia of the several States, when called into the actual Service of the United States; he may require the Opinion, in writing, of the principal Officer in each of the Executive Departments, upon any Subject relating to the Duties of their respective Offices, and he shall have Power to grant Reprieves and Pardons for Offenses against the United States, except in Cases of Impeachment.

[2] He shall have Power, by and with the Advice and Consent of the Senate to make Treaties, provided two thirds of the Senators present concur, and he shall nominate, and by and with the Advice and Consent of the Senate, shall appoint Ambassadors, other public Ministers and Consuls, Judges of the supreme Court, and all other Officers of the United States, whose Appointments are not herein otherwise provided for, and which shall be established by Law; but the Congress may by Law vest the Appointment of such inferior Officers, as they think proper, in the President alone, in the Courts of Law, or in the Heads of Departments.

[3] The President shall have Power to fill up all Vacancies that may happen during the Recess of the Senate, by granting Commissions which shall expire at the End of their next Session.

Section 3.   He shall from time to time give to the Congress Information of the State of the Union, and recommend to their Consideration such Measures as he shall judge necessary and expedient; he may, on extraordinary Occasions, convene both Houses, or either of them, and in Case of Disagreement between them, with Respect to the Time of Adjournment, he may adjourn them to such Time as he shall think proper; he shall receive Ambassadors and other public Ministers; he shall take Care that the Laws be faithfully executed, and shall Commission all the Officers of the United States.

Section 4.   The President, Vice President and all civil Officers of the United States shall be removed from Office on Impeachment for, and Conviction of, Treason, Bribery, or other high Crimes and Misdemeanors.

ARTICLE III

Section 1.   The judicial Power of the United States, shall be vested in one supreme Court, and in such inferior Courts as the Congress may from time to time ordain and establish. The Judges, both of the supreme and inferior Courts, shall hold their Offices during good Behaviour, and shall, at stated Times, receive for their Services a Compensation, which shall not be diminished during their Continuance in Office.

Section 2.   [1] The judicial Power shall extend to all Cases, in Law and Equity, arising under this Constitution, the Laws of the United States, and Treaties made, or which shall be made, under their Authority;—to all Cases affecting Ambassadors, other public Ministers and Consuls;—to all Cases of admiralty and maritime Jurisdiction;—to Controversies to which the United States shall be a Party;—to Controversies between two or more States;—between a

State and Citizens of another State;—between Citizens of different States;—between Citizens of the same State claiming Lands under the Grants of different States, and between a State, or the Citizens thereof, and foreign States, Citizens or Subjects.

[2] In all Cases affecting Ambassadors, other public Ministers and Consuls, and those in which a State shall be a Party, the supreme Court shall have original Jurisdiction. In all the other Cases before mentioned, the supreme Court shall have appellate Jurisdiction, both as to Law and Fact, with such Exceptions, and under such Regulations as the Congress shall make.

[3] The trial of all Crimes, except in Cases of Impeachment, shall be by Jury; and such Trial shall be held in the State where the said Crimes shall have been committed; but when not committed within any State, the Trial shall be at such Place or Places as the Congress may by Law have directed.

Section 3. [1] Treason against the United States, shall consist only in levying War against them, or, in adhering to their Enemies, giving them Aid and Comfort. No Person shall be convicted of Treason unless on the Testimony of two Witnesses to the same overt Act, or on Confession in open Court.

[2] The Congress shall have Power to declare the Punishment of Treason, but no Attainder of Treason shall work Corruption of Blood, or Forfeiture except during the Life of the Person attainted.

ARTICLE IV

Section 1. Full Faith and Credit shall be given in each State to the public Acts, Records, and judicial Proceedings of every other State. And the Congress may by general Laws prescribe the Manner in which such Acts, Records and Proceedings shall be proved, and the Effect thereof.

Section 2. [1] The Citizens of each State shall be entitled to all Privileges and Immunities of Citizens in the Several States.

[2] A Person charged in any State with Treason, Felony, or other Crime, who shall flee from Justice, and be found in another State, shall on demand of the executive Authority of the State from which he fled, be delivered up, to be removed to the State having Jurisdiction of the Crime.

[3] No Person held to Service or Labour in one State, under the Laws thereof, escaping into another, shall, in Consequence of any Law or Regulation therein, be discharged from such Service or Labour, but shall be delivered up on Claim of the Party to whom such Service or Labour may be due.

Section 3. [1] New States may be admitted by the Congress into this Union; but no new State shall be formed or erected within the Jurisdiction of any other State; nor any State be formed by the Junction of two or more States, or Parts of States, without the Consent of the Legislatures of the States concerned as well as of the Congress.

[2] The Congress shall have Power to dispose of and make all needful Rules and Regulations respecting the Territory or other Property belonging to the United States; and nothing in this Constitution shall be so construed as to Prejudice any Claims of the United States, or of any particular State.

Section 4. The United States shall guarantee to every State in this Union a Republican Form of Government, and shall protect each of them against Invasion; and on Application of the Legislature, or of the Executive (when the Legislature cannot be convened) against domestic Violence.

ARTICLE V

The Congress, whenever two thirds of both Houses shall deem it necessary, shall propose Amendments to this Constitution, or, on the Application of the Legislatures of two thirds of the several States, shall call a Convention for proposing Amendments, which, in either Case, shall be valid to all Intents and Purposes, as part of this Constitution, when ratified by the Legislatures of three fourths of the several States, or by Conventions in three fourths thereof, as the one or the other Mode of Ratification may be proposed by the Congress; Provided that no Amendment which may be made prior to the Year One thousand eight hundred and eight shall in any Manner affect the first and fourth Clauses in the Ninth Section of the first Article; and that no State, without its Consent, shall be deprived of its equal Suffrage in the Senate.

ARTICLE VI

[1] All Debts contracted and Engagements entered into, before the Adoption of this Constitution shall be as valid against the United States under this Constitution, as under the Confederation.

[2] This Constitution, and the Laws of the United States which shall be made in Pursuance thereof; and all Treaties made, or which shall be made, under the Authority of the United States, shall be the supreme Law of the Land; and the Judges in every State shall be bound thereby, any Thing in the Constitution or Laws of any State to the Contrary notwithstanding.

[3] The Senators and Representatives before mentioned, and the Members of the several State Legislatures, and all executive and judicial Officers, both of the United States and of the several States, shall be bound by Oath or Affirmation, to support this Constitution; but no religious Test shall ever be required as a Qualification to any Office or public Trust under the United States.

ARTICLE VII

The Ratification of the conventions of nine States shall be sufficient for the Establishment of this Constitution between the States so ratifying the Same.

ARTICLES IN ADDITION TO, AND AMENDMENT OF, THE CONSTITUTION OF THE UNITED STATES OF AMERICA, PROPOSED BY CONGRESS, AND RATIFIED BY THE LEGISLATURES OF THE SEVERAL STATES PURSUANT TO THE FIFTH ARTICLE OF THE ORIGINAL CONSTITUTION.

AMENDMENT I [1791]

Congress shall make no law respecting an establishment of religion, or prohibiting the free exercise thereof; or abridging the freedom of speech, or of the press; or the right of the people peaceably to assemble, and to petition the Government for a redress of grievances.

AMENDMENT II [1791]

A well regulated Militia, being necessary to the security of a free State, the right of the people to keep and bear Arms, shall not be infringed.

AMENDMENT III [1791]

No Soldier shall, in time of peace be quartered in any house, without the consent of the Owner, nor in time of war, but in a manner to be prescribed by law.

AMENDMENT IV [1791]

The right of the people to be secure in their persons, houses, papers, and effects, against unreasonable searches and seizures, shall not be violated, and no Warrants shall issue, but upon probable cause, supported by Oath or affirmation, and particularly describing the place to be searched, and the persons or things to be seized.

AMENDMENT V [1791]

No person shall be held to answer for a capital, or otherwise infamous crime, unless on a presentment or indictment of a Grand Jury, except in cases arising in the land or naval forces, or in the Militia, when in actual service in time of War or public danger, nor shall any person be subject for the same offence to be twice put in jeopardy of life or limb; nor shall be compelled in any criminal case to be a witness against himself, nor be deprived of life, liberty, or property, without due process of law; nor shall private property be taken for public use, without just compensation.

AMENDMENT VI [1791]

In all criminal prosecutions, the accused shall enjoy the right to a speedy and public trial, by an impartial jury of the State and district wherein the crime shall have been committed, which district shall have been previously ascertained by law, and to be informed of the nature and cause of the accusation; to be confronted with the witnesses against him; to have compulsory process for obtaining witnesses in his favor, and to have the Assistance of Counsel for his defence.

AMENDMENT VII [1791]

In Suits at common law, where the value in controversy shall exceed twenty dollars, the right of trial by jury shall be preserved, and no fact tried by jury, shall be otherwise re-examined in any Court of the United States, than according to the rules of the common law.

AMENDMENT VIII [1791]

Excessive bail shall not be required, nor excessive fines imposed, nor cruel and unusual punishments inflicted.

AMENDMENT IX [1791]

The enumeration in the Constitution, of certain rights, shall not be construed to deny or disparage others retained by the people.

AMENDMENT X [1791]

The powers not delegated to the United States by the Constitution, nor prohibited by it to the States, are reserved to the States respectively, or to the people.

AMENDMENT XI [1798]

The Judicial power of the United States shall not be construed to extend to any suit in law or equity, commenced or prosecuted against one of the United States by Citizens of another State, or by Citizens or Subjects of any Foreign State.

AMENDMENT XII [1804]

The Electors shall meet in their respective states and vote by ballot for President and Vice-President, one of whom, at least, shall not be an inhabitant of the same state with themselves; they shall name in their ballots the person voted for as President, and in distinct ballots the person voted for as Vice-President, and they shall make distinct lists of all persons voted for as President, and of all persons voted for as Vice-President, and of the number of votes for each, which lists they shall sign and certify, and transmit sealed to the seat of the government of the United States, directed to the President of the Senate;— The President of the Senate shall, in the presence of the Senate and House of Representatives, open all the certificates and the votes shall then be counted;—The person having the greatest number of votes for President, shall be the President, if such number be a majority of the whole number of Electors appointed; and if no person have such majority, then from the persons having the highest numbers not exceeding three on the list of those voted for as President, the House of Representatives shall choose immediately, by ballot, the President. But in choosing the President, the votes shall be taken by states, the representation from each state having one vote; a quorum for this purpose shall consist of a member or members from two-thirds of the states, and a majority of all the states shall be necessary to a choice. And if the House of Representatives shall not choose a President whenever the right of choice shall devolve upon them before the fourth day of March next following, then the Vice-President shall act as President, as in the case of the death or other constitutional disability of the President.—The person having the greatest number of votes as Vice-President, shall be the Vice-President, if such number be a majority of the whole number of Electors appointed, and if no person have a majority, then from the two highest numbers on the list, the Senate shall choose the Vice-President; a quorum for the purpose shall consist of two-thirds of the whole number of Senators, and a majority of the whole number shall be necessary to a choice. But no person constitutionally ineligible to the office of President shall be eligible to that of Vice-President of the United States.

AMENDMENT XIII [1865]

Section 1.   Neither slavery nor involuntary servitude, except as a punishment for crime whereof the party shall have been duly convicted, shall exist within the United States, or any place subject to their jurisdiction.

Section 2.   Congress shall have power to enforce this article by appropriate legislation.

AMENDMENT XIV [1868]

Section 1.   All persons born or naturalized in the United States, and subject to the jurisdiction thereof, are citizens of the United States and of the State wherein they reside. No State shall make or enforce any law which shall abridge the privileges or immunities of citizens of the United States; nor shall any State deprive any person of life, liberty, or property, without due process of law; nor deny to any person within its jurisdiction the equal protection of the laws.

Section 2.   Representatives shall be apportioned among the several States according to their respective numbers, counting the whole number of persons in each State excluding Indians not taxed. But when the right to vote at any election for the choice of electors for President and Vice President of the United States, Representatives in Congress, the Executive and Judicial officers of a State, or the members of the Legislature thereof, is denied to any of the male inhabitants of such State, being twenty-one years of age, and citizens of the

United States, or in any way abridged, except for participation in rebellion, or other crime, the basis of representation therein shall be reduced in the proportion which the number of such male citizens shall bear to the whole number of male citizens twenty-one years of age in such State.

Section 3. No person shall be a Senator or Representative in Congress, or elector of President and Vice President, or hold any office, civil or military, under the United States, as a member of any State, who having previously taken an oath, as a member of Congress, or as an officer of the United States, or as a member of any State legislature, or as an executive or judicial officer of any State, to support the Constitution of the United States, shall have engaged in insurrection or rebellion against the same, or given aid or comfort to the enemies thereof. But Congress may by a vote of two-thirds of each House, remove such disability.

Section 4. The validity of the public debt of the United States, authorized by law, including debts incurred for payment of pensions and bounties for services in suppressing insurrection or rebellion, shall not be questioned. But neither the United States nor any State shall assume or pay any debt or obligation incurred in aid of insurrection or rebellion against the United States, or any claim for the loss or emancipation of any slave; but all such debts, obligations and claims shall be held illegal and void.

Section 5. The Congress shall have power to enforce, by appropriate legislation, the provisions of this article.

AMENDMENT XV [1870]

Section 1. The right of citizens of the United States to vote shall not be denied or abridged by the United States or by any State on account of race, color, or previous condition of servitude.

Section 2. The Congress shall have power to enforce this article by appropriate legislation.

AMENDMENT XVI [1913]

The Congress shall have power to lay and collect taxes on incomes, from whatever source derived, without apportionment among the several States, and without regard to any census or enumeration.

AMENDMENT XVII [1913]

[1] The Senate of the United States shall be composed of two Senators from each State, elected by the people thereof, for six years and each Senator shall have one vote. The electors in each State shall have the qualifications requisite for electors of the most numerous branch of the State legislatures.

[2] When vacancies happen in the representation of any State in the Senate, the executive authority of such State shall issue writs of election to fill such vacancies: *Provided,* That the legislature of any State may empower the executive thereof to make temporary appointments until the people fill the vacancies by election as the legislature may direct.

[3] This amendment shall not be so construed as to affect the election or term of any Senator chosen before it becomes valid as part of the Constitution.

AMENDMENT XVIII [1919]

Section 1. After one year from the ratification of this article the manufacture, sale, or transportation of intoxicating liquors within, the

importation thereof into, or the exportation thereof from the United States and all territory subject to the jurisdiction thereof for beverage purposes is hereby prohibited.

Section 2. The Congress and the several States shall have concurrent power to enforce this article by appropriate legislation.

Section 3. This article shall be inoperative unless it shall have been ratified as an amendment to the Constitution by the legislatures of the several States, as provided in the Constitution, within seven years from the date of the submission hereof to the States by the Congress.

AMENDMENT XIX [1920]

[1] The right of citizens of the United States to vote shall not be denied or abridged by the United States or by any State on account of sex.

[2] Congress shall have power to enforce this article by appropriate legislation.

AMENDMENT XX [1933]

Section 1. The terms of the President and Vice President shall end at noon on the 20th day of January, and the terms of Senators and Representatives at noon on the 3d day of January, of the years in which such terms would have ended if this article had not been ratified; and the terms of their successors shall then begin.

Section 2. The Congress shall assemble at least once in every year, and such meeting shall begin at noon on the 3d day of January, unless they shall by law appoint a different day.

Section 3. If, at the time fixed for the beginning of the term of the President, the President elect shall have died, the Vice President elect shall become President. If the President shall not have been chosen before the time fixed for the beginning of his term, or if the President elect shall have failed to qualify, then the Vice President elect shall act as President until a President shall have qualified; and the Congress may by law provide for the case wherein neither a President elect nor a Vice President elect shall have qualified, declaring who shall then act as President, or the manner in which one who is to act shall be selected, and such person shall act accordingly until a President or Vice President shall have qualified.

Section 4. The Congress may by law provide for the case of the death of any of the persons from whom the House of Representatives may choose a President whenever the right choice shall have devolved upon them, and for the case of the death of any of the persons from whom the Senate may choose a Vice President whenever the right of choice shall have devolved upon them.

Section 5. Sections 1 and 2 shall take effect on the 15th day of October following the ratification of this article.

Section 6. This article shall be inoperative unless it shall have been ratified as an amendment to the Constitution by the legislatures of three-fourths of the several States within seven years from the date of its submission.

AMENDMENT XXI [1933]

Section 1. The eighteenth article of amendment to the Constitution of the United States is hereby repealed.

Section 2. The transportation or importation into any State, Territory, or possession of the United States for delivery or use therein of intoxicating liquors, in violation of the laws thereof, is hereby prohibited.

Section 3.   This article shall be inoperative unless it shall have been ratified as an amendment to the Constitution by conventions in the several States, as provided in the Constitution, within seven years from the date of the submission hereof to the States by the Congress.

AMENDMENT XXII [1951]

Section 1.   No person shall be elected to the office of the President more than twice, and no person who has held the office of President, or acted as President, for more than two years of a term to which some other person was elected President shall be elected to the office of President more than once. But this Article shall not apply to any person holding the office of President when this Article was proposed by the Congress, and shall not prevent any person who may be holding the office of President, or acting as President, during the term within which this Article becomes operative from holding the office of President or acting as President during the remainder of such term.

Section 2.   This article shall be inoperative unless it shall have been ratified as an amendment to the Constitution by the legislatures of three-fourths of the several States within seven years from the date of its submission to the States by the Congress.

AMENDMENT XXIII [1961]

Section 1.   The District constituting the seat of Government of the United States shall appoint in such manner as the Congress may direct:

A number of electors of President and Vice President equal to the whole number of Senators and Representatives in Congress to which the District would be entitled if it were a State, but in no event more than the least populous state; they shall be in addition to those appointed by the states, but they shall be considered, for the purposes of the election of President and Vice President, to be electors appointed by a state; and they shall meet in the District and perform such duties as provided by the twelfth article of amendment.

Section 2.   The Congress shall have power to enforce this article by appropriate legislation.

AMENDMENT XXIV [1964]

Section 1.   The right of citizens of the United States to vote in any primary or other election for President or Vice President, for electors for President or Vice President, or for Senator or Representative in Congress, shall not be denied or abridged by the United States, or any State by reason of failure to pay any poll tax or other tax.

Section 2.   The Congress shall have power to enforce this article by appropriate legislation.

AMENDMENT XXV [1967]

Section 1.   In case of the removal of the President from office or of his death or resignation, the Vice President shall become President.

Section 2.   Whenever there is a vacancy in the office of the Vice President, the President shall nominate a Vice President who shall take office upon confirmation by a majority vote of both Houses of Congress.

Section 3.   Whenever the President transmits to the President pro tempore of the Senate and the Speaker of the House of Representatives his written declaration that he is unable to discharge the powers and duties of his office, and until he transmits to them a written declaration to the contrary, such powers and duties shall be discharged by the Vice President as Acting President.

Section 4.   Whenever the Vice President and a majority of either the principal officers of the executive departments or of such other body as Congress may by law provide, transmit to the President pro tempore of the Senate and the Speaker of the House of Representatives their written declaration that the President is unable to discharge the powers and duties of his office, the Vice President shall immediately assume the powers and duties of the office as Acting President.

Thereafter, when the President transmits to the President pro tempore of the Senate and the Speaker of the House of Representatives his written declaration that no inability exists, he shall resume the powers and duties of his office unless the Vice President and a majority of either the principal officers of the executive department or of such other body as Congress may by law provide, transmit within four days to the President pro tempore of the Senate and the Speaker of the House of Representatives their written declaration and the President is unable to discharge the powers and duties of his office. Thereupon Congress shall decide the issue, assembling within forty-eight hours for that purpose if not in session. If the Congress, within twenty-one days after receipt of the latter written declaration, or, if Congress is not in session, within twenty-one days after Congress is required to assemble, determines by two-thirds vote of both Houses that the President is unable to discharge the power and duties of his office, the Vice President shall continue to discharge the same as Acting President; otherwise, the President shall resume the powers and duties of his office.

AMENDMENT XXVI [1971]

Section 1.   The right of citizens of the United States, who are eighteen years of age or older, to vote shall not be denied or abridged by the United States or by any State on account of age.

Section 2.   The Congress shall have power to enforce this article by appropriate legislation.

AMENDMENT XXVII [1996]

No law, varying the compensation for the services of the Senators and Representatives, shall take effect, until an election of Representatives shall have intervened.

INCOTERMS 2000 OVERVIEW*

Term	Mode of Transport	Delivery Obligation; Risk of Loss	Seller's Insurance Obligation
Ex Works (EXW)	Any	Make goods available to buyer at named place of delivery in seller's country, usually seller's premises	None
Free Carrier (FCA)	Any	Deliver goods to carrier nominated by buyer	None
Free Alongside Ship (FAS)	Sea or inland waterway transport only[c]	Place goods alongside vessel nominated by buyer at named port of shipment, either on wharf or in lighters	None
Free on Board (FOB)	Sea or inland waterway transport only[c]	Deliver goods on board vessel nominated by buyer at named port of shipment. Risk passes when goods have passed ship's rail.	None
Cost and Freight (CFR)	Sea or inland waterway transport only[c]	Deliver goods on board vessel chosen by seller at point of shipment. Risk passes when goods have passed ship's rail.	None
Cost, Insurance, and Freight (CIF)	Sea or inland waterway transport only[c]	Deliver goods on board vessel chosen by seller at point of shipment. Risk passes when goods have passed ship's rail.	Minimum cover
Carriage Paid To (CPT)	Any	Deliver goods to carrier. Risk passes on delivery to first carrier if more than one.	None
Carriage and Insurance Paid To (CIP)	Any	Deliver goods to carrier. Risk passes on delivery to first carrier if more than one.	Minimum cover
Delivered at Frontier (DAF)	Any, but usually land transport—rail or truck	Place goods at disposal of buyer at frontier (border)	None
Delivered Ex Ship (DES)	Sea or inland waterway transport only[c]	Place goods at disposal of buyer on board ship at named port of destination	None
Delivered Ex Quay (DEQ)	Sea or inland waterway transport only[c]	Place goods at disposal of buyer on quay (wharf) at named port of destination	None
Delivered Duty Unpaid (DDU)	Any	Place goods at disposal of buyer at named port of destination	None
Delivered Duty Paid (DDP)	Any	Place goods at disposal of buyer at named port of destination	None

*This table is reprinted with permission of the Uniform Commercial Code Law Journal from Mark E. Roszkowski, *Shipping Terms Based on Incoterms 2000: A Statutory Proposal,* 34 U.C.C.L.J. 169, 173–175 (Fall 2001).

Payment for Carriage	Export Clearance Obligation	Import Clearance Obligation[d]	Comments
Buyer	Buyer	Buyer	• Minimum obligation of seller
Buyer	Seller	Buyer	• If delivery is to carrier's terminal in or outside port, rather than to ship, use FCA rather than FOB.[a]
Buyer	Seller	Buyer	• Buyer bears risks and costs of loading goods on board
Buyer	Seller	Buyer	• Seller bears risks and costs of loading goods on board
Seller	Seller	Buyer	• Requires use of bill of lading or other maritime transport document. • Should not be used if goods do not pass ship's rail; instead, use CPT.
Seller	Seller	Buyer	• Should not be used for manufactured goods because only minimum insurance coverage required. • Should only be used when goods are to be sold in transit; otherwise, buyer should obtain own insurance.[b] • Requires use of bill of lading or other maritime transport document.
Seller	Seller	Buyer	• Unlike CFR and CIF, delivery obligation not tied to means of conveyance. • Use, for example, if goods shipped by road or rail for future carriage by sea.
Seller	Seller	Buyer	• Unlike CFR and CIF, delivery obligation not tied to means of conveyance. • Should only be used when goods are to be sold in transit; otherwise, buyer should obtain own insurance.[b] • Like CIF, suitable only for bulk cargoes because only minimum insurance coverage required.[b] • Like CPT, useful when goods not delivered directly to vessel.
Seller	Seller	Buyer	• "Frontier" includes any border, including that of country of export.
Seller	Seller	Buyer	• Buyer bears risk and expense of unloading goods from ship.
Seller	Seller	Buyer	• Seller bears risk and expense of unloading goods from ship onto wharf.
Seller	Seller	Buyer	• Manufactured goods rarely picked up out of ship DES or DEQ. Usually taken to cargo terminal. Should use DDU or DDP.[a]
Seller	Seller	Seller	• Whereas EXW represents the minimum seller's obligation, DDP is the maximum obligation.

[a]Ramberg, International Chamber of Commerce, Pub. No. 620, ICC Guide to Incoterms 2000: Understanding and Practical Use 20 (1999) (*"Incoterms Guide"*).

[b]*Incoterms Guide,* at 18.

[c]Maritime terms rarely are appropriate for manufactured goods that are usually containerized; use instead EXW or FCA, or DDU or DDP. *Incoterms Guide,* at 18, 20.

[d]As a general rule, the party domiciled in the country of import or export undertakes these duties. Exceptions are EXW and DDP. *Incoterms Guide,* at 24.

COMPARISON OF FORMS
OF BUSINESS ORGANIZATION

Type of Organization	Ownership	Formalities of Creation and Operation	Owner's Liability for Business Debts
Sole Proprietorship	By one person, the proprietor.	No formalities required: proprietorship automatically created if one owner and no other form is selected.	Proprietor has unlimited liability.
General Partnership	By two or more partners.	No formalities: general partnership automatically created if two or more owners and no other form is selected.	Partners have unlimited liability, unless partners elect Limited Liability Partnership (LLP) status.
Limited Partnership	By one or more general partners and one or more limited partners.	Formalities including: applying to state for formation, filing limited partnership certificate and amendments with state, maintaining registered office and agent in state, registering to transact business in other states, and keeping some records of ownership interests.	General partners have unlimited liability. Limited partners' liability is limited to their investment in the business. If partnership elects Limited Liability Limited Partnership (LLLP) status, all partners, general and limited, have limited liability.
Limited Liability Company	By one or more members.	Formalities including: applying to state for formation, filing articles of organization and amendments with state, maintaining registered office and agent in state, and obtaining a certificate of authority to transact business in other states.	Members' liability is limited to their investment in the business.
Corporation	By one or more shareholders.	Significant formalities including: applying to state for incorporation, filing articles of incorporation and amendments with state, maintaining registered office and agent, adopting bylaws, holding regular shareholders' and directors' meetings, keeping minutes and other records, paying annual franchise taxes, and obtaining a certificate of authority to transact business in other states. Also may be subject to regulation under federal and state securities laws.	Shareholders' liability is limited to their investment in the business.

Management and Control	Continuity of Existence	Transferability of Ownership	Federal Income Tax Considerations
Proprietor has exclusive right to manage the business.	Terminates when proprietor dies or abandons business.	Proprietorship assets freely transferable by proprietor.	Business not taxed as separate entity; business income/loss taxed on proprietor's individual return.
All partners have equal rights to participate in management.	Upon dissociation of partner, partnership either dissolves and is liquidated, or continues with buyout of dissociated partner's interest. Partnership agreement may provide for continuity.	Entire partnership interest cannot be transferred without consent of other partners.	Business not taxed as separate entity; proportionate shares of business income/loss taxed on partners' individual returns.
General partners share management rights equally; limited partners have no management rights but may be entitled to vote on extraordinary matters.	Similar to general partnership, except death or withdrawal of limited partner does not affect continuity. Limited partnership agreement may provide for continuity.	Entire partnership interest cannot be transferred without consent of other partners; agreement may allow free transferability of limited partnership interest.	Business not taxed as separate entity; proportionate shares of business income/loss taxed on partners' individual returns.
Members must choose either management by members or centralized management by managers (who may be members).	Upon dissociation of member, company either dissolves and is liquidated, or continues with buyout of dissociated member's interest. Operating agreement may provide for continuity.	Varies by state. Under the ULLCA, transferee of distributional interest does not become member unless authorized in operating agreement or all remaining members consent.	Business not taxed as separate entity; proportionate shares of business income/loss taxed on members' individual returns.
Shareholders elect directors who appoint officers to manage business. Closely-held corporations may operate by shareholder agreement that alters statutory control scheme.	Perpetual unless terminated as prescribed by statute.	Generally freely transferable, except that transfer of shares in a closely-held corporation generally is restricted by agreement.	Generally subject to double taxation: corporation taxed as separate entity and dividends paid to shareholders taxed on shareholders' individual returns. If operated as "S corporation," corporation not taxed as entity and proportionate share of business income/loss taxed on shareholders' individual returns.

Part 1—Alphabetical Listing

Part 2—Listing by Topic